DISCARDED

The BIOGRAPHICAL DICTIONARY of WOMEN in SCIENCE

The BIOGRAPHICAL DICTIONARY of WOMEN in SCIENCE

Pioneering Lives from Ancient Times to the Mid-20th Century

MARILYN OGILVIE
AND JOY HARVEY,

EDITORS

Volume 1
A–K

ROUTLEDGE

New York and London

*We dedicate these volumes to the memory of
Kerry Meek Whitney, who was an enthusiastic
supporter and contributor to this work.*

Published in 2000 by
Routledge
29 West 35th Street
New York, NY 10001

Published in Great Britain by
Routledge
11 New Fetter Lane
London, EC4P 4EE

Copyright © 2000 by Marilyn Ogilvie
Interior Design by Publisher's Studio/Stratford Publishing Services
Printed in the United States on acid-free paper.

Library of Congress Cataloging-in-Publication Data

The biographical dictionary of women in science: pioneering lives
from ancient times to the mid-20th century. / Marilyn Ogilvie and Joy
Harvey, editors.
     p. cm.
    Includes bibliographical references and index.
    ISBN 0-415-92038-8 (set : alk. paper). — ISBN 0-415-92039-6
(vol. 1 : alk. paper). — ISBN 0-415-92040-X (vol. 2 : alk. paper)
    1. Women scientists—Biography—Dictionaries.   I. Ogilvie,
Marilyn Bailey.   II. Harvey, Joy Dorothy.
Q141.B5285   2000
509′ 2′2—dc21   99-17668
[b]   CIP

*R 509.2
v.1*

CONTENTS

FOREWORD

It used to be said that there had never been any women scientists—even Marie Curie with her two Nobel Prizes had been a drudge who merely stirred the pitchblende for her husband's discovery of radium. Then it was admitted that there had been a few outstanding women scientists—the German chemist Lise Meitner, and the Americans Barbara McClintock, Rachel Carson, and Margaret Mead—but they were dismissed as "exceptions" to the general rule that there had been none of consequence. Accordingly, coverage of, or space devoted to, women in major biographical works on scientists was minimal, and it was difficult to find out anything about them. Somehow there was never enough room to include more than a small number, as was the case in encyclopedias of the 1960s (as the *McGraw-Hill Modern Men of Science*) and even the *Dictionary of Scientific Biography* (1970–80), whose sixteen volumes included just twenty-five women.

But from the 1970s onward, as the women's movement in the United States progressed, scholars began to explore women's history and as they did found more and more women scientists. Their definition of who had been a scientist also expanded to include women who previously had been dismissed as mere illustrators, popularizers, visionaries, patronesses, translators, collectors, helpmates, home economists, and others. In 1986 Marilyn Ogilvie astonished everyone with the 186 women scientists listed in her landmark *Women in Science, Antiquity through the Nineteenth Century: A Biographical Dictionary with Annotated Bibliography* that covered Western Europe as well as the United States and Canada.

Now with the help of Joy Harvey she has extended this work twenty-fold. These volumes include approximately twenty-five hundred women scientists and cover a wide range of fields—engineers and physicians, mathematicians and home economists, botanists and zoologists, psychologists, anthropologists, and others. Unlike many other bio-bibliographical dictionaries devoted to particular fields (as mathematics, psychology, or anthropology) that have appeared in the last two decades, this one cuts across all fields and all nationalities and

thus includes persons of all employment categories and walks of life. The coverage accordingly goes beyond the now well-known or award-winning women to others who have remained obscure, even though, as we learn here, they were often the mainstays of their government bureaus, colleges, nonprofit institutions, local or regional groups, and specialties. So varied have been their accomplishments that reading about them broadens one's notion of what constitutes a contribution to science—there is a lot more to science than winning the Nobel Prize.

One particular feature of this work is the wide international coverage. Russians, Turks, Filipinos, Latin Americans, and Asians, as well as western Europeans, Americans, and Canadians fill these pages. This is particularly notable and exciting, since so little is otherwise available in English on these women. At times the language barrier has been so formidable that it has not even been clearly discernible if they indeed were women.

Besides being comprehensive this work is also authoritative, because the two compilers are both established scholars with previous works in the area, and because they have been so thorough in locating and checking the materials they have used. This is painstaking and exasperating work, because two sources on the same person may often disagree, and some pioneers followed informal and circuitous paths to success.

The coverage is from antiquity to the recent past, and some of the scientists who were born before 1910 are only recently deceased or still alive at the time of printing. Each entry has a short biographical summary of educational attainments and work history, followed by a description of her most important accomplishments, and then lists of her most important publications and references to biographical works that one can use to pursue the subject further. The length of each entry varies and reflects what is currently known. More could have been said about some of these women, and others might have been included, but anyone holding these two hefty volumes will agree that there is already plenty here.

As a result this state-of-the-art set of volumes will be an invaluable resource to those seeking information on individual women of science (especially so when there are more than one with a slightly similar name—as with the several Andersons or MacCrackens). It will also be useful to those students who need biographical information for papers, and it is an authoritative reference for those pursuing particular topics or seeking to study subgroups, such as Russian women physicians or British women botanists. One can also use the entries to examine other collectivities, such as married women scientists before 1920 or friendship networks among women scientists, since some of their collaborators were women scientists who are included here and cross-referenced.

It will also be of interest to those who just want to browse, and expand their horizon. It will be a particular feast for scientists or others who want to know who was out there before them. To read these pages is to inhabit the inspirational realm of those who rose above obstacles to triumph and accomplishment despite adversity.

Margaret W. Rossiter

ACKNOWLEDGMENTS

This dictionary could not have been compiled without the help of the many individuals who supplied us with sources, pointed us in the direction of important materials, and gave us moral support. We are indebted to so many people that we hesitate to mention them by name, for fear of leaving some out, but we want to thank the following people for their help.

Among the many librarians and archivists who made this effort more effective, we thank Paul G. Anderson, associate professor and archivist, Washington University Library; Margaret R. Bollick, University of Nebraska Library; Joanne Day, reference librarian, Albertus Magnus College; Nick Gill, University of Cambridge Library; Andrew J. Harrison, processing archivist, Alan Mason Chesney Medical Archives, Johns Hopkins Medical Institutions; Tanya Hollis, assistant librarian, California Historical Society, North Baker Research Library; Diane E. Kaplan, archivist, Yale University; Ginny Kieler, Curator of Special Collections, Tuft Library, Colorado College; Claren Kidd, Professor of Bibliography and head, Youngblood Library for the Geosciences, University of Oklahoma; David Koch, Associate Dean and Curator of Special Collections, Southern Illinois Universitity; Kathy Kraft, archivist, Radcliffe Institute for Advanced Study; Margret Helgadóttir Næss, senior executive officer/web editor, KILDEn, Norwegian Information and Documentation Center for Women's Studies; Debora A. Rougeux, University of Pittsburgh Archives Service Center; Wilma R. Slaight, Wellesley College Archives; the Stanford University archivist; Wolfgang Smolka, University archives, Ludwig-Maximilian University; Bill Tully, Senior Reference Librarian, National Library of Australia; the UCLA Biomedical Library; Michele Wellck, Academy Archivist and Karren Elsbend, assistant archivist, California Academy of Sciences; Geoffrey P. Williams, University Archivist, State University of New York (SUNY) at Albany; the archivist for Agnes Scott College; and, reference librarians at the Widener Library, Harvard University.

We especially want to thank historian of botany Ronald Stuckey, who supplied us with valuable material on women in botany, and historian of science Annette Vogt of the Max Planck Institute for the History of Science, who has been very helpful in providing information on the German women. Marian Bruinvels, historian of medicine, and Ida Stamhuis, historian of science, gave us invaluable help on the Dutch women. Renate Strohmeier provided us with excellent information on European women scientists.

We had help in translation from Vladimir E. Andrusevich, Jeannie O'Connell, Irene Erdoes, Professor Tibor Herczeg, and Professor Lawrence Larsen. We also thank those who provided us with information that arrived too late to incorporate into this edition, especially Catherine Goldstein on French women mathematicians, Jane Carey on Australian scientists, Carmen Margallon on Spanish women scientists, and Marian Bruinvels on Dutch scientists. Others provided us with additional help in different ways. Gabrielle Netchine supplied us with names of French psychologists, Marsha Richmond pointed our way through the literature of the Balfour Laboratory at Cambridge University, and Ilse Jahn sent us material on a German naturalist. Cambridge University professor and physiologist Horace Barlow provided us with information on his mother, Nora. Henry Harvey spent several weeks helping us locate subjects on the Internet. We especially want to thank Ursula Dunlap, Kelly Lankford, Maureen McCormick, Sylvia Patterson, and Erika Tracy, students at the University of Oklahoma, for their help.

INTRODUCTION

PURPOSE

The purpose of this dictionary is to provide biographical and bibliographical information on approximately twenty-five hundred women scientists. As impossible as it is to create a truly inclusive biographical dictionary, we have made every effort in that direction, covering a longer time frame, more countries, and a greater number of fields than previous works of this kind. These volumes integrate material from earlier collective biographies as well as provide new biographies. Ideally, this dictionary will contribute something unique— an opportunity to study women scientists in a more comprehensive manner. The subjects can be viewed longitudinally within fields over a long period of time or horizontally across fields within a restricted time period. This kind of cross-comparison offers a unique perspective and provides new connections between scientific disciplines, patterns of education, and professionalization. We hope to demonstrate the wide variety of science-related activities in which women have been involved throughout history.

SCOPE

Temporal Scope

The temporal scope of this dictionary is broad and includes women scientists from ancient times to living scientists born before 1910 or those born more recently but who have since died. For several reasons, biographers cannot always trust accounts contemporary with the events. The farther back in time biographers go, the more they are at the mercy of the reporters' biases. Researchers do not know the politics, socioeconomic status, or religious beliefs of these early writers, and any of these factors could skew the way they reported history. Much of the early documentary evidence may have been lost and the extant sources may be anything but typical. For example, different sources alternately described the Pythagorean Theano as the wife and the sister of Pythagoras. Even her father's name varies in different accounts. Although

we do not have any sure way to sort out the correct interpretation, the conflicting evidence still indicates the important role of women in early Greek culture. As we move forward in time, we find not only the same problems of bias and missing and conflicting sources, but we encounter additional ones based on gender, race, and class.

The scope of science has changed throughout time, as has the understanding of what constitutes science and who has practiced it. These changes have affected our selection of subjects. We moved from antiquity, where the very existence of the woman scientist may be questionable, to the twentieth century, where science has become a sophisticated enterprise with practitioners of both sexes asking difficult questions. Between these two extremes we see the evolution of science produced by women. Thus, while the dictionary includes queens, nuns, and saints from the Middle Ages and learned ladies of the Renaissance through the Enlightenment, we held women in the later periods to a higher standard of the "scientific." From the eighteenth century we found an important group of women who specialized in scientific illustration, ornithological observations, and plant collecting. Others observed the stars and planets, taught science and mathematics in girls' schools, served as science bibliographers, wrote popular books, and worked in museums. Some acted as assistants to fathers, brothers, or husbands who collected scientific specimens. Different criteria for inclusion were needed for these eighteenth- and nineteenth-century women than were appropriate for earlier periods. As science became more professionalized in the nineteenth and early twentieth centuries, it became, if anything, more difficult for a women to succeed in science. Those who were fortunate enough to earn degrees still had a difficult time finding professional positions. However, a woman interested in chemistry and physiology might make a place for herself within an appropriate "woman's field" such as home economics. Not all women interested in science chose that path. Sometimes a woman satisfied every qualification for professional scientific status and was limited only by gender. These women have been termed "obligatory amateurs" by Ogilvie because, for despite their qualifications, they were never accepted as professionals. At the same time, however, there were a few women who made theoretical contributions and were recognized by exceptional men for these accomplishments. In the twentieth century, although the education and training of women became comparable to that of men, the importance of womens' positions has not.

The world has changed even since 1990, when the editor of the *Dictionary of Scientific Biography Supplement* was able to excuse the addition of only ten women to its new volumes with the comment that the editors had decided not to engage in "retrospective affirmative action," since the small number of women reflected the historical reality of women's entrance into science. Some decades earlier, the German reference *Biographisch-literarisches Handworterbuch der Exakten Naturwissenschaften,* by J. C. Poggendorff, regularly included women working in the exact sciences in Europe and England, as did the *Catalogue of the Royal Society.* Recently, the editor of *Notable Twentieth Century Scientists* included more than 150 women from the modern period, reflecting a new awareness of the lacunae.

Margaret Rossiter, examining reasons why so many women scientists remained obscure in spite of the enormous increase in their numbers by the mid-twentieth century, refers to them as being "camouflaged" as housewives, mothers, and "others" and as being "stockpiled" in cities and college towns. They also have suffered from Rossiter's "Mathilda Effect," in which women scientists, cast in the role of handmaiden, could not profit from Robert Merton's "Matthew Effect," which is that recognition and citation lead to further recognition and citation. More than once we have found that in searching out information and writing a brief biographical account of a person who appeared to be an obscure woman scientist, we uncovered additional references in the literature that indicated her importance to later scientific workers.

During the last five years we have seen the publication of excellent specialized collective biographies on women scientists in the biological, physical, and social sciences, but the length of the articles necessarily limited the number of accounts in each volume. Because of the large number of women included and the enhanced time period it covers, our dictionary is able to reflect changes in women's contributions to science through time and across fields.

Geographical Scope

We attempted universal geographical coverage, but we realize that we have excluded or given minimal coverage to certain areas of the world. This occured simply because information was not available to us or arrived too late to be included in this edition of the dictionary, so although the scope is worldwide, the coverage is skewed toward the United States and Great Britain. Other nations do not have an equivalent of *American Men of Science* and *American Men and Women of Science.* These sources are unique in scope, covering both famous women and those engaging in "normal" scientific activities. Rossiter's seminal work on American women scientists was based on individuals first identified through this source. She was able to move from these sources into specialized archives. Even without a comparable type of reference, Britain recently has included many women in its *Dictionary of National Biography* and other collective biographical sources. For example, Ray Desmond, in *British and Irish Botanists,* includes women as well as men who have contributed to botany, botanical illustration, and horticulture.

Standard biographical sources do not always reflect the number of women working in science. For example, the *Belgian National Biographical Dictionary* includes only one or two women scientists in its multiple volumes. The Danish and Dutch biographical dictionaries are somewhat better, but still it can be very difficult to find publications and dissertations written by women between 1890 and 1930.

Some European countries did not memorialize their women scientists with obituaries in the major scientific journals because they did not serve as heads of laboratories or hold full professorships. However, this situation has been remedied by archival projects in Germany and to some degree in France, the Netherlands, Spain, and the Scandinavian countries. During international conferences, we have met historians of science from many countries who have supplied us with information. Through Dutch historians of science we collected additional information, though not in time for inclusion in these volumes. The situation in Russia, the other countries of the former Soviet Union, and the former eastern block is somewhat different. There, many women are included in biographical sources, and we found that obituaries were written on women scientists as well as on men. Although we included some women from South America, Mexico, the Far East, and the Middle East, there is much work to be done here in the future. We hope that responses to this dictionary from researchers and archivists working in those countries will provide us with names of women scientists and information that we can incorporate into future editions.

Disciplinary Scope

We have featured a wide range of scientific disciplines, including most areas of science and science-related activities in which women have worked. We have considered those women who have made major contributions to experimental and theoretical science, as well as many others who have added to the scientific enterprise. The women displayed a wide range of educational backgrounds, and their disciplines range from mathematics and physics to field biology and natural history. We made an early decision to include physicians, psychologists (including those working in Freudian psychiatry), anthropologists, and, to a lesser extent, sociologists, in recognition of the strength of women in these fields. Many historians have noted that women gravitate toward in certain scientific professions. Health-related fields, particularly, have engaged women from the earliest times. Even though women are found in all areas of science, they still cluster in larger numbers within the biological and social sciences. The data in this dictionary may provide material that will illustrate these trends.

METHODOLOGY

Individual and collective biographies call for different approaches. When researching the life of an individual, a biographer has the luxury of exploring a life intensively. Collective biography by its very nature requires the biographer to select a more restricted set of events in the lives of its subjects. For this dictionary we first drew up a list of names gleaned from multiple sources. Our list constantly expanded through our use of secondary sources that mentioned women for whom there was little detailed biographical information. We then contacted historians, historians of science, librarians, and others to write biographical accounts. The large number of entries, as well as time constraints, obliged us to write many of these biographical entries ourselves.

Unlike in some biographical dictionaries, these entries vary considerably in length. The perceived importance of the scientist is the most obvious reason for this variation, yet this is not always the case. Where sources and detailed biographies are readily available for a well-known figure, we have often given more abbreviated accounts. On the other hand, we have offered longer biographical entries for less well-known women whose scientific contributions have been significant but about whom few biographical articles have been written. Still others were members of collective efforts and deserve identification whether or not good sources exist on their personal lives. For those women scientists whose accounts are briefer than we felt appropriate, we hoped that by placing together whatever sources were available the door would be opened for later, more fully realized biographies. Science depends on collective activities, and we must always include less well-known individuals to give a balanced view.

As we came to the end of compiling these accounts, we began to find that the Internet had made available new sources of information, providing ready access to biographies hidden within finding aids of archives throughout the world. Scientific societies, scientific centers, colleges, and universities producing memorial Web sites in honor of particular women scientists offered excellent additional materials. Although we were able to utilize these sources only toward the end of this work, the promise that they hold for present and future historians and biographers will enhance subsequent editions of this biographical source.

In contrast to Billy the Kid's admonition to "die young and leave a good-looking corpse," many women scientists have outlived their male colleagues, leaving no one to write their obituaries by the time they died, often well into their nineties, possibly in a nursing home in some obscure town far from academic centers. This may partially explain why information, including the death dates, for women who achieved some notability during their life is so often difficult to find.

AUDIENCE

The audience for this biographical dictionary is as varied in its nature, background, and interests as the women it portrays. It provides information for use by scientists, students, educators, professional historians, sociologists, historians of science, and women's studies professionals. Scientists should find it useful for examing the history of their discipline and the recovery of their women predecessors, a process already begun by excellent autobiographical sources and collective biographies within specialities. For young women scientists, the sense of a long genealogical lineage of other women who have overcome handicaps and reached out to male and female colleagues may provide both historical precedents and a sense of continuity, not only in their own field but in adjoining and distant disciplines. For students of all ages, from middle school through graduate school, this dictionary should serve as an important reference tool. Their teachers will be able to have a ready reference for women scientists and be able to provide role models for their female students. For those historians interested not only in science but in its broader cultural context, the inclusion of women who spanned a variety of fields of intellectual and artistic endeavor well into the twentieth century offers a chance to rethink the close interaction between private and public spheres and a redefinition of public spheres. It also offers a tool to enumerate the platforms used for expression and the multiple numbers of women who popularized as well as practiced science, a popularization that accompanied the movement into ever more specialized subdisciplines. For sociologists, the far larger core of women scientists that this biographical dictionary includes provides data to underscore the presence of women in governmental agencies ranging from agriculture to radiation laboratories, as well as the role of professional women in the life of their social and intellectual communities. We hope that this source will help

Introduction

historians to refocus science from the former emphasis on a few notables to the real community of scholars that research projects have always demanded. The role of a male or female mentor, the encouragement or staffing practices by some scientists in contrast to others, the importance of career trajectories from college to university, from state to state, from country to country, and the growing importance of post-doctoral work can be found in many of the late- and early-twentieth century biographies. The indices may be used to provide ready cross-cultural contrasts between and among women from different cultures. Those people involved in gender studies will have a new core of data from which they can illuminate theories about gender and science.

HOW TO USE THIS BOOK

Arrangement

The biographies are divided into three major sections: the data section, the biographical narrative, and the bibliography. This use of collective biography allows the user to cross-reference far more extensively and pass beyond the studies of individuals to that of interacting collectives of scientists. The data section includes concise personal information such as birth and death dates and places, parents' names, marital status, number of children, education, professional experience, honors, and memberships in scientific and honor societies. In many cases, only a part of this standard material is available. Following the italicized data section is the biographical narrative that may vary from a few sentences in one entry to several pages in another. Finally, a bibliographic section follows the narrative biography and includes primary, sec-

ondary, and standard sources. In some cases no primary sources were found, whereas in others, they are so numerous that we have had to include just a few. This material includes scientific publications as well as autobiographical or archival materials, if any. Secondary sources included obituaries, other biographical sources, and in some cases, books on a general topic with sufficient biographical detail. References are made to the biography of a husband scientist or male mentor when this illuminates the life of a woman scientist. As we worked on the accounts, we found that certain secondary sources appeared over and over, and those have been included in a separate category entitled standard sources, along with more comprehensive standard sources such as *American Men and Women of Science, Who's Who* volumes, and other similar biographical dictionaries and encyclopedias.

Use

Although a biographical dictionary provides easy access to those who know the name of the individual they seek, this edition has made every attempt to mention and index colleagues both male and female, although only biographies of other women scientists are cross-referenced.

Beyond this alphabetical use, indices are provided at the end of the volumes to allow the location of a scientist by geographical area, by specialty, and by time period. These lists are intended for use with the general index, which is organized by name and subject.

Marilyn Bailey Ogilvie
Joy Harvey

STANDARD SOURCES

ADELMAN Adelman, Joseph. *Famous Women*. New York: Lonow, 1926.

AINLEY Ainley, Marianne Gosztonyi, ed. *Despite the Odds: Essays on Canadian Women and Science*. Montreal: Vehicule Press, 1990.

ALIC Alic, Margaret. *Hypatia's Heritage: A History of Women in Science from Antiquity through the Nineteenth Century*. Boston: Beacon Press, 1986.

AMERICAN WOMEN *American Women*. Ed. Durward Howes. Los Angeles: Richard Blank, 1935–1940.

AMERICAN WOMEN 1974 *American Women: The Standard Biographical Dictionary of Notable Women*. Ed. Durward Howes. Teaneck, N.J.: Zephyrus Press, 1974.

AMS *American Men of Science: A Biographical Dictionary*. New York: Bowker 1–11th, 1906–1968. Eds. 1–8 published by the Science Press, 9th ed. published by Bowker and Science Press, 10th and 11th ed. published by Jacques Cattell Press. 9th ed. issued in 3 vols.: vol. 1, *Physical Sciences;* vol. 2, *Biological Sciences;* and vol. 3, *Social Sciences*. 10th ed. issued in 5 vols.: vols. 1–4, *Physical and Biological Sciences,* A–Z; vol. 5, *Social and Behavioral Sciences*. 11th ed. issued in 8 vols.: vols. 1–6, *Physical and Biological Sciences;* vols. 7–8, *Social and Behavioral Sciences,* A–Z. Supplements issued between some editions. Continues as *American Men and Women of Science*. Titles of the 12th–19th eds. vary. The abbreviations for all citations, whether *American Men of Science* or *American Men and Women of Science,* will be *AMS*.

ANB *American National Biography*. New York: Oxford University Press, 1999.

ANNUAL OBITUARY *The Annual Obituary* (1980–1993). [editor varies with each volume.] 14 vols. New York: St. Martin's Press, 1981–1994.

AOU BIOGRAPHIES Palmer, T.S. *Biographies of Members of the American Ornithologists' Union*. Washington, D.C.: American Ornithologists' Union, 1954.

APA DIRECTORY *American Psychological Association Directory*. Washington, D.C.: American Psychological Association, annual.

APA MEMBERSHIP REGISTER *American Psychological Association Membership Register*. Washington, D.C.: American Psychological Association, annual.

APPIGNANESI Appignanesi, Lisa, and Forrester, John. *Freud's Women*. New York: Basic Books, 1992.

APPLETON'S CYCLOPAEDIA *Appletons' Cyclopaedia of American Biography*. Ed. James Grant Wilson and John Fiske. New York: D. Appleton and Co., 1888.

ARNOLD Arnold, Lois Barber. *Four Lives in Science: Women's Education in the Nineteenth Century*. New York: Schocken Books, 1984.

BAILEY Bailey, Martha J. *American Women in Science: A Biographical Dictionary*. Denver, Colo: ABC-CLIO, 1994.

BALLARD Ballard, George. *Memoirs of Several Ladies of Great Britain Who Have Been Celebrated for their Writings or Skill in the Learned Languages, Arts and Sciences*. London: Edwards, 1775.

BARNHART Barnhart, John Hendley. *Biographical Notes upon Botanists in the New York Botanical Garden Library*. Boston: G. K. Hall, 1965.

BARR Barr, Ernest Scott. *Index to Biographical Fragments in Unspecialized Scientific Journals*. University of Alabama Press, 1973.

BAUDOUIN Baudouin, Marce. *Femmes médecins d'autrefois*. Paris: Librairie Médicale et Scientifique Jules Rousset, 1906.

BDAS Elliott, Clark. *Biographical Dictionary of American Science: The Seventeenth Through the Nineteenth Centuries*. Westport, Conn: Greenwood Press, 1979.

BIBLIOGRAPHIE ASTRONOMIQUE Lalande, Jérôme de. *Bibliographie astronomique avec l'histoire de l'astronomie depuis 1781 jusqu'à 1802*. Paris: Imprimerie de la République, 1803.

BIOGRAFISCH WOORDENBOEK *Biografisch Woordenboek van Nederland*. Ed. by J. Charite. 4 vols. 's-Gravenhage: Nijhoff, 1979–1994.

BIOGRAPHICAL MEMOIRS Royal Society of London. *Biographical Memoirs of Fellows of the Royal Society*. London: Royal Society 1–44, 1955–1998.

BIOGRAPHIE UNIVERSELLE *Biographie universelle, ancienne et moderne*. 85 vols. Paris: L. G. Michaud, 1811–1826.

BOASE Boase, Frederic. *Modern English Biography*. 6 vols. London: Truro, Netherton and Worth, for the author, 1892–1921.

BONNER Bonner, Thomas Neville. "Rendezvous in Zürich: Seven Who Made a Revolution in Women's Medical Education, 1864–1874." *Journal of the History of Medicine* 44, no. 1: 7–27.

BONNER 1992 ———. *To the Ends of the Earth: Women's Search for Education in Medicine*. Cambridge, Mass: Harvard University Press, 1992.

BONTA Bonta, Marcia Myers. *Women in the Field: America's Pioneering Women Naturalists*. College Station: Texas A&M University Press, 1991.

BRINK Brink, J. R., ed. *Female Scholars: A Tradition of Learned Women before 1800*. Montreal: Eden Press, 1980.

BROOKE BAILEY Bailey, Brooke. *The Remarkable Lives of 100 Women Healers and Scientists*. Holbrook, Mass: Bob Adams, 1994.

CARR AND CARR Carr, D. J. and S. G. M. Carr. *People and Plants in Australia*. Sydney: Academic Press, 1981.

CATALOGUE ROYAL SOCIETY Royal Society of London. *Catalogue of Scientific Papers (1800–1900)*. London: Royal Society, 1867–1925.

COLUMBIA ENCYCLOPEDIA *New Columbia Encyclopedia*. New York: Viking Press, 1953.

CONCISE UNIVERSAL BIOGRAPHY *Concise Universal Biography*. Ed. John Alexander Hammerton. London: Educational Book Company, 1934–1935.

CREATIVE COUPLES Pycior, Helena M., Nancy G. Slack, and Pnina G. Abir-Am, eds. *Creative Couples in the Sciences*. New Brunswick, N.J.: Rutgers University Press, 1996.

CREESE 1991 Creese, Mary R. S. "British Women and Research in the Chemical Sciences." *The British Journal for the History of Science*. 24 (September 1991): 275–305.

CREESE Creese, Mary R. S. *Ladies in the Laboratory? American and British Women in Science, 1800–1900*. Lanham, Md.: Scarecrow Press, 1998.

CREESE AND CREESE Creese, Mary R. S., and Creese, Thomas M. "British Women Who Contributed to Research in the Geological Sciences in the Nineteenth Century." *The British Journal for the History of Science* 27 (March 1994): 23–54.

CURRENT BIOGRAPHY *Current Biography*. New York: H. W. Wilson, *1940–*.

CYCLOPEDIA *A Cyclopedia of Female Biography*. Ed. H. G. Adams. Glasgow: Robert Forrester, Stockwell, 1866.

DAB *Dictionary of American Biography*. Ed. by Allen Johnson and Dumas Malone. 11 vols. New York: Scribner, 1964.

DANSK BIOGRAFISK *Dansk Biografisk Leksikon*. 16 vols. Engelstoft: Porl, 1876–.

DAS DEUTSCHE WW *Wer ist Wer?: Das Deutsche Who's Who*. Berlin: 1954–.

DBE *Deutsche Biographische Enzyclopadie*. Munich: K. G. Sour.

DBF *Dictionnaire de Biographie Française*. Paris: Letouzey, 1933–.

DEBUS *World Who's Who in Science: A Biographical Dictionary of Notable Scientists from Antiquity to the Present*. Ed. Allen G. Debus. Chicago: Marquis, 1968.

DESMOND Desmond, Ray. *Dictionary of British and Irish Botanists and Horticulturists*. London: Taylor and Francis, and the Natural History Museum (London), 1994.

DFC *Dictionnaire des femmes celebres, de tous les temps et de tous les pays*. Ed. Lucienne Mazenod and Ghislain Schoeller. Paris: R. Laffont, 1992.

DIB *Dictionary of International Biography*. Cambridge: International Biographical Centre, 1963–.

DICTIONARY OF SCIENTIFIC BIOGRAPHY *Dictionary of Scientific Biography*. Ed. Charles Coulston Gillispie. 16 vols. New York: Charles Scribner's Sons, 1970–1980. Supplement II, ed. Frederic L. Holmes. 2 vols. 1990.

DIZIONARIO ITALIANI *Dizionario biografico degli Italiani*. Ed. by Alberto Mario Ghisalberti. Rome: Instituto della Enciclopedia Italiani, 1964–.

DNB *The Dictionary of National Biography:* London: Oxford University Press, 1882–.

DNB, MISSING PERSONS *The Dictionary of National Biography: Missing Persons*. Oxford: Oxford University Press, 1994.

DOLAN Dolan, Josephine A. *Goodnow's History of Nursing*. 10th ed. Philadelphia: W. B. Saunders, 1958.

DORLAND Dorland, William Alexander Newman. *The Sum of Feminine Achievement: A Critical and Analytical Study of Woman's Contribution to the Intellectual Progress of the World*. Boston: Stratford, 1917.

DUBREIL-JACOTIN Dubreil-Jacotin, Marie Louise. "Women Mathematicians." In *Mathematics: Concepts and Development,* 168–180. Vol. 1 of *Great Currents of Mathematical Thought*. Ed. F. LeLionnais. New York: Dover, 1971.

ECHOLS AND WILLIAMS Echols, Anne and Marty Williams. *Annotated Index of Medieval Women*. New York: Markus Wiener Publishing, 1992.

ECKENSTEIN Eckenstein, Lina. *Woman Under Monasticism*. New York: Russell and Russell, 1963.

ENCYCLOPEDIA BRITTANICA *Encyclopedia Britannica: A Dictionary of Arts, Sciences, Literature and General Information.* 11th ed. 29 vols. Cambridge: Cambridge University Press, 1910.

ENCYCLOPEDIA OF PSYCHOLOGY *Encyclopedia of Psychology.* Ed. Raymond J. Corsini. 4 vols. New York: John Wiley and Sons, 1994.

EUROPA *The Europa Biographical Dictionary of British Women.* Ed. Anne Crawford, et al. London: Europa, and Detroit, Mich.: Gale Research, 1983.

FRS OBITUARY NOTICES Royal Society of London. *Obituary Notices of the Fellows of the Royal Society.* London: Royal Society, 1–9, 1932–1954.

GACS Gacs, Ute, et al., eds. *Women Anthropologists: A Biographical Dictionary.* New York: Greenwood Press, 1988.

GIRTON *Girton College Register* 1869–1946. Cambridge: privately printed for Girton College, 1948.

GREAT SOVIET ENCYCLOPEDIA *Great Soviet Encyclopedia* (Bol'shaia sovetskaia entsiklopediia). Ed. by A. M. Prokhorov, New York: Macmillan, 1973–1983. 31 vols.

GRINSTEIN 1993 Grinstein, Louise S., Rose K. Rose, and Miriam H. Rafailovich, eds. *Women in Chemistry and Physics: A Biobibliographic Sourcebook.* Westport, Conn: Greenwood Press, 1993.

GRINSTEIN 1997 Grinstein, Louise S., Carol A. Biermann, and Rose K. Rose, eds. *Women in the Biological Sciences: A Biobibliographic Sourcebook.* Westport, Conn: Greenwood Press, 1997.

GRINSTEIN AND CAMPBELL Grinstein, Louise S. and Paul J. Campbell, eds. *Women of Mathematics: A Biobibliographic Sourcebook.* New York: Greenwood Press, 1987.

GUNN AND CODD Gunn, Mary, and L. E. W. Codd. *Botanical Exploration of Southern Africa: An Illustrated History of Early Botanical Literature on the Cape Flora: Biographical Accounts of the Leading Plant Collectors and Their Activities in Southern Africa from the Days of the East India Company until Modern Times.* Cape Town: Botanical Research Institute by A.A. Balkema, 1981.

HABER Haber, Louis. *Women Pioneers of Science.* New York: Harcourt Brace Jovanovich, 1979.

HACKER Hacker, Carlotta. *The Indomitable Lady Doctors.* Toronto: Clarke, Irwin & Co., 1974.

HARLESS Harless, Johann Christian Friedrich. *Die Verdienste der Frauen um Naturwissenschaft und Heilkunde.* Göttingen: Vandenhoeck-Ruprechtschen Verlage, 1830.

HELLSTEDT, AUTOBIOGRAPHIES Hellstedt, Leone. *Women Physicians of the World: Autobiographies of Medical Pioneers.* Washington, D.C.: Hemisphere Publ., 1978.

HERZENBERG Herzenberg, Caroline. *Women Scientists from Antiquity to the Present: an Index.* West Cornwall, Conn: Locust Hill Press, 1986.

HØYRUP Høyrup, Else. *Women of Science, Technology, and Medicine: A Bibliography.* Roskilde, Denmark: Roskilde University Library, 1987.

HUGHES Hughes, Muriel Joy. *Women Healers in Medieval Life and Literature.* Oxford: Oxford University Press, 1943.

HUNT INSTITUTE Hunt Institute for Botanical Documentation. *Biographical Dictionary of Botanists Represented in the Hunt Institute Portrait Collection.* Boston: G.K. Hall, 1972.

HURD-MEAD 1933 Hurd-Mead, Kate Campbell. *Medical Women of America.* New York: Froben, 1933.

HURD-MEAD 1938 Hurd-Mead, Kate Campbell. *A History of Women in Medicine: From the Earliest Times to the Beginning of the Nineteenth Century.* Haddam, Conn.: The Haddam Press, 1938.

IDA *International Dictionary of Anthropologists.* New York: Garland, 1991.

INTERNATIONAL WW *The International Who's Who of Women.* London: Europa Publications, 1992.

IRELAND Ireland, Norma Olin. *Index to Women of the World from Ancient to Modern Times: Biographies and Portraits.* Boston: Faxon, 1962.

JEWS IN MEDICINE Schreiber, Emanuel. *Jews in Medicine.* Chicago: n.p., 1902.

JONES AND BOYD Jones, Bessie Zaban, and Lyle Gifford Boyd. *The Harvard College Observatory: The First Four Directorships, 1839–1919.* Cambridge, Mass.: Harvard University Press, 1971.

KASS-SIMON AND FARNES Kass-Simon, G., and Patricia Farnes, eds. *Women of Science: Righting the Record.* Bloomington, IN: Indiana University Press, 1990.

KERSEY Kersey, Ethel M. *Women Philosophers: A Bio-Critical Source Book.* New York: Greenwood Press, 1989.

LA GRAN ENCICLOPEDIA DE PUERTO RICO *La Gran Enciclopedia de Puerto Rico.* Madrid: n.p., 1976.

LAROUSSE BIOGRAPHICAL DICTIONARY *Larousse Biographical Dictionary.* New York: Larousse, 1994.

LEXICON DER FRAU *Lexikon der Frau.* 2 vols. Zürich: Encyclios Verlag AG, 1953.

LIPINSKA 1900 Lipinska, Melanie. *Histoire des femmes médecins depuis l'antiquité jusqu'à nos jours.* Paris: Librairie G. Jacques, 1900.

LIPINSKA 1930 Lipinska, Melanie. *Les femmes et le progrès des sciences médicales.* Paris: Masson, 1930.

LKW Golemba, Beverly E. *Lesser Known Women: A Biographical Dictionary.* Boulder, Colo.: Lynne Rienner, 1992.

LOVEJOY Lovejoy, Esther Pohl. *Women Doctors of the World.* New York: Macmillan, 1957.

MALLIS Mallis, Arnold. *American Entomologists.* New Brunswick, N.J.: Rutgers University Press, 1971.

McGRAYNE McGrayne, Sharon Bertsch. *Nobel Prize Women in Science: Their Lives, Struggles, and Momentous Discoveries.* New York: Birch Lane Press, 1993.

MEDICAL WOMEN Jex-Blake, Sophia. *Medical Women: A Thesis and a History.* 2d ed. Edinburgh: Oliphant, Anderson and Ferrier, 1886.

MÉNAGE Ménage, Gilles. *The History of Women Philosophers.* Trans. Beatrice H. Zedler. Lanham, Md.: University Press of America, 1984.

MEYER Meyer, Gerald Dennis. *The Scientific Lady in England, 1650–1760: An Account of Her Rise, with Emphasis on the Major Roles of the Telescope and Microscope.* Berkeley: University of California Press, 1955.

MEYER AND VON SCHWEIDLER Meyer, Stefan, and Egon von Schweidler. *Radioaktivität.* Leipzig: B. G. Teubner, 1927.

MODERN SCIENTISTS AND ENGINEERS McGraw-Hill *Modern Scientists and Engineers.* New York: McGraw-Hill, 1980.

MOLLAN AND FINUCANE Mollan, William Davis, and Brandan Finucane, eds. *Some People and Places in Irish Science and Technology.* Dublin: Royal Irish Academy, 1985.

MORANTZ-SANCHEZ Morantz-Sanchez, Regina Markell. *Sympathy and Science: Women Physicians in American Medicine.* New York: Oxford University Press, 1985.

MOTHERS AND DAUGHTERS Stanley, Autumn. *Mothers and Daughters of Invention: Notes for a Revised History of Technology.* Metuchen, N.J.: Scarecrow Press, 1993.

MOZANS Mozans, H. J. *Woman in Science.* Notre Dame: University of Notre Dame Press, 1991.

MUNK'S ROLL *Lives of the Fellows of the Royal Society of Physicians: Continued to 1983* (Munk's Roll). Oxford: IRL Press, 1984.

NALIVKIN Nalivkin, D. V. *Nashi Pervye Zhenshchinye-geologi* (Our First Women Geologists). Leningrad: Nauka, 1979.

NBG Nouvelle biographie générale: Depuis les temps les plus reculés jusqu'à nos jours. 46 vols. Paris: Firmin Didot Frères, 1856.

NAW James, Edward T., ed. *Notable American Women, 1607–1950: a Biographical Dictionary.* 3 vols. Cambridge, Mass.: Belknap Press of Harvard University Press, 1973.

NAW(M) Sicherman, Barbara, and Carol Hurd Green, eds., *Notable American Women: The Modern Period: A Biographical Dictionary.* Cambridge, Mass.: Belknap Press of Harvard University Press, 1980.

NAW(UNUSED) *Notable American Women: The Modern Period Records, 1975–1980.* Schlesinger Library, Radcliffe Institute. MC 307, IV, series III.

NBAW Smith, Jessie Carney, ed. *Notable Black American Women.* 2 vols. Detroit: Gale, Research, 1992–1996.

NCAB National Cyclopedia of American Biography. Clifton, N.J.: J. T. White, 1891–.

NDB Neue Deutsche Biographie. Berlin: Duncker and Humblot, 1953–.

NEWNHAM Newnham College Register. 3 vols. Cambridge: Newnham College, 1871–1971.

NEWNHAM ROLL Newnham College Roll Letter. Cambridge: printed for private circulation, 1957.

NOTABLE MATHEMATICIANS Notable Mathematicians from Ancient Times to the Present. Ed. Robyn V. Young. Detroit: Gale, 1998.

NOTABLE/NOTABLE SUPPL. *Notable Twentieth-Century Scientists.* Ed. Emily McMurray. 4 vols. New York: Gale Research, 1995. Supplement, ed. K. M. Krapp, 1998.

O'CONNELL AND RUSSO 1988 O'Connell, Agnes N., and Nancy Felipe Russo. *Models of Achievement.* New York: Columbia University Press, 1983–1988.

O'CONNELL AND RUSSO 1990 O'Connell, Agnes N., and Nancy Felipe Russo. *Women in Psychology: A Bio-Bibliographic Sourcebook.* New York: Greenwood Press, 1990.

O'CONNOR O'Connor, W. J. *British Physiologists 1885–1914: A Biographical Dictionary.* Manchester: Manchester University Press, 1991.

OGILVIE 1986 Ogilvie, Marilyn Bailey. *Women in Science: Antiquity through the Nineteenth Century: A Biographical Dictionary with Annotated Bibliography.* Cambridge, Mass.: MIT Press, 1986.

OGILVIE 1996 ———. With Kerry Meek. *Women and Science: An Annotated Bibliography.* New York: Garland, 1996.

O'HERN O'Hern, Elizabeth Moot. *Profiles of Pioneer Woman Scientists.* New York: Acropolis Books: 1985.

O'NEILL O'Neill, Lois Decker, ed. *The Women's Book of World Records and Achievements.* Garden City, N.Y.: 1979.

OPFELL Opfell, Olga S. *The Lady Laureates: Women Who Have Won the Nobel Prize.* 2d ed. Metuchen, N.J.: Scarecrow Press, 1986.

OSBORN Osborn, Herbert. *A Brief History of Entomology.* Columbus, Ohio: Spahr and Glenn Company, 1952.

PAULY-WISSOWA Pauly, August Friedrich von. *Paulys Real-Encyclopädie der classichen Altertumswissenschaft.* Ed. G. Wissowa. Stuttgart: J. B. Metzler, 1891–.

PHILLIPS Phillips, Patricia. *The Scientific Lady: A Social History of Women's Scientific Interests, 1520–1918.* New York: St. Martin's, 1990.

POGGENDORFF Poggendorff, J.C. *Biographisch-literarisches Handworterbuch der Exakten Naturwissenschaften.* 7 vols. Berlin: Akademie-Verlag, 1863–1992.

PRAEGER Praeger, R. Lloyd. *Some Irish Naturalists: A Biographical Notebook.* Dundalk, W. Tempest: Dundalgen Press, 1949.

PSYCHOLOGICAL REGISTER Psychological Register. Ed. Carl Murchison. Worcester, Mass.: Clark University Press, 1929–.

RAYNER-CANHAM 1997 Rayner-Canham, Marelene F., and Geoffrey W. Rayner-Canham. *A Devotion to Their Science: Pioneer Women of Radioactivity.* Philadelphia, Penn.: Chemical Heritage Foundation, 1997.

RAYNER-CANHAM 1998 Rayner-Canham, Marelene F., and Geoffrey W. Rayner-Canham. *Women in Chemistry*. American Chemical Society and Chemical Heritage Foundation, 1998.

REP *Routledge Encyclopedia of Philosophy*. Ed. Edward Craig. 10 vols. London: Routledge, 1998.

REBIÈRE Rebière, A. *Les femmes dans la Science*. Paris: Nony, 1897.

ROSSITER 1982 Rossiter, Margaret. *Women Scientists in America: Struggles and Strategies to 1948*. Baltimore: Johns Hopkins University Press, 1982.

ROSSITER 1995 Rossiter, Margaret. *Women Scientists in America: Before Affirmative Action, 1940–1972*. Baltimore: Johns Hopkins University Press, 1995.

SARJEANT Sarjeant, William Antony S. *Geologists and the History of Geology: An International Bibliography from the Origins to 1978*. New York: Arno Press, 1980; 1987; 1996.

SCHIEBINGER Schiebinger, Londa. *The Mind Has No Sex? Women in the Origins of Modern Science*. Cambridge, Mass.: Harvard University Press, 1989.

SHEARER AND SHEARER 1996 Shearer, Benjamin F. and Barbara S. Shearer, eds. *Notable Women in the Life Sciences: A Biographical Dictionary*. Westport, Conn.: Greenwood Press, 1996.

SHEARER AND SHEARER 1997 Shearer, Benjamin F., and Barbara S. Shearer, eds. *Notable Women in the Physical Sciences. A Biographical Dictionary*. Westport, Conn.: Greenwood Press, 1997.

SHTEIR Shteir, Ann B. *Cultivating Women Cultivating Science: Flora's Daughters and Botany in England 1760–1860*. Baltimore: Johns Hopkins Press, 1996.

SIEGEL AND FINLEY Siegel Patricia Joan and Kay Thomas Finley. *Women in the Scientific Search: An American Bio-bibliography, 1724–1979*. Metuchen, N.J.: Scarecrow Press, 1985.

SOUTH AFRICAN DNB Rosenthal, R. *Southern African Dictionary of National Biography*. N.p., 1966.

SOVIET UNION *The Soviet Union: A Biographical Dictionary*. New York: Macmillan, 1990.

SPENDER Spender, Dale, and Janet Todd, eds. *British Women Writers: An Anthology from the Fourteenth Century to the Present*. New York: P. Bedrick Books, 1989.

STAFLEU AND COWAN Stafleu, Frans A, and R.S. Cowan, eds. *Taxonomic Literature: A Selective Guide to Botanical Publications and Collections with Dates, Commentaries and Types*. Utrecht: Bohn, Scheltema & Holkema, 1976–1988. Supplement, Ed. F. A. Stafleu and E. A. Mennega. Königstein, Germany: Koeltz Scientific Books, 1992.

STEVENS AND GARDNER Stevens, Gwendolyn, and Sheldon Gardner. *Women of Psychology*. Cambridge, Mass.: Schenkman, 1982.

STROHMEIER Strohmeier, Renate. *Lexikon der Naturwissenschaftlerinnen und naturkundigen Frauen Europas von der Antike bis zum 20. Jahrhundert*. Thun and Frankfurt am Main: Harri Deutsch, 1998.

STUCKEY Stuckey, Ronald. *Women Botanists of Ohio Born Before 1900*. Columbus, Ohio: Ohio State University, 1992.

TURKEVICH AND TURKEVICH Turkevich, John, and Turkevich, Ludmilla, comp. *Prominent Scientists of Continental Europe*. New York: American Elsevier Publishing Co., 1968.

TUVE Tuve, Jeanette E. *The First Russian Women Physicians*. Newtonville, Mass.: Oriental Research Partners, 1984.

UGLOW 1982 Uglow, Jennifer S., ed. *International Dictionary of Women's Biography*. New York: Continuum, 1982; 1989.

UGLOW 1989 Uglow, Jennifer S., ed. *Macmillan Dictionary of Women's Biography*. 2d. ed. New York: Macmillan, 1989.

UNEASY CAREERS Abir-Am, Pnina, and Dorinda Outram, eds. *Uneasy Careers and Intimate Lives: Women in Science, 1787–1979*. New Brunswick: Rutgers University Press, 1987.

VARE AND PTACEK Vare, Ethlie Ann, and Ptacek, Greg. *Mothers of Invention*. New York: Morrow, 1988.

VOGT Vogt, Annette, "The Kaiser-Wilhelm-Gesellschaft and the Career Chances for Female Scientists Between 1911 and 1945." Paper for International Congress for the History of Science, Liége, Belgium, 1997.

WAITHE Waithe, Mary Ellen. *Ancient Women Philosophers, 600 B.C.–500 A.D.* Dordrecht: Kluwer, 1987.

WALSH Walsh, James Joseph. *Medieval Medicine*. London: A. and C. Black, 1920.

WHO'S WHO OF AMERICAN WOMEN *Who's Who of American Women*. Chicago: Marquis Who's Who.

WOMAN'S WHO'S WHO OF AMERICA *Woman's Who's Who of America: A Biographical Dictionary of Contemporary Women of the United States and Canada*. Ed. John William Leonard. New York: American Commonwealth, 1914.

WOMEN PHYSIOLOGISTS Bindman, Lynn, Alison Brading, and Tilli Tansey eds. *Women Physiologists: An Anniversary Celebration of their Contributions to British Physiology*. London: Portland Press, 1992.

WOMEN IN WHITE Marks, Geoffrey, and Beatty, William K. *Women in White*. New York: Scribner, [1972].

WORLD WW OF WOMEN *World Who's Who of Women*. Cambridge: Melrose Press, 1973–.

WW *Who's Who*. London: A. and C. Black, 1849–.

WW IN AMERICA *Who's Who in America*. Chicago: Marquis Who's Who, 1899–.

WW IN AMERICAN EDUCATION *Who's Who in American Education*. Nashville, Tenn.: Who's Who in American Education, 1928–.

WW IN EDUCATION *Who's Who in Education*. Ed. G. E. Bowman and Nellie C. Ryan. Greeley, Colo.: 1927–.

WW IN FRANCE *Who's Who in France.* Paris: J. LaFitte, 1953–.

WW IN ITALY *Who's Who in Italy.* London: Eurospan, 1994.

WW IN THE MIDWEST *Who's Who in the Midwest.* Chicago: Marquis Who's Who, 1949–.

WW IN NEW YORK *Who's Who in New York City and State.* New York: L.R. Hamersly Co., 1904–.

WW IN SCIENCE IN EUROPE *Who's Who in Science in Europe.* Vol. 3. London: Francis Hogson, 1967.

WW IN SOVIET SCIENCE *Who's Who in Soviet Science.* Ed. Ina Telberg. New York: Telberg Book Co., 1960.

WW IN SWITZERLAND *Who's Who in Switzerland.* Zurich: Central European Times Publishing Co., 1952–.

WWW *Who Was Who.* Vols. 1–9. London: A. and C. Black, 1920–1996.

WWW(A) *Who Was Who in America.* Chicago, Marquis Who's Who.

WWW(UUSR) *Who Was Who in the USSR: A Biographic Directory Containing Biographies of Prominent Soviet Historical Personalities.* Ed. Heinrich E. Schulz, Paul K. Urban, and Andrew I. Lebed. Metuchen, N.J., Scarecrow Press.

YOST Yost, Edna. *Women of Modern Science.* New York: Dodd, Mead & Co., 1959.

ZUSNE Zusne, L. *Names in the History of Psychology.* Washington, D.C.: Hemisphere, 1975.

ADDITIONAL REFERENCES

Allgemeine deutsche biographie. Ed. Rocus von Liliencron. 56 vols. Leipzig: Verlag von Duncker and Humblot, 1875–1912.

Allibone, S.A. *A Critical Dictionary of English Literature.* Philadelphia: Lippincott, 1872.

Burke's Peerage and Baronetage. 105th ed.; London: Burke's Peerage, 1980.

Crone, John S. *Concise Dictionary of Irish Biography.* Dublin: Talbot Press, 1928,

Cyclopedia of American Medical Biography. Philadelphia: W. B. Saunders, 1912.

Hall, Diana Long. "Academics, Blue Stockings and Biologists: Women at the University of Chicago, 1892–1932." *Annals of the New York Academy of Sciences* 323 (1979).

La Grande Encyclopédie, inventaire raisonné des sciences, des lettres et des arts, par une société de savants et de gens de lettres. Ed.

A. Berthelot. 31 vols. Paris: Lamirault et cie; vols. 23–31 published by the Societe anonyme de la grande encyclopédie, [1886–1902].

Leaders in American Science. Ed. Robert C. Cook. Who's Who in American Education, Inc., [1953–].

Larousse Biographical Dictionary of Scientists. Ed. Hazel Muir. New York: Larousse, 1994.

Lovejoy, Esther. *Women Physicians and Surgeons.* Livingston, N.Y.: Livingston Press, 1939.

Magill, Frank N., ed. *Physics,* 831–839. Vol. 2 of *The Nobel Prize Winners.* Pasadena, Calif. and Englewood Cliffs, N.J.: Salem Press, 1989.

National Academy of Sciences. *Biographical Memoirs (National Academy of Sciences).* New York: Columbia University Press, 1960.

National Union Catalog, Pre-1956 Imprints: A Cumulative Author List Representing Library of Congress Printed Cards and Titles Reported By Other American Libraries. Comp. and ed. with the cooperation of the Library of Congress and the National Union Catalog Subcommittee of the Resources and Technical Services Divisions, American Library Association. London: Mansell, 1968–1980.

Osborn, Herbert. *Fragments of Entomological History.: Including Some Personal Recollections of Men and Events.* Columbus, Ohio: privately printed, 1937.

Royal Society of London. 1902–1921. *International Catalogue of Scientific Literature, 1901–1914.* 14 vols. London: Royal Society, n.d. Reprint, 32 vols, New York: Johnson, 1968–1969.

Rudolph, E. D. "Women Who Studied Plants in the Pre-Twentieth Century United States and Canada." *Taxon,* 39, no. 2, 1990: 151–205.

Sammons, Vivian O. *Blacks in Science and Medicine.* New York: Hemisphere, 1990.

Sheehy, Noel, J. Chapman, and Wendy A. Conroy, eds. *Biographical Dictionary of Psychology.* London: Routledge, 1997.

Turkevich, John. *Soviet Men of Science: Academicians and Corresponding Members of the Academy of Sciences of the USSR.* Westport, Conn.: Greenwood, 1963.

Yost, Edna. *American Women of Science.* Philadelphia: Frederick A. Stokes Co., 1943.

CONTRIBUTORS

TATIANA BRESINSKY

Tatiana Bresinsky has a B.S. in History from the University of Maine, a B.S. in Religious Studies from Boston University, and an MLIS from the University of Oklahoma. She has been the science librarian at the Nantucket Maria Mitchell Association, assistant librarian at the Burndy Library, and is now a science reference librarian at MIT. Her research interests are in women in science, science in religion, science in literature, and the history of modern astronomy and cosmology.

CECILIA BROWN

Cecilia Brown holds a Ph.D. in nutritional sciences from the University of Illinois, Urbana-Champaign, and an M.L.I.S. (master's degree in library and information studies) from the University of Oklahoma. She currently is an Assistant Professor of Bibliography and the Chemistry-Mathematics Librarian at the University of Oklahoma and is a co-author of *The Biographical Encyclopedia of Women Healers,* to be published by ORYX Press in 2001.

JOANN EISBERG

JoAnn Eisberg earned both her bachelor's and her doctoral degree from Harvard University. She teaches at the University of California, Santa Barbara, in the physics department and is affiliated with the history of science department. She won the Pollock prize from the Dudley Observatory.

PATRICIA FARA

Patricia Fara holds an honours bachelor's degree in Physics from Oxford University and both an M.Sc. and Ph.D. in the history of science from Imperial College, London. She is a fellow of Clare College, Cambridge University, and she lectures in the Department of History and Philosophy of Science, also at Cambridge. Her major book is *Sympathetic Attractions: Magnetic Practices, Beliefs, and Symbolism in Eighteenth-Century England* (Princeton, 1996). She has also coedited two collections of essays, *Memory and The Changing World* (both from

Cambridge University Press). She is currently writing *Under Newton's Apple Tree* (to be published by Picador Press), an examination of how Newton became a scientific and national hero and of what it means to be a genius.

MARGOT FUCHS

Margot Fuchs earned a B.A. in modern history from the University of York in Great Britain and an M.A. in modern and medieval history and English literature from the University of Munich. Currently, she is Head of the Archive at the Technical University of Munich. Among her publications is the book *Wie die Väter so die Töchter: Frauenstudium an der Technischen Hochschule München* (1994).

INGRID GUENTHERODT

Ingrid Guentherodt earned her first degrees in Germany. She holds a Ph.D. from the University of Texas. She has taught in both the United States and Germany, and since 1972 she has held a tenured position at the University of Trier. She has published extensively on women in science, including "'Dreyfache Verenderung' und 'Wunderbare Verwandelung': Zu Forschung und Sprache der Naturwissenschaftlerinnen Maria Cunitz (1610–1664) und Maria Sibylla Merian (1647)" in *Deutsche Literatur von Frauen.* (1988); "Maria Cunitia: Urania Propitia. Intendiertes, erwartetes und tatsächliches Lesepublikum einer Astronomin des 17. Jahrhunderts" in *Daphnis* (1991); and a contribution to *Religion und Religiosität in Zeitalter des Barock* (1995).

JOY HARVEY

Joy Harvey earned her doctorate in history of science from Harvard University and has taught at Harvard University, Skidmore College, Sarah Lawrence College, and Virginia Polytechnic Institute. She was an associate editor with the Darwin Correspondence Project at the Cambridge University Library. Her biography of Darwin's first French translator, Clémence Royer, *Almost a Man of Genius: Clémence*

Royer, Feminism and Nineteenth Century Science, was published by Rutgers University Press in 1997. She has published extensively and is now preparing a biography of the nineteenth-century American woman physician Mary Putnam Jacobi.

ANNE C. HUGHES

Anne Hughes is an alumna of Radcliffe College and a graduate of the University of Lancaster, England. She received a Ph.D. in 1978 from the University of Lancaster and a Postgraduate Diploma in Librarianship in 1980 from Liverpool Polytechnic. She has worked as a librarian at Harvard University, at Somerville Hospital, and at an engineering firm, Haley & Aldrich, Inc., and she has various publications in the field of Soviet literature.

CLAREN KIDD

Claren Kidd earned both her B.A. and M.A. from the University of Oklahoma and an M.L.S. degree from the University of Pittsburgh. She is Professor of Bibliography and librarian for the L.S. Youngblood Energy Library at the University of Oklahoma. She has published bibliographical reference books on Oklahoma geology, geological field trip guidebooks, works on the redistribution of geological literature, and the "Union List of Geological Field Excursions of Australia." She is a member and past president of the Geoscience Information Society.

SHARON SUE KLEINMAN

Sharon Sue Kleinman is a doctoral student in the Department of Communication at Cornell University, with research interests focusing on gender and communication, especially with regard to science and emerging communication technologies. Her publications include biographical essays on women in science, articles on communications theory, and interviews with literary figures.

SALLY GREGORY KOHLSTEDT

Sally Gregory Kohlstedt holds a B.A. from Valparaiso University and a Ph.D. from the University of Illinois. She is currently professor in the History of Science and Technology Program at the University of Minnesota, where she has also served as Director of Feminist Studies. Among her recent publications relating to women in science are several edited books, including *Gender and Scientific Authority,* with Barbara Laslett, Helen Longino, and Evelyn Hammons (University of Chicago Press, 1996); "Women, Gender, and Science: New Directions," with Helen Longino, in *Osiris* (1997); and *Women in Science: An Isis Reader* (1999).

GERIT VON LEITNER

Gerit von Leitner earned her Ph.D. from the University of Munich and degrees in pedagogy from the University of Cologne. Since 1987 she has worked as a historian, writer, filmmaker, and radio feature writer. She has published numerous works on women in science, including a biography of Clara Immerwahr, *Der Fall Clara Immerwahr: Leben für eine humane Wissenschaft* (1993); "Frauenraum Naturwissenschafter? Clara Immerwahr und Gertrud Woker." in *Friedensentwürfe* (1995); and a biography of Gertrud Woker, *Wollen wir unsere Hände in Unschuld waschen? Gertrud Woker (1878–1968)* (1998).

BERNARD LIGHTMAN

Bernard Lightman received his Ph.D. in the history of ideas from Brandeis University. Currently he is Professor of Humanities at York University in Toronto, Canada. Among his publications are "The Origins of Agnosticism"; Victorian Faith in Crisis," co-edited with Richard Helmstadter; and "Victorian Science in Context."

SYLVIA MCGRATH

Sylvia McGrath holds a B.A. from Michigan State University, an M.A. from Radcliffe College, and a Ph.D. from the University of Wisconsin, Madison. She is Professor of History at Stephen F. Austin State University, was Regents' Professor for 1994–1995, and will become chair of the department in 2000. She has published extensively and is currently researching the life and work of Frieda Cobb Blanchard, a plant geneticist and zoologist who worked during the first half of the twentieth century.

MARJORIE MALLEY

Marjorie Malley earned a B.S. in physics and philosophy from the Massachusetts Institute of Technology, an M.A.T. from Harvard University, and a Ph.D. from the University of California, Berkeley. She has been active in various capacities in the field of science and mathematics education. Her publications include papers on the history of radioactivity and the history of optical luminescence, reviews, and numerous biographical and topical articles in the history of science.

KERRY L. MEEK (WHITNEY)

Kerry L. Meek holds a B.A. in French and a master's degree in library science. With Marilyn Ogilvie she published *Women and Science: An Annotated Bibliography* (Garland, 1996).

ANNA E. MOORE

Anna Moore holds an A.B. *cum laude* degree in English and an M.L.I.S. (master's degree in library and information studies) from the University of Oklahoma. She has worked as a temporary instructor at the University of Oklahoma Libraries, was the Information Services Librarian for the Norman (Oklahoma) Public Library, and is currently the Library System Trainer for the Pioneer Library System and Young Adult Librarian for the the Norman Public Library.

SIBYLLE NAGLER-SPRINGMANN

Sibylle Nagler-Springmann studied history and French in Düsseldorf, Cologne, and Paris, followed by attendance at journalism school in Cologne. She works as a free lance journalist and on historical projects. She publishes on science in secondary education and women's history, in German newspapers and magazines. Among her publications about women in the natural sciences are a chapter in an exposition and catalogue, "Stieftöchter der Alma Mater, 90 Jahre Frauenstudium in Bayern am Beispiel der Universität München" (1993) and an article on Ruth Beutler in *Bedrolich Gescheit: Ein Jahrhundert Frauen und Wissenschaft in Bayern* (1997).

MARILYN BAILEY OGILVIE

Marilyn Ogilvie holds an A.B. from Baker University, an M.A. in zoology from the University of Kansas, and an M.A. in library science and a Ph.D. in the history of science from the University of Oklahoma. She is Professor and Curator of the History of Science Collections at the University of Oklahoma. Her publications include *Women in Science: An Annotated Bibliography, A Dame Full of Vim and Vigor: A Biography of Alice Middleton Boring* (with Clifford Choquette), and *Women in Science: Antiquity through the Nineteenth Century.* She has contributed numerous chapters in books and articles in journals.

SYLVIA PATTERSON

Sylvia Patterson earned a B.A. and is doing advanced work in art history/museum studies and film studies.

MARITA A. PANZER

Marita Panzer earned her doctor of philosophy degree and worked at the Universities of Munich and Regensburg. She now works as a freelance historian and author in Munich and Regensburg. Among her publications are *Barbara Blomberg (1527–1597): Bürgerstochter und Kaisergeliebte* (1995) and *Bavarias Töchter: Frauenporträts aus fünf Jahrhunderten* (1997).

MARJA LEENA ROGERS

Marja Leena Rogers received a B.A. from Brigham Young University and did post-graduate work in museology and the history of science at the University of Oklahoma. Now Executive Assistant to the CEO and President of PowerQuest Corporation in Orem, Utah, she is continuing her research on Hildegarde Howard Wylde, an early Avian paleontologist.

NINA MATHENY ROSCHER

Nina Roscher received her bachelor's degree from the University of Delaware and her Ph.D. from Purdue University. She is Professor and Chair of the Department of Chemistry at American University in Washington, D.C. Roscher's research interests are in physical organic chemistry. She is active in the American Chemical Society and was chair of the Women Chemists Committee. In September 1998 she received a Presidential Award for Excellence in Science, Mathematics, and Engineering Mentoring. Roscher recently completed the book *Women Chemists 1995* for the American Chemical Society.

MARGARET ROSSITER

Margaret W. Rossiter is the Marie Underhill Noll Professor of History of Science at Cornell University and the editor of *Isis* and *Osiris.* She is the author of numerous publications, including *Women Scientists in America: Struggles and Strategies to 1940* and *Women Scientists in America: Before Affirmative Action, 1940–1972.*

ANNE SECORD

Anne Secord was trained in history of science at London University. She worked as assistant editor of *The Correspondence of Charles Darwin* for the first seven volumes and is currently an Affiliated Research Scholar in the Department of History and Philosophy of Science, Cambridge University. Her research focuses on popular, particularly working-class, natural history in nineteenth-century Britain.

SUZANNE LE-MAY SHEFFIELD

Suzanne Le-May Sheffield received an Honours B.A. and an M.A., and a Ph.D. in history from York University. She is currently Assistant Professor of History at Dalhousie University. Her book on Margaret Gatty, Marianne North, and Eleanor Ormerod is being published by Harwood Academic.

RUTH LEWIN SIME

Ruth Sime received a B.A. in mathematics from Barnard College and a Ph.D. in physical chemistry from Harvard University. At present, she is Professor of Chemistry at Sacramento City College. Her educational focus is on increasing the participation of women and nontraditional minorities in the math-based sciences. Her research interests are in the history of science. She is the author of *Lise Meitner: A Life in Physics* (1996).

RENATE TOBIES

Renate Tobies studied mathematics and chemistry at the University of Leipzig and earned her doctoral and postdoctoral degrees there. She is presently employed in the mathematics department at the University of Kaiserlautern and holds the Sofia-Kovalevskaia Guest Professorship. She is managing editor of the *International Journal of History and Ethics of Natural Sciences, Technology, and Medicine.* She has published six books and more than fifty articles, including works on the mathematician Felix Klein and a book on women in mathematics and natural sciences, *"Aller Männerkultur Zum Trotz": Frauen in Mathematik und Naturwissenschaften* (1997).

ALPHABETICAL
LIST OF ENTRIES

Bailey, Florence Augusta (Merriam)
Baker, Anne Elizabeth
Baker, Sara Josephine
Baker, Sarah Martha
Bakwin, Ruth (Morris)
Balaam, Ellen
Balfour, Margaret Ida
Balk, Christina (Lochman)
Ball, Anne Elizabeth
Ball, Josephine
Ball, Mary
Ballard, Julia Perkins Pratt
Bancroft, Nellie
Bang, Duck-Heung
Banga, Ilona
Banham, Katherine May
Banks, Sarah Sophia
Barbapiccola, Giuseppa Eleonora
Barbarshova, Zoya
Barber, Helen Karen
Barber, Mary Elizabeth (Bowker)
Bari, Nina Karlovna
Barkly, Lady Anna Maria (Pratt)
Barkly, Lady Elizabeth Helen (Timins or
    Timmins)
Barlett, Helen Blair
Barlow, Lady Emma Nora Darwin
Barnard, Alicia Mildred
Barnard, Edith Ethel
Barnard, Lady Anne (Henslow)
Barnard, Lady Anne (Lindsay)
Barnes (Berners), Juliana
Barney, Ida
Barney, Nora Stanton (Blatch) De Forest
Barnothy, Madeleine (Forro)
Barnum, Charlotte Cynthia
Barrera, Oliva Sabuca de Nantes
Barringer, Emily Dunning
Barrows, Katherine Isabel Hayes Chapin
Barry, James (pseudonym)
Barton, Clara Harlowe
Barton, Lela Viola
Bascom, Florence
Bass, Mary Elizabeth
Bassi, Laura Maria Caterina
Batchelder, Esther Lord
Bate, Dorothea Minola Alice
Bates, Mary E.
Bateson, Anna
Bateson, Beatrice
Battle, Helen Irene
Bauer, Grace M.
Baum, Marie
Baumann, Frieda
Baumgarten-Tramer, Franziska
Baumgartner, Leona
Baxter, Mildred Frances
Bayern, Therese von
Bayley, Nancy
Baynard, Anne
Beanland, Sarah
Beatley, Janice Carson
Beatrice of Savoy, Countess of Provence
Beatrice, Medica of Candia
Beaufort, Countess Margaret

Beaufort, Harriet Henrietta
Beausoleil, Martine de Bertereau
Beauvallet, Marcelle Jeanne
Beck, Sarah Coker (Adams)
Becker, Lydia Ernestine
Becker- Rose, Herta
Beckman, A.
Beckwith, Angie Maria
Beckwith, Cora
Beckwith, Martha Warren
Beecher, Catharine Esther
Beers, Catherine Virginia
Beever, Mary
Beever, Susan
Behn, Aphra
Behre, Ellinor H.
Beilby, Winifred
Belaeva, Elizaveta Ivanovna
Belar, Maria
Bell, Julia
Belota [Johanna Belota]
Belyea, Helen Reynolds
Bender, Hedwig
Bender, Lauretta
Bender, W.
Benedek, Therese F.
Benedict, Ruth (Fulton)
Benett, Etheldred
Bengston, Ida Albertina
Bennett, Alice
Bennett, Dorothea
Benson, Margaret Jane
Bentham, Ethel
Bentham, Lady Mary Sophia (Fordyce)
Bentinck, Margaret Cavendish (Harley),
    Duchess of Portland
Berger, Emily V.
Berger, Katharina Bertha Charlotte
Berners, Juliana See Barnes, Juliana
Beronice
Berridge, Emily Mary
Bertereau, Martine de, Baroness de
    Beausoleil
Berthagyta, Abbess
Berthildis of Chelles
Bertile of Chelles
Bertillon, Caroline Schultze
Besant, Annie (Wood)
Beutler, Ruth
Bevier, Isabel
Bhatia, Sharju Pandit
Bibring, Grete Lehner
Bickerdyke, Mary Ann (Ball)
Bidder, Anna McClean
Bidder, Marion Greenwood
Biheron, Marie Catherine
Bilger, Leonora (Neuffer)
Billings, Katharine Stevens (Fowler– Lunn)
Bingham, Millicent (Todd)
Bird, Grace Electa
Bird, Isabella See Bishop, Isabella Bird
Birdsall, Lucy Ellen
Birstein, Vera
Biscot, Jeanne
Bishop, Ann

Bishop, Isabella Lucy Bird
Bishop, Katharine Scott
Bissell, Emily P.
Bitting, Katherine Eliza (Golden)
Black, Florence
Black, Hortensia
Blackburn, Kathleen Bever
Blackburne, Anna
Blacker, Margaret Constance Helen
Blackwell, Antoinette Louise (Brown)
Blackwell, Elizabeth
Blackwell, Elizabeth
Blackwell, Elizabeth Marianne
Blackwell, Emily
Blackwood, Beatrice Mary
Blagg, Mary Adela
Blake, Mary Safford
Blanchan, Neltje (pseud.)
Blanchard, Frieda Cobb
Blanchard, Phyllis
Blanquies, Lucie
Blatchford, Ellen C.
Blau, Marietta
Bledsoe, Lucybelle
Blinova, Ekaterina Nikitichna
Bliss, Dorothy Elizabeth
Bliss, Eleanor, Albert
Bliss, Mary Campbell
Block, Jeanne (Humphrey)
Blodgett, Katharine Burr
Bluhm, Agnes
Bluket, Nina Aleksandrovna
Blunt, Katharine
Bocchi (Bucca), Dorotea
Bochantseva, Zinaida Petrovna
Bodley, Rachel Littler
Bogdanovskaia, Vera Evstaf'evna
Böhm- Wendt, Cäcilia
Boivin, Marie Gillain
Bokova– Sechenova, Mariia Aleksandrovna
Boley, Gertrude Maud
Bolschanina, M. A.
Bolton, Edith
Bolus, Harriet Margaret Louisa (Kensit)
Bomhard, Miriam Lucile
Bonnay, Marchioness du
Bonnevie, Kristine
Boole, Mary (Everest)
Boos, Margaret Bradley (Fuller)
Booth, Mary Ann Allard
Boring, Alice Middleton
Borisova- Bekriasheva, Antoniia
    Georgievna
Boron, Elizabeth (Riddle) Graves
Borromeo, Clelia Grillo
Borsarelli, Fernanda
Boswell, Katherine Cumming
Bourdel, Léone
Bourgeoise, Louyse
Bouteiller, Marcelle
Bouthilet, Lorraine
Boveri, Marcella Imelda O'Grady
Bowen, Susan
Boyd, Elizabeth Margaret
Boyd, Louise Arner

Boyer, Esther Lydia
Bracher, Rose
Bradley, Amy Morris
Bradley, Frances Sage
Brahe, Sophia
Branch, Hazel Elisabeth
Brand, Martha
Brandegee, Mary Katharine Layne
Branham, Sara Elizabeth
Brant, Laura
Braun, (Emma) Lucy
Braun, Annette Frances
Brazier, Mary Agnes Burniston (Brown)
Breckinridge, Mary
Bredikhina, Evgeniia Aleksandrovna
Breed, Mary (Bidwell)
Brenchley, Winifred Elsie
Brenk, Irene
Brès Madeleine (Gébelin)
Breyer, Maria Gerdina (Brandwijk)
Brezina, Maria Aristides
Bridget, Saint, of Ireland
Bridget, Saint, of Scandinavia
Bridgman, Olga Louise
Brière, Nicole-Reine Etable de la.
Brière, Yvonne
Brightwen, Eliza (Elder)
Britten, Lilian Louisa
Britton, Elizabeth Knight
Broadhurst, Jean
Brock, Sylvia (DeAntonis)
Bromley, Helen Jean (Brown)
Bronner, Augusta Fox
Brooke, Winifred
Brooks, Harriet T.
Brooks, Matilda (Moldenhauer)
Brooks, Sarah Theresa
Broomall, Anna Elizabeth
Brousseau, Kate
Brown, Charlotte Amanda Blake
Brown, Dame Edith Mary
Brown, Elizabeth
Brown, Fay Cluff
Brown, Mabel Mary
Brown, Nellie Adalesa
Brown, Rachel Fuller
Browne, Ida Alison (Brown)
Browne, Lady Isabel Mary (Peyronnet)
Browne, Marjorie Lee
Bruce, Catherine Wolfe
Bruce, Eileen Adelaide
Brüch, Hilde
Brückner, Frau Dr.
Brunetta
Brunetti, R.
Brunfels, Frau Otto
Brunswick, Ruth Jane (Mack)
Bryan, Alice Isabel (Bever)
Bryan, Margaret
Bryan, Mary Katherine
Bryant, Louise Stevens
Bryant, Sophie (Willock)
Bucca, Dorotea.
Buchanan, Florence

Buchbinder, Laura G. Ordan
Buckel, Chloe A.
Buckland, Mary Morland
Buckley, Arabella
Buell, Mary Van Rensselaer
Buerk, Minerva (Smith)
Bühler, Charlotte Bertha (Malachowski)
Bülbring, Edith
Bull, Nina Wilcox
Bunch, Cordia
Bunting, Martha
Bunting-Smith, Mary (Ingraham)
Bunzel, Ruth Leah
Burges, Mary Anne
Burgess, May (Ayres)
Burkill, Ethel Maud (Morrison)
Burlingham, Dorothy (Tiffany)
Burlingham, Gertrude Simmons
Burns, Eleanor Irene
Burns, Louisa
Burr, Emily Thorp
Burrell, Anna Porter
Burton, Helen Marie Rousseay
   (Kannemeyer)
Burtt Davy, Alice (Bolton)
Bury, Elizabeth (Lawrence)
Bury, Priscilla Susan (Falkner)
Bush, Katharine Jeannette
Busk, Lady Marian (Balfour)
Bussecker, Erna
Buttelini, Marchesa
Bykhovskaia, Anna Markovna
Byrd, Mary Emma
Byrnes, Esther Fussell
Byron, Augusta Ada, Countess of Lovelace
Cadbury, Dorothy Adlington
Cadilla de Martínez, María
Cady, Bertha Louise Chapman
Caerellia (Caerelia)
Caetani-Bovatelli, Donna Ersilia
Calderone, Mary S.
Caldwell, Mary Letitia
Cale, F. M.
Calenda, Constanza or Laurea Constantia
Calkins, Mary Whiton
Callcott, Lady Maria Graham
Calvert, Catherine Louisa Waring
   (Atkinson)
Calvert, Emily Amelia (Adelia)
Cambrière, Clarisse
Campbell, Dame Janet Mary
Campbell, Helen Stuart
Campbell, May Sherwood
Campbell, Persia Crawford
Cannon, Annie Jump
Capen, Bessie
Carlson, Elizabeth
Carlson, Lucille
Carne, Elizabeth Catherine (Thomas)
Carothers, Estrella Eleanor
Carpenter, Esther
Carr, Emma Perry
Carroll, Chris tiane (Mendrez)
Carroll, Dorothy

Carson, Rachel Louise
Carter, Edna
Carter, Elizabeth
Cartwright, Dame Mary Lucy
Carus, Mary Hegeler
Carvajales y Camino, Laura M. de
Castle, Cora (Sutton)
Castra, Anna de
Catani, Giuseppina
Catherine of Bologna, Saint
Catherine of Genoa, Saint
Catherine of Siena, Saint
Catherine Ursula, Countess of Baden
Catherine, Medica of Cracow
Catlow, Maria Agnes
Cattell, Psyche
Cattoi, Noemí Violeta
Cauchois, Yvette
Caughlan, Georgeanne (Robertson)
Cauquil, Germaine Anne
Cavendish, Margaret, Duchess of
   Newcastle
Cellier, Elizabeth
Cesniece-Freudenfelde, Zelma
Chaix, Paulette Audemard
Chalubinska, Aniela
Chamié, Catherine
Chandler, Elizabeth
Chandler, Marjorie Elizabeth Jane
Chang, Moon Gyung
Chang, Vivian
Charles, Vera Katherine
Charlotte Sophia, Queen
Charsley, Fanny Anne
Chase, Mary Agnes Meara
Chasman, Renate Wiener
Châtelet, Gabrielle-Emilie Le Tonnelier de
   Breuteuil, Marquise du
Chauchard, B.
Chaudet, Maria Casanova de
Cheesman, Lucy Evelyn
Chenoweth, Alice Drew
Chesser, Elizabeth (Sloan)
Chick, Dame Harriette
Child, Lydia Maria (Francis)
Chinchon, Countess of
Chinn, May Edward
Chisholm, Catherine
Chisholm, Grace Emily
Chmielewska, Irene
Chodak-Gregory, Hazel Haward
   (Cuthbert)
Christen, Sydney Mary (Thompson)
Christina, Queen of Sweden
Church, Elda Rodman (MacIlvaine)
Chute, Hettie Morse
Cilento, Lady Phyllis
Cinquini, Maria dei Conti Cibrario
Cioranescu-Nenitzescu, Ecaterina
Clapp, Cornelia Maria
Clappe, Louisa Amelia (Smith)
Clara (Clare) of Assisi, Saint
Clarisse of Rotomago (or Clarice of
   Rouen)

Clark, Bertha
Clark, Frances N.
Clark, Janet Howell
Clark, Jessie Jane
Clark, Lois
Clark, Mamie Katherine (Phipps)
Clark, Nancy Talbot
Clarke, Cora Huidekoper
Clarke, Edith
Clarke, Lilian Jane
Clarke, Louisa (Lane)
Clay-Jolles, Tettje Clasina
Claypole, Agnes Mary
Claypole, Edith Jane
Clea
Cleachma
Clemens, Mary Knapp (Strong)
Clements, Edith Gertrude (Schwartz)
Clements, Margaret
Cleobulina of Rhodes
Cleopatra
Clerke, Agnes Mary
Clerke, Ellen Mary
Cleve-Euler, Astrid
Cleveland, Emeline Horton
Clifford, Lady Anne
Clinch, Phyllis E. M.
Clisby, Harriet Jemima Winifred
Clothilde of Burgundy
Coade, Eleanor
Coates, Sarah J.
Cobb, Margaret Vera
Cobb, Rosalie M. Karapetoff
Cobbe, Anne Phillipa
Cobbe, Frances Power
Cobbe, Margaret
Cochran, Doris Mabel
Cockburn, Catharine (Trotter)
Cockrell, Wilmatte (Porter)
Cohn, Essie White
Coignou, Caroline Pauline Marie
Colby, Martha Guernsey
Colcord, Mabel
Colden, Jane
Cole, Emma J.
Cole, Rebecca J.
Collet, Clara Elizabeth
Collett, Mary Elizabeth
Collins, Katharine Richards
Colvin, Brenda
Comnena (Comnenos), Anna
Comstock, Anna Botsford
Comyns-Lewer, Ethel
Cone, Claribel
Conklin, Marie (Eckhardt)
Conklin, Ruth Emelene
Converse, Jeanne
Conway, Anne
Conway, Elsie (Phillips)
Cook, A. Grace
Cook, Margaret C.
Cooke, Alice Sophia (Smart)
Cookson, Isabel Clifton
Cooley, Jacquelin Smith

Coombs, Helen Copeland
Cooper, Clara Chassell
Cooper, Elizabeth Morgan
Cooper, Susan Fenimore
Cooper, Sybil
Cooper-Ellis, Katharine Murdoch
Copeland, Lennie Phoebe
Cordier, Marguerite Jeanne
Cori, Gerty Theresa Radnitz
Cornaro (Cornero), Elena (Helena)
    Lucretia
Cornelius-Furlani, Marta
Coryndon, Shirley (Cameron)
Coste Blanche, Marie de
Cotelle, Sonia
Cotter, Brigid M.
Coudreau, Octavie
Cowan, Edwina Abbott
Cox, Gertrude Mary
Cox, Rachel (Dunaway)
Coyle, Elizabeth Eleanor
Cram, Eloise Blaine
Cramer, Catherine Gertrude du Tertre
    Schraders
Crandall, Ella Phillips
Crane, Agnes
Crane, Jocelyn
Cranwell, Lucy May
Cremer, Erika
Crespin, Irene
Crocker, Lucretia
Croll, Hilda M.
Crosbie, May
Crosby, Elizabeth Caroline
Crosfield, Margaret Chorley
Csepreghyné-Meznerics, Ilona
Cuffe, Lady Charlotte Wheeler (Williams)
Cullis, Winifred
Cumming, Lady Gordon (Eliza Maria
    Campbell)
Cummings, Clara Eaton
Cummings, Louise Duffield
Cunio, Isabella
Cunitz, Maria
Cunningham, Bess Virginia
Cunningham, Gladys Story
Cunningham, Susan
Curie, Marie (Maria Sklodowska)
Currie, Ethel Dobbie
Curtis, Doris Sarah (Malkin)
Curtis, Natalie
Cushier, Elizabeth
Cushing, Hazel Morton
Cushman, Florence
Cuthbert-Browne, Grace Johnston
Cutler, Catherine
Czaplicka, marie antoinette
Czeczottowa, Hanna (Peretiatkowicza)
Dalai, Maria Jolanda (Tosoni)
Dalby, Mary
Dale, Elizabeth
Dallas, A. E. M. M.
Dalle Donne, Maria
Damo

Dane, Elisabeth
Daniel, Anne Sturges
Daniels, Amy L.
Danti or Dante, Theodora
Darwin, Emma (Wedgwood)
Dashkova, Princess Ekaterina Romanovna
Daulton, Agnes Warner McClelland
Davenport, Gertrude (Crotty)
David, Florence N.
Davidson, Ada D.
Davis, Adelle
Davis, Alice (Rohde)
Davis, Frances (Elliott)
Davis, Grace Evangeline
Davis, Katharine Bement
Davis, Marguerite
Davis, Olive Griffith Stull
Davis, Rose May
Davy, Lady Joanna Charlotte (Flemmich)
Dawson, Maria
Day, Dorothy
Day, Gwendolen Helen
Day, Mary Anna
De Almania, Jacqueline Felicia
De Bréauté, Eléonore-Nell-Suzanne
De Chantal, Mme.
De Fraine, Ethel Louise
De Gorzano, Leonetta
De Graffenried, Mary Clare
De la Cruz, Juana Inés
De la Marche, Marguerite du Tertre
De Laguna, Fredericka Annis Lopez de
    Leo
De Lange, Cornelia Catharina
De Lebrix, Françoise
De Marillac, Louise, Mlle, Le Gras.
De Milt, Clara Marie
De Mole, Fanny Elizabeth
De Staël Holstein, Anne Louise Germaine
    Necker
De Valera, Mairin
De Valois, Madame
De Vesian, Dorothy Ellis
De Witt, Lydia Maria Adams
Decker, Jane Cynthia (McLaughlin)
Deflandre-Rigaud, Marthe
Deichmann, Elisabeth
Déjerine-Klumpke, Augusta
Delaney (or Delany), Mary (Granville),
Delap, Maude Jane
Delauney, Marguerite de Staël
Delf-Smith, Ellen Marion
Deloria, Ella Cara
Dembo, Tamara
Dempsey, Sister Mary Joseph
Demud
Dengel, Anna Maria
Denis, Willey Glover
Dennett, Mary Ware
Dennis, Olive Wetzel
Densmore, Frances Theresa
Derick, Carrie M.
Derscheid-Delcourt, Marie
Detmers, Frederica

Deutsch, Helene Rosenback
Dewey, Jane Mary (Clark)
Di Novella, Maria
Diana of Poitiers
Dick, Gladys Rowena Henry
Dickerson, Mary Cynthia
Dietrich, Amalie
Diggs, Ellen Irene
Dimock, Susan
Dimsdale, Helen Easdale (Brown)
Dinnerstein, Dorothy
Diotima of Mantinea
Dix, Dorothea Lynde
Dobrolubova, Tatiana A.
Dobroscky, Irene Dorothy
Dobrowolska, H.
Dobson, Mildred E.
Dock, Lavinia Lloyd
Dodd, Katharine
Dodds, Mary Letitia
Dodgson, Sarah Elizabeth
Dodson, Helen Walter
Doering, Kathleen Clara
Dohan, Edith Haywood Hall
Dokhman, Genrietta Isaakovna
Dolgopol de Saez, Mathilde
Dolley, Sarah Read Adamson
Dombrovskaia, Iuliia Fominichna
Donnay, Gabrielle (Hamburger)
Dooley, Lucile
Dorabialska, Alicja Domenica
Doreck, Hertha (Walburger Doris Sieverts)
Dorenfeldt, Margot
Dorety, Angela
Dormon, Caroline
Doubleday, Neltje Blanchan (De Graff)
Dougal, Margaret Douie
Douglas, Alice Vibert
Dover, Mary Violette
Downey, June Etta
Downey, K. Melvina
Downie, Dorothy G.
Downs, Cornelia Mitchell
Drake, Judith
Drant, Patricia (Hart)
Draper, Mary Anna Palmer
Drebeneva-Ukhova, Varvara Pavlovna
Drew, Kathleen Mary
Drinker, Katherine (Rotan)
Drummond, Margaret
Du Bois, Cora
Du Châtelet, Gabrielle-Emilie Le
  Tonnelier de Breteuil (Marquise)
Du Coudray, Angelique (Marguerite le
  Boursier)
Du Luys, Guillemette
Dubuisson-Brouha, Adele
Duffy, Elizabeth
Duges, Marie-Louise
Dumée, Jeanne
Dummer, Ethel (Sturges)
Dunbar, Helen Flanders
Duncan, Catherine (Gross)
Duncan, Helen

Duncan, Ursula Katherine
Dunham, Ethel Collins
Dunlop, Janette Gilchrist
Dunn, Mary Douglas
Dunn, Thelma Brumfield
Dunning, Wilhelmina Frances
Dupré, Marie
Durham, Mary Edith
Durocher, Marie (Josefina Mathilde)
Duryea, Nina
Dutcher, Adelaide
Dutton, Bertha Pauline
Dutton, Loraine Orr
Dye, Marie
Dyer, Helen Marie
Dylazanka, Maria
Earle, Marie Theresa (Villiers)
Eastwood, Alice
Eaves, Elsie
Ebers, Edith (Knote)
Eccello of Lucania
Echecratia the Philiasian
Echols, Dorothy Jung
Eckerson, Sophia Hennion
Eckstorm, Fannie Pearson (Hardy)
Eddy, Bernice Elaine
Edge, Rosalie Barrow
Edgell, Beatrice
Edgerton, Winifred Haring
Edgeworth, Maria
Edinger, Johanna Gabrielle Otellie (Tilly)
Edkins, Nora Tweedy
Edson, Fanny Carter
Edwards, Emma Ward
Edwards, Lena Frances
Edwards-Pilliet, Blanche
Efimenko, Aleksandra Iakovlevna
Eggleton, Marion Grace (Palmer)
Ehrenfest-Afanassjewa, Tatyana Alexeyevna
Eichelberger, Lillian
Eigenmann, Rosa Smith
Eimmart, Marie Claire
Einstein, Elizabeth Roboz
Einstein-Maric, Mileva
Eisele, Carolyn
Elam, Constance Fligg Tipper
Elderton, Ethel
Eleanora, Duchess of Mantua
Eleanora, Duchess of Troppau and
  Jagerndorf
Elephantis
Elgood, Cornelia Bonté Sheldon (Amos)
Elion, Gertrude Belle
Eliot, Martha May
Elizabeth of Bohemia
Elizabeth of Poland, Queen of Hungary
Elizabeth of Portugal, Saint
Elizabeth of Schönau
Elles, Gertrude Lilian
Elliott, Charlotte
Ellis, Florence Hawley
Ellisor, Alva Christine
Elsom, Katharine (O'Shea)
Emerson, Gladys Ludwina (Anderson)

Eng, Helga
Engelbrecht, Mildred Amanda
Erdmann, Rhoda
Erdmuthe, Sophie
Ermol'eva, Zinaida Vissarionovna
Erxleben, Dorothea Christiana (Leporin)
Esau, Katherine
Esdorn, Ilse
Etheldrida, Queen
Euphemia, Abbess of Wherwell
Evans, Alice Catherine
Evans, Alice Margaret
Everard, Barbara Mary Steyning
Everett, Alice
Evershed, Mary Orr
Eves, Florence
Ewing, Elizabeth Raymond (Burden)
Eyton, Charlotte
Fabiola
Fage, Winifred E.
Farenden, Emma
Farnsworth, Alice
Farnsworth, Vesta J.
Farquharson, Marian Sarah (Ridley)
Farr, Wanda Kirkbride
Farrar, Lillian K. P.
Fátima
Faustina
Favilla
Fawcett, Phillipa Garrett
Fearn, Anne Walter
Fedchenko, Ol'ga Aleksandrovna
Feichtinger, Nora
Felicie, Jacobina
Fell, Honor Bridget, Dame
Fenchel, Käte (Sperling)
Fenwick, Florence
Ferguson, Margaret Clay
Fernald, Grace Maxwell
Fernald, Maria Elizabeth (Smith)
Ferrand, Elizabeth M.
Ferrand, Jacqueline
Ferrero, Gina (Lombroso)
Fielde, Adele Marion
Fielding, Mary Maria (Simpson)
Fiennes, Celia
Fieser, Mary
Figner, Vera
Finch, Louisa (Thynne), Countess of
  Aylesford
Findlater, Doris
Finkler, Rita V. (Sapiro)
Fischer, Irene Kaminka
Fish, Margery
Fish, Marie Poland
Fishenden, Margaret White
Fisher, Edna Marie
Fisher, Elizabeth Florette
Fisher, Sara Carolyn
Fitton, Sarah Mary
FitzGerald, Mabel Purefoy
Flammel, Perrenelle
Fleming, Amalia Coutsouris, Lady
Fleming, Williamina Paton Stevens

Fletcher, Alice Cunningham
Flock, Eunice Verna
Flood, Margaret Greer
Florendo, Soledad Arcega
Flügge-Lotz, Irmgard
Foley, Mary Cecilia
Folmer, HerminE Jacoba
Fomina-Zhukovskaia, Evdokiia
    Aleksandrovna
Fonovits-Smereker, H.
Foot, Katharine
Forbes, Helena Madelain Lamond
Forster, Mary
Fossey, Dian
Fossler, Mary Louise
Foster, Josephine Curtis
Foster, Margaret D.
Fouquet, Marie de Maupeou, Vicomtesse
    de Vaux
Fowler, Lydia Folger
Fowler-Billings, Katharine Stevens
Fox, Ruth
Fraine, Ethel Louise de
Frampton, Mary
Frances of Brittany
Francini, Eleonora Corti
Françoise, Marie-Thérèse
Frank, Margaret
Franklin, Rosalind Elsie
Frantz, Virginia Kneeland
Freeman, Joan Maie
Freidlina, Rakhil' Khatskelevna
Frenkel-Brunswik, Else
Freud, Anna
Freund, Ida
Friant, M.
Friedlander, Kate
Friedmann, Friederike
Friend, Charlotte
Fritz, Madeleine Alberta
Fromm, Erika Oppenheimer
Frostig, Marianne Bellak
Fulford, Margaret Hannah
Fulhame, Elizabeth
Furness, Caroline Ellen
Fuss, Margarita
Gabler, Anna
Gage, Catherine
Gage, Susanna Phelps
Gaige, Helen (Thompson)
Galabert, Renée
Galindo, Beatrix
Galvani, Lucia (Galeazzi)
Gamble, Eleanor Acheson McCulloch
Gantt, Love Rosa
Gaposchkin, Cecilia Payne
Gardiner, Edith Gertrude (Willcock)
Gardiner, Margaret Isabella
Gardner, Elinor Wight
Gardner, Julia Anna
Gardner, Mary Sewall
Garfield, Viola Edmundson
Garlick, Constance
Garnett, Alice

Garnjobst, Laura Flora
Garretson, Mary (Welleck)
Garrett, Elizabeth
Garrod, Dorothy Anne Elizabeth
Gàta, Elena (Stefanescu)
Gates, Fanny Cook
Gatty, Margaret (Scott)
Gaw, Esther Allen
Gaw, Frances Isabel
Geiringer Hilda
Geldart, Alice Mary
Genet-Varcin, Emilienne
Genung, Elizabeth Faith
Gepp, Ethel Sarel (Barton)
Geppert, Maria Pia
Germain, Sophie
Gerould, Elizabeth Wood
Gerry, Eloise B.
Gey, Margaret Lewis
Ghilietta
Giammarino, Pia
Gibbons, E. Joan
Gibbons, Vernette Lois
Gibbs, Lilian Suzette
Gifford, Isabella
Gilbert, Ruth
Gilbreth, Lillian Evelyn Moller
Gilette of Narbonne
Giliani, Alessandra
Gilkey, Helen Margaret
Gill, Jocelyn Ruth
Gillett, Margaret (Clark)
Gilmore, Jane Georgina
Gilroy, Helen (Turnbull)
Giraud, Marthe
Gitelson, Frances H.
Gjellestad, Guro Else
Glagoleva-Arkad'yeva, Aleksandra
    Andreyevna
Glascott, Louisa S.
Glasgow, Maude
Glass, Jewell Jeanette
Gleason, Josephine Mixer
Gleason, Kate
Gleason, Rachel Brooks
Gleditsch, Ellen
Glueck, Eleanor (Touroff)
Gocholashvili, Mariia Mikievna
Godding, D. W.
Godfery, Hilda Margaret
Goeppert Mayer, Maria Gertrud Käte
Goldfeder, Anna
Goldfrank, Esther Schiff
Goldhaber, Sulamith
Goldman, Hetty
Goldring, Winifred
Goldschmidt, Frieda
Goldsmith, Grace Arabell
Goldsmith, Marie
Goldthwaite, Nellie Esther
Golinevich, Elena Mikhailovna
Goodenough, Florence Laura
Goodrich, Sarah Frances
Goodyear, Edith

Gordon, Kate
Gordon, Maria Matilda Ogilvie
Gorinevskaya, Valentina Valentinovna
Gorizdro-Kulczycka, Zinaida
Gorshkova, Tat'yana Ivanovna
Götz, Irén Julia (Dienes)
Gracheva, Yekaterina Konstantinovna
Graham, Helen (Treadway)
Graham, Maria Dundas (Lady Calcott)
Grainger, Jennie
Gravatt, Annie Evelyn (Rathbun)
Graves, Elizabeth (Riddle)
Gray, Etta
Gray, Maria Emma (Smith)
Gray, Susan Walton
Green, Arda Alden
Green, Mary Letitia
Green, Vera Mae
Greene, Catherine (Littlefield)
Greenwood, Marion
Gregory, Eliza Standerwick (Barnes)
Gregory, Emily Lovira
Gregory, Emily Ray
Gregory, Lady Isabella Augusta (Persse)
Gregory, Louisa Catherine (Allen)
Gregory, Louise Hoyt
Greig, Margaret Elizabeth
Greisheimer, Esther Maud
Griffin, Harriet Madeline
Griffiths, Amelia Elizabeth
Griffiths, Amelia Warren (Rogers)
Griggs, Mary Amerman
Grignan, Françoise Marguerite de Sévigné,
    Comtesse de
Grinnell, Hilda Wood
Griswold, Grace Hall
Gromova, Vera Isaacovna
Gruhn, Ruth
Grundy, Clara
Grundy, Ellen
Grundy, Maria Ann
Grzigorzewska, Marja
Gsell, Maria Dorothea Henrica (Graf)
Gualco, Sellina
Guarna, Rebecca
Guldberg, Estrid
Gullett, Lucy E.
Gundersen, Herdis
Gunn, Mary Davidson
Gunther, Erna
Guthrie, Mary Jane
Guyton de Morveau, Claudine Poullet
    Picardet
Gwynne-Vaughan, Dame Helen Charlotte
    Isabella (Fraser)
Haber-Immerwahr, Clara
Haccius, Barbara
Hagood, Margaret Loyd Jarman
Hahn, Dorothy Anna
Hainault, Countess of
Haldorsen, Inger Alida
Halicka, Antonina (Yaroszewicz)
Halket, Ann Cronin
Halket, Lady Anne (Murray)

Alphabetical List of Entries

Hall, Agnes C.
Hall, Dorothy
Hall, Edith Hayward
Hall, Julia Brainerd
Hall, Kate Marion
Hall, Rosetta Sherwood
Hall-Brown, Lucy
Halliday, Nellie
Hallowell, Susan Maria
Hamburger, Erna
Hamerstrom, Frances (Flint)
Hamilton, Alice
Hamilton, Peggy-Kay
Hammer, Marie Signe
Hanfmann, Eugenia
Hanks, Jane Richardson
Hansen, Hazel D.
Hansen, Julie Marie Vinter
Hanson, Emmeline Jean
Haoys (la meresse)
Hardcastle, Frances
Hardesty, Mary
Harding, Anita
Hardwick, Rose Standish
Hardy, Harriet
Hardy, Thora Marggraff Plitt
Harmon, Élise F.
Harrison, Jane Ellen
Harrison, Janet Mitchell Marr (Dingwall)
Harrower, Molly R.
Hart, Esther Hasting
Hart, Helen
Hart, J. B.
Hartt, Constance Endicott
Harvey, Elizabeth
Harvey, Ethel Nicholson Browne
Harwood, Margaret
Haslett, Dame Caroline
Hassall, Bessie Florence (Cory)
Hastings, Barbara, Marchioness of
Hathaway, Millicent Louise
Hatshepsut, Queen
Hausser, Isolde (Ganswindt)
Hawes, Harriet (Boyd)
Hawkes, Jacquetta (Hopkins)
Hawkins, Kate
Hawkins, Mary Esther (Sibthorp)
Hawn Mirabile, Margaret H.
Hayes, Ellen Amanda
Hayner, Lucy Julia
Hayward, Ida Margaret
Haywood, Charlotte
Hazen, Elizabeth Lee
Hazlett, Olive Clio
Hearst, Phoebe (Apperson)
Heath, Daisy Winifred
Hebb, Catherine Olding
Hebel, Medicienne
Heckter, Maria
Hedges, Florence
Hedwig of Silesia, Saint
Heermann, Margareta
Hefferan, Mary
Heidbreder, Edna Frances

Heim-Vögtlin, Marie
Heimann, Berta
Heimann, Paula
Heinlein, Julia Elizabeth Heil
Hélène, Duchess of Aosta
Hellman, Johanna
Hellstedt, Leone McGregor
Héloise
Henderson, Nellie Frater
Hendricks, Eileen M.
Hennel, Cora Barbara
Henrey, Blanche Elizabeth Edith
Henry, Caroline (Orridge)
Henshaw, Julia Wilmotte
Heppenstall, Caroline A.
Herford, Ethilda B. Meakin
Herrad of Hohenburg
Herrick, Christine (Terhune)
Herrick, Julia Frances
Herrick, Sophia McIlvaine (Bledsoe)
Herschel, Caroline Lucretia
Hersende. Abbess of Fontevrault
Herskovits, Frances S. (Shapiro)
Hertwig, Paula
Hertz, Mathilde
Herwerden, Marianne van
Herwerden, Marianne van
Herxheimer, Franziska
Heslop, Mary Kingdon
Hesse, Fanny
Hetzer, Hildegard
Hevelius, Elisabetha Koopman
Hewer, Dorothy
Hewitt, Dorothy Carleton
Hibbard, Hope
Hickey, Amanda Sanford
Hicks, Beatrice Alice
Higgins, Vera (Cockburn)
Hightower, Ruby Usher
Hildegard of Bingen
Hildreth, Gertrude Howell
Hilgard, Josephine Rohrs
Hill, Dorothy
Hill, Justina Hamilton
Hill, Mary Elliott
Hines, Marion
Hinman, Alice Hamlin
Hinrichs, Marie Agnes
Hirschfeld-Tiburtius, Henriette (Pagelsen)
Hitchcock, Fanny Rysam Mulford
Hitchcock, Orra White
Hitchens, Ada Florence R.
Hitzenberger, Annaliese
Hoare, Sarah
Hobby, Gladys Lounsbury
Hoby, Lady
Hodgkin, Dorothy Mary Crowfoot
Hodgson, Eliza Amy
Hodgson, Elizabeth
Hoffleit, Ellen Dorrit
Hofmann, Elise
Hogg, Helen Sawyer
Hoggan, Ismé Aldyth
Hohl, Leonora Anita

Hoke, Calm ,(Morrison)
Hol, Jacoba Brigitta Louisa
Holley, Mary Austin
Hollingworth, Leta Anna Stetter
Holm, Esther (Aberdeen)
Holmes, Mary Emilee
Holton, Pamela Margaret (Watson-Williams)
Homer, Annie
Hoobler, Icie Gertrude Macy
Hooker, Frances Harriet Henslow
Hooker, Henrietta Edgecomb
Hooker, Marjorie
Hopkins, Esther (Burton)
Hopper, Grace (Brewster Murray)
Horenburg, Anna Elizabeth von
Horney, Karen Clementine (Danielsen)
Horowitz, Stephanie
Hough, Margaret Jean Ringier
Howard Beckman, Ruth Winifred
Howard Wylde, Hildegarde
Howard, Louise Ernestine (Matthaei), Lady
Howe Akeley, Delia Julia Denning
Howes, Ethel Dench Puffer
Howitt, Mary (Botham)
Hroswitha of Gandersheim
Hubbard, Marian Elizabeth
Hubbard, Ruth Marilla
Hubbs, Laura Cornelia (Clark)
Hudson, Hilda Phoebe
Hug-Hellmuth, Hermine von
Huggins, Margaret Lindsay (Murray)
Hughes, Ellen Kent
Hughes, Mary Caroline (Weston)
Hughes-Schrader, Sally Peris
Hugonnai-Wartha, Vilma
Hummel, Katharine Pattee
Hunscher, Helen Alvina
Hunt, Caroline Louisa
Hunt, Eva Verbitsky
Hunt, Harriot Kezia
Hurler, Gertrud (Zach)
Hurlock, Elizabeth Bergner
Hurston, Zora Neale
Hussey, Anna Maria (Reed)
Hussey, Priscilla Butler
Hutchins, Ellen
Hutchinson, Dorothy (Hewitt)
Hutton, Lady Isabel Emilie
Huxley, Henrietta Heathorn
Hyde, Ida Henrietta
Hyman, Libbie Henrietta
Hynes, Sarah
Hypatia of Alexandria
Ianovskaia, Sof'ia Aleksandrovna
Ibbetson, Agnes (Thomson)
Ide, Gladys Genevra
Ilg, Frances Lillian
Inglis, Elsie (Maude)
Irwin, Marian
Isaacs, Susan Sutherland (Fairhurst)
Iusupova, Saradzhan Mikhailovna
Ivanova, Elena Alekseevna

Ives, Margaret
Iwanowska, Wilhelmina
Jacobi, Mary Corinna Putnam
Jacobina Medica of Bologna
Jacobs, Aletta Henrietta
Jacobson, Clara
Jacopa of Passau
Jacson, Maria Elizabeth
Jahoda, Marie
James, Lucy Jones
Janaki Ammal, Edavaleth Kakkat
Janssen, Mme.
Janssen, Mme.
Jeanes, Allene Rosalind
Jekyll, Gertrude
Jensen, Estelle Louise
Jérémine, Elisabeth (Tschernaieff)
Jermoljeva, Zinaida Vissarionovna
Jesson, Enid Mary
Jex-Blake, Sophia
Jězowska-Trzebiatowska, Boguslawa
Jhirad, Jerusha
Johanna (Johanne, Joanna)
Johnson, Dorothy Durfee Montgomery
Johnson, Hildegarde (Binder)
Johnson, Mary
Johnson, Minnie May
Johnston, Mary Sophia
Joliot-Curie, Irène
Jonas, Anna I.
Jones, Amanda Theodosia
Jones, Eva Elizabeth
Jones, Katharine, Viscountess Ranelagh
Jones, Lorella Margaret
Jones, Mary Amanda Dixon
Jones, Mary Cover
Jordan, Louise
Jordan, Sara Claudia (Murray)
Jordan-Lloyd, Dorothy
Joslin, Lulu Broadbent
Josselyn, Irene (Milliken)
Joteyko, Joséphine
Joyce, Margaret Elizabeth
Juhn, Mary
Julian, Hester Forbes (Pengelly)
Justin, Margaret M.
Kaan, Helen Warton
Kaberry, Phyllis Mary
Kablick [Kablíková], Josephine (Ettel)
Kaczorowska, Zofia
Kahn, Ida
Kaltenbeiner, Victorine
Kane, Lady Katherine Sophia (Baily)
Kanouse, Bessie Bernice
Karamihailova, Elizabeth/Elizaveta [Kara-
    Michailova]
Kardymowiczowa, Irena
Karlik, Berta
Karp, Carol Ruth (Vander Velde)
Karpowicz, Ludmila
Karrer, Annie May Hurd
Kashevarova-Rudneva, Varvara
    Aleksandrovna
Katherine, la Surgiene (the Surgeon)

Katz, Rosa Heine
Kaye-Smith, A. Dulcie
Keeler, Harriet Louise
Keen, Angeline Myra
Keeney, Dorothea Lilian
Keil, Elizabeth Marbareta
Keil, Elsa Marie
Keith, Marcia Anna
Keldysh, Liudmila Vsevolodovna
Keller, Ida Augusta
Kellerman, Stella Victoria (Dennis)
Kelley, Louise
Kellogg, Louise
Kellor, Frances A.
Kelly, Agnes
Kelly, Isabel Truesdell
Kelly, Margaret G.
Kelly, Margaret W.
Kendall, Claribel
Kendrick, Pearl (Luella)
Kennard, Margaret Alice
Kennedy, Cornelia
Kenny, Elizabeth (Sister Kenny)
Kent, Elizabeth
Kent, Elizabeth Isis Pogson
Kent, Grace Helen
Kent, Kate Peck
Kenyon, Kathleen Mary
Kerling, Louise Catharina Petronella
Keur, Dorothy Louise (Strouse)
Kharuzina, Vera Nikolaevna
Kielan-Jaworowska, Zofia
Kil, Chung-Hee
King, Anastasia Kathleen (Murphy)
King, Georgina
King, Helen Dean
King, Jessie Luella
King, Louisa Boyd (Yeomans)
King, Martha
King, Susan (Raymond)
Kingsley, Louise
Kingsley, Mary Henrietta
Kirby, Elizabeth
Kirch, Christine
Kirch, Margaretha
Kirch, Maria Margaretha Winkelmann
Kirkbride, Mary Butler
Kirkham, Nellie
Kittrell, Flemmie Pansy
Kleegman, Sophia
Klein, Marthe
Klein, Melanie (Reizes)
Kletnova, E. N.
Klieneberger-Nobel, Emmy
Kline, Virginia Harriett
Klosterman, Mary Jo
Kluckhohn, Florence Rockwood
Klumpke, Dorothea
Knake, Else
Knight, Margaret
Knopf, Eleanora Frances (Bliss)
Knott-Ter Meer, Ilse
Knowles, Matilda Cullen
Knowles, Ruth Sheldon

Knull, Dorothy J.
Kobel, Maria
Koch, Helen Lois
Koch, Marie Louise
Kochanowská, Adéla
Kochina, Pelageia Iakovlevna
Kohler, Elsa
Kohn, Hedwig
Kohts, Nadie (Ladychin)
Kolaczkowska, Maria
Komarovsky, Mirra
Koprowska, Irena Grasberg
Korn, Doris Elfriede
Korobeinikova, Iuliia Ivanovna
Korringa, Marjorie K.
Korshunova, Olga Stepanovna
Koshland, Marian (Elliott)
Kovalevskaia, Sofia Vasilyevna
Kovrigina, Mariia Dmitrievna
Kozlova, Ol'ga Grigoriyevna
Krasnosel'skaia, Tat'iana Abramovna
Krasnow, Frances
Kraus Ragins, Ida
Kroeber, Theodora Kracaw
Krogh, Birthe Marie (Jorgensen)
Krupskaia, Nadezhda Konstantinovna
Krutikhovskaia, Zinaida Aleksandrovna
Kunde, Margarethe Meta H.
L'Esperance, Elise Depew Strang
La Chapelle, Marie Louise Dugès
La Mance, Lora Sarah (Nichols)
La Sablière, Marguerite Hessein, Madame
    de
La Vigne, Anne de
Ladd-Franklin, Christine
Ladygina-Kots, Nadezhda Nikolaevna
Laird, Carobeth (Tucker)
Laird, Elizabeth Rebecca
Laïs
Lalande, Marie Jeanne Amélie Harlay
    Lefrançais de
Lamarck, Cornelié
Lambin, Suzanne
Lamme, Bertha
LaMonte, Francesca Raimonde
Lampe, Lois
Lampl-de Groot, Jeanne
Lancefield, Rebecca Craighill
Landes, Ruth (Schlossberg)
Lane-Claypon, Janet Elizabeth
Langdon, Fanny E.
Langdon, LaDema M.
Lange, Linda Bartels
Lange, Mathilde Margarethe
Langecker, Hedwig
Langford, Grace
Langsdorff, Toni von
Lankester, Phoebe (Pope)
Lansdell, Kathleen Annie
Lapicque, Marcelle (de Heredia)
Larsson, Elisabeth
Larter, Clara Ethelinda
Laskey, Amelia (Rudolph)
Laski, Gerda

Lassar, Edna Ernestine (Kramer)
Lasthenia of Mantinea
Latham, Vida Annette
Latimer, Caroline Wormeley
Laubenstein, Linda
Laughlin, Emma Eliza
Laurie, Charlotte Louisa
Lavoisier, Marie Anne Pierrette Paulze
Law, Annie
Lawder, Margaret
Lawrence, Barbara
Lawrence, Penelope
Lawrenson, Alice Louisa
Lawton, Elva
Lazarus, Hilda Mary
Le Beau, Désirée
Le Breton, Elaine
Le Maître, Dorothée
Leach, Mary Frances
Leacock, Eleanor Burke
Leakey, Mary Douglas (Nicol)
Leavitt, Henrietta Swan
Lebedeva, Nataliia Ivanova
Lebedeva, Vera Pavlovna
Lebour, Marie Victoire
Leclercq, Suzanne (Céline)
Ledingham, Una Christina (Garvin)
Lee, Julia Southard
Lee, Rebecca
Lee, Rose Hum
Lee, Sarah Wallis Bowdich
Leebody, Mary Elizabeth
Lees, Florence Sarah
Lefroy, Helena (Trench)
Lehmann, Inge
Lehmus, Emilie
Lehr, Marguerite (Anna Marie)
Leighton, Dorothea (Cross)
Leland, Evelyn
Lemmon, Sarah Plummer
Leontium
Leoparda
Lepaute, Nicole-Reine Hortense (Etable
    de la Brière)
Lepeshinskaia, Ol'ga Borisovna
Lepin, Lidiia Karlovna
Lermontova, Ekaterina Vladimirovna
Lermontova, Iuliia Vsevolodovna
Leschi, Jeanne
Leslie (Burr), May Sybil
Leverton, Ruth Mandeville
Levi, Hilde
Levi-Montalcini, Rita
Levine, Lena
Levyns, Margaret Rutherford Bryan
    (Michell)
Lewis, Florence Parthenia
Lewis, Graceanna
Lewis, Helen Geneva
Lewis, Isabel (Martin)
Lewis, Lilian (Burwell)
Lewis, Madeline Dorothy (Kneberg)
Lewis, Margaret Adaline Reed
Lewis, Mary Butler

Leyel, Hilda Winifred Ivy (Wauton)
Libby, Leona Woods Marshall
Libert, Marie-Anne
Lieber, Clara Flora
Lieu, K. O. Victoria
Lin Qiaozhi (Lin Chiao-chi)
Lincoln, Almira Hart
Lind-Campbell, Hjördis
Lindsten- Thomasson, Marianne
Lines, Dorolyn (Boyd)
Linton, Laura Alberta
Lipinska, Mélanie
Lisitsian, Srbui Stepanova
Lisovskaia, Sofiya Nikolaievna
Lister, Gulielma
Litchfield Henrietta Emma (Darwin)
Litvinova, Elizaveta Fedorovna
Litzinger, Marie
Lloyd, Dorothy Jordan
Lloyd, Rachel
Lloyd-Green, Lorna
Lochman-Balk, Christina
Loewe, Lotte Luise Friedericke
Logan, Martha Daniell
Logan, Myra Adele
Logsdon, Mayme (Irwin)
Lomax, Elizabeth Anne (Smithson)
Longfield, Cynthia
Longshore, Hannah E. (Myers)
Longstaff, Mary Jane (Donald)
Lonsdale, Kathleen (Yardley)
Losa, Isabella
Löser, Margaret Sibylla von
Loudon, Jane (Webb)
Lovejoy, Esther Pohl
Lovelace, Augusta Ada Byron, Countess of
Loveless, Mary Hewitt
Lowater, Frances
Lowell, Frances Erma
Lozier, Clemence Sophia (Harned)
Lu Gwei Djen
Lubinska, Liliana
Lukanina, Adelaida N.
Lunn, Katharine Fowler
Luomala, Katharine
Lutwak-Mann, Cecelia
Lwoff, Marguerite (Bourdaleix)
Lyell, Katharine Murray (Horner)
Lyell, Mary Elizabeth (Horner)
Lynn, Mary Johnstone
Lyon, Mary
Lyubimova, Yelena Aleksandrovna
Maass, Clara Louise
Macaulay, Catharine (Sawbridge)
MacCallum, Bella Dytes (MacIntosh)
Macdonald, Eleanor Josephine
MacDougall, Mary Stuart
MacGill, Elsie Gregory
MacGillavry, Carolina Henriette
Macintyre, Sheila Scott
Mack, Pauline Beery
Mackay, Helen Marion MacPherson
Macklin, Madge (Thurlow)
Mackowsky, Marie-Therese

MacLaughlin, Florence Edith Carothers
MacLean, Ida (Smedley)
MacLeod, Annie Louise
MacLeod, Grace
Macrina
MacRobert, Rachel (Workman), Lady of
    Douneside and Cromar
Maddison, Ada Isabel
Mahler, Margaret Schönberger
Mahout, Countess of Artois
Mair, Lucy Philip
Makemson, Maude (Worcester)
Maling, Harriet Florence (Mylander)
Malleson, Elizabeth
Mallory, Edith (Brandt)
Maltby, Margaret Eliza
Man, Evelyn Brower
Mangold, Hilde (Proescholdt)
Mann, Harriet
Manning, Ann B. (Harned)
Manson, Grace Evelyn
Mantell, Mary Ann (Woodhouse)
Manton, Irene
Manton, Sidnie Milana
Manzolini, Anna Morandi
Maracineanu, Stefania
Marcella
Marcet, Jane Haldimand
Marche, Marguerite du Tertre de la
Margery
Margulova, Tereza Kristoforovna
Marianne Plehn
Maric, Mileva
Marillac, Louise de
Marinov, Evelina
Marks, Hertha
Marlatt, Abby Lillian
Marriott, Alice Lee
Marsh, Mary Elizabeth
Marshall, Clara
Marshall, Sheina Macalister
Martin, Ella May
Martin, Emilie Norton
Martin, Lillien Jane
Martineau, Harriet
Martinez-Alvarez, Josefina
Mary the Jewess
Mason, Carol Y.
Mason, Marianne Harriet
Massee, Ivy
Massevitch, Alla Genrikhovna
Massey, Patricia
Massy, Anne L.
Masters, Sybilla (Righton)
Mateer, Florence Edna
Mateyko, Gladys Mary
Mather, Sarah
Mathias, Mildred Esther
Mathisen, Karoline
Matikashvili, Nina
Matilde
Maunder, Annie Scott Dill Russell
Maury, Antonia Caetana de Paiva
Maury, Carlotta Joaquina

Maver, Mary Eugenie
Maxwell, Martha Dartt
May, Caroline Rebecca
Mayer, Maria Goeppert
Mayo, Clara Alexandra (Weiss)
McAvoy, Blanche
McBride, Katharine Elizabeth
McCarthy, Dorothea Agnes
McClintock, Barbara
McConney, Florence
McCracken, Eileen May
McCracken, Elizabeth (Unger)
McCracken, Mary Isabel
McCrea, Adelia
McDonald, Janet
McDowell, Louise Sherwood
McGee, Anita (Newcomb)
McGlamery, Josie Winifred
McGraw, Myrtle Byram
McGuire, Ruth Colvin Starrett
McHale, Kathryn
McKeag, Anna Jane
McKinney, Ruth Alden
McLaren, Agnes
McLean, Helen (Vincent)
McNab, Catherine Mary
McVeigh, Ilda
Mead, Kate Campbell (Hurd)
Mead, Margaret
Measham, Charlotte Elizabeth (Cowper)
Mechthild of Magdeburg
Medaglia, Diamante
Medes, Grace
Medvedeva, Nina Borisovna
Mee, Margaret Ursula (Brown)
Meek, Lois Hayden
Meigler, Marie J.
Meitner, Lise
Melissa
Mellanby, May (Tweedy)
Memmler, Ruth Lundeen
Mendenhall, Dorothy (Reed)
Mendrez-Carroll, Christiane
Menten, Maud L.
Mentuhetep, Queen
Mercuriade
Meredith, Louisa Anne (Twamley)
Mergler, Marie
Merian, Maria Sibylla
Meritt, Lucy Taxis (Shoe)
Merriam, Florence
Merrifield, Mary Philadelphia (Watkins)
Merrill, Helen Abbot
Merrill-James, Maud Amanda
Messina, Angelina Rose
Metchnikova, Olga (Belokopytova)
Metrodora
Metzger, Hélène (Bruhl)
Meurdrac, Marie
Mexia, Ynes
Meyer, Margaret Theodora
Meyer-Bjerrum, Kirstine
Meyling-Hylkema, Elisabeth
Meznevics, Ilona

Michael, Helen Cecilia DeSilver Abbott
Michelet, Athénaïs (Mialaret)
Mildmay, Grace Sherrington
Miles, Catherine Cox
Mill, Harriet Hardy Taylor
Miller, Bessie Irving
Miller, Elizabeth Cavert
Miller, Olive Thorne
Minoka-Hill, Lillie Rosa
Minor, Jessie Elizabeth
Minot, Ann Stone
Mirchink, Maria E.
Mises Geiringer, Hilda von
Missuna, Anna Boleslavovna
Mitchell, Anna Helena
Mitchell, Evelyn Groesbeeck
Mitchell, Helen Swift
Mitchell, Maria
Mitchell, Mildred Bessie
Miyaji, Kunie
Mockeridge, Florence Annie
Moffat, Agnes K.
Mohr, Erna W.
Molesworth, Caroline
Molza, Tarquinia
Monin-Molinier, Madeline
Monson, Lady Anne Vane
Montague, Lady Mary Wortley
Montel, Eliane
Montessori, Maria
Moody, Agnes Claypole
Moody, Mary Blair
Mooney-Slater, Rose Camille LeDieu
Moore, Anne
Moore, Charlotte Emma
Moore, Emmeline
Moore, Lillian Mary
Moore, Mary Mitchell
Moore, Ruth Ella
Morehouse, Kathleen M.
Morgan, Agnes Fay
Morgan, Ann Haven
Morgan, Elizabeth Frances
Morgan, Lilian Vaughan Sampson
Moriarity, Henrietta Maria
Morozova, Valentina Galaktionovna
Morris, Margaretta Hare
Morse, Elizabeth Eaton
Morse, Meroë Marston
Morton, Emily L.
Morton, Rosalie Slaughter
Moser, Fanny
Mosher, Clelia Duel
Mottl, Mária
Moufang, Ruth
Mueller, Kate Heuvner
Muir-Wood, Helen Marguerite
Muller, Marie Claire Eimmart
Murphy, Lois Barclay
Murray, Amelia Matilda
Murray, Lady Charlotte
Murray, Margaret Alice
Murray, Margaret Mary Alberta
Murray, Margaret Ransone

Murrell, Christine Mary
Murtfeldt, Mary
Muszhat, Aniela
Myers, Mabel Adelaide
Myia or Mya
Nance, Nellie Ward
Napper, Diana Margaret
Nasymuth, Dorothea Clara (Maude)
Naumova, Sofiya Nickolaevna
Naylor, Bertha
Neal, Marie Catherine
Necker, Susanne (Curchod)
Needham, Dorothy Mary (Moyle)
Neiburg, Maria Feodorovna
Nelson, Katherine Greacen
Nemcová-Hlobilová, Jindriska
Nemir, Rosa Lee
Netrasiri, Khunying Cherd-Chalong
Neuburg Maria Feodorovna
Neumann, Elsa
Neumann, Hanna (von Caemmerer)
Nevill, Lady Dorothy Frances (Walpole)
Newbigin, Marion Isabel
Newson, Mary Frances Winston
Newton, Margaret
Nice, Margaret Morse
Nicerata, Saint
Nichols, Mary Louise
Nichols, Mary Sargeant Neal Gove
Nicholson, Barbara Evelyn
Nickerson, Dorothy
Nickerson, Margaret (Lewis)
Nicosia, Maria Luisa
Nieh, Chung-en
Nightingale, Dorothy Virginia
Nightingale, Florence
Nihell, Elizabeth
Noddack, Ida Eva Tacke
Noel, Emilia Frances
Noether, Amalie Emmy
Nolde, Hélène Aldegonde de
Nolte, Margarethe
Norsworthy, Naomi
North, Marianne
Northrup, Ann Hero
Novoselova, Aleksandra Vasil'evna
Noyes, Mary Chilton
Nuttall, Gertrude (Clarke)
Nuttall, Zelia Maria Magdalena
Nutting, Mary Adelaide
O'Brien, Charlotte Grace
O'Brien, Ruth
O'Connell, Marjorie
O'Malley, Lady Emma Winifred
    (Hardcastle)
O'Reilly, Helen
O'Shea, Harriet Eastabrooks
Obrutsheva, A.
Occello of Lucania
Odlum, Doris
Ogilvie, Ida Helen
Ogilvie-Gordon, Dame Maria Matilda
Ogino, G.

Quiroga, Margarita Delgado de Solis
Rabinoff, Sophie
Rabinovitch-Kempner, Lydia
Radegonde
Radnitz, Gerty.
Rafatdjah, Safieh
Ragins, Ida.
Raisin, Catherine Alice
Ramart-Lucas, Pauline
Ramirez, Rosita Rivera
Ramsay, Christina (Broun), Countess of
    Dalhousie
Ramsey, Elizabeth Mapelsden
Ramstedt, Eva Julia Augusta
Rancken, Saima Tawast
Rand, Marie Gertrude
Randoin, Lucie Gabrielle (Fandard)
Randolph, Harriet
Rasskazova, Yelena Stepanovna
Rathbone, Mary May
Rathbun, Mary Jane
Ratnayake, May
Ratner, Sarah
Rauzer-Chernousova, Dagmara M.
Ray, Dixy Lee
Raymond-Schroeder, Aimee J.
Rayner, Mabel Mary Cheveley
Rea, Margaret Williamson
Reames, Eleanor Louise
Reddick, Mary Logan
Reder, Ruth Elizabeth
Redfield, Helen
Reed, Eva M.
Rees, Florence Gwendolen
Rees, Mina Spiegel
Refshauge, Joan Janet
Reichard, Gladys Amanda
Reid, Eleanor Mary (Wynne Edwards)
Reid, Mary Elizabeth
Reimer, Marie
Reinhardt, Anna Barbara
Remond, Sarah Parker
Renooz, Céline
Reynolds, Doris Livesey
Rhine, Louise Ella (Weckesser)
Rhodes, Mary Louise
Rice, Elsie (Garrett)
Rice-Wray, Edris
Rich, Mary Florence
Richards, Audrey Isabel
Richards, Clarice Audrey
Richards, Ellen Henrietta Swallow
Richards, Mary Alice Eleanor (Stokes)
Richards, Mildred Hoge (Albro)
Richter, Emma (Hüther)
Richter, Grete
Riddle, Lumina Cotton
Ridenour, Nina
Rigas, Harriett B.
Ring, Barbara Taylor
Rioch, Margaret J.
Ripley, Martha (Rogers)
Rising, Mary Meda
Risseghem, Hortense van

Ritter, Mary Elizabeth (Bennett)
Riviere, Joan (Verrall)
Rob, Catherine Muriel
Robb, Jane (Sands)
Robb, Mary Anne (Boulton)
Roberts, Charlotte Fitch
Roberts, Dorothea Klumpke
Roberts, Edith Adelaide
Roberts, Lydia Jane
Roberts, Mary
Robertson, Florence
Robertson, Jeannie (Smillie)
Robertson, Muriel
Robeson, Eslanda Cordoza (Goode)
Robinson, Daisy Maude (Orleman)
Robinson, Gertrude Maud (Walsh)
Robinson, Harriet May Skidmore
Robinson, Julia (Bowman)
Robinson, Margaret (King)
Robinson, Pamela Lamplugh
Roboz-Einstein, Elizabeth
Robscheit-Robbins, Frieda Saur
Rockley, Lady Alicia Margaret (Amherst)
Rockwell, Alice Jones
Rockwell, Mabel Macferran
Rodde, Dorothea von (Schlözer)
Roe, Anne
Roe, Josephine Robinson
Roger, Muriel
Rogers, Agnes Lowe
Rogers, Julia Ellen
Rogers, Marguerite Moillet
Rogick, Mary Dora
Rohde, Eleanour Sinclair
Róna, Elisabeth
Ronzoni, Ethel (Bishop)
Roper, Ida Mary
Roper, Margaret
Rose Stoppel
Rose, Flora
Rose, Glenola Behling
Rose, Mary Davies Swartz
Rosenberg, Mary Elizabeth
Rosenfeld, Eva
Ross, Joan Margaret
Ross, Marion Amelia Spence
Ross, Mary G.
Rosse, Mary, Countess of
Rothschild, Miriam
Roupell, Arabella Elizabeth (Piggott)
Royer, Clémence
Rozanova, Mariia Aleksandrovna
Rozovna, Evdokia Aleksandrovna
Rubin, Vera (Dourmashkin)
Rucker, Augusta
Rudnick, Dorothea
Rumbold, Caroline (Thomas)
Russell, Anna (Worsley)
Russell, Annie
Russell, Dorothy
Russell, Jane Anne
Ruth Tunnicliff
Ruys [Ruijs], Anna Charlotte
Ruysch, Rachel

Rydh, Hanna
Sabin, Florence Rena
Sablière, Marguerite (Hessein) de la
Sabuco Banera D'Alcaraz, Olivia
Sackville-West, Victoria Mary
Safford, Mary Jane
Sager, Ruth
Salbach, Hilde
Sale, Rhoda
Salmon, Eleanor Seely
Salpe
Sampson, Kathleen Samuel
Sanborn, Ethel
Sandford-Morgan, Elma (Linton)
Sandhouse, Grace Adelbert
Sandiford, Irene
Sanford, Vera
Sanger, Margaret Higgins
Sara of Saint-Gilles
Sara of Würzburg
Sargant, Ethel
Sargent, Winifred
Satur, Dorothy May
Saunders, Edith Rebecca
Savulescu, Olga
Sawin, Martha
Say, Lucy (Sistare)
Scarpellini, Caterina
Schaffner, Mabel (Brockett)
Schantz, Viola Shelly
Scharlieb, Dame Mary Ann Dacomb
    (Bird)
Scharrer, Berta (Vogel)
Schiemann, Elisabeth
Schliemann, Sophia (Kastromenos)
Schmid, Elisabeth
Schmideberg, Melitta (Klein)
Schmidt, Johanna Gertrud Alice
Schmidt-Fischer, Hildegard
Schoenfeld, Reba Willits
Schoental, Regina
Schofield, Brenda Muriel
Schraders, Catharina Geertruida
Schubert, Anna
Schulze, Caroline M. (Bertillon)
Schurman, Anna Marie van
Schwidetsky, Ilse
Scotland, Minnie (Brink)
Scott, Charlotte Angas
Scott, Flora Murray
Scott, Henderina Victoria (Klaassen)
Scudder, Ida Sophia
Seaman, Elizabeth Cochrane
Sears, Pauline Snedden
Seegal, Beatrice Carrier
Seibert, Florence Barbara
Seligman, Brenda Zara
Semikhatova, Sofia Viktorovna (Karpova)
Semple, Ellen Churchill
Serment, Louise-Anastasia
Sessions, Kate Olivia
Sewall, Lucy
Seward, Georgene Hoffman
Shabanova, Anna Nikolaevna

Teagarden, Florence Mabel
Tebb, Mary Christine
Telfair, Annabella (Chamberlain)
Telkes, Maria
Tenenbaum, Estera
Terent'eva, Liudmila Nikolaevna
Terry, Ethel Mary
Terzaghi, Ruth Doggett
Tessier, Marguerite
Tetsuo, Tamayo
Theano
Thelander, Hulda Evelin
Thelberg, Elizabeth (Burr)
Thelka, Saint
Theodora, Empress
Theodosia, Saint
Theosebeia
Thiselton-Dyer, Lady Harriet Ann
    (Hooker)
Thoday, Mary Gladys Sykes
Thomas, Caroline (Bedell)
Thomas, Dorothy Swaine (Thomas)
Thomas, Ethel Nancy Miles
Thomas, Mary Frame (Myers)
Thome, Frances
Thompson, Caroline Burling
Thompson, Clara Mabel
Thompson, Helen
Thompson, Laura
Thompson, Mary Harris
Thompson, Rachel Ford
Thompson, Rose Elizabeth (Paget)
Thompson, Sydney Mary
Thoms, Adah B. (Samuels)
Thomson, Agnes C.
Thomson, Jane Smithson
Thring, Lydia Eliza Dyer (Meredith)
Thurstone, Thelma Gwinn
Tiburtius, Franziska
Tilden, Evelyn Butler
Tilden, Josephine Elizabeth
Timofe'eff-Ressovsky, Elena
    Aleksandrovna (Fiedler)
Tindall, Isabella Mary
Tinne, Alexandrina Petronella Francina
Tinsley, Beatrice Muriel (Hill)
Tipper, Constance Fligg (Elam)
Tisserand, M.
Todd, Emily Sophia
Todd, Mabel Loomis
Todd, Ruth
Todtmann, Emmy Mercedes
Tolman, Ruth (Sherman)
Tomaszewicz-Dobrska, Anna
Tompkins, Sally Louisa
Tonnelat, Marie-Antoinette (Baudot)
Toops, Laura Chassell (Merrill)
Towara, Hélène
Town, Clara Harrison
Tracy, Martha
Traill, Catharine Parr (Strickland)
Treat, Mary Lua Adelia (Davis)
Trimmer, Sarah (Kirby)
Tristram, Ruth Mary (Cardew)

Trizna, Valentina Borisovna
Trotter, Mildred
Trotula
Trower, Charlotte Georgiana
Tsvetaeva, Maria
Tum-Suden, Caroline
Tumanskaya, Olga G. (Shirokobruhova)
Tunakan, Seniha (Hüsnü)
Turnbull, Priscilla Freudenheim
Turner, Abby Howe
Turner, Mary (Palgrave)
Twining, Elizabeth Mary
Tyler, Leona Elizabeth
Tyler, Martha G.
Tyndall, A. C.
Tyng, Anita E.
Tyska, Maria
Ubisch, Gerta von
Underhill, Ruth Murray
Ushakova, Elizaveta Ivanovna
Uvarova, Countess Praskov'ia Sergeevna
Vachell, Eleanor
Valentine, Lila Hardaway (Meade)
Van Beverwijk, Agathe L.
Van Blarcom, Carolyn (Conant)
Van Deman, Esther Boise
Van Hoosen, Bertha
Van Rensselaer, Martha
Van Wagenen, Gertrude
Varsanof'eva, Vera Aleksandrovna
Vasilevich, Glafira Makar'evna 1895–1971
Vaughan, Dame Janet
Vavrinova, Milada
Veil, Suzanne Zélie Pauline
Veley, Lilian Jane (Nutcombe)
Venning, Eleanor (Hill)
Verder, Ada Elizabeth
Veretennikova, Anna Ivanovna
Vernon, Magdalen Dorothea
Vesian, Dorothy E. de
Vickers, Anna
Vilar, Lola
Vilmorin, Elisa (Bailly)
Vivian, Roxana Hayward
Vogt, Cécile (Mugnier)
Vogt, Marthe Louise
Vold, Marjorie Jean Young
Volkova, Anna Fedorovna
Von Schroeder, Edith
Vyssotsky, Emma T. R. (Williams)
Vytilingam, Kamala Israel
Waelsch, Salome Glueksohn
Wakefield, Elsie Maud
Wakefield, Priscilla (Bell)
Walcott, Helene B. (Stevens)
Walcott, Mary Morris (Vaux)
Wald, Lillian D.
Walker, Eliza
Walker, Elizabeth
Walker, Harriet Ann
Walker, Helen Mary
Walker, Mary Edward
Walker, Norma (Ford)
Wall, Florence

Wallace, Louise Baird
Wallis, Ruth Sawtell
Walworth, Ellen Hardin
Wang Chi Che
Wang Zhenyi
Ward, Mary (King)
Warga, Mary Elizabeth
Waring, Sister Mary Grace
Warren, Elizabeth Andrew
Warren, Madeleine (Field)
Washburn, Margaret Floy
Washburn, Ruth
Wassell, Helen Erma
Watkins, Della Elizabeth (Ingram)
Watson, Janet Vida
Watt, Helen Winifred Boyd (de Lisle)
Watt, Menie
Watts, Betty (Monaghan)
Way, Katharine
Webb, Jane
Weber, Anne Antoinette (van Bosse)
Webster, Mary McCallum
Wedderburn, Jemima
Wedgwood, Camilla Hildegarde
Wedgwood, Mary Louisa (Bell)
Weeks, Alice Mary (Dowse)
Weeks, Dorothy W.
Weeks, Mary Elvira
Weightman, Mary
Weinzierl, Laura (Lane)
Weishaupt, Clara Gertrude
Weiss, Marie Johanna
Weiss, Mary Catherine (Bishop)
Welch, Betty
Welch, Winona Hazel
Weld, Julia Tiffany
Wellman, Beth Lucy
Wells, Agnes Ermina
Wells, Charlotte Fowler
Wells, Louisa D.
Welser, Philippine
Welsh, Jane Kilby
Welsh, Lilian
Weltfish, Gene
Wertenstein, Mathilde
Wessel, Bessie (Bloom)
West, Ethel
Westall, Mary
Westcott, Cynthia
Westover, Cynthia May
Wharton, Martha Lucille
Whedon, Frances Lovisa
Wheeler, Anna Johnson Pell
Wheeler, Elizabeth Lockwood
Wheeler-Voeglin, Erminie Brooke
White, Edith Grace
White, Eliza Catherine (Quekett)
White, Elizabeth Juanita (Greer)
White, Florence Roy
White, Frances Emily
White, Margaret Pirie
White, Marian Emily
Whitehead, Lilian Elizabeth
Whiteley, Martha Annie

A

ABBOTT, MAUDE ELIZABETH SEYMOUR (1869–1940)

Canadian physician and medical historian. Born 18 March 1869 in St. Andrews East, Quebec, Canada, to Frances Elizabeth (Seymour) Abbott and Jeremiah Babin, clergyman. One older sister, Alice. Educated McGill University (B.A., 1890); Bishop's College (M.D., 1894); Edinburgh, graduate studies in internal medicine (L.R.C.P., L.R.C.S., 1897). Professional experience: Medical Museum at McGill, assistant curator (1899–1901), curator (1901–1932); McGill Medical School, research fellow in pathology (1905–1912), lecturer in pathology (1912–1923), assistant professor of medical research (1925–1937); Woman's Medical College of Pennsylvania, professor of pathology and bacteriology (1923–1925); Canadian Army Medical Museum, acting curator (1919– ?). Honors and memberships: Royal College of Physicians, Royal Society of Medicine, Canada, Fellow; New York Academy of Medicine, honorary fellow; McGill University, honorary M.D. (1910), honorary LL.D. (1936); Canadian Medical Association; Montreal Medico-Chirurgical Society; British Pathological Society; International Association of Medical Museums; International Association of Medical History. Died 2 September 1940.

Maude Elizabeth Abbott spent her life both making and preserving medical history. After her mother died, her father, Jeremiah Babin, immigrated to the United States and left his two small daughters to be raised by their maternal grandmother, who had their name legally changed to Abbott. Maude had an intense yearning for education throughout her life. After high school, she entered the McGill Faculty of Arts—or rather, the Donelda Department for Women, since the sexes were segregated; she graduated valedictorian and received the Lord Stanley Gold Medal. She and others petitioned for admission to the McGill Medical School, but were denied. Instead Abbott attended the University of Bishop's College Medical School where she received her M.D. with honors in 1894. During most of her years in higher education, Abbott and other women were taught separately from men and suffered from the intense prejudice of both male students and faculty, and from the traditional stereotype that women's sphere was domestic. Especially in the field of medicine, women practitioners were stigmatized as unfeminine, immodest, and physically and emotionally incapable.

Abbott went to Edinburgh for postgraduate training (1894–1897) and returned to Montreal to begin private medical practice. She received a part-time appointment at the Royal Victoria Hospital and was soon engaged in research on heart murmurs that resulted in a significant paper. When this paper was read (by a male colleague) at the Medico-Chirurgical Society, Abbott was proposed and accepted as the society's first woman member. Working under a governor's fellowship for research, Abbott became a world authority on congenital heart disease; William Osler, one of Canada's most distinguished physicians, asked her to contribute the chapter on congenital heart diseases for the medical textbook he was preparing.

Both her interest in the history of medicine and her frequent use of real objects and exhibits in teaching led her into a concurrent career at the Medical Museum at McGill. She was appointed assistant curator of the museum in 1899 and full curator in 1901, a position she held through 1932, when the museum became The History of Medicine Museum. Her duties included classifying and cataloging all the specimens collected by the medical school since its inception. She produced a monumental catalogue of the McGill holdings and was instrumental in organizing the International Association of Medical Museums. Her expertise led to an additional appointment as acting curator of the Canadian Army Medical Museum. Osler called her the "most perfect director of museums in the world" (Hurd-Mead).

Due to her status as an authority in pathology and heart disease, Abbott was sought after by medical institutions around the world. Most she turned down, since she was held in Canada by both her love of McGill and her dedication to the care of her invalid sister, Alice. However in 1923 she was persuaded to accept a two-year "loan" to the Woman's Medical College of Pennsylvania as professor of pathology and bacteriology. She returned to McGill and the post of assistant professor, where she remained until her forced retirement at age 65. During her career, Abbott published more than one hundred papers and books, edited the *Canadian Medical Association Journal,* and was internationally acclaimed for her work in both heart disease and the history of medicine. It is almost incomprehensible that in her more than 35 years at McGill her requests for promotion, salary increases, assistance or equipment for research, and "one final favour: namely that I be retired with the status of Professor of Medical Research" were routinely denied (Gillett). McGill did present her with honorary degrees: the M.D. in 1910 and the LL.D. in 1936. Abbott died in 1940, still working to complete a new medical textbook.   KM

PRIMARY SOURCES

Abbott, Maude E. *Historical Sketch of the Medical Faculty of McGill University.* Montreal, 1902.

———. "Congenital Heart Disease." In *Modern Medicine, Its Theory and Practice, In Original Contributions by American and Foreign Authors,* ed. William Osler, vol. 4. Philadelphia: Lea & Febiger, [1908].

———. *Statistics of Congenital Cardiac Disease: 400 Cases Analyzed.* Boston: [n.p., 1908].

———. *Descriptive Catalogue of the Medical Museum of McGill University Arranged on a Modified Decimal System of Museum Classification.* Oxford: Clarendon, 1915.

———. *Diagnosis of Congenital Cardiac Disease.* Philadelphia: Saunders, 1928.

———. *History of Medicine in the Province of Quebec.* Montreal: McGill University, 1931.

———. *Atlas of Congenital Cardiac Disease.* New York: American Heart Association, 1936.

STANDARD SOURCES

Ainley; *AMS* 2–6; Hacker; Hurd-Mead 1933; *LKW*; Lovejoy.

ABEL, MARY HINMAN (1850–1938)

U.S. home economist and nutritionist. Married John J. Abel, professor and pharmacologist at Johns Hopkins University (10 July 1883). Professional experience: New England Kitchen (with Ellen Swallow Richards, ca. 1890); Lake Placid Conferences (on home economics), founding member; Journal of Home Economics, editor (1908–?); United States Department of Agriculture, writer and editor on home economics and nutrition; American Home Economics Association charter member and councilor-at-large. Honors and memberships: Lomb Prize, American Public Health Association, 1890. Died in 1938.

Little is known about Mary Hinman Abel's early life. She married John J. Abel (1857–1938) in 1883, soon after he received his master's degree from the University of Michigan. After spending his postgraduate year at Johns Hopkins, the young couple went to Europe where John Abel studied chemistry and medicine in Vienna, Berne, Leipzig, Würzburg, and Strassburg (M.D., 1888). They returned to the United States in 1891. Mary Abel acquired enough facility in the German language to write a little book in both German and English, *Practical Sanitary and Economic Cooking.* The book was awarded the Lomb prize by the American Public Health Association in 1890, the same year it was published.

Upon their return, her husband lectured on *materia medica* at the University of Michigan. Mary Abel, who had become intrigued by comparative methods of domestic economy while in Europe, chose to work with ELLEN SWALLOW RICHARDS at the newly established New England Kitchen. In 1892, Abel published with Richards, Edward Atkinson, and others on the science of nutrition. The following year, she produced popular pamphlets for the Rumford Kitchen, set up by Richards, at the Chicago World's Fair. When her husband was appointed professor of pharmacology at Johns Hopkins in 1893, Abel joined him in Baltimore. She was soon writing pamphlets on the nutritional value of various foods for the United States Department of Agriculture, and on children's nutrition for the American Public Health Association.

Abel was a founding member of the Ellen Swallow Richards Lake Placid Conferences, held during the summers from 1899 to 1908. Created to discuss the "betterment of the home," these conferences provided the impetus for the newly designated home economics movement.

Abel was an early member of the American Home Economics movement and became an editor of the *Journal of Home Economics,* founded in 1908 by Richards. By 1909, she was publishing pamphlets on methods to prevent infection by diseases such as typhoid fever as part of the Health Education series.

In her early seventies, Abel published her best-known book, *Successful Family Life on the Moderate Income* (1921). This book, published by a commercial publisher, attempted to detail how individuals with limited means could live well. According to one of her few biographers, Abel practiced these methods effectively in her own home, with a successful mixture of "comfort, beauty, simplicity, and friendliness." She and her husband both died in the same year.   JH/MBO

PRIMARY SOURCES

Abel, Mary Hinman. *Practical Sanitary and Economic Cooking Adapted to Persons of Moderate and Small Means. Praktikische sanitäre und ökonomische Küche.* Rochester: American Public Health Association, 1890.

———. With Edward Atkinson, Ellen Swallow Richards, et al. *The Science of Nutrition: Treatise upon the Science of Nutrition.* Boston: Damrell & Upham, 1892.

———. *Beans, Peas and other Legumes as Food.* Washington, D.C.: U.S. Dept of Agriculture (Farmers Bulletin), 1900.

———. *Typhoid Fever, Infection and Prevention.* Boston, 1909. No. 22 of Health Education Series.

———. *Successful Family Life on the Moderate Income: Its Foundation in a Fair Start. The Man's Earnings. The Woman's Contribution. The Cooperation of the Community.* Philadelphia and London: Lippincott, 1921; 2d ed., rev., 1927.

SECONDARY SOURCES
Committee of the Home Economics Association, *Home Economists: Portraits and Brief Biographies of the Men and the Women Prominent in the Economics Movement in the United States.* Baltimore: Home Economics Association, 1929, pp. 12–13.

STANDARD SOURCES
Debus (under John J. Abel).

ABEL, THEODORA MEAD (1899–?)

U.S. clinical psychologist. Born 9 September 1899 in Newport, R.I., to Elsie Cleveland and Robert Mead, Jr., an attorney. Educated Vassar College (A.B., 1921); Institut de Psychologie at the Sorbonne, Diploma in Psychology, 1923); Columbia University (A.M., 1924; Ph.D., 1925). Married Theodore Abel (1923). Three children: Peter, Caroline, and Zita. Professional experience: Cornell University, research fellow in psychology, National Research Council (1926–1927); University of Illinois, research fellow (1927–1929); Sarah Lawrence College, fellow in psychology (1929–1935); Laura Spelman Rockefeller Fund research fellow (1935–1936); Miss Chapin's School, New York, instructor (1930–1936); Manhattan Vocational High School, New York, director of research (1937–1940); Letchworth Village, Thiells, New York, research psychologist (1940–1946); Office of Naval Research Project in Contemporary Culture, Columbia University, researcher (1946–1949); New York Postgraduate Center for Mental Health, director of psychology (1947–1971); Long Island University, instructor (1951–1965); private practice in Albuquerque, New Mexico (1971–?); School of Medicine, University of New Mexico, clinical associate in psychiatry (1971–?); Child Guidance Center, Albuquerque, chief of family therapy service (1971–?). Honors and memberships: American Association for the Advancement of Science; American Psychological Association; American Group Psychotherapy Association; World Association for Social Psychiatry; Society of Personality Assessment, New York State Psychology Association (Psychologist of the Year Award, 1972).

Born the only child of affluent and socially active parents, Theodora Mead was given early opportunities to study languages and the violin. She traveled frequently to Europe and spent her sixth-grade year in Geneva. Her mother, Elsie Cleveland Mead, who had been decorated by the French government for her work with the YWCA in Paris during World War I, was a dynamic role model for Theodora. Together with her father, she helped found the American Cancer Society. She also helped raise the money to purchase a gram of radium for MARIE CURIE, who became a friend of the family. While studying in Paris, Theodora spent evenings with the Curie family. Music played a role in her first real project in psychology when, as a student of MARGARET WASHBURN at Vassar, she collaborated in a study of the subjective effect of immediate repetition of music.

At Columbia University, Mead studied physiological psychology with Robert Woodworth, and exceptional children with LETA HOLLINGWORTH. After receiving her doctorate from Columbia University, she spent a year at the University of Illinois, working under Madison Bentley on a research grant to study the use of the galvanometer to measure emotional responses. Moving to Cornell University, where her husband Theodore Abel had been appointed to the sociology faculty, Mead completed her research on galvanic skin reflexes and wrote an article on Washburn's "motor theory" that brought her professional recognition. Because of personal conflict with E. B. Tichener, head of Cornell's psychology department, Mead's paper on galvanic skin reflex was not published until 1930. Its conclusion, that the galvanometer did not provide an accurate estimation of changes in emotional states, ran counter to the hopes of many researchers, including anthropologist MARGARET MEAD (no relation).

Theodora Abel developed a range of research and clinical skills that enabled her to succeed in several different areas of psychological study: mental testing, cultural and racial differences, tactual perception of movement, galvanometric response, individual differences in thinking processes, social facilitation at different intelligence levels, and measurement of dynamic aspects of behavior. Her writings were broad in scope, since she continually sought to educate herself in new procedures. She studied Gestalt psychology with Max Wertheimer and later studied psychoanalysis with Lewis Wolberg (completing her own analysis in 1952 and becoming a training analyst in 1960).

After being introduced to the Polish emigré Zygmunt Piotrowski, a renowned expert on the Rorschach test, Abel studied his projective techniques and those of Bruno Klopfer of UCLA. She was elected president of the Society of Projective Techniques in 1947. She used the Rorschach in studies and personality assessments of subnormal and delinquent girls at the Letchworth Village Institution operated by the

New York State Department of Mental Hygiene. Her first book (with Elaine F. Kinder) was *The Subnormal Adolescent Girl* (1942), which dealt with juvenile delinquency and the personality and culture of mentally deficient girls.

A friend of Margaret Mead since they were classmates at Columbia, Abel joined with Mead and Mead's collaborator, Rhoda Métraux, in the Columbia "Research in Contemporary Cultures" project in 1947. Her skills in projective techniques and clinical observation made her the perfect psychologist to complement the anthropologists. Their joint work produced widely recognized books and a landmark article on the acculturation process of Chinese immigrants in the United States (with Francis Hsu). She also wrote on projective testing in Mexican and Caribbean cultures.

In 1947, Theodora Abel began her long association with the New York Postgraduate Center for Mental Health. As director of psychology she provided special training for psychologists and psychoanalysts until 1971. Between 1949 and 1951, Abel worked in a special interdisciplinary study on psychological and social aspects of physical disfigurement and plastic surgery at Bellevue Hospital in New York City. In 1951, Abel became an instructor at Long Island University. She also began to train in family therapy under Nathan Ackerman, a pioneer in that movement. From 1968 to 1971, Abel codirected the family therapy training program at Columbia University's Postgraduate Center. She began to write and lecture worldwide on the topic.

From 1971 on, Abel lived in Albuquerque, New Mexico, where she was associated with the University of New Mexico Department of Psychiatry. She served as chief of family therapy at the Child Guidance Center and practiced privately.   KM

PRIMARY SOURCES

Abel, Theodora Mead. "Tested Mentality as Related to Success in Skilled Trade Training." Ph.D. diss., Columbia University, 1925.

———. With Elaine F. Kinder. *The Subnormal Adolescent Girl.* New York: Columbia University Press, 1942.

———, et al. *Facial Disfigurement.* National Institute of Mental Health, 1952.

———. *Psychological Testing in Cultural Contexts.* New Haven: College & University Press, 1973.

———. With Rhoda Métraux. *Culture and Psychotherapy.* New Haven: College & University Press, 1974. Enlarged and expanded in 1987.

STANDARD SOURCES

AMS 4–8, S&B 10–13; *Psychological Register*, vols. 2–3; Stevens and Gardner; *Who's Who of American Women*, 1985–1986.

ABELLA (fl.14th century)

Italian teacher of medicine who flourished in the fourteenth century. Lecturer, medical school, Salerno.

Biographical information about Abella is scant. Renatus Moreau reported in the *Schola Salernitano de Valetudine* (1625) that Abella was a Roman who taught at the medical school at Salerno. She reputedly wrote medical treatises in verse, and lectured on bile and on the nature of women. She published two treatises, *De atrabile* and *De natura seminis humani,* neither of which have survived.   JH/MBO

SECONDARY SOURCES

Harington, John. *The School of Salernum. Regimen salernitanum.* The English version by Francis R. Packard, M.D., with a note on the prehistory of the *Regimen sanitatus* by Fielding H. Garrison, M.D. New York: Augustus M. Kelley, 1970, p. 17.

STANDARD SOURCES

Hurd-Mead 1938; Lipinska 1900; Ogilvie 1986.

ABERLE, SOPHIE BLEDSOE (1899–?)

U.S. anthropologist, physician, and nutritionist. Born 21 July 1899 in Schenectady, N.Y. Married William A. Brophy (1940). Educated Stanford University (A.B., 1923; M.S., 1925; Ph.D., 1927); Yale University (M.D., 1930). Professional experience: Stanford University, assistant histologist (1924–1925), assistant embryologist and neurologist (1925–1926); Yale University, Institute of Human Relations, instructor (1927–1930); Yale University School of Medicine, Sterling Fellow (1930–1931), instructor (1930–1934); Carnegie Institute, associate in research (1934–1935); Bureau of Indian Affairs, superintendent of Pueblo Indians; Southwest Superintendents Council, secretary (1935–1944); National Research Council, Division of Medical Science (1944–1949); University of New Mexico, special research director (1949–1954); Bernalillo County Indian Hospital, chief nutritionist (1953–1966); University of New Mexico, Department of Psychiatry, medical school, member of staff (1966–1969), and law school, member of staff (1970–?). Death date unknown.

A Native American, Sophie Aberle had a varied career spanning the fields of nutrition, anthropology, medicine, and psychiatry. While Aberle studied at Stanford, she worked as an assistant in histology, embryology, and neurology. Aberle studied in a number of departments, ultimately receiving her master's and her doctorate in genetics.

During her years at Yale, Aberle was an instructor in anthropology and human relations and was awarded the Sterling Fellowship from the School of Medicine. After leaving Yale in 1934 she became a research associate at the Carnegie Institution. She then moved to the Southwest, where she took a position with the Bureau of Indian Affairs, from 1935–1944. From 1944–1949, Aberle worked in the division of medical science, National Research Council, and from 1949–1954 was special resident director at the University of New Mexico. She became the chief nutritionist for the Bernalillo County Indian Hospital, then a staff member of the department of psychiatry at the university's medical school. In 1970, she replaced medicine with law, and became a member of the law school staff at the University of New Mexico. During the time she was officially employed at these positions, she held numerous concurrent positions that affected the lives of the Pueblo Indians.

A visible advocate for Native Americans, Aberle applied her skills in a number of different areas. Although her doctorate was in genetics and her first jobs were related to work she had done in graduate school, most of her professional career was spent with activities on behalf of southwestern Native Americans.

Aberle provided important statistical information on the Pueblo Indians of the Southwest, including data on natality, fertility, and mortality. She believed that understanding the biological and sociological phenomena could enhance the research of historians and anthropologists. Aberle was one of two women appointed to the first National Science Board by President Harry S. Truman. JH/MBO

PRIMARY SOURCES
Aberle, Sophie B. "Frequency of Pregnancies and Birth Interval among Pueblo Indians." *American Journal of Physical Anthropology* 16 (1931): 63–80.
———. "Child Mortality Among Pueblo Indians." *American Journal of Physical Anthropology* 16 (1932): 339.
———. With J. H. Watkins, and E. H. Pitney. "Vital Statistics of the Pueblo Indians." *American Journal of Public Health* 29 (1939): 753–760.
———. With J. H. Watkins, and E. H. Pitney. "The Vital History of San Juan Pueblo." *Human Biology* 12 (1940): 141–187.
———. *The Pueblo Indians of New Mexico: Their Land, Economy and Civil Organization.* Memoir Series of the American Anthropological Association, no. 70. Menasha, Wis.: American Anthropology Association, 1948.

STANDARD SOURCES
AMS 5–8, B 9, P&B 10–11, and supp. 4, 12–14; Bailey; Rossiter 1995.

ABOUCHDID, EDNA (fl. 1947)
Lebanese physician. Educated American University, Beirut (graduated in medicine 1931); Johns Hopkins University (postgraduate studies 1947). Professional experience: American University, member of medical faculty.

Abouchdid was the first Lebanese woman to graduate in medicine from the American University at Beirut (1931). She did postgraduate work at Johns Hopkins in 1947 and returned to the American University as a member of the medical faculty. In 1953, she attended a conference in New York. On another occasion, she praised American women doctors who had served in Lebanon. JH/MBO

STANDARD SOURCES
Lovejoy.

ABRAMSON, JADWIGA (1887–?)
Polish/French child psychologist. Born 17 February 1887 in Poland. Educated in Poland; University of Paris, Sorbonne, Medical faculty (Diplôme Philosophie). Professional experience: Clinic of Pediatric Neuro-Psychiatry, Paris, chief of psychology.

Jadwiga Abramson was reared and educated in Poland. For her medical degree, she went to the University of Paris, Sorbonne, and remained in France to pursue a career in neuropsychiatry. She was appointed Chief of Psychology at the Clinic of Pediatric Neuro-Psychiatry in Paris. JH/MBO

PRIMARY SOURCES
Abramson, Jadwiga. "L'Enfant et L'Adolescent Instables."
Etudes Cliniques et Psychologiques. Paris: Presses Universitaires de France, 1940.

STANDARD SOURCES
Psychological Register, vol. 2.

ABROTELIA (fl. 5th century B.C.E.)
Greek Pythagorean philosopher. Born in Tarentum. Father, Abroteles of Tarentum.

Abrotelia was one of the fifteen female Pythagoreans listed by Iamblichus in his *Life of Pythagoras*. She reputedly was born in Tarentum, a Greek colony in southern Italy.
JH/MBO

SECONDARY SOURCES
Iamblichus of Chalcis. *Life of Pythagoras.* London, 1818.

STANDARD SOURCES
Kersey; Ménage.

ACHILLES, EDITH MULHALL (1892–?)
U.S. psychologist. Born 6 August 1892 in Boston, Mass. Educated Barnard College, Columbia University (B.S., 1914); Columbia University (A.M., 1915; Ph.D., 1918). Married Paul Strong Achilles

(Ph.D., Columbia University 1923). One daughter. Professional experience: The Psychological Corporation, Grand Central Terminal Building, New York, director (1926–?); Columbia University, faculty (1917–?). Honors and memberships: American Association for the Advancement of Science, Fellow; New York Academy of Medicine, Associate Fellow; Home Study Department American Psychological Association, Member.

Edith Mulhall married fellow student Paul Strong Achilles in 1917 and received her doctorate from Columbia University a year later. She taught at Columbia University and worked specifically in school and clinical psychology. She worked under the shadow of her ambitious husband at Columbia and at the Psychological Corporation, which he joined in 1926 and directed from 1932 to 1946. The couple divorced in the 1930s and Edith Achilles continued to raise their daughter and practice psychology. She consulted at Oxford School and was a trustee of Barnard College, Columbia, for several years. One interest she pursued throughout her career was the development of memory and recognition in children along with test methods for measuring those skills.   KM

PRIMARY SOURCES
Achilles, Edith Mulhall. *Experimental Studies in Recall and Recognition.* New York, 1920.
———. With Clairette Papin Armstrong, and M. J. Sacks. *Report of the Special Committee on Immigration and Naturalization of the Chamber of Commerce of the State of New York Submitting a Study on Reactions of Puerto Rican Children in New York City to Psychological Tests.* New York: The Special Committee . . . , 1935.

STANDARD SOURCES
AMS 3–6, S&B 9; Psychological Register, vol. 3, 1932.

ACOSTA-SISON, HONORIA (1848–?)

Philippine physician. Born 1888 in the Philippines to Paslora (Dixon) and Mariano Acosta. Married Antonio P. Sison (10 October 1910); two children (Antonio and Honora). Educated Drexel Institute, Pa. (1904–1905); Woman's Medical College of Pennsylvania (M.D., 1909). Professional experience: St. Paul's Hospital, Manilla, first assistant in obstetrics (1912–1914); University of Philippines, faculty member (1914–1955), emerita (1955–?). Honors and memberships: Philippine Obstetric and Gynecologic Society, Fellow and first president; Philippine Academy of Sciences and Humanities, founding member; College of Surgeons, charter member; National Research Council, member board of directors; Acta Medica Philippina, editor; Women's Medical Association, honorary member; University of the Philippines, College of Medicine, honorary alumna; Pi Gamma Mu; Phi Kappa Phi; University of Philippines Medical Association, citation (1951); medical research,

presidential medal (1953); Board of Regents, University of Philippines, citation (1963). Death date unknown.

Honoria Acosta-Sison was the first woman doctor from the Philippines. Since the medical school at the University of the Philippines did not admit women until 1930, she entered the Woman's Medical College of Pennsylvania in 1905. On her return to the Philippines, she married Antonio G. Sison, dean of the College of Medicine of the University of the Philippines and director of the Philippine General Hospital at Manilla. She first worked as assistant in obstetrics at the hospital where her husband was director (1910–?) and then was first assistant in obstetrics at St. Paul's Hospital in Manila. Acosta-Sison became a faculty member at the University of the Philippines in 1914 and rose to the rank of professor of obstetrics and gynecology and head of the department of obstetrics by 1940.

Acosta-Sison's research and publications focused on eclampsia and other disease states in pregnancy, choriocarcinoma, difficulties in partruition, comparative obstetric and gynecologic practices in different countries, and on sex education in the Philippines.   JH/MBO

STANDARD SOURCES
Debus; Lovejoy (includes photograph).

ACTON, FRANCES (KNIGHT) (ca. 1793–1881)

British botanist. Born ca. 1793 in Elton, England. Father Thomas Andrew Knight (1759–1838). Married T. P. Stackhouse Acton (1812). Died 24 January 1881 in Acton Scolt, Shropshire.

Frances Acton was the eldest daughter of Thomas Andrew Knight, well-known botanist and pomologist. She assisted her father in his plant breeding experiments. She also illustrated his books, drawing three plates for his book on apple varieties, *Pomono Herefordiensis* (1811), and another many years later for the first volume of an updated book on this topic, *Herefordshire Pomona* (1876–1885).   JH/MBO

PRIMARY SOURCES
Knight, Thomas A. *Pomono Herefordiensis,* 1811. Includes three plates by Acton.
Hogg, R., and G. Bull, *Herefordshire Pomona.* Hereford: Jakeman and Carver, 1876–1885. Includes plates by Acton.

STANDARD SOURCES
Desmond.

ADAMETZ, LOTTE (1879–1966)

Austrian geologist. Born 25 July 1879 in Vienna. Father Heinrich Adametz. Four siblings. Educated St. Ursula's School of Art; business school; technical school. Professional experience: Vienna Natural History Museum, geological and paleontological department (1898–1945). Died 3 June 1966.

After a fine general education, Lotte Adametz attended art and then business school. Her varied interests made her eager to attend Ernst Kittl's lectures at the technical school for several semesters. During countless excursions under his direction she became thoroughly familiar with the environments of Vienna and Lower Austria. Kittl helped Adametz to be admitted to the geological/paleontological department of the Natural History Museum. On geological excursions, she acquired information that was of great use to students, museum visitors, and geologists. In 1900, Max von Gutmann asked Kittl to record the geology of an area in the Rottmanner Tauern. Adametz assisted with the excursions, did photography, and produced geological reliefs. After Kittl's sudden death she herself finished a relief that became a long-term exhibit in the Natural History Museum. Adametz performed administrative and inventory work at the museum under the direction of F. X. Schaffer, in addition to assisting the museum's visitors. Her many talents proved useful to Schaffer, as well as to students, colleagues, and visitors. She produced all of the illustrations and photographs for Schaffer's text. She also took many of the photographs for J. Bayer's *Der Mensch in Eiszeitalter.* Adametz later produced a series of "ideal pictures" of the Viennese Valley, which were exhibited in the museum. In addition to her geological and paleontological interests, Adametz had expertise in related fields. In 1920 she accompanied Joseph Bayer, the director of the prehistoric part of the Natural History Museum, to excavations in Lower and Upper Austria and in the Burgenland. She also took part in excursions with Dr. Brodar of the Universität Ljubljana until 1938. Adametz retired in the museum after forty-eight years of service, but remained active in the geology/paleontology department.   JH/MBO

PRIMARY SOURCES

Adametz, Lottie. "Eine Mammutjägersstation." *Die Umschau* 29, no. 24 (1925).

———. "Ergänzungen zu dem vorhergehende Bericht von Kyrie un Zusammenfassung der alt-und jungpaläolothischen Höhlenstationen Osterreichs auf Grund der Ausgrabungen von Josef Bayer." *Report 16. International Geological Congress.* Washington, 1933.

———. With J. Pia. "Ein rätselhaftes Quecksilbervorkommen bei Haugsdorf im Weinviertel." *Anzeiger Akademie Wissenschaften in Wein, Mathematische-Naturwissenschaftliche Klasse 79* (1942): 33–36.

SECONDARY SOURCES

Kühn, Othmar. "Lottie Adametz." *Geologische Gesellschaft in Wien* 59 (1966): 255–257.

ADAMS, AMY ELIZABETH KEMPER (ca. 1892–1962)

U.S. embryologist and endocrinologist. Born ca. 1893 in Delaware, New Jersey. Never married. Educated Mount Holyoke College (A.B., 1914); University of Chicago (1916); Columbia University (A.M., 1918); Yale University (honorary fellow, 1922–1923; Ph.D. in zoology, 1923); University of Edinburgh (1930–1931). Professional experience: Mount Holyoke College, assistant in zoology (1914–1915), instructor (1915–1917, 1918–1919), associate professor (1919–1928), professor (1928–1957), chairman of department (1947–1957). Grants awarded: U.S. Rockefeller Foundation (1937); Sigma Xi; National Research Council; National Academy of Sciences. Fellowships: New York Academy of Science; American Association for the Advancement of Science. Memberships: Phi Beta Kappa; Sigma Xi; American Association of Anatomists and other scientific commissions, executive committee. Retired 1957. Died 15 February 1962.

Amy Adams received an excellent education at Mt. Holyoke, the University of Chicago, and Columbia University. Unlike many American women scientists, she was effective in getting grants; none, however, exceeded $5,000. Adams taught for over forty years at Mt. Holyoke College and during that time inspired and encouraged many women to pursue a profession in the sciences. Her textbook in zoology went through several editions. She produced several studies in endocrinology, experimental embryology and administration of sex hormones.   JH/MBO

PRIMARY SOURCES

Adams, A. Elizabeth. *Studies in Experimental Zoology* (Regeneration, Experimental Embryology, Endocrinology). Ann Arbor: Edwards Brothers, 1936.

Numerous articles in scientific journals.

STANDARD SOURCES

AMS 4–8, B 9, P&B 10; Bailey; *NAW* unused; Rossiter 1982.

ADAMS, MILDRED (1899–?)

U.S. biological chemist and nutrition researcher. Born 21 July 1899 in Manchester, N.H., to Grace (Gibson) and James Edward Adams. Educated Smith College (B.A., 1921); Columbia University (M.A., 1923; Ph.D., 1927). Professional experience: Columbia University, Carnegie research assistant (1923–1929); Centenary Junior College, Hackettstown, N.J., instructor (1929–1930); University of Minneapolis Mayo Foundation, assistant professor

(1930–1936); Mayo Clinic, consultant in clinical metabolism (1930–1936); National Institutes of Health, biochemist (1936–1942); Takamine Laboratories, vice-president in charge of research (1942–1949); U.S. Department of Agriculture, Agricultural Research Service, chief of experimental human nutrition laboratory (1950 to post-1968). Honors and memberships: American Association for the Advancement of Science; New York Academy of Sciences; American Chemical Society; American Society of Biological Chemists; Institute of Nutrition; Society for Experimental Biology and Medicine; Phi Beta Kappa; Sigma Xi.

Mildred Adams graduated from Smith College and continued her education at Columbia University, where she earned her two advanced degrees in biochemistry. During her graduate years, she held a Carnegie research assistantship that continued for two postgraduate years.

Adams taught at a junior college in New Jersey for a year, then joined the faculty of the Mayo Foundation at the University of Minnesota as an assistant professor; she held the concurrent position of consultant in clinical metabolism at the Mayo Clinic. She remained for the next six years, developing her interests in muscular weakness disorders. In 1936, Adams moved to Maryland, where she worked for the National Institutes of Health at Bethesda, Maryland, as a biochemist until 1942. In the middle of World War II, she was appointed vice-president in charge of research at the Takamine Laboratories in Clifton, New Jersey, a position she held until 1949.

Adams returned to government research in 1950, taking a position in the Human Nutrition Research Division of the Department of Agriculture, where she was chief of a nutrition laboratory until her retirement. Here Adams continued to research basic nutrition and publish on the amylases. She contributed numerous articles to scientific journals on her various topics, and wrote chapters for biochemical texts.

JH/MBO

PRIMARY SOURCES

Adams, Mildred. "Diet as a Factor in Length of Life and in Structure and Composition of Tissues of the Rat with Aging." Washington, D.C.: Government Printing Office, 1964.

STANDARD SOURCES

Debus.

ADAMSON, JOY (GESSNER) (1910–1980)

Austrian/Silesian artist and writer on natural history. Born Joy-Friedericke Victoria Gessner 20 January 1910 in Troppau, Silesia (now Opava, Czechoslovakia), to Traute and Victor Gessner. Married Victor von Klarvill (divorced 1937); Peter Bully (1938; divorced); George Adamson (1943). Educated in Vienna, Austria; later studied psychology and biology. Professional experience: Colonial government, Kenya, portraitist of native peoples; Royal Horticultural Society, director of exhibit of plant studies (ca. 1940). Awarded the Grenfell Gold Medal (1947). Popular science writer, 1959–1978. Died 3 January 1980.

Joy Adamson, popular natural history writer and conservationist, was born Joy-Fredericke Victoria Gessner in Silesia. Educated in Vienna, she studied various practical and fine arts including dressmaking, art, metal work, sculpture, photography, and piano. As a young woman, she married Victor von Klarvill, an Austrian businessman.

While on vacation in Kenya to recover from a miscarriage, she met the botanist Peter Bully, who was taking the boat to Mombasa, Kenya. She began accompanying him on his botanical expeditions and, after obtaining a divorce from her husband in 1937, she married Bully. She continued to travel with Bully on his collecting trips, providing excellent illustrations of his specimens. In 1947 the Royal Horticultural Society exhibited some of her seven hundred illustrations of African trees, flowers, and shrubs in London and awarded her the Grenfell Gold Medal. Adamson contributed illustrations to Arthur Jex-Blake's *Gardening in East Africa* (1939), to Jex-Blake's wife's *Some Wild Flowers of Kenya* (1948) by Muriel Katherine Jex-Blake (Arthur's wife), and to H. J. Beentje's *Kenya Trees, Shrubs, and Lianas* (1994).

Adamson was commissioned by the Kenyan government to paint individuals from twenty-two of the country's tribes as part of an anthropology project to record the vanishing peoples and wildlife of Kenya. She made six hundred studies of members of those tribes, and these paintings were placed in the National Museum of Kenya.

Adamson's second marriage disintegrated; in 1943, she married George Adamson, the British game warden in the North Frontier District of Kenya. He was dedicated to ecological responsibility and conservation of wildlife, a dedication she came to share.

In 1956, George Adamson shot a lioness in self-defense. The Adamsons kept and raised one of her cubs, teaching her to hunt and survive in the wild, then released "Elsa" when she was two years old. Joy Adamson described this experience in the book *Born Free*, which was an immediate international success. This book and those that followed (*Elsa and Her Cubs, Living Free, Forever Free*), provided Adamson with a large audience to whom she could address conservation issues, educating the public on the plight of large game animals in the modern world. They established the Elsa Wild Animal Appeal to publicize and fund environmental projects. Following these successes, Adamson wrote her autobiography in 1978.

On 3 January 1980, Joy Adamson was found dead. She was believed to have been mauled by a lion. After investigation, a former employee was accused of her murder. JH/MBO

PRIMARY SOURCES

Adamson, Joy. *Born Free, a Lioness of Two Worlds.* With extracts from George Adamson's letters, preface by Lord William Percy, and foreword by Charles Pitman. London: Collins & Harvill Press, 1960.

———. *Born Free: Elsa, the True Story of a Lioness.* London: Collins & Harvill Press, 1961.

———. *Forever Free: Elsa's Pride.* London: Collins & Harvill Press, 1962.

———. *Elsa and Her Cubs.* London: Collins & Harvill, 1965.

———. *The Peoples of Kenya.* With an epilogue by G. W. Huntingford. London: Collins & Harvill, 1967.

———. *Living Free: the story of Elsa and Her Cubs.* London: Collins & Harvill, 1970.

———. *The Searching Spirit: An Autobiography.* With a foreword by Elspeth Huxley. London: Collins & Harvill, 1978.

SECONDARY SOURCES

Adamson, George. *My Pride and Joy.* New York: Simon and Schuster, 1987.

Browne, Ray B., ed. *Contemporary Heroes and Heroines.* Detroit; London: Gale Research, 1990.

House, Adrian. *The Great Safari: The Lives of George and Joy Adamson.* 1st. ed. New York: W. Morrow, 1993.

STANDARD SOURCES

Notable (article by Margaret DiCanio), 7–8; Uglow 1989.

ADDAMS, JANE (1860–1935)

U.S. social reformer and social thinker, founder of social sciences. Born 6 September 1860 in Cedarville, Ill., to Sarah Weber and John Huy Addams. Nine siblings. Never married. Educated Rockford (Ill.) Female Seminary (B.A., 1882); Woman's Medical College (1881–1882); postgraduate courses, Johns Hopkins University. Professional experience: founded Hull House, Chicago, 1889; studied the immigrant population of Chicago and offered social services for forty years. Honors and memberships: first president, National Conference of Charities and Corrections; first woman to receive honorary degree from Yale (1910); first head of the National Federation of Settlements; delegate of the National American Woman Suffrage Association; first president of the Women's League of Peace and Freedom; recipient of the Nobel Peace Prize (1931). Died 21 May 1935 at Hull House.

Born and educated before sociology or social sciences existed in a formal sense, Jane Addams is regarded as founder of those disciplines. She was the youngest of four surviving children of a mother who died two years after her birth. Both her parents were originally from Pennsylvania. Her father, a banker, was active in Republican politics, a friend of Abraham Lincoln and an ardent abolitionist.

Addams went to Rockford Female Seminary, which her oldest sisters had attended. Although she resisted her teachers' desire to turn her into a Christian missionary, she planned to study medicine and live with the poor. But depressed by her father's death and realizing that she had no real gift for the field, Addams ultimately decided not to take a medical degree. Recovering from a spinal injury that required surgery, she traveled from 1883 to 1885 with her stepmother in Europe, where she reacted to the plight of the poor as much as to the culture and art. After two years in Baltimore, where she took classes at Johns Hopkins and worked among the African American poor, Addams returned to London in 1887. A strike by the impoverished matchgirls of London's East End had a profound effect upon Addams. She traveled with a former classmate, Ellen Starr, with whom she would formulate the idea for Hull House. She met the famous positivist Frederic Harrison, whose Comtean ideas appeared to promise the synthesis of many religions and the future of scientific thinking. After touring Madrid (where she reacted badly to the cruelty of a bullfight) and visiting the catacombs in Rome, Addams returned to London. Here a visit to Toynbee Hall, a settlement house founded by social theorists from Oxford University, convinced her to open a similar house in order to temper the human misery caused by industrial society.

In Chicago, Addams and Ellen Starr rented a decaying mansion in the middle of the growing immigrant area in February 1889. Here they instituted a place where overprivileged young women (and some young men) could "learn from life itself" and make themselves useful by offering a wide choice of clubs, infant nurseries, dispensaries, playgrounds, and cooking and sewing courses for the local poor. They even provided a cooperative boarding house for working girls and opened an art gallery, a theater, and a music school for the local residents, attracting creative talent from all over the country.

The residents at Hull House made some of the first sociological studies of the immigrant area, with its tenements, sweatshops, and child labor. Notable residents included ALICE HAMILTON, who studied occupational diseases, and social worker Florence Kelley. A future president of General Electric lived there in his youth, as did John Dewey and various literary figures. Hull House challenged corrupt politicians and improved conditions throughout Illinois and the country by agitating to have labor unions recognized, child labor laws instituted, limited work hours for women, protection for immigrants, and compulsory school attendance. Since all manner of ideas were openly debated in Hull House's Working People's Social Science Club, including those of the anarchistic Peter Kropotkin and the socialist thinkers Stanley and Beatrice Webb, some of the wealthy citizens feared Addams as a dangerous radical and withdrew financial support.

Jane Addams served as the glue that held very diverse

people together and made Hull House an exciting place to live and work. She became an inspiring lecturer and writer, and in 1910 published her account of the development of Hull House in a remarkable book that has never gone out of print, *Twenty Years at Hull House*. Addams was the first president of the National Conference of Charities and Corrections (later the National Conference of Social Work); the first woman to receive an honorary degree from Yale (1910); and the first head of the National Federation of Settlements, a position she retained until her death. As delegate of the National American Woman Suffrage Association, she seconded Theodore Roosevelt's nomination for the presidency at the 1912 Progressive Party convention.

During World War I, Addams remained firm in her pacifism in the face of widespread antagonism to this position. She became the first president of the Women's League of Peace and Freedom. Addams's name was submitted to the Nobel Prize Committee almost every year between 1920 and 1930; in 1931 she was awarded the Nobel Peace Prize. Following the war, Addams and Hull House had great influence on the subsequent social commitment of the New Deal under Franklin Roosevelt, although Addams did not live to see this. She died of cancer at Hull House, 21 May 1935.

JH/MBO

PRIMARY SOURCES

Addams, Jane. *Function of the Social Settlement*. Philadelphia: American Academy of Political and Social Science, 1899.
———. *Democracy and Social Ethics*. New York: Macmillan, 1902.
———. *Housing Problem in Chicago*. Philadelphia: American Academy of Political and Social Science, 1902.
———. *Newer Ideals of Peace*. New York and London: Macmillan, 1907.
———. *Spirit of Youth and the City Streets*. New York: Macmillan, 1909.
———. *Twenty Years at Hull House, with Autobiographical Notes.* New York: Macmillan, 1910.
———. With Emily G. Balch and Alice Hamilton. *Women at the Hague: The International Congress of Women and Its Results, by Three Delegates to the Congress from the United States.* New York: Macmillan, 1915.
———. *Peace and Bread in Time of War*. New York: Macmillan, 1922.
———. *Second Twenty Years at Hull House, September 1909 to September 1929, with a Record of a Growing World Consciousness.* New York: Macmillan, 1930.

SECONDARY SOURCES

Davis, Allen F. *American Heroine: The Life and Legend of Jane Addams*. New York: Oxford, 1973.
Deegan, Mary Jo. *Jane Addams and the Men of the Chicago School, 1892–1918*. New Brunswick, N.J.: Transaction Books, 1990.

Harvey, Bonnie Carman. *Jane Addams: Nobel Prize Winner and Founder of Hull House*. Springfield, N.J.: Enslow, 1999.
Mitchard, Jacquelyn. *Jane Addams: Pioneer in Social Reform and Activist for World Peace*. Milwaukee: Gareth Stevens, 1991. Juvenile literature.
Spender, Dale. *Women of Ideas and What Men Have Done to Them*. London: Pandoro, 1982.

STANDARD SOURCES
NAW (article by Anne Firor Scott).

ADELBERGER OF LOMBARDY (fl. 760)
Italian physician. Born in Lombardy. Father King Desiderius. Educated by Paul of Lombardy.

The scant information available on Adelberger indicates that she was among several lay medical women who had been taught by the historian Paul of Lombardy (720–800). Paul was a Benedictine monk from Como. Adelberger's father was Desiderius (ruled 756–774), the last ruler of the Lombards.

JH/MBO

STANDARD SOURCES
Hurd-Mead 1938.

ADELLE OF THE SARACENS (fl. 12th century)
Italian physician. Lay teacher of the medical faculty at Salerno.

Twelfth-century records of the university of Salerno yielded the name of Adelle of the Saracens [Saracins], or the Saracinesca family.

JH/MBO

STANDARD SOURCE
Hurd-Mead 1938.

ADELMOTA OF CARRARA (fl. 14th century)
Italian physician. Born in Padua in the first quarter of the fourteenth century. Married James, Prince of Carrara.

According to the seventeenth-century writer Rhodius, Adelmota was a learned physician of Padua. Observers attested to her skill as an obstetrician.

JH/MBO

STANDARD SOURCES
Hurd-Mead 1938; Lipinska 1930.

ADKINS, DOROTHY CHRISTINA (1912–1976)
Educational psychologist and pioneer in psychometric research in education. Born 6 April 1912 in Atlanta, Georgia. Educated Ohio

State University (B.S., 1931; Ph.D., 1937). *Professional experience: University of Chicago, assistant examiner psychometrics (1936–1938), research associate (1938–1940); United States Social Security Board, chief research and test constructor (1940–1944); United States Civil Service Commission, chief of social sciences and administrative testing, policy consultant, and chief test developer (1944–1948); University of North Carolina, Chapel Hill, professor of psychology (1948–1965), department chair (1950–1961); University of Hawaii, Center for Research in Early Childhood Education, researcher and professor of education research and educational psychology (1966–1973). Honors and memberships: American Psychological Association; Psychometric Society (president, 1949). Died 1976.*

Adkins was the only woman department chair at the University of North Carolina (1950–1961) and one of the very few female heads of coeducational departments in any university during the 1950s. She moved to the University of Hawaii late in her career and became head of the Center for Research in Early Childhood Education (1966–1973). In that position she wrote grant applications that yielded ten successive awards, totaling $1.3 million for the United States Office of Equal Economic Opportunity.

Adkins's research topics include the measurement of affective traits in young children; the development of circular modules for preschool children; and the evaluation of education research programs.   JH/MBO

PRIMARY SOURCES

Adkins, Dorothy Christina. *Construction and Analysis of Achievement Tests: The Development of Written and Performance Tests of Achievement for Predicting Job Performance of Public Personnel.* Washington, D.C.: U.S. Civil Service Commission, 1947.

———. With John C. Flanagan and Dorothy H. B. Cadwell. *Major Developments in Examining Methods.* Chicago: Civil Service Assembly [of the United States and Canada], 1950.

———. With Samuel B. Lyerly. *Factor Analysis of Reasoning Tests.* Chapel Hill: University of North Carolina Press, 1952.

———. *Test Construction: Development and Interpretation of Achievement Tests.* Columbus, Ohio: C. E. Merrill, 1960.

———. *Statistics: An Introduction for Students in the Behavioral Sciences.* Columbus, Ohio: C. E. Merrill, 1964.

SECONDARY SOURCES

American Psychologist 4, no. 32 (June 1977): 410.

Thurstone, L. G. "Dorothy Adkins." *Psychometrika* 41, no. 4 (December 1976): 435–437. Obituary notice.

STANDARD SOURCES

AMS 7–8, S&B 9–12; Rossiter 1995.

AELFLEDA (fl. 680)

British physician. Probably born in Whitby. Father Oswy (or Oswiu), a Saxon king. Professional experience: Abbess of Whitby.

Aelfleda, from a royal Saxon family, was known for her skill in medicine and surgery. Her great-grandfather was the Saxon King Edwin; her grandfather, King Ecgfrith; and her father, King Oswy. Her father requested Hilda of Whitby, the niece of Edwin of Northumbria, to take over his estates and to take charge of his young daughter, Aelfleda. Hilda and her nuns were known for their medical skill. Upon Hilda's death in 680, Aelfleda succeeded her as abbess. As did Hilda, she gave personal attention to her patients.   JH/MBO

STANDARD SOURCES

Hurd-Mead 1938.

AEMILIA (d. ca. 363)

French/Roman physician. Born early fourth century in Moselle, France. At least one brother. Nephew, Ausonius. Died ca. 363.

Aemilia was the aunt of the poet Ausonius, a Gallo-Roman who became tutor to the Emperor Gratian. In describing his childhood, he recorded the work of his aunt, Aemilia, a physician who lived near the Moselle and helped him with his education. He described her as a skilled and honest physician who had studied medicine in order to assist her physician brother. Ausonius explained that she wrote books on gynecology. He described his aunt as "a *virgo devota;* and though in kinship's degree an aunt, she was to me a mother, bright and happy like a boy, and busied in the art of healing like a man."   JH/MBO

SECONDARY SOURCES

Ausonius, Decimus Magnus. *Opuscula.* Part 3, *Domestica,* 33. Ed. Rudolfus Peiper. Leipzig, 1886. Trans. H. A. Evelyn White. London, 1919.

STANDARD SOURCES

Hurd-Mead 1938.

AESARA OF LUCANIA
(fl. 5th–4th centuries B.C.E.)

Greek/Italian Pythagorean philosopher. Born in Lucania.

Aesara probably flourished in fourth-century B.C.E., and thus lived later than many Pythagoreans. Although little is known about her life, a fragment of her *Book on Human Nature* is extant. In this fragment, she described the soul as consisting of three parts: mind, "spiritedness," and desire, with the principal of *harmonia* (correct proportion) governing the functioning of these parts. According to Aesara, the bases of individual and social moral law can be found through studying the human soul. JH/MBO

PRIMARY SOURCES

Aesara of Lucania. Fragment from *Book on Human Nature.* Trans. Vicki Lynn Harper. In Waithe, 20–21.

SECONDARY SOURCES

Beard, Mary R. *Women as Force in History.* New York: Farrar, Straus, and Giroux, 1976.

STANDARD SOURCES

Kersey; Waithe.

AGAMEDE (12th c. B.C.E.)

Greek physician who used plants for medicinal purposes. Born at Elis to Augeas, king of the Epeans. Married Mulius.

Most of the information about Agamede comes from Homer, who reported that she lived before the Trojan War, "when the Pylians and th' Epeans met," and was the "yellow-hair'd" eldest daughter of Augeas, king of the Epeans in Elis, the son of Helios. According to Homer, her husband was the "bold spearman, Mulius," who was killed by Nestor in battle. Agamede reputedly was skilled in the use of plants for healing purposes. Homer reported that she "all the virtues knew of each medicinal herb the wide world grows." Some of the sources refer to her as Perimede. Although it is difficult to sort myth from fact, reports indicate the existence of a specific woman, skilled in herbal medicine. JH/MBO

SECONDARY SOURCES

Homer. *Iliad* 2:740.

Hyginus. *Fabulae* 157.

Propertius. *Elegies* 2.4. Refers to Agamede using the name Perimede.

Theocritus. *Idyls* 2.16. Refers to Agamede, using the name Perimede.

STANDARD SOURCES

Pauly-Wissowa; Ogilvie 1986.

AGASSIZ, ELIZABETH CARY (1822–1907)

U.S. writer on natural history. Born 5 December 1822 in Boston, Mass., to Mary Ann (Perkins) Cary and Thomas Cary. Married Louis Agassiz (1850). Educated at home. Professional experience: Radcliffe College, first president. Died 1907 in Arlington Heights, Mass.

Elizabeth Agassiz was a natural history popularizer from "excellent Massachusetts stock." She spent most of her childhood in her grandfather Perkins's large house at Temple Place, Boston. Her parents hired a governess to teach their children until the age of fourteen, when they were to go to school. Elizabeth, who was considered to have delicate health, was kept at home. She studied languages, drawing, and music.

In 1846 Louis Agassiz (1807–1873), professor at the University of Neuchâtel, Switzerland, arrived in Boston to study North American natural history. While he was in Boston, he presented a popular series of lectures at the Lowell Institute, where Elizabeth's mother met him. Louis Agassiz left his wife and children in Switzerland and immigrated to the United States, accepting the chair of natural history at the Lawrence Scientific School of Harvard University. When Agassiz's wife died, his three children remained in school in Europe. Elizabeth was introduced to Agassiz by her sister, Mary, whose husband was Cornelius C. Felton, professor at Harvard. Elizabeth Cary married Agassiz in 1850.

Agassiz's children came to the United States, and a special relationship developed between them and their stepmother. She was particularly close to the oldest boy, Alexander (who was to become an eminent marine zoologist); he wrote after her death that "she was my mother, my sister, my companion and friend, all in one" (A. Agassiz, 441).

Elizabeth Agassiz set up a school for girls in her Cambridge home in 1856 in which her husband became involved. The school operated successfully until 1863, when financial considerations forced them to abandon the venture. During this time Elizabeth, with no previous scientific training, began to take notes on her husband's lectures.

Elizabeth accompanied her husband on a trip to Brazil (April 1865–August 1866) to study the fauna of that region for the benefit of the fledgling Museum of Comparative Zoology (now the Agassiz Museum) at Harvard. Elizabeth served as a recorder for the expedition and kept a detailed journal, including anecdotes about their companions, one of whom was the youthful psychologist William James.

In 1871 Louis Agassiz formed an expedition for deep-sea dredging along the Atlantic and Pacific coasts of the Americas aboard the U.S. Coast and Geodetic Survey vessel *Hassler.* The voyage began in December of that year and ended in August 1872. Again Elizabeth accompanied her husband and made detailed notes. In their last project together (1873), Elizabeth helped Louis plan and administer the coeducational Anderson School of Natural History, a summer school and marine laboratory, on Penikese Island in Buzzard's Bay.

After Louis's death in 1873, Elizabeth Agassiz entered a different phase in her life. She spent her time working on a biography of Louis and caring for her stepson Alexander's three children after the death of his young wife. During her later years Elizabeth returned to her earlier interest in the education of girls and women. She was active in the establishment of Radcliffe College and served as its first president (1894–1903). She suffered a cerebral hemorrhage in 1904 and died from a second attack in 1907.

Elizabeth Agassiz' interest in science was derived from her husband's. She was important in preserving, elucidating, and popularizing his ideas. Lacking scientific training, she received all her information through her association with Louis. Her first book, *Actaea, a First Lesson in Natural History* (1859), was prepared under his direction. Revised and published in 1865 in collaboration with Alexander Agassiz as *Seaside Studies,* the book is a text and field guide on marine zoology. In addition to drawings of specimens (made by Alexander) with descriptions and accounts of the animals' geographical distribution, the book includes information on the best mode of catching jellyfish, a consideration of the embryology of echinoderms, a discussion of the distribution of life in the ocean, and a general description of the radiates. In her preface, Elizabeth states that she has endeavored to supply "a want often expressed for some seaside book of popular character, describing the marine animals common to our shores."

Elizabeth Agassiz' diary provided information for both a short account for the *Atlantic Monthly* (October and November 1869) and a long account, *A Journey in Brazil,* written in collaboration with Louis. Her record-keeping abilities were important when she accompanied Louis in the Hassler Expedition to the Straits of Magellan. Louis Agassiz had theorized that the entire South American land mass had once been covered by a vast ice sheet. His idea of a continuous former glacial chain extending from south to north was supported by the evidence of past glaciation they encountered around the Straits of Magellan. The only published reports of these findings were Elizabeth's articles in the *Atlantic Monthly* in 1872 and 1873.

The two-volume biography of Louis that Elizabeth compiled after his death is an important source of information about his life. It has, however, as the author herself states, "neither the fullness of personal narrative, nor the closeness of scientific analysis, which its too comprehensive title might lead the reader to expect" (*Louis Agassiz: His Life and Correspondence,* 1:[iii]). Little of the personality of the author, and few details of her life, appear in the narrative.

Elizabeth Agassiz was thrust into the world of science. Her role as scribe and popularizer of Louis Agassiz' work enabled her to make real contributions to science and education in the United States. MBO

PRIMARY SOURCES

Agassiz, Elizabeth. *A First Lesson in Natural History.* Boston: Little, Brown & Co. [1859].

———. "An Amazonian Picnic." *Atlantic Monthly* 17 (March 1866): 313–323.

———. With Louis Agassiz. *A Journey in Brazil.* Boston: Ticknor and Fields, 1868.

———. With Alexander Agassiz. *Seaside Studies in Natural History. Marine Animals of Massachusetts Bay. Radiates.* 2d printing. Boston: Houghton Mifflin, 1871.

———. "The Hassler Glacier in the Straits of Magellan." *Atlantic Monthly* 30 (October 1872): 472–478.

———. "In the Straits of Magellan." *Atlantic Monthly* 31 (January 1873): 89.

———. "A Cruise through the Galapagos." *Atlantic Monthly* 31 (May 1873): 579.

———. *Louis Agassiz: His Life and Correspondence.* 2 vols. London: Macmillan, 1885.

SECONDARY SOURCES

Agassiz, Alexander. *Letters and Recollections of Alexander Agassiz. With a Sketch of His Life and Work.* Ed. by G. R. Agassiz. Boston: Houghton Mifflin, 1913. Includes biographical material on Elizabeth Agassiz.

Burstyn, Joan N. "Early Women in Education: The Role of the Anderson School of Natural History." *Journal of Education* 159 (1977): 50–64. Describes the summer school on Penikese Island founded by Louis Agassiz, which provided women with a postgraduate education.

Lurie, Edward. *Louis Agassiz: A Life in Science.* Chicago: University of Chicago Press, 1960. Information on Elizabeth Agassiz included in this biography of her husband.

Paton, Lucy Allen. *Elizabeth Cary Agassiz: A Biography.* Boston: Houghton Mifflin, 1919. A biography of Elizabeth begun by her younger sister and completed by Lucy Paton, who had access to letters and papers left to Radcliffe College.

Tharp, Louise Hall. *Adventurous Alliance: The Story of the Agassiz Family of Boston.* Boston: Little, Brown & Co., 1959. Elizabeth Agassiz plays an important part in this study of the Agassiz family.

STANDARD SOURCES

DAB; NAW (article by Hugh Hawkins); Ogilvie 1986.

AGLAONIKE (dates unknown)

Greek astronomer of antiquity, probably born in Thessaly to Hegetor of Thessaly (sometimes Hegemon).

Very little is known about Aglaonike's life or works. Two statements, one by Plutarch and the other by a scholiast of Apollonios of Rhodes, tersely refer to her origins. Although both sources mention her father—Hegetor of Thessaly, according to the scholiast—neither a Hegemon nor a Hegetor who might have been her father appears elsewhere in extant sources. Aglaonike's contemporaries regarded her as a sorceress, for she reputedly possessed the occult power traditional to certain Thessalian women, the ability to make the moon disappear at will. Plato, Horace, and Virgil all refer to this belief: Plato alludes to "the Thessalian enchantresses, who, as they say, bring down the moon from heaven at the risk of their own perdition"; Horace, to a "Thessalian incantation [that] bewitches stars and moon and plucks them down from heaven"; and Virgil, to "songs [that] can even draw the moon down from heaven." Aglaonike's abilities may have gone beyond the purely magical into the realm of eclipse prediction, for she seemed to be familiar with the periodic recurrence of lunar eclipses. Plutarch in his "Advice to Bride and Groom" explained that Aglaonike's knowledge of the lunar cycle and its eclipses "imposed upon the women, and made them all believe that she was drawing down the moon."

Aglaonike's reputation makes it likely that she was interested in celestial phenomena and had mastered the skill of eclipse prediction. This was an ancient skill and one that she did not originate. Still it is appropriate to distinguish Aglaonike as an important symbol in the history of science, the first woman astronomer.   JH/MBO

SECONDARY SOURCES
Apollonios of Rhodes. *Argonautica* (scholiast) 59.26–34.
Davis, Herman S. "Women Astronomers, 400 A.D.–1750."
    Popular Astronomy 6 (1898): 211–228.
Horace. *Epodes* 5.45.
Plato. *Gorgias* 513.
Plutarch. *Morals,* "Advice to Bride and Groom" 31.
Plutarch. *Morals,* "The Obsolescence of Oracles" 13.
Virgil. *Ecologues* 8.69.

STANDARD SOURCES
Pauly-Wissowa, vol. 1; Mozans; Ogilvie 1986.

AGNES, COUNTESS OF AIX
(ca. 1080–ca. 1120)
Spanish/French physician. Born eleventh century.

This twelfth-century Agnes was a royal healer. She was the Countess of Aix and a prioress known for her piety and gentleness in caring for the sick. Agnes retired to Fontevrault and was instrumental in establishing several other houses dependent on Fontevrault.   JH/MBO

STANDARD SOURCES
Echols and Williams; Hurd-Mead 1938.

AGNES OF BOHEMIA (ca. 1205–1282)
Bohemian physician. Born ca. 1205 in Bohemia. Daughter of Constance (of Hungary) and King Premysl Ottokar I of Bohemia. At least one sister, Anna. Died 1282.

Agnes was the sister of ANNA, a princess of Bohemia. After the violent death of her husband, Anna devoted her entire life to medical work as did Agnes. Agnes was betrothed to Emperor Frederick II, who died before they could be married. She petitioned Pope Gregory IX to allow her to become a Poor Clare nun, then founded a convent in Prague. Agnes lived in the castle in Prague and worked in the convent and hospital. Reputedly she cooked and cleaned like the humblest of servants. Reports indicate that both Agnes and Anna were friends of St. Francis of Assisi and St. Clare. Agnes was noted for her tenderness in caring for the sick.   JH/MBO

STANDARD SOURCES
Echols and Williams; Eckenstein; Hurd-Mead 1938.

AGNES OF JERUSALEM (fl. late 11th century)
Physician, probably Palestinian. Born ca. 1070. Member of the Knights of St. John of Jerusalem.

It is difficult to distinguish between the many medical women of the twelfth century named Agnes. However, this Agnes was apparently a member of the Knights of St. John of Jerusalem, an order established to care for the sick and wounded Crusaders in Jerusalem. A report of crusader Godfrey of Bouillon indicated that the hospitals were greatly overcrowded but the patients were well cared for by a physician named Agnes.   JH/MBO

STANDARD SOURCES
Hurd-Mead 1938.

AGNES OF SILESIA (b. ca. 1170)
Silesian physician. Sister of Hedwig of Silesia (b. 1174). Married Philip Augustus of France.

Agnes was a twelfth-century royal healer. Her daughters-in-law, ANNA and AGNES, were also noted healers.   JH/MBO

STANDARD SOURCES
Hurd-Mead 1938.

AGNESI, MARIA GAETANA (1718–1799)
Italian mathematician. Born 16 May 1718 in Milan to Anna (Brivio) and Pietro Agnesi. Twenty-three siblings and half-siblings.

Unmarried. Educated at home. University of Bologna, (honorary) professor of mathematics and natural philosophy. Died 9 January 1799 in Milan.

Maria Agnesi was a child prodigy whose wealthy father recognized his daughter's intellectual talents and encouraged her to develop them. Pietro Agnesi, a professor of mathematics at the University of Bologna, provided Maria and her younger sister Teresa Maria with the best tutors that he could find locally. The sisters were tutored in languages, philosophy, mathematics, natural science, and music. Maria spoke French fluently by age five, had an excellent command of Latin by nine, and by the time she was eleven was known as the "Seven-Tongued Orator," for competence in Italian, Latin, French, Greek, Hebrew, German, and Spanish. Her facility in Greek became legendary.

Agnesi suffered from ill health, and her physicians blamed an "obstinate" illness with which she was afflicted in 1730 on an overabundance of study and a sedentary life. Her physicians prescribed dancing and horseback riding; however, she committed herself so completely to these activities that she again became ill. The doctors next suggested that she moderate these activities. Moderation, however, was not characteristic of Agnesi, and she replaced her curtailed pastimes with religious fervor.

Agnesi's reputation as a scholar and debater spread. Her disputations ranged through logic, physics, mineralogy, chemistry, botany, zoology, and ontology. Her father constantly displayed his daughter's talents to groups of people who gathered in his home. On one of these occasions, held in 1738 as a finale for her studies, she defended 190 theses. A compilation of these arguments, published as the *Propositiones philosophicae* (1738), does not contain any of her strictly mathematical ideas. Other documents, however, indicate her early interest in mathematics. By the time she was fourteen, she was solving difficult problems in ballistics and geometry.

After the publication of the *Propositiones philosophicae,* Agnesi announced that she intended to go into a convent. This proclamation was greeted by a storm of protest from her teachers. Her father's reaction caused her to reconsider. She promised him that she would not enter the order if he would submit to three conditions: she must be allowed to dress simply and modestly, to go to church whenever she desired, and to abandon dancing, the theater, and other secular pursuits. Relieved, her father agreed to all three demands.

Freed from her social obligations, Agnesi spent most of her time in study and contemplation. She dedicated herself to a work designed to present an integrated discussion of algebra and analysis, emphasizing the mathematical concepts that were new to her day. The research resulted in the two-volume *Instituzioni analitiche ad uso della gioventù* (1748), dedicated to Empress Maria Theresa of Austria, who responded by sending Agnesi a diamond ring and a letter in a crystal case encrusted with diamonds. The clarity of its presentation resulted in a recommendation by the French Academy in 1749 that the book be translated into French. Laudatory letters bombarded the Agnesi household. In addition to those from scientists and mathematicians, she received a letter from Pope Benedict XIV accompanied by a gold medal and a wreath containing precious stones set in gold. In 1750 Benedict appointed her to the chair of mathematics and natural philosophy at the University of Bologna. Although she never taught at Bologna, Agnesi accepted the position as an honorary one.

In spite of the wide acclaim given to her book, Agnesi increasingly directed her attention away from mathematics and toward the church. Her health became uncertain again, and she reported in a letter in 1751 that the doctors had forbidden her to study because of a persistent headache. She spent much of her time working at the parish hospital. When she was at home she segregated herself from the rest of her large family (by 1748 she had twenty-three siblings and half-siblings), having persuaded her father to give her rooms in a remote part of the house.

After her father's death in 1752, Agnesi increased her isolation from the world, refusing to correspond with or visit men from the academic world. Little by little she gave away her inheritance to the poor, including the crystal box and ring given to her by Maria Theresa. When her own resources were exhausted, she begged money from others to make goods and services available to the poor. In 1783 she founded the Opera Pia Trivulzi, a charitable home for the aged in Milan, and resided there as its director for the rest of her life. Although she never became a nun herself, she lived under the same restrictive rules.

Failing health dominated her last years. Shortly before her death she became obsessed with the state of her soul, fearing that in her senility she might forget to say her prayers.

Any evaluation of Maria Agnesi's work must be filled with probabilities. *If* she had continued to produce in mathematics, *then* she might be ranked as one of the century's outstanding mathematicians. Much of the praise that she received from her contemporaries was a tribute to her youthful promise, never fulfilled because of her decision to abandon mathematics. An interest in the education of the young motivated much of Agnesi's mathematical work. Her major mathematical publication, the *Instituzioni analitiche,* was written to provide a handy compilation for students. Fontenelle reported that it would have produced her admission to the French Academy of Science, if the laws of that body "allowed us to accept women" (Frisi, 58). Most authors agree that while some of her methods are original and some of her ideas were new, the work contains no original discoveries. Even the so-called "Witch of Agnesi," the cubic curve with an equation of $x^2 y = a^2(a - y)$ usually credited to Agnesi, had actually been formulated by Pierre de Fermat (1601–1665), and the name *versiera* (meaning *versed sine curve,* but also the Italian for *witch*) had been used for it by Guido Grandi in 1703.

Maria Agnesi's greatest importance to the history of science is symbolic. She made no discoveries, yet her reputation for brilliance convinced many of her contemporaries of the capacity of women for abstract mathematical thinking.   MBO

PRIMARY SOURCES
Agnesi, Maria. *Propositiones philosophicae.* Milan: In Curia Regia, per Joseph Richinum Malatestam, 1738.
———. *Analytical Institutions.* Trans. John Colson. London: Taylor and Wilks, 1901. Includes biographical information and an English translation of *Instituzioni analitiche.*

SECONDARY SOURCES
Anzoletti, Luisa. *Maria Gaetana Agnesi.* Milan: L. F. Cogliati, 1900. Biography of Agnesi in Italian.
Frisi, Antonio Francesco. *Elogio storico di Maria Gaetana Agnesi, Milanese. Dell'instituto delle scienze, e lettrice onoraria di matematiche nella Università di Bologna.* Milan: Giuseppe Galeazzi, 1979. The best available source on the life and work of Agnesi. In Italian.
Masotti, Arnaldo. "Maria Gaetana Agnesi." *Rendiconti del Seminario matematico e Fisico di Milano* 14 (1940): 39 pp.
Tilche, Giovanna. *Maria Gaetana Agnesi.* Milano: Rizzoli, 1984.
Truesdell, C. "Maria Gaetana Agnesi." *Archive for History of Exact Sciences* 9 (1989): 113–142. An English biographical article that contains information found in the Italian biographies.

STANDARD SOURCES
DSB; Ogilvie 1986.

AGNODIKE (late 4th century B.C.E.)
Greek physician. Born in Athens. Studied under the physician Herophilus. Died in Athens.

Little is known about the Greek physician Agnodike. In *Fabulae,* Hyginus tells a story of this Athenian maiden, who disguised herself as a man and who reputedly studied under the physician Herophilus. Since slaves and freeborn Athenian women were forbidden to practice medicine, many women died needlessly in childbirth and from "private diseases" rather than submit to the embarrassment of confiding in a male physician. Agnodike changed this pattern. After her training she committed herself to the practice of medicine. Disguised

as a man, she attempted to attend a woman in labor. Her services were refused until Agnodike confessed that she herself was a woman, with the result that she "cured her perfectly." Agnodike was brought to trial before the Aereopagus for flouting the law. Although a conviction could have resulted in her death, throngs of protesting women moved the judge to abandon the old law and replace it with a new one permitting gentlewomen to practice medicine on their own sex, and awarding stipends to those "that did it well and carefully."

After the restrictive law was nullified, the medical field was open to Athenian women and formal barriers to female creativity in this field were lowered.   JH/MBO

SECONDARY SOURCES
Hyginus. *Fabulae* 274.

STANDARD SOURCES
Mozans; Pauly-Wissowa; Ogilvie 1986.

AITKEN, JANET KERR (1886–1982)
British physician. Born 3 January 1886 in Buenos Aires to Scottish parents. Four sisters. Moved permanently to Lancashire, England (1890). Never married. Educated St. Leonard's School; St. Andrew's (L.R.A.M.[piano], 1905); Manchester College of Music (voice); London School of Medicine for Women (qualified 1922; M.D., 1924); and member Royal College of Physicians, 1926. Professional experience: Elizabeth Garrett Anderson Hospital, Casualty Clearing Station (1919), house physician (1924?), clinical assistant (1925?–1929), consultant physician (1929–1933); Kensington Supervisory Rheumatic Clinic for Children (1929); Royal Free Hospital, vice-dean (1934–?), dean until retirement; Casualty Clearing Unit, chief (ca. 1939–1945). Honors and memberships: Royal College of Physicians, Fellow (1943); Commander of the British Empire (1950); Central Health Services Council of the Ministry of Health, first woman elected to sit on the General Medical Council; Medical Women's Federation, president (1942–1944); Medical Women's International Association (MWIA) honorary secretary (1950–), president (1958–1962). Died 21 April 1982.

Janet Aitken was the second of five daughters of a Scottish shipping merchant. The family moved permanently to Lancashire, England, in 1890. Since they were financially well-off, there was no pressure on the girls to prepare for a career. Janet, who loved music and played piano well, attended St. Leonard's School and St. Andrew's University and received her degree in piano in 1905. She went to Paris to study French and voice, planning a career as a singer. In order to study with Mme. Fillunger, a friend of Robert Schumann, she returned to Manchester College of Music, taking a gold medal in voice. She began her singing career in London in 1913.

The outbreak of war in 1914 completely changed the direction of Aitken's life. Many friends died and others were wounded. Aitken determined to do something to help. Thinking she would become a masseuse, she studied for the exam of the Incorporated Society of Masseurs and became interested in anatomy and physiology. With the loss of many young men physicians on the front, women were encouraged to enter the profession, and Aitken decided to become a doctor. Since Latin and the sciences were not part of her earlier education, she "crammed" to pass the entrance exams for London School of Medicine for Women and entered the school in 1917. By 1919, she was head of the casualty clearing station. Receiving her M.D. in 1924, she was elected a member of the Royal College of Physicians in 1926. She worked as a physician at the Royal College's associated women and children's hospital, Elizabeth Garrett Anderson Hospital. Aitken developed an interest in rheumatic hearts (her youngest sister had died of this disease), and from 1929 she was also a consultant physician at the Kensington Supervisory Rheumatic Clinic for Children.

Aitken was made vice-dean in 1934, and then dean of the Royal Free Hospital School of Medicine, which had incorporated the London School of Medicine for Women. She successfully developed the school. During World War II, she served as the head of the casualty clearing unit at the Elizabeth Garrett Anderson Hospital, where her quiet, assured manner did much to keep up the spirits of the residents, medical staff, and patients during the London blitz.

Aitken did much to improve the position of women in medicine. She served as president of the Medical Women's Federation from 1942 to 1944. In 1950, she began serving as honorary secretary of the Medical Women's International Association (founded in 1919); her home became the office for the organization. As the organization's president from 1958 to 1962, she traveled throughout the world to administer its agencies.

A tall, handsome, dignified woman, Aitken had an undeniable presence. She gave freely of her time, money, and personal concern. She never completely gave up music, singing as a soloist at the Queen's Proms, and enriching performances of Gilbert and Sullivan at the Royal Free Hospital. Never married, Aitken lived in her later years with a companion and friend, Althea Jackson and her niece Lillas Grey-Turner. She died on 21 April 1982 at the age of eighty-four.

JH/MBO

PRIMARY SOURCES
"Aitken, Janet." In *Women Physicians of the World*, ed. Leone Hellstedt. New York: McGraw-Hill, 1978. Autobiographical sketch.

STANDARD SOURCES
Munk's Roll, vol. 7, 1984.

AKELEY, DELIA JULIA DENNING (HOWE) (1872–1970)
See Howe, Delia Julia Denning Akeley.

AKELEY, MARY LEE (JOBE) (1878–1966)
U.S. explorer, photographer, and conservationist. Born 29 January 1878 in Tappan, Ohio to Sarah Jane Pittis and Richard Watson Jobe. Educated Scio College, Ohio (Ph.B., 1897); Bryn Mawr College (graduate study, 1902–1903); Columbia University (A.M., 1909). Married Carl Akeley (1924; he died 1925). Professional experience: Temple College, instructor (1902–1903); Normal College City of New York (later Hunter College), instructor in history (1909–1916); Camp Mystic, founder, director (1914–1930); Great African Hall, American Natural History Museum, New York, special advisor (1927–ca. 1950). Explored British Columbia (summers 1909, 1913, 1914, and 1915; winters 1917, 1918, 1938, and 1941); explored Africa (1926; 1935). Honors and memberships: Royal Geographic Society of London, Fellow. Died 19 July 1966 in Stonington, Conn.

Mary Lee (Jobe) Akeley became known as an explorer and an advocate of national game parks and the conservation of large African mammals. She did graduate work in history at Bryn Mawr College in 1902, and finished a master's degree in history from Columbia University in 1909. From 1909 through 1918, Akeley spent almost every summer or winter exploring in British Columbia or the Canadian Rockies, where she collected botanical specimens, climbed mountains, and practiced the art of photography, which was to become one of her major professional skills. She was commissioned by the Canadian government to explore and map the area at the head of the Fraser River. She also made attempts to scale one of the highest peaks of the Canadian Rockies. Another mountain in the area was later named Mt. Jobe in her honor. In 1915, Akeley wrote about her adventures in *Harper's Magazine*, the *Bulletin of the American Geographical Society*, and the *Canadian Alpine Journal*.

In 1924, Mary Lee Jobe married well-known explorer Carl Akeley, who was collecting specimens for the Great African Hall of the American Natural History Museum. The couple went to the Belgian Congo in Africa for this purpose in 1925, with Mary Jobe Akeley acting as safari organizer and photographer. Carl Akeley had long been interested in the gorilla, and he had been commissioned by the Belgian king to study the Parc National Albert as a possible site for a gorilla sanctuary. After her husband died from a fever in November 1925, Akeley took over the expedition, mapped the region of Kenya, Taganyika, and the Congo, photographed the habitat, and collected plants for the projected Great Hall. She then went to Uganda to photograph the famed pink flamingos, returning to New York in 1927. In recognition of her work, the American Natural History Museum made her a special advisor and assistant at the Great African Hall, which was dedicated in 1936 as Carl Akeley Hall.

Akeley was invited to Belgium in 1928 to revise her and her husband's notes and to provide a full report of the African expedition. She was asked to help with plans to expand the game park and to map out a plan to preserve gorillas. Akeley became an ardent advocate of game preserves, and urged the protection of African pygmies in the area of the Parc National Albert. For her work she received the Cross of the Knight and Order of the Crown from the Belgian government and king.

Returning to New York, Mary Akeley published her expedition report to the museum and Carl Akeley's journal up to his death as *Carl Akeley's Africa* (1929), followed by further material from Carl Akeley's investigations: *Adventures in the African Jungle* (1930), and *Lions, Gorillas and Their Neighbors* (1932). She headed her own expedition to Africa for the American Natural History Museum in 1935. Journeying to the Transvaal in Southern Rhodesia and to Portuguese East Africa, she sent back materials for the museum, surveyed wildlife in Kruger National Park and studied the Zulu and Swazi people, taking ethnographic films. Akeley emphasized her belief in wildlife conservation and her recognition of the need to preserve vanishing species in five more books, written between 1936 and 1950.

After World War II, Akeley returned to Africa, where she completed a second survey of wildlife sanctuaries and parks in the Congo for the Belgian government in 1947. She also filmed threatened mammal species and collected plant specimens for the museum.

From 1914 to 1930, Akeley founded and directed a summer camp for girls in Mystic, Connecticut, to which she brought explorers to talk about the excitement and challenge of outdoor life. In the 1960s she retired to that area. She died of a stroke in Stonington, Connecticut, 19 July 1966.   JH/MBO

PRIMARY SOURCES

Akeley, Mary Jobe. "My Quest in the Canadian Rockies."
      Harpers Magazine 130 (15 May 1915).
————. *Carl Akeley's Africa: The Account of the Akeley-Eastman-
      Pomeroy African Hall Expedition.* New York: Dodd, Mead &
      Company, 1929.
————. *Adventures in the African Jungle.* New York: Dodd,
      Mead & Company, 1930.
————. *Lions, Gorillas and Their Neighbors.* New York: Dodd,
      Mead & Company, 1932.
————. *The Restless Jungle.* New York: R. McBride, 1936.
————. *The Wilderness Lives Again: Carl Akeley and the Great
      Adventure.* New York: Dodd, Mead & Company, 1940.
————. *Rumble of a Distant Drum.* New York: Dodd, Mead &
      Company, 1946.

STANDARD SOURCES
NAW(M) (article by Mary MacCay).

ALBERTSON, MARY (d. 1914)

U. S. botanist and astronomer. Never married. Librarian and curator, Maria Mitchell Memorial, Nantucket Island, Mass. Died 1914 at Nantucket.

Little information is available on Mary Albertson's life. She worked as a librarian and curator at the Nantucket Maria Mitchell Memorial for ten years, until her death. While working for the observatory, Albertson organized a botany department. She was a friend of astronomer MARIA MITCHELL and shared Mitchell's love for flowers. Albertson collected a complete herbarium of Nantucket flora.   TB

SECONDARY SOURCES
"Albertson, Mary A." *Science* 40 (1914): 314. Obituary notice.

ALBRECHT, ELEONORE (fl. 1919)

German or Austrian Physicist. Professional experience: Institute for Radium Research in Vienna.

Nothing is known about Eleonore Albrecht's early life or education. According to Marelene and Geoffrey Rayner-Canham, the Austro-German group to which she would have belonged was more of a research circle than a research school. Stefan Meyer was considered the overall leader. The Vienna researchers were chiefly oriented toward physics, whereas both the British and the French schools worked in the middle ground between physics and chemistry. After the fall of the Austro-Hungarian Empire much of the work moved to Berlin.

Working at the Institute for Radium Research in Vienna, Albrecht determined the periods of the thallium isotopes produced by branched disintegration in the radium, thorium, and actinium series. She also determined the relative amounts of these isotopes produced in the radium and actinium series, confirming results that another researcher had obtained using a different method.   JH/MBO

PRIMARY SOURCES
Albrecht, Eleonore. "Über die Verzweigungsverhältnisse bei Ra
      C, Ac C, Th C und die Zerfallskonstanten der C-Produkte."
      Akademie der Wissenschaften, Vienna. Sitzungsberichte 2a 128
      (1919): 925–944.

STANDARD SOURCES
Meyer and von Schweidler; Rayner-Canham 1997.

ALBRECHT, GRETE (1893–?)

German neurologist. Born 17 August 1893. Two older brothers. Married. Two children. Educated Verein für Mädchenbildung und Frauenstudium; Universities of Munich, Freiburg, and Kiel (Physikum, 1915); licensed (1918). University Clinic in Marburg, specialty training in neurology (1928–1929); University Clinic in Eppendorf. Professional experience: University Surgical Clinic at Kiel, laboratory assistant; Berlin hospital, assistant and intern; national health insurance system, neurologist, psychotherapist; later in private practice. Honors and memberships: Hamburg Medical Board (1945–1963); Medical Women's International Association, vice-president (1958–1963).

Grete Albrecht first announced at age twelve that she wanted to study medicine. Her father flatly forbade her to think of such a profession, but after he died when she was fifteen, Grete convinced her mother to allow her to attend a private girls' gymnasium. It was so poorly equipped that the girls walked long distances to the boys' school in order to learn chemistry and physics in laboratories made available to them for one hour a day. Even the matriculation exam (*Arbitur*) was given at the boys' school. In spite of these obstacles, Grete studied medicine at Munich and Freiburg before settling down at the University in Kiel (summer 1914). She registered at the University Surgical Clinic at the outbreak of World War I in August 1914, working in the laboratory while continuing to attend lectures. She passed the *Physikum* in 1915 and began clinicals in Berlin. There she worked as a medical assistant at the University of Berlin Surgical Clinic and was assistant and intern in a Berlin Hospital. In 1918, she was licensed by the state and for a year took over the practice of a general practitioner who was stationed at the front.

Marriage and the birth of two children interrupted Albrecht's practice. The family moved to Hamburg and she volunteered as a counselor at a baby and infant welfare service and at a Hamburg hospital in the internal medicine and dermatology wards. During this time she developed a special interest in mental and neurological illnesses. In 1928–1929, Albrecht trained with Professor Kretschmer at the University Clinic in Marburg then completed her specialty training at the neurological department of the University Clinic in Eppendorf. She practiced in Hamburg as a neurologist from 1931. She was under contract with the national health insurance system until the Nazi period, when women doctors were forbidden to remain under contract if their husbands were wage earners. After 1945, Albrecht helped to reestablish the Hamburg Medical Board and served on its directorate until 1963. She helped organize the German Medical Women's Association and served as vice-president of the Medical Women's International Association (1958–1963).

KM

PRIMARY SOURCES
Albrecht, Grete. In Hellstedt, *Autobiographies.*

ALCOCK, NORA LILIAN LEOPARD (ca. 1875–1972)

British botanist and mycologist. Professional experience: Plant Pathology Laboratory, Royal Botanic Gardens, Kew and Harpenden (1917–1924); Department of Agriculture, Scotland, plant pathologist (1924–1937). Died 1 April 1972.

Alcock performed pioneer research on the red core disease of strawberries. She contributed to the *Transactions of the Botanical Society,* Edinburgh, and was a member of the British Mycological Society.   JH/MBO

PRIMARY SOURCES
Articles, *Transactions of the Botanical Society,* Edinburgh.

SECONDARY SOURCES
Botanical Society of Edinburgh News no. 10 (1973): 10–11.
Bulletin British Mycological Society 8 (1972): 81.
Journal Kew Guild 1974: 342.

STANDARD SOURCES
Desmond.

ALDRICH-BLAKE, LOUISA BRANDRETH (1865–1925)

British surgeon and medical school dean. Born 15 August 1865 in Chingford, Essex, to Louisa Blake (Morrison) and Frederick Aldrich, rector of Chingford. Five siblings. Educated secondary schools in Great Malvern (1881), Neuchâtel, Switzerland (1884–1886), St. Hilda's College, Cheltenham (1886–1887). London School of Medicine for Women (1887–1892); London University (M.B., 1892, with first class honors; B.S., 1893, with first class honors; M.D, 1894; master in surgery, 1895). Professional experience: Eizabeth Garrett Anderson Hospital, assistant, surgeon, consulting surgeon (1895–1914); London School of Medicine for Women (later incorporating the name of the Royal Free School of Medicine), dean (1914–1923); Royal Free Hospital, surgeon, consulting surgeon. Honors and memberships: Gold medal for surgery (1893); Fellow of Royal Society of Medicine (1910); Dame of the British Empire (DBE, 1925). Died in London in 1925.

Louise Brandreth Aldrich-Blake was born in Chingford, Essex, where her father was rector. The family soon moved to Welsh Bicknor, Herefordshire, where they lived for the rest of her childhood. She was the oldest daughter but second child of six, and she spent much time at sports. Aldrich-Blake was sent away to school, first to Great Malvern, then to a school in Switzerland; she finished by spending her last year at St. Hilda's College, Cheltenham, from 1886 to 1887.

After leaving school, she decided to study medicine, entering the London School of Medicine for Women in 1887. Her interest had been fired, and instead of the rather indifferent work she had produced during her secondary education, she began to achieve at a very high level, winning every available prize. She passed from M.B. to B.S., and received a gold medal for surgery in 1893. In 1894, she received her M.D. (awarded by the University of London); in 1895, she became the first woman to qualify in surgery as a master of surgery.

Entering the Elizabeth Garrett Anderson Hospital as an assistant surgeon, she soon became surgeon and then consultant surgeon, positions she also held concurrently at the Royal Free Hospital. In 1914, she was appointed dean of her former medical school, the London School of Medicine for Women; she is credited for much of its expansion during the following years, as it merged with the Royal Free School of Medicine.

She was elected a Fellow of the Royal Society of Medicine in 1910, and created Dame of the British Empire in January 1925. She died that same year, in December, at her home in London. A portrait of her, painted by Sir William Orpen in 1923, hung in the London School of Medicine for Women before its closure.   JH

SECONDARY SOURCES
Riddell, G. A., *Dame Louise Aldrich-Blake.* London: Hodder and Stoughton, 1926.

STANDARD SOURCES
DNB; Europa.

ALEXANDER, ANNIE MONTAGUE
(1867–1950)

U.S. zoologist. Born 29 December 1867 in Honolulu, Hawaii. Father Samuel Thomas Alexander. Educated Oakland, Calif., public grammar and high schools; La Salle Seminary for Girls in Auburndale (M.A., 1888); Paris, studied art (from 1888); University of California, Berkeley, attended John C. Merriam's lectures on paleontology (ca. 1900). Professional experience: Paleontological field trip to Fossil Lake region of Oregon (1901); expedition led by Vance C. Osmont to Shasta County, Calif. (1902); hunting safari to British East Africa (1904); expedition to Humboldt Range in Nevada (1905); expedition to Kenai Peninsula in search of Alaskan bears (1906); two additional collecting trips to Alaska; established Museum of Vertebrate Zoology (1909); worked as a team with LOUISE KELLOGG (1909–1949). Charter member American Society of Mammalogists. Died 1950.

Annie Alexander was born in Hawaii, where she lived until she was fifteen years old. Her early education was with a governess, after which she was sent to Honolulu to attend school for the children of missionaries. Her mother is never mentioned in accounts of Alexander's life. Annie worshipped her adventurous father, who apparently developed a successful sugar cane business with his brother-in-law. He moved the family to Oakland, California, in 1882, where Annie attended school. In 1886 she was sent to Auburndale, Massachusetts, to complete her formal education. She accompanied the family on a tour of Europe and was left to study art in Paris. But her eyes began to bother her and she was told that if she continued with art, she would go blind. She next tried to become a nurse, but her weak eyes also prevented that career. She became her father's traveling companion during this period, but, as she told her best friend, Martha Beckworth, she was restless and dissatisfied, always hunting for something that would interest her. Martha introduced her to a study of fossils. To better prepare herself in this area, she attended lectures at Berkeley by John C. Merriam. By this time, she seems to have had an independent income and was able to finance expeditions under Merriam's supervision. Only her very close friends realized that she was financing the expeditions herself. Several women, including Beckwith, Mary Wilson, and Katherine Jones, accompanied Alexander and the men on the expeditions. Alexander soon gained the reputation for choosing the right place to dig for fossils. During an expedition to the black limestone region of Shasta County, she discovered a new reptile from the upper Triassic, named *Thalattosaurus alexandrae* in her honor.

In 1903, she took up a new pursuit, collecting mammalian skulls. On a hunting Safari to East Africa in 1904 with her father, they hiked many miles collecting skulls as they explored. However, tragedy struck as they stopped at Victoria Falls. As workmen were excavating a bridge foundation they threw rocks over the edge. One of the rocks hit her father and he died the same night. Although devastated by her father's death, she continued her paleontological expeditions the next year.

During the fall of 1904, Alexander met the head of the United States Biological Survey, C. Hart Merriam, John C. Merriam's cousin. He encouraged her to organize a trip to collect Alaskan grizzly bears. The collection amassed on that trip as well as a second one, was one of the best in the world. She also learned to make study skins of mammals and birds. After accumulating great numbers of museum specimens, Alexander finally understood the nature of her life work. At this time she met Joseph Grinnell, a mammalogist who had also collected in Alaska. After he showed her his private museum and talked to her about the need for a museum of natural history in California, she provided the money for what became the Museum of Vertebrate Zoology at the University of California at Berkeley. Grinnell became the permanent director of this museum. She also was influential in developing and financing the Department of Paleontology at the university.

After the founding of the museum, Alexander planned another trip to Alaska. It was while seeking a female companion for this trip that she met LOUISE KELLOGG, with whom she collaborated for forty years. She and Kellogg contributed more than 34,000 specimens of fossils, plants, and animals to museums of the University of California. This number included 16,000 species of birds and mammals. Alexander and Kellogg purchased a large farm in the California Suisun marshes on Grizzly Island in central California near San Pablo Bay in 1911. They began by raising cattle but found this to be too labor-intensive and switched to growing asparagus. With this new spring crop, they had time to go on field trips in the summer and to Hawaii or the desert in the winter. The farm episode only lasted until 1922, when they resumed their full-time field trips. They left the bears behind on these trips and concentrated on trapping and collecting small mammals.

Disappearing into the desert for long periods of time, they ate kangaroo rat, noosed rattle snakes, and endured freezing weather (entailing a rescue). After Grinnell's death in May 1939, Alexander and Kellogg gave up most of their mammal collecting and turned to collecting botanical specimens. They were still collecting when Alexander celebrated her eightieth birthday. She continued to go on field trips for the next two years, until she suffered a stroke and remained in a coma until she died the following September, in 1950. A charter member of the American Society of Mammalogists, not enough can be said about the contributions to mammalogy of Annie Alexander.

MBO

PRIMARY SOURCES
Alexander, Annie. *Field Notebooks. Museum of Vertebrate Zoology.* Berkeley, Calif.: University of California.
———. Papers. Bancroft Library. University of California, Berkeley, Calif.

SECONDARY SOURCES
Grinnell, Hilda W. *Annie Montague Alexander.* Berkeley, Calif.: Grinnell Naturalists Society, 1958.
Kaufman, Dawn M., Donald W. Kaufman, and Glennis A. Kaufman. "Women in the Early Years of the American Society of Mammalogists (1919–1949)." *Journal of Mammalogy* 77, no. 3 (1996): 642–654.
Kellogg, Louise. *Field Notebooks. Museum of Vertebrate Zoology.* University of California, Berkeley, Calif.
Merriam, C. Hart. "The Museum of Vertebrate Zoology of the University of California." *Science* 40 (November 13, 1914): 703–704.
Smith, Felisa A., and Brown, James H. "The Changing Role of Women in North American Mammalogy." *Journal of Mammalogy* 77, no. 3 (1996): 609–612.

Smith, Felisa A., and Kaufman, Dawn M. "A Quantitative Analysis of the Contributions of Female Mammalogists from 1919 to 1994." *Journal of Mammalogy* 77, no. 3 (1996): 613–628.
Stein, B. R. "Women in Mammalogy: The Early Years." *Journal of Mammalogy* 77, no. 3 (1996): 629–641.
Zullo, Janet Lewis. "Annie Montague Alexander: Her Work in Paleontology." *Journal of the West* 8 (1969): 183–199.

ALEXANDER, FRANCES ELIZABETH SOMERVILLE (CALDWELL) (1908–1958)

British geologist. Born 13 December 1908 in Surrey, England, to Gertrude Sailman and K. C. Caldwell. Married Norman Stanley Alexander (1936). Three children. Educated Nuneaton High School; St. Swithun's School, Winchester; Newnham College, Cambridge (first-class degree in geology in Part II of the Natural Science Tripos, 1931); Cambridge University (Ph.D., 1934). Professional experience: Singapore Intelligence Section, consultant geologist (1940–1941); New Zealand Department of Scientific and Industrial Research, scientific officer of the Radio Development Laboratory and founder of the first operational research group in New Zealand on the performance of radar installations; development of radio-meteorological studies; Canterbury Project, a large-scale radio-meteorological experiment (1942–1946); Geological work in Singapore; Malaya University, temporary registrar (1947–1949); Government of Singapore, geologist (1949–1950); government geologist and consultant (1949–1952); University College, Ibadan, lecturer in the department of agriculture (1958–1958). Died 23 October 1958 in Ibadan, Nigeria.

Frances Caldwell's parents moved to India when she was a one-year-old, for her father was professor of chemistry at Patna Science College and later its principal. In 1918, Frances returned to England and attended Nuneaton High School and St. Swithun's School, Winchester. She received the Charlotte Mary Yonge Scholarship in 1928 and entered Newnham College, Cambridge, where she took a first-class degree in the second part of the Natural Science Tripos and earned the Harkness Prize. She received a doctorate in 1934.

Frances Elizabeth Alexander's career followed that of her husband, physicist Norman S. Alexander. In 1936 after their marriage, he was appointed professor of physics at Raffles College, Singapore, and she accompanied him. On Singapore, she studied the geology of the island, particularly the tropical weathering of rocks. The couple's three children were born there. During 1940 and 1941, she became involved in scientific wartime work concerned with radio direction finding. In 1942, she took the children and left for New Zealand. Her husband remained in Singapore where he was interned until the end of the war. In New Zealand, she had a number of radio-related jobs.

After the war, she rejoined her husband and resumed her geological work in Singapore. She was appointed registrar of the new University of Malaya during the period of its formation. As soon as the organizational details were taken care of, Alexander left to become geologist to the Government of Singapore. Her main task was to conduct a survey of the island's resources of useful stones. In 1950, she published a report that included the first complete geological map of Singapore Island. Subsequently, she worked as a consultant to the Singapore City Council as well as commercial firms on problems of quarrying and water supply. Later, she moved to Ibadan, Nigeria, where her husband became chair of physics at University College. She was appointed lecturer in the Department of Agriculture and organized and taught geology in the Department of Geology.

Alexander's research for her doctorate was on the main outcrop of the Aymestry Limestone. She published an account of her stratigraphical research in the *Quarterly Journal* in 1936. Although all of her conclusions were not accepted, her research was still one of the foundations for later research of the shelf deposits of the Ludlovian. She then published a series of paleontological papers on brachiopods and corals based on her earlier work.   JH/MBO

SECONDARY SOURCES
Butler, A. J. "Frances Elizabeth Somerville Alexander (née Caldwell)." *Proceedings of the Geological Society* no. 1572 (1959): 140–141.

ALEXANDER, HATTIE ELIZABETH (1901–1968)

U.S. pediatrician and microbiologist. Born 5 April 1901 in Baltimore, Md. to Elsie May (Townsend) and William Bain Alexander. Seven siblings. Companion of Elizabeth Ufford. Educated Western High School for Girls; Goucher College (A.B., 1923); Johns Hopkins Medical School (M.D., 1930). Professional experience: U.S. Public Health Service (1923–1926); Johns Hopkins University, Harriet Lane Home, intern (1930–1931); Columbia-Presbyterian Medical Center, Babies Hospital, and Vanderbilt Clinic, pediatrician and head of microbiological laboratory (1931–1951), attending pediatrician (1951–1966). Columbia University, College of Physician and Surgeons (fellow, 1930–1934; assistant 1933–1935; instructor 1935–1948; associate professor 1948–1958; professor 1958–1966; professor emeritus 1966–1968). Honors and memberships: E. Mead Johnson Award for Research in Pediatrics (1942); she received the Elizabeth Blackwell Award from the New York Infirmary (1956); she was the first woman to receive the Oscar B. Hunter Memorial Award of the American Therapeutic Society (1961); and was the first woman head of the American Pediatric Society (1964). At the time of her death she had published some 150 articles. Died from cancer 24 June 1968 in New York City.

Interested in hygiene from her early college days, Hattie Alexander took the courses in bacteriology and physiology that enabled her to work as a microbiologist for the U.S. Public Health and the Maryland Public Health services between her graduation from Goucher College (1923) and her entrance as a medical student into Johns Hopkins. After her graduation from medical school in 1930, Alexander interned at Babies Hospital, Columbia-Presbyterian Medical Center, where she would spend the rest of her working life. She soon became head of the microbiological laboratory at Babies Hospital, and taught clinical medicine at the hospital.

Alexander's research focused on the bacterial influenza meningitis, and she devoted much of her research to exploring serum immunization and, later, DNA manipulation of the bacterium *Hemophilus influenzae*. In the late 1930s, she worked with the scientist Michael Heidelberger on an anti-influenza serum developed to cure infants critically ill with influenza meningitis. In the 1940s, with the development of sulfa drugs and other antibiotics, Alexander began to do research and clinical trials that succeeded in drastically reducing mortality from this infection. She was one of the first to note the rapid genetic mutation of the bacillus that produced resistance to various antibiotics.

Alexander focused on microbial genetics following the 1944 Rockefeller Institute report on genetic change in pneumococci. She subsequently published with Grace Leidy studies of genetic change in the DNA of *Hemophilus influenzae*. While researching DNA and genetic change in various bacterial species and viruses in the laboratory, she continued her clinical work on the wards, extending her studies to tuberculosis.   JH/MBO

PRIMARY SOURCES
Alexander, Hattie. "Response to Antiserums in Meningococcic Infections of Human Beings and Mice. A Comparative Study." *American Journal of Diseases of Children* 58 (1919): 746–752.
———. "Type 'b' Anti-influenzal Rabbit Serum for Therapeutic Purposes." *Proceedings of the Society for Experimental Biology and Medicine* 40 (1930): 313–314.
———. With Michael Heidelberger. "Chemical Studies on Bacterial Agglutination. Agglutin and Precipitin Content of Antisera to *Haemophilus influenzae*, type b." *Journal of Experimental Medicine* 71 (1940): 1–11.
———. With Grace Leidy. "Induction of Streptomycin Resistance in Sensitive *Hemophilus influenzae* by Extracts Containing Desoxyribonucleic Acid from Resistant *Hemophilus influenzae*." *Journal of Experimental Medicine* 97 (1953): 17–31.
———. "Infectivity of Ribonucleic Acid of Poliovirus on HeLa Cell Monolayers." In *Viral Infections of Infancy and Childhood*, ed. H. M. Rose, 1–9. New York: Hoeber, 1960.

———. "Genetic Modifiers of the Phenotypic Level of De-oxyribonucleic Acid-Conferred Novobiocin Resistance in *Haemophilus.*" *Journal of Bacteriology* 92 (1966): 1464–1468.

Full bibliography of articles held in archives Columbia-Presbyterian Medical Center and Goucher College Archives.

SECONDARY SOURCES
"Dr. Hattie Alexander, 67, Dies: Columbia Research Pediatrician." *New York Times,* 25 June 1968, 41.
Ghayourmanesh-Svoronos, Soraya. "Hattie Elizabeth Alexander (1901–1968). In Grinstein 1997. Includes excellent bibliography.
Hogue, J. "The Contribution of Goucher Women to the Biological Sciences." *Goucher Alumnae Quarterly* (Summer 1951): 21–22.

STANDARD SOURCES
NAW(M) (article by René Dubois); *Notable* (article by Miyoko Chu).

ALI, SAFIEH (b. early 1900s)
Turkish physician. Studied medicine in Germany.

Many consider Safieh Ali to be the first Turkish woman doctor. She attended the Medical Women's International Association in London in 1924 and helped publicize the opening of the medical school of the University of Istanbul to women and the emergence of well-trained and qualified women doctors in Turkey.   JH/MBO

STANDARD SOURCES
Lovejoy.

ALIMEN, HENRIETTE (1900–   )
French paleontologist and stratigrapher. Born in 1900. Professional experience: Laboratoire de geologie, centre national de la recherche scientifique (1950s).

Little is known about the life of Henriette Alimen, except that she worked on Tertiary strata and fossil vertebrates. During the 1950s, she was employed at the Laboratoire de geologie, centre national de la recherche scientifique (Hauts-de Seine). She was a prolific writer, authoring more than ninety publications.   JH/MBO

PRIMARY SOURCES
[Alimen, Henriette]. *Notice sur les titres et travaux scientifiques de Henriette Alimen.* Paris: Centre de Documentation Universitaire. An eight-page summary of her degrees and bibliography.

———. With A. Vatan. "Contribution a l'etude petrographique des sables stampiens." *Bulletin de la societé geologique de France* series 5, no. 7 (1937): 141–162.
———. "Le Quaternary des Pyrenees de la Bigorre." *Memoire service carte geologie France.* Paris: Service Carte Geologique, 1964.
———. "The Quaternary of France." In *The Geologic Systems: the Quaternary,* ed. Kalervo Rankama, 89–238. New York: Interscience Publishers, 1967.
———. "Quaternary Research in France." *Quaternary Research* 1:369–388, 1971.
———. "Le Sahara; grande zone desertique nord-africaine." In *Striae* 17, 35–51. Uppsala: Societas Uppsaliensis pro Geologia Quaternaria, 1982.

STANDARD SOURCES
Sarjeant.

ALLAN, MARY ELEANOR (MEA) (1909–1982)
British writer on botanical subjects, journalist, historian of science. Born in Bearsden, Dumbartonshire, 23 June 1909. Died Walberswick, Suffolk, 29 August 1982.

Mary Eleanor Allan, known as Mea, wrote a series of popular studies of famous English botanists. She is best known for her life and work of William and Joseph Hooker and their families (1967), and the botanical studies of Charles Darwin (1977). She also wrote on the effect of the introduction of plants on British gardens. Her last study on William Robinson, a "natural gardener" at Kew, was published just before her death in 1982 in Walberswick, Suffolk.   JH/MBO

PRIMARY SOURCES
Allan, Mea. *The Hookers of Kew, 1785–1911.* London: Joseph, 1967.
———. *Plants That Changed Our Gardens.* Newton Abbot, North Pomfret, Vt.: David and Charles, 1974.
———. *Darwin and His Flowers: The Key to Natural Selection.* London: Faber and Faber, 1977.
———. *Weeds: The Gardener's Book of Weeds.* London: Macdonald and Jane's, 1978.
———. *William Robinson, 1838–1935: Father of the English Flower Garden.* London: Faber and Faber, 1982.

SECONDARY SOURCES
"Allan, Mary Eleanor." (London) *Times,* 2 September 1982. Obituary notice.
"Allan, Mary Eleanor." *Gardeners Chronicle.* Obituary notice.

STANDARD SOURCES
Desmond.

ALLEN, DORIS TWITCHELL (1901–)

U.S. clinical psychologist. Born 8 October 1901 in Old Town, Maine. Educated at local schools; University of Maine (A.B., 1923; M.A., 1926); University of Michigan (Ph.D., 1930); University of Munich (1931); University of Berlin (1931–1932). Married patent attorney Erastus Smith Allen (1935 or 1936). One son, E. R. Allen. Professional experience: University of Maine, instructor (1923–1925); University of Michigan, research assistant (1926–1931); Child Education Foundaton, New York City, director of the field laboratory, (1932–1935); Out-of-Door-School, New York City, director (1934–1935); Children's Hospital, Cincinnati, psychologist (1936–1947); Child Convalescent Home, Cincinnati, consulting psychologist (1936–1948); Longview State Hospital, Cincinnati, chief psychologist (1946–1957); University of Cincinnati, associate professor (1949–1962), professor (1962–1972); University of Maine at Orono, adjunct professor (1962–1972); University of Cincinnati, professor emeritus (1972–). Honors and memberships: Children's International Summer Villages, Inc., founder and national president (1951–); American Psychological Association, divisions 9, 13, 29, member; American Board of Professional Psychology, diplomate.

Doris Twitchell Allen was nominated for the Nobel Peace Prize in 1979 for her organizational work for the cause of world unity and world peace through the Children's International Summer Villages (CISV), which she helped found. The villages brought together two eleven-year-old representatives and one adult advisor from each nation that wished to participate. At the camps, the children were encouraged to develop methods of communication with each other. Their activities were observed and recorded by psychologists who focused on attitudes involving prejudice, interest in international relations, war, and confidence in international communication and understanding. Data compiled from follow-up studies of participating children shows that CISV children tend to be significantly less prejudiced against other societies, more interested in international events and problems, and more confident about the possibility of nonviolent settlement of international disputes.

Doris Twitchell Allen's interest in peace was formed during the years in which she studied behavior and personality. Her father was a physician who specialized in diseases of women and children and her mother had been an elementary school teacher. Allen was the youngest daughter in a family that valued education and creative expression. She attended local schools and entered the University of Maine to study biology, hoping eventually to enter medical school. When her father became terminally ill, she instead remained at Maine for a master's degree in biology and accepted a research fellowship at the University of Michigan, where her mentor, C. C. Little, had become president. Twitchell became interested in thinking and behavior while at Maine, where

she studied educational psychology with Professor Halverson and learned about the laboratory techniques applied at Yale University's Laboratory of Child Development.

Interested in group work in education, she organized several groups of adolescents in which leadership and interpersonal skills were taught. After one year at the Bureau for Educational Research conducting field studies in education from elementary levels through college, Twitchell decided to study for her doctorate. Her dissertation adviser was Clarence Yoakum, the psychologist and pioneer in intelligence testing. At Michigan, she studied with Louis Thurstone and Walter Pillsbury, and was influenced by the German Gestalt psychologist Wolfgang Kohler and by the vector psychology of Kurt Lewin.

After completing her doctorate, Twitchell still found the theories of Kohler and Lewin compelling. She worked for a year, borrowed against her insurance policy, and departed for Berlin. When she first arrived, she lived in the home of a German couple who tutored her in German. Afterward, she moved into Lewin's home and tutored him in English. At the Psychological Institute she became involved with Lewin's field theory research. In addition to her studies, she worked with children in an orphanage and attended lectures with Lewin's wife.

Twitchell returned after one year to accept a position as Director of the Field Laboratory of the Child Education Foundation in New York City, where she supervised interns in an early childhood education program. There, during the depths of the Great Depression, she met Erastus Allen, a young patent attorney from Cincinnati. They were married in 1935 or 1936.

Through her sister-in-law, who was chief social worker there, Doris Allen became associated with the Children's Hospital in Cincinnati, and introduced the first psychological service unit in both the hospital and the Children's Convalescent Home. She also initiated developmental and personality assessment of children in conjunction with their routine physical care. For eleven years she built and developed programs there while rearing her own son. In 1944, she accepted a position as chief psychologist at Longview State Hospital, Cincinnati, where she stayed until 1957. In 1948, she published a personality test, *The Three Dimensional Apperception Test* (later renamed the *Twitchell-Allen Three Dimensional Personality Test*). At Longview, Allen began using the group treatment developed by Moreno known as "psychodrama," which she integrated with Kurt Lewin's topological vector psychology. This synthesis became the hallmark of Allen's work in clinical psychology. She taught classes in psychodrama at the University of Cincinnati as associate professor in the Department of Psychology.

In 1951, Allen realized her vision for creating an environment to promote global peace and understanding among diverse cultures when the first Children's International Summer Village was held in Cincinnati. She was awarded the Ordre de Palmes Academiques from France (1961), the Placque Award of the International Council of Psychologists (1962), and the Gold Medal of the City of Stockholm. In 1976, to celebrate twenty-five years of operation with thirty-one countries participating as CISV members, the mayor of Cincinnati declared "Doris Allen Day." A school in Guatemala was dedicated to Allen in recognition of her international dedication as educator and psychologist.

After her husband's death, Allen returned to Maine (1962) and continued to teach, serving as adjunct professor at the University of Maine as well as at the University of Cincinnati. She became contributing editor to the journal *Group Psychiatry*, originated a publication of research studies in CISV called *Research Remarks* (1963), held offices in the American Society of Group Psychotherapy and in the International Council of Psychologists (including several years as president). She continued to write and practice group therapy using psychodrama. In her late seventies, Allen took on a full-time position as psychologist at the State Hospital in Bangor, Maine. She received honorary doctorates from the University of Maine at Orono, Xavier University (Ohio), and Wilmington College (Ohio).

Allen was popular with her peers, and her positive attitude and contagious enthusiasm endeared her to people of all kinds. Her efforts to fight prejudice and influence world peace through the Children's International Summer Villages left a legacy that continues today. KM

PRIMARY SOURCES
Allen, Doris Twitchell. "Essence of Psychodrama." *Group Psychotherapy* 13, nos. 3–4 (Sep.–Dec. 1960): 188–194.
———, and William P. Matthews, Jr., eds. *Handbook of Procedure for Children's International Summer Villages.* Oslo, Cincinnati: CIV International, 1961.
———. "Crib-Scene, a Psycho-Dramatic Exercise." *Psychotherapy: Theory, Research & Practice* 6, no. 3.
———. "Social Scientists Examine the Middle East Conflict: A Symposium." In *International Understanding.* Ed. Leah Gold Fein. (New York: International Council of Psychologists, 1974). Presented as part of symposia of the same title.
———. *Pattern for Survival: Educating Children for Peace* [sound recording] New York, McGraw-Hill.
———. *Rationale of the Twitchell-Allen Three Dimensional Personality Test.* [Sound recording] New York, J. Norton.
———. *Social Learning in the Schools through Psychodrama.* Old Town, Me.: Old Town Teacher Corp., 1978.

SECONDARY SOURCES
Archives of the History of American Psychology. Bierce Library, University of Akron (Ohio).

Mikols, Patricia Elaine. "Biographical Profiles of Ten Eminent Women Psychologists." Ph.D. diss., University of Pennsylvania, 1981.

STANDARD SOURCES
AMS 6–8, S&B 13–19; *Who's Who of American Women.*

ALLEN, ELIZA (STEVENS) (1842–?)
British botanical illustrator. Married.

Allen illustrated C. A. Johns's *Flowers of the Field* in 1853.

JH/MBO

PRIMARY SOURCES
Johns, C. A. *Flowers of the Field.* London: Society for promoting Christian Knowledge, 1853. Illustrations by Allen.

STANDARD SOURCES
Desmond.

ALLEN, RUTH FLORENCE (1879–1963)
U.S. plant pathologist. Born 1879 in Sturgeon Bay, Wisconsin, to Annie M. (Cox) and Gideon W. Allen. No siblings. Marital status unknown. Educated University of Wisconsin (A.B., 1905; A.M., 1907; Ph.D., 1909). Professional experience: University of Wisconsin, assistant botanist (1905–1910); Michigan State College, instructor (1910–1914); Wellesley College, instructor and assistant professor (1914–1918); Bureau of Plant Industry, U.S. Department of Agriculture and Genetics Department, associate pathologist; and University of California, Berkeley, pathologist (1918–1936). Retired 1936. Died 30 November 1963.

Ruth Florence Allen was the daughter of a lawyer and district attorney in Sturgeon Bay, Wisconsin. After attending the local public high school, she waited five years to attend college while caring for an ailing mother and brother. After attending the University of Wisconsin from 1901–1909, Allen received her Ph.D. degree for studies on spermatogenesis and apogamy in ferns. These studies were published in the *Wisconsin Academy of Sciences, Arts and Letters* (1914). The same year she published a study of light reactions in *Pilocolus* with Holly D. M. Johnson. She took a job in the U.S. Department of Agriculture in 1918, which she combined with a position in the Genetics Department, University of California, Berkeley. In an obituary in 1964, Allen is commended as the "most cited woman in past 30 years, mainly for her cytological studies of rust infections [in wheat]." Her salary was halved during the depression years by the USDA, a fate that did not happen to male members of her department. Two years later she retired (at age fifty-seven) because of her pollen allergies, recurring tuberculosis, and mild diabetes. Allen built up a fortune in the stock market. In 1965, her heirs funded a yearly award in her name to the American Phytopathological Society, of which she had been an early member.   JH/MBO

PRIMARY SOURCES

Allen, Ruth Florence. "Studies in Spermatogenesis and Apogamy in Ferns" (1909 Ph.D. Thesis). *Transactions of the Wisconsin Academy of Sciences, Arts and Letters.* 17, no. 1 (1914): 1–56.

———. "Resistance of Stem Rust in Kanred Wheat." *Science* 53 (1921): 575–576.

———. "A Cytological Study of Infection of Baart and Kanred Wheats by *Puccinia graminis tritici.*" *Journal of Agricultural Research* 23 (1923): 131–151.

———. "A Cytological Study of Orange Leaf Rust, *Puccinia triticina,* Physiological Form 11, on Malakoff Wheat." *Journal of Agricultural Research* 34 (1927): 697–714.

———. "Concerning Heterothallism in *Puccinia graminis.*" *Science* 70 (1929): 308–309.

———. "A Cytological Study of Heterothallism in Flax Rust." *Journal of Agricultural Research* 49 (1934): 765–791.

SECONDARY SOURCES

NAW unused files, MC 307. Notable American Women Series III, box 19, folder 16.

Reynolds, Anne. 13 December 1976, unpublished manuscript in Schlesigner Archives.

Yarwood, C. E., and Mabel Nebel. *Phytopathology* 54 (1964): 885. Obituary notice.

STANDARD SOURCES

Bailey; Rossiter 1982.

ALPER, THELMA GORFINKLE (1908–)

U.S. clinical psychologist. Born 24 July 1908 to Millie (Hermann) and David Gorfinkle in Chelsea MA. One sister. Married Abraham T. Alper (1933; he died 1953). Educated at Wellesley College (B.A., 1929; M.A., 1933); Radcliffe College (Harvard University) (Ph.D., 1942). Board of Clinical Psychologists, diplomate. Professional experience: Wellesley College, tutor and assistant in psychology (1929–1938); Remedial Reading program, director (1938–1942); psychology department associate professor (1952–1954), professor (1954–1973), chair (1963–post 1968). Harvard University, lecturer in clinical psychology (1946–1948). Clark University, Worcester Mass., associate professor (1948–1952). Judge Baker Guidance Clinic (1959–1979). Honors and memberships: Massachusetts Psychological Association, president (1952–1954); Phi Beta Kappa, Radcliffe chapter, president (1952–1954), Wellesley chapter, president (1963–1967).

Growing up in an achievement-oriented Jewish family, Thelma Gorfinkle took her sister Bertha as her model, although her sister was ten years older and chose business over academics. Her sister, rather than her parents, decided that the younger sister should pursue an academic program in high school and attend college. At first she intended to become a kindergarten teacher, but soon changed her studies to German, although she took other courses, including psychology. She also began to volunteer to test young patients at the newly opened Judge Baker Guidance Clinic during the summer of her junior year. Upon graduation she declined offers to teach German or to serve as a translator. Her sister had died, leaving a small child with her mother, and Thelma accepted an opportunity to serve as an assistant to the psychology instructor and then a departmental assistant at Wellesley while she helped with the two-year-old boy. This position also allowed her to begin graduate work, tuition free.

At the age of twenty-three, she married Abraham T. Alper, and the following year received her master's degree in psychology. Although she continued to serve as an assistant in the department at Wellesley, she realized after four years that she would have to get her doctorate in order to obtain a better position. She began graduate work in psychology at Harvard (enrolling in Radcliffe College as all women graduate students were required to do). Warned that women were "given a hard time at Harvard" by Edwin G. Boring, head of the psychology department and brother of ALICE BORING, Alper began part-time study in 1941. She finished her degree in 1943, with a dissertation on learning memory, only the eleventh woman to graduate from Harvard's psychology department. In her last year of graduate work she left her Wellesley position and began to serve first as tutor then as instructor in psychology at Harvard, the only woman in the department. During her years at this institution, she found Boring to be stimulating and supportive, and she worked closely with him, editing two psychology books written for the military, *Psychology for the Fighting Man* and *Psychology for the Returning Veteran.* She taught the child psychology class to both Harvard and Radcliffe students in separate classes and did not experience the severe drop in male enrollment predicted by the faculty. In her later autobiographical account she provides anecdotes underlining the lowly status of women students and faculty at Harvard at that time. Among other problems, Harvard, like Boston University and Tufts in the same period, made it clear that they were willing to appoint her as instructor but could never offer tenure to a woman.

In 1948, Alper resigned her Harvard appointment (expressing her displeasure both in a letter to the dean and by marching out the front door of the faculty club in defiance of custom). She then accepted a position as associate professor at Clark University, where she found faculty and staff very welcoming in spite of her position as the only woman faculty member. The distance from Boston made the position difficult to hold after her husband became ill in 1951, and she returned to Wellesley as associate professor with the promise of rapid tenure and the use of the Nursery School for research in child psychology.

While teaching at Wellesley, Alper reestablished her connection with the Judge Baker Guidance Clinic, where she continued to do clinical research and furthered her training in therapy one day a week. Even after she retired from Wellesley, she continued her work at the clinic, participating as a consultant to the creation of a Head Start group in Charleston, Massachusetts.

In her research, she developed a role-oriented measure to study achievement motivation in women in 1974 to challenge the pattern claimed by Matina Horner of fear of success in relationship to men and found that women fell into two groups: those that accepted a traditionally role-oriented position and those who did not. The non-traditionalists did not follow the pattern.   JH/MBO

PRIMARY SOURCES

Alper, Thelma, "Memory for Completed and Incompleted Tasks." Ph. D. diss., Radcliffe College, 1943.

———. "Task-orientation versus Ego-orientation in Learning and Retention." *Journal of Experimental Psychology* 38 (1948): 224–238.

———. "Predicting the Direction of Selective Recall: Its Relation to Ego-Strength and *n* Achievement." *Journal of Abnormal and Social Psychology* 55 (1957): 149–165.

———. "Achievement Motivation in College Women. A Now-you-see it, Now-you-don't Phenomenon." *American Psychologist* 29 (1974): 194–203.

STANDARD SOURCES

APA Membership Register; O'Connell and Russo 1988 (article by Thelma Alper) (with portrait).

ALTMANN, MARGARET (1900–1984)

German/U.S. biologist. Born 1900 in Berlin. Educated in local schools; University of Bonn (Ph.D., 1928); Cornell University (Ph.D., 1938). Marital status unknown. Professional experience: Farm manager, Germany (1921–1930); dairy researcher; German government specialist (1932–1933); Cornell University, assistant in animal breeding (1933–1938), research associate in psychobiology (1938–1941); Hampton Institute, associate professor of biology and animal husbandry, department chair (1941–1945), professor (1945–1956); Kenyon College, visiting lecturer in psychology and biology (1959); University of Colorado, professor of psychology (1959–1969), emerita professor (from 1969).

Born and trained in Germany, Margaret Altmann began by working on farms and studying farm management. She received her Ph.D. in rural economics from the University of Bonn in 1928 and worked as a specialist in dairy breeding for the German government until the rise of Hitler in 1933. She then came to the United States and took a second Ph.D. in animal breeding from Cornell University, where she worked in the animal breeding program. Altmann then became an associate professor of animal husbandry and genetics at Hampton Institute and, later, professor. She continued her research, switching from farm animals to big game animals at the Biological Research Station, Colorado, where she worked from 1948 to 1956. At the station, she worked on the behavior of ungulates and carnivores. Altmann began to combine genetics research with an interest in psychology, doing research in psychobiology at Cornell and then teaching psychology and biology at Kenyon College. She finished her career at the University of Colorado, where she was psychology professor from 1959 to 1969. She joined the American Society of Mammalogists, where she remained a member for more than twenty years. She published three papers in the *Journal of Mammalogy* on moose, and gave two presentations, one on wapiti and one on dog packs at the annual meeting of the society in 1950. Altmann was well known for her skills as a field biologist.   JH/MBO

PRIMARY SOURCES

Altmann, Margaret. "Group Dynamics in Wyoming Moose During the Rutting Season." *Journal of Mammalogy* 40 (1959): 420–424.

SECONDARY SOURCES

Kaufman, Dawn M., Donald W. Kaufman, and Glennis A. Kaufman. "Women in the Early Years of the American Society of Mammalogists (1919–1949)." *Journal of Mammalogy* 77, no. 3 (1996): 642–654.

STANDARD SOURCES

AMS 7–8, B 9, P&B 10–12; Bailey.

ALUWIHARE, FLORENCE KAUSHALYA (RAM) (1905–   )

British/Indian physician. Born 16 September 1905 in Edinburgh, to Sukhda Ram and Labbhu Ram. Married Bernard Herbert Aluwihare (12 October 1932). One son and one daughter. Educated Mexborough Secondary School; Newnham College, Cambridge (1923–1926); Sheffield University (B.Chir., Cambridge, 1929). Professional experience: Weston sur Mare, house surgeon (1929–1930); Edinburgh Hospital for Women and Children, house physician (1930); Lady Hardinge Medical College, New Delhi, assistant to professor of physiology (1932–1933); Colombo, Sri Lanka, various posts (1935–1937); general practice (1938–1956); Ceylon University, part-time physician (1956–1967); Ealing, Hammersmith, and Brent, England, various appointments (1969–1970); Sessional Medical Officer, Brent (1970–?).

Florence Ram Aluwihare was born and educated in Great Britain. After practicing in Scotland, she went to Ceylon (Sri Lanka) where she spent the greater part of her career. Her work in orphanages and in family-planning clinics was especially important. Aluwihare volunteered as a member of the Management Committee of the Children's Hospital of Colombo (Sri Lanka) Hospital Board. She published a "family doctor" column in the *Times* of Ceylon from 1954 to 1957. Aluwihare left Ceylon in 1968 to return to England, where she worked in various positions. JH/MBO

PRIMARY SOURCES
Aluwihare, Florence Ram. Articles in Ceylonese journals and contributions to *Sinhalese Encyclopaedia*.

STANDARD SOURCES
Newnham vol. 1.

AMALITSKIYA, ANNA P. (1861–1939)

Russian/Soviet Geologist. Born 1861. Married V. P. Amalitskiya. Educated Gymnasium. Professional experience: assistant to her husband. Honors and memberships: St. Petersburg Society of Experimental Natural Scientists (elected); Paleontological Society (elected). Died Leningrad, 1939.

Although Anna P. Amalitskiya was not trained as a geologist, she made many contributions to the science by assisting her husband, V. P. Amalitskiya, a professor at Warsaw University. After their wedding, they immediately went on a scientific expedition, with Anna acting as her husband's secretary. From that time on, she dedicated herself to her husband's work. She was especially well known for creating a unique collection of Permian reptiles from North Dvina. She continued to work on this collection for twenty years after Amalitskiya's death.

In 1895, Amalitskiya discovered lenses of sandstones containing tons of concretions of different sizes in Upper Permian species on the coast of northern Dvina. When they opened these concretions, they found that each one contained one or more animal bones. Amalitskiya found that that the concretions lay in accumulations, and that one such accumulation consisted of a whole skeleton of an animal wonderfully preserved. He described and identified these animals and determined that they were previously unknown forms. These fossils became the central focus of his scientific work. Anna accompanied her husband to northern Dvina, lived in difficult field conditions, and assisted him in every aspect of the work. Soon Anna could identify the reptiles and amphibians with as much skill as her husband. She was always subordinate to her husband, and although he praised her skill, he did not add her name to his papers. He did, however, name a new animal after her, *Anna Petri*. They mounted the collection and kept it at first at Warsaw University. After Amalitskiya died, Anna devoted herself to the collection. She saved the existing collection and then worked to enlarge and better it. She mounted the collection in Leningrad in the Geological Museum of the USSR Academy of Sciences. Her work was recognized by several awards, and in 1937, at the International Geological Congress in Moscow, where the Amalitskiya collection was one of the highlights. After the Congress she returned to Leningrad, where she lived in a retirement home for scientists until she died. JH/MBO

STANDARD SOURCES
Nalivkin.

AMALOSUNTA (b. 1400s)
Italian healer.

Amalosunta was a Lombard princess from northern Italy who is reputed to have performed medical miracles. JH/MBO

SECONDARY SOURCES
Lemoyne, Pierre. *Gallerie of Heroick Women*. Trans. Marquess of Winchester. 1652.

STANDARD SOURCES
Hurd-Mead 1938.

AMELINE (fl. 1313–1325)
French physician.

Ameline, *la miresse*, practiced in Paris in 1313 on the rue Guillaume Porée. She was later charged with illegally practicing medicine. JH/MBO

STANDARD SOURCES
Echols and Williams.

AMES, BLANCHE (AMES) (1878–1969)

U.S. botanical illustrator, inventor, and author. Born 1878 to Adelbert and Blanche (Butler) Ames. Five siblings. Married Oakes Ames (1900). Four children: Pauline (1901), Oliver (1903), Amyas (1906), Evelyn (1910). Educated Smith College (B.A., 1899). Professional experience: Spanish-American War, served briefly as nurse; Birth Control League of Massachusetts, cofounder (1916); World War II, patented device to ensnare low-flying aircraft; botanical works of Oakes Ames, illustrator. Died 1969 at the family home, Borderland, near North Easton, Massachusetts.

Blanche Ames was a progressive and creative woman who had the opportunity through her wealth, education, and marriage to an open-minded and supportive husband, to pursue a variety of interests to the fullest. After graduating as president of her class at Smith College in 1899, she married Oakes Ames, who introduced her to his world of botany (especially orchids). They began a lifetime of collaboration. He would eventually become research professor and director of the Botanical Museum at Harvard University, and originator of the field of economic botany (the study of the conservation and economic impact of natural resources). Blanche Ames illustrated his seven-volume treatise on orchids, and it was her illustrations that made the book so significant. An accomplished artist, she produced an extensive body of portrait work, botanical etchings, drawings, and watercolor illustrations, and created a detailed system of color tabs for matching any shade of color. An active suffragist and feminist, she also drew biting political cartoons that received national attention in support of the movement.

Blanche Ames's suffragist activities began in college and continued throughout her life. Both Republicans, Blanche and Oakes Ames together lobbied at the 1914 National Convention for a suffrage plank. She worked with the Massachusetts Woman Suffrage League, he with a men's suffrage group. Central to her women's rights beliefs was birth control. In 1916, she cofounded the Birth Control League of Massachusetts (BCLM), which sought to make birth control a public issue. When their attempts to modify a law prohibiting the dissemination of birth control information failed, Ames urged mothers to educate their daughters and gave them methods for the construction of homemade diaphragms and spermicidal jellies. Concern for the education and health care of women led Ames in 1941 to become a member of the corporation of the New England Hospital for Women and Children—founded in 1862 to provide services to women by women and to train female physicians and nurses. When financial difficulties in the 1950s led the board to consider including men on the staff, Ames began a successful fund-raising campaign in order to maintain the original premise and unique character of the hospital. She also helped found the birth control movement in Massachusetts.

Blanche and Oakes Ames began to aquire land soon after marriage, buying up small farms along the edge of their property. Besides being a working farm, Borderland (as they named the estate) was developed as a game and forest preserve and was managed as a wildlife sanctuary during their later years. Borderland is now a state park renowned for its wide variety of habitat and wildlife. When an architect would not produce the style of fireproof ediface the Ameses desired, Blanche redesigned the house herself and supervised its construction. She used stones from walls left elsewhere on the property and concrete for the floors so that her husband's vast library would be protected. In order to salvage swampy areas on the estate, Blanche Ames designed and built a system of dams and ponds, sometimes with the help of her children. Using large granite stones from Oakes's grandfather's shovel manufactory, she built an unusual swimming pool, which was kept filled by a spring and a sump pump in a nearby stream. After she died, no one could figure out how to make the system work and the pool was finally filled in and landscaped as a water garden.

Blanche Ames was also involved in agriculture. She raised turkeys to sell in Boston and invented a system of keeping the birds on wire off the ground so they would not contract disease. She contributed scientific articles concerning her experiments on disease prevention.

Blanche Ames's daughter Pauline wrote that "whenever an idea would occur to my mother, she would usually carry it out." During World War II, after noticing how a single thread snarled in the works would stop a sewing machine, Ames conceived the idea of protecting London by hanging ordinary strings from balloons over the city, which would snare bombers by snarling and stopping their propellers. She rented an aeroplane and a windmill, and designed machinery to wind the string onto huge spools. Ames invited several Pentagon officials and the president of MIT to witness her experiment, which stopped the test plane in short order. Her idea was accepted by the army and patented in Washington but was too late for practical application.

When she was eighty years old, Blanche Ames became angered by a passage in John F. Kennedy's *Profiles in Courage* criticizing her father as a "carpetbagger." To set the record straight, she undertook a six-year research project that culminated in an important book. She died in 1969 at the age of ninety-one.

JH/MBO

PRIMARY SOURCES
Blanche Ames's papers are at Sophia Smith Archives, Smith College.
Ames, Blanche. *Drawing of Florida Orchids, with Explanatory Notes by Oakes Ames.* Cambridge, Mass.: Printed at the Botanical Museum, 1947.
———. *Adelbert Ames, 1835–1933: General, Senator, Governor, the Story of His Life and Times and His Integrity as a Soldier and Statesman.* New York: Argosy-Antiquarian, 1964.
Ames, Oakes. *Orchidiceae: Illustrations and Studies of the Family Orchidaceae.* 7 vols. Boston: Merrymount Press, 1905–1922. Drawings and plates by Blanche Ames.

SECONDARY SOURCES

Ames, Oakes. *Broken Oaths and Reconstruction in Mississippi,* 1964.

———. *Oakes Ames, Jottings of a Harvard Botanist, 1874–1950.* Cambridge, Mass.: Botanical Museum of Harvard University, 1979. Autobiographical writings, with introduction by Pauline Plimpton Ames.

"Borderland State Park." Brochure. North Easton, Mass.: Massachusetts Department of Environmental Management, n.d. Biographical information on Oakes and Blanche Ames with history and description of their estate, which is now Borderland State Park.

Plimpton, Pauline Ames. "Ramblings about Borderland," N.p., [1986]. Reminiscences by the oldest child of Blanche and Oakes Ames; includes anecdotes about her parents and family life at Borderland.

STANDARD SOURCES

NAW(M) (article by Janet Nelson Friedel).

AMES, LOUISE BATES (1908–)

U.S. developmental and educational psychologist. Born 29 October 1908 in Portland, Maine, to Anne Earle (Leach) and Samuel Lewis Bates. Married Smith Ames (1930); divorced (1937). One daughter. Educated University of Maine (B.A., 1930; M.A., 1933); Yale University (Ph.D., 1936). Professional experience: Yale University Medical School, research assistant in child development (1933–1936), instructor and assistant professor (1936–1950); Yale Films, curator (1944–1950); Gesell Institute of Child Development, cofounder and director of research in child development (1950–1963), associate director (1963–1971), chief psychologist and codirector of child development (1971–?). Honors and memberships: University of Maine (1957) and Wheaton College (1967), honorary Sc.D.; Bruno Klopfer Distinguished Contribution Award of the Society of Personality Assessment; University of Maine Alumni Career Award, recipient (1974).

After receiving her B.A. and M.A. from the University of Maine, Louise Bates Ames earned a Ph.D. in psychology at Yale University. At Yale, Ames became secretary and research assistant to Arnold Gesell, director of the Clinic of Child Development. This clinic was one of the most progressive child-study laboratories in the nation and provided ample opportunities for study of children from birth through preschool age. Ames progressed from instructor to assistant professor, becoming full professor of psychology in 1948. In 1944, she was appointed curator of the Yale Films of Child Development and became an expert on behavior patterns in children. Without their knowledge, the films recorded children at play, work, meals, and during sleep. They became the basis for a weekly television series in Boston.

Ames's first collaboration with Gesell and FRANCES LILLIAN

ILG produced *The Infant and Child in the Culture of Today,* based on clinical observations of infants and children up to four years old. When the Yale Clinic affiliated with the New Canaan Country School (New Canaan, Connecticut), the team was able to extend its studies to older children. They educated the parents of the children according to the developmental point of view and taught them to report day-to-day observations. More than fifty children from five to ten years were included in this study and their case histories resulted in *The Child from Five to Ten.* Ames's books were tremendously popular, giving practical guidance and reassurance concerning typical normal growth patterns and fluctuations. After Gesell retired in 1950, Ilg and Ames founded the Gesell Institute of Child Development to carry on the Gesell programs, with Gesell acting as consultant until his death in 1961.

Ames and Ilg coauthored the popular syndicated newspaper column, *Child Behavior,* which appeared in more than fifty newspapers nationwide. The column gave advice on basic child-rearing as well as on specific behavior problems. The book *Child Behavior* was an outgrowth of the column and was the first Gesell publication to address specific behavior problems of children. In 1956, in *Youth: The Years from Ten to Sixteen,* Gesell, Ames, and Ilg reported several thousand adolescent behavior patterns they had identified and codified in forty areas of behavior.

In 1947, Ames completed a study with Harriett Field in which the 1,400 women in the American Psychological Association Yearbook responded to the question, "In what ways has the fact that you are a woman affected your career?" The results were published in the *Journal of Social Psychology* in 1950. The report revealed that there were two kinds of women psychologists: those working in "men's work" (universities, miscellaneous) where they felt generally frustrated, unequally paid, and unequally compensated professionally; and those in "women's work" (clinics, public education) where they felt generally appreciated and optimistic about their future. Despite the 40 percent of respondents who felt their sex hindered their careers, and the many who expressed dissatisfaction, isolation, and worse, Ames and Field concluded that women found psychological work a "satisfying profession."

Ames was a recognized authority on the Rorschach tests and published a monumental normative study of children's Rorschach responses in 1952. One of the most prolific writers in the history of psychology, she authored twenty-two books, hundreds of technical articles, scores of features for popular journals, and years of syndicated newspaper columns. Ames was a Fellow of the American Psychological Association, a charter member of the Connecticut State Psychological Society, and a member of the International Council of Women Psychologists, the Society for Research in Child Development, the Society of Personality Assessment, the International Society for the Study of Behavior Development, and Sigma Xi.   JH/MBO

PRIMARY SOURCES

Ames, Louise Bates. *The Sequential Patterning of Prone Progression in the Human Infant.* Provincetown, Mass.: Journal Press, 1937.

———. With Arnold Gesell and Frances Ilg. *The Child from Five to Ten.* New York and London: Harper & Brothers, 1946.

———. With others. *Child Rorschach Responses: Developmental Trends from Two to Ten Years.* New York: P. B. Hoeber, 1952.

———. With Frances Ilg. *Child Behavior.* New York: Harper, 1955.

———. With Ruth W. Métraux and Richard N. Walker. *Adolescent Rorschach Responses: Developmental Trends from Ten to Sixteen Years.* New York: P. B. Hoeber, 1959. Rev. ed. 1995.

———. *School Readiness: Behavior Tests Used at the Gesell Institute.* New York: Harper & Row, 1965.

———. With Janet Learned, Ph.D.; Ruth W. Métraux, M.A.; Richard N. Walker, M.A. *Rorschach Responses in Old Age.* New York: Hoeber-Harper, 1954. 2d. edition, 1973.

———. With Clyde Gillespie and John. W. Streff. *Stop School Failure.* New York: Harper, 1972. Rev. ed., 1985.

SECONDARY SOURCES

Murstein, B.I. "Louise Bates Ames." *Journal of Personality Assessment* 386 (1974): 505–506.

STANDARD SOURCES

AMS 8, S&B 9–13; *Current Biography* 1956; Rossiter 1995; Stevens and Gardner; *Who's Who of American Women.*

AMES, MARY E. PULSIFER (1843–1902)

U.S. botanist. Born 1843. Died 21 March 1902 in San Jose, Calif.

Mary E. Pulsifer Ames was a California botanical writer who was a friend of botanist REBECCA AUSTIN. She helped Austin with her *Darlingtonia* studies and was also a dedicated collector. The pollinating agent of *Darlingtonia* was unknown and Austin, her daughter Mrs. C.C. Bruce and Mary Ames attempted to solve the mystery. Austin concluded that spiders were the pollinators. Ames was important in providing a foundation to the knowledge of the vegetation of northeastern California. She was recognized by having a plant named for her, *Astragalus pulsiferae.* Ames died at the age of fifty-seven in San Jose, CA.   JH/MBO

SECONDARY SOURCES

"Scientific Notes." *Science* 15, 2nd series (1902): 517.

STANDARD SOURCES

Barnhardt; Barr; Bonta.

AMHERST, SARAH (ARCHER), COUNTESS. (1762–1838)

British natural historian and botanist. Born 1762. Married Lord Amherst in 1823. At least one daughter? Traveled and collected plants in India from 1823 to 1824. Died 1838.

Sarah Amherst traveled with her husband, governor general of India, from 1823–1824, collecting plants on these trips. She is noted for the introduction of *Clematis montana* and other plants to Europe. Her Indian plant collection is at Kew. Amherst was a patron of natural history, especially botany. Her daughter, Lady Sarah Amherst, followed her mother's interests. Amherst is commemorated by the plant name, *Amherstia nobilis Wall.*

Amherst's plant collection from the Himalayas (1823–1828) was found in the herbarium of Aylmer Bourke Lambert (1761–1842), which was sold at auction after his death. An article in *Taxon,* 1970, discusses the probable disposition of these plants.   JH/MBO

SECONDARY SOURCES

Miller, Hortense S. "The Herbarium of Aylmer Bourke Lambert. Notes on Its Acquisition, Dispersal, and Present Whereabouts." *Taxon,* vol. 19 (1970): 489–553. See page 511 for a discussion of Amherst's herbarium.

Ritchie, Anne Thackeray. *Lord Amherst and the British Advance to Burma.* Oxford: Clarendon Press, 1894.

STANDARD SOURCES

Desmond.

ANDERSEN, DOROTHY HANSINE (1901–1963)

U.S. pathologist and pediatrician. Born 15 May 1901 in Asheville, N.C., to (Mary) Louise (Mason) and Hans Peter Andersen. Never married. Educated at Saint Johnsbury Academy (1918); Mount Holyoke (A.B., 1922); Johns Hopkins Medical School (M.D., 1926); Columbia University (D.Med.Sc., 1935). Professional experience: University of Rochester, anatomy instructor (1927), instructor (1929–1930); Babies Hospital, Columbia-Presbyterian Medical Center, assistant pathologist (1935–1944), assistant attending pediatrician (1945–1951), chief of pathology (1952–1957); College of Physicians and Surgeons, professor of pathology (1958–1962). Honors and memberships: E. Mead Johnson Award (1938). Died 3 March 1963, of lung cancer, in New York City.

Born in Asheville, North Carolina, Dorothy Hansine Andersen was the daughter of a Danish-born farmer who was an activist in the YMCA and a mother with historical roots in Vermont. Her father died when she was thirteen years old. Mother and daughter returned to Vermont where Andersen attended the St. Johnsbury Academy. She then entered Mount Holyoke College and completed her education in 1922, in spite of her mother's early death in 1920. Andersen entered Johns Hopkins Medical School in 1923 and began research under FLORENCE SABIN, publishing a paper on the blood vessels and lymphatics of swine Fallopian tubes and ovaries while she was still a student.

After receiving her medical degree in 1926, Andersen taught anatomy at the Rochester School of Medicine, then interned in surgery at the Strong Memorial Hospital in Rochester. Denied a residency in surgery or an appointment in pathology at Rochester because she was a woman, Andersen went to Columbia University where she served as assistant in the Department of Pathology at the College of Physicians and Surgeons. She continued her research interests in female reproduction by studying the endocrine glands. From 1930 to 1935, Andersen was an instructor in pathology at the medical school. On the basis of her research, she was awarded a doctorate in medical sciences from Columbia in 1935.

In 1935 Andersen moved to Babies Hospital at Columbia-Presbyterian Medical Center where she served first as assistant pathologist, next as assistant attending pediatrician, then as chief of pathology. During the first three years she collected cases of children with celiac disease who had lesions of the pancreas. From these observations she described a new disease entity that she named cystic fibrosis. For this discovery she was awarded the E. Mead Johnson Award in 1938. Continuing her studies of cystic fibrosis, she developed tests for its early diagnosis based on enzymes in the duodenal fluid. By the 1940s, she began to write articles on chemotherapy for respiratory tract infections in cystic fibrosis and on the genetic aspects of this disease.

In 1952 Andersen was appointed chief of pathology, a position she held until 1958. Her studies on congenital heart disease in infants and her collection of pathological examples served as crucial aids to the early work on open heart surgery being pioneered at Columbia. In 1958, Andersen was made full professor at the College of Physicians and Surgeons. Because of her investigations, cystic fibrosis patients began to survive into young adulthood. This age group was the subject of her last major paper in 1959. She published several papers on cardiac malformations in her last years. An energetic and enthusiastic athlete, she brought friends and colleagues to spend weekends at her farm in northwest New Jersey. She developed lung cancer and died in 1963.   JH/MBO

PRIMARY SOURCES

Anderson, Dorothy Hansine. *Lymphatics and Blood Vessels of the Sow.* Washington, D.C.: Carnegie Institution, 1926.

Autobiographical sketch. Archives, Mount Holyoke College.
List of publications, Columbia University College of Physicians and Surgeons.
Papers privately held.

SECONDARY SOURCES

Journal of the American Medical Association, 25 May 1963: 670. Obituary notice.
Journal of Pediatrics (October 1964): 477–479. Obituary notice.
The Stethoscope (April 1963). Obituary notice.

STANDARD SOURCES

NAW (M) (article by Libby Machol); *Notable.*

ANDERSON, CAROLINE VIRGINIA (STILL) WILEY (1848–1919)

U.S. physician and educator. Born 1848 in Philadelphia, Pa., to Lucy and William Still. Married Edward Wiley (1869) and Matthew Anderson (1880). Two children by Wiley and three surviving children by Anderson. Educated in Philadelphia at Mrs. Gordon's Private School; The Friends' Raspberry Alley School; the Institute for Coloured Youth (now Cheyney State College); Oberlin College (1865–1868 and 1874–1876); Howard Medical School (one year); Women's Medical College of Philadelphia (M.D., 1878). Professional experience: New England Hospital for Women and Children, Boston, intern (1878–1879); private practice; Berean Manual Training and Industrial School, teacher of elocution, physiology, and hygiene. Honors and memberships: Women's Medical College Alumnae Association; Bureau Women's Christian Temperence Union. Died in 1919.

Caroline Still Anderson was the daughter of William Still, whose parents were fugitive slaves. Still was a successful businessman, abolitionist, and prominent figure in the Underground Railroad. He wrote *The Underground Railroad,* a book that recorded many of the names and events regarding escaped slaves. Comfortably established in the coal industry, he was able to send Caroline to Mrs. Henry Gordon's Private School and the Friends' Raspberry Allen School. In 1861, Caroline entered the Institute for Coloured Youth in Pennsylvania to finish her high school education. Sources disagree on the dates of her attendance and graduation from Oberlin College. At graduation she was elected to preside over the annual meeting of the Ladies' Literary Society of Oberlin, the first African American to have this honor. Returning to Philadelphia, she taught a year and married Edward A. Wiley, a former slave who had also attended Oberlin College. Edward died in 1873, leaving Caroline with two children, William and Letitia.

After Edward Wiley's death, Caroline Wiley matriculated at Howard University in Washington D.C. To help pay expenses, she taught drawing and speech. In 1875 she enrolled in the University Medical College. The next year she transferred to the Woman's Medical College of Pennsylvania, where she graduated on 14 March 1878, under RACHEL BODLEY. Wiley was one of two black women in the graduating class. Although initially refused admittance to the New England Hospital for Women and Children in Boston due to her race, Caroline appealed to the hospital board and was accepted in 1878. After completing two years of internship, she returned to Pennsylvania and began her medical practice.

In 1880, Wiley married Matthew Anderson, who had attended Oberlin (B.A., 1874) and received his doctorate of divinity from Lincoln University near Philadelphia. Soon after graduation, he helped found the Berean Presbyterian Church in Philadelphia. In 1899, with Caroline's support, he helped found the Berean Manual Training and Industrial School. Caroline became the school's assistant principal and instructor in elocution, hygiene, and physiology. She also worked at the clinic and dispensary connected to the Berean Presbyterian Church, where her husband was minister. She and Matthew had five children, three of whom survived (Helen, Maude, and Margaret). Until she suffered a stroke that left her paralyzed, Anderson was an active presence in the school and community, serving as treasurer of Women's Medical College Alumnae Association, as a member of Women's Medical Society, Philadelphia, and as president of Berean WCTU. She founded the first black YWCA in Philadelphia. Caroline Anderson died in 1919.   JH/MBO

PRIMARY SOURCES
Papers in Archives and Special Collections on Women in Medicine, Medical College of Pennsylvania; Berean Institute; Charles L. Blockson Afro-American Historical Collection, Temple University; Historical Society of Pennsylvania (includes photographs); and Oberlin College Archives (includes photographs).

SECONDARY SOURCES
Hine, Darlene Clark. "Co-Laborers in the Work of the Lord: Nineteenth Century Black Women Physicians." In *Send Us a Lady Physician*, ed. Ruth J. Abram. New York: Norton, 1985.

STANDARD SOURCES
Ireland; *LKW; NBAW.*

ANDERSON, ELDA EMMA (1899–1961)

U.S. physicist. Born 5 October 1899 in Green Lake, Wis., to Lena (Heller) and Edwin A. Anderson. Three siblings. Educated high school in Greenlake; Ripon College, Wis. (A.B., 1922); University of Wisconsin (A.M., 1924; Ph.D., 1941). Professional experience: Estherville Junior College, Iowa, dean of chemistry, physics

and math (1924–1927); Menasha High School, science teacher (1927–1929); Milwaukee-Downer College, professor of physics (1929–1943), chair of physics department (1934–1943; 1947–1949); Princeton University, Office of Scientific Research and Development, scientific staff member (1941); Los Alamos Scientific Laboratory, Manhattan Project (1943–1947); Oak Ridge National Laboratory, Tennessee, chief of education and training (1947–1961). Honors and memberships: Health Physics Society (1950), secretary pro tem, charter secretary, president (1959–1960); American Board of Health Physics, secretary and chair (1960–1961); Sigma Xi; Sigma Delta Epsilon; American Association for the Advancement of Science, Fellow; Elda E. Anderson Award established in her honor. Died 17 April 1961 in Oak Ridge, Tenn., of breast cancer and leukemia.

A warm friendly woman, Elda Emma Anderson was one of the founders of the science of health physics, involving the study of radiation protection. Educated in the state of Wisconsin, she did not get her Ph.D. until 1941, long after she had become professor of physics and department chair at Milwaukee-Downer College. During a sabbatical leave in 1941, she worked for the Office of Scientific Research and Development at Princeton University, the forerunner of the Manhattan Engineering District. She returned to Milwaukee-Downer for two years and then joined the Manhattan project at Los Alamos, New Mexico. Working as a part of the cyclotron group, she researched spectroscopy and experimental measurement of neutron cross-sections. This research was essential to the development of the atomic bomb. She observed the "Trinity event," the explosion of the first atomic bomb, in the New Mexican desert. After the war she returned to her former position as a chair of the physics department and also held a concurrent position at Wisconsin State Teachers College.

Anderson remained at the university for only two more years, after which she moved to Tennessee, where she became the Oak Ridge National Laboratory's first chief of education and training. In this position, she worked tirelessly to make the field of health physics recognized. After both physicists and those in the health professions recognized the dangers of radiation, they accepted the need to protect people and their environment from radiation. Anderson's job was to educate people as to the potential dangers of radiation. In doing this she promoted health physics as a profession, establishing a training program at Oak Ridge and even cooperating with Vanderbilt University to begin a master's degree program in the field. Not only did Anderson work in the United States, she also organized international courses in Stockholm, Belgium, and Bombay. She encouraged her students at Oak Ridge to form a Health Physics Society. She also established a professional certifying agency, the American Board of Health Physics. Ironically, Anderson contracted leukemia and later breast cancer, perhaps because of her work with radioactivity.　　　　　　　JH/MBO

PRIMARY SOURCES

Anderson's papers are deposited in the Center for the History of Physics at the American Institute of Physics in New York City.

Anderson, Elda. "Education and Training of Health Physicists." *Radiology* (January 1954): 83–87.

———. "Isotope Milker Supplies Ba-137 from Parent Cs-137." *Nucleonics* (May 1957): 122–125.

———. L. J. Beaufait, Jr., and Paul Peterson. "Development and Preparation of a Set of Gamma Spectrometer Standards." *Analytical Chemistry* 30 (1958): 1762–1764.

SECONDARY SOURCES

"Anderson, Elda Emma." *Physics Today* (July 1961): 68. Obituary notice.

STANDARD SOURCES

Brooke Bailey; *NAW* (M) (article by Ronald L. Kathren); *NCAB.*

ANDERSON, ELIZABETH GARRETT (1836–1917)

British physician. Born 9 June 1836 in London to Louisa and Newson Garrett. Married James G. Skelton Anderson. Three children: Louisa Garrett, Margaret Skelton, and Alan Garrett. Educated at Blackheath Boarding School (finished 1851); Apothecaries' Hall (L.S.A., 1865); and the University of Paris (M.D., 1870). Professional experience: physician for women and children, London; London School of Medicine for Women, dean. Died 17 December 1917.

Elizabeth Garrett was born in Whitechapel, an undesirable section of London, the daughter of a pawnbroker. Her father prospered after buying a small business and moved his family to a better neighborhood.

Elizabeth was sent with her sister Louisa to a "boarding school for ladies" at Blackheath, near London. Strong-willed Elizabeth abhorred the finishing school atmosphere and later complained that she was not taught science or mathematics. Nevertheless, she had excellent instruction in English literature, French, Italian, and German.

After being "finished" in 1851, Elizabeth and Louisa took a short tour on the Continent. Elizabeth became interested in the embryonic women's movement. In *The Englishwoman's Journal* she first read of the American physician ELIZABETH BLACKWELL. When Garrett heard that Blackwell was in England (1859), she arranged to meet her through Emily Davies (an important figure in the women's education

movement) and the eccentric feminist Barbara Bodichon. After talking to Blackwell, Garrett decided to become a physician.

Enormous legal difficulties had to be overcome before any woman could obtain a medical education in England. In spite of the obstacles, Garrett set herself the goal of opening the medical profession to women in England. With the help of Davies, she began to fill the gaps in her own education. Her father's first reaction to her "disgusting" idea was rage, and her mother wept over the coming "disgrace." Eventually, however, Newson Garrett became his daughter's ally and agreed to help her. Garrett underwent a trial period (August 1860–January 1861) as a surgical nurse at the Middlesex Hospital in London. Obviously she was competent, and sympathetic physicians permitted her to follow them into the wards. Although the dean supported her attempts to establish herself as a regular student, the students produced a petition protesting her presence. Garrett attempted to locate an English university that would allow her to matriculate. After the universities of London, Edinburgh, and St. Andrews refused her, she worked outside the regular system to gain licensing through the Apothecaries' Hall, receiving her L.S.A. (Licentiate of the Society of Apothecaries) in 1865.

Since many aspects of medicine were closed to Garrett, she decided to become a physician for women and children in London, helped by subsidies from her father. Garrett's practice grew during the cholera epidemic of 1866, when people were grateful for any medical attention. She established a dispensary staffed by women, and as it prospered, people forgot their hostility to women physicians.

Garrett became one of the 1,498 women members of the first British Women's Suffrage Committee in 1866. She supported the committee's work, but did not engage in politics actively for fear of prejudicing the case of women in medicine. When she was elderly she again became involved in the suffrage movement.

Informed by MARY PUTNAM JACOBI in 1868 that women would be allowed to pursue degrees in France, Garret applied and, after additional controversy, received an M.D. in 1870.

Garrett's former supporter in the Middlesex Hospital, Nathaniel Heckford, had opened a children's hospital and proposed Garrett as the visiting medical officer. In spite of some opposition, she was accepted. One of the opponents to her appointment, James G. Skelton Anderson, the hospital's vice-president and financial adviser, reversed his position after Garrett appeared before the board. Garrett and Skelton Anderson often worked together during her successful campaign for the London School Board in 1870. In 1871 they were married in an unconventional ceremony, Elizabeth insisting that she would not promise "to obey" and refusing to be "given away."

Elizabeth Garrett Anderson's activities were not slowed down by marriage. In addition to her duties as a physician, she "fulfilled, and enjoyed, the duties of an ordinary housewife"; worked on the London School Board, to whose Statistical, Law, and Parliamentary Committee she was elected; and was active on the committee that proposed to move Emily Davies' college from Hitchin to a site at Girton, only two miles from Cambridge. In 1873 she gave birth to her first child, LOUISA GARRETT ANDERSON, and in 1874 to a second, Margaret, who died of meningitis as a baby. Her son, Alan, was born in 1877.

Anderson became involved in the establishment of the London School of Medicine for Women. She was elected dean over SOPHIA JEX-BLAKE in 1883. From 1886 to 1892 she was occupied with building and staffing the New Hospital for Women, the teaching institution connected with the school. Retiring from the staff of this hospital in 1892, she continued as a consultant and remained dean of the medical college until 1902. Her administrative abilities assured the school of full university status: it became a college of the University of London, and its graduates received hospital appointments, positions in public health services, and medical society memberships.

Anderson's husband succeeded her father as mayor of the village of Aldeburgh in Suffolkand. After Skelton Anderson died in 1907, Elizabeth, at age seventy-one, successfully stood for mayor. As active in supervising the details of running the village as she had been in managing the hospital, she lost popularity toward the end of her tenure because of her support for the militant wing of the suffrage movement. She, who had proposed moderation in the medical struggle, even quarreled with Millicent Fawcett, her sister, who led the moderate faction.

After her second term as mayor ended in 1909, Anderson spent more time on her hobbies of gardening and travel, and observed with pleasure her children's careers: Louisa, who received an M.D. in 1905, became an eminent physician and an active suffragist; Alan served as controller of the navy and received a knighthood in 1917.

Elizabeth Garrett Anderson was a practical physician and a social activist, not a theoretical scientist. Because this determined crusader began the opening of the British medical schools to women, she is vital to the history of medicine. In addition to persistence, Anderson possessed practical skills and tact; although she single-mindedly worked toward her goal, she did not represent the stereotype of an aggressive woman. She was able to recruit powerful male allies in spite of what sometimes seemed overwhelming opposition. Later when she married, had children, yet continued with her work, her reputation was enhanced further. Elizabeth Garrett Anderson's publications reflect the nature of her contributions to science. Her medical works are descriptive and practical rather than theoretical. Even though she never published her lectures, she revised her notes continually and

stressed the importance of observation to her students. Although she was a skilled physician and surgeon, it is her interest in the medical education of women that remains significant. MBO

PRIMARY SOURCES
Anderson, Elizabeth Garrett. *On the Progress of Medicine in the Victorian Era*. London: Macmillan, 1897.

SECONDARY SOURCES
Manton, Jo. *Elizabeth Garrett Anderson*. New York: Dutton, 1965. This biography contains a collection of previously unpublished papers.

STANDARD SOURCES
DNB, Supplement 3; *WWW* 1916–1928; Ogilvie 1986.

ANDERSON, EVELYN M. (1899–1985)

U.S. physiologist and biochemist. Born 20 March 1899 in Willmar, Minnesota. Married Webb E. Haymaker (1936). Educated Carleton College, Northfield, Minnesota; University of California, Berkeley, School of Medicine (M.D., 1928); internship and residency in medicine at University of California Hospital, San Francisco; postgraduate fellow, McGill University (Ph.D., 1934). Professional experience: University of California at Berkeley, instructor, assistant professor (1935–1946), associate professor of medicine (1946–1947); Section on Endocrinology in the National Institute of Arthritis and metabolic Diseases (NIAMD) at National Institutes of Health (NIH), chief (1947–1962); Howard University, visiting professor (1955); Neuroendocrinology unit, NASA, Ames Research Institute, head (1962–1969). Retired in 1969. Honors and memberships: Guggenheim Fellowship (1946); Woman's Medical College of Pennsylvania (1961); Carleton College (1954), honorary doctorate; Federal Woman's Award (1964).

The daughter of Swedish immigrants, Evelyn M. Anderson attended Carleton College in Northfield, Minnesota, where she was encouraged by the dean of women, who helped her gain admittance to the University of California School of Medicine. She spent her research year in the laboratory of Herbert M. Evans at Berkeley from 1924 to 1925. Her research resulted in two papers on vitamin A and nutrition, which Evans introduced at the annual meeting of anatomists. She received her M.D. in 1928, graduating at the head of her class. After graduating, Anderson did an internship and residency in medicine at the University of California Hospital in San Francisco. During this period she published papers with three of the hospital clinicians.

Not content with an M.D., Anderson went to McGill University in Montreal with the intention of obtaining a Ph.D. in biochemistry. She trained with J. B. Collip, who was working on hormone isolation from pituitary glands. Her dissertation in biochemistry (under Collip) was on the anterior hypophysis and thyroid (1934). Anderson was codiscoverer, with Collip and D. L. Thomson, of ACTH (adrenocortical thyroid hormone). The paper, published in the *Lancet* in 1933, demonstrated that the extract they obtained from the anterior pituitary contined an adrenotropic hormone. In 1934 Anderson and Collip produced a paper showing the existence of an anti-thyroid stimulating hormone capable of countering TSH and contributing to understanding of antihormones. In 1935, Anderson returned to the University of California at Berkeley as an instructor, progressing to assistant professor, then to associate professor of medicine in 1946.

Anderson continued to research hormone-related disorders. She investigated evidence with Webb E. Haymaker (whom she married in 1936) that Cushing's disease was the result of hyperfunction of the adrenal cortex. After World War II, Anderson worked with emeritus professor of zoology Joseph A. Long in the Institute for Experimental Biology to develop apparatus to study the secretion of insulin by the isolated rat pancreas. This technique was revived later by other researchers and used with an improved immunochemical assay for insulin.

Anderson spent a year on a Guggenheim Fellowship in the laboratory of Philip Bard at Johns Hopkins in 1946. From there she moved to the National Institute of Arthritis and Metabolic Diseases (NIAMD) at the National Institutes of Health as the first chief of the Section on Endocrinology. From 1955 she served as Visiting Professor of Physiology at Howard University. Her research focused on the hypothalmic regulation of metabolism. In 1962, Anderson and her husband (now a noted neurologist and neuropathologist) moved back to California where she was made head of the neuroendocrinology unit at NASA's Ames Research Institute. She retired in 1969.

Anderson published over one hundred research papers. She received honorary doctorates from the Woman's Medical College of Pennsylvania (1961) and Carleton College (1954). She was one of six women who received the Federal Woman's Award in 1964. She chaired a number of groups in professional societies and was vice-president and program chairman of the Endocrine Society in 1951 to 1952. Anderson had three children and eight grandchildren. She died in 1985.

JH

PRIMARY SOURCES

Anderson, Evelyn M. "Anterior Hypophysis and Thyroid [exact title] (1934)." Ph.D. diss., McGill University, 1934.

———. With J. B. Collip. "Antithyroid Stimulating Hormone Capable of Countering TSH." *Lancet* 1 (1934): 76–78 and 1 (1934): 784–786.

———. With Webb Haymaker. "Cushing's Disease Caused by Hyperfunction of Adrenal Cortex." *Science* 86 (1937): 545–546.

———. With Joseph A. Long. "Apparatus to Study the Secretion of Insulin by the Isolated Rat Pancreas." *Endocrinology* 40 (1947): 92–103.

SECONDARY SOURCES

"Evelyn M. Anderson." *The Physiologist* 28, no. 6 (1985): 474. Obituary notice.

ANDERSON, LOUISA GARRETT (1873–1943)

British physician. Born 28 July 1873 in London to Elizabeth (Garrett) and James George Skelton Anderson. Two siblings, one daughter. Never married. Educated St. Leonard's School, St. Andrews; London (Royal Free Hospital) School of Medicine for Women (B.S.; M.D.). Professional experience: private practice and hospital work (ca. 1909–1917); Women's Hospital Corps, joint-organizer and chief surgeon in France (Voluntary Unit); Military Hospital, London, chief surgeon (1915–1918). Honors and memberships: Fellow Royal Academy of Medicine, Commander of the British Empire (1917). Died 15 November 1943.

Louisa Garrett Anderson is now remembered chiefly for her biography of her famous mother, ELIZABETH GARRETT ANDERSON, a pioneer British woman physician. Her father, James Skelton Garrett, was a distinguished businessman and shipowner. When she was very young, her older sister died from an infection. The result was a constant worry about her health on the part of her parents.

For her secondary education, she went away to St. Leonard's School, in St. Andrews, Scotland, close to her father's ancestral home. She decided to follow her mother in the study of medicine, and entered the London School of Medicine for Women (set up by her mother) where she took her B.S. and M.D. degrees. Following her qualification in medicine, she went into private and hospital practice until the outbreak of World War I.

Anderson formed a voluntary unit and went to France as part of the Women's Hospital Corps where she served as Chief Surgeon, and was also attached to the Military Hospital in London during this period. Her excellent organizational and medical skillls brought her the award of a CBE in 1917. After the war she began to look through her mother's papers, and published a biography of her mother's life in 1939. She died in London, 15 November 1943.

JH/MBO

PRIMARY SOURCES

Anderson, Louisa Garrett. *Elizabeth Garrett Anderson 1836–1917*. London: Faber & Faber, 1939.

SECONDARY SOURCES
Manton, Jo. *Elizabeth Garrett Anderson.* New York: E. P. Dutton, 1965.

STANDARD SOURCES
Lipinska 1930; *WWW* 1941–1960.

ANDERSON, ROSE GUSTAVA (1893–?)

U.S. psychologist. Born 23 June 1893 in Gothenburg, Nebr. to Emily (Axing) and Matthew Anderson. Educated University of Chicago (1913–1914); University of Nebraska (1914–1918, A.B.; A.M.); Columbia University (Ph.D., 1925). Marital status unknown. Professional experience: Board of Education, Cleveland, Ohio, assistant psychologist (1918–1919); Research Bureau, State Board of Control, Minnesota, assistant and mental examiner (1919–1923); Minneapolis Child Guidance Clinic, Board of Education, chief psychologist (1925–1930); Educational Adjustment Bureau of the Westchester County Children's Association, New York, director and psychologist (1930–1932); Psychological Services Center, director of the Children's Division and Consultant to Women, (1932–1942), director (1942–1958); Psychological Corporation, vice-president (1944–1955); private research (1958–?). Honors and memberships: American Board of Examiners, Professional Psychologists; Personnel & Guidance Association; American Psychological Association; American Orthopsychiatric Association, Fellow.

Rose Gustava Anderson was born and reared in Nebraska and educated in local schools. After completing high school, she left home to attend the University of Chicago (1913–1914), but lasted only a year before returning to her roots and the University of Nebraska. She worked in assistant psychologist positions for several years and realized that she would need a Ph.D. to advance in her chosen field of educational psychology. She went to Columbia University for that degree and graduated in 1925. Her first appointment as a Ph.D. was as chief psychologist at the Minneapolis Child Guidance Clinic, governed by the Minneapolis Board of Education.

In 1930, Anderson made the move to New York City, where she would spend the remainder of her professional life. She was appointed director and psychologist of the Educational Adjustment Bureau of the Westchester County Children's Association and, shortly afterwards, director of the Children's Division and Consultant to Women at the Psychological Services Center. She became director of the center in 1942 and remained in that position for twelve years.

In New York, she began her efforts, along with Frederick Kuhlmann, to develop tests to measure an individual's academic potential through assessing cognitive skills related to the learning process. During this time she also served as vice-president of the Psychological Corporation. After leaving the Psychological Services Center, Anderson continued personal and vocational counseling and conducted private research.   KM

PRIMARY SOURCES
Anderson, Rose Gustava. "Study of Learning with Visual and Auditory Stimuli." Master's thesis. Lincoln, Neb.: University of Nebraska, 1918.
———. *Methods and Results of Mental Surveys.* N.p. [1922].
———. *A Critical Examination of Test-Scoring Methods.* New York, 1925.
———. With Frederick Kuhlmann. *Intelligence Tests for Ages Six to Maturity.* 4th ed. Princeton, N.J.: Personnel Press, 1942. Reedited numerous times; issued in seven volumes by Scholastic Testing Service, 1981–1982.

STANDARD SOURCES
AMS 5–8, S&B 9–11; *Psychological Register,* vol. 3, 1932.

ANDERSON, VIOLET LOUISE (1906–1990)

Canadian mineralogist. Born 16 November 1906 in Dundas, Ont. Married Ross Anderson. Educated Hamilton Collegiate Institute; Ontario Ladies College, Whitby, Ontario; University of Toronto (first class honors, 1930; graduate work 1931). Professional experience: Royal Ontario Museum, research associate. Died 13 August 1990.

Violet Anderson trained in psychology and English and was also an accomplished pianist. She became fascinated by minerals and crystals and applied her artistic sensibilities to the subject. This interest did not surface until late in life after she received a microscope as a birthday gift and became fascinated with photomicrography. Anderson excelled at the work and became a research associate at the Royal Ontario Museum and photographed hundreds of specimens in the collection. She also developed exhibits for the museum. Combining literary, artistic, and photographic talents, she wrote columns for the *Mineralogical Record* and *Monde and Minéraux,* in which she described the forms of her exquisite microcrystals. Anderson coauthored and illustrated a book with J. A. Mandarino. She and her husband donated her entire collection of 35mm slides and her mineral collection (including photographed collections and micromounts) to the Royal Ontario Museum.   JH/MBO

PRIMARY SOURCES
Anderson, Violet Louise. *Monteregian Treasure—The Minerals of Mont Saint-Hilaire, Quebec.*

SECONDARY SOURCES
Gait, Robert I. "In Memoriam; Violet Louise Anderson." *Rocks and Minerals* 66, no. 1 (1991): 47.

ANDERTON-SMITH, MRS. W. (fl. 1850s)
British botanist. Flourished in 1850s in Herefordshire.

Little information is available on Mrs. W. Anderton-Smith. We know that she lived in Tedstone Delamere, Herefordshire, where she discovered *Epipogium gmelini* in 1854.   JH/MBO

PRIMARY SOURCES
Anderton-Smith, Mrs. W. *Hooker's Journal of Botany* 1854: 318–319.
———. *Botanical Magazine* no. 4821: 1854.

STANDARD SOURCES
Desmond.

ANDREAS-SALOMÉ, LOUISE LELIA (1861–1937)
Russian/German psychoanalyst, writer, and literary critic. Born February 1851 in St. Petersburg to Gustav von Salomé. Married Frederick Andreas (1887). Educated University of Zurich; studied psychoanalysis with Karl Abraham, Karl Adler, and Sigmund Freud. Professional experience: practiced psychoanalysis from 1913. Died in Göttingen in 1937 of cancer.

Louise (Lou) Gustav von Salomé, a Baltic German of Huguenot extraction, was the youngest child and only daughter in a family of six children (two of whom died young). Her father was a general in the army of Tsar Nicholas I. The family occupied a large apartment in the General Staff Building near the Winter Palace and circulated in top levels of society. Lou von Salomé was educated privately and at the Petrischule or Gymnasium until, at seventeen, she became a special student of the Dutch-Reform preacher, Hendrik Gillot. Gillot introduced her to philosophy, literature, logic, and religious history and exerted a powerful influence on her life. In 1880, after rejecting Gillot's proposal of marriage, she and her mother moved to Zürich where Salomé attended the university and studied philosophy and religion. After moving to Rome she met the positivist philosopher Paul Rée who introduced her to Friedrich Nietzsche. Nietzche inspired Salomé to write essays, fiction, drama, and diaries. Her first novel, *Struggling for God* (1885), was largely drawn from conversations with Nietzche. Salomé and Rée lived together in Berlin for four years while maintaining an active friendship with Nietzche. Both men offered her marriage but she felt that sexual love would be destructive to the idealized intellectual friendship she desired. When she abandoned Rée and married Frederick Andreas, a famous orientalist and philologist, she swore the marriage would never be consummated; they lived in a mutually fulfilling companionship until Frederick's death.

During the 1890s, Salomé wrote and published over fifty essays and reviews. She explored, in several works, the sphere of woman and the meaning of womanhood. Fraisse and Perrot call her "the apostle of the self-fulfillment of women as women, allowing for their differences from men." From 1897 to 1901, she had an affair with the poet Rainer Maria Rilke, going to Russia with him in 1899 and 1901 where they met Tolstoy and the poet Drozhzhin, among others. She was to affect Rilke and his work intensely throughout his life.

In 1911, Andreas-Salomé attended the Third Psychoanalytical Congress and met Sigmund Freud. She began studying psychoanalysis with him in 1912 and attended meetings of the Vienna Psychoanalytical Society. She worked with Karl Abraham, Sandor Ferenczi, Viktor Tausk, and Karl Adler, but later turned against Adler, who was a critical rival of Freud. The copious diary of reflections and observations she kept during her psychoanalysis (October 1912 to November 1913) was translated into English as *The Freud Journal* (1964). After 1913, Andreas-Salomé worked briefly in various clinics and wrote two books on psychoanalysis. Her interest centered on the relation of mind and body in the experience of love especially as interpreted by woman. She made a major contribution in extending Freud's concept of narcissism from love of one's image to love of one's self—a cornerstone of her philosophy of wholeness and acceptance of feminism. The friendship, correspondence, and intellectual exchange of Andreas-Salomé with Freud and his daughter, ANNA FREUD (whom she met in 1921), continued until Salomé's death and enriched all three lives.   JH

PRIMARY SOURCES
Andreas-Salomé, Lou. *Henrik Ibsen's Frauen-Gestalten.* Berlin, 1892. A study of Ibsen's female characters; one of four studies of Ibsen's work that she wrote.
———. *Friedrich Nietzsche in seinen Werken.* Wien, 1894. Later translated into Russian and French.
———. *Im Zwischenland; (Fünf Geschichten aus dem Seelenleben halbwüchsiger Mädchen).* Stuttgart and Berlin, 1902. A collection of stories set in Russia.
———. *Die Erotik.* Frankfurt, 1910. 2nd ed., 1979. Her thoughts on love, individualization, idealization, and womanhood.
———. *Rainer Maria Rilke.* Leipzig, 1928.
———. *Mein Dank an Freud.* Wien, 1931. A rambling letter of thanks to Freud in honor of his seventy-fifth birthday.
———. *Lebensrückbild; Grundriss einiger Lebenserrinerungen.* E. Pfieffer, ed. Zurich and Wiesbaden: Basic Books, 1951. A retrospective meditation on the main moments of her life, literally "A Look Back at Life," completed by the author in 1933–1934.
———. *In der Schule bei Freud.* Ernst Pfeiffer, ed. Zurich:

M. Niehans, 1958. (*The Freud Journal of Lou Andreas-Salomé*. Transl. Stanley Leavy. New York: M. Niehans, 1964.)

SECONDARY SOURCES
Fraisse, Geneviève, and Michelle Perrot, eds. *History of Women in the West. IV. Emerging Feminism from Revolution to World War*. Cambridge, Mass.: Belknap/Harvard University Press, 1993.
Livingstone, Angela. *Salomé: Her Life and Work*. Mt. Kisco, NY: Moyer Bell Limited, 1984.
Martin, Biddy. *Woman and Modernity: The (Life) Styles of Lou Andreas-Salomé*. Ithaca: Cornell University Press, 1991.

STANDARD SOURCES
Appignanesi; Uglow 1982.

ANDREWS, ELIZA FRANCES (1840–1930)

U.S. teacher, writer, and botanist. Born 1840 in Haywood, Ga., to Annulet (Ball) and Garnet Andrews. Educated at Washington Seminary for Girls, La Grange (Georgia) Female College (A.B., 1857). Died in Rome, Ga., in 1930.

Eliza Andrews was a writer who wrote a number of popular novels in the 1870s and 1880s under the nom de plume Elizey Hay. Later she wrote about her experiences during the Civil War in the South, publishing *The War-Time Journal of a Georgia Girl* (1906), a socialist view of her life during that period. Andrews taught at the Girl's High School, Yazoo, Missouri, then became principal at Washington Girl's Seminary. From 1885 to 1903, Andrews taught French then literature at Wesleyan Female College, Macon. In 1896–1903, Andrews taught botany and produced two textbooks. She wrote an article on "Socialism in the Plant World" for the *International Socialist Review* in June 1916. Andrews continued writing on botany until the end of her life.   JH/MBO

PRIMARY SOURCES
Andrews, Eliza. *Botany All the Year Around*. New York: American Book Co., 1903.
———. *The War-Time Journal of a Georgia Girl*. New York: Appleton, 1908.
———. *A Practical Course in Botany*. New York: American Book Co., 1911.
———. "Socialism in the Plant World." *International Socialist Review* (June 1916).
Letters and scrapbook, Garnett Andrews papers, Southern Historical Collection, North Carolina Library, University of North Carolina, Chapel Hill.

SECONDARY SOURCES
New York Times 23 January 1931. Obituary notice.

King, Spencer Bidwell, Jr. Introduction to *War-Time Journal*. Macon, Ga., Ardivan Press.
Willard, Frances, and Mary Livermore. *Woman of the Century*. Buffalo, N.Y.: C. W. Moulton, 1893.

STANDARD SOURCES
Barnhart; *NAW* (article by James Patton); *Woman's Who's Who in America*.

ANDREWS, GRACE (1869–?)

U.S. mathematician. Born 30 May 1869 in Brooklyn, N.Y. Educated Wellesley (B.S., 1890); Columbia (A.M., 1899; Ph.D., 1901). Marital status unknown. Professional experience: Barnard College (Columbia), assistant in mathematics (1901–1902).

Grace Andrews is apparently one of those women who, after getting a Ph.D., did little that is recorded professionally. She does not appear in *AMS* after the fourth edition. All that is known about her is that she worked on the primitive double minimal surface of the seventh class and its conjugate.

JH/MBO

STANDARD SOURCES
AMS 1–4; Bailey.

ANDROMACHE (fl. mid-6th century)

Egyptian physician.

According to her contemporary Aëtius, Andromache was an expert at obliviating pain. Aëtius quotes various remedies for toothache, bruises, and ulcers. Pliny apparently was the source for many of her remedies, and she developed others from both Egyptian and Indian folk medicine. She also believed in the efficacy of magic words to exorcise devils.

JH/MBO

SECONDARY SOURCES
Aëtius. *Tetrabiblion*. 1534.
Cumston, Charles Green. *Introduction to the History of Medicine*. 1926.

STANDARD SOURCES
Hurd-Mead 1938.

ANDRUS, RUTH (1886–?)

U.S. psychologist. Born 12 March 1886 in Syracuse, New York. Educated Vassar College (A.B., 1907); Columbia University (A.M., 1908–1909); Columbia University, Teacher's College (Ph.D., 1924). Professional experience: Columbia University Teachers College, lecturer (1924–1928); Institute of Child Welfare

Research, associate professor of education and acting director (1928–1929); State of New York, director of the Child Development and Parental Education Bureau (1928–1952); Cold Spring Institute, Long Island, director (1952–1955), program coordinator (1955–1957); Dutchess County Mental Health Clinic, psychotherapist (1957–1971); Russell Sage College, trustee (1933–1938); Bard College, trustee (1949–1955); Mills College, trustee (1952–1965); Section III, White House Conference on Children in a Democracy, chairman (1929); White House Conference on Aging, member (1961). Honors and memberships: American Psychological Association, Fellow; Society for Research in Child Development, Gerontological Society, Sigma Xi, member.

Ruth Andrus was born in New York, but for her higher education went to Vassar College (A.B., 1907) then to Columbia University for her M.A. and Ph.D. (1924). She continued at Columbia University Teachers College as lecturer until 1928. In 1928, Andrus was appointed associate professor of education and acting director of the Institute of Child Welfare Research. JH/MBO

PRIMARY SOURCES

Andrus, Ruth. *An Inventory of the Habits of Children from Two to Five Years of Age.* New York: Teachers College, Columbia University, 1928.

State University of New York. *Report on the Work in Child Development and Parental Education Supported by Grant from the Spelman Fund to the State Education Department.* Ruth Andrus, Director. Albany, New York, 1933.

Andrus, Ruth. With Elinor Lee Beebe, Margaret C. Holmes, Marie L. Schaefer, Grace Allen, Rhoda E. Harris, Martha May Reynolds, Maud C. Stewart. *Curriculum Guides for Teachers of Children from Two to Six Years of Age.* New York: Reynal & Hitchcock, [1936].

———. *The Education of Children under Six in Public Schools: Programs and Standards.* Chicago: National Association for Nursery Education, 1951.

STANDARD SOURCES
AMS 5–8, S&B 9–12; *Psychological Register,* vol. 3.

ANGST-HORRIDGE, ANITA (1897–?)

English/Swiss physician and gynecologist. Born 1 August 1897 near London. Married (1928; divorced 1945). One son. Educated at schools in Germany and Brussels; Medical Faculty of the University of Lausanne (1917, M.D., 1923); University of Strasbourg; University Maternity Hospial in Basel, gynecological training; Institute of Pathology in Zurich. Professional experience: Lariboisière Hospital and Hôpital de la Pitié, Externe; Sanatorium at Davos, assistant in tuberculosis; private practice in Zurich (to 1964); Maternity Hospital of the University of Zurich, organizer and director of family planning clinic (to 1972). Honors and memberships: Swiss

Medical Women's Association, Medical Women's International Association, International Planned Parenthood Federation.

Anita Angst received her early education at home from a French-Swiss governess. She continued her education at schools in Germany and Brussels and completed the Lyceum in Hanover in 1914. To help with the war effort, she worked as "bandage nurse" at the military hospital of the Sixteenth Army Corps at Narbonne, France. This experience inspired her to become a doctor. She entered the medical faculty of the University of Lausanne in 1917, studied three semesters at the University of Strasbourg and returned to Lausanne for her M.D. in 1923.

Angst worked at the Lariboisière Hospital and Hôpital de la Pitié before becoming an assistant in tuberculosis at the Sanatorium at Davos. She attended University Maternity Hospial in Basel for gynecological training and the Institute of Pathology in Zurich. Angst married a general practitioner in 1928 (divorced 1945), and remained in Zurich in the private practice of gynecology and obstetrics for thirty-four years, until 1964.

In Zurich, Angst-Horridge organized a family planning clinic at Maternity Hospital of the University of Zurich and served as its director until 1972. She was active in the Swiss Medical Women's Association, Medical Women's International Association, and the International Planned Parenthood Federation. JH/MBO

PRIMARY SOURCES
Angst-Horridge, Anita. In Hellstedt. *Autobiographies.*

STANDARD SOURCES
Rebière.

ANICIA OR AMYTE (fl. 300 B.C.E.)
Greek physician.

Described by Pausanias as a woman doctor of Epidaurus who was also a poet and writer. Tradition indicates that Anicia, as a physician at the Aesculapian institution of Epidaurus, was skilled at bleeding and in performing minor operations. Anicia wrote oracles of the god Aesculapius in verse. JH/MBO

STANDARD SOURCES
Hurd-Mead 1938.

ANN MEDICA OF YORK (fl. 1476)
British hospital administrator.

Ann Medica illustrates the use of women as hospital "officers." She was an officer in the hospital of York, which, at that time, had 224 adult patients and twenty-three children.   JH/MBO

STANDARD SOURCES
Hurd-Mead 1938.

ANNA OF BOHEMIA (1210–ca. 1255)

Born 1210 to Constance of Hungary and King Premysl Ottakar I of Bohemia. Married Heinrich of Silesia and Poland.

Anna reputedly was very pious and interested in the care of the sick, particularly children (orphans) and those with fevers. In 1253 she founded a hospital and convent at Kreuzberg and another at Neumarkt.   JH/MBO

STANDARD SOURCES
Echols and Williams; Hurd-Mead 1938.

ANNA SOPHIA OF DENMARK (fl. 1543)

Danish botanist. Married Kurfürst August I of Saxony (1543).

Anna Sophia was well known for her botanic garden in which she raised her own medicinal herbs. She founded an apothecary shop which remained in existence for three hundred years.   JH/MBO

STANDARD SOURCES
Hurd-Mead 1938.

ANNA SOPHIA OF HESSE (fl. 1685)

German botanist.

Anna Sophia was the abbess of Quedlinburg. She published a well-received book on natural history in 1685.   JH/MBO

STANDARD SOURCES
Hurd-Mead 1938.

ANNE, ELECTRESS OF DENMARK
(17th century?)

Danish alchemist.

The Electress Anne (or Anna) was a member of the Danish royal family who experimented in alchemy. Anne built a laboratory on her estate at Annaberg, described by the German alchemist Kunckel as the "largest and finest he had ever seen."   JH/MBO

STANDARD SOURCES
Alic.

ANNING, MARY (1799–1847)

British paleontologist. Born 21 May 1799 in Lyme Regis, Dorset, to Mary and Richard Anning. Nine siblings, only two of whom reached maturity. Never married. Educated at the local parish school. Died 9 March 1847 at Lyme Regis.

Of the approximately ten children born to Mary and Richard Anning, only two survived past childhood: Joseph (1796–1849) and Mary. Mary Anning was named for her mother, Mary, and for an older sister who died in a fire. Mary suffered a traumatic experience when she was fourteen months old that almost resulted in her death. A tree, under which she and three others had taken shelter, was struck by lightning, and Mary was the only survivor.

Mary Anning derived her scientific interests from her father, a cabinetmaker whose hobby was fossil collecting. He died in 1810 and left the family in debt. The three remaining Annings were almost destitute when a collector, Thomas James Birch, visited Lyme and engineered a sale of the fossils. Anning's fossil collecting eventually provided her with a small income, part of it in the form of a government grant. The entire family seems to have been involved in the enterprise. Mary's mother died in 1842 and Mary herself died from breast cancer in Lyme in 1847. According to a local guidebook, her "death was in a pecuniary sense a great loss to the place, as her presence attracted a large number of distinguished visitors."

Anning's reputation was built upon five major discoveries. The first, probably not as important as her later ones, established her reputation. When she was between nine and twelve years old, she and her brother discovered the complete skeleton of an ichthyosaur. Although other specimens had been reported as early as 1804 in other localities, it was this discovery of the *Ichthyosaurus* that brought her name to the attention of scientists and the specimen's official description and name (1817) was based on Mary and Joseph's finding. Anning's second major discovery was of a virtually complete specimen of the little-known plesiosaur. This discovery, which was praised most highly by many scientific contemporaries, gave rise to an acrimonious debate about the authenticity of the specimen. Cuvier first claimed that the fossil was a forgery, but it was soon established to be genuine. Her third discovery, that of the pterodactyl, most appealed to the public. The type specimen of her fourth discovery, the fossil fish *Squaloraja,* no longer exists. Her final discovery was *Plesiosaurus macrocephalus,* named by William Buckland and described by Richard Owen.

Although she had no formal training, Anning was an

astute observer and collector who provided materials to be interpreted by theoreticians. Although she furthered the studies and enriched the collections of a number of contemporary paleontologists, she was not credited with the discoveries. Anning, as a woman collector, was a curiosity who became the subject of popularizers and writers of children's books. Hugh Torren's research has led to a reappraisal of Mary Anning, her contributions to paleontology, and the place of the scientific collector in paleontology.   MBO

PRIMARY SOURCES
Letter in the Wellcome Library for the History of Medicine.
Specimens in the Sedgwick Museum.

SECONDARY SOURCES
Taylor, Michael A., and Hugh S. Torrens. "Saleswoman to a
    New Science: Mary Anning and the Fossil Fish *Squaloraja*
    from the Lias of Lyme Regis." *Proceedings of the Dorset Natu-*
    ral History and Archaeological Society 108 (1986): 135–148.
Torrens, Hugh. Presidential Address. "Mary Anning (1799–
    1847) of Lyme; 'the Greatest Fossilist the World Ever
    Knew.'" *The British Journal for the History of Science* 28, 1995:
    257–284. An excellent critical study of Mary Anning that
    debunks many of the myths surrounding her. Most of the
    writings about Anning, both popular, fictional, and histori-
    cal, are included in the body of the paper and in the foot-
    notes.

STANDARD SOURCES
DNB.

ANSLOW, GLADYS AMELIA (1892–1969)

U.S. physicist. Born 1853 in Kidderminster, England, to Amelia
and William Anslow. Four stepsisters by Elizabeth Jane Mathews;
one sister. Educated Springfield Central High School, Conn.; Smith
College (A.B., 1914; A.M., 1917); University of Chicago, grad-
uate courses (1921); Yale University (Ph.D., 1924). Professional
experience: Smith College, demonstrator in physics (1914–1915),
assistant (1915–1917), instructor (1918–1919), assistant profes-
sor (1924–1930), associate professor (1930–1936), professor
(1936–1948); endowed professorship (1948–1960), research pro-
fessor (1960–1969); chair of physics department (several terms be-
ginning in 1933); director of graduate studies (1941–1959).
Honors and memberships: Sigma Xi, president (1935); American
Academy of Arts and Sciences, Fellow; American Association for the
Advancement of Science, Fellow; American Physical Society, Fellow
(offices in the New England Section); American Association of
Physics Teachers, associate editor and member of the AAPT Execu-
tive Board; Smith College, honorary D.Sc. (1950); Sigma Delta
Epsilon, Woman in Science Award (1950). Died of cancer 31
March 1969 in Brookline, Mass.

Gladys Anslow's career was enhanced by both supportive home and work environments. She was a part of the second family of William Anslow. The death of her mother in Anslow's second year at Smith College necessitated her returning home for the second semester. She reentered in February 1912 and received her bachelor's degree two years later. She was both impressed by and impressed the professor Frank Allan Waterman. He supported her appointments as demonstrator and assistant in physics. The advantage of this position was that while she was obtaining teaching experience, she was able to take additional courses in physics. One of these courses was spectroscopy, taught by JANET T. HOWELL (later CLARK). Accepted for the master's program, she did her research under Howell on the emission spectra of radium. After she received her degree, Waterman suggested that she be appointed instructor, to forestall an expected attempt by Vassar College to hire her away. During the summer of 1921, she took graduate courses at the University of Chicago. Waterman and his son Alan Tower Waterman convinced her to enter the Ph.D. program at Yale University. The younger Waterman was appointed to the Yale physics faculty in 1919. Anslow began this program in 1922 and received her degree in 1924.

After she became an associate professor, Anslow's family moved in with her in Northampton. What could have been a stressful situation appeared to be helpful for all. Her seventy-two-year-old father (who lived to be ninety-five) and her sister, Sadie, moved in first. Then her half-sister Evelyn moved in with her husband, William, and their son, Joseph. William died in 1935. Another half-sister, Rhoda, joined them in 1942. Apparently the family took away the pressure of day-to-day household duties, particularly when Gladys was involved with research projects.

When she entered college, she listed Christian Science as her religious preference, but later became an active member of the Unitarian Society of Northampton. She was a member of the Northampton Republican City Committee.

During her time as assistant professor, Anslow collaborated with Mary Louise Foster on a research program involving the chemistry and absorption spectra of amino acids. This work resulted in four publications in the *Journal of Biological Chemistry* and the *Physical Review*. Anslow's graduate research at Yale had been on high-energy physics. Ernest O. Lawrence, Nobel laureate and inventor of the cyclotron, invited her to his laboratory at Berkeley to continue with her research during the summer of 1939. At Berkeley she observed the Berkeley plan of focused group research, which she attempted to apply at Smith when she returned. However, the effective program that she had developed at Smith screeched to a halt at the advent of World War II. Several key faculty members joined the MIT Radiation Laboratory under the National Defense Research Committee, where defensive warfare devices, including radar, were developed. Alan Waterman, who had left Yale in 1942 to become chief of the Office of Field Service of the Office of Science and Research Development (OSRD), asked Anslow to serve as a special consultant to him from July 1944 to December 1945. She accepted and became chief of the Communications and Information Section, in charge of supplying scientific and technical information to specialists throughout the world. She retained her position at Smith during her War Service. She was awarded the Presidential Certificate of Merit by Harry Truman in 1948.

After the war, the possibility of building the type of research center that she had previously envisioned was slim. Therefore, she organized a Smith College research program, which would take advantage of the new federal support of scientific research. One of the benefits of this program was the loan of various instruments, putting Smith on the cutting edge of research. They were able to attack a fundamental biochemical problem, the structure of proteins. She and DOROTHY WRINCH began a two-decade collaboration focusing on spectral investigation of the amino acid protein subunit, small polymers of these amino acids, and the proteins hemoglobin and insulin.

Anslow convinced the Smith trustees of the need for a new science building. Fund-raising was slow, so instead of the new building, a basement was renovated for a new spectroscopy laboratory. The new laboratory was very effective and produced some spectacular research papers. A paper that she gave at the Faraday Society, Cambridge University, was very well accepted and resulted in her being given the 1950 Sigma Delta Epsilon Woman in Science award. In 1958, she was awarded the first of a series of National Science Foundation grants, which supported her research for the rest of her life. Her dream of a new science center finally came to fruition by the time she retired. Anslow's main scientific strength was her ability to collaborate with others. She also recognized the importance of interdisciplinary applications of physics.   JH/MBO

PRIMARY SOURCES
Anslow, Gladys Amelia. "Spectroscopic Evidence for the Electron Theory of Matter." Master's thesis, Smith College, 1917.
———. With J. T. Howell. "The Triplet Series of Radium." *Proceedings of the National Academy of Science* 3 (1917): 409–412.
———. "The Total Ionization Product in Air by Electrons at Various Energies." Ph.D. diss., Yale University, 1924.
———. With M. D. Watson. "The Total Ionization of Nitrogen by Electronic Collisions." *Physical Review* 50 (1936): 162–169.
———. With P. C. Aebersold. "Fast Neutron Energy Absorption in Gases, Wall, and Tissue." *Physical Review* 69 (1946): 1–21.

———. With O. Glaser. "Copper and Ascidian Metamorphosis." *Journal of Experimental Zoology* 111 (1949): 117–139.

SECONDARY SOURCES
"Gladys A. Anslow '14, Professor Emeritus of Physics." *Smith Alumnae Quarterly* (April 1969): 62.
"Prof. Gladys Anslow, Physics Field Leader, Dies in 78th Year." *Daily Hampshire Gazette,* 1 April 1969. Obituary notice, with photograph.

STANDARD SOURCES
AMS 6–11; Bailey; Debus; Grinstein 1993; Rossiter 1982.

ANTIPOFF, HELENE (1892–?)

Russian/Swiss psychologist. Born 1892 in Russia. Educated University of Paris (1910–1912); University of Geneva, Institute of Science and Education (1912–1914, diploma). Professional experience: Station medico-psychologiques Viatka, Petersburg, Russia (1919–1924); Laboratory of Experimental Psychology, Petersburg, collaborator; Laboratory of Psychology at University of Geneva, assistant to Edouard Claparède (1926–1929); Institut J. J. Rousseau, professor of child psychology (1926–1929); Ecole de Perfectionnement Pedagogique, Bello Horizonte, Brazil, director (1929–?). Death date unknown.

Helene Antipoff was born in Russia but was educated in Paris and Geneva. After graduation she worked at the Station medico-psychologiques Viatka, Petersburg, Russia, then at the Laboratory of Experimental Psychology, founded by experimental pedagogist, Alexander Petrovich Netschaieff. Although she began her work in experimental psychology in St. Petersburg, she returned to Geneva to the Laboratory of Psychology at University of Geneva as Assistant to Edouard Claparède. In 1926, she became Professor of Child Psychology at the Institut J. J. Rousseau.

In 1929, Antipoff became Director of the Ecole de Perfectionnement Pedagogique in Bello Horizonte, Brazil.

JH/MBO

STANDARD SOURCES
Psychological Register, vol. 3, 1932.

ANTOINE, LORE (1895–?)

Austrian physician. Born 1895 in Austria-Hungary to a Yugoslavian mother and Austrian engineer father. One sister; one stepbrother. Married Tassilo Antoine (1919 or 1920). One daughter (born 1921). Educated at home; Catholic boarding school in Lindau (one term); private school in Vienna; boarding house for girls; Red Cross nursing school; secondary school for boys in Klagenfurt (audit for exams); university in Graz; University of Vienna (1918–1923,

M.D.); *St. Louis Hospital, Paris, postdoctorate studies in dermatology and plastic surgery. Professional experience: Vienna hospital, internal medicine (1923–1924), surgeon (1924–1925), gynecologist-anesthetist; University Hospital, specialist in dermatology; Vienna, private practice (from 1930); private hospital, assistant (1930–?); University Institute, Vienna (1940–1965), teacher of hygiene. Honors and memberships: Austrian Medical Women's Association (from 1924); League of United Nations Associations; Soroptimists; Medical Women's International Association (president, 1966–1968); Vienna Medical Association (first woman president, 1952). Death date unknown.*

Antoine was born into an affluent family and grew up in a large house with extensive grounds, a working farm, gardens, and hunting lodges. She and her sister were tutored at home, taking their examinations at a nearby German school. From the time she was nine years old, Antoine wanted to become a doctor.

After begging to continue in higher education, which was still considered unnecessary for an aristocratic lady, Antoine was sent to a Catholic boarding school at age fourteen, where the strict convent routine and discipline were foreign to her. She left before the end of the first semester and was sent to a private school in Vienna. Having no solid background in grammar, mathematics, or classics, Antoine fell behind in spite of being encouraged by the headmistress, a Dr. Schwarzwald. Antoine was transferred to a girls' boarding house where she stayed until 1914.

When World War I broke out, Antoine's mother became active in the war effort and involved her daughter. While running an errand in Ljubljana, Antoine heard that Red Cross courses for nurses had been started. She joined and was soon nursing wounded soldiers. When their home was overrun, Antoine and her family moved to Honnef, then to Klagenfurt, Germany. There, Antoine renewed her efforts to become a doctor, entering a boys' secondary school to study for the examinations for university. She passed the examinations and entered a local university. When her father died of cancer the next year, he provided for her to continue her education and she spent the next term in Graz taking highest marks on her exams. With that, she was accepted at the University of Vienna in 1918.

There she met and married Tassilo Antoine, a Viennese student in gynecology. Their daughter was born in 1921. Antoine received her doctor of medicine degree in 1923 but found it difficult to obtain a job due to ingrained sex discrimination and the return of male medical refugees and soldiers, who received first consideration for positions. For a year she worked as a "guest doctor" without pay. Later, she was promised a salaried position in a town hospital as surgeon/gynecologist, but was assigned mostly to giving anesthetics. After five months, she had not received the

promised pay, so she resigned and went back to the Vienna University hospital to specialize in dermatology. In 1927, she went to Paris to continue her study of dermatology and plastic surgery at St. Louis Hospital. Returning to Vienna, she began her dermatology practice and worked as a volunteer in a private hospital.

Antoine joined the International Association of University Women and was selected chairperson of international relations. In this capacity, she traveled to the United States where she saw for the first time skin diseases in the black population. When the Nazis occupied Austria, Antoine and many of her friends in the Austrian Medical Women's Association helped their Jewish coworkers and friends to emigrate. Antoine's husband went to Innsbruck for three years while she stayed in Vienna and taught hygiene at the university's institute for domestic science. In 1943, she served as air-raid physician for the university. The period of Nazi and Russian occupations was very difficult. Antoine's home was damaged and food and medication were scarce.

After the war, Antoine worked intensively with several international organizations to reaffiliate scattered chapters. The Austrian Medical Women's Association was refounded. Antoine was sent to inform Mrs. John Foster Dulles of the activities of women's organizations in Austria. In 1947, Antoine went to Amsterdam for reaffiliation of Austria with the Medical Women's International Association. She spoke at many meetings of the German and Austrian dermatology associations and traveled with her husband to Venezuela and Columbia and other locations in connection with his specialty of gynecology. For many years, Antoine continued working with various associations to improve opportunities for women in medicine.   JH/MBO

PRIMARY SOURCES
Antoine, L. In Hellstedt, *Autobiographies.*

ANTOINETTE DE BELLEGARDE (fl. 1360)
French physician.

Antoinette de Bellegarde was accused in 1360 of practicing medicine illegally. In spite of being fined, she continued to practice and later was fined again for practicing surgery without a license.   JH/MBO

STANDARD SOURCES
Echols and Williams.

ANTONIA, MAESTRA (fl. 1386–1408)
Italian healer. Born probably in Florence. Professional experience: Medical School University of Florence, registra (1386–1408).

Although she was a Jew and Ferdinand of Aragon forbade Jews to practice medicine among the Christians (from 1415), Antonia Daniello was honored by the faculty of the medical school at Florence and given the position as *registra* from 1386 to 1408. After Ferdinand's decree, Jews continued to practice but they did so in secret.　　　　JH/MBO

STANDARD SOURCES
Hughes; Hurd-Mead 1938.

APGAR, VIRGINIA (1909–1974)

U.S. physician. Born 7 June 1909 in Westfield, N.J., to Helen May (Clarke) Apgar and Charles Emory. Two brothers (one died 1903). Educated Westfield High School; Mt. Holyoke College (B.A., 1929); Columbia University (M.D., 1933); surgical internship, Presbyterian Hospital, New York City; residency in anesthesiology, University of Wisconsin and Bellevue Hospital, New York City (1937); Johns Hopkins University (masters degree in public health, 1959). Professional experience: Columbia University, instructor of anesthesiology (1936–1938), assistant professor (1938–1942), associate professor (1942–1949), professor (1949–1959); Presbyterian Medical Center, clinical director of anesthesia; Presbyterian Hospital, New York City, attending anesthesiologist; Valley Hospital, Ridgewood, N.J., consulting anesthesiologist; Goldwater and Triborough hospitals, New York City, consulting anesthesiologist; National Foundation March of Dimes for Infantile Paralysis, director of the division of congenital malformations (1959–1968), director of basic research and vice-president of medical affairs (1968–1974); Medical College at Cornell University, lecturer (from 1965). Honors and memberships: Mt. Holyoke College, Alumnae Award (1954); New York Infirmary, Elizabeth Blackwell Citation (1960); American Society of Anesthesiologists, Distinguished Service Award (1961); Woman's Medical College of Pennsylvania, honorary M.D. (1964); Mt. Holyoke, Honorary Sc.D. (1965). Died in 1974.

Virginia Apgar may personally have saved millions of newborns. One of the first women to be granted a surgical internship at Presbyterian Hospital in New York and the first female full professor at Columbia's medical school, she made a great contribution to neonatal survival rate by developing the definitive system for measuring vital signs in the first minute after birth (the Apgar Score).

After graduation from Westfield High School, she attended Mt. Holyoke College (B.A., 1929) where she was a newspaper reporter, a violinist in the orchestra, and winner of eleven letters in athletics while working part-time and completing a pre-med zoology major degree. She received her M.D. with honors in 1933 from Columbia College of Physicians and Surgeons and went straight into surgical internship at Presbyterian Hospital, New York City—the fifth woman to be granted that privilege. "Two hundred operations later"

at the end of her internship, she was encouraged to switch to the newly developing specialty of anesthesiology for economic reasons. She went into residency in anesthesiology at the University of Wisconsin, then Bellevue Hospital in New York City and in 1937 became the fiftieth physician certified by the American Board of Anesthesiology.

Apgar began her professional career at Columbia University Medical College as an instructor in 1936. She worked her way up the ranks, serving finally as full professor until leaving Columbia in 1959. While on faculty at Columbia, Apgar also worked as director of anesthesia at the Presbyterian Medical Center. It was there that she became concerned with the need for a notation system for vital signs in newborns, and in 1952 developed the Apgar Score System used to evaluate infants within the first moments following birth for heart rate, respiratory effort, muscle tone, reflexes, and color, measured on a scale of zero to ten. This test became standard procedure in hospitals in the United States and in many countries around the world, alerting attendants to any need for emergency treatment.

At age fifty, Apgar returned to school to take a master's degree in Public Health at Johns Hopkins University (1959). The National Foundation-March of Dimes was just beginning an intensive research program on two of the nation's greatest health hazards—birth defects and arthritis. They asked Apgar to direct the Division of Congenital Malformations while she was still at Johns Hopkins. Though she protested that she knew little about birth defects, she proceeded to learn as much as possible, then taught, lectured, and wrote articles to educate the public about birth defects and congenital anomalies. Apgar authored more than fifty papers or articles on birth defects and anomalies and on precautionary measures for pregnant women. She became vice-president of medical affairs for the foundation (1968–1974) and traveled thousands of miles each year to lecture in many countries on birth defects and the importance of prenatal care. She also lectured on teratology (malformations) in the pediatrics department at the Cornell University Medical College. Apgar was granted many awards and honorary degrees throughout her career. Additionally she was a Fellow of the American Medical Association and the New York Academy of Medicine and a member of many other medical, pediatric, and public health associations. Her active membership reflected her involvement in many aspects of medicine and her desire to communicate with and share her findings. In spite of her heavy work load, Apgar found time to play the violin in amateur groups and also to learn the craft of making stringed instruments. Over the years she constructed a violin, a viola, and a cello, all of which she played expertly. Additionally, she was an avid stamp collector and somehow found time for fishing, gardening, and (in her sixties) golf.　　　　JH/MBO

PRIMARY SOURCES

Apgar, Virginia. *Notes on Anesthesia.* New York: College of
Physicians & Surgeons, Columbia University, 1949.

———, ed. *Down's Syndrome (Mongolism). Annals,* vol. 171.
New York: New York Academy of Sciences, 1970. Papers
resulting from a conference on Down's syndrome held
24–26 November 1969, authored by Virginia Apgar and
others.

———. With Joan Beck. *Is My Baby All Right?* New York:
Trident Press, 1972.

Teaching video recordings:

———. *Apgar on Apgar.* Detroit: Wayne State University
Medical School, 1966. Application of the Apgar Score
System to the Neonate in the First Ten Minutes of Life.

———. *Obstetrical Anesthesia: The Mother and the Newborn.*
New York, 1972.

"Apgar." Newark *Sunday News* interview, 1967.

Papers: Correspondence, writings, and speeches, which reflect
Apgar's interest in anesthesiology, birth defects, and problems
of newborn infants; clippings; professional diaries, 1959–
1973; personal diaries and travel logs, 1937–1974; etc. Mount
Holyoke College Library/Archives. South Hadley, Mass.

STANDARD SOURCES

AMS 8, B 9, P&B 10–12; *Current Biography,* vol. 1968; *LKW;*
NAW(M) (article by Robert J. Waldinger).

APPLIN, ESTHER (RICHARDS) (1895–1972)

*U.S. petroleum geologist. Born 24 November 1895 in Newark,
Ohio, to Jennie (DeVore) and Gary F. Richards. Married Paul Ap-
plin. Two children, daughter Louise and son Paul Jr. Educated Girls'
High School, San Francisco. University of California (B.A., 1919;
M.A., 1920). Professional experience: Rio Bravo Oil Company,
head of paleontology laboratory (1920–1927); various oil companies, consulting geologist (1927–1944); University of Texas,
Austin, assistant professor of geology (1944–1945); U.S. Geological Survey (1944–1962). Honors and memberships: Gulf Coast
Association of Geological Societies, a plaque in honor of her accomplishments; from the U.S. Department of the Interior, citation for
meritorious service; Geological Society of American, Fellow; Society
of Economic Paleontologists and Mineralogists, charter member; Mississippi Geological Society, charter member. Died 23 July 1972.*

Esther Richards was born into a peripatetic family. Her father was a civil engineer leading the family to various cities
in Ohio, to Fort Des Moines, Iowa, and to San Francisco. In
San Francisco her father directed the building of the prison
on Alcatraz Island. The island became their home from 1907
to 1920 and Richards commuted to school (both high
school and later the University of California, Berkeley) by
ferry. She graduated with honors in paleontology from the
University of California. After earning her bachelor's degree
and a master's degree in paleontology, geology, and physiography, Richards was hired by the Rio Bravo Oil Company to
take charge of its paleontological laboratory in Houston.
There she met and married a young geologist, Paul L. Applin. The couple collaborated both professionally and do-
mestically.

At the beginning of her career with Rio Bravo, Applin
investigated fossils present in samples recovered from oil
wells drilled in the Gulf Coast. She realized that the macro-
fossils that she had studied were too badly broken in well
cuttings to be identifiable as to species. She therefore turned
to microfossils.

In a paper presented at a Geological Society meeting in
1921 by her supervisor at Rio Bravo, Applin suggested that
microfossils could be used to date strata. She was ridiculed by
more experienced geologists for her audacity in claiming that
foraminifera could be used to date strata. To verify her claim,
Applin worked with Alva Ellisor and Hedwig Kniker to find
ways to separate the fossils from the matrix of the cuttings. In
1925, the three coauthored a paper that detailed the sequence
and oil-bearing zones in the Gulf Coast using microfossils.

While she was raising Louise (born in 1926) and Paul Jr.
(born in 1927), Esther continued to work as a consulting paleontologist and subsurface geologist in Fort Worth, conducting research on the surface and subsurface stratigraphy
of the Coastal Plain in Texas, Arkansas, Louisiana, and Florida. She continued this work until 1944 when the family
moved to Tallahassee, Florida, and she joined the U.S.
Geological Survey. After the decline of the "oil boom" in
Florida, the Applins moved to Jackson, Mississippi, where
she continued to publish papers on the stratigraphy and
structure of the southeastern states, also writing papers on
the foraminifera. She retired from the survey in 1962 but
continued to publish and do research.   JH/MBO

PRIMARY SOURCES

Applin, E. R. With A. E. Ellisor and H. T. Kniker. "Subsurface
Stratigraphy of the Coastal Plain of Texas and Louisiana."
American Association of Petroleum Geologists Memoir 9, no. 1
(1925): 79–122.

———. With Paul Livingston Applin. "Regional Subsurface
Stratigraphy and Structure of Florida and Southern Georgia." *Bulletin of the American Association of Petroleum Geologists*
28, no. 12 (1944): 1673–1753.

———. With Louise Jordan. "Diagnostic Foraminifera from
Subsurface Formations in Florida." *Journal of Paleontology* 19,
no. 2 (1945): 129–148.

———. With W. S. Cole. "Analysis of some American Upper
Cretaceous Larger Foraminifera." *Bulletin of American Paleontology* 258, no. 58 (1970): 39–80.

———. With John C. Maher. "Geologic Framework and Petroleum Potential of the Atlantic Coastal Plain and Continental Shelf." *U.S. Geological Survey Professional Paper* 659, 1971.

SECONDARY SOURCES
Aldrich, Michele L. "Women in Geology." In Kass-Simon and Farnes.
Berdan, Jean M. "Memorial to Esther Richards Applin 1895–1972." *Geological Society of America Memorials* 4 (1975): 14–18. Includes bibliography.

STANDARD SOURCES
Rossiter 1995.

APSLEY (HUTCHINSON), LADY LUCY (1620–1675)

British physician. Born in London to a "universal nurse and doctor" and a noble family of Apsley. Nine siblings; five survived until maturity. Married Colonel Hutchinson (1638). Four sons (at least two died before they were six years old). Educated by tutors; taught medicine by her mother. Died 1675.

Although Lucy Apsley Hutchinson is probably best known for her biography of her husband, Colonel Hutchinson, she was important in medicine during the seventeenth century. As a child prodigy, who was reputed to have learned five languages by the time she was five years old, she translated Lucretius into verse at an early age. Her medical training came from her mother, Lady Apsley, who had read the latest books on pediatrics as well as learning about pharmacology from Sir Walter Raleigh while he was imprisoned in the Tower of London. Even with this "up-to-date" knowledge, four of her nine children died very young. Lady Apsley taught her daughters the pharmacology of pain relief and the dressing of wounds. Lucy, who had had a severe case of smallpox as a child leaving her face pocked, was the only one to absorb her mother's teachings. Lucy married Colonel Hutchinson when she was eighteen years old and, as was the case with many women of that period, had a difficult time with childbirth. Even when the children were born successfully, survival was very uncertain. In her first pregnancy, she miscarried twins and in the following year, she survived the birth of twin sons. Two other sons died, one at six and the other at four.

Colonel Hutchinson was imprisoned as a regicide in Nottingham in 1643 where his family lived with him. Lucy tended the sick and wounded soldiers. Without her husband's approval, she cared for enemy soldiers and tried to improve the living conditions of the prisoners.   JH/MBO

PRIMARY SOURCES
Hutchinson, Lucy. *Memoirs of the Life of Colonel Hutchinson by his Widow, Lucy.* The Reverend Julius Hutchinson, 1806.

STANDARD SOURCES
Hurd-Mead 1938.

ARBER, AGNES (ROBERTSON) (1879–1960)

British botanist, historian, and philosopher of botany. Born London, 1879, to Agnes Lucy (Turner) and Henry Robert Robertson. Three siblings. Married E. A. N. Arber (1909). One daughter. Educated North London Collegiate School for Girls; University College London (B.Sc., D.Sc., 1905); Newnham College, Cambridge (1899–1902, College Scholar; Natural Science Tripos, Part I, class 1, 1901; Part II, class 1, 1902; M.A., 1926). Professional experience: University College, research assistant (1902), lecturer in botany (1905–c. 1909); Newnham College, teacher (1909–1912), research fellow (1912–1913). Keddy Fletcher-Warr student (1920–1923); private botanical laboratory, Cambridge (1927–1959). Honors and memberships: Linnean Society, Fellow; Royal Society, Fellow. Died 22 March 1960.

Agnes Robertson Arber's family environment was rich culturally, but more in the arts than the sciences. Agnes learned about plants from her mother, and took lessons in drawing from her earliest years. At the age of eight she went to North London Collegiate School for Girls. This school was run by Miss Frances Buss, who was one of the leading proponents of education for girls. She insisted that girls from the "wealthy" classes be provided with a serious education, not one that merely taught the social graces. Her school had a strong commitment to teaching science. Although Agnes spoke well of the school generally, she did note an overabundance of rules and excessive stress on outside examinations. In spite of this, Agnes obtained first place in the botany examinations and won a scholarship.

Robertson trained as a botanist, working as research assistant to ETHEL SARGANT in 1902, later a lifelong friend. Sargant had a great influence upon Arber's research style. Their backgrounds were similar in that Sargant had also been educated at North London Collegiate School and subsequently attended Cambridge University, although she went to Girton, the other women's college. Sargant carried out her work at her home laboratory in Reigate where Robertson assisted her. She continued to work in Sargant's laboratory during vacations while she studied for her degree at University College London, where she studied under Francis West Oliver and Arthur Tansley. Unlike Cambridge, this university had admitted women students since 1878. She received a first class degree from University College, but then went to Newnham College, Cambridge, where she took an additional degree. When she went to Cambridge in 1899 women were not members of the university and were not admitted to the university's laboratories nor awarded official degrees. She, however, excelled at Newnham as she had at University

College and got two "firsts" in her Tripos examinations. She received an excellent background in botany from both Oliver at University College London and then Sargant at Cambridge. The so-called new Botany that Robertson learned from her teachers introduced an experimental approach to plant study, including plant morphology and physiology, rather than relying on the former systematic approach.

After she finished her Tripos, Robertson returned to Sargant's laboratory in Reigate. Her first paper was published in 1903 in the *Proceedings of the Cambridge Philosophical Society*. In 1903 she returned to University College London to become a lecturer in botany. She received a University College London Quain studentship and carried out research on gymnosperms in Oliver's laboratory. She was awarded a D.Sc. in 1905.

Robertson remained in London until 1909. However, shortly after she was appointed lecturer, she left in order to marry. Her husband was a demonstrator in palaeobotany in the Geology Department at Cambridge, where she may have met him. After her marriage to Edward Alexander Newell Arber, she moved to Cambridge (1909). Often after marriage a woman scientist gave up her career. Agnes Arber was an exception. She converted part of her house into a laboratory (as Sargant had done earlier) and published articles on the form and structure of plants. Her major study, *Monocotyledons: A Morphological Study* (1925) was followed by a study of grasses and cereals (*The Graminae*). It was Sargant who, shortly before her death, asked Arber to take over the production of a book on monocotyledons for the Cambridge Botanical Handbooks series. It consists both of careful investigations and a survey of the general principles of plant morphology and the philosophy behind these principles.

Arber was made a Fellow of the Linnean Society in 1908. She also began research in the history of herbals, publishing in 1912 her study of Renaissance and early modern herbals (later enlarged and republished), which became the classic in that field. She was appointed to a one-year research fellowship at Newnham to work on this book.

Newell and Agnes's only child, Muriel, was born in July 1912. In the years immediately following Muriel's birth, Arber's scientific productivity barely diminished. She only published two articles in 1916 and 1917, in the middle of World War I. One of these papers was simply titled "Science" and was the first time that she, in print, reflected on the nature of science in the broadest sense.

Newell Arber died at the age of forty-eight. According to one of her obituarists, Arber was a superwoman, juggling family, housework, and research successfully. Muriel Arber, on the other hand, noted that the obituary had been written by someone who did not know her mother very well. Her writing definitely had priority status and they usually had help with the housework and cooking. When she did do the cooking, "it was the simplest possible."

Arber also published on Goethe's botany (1946) and on the famous seventeenth-century plant anatomist Nehemiah Grew. She wrote two books on the philosophy of science late in her life. She was made a Fellow of the Royal Society in 1946 and received a number of grants and honors including the Gold Medal of the Linnean Society in 1948.   JH

PRIMARY SOURCES

Arber, Agnes. "Notes on the Anatomy of *Macrozamia heteromera." Proceedings of the Cambridge Philosophical Society*, 1903.
———. *Herbals: Origin and Evolution*. 1912.
———. *Water plants: A Study of Aquatic Angiosperms*. Cambridge: Cambridge University Press, 1920.
———. *Monocotyledons: A Morphological Study*. Cambridge: Cambridge University Press, 1925.
———. *The Graminae: A Study of Cereal Bamboo and Grass*. Cambridge: Cambridge University Press, 1934.
———. *The Mind and the Eye: A Study of the Biologists' Stand Point, Natural Philosophy of Plant Form*. Cambridge: Cambridge University Press, 1954.
———. *The Manifold and the One*. London: J. Murray, 1957.
Manuscripts and portrait in the Hunt Library, Pittsburgh, Pennsylvania.

SECONDARY SOURCES

"Agnes Arber." *Phytomorphology* 11 (1961): 197–198.
"Agnes Robertson Arber, 1879–1960." *Biographical Memoirs of Fellows of the Royal Society,* vol. 6, 1960: 1–11. Includes bibliography.
Arber, M. A. "List of Published Works of Agnes Arber, E. A. N. Arber and Ethel Sargant." *Journal of the Society for the Bibliography of Natural History* 4 (1968): 370–384.
Packer, Kathryn. "A Laboratory of One's Own: The Life and Works of Agnes Arber, F.R.S. (1879–1960)." *Notes and Records of the Royal Society of London* 51, no. 1 (1997): 87–104.
Stearn, W. T. "Mrs. Agnes Arber." *Taxon* 6 (1960): 261–263.
Thomas, H. Hamshaw. "Dr. Agnes Arber, F.R.S." *Nature* 186, 11 June 1960: 847.

STANDARD SOURCES

DSB (includes bibliography); Grinstein 1997; *Newnham* vol. 1; *Notable; WWW,* 1951–1960.

ARBUTHNOT, ISOBEL AGNES (1870–1963)

Irish/South African botanist. Born 1870 in Belfast, County Antrim. Married Henry Bolus. Professional experience: Henry Bolus Herbarium, Capetown, South Africa, assistant (1918–1938); Compton Herbarium, botanist (1938–1945). Died 1963 in Newlands, Cape Province.

Isobel Arbuthnot went to South Africa in 1888 as companion to the wife of the botanist Henry Bolus. Later she worked as assistant in the Henry Bolus Herbarium in Capetown from around 1918 to 1938. She then worked in the Compton Herbarium until 1945. Arbuthnot developed her own herbarium, now in Bolus Herbarium. She is commemorated by the plant name *Lampranthus arbuthnotiae,* L. Bolus.

JH/MBO

STANDARD SOURCES
Desmond; Gunn and Codd.

ARCONVILLE, GENEVIÈVE CHARLOTTE D' (1720–1805)

French anatomist. Born 1720. Married M. Thiroux, conseiller au parlement. Educated Jardin du Roi. Professional experience: Translated Alexander Monro's two-volume Osteology *1759. Died 1805.*

Geneviève Charlotte d'Arconville, an eclectic scientist, was a friend of Lavoisier. Although she is best known for her work in anatomy, she also carried on research in chemistry, physics, natural history, and medicine. Sandwiched between her anatomical studies was a course in medicine at the Jardin du Roi. Much of her social life revolved around famous personalities including scientists such as Macquer, Chantal, Lacépède, and Fourcroy. In addition to her scientific writings, she published a three-volume life of Marie de Medicis and another work on the husband of Mary Queen of Scots, Francis II.

D'Arconville translated Shaw's *Leçons de Chimie* in 1759. Probably her most important work, though, was her translation of Alexander Monro's *Osteology,* also in 1759. She supervised the beautiful illustrations drawn from a cadaver and included them in this translation. In addition to these popular translations, she also studied and published on putrefaction, a work extolled by her contemporaries. D'Arconville published more than sixteen titles on scientific subjects, including a "Description of the Movements of Systole and Diastole of the Heart," "Description of the Lacteals," "A Tumor in the Loins of an Infant," and "On a Young Boy Who Lived a Considerable Time without Food." JH/MBO

PRIMARY SOURCES
Arconville, Geneviève-Charlotte, translator. Shaw, Peter. *Leçons de Chimie,* Paris: Jean Thomas Herissant, 1759.
———. *L'essai pour servir a l'histoire de la putréfaction.* Paris: Chez Fr. Didot le jeune, 1766. Probably her most important original work, based on a series of experiments. Noted thirty-two substances that either retarded or produced putrefaction. Second half includes her original research on human and bovine bile.

STANDARD SOURCES
Alic; Hurd-Mead 1938; Lipinska 1900.

ARDEN, LADY MARGARET ELIZABETH (SPENCER WILSON) (d. 1851)

British botanist and mycologist. Married. Lived in Nork, Epsom, Surrey. Contributed plants to Sowerby and Smith. Died 1851.

Lady Arden is known to have contributed to J. Sowerby and J. E. Smith's *English Botany.* JH/MBO

PRIMARY SOURCES
Sowerby, J., and J. E. Smith. *English Botany.* Arden's contribution can be found page 461, tabula 2659.

STANDARD SOURCES
Desmond.

ARDINGHELLI, MARIA ANGELA (fl. 1756)
Italian physicist and mathematician. Born in Naples.

Little is known of the life of Maria Ardinghelli, except that she was born in Naples and was recognized for her abilities in physics and mathematics as well as languages.

Ardinghelli is known for her translations into Italian of Stephen Hales's (1677–1761) works, the *Hemastaticks* (1750, 1756, and 1776) and the *Vegetable Staticks.* Some clues about Ardinghelli's abilities in physics and mathematics emerge in the preface "To the Reader" in her Italian translation of the *Vegetable Staticks.* She stated that while she was working with the English original, she also used the French translation by Buffon to elucidate difficult concepts, such as an experiment performed by Hales illustrated by Buffon. Ardinghelli included this illustration in her translation. In addition she inserted an appendix of experiments explicating Hales's and Buffon's work. She also noted that her translation in some cases differed from Buffon's since his differed from the original, and he had omitted at least one experiment (experiment 93). Ardinghelli did not simply translate Hales's work but brought her understanding to it, correcting some calculations that were incorrect in both the French translations and the English original. She also added numerous explanatory footnotes with additional calculations. JH/MBO

PRIMARY SOURCES
Hales, Stephen. *Statica de' vegetabili, ed analisi dell' tradotta dall' Inglese con varie annotazioni.* Transl. Maria Ardinghelli. Naples: G. Raimondi, 1756. Translation of the *Vegetable Staticks* of Stephen Hales. Includes a section, "To the Reader," explaining changes in her translation. The footnotes are also Ardinghelli's.

STANDARD SOURCES
Mozans; Ogilvie 1986.

ARETE OF CYRENE (fl. late 5th–early 4th centuries B.C.E.)

Greek philosopher. Born in Cyrene. Father was Aristippos. Teacher in schools and academies of Attica.

Arete was a member of a family noted for scholarly pursuits. Her father, Aristippos, was a pupil of Socrates and founder of the Cyrenaic or Hedonistic school of philosophy. Her son, also named Aristippos, was a scholar who received his education from her. Arete was known for the breadth of her knowledge, which reputedly encompassed natural as well as moral philosophy. H. J. Mozans, quoting from Boccaccio's *De laudibus mulierum,* reports that she "is said to have publicly taught natural and moral philosophy in the schools and academies of Attica for thirty-five years, to have written forty books, and to have counted among her pupils one hundred and ten philosophers." No fragments of her works are extant, nor are reliable accounts of their contents available. Diogenes Laertius provided the information that Arete was the daughter of Aristippos and had for her pupil Aristippos. Strabo, Clement of Alexandria, and Eusebius noted Arete's role as the successor to her father in the Hedonistic school. JH/MBO

SECONDARY SOURCES
Diogenes Laertius. *Lives of the Eminent Philosophers, Life of Aristippus,* 2.72.86.
Themistius. *Orationes,* 21.24.

STANDARD SOURCES
Mozans; Pauly-Wissowa; Waithe.

ARIGNOTE OF SAMOS (fl. 6th century B.C.E.)

Greek Pythagorean philosopher. Born in Croton to Theano and Pythagoras.

Reputedly Arignote was the daughter of Theano and Pythagoras, but this information must be viewed cautiously because of the aura of mystery surrounding Pythagoras. She was said to have been educated in the Pythagorean school in Croton. She is quoted in an apothegm as saying that "the eternal essence of numbers is the most providential cause of the whole heaven, earth, and the region in between. Likewise it is the root of the continued existence of the gods and daimones, as well as that of divine men" (Waithe, 12). This attributed statement is congruent with the Pythagorean belief that the nature of the universe is mathematical. JH/MBO

STANDARD SOURCES
Kersey; Ménage; Waithe.

ARKHANGEL'SKAIA, ALEKSANDRA GAVRIILOVNA (1851–1905)

Russian physician. Born 1851 in Krapivno, daughter of Gavriil Arkhangel'skii, a priest. Educated at Tula Women's gymnasium; Women's Medical Courses in St. Petersburg. Professional experience: Nizhegorod Province, hospital work; district physician at Petrovsk. Died in Petrovsk in 1905.

Aleksandra Gavriilovna Arkhangel'skaia was the daughter of a village priest. She had no formal education as a child, but taught herself how to read and write. Despite pressure from her family to marry young, Arkhangel'skaia was determined to pursue a career. Her original intention had been to enter a course for midwives, but as it was full by the time she had obtained permission from her parents to enter, she enrolled in Tula Women's gymnasium, although she was ten years older than the other students. Here, her lack of preparation became apparent and she was obliged to drop out and study on her own to catch up. When she completed the course in 1873, she prepared to enter the Women's Medical Courses in St. Petersburg and enrolled there in 1874.

In St. Petersburg, Arkhangel'skaia studied various nonmedical subjects and wrote several stories that were published. In her third year she was involved in a political event as a result of which she was arrested and sent back to Krapivno for a whole school year. Upon her return, she seriously pursued her medical studies and, to finance herself, worked in the summer at a cottage hospital in Nizhegorod.

Arkhangel'skaia completed her medical courses in 1881 and, after a year as assistant to the professor of surgery K. K. Reier, a pioneer in the use of antiseptic methods, and after a trip to Paris, she began practice in a salaried post as a zemstvo (district) physician at Petrovsk near Moscow. There she remained for the rest of her life.

Fortunate in having an enlightened zemstvo council desirous of improving medical care in the area, Arkhangel'skaia now had scope to develop all her talents, both medical and administrative. Her first assignment was to plan and build a hospital. The original fifteen-bed hospital was completed in 1885 but, over the years, there was much expansion and many additions. Arkhangel'skaia administered the whole facility herself and succeeded in creating a model hospital, which was visited by doctors from Russia and abroad.

Arkhangel'skaia's primary interest in medicine was surgery. She performed increasingly complex operations using the most modern methods then developed. She perfected operations for the removal of gallstones and cataracts, and also a procedure for bladder operations.

Arkhangel'skaia has been criticized for her enthusiasm for surgery and it is undoubtedly true that she considered it a cure for many conditions for which other treatments now exist. However, in the context of her time, given the increasing skill of surgeons and their knowledge of antisepsis, this bias toward surgery was not unusual.

Arkhangel'skaia was actively involved in all aspects of her profession. She wrote numerous articles, headed many committees and supported progressive causes. In 1902 she was elected president of the surgery section of the Pirogov Society. She was particularly concerned with the improvement of the rural health services and with popular medical education and was the author of several publications intended for the general public. She recommended improvements in the training of feldshers or surgeon's assistants (somewhat akin to nurse practitioners), training for nurses and refresher courses for physicians. Well known for her dedication and total commitment to public health, Arkhangel'skaia was widely respected both as a surgeon and as a pioneer in the development of zemstvo medicine, which ultimately served as a model for the public health system of the Soviet era.   ACH

PRIMARY SOURCES

Arkhangel'skaia, Aleksandra Gavriilovna. *Dlia chego doktora delaiut operatsii.* 1897. Reprinted 1900, 1903, 1908, 1924, 1925.

————. *Pervaia pomoshch' v neschastnykh sluchaiakh i pri vnezapnom zabolevanii liudei.* 1899. Reprinted 1901, 1903, 1912.

SECONDARY SOURCES

Tuve, Jeanette E. *The First Russian Women Physicians.* Newtonville, Mass.: Oriental Research Partners, 1984.

ARLITT, ADA HART (1889–1976)

U.S. educational psychologist. Born 17 July 1889 in New Orleans. Educated Tulane University (A.B., 1913); University of Chicago (Ph.D., 1917). Professional experience: Bryn Mawr College, associate educational psychologist (1917–1923); Central Clinic, Cincinnati, psychologist (1923–1925); University of Cincinnati, professor and head of the Department of Child Care and Training (1925–1951), emeritus professor of psychology and child care and training (from 1951). National Congress of Parents and Teachers, national chairman of parent education (1928–1943); Childhood Education, board of editors; Child Welfare, associate editor (1929–?). Honors and memberships: American Psychological Association; American Society for the Advancement of Science, Fellow. Died 1976.

Ada Hart Arlitt was born in New Orleans, Louisiana, and educated at Tulane. After receiving her A.B. in 1913, she went to the University of Chicago where she received her Ph.D. Her thesis was a study of the effects of alcohol on the intelligence of white rats and their progeny. From Chicago,

she went to Bryn Mawr College as associate educational psychologist, moving to a position at the Central Clinic of Cincinnati (1923–1925). She was appointed professor and department head of Child Care and Training at the University of Cincinnati, a position she held until her retirement in 1951. Throughout her career, Arlitt published books on child and adolescent psychology.

Arlitt's interest in parent education is shown by her position as National Chairman of the National Congress of Parents and Teachers (PTA) from 1928 to 1943. She was on the board of editors of the journal *Childhood Education* and an associate editor of *Child Welfare* from 1929 until her retirement. Her work reflects a life-long interest in the behavior problems of young children, the psychological aspects of family life, and child and adolescent psychology.   KM

PRIMARY SOURCES

Arlitt, Ada Hart. *The Effect of Alcohol on the Intelligent Behavior of the White Rat and Its Progeny.* Princeton, N.J.: Psychological Review Co., 1919. Reprint, Johnson Reprint Corp. New York: Kraus, 1970.

————. *Psychology of Infancy and Early Childhood.* New York: McGraw-Hill, 1928.

————. *The Child from One to Six.* New York: McGraw-Hill, 1930.

————. *Adolescent Psychology.* New York: American Book Company, 1933.

————. *The Adolescent.* New York, London: Whittlesey House, McGraw-Hill, 1938.

————. *Family Relationships.* New York; London: McGraw-Hill, 1942.

SECONDARY SOURCES

American Psychologist (June 1977): 410.

STANDARD SOURCES

AMS 3–8, S&B 9–11; *Psychological Register*, vol. 3, 1932.

ARMITAGE, ELEANORA (1865–1961)

British botanist. Born 11 December 1865 in Dadnor, England, Never married. Died 24 October 1961.

Armitage studied the flora of Herefordshire, specializing in the iris. She contributed to *Journal Royal Horticultural Society.* Her plants are held at Bristol and Manchester University, and the iris drawings are at Royal Botanic Gardens, Kew. She was a member of the Woolhope Natural Field Club and the British Bryological Society.   JH/MBO

PRIMARY SOURCES

Armitage, Eleanora. Articles in *Journal Royal Horticultural Society.* Her plants are at Bristol and Manchester Universities.

SECONDARY SOURCES
Review of Bryology and Lichenology 1963: 296–297. With portrait.
Transactions Woolhope Natural Field Club 34 (1954): 257.
Transactions of the British Bryological Society 1962: 338–340. With portrait. Obituary notice.

STANDARD SOURCES
Desmond.

ARMITAGE, ELLA SOPHIA A. (BULLEY) (1841–1931)

Medieval archeologist. Born 3 March 1841 in Liverpool to Mary (Raffles) and Samuel Marshall Bulley. Married Reverend Elkanah Armitage (1874). Two children (son and daughter). Educated at home; Newnham College (1871–ca. 1874); research student (1874–ca. 1877); Manchester University (honorary M.A., 1919). Professional experience: Owen College, Manchester, history instructor (1877–1879). Other experience: Rotterham, school board member (1887); Bradford and West Riding Education Committee, school board member (1890); Royal Commission on Secondary Education, assistant commissioner; research on earthworks and medieval castles. Died 20 March 1931 in Middlesbrough.

Ella Sophia Armitage was born on 3 March 1841 to Mary (Raffles) and Samuel Marshall Bulley in the city of Liverpool where her father was a cotton broker and justice of the peace. She was the second daughter of a family of four sons and ten daughters. Having been educated privately at home, she was expected in turn to teach her younger siblings. She mastered a wide range of languages, including French, German, Italian, and Latin, and learned to read Spanish, Norwegian, Danish, Welsh, and Early English.

At thirty years of age she was one of the first five women to enter Newnham College, Cambridge. She continued her education as the college's first research student in 1874. That same year she married Reverend Elkanah Armitage, a Nonconformist minister. The couple had one son and one daughter. When her husband moved the family to Manchester, an important center for the Unitarian ministry, Armitage taught history at Owen College, Manchester, from 1877 to 1879, and became intrigued by the history of ancient medieval earthworks and castles. Her view, that these were not Anglo-Saxon but Norman, was at first controversial, but her further research and publications marshaled additional evidence for her position. A significant paper was read on her behalf by a male cousin, Gerrard Baldwin Brown, before the Society of Antiquities of Scotland in 1900. By 1912, her most important book, *The Early Norman Castles of the British Isles,* was published by the well-respected publishing house John Murray.

Armitage had a lifelong interest in secondary education. She served on a number of school boards and education committees from 1887 through 1894. In that year she was appointed to the Royal Commission on Secondary Education as Assistant Commissioner to investigate girls' secondary education in Devon.

She was also a frequent speaker for the London Missionary Society throughout the country. Her musical talents were evident from her accomplished performances on the piano, as well as in the composition of a number of hymns. A tall, stately woman, she was seen by some as rather forbidding, but intimate friends appreciated her for her humor. She died at the age of ninety at the home of her daughter in Middlesex, retaining her sharp intellect to the end.   JH/MBO

PRIMARY SOURCES
Armitage, Ella. [On earthworks]. *Journal Society of Antiquaries,* 1900.
———. *The Early Norman Castles of the British Isles.* London: John Murray, 1912.

SECONDARY SOURCES
Counihan, Jean. "Mrs Ella Armitage, John Horace Round, G. T. Clark and Early Norman Castles." Anglo Norman Studies VII, 1985.

STANDARD SOURCES
DNB Missing Persons.

ARMITT, ANNIE MARIA (1850–1933)

British naturalist.

Annie Maria Armitt was one of three naturalist sisters from Rydal in Cumbria. She apparently was connected with BEATRIX POTTER.   JH/MBO

PRIMARY SOURCES
Kendal Cumbria Natural History and Scientific Society. Archives.

ARMITT, MARY LOUISA (1851–1911)

British ornithologist/musicologist. Born 24 September 1851 in Salford. Died 1911.

Mary Louisa was a member of a family that lived in Rydal in Cumbria. She produced eleven volumes of notes on birds of Lakeland from 1890 to 1907. She was also known as a musicologist and her musicology is discussed in Browon and Stratton, *British Musical Biography,* 1897.   JH/MBO

PRIMARY SOURCES
Maria Louisa Armitt's manuscripts are found in the Kendal Cumbria Natural History and Scientific Society.

SECONDARY SOURCES

Bridson, Gavin D. R. Natural History Manuscript Resources in the British Isles. London: Mansell, 1980.

Browon, James Duff, and Stratton, Stephen S. *British Musical Biography*. Birmingham: S. S. Stratton, 1897.

ARMITT, SOPHIA (1847–1908)

British botanist. Born 1847. Died 1908.

Sophia Armitt was a sister of MARIA and ANNIE ARMITT. She was the botanist of the trio and produced botanical notes between 1870 and 1892 as well as a book of drawings and watercolors of fungi in 1906.   JH/MBO

PRIMARY SOURCES

Archives of the Armitt Family of Rydal. Notes, proofs, sketches etc. Contains two small sketchbooks, one by Sophia Armitt.

SECONDARY SOURCES

Natural History Manuscripts in the British Isles.

ARNOLD, MAGDA BLONDIAU (1903–   )

Austrian/U.S. psychologist. Born 22 December 1903 in Mahr-Trubau, Austria (later Czechoslovakia), to Marie Blondiau and Rudolf Barta. Educated University of Toronto (B.A., 1939, M.A., 1940; Ph.D., 1942). Professional experience: University of Toronto, lecturer in psychology (1942–1947); Department of Veterans Affairs, Ottawa, Canada, director of research and training (1946–1947); Wellesley College, visiting lecturer (1947–1948); Bryn Mawr College, associate professor and department head (1948–1950); Barat College of the Sacred Heart, professor and department head (1950–1952); Loyola University, Chicago, professor and director of the experimental division (1952–1972); Spring Hill College, director of the social science division (1972–?); Fulbright Residential Professor, Munich, Germany (1962–1963). Honorary Degrees from St. Mary's College, California (LL.D., 1959); Loyola University, Chicago (L.H.D., 1973). Honors and memberships: American Psychological Association, member.

Magda Arnold was born in Europe but received all three of her college degrees in Canada. As did many women in the first three-quarters of the twentieth century, Arnold held numerous academic positions. Her research involved personality, emotion, projective technique, and brain function in memory and emotion. Arnold authored several books and contributed many articles to professional journals.   JH/MBO

PRIMARY SOURCES

Arnold, Magda. *Emotion and Personality*. 2 vols. New York: Columbia University Press, 1960.

———. *Story and Sequence Analysis*. New York: Columbia University, 1962.

———. *The Nature of Emotions*. New York: Penguin, 1968.

STANDARD SOURCES

AMS 7–8, S&B 9–13; Stevens and Gardner, vol. 2.

ARNSTEIN, MARGARET GENE (1904–1972)

U.S. public health nurse and nursing educator. Born 27 October 1904 in New York City to Leo and Elsie (Nathan) Arnstein. Educated Ethical Culture School, New York (1921); Smith College (A.B., 1925); New York Presbyterian Hospital School of Nursing (1928); Teachers College, Columbia University (A.M. in public health, 1929); Johns Hopkins University (M.S. in public health, 1923). Professional experience: Westchester County Hospital, White Plains, N.Y., staff nurse, later supervisor (1929–ca. 1933); New York State Department of Health, Communicable Disease Division, consultant nurse (1934–1937); University of Minnesota, Department of Preventive Medicine, teacher of public health and nursing (1938–1940); New York Department of Health (1940–1946); United States Public Health Service (1946–1966); University of Michigan, professor of public health nursing (1966–1967); Yale School of Nursing, dean (1967–1972); United Nations Relief and Rehabilitation Administration, nurse training advisor in Balkan countries (1943–1945). Honors and memberships: first holder of the Annie W. Goodrich Chair of Nursing at Yale (1958); Rockefeller Public Service Award (1965); Sedgwick Memorial Medal (1971); several honorary degrees. Died of cancer at her apartment in New Haven, Conn., 8 October 1972.

Margaret Arnstein was born into a family actively engaged in health education and concerns. Her father was a successful businessman who later became president of Mt. Sinai Hospital. Both parents were closely associated with the Henry Street Settlement, a visiting nurses service founded by LILLIAN WALD. Wald, a family friend and leader in public health nursing, encouraged Margaret's interest. Arnstein eventually earned two master's degrees in public health and spent her career using field studies and applied research to increase public health nurses' participation in the development and modernization of their field.

Arnstein worked at different times as nurse and as teacher but her real passion was field work. She designed studies to analyze and systematize the observations and insights of working public health nurses, who she felt had "an intuitive grasp of the ways in which their patient might fare better." During her long career in the United States Public Health Service, she directed national field studies on nursing and helped individual hospitals conduct their own research on how to improve patient care. She prepared *A Guide for National Studies of Nursing Resources* (1953) for the World Health

Organization and directed the first International Conference on Nursing Studies (1956) in Sevres, France. Supported by the Rockefeller Foundation and the Agency for International Development, she joined U.S. and British physicians to study health service needs in developing countries. Over the years, Arnstein consulted in the Balkan countries and in India, as well as in Appalachia and the urban ghettos of the United States.

Arnstein passed her final years in academia, as professor of public health nursing at the University of Michigan, then as dean of the Yale School of Nursing until her retirement a year after being diagnosed with cancer. She died in 1972. Her contributions to public health nursing were widely lauded and she received several honorary degrees. She was the first woman to receive the $10,000 Rockefeller Public Service Award (1965); she also received the Sedgwick Memorial Medal, the highest honor of the American Public Health Association (1971).   JH/MBO

STANDARD SOURCES
NAW(M) (article by Nancy Milio).

ARSENJEWA, A. (fl. 1926)

Russian? physicist. Professional experiece: Physical-Technical Institute, Leningrad, researcher.

Biographical information is lacking on Arsenjewa. Nevertheless, what is known about her work is intriguing. Working at the Physical-Technical Institute in Leningrad under Abram Joffé, Arsenjewa investigated the photoelectric effect in rock salt that had been previously exposed to X-rays. She found that the electrical conductivity produced by light depended on intensity, but not on wavelength. This result, which conflicted with the quantum interpretation of the photoelectric effect, suggested the presence of secondary ionization. Arsenjewa proposed that the quantum law applied only to primary photoelectrons, and not to secondary ionization.   MM

PRIMARY SOURCES
Arsenjewa, A. "Über die lichtelektrische Leitfähigkeit im Steinsalz." *Zeitschrift für Physik* 37 (1926): 701–704.

STANDARD SOURCES
Meyer and von Schweidler.

ARTEMISIA OF CARIA II (fl. 350 B.C.E.)

Greek botanist and pharmacologist. Married Mausolus.

Artemisia is known for her great love for her brother/husband, and the celebrated tomb, the Mausoleum, that she ordered built at his death. It was considered one of the seven wonders of the world. In spite of her grief, she commanded an army against the Rhodians, where she was recognized for unusual bravery. Artemisia of Caria was praised by Strabo, Pliny, Suidas, and Theophrastus for her knowledge of herbal medicine. Soranus of Ephesus noted that the herb *Artemisia,* which she named for herself, was used in the bath to prevent abortion and as a treatment in "retarded menses" and retained placenta. Another species of artemisia was used to cause abortions. According to Pliny, Artemisia discovered the value of wormwood as a drink. She also named the cyclamen, gentian, and lysimachia for the kings of Arcadia, Thrace, and Ilium.   JH/MBO

STANDARD SOURCES
Cyclopaedia of Female Biography; Hurd-Mead 1938.

ARTHUR, MARY GRACE (1883–?)

U.S. educational psychologist. Born 22 May 1883 in St. Paul, Minn. Never married. Educated Hamline College (B.S., 1917); University of Minnesota (A.M., 1919; Ph.D., 1924). Professional experience: Minnesota public schools, psychological examiner and teacher (1917–1920); St. Paul Child Guidance Center, psychologist (1920–1923; 1924–1942), consulting psychologist (from 1942); University of Minnesota, teaching fellow in psychology (1923–1924), director of research projects with rank of assistant professor (1926–1928); Office of Indian Affairs (1942–1947). Honors and memberships: American Psychological Association, member; Minnesota Psychological Society, member; Orthopsychiatric Association, Fellow.

Mary Grace Arthur spent her entire life in Minnesota, working in educational psychology, first at the St. Paul Child Guidance Center and then at her alma mater, the University of Minnesota. She was forty-three years old when she was appointed director of research projects and she remained at that position only two years. Her primary interest was in devising intelligence (or performance) tests for non-English-speaking persons, illiterates, and children with speech and hearing handicaps. She published her own point scale of performance tests in two volumes between 1930 and 1933 and adapted the Leiter International Performance Scale in 1952. In 1969, Arthur and Russell G. Leiter together reissued the Leiter scale as a kit of blocks and cards. This kit was revised and reissued in about 1980 and is still in use. She also questioned the relation of intelligence quotient to position in family and the stability of IQ over a long period of time. When she was appointed to the Office of Indian Affairs, she studied the intelligence of Indian children and developed a nonverbal test of logical thinking.   KM

PRIMARY SOURCES

Arthur, Mary Grace. *A Point Scale of Performance Tests.* Vol. 1. New York: Commonwealth Fund, 1930. 2d. edition, 1943.

———. *Tutoring as Therapy.* New York: Commonwealth Fund, 1946.

———. *The Arthur Adaptation of the Leiter International Performance Scale.* Washington, D.C.: Psychological Service Center Press, 1952.

———. With Russell Graydon Leiter. *Leiter International Performance Scale: Arthur Adaptation.* Chicago and Stoelting: distributed by Western Psychological Services, 1969.

STANDARD SOURCES

AMS 4–8, S&B 9–10; *Psychological Register,* 1932.

ARTNER, MATHILDE (fl. 1921)

Austrian?/German physicist. Professional experience: Institute for Radium Research, Vienna, researcher.

Mathilde Artner was one of the women who was a part of the Austro-German group that studied radioactivity. Nothing is known about her education and early life, but she did some important work. At the Institute for Radium Research in Vienna, Artner determined the spatial variation of the potential gradient in air ionized by alpha rays and the gradient's dependence upon experimental variables.   MM

PRIMARY SOURCES

Artner, Mathilde. "Untersuchung des Spannungsgefälles im Plattenkondensator bei Ionisation durch α-Strahlen." *Akademie der Wissenschaften, Vienna. Sitzungsberichte 2a* 130 (1921): 253–264.

STANDARD SOURCES

Meyer and von Schweidler.

ASCLEPIGENIA (4th century)

Greek Neoplatonist. Father Plutarch the Younger.

The Athenian Neoplatonic school was later taken over by Asclepigenia's daughter, Asclepigenia the Younger. This eastern branch of Neoplatonism also included many other women.   JH/MBO

STANDARD SOURCES

Kersey; Waithe.

ASHBY, WINIFRED MAYER (1879–?)

British/U.S. immunologist. Born 1879 in London. Educated University of Chicago (B.A., 1903); Washington University at St. Louis (M.S., 1905); University of Minnesota (Ph.D., 1921). *Professional experience: Mayo Foundation, researcher (1921–1923); Mayo Clinic (1923–1924); St. Elizabeth's Hospital, immunologist (1924–1948), guest researcher until 1958; United States Federal Security Agency, advisor. Honors and memberships: Society of Bacteriology; Society of Immunology; Society of Experimental Biology; New York Academy of Medicine.*

Winifred Ashby was born in 1879 in London, but she was educated and lived most of her life in the United States. She received a B.S. at the University of Chicago and an M.S. at Washington University at St. Louis. The field of immunology caught her interest at Washington University and she continued her education in immunology at the University of Minnesota, where she received her Ph.D..

Immediately after graduating from Minnesota, she began her research in the division of experimental bacteriology at the Mayo Foundation, working there for two years. From the foundation, she went to the Mayo Clinic for a year. Ashby then began her long career as immunologist at St. Elizabeth's Hospital. After her retirement, she continued as guest researcher there until 1958. Concurrently she served as advisor with the United States Federal Security Agency.

Ashby's specialities were blood destruction and changes in blood volume. She was interested in colloidal gold, brain enzyme chemistry, and the pattern of enzyme distributions in the brain and mental functions.   JH/MBO

STANDARD SOURCES

AMS 4–8, B 9, P&B 10; Herzenberg.

ASPASIA OF MILETUS (d. ca. 401 B.C.E.)

Greek rhetorician and philosopher. Born after 470 B.C.E. in Miletus. Father Axiochus. Hetaera (consort) of Pericles. Usually assumed to have married Lysicles. Two sons, one by Pericles and one by Lysicles. Probably died in Athens in 401 B.C.E.

Although Aspasia is probably one of the most important women in fifth-century Greece, so many myths surround her that it is difficult to arrive at facts. She is memorialized in a fresco over the portal at the University of Athens where she is shown in the company of Pericles, Socrates, and famous men from a variety of previous eras. Aspasia apparently held a popular salon frequented by Socrates, Phidius, Anaxagoras, and Euripides. Tradition says that she was the teacher of Socrates and Pericles.

Plutarch's *Life of Pericles* tells us that Aspasia came from Miletus and that her father's name was Axiochus. Other ancient sources provide other, often contradictory, information about her. No fifth-century source presents factual evidence about Aspasia's life. She became a "companion" or hetaera of

Pericles after his divorce from his Athenian wife. As a member of the hetaerae, Aspasia could participate in the intellectual life of Athens, whereas the wives of Athenian citizens were excluded. Her union with Pericles presumably produced a son. She also supposedly married Lysicles, an Athenian politician, and produced a son by him. Peter Bicknell proposes that Aspasia could have been born any time after 470 B.C.E. and came to Athens about 450 B.C.E. Although he tentatively identifies her as a dependent relative of an Athenian aristocrat, she was still a resident alien.

Aspasia allegedly wrote some of Pericles' best speeches, including his famous funeral oration over those who had died in the battle of Potidaea. Plato's dialogue, the *Menexenus,* includes a funeral oration said to have been composed by Aspasia. This dialogue differs from the well-known Periclean oration that Socrates ascribed to Aspasia. The account in the *Menexenus* is filled with historical misstatements, and it may well be that this is Plato's way of condemning current oratory and its sometimes gross fabrications. Aspasia certainly was not a scientist, but was apparently an influential advocate for women's rights. If she indeed taught Socrates, as Plato claimed, she was a respected scholar and the fact that she was a woman may have been significant for his views and for his student Plato. Aspasia was clearly an important figue in fifth-century Athenian intellectual history. This importance is reflected in the views of others in antiquity, for although she left no books of her own she was satirized in Greek comedy, was considered an important personage in Greek philosophical dialogue, and was the subject of colorful, unverifiable anecdotes. Mozans reports that it is probable that Aspasia strongly influenced Plato's views on women as found in the *Republic.* She is thought to have insisted that women should be more than mothers and housewives and urged them to improve their minds.   MBO

SECONDARY SOURCES
Henry, Madeleine M. *Prisoner of History: Aspasia of Miletus and Her Biographical Tradition.* New York: Oxford University Press, 1995. An excellent treatment of Aspasia, investigating her life by tracing the evolution of her *bios* from late antiquity to the present. Very well documented with endnotes and a bibliography.
Plato. *Menexenus.* In *Plato in Twelve Volumes.* Vol. 9. Loeb Classical Library. Cambridge, Mass.: Harvard University Press, 1981. The introduction on pages 330–331 provides an interesting background to the *Menexenus.*

STANDARD SOURCES
Mozans; Waithe (discusses various views of Aspasia).

ASPASIA THE PHYSICIAN (fl. first centuries C.E.)
Greek physician.

Although nothing is known about the life of Aspasia the Physician, fragments cited by a physician to an emperor of Byzantium indicate that she was not the celebrated consort of Pericles but rather that she lived in an early century of the Christian era. Her major medical contributions were in the areas of obstetrics and gynecology. There is no extant evidence to suggest that she went beyond practical solutions to medical problems. Even the very important technique of rotating the fetus in a breech presentation was a procedural advance—a specific solution to a specific problem. It was in her discussion of the importance of preventive medicine during pregnancy that she made her nearest approach to theoretical science; here too, however, her suggestions were based on a common-sense approach rather than on the consideration of an abstract principle.   JH/MBO

STANDARD SOURCES
Lipinṣka 1930.

ASTELL, MARY (1668–1731)
British natural philosopher and writer on social science. Born 1668 in Newcastle to landed gentry parents. At least one sibling, a younger brother. Never married. Educated by a clergyman uncle who was a Platonist. Professional experience: established a charity school for girls in Chelsea (1709). Died 1731.

Mary Astell's father was a Royalist during the Civil War and a prosperous coal merchant. Although she never attended school, Astell was educated by an alcoholic clergyman uncle who had been fired from his post as assistant curate. A graduate of Cambridge University, he had absorbed many of the tenets of Platonism, and passed these ideas on to Astell. She also learned Latin, English literature, and some theology from him. Her father died in 1680 (placing the family in financial difficulties), her uncle the following year, and her mother six years later. Upon the death of her mother, she was left with enough money to support herself for a year. She did the unthinkable—went off on her own, something a young lady simply did not do. She established herself in Chelsea with a group of wealthy aristocratic women friends who shared her concern for women's education. These women and other friends helped her financially. From these experiences, she discovered the need for a college for women, and so proposed a school along the lines of a medieval convent where women could receive an education, including scientific study. After her efforts were frustrated, she organized a charity school for girls in Chelsea. She found backers, selected the staff, and generally supervised the school. She died at the age of sixty-five from breast cancer after a mastectomy without anesthesia.

Mary Astell is considered one of the women founders of social science. A recent book calls her the first English feminist. Her works were a blend of Cartesian doubt and Lockean caution. Astell was basically a conservative politically, following her family's Royalist views. Not wanting to violate the conventions of class and sex, Astell published her books anonymously. The radical part of her position was her treatment of women as men's intellectual and moral equals. Her case for this was a part of a general argument that all people had been given rational minds, which God intended for them to use. She was in agreement with Montaigne, Bacon, and the scientists of the Royal Society in her view that reason was vitally important to knowledge, but it must not be allowed to undermine faith, which could only be known by revelation. Her many publications indicate that she may very well be the first systematic feminist theoretician as well as a pioneer methodologist.   JH/MBO

PRIMARY SOURCES
[Astell, Mary]. *A Serious Proposal to the Ladies.* 1694, 2nd ed., 1695. The author of this book was "By a Lover of her Sex."
———. *Six Familiar Essays upon Marriage, Crosses in Love.* 1696.
———. *An Essay in Defence of the Female Sex.* (3d edition, London: 1697.
———. *Some Reflections upon Marriage.* London: Parker, 1700.
———. *Moderation Truly Stated.* London: Rich, Wilkin, 1704.
———. *The Christian Religion.* London: Wilkins, 1705.
———. *An Enquiry after Wit.* London: Bateman, 1709.
———. *The Plain Dealer,* no. 30 (July 1724): 239–248.

SECONDARY SOURCES
Hill, Bridget, ed. *The First English Feminist: Reflections upon Marriage and Other Writings by Mary Astell.* New York: St. Martin's Press, 1986.
McDonald, Lynn. *Women Founders of the Social Sciences.* Ottawa, Canada: Carleton University Press, 1994.
Perry, Ruth. *The Celebrated Mary Astell.* Chicago: University of Chicago Press, 1986.
Smith, Florence Mary. *Mary Astell.* Reprint, New York: Columbia University Press, 1966. This work originally was published in 1916.

STANDARD SOURCES
Alic; *DNB*; Uglow.

ATKINS, ANNA (1799–1871)
British botanist/photographer. Born 16 March 1799 in Tonbridge, Kent, to Hester Anne Holwell and John George Children. Married John Pelly Atkins. Died 9 June 1871.

The only child of John George Children, FRS, botanist at the British Museum, Anna Children worked with her father. Since her mother died shortly after Anna was born, father and daughter established an especially close relationship. Her father's position in the British Museum and the Royal Society probably assured his daughter's acceptance in these circles. She was a highly skilled draughtsperson and contributed two hundred illustrations to her father's translation of Lamarck's *Genera of Shells* (1823).

Anna Children, a member of the Botanical Society of London, was a pioneer in the application of photography to science. John George Children chaired the Royal Society meeting in 1839, where William Henry Fox Talbot demonstrated a photographic process. Both father and daughter experimented with the process. Anna recognized the usefulness of photography to record complex data, and applied it to publication. She independently published *Photographs of British Algae,* which were reproduced by the blueprint process. Her photographs were published also after her death in the *Journal of Photography* (1889). Her British plants are at the British Museum (Natural History). She also wrote a memoir of her father in 1853.   JH/MBO

PRIMARY SOURCES
Atkins, Anna. *Photographs of British Algae.* Halstead Place, Sevenoaks, England: Anna Atkins. 1843–1859.
———. *Memoir of John George Children.* Westminster: privately printed, 1853.
———. *Journal of Photography* (1889): 702–703; 787. Atkins's photographs, published posthumously.

SECONDARY SOURCES
Proceedings of the Philosophical Society of Glasgow 21 (*1889–1890*): 155–157.
Schaaf, Larry J. *Sun Gardens: Victorian Photograms by Anna Atkins.* New York: 1985. A recent publication of her "photograms" with some biographical material.

STANDARD SOURCES
Boase; Desmond; *DNB Missing Persons.*

ATKINS, LOUISA CATHERINE FANNY (fl. late 19th century)
British physician. Married and widowed. Educated London; University of Zurich (entered 1867; M.D., 1872). Professional experience: private practice, England.

Louisa Atkins had little education in the sciences when she entered the University of Zurich along with fellow Englishwoman Elizabeth Morgan. It was "only by dint of extraordinary self-discipline" that she was able to complete her M.D. in five years. Her thesis was on pulmonary gangrene in children. She returned to England to establish a practice.

JH/MBO

SECONDARY SOURCES
Bonner, Thomas Neville. "Rendezvous in Zurich: Seven Who Made a Revolution in Women's Medical Education, 1864–1874." In *Journal of the History of Medicine* 44, no. 1 (1989): 7–27.

ATKINSON, LOUISA (CALVERT) (1832–1874)
Australian natural historian, botanical illustrator and popular writer on botany. Born 1832 near Berrima, New South Wales. Married James Calvert in 1869. Daughter (b. ca. 1872). Died 1874, probably in Sydney.

Self-taught in science, Louisa Atkinson began by writing popular fiction for a Sydney paper, but soon began to write a regular column on natural history, contributed from 1861 to 1872, describing her rambles in the Kurrajong area. Atkinson began as an associate of William Woolls, a clergyman and botanist, who helped her develop her scientific studies and accompanied her on her excursions. Through Woolls, she became a correspondent of the German-born Australian government botanist Ferdinand Müller, for whom she collected ferns and other plants around Kurrajong. She also learned to stuff birds and other specimens.

Atkinson carefully recorded and illustrated her observations in a series of notebooks, and sent information and plants to Müller, who incorporated them into his *Flora Australiensis*. She also contributed articles to the *Horticultural Magazine*. At the time of her death in 1872, she was planning to publish a natural history of the area. She is commemorated in the genus *Atkinsonia,* and the distinctive fern, *Doodia atkinsonia*.

Atkinson died from tuberculosis soon after the birth of her daughter.

JH/MBO

PRIMARY SOURCES
Bentham, George, and Muller, Ferdinand Jacob Heinrich von. *Flora australiensis*. London: L. Reeve & Co., 1863–1873. Includes materials by Atkinson.
Her notebooks, clippings from her columns, and correspondence are preserved in the Mitchell Library, Sydney.

STANDARD SOURCES
Carr and Carr.

ATTERSOLL, MARIA (1793–1877)
British botanist. Born 1793. Never married. Educated privately. Died 12 February 1877.

Maria Attersoll spent her life in Weymouth, Dorset, where she collected plants and recorded information on specimens. Her records were included in T. B. Slater's historical appendix to J. Syndenham's *History of Poole,* 1839. She was elected a member of the Botanical Society of London in 1839. Her plants are located at Cambridge.

JH/MBO

PRIMARY SOURCES
Slater, T.B. *Botanical Appendix.* In J. Syndenham, *History of Poole,* 1839. Contains some of Attersoll's plant records.

SECONDARY SOURCES
British Journal for the Historical Society 13 (1980): 240–254.
Allen, David Elliston. *The Botanists: A History of the Botanical Society.* Winchester, U.K.: St. Paul's Biographies, 1986.

STANDARD SOURCES
Desmond.

ATWATER, HELEN WOODARD (1876–1947)
U.S. home economist and nutritionist. Born 29 May 1876 in Somerville, Mass., to Marcia (Woodard) and Wilbur Olin Atwater. One brother. Never married. Educated Smith College (B.L., 1897). Professional experience: assistant to her father (1897–1906); United States Department of Agriculture, scientific staff of the Office of Home Economics (1909–1923); Journal of Home Economics, full-time editor (1923–1941). Honors and memberships: The American Home Economics Association established the Helen Atwater International Fellowship Award in her memory. Smith College honorary Sc.D. (1943). Died 26 June 1947 in Washington, D.C.

Although Helen Atwater's father was a pioneer in agricultural and food chemistry, and a professor at Wesleyan University, she had no intention of pursuing a career in this area. She grew up in Middletown, Connecticut, and had one brother. During the time that she was growing up, her father often went to Europe and took his family with him. Helen received much of her early education abroad and became fluent in French and German.

After graduating from Smith College, Helen spent the next nine years as her father's assistant. Much of his research was concerned with calorimetry and his work resulted in two bulletins, *The Chemical Composition of American Food Materials* (1896) and *Principles of Nutrition and Nutritive Value of Food* (1902). Although she had not studied chemistry formally, she became proficient during the time that she worked with her father. After his death in 1907, she prepared an extensive bibliography of her father's writings on nutrition. The bibliography completed and her own credentials established, Atwood took a scientific position with the United States Department of Agriculture in Washington, D.C., where she remained for fourteen years. She frequently published in the *Journal of Home Economics*.

In 1923, Atwater was offered a position as the first full-time editor of the *Journal of Home Economics*. She remained at this position until she retired in 1941. During these years, Atwater was engaged in civic and Congregational church work. In World War I, she was executive chairman of the deparment of food production and home economics of the Woman's Committee of the United States Council of National Defense. In 1930, she served on the committee for the White House Conference on Child Health and Protection and in 1931 was a participant in the President's Conference on Home Building and Home Ownership. She was active for twenty years in the Women's Joint Congressional Committee formed as a clearinghouse for diverse organizations that promoted federal measures of interest to women, and chaired this organization from 1926 to 1928. She also was a member of the American Public Health Association and in 1942 chaired its committee on the hygiene of housing.

A small, lively woman, Atwater had a keen sense of humor. Her early background in foreign languages inspired her to work with foreign students who wanted to study home economics in the United States.   JH/MBO

PRIMARY SOURCES
Atwater, Helen Woodward. Numerous articles in the *Journal of Home Economics*.

SECONDARY SOURCES
Smith Alumnae Quarterly November 1947; February 1948.

STANDARD SOURCES
AMS 3–7; Bailey; *NAW*; *Woman's Who's Who of America*; *WWW*(A).

ATWOOD, MARTHA MARIA (1810–1880)

British botanist, bryologist, and lichenologist. Born 1810. Lived in Bristol and Bath. Collected lichens and mosses. Died 1880 in Worcester.

Martha Maria Atwood lived in Clifton, Bristol, and Bath, where she collected specimens of moss and lichens. These were included in nineteenth-century reference works. She also contributed to the journal *Phytologist*.   JH/MBO

PRIMARY SOURCES
Atwood, Martha Maria. Various articles in *Phytologist*.

Swete, E. H. *Flora Bristoliensis*. 1854. Atwood's specimens are included.
Leighton, W. A. *Lichen Flora*. 1879. Atwood's specimens are included.
Letters are in William Wilson correspondence, British Museum of Natural History.

SECONDARY SOURCES
Riddelsdell, H. J. *Flora Gloucestershire* (1949): cxxix.
White, J. W. *Flora Bristol* (1912): 96–97.

STANDARD SOURCES
Desmond.

AUERBACH, CHARLOTTE (1899–1994)

German-born, British geneticist. Born 14 May 1899 in Krefeld, Germany, to Selma (Sachs) and Frederich Auerbach. Never married. Educated Auguste-Victoria Schule (Realgymnasium), Berlin; science studies in Berlin, Würzburg, and Freiburg (1919–1924); University of Berlin (science degree, 1924); postgraduate studies in biology, Kaiser Wilhelm Institute, Berlin (1926–1929; secondary teaching certificate, 1929); University of Edinburgh (Ph.D., 1936; D.Sc., 1947). Professional experience: Heidelberg and Freiburg secondary schools, science teacher (1924–1925); Berlin secondary schools, science teacher (1929–1933); University of Edinburgh, reader and lecturer in genetics (1947–1967); University of Edinburgh, Unit of Mutagenesis research (Medical Research Council), honorary director (1959–1969); University of Edinburgh, Institute of Genetics, researcher (1967). Honors and memberships: Royal Society of Edinburgh, Fellow; Royal Society, Fellow; Royal Society of Edinburgh, Keith prize (1948). Died 1994.

Charlotte Auerbach was the daughter of a noted chemist, Friedrich Auerbach, the niece of a physicist, and the granddaughter of a noted physician, Leopold Auerbach. Soon after her birth, the family moved from Krefeld to Breslau and then to Berlin, where her father held a high position in the government health service. She was educated in the girl's gymnasium in Berlin, and later at the Universities of Berlin, Würzburg, and Freiburg. Auerbach obtained her degree in biology, chemistry, and physics in 1924. In Freiburg, she had studied develpmental biology with Hans Spemann, and she hoped to continue her studies, but she had little hope as a Jewish woman of obtaining a position at a German university. After obtaining a certificate in secondary education, she taught science for a year in private girls' secondary schools in Heidelberg and Frankfurt. After receiving a small legacy, she was able to return to biology. In 1926, she began to study for an advanced degree with Otto Mangold and attended lectures in genetics by Curt Stern at the Kaiser Wilhelm Institute. However, Mangold's dogmaticism and growing Nazi sympathies made her studies unpleasant, so she abandoned her studies and returned to teaching biology at the secondary level in Berlin.

In April 1933, following the rise of Hitler, Auerbach was dismissed from her post because of her Jewish ancestry. Her mother persuaded her not to take a position in a Jewish school (the only position in teaching she could then legally hold). Instead, on the recommendation of a half-English friend of her father, Herbert Freundlich, she went to study with F. A. E. Crew, head of the Institute of Genetics at the University of Edinburgh. Under him, in 1936, she earned a Ph.D. on genetic mutations and developmental abnormalities.

Auerbach began to do research on chemically caused mutations at the suggestion of H. J. Müller, who was then at the Institute of Genetics. She is most noted for her classic study on the chemical production of mutation in the fly (*Drosophila*), the first animal in which such mutation was demonstrated. Similarities between effects on mammals caused by mustard gas and X-rays suggested a similar process of mutagenesis in both, so she proceeded to expose drosophila to nitrogen and sulphur mustards. This study, made during World War II, was classified until 1946, and her preliminary reports could not name the chemical agent. Her work is cited in almost every genetics textbook. As a result of this work, she obtained a D.Sc. from the University of Edinburgh in 1947.

Auerbach's later research included a study of the relationship of gene mutations to changes in nucleotide sequences, following the new understanding of molecular biology. She also began to use other mutagenic agents such as formaldehyde, following the work of Rappoport, and did studies on mutagenesis in mice, on *Neurospora,* on the intestinal bacterium *Escherichia coli,* and on phage. Auerbach observed that her mutants were mosaics, made up of both mutant and non-mutant cells. Over the next twenty years she and her colleagues were able to show that chemical mutagens and ultraviolet light produced mosaics in a wide variety of organisms, while X-rays did not. Her research on these topics resulted in a series of books as well as articles. She was awarded a chair in genetics at the Institute of Genetics, University of Edinburgh, in 1967. Auerbach was made a Fellow of the Royal Society of Edinburgh and then a Fellow of the Royal Society in 1957. Among her many awards was the Darwin Prize in 1972 from the Royal Society of London.

In her personal life, Auerbach was a strong opponent of atomic bomb research and the widespread use of medical and industrial radiation. She opposed apartheid in South Africa, refusing to lecture there unless all racial groups were admitted.

Auerbach brought her mother to Edinburgh before the start of World War II. Although she never married, she unofficially adopted two boys, one the son of a German-speaking woman who served as a companion to her mother, and the other a poor Sicilian child, Angelo Alecci, whom she befriended through Save the Children. She learned Italian so she could meet him and encourage him in his studies. He later had an academic career as a professor in an agricultural college. Having been raised in a nonobservant family, Auerbach experienced her first seder in 1980 in Jerusalem and was apparently quite moved by the experience. In 1989, at the age of ninety, she gave up her home to her adopted son, Michael Alvern, and his family, and entered a retirement home run by the Church of Scotland, where she lived until her death, 15 January 1994.   JH/MBO

PRIMARY SOURCES

Auerbach, Charlotte. With J. M. Robson. "Chemical Production of Mutation." *Nature* 157 (1946): 302.

Auerbach, Charlotte. "Chemical Induction of Mutations *Hereditus* (Lund) *Supplementary Collection*." *Proceedings of the 8th International Congress of Genetics* (1948): 128–147.

———. *Genetics in the Atomic Age.* Edinburgh: Oliver and Boyd, 1956, 1962.

———. *Science of Genetics.* New York: Harper, 1961.

———. *Mutation Research: Problems, Results and Perspectives.* London: Chapman & Hill, 1976.

SECONDARY SOURCES

Beale, G. H. "Charlotte Auerbach." *Biographical Memoirs of the Fellows of the Royal Society* 41 (1995): 19–42. With photographs.

STANDARD SOURCES

Grinstein 1997; Roach, Linda, and Scott Roach, "Charlotte Auerbach (1899–1994)"; *Modern Scientists; Notable.*

AUKEN, KIRSTEN (LOMHOLT) (1913–1968)

Danish physician, sexologist. Born 25 June 1913 in Copenhagen to Marie Kirstine (Beck) and Svend Lomholt. Married Niels Gunnar Jensen Auken (20 March 1940). One son. Educated Rysensteens Gymnasium, Copenhagen; Univeristy of Copenhagen Medical School (M.D., 1941). Professional experience: Kristeligt studenter settlement, Saxogade. (1934–1941); Danish Red Cross (1940); University of Copenhagen Medical School, researcher (1953–1962); Montebello Hospital, Glostrop, Social Psychiatric Clinic, psychiatrist (1962–1966). Died 21 January 1968 in Fredericksberg.

Kirsten Auken, a noted Danish sexologist, came from a strongly religious home in Copenhagen which contributed to her lifelong social conscience. She was educated in a Copenhagen secondary school and then attended the university medical school. Interested in social work, she worked with the Kristelight student settlement before finishing her medical degree. She worked for some months with the Danish Red Cross during the Finnish-Russian war, around which time she married a fellow physician, Niels Gunnar Jensen Auken, with whom she had one son, Sven. Her son later would become an important political figure in Denmark.

Auken wrote her dissertation on early sexual behavior in young children, eventually helping to establish the field of sexology in Denmark. She worked as a researcher in that field at the University of Copenhagen Medical School. After the publication of a major study of the family with three other colleagues, Auken was appointed psychiatrist in a social psychiatric clinic, where she pursued her studies and clinical work. She died at the age of fifty-five in Fredericksberg, not far from Copenhagen.   JH/MBO

PRIMARY SOURCES
Auken, Kirsten. "Undersøgelser over Unge Kvinders Seksuelle Adfoerd." University of Copenhagen Medical School. Medical thesis, 1941.
———. With Vagn Christensen, Ingrid Jørgensen, and Otto Krabbe. *Familien Lever: En Familienundersogelse.* Copenhagen: G.E.C. Gad, 1962.

SECONDARY SOURCES
Cedergreen Bech, Svend, ed. "Kirsten Auken." *Biografisk Dansk Lexicon.* vol. 1. Copenhagen: Glydendal, 1979.

AUSTIN, MARY LELLAH (1896–?)

U.S. protozoologist and geneticist. Born 12 April 1896 in Austinburg, Ohio, to Harriet (Phillips) and Henry Lewis. Educated Wellesley College (A.B., 1920; M.A., 1922); Columbia University (Ph.D., 1928). Professional experience: Wellesley College, assistant custodian in zoology (1920–1922), instructor (1928–1931), assistant professor (1931–1940), associate professor (1940–1952), professor (1952–1961); Barnard College, instructor (1925–1926), lecturer (1926–1928); Indiana University, Bloomington, research scholar in zoology (from 1961); Isabella Thoburn College, Luchnow, India, exchange lecturer in zoology (1932–1933, 1935–1936). Honors and memberships: American Association for the Advancement of Science, Fellow; Phi Beta Kappa; Sigma Xi; American Society for Human Genetics; Genetics Society of America; Society of Protozoologists.

Mary Lellah Austin was born in the Midwest. She attended Wellesley College, where she received her A.B. and then her M.A. in biology. During the period between her undergraduate and first graduate degree, she served as the assistant custodian in zoology at Wellesley. She then went to Columbia University to study for a Ph.D. in protozoology, while lecturing in zoology at Barnard College. She returned to Wellesley after receiving her degree and was appointed first

as an instructor and then as an assistant professor. During this period, Austin had two opportunities to go to Isabella Thoburn College as an exchange lecturer in zoology. Working in an entirely different ecological system must have provided her with important material for her research in protozoology and human serotypes, quite apart from the stimulation she must have gotten from simply living in another culture. She returned to Wellesley and was appointed associate professor, then full professor in zoology (1951).

As Austin approached her mid-sixties, both her desire to do more intensive research and her wish to return to the Midwest increased. In 1961, she took early retirement from Wellesley, leaving the East Coast for a position as a research scholar at the University of Indiana at Bloomington. Here she continued to work in protozoology, examining the antibiotic response of *Paramecium aurelia,* as well as maintaining her research interests in physiology and genetics.   JH/MBO

STANDARD SOURCES
AMS 5–8, B 9, P&B 10–14; Debus; *WWW*(A), 1929–1940.

AUSTIN, REBECCA (fl. 1875)

U.S. botanist. Born in Plumas County, Calif. At least one daughter, Mrs. C. C. Bruce.

Rebecca Austin collected plants in California, particularly the California pitcher plant, *Darlington.* She sent specimens to William M. Canby of Willmington, Delaware. Canby supplied her with a pocket lens and botanical papers including Darwin's book on insectivorous plants. She corresponded with him from 1875 to 1877 and then moved to Modack where she continued collecting with her daughter, Mrs. C. C. Bruce. She had a plant named after her, *Scutelaria austini.* Early in her career she had been visited by another itinerant collector, John Gill Lemmon, who recommended her to Canby. Asa Gray acknowledged her observations of the pitcher plant, *Darlingtonia californica,* in his book *Darwiniana.* C. Keck and Joseph Dalton Hooker also were aware of her discoveries.   JH/MBO

PRIMARY SOURCES
Letters of Rebecca Austin to William M. Canby. Library of the Academy of Natural Sciences, Philadelphia.

SECONDARY SOURCES
Ewan, Joseph. *A Century of Progress in the Natural Sciences 1853–1953.* San Francisco, Calif.: California Academy of Sciences, 1955.
Rudolph, Emmanuel D. "Women in Nineteenth Century American Botany; a Generally Unrecognized Constituency." *American Journal of Botany* 69 (September 1982): 1346–1355.

AXIOTHEA OF PHLIUS (fl. ca. 350 B.C.E.)

Greek philosopher. Born at Phlius. Educated with Plato and Speusippus.

According to Diogenes Laertius, Axiothea was one of two female disciples of Plato; she dressed as a man in her role as his student, according to Dicaearchus. Themistius announced that after Axiothea read the *Republic* she traveled from Arcadia to Athens and became his follower. After Plato's death she attended the lectures of his nephew and successor, Speusippus. It was her presence as a female in the company of male scholars, rather than her intellectual accomplishments, that impressed the sources. It is significant that a woman, whether actually or apocryphally, was a part of the entourage of Plato, one of the most significant contributors to the form of modern science.   JH/MBO

SECONDARY SOURCES

Diogenes Laertius. *Lives of Eminent Philosophers.* Trans. by R. D. Hicks. 2 vols. Cambridge, MA: Harvard University Press, 1980, 3:46.

Themistius. *Orationes,* 1:23.295c.

STANDARD SOURCES

Pauly-Wissowa; Waithe.

AYRTON, HERTHA (MARKS) (1854–1923)

British physicist. Born Phoebe Sarah Marks 28 April 1854 in Portsea, England, to Alice Theresa and Levi Marks, a clockmaker and jeweler. Seven siblings. Married W. E. Ayrton, F.R.S. One child, Barbara Bodichon. Educated at boarding school, London; Girton College, Cambridge (1876–1880); Finsbury Technical College (1884–1885). Died 27 August 1923.

Hertha Ayrton was born Phoebe Sarah Marks, the third child of Alice (Moss) and Levi Marks. Her father was a Jewish refugee from Poland who constantly struggled for solvency in his clock-making and jewelry trade in Portsea, near Portsmouth, England. After his death in 1861, his widow attempted to support the family with her needlework. Sarah was able to attend school only because she had an aunt, Marion Hartog, who ran a school in London. Independent and stubborn, Sarah shocked many of her teachers with her "crudities." She received a broad education in mathematics, music, and ancient and modern languages from her aunt's talented family, and learned some social skills from her five cousins.

After discussions with her cousin Marcus Hartog, a freethinking graduate student at Cambridge, she renounced Judaism but continued to express pride in her Jewishness for the rest of her life. As a gesture of independence she adopted a new name, Hertha, suggested by her friend Ottilie Blind and inspired by Swinburne's poem *Hertha.* Blind thought that Sarah physically resembled the Teutonic goddess Erda.

After teaching in London to support her mother and later her invalid sister, Marks passed the Cambridge University Examination for Women (later merged into the Higher Local Examination) in 1874, with honors in English and mathematics. Through friends she heard of the progress of the new women's college that had opened at Hitchin in 1869 and had been incorporated in 1872 as Girton College. In 1876 she took the Girton scholarship examinations but did not win either of the two openings. Examinations were her lifelong nemesis. Her friends scraped together enough money to allow her to enter Girton as a student in October 1876. Barbara Bodichon, a wealthy philanthropist interested in women's causes, became her benefactress. A short time after Marks entered Girton, she became ill and was forced to rest. Again the loyalty of friends made her return possible.

Until the Cambridge University baccalaureate honors (Tripos) examinations were opened to women in 1881, students at Girton College had to sit for them unofficially in a room in their own college. The papers were then sent out in a sealed packet to be read. Although the mistress received the names of the successful women, the names were not printed with the list of successful male candidates. Marks took her Tripos examination in 1880, again with disappointing results. To Barbara Bodichon she wrote, "I am only fifteenth in the Third Class. I am sorry. I am afraid you will be very disappointed." After leaving Girton, Marks taught mathematics, had an active social life, and set up classes to prepare ladies for the London University Matriculation Examination and for part of the Cambridge Local Examinations.

As a student she invented and patented an instrument for dividing a line into any number of equal parts (1884). She also constructed a sphygmometer for recording the pulse in arteries. During her student days, Marks was leader of the College Choral Society and the founder of the Girton Fire Brigade. She decided to pursue a career of research and invention, again financed by Bodichon. She became a student at Finsbury Technical College, where W. E. Ayrton, Fellow of the Royal Society, was professor of physics. W. E. Ayrton's wife, MATILDA CHAPLIN AYRTON, had died in 1883, leaving him with a daughter, Edith. Hertha and Will Ayrton were married in 1885, and for a period after their marriage Hertha continued her scientific work. Although she gave a series of six elementary lectures on electricity in 1888, most of her early married life was occupied with domestic considerations. She and W. E. Ayrton lavished attention on their daughter, Barbara (Barbie) Bodichon Ayrton.

Hertha Ayrton began to experiment again in 1893. She presented two papers to the British Association, published papers in the *Electrician,* and made plans to publish a book. She read a paper, "The Hissing of the Electric Arc," to the

Institution of Electrical Engineers (1899), presided over the physical science section of the International Congress of Women in London (1899), and spoke at the International Electrical Congress in Paris (1900). The Royal Society, which would not allow a woman to read a paper, compromised by having John Perry, an associate of W. E. Ayrton's and a Fellow of the society, read Ayrton's "The Mechanism of the Electric Arc" in 1901.

During a stay at Margate in the autumn of 1901, Ayrton began work on a new project, investigating the causes of ripple marks in sand, and put most of the finishing touches on her book, *The Electric Arc,* which was published in 1902 and quickly became the accepted textbook on the subject. During the summer of 1903, Ayrton met MARIE CURIE, and the two women became good friends.

When in 1904 Ayrton read a paper, "The Origin and Growth of Ripple Marks," before the Royal Society, she was the first woman ever to have done so. John Perry proposed her as a candidate for the Royal Society in 1902. She had considerable support from other Fellows but was opposed by Henry Armstrong, who also led the opposition to the admission of women to the Chemical Society. Ayrton was finally declared ineligible for the fellowship because she was a married woman. Although she could not become a Fellow of the society, she was eligible for its medals, and in 1906 she received the Hughes Medal for original research for her investigations on the electric arc and sand ripples.

As she grew older, Aryton became increasingly interested in the suffrage cause. She had always found the idea of sex discrimination galling. Toward the end of her life she remarked to a journalist, "Personally I do not agree with sex being brought into science at all. The idea of 'women and science' is entirely irrelevant. Either a woman is a good scientist, or she is not; in any case she should be given opportunities, and her work should be studied from the scientific, not the sex, point of view." After her husband's death in 1908, Ayrton continued her work as scientist and suffragist, growing ever more militant in her views.

Ayrton applied her inventiveness during World War I to devising a fan that would make it possible "for our men to drive off poisonous gases and bring in fresh air from behind by simply giving impulses to the air with hand fans." After the war she continued to experiment; most of her work involved various applications of the fan principles. She remained active in both scientific and political causes until her death in 1923.

Hertha Ayrton's scientific career began with invention—her line divider. From an idea supplied by her cousin, Ansel Leo, she worked for a year on the design of her line divider, obtaining a patent in 1884. This device was favorably reviewed in *Nature,* the *Academy* and the *Revue Scientifique.* Architects, artists, and engineers found the instrument useful, and it was manufactured by W. F. Stanley of Great Turnstile, Holborn, in London. Her lifelong interest in the electric arc began when her husband left to read a paper in Chicago, suggesting that she continue the experiments in which he was engaged at the college. Soon she wanted to "solve the whole mystery of the arc from beginning to end." In 1895 she accepted an offer to write a series of articles on the arc for the *Electrician.* These twelve papers formed the basis of her book.

In addition to the electric arc and the formation of sand ripples (the latter occupying her from 1901 to 1905), Ayrton was involved in several other areas of research. After his 1905 illness, her husband increasingly relied on her to complete his scientific commissions. One project, assigned by the admiralty, involved supplying specifications for carbon that would burn successfully in searchlight projectors. Hertha Ayrton inherited the project and wrote four reports (1904–1908), which were officially credited to her husband; he insisted, however, that his wife's name be included as the co-author of the fourth report. The invention of her fan represented the last major area of scientific involvement for Hertha Ayrton.   MBO

PRIMARY SOURCES

Ayrton, Hertha. "The Drop of Potential at the Carbons of the Electric Arc." *Report of the Bristol Association for the Advancement of Science* 68 (1899): 805–807.

———. "The Mechanism of the Electric Arc." *Philosophical Transactions of the Royal Society of London,* ser. A, 19 (1901–1902): 299–336.

———. "The Electric Arc." In *The Electrician.* London: Printing and Publishing Company, Ltd., 1902.

———. "Local Differences of Pressure Near an Obstacle in Oscillating Water." *Proceedings of the Royal Society of London,* ser. A, 91 (1915): 405–510.

———. "On a New Method of Driving Off Poisonous Gases." *Proceedings of the Royal Society of London,* ser. A, 96 (1919): 249–256.

SECONDARY SOURCES

Mason, Joan. "Hertha Ayrton (1854–1923) and the Admission of Women to the Royal Society of London." *Notes and Records of the Royal Society of London* 45 (1991): 201–220.

Ogilvie, Marilyn. "Marital Collaboration: An Approach to Science." In *Uneasy Careers and Intimate Lives.*

Sharp, Evelyn. *Hertha Ayrton, 1854–1923: A Memoir.* London: Edward Arnold, 1926. The traditional biography of Ayrton.

Trotter, A. P. "Mrs. Ayrton's Work on the Electric Arc." *Nature* 13 (12 January 1924): 48–49.

STANDARD SOURCES

DNB Missing Persons; DSB; Grinstein 1993; *Notable;* Ogilvie 1986.

AYRTON, MATILDA (CHAPLIN) (1846–1883)

British physician. Born 1846 at Honfleur. Married William Edward Ayrton (1872). One child, Edith. Educated first in art; London Medical College for Women (1867–1869); University of Edinburgh (high honors in anatomy and surgery at extramural examinations 1870–1871, Surgeons' Hall, Edinburgh); University of Paris (Bachelier ès-Sciences and Bachelier ès-Lettres; M.D., 1879); London Obstetric Society (certificate in midwifery, 1873); King and Queen's College of Physicians in Ireland (ca. 1880); Royal Free Hospital, London (1880); Hospital of Algiers and Montpelier, physiological laboratory, continued studies. Died 19 July 1883 in London.

Matilda Ayrton spent her short life pioneering the cause of women in medicine. She was the first wife of the scientist W. E. Ayrton and the mother of Edith, who married Israel Zangwill. Although she did not practice privately, she continually studied medicine. Her search for a medical education was fraught with obstacles from the very beginning. After two years at the London Medical College for Women and having passed the preliminary examination at Apothecaries' Hall in 1869, she attempted to enroll in the later examination but was refused because she was a woman. She then went to Edinburgh and matriculated there, but was again refused instruction in the highest branches of medicine. Although the situation was protested the legal decision issued in 1872 went against the women students.

Ayrton, nevertheless, earned high honors in anatomy and surgery at the extramural examinations at Surgeons' Hall. In spite of her excellent academic record, most medical classes in England and Scotland remained unavailable to her as a woman. She went to Paris to continue her education but did not sever her connection with Edinburgh and attended those classes that were available to her there.

In the same year that she married W. E. Ayrton, an Edinburgh student who was to become a well-known physicist, she obtained a certificate in midwifery from the London Obstetric Society, the only medical qualification then open to women in England. W. E. Ayrton was appointed to a professorship in the Imperial College of Engineering in Japan, and Matilda followed him. In Japan she did some anthropological research and opened a school for native midwives.

Undaunted by the symptoms of tuberculosis that she began to exhibit in 1877, Ayrton returned to Europe and was awarded the M.D. that she had so richly deserved. The situation in the British Isles had definitely improved for women in medicine by the latter part of the century. She became a licentiate of the King and Queen's College of Physicians in Ireland. The only female candidate, she came out first in the examination. Ayrton continued to study, working with diseases of the eye at the Royal Free Hospital in London. Her health was failing and she spent the winters of 1881 and 1882 in warmer climates. However, she continued to improve her knowledge during these two winters, spending the first one at the hospital of Algiers and the second in the physiological laboratory at Montpelier. At the age of thirty-seven, Ayrton, an activist in improving the educational opportunities for women, died in London.   JH/MBO

PRIMARY SOURCES

Ayrton, Matilda Chaplin. "Plants Used in New Year Celebrations by the Japanese." *Transactions Botanical Society Edinburgh* 13 (1870), xiv–xvi.

———. "Recherches sur les dimensions généales et sur le développement du corps chez les Japonais." M.D., University of Paris, 1879.

———. *Child Life in Japan.* London, 1879.

SECONDARY SOURCES

Orme, Eliza. Memorial Notice. *Englishwoman's Review,* 15 August 1883.

Rémy, Charles. *Le XIXe Siècle,* 23 August 1883.

STANDARD SOURCES

Desmond; *DNB.*

B

BABCOCK, HARRIET (1877–1952)

U.S. psychologist. Born 1877 in Westerly, Rhode Island. Married H. Hobert Babcock, psychologist at Manhattan State Hospital (1923–1925). Educated Columbia University (A.B.; M.A; Ph.D., 1930). Professional experience: Manhattan State Hospital, psychologist (1923–1925); Bellevue Hospital, chief psychologist (1926–1928); New York University, department of psychology, research in personality training (1931–1952). Honors and memberships: American Psychological Association; New York Association of Consulting Psychologists; International Council of Women Psychologists; New York Academy of Science; Eastern Psychological Association. Diplomate of the American Board of Examiners in Professional Psychology (Clinical). Died 12 December 1952.

Although little has been published concerning her personal life, psychologist Harriet Babcock apparently married and spent many years in a traditional family role before earning her three degrees from Columbia University. Her first positions before she received her doctorate were in mental hospitals. She researched and published on mental deficiency and dementia praecox and joined the search for a definitive means of measuring both intelligence and abnormal mental functioning.

In 1931, after finishing her doctorate, she began working at the Department of Psychology, New York University, where she remained for the rest of her career. She served as a special consultant to the New York City Guidance Bureau. Working with EMILY BURR at the Guidance Center for Girls, she developed the Babcock Test of Mental Efficiency. Besides measurement and analysis of mental efficiency, she was interested in the time and mind theory and level-efficiency theory of intelligence.

A late starter, Babcock showed a passion for her field and a remarkable capacity for achievement. She originated a method of measuring and evaluating the efficiency of mental functioning in normal and abnormal mental conditions by controlling abstract verbal development. She determined the position of psychogenic psychoses. These disorders were between the normal and definitely abnormal. In other research, she stated a level-efficiency theory of intelligence and showed the relation of personality to basic mental functioning.

KM

PRIMARY SOURCES

Babcock, Harriet. "An Experiment in the Measurement of Mental Deterioration." Thesis, Columbia University, 1930. (Archives of Psychology, no. 117)

———. *Dementia Praecox: a Psychological Study.* [film] New York, 1933.

———. *The Babcock Test of Mental Efficiency: a Measure of the Efficiency Variable both in Mental Functioning and Mental Deterioration.* Beverly Hills, Calif.: Western Psychological Services, 1940. Manual revised; test kit reissued 1964, Western Psychological Services, Beverly Hills, Calif.

———. *Time and the Mind: Personal Tempo—The Key to Normal and Pathological Mental Conditions.* Cambridge, Mass.: Sci-Art, 1941.

———. *The MacQuarrie Test as a Clinical Instrument; Validity of Vocabulary—MacQuarrie Deviations as a Measure of Abnormal Mental Functioning When Scored in Psychological Units.* Lancaster, Pa.: Science Press, 1950.

———. *Measuring the Efficiency Variable.* Chicago: C. H. Stoelting, [ca. 1950].

STANDARD SOURCES

AMS 5–8; APA Directory; Debus; O'Connell and Russo 1988; *Psychological Register* vol. 3, 1932.

BABER, ZONIA (1862–ca. 1920)

U.S. geographer. Born 1862. Educated University of Chicago (B.S., 1904). Professional experience: Private school, principal (1886–1888); Cook County Normal School, teacher (1888–1890), Department of Geography, head (1890–1899); University of Chicago,

Department of Education, associate professor and head of geography and geology department (1901–1921); elementary school, principal (1901–1921); emerita associate professor. Honors and memberships: instrumental in the founding of the Chicago Geographic Society, served as president of this organization.

One of the few women to be listed as a geographer in the first few editions of *American Men of Science,* Zonia Baber was first educated as a teacher and then attended the University of Chicago, where she received her bachelor of science degree in 1904. In the late 1880s, she worked as a principal in a private school and then as a teacher and head of the geography department in the Cook County Normal School before she was appointed as an associate professor and head of geology and geography in the University of Chicago Department of Education. Concurrently, she was a principal of the laboratory elementary school associated with the university.   JH/MBO

STANDARD SOURCES
AMS 1–4; Bailey; Siegel and Finley.

BACHMAN, MARIA MARTIN (1796–1863)

U.S. natural history painter. Born 1796 in Charleston, S.C., to Rebecca (Murray) and John Jacob Martin. Married John Bachman (1848). Educated privately. Professional experience: contributed background insects and plants to J. J. Audubon's books. Died 1863 in Columbia, S.C.

Maria Martin developed an interest in natural history from her brother-in-law John Bachman, pastor of St. John's Lutheran Church, Charleston, who became a noted naturalist. He (and later she) were close friends of John James Audubon from 1831 until Audubon's death in 1851. Audubon's sons later married two of John Bachman's daughters, making the link still closer. Martin was trained by Audubon and soon began to assist him in drawing the backgrounds for his illustrations, including associated insects, flowers, and plants for Audubon's *Birds of America.* Martin married John Bachman two years after her sister's death, in 1848, and assisted him with color and other details for his joint publication with Audubon, *Viviparous Quadrupeds of North America,* published in three volumes (1846–1854). She also contributed a number of drawings of Carolina reptiles to John Edward Holbrook who used them with acknowledgment in *North American Herpetology.* Audubon named a subspecies of hairy woodpecker after her: "Maria's woodpecker," *Picus martinae.*

She fled from Charleston to Columbia with her family to escape shelling during the Civil War, and died soon afterward in that city.   JH/MBO

PRIMARY SOURCES
John Bachman papers, Charleston Museum, Charleston, S.C. In the 1960s, Maria Martin Bachman's papers, original sketches, and watercolors were still in the hands of her family in Charleston, S.C.
Corning, Howard, ed. *Letters of John James Audubon (1826–1840).* Includes letters to and from Bachman.

SECONDARY SOURCES
Arnold, Lois B. *Four Lives in Science.* Boston: The Club of Odd Volumes, 1929.
Coffin, Annie Roulhac. *Art Quarterly* (January 1965).
———. *New York Historical Society Quarterly* (January 1965).
Herrick, Francis H. *Audubon the Naturalist.* 2 vols. New York: Appleton, 1917.

STANDARD SOURCES
Bailey; Kass-Simon and Farnes; *NAW* (listed under Martin); Siegel and Finley.

BACON, CLARA (LATIMER) (1866–1948)

U.S. mathematician. Born 13 August 1866 in Hillsgrove, Ill. Educated Wellesley College (A.B., 1890); University of Chicago (A.M., 1904); Johns Hopkins University (Ph.D., 1911). Professional experience: Secondary schools, teacher (1890–1897); Goucher College, instructor in mathematics (1897–1905), associate professor (1905–1914), professor (1914–1934), emerita professor (1934–1948). Honors and memberships: Mathematics Society, Mathematics Association, member. Died 1948.

After Clara Bacon earned her A.M. from the University of Chicago she was promoted from assistant to associate professor. She became professor at Goucher after she obtained her Ph.D. from Johns Hopkins University and remained at that rank until she retired. Her field of study in mathematics was geometry.   JH/MBO

SECONDARY SOURCES
New York Times, 16 April 1948. Obituary notice.
School and Society 67 (1948): 313. Obituary notice.

STANDARD SOURCES
AMS 3–7, Necrology 8; Grinstein and Campbell; *WWW(A),* vol. 2, 1943–1950.

BAETJER, ANNA MEDORA (1899–?)

U.S. physiologist, toxicologist. Born 1899. Educated Wellesley College (A.B., 1920); Johns Hopkins (Sc.D., 1924). Professional experience: Johns Hopkins University, School of Hygiene and Public Health, assistant (1923–1924), instructor (1924–1927), research

associate (1927–1945), assistant professor (1945–1950), consultant, U.S. Surgeon General's Office (1947); position at School of Environmental Medicine (1950–1952), associate professor (1952–1961); professor (1962–1970); emerita professor (1972– ca. 1995). Honors and memberships: president of the American Industrial Hygiene Association (1954); Kehoe Award of the American Academy of Occupational Medicine (1974); Stokinger Award of the American Conference of Government Industrial Hygienists (1980); several honorary degrees, including one from Johns Hopkins (1979). Died 21 February 1984.

Anna Medora Baetjer spent her entire professional career at Johns Hopkins University. Active in early work on radiology and radiation in the environment, Baetjer served as a consultant to the U.S. Surgeon General's Office beginning in 1947, where she emphasized the role of preventive medicine and investigated the health of women in the environment. She contributed important chapters to books on these topics as well as numerous articles. She sat on FDA committees where she studied residues of pesticides in the environment (1966–1970). An extensive archive collection on her work is held at Johns Hopkins University.   JH/MBO

PRIMARY SOURCES

Baetjer, Anna Medora. *Women in Industry: Their Health and Efficiency.* Philadelphia: W. B. Saunders, 1946.

———. *Results of Influenza Vaccination in Industry during the 1947 Epidemic.* Preventative Medicine and Public Health. Pittsburgh: Industrial Hygiene Foundation, 1948.

SECONDARY SOURCES

Corn, J. K. "An Impression of Anna M. Baetjer." *American Industrial Hygiene Association Journal* 53 (September 1992): A441–444.

STANDARD SOURCES

AMS 4–8, B 9, P&B 10–16; Bailey; Debus; Rossiter 1982; *WWW*(A), vol. 10, 1989–1993.

BAGLEY, FLORENCE (WINGER) (1874–1952)

U.S. psychologist. Born 7 January 1874 in Clay Lick, Pa. Educated University of Nebraska (A.B., 1895; A.M., 1898); Cornell University (1898–1901). Married William C. Bagley (1901). Professional experience: University of Nebraska, unofficially employed as assistant psychologist; Cornell University, unofficially employed. Member Western Philosophical Association. Died 1952.

Florence Winger attended the University of Nebraska and Cornell University. In 1901 she married William C. Bagley, an educational psychologist, who became the director of education at the University of Illinois. Her professional posi-

tions were all unofficial. Her research was in the area of color aesthetics and on Fechner's color rings.   JH/MBO

STANDARD SOURCES

AMS 1–2; Bailey.

BAGSHAW, ELIZABETH CATHERINE (1881–ca. 1976)

Canadian physician. Born 1881 in Mariposa Township, Victoria County, Canada. Three sisters. Never married. Two adopted children. Educated local public schools; Lindsay Collegiate High School; Toronto University, Women's Medical College (M.D., 1905). Professional experience: Hamilton, Victoria, Canada, private practice in general medicine, (1906–1976); Planned Parenthood Association, Hamilton, director, staff physician. Honors and memberships: Order of Canada Medal (1973); honorary LL.D. from McMaster University (1974); Citizen of the Year for Hamilton (1970); life membership of the College of Family Physicians of Canada; charter and honorary life member of the Canadian Federation of Medical Women; honorary member of the Hamilton Academy of Medicine; and senior member of the Canadian Medical Association.

Elizabeth Catherine Bagshaw grew up on a farm with her three older sisters. After attending local schools, she went to Lindsay Collegiate High School. She decided to follow her interests and study medicine. Her father encouraged her interest, but did not live to see her receive her degree. Along with seven others, she obtained her M.D. from Toronto University Women's Medical College. After graduation, Bagshaw went into general practice—a common career path for female medical graduates, since specialty internships were rarely awarded to them.

Bagshaw took over the practice of Mabel Henderson, an early woman graduate of Queen's University Medical School, and remained in Hamilton, Victoria, Canada, for the rest of her career. She had a successful practice and was on the staff of the Hamilton Civic (General) Hospital Skin Clinic. She directed the first birth-control clinic in Canada, the Planned Parenthood Association. She attended over three thousand maternity cases, delivering many babies in the home.

At the age of forty-two, Bagshaw adopted two children, a boy and a girl (the boy was son of a distant cousin) and began a family life of her own. Her son became a physician and practiced with her for many years. In 1976, Bagshaw retired from medicine at the age of ninety-five, but continued to be active in civic and professional organizations.   JH/MBO

PRIMARY SOURCES

Bagshaw, Elizabeth Catherine. In Hellstedt, *Autobiographies.*

BAHR-BERGIUS, EVA VILHELMINA JULIA VON (1874–1962)

Swedish physicist. Born 16 September 1874 in Mälby at Östanå, Stockholm province, Sweden, to Maria Elisabet (Boström) and Karl Fredrik Oskar von Bahr, an accountant secretary. Educated Åhlinska School, Uppsala/School for Domestic Technology, and in Stockholm; University of Uppsala (B.A., 1903; licentiate, 1907; Ph.D., 1909); Freiburg and Berlin (1911, 1913, 1914). Married Georg Niklaus Josef Bergius (19 June 1917). Professional experience: Uppsala School for Domestic Technology, teacher (1896–1898); docent (1909–1915); Technical Institute 1910, University of Uppsala, amanuensis; Brunnsviks Volkshochschule, teacher (1914–1927). Died 28 February 1962.

Von Bahr completed a dissertation on the effect of pressure on absorption of infrared radiation by gases under the physicist Knut Ångström. She then worked in Berlin under Heinrich Rubens, well known for his work with infrared radiation. Von Bahr was a Privatdozent (assistant professor, usually unpaid) at Uppsala until 1915, leaving soon after she took a position at the Brunnsviks College in Sörvik, Sweden. There she taught physics, chemistry, and mathematics. On 19 June 1917 she married Georg Niklaus Josef Bergius, a bookseller and fellow teacher at the college. The couple remained at their teaching positions until 1927, then retired to the small town of Kungälv. A former Jesuit seminarian, Bergius had converted to Catholicism in his youth. Von Bahr-Bergius took that step in 1930, a process that led her to publish two books about Catholicism and her experience.

Von Bahr-Bergius became a close friend of the physicist LISE MEITNER, who worked in Berlin. After escaping from Nazi Germany in 1938, Meitner stayed temporarily with von Bahr-Bergius and her husband. Meitner and her nephew Otto Frisch (who visited during Christmas 1938) developed the theoretical explanation of nuclear fission in Küngalv.

Von Bahr-Bergius's first publications concerned the effects of pressure and temperature on infrared absorption in gases, as well as the effect of ultraviolet light on ozone. She found that increasing the temperature caused the absorption bands in gases to become smoother and wider, perhaps continuous. With Johann Koenigsberger of the University of Freiburg, she made a classical analysis of the relation of color to vibrational energy. She continued to investigate infrared absorption, and searched with James Franck for a minimum ionization potential for positive ions, analogous to that found by Franck and Hertz for electrons. Von Bahr-Bergius was one of the pioneering physicists who applied quantum theory to ionization and to molecular theory. The combination of the world war and her move to Brunnsviks reduced her research opportunities, and she did not publish much afterward.   JH/MBO

PRIMARY SOURCES

Bahr–Bergius, Eva von. "Über die Einwirkung des Druckes auf die Absorption ultraroter Strahlung durch Gase." Ph.D. diss., Uppsala University, 1908.

———. "Über die Zersetzung des Ozons durch ultraviolettes Licht." *Annalen der Physik* 33 (1910): 598–606.

———. With J. Koenigsberger. "Über die Farbe anorganische Salze und die Berechnung der schwingenden Teile." *Sitzungsberichte der Heidelberger Akademie der Wissenschaften* 1911, 2A: 1–26.

———. "Über den Einfluss der Temperatur auf die ultrarote Absorption der Gase." *Annalen der Physik* 38 (1912): 206–222.

———. "On the Quantum-Theory and the Rotation-Energy of Molecules." *Philosophical Magazine* 28 (1914): 71–73.

———. With James Franck. "Über Ionization durch positive Ionen." *Verhandlungen der Deutschen Physikalischen Gesellschaft* 16 (1914): 57–68.

Correspondence with Lise Meitner, Meitner Collection, Churchill College Archives Centre, Cambridge, England.

SECONDARY SOURCES

Ångström, Anders. In *Svenskt biografiskt lexikon.* Vol. 3: 575–577. Stockholm: A. Bonnier, 1922.

Johansson, Sigurd. *Atomålderns vagga stod i. Kungälv.* Unpublished manuscript, no date.

Konen, Heinrich. *Das Leuchten der Gase und Dämpfe.* Braunschweig: Friedrich Vieweg & Sohn, 1913.

Krafft, Fritz. *Im Schatten der Sensation. Leben und Wirken von Fritz Strassmann.* Weinheim, Deerfield Beach, Florida, and Basel: *Verlag Chemie,* 1981, pp. 250, 257.

Lindgvist, Svante, ed. *Center on the Periphery: Historical Aspects of 20th-Century Swedish Physics.* Canton, Mass.: Science History Publications, 1993.

Rhodes, Richard. *The Making of the Atomic Bomb.* New York: Simon & Schuster, 1986.

Sime, Ruth. *Lise Meitner. A Life in Physics.* Berkeley, Los Angeles, and London: University of California Press, 1996.

Steenberg, Börje. In *Svenska män och kvinnor.* Stockholm: A. Bonnier, 1942, vol. 1, p. 249.

Warner, Yvonne Maria. *Världsvid men främmande.* Uppsala: Katolska Bokförlaget, 1996.

STANDARD SOURCES

Poggendorff, vols. 5, 6.

BAILEY, ETHEL ZOE (1890–1983)

U.S. horticulturist and compiler. Born 1890 in Ithaca, N.Y., to Annette (Smith) and Liberty Hyde Bailey. Professional experience: Liberty Hyde Bailey, assistant and associate; Gentes Hortorium, editor (1920–1928); Liberty Hyde Bailey Hortorium, Cornell University, curator (1935–57). Died 1983.

Born and raised in Ithaca, New York, Ethel Zoe Bailey's work was closely associated with that of her father. From 1888 to 1935, her father, Liberty Hyde Bailey, was professor of experimental botany at the College of Agriculture at Cornell, which he helped to develop. She assisted her father with his work, accompanying him on numerous collecting expeditions and working as coworker and sometimes as coauthor, most notably with publications in the journal *Hortus* (which carry her name as coauthor) but also in the production of his *Standard Cyclopedia of Horticulture* (1914–1917) and the *Manual of Cultivated Plants.* She was editor of the first eight volumes of his journal *Gentes Hortorium,* founded in 1920. She became curator of the Liberty Hyde Bailey Hortorium of Cornell College of Agriculture, founded and given to the state by her father in 1935. (It was designated a department of the university at its inception.) She remained in that position from 1935 until her retirement in 1957, but she continued to work informally with the herbarium and library at the hortorium until her death in 1983. She developed and updated an index of over 200,000 references to cultivated plants that served as the basis for subsequent editions of *Hortus.* Her contributions are recognized in the introduction to *Hortus Third* (1976) and more extensively in the biographical article on her father in Harlan P. Banks's *Biographical Memoirs of the Academy of Sciences.* JH

PRIMARY SOURCES

Bailey, Ethel Zoe. With Liberty Hyde Bailey. *Hortus.* New York: Macmillan, 1930.

SECONDARY SOURCES

Banks, Harlan P. "Liberty Hyde Bailey." *Biographical Memoirs of the Academy of Sciences.* 1994, 64: 3–32.

Lawrence, George H. M. *Nature* 175 (1955): 451.

Rodgers, Andrew Denny. *Liberty Hyde Bailey: A Story of American Plant Sciences.* Princeton: Princeton University Press, 1949.

STANDARD SOURCES

AMS 6–8; B 9; P&B 10; DSB (under Liberty Hyde Bailey).

BAILEY, FLORENCE AUGUSTA (MERRIAM) (1863–1948)

U.S. naturalist and ornithologist. Born 8 August 1863 in Locust Grove, N.Y. to Caroline (Hart) and Clinton Merriam. Three siblings, including naturalist brother, C. Hart. Married Vernon Bailey. Educated at home; Miss Piatt's School, Ithaca, N.Y.; Smith College (bachelor's 1882–1886). Professional experience: studied birds; wrote books and popular articles; collaborated with Vernon Bailey; conservation activities. Honors and memberships: honorary LL.D. degree from the University of New Mexico (1921); American Ornithologists' Union (AOU) awarded Brewster Medal for Birds of New Mexico *(1931); became first regular member of the AOU (1901); first woman Fellow of the AOU (1929). Died 22 September 1948 of myocardial degeneration in Washington, D.C.*

Florence Merriam Bailey, the youngest of four children of a banker, grew up on the family country estate of Homewood in Locust Grove, New York, just west of the Adirondack Mountains. Her mother, Caroline Hart, was interested in astronomy, and encouraged Florence to observe the constellations. Florence had two older brothers, Charles Collins and Clinton Hart, but her sister, Gertrude, died at age five, one year before Florence's birth. Her father had retired to Locust Grove shortly after the birth of Florence. From an early age, encouraged by her father and her brother Clinton Hart, Merriam showed an interest in natural history. After attending a private preparatory school in Utica, New York, she went to Smith College as a special student (1882–1886). Because of this status she did not receive a bachelor's degree at the end of four years; in 1921, however, Smith awarded her one. Her favorite teacher was a Miss Jordan, a cousin to the biologist David Starr Jordan. While at Smith, Merriam became interested in ornithology, established a chapter of the Audubon Society, and began to publish articles in the *Audubon Magazine,* as well as popular books on birds.

Her *Audubon Magazine* articles were collected as the centerpiece of her first book, *Birds through an Opera Glass.* The book's purpose was to provide hints to laypersons on bird identification. She provided autobiographical recollections and included quotations from Mary Treat, Thomas Nuttal, Henry David Thoreau, and John Burroughs.

Merriam's other sphere of activity was social reform. In 1891 she spent a month in a summer school for Chicago working girls, and during the following winter she was an employee of one of Grace Dodge's working girls' clubs in New York City.

After contracting tuberculosis, Merriam went to Utah with her friend Olive Thorne Miller. From Utah she went alone to Palo Alto, California, where she attended Stanford University for six months. She left Stanford for San Diego County, California, where she lived on her uncle's ranch and observed birds. She spent three years in the Southwest (1893–1896), during which time she wrote several popular books on natural history. She then settled in Washington, D.C., at the home of her brother, who was then chief of the U.S. Biological Survey. Through him she met Vernon Bailey (1864–1942), a naturalist with the survey; after their marriage in 1899 she accompanied her husband on many of his field trips. Although they were often in the field, the Baileys kept a home in Washington, D.C. They had a symbiotic collaborative marriage: he was interested in mammals, reptiles, and plants, whereas she was interested in birds. The couple spent the next thirty springs and summers in the West collecting data for the U.S. Biological Survey. They wrote their articles and books at their home in Washington in the fall, after the collecting trips.

Florence Merriam Bailey was a popularizer of natural history. Notable among her sensitively written accounts of animals, particularly birds, is a comprehensive report on the birdlife of the Southwest, *Birds of New Mexico*. She also contributed sections on birds for many of her husband's writings. However, she also published in well-known ornithological journals such as the *Auk* and the *Condor*. Her career can be divided into two phases: in the first she was chiefly a nature writer, and in the second a field naturalist and collaborator with her husband. During this latter phase, her works became more "scientific" and less anecdotal. In 1939, the National Park Service published her last book, *Among the Birds in the Grand Canyon National Park*.   MBO

PRIMARY SOURCES
Bailey, Florence Merriam. *Birds Through an Opera Glass*. Boston: Houghton-Mifflin, 1889. A chatty popular book on bird collecting.
————. *Birds of Village and Field*. Boston: Houghton-Mifflin, 1898.
————. *Handbook of Birds of the Western United States*. Boston: Houghton-Mifflin, 1902. Includes thirty-three full-page plates by Louis Agassiz Fuertes and six hundred drawings in the text. A companion volume to Frank Chapman's *Handbook of Birds of Eastern North America*.
————. *Birds of New Mexico*. Washington, D.C.: Judd and Detweiler [1928].
————. "Abert Squirrel Burying Pine Cones." *Journal of Mammalogy* 13 (1932): 165–166.

SECONDARY SOURCES
Ainley, Marianne Gosztonyi. "Field Work and Family. North American Women Ornithologists, 1900–1950." In *Uneasy Careers and Intimate Lives: Women in Science 1789–1979*. Ed. Pnina G. Abir-Am and Dorinda Outram. New Brunswick, N.J.: Rutgers University Press, 1987.
Kofalk, Harriet. *No Woman Tenderfoot: Florence Merriam Bailey, Pioneer Naturalist*. College Station: Texas A&M University Press, 1989.

STANDARD SOURCES
AMS 2–7 (listed as Mrs. Vernon Bailey in editions 2–5); Bailey, 18–19; Bonta; *DAB*; Grinstein 1997; *NAW; Notable*.

BAKER, ANNE ELIZABETH (1786–1861)
British plant collector and illustrator. Born in Northampton 16 June 1786. Never married. Educated privately. Died 22 April 1861 in Northampton.

Baker supplied botanical notes and many drawings and plant lists to her brother George Baker (1781–1851), which were included in his *History and Antiquities of Northampton*.

JH/MBO

PRIMARY SOURCES
Baker, George. *History and Antiquities of Northampton*. 2 vols. London: 1822–1830. Illustrations by Anne Elizabeth Baker. Never completed.

SECONDARY SOURCES
Northampton Mercury, 13 October 1851.
Druce, G. C. *Flora Northamptonshire* 1930: lxxxviii–ix.

STANDARD SOURCES
Desmond.

BAKER, SARA JOSEPHINE (1873–1945)
U.S. physician and public health advocate. Born 15 November 1873 in Poughkeepsie, N.Y. to Jenny Harwood (Brown) and Orlando Daniel Mosher Baker. Three siblings. Never married. Educated Woman's Medical College of the New York Infirmary for Women and Children (M.D., 1898, D.P.H., 1917). Professional experience: New York Department of Health, medical inspector (1901–1907); Commissioner for Public Health of New York City, assistant (1907–1908); Department of Health, head (1908–1933). Honors and memberships: Health Committee of the League of Nations, United States representative (1922–1942); American Medical Women's Association, president (1935–1936); Child Hygiene Association, president (1918). Died 22 February 1945 of cancer.

Sara Josephine Baker's father was a well-to-do lawyer of Quaker stock, and her mother was a member of the first class of Vassar College. Sara was the third daughter of four children; her father and brother died of typhoid when she was sixteen.

Baker resolved to become a doctor after the deaths of her father and brother, giving up her plans to attend Vassar. She was tutored privately in order to prepare her for the entrance examination to the Woman's Medical College of the New York Infirmary for Women and Children, where she received her medical degree in 1898. Some eighteen years later (1917) she received a doctorate in public health (the first awarded to a woman), writing a thesis on classroom ventilation and respiratory disease among schoolchildren.

After graduation from Woman's Medical College, Baker tried private practice for a year but was financially unsuccessful. She became a medical inspector for the New York Department of Health (1901–1907), and was assistant to the commissioner for public health of New York City. She was appointed head of the Department of Health the following year, a position she held for twenty-five years.

While working for the health department (in "Hell's Kitchen"), she witnessed firsthand high infant mortality and rampant disease. She helped to apprehend and isolate Mary Mallon, "Typhoid Mary," during the typhoid epidemic, an action that has since been questioned. In 1908, she designed a controlled experiment to look at methods to reduce infant mortality. Baker and her team of thirty trained nurses taught women in an East Side district the basics of preventive child care, which remarkably reduced infant deaths in that district.

Baker pioneered public health education, using educational pamphlets; free prenatal instruction; and school testing for diphtheria, influenza, and other infectious diseases. She set up free milk clinics, trained and licensed midwives, and taught the use of silver nitrate to prevent blindness in newborns. This work eventually made the infant mortality rate in New York City the lowest in the United States or Europe at the time.

Noting the high hospital death rate among foundlings, Baker saved many by boarding them with foster mothers. She organized the Little Mother's League, which taught proper child care and basic hygiene and first aid to siblings and young untrained caretakers. Baker founded the Bureau of Child Hygiene, the first tax-supported agency devoted exclusively to improving the health of children (first called the Babies Welfare Association). She directed the life-saving work of the bureau until her retirement in 1923. By then a Children's bureau had been created within the U.S. Department of Labor and similar agencies were installed in every state and in several foreign countries.

Because of her work with the health department she was increasingly recognized as an authority on children's health. When she refused a lectureship at New York University because of their non-admittance of women as postgraduate students, they changed the policy. Beginning in 1916, she lectured annually for fifteen years at New York University–Bellevue Hospital Medical School on child hygiene. Baker was a founding member of the College Women's Equal Suffrage League (begun in 1908 under the auspices of the National American Woman Suffrage Association) and she spoke on many occasions for the woman suffrage movement although she did not see herself as a "militant" feminist.

After her retirement from the bureau, she served as a member of over twenty-five committees and as a consultant to federal and state health agencies. From 1922 to 1924 she represented the United States on the Health Committee of the League of Nations, and in 1935–1936 served as president of the American Medical Women's Association. She was also president of the Child Hygiene Association in 1918 and a Fellow of the New York Academy of Medicine. Her literary output included over 250 journal articles.

Sara Josephine Baker died of cancer 22 February 1945, in New York Hospital, having spent her retirement at her Trevenna Farm in Bellemead, New Jersey. She is buried in Poughkeepsie, New York.   KM

PRIMARY SOURCES

Baker, Sara Josephine, et al. *A Child Health Survey of New York State: An Inquiry into the Measures Being Taken in the Different Counties for Conserving the Health of Children*. Conducted by the Child Welfare Committee of the New York State League of Women Voters. New York: New York State League of Women Voters, 1922. The seminal study that led to the formation of state supported child service agencies.

Baker, Sara Josephine. *Healthy Babies; Healthy Mothers; Healthy Children*. Boston: Little, Brown and Company, 1923. A trilogy of separate books devoted to explaining basic health care for expectant mothers, infants, and young children.

———. *The Growing Child*. Boston: Little, Brown and Company, 1923.

———. *Child Hygiene*. New York and London: Harper, 1925.

———. *Fighting for Life*. New York: Macmillan, 1939. Baker's autobiography. Reprinted in 1980. Includes historical introduction.

SECONDARY SOURCES

"Baker, Sara Josephine." *Journal of the American Medical Association,* 17 March 1945. Obituary notice.

Fabricant, Noah. *Why We Became Doctors*. New York: Grune & Stratton, 1954.

Ptacek, Greg. *Champion for Children's Health*. Minneapolis: Carolrhoda Books, 1994.

Rosen, George. *400 Years of a Doctor's Life*. New York: Schuman, 1947.

STANDARD SOURCES

AMS 3–7; *Current Biography* 1945; *NAW* (article by Leona Baumgartner); *NCAB; Notable;* O'Hern; Uglow 1982; *Woman's Who's Who of America; WWW(A)* 2: 1950.

BAKER, SARAH MARTHA (1887–1917)

British botanist. Born 4 June 1887. Educated University College, London (D.Sc., 1913). Linnean Society, Fellow (1914); Ecological Society, member. Died 29 May 1917.

Sarah Martha Baker earned a D.Sc. from University College, London, and was made a Fellow of the Linnean Society the following year. Her major research interest was the salt marsh Fucaceae. She also wrote on vegetable dyes for a book on plant uses.   JH/MBO

PRIMARY SOURCES

Baker, Sarah Martha: "Fucaceae of the Salt Marsh." *Journal of the Linnean Society* 1911–1912: 275–291; 1916: 325–380.

———. "Vegetable Dyes." In *Exploitation of Plants,* ed. Francis W. Oliver, 99–119. London: J. M. Dent & Sons, Ltd., 1917.

SECONDARY SOURCES

"In Memoriam: Sarah Martha Baker," *Journal of Ecology* 1917: 222–223. Obituary.

Nature 99 (1917): 329. Obituary.

Proceedings of the Linnaean Society 1916–1917: 41–42. Obituary.

STANDARD SOURCES

Desmond.

BAKWIN, RUTH (MORRIS) (1898–?)

U.S. pediatrician. Born 3 June 1898 in Chicago, Ill., to Helen (Swift) and Edward Morris. Married Harry Bakwin (2 February 1924). Four children: Edward, Patricia, Barbara, and Michael. Educated Wellesley College (A.B., 1919); Cornell Medical College (M.D., 1923); Columbia University (M.A., 1929). Professional experience: Fifth Avenue Hospital, New York City, assistant pediatrician (1925–1935); Bellevue Hospital, New York City, assistant pediatrician (1927–1943); Children's Medical Service, assistant visiting physician (1943–1948), associate visiting physician (1948–1955), visiting physician (from 1955). Concurrent experience: Child Guidance Clinic (1927–1966); University Hospital, attending physician in pediatrics (from 1962); New York University, professor of clinical pediatrics (from 1961); New York Infirmary, member of staff (from 1929), director, department of pediatrics (1936–1954), director emerita (1955–1956), codirector (1966–1967). Honors and memberships: Advisory Council on Mental Illness, member (from 1962); Elizabeth Blackwell Award (1950); New York Infirmary Merit Award (1960); American Academy of Pediatrics, New York state chairman (1965–1967); American Medical Women's Association, councilor (1962–1965); American Medical Society; Women's Medical Society.

In addition to the many articles that Ruth Bakwin contributed to professional journals, she authored two books coedited with her physician husband, Harry Bakwin. One of these books, *Clinical Management of Behavior in Children,* went through three editions. Bakwin managed a distinguished medical career while raising four children. Her entire career was spent in New York City. Although her main position was with the New York Infirmary, she held numerous concurrent positions. She was the recipient of the coveted Elizabeth Blackwell medal and New York Infirmary Medical Board Merit Award.   JH/MBO

PRIMARY SOURCES

Bakwin, Ruth, and Harry Bakwin. *Psychological Care During Infancy and Childhood.* New York: D. Appleton-Century, 1942.

———. *Clinical Management of Behavior Disorders in Children.* Philadelphia: Saunders, 1953.

STANDARD SOURCES

Debus.

BALAAM, ELLEN (1891–?)

Australian physician. Born 30 November 1891 in Melbourne Australia. Eight siblings (one died in childhood). Married (June 1916). Educated public schools Melbourne; Continuation School (1906–1910); Melbourne University (M.D., 1915). Professional experience: Melbourne, private practice and general surgery (1917–1952).

Ellen Balaam was an Australian physician born to British pioneer descendants. She was the second oldest in a family of nine (one of whom died) and the first of six girls in a family of moderate means. By age seven, Ellen knew she wanted to "be a doctor, own my own home, and to see the world." She continued to attend the best primary school in the area even after a move put her a long walk away. Her efforts paid off when an excellent male teacher encouraged her to study medicine. He was instrumental in persuading her parents to allow Ellen to use the scholarship she received on graduating from normal school to go on to secondary school. From 1906 to 1910 she attended "Continuation School" in Melbourne, where she won a senior scholarship for entrance to the university. After a year, she was awarded a scholarship that entitled her to attend tutorials in all subjects in first-year medicine. In 1910, she entered Melbourne University, augmenting her scholarship allowance by tutoring mathematics at one of the public schools in Melbourne for three of her five years of course work. She graduated with second class honors in all subjects in 1915. Her honor degree led to her appointment as resident medical officer at Melbourne Hospital for a year.

In June 1916, Ellen married the classmate who had received first class honors and was also a resident medical officer. They began their practices immediately as there was no money available for overseas postgraduate study. Ellen Balaam was appointed clinical assistant to Queen Victoria Hospital for women in July 1917, then full member of the staff in April and honorary surgeon in January 1924, making her the first woman to do general surgery in Melbourne. Her private practice in general medicine and surgery grew and prospered until her retirement in 1952 at age sixty, after thirty-five years of practice. Her husband died in 1964. Balaam spent her retirement years enjoying her home and garden, reading, music, theater and opera, and travel.   JH/MBO

STANDARD SOURCES
Balaam, Ellen. In Hellstedt, *Autobiographies.*

BALFOUR, MARGARET IDA (ca. 1870–1945)

British (Scottish) physician. Professional experience: Ludhiana Christian Medical College and Hospital for Women, established, with EDITH BROWN in the 1890s; Ludhiana, India, The Women's Medical Service in India, director (fr. 1930); Standing Committee of the Medical Women's International Association (MWIA), chair. Died 1945.

Little is known about Balfour's life and education. In her capacity as chairman of the Standing Committee of the Medical Women's International Association, she conducted a survey of medical missionaries and the women doctors employed by colonial governments in remote parts of the world (in cooperation with the British Medical Women's Federation). The purpose of the survey was to ascertain the health of native women and children in "exotic" countries. The MWIA Bureau of Information hoped to succeed in publicizing the problems of hygiene and health faced by medical personnel in these countries; gather the women working in these countries for discussions and consultations to share information and solutions; facilitate organization and best use of trained medical women. A meeting of women doctors under the MWIA was held at the School of Tropical Medicine in London in 1935 under Balfour's direction.   JH/MBO

STANDARD SOURCES
Lovejoy; *WWW.*

BALK, CHRISTINA (LOCHMAN) (1907–   )
See Lochman-Balk, Christina.

BALL, ANNE ELIZABETH (1808–1872)

Irish botanist and amateur algologist. Born 1808 in Younghal, County Cork, Ireland. Father Bob Stawell Ball. Two siblings. Educated at home. Died 1872.

Like her sister MARY BALL and her brother, Anne Elizabeth Ball became interested in natural history through the enthusiasm of their father for the subject. Anne Elizabeth studied marine life, particularly algae. She assisted William H. Harvey in the preparation of his *Phycologia Britiannica* (1846–1851). She collected specimens of algae, which now are at the National Museum, Dublin. Her letters and Irish plants are at Kew. She is commemorated by the plant genus, *Ballia* Harvey.   JH/MBO

PRIMARY SOURCES
Harvey, William H. *Phycologia Britiannica* 1846–1851. t. 356.
Letters and Irish plants are at Royal Botanic Gardens, Kew.

STANDARD SOURCES
Desmond.

BALL, JOSEPHINE (1898–?)

U.S. psychologist. Educated Columbia University (A.B., 1922); University of Minnesota (1923–1926); University of California (Ph.D., 1929); University of California, field study of anthropoid apes with Yerkes Expedition to Cuba; diplomate, American Board of Examiners of Professional Psychologists. Professional experience: University of Minnesota, assistant in psychology (1923–1926); University of California, research assistant in anatomy, teaching fellow in psychology (1927–1929); Phipps Psychiatric Clinic, Johns Hopkins University Hospital, assistant psychobiologist (1929–1942); Cornell University College of Home Economics, research associate (1942–1943); Vassar College, assistant professor (1943–1945); Hartford Junior College, assistant professor (1945–1947); University of Connecticut Institute of Living, psychologist (1945–1947); Rockland State Hospital, senior psychologist (1948–1950); Psychological Intern Training Program, New York State field supervisor (1950–1955); New York State Department of Mental Hygiene, assistant director psychological services (1954–1955); Veterans Administration Hospital, Perry Point, Md., lobotomy research project, research psychologist (1955–1959), clinical psychologist (1959–1967). Honors and memberships: Gerontological Society, Fellow; Sigma Xi, Fellow; American Psychological Association, member.

Josephine Ball had a long and varied career as both a clinical and research psychologist. From Columbia University, where she received her A.B., she moved to the University of Minnesota, where she earned a doctorate in psychology. After working as an assistant in psychology, she moved to the University of California, serving first as an assistant in anatomy and then as a teaching fellow in psychology. While doing her graduate work, she accompanied the University of California–sponsored Yerkes Expedition to Cuba. The goal of this expedition was to establish a long-term colony to study anthropoid apes.

After Ball received her Ph.D., she moved from California to Baltimore, accepting a position at the Phipps Psychiatric Clinic at Johns Hopkins. She remained at Hopkins for thirteen years until she was offered a research position in the College of Home Economics at Cornell University, where she remained for a year before accepting an opportunity to teach at Vassar College in the psychology department. Her next position, at Hartford Junior College in Connecticut, enabled her to combine teaching with a clinical position at the University of Connecticut Institute for Living, through 1947.

In 1948, Ball began a seven-year association with the New York State health system, serving first as a senior psychologist at Rockland State Hospital and then as field supervisor of the New York intern program for psychologists. From 1954 to 1955, she served as assistant director of psychological services for the New York State Department of Mental Hygiene.

Ball moved again in 1955 to the Veterans Administration Hospital, Perry Point, Maryland. This was the era of psychosurgery, and Ball served as research psychologist for the lobotomy research project, from 1955 to 1959. She then became a VA clinical psychologist in that hospital from 1959 until her retirement in 1967.

During this period, she kept up her research interests in the physiological mechanism of sex behavior; in psychosomatic relationships in the menstrual cycle of women; and in the general field of clinical psychology. Based at the Veteran's Hospital, she was also interested in gerontological research, and was made a fellow of the Gerontological Society.   K M

PRIMARY SOURCES
Ball, Josephine. "Test for Measuring Sexual Excitability in the
    Female Rat." *Comparative Psychology* (monograph edition).
    Baltimore: Johns Hopkins, 1937.
Numerous journal articles.

STANDARD SOURCES
AMS 5–8 S&B 9–11; *Psychological Register*, vol. 3, 1932

BALL, MARY (1812–1898)

Irish entomologist, nature scientist, and collector. Born 15 February 1812 in Queenstown, Cobh, County Cork, Ireland. Father Bob Stawell Ball. Two siblings, one older brother and one older sister. Educated at home. Professional experience: provided natural history materials to leading scientists. Entomological collection extant in Dublin. Died 17 July 1898 in Dublin.

Mary Ball's father, Bob Stawell Ball, a customs officer, was a student of natural history who transmitted an enthusiasm and curiosity for knowledge and plants and animals to his three children. Along with their brother, Robert, Mary and her sister, Anne Elizabeth, were encouraged in the study of nature, as this was considered a proper pursuit for women. Mary received no formal education beyond elementary tutoring. Her sister, ANNE ELIZABETH (1808–1872), studied marine life and seaweeds and contributed a number of discoveries to the publications of William H. Harvey and William Thompson. Her brother, Robert (1802–1857), who was interested in all aspects of natural history, became a

Fellow of the Royal Society and director of Trinity College Museum. Through his interests and acquaintances, the sisters gained knowledge and contacts for their own studies and observations.

Mary Ball started to collect and study butterflies and moths from age twenty and became an ardent student of insects. She communicated details and discoveries resulting from her observations to her friend, one of the foremost nineteenth-century entomologists, A. H. Haliday, who included them in his papers. She also reported her accurate observations to Baron de Selys-Longchamps, the Belgian authority on dragonflies. By 1834 her collections of insects and shells were among the notable Irish collections listed by William Thompson, who also included details of her zoological collection in his book *The Natural History of Ireland*. She was the first recorder (in a paper published by her brother, Robert) of *stridulation,* the production of a harsh grating noise, in corixid water bugs. When Mary was only three years old, the Ball family moved to the seaport community of Youghal, County Cork, so apart from insects, Mary studied a wide range of marine invertebrates, often no doubt on the heels of her older sister, Anne. With the death of William Thompson (1805–1852) and her brother, Ball's interest in nature study waned. She died in Dublin, 17 July 1898, at the age of eighty-six, having made a number of substantial contributions to the natural sciences. Part of her entomological collection still resides in Trinity College Museum, but her shell collection has been dispersed.   JH/MBO

SECONDARY SOURCES
Chesney, Helena C. G. "Ireland's Pioneering Malacologists—
    From Dredging to *drummondi*." *Archives of Natural History
    Journal*, 22, 3 (1995): 321–331.

STANDARD SOURCES
Desmond; Mollan and Finucane.

BALLARD, JULIA PERKINS PRATT (1824–1894)

U.S. nature writer. Born 1828. Married Addison Ballard (7 August 1851). One child, Harlan Hoge Ballard (b. 26 May 1853). Professional experience: published popular science for children. Died 1894.

Sometimes writing under the name of Kruna, Julia Ballard was a children's author, writing about moths and butterflies, scriptural works, poetry, and many works on temperance for the National Temperance Society and Publishing House. Her son, Harlan Hoge Ballard, was an educator, and founded the Agassiz Association, which was devoted to the study of science.   AEM

PRIMARY SOURCES

Ballard, Julia. *The Scarlet Oak and Other Poems.* New York: G. P. Putnam's Sons, 1878.

———. *Insect Lives, or Born in Prison.* Cincinnati: R. Clarke and Co., 1879. This book gives an overview of the lives and stages of moths and butterflies with illustrations. It also gives advice to young collectors on observing these creatures in their natural habitat as well as in an environment created by the reader, therefore the "prison" of the title. This book was later revised and published as *Among the Moths and Butterflies* (New York: G. P. Putnam's Sons, 1884).

BANCROFT, NELLIE (1887–1950)

British botanist. Born 30 September 1887 in Derby, England. Married Charles Eyres Simmons (20 March 1939). Educated Derby Girls' Secondary School; University College, Nottingham; University College, London (B.Sc., ca. 1910). Research student, Newnham College (1911–1914); Cambridge University of London (D.Sc., 1915); Oxford (M.A., 1927). Professional experience: Bedford College, London, demonstrator in botany (1916); Westfield College, London, acting head of botany department (1916–1918); Oxford University, demonstrator in school of rural economy (1918–1927), university demonstrator (1927–1932); Imperial Forestry Institute (from 1932). Le Vieux Manoir, Barneville France, research worker (1939–1940); interned in France (1940–1944). Honors and memberships: Linnean Society, Fellow (1910); Royal Society, Fellow (1936); General Committee of the British Association for the Advancement of Science, member (1933). Died 2 October 1950.

Botanist Nellie Bancroft was trained at Newnham College, Cambridge, London, and Oxford. She held a variety of professional positions. After working for the Imperial Forestry Institute, she went to France as a research worker. While she was there, she was interned by the Germans and spent four years in an internment camp. She lived for only six years after that experience.

Bancroft contributed numerous works to botanical and agricultural journals, including illustrating *How a Tree Grows* (1927) by Sir William Somerville.   JH/MBO

PRIMARY SOURCES

Bancroft, Nellie. *A Review of Literature Concerning the Evolution of Monocotyledons.* Cambridge, England: Botany School, 1914.

———. *Outline of Elementary Botany for Students of Agriculture.* 1927.

———. "The Dipterocarpaceae." In *Conspectus Florae Angolensis,* ed. W. Carosso. Portugal, 1937.

STANDARD SOURCES

Desmond; Newnham.

BANG, DUCK-HEUNG (1908–   )

Korean pediatrician. Born 6 July 1908 in rural Korea. Married Sun Keun Lee. Eight children (four from his previous marriage). Educated public schools in Seoul; teacher-training school; Tokyo Women's Medical College (M.D., 1934). Professional experience: Seoul University Hospital, pediatric training; private practice and pediatric clinic (1936–1971).

When Duck-Heung Bang was in high school in Seoul, her two-year-old brother died of acute dysentery, an event that strongly influenced her decision to enter medicine. For a woman in Korea, getting a medical education was nearly impossible; there were no medical schools that admitted women, and even in Japan there was only one women's medical school. Duck-Heung finished at a teacher-training school and taught for four years, saving money and studying on her own in anticipation of attending the Tokyo Women's Medical College. In 1929, she succeeded in entering the medical college and graduated in 1934 after much financial hardship.

She returned to Seoul, to the Seoul University Hospital, one of the few women physicians in Korea. Because of the social pressure in Korea to marry young and have children, Duck-Heung Bang married the chief of the pediatric department, Sun Keun Lee, a widower with four children. In time the couple had four children of their own and Duck-Heung raised all eight while maintaining an active pediatric practice and fourteen bed clinic, especially difficult in the years following Korea's liberation from Japan. In 1954 the war with North Korea devastated Seoul and caused many personal and financial problems. Lee died in 1967 after many months of illness; Duck-Heung Bang kept the practice until 1971 when her own failing health convinced her to retire. She suffered from diabetes (from 1954 on) and decreased hearing and eyesight. She took the opportunity to visit her two sons in the United States, while undergoing treatment.   JH/MBO

PRIMARY SOURCES

Bang, Duck-Heung. In Hellstedt, *Autobiographies.*

BANGA, ILONA (b. 1906)

Hungarian biochemist. Born 3 February 1906 in Hungary to Maria Róza and Samuel Berényi. Married Joseph Baló (26 May 1945). One son, Joseph Matthias. Educated University of Szeged, Hungary (doctorate in chemistry, summa cum laude, 1929); University of Vienna (1925–1927); Medical University Budapest, Hungary (D. Biol. Sciences, 1956). Professional experience: University of Szeged, Medical Chemical Institute, staff (1930–1946); titular assistant professor (1944–1946); University of Budapest, Biological-Chemical Institute, professor (1946–1950); Medical University of Budapest, assistant professor, first department of pathological anatomy and experiment cancer research (from 1950). Honors and memberships:

Kossuth Prize II Degree, recipient with Joseph Baló (1956); International Union of Biochemistry, member of national committee (from 1955); Deutsche Akademie der Naturforscher Leopoldina.

Hungarian biochemist Ilona Banga earned a doctorate in chemistry and a doctorate in biological sciences. She was married and had one son. She published numerous articles on the large-scale preparation of ascorbic acid from Hungarian pepper, and the catalytic role of C4-dicarboxylic acids in tissue respiration. With her husband, Joseph Baló, she discovered actomyosine. She demonstrated the role of mucoproteins covalently bound to fibers in the functioning of elastic and collagen fibers. JH/MBO

PRIMARY SOURCES
Banga, Ilona. *Structure and Function of Elastin and Collagen.* Budapest: Akademiai Kiadó, 1966.

STANDARD SOURCES
Debus.

BANHAM, KATHERINE MAY (1897–?)

British/Canadian clinical psychologist. Born 26 May 1897 in Sheffield, England. Educated University of Manchester, England (B.S., 1919; diploma 1920); Cambridge University (1920–1921); University of Toronto (M.A., 1923); University of Montreal (Ph.D. in psychology, 1934). Professional experience: University of Toronto, lecturer in psychology (1921–1924); McGill University nursery school, psychologist (1925–1930); McGill University, lecturer in psychology and abnormal psychology (1929–1936); Leicester Education Department, England, psychologist (1936–1942); Montreal Mental Hygiene Institute, clinical psychologist (1942–1943); Board of Control, State Institutions, Iowa, Division of Psychological Services, acting director (1943–1945); State Board of Children's Guardians, New Jersey, psychologist (1945–1946); Duke University, associate professor of psychology (1946–1967), emerita associate professor (from 1967). Awarded North Carolina Cerebral Palsy Hospital, National Institute of Health research grant (1967–1968). Concurrent experience: psychologist, Montreal Research Division Canadian National Committee on Mental Hygiene (1924–1930); Montreal Foundling Hospital (1932–1936), State Department of Public Welfare, North Carolina, senior psychologist (1950–1951). Honors and memberships: American Board of Examiners of Professional Psychologists, diplomate (1948); American Psychological Association, Fellow; British Psychological Society, Fellow; Gerontological Society, member; International Counseling Psychologists, member; American Association for the Advancement of Science, member.

Psychologist Katherine Banham was born and received her early education in England. For her advanced degrees, she

came to Canada, receiving her Ph.D. from the University of Montreal. Her career as a psychologist was varied. Before she got her Ph.D., she was a lecturer in psychology at the University of Toronto and a psychologist at the McGill University nursery school. During the latter part of her Ph.D. research, and for two years after she received the degree, she was a lecturer in psychology and abnormal psychology at McGill University. She then returned to England as a psychologist at the Leicester Education Department. As the war in Europe escalated, Banham returned to Canada to serve as a clinical psychologist for the Montreal Mental Hygiene Institute. After a year at Montreal, she moved to Iowa as the acting director of the Division of Psychological Services of the Board of Control of the State Institutes of Iowa. From Iowa she moved first to New Jersey as psychologist for the State Board of Children's Guardians, and then to Duke University, where she was an associate professor until 1967, when she was named emerita.

Her research topics included changes in social and emotional behavior from infancy to old age. These topics involved devising tests of behavioral development in both infancy and senescence. KM

PRIMARY SOURCES
Banham, Katherine. *The Social and Emotional Development of the Preschool Child.* Circle Pines, Minn.: Kegan Paul, 1931.
———. *Maturity Level for School-Entrance and Reading Readiness.* Circle Pines, Minn.: American Guidance Service, 1959.
———. *Quick Screening Scale of Mental Development.* Psychometric Affiliates, 1963.

STANDARD SOURCES
AMS 8; S&B 9–11, O'Connell and Russo 1988.

BANKS, SARAH SOPHIA (1744–1818)

British naturalist's assistant. Born 1744 in Revesby Abbey, Lincolnshire, to Sarah (Bate) and William Banks. One brother, Joseph Banks. Never married. Died 27 September 1818 in London.

Sarah Sophia Banks, the only sister of botanist Joseph Banks (1743–1820), although not a scientist herself, contributed to science through assisting her brother, for the two had remarkably similar interests. Joseph Banks lived with his sister before his marriage, and afterward the three of them, Joseph Banks, his wife, and Sarah Sophia, lived together in what Hector Charles Cameron, a biographer of Sir Joseph Banks, described as "complete harmony for the rest of their long lives." Sarah Sophia's personality was abrasive, and Cameron remarked that she was blunt and "disconcertingly rude to those whom she disliked" and eccentric in appearance. Sophia had an inquiring mind, discussed scientific questions with her brother, and added her own interpretations, which made their way into his writings. She acted as his amanuensis; one of her most laborious tasks was copying the entire manuscript of Banks's Newfoundland voyage journal (1766).   JH/MBO

SECONDARY SOURCES
Cameron, Hector Charles. *Sir Joseph Banks, K.B., P.R.S., the Autocrat of the Philosophers.* London: Batchworth Press, 1952. Information about Sophia Banks is found within this biography of Joseph Banks.

STANDARD SOURCES
DNB.

BARBAPICCOLA, GIUSEPPA ELEONORA (fl. 1731)
Italian natural philosopher and translator.

Giuseppa Barbapiccola translated René Descartes's *Principles of Philosophy* into Italian and reputedly was accomplished in science, design, and languages. She used Descartes's dedication of his *Principles of Philosophy* to Elizabeth of Bohemia (1644) as support for her view that women are capable philosophers. Although nothing is known of her formal education, much of her knowledge may have been acquired and assimilated during conversations in Neapolitan salons, particularly in the home of the philosopher Giovanni Battista Vico, whose daughter, Luisa, was her close friend. Vico's resistance to Descartes's ideas may have spurred her translation of his work. Barbapiccola insisted that those who objected to Descartes because he had separated himself from antiquity had not read his works carefully. While noting Aristotelian precedents for the Cartesian theories of doubt, form, and motion, she averred Descartes had assimilated and Christianized the "godless" philosophies of Aristotle, Plato, and Epicurus.   JH/MBO

PRIMARY SOURCES
Descartes, René. *I principi della filosofia.* Trans. Giuseppa Eleonora Barbapiccola. Torino: Mairesse, [1722].

SECONDARY SOURCES
Vico, Giambattista. *The Autobiography of Giambattista Vico.* Trans. Max Harold Fisch and Thomas Goddard Bergin. New York: Cornell University Press, 1944.

STANDARD SOURCES
Dizionario Italiani; Ogilvie 1986.

BARBARSHOVA, ZOIA IVANOVNA (d. 1980)
Russian physiologist. Professional experience: Institute of Evolutionary Physiology, Leningrad, member. Died 8 January 1980.

Zoia Barbashova was a Russian physiologist who worked at the Institute of Evolutionary Physiology in Leningrad on topics of human ecology and physiological adaptation. She contributed an excellent article to the *Handboook on Physiology* (ca. 1962) edited by David Bruce Dill. Dill recalled meeting her in 1961 at a meeting of physiologists in Leningrad, and remained in correspondence with her.   JH/MBO

PRIMARY SOURCES
Barbashova, Zoia. [article]. In *Handbook on Physiology,* ed. David Bruce Dill. Washington, D.C.: American Psychological Society, 1964.
———. *Akklimatizatsiia Kgipoksii i ee Fiziologicheske Mekhanizmy.* Leningrad: Nauka, 1960.

SECONDARY SOURCES
Dill, David Bruce. "Zoya Barbashova," *The Physiologist* (April 1980): 8. Obituary notice.

BARBER, HELEN KAREN (1922–1980)
Canadian geologist. Born 1922 in Vancouver, British Columbia. Married Douglas Barber. Three children: two sons, Howard and John, and a daughter, Patricia. Educated University of British Columbia (bachelor's degree, 1943) and University of Calgary (B.S., 1976). Professional experience: Pacific Petroleum, programmer (1965), exploration department (1976). Died 14 February 1980 in Vancouver.

Helen Barber is representative of a group of college-educated women who married and raised a family, later to return to the university to acquire scientific training. In 1943, she graduated with a mathematics degree from the University of British Columbia. Upon graduation, she worked for Boeing and the YMCA war services. During this time she met her husband, Douglas, and spent from 1946 to 1960 working as a homemaker and raising three children. In 1961, she became involved with the fledgling computer industry and worked at the University of Calgary and with Univac in Calgary. She joined a data processing group as a programmer for Pacific Petroleum in 1965. She became interested in the geology done by the company and took evening courses at the University of Calgary, attaining a B.S. in geology in 1976. This degree and the knowledge that she acquired in pursuing it made it possible for her to move from computer programming to work in the exploration department. She continued this work until her death at age fifty-eight.   JH/MBO

SECONDARY SOURCES
"In Memoriam. Helen Karen Barber 1922–1980." *Bulletin of Canadian Petroleum Geology* 30 (September 1982): 238–239.

STANDARD SOURCES
Sarjeant, supplement.

BARBER, MARY ELIZABETH (BOWKER) (1818–1899)

British/South African botanist. Born 1818 in Gateshead, Durham, England. Father, Miles Bowker. Family went to South Africa in 1820. Married Frederick Elliam Barber (1813–1892) in 1845. Two sons. Professional experience: collected plants and insects in South Africa; collected information for Charles Darwin on native peoples (1868). Died August 1899 in Pietermaritzburg, South Africa.

No information exists about the early life or education of Mary Elizabeth (Bowker) Barber, but her younger brother, J. W. Bowker, also became a botanist. She moved to Johannesburg from Grahamstown in 1886, returning to Grahamstown in 1889. She collected both plants and insects in South Africa and contributed to *Journal of the Linnean Society* in 1869–1871. She was a correspondent of Charles Darwin, W. H. Harvey, and both William and Joseph Dalton Hooker.

In 1868, she provided detailed observations replying to Charles Darwin's queries about the expression of emotions in native people of South Africa (letter in DAR 160), incorporated by Darwin in *Expression of the Emotions* (1872).

In 1869, Darwin wrote a favorable report recommending that her article on a South African plant be published because it was unique in describing what he termed "fertilization" (pollination) of a plant by a single insect that included a description of the mechanism that excluded other insects. Her article was then published in 1870 in the *Journal of the Linnean Society.* The following year she published a second paper on plant pollination. She discovered *Stapelia glabricaulis* and *S. jucunda,* specimens of which she sent to Kew.

Barber's herbarium is held by the Albany Museum, Grahamstown, South Africa. Her drawings of stapelias are at both Kew and the Albany Museum, Grahamstown. She is commemorated by a number of South African plant names: *Barbaretta* Harv.; *Bracystelma barberae* Harv.; *Iboza barberae* N.E. Br., *Ceropegia sororia,* Harv. (the name refers to the earlier discovered species *C. bowkeri,* named after her brother J. W. Bowker). The genus *Bowkeri* is named after both her and her brother. JH/MBO

PRIMARY SOURCES
Barber, Mary Elizabeth. *Journal of the Linnean Society* 1870.
    Other articles are listed in *Royal Society Catalogue* 5:89;
    9:118; 12:48.
———. "On the Fertilisation of a Species of *Salvia.*" *Proceedings of the Linnean Society* (1871–1872): xxxi.
Letters and drawings at Royal Botanical Garden, Kew.

Letter [ca. 1868] in DAR 160, Charles Darwin Archive, Cambridge University Library.

SECONDARY SOURCES
Darwin, Charles, "Report [on paper of Mary Elisabeth Barber] to the Linnean Society," 10 May 1869, Archives of the Linnean Society.
Harvey, W. H. *Thesaurus Capensis.* Vol. 1, 1859: 24–25. *Records of the Albany Museum* 1903: 95–108.
Mitford-Baberton, Ivan. *Barbers of the Peak.* Cambridge: Oxford University Press, 1934.
White, A., and B. Sloane. *Stapleiae.* Vol. 1. 100 portraits.

STANDARD SOURCES
Gunn and Codd (includes portrait); *Southern African DNB.*

BARI, NINA KARLOVNA (1901–1961)

Russian mathematician. Born 19 November 1901 in Moscow to Ol'ga Eduardovna and Karl Adol'fovich Bari, a doctor. Married Viktor Vladimirovich Nemitskii. Educated L. O. Viazemskaia's private high school for girls; Moscow State University (Ph.D., 1926; D.Sc., 1935); the Sorbonne and College de France. Professional experience: Moscow Forestry Institute, lecturer; Moscow Polytechnic Institute, lecturer; Sverdlov Communist Institute, lecturer; Moscow State University, professor. Died 15 July 1961 in Moscow.

Nina Karlovna Bari had an excellent private education. She showed mathematical promise from an early age and was the first woman to enter the faculty of physics and mathematics at Moscow University when it reopened after the Russian Revolution of 1917. She was an original member of the "Luzitania" group centered around Nikolai Nikolaevich Luzin, whose primary interest was function theory. Upon graduation, Bari went into teaching but also continued her own research into the theory of trigonometric series. Her thesis, which she defended in 1926, received the Glavnauk Prize. In 1927 she had the opportunity to study in Paris and later to travel to Poland and Italy. She was awarded a Rockefeller grant and continued her studies in Paris until 1929. In 1932 she became a full professor at Moscow State University, where her husband, V. V. Nemitskii, was also a mathematician and professor, and continued to teach there for the rest of her life. In 1935 she was awarded the degree of doctor of physical-mathematical sciences. Bari was the author of numerous publications and the editor of several mathematical journals. She died as the result of an accident in the Moscow metro in 1961.

Bari started her career in mathematics during a period when Russian mathematics as well as all other areas of Russian life were undergoing profound changes. More abstract areas of mathematics such as topology, abstract algebra, and function theory were replacing classical mathematics. Sometimes referred to as "descriptive mathematics," these studies were derided by those who thought that they had no application to problems in the real world. Bari convincingly disproved this by solving a number of famous problems using the constructive method of proof that she had learned from Luzin.

Bari's lifelong interest was trigonometric series and she was an acknowledged expert in this field. Among over fifty publications, of particular note was a survey article she wrote in 1949 on the uniqueness problem, and her final work, a monograph on trigonometric series, which has become a standard reference. ACH

PRIMARY SOURCES

Bari, N.K. *Teoriia riadov.* Moscow: Ushpedgiz, 1936. 2nd ed., 1938.

———. *Trigonometricheskie riady.* Moscow: Gos.Izd.Fiz.Mat.Lit., 1961. Translated by Margaret F. Mullins as *A Treatise on Trigonometric Series.* 2 vols. New York: Macmillan, 1964.

SECONDARY SOURCES

Men'shov, D. E., S. B. Stechkin, and P. L. Ul'ianov. "Nina Karlovna Bari: necrolog." *Uspekhi matematicheskikh nauk* 17, no. 1 (1962): 121–133. Translation by Roy O. Davies as *Russian Mathematical Surveys* 17, no. 1 (1962): 119–131.

STANDARD SOURCES

Grinstein and Campbell.

BARKLY, LADY ANNA MARIA (PRATT) (1838–1932)

British Botanist. Born 1838 in England. Second wife of Sir Henry Barkly (1815–1898), Fellow of the Royal Society. Died 10 September 1932.

Lady Anna Maria Barkly collected plants in Mauritius, Bourbon, Cape, South Africa (1867–1878), and published her revised list of ferns in 1875. Her fern collections are in the British Museum (Natural History) and the Royal Botanic Gardens, Kew. The plants and letters of her husband, Sir Henry Barkly, are also at Kew. JH/MBO

PRIMARY SOURCES

Barkly, Lady Anna Maria. "Revised List of Ferns of South Africa" *Cape Monthly Magazine* n.s. 10 (1875): 193–207.

SECONDARY SOURCES

"Barkly, Lady Anna Maria." (London) *Times,* 10 September 1932. Obituary notice.

Curtis Botanical Magazine Dedications 1827–1927; 102–103. On Henry Barkly.

STANDARD SOURCES

Gunn and Codd; *WWW* vol. 1, 1897–1916 (on Henry Barkly).

BARKLY, LADY ELIZABETH HELEN (TIMINS or TIMMINS) (ca. 1820–1857)

English botanist/illustrator. Born ca. 1820. First wife of Sir Henry Barkly (1815–1898). One daughter, Emily Blanche Barkly. Died 17 April 1857 in Melbourne.

Lady Elizabeth Barkly drew plants of British Guiana and Jamaica that were sent to the Royal Botanic Gardens, Kew, along with the original plants. Her daughter, Emily Blanche Barkly, helped her in this work. She also collected ferns in Jamaica. JH/MBO

PRIMARY SOURCES

Barkly, Lady Elizabeth. With Emily Blanche Barkly. Drawings of plants, Royal Botanic Gardens, Kew.

SECONDARY SOURCES

Kew Bulletin 1918: 342.

Father J. T. Timins. *Proceedings Royal Society* 75 (1904): 23–24.

J. D. H. "Sir Henry Barkly. 1815–1898. *Proceedings of the Royal Society* 75 (1905): 23–25.

STANDARD SOURCES

Desmond; Gunn and Codd.

BARLETT, HELEN BLAIR (1901–1969)

U.S. geologist and mineralogist. Born 14 December 1901 at Sharpsville, Pa. Educated Ohio Wesleyan (B.S., 1927); Ohio State University (Ph.D., 1931). Professional experience: American Ceramics, (AC) Ceramic Research Department, ceramic research specialist (1955), supervisor, ceramic research (1956), and ceramic scientist (1959). Honors and memberships: Mineralogical Society of America, Fellow; American Ceramic Society, Fellow; American Chemical Society, American Association for the Advancement of Science, member. Died 25 August 1969 at Southern Pines, North Carolina.

Helen Blair Barlett spent her entire working career in the General Motors organization and was the first woman to attain a top technical position there. While she was working on her doctorate, she served as petrographer in the Ceramic Laboratory at American Ceramics (AC), a division of General Motors, and, after graduation, held full-time positions in the AC Ceramic Research Department, advancing from a research specialist to supervisor and finally ceramic scientist. During World War II, Barlett was granted a leave in order to work on the Manhattan Project at the Massachusetts Institute of Technology under John Chipman, and received a citation for this work. After retirement she taught mineralogy to a group of students and became involved in Campbell College, Buies Creek, North Carolina. To recognize this interest, a memorial was set up at Campbell College.

Several of Barlett's discoveries involved her work with alumina ceramics, including the discovery that high alumina melts containing about 0.35 percent lithium oxide precipitated zeta alumina, $Li_2O.5Al_2O_3$. Other discoveries throughout her career were based on her work on sintered alumina ceramic structures, especially those related to spark plug insulators. She received seven patents for her ceramics work. CK

PRIMARY SOURCES

Barlett, Helen Blair. "X-ray and Microscopic Studies of Silicate Melts Containing ZrO_2." *Journal of the American Ceramic Society* 14 (1931): 837–843.

———. "Rate of Decomposition of Kyanite at Various Temperatures." *Journal of the American Ceramic Society* 23 (1940): 249–251.

———. With Karl Schwartzwalder. "Trends in the Chemical Mineralogical Constitution of Spark Plug Insulators." *Journal of the American Ceramic Society* 28 (1949): 462–470.

SECONDARY SOURCES

Schwartzwalder, Karl. "Memorial of Helen Blair Barlett." *The American Mineralogist* 56 (March-April 1971): 669–670.

STANDARD SOURCES

AMS 6–8, P 9, P&B 10; Sarjeant

BARLOW, EMMA NORA (DARWIN) (1885–1989)

British botanist, geneticist, historian of science. Born 22 December 1885 in Cambridge, England, to Ida (Farrar) and Horace Darwin. Educated Cambridge. Married James Alan Noel Barlow (1911). Four sons, two daughters. Professional experience: John Innes Institute, research assistant (1905–1926?); popular writer on Charles Darwin and history of biology. Died 29 May 1989 in Cambridge, England.

Nora Darwin Barlow, a granddaughter of Charles Darwin, was born and educated in Cambridge, England. Her father, Horace Darwin (Charles Darwin's youngest son), founded the Cambridge Scientific Instrument Company, which made instruments for scientific research. Nora studied botany and became interested in plant genetics. In her twenties, she and other Cambridge women assisted William Bateson in his genetic research at the John Innes Institute near Cambridge.

Although Nora Darwin continued research until Bateson's death in the mid 1920s, her work slowed and stopped some years after her marriage to Alan Barlow. The birth of six children brought an end to her work in this field. As a British civil servant, her husband attributed his understanding and sympathy with scientists to his wife's scientific knowledge and connections.

In the early 1930s, Nora Barlow began to edit the manuscripts of Charles Darwin. Her investigations led to a new edition of his *Voyage of the Beagle*. She later worked on the first publication of Darwin's unexpurgated autobiography and edited an edition of letters by Darwin and J. S. Henslow, which stimulated interest in the Darwin correspondence. She contributed to the endowment of Darwin College, Cambridge, part of which was the home of her uncle George Darwin, and placed a number of family portraits and sculptures in the college. A portrait of her in old age hangs in Cambridge University Library. She died in 1989 at the age of 104. JH/MBO

PRIMARY SOURCES

Barlow, Nora, ed. *Charles Darwin and the Voyage of the Beagle,* by Charles Darwin. Cambridge: Cambridge University Press, 1934.

———, ed. *Darwin and Henslow: The Growth of an Idea: Letters, 1831–1860.* London: Murray for Bentham-Moxam Trust, 1967.

———, ed. *The Autobiography of Charles Darwin.* New York: W. W. Norton, 1969.

Cambridge University Library, Darwin Archive.

Cambridge University Library. Ida (Farrar) Darwin collection, Charles Darwin Archive. Letters and photographs.

SECONDARY SOURCES

Barlow, Thomas, et al. *Nora Barlow, 1885–1989.* Cambridge: privately printed, 1992.

Schweber, Sylvan. "John Herschel and Charles Darwin: A Study in Parallel Lives." *Journal of the History of Biology,* 22, 1, (Spring 1989): 1–71.

Ruse, Michael. *History of Science* 5 (1990): 119–124. With references.

STANDARD SOURCES

DNB 1861–1970 (James Alan Noel Barlow).

BARNARD, ALICIA MILDRED (1825–1911)

British plant collector and illustrator. Born 22 March 1825. Grandniece of botanist Sir J. E. Smith (1759–1828). Professional experience: specialized in the study of bryophytes. Died 1 May 1911 in Norwich, Norfolk.

Alicia Mildred Barnard collected and illustrated Norfolk bryophytes (mosses and liverworts). The list of her bryophytes appears in R. H. Mason's *History of Norfolk,* 1884. She named the species *Bromus pseudo-velutinus.* Her herbarium is at Norwich Museum and her letters at the Royal Botanic Gardens, Kew.   JH/MBO

PRIMARY SOURCES
Barnard, Alicia Mildred. Correspondence, Royal Botanic
    Gardens, Kew.
————. Created herbarium at Norwich Museum.

SECONDARY SOURCES
List of bryophytes in R. H. Mason's "History of Norfolk
    1884." *Phytologist* vol. 3 (1850): 807–808.

STANDARD SOURCES
Desmond.

BARNARD, LADY ANNE (HENSLOW) (d. 1899)
British botanical illustrator. Birth date unknown. Father John S. Henslow. Married. Died 1899.

Anne Barnard was the daughter of botanist J. S. Henslow (1796–1861), who was professor of Botany at Cambridge and then vicar at Hitchin. She was the sister-in-law of the botanist Joseph Dalton Hooker, director of Royal Botanic Gardens, Kew. She illustrated Daniel Oliver's student guide, *Lessons in Elementary Botany* in 1864. She also contributed plates to *Botanical Magazine* from 1879 to 1886.   JH/MBO

PRIMARY SOURCES
Barnard, Anne. Illustrations throughout *Botanical Magazine,*
    1879–1886.
Oliver, Daniel. *Lessons in Elementary Botany.* 1864. Several illus-
    trations by Anne Barnard.

SECONDARY SOURCES
Kew Bulletin 1899: 19–20.

STANDARD SOURCES
Desmond.

BARNARD, LADY ANNE (LINDSAY) (fl. 1790s–1800s)
British botanist and plant collector. Born in Balcarres, Saskatchewan, 1790. Father, James, Earl of Balcarres. Married Andrew Barnard, who was appointed Colonial Secretary to the Cape, (South Africa) 1797–1802. Educated privately. Professional experience: botanical illlustrations (sent to Kew).

Lady Anne Barnard was the daughter of the Earl of Balcarres. She married Andrew Barnard, then appointed Colo-

nial Secretary to the Cape (South Africa), where they lived from 1797 to 1802. She botanised on Table Mountain and drew Cape flora, especially members of the family *Stapelieae.* Her illustrations of Cape flora are in the Royal Botanic Gardens, Kew.   JH/MBO

PRIMARY SOURCES
Barnard, Anne. Illustrations of Cape flora in Royal Botanic
    Gardens, Kew.
————. *The Cape Journals of Lady Anne Barnard.* A. M.
Lewin Robinson, ed. Cape Town: Van Riebeeck Society,
1994.

SECONDARY SOURCES
Country Life 1963: 360–361. Portrait.
Fairbridge, D. *Lady Anne Barnard at the Cape of Good Hope
    1797–1802.* Oxford: Clarendon Press, 1924.
White, Alain, and B. L. Sloane. *The Stapelieae.* Abbey San En-
    cino Press, 1937.

STANDARD SOURCES
Desmond; Gunn and Codd.

BARNARD, EDITH ETHEL (1880–?)
U.S. chemist. Born 20 October 1880 in Seville, Ohio. Educated University of Chicago (B.S., 1903; M.S., 1905; Ph.D., 1907). Professional experience: University of Chicago, assistant chemist (1903–1906), associate (1906–1907), instructor (1907–?).

No information is available as to what happened in Edith Barnard's career after she became an instructor at the University of Chicago. Her entire academic career, as far as can be ascertained, was at that university. However, she is only listed in one edition of *AMS* so it is possible that she married and discontinued her career.   JH/MBO

STANDARD SOURCES
AMS 2.

BARNES (BERNERS), JULIANA (fl. 1460)
British writer on hawking, hunting, and fishing. Born At Berners Roding, Essex. Father, Sir James Berners. Brother, Richard Lord Berners. Professional experience: prioress of Sopewell Nunnery.

According to tradition, Juliana Barnes (Berners) was the daughter of Sir James Berners of Berners Roding and the sister of Richard Lord Berners. George Ballard reported that she was well educated and known for her "uncommon learning; and likewise for her other fine accomplishments." As prioress of Sopewell Nunnery, the reputedly beautiful Juliana was known for her love of hawking, hunting, and fishing, as well as her skill in these "innocent diversions." It is possible, though, that the historic and the legendary Juliana Barnes are quite different. The *Boke of St. Albans* (1486), which includes treatises on hawking, hunting, fishing, and heraldry, is the source for the interpretations. One scholar concludes that the most one can assume from the brief mention of Barnes in the original edition is that "she probably lived at the beginning of the fifteenth century, and she possibly compiled from existing MSS some rhymes on hunting." However, the reprint of the *Boke* ten years later indicates that at least the hunting treatise can be attributed to "Julyans Bernes." Since the authentic pedigree of the Berners family does not include a Juliana, an additional historical problem appears.

Whether or not Juliana Barnes actually published treatises on hawking, hunting, fishing, and heraldry, it is not as a creative scientist but as an oddity—a fifteenth-century nun interested in natural history—that she will be remembered. MBO

STANDARD SOURCES
Ballard; *DNB*; Ogilvie 1986.

BARNEY, IDA (1886–1982)

U.S. astronomer. Born 6 November 1886 in New Haven, Conn., to Ida Bushnell and Samuel Eben Barney. Educated Smith College (B.A., 1908); Yale University (Ph.D. in mathematics, 1911). Professional experience: Rollins College, Winter Park, Fla., professor of mathematics (1911–1912); Smith College, instructor in mathematics (1912–1917), assistant professor 1920–1921; Lake Erie College, Plainsville, Ohio, instructor (1917–1919); Yale University Observatory, research assistant (1922–1949); research associate (1949–1955). Honors and memberships: awarded Annie Jump Cannon Prize. Died 7 March 1982.

Ida Barney was an excellent student, and was initiated into Phi Beta Kappa and Sigma Xi. Her doctorate at Yale was in mathematics, which she taught for ten years at various colleges. In 1922, she began the career in astronomy for which she is known. She became a member of the Yale Observatory staff. New technical advances had made astronomy an exciting subject at this time. Increased funding and cameras mounted on telescopes made massive measurement programs possible. The measurement of stars on photographic plates and the determination of their exact positions became Barney's job. She measured the images and supervised the mathematical computations necessary in order to translate the positions into celestial coordinates. Her supervisor was Frank Schlesinger, who believed that women in astronomy were not supposed to make any large innovations. Any improvements that she made were to be minor and based on

practical, not theoretical considerations. Thus the measurements and calculations remained tedious tasks. JH/MBO

STANDARD SOURCES
Shearer and Shearer 1997.

BARNEY, NORA STANTON (BLATCH) DE FOREST (1883–1971)

U.S. civil engineer, architect, political activist. Born 30 September 1883 in Basingstoke, England, to Harriot (Stanton) and William Henry Blatch. One sibling (died in childhood). Married Lee De Forest (February 1908; divorced 1912). Married Morgan Barney (1919; he died 1943). One daughter, Harriet, by first husband, two children, Rhoda and John, by second husband. Educated Horace Mann High School, N.Y.C.; Cornell University (1905 with honors in civil engineering); Columbia University, postgraduate studies in physics, with Michael Pupin (1907). Professional experience: American Bridge Company, draftsman (1905–1906); New York City Board of Water, radio equipment company (De Forest), laboratory assistant; Radley Steel Construction Company, assistant engineer, chief draftsman (ca. 1909–1911). New York Public Service Commission, assistant engineer (ca. 1912). Women's Political World, editor; Architect and Real Estate Developer (1914–1971). Honors and memberships: American Society for Civil Engineers (ca. 1905 to 1916); Sigma Xi.

Nora Stanton Blatch was born in 1883 in England. Although her father was English and owned a brewery in Basingstoke, her mother was an American of Colonial descent. Nora's mother, Harriot Stanton Blatch, and her grandmother, Elizabeth Cady Stanton, were dedicated women's rights leaders of note, and Nora would also become involved in this movement. The family traveled between the U.S. and England frequently and then permanently settled in New York in the 1890s.

As a young woman, Nora Blatch showed a marked interest in science, and in 1901 she entered the engineering school of Cornell University. In 1905, she was the first woman to graduate in the field of civil engineering, receiving honors and later being inducted into the American Society for Civil Engineers as a junior member. For the first two years after graduation, she worked as draftsman for the American Bridge Company and then for the New York City Board of Water Supply.

Lee De Forest, who had invented and developed the radio tube when this was cutting-edge technology, influenced her to return for postgraduate work in electricity and mathematics at Columbia University, studying with Michael Pupin. She married De Forest in 1908 and at first worked with him, traveling to Europe to display radio equipment manufactured by him. Soon they began to disagree about the management of the company, and the couple parted just before the birth of their only daughter, Harriet, in 1909.

The next move for Nora De Forest was to return to engineering work. She worked for the Radley Steel Construction Company and then the New York Public Service Commission in New York City. During this period (1909–1917), she obtained her divorce from De Forest. She also conducted a famous suit against the American Society of Civil Engineers who had initially admitted her as a junior member when she obtained her engineering degree, but dropped her from membership after ten years, refusing to advance her (or any woman student). Although she lost the suit, she continued to work for the vote and improved status for women. She took over the editorship of *Women's Political World* when her mother resigned in 1915. With her mother, she also worked for a protective Equal Rights Amendment for working women even after the vote was achieved. She also moved into a new field that could use her drafting abilities, designing and building homes on Long Island.

Nora De Forest married again in 1919, this time to a naval architect, Morgan Barney. This appears to have been a happy marriage, and the couple had two children, a boy and girl. She continued her new life as an architect and land developer in Connecticut, but did not completely cease to work as an engineer. Under the New Deal, in 1934, she took a position as engineering inspector for the New Deal Public Works Administration in Connecticut and Rhode Island.

She also continued her political activism, supporting the Progressive Party in 1948, and working with the Congress of American Women. When investigated by Senator McCarthy's notorious House Un-American Activities Committee, she replied with a dramatic letter insisting on the importance of American movements for racial and sexual equality.   JH/MBO

PRIMARY SOURCES
Barney, Nora Stanton Blatch (under Blatch). "Discussion on Works for the Purification of the Water Supply of Washington." *Transactions of the American Society of Civil Engineering* December 1906: 400–408.
———. *Women as Human Beings.* Pamphlet. 1946.
———. *Life Sketch of Elizabeth Cady Stanton.* Pamphlet. 1948.
De Forest, Lee. *Father of Radio: The Autobiography of Lee De Forest.* Chicago: Wilcox and Follett, 1950.
Correspondence and photographs held by family.

STANDARD SOURCES
Mothers and Daughters; NAW(M) (article by Terry K. Rockefeller).

BARNOTHY, MADELEINE (FORRO) (b. 1904)

Hungarian/U.S. physicist. Born 21 August 1904 in Zsambok, Hungary, to Margit (Somlo) and Robert Forro. Married Jeno M. Barnothy. Educated Royal Hungarian University, Budapest (Ph.D., 1927). Naturalized U.S. citizen (1954). Professional experience: Royal Hungarian University, faculty (1929–1948), associate professor (1940–1948); Barat College, Lake Forest, Ill., professor (1948–1953); Northwestern University, Evanston, Ill., research associate (1953–1959); University of Illinois, College of Pharmacy, Chicago, researcher (1955–?); professor of physics (1964–?). Awards: Royal Hungarian Academy of Sciences, medal (1937); Eovos Medal (1947); American Association of University Women, Fellow (1954–1955). Honors and memberships: American Physical Society; Biophysical Society; American Astronomical Society, AAAS; Sigma Xi.

Born in Hungary, Madeleine Forro received her Ph.D. from the Royal Hungarian University in Budapest. She married physicist Jeno Michael Barnothy, who also earned his Ph.D. from that university. They both were on the faculty there until they came to the United States in 1948. Jeno went to work for industry while Madeleine held academic posts. They both became naturalized U.S. citizens in 1954. She became the editor of *Biological Effects of Magnetic Fields,* 1964. She also published numerous papers on absorption spectra alkali halides, cosmic ray telescope measurements, neutrino component at great depths, lifetime mu-meson, meterological factor influencing cosmic ray intensity, and extragalactic origin of cosmic radiation. In biophysics she worked on hematological changes, counteraction radiation syndromes, inhibition of bacterial growth, and genetic changes produced by static magnetic fields.   JH/MBO

PRIMARY SOURCES
Barnothy, Madeleine F., ed. *Biological Effects of Magnetic Fields.* New York: Plenum Press, 1964.

STANDARD SOURCES
Debus.

BARNUM, CHARLOTTE CYNTHIA (1860–1934)

U.S. mathematician/science editor. Born 17 May 1860 in Phillipston, Mass. Educated Vassar College (A.B., 1881); Johns Hopkins University (1890–1892); Yale University (Ph.D., 1895). Professional experience: Betts Academy, Connecticut, teacher (1881–1882); high school teacher (1883; 1885–1886); Yale Observatory, computer (1883–1887); Smith College, astronomy teacher (1889–1900); Carleton College, mathematician (1895–1896); Massachusetts Mutual Life Insurance Co. (1898); Fidelity Mutual Life Insurance Co. (1900–1901); U.S. Naval Observatory (1901); U.S.

Coast and Geodesic Survey (1901–1908); U.S. Department of Agriculture, editor biological survey (1908–1913); Yale University, editor and proofreader scientific works (1914–1926); assistant editor Webster's International Dictionary (1886–1900; 1897).

Charlotte Barnum, a Ph.D. from Yale, had a varied career. After she earned her undergraduate degree, she taught school for seven years. She then worked as a computer for the Yale University Observatory, assisted in the preparation of the *Webster's International Dictionary,* taught astronomy at Smith College, and worked for two life insurance companies. Additionally, she taught mathematics at Carleton College, served as editor for the Biological Survey, and as an editor and proofreader for scientific publications. Her research interests were in functions having lines or surfaces of discontinuity, tides and currents, annuities, and social legislation—an extremely varied set of interests. JH/MBO

STANDARD SOURCES
AMS 1–5; Bailey; Dorland; Siegel and Finley.

BARRERA, OLIVA SABUCA DE NANTES (1562–1625)
Spanish philosophical writer on mental states. Born 1562. Died 1625.

Barrera wrote a treatise on human physiological and mental states entitled *A New Philosophy of the Nature of Man, Not Known or Achieved by the Ancient Philosophers, Which Will Improve Human Life and Health.* It was written in Spanish and Latin and cited authorities from antiquity, including Hippocrates, Plato, Pliny, and Galen. Barrera believed that the passions (fear, anger, despair, unrequited love, shame, anxiety, compassion, etc.) stimulated the secretions of the brain, affecting health and initiating disease. Her work was printed in Madrid in 1587 and again in 1588. The Inquisition attempted to destroy all available copies but two survived and the treatise was republished in 1728. JH/MBO

PRIMARY SOURCES
Sabuca de Nantes, Barrera, Oliva. *Nueva Filosofia de la Naturaleza del hobre [sic], No Conocida Ni Alançado de los Grandes Filosofos Antiguos.* Madrid: P. Madrigal, 1588. It is possible this book was written by Oliva Barrera's father, Miguel Sabuco, who published it under his daughter's name.

STANDARD SOURCES
Alic; Waithe.

BARRINGER, EMILY (DUNNING) (1876–1961)
U.S. physician, surgeon, gynecologist. Born 1876. Educated Cornell University; Woman's Medical College of New York (M.D., 1901); New York medical license (1903). Married Benjamin S. Barringer, a physician (December 1904). Two children, a son and a daughter. Professional experience: medical assistant to Mary Putman Jacobi; first woman ambulance physician (1902–1904); postgraduate work in Vienna (1905–?); New York Infirmary for Women and Children, attending surgeon; New York Polyclinic, assistant attending gynecologist; New York Board of Health, head of female venereal service (1918); Department of Hospitals, New York City; Kingston Avenue Hospital, director of gynecology; on retirement, consultant in obstetrics and gynecology to New York City hospitals. Honors and memberships: New York State Medical Society, delegate; American Medical Association, delegate; American Medical Women's Association, president (1941–1942). Died 1961.

Emily Dunning Barringer devoted much of her career to helping the poor. She was born in New York in 1876 to parents who were good friends of influential physicians, including MARY PUTNAM JACOBI, who encouraged Emily to enter medicine. Upon graduation from the Woman's Medical College of New York, she applied as a resident to many hospitals, but was denied admission because of her sex. She then worked for a year as assistant to Jacobi in 1894. Finally she was admitted as house doctor to Gouvenour Hospital in New York, where she worked as an ambulance doctor from 1902 to 1904. After two exciting years as the first woman ambulance doctor in the United States, she married fellow resident Benjamin Barringer in December 1904; with him she spent the next couple of years doing postgraduate work in medicine in Vienna.

On her return, in spite of the birth of two children, she continued her work in medicine, first as attending surgeon at the New York Infirmary for Women and Children (the hospital associated with her former medical school), then as assistant attending gynecologist, at the New York Polyclinic. She began to work with the New York Board of Health as head of the Female Venereal Department, associated with another former student of Jacobi's, the microbiologist ANNA WESSELS WILLIAMS. Barringer later became chief of gynecology at the Kingston Avenue Hospital and chief of gynecology at the Gouvenour Hospital.

Efforts to have women physicians commissioned in the military had been ongoing since World War I, and as president of the American Medical Women's Association (1941–1942), Barringer continued the fight. Backed by the American Legion, as well as many women's organizations and state medical societies, she sought support of a bill authorizing commissions. This battle was won in 1943 when the U.S. Senate voted to pass the bill.

After her retirement, Barringer continued to act as consultant in obstetrics and gynecology to New York hospitals. Toward the end of her life, she wrote an autobiographical account of her early medical years.   KM

PRIMARY SOURCES

Barringer, Emily. *Bowery to Bellevue: The Story of New York's First Woman Ambulance Surgeon.* New York: Norton, 1950.

SECONDARY SOURCES

Fabricant, Noah. *Why We Became Doctors.* New York: Grune & Stratton, 1954, 101–103.

STANDARD SOURCES

Current Biography; Haber, *Women Pioneers;* Lovejoy; *Women in White.*

BARROWS, KATHERINE ISABEL (HAYES) CHAPIN (1845–1913)

U.S. opthamologist/reformer. Born 17 April 1845 in Irasburg, Vt., to Anna (Gibb) and Henry Hayes. Six siblings. Married (1) William Wilberforce Chapin (26 September 1863; he died in India 1865); (2) Samuel June Barrows (28 June 1867; he died in 1909). Daughter, Mabel Hay (b. 1873). Son, William Burnet (adopted 1885). Educated local schools; Adams Academy, Derry, N.H. (1862); James Caleb Jackson, apprentice in hydropathy (1865); Woman's Medical College of the New York Infirmary (1868–1869); University of Vienna Medical School (1869–1870). Professional experience: Danville, N.Y., hydropathy bath assistant (1865–1866); Howard University, Washington, D.C., teacher; private practice; Congressional stenographer (ca. 1872); Christian Register, volunteer assistant editor; National Conference of Charities and Corrections, reporter and editor (1884–1904); Lake Mohonk Conferences, reporter (1880s–1890s); National Prison Association, reporter. Died in 1913 of cirrhosis of the liver.

Katharine Isabel Hayes was the fifth of seven children of a physician father and schoolteacher mother. Both parents were Presbyterians and Scottish emigrants. Dr. Hayes advocated health through diet and temperance. He allowed Isabel to act as his lay nurse and dental assistant. After attending village schools, she graduated from Adams Academy in Derry. At the age of eighteen, she married a congregational minister, William Wilberforce Chapin, and sailed with him to India, intending to complete a ten-year missionary assignment. Unfortunately, William Chapin died of diptheria little more than a year after they arrived. Isabel stayed for another ten months teaching Hindu girls, but then returned to the United States, planning to become a physician and then return to India.

However, instead of immediately going to medical school, she took a position as a bath assistant at a water-cure sanatorium in Danville, New York, where she met Samuel June Barrows whom she later married. Barrows was an expert stenographer with long-range plans to become a missionary. However, ill health caused a delay in his plans and he paid off his medical debts by working as a secretary at the sanatorium.

At the sanatorium, Isabel Barrows received some training in hydropathy. The couple married and moved to New York City, where she learned shorthand while continuing her medical studies. They moved to Washington, D.C., when Samuel Barrows was offered the position of stenographic secretary to Secretary of State William H. Seward. Samuel fell ill and Isabel took his place, becoming the first woman to work for the State Department.

She returned to New York in 1868 to enroll in the new Woman's Medical College of New York of the New York Infirmary for Women and Children. Samuel remained in Washington as a government stenographer. With his endorsement, Isabel went to Vienna to study ophthalmology, where she learned to perform delicate eye operations. Upon her return, she set up a private practice and taught at the School of Medicine at Howard University. She also worked as a stenographer for congressional committees.

According to their agreement, after Isabel finished her education, Samuel would complete his. Thus he entered the Harvard Divinity School in the fall of 1871. Both of the Barrowses had become Unitarians. Until shortly before the birth of their child, Mabel Hay, the couple lived separately, Isabel continuing with her work in Washington, and Samuel in Cambridge. Before the birth of Mabel, she moved to Cambridge. Isabel, Samuel, and Mabel went to Leipzig for a year for general studies. Upon their return, Samuel Barrows held a pastorate for a short time and then became an editor of the Unitarian weekly, the *Christian Register.* Isabel helped with the journal and by 1885 had given up medical practice.

They gathered a group of reformers around them, and devoted themselves to social causes. In 1896, Samuel Barrows left his editorial work and ran for Congress as a Republican. Elected for a first term, he was defeated for a second. Isabel was in Russia, attempting to win freedom for a Russian revolutionary when Samuel Barrows died. She continued with his work on reform, particularly in women's prison reform.   KM

PRIMARY SOURCES

Barrows, Isabel C. *A Sunny Life: The Biography of Samuel June Barrows.* Boston: Little, Brown, and Co., 1913.

SECONDARY SOURCES

Arnold, Lois Barber. *Four Lives in Science: Women's Education in the Nineteenth Century.* New York: Schocken Books, 1984.

———. *The Wissahickon Controversy: Florence Bascom vs. Her Students.* Newton, Mass.: Allyn and Bacon, Inc., 1983.

Blackwell, Alice Stone. *Woman's Journal* 8 November 1913. Obituary notice.

Stern, Madeleine B. *We the Women.* New York: Schulte Pub. Co., 1963.

———. *So Much in a Lifetime: The Story of Dr. Isabel Barrows.* New York: Messner, [1964].

STANDARD SOURCES
NAW.

BARRY, JAMES (1795–1865)
See Stuart, Miranda.

BARTON, CLARA HARLOWE (1821–1912)

U.S. nurse/founder of American Red Cross. Born 1821 in North Oxford, Mass., to Sarah (Stone) and Stephen Barton. Educated local schools; Liberal Institute, Clinton N.Y. Professional experience: Bordentown, N.J., teacher, public school founder (1852–1854); U.S. Patent Office, clerk (1854–1857, 1860–ca. 1862); Army of the James (under Benjamin Butler), head nurse (1864); Office for Missing Soldiers, Annapolis (1865–1868); International Red Cross in Strassbourg (1870–1871); American Red Cross, founder (1882); Women's Reformatory Prison, Sherborn, Mass., superintendent (1883); American Red Cross, president (1882–1904); National First Aid Association, Boston, organizer (1906). Died 1912 in North Oxford, Mass.

Much of Clara Barton's nursing began initially as volunteer work. During the Civil War, she volunteered as a nurse independently of Dorothea Dix's group of nurses and the U.S. Sanitary Commission. Barton distributed needed supplies to difficult-to-reach areas and ministered to the sick. She called the authorities' attention to neglect and poor medical treatment. In the same way, her work with the International Red Cross began as volunteer work in Switzerland and then Strassbourg. She pushed for the adoption of the Geneva Convention by the United States from 1878 to 1882, when it was finally ratified. Her founding of the American Red Cross was not formally recognized by the federal government until 1900.

During the Spanish-American War, she tried to distribute supplies with mule trains and set up soup kitchens and orphan asylums in Cuba much in the same way as she had during the Civil War, but she was criticized for this, especially for her inability to delegate authority. She was forced to resign her position as president of the Red Cross in 1904. However, her work ensured the adoption by the International Red Cross of peacetime relief following catastrophes (the "American amendment"). She was awarded many medals and other honors by governments of Germany, Serbia, Russia, and Turkey, among others, and recognized more widely outside the U.S. Barton died in North Oxford, Massachusetts, in 1912.   JH/MBO

PRIMARY SOURCES
Barton, Clara. *A Story of the Red Cross.* Appleton, 1904.
———. *The Story of My Childhood.* 1907. Reprint, New York: Arno Press, 1980.
Diaries in 35 volumes from 1866 to 1910, correspondence, and other archival materials, Library of Congress.
Archival materials, Sophia Smith Collection, Smith College.
Archival materials, National Headquarters of the American Red Cross.

SECONDARY SOURCES
Epler, Percy Harold. *The Life of Clara Barton.* New York: Arno Press, 1980.
Oates, Stephen B. *Clara Barton and the Civil War.* New York: Free Press, 1944.
Pryor, Elizabeth Brown. *Clara Barton: Professional Angel.* Philadelphia: University of Pennsylvania Press, 1987.

STANDARD SOURCES
NAW (article by Merle Curti); *Women in White.*

BARTON, LELA VIOLA (1901–1967)

U.S. plant physiologist. Born 14 November 1901. Educated University of Arkansas (B.A., 1922); Columbia University (M.A., 1927; Ph.D., 1939). Companion, Clyde Chandler. Professional experience: Van Buren and Little Rock, Ark., biology teacher (1922–1927); Boyce Thompson Institute for Plant Research, plant physiologist (hired 1928). Honors and memberships: award from American Seed Research Foundation. Died 31 July 1967.

All her life, Lela Barton worked in close association with another woman botanist, the geneticist Clyde Chandler. Both women received their bachelor degrees from University of Arkansas and went on to attend Columbia University, joined the Boyce Thompson Institute for Plant Research; they shared a house as well. Barton first worked with William Crocker as his assistant in a laboratory for seed germination and physiology in 1928. The organization she joined, the Boyce Thompson Institute for Plant Research, was itself only a little over three years old. Soon she took over complete charge of the work on seed physiology.

From 1949, Barton held the title plant physiologist until her retirement in late 1966. She was active in such major botanical and graduate research societies as the Torrey Botanical Club (president, 1956), Sigma Delta Epsilon (national sectretary, 1943–1946, and national president, 1947). She was awarded National Honorary Membership in that organization in 1964 and was made a Fellow of AAAS. She won an award for *A Bibliography of Seeds* given by American Seed Research Foundation.

Barton and Chandler moved to Tucson, Arizona, in hope

of improving the arthritis that afflicted Barton, but she died seven months later.

Barton had over ninety publications, including articles in the *Encyclopedia Americana and Dictionary of Gardening (England)*.   JH/MBO

PRIMARY SOURCES

Barton, Lela. With William Crocker. *Twenty Years of Seed Research*. London: Faber and Faber, 1948.
———. With William Crocker. *Physiology of Seeds: Introduction to the Experimental Study of Seed and Germination Problems*. Waltham, Mass.: Chronica Botanica, 1953.
———. "Dormancy in Seeds and Seed Germination" and "Longevity in plants and its limitations." In *Handbuch der Pflanzenphysiologie,* vol. 15. Berlin: Springer-Verlag, 1955.
———. *Seed Preservation and Longevity.* Leonard Hill: London, 1961.
———. *A Bibliography of Seeds.* New York: Columbia University Press, 1967.

SECONDARY SOURCES

Schlesinger Library, Radcliffe College. *NAW* (unused).
Small, John. "Lela Viola Barton." *Bulletin Torrey Botanical Club* 95 (1967): 103–110. Includes portrait.

BASCOM, FLORENCE (1862–1945)

U.S. geologist. Born 14 July 1862 in Williamstown, Mass., to Emma Curtiss Bascom and John Bascom. Educated University of Wisconsin (B.A., B.L., 1882; M.S., 1887); Johns Hopkins University (Ph.D., 1893). Professional experience: Ohio State University, instructor, associate professor (1893–1895); Bryn Mawr College, reader (1898–1903), associate professor (1903–1906), professor (1906–1928), professor emerita (1928–1945); U.S. Geological Survey, geological assistant (1896–1901). Died 18 June 1945 in Northampton, Mass.

Until she was twelve years old, Florence Bascom lived in Williamstown, Massachusetts, where her father was professor of oratory and rhetoric. Both of her parents were well educated; her mother had studied at the Patapsco Institute of Almira Hart Lincoln Phelps and had been a former school teacher, suffragist, and reformer. Her father was a graduate of Williams College and the Auburn Theological seminary and, at one time, had considered becoming a minister. In 1874, the family moved to the University of Wisconsin, where Bascom's father became president. Both parents were social and educational activists, advocating educational reform and suffrage for women.

Bascom received much of her education from the University of Wisconsin, where she began her study of geology.

While working on her master's degree under Roland Irving and Charles R. Van Hise, her interest in geology increased. Although she respected Irving's teaching and research abilities, she noted that he was was not inclined toward coeducation. Therefore, after she received her master's degree, she left Wisconsin and accepted a teaching position at Rockford College in Illinois. When Johns Hopkins opened its graduate school to women, Bascom entered, studied petrology, and received her Ph.D. (1893), a degree granted by a special dispensation, since women were not admitted officially until 1907. Her teaching experience began at Ohio State University, where she was instructor and associate professor in geology and petrography from 1893 to 1895. Upon leaving Ohio State, she went to Bryn Mawr College, where she advanced rapidly.

During part of her time at Bryn Mawr, Bascom worked as a geological assistant for the U.S. Geological Survey. She was the first woman to serve as a geologist for the survey, the first woman to be elected to fellowship in the Geological Society of America, and the first woman to become vice-president of that organization. Her work for the survey involved mapping formations in Pennsylvania, Maryland, and New Jersey during the summers and analyzing microscope slides during the winters. The results were published in folios and bulletins of the U.S. Geological Survey.

Bascom's research consisted chiefly of work on the petrography of the areas that she studied for the U.S. Geological Survey. Her bibliography includes over forty titles.

Bascom was a pioneer among women in geology. After her experience with Irving at Wisconsin, she accomplished the difficult task of being admitted to Johns Hopkins. The strongly conservative attitude of German universities pervaded Hopkins, and to be admitted, a woman had to prove that she was not able to receive equivalent instruction elsewhere and, even then, she was not admitted as a regular student. A friend of her father's interceded for Bascom and she was admitted but without being enrolled as a student and without paying tuition. She attended classes while sitting behind a screen. George Huntington Williams, whose specialty was microscopic petrography, became her advocate. After spending a summer in field work with Williams, she applied to the Ph.D. program and was admitted. Probably her most important accomplishment was that of a mentor to an entire generation of young women geologists.   MBO

PRIMARY SOURCES

Bascom, Florence. "The Sheet Gabbros of Lake Superior." Master's thesis, University of Wisconsin, 1884.
———. "A Contribution to the Geology of South Mountain, Pennsylvania." Ph.D. diss. Johns Hopkins University, 1893.
———. *The Ancient Volcanic Rocks of South Mountain, Pennsylvania.* Washington, D.C.: U.S. Government Printing Office, 1896.

———. "Cycles of Erosion in the Piedmont Province of Pennsylvania." *Journal of Geology* 29 (1929): 540–559.

———. With George Willis Stose. "Geology and Mineral Resources of the Honeybrook and Phoenixville Quadrangles, Pennsylvania." *U.S. Geological Survey Bulletin* (1938) 891.

SECONDARY SOURCES

Arnold, Lois Barber. *Four Lives in Science: Women's Education in the Nineteenth Century.* New York: Schocken Books, 1984.

———. *The Wissahickon Controversy: Florence Bascom vs. Her Students.* Newton, Mass.: Allyn and Bacon, 1983.

Ogilvie, Ida. "In Memoriam Florence Bascom." *Bryn Mawr Alumnae Bulletin* 1945: 12–13.

Smith, Isabel Fothergill. *The Stone Lady: A Memoir of Florence Bascom.* Bryn Mawr, Pa.: Bryn Mawr College Library, 1981.

Thwaites, Reuben Gold. *The University of Wisconsin: Its History and Its Alumnae.* Madison, Wis.: J. N. Purcell, 1900. Includes a partial bibliography in the sketch of Bascom.

STANDARD SOURCES

AMS 1–7; *DAB; NAW; Notable; Ogilvie* 1986.

BASS, MARY ELIZABETH (1876–1956)

U.S. physician. Born 5 April 1876 in Carley, Marion County, Mich., to Mary Eliza (Wilkes) and Isaac Esau Bass. Seven siblings. Educated Columbia, Mich., High School (graduated 1893); normal schools (certificates 1892 and 1896); Medical College of Pennsylvania (M.D., 1904). Professional experience: New Orleans Hospital and Dispensary for Women and Children (later the Sara Mayo Hospital) (1905–1911); Tulane University, School of Medicine, assistant demonstrator of surgical pathology, nonsalaried (1911–1914), laboratory of clinical medicine, instructor (1914–1920), professor (1920–1941). Honors and memberships: Orleans Parish Medical Society (1923); Women's Physicians of the Southern Medical Association (1925–1927); Medical Women's National Association (1921–1922); delegate to international conferences; Elizabeth Blackwell Centennial Medal (1956). Died 26 January 1956.

After she retired from Tulane, Mary Elizabeth Bass made some of her most important contributions to medicine. She collected thousands of documents that make up the Elizabeth Bass Collection at Tulane University. From her research, she wrote a column from 1946 to 1956 entitled "These Were the First" for the *Journal of the American Women's Medical Association.*

Born in Mississippi to a devout Baptist family, Elizabeth earned teaching certificates after attending local schools. She taught in Mississippi and Texas public schools for several years when she was in her early twenties. Her older brother Charles had graduated from the Tulane School of Medicine and he encouraged Mary and her younger sister Cora when they announced that they wanted to attend medical school. Since southern schools did not accept women students, both sisters matriculated at the Woman's Medical College of Pennsylvania in 1900. After they graduated, both women moved to New Orleans to be near their brother who practiced there. Women were excluded from practicing in New Orleans hospitals, so Bass established a free dispensary for women and children, which by 1908 developed into the New Orleans Hospital for Women and Children. Three years later, Bass became one of the first two women appointed to the faculty of medicine at Tulane; however, the position was not a paid one. This position was transformed into a paying position, although it originally paid only $500 a year. She apparently advanced through the academic ranks, for she became a full professor in 1920.

At Tulane, Bass taught bacteriology, pathology, and clinical medicine. She was recognized as a caring teacher and mentored many of her women students. She remained at Tulane until 1941, when she resigned, returning to private practice and collecting information on women physicians. Bass retired from medicine in 1949.

Always interested in women's rights, Bass lobbied strongly for women's suffrage and improved child labor laws. She also did much to advance the cause of women physicians through her work in professional and social organizations.

JH/MBO

PRIMARY SOURCES

Bass, Mary Elizabeth. "Dispensaries Founded by Women Physicians in the Southland." *Journal of the American Medical Women's Association* (December 1947): 560–561. Additional works by Bass published in various issues of this journal.

See the Sophia Smith Collection, Smith College for correspondence between Elizabeth Bass and FLORENCE SABIN. See also the alumnae file of the Medical College of Pennsylvania for information.

SECONDARY SOURCES

Healers and Scientists. Holbrook, Mass.: Bob Adams, Inc., 1994.

"In Memoriam." *Journal of the American Medical Women's Association,* 9 September 1956.

"In Memoriam Elizabeth Bass, 1876–1956." *Bulletin of the Orleans Parish Medical Society,* 9 April 1956.

STANDARD SOURCES

Brooke Bailey; *NAW*(M) (article by Chester Burns and Melissa Nelson); *NCAB.*

BASSI, LAURA MARIA CATERINA (1711–1778)

Italian anatomist and natural philosopher. Born 29 October 1711 at Bologna to Giuseppe Bassi and Rosa (Cesari) Bassi. Married

Giuseppe Veratti, a doctor. At least five children. Educated at home and at the University of Bologna (Ph.D., 1731 or 1732). Professional experience: professor of anatomy, University of Bologna. Died 1778 at Bologna.

Surrounded by doting relatives, child prodigy Laura Bassi had educational opportunities denied to most early-eighteenth-century girls. The well-to-do Bassi family's house where Laura lived from birth to her marriage in 1732 was a meeting place for Bologna's intelligentsia. A priest cousin taught her elementary Italian grammar and introduced her to Latin. The family physician, Gaetano Tacconi, surprised at Laura's precociousness, asked for and received her parents' permission to tutor her. After seven years of tutoring, Tacconi invited his colleagues to examine the young woman using the traditional scholastic disputational form. Bassi's performance exceeded expectations, and she became a popular curiosity, discussing and debating philosophical questions. Semipublic displays of her abilities, some involving scientific experiments, convinced the academic scientists to admit her to the Academy of Science (20 March 1732).

Cardinal Lambertini (later Pope Benedict XIV), a Bassi family friend, insisted that Laura's talents be made public; he arranged for a public disputation in the Hall of the Elders. Following the disputation, Lambertini informed her that she would be eligible for a doctoral degree and a professorship at the university. After a second formal degree examination, she was awarded a doctorate. A third disputation earned Bassi a professorship in philosophy, with a rather handsome honorarium of one hundred *scudi* annually and a medal with her portrait and a motto.

On 6 February 1738, Bassi married a young physician, Giuseppe Verati. Complete strangers were convinced that they had a stake in the marriage, and freely offered advice and opinions about Verati's suitability. Those who approved believed married life would be more proper for Bassi, exposed as she was to foreign admirers, students, and curiosity seekers. Although certain sources indicate that Bassi and Verati had twelve children, more reliable sources place the number at eight, with five surviving past childhood. Bassi's health was poor throughout much of her life. In letters, she referred to various "domestic diseases" that did not allow her to go out. She died at the age of sixty-seven in Bologna.

Bassi was important to the scientific culture of Enlightenment Italy, but we know little about the precise nature of her intellectual contributions because few have survived. We know that her published works represent only a small part of her total output. She published only four works during her lifetime and, as Alberto Elena noted, they tell us little about her experimental and pedagogical activities. An additional work was published posthumously. Paula Findlen notes Bassi's position as a "centerpiece" of a network that "linked the university, the salon, and the urban patriciate," able to use patronage to her own advantage as well as to dispense it to others.

The hesitation of the Bolognese professors to allow a woman to give lectures regularly at the university and her own family responsibilities caused Bassi to do most of her experiments and teaching at home, a not wholly satisfactory situation. She supplied most of the apparatus herself and offered well-attended courses in experimental physics daily. Charles de Brosses (1709–1777) and Joseph-Jérome Le Française de Lalande (1732–1807) attended her classes on a visit from France. De Brosses noted that she occasionally presented public lectures wearing her robe and ermine mantle.

Throughout her letters, Bassi implied that she encountered numerous obstacles because of her sex. One example involved the nomination of twenty *pensionari* each year to give dissertations. Bassi was not selected, but devised a diplomatic solution whereby she, as a member of the university, was selected as a supernumerary member.   MBO

PRIMARY SOURCES
Bassi, Laura. "De problemate quodam hydrometrico." *De Bononiensi scientiarum et artium. Instituto atque academia commentarii* 4 (1757): 61–73.
———. "De problemate quodam mechanico." *De Bononiensi scientiarum et artium. Instituto atque academia commentarii* 4 (1757): 74–79.
———. *Alcune lettere di Laura Bassi Veratti al Dottor Flaminio Scarleselli.* Bologna: Tipi della volpe al sassi, 1836.

SECONDARY SOURCES
Comelli, G. B. "Laura Bassi e il suo primo trionfo." In *Studi e memorie per la storia dell' Universita a di Bologna.* Bologna: Università di Bologna, 1907.
Elena, Alberto. "'In lode della filosofessa di Bologna': An Introduction to Laura Bassi." *Isis* 82 (1991): 510–518.
Findlen, Paula. "Science as a Career in Enlightenment Italy: The Strategies of Laura Bassi." *Isis* 84 (1993): 441–469.
Magnani, A. *Elogio di Laura Bassi Bolognese.* Venice: Stamperia Palese, 1806.

STANDARD SOURCES
Ogilvie 1986; Grinstein.

BATCHELDER, ESTHER LORD (1897–?)

U.S. chemist. Born 19 May 1897 in Hartford, Conn. Educated Connecticut College (B.A., 1919); Columbia University (A.M., 1925; Ph.D., 1929). Professional experience: East Malleable Iron Co., chemist (1919–1920); Henry Souther Engineering Company (1920–1924); Columbia University, assistant chemist (1924–1929), assistant specialist, "Delineator" (1929–1932); Washington State College, assistant professor nutrition (1932–1934); University of Arizona (1934–1936); Rhode Island State College, head of department of home economics (1936–1942); U.S. Department of Agriculture, human nutrition researcher (1942–1956), director of clothing and housing, research division (1956–?). Honors and memberships: U.S. Department of Agriculture, distinguished service award (1954).

Esther Batchelder was a chemist who, after working in industry, spent the remainder of her career in home economics. After she received her Ph.D. she held several university positions and then went to the U.S. Department of Agriculture, where she researched nutrition and eventually became the director of the clothing and housing research division. After World War II, she was a member of a food mission to Germany (1947) and one to Japan (1949). She was a trustee of Connecticut College from 1936 and a member of the Institute for Nutrition, the Dietetic Association, the Home Economic Association, the Public Health Association, the Association for Textile Chemistry and Colorists, and the Royal Society for Health. Her research interests were in consumers' needs and use of food, clothing, and housing.

JH/MBO

STANDARD SOURCES
AMS 5–9, P&B 10–11.

BATE, DOROTHEA MINOLA ALICE (1879–1951)

British vertebrate paleontologist and prehistorian. Born 1879. Professional experience: Geological Department of the British Museum of Natural History, associate. Died 13 January 1951.

Dorothy Minola Bate began her more than fifty-year affiliation with the British Museum of Natural History in the Bird Room as an unsolicited volunteer at the age of seventeen. She found that her interests lay primarily in paleontology and, in 1901–1902, while exploring the caves of Cyprus, she discovered the remains of pygmy elephants. She extended her explorations to cave deposits in Crete, the Balearics, Malta, and Sardinia. At the invitation of DOROTHY GARROD, she worked several seasons in the Mount Carmel and Bethlehem areas. Her Palestinian collections formed the basis of one of her most important monographs, *The Fossil Fauna of the Wady-el-Mughara Caves*. This volume was an example of a paleo-ecological interpretation. After completing this work, she studied the African faunas, particularly those of the Sudan.

By the time she joined the Geologists' Association in 1915, Dorothy Bate was already an authority on the Pleistocene avian and mammalian faunas of Cyprus, Crete, the Balearic Islands, England, Corsica (France), Sardinia (Italy), Israel, Sweden, and of Tertiary Suidae. When she was sixty-

eight years old she went to Rusinga Island in Lake Victoria with Dr. Louis Leakey. Bate published approximately eighty titles on natural history subjects, particularly birds, and contributed information to other geologists for publication. Archaeologists from different countries often consulted her for information concerning fragments of animal remains.

Her careful methodology and her many years of experiences enabled Bate to glean significant information from what others had discounted as unimportant fragments. She was associated with the Geological Department of the British Museum of Natural History.

JH/MBO

PRIMARY SOURCES
Bate, Dorothea Minola Alice. "Further Note on the Remains of Elephas Cypriotes from a Cave Deposit in Cyprus." *Philosophical Transaction of the Royal Society,* Series B, vol. 197, 347–360; ca. 1904.
———. "Note on the Animal Remains From Willington." *Proceedings of the Geologists' Association* 37 (1926): 418–419.
———. "A Fossil Wart-Hog from Palestine." *Annals and Magazine of Natural History* series 10, vol. 13; no. 73 (1934): 120–129.
———. "The Stone Age of Mount Carmel." *Joint Expedition of the British School of Archaeology in Jerusalem and the American School of Prehistoric Research.* 2 vols. Oxford: Clarendon Press, 1937–1939.
———. "The Fossil Antelopes of Palestine in Natufian (Mesolithic) Times, with Descriptions of New Species." *Geological Magazine* 77 (1940): 418–443.
———. "New Pleistocene Murinae from Crete." *Annals and Magazine of Natural History* series 11, vol. 9; no. 49 (1942): 41–49.
———. "Pleistocene Moles of Sardinia." *Annals and Magazine of Natural History* series 11, vol. 12; no. 91 (1945): 448–461.

SECONDARY SOURCES
[Edwards, Wilfred N.]. "Dorothea Minola Alice Bate." *Proceedings of the Geological Society of London* 1951: lvi–lviii.
———. "Dorothea Minola Alice Bate." *Proceedings of the Geologists' Association* 63 (1952): 106–107.
White, Errol Ivor. "Miss D. M. A. Bate." *Nature* 167, no. 4243 (1951): 301–302.

STANDARD SOURCES
Sarjeant.

BATES, MARY E. (1861–1954)

U.S. physician. Born 1861. Educated Women's Hospital Medical College (M.D., 1881). Cook County Hospital, internship (1881–1882); postgraduate study, Heidelberg and Vienna (1883–1885). Professional experience: Women's Hospital Medical College, Chicago, professor of anatomy (1885–1890). Died 1954 in Denver, Colo.

Mary Bates graduated from the Women's Hospital Medical College, Chicago, in 1881. She was the first woman to win an internship at Cook County Hospital (April 1881–October 1882), where she overcame initial skepticism and prejudice with her good spirits, hard work, and intelligence. She finished her internship with a standing second highest among her fellow interns, then went to study at Heidelberg and Vienna. In 1885, she was appointed professor of anatomy at her alma mater, a position that she held until 1890.

Bates moved to Denver, Colorado, in 1891, for health reasons. There she participated in social welfare activities and promoted the passage of laws for the protection of women and children and the prevention of cruelty to animals.　KM

STANDARD SOURCES
Lovejoy.

BATESON, ANNA (1863–1928)

British botanist and horticulturist. Born 1863 to Anna (Aikin) and William Henry Bateson. Five siblings. Never married. Educated privately; Cambridge Day School; Karlsruhe, Germany (one year); Newnham College, Cambridge (Natural Science Tripos, Parts I and II [Class 2] 1884, 1886). Professional experience: Newnham College, Cambridge, assistant demonstrator in botany (1887–1889); University Botanical Laboratories, assistant (to Sir Francis Darwin); market gardener apprentice (1890–1892); New Milton, Hants, market gardener (1892–1928). Concurrent experience: Milton Parish Council, member of Lymington D.C. Poor Law Guardian; Milton District Nursing Association, president; New Forest Suffrage Association, secretary; Military Service Tribunal (Milton), member (1914–1918). Died 27 May 1928.

Anna Bateson was the older of two daughters of William Henry Bateson, who was Master of St. John's College, Cambridge. Her older brother, the geneticist William Bateson, shared her interest in science. After her early education, both privately and in a Cambridge day school, she spent a year in Karlsruhe. In 1882, a year after her father died, she entered Newnham College and began to study for the Natural Science Tripos, apparently at the urging of her brother, who had just achieved first class honors. She sat for both parts of the Tripos and took second class honors in 1884 and 1886, which, although respectable, disappointed her. William consoled her for her disappointment but suggested she would have taken first honors had she studied history like her sister Mary. On completion of her undergraduate work, she was made a Bathurst Student, and served as an assistant demonstrator in botany for two years, from 1887 to 1889. At the same period, she worked as assistant to Sir Francis Darwin in the University Botanical Laboratories (1886–1890). Her sister, Mary, just two years younger than she was, followed

her to Newnham but studied Medieval History, receiving first class honors and prizes. Mary Bateson, later a research fellow, was then appointed to the Newnham College faculty, where she taught until her death in 1906.

Anna left the academic world in 1890 and apprenticed herself to a market gardener for two years. She then set herself up as a market gardener, putting her botanical skills to practical use, and following this new profession in Milton, Hants, until her death in 1928. She was active in the local affairs of Milton, serving on the Milton Parish council, as Poor Law Guardian and during World War I sat on the local Military Service Tribunal. She was president of the Milton District Nursing Association and acted as secretary of the New Forest Suffrage Association, indicating her interest in women's professional concerns and suffrage.　JH

SECONDARY SOURCES
Bateson, Beatrice. *William Bateson, F.R.S. Naturalist: His Essays and Addresses Together with a Short Account of His Life.* Cambridge: Cambridge University Press, 1928. Contains some letters to Anna Bateson, and also quotes some of her remarks on the family history.

STANDARD SOURCES
Newnham, vol. 1.

BATESON, BEATRICE (d. 1941)

British scientific associate in hybridization and breeding experiments. Married William Bateson (June 1896). Three sons. Died 1941.

Beatrice Bateson, wife of the geneticist William Bateson, served as her husband's associate and wrote a memoir of his life that included letters and unpublished essays. The couple had three sons, only one of whom survived World War I. The oldest boy was killed in the war and the second died in London shortly afterward. Bateson's third son, Gregory, became an anthropologist and worked in the United States. Beatrice Bateson was an important part of the intellectual community surrounding William Bateson. On her own, she was a gardener and a fine pianist.　JH/MBO

PRIMARY SOURCES
Bateson, Beatrice. *William Bateson FRS, Naturalist. His Essays and Addresses, Together with a Short Account of His Life.* London: Cambridge University Press, 1928.

SECONDARY SOURCES
Nature 147 (1941): 703. Obituary notice.

STANDARD SOURCES
Desmond.

BATTLE, HELEN IRENE (1903–1994)

Canadian zoologist. Born 1903. Never married. Educated University of Toronto (Ph.D., 1928). Professional experience: University of Western Ontario, assistant professor (1929–1933), associate professor (1933–1947), professor (1947). Honors and memberships: American Association for the Advancement of Science, Fellow; Canadian Society of Zoologists, president (1962–1963).

The first woman to obtain a Ph.D. in marine zoology, Helen Battle had a successful career at the University of Western Ontario, where she eventually became a full professor. She attributed her own rather smooth climb up the academic ladder to the fact that she had never married. She, however, realized that many women had severe problems when they tried to pursue a scientific career, so she embarked upon a campaign to encourage them.

Battle's research was in experimental zoology. In addition to her work in marine biology, one of her main topics was an investigation of the embryological effects of carcinogens.

JH/MBO

PRIMARY SOURCES
Battle, Helen I. "Effects of Extreme Temperatures on Muscle and Nerve Tissue in Marine Fishes." *Transactions of the Royal Society of Canada* 3d series, 20 (1926): 127–143. Contains tables and diagrams.

SECONDARY SOURCES
Judd, William W., ed. *Memorabilia of Helen Irene Battle, 1903–1994.* London, Ontario: Phelps, 1995.

STANDARD SOURCES
Ainley, Marianne Gosztonyi. "Last in the Field? Canadian Women Natural Scientists, 1815–1965." In Ainley.

BAUER, GRACE M. (1878–1965)

British geologist. Born 1878. Honors and memberships: Geological Association, member (Midlands Group). Died 1965.

Bauer was an amateur geologist who was active in the Midlands Group of the Geologists' Association. JH/MBO

SECONDARY SOURCES
S. I. "Grace M. Bauer." *Proceedings of the Geologists' Association,* 77, pt. 1 (1966): 159–160.

STANDARD SOURCES
Sarjeant.

BAUM, MARIE (1874–1964)

German chemist. Born 23 March 1874 in Danzig. Father was director of municipal hospital. Five siblings. Educated Zürich; teaching examination in Zürich (passed, 1897); doctorate in chemistry (1899). Professional positions: AGFA patent division in Berlin, chemist (1899–1902); Karlsruhe, faculty inspector (1902–1907); "Soziale Frauenschule," and the "Sozialpädagogisches Institut" in Berlin, director with Gertraud Bäumer (1916–1919); "Reichsverbänden, social science research"; University of Heidelberg, special teaching post (1928–1933 and 1946–1951). Vassar College with Marian Whitney, guest lecturer (1931). Died 8 August 1964 in Heidelberg.

Marie Baum made a name for herself not as much in her chosen field of study, chemistry, as for her participation in the German women's movement, as a social worker, and as a social scientist. As a factory inspector she traveled through the country and observed the working conditions of women and young people. It was during this time that she produced her social science publications. She worked for private and public welfare and as a *Dozentin.* When she lost her teaching certificate she became actively involved in the cause of the Nazi regime victims.

After the war she took up her *Dozentin* activities after a long hiatus. Until her death in 1964 she never tired of active participation in political and social issues. SNS

PRIMARY SOURCES
Baum, Marie. *Fabrikarbeit und Frauenleben.* Göttingen, 1910.
———. *Familienfürsorge: Eine Studie.* Karlsruhe: G. Braun, 1927.
———. *Rückblick auf mein Leben.* Heidelberg: F. H. Kerle, 1950.

SECONDARY SOURCES
Schulz, Susanne. "Dr. Marie Baum–Lebensweg einer Naturwissenschaftlerin." In *21. Kongress von Frauen in Naturwissenschaft unt Technik.* Karlsruhe, 1995.

BAUMANN, FRIEDA (1887–?)

U.S. physician. Born 28 April 1887 in Scranton, Pa. to Ida E.(Hooker) Baumann and Anthony Baumann. Two siblings. Educated at home; Mansfield State Teachers' College; Baptist Institute (later Cushing Junior College); Woman's Medical College of Pennsylvania (M.D. cum laude, 1917); New York Infirmary for Women and Children, intern; Bellevue Hospital, New York City, chief resident, lung diseases; Scranton (Pennsylvania) State Hospital, surgical resident; Pennsylvania State Board examination (1920). Professional experience: public schools, teacher; Pennsylvania State Reformatory at Morganza, proctor; Western Pennsylvania, parole officer; Woman's Medical College of Pennsylvania, instructor in internal medicine, assistant professor of medicine, and associate professor of applied therapeutics, professor of therapeutics and then professor of medicine in charge of nutrition and metabolism; Philadelphia Gen-

eral Hospital, Hannah E. Longshore Professor of Medicine, and the first woman president of the medical department staff (1952); private practice (internal medicine) in association with pediatricians Emily Bacon and Jean Crump (1923–1963); Woman's Medical College of Pennsylvania, attending physician; tuberculosis division at Philadelphia General Hospital, physician (two years); member of the A.T.& T. corporation medical department; Journal of the American Medical Women's Association, editor (1957–1962). Retired from medical practice, 1963. Died in Philadelphia.

Frieda Baumann's father was a lawyer who also taught courses in German and Spanish as a young man. He moved the family away from Frieda's urban birthplace to nearby Elmhurst so the children could experience country life and become familiar with nature. Ida Baumann was a teacher and instructed Frieda, Frieda's older brother, Carl, and younger sister, Hilda, at home until the family moved back to Scranton (Frieda was about eight years old) so that Anthony Baumann could receive medical care for his "heart disease." He died in 1900 and the family moved to Mansfield, where Ida Baumann became an associate principal in the Model School of the Mansfield State Teachers' College. Frieda was admitted to the teachers' college at age sixteen, finished in 1906, and went to teach school, first in Lancaster County, then in Shinglehouse, then to Punxatawney. Not wishing to burden her mother during the off months of public school, Frieda took a year-round teaching position at the Pennsylvania State Reformatory at Morganza and was put in charge of a new rehabilitation cottage for thirty girls. She found this job inspirational, believing that she could help the girls begin a new life. After two years, she was made first parole officer for Western Pennsylvania.

Feeling a need for further education, Baumann entered the Baptist Institute (later Cushing Junior College) to study social service, but decided after a year to go into medicine, so that she could attend to the girls' "physical, as well as spiritual, health." She entered the Woman's Medical College of Pennsylvania in 1913, graduating cum laude in 1917 in a class of seventeen. She interned at the New York Infirmary for Women and Children, then, after consulting with James Alexander Miller, chief of tuberculosis service, Bellevue Hospital, she was given a residency in lung diseases. As chief resident she stayed there for eighteen months, then became a surgical resident at Scranton State Hospital so that she could practice in Pennsylvania. She took her State Board examinations in 1920, intending to go into internal medicine practice.

On a casual visit to the Woman's Medical College campus, she met a classmate, by then a professor of gynecology, who suggested Baumann consider teaching; the college was in need of medical faculty with a teaching background. Baumann returned to the classroom, first as instructor in internal

medicine, then as assistant professor of medicine and associate professor of applied therapeutics. Later she was appointed professor of therapeutics and then professor of medicine in charge of nutrition and metabolism. In 1952, she was named Hannah E. Longshore Professor of Medicine at the Woman's Medical College of Pennsylvania and the first woman president of the medical department staff of Philadelphia General Hospital. Concurrently with her teaching, she served as attending physician at the college hospital and for two years as a physician in the tuberculosis division of Philadelphia General Hospital. She was a consultant to the medical department of the American Telephone and Telegraph Corporation. From 1923 until her retirement in 1963, she maintained a private practice in association with pediatricians Emily Bacon and Jean Crump.

Frieda Baumann was active in women's medical organizations and stressed their importance for support and professional communication for female physicians during the years when they were not accepted by the men's organizations. She was local chapter president and later national president of Zeta Phi medical fraternity, and active in the Medical Women's International Association. From 1957 to 1962, she was editor of the *Journal of the American Medical Women's Association.* Among her honors were the Elizabeth Blackwell Award of the American Medical Women's Association (1970) and the Commonwealth Committee award for distinguished teaching from the Woman's Medical College of Pennsylvania (1967). JH/MBO

PRIMARY SOURCES
Baumann, Frieda. In Hellstedt, *Autobiographies.*

BAUMGARTEN-TRAMER, FRANZISKA (1883–1970)

Polish/Swiss psychologist. Born 26 November 1883 in Lodz, Poland, to Eleanor (Lubliner) and Raphael Baumgart. Married M. Tramer 17 May 1924. Educated universities of Cracow, Paris, Zürich, Bonn, Berlin; University of Zürich, Switzerland (Ph.D., 1910). Professional experience: University of Bern, faculty (1929–1960?); Institute for Psychotechnology (1930–?); Schweizerischen Stiflung für Psychotechnik, board member.

Franziska Baumgarten-Tramer, an important Swiss psychologist, was a contributor to *Psychotechnische Zeitschrift,* and *Gesellschaft für experimentelle Psychologie.* In addition, she was a corresponding member of the Pedagogical Commisssion of the Ministry of Public Instruction in Poland; *Schweiserischen Arbeitgemeinschaft für praktische Psychologie*; and the *Internationalen Kommission sur Vereinheitlichung der psychotechnischen Terminologie.* She wrote numerous articles in her field of developmental and child psychology. A recent biography depicts her work divided between academic and practical psychology. JH/MBO

PRIMARY SOURCES

Baumgarten-Tramer, Franziska.*Perceptual and Motor Skills* 41, 479–486, 487–490. In Stevens and Gardner, 82–I, 212–15.

SECONDARY SOURCES

Daub, Edelgard. *Franziska Baumgarten-Tramer: Eine Frau Zwischen Akademischer und Praktischer Psychologie.* Frankfurt; New York: P. Lang, 1996.

STANDARD SOURCES

O'Connell and Russo 1990.

BAUMGARTNER, LEONA (1902–1991)

U.S. physician/government official. Born 18 August 1902 in Chicago, Ill., to Olga (Leisy) and William J. Baumgartner. Married Nathaniel M. Elias (1942). Two children, Peter and Barbara. Educated Lawrence (Kansas) High School; University of Kansas (B.A., 1923; M.A., 1925); Yale University fellowship (1930). Professional experience: Kansas City (Missouri) Junior College, director of nursing education (1924–1926); University of Montana, head of division of bacteriology and hygiene (1926–1928); Kaiser Wilhelm Institute, Munich, Rockefeller Research Fellow; Sterling Fellowship (1931, Ph.D., 1932); Yale University Medical School (M.D., 1932), internship in pediatrics; New York Hospital and Columbia Medical School, assistant resident and assistant in pediatrics; Cornell University Medical College, instructor in public health, preventive medicine, and pediatrics, assistant professor of public health (1940), assistant professor of preventive medicine (1944); Columbia University Teachers College, lecturer in nursing education (1939–1942); Harvard School of Public Health, visiting lecturer, Department of Maternal and Child Health (1938–ca. 1954); United States Public Health Service, acting assistant surgeon (1936), medical instructor in child and school hygiene, director of public health training (1938–1939), district health officer (1939–1940); New York City Health Department, director of the Bureau of Child Hygiene (1941–1947); New York Hospital, assistant pediatrician (1940); pediatrician (1942); Maternal and Child Health for New York City, assistant commissioner (1948–1953); New York City Department of Health, commissioner (1954–1962). U.S. Children's Bureau, Washington, D.C., associate chief (from 1949); New York Foundation, executive director; U.S. Agency for International Development, head, Office of Technical Cooperation and Research (1962–1966); Cornell University Medical School, professor of public health (1958–1966); Harvard Medical School, visiting professor of social medicine (1966–1972). Honors and memberships: John Lovett Morse Prize (1934); honorary degrees from various colleges and universities; citations for distinguished service in immunology and in public health from the

University of Kansas Alumni Association (1947); honorary member of the Eugene Field Society (1945). Died 15 January 1991 in Chilmark, Mass.

One of those amazing women who managed to juggle several appointments and careers while maintaining a family and social life, Leona Baumgartner spent her life in the service of children and her country. Born in Chicago, Illinois, Leona moved with the family to Lawrence, Kansas, when her father was a zoology professor at the University of Kansas. She attended the local schools, graduating from Lawrence High School in 1919, and took her bachelor and master's degrees in bacteriology and immunology from the University of Kansas. During this time she also taught biology at Colby, Kansas High School (1923–1924) and directed nursing education at Kansas City Junior College (1924–1926). Between 1926 and 1928, Baumgartner headed the division of bacteriology and hygiene at the University of Montana. On a 1928 Rockefeller research fellowship, she spent a year studying the effects of Vitamin D at the Kaiser Wilhelm Institute in München. Her studies were rewarded with a Yale University fellowship (1929) and a Sterling Fellowship (1930) to continue research in the relationship of age to resistance. After receiving her Ph.D. at Yale in 1932, she went on to receive her M.D. in 1934 and was given the John Lovett Morse Prize, presented by the New England Pediatric Society in honor of the best paper by a fourth-year medical student on a subject of scientific interest in connection with the health of children. Baumgartner's thesis was on age and antibody production. On completion of her medical schooling, Leona married Nathaniel M. Elias, a chemical engineer.

In 1936, Baumgartner began what was to be a long and illustrious career in public health service when she was appointed acting assistant surgeon with the United States Public Health Service. The following year she joined the New York City Health Department, where she progressed to Director of Public Health Training and, in 1941, became head of the Bureau of Child Hygiene. In this capacity she was engaged in supplying health services for students in vocational high schools, providing mothers with scientific health information, and overseeing maternal and child health services. During this time, Baumgartner was also associated with the pediatric staff of the New York Hospital as assistant pediatrician, then as staff pediatrician (from 1942). In 1948, she was appointed assistant commissioner in charge of Maternal and Child Health for New York City. She served as delegate to the National Council of Women, International Congress of Women (1938) and as chairman of the International Committee of American Women in Public Health. In 1940, she was appointed chair of the maternal and health section of the National Health Assembly, and committee member of the National Commission of Children and Youth.

Baumgartner succeeded MARTHA M. ELIOT as chief of the United States Children's Bureau in Washington, D.C. (from 1949)—an agency covering a wide range of services, grants, and educational studies—becoming the U.S. representative on the executive board of the United Nations International Children's Emergency Fund (UNICEF). In 1954 she was appointed commissioner for the New York City Department of Health and took the opportunity to strengthen the New York City sanitary code, expand research, and upgrade treatment of a wide range of health problems. In 1962, she left the city post to become head of the office of technical cooperation and research of the United States Agency for International Development (1962–1965). Simultaneously, she was professor of public health at the medical college of Cornell University (1958–1966). After "retirement" she was a visiting professor of social medicine at Harvard Medical School until 1972 and continued contributing articles to professional journals.

In 1942 Baumgartner was made a diplomate of the American Board of Pediatrics; in 1949, a diplomate of the American Board of Preventive Medicine and Public Health. She served on various advisory boards and held many offices in professional organizations throughout her career, including New York Academy of Medicine; American Public Health Association; Association for Aid of Crippled Children; Medical Society of the County of New York; Child Study Association; Pi Beta Phi, Sigma Xi, Phi Beta Kappa, and Phi Sigma. Her hobby was the study of the history of medicine and collecting old medical works. She died 15 January 1991 in Chilmark, Massachusetts.   KM

PRIMARY SOURCES
Baumgartner, Leona. "Leonardo da Vinci as a Physiologist." In *Annals of Medical History.* 4, no. 2 (March 1932): 155–171.
———. With Elizabeth Mapelsden Ramsey. *Johann Peter Frank and His "System einer vollständigen medicinischen Polizey."* New York: P. B. Hoeber, 1933.
———. With John F. Fulton. *A Bibliography of the Poem Syphilis, sive Morbus gallicus by Girolamo Fracastoro of Verona.* New Haven: Yale University Press, 1935.
———. *The Emerging Adventure in World Health.* [New York]: American Public Health Association, 1963.
———. With Susan Aukema and Marilyn Kostick. *The Parents' Guide to Baby Care.* New York: Grosset and Dunlap, 1977.

STANDARD SOURCES
AMS 6–8, B 9, P&B 10–11 (supp. 4), P&B 12–14; *Current Biography* 1950, March 1991 (obituary notice); Lovejoy.

BAXTER, MILDRED FRANCES (1894–?)
U.S. psychologist. Born 16 June 1894 in Springfield, Mass. Educated Vassar College (A.B., 1916); classes at Harvard University and Columbia University; University of Michigan (A.M., Ph.D., 1925). Professional positions: Pennsylvania State Reformatory for Girls, Child Study Department, psychologist and director (1918–1919); Department of Public Instruction, Rochester, N.Y., psychologist (1919–1921); Board of Education, Cleveland, Ohio, psychologist (1924–1954). G.&C. Merriam Publishing Company, assistant editor (1954–1961), Fellow (1946). Memberships: American Psychological Association; American Association for the Advancement of Science; American Association of University Women.

Mildred Baxter contributed to applied psychology through her studies of affective processes, temperament, and intelligence, especially in relation to school placement and performance. Her Ph.D. dissertation was on temperament. She spent most of her professional life (1924–1954) working for the Cleveland Board of Education. When she retired from the board at age sixty, she became an assistant editor for Merriam Publishers, and stayed with them for another seven years. She retired to Springfield, Massachusetts.   KM

PRIMARY SOURCES
Baxter, Mildred Frances. With Yamaka, K., and Washburn, M.F. "Directed Recall of Pleasant and Unpleasant Experiences." *American Journal of Psychology* vol. 28 (1917): 155–157.
———. "Opportunities for College Graduates in Psychological Examining in Social Service Work and Education." *Journal of Applied Psychology* vol. 4 (1920): 207–218.
———. "An Experimental Study of the Differentiation of Temperaments on a Basis of Rate and Strength." Ph.D. diss., University of Michigan, 1925.

STANDARD SOURCES
AMS 4–8, S&B 9–10; *APA Membership Register*, 1992; *Psychological Register* vol. 3, 1932.

BAYERN, THERESE VON (1850–1925)
German natural scientist (botanist, zoologist, minerologist, ethnologist, anthropologist, and geographer). Born 12 November 1850 in Munich, to Auguste Ferdinand and Prince Luitpold of Bavaria. Born Princess of Tuscany, Countess of Austria. Three siblings. Never married. Abbess of the Royal "Womens' Cloister" to Holy Anna in Munich. Educated privately. Honors and memberships: awarded honorary memberships in the Bavarian Academy of Sciences (1892); the Geographic Societies of Munich (1892), Lisbon (1897), and Vienna (1898); the University of Munich honored her as first woman recipient of an

honorary doctorate, Dr.Phil.H.C. (9 December 1897); the Anthropological Society of Vienna (1900–1901); the German Association of Researchers (1910); the German Society of Anthropology, Ethnology, and Ancient History (1913); the Anthropological Society in Munich (1920); Austro-Hungarian Award for Science and Art (1908); granted title of "officer of public instruction" in France (1909).

Theresa Charlotte Maria Anna, royal princess of Bavaria, was the third of four children of Prince Luitpold and his wife, Auguste Ferdinand, and the first woman to receive an honorary doctorate from the University of Munich. In her handwritten notes, Therese remarks that from childhood she had a passion for natural sciences, and little interest in, or talent for, obligatory feminine handwork. She had private tutors and taught herself; women were first able to apply to the Bavarian University in the fall of 1903. She felt she was not particularly musically talented but she showed talent in drawing as well as in learning foreign languages. Through her travels over the years she gathered knowledge of eleven languages, written and spoken. She was also athletic, enjoying swimming and biking, which kept her fit for her strenuous expeditions.

Von Bayern was not the ideal image of a nobleman's daughter; she was stubborn and did not fit into her society. She lived a rather isolated life and did not often go out in society. But her life was not uneventful. She established herself as a natural scientist and respected researcher through her travels and publications. Her studies led her through Russia, the polar regions, Brazil, Mexico, North America, North Africa, and Asia Minor. She also traveled throughout Europe, from Scandanavia to the Mediterranean countries, from Ireland to the Balkan Sea.

Von Bayern first published under the pseudonym of Th.v. Bayer, about twenty works on the methods of descriptive natural science. Her observations and examinations, which she recorded in a daily journal with handwritten illustrations and photographs, give us a picture of the often extreme conditions of expeditions into unknown regions at that time. Von Bayern usually went out incognito, together with only a few hand-picked companions. She researched the natural conditions and described the social relationships of the countries; she collected, drew, notated, interviewed, observed, photographed, and brought much home with her. She exhibited her "finds" in a private museum. After her death, the Museum für Völkerkunde in Munich was given her richly varied collection of over two thousand objects of North and South American Indians. The remainder became the property of the Bavarian State Natural Sciences Collection.

The self-taught scholar was recognized in her field by Europe's many scientific organizations.

Therese died September 19, 1925 in her home in Lindau am Bodensee. Her contemporaries saw in her a female

Alexander von Humboldt. This comparison was meant as praise. The Botanical Council named Melastomaceenart "Macairea Theresia" for Therese von Bayern.   MP

PRIMARY SOURCES

Bayern, Therese von/Th.v. Bayer (pseudonym). *Ausflug nach Tunis.* Munich: Wolf & Sohn, 1880.
———. *Reiseeindrücke und Skizzen aus Russland.* Stuttgart: Cotta, 1885.
———. *Über den Polarkreis.* Leipzig: Brockhaus, 1889.
———. *Meine Reise in den Brasilianischen Tropen.* Berlin: Dietrich Reimer, 1897.
———. *Reisestudien aus dem westlichen Südamerika.* 2 vols. Berlin: Dietrich Reimer, 1908.

SECONDARY SOURCES

Bayern, Adalbert von. *Die Wittelsbacher, Geschichte unserer Familie,* 242–243, 364–365. Munich: Prestel, 1979.
Doering, Oscar. *Das Haus Wittelsbach.* Munich: Parcus, 1924.
Eulenberg, Herbert. *Die letzten Wittelsbacher.* Wien: Phaidon-Verlag, 1929.
Hildebrandt, Irma. *Bin halt ein zähes Luder, 15 Münchner Frauenportrats,* 43–54. Munich: Diederichs, 1990.
Nachlass, Therese von Bayern. Geheimes Hausarchiv Munchen.
Panzer, Marita Al. "Prinzessin Therese von Bayern." In Stieftöchter der Alma mater, ed. Hadumod Bussmann, 106–107. Munich: Verlag Antje Kunstmann, 1993.
Theresiana. Bayerische Staatsbibliothek München. Handschriftenabteilung.

BAYLEY, NANCY (1899–?)

U.S. child psychologist. Born 28 September 1899 in The Dalles, Oregon, to Prudence (Cooper) and Frederick W. Bayley. Four siblings. Married John Reid (1929). Educated University of Washington (1918–1924, B.S., M.S.) and the State University of Iowa (Ph.D., 1926). Professional experience: University of Wyoming, staff (1926–1928); University of California, Berkeley, Institute of Child Welfare (1928–1954); National Institute of Mental Health, Bethesda, Md., chief of the section on child development; Berkeley National Collaborative Perinatal Project and administrator of the Harold E. Jones Child Study Center (1964–1968); University of California, Berkeley, Institute of Human Development, consulting psychologist (from 1968). Honors and memberships: Fellow of the American Psychological Association and the American Association for the Advancement of Science; member Sigma Xi; president of the Society for Research in Child Development (1961–1963), recipient of its Distinguished Scientific Contribution Award (1983); G. Stanley Hall Award (1971); American Psychological Association Distinguished Scientific Contribution Award (1966) (first woman); Institute of Human Development Award (1969); Society for Re-

search in *Child Development Distinguished Scientific Contribution Award (1983); California State Psychological Association Award (1976); American Psychological Foundation Gold Medal (1982); American Psychological Association, Fellow (1937).*

Nancy Bayley, who contributed several landmark techniques for measuring infant and child development, was the child of a grocer and a community volunteer. She had two older sisters, Dorothy and Prudence, a younger brother, Alfred, and a younger sister, Katharine. Her aunt Belle, a physician who drove her early model car across the countryside to make house calls, was a major influence in her life

Bayley wrote her thesis on the construction of performance tests for preschool children. At what is now the University of Iowa she wrote a Ph.D. dissertation on the use of the galvanometer to study children's fears (psychogalvanic skin response). Her thesis study of fear inspired numerous other studies and helped to generate technological advances in the development of electronic instrumentation for recording bioelectric responses.

Her first professional job was at the University of Wyoming, (1926–1928) where she was an instructor in psychology. It was at the University of California, Berkeley, at the Institute of Child Welfare (now Institute of Human Development) that she really set down professional and personal roots. On 27 April 1929, Bayley married John R. Reid, who had earned his Ph.D. in philosophy at University of California, Berkeley, and was also employed by the Institute of Child Welfare. Bayley stayed on faculty of the institute until 1958.

Her next position was at the National Institute of Mental Health at Bethesda, Maryland, as chief of the section on child development. Returning to Berkeley, Bayley worked with the National Collaborative Perinatal Project and served as administrator of the Harold E. Jones Child Study Center (1964–1968). She continued as consulting psychologist at the newly named Institute of Human Development, Berkeley, from 1968 until her retirement.

Bayley conducted landmark studies of developmental regularities and handicapping conditions, which became the Berkeley Growth Study. She developed the Bayley Scales of Mental and Motor Development, recognized as the best standardized measures of infant development and used internationally. Her paper with Mary Cover Jones in 1950 on the association of behavior with the rate of physical maturation, followed by her paper on the psychological correlates of somatic androgyny, pioneered research by anatomists, physicians, and anthropometrists concerned with morphological maturation. James Tanner, an internationally renowned authority on human growth, credits Bayley's contributions as being seminal in research producing standards for height, correlations relating infant size to adult size, and relationships

between height and academic ability. Bayley contributed over two hundred papers, chapters, and books to the field of child development.   KM

PRIMARY SOURCES

Bayley, Nancy. *The California First-Year Mental Scale.* Berkeley: University of California Press, 1933.

———. *Mental Growth During the First Three Years: A Developmental Study of Sixty-One Children by Repeated Tests; from the Institute of Child Welfare, University of California.* Worcester, Mass.: Clark University, 1933.

———. *Development of Motor Abilities During the First Three Years.* Washington, D.C.: Society for Research in Child Development, 1935.

———. With Earl S. Schaefer. *Correlations of Maternal and Child Behaviors with the Development of Mental Abilities: Data from the Berkeley Growth Study.* Chicago: Child Development Publications, 1964.

———. *Bayley Scales of Infant Development.* New York: Psychological Corporation, 1966.

———. With Leona M. Bayer. *Growth Diagnosis: Selected Methods for Interpreting and Predicting Physical Development from One Year to Maturity.* 2nd. ed. Chicago: University of Chicago Press, 1976.

Nancy Bayley research papers, 1961–1982. The Bancroft Library, University of California, Berkeley. Includes much of Bayley's research in child development done while working as research psychologist at the Institute of Human Development.

STANDARD SOURCES
AMS 5–8; S&B 9–13; *Encyclopedia of Psychology;* O'Connell and Russo 1990; *Psychological Register,* vol. 3, 1932.

BAYNARD, ANNE (1672–1697)

British natural philosopher. Born 1672 at Preston, Lancashire. Father Edward Baynard. Educated by her father and tutors. Died 1697 at Barnes in Surrey.

Anne Baynard was an example of a Renaissance woman who was skilled in a number of subjects. Like LADY ANNE CLIFFORD, she was beautifully educated and simple in her needs. The only daughter of an eminent physician, she was instructed at his insistence in the classics and sciences. She asserted that it was a sin to be content with a little knowledge. By the age of twenty-three, she was considered a profound philosopher.   JH/MBO

STANDARD SOURCES
Cyclopaedia.

BEANLAND, SARAH (1959–1996)

New Zealand geologist. Born 24 January 1959 in Epsom, England. Moved to New Zealand, 1966. Married. Two children. Educated Kapiti College (Head Girl, 1976); University of Otago (B.Sc., honors 1981); Victoria University of Wellington (Ph.D., 1996). Professional experience: Institute of Geological and Nuclear Sciences, Lower Hutt (formerly DSIR Geology and Geophysics), and the New Zealand Geological Survey (1982–1996). Honors and memberships: the Bronze (1973), Silver (1974), and Gold (1977) Duke of Edinburgh Awards; the University of Otago Award in Science (1980); the P.G. Morgan Award from the Wellington Branch of the Royal Society of New Zealand; Geological Society of New Zealand, member and honorary treasurer; Geophysical Society of New Zealand, member; New Zealand Geological Survey, member; task group on the World Map of Active Faults of the interunion commission of the lithosphere, member; New Zealand National Society for Earthquake Engineering, member. Died 1 July 1996 in the Mangahao River region of the Tararua State Forest Park.

In Sarah Beanland's short career, she produced twenty-two scientific publications, a 340-page Ph.D. thesis, over sixty research and commercial reports, and numerous additional minor publications and conference presentations. She was active in the Geological Society of New Zealand and with speaking engagements.

Although she was born in England, from the time she was seven years old she lived in New Zealand. When she was not working as a geologist, Beanland's leisure activities revolved around her young children. Her potential as both a mother and as a geologist was cut short when she drowned in the flooding Mangahao River.

Beanland's research interests involved active faults, paleoseismicity, Quaternary and structural geology, and earthquake hazards. Her early research involved geological mapping and earthquake hazard assessments for the Clyde, Upper Clutha, and Kawarau River hydroelectric power investigations. She spent from 1985 to 1986 in California with the U.S. Geological Survey investigating the 1872 Owens Valley earthquake. Her work became the standard reference on the faulting that caused California's third largest earthquake. When she returned to New Zealand she had the opportunity to investigate another earthquake, the Edgecumbe, Bay of Plenty, earthquake that occurred in 1987. After 1991, her work centered on the geologically recent structures in the eastern part of the North Island of New Zealand. Her work led to a new understanding of the relationships of these structures to the movement of the Pacific and Australian tectonic plates. From this she was able to identify which structures were important for assessing earthquake hazards.   CK

PRIMARY SOURCES

Beanland, Sarah. *Curriculum vitae.* [unpublished]

———, et al. "Late Quaternary Deformation at the Dunstan Fault, Central Otago, New Zealand." *Royal Society of New Zealand Bulletin* 24: 293–306.

———. With Malcolm M. Clark. "The Owens Valley Fault Zone, Eastern California and Surface Faulting Associated with the 1872 Earthquake." *United States Geological Survey Bulletin.* Washington, D.C.: Government Printing Office, 1982. Includes 1:24,000-scale maps of the rupture and other faults of the Owens Valley Fault Zone. Gives detailed descriptions of forty sites that show late Quaternary deformation. Also discusses how the Owens Valley fault zone relates to other tectonic elements of the region.

———. With K. R. Berryman. "Holocene Coastal Evolution in a Continental Rift Setting: Bay of Plenty, New Zealand." *Quaternary International* 15/16 (1992): 151–160.

SECONDARY SOURCES

Little, Tim, and Gamble, John. "Sarah Beanland." *Geological Society of New Zealand Newsletter* no. 3 (November 1996): 9–18. Includes photographs and a bibliography. The account was an expansion of an obituary prepared for the Wellington Post by Desmond Darby and Kelvin Berryman.

BEATLEY, JANICE CARSON (1919–1987)

U.S. botanist. Born 18 March 1918 in Columbus, Ohio, to Alice Elizabeth (Carson) and Earle Beatley. Educated Columbus public school system (graduated North High School, 1935); Ohio State University (B.A., cum laude, 1940; M.S., 1948; Ph.D., 1953). Professional experience: McArthur High School in Ohio, teacher (1943–1945); East Carolina College, Greenville, assistant professor (1954–1955); Ohio State University general botany, instructor (1955–1956); North Carolina State University, Raleigh, acting assistant professor (1956–1957); Mary S. Muelhaupt Post-doctoral Scholarship (1957–1958); New Mexico Highlands University research associate (1959); University of Tennessee, instructor (spring–summer, 1952; summers 1953–1955), acting assistant professor (summers, 1957, 1959, 1960), assistant (1960–1967), associate (1967–1973); University of California, Los Angeles, Laboratory of Nuclear Medicine and Radiation Biology and the Nevada Test Site at Mercury, Nevada, research ecologist (1960–1973); University of Cincinnati associate professor (1973–1977), professor (1977–1987); Ohio State University, research associate, herbarium (1983–1987). Honors and memberships: Ecological Society of America; the American Society of Plant Taxonomists; the Ohio, Kentucky, and Tennessee Academies of Science; the California Botanical Society; the Sierra Club, Nature Conservancy, life memberships; Phi Beta Kappa and Sigma Xi, member. Died 14 November 1987.

Janice Carson Beatley was born in, received all of her education in, and died in Ohio. After working at five different academic or research institutions she returned to Ohio to teach at the University of Cincinnati and as a reseach associate at Ohio State University. She had an older brother, Charles E. Beatley, and at least one younger sister, Mary Alice (Beatley) Jordan. While she was working on her Ph.D., she had a predoctoral university scholarship; then she had a postdoctoral fellowship.

Her research work for both graduate degrees was directed by John N. Wolfe. Her master's thesis, "The Wintergreen Herbaceous Angiosperms of Ohio," was published, as was her doctoral dissertation, "The Primary Forests of Vinton and Jackson Counties, Ohio." Beatley did most of her career research at the Nevada Atomic Test Site in Nevada. Over thirty-six published papers and eleven abstracts resulted from this research. She also published a comprehensive study, *Vascular Plants of the Nevada Test Site and Central-Southern Nevada: Ecologic and Geographic Distributions.* For these projects she studied the region's ecological-floristic relationships. She also published on Tennessee sunflowers and Ohio buckeyes.

Some of her ideas about ecological concepts and processes were contrary to the botanical establishment. For example, she did not believe in the concept of competition, declaring that it had not been proven under field conditions.

JH/MBO

PRIMARY SOURCES

Beatley, Janice Carson. "The Wintergreen Herbaceous Angiosperms of Ohio." *Ohio Journal of Science,* 1956.
———. "The Primary Forests of Vinton and Jackson Counties, Ohio." *Bulletin of the Ohio Biological Survey,* 1959.
———. *Vascular Plants of the Nevada Test Site and Central-Southern Nevada: Ecologic and Geographic Distributions.* 1976. Prepared for the Division of Biomedical and Environmental Research, Energy Research, and Developmental Administration.

SECONDARY SOURCES

Stuckey, Ronald L. "Janice Carson Beatley (1919–1987)." *Ohio Journal of Science* 88 (December 1988): 207.
———. "Janice Carson Beatley (1919–1987): Taxonomist and Ecologist." *Taxon* 39, no. 2 (1990): 212–217. Includes portrait and photograph. A good discussion of Beatley's contributions.
———. *Women Botanists of Ohio Born Before 1900.* Columbus: Ohio State University, 1992.

STANDARD SOURCES

AMS, B 9, P&B 10–14.

BEATRICE, MEDICA OF CANDIA (fl. 14th century)

Italian physician. Flourished in fourteenth century. Married Gherardo di Candia. Widowed.

As the widow of Gherardo di Candia, Beatrice was known in Venice as an excellent doctor.
JH/MBO

STANDARD SOURCES

Echols and Williams; Hurd-Mead 1938.

BEATRICE OF SAVOY, COUNTESS OF PROVENCE (ca. 1220–1266)

French scholar, patron. Born ca. 1220 to Beatrix de Genève and Thomas I, Count of Savoy. Married Raymond Berengar of Provence (d. 1245). Four daughters. Professional experience: patron of medical encyclopedia. Died ca. 1266.

The daughter of Beatrix de Genève and Thomas I, Count of Savoy, Beatrice married Raymond Berengar of Provence who left her a widow in 1245. The arranged marriages of their four daughters helped ally Savoy with the kings of England, France, and Naples. Interested in the study of medicine, Beatrice commissioned Aldobrandino of Siena to write an encyclopedia for her. This encyclopedia, called the *Regime du Corps,* contained material from Rhazes, Avicenna, and Constantine, and included information on hygiene, gynecology, and skin care.
JH/MBO

STANDARD SOURCES

Echols and Williams; Hurd-Mead 1938.

BEAUFORT, HARRIET HENRIETTA (1778–1865)

British botanist. Born 1778 in Ireland. Father Reverend Daniel Beaufort. Three siblings. Never married. Died 1865.

Harriet Henrietta Beaufort became interested in botany through her father, the Reverend Daniel Beaufort. He was a founding member of the Royal Irish Academy and she became involved in many of his scientific projects. Other members of her family in addition to her father were interested in science. Her older brother, Francis, had an important career as a hydrographer for the admiralty and was responsible for marine chartmaking. Her sister Louisa wrote the popular book *Dialogues on Entomology* (1819), published anonymously, and Harriet wrote a popular book on botany. Harriet was related to MARIA EDGEWORTH through marriage. Frances, her older sister, was the fourth wife of Maria Edgeworth's father, Richard Lovell Edgeworth.

The two unmarried sisters, Louisa and Harriet, kept house for their parents and other family members. One inspiration behind Harriet's publishing her popular volume was to help the family with its financial difficulties. In 1818, her father gave up his clerical position and became increasingly burdened by debt. Both her book on botany and her sister's book on entomology were published by Rowland Hunter, Maria Edgeworth's publisher. Edgeworth also helped to arrange annuities for Harriet, Louisa, and their mother after Daniel Beaufort died.

In *Dialogues on Botany*, Harriet Beaufort proposed to teach plant physiology to young readers. She considered it important to delay teaching the fundamentals of the Linnaean system of classification until she first provided the basis, physiology. As did many of her contemporaries, such as Jane Marcet and Maria Edgeworth, she chose the dialogue form as appropriate for children. She did not include pictures, for she wanted children to study nature, not a representation of it. She was criticized for this omission, which was considered unforgivable. Instead of giving them photographs to look at, she had her young readers dissect plants and work with microscopes.   JH/MBO

PRIMARY SOURCES
Beaufort, Harriet. *Dialogues on Botany*. London: Hunter, 1819.

SECONDARY SOURCES
Mitchell, M. E. *Irish Naturalists Journal* vol. 19, no. 11 (1979): 407.

STANDARD SOURCES
Desmond; Shteir.

BEAUFORT, COUNTESS MARGARET (1443–1509)

British learned scholar, patron of arts, education and hospitals. Born in 1443 to Margaret (Beauchamp) and John Beaufort, Duke of Somerset. Married (1) John de la Pole (annulled 1453); (2) Edmund Tudor, Duke of Richmond (he died in 1456); (3) Henry Stafford (he died in 1482); and (4) Thomas, Lord Stanley (he died in 1504). Son Henry (later Henry VII, king of England), by the Duke of Richmond. Died 1509.

Daughter of John Beaufort, Duke of Somerset, and Margaret (Beauchamp), Margaret was well educated, cultured, and pious. Notable for a long sequence of marriages, she also produced a son, Henry Richmond, who became Henry VII, king of England. Margaret was an art patron. She also endowed many schools and hospitals.   JH/MBO

STANDARD SOURCES
Echols and Williams.

BEAUSOLEIL, MARTINE DE BERTEREAU
See Bertereau, Martine de (Baroness de Beausoleil).

BEAUVALLET, MARCELLE JEANNE (1905–   )

French physiologist and neuropharmacologist. Born 26 December 1905 in Fleury–les Aubrais to Alice Bruneau and Aristede Armand Beauvallet. Educated Ecole Normale Supérieure, Sèvres; Faculté des Sciences, Paris, (License ès Sciences naturelles, 1930; doctor of sciences, 1935). Professional experience: Faculté de Médecine, assistant (1941–1944); Sorbonne, assistant (1946–1955), head of special projects, (1955–1959), assistant lecturer (from 1959); Centre Nationale Recherche Scientifique (C.N.R.S.), fellow (1933–1944), maître de recherche (1954), directeur de recherche (1961 to retirement); Faculté des Sciences d'Orsay (France), research staff in cardiovascular physiology (1965 to retirement). Honors and memberships: Académie de Médecine, prize-winning laureate (several times); multiple other honors.

Marcelle Jeanne Beauvallet was born in Fleury–les Aubrais, but went to study at the prestigious Ecole Normale Supérieure in Sèvres. After graduation, she began to consider science seriously. She studied under the famous French physiologist Louis Lapicque at the Sorbonne, investigating the electrophysiology of the pigmentary cells in fish scales. She discovered the adrenergic fibers that controlled their contraction, for which she was named laureate of the Academy of Medicine. Later she moved to cardiovascular research in the Faculty of Sciences at Orsay. Interested in neuropharmacology and neurotransmission, she focused on the sympathetic system and its mediators, studying variations in catecholamines under changing physiological and pharmacological conditions. She was a member of the Société de Biologie from 1952.   JH/MBO

PRIMARY SOURCES
Beauvallet, Marcelle Jeanne. *L'excitabilité des cellules pigmentaires des écailles de poissons*. Paris: Imperial Chantenay, 1935.

STANDARD SOURCES
Debus.

BECK, SARAH COKER (ADAMS) (1821–1915)

British botanist. Born 20 January 1821 in Anstey, Warwickshire. Married. Died 8 November 1915, Monk's Risborough, Buckinghamshire.

A sister of the botanist Daniel Charles Octavius Adams (1822–1914), Beck contributed records of fungi to G. D. Druce's *Flora Oxfordshire* (1886).   JH/MBO

PRIMARY SOURCES
Druce, G. D. *Flora Oxfordshire*. Oxford: Parker, 1886. Includes Beck's records of fungi.

SECONDARY SOURCES
Botanical Society Exchange Club British Isles Reports 1915: 249–250.

STANDARD SOURCES
Desmond.

BECKER, LYDIA ERNESTINE (1827–1890)

British botanist. Born Manchester 24 February 1827 to Mary (Duncuft) and Hannibal Leigh Becker. Educated at home and in Germany (1844). Professional experience: corresponded with Charles Darwin; Women's Suffrage Journal, *editor (1870–1890). Honors and memberships: Manchester Women's Literary Society (1866); Manchester Women's Suffrage Association (1867); Manchester school board, member (1870–1880?). Died 18 July 1890 in Geneva, Switzerland.*

Lydia Becker became interested in botany in the early 1860s, and in the process of educating herself, wrote *Botany for Novices* (1864). She won the Horticultural Society Gold Medal in 1865 for the best dried herbarium. She corresponded with Charles Darwin, from 1863 to 1877, making observations on unusual varieties of dimorphic plants, and, at his request, studying the proportions of male, female, and bisexual forms of *Lychnis*. Darwin encouraged her to investigate the effect of a fungus on the plant. She followed up this problem for a paper she then presented at the British Association for the Advancement of Science, Exeter (1869), unusual for a woman at the time. She founded the Manchester Women's Literary Society at the end of 1866, in reaction to her exclusion from local scientific associations on the grounds of her sex. Her first speech as president of that society at the Royal Institution of Manchester urged women to study and contribute to science. She concluded with two papers written by Darwin and sent to her at her request, one on the trimorphic species of *Lythrum* (1865), and one on climbing plants (1867). Darwin had added a note conveying his wishes for the success of her society. Judging by her letter to Darwin written soon after the first meeting (6 February 1867), she copied his diagrams in large format and brought out examples of each plant from her own herbarium to illustrate her discussion of his papers.

In 1867, Becker founded the Manchester Women's Suffrage Association, stimulated by a talk on suffrage by Barbara Bodichon before the Social Science Association in Manchester in 1866, and by Bodichon's visit to the women's group in 1867. The same year Becker read a paper entitled, "Some Supposed Differences in the Minds of Men and Women with Regard to Educational Necessities," at the British Association at Norwich. It caused extensive discussion at the meeting.

Becker became a feminist activist, writing, lecturing, and working with politicians on behalf of women's suffrage. A tireless worker, she founded and served as editor of the *Women's Suffrage Journal* (1870–1890). At the first Manchester election for a school board, she was elected a member (1870) and was re-elected seven times as an independent. Shortly before her death, she traveled to Geneva, Switzerland in search of a cure for her acute illness, possibly diptheria.

JH/MBO

PRIMARY SOURCES
Becker, Lydia E. *Botany for Novices. A Short Outline of the Natural System of Classification of Plants*. London: Whittaker, 1864.
———. "Speech before the Manchester Women's Literary Society, (1867)." Quoted in Helen Blackburn, *Woman's Suffrage with Biographical Sketches of Miss Becker*, 32–39. London: Williams & Norgate, 1902.
———. "On Alteration in the Structure of *Lychnis diurna* Observed in the Connection with the Development of a Parasitic Fungus. *Journal of Botany*, vol. 7 (1869):291–292.
——— ed. *Women's Suffrage Journal*. London: Trübner, 1870–1890.
Unpublished letters from Lydia E. Becker in Darwin Archive, Cambridge University. See Frederik Burkhardt and Sydney Smith, eds. *A Calendar of the Correspondence of Charles Darwin*, 2nd edition. Cambridge: Cambridge University Press, 1994. Her archives on suffrage are in Manchester.

SECONDARY SOURCES
Journal of Botany 1865, 264; 1890, 320, obituary notice.
Manchester Examiner and Times, July 1980, obituary notice.
Transactions of the Liverpool Botanical Society 1909: 60, obituary notice.
Blackburn, Helen. *Woman's Suffrage with Biographical Sketches of Miss Becker*, London: Williams & Norgate, 1902. A biography of her by a contemporary with two portraits.

STANDARD SOURCES
DNB supplement; Europa; Shteir; Spender, 420–429.

BECKER-ROSE, HERTA (fl. 1920s)

German physicist. Professional experience: Osram–Konzern, Berlin, researcher.

Herta Becker-Rose was one of the women who worked in the Austro-German school on radioactivity. Working with division director Karl Becker at the Educational Society for

Electrical Lighting at Osram-Konzern, Berlin, Becker-Rose showed that exposure to X-rays increased the duration of calcium tungstate's phosphorescence in geometric proportion to the time of exposure. The phosphorescence of this preparation, used in screens designed to count particles ejected from radioactive substances, was affected by heating in a similar manner to some other phosphors.   MM

PRIMARY SOURCES

Becker-Rose, Herta. With Karl Becker. "Notiz über das Nach-leuchten Calsiumwolframats nach der Bestrahlung mit Röntgenstrahlen." *Zeitschrift für Physik* 29 (1924): 343.

STANDARD SOURCES

Meyer and von Schweidler.

BECKMAN, A. (fl. 1920s)
German?/Dutch? physicist.

A. Beckman was one of the women who worked in the Austro-German circle on radioactivity. The only information available on Beckman revolves around her research on piezoelectricity, for which she found a temperature dependence. She contributed to a Festschrift for the Dutch scientist H. Kammerlingh Onnes upon his retirement from the laboratory at the State University of Leiden.   MM

PRIMARY SOURCES

Beckman, A. *Het Naturkundig Laboratorium der Rücksuniversiteit te Leiden de jaren 1904–1922.* Leiden: Rejsuniversiteit, 1922. Festschrift for H. Kammerlingh Onnes, 1922, 454.

STANDARD SOURCES

Meyer and von Schweidler.

BECKMAN, RUTH WINIFRED (HOWARD) (1900–)
See Howard Beckman, Ruth Winifred.

BECKWITH, ANGIE MARIA (1881–1945?)
U.S. plant pathologist. Born 1881. Educated University of Michigan (A.B., 1904); University of Chicago (1904–1905). Professional experience: Biological Laboratory, Vassar College, assistant (1906–1908); U.S. Forest Service, xylotomist (wood specialist) (1908–1910); U.S. Department of Agriculture, scientific assistant, USDA Bureau of Plant Industry junior pathologist (1910–1940s). Honors and memberships: American Phytopathological Society, member. Probably died 1945.

Trained at the University of Michigan and the University of Chicago, Beckwith taught for two years in the biology laboratories at Vassar and then became one of the first women to join the U.S. Forest Service. Within two years she moved to the United States Department of Agriculture where she worked as a plant pathologist until the mid-1940s, studying rubus and grape fungi and the control of insect and plant parasites.   JH/MBO

PRIMARY SOURCES

Beckwith, Angie. "Life History of the Grape Root Rot Fungus *Roselaeria hypogaea.*" *USDA Journal of Agricultural Research* 27 (1924): 609–616.

STANDARD SOURCES

AMS 3–7; Bailey.

BECKWITH, CORA (1875–?)
U.S. zoologist. Born 24 March 1875 in Grand Rapids, Mich. Never married. Educated University of Michigan (B.S., 1900); Columbia University (A.M., 1908; Ph.D., 1914). Professional experience: Vassar College, assistant in biology (1900–1902), instructor (1902–1913), assistant professor (1914–1915), associate professor (1915–1928), professor (1928–1940), emeritus professor (1940–?). Honors and memberships: Society of Naturalists; Society of Zoologists. Death date unknown.

Cora Beckwith spent her entire professional career at Vassar College, where she moved from assistant through the ranks to professor. She did research on the lateral line organ in *Amia calva.* She also worked on the cytology of hydroid germ cells and lens removal in the eye of *Amblystoma.*   JH/MBO

STANDARD SOURCES

AMS 3–8; B 9.

BECKWITH, MARTHA WARREN (1871–1959)
U.S. folklorist and anthropologist. Honors and memberships: American Folklore Society, president (1932). Died 1959.

Martha Beckwith was professor of anthropology at Vassar, but spent most of her time in the field, in Hawaii and Jamaica, collecting folklore materials. She was president of the American Folklore Society in 1932. Her collections are still in print.   JH/MBO

PRIMARY SOURCES

Beckwith, Martha Warren. *Notes on Jamaican Ethnobotany.* Poughkeepsie, N.Y.: Vassar College, 1927.

———. *Jamaica Folk-Lore, with Music Recorded in the Field by Helen H. Roberts.* New York: The American Folk-Lore Society, G. E. Stechert and Co., 1928.

———. *Folklore in America, Its Scope and Method.* Poughkeepsie, N.Y.: Vassar College Folklore Foundation, 1931.

STANDARD SOURCES
Rossiter 1982.

BEECHER, CATHARINE ESTHER (1800–1878)

U.S. educator, home economist, and author. Born 8 September 1800 in East Hampton, Long Island, to Roxana Foote and Lyman Beecher. Eight siblings. Never married. Educated Miss Sarah Pierce's School in Litchfield, Conn., and later by independent study. Professional experience: New London, Conn., small private school, teacher; Hartford Female Seminary and the Western Female Institute, founder and teacher. Honors and memberships: organized American Woman's Educational Association. Died 12 May 1878 of "apoplexy" in Elmira, N.Y.

Catharine Esther Beecher was the eldest surviving child of a family well known for its work in various reform movements. Her Presbyterian minister father supported temperance and other moral reform movements, her sister was Harriet Beecher Stowe, author of *Uncle Tom's Cabin*, and her two brothers were prominent abolitionists Henry Ward Beecher and Edward Beecher. Her early education was at home, but when she was ten, her father enrolled her in a small private school in Litchfield, Conn., where she received a traditional education in subjects considered suitable for girls, including drawing, painting, and music. It was chiefly through independent study that she gained a knowledge of mathematics, Latin, and philosophy. She had learned much about domestic subjects from her gentle mother, who died when Catharine was sixteen years old. During the two years before her father remarried, she, as the oldest child, shared the duties of the household with her aunt.

After her fiancé, Yale professor Alexander Metcalf Fisher, died at sea four months after they had become engaged, Beecher fell into a deep depression and rejected the Calvinism of her father, maintaining that humans were not naturally depraved and could, through education, be made perfect. But to Lyman Beecher, Fisher's death meant that God had placed his daughter among the elect and was preparing her for a different vocation.

In 1823, Beecher and her sister Mary opened a girls' school in Hartford, where their brother Edward was master of a grammar school. Incorporated as the Hartford Female Seminary, the school did well and downplayed traditional forms of female education, adding innovations such as calisthenics to the curriculum. Beecher produced a fund-raising pamphlet in 1829 in which she proposed that schools for women be endowed, and that girls be trained in domestic science (she had learned at an early age the importance of a well-run household) and in methods of teaching. The frenetic activity into which she had thrown herself took its toll, and she suffered a kind of mental collapse in 1828. In 1831, she resigned her position and accompanied her father to Cincinnati, where he assumed the presidency of the Lane Theological Seminary.

In Cincinnati, Beecher opened another school, the Western Female Institute, but was still mentally unstable, although she continued to carry on with her school. The school collapsed in 1837, allowing Beecher freedom to pursue her other interests. Previously she had published numerous articles and several elementary textbooks. Surprisingly, given the interests of her family, she was not a strong supporter of abolitionism, opposing activities that throw women into the position of a combatant, because such a position was outside her appropriate sphere.

She gave numerous lectures throughout the country. One of her major projects was securing adequate education for women in the West. She was instrumental in the formation of "female colleges" in Burlington, Iowa, Quincy, Illinois, and Milwaukee, Wisconsin. While she was one of the early advocates of the opportunity for the higher education of women in this country, she was a vocal opponent of women's suffrage. On the suffrage question, she and her sister Harriet sided against their brother Henry Ward and their half-sister Isabella Beecher Hooker.

One of her most important accomplishments was the advocacy of domestic science in the schools. Her support helped to create a public opinion favorable to the introduction of home economics into the curriculum. SP

PRIMARY SOURCES
Beecher, Catharine. *Treatise on Domestic Economy for the Use of Young Ladies at Home and at School.* New York: Marsh, Capen, Lyon, and Webb, 1841.

———. *Miss Beecher's Domestic Receipt Book.* 3rd ed. New York: Harper, 1851.

———. *Physiology and Calisthenics for Schools and Families.* New York: Harper & Brothers, 1856.

———. *Calisthenic Exercises for Schools, Families and Health Establishments.* New York: Harper, 1860.

———. *The American Woman's Home.* New York: J. B. Ford and Co., 1869.

———. *Woman Suffrage and Woman's Profession.* Hartford, Conn.: Brown and Gross, 1871.

Catharine Beecher's letters are at the Schlesinger Library at Radcliffe College.

SECONDARY SOURCES

Biester, Charlotte Elizabeth. "Catharine Beecher and Her Contributions to Home Economics." Master's thesis, Colorado State College of Education, Division of Education, 1950.

Chambers, Carol. "Heavenly Influences: Catharine Beecher and the Moral Sphere of Nineteenth-Century Women." Master's thesis, Indiana University, 1984.

Harveson, Mae E. *Catharine Esther Beecher, Pioneer Educator.* Ph.D. diss. University of Pennsylvania, 1932. Includes a complete bibliography.

Lindley, Susan Hill. "Woman's Profession in the Life and Thought of Catharine Beecher: A Study of Religion and Reform." Ph.D. diss., Duke University, 1974.

Mahoney, Margaret Ward. "Catharine Beecher: Champion of Female Intellectual Potential in Nineteenth-Century America." Ph.D. diss., Drew University, 1993.

Sklar, Kathryn K. *Catharine Beecher: A Study in American Domesticity.* New Haven: Yale University Press, 1973.

STANDARD SOURCES
Bailey; *NAW;* Rossiter 1982.

BEERS, CATHERINE VIRGINIA (1892–1949)

U.S. zoologist. Born 3 June 1892 in Chicago, Ill. Educated Northwestern University (A.B., 1914; A.M., 1915); University of California (1918); Columbia University (1924–1925). Professional experience: Northwestern University, assistant in zoology (1912–1915); Illinois public high school, teacher (1915–1916); University of Southern California, assistant professor of zoology (1916–1942), associate professor (from 1942); Washington Square College, New York University, instructor (1924–1925); Hunter College, extension department, faculty member (1924–1925). Honors and memberships: the Genetic Association, the Genetics Society, the Eugenics Society, and the Western Society of Naturalists. Died 1949.

Zoologist Catherine Beers earned her master's degree at Northwestern University and did some additional graduate work at the University of California and Columbia University. However, she did not complete a doctorate. The lack of this degree probably accounts for the fact that she remained at the rank of assistant professor for twenty-six years before being promoted to associate professor. She spent summers doing research at the Puget Sound Biological Station (1912), the Marine Biological Laboratory, Woods Hole (1913; 1924) and Cold Spring Harbor (1914). JH/MBO

SECONDARY SOURCES
Records of the Genetics Society of America 18 (1949): 17. Obituary notice.

STANDARD SOURCES
AMS 5–7.

BEEVER, MARY (1802–1883)

British botanist. Born 1802 in Ardwick, Manchester. Professional experience: supplied plant specimens to various British botanists; corresponded with J. G. Baker and John Ruskin. Died 31 December 1883, Coniston, Lancashire.

Mary Beever sent specimens of *Gentiana pneumonathe* to W. Baxter in 1836, and also ferns to the botanists E. Newman and E. J. Lowe. She was a correspondent of J. G. Baker, who wrote *Flora of the English Lake District* (1885), and also corresponded with the famous art critic and botanist John Ruskin. He includes her letters in *Hortus Inclusus* (1887). Her sister, SUSAN BEEVER, was also an active amateur botanist.

She is commemorated in the species *Lastraea felix-mas* var. *Beevorii.* She died 31 December 1883, in Coniston, Lancashire. JH/MBO

PRIMARY SOURCES
Beever, Mary. Letters to John Ruskin. *Hortus Inclusus.* New York: Thomas Y. Crowell and Co., 1887.

SECONDARY SOURCES
Transactions Liverpool Botanical Society (1909): 60.

Baxter, W. *British Phaenogamous Botany.* 1834–1843. Beecher's contributions noted in tables 185–187. Oxford, 1834–1843.

Beever, John. *Practical Fly-Fishing.* Memoir of the author by W. G. Collingwood. New edition. London: Methuen, 1893.

Collingwood, W. G. *John Beever's Practical Fly Fishing.* 1893. Beever's work noted in preface.

STANDARD SOURCES
Desmond.

BEEVER, SUSAN (1805–1893)

British botanist. Born 27 November 1805 in Manchester. Sister of Mary Beever. Died 29 November 1893 in Coniston, Lancashire.

Susan Beever sent specimens of *Radiola linoides* to William Baxter. She was a correspondent of John Ruskin and her letters to him are included in his *Hortus Inclusus;* in the *Naturalist,* 1894: 290, and in the *Transactions of the Liverpool Botanical Society* 1909: 60. She died in Coniston, Lancashire, 29 November 1893, a month before her sister, MARY BEEVER. JH/MBO

PRIMARY SOURCES

Baxter, W. *British Phaenogamous Botany,* 1823–1843. Beever is mentioned on table, p. 188. Oxford, 1834–1843.

Beever, Susan. Letters to John Ruskin. In his *Hortus Inclusus,* 1887: 155–172.

SECONDARY SOURCES

Naturalist, 1894:290.

Transactions of the Liverpool Botanical Society, 1909:60.

STANDARD SOURCES

Desmond.

BEHN, APHRA (?) (ca. 1640–1689)

English writer and popularizer of science. Born Eaffrey Johnson(?), the daughter of a barber and wet nurse, Bartholomew Johnson and Elizabeth Denham. Baptism registered 14 December 1640 in St. Michael's Church, Harbledown (circumstances of birth and family uncertain). May have had one sister and one brother. Means of education unverifiable. Probable marriage to Behn (first name unknown), a Dutch merchant, in 1664 or 1665; apparently widowed in or before 1666. No known children. Professional experience: supported herself as a professional writer. Often honored as "the first" woman writer to earn her own living. Died April 1689, buried in the Cloisters of Westminster Abbey.

The basic facts of Aphra Behn's life are vague and contested. Autobiographical statements, biographical accounts published a few years after her death (1696–1698), and recent biographical scholarship do not agree on details. The early biographies indicate that she was born a gentlewoman in Canterbury, Kent, into the Johnson family, who were related to Lord Willoughby of Parham. Claims that her surname was Amis have been proven erroneous, but questions remain about her first name, which is variously given as Afra, Aphara, Ayfara, Ann, and Astrea. Astrea was almost certainly a "code" name that Behn used for herself, but Aphra may also be an adopted pen or stage name. Research by Maureen Duffy disputes the class status granted by the early biographies, suggesting that Behn may have entered life as Eaffrey Johnson, the daughter of a barber and a wet nurse. An alternative theory proposed by Sharon Valiant is that Behn was born to the illegitimate daughter of Lady Mary Sidney Wroth by William Herbert, third Earl of Pembroke (her cousin), and through this connection had ties to the Howard and Willoughby families as well as to the women writers the Countess of Pembroke and Lady Mary Wroth. If so, these connections may explain how and why she attained a level of literacy and learning far superior to the average early modern Englishwoman.

Behn's own accounts mention her father's appointment, through Lord Willoughby, as lieutenant-general of Surinam (although he did not survive the journey to take up his post). She recounts her experiences in Surinam with her mother, sister, and brother. She also describes her work as a royal spy reporting on Dutch naval operations in the Netherlands and alludes to her marriage. Mr. Behn may have died in the plague outbreak of 1666, been separated from his wife by his work, or been lost at sea. Widowed, without father's support or hope of dowry, and not compensated as she expected for her spy mission, upon her return to London at the end of 1666, Behn was threatened with debtors' prison. Whether she was actually imprisoned is not known for certain. As a young widow, by all accounts attractive and energetic, she sought to support herself (and probably her mother as well) by her wit and pen. Although long-established social attitudes generally allowed widows to seek employment, this was a bold and exceptional choice at a time when even most successful male writers were independently wealthy or heavily subsidized by patrons. For a woman, a career as a professional writer was without any close precedent. Allusions in her poems, plays, and novels offer further evidence of her persistent struggle against poverty, consistent support of Tory politics and the Stuarts, as well as substantial indications that she was born and raised a Catholic.

As a woman writer and outspoken Tory and Catholic, she had three strikes against her gaining acceptance in what had been the exclusively male world of English drama and what was still the male-dominated domain of educated letters. All three points were exploited by contemporaries who criticized her as a woman for writing "bawdy," political, social satire after the fashion of male dramatists and poets. Behn became expert at appealing to the tastes of a popular audience, who enjoyed farcical sex comedies featuring rakish heroes, sexual intrigue, and dialogue replete with innuendo. She was attacked as "whorish" both in regard to her personal behavior and for her expression of female sexuality in her plays and poems. She was dismissed as generally uneducated and ignorant of classical dramatic unities, and was accused of plagiarism and political slander. She defended herself deftly in prefaces, prologues, and epilogues. She criticized the double standard she was being held to as a female playwright, reminding her critics that her models for sexual content in drama and poetry were works by acclaimed male writers who felt free to adapt material from other plays and pointedly satirize the politics of the age. She decried the fact that as a woman she had been denied opportunities for a classical education, but that even so, the great Shakespeare himself had "little Latin and less Greek" and he managed to write critically acceptable plays. Throughout her career, Behn defended women's right to exercise their wit and offered sophisticated theories of translation and drama. In her writing, she explored such topics as love, lust, marriage, politics, morality, and science. She often provided a female perspective on these topics, exposing their effects upon women in society and at home.

Her relatively rapid rise and long run in the theater world have been variously explained. Some, casting aspersions on her talent as a writer, claim that she owed her success to a wealthy lover who supported her work or wrote it for her. Others suggest that she might have been an actress (women being allowed on stage after the Restoration) or worked as a dramatic adapter. This last seems most likely. Her first play was produced in 1670. During the next nineteen years, she wrote over two dozen plays, often adapting themes and ideas from other English plays, as well as French and Italian sources. She also wrote over one dozen novels and many poems and translations. Many of her plays were tremendously successful; some were performed hundreds of times during the seventeenth century, regularly well into the eighteenth, and still enjoy revival on twentieth-century stages.

Probably around 1682 Behn began to suffer from a type of dystrophic disease. Her weakened condition, along with fallout from the Popish Plot and coincidental drop in theater attendance, caused her to earn a comparatively meager living by contributing verses and lyrics to best-selling miscellanies and by producing prose fiction and translations. She had a working knowledge of French, some ability with Spanish and Italian, and may have also spoken Dutch. She probably did not know Latin and her "translations" from that language were most likely poetic paraphrases of rough English prose prepared by another translator (among them Lucretius's *De re natura* (1683) and Abraham Cowley's *Of Plants,* 1689). Even so, these works were complimented by such expert translators as John Dryden for their grace and aptness of expression. She continued to write poetry until a few weeks before her death.

Her most important works from the perspective of the history of science are the paraphrase translations mentioned above, the plays *Sir Patient Fancy* (1678) and *The Emperor of the Moon* (1687), the novel *Oroonoko* (1688), and her translation of Bernard le Bovier de Fontenelle's *Entretiens sur la pluralité de mondes* (1686), first entitled in English *The Discovery of New Worlds* (1688) and later, *A Theory of the System of Several New Inhabited Worlds*.

Behn's life and works have received much recent attention by literary and cultural critics who herald her as an apologist for female education, early abolitionist, and an intrepid social and political commentator who urged sexual and marital equality for women as well as tolerance for political and religious minorities. Her work as a scientific satirist and popularizer has just begun to attract serious scholarly appreciation. Behn's poetic paraphrases indicate a long interest in ancient atomist and materialist philosophy and contemporary natural history. Her literary treatments of scientific themes and discoveries served at once to popularize and critique contemporary natural philosophy.

In *Sir Patient Fancy,* Behn elaborates upon the theme of Moliere's *La malade imaginaire* with emphasis upon the central character's hypocritical godliness, constant intoxication by "medicinal" potions, and the social inequity of his marriage to his much younger wife, who, despite loving another man, was forced to marry him because of her financial situation. Fancy's selfish obsession with medicine and physical and spiritual disease leads him to neglect his proper social role and family duties. According to Behn's comic standard, the flaws in Fancy's character and behavior, teamed with the injustice of social mores, excuse his wife's liaisons with her true love. In associating lack of moderation with scientific or medical endeavors, Behn's reproach employs an already common stereotype of contemporary natural philosophers as mad doctors possessed by intellectual mania. She draws upon similar characterization again in her highly successful and entertaining *The Emperor of the Moon*.

In that play, Behn adapts popular astronomy from diverse sources such as Lucian, Francis Godwin, John Wilkins, Ben Jonson, and Samuel Butler, to satirize mechanical philosophy, hermeticism, enthusiasm, and the "lunatic" antics of a "learned" doctor who has lost all "perspective" in his lunar observations. Despite the aid of "his microscope, his horoscope, his telescopes, and all his scopes," he is blind to the realities of what would make his niece and daughter happy—freedom to choose their own marriage partners. Although Behn's characterization of their beaux indicates that they may not make the best husbands, she values her female characters' freedom to choose—and to make their own mistakes—above even ideal arranged marriages.

The main focus of the stage action is on the fantastic theatrical illusions the comic characters prepare for Doctor Baldiardo to "cure" him of his scientific delusions. The idea is to trick him into believing he is meeting the Emperor of the Moon and Prince of Thunderland for the purposes of blessing their marriages to his female wards and then, by shattering the fraud, shock him into seeing how far his own astronomical "visions" have carried him away. In some of the most elaborate staging then present in the English theater (rivaling that of royal masques and new French and Italian operas), Behn dazzles the duped doctor and the audience. She builds up to her trademark "discovery" scene with a living tapestry, glittering costumes, pageantry, orchestra music, choral interludes, troupes of dancers, and exciting stage machinery, including a twenty-foot perspective glass, chariots descending from the heavens (carrying Kepler and Galileo with their telescopes), large flying moons bearing the lunar bridegrooms, a huge display of the zodiac passing overhead, and a working model of the moon passing through its phases. With Kepler serving as an astronomical master of ceremonies, the lunar pageantry proceeds to the traditional happy ending—the wedding. As the layers of dramatic illusion are peeled away, the doctor sees the down-to-earth truth for the first time.

The play provides a popular critique of contemporary engagement with the novelty and excitement of science. Astronomy, in particular, could be both enlightening and richly entertaining, but proved a foolish diversion when carried to extremes. The most powerful telescopes do not guarantee useful perspective when the images they reveal are misinterpreted by their users. However much we may yearn for the existence of an ideal realm of extraterrestrial life, it is our job to learn to appreciate the mundane human world around us.

Behn's metaphoric association of the theater and science in *The Emperor of the Moon* may reflect her knowledge of Fontenelle's prominent use of the trope a year earlier. In *The Discovery of New Worlds,* she not only translates his "conversations" on the plurality of worlds, but adds her own commentary in the preface. Behn criticized Fontenelle's inconsistent characterization of the female lead, remarking that the marquise did not demonstrate the gradual acquisition of real learning but suddenly was able to grasp difficult astronomical concepts without prior preparation and could speak like "the greatest Philosophers in Europe." Behn hinted that had her health not been failing, instead of translating, she might have written an original work of popular astronomy that would have greatly differed from Fontenelle's treatment. She defends the Copernican system by restating Galileo's argument about the "two books" of revelation and nature, warning, however, that error creeps into the interpretations of both. Her translation was (and still is) preferred by many to that of Glanvil both for its accurate rendering of the technical material and true-to-life reproduction of courtly and flirtatious talk.

Behn's translation of Fontenelle contributed to the popularization of contemporary astronomy by providing an English version of the long-lived French original. In subtler ways, her best-known work, the novel *Oroonoko,* also participated in the popularization process by recounting details of the natural history of "exotic" lands and peoples within a narrative that recognizes the moral values of cultural "others." Drawing upon her own firsthand observation of native villages in Surinam (and perhaps enhancing her story with that of other travel accounts), Behn crafts an ironic narrative that reveals the savagery and ignorance of "civilized" man in comparison with the heroism of the enslaved title character, who values freedom and honor above his life.

Because literature has traditionally been undervalued in its importance to the history of science, Behn's work as a literary popularizer, scientific satirist, and translator have not received the attention they deserve. As a woman writer, Behn wrote successfully in all major genres except epic. The fact

that her literary output also included popular science attests to her commitment to educate a mass audience and female readers about the social and moral implications of science. Behn transcended conventional constraints of gender to participate and comment upon the predominately male endeavors of literature and science. By her example, she encouraged other women to do the same.   P G

PRIMARY SOURCES

Behn, Aphra. *The Works of Aphra Behn*. Ed. Montague Summers. New York: Phaeton Press, 1967. Incomplete; contains early biographical "memoir."

———. *The Complete Works of Aphra Behn*. 6 vols. Ed. Janet Todd. Columbus: Ohio State University Press, 1992+. Quickly establishing itself as the new standard edition.

———. *The Rover and Other Plays*. Ed. Jane Spencer. Oxford: Clarendon Press, 1995. Contains a carefully annotated edition of *The Emperor of the Moon.*

SECONDARY SOURCES

Duffy, Maureen. *The Passionate Shepherdess: Aphra Behn 1640–1689*. London: Jonathan Cape, 1977. Most reliable biography to date.

Goreau, Angeline. *Reconstructing Aphra: A Social Biography of Aphra Behn*. Oxford: Oxford University Press, 1980. Lively, politically charged account; good social context; interpretations occasionally unreliable.

Hutner, Heidi, ed. *Rereading Aphra Behn: History, Theory and Criticism*. Charlottesville and London: University Press of Virginia, 1993. Collection of exciting new scholarship on Behn's literature.

Jones, Jane, "New Light of the Background and Early Life of Aphra Behn." *Notes and Queries,* new series 37, no. 3 (September 1990): 288–293.

Link, Frederick. *Aphra Behn*. New York: Twayne, 1968. Still valuable discussion of Behn's literature, especially her plays and their performance history. Brief mention of translations.

Mendelson, Sara Heller. *The Mental World of Stuart Women*. Brighton: Harvester, 1987.

O'Donnell, Mary Ann. *Aphra Behn: An Annotated Bibliography of Primary and Secondary Sources*. New York and London: Garland, 1986. The standard bibliography, useful for secondary sources up to 1985.

———. "Tory Wit and Unconventional Woman: Aphra Behn," In *Women Writers of the Seventeenth Century,* ed. K. M. Wilson and F. J. Warnke, 341–354. Athens: University of Georgia Press, 1989. Good overview of current biographical scholarship.

Phillips, Patricia. "Science and the Ladies of Fashion." *New Scientist* (12 August 1982): 416–418. Discussion of Behn's translation of Fontenelle in relation to other contemporary women popularizers.

Turner, Margaret. "A Note on the Standard of English Translation from the French, 1685–1720." *Notes and Queries* new series 1 (December, 1954): 516–521.

STANDARD SOURCES
DNB; see also many standard dictionaries of literary biography.

BEHRE, ELLINOR H. (1886–post-1968)

U.S. biologist. Born 28 September 1886, Atlanta, Ga., to Emilie Schumann and Charles H. Behre. Educated Radcliffe College (A.B., 1908); Tulane University, postgraduate study; University of Chicago (Ph.D., 1918). Never married. Adopted two children. Professional experience: Private school, Atlanta, teacher (1908–1912); Newcomb College, New Orleans, faculty member (1912–1918?); Cold Spring Harbor for Experimental Evolution, staff (1919–1920); Louisiana State University, Baton Rouge, faculty member (1920–1957), emerita professor (1957–1968); Marine Laboratory, Gulf of Mexico, founder and director (1928–1946); Mount Holyoke College, visiting professor (1936–1937); Inter-American University, San German, Puerto Rico, visiting professor (1964–1965). Honors and memberships: American Association for the Advancement of Science, Fellow. Retired to North Carolina. Died sometime after 1968.

Ellinor Behre was that rare creature, a Southern-born woman scientist. She was born in Atlanta, Georgia, in 1886 but went to Radcliffe College where she received her bachelor's degree in 1906 in biology. She returned to Georgia to teach in a private school from 1908 to 1912. She then went to Tulane University in New Orleans where she began postgraduate studies in biology, while acting as an instructor in biology at Newcomb College, Tulane, from 1912 to 1915. She went next to the University of Chicago to work toward a doctorate in marine biology while working in the Department of Biology as an assistant in zoology from 1915 to 1918.

Once Behre had completed her dissertation, she started research at Cold Spring Harbor for Experimental Evolution in New York, then linked to the Carnegie Institution, where she remained on the staff for a little over a year. She then was offered a position on the faculty in Louisiana, at the State University in Baton Rouge, and remained there, rising through the ranks until she was made full professor in 1932.

Behre was interested in marine littoral fauna, particulary crustacea, fish, and snakes, as well as other shore-dwelling vertebrates and invertebrates. She founded a marine biological laboratory by the Gulf of Mexico, and directed it herself, from 1926 to her retirement.

Although based in Louisiana, Behre took opportunities to teach as visiting faculty, first at Mount Holyoke College in 1936 to 1937, and twice in Puerto Rico, at the College of Agriculture and later at the Inter-American University at San German after her retirement, in 1964 to 1965. After she retired from teaching, she left Louisiana and retired to North Carolina.   JH/MBO

STANDARD SOURCES
AMS 3–8, B 9, P&B 10–11; Debus; Yost.

BEILBY, WINIFRED
See Soddy, Winifred Moller (Bielby)

BELAEVA, ELIZAVETA IVANOVNA (1894–1983)

Soviet Geologist. Born 25 October 1894 in Petrograd. Higher education in Petrograd (doctorate?). Professional experience: Museum of the Mining Institute, Leningrad curatorial assistant (1919); Soviet Academy of Sciences osteological department of the Geological Museum, researcher (1921–1930); Soviet Academy of Sciences, Paleontological Institute, researcher (1930–?). Honors and memberships: the Moscow Naturalists' Society of the Quaternary Committee; the Paleogene Commission of the Interdepartmental Stratigraphic Committee; honorary member of the All-Union Paleontological Society, member of the (American) Society of Vertebrate Paleontology. Died 1983.

Elizaveta Belaeva was born and educated in Petrograd. Beginning as a curatorial assistant in the Museum of the Mining Institute in Leningrad, she moved to the osteological department of the Geological Museum of the Soviet Academy of Sciences. In 1930 she moved to the Paleontological Institute of the Academy. Sources on her do not mention when she retired.

Her area of research was fossil mammals of the Soviet Union and Mongolia. Her research was very broad, comprising Tertiary and Quaternary mammal faunae, systematics, morphology, phylogeny, and paleozoogeography. She worked with Proboscideans, Perissodactyls, and Artiodactyls, and published over eighty works. She also classified, cataloged, and housed the Paleontological Institute's fossil vertebrate collections. She was a member of many paleontological expeditions, going to Kazakhstan, Middle Asia, European U.S.S.R., and the Caucasus and Siberia.   CK

PRIMARY SOURCES
Belaeva, Elizaveta Ivanovna. "Materialy k kharakteristike verkhnetretichnoy fauny mlekopitayushchikh Severo-Zapadnoy Mongolii" (Materials for the Characterization of the Upper Tertiary Mammalian Fauna of Northwestern Mongolia). *Trudy Mongol'skoy Komissii* 33 (1937): 54.

———. "O nakhodke *Elephas* (*Archidiskodon*) *meridionalis* Nesti i *Mastodon borsoni* Hays v Chkalovskoy oblasti." (Concerning the Find of an *Elephas [Archidiskodon] meridionalis Nesti* and a *Mastodon borsoni Hays* in Chkalov Oblast.) *Biulleten' Komissii po Izucheniiu Chetvertichnogo Perioda* 12 (1948): 78–84.

———. "Novyye dannyye po aminodontam SSSR." (New Data on Amynodonts of the USSR.) *Trudy Paleontologicheskogo Instituta* 130 (1971): 39–60.

———. "K istorii tretichnykh muntzhaknov Azii." (To the History of Asiatic Tertiary Montiacinae.) *Fauna i biostratigrafiia mezozoiz i kaynozoia Mongolii. Trudy Sovmestnaia Sovetsko-Mongol'skaia Paleontologicheskaia Ekspeditsiia* 1 (1974): 80–86; 365–366.

SECONDARY SOURCES

Gekker, Roman Fedorovich, et al. "Elizaveta Ivanovna Belaeva (1894–1983)." *Paleontologicheskii Zhurnal* 4 (1983): 121–122.

Trofimov, B. A., and Reshetove, V. Ju. "Elizaveta Ivanovna Belajeva 1894–1983." *Society of Vertebrate Paleontology News Bulletin* no. 129 (1983). Obituary with portrait.

BELL, JULIA (1879–1979)

British geneticist. Born 1879 in Nottingham to Katherine Thomas (Heap) and James Bell. Educated Nottingham High School; Girton College, Cambridge (Mathematical Tripos, Part I, 1901), postgraduate fellow (1902–1907); Trinity College, Dublin (B.A., 1901; M.A., 1907); London School of Medicine for Women (1914–1920). Professional experience: Cambridge Observatory, assistant to A. R. Hinks; Galton Laboratories, University College, London, statistical assistant to Karl Pearson (1908–1914), medical researcher (1920–1933), research fellow (1933–1944), honorary research associate (1944–1965). Retired 1965. Honors and memberships: Galton Research Fellow, Medical Research Council (1926); Royal College of Surgeons, member; Royal College of Physicians, London, licentiate (1920), member (1926); Medical Research Council, member (1933–1944); Royal College of Physicians, Fellow (1938); Weldon prize for biometric science, Oxford (1941). Died 26 April 1979.

Julia Bell was born in Nottingham and attended Nottingham High School before going to Girton College, Cambridge. At Cambridge, she read mathematics and took the Mathematical Tripos exam (Part I) in 1901. Since at that time, women could not officially receive degrees from Oxford or Cambridge, she was awarded a master's degree from Dublin University for her work done with A. R. Hinks at the Cambridge Observatory on solar parallax.

After working at the observatory from 1902–1908, as a postgraduate, Bell went to London to use her mathematical and scientific skills as Karl Pearson's statistical assistant in the Galton Laboratories at University College, London. Here she remained for most of her life. At Pearson's suggestion, in order to strengthen the research the laboratory was doing on inherited diseases, Bell began to study for a medical degree, entering the London School of Medicine in 1914, receiving her license from and membership in the Royal College of Physicians in 1920.

In the work that made her famous, she applied statistical analysis to hereditary medical disorders, writing on inherited diseases of the nervous system, the eye, muscle, hands, and feet. These articles appeared from 1926 to 1951 in Pearson's *Treasury of Human Inheritance* and brought her the greater part of her fame. She also published an important study with J. B. S. Haldane on consanguinity and inherited disease in 1937.

Bell outlived three heads of the Galton Laboratories, Pearson, Penrose, and Fischer, but, in spite of her importance, she was never made head of the laboratory. She remained active, publishing studies well into her seventies and even one piece at the age of eighty on the effects of rubella in pregnancy. She was awarded Oxford University's Weldon medal and prize for her biometric research in 1941.

She actively suported the women's suffrage movement, although her major contribution to the women's movement was as a role model to many other young professional women through the excellence of her science. She died in London at the age of one hundred, 26 April 1979.   J M

PRIMARY SOURCES

Bell, Julia. With A. R. Hinks. *Solar Parallax.* Master's thesis. Dublin University.

———. "Anomalies and Diseases of the Eye." In *Treasury of Human Inheritance*, series ed. Karl Pearson. Vol. 2. 1922–1932. Also separately printed. Produced at University of London, Francis Galton Laboratory for National Eugenics. London, Dulan.

———. "Huntington's Chorea." In *Treasury of Human Inheritance*, vol. 4, pt. 1, 1934.

———. With E. Michael Carmichael. "Hereditary Ataxia and Spastic Paralysis." In *Treasury of Human Inheritance*, vol. 4, pt. 3, 1939. University of London, Francis Galton Laboratory for National Eugenics. London, Dulan.

———. "Pseudohypertrophic and Allied Types of Muscular Dystrophy." *Treasury of Human Inheritance*, vol. 4, pt. 4, 1943.

———. "Rubella in Pregnancy." *British Medical Journal* (1960).

SECONDARY SOURCES

"Julia Bell." *British Medical Journal* 1 (1979): 1239.

"Julia Bell." *Lancet* 1 (1979): 1152.

"Julia Bell." *Nature* 281 (1979): 163.

Beighton, Peter, and Beighton, Greta. *The Man Behind the Syndrome.* Berlin: Springer-Verlag, 1986.

Robson, Elizabeth B. and Gordon Wolstenholme, "Julia Bell." *Munks Roll 6* (1976–1983): 31–33. With portrait.

BELAR, MARIA (fl. 1926)
Hungarian physicist.

A member of the Austro-German circle that investigated properties of radioactivity, Belar investigated the effects of radiation from radioactive materials on the color of substances. She used spectrophotometric methods to produce quantitative results. No information is available on her life.　　M M

PRIMARY SOURCES

Belar, M. "Über Beeinflussung der Ionenbeweglichkeit in Luft Durch Dämpfe." *Akademie der Wissenschaften*, Vienna. *Sitzungsberichte* 2a, 130 (1921): 373–381.

———. "Spektrophotometrische durch Becauere Istrahlen." *Akademie der Wissenschaften*, Vienna 132 (1923):45–54; 261–277.

SECONDARY SOURCES

Hevesy, Georg von, and Fritz Paneth. *A Manual of Radioactivity*. Trans. Robert W. Lawson. London: Oxford University Press/Humphrey Milford, 1926.

STANDARD SOURCES

Meyer and von Schweidler.

BELOTA [JOHANNA BELOTA] (fl. 1320s)
French physician.

Johanna Belota, a Jewish physician of the mid-fourteenth century, was arrested in Paris for practicing medicine illegally and prohibited from further practice.　　J H / M B O

STANDARD SOURCES

Echols and Williams.

BELYEA, HELEN REYNOLDS (1913–1986)
Canadian geologist. Born 11 February 1913 in St. John, New Brunswick, to parents of French Huguenot origin. Educated St. John; Dalhousie University (B.A.; M.A.); Northwestern University (Ph.D.). Professional experience: Private high schools in Victoria and Toronto, teacher (1940?–1943); Women's Royal Canadian Naval Service, lieutenant (1943–1945); Geological Survey of Canada, sub-surface stratigrapher (1945–1971); officially retired (1971); research scientist emeritus (1971–1986). Honors and memberships: Royal Society of Canada, Fellow (1964); Canadian Society of Petroleum Geologists, honorary member; Canadian Institute of Mining and Metallurgy, Barlow Memorial Medal (1956); University of Windsor and Dalhousie Universities, honorary degrees; Officer of the Order of Canada (1976).

After a brief stint as a high school teacher and as a member of the Canadian women's navy during World War II, Helen Belyea used her Ph.D. in geology when she joined the Canadian Geological Survey in 1945. In 1947, oil was discovered in the Devonian rocks at Leduc, Alberta. Inspired by the discovery, the Geological Survey opened an office in Calgary in 1950. Helen Belyea was one of the first geologists at that office. From this beginning, the Institute of Sedimentary and Petroleum Geology was opened in 1967. Belyea developed into a field geologist of great ability. Since oil had been found in the Leduc Devonian, Belyea began work on other Devonian rocks. Her work involved two of the most important aspects of science, explaining and synthesizing. She spent much of her research life attempting to make sense of the western plains Devonian rocks. In her first two papers she won the respect of her colleagues. In the 1950s she became involved in establishing a stratigraphic framework of an area west of the Hay River and south of the Mackenzie. Her work in this area was recognized when she was asked to contribute to the volume on the "Geological History of Western Canada," known as "The Atlas." Because of the oil boom, she was sent to Calgary with R. T. D. Wickenden to open an office. This soon led to the establishment of the Institute of Sedimentary and Petroleum Geology in 1967, the same year that the First International Devonian Symposium, sponsored by the Alberta Society of Petroleum Geologists, met in Calgary. Belyea wrote over thirty scientific papers.

Belyea had many other interests in addition to geology. A good athlete, she enjoyed skiing, walking, mountain climbing, and horseback riding. Although she was not always tolerant of those whom she considered misguided, she had a wide circle of friends both inside and outside of the geological community. She loved to travel, particularly in France, and was interested in art and music. She claimed never to have been discriminated against because of her gender from the time that she was the only girl in a geology class at Dalhousie University through her years at the Geological Survey, the second woman to join this service.　　C K

PRIMARY SOURCES

Belyea, Helen. "The Geology of the Musquash Area, New Brunswick." Ph.D. diss., Northwestern University, 1939.

———. "Notes on the Devonian System of the North Central Plains of Alberta." Geological Survey of Canada vol. 52-27. Ottawa: Department of Mines and Technical Surveys, 1952. Her first paper. Dealt with the difficult problem of understanding the facies relations in the upper Devonian and the meaning of the reef-off-reef sequences.

———. "Cross-Sections through the Devonian System of the Alberta Plains." Geological Survey of Canada vol. 55-3. Ottawa: Department of Mines and Technical Surveys, 1955.

Outlined the southern margin of the reef complexes and sought an answer to the problems of relationships in the upper part of the succession.

———. With B. S. Norford. "The Devonian Cedared and Harrogate Formates in the Beaverfoot, Brisco, and Stanford Ranges, Southeast British Columbia." *Bulletin of the Geological Survey of Canada* 1962: 82 pp.

———. "Middle Devonian Tectonic History of the Tathlina Uplift, Southern District of Mackenzie and Northern Alberta, Canada." Geological Survey of Canada vol. 70-14. Ottawa: Department of Energy, Mines, and Resources, 1971.

SECONDARY SOURCES

Fleming, Iris. "Rocks are Her Forte." *Geosciences* (Fall 1975): 12–14.

McLaren, Digby J. "Helen Belyea, 1913–1986." *Transactions of the Royal Society of Canada* ser. 5, vol. 2 (1987): 198–201.

BENDER, HEDWIG (fl. 1914)

Educated University of Breslau (Ph.D., 1913).

Bender did research on spectroscopy. In her inaugural dissertation, Bender showed the flicker spectrometer was a reliable instrument for comparing brightness in different spectral sources, and thus was potentially useful for determining temperatures of light sources in optical pyrometry. Bender measured the visual sensitivity of normal and color-blind subjects (which she found to be a maximum in the green region) under different conditions.   JH/MBO

PRIMARY SOURCES

Bender, Hedwig. "Untersuchen am Lummer—Pringsheimschen Spectralflickerphotometer," *Annalen der Physik* 45 (1914): 105–132.

SECONDARY SOURCES

Kohn, Hedwig. "Photometrie." In *Müller-Pouillet's Lehrbuch der Physik*, 11th ed., vol. 2, 1104–1320. Brunswick: Friedrick Vieweg & Son, 1929.

BENDER, LAURETTA (1897–1987)

U.S. child psychiatrist. Born 9 August 1897 in Butte, Mont., to Katherine (Irvine) and John Oscar Bender. Three siblings. Married (1) Paul F. Schilder (1936; he died ca. 1942); (2) Henry Parks. Three children. Educated Leland Stanford University; University of Chicago (B.S., 1922; M.A. in pathology, 1923); University of Iowa Medical School (M.D., 1926). University of Amsterdam (1926–1927); Albert Merritt Billings Hospital, University of Chicago, internship and residency, neurology; Boston Psychopathic Hospital, residency, psychiatry (1928–1929). Professional experience: University of Chicago, research associate (1920–1923); University of Iowa, assistant instructor (1923–1926); Johns Hopkins University, Phipps Psychiatric Clinic, resident research associate (1929–1930); Bellevue Hospital, senior psychiatrist, children's service, (1930–1956); New York University College of Medicine, professor (1941–1958). State Department of Mental Hygiene, New York, principal resident scientist in child psychiatry, (1956–1960); Creedmoor State Hospital, director of Psychiatric research, children's unit (1960–1969); College of Physicians and Surgeons, Columbia University, professor of clinical psychiatry (1959–1962); attending psychiatrist (1969–1974); University of Maryland School of Medicine, clinical professor of psychiatry (from 1975). Honors and memberships: American Psychopathological Association, president (1961–1962); Society of Biological Psychiatry, president (1951–1962); Schilder Society, president (1942–1944); American Medical Association, Fellow; American Neurological Association, American Psychiatric Association, American Orthopsychiatric Association, member.

Lauretta Bender was one of the most prominent women psychiatrists of the mid-twentieth century. Her Visual Motor Gestalt Test, which provides a device for screening neurological impairment through psychological deficits, is considered a major contribution to the field of psychology. Equally important are her contributions to the diagnosis, treatment, and understanding of brain-injured persons and her studies on childhood schizophrenia; she became the world authority on these subjects. She was a leading authority in several different areas of medicine and psychology: pathology, neuropathology, pediatric neurology, child psychiatry, developmental psychology, and Gestalt psychology.

Born in Butte, Montana, 9 August 1897, the only girl and youngest of four children of John Oscar and Katherine (Irvine) Bender, Lauretta repeated first grade three times and was considered mentally retarded due to her *strephosymbolia* or tendency to reverse letters in reading and writing—a common problem especially in left-handed children. In spite of this and frequent family moves, Bender worked her way to the top of her classes. She became interested in biological research early and her first publications as an undergraduate were on "hemotological studies on experimental tuberculosis of the guinea pig" at University of Chicago. The year Bender received her M.D. at the University of Iowa (1926) she published four papers (dealing with experimentally-induced cancerous tumors and central nervous system lesions in laboratory animals), a productivity she kept up throughout her working life, leading to over 275 contributions to scientific literature.

Bender was awarded a Laura Spelman Rockefeller traveling fellowship, which she used to study neuropathology, physiology and anatomy at the University of Amsterdam. Her research there, on cerebellar control of the vocal organs, was published by the Royal Academy of Science of Amsterdam. Following residencies in neurology and psychiatry, she accepted an appointment at the Henry Phipps Psychiatric Clinic, Johns Hopkins Hospital, to do research on schizophrenia under Adolf Meyer.

In 1930, while at Johns Hopkins, she fell in love with Paul Schilder, a renowned psychoanalyst and neurologist from Vienna. They shared many personal characteristics and interests and worked together completing a study on pain reactions among schizophrenics before both taking positions at Bellevue Hospital, New York City. Schilder was married at this time but soon divorced and he and Lauretta were married 27 November 1936. Despite a full schedule of research and collaboration at Bellevue, the couple had two sons and a daughter born within the first four years of their marriage. Bender also published papers on a wide range of subjects, and began to develop the Bender Visual Motor Gestalt Test.

Paul Schilder was tragically killed by a car as he was leaving the hospital where he had been visiting Lauretta and their new daughter, Jane. This loss led Bender to an even greater immersion in her work. She published several of Schilder's works, served as president of the New York Society for Psychopathology and Psychotherapy (renamed the Schilder Society) and went into psychoanalysis. Besides remaining senior psychiatrist at Bellevue, she taught clinical psychiatry at New York University from 1941 to 1958 and then was professor of Clinical Psychiatry at the College of Physicians and Surgeons, Columbia University, from 1959 to 1962. She served as consultant to the Veteran's Administration, Irvington House, and the New Jersey State Neuropsychiatric Institute.

She was editor of *Nervous Child* and editorial advisor to *Action Comics* (after publishing "The Psychology of Children's Reading and the Comics" in 1945). She served as principal resident scientist in child psychiatry, State Department of Mental Hygiene, New York (1956–1960). In 1975, she took a position as professor of Psychiatry at the University of Maryland, which she held until her retirement.

For over forty years Lauretta Bender worked with patients and designed and conducted studies to improve diagnosis, treatment techniques, and determination of causes for psychological and neuropathological conditions. She died in Maryland in 1987. KM

PRIMARY SOURCES

Bender, Lauretta. *A Visual Motor Gestalt Test and Its Clinical Use.* New York: The American Orthopsychiatric Association, 1938.

———. *Child Psychiatric Techniques: Diagnostic and Therapeutic Approach to Normal and Abnormal Development through Pat-*

terned, Expressive and Group Behavior. Springfield, Ill.: Thomas, 1952.

———. *Aggression, Hostility, and Anxiety in Children.* Springfield, Ill.: Thomas, 1953.

———. *A Dynamic Psychopathology of Childhood.* Springfield, Ill.: Thomas, 1954.

———. *Psychopathology of Children with Organic Brain Disorders.* Springfield, Ill.: Thomas, 1955.

SECONDARY SOURCES

Knapp, Sally. *Women Doctors Today.* New York: Crowell, 1947.

STANDARD SOURCES

AMS 8, B 9, P&B 10–12; Stevens and Gardner; Zusne.

BENDER, WILMA (fl. 1915)

German chemist/physicist. Educated Heidelberg University (Ph.D., 1915). Professional experience: Heidelberg University, chemical laboratory, research.

Wilma Bender did her dissertation at Heidelberg University on radioactive chlorides. Working at Heidelberg University's Chemical Laboratory, Bender and E. Ebler developed a new method for extracting radium from minerals using adsorption, which simplified the process. They suggested that this method could be used to separate other rare elements. Bender performed some of this research at the Society for Electro-Osmosis Laboratory in Frankfurt (am Main). MM

PRIMARY SOURCES

Bender, Wilma. *Neue Methode zur Gewinnung der Radium Chlorids aus Uranerzen.* Leipzig: Spanen, 1915. Heidelberg Ph.D. dissertation, 1915.

———. With E. Ebler. "Purification and Enriching of Crude Radium Barium Chlorides." *Berichte des Deutschen chemischen Gesellschaft* 46 (1913): 1571–1573.

———. With E. Ebler. "Neue Methoden zur Gewinnung des Radiums aus Uranerzen." *Zeitschrift für angewandte Chemie* 28 (1915): 25–40, 41–48.

SECONDARY SOURCES

Henrich, Ferdinard. *Chemie und chemische Technologie radioaktiver Stoffe.* Berlin: Julius Springer, 1918.

STANDARD SOURCES

Meyer and von Schweidler.

BENEDEK, THERESE F. (1892–1977)

Hungarian/U.S. psychologist and psychoanalyst. Born 8 November 1892 in Eger, Hungary. Married (1919). Two children. Educated

Budapest (M.D., 1916); Budapest City General Hospital, intern (1916–1917); Epidemic Hospital, resident (1917–1918). Professional experience: University of Hungary, clinical pediatrics, instructor (1918–1919); Leipzig Clinic, assistant psychiatrist (1920–1925); Institute of Psychoanalysis, Chicago, staff member (1936–1968). Died 1977.

Although Therese Benedek received her education in her native Hungary, she moved to the United States in 1936, where she practiced psychiatry at the Institute of Psychoanalysis in Chicago. She was a member of both the American Psychiatric Association and the Psychoanalytic Association.   KM

PRIMARY SOURCES
Benedek, Therese. *Insight and Personality Adjustment.* New York: Ronald Press Co., 1946.
———. *Psychosexual Function in Women.* New York: Ronald Press Co., 1952.
———. With Joan Fleming. *Psychoanalytic Supervision: A Method of Clinical Teaching.* New York: Grune and Stratton, 1966.
———. With E. James Anthony. *Parenthood: Its Psychology and Psychopathology.* Boston: Little, Brown, 1970.

SECONDARY SOURCES
Quack, Sibylle, ed. *Between Sorrow and Strength: Women Refugees of the Nazi Period.* German Historical Institute and Cambridge University Press, 1995, p. 263.

STANDARD SOURCES
AMS 8, S&B 9–11; Stevens and Gardner.

BENEDICT, RUTH (FULTON) (1887–1948)

U.S. anthropologist. Born 5 June 1887 in New York City to Beatrice (Shattuck) and Frederick Fulton. Married Stanley Rossiter Benedict (1914). Divorced (1930?). Educated St. Margaret's Academy, Buffalo, N.Y.; Vassar College (A.B., 1909); Columbia University (Ph.D., 1923). Professional experience: Columbia University, Office of War Information (WWII); Columbia University, professor of anthropology. Died 17 September 1948 in New York City.

Ruth Benedict was born in New York City to Beatrice (Shattuck) and Frederick Fulton. Her parents then moved to Buffalo where she attended St. Mary's Academy. She attended Vassar College (1904–1909) and in 1914 married Stanley Rossiter Benedict, whom she would divorce in 1930. Moving to New York, she began to study anthropology at Columbia with ELSIE CLEWS PARSONS, Franz Boas, and Edward Sapir. Benedict received her Ph.D. in 1923 from Columbia with a thesis on North American Indian vision

quests after spending some time in the field with the Serrano Indians (1922). Fired by Elsie Parsons's interest in the American Indian pueblos of the Southwest, she spent her summers in field work with the Zuni (1924–1925, 1935), the Cochiti (1925, 1931), and the Pima (1926). She also served as editor of the *American Journal of Folklore* (1925–1939) and taught with Franz Boas at Barnard College and Columbia University.

In Benedict's analysis, the calm personalities of Pueblo people, whom she saw as Apollonian, were contrasted with other Native American peoples whom she described as Dionysian, adopting Nietzsche's terminology. This approach, identifying various aspects of culture and personality according to a characteristic pattern in different societies, emerged about 1928 and culminated with her book *Patterns of Culture* (1934). This book came to define a new "configurational" style in anthropology.

Benedict formed close friendships, first with Edward Sapir then with MARGARET MEAD, who considered herself preeminently Benedict's student, becoming her colleague and later her close friend and biographer.

Other important work by Benedict included her reexamination of the definition of race at the outbreak of World War II, *Race: Science and Politics* (1940), a classic study often referred to in the postwar period. Her study of Japanese culture "at a distance," during World War II resulted in her book *The Chrysanthemum and the Sword* (1946), and set a model for the study of societies that could not be investigated directly for political or other reasons. She had an enormous impact on the anthropologists of her own and the next generation, but fell out of favor for a period in the 1960s and 1970s, although her writings remained well known. Her work became of interest to anthropologists again in the 1980s.   JH

PRIMARY SOURCES
Benedict, Ruth. *Patterns of Culture.* Boston: Houghton Mifflin Company, 1934.
———. *Zuni Mythology,* 2 vols. New York: Columbia University Press, 1935.
———. *Race: Science and Politics.* New York: Modern Age Books, 1940.
———. *The Chrysanthemum and the Sword.* Boston: Houghton Mifflin Co., 1946.

SECONDARY SOURCES
Mead, Margaret. *An Anthropologist at Work: The Writings of Ruth Benedict.* Boston: Houghton Mifflin, 1959.
———. *International Encyclopedia of the Social Sciences,* vol. 2, 48–52.

STANDARD SOURCES
AMS 4–7; Gacs; *NAW.*

BENETT, ETHELDRED (1776–1845)

British geologist. Born 1776 at Tisbury. Father Thomas Benett. At least one brother, John Benett. Never married. Died Norton House, Norton Bavant, on 11 January 1845.

Etheldred Benett's father, Thomas Benett (d. 1797), was a Wiltshire squire of Pyt House, an interesting geological area with exposures ranging from the Upper Jurassic Kimmeridge Clay to the higher Cretaceous strata. Benett's interest in fossils was piqued by these physical surroundings.

Although concrete early evidence of Benett's geological interests is unavailable, we know from a letter she had written to James Sowerby (1810) that she had collected a cabinet of fossils. This cabinet was reported to have been very extensive by 1813, and she soon had her fossils illustrated in Sowerby's *Mineral Conchology*. Since Benett never married, she had the freedom to devote her energies to fossil collecting. Financially independent, she employed collectors and quarrymen. She died on 11 January 1845 at Norton House and was buried at Boynton Church.

Benett was a contemporary of William Smith, one of the founders of stratigraphical geology, and was influenced by his careful work. As she logged quarry sections and collected stratigraphically controlled series of fossils for members of the Geological Survey, she was scrupulous about supplying documentation for all of her specimens. Hugh Torrens reports that she provided a bed-by-bed description of her finds. She meticulously indicated cases in which she lacked sufficient information to locate the fossils accurately. On 21 March 1815 she supplied a note to the Geological Society of London reporting on the many fossils of fish scales, ammonites, and various other organic remains found in the Chicksgrove Quarry in Tisdale. James Sowerby used her data without permission in his *Mineral Conchology of Great Britain* (1816, 2:57–59) to draw what she thought were erroneous conclusions. She claimed that she had not been able to locate the fossils in their proper position in the beds. Her persistence eventually allowed her to place the fossils in their proper location.

Although she had planned to publish a catalog of her collection around 1818, it was not published until 1831. The catalog was well received at the time and contained a number of new taxa. Benett corresponded with and loaned specimens to many of the important geologists of the time, including William Smith, William Buckland, Charles Koening, Gideon Mantell, John S. Miller, James Parkinson, and Samuel Woodward. Lindley and Hutton, Richard Owen, and J. de C. Sowerby named new taxa based on these specimens. Benett's collection of fossils has been relocated to the Academy of Natural Sciences of Philadelphia.

After Benett's death, the collection was dispersed and the location of the central part was unknown. It seems that it was purchased by a patron of the academy between 1845 and 1847 and was ignored and eventually forgotten until it was rediscovered in 1980. It contains most of Benett's type specimens. A paper in the *Proceedings of the Academy of Natural Sciences* by Spamer, Bogan, and Torrens documents the history of the collection, and provides a catalog as well as plates of the specimens.

MBO

PRIMARY SOURCES

Benett, Etheldred. "A Slight Sketch of the Geology of South Wilts." In *Modern History of South Wiltshire*, ed. Richard Colt Hoare. vol. 3, *Hundred of Warminster*, London, 1831. 117–127. This catalog was a stratigraphic catalog of the species in her collection of local fossils.

———. *Catalogue of Organic Remains of the County of Wiltshire*. Warminster: J. L. Vardy, 1831. Private reissue with some revisions of the first catalog. Included eighteen new lithographic plates.

SECONDARY SOURCES

Kasper, Betty. "The First Lady Geologist." *Earth Science* vol. 27, no. 1 (1974): 35.

Spamer, Earle E., Arthur E. Bogan, and Hugh S. Torrens. "Recovery of the Etheldred Benett Collection of Fossils Mostly from Jurassic-Cretaceous Strata of Wiltshire, England, Analysis of the Taxonomic Nomenclature of Benett (1831), and Notes and Figures of Type Specimens Contained in the Collection." *Proceedings of the Academy of Natural Sciences of Philadelphia* 141 (1989): 115–180.

Torrens, Hugh. "Women in Geology. 2: Etheldred Benett." *Open Earth* 21 (1985): 12–13.

BENGSTON, IDA ALBERTINA (1881–1953)

U.S. bacteriologist. Born 17 January 1881 in Harvard, Nebr. Educated University of Nebraska (A.B., 1903); University of Chicago (M.S., 1913; University Scholar, 1913–1915; Ph.D., 1919). Professional experience: Department of Health, Chicago, bacteriologist (1915–1916); U.S. Public Health Serivice, from assistant bacteriologist to senior bacteriologist (1916–1946). Honors and memberships: Society of American Bacteriologists, Society for Experimental Biology and Medicine, Washington Academy of Sciences, and Sigma Xi. Fellow, American Association for the Advancement of Science. Honors: elected president, Washington branch of the Society of American Bacteriologists (1943); awarded Typhus Medal, American Typhus Commission. Died 6 September 1952.

Born of Swedish immigrant parents, Bengston attended the University of Nebraska where she majored in languages and mathematics and was elected Phi Beta Kappa. After graduation, she went to Washington, D.C., to be a cataloger in the library of the U.S. Geological Survey. After talking with a friend, she decided that it would be more interesting to be a scientist than a cataloger of scientific works. In response to this decision she resigned her position at the survey and entered the University of Chicago, where she majored in bacteriology and minored in chemistry and physiology. She earned her master's degree in 1913, held a university scholarship for two years, and received her doctorate in 1919.

After she earned her degree she went to work for the United States Public Health Service (now National Institutes of Health) as its first woman scientist. Although her salary seemed very low ($1,800 a year), her colleagues were amazed that she, as a woman, obtained such a lucrative position. She received regular promotions and eventually became a senior bacteriologist.

Bengston was the author of many papers, many of which were published in Public Health Reports or in bulletins of the Hygienic Laboratory. Her research was basically on three topics, anaerobes and their toxins, trachoma, and rikettsial disease. While she was working on anaerobic bacteria, she identified a new variety of *Clostridium*. The toxin from this organism was responsible for causing a paralytic disease (limberneck) in chickens. In 1924 she went to Rolla, Missouri, where she studied the etiology of trachoma in the United States Public Health Service Trachoma Hospital for seven years. They did not solve the problem, but suspected that the causal agent might be a rickettsia. In 1937, she became a part of a unit that studied the rickettsial disease, Rocky Mountain spotted fever, and endemic and epidemic typhus. They later added "Q" fever and Tsutsugamushi disease to the study. Her work on rikettsial infections represented her greatest accomplishments. She used the newly discovered ways to grow the rickettsia *in vitro* and was able to adapt it to a number of situations.

Bengston was a member of numerous scientific organizations, including the Society of American Bacteriologists, the Society for Experimental Biology and Medicine, the Washington Academy of Sciences, and Sigma Xi. She was a Fellow of the American Association for the Advancement of Science. In 1943–1944, she was president of the Washington branch of the Society of American Bacteriologists. In 1947, she was awarded the Typhus Medal of the American Typhus Commission.

For recreation, she would escape to her 370-acre farm with its large colonial house in the foothills of the Blue Ridge Mountains of Virginia. She was also interested in historic homes. A gentle, reserved person, she was known for her sense of humor.   JH/MBO

SECONDARY SOURCES
Evans, Alice. "Obituary: Ida Albertina Bengston." *Journal of the Washington Academy of Sciences* 43 (1953): 238–240.

Williams, Ralph Chester. *U.S. Public Health Service.* Washington, D.C.: Commissioned Officers Association of the U.S. Public Health Service, 1951, pp. 244–245.

STANDARD SOURCES
AMS 4–8.

BENNETT, ALICE (1851–1925)

U.S. physician. Born 31 January 1851 in Wrentham, Mass., to Isaac Francis Bennett and Lydia Hayden Bennett. Five siblings. Never married. Educated Day's Academy, Wrentham; Woman's Medical College of Pennsylvania, Philadelphia (M.D., 1876); University of Pennsylvania (Ph.D., 1880). Professional experience: Woman's Medical College, demonstrator of anatomy (1876); Pennsylvania State Hospital for the Insane, Department for Women, medical superintendent (1880–1896); private practice; New York Infirmary for Women and Children, physician (1910–1925). Died 1925 at the New York Infirmary, of angina pectoris.

Alice Bennett, the youngest of six children, was educated in her hometown, Wrentham, Massachusetts, and taught in local district schools for four years after her graduation. In 1872 she entered the Woman's Medical College of Pennsylvania in Philadelphia. She worked briefly in a dispensary in the Philadelphia slums, after which she was appointed demonstrator of anatomy in the Woman's Medical College (1876). She continued with her anatomical studies and received a Ph.D. degree in anatomy from the University of Pennsylvania in 1880 (the first given a woman). With the help of Hiram Corson, a physician who supported women in medicine, Bennett was appointed medical superintendent of the Department for Women at the Pennsylvania State Hospital for the Insane at Norristown (1880–1896). She became an advocate of more humane treatment for patients—undertaking to abolish physical restraint and to introduce occupational therapy (handicrafts, music, and art). Her innovations in the care of the insane were adopted by other institutions, and she won widespread professional recognition through her results and the numerous articles and papers on the nature and characteristics of mental illness that she wrote.

After leaving the state hospital (probably for health reasons), she maintained a private practice back in Wrentham until 1910, when she began working in Emily Blackwell's New York Infirmary for Women and Children. She served voluntarily as head of the outpatient department of obstetrics for fifteen years. Bennett never married. She died in 1925 of angina pectoris at the New York Infirmary and was buried in Wrentham.   JH/MBO

STANDARD SOURCES
Lovejoy; *NAW* (article by Stanley I. Kutler).

BENNETT, DOROTHEA (1929–1990)

U.S. immunogeneticist. Born 27 December 1929 in Honolulu to Anna (Schorling) and James William Bennett. Educated Barnard College (A.B., 1951); Columbia University (Ph.D., 1956). Professional experience: Columbia University, Department of Zoology, research associate (1956–1962); Cornell University Medical College, faculty (from 1962), associate professor of anatomy (from 1965). Honors and memberships: American Society for Human Genetics, American Society of Naturalists, American Society of Zoologists, Genetics Society of America, American Society for the Study of Development and Growth, member. Died 1990.

Dorothea Bennett was a geneticist who earned her doctorate from Columbia University. After six years as a research associate, she went to the Cornell Medical College, where she remained on the faculty until her death. Her research and publications were on effects of mutant genes on development and growth of the mammalian embryo. JH/MBO

SECONDARY SOURCES
"In Memoriam: Dorothea Bennett, 1929–1990." *Immunogenetics* 33 (1991): 1.
Mammalian Genome 1 (1991): 68–70. Obituary notice.

STANDARD SOURCES
Debus.

BENSON, MARGARET JANE (1859–1936)

British paleobotanist. Born 20 June 1859 in London to Edmunda Bourne and William Benson. Eight siblings. Never married. Educated privately; Newnham College, Cambridge (1878–1879); University College, London (B.Sc., 1881; Research Fellowship (1892–1893; D.Sc., 1894). Professional experience: assistant mistress, Exeter High School (1879–1887); Department of Botany, Royal Hollaway College, head (1893–1912), professor (1912–1922). Linnean Society, Fellow (1904). Died 20 June 1936 in Hertford.

Margaret Jane Benson was the daughter of an architect and civil engineer who was interested in botany and introduced all of his children to field botany. Her mother was a painter whose works were exhibited at the Royal Academy of Art. She was first educated at home by her sister who had studied at Queen's College and then attended Newnham where she studied classics. After passing the Cambridge Higher Local Examinations she went as assistant mistress to Exeter High School until she had saved enough money to enter University College, London (1887). She earned her bachelor's degree in 1891 and was awarded a research fellowship at Newnham. She worked on the embryology of the *Amentiferae*, which earned her a doctorate from the University of

London. The result of this study was her first paper, which was communicated to the Linnaean Society in 1893. She collaborated with D. H. Scott and F. W. Oliver in paleobotanical research. She continued to study the embryology of *Amentiferae*. Her articles appear in *Annals of Botany* and *New Phytologist*.

In October 1893 Benson was appointed head of the newly founded Department of Botany at the Royal Holloway College. The department prospered under her leadership and in 1912 conferred upon her the title of University Professor of Botany. She held this chair until she resigned. At Royal Holloway College she began to work with ETHEL SARGANT and traveled with her through Europe to gather information and equipment to establish the botanical laboratory. In order to do this, she was granted a leave of absence during the Michaelmas term of 1897 to visit the professors of botany at Brussels, Heidelberg, Tübingen, Basle, Strasbourg, and Paris. Benson continued traveling throughout the world to collect specimens. In 1905 she made a world tour, and in her later years, she made two journeys to the Antipodes and brought back quantities of valuable specimens. In 1927 a botanical laboratory was established in her honor at Royal Holloway College. Many of her students attended the dedication, including Dame HELEN GWYNNE-VAUGHAN and Nesta Ferguson. JH/MBO

PRIMARY SOURCES
Benson, Margaret. "Contributions to the Embryology of the Amentiferae." *Transactions of the Linnaean Society of London: Botany*. Part I, ser. 2, vol. 3, 1893; Part II, ser. 2, vol. 7, 1905.
———. "The Sporangiophore; a Unit of Structure in the Pteridophyta." *New Phytologist* 7 (1908): 143–149.
———. "*Sphaerostoma ovale*, a Lower Carboniferous ovule from Pettycur, Fifeshire, Scotland." *Transactions of the Royal Society of Edinburgh* 50 (1914): 1–15.
———. "*Heterotheca grievii*, the microsporange of *Heterangium Grievii*." *Botanical Gazette* 74 (1922): 121–142.
———. "The Roots and Habits of *Heterangium Grievii*." *Annals of Botany* 186 (1933): 313–316.
Herbarium and fossil slides are at Royal Holloway College, as is Benson's portrait.

SECONDARY SOURCES
"Benson, Margaret Jane." *Nature* 138 (1936): 17. Obituary notice.
"Benson, Margaret Jane." *Chronica Botanica* 1937: 159–160. Obituary notice.
B., M. E. "Margaret Jane Benson." *Newnham College Roll Letter*. Cambridge, England: Printed for Private Circulation, 1937.
Blackwell, E. M. "Benson, Margaret Jane." *Proceedings Linnean Society* 1937: 186–189.

STANDARD SOURCES
Desmond; *WWW*, vol. 3, 1929–1940.

BENTHAM, ETHEL (d. 1931).

British/Irish physician. Born in England. Educated Alexandra School and College, Dublin; London School of Medicine for Women; hospitals in Brussels and Paris, practical work. Professional experience: Newcastle-upon-Tyne and Gateshead, medical practice (to 1909); London, North Kensington, medical practice; Margaret O. MacDonald Memorial Clinic for Children under School Age, North Kensington, principal supporter and organizer. Honors and memberships: Executive of the National Union of Women's Suffrage Societies; Fabian Society (from 1907); Fabian Women's Group, lecturer at summer schools (from 1908); Independent Labour Party; Women's Labour League; Kensington Borough Council (1912–1925); Labour Party Executive (1917); Standing Joint Committee of Industrial Women's Organizations; Labour Party Candidate for East Islington (1929); Executive of the Labour Party (1929). Died 1931.

Although Ethel Bentham was born in England, she grew up in Ireland. She studied medicine at the London School of Medicine for Women, then opened up a private practice in Newcastle-upon-Tyne and Gateshead. She left these practices for London in 1909, and opened a practice there. She was very active in liberal political causes. In 1912, she published a text with Margaret McMillan on the needs of young children. Another of her achievements was to organize and support the MacDonald Memorial Clinic for Children under School Age. She was a strong believer in providing public health benefits for mothers and preschool children.

Her activism took her into the realm of politics, where she held various positions within the Fabian organization and worked hard for women's suffrage. A staunch member of the Labour Party, she stood as its candidate at East Islington in the 1922 general election and in each subsequent election until she was finally successful in 1929.   JH/MBO

PRIMARY SOURCES
Bentham, Ethel. With Margaret McMillan. "The Needs of
    Little Children." 1912.

STANDARD SOURCES
Europa.

BENTHAM, LADY MARY SOPHIA (FORDYCE) (ca. 1765–1858)

British botanist. Born ca. 1765. Father G. Fordyce. Married Sir Samuel Bentham (1796). Mother of George Bentham (1800–1884). Died 18 May 1858.

Mary Sophia Fordyce Bentham was the mother of the famous botanist George Bentham (1800–1884). Her son considered her to have been a very fine botanist; she collected throughout Europe when her husband traveled to France and Russia.

She had an herbarium that was probably absorbed into George Bentham's collections at Kew. She died 18 May 1858.   JH/MBO

PRIMARY SOURCES
Gray, Asa. *Letters*. London: Macmillan and Co., 1893. Reference to Bentham in vol. 1, p. 188.
Bentham, George. Papers and diaries, Royal Botanic Gardens, Kew.

SECONDARY SOURCES
Journal of Botany 32 (1894): 314.
Hooker, J. D. "George Bentham, F.R.S." *Annals of Botany* 12 (1898) ix–xxx.
Bentham, George. *George Bentham: Autobiography*. Toronto: University of Toronto Press, 1997.

STANDARD SOURCES
Desmond; *DSB* (under George Bentham).

BENTINCK, MARGARET CAVENDISH (HARLEY), DUCHESS OF PORTLAND (1715–1785)

British natural historian and patron of natural science. Married William Bentinck Cavendish, 2nd duke of Portland (1734). Professional experience: hired famous scientists to describe and publish catalogues of her collection. Died 1785 in Bulstrode, Buckinghamshire.

The duchess of Portland was renowned for her patronage of science, spending most of her money in establishing fine collections of shells, plants, and other specimens. She hired a number of famous natural historians to work in her herbarium, library, and museum at Bulstrode at a time before any other collections were publicly open. Among these were Daniel Solander, the Swedish-born natural historian and botanist associated with Joseph Banks. John Lightfoot, who dedicated his *Flora Scotia* to her in 1777, taught her botany and produced a catalogue for her museum. Jean-Jacques Rousseau visited her museum while in Britain and provided plant specimens for her botanical collection.

Her friend and fellow enthusiast, Mary Granville Delaney, a remarkable practitioner of the art of cut-paper flowers, described their mutual enthusiasm for mushroom and puff-ball collecting, filling all containers and every chair in the drawing room (quoted by Shteir). The debts the duchess incurred in forming her collections forced her estate to sell them at auction after her death. She died in Bulstrode, Buckinghamshire, in 1785.   JH/MBO

PRIMARY SOURCES
A Catalogue of the Portland Museum, Lately the Property of the
    Duchess Dowager of Portland. London: Skinner & Co., [1786].
Lightfoot, John. *Flora Scotia.* London: 1777. Dedicated to the
    duchess.
Papers at Longleat and Nottingham University.

SECONDARY SOURCES
Dance, S. P. "The Authorship of the *Portland Catalogue* (1786)."
    Journal of the Society for the Bibliography of Natural History 1962:
    30–32.

STANDARD SOURCES
Desmond; Shteir.

BERGER, EMILY V. (d. ca. 1922)
U.S. chemist.

Although no biographical information is available on E. V.
Berger, we know that she was a chemist who worked on the
solubility of noble gases. Even though she did research at
the University of Kansas and published in the *Journal of the
American Chemical Society*, we do not know whether she was
born in the United States or whether she immigrated to the
United States. Working at the University of Kansas, Berger
and her colleagues made careful determinations of helium's
solubility, in order to shed light on anomalous and conflicting results of other experimenters. They were able to attribute the latter results to various sources of experimental
error.   MM

PRIMARY SOURCES
Berger, Emily V. With Hamilton P. Cady and Howard M. Elsey.
    "The Solubility of Helium in Water." *Journal of the American
    Chemical Society* 44 (1922): 1456–1461.

STANDARD SOURCES
Meyer and von Schweidler

BERGER, KATHARINA BERTHA CHARLOTTE (1897–?)
*German zoologist. Born 4 February 1897 in Breslau to Emma
(Schüller) and Georg Berger. Married Osk Heinroth (13 December
1933). Educated University of Breslau; University of Munich
(Ph.D.). Professional experience: Munich, assistant in zoology to
Professors Koehler and von Frisch; collaborated with husband;
Berlin, director of zoological gardens (1945–1956); Technical Uni-
versity of Berlin, instructor in zoology (1953–ca. 1968). Honors*

*and memberships: International Association of Zoo Directors, Ger-
man Society of Ornithologists, Federation for the Protection of Nature, German Zoological Society, Association for the Protection of
Birds. Death date unknown.*

Katharina Berger earned her doctorate from the University
of Munich, and was a zoological assistant to the well-known
zoologists Otto Koehler and Karl von Frisch. After doing
some collaborative work with her husband, she became the
director of the Berlin Zoo immediately after World War II.
She remained at the zoo until 1956, but began teaching
at the Technical Institute of Berlin in 1953, until at least
1968.   JH/MBO

STANDARD SOURCES
Debus.

BERNERS, JULIANA See Barnes, Juliana

BERONICE (1st c. C.E.)
Roman philosopher. First century C.E.

Although little is known about Beronice, she is reputed to be
the source for Stobaeus' apothegms, listed in his *Bibliotheca.*
She is sometimes known as Pherenice or Berenice.
                                                             JH/MBO

SECONDARY SOURCES
Ménage, Gilles. *The History of Women Philosophers.* Trans. Beat-
    rice H. Zedler. Lanham, Md.: University of America, 1984.

STANDARD SOURCES
Kersey; Rebière.

BERRIDGE, EMILY MARY (1872–1947)
*British botanist. Born 20 February 1872 in Bromley, Kent. Edu-
cated University of London (B.Sc., 1898; D.Sc., 1914). Professional experience: Royal Holloway College, research on Gnetales
and Amentiferae under Margaret Benson. Died 8 October 1947.*

Emily Berridge held an unpaid research position at the
Royal Holloway College where she worked on the fossil
plants *Gnetales* and *Amentiferae.* She contributed to the
Annals of Botany, the *New Phytologist*, and *Annals of Applied
Biology.*   JH/MBO

PRIMARY SOURCES
Berridge, Emily. "The Structure of the Female Strobilus in
    Gnetum gnemon." *Annals of Botany* 26 (1912): 987–992.

SECONDARY SOURCES

Blackwell, G. M. "Obituaries: Dr. Emily Berridge." *Nature* 161 (1948): 87.

——. "Obituaries: Emily M. Berridge." *Proceedings of the Linnaean Society* 160 (1947–1948): 68–70.

BERTEREAU, MARTINE DE, BARONESS DE BEAUSOLEIL (fl. 1600–1630)

French metallurgist and alchemist. Born in Tours or in the Berry District of France. Married Jean du Châtelet, Baron de Beausoleil. At least one child, Anne.

Little is known about the baroness de Beausoleil. She was born Martine de Bertereau in either Tours or in the Berry District of France. She married Jean du Châtelet, Baron de Beausoleil, in 1601, and aided him in his work. Du Châtelet was a Belgian metallurgist, alchemist, and prospector who was employed by several European rulers to find and exploit mines. His alchemical experiments engaged upon during a prospecting trip to Brittany in 1628 prompted his arrest on charges of sorcery. He was released after a short term in prison, but his apparatus was destroyed.

Martine is considered to have written reports on their joint work. She presented two memoirs to the French court to inform the king how he could make himself and his countrymen independent of other countries by using the mineral resources of France. She never received a response to these reports, and apparently the couple's persistence annoyed Cardinal Richelieu to the extent that he had the pair imprisoned in the Bastille, where du Châtelet died in 1645. The archives do not contain any official record either of his imprisonment or death. After her husband's death, Martine and her daughter Anne were imprisoned at the Chateau de Vincennes.

According to Mozans, the baroness's memoirs discuss various types of mines, the assaying and smelting of ores, and the general principles of metallurgy. She also provides a description of the qualifications of a mining engineer—a person who was knowledgeable in chemistry, mineralogy, mechanics, and hydraulics. She assured her readers that she devoted thirty years of study to these branches of knowledge.

JH/MBO

PRIMARY SOURCES

Beausoleil, Martine de Bertereau. *Véritable Déclaration de la découverte des mines et minières par le Moyen desquelles sa majesté et sujets se peuvent passer des pays etrangers.* Paris: 1632.

——. *Restitution de Pluton.* Paris: 1640.

SECONDARY SOURCES

Descoqs, Albert. "La Bretagne minière et les prospections du bon et de la Bne de Beausoleil." *Bulletin de la Société géologique et Mineralogique de Bretagne* 1, no. 4 (1920): 227–239.

Elder, Eleanor S. "Women in Early Geology." *Journal of Geological Education* 30 (1982): 287–293.

STANDARD SOURCES

Debus; Mozans; Sarjeant.

BERTHAGYTA, ABBESS (d. ca. 616)

British healer. Born in England to Ingeberg and Haribert, King of the Franks. Married Ethelbert of Kent. Died ca. 616.

Berthagyta was a daughter of the Frankish king Haribert and his Saxon wife, Ingeberg. She married Ethelbert of Kent and began to correspond with Pope Gregory the Great. She, her husband, the king, and ten thousand converts were baptized by Saint Augustine during his visit to England in 597. Berthagyta was important in preparing for Augustine's visit. She became known for her wisdom and established the first Benedictine nunnery in England, at Barking in Essex. The Venerable Bede noted that she governed wisely for the rest of her life and taught medicine to the women under her care. She was said to have tended the sick with great skill.

JH/MBO

SECONDARY SOURCES

Bede. *Ecclesiastical History of England.* 2d ed. London: Bohn Library, 1849.

STANDARD SOURCES

Hurd-Mead 1938.

BERTHILDIS OF CHELLES (d. 680)

French healer. Widow of Clovis II. Died 680.

Berthildis of Chelles restored the Abbey of Chelles, near Paris, and placed BERTILE in charge of it. The two carried on numerous reforms, putting an end to slavery in the region, and abolishing the oppressive head tax on men and cattle. The reforms were unpopular among the wealthy, and Berthildis and Bertile endured much opposition. She retired to the monastery of Chelles and devoted herself to medical work until her death in 680.

JH/MBO

SECONDARY SOURCES

Bede. *Ecclesiastical History.* 2d ed. London: Bohn Library, 1849.

STANDARD SOURCES

Eckenstein; Hurd-Mead 1938.

BERTILE OF CHELLES (652–702)
French healer and general scholar. Born 652 near Soissons.

Bertile was a scholarly woman whom the Abbess BERTHILDIS chose to govern the convent of Chelles, near Paris. With Berthildis, she carried on numerous reforms and met with strong opposition. She later devoted herself to medical work.

JH/MBO

SECONDARY SOURCES
Bede. *Ecclesiastical History*. 2d ed. London: Bohn Library, 1849.

STANDARD SOURCES
Hurd-Mead 1938.

BERTILLON, CAROLINE SCHULTZE (1867–1900s)
Polish/French physician. Born 20 May 1867 in Warsaw, Poland. Married Jacques Bertillon, physician and statistician for the City of Paris (1893). Educated University of Paris, Medical School (M.D., 1888). Daughter (Suzanne). Professional experience: Lycée Racine, physician; Paris Postal Service, physician for female employees. No information about her exists after 1901.

Polish-born, Caroline Schultze entered the Paris faculty in the 1880s and wrote a controversial thesis under the physician Paul Reclus on women in medicine. The famous physician Jean Charcot challenged this subject as not appropriate for a medical degree. The thesis was, however, published in German the following year and provides excellent information on the numbers and in some cases the specific theses written by women physicians throughout Europe over a period of thirty years. For the one year of its existence, she helped CÉLINE RENOOZ to edit the journal *Revue Scientifique des Femmes* (1889), which announced women's accomplishments in the sciences. At the time of her marriage, it was incorrectly noted that she was the first woman to be made physician in France. In correcting this error, she commented that she was probably the first physician to marry a physician in France. She became a physician to the girls at Lycée Racine and to the women employees of the Paris Postal Service. She is mentioned by a contemporary woman physician, Dr. BLANCHE EDWARDS-PILLIET during the Congrès des oeuvres feminins in 1900, and by MÉLANIE LIPINSKA (1900). Curiously, her daughter, Suzanne Bertillon, although discussing her father and the history of the Bertillon family in the book she wrote about her uncle Alphonse Bertillon, never mentions her mother, nor do Jacques Bertillon's biographers.

JH

PRIMARY SOURCES
Schultze, Caroline. "Le femme-medecin au XIXe Siècle." Thesis, Paris Medical School, 1888.
———. *Die Aerztin im 19.Jahrhundert*. Leipzig: 1889.
Articles in *Revue scientifique des femmes*.
Letter to *Le Figaro* from Caroline Schultze Bertillon 1893 in Wellcome Library of the History of Medicine.

SECONDARY SOURCES
Bertillon, Suzanne. *Vie de Alphonse Bertillon, inventeur de l'anthropometre*. 8th ed. [Paris?]: Gallimard, [1941].
Renooz, Céline. Archives. Bougle Collection, Bibliotheque Historique de la Ville de Paris.

STANDARD SOURCES
Lipinska 1900.

BESANT, ANNIE (WOOD) (1847–1933)
British birth control advocate, controversial social reformer, inventor of quinine-soaked contraceptive sponge. Born 1847 of Irish parents. Married and separated from the Reverend Frank Besant. Died 1933.

After Annie Besant separated from her clergyman husband, she became vice-president of the National Secular Society. She was an ardent proponent of birth control, and was a close associate of Charles Bradlaugh. She became interested in theosophy after meeting Madame Blavatsky, the U.S. theosophist. She went to India and immediately became involved in politics; she was elected president of the Indian National Congress (1917–1923).

JH/MBO

PRIMARY SOURCES
Besant, Annie. *The Gospel of Atheism: A Lecture*. London: Freethought Publishing Company, London, Theosophical Publishing Society, 1877.
———. *Theosophy and the New Psychology: A Course of Six Lectures*. 1904.

SECONDARY SOURCES
"Besterman, Theodore. *Mrs. Annie Besant: A Modern Prophet*. London, Kegan Paul & Co., 1934.

STANDARD SOURCES
Europa; Stanley; Uglow 1989.

BEUTLER, RUTH (1897–1959)
German zoologist. Born 16 July 1897 in Chemnitz in Saxony. Father a lawyer and notary. Two siblings. Never married. Educated in

natural sciences at the universities of Jena, Leipzig, Munich, and Rostock (Ph.D., 1923). *Professional experience: Zoological Institute of the University of Munich, fundamental research in comparative physiology and zoology; qualified as a university lecturer in 1930; University of Munich, professor and curator (1937–1959). Died 22 October 1959 in Munich.*

Ruth Beutler came from a middle-class family in Chemnitz. Her father was a lawyer and notary and owned a manor in Thum in Saxony. As a young girl she suffered from tuberculosis of the bone, which resulted in the loss of a lower leg. Because she was confined to her bed, she became interested in intellectual endeavors at an early age. The physical work associated with the study of agriculture proved to be too strenuous for her. She chose instead to study the natural sciences.

Inspired by Karl von Frisch, who became her teacher in Munich and who would later receive a Nobel Prize, she conducted research in the field of comparative physiology, a field that was just becoming an independent branch of zoology. In her habilitation thesis in 1930, she discussed the makeup and concentration of flower nectar. She later allowed Karl von Frisch to publish the results of her work on the language of the bees.

Ruth Beutler became a professor of zoology in 1937. A beloved teacher, she knew how to inspire her students. During World War II she did extensive research on the Nosema plague, an epidemic in bee populations.

Beutler was never a fighter for a feminist science, rather "only" a scientist and academic teacher. During her academic life she was bound by traditional thinking and never dared to step outside the shadow of her professor. She remained the deft and meticulous helpmate to the male scientist who applied her practical research.   SNS

PRIMARY SOURCES
Beutler, Ruth. "Experimentelle Untersuchungen über die Verdauung bei Hydra." *Zeitschrift für vergleichende Physiologie* 1 (1924): 1–56.
———. "Biologisch-chemische Untersuchungen am Nektar von Immenblumen." *Zeitschrift für vergleichende Physiologie* 12 (1930): 72–176.
———. "Die wissenschaftliche Mitarbeit von Frauen in der 'Bienenkunde.'" *Der deutsche Imkerführer* nos. 9, 10 (1936).

SECONDARY SOURCES
Frisch, Karl von. "Ruth Beutler." In *Verhandlungen der Deutschen Zoologischen Gesellschaft.* Leipzig: Academische Verlagsgesellschaft, 1961, p. 545.
Nagler-Springmann, Sibylle. "Ihr Leben hatte sie der Wis-

senschaft verschrieben." Professorin im Schatten ihres Lehrers. Ruth Beutler (1897–1959). In *Bedrohlich gescheit: Ein Jahrhundert Frauen und Wissenschaft in Bayern*, ed. Hiltrud Haentzschel and Von Hadumod Bussmann. Munich: Beck, 1997.

BEVIER, ISABEL (1860–1942)
U.S. chemist and home economist. Born 14 November 1860 on a farm near Plymouth, Ohio, to Cornelia (Brinkerhoff) and Caleb Bevier. Eight siblings. Never married. Educated Plymouth High School; Wooster (Ohio) Preparatory School; University of Wooster (Ph.B., 1885; M.A., 1888); Case School of Applied Science, Cleveland (summer of 1888?); Harvard University and Wesleyan University (summers); Western Reserve University and MIT (1897–1898). Professional experience: country schools in Ohio, teacher (three summers); high school teacher and principal (1885–1888); Pennsylvania College for Women, Pittsburgh, natural science teacher (1888–1897); Lake Erie College, Painesville, Ohio, chemistry professor (1897–1900); University of Illinois, professor of household science (1900–1920; 1928–1930); Illinois Council of National Defense, chair of conservation department (World War I); UCLA, chair department of home economics (1921–1923?); University of Arizona, lecturer (1925). Died 17 March 1942 in Urbana, Ill. of arteriosclerotic heart disease.

Born to a French Huguenot family on her father's side and Dutch ancestors on her mother's, Bevier was the youngest of four sons and five daughters. After earning her bachelor's degree from the University of Wooster (now Wooster College), she became a high school principal and language teacher. She received a master's degree in Latin and German from Wooster in 1888. The course of her career changed in that year, for her fiancé was accidentally drowned. In that same year she became a natural science teacher at Pennsylvania College for Women in Pittsburgh, preparing herself to teach the subjects by attending Case School of Applied Science. However, she was never satisfied with teaching in a women's college and decided that the most interesting available career for a woman was food chemistry. During the summers, she attended Harvard and Wesleyan University. She worked with Wilbur O. Atwater, a pioneer in agricultural chemistry, and conducted nutrition studies in Pittsburgh and among blacks in Hampton, Virginia. These studies were published in 1899 and 1900 in the Bulletins of the Office of Experimental Science, U.S. Department of Agriculture. She resigned from Pennsylvania College, and studied at Western Reserve University and at MIT in sanitary chemistry under ELLEN SWALLOW RICHARDS. She became a professor of chemistry at Lake Erie College in Ohio, but still yearned for a different type of position.

The opportunity presented itself in 1900, when she was offered a position at the University of Illinois, where she organized the new department of household science. Rather than treat home economics as merely a cooking and sewing school, she billed it as a part of both a liberal and a professional education. She ran into some difficulty at first, because she refused to offer sewing and dressmaking courses. The administration supported her, while commenting on her lack of tact.

In 1921, Bevier resigned from the University of Illinois to become chair of the department of home economics at UCLA, where she remained for only two years. She taught one semester at the University of Arizona before returning to Illinois as a professor of home economics. In 1929, she became acting vice-director of home economics extension, a position that she held until she retired in 1930.

Bevier published numerous journal articles, sat on the editorial board of the *Journal of Home Economics*, and was a sought-after speaker. She established a laboratory house on campus for study, participated in the annual Lake Placid Conferences on Home Economics (forerunner of the American Home Economics Association), was the second president of the American Home Economics Association, and vice-director of home economics extension work at the University of Illinois. During World War I, she was chair of the conservation department in the Illinois Council of National Defense. She also served as chair of the Home Economics Committee of Herbert Hoover's Food Administration. She received honorary doctorates from the College of Wooster and Iowa State College. Brusque and sometimes abrasive, Bevier had a domineering personality; people either liked her very much or resented her.   JH/MBO

PRIMARY SOURCES
Bevier, Isabel. With Susannah Usher. *The Home Economics Movement*. Boston: Whitcomb and Barrows, 1906.
———. *The House: Its Plan, Decoration and Care*. Chicago: American School of Home Economics, 1907.
———. *Home Economics in Education*. Philadelphia: J. B. Lippincott Company, 1924.
Bevier's archives are located in the Department of Home Economics, Bevier Hall, University of Illinois. Her official correspondence is in the papers of Presidents Draper and James in the University Archives.

SECONDARY SOURCES
Bane, Lita, and Van Meter, Anna R. "Isabel Bevier: Pioneer Home Economist." *Journal of Home Economics* 34, no. 6 (June 1942): 341–344.
Davenport, Eugene. "Home Economics at Illinois." *Journal of Home Economics* 13, no. 8 (August 1921): 337–341.

Moores, Richard G. "Isabel Bevier, Lady with a Mission." In *Fields of Rich Soil: The Development of the University of Illinois College of Agriculture*. Urbana: University of Illinois Press, 1970.

STANDARD SOURCES
Bailey; Høyrup; *NAW* (long article by Winton U. Solberg); Rossiter 1982.

BHATIA, SHARJU PANDIT (1907–)

Indian physician and public health advocate. Born 19 June 1907 in Gwalior, India. Four siblings. Married Major General S. L. Bhatia. Educated Canadian Baptist Mission School, Indore; Lady Hardinge Medical College for Women, New Delhi (1923); Grant Medical College, Bombay (M.D., 1931). All India Institute of Hygiene and Public Health (postgraduate training in obstetrics); Rockefeller fellowship, Harvard School of Public Health (master's degree in Public Health, 1935?). Professional experience: Women's Medical Service of India, assistant physician; medical school outpatient clinic, Agra, director; Indian Red Cross Society, Bengal, medical officer (1938), superintendent of maternity and child welfare (1939– 1941); bureaus of maternity and child welfare in Orissa, then Delhi, director; state government, adviser for maternity and child welfare (1946–1961). Retired 1961, settled in Bangalore.

Sharju Pandit was born into an orthodox Brahmin farming family in the princely state of Gwalior in India. A plague epidemic when Sharju was three months old killed her father but her mother and four siblings, who had fled to another area, lived. Both sisters and an older brother later died of plague. The family went to live with Sharju's maternal grandfather, an astrologer, as did an uncle, a physician, and his family. When her uncle moved to the medical school at Indore in 1915, Sharju went along to join the first class of the Canadian Baptist Mission School there.

In 1916 the Lady Hardinge Medical College for Women opened in New Delhi, and Sharju was told she could go if she did well in school. She entered in 1923 and later attended the Grant Medical College in Bombay where her brother was also a student. In 1927 her mother died of typhoid fever and Sharju turned to the National Association of Women for scholarship aid. She obtained the medical degree in 1931, and won a gold medal and cash prize in the ophthalmology competition.

Pandit began her professional career in the Women's Medical Service of India, established in 1914, as assistant in a small women's hospital. Then she transferred to Agra as director of the medical school outpatient clinic. In 1933 the All India Institute of Hygiene and Public Health was established in Calcutta with the help of the Rockefeller Foundation. Pandit applied for the special course in maternity and child welfare, which required that she promise to continue in public health after graduation. She pointed out to the board of the institute that, unless there were posts in public health for women, it would not be possible to use the training fully. The board decided that she should do postgraduate work in obstetrics followed by tours of maternity and child welfare facilities overseas.

On a Rockefeller fellowship, she traveled to New York, Harvard School of Public Health, took classes and fieldwork, and passed the Masters in Public Health examination with distinction in child health. Study visits to New York, Philadelphia, Chicago, Washington, and Canada followed, and she returned to India at the end of 1936 full of ideas for administering health services in urban and rural areas in India. Her first assignment in Calcutta was to conduct an inquiry into the causes of maternal deaths. As she grew to appreciate the role of the midwife or *dai* she developed a training program for midwives which was adopted under India's first Five-Year Plan. In 1938 she worked as a medical officer for the Indian Red Cross Society in Bengal, and a year later became superintendent of maternity and child welfare. For two years Pandit spent part of each month traveling to remote villages to explain the maternity and child care services, conduct clinics, and train indigenous midwives and to establish an administrative bureau under the auspices of the State Department of Health. The system was a success and Pandit was asked to direct bureaus of maternity and child welfare in the state of Orissa, then in Delhi. The bureau in Delhi was under the Indian Red Cross Society and handled referrals from all over India. In 1946, Pandit accepted the post of adviser for maternity and child welfare with the state government.

In 1947 Pandit was asked to assist at the reception camp for the ten thousand Hindus who migrated into India following the partitioning of Pakistan. Over several months, the population of the camp grew to three million and health services, especially to children and pregnant women, were critical. As government advisor, Pandit initiated or influenced many helpful programs. The United Nations' Children's Fund (UNICEF) gave aid for promoting direct services to children; the Department of Maternity and Child Welfare was expanded; additional schools for training of health personnel and *dais* were established; pediatric clinics and training at medical schools were developed.

At the age of forty-four, Pandit married Major General S. L. Bhatia and in 1961 retired and settled in Bangalore. She remained active in social work through the Social Welfare Board and State Council for Child Welfare; she was also involved with the Cheshire Home and Chinmaya Mission Hospital in Bangalore.   K M

PRIMARY SOURCES
Bhatia, Sharju Pandit. In Hellstedt, *Autobiographies*.

BIBRING, GRETE LEHNER (1899–1977)

Austrian/U.S. psychiatrist. Born 11 January 1899 in Vienna, Austria, to Victoria (Stengel) and Moritz Lehner. Educated University of Vienna (M.D., 1924). Married Edward Bibring (d. 1959), 18 December 1921. Two sons, George and Thomas. Naturalized U.S. citizen (1946). Professional experience: Vienna Psychoanalytic Clinic, training analyst (1926–1938); British Psycho-analytical Society, training analyst (1938–1941); Boston Psychoanalytic Society, training analyst (1941–1977), president (1955–1958); Harvard Medical School, faculty (1946–1977), clinical professor of psychiatry (1961–1965), emerita professor (1965–1977). Concurrent experience: Beth Israel Hospital, Boston psychiatric staff (1946–1965), psychiatrist-in-chief (1955–1965), director of psychiatric research (1958–1977); Simmons College, School of Social Work, special lecturer in analytic psychiatry (1942–1965); Brandeis University and Radcliffe Institute, consultant. Honors and memberships: American Psychoanalytic Society, president (1962–1963); International Psychoanalytic Society, vice-president (1959–1963). Died 1977.

Grete Lehner Bibring was born in Vienna, Austria, in 1899, to a middle-class Jewish family. She studied medicine at the University of Vienna, obtaining her medical degree in 1924. Three years before she finished, she married Edward Bibring, with whom she had two sons, George and Thomas. Bibring decided to become a psychiatrist, and was very much influenced by the Viennese psychoanalytic movement begun by Sigmund Freud. She served as the assistant director to the Viennese Psychoanalytic Clinic from 1926 to 1938, during which period both HELENE DEUTSCH and MELANIE KLEIN were active in the clinic. Bibring acted as one of the training analysts during this period.

In 1938, with the move of German forces into Austria, the family left for Britain, where they remained for the next three years. In London, Bibring worked as a training analyst for the British Psychoanalytic Society until the family moved to the U.S. in 1941. Rather than establish themselves in New York, the Bibrings chose Boston, where Grete Bibring served as a training analyst for the Boston Psychoanalytic Society from 1941. She would be president of that organization from 1955 to 1958.

Naturalized as a U.S. citizen by 1946, Bibring began to teach at Harvard Medical School and to serve as a staff psychiatrist at Beth Israel Hospital, one of Harvard's training hospitals, where she became psychiatrist-in-chief in 1955. She lived with her family in a pleasant part of Cambridge, and her children went to the local schools. During the mid-fifties (1955–1957), she carried out extensive research on the psychological response of fifteen women to pregnancy and early motherhood. The women were chosen to represent a range of class and race backgrounds at one of the City Hospitals of the Boston area, given extensive batteries of standard projective tests, and followed over the course of two full years. In 1959, Bibring's husband, Edward, died. Only in 1961 did Harvard appoint her as clinical psychiatrist, a post she retained until she retired in 1965. After retirement, she continued to work as emerita professor both at Harvard and at the hospital, writing a book that pulled together her lectures in medical psychology and her research, which included research on the psychological reaction to heart attacks.

Bibring recognized the need to reappraise the goals and techniques of teaching psychoanalytic psychiatry and, in October 1964, just before her retirement, organized a symposium at Harvard University that raised this question. The resulting essays were edited in a book by Bibring in 1968. She died in 1977 in Cambridge. Her family collected her papers from the years 1955 to 1977 and deposited them in the Rare Book Department of the Countway Medical Library, Harvard Medical School. These remain as yet uncatalogued. Her unpublished psychological evaluation of fifteen pregnant women and their responses to various standard objective and projective tests are in the Henry A. Murray Research Library, Radcliffe College.   JH

PRIMARY SOURCES

Bibring, Grete, ed. *Teaching of Dynamic Psychiatry: A Reappraisal of the Goals and Techniques in Teaching of Psychoanalytic Psychiatry.* New York: International Universities Press, 1968.

———. *Lectures in Medical Psychology: An Introduction to the Care of Patients.* New York: International Universities Press, 1969.

———. Papers, 1955–1975 (uncatalogued). Countway Medical Library, Harvard Medical School Rare Books Department.

STANDARD SOURCES
Debus.

BICKERDYKE, MARY ANN (BALL) (1817–1901)

U.S. Civil War hospital nurse. Born 19 July 1817 in Knox County, Ohio, to Annie Rodgers and Hiram Ball. Educated informally. Married Robert Bickerdyke (27 April 1847). Two sons, one daughter. Widowed 1859. Professional experience: Cairo, Ill., military hospital nurse (1861); General Hospital, matron (1862); labored at scattered Union field hospitals after the battle of Shiloh; Northwestern Sanitary Commission in Chicago, "agent in the field" (1862); San Francisco, Salvation Army worker (1876–1887); helped organize the California branch of the Woman's Relief Corps. Died 1901 in Bunker Hill, Kans.

Mary Ann Ball had the usual education of a female in the nineteenth century; she was "schooled" in only those practical subjects that would enable her to marry and raise a family. Her mother died when Mary Ann was only seventeen months old and she was cared for by her maternal grandparents in Richland County, Ohio, until her father's remarriage several years later. When she was twelve, she was again sent to live on the Rodgers's farm until her grandparents' death, then with other relatives, then in Hamilton County near Cincinnati, Ohio, where her uncle and his family lived. She apparently did domestic work and may have picked up additional knowledge of herbal or "botanic" medicine. She may have attended a Physio-Botanic school, run by Zimri Hussey, in Cincinnati, which lectured on the *materia medica* and popular therapeutic practices including the generous use of hot water and fresh air, the drinking of copious amounts of water and clear liquids, a moderate diet with fresh fruits and vegetables, and judicious use of nature's pharmacopoeia. Mary Ball was married late (at age thirty) to an Englishman, Robert Bickerdyke, who was a widower with at least three children. The couple had two sons of their own, James and Hiram (and in 1858 a daughter who died at the age of two). When Robert's sign and housepainting business in Cincinnati failed, the Bickerdykes left Robert's older children with relatives in Kentucky and took their sons to Galesburg, Illinois. In 1859, "Professor" Bickerdyke (so called in recognition of his gifts as an amateur bass violist) suddenly died. Mary Ann Bickerdyke supported her family with her folk medicine practice and was a respected and resourceful member of her community and her church, the Galesburg Congregational Church. Through the church, she found an outlet for her considerable energies and organizational talents.

In 1861, a letter arrived at the Congregational Church from Benjamin Woodward, a Galesburg doctor serving at the Cairo, Illinois, battleground hospital. The letter graphically detailed the horrors of the filthy, ill-supplied hospital and begged for assistance, since the army seemed unable or unwilling to make improvements. Mary Bickerdyke agreed to oversee the distribution of a relief fund for the Illinois Union Army volunteers who were reported to be suffering from typhoid, dysentery, and worse at the camp in Cairo. Leaving her young sons in the care of the congregation, she began what would become four years of unceasing effort on behalf of the sick soldiers. She became matron of the general hospital established at Savannah, Tennessee. With the most primitive equipment, Bickerdyke labored at scattered Union field hospitals after the battle of Shiloh, nursing, laundering, cleaning, preparing food, and distributing supplies. She became known by the soldiers as "Mother" Bickerdyke. In 1862 she was appointed "agent in the field" by the Northwestern Sanitary Commission in Chicago, whose food and medical supplies she had been informally distributing since

1861. She was highly publicized by newspaper correspondents after news of her midnight visit to the battlefield of Fort Donelson, looking for wounded men among the dead. "Colorful and unpredictable" *(NAW)* she was soon recognized as a valuable spokesperson by leaders of the Sanitary Commission and was sent to conduct public speaking tours on their behalf.

In 1863, she became matron of the Gayoso Military Hospital in Memphis, Tennessee, and greatly raised the standard of care by replacing the convalescent soldiers used as nurses with healthy ex-slave women whom Bickerdyke trained in patient care. She also promptly began a food-procurement tour of Illinois farms that resulted in donations to a surprised Chicago Sanitary Commission of large numbers of live chickens and cows (for fresh eggs and milk), which Bickerdyke then shipped off to Memphis. Soon she returned to the battlefields, serving with both Grant (Vicksburg, 4 July 1863) and Sherman (on the battlefield at Lookout Mountain and Missionary Ridge). From November 1863 for nine months, she and Eliza Porter worked in field hospitals, bearing freezing mud and rain to comfort the men and distribute what supplies came to them. She spent June to September at a tent hospital in Marietta, Georgia, within sight of Atlanta when it fell 1 September 1864. She spent two months on hospital trains, did some speaking for the Sanitary Commission, then set out with a steamer of supplies to join Sherman's main army at Savannah. Stopping for a time to help a group of emaciated soldiers who had just been released from Andersonville prison, she met with Sherman's main army at Beaufort, North Carolina, where she stayed until the war ended in April 1865. She was given a position of honor in the great victory parade on 24 May 1865. In March 1866, she resigned from the Sanitary Commission.

Bickerdyke worked at various short-term positions and was involved in an unsuccessful project for resettling veterans in the farmlands of Kansas before moving in 1876 to San Francisco for her health. Here she lived eleven years, working for the Salvation Army and other benevolent organizations, and helped organize the California branch of the Woman's Relief Corps, an auxiliary of the Grand Army of the Republic. Her great concern in her later years was the fate of the Union veterans and she visited soldiers' homes and made regular trips to Washington, D.C., to advocate pension claims of men she had known at the front. In 1865, Congress gave her a pension of twenty-five dollars a month. She returned to central Kansas (Salina and Bunker Hill) in 1887 to be near her son James. She died in 1901 in Bunker Hill and is buried in Linwood Cemetery at Galesburg, Illinois.   K M

SECONDARY SOURCES
Baker, Nina Brown. *Cyone in Calico: The story of Mary Ann Bickerdyke.* Boston: Little, Brown and Company, 1952.

Brockett, L. P. *Woman's Work in the Civil War: A Record of Heroism, Patriotism and Patience.* Philadelphia: Zeigler, McCurdy & Co., 1867, pp. 172–186.

STANDARD SOURCES
NAW (long article by George Adams).

BIDDER, ANNA McCLEAN (1903–   )

British conchologist. Born 1903 in Cambridge, England, to Marion Greenwood and George Parker Bidder. Educated Perse Girls' School; University College London; Newnham College, Cambridge (1922–1926. M.A., 1930; Ph.D., 1933). Professional experience: Newnham College, associate in zoology (1944–1957); supervisor in zoology (1929–1963); Hugh Watson Curator of Mollusca (1963–1970). Death date unknown.

Anna McClean Bidder followed in the footsteps of her mother, MARION GREENWOOD BIDDER. Like her mother, she was a member of Newnham College. She earned all three of her degrees from Cambridge, although she first attended University College, London.   J H / M B O

STANDARD SOURCES
Newnham, vol. 1.

BIDDER, MARION GREENWOOD (1862–1932)

British physiologist. Born 24 August 1862 at Oxenhope, Yorkshire, to Agnes Hamilton and George Greenwood. Married George Parker Bidder (1899). Two daughters, Caroline Greenwood Bidder and Anna McClean Bidder. Educated Bradford Grammar School; Girton College (Natural Science Tripos, Part I, class 1, 1882; Part II, class 1, 1883). Professional experience: Newnham College, Bathurst Student (1883–1884); Balfour Laboratory, demonstrator (1885–1887); Newnham and Girton colleges, lecturer in physiology and botany (1888–1899); Balfour Laboratory, head (1890–1899), associate (1893–1904), member of council (1894–1896); Girton College, member (1892–1898), governor (1924–1932). Died 25 September 1932.

Marion Greenwood's father was a businessman and lay preacher. She grew up in the Yorkshire moor country and whenever she had the opportunity went tramping in the English Lake district, often with one of her brothers. Her mother trained her to be a competent housewife and cook. After achieving first class honors in both sections of the Natural Sciences Tripos, she was awarded a Bathurst Studentship for research at Newnham College. After holding the studentship for a year, she was appointed a demonstrator in physiology at Newnham. Since at that time women were not allowed to use the Cambridge University laboratory facilities, she worked in the new Balfour Laboratory. This laboratory, originally a Nonconformist Chapel, provided at first for the teaching of biology, zoology, and physiology. The college later added botany, and Greenwood taught both botany and physiology.

Greenwood had a wide variety of interests outside of teaching. She was a personable woman who enjoyed having readings of Browning and other poets in her room and got to know many students in that way. She also indulged her continuing love for the out-of-doors. Never particularly interested in athletics, Greenwood found rowing to be a sport that pleased her.

She continued her research on the processes of digestion for sixteen years. Some of these studies have become classic. Greenwood was the first woman to communicate the results of her work in person to the Royal Society.

After she married biologist G. P. Bidder, her research ended. She devoted herself to her husband and family and became quite involved in social causes, although she maintained her interest in science and kept up with new developments in physiology. For many years she was a Poor Law Guardian and a school manager and was a member of the Body of Trustees of Homerton College for eighteen years. She also was involved in supporting the Liberal cause and was president of the Cambridge Women's Liberal Association and she opened her home to all people who needed help. She had heart problems in later life, but lived to see her two daughters, particularly ANNA MCLEAN BIDDER, follow in her footsteps.   JH/MBO

PRIMARY SOURCES

Greenwood, Marion. "Observations on the Gastric Glands of the Pig." *Journal of Physiology (London)* 5 (1884): 195–208.

———. "On the Digestive Process in Some Rhizopods." *Journal of Physiology (London)* 7 (1886): 253–273.

———. "On Digestion in *Hydra*, with Some Observations on the Structure of the Endoderm." *Journal of Physiology (London)* 9 (1888): 317–344.

———. "On the Action of Nicotin upon Some Invertebrates." *Journal of Physiology (London)* 11 (1890): 583–605.

———. "On Retractile Cilia in the Intestine of *Lumbricus terrestris*." *Journal of Physiology (London)* 13 (1892): 239–259.

STANDARD SOURCES

Newnham, vol. 1; *Newnham Roll* (long article by E. R. S.); *Women Physiologists*.

BIHERON, MARIE CATHERINE (1719–1786)

French anatomist. Born 1719 in Paris. Father an apothecary. Never married.

Marie Biheron studied illustration with Madeleine Basseport, an illustrator at the Jardin Royal des Herbes Médicinales, and represents a unique example in this time period of a woman mentoring another woman. Although Basseport reputedly encouraged Biheron to turn her artistic skills to preparing anatomical models from wax, little is known about how Biheron gained her education in anatomy. Little is known about their collaboration, for none of their correspondence is extant. As Londa Schiebinger notes, only Biheron's four-page advertisement and Basseport's drawings have survived; reports about their work are known only from the memoirs of contemporaries.

Biheron won considerable renown for her creation of realistic anatomical models. Her models were famous for replicating the texture, color, appearance, and position of the actual organs. According to a contemporary, the models were so perfect that they lacked only "the odor of the natural object." Biheron sold only completed models, keeping secret her formula for their material. On several occasions she presented her models before the French king's academicians. During his 1771 visit to Paris, the crown prince of Sweden invited both Biheron and the chemist Lavoisier to lecture before him at the Royal Academy of Sciences at a later time.

Because of a shortage of cadavers for the use of students in the sixteenth and seventeenth centuries, there was a market for accurate models, many of which were gynecological in nature. Biheron's models were used by midwives to teach their craft to students.   JH/MBO

SECONDARY SOURCES

Schiebinger, Londa. *The Mind Has No Sex? Women in the Origins of Modern Science.* Cambridge, Mass.: Harvard University Press, 1989. An excellent discussion of Biheron within the context of women at the periphery of institutions.

STANDARD SOURCES

DFC; Hurd–Mead 1938; Ogilvie 1986.

BILGER, LEONORA (NEUFFER) (1893–?)

U.S. chemist. Married Earl Mathias Bilger (1928). Educated University of Cincinnati (A.B.; A.M.; Ph.D., 1916); Cambridge University (1924–1935). Professional experience: Sweetbriar College, professor of chemistry (1916–1918); University of Cincinnati, instructor and assistant professor (1918–1925); Basic Science Research Laboratory, director of chemical research (1924–1929); University of Hawaii, dean of women (1929–1937); Experimental Station, research chemist (1919–1937), professor of chemistry (1937–1954), head of department (1943–1954), emerita professor (from 1954). Honors and memberships: Sara Berliner fellow;

Chemical Society, Garvan Metal (1950); AAAS; Chemical Society; New York Academy of Sciences. Death date unknown.

Leonora Bilger was a recipient of the prestigious Garvan medal of the Chemical Society. Her husband was also a chemist and they both went to the University of Hawaii where Leonora became a full professor and a department head.

Her research was on asymmetric structures, hydroxylamines, and hydroxamic acids. She also did toxicity studies of substances used in cancer treatment. She studied the pigments of red peppers, radiation and asymetric molecules, and sterols of tropical oils.   JH/MBO

STANDARD SOURCES
AMS 5–9, P 9, P&B 10–11; O'Neill.

BILLINGS, KATHARINE STEVENS (FOWLER–LUNN) (1902–   )

U.S. geologist. Born 1902. Married Rhodesian economic geologist Marland Pratt Billings. Educated University of Wisconsin.

An American, educated at the University of Wisconsin, Katharine Stevens Billings married a Rhodesian economic geologist and proceeded to become an excellent geologist herself. Billings participated in prospecting work on the Gold Coast (Ghana) and in Sierra Leone.   JH/MBO

PRIMARY SOURCES
Fowler-Lunn, Katharine S. "Hematite Iron Ores of Sierra Leone, West Africa." *Economic Geology* 28 (1933): 59–67.
———. "Molybdenite in Sierra Leone." *Mining Magazine* 51 (1934): 73–75.
———. "Geology of the Cardigan Quadrangle, New Hampshire." *Geological Society of America, Bulletin* 48 (1937): 1363–1386.
———. *The Gold Missus: A Woman Prospector in the Sierra Leone.* New York: Norton, 1938.

STANDARD SOURCES
Sarjeant.

BINGHAM, MILLICENT (TODD) (1880–1968)

U.S. geographer and literary editor. Born 5 February 1880 to Mabel Loomis and David Peck Todd. Married Walter van Dyke Bingham. Educated Radcliffe (A.M., 1917; Ph.D., 1923). Professional experience: Columbia University, instructor in urban geography (1929); Sarah Lawrence College, lecturer in geography. Put aside scientific work to complete editions of Emily Dickinson poems and letters (1930 to death). Honorary doctorate from Amherst College. Died 1 December 1968.

Millicent Todd Bingham was the daughter of a noted Amherst astronomer, David Peck Todd, and an important literary figure, Mabel Todd, who produced the first edition of Emily Dickinson's poetry. She and her mother accompanied her father's expeditions to observe eclipses of sun in Japan, Tripoli, the Dutch East Indies, Chile, and Russia between 1897 and 1914. This gave her a taste for science and a keen interest in geography.

From 1917 until 1923, Todd did graduate work at the University Museum, Harvard, writing her dissertation on an investigation of geographic controls in Peru. She received her Ph.D. in geography from Radcliffe College in 1923 with the approval of the Harvard Department of Geology and Geography, since at that time, women could not receive Harvard degrees. Soon after she received her degree, she married psychologist Walter van Dyke Bingham. She served as instructor in urban geography at Columbia in 1929 and lectured at Sarah Lawrence College. Interested in some of the French geographers, she translated *Principes de Géographie Humaine* by Paul Vidal de la Blache and contributed an article on Miami, Florida, for a book of geographical studies in honor of Raoul Blanchard.

Since her mother was partially paralyzed from a cerebral hemorrhage, Todd put aside her scientific work in 1930 to help her mother with a new edition of Emily Dickinson letters. Following her mother's death in 1932, she felt an obligation to continue that work and explain the complexities of the Dickinson texts and the important role her mother had played in bringing the Dickinson poems to international recognition. She would eventually acquire her own reputation for Dickinson scholarship, and published the intimate letters of Dickinson to Otis Philipps Lord in 1954. Her work was honored by an honorary doctorate degree in letters from Amherst College.   JH/MBO

PRIMARY SOURCES
Bingham, Millicent Todd. "An investigation of Geographic Controls in Peru." Ph.D. diss., Radcliffe College, 1923.
———, trans. *Principles of Human Geography*, by Paul Vidal de la Blache. New York: H. Holt, [1926].
———. "Le Floride du sud-est et la ville de Miami." *Mélanges geographiques offerts à Raoul Blanchard.* Grenoble: University de Grenoble, Institut de Geographie Alpine, [1932?].
———. With Mabel Todd. *Bolts of Melody: New Poems of Emily Dickinson.* New York: Harper, 1945.
———. *Ancestors Brocades.* New York: Harper and Brothers, 1945.

―――. *Emily Dickinson—A Revelation.* New York: Harper, 1954.

Autobiographical account in Schlesinger files, Radcliffe College.

SECONDARY SOURCES
Explorers file, Schlesinger Library, Radcliffe College.

STANDARD SOURCES
NAW (unused).

BIRD, GRACE ELECTA (b. 1880s)

U.S. psychologist. Born late 1800s in Brooklyn, N.Y. Educated University of Chicago (Ph.B); Columbia University (A.M., 1916); Brown University (Ph.D., 1918). Professional positions: Rhode Island College of Education, professor of educational psychology (from 1914). Honors and memberships: American Society for the Advancement of Science, fellow; Rhode Island Society for Mental Hygiene, fellow; National Economic League, member; American Psychological Association, member. Death date unknown.

Although little is known about Grace Electa Bird, she was a well-educated psychologist who made the most of her education. She received degrees from the University of Chicago, Columbia University, and Brown University. She became a professor of educational psychology and was a Fellow of the American Society for the Advancement of Science and of the Rhode Island Society for Mental Hygiene. Bird used her psychological training to write historical plays for children. Her plays went through numerous editions.   JH/MBO

PRIMARY SOURCES
Bird, Grace Electa. *Historical Plays for Children.* New York: Macmillan, 1914.

STANDARD SOURCES
AMS 3–8, *Psychological Register*, vol. 3, 1932.

BIRD, ISABELLA See Bishop, Isabella Lucy Bird

BIRDSALL, LUCY ELLEN (1914–1990)

U.S. geologist. Born 1914 in Mansfield Depot, Conn., to Lucy Ellen Storrs and Rollin L. Birdsall. Five siblings. Never married. Educated University of Connecticut (B.S., 1950?). Professional experience: Women's Army Auxiliary Corp of the U.S. Army (1943–1945); U.S. Geological Survey (1950?) Public Inquiries Office for geological publications 1953–1983). Honors and memberships: Department of Interior's Distinguished Service Award *(1984); Distinguished Alumnus Award, University of Connecticut (1985). Died 21 October 1990 in Los Angeles, Calif.*

Lucy Birdsall traced her lineage on her mother's side to two brothers who came from England and settled in Connecticut. Their descendants founded Storrs Agricultural College, later Storrs College, which became the University of Connecticut. After Lucy graduated from high school (1933), she enlisted in the Women's Army Auxiliary Corp of the U.S. Army and remained there throughout the war. She was sent to signal corps school where she learned cryptography. She remained in the Philippines for eight months after she was discharged as a civilian worker in the signal corps. When she returned home she took advantage of the G.I. Bill and enrolled at the University of Connecticut, intending to major in mathematics. During her first mathematics class, according to her biographer, she fell asleep and when she awoke a different person was lecturing. Not wanting to disturb the class, she remained and got keenly interested in his lecture on geology. She changed her major and was the first woman to graduate with a geology major from the University of Connecticut. Her entire career was with the U.S. Geological Survey. She began by working in the geophysical branch in Washington, D.C., but in 1953 moved to Los Angeles where she opened the Public Inquiries Office for geological publications and served there for thirty-four years.

When California initiated the registration of geologists, she became registered geologist 2146. She attended professional meetings regularly and brought literature to distribute to interested people. In 1957 she began a monthly column for the *Pacific Petroleum Geologist Newsletter*—a publication of the AAPG Pacific Section. She was given honorary membership in the organization in 1979 and was elected the first woman president in 1984. She was active in the many professional organizations to which she belonged. For example she served in every office for the Los Angeles Minerals Society and was elected president of the Los Angeles Basin Geological Society in 1981. She was recognized nationally for her service, receiving the Department of Interior's Distinguished Service Award in 1984 for meritorious service to the U.S. Geological Survey, and a Distinguished Alumnus Award in 1985 from the University of Connecticut.   JH/MBO

PRIMARY SOURCES
Birdsall, Lucy E. "Sources of Geologic Data." In *Geology, Seismicity, and Environmental Impact*, ed. Douglas E. Moran, et al., 57–63. Los Angeles: Association of Engineering Geologists, 1973.
―――. With Kikuye Yanaihara. "Sources of Geological Literature and Mine Data for the California Desert." In *Geology and Mineral Wealth of the California Desert*, Diblee volume, ed.

Donald L. Fife and Arthur R. Brown, 537–540. Santa Ana, Calif.: South Coast Geological Society, 1980.

———. With Kikuye Yanaihara. "Sources of Geological Literature and Mine Data for the California Transverse Ranges." In *Geology and Mineral Wealth of the California Transverse Ranges*, Mason Hill volume, ed. Donald L. Fife and John A. Minch, 685–687. Santa Ana, Calif.: South Coast Geological Society, 1982.

———. "Selected Bibliography of Death Valley." In *Geology of the Death Valley Region*, ed. Jennifer L. Gregory and Joan E. Baldwin, 417–420. Santa Ana, Calif.: South Coast Geological Society, 1988.

SECONDARY SOURCES

Stout, Dorothy L. "Lucy E. Birdsall (1914–1990)." *American Association of Petroleum Geologists Bulletin* 75, no. 7 (1991): 1264–1265.

BIRSTEIN, VERA (1898–?)

German chemist. Educated University of Berlin, Philosophical Faculty (thesis, 1926). Professional experience: Kaiser Wilhelm Institute for Physical Chemistry and Electrochemistry (1923–1933?). Death date unknown.

Little is known about the German chemist Vera Birstein. Her degree is from the Philosophical Faculty of the University of Berlin. She is listed in the *Handbook of the KWG* (Kaiser Wilhelm Gesellschaft) for 1928 as one of two women among twenty-one "miscellaneous co-workers." She apparently lost her position in the KWI (Kaiser Wilhelm Institute) for Fiber Research in 1933, and nothing more is known about her. JH/MBO

SECONDARY SOURCES

Handbook of the KWG, 1928: 178.

Vogt, Annette. "The Kaiser-Wilhelm-Gesellschaft and the Career Chances for Female Scientists between 1911 and 1945." Paper presented at the International Congress for the History of Science, Liège, Belgium, 23 July 1997.

BISCOT, JEANNE (1601–1664)

French physician. Born 1601. Educated in languages, literature, and medicine. Founded hospital in Arras. Died 1664.

Jean Biscot is an example of a woman who was born wealthy and was well educated for her time who dedicated her life to the care of the sick. She founded a hospital in Arras, and was especially interested in caring for sick children and for soldiers who had been wounded. After being besieged by the Germans, Arras was crowded with victims of dysentery and after the war the plague. Biscot worked tirelessly to relieve suffering. JH/MBO

STANDARD SOURCES

Hurd-Mead 1938.

BISHOP, ANN (1899–1990)

British protozoologist and parisitologist. Born 19 December 1899 in Manchester to Ellen (Ginger) and James Kimberly Bishop. One brother. Educated Fielden School, Manchester; University of Manchester (B.S. with honors, 1921; M.S., 1922), (D.Sc., 1932); Cambridge University (Ph.D., 1926; D.Sc. [titular], 1941). Professional experience: Manchester University, honorary research fellow (1923); Cambridge University, Department of Zoology, part-time teacher (1924–1926); National Institute of Medical Research, researcher under Clifford Dobell (1926–1929); Molteno Institute for Parasitology, Cambridge, researcher (1929–1967); Girton College, Yallow Fellow (1932–1990); Girton College Council, college governor, Yarrow Board. Honors and memberships: Beit Fellowship (1929–1932); Royal Society, Fellow (1959).

Ann Bishop was born in Manchester in midwinter, 1899. Her father, of Lancastershire origins, had followed his father into their successful furniture factory, attached to a lumber mill, and Ann's early desire was to enter that business. She was an only child for thirteen years, until the birth of her only brother. Her father urged her from her earliest years to try for a university education. She first attended the Fielden School, an early experimental school under the University of Manchester education department. Fearing that this would not be disciplined enough to prepare his daughter for advanced education, her father sent her at age twelve to the Manchester High School for Girls. There she studied both history and science, hoping to train in chemistry at the university.

In 1918, Bishop entered Manchester University to prepare for a bachelor of science degree, with courses in chemistry, botany, and zoology. Although she had first been interested in training for a career in industrial chemistry, reading Charles Darwin, Thomas Henry Huxley, and Alfred R. Wallace on evolution made her interested in studying biology. She was accepted in the Honors School of Zoology, where she became intrigued by the work of two of her professors, R. A. Wardle, a helminthologist, and Geoffrey Lapage, a protozoologist who had looked at parasitic protozoa that cause human disease. After winning the John Dalton Natural History Prize in her second year, she was given space in the laboratory of S. J. Hickson, who also did some protozoology, and was a Fellow of the Royal Society. She was able to begin her own undergraduate research project on ciliates, and received her honors degree in zoology in 1921.

She stayed on as an honorary research fellow for the following year, backed by Hickson, in order to assist in the large classes, swollen with the returning soldiers from the World War I. She developed methods of cultivating *Spirostomum*, a large wormlike ciliate with an undefined bacterial flora, and studied its division and conjugation. For this she received her master's degree in 1922.

The only academic position she could find in zoology was as a part-time demonstrator in the Zoology Department of Cambridge University, where she also prepared for her Ph.D., doing further studies of *Spirostomum*, in spite of the fact that no one on the faculty was interested in protozoa. She received the degree in zoology in 1926, soon after it was instituted.

Having obtained her degree, she became an assistant to the protozoologist and historian of science Clifford Dobell, in the laboratories of the National Institute of Medical Research in Hampstead. There she studied amoeba that were parasites in the human digestive system. She would later name a genus of parasitic amoeba after Dobell.

By 1929, Bishop won a Beit fellowship, and she returned to Cambridge with her grant and allied herself wth the Molteno Institute for Parasitology. She remained there for the rest of her professional life. Working under David Keilin, also a Fellow of the Royal Society, she began to study systematically the flagellate and amoebic parasites of both vertebrates and invertebrates. Bishop was particularly interested in the mechanisms for primitive nuclear divisions in these organisms, now recognized as aerotolerant anerobic protozoa. She had continued her interest in the ciliates and flagellates, particularly intrigued by non-parasitic forms that were closely related to the parasitic form. She also isolated the flagellate that caused blackhead in turkeys. For her work on these protozoan parasites, she received a doctorate from Manchester University in 1932.

When her Beit fellowship ended, she was offered the Yarrow fellowship connected to Girton College, which allowed her to continue at the Molteno Institute. She also took up residency at the college and this began a close relationship with Girton that would last to the end of her life. She remained a research fellow for the next thirty-eight years, becoming a "Girtonian of Girtonians." Bishop submitted her work on flagellates and amoebae in 1941 for a Cambridge doctorate (titular at that time for women at Cambridge).

With the beginning of World War II, her work took another turn. She had already received a Medical Research Council grant in 1937 to investigate the chemotherapy of malaria and the biology of malaria parasites. By 1942, she was a member of the MRC staff, and produced a critical review of previous work on antimalarial compounds, recognized as important in helping the search for new anti-

malarials. She investigated in turn the technique for feeding the mosquito *Aedes aegypti* (the vector for chicken malaria) with a membrane of chicken skin, and was able to investigate the effect of temperature, whole blood fractions, and other substances on the feeding behavior of those parasites. She also investigated the conditions triggering the development of malaria gametes. During this period she worked with three coworkers successively, and in 1948, after the war, she was made director of the unit, although she was always happier working with only a single coworker whom she knew well.

Bishop also began to investigate the phenomenon of drug resistance to the new malarial compounds being developed. Although parasites did not appear to be resistant to quinine, young chicks rapidly developed a resistance to proguanil (Paludrine), a new antimalarial. This finding, corroborated by field trials on patients with malignant tertian malaria treated with that drug in 1950, led Bishop to focus for her remaining research years on the study of this phenomenon in malaria parasites. Her work led to her election as a Fellow of the Royal Society.

Ann Bishop has been credited as the major force behind the founding of the British Society for Parasitology first within the Institute of Biology in the 1950s and then independently. However, when asked to stand for president of the institute as a whole in the early 1960s, she declined on grounds of her unsuitablity for public office. This is unfortunate from the point of view of women's representation among the presidents of that body, since no woman has yet held the position.

Two years before her retirement in 1967, she moved out of Girton College to Sherlock Close in Cambridge. Impeded in her activity by arthritis, she spent much of her time reading on the history of medicine and biology, but unfortunately did no work in those fields. She died 7 May 1990, after a brief bout with pneumonia.   JH/MBO

PRIMARY SOURCES

Bishop, Ann. "Some observations upon *Spirostomum ambiguum* (Ehrenberg)." *Quarterly Journal of the Microscopical Society* 67 (1923): 391–434.

———. "The Cytoplasmic Structures of *Spirostomum ambiguum* (Ehrenberg)." *Quarterly Journal of the Microscopical Society* 71 (1927): 147–172.

———. With Clifford Dobell. "Researches on the Intestinal Protozoa of Monkeys and Man. III: The Action of Emetine on Natural Amoebic Infections in Macaques." *Parasitology* 21, no. 4 (1929): 446–468.

———. "Experiments on the Action of Emetine in Cultures of *Entamoeba coli*." *Parasitology* 21, no. 4 (December 1929): 481–486.

———. "The Morphology and Division of *Trichomonas.*" *Parasitology* 23 (1931): 129–156.

———. "Chemotherapy and Avian Malaria." *Parasitology* 34 (1942): 1–54.

———. "Drug Resistance in Protozoa." *Biological Reviews* 34 (1959): 334–500.

SECONDARY SOURCES
Goodwin, L. G., and Vickerman, K. "Ann Bishop, 19 December 1899–7 May 1990." *Biographical Memoirs of Fellows of the Royal Society* 35 (1992): 27–40

STANDARD SOURCES
Newnham, vol. 1.

BISHOP, ISABELLA LUCY BIRD (1831–1904)

British naturalist, geographer, and travel writer. Born 15 October 1831 at Boroughbridge Hall, Yorkshire, to Dora (Lawson) and Reverend Edward Bird. One sister. Married John Bishop. Died 7 October 1904 in Edinburgh.

Isabella Bird was born into a family of evangelical Christians; her father was a cleric and her mother from a family of clerics. Her childhood in her father's various benefices nurtured her own evangelical tendencies. Throughout her life, she suffered from a "spinal complaint" and her doctors advised her to spend as much time as possible out-of-doors. She became a superb horsewoman and became competent at rowing. Equally important, she trained herself to observe natural objects. When she was twenty-two, she had back surgery. During her recovery period she began a series of travels that eventually took her all over the world, including Canada, the United States, Australia, New Zealand, Hawaii, the Malay Peninsula, Japan, Egypt, Tibet, Persia, Kurdistan, Armenia, Korea, and China. Bird became involved in geography and natural history through her travels. Her interests varied from microscopy to the establishment of a training college for medical missionaries. Her father died in 1858, after which she moved to Edinburgh to live with her sister, Henrietta, and her mother. After her mother's death, she continued to live with her sister until Henrietta's death in 1880. On 8 March 1881, Isabella married John Bishop, her sister's medical adviser. After the marriage she continued to travel and to write books about her travels; she produced at least one volume from each of her journeys. After John Bishop's death in 1886, much of Isabella's work centered around medical missionary work. She studied medicine at St. Mary's Hospital and advocated the establishment of hospitals and medical missions in different parts of the world. However, she continued her interest in the geography and natural history of foreign lands. Her knowledge in these areas was recognized, for in 1891, 1892, and 1898 she addressed the British Association and in 1892 was made the first female Fellow of the Royal Geographical Society.

Her willingness to explore new areas and her accurate record-keeping make Isabella Bishop significant to the history of science. Although not herself a scientist, Bishop made observations that were useful to geographers and naturalists. Her writings included missionary tracts, social commentaries, and books and articles including material on natural history. After a six-month trip to Morocco, Bishop's health worsened, and in 1904 she died.   JH/MBO

PRIMARY SOURCES
Bishop, Isabella Bird. *The Golden Chersonese and the Way Thither.* New York: G. P. Putnam's, 1883.

———. *Journeys in Persia and Kurdistan: Including a Summer in the Upper Kurun Region and a Visit to the Nestorian Rayas.* New York: G. P. Putnam's Sons, 1891.

———. *Among the Tibetans.* New York: F. H. Revell Company [ca. 1894].

———. *A Lady's Life in the Rocky Mountains.* Norman, Okla.: University of Oklahoma Press, 1976. An autobiographical record, in the form of letters, of Bishop's travels in the Rocky Mountains; introduction by Daniel J. Boorstin.

SECONDARY SOURCES
Chappell, Jennie. *Women of Worth: Sketches of the Lives of "Carmen Sylva," Isabella Bird Bishop, Frances Power Cobbe, and Mrs. Bramwell Booth.* London: W. W. Partridge, [1908].

Stoddart, Anna M. *The Life of Isabella Bird (Mrs. Bishop).* London: John Murray, 1907. Biography of Bishop, including maps showing her various voyages. Includes quotation from correspondence and other writings.

Williams, Constance. *The Adventures of a Lady Traveller: The Story of Isabella Bishop.* London: Sunday School Union, [1909].

STANDARD SOURCES
DNB.

BISHOP, KATHARINE SCOTT (1889–1975)

U.S. anatomist, physician, and histopathologist. Born 23 June 1889 in New York City to Katherine Emma and Walter Scott. Married Tyndall Bishop (d. 1938). Two daughters. Educated Somerville Latin School; Wellesley College (A.B., 1910); Radcliffe College, premedical courses (1911); Johns Hopkins (M.D., 1915); University of California Medical School, postgraduate public health (1930s). Professional experience: University of California Medical School, lecturer in histology (1915–1923); George William Hooper Institute of Medical Research, San Francisco, histopathologist (1924–1929);

St. Luke's hospital, San Francisco, anesthesiologist and private practice (late 1930s–1939); Alta Bates Hospital in Berkeley, Calif. (1940–1953). Died 20 September 1975 in Berkeley, Calif.

Katharine Scott Bishop was the codiscoverer of Vitamin E with anatomist Herbert McLean Evans. After receiving her medical degree, she taught histology for seven years during which period she studied vitamin deficiencies in laboratory rats, observing that the deprivation of a "substance X" disturbed the ability of the rats to reproduce. Although Evans went on to isolate pure Vitamin E ten years later, Bishop's marriage to the attorney Tyndall Bishop caused a break in her career. Bishop pursued a new interest in public health in the 1930s while she was raising her two daughters.

Although she was one of the few women to pursue medical research in the early twentieth century, she found it necessary to practice medicine in order to earn a living following the illness and death of her husband. She changed career strategies and became an anesthesiologist. She retired in 1953 and died twenty-two years later.   JH/MBO

PRIMARY SOURCES

Scott, Katharine. With Herbert Evans. "Existence of a Hitherto-Unknown Dietary Factor Essential for Reproduction." *Journal of the American Medical Association* 81 (1923): 889–892.

SECONDARY SOURCES

Apple, Rima D., ed. *Women, Health and Medicine in America: A Historical Handbook.* New York: Garland, 1990.

STANDARD SOURCES

AMS 4–8; *Notable* (long article by Valerie Brown); Rossiter 1982.

BISSELL, EMILY P. (1861–1948)

U.S. social activist. Born 31 May 1861 in Wilmington, Del. to banker Champion Aristarcus Bissell and Josephine Wales Bissell. Three siblings. Never married. Educated privately. Professional experience: initiator of use of Christmas Seals to fund tuberculosis research in the United States; began the first Red Cross chapter in Delaware. Died 8 March 1948 in Wilmington, Del. of a stroke.

Emily Bissell was the first daughter and second of four children of Champion Aristarcus Bissell, a banker, and Josephine Wales Bissell. Financially comfortable, Emily was educated by tutors and attended a private school in Wilmington. Like most girls of her time and class, she was not encouraged to attend university and never completed a higher degree. Although she never married, she apparently was especially sensitive to the needs and problems of children. Her sense of

responsibility to the Wilmington community where she spent her entire life was strong. In 1889, she founded the West End Reading Room, which sponsored Wilmington's first free kindergarten. She also founded the Boys' Brigades (a forerunner of the Boy Scouts), a boys' gymnasium, and the first public playground in Delaware. Desiring to improve public access to health treatment, Bissell played an important part in organizing Delaware's first Red Cross chapter (1904) and became its secretary for many years.

She heard about the success in Denmark of funding tuberculosis research through the sale of special stamps and became an initiator of the Christmas Seal in America to raise funds, designing and printing the first issue herself (1908). The funds from the stamp sales were used to provide a hospital for the care of tuberculosis sufferers (renamed in Bissell's honor in 1953). The printing and sale of the stamps was later taken over by the National Tuberculosis Association.

Emily Bissell was instrumental in securing passage of Delaware's first child labor laws and of the state's first maximum-hour law for women in industry. She was an active antisuffragist, believing the ballot would add to women's burdens, lead to family discord, and double the Negro and immigrant vote. She felt women could make their influence known through economic pressure, church activity, and moral persuasion. She also supported temperance; worked to promote new school facilities and educational opportunities among immigrants; and attempted to improve public health practices. In 1942, she received the Trudeau Medal of the National Tuberculosis Association. She died of a stroke in her home in Wilmington in 1948.   KM

SECONDARY SOURCES

Handbook of Scientific and Technical Awards. New York: Special Library Association. Trudeau.

STANDARD SOURCES

LKW (long article by Beverly E. Colemba) *NAW* (article by W. David Lewis).

BITTING, KATHERINE ELIZA (GOLDEN) (1869–1937)

U.S. botanist, microbiologist. Educated Purdue University (B.S., 1890; M.S., 1892). Married A. W. Bitting (1904). Professional experience: Indiana Experiment station, assistant botanist (1890–1893); Purdue University, instructor in biology (1893–1901), assistant professor (1901–1905); USDA, microanalyst (1907–1913); National Canners Association, microanalyst; Glass Container Assocation, bacteriologist (1919–1923). Died 1937 in Indiana.

Katherine Eliza Golden trained in biology at Purdue University. She worked closely with the botanist J. C. Arthur at the Indiana Experiment Station from 1890 to 1893. She then began to teach biology at Purdue University first as instructor, and then assistant professor from 1893 to 1905, when her marriage to another member of the faculty, A. W. Bitting, meant that she could not continue in a faculty position. Since their work was closely connected, he left Purdue as well, and they continued to work together first for the USDA and then for the National Canners Association and the Glass Container Association. Husband and wife published extensively together, and both received honorary degrees from Purdue in 1935 at his insistence: Purdue contacted A. W. Bitting about receiving an honorary degree, and he insisted that Katherine deserved the degree more than he. After her death in 1937, her husband arranged for the publication of her *Gastronomic Bibliography* (1937), still a basic reference tool, which derived from a library of books they collected. He presented those books to the Library of Congress as a memorial to her.   JH/MBO

PRIMARY SOURCES
Bitting, Katherine. *The Effect of Certain Agents on the Development of Some Moulds*. Washington, D.C.: National Capitol Press, 1920.
———. *Gastronomic Bibliography*. San Francisco, 1939. Rpt., Ann Arbor: Graphon Books, 1971.
Letters in the J.C. Arthur collection, Arthur Herbarium, Purdue University.

SECONDARY SOURCES
"Bitting, Katherine." *Proceedings of the Indiana Academy of Science* 48 (1939): 3–4. Obituary notice.

STANDARD SOURCES
AMS 2–5; Bailey; Rossiter 1982.

BLACK, FLORENCE (1889–1974)

U.S. mathematician. Born 22 November 1889 in Meade, Kans., to Mary Ellen and Moses Black. Educated Lawrence High School (graduated 1909); Kansas University (A.B., 1913; A.M., 1921; Ph.D., 1926). Professional experience: Anthony (Kans.) High School, teacher (1913–1915); Wichita High School, teacher (1915); University of Kansas, instructor (1918), assistant professor (1926), associate professor (1940–1960), emerita professor (1960–1974). Died 11 September 1974 in Lawrence, Kans.

Born in western Kansas, Florence Black was proud of her heritage as the child of a cattleman; she would even write a biography of her father. She attended Lawrence High

School, and then went to the University of Kansas where she received her bachelor's degree in 1913. She taught from 1913 to 1918 in Kansas high schools until she earned enough to return to the University of Kansas, where she ultimately obtained a Ph.D. in mathematics in 1926. Her research centered on differential equations for the invariants of ternary forms. She began to teach mathematics at the University of Kansas in 1918 and rose to professor of mathematics in 1940. She remained at Kansas until her retirement in 1960. Black was remembered mostly as an outstanding teacher.   JH/MBO

PRIMARY SOURCES
Black, Florence. "A Reduced System of Differential Equations for the Invariants of Ternary Forms." *University of Kansas Science Bulletin* 19, no. 2 (November 1929): 18–25. This was the topic of her thesis as well.
———. "Life on the Cattle Range in the Early Days of Western Kansas." *University of Kansas Alumni Magazine* Spring 1975.

STANDARD SOURCES
NAW unused.

BLACK, HORTENSIA (fl. 1893)
U.S. ornithologist.

Hortensia Black is known only for a paper that she read on bird protection to the World's Congress on Ornithology held as part of the World's Columbian Exposition in 1893.
                                 JH/MBO

STANDARD SOURCES
Rossiter 1982.

BLACKBURN, KATHLEEN BEVER (1892–1968)
British cytologist and palynologist. Born 1892. Educated Bedford College (A.B. with honors, 1913); Southlands Training College (M.Sc., 1916); University of London (D.Sc., 1924). Professional experience: Southlands Training College, Battersea, lecturer in botany (1914–1918); Armstrong College (later King's College), Newcastle-upon-Tyne, lecturer (1918–1947), reader in cytology (1947–1957). Honors and memberships: Linnean Society, Fellow (1922); Trail Medal, Linnean Society (1930); Northern Naturalists Union, president (1935), secretary (1948–1955). Retired, 1957. Died 20 August 1968, Newcastle-upon-Tyne.

There is little available on the early family life of Kathleen Bever Blackburn. She appears to have been interested in botany from an early age. She graduated from Bedford College in London with honors in Botany in 1913. She was soon appointed as lecturer in Botany at Southlands Training

College in Battersea, from 1914 to 1918, lecturing during part of the period that she was also writing her thesis on plant anatomy, for which she received a master's from the same institution. She then moved to Newcastle-upon-Tyne in 1918 to begin a lectureship at Armstrong College (which would later be renamed King's College).

She continued her research in botany, working in close collaboration with J. W. Heslop Harrison on evolution and taxonomy of flowering plants. While his work emphasized genetics and biosystematics, her work was focused on cytology. Together they looked at the Salicaceae and then forms of British roses as determined by their cytology, producing a series of genetic and cytological studies of various hybrids in the genus *Rosa* (1921 to 1924).

In 1923, Blackburn wrote a remarkable paper, producing the first report of sex chromosones in plants, published in *Nature*. It was this work on sex in plants that earned her a doctorate of science at University of London in 1924. She went on with Harrison to demonstrate this in the genus *Populus*, and then Blackburn produced convincing evidence somewhat later in two species, *Silene dioica* and *Silene alba*. Her work earned her an international reputation, and she went on to suggest the origin of sex chromosones in flowering plants and to theorize about its origin. Intersted in problems that Charles Darwin had posed but not solved some sixty-five years before, she investigated dioecious forms and hermophrodites and she worked on polyploidy in plants. In 1930, she was awarded the Trail Medal of the Linnean Society. In 1947, she was appointed reader in cytology, a position she held until her retirement in 1957.

Blackburn stimulated her postgraduate students to undertake similar kinds of studies, managing to pass her excellent technique on to them. She was considered a pioneer in the teaching of practical plant cytology, and her course was widely known and respected. As a university tutor she also was in wide demand and was greatly liked by all her pupils and colleagues. An excellent field botanist, she often collected materials for her classes and for her own research. Later in her research life, she became interested in pollen analysis as a method of dating peats in the Hebrides and the North of England.

Blackburn was an active member of the Northern Naturalists Union, serving as its secretary from 1940 until 1955. She also was on the management committee of the Hancock Museum. Soon after she retired, she became seriously ill, which kept her first from botanical trips and eventually from any kind of research. She died in August 1968.

JH/MBO

PRIMARY SOURCES

Blackburn, Kathleen Bever. With J. W. H. Harrison. "The Status of British Rose Forms as Determined by their Cytological Behavior." *Annals of Botany* 35 (1921): 159–187.

Blackburn, Kathleen Bever. "Sex Chromosones in Plants." *Nature* 112 (1923): 687–688.

———. With J. W. Harrison. "Genetical and Cytological Studies in Hybrid Roses. 1. The Origin of a Fertile Hexaploid Form in the *Pipinellifoliae-Villosae Crosses*." *Journal of Experimental Biology* 1 (1924): 557–570.

———. "Notes on the Chromosomes of Duckweed (Lemnaceae) Introducing the Question of Chromosome Size." *Proceedings of the University of Durham Philosophical Society* 9 (1933): 84–90.

———. With J. K. Morton. "The Incidence of Polyploidy in the Caryophyllaceae of Britain and Portugal." *New Phytologist* 56 (1957): 344–351.

Kathleen Bever Blackburn Papers, Hancock Museum, Newcastle-Upon-Tyne.

Portrait at Hunt Library.

SECONDARY SOURCES

Lunn, A. G., ed. *History of Naturalists in North East England*. Newcastle-upon-Tyne: Department of Adult Education, University of Newcastle-upon-Tyne, 1983, pp. 30–31. Obituary notice; includes portrait.

Valentine, D. H. *Watsonia* 1970: 69–70. Obituary Notice.

STANDARD SOURCES

Desmond.

BLACKBURNE, ANNA (1726–1793)

British botanist and natural historian. Born 1726 (often incorrectly given as 1740) at Orford Hall, Warrington, Lancashire, to Katherine (Ashton) and John Blackburne. Nine siblings. Never married. Educated privately. Professional experience: developed important museum of natural history specimens. Died 30 December 1793 at Fairfield house, Warrington.

Anna Blackburne was the fifth daughter of John Blackburne, a wealthy salt merchant who studied natural history and set up remarkable hothouses at his home, Orford Hall. He was famous for his palm trees, for his exotic hothouse plants, and for his cultivation of some rare fruits, like the pineapple. He included carefully arranged aquatic plants in his garden as well, in a manner that impressed the botanist Thomas Pennant in 1771.

Anna Blackburne learned much of her natural history initially from her father, but she extended that knowledge. Virtually mistress of the house after the death of her mother when Anna was about seventeen, she began to learn about plants, shells, and insects, adopting a systematic approach. By the mid-1860s, she began to develop plans for extensive collections. Wishing to establish these on the new Linnean classification system, she began to study Latin, as she later explained to Linnaeus himself. Her father, then in his seventies, felt it was too late for him to learn a new system, so she essentially had to teach herself both the language and the Linnean system. By 1868 she was obtaining significant help in identification of insects from the German naturalist Johann Reinhold Foster, later naturalist on the Cook voyages. He also read his unpublished lectures on entomology to her, which she urged him to have printed.

Blackburne's younger brother, Ashton, was living in North America. At her request, he sent numerous birds for her museum, collecting well over a hundred species from New York, New Jersey, and Connecticut, many of which were later described by Pennant, who thanked Blackburne for providing him with a substantial number of new species for his *Arctic Zoology*. Ashton Blackburne also sent over fifty insects and a few miscellaneous reptiles from the same area, also described and named by Pennant.

In 1771, Anna Blackburne approached Linnaeus and offered him some rare North American birds and insects not included in his *Systema Naturae*. He thanked her profusely and indicated that he had already heard her named as a very knowledgeable "botanical lady." A third letter from her explained her interest in his system of classification, her own self-education in both Latin and his system, and the fact that many Englishwomen were knowledgeable about plants. One woman of her acquaintance she mentioned as an example was LADY ANN MONSON, who had a "scientific knowledge" of botany. Linnaeus appeerently sent his student J. C. Fabricius to England a few years later to examine her insect collection. Fabricius named a new species of beetle after her (*Scarabaeus blackburnii*, since renamed) and memorialized both father and daughter in the genus of a plant he called *Blackburnus* (later placed in that genus). A bird from the northeastern United States that is popularly known as the Blackburnian warbler also memorialized Anna. *Blackburnei* was reclassified and renamed (another bird among this groups still bears her name).

After the death of her father, in 1786, Blackburne had to re-establish herself and her museums elsewhere. She settled in "Fairfield," Warrington, where she died 30 December 1793.   JH/MBO

PRIMARY SOURCES

Letters from Anna Blackburne are in Linnaeus correspondence and have been published in Sweden.

The Foster-Pennnant correspondence is held in the Peabody Museum, Salem, Mass.

Urness, Carol, ed. *A Naturalist in Russia: Letters from Peter Simon Pallas to Thomas Pennant*. Minneapolis: University of Minnesota Press, 1967.

SECONDARY SOURCES

Wystrach, V. P. "Anna Blackburne—A Neglected patroness of Natural History." *Journal of the Society for the Bibliography of Natural History* 8 (1977): 148–168.

STANDARD SOURCES

Desmond; *DNB*; Shteir.

BLACKER, MARGARET CONSTANCE HELEN (1902–1981)

British mycologist. Born 29 August 1902 in Arnside, Westmorland. Educated University of Liverpool (B.Sc., 1925). Professional experience: Liverpool Museum, affiliate; St. Andrews University, lecturer (1947–1968). Died 1981.

Margaret Blacker, a founding member of the Mycological Society, was born in Arnside, Westmorland, and educated at Liverpool, where she received a bachelor's degree. She was affiliated with Liverpool Museum and in 1947 was appointed a lecturer at St. Andrews University, a position she held until 1968. She contributed to the *British Phycological Bulletin* and the *Transactions of the Botanical Society of Edinburgh*.   JH/MBO

STANDARD SOURCES

Desmond.

BLACKWELL, ANTOINETTE LOUISE (BROWN) (1825–1921)

U.S. Congregationalist/Unitarian minister, science lecturer and writer. Born 20 May 1825 in Henrietta, N.Y., to Abby (Morse) and Joseph Brown. Educated Monroe County Academy; Oberlin College (1846–1850). Honors and memberships: Oberlin College, honorary M.A. (1878), honorary D.D. (1908). Married Samuel Charles Blackwell (24 January 1856). Five daughters. Died 1921 in Elizabeth, N.J.

Antoinette Brown came from a very religious family of Congregationalists and became the first woman minister in the United States. After a precocious interest in learning, she trained in theology at Oberlin College and became a Congregationalist minister, but left her ministry for Unitarianism in 1855, when she began to work among the mentally disturbed poor in New York. She published articles on what she observed, which were collected into a book in 1856 (*Shadows of Our Social System*). She became very interested in Darwinism in the late 1860s and published a general science book (*Studies in General Science*, 1869), a copy of which she sent to Charles Darwin. She later challenged Darwin's view of sexual selection, and his interpretation of the limits of female mental capacity in her book *The Sexes throughout Nature* (1875), parts of which had originally been published in *Woman's Journal* and *Popular Science Monthly*. She argued that the male perspectives of both Darwin and Spencer had led them to take the male as the representative type of the species. Spencer, she said "scientifically *subtracts from the female* and Mr Darwin as scientifically *adds to the male*" (*The Sexes*, p.18–19). The following year she wrote another book on science, *The Physical Basis of Immortality* (1876). She joined Maria Mitchell in encouraging young women to study science.

After marrying Samuel Charles Blackwell, she traveled and lectured extensively on woman's suffrage from 1879 to 1880, and served as the vice-president of the Association for the Advancement of Women, under the directorship of Julia Ward Howe.

In the 1890s, Blackwell began to explore the connections between mind and matter, working out a complicated cosmology that would link "the relative to the absolute," and which she illustrated with diagrams of vibrating atoms (*The Philosophy of Individuality*, 1893). The Blackwells returned to New York City in 1896. They had five daughters, Florence, Edith, Grace, Agnes, and Ethel, two of whom became physicians. After her husband's death in 1901, Blackwell helped to found a Unitarian church in Elizabeth, New Jersey, where she served as pastor emeritus from 1908 to 1915. She also issued condensations of her earlier books of philosophy in 1914 and 1915. She continued to support suffrage during this period and cast her first vote in 1920 at the age of ninety-five. She died in 1921 in Elizabeth, New Jersey, at the age of ninety-six.

JH

PRIMARY SOURCES

Blackwell, Antoinette Louise. *Woman's Right to Preach the Gospel*. Syracuse, N.Y., 1853.

———. *Studies in General Science*. New York: G. P. Putnam and Son, 1869.

———. *The Sexes throughout Nature*. New York: G. P. Putnam's Sons, 1875.

———. *The Physical Basis of Immortality*. New York: G. P. Putnam's Sons, 1876.

———. *The Philosophy of Individuality*. New York: Putnam, 1893.

Letters in the Blackwell Papers, Schlesinger Library, Radcliffe College.

Letter from Antoinette Brown Blackwell to Charles Darwin in Charles Darwin Archives, Cambridge University Library.

STANDARD SOURCES

NAW (long article by Barbara M. Solomon).

BLACKWELL, ELIZABETH (1821–1910)

British/U.S. physician. Born 3 February 1821 in Bristol, England, to Hannah (Lane) and Samuel Blackwell. Eleven siblings; three died in infancy. Educated by private tutors; attended school in New York City; Geneva College, New York (M.D., 1849). Professional experience: New York Infirmary for Women and Children, founder and physician. Died 31 May 1910 at Hastings, England.

Elizabeth Blackwell was one of nine children who survived infancy. Her father, a sugar refiner, was a Dissenter by religion and an advocate of social reform. He was supported in his ideas by his wife. The children seemed to benefit from the open family atmosphere: one of Elizabeth's sisters, Anna, became a newspaper correspondent; another, EMILY, a physician; and a third, Ellen, an author and artist. Two brothers, Samuel and Henry, were reformers and married women who became active in the women's movement: ANTOINETTE BROWN BLACKWELL, the first woman minister in America, and Lucy Stone Blackwell, abolitionist and women's rights advocate.

The Blackwell children, both boys and girls, were taught by private tutors. In 1832, after his sugar refinery was destroyed by fire, Samuel Blackwell emigrated with his family to the United States, spending the first six years in New York City and Jersey City. Despite financial pressures, Elizabeth was able to attend daily "an excellent school in New York" (*Pioneer Work*, 9). All the Blackwells became involved in the antislavery movement. Crusader William Lloyd Garrison was a frequent visitor to their house, which often served as a haven for fugitives.

When Elizabeth was seventeen years old, the family moved to Cincinnati, Ohio. Samuel Blackwell's death shortly thereafter left his widow and nine surviving children in financial difficulties. The girls opened a boarding school and took private pupils; after participating in this venture for four years, Elizabeth accepted a teaching position at a girls' school in western Kentucky. School teaching did not appeal to her, however; nor did marriage. She noted in her autobiography that she had despised anything connected with the body from childhood and that her interest in becoming a doctor had arisen from her wish to discourage a tenacious suitor and to express indignation over social inequalities.

"The idea of winning a doctor's degree," Blackwell later reflected, "gradually assumed the aspect of a great moral struggle, and the moral fight possessed immense attraction for me" (*Pioneer Work*, 29). After being turned down by schools in Philadelphia and New York and by Harvard, Yale, and Bowdoin, she was finally accepted by Geneva College in New York. Even her admission to this school was accidental; the professors referred her application to the students for action, and, believing it to be a hoax perpetrated by a rival school, the students voted to accept her. "When the *bonifide* student actually appeared, they gave her a manly welcome, and fulfilled to the letter the promise contained in their invitation" (*Pioneer Work*, 29). It was the doctors' wives and the townspeople who were unpleasant.

Blackwell's experiences at Philadelphia Hospital in 1848 were not positive. Although the medical head of the hospital was kind to her, "the young resident physicians, unlike their chief, were not friendly . . . throwing me entirely on my own resources for clinical study" (*Pioneer Work*, 80–81).

After receiving her degree in 1849, Blackwell went to Europe for additional training (1849–1851). On this trip she contracted ophthalmia, which later led to the loss of one eye. Tempted to remain in London to practice, "for I was strongly attracted to my native land," she was urged back to the United States by the lack of capital and of supportive friends.

Arriving in New York in 1851, she found that her attempts to practice medicine were consistently blocked. She offered a series of lectures on hygiene (published in 1852), which, because of the social and professional connections that resulted, gave her her first start in the practicalities of medical life. They were attended by a small but very intelligent audience of ladies, and amongst them were some members of the Society of Friends, "whose warm and permanent interest was soon enlisted" (*Pioneer Work*, 194).

Blackwell opened a dispensary in a tenement district in New York City in 1853. The New York Infirmary for Women and Children evolved from this beginning. Assisted by two other women doctors—her sister Emily Blackwell and Marie Zakrzewska—and supported in this venture by Lady Byron (the wealthy widow of the poet), she began to build a clientele among those who lacked other options. The Civil War blocked the early implementation of Blackwell's plan to expand the infirmary to include a medical college and nursing school for women. Meanwhile, she continued to advance the cause of women in medicine and to broaden her own experience. In 1868 the new institution was opened, and it functioned until 1899. Elizabeth, however, left its operation to her sister Emily, and in 1869 returned to England, where she developed a flourishing practice. As she grew older, she spent an increasing amount of time in a retreat in the Highlands of Scotland. She never fully recovered from the results of a fall in 1907 and died in 1910 at Hastings.

To Elizabeth Blackwell, medicine was not an end in itself but a tool for fighting social injustice. By making medicine a more acceptable profession for women, emphasizing the importance of personal hygiene, crusading for moral reform, and attempting to combat Victorian inequities, Blackwell assumed an important place in social history and in the history of science. MBO

PRIMARY SOURCES

Blackwell, Elizabeth. *The Laws of Life with Special Reference to the Physical Education of Girls*. New York: G. P. Putnam, 1852.

———. *Pioneer Work in Opening the Medical Profession to Women: Autobiographical Sketches*. London: Longmans, Green, 1895. Autobiography, with bibliography; later editions appeared under the title *Pioneer Work for Women*.

———. "The Influence of Women in the Profession of Medicine." In *Essays in Medical Sociology* ed. Elizabeth Blackwell. London: Bell, 1902. Rpt., New York: Arno, 1972.

SECONDARY SOURCES

Baker, Rachel. *The First Woman Doctor: The Story of Elizabeth Blackwell, M.D*. New York: Messner, 1944.

Morantz–Sanchez, Regina. "Feminist Theory and Historical Practice: Rereading Elizabeth Blackwell." *History and Theory* 31 (1992): 51–69.

———. *Sympathy and Science: Women Physicians in American Medicine*. New York: Oxford University Press, 1985.

Sanes, Samuel. "Elizabeth Blackwell: Her First Medical Publication." *Bulletin of the History of Medicine* 16 (1944): 83–88.

STANDARD SOURCES

DAB; *DNB*; *NAW* (long article by Elizabeth Thomson).

BLACKWELL, ELIZABETH (ca. 1700–1758)

British botanical illustrator. Married Alexander Blackwell. Died Chelsea, London, October 1758.

Blackwell published a famous herbal, *A Curious Herbal* (1739) in which she drew, engraved, and colored the plants herself in order to clear the debts of her botanist printer husband, Alexander Blackwell (1709–1749). Alexander Blackwell was trained in medicine but was a printer in London. He later served as physician to the King of Sweden. He was involved in political as well as printing activities in which Elizabeth also took an interest. Her herbal was a great success and also appeared in a German edition. JH/MBO

PRIMARY SOURCES

Blackwell, Elizabeth. *A Curious Herbal*. 2 vols. London: printed for S. Harding, 1737–1739.

SECONDARY SOURCES

Tjaden, W. L. "Herbarium Blackwellianum Emendatum et Auctum . . . Norimbergae 1747–1773." *Taxon* 21, no. 1 (1972): 147–152. This article discusses the greatly expanded German version of *A Curious Herbal* and argues that the German botanist Trew should be properly listed the author of that work.

STANDARD SOURCES
DNB (under Alexander Blackwell); Desmond; Shteir; Stafleu and Cowan.

BLACKWELL, ELIZABETH MARIANNE (1889–1973)

British botanist. Born 8 January 1889. Educated University of Liverpool (B.Sc.; M.Sc., 1912). Professional experience: University of Liverpool, demonstrator in botany (1912); Royal Holloway College, head, botany department (1922–1949). Died 25 May 1973.

Blackwell's major interest was in *Phytophthora*. She contributed many articles to the *Transactions of the British Mycological Society*. She was president of the British Mycological Society in 1942. She studied both plant anatomy and physiology.   JH/MBO

PRIMARY SOURCES
Blackwell, Elizabeth Marianne. *Terminology in Phytophthora.* Kew, Surrey: Commonwealth Mycological Institute, 1949.
———. With Grace M. Waterhouse. *Key to the Species of Phytophthora Recorded in the British Isles.* Kew, Surrey: Commonwealth Mycological Institute, 1954.
Blackwell family papers, Schlesinger Library, Radcliffe.

SECONDARY SOURCES
"Blackwell, Elizabeth.*" Transactions of the British Mycological Society* (1973): 611–614. Obituary notice, with portrait.
"Elizabeth Marianne Blackwell." *Naturalist* (1973): 113. Obituary notice.

STANDARD SOURCES
Desmond.

BLACKWELL, EMILY (1826–1910)

British/U.S. physician. Born 8 October 1826 in Bristol, England to Hannah (Lane) and Samuel Blackwell. Eleven siblings; three died in infancy. Never married. Adopted a daughter, Anna. Educated by private tutors; Rush Medical College; Western Reserve University. Professional experience: founder with sister Elizabeth Blackwell, Woman's Medical College of New York and New York Infirmary for Women and Children; physician and surgeon at New York Infirmary for Women and Children; dean and professor of obstetrics and diseases of women. Died 7 September 1910 at York Cliffs, Maine.

Like her older sister, ELIZABETH BLACKWELL, Emily Blackwell was important in opening the medical profession to women. Her parents exposed her to liberal causes (see account of Elizabeth Blackwell), and she, as well as her successful brothers and sisters, showed the results of their stimulating home atmosphere. The family moved to the United States when Emily was only five years old; the family moved from New Jersey to Cincinnati shortly before her father died. As were all the Blackwell children, Emily was educated primarily at home. A good student, Emily decided to follow her older sister's example and study medicine. Rebuffed in her applications to medical schools, she was eventually accepted by the Rush Medical College in Chicago. After the State Medical Society censured Rush for having admitted a woman, she was not allowed to return for a second year. However, she was able to continue her medical education at Western Reserve University in Cleveland, from which she graduated with honors in 1854. After graduation, she went to Britain, where she gained important postgraduate experience in surgery.

Returning to the United States in 1856, she codirected the New York Infirmary for Women and Children, founded by her sister Elizabeth. Emily exhibited important managerial skills and it was largely because of her that the successful infirmary needed larger quarters. She was vitally important in helping to establish training courses for nurses and, soon after, the Woman's Medical College of the New York Infirmary.

After 1869, Elizabeth returned to live in Britain, leaving Emily to run the hospital and the college. She served as professor and dean of the college for thirty years, and was both physician and surgeon at the hospital. Although the two sisters had established a woman's medical college, both Emily and Elizabeth Blackwell firmly believed that medical education should strive to become coeducational. After 1898, when the new Cornell University Medical College in New York was induced to accept women on equal terms, Emily Blackwell arranged for the transfer of her students to Cornell and the Woman's Medical College closed its doors in 1899, although the hospital remained open. The unforeseen consequence of the closing of many women's medical colleges in this period, was the marked decline in the number of available positions for women physicians to teach in medical schools.

Emily never married but adopted a daughter, Anna. In 1882 she and her colleague ELIZABETH CUSHIER set up housekeeping together and established a companionable relationship. Emily died of enterocolitis in her summer home at York Cliffs, Maine, in 1910.

Although Elizabeth Blackwell is better known than her sister because she was the "pioneer" woman physician and the more prolific writer and educator, Emily Blackwell should not be forgotten for her successful use of medical, surgical, and administrative skills.   JH

PRIMARY SOURCES
Blackwell, Emily. With Elizabeth Blackwell. *Medicine as a Profession for Women.* New York: New York Infirmary for Women, 1860.

———. "The Industrial Position of Women." *Popular Science Monthly* 23 (1883): 388–399.
Blackwell family papers, Schlesinger Library, Radcliffe.
Blackwell collection, Library of Congress.

SECONDARY SOURCES
Morantz-Sanchez, Regina. *Sympathy and Science: Women Physicians in American Medicine.* New York: Oxford University Press, 1985.

STANDARD SOURCES
NAW (long article by Elizabeth H. Thomson).

BLACKWOOD, BEATRICE MARY (1889–1975)

British social anthropologist. Born 1889. Father James Blackwood. Educated British and German secondary schools; Somerville College, Oxford University (A.B., earned 1912, awarded 1920; diploma in anthropology, 1918; M.A., 1920; B.Sc. in embryology, 1923). Professional experience: Oxford University, anatomy assistant (1912–1923); demonstrator and lecturer in ethnology (1923–1959); Pitt Rivers Museum, curatorial staff (1935–1975). Honors and memberships: Rockefeller Foundation grant (1920s). Died 1975.

Educated in England and in a finishing school in Germany, Blackwood continued her education at Somerville College, Oxford, finishing in 1912 although Oxford awarded the actual degree with her M.A. only in 1920 because its policy before that date had denied the actual award of earned degrees to women. Although her real interest was anthropology, Blackwood had studied anatomy as part of her work in physical anthropology, and served as an anatomical demonstrator at Somerville College from the time she finished her undergraduate work until 1923 when she received a bachelor's of science degree in embryology. She then changed positions to serve as demonstrator and then lecturer in physical anthropology at Oxford University, a position that she held until 1959.

She obtained a Rockefeller Foundation grant in the 1920s that took her to work with Clark Wissler at the American Museum of Natural History and with psychologist [?] Brigham at Princeton. She traveled throughout America and Canada, studying individuals on Indian reservations and in the American South, collecting genealogical and intelligence test data (published in 1927 and 1930).

On a later field trip to Melanesia, she studied the ethnology of New Guinea island people from 1929 to 1930 and published these results in her book *Both Sides of the Buka Passage* (1935). She returned a few years later to mainland Melanesia and studied the little-known Kukukuku. She also produced a documentary film on this New Guinea group.

Blackwood took up a position at the Pitt Rivers Museum under T. K. Penniman and remained on the staff until her death. In 1970, she published a monograph on the artifacts in the museum. Throughout her life, Blackwood received various honors. She was also an active participant in her many professional organizations.   JH/MBO

PRIMARY SOURCES
Blackwood, Beatrice. "A Study of Mental Testing in Relation to Anthropology." *Mental Measurement Monographs.* No. 3. Baltimore: Williams and Wilkins, 1927.
———. *Both Sides of the Buka Passage.* Oxford: Oxford University Press, 1935.
———. "Use of Plants Among the Kukukuku of Southeast-Central New Guinea." *Proceedings of the Sixth Pacific Conference* 4 (1939): 111–126.
———. "The Technology of a Modern Stone Age People in New Guinea." *Occasional Papers on Technology* 3 (1950): 3–59.
Diaries, letters, and field notebooks are in the Pitt River Museum, Oxford.

SECONDARY SOURCES
"Beatrice Mary Blackwood." *American Anthropologist* 78 (1976): 321–322. Obituary notice.
"Beatrice Mary Blackwood." *Oceania* 46 (1976): 235–237. Obituary notice.

STANDARD SOURCES
Gacs.

BLAGG, MARY ADELA (1858–1944)

British astronomer. Born 17 May 1858 in Cheadle, North Staffordshire. Father, Charles Blagg, a solicitor. Educated at home and in a private boarding school, London. Never married. Died 14 April 1944 at Cheadle.

Mary Blagg was the daughter of a lawyer. She received her formal education at a private boarding school in London. Blagg became involved in a variety of community service activities, which eventually included the care of Belgian children during World War I. Her active mind found expression in mathematics and astronomy. Because she found mathematics intriguing, Blagg borrowed her brother's school books and taught herself as much of the subject as she could understand. Her increasing mathematical competence prepared her to understand basic astronomy. However it was only when she reached middle age that she became seriously interested in astronomy.

Her interest was piqued by a lecture given by astronomer J. A. Hardcastle, whose arguments convinced her of the need to standardize lunar nomenclature, underscoring the inconsistencies in the literature in the use of names describing lunar formations. Other astronomers had also recognized the need to reform the nomenclature, and in 1907 an international committee was formed. Blagg was appointed to collate the names given to lunar formations on existing maps of the moon. The collated list was published in 1913 under the auspices of the International Association of Academies. In 1920 Blagg was appointed to the Lunar Commission of the newly founded International Astronomical Union. She served on a subcommittee that prepared a definitive list of names, which on its publication became the standard authority in matters of lunar nomenclature.

During the same period, Blagg was involved in a study of variable stars. The astronomer H. H. Turner had acquired a manuscript of Joseph Baxendell's original observations of variable stars, and was having difficulty analyzing these observations because of the raw state of the data. Turner appealed to skilled volunteers for assistance. Mary Blagg responded, and a series of ten papers in the *Monthly Records* (vols. 73–78, 1912–1918) resulted. Although the papers appeared under their joint authorship, Turner noted that "practically the whole of the work of editing has been undertaken by Miss Blagg. The difficulties of identification have been noted frequently; they could scarcely have been overcome without her patience and care." Blagg studied the eclipsing binary Lyrae and the long period variables RT Cygni, V Cassiopeiae and U Persei. She deduced new elements for these stars and harmonically analyzed the light waves obtained from the observations of other astronomers.

Mary Blagg might well have become a professional astronomer if the opportunity had presented itself. During her lifetime, professionalization became the norm rather than the exception for astronomers, although amateurs continued to make important contributions to astronomy. Men had the opportunity to choose amateur or professional status, but women had fewer options. Blagg was a member of a group of women that can be termed obligatory amateurs—women for whom a profession was not an option. Blagg managed to succeed in astronomy partially because of her willingness to work under the direction of others and to undertake tedious problems. However, her originality, skill, and good judgment in approaching these problems assure that her contributions transcended fact collecting. Her importance to astronomy was recognized in her election to the Royal Astronomical Society (1915); following her death in 1944, the International Lunar Committee assigned the name Blagg to a small lunar crater.

JH/MBO

PRIMARY SOURCES

International Association of Academies, Lunar Nomenclature Committee. *Collected List of Lunar Formations Named or Let-tered in the Maps of Nelson, Schmidt, and Madler.* Compiled and edited by Mary A. Blagg. Edinburgh: Neill, 1913.

Blagg, Mary. With K. Muller. *Named Lunar Formations.* London: Percy Lund Humphries, 1935. Became standard authority for matters of lunar nomenclature.

SECONDARY SOURCES

Kidwell, Peggy Aldrich. "Women Astronomers in Britain, 1780–1930." *Isis* 75 (1984): 534–546.

Ryves, P. M. "Mary Adela Blagg." *Monthly Notices of the Royal Astronomical Society* 105 (1945): 65–66.

BLAKE, MARY SAFFORD (1834–1891)

U.S. Civil War nurse and physician. Born 31 December 1834 in Hyde Park, Vt., to Diantha (Little) and Joseph Safford. Four siblings. Married James Blake (1872). Two adopted daughters. Educated Bakersfield, Vermont; informal nursing training; New York Medical College for Women (M.D., 1869); General Hospital of Vienna; German medical centers, including the University of Breslau. Professional experience: Chicago and Boston, private practice; Boston University School of Medicine, professor of women's diseases; Massachusetts Homeopathic Hospital, staff. Retired 1886. Died 8 December 1891 in Tarpon Springs, Fla.

Mary Safford was the second of five children of Joseph and Diantha (Little) Safford. When she was three, the family moved to Crete, Illinois (near Chicago), where her father farmed. Mary was educated in Bakersfield, Vermont, and learned French in Canada and German by living with a German family. After her mother died, Mary chose to live with her brother, Alfred Boardman Safford, in Jolliet, Illinois. They moved next to Shawneetown, Illinois, where Mary established and taught in a public school built by her brother. In 1858, they moved to Cairo where Alfred Safford became a wealthy banker and community benefactor.

With the outbreak of the Civil War, Cairo became a major military supply depot and training center. When sickness broke out in the crowded camps, crude hospitals were set up and Mary Safford began visiting the sick. Seeing the need for food and other supplies, she obtained permission to bring in what was needed, bought first with money from her brother and later, due to her astute management, supplied by the United States Sanitary Commission. She made the acquaintance of MARY ANN BICKERDYKE, who trained her in nursing techniques. The two cared for the first battle victims transported into Cairo.

Petite and fragile in spite of her energy and courage, Mary Safford was forced to take a leave for a time but returned to service during the battle at Shiloh. This exhausting duty led to complete collapse. She joined a party of friends on an extensive trip to Europe and took the opportunity to visit foreign hospitals. On her return to the United States, Safford entered the New York Medical College for Women. She graduated in 1869 and returned to Europe for nearly three years of surgical training, first in the General Hospital of Vienna and then at German medical centers, including the University of Breslau. There she was credited with the first ovariotomy performed by a woman. Safford began practice in Chicago in the spring of 1872 and quickly established a reputation as a surgeon and also as an advocate of dress reform, routinely wearing a sensible plain dress with no stays or flounces, one inch above floor level, revealing sturdy, flat, squared-toed shoes.

In 1872, Mary Safford married James Blake of Boston and soon joined the faculty of Boston University School of Medicine as a professor of women's diseases. She served on staff at the Massachusetts Homeopathic Hospital, maintained a private practice, and lectured throughout the community on hygiene, exercise, dress, and the working conditions for girls. Probably this marriage ended in divorce, for Mary returned to her maiden name in 1880. In 1886, frail health forced her to retire and she moved with her two adopted daughters to Tarpon Springs, Florida, where another brother, Anson P. K. Safford, resided. She died there on 8 December 1891, shortly before her fifty-seventh birthday.   JH/MBO

STANDARD SOURCES
NAW (under Safford).

BLANCHAN, NELTJE (1865–1918)

See Doubleday, Neltje Blanchan (De Graff).

BLANCHARD, FRIEDA COBB (1889–1977)

U.S. plant and animal geneticist. Born 2 October 1889 in Sydney, Australia, to Alice Vara (Proctor) and Nathan Augustus Cobb. Six siblings. Married Frank Nelson Blanchard (12 June 1922). Three children: Dorothy, Grace, and Frank Nelson. Educated at local schools in Sydney, Australia; Worcester and Cambridge, Mass.; Washington, D.C.; Radcliffe College; University of Illinois; University of Michigan (Ph.D., 1920). Professional experience: University of Michigan Botanical Gardens, assistant director. Honors and memberships: American Association for the Advancement of Science, Fellow; Board of Governors, American Society of Ichthyology and Herpetology; Michigan Academy of Sciences, Section of Botany, chair; Botanical Society of America, member; Chicago Academy of Sciences, honorary life member. Died 29 August 1977 at Ann Arbor, Mich.

Frieda Cobb was the fifth child in a scientifically oriented family. Her father was a pioneer plant pathologist and nematologist whose career included research on three continents. In 1887 N. A. Cobb left a teaching post in Massachusetts and

moved with his wife and three small children (one son had died) to Germany where he earned a Ph.D. with a dissertation on parasitic and free-living nematodes. In 1889 he went to Australia where he became the first full-time plant pathologist in the British overseas government. In Australia the Cobbs had three more children, all girls, of whom Frieda was the first. In 1905 the Cobbs returned permanently to the United States, moving first to Hawaii and then to Washington, D.C., where Cobb accepted a position in the U.S. Department of Agriculture and developed the new science of nematology.

Growing up in the Cobb family shaped Frieda's attitudes and career. Cobb always had a home laboratory where he did some of his research. Alice Cobb shared her husband's love of science, helped him in his work, and organized the household to support that work. The children, especially the girls, became their father's assistants, and Frieda developed an enthusiasm for science and a love for plants and animals. In Hawaii, where her father studied the diseases of sugar cane, Frieda worked in the laboratory he organized. She later completed high school in Washington, D.C., attended Radcliffe College for three years, assisted her father in his home laboratory in Falls Church, Virginia, for another three years, and then completed her bachelor's in general science at the University of Illinois in 1916.

In the fall of 1916, after a summer helping her father with nematode research at Woods Hole, Massachusetts, Frieda Cobb moved to Ann Arbor, Michigan, at the request of Harley Harris Bartlett, director of the University of Michigan Botanical Gardens, and a pioneer in plant genetics. There she became not only his graduate student but also, in 1919, the assistant director of the gardens. Together, Bartlett and Cobb developed the gardens as a major center for *Oenothera* (evening primrose) research as they tried to solve some of the puzzles in the newly developing science of genetics. Cobb earned her doctorate in 1920 with a study of Mendelian inheritance in certain strains of *Oenothera*. Because Bartlett was often away from Ann Arbor, Cobb became the active administrator at the gardens, maintaining facilities for scientific research and an atmosphere conducive to such research. That arrangement continued until the 1950s when both retired.

In 1922 Cobb married Frank N. Blanchard, a herpetologist, who had come to Michigan as a graduate student in 1915 and had later become a faculty member in zoology. The two worked together in several areas, including studies of garter snakes; Frank concentrated on life history, Frieda on genetics. Their work, carried on over many years, provided the first demonstration of Mendelian inheritance in a reptile. When Frank Blanchard died, unexpectedly, in 1937, Frieda Blanchard continued their work as well as her other research and raised their three children. Several generations of Michigan students appreciated her high intellectual standards and her kindness toward others.   SM

PRIMARY SOURCES

Cobb, Frieda. With H. H. Bartlett. "On Mendelian Inheritance in Crosses between Mass-Mutating and Non-Mass-Mutating Strains of *Oenothera pratincola.*" *Journal of the Washington Academy of Sciences* 9 (1919): 462–483.

———. "A Case of Mendelian Inheritance Complicated by Heterogametism and Mutation in *Oenothera pratincola.*" *Genetics* 6 (1921): 1–42.

Blanchard, Frieda Cobb. "Tuatara: 'Living Fossils' Walk on Well-Nigh Inaccessible Rocky Islands off the Coast of New Zealand." *National Geographic Magazine* 67 (1935): 649–666. The article resulted from a research and collecting trip that the Blanchards took to Australia and New Zealand in 1927 and 1928 when both obtained sabbatical leave from the University.

Blanchard, Frank N., and Frieda Cobb Blanchard, "The Inheritance of Melanism in the Garter Snake *Thamnophis sirtalis sirtalis* (Linnaeus), and Some Evidence of Effective Autumn Mating." *Papers of the Michigan Academy of Science, Arts, and Letters* 26 (1940): 177–193.

Blanchard, Frieda Cobb. "Nathan A. Cobb, Botanist and Zoologist, a Pioneer Scientist in Australia," *Asa Gray Bulletin,* n.s. 3: (1957) 205–272.

SECONDARY SOURCES

McGrath, Sylvia W. "Frieda Cobb Blanchard." In *Encyclopedia USA*, vol. 6, ed. A. P. McDonald, 156–158. Gulf Breeze, Fla.: Academic International Press, 1985.

———. "Unusually Close Companions: Frieda Cobb Blanchard and Frank Nelson Blanchard." In *Creative Couples in the Sciences*, ed. Helena M. Pycior, Nancy G. Slack, and Pnina G. Abir-Am, 156–169. New Brunswick, N.J.: Rutgers University Press, 1996.

STANDARD SOURCES

AMS 5–8, B 9.

BLANCHARD, PHYLLIS (1895–?)

U.S. psychologist. Born 14 March 1895 in Epping, N.H. Educated New Hampshire State College (A.B., 1917); Clark University (A.M., Ph.D. 1919). Professional experience: New York State Reformatory for Women, psychologist (1920); Bellevue Hospital, psychologist (1920–1922); National Committee for Mental Hygiene, psychologist (1922–1925); University of Pennsylvania, Graduate School of Medicine, instructor in psychology; Philadelphia Child Guidance Clinic, psychologist (1925). Honors and memberships: American Psychological Association, member; American Society for the Advancement of Science, Fellow. Death date unknown.

Phyllis Blanchard attended New Hampshire State College where she received her bachelor's degree and continued at Clark University for her master's and doctorate. From working as a psychologist at a reformatory for women, a mental hospital, and the National Committee for Mental Hygiene, Blanchard moved to the University of Pennsylvania as an instructor. In Philadelphia, she also worked at the Philadelphia Child Guidance Clinic. Her research interests focused on child and adolescent mental health, particularly on the development of girls.   JH/MBO

PRIMARY SOURCES

Blanchard, Phyllis. *The Adolescent Girl.* New York: Dodd, Mead, 1920.

———. *The Child and Society.* New York: Longmans, Green, 1928.

———. With M. M. Knight and I. L. Peters. *Taboo and Genetics.* New York: Moffat, Yard, 1920.

———. With I. J. Sands. *Abnormal Behavior.* New York: Dodd, Mead, 1923.

———. With C. Manasses. *New Girls for Old.* New York: Macaulay, 1930.

———. With E. R. Groves. *An Introduction to Mental Hygiene.* New York: Holt, 1930.

STANDARD SOURCES

AMS 3–8, S&B 9, 10; *Psychological Register*, vol. 3, 1932.

BLANQUIES, LUCIE (fl. 1908)

French physicist.

Little is known about Lucie Blanquies' life. She worked in MARIE CURIE's laboratory in Paris during 1908–1910. She measured the range of alpha particles from different radioactive substances, which enabled her to compare the initial energies of the particles. Blanquies used these techniques to analyze decay products of actinium, finding that actinium C was probably complex. Other reachers were unable to reproduce her results. However, actinium C was later found to decay in two ways, producing a branching in the series.   MM

PRIMARY SOURCES

Blanquies, Lucie. "Comparison entre les rayons α produits par différentes substances radioactives." *Le Radium* 4 (1907): 213–218.

———. "Comparison entre les rayons α produits par différentes substances radioactives." *Comptes Rendues* 148 (1909): 1753–1756.

———. "Comparison entre les rayons α produits par différentes substances radioactives." *Le Radium* 6 (1909): 230–232.

———. "Sur les constituants de l'radioactivité induite de l'actinium." *Comptes Rendues* 151 (1910): 57–60.

———. "Recherches sur les constituants de l'activité induite de l'actinium." *Le Radium* 7 (1910): 159–162.

SECONDARY SOURCES

Davis, J. L., "The Research School of Marie Curie in the Paris Faculty, 1907–14." *Annals of Science* 52 (1995): 321–355.

Malley, Marjorie. "From Hyperphosphorescence to Nuclear Decay: A History of the Early Years of Radioactivity, 1896–1914." Ph.D. diss., University of California, Berkeley, 1976, p. 228.

Rayner-Canham, M. F. and G. W. "Pioneer Women in Nuclear Science." *American Journal of Physics* 58 (1990): 1036–1043.

Rutherford, Ernest. *Radioactive Substances and Their Radiations.* Cambridge: Cambridge University Press, 1913.

BLATCHFORD, ELLEN C. (1900–)

Canadian physician. Born 17 October 1900 in Maple Valley, Wis., to Canadian parents. Three siblings. Married Douglas Blatchford (July 1925). Two children: Bob (1933) and Ann (1934). Educated public schools; University of Toronto (M.D., 1923); Philadelphia Hospital for Women, resident intern. Certified in anesthesia by the College of Physicians and Surgeons (1937). Professional experience: Women's College Hospital, Philadelphia, anesthetist, chief of department of anesthesia (1932–1955), active consultant in anesthesia (to 1967).

Ellen Blatchford's Canadian family moved from Wisconsin back to Canada in 1901 to a northern Ontario mining town. There they lived a rugged life in a small apartment over the store they owned. Ellen's memories of that town of dynamite blasts, fires, and two-mile walks to school with her younger brother were not happy ones. When she was eight, the family moved to Aurora where two more children were born and Ellen continued her schooling. After reading a book about a woman doctor, Ellen asked if it would be possible for her to eventually go to the university for a medical degree; to her surprise her parents encouraged her.

In Richmond Hill, where the family moved in 1918, Ellen met Lilian Langslaff, who was in medical practice with her husband and who became Ellen's inspiration. She entered the University of Toronto in the spring of 1918 along with 32 other women in a class of 250. Only 12 of the original 33 finally graduated in 1923; Ellen accepted an internship at the Philadelphia Hospital for Women. In July 1925, she married Douglas Blatchford.

Hearing of an opening for an anesthetist at the Women's College Hospital, Blatchford, who had taken coursework and interned in anesthesia at St. John's Hospital, joined the staff; she soon found herself involved in a campaign to begin a new teaching hospital. Evelyn Bateman joined the anesthetic staff in the early 1930s and the two worked together.

Blatchford received her certification diploma in anesthesia from the College of Physicians and Surgeons in 1937. The anesthesia department of the Women's College Hospital grew and Blatchford served as chief of the department until 1955 when she became active consultant (to 1967). The Blatchfords had two children, Bob (b. 1933) and Ann (b. 1934). After Douglas Blatchford retired from teaching in 1953, the couple arranged for a two-month leave each year to travel to various parts of the world.   KM

PRIMARY SOURCES

Blatchford, Ellen C. In Hellstedt, *Autobiographies.*

BLAU, MARIETTA (1894–1970)

Austrian/U.S. physicist. Born 29 April 1874 in Vienna to Florentine (Goldenzweig) Blau and Mayer (Marcus) Blau, an attorney and publisher. One brother. Educated University of Vienna (Ph.D., 1919). Professional experience: worked briefly in industry in Berlin; University of Frankfort am Main, assistant (1921–1923); Institute for Radium Research, Vienna, and Second Physical Institute, University of Vienna, unpaid positions (1923–1938); University of Göttingen and Institute of Radium, Paris, researcher (1933–1934); Bohr Institute, Copenhagen, and Institute for Organic Chemistry, Oslo, researcher (1938–1939); Technical University of Mexico City, professor of physics (1939–1944); Canadian Radium and Uranium Corporation, researcher (ca. 1944–1948); Columbia University, research physicist (1948–1950); Brookhaven National Laboratory, associate physicist (1950–1955); University of Miami, associate professor (1955–1960). Honors and memberships: Vienna Academy of Sciences, Lieben Prize; Austrian Academy of Sciences (with H. Wambacher) Haitinger Prize; Schrödinger Prize (with H. Wambacher). Died 27 January 1970, probably in Vienna.

Blau made her most significant innovations during her time as an unpaid researcher in Vienna. She was assisted in some of her researches by Hertha Wambacher, who had been a law student. Blau's sex and her Jewish background impeded her professional advancement in Austria. Since her family could support her, Blau could afford to work without pay, but consequently she later received no retirement benefits for her many years of volunteer work.

When the Nazis annexed Austria in 1938, Blau, who was out of the country at the time, did not return. She worked briefly in Oslo at the invitation of her friend Ellen Gleditsch, then relocated to Mexico City. In 1944 Blau moved to New York, where she worked on radioactivity and took out several patents. She then did research at Columbia University and at Brookhaven National Laboratory. Afterward she took a position at the University of Miami.

Due to the brevity of her employment in the United States, Blau's retirement income was very low. In order to economize on expenses, she returned to Austria for an eye operation. Poor health caused in part by radiation exposure prevented her from returning to the United States, and she died impoverished in Vienna.

Blau's first research concerned gamma and X-ray absorption. At Vienna she investigated ionization and photographic action of hydrogen particle beams (protons), then extended these studies to alpha particles. Prompted by a suggestion from Hans Petterson, Blau developed a method to capture particle tracks on photographic emulsions, which would record different kinds of nuclear reactions. She used this method to search for heavy particles in cosmic rays. Working with Hertha Wambacher, Blau found high energy tracks produced by heavy particles, including the famous Blau–Wambacher stars, tracks which meet at a point and therefore resemble a star shape. These tracks are created when cosmic rays cause atoms in the emulsion to disintegrate, releasing as many as nine long-range subatomic particles at once. Blau and Wambacher received funding to conduct further studies using balloon flights, but were interrupted by the *Anschluss*.

In Mexico Blau investigated radioactivity in rocks, springs, and sediments, and invented new methods for developing emulsions and measuring ionization. She continued studying radioactivity and cosmic rays at Columbia University, and investigated meson production at Brookhaven. Blau developed ways to use photomultipliers, which became very important to researchers. She did further research on subatomic particles at the University of Miami. JH/MBO

PRIMARY SOURCES

Blau, Marietta. "Photographische Wirkung von H–Strahlen II." *Sitzungsberichten der Akademie der Wissenschaften zu Wien* 136 (1927): 469–480.

———. With H. Wambacher. "Disintegration Processes by Cosmic Rays with the Simultaneous Emission of Several Heavy Particles." *Nature* 140 (1937): 585.

———. With H. Wambacher. "Mitteilung über photographische Untersuchungen der schweren Teilchen in der kosmischen Strahlung." *Sitzungsberichten der Akademie der Wissenschaften zu Wien* 146 (1937): 623–641.

———. "Bericht über die Entdeckung der durch kosmische Strahlung erzeugten 'Sterne' in photographischen Emulsionen." *Sitzungsberichten der Akademie der Wissenschaften zu Wien* 159, no. 2a (1950): 53–57.

———. "Photographic Emulsions," "Charge Determination of Particles in Photographic Emulsions," "Momentum Measurement in Nuclear Emulsions," "Detection and Measurement of Gamma–Rays in Photographic Emulsions," and "Determination of Mass of Nucleons in Emulsions." In *Methods of Experimental Physics—Nuclear Physics*, ed. L. C. L.

Yuan and C.-S. Wu, 5A: 208–264, 298–307, 388–408, 676–682, and 5B: 37–44. New York: Academic Press, 1961, 1963.

SECONDARY SOURCES

"Blau, Marietta." *Physics Today* 23 (July 1970): 81. Obituary notice.

Frisch, Otto. *What Little I Remember*. Cambridge: Cambridge University Press, 1979, 1980.

Moore, Walter. *Schrödinger: Life and Thought*. Cambridge: Cambridge University Press, 1989.

Stetter, Georg, and Hans Thirring. "Hertha Wambacher." *Acta Physica Austriaca* 3 (1950): 318–320.

STANDARD SOURCES

Grinstein 1993 (long article by Leopold Halpern); Poggendorff, vol. 6.

BLEDSOE, LUCYBELLE (1923–1966)

U.S. editor of geological publications. Born 1923 in Pocahontas, Ark. Never married. Educated Hendrix College, Arkansas; University of Arkansas (A.B., 1944); Columbia University (M.A., 1945). Professional experience: Geological Society of America, editorial assistant; SIPRE, editor (1956–1961); CRREL and SIPRE, editor (1961–1966). Died 29 September 1966.

Lucybelle Bledsoe was not a scientist but became very knowledgeable in geology through her editorial duties. Born in Arkansas, her degrees were in English. In 1946, she joined the staff of the Geological Society of America as an editorial assistant. Her work impressed the director of the Snow, Ice and Permafrost Research Establishment (SIPRE) where she joined the staff in 1956. SIPRE became part of the Cold Regions Research and Engineering Laboratory (CRREL) in 1961, and during that time she personally edited most of the reports that emerged from these organizations. Bledsoe died in an apartment fire.

Although Bledsoe was not a scientist, she is a good example of women doing the work and not getting much of the credit. She was the unlisted coauthor of many of the reports that emerged from SIPRE and CRREL and the "informal teacher of many scientists." James Bender, the author of her obituary notice, writes:

"Too often we, as authors of scientific reports, take for granted the careful work of good technical editors and seldom do we give them the proper credit which they so rightly deserve. So it was with Lucybelle Bledsoe. Although you will not find her name listed as author or co-author of any research papers, she has been a full-time worker in the field of glaciology for the last ten years. We believe that she contributed a great deal to the field of glaciology, especially in the all-important aspects of written communication" (Bender, 756). JH/MBO

SECONDARY SOURCES

Bender, James A. "Lucybelle Bledsoe, 1923–1966." *Journal of Glaciology* 6 (1967): 755–756.

STANDARD SOURCES

Sarjeant.

BLINOVA, EKATERINA NIKITICHNA (1906–)

Russian meteorologist. Born 7 December 1906 in Kamensk-Shakhtinskii, Rostov region. Educated North Caucasus University (Rostov-on-Don). Professional experience: Main Geophysical Observatory, staff (to 1943); Central Institute of Weather Forecasting, staff (to 1958); Institute of Applied Geophysics, staff (to 1961); Meteorological Computer Center, head of department. Honors and memberships: Soviet Academy of Sciences, corresponding member; Badge of Honor.

Ekaterina Nikitichna Blinova graduated from the North Caucasus University in Rostov-on-Don in 1928. From 1935, she held a series of appointments: in the Main Geophysical Observatory, in the Central Institute of Weather Forecasting, and in the Institute of Applied Geophysics. In 1961, she became head of a department in the Meteorological Computer Center.

Blinova's work has been largely concerned with long–range weather forecasting. Continuing the work of the mathematician N. E. Kochin, she conducted research on atmospheric front stability, developed a theory of radiative equilibrium in the atmosphere, and quantitatively explained the existence of centers of atmospheric action. She studied wave disturbances in the east-west atmospheric flow and used this method to analyze large-scale atmospheric processes. She suggested mathematical methods of long-range weather forecasting that are now widely used with the aid of computers.

In 1953, she was elected a corresponding member of the Soviet Academy of Sciences. She was also awarded the Badge of Honor and other medals. ACH

PRIMARY SOURCES

Blinova, Ekaterina Nikitichna. "Obshchaia tsirkuliatsiia atmosfery i gidrodinamicheskii dolgosrochnyi prognoz pogody." In *Meteorologiia i gidrologiia za 50 let sovetskoi vlasti*, ed. E. K. Fedorov. Leningrad: Gidrometeoizdat, 1967.

SECONDARY SOURCES

Bol'shaia sovetskaia entsiklopedia. 3rd ed. Moscow: Izd-vo "Sovetskaia entsiklopediia," 1973.

STANDARD SOURCES

Turkevich and Turkevich.

BLISS, DOROTHY ELIZABETH (1916–1987)

U.S. invertebrate zoologist. Born 13 February 1916 in Cranston, R.I. Educated Brown University (A.B., 1937; Sc.M., 1942); Radcliffe College (Ph.D., 1952). Professional experience: Milton Academy, Mass., teacher (1942–1947); Harvard University, resident fellow in biology (1952–1955); Albert Einstein College of Medicine, research assistant professor of anatomy (1956–1964), visiting research associate professor (1964–1966), from assistant curator to curator, living invertebrates (1956–1974); American Museum of Natural History, chair and curator, department of fossil and living invertebrates (from 1974). Died 1987.

Dorothy Bliss earned her first two degrees from Brown University and her doctorate from Radcliffe College. From 1956 to 1974, she worked at the Albert Einstein College of Medicine, both as a research professor of anatomy and as the curator of living invertebrates. She left this position in 1974 to become the curator of the department of fossil and living invertebrates. Concurrently, she had a National Science Foundation research grant in 1957, and was adjunct professor at the City University of New York in 1971. She was a Fellow of the AAAS and a member of the American Society of Zoologists and the American Institute of Biological Sciences. JH/MBO

PRIMARY SOURCES

Bliss, Dorothy Elizabeth. "Endocrine Control of Metabolism in the Decapod Crustacean, *Gecarcinus lateralis*." Ph.D. diss., Radcliffe College, 1952.

———. With Dorothy M. Skinner. *Tissue Respiration in Invertebrates*. New York: American Museum of Natural History, 1963.

———. With Lawrence G. Abele, David C. Sandeman, and Harold C. Atwood. *The Biology of Crustacea*. New York: Academic Press, 1982.

SECONDARY SOURCES

"Dorothy Elizabeth Bliss." *Harvard Magazine* 90 (1988): 129. Obituary notice.

"Dorothy Elizabeth Bliss." *Radcliffe Quarterly* 79 (1988). Obituary notice.

Mantel, Linda H. "Dorothy E. Bliss." *Journal of Crustacean Biology* 9 (1988): 706–709. Obituary notice.

STANDARD SOURCES

AMS, P&B 10–14; Rossiter 1995.

BLISS, ELEANOR ALBERT (1899–1987)

U.S. bacteriologist and immunologist. Born 16 August 1899 in Jamestown, R.I., to Edith G. (West) and William J. A. Bliss. Educated Bryn Mawr College (A.B., 1921); Johns Hopkins University (Sc.D., 1925; fellow in medicine, 1925–1935). Professional experience: Johns Hopkins University, faculty member (1936–1952); U.S. Army Chemical Corps, advisor (1945–1950); Bryn Mawr College, professor of biology and dean of graduate school (1952–1966); University of Pennsylvania, board member (1954–1959). Died 1987.

Eleanor Bliss trained as a bacteriologist at Bryn Mawr and then went on to take her doctorate in science at Johns Hopkins where she was made a fellow in medicine, working in the field of bacteriology from 1925 to 1935. Made a member of the Johns Hopkins faculty, she soon made her name with a major book on the clinical and experimental use of sulfa drugs. She left to work with the U.S. Army Chemical Corps during World War II. After the war, she returned to Hopkins but soon accepted a position as dean of the graduate school at Bryn Mawr, which she combined with a professorship in biology.

Bliss did significant research on the hemolytic streptococcus. She discovered group F, a minute hemolytic streptococcus of the serological group, and became an authority on sulfa drugs. She published numerous papers in her field during her lifetime. She was a Fellow of the American Academy of Microbiologists, a Fellow of the AAAS, and received an honorary degree from Drexel University in 1956.   JH/MBO

PRIMARY SOURCES
Bliss, Eleanor. With Perrin H. Long. *Clinical and Experimental Use of Sulfanilamide, Sulfapyridine and Allied Compounds.* New York: MacMillan, 1939.

STANDARD SOURCES
AMS 5–8, B 9, P&B 10–11; Bailey; Debus; Rossiter 1995.

BLISS, MARY CAMPBELL (1877–1948)

U.S. botanist. Born 19 April 1877 in Newburyport, Mass. Educated Wellesley College (A.B., 1899; A.M., 1904); Radcliffe College (Ph.D., 1922). Professional experience: Massachusetts public high school, teacher (1900–1901); Wellesley College, assistant in botany (1904–1905), instructor (1905–1915), assistant professor (1915–1922), associate professor (1922–1940), professor (from 1940). Died 1948.

Mary Campbell Bliss earned her bachelor's degree from Wellesley College and then taught high school for a year. She returned to Wellesley for her master's degree. She was an assistant in botany at Wellesley while she was working on this

degree. She proceeded through the academic ranks from instructor to professor. After she received her doctorate, she was promoted to associate professor. She was a member of the Botanical Society and did research in plant morphology, specifically on the vessel in seed plants and tracheal elements in ferns.   JH/MBO

PRIMARY SOURCES
Bliss, Mary Campbell. "Part 1: The Vessel in Seed Plants; Part 2: The Tracheal Element in Ferns." Ph.D. diss., Harvard (Radcliffe), 1922.

STANDARD SOURCES
AMS 3–7.

BLOCK, JEANNE (HUMPHREY) (1923–1981)

U.S. psychologist. Born 17 July 1923 in Tulsa, Okla., to Louise Lewis and Charles Joseph Humphrey. One younger brother. Married Jack Block. Four children. Educated public schools; Oregon State College (1941–1942); Reed College (1946–1947); Stanford University (Ph.D. 1951). Professional experience: SPARS (women's reserve of the U.S. Coast Guard), enlisted (1943), commissioned as ensign (1944); Veterans Administration, clinical psychology, intern (1948); Stanford Child Guidance Clinic, psychometrician and therapist; Stanford University Department of Psychology, instructor (1951–1952); University of California Medical School, Department of Psychiatry, researcher; Children's Hospital at East Bay, childhood asthma researcher; University of California, Berkeley, adjunct professor (1979–1981). Honors and memberships: National Institute of Mental Health, special research fellowship at the Norwegian Institute for Social Research, Oslo; Rosenberg Grant, Institute of Human Development, Berkeley (1965); NIMH Research Scientist Development Award (1968, 1973, 1978). Died 4 December 1981, at Berkeley, Calif., of pancreatic cancer.

Jeanne Humphrey Block, known for her longitudinal studies of personality and cognitive development, contributed brilliantly in several areas of clinical psychology. Her father, Charles Joseph Humphrey, a building contractor, and mother, Louise Lewis Humphrey, a tax analyst and future lobbyist, moved to Portland, Oregon, when Jeanne was four months old. There her younger brother, Richard, was born. Jeanne grew up on a small farm that was largely self-providing and went through the local schools with the same set of friends until high school graduation (1941). After graduation, she attended Oregon State College for one year, majoring in home economics, but quit to work in a local department store. By then, the United States was at war and Jeanne's life, like many others', was affected. In 1943 she enlisted in the women's unit of the coast guard, serving with distinction. In 1945, she was severely scalded and spent weeks undergoing treatment and many painful skin grafts before returning to duty. When demobilized in 1946, Humphrey enrolled in Reed College, near her home, majoring in psychology. She graduated with honors and planned to attend Harvard until she happened to visit Stanford University. There she met the learning psychologist Ernest Hilgard, who invited her to come to Stanford. Maud Merrill James, Humphrey's mentor at Stanford, and Howard Hunt led the clinical psychology department which was in the development stages. Other psychology courses were taught by Ernest Hilgard (learning), Quinn McNemar (statistics), Calvin Stone (comparative psychology), Donald Taylor (experimental methods), and Paul Farnsworth (history of psychology), among others. She was given the opportunity to intern at the Veterans Administration Hospital, an experience that exposed her to a full range of psychopathology. Concurrently, she served in the Stanford Child Guidance Clinic, first as a psychometrician and later as a therapist with children and parents.

Another intelligent and intense postwar student interested in Lewinian psychology and psychoanalytic theory was Jack Block. The two completed joint theses on a concept they called ego control and ego resiliency and married in 1950 after Jack received his Ph.D. Jeanne Block was already pregnant with the first of their four children when she completed her doctoral thesis in 1951. After Susan Dale (1952), came Judith Lynne (1953), David Lewis (1956), and Carol Ann (1959). As was expected of even career women in the 1950s, Block left academic life for child-rearing and homemaking but kept intellectually involved in psychology by writing and researching part-time. She was a key figure in the University of California Medical School study comparing the parents of schizophrenic children with the parents of neurotic children. For the California Medical Association, she interviewed a group of physicians who had been sued for malpractice and wrote an analytical report that was never publicly released. She served as consultant at a mental health clinic, began her influential work on the psychology of childhood asthma, and wrote several papers with her husband. Along with being a model mother, homemaker, and community figure, she underwent a personal psychoanalysis. A social activist, she protested the Vietnam War, helped start the Committee for Social Responsibility (which later became Physicians for Social Responsibility), and supported feminist issues. She was widely sought after as a consultant and lecturer.

In 1963, Jeanne Block received a Special Research Fellowship from the National Institute of Mental Health and the entire family spent a year in Oslo, where Jack Block did sabbatical research and Jeanne Block held an appointment at the Norwegian Institute for Social Research. Soon after the family returned to the United States, she returned to work full-time and completed several studies comparing the socialization practices of the four Scandinavian countries, America, and England, and subsequently developed her widely used assessment instrument, the Child Rearing Practices Report (1965). Returning to Berkeley in 1965, Block began studies of the personalities, the moral orientations, and the parenting of different types of student activists. She published her first single-author paper (on asthmatic children and their parents) in 1968 and received a National Institute of Mental Health Research Scientist Career Development Award (renewed in 1973 and in 1978), sited within the Institute of Human Development, where her husband worked. Together they started the ambitious longitudinal study of personality development that both controlled and fulfilled their career futures.

The Block and Block Longitudinal Study combined concepts and issues that were challenging and exciting in a format designed to provide empirical knowledge and define biological and cultural factors in behavior/personality development. The study observed and tested 130 children at ages three, four, five, seven, eleven, and fourteen (later extended to ages eighteen and twenty-three as well). In spite of frequent hospitalizations due to a disease of the autoimmune system (probably dating from her severe burns in the 1940s), Block devoted herself wholly to the continuation of this huge enterprise. She generated many scientific papers revealing findings in regard to such diverse issues as sex role and socialization patterns, intolerance of ambiguity in young children, sex differences in cognitive functioning, effects of delay of gratification, effects of family stress, creativity, early antecedents of low self-esteem in adolescents, and many others. Perhaps her primary contribution was the series of essays she wrote during the 1970s on sex role development, culminating in her posthumously published book, *Sex Role Identity and Ego Development* (1984). This series of insightful and fully documented findings pulled together previously explored issues of biological and cultural factors with contemporary technical and societal influences resulting in a revision of understanding gender role development. Her seminal work led to studies by others in sex role and socialization, sex role stereotyping, ego control and ego resiliency, and influence of parental disagreement or family stress on personality development of children.

Block served on numerous professional committees of the American Psychological Association (APA); was elected Fellow of the AAAS (1980) and of four APA divisions; served on National Institute of Mental Health committees; received APA Hofheimer Prize for Research 1974 (childhood asthma study). She was valued as a thoughtful and strong resource for conferences, dissertation committees, and advisory boards. In 1979 she was made an adjunct professor in the department of psychology at Berkeley and, that same year, gave a master lecture at APA on the differential socialization of males and females.

Jeanne Block lived in an era when society's expectations dictated that the role of wife and mother supersede career development for women, yet she managed to excel in both areas. Most of her contributions were made after raising her four children, after remastering confidence in herself and her field as well as gaining personal recognition in the shadow of an outstanding and established husband. Proving herself highly capable and an equal partner in a complementary and supportive professional marriage, Block was just beginning to reap the harvest of her hard work when she succumbed to cancer 4 December 1981.   JH/MBO

PRIMARY SOURCES
Block, Jeanne H. "Sex-Role Typing and Instrumental Behavior: a Developmental Study." *Resources in Education*, February 1976. Abstract no. 113 014
———. "Another Look at Sex Differentiation in the Socialization Behaviors of Mothers and Fathers." In *Psychology of Women: Future Directions for Research*, ed. F. L. Denmark & J. Sherman. New York: Psychological Dimensions, 1978.
———. With J. Block. "The Role of Ego-Control and Ego-Resiliency in the Organization of Behavior." In *The Minnesota Symposia on Child Psychology*, vol. 13, ed. W. A. Collins, 39–101. Hillsdale, N.J.: Lawrence Erlbaum Associates, 1978.
———. With P. H. Jennings, E. Harvey, and E. Simpson. "The Interaction between Allergic Predisposition and Psychopathology in Childhood Asthma." *Psychosomatic Medicine* 4, 307–320.
———. *Sex Role Identity and Ego Development*. San Francisco: Jossey-Bass, 1984.
———. With J. Block, and P. F. Gjerde. "The Personality of Children Prior to Divorce." *Child Development* 57, no. 4 (August 1986): 827–840.

SECONDARY SOURCES
Helson, Ravenna. "Jeanne Block (1923–1981)" *American Psychologist* 38 (March 1983): 338–339. Obituary notice.

STANDARD SOURCES
AMS, S&B 9–13; O'Connell and Russo 1990; *Psychological Register*, vol. 3, 1932.

BLODGETT, KATHARINE BURR
(1898–1979)

U.S. physicist. Born 10 January 1898 in Schenectady, N.Y., to Katharine Buchanan (Burr) and George Bedington Blodgett. One brother. Never Married. Educated Saranac Lake, N.Y.; Rayson School, New York City; Bryn Mawr College, (A.B., 1917); University of Chicago (M.S., 1918); Cambridge University (doctorate

in physics, 1926). Professional experience: General Electric, researcher (1918–1924; 1926–1932; 1933–1963). Honors and memberships: honorary doctorates Elmira College (1939), Western College (1942), Brown University (1942), Russell Sage College (1944); Independent Woman cited her among "Women of 1939"; AAUW, Annual Achievement Award (1945); American Chemical Society, Garvan Medal (1951); Photographic Society of America, Annual Achievement Award (1972). Died 12 October 1979 in Schenectady, N.Y.

Katharine Burr Blodgett's father was a respected patent attorney at General Electric in Schenectady, New York. George Blodgett died before Katharine was born. After his death, her mother moved Katharine and her brother to New York City. The family moved to France for four years so that the children would be exposed to French language and culture. They returned to New York for a short time and then went to Europe again. It was not until Katharine was eight years old that she enrolled in a school. Blodgett was awarded a scholarship to Bryn Mawr where she had two teachers, mathematician CHARLOTTE ANGAS SCOTT and physicist James Barnes, who especially impressed her. During the 1917 Christmas season, Irving Langmuir, who would later become a Nobel Laureate, escorted Katharine on a tour of the General Electric research laboratories and agreed that the daughter of his former colleague could have a job there after she had studied more science. Consequently, after she got her bachelor's degree in 1917, she went to the University of Chicago where she worked with Harvey B. Lemon on a problem involving the adsorption of gases. She and Lemon jointly published a paper on this subject, which appeared in the *Proceedings of the National Academy of Sciences*. Since papers had to be communicated by a member of the academy, Nobel Prize Winner Albert Abraham Michaelson agreed to do so. Langmuir kept his word and Blodgett got her job at General Electric. From 1918 to 1924, she and Langmuir formed a creative team and carried out some fine research. Realizing that Blodgett was talented and looking out for her best interests, Langmuir suggested that she work with Sir Ernest Rutherford at the Cavendish laboratory, Cambridge. Blodgett became the first woman to receive a doctorate in physics from Cambridge University. She returned to Schenectady and again collaborated with Langmuir for the next six years. In 1932, Langmuir received the Nobel Prize and asked Blodgett to work on the problems associated with his thin films. They published some results collaboratively, but as Blodgett matured as a scientist she published more individually. She was not concerned with her title as long as she was with GE. All she wanted to do was her research. She received recognition, however, from her invention of nonreflecting glass. In 1938, GE announced that Blodgett had produced a glass that allowed 99 percent of the light striking it to pass through. A similar accomplishment but a different method of achieving it was announced at MIT the following day. Blodgett's accomplishment appealed to the media and to the public and her name and picture appeared in *Time* magazine. Her process involved building up one at a time more than two hundred successive monomolecular layers on glass and metal surfaces. These techniques were expanded in a series of publications and her interests changed from the fatty acids and metallic ions that were deposited to the films themselves. Studying the brilliant colors produced and the ways in which they varied with successive additions, she realized she could reduce the quantity of light reflected from the surface of glass. She also realized that this technique would provide a sensitive tool for making measurements of very thin films.

Blodgett was a quiet, unassuming person, who seldom talked about herself. She was a member of the Presbyterian church but was not politically active. With a reputation as an excellent cook, an amateur astronomer, and a competent gardener, she enjoyed quiet activities at home as well as out of doors, where she spent as much time as possible at her house at Lake George, New York. JH/MBO

PRIMARY SOURCES

Blodgett, Katharine Burr. With H. B. Lemon. "The Relative Adsorption of Mixtures of Oxygen and Nitrogen in Coconut Shell Charcoal." *Proceedings of the National Academy of Sciences* 5 (1919): 289–295.

———. "Monomolecular Films on Fatty Acids on Glass." *Journal of the American Chemical Society* 56 (1934): 313–315.

———. "Films Built by Depositing Successive Monomolecular Layers on a Solid Surface." *Journal of the American Chemical Society* 57 (1935): 1007–1022.

———. With I. Langmuir. "A New Method of Investigating Unimolecular films." *Kolloid Zeitschrift* 73 (1935): 258–263.

———. "Use of Interference to Extinguish Reflection of Light from Glass." *Physical Review* 55 (1939): 391–404.

SECONDARY SOURCES

Clark, A. E. "Dr. Katharine Burr Blodgett, 81, Developer of Nonreflecting Glass." *New York Times*, 13 October 1979.

Goff, A. C. "Katharine Burr Blodgett." In *Women Can be Engineers*, 177–182. Youngstown, Ohio, 1946.

STANDARD SOURCES

AMS 6–8, P 9, P&B 10; Bailey; *Current Biography* 1940; Grinstein 1993; *Notable*; Rossiter 1995; Yost.

BLUHM, AGNES (1862–1944)

German physician and eugenicist. Born 9 January 1862. Father, military officer. Educated in preparation for teaching; University of Zürich, Medical studies (M.D., 1890); Königliche Frauenklinik in Munich, special medical training. Professional experience: Berlin, private physician (from 1890); Berliner Gesellschaft für Rassenhygiene, founded in 1905, member; Archiv für Rassen- und Gesellschaftsbiologie, coeditor; Kaiser-Wilhelm Institute in Berlin, conducted experimental research on mutation (1919). Honors and memberships: Silver Leibnitz medal for her work, "Alkohol und Nachkommenschaft" (1932). Goethe Medal for the Arts and Sciences (1940). Died in Berlin in 1944.

Agnes Bluhm was one of the first women in Germany to fight her way into the masculine domain of the medical profession and medical science. Her image as a pioneer of women's studies, however, takes on a different perspective when one is made aware of the impetus that drove Bluhm's professional work and her political activity in the women's movement: her interests centered primarily on the improvement of "the Race" through "racial hygiene."

Bluhm had originally intended to become a teacher. She finished her professional training in Zurich in 1884 and immediately gained admission to the university there. Through her friendship with medical scientist Alfred Ploetz she was confronted for the first time in her studies with the views and politics of racial hygiene. Over time she became convinced that equality for all people would result in degeneration.

After receiving her medical degree at age twenty-eight, she volunteered at the Königliche Frauenklinik (Royal Women's Clinic) in Munich. Late in 1890 she opened her medical practice in Berlin. She was the third woman in Berlin to do so, following EMILIE LEHMUS and FRANZISKA TIBURTIUS. Due to the fact that her doctor's degree had been obtained in a foreign country, she came into conflict with city officials and the medical community, who raised questions concerning its legitimacy. However, the laws at that time did not yet limit the practice of medicine to an academic degree.

In 1895 Agnes Bluhm had the opportunity to be the first female doctor to contribute to the *Deutsche Medizinische Wochenschrift* with her article "Die Entwicklung und der gegenwartige Stand des medicinischen Frauenstudiums in den europäischen und aussereuropäischen Ländern." In this essay she called for the admission of women to the study of medicine.

In 1905 severe ear problems forced her to give up her medical practice. She then turned her energies to the formulation of demands on the state and on employers for the protection of women workers and expectant mothers. The unseen motive behind her enthusiastic engagement was a eugenically related interest in women's fertility.

Bluhm was among the early members of the Berliner Gesellschaft für Rassenhygiene (Berlin Society for Race Hygiene), founded in 1905. This organization gave rise to the

Deutsche Gesellschaft für Rassenhygiene (German Society for Race Hygiene), established in 1910. The goal of this order of biologists, medical scientists and physicians was the preservation of "the Race." Bluhm participated in the scientific founding of "race biology" which provided the groundwork for eugenics. In numerous articles in *Die Archiv für Rassenhygiene und Gesellschaftsbiologie*, of which she was coeditor, she defined "race" as the "preservation of and developmental unity of life," therefore defining it as a purely biological term. She also related physical and psychological characteristics to genetic make–up, assigning them to individual types as well as different races and drawing conclusions concerning their superiority and inferiority. Such concepts were based on ideas of selection as drawn from social Darwinism.

In her contributions to the magazine *Die Frau*, the mouthpiece of the Bundes Deutscher Frauenverein [Federal German United Women's Movement], Bluhm promoted the idea that the reproductive behavior of German women would guarantee the quantitative and qualitative preservation of "the Race." She embraced "fertility selection" in the form of eugenically indicated, forced sterilization as an effective measure toward the "eradication of inferiors." Involuntary sterilization was later legally ordered and carried out by the Nazis.

After World War I Bluhm began experimental work in mutation research at the Kaiser-Wilhelm Institute in Berlin. Behind the genotypical experiments lay an ambition to master "gene manipulation" for the purpose of "the improvement of the Race." For her research Agnes Bluhm was presented with numerous awards and honors. For her work "Alchohol und Nachkommenschaft" (Alcohol and the Next Generation), she was awarded the silver Leipzig medal in 1932. In 1940 she received the Goethe award in Arts and Sciences—the first German woman to do so.

Bluhm's autobiographical accounts of her work read as if she pioneered the professional emancipation of women. The image of women as propagated by her did not, however, indicate an advocacy for emancipation: she saw motherhood as a woman's duty and sacrifice. A woman's occupation would stand in the way of this duty. Bluhm justified the study of medicine by women and women's participation in the medical profession by pointing to the special role of the female physician. In her book *Die rassenhygienischen Aufgaben des weiblichen Arztes* (The Race Hygiene Problem for Women Physicians), published in 1936, she pictured the professional woman physician as an instrument of racial hygiene. Here she asserts that the specifically "feminine psyche" is especially suited to the dissemination and implementation of racial hygiene, a chilling suggestion in view of the tragic consequences of Nazi eugenics.   SNS

PRIMARY SOURCES

Bluhm, Agnes. *Zur Aetiologie des Morbus Brightii*. Leipzig, 1890.
———. "Mutterschutz und Rassenhygiene." In *Archiv für Rassen- und Gesellschaftsbiologie* 6 (1909).
———. With Marie Baum. *Der Einfluss der gewerblicher Arbeit auf das personliche Leben der Frau*. Jena: G. Fischer, 1910.
———. *Zum Problem Alkohol und Nachkommenschaft*. Munich: J. F. Lehmanns, 1930.
———. *Die rassenhygienischen Aufgaben des weiblichen Artztes*. Berlin: A. Metzer, 1936.

SECONDARY SOURCES

Just, Günther. "Agnes Bluhm und ihr Lebenswerk" *Die Ärtzin* 17 (1941): 516–526.
Kuhlo, Ulla. "Dr. Agnes Bluhm" *Deutsches Ärzteblatt* 72 (1942): 32.
Siebertz, Karin. "Agnes Bluhm: Ärztin und Rassenhygienikerin." In *Pionierinnen Feministinnen Karrierefrauen? Zur Geschichte des Frauenstudiums in Deutschland*, ed. Anne Schluter. Pfaffenweiler: Centaurus, 1992.

STANDARD SOURCES

Deutsche Biographische Enzyclopädie, vol. 1, 1995.

BLUKET, NINA ALEKSANDROVNA (1902–)

Russian botanist. Born 1902 in Oboyan (now Kursk Oblast), Russia. Educated Agronomical Faculty, Timiryazev Agricultural Academy (1924); higher pedagogical courses (completed 1928); (D.Biol.Sci., 1960). Professional experience: Moscow Political Educational Institute, staff member (1926–1929), instructor (1929–1931); various Moscow institutions, director of correspondence courses in botany (1930–1931); Academy of Socialist Agriculture, instructor (1931–1932); Timiryazev Biological Museum, head botany department; Moscow Timiryazev Agricultural Academy, professor (after 1943).

Nina Aleksandrovna Bluket was educated at the Timiryazev Agricultural Academy where she returned to work, first as head of the botany department of its biological museum and then the Timiryazev Agricultural Academy where she advanced to the rank of professor.   JH/MBO

PRIMARY SOURCES

Bluket, Nina. *Practical Laboratory Work on Botany*. 1934.
———. *The Plant and Its Life*. 1936.
———. *Starch in the Vegetative Organs of Angiospermae*. 1960.
———. *The Study of the Elimination System in Plants*. 1962.

STANDARD SOURCES

Debus.

BLUNT, KATHARINE (1876–1954)

U.S. nutritionist and educator. Born 28 May 1876 in Philadelphia, Pa., to Fanny (Smythe) and Stanhope English Blunt. Never married. Two sisters. Educated "the Elms," Miss Porter's School, Springfield, Mass.; Vassar College (A.B., 1898); MIT (1902–1903); University of Chicago (Ph.D., 1907). Professional experience: Vassar College, assistant in chemistry (1902–1905); Pratt Institute, N.Y., instructor in chemistry (1907–1913); University of Chicago, assistant professor, then associate professor, home economics (1913–1925), professor and chair of department (1925–1929); Connecticut College for Women, president (1929–1943). Honors and memberships: Home Economics Association, president (1924–1926); Connecticut State Board of Education, board member (1931–1940); member, Sigma Xi, Phi Beta Kappa, and many professional organizations. Honorary degrees: Connecticut College (LL.D., 1943), Wesleyan University (LL.D., 1936), Mount Holyoke College (1937), University of Chicago (1941). Died 29 July 1954.

Katharine Blunt, college president and nutritionist, was the oldest of three daughters of a professional soldier, Stanhope English Blunt, who taught as a young man at West Point, and was an expert in gunnery and small arms, retiring as a colonel. Like her female relatives, Blunt went to a finishing school, the Porter School, but then she went on to Vassar College where she became interested in science. After graduating in 1898, she followed her parents' wishes and returned home to do volunteer church and civic work. Influenced by the new field of home economics that another Vassar graduate, ELLEN SWALLOW RICHARDS, was creating at the Massachusetts Institute of Technology, Blunt spent a year at MIT and then returned to teach at Vassar as an assistant in chemistry for three years (1902–1905). She then spent two years at the University of Chicago, obtaining her doctorate in organic chemistry in 1907.

Blunt then taught chemistry at the Pratt Institute in Brooklyn from 1907 to 1913. Her involvement in nutritional studies and her emphasis on research brought her back to the University of Chicago to the department of home economics as an assistant professor in 1913. Here she remained until 1929, rising to associate professor in 1918. Her excellent organizational skills meant that she served as the informal head of the department from this period onward. Only when she was made full professor in 1925 did she also receive the formal title of department head. During World War I, she was asked by the U.S. Department of Agriculture and the Food Administration to work on pamphlets on food conservation. This mission resulted in not only pamphlets but also a textbook, *Food and the War* (1918), written with Florence Powdermaker. In the 1920s she also published a series of articles on food chemistry and nutrition in various

scholarly journals, served as president of the American Home Economics Association from 1924 to 1926 and edited the home economics series published by the University of Chicago Press. Her work culminated in a well-received summary of her research, *Ultraviolet Light and Vitamin D in Nutrition*, published in 1930 with Ruth Cowan.

A change of direction came with her appointment as third president of Connecticut College for Women in 1929. She helped to place the college on a secure financial basis and a strong academic accreditation. She also brought many outstanding women to speak on campus, including JANE ADDAMS, Eleanor Roosevelt, and ALICE HAMILTON. Blunt retired in 1943, but was brought back to serve as president again in 1945. Blunt never married but had many friends. As a young woman she traveled widely and enjoyed mountain climbing. She also traveled after her retirement, as far as Turkey and Israel, but her increasing blindness caused her to fall and break her hip in 1954. She died on 29 July from a pulmonary embolism in a New London hospital.

JH/MBO

PRIMARY SOURCES

———. With Florence Powdermaker. *Food and the War: A Textbook for College Classes.* Boston and New York: Houghton Mifflin, 1918.

———. With Ruth Cowan. *Ultraviolet Light and Vitamin D in Nutrition.* Chicago: University of Chicago Press, 1930.

SECONDARY SOURCES

Noyes, Gertrude. "Katharine Blunt." *Connecticut Teacher* January 1950.

Nye, Irene. *Home Economics at the University of Chicago 1892–1956.* Chicago: University of Chicago Press, 1982.

STANDARD SOURCES

Current Biography 1946; *NAW* (M) (long article by Janice Law Trecker); *NCAB*.

BOCCHI (BUCCA), DOROTEA (fl. 1390)

Italian teacher of medicine. Professor of medicine, University of Bologna.

Dorotea Bocchi was appointed professor of medicine at the University of Bologna in 1390 to succeed her father. She remained in this post for forty years. JH/MBO

SECONDARY SOURCES

Fantuzzi, Giovanni. *Notizie degli scrittori bolognesi, raccolte da Givanni Fantuzzi.* 9 vols. Bologna: S. Tommasco d'Aquino, 1781–1794.

BOCHANTSEVA, ZINAIDA PETROVNA
(1907–)

Russian cytologist and plant embryologist. Born 1907 in Verny (now Alma-Ata, Kazakhstan). Educated Central Asian University, Tashkent. biological sciences, candidate (1945). Professional experience: faculty of biology, Central Asian University, assistant, then lecturer; Tashkent Botanical Gardens, associate.

Zinaida Petrovna Bochantseva worked at the Central Asian University in Tashkent, Uzbekistan, from 1926 to 1941, first as an assistant, then as a lecturer. She graduated from the university in 1930 and in the same year became an associate of the Tashkent Botanical Gardens. She was awarded the degree of candidate of biological sciences (similar to a Ph.D.) in 1945.

Bochantseva's main field of research was intergeneric hybridization, caryosystematics, embryology, spermatogenesis, and the biology of florescence. She took part in expeditions to study decorative export plants from many areas of Central Asia including areas in Kazakhstan, the Ferghana Mountains, and Karmine area. She has written extensively on tulips.   ACH

PRIMARY SOURCES
Bochantseva, Zinaida Petrovna. *Novye sorty tiul'panov selektsii Botanicheskogo sada AN USSR.* Tashkent: "Fan," 1969.

———. *Tiul'pany: morfologiia, tsitologiia i biologiia.* Tashkent: Izd-vo Akademii nauk Uzbekskoi SSR, 1962.

STANDARD SOURCES
Debus.

BODLEY, RACHEL LITTLER (1831–1888)

U.S. chemist and botanist. Born 7 December 1831 in Cincinnati, Ohio, to Rebecca (Talbott) and Anthony Prichard Bodley, a carpenter. Four siblings. Educated at a private school in Cincinnati; Wesleyan Female College, Cincinnati (classical diploma, 1849); Polytechnic College, Philadelphia (1860). Cincinnati Female Seminary, teacher (1862–1865), professor (1865–1874), dean (1874–1888); Female Medical College, Philadelphia. Honors and memberships: Academy of Natural Sciences of Philadelphia (1871), New York Academy of Sciences (1876); Franklin Institute (1880); honorary M.D. degree from the Woman's Medical College (1879). Died 15 June 1888 in Philadelphia.

Raised a Presbyterian, Rachel Bodley, the third of five children, decided to become a medical missionary but was rejected because of frail health. After first studying at a private school run by her mother in Cincinnati she attended Wesleyan Female College. When she left Wesleyan, Bodley continued her studies in the natural sciences at the Polytechnic College in Philadelphia (1860). In 1862 she returned to

Cincinnati to teach at the Cincinnati Female Seminary. She was later (1865) appointed to the first chair of chemistry at the Female Medical College (later named the Woman's Medical College) in Philadelphia. She became dean of the college in 1874. In addition to teaching and research, Bodley was an elected school director in Philadelphia's 29th School Section (1882–1885, 1887–1888) and was one of the women visitors appointed (1883) by the State Board of Public Charities to inspect local charitable institutions. She died unexpectedly of a heart attack at the age of fifty-six.

Bodley was the recipient of numerous honors during her lifetime, including membership in the Academy of Natural Sciences of Philadelphia (1871), a corresponding membership in the New York Academy of Sciences (1876), a charter membership in the American Chemical Society (1876), and a membership in Philadelphia's Franklin Institute (1880). In 1879 the Woman's Medical College awarded her an honorary M.D. degree.

Although most of Rachel Bodley's time was occupied in teaching chemistry and botany and in administrative responsibilities, she was also interested in the classification of plants. While teaching in Cincinnati, she classified and mounted an extensive collection (the plant collections of Joseph Clark), and during her years at the Woman's Medical College she continued to collect and classify plant materials. Bodley made no theoretical scientific advances but was nonetheless important in the history of women in science. A statistical survey she conducted in 1881, concerning the careers of graduates of the Woman's Medical College (published in pamphlet form as *The College Story*), was one of the first collections of facts relative to women and the professions. Two of her lectures have also been published. By writing and teaching as well as participating in scientific societies and delivering lectures, Bodley helped to establish an image of woman in science.   MBO

PRIMARY SOURCES
Bodley, Rachel. *Catalogue of Plants, Contained in [the] Herbarium of Joseph Clark.* Cincinnati, Ohio: R. P. Thompson, 1865.

———. *Introductory Lectures to the Class of the Woman's Medical College of Pennsylvania: Delivered at the Opening of the Nineteenth Annual Session, October 15, 1868.* Philadelphia: Merrihew and Son, 1868.

———. *The College Story: Valedictory Address to the Twenty–ninth Graduating Class of the Woman's Medical College of Pennsylvania, March 17th, 1881.* Philadelphia: Grant, Faires, and Rodgers, 1881.

SECONDARY SOURCES
Alsop, Gulielma Fell. "Rachel Bodley: Professor of Chemistry (1865–1874)," "Rachel Bodley: Dean (1874–1888)," "The College Story," "Pioneer Women Missionaries of the

Woman's Medical College." In *History of the Woman's Medical College, Philadelphia, Pennsylvania 1850–1950,* 101–109, 110–126, 127–134, 135–144. Philadelphia, Pa.: J. B. Lippincott, 1950.

Drachman, Virginia G. "The Limits of Progress: The Professional Lives of Women Doctors, 1881–1926." *Bulletin of the History of Medicine* 60 (1986): 58–72.

Rossiter, Margaret. "Women Scientists in America before 1920." *American Scientist* 62 (1974): 312–323.

STANDARD SOURCES
BDAS; Grinstein 1997; *NAW* (long article by Gulielma Fell Alsop); Ogilvie 1986.

BOGDANOVSKAIA, VERA EVSTAF'EVNA (1867–1896)

Russian chemist. Born 17 September 1867 in St. Petersburg, daughter of Evstaf I. Bogdanovskii, a professor of surgery. Two siblings. Married Ia. K. Popov. Educated Smol'nii Institute in St. Petersburg; St. Petersburg Higher Women's Courses; University of Geneva (Ph.D., 1892). Professional experience: Lectured at Higher Women's Courses in St. Petersburg. Died 8 May 1896 at Izhevskii Zavod.

Vera Evstaf'evna Bogdanovskaia was the second of the three children of E. I. Bogdanovskii, a professor of surgery in St. Petersburg. With her older brother and younger sister, she was educated at home on progressive lines. She was a lively and witty girl with both scientific and artistic abilities. In 1878 at the age of eleven she entered the Smol'nii Institute in St. Petersburg and from 1883 to 1887 she studied in the physical-mathematical department of the Higher Women's Courses, where she impressed her professors with her ability. Following her graduation, she worked for two years in the laboratory of the courses and also in the laboratories of the Academy of Sciences and the Military Surgical Academy.

In 1889 Bogdanovskaia went to the University of Geneva to study under a Professor Groebe. She originally intended to work on obtaining a combination analogous to prussic acid in which phosphorus would be substituted for nitrogen, but Groebe dissuaded her. Instead she conducted research on dibenzyl ketone, which was the subject of the dissertation she defended in 1892.

In 1892, she returned to Russia as an assistant to a Professor L'vov at the Higher Women's Courses. She taught chemistry to beginners and delivered a series of lectures on stereochemistry, the first that had ever been given in Russia. Bogdanovskaia was considered a brilliant lecturer and dedicated teacher. In 1897, she published a beginners' chemistry textbook, which was widely used. She also assisted L'vov in the posthumous publication of A. M. Butlerov's *Vvedeniia k pol-*

nomu izucheniiu organicheskoi khimii, translated chemical publications, and wrote critical reviews.

Bogdanovskaia was interested in entomology, particularly in bees, about which she wrote an article in 1889. She was also interested in literature; she translated Maupassant and wrote short stories.

In 1895 Bogdanovskaia married Ia. K. Popov, an artillery general. She left St. Petersburg for Izhevskii Zavod in the Viatsk Province. This was a large factory town, administered by the military authorities, and dedicated to the manufacture of rifles and other weapons. Here she set up a small laboratory to continue her research and returned to her original interest in the phosphorous analogues of prussic acid. She died in 1896 at age twenty-nine as the result of the aftereffects of an explosion in her laboratory.

Bogdanovskaia's tragic death left a profound impression on chemistry circles. Her portrait was hung in the laboratory of the Higher Women's Courses and her husband gave fifteen thousand rubles to help needy women students.

Bogdanovskaia did much original research in the field of organic chemistry. Her dissertation was concerned with the structure and properties of dibenzylketone and dibenzylcarbinol. She proved that dibenzylketone occupied an intermediate position between the fatty and the aromatic ketones. Between 1891 and 1894, she wrote a series of articles on these chemicals and their reactions. Much of her work served as a basis for such future organic chemicals as synthetic resin. ACH

PRIMARY SOURCES
Bogdanovskaia, Vera Evstaf'evna. *Über Dibenzylketon und Dibenzylkarbinol.* Berlin: 1892. Band.25, S. 1276.
———. *Ocherki, Stat'l l Otryvki.* 1898. (Two-volume work with portraits.) Held by CGU, Ill.

SECONDARY SOURCES
Andreevskii, I. E., ed. *Entsiklopedicheskii slovar'.* St. Petersburg: Tip. I. A. Efron, 1890–1906.
Musabekov, Iu. S. *Iuliia Vsevolodovna Lermontova: 1846–1919.* Moscow: Nauka, 1967.

BÖHM-WENDT, CÄCILIA (fl. 1909)

German?/Austrian? physicist. Professional experience: Physical Institute in Vienna, researcher.

Cäcilia Böhm-Wendt was one of a coterie of women doing research on radioactivity in Vienna. Working at the Physical Institute with the physicist Egon von Schweidler, Böhm-Wendt investigated the conductivity produced in two liquid dielectrics (petroleum ether and vaseline oil) by radium rays, and determined the order of magnitude of the mobility of the resulting ions. MM

PRIMARY SOURCES

Böhm-Wendt, Cäcilia. With Egon von Schweidler. "Über die spezifische Geschwindigkeit der Ionen in flüssigen Dielektrikas." *Physikalische Zeitschrift* 10 (1909): 379–382.

SECONDARY SOURCES

Rutherford, Ernest. *Radioactive Substances and Their Radiations.* Cambridge: Cambridge University Press, 1913.

STANDARD SOURCES

Meyer and von Schweidler.

BOIVIN, MARIE GILLAIN (1773–1841)

French midwife. Born 1773 in Montreuil. Married Louis Boivin. One daughter. Educated by nuns in hospital at Etampes. Professional experience: General Hospital for Seine and Oise (1814), codirector; temporary military hospital, director (1815); Hospice de la Maternité, Bordeaux, and Maison Royal de Santé, director. Died 1841.

French midwife, Marie Gillain, who received an honorary M.D. from the University of Marburg, was born in Montreuil. According to H. J. Mozans, if the French Royal Academy of Medicine had accepted female members, she would have been selected. In 1814 she was appointed codirector of the General Hospital for Seine and Oise; in 1815 she directed a temporary military hospital; she later directed the Hospice de la Maternité and the Maison Royal de Santé.

Boivin wrote a treatise on her specialty, gynecology and obstetrics, and reputedly was a skilled diagnostician. This book, used as a text, had a popular following in both Germany and France. In 1814 the king of Prussia invested her with an order of merit. JH/MBO

PRIMARY SOURCES

Boivin, Marie. *Mémorial de l'art des accouchements: ou principes fondés sur la pratique de l'Hospice de la Maternité de Paris et sur celles des célèbres praticiens nationaux et étrangers. Suivis des aphorismes de Mauriceau [et] de ceux d'Orazio Valota.* 2d ed. Paris: Méquignon, 1817.

———. With A. Dugès. *Traité pratique des maladies de l'utérus et ses annexes fondé sur un grand nombre d'observations cliniques.* 2 vols. and atlas. Paris: Baillière, 1833. Dugès was her son-in-law, a member of Paris medical faculty until he became professor of obstetrics at University of Montpellier in 1825. Garrison says of this book that it is the first to describe cancer of the urethra, and that it describes the practice of amputation of the cervix for chronic inflammation. Boivin did the illustrations for the plates.

SECONDARY SOURCES

Jex-Blake, Sophia. *Medical Women: A Thesis and a History.* Edinburgh: Oliphant, Anderson, and Ferrier, 1886.

STANDARD SOURCES

Hurd-Mead 1938; Mozans.

BOKOVA–SECHENOVA, MARIIA ALEKSANDROVNA (1839–1929)

Russian ophthalmologist. Born 1839. Daughter of General Aleksandr Obruchev. One brother. Married Petr Ivanovich Bokov; Ivan M. Sechenov. Educated Petersburg Institute for Young Noblewomen; Petersburg Medical Surgical Academy, auditor; University of Zurich (M.D., 1871). Professional experience: worked in clinic in Kiev. Died in 1929.

Mariia Aleksandrovna (Obrucheva) Bokova–Sechenova was the second Russian woman to become a doctor of medicine (after Nadezhda Suslova). She was born into the family of the honorable but despotic General Aleksandr Obruchev in 1839. At the Petersburg Institute for Young Noblewomen, she became acquainted with NADEZHDA SUSLOVA and like her, wished to continue her education. Anticipating objections and to escape parental control, Bokova entered into a fictitious marriage with Petr Ivanovich Bokov, a young doctor and friend of her brother, Vladimir, and also of the writer Nikolai G. Chernyshevskii, later to become the author of the influential novel *What Is to Be Done?* Bokova was one of the earliest to adopt this escape route. It is said that the heroine of the novel, Vera Pavlovna, is partially based on Bokova. Bokov encouraged Bokova's studies; he particularly wanted her to learn English so that she could translate Darwin into Russian.

Like Suslova, Bokova enrolled as an auditor at the Petersburg Medical Surgical Academy hoping that the question of whether or not to admit women students would be decided in their favor. There she fell in love with the young physiologist, Ivan M. Sechenov, who at that time had just returned from his studies abroad and was teaching at the academy. She divorced Bokov to marry him. When, in 1863, the decision was made to bar women, even as auditors, from the universities, Bokova followed Suslova to Zurich. At twenty-nine, she was the oldest of the early women at the University of Zurich medical school and fourth to be admitted to the degree program. She became interested in opthalmalogy and studied with Friedrich Horner, working with him on an extensive study of hypopyon-keratitis. In 1871, before graduating, she volunteered (along with psychiatrist August Forel, surgeon Edmond Rose, and others) to go with a medical team to the Franco-Prussian battlefield. There she showed her determination, skill, and compassion working with the wounded. She obtained her medical degree in 1871. Returning to Russia, she passed the examinations that gave her the right to practice and then went on to Vienna for a year of further study. When she returned to Russia, she worked in a clinic in Kiev while Sechenov worked in Odessa.

In 1876, Sechenov was appointed professor at Petersburg University. Bokova left Kiev and returned to St. Petersburg to live with Sechenov. Retiring into private life, she worked on scientific translations and on putting her family estate in order. She died in 1929.

Although Bokova practiced medicine successfully and even received the thanks of the local zemstvo [district] council for her work improving medical conditions at her estate, she is best known as a translator of scientific works on physiology and the works of Charles Darwin. Her mastery of foreign languages was so great and her standards were so high that her work required no editing.

Like her close friend, Nadezhda Suslova, Bokova was a pioneer and an inspiration to the future generations of Russian women who followed in her footsteps.   JH/MBO

SECONDARY SOURCES
Bonner, Thomas Neville. "Rendezvous in Zurich: Seven Who Made a Revolution in Women's Medical Education, 1864–1874." *Journal of the History of Medicine* 44, no. 1 (January 1989): 7–27.
Sechenov, Ivan M. *Avtobiograficheskie zapiski Ivana Mikhailovicha Sechenova.* Moscow: Izd-vo AN SSSR, 1945.

STANDARD SOURCES
Tuve.

BOLEY, GERTRUDE MAUD (ca. 1877–1965)
British botanist and ecologist. Born 1877. Died 15 June 1965, probably in Bristol.

Active in the Bristol Natural History Society, Gertrude Boley contributed studies of plant ecology of north Somerset to the *Proceedings* of that society.   JH/MBO

PRIMARY SOURCES
Boley, Gertrude Maud. *Proceedings of the Bristol Natural History Society.* Numerous articles.

SECONDARY SOURCES
"Gertrude Maud Boley." *Proceedings of the Bristol Natural History Society*, 1965. Obituary notice.

STANDARD SOURCES
Desmond.

BOLSCHANINA, M. A. (fl. 1925)
Russian chemist.

M. A. Bolschanina is one of the women who worked on radioactivity in its early days. Very little is known about her. She worked on the chemical effects of radioactive substances.   MM

PRIMARY SOURCES
Bolschanina, M. A. With W. D. Kosnezow. *Russian Physical and Chemical Society Journal* 57 (1925): 15.

STANDARD SOURCES
Meyer and von Schweidler.

BOLTON, EDITH (1893–?)
British botanist. Born 1893. Father, Herbert Bolton. Educated Bristol University (B.Sc., 1916; M.Sc., 1920). Professional experience: Natural History Museum Bristol, assistant curator. Death date unknown.

Edith Bolton was educated at Bristol University, obtaining her bachelor's degree in 1916 and her master's degree in 1920. She worked under her father, Herbert Bolton (1863–1936), the curator of the Natural History Museum, Bristol, as his assistant curator from 1920 until his retirement in 1930. At that point Edith Bolton ceased to work for the museum as well.   JH/MBO

SECONDARY SOURCES
"Bolton, Herbert." *Quarterly Journal of the Geological Society* 92 (1936): lxxix–cxxi.

STANDARD SOURCES
Desmond.

BOLUS, HARRIET MARGARET LOUISA (KENSIT) (1877–1970)
South African botanist. Born in Burgesdorp 31 July 1877. Married her cousin, Frank Bolus. Educated Girls' Collegiate School, Port Elizabeth; South African College, Cape Town (B.A.); Stellenbosch University (hon D.Sc.). Professional experience: Henry Bolus Herbarium, curator (ca. 1902–1955). Died 5 April 1970 in Cape Town.

Bolus studied Cape flora especially Eriraceae and Orchidaceae. She wrote numerous scientific publications and wrote popular gardening articles and books, notably *A Book of South African Flora*. She traveled to other major herbaria in Europe. She was elected a Fellow of the Royal Society of South Africa in 1920. She was appointed by great uncle Henry Bolus to the position of curator of his private herbarium, a position which she retained after it was incorporated in University of Cape Town, until her retirement at age seventy-seven. She is commemorated in the genus Bolusantheum Schwantes and in *Geissorhiza Louisa bolusiae*, Foster. JH/MBO

PRIMARY SOURCES

Bolus, Harriet. *A First Book of South African Flowers.* Capetown: Specialty Press, 1928.

————. *Notes on Mesembriathemum and Some Allied Genera.* Capetown: Specialty Press, 1928.

————. *A Second Book of South African Flowers.* Capetown: Specialty Press, 1936.

SECONDARY SOURCES

Glen. *Aloe* 13 (1975): 84, 87.

Herre. *Kakt und Sukk* 12 (1961):1–3.

Oliver. *Forum Botanicum* 8 (1970): 68–69.

STANDARD SOURCES

Gunn and Codd.

BOMHARD, MIRIAM LUCILE (1898–1952)

U.S. range conservationist. Born 24 July 1898 in Bellevue, Ky., to Emma (Koch) and Reverend W. A. Bomhard. Never married. Educated Sharpsburg (Pa.) High School (graduated valedictorian 1917); University of Pittsburgh (B.S. cum laude, 1921; M.A., 1921; Ph.D., 1926). Professional experience: University of Pittsburgh, graduate assistant; instructor (1921–1925); Carnegie Museum Herbarium (1925–1926); Newcomb College, instructor (1926–1927), assistant professor (1927–1932); Bureau of Plant Industry, Washington, D.C., junior pathologist (1933–1934); U.S. Forest Service in what is now the Division of Dendrology and Range Forage Investigations (1934–1952). Honors and memberships: American Association for the Advancement of Science; American Society of Plant Taxonomists; the Botanical Society of America; the Botanical Society of Washington; the Ecological Society of America; the International Association for Plant Taxonomy; and the Washington Academy of Sciences. Died 16 December 1952 at her home in Glenshaw, Pa., after an extended illness.

An outstanding student, Miriam Bombard earned her bachelor's and master's degrees in the same year, the first in February and the second in June. She spent a summer at the Cold Springs Harbor, Long Island Laboratory of Biological Research. From 1921 to 1925 she was first a graduate student and then an instructor in the botany department of the University of Pittsburgh. She wrote her doctoral thesis

on the identification of seeds of Allegheny County, Pennsylvania, including illustrations and keys. This work was never published except as an abstract. Bomhard was the first woman to receive a doctorate from Pittsburgh. After she got her doctorate, she took a position as instructor in biology in Newcomb College, New Orleans, and was promoted to assistant professor. In 1932, she resigned her position to travel around the world and specifically to go to Malaya. When she returned to the United States, she could not find a college teaching job in the very tight market, so she took a position with the Bureau of Plant Industry as a junior pathologist. She never returned to academia. She went to work for the U.S. Forest Service where she completed her career.

Bomhard was a member of a number of professional organizations, including the American Association for the Advancement of Science, the American Society of Plant Taxonomists, the Botanical Society of America, the Botanical Society of Washington (corresponding secretary, 1940), the Ecological Society of America, the International Association for Plant Taxonomy, and the Washington Academy of Sciences. In 1930 she was secretary and in 1931 president of the New Orleans Society of Plant Sciences, a society she cofounded.

Bomhard concentrated her research on the taxonomy and ecology of United States range plants of the southeast and on the taxonomy, distribution, and economic importance of palms. The latter interest brought her to the attention of governmental agencies in Washington.

Certainly not a one-dimensional person, Bomhard was a vocalist in her early days and sang on the radio. She was personable, intelligent, and vivacious. These qualities well-suited her to her job as a guide to the AAAS meeting in New Orleans in 1931. JH/MBO

PRIMARY SOURCES

Bomhard, Miriam Lucile. "Taxonomic Studies of Seeds of Selected Groups of the Plants of Western Pennsylvania, With Keys and Descriptions." Ph.D. diss., University of Pittsburgh, 1926.

————. *The Wax Palms.* In Smithsonian Institution Annual Report, 1936. Washington, D.C.: 1937.

————. *Palm Trees in the United States.* Washington, D.C.: U.S. Department of Agriculture Forest Service, 1950.

————. *Pine—Bluestem Ranges of Louisiana.* 1953.

SECONDARY SOURCES

Dayton, W. A. "Obituary." *Taxon* 2 (1953): 133–134.

BONNAY, MARCHIONESS DU (fl. ca. 1741)

French botanist. Married the French ambassador to Berlin.

The Marchioness du Bonnay, wife of the French Ambassador to Berlin, was an author of a book on herbs. JH/MBO

STANDARD SOURCES
Harless; Hurd-Mead 1938.

BONNEVIE, KRISTINE (1872–1949)

Norwegian cytologist and geneticist. Born 8 October 1872 to Anne Johanne (Daae) and Jacob Aal Bonnevie in Trondheim, Norway. Educated University of Oslo (entered 1892). Studied in Zurich with Arnold Lang (1900); studied with Theodor Boveri in Würzburg (Ph.D., 1906). Professional experience: University Zoological Museum and Zoological Laboratory, conservator (1900–1912); University of Oslo, professor of zoology (1912–1916); Institute of Human Heredity (later Genetics), Oslo, professor and head. Norwegian North Sea Expedition, collaborator (1896–1899). Honors and memberships: head of the Academic Women's Society (1920–1925); royal medal for work on behalf of student welfare (1920); and St. Olof Knight, First Class, for organizing food delivery during World War II. Died 30 August 1949.

The first woman member of the Norwegian Academy of Sciences (1911), Kristine Bonnevie, was the daughter of a well-known Norwegian educator, Jacob Aal Bonnevie, and his first wife, Anne Johanne Daae. She entered the University of Christiana (Oslo) in 1892. In 1895, she published an article with her zoology professor Johan Hjort. She then collaborated with the Norwegian North Sea Expedition from 1896 to 1899.

In 1900, she was appointed conservator of the University Zoological Museum and that same year went to study with Arnold Lang in Zürich. Then she went to study with Theodor Boveri in Würzburg, Germany, and received her doctorate in 1906 writing her dissertation on a detailed study of sex cells in the gastropod, *Enteroxenos stergreni*. The dissertation was published the same year. The problem of chromosome halving in the sex cells was not well understood at the time, and her work challenged the classic work of the Norwegian cytologists Alette and Kristian Emil Schreiner.

In response to criticism by the Schreiners about her chromosomal work, Bonnevie went to Columbia University where she worked on sex chromosones in the sea snake, under E. B. Wilson, verifying her earlier work on *Enteroxenos*. In 1908, she extended her work to non–dividing chromosones in related organisms. She continued work on mitosis even after she gave up other work in cytology.

Returning to Norway, she was made professor of zoology at the University of Christiana (Oslo) in 1912, and turned to problems of human heredity in 1914. From 1916, she was made head and professor of the newly founded Institute for Human Heredity (later Genetics) at Oslo. With the help of district physicians and local medical boards, she examined the genetic diseases in remote Norwegian village communities, especially abnormalities such as dwarfing, polydactylism, and multiple births. This resulted in a major publication on twin births with Aslaug Sverdrup in 1926, demonstrating that the tendency toward dizygotic twins was hereditary.

Bonnevie also used statistical methods to study fingerprints from materials in the collection of the Oslo police department, often from large family groups, to describe three basic elements that combined to form fingerprint patterns. She published the first account of the embryological orgin of "papillary patterns" of human fingers. She also did related work on mice embryos, tracing the inheritance of abnormalities to their early manifestation of the mutated gene. Another study on hydrocephaly was partly funded by the Rockefeller Foundation. After her retirement, she continued to work at the zoological laboratory until her death in 1949, publishing her last contribution (on murine embryology) in an American journal shortly before her death.

An excellent teacher, Bonnevie, along with her teacher John Hjort, introduced modern individual attention to practical laboratory instruction in microscopy and comparative zoology. By 1949, almost every Norwegian cytologist had been trained by her. Her lectures often ran well beyond the traditional forty-five-minute time limit. She also gave popular lectures throughout Norway, dedicated not only to science but to nutritional and psychological issues.

Besides her scientific and academic life, Bonnevie participated in government at the local and national level. She served as a member of the Christiana city council (1909–1919), as a deputy member to the Norwegian Parliament, as a member to the Committee for Intellectual Cooperation (1922–1930), and as the head of the Academic Women's Society (1920–1925). In 1920, she received a royal medal for her work on behalf of student welfare. In 1946, she became a St. Olaf knight, First Class, for organizing food delivery for the Norwegian underground during World War II. JH/MBO

PRIMARY SOURCES
Bonnevie, Kristine. "Zur Kentneiss der Spermiogenese bei den Gastropoden (*Enteroxenos oestergreni*) aus einem Vortrag gehaten in der biologischen Geselschaft su Kra." *Biologischen Centralblatt* 24 (1904): 267.
———. "Unterzuchen über Keimzellen." Ph.D. thesis, University of Würzburg, 1906.
———. "Chromosomenstudien I. Chromosomen von *Acaris, Allium*, und *Aphiuma*. Ein Beitrag zur Lehre der Chromosomenindividualität." *Archiv für Zellforschung* 1 (1908): 450–514.
———. "Chromosomenstudien II. Heterotypische mitose als Reifungscharacter. Nach Unterschungen an *Nereis limbata* Ehlers, *Thalassemia mellita* Conn. und *Cerabratulus lacteus*

Hubr." *Archiv für Zellforschung* 2 (1908): 201–278, plates XIII–XIX.

———. "Chromosomenstudien III. Chromatinreifung in *Allium cepa* (male)." *Archiv für Zellforschung* 1 (1911): 1–35.

———. "Arkvelighetsunderso/kelser i norske bygdeslekter." *Naturens Verden, Copenhagen* (July 1920): 317–326.

SECONDARY SOURCES

Over, Minnetale. "Professor Kristine Bonnevie." *Norwegian Academy of Sciences Journal* (30 September 1949).

BOOLE, MARY (EVEREST) (1832–1916)

British mathematics writer and educator. Born 1832 in Wickwar, Gloucestershire. Father Thomas Roupell Everest, rector of Wickwar. Married George Boole (he died in 1864), 11 September 1855. Five daughters. Educated privately, near Paris, France; studied acoustics and later mathematics with George Boole (1850–1852). Professional experience: Queen's College, matron (1865–1873); secretary to James Hinton (from 1873); professional journalist and popular writer on mathematics and philosophy; creator of Boole's Sewing Cards. Died 1916.

Mary Everest Boole was born in Wickwar, Gloucestershire, where her father was rector, but grew up near Paris, France. Her father, a follower of Samuel Hahnemann's homeopathy, moved to Paris with his family to be nearer Hahnemann's clinic in an attempt to improve his health. Mary followed her father's interest in mathematics, studying at a very young age with a mathematics tutor. When the family returned to England in 1843, she continued the study of mathematics under her father's direction.

George Boole, already famous for his book on mathematical logic, met her when she was eighteen, and began to instruct her in acoustics. She wrote later that it was his book on logic that made her fall in love with him. They corresponded on mathematics and science from 1850 to 1852, and he then began to teach her differential calculus in 1852. She reported to him that she found fluxions easier to understand than differential calculus, and he agreed with her that this was the more logical approach.

When her father died in 1855, she was left destitute. George Boole proposed marriage that same year and they were married in her father's former parish church in Wickwar, on 11 September 1855. The couple then went to Cork, Ireland, where he was teaching mathematics at the university. The couple had five daughters, two of whom were later to show marked abilities in mathematics and science. George Boole encouraged her to attend his lectures and improve her knowledge of mathematics. He read his book on differential equations to her, altering it until the language was completely clear to her. He also shared his interest in F. D. Mau-

rice's ideas of Christian Socialism and Judaic thought with his wife.

When George Boole died in December 1864, Mary Boole was again without financial resources, but was awarded a small Civil List pension of one hundred pounds and given a position by F. D. Maurice as matron at Queen's College. She took over the tenancy of the building at 68 Harley Street, which she ran as a boarding house for students until 1873. Perhaps because of the difficulties of raising children in this situation, her daughters were raised by various relatives, and resented her absence from their life. She also challenged the students in her care with a mixture of psychology, mathematics, Judiasm, logic, and a form of problem encounter groups. Her two oldest children attended the junior school of the college in 1873, but the college began to feel that her ideas were disruptive, and she was dismissed in that year.

Mary Boole wrote a biographical account of the life of George Boole, *Home Side of a Scientific Mind*, but was discouraged from publishing it by Maurice who featured in her account. Maurice's objections meant that the book did not appear until 1878, some years after his death.

Boole then served as secretary to James Hinton, surgeon and friend of her father, who held unconventional ideas on psychology, philosophy, and science. Among these were the interesting proposal that the effects of Hahnemann therapies were due to the imagination of the patient acted upon by silent suggestion from the doctor. Boole considered Hinton's ideas to be in accord with her husband's ideas of the laws of thought, a conclusion recently contested by George Boole's biographer.

Boole was interested not only in Christian Science but in Judiasm and wrote articles for many Jewish papers. She corresponded with Charles Darwin to ask him to assure her that his ideas did not conflict with morality. Her home became a meeting place for anti-vivisectionists, vegetarians, and unconventional educational theorists. She was a friend of a number of brilliant men of the period, including the psychiatrist Henry Maudsley and the scientific journalist and science fiction novelist H. G. Wells.

In 1897, Boole wrote a detailed analysis of the philosophical writings of the French writer P. Gratry (whom George Boole had admired), comparing them with her husband's mathematical concepts which she tried (not entirely successfully) to explain using simple geometic concepts. This book also tried to investigate what she termed "mathematical psychology," the importance of logical thinking, and the nature of genius.

She began to outline a new mathematical approach to learning. Her collected works, published after her death in 1931, reprinted interesting articles on mathematical education that include the idea that a child should construct a mathematical table before he or she uses it, and emphasize the need for logical thinking.

She marketed *Boole Sewing Cards* that contain grids on which many geometric concepts could be illustrated and constructed, and published a series of books on preparing the child to do mathematics and science. Her methods of teaching mathematics and logic to young people has been taken up again in recent years, and her books on those topics republished by the Association of Teachers of Mathematics and the International Society for General Semantics.   JH

PRIMARY SOURCES

Boole, Mary Everest. "Home Life of a Scientific Mind." *University Magazine* 1 (1878): In four parts. Included in *Collected Works*.

————. *The Mathematical Psychology of Gratry and Boole Translated from the Language of the Higher Calculus into that of Elementary Geometry.* London: Swan Sonneschein; New York: G. P. Putnam's Sons, 1897. This book is dedicated to the physician and psychiatrist Henry Maudsley.

————. *The Preparation of the Child for Science.* Oxford: Carendon Press, 1904; reprint, San Franciso: International Society for General Semantics, 1978.

————. *Collected Works.* Ed. E. M. Cobham. Essex: C. W. Daniel, 1931. The collected works include the above articles and books and some unpublished work and poems by George Boole.

————. *A Boolean Anthology: Selected Writings of Mary Boole on Mathematical Education.* Comp. D. G. Tahta. Association of Teachers of Mathematics, 1972.

SECONDARY SOURCES

Dummer, Ethel Sturges. *Mary Everest Boole: A Pioneer Student of the Unconscious.* n.p., n.p. [1931?]

MacHale, Desmond. *George Boole: His Life and Work.* Dublin: Boole Press, 1985.

BOOS, MARGARET BRADLEY (FULLER) (1892–1978)

U.S. petroleum geologist. Born 17 June 1892 in Beatrice Nebr. Married C. Maynard Boos (1927). Educated Northwestern University (B.A. 1913); University of Chicago (M.A., 1919; Ph.D., 1924). Professional experience: Centralia High School, Centralia, Ill., teacher; Smith College, instructor in geology; Northwestern University, instructor in geology; University of Denver, founder of geology department and head (from 1935); several oil companies, geologist (1932–1970); U.S. Bureau of Mines, strategic minerals program, pegmatite minerals specialist (1943–1945); U.S. Bureau of Reclamation, engineer-geologist (1945–1947); University of Illinois, visiting professor (1949); South Dakota School of Mines, field course teacher (1952–1955); oil and gas companies, consul-

tant (1950–1970). Honors and memberships: Geological Society of America, Fellow (1928); Mineralogical Society of America, Fellow (1953); Rocky Mountain Association of Geologists, honorary member (1970); Northwestern University, Distinguished Alumnus Award (1970); Denver Section of the Society of Women Engineers, outstanding senior member (1975); Colorado Society of Engineers, life membership (1975). Died 20 April 1978 in Denver, Col.

Margaret Fuller Boos, known as Peggy to her students, colleagues, and friends, received a doctorate in geology from the University of Chicago in 1924. Before she married geologist C. Maynard Boos and after teaching high school and at Smith College she was accepted at the University of Chicago where she earned a master's and then a Ph.D. degree. Her doctoral thesis was on the geology of the Big Thompson River Valley, Colorado, from the foothills to the continental divide. During the summers of 1926 and 1927, she was acting Park Naturalist at Rocky Mountain Natural Park, Colorado. In 1927, she married C. Maynard Boos, and the two of them collaborated on research. Both Margaret and Maynard Boos did postdoctoral work and research at the University of Wisconsin and she continued her studies at the University of California, Berkeley, and at the University of Chicago. In 1935, she established the Department of Geology at the University of Denver and was department head until 1943. During the time that she was department head at the University of Denver, she held other positions. She worked for several oil companies, but is best known for the work she and her husband did on the structure and stratigraphy of the Front Range of the Rockies in Colorado. This research was useful to oil companies, and also helped geologists studying the general scientific problems associated with mountain building. As a result of her work, she was invited to Washington, D.C., to work on the strategic minerals program of the U.S. Bureau of Mines during World War II. After the end of the war, she worked for the U.S. Bureau of Reclamation for two years, was a visiting professor at the University of Illinois, and taught courses at the South Dakota school of mines. Boos and her husband maintained an office in Denver where they worked as consultants for mining, oil, gas, and coal companies.

In 1975, the U.S. Board of Geographic Names named a previously unclimbed mountain in central Alaska Peggy's Peak in honor of Boos. Her grandnephew, who later climbed the peak, suggested that it would be a suitable memorial for his aunt. In 1978, the Rocky Mountain Association of Geologists dedicated its volume *Energy Resources of the Denver Basin* to Boos. Boos was very interested in supporting women students studying geology at Northwestern University; following her death, the Margaret Fuller Boos Scholarship was established as a permanent endowed fund for women graduate students at Northwestern. After her death, her rock collection and her geological library were donated to the geology department of the University of Northern Colorado at Greeley. JH/MBO

PRIMARY SOURCES

Fuller, Margaret Bradley. "The Physiographic Development of the Big Thompson River Valley in Colorado." *Journal of Geology* 13, 2: 126–137.

———. "Early Quaternic Drainage Diversions around Mount Olympus, Colorado." *Pan American Geologist* 43, no. 1 (1925): 51–54.

Boos, Margaret Fuller. "Stratigraphy and Fauna of the Luta Limesone (Permian) of Oklahoma and Kansas. *Journal of Paleontology* 3, no. 3 (1929): 241–253.

———. "Genesis of Precambrian Granitic Pegmatites in the Denver Mountain Parks Area, Colorado." *Geological Society of America Bulletin* 65, no. 2 (1954): 115–141.

———. With C. Maynard Boos. "Tectonics of the Eastern Flank and Foothills of the Front Range, Colorado." *American Association of Petroleum Geologists Bulletin* 41, no. 12 (1957): 2603–2676.

SECONDARY SOURCES

Byers, Virginia, and Osterwald, Doris. "Memorial to Margaret Fuller Boos, 1892–1978." *Geological Society of America Memorials* 11 (1981): 1–3.

STANDARD SOURCES

Kass-Simon and Farnes; Rossiter 1995.

BOOTH, MARY ANN ALLARD (1843–1922)

U.S. microscopist, photographer. Born 1843 in Longmeadow, Mass. Educated privately at home; Wibraham Academy. Married. Professional experience: lectured and gave public exhibitions of photomicrographs. Died 1922.

During a period of chronic illness, Mary Ann Allard Booth acquired great skill in preparing slides for the microscope of a wide variety of human parasites, from which she made unusually fine photomicrographs. From her own home laboratory she collected and prepared parasites, slides, and photographs. She was considered to have the largest private American collection of these parasites. Her photomicrographs won her many awards at the international expositions between 1885 and 1915, winning medals in the New Orleans Exposition (1885), the St. Louis Exposition (1904), and the San Francisco Exposition (1915). She edited *Practical Microscopy* from 1900 to 1907, and was elected a Fellow of the Royal Microscopical Society and the Royal Photographic Society. JH/MBO

PRIMARY SOURCES

Practical Microscopy, 1900–1907. Ed. Mary Ann Allard Booth. A monthly magazine of microscopical science.

STANDARD SOURCES

AMS 1–3; Bailey; *NCAB.*

BORING, ALICE MIDDLETON (1883–1955)

U.S. cytologist, geneticist, and zoologist. Born 22 February 1883 in Philadelphia to Elizabeth (Truman) and Edwin Boring. Never married. Educated at Friends' Central School, Philadelphia (graduated 1900); Bryn Mawr College (B.A., 1904; M.A., 1905; Ph.D., 1910); University of Pennsylvania (1905–1906). Professional experience: Vassar College, instructor in biology (1907–1908); University of Maine, instructor of zoology (1911), assistant professor (1911–1913), associate professor (1913–1918); Peking Union Medical College, assistant professor of biology (1918–1920); Wellesley College, professor of zoology (1920–1923); Yenching University, professor of zoology (1923–1950); Smith College, part–time professor of zoology (1951–1953). Died 18 September 1955 in Cambridge, Mass.

Alice Middleton Boring's career diverged in a radical way from that of most women scientists. After pursuing a traditional career in biology, she became a part of a new trend in early twentieth-century biology—the export of science to Asia. Boring remained in China from 1918 through 1950, distracted and interrupted from science by civil war; revolution; the Japanese occupation; World War II, involving her internment and repatriation; and the final Chinese upheaval, resulting in the creation of a new socialist society.

One of four children of the pharmacist Edwin Boring and his wife Elizabeth, Alice graduated from Friends' Central School, a coeducational college preparatory school. Then she attended Bryn Mawr College, where she received all of her degrees, culminating in a doctorate. Bryn Mawr was an excellent choice for a potential cytologist or geneticist; the faculty included the noted cytogeneticists NETTIE STEVENS and Thomas Hunt Morgan (1866–1945). Boring studied with Morgan from 1902 to 1904 and, as his junior coauthor, published the first of her thirty-six works.

Although Boring remained at Bryn Mawr to work on her master's degree, this first graduate year may have been anticlimactic, for Morgan had left for Columbia University. Therefore, when the time came for her to continue her graduate work, Boring studied for a year at an institution near home, the University of Pennsylvania, under another outstanding biologist, Edwin Conklin (1863–1942), who remained a close friend throughout her life. In 1906 she returned to Bryn Mawr to complete her doctoral work. During her years at Bryn Mawr and the University of Pennsylvania, Boring's research moved from purely descriptive work on regeneration and embryology to investigation of the behavior of the chromosomes during spermatogenesis. Stevens, known for her theory of sex determination by chromosomes (1905), suggested Boring's dissertation project—following the course of spermatogenesis in various groups of insects.

Boring worked as an instructor in the biology department at Vassar College during 1907 and 1908 and, like KRISTINE BONNEVIE, studied with histologist Theodor Boveri (1862–1915), at the University of Würzburg and at the Naples Zoological Station during 1908 and 1909. After she received her doctorate from Bryn Mawr (1910), she accepted a position as instructor in zoology at the University of Maine, which she maintained until 1919. Here her research was influenced by biologists Gilman Drew (1864–1934) and Raymond Pearl (1879–1940).

By 1918, although Boring had added to the body of data available to scientists, she perceived that she had not made outstanding original theoretical contributions. Thus it was not surprising that when she accepted a two-year job as assistant professor of biology in the premedical division of the Peking Union Medical College (1918–1920), she changed the course of her career. Henceforth she was not satisfied with teaching and research in the United States. Although she returned for a brief tenure as professor of zoology at Wellesley College (1920–1923), as soon as the opportunity arose—in the form of a temporary position teaching biology in a proposed new institution, Peking (later Yenching) University—she departed for China, at first asking only for a two-year leave of absence from Wellesley.

Boring involved herself immediately in Chinese educational and political causes. Indignant over the interference of the "great powers" in Chinese affairs, she believed that at times school and science should be secondary to social and political concerns. Her two-year term expanded into a life's work in China. The decision to remain there permanently was probably made before the years 1928–1929, which she spent on furlough in the United States. Boring's research interests had changed by this time, too—from cytogenetics to amphibian and reptile taxonomy.

The Japanese invasion of 1937 changed the nature of both Boring's research and her personal life. Although the Yenching University campus was exempt from many of the "petty tyrannies" perpetrated by the occupying force, she reported that a sense of foreboding hung over all of her activities. By 1939 it was very difficult either to receive or to send mail, and finances were a problem for everybody. Boring loaned money to friends until she had none left. Plans were made to evacuate foreigners from China, but Boring elected to remain, explaining that "this is home" (Ogilvie 1999).

In December 1941, following their attack on Pearl Harbor, the Japanese closed Yenching University; a few months later the British and American faculty were moved to a concentration camp in Shantung. Boring's family lost contact with her for over a year; but in the autumn of 1943 she was among a group of Yenching University staff sent back to the United States. In a letter written during the voyage, Boring announced with characteristic cheerfulness that "we have been marvelously well . . . We shall not look like physical wrecks when you see us in New York, even if our clothes may be rather dilapidated" (Boring to Charles Corbett, 9 November 1943).

Boring took a post as instructor in histology, with a research assistantship, in the College of Physicians and Surgeons, Columbia University (1944–1945), then spent a year as visiting professor in zoology at Mount Holyoke College (1945–1946). She availed herself of the first opportunity to return to China, taking up her duties at Yenching University in the autumn of 1946. Although the university had made "a marvelous comeback," (Ogilvie 1999) politics again intruded on the educational scene. The conflict between the Communists and the Nationalists grew into a war. Boring eventually accepted and even felt some enthusiasm for the Communists' approach: in 1949 she wrote that she was surprised to find that "in spite of my opposition in the past, I now am full of hope!" (Boring to family, 9 January 1949).

It was not disenchantment with the new regime but the ill health of her sister that caused Boring to return to the United States in 1950. She settled in Cambridge, Massachusetts, but took on a part-time professorship of zoology at Smith College in Northampton, Massachusetts, during 1951–1953. She died in 1955 of cerebral arteriosclerosis.

It is not sufficient to measure Alice Boring's contributions to science by her creation of new theoretical constructs, her accumulation of new facts, or her output of scientific publications. To these we must add her success in acquainting her Chinese students with Western science, her reports on the fauna of an area previously unknown, her help to American taxonomists on collecting trips to China, her provision of specimens and notes to museums and universities in the United States, and her documentation of the interaction between science and politics in China. Measured only by her theoretical originality and her output, she would be considered unexceptional. She, nevertheless, provided confirmation for existing theories and data for her successors to assimilate. When considered in the context of the political turmoil within which she operated, her productivity is impressive.

In her early work in cytogenetics and embryology, Boring reflected the research interests of her associates. Although she added data to confirm existing theories of the chromosomal basis of heredity and information about the course of regeneration in certain species, she did not create any novel explanations. Whether she might have made any such generalizations had she remained in the United States must be left to speculation, for when she went to China, pragmatism dictated a change in research areas.

Boring's science became inextricably intertwined with the politics of China. A part of the Western world's effort to supply its culture to the East, she was confronted by mission politics, funding institution politics, and university politics, as well as by the overriding unstable condition of China in an unstable world. Within this context she taught biology to several generations of Chinese, many of whom became well known in the field of herpetology, while others spread the tradition that Boring had taught them to their own students. By supplying information to American collectors in China and by her own publications on the herpetofauna of the area, she contributed concretely to the faunal understanding of China. MBO

PRIMARY SOURCES

Boring, Alice Middleton. "A Study of the Spermatogenesis of Twenty-Two Species of the Membracidae, Jassidae, Cercopidae, and Fulgoridae, with Especial Reference to the Behavior of the Odd Chromosome." *Journal of Experimental Zoology* 4 (1907): 469–512.

———. "A Small Chromosome in Ascaris megalocephala." *Archiv zur Zellforschung* 4 (1909): 120–131.

———. "A Checklist of Chinese Amphibia with Notes on Geographical Distribution." *Peking Natural History Bulletin* 4 (December 1929): 15–51.

SECONDARY SOURCES

Ogilvie, Marilyn Bailey. "'The New Look.' Women and the Expansion of American Zoology: Nettie Maria Stevens (1861–1912) and Alice Middleton Boring (1883–1955)." In *The Expansion of American Biology*, ed. Keith R. Benson, Jane Maienschein, and Ronald Rainger, 52–79. New Brunswick, N.J.: Rutgers University Press, 1991.

Ogilvie, Marilyn Bailey and Clifford J. Choquette. *A Dame Full of Vim and Vigor, a Biography of Alice Middleton Boring: Biologist in China.* Amsterdam: Harwood Academic Publishers, 1999.

———. "Western Biology and Medicine in Modern China: The Career and Legacy of Alice M. Boring (1883–1955)." *Journal of the History of Medicine and Allied Sciences* 48 (1993): 198–215.

BORISOVA-BEKRIASHEVA, ANTONIIA GEORGIEVNA (1903–)

Russian geographical botanist. Born 1903 in St. Petersburg. Educated Leningrad University. Professional experience: Botanical Institute of the Soviet Academy of Sciences, Leningrad, associate; senior associate.

Antoniia Georgievna Borisova-Bekriasheva graduated from the geography department of Leningrad University in 1927. She completed a postgraduate course in 1931 and received the degree of candidate of biological sciences (similar to a Ph.D.) in 1935.

From 1927 to 1941, Borisova worked as an associate at the Botanical Institute of the Soviet Academy of Sciences in Leningrad. In 1941, she became a senior associate.

Between 1925 and 1944, Borisova was a member of many expeditions to study the flora of different parts of the Soviet Union. Areas explored include Kazakhstan, the South Urals, and the Novosibirsk area as well as the Leningrad and Iaroslavl' regions.

Borisova was a specialist in floristic systematics and the author of a number of works on this subject. JH/MBO

PRIMARY SOURCES

Borisova-Bekriasheva, Antoniia Georgievna. *Novye dlia kultury vidy espartseta.* Moscow: Izd-vo Akademii nauk SSSR, 1952.

STANDARD SOURCES

Debus; *WW in Science*, 1968.

BORON, ELIZABETH (RIDDLE) GRAVES (1916–1972)

U.S. physicist. Born 23 January 1916 in Nashville, Tenn. Mother Clymetra Riddle. One brother, John B. Riddle. Married Alvin R. Graves (1940). Three children, Marilyn Elizabeth, Elizabeth Anne, and Alvin Palmer. University of Chicago (B.S., 1936; Ph.D., ca. 1940). Professional experience: Los Alamos, Metallurgical Laboratory (1943–1950), research group leader (from 1950). Died 10 January 1972 in Bataan Memorial Hospital in Albuquerque, N.M., of cancer.

Elizabeth Riddle married Alvin nearly a year after she received her doctorate in Physics from the University of Chicago. The couple went to Los Alamos in April 1943, where her husband became a division leader, a position he held from 1943 until his death of a heart attack in April 1965. Elizabeth was a member of the Metallurgical Laboratory with Enrico Fermi in 1943 and became a group leader in 1950.

She held a University of Chicago fellowship while working on her Ph.D. under S. K. Allison. Her thesis was on energy release from Beryllium, lithium 7, and the production of lithium 7. She received a Department of Defense medal for her husband.

JH/MBO

PRIMARY SOURCES

Graves, Elizabeth Riddle. "Energy Release from Be 9 (d, a) Li 7 and the Productionof Li 7." *Physical Review* 57 (1940). Ph.D. dissertation.

STANDARD SOURCES

AMS 8, P 9, P&B 10–12; *NAW* (unused).

BORROMEO, CLELIA GRILLO (fl. 18th century)

Italian natural philosopher. Born probably in Genoa.

Clelia Grillo Borromeo was distinguished in science, mathematics, mechanics, and languages, and a medal with the inscription *Gloria Genuensium* was struck in her honor. It was claimed that no problem in mathematics or science was beyond her comprehension.

JH/MBO

STANDARD SOURCES

Mozans.

BORSARELLI, FERNANDA (1904–)

Italian physician. Born 28 September 1904 in Turin, Italy. Three siblings.

Fernanda Borsarelli's father was an engineer with the provincial government and her mother was a teacher with degrees in both literature and philosophy. Fernanda was the second of four children and was particularly close to her older brother, Paolo Emilio, who died of pneumonia at age twenty-two. Fernanda's uncle and great-grandfather were physicians; among the large library of her home were many medical books. The home was filled with love, laughter, and encouragement to learn. During her high school years, she decided to study medicine, partly because of the acute shortage of doctors due to the First World War. She enrolled at the Faculty of Medicine at the University of Turin in October 1922.

JH/MBO

PRIMARY SOURCES

Borsarelli, Fernanda. In Hellstedt, *Autobiographies.*

BOSWELL, KATHERINE CUMMING (1888–1952)

*British geomorphologist. Born 1888. Never married. Educated University College, Southampton (1926–1944). Professional experi-*ence: University College, Southhampton, lecturer; Friends' College, Highgate, Jamaica, Co-Principal (1945–1949). Died 18 September 1952 at Beni Abbes in the Sahara.*

Katherine Boswell was educated as a geographer at University College, Southampton. She received a master's degree for her work on the geography of the Port of Southampton, but, although she was a fine geographer, she was always interested in geomorphology. She published in the *Proceedings of the Geologists' Association*. She went to Jamaica for four years and then returned to England. In connection with the nineteenth International Geological Congress, she went to Algiers, satisfying a lifelong ambition to see the Sahara desert. As she explored the Sahara with a field excursion from the International Congress, she suffered a fatal heat stroke.

Much of her work was on the geomorphology of Hampshire.

JH/MBO

PRIMARY SOURCES

Boswell, Katherine. "A Detailed Profile of the River Test." *Proceedings of the Geologists' Association* 57, no. 2 (1946): 102–116.

SECONDARY SOURCES

[Wisden, D. E.]. "Katharine Cumming Boswell." *Proceedings of the Geologists' Association* 64 (1953): 59–60.

STANDARD SOURCES

Sarjeant.

BOURDEL, LÉONE (1907–)

French psychologist and anthropologist. Born 20 December 1907 in Paris, France to Marie (Donnadieu) and Léone Bourdel. Married Jacques Genevay. One son, Richard-Olivier. Educated Sorbonne (M.A.). Professional experience: National Institute of Professional Orientation, researcher (1928–1937); School of Scientific Organization of Work, professor (1935–1948); Superior School of Anthrobiology, professor (1948); Laboratory of Applied Psychology, director (from 1937). Honors and memberships: Joseph Saillet Prize in Academic Moral and Political Science, recipient; Association of Directors of Social Statistics, Paris, member; Society of Men of Letters, member; Association of Counselors of Private Economy, member.

Born in Paris, psychologist and anthropologist Léone Bourdel was married and had one son. She earned a master's degree at the Sorbonne, and then began work at various institutes in applied psychology and anthrobiology. She was a member of several societies, and published on psychological differences, especially temperament, between people of different races.

JH/MBO

PRIMARY SOURCES

Bourdel, Léone. *La mission de la France.* Paris: Editions Médicis, 1945.

———. *La Connaissance des hommes par la psychobiologie.* Paris: Editions Médicis, 1946.

———. *Sang, tempéraments, travail et races.* Paris: Librairie Malonie, 1946.

STANDARD SOURCES

Debus.

BOURGEOISE, LOUYSE (1563–1636)

French surgeon, obstetrician, gynecologist. Born 1563. Married Martin Boursier, army surgeon, then widowed. Three children. Friend and pupil of French surgeon Ambroise Paré. Died 1636.

Louyse or Louise Bourgeoise (sometimes written as Bourgeois) wrote a series of books on childbirth. She was a pupil and a friend of French surgeon Ambroise Paré. The most famous of her books is *Observations* (1610), which included descriptions of pregnancy, problems in labor and delivery, abortion, and aftercare for mother and child, based on two thousand cases. She developed a number of new techniques and instituted the practice of inducing labor in cases of placenta praevia. She was called in for confinements of two queens of France, and attended the birth of Louis XIII in 1601.   JH/MBO

PRIMARY SOURCES

Bourgeoise, Louise. *Observations.* Frankfurt: Matthea Merrian, 1610.

STANDARD SOURCES

Hurd-Mead 1938; Ireland; Lipinska 1900; Lovejoy; *Women in White.*

BOUTEILLER, MARCELLE (1904–1990)

French anthropologist. Never married. Professional experience: Musée de l'Homme, assistant, Centres Nationales Recherches Scientifiques (CNRS), master of research (from 1956). Honors and memberships: Société d'Anthropologie, member (1944–1990). Died 1990.

Marcelle Bouteiller was a French anthropologist and ethnologist who was first elected to the Société d'Anthropologie in 1944 when she was an assistant in ethnology at the Musée de l'Homme, Paris. By 1956 she had been appointed master of research of the CNRS, which allowed her to teach seminars and conduct research. This research included a study of the religious significance of tatooing among native peoples of Indochina. She also investigated the history of early French anthropology with her study of the late-eighteenth-century society Observateurs de l'Homme. She died at the age of eighty-six.   JH/MBO

PRIMARY SOURCES

Bouteiller, Marcelle. "La Tatouage: technique et valeur sociale! ou magico-religieuse dans quelques société d'Indochine (Laos, Siam, Burmanie et Cambodge)." *Bulletins et Mémoires Société d'Anthropologie de Paris.* 4 (1953): 515–534.

———. "La Société des Observateurs de l'Homme (1800–1805), ancestre de la Société d'Anthropologie de Paris." *Bulletins et Mémoires Société d'Anthropologie de Paris.* 7 (1956): 448–465.

———. "Traditionnalisme et évolution dans un petit port saumurois: le Thoureil (Maine-et-Loire)." *Ethnographie,* 57 (1963): 118–130.

SECONDARY SOURCES

Ethnologies françaises 22 (1992): 84–91. Obituary notice.

BOUTHILET, LORRAINE (1915–1984)

U.S. psychologist. Born 7 November 1915 in St. Paul, Minn. Five siblings. Educated Minnesota public schools; University of Minnesota (B.A. 1936); University of Chicago (M.A., 1947, Ph.D., 1948). Professional experience: University of Chicago, research assistant (1941–1945); Encyclopedia Britannica, editorial reviewer (1943–1945); American Psychologist, managing editor (1946–1956); Behavioral Science, cofounder and managing editor (1956–?). Science Research Associates of Chicago, associate test editor (1947–1948); Department of Psychology, University of Chicago, instructor and executive secretary (1948–1951); publications for the American Psychological Association, managing editor (1951–1957); Psychopharmacology Service Center, National Institute of Mental Health, medical research program specialist (1957–1962); National Clearinghouse for Mental Health Information, program director (1962–1977); Surgeon General's Report on Television and Behavior, coeditor; Publications Board of the APA, chair (1983–1984). Died 5 May 1984 in Washington, D.C.

Lorraine Bouthilet entered the study of psychology with a background in English and a strong spirit of commitment and high standards. Her dissertation topic at the University of Chicago was a comparative study of intuitive cognition in women and men. She demonstrated her hypothesis that women made more intuitive decisions than men. She was first exposed to the publication field as an undergraduate when she worked as an editorial reviewer for *Encyclopedia Britannica* (1943–1945). Her attention to detail and sound judgment were rewarded with the job of managing editor of

American Psychologist in 1946. In 1947–1948, she was the associate test editor of Science Research Associates (SRA) of Chicago. She worked closely with L. L. Thurstone and his wife in the construction and publication of the Primary Mental Abilities Intelligence Test, which became one of the most widely used intelligence tests in the world. After completing her doctorate in 1948, Bouthilet was an instructor and the executive secretary of the Department of Psychology at the University of Chicago. In 1951, she was named managing editor of publications for the American Psychological Association, and also became medical research program specialist of the Psychopharmacology Service Center at the National Institute of Mental Health (NIMH), then directed by Jonathan Cole.

One of her major contributions in the field of editorial work was the preparation of the first edition in 1952 of the *Publication Manual of the APA*, which has become a standard in the social sciences and has had many subsequent editions. In 1956, she became the first managing editor of *Behavioral Science*, a journal she helped found. The Psychopharmacology Service Center served so successfully in providing information to professionals on published basic and clinical research on psychoactive drugs that Bouthilet's system was expanded into a National Clearinghouse for Mental Health Information, covering the full range of mental health research and practice. In 1962, Bouthilet became program director for the clearinghouse within NIMH.

Bouthilet retired in 1977 but continued to write and edit on a part-time basis. She was one of the editors of the 1982 publication *Television and Behavior: Ten Years of Scientific Progress and Implications for the Eighties*, an elaboration and update of the 1972 Surgeon General's Advisory Committee report. She continued to be active on the Publications Board of the APA, serving as chair at the time of her death in 1984.

Lorraine Bouthilet found fulfillment and respect in areas often dominated by men. She was admired for her intelligence, keen intuition, perfectionism in regard to the written word, gentle tenacity in upholding her high standards, and warmth as a teacher and friend. In the field of professional communication and dissemination of information, she made important pioneering advances, helping bring psychological publications into the electronic era.   JH/MBO

PRIMARY SOURCES
Bouthilet, Lorraine. "Measurement of Intuitive Thinking."
  Ph.D. diss., University of Chicago, 1948.
———. With Katherine Byrne. *You and Your Mental Abilities.*
  Chicago: Science Research Associates, 1948.
———. With Jerome Levine and Burtrum C. Schiele. *Principles and Problems in Establishing the Efficacy of Psychotropic Agents.*
  [Chevy Chase, Md.: NIMH, 1971].

———, ed. *Television and Behavior: Ten Years of Scientific Progress and Implications for the Eighties.* 2 vols. Rockville, Md.: U.S. Dept. of Health and Human Services, NIMH, 1982. An elaboration and update of the 1972 Surgeon General's Advisory Committee report on television and behavior.

SECONDARY SOURCES
Miller, James Grier. "Lorraine Bouthilet (1915–1984)." *American Psychologist* 42 (1987): 817. Obituary notice.

BOVERI, MARCELLA IMELDA O'GRADY (1863–1950)

U.S./German biologist. Born 7 October 1863 in Boston, Mass., to Anne and Thomas O'Grady. Educated Girls' High School, Boston; Massachusetts Institute of Technology (B.S., 1885); Bryn Mawr College (fellowship for advanced study, 1887–1889; doctoral work, 1887–1890; Marine Biological Laboratories, Wood's Hole summer research (1885–1896); University of Würzburg, Institute of Zoology, postgraduate study (1896–1897). Married Theodor Boveri (June 1897; he died in 1915). One daughter (Margret, born 1900). Professional experience: Bryn Mawr, demonstrator in biology (1888–1890); Vassar College, instructor in biology (1890–1891), associate professor (1892), professor (1893–1896); University of Würzburg, unpaid research associate (1897–1915); Albertus Magnus College, New Haven, Conn., professor (1927–1943). Died 24 October 1950 at Wickatunk, N.J.

Marcella O'Grady Boveri was involved in much of the exciting biological research on embryological development and genetics at the end of the nineteenth and the beginning of the twentieth century. She was born in Boston, Massachusetts, to a prosperous family of Irish ancestry. Her father, Thomas O'Grady, and her brother were both architects. As a young girl, she attended Girls' High School in Boston; she then went on to study at MIT, where she received her bachelor's degree in biology in 1885. Her professor there, W. T. Sedgwick, introduced her to a number of important biologists, including the cell biologist E. B. Wilson, then teaching at Bryn Mawr College.

After her graduation, Wilson recommended O'Grady (with some qualification) for advanced graduate study and a position as demonstrator in biology at Bryn Mawr College. She was subsequently appointed, with a fellowship. Much of her original research was conducted at the Marine Biological Laboratories (MBL), at Wood's Hole during the summer months. She began to do embryological research, particularly on Kupffer's organ in the embryo teleost, working under Charles O. Whitman, director of the MBL. Her work would result in the discovery of a rudimentary neuroenteric canal. She also studied invertebrate embryology, looking at development in the small crustacean group of isopods.

With the expiration of her fellowship at Bryn Mawr, in 1890, O'Grady began to look for a new position that would afford her more scope in teaching. She was aware that any new teaching job would delay the award of her doctorate, but this did not deter her. Vassar was looking for a new teacher to replace the botanist Isabelle Mulford. Strongly supported by Wilson and Whitman, O'Grady was offered the position.

For seven years, O'Grady showed herself to be an excellent teacher, and was recognized as such by the administration at Vassar College. She was promoted to associate professor in 1892, and although she had not completed her doctorate, she was made full professor the following year. Her teaching was memorable, and many of her students later testified to the impact she had upon them as she conveyed the excitement of research. O'Grady taught Darwinism, new theories of heredity, and the new experiments in embryology from the just-published textbook of her former professors. She instituted a research table for her students at the MBL every summer, in order to educate them about scientific research. In her department, as her course size rose, she gathered a small staff of three under her.

In 1896, O'Grady was anxious to travel to the University of Würzburg, Germany, to do research on chromosomes, and obtain a German doctorate. She had read the exciting experimental work on the cell nucleus and development issuing from the laboratory of the new dynamic professor of biology, Theodor Boveri. Her former professor, E. B. Wilson, had worked with him at Anton Dohrn's Naples Zoological Station and had lectured about his work to her students. Studying German in her spare time, O'Grady left the biology department to be administered in her absence by her instructor, Elizabeth Bickford, who had a similar educational background.

In Germany, with E. B. Wilson's recommendation, O'Grady was able to enter the University of Würzburg to work at Boveri's Institute of Zoology. She soon impressed Theodor Boveri with her intelligence and her interest in his work. Within a short time they were engaged to be married, with the approval of his closest friends, who included William Roentgen and his wife. Marcella Boveri began to work closely with her husband, serving as his research associate. In August 1900, their first and only child, Margret, was born, and the next summer the couple, taking the baby along, went to work at the Naples Zoological Station, run by Anton Dohrn, where many distinguished scientists from around the world came. Although Marcella Boveri was actually her husband's close collaborator, she held no formal position, and her name did not appear on his publications. She published only one paper independently on chromosome mitosis in 1903, intended as the research for her doctoral degree at Würzburg. She never finished that degree.

In 1904, she urged her former student and friend EDNA CARTER to study physics at the University of Würzburg and stay with her family. Carter did so, obtaining her doctoral degree in 1906. She brought Boveri a sense of her former world, and Carter also developed a close bond with young Margret. In 1911 and 1913, the couple worked again at Naples. Theodor Boveri was increasingly ill and died from tuberculosis at the beginning of World War I. During his last illness, Marcella Boveri worked hard to help him complete his last book, which examined the possibility that there was a chromosome irregularity that could explain the cellular origin of malignant tumors. The book was published in Jena in 1914, shortly before his death. Marcella Boveri would translate it into English in 1929.

Marcella Boveri remained in Germany after her husband's death, working through his papers, but cut off from active biological research. She collected her husband's letters together from many sources, but these, left in Germany, were all destroyed during World War II. Clearly, she missed science. On a visit to the United States in 1926, she was offered the unexpected opportunity to develop the biological sciences at Albertus Magnus College, a small Catholic women's college in New Haven. She accepted and began months of preparation, working at the Naples station for three months, attending the International Congress in Zoology, working in Hans Spemann's laboratory in Freiburg (he had been on the staff of the Zoological Institute at Würzburg during Theodor Boveri's directorship) and making many slides and preparing specimens to send to the college. She was also offered the support of the Yale University biologists, especially Ross Harrison.

After some problems because of her now-lapsed American citizenship, she arrived in the United States in September of 1927 and began a fifteen-year, highly successful professorship at Albertus Magnus. Not only did she organize the laboratories and give exciting lectures, but she arranged for important German scientists to lecture in the United States, and to stop at her college as well. She persuaded Spemann and the insect behaviorist Otto von Frisch to come, among others.

Her daughter, Margret, who had served as secretary to the director of the Naples Station, went on to complete a doctorate in English and then joined the *Frankfurter Zeitung* as the American correspondent, coming to the United States in 1940. As a German national, she was interned in 1941 at the outbreak of World War II and then deported to Lisbon in 1942, and she returned to Germany in 1944. After the war, Margret became an important political journalist.

Marcella Boveri retired from teaching at the age of eighty, in 1943. She was succeeded by the important embryologist DOROTHEA RUDNICK. Boveri was tended through her last illness at the convent where her sister had been a nun. Since her daughter was not granted a visa immediately after the war, she never saw her mother again. Boveri died in Wickatunk, New Jersey, in 1950. Her surviving archives are in the Albertus Magnus College library.   JH

PRIMARY SOURCES
Boveri, Marcella. "Ueber Mitosen bei einseitiger Chromosomenbindung." *Jenaischen Zeitschrift Naturwissenschaft* 37 (1903): 401–44.
Boveri, Theodor. *The Origin of Malignant Tumors.* (Baltimore: Williams & Wilkins, 1929). Translated by Marcella Boveri.
Marcella Boveri Archive at Albertus Magnus College Library, Bryn Mawr College, and Vassar College.

SECONDARY SOURCES
Baltzer, Fritz. *Theodor Boveri: Life and Work of a Great Biologist* (1962) (Berkeley: University of California Press, 1967). Translated by Dorothea Rudnick.
McKusick, Victor. "Marcella O'Grady Boveri (1865–1950) and the chromosome theory of cancer." *Journal of Medical Genetics* 22 (1985): 431–440.
Rudnick, Dorothea. "Madame Boveri and Professor Boveri," *Albertus Magnus Alumna* 4 (1967): 8–11, 14.
Wright, Margaret R. "Marcella O'Grady Boveri (1863–1950): Her Three Chapters in Biology." *Isis* 88 (December 1997): 627–652.

STANDARD SOURCES
Rebière; Rossiter 1982. Rossiter lists Marcella O'Grady Boveri and Theodor Boveri as one of her notable American scientific couples.

BOWEN, SUSAN (d. 1886)
U.S. zoologist and educator. Probably educated at Mount Holyoke. Professor of zoology, Mount Holyoke. Married David Starr Jordan in 1870s. Died in 1886.

Although Susan Bowen did no research in zoology, according to Rossiter, she trained important women scientists. She married David Starr Jordan, who became president of Stanford after her death, in the 1890s.   JH/MBO

STANDARD SOURCES
Rebière; Rossiter 1982.

BOYD, ELIZABETH MARGARET (1908–)
U.S. zoologist. Born 8 July 1908 in Liverpool, England. Naturalized U.S. citizen. Educated University of Edinburgh (B.Sc., 1930); Mt. Holyoke College (M.A., 1933); Cornell University (Ph.D., 1946). Professional experience: University of Edinburgh, assistant

in zoology (1930–1931); Mt. Holyoke College, assistant (1931–1933; 1937–1939), instructor (1939–1944), assistant professor (1944–1948), associate professor (1948–1964?), Alumnae Foundation professor (1964–1974), emerita professor (1974–?); McGill University, teacher (1933–1937 and 1937–1964).

Born in Liverpool, England, Elizabeth Boyd became a naturalized U.S. citizen and spent the greater part of her career at Mt. Holyoke College. She moved through the academic ranks to professor at Holyoke, and was the recipient of a named professorship. She was U.S. Public Health Fellow during 1963–1964 and was a Fellow in tropical medicine and parasitology in 1964. She was a Fellow of the American Association for the Advancement of Science, and a member of the American Society of Zoologists, the National Audubon Society, the American Society of Parasitology, and the American Ornithologists Union. Her research was both in parasitology and ornithology.   JH/MBO

STANDARD SOURCES
AMS 8, B 9, P&B 10–14.

BOYD, LOUISE ARNER (1887–1972)
U.S. geographer and scientific explorer. Born 1887. Educated private schools. Professional experience: sponsored seven trips to the Arctic (from 1926). U.S. war department, consultant. American Geographical Society, first councilor. Died 1972.

Louise Boyd Arner was not trained as a scientist. However, she was more than an ordinary patron of science because of her involvement in collecting botanical specimens, photographing the regions, and selecting the scientists and the equipment. She became interested in the polar regions while she was on a vacation with friends. She sponsored six additional expeditions to the polar regions, carefully consulting with the staff of the American Geographical Society before choosing scientists and equipment. In 1955, Boyd became the first woman to reach the North Pole in an airplane. She traveled to the International Geographical Congress in Warsaw (1934) where she served as a delegate, representing the United States government and the American Geographical Society. Boyd received honorary degrees from the University of California and Mills College.   JH/MBO

PRIMARY SOURCES
Boyd, Louise Arner. *Fiord Region of East Greenland.* New York: American Geographical Society, 1935. Contains the results of her 1931 and 1933 trips.
———. *Polish Countrysides.* New York: American Geographical Society, 1937. Describes her trip to Poland for the International Geographical Conference.

———. *The Coast of Northeast Greenland with Hydrographic Studies in the Greenland Sea.* New York: American Geographical Society, 1948.

SECONDARY SOURCES
Olds, Elizabeth F. *Women of the Four Winds.* Boston: Houghton Mifflin, 1985. Description of Boyd's first three expeditions.

STANDARD SOURCES
Current Biography (1960); Debus; Ireland; *LKW*; Rossiter 1982.

BOYER, ESTHER LYDIA (1902–1948)
U.S. anatomist. Born 27 March 1902 in Reddick, Ill. Educated West Union College (A.B., 1923); University of Wisconsin (A.M., 1930; Ph.D., 1933; M.D., 1939). Professional experience: University of Wisconsin, assistant in zoology (1929–1934), medical school anatomist (1934–1939); Madison General Hospital, Wisconsin, intern (1939–1940); Woman's Medical College of Pennsylvania, instructor in anatomy (1940–1942); Student Health Service, University of Missouri, assistant physician (1942). Died 1948.

Esther Boyer earned both a doctorate and a medical degree from the University of Wisconsin. Since she died at the age of forty-six, she did not have the opportunity to use her skills for very long. She worked as an anatomist for several years before she took a position as an assistant physician. Her research interests were in vertebrate morphology.

JH/MBO

PRIMARY SOURCES
Boyer, Esther Lydia. *The Musculature of the Inferior Extremity of the Orange-Utan,* Simia Satyrus. Philadelphia: The Wistar Institute Press, 1935. Ph.D. dissertation at the University of Wisconsin.

STANDARD SOURCES
AMS 6–7.

BRACHER, ROSE (1894–1941)
British botanist and mycologist. Born 1894 in Salisbury, Wiltshire. Educated Bristol University (B.Sc., 1917; M.Sc., 1918; Ph.D., 1927). Marital status unknown. Professional experience: London School of Medicine for Women, demonstrator (1918–1920); East London College, lecturer (1921–1924); Bristol University, lecturer (1924-1941). Died 15 July 1941 at Bristol.

Rose Bracher studied the ecology of mud banks of the river Avon and species of Euglena. She was elected a fellow of the Linnean Society in 1938. In addition to her books, she also published in the *Proceedings of the Bristol Naturalists' Society,* the *Journal of the Linnean Society,* and *Annals of Botany.*   JH/MBO

PRIMARY SOURCES
Bracher, Rose. *Field Studies in Ecology.* Bristol, London: J.W. Arrowsmith, 1934.
———. *Ecology in Town and Classroom.* Bristol, London: J.W. Arrowsmith, 1937.
———. *Book of Common Flowers.* Oxford: Oxford University Press, 1941.

SECONDARY SOURCES
"Dr. R. Bracher." *Nature* 148 (1941): 134. Obituary notice.
"Rose Bracher." *Proceedings of the Linnean Society* 1941–1942: 270. Obituary notice.

BRADLEY, AMY MORRIS (1823–1904)
U.S. nurse and educator. Born 12 September 1823 in East Vassalboro, Maine, to Jane (Baxter) and Abired Bradley. Seven siblings. Educated East Vassalboro Academy. Professional experience: private school, teacher (1838–1839); public country schools, teacher (1939–1943); Gardiner, Maine, grammar school principal (from 1944); Charleston, Mass., grammar school teacher; East Cambridge, Mass., grammar school teacher; San José, Costa Rica, tutor and founder of an English school; Fifth Maine Regiment Civil War nurse; United States Sanitary Commission, superintendent (1861–1862); home for convalescent soldiers, matron (1862–1865); Wilmington, N.C., organized schools for poor white children (1865–1904). Died 15 January 1904 in Wilmington, N.C.

Amy Bradley was not trained as a nurse. Before the beginning of the Civil War, she had been a schoolteacher. Her own precarious health and her passionate adherence to the Union cause impelled her to offer to nurse the war wounded. A surgeon friend accepted her offer, and she was attached to the Fifth Maine Regiment. She soon showed a flair for administration. Her regimental hospital was clean and well organized, so much so that General Henry W. Slocum named her superintendent of a brigade hospital. She called upon the United States Sanitary Commission for supplies and after the brigade hospital was dismantled worked for the Sanitary Commission. Throughout the war, she held several different positions with the commission, administering each with great skill.

After the war, she returned to education, founding schools in the South for poor white children. At first she met considerable resistance, but she soon won the support of the communities. In Wilmington, North Carolina, she won the support of Mary Porter Tileston Hemenway, a Boston philanthropist, who provided funds for another school. In 1872 the Tileston Normal School opened at Wilmington.

JH/MBO

SECONDARY SOURCES

Howe, Julia Ward, ed. *Sketches of Representative Women of New England*. Boston: New England Historical Publishing, 1904.

Willard, Frances E. and Livermore, Mary A., eds. *A Woman of the Century*. Buffalo, N.Y.: C.W. Moulton, 1893.

STANDARD SOURCES

NAW (long article by Mary R. Dearing).

BRADLEY, FRANCES SAGE (1862–1949)

U.S. physician and pioneer in child hygiene. Educated Cornell Medical School (M.D.). Professional experience: Atlanta, Ga., private practice; Fulton County, Ga., worked in prevention of infant death; North Carolina State Board of Health, physician; Federal Children's Bureau, administrator. Died 1949.

Frances Sage Bradley was a pioneer in child hygiene. She received her medical degree from Cornell Medical School and went on to practice in Atlanta, Georgia. She worked in Fulton County, Georgia, to prevent infant death, after learning that in rural America, professional staffs and adequate facilities were virtually nonexistent.

One of the earliest specialists in rural medicine, she believed that medical practice and research should lead to the positive reconstruction of society—that the physician was obliged to protect the community as well as the individual patient. For Bradley, the key to reconstruction was education. In 1913, she took advantage of the National Conservation Exposition in Knoxville, Tennessee, to organize the first child health exhibition and conference. Supplementing funds from the Children's Bureau with gifts from the Russell Sage Foundation, the National Child Labor committee, and the New York Child Welfare Exhibit Committee, she set up a multifaceted display that emphasized the interrelationship of social conditions and children's health. Using stereopticon slides, pamphlets, a free health critique for children under age fifteen, and personal interviews, she educated attendees on nutrition, elemental bedside care, first aid, and the importance of environmental and personal hygiene.

Appointed special agent of the rural medical program of the Federal Children's Bureau in 1915, she began an aggressive program of investigation and education. In 1916, she began a social-medical survey in North Carolina. Choosing two counties that represented both geographic-topographic extremes of the state (coastal plain and mountain), she began with a house-to-house study in a town where sharecropping was the principal means of support. Her report, thanks to her sharp eye and fine descriptive style, presented an accurate and alarming picture of the state of rural health. Bradley found that the ignorance of sanitation and nutrition com-

bined with physical work habits resulted in reduced stamina, greater liability to infection, and restricted intellectual capacity. In the mountain, inaccessibility of physicians contributed to the high mortality rate, as did lack of knowledge concerning sanitation and nutrition. As the State Board of Health and the University of North Carolina worked to create a rural health care and health education program, Bradley served as consultant and coordinator.

Bradley also took advantage of the terrible influenza epidemic that broke out in 1919 at Berea College in Kentucky. As the cases mounted, nearby townspeople had to be called into service to care for and house the ill. When a small hospital was commandeered, the staff had to overcome prejudice and superstition to properly care for the sick and avoid further contagion, but when the crisis was over, those who were saved, along with their families and friends, became converts who helped initiate public health programs in 1900 of the 2500 counties of Appalachia.

Another of Bradley's concerns was the mountain tradition that reduced the woman to a beast of burden. She saw repeatedly the physical results of repressive treatment of women combined with lack of prenatal and delivery care, and she worked to instill in the younger generations a desire for social reform. Her educational campaign concentrated on winning over the young married group to the idea of social rehabilitation. She wrote a series of pamphlets that took into consideration the traditions and problems of the rural community. They became part of the standard literature distributed by the county agents and home demonstrators of the State Department of Agriculture. In them, she discussed principles of good hygiene; the economic ramifications of illness; the meaning of good citizenship in contributing to a health environment; child welfare (from prenatal care through normal childhood development); and public and private agencies available to help with care and education.

By spending much of her time actually visiting backroads areas and personally interviewing the people of rural America, Bradley was able graphically to support her campaign for upgrading rural medical services, which she found often to be rampant with malpractice and quackery. She also began a program to train and register midwives. Bradley then organized a pilot program of social reform in a single county to prove the difference local residents could make if directed by the state and federal agents and physicians. The physical environment was cleaned up, home demonstration classes for canning, cooking, and first aid were offered, and public health nurses made regular rounds of the schools teaching hygiene and making appointments for doctor and dentist visits. The county government voted the first appropriation for public health work, enabling the authorities to drain swamps and install modern water and sewage systems. This pilot program proved the feasibility of real reform with limited financial resources and limited professional staff and gave hope to the depressed rural sections of the nation. JH/MBO

SECONDARY SOURCES
Taylor, Lloyd C. *The Medical Profession and Social Reform, 1885–1945.* New York: St. Martin's Press, 1974. Bradley is discussed pp. 63–84.

BRAHE, SOPHIA (1556–1643)

Danish student of astronomy and chemistry. Born 1556 to Beate (Bille) and Otto Brahe. Nine siblings, including brother, Tycho Brahe. Married Otto Thott (d. 1588); and Erik Lange. One child.

Sophie was the youngest of ten children of Otto Brahe and Beate Bille Brahe. Her oldest brother was the astronomer Tycho Brahe (1546–1601). Highly educated, she was knowledgeable in classical literature, astrology, and alchemy. She assisted Tycho with the observations that led to his computation of the lunar eclipse of 8 December 1573, and frequently visited her brother when he lived on the island of Hveen, where he had a fine observatory. When she was nineteen or twenty, Sophia Brahe married Otto Thott of Ericksholm in Scania; they had one child. After her husband died in 1588, she managed the property at Ericksholm, became an excellent horticulturist, and studied chemistry and medicine. Eventually she was remarried to the impecunious Erik Lange. Although Sophia Brahe was not an astronomer herself, her position as an occasional assistant to Tycho Brahe makes her of some importance to the history of science. One statement in Gassendi's *De Tychonis Brahei Vita* may be the origin of every mention of Sophia as an astronomer: "Ea fuit perita Matheseos, et Astronomiam cum diligeret, tum Astrologiam praesertim deperit: unde et expeditissima in erigendis Thematibus fuit" (She had been exposed to [the study of] mathematics, and [as a result] not only did she love astronomy but she was especially ready to engage in these exciting [astrological] studies). JH/MBO

SECONDARY SOURCES
Dreyer, J. L. E. *Tycho Brahe: A Picture of Scientific Life and Work in the Sixteenth Century.* Edinburgh: Adam and Charles Black, 1890. Includes information on Sophia Brahe.

STANDARD SOURCES
Ogilvie 1986; Rebière.

BRANCH, HAZEL ELISABETH (1886–post-1957)

U.S. entomologist. Educated University of Kansas (A.B., A.M., 1908); Cornell University (Ph.D., 1921). Professional experience:

Collegiate Sisters of Bethany, preceptress (1914–1918); Cornell, assistant in biology (1918–1922); Fairmont College, professor (1922–1926); Wichita State University, professor of zoology (1926–1956), emerita professor. Death date unknown.

Hazel Branch published on three groups of insects, the Membracidae, Trichoptera, and Chironomidae. Bailey gives no personal details but mentions her presidency of the Kansas Academy of Science, which surely has a biography of her. She was a member of the American Public Health Association and the Entomological Society of America and a Fellow of the AAAS. JH/MBO

PRIMARY SOURCES
Branch, Hazel Elisabeth. *Morphology and Biology of the* Membracidae *of Kansas.* Lawrence, Kan.: University of Kansas, 1913.
———. *A Contribution to the Knowledge of the Internal Anatomy of* Trichoptera. Columbus, Ohio: n.p., 1922.
———. *A Laboratory Manual of* Cryptobranchus Allegheniensis, daubin. St. Louis: J.S. Swift, 1935.

SECONDARY SOURCES
Osborn, Herbert. *A Brief History of Entomology. Including Time of Demosthenes and Aristotle to Modern Times with Over Five Hundred Portraits.* Columbus, Ohio: The Spahr & Glenn Co., 1952. Includes a portrait of Branch (plate 31).

STANDARD SOURCES
AMS 4–8, B 9, P&B 10; Bailey.

BRAND, MARTHA (1755?–1814)

U.S. physician. Probably born in 1755 in Philadelphia to Mary (Gardiner) Brand. Stepfather, Alexander Elmslie. Professional experience: "doctoress." Died 24 March 1814 in Philadelphia.

Very little is known about Martha Brand. She was born of Quaker parents. Her father died and her mother remarried a widower in 1771. In the *Philadelphia City Directory* of 1795, 1796, 1798, and 1799, Brand is listed as "Doctoress." Her occupation is not given in 1801 and 1802. From 1803 to 1810 she is listed as "gentlewoman." In the *Census Directory* of 1811 she is identified as "doctoress," as she is in John A. Paxton's *Philadelphia Directory and Register* for 1813 and in B. and T. Kite's *Philadelphia Directory* for 1814. There is no hint as to where she received her medical training and the nature of the practice that earned her the appellation of "doctoress." The available evidence comes from a series of wills, reported on by Whitfield J. Bell, Jr., in the *Journal of the History of Medicine.* Dr. Benjamin Rush received two wills and several letters from Dr. Peter Fassoux of Charleston, South Carolina. Two of Fassoux's daughters had contracted a disfiguring skin disease as children, and Fassoux was unable to help them. He appealed to Rush for advice. Bell thinks it possible that the girls' mother recommended Martha Brand as a sympathetic physician. This can be concluded from the two girls' wills. Martha Brand witnessed Frances Sarah Fassoux's will on 6 March 1797 and Frances's sister Mary's on 12 June 1804. Mary states that Brand had given her tender care throughout her illness.

Martha Brand is listed in *The New Trade Directory for Philadelphia, Anno 1800* not as a midwife but among the physicians. She may have run some kind of a nursing home. She died at the age of fifty-nine after a brief but painful illness.

JH/MBO

SECONDARY SOURCES

Bell, Whitfield J., Jr. "Martha Brand (ca. 1755–1814): "An Early American Physician." *Journal of the History of Medicine* 33 (1978): 218–219.
Philadelphia Will Book No. 5, 233. Philadelphia.
Philadelphia Will Book 10, 560. Philadelphia.
Philadelphia Will Book No. 1, 228. Philadelphia.

BRANDEGEE, MARY KATHARINE LAYNE (1844–1920)

U.S. botanist. Born 28 October 1844 in western Tennessee to Mary (Morris) and Marshall Layne. Nine siblings. Married Hugh Curran (d. 1874); Townshend Brandegee. Educated University of California, San Francisco (M.D., 1878). Professional experience: curator of botany, California Academy of Sciences (1883–1893). Died 30 April 1920 in Berkeley, Calif.

Katharine Layne was the second of ten children of a peripatetic father. After numerous moves the family ended up on a farm near Folsom, California, before Katherine's ninth birthday. In 1866 she married Hugh Curran, an Irish native and a constable at Folsom, who died in 1874.

After Curran's death, Layne went to San Francisco and entered the medical department of the University of California. In 1878 she received a medical degree. She became interested in *materia medica* and began to learn about plants, at first concentrating on those with medicinal values and then expanding her interests to plants in general. Through her mentor, Hans Herman Behr, she met people who were active in the California Academy of Sciences and began to work there by stages; she served as the academy's curator of botany from 1883 to 1893.

In 1889 she married Townshend Brandegee, a civil engineer and avid plant collector. Together they established a series of bulletins of the California Academy of Sciences, with Katharine as editor. They also founded *Zoe*, a journal of botanical observations from the western United States. Most of Katharine Brandegee's published work appeared in *Zoe*, which was issued, with increasing irregularity, until 1908.

Katharine Brandegee's extensive collections were important in determining range boundaries. She was especially interested in locating intermediate forms of newly described species, thereby demonstrating that the new "species" were actually only subspecifically different. Two new species of plants, *Astragalus laynea* and *Mimulus layneae*, were named for her.

JH/MBO

PRIMARY SOURCES

Brandegee, Mary Katharine Layne. *Variation in* Oneothera Ovata. Berkeley: University of California Press, 1914.

SECONDARY SOURCES

Ewan, Joseph. "Bibliographical Miscellany—IV. A Bibliographical Guide to the Brandegee Botanical Collections." *American Midland Naturalist* 27, 1942: 772–789. Includes brief biographies of Mary Katharine Brandegee and Townshend Brandegee as well as information on the collections.
Jones, Marcus E. "Mrs. T. S. Brandegee." *Contributions to Western Botany* 18 (1935): 12–18. Includes many unsupportable statements but, in addition to a biographical sketch, contains a photograph of both Brandegees.
Setchell, William Albert. "Townshend Stith Brandegee and Mary Katharine (Layne)(Curran) Brandegee." *University of California Publications in Botany* 13 (1926): 155–178. Contains complete bibliographies of the Brandegees' writings and the most complete account of their lives. Includes autobiographical material, portraits, and other illustrations.

STANDARD SOURCES

NAW (article by Hunter Dupree and Marian L. Gade).

BRANHAM, SARA ELIZABETH (1888–1962)

U.S. microbiologist. Born 1888 in Oxford, Miss. Educated Wesleyan College, Macon, Ga.; University of Colorado (Ph.D., 1923); University of Colorado Medical School (M.D., 1934). Professional experience: Atlanta, Ga., biology teacher (until 1917); University of Colorado, assistant in bacteriology (1917–1923); Hygienic Laboratories of the United States Public Health Service (now the National Institutes of Health (NIH), division of biological standards, senior bacteriologist (1927–1954); division chief (1955–1958). Honors and memberships: American Medical Women's Association, Woman of the Year (1959). Died 1962.

After Sara Elizabeth Branham earned her doctorate she decided to work on a medical degree as well. Before she obtained the latter degree, she took a job with what later became the National Institutes of Health. From 1955 to 1958, she was chief of the Division of Biological Standards.

During the thirty years that she was at the NIH, she did outstanding work on meningitis. She was the first to demonstrate that sulfa drugs inhibited the activity of the meningitis causal agent, the meningococcal bacteria. Branham had previously worked with *bacterium enteritidis,* a bacterium that causes food poisoning. However an epidemic of meningitis had broken out in the United States in the late 1920s, and the NIH became involved in the search for a treatment.

A new strain of bacteria, *Neisseria meningitidis,* was responsible for the new epidemic. This strain apparently was immune to the antiserum that had been developed to fight an earlier epidemic. Working with the meningococcus bacteria was very difficult, for the cultures had to be subcultured every other day to insure that the strain remained viable. After becoming an expert in identifying various strains of the bacteria, Branham discovered that sulfa drugs provided an effective treatment.

Branham retired from the NIH at the age of seventy, but continued to study the effects of various toxins in mice, chickens, and monkeys. JH/MBO

PRIMARY SOURCES

Branham, Sara Elizabeth. "I. The Toxic Products of *Bacillus enteritidis.* II. The Production of Lung Hemorrhages and Associated Phenomena in Rabbits and Guinea Pigs." Ph.D. diss., University of Chicago, 1923.

————. With Clara E. Taft. *Studies on Meningococci Located in the United States 1928–1930.* Washington, D.C.: Government Printing Office, 1931.

————. With Anna Pabst. *Serum Studies in Experimental Meningitis.* Washington, D.C.: Government Printing Office, 1937.

————. With Edward R. Stitt and Paul Clough, eds. *Practical Bacteriology, Hematology and Parasitology.* 10th ed. Philadelphia: Blakiston, 1948.

National Library of Medicine in Bethesda, Maryland, has a Branham File.

SECONDARY SOURCES

New York Times, 19 November 1962. Obituary notice.

Greiner, Mary. "Women Scientists Resemble Housewives in Making Things Do" [interview with Branham]. *Washington Post,* 18 May 1934.

O'Hern, Elizabeth Moot. "Women Scientists in Microbiology." *BioScience* 23 (September 1973): 539–543.

————. *Profiles of Pioneer Women Scientists.* New York: Acropolis Books, 1985.

Pittman, M. "Sarah Elizabeth Branham (Matthews): A Biographical Sketch." *ASM News* 42: 420–422.

Radcliff, J. D. "Lady of the Lab." *McCall's* 66 (April 1939): 7–8.

————, ed. In Stitt, Edward Rhodes, *Practical Bacteriology, Hematology, and Parasitology.* 10th ed. Philadelphia: Blakiston, ca. 1948.

STANDARD SOURCES

Brooke Bailey; O'Hern; Rossiter 1982.

BRANT, LAURA (1883–?)

U.S. physicist. Born 4 February 1883 in Kent County, R.I. Educated Brown University (A.B., 1908; A.M., 1909); Columbia University (Ph.D., 1921). Professional experience: Brown University, assistant to the dean (1908–1909); Smith College, physics teacher (1909–1912); Barnard College, Columbia, researcher (1912–1917), lecturer (1917–1919); Vassar College, instructor (1919–1925); Judson College, professor of mathematics and physics and department head (1925–1929); Oauchita College, acting head of the mathematics department (1929–1930), head of the department (1930–1931). Honors and memberships: International Exposition and 50th Congés Association Francaise pour l'Avancement des Sciences; Physical Society; Mathematical Society.

Information about the career of Laura Brant ends when she was forty-eight years old, after her term as head of the mathematics department at Oauchita College. She had an excellent education at Brown and Columbia universities and then taught at several colleges. She was involved in international activities and did research on the magnetic susceptibility of paramagnetic salts in solution and the softening of cold glass-hard steel. JH/MBO

STANDARD SOURCES

AMS 3–8, P 9, P&B 10.

BRAUN, ANNETTE FRANCES (1884–1978)

U.S. entomologist. Born 1884 to Emma Morah (Wright) and George Frederick Braun. Educated Cincinnati public schools; University of Cincinnati (A.B., 1906; A.M., 1908; Ph.D., 1911). Professional experience: University of Cincinnati, assistant in zoology (1911–1916); independent research (1916–1978). Died 1978.

The elder sister of LUCY BRAUN, the entomologist Annette Frances Braun learned from her parents to appreciate the Ohio woodlands, plants and insects. She attended the Cincinnati public schools and the University of Cincinnati, obtaining her doctorate in 1911. She was an assistant in zoology at the University of Cincinnati from 1911 to 1916, but dropped out to do private research when her sister Lucy Braun was appointed instructor in botany, possibly because of the same rules against nepotism in hiring that affected the lives of husbands and wives.

Annette Braun continued her own research on North American moths while keeping house for her sister and assisting her in her research, working closely with her in their experimental garden, and traveling with her as she made extensive surveys of Ohio and Kentucky forests. She became the vice-president of the Entomological Society of America in 1926 and published a major contribution on a group of moths (Microlepidoptera) for that society in 1948. She also published numerous papers on this group in the *Transactions of the Philadelphia Academy of Science*. After her sister's death, she served as a major source for Ronald Stuckey's biographical article on her for the *Notable American Women (Modern)*. Annette Braun died seven years after her sister.   JH/MBO

PRIMARY SOURCES
Elaschistidae of North America *(Microlepidoptera), American Entomological Society Memoirs* 13, 1948.

SECONDARY SOURCES
Osborn, Herbert. *A Brief History of Entomology. Including Time of Demosthenes and Aristotle to Modern Times with Over Five Hundred Portraits.* Columbus, Ohio: The Spahr & Glenn Co., 1952. Includes a portrait of Braun (plate 17).
Stein, Lisa K. The Sisters Braun: Uncommon Dedication. *Cincinnati Museum of Natural History* 21, 2 (1988): 9–13.
Stuckey, Ronald L. "Emma Lucy Braun." *NAW*(M) 102–103. See also other articles by R. L. Stuckey on her sister, Emma Lucy Braun.

STANDARD SOURCES
AMS 3–8, B 9, P&B 10–11; Bailey.

BRAUN, (EMMA) LUCY (1889–1971)

U.S. botanist, ecologist, conservationist. Born 19 April 1889 in Cincinnati, Ohio, to Emma Morah (Wright) and George Frederick Braun. Never married. Cincinnati public schools, University of Cincinnati (A.B., 1910; A.M. in geology; Ph.D. in botany, 1914). Professional experience: University of Cincinnati, assistant in geology (1910–1913), assistant in botany (1914–1917), instructor in botany (1917–1923), assistant professor (1923–1927), associate professor (1927–1946), professor of plant ecology (1946–1948); emerita professor (1948–1971); edited Wild Flower, *journal of the Wild Flower Preservation Society (1928–1933); Ohio Academy of Sciences, president (1933–1934); Ecological Society of America, president (1950). Died 5 March 1971.*

E. Lucy Braun, plant ecologist, and her older sister, ANNETTE FRANCES BRAUN, an entomologist, were encouraged in their nature studies from early childhood by their parents. Walking and observing in the surrounding area of the Ohio woods, both sisters developed a lasting love for the study of plants and the insects they interact with. Braun first studied geology, but changed to botany, obtaining her doctorate in botany at the University of Cincinnati in 1914. She taught for many years at the University of Cincinnati, beginning as an assistant in geology, then as an assistant in biology. She was made an instructor in 1917 and rose through the academic ranks until she was made full professor in plant ecology two years before her retirement (1948). Many of her important publications appeared between 1950 and 1967, during her years as emerita professor. Her first studies were in the unique vegetation of the unglaciated limestone of Adams County, Ohio, and the physiographic ecology and vegetation of the Cincinnati region. She extended this to study the forests in southwestern Ohio and the plateau and mountain regions of Kentucky. This study led to her classic book *Deciduous Forests of Eastern North America* (1950), published after she had taken early retirement from the University of Cincinnati.

Braun also made important contributions to the study of taxonomy of vascular plants, cataloguing the flora of Cincinnati area, comparing it with the flora a hundred years earlier. This historical comparison was a model for comparing the changes in flora over time. She also provided a key to the deciduous trees of the Ohio and Kentucky areas. She proposed and chaired a committee to study the flora of Ohio within the Ohio Academy of Science, and soon after published two books, one on woody plants and vascular flora (1961) and the other on the monocotyledons (1967).

Her work led her to study plant distribution and migration with the resulting publication of an extensive analytical summary of phytogeography of the Eastern United States (1955). She calculated that she had traveled more than 65,000 miles in her surveys. In this work, as in all her work, she proposed new and innovative methods and equally innovative points of view.

Braun spent much time popularizing the need for conservation, editing the magazine for the Wild Flower Preservation society, *Wild Flower*. She also fought for prairie conservation and urged the establishment of preserves. She was the first woman president of the Ohio Academy of Science (1933–1934) and of the Ecological Society of America. She received a number of awards, including the Mary Soper Pope Medal for achievement in botany, and the Certificate of Merit from the Botanical Society of America (1956).

Braun's work was extensive and thorough. She integrated the work of many other scientists, adding her own original methods and theory. She died at Mount Washington, Ohio, 5 March 1971, seven years before her older sister, the entomologist Annette Braun, with whom she had worked closely and lived throughout her life.   JH/MBO

PRIMARY SOURCES
Braun, Emma Lucy. *The Physiographic Ecology of the Cincinnati Region.* Ph.D. diss., Cincinnati, Ohio, University of Cincinnati, 1914.

———. "Glacial and Post-Glacial Plant Migrations Indicated by Relic Colonies of Southern Ohio." *Ecology* 9 (1928): 284–302.

———. *An Annotated Catalogue of the Spermatophytes of Kentucky.* Planographed by John S. Swift, 1943.

———. *Deciduous Forests of Eastern North America* (1950) reprinted in 1964, 1967, 1972.

———. *The Woody Plants of Ohio: Trees Shrubs, and Weedy Climbers, Native, Naturalized, and Escaped.* Columbus: Ohio University Press, 1961. Facsimile edition 1969, Hafner, New York. Reissued Ohio University Press, 1991.

———. *The* Monocotyledoneae; *Cat-tails to Orchids with* Gramineae *by Clara G. Weishaupt.* Columbus: Ohio State University Press, 1967. For full bibliography see Stuckey.

SECONDARY SOURCES

Stein, Lisa K. The Sisters Braun: Uncommon Dedication. *Cincinnati Museum of Natural History* 21, 2 (1988): 9–13.

Stuckey, Ronald L. "E. Lucy Braun (1889–1971). Outstanding Botanist and Conservationist: A Biographical Sketch with Bibliography." *Michigan Botanist* 12 (1973): 83–106.

———. "Emma Lucy Braun (1889–1971)." In Grinstein 1997.

STANDARD SOURCES

AMS 3–8, B 9; P&B 10–11; Bailey; *NAW*(M)

BRAZIER, MARY AGNES BURNISTON (BROWN) (1904–1995)

British-U.S. neurophysiologist and historian of science. Born 1904 in Weston-super-Mare, England. Married Leslie J. Brazier (1928). One son, Oliver. Naturalized U.S. citizen. Educated Bedford College (B.Sc., 1926); University of London (Ph.D. in biochemistry, 1929; E.Wd. in neurophysiology, 1960). Professional experience: Maudsley Hospital, London, research fellow (1930–1940); Massachusetts General Hospital and Massachusetts Institute of Technology (MIT), neurophysiologist (1940–60); University of California, Los Angeles, Brain Research Institute, professor of anatomy, physiology, biophysics (1961–1988). Concurrent experience: Journal of Electroencephalography and Clinical Neurophysiology, *editor for the Americas and the Far East (1972–1987); Editor-in-Chief (1975–1984). Honors and memberships: Rockefeller Fellowship (1940–1945); American Academy of Arts and Sciences, Fellow; American Physiological Society, president; American Electroencephalographic Society, president (1955); International Federation of Electroencephalographic Societies, treasurer (1953–1957), secretary (1957–1961), president (1961–1965), honorary president; University of London, Hon. D.Sc. (1960); University of Utrecht, honorary M.D. (1976); International Brain Research Organization, secretary general (1978–1982); British EEG Society, Grey Walter Medal (1985); National Institutes of Health, Neurol-*

ogy Institute, Research Career Award. Died in East Falmouth, Mass., 5 May 1995.

Mary Agnes Burniston (Brown) Brazier was a distinguished neurophysiologist, editor, and historian of science. Born in England near Bristol, she came from a scientific family that included a physicist brother. Her father was a cousin of the physicist Arthur Eddington, and he treasured photographs of Einstein's meetings with his distinguished relative. As a young woman, Mollie (as she preferred to be called) Brown was trained at Bedford College, later part of the University of London, where many women physiologists were educated. She went on to study both physiology and biochemistry at the University of London, where she received her doctorate one year after marrying an electrical engineer, Leslie J. Brazier.

During the next twelve years, her work at Maudsley Hospital in London centered on endocrinology, but she used her physiological training to follow electrical changes of the skin to demonstrate changes in thyroid disease. This work earned her a Gold Medal from the Institute of Electrical Engineers (in Britain) and the Van Meiter Prize from the American Association for the Study of Goiter in 1934, and encouraged her to study the electrical activity of the nervous system as her lifelong research interest.

With the outbreak of World War II, she became concerned with the safety of her son, Oliver, in London, and took the opportunity to travel to the United States with her child on a Rockefeller Fellowship. Her husband remained behind in England. Brazier entered the laboratory of Stanley Cobb at Massachusetts General Hospital (MGH), affiliated with Harvard Medical School. She later moved to other laboratories, including that of Dr. Robert Schwab with whom she studied peripheral nerve injuries, war neuroses, and muscle function. Increasingly, Brazier used the electroencephalograph (EEG) as a diagnostic tool to study the effects of anesthesia. She was for a time acting director of Schwab's EEG laboratory at MGH and helped develop the use of computers for frequency analysis of the EEG.

After World War II, she joined another colleague, James Casby, in working with Norbert Wiener at Massachusetts Institute of Technology (MIT) and then with Walter Rosenblith, who formed the Communication Biophysics Laboratory there. The combined group developed an analog correlator specifically to analyze EEG and other nerve potentials. Brazier presented the results of this work at the Third International EEG Congress held in Cambridge, Massachusetts, in 1953. For her work, she also used the general purpose digital computers then being developed at MIT.

Soon after Horace Magoun established the Brain Research Institute at the University of California, Los Angeles

(UCLA), Brazier moved to California to join his group and spearhead the development of its computer facilities for the analysis of the nervous system. There she was appointed professor of anatomy, physiology, and biophysics. As editor of the important new journal in her field, she published an important bibliography of EEG publications ranging from 1875–1948, and served as a guide to students and researchers. Her later work on the history of her field explored these early publications and extended back into the beginning of neurophysiology in the seventeenth century.

Brazier was a strong believer in international cooperation in science and worked with the international organizations in neurophysiology and electroencephalography, serving as officer and president of a number of them. Her activities meant that she also organized collaboration between scientists from both sides of the Iron Curtain and edited or coedited symposia volumes that resulted from this cooperation with help from the International Brain Research Organization and UNESCO.

Toward the end of her life, she was awarded a prestigious Research Career Award by the National Institutes of Health and received an honorary medical degree from the University of Utrecht. In her mid-eighties, she left California to return to the east coast where she had built a house on Cape Cod during her years in Boston. She also was able to be near her son, who had become an oceanographer at Woods Hole. She continued active work even after her eyesight began to fail. In her lifetime, Brazier published nearly 250 papers and books. Her last paper, on the Abbe Nollet's contributions to early electrotherapy in the eighteenth century, was published when she was eighty-nine.   JH/MBO

PRIMARY SOURCES

Brazier, Mary Agnes Burniston. *The Physiological Effects of Carbon Dioxide on the Activity of the Central Nervous System in Man with Special Reference to the Problem of High Altitude Flying.* [New York]: Josiah Macy, Jr., Foundation, 1943.

———. *The Electrical Activity of the Nervous System: A Textbook for Students.* New York: MacMillan, 1951.

———. *Epilepsy: Its Phenomena in Man.* UCLA Forum in Medical Sciences, 17. New York: Academic Press, 1973.

———. *Growth and Development of the Brain: Nutritional, Genetic, and Environmental Factors.* Monograph Series, International Brain Research Organization, 1. New York: Raven Press, 1975.

———. *The Evolution of Protein Structure and Function: A Symposium in Honor of Professor Emil L. Smith.* UCLA Forum in Medical Sciences, 21. New York: Academic Press, 1980.

———. *Developmental Immunology: Clinical Problems and Aging.* UCLA Forum in Medical Sciences, 25. New York: Academic Press, 1982.

———. *A History of Neurophysiology in the 17th and 18th Centuries: From Concept to Experiment.* New York: Raven Press, 1984.

———. *A History of Neurophysiology in the 19th Century.* New York: Raven Press, 1988.

———. "The Abbe Nollet (1700–1770): The Beginnings of Electrotherapy." *Journal for the History of Neuroscience* 2 (1993): 53–64.

SECONDARY SOURCES

Barlow, John, Robert Nacquet, and Hans van Dujin. "In Memoriam M.A.B. Brazier." *Journal of Electroencephalography and Clinical Neurophysiology* 1996, 98: 1–4. Includes portrait.

Marshall, Louise H. With Horace W. Magoun. *Discoveries in the Human Brain: Neuroscience Prehistory, Brain Structure, and Function.* Totowa, N.J.: Humana, 1998. Has passim references to Brazier's books and editorial work, as well as portraits with colleagues.

STANDARD SOURCES

AMS 8–19; *WW in America*, 1981–1982.

BRECKINRIDGE, MARY (1881–1965)

U.S. nurse, public health activist. Born 17 February 1881 in Memphis, Tenn., to Katherine (Carson) and Clifton Rodes Breckinridge. Married Henry Ruffner Morrison (1904) (d. 1906); Richard Ryan Thompson (1912) (divorced 1920). One son and daughter (both died in childhood). Educated Rosemont-Dézaley School, Lausanne, Switzerland; Low and Heywood, Conn.; St. Luke's Hospital School of Nursing, New York City (R.N., 1910); Teacher's College, Columbia University, studies in public health; British Hospital for Mothers and Babies (London) and York Road General Lying-In Hospital (London), postgraduate work. Professional experience: Crescent College for Young Women, Eureka Springs, Ark., teacher, French and hygiene (1912–1918?); Boston and Washington, D.C., public health nurse (1918); American Committee for Devastated France, nursing supervisor (1919); Kentucky Committee for Mothers and Babies (which became the Frontier Nursing Service), founder and director (1924–1965). Died 1965 in Hyden, Ky.

Mary Breckinridge was born into a wealthy southern family. Her grandfather John Breckinridge had been both vice-president of the United States and a Confederate general; her father was a congressman from Arkansas, where her parents had moved soon after her birth, but she spent her childhood in Washington, D.C. When her father went as a diplomat to Russia, she was sent to a school in Lausanne for two years, returning to Connecticut in 1899 to spend her final year of school there. On return to Fort Smith,

Arkansas, where her parents were living, she married Henry Ruffner Morrison, in 1904, but her husband died within two years from a ruptured appendix. Perhaps for this reason, she took up nursing, studying at a New York City hospital (St. Luke's), and graduated as registered nurse in 1910. Upon returning again to Arkansas, she married for a second time and taught French and hygiene in the school where her husband, Richard Ryan Thompson, was president (Crescent College and Conservatory for Young Women) in Eureka Springs. Following the early childhood deaths of first a daughter and then a son, she separated from her husband and returned to full-time nursing, obtaining a divorce in 1920.

Anxious to do something for the civilians in Europe toward the end of World War I, she first spent a year training as a public health nurse in hospitals in Boston and Washington. She went to France after the armistice as part of the American Committee for Devastated France, based near Versailles and headed by an American philanthropist, Anne Morgan. She quickly organized a program to bring food and medical help to pregnant and nursing women and their children. This served her as excellent preparation for her later organizational work in providing similar services to mothers and children in the rural South. She returned to the United States in 1921 to train in public health at Columbia University Teachers College and then spent time studying at a number of hospitals in London. She also observed the medical and nursing service in Scotland, which delivered care to a widely scattered rural population, using well-trained nurse midwives.

When she returned to the United States, she chose the Kentucky mountains as an appropriate place to begin the kind of pioneer nursing she envisaged. A number of her distant female cousins were active in Kentucky as nationally recognized social reformers, and she was able to enlist the support of prominent families in organizing the Kentucky Committee for Mothers and Children in 1925. This developed into the Frontier Nursing Service, much of which was initially funded by Breckinridge from the inheritance left to her by her mother. She developed a system of trained nurse midwives who were stationed in outposts ten miles apart who could reach their patients on horseback. A hospital based in Hyden with an attending physician served as the center for this service. In 1925, Breckinridge began to publish the *Frontier Nursing Service Quarterly Bulletin* which continued under her editorship until her death. She never remarried, but brought her widowed father to live with her in Hyden. She continued to be the main fundraiser for the FNS and also established a flourishing graduate program in training nurse midwives. She received many honors throughout her life, dying of leukemia and a stroke in Hyden, Kentucky, at the age of eighty-four.   JH/MBO

PRIMARY SOURCES

Breckinridge, Mary. "The Nurse-Midwife, a Pioneer." *American Journal of Public Health,* November, 1927.

———. *Wide Neighborhoods: The Story of the Frontier Nursing Service.* Autobiography. New York: Harper, 1952.

———. Various articles in *Frontier Nursing Service Quarterly Bulletin* (1925–1965).

SECONDARY SOURCES

Faust, Drew Gilpin. "Mary Breckinridge." In *NAW*(M).

New York Times, 17 May 1965. Obituary notice.

Wilkie, Katherine E. and Elizabeth R. Mosely. *Frontier Nurse: Mary Breckinridge.* New York: Messner, 1969.

BREDIKHINA, EVGENIIA ALEKSANDROVNA (1922–1974)

Russian mathematician. Born 2 January 1922 in Chistovok to Anna Sergeevna Kitaeva, a teacher, and Aleksandr Fomich Kitaev, a doctor. Married with children and grandchildren. Educated at schools in Kuibyshev; University of Kazan; University of Leningrad; Kuibyshev Polytechnic Institute (graduated 1945); University of Leningrad (Ph.D., 1955); University of L'vov (D.Sc., 1972). Professional experience: Kuibyshev Polytechnic, teacher; Kuibyshev Institute of Aviation, department of higher mathematics, head. Died 6 October 1974.

Evgeniia Aleksandrovna Bredikhina was born in the village of Chistovok in the Kuibyshev region. In 1939, she graduated with honors from the middle school there and entered the mathematical-physical department of the University of Kazan. In 1940, she transferred to the department of mathematics and mechanics of the University of Leningrad. When war with Germany broke out, Bredikhina worked on fortifications for the city and then in a hospital in the besieged city. In April 1942, she was evacuated to Kuibyshev and was able to return to her studies, graduating with honors in 1945 from the department of mathematics and mechanics of the Kuibyshev Pedagogical Institute.

After graduation, Bredikhina worked at the Kuibyshev Polytechnic and then moved to the Kuibyshev Institute of Aviation, first as an assistant and then in increasingly senior positions until she became head of the department of higher mathematics.

Bredikhina continued her studies as an external student at the University of Leningrad, where she worked under the supervision of I. P. Natanson. In 1955, she defended her doctoral thesis in the field of almost periodic functions. Further research on this subject led to her doctor of science dissertation in 1972. Bredikhina died after a long illness in 1974.

Bredikhina's talents lay in a specialized and theoretical branch of mathematics. Her research was devoted exclusively to the study of the theory of almost periodic functions. She published thirty-five papers on this topic. Among other related subjects, she studied the uniform and absolute convergence of Fourier series of almost periodic functions; Fourier gap series; questions of simultaneous approximations of almost periodic functions and their derivatives by finite trigonometrical sums and entire functions of finite degree.

Bredikhina was an outstanding teacher and lecturer. She also took an active part in the Third and Fourth All-Union Mathematical Congresses (1957 and 1961) and the International Congress of Mathematics in Moscow in 1966. She received several medals for her work.   ACH

PRIMARY SOURCES

Bredikhina, Evgeniia Aleksandrovna. "K voprosu ob otsenke posledovatel'nykh integralov periodicheskikh funktsii." *Izv. vuzov. Matematika* 4 (1967): 19–25.

———. "K voprosu o raskhodimosti riadov Fur'e pochtiperiodicheskikh funktsii." *Izv. vuzov. Matematika* 8 (1970): 27–32.

———. "Ob okonchatel'nosti priznakov skhodimosti riadov Fur'e pochti-periodicheskikh funktsii." *DAN* 194 (1970): 489–492.

SECONDARY SOURCES

Levitan, B. M., et al. "Evgeniia Aleksandrovna Bredikhina: necrolog." *Russian Mathematical Surveys* 30, no. 3 (1975): 129–133. Translated from the Russian; includes bibliography.

BREED, MARY (BIDWELL) (1870–?)

U.S. chemist. Born 15 September 1870 in Pittsburgh, Pa. Educated Bryn Mawr College (A.B., 1894; European fellowship, 1894–1895; A.M., 1895; Ph.D., 1901); University of Heidelberg (1895–1896). Professional experience: Bryn Mawr College, assistant chemical laboratory (1894–1895); Pennsylvania College for Women, science department, head (1897–1899); Indiana University, assistant professor of chemistry and dean of women (from 1901). Death date unknown.

Mary Bidwell Breed's career is not well documented after 1906. The first edition of *American Men of Science* was published in this year and it is the only edition in which Breed appears. At this time she was assistant professor of chemistry and dean of women at the University of Indiana. Before she went to Indiana, she had received three degrees at Bryn Mawr University and had studied overseas at Heidelberg. Before she finished her doctorate, she was head of the sci-

ence department at Pennsylvania College for Women. Her research was on the atomic weight of palladium and polybasic and diortho substituted aromatic acids. She was a member of the Chemical Society and Chemical Gesellschaft.

JH/MBO

STANDARD SOURCES
AMS 1; Rossiter 1982.

BRENCHLEY, WINIFRED ELSIE (1883–1953)

British botanist. Born 10 August 1883 at Harpenden, Hertfordshire. Educated Swanley Horticultural College; University College, London (B.Sc., 1905; D.Sc., 1911). Professional experience: Rothamsted Experimental Station, head of the botany department (1907–1948). Honors and memberships: University College; Linnean Society; Royal Entomological Society. Died 27 October 1953.

Winifred Brenchley was originally trained in horticulture and then studied botany at University College, London. She spent her entire professional career at the Rothamsted Experimental Station, where she was head of the botany department. She wrote several books and contributed numerous articles to professional journals.   JH/MBO

STANDARD SOURCES
Debus; Desmond; *WWW,* vol. 5.

BRENK, IRENE (1902–)

Swiss physician born in Zurich, Switzerland. Only child. Married H. Brenk (August 1929). Three children. Educated girls' gymnasium of Zurich (from 1918); University of Zurich. Professional experience: Polyclinic of Internal Medicine, Zurich, associate (1928); psychiatric clinic of Professor Stachelin, Basel, associate (1928–1929); Basel, private practice.

Irene Brenk was born and educated in Zurich, Switzerland. The only child of highly educated parents, she was well tutored and especially enjoyed music and playing piano in various ensembles. She entered the girls' gymnasium of Zurich in 1918 with an interest in the natural sciences. At the close of the nineteenth century, the gymnasiums (high schools or preparatory schools) of Switzerland attracted girls especially from Russia and Germany where universities were still closed to them. Zurich was a center of open-minded education, where girls could learn mathematics, sciences, classical and modern languages, and modern literature, and participate in sports with the possibility of proceeding to a university. Irene's father had suggested that she study medicine. She decided finally to do so when she attended a lecture by a woman doctor who explained the barriers for women in medicine as well as the opportunities, especially in private practice. After the matriculation examination, Irene entered medical studies, but that year her father, with whom she had been exceptionally close since her parents had separated, became ill. He died in January 1928. Irene was devastated and might have left medicine for more immediate financial stability had not her internal medicine professor, Professor Loffler, asked her to join his polyclinic to work half days and research her dissertation topic, lymphogranulomatosis, under his supervision.

In 1928 at Loffler's suggestion, Irene began working as a volunteer in the psychiatric clinic under Professor Maier. Here she met H. Brenk, a young neurologist; the two were married August 1929. They both found positions in the psychiatric clinic of Professor Stachelin in Basel and Irene continued training in psychiatry while her husband set up private practice. The couple had three children between 1932 and 1940 and Irene devoted herself to her household. When World War II broke out and the German army marched into France, the Swiss government called all medical personnel into duty. The women doctors were given civil service duties in the cities and countryside, while the men were sent to field hospitals. Basel, on the Swiss border, was heavily exposed and experienced bombing and food shortages. Brenk took over her husband's practice in general medicine, did minor surgery, pediatric and emergency cases, and shared duty at bomb-shelter hospital facilities. Her husband returned from military duty with chronic bronchitis and fever, which made it impossible for him to return to his practice regularly. The couple finally retired around 1969 to an area near the Lake of Zurich. Their eldest daughter is a physician.   KM

PRIMARY SOURCES
Brenk, Irene. In Hellstedt, *Autobiographies.*

BRÈS, MADELEINE (GÉBELIN) (1839–1925)

French physician. Married and widowed shortly after the marriage. Educated as midwife; baccalaureate; School of Medicine, Paris (M.D., 1875). Professional experience: Paris, head of creche infant nurseries; L'Hygiene de la Femme et l'Enfant, founder and editor. Died 1925 in Paris.

Daughter of an artisan named Gébelin (a wheelwright) who worked in the provincial hospitals, Brès grew up with a strong desire to be a physician. Married at age fifteen and then widowed soon after, Brès trained initially as a midwife. She wrote to the dean of the Paris medical school, Adolphe Wurtz, in 1866 asking for admission to the Paris School of Medicine. Wurtz and the minister of education, Victor Duruy, were looking for an opportunity to admit women in order to counteract Empress Eugenie's request to open a school for women missionary physicians. Brès was told that even if the faculty were to overcome the exclusion of women, she would still be required to obtain the equivalent of a baccalaureate degree. After she qualified herself, she was admitted to the school in 1868, along with the American MARY PUTNAM JACOBI, the Englishwoman ELIZABETH GARRETT ANDERSON, and a Russian woman, Goncharev, all three of whom had first qualified as physicians in their own countries. Delayed by the siege of Paris by the Prussian army, and the Paris Commune that followed, Brès completed her medical degree on 3 June 1875 with a thesis on the breast and breastfeeding, the first Frenchwoman to receive her degree from the Paris Medical School.

During the Franco-Prussian war and the Commune, Brès served as a provisional *interne* (resident) at La Pitié under Paul Broca, raised to that position because of the need for additional physicians. In spite of Broca's support for her application, the faculty of the Paris medical school refused to recognize her qualifications as hospital resident or let her take the examinations to properly qualify herself for hospital work. Only by 1886 were two women, AUGUSTA DÉJERINE-KLUMPKE and BLANCHE EDWARDS-PILLIET, allowed to take the prestigious examinations for the *internat,* and this required Paul Bert, then minister of public instruction, to supersede the authority of the medical faculty.

Brès then founded a famous creche, or infant care nursery, where she worked until the end of her life, pouring most of her earnings into it. She edited a journal on the hygiene of women and children from 1883 to 1895 (*L'hygiene de la femme et l'enfant*). She wrote a book about bottle-feeding (*L'allaitement artificiel et le biberon*) and another about childcare (*Mamans et bébés,* 1899) and was celebrated as the "dean" of women physicians in France. She died poor and almost blind at Montrouge, Paris, in 1925.   JH

PRIMARY SOURCES
Brès, Madeleine. "De la mammelle et de l'allaitement." Thesis, Facuté de Medicine, Paris, 1875.
———. *L'allaitement artificiel et le biberon.* Paris: Masson, 1889.
———. *Mamans et bébés.* Paris: 1899.
———, ed. *L'hygiene de la femme et l'enfant.* (journal editor, 1883–1895).

SECONDARY SOURCES
Harvey, Joy. "'La Visite': Mary Putnam Jacobi and the Paris Medical Clinic." In *French Medical Culture in the Nineteenth Century,* ed. Ann La Berge and M. Feingold. Amsterdam: Rodope, 1994.

Schultze, C. "La femme-médecin au XIX siècle." Thesis, Paris School of Medicine, 1888; *Biographie des Françaises.*

STANDARD SOURCES
DFC; Lipinska 1900; Lipinska 1930.

BREYER, MARIA GERDINA (BRANDWIJK) (1899–?)

Dutch/South African biochemist. Born 21 November 1899 in Culemborg, Netherlands, to Judith (Pijselman) and Nicolaas Brandwijk. Married Jan Hendril Breye (25 June 1927). One daughter, Judith. Educated University of Utrecht, Netherlands (Ph.D., 1923); State Exam, pharmacy (1924); University of Witwatersrand, South Africa (D.Sc., 1935). Professional experience: University of Witwatersrand, medical faculty, lecturer in pharmacology (1925–1940); Transvaal and Orange Free State Chamber Mines, South Africa, chemist in research laboratories (1943–1965); Johannesburg, private consulting work (from 1965). Death date unknown.

Maria was born in the Netherlands but moved with her husband to South Africa. She completed another degree at Witwatersrand University and became a lecturer in pharmacy on the medical faculty for fifteen years. She worked as a chemist in mines and later did consulting work. She was a member of the Royal Society of South Africa, the South African Association for the Advancement of Science, the South Africa Chemical Institute, and the International Federation of University Women. In addition to two books she wrote numerous articles. She did research on phytochemistry, biochemical toxicology, anatomy and allergic problems of plants, folk and native medicines, and the protection of timber and textile materials in mines from fungal organisms.   JH/MBO

PRIMARY SOURCES
Breyer, Maria. With J. M. Watt. *The Medicinal and Poisonous Plants of Southern Africa.* Edinburgh: E.&S. Livingstone, 1932.
———. With John Mitchell Watt. *The Medicinal and Poisonous Plants of Southern and Eastern Africa.* Edinburgh: E.&S. Livingstone, 1962.

STANDARD SOURCES
Debus.

BREZINA, MARIA ARISTIDES (1848–1909)

Austrian mineralogist and crystallographer. Born 1848. Professional experience: Natural History Museum, Vienna. Died 1909.

Brezina worked extensively on meteorites.   JH/MBO

SECONDARY SOURCES
Hlawatsch, C. [Maria Aristides Brezina]. *Abhandlungen der Kaiserlich-Koniglichen Geologischen Reichsanstatt.* 1909: 181–187.
[Spencer, Leonard]. "Maria Aristides Brezina (1848–1909)."

STANDARD SOURCES
Sarjeant.

BRIDGET, SAINT, OF IRELAND (453–525)

Irish healer. Born in 453; said to be the daughter of a druidess.

Bridget of Ireland was said to have practiced medicine and midwifery in that country shortly after the death of Saint Patrick (d. 469). Legend tells us that she was the daughter of a druidess who was converted to Christianity and who could perform miracles of healing. In her care of the sick she convinced the rulers that obvious quacks should be expelled from the country.   JH/MBO

STANDARD SOURCES
Hurd-Mead 1938; Uglow 1989.

BRIDGET, SAINT, OF SCANDINAVIA (1302?–1373)

Swedish physician (Saint Birgitta). Born in 1302 or 1304 to Birger Persson. Married Ulf Gudmarsson of Narke (d. ca. 1343). Eight children. Died 1373.

Little is known of Saint Bridget, except that she was the daughter of Birger Persson, married a knight, Ulf Gudmarsson of Narke, at the age of thirteen, and produced eight children. After her husband's death, she reputedly began her holy work, which consisted of caring for the sick. She founded the first Birgittine house at Vadstena in 1346, took a pilgrimage to Jerusalem; wrote letters to rulers admonishing them to behave in a more Christian fashion; had visions; performed miracles; and helped pester Pope Urban V into returning from Avignon to Rome.   JH/MBO

SECONDARY SOURCES
Andersson, Ingvar. *History of Sweden.* Trans. Caroline Hannay. New York: Praeger, [1956] 1968. Saint Bridget discussed on pp. 53–62.

STANDARD SOURCES
Echols and Williams; Hurd-Mead 1938.

BRIDGMAN, OLGA LOUISE (1886–?)

U.S. pediatric psychologist. Born 30 March 1886 in Jackson, Mich. Never married. Educated University of Michigan (A.B., 1908; M.D., 1910); University of California (Ph.D., 1915). Professional experience: State School for Girls, Geneva, Ill., resident physician (1910–1912); Lincoln State School for Feeble-minded and Epileptics, physician (1912–1913); University of California, instructor of pediatrics and mental abnormalities of childhood (1915–1919), assistant clinical professor (1919–1922), associate professor of abnormal psychology (1922–1926), professor of psychology and pediatrics (1926–1954), professor emerita (from 1954); San Francisco Department of Public Health, director of division of mental hygiene (1919–1952), Child Guidance Clinic, director. Honors and memberships: American Orthopsychiatric Association; American Psychological Association (Fellow); American Medical Association; American Psychiatric Association. Death date unknown.

Olga Bridgman began working with mentally handicapped children early in her career and never lost her interest in their special problems and development traits. On the faculty of the University of California for almost forty years and director of the Child Guidance Clinic (San Francisco Department of Public Health), Bridgman conducted research on mental deficiency and the problems of physically handicapped children. She never married but filled her life with her students and the children in her studies.   JH/MBO

PRIMARY SOURCES
Bridgman, Olga Louise. "Effects of Environment on the Mental Development of Dependent Children." Masters' thesis, University of California, Berkeley, 1914.
———. *An Experimental Study of Abnormal Children, with Special Reference to the Problems of Dependency and Delinquency.* Berkeley: University of California Press, 1918.
———. *Mental Training of the Young Child.* Sacramento: California State Printing Office, 1918. Reprinted 1927.

STANDARD SOURCES
AMS 3–8, S&B 9; *Psychological Register,* vol. 3, 1932.

BRIÈRE, NICOLE-REINE ETABLE DE LA
See Lepaute, Nicole-Reine.

BRIÈRE, YVONNE (fl. 1926)
French geologist and mineralogist.

Yvonne Brière was interested in radioactive phenomena, but she approached the problem from the standpoint of a geologist. Brière began her research career by studying problematic Permian fossils in Madagascar. She examined mineral deposits in Madagascar, which appeared similar to uranium bearing deposits in North Carolina. She found uranite in at least one region and measured the radioactivity of samples.   MM

PRIMARY SOURCES
Brière, Yvonne. Fossiles Problématiques de Permian. *Paleontologie de Madagascar.* no. 11, Paris: 1923. Reprinted from *Annales de Paléontologie* 12, 1923.

STANDARD SOURCES
Meyer and von Schweidler.

BRIGHTWEN, ELIZA (ELDER) (1830–1906)
British naturalist. Born 30 October 1830 in Banff. Died 5 May 1906 in Stanmore, Middlesex.

Eliza Brightwen studied botany at her home at Stanmore. She wrote one book on plants, *Glimpses into Plant Life* (1898), but her journals were published after her death as *Eliza Brightwen: The Life and Thoughts of a Naturalist* (1909).   JH/MBO

PRIMARY SOURCES
Brightwen, Eliza. *Glimpses into Plant Life.* London: T. Fisher Unwin, 1897.
———. *Eliza Brightwen: The Life and Thoughts of a Naturalist.* London: T. Fisher Unwin, 1909. Posthumously published autobiography.

SECONDARY SOURCES
Gosse, Edmund. "Introduction and Epilogue." Eliza Brightwen: *The Life and Thoughts of a Naturalist.* ed. W.H. Chesson. London: T. Fisher Unwin, 1909.

STANDARD SOURCES
Desmond.

BRITTEN, LILIAN LOUISA (1886–1952)
South African botanist. Born December 1886 in Grahamstown, South Africa. Educated Rhodes University College (B.Sc., 1907); further studies at Cambridge, Oxford, and London. Professional experience: Rhodes University College, lecturer and senior lecturer in botany. Died 1 January 1952 at Grahamstown.

Lilian Britten was educated in South Africa at Rhodes University College. Her family returned to England where she pursued further studies in botany at the botanical departments at Cambridge, Oxford, and London. Upon returning to South Africa, she taught botany at Rhodes University College for many years. She collected extensively and her plant collections are in a number of museums in South

Africa, but she published little. She was highly knowledge-able about Eastern Cape flora.   JH/MBO

STANDARD SOURCES
Gunn and Codd.

BRITTON, ELIZABETH KNIGHT (1858–1934)

U.S. botanist. Born 9 January 1858 in New York City to Sophie (Compton) and James Knight. Four sisters. Married Nathaniel Britton in 1885. Elementary education in Cuba; Normal (later Hunter) College, New York (graduated 1875). Professional experience: Hunter College Model School, teacher (1875–1885); Bulletin of the Torrey Botanical Club, editor (1886–1888); Columbia University, moss collection, unofficial curator. Died 25 February 1934 in New York City.

One of five daughters, Elizabeth Knight spent much of her childhood in Cuba, where her father operated a furniture factory and a sugar plantation. Although she attended elementary school there, when she was older she divided her time between Cuba and New York, where she stayed with her grandmother. After graduating from Normal (later Hunter) College in 1875, she served on its staff (1875–1885). Increasingly interested in botany, she became a member of the Torrey Botanical Club in 1879 and published the first of many scientific papers in 1883.

In 1885 Knight married Nathaniel Britton, then an assistant in geology at Columbia College, who shared her interest in botany and from 1886 taught that subject. Elizabeth Britton became the unofficial curator of the moss collection at Columbia. She has been credited with the inspiration that resulted in the establishment of the New York Botanical Garden in 1891; her husband served as its first director. From 1886 to 1888 she was editor of the *Bulletin of the Torrey Botanical Club.*

Turning away from original research in her later years, Britton became involved in efforts to conserve wild flowers. She participated in the founding of the Wild Flower Preservation Society of America and through lectures and publications attempted to push conservation measures through the New York legislature. In 1934 she died of a stroke.

Enormously productive (she published 346 scientific papers between 1881 and 1930), Britton was a meticulous observer. She accompanied her husband on numerous collecting expeditions and amassed a formidable amount of taxonomic information about mosses. Although she held no official academic position at Columbia, she acted as advisor to doctoral students in bryology. The general respect in which she was held by the scientific community is reflected in the fact that fifteen species of plants and the moss genus *Bryobrittonia* were named for her. Although Britton was rec-ognized as America's foremost bryologist, she was also interested in ferns and in the flowering plants.   MBO

PRIMARY SOURCES
Britton, Elizabeth Gertrude [Knight]. "Albinism." *Bulletin of the Torrey Botanical Club* 8 (1881): 125. Britton's first botanical paper. Describes finding atypical plants of *Pontederia cordata* (pickerelweed) that had white flowers instead of the usual blue flowers.
———. "An Enumeration of the Plants Collected by Dr. H. H. Rusby in South America. 1885–1886. III. Pteridophyta." *Bulletin of the Torrey Botanical Club* 15 (1888): 247–253.
———. "Contributions to American Bryology. I, 1889; II, 1891; III, 1893; IV, V, VI, VII, VIII, 1894; IX, X, XI, 1895; *Bulletin of the Torrey Botanical Club.*

SECONDARY SOURCES
Barnhart, John Hendley. "The Published Works of Elizabeth Gertrude Britton." *Bulletin of the Torrey Botanical Club* 62 (1935): 1–17. Nathaniel Lord Britton requested that the bibliography be prepared and published in the *Bulletin.* The bibliography represents a complete list of her published works.
Gager, C. S. "Elizabeth G. Britton and the Movement for the Preservation of Native American Wild Flowers." *Journal of the New York Botanical Garden* 41 (1940): 137–142.
Howe, Marshall A. "Elizabeth Gertrude Britton." *Journal of the New York Botanical Garden* 35 (1934): 97–103.
"Obituary Notice, Elizabeth G. Knight Britton." *Bryologist* 37 (1934): 64.
Slack, Nancy G. "Nineteenth-Century American Botanists: Wives, Widows, and Work." In *Uneasy Careers,* p. 42.

STANDARD SOURCES
AMS 1–5; Bonta (article by M. Bonta); *NAW;* Ogilvie 1986.

BROADHURST, JEAN (1873–?)

U.S. bacteriologist. Born 29 December 1873 in Stockton, N.J. Educated Columbia University (B.S., 1903; A.M., 1908); Cornell University (Ph.D., 1914). Professional experience: New Jersey State Normal School, teacher (1903–1906); Teachers' College, Columbia University, biology teacher (1906–1914), assistant professor (1914–1920), associate professor (1920–1928), professor (1928–1939), emerita professor (1939–?). Death date unknown.

After receiving her undergraduate and master's degrees from Columbia University, Jean Broadhurst earned her Ph.D. from Cornell University. After a short stay at the New Jersey Normal School, she returned to Teachers College, Columbia, where she spent thirty-three years of active teaching. She belonged to the Society of Bacteriologists and studied problems relating to human resistance to disease, home and community hygiene and the applications of microbiology to nursing.   JH/MBO

STANDARD SOURCES
AMS 2–8; Rossiter 1982.

BROCK, SYLVIA (DᴇANTONIS) (1925–1994)

U.S. chemist. Born 21 October 1925 in Newton Hook, New York, to Assunta (Cristini) and Joseph DeAntonis. One sister, Lydia. Married Bernard Brock; five children, Anthony, Ann, Alan, Christine, and Andrew Brian. Educated Castleton, New York; College of St. Rose, Albany, New York (B.S., 1947); Smith College (A.M., 1949). Professional experience: AT&T telephone operator (1950–1952); Avila College, Kansas City, Kans., chemistry teacher (1969–1972); Department of Energy, Bartlesville, Okla., chemist (1983–1986). Honors and memberships: Sigma Xi. Died 18 December 1994 in Bartlesville, Okla.

Sylvia DeAntonis Brock received her early education in Castleton, New York, graduating from high school as class valedictorian in 1943. Her father was a foreman for the New York Central Railway and her mother, a homemaker. Coming from a poor immigrant family where they spoke Italian at home, DeAntonis and her sister struggled against prejudice. Fortunately, DeAntonis's teachers noticed her intellectual ability. After placing first in the New York State Regents Examination, she received a full scholarship to the College of Saint Rose, a small women's college in Albany, New York, where she majored in chemistry.

DeAntonis continued her studies in chemistry with a fellowship at Smith College. She completed her master's thesis on synthetic intermediaries of morphine under Milton Soffer. With the intent of obtaining a doctorate in chemistry, she took a laboratory position at the University of Kansas Medical Center in the area of cancer research. There she met the medical student Bernard Brock, whom she married on 13 April 1950 in Kansas City. Sylvia Brock gave up her career plans and took a job as an AT&T operator to enable her husband to finish his medical training. In 1959 the Brocks (now with five children) moved to Windsor, Missouri, where Sylvia Brock tutored students. They returned to Kansas City in 1967. From 1969 to 1972, Brock taught chemistry at Avila College in Kansas City. In 1971 the family moved to Bartlesville, Oklahoma.

After Bernard Brock's death in 1979, Sylvia Brock undertook a new career working on enhanced oil recovery at the Department of Energy. Her work included investigations of the behavior of polymers and surfactants under a variety of physical and chemical conditions, with the goal of developing improved oil recovery agents for the petroleum industry.

Warm, witty, ebullient, a lifelong Catholic and political liberal, Brock was a "practical visionary" (as characterized in her college yearbook) who spent much time helping others by working in charitable organizations (Meals on Wheels, Birthright), as a Vista Volunteer (1985–1988), and as project director of the Bartlesville Literacy Council (1988–1992). She was a gifted amateur actress who was active in community and church theater associations. Brock died in Bartlesville, Oklahoma, on 18 December 1994.   JH/MBO

PRIMARY SOURCES
Brock, Sylvia. With P. B. Lorenz, M. K. Tham, A. F. Bayazeed, and F. W. Burtch. "Observations on Tailoring Chemical Slugs and Simulating Reservoir Cores for an Oil-Wet Reservoir." *Proceedings of the SPE/DOE Fourth Symposium on Enhanced Oil Recovery* 2 (1984): 431–438.
———. With H. W. Gao and P. B. Lorenz. "Viscoelastic Behavior of Hydrolyzed Polyacrylamide Solutions in Porous Media: Some Preliminary Observations." *Proceedings of the 192nd ACS National Meeting* 55 (1986): 685–693.
———. With H. W. Gao and P. B. Lorenz. "The Effects of Polymer and Salt Concentrations on the Flow Behavior of Hydrolyzed Polyacrylamide Solutions in Porous Media." *192nd ACS National Meeting.* Abstract. 1986, No. PMSE 149.
———. With H. W. Gao and P. B. Lorenz. "Rheological Behavior of Pusher 500 under a Variety of Chemical and Thermal Conditions: Topical Report." *DOE Report Niper-225.* November 1986.
———. With P. B. Lorenz. "Surfactant and Cosurfactant Properties of Mixed and Polysulfonated Surfactant by Phase Volume Measurements: Topical Report." *DOE Report Niper-256.* July 1987.

STANDARD SOURCES
Stuckey.

BROMLEY, HELEN JEAN (BROWN) (1903–1982)

U.S. botanist. Born 9 August 1903 in Beaumont, Tex. Married Stanley Willard Bromley (1935). One son, James Robert Bromley. Educated Ohio State University (B.A.; M.A.; and Ph.D., 1929). Professional experience: College of St. Mary of the Springs (now Ohio Dominican College) Columbus, Ohio, teacher (1925–1928); Ohio State University, instructor in botany (1928–1935); University of Connecticut, instructor (1935–1952), registrar (1952–1970). Died 16 June 1982.

Helen Jean Brown was born in Beaumont, Texas, educated in Ohio, and spent most of her career in Connecticut. She did her doctoral work under Edgar N. Transeau, with whom she studied algae. Publishing under her maiden name of Helen Jean Brown, she did descriptive work on the algal family Vaucheriaceae. For an eight-year period she published papers in algalogy. However, in 1935, she moved with her husband, Stanley Willard Bromley, an entomologist, to Stamford. She had one son, James Robert Bromley. At first she served as an instructor in botany for the University of Connecticut, but in 1952 was named registrar. This appointment signaled the end of her botanical career. She remained in Stamford until her death in 1982.

Even though she was no longer in the field she retained her membership in professional organizations. These organizations included the American Association for the Advancement of Science and the Ohio Academy of Science. She served twice as the national president of Sigma Delta Epsilon, the Graduate Women's Scientific Society (1930; 1935). JH/MBO

PRIMARY SOURCES

[Bromley] Brown, Helen Jean. *Transactions of the American Microcopic Society.* Contributor 1929–1937.

SECONDARY SOURCES

[Stuckey, Ronald L.]. "Helen Jean (Brown) Bromley (1903–1982)." *Ohio Journal of Science* 83 (1983): 276.

———. *Women Botanists of Ohio Born Before 1900.* Columbus: Ohio State University Press, 1992.

BRONNER, AUGUSTA FOX (1881–1966)

U.S. clinical psychologist and criminologist. Born 22 July 1881, in Louisville, Ky., to Hannah (Fox) and Gustav Bronner. Two siblings. Married William Healey (September 1932). Educated Louisville and Cincinnati public schools; Louisville Normal School (graduated 1901); Columbia University Teachers College, (B.S., 1906; A.M., 1909; Ph.D., 1914). Professional experience: Columbia University Teachers College, grader (1903–1906); Louisville Girls' High School, teacher (1906–1911); Teacher's College, Columbia, graduate assistant (1911–1914); Chicago Juvenile Psychopathic Institute, researcher (1914–1917); Judge Baker Foundation, Boston, assistant director (1917), codirector (1930). Honors and memberships: American Orthopsychiatric Association, president (1932). Retired 1946. Died December 1966 in Clearwater, Fla.

Born in Louisville, Kentucky, Augusta Fox Bronner was of German ancestry. During her early childhood the family lived in Cincinnati and then returned to Louisville where she completed her high school education in 1898. She then entered Louisville Normal School, but dropped out because of eye problems and spent a year traveling with her aunt in Europe. She returned and completed her teaching diploma

in 1901. In 1903 she went to Columbia University Teachers College, where she received her bachelor's and master's degree and briefly held a position as a grader for the psychologist Edward L. Thorndike. She returned to Louisville in 1906 and taught in the girls' high school in 1911. After her father died she returned to Teachers College and worked again with Thorndike. Her dissertation discussed the relation between mental defects and delinquency in groups of girls. This dissertation was published the same year that she completed it.

During a summer school course at Harvard, she met Chicago neurologist William Healey, who was interested in the motivation of juvenile offenders. Healey was impressed by Bronner and offered her a position at the Chicago Juvenile Psychopathic Institute. They soon learned that a group of Boston philanthropists wanted to open a new child guidance clinic, the Judge Baker Foundation. This institution opened in 1917 with Healey as director and Bronner as assistant director. They divided the work so that Healey supervised the medical workups and Bronner did the testing. By 1930 Bronner was appointed codirector. After Healey's wife died, Healey and Bronner married. Together, they had an impact on criminology and criminal psychology, publishing an important guide, *A Manual of Individual Tests and Testing.* The Judge Baker Guidance Center, as it is now called, became a model child guidance clinic in the United States. They developed the team concept in which psychologist, psychiatrist, and social worker met together in a case conference. Although Bronner had no formal university position, she lectured in Boston area colleges and universities. Bronner and Healey retired to Florida in 1946, where she died twenty years later. JH/MBO

PRIMARY SOURCES

Bronner, Augusta F. *The Psychology of Special Abilities and Disabilities.* Boston: Little Brown, 1917.

———. With William Healey. *A Manual of Individual Mental Tests and Testing.* Boston: Little Brown, 1927.

———. With William Healey. "The Child Guidance Clinic: the Birth and Growth of an Idea." In *Orthopsychiatry 1923 to 1948, Retrospect and Prospect,* ed. L. G. Lowery and Victoria Sloan. New York, 1948. This account is autobiographical.

Some of Bronner's papers are in the Judge Baker Guidance Center Archive, Countway Library of Medicine, Harvard.

SECONDARY SOURCES

American Journal of Psychology 11, 1–29; S&G-82-1, 198–203.

STANDARD SOURCES

AMS 3–8, S&B 9; *NAW*(M) "Bronner, Augusta Fox," by John C. Burnham; O'Connell and Russo 1990.

BROOKE, WINIFRED (1894–1975)
British botanical collector and artist. Born 1894 in Alton, Hants. Died in 1975.

By the early 1950s, Brooke was widely recognized as an authority on Bolivian plants. She traveled throughout Europe, South Africa, South America, and the East Indies. She published a book of her sketches from nature while traveling in Ireland (1935) and sent her collections to the Royal Botanic Gardens, Kew. JH/MBO

PRIMARY SOURCES
Brooke, Winifred. *Sketches from Nature in the North of Ireland.* Belfast: Carswell, 1935.
———. "Some Bolwean Plants." *Proceedings of the South London Entomological and Natural History Society.* 1951–1952: 137–143.
Drawings and collections are in the Royal Botanic Gardens, Kew.

SECONDARY SOURCES
Biological Journal of the Linnean Society 8 (1976): 368. "Winifred Brooke." Obituary notice.
Hawkes, J. G. and J. P. Hjerting. *Potatoes of Bolivia.* Oxford: Oxford University Press, 1989. Brooke mentioned on page 103.

STANDARD SOURCES
Desmond.

BROOKS, HARRIET T. (1876–1933)
Canadian physicist. Born 2 July 1876 in Exeter, Ontario, to Elizabeth Agnes (Worden) and George Brooks, flour salesman. Eight siblings. Married Frank Pitcher, a physicist. Three children. Educated Seaforth Collegiate Institute, Seaforth, Ontario; McGill University (graduated 1898, M.A., 1901); Newnham College, Cambridge (1902); graduate work at Bryn Mawr, Cavendish Laboratory, Curie Laboratory. Professional experience: Royal Victoria College at McGill University, nonresident mathematics tutor; Barnard College, tutor in physics (1904–1906). Died 17 April 1933 in Montreal.

Brooks was an excellent student at McGill, where she earned several scholarships. She graduated with an honors degree in mathematics and natural philosophy. At the same time she received a teaching diploma from the associated normal school. She then began research in radioactivity as Ernest Rutherford's first graduate student.

For Brooks's first research project she examined the effects that an electrical discharge conducted through steel needles had on their magnetization. This question was related to wireless (radio) transmission, an early interest of her mentor, Ernest Rutherford. Later, Brooks submitted this research for

her master's thesis. Next, Brooks and Rutherford investigated the mysterious radium "emanation" and determined from its diffusion that it was a gas whose molecular weight was much lower than radium's. This meant the emanation was chemically different from radium, a clue that pointed Rutherford and Frederick Soddy toward a theory of atomic transmutation. It was natural to ask whether the different radioactive elements emitted the same kinds of radiations. By studying the absorption, behavior in a magnetic field, and decay of emissions from radioactive substances, Brooks and Rutherford found that, although some similarities existed, radioactive processes generally differed in different substances.

In 1901 Brooks entered Bryn Mawr. There she won a President's European Fellowship, which she took at the Cavendish Laboratory, Newnham College, Cambridge, the next year. Working under J. J. Thomson, she determined the half life of thorium emanation [radon] and studied its behavior over time, as well as other aspects of radium and thorium decay. Brooks did not complete a doctorate, possibly because she was dissatisfied with the laboratory. In 1903 Brooks returned to Rutherford's laboratory at McGill, where she studied the decay product of radium emanation. While working with this material she noticed that it seemed to make the walls of the container radioactive. Brooks thought the substance must be volatile, and Rutherford agreed. But soon afterward he decided these results were due to recoil of radioactive atoms which had emitted heavy α particles. Radioactive recoil was used later to separate different substances produced by radioactive decay. Brooks also analyzed the decay of products from thorium, radium, and actinium, finding that two successive changes were involved in each case. Taking a position at Barnard College in 1904, Brooks became engaged to a physicist at Columbia whom she had met in Cambridge. However, Barnard's dean was opposed to retaining a married woman. In the summer of 1906 Brooks ended her engagement for unspecified reasons and resigned from Barnard.

During 1906 Brooks met Prestonia Martin, a social reformer, and Maxim Gorky. She spent time at Martin's collectivist community in upstate New York. Later that year she accompanied Gorky and his entourage to Europe, where she spent part of 1906–1907 working in Marie Curie's laboratory in Paris. Brooks investigated radioactive recoil, radioactive gases, and the decay rate of actinium B, but she did not publish this work.

Rutherford had a high opinion of Brooks as an experimenter. He used her results when developing the transmutation theory of radioactivity with Frederick Soddy. She was regarded as one of the most significant contributors to the early research on this subject. In 1907 Rutherford was preparing to move to the University of Manchester and recommended Brooks for a fellowship there. Brooks moved to London and awaited word on the fellowship. There she became engaged to Frank Henry Pitcher, a physicist whom she had met at McGill. They were married in London on 13 July 1907.

The couple returned to Montreal, where Harriet Brooks Pitcher was active in community organizations and with gardening. She did not return to research. Their children were born on 19 October 1910 (Barbara Anne), 17 January 1912 (Charles Roger), and 5 August 1913 (Paul Brooks). Charles died of meningitis at age ten, while Barbara drowned at age eighteen. Harriet Brooks Pitcher died in 1933 of a blood disorder, possibly caused by her earlier exposure to radiation.

MM

PRIMARY SOURCES

Brooks, Harriet. "Damping of Electrical Oscillations." *Transactions of the Royal Society of Canada*, section 3 (1899): 13–15.

———. With E. Rutherford. "The New Gas from Radium." *Transactions of the Royal Society of Canada* 7 (1901): 21–25.

———. With E. Rutherford. "Comparison of the Radiations from Radioactive Substances." *Philosophical Magazine* 4 (1902): 1–23.

———. "The Decay of the Excited Radioactivity from Thorium, Radium, and Actinium." *Philosophical Magazine* 8 (1904): 373–384.

———. "A Volatile Product from Radium." *Nature* 70 (1904): 270.

SECONDARY SOURCES

Blanquies, Lucie. "Comparison entre les rayons α produits par différentes substances radioactives." *Le Radium* 6 (1909): 230–232.

Debierne, André. "Sur le *Le Radium*" 4 (1907): 213–218.

———. "Sur le *Le Radium*" 6 (1909): 97–106.

Heilbron, John. "Physics at McGill in Rutherford's Time." In *Rutherford and Physics at the Turn of the Century*. Ed. Mario Bunge and William R. Shea, 42–73. London and New York: Dawson and Science History, 1979. On 50f.

Malley, Marjorie. *From Hyperphosphorescence to Nuclear Decay: A History of the Early Years of Radioactivity, 1896–1914.* Berkeley, 1976; Ann Arbor, University Microfilms. On pp. 153, 154–155.

Rayner-Canham, Marelene F. and Geoffrey Rayner-Canham. "Canada's First Woman Nuclear Physicist, Harriet Brooks." Ainley.

Rayner-Canham, Marelene F. and Geoffrey Rayner-Canham. *Harriet Brooks Pioneer Nuclear Scientist.* Montreal & Kingston, London, and Buffalo: McGill-Queens University Press, 1992, 1994.

Rayner-Canham, Marelene F. and Geoffrey Rayner-Canham. *Harriet Brooks Pioneer Nuclear Scientist.* Montreal & Kingston, London, and Buffalo: McGill-Queens University Press, 1992, 1994.

Rutherford, Ernest. *Radio-activity.* Cambridge: Cambridge University Press, 1904, 1905.

Rutherford, Ernest. *Radioactive Substances and Their Radiations.* Cambridge: Cambridge University Press, 1913. On pp. 175, 525, 526, 146, 383, 487, 536.

Rutherford, Ernest. "Obituary: Harriet Brooks (Mrs. Frank Pitcher)." *Nature* 131 (1933): 865.

Trenn, Thaddeus J. "Rutherford and Recoil Atoms: The Metamorphosis and Success of a Once Stillborn Theory." *Historical Studies in the Physical Sciences* 6 (1975): 513–547.

Weeks, Mary Elvira. Discovery of the Elements. Easton, Pa.: Journal of Chemical Education, 1956: 815.

BROOKS, MATILDA (MOLDENHAUER) (1890–?)

U.S. physiologist. Born 1890 in Pittsburgh, Pa., to Selma (Neuffer) and Rudolph Moldenhauer. Married Sumner Cushing Brooks in 1920. Educated Girl's High School, Philadelphia; University of Pittsburgh (B.A. and M.A.); Radcliffe College, Harvard University (Ph.D., 1920); summer research courses, Marine Biological Laboratories, Woods Hole. Professional experience: Research Institute, American Dental Association, bacteriologist (1917–1920); United States Public Health Service, Hygienic Laboratory, assistant biologist (1920–1924), associate biologist (1925–1927); University of California, research associate (1927–?), lecturer in zoology (1934, 1936); Naples Marine Biological Station, Woman's Table (1932); Marine Biological Laboratories, corporation member. Honors and memberships: Phi Beta Kappa (hon.), Sigma Xi. Death date unknown.

Born in Pittsburgh, Pennsylvania, to a family of German origin, Mathilda Moldenhauer lost her father when young. She attended the Girl's High School of Philadelphia and then entered the University of Pittsburgh, where she received her bachelor's and master's degrees in zoology. While she worked on her doctorate at Harvard University, she took a position as bacteriologist with the research wing of the American Dental Association. For her Harvard doctoral degree, awarded in those years by Radcliffe College (which had no independent faculty), Moldenhauer made a quantitative study of the respiration of the bacterium *Bacillus subtilis*.

The year that she completed her degree (1920), Moldenhauer married Sumner Cushing Brooks, a fellow graduate student of zoology, whose father had founded the first agricultural college in Japan. They both took positions soon after with the Public Health Service, where she worked in the hygienic laboratories first as assistant biologist and then as associate biologist, studying the permeability of living and dead cells to various substances.

When her husband was appointed professor of zoology at University of California, Berkeley, in 1927, Brooks could not hold a comparable position because of rules against nepotism. She was hired as a research associate, and depended on a series of grants, beginning with a five-year Bache grant from the National Academy of Sciences. Only when he was incapacitated in 1934 and in 1936 could she teach in his place.

Brooks's important discovery of the treatment of cyanide and carbon monoxide poisoning through the use of methylene blue brought her to national attention in 1932, when she first published her research, and again in 1941, when a biographical article appeared. After that period she continued to investigate the mechanism of methylene blue on cell respiration and continued her general research interest in oxidation reduction within living cells.

She was an honorary member of Phi Beta Kappa, and a member of Sigma Xi.   JH/MBO

PRIMARY SOURCES

Brooks, Matilda Moldenhaeur. *Quantitative Studies on the Respiration of Bacillus subtilis (Ehrenberg) Cohn.* Ph.D. diss., Radcliffe College, 1920; in Harvard University Archives.

———. "Studies on the Permeability of Living and Dead Cells. 2. Observations on the Penetration of Alkali Bicarbonates into Living and Dead Cells." *Public Health Service Reports* no. 846. Washington, D.C.: Public Health Service, 1923.

———. [Methylene blue as a treatment for carbon monoxide and cyanide poisoning] 1932.

STANDARD SOURCES

AMS 4–8, B 9, P&B 10–14. *Current Biography* 1941; *Mothers and Daughters; Who's Who of American Women.*

BROOKS, SARAH THERESA (1850–1928)

Irish/Australian botanist and artist. Born 1850 in Ireland. Emigrated to Australia. Died 28 September 1928 in Norseman, Western Australia.

Sarah Theresa Brooks was born in Ireland and emigrated with her parents to Australia. She collected plants in western Australia and corresponded with the great German-born naturalist Ferdinand von Müller, who directed the Botanic Garden at Melbourne and later was president of the Australian Association for the Advancement of Science. Brooks also drew plants and was recognized as an Irish woman artist. She is remembered by a plant named for her, *Scaevola brooksiana.*   JH/MBO

SECONDARY SOURCES

Early Days Journal 7, no. 4 (1974): 35–48.

Irish Women Artists from the Eighteenth Century to the Present Day. Dublin: National Gallery of Ireland, 1987. Brooks is mentioned on page 152 of the exhibition catalog.

Victorian Naturalist (1970): 145.

STANDARD SOURCES

Desmond.

BROOMALL, ANNA ELIZABETH (1847–1931)

U.S. physician. Born 4 March 1847 in Upper Chichester Township, Delaware County, Pa., to Elizabeth (Booth) and John Martin Broomall; older brother. Educated private school in Chester; Kennett Academy; Bristol Boarding School in Bristol, Pa. (graduated 1866); Woman's Medical College of Pennsylvania (1867–1868); clinics at the Pennsylvania Hospital (1869; M.D., 1871); Vienna and Paris, postdoctoral study. Professional experience: Woman's Hospital in Philadelphia, chief resident physician (1875–1883); instructor of obstetrics (1875–1879); chair of obstetrics (1879). Died 1931.

Anna Broomall's father was a lawyer who later turned to farming and eventually served in Congress. Her mother died when Anna was one year old. Anna and her older brother were raised by their mother's brother and his wife, who was Anna's father's twin sister, until their father remarried in 1853. The family were Quakers (Society of Friends), a group notable for their belief in equal opportunity and education for women, and Anna's father was a supporter of woman's suffrage.

Broomall was educated at a private school in Chester, then at Kennett Academy, and finally at the Bristol Boarding School in Bristol, graduating in 1866. She first was interested in law but decided medicine would offer more opportunity. She entered the Woman's Medical College of Pennsylvania, and in 1869 was admitted to clinics at the Pennsylvania Hospital (which occasioned riotous protest from the male students); she received her medical degree in 1871. Broomall went to Vienna to study skin, nose, and throat diseases; then to Paris to study gynecology under the noted French obstetricians of the day.

Broomall worked at the Woman's Hospital in Philadelphia before going to Europe, where she decided to specialize in gynecology and obstetrics (learning she might succeed her teacher Emeline Horton Cleveland at Woman's Medical College). She served as chief resident physician at the Woman's Hospital in Philadelphia from 1875 to 1883. There she contributed to advances in nurses training, organization, and high-quality patient care. She began teaching at the Woman's Medical College, was appointed instructor of obstetrics in 1875, and took the chair of obstetrics in 1879 after Cleveland's death. She was an outstanding teacher and served as professor of obstetrics from 1880 to 1903, making many improvements in the department. In 1888 she established an out-practice department (clinic) in South Philadelphia, where students were assigned to actual patient care, including prenatal care, home confinement, and postnatal visits. They performed deliveries and provided high-quality obstetrical care. The facility eventually expanded to provide inpatient care for difficult cases as well.

Broomall sought to instill the standards of the great medical teaching centers of Europe, i.e., scrupulous attention to antisepsis, thorough prenatal care including pelvimetry; up-to-date obstetrical procedures such as episiotomy to prevent ruptures of the birth canal, Caesarean section, and symphysiotomy. The mortality rate at the Maternity Hospital of the Woman's Medical College was phenomenally low for that time due to strict adherence to her advanced practices.

Broomall established her private practice on Walnut Street in Philadelphia. In 1883 she was appointed gynecologist to the Friends' Asylum for the Insane. Although barred against admission to the Philadelphia Obstetrical Society because of her sex until 1892, two of her papers were read to the assembly by a male colleague and published in their *Transactions*. In 1890, she began an extensive lecture tour, visiting former students on medical missionary duty in Asia and India. After her retirement from medical practice in 1903, Broomall devoted herself to community historical work in Chester, Pennsylvania, where she settled. She served as curator of the Delaware County Historical museum and library from 1923 until her death on 4 April 1931.   KM

PRIMARY SOURCES
Broomall, Anna. "The Operation of Episiotomy as a Prevention of Perineal Ruptures during Labor." *American Journal of Obstetrics and Diseases of Women and Children* 11 (1878): 517–527.
———. "Three Cases of Symphysiotomy, with One Death from Sepsis" in *American Journal of Obstetrics and Diseases* 28 (1893).
Numerous other journal articles.

STANDARD SOURCES
Hurd-Mead 1933; *NAW* (long article by Patricia Spain Ward).

BROUSSEAU, KATE (1860s–1938)

U.S. psychologist. Born 1860s in Ypsilanti, Mich. Educated Leipzig; Göttingen; Collège de France (1891–1892 and 1894–1897); Université de Paris (doctorate 1904); universities of Chicago (Law School, 1912–1913), Minnesota, California; École d'Anthropologie, Paris. Professional experience: California high schools, teacher; State Normal School, Los Angeles, instructor in psychology (1897–1903); Mills College, professor (1907–1928); Institute of Family
Relations, Los Angeles, director of psychological services; Sonoma State Home for the Feeble-Minded, California, surveyor (1914–1916); assistant to Dr. Toulouse, Paris (1917); French Army, director, foyers du soldat, or soldier's home (1917–1919). Honors and memberships: American Psychological Association; Southern California Society of Mental Hygiene (treasurer and director); Southern California Academy of Criminology; Ligue d'Hygiene Mentale, Paris.*

Although she was born in Ypsilanti, Michigan, Kate Brousseau divided both her education and work experience between the United States and Europe. After spending some time at the Collège de France she went to the University of Paris where she received her doctorate in 1904 with high honors. Her thesis, a lengthy study on the education of African-Americans, was published in French that year. Brousseau had worked at several previous jobs in the United States, but after she earned her doctorate obtained a position at Mills College, where she became a professor. She was a member of the École d'Anthropologie in Paris.

During World War I, she returned to France where she worked as an assistant to the psychiatrist Dr. Edward Toulouse and held several positions with the French army.

Brousseau's later research interests were the mental and physical characteristics of "Mongolian Imbeciles" (children with Downs Syndrome), and exceptional children. A member of the Southern California Society for Mental Hygiene, she was a member of its board of directors. She was a Fellow of the American Association for the Advancement of Science.   JH/MBO

PRIMARY SOURCES
Brousseau, Kate. *L'éducation des nègres aux États-Unis.* Paris: Alcan, 1904.
———. *Mongolism, a Study of the Physical and Mental Characteristics of Mongolian Imbeciles.* Revised by H.G. Brainerd. Baltimore: Williams and Wilkins, 1928.

STANDARD SOURCES
AMS 4–6; Herzenberg; *Psychological Register*, vol. 2.

BROWN, CHARLOTTE AMANDA BLAKE (1846–1904)

U.S. physician. Born 22 December 1846 in Philadelphia, Pa., to Charlotte A. (Farrington) and Charles Morris Blake. Four siblings. Married Henry Adams Brown (1867). Two daughters, one son. Educated Elmira College, N.Y. (B.A., 1866); Woman's Medical College of Pennsylvania (M.D., 1874). Professional experience: Pacific Dispensary for Women and Children (later renamed San Francisco Hospital for Children and Training School for Nurses), founder and attending physician and surgeon (1875–1895); private hospital (with Amanda and Philip Brown), physician (1895–1904). Died 19 April 1904 in San Francisco, Calif., of intestinal paralysis.

Charlotte Amanda Blake was the second child and first daughter of a teacher and later a Presbyterian minister originally from Maine. Her father, Charles Blake, set out for California in 1849, where he founded and headed a short-lived "collegiate institute" for boys in Benicia, California, then five years later moved the family to Chile, to serve as a missionary for two years.

Charlotte attended high school in Bangor, Maine, while living with relatives, and then went to Elmira College in New York. After graduation, she went to Arizona, where her father was serving as a chaplain to an army regiment in the post–Civil War years. There she met and married Henry Adams Brown. Both families moved to Napa, California, where her three children were born. Brown had begun to study medicine as an apprentice to a family physician; soon after the birth of her third child, she left for Philadelphia to attend the Woman's Medical College of Pennsylvania, receiving her medical degree in 1874. The family moved to San Francisco where she opened her medical practice. Possibly influenced by her example, her father returned to medical school (he had briefly studied medicine in Pennsylvania) and received a medical degree from the University of California in 1876. Charlotte's older brother, Charles E. Blake, also became a physician and surgeon.

In 1875, Brown joined another woman physician, Martha E. Bucknell, and several others to found the Pacific Dispensary for Women and Children. They were joined by Dr. Sara E. Browne. In 1878, the dispensary was reorganized as a hospital and two years later introduced the first nurses' training program in California. Seven years later, the hospital limited its care to children and was renamed the Children's Hospital of San Francisco.

Denied admittance to the San Francisco Medical Society, Brown was received into the California Medical Society (1876) and appointed with four other women physicians, including Bucknell and Browne, to a special committee on diseases of women and children. When she demonstrated her skill in performing the first ovariotomy by a woman surgeon in the California area, the objections to her admission in the San Francisco Medical Society were withdrawn.

Brown was active in her profession and aware of current advances in medicine. She suggested the establishment of a "tumor registry," advocated the use of Parisian-style incubators for premature babies, and introduced a milk sterilizing apparatus that she designed. She believed in educating the public about a variety of public health concerns. She fought for improved training for nurses and doctors, urging estab-

lishment of postgraduate schools to expand specialty expertise.

After almost twenty years at the Children's Hospital, Charlotte Brown left to open a small private hospital with one of her daughters and her son, who had also trained as physicians. She devoted much of her time to the California branch of the National Conference of Charities and Correction, which she helped to organize.

Brown died at age fifty-seven of intestinal paralysis. The San Francisco Children's Hospital was rebuilt and enlarged after the earthquake of 1906 but Brown's papers and manuscripts, unfortunately, were destroyed.　　　KM

PRIMARY SOURCES

Brown, Charlotte. "Report on Diseases of Women and Children." *Transactions of the California Medical Society* 1883: 252–260.

———. "A Bureau of Information: The Need of a Postgraduate School for Nurses." *Proceedings of the National Conference of Charities and Correction* 1890: 147–154.

———. "Report on Obstetrics." *Transactions of the California Medical Society* 1893: 129–139.

———. "Practical Points in Obstetrics." *Occidental Medical Times* 14 (1900): 12–16.

SECONDARY SOURCES

Brock, Lois. "The Hospital for Children and the Training School for Nurses 1874–1949." *Journal of the American Medical Women's Association* (January 1950).

Brown, Adelaide. "A History of the Development of Women in Medicine in California." *California and Western Medicine* (May 15, 1925): 17–20. Written by Charlotte Brown's daughter, herself a physician; includes a biographical sketch of her mother. Reprinted in *History of Women* [microform] no. 8624.

STANDARD SOURCES

Lovejoy; *NAW* (long article by Joan Jensen).

BROWN, DAME EDITH MARY (1864–1956)

British physician. Born 1864. Educated Girton College Cambridge (honors degree 1882); Edinburgh and Brussels (studied medicine). Professional experience: India, medical missionary; established Ludhiana Christian Medical College and Hospital for Women. Died 1956.

Educated at Girton College, Brown took the Honours Degree Examination at Cambridge University (1882), then studied medicine at Edinburgh and Brussels. She was sent to India by the Baptist Zanana Mission and devoted her life to her medical work there. In the 1890s with other missionaries, including Maud Allen and M. IDA BALFOUR, she established the Ludhiana Christian Medical College and Hospital for Women in Ludhiana, India. Under her guidance, this facility trained nurses, midwives, hospital aides, and licensed medical practitioners, becoming coeducational three years before Brown's death. On Brown's ninetieth birthday, the foundation stone of an enlarged hospital was laid by the first woman Minister of Health of India. Edith Brown was recognized for her service with the Kaiser-i-Hind Gold Medal and the title, Dame of the British Empire.   JH/MBO

STANDARD SOURCES
Lovejoy; 5 *WWW*.

BROWN, ELIZABETH (?–1899)
British astronomer. Born in Cirencester. Liverpool Astronomical Society, head of solar section (1882–1890); British Astronomical Association, director of the solar section (1890–1899). Died 1899.

Amateur astronomer Elizabeth Brown published both scientific and popular accounts of solar phenomena, including descriptions of the total eclipses of the sun in 1887, 1889, and 1896. Brown joined a new organization formed in 1882, the Liverpool Astronomical Society, which catered to amateurs and allowed women members. (The Royal Astronomical Society, although it had recently declared women eligible and had received several nominations of women—including Brown—had so far elected none to fellowship.) The society was divided into sections in order to facilitate observations. Brown became the head of the solar section, collected sunspot observations, and engaged in solar eclipse expeditions to Russia and the West Indies. She published two books anonymously on her travels. With the demise of the Liverpool Astronomical Society in 1890, Brown joined the British Astronomical Association, which also catered to amateurs and encouraged women members.

She was head of the solar section of this organization from 1890 to 1899. Known for her enthusiasm and skill in drawing she also had the ability to encourage beginners. In an appeal to women to join the solar section, she wrote, "for ladies, many of whom have ample time at their disposal, and who are often skilful in the use of the pencil, this branch of astronomy ought to have special attraction. The Sun is always at hand. No exposure to the night air is involved." The result is "an ever-increasing pleasure, previously little dreamed of" (*The British Astronomical Association: The First Fifty Years*, 65). The *Journal of the British Astronomical Association* published numerous observational reports by Brown. Convinced of the importance of methodical data collecting, Brown advised

potential observers to "look for no great or stirring discoveries; be prepared for long periods when there will be little or nothing to record; but persevere." The meticulous observer would eventually find it "worth the labor involved, and the laborer who once begins to cultivate his field will rarely, if ever, leave it in disappointment or disgust."   JH/MBO

PRIMARY SOURCES
Brown, Elizabeth. *Caught in the Tropics.* London: Griffin, Farran, Okeden, and Welsh, 1890.
———. "A Few Hints to Beginners in Solar Observation," *Publications of the Astronomical Society of the Pacific* 3 (13 June 1891): 172–175.
———. *In Pursuit of a Shadow.* London: Turbner, 1887.
———. "The Recent Aurora," *Nature* 5, no. 26 (October 1882): 548–549.
———. "Scientific Notes and News." *Science* 7 (April 1899): 528, 598.
———. "Solar Section." *Journal of the British Astronomical Association* 1 (1891): 172.

SECONDARY SOURCES
Kidwell, Peggy Aldrich. "Women Astronomers in Britain, 1780–1930." *Isis* 75 (1984): 534–546.
"The Solar Section." *The British Astronomical Association: The First Fifty Years*, ed. Richard McKim. *B.A.A. Memoirs* 42 (1989): 65–72.

BROWN, FAY CLUFF (1881–?)
U.S. physicist.

Fay Cluff Brown was perhaps a student of the physicist Ernest Merritt at the University of Illinois at Urbana. Brown met Professor Rutherford when he visited the university in 1905 or 1906. He loaned her some radium, which she used to test the effects of its rays on light sensitive (photoelectric) selenium cells. She worked with Joel Stebbins, later an astrophysicist.   MM

PRIMARY SOURCES
Brown, F. C. With Joel Stebbins. *Physical Review* 26 (1908): 273–298.
———. "Evidence that Sodium Belongs to a Radioactive Series of Elements." *Science* 37 (1913): 72-75; also *Le Radium* 9 (1912): 352–355.
———. "An Extension toward the Ultra-Violet if the Wave-Length-Sensibility Curves for Certain Crystals of Metallic Selenium." *Physical Review* 5 (1915): 65.
———. "Some Fundamental Electro-Mechanical and Photo-Electrical Relations in Isolated Crystals of Selenium."

Physical Review 5 (1915): 74–75 (summary). Proceedings from American Physical Society meeting, Chicago, November 1914.

———. "The Electrical, the Photo-Electrical and the Electro-Mechanical Properties of Certain Crystals of Metallic Selenium, with Certain Applications to Crystal Structure." *Physical Review* 5 (1915): 167–175.

———. "Isolated Crystals of Selenium of the Second and Fifth Systems, and the Physical Conditions Determining their Production." *Physical Review* 5 (1915): 236–237.

———. "On the Reflecting Power of a Certain Selenium Crystal." *Physical Review* 5 (1915): 341.

———. "An Extension toward the Ultra-Violet of the Wave-Length-Sensibility Curves for Certain Crystals of Metallic Selenium." *Physical Review* 5 (1915): 65.

———. "The Nature of Electric Conduction as Required to Explain the Recovery of Resistance of Metallic Selenium Following Illumination." *Physical Review* 5 (1915): 395–403. More on theory of electron conduction. Of J.J.T.'s ideas likes idea of the electron tied up with the atom in the form of a doublet.

———. "Some Experiments on the Nature of Transmitted Light-Action in Crystals of Metallic Selenium." *Physical Review* 5 (1915): 404–411.

———. "The Frequent Bursting of Hot Water Pipes in Household Plumbing Systems." *Physical Review.* 8 (1916): 500–503.

Rutherford correspondence, Cambridge: letter to Rutherford, 28 May 1906.

SECONDARY SOURCES
Badash. *Le Radium* Oct. 1912, 9: 352–355; *Science* (10 Jan. 1913) 37:72–76.

STANDARD SOURCES
Rayner-Canham 1997.

BROWN, MABEL MARY (1890–1927)

U.S. botanist. Born 1890 in Belmont, Wis. Educated University of Wisconsin (A.B., 1915; A.M., 1916; Ph.D., 1919). Professional experience: University of Wisconsin, assistant in botany (1915–1918); University of Missouri, instructor (1919–1920); University of New Hampshire, assistant professor (1920–?).

Mabel Mary Brown got all three of her degrees from the University of Wisconsin. The last *American Men of Science* in which she appears is the fourth edition. At that time she was an assistant professor at the University of New Hampshire. Her research was in plant morphology and cytology and she was a member of the Botanical Society, the Phytopathology Society, and the Wisconsin Academy of Science. JH/MBO

STANDARD SOURCES
AMS 3–4.

BROWN, NELLIE ADALESA (1877–1956)

U.S. plant pathologist. Born 1877. Educated University of Michigan (A.B. 1901). Professional experience: High school teacher (1901–1905); U.S. Department of Agriculture, Bureau of Plant Industry, scientific assistant (1906–1910), assistant pathologist (1910–1925), associate pathologist (1925–1941). Died 1956.

Nellie Adalesa Brown was educated in botany at the University of Michigan. The midwestern universities provided an excellent place for fundamental training in plant pathology. After teaching science for five years in high schools in Michigan and Florida, Brown entered the Bureau of Plant Industry (U.S. Department of Agriculture) as a scientific investigator in 1905. The plant pathologist who was in charge of the laboratory, Erwin Frink Smith (1854–1927), was known to encourage women scientists, and hired more than twenty women over twenty-five years.

After she rose to the rank of assistant pathologist, Brown appeared as the second author (with Smith) of two major studies on crown-galls in plants in 1911 and 1912. Between 1915 and 1918, she had begun to study bacterial disease in lettuce, publishing this research under her own name. She returned to the problem of plant tumors in 1924 with an investigation of an apple stem-tumor, which she carefully differentiated from crown-gall.

In the mid-twenties, around the time of Smith's retirement, Brown was advanced to associate pathologist, a position she would hold until her own retirement. Her contemporary and colleague RUTH F. ALLEN, who had received a doctorate from Michigan in 1909, was raised at the same period to the higher rank of pathologist. Allen's more widely recognized work centered on the problem of leaf rust in plants and her far more prolific publication rate contrasts with Brown's more modest total output of fourteen or so papers.

Little information is available about the personal life of Brown. She did not appear to be active in the scientific organizations to which she belonged, and therefore remains only briefly mentioned in a number of sources. She died in 1956.

JH/MBO

PRIMARY SOURCES
Brown, Nellie Adalesa. With Erwin F. Smith and C. O. Townsend. *Crown-Gall Disease in Plants: Its Cause and Remedy.* USDA Bureau of Plant Industry Bulletin no. 213. Washington, D.C.: Government Printing Office, 1911.

———. With Erwin F. Smith and Lucia McCulloch. *The Structure and Development of Crown-Gall: A Plant Cancer.* USDA

Bureau of Plant Industry Bulletin no. 255. Washington, D.C.: Government Printing Office, 1911.

⸺. "An Apple-Stem Tumor Not Crown-gall." U.S.D.A. *Journal of Agricultural Research* 27 (1924): 695–698.

⸺. "Some Bacterial Diseases of Lettuce." U.S.D.A. *Journal of Agricultural Research* 13 (1918): 367–388.

STANDARD SOURCE

AMS 3–7; Bailey; Rossiter 1982; Stanley.

BROWN, RACHEL FULLER (1898–1980)

U.S. biochemist. Born 23 November 1898 in Springfield, Mass., to Annie (Fuller) and George Hamilton Brown. One brother. Educated Webster Groves grammar school; Springfield, Mass., High School; Mount Holyoke College (A.B., 1920); University of Chicago (M.A., Ph.D. 1926). Professional experience: Francis Shimer School near Chicago, teacher (ca. 1922–1925); Division of Laboratories and Research, New York State Department of Health, Albany, assistant chemist (1926–1951); associate chemist (1951–1968). Died 14 January 1980.

Rachel Fuller Brown's early home life was unstable. Her real estate and insurance agent father moved from Massachusetts to Webster Groves, Missouri, where Rachel attended elementary school. In 1912, George Brown deserted his family. Rachel, her mother, and Rachel's younger brother returned to Massachusetts where she finished high school. After she graduated from high school, a wealthy family friend financed Brown's college education at Mount Holyoke. Although she was originally a history major, Brown became fascinated by chemistry after she took a required course. She double majored in history and chemistry. After she completed her bachelor's degree she went to the University of Chicago, where she completed her master's degree in organic chemistry.

Finances dictated much of Brown's academic career. Because of insufficient funds to continue directly for her doctorate, she took three years off to teach chemistry and physics at the Francis Shimer School near Chicago and save money. She returned to the university and submitted her thesis in 1926. However, again because of lack of funds, there was a delay in arranging her oral examinations. Again, she took a job to tide her over, this time as an assistant chemist at the Division of Laboratories and Research at the New York State Department of Health. She returned to Chicago seven years later to take her oral examinations and was finally awarded her degree.

Brown, along with her colleague ELIZABETH HAZEN, developed a pneumonia vaccine still used. Again working with Hazen, Brown worked on antifungicidal antibiotics. She and Hazen purified this new antifungal agent and named it "nys-

tatin" after New York State. The patent license was issued to E. R. Squibb and Sons who developed a way to mass produce the substance. They named the original nystatin, mycostatin. Brown remained an assistant chemist until 1951, when she was finally promoted to associate. She continued to work with Hazen discovering the antibiotics phalamycin and capacidin. In response to these discoveries, Brown and Hazen were awarded the Squibb Award in Chemotherapy in 1955. When Brown retired, still at the rank of associate chemist, she was awarded the New York State Department of Health's Distinguished Service Award and in 1972 the Rhoda Benham Award of the Medical Mycological Society of the Americas. With Hazen, Brown became the first woman to receive the Chemical Pioneer Award from the American Institute of Chemists.

Active in the Episcopalian church, she became the first female vestry member of her church. By the time of her death, she had paid back the wealthy woman who made her education at Mount Holyoke possible. With her royalties from nystatin, she helped designate new funds for scientific research and scholarships.   JH/MBO

PRIMARY SOURCES

Brown, Rachel Fuller. "Rachel Fuller Brown, Retired Scientist, New York State Department of Health." *Chemist* (January 1980): 8.

Archival sources at Schlesinger Library, Radcliffe College.

SECONDARY SOURCES

Baldwin, Richard S. *The Fungus Fighters: Two Women Scientists and Their Discovery.* Ithaca, NY: Cornell University Press, 1981.

Jones, Stacey V. "Antibiotic Said to Be Effective Against Some Fungus Diseases." Includes photo of Brown and Hazen. *New York Times,* 29 June 1957.

New York Times, 16 January 1980. Obituary notice.

STANDARD SOURCES

Annual Obituary 1980; *Notable* (long article by Miyoko Chu); Uglow 1989; Vare and Ptacek; Yost.

BROWNE, IDA ALISON (BROWN) (1900–1976)

Australian geologist. Born 16 August 1900 at Paddington, Sydney, to Alison (Logan) and William George Brown. Married William Rowan Browne. Educated Fort Street Girls' High School; University of Sydney (B.Sc., 1922; D.Sc., 1932). Professional experience: University of Sydney, demonstrator (1923?–1927; 1934); Linnean Macleay Fellowship (1927–1934); assistant lecturer in paleontology (1935–1940), lecturer (1941–1945), senior lecturer (1945–1950). Resigned August 1950; worked from home 1950–1970? Died 21 October 1976.

Ida Alison Brown had to change only the spelling of her name when she married William Rowan Browne, a well-known Australian geologist. Brown was born in Sydney, to which her mother was native; her insurance clerk father was from New Zealand. Graduating with first-class honors and the university medal in geology, Brown became a demonstrator in geology after she graduated. In 1927 she was awarded a Linnean Macleay Fellowship, which allowed her to investigate the geology of the southern coast of Australia. She combined mapping in the field with laboratory work in petrology. When her fellowship ended, she returned as a demonstrator to the university. She continued to be promoted until she was named a senior lecturer. She resigned after five years at that level and the Brownes worked from home after 1950, and led field trips during the summers.

Ida was a vice-president of the Royal Society of New South Wales from 1942 to 1950, honorary editorial secretary from 1950 to 1953, and president from 1953 to 1954. She also belonged to the Australian National Research Council and to the Australian and New Zealand Association for the Advancement of Science. She had a long association with the Geological Society of Australia.

Ida and William Browne are another example of the importance of collaboration between spouses. They belonged to the same scientific societies and held offices in them. They sometimes collaborated on their geological work, but Ida Browne was also independent in her work.

William Browne died on 1 September 1975 and Ida one year later. Her last years were painful because of a paralyzing illness requiring the attention of nurses and of her husband until he died.

JH/MBO

PRIMARY SOURCES

Browne, Ida Alison. "Ordovician Limestone at Bowan Park, N.S.W." *Australian Journal of Science* 15, no. 1 (1952): 29–30. This study confirmed the Ordovician age of brachiopods from limestones in the Owan Park region, New South Wales. Established an Ordovician age for the limestones which had formerly been considered Silurian.

———. "Permian Spirifers from Tasmania." *Journal and Proceedings of the Royal Society of New South Wales* 86, no. 2 (1953): 55–62. Describes an organism, *Trigonotreta stokesii,* and shows *Spirifer tasmaniensis* to be synonymous. Also describes a new species from the Berriedale limestone, a Permian area near Hobart, Tasmania.

———. "*Martiniopsis Waagen* from the Salt Range, India." *Journal and Proceedings of the Royal Society of New South Wales* 86, 4 (1953): 100–107. Describes external and internap characters of the Permian brachiopod *Martiniopsis waagen* based on complete and serially sectioned specimens from the Permian Productus limestone from Sal Range India.

———. "A Study of the Tasman Geocyncline in the Region of Yass, New South Wales [presidential address]. *Journal and Proceedings of the Royal Society of New South Wales* 88, 1 (1954): 3–11.

———. "Stratigraphy and Structure of the Devonian Rocks of the Taemas and Cavan Areas, Murrumbidgee River, South of Yass, N.S.W." *Journal and Proceedings of the Royal Society of New South Wales,* Part 4, 92 (1958). Showed that there are two major faults rather than four as previously postulated and the strains set up by the intense folding have produced cleavages which cut the bedding planes at a high angle.

———. "A New Cystoid (Pelmatozoa, Echinodermata) from the Silurian of New South Wales." *Proceedings of the Linnean Society of New South Wales,* Part 3, *Proceedings* 88 (1963). Description of a new genus and new species.

SECONDARY SOURCES

Lankford-Smith, T. "William Rowan Brown: An Appreciation." *Australian Geographer* 13 (1976): 237–238.

Linnean Society of New South Wales, *Proceedings* 102 (1977): 76.

Records of the Australian Academy of Science 4 (1979): 65. Contains a list of publications and personal information.

Vallance, T. G. *Australia Dictionary of Biography,* vol. 13, 1940–1980. Melbourne: Melbourne University Press, 1993. The article is on William Rowan Browne, but has considerable information on Ida.

BROWNE, LADY ISABEL MARY (PEYRONNET) (1881–1947)

British botanist. Born 6 November 1881 in London to Lady Sligo, a daughter of Baron (afterward Vicomte) Jules de Peyronnet and the third Marquess of Sligo. Twin sister, Mary. Died 1947.

Isabel Peyronnet and her twin sister, Mary, were greatly influenced in their youth by their mother, Lady Sligo, who read Shakespeare to the girls, and instilled a Gallic sense of *joie de vivre* in them. They celebrated Napoleon III's coup d'etat and read great tomes of French history. Isabel became fascinated at an early age by Milton and other English authors. Lady Sligo was her father's third wife, and by the time the twins were five years old he was more or less an invalid, unable to influence the course of the twin's intellectual development. Another important intellectual influence on the twins was the English wife of Lady Isabel's grandfather, who debated many aspects of political theory with the girls.

Isabel became interested in botany through her cousin Harold Russell, who also discussed other scholarly topics with her. By the time the twins were nine years old, they received lessons in botany, zoology, geology, and some astronomy weekly, from a tutor, W. F. Gwinnell. On Isabel's fifteenth birthday, her tutor gave her a copy of D. H. Scott's *Structural Botany*, a book that was to influence her greatly. She attended several of Scott's lectures at University College, London, on fossil botany and was fascinated by the subject. Scott evidently thought that she had potential, for he invited her in 1916 to collaborate with him on a book. The book, however, failed to materialize, because she refused to jeopardize her war work for her private interests.

After hearing another of Scott's lectures, this time on the Lycopsida, Browne began to read regularly at the British Museum of Natural History on the structure and phylogenetic relations of different vascular cryptogams. She compiled these studies into what she hoped would be a book. The publisher to whom she had submitted it gave it to Scott to review. Although Scott did not recommend its publication as a book, he suggested that the more general chapters be used as an essay in a scientific journal. The *New Phytologist* accepted it and it was later reprinted as one of the *New Phytology Reprints*. This work was considered little short of amazing for one who had not had academic training in the field and who had not been inside a laboratory.

Browne remedied her lack of laboratory experience by enrolling in University College, London, where AGNES ARBER served as her individual tutor in botanical technique. After she mastered laboratory methods, she continued to do research at the Botanical Department of University College. She chose to study *Equisetum* (horsetails). She published the result of these studies over a period of thirty years in the *Annals of Botany* and the *Botanical Gazette*. She was meticulous in her laboratory work and insisted on having complete microtome sections of her specimens before she would make generalizations.

In addition to her work on *Equisetum*, she worked on sections of *Calamostachys* at the Muséum d'Histoire Naturelle at Paris or owned by the Société d'Histoire Naturelle d'Autun. She published her notes in the *Annals of Botany*, in the *Bulletin du Muséum d'Histoire Naturelle*, and the *New Phytologist*.

Browne published not only the results of her careful laboratory work, she also published several very theoretical papers on the interrelationships and the phylogeny of the Pteridophyta. These general papers indicate a thoughtful, critical scientist who can postulate generalizations using the factual data as it became available.   JH/MBO

PRIMARY SOURCES

Browne, Isabel M. P. "The Phylogeny and Inter-relationships of the Pteridophyta." *New Phytologist* 7 (1908): 93–113; 150–166; 181–197; 230–253; and vol. 8 (1909): 13–31; 51–72. Reprinted as *New Phytologist Reprints*, no. 3.

————. "Contributions to Our Knowledge of the Anatomy of the Cone and Fertile Stem of Equisetum." *Annals of Botany* 26 (1912): 663–703.

————. "A Second Contribution to Our Knowledge of the Anatomy of the Cone and Fertile Stem of Equisetum." *Annals of Botany* 29 (1915): 231–265.

————. "Anatomy of *Equisetum giganteum*." *Botanical Gazette* 78 (1922): 447–468.

————. "Anomalous Traces in the Cone of *Equisetum maximum* Lam." *Annals of Botany* 37 (1923): 594–604.

————. "A New Theory on the Morphology of the Calamarian Cone." *Annals of Botany* 41 (1926).

SECONDARY SOURCES

Arber, Agnes. *Proceedings of the Linnaean Society of London* 159 (1946–1947): 154–158. A long obituary notice on Browne. Includes a bibliography.

BROWNE, MARJORIE LEE (1914–1979)

U.S. mathematician. Born 1914 in Memphis, Tenn. Father Lawrence Johnson Lee. Educated LeMoyne High School, Memphis (graduated 1931); Howard University (B.S., 1935); University of Michigan (M.S., 1939; Ph.D., 1949). Professional experience: Gilbert Academy, New Orleans (1935–1936); Wiley College, Marshall, Tex., instructor (1942–1945); North Carolina Central University, instructor (1949–1951). Died 1979 in Durham, N.C.

Topologist Marjorie Lee Browne was one of the first African American women to be awarded a doctorate. Educated in Memphis and New Orleans she was influenced by her stepmother, Lottie Taylor Lee, who was a schoolteacher. Her doctoral dissertation from the University of Michigan was on one-parameter subgroups in selected topological and matrix groups; she published on this topic in 1955. She received a fellowship from the Ford Foundation to travel to Cambridge, England, in 1952–1953.

After teaching at an academy in New Orleans and a college in Texas, she was appointed to the department of mathematics at North Carolina Central University. Here she served as the first head of the department and rose to the rank of professor. Browne was instrumental in coordinating a program in secondary school science and mathematics teaching at the university, for which she was awarded a National Science Foundation grant and Shell Foundation Scholarship grants.

As a minority holder of a doctorate in 1949, she was unable to obtain any position in a major research institution. This experience fueled her decision to develop programs to prepare students and teachers for careers in mathematics and science. For this work she received recognition from the North Carolina Council of Teachers of Mathematics and served as a faculty consultant for the Ford Foundation.

                                                    JH/MBO

PRIMARY SOURCES

Browne, Marjorie Lee. "A Note on the Classical Groups."
American Mathematical Monthly vol. 26, no. 6 (June–July
1955): 424–427.

SECONDARY SOURCES

"$57,500 Granted for High School Teachers Summer Institute
at NCC." Article in the *Durham Sun,* 21 December 1956.

STANDARD SOURCES

Notable (long article by William T. Fletcher).

BRUCE, CATHERINE WOLFE (1816–1900)

*U.S. philanthropist and patron of astronomy. Born 22 January
1816 in New York City to Catherine (Wolfe) and George Bruce.
Four siblings. Never married. Educated privately in New York; extensive travel. Donor of George Bruce Free Library, New York
(1887); Harvard College Observatory, Bruce Telescope (1889); Astronomical Society of Pacific, donor of Bruce Medal award; donor,
Heidelberg Observatory. Honors and memberships: Grand Duke of
Baden, gold medal; memorialized by Bruce asteroid. Died 13 March
1900.*

A remarkable patron of astronomy, Catherine Bruce supported research with gifts to individual scientists and observatories in the United States and Germany.

Catherine Bruce inherited money from her parents. Her
father, who had emigrated from Scotland, in partnership
with his brother, became a leading printer and type founder.
When he died in 1866 he was a respected citizen of New
York and the country's leading typographer. Her mother also
had money and also reflected a tradition of philanthropy; the
philanthropist Catharine Lorillard Wolfe was her first cousin.
Blessed with wealth and culture, Catherine was educated
privately and through extensive European travel became fluent in several languages, including Latin. She delighted in
collecting rare art works and gave money and an endowment
to the George Bruce Branch of the New York Free-Circu-
lating (later the New York Public) Library. She also translated
and printed a fine edition of the *Dies Irae* of Tommaso da
Celano.

It was not until she was seventy-three years old that Bruce
became a patron of astronomy. Although she had long been
fascinated by the heavens, she lacked formal training in astronomy. However, in the February 1888 edition of a popular astronomical journal *Sidereal Messenger,* she read an article
by Simon Newcomb that upset her. Newcomb had suggested that most significant astronomical discoveries had already been made. This view was totally opposed to Bruce's
ideas. She was convinced that science was an open frontier
and was incensed by Newcomb's assertions to the contrary.

She wrote to Newcomb to object to his ideas. Bruce then
approached the scientific community with an offer of aid,
first giving $50,000 to the Harvard College Observatory to
finance a powerful photographic telescope. Later she gave an
additional $124,275 to astronomy. Much astronomical
equipment was purchased with Bruce's money. The money
generated by this endowment was not huge, but by providing Bruce Grants to young astronomers it assisted many
people in critical stages in their careers. The money was used
to subsidize salaries and publications. Bruce also provided an
endowment for a gold medal to be given by the Astronomical Society of the Pacific. She died at age eighty-four.

JH/MBO

PRIMARY SOURCES

Correspondence with professional astronomers in the Simon
Newcomb Papers, Library of Congress and the Edward C.
Pickering Papers in the Harvard University Archives.

SECONDARY SOURCES

"Catherine Wolfe Bruce," *Astrophysical Journal* (March 1900):
Obituary notice.
"Catharine Wolfe Bruce," *New York Tribune,* 23 March 1900.
Obituary notice.
"Catherine Wolfe Bruce," *Popular Astronomy* (May 1900):
Obituary notice. Includes a complete list of her bequests to
astronomy.

STANDARD SOURCES

NAW (long article by Howard S. Miller).

BRUCE, EILEEN ADELAIDE (1905–1955)

*British botanist. Born 1905 in Petersham, England. Educated Uni-
versity College, London (B.Sc., 1920s). Professional experience:
Royal Botanical Gardens, staff (1930–1939; 1952–1955).
National Herbarium, Pretoria, South Africa (1946–1951?). Died
6 October 1955, Kingston upon Thames.*

Eileen Bruce was on the staff of Royal Botanical Gardens,
Kew, from 1930 until 1939(?). During World War II, she
served as a commissioned officer in the Anti-Aircraft Command of the Territorial Army. In 1946, she went to the National Herbarium, Pretoria, where she revised the genus
Kniphofia. Bruce published in *Bothalia* and in *Flowering Plants
of South Africa.* She rejoined the Kew staff in 1952 and
worked on *Pedaliceae* and *Longaniceae* for Flora of Tropical
East Africa. Her plant specimens are in Pretoria and Kew.

JH/MBO

PRIMARY SOURCES

Articles in *Bothalia* and in *Flowering Plants of South Africa.*

SECONDARY SOURCES
Kew Bulletin (1956): 39.

STANDARD SOURCES
Desmond; Gunn and Codd.

BRÜCH, HILDE (1904–)

German/U.S. psychiatrist. Born 11 March 1904, Duelken, Germany, to Hirsch and Adele Rath Brüch. Never married. Educated University of Freiburg (M.D., 1929). Emigrated to the United States. Professional experience: Columbia University, instructor in pediatrics (1934–1943); Rockefeller Fellow (1941–1942); Johns Hopkins University Hospital, assistant (1941–1943); College of Physicians and Surgeons, Columbia University, associate psychiatrist (1943–1954), associate clinical professor (1955–1959), clinical professor (1959–1964); Baylor College of Medicine, professor (1964–?). Concurrent experience: Psychoanalytic Clinic for Training and Research, associate psychoanalyst (1948–1965); Food Committee, National Research Council, member (1942–1944). Honors and memberships: American Psychiatric Association, Fellow; American Academy of Child Psychiatry, Fellow; American Psychoanalytic Association, member.

Hilda Brüch was at one time the world's leading authority on eating disorders. Her early work on obesity and anorexia brought to light a "hidden" disorder of epidemic proportions. She was also an educator in psychiatry and psychoanalysis, recognized professionally with many awards, including the President's Citation for Meritorious Contributions to the Clinical Services, Baylor College; William A. Schonfeld Award for Contribution to Psychiatry, American Society for Adolescent Psychiatry; Gold Doctor Diploma, Medical Faculty, University of Freiburg, Germany; Mount Airy Gold Medal Award for Distinction and Excellence in Psychiatry.

After receiving her medical degree from the University of Freiburg in 1929, Brüch studied and conducted research in psychology and pediatrics at the university clinics at Kiel and Leipzig. As did many other women psychologists, she fled Nazi-occupied Germany in 1933. She worked at the East End Child Guidance Clinic in England for a year, then emigrated to America where she became an instructor in pediatrics at Columbia University (1934–1943). She obtained psychiatric training at Johns Hopkins Hospital on a Rockefeller Fellowship, and psychoanalytic training at the Washington-Baltimore Institute. After her psychiatric residency, she returned to Columbia University and joined the clinical staff at the College of Physicians and Surgeons. She was at Columbia from 1943 to 1964 and became full professor of psychiatry in 1959.

Besides her clinical duties, Brüch maintained a private practice in psychoanalysis from 1943 until 1964 when she moved to Baylor College of Medicine in Houston, Texas. At Baylor, continuing her overall research on concepts of self-awareness and body image, Brüch did specific studies on eating disorders and published her most popular and controversial books, *Eating Disorders: Obesity, Anorexia Nervosa and the Person Within* (1973) and *The Golden Cage: The Enigma of Anorexia Nervosa* (1978). Early topics for her research were elements and interaction in the process of parent education (*Don't Be Afraid of Your Child: A Guide for Perplexed Parents*).

JH/MBO

PRIMARY SOURCES
Brüch, Hilde. *Don't Be Afraid of Your Child: A Guide for Perplexed Parents.* New York: Farrar, Straus and Young, 1952.
———. *The Importance of Overweight.* New York: Norton, 1957.
———. *Studies in Schizophrenia.* Copenhagen: Munksgaard, 1959.
———. *Eating Disorders: Obesity, Anorexia Nervosa and the Person Within.* New York: Basic Books, 1973.
———. *Learning Psychotherapy: Rationale and Ground Rules.* Cambridge: Harvard University Press, 1974.
———. *The Golden Cage: the Enigma of Anorexia Nervosa.* Cambridge: Harvard University Press, 1978.
———. *Conversations with Anorexics.* New York: Basic Books, 1988. Case studies.

SECONDARY SOURCES
Quack, Syblle, ed. *Between Sorrow and Strength: Women Refugees of the Nazi Period.* Cambridge and New York: Cambridge University Press, 1995.

STANDARD SOURCES
AMS B 9; P&B 10–14; *Encyclopedia of Psychology*, 1994; Stevens and Gardner.

BRÜCKNER, FRAU DR. (fl. 1794)

German/Swiss physician. Married Dr. Brückner. Professional experience: practiced in Eisenach.

Frau Dr. Brückner was the widow of a court physician in Gotha who studied orthopedics. In 1794, she began to treat club foot and other bone deformities. She then practiced in Eisenach for many years.

JH/MBO

SECONDARY SOURCES
Harless, Christian F. *Die Verdienste der Frauen um Naturwissenschaft und Heilkunde.* Göttingen: Vandenhoeck-Ruprechtschen Verlag, 1830.

STANDARD SOURCES
Hurd-Mead 1938.

BRUNETTA (fl. 1475)
German Jewish physician.

The only information available on this German Jewish physician is that she was charged with complicity in the death of a child in Germany in the late 1400s.   JH/MBO

STANDARD SOURCES
Echols and Williams; *Jews in Medicine.*

BRUNETTI, R. (fl. 1921–1924)
Italian physicist and chemist.

R. Brunetti was an early experimenter who worked in radioactivity. No information is available on her life. She worked on possibilities for separation of isotopes based on differences in fine structure of spectra or diffusion constants.
                                                    MM

PRIMARY SOURCES
Brunetti, R. *Nuov. Cimento* 22 (1921): 5, 216.
——. *Nuov. Cimento* 1 (1924): 185.

STANDARD SOURCES
Meyer and von Schweidler.

BRUNFELS, FRAU OTTO (fl. 1534)
Swiss physician. Married Otto Brunfels (1464–1534). Educated Montpellier (1557); Basel. Professional experience: Berne, city physician.

The widow of botanist Otto Brunfels studied medicine in Montpellier long after his death. Apparently much younger than Brunfels, she studied medicine in the same class as Felix Plater, who kept a diary of his medical education experience and wrote that there were women students at Montpellier. According to Plater, she was a good student and had an excellent reputation as a physician. She continued her medical studies at Basel and then was appointed city physician of Berne.   JH/MBO

SECONDARY SOURCES
Plater, Felix and Cole, Abdiah. *A Bolden Practice Physic.* London: Peter Cole, 1662.

STANDARD SOURCES
Hurd-Mead 1938.

BRUNSWICK, RUTH JANE (MACK) (1897–1946)
U.S. psychiatrist and psychoanalyst. Born 17 February 1897 in Chicago, Ill., to Jessie (Fox) and Julian William Mack. No siblings. Married (1) Herrman Ludwig Blumgart (1917; divorced 1924); (2) Mark Brunswick (1928; divorced). One daughter. Educated University High School, Chicago; Radcliffe College (graduated 1918); Tufts Medical School (M.D. cum laude, 1922). Psychoanalysis by Sigmund Freud in Vienna. Professional experience: Vienna, Psychoanalytic practice (to 1938); Vienna Psychoanalytic Society; Psychoanalytic Institute, training analyst; New York Psychoanalytic Institute, New York City, instructor (1938–1946). Died 24 January 1946 in New York City of myocarditis following pneumonia.

Ruth Jane Mack was the only child of old American German-Jewish families on both sides. Her father, a graduate of Harvard Law School, was a liberal jurist who served on state and federal courts and was prominent in social welfare and Zionist organizations. Ruth Mack attended University High School in Chicago and received her undergraduate degree from Radcliffe College. She married Herrman Ludwig Blumgart in 1917, while still at Radcliffe (he was at Harvard and later became a distinguished cardiologist). She took advanced coursework in medical psychology with Elmer Ernest Southard, Harvard's professor of neuropathology, who agreed to sponsor her for Harvard Medical School; because of her sex, though, she was not admitted. She went to Tufts Medical School, receiving her medical degree with honors in 1922. Her marriage to Herrman Ludwig Blumgart ended in divorce in 1924. After medical school graduation, she went to Vienna to be analyzed by Sigmund Freud, ultimately becoming a member of the intimate circle of psychoanalysts around Freud and participating in the Vienna Psychoanalytic Society. In 1928, she married Mark Brunswick, a composer. This marriage also ended in divorce. She and Brunswick had a daughter, Mathilda Juliana Brunswick.

Until 1938 (except for one year when she returned to the States for the birth of her child) Ruth practiced psychoanalysis in Vienna and taught in the Psychoanalytic Institute. Her special interest was the treatment of severe mental illnesses. She was admired as a brilliant clinician and therapist who was thorough in both her analytic work and her written contributions. When Hitler took over Austria, she helped many of her colleagues leave the country. She left for the United States in 1938, settling in New York City. Here she resumed her practice, teaching courses in dream analysis and psychoanalytic technique at the New York Psychoanalytic Institute and working with borderline and psychotic patients.

She made significant contributions to psychoanalytic and psychiatric theory. Of her four major articles, three are classics in the field of psychoanalytic literature. She added to the understanding of the psychological processes involved in psychoses. Using clinical evidence, she worked out, in collaboration with Freud, the dynamics of the growth of the emotional relationship of the very young child to his mother (libido development) and the role of this relationship in later mental illness.

Ruth Brunswick died 24 January 1946 in New York City of myocarditis following pneumonia.   KM

PRIMARY SOURCES

Brunswick, Ruth Mack. *Die Analyse Eines Eifersuchtswahnes.* Leipzig: Internationaler Psychoanalytischer Verlag, 1929. Case study of jealousy.

———. *Ein Nachtrag zu Freuds "Geschichte Einer Infantilen Neurose."* Leipzig: Internationaler Psychoanalytischer Verlag, 1929.

———. "Supplement to the Case of the Wolf Man," in *The Wolf Man and Sigmund Freud.* Ed. Muriel Gardner. London: Hogarth Press and the Institute of Psychoanalysis, 1972.

SECONDARY SOURCES

"Brunswick, Ruth." *New York Times,* 26 January 1946. Obituary notice.

Nunberg, Herman. "In Memoriam: Ruth Mack Brunswick." *Psychoanalytic Quarterly* vol. 15, no. 2 (April 1946): 141–143. Obituary notice.

STANDARD SOURCES

Appignanesi; *NAW* (long article by John Chynoweth Burnham).

BRYAN, ALICE ISABEL (BEVER) (1902–1993)

U.S. psychologist. Born 11 September 1902 in Arlington, N.J., to Caroline and Ewald Bever. Two brothers. Married (1) Chester Ward Bryan (1924; divorced); (2) Frank Marvin Blasingame (1936; divorced); (3) Colonel George Virgil Fuller (1956). Educated Columbia University (B.S., 1929; A.M., 1930; Ph.D., 1934); University of Chicago (M.A., 1951). Professional positions: Child Education Foundation, instructor of psychology (1929–1939); Sarah Lawrence College, instructor (1934–1935); School of Library Services, Columbia University, consulting psychologist (1936–1939), assistant professor (1939–1953), associate professor (1953–1959), professor (1959–1971); Pratt Institute, Department of Psychology, head (1936–1939); Social Science Research Council, Public Library Inquiry, director of personnel study (1948–1950); Russell Sage Community Study, associate director (1950–1956); Library Extension Division, State Education Department, New York, consultant (1947–1949). Memberships: AAAS; APA; Association of Applied Psychology; Library Association. Died 1992.

Alice Bever's interest in art and music was encouraged by her mother and grandmother. She grew up in an extended family in Kearney, New Jersey, where she attended public schools. When she started school, she could already read and write, so she was advanced to the second grade at the age of five. She also skipped the seventh grade. After graduating from high school, she attended Columbia University Extension Division where she took secretarial courses. Since she lacked money to attend the university, she worked at the American Book Company while taking evening classes at Columbia and New York universities. There she met author Paul Gallico, who became a lifelong friend, and Marc Edmund Jones, who introduced Bryan to occult philosophy and parapsychology.

An advertising course that Bever taught through the YMCA used a text entitled *The Psychology of Advertising and Selling.* This book motivated her to study psychology. At this point she decided to become a psychologist and earned her three degrees at Columbia University. Her dissertation was written on the correlation between memory and verbal ability in five-year-olds.

Interestingly, she worked with Edwin Boring, well-known professor of psychology at Harvard and Radcliffe, on a series of articles on the status of women in psychology. Bryan was a feminist, whereas Boring was not. Consequently the two did not entirely agree upon their conclusions. Boring insisted that women were already being treated equally. Bryan was the founder of the National Council of Women Psychologists and, during the time of their collaboration, worked at the Columbia School of Library Services.

Most of Bryan's research at Columbia involved the idea of bibliotherapy—reading as a way to improve mental health. Although the concept was developed for the mentally ill in veterans' hospitals during and after World War I, she used bibliotherapy for both well and ill people as a preventative. The results of her studies were exported to many public libraries nationwide. She won an appointment to conduct a nationwide study of public libraries; the study resulted in a book in 1952 and promotion to full professor.

Bryan married three times; the first two marriages ended in amicable divorces and the third ended with the death of her Air Force colonel husband. She did not have children of her own, although her second husband was a single parent.

JH/MBO

PRIMARY SOURCES

Bryan, Alice. "Organization of Memory in Young Children." *Archives of Psychology* no. 162. Ph.D. diss., Columbia University, 1934.

———. "Personality Adjustment Through Reading." *Library Journal* 64 (1939): 573–576.

———. With Edwin G. Boring. "Women in American Psychology: Prolegomenon." *Psychological Bulletin* 41 (1944): 447–454.

———. "Legibility of Library of Congress Cards and Their Reproductions." College and Research Libraries 6 (1945): 447–464.

———. With Edwin G. Boring. "Women in American Psychology: Factors Affecting Their Careers." *Transactions of the New York Academy of Sciences*, ser. 2, no. 9 (1946): 19–23.

———. With Edwin G. Boring. "Women in American Psychology: Factors Affecting Their Professional Careers." *American Psychologist* 2 (1947): 3–20.

———. *The Public Librarian*. New York: Columbia University Press, 1952.

STANDARD SOURCES
AMS 9–11; O'Connell and Russo 1988; Rossiter 1995.

BRYAN, MARGARET (b. ca. 1760)

British educator and writer on natural philosophy. Married with two daughters. Professional experience: operated boarding schools for girls.

Very little is known about the life of Margaret Bryan, and the information that is available comes from her own books. According to the *DNB,* she was "a beautiful and talented schoolmistress . . . the wife of a Mr. Bryan." From the frontispiece of *A Compendious System of Astronomy,* we know that she had two daughters. Bryan ran a boarding school for girls at Blackheath from 1795 to 1806, opened a school in London in 1815, and moved to Margate in 1816. The curriculum in her schools differed from that of most peer institutions by including mathematics and science as suitable subjects for girls. In 1797 she published her early lecture notes as *A Compendious System of Astronomy.* In the preface to this book, she denied demonstrating any originality, proclaiming that the subject had already been extensively considered "by the ablest mathematicians and by philosophers of the most penetrating genius." Perhaps she hoped to defuse criticism of her work as a woman dabbling in the public sphere by stressing the accomplishments of the male mathematicians who had previously written on the subject. She explained that her goal was to make obtuse subjects clear, and, continuing in an apologetic tone, stated that if she had failed "through the imbecility of my judgment, I hope the motive may be my apology." She appeared anxious not to offend her male critics, noting that her lectures were not written for publication but for her students. Explaining that she had published these notes at the insistence of friends, she expected censure from those with "false and vulgar" prejudices but expected fair treatment by those who acknowledged "truth, although enfeebled by female attire."

Commenting on this work, Charles Hutton, Fellow of the Royal Society of London and Edinburgh and then professor of mathematics at Woolwich Royal Military Academy, noted that, "I have read over your lectures with great pleasure and the more so, to find that even the learned and more difficult sciences are thus beginning to be successfully cultivated by the extraordinary and elegant talents of the female writers of the present day." Hutton noted that he was honored to have encouraged Bryan in her work. This praise encouraged Bryan to publish her *Lectures on Natural Philosophy* (1806), a work consisting of thirteen lectures on hydrostatics, optics, pneumatics, and acoustics. In this work, she was anxious to impress upon her students the mutual relationship between religion and science as expressed by William Paley in his *Natural Theology.* Since her first book had gotten such good reviews, she was more confident and less apologetic in this work. In 1815 she published *An Astronomical and Geographical Class Book for Schools.* Her work was often confused with that of JANE MARCET, who sometimes published anonymously.

In no way was Margaret Bryan denigrating the two spheres concept—the idea that women and men have separate spheres. As she mentioned in her *Lectures on Natural Philosophy,* she was pleased with her domestic responsibilities and saw her teaching as an extension of her role as "Parent and Preceptress." Still in her first book she felt the need to explain why she might appear to be overstepping the line of propriety and venturing into the public sphere. Her reasons were that to do so was to engage in responsible motherhood and to follow the advice of her friends who urged her to publish. Unlike strident "scientific women," Bryan appeared to retain the values admired in the domestic sphere and thus was not seen as a threat to her male colleagues. Although her approach probably did not represent a deliberate strategy, it nevertheless served as a means to open scientific education to girls.   MBO

PRIMARY SOURCES
Bryan, Margaret. *A Compendious System of Astronomy in a Course of Familiar Lectures.* 3rd ed. London: Wynne and Scholey, 1805.

———. *Lectures on Natural Philosophy.* London: T. Davison, 1806.

———. *An Astronomical and Geographical Class Book for Schools.* 1815.

SECONDARY SOURCES
Benjamin, Marina. "Elbow Room: Women Writers on Science, 1790–1840."

Hans, Nicholas. *New Trends in Education in the Eighteenth Century.* London: Keegan Paul, 1951. Chapter 10 provides information on Margaret Bryan.

Krupp, E. C. "Astronomical Musings." *Griffith Observer* 39 (1975): 8–18.

STANDARD SOURCES
DNB; Ogilvie 1986.

BRYAN, MARY KATHERINE (1877–?)

U.S. plant pathologist. Born 13 February 1877 in Prince George Co., Md. Educated Stanford University (A.B., 1908). Professional experience: Bureau of Plant Industry, U.S. Department of Agriculture, scientific assistant (1909–1918), assistant pathologist (1909–1918). Death date unknown.

Mary Katherine Bryan was one of several women who made a career with the Bureau of Plant industry, U.S.D.A. She worked with Erwin Frink Smith at the U.S Department of Agriculture on bacterial diseases of fruits and vegetables. NELLIE ADALESA BROWN also worked with Smith.

JH/MBO

PRIMARY SOURCES
Bryan, Mary Katherine. "A Nasturtium Wilt Caused by *Bacterium solanacearum.*" USDA *Journal of Agricultural Research* 4 (1915): 451–458.

———. With Erwin E. Smith. "Angular Leaf Spot of Cucumbers." USDA *Journal of Agricultural Research* 5 (1915): 465–475.

———. "A Bacterial Budrot of Cannas." USDA *Journal of Agricultural Research* 21 (1921): 143–152.

———. "Bacterial Leafspot of Delphinium." USDA *Journal of Agricultural Research* 27 (1924): 251–273.

———. "Bacterial Canker of Tomatoes." Washington D.C.: USDA, 1928. Published as a circular from the Bureau of Plant Industry.

SECONDARY SOURCES
Benjamin, Marina. "Elbowroom: Women Writers on Science, 1790–1840." In *Science and Sensibility: Gender and Scientific Enquiry 1780–1945.* Ed. Marina Benjamin. Oxford: Basil Blackwell, 1991.

STANDARD SOURCES
AMS 3–6; Rossiter 1982.

BRYANT, LOUISE STEVENS (1885–1956)

U.S. physician. Born 19 September 1885 in Paris, France. Educated Smith College (A.B., 1908); University of Pennsylvania (Ph.D., 1914). Professional experience: American Museum Natural History Department of Physiology (1908–1909); Russell Sage Foundation, research in school feeding (1909–1911); Psychological Clinic, Pennsylvania, social service and instructor in clinical psychology (1911–1914); Pennsylvania School for Social Work, lecturer (1915–1917); Municipal Court, Philadelphia, director of statistics and records (1914–1918); statistics branch of the U.S. Army, general staff (1918–1919); National Committee on Maternal Health, Inc., executive director (1927–1935).

Although Bryant began her career in academics, she gradually moved to administrative areas. For example, she worked in the statistics branch of the U.S. Army (1918–1919) and became executive director of the National Committee on Maternal Health, Inc. (1927–1935). She was a Fellow of the Eugenics Society, England, and an associate Fellow of the New York Academy of Sciences. She was a member of the AAAS and the Statistical Association. Her special interests were school feeding, clinical psychology, social court organization and statistics, outpatient service, hospital social service, and the medical control of fertility. She also applied her skills to supporting the Girl Scouts, the United Hospital Fund, the National Committee on Maternal Health, Inc., and the International Congress of Social Hygiene. KM

PRIMARY SOURCES
Bryant, Louise, editor. *Havelock Ellis's Studies on the Psychology of Sex.* New York: Random House, 1936.

SECONDARY SOURCES
Tansey, E. M. (Tilli) "'To Dine with Ladies Smelling of Dog'? A Brief History of Women and the Physiological Society." In *Women Physiologists: An Anniversary Celebration of Their Contributions to British Physiology,* Lynn Bindman, et al., 3–17, esp. 8–9. London: Portland Press, 1992.

STANDARD SOURCES
AMS 5–7.

BRYANT, SOPHIE (WILLOCK) (d. 1922)

British mathematician. Born in Ireland in County Fermanagh. Father a clergyman of the Church of Ireland. Married and widowed young. Educated Senior Cambridge Local Examination, distinction in mathematics; Bedford College, Arnott scholarship; London University (B.Sc., 1881; doctorate, 1884). Professional experience: North London Collegiate School, staff (from 1875), headmistress (from 1895); Royal Commission for Secondary Education (1894); Consultative Committee of the Board of Education (1900); London University, Senate, member (1900); London Education Committee, member (1908–1914). Died 1922 in the Alps.

Sophie Bryant was not only a mathematician but a philosopher, Irish patriot, suffragist, and educational pioneer. Born in Ireland, when her clergyman father died, she and her family moved to London. Sophie performed brilliantly on her Senior Cambridge Local Examination, earning first-class honors with distinction in mathematics. She married and was widowed early. After her husband died, she met the famous "Miss Buss," headmistress of the North London Collegiate School, and joined its staff. London University opened its degrees to women, and Bryant was one of the first women to take advantage of the new possibilities. She matriculated with honors in 1879 and earned both a bachelor's (with honors in mathematics and moral sciences) and a doctorate from that institution. She replaced Miss Buss as headmistress in 1895, and became more of an administrator than a teacher. Her ideas, however, permeated the school and she impressed her views of moral virtues on all of the students—explicitly through the scriptures and implicitly through her life.

She was a member of a number of very important education committees and commissions and worked tirelessly to promote educational superiority in Great Britain. She published several books on morality and Irish history. She was supportive of Irish causes; Trinity College, Dublin, when it first opened its degrees to women, gave her the degree of doctor of literature, *honoris causa.*   JH/MBO

PRIMARY SOURCES
Bryant, Sophie. *The Genius of Gael.* London: Leipzig, T. F. Unwin, 1913.
———. *Moral and Religious Education.* New York: Longmans, Green and Co., 1920.

SECONDARY SOURCES
"Dr. Sophie Bryant." *Nature* 110 (1922): 458.
Valentin, G. "Die Frauen in den exakten Wissenschaften." *Bibliotheca Mathematica* 9 (1895): 65–76.

STANDARD SOURCES
Grinstein and Campbell; Rebière.

BUCCA, DOROTEA
See Bocchi, Dorotea.

BUCHANAN, FLORENCE (fl. 1899–1929)
British physiologist. Born second half nineteenth century. Lived in Oxford. Professional experience: contributed twelve communications to the Physiological Society on electrical properties of contracting and resting skeletal muscle, comparative studies of cardiovascular function. Honors and memberships: elected as one of first six women members of the Physiological Society, on proposal of J. S. Haldane. No other biographical details available.

Although according to historian of modern medicine Tilli Tansey there are no biographical details known about Florence Buchanan, one of the first women members of the

Physiological Society, her work on electrical properties of contracting skeletal muscle and comparative studies of cardiovascular function attracted the attention of contemporary physiologists. She was proposed as a member of the Physiological Society as early as 1912 by Haldane, but in spite of the support from thirty additional members of the society, the vote to elect women members was not passed until 1915, when Buchanan entered the society along with Winifred Cullis, Sarah Sowton, and two other women. The number of her final supporters totaled forty-nine. She had contributed twelve papers to the Physiological Society and a number were published before she was elected. Along with the above-mentioned investigations of muscle and cardiovascular function, she studied the effects of hibernation. She was the most prolific woman contributor to the Physiological Society before the entrance of women to that society.

JH/MBO

SECONDARY SOURCES
Tansey, E. M. (Tilli). "To Dine with Ladies Smelling of Dog?" In *Women Physiologists: An Anniversary Celebration of Their Contributions to British Physiology,* Lynn Bindman et al. London: Portland Press, 1992. See especially pages 8–9.

BUCHBINDER, LAURA G. ORDAN (1951–1984)
U.S./Israeli geologist. Born 1951 in the Bronx, New York. Married Binyamin Buchbinder. Two children 'Oded and Ya'el. Educated Brooklyn College; Rensselaer Polytechnic Institute (master's degree, 1974); Hebrew University (doctoral candidate, 1981). Professional experience: Oil Division of the Geological Survey of Israel, geologist (1974). Died 1984.

Laura Ordan was born in the Bronx and received not only a strong general education but a thoroughly Orthodox Jewish and Zionist upbringing as well. She graduated from Brooklyn College where she majored in geology and then went to Rensselaer Polytechnic Institute, Troy, New York, where she earned her master's degree. Soon after receiving her degree she went to Israel, where she found employment with the Oil Division of the Geological Survey of Israel. She became interested in the area of sedimentology, especially carbonate petrography. She married Binyamin Buchbinder in 1976.

Although Laura Buchbinder enrolled at Hebrew University as a doctoral candidate, she found that she had leukemia in 1983 and was unable to complete the degree. She showed extreme courage in submitting to experimental techniques, hoping that she might be among the few who survived. She died at the age of thirty-three.

Although her career was very short, it was impressive. She contributed to both applied and theoretical geology. As a Zionist in Israel, she especially felt the importance of the applied side of her science to the development of the new country's natural resources. When oil was discovered at Ashdod and Yavneh, the geology was not clearly understood. She studied the questions of sedimentologic control that led to oil accumulation on these coastal plain locations and constructed a model based on her new observations. This model demonstrated not only the originality of her thought but its applicability to future drilling. As she continued her research, she became an expert in the field of low temperature diagenesis and epigenesis of carbonates.   CK

PRIMARY SOURCES

Buchbinder, L. C. "Diagenesis-epigenesis of the Middle-Upper Jurassic Section in the Ashdod-Gan Yavneh area." *Israeli Geological Survey Current Research* (1980): 44.

———. "Dolomitization, porosity development and late mineralization in the Jurassic Zohar and Sederot formations in the Ashdod." *Israeli Journal of the Earth Sciences* 30 (1981): 64–80.

———, M. Magaritz, and M. Goldberg. "Stable Isotope Study of Karstic-Related Dolomitization: Jurassic Rocks from the Coastal Plain, Israel." *Journal of Sedimentary Petrolology* 54 (1984): 236–256.

SECONDARY SOURCES

Gvirtzman, Gedaliahu. "In Memoriam. Laura G. (Ordan) Buchbinder." *Current Research Geological Society of Israel* (1984): 11–13.

BUCKEL, CHLOE A. (1833–1912)

U.S. physician, Civil War nurse. Born 25 August 1833 in Warsaw, NY to ?(Bartlett) and Thomas Buckel. Educated in local schools; further public schooling nearby; Woman's Medical College of Pennsylvania (M.D., 1858); New York Infirmary for Women and Children, postgraduate study. Professional experience: Chicago, Ill., Dispensary for Women and Children, joint practice with another woman doctor (from 1859); established numerous field hospitals (1863–1864); agent for Dorothea Dix in the selection and assignment of army nurses; Jefferson General Hospital in Jeffersonville, Ind., chief of female nurses (1864–1865); Evansville, Ind., private practice (1865–1866); New England Hospital for Women and Children in Boston, assistant physician; resident physician specializing in respiratory ailments (1866–1872); New England Hospital, attending surgeon (1875–1877); Pacific Dispensary for Women and Children, Oakland, Calif., consulting physician (from 1877). Died 17 August 1912 in Piedmont, Calif., of arteriosclerosis.

Chloe Buckel's parents both died less than a year after her birth. She was raised by her grandparents until their death when she was four. Two aunts who were stern and rather cold disciplinarians took over the task of caring for the little girl. She had her primary schooling in the local district school and then went to a nearby town to complete her education. When she was fourteen, she began to teach at a local elementary school. Having resolved to study medicine when she was in her teens, she saved money for this purpose by working in a Connecticut burnishing factory. In order to pay her tuition to the Woman's Medical College of Pennsylvania, she borrowed money on her life insurance. After she earned her medical degree in 1858, she studied for a year with MARIE ZAKRZEWSKA at the New York Infirmary for Women and Children. After that year, she opened a practice with another woman physician in Chicago. During the Civil War, she volunteered her services to the governor of Indiana. She is reported to have set up six field hospitals. Shortly thereafter, she was appointed as an agent for DOROTHEA DIX in the selection and assignment of army nurses. Later in the fall of 1863, she became chief of female nurses at the Jefferson General Hospital, where she remained until 1865.

After the war, Buckel practiced for a short time in Evansville, Indiana, but the next year became a member of the staff of the New England Hospital for Women and Children in Boston headed by Zakrzewska. She was first an assistant physician and then a resident physician specializing in respiratory problems. Her health began to fail and she took a two-year leave of absence, during which time she toured Europe. While she was gone, she observed surgical techniques in hospitals in Vienna and Paris. When she returned she was appointed attending surgeon at the New England Hospital.

Buckel's health continued to deteriorate, so she moved to the San Francisco Bay area and settled in Oakland, where she opened a medical practice. She was the first woman to be admitted to the Alameda County Medical Association and was appointed a consulting physician at the Pacific Dispensary for Women and Children. Her work increasingly concentrated on problems of child welfare and health. She worked to exclude dairies with tuberculin cows from supplying milk to Oakland. Her hobbies were astronomy, music, and nature study. In her later years she founded a local Agassiz Society and created a Chautauqua circle for her friends. She moved with her friend Charlotte Playter to Piedmont, Calif., in 1906 and died there in 1912. Her generous will left her estate in trust to benefit mentally handicapped children. From this bequest, a grant to Stanford University established the Buckel Foundation research fellowship in this special area of child psychology.   JH/MBO

PRIMARY SOURCES

Some of Buckel's papers are at the California Historical Society in San Francisco.

SECONDARY SOURCES

Brown, Adelaide. "A History of the Development of Women in Medicine in California." *California and Western Medicine,* May 1925.

Mosher, Eliza M. *Medical Woman's Journal* (January 1924): 15–16.

STANDARD SOURCES

NAW (article by Joan M. Jensen).

BUCKLAND, MARY MORLAND (d. 1857)

British naturalist. Born at Sheepstead House, near Abington, Berkshire, to Benjamin Morland. Married William Buckland (1825). One son, two? daughters. Died in 1857.

Mary Morland's mother died when Mary was a baby. Her father remarried shortly thereafter, and produced a large family of half-brothers and sisters. She spent much of her childhood in Oxford, living with the physician Sir Christopher Pegge and his wife. Childless, yet loving children, the Pegges encouraged many of Mary's interests, including natural science.

In 1825 Mary married naturalist William Buckland (1784–1856). Throughout her life she helped her husband with his work, both serving as his amanuensis and illustrating specimens for his books. She also took notes on their observations. In addition to her interest in natural history, Mary Buckland was concerned with social problems. The main emphasis in her life, however, remained her home and family.

Dr. Buckland's bias against women in science makes his acceptance of his wife's help incongruous. In 1832, in a letter to Sir Roderick Murchison (1792–1871) discussing the proposed June meeting of the British Association, he remarked, "Everybody whom I spoke to on the subject agreed that, if the meeting is to be of scientific utility, ladies ought not to attend the reading of the papers . . . as it would at once turn the thing into a sort of Albemarle dilettanti-meeting, instead of a serious philosophical union of working men" (Buckland, p. 123).

It is difficult to evaluate Mary Buckland's contributions to science, since her work was so involved with that of her husband. According to her son Frank, "Not only was she a pious, amiable, and excellent helpmate to my father; but being naturally endowed with great mental powers, habits of perseverance and order, tempered by excellent judgment, she materially assisted her husband in his literary labors, and often gave them a polish which added not a little to their merits. During the long period that Dr. Buckland was engaged in writing the Bridgewater Treatise, my mother sat up night after night for weeks and months consecutively, writing to my father's dictation; and this, often till the sun's rays, shining through the shutters at early morn, warned the husband to cease from thinking, and the wife to rest her weary hand" (Buckland, p. 193).

Not only did Mary contribute illustrations to William Buckland's publications, she also added drawings to a work by geologist William Conybeare (1787–1857). MBO

SECONDARY SOURCES

Buckland, Mrs. Gordon. *The Life and Correspondence of William Buckland, D.D., F.R.S., Sometime Dean of Westminster, Twice President of the Geological Society and First President of the British Association.* New York: Appleton, 1894. Contains information on Mary Buckland.

STANDARD SOURCES

DNB (the article on William Buckland contains information about Mary); Ogilvie 1986.

BUCKLEY, ARABELLA (1840–1929)

British naturalist. Born 1840. Married Fisher. Professional experience: secretary to Charles Lyell; author of popular science books. Died 1929.

For many years toward the end of his life, Arabella Buckley served as Sir Charles Lyell's secretary. Inspired by what she learned in his employ, she decided to write popular accounts for school children. Through Lyell, she was personally acquainted with well-known scientists. Buckley was convinced that through writing on scientific subjects, she could convey ideas of morality, which she, as a woman, felt was her responsibility. Her first book, *A Short History of Natural Science* (1876), predicted that scientific knowledge not only should be a part of every person's life for its own sake, but was important in building character. Her book, she explained, would form a basis for those who wished to continue in scientific study. She continued to inspire popular readers with *The Fairy-Land of Science* (1879). In this book and its sequel, *Through Magic Glasses* (1890), she employs the language of fairy stories to reinforce her ideas about the "fairyland of science."

In other books, her favorite topic was evolution, and she narrated fascinating accounts of the struggle for survival. Charles Darwin praised her popular accounts in letters found in the Darwin project, Cambridge University Library. In her next two books, *Life and Her Children* (1881) and *Winners in Life's Race* (1883), she described sensitively invertebrate and vertebrate life groups, respectively. Buckley parts company with Darwin when she insists that vertebrates continue life for other reasons than the continuation of their species. This view contrasts with her authoritative chapter on ants, where she concludes that although ants are devoted to their community, they do not have sympathy for each other—a characteristic that she reserves for the vertebrates. To Buckley, the reason for evolution was to move toward the ideal of the vertebrates—animals that could be sympathetic and that could exhibit kindness. Barbara Gates indicates that Buckley dealt with the problem that gave Darwin so much grief in *The Descent of Man.* Darwin, while noting that competitive advantage derived from a well-developed social instinct, did not offer a satisfactory explanation for it, especially in regard to parenting. Buckley made parenting her central metaphor in *Life and Her Children* and stressed the evolutionary benefits of mutualism. Gates also notes another "modern" idea proposed by Buckley: her discussion of the life force is similar to the Gaia hypothesis proposed by Lynn Margulis and James Livelock. Buckley's last work was *Moral Teachings of Science* (1891).

It is surprising that so little work has been done on Buckley. At this point, biographical information on this fascinating woman is extremely sparse. Even biographers of Sir Charles Lyell say very little about her.   JH/MBO

PRIMARY SOURCES

Buckley, Arabella Fisher. *A Short History of Natural Science and of the Progress of Discovery from the Time of the Greeks to the Present Day. For the Use of Schools and Young Persons.* London: John Murray, Albemarle Street, 1876.

———. *Life and Her Children: Glimpses of Animal Life from the Amoeba to the Insects.* New York: D. Appleton and Company, 1881.

———. *Winners in Life's Race.* New York: Appleton and Co., 1883.

———. *The Fairy-Land of Science.* London: 1879. U.S. edition, New York: D. Appleton and Company, 1888.

———. *Through Magic Glasses.* London: E. Stanford, 1890.

SECONDARY SOURCES

Gates, Barbara T. "Revisioning Darwin with Sympathy." In *Natural Eloquence,* ed. Barbara Gates and Ann Shteir. Madison: University of Wisconsin Press, 1997. An excellent account of Buckley's work.

BUELL, MARY VAN RENSSELAER (1893–?)

U.S. biochemist. Born 14 June 1893 in Madison, Wis., to Martha (Merry) and Charles Edwin Buell. Educated University of Wisconsin (B.A., 1914; M.A., 1915; Ph.D., 1919). Professional experience: University of Illinois, assistant in general chemistry (1915–1916); University of Wisconsin, instructor (1917–1919); University of Iowa, assistant professor (1920–1921); Johns Hopkins University, school of medicine, assistant (1921–1922), associate (1922–1930); department of medicine (1930–1946); University of Wisconsin Enzyme Institute, research associate (1948–1950); Washington University, St. Louis, school of medicine (1950–

1954); University of Chicago, school of medicine (1954–1957), professor of biochemistry (1957–1960); University of Wisconsin Enzyme Institute, project associate (from 1960); Johns Hopkins Medical School, associate in medicine. Honors and memberships: Phi Beta Kappa and Sigma Xi. Death date unknown.

Mary Buell had a long professional career from the time that she got her doctorate from the University of Wisconsin until she was quite elderly, working as an associate in the Johns Hopkins University Medical School. She was an assistant professor at the University of Iowa for a year and then went to the Johns Hopkins University school of medicine, first as a research assistant and then as an associate. She worked at the Enzyme Institute at the University of Wisconsin two separate times, leaving it the last time to return to Johns Hopkins. After the first time at the Enzyme Institute, Buell went to the Washington University, St. Louis, Medical School for four years and then went to the University of Chicago, where she remained until she went to the Enzyme Institute for a second stint. Buell was a member of the American Society of Biological Chemists. She published prolifically on the chemistry of nucleic acids and nucleotides, the relation of hormones to the metabolism of carbohydrates, and the development of ultramicroscopic procedure for the analysis of enzyme activity.   JH/MBO

STANDARD SOURCES

AMS 3–8, P 9, P&B 10–11; *American Women*; Debus.

BUERK, MINERVA (SMITH) (1909–)

U.S. physician, dermatologist. Born 4 February 1909 on a farm in Brant County, Ontario, Canada, to Sarah (Russell) and William Smith. Nine siblings. Married (widowed 1936). Educated local primary school; New York State School of Nursing; University of Buffalo (B.A. in medical technology, 1941); Woman's Medical College of Pennsylvania (M.D., 1946); Detroit City Hospital, intern (1946–1948?); Johns Hopkins Hospital, fellowship in dermatology (1948–1950); board certification (1950). Professional experience: Bryn Mawr, Pennsylvania, private practice (from 1950); University of Pennsylvania, instructor and associate in dermatology; Woman's Medical College, visiting associate professor; Bryn Mawr Hospital, chief of the dermatology service. Honors and memberships: American Medical Women's Association, scholarship committee; president (1971); one of six distinguished American women invited as guests of France in their Cultural Division of Foreign Affairs; Medical Women's International Association (MWIA), national corresponding secretary for the United States (1972), vice-president for North America (1974–1976, 1976–1978); Woman's Medical College of Pennsylvania, Alumnae Association Achievement Award (1976); National Society of the Daughters of the American Revolution, the Americanism Medal (1977).

Minerva Smith Buerk was born and educated in Ontario but became a naturalized U.S. citizen. She attended a school of nursing in New York State where she met her future husband. The marriage was cut short by her husband's death when she was twenty-seven years old. At this time, she became determined to study medicine, and passed the entrance examinations for the University of Buffalo. She graduated as the first candidate with a bachelor's degree in medical technology. When she was thirty-two years old, she entered the Woman's College of Pennsylvania. Since she had to work, she could only attend medical school part time. After a series of illnesses, she was assigned a less stressful job that allowed her to attend medical school full time, and she graduated in 1946. After her internship and residency (in syphilology and dermatology at Johns Hopkins), she held a fellowship in dermatology at the hospital of the University of Pennsylvania in Philadelphia. After thirteen years of study she passed her board examinations and qualified as a certified dermatologist. She opened a private practice in Bryn Mawr, Pennsylvania, and at various times taught at the University of Pennsylvania and the Woman's Medical College. Late in her career she was appointed a consultant to the Federal Drug Administration in the United States Department of Health, Education, and Welfare for reviewing the safety of over-the-counter drugs.

Buerk had a number of hobbies, including playing the piano, collecting antiques, traveling, photography, and shell collecting. She spent free time as a volunteer in the mollusk department at the Academy of Natural Sciences of Philadelphia and was able to participate in several of its scientific expeditions to the tropics to collect living marine mollusks. She became interested in the anatomy and microanatomy of marine mollusks.   KM

PRIMARY SOURCES
Buerk, Minerva. In Hellstedt, *Autobiographies.*

BÜHLER, CHARLOTTE BERTHA (MALACHOWSKI) (1893–1974)

German/U.S. developmental psychologist. Born 20 December 1893 in Berlin, Germany, to Rose (Kristeller) (a musician) and Walter Malachowski (an architect). One younger sibling. Married Karl Bühler, psychologist (4 April 1916) (d. 1963). Two children. Educated universities of Freiburg, Kiel, Berlin (1913–1915); Munich (Ph.D., 1918). Professional experience: Dresden Institute of Technology, Privatdozent (1920–1922); Munich school board, researcher (1920–1922); Vienna Psychological Institute, lecturer (1923), associate professor (1929); Columbia University, New York, N.Y., Laura Spelman Memorial Rockefeller Fellow (1924–1925); Rockefeller-supported researcher in Vienna (1925–1935); College of St. Catherine, St. Paul, Minn., psychology faculty

(1940–1941); Clark College, Worcester, Mass., faculty; Worcester Child Guidance Clinic, psychologist (1942–1943); City College of New York, faculty; Minneapolis General Hospital, chief clinical psychologist (1943–1945); Los Angeles County Hospital, California, clinical psychologist (1945–1953); University of California Medical School, assistant clinical professor of psychiatry (1945–1959); private practice, Los Angeles (1953–1972). Died 3 February 1974 in Stuttgart, West Germany.

Charlotte Malachowski began her study of human thought processes as early as high school, completing a paper that presaged her doctoral research. Between 1913 and 1918, she attended universities in Freiburg, Kiel, Berlin, and Munich. At the University of Munich she was assigned to psychology professor Karl Bühler, whose work she had admired previously. They were married in 1916, producing their first child, Ingeborg, in 1917, the year before Charlotte Bühler received her doctorate. Their son, Rolf, was born in 1919. The family moved to Vienna in 1923 where Karl Bühler had an appointment at the university. Charlotte Bühler was employed at the Vienna Psychological Institute, as lecturer (1923) then as associate professor (1929). During those years, she made her first trip to the United States, attending Columbia University on a Laura Spelman Rockefeller Fellowship (1924–1925). Back in Vienna she continued her research on infant development with her collaborator HILDEGARD HETZER. Together they devised the Bühler-Hetzer tests of infant development, which were standardized (1932) and used to quantify six sectors of personality development and maturation. During her years in Vienna, she was guest professor at Barnard College, Columbia University (1929), and consultant at child guidance centers in England, Holland, and Norway. Her research in Vienna was partially supported by a ten-year grant from the Rockefeller Foundation. She was in England when Nazis invaded Vienna in 1938. A vocal anti-Nazi, Karl Bühler was imprisoned, but Charlotte Bühler successfully negotiated her husband's release and transport to Norway where they lived for the next two years. They moved to the United States in 1940.

Bühler's first appointment in the United States was at the College of St. Catherine in St. Paul, Minnesota, as a member of the faculty of psychology. She soon transferred to Minneapolis General Hospital as chief clinical psychologist (1943–1945). Displaced and uncomfortable, the Bühlers searched for a place they could feel at home and resume their research and publication. They moved to California in 1945 and Charlotte Bühler took a position at Los Angeles County Hospital, where she stayed as chief clinical psychologist until 1953. She also affiliated with the University of Southern California Medical School as assistant professor of clinical psychiatry.

Charlotte Bühler became one of the early leaders in humanistic and life-span developmental psychology, developing techniques based on observation and naturalism (rather than on experiment) for investigating the human person as a continually developing totality. She developed the Life Goal Inventory coding system for personality characteristics. She conducted a private practice in Los Angeles between 1953 and 1972, returning to Germany in 1970 because of illness. She was one of the organizers, with Abraham Maslow and Carl Rogers, of the American Association for Humanistic Psychology, and chaired the First International Conference on Humanistic Psychology (Amsterdam, 1970). Her husband died in 1963 as the humanistic psychology movement was beginning.   KM

PRIMARY SOURCES

Bühler, C. *Das Seelenleben des Jugendlichen (Psychology of Adolescence)*. Jena: Gustav Fischer, 1922.

———. *Soziologische und psychologische Studien über das erste Lebensjahre*. 1927.

———. *Personality Types Based on Experiments with Children*. Report of Ninth International Congress of Psychology. New Haven, Conn., 1930.

———. *Der menschliche Lebenslauf als psychologisches Problem*. Leipzig: Hirzel, 1933.

———. *From Birth to Maturity*. London: Kegan Paul, Trench, & Trubner, 1935.

———. *The Child and His Family*. trans. by H. Beaumont. London: Kegan Paul, Trench, & Trubner, 1940.

———. *The Course of Human Life: A Study of Goals in the Humanistic Perspective*. ed. with F. Massarik. New York: Springer, 1968.

———. *Values in Psychotherapy*. New York: Free Press of Glencoe, 1962.

———. With M. Allen. *Introduction to Humanistic Psychology*. Belmont, Calif.: Brooks Cole, 1972.

STANDARD SOURCES

AMS S&B 9–12; *NAW*(M) (article by Melanie Allen); *Notable*; O'Connell and Russo 1990.

BÜLBRING, EDITH (1903–1990)

German/British physiologist. Born 27 December 1903 in Bonn, Germany. Educated Bonn schools; Bonn University (M.D.); Berlin University, postgraduate pharmacology (1929–1931). Professional experience: Jena, pediatrician (1932); Virchow Krankenhaus, research assistant and clinician (1933); Pharmaceutical Society of Great Britain, University of London, Pharmacological Laboratory (1933–1938). Department of Pharmacology, Oxford University (departmental demonstrator from 1946) (1938–1971), university reader (1960–1967), professor of pharmacology (1961–1967), emerita professor (1971–1990). Fellow Royal Society (1958), and

many international societies. Honors and memberships: University of Gröningen, Netherlands, honorary M.D. (1979); University of Leuwen, Belgium (1981); University of Homburg Saar, Germany; Wellcome Gold Medal Pharmacology (1985). Died July 1990.

As a young woman, Edith Bülbring was proficient in languages and music, encouraged by her father, who was professor of English at Bonn University. Bülbring left Germany at the rise of Hitler; she was dismissed from the university because her mother was Jewish. She went first to Holland and then to Britain. There she first worked with J. H. Burn in the laboratories of the Pharmaceutical Society and accompanied him on his move to Oxford. She went to the United States on a Rockefeller fellowship to Johns Hopkins, then returned to Oxford to work in the department of pharmacology, becoming university reader in 1960, professor of pharmacology in 1961, and finally professor emerita. Bülbring became a Fellow of the Royal Society in 1958 and was awarded many honorary degrees throughout Europe. She was first to record electrical activity of smooth muscle, in intestines, stomach, and uterus. By using micro-electrodes she showed that tension within muscle tissue is proportionate to frequency of discharge of action potential. In the 1960s, she demonstrated that smooth muscle action potential was due to the influence of calcium ions, while action potential of skeletal and cardiac muscle was due to sodium ions. A considerable number of international scientists did their postdoctoral training with her. She died in Oxford, July 1990.   JH

SECONDARY SOURCES

Women Physiologists: An Anniversary Celebration. Eds. Lynn Bindman, Alison Brading, Tilli Tansey. Chapel Hill, N.C.: Portland Press, 1993.

Biographical Memoirs of Fellows of the Royal Society. London: Royal Society, 1992.

STANDARD SOURCES

Annual Obituary, 1990.

BULL, NINA WILCOX (1880–?)

U.S. psychologist. Born 4 November 1880 in Buffalo, N.Y. Married (1901). Three children. Professional experience: Brain Research Foundation, Inc., president (1930–1940); Columbia University College of Physicians and Surgeons, associate in psychiatry (1940–1950); Psychiatric Institute, project to study motor attitudes (1950–1960); personal research and writing (from 1960).

Nina Bull, a psychologist who specialized in the attitude theory of emotion, was married and had three children. She was a Fellow of the New York Academy of Sciences and a member of the AAAS and the APA. She did research on body-mind relation in emotion, the role of motor attitude in emotion and purpose, and goal-oriented attitudes and their breakdown. She believed that this breakdown led to a complex of frustration and depression and served as the physiological basis of resentful feelings and pride. JH/MBO

PRIMARY SOURCES

Bull, Nina W. *The Body and Its Mind: An Introduction to Attitude Psychology.* New York: Las Americas, 1962.

———. *Attitude Theory of Emotion.* Nervous and Mental Disease Monograph, 1951, and Johnson reprint, 1968.

Numerous journal articles.

STANDARD SOURCES

AMS S&B 10–11; Debus.

BUNCH, CORDIA (1885–1942)

U.S. otologist/psychologist. Born 30 April 1885 in Tama County, Ia. Educated Iowa State Teachers College (A.B., 1916); State University of Iowa (A.M., 1917; Ph.D., 1920). Professional experience: State University of Iowa, Psychology-Otology, assistant (1917–1924), associate professor of otolaryngology (1924–1927); Johns Hopkins Medical School, associate professor of research otology (1927–1930); Washington University Medical School, professor of applied physics of otology, head of physics division (1930–1942). Died 1942.

Cordia Bunch was born in Iowa and educated at Iowa State Teachers College, where she received her bachelor's degree. Her higher degrees were from the University of Iowa. While she was working on her dissertation, she served first as an assistant in psychology-otology and then became associate professor in 1924. She was appointed to the Johns Hopkins Medical School, where she held a three-year appointment in research otology. She then moved to the Washington University Medical School where she held a professorship in the applied physics of otology until her death in 1942. She wrote numerous articles on audition, auditory testing, hearing acuity, and disease processes. JH/MBO

PRIMARY SOURCES

Bunch, Cordia C. *Clinical Audiometry.* St. Louis: C.V. Mosby, 1943. With seventy-four illustrations.

STANDARD SOURCES

AMS 4–6; *Psychological Register,* vol. 2

BUNTING, MARTHA (1861–1944)

U.S. plant and aquatic biologist. Educated Swarthmore College (B.L., 1881); University of Pennsylvania (B.S., 1890); Bryn Mawr College (Ph.D., 1895); Columbia University (postdoctorate, 1898–1899). Professional experience: Goucher College, instructor in biology (1893–1897); high school teacher (1897–1898, 1900–1910); University of Pennsylvania, research assistant (1910–1916, 1918–1919). Honors and memberships: University of Pennsylvania, honorary Fellow (1919–1924, 1926–1927, 1920–1931); Academy of Natural Sciences of Philadelphia, member. Died 1944.

Martha Bunting was one of those well-educated women who spent the majority of her professional career teaching high school after she received her doctorate. She worked for a short time as an instructor of biology at Goucher College and later worked as a research assistant at the University of Pennsylvania. Her lack of professional recognition did not keep her from interesting research; during this time she conducted research on photozoology, sex cells in *Hydractinia,* and Podocoryne. She also studied otoliths, the geotropic functions of *Astacus,* and the life cycle of *Tetramitus rostratus.* She was recognized as an important member of the community of biologists, for she was elected a member of the Academy of Natural Sciences of Philadelphia. JH/MBO

PRIMARY SOURCES

Bunting, Martha. The Origin of Sex Cells in Hydractinia and Podocoryne, and the Development of Hydractinia. *Journal of Morphology* 9 (1894): 203–232.

SECONDARY SOURCES

Harshberger, John W. *The Botanists of Philadelphia and Their Work.* Philadelphia: Press of T. C. Davis & Son, 1899.

STANDARD SOURCES

AMS 1–7; Bailey; Siegel and Finley; *WWW(A).*

BUNTING-SMITH, MARY (INGRAHAM) (1910–1998)

U.S. microbiologist and Radcliffe College president. Born 1910 in Brooklyn to Mary (Shotwell) and Henry A. Ingraham. Married (1) Henry Bunting, 1937 (d. 1954); (2) Dr. Clement A. Smith, 1979 (d. 1988). Three sons, one daughter. Educated Packer Collegiate Institute; Vassar College (A.B. in physics, 1931); University of Wisconsin, (M.A., 1932; Ph.D., 1934). Professional experience: Bennington College, assistant professor (1934–1935); Goucher College, lecturer in physiology and hygiene (1935–1937); Yale University Medical School, part-time research assistant (1937–1940), full-time research assistant (1947–1952), lecturer (1952–1954); Wellesley College, lecturer (1946–1947); Douglass College (Rutgers University), dean of women (1955–1959); Rutgers University, professor of bacteriology (1954–1959) (concurrent); Radcliffe College (Harvard University), president (1959–1972);

Princeton University, special assistant to president (1972–1975). Honors and memberships: National Science Foundation, Committee for Scientific Personnel and Education (1957–1959); Phi Beta Kappa; American Academy of Arts and Sciences, vice-president (1963). Society of American Bacteriologists. Died 21 January 1998 in Hanover, New Hampshire.

Mary Ingraham Bunting-Smith, known as Polly throughout her life, can be said to have had two major careers as a microbiologist and as the president of Radcliffe College. In her second role she made a significant difference in the life of postgraduate women, enabling them to return to further their professional lives in both the liberal arts and sciences through her establishment of the Radcliffe Institute for Independent Study (now the Bunting Institute).

Polly Ingraham was born in Brooklyn, to energetic parents who were both involved in community affairs. Her mother was president of the Brooklyn YMCA and on the New York Board of Higher Education. Her father, a lawyer, was a founder of the Long Island College of Medicine. As a child, Ingraham's ill health kept her from regular attendance at school, but after high school, she became interested in science. She attended Vassar College (her mother's college) where she majored in physics. She soon changed her interest to bacteriology, and, on receipt of a Vassar scholarship, went to the University of Wisconsin to pursue first a master's and then a doctorate in agricultural bacteriology and agricultural chemistry. There she met her future husband, Henry Bunting, who was training as a physician. During his internship and then residency, Ingraham lectured at Bennington College and then Goucher College, teaching physiology and hygiene while her fiancé finished his studies at Johns Hopkins Medical School.

Following her wedding in 1937, she accompanied her husband to Connecticut, where he had a position on the faculty of Yale School of Medicine. For some years, she continued her research in a part-time position as research assistant, studying the genetic effects of ultraviolet light and radiation on color mutations in the bacterium *Serratia marcescens*. During World War II, her four children began to absorb her time and energy, but she still found time to serve as a 4-H leader, and sit on library and school boards. She also contributed her expertise in bacteriology to organizing and directing the Public Health Nursing Association. In the year following the war, she accompanied her husband to the Boston area where he had a visiting appointment at Harvard, and she taught part-time at Wellesley College. On return to New Haven, she began to work in the laboratory as a full-time research assistant and then as a lecturer. During this period, her research was funded by the Atomic Energy Commission.

Her husband's early death from a brain tumor in 1954 left her in need of a job that could provide for her family. With the help of a former Vassar classmate, married to the then president of Rutgers University, she obtained a position as dean of women at Douglass College (the women's college of Rutgers University). There she began to explore the problem of married women scholars keen to reenter the workplace as academics and scientists following their child-raising years. Bunting soon became a leader in the movement for "continuing education."

While serving on the Committee for Scientific Personnel and Education at the National Science Foundation in 1957, she found to her surprise that the figures on the top-ranking women students graduating from high school indicated that 97 to 99 percent did not continue on to college. Even more astonishing was the suppression of this figure by the NSF. This experience brought home to her the negative expectation regarding women's contributions to science, or to any intellectual endeavor. The pressure from the Sputnik alarm in the government made it a priority to train more women in science and education, but as Margaret Rossiter points out, the attitudes of both foundations and scientific or academic employers toward the hiring of women scientists was still hostile.

When Bunting was appointed president of Radcliffe College in 1959, she began to work toward the full acceptance of women in the life of Harvard University and toward the establishment of a new institute for returning women scholars that would include as well both artists and scientists. The Radcliffe Institute for Independent Study, opened in 1961, also focused on the study of both psychological and cultural factors that affected women's status in society. During the late sixties, Bunting dealt with protests from minority women when twenty black women students staged a sit-in, demanding greater representation in the student body.

After thirteen important years as president, Bunting left Radcliffe College at the age of sixty-two. For three subsequent years, she worked as special assistant to William Bowen, president of Princeton University, developing a plan for coeducation there. Although she continued to be called upon for her advice during her retirement years, she ceased to be the vocal presence she had been during the sixties. In 1979, she married a Harvard Medical School pediatrician, Clement A. Smith, and became close to his four children. Following his death in 1988, she spent her final years in a continuing care community, Kendal, in Hanover, New Hampshire. JH/MBO

PRIMARY SOURCES

"Mary Ingraham Bunting, Oral Memoir." Recorded by Jeannette Bailey Cheek, September–October 1978. Schlesinger Library, Radcliffe College.

Bunting, Mary Ingraham. "From *Serratia* to Women's Lib and a Bit Beyond." *American Society of Microbiology News (ASM News)* 37, no. 3 (1971): 46–52.

SECONDARY SOURCES

Arenson, Karen W. "Mary Ingraham Bunting-Smith, Ex President of Radcliffe, Dies at 87." *New York Times,* 23 January 1998. Obituary notice with portrait.

"One Woman, Two Lives." *Time Magazine* 78, no. 3 (November 1961): 68–73. Cover story, with portrait.

STANDARD SOURCES

AMS 6–8, B 9, P&B 10–14; *Current Biography* 1967; Debus; Rossiter 1995.

BUNZEL, RUTH LEAH (1898–1990)

U.S. anthropologist. Born 1898 in New York City to Hattie (Bernheim) and Jonas Bunzel. Educated New York City public schools; Columbia University (A.B., 1918; Ph.D., 1927). Professional experience: U.S. Office of War Information, England (1941–1945); Columbia University, Department of Anthropology, instructor (1946–1954), adjunct professor (1954–1972). Died 14 January 1990 in New York City.

Bunzel began her career as a secretary to Franz Boas, following another woman anthropologist, ESTHER GOLDFRANK, in that position. She then began to do graduate work with Boas and the many women anthropologists around him. For her field work, she went to the American Southwest with RUTH BENEDICT in the summer of 1924, and returned alone for four more consecutive summers to study pottery making and ritual at Zuni. Some of her subsequent trips were funded by the anthropologist ELSIE CLEWS PARSONS, who shared her interest in the Southwest.

Bunzel wrote her dissertation on the pueblo potter, and received her degree from Columbia University in 1927. One part of this study was published two years later as *The Pueblo Potter* (1929), and remains a classic in the field, combining art with observations on the psychology of the potter. This was followed by the publication of her studies of Zuni ceremonialism in a series of Bureau of American Ethnology monographs in 1932. She went to Chiapas, Mexico, and to highland Guatemala where she made an ethnographic study of small village life in the two cultures, supported by a Guggenheim grant (1930–1932). Only one part of this study, examining alcoholism in the two cultures, was published before World War II. Intrigued by Spanish culture, she went to Spain in the early 1930s, and was caught up in the Spanish Civil War. During the war she worked for the Office of War Information, while based in England, translating Spanish broadcasts.

Bunzel returned to the United States after the war and taught at Columbia. She was appointed adjunct professor in 1954, remaining at Columbia until her retirement in 1972. From 1946 to 1954 she participated in the Research in Contemporary Cultures Project at Columbia, funded by the Office of Naval Research under the directorship of Ruth Benedict. Bunzel became the director in 1954. She finally published a book on her many years of research on Guatemala in 1952. She also published a retrospective collection of classic anthropological articles with MARGARET MEAD. Her work was the first to combine a study of the creative arts with anthropological and psychological techniques.

JH/MBO

PRIMARY SOURCES

Bunzel, Ruth L. *The Pueblo Potter.* New York: Columbia University Press, 1929.

———. "Introduction: Zuni Ceremonialism." *Bureau of American Ethnology (BAE) Annual Report* 47 (1932): 467–544.

———. "Zuni Origin Myths." *Bureau of American Ethnology (BAE) Annual Report* 47 (1932): 545–609.

———. "Zuni Ritual Poetry." *Bureau of American Ethnology (BAE) Annual Report* 47 (1932): 611–835.

———. "The Nature of Katsinas." *Bureau of American Ethnology (BAE) Annual Report* 47 (1932): 837–1006. (Reprinted in *Reader in Comparative Religion.* Ed. A.W. Lessa and E.V. Vogt, 1958: 401–404.

———. *Chichicastenango: A Guatemalan Village.* Locust Valley, N.Y.: J. J. Augustin, 1952.

———. *Zuni Texts.* New York: G. E. Steichert, 1958.

———. "The Role of Alcoholism in Two Central American Cultures." *Psychiatry* 3: 361–387.

———. With Margaret Mead. *The Golden Age of American Anthropology.* New York: George Braziler, 1960.

SECONDARY SOURCES

"Ruth Leah Bunzel." *Anthropology Newsletter* 31, no. 4 (1990): 5. Obituary notice.

Babcock, Barbara, and Nancy J. Parezo. "Ruth Bunzel." In *Daughters of the Desert.* Tucson, Ariz.: University of New Mexico Press, 1988.

Fawcett, David M., and Teri McLuhan. "Ruth Leah Bunzel." In Ute Gacs et al., 28–36.

STANDARD SOURCES

IDA.

BURGES, MARY ANNE (1763–1813)

British naturalist. Born 6 December 1763 in Edinburgh to the Hon. Anne Whichnour Somerville and George Burges. Educated privately. Professional experience: writing; geology; botany. Died 10 August 1813 at Ashfield, near Honiton.

Mary Anne Burges was an accomplished eighteenth-century woman, who knew Greek, Latin, French, Italian, and Spanish, as well as some Swedish and German. She was knowledgeable in geology and was a friend of French geologist, Jean André De Luc. She contributed to his last publication, *Histoire du Passage des Alpes par Annibal.* She was also proficient in botany; although it apparently was never published, she prepared an exhaustive account of British Lepidoptera. Burges was typical of the "learned lady" of her period. She, however, is best known for a book that she wrote extending John Bunyan's *Pilgrim's Progress.* This book went through three editions in 1800, four more in 1801, plus several editions in Dublin and in the United States.   JH/MBO

PRIMARY SOURCES
[Burges, Mary Anne]. *The Progress of the Pilgrim Good Intent.* New Haven, Conn.: William W. Morse, 1802.

STANDARD SOURCES
DNB.

BURGESS, MAY (AYRES) (1885–1953)

U.S. mathematician. Born 17 May 1888 in Newton Highlands, Mass., to Georgiana (Gall) and Milan Church Ayres. Married W. Randolph Burgess (17 May 1917). Two sons, Leonard Randolph (b. 1919) and Julian Ayres (b. 1921). Educated Normal School, University of Puerto Rico; Oberlin, Ohio; Simmons College (B.S., 1911); Columbia University (Ph.D., 1920); University of Pennsylvania, special graduate work; Teachers College, Columbia, Dodge Fellow. Professional experience: Russell Sage Foundation, Division of Education, statistician; University of Pennsylvania, psychological clinic; U.S. Food Administration; war department, general staff, statistics branch; education and health research.

May Ayres Burgess was a statistician who did educational research. She married the vice-president of the New York Federal Reserve Bank and the couple had two sons. The dates of her various positions are not known, but most of her work involved applying statistical techniques to such areas as grading of nursing schools, working with department of education statistics, and applying her mathematical skills to practical problems in educational and health needs. Her hobbies were sewing, reading, and music.   JH/MBO

PRIMARY SOURCES
Burgess, May Ayres. With L. P. Ayres. *Health Work in the Public Schools.* Cleveland: Survey Committee of the Cleveland Foundation, 1915.
———. *Healthful Schools—How to Build, Equip and Maintain Them.* Boston: Houghton Mifflin, 1918.
———. *The Measurement of Silent Reading.* New York: Department of Education, 1921.
———. *Nurses, Patients, and Pocketbooks.* New York, 1928.

———. *Results of the First Grading Study of Nursing Schools.* New York, 1930–1931.
———. *Results of Second Grading Study of Nursing Schools in the U.S.* New York, 1933.
———. *Nursing Schools Today and Tomorrow.* New York, 1934. The final report of the Committee on Grading of Nursing Schools.

STANDARD SOURCES
American Women; Grinstein and Campbell; *WWW(A).*

BURKILL, ETHEL MAUD (MORRISON) (1874–1956)

British botanical collector, illustrator. Born 28 February 1874 in Wakefield, Yorkshire. Married Isaac Henry Burkill. Died 1956.

Ethel Maud Burkill collected plants from Calcutta in 1911, while her husband, the botanist Isaac Henry Burkill (1870–1965), held a position at the Indian Museum in Calcutta. Isaac Burkill published prolifically, while Ethel Burkill collected on the Malay peninsula (1912) and Sumatra (1921). When he became director of the botanic gardens in Singapore, she made collections and drew fungi for the botanic gardens.   JH/MBO

PRIMARY SOURCES
Specimens and illustrations in Royal Botanic Gardens, Kew.

STANDARD SOURCES
Desmond.

BURLIN, NATALIE CURTIS (1875–1921)
See Curtis, Natalie.

BURLINGHAM, DOROTHY (TIFFANY) (1891–1979)

U.S./British child psychoanalyst. Born 1891. Married, then divorced. Four children. Educated Psychoanalytic Institute, Vienna (from 1925). Professional experience: Psychoanalytic Institute, Vienna, child analyst; Hampstead Wartime Nursery for Homeless Children, London (later Hampstead Child Therapy Clinic), cofounder and codirector. Died 1979.

Dorothy Burlingham was ANNA FREUD's closest friend and constant companion after Sigmund Freud died. The youngest daughter of glass millionaire Louis Comfort Tiffany, she was brought up in an affluent but not particularly happy home. Her mother Louise, Tiffany's second wife, was a vivacious feminist and intellectual who died when Dorothy was twelve. Her father was eccentric, autocratic, and alcoholic; Dorothy felt frightened and alienated by him, and by her half siblings. Next to her in age were beautiful twins, talented and self-absorbed. It was through the influence of her mother's friend, Julia de Forest, that Dorothy was sent (against her father's wishes) to a private boarding school for a good education.

In 1914, Dorothy Tiffany married Robert Burlingham and within ten months bore their first son, Bob. Three more children followed, in spite of the fact that Robert Burlingham's sequence of violent nervous breakdowns quickly brought on such fear and apprehension over the mental stability of her children that Dorothy left him on several occasions. Under the strain of her disintegrating marriage and obsessive concern for the children, Burlingham fled to Vienna in 1925. She purposefully sought out Anna Freud, whose work she knew, for psychoanalytic help for herself and the older children.

Anna Freud accepted young Bob Burlingham into analysis and referred Dorothy to Theodor Reik. The two women quickly bonded in a friendship that soon included Sigmund Freud. When her analysis with Reik faltered in 1927, Burlingham was accepted into an analysis by Sigmund Freud, which continued for twelve years. She became an early and loyal member of the Vienna child analysis school; she audited Anna Freud's lectures on child analysis (1926–1927), presented a paper to the Vienna Society in order to become an Associate Member in 1932, and became a highly proficient and intuitive child analyst. Her husband, Robert, who during his lucid periods was loving and devoted to his children and tormented by the divorce, committed suicide in May 1938.

One month later, following the Anschluss, Anna and Sigmund Freud emigrated to London; Burlingham went with them. Sigmund Freud died less than four months after the move, so Anna Freud and Dorothy Burlingham established a residence and basically a marriage, in which they co-mothered Burlingham's children and began their work to institute a child care and research center. The Hampstead Wartime Nursery for Homeless Children served as a home for children evacuated from residences during the bombing of London and as a child research laboratory. Burlingham was partner and analyst, contributing especially to techniques with blind children. She wrote several books with Freud: *Young Children in War-Time* (1942), *War and Children* (1943), and *Infants Without Families* (1944). The postwar Hampstead Child Therapy Clinic was the descendant of the Hampstead nurseries and produced the next generation of Freudian trained analysts. JH/MBO

PRIMARY SOURCES
Burlingham, Dorothy. With Anna Freud. *War and Children.* New York: Medical War Books, 1943.

———. *Infants without Families.* New York: Medical War Books, 1944.
———. *Psychoanalytic Studies of the Sighted and the Blind.* New York: International Universities Press, 1972.

SECONDARY SOURCES
Burlingham, Michael John. *The Last Tiffany: A Biography of Dorothy Tiffany Burlingham.* New York: Atheneum, 1989.
Young-Bruehl, E. *Anna Freud: A Biography.* London: Macmillan, 1989.

STANDARD SOURCES
O'Connell and Russo 1983.

BURLINGHAM, GERTRUDE SIMMONS (1872–1952)

U.S. mycologist. Born 21 April 1872 in Mexico, New York. Educated Syracuse University (A.B.); Columbia University (Ph.D., 1908). Professional experience: Eastern District High School, Brooklyn, N.Y., biology teacher (to 1934); New York Botanical Gardens, independent researcher (1907–1945). Died 11 January 1952 in Winter Park, Fla. (Stafleu reports instead that she died at Syracuse University).

Gertrude Simmons Burlingham was educated at Syracuse University, where she received her bachelor's degree. She went on to take a doctorate at Columbia in 1908, but continued to teach biology at Eastern District High School throughout her career. She summered in Vermont (Newfane Hill, built in 1913), but went along the coast in Massachusetts collecting specimens of *Russula* and *Lactaria*. She also traveled to the Pacific Coast to collect *Lactariae*. She worked on the material collected in summers, using the herbarium at the New York Botanical Garden. She retired to Florida in 1934, but continued to work on plants she collected there. Her extensive publications from 1907 until 1945 were on new and noteworthy species of *Russulae* and *Lactariae* (her major interest). Her extensive collections of these plants were left to the New York Botanical Garden. JH/MBO

PRIMARY SOURCES
Burlingham, Gertrude. "A Study of Lactariae of the U.S." *Memoirs of the Torrey Botanical Club,* 14 (1908): 1–109.
———. "The Lactariae of the Pacific Coast." *Mycologia* 5 (1913): 305–311.
———. "New or Noteworthy Species of *Russula* and *Lactaria*." *Mycologia* 28 (1936): 263–267.
———. "New Species of *Russula* from Massachusetts." *Mycologia* 10 (1918): 93–96.
———. With Henry Curtis Beardslee. "Interesting Species of *Lactariae* from Florida." *Mycologia* 32 (1940): 575–586.

Collections of *Russulae* and *Lactariae* to New York Botanical Garden.

SECONDARY SOURCES
Seaver, Fred. "Gertrude Simmons Burlingham, 1872–1952." *Mycologia* 45 (1953): 136–138. Obituary notice, with portrait.

BURNS, ELEANOR IRENE (1883–1952)

U.S. physicist and meteorologist. Born 16 July 1883 in Philadelphia, Pa., to Mary Lucretia (Harvey) and Charles Edward Burns. Educated Philadelphia Normal School; Cornell University (A.B., 1904); Lafayette College (honorary Sc.D., 1914). Professional experience: Wellesley College, instructor of physics (1905–1908); Istanbul American College for Girls, professor (1908–1924), dean (from 1924).

As did ALICE BORING, Eleanor Irene Burns chose to pursue her career outside of the United States after an initial position at a woman's college. Her situation, however, differed from Boring's, as she did not have a doctoral degree. After sixteen years as professor, she became dean at the Istanbul American College. She was a member of the Genetics Society of America and the Academy for Political Science. She researched past and present meteorological conditions of Constantinople and the west coast of Asia Minor. She was also involved in adult education in Turkey and in the modern Turkish educational program. Burns was the recipient of a Simon Muhr Scholarship and a member of Sigma Xi.

JH/MBO

SECONDARY SOURCES
New York Times, 2 February 1952. Obituary notice.
School and Society 75 (1952): 93. Obituary notice.

STANDARD SOURCES
AMS 2–8; *American Women*; Rossiter 1982.

BURNS, LOUISA (1869–1958)

U.S. osteopathic physician. Born 18 March 1869 in Saltiloville, Ind., to Mary Lois (Littell) and William Nathan Burns. Educated Borden Institute (B.S., 1891; M.S., 1906); Pacific College of Osteopathy (D.O., 1903; Sc.D., 1906). Professional experience: Pacific College of Osteology, faculty of physiology (1906–1914); Still Research Institute, head (1914–1936); Louisa Burns Osteopathic Research Institute, head (1936–1957). Died 19 January 1958 in Whittier, Calif.

Louisa Burns was an osteopath who received her degree from the Pacific College of Osteopathy in 1903. Three years later, she earned a doctoral degree. Her research was on the physiological and anatomical effects of structural abnormalities in animals and humans. She also worked on vertebral strains and their effects, articular sprains, fibrinolysis and fibrin studies of the blood, and apthogenesis of viscera affected by vertebral lesions. She received the Distinguished Service Certificate of the American Osteopathic Association in 1929, and was a member of this association and the American Association for the Advancement of Science. JH/MBO

PRIMARY SOURCES
Burns, Louisa. *Basic Principles*. Los Angeles: Occident Printery, 1907.
————. *The Nerve Centers*. Cincinnati: Monfort & Co., 1911.
————. *The Physiology of Consciousness*. Cincinnati: Monfort & Co., 1911.
————. *Cells of the Blood*. Los Angeles: A. T. Still Research Institute, 1931.

STANDARD SOURCES
AMS 6–8; B 9; *American Women*; Debus addendum.

BURR, EMILY THORP (1880–?)

U.S. industrial psychologist. Born 1880. Educated Cornell University (1912–1913); Barnard College (A.M., Ph.D., 1922). Professional experience: Post-Graduate Hospital, psychologist (1909–1912); New York Department of Public Welfare, clinical psychologist (1911–1913); Bellevue Hospital, clinical psychologist (1913–1922); Cornell Medical School, assistant neuropathologist (1914–1922); Vocational Adjustment Bureau, assistant neuropathologist (from 1923), director, psychologist. Honors and memberships: American Psychological Association, American Association for the Advancement of Science, Association of Consulting Psychologists, Vocational Guidance Association, American Vocational Guidance Association, American Vocational Association.

Industrial psychologist and neuropathologist, Emily Burr began her education at Cornell University and continued at Barnard College where she received a master's and a doctoral degree. She began her professional career at the New York Department of Public Welfare. She then moved to the Cornell University Medical School, where she was an assistant neuropathologist. After eight years in this position, she moved to the Vocational Adjustment Bureau, where she was an assistant neuropathologist and later advanced to director and psychologist. She was a member of several professional organizations.

Her research consisted of producing articles on testing and training the "feebleminded" for jobs in industry. KM

STANDARD SOURCES
AMS S&B 10.

BURRELL, ANNA PORTER (b. ca. 1902)
U.S. psychologist and human relations specialist. Born in Knoxville, Tenn. Educated University of Pennsylvania (B.S., 1923; M.S., 1926); Columbia University (1939–1941); New York University (Ph.D., 1949). Professional experience: Lincoln, Missouri, instructor (1923–1925); Howard Medical School, instructor of bacteriology (1926–1929); New York City high schools, teacher (1930–1948); State University of New York, Buffalo, professor of psychology, education, and human resources (from 1948); India, Fulbright Professor (1959–1960); human relations workshops, director of workshops and lecturer (summers 1949, 1952, 1959, 1961); Rutgers University, human relations workshops, director (1955–1956); State of New York, Board of Education, consultant (1945–1948).

Born in Knoxville, Tennessee, psychologist and human relations specialist Anna Burrell was educated at the University of Pennsylvania, Columbia University, and New York University. After receiving her bachelor's degree from Pennsylvania, she was an instructor in Lincoln, Missouri, followed by a position as an instructor of bacteriology at Howard University. She then served as a high school teacher in New York for eighteen years, during which time she was working on her doctorate at New York University. After receiving this degree (1948), she became professor of psychology at the University of New York, Buffalo, a position that she held until retirement. Burrell also sat on the Board of Education for New York State, and was a consultant for other cities' boards of education. She ran numerous human relations workshops, directed many projects, and was a member of the President's Committee on Civil Rights (1958–1961). From 1964 she was a member of the College Committee on the Disadvantaged. Much of her research involved the study of social issues from the standpoint of social psychology.

JH/MBO

PRIMARY SOURCES
Burrell, Anna. *Do's and Don'ts of the Needs Theory.* Bronxville, N.Y.: Modern Education Service, 1951.
———. With Louis Edward Raths. *Understanding the Problem Child.* West Orange, N.J.: Economics Press, 1963.

STANDARD SOURCES
AMS S&B 10–12.

BURTON, HELEN MARIE ROUSSEAY (KANNEMEYER) (1878–1973)
South African patron of botany, botanical collector. Born in Burgerdorp, Cape Province. Married Henry Burton, K.C. Died 1973 in Cape Town, South Africa.

Helen Marie Rousseay Kannemeyer was married to the Honorable Henry Burton, who became minister of railways in an early South African parliament. She negotiated with leading politicians to establish Kirstenbosch as a national botanic garden. She was a founding member of the Botanical Society of South Africa. She is commemorated in *Oxalis burtoniae* Salter.

JH/MBO

SECONDARY SOURCES
Louis, Thomas Henry. *Women of South Africa.* Cape Town: Le Quesne and Hooten-Smith, 1913: 49.
Rand Daily Mail, 4 (1916): 5.

STANDARD SOURCES
Gunn and Codd.

BURTT DAVY, ALICE (BOLTON) (1863–1953)
U.S./British botanical illustrator. Born 1863 in California. Married Joseph Burtt Davy (1896?). Died Haywards Heath, Sussex, 1953.

Alice Bolton met her future husband, Joseph Burtt Davy, while he was lecturing on botany at the University of California from 1893 to 1896. After he worked for some years for the United States Department of Agriculture, they moved to South Africa in 1903. She illustrated his *Manual of Flowering Plants and Ferns of Transvaal* (1920–1932). They returned to England upon his appointment as lecturer in Tropical Forestry and Botany at Oxford in 1925. She died in Sussex in 1953.

JH/MBO

PRIMARY SOURCES
Burtt Davy, Joseph. *Manual of Flowering Plants and Ferns of Transvaal with Swaziland.* London: Longman's, Green, and Co., 1926. Illustrated by Alice Burtt Davy and W. E. Trevithick.

STANDARD SOURCES
Gunn and Codd.

BURY, ELIZABETH (LAWRENCE) (1644–1720)
British feminist scholar and physician. Born March 1644 in the county of Suffolk, England, to Elizabeth Cutts and Captain Adams Lawrence of Lynton. Educated informally. Married (1) Griffith Lloyd of Hemmingford Grey in Huntingdonshire (1 February 1667; widowed 1682); (2) Samuel Bury, a minister (29 May 1697). Died 11 May 1720 after a brief illness.

Elizabeth Lawrence was a scholar and physician renowned and loved for her intelligence, piety, and charity. She was born in March 1644, in the county of Suffolk, England, to Captain Adams Lawrence of Lynton and Elizabeth Cutts, who apparently encouraged her desire to learn. Of quick and inquisitive mind and prodigious memory, she sought knowledge from whomever would teach her. She was interested in everything from philosophy to music, religion, and history. She learned French, which she used especially in conversing with French refugees to whom she was a benefactress; Latin, for translating the classics; and Hebrew, which she perfected to the point of translating scriptures from the original and writing commentaries on the language. Of fragile health herself, she soon turned to the study of anatomy and medicine, becoming so knowledgeable about anatomy and the *materia medica* that Ballard states "in [medicine] she improved so much, that many of the greatest masters of the faculty have been often startled, by her stating the most nice and difficult cases, in such proper terms, as could have been expected only from men of their own profession."

Her first marriage was to Griffith Lloyd of Hemmingford Grey in Huntingdonshire, in February 1667, when she was twenty-three years old. They lived together happily until his death in April 1682. During this time she continued the charitable works for which she was already noted, such as aiding refugees and religious exiles, erecting charity schools for the education of the poor, and giving medical assistance to her neighbors. She was of the opinion that everyone should donate a part of his or her estate to "pious and charitable uses," and did so herself throughout her life. Deeply religious, she wrote many religious works, including *Meditations on the Divinity of the Holy Scriptures, A Believer's Union With Christ,* and *Duty and Happiness of Man.* Her second marriage was to Samuel Bury, a minister, in May 1697, another happy union, which lasted until her death on 11 May 1720, at age seventy-six, after a brief illness. She left an extensive diary, which was abridged and published by her husband.

Bury frequently commented on the limitations of her own considerable knowledge and bewailed the lack of opportunity for women to receive an education. According to Ballard, "She would often regret, that so many learned men should be so uncharitable to her sex, as to speak so little in their mother tongue, and be so loath to assist their feebler faculties."

JH/MBO

PRIMARY SOURCES

Bury, Elizabeth Lawrence. *An Account of the Life and Death of Mrs. Elizabeth Bury, Who Died, May the 11th, 1720, Aged 76: Chiefly Collected Out of Her Own Diary, Together With Her Funeral Sermon, Preached at Bristol, May 22, 1720, by the Reverend Mr. William Tong, and Her Elegy by the Reverend Mr. Watts.* Bristol: Printed by and for J. Penn, and sold by J. Spring, 1720.

STANDARD SOURCES

Alic; Ballard.

BURY, PRISCILLA SUSAN (FALKNER)
(ca. 1794–post-1869)

British botanical illustrator and microscopist. Born ca. 1794 at Fairfield House, Liverpool, to Bridget (Tarleton) and Edward Dean Falkner. Educated privately. Married Edward Bury (1794–1858) ca. 1830. One son. Died after 1869, probably at Fairfield, Thornton Heath, Croydon.

Priscilla Susan Falkner, listed in sources as Mrs. Edward Bury, was born sometime after 1793 to a well-placed family in Liverpool. Her father was a justice of the peace, a high sheriff of Lancashire, and a wealthy merchant; her mother's family were large landholders, active in national politics. The elegant house she was raised in was noted for its hothouses.

Falkner painted flowers, specializing in lilies and related plants, and corresponded with the botanist William Roscoe about her intention to publish these as lithographs in an edition modeled on his recently issued *Monandrian Plants* (1823–1829). The subjects were culled from the hothouses in her home, from specimens carefully chosen from bulbs sent to her father by known bulb breeders. Her illustrations included representations of the seedlings. Although she planned to issue these in 1829, her marriage to the renowned engineer Edward Bury intervened, as did the birth of her only son in 1831. The large, hand-colored lithographed plates of her paintings were issued as a subscription series between 1831 and 1834. Bury continued to do botanical illustrations for botanists, contributing to later volumes of Benjamin Maund's series, *Botanic Garden* (1825–1850) and *The Botanist* (1837–1846).

Her husband, Edward Bury, was a partner in the firm that made railroad locomotives and also served as superintendent for the London and North West Railway. In 1846 he retired and the couple went to live at Crofton Lodge, Windemere. In 1848 he was made a Fellow of the Royal Society. After her husband's death in 1858, Bury issued a memoir describing her husband's life as an engineer. She also turned from botanical illustration to the newer method of photography, using both drawings and photographic plates to record images seen through a microscope of polycistins and diatoms from Barbados chalk deposits. Bury appears to have been inspired by reading the discussion of these forms as discussed in a lecture delivered by John Davy in Barbados in 1846. In 1865, she issued twelve mounted photographs accompanied by some thirteen lithographs of her drawings. She supplemented these with various addenda and reissued the book in 1869 with a further added photographic plate of diatoms signed by her. Her exact death date is not known, but her home as of the late 1860s was at Fairfield (named after her natal house), Thornfield, Croydon.

JH/MBO

PRIMARY SOURCES

Bury, Mrs. Edward (Priscilla Susan). *A Selection of Hexandrian Plants Belonging to the Natural Orders of Amaryllidae and Liliaceae.* London: R. Havel, 1831–1834. This book has a text of 51 pages as well as the plates.

———. *Figures of Remarkable Forms of Polycystins or Allied Organisms in the Barbados Chalk Deposit (Chiefly from That Collected by Dr. Davy and which He Had Noticed in a Lecture Delivered to the Agricultural Society of Barbados in July 1846) Drawn by Mrs. Bury as Seen in Her Microscope on Slides Prepared by Chr. Johnson, Esq. of Lancaster, 1860 and 1861.* [Windemere: John Garnett, 1862].

Letters between Bury and William Roscoe are in the Liverpool City Library.

SECONDARY SOURCES

McMillan, Nora F. "Mrs Edward Bury (née Priscilla Susan Falkner), Botanical Artist." *Journal of the Society for the Bibliography of Natural History* 5 (1968): 71–75. The letters between P. S. Bury and William Rosoe are published in this article.

STANDARD SOURCES

Desmond.

BUSH, KATHARINE JEANNETTE (1855–1937)

U.S. marine biologist. Born 30 December 1855 in Scranton, Pa., to Eliza Ann Clark and William Henry Bush. Educated New Haven, Conn., public and private schools; graduated Hillhouse High School; Sheffield Scientific School, Yale University, special student (with Addison E. Verrill [conchologist] and others) (1885–?); Yale University (Ph.D., 1901). Professional experience: zoological department, Yale University Museum, assistant (1879–1910?); U.S. Fish Commission, assistant (1881–1888); U.S. National Museum (1891–1892, 1894–1898), with work carried out at Yale. Died 19 January 1937.

Katharine Jeanette Bush was born in Scranton, Pennsylvania, and educated in the local schools. She became interested in science and worked at the Peabody Museum of Natural History with the conchologist Addison Emery Verrill for six years, beginning at the age of twenty-three as his assistant. She then obtained the equivalent of a bachelor's degree, studying in Yale's Sheffield Scientific School, beginning in 1885 as a special student. Studying with Verrill and others at Yale, she began graduate work in 1899; by 1901 she had obtained her doctorate in zoology, the first woman to do so. She continued to take postdoctoral classes from 1901 to 1904 and from 1908 to 1909, apparently eager to expand her knowledge of science. Although she first worked with collections of molluscs and enchinoderms, by 1911 Bush had begun to help with both vertebrate and invertebrate museum exhibits, working with Stanley Ball and others. She worked on the storage collections at the Peabody with A. M. Chickering between 1911 and 1912. She became ill and by 1914, increasing illness required two assistants to replace her. Sometime in that year she entered the Hartford Retreat for treatment of a neuropsychiatric illness. She may have stayed there for six years, since evidence indicates that she lived in Farmington (Massachusetts) from 1920 to 1924. Sometime in the 1930s she returned to the Hartford Retreat and remained there with increasingly declining health. She died from pneumonia and pernicious anemia at the beginning of 1937.

Bush's main field of research was the taxonomy and systematic classification of marine invertebrates and she published on this subject. Part of Bush's funding came from her position as an assistant on the U.S. Fish Commission (1881–1888), although the work was done at the Yale museum. She published articles on this and related topics in publications of the Smithsonian, the Museum of Comparative Zoology, Harvard, and the *Proceedings of the Academy of Natural Sciences of Philadelphia.* In her doctoral dissertation, Bush described the marine molluscs and annelids from the Harriman Alaska expeditions for the U.S. National Museum, 1894–1899, and this was later published in 1905 in an expanded form as part of the volumes of the Harriman Alaska expedition. In 1910, her final publication examined related species provided by the Harriman Bermuda expedition.   JH/MBO

PRIMARY SOURCES

Bush, Katharine Jeannette. "Catalogue of Mollusca and Echinodermata dredged on the coast of Laborador by the expedition under the direction of Mr. W. A. Stearns in 1882." *Proceedings U.S. National Museum* 1883 [1884] 6:236–247, pl. 9.

———. "Report on the Mollusca Dredged by the 'Blake' in 1880, Including Descriptions of Several New Species." *Bulletin Museum Comparative Zoology* 23 (1893): 197–284.

———. With A.E. Verrill. "Revision of the Deep-Water Mollusca of the Atlantic Coast of North America with Descriptions of New Genera and Species, Part 1. Bivalvia." *Proceedings U.S. National Museum* 20 (1898): 775–901, pl. 71–97.

———. "Descriptions of New Species of *Turbonilla* of the Western Atlantic Fauna With Notes on Those Previously Known." *Proceedings Academy Natural Sciences of Philadelphia* 56 (1907): 156–179, pl. 11,12.

———. "Tubicolous Annelids of the Tribes Sabellidae and Serpulides from the Pacific Ocean." 1905. Smithsonian Institution Harriman Alaska Expedition Series, vol. 12. Washington, D.C., 1999.

———. "Description of New Serpulids from Bermuda with Notes on Known Forms from Adjacent Regions." *Proceedings Academy of the Natural Sciences of Philadelphia* 62 (1910): 490–501.

SECONDARY SOURCES
Remington, Jeanne E. "Katharine Jeanette Bush: Peabody's Mysterious Zoologist." *Discovery* 12 (1977): 3–8.

STANDARD SOURCES
AMS 1–5; Bailey.

BUSK, LADY MARIAN (BALFOUR) (1861–1941)

British botanist. Born in 1861. Educated University College, London (B.Sc.). Honors and memberships: Linnean Society, Fellow (1905). Died 1941.

Lady Marian Busk assisted F. W. Oliver in translating A. Kerner von Marilaun's *Natural History of Plants* (1894). JH/MBO

PRIMARY SOURCES
Von Marilaun, A. Kerner. *Natural History of Plants.* Trans. F. W. Oliver, with the assistance of Marian Busk. London: Blackie, 1894–1895.

SECONDARY SOURCES
Proceedings of the Linnean Society, 154th session. 1941–1942: 271–272. Obituary notice.

STANDARD SOURCES
Desmond.

BUSSECKER, ERNA (fl. 1928)

German?/Austrian? Physicist. Professional experience: Vienna Institute for Radium Research, researcher.

No information was available on Erna Bussecker's life or education. She is an example of the many women working on radioactivity in Vienna during the first part of this century. Working at the Vienna Institute for Radium Research, she determined that some variations in vaporization of radium decay products were caused by alloy formation. She used radioactive recoil to create these alloys with gold. MM

PRIMARY SOURCES
Bussecker, Erna. "Verflüchtigungskurven von RaB und RaC, die auf Gold bei einfachem und bei zweifachem Rückstoss niedergeschlagen sind." *Akademie der Wissenschaften, Vienna, Sitzungsberichte* 2a 137 (1928): 117–126.

BUTTELINI, MARCHESA (fl. mid-1700s)

Italian physician. Professional positions: medical practice in Rome under the patronage of Benedict XIV.

All that is known of Buttelini is that she apparently had a medical degree and practiced in Rome under the patronage of Pope Benedict XIV. At Benedict's command she spent most of her time inoculating patients with smallpox. LADY MARY MONTAGUE also used this technique. JH/MBO

STANDARD SOURCES
Hurd-Mead 1938.

BYKHOVSKAIA, ANNA MARKOVNA (1901–)

Russian zoologist. Born 1901. Graduated Moscow University (1927); graduate work under G. O. Roskin. Professional experience: Zoological Research Institute of Moscow State University, dean, then director of department of biology. Politically repressed by government, 1937.

Owing to lack of financial resources, Anna Markovna Bykhovskaia was unable to attend a gymnasium, but managed to pass the examinations as an external student. She was self-supporting from the age of fifteen, first giving private lessons and later working as a primary school teacher. In 1920 she joined the Communist Party, which probably played a role in her admittance to Moscow University, where she graduated from the physical-mathematical department in 1927. She continued postgraduate studies under G. O. Roskin, working in the field of histology. She was particularly interested in questions of the formation and differentiation of tissues.

In 1930 Bykhovskaia was appointed dean of the biology department of Moscow State University and also director of the Zoological Research Institute, which at that time was working intensively on problems of agricultural pests, particularly those affecting grain.

Bykhovskaia was very young to hold two such important posts, but it was not uncommon in that era for a candidate of suitable proletarian background and party affiliation to be appointed over the heads of more experienced people. Such individuals (or *vydvizhentsi*), although privileged in one way, were vulnerable to political crossfire and expendable in a way more established specialists were not.

The 1930s were a critical period in Soviet agriculture. Collectivization had been introduced in 1929 and grain harvests had dropped. Against this background the ambitious and unscrupulous agronomist Trofim D. Lysenko came out with the first "discoveries" of what would develop into the obscurantist pseudoscience known, among other things, as

"Michurinist biology" (after the plant breeder Ivan V. Michurin). This doctrine in time received official sanction as dogma with which it became increasingly dangerous to disagree.

The first wave of the Lysenkoist onslaught came in the years 1936 to 1937. The Lysenko doctrine was not as highly developed at this period as it became later when it led to the banning of the science of genetics, but it exerted a strong influence particularly in the agricultural sciences. Lysenko had promised a quick fix to the grain problem in the country, something that would be much faster than the time-honored methods of breeding, selection, and hybridization practiced in "bourgeois" countries where, supposedly, scientists had no interest in increasing harvests as that would lower the price of grain.

Scientists working in a traditional manner were therefore depicted as sabotaging the country's efforts and branded as "enemies" and "wreckers."

There is no evidence that Bykhovskaia took any position in regard to Michurinist biology, but as a young *vydvizhenka* she was a safe and easy target. In an article published 17 June 1937 in *Za proletarskie kadry*, Bykhovskaia was criticized for being soft on enemies; in a further article of 17 October 1937, she was accused of being an enemy herself. She was subsequently arrested and disappeared into the Gulag. ACH

PRIMARY SOURCES

"A.M. Bykhovskaia: Doktor Zoologicheskogo instituta. Dekan biofaka MGU." Front nauki i truda 3 (1936): 71. Autobiographical sketch.

SECONDARY SOURCES

Joravsky, David. *The Lysenko Affair.* Cambridge, Mass.: Harvard University Press, 1970.

BYRD, MARY EMMA (1849–?)

U.S. astronomer. Born 15 November 1849 in Le Roy, Mich. Educated University of Michigan (A.B., 1878); Harvard College Observatory (1882–1883); Carleton College (Ph.D., 1904). Professional experience: Indiana High School, principal (1879–1882); Carleton College, first assistant, observatory (1883–1887); Smith College, observatory director (1887–1906), professor of astronomy (1898–1906). Death date unknown.

Mary Byrd did her undergraduate work at the University of Michigan, and worked in an Indiana high school as principal for four years after graduation. After a year at the Harvard College Observatory she went to Carleton College to work on her doctorate and also served as the first assistant at the College Observatory. After four years as assistant, Byrd became the director and remained in that position for nineteen

years. She also was professor of astronomy from 1898 to 1906. Byrd was a member of the Astronomical Society and did research on comet positions using a filar micrometer.

PRIMARY SOURCES

Byrd, Mary Emma. *A Laboratory Manual in Astronomy.* Boston: Ginn, 1899.

———. "Anna Winlock." Reprinted from *Popular Astronomy* no. 114, April 1904.

———. *First Observations in Astronomy: A Handbook for Schools and Colleges.* Concord, N.H.: Rumford Press, 1913.

SECONDARY SOURCES

Hoblit, Louise Barber. "Mary E. Byrd." *Popular Astronomy* 42 (1934): 496–498.

"Miss Mary E. Byrd's Resignation." *Popular Astronomy* 14 (1906): 447–448.

STANDARD SOURCES

AMS 1–5; Rossiter 1982.

BYRNES, ESTHER FUSSELL (1866–1946)

U.S. biologist. Born 1866. Educated Bryn Mawr (A.B., 1891; M.A., 1894; Ph.D., 1898); Marine Biological Laboratories, Woods Hole (1891). Professional experience: Vassar College demonstrator in biology (1891–1893); Philadelphia Girls' High School, senior instructor in physiology and biology (1898–1932); Mount Desert Biological Laboratory, director. Honors and memberships: New York Academy of Sciences, Fellow. Died 1946.

Esther Fussell Byrnes received all three of her degrees from Bryn Mawr College between 1891 and 1898, during the period in which this institution was establishing its graduate programs, with some of the most important experimental biologists of the time. In the period between her master's and doctoral degrees, she was a demonstrator in biology at Vassar College, when MARCELLA O'GRADY BOVERI was professor of zoology. After getting her doctoral degree, Byrnes was appointed senior instructor in physiology and biology at the Philadelphia Girls' High School and trained many young women who then went on to significant research careers in biology. She was also director of the Mount Desert Biological Laboratory, and a Fellow of the New York Academy of Sciences. JH/MBO

PRIMARY SOURCES

Byrnes, Esther Fussell. "Heterogeny and Variation in Some of the Copepoda of Long Island." *Biological Bulletin* 5 (1903): 152–168.

———. "On the Skeleton of Regenerated Anterior Limbs in the Frog." *Biological Bulletin* 7 (1904): 166–169.

———. "Regeneration of the Anterior Limbs in the Tadpoles of Frogs." *Archiv Für Entwicklungsmechanik der Organismen* 18 (1904): 171–177.

———. *The Fresh Water Cyclops of Long Island.* Brooklyn, N.Y.: Brooklyn Institute of Arts and Sciences (Cold Spring Harbor Monographs), 1909.

STANDARD SOURCES
AMS 1–7.

BYRON, AUGUSTA ADA, COUNTESS OF LOVELACE (1815–1852)

British mathematician. Born 10 December 1815 in London to Anne Isabella (Annabella) (Milbanke) and George Gordon, Lord Byron. Married William, 8th Lord King, later Earl of Lovelace. Three children: Byron, Annabella, Ralph. Educated by governesses and tutors. Died 27 November 1852.

Ada Byron, daughter of the poet George Gordon, Lord Byron, managed, in spite of family scandals and a series of debilitating illnesses, to become an accomplished mathematician. The scandals involved her father. Byron told his bride, Annabella, of his incestuous relationship with his half-sister, Augusta, and of his homosexual loves; with this knowledge and with her own experience of his violence, drunkenness, and disordered financial affairs, Lady Byron endured the pregnancy that produced Ada. A month after Ada's birth, Lady Byron took the child and left her husband's house, eventually obtaining a legal separation. Byron departed for the Continent, where he remained for the rest of his life.

A scholarly, quiet child, Ada was educated by her mother (whose special interest was mathematics) and by tutors closely superintended by her mother. At the age of eight, Ada was intrigued by crafts, such as building model boats; mathematics and music became her most serious lifelong pursuits. Society, courts, and fine gowns all bored her. Nevertheless, she allowed herself to be presented at court during the season of 1833. In that same year her "greatest delight was to go to the Mechanics Institute to hear the first of Dr. Dionysius Lardner's lectures on the difference engine . . . Miss Byron, young as she was, understood its working and saw the great beauty of the invention" (Strickland, 197). The "engine" was a calculating machine, the invention of Charles Babbage (1791–1871), and Ada's interest in it led to an introduction to Babbage that initiated a lifelong friendship. At about this time (1834), Ada began corresponding with the fifty-four-year-old scientist Mary Somerville, who was impressed by her knowledge of mathematics and astronomy. A third mentor was the mathematician and logician

Augustus De Morgan (1806–1871), who, in a series of letters (1840–1842), instructed her in calculus.

In 1835 Ada married William, eighth Lord King, who in 1838 became earl of Lovelace. Lovelace was tolerant of his wife's intellectual interests, and they spent most of their time in the country, where they could read and study. Although they had three children, Ada was little involved in their upbringing. Motherhood interested her far less than mathematics, and her own mother often took care of the children.

Mathematician Charles Babbage was a frequent guest in the Lovelace household; the middle-aged man was flattered by Ada's attention, and she encouraged his chivalrous attachment to herself. By 1842 she had developed enough confidence in her mathematical abilities to undertake a translation of a treatise on Babbage's analytical engine (the successor to the difference engine) that had been published that year in French by the Italian mathematician Luigi Menabrea. The result was more than a translation: Ada's commentary expanded the treatise to three times its original size. Although Babbage advised her on substantive matters, Ada was very proprietary about their writing, chastising Babbage when he suggested a change. "I cannot endure another person to meddle with my sentences," she insisted. Ada's husband also helped with the work by copying and making "himself useful in other ways" (Strickland, 205). The *Sketch of the Analytical Engine,* translated and with notes by "A.A.L.," appeared in 1843. Ada was satisfied with her work, praising her own "masterly" style "and its superiority to that of the memoir itself" (Strickland).

In 1850 Ada took up betting at horse races and was soon dangerously in debt. At one point "she pawned the [Lovelace] family jewels, and then implored the help of her mother in redeeming them, and in concealing the whole of the transaction from her husband" (Strickland, 210). She died of cervical cancer in 1852, at the age of thirty-six. MBO

PRIMARY SOURCES
Menabrea, Luigi. "Sketch of the Analytical Engine Invented by Charles Babbage," *Taylor's Scientific Memoirs* 3 (1843): 666–731. Translated and with notes by Ada Byron.

SECONDARY SOURCES
Anguluin, Dana. "Lady Lovelace and the Analytical Engine." *Newsletter of the Association for Women in Mathematics* 1 (1976): 5–10; 6, 2: 6–8.
Baum, Joan. *The Calculating Passion of Ada Byron.* Camden, Conn.: Archon Books, 1986.
Stein, Dorothy. *Ada: A Life and a Legacy.* Cambridge, Mass.: MIT Press, 1985. Biography of Ada Byron.
Strickland, Margot. *The Byron Women.* London: Peter Owen, 1974. Includes biographical information on Ada Byron.

C

CADBURY, DOROTHY ADLINGTON
(1892–1987)

British botanist and candy manufacturer. Born 14 October 1892. Educated privately. Professional experience: Cadbury Brothers, Bournville, director. British Museum of Natural History, collector. Worked on flora of Birmingham. Died 21 August 1987 at Edgsbaston Park.

As a child, Dorothy Adlington Cadbury studied every example she and her mother could find of the flowering plants illustrated in George Bentham and Joseph Hooker's *Flora of the British Isles.* She then carefully colored the plate, copying the natural colors. As an adult, she made significant studies of the pond weed genus *Potamogeton,* which she also collected for the British Museum of Natural History, making four hundred collections of this plant from all over Britain. She also worked on a revision of the *Flora of Warwickshire* for over twenty years with J. G. Hawkes, a joint project with the Birmingham Natural History Society and the Botany Department of the University of Birmingham. This was published in 1971.

She served as director of her family company, Cadbury Brothers, at Bournville for many years, but continued her interest in botany. She was a member of the Wild Flower Society from 1937, the Birmingham Natural History Society from 1950. Like many of the Cadbury family, she was a devout Quaker, and had a strong commitment to the Society of Friends.

She is commemorated by having a plant named after her, *Potamogeton cadburyae* Dandy and Taylor.   JH/MBO

PRIMARY SOURCES

Cadbury, Dorothy Adlington. With J. G. Hawkes, and R. C.
    Readett. *A Computer-Mapped Flora, a Study of the County of
    Warwickshire.* London: Academic Press, 1971.

SECONDARY SOURCES

"Dorothy Adlington Cadbury," *Times,* 3 September 1987.
    Obituary notice.
Hawkes, J. G. "Dorothy Adlington Cadbury (1892–1987)."
    Watsonia 17 (1988): 208–209. Obituary notice.

STANDARD SOURCES
Desmond.

CADILLA DE MARTÍNEZ, MARÍA
(1886–1951)

American / Puerto-Rican folklorist and anthropologist. Born 21 September 1886 in Arecibo, Puerto Rico, to Catalina Cólon y Nieves and Armindo Cadilla y Fernández. Married Julio Tomas Martínez Mirabal (1903). Two daughters. Educated Arecibo; U.S. normal school (1902); University of Puerto Rico, teaching license; College of Mechanical and Agricultural Arts, Mayaguez (1913); University of Puerto Rico (A.B., 1928; A.M., 1930); Universidad Central (Madrid) (Ph.D., 1933). Professional experience: Puerto Rico, rural teacher (1903–1916); University of Puerto Rico, professor (1916–1951?). Died 23 August 1951 of cancer.

María Cadilla de Martínez's father was from Spain and her mother from Puerto Rico. She attended a private school in Arecibo and then went to the United States to a normal school to prepare her to teach. She was licensed to teach in both primary and secondary schools and became a rural teacher. She married a surrealist painter and taught at a preparatory school that he founded. She studied agriculture and home economics and then completed a bachelor's in education in 1928 and a master's in 1930. Cadilla de Martínez became interested in her local folk culture and wrote on popular poetry in Puerto Rico for a dissertation in philosophy and literature from the University of Madrid. She studied and practiced art and music at an advanced level. She continued to teach at all levels for thirteen years after her marriage and then was appointed to teach Hispanic history and literature at the University of Puerto Rico, through which position she encouraged the preservation of folkloric traditions of Puerto Rican culture. She collected children's songs and games and various stories and legends, which she published and retold. She also did research on nineteenth-century modes of dress to provide insights into folk customs. Cadilla de Martínez was a dedicated feminist, serving as vice-president of the Suffrage Association of Puerto Rico. She was active in numerous civic clubs and international and national organizations. She was elected as the only female member of the Puerto Rico Historical Academy (1934). For her essay on the ethnology of Puerto Rico, she won a gold prize from the French Academic Society of International History held at the Sorbonne in 1921. Throughout her life she was awarded many international honors. She died of cancer 23 August 1951 in Arecibo.   JH/MBO

PRIMARY SOURCES
Cadilla de Martínez, María. "Ethnography of Puerto Rico." *Raices de la Tierra*. Arecibo, Puerto Rico: Puerto Rico Illustrado, 1921.
————. *Cuentos a Lillien*. San Juan, Puerto Rico: Puerto Rico Illustrado, 1925.
————. *Costumbres y tradicionalismos de mi tierra*. Puerto Rico: Imprenta Venezula, 1938.
————. *Juegos y canciones infantiles de Puerto Rico*. San Juan: Baldrich, 1940.

SECONDARY SOURCES
Votaw, Carmen Delgado. *Puerto Rican Women: Some Biographical Profiles*. Washington: National Conference of Puerto Rican Women, 1978.

STANDARD SOURCES
La Gran Enciclopedia de Puerto Rico, 1976; *NAW* (M) (long article by Carmen Delgado Votaw).

CADY, BERTHA LOUISE CHAPMAN (1876–1956)

U.S. entomologist and science educator. Educated Stanford University (A.B.; A.M.; Ph.D., 1923); University of Chicago; Columbia University. Married Vernon Mosher Cady. Professional experience: high school teacher (1907–1909); University of Chicago, assistant, nature study; California State Teacher's College, faculty (1918); Stanford University, lecturer (1921–1923); Girl Scouts, naturalist (1924–1936); American School for the Air, Columbia Broadcasting Company, advisory board. American Nature Study Society, president (1926–1929). Died 1956.

Trained as an entomologist and science educator, Bertha Cady devoted much of her energy to lecturing on nature study for girls and serving as naturalist and advisor to the U.S. Girl Scouts (1924–1936). She wrote a popular introduction to sex education titled *The Way Life Begins* with her husband, psychologist Vernon Mosher Cady, in 1917. In the early years of radio broadcasting she was on the advisory science board of Columbia Broadcasting Company's American School for the Air. She was president of the American Nature Study Society from 1926 to 1929.   JH/MBO

PRIMARY SOURCES
Cady, Bertha Louise Chapman. With Vernon Mosher Cady. *The Way Life Begins*. New York: American Social Hygiene Association, 1917.
————. *Animal Pets: A Study in Character and Nature Education*. 1930.
————. *Nature Guides for Schools, Volunteer Organizations, Camps and Clubs*. Ithaca, N.Y.: Slingerland-Comstock Co., 1930.

STANDARD SOURCES
AMS 4–8; Bailey.

CAERELLIA (CAERELIA) (ca. 45 B.C.E.)
Roman academician.

Caerellia is known for her association with Cicero, although there are differences in opinion as to whether or not she was his mistress. She apparently was a longtime friend, perhaps a widow or divorcée who was fascinated by philosophy. She copied Cicero's *De finibus*, which may have indicated her interest in the Platonism of the New Academy School of which Cicero was a member. This school espoused an eclectic Platonism.   JH/MBO

SECONDARY SOURCES
Austin, Lucy. "The Caerellia of Cicero's Correspondence." *Classical Journal* vol. 41, no. 7 (April 1946): 305–309.

STANDARD SOURCES
Kersey; Ménage.

CAETANI-BOVATELLI, DONNA ERSILIA (fl. 1879)

Italian classical archeologist. Born ca. 1840 in Rome. Father Don Michel Angelo Caetani-Sermonetta. Married Bovatelli (d. 1879). Children. Educated privately. Member of the Accademia dei Lincei.

Born ca. 1840 in Rome to an Italian nobleman who was a Dante authority and well versed in archeology and philology, young Donna Ersilia learned Greek, Latin, and Sanscrit. Although she married young and bore a number of children, her husband's early death freed her to pursue classical archeology. She held a notable salon for historians and archeologists and regularly published in the *Nuova antologia* and the bulletins of the archeological commissions.

JH/MBO

STANDARD SOURCES
Mozans.

CALDERONE, MARY S. (1904–1983)

U.S. physician. Born 1904 in New York City. Father Edward Steichen. (1) Married and divorced; (2) married Dr. Frank Calderone (1941). Educated Vassar College (A.B., 1925); University of Rochester (M.D., 1939); Columbia University (Master of Public Health 1942). Professional experience: Planned Parenthood Federation of America, medical director (1953–1964). Died 1983.

Born to an internationally known photographer Edward Steichen, Mary Calderone attended Vassar College, where she majored in chemistry. After an early marriage that ended in divorce, she decided to study medicine. The facet of medicine that she found most interesting was public health, so in addition to her medical degree, she earned a master's degree in public health at Columbia. In the meantime, she had married Frank Calderone, a physician, whom she met during her graduate study. While she was director of the Planned Parenthood of America, she became more and more convinced of the importance of sex education for children and was a part of the group that established the Sex Information and Education Council of the United States (SIECUS) in 1964. She advocated the inclusion of information on biological reproduction with discussions of responsible human relationships.

JH/MBO

PRIMARY SOURCES
Calderone, Mary. *Autobiography.* In *Annals of the New York of Science* 208 (1973): 47–51.
Schlesinger Papers, 5 vols. Volume 1, biographical and personal, vols. 2–5, 1955–1971, professional. Schlesinger Library, Radcliffe College.

STANDARD SOURCES
Kass-Simon and Farnes.

CALDWELL, MARY LETITIA (1890–1972)

U.S. biological chemist and nutritionist. Born 18 December 1890 in Bogota, Colombia, to Susanna (Adams) and Milton Etsil Caldwell. Four siblings. Never married. Educated high school in U.S.; Western College for Women, Oxford, Ohio (B.A., 1913); Columbia University (M.A., 1919; Ph.D., 1921). Professional experience: Western College, instructor (1914–1917), assistant professor (1917–1918); Columbia University, Department of Chemistry, instructor, assistant professor, associate (1921–1948), and professor (1948–1959). Retired 1959. Honors and memberships: Garvan Medal (1960); Columbia University, Honorary D.Sc. (1961); New York Academy of Sciences, Fellow; American Association for the Advancement of Science, fellow. Died 1 July 1972 in Fishkill, N.Y.

Mary Letitia Caldwell, the daughter of Presbyterian missionaries working in Colombia, was educated in the United States. She attended Western College for Women, graduating in 1913, and then taught there for the following five years. Deciding to pursue chemistry at an advanced level, she went to Columbia University, where she studied with Henry C. Sherman. She received a fellowship that allowed her to obtain both a master's and a doctoral degree in organic chemistry. She remained at Columbia University as a faculty member, rising through the ranks from instructor until she was appointed professor in 1948.

Dedicated to her teaching and research, Caldwell studied starch enzymes (amylases). She developed important techniques in the late 1940s and was the pioneer in purifying crystalline porcine pancreatic amylase, a substance important to industry as well as to pure research. She showed that amylases were proteins and demonstrated their activity with various chemical groups. Her specialty course was Chemistry of Food and Nutrition. As the main advisor to graduate students, she served also as secretary of the department. More than eighteen graduate students earned their doctorates under her supervision.

JH/MBO

PRIMARY SOURCES
Caldwell, Mary Letitia. "An Experimental Study of Certain Amino Acids." Ph.D. diss., Columbia University, 1921.
———. "A Study of the New Sulfur-Containing Amino Acid on the Activity of Pancreatic Amylase." *Journal of Biological Chemistry* 59 (1924): 661–665.
———. With H. C. Sherman. "Enzyme Purification: Further Experiments with Pancreatic Amylase." *Journal of Biological Chemistry* 88 (1930): 295–304.
———. With J. W. Van Dyke. "Spectophotometric Method for Quantitative Evaluation of Early Stages of Hydrolyses of Branched Components of Starches by Alpha Amylases." *Analytical Chemistry* 28 (1956): 318–320.

SECONDARY SOURCES
"Garvan Medal. Dr. Mary L. Caldwell." *Chemical and Engineering News* 38 (18 April 1960): 86. Includes photograph.
"Mary L. Caldwell." *New York Times,* 3 July 1972. Obituary notice.

STANDARD SOURCES
Grinstein 1993 (article by Soraya Svoronos).

CALE, F. M. (fl. 1922)

Canadian? physicist. Probably educated at University of Toronto (M.A.). Professional experience: University of Toronto, researcher.

Little is known about F. M. Cale's life. She held an M.A. degree and did research on fluorescence at the University of Toronto with the physicist J. C. McClennan. Her investigations showed that fluorescence in an organic substance was not generally caused by destruction of the substance. She also contributed to analysis of the spectrum of mercury. By adjusting Niels Bohr's atomic theory, the fine structure was matched to mercury isotopes. She was one of the early workers in radioactivity.   MM

PRIMARY SOURCES
Cale, F. M. With J. C. McClennan. "On the Fluorescence of Aesculin." *Royal Society of London. Proceedings A,* 102 (1922): 256–268.
———. With J. C. McClennan and D. S. Ainslie. "Absorption of λ 5460. 97A by Luminous Mercury Vapour." *Royal Society of London. Proceedings A,* 102 (1922): 33–45.

SECONDARY SOURCES
Baly, E. C. C. *Spectroscopy.* Vol. 2. London: Longmans, Green and Co., 1927.

STANDARD SOURCES
Meyer and von Schweidler.

CALENDA, CONSTANZA OR LAUREA CONSTANTIA (fl. 1415–1423)

Italian physician. Father Salvator Calenda, dean of medicine at the University of Salerno. Married Baldassare de Sancto Magno. Educated University of Salerno. Professional experience: University of Naples, teacher (1423).

Constanza Calenda's father, Salvator, was the dean of medicine at the University of Salerno. He taught his daughter and because of his teaching she was able to obtain a medical degree. In the archives of Naples, a document from the king exists that gives her permission to marry Baldassare de Sancto Magno.   JH/MBO

STANDARD SOURCES
Echols and Williams; Lipinska 1900.

CALKINS, MARY WHITON (1863–1930)

U.S. psychologist and philosopher. Born 30 March 1863 in Hartford, Conn., to Charlotte (Whiton) and Wolcott Calkins. Four siblings. Never married. Educated Smith College (B.A., 1885; M.A., 1888); Harvard University, informally (1890–1895). Professional experience: Wellesley College, instructor in Greek and philosophy (1887–1890), instructor in psychology (1890–1894), associate professor of psychology and philosophy (1894–1898), professor of psychology and philosophy (1898–1929), research professor (1928–1930). Honors and memberships: American Psychological Association, fourteenth president; American Philosophical Association, president (1918); British Psychological Association, first woman to receive honorary membership. Died of cancer 26 February 1930 in Newton, Mass.

Mary Whiton Calkins was the eldest of five children of Wolcott Calkins, a Presbyterian minister, and spent most of her childhood in Buffalo, New York. The closeness of the family and Mary's devotion to her siblings and especially to her mother, Charlotte Whiton, remained prominent in her personal life. In 1880 the family moved to Newton, Massachusetts, and the house where Mary would live the rest of her life. After graduating from Newton High School, Calkins attended Smith College, where she studied classics and philosophy. Thanks to her father's attention and guidance in her studies, she was able to enter Smith with advanced standing as a sophomore. The death of her closest sister, Maud, in 1883 had a profound effect on her and she spent the following year studying at home. She graduated from Smith with her bachelor's degree in 1885 and received her master's in classics and philosophy in 1888.

Calkins's long teaching career at Wellesley College began with a position as tutor in Greek in 1887. During her first three years there, the philosophy department decided to begin offering courses in the new field of psychology and proposed that Calkins teach the first classes, after spending a year in preparation. Immediately there were two obstacles to this opportunity: few psychology departments or psychological laboratories existed and those that did were reluctant to offer advanced work to one of her sex. After considering several options, Calkins studied experimental psychology with Edmund Sanford at Clark University in 1890 and with William James, Hugo Münsterberg, and Josiah Royce at Harvard University between 1890 and 1895. Her admittance to seminars at Harvard came only after the initial refusal by Harvard's President Eliot was reversed following petitions from her father, Wolcott Calkins, and the president of Wellesley. Still commuting to Harvard seminars, Mary Calkins returned to teaching at Wellesley in the fall of 1891 and established her psychological laboratory, the first at any women's college.

In 1892, Calkins published her first professional article

(on association) and began her long and steady stream of contributions to psychological literature. By 1896 she had fulfilled all the requirements for the doctorate degree. At her doctoral examination, professors James, Royce, Münsterberg, Palmer, Harris, and Santayana voted unanimously that she satisfied all the requirements for the degree. Their recommendation was refused; Harvard would not grant a doctorate to a woman. Calkins was named associate professor of psychology and philosophy at Wellesley in 1895, and professor in 1898.

During the nineteenth century, there was a strong societal norm that prohibited women from combining a career and marriage; however, strong friendships and supportive emotional ties between educated professional women were acceptable and cultivated in a place such as Wellesley (where Calkins spent forty years). She and other members of the all-single, all-female faculty envisioned Wellesley as a model community that would set a standard for the uplifting of women through higher education, and consequently the uplifting of the entire society. From this environment grew Calkins's commitment to a theory of psychology that radically opposed the atomistic, impersonal conception of mainstream classical experimental psychology. She developed the theory of self-psychology, that is, emphasis on the self in relation to other selves in everyday experience. In addition to her teaching responsibilities, she did research in the areas of dreams (her dream research was cited by Freud), association, supplementary images in recognition, and Hegelian categories. She was the first to present the methodology of paired-associates learning and memory (reinvented later by Georg Müller at Göttingen and widely used).

She stood firmly in opposition to the belief that there were inherent sex differences in mental abilities and condemned unwarranted unequal treatment of the sexes. She challenged popular studies purporting to prove the inability or unsuitability of women to pursue logical or scientific studies, pointing out the effect of environment and differences in training prescribed by society from a child's earliest months throughout life. She maintained denying women the right to vote was "artificial and illogical," and chastised Smith College for considering adopting a course of study different from that found in colleges for men, asking if it was not as futile to differentiate male and female studies as to distinguish between women's and men's foods. Her belief in the fundamental right of women to equal recognition for equal achievement led her to steadfastly refuse the offer by Radcliffe of a doctoral degree (in spite of persuasion by her former mentor Hugo Münsterberg and others). Again in 1927, Harvard stubbornly refused to grant Calkins the degree she had earned, this time in response to a request outlining her significant achievements and international reputation signed by thirteen Harvard graduates, many of whom were professors of psychology or philosophy at prestigious institutions.

Publications by Calkins began to appear in the psychological literature as early as 1892; between 1901 and 1930, she published several influential textbooks, more than one hundred papers, and numerous notes and reviews. Her writing was divided between the disciplines of psychology and philosophy, with her initial interest in philosophy reasserting itself more strongly later in her life. Columbia University awarded her a doctor of letters degree in 1909 and Smith College a doctor of laws degree in 1910; both offered her teaching positions, which she declined in order to remain with her aging parents. Among other honors bestowed on her were the first woman presidencies of the American Psychological Association (1905) and the American Philosophical Association (1918) and the first honorary membership in the British Psychological Association given to a woman. Calkins retired from Wellesley College in 1929 with the title of research professor and planned to continue writing and enjoying time with her mother. Sadly she died less than a year later from an inoperable cancer, on 26 February 1930.

MBO

PRIMARY SOURCES

Calkins, Mary Whiton. "Statistics of Dreams." *American Journal of Psychology* 5 (1893): 311–343.
———. "Association I." *Psychological Review* 1 (1894): 476–483.
———. "Association II." *Psychological Review* 3 (1896): 32–49.
———. "Psychology as a Science of Selves." *Philosophical Review* 9 (1900): 490–501.
———. *An Introduction to Psychology*. New York: Macmillan, 1901.
———. *A First Book in Psychology*. New York: Macmillan, 1909.
———. In *The History of Psychology in Autobiography*, ed. C. Murcheson. Vol. 1. Worcester, Mass.: Clark University Press, 1930.

SECONDARY SOURCES

Furumoto, Laurel. "From 'Paired Associates' To a Psychology of Self: The Intellectual Odyssey of Mary Whiton Calkins." In *Portraits of Pioneers in Psychology*, ed. Gregory Kimble, Michael Wertheimer, and Charlotte White (57–72). Washington, D.C.: American Psychological Association, 1991.
———. "Mary Whiton Calkins (1863–1930)." In *Psychology of Women Quarterly, Special Issue*, ed. Agnes N. O'Connell and Nancy Felipe Russo. Vol. 5 (1980): 55–68.
Mary Whiton Calkins Collection, Smith College Archives. Includes memorial booklet, 1885 essay, memorial service program, explanation of visiting professorship created at Wellesley, photographs, letters, publication notices, honorary degree citation, article in *Smith College Monthly,* and

lecture synopses. *In Memoriam, Mary Whiton Calkins, 1863–1930* (1931), found in this collection, is a pamphlet containing a biographical sketch by her brother the Reverend Raymond Calkins, and several other tributes.

STANDARD SOURCES
AMS 1–4; *DAB; NAW* (long article by Virginia Onderdonk); O'Connell and Russo; Ogilvie 1986; Zusne.

CALLCOTT, LADY MARIA GRAHAM (1785–1842)

British traveler, writer, botanical collector, plant illustrator. Born 19 July 1785 in Cockermouth, Cumberland. Father Rear Admiral Dundas. Married Thomas Graham (1809); he died 1822. Married Sir Augustus Wall Callcott (1827). Privately educated. Traveled in India, Brazil, Chile. Collected plants in Brazil. Wrote a series of books on her travels. Memorialized by Graemia *(Hook) and* Escallonia callcottiae *(H&A). Letters and drawings at Royal Botanical Gardens, Kew. Died 1842.*

Maria Graham, later Lady Callcott, was the daughter of a rear admiral. While accompanying her father on a long voyage in 1809, she met and married Captain Thomas Graham. In 1822 she accompanied her husband on his own ship which was to go to Brazil and then Valparaiso, Chile. Before they could reach their destination, Graham died of fever. Maria, however, arrived in Valparaiso and stayed there for a year in the British community. That year, 1822, was the year of a mammoth earthquake and Graham kept a journal that was later published.

Maria Graham and George Greenough, the president of the Geological Society, engaged in a dispute over the elevation of Chilean land after the earthquake of 1822. Callcott was traveling in Chile during the time of the quake and took extensive notes, recording the time, frequency, severity, and results. She published her account in the *Transactions* of the Geological Society of London and immediately was challenged by Greenough. He became angry at the temerity of a non-geologist writing on a geological subject and disputed her results. He was particularly vehement about her conclusion that the land had risen after the quake. Callcott refuted his claims by referring to her journal as well as using evidence from other observers. She effectively challenged the statement that her account was worthless because she was not a geologist by noting that she had no preconceived ideas and her testimony was far less biased than that of geologists.

JH/MBO

PRIMARY SOURCES
Callcott, Lady Maria Graham (Dundee). *Journal of Residence in India.* Edinburgh: A. Constable, 1812.

———. *Letters on India.* London: Longman, 1814.
———. *Journal of Voyage to Brazil.* London: Longman, 1824.
———. *Journal of Residence in Chile.* London: Longman, 1824.
———. As Callcott, Maria. "On the Reality of the Rise of the Coast of Chili [*sic*] in 1822." *American Journal of Science* 2 (1835): 236–247.
———. *Scripture Herbal.* London: Longman, 1842.

SECONDARY SOURCES
Davison, Charles. *The Founders of Seismology.* Cambridge: Cambridge University Press, 1927: 34–35.
Gotch, R. B. *Maria, Lady Callcott.* London: J. Murray, 1937.
Lyell, K. M. *Life, Letters and Journals of Sir C. J. F. Bunbury.* Vol. 1. London: J. Murray, 1906.
Howe, B. *A Galaxy of Governesses.* London: D. Verschoyle, 1954.
Mavor, E., ed. *The Captain's Wife.* 1993.

STANDARD SOURCES
Desmond; Sarjeant.

CALVERT, CATHERINE LOUISA WARING (ATKINSON) (1834–1872)

British/Australian plant collector and illustrator. Born 25 February 1834 in Oldbury, Argyle County, New South Wales. Married J. S. Calvert (1870). Professional experience: collected and illustrated Australian plants for the botanists William Woolls and Ferdinand von Mueller. Died 1872.

Catherine Louisa Calvert was born in New South Wales, Australia, to British parents. From her early years, she collected plants. At the age of thirty-six, she married explorer and plant collector J. S. Calvert, who had traveled with the German explorer Ludwig Leichhardt. She traveled around Australia collecting plants for the botanists William Woolls and Ferdinand von Mueller. She illustrated the plants she collected. Von Mueller memorialized Calvert by naming several plants after her, using both her maiden and married names (*Atkinsonia* F. Muel and *Epacris calvertiana* F. Muel).

JH/MBO

PRIMARY SOURCES
Von Mueller, Ferdinand. *Fragmenta Phytographie Australiae* 5 (1865): 34; 8 (1872): 52–53.

SECONDARY SOURCES
Carr, D. J., and Carr, S. G. M. *People and Plants in Australia.* Sydney: Academic Press, 1981: 342–346.
Proceedings of the Royal Society, New South Wales (1908): 83.

STANDARD SOURCES
Boase.

CALVERT, EMILY AMELIA (ADELIA) (SMITH) (fl. 1885–1905)

U.S. zoologist. Married Philip Powell Calvert (1901). Educated University of Pennsylvania (B.S., biology); Bryn Mawr College, Fellow (1900–1901).

Little information is available on Emily Adelia (Smith) Calvert. Although she apparently did not earn an advanced degree, she received a bachelor's in biology from the University of Pennsylvania. According to Bonta, Emily Smith was an entomologist who contributed papers in the 1880s to the *Transactions* of the Illinois Department of Agriculture and to the *North American Entomologist*. She married entomologist Philip Powell Calvert (1871–1961), who spent his academic career at the University of Pennsylvania. Six years after he received his doctorate from that institution, he married Smith. They had apparently met at the University of Pennsylvania, and after she returned from Illinois, lived the rest of their lives in a modernized old Pennsylvania farmhouse. The couple collaborated on entomological projects, and their home became a center for intellectuals in the area. Edith Patch wrote a short history of early women entomologists and mentioned Smith. Patch also wrote a paper on "Entomology as a Vocation for Women" in 1939. Calvert's research was on the structure and parasitic habits of *Aphyllon univlorum,* the reactions of *Allolobophora foetida,* and the natural history of Costa Rica, where she went with her husband.

JH/MBO

STANDARD SOURCES
AMS 1–6; Bonta (under Smith); Mallis; Osborn; Rossiter 1982.

CAMBRIÈRE, CLARISSE (fl. 1322)

French physician. Flourished early fourteenth century.

Clarisse Cambrière refused to abide by a document produced at the University of Paris that denied the right of women to practice medicine. In 1312, the Prior of Sainte-Geneviève excommunicated another physician, Clarisse de Rotomago, for practicing medicine in defiance of the edict. Clarisse Cambrière along with others suffered the same fate between 1322 and 1327.

JH/MBO

STANDARD SOURCES
Hurd-Mead 1938; Lipinska 1900.

CAMPBELL, HELEN STUART (1839–1918)

U.S. home economist. Born 4 July 1839 in Lockport, N.Y., to Jane E. (Campbell) and Homer H. Stuart. Married Grenville Mellen Weeks (ca. 1860; divorced 1871). Educated New York public schools; Gammell School of Rhode Island; Mrs. Cook's Seminary, Bloomfield, N.J. Professional experience: Published children's stories (1862–1869); Raleigh, N.C., Cooking School, teacher (1878–1880); Mission Cooking School, founder with Mrs. Anna Lowell Woodbury, Washington, D.C. (1880–1882?); Our Continent magazine, literary and household editor (1882–1884); freelance writer about the poor (from 1882); University of Wisconsin, lecturer (spring 1895); Unity Settlement, later Eli Bates House, Chicago, head resident (1895–1896); Kansas State Agricultural College, professor of home economics (1897–1898); freelance writer (1898–1900). Died 1918 in Dedham, Mass., of endocarditis and nephritis.

Born to Vermont parents of Scottish descent, Helen Stuart Campbell was born in New York City where her father was a lawyer and at one time was president of the Continental Bank Note Company. She received her education in the New York City public schools and in two private girls schools in Rhode Island and New Jersey. Her marriage to Grenville Mellen Weeks, a graduate of the University Medical College (now part of New York University) was short-lived. He served as a surgeon aboard the U.S.S. *Monitor* during the Civil War and an Indian agent and surgeon in the West. When he returned home as a civilian the marriage ended in divorce. In the meantime, Helen had published numerous children's stories and several novels, some under her married name and others under the names Helen Stuart Campbell and Campbell Wheaton.

After the divorce, she held several professional positions in home economics. After taking cooking lessons from Juliet Corson, she began teaching in the Raleigh Cooking School and while she was there wrote a textbook, *The Easiest Way in House-Keeping and Cooking.* With Anna Lowell Woodbury she founded a diet kitchen and mission cooking school in Washington, D.C. She was the literary and household editor of a magazine, *Our Continent,* which had a short life. In 1893, she was one of the organizers of the National Household Economics Association, an organization that grew out of the Women's Congress of the World's Columbian Expositions. In 1903, this organization merged into the committee on household economics of the General Federation of Women's Clubs.

Campbell's interest in home economics seemed to wane for a while and to be replaced by the social problems faced by the poor, particularly in New York City. She wrote several books dealing with poverty, and also contributed a column on "Women's Work and Wages" to *Good Housekeeping* magazine and to the *New York Tribune.*

Although Campbell continued to write about the poor, she returned to home economics when Richard T. Ely, an economist at the University of Wisconsin, invited her to give two lecture series in the spring of 1895. She had hoped that the lectures would result in a permanent position, but they did not. She then took a one-year position as head resident of Unity Settlement. Again through the good offices of Ely, she was offered a position at Kansas State Agricultural College as professor of home economics. By the time she got this position, her health was failing and she stayed for only one year, after which she resumed her freelance writing career. After she left Kansas, she moved with reformer Charlotte Perkins Gilman back to New York City, and then moved to the Boston area. Her final illness was long drawn out. The endocarditis and nephritis from which she suffered finally caused her death in 1918. She had become a follower of the Baha'i religion and had attended a retreat at Eliot, Maine, where her remains were taken after her death.　　　　JH/MBO

PRIMARY SOURCES

Campbell, Helen Stuart. *The Easiest Way in House-Keeping and Cooking.* New York: Fords, Howard, & Hulbert, 1881.

————. *The Problem of the Poor.* New York: Fords, Howard, & Hulbert, 1882.

————. *Mrs. Herndon's Income.* Boston: Roberts Brothers, 1886.

————. *Prisoners of Poverty.* Boston: Roberts Brothers, 1887. A compilation of the weekly articles in the *New York Tribune,* which commissioned her to study conditions among women in New York City.

————. "Women Wage-Earners." 1891.

SECONDARY SOURCES

Boston Transcript, 23 July 1918. Obituary notice.

Mott, Frank L. *A History of American Magazines* 3 and 4. 1938–1968. Cambridge: Harvard University Press.

Willard, Frances E., and Livermore, Mary A., eds. *A Woman of the Century.* Buffalo, N.Y.: Moulton, 1893.

STANDARD SOURCES

NAW (long article by Ross E. Paulson); *NCAB.*

CAMPBELL, DAME JANET MARY (1877–1954)

British medical officer. Born 5 March 1877 in Brighton to Mary Letitia (Rowe) and George Campbell. Married Michael Heseltine (died 1952). Educated Brighton High School; Germany; London School of Medicine for Women (M.B., 1901; M.D., 1904; M.S., 1905). Professional experience: Royal Free Hospital, house appointments; Belgrave Hospital for Children, senior medical officer; London School Medical Service, assistant school medical officer (1904–1907); Board of Education, first full-time woman medical officer (1907–1919; retained connection with the board thereafter); War Cabinet, medical member (1914–1918); Ministry of Health, senior medical officer in charge of maternity and child welfare (from 1919). Honors and memberships: Dame of the British Empire

(D.B.E.) (1924); Durham University, honorary doctorate (1924); Medical Women's Federation, member and eventually president; Dartford Physical Training College, honorary secretary and chair. Died 27 September 1954 in Chelsea.

Dame Janet Campbell, an imposing, attractive woman, was born and raised in Brighton. After attending high school there, she spent some time in Germany, where she became proficient in the language. She attended the London School of Medicine for Women, where she earned three degrees in a very short time. She then had two desirable appointments, one in particular that was sought after by women graduates since it was one of a small number of London hospitals that would employ them. The British government had become very interested in issues of physical fitness among its young people after the Boer War and established the Education Act of 1902, which had among its provisions the introduction of systematic medical checkups of children in elementary schools. In 1904, Campbell got a position as an assistant school medical officer. In 1907, she joined the Board of Education as its first full-time medical officer.

One of the problems that disturbed Campbell was the high rate of infant mortality. The authorities were also concerned about this situation and appointed Campbell as senior medical officer in charge of maternity and child welfare. However, she did not give up her position with the Board of Education. During World War I, she was a medical member of the war cabinet and later served on the health committee of the League of Nations.

Campbell wrote a critically important report on the physical welfare of mothers and children in 1917 for the Carnegie United Kingdom Trust. She also produced many official reports on the recruitment and training of midwives and on the teaching of obstetrics and gynecology in the medical schools. After her well-received report on maternal mortality was published in 1924 she was appointed Dame of the British Empire and given an honorary degree from Durham University. Her work had a profound influence on public health, particularly of women and children in England.

Campbell married quite late, in 1934. Her husband, Michael Heseltine, was registrar of the General Medical Council. After marriage, Civil Service nepotism rules precluded her from keeping her office. Dame Janet had a number of hobbies, including horseback riding, gardening, literature, and politics. She died in Chelsea after a long illness.　　　　JH/MBO

SECONDARY SOURCES

"Dame Janet M. Campbell, D.B.E., M.D., M.S." *British Medical Journal* (9 October 1954): 874–875.

Lancet (9 October 1954).

STANDARD SOURCES
DNB (article by Margaret Hogarth).

CAMPBELL, MAY SHERWOOD (1903–1982)

British botanist. Born 9 March 1903 in Streatham, London, to May and J. W. Campbell. One brother. Never married. Educated Belstead House, Aldeburgh. Professional activities: Lived in both Britain and France. Studied the flora of the Outer Hebrides. Specialist on Salicornia. Botanical Society and Exchange Club of British Isles, secretary; British Museum of Natural History, herbarium. Died 11 August 1982 in Roquebrune-Cap-Martin. Memorialized by Euphrasia campbelliae Pugsley.

Although May Campbell was born near London of Scottish parents, her father, during the season, was doctor for the British community of Menton along the Riviera, where she collected wild flowers. Her brother became a well-known Scottish ornithologist. She was known throughout her life as Maybud, since her mother was also named May. In the 1920s she joined the Wild Flower Society and then the Botanic Society Exchange Club, where she was introduced to scientific field and herbarium botany by Gertrude Foggitt, who also introduced her to A. J. Wilmott of the British Museum (natural history) in the 1930s. She collaborated with Wilmott on annual botanizing expeditions to the Outer Hebrides and published *Flora of Uig* (1945). Assisted by Wilmott, she led a successful field meeting on Pitlochry in 1946 for the Botanic Society of the British Isles (BSBI), formerly the Botanic Society Exchange Club. She became honorary general secretary of that body in 1947 until 1950. She led the Glen Affric field meeting in Scotland, one of the most successful meetings of the BSBI, which saved specimens about to be flooded by a hydroelectric plant. Campbell edited the first yearbook of the BSBI in 1949. In March of 1950, she was elected vice-president of the society and made an honorary life member. She held fellowships in the Linnaean Society and the Royal Horticultural Society.

After her mother died, she moved to Menton, where her father had practiced. She inherited her father's collection of citrus species and cultivars and exhibited them, and small parties of students interested in taxonomic botany would come to visit. In the 1970s, she sold her villa and gardens to the Jardin des Plantes, Paris, which used it as a field station. She retained a small pavillion on the grounds. She bought a second house in the Swiss Alps, but returned every summer to Britain to visit and to botanize. JH/MBO

PRIMARY SOURCES
Campbell, May. *Flora of Uig.* Arbroath, Scotland: T. Buncle, 1945.

SECONDARY SOURCES
Milne-Redhead, E. "Maybud Sherwood Campbell (1903– 1982)." *Watsonia* 15 (1984): 157–160; 519. Obituary notice.

STANDARD SOURCES
Desmond.

CAMPBELL, PERSIA CRAWFORD (1898–1974)

Australian/U.S. economist. Born 15 March 1898 near Sydney, Australia, to Beatrice (Hunt) and Rodolphe Campbell. Married Edward Rice, Jr. (1933, d. 1939). One son, Edward Boyden, and one daughter, Sydney. Naturalized U.S. citizen (1938). Educated local public schools; Sydney University (A.B., 1918; A.M.); London School of Economics (M.Sc., 1923); Bryn Mawr College, fellowship (1924); Rockefeller International Fellowship in Economics, Harvard University (1930–1932); Columbia University, graduate courses in public law (Ph.D., 1940?). Professional experience: Australian Encyclopedia, assistant editor (1924–1926); Industrial Commission of New South Wales, research economist (1926– 1930); Queens College, advancing to professor and head of the department of social science (1939–1965); emerita professor of economics (1965). University of North Carolina, Bryan Professor of Economics (1965–1966). Died 2 March 1974.

Persia Campbell emigrated to the United States from Australia, where she was born and received her education through a master's degree. After a two-year fellowship at the London School of Economics, she completed a master's and published her first book. After receiving this degree, she went to Bryn Mawr College on a fellowship to study American immigration problems. She returned to Australia, where she had several jobs, but in 1930 returned to the United States on a two-year Rockefeller International Fellowship. During her fellowship years, at Harvard University, she studied U.S. agricultural policy and published a book on the subject.

In the United States, Campbell met and married an American electrical engineer, Edward Rice, Jr., and became a U.S. citizen five years later. The couple had two children, but Rice died shortly after their son was six years old and their daughter was five.

Campbell took a position at Queens College, where she remained, advancing through the academic ranks to full professor and head of the department of social sciences. Much of her research involved consumer questions. While continuing with her academic position, she served as an advisor to various government agencies, being especially interested in the problems of the poor. In addition to her academic publications, she wrote popular pamphlets and conducted weekly radio broadcasts, *Report to Consumers,* and the first series for public television, *You, the Consumer*. Appointed the first consumer counsel of New York state by Governor Averell Harriman, she took a leave of absence from Queens and spent four years in Albany working to promote legislative action for consumer abuse. She continued to work as a consultant and advisor to the local, state, and federal governments. President John F. Kennedy appointed her to the President's Council of Economic Advisors (1962) and in 1964 Campbell was reappointed by President Lyndon Johnson.

Campbell also became involved in numerous international programs. She arranged international conferences on women, education, and the consumer, carried out three missions for UNESCO, and in 1958 and 1961 led the United States delegation to the Eighth Triennial Conference of the Pan-Pacific and Southeast Asia Women's Association in Tokyo. She spent a considerable amount of her time representing the International Organization of Consumers Unions at the United Nations.   JH/MBO

PRIMARY SOURCES
Campbell, Persia. *Chinese Coolie Emigration*. London: P. S. King, 1923.
———. *American Agricultural Policy*. London: P. S. King, 1933.
———. *Consumer Representation in the New Deal*. New York: Columbia University Press, 1940.
———. *The Consumer Interest*. New York: Harper, 1949.
———. *Mary Williamson Harriman*. New York: Columbia University Press, 1960.
Many of Campbell's papers are located at the Center for the Study of the Consumer Movement, Mount Vernon, N.Y.

SECONDARY SOURCES
"Persia Campbell: Pioneer Consumer Advocate, Dies." *Consumer Reports* vol. 39, no. 5 (May 1974): 365. Includes photo.
New York Times, 3 March 1974. Obituary notice.
Washington Post, 4 March 1974. Obituary notice.

STANDARD SOURCES
NAW (M) (long article by Sybil Shainwald).

CANNON, ANNIE JUMP (1863–1941)

U.S. astronomer. Born 11 December 1863 in Dover, Del., to Mary (Jump) and Wilson Cannon. Four older half-siblings. Never married. Educated public schools and Wilmington Conference Academy, Dover; Wellesley College (B.S., 1884; M.A., 1907); Radcliffe College, special student (1895–1897). Professional experience: Harvard College Observatory, astronomer (1896–1940), curator of astronomical photographs (1911–1938); Harvard University, William Cranch Bond Astronomer (1938–1940). Died 13 April 1941 in Cambridge, Mass.

Annie Cannon, the oldest of three siblings (there were four other half-brothers and sisters in the family), was the daughter of a shipbuilder, Wilson Cannon. He was the Delaware state senator who had broken with the Democratic Party at the outbreak of the Civil War and cast the deciding vote against secession. Annie's mother, Mary, had been interested in astronomy since her school days, and she and her daughter observed the skies from a makeshift observatory in the attic of their house.

Educational opportunities for girls born in the last half of the century had increased greatly, and Cannon profited from the change. After attending public school and the Wilmington Conference Academy in Dover, she entered the five-year-old Wellesley College in 1880. Astronomer SARAH WHITING guided her astronomical studies and interested her in spectroscopy. After her graduation in 1884, she returned home. Attractive and popular, Cannon spent much of her time engaged in Dover social affairs. After her mother's death in 1893, however, she returned to Wellesley as a postgraduate student and assistant to Sarah Whiting. Following this experience, she was a special student in astronomy at Radcliffe for two years (1895–1897).

In 1896 Cannon became an assistant at the Harvard College Observatory as part of Edward Pickering's (1846–1919) team. Along with WILLIAMINA FLEMING and ANTONIA MAURY, she became intensely involved in the investigations of the observatory, specializing in the study of stellar spectra. Cannon worked at the Harvard Observatory until her retirement in 1940. She succeeded Williamina Fleming as curator of the observatory's astronomical photographs (1911–1938) and in 1938 was made William Cranch Bond Astronomer at Harvard University—one of the first appointments of women by the Harvard corporation.

Cannon was a popular lecturer, enjoyed travel, and regularly attended meetings of the International Astronomical Union. A member of the National Woman's Party, she supported women's suffrage. She received six honorary degrees, including one from the University of Groningen (1921) and one from Oxford (1925). She was made an honorary member of the Royal Astronomical Society in 1914 and received several prizes, including the Nova Medal of the American Association of Variable Star Observers (1922), the Draper Medal of the National Academy of Sciences (1931), and the Ellen Richards Prize of the Society to Aid Scientific Research by Women (1932). Cannon died of cardiovascular disease in 1941.

Most of Annie Cannon's scientific career involved the observation, classification, and spectroscopic analysis of stars. Although she did not create the concept nor invent the methodology for studying stellar spectra, she simplified and perfected the system currently in use, applying it to a comprehensive survey of the heavens. The sheer volume of her work on spectral classification is impressive. Her major publications, *The Henry Draper Catalogue* (1918–1924) and *The Henry Draper Extension* (1925–1949), represent a classification of 350,000 stars; in addition, she published nine smaller catalogues and numerous short papers. Especially fascinated by variable stars, she catalogued many of them. Her work provided a great quantity of data for subsequent investigation. Cannon's own assertion that patience was the major component of her success must be considered; yet her skill as an observer reflected a thorough grasp of principles. MBO

PRIMARY SOURCES

Cannon, Annie Jump. "Williamina Paton Fleming." *Science* n.s. 33 (30 June 1911): 987–988. Obituary of Fleming.

———. With Edward Pickering. *The Henry Draper Catalogue,* vols. 91–99 of *Annals of the Astronomical Observatory of Harvard College,* Cambridge, Mass.: The Observatory, 1918–1924.

SECONDARY SOURCES

Gaposchkin, Cecilia Payne. "Dr. Annie J. Cannon." *Nature* vol. 147, no. 3737 (1941): 738. Obituary notice.

Lankford, John, and Slavings, Rickey L. "Gender and Science: Women in American Astronomy 1859–1940." vol. 43, no. 3, *Physics Today* (March 1990): 58–65.

New York Times, 14 April 1941. Obituary notice.

STANDARD SOURCES

AMS 2–3; *DAB; DSB;* Jones and Boyd; *NAW; Notable;* Ogilvie 1986.

CANNON, LILLIAN (EICHELBERGER) (1897–?)

See Eichelberger, Lillian.

CAPEN, BESSIE (fl. 1874)

U.S. chemist. Professional experience: Girls' High School, Boston; Wellesley College.

Little information is available on Bessie Capen. She was one of the women chemists to attend the first meeting of the American Chemical Society. JH/MBO

STANDARD SOURCES

Rossiter 1982.

CARLSON, ELIZABETH (1896–?)

U.S. mathematician. Born 2 October 1896 in Minneapolis, Minn., to Alice (Johnson) and Carl Emil Carlson. Educated University of Minnesota (B.A., 1917; M.A., 1918; Ph.D., 1924). Professional experience: Knox College, Galesburg, Ill., instructor (1919–

1920); *University of Minnesota, faculty (1924–1965?); professor emerita (from 1965); Macalester College, professor of mathematics (from 1965). Honors and memberships: Phi Beta Kappa, Sigma Xi. Death date unknown.*

Although it is known that Elizabeth Carlson taught at the University of Minnesota for about forty-one years, her progress through the academic ranks has not yet been documented. We know that she was made professor emerita in 1965, after which she continued to teach mathematics at Macalester College until she retired again. JH/MBO

STANDARD SOURCES

Debus.

CARLSON, LUCILLE (1904–)

U.S. geographer and educator. Born 23 January 1904 in Minot, N.D., to Anna C. (Clambey) and John August Carlson. Educated State College, Minot (B.A., 1931); University of Washington (M.A., 1942; Ph.D., 1947). Professional experience: University of Washington, faculty (1947–1948); Western Reserve University, Cleveland, faculty (from 1948), associate professor, geography (1960); chemistry department (from 1961). Honors and memberships: Journal of Geography, Whitbeck Prize (1954); Association of American Geographers; African Studies Association; American Geographic Society, American Association of University Professors, and Phi Beta Kappa.

Born in Minot, North Dakota, Lucille Carlson did her undergraduate work at Minot State College. She then went to the University of Washington for her advanced degrees. After earning her doctorate, she was on the faculty at Washington for a year before moving to Western Reserve University, where she advanced to associate professor, but never made full professor. She published on her research interests, the European Arctic and Africa. JH/MBO

PRIMARY SOURCES

Carlson, Lucille. *Geography and World Politics.* Englewood Cliffs, N.J.: Prentice Hall, 1958.

———. *Africa's Land and Nations.* New York: McGraw Hill, 1967.

STANDARD SOURCES

Debus.

CARNE, ELIZABETH CATHERINE (THOMAS) (1817–1873)

British geologist and author. Born 6 December 1817 in Phillack, Cornwall, to Mary (Thomas) and Joseph Carne, Fellow of the

Royal Society (F.R.S.). Four siblings. Never married. Head of Bank of Batton, Carne and Carne, Penzance (1858–1873). Died 7 September 1873 in Penzance.

Elizabeth Carne was an amateur geologist who absorbed her F.R.S. father's interest in the subject. Upon her father's death in 1858, she inherited his money and gave considerable amounts to various charities. She gave the sites for two schools that were opened at Penzance and founded schools at Wesley Rock, Carfury, and Bosullow. She inherited a collection of minerals from her father and built a museum in which to exhibit it publicly. She was the head of the Penzance bank from 1858 until her death. Carne published a book, *Three Months' Rest at Pau in the Winter and Spring of 1859,* under the pseudonym John Altrayd Witterly, in addition to three other books.

Carne wrote four papers on the geology of Cornwall describing studies that were carried out in the 1860s; they appeared in the *Transactions of the Royal Geological Society of Cornwall.* She also contributed numerous articles to the *London Quarterly Review.*   JH/MBO

PRIMARY SOURCES
Carne, Elizabeth. "Cliff Boulders and the Former Condition of the Land and Sea in the Land's End District." *Transactions of the Royal Geological Society of Cornwall.*
———. "The Age of the Maritime Alps Surrounding Mentone." *Transactions of the Royal Geological Society of Cornwall.*
———. "On the Transition and Metamorphosis of Rocks." *Transactions of the Royal Geological Society of Cornwall.*
———. "On the Nature of the Forces that Have Acted on the Formation of the Land's End Granite." *Transactions of the Royal Geological Society of Cornwall.*

SECONDARY SOURCES
"Carne, Elizabeth Catherine Thomas." *Daily News* (London), 10 September 1873.
"Miss Carne." *Geological Magazine* 10 (1872): 480, 524–525. Obituary notice on Carne's death noted at the annual meeting of the Royal Cornwall Geological Society at the Museum, Penzance. In his presidential address, Warington Smyth, F.R.S., praised Carne for her devotion to geology and to the society.
Creese, Mary R. S., and Thomas M. Creese. "British Women Who Contributed to Research in the Geological Sciences in the Nineteenth Century." *British Journal for the History of Science* 27 (March 1994): 23–54.

STANDARD SOURCES
DNB.

CAROTHERS, ESTRELLA ELEANOR (1882–1957)

U.S. geneticist and cytologist. Born 4 December 1882 in Newton, Kans., to Mary (Bates) and Z. W. Carothers. Educated Nickerson Normal College, Kans.; University of Kansas (B.A., 1911; M.A., 1912); University of Pennsylvania (Ph.D., 1916). Professional experience: assistant professor of zoology, University of Pennsylvania (1913); State University of Iowa, (now the University of Iowa), research associate for the Department of Zoology. Died 1957 in Murdoch, Kans.

Little information is available on Eleanor Carothers's early life. Her parents, Mary and Z. W. Carothers, saw to it that she attended Nickerson Normal College. After this experience, she attended the universities of Kansas, where she received her bachelor's and master's degrees, and Pennsylvania, where she received her doctoral degree. In 1916, the year in which she received her doctorate, she became assistant professor of zoology at the University of Pennsylvania. During 1915 and 1919 she was a member of the University of Pennsylvania's scientific expeditions to the southern and southwestern states. During most of her career, she was an independent investigator. She returned to Kansas from Iowa in 1941.

Carothers specialized in orthopteran genetics and cytology, with special reference to heteromorphic homologous chromosomes. She received a grant from the Rockefeller Foundation Fund for research on the physiology and cytology of the normal cell. With this grant, she was able to conduct research on grasshopper cells. A careful research scientist, she contributed both data and explanations to the question of the cytological basis of heredity; her findings were published in the *Journal of Morphology,* the *Quarterly Review of Biology,* the *Proceedings of the Entomological Society,* and the *Biological Bulletin.* She was listed as an independent investigator for nearly twenty years in the Marine Biological Laboratory's annual report. From 1920 to 1956 she was listed as a regular member of the Marine Biological Laboratory in Woods Hole, Massachusetts.   JH/MBO

PRIMARY SOURCES
Carothers, E[strella] Eleanor. *The Segregation and Recombination of Homologous Chromosomes as Found in Two Genera of Acrididae (Orthoptera).* Baltimore: Waverly Press, 1917.
———. Various publications in *Journal of Morphology* and *Biological Bulletin.*

SECONDARY SOURCES
Chadwell, Faye A. "E. (Estrella) Eleanor Carothers (1882–1957)." In Shearer and Shearer 1996.
Rossiter, Margaret. "Women Scientists in America before 1920." *American Scientist* 62 (1974): 312–323.

CARPENTER, ESTHER (1903–?)

U.S. zoologist. Born 4 June 1903 in Meriden, Conn., to Nettie Jane (Hale) and Ernest Charles Carpenter. Educated Ohio Wesleyan University (B.A., 1925); University of Wisconsin (M.S., 1927); Bryn Mawr College, fellow, biology (1927–1928); Yale University (Ph.D., 1932). Professional experience: Carnegie Institute of Technology, research assistant, embryology (1932–1933); Albertus Magnus College, part-time instructor (1933–1934); Smith College, faculty member (from 1933), professor of zoology (from 1953), chemistry department, professor (1955–1960); Myra M. Sampson Professor of Zoology (from 1963). Death date unknown.

Esther Carpenter did research on embryonic thyroid, its stimulation, and its tissue culture. In the 1920s she received both her bachelor's and master's degrees at midwestern universities and then went east to Bryn Mawr as a fellow in biology. Immediately after Esther Carpenter received her doctoral degree from Yale University, she became a research assistant for one year at the Carnegie Institute of Technology. The next year, she worked as a part-time teacher at Albertus Magnus. During the same year she became a faculty member at Smith, where she eventually was named Myra M. Sampson Professor of Zoology. In the early 1930s she was a part-time instructor at Albertus Magnus College where MARCELLA BOVERI had just developed an excellent program in biology and embryology.

Campbell received a number of research fellowships. Twice traveling to England she did research at Strangeways Research Laboratories during 1953–1954. She was a member of numerous organizations, including the Tissue Culture Association, the Growth Society, the American Society for Cell Biology, the American Society of Zoologists, the American Association of Anatomists, and Sigma Xi. Much of her research was on endocrine glands and the relationship of vitamin A to their function, particularly in developmental stages. She contributed articles on the thyroid and pituitary glands and the way in which vitamin A functioned. She also worked with differentiation, specifically the onset of functioning in embryonic thyroids of chick and rat and the effect of excess vitamin A in the diet of young rats on the thyroid gland and on the thyroid-stimulating cells in the pituitary glands.   JH/MBO

PRIMARY SOURCES

Carpenter, Esther. "Differentiation of Chick Embryo Thyroids in Tissue Culture." *Journal of Experimental Zoology* 89, no. 3 (1942): 407–426.

———. With Ursula Rothfels. "A Comparison of Growth and Differentiation of Avian Femur Rudiments on Clots of Partially or Completely Known Constituents." *Anatomical Record* 97, no. 3 (1947): 412–413.

STANDARD SOURCES

AMS 6–8, B 9; P&B 10–19; Debus.

CARR, EMMA PERRY (1880–1972)

U.S. physical chemist. Born 23 July 1880 in Holmsville, Ohio, to Anna Mary (Jack) and Edmund Carr. Four siblings. Never married. Educated at Ohio State University (1898–1899); Mount Holyoke College; University of Chicago (B.S., 1904); graduate work at University of Chicago (Ph.D., 1910); postdoctoral research at Queens University, Belfast (1919); University of Zurich (1929–1930); University of Mexico (1944). Professional experience: Mount Holyoke, head of chemistry department (1913–1946). Honorary degrees: D.Sc.: Allegheny College (1939); Russell Sage College (1941); Mount Holyoke College (1952); Hood College (1957). Honors and memberships: Garvan Medal from the American Chemical Society (1937); Northeastern Section of the American Chemical Society, Norris Award (1957); Phi Beta Kappa, Iota Sigma Pi, and Sigma Delta Epsilon, honorary memberships; American Association for the Advancement of Science, Fellow. Died 7 January 1972 at Evanston, Ill.

Emma Carr was the third of five children of Edmund and Anna Mary Carr. After her birth, the family decided to move to Coshocton, Ohio. Here Emma's father was a general practitioner and pediatrician. Her mother became active in the matters of the community, especially the Methodist Church. Because Mrs. Carr was the center of the community, the Carr children also became involved. Emma herself played the organ in the Methodist Church. This is where she began to gain a great appreciation for music and came to cherish the cello, which she later played. Not only did Emma show enthusiasm toward such daily life activities, but throughout her life she continued her enthusiastic approach toward her studies and her teaching.

At Ohio State University, Carr began her study of chemistry under William McPherson. After her first year she transferred from Ohio State to Mount Holyoke College, where, after her junior year, she became an assistant in the chemistry department. She then went to the University of Chicago to complete her bachelor's degree. She returned to teach chemistry as an instructor at Mount Holyoke from 1905 to 1907. She then returned to the University of Chicago where she completed her doctorate. Carr came back to Mount Holyoke as an associate professor from 1910 to 1913. At age thirty-three she became a full professor and head of the chemistry department. While teaching she did research by herself, with faculty, and with students. Before Carr began her research, she undertook learning how to work cooperatively. She saw research as an essential part of both the learning and the teaching of chemistry, so she decided to combine the two. The year that she became full professor, she developed a departmental research program designed to teach students, those with honors and those working toward their master's degrees, through cooperative research work with the faculty of Mount Holyoke. These cooperative projects combined the concepts and techniques of organic and physical chemistry. Carr understood the impact of combining minds when doing research and she was recognized for her leadership in developing the group research efforts. Her recognition for being a great teacher was based not only on her leadership of group research, but also on her ability to share her enthusiasm with her students. This enthusiasm went beyond chemistry to any activity or project in which she was involved.

From her research, Carr became renowned in the scientific world. In 1919, she worked at Belfast, where she learned the most advanced ultraviolet techniques of the post–World War I period. She took advantage of the wartime demand for chemists and scientists to secure trustee approval and funding for research. Carr built up a well-equipped spectrographic laboratory at Mount Holyoke. She did this through grants that she secured from the National Research Council and the Rockefeller Foundation and from support of the trustees. The research involving ultraviolet spectroscopy led to numerous awards and continued funding.

Carr's research in vacuum spectroscopy also led to the application of physical chemistry to organic problems. Her studies made her a pioneer in the field of absorption of organic chemical compounds. Her work involved the analysis of unsaturated hydrocarbons by ultraviolet absorption spectra. She examined the molecular patterns of the hydrocarbons through ultraviolet spectroscopy. This work was a theoretical study of the absorption spectra of highly purified hydrocarbons. Although it was only theoretical, petroleum chemists had already found this research to have an important use. From this and other research Mount Holyoke became one of the first American research centers to make use of spectroscopy to study organic molecules.

Carr achieved national and international prestige. A few of Carr's honors for her work included serving as an official delegate to the meetings of the International Union of Pure and Applied Chemistry in 1925, 1926, and 1936. She was also a consulting expert on spectra for the International Critical Tables. Other honors include the Mary Woolley and Lowenthal Fellowships that she held along with the Alice Freeman Palmer Fellowship from 1929–1930, awarded by the American Association of University Women. Carr and MARY SHERRILL were jointly awarded the James Flack Norris award on 9 May 1957, for their outstanding achievement in the teaching of chemistry as well as in research. One of Carr's greatest honors was the receipt of the Garvan Medal in 1937. This medal is given by the American Chemical Society to honor an American woman for distinguished service

in chemistry. This was the first annual award of its kind and Carr was the first woman to receive this great honor. The award was established by Francis Garvan because of his knowledge of Carr and his desire to encourage women chemists. She received this award for her research in physical chemistry, especially on the structure of organic molecules through the use of absorption spectra in the far ultraviolet, as well as her development of the group research technique. Carr's work at the time she received the Garvan Medal was described as an "incomparable contribution to American chemistry" [*NAW* (M)].

In honor of her contributions to American chemistry and Mount Holyoke, the chemistry laboratory at Mount Holyoke was given her name in 1955. Carr belonged to numerous committees and organizations. She was a member of Phi Beta Kappa, Sigma Xi, American Association of University Women, American Chemical Society, and American Physical Society; she was Fellow of the American Association for the Advancement of Science and an honorary member of Sigma Delta Epsilon and Iota Sigma Pi. She was named an emerita professor at Mount Holyoke when she retired in 1946.

Carr was recognized as a distinguished teacher throughout her career at Mount Holyoke. She felt a duty to take interest in political and everyday life as well as her studies, which she did zealously, showing her students, who were all women, the way to live and act in the world. While Carr taught there, the number of women chemistry graduates from Mount Holyoke who went on to earn doctorates was greater than at any other American institution. Carr showed her students that training, motivation, and persistence were the means to full acceptance of women in the chemistry field. Each succeeding year, Carr's students built upon her work and studies and in turn taught others about the chemistry field, always with the enthusiasm that Carr had showed them. Carr moved to Evanston, Illinois in 1964, where she lived until heart failure took her from the chemistry world in 1972. Carr's work continues today to be a foundation of our most basic understanding of molecules.   N R

PRIMARY SOURCES

Carr, Emma P. "Isomers of 2-Pentane. III. The Ultraviolet Absorption Spectra of the Isomeric 2-Pentenes." *Journal of the American Chemical Society* 51 (1929): 3041–3053. Three articles on the isomers of 2-Pentane were published by the Mount Holyoke research group in this issue with Carr as the author of the third article. The article focuses on the ultraviolet absorption spectra and isomerism.

———. "One Hundred Years of Science at Mount Holyoke College." *Mount Holyoke Alumnae Quarterly* (1936): 135–138. A radio talk show at Mount Holyoke of 19 May 1936. Emma Perry Carr speaks of the many inspiring women that contributed greatly to Mount Holyoke's uniqueness in science and of the college itself.

———. "The Ultraviolet Absorption Spectra of the Isomers of Butene-2 and Pentene-2." *Journal of the American Chemical Society* 59 (1937): 2138–2141. In this paper Carr brings together all of the theory and experimental work on the ultraviolet absorption spectra and provides the interpretation of the earlier discussions on isomerism.

———. "Electronic Transitions in Simple Unsaturated Hydrocarbons." *Chemical Reviews* 41 (1947): 293–299. In this paper published the year after she retired, she reviews not only the work from Mount Holyoke, but all of the work in the field to that time.

SECONDARY SOURCES

"In Memoriam. Carr, Emma Perry." *Mount Holyoke Alumnae Quarterly* (Spring 1972): 23–25.

Doolittle, Martha Bailey. "Women in Science." *Journal of Chemical Education* 22 (1945): 171–174.

Hallock, Grace Taber. "Emma Perry Carr, Professor Emeritus of Chemistry." *Mount Holyoke Alumnae Quarterly* 30 (August 1946): 53–55.

Jennings, Bojan Hamlin. "The Professional Life of Emma Perry Carr." *Journal of Chemical Education* 63 (1986): 923–927.

Miles, Wyndham N., ed. *American Chemists and Chemical Engineers.* Washington, D.C.: American Chemical Society, 1976.

Sherrill, Mary L. "Group Research in a Small Department." *Journal of Chemical Education* 34 (1957): 467–468.

STANDARD SOURCES

AMS 3–8, P 9, P&B 10–11; *Current Biography;* Debus; Herzenberg; Kass-Simon and Farnes; *NAW* (M); O'Neill; Rossiter 1982; Rossiter 1985; Siegel and Finley.

CARROLL, CHRISTIANE (MENDREZ) (1937–1978)

French geneticist, anthropologist, and vertebrate paleontologist. Born 24 September 1937 in Paris. Married Robert Carroll. One son, Roland. Educated Sorbonne (Doctorat de 3ᵉ, cycle, 1962, a degree short of a Ph.D. and beyond a master's). Died November 1978.

Carroll was born in Paris where she lived for most of her life. Before she became interested in vertebrate paleontology, she taught genetics and physical anthropology at the Sorbonne. Afterward, she worked on Pleistocene mammals for her doctorate, which she earned in 1962. In 1974, she married Robert Carroll and their son, Roland, was born in 1975. Although information is not available as to the cause of her death, it is probable that both Cristiane and Roland died in an accident.

Carroll studied Pleistocene mammals, but her major interest was on South African therocephalians. At the time of her death she was working on a doctorate from the University of the Witwatersrand at Johannesburg. Although her life was short, she established herself as an expert in classical morphology while working with therapsid reptiles. She was meticulous in her research, and in her descriptions of these animals combined a morphological with a functional approach, departing from the standard approach, which stressed the mammal-like characteristics of the therapsids. Before her death she expanded her taxonomic studies to Russian, Chinese, and East African therocephalians, making it possible to provide a broader interpretation of the paleozoogeography and evolution of this group.   JH/MBO

SECONDARY SOURCES

Hotton, Nick. *News Bulletin of the Society of Vertebrate Paleontology* no. 116 (June 1979): 63–64. Obituary notice. Includes photo.

STANDARD SOURCES

Sarjeant.

CARROLL, DOROTHY (1907–1970)

Australian/U.S. geologist. Born 7 June 1907 in western Australia, to an English mother and Scotch-Irish father. Three siblings. Never married. Educated University of Western Australia (B.A. with honors in geology); Imperial College, University of London (Ph.D., 1936). Professional experience: University of Western Australia, lecturer (1936–1941); Government Chemical Laboratories of Western Australia, mineralogist (1941 until post–World War II); Linnean Society of New South Wales, secretary; University of Sydney, lecturer; Bryn Mawr College, research fellow; Geochemistry and Petrology Branch of the U.S. Geological Survey, researcher (1952–1963); USGS in Menlo Park, California, researcher; administrator (1963–1967). Died 30 January 1970.

Dorothy Carroll was a native Australian. Her childhood was spent in a large house by the sea in western Australia, and her life was filled with pets, farm animals, agricultural shows, and outdoor life in general. Her father was the local manager of a stock company. Although Dorothy grew up believing that women could do anything that men could, her upbringing was traditional with its stress on manners, duty, books, painting, and music. She received a science scholarship to the University of Western Australia but, unaware of the mathematics entrance requirement, received an arts degree in zoology. She then entered the science faculty, became interested in geology, and took an honors degree. After earning this degree, Carroll was awarded a scholarship to complete her doctoral work at the University of London, becoming in 1936 the first woman from western Australia to obtain a doctorate in geology. After working for several years in Australia, she accepted a research fellowship at Bryn Mawr College. After a hassle with the immigration authorities, Carroll was given the necessary documentation to work at a federal job. For the remainder of her career, she worked with the U.S. Geological Survey, first in Washington, D.C., and then in Menlo Park, California. However, when the laboratory of the survey was moved from Washington, D.C., to Denver, Colorado, Carroll relinquished her position as its head in order to remain in Washington. During her last year in Washington, Carroll was diagnosed as having a cyst on the cerebellum. This cyst was successfully removed. However, she later died of cancer.

Carroll was a Fellow of the Geological Society of America and the Mineralogical Society of America. She was a member of a host of other scientific organizations.

As a research fellow at Bryn Mawr, Carroll had the opportunity to explore chemical-geological relationships in sediments and soils. Previously, she had worked mainly with mechanical analysis. Her work with the U.S. Geological Survey was on marine sediments and clay mineralogy on which she published extensively. Dorothy Carroll was a good administrator and at the USGS organized the laboratory personnel and procedures. CK

SECONDARY SOURCES

Hooker, Marjorie, and Helen L. Foster. Memorial of Dorothy Carroll, April 7, 1907–January 30, 1970. *American Mineralogist* 57, parts 3–4 (1972): 631–635.

STANDARD SOURCES

Sarjeant.

CARSON, RACHEL LOUISE (1907–1964)

U.S. biologist, conservationist, science writer. Known for her important biological observations and attention to the hazards of insecticides. Born 27 May 1907 in Springdale, Pa., to Maria Frazier (McLean) and Robert Warden Carson. Educated Pennsylvania College for Women, later Chatham College (A.B., 1929; D.Litt., 1952); Johns Hopkins University (M.A., 1932); Oberlin College (D.Sc., 1952); Marine Biological Laboratories, Woods Hole, summers (1929–1964). Professional experience: University of Maryland, zoology department, faculty (1931–1936); Johns Hopkins summer school, faculty (1930–1936); U.S. Bureau of Fisheries, junior aquatic biologist; Fish and Wildlife Service, biologist (1936–1948), and editor-in-chief (1949–1952). Guggenheim Fellowship (1951–1952). Various awards and honors 1951–1962. Died 14 April 1964.

From her early childhood in Springdale, Pennsylvania, Rachel Carson was determined to be a writer. Consequently, when she attended Pennsylvania College for Women, she majored in English where she graduated *magna cum laude.* Encouraged by her mother, she was also intrigued by natural history, an interest that was magnified when she took a required college zoology course. Assuming that her two interests were mutually exclusive, Carson accepted that by attending graduate school in biology she would have to give up writing. In the fall of 1929, she enrolled at Johns Hopkins University after spending a summer at the Marine Biological Laboratory, Woods Hole, Massachusetts. In 1932, she earned a master's degree in marine biology. After teaching part-time at Johns Hopkins and the University of Maryland, Carson sought a better paying and more reliable job. After scoring higher than the other candidates on the Civil Service examination, she accepted a position as a junior aquatic biologist with the U.S. Bureau of Fisheries, where she had previously worked part-time.

During the times when she was not working, Carson wrote. She published her first article, "Undersea," in the *Atlantic Monthly.* This article later formed the basis of her first book, *Under the Sea Wind.* During World War II, Carson wrote conservation bulletins urging people to eat fish. After the war, she remained at the renamed U.S. Fish and Wildlife Service. In 1949 she was promoted to biologist and became chief editor of the journal of the U.S. Fish and Wildlife Service. Her small income enabled her to continue with her own writing, and in 1951 *The Sea Around Us* was published. This book was a great success, partly because it had been serialized in the *New Yorker;* it remained on the best-seller list for eighty-six weeks. The success of this book caused *Under the Sea Wind* to be reissued, and it, too, was a success this time. After the success of these books and the film version of *The Sea Around Us,* Carson resigned her position with the Fish and Wildlife Service and devoted her time exclusively to writing, living in a small cottage in West Southport, Maine. *The Edge of the Sea* resulted from this effort.

The domination of the human species over all others increasingly disturbed Carson. This type of shortsighted thinking, she asserted, would mean the destruction of life as we knew it. To convince people of the necessity of changing our way of dealing with the natural world, she produced one of the most poignant and influential books of all time—the book that, in essence, began the environmental movement. *Silent Spring,* published in 1962, expressly addressed the problem of insecticides and herbicides, especially DDT. Beautifully written, it engaged its sympathetic readers and infuriated its opponents, in particular members of the pesticide industry. Industry scientists accused Carson of launching an unscientific polemic. Her story, however, was so powerful that the public's awareness of the problem ballooned and the environmental movement moved from an esoteric discipline to a burgeoning popular movement. The person who thought that writing and science were mutually incompatible proved that through writing, scientific ideas could become relevant to nonscientists and, consequently, become the instruments of change. Carson died in 1964 of cancer and heart failure.   J H

PRIMARY SOURCES

Carson, Rachel Louise. "The Development of the Pronephros during the Embryonic and Early Larval Life of the Catfish *(Ictalurus punctatus)*." Master's thesis, Johns Hopkins University, 1931.

———. *Under the Sea Wind.* New York: Simon and Schuster, 1941.

———. *The Sea Around Us.* New York: Oxford University Press, 1951.

———. *The Edge of the Sea.* Boston: Houghton Mifflin, 1956.

———. *Silent Spring.* Boston: Houghton Mifflin, 1962.

SECONDARY SOURCES

Brooks, Paul. *Rachel Carson at Work: The House of Life.* Boston: G. K. Hall, 1972; 1985.

Gartner, C. B. *Rachel Carson.* New York: Ungar, 1983.

Graham, Frank, Jr. *Since Silent Spring.* Boston: Houghton Mifflin, 1970.

Hynes, H. Patricia. *The Recurring Silent Spring.* New York: Pergamon Press, 1989.

Lear, Linda J. *Rachel Carson: Witness for Nature.* New York: Henry Holt, 1997.

McCay, Mary A. *Rachel Carson.* New York: Twayne, 1993.

Sabin, Francene. *Rachel Carson: Friend of the Earth.* Mahwah, N.J.: Troll, 1998.

Sterling, P. *Sea and Earth: The Life of Rachel Carson.* New York: Crowell, 1970.

STANDARD SOURCES

Bailey; Debus; *DSB;* Grinstein (long article by Randy Moore); *Notable* (long article by Tom Crawford); Uglow 1989.

CARTER, EDNA (1872–?)

U.S. physicist. Born 29 January 1872 in High Cliff, Wis. Educated Vassar College (A.B., 1894); University of Chicago (1898–1899); University of Würzburg (Ph.D., 1906); also in Würzburg 1911–1912. Professional experience: public high school, Wisconsin, assistant principal (1895–1896); Vassar College, assistant in physics (1896–1898), associate professor (1912–1920), professor (1920–1941), emerita professor (from 1941); Wisconsin State Normal School, Oshkosh, Wis., teacher (1899–1904).

Physicist Edna Carter was born in Wisconsin, but received her education at Vassar, the University of Chicago, and

Würzburg. She advanced through the academic ranks at Vassar, eventually becoming full professor. She was a member of the Physical Society and the Optical Society. In her research she studied the relation of the energy of Roentgen rays to the energy of the cathode rays producing them. She also worked on the discharge potentials across very short distances, metallic spectra produced in high vacua, electric furnace spectra, and thermoluminescence.   M M

STANDARD SOURCES

AMS 1–3; Rossiter 1982.

CARTER, ELIZABETH (1717–1806)

British natural philosopher, classicist, and miscellaneous writer. Born 16 December 1717 at Deal in Kent to Margaret and the Reverend Nicholas Carter. Never married. Educated in classical languages by father; tutored by the astronomer Thomas Wright. Died 19 February 1806 in Clarges Street Piccadilly.

Though not naturally a quick learner, judging from statements made by her father as he taught her classical languages, by her perseverance Elizabeth Carter eventually succeeded. Before she was seventeen she was writing verses. Her first published piece was a riddle that appeared in the 1734 *Gentleman's Magazine.* She continued to contribute to this magazine, usually under the name of Eliza. She published numerous works on a variety of subjects throughout her life.

Elizabeth Carter was a part of a group of intellectual women, the Bluestockings. The Italian Francesco Algarotti had written an explanation of Newton's *Opticks* based on Fontenelle's work. Algarotti's *Il Newtonianismo per le dame,* however, was geared especially to women. Carter translated this book under the title of *Sir Isaac Newton's Philosophy Explained for the Use of the Ladies in Six Dialogues on Light and Colours.* Although Carter devoted much time to the study of science, she still considered the classics to be of greater importance and became an internationally known classical scholar. Part of her classical studies included astronomy and mathematics, two parts of the old mathematical quadrivium. She employed the well-known astronomer Thomas Wright of Durham, a scientific instrument maker who supplemented his income by teaching mathematics and science to young men and women. Carter met her good friend Catherine Talbot, with whom she shared many interests, through Wright.

Although she never married, she was called "Mrs. Carter" by the author of the *DNB.* During the latter part of her life her health was poor, but she was eighty-eight years old when she died.   J H / M B O

PRIMARY SOURCES

Carter, Elizabeth. *Memoirs of the Life of Mrs. Elizabeth Carter.* Ed. Montagu Pennington. London: F. C. and J. Rivington, 1807.

———. *Letters.* 2 vols. London: F. C. and J. Rivington, 1809.

SECONDARY SOURCES

Pennington, Montagu. *Memoirs of the Life of Mrs. Elizabeth Carter.* 2d. ed. Boston: Oliver C. Greenblatt, 1808.

STANDARD SOURCES

DNB; Encyclopaedia Britannica, 9th ed., vol. 141.; Meyer; Phillips; Rebière; Uglow 1989.

CARTWRIGHT, DAME MARY LUCY (1900–?)

British mathematician. Born 17 December 1900 in Aynho, Northampshire, England, to Lucy (Bury) and Digby Cartwright. Educated St. Hugh's College, Oxford (B.A., 1919; M.A., 1923; Ph.D., 1930); Cambridge University (Sc.D., 1949). Professional experience: Alice Ottley School, Worcester, England, assistant mistress (1923–1924); Wycombe Abbey School, Buckinghamshire, England, assistant mistress (1924–1927); Girton College, Cambridge, research fellow (1930–1934), fellow and lecturer in mathematics (1934–1949), mistress (1949–1968); Cambridge University, university lecturer in mathematics (1935–1959), reader, theory of functions (1959–1968), emerita reader (from 1968); Brown University, R.I., visiting professor (1968–1969); Claremont Graduate School (1969–1970); Case Western Reserve University (1970); Levelhume visiting professor, Poland (1970); University of Wales, visiting professorial fellow (1971). Honors and memberships: Order of Dannebrog, Commander (1961); Royal Society, Sylvester Medal (1964); London Mathematical Society, Morgan Medal (1968); Mathematical Association, London; Cambridge Philosophical Society; Institute of Mathematics and Its Applications; American Mathematical Society. Honorary degrees: Edinburgh (Ll.D., 1953); Leeds (D.Sc., 1958); Hull (1959); Oxford (1966); Wales (1967); Brown (1969). Death date unknown.

Mary Cartwright earned her bachelor's, master's, and doctoral degrees from Oxford University. After she received her degrees, she taught in two girls' schools before going to Cambridge, where she was a fellow of Girton College and later mistress. From 1933 she was on the faculty at Cambridge, finally becoming a reader in the theory of functions in 1959. She published numerous articles and authored a book on integral functions. Much of her research was on the theory of analytic functions and series. She also worked on the theory of nonlinear differential equations, with J. E. Littlewood, especially the consideration of equations connected with radio and stability problems of automatic control.

Cartwright was a Fellow of the Royal Society of Edinburgh, a Fellow and council member of the Royal Society of London, and the recipient of seven honorary degrees. She was made a Dame Commander of the British Empire in 1969.

JH/MBO

PRIMARY SOURCES

Cartwright, Mary Lucy. *The Mathematical Mind.* New York: Oxford University Press, 1955.

———. *Integral Functions.* Cambridge, England: Cambridge University Press, 1956.

STANDARD SOURCES

Debus; *World Who's Who of Women.*

CARUS, MARY HEGELER (1861–1936)

U.S. mathematical editor. Born 10 January 1861 in La Salle, Ill., to Camilla Weisbach and Edward C. Hegeler. Nine siblings. Married Paul Carus. Six children. Educated La Salle public schools; University of Michigan (A.B., 1882); Freiberg Mining Academy (attended lectures on metallurgy). Professional experience: collaborated with her husband in editing Open Court, *associate editor (1890–1936); arranged for financing the Carus Mathematical Monographs (from 1925); Matthiessen and Hegeler Zinc Company, vice-president and president (1903–1936). Died 27 June 1936.*

Mary Hegeler was not a mathematician herself, but served with her husband as an associate editor for *Open Court*, and *Monist*, journals that included many mathematical articles. Although her father had come from Bremen, Mary was born in the United States, where he had emigrated. Before he left Saxony, he met his future wife, Camilla, the daughter of a professor at the School of Mines, Freiberg. With the intention of building a zinc plant, Edward Hegeler settled on La Salle, Illinois, a likely location because of its proximity to both coal fields and zinc mines. Mary Hegeler attended school at La Salle and when she was sixteen years old worked in her father's zinc plant. She then went to the University of Michigan, where she studied mathematics and chemistry. After graduating in 1882, she went to Freiberg, where she attended lectures at the Freiberg Academy. She also assisted in the laboratory of her uncle, the chemist Clemens Winkler, who discovered the chemical element Germanium (Ge). When she returned to the United States, she again worked for her father, taking on more and more responsibilities at the plant.

Her father had met a young German scholar, Paul Carus, whom he had hired to tutor his children and to edit the magazine *Open Court*, which Hegeler had established in 1887. In 1888, Carus and Mary Hegeler were married, and collaborated on projects involving *Open Court* and *Monist.* Later, through her financial support, she assured the publication of the Carus Mathematical Monographs under the auspices of the Mathematical Association of America.

Edward Hegeler founded *Open Court* in many ways to buttress his monistic conceptions of science and God. To him God was in nature and morality was that which could stand the test of continued experience. Paul Carus had similar ideas, and both men were important influences on Mary. By 1890, *Open Court* had evolved into a more popular magazine and a new quarterly, the *Monist,* was established. Paul Carus served as editor and Mary Hegeler and her father served as associate editors of the magazines and books issued by the Open Court Publishing Company. After the death of Paul Carus in 1919, Mary with able assistants continued her husband's work. Monism was closely related to mathematics, and because of Mary Carus's sympathies for monism, many of Open Court's publications were on mathematics.

JH/MBO

SECONDARY SOURCES
Smith, David Eugene. "Mary Hegeler Carus, 1861–1936."
    American Mathematical Monthly 44 (1937): 280–283.

STANDARD SOURCES
Rossiter 1982.

CARVAJALES Y CAMINO, LAURA M. DE (b. ca. 1866)
Cuban physician. Born ca. 1866. Educated Havana, Cuba, medical school (M.D., 1889).

Laura M. de Carvajales y Camino was one of several women awarded medical degrees from Latin American schools. The admission of women to medical school in Havana, Cuba, followed that of women in the home country of Spain. In 1889, Manuela Solis, the first woman physician in Spain, received her degree from the Medical Faculty at Valencia; in the same year, Laura de Carvajales y Camino received hers from the University of Havana. No other information is known about Carvajales y Camino.   JH/MBO

STANDARD SOURCES
Lovejoy.

CASTLE, CORA (SUTTON) (b. 1880)
U.S. psychologist and statistician. Married H. E. Castle, M.D. Educated Columbia University (Ph.D. in psychology, 1913). Professional experience: private practice in psychology.

Cora Sutton made a name for herself because of her dissertation, which was later published as a book. She received a doctorate in psychology at Columbia University under James McKeen Cattell and Robert S. Woodworth. Her dissertation, a compilation of 868 eminent women in psychology, was published and received considerable attention. She used Cattell's methods to rank her women on the basis of the length of their encyclopedia entries. Her sample was skewed toward royalty and writers, so she failed to make any conclusions from her samples regarding social versus biological factors. There were those then and later who considered the small number deemed "eminent" by the definition of "holding high rank, office, or worth" to be a negative judgment of women psychologists. The book as a whole was considered antifeminist. Cora Sutton was married to H. E. Castle, M.D., and became a prominent private psychologist.   JH/MBO

PRIMARY SOURCES
Castle, Cora S. "A Statistical Study of Eminent Women."
    Archives of Psychology 4, no. 27 (August 1913).
———. "A Statistical Study of Eminent Women." *Popular
    Science Monthly* 82 (1913): 593–611. A shortened version of
    the above.

STANDARD SOURCES
Rossiter 1982; Stevens and Gardner.

CASTRA, ANNA DE (fl. 1629)
Spanish natural philosopher.

Little is known of Anna de Castra, except that she published several philosophical works, one of which is entitled *Etergidad del rey Felippe III.*   JH/MBO

PRIMARY SOURCES
Castra, Anna de. *Etergidad del rey Felippe III.* Madrid, 1629.

STANDARD SOURCES
DFC, vol. 2, 29; Hurd-Mead 1938; Lipinska 1900.

CATANI, GIUSEPPINA (fl. ca. 1890)
Italian pathologist. Educated University of Bologna (M.D., 1884). Professional experience: University of Bologna, faculty of medicine, privat docent of general pathology (1889).

Giuseppina Catani received the first medical diploma from the University of Bologna's faculty of medicine in modern times. After she received her degree, she was named *privat-docent* of pathology at the Faculty of Medicine of Bologna.

The students gave Catani an ovation after her first lecture. She was known for her ability to lecture and for her talent with words.   JH/MBO

STANDARD SOURCES
Lipinska 1900; Mozans.

CATHERINE, MEDICA OF CRACOW (fl. ca. 1400)
Polish medical woman. Flourished last part of fifteenth century.

Catherine, Medica of Cracow, was one of several noble-women in Poland who practiced medicine.   JH/MBO

STANDARD SOURCES
Hurd-Mead 1938.

CATHERINE OF BOLOGNA, SAINT (1413–1463)
Italian medical woman. Born 1413 in Bologna[?] Professional experience: Abbess of Poor Clares of Bologna; artist (mostly miniatures) and musician; cared for the poor and sick.

Catherine of Bologna was an important fifteenth-century Italian medical woman who became a saint. As abbess of the monastery of the Poor Clares, she taught the sisters medicine so that they could prescribe for as well as nurse their patients. They were taught to diagnose diseases and understand the significance of urine and the pulse. They knew the signs of death and when further treatment was hopeless.   JH/MBO

STANDARD SOURCES
Echols and Williams; Hurd-Mead 1938.

CATHERINE OF GENOA, SAINT (1447–1510)
Noblewoman of Fleschi. Married Julio Adorno. Professional experience: cared for the sick; founded a hospital in Genoa in 1477.

Catherine of Genoa was forced to marry Julio Adorno. After the marriage she became very pious, had visions, and wore a hairshirt. She founded a hospital in Genoa in 1477 and trained helpers to care for the sick. She worked during the plague outbreak.   JH/MBO

STANDARD SOURCES
Echols and Williams; Hurd-Mead 1938.

CATHERINE OF SIENA, SAINT (1347–1380)
Italian medical woman. Born 1347 in Siena. Educated Dominican order (from 1367). Professional experience: Dominican. Taught nuns to diagnose diseases. Worked to push the papal court out of Avignon and back to Rome. Died 1380 in Siena.

Born in a small house which still stands on a hillside in Siena, Catherine was the daughter of a tanner. As a young girl, she refused marriage and dedicated her life to Christ. When she was twenty years old, she joined the Dominican order. Catherine was a mystic who had received the stigmata by the time she joined the order. She devoted her life to the care of the sick. She was especially involved with those who had the plague. In 1372, she cared for its victims for a year without contracting the disease herself. She showed no revulsion as she dressed the sores of lepers, and daily washed the sores of a woman who was dying of a "bad-smelling cancer."
                                                      JH/MBO

STANDARD SOURCES
Echols and Williams; Hurd-Mead 1938.

CATHERINE URSULA, COUNTESS OF BADEN (b. 1600s)
German medical woman. Born ca. 1600.

Catherine Ursula of Baden is another example of a noble-woman who became a physician.   JH/MBO

STANDARD SOURCES
Hurd-Mead 1938.

CATLOW, MARIA AGNES (1807?–1889)
British botanist born ca. 1807. Published on botanical subjects. Died 10 May 1889 in Addlestone, Surrey.

British popular botanical writer, Maria Catlow wrote books on field, garden, and greenhouse botany between 1847 and 1857. She died in Addlestone, Surrey, 10 May 1889.
                                                      JH/MBO

PRIMARY SOURCES
Catlow, Maria Agnes. *Popular Field Botany.* London: Reeve, Benham, and Reeve, 1848.
———. *Popular Garden Botany.* London: Lovell Reeve, 1855.
———. *Popular Greenhouse Botany.* London: Lovell Reeve, 1857.

STANDARD SOURCES
Desmond.

CATTELL, PSYCHE (1893–1989)

U.S. psychologist and creator of the Cattell Infant Intelligence Scale. Born 2 August 1893 in Garrison, N.Y., to Josephine (Owen) and James McKeen Cattell. Six siblings. Never married. One adopted son; one adopted daughter. Educated Columbia University, Barnard College (1912–1914); Sargent School (1913–1917); U.S. Marine Laboratory, Woods Hole (summer 1915); Harvard University (1916, 1921–1927; M.Ed.; Ph.D. in education, 1927); University of Vienna (summer 1930). Professional positions: Third edition of American Men of Science, *assistant statistician (1919–1921); Psycho-Education Clinic, Harvard University, assistant (1922–1925; 1926–1927); Stanford University, psychologist (1925–1926); Harvard University School of Education, research associate (1927–1936); School of Public Health, research fellow (1932–1937); Mental Health Clinic, Lebanon, Pa., psychologist (1939–1942); Cattell School, director (from 1942); private psychology practice (from 1939). Memberships: American Psychological Association; American Association for the Advancement of Science; National Society for the Study of Education; Educational Research Association. Died 17 April 1989 at Lititz, Pa., at age ninety-five.*

Born 2 August 1893 to James McKeen Cattell, eminent psychologist, educator, and author at Columbia University, and Josephine Owen Cattell, Psyche had an unconventional childhood. She and her six brothers and sisters were allowed to run free on the acreage of the family home in Fort Defiance in Garrison-on-Hudson, New York. The children were educated in part by graduate students from James Cattell's Columbia University classes, but received no formal schooling up to the college level. Psyche took classes at area colleges and became sufficiently capable in mathematics to perform statistical analyses for the third edition of *American Men of Science* (1919–1921), which her father edited.

When Psyche and her sister Quinta finished their bachelor degree classwork, their lack of high school diplomas made them ineligible for the undergraduate degree, so their master's degrees, earned in 1925, were their first academic credentials. Psyche Cattell enrolled at Harvard University in education and began working at the Psycho-Education Clinic. There, she collaborated with Walter F. Dearborn on the Harvard Growth Study and soon focused on dentition as a measure of maturity. Her studies led to a master of education in 1925 and a doctor of education in 1927. Measurement of intelligence became Cattell's primary interest for the next several years; she used the Harvard Growth Study's data as well as that she collected at the Center for Research in Child Health and Development at the Harvard School of Public Health to produce significant papers on the subject.

Never married, Psyche Cattell was one of the first unmarried women to adopt a child, a son (Hudson, 1931) and later a daughter (Jowain). Her studies convinced her that contemporary measures of infant intelligence could be improved dramatically and she worked to extend the Stanford-Binet downward. The resulting Cattell Infant Intelligence Scale, which appeared in her *Measurement of Intelligence in Infants and Young Children* (1940), could be used with infants as young as three months.

In 1939, Cattell joined the staff of the Lancaster Guidance Clinic, where she remained through 1963, eventually becoming its chief psychologist. Her services in improving psychological clinical service to Lancaster included acting as psychologist with the Lebanon County Mental Health Clinic and opening the West End Nursery School and Kindergarten (which become formally the Cattell School in 1945). She authored a regular column on child rearing in the *Lancaster New Era,* a local newspaper, after she was forced to retire from the clinic at age seventy. In retirement, she continued writing, including a popular book, *Raising Children with Love and Limits* (1972), which was seen by many as a common-sense alternative to the popular permissiveness of Benjamin Spock's *Baby and Child Care.* Cattell spent her final years in seclusion at the Moravian Manor in Lititz, where she died at age ninety-five.

JH/MBO

PRIMARY SOURCES

Cattell, Psyche. *Measurement of Intelligence in Infants and Young Children.* New York: Psychological Corp., 1940; Reprint: New York: Johnson Reprint Corp., 1966.

———. *Raising Children with Love and Limits.* Chicago: Nelson-Hall, 1972.

SECONDARY SOURCES

Sokal, Michael M. "Psyche Cattell (1893–1989)." *American Psychologist,* vol. 46, no. 1, (January 1991): 72. Obituary notice.

STANDARD SOURCES

AMS 6–8, S&B 9–13; O'Connell and Russo.

CATTOI, NOEMÍ VIOLETA (1911–1965)

Argentinian vertebrate paleontologist. Born 23 December 1911. Educated la Universidad Nacional de Buenos Aires (1939). Instituto Superior del Profesorado de la Capital Federal (1948–1965). Died 29 January 1965.

Noemí Cattoi was born in Buenos Aires and received a doctorate in natural sciences at the National University of Buenos Aires. Her thesis was of exceptionally high caliber. Before her graduation, she was trained as a part of the group of investigators at the Museo Argentio de Ciencias Naturales "Bernardino Rivadavia." Before she was actually appointed section chief she shouldered all of the burdens of the job. From 1948 until her death, Cattoi was a professor of geology and paleontology at the Instituto Superior del Profesorado de la Capital Federal. In addition she was an adjunct professor in the faculty of natural science at the Museo de La Plata. Cattoi was a delegate to many congresses and participated in numerous scientific meetings. She presented papers at many of them.

On her numerous voyages of exploration, she collected paleontological specimens for the Museo Argentino de Ciencias Naturales. Her published scientific works refer mainly to extinct birds and mammals (typotheres, and fossil tapirs) of South America.   JH/MBO

PRIMARY SOURCES
Cattoi, Noemí V. "Craneología y craneometrí comparada de los géneros *Typotheriodon y Typotherium." Physis. Revista de la Sociedad de Ciencias Naturales.* 14 (1939).
———. "Contribución al estudio de la avifauna extinguida del Pleistoceno de la República Argentina." *Ameghiniana.* vols. 1 and 2 (January 1957): 17–24.
———. Una especie extinguida de *Tapirus* Brisson (*Tapirus rioplatensis* nov. sp.)." *Ameghiniana* 1, no. 3 (1957): 15–21.

SECONDARY SOURCES
"La Comisíon Directiva. Doctora Noemí V. Cattoi, 1911–1965." *Ameghiniana* 4, no. 1 (1965): 3–5.

CAUCHOIS, YVETTE (1908–)
French physicist. Educated University of Paris (Ph.D., 1933?). Professional experience: University of Paris, professor; Laboratoire de Chimie-Physique, director (to 1990).

As Lorella M. Jones wrote in "Intellectual Contributions of Women in Physics," Cauchois courted anonymity and did not provide information about her life to biographers. Most of the information about her comes from the Science Citation Index, which lists a thesis from Paris in 1933, thus approximately dating her doctorate, and references to papers dating from 1932 to at least 1990. In 1990 she was still a professor at the University of Paris, although the time of her promotion to this rank is unknown.

Her research has been in X-ray spectroscopy, where she applied the techniques of spectroscopy to solids. It is a generally accepted theory that properties of solids are determined by the energy levels inside them. These energy levels are related both to the energy levels of the electrons in individual atoms and to the way in which the atoms combine to form the specific solid. In order to learn about the energy levels, the investigator bombards the atom or the solid being investigated with radiation of the "right" wavelength to stimulate transitions between levels. In her research, Cauchois concentrated on this type of measurement in solids.

Cauchois's monograph, *Les spectres de Rayons X et la structure electronique de la matière,* is interesting from a historical point of view, for it reports the thinking in solid state physics in 1946. It was often cited. Her interest in the subject continued and she continued to write papers in this area. In 1964, she published a coauthored text, *Cheminement des particules chargées.*   JH/MBO

PRIMARY SOURCES
Cauchois, Yvette, "Les niveaux d'energie des atomes Lourdes." *Le Journal de Physique et le Radium* 13 (1952): 113.
———. "Les niveaux d'energie des atomes de numero atomique infériéure à 70." *Journal Phys. Radium* 16 (1955): 233.
———. With C. Bonnelle and G. Missoni. "Premiers spectres X du synchrotron de Frascati." *Comptes rendus de l'Academie des Sciences* 257 (1963): 409.

STANDARD SOURCES
Kass-Simon and Farnes (long article by Lorella M. Jones).

CAUGHLAN, GEORGEANNE (ROBERTSON) (1916–1994)
U.S. physicist. Born 25 October 1916. Married Charles Norris Caughlan, 1936. Four children. Educated University of Washington (B.S., 1937; Ph.D., 1964). Professional experience: Montana State University, instructor through associate professor (1957–1974), professor (1974–1984), professor emerita (1984). Died 3 January 1994 in Bozeman, Mont. (?).

Georgeanne Caughlan's academic career was divided, for she earned her bachelor's degree in physics from the University of Washington in 1939, married, raised her children, and then worked on her doctorate (also from the University of Washington). During this time she moved from instructor to associate professor at Montana State University; in 1974, she was promoted to professor. Her research interests were in nuclear astrophysics and the analysis of the synthesis of elements in the stars. She was a member of the American Physical Society, the American Astronomical Society, the American Association of Physics Teachers, the International Astronomical Union, and Sigma Xi.

William A. Fowler of the California Institute of Technology worked with Georgeanne Caughlan, known as Jan, on the study of thermonuclear reactions in stars and supernovae. She began this study at the Kellogg Radiation Laboratory at California Institute of Technology and worked with Fowler, who received the 1983 Nobel Prize in physics. He credited her with invaluable help in the theoretical part of the studies of reactions important for nucleosynthesis. With Fowler, Caughlan developed a standard format for presenting the reaction rates of protons, deuterons, and alpha particles that would be relevant to the nuclear reactions in stars and supernovae.   JH/MBO

SECONDARY SOURCES

Fowler, William A. "Georgeanne Robertson Caughlan." *Physics Today* 47 (October 1994): 88. Obituary notice.

STANDARD SOURCES
AMS 12–14.

CAUQUIL, GERMAINE ANNE (1897–?)

French chemist. Born 1897 in Montpellier, France, to Germain and Augustine Banau Cauquil. Educated University of Montpellier (Ph.D., physical science and chemistry). Professional experience: University of Montpellier, lecturer, professor of chemistry. Honors and memberships: laureate, Academie des Sciences; laureate, Chemical Society of France; member, Society of Physical Chemistry, London, and American Chemical Society. Death date unknown.

Germaine Cauquil received her doctoral degree from Montpellier University, where she later began her academic career as a lecturer advancing to professor. She was the recipient of several prizes: the Taupie prize for the physical sciences, the Berthelot prize, and Berthelot physician. She was a member of the Chemical Society of France (laureate), the Society of Physical Chemistry, London, and the American Chemical Society.   JH/MBO

STANDARD SOURCES
Debus.

CAVENDISH, MARGARET, DUCHESS OF NEWCASTLE (1623–1673)

British writer on natural philosophy. Born 1623 or 1624 at St. John's, near Colchester, Essex, to Elizabeth (Leighton) and Sir Thomas Lucas. Married William Cavendish, marquis and later duke of Newcastle. Educated by tutors. Died 1673 in London.

Margaret Cavendish was eccentric, individualistic, and fascinated by a poetic form of natural philosophy. "After her time," and "thanks in part to her efforts, it became fashionable to make science intelligible, and therefore accessible to 'those of meaner capacities'—the ladies" (Meyer, 2). The youngest of eight children of a wealthy landowner, she received an education that was, by her own account, "no worse than that given to other girls of her class and time" (Grant, 27–32). Although she once asserted, "I do not repent that I spend not my time in learning, for I consider it better to write wittily than learnedly" (Meyer, 2), on another occa-

sion she pronounced women's stupidity to be the result of an education such as hers—of "women breeding up women, one fool breeding up another; and as long as that custom lasts there is no hope of amendment, and ancient customs being a second nature makes folly hereditary in that sex" (Grant, 38).

Margaret Lucas's brothers joined the Royalist side in the civil war that began in 1642. She herself entered the service of Queen Henrietta Maria, whom she followed into exile in Paris in 1644. In Paris, she met William Cavendish, then marquis of Newcastle, a Royalist commander. They were married in 1645. Although her husband took an interest in science and mathematics (he himself was poorly educated), it was his physically deformed brother, Sir Charles, who was the serious scientist and who helped develop Margaret's scientific interests.

The exiled Newcastle, who had contributed heavily to the king's cause from his own estates, was in a precarious financial situation. During the time that he traveled attempting to raise funds, Margaret ventured into print with her first book, *Poems and Fancies* (1653). After the Restoration (1660), the Newcastles returned to England; William was made a duke, but most of his earlier influence with the court was gone. The couple retired to the country and attempted to restore William's wasted estates.

Margaret Cavendish greatly admired the Royal Society and longed to attend one of its meetings. In 1667 an invitation was extended, "experiments [were] appointed for her entertainment" (Birch, 2:175), and contemporaries record that her visit fully bore out the members' fear that her mannerisms and penchant for fantastic dress would provide opponents of the society with a subject for mockery.

Cavendish's later life was overshadowed by a plot by the children of Newcastle's first marriage to undermine her influence with their father. The plot was unsuccessful, and relations with her husband's family gradually improved.

Cavendish was interested in medicine and applied techniques she had read about or devised to her own medical problems. This habit of doctoring herself may, according to one biographer, have shortened her life. She died suddenly at age fifty and was buried in Westminster Abbey. As a memorial, Newcastle arranged for the publication in 1676 of all of the letters and poems that had been written in her praise, *Letters and Poems in Honor of the Incomparable Princess, Margaret, Duchess of Newcastle.*

Cavendish's participation in the intellectual life of the émigré community in Paris during the 1640s and 1650s was important to her interest in science—in particular, in atomism. Atomism as a system of thought had enjoyed a limited success in England from the time of the Oxford-educated Thomas Hariot (1560–1621), but it failed to take root there until Thomas Hobbes and a group of displaced Englishmen—a part of the "Newcastle Circle"—fused their ideas with the mechanistic explanations of Descartes and Pierre Gassendi (1592?–1655). The character of Cavendish's philosophical works resulted from her imaginative processing of ideas absorbed in discussion and correspondence with her atomist contemporaries. In *Poems and Fancies,* she expounded an Epicurean atomism "at once so extreme and so fanciful that she shocked the enemies of atomism, and embarrassed its friends" (Grant, 126). Cavendish wrote in "rhymed, almost jingled, couplets" (Perry, 174), explaining that she had chosen verse "because I thought *Errours* might better passe there than in *Prose; since Poets* write most *Fiction,* and *Fiction* is not given for *Truth,* but *Pastime,* and I fear my *Atomes* will be as small passtime, as themselves; for nothing can be lesse than an *Atome*" (*Poems and Fancies,* n.p.). The system that Cavendish poetically proposed was a mechanistic one in which all phenomena could be explained as matter in motion. Even the soul, though composed of rare atoms, was corporeal in nature.

Untrammeled, undisciplined speculation characterized Cavendish's scientific pronouncements; yet she was vaguely aware of the importance of experimentation. She received Robert Hooke's publication of the *Micrographics* in 1665 with hostility. Arguing that "the best optic is a perfect natural eye, and a regular sensitive perception; and the best judge is reason, and the best study is rational contemplation, joined with the observations of regular sense, but no deluding arts," she disapproved of Hooke's reliance on the microscope (Grant, 205).

Cavendish's atomism contained little that was new or original. Even her use of poetry as a device to express her atomistic ideas is reminiscent of Lucretius. However, as a popularizer, as a woman interested in a "man's field," and as a correspondent of influential natural philosophers, she holds a place in the history of science.   MBO

PRIMARY SOURCES

Cavendish, Margaret. *The Life of William Cavendish, Duke of Newcastle: To Which Is Added the True Relation of My Birth, Breeding, and Life.* Ed. C. H. Firth. London: Routledge, 1906. Includes Margaret Cavendish's autobiography. This definitive edition has been reprinted many times.
———. *Poems and Fancies.* London, 1653. Reprint, ed. Menston, Yorkshire, England: Scolar Press, 1952.
———. *Nature's Pictures Drawn by Fancies Pencil to the Life.* London: J. Martin & J. Allestrye, 1656.
———. Observations upon Experimental Philosophy: To Which is Added, the Description of a New World. Written by, &c. the Lady Marchioness of Newcastle." Folio. London, 1663.

SECONDARY SOURCES

Birch, Thomas. *The History of the Royal Society of London for Improving of Natural Knowledge, from its First Rise in Which the Most Considerable of Those Papers Communicated to the Society, Which Have Hitherto Not Been Published, are Inserted in Their Proper Order, as a Supplement to the Philosophical Transactions.* Vol. 2. London: A. Millar, 1756. Gives notice of Margaret Cavendish's proposed visit to the Royal Society. Describes the entertainment planned for her as well as her entrance on the meeting day.
Evelyn, John. *The Diary of John Evelyn.* London: Oxford University Press, 1959. Describes Cavendish and her visit to the Royal Society.
Grant, Douglas. *Margaret the First: A Biography of Margaret Cavendish, Duchess of Newcastle, 1623–1673.* London: University of Toronto Press, 1957.
Pepys, Samuel. *The Diary of Samuel Pepys.* Ed. Robert Latham and William Matthews. Vol. 8, 1667. Berkeley, Calif.: University of California Press, 1974. Information about Cavendish's visit to the Royal Society.
Perry, Henry Ten Eyck. *The First Duchess of Newcastle and Her Husband as Figures in Literary History.* Boston: Ginn, 1918. In addition to biographical information, considers the revisions she made in her various books.

STANDARD SOURCES
Ballard; *DNB;* Meyer; Phillips.

CÉLINE, SUZANNE (1907–   )
See Leclercq, Suzanne (Céline).

CELLIER, ELIZABETH (fl. 1680)
British midwife. Family named Dormer. Married Peter Cellier.

Elizabeth Cellier was the daughter of a well-to-do family by the name of Dormer. She converted to Catholicism following her marriage to a Frenchman, Peter Cellier. She was tried for high treason after attempting to help prisoners in Newgate who had been implicated in the "popish plot" fabricated by Titus Oates. Although she was acquitted, a pamphlet that she published in vindication of herself contained allegations that occasioned a new trial, for libel. This time she was found guilty, fined £1,000, and made to stand in the pillory.

Cellier was a competent midwife, not a theoretical scientist. She compiled statistics demonstrating the high mortality rates of mothers and infants due to inadequate obstetrical care, and published (1687) a plan for a hospital that would care for mothers, educate nurses, and find homes for illegitimate children. She became a militant advocate of the education of women and midwives, stressing the need to elevate the profession through licensing procedures based on skill rather than money.   JH/MBO

STANDARD SOURCES
DNB; Hurd-Mead 1938; Mozans; Ogilvie 1986.

CESNIECE-FREUDENFELDE, ZELMA (1892–1929)

Latvian physician. Born 17 February 1892 in Courland, Latvia. Married J. Freudenfelde. Educated high school for girls at Mitau; Moscow University (M.D., 1919). Professional experience: "Mother and Child" Consultation Center, head; Latvian National Women's League, president; National Center in Constitutent Assembly, representative. Died 1929.

Zelma Cesniece-Freudenfelde was born on Zalenieku Farm in Courland, Latvia, at that time part of the Russian Empire. After finishing school at Mitau near Riga, Cesniece-Freudenfelde went to Moscow, where she studied medicine. On completing the course, she returned to Riga and married the barrister J. Freudenfelde. As a result of the Russian Revolution of 1917, Latvia became independent. Cesniece-Freudenfelde became head of the medical department of the "Mother and Child" Consultation Center formed in Latvia by Lady Muriel Paget. She was also the first president of the Latvian National Women's League.

In 1920, Cesniece-Freudenfelde was elected to the Constituent Assembly as a representative of the National Center and worked there in the Commission of Social Law. She died at the age of thirty-seven.   ACH

SECONDARY SOURCES
Schmidt, Minna Moscherosch. *400 Outstanding Women of the World.* Chicago: Minna M. Schmidt, 1933.

CHAIX, PAULETTE AUDEMARD (1904–)

French biochemist. Born 9 June 1904. Educated (M.D.; D.Sc.). Professional experience: Centre National de la Recherche Scientifique, Chargé de recherche; maitresse de recherche. University of Lyon, Faculté des Sciences, University of Paris, master of research, University of Paris, Faculté des Sciences, professor.

Paulette Chaix was a French biochemist who earned both medical and doctoral degrees. She worked for the Centre National de la Recherche Scientifique, where she was first chargé de recherche and then maitresse de recherche. After doing research at the University of Lyon, she moved to the University of Paris, where she became a faculty member in the faculty of sciences. Her research was on hematic enzymes.   JH/MBO

STANDARD SOURCES
Turkevich and Turkevich.

CHALUBINSKA, ANIELA (1902–)

Polish geographer. Born 1 October 1902 in Lemberg (now Lwow), variously part of the Austro-Hungarian Empire, Poland, and the Ukraine. Educated Jan Kazimierz University in Lemberg (1921–1926). Professional experience: secondary school (Oberschule) in Lublin, teacher (ca. 1926–1950); Marie Curie Sklodowska University, professor and director of the Regional Geographical Section. Honors and memberships: Golden Distinguished Service Award (1956); Order of the Rebirth of Poland (1973); Medal of the People's Commission (Volksbildungskommission) (1982); University of Lublin, honorary doctorate (1992).

Born in a part of the world that belonged to different political entities at different times, Aniela Chalubinska spent her youth in Zakopane and Cracow. She studied geography and geology at the Jan Kazimierz University in Lemberg, where she wrote two scientific papers before she graduated. Her record seemed to predestine her for a university career. However, her life took a different turn when she became a teacher at a secondary school *(Oberschule)* in Lublin. She not only taught, but worked on developing her skills as a teacher. During the German occupation, she studied in secret as did so many other of her colleagues. After World War II she attended lectures at the Marie Curie-Sklodowska University in Lublin. In 1950, she was suspended from her position at the secondary school for political reasons. At this point, she went to the university, became a professor, and was director of the Regional Geography Section.

Chalubinska became interested in questions posed by physical geography. She developed a new method, still in use today, of determining the thickness of the water nets *(Wassernetzes)*. She published both by herself and with collaborators.   JH/MBO

PRIMARY SOURCES
Chalubinska, Aniela. *Ignacy Domeyko i jego wkllad do geografii Polski.* Warsaw: Naukowe, 1969. Summaries in French.

SECONDARY SOURCES
Buraczynski, Jan. "Professor Dr. Aniela Chalubinska emerytowany professor Zakladu." In *Ksiega Pamiatkowa Wydzialu,* Lublin: Biologii i Nauk o Ziemi Universytetu Marii Vurie Sklodowskiej w Lublinie, 1995.

STANDARD SOURCES
Strohmeier, 1998. *WhW in Science in Europe.*

CHAMIÉ, CATHERINE (1888–ca. 1950)

Syrian/Russian/French physicist. Born 13 November 1888 in Odessa to Hélène Golovkine and Antoine Chamié, a notary. Educated in Odessa; University of Geneva (D.Sc., 1913); University of Petrograd (1913–1914); University of Odessa (1916–1919); College de France (1919–1920). Professional experience: University of Odessa Clinic, nurse (1914–1916); University of Odessa, assistant; Polytechnical Institute, Odessa, assistant lecturer (1916–1919); Russian Secondary School, Paris, professor (from 1920). Radium Institute, Paris, researcher (from 1921); Department of Measures, manager (1933–1950).

A native of Damascus, Syria, Chamié's father studied in Russia, and married a Russian woman. Chamié returned to Russia after she received her doctorate in Geneva with a thesis on hysteresis in a changing magnetic field. She began an investigation at the University of Petrograd on the distribution of potential in an evacuated tube during passage of a current. This work was interrupted in 1914 by World War I. Chamié spent the next two years working in a clinic for the wounded. During 1916–1919 she became a member of the Society of Mathematicians at the University of Odessa and began another research project, on singular solutions of differential equations. During this period, Chamié worked as assistant to Timtchenko and tutored mathematics students at the Polytechnic Institute. She also began a dissertation on the methodology of the sciences.

During the Russian Revolution, in 1917, Chamié fled Odessa with her family, leaving her research notes behind. After spending five months in a refugee camp in France, Chamié went to Paris, hoping to find a way to support herself and her family. She attended courses at the College de France and MARIE CURIE's lectures on radioactivity, and taught at a Russian secondary school for a number of years. Chamié began work at M. Curie's laboratory in 1921, where she received a Carnegie scholarship. She was given the responsibility of storing the laboratory's radium preparations and put in charge of the measurement service in 1933, a position she held until 1950.

Chamié's first investigations in Paris reflected longstanding concerns of M. Curie to distinguish radioactivity from chemical phenomena and to prove the existence of new radioactive elements. Chamié showed that the ionization produced by quinine sulfate was due to hydration, rather than to radioactivity (a question examined earlier by F. C. Gates). She also worked briefly with E. Gleditsch on separation of actinium from rare earths, using the actinium isotope mesothorium 2 to trace the process. Gleditsch and Chamié concluded that both actinium and mesothorium 2 behaved like chemical elements. With I. Curie, Chamié redetermined the half life of radon in response to published work that differed from earlier results of M. Curie and others.

Chaimé used photographic plates to investigate the distribution of radioactive atoms in diverse media. Testing different radioactive substances under various experimental conditions, she found that the radioactive atoms associated in distinct groups, as evidenced by the discrete starlike patterns which their α particle tracks produced on the plates. Chamié's photographic method was employed by E. Róna and M. Blau in Vienna. Chamié also wrote two books on psychology.   MM

PRIMARY SOURCES
Chaimé, Catherine. With A. Schidlof. "Influence de la rapidité des variations du champ magnétisant sur l'hystérésis alternative." *Archives des sciences physiques et naturelles* 36 (1913): 13–40.
———. "Ionisation produite par l'hydration du sulfate de quinine." *Comptes rendus* 176 (1923): 251–253.
———. With I. Curie. "Sur la constante radioactive du radon." *Comptes rendus* 178 (1924): 1808–1810.
———. With E. Gleditsch. "Contribution à l'étude des propriétes chimiques du mésothorium 2 et de l'actinium." *Comptes rendus* 182 (1926): 380–381.
———. "Sur les groupements d'atomes d'éléments radioactifs dans le mercure." *Comptes rendus* 184 (1927): 1243–1245.

SECONDARY SOURCES
Curie, Eve. *Madame Curie.* Trans. Vincent Sheean. Garden City, N.Y.: Doubleday, Doran & Co., 1937: 373, 374.
Quinn, Susan. *Marie Curie: A Life.* New York: Simon and Schuster, 1995.
Róna, Elizabeth. *How It Came About: Radioactivity, Nuclear Physics, Atomic Energy.* Oak Ridge, Tenn.: Oak Ridge Associated Universities, 1978: 28.
Records and communications from Monique Bordry, director, and Ginette Gablot, Musée et Archives de l'Institut du Radium, Paris.

STANDARD SOURCES
Rayner-Canham.

CHANDLER, ELIZABETH (1818–1884)

British botanist. Born 28 April 1818 in Hinton-in-the-Hedges, Northants. Educated privately. Buckinghamshire and Gloucestershire, plant collector. Cited in two sources on local flora. Died 29 April 1884 in Isleworth, Middlesex.

Elizabeth Chandler, born in the second decade of the nineteenth century, collected plants in Buckinghamshire and Gloucestershire for which she was cited in Druce's *Flora of Buckingham* and Riddelsdell's *Flora of Gloucestershire.* She herself published on the plants of High Wycombe. Her collection of Buckinghamshire plants is in the British Museum (Natural History). JH/MBO

PRIMARY SOURCES
Chandler, Elizabeth. "Plants of High Wycombe." *Botanist's Chronicle* (1864): 81–84.

SECONDARY SOURCES
Druce, G. C. *Flora of Buckinghamshire.* Abroath, Scotland: T. Buncle, 1926. Chandler cited page 102.
Riddelsdell, H. *Flora of Gloucestershire.* Cheltenham: Cotteswold Naturalists' Field Club, 1948. Chandler cited page 131.

STANDARD SOURCES
Desmond.

CHANDLER, MARJORIE ELIZABETH JANE (1897–?)

British paleobotanist. Born 18 May 1897 at Leamington Spa (Warwickshire) to Alice Sarah (Roberts) and Frederick August Chandler. Six siblings. Educated Leamington Secondary School; Newnham College, Cambridge (1915–1919); Natural Science Tripos (1918); Cambridge University (M.A., 1948). Funded independent research in Milford, Hampshire (1923–1924); Girton College, Yarrow Fellow (1924–1927). Professional experience: British Museum Geology Department, research worker in palaeobotany (1927–1956).

Marjorie Chandler was the daughter of a jeweler and the oldest of seven children. Absorbing her father's interest in music, she became skilled at playing the violin. While she was at Cambridge she joined the university orchestra; she also played chamber music with members of the Darwin family. She began her formal education at a dame school, but later moved to a newly founded girls' high school in Leamington. Since her early goal was to study geology and this school was insufficiently equipped to teach science to scholarship standard, she had to get an arts scholarship in order to reach the university and study geology. She began in English and changed to science when she entered Newnham College. At Newnham, she studied under geologist GERTRUDE ELLES and at Cambridge under John Marr of the Sedgwick and A. C. Seward in the Botany School. She won a series of scholarships, beginning with the Sedgwick prize at Cambridge which allowed her to survive in a frugal manner. World War I prohibited Chandler from attempting a double

first. She had earned a first in Part I of the Tripos, but since she was the only candidate for Part II, the authorities refused to set her a paper. Reluctantly, she applied for a master's degree after Cambridge granted degrees to women.

A. C. Stewart introduced Chandler to Mrs. ELEANOR MARY REID, which led to a productive collaboration. Mrs. Reid, a mathematics teacher, was married to a member of the Geological Survey, and she helped him with his work on fossil fruits and seeds. By the time of his death in 1916, she was the more important partner in the collaboration. Chandler's partnership with Reid led to the publication of *The Bembridge Flora* (1926) and *The London Clay Flora* (1933). The situation was far from ideal, and Chandler was forced to work with antiquated equipment in a house that was very hot in the summer and so cold in the winter that the windows were sheets of ice. She also collected fossil material from herbaria after which she and Reid macerated and dissected the fruits and seeds.

After the publication of the *London Clay Flora,* Reid retired from active work. Chandler remained with her and continued her research (including active field collecting), but also took over the role of housekeeper. After Reid's death, she joined the Geological Department staff in the British Museum. She continued with the museum until 1970. At that time, the museum dispensed with her services, declaring that she was too old to continue. After her retirement, she spent most of her time on gardening, on church affairs, and in corresponding with geologists from all over the world. JH/MBO

PRIMARY SOURCES
Chandler, Marjorie. With Reid, E. M. "A Note on Certain Plants from a Clay-Bed in the Bembridge Limestone Near Gurnard, Isle of Wight." *Proceedings of the Island of Wight Natural History Society* 1 (1926): 378.
———. *The London Clay Flora.* London: British Museum of Natural History, 1933.
———. *The Lower Tertiary Floras of Southern England. I. Paleocene Floras.* London Clay Flora (supplement); text and atlas. London: British Museum of Natural History, 1961.
———. *The Lower Tertiary Floras of Southern England. II. Flora of the Pipe-Clay Series of Dorset (Lower Bagshot).* London: British Museum of Natural History, 1962.
———. *The Lower Tertiary Floras of Southern England. III. Flora of the Bournemouth Beds; the Boscombe and the Highcliff Sands.* London: British Museum of Natural History, 1963.
———. *The Lower Tertiary Floras of Southern England. IV. A Summary and Survey of Findings in the Light of Recent Botanical Observations.* London: British Museum of Natural History, 1964.

SECONDARY SOURCES
Chesters, K.I.M. "Marjorie E. J. Chandler." *Tertiary Research* 9 (1987): 1–5.

STANDARD SOURCES
Newnham, vol. 1.

CHANG, MOON GYUNG (1904–)

Korean obstetrician and gynecologist. Born in Jinju, Korea. One much older sister. Father died when she was eight. Married. No children. Educated local elementary school; Jong Wha Girls' High School, Tokyo; Imperial Women's Medical College. Professional experience: Imperial Women's Medical College, obstetrics service (fifteen months); Jong Wha Doctor's Clinic, Seoul, private practice (1934–retirement). Honors and memberships: Seoul Medical Association, director (1964); Seoul Medical Women's Association, president; Korean Obstetrics Institute, vice-president; Seoul chapter of Korean Tuberculosis Association, president; Korean Women Bachelor's Association, vice-president; Seoul chapter Korean Red Cross, vice-president.

Born in Jinju, Korea, when her mother was forty-five years old, Moon Gyung was initially told she would not be allowed to attend the newly established primary schools because many of the first students there were adult women of dubious reputation, and because her father thought education for women to be of little use. After her father died, when she was eight years old, Moon Kyong convinced her mother of her overwhelming desire to attend school. She used a slate board for school work until she graduated and sold her honors prize in order to buy paper and supplies. Because of her own extreme poverty, one of the guiding purposes of Moon Gyung Chang's life was to help poor students finance their higher education. She established the Moon Gyung Educational Council to provide financial aid to college students. Most of her medical work was clinical.   KM

PRIMARY SOURCES
Chang, Moon Gyung. In Hellstedt, *Autobiographies.*

CHANG, VIVIAN (1931–1990)

U.S. Physician. Born 1931 in Shanghai. Never married. Educated University of Utah School of Medicine (M.D., 1955); University of California, Berkeley (Master of Public Health, 1969). Professional experience: Public Health Service, Peace Corps physician (from 1964), rear admiral (1978); health administrator of region II (1984–1990). Died 1990 south of Wilmington, Del., on Interstate 95 in an automobile accident.

Vivian Chang's life was cut short by an automobile accident. After leaving a friend's wedding in Philadelphia, she was killed on her way to Washington, D.C., to see the AIDS quilt.

Born in Shanghai, Chang grew up in Utah and attended the University of Utah Medical School. Her major passion was public health. Her career with the Public Health Service was challenging and her insights often brilliant. She was an untiring advocate for the dispossessed and minorities. She strongly supported the Women with AIDS initiatives.

JH/MBO

SECONDARY SOURCES
Harris, David. "Tribute to Vivian Chang, M.D." *Bulletin of the New York Academy of Medicine* 67 (May–June 1991): 193–195. Includes portrait.

CHARLES, VERA KATHERINE (1877–1954)

U.S. mycologist and plant pathologist. Born 1877. Educated Mount Holyoke College (A.B.); Cornell University (Ph.D., 1903). Professional experience: Bureau of Plant Industry, U.S. Department of Agriculture, mycologist (1903–1942). Died 1954.

As a graduate of Mount Holyoke during the early period when CORNELIA CLAPP stimulated the interest of young women in biology, Vera Charles made a decision to continue for an advanced science degree, studying for her doctorate at Cornell, where she trained in mycology and plant pathology at the Agriculture School. After receiving her doctorate in 1903, she joined the U.S. Department of Agriculture as a mycologist with the first cohort of highly trained women in that department. She soon became an expert on plant fungi. Before 1912 she inspected much of the imported plants brought into the department for fungus diseases. The Plant Quarantine Act of 1912 made this kind of inspection no longer necessary. In 1915, she coauthored a study of mushrooms and common fungi for the USDA with FLORA PATTERSON, revised in 1917 and 1931 with Charles's name as sole author.

Charles also collected mycological specimens in Florida, and wrote a popular book on mushroom collecting in 1931. In 1935, she wrote another popular account, in a book by Catherine Filene on women's careers, suggesting that the position as government mycologist offered a good career for young women. By 1942, she retired from her government position, but continued to work in the division of mycology until her failing sight made microscope work impossible.

JH/MBO

PRIMARY SOURCES
Charles, Vera. Occurrence of *Lasiodiplodia* on *Thebroma cacao* and *Mangifera indica. Journal Mycology* 12 (1906): 145–146.
———. With Flora W. Patterson. "Some Fungus Diseases of Economic Importance in Miscellaneous diseases II Pineapple Rot Caused by *Thielaviopsis paradoxa." USDA Bureau Plant Industry Bulletin* 171 (1910): 41 pp.

———. With Flora W. Patterson. "Mushrooms and other Common Fungi." *Bulletin U.S. Department of Agriculture* no. 175, 1915; revised 1917, 1931, under Charles alone.

———. With G. H. Martin. "Preliminary Studies of the Life History of *Erostrotheca multiformis,* the Perfect Stage of *Cladosporim album* Dowson." *Phytopathology* 18 (1928): 839–846.

———. "Flora Wambaugh Patterson." *Mycologia* 21 (1928): 1–4. Includes portrait.

———. *Introduction to Mushroom Hunting.* 1931; New York: Dover, 1974.

———. "The Mycologist." In *Careers for Women,* ed. Catherine Filene. New York: Houghton Mifflin Company, 1934.

———. "A Preliminary Check List of the Entomogenous Fungi of North America." *Insect Pest Survey Bulletin* 21, supplement to no 9: 707–785.

SECONDARY SOURCES
Baker, Gladys L. "Women in the U.S. Department of Agriculture: Vera Charles." *Mycologia* 47 (1955): 263–265. Includes her scientific bibliography.

STANDARD SOURCES
Bailey (includes portrait); Barnhart.

CHARLOTTE SOPHIA, QUEEN (1744–1818)

British patroness of botany. Born in Mirow, Mecklenberg-Strelitz in 1744. Married future King George III in 1761. Educated in botany and flower painting. Developed gardens at Kew, now Royal Botanical Gardens. Died in 1818.

The Princess of Mecklenberg, Charlotte Sophia, married King George III in 1761. Educated in botany by British botanist Reverend James Lightfoot and by Sir. J. E. Smith, she became interested in establishing gardens that would include exotic as well as native plants at her home in Kew. Queen Charlotte was trained in flower painting by Francis Bauer, and her works are still on display at the Royal Botanical Gardens, Kew.   JH/MBO

SECONDARY SOURCES
Journal of Botany (1910): 269–271.
Hedley, Owen. *Queen Charlotte.* London: Murray, 1975.
Strong, Roy C. *Royal Gardens.* London: BBC Books, 1992.
    Charlotte Sophia discussed on pages 64–76.

STANDARD SOURCES
DNB.

CHARSLEY, FANNY ANNE (1828–1915)

British botanist. Born 23 July 1828 in Beaconsfield, Bucks. Died 21 December 1915 in Hove, Sussex.

Fanny Charsley went to Melbourne, Australia, in 1856, where she spent ten years before returning to England. While in Melbourne she drew plants, and published a book about the wildflowers of the area in 1867. She also corresponded with botanist F. von Müller. A species of plant is named after her, *Hepipterum charsley* F. Muell.   JH/MBO

PRIMARY SOURCES
Charsley, Fannie Anne. *Wild Flowers around Melbourne.* London: Day & Son, 1867.

SECONDARY SOURCES
Victorian Naturalist (1908): 105; (1933): 261; (1983): 21–24.

CHASE, MARY AGNES MEARA (1869–1963)

U.S. botanist, agrostologist. Born 20 April 1869 in Iroquois Country, Ill., to Mary (Cassidy) (Brannick) and Martin Meara. Five siblings. Married William Ingraham Chase (d. 1889). Educated public grammar school, Chicago. Professional experience: proofreader for periodical (1888–1889); various positions including Field Museum, Chicago, botanist; professional proofreader; botanical illustrator; U.S. Department of Agriculture, Washington, D.C., meat inspector (1901–1903); Division of Forage Plants, collaborator, senior botanist (1903–1939). Honors and memberships: Botanical Society of America, Certificate of Merit (1956); University of Illinois, honorary degree (1958); Smithsonian Institution Honorary Fellow (1958). Died 24 September 1963 in Bethesda, Md.

Agnes Chase was an important botanical illustrator and botanist whose specialty was the study and illustration of grasses. Agnes was one of six children of a railroad blacksmith. She was named Mary Agnes Meara at birth, but when her father died, her mother moved Agnes and the four other surviving children to Chicago and changed the family name to Merrill. Agnes herself soon dropped her first name. She attended the local public grammar schools and, together with her brothers and sisters, took jobs to help with expenses. Because of the financial necessity to find work, Agnes had no formal education past elementary school. In 1888 she married William Chase, the editor of a periodical for which she worked as a proofreader. After his premature death in 1889 she held various jobs and became interested in botany as a hobby. During a plant collecting trip in 1898 she met bryologist Ellsworth Hill, who served as her mentor.

Hill instructed Chase in plant lore and in the use of the microscope, and employed her to illustrate the new species that he described. She also illustrated two publications of the

Field Museum of Natural History, *Plantae Utowanae* (1900) and *Plantae Yucatanae* (1904). Chase began her long association with the United States Department of Agriculture, through Hill's urging, beginning as a meat inspector at the Chicago stockyards (1901–1903). In 1903 she moved to the Bureau of Forage Plants, where she worked as a collaborator with Albert Speak Hitchcock in charge of the systematic study of grasses (agrastology). Before Hitchcock's retirement, Chase had progressed to associate botanist; she succeeded him as senior botanist and principal scientist in charge of systematic agrostology. She and Hitchcock made extensive contributions to the collections of the U.S. National Herbarium. Alone, she produced more than seventy articles, primarily on grass species and updated and augmented the grass herbarium, donating her own library to the Smithsonian.

Throughout her life Chase was identified with reform movements. She was a suffragist, a prohibitionist, and a socialist. She contributed to the Fellowship of Reconciliation, the NAACP, the National Woman's Party, and the Women's International League for Peace and Freedom. A woman of unflagging energy, she maintained a strenuous schedule long after her official retirement in 1939; at age seventy-one she traveled to Venezuela to help develop a program of range management. Until her death of congestive heart failure, she worked at the herbarium.

An important contributor to the systematics of grasses, Chase made collecting trips in the United States, northern Mexico, Puerto Rico, and Brazil; she deposited her collections in the U.S. National Herbarium. She collected many new species and extended the ranges of previously described ones. Much of her distribution information was incorporated into Hitchcock's range maps in *Manual of Grasses of the United States* (1935). Chase extended her work from the New World to Europe when she visited European herbaria in 1922 and 1923.

Chase's service to plant taxonomy was recognized by a certificate of merit from the Botanical Society of America (1956), an honorary doctorate from the University of Illinois (1958), a medal for service to the botany of Brazil (1958), an honorary fellowship in the Smithsonian Institution (1958), and a fellowship in the Linnean Society (1961).   MBO

PRIMARY SOURCES

Chase, Mary Agnes Meara. With C. F. Millspaugh. "Plantae Utowanae." *Field Columbian Museum Botanical Series,* no. 50 (1900): 113–124.

———. "Plantae Yucatanae." *Field Museum of Natural History, Botanical Series,* no. 69 (1903): 14–84; no. 92 (1904): 85–151.

———. *The First Book of Grasses: The Structure of Grasses Explained for Beginners.* New York: Macmillan, 1922.

———. With A. S. Hitchcock. *The Genera of Grasses of the*

United States, with Special Reference to the Economic Species, rev. ed. Washington, D.C.: U.S. Government Printing Office, 1936.

SECONDARY SOURCES

Fosberg, F. R., and J. R. Swallen. "Mary Agnes Chase." *Taxon* 8 (1959): 145–151. Bibliography of Chase's articles.

"Mary Agnes Chase." *Taxon* 27 (1978): 373–374.

Rudolph, Emanuel. "Women in Nineteenth Century Botany: A Generally Unrecognized Constituency." *American Journal of Botany* 69 (1982): 1346–1355.

STANDARD SOURCES

AMS 2–8, B 9, P&B 10–11; Bonta; Grinstein 1997 (article by Lesta J. Cooper-Freytag); *NAW* (M) (article by Michael T. Stieber); Ogilvie 1982; Shearer and Shearer 1996.

CHASMAN, RENATE WIENER (1932–1977)

German/U.S. physicist. Born 10 January 1932 in Berlin, Germany, to Else (Scheyer) and Hans Wiener, an attorney. One sibling. Married Chellis Chasman. Two children, Danial Ian and Deborah Lynn. Educated Sweden; Hebrew University, Jerusalem (M.Sc., 1955; Ph.D., 1959). Professional experience: Columbia University, research associate; Yale University, researcher (1962–1963), assistant physicist (1963–1967), associate physicist (1967–1969), physicist (1969–1977); Brookhaven National Laboratory. Visiting scientist at Centre Européen de Recherche Nucléaire. Died 17 October 1977.

Renate Wiener was born into a Jewish family that valued education. Her father was a founder of the German Social Democratic Party. The Wieners fled Hitler's Germany in 1938 and settled in Sweden. Since Hans Wiener could not practice law in Sweden, the family experienced economic problems for several years. He died in 1944. Else Wiener worked first as a cleaning woman, then as a bookseller. Renate and her twin sister, Edith, were educated at a girls' home north of Stockholm, then at the public girls' school in Stockholm.

In high school Wiener discovered her calling. Encouraged by a teacher, she studied advanced physics and mathematics texts with his guidance. After graduation, Wiener registered at Hebrew University, Jerusalem, where she majored in physics and minored in chemistry and mathematics. She was awarded a Faculty Research Prize for her master's thesis. Four years later Wiener received a doctorate in experimental physics from the university.

Wiener came to Columbia University in 1959 after being offered a position by Chien-Shiung Wu, codiscoverer of the effect Wiener investigated in her doctoral research. One of her coworkers was Chellis Chasman, who was completing his doctoral research. On 4 February 1962 Wiener and Chasman were married in New York City, and Renate Chasman took a research position at Yale, where her husband had been an instructor since the previous summer.

The family's size increased rapidly with the birth of Daniel Ian on 14 September 1962 and Deborah Lynn on 24 August 1963. The children were entrusted to sitters, occasionally accompanying their mother to work and to conferences. Chellis Chasman took a position in the Department of Physics at Brookhaven in 1963. The department was uncomfortable with hiring a married couple, so Renate Chasman found a position in Brookhaven's Department of Nuclear Engineering. In 1965 she transferred to the Accelerator Department, where she was able to use her theoretical training. She advanced rapidly, designing components of several major accelerator projects. In spite of a serious illness diagnosed in 1972, Chasman continued to work, finally succumbing to melanoma in 1977.

In her dissertation, Chasman studied the newly discovered violation of parity in beta decay. She investigated beta decay and positron emission at Columbia and nuclear spectroscopy at Yale. At Brookhaven Chasman compiled neutron cross-section data for the Department of Nuclear Engineering, work that she did not enjoy. In Brookhaven's Accelerator Department, Chasman participated in developing a linear accelerator, a colliding beam accelerator, and a storage ring for the National Synchrotron Light Source. With G. Kenneth Green, Chasman developed a design that greatly increased the intensity of ultraviolet light and X-rays emitted from synchrotrons. She received international recognition for her work on accelerator design.　　MM

PRIMARY SOURCES

Chasman, Renate. With S. G. Cohen. "Search for Pseudoscalar Interaction in Beta Decay." *Nuclear Physics* 15 (1960): 79–88.

———. "Numerical Calculations of the Effects of Space Charge on Six-Dimensional Beam Dynamics in a Proton Linear Accelerator." *Proceedings of 1968 Brookhaven Linear Accelerator Conference.* BNL 50120. Brookhaven National Laboratory, 1968, 372–388.

———. With R. L. Gluckstern. "Extrapolation of ISABELLE Design to 400x400 GeV." *IEEE, Transactions on Nuclear Sciences,* nos. 22, 23 (1975): 1435–1438.

———. With G. K. Green. *Design of a National Dedicated Synchrotron Radiation Facility.* BNL-21849. Brookhaven National Laboratory, 1976.

SECONDARY SOURCES

"Chasman, Renate W." *New York Times,* 19 October 1977.
Physics Today 31, no. 2 (1978): 64. Obituary notice.

CHÂTELET, GABRIELLE-EMILIE LE TONNELIER DE BREUTEUIL, MARQUISE DU

See Du Châtelet, Gabrielle-Emilie.

CHAUCHARD, B. (fl. 1935)

French biologist. Married A. E. Chauchard. Professional positions: Laboratoire des hautes etudes, associate director; faculty of sciences, associate. Member of Société de biologie (from 1935).

B. Chauchard was an associate director in her husband's laboratory. She was a member of the Société de biologie.
　　　　　　　　　　　　　　　　　　JH/MBO

SECONDARY SOURCES

Société de biologie membership list included as front matter of text, 1935.

CHAUDET, MARIA CASANOVA DE (d. 1947)

Argentinian geologist. Born in Italy. Educated in Italy (doctorate in chemistry and in natural sciences). Professional experience: Direccion General de Yacimientos Petroliferos Fiscales of Argentina; University of Buenos Aires (teacher). Died 8 November 1947.

Maria Casanova de Chaudet was born and educated in Italy, earning her doctorate in that country. She emigrated to Argentina where she worked for the Direccion General de Yacimientos Petroliferos Fiscales of Argentina.

Chaudet was chiefly a sedimentary petrographer. She is best known for her work on the coals and asphalts of Argentina.
　　　　　　　　　　　　　　　　　　JH/MBO

PRIMARY SOURCES

Chaudet, Maria Casanova de. "Aguas, rocas ye minerales del Campamento Tupungato." *Boletin de Informaciones Petroliferas* (1924): 125; (1935): 79–98.

———. "Carbones ye asfaltitas." *Boletin de Informaciones Petroliferas* (1924): 215; (1942): 59–75.

SECONDARY SOURCES

"Doctora Maria Casanova de Chaudet." *Revista de la Sociedad Geologica Argentina* vol. 3, no. 1 (1948): 71.

CHEESMAN, LUCY EVELYN (1881–1969)

British entomologist and botanist. Born 1881 in Westwell, Kent. Educated at Ashford and Brighton. Professional experience: Murray-Smith family, Leicestershire, governess; botanized in Leicestershire; civil servant (1914–1918); London Zoological Society, keeper of insects (1920–1927). British Museum, Department of Entomol-

ogy, honorary associate (1925–ca. 1960); insect and plant collecting, South Pacific (1924–1925); New Hebrides (1929–1931, 1954–1955); Papua, New Guinea (1933–1934, 1936, 1938–1939); New Caledonia (1949–1950). Honors and memberships: Royal Entomological Society, Fellow. Died 15 April 1969.

Evelyn Cheesman began her work as an entomologist and botanist as governess to the Murray-Smith family in Leicestershire. Botanizing in rural England spurred her to study first plants and then insects. Working as a canine nurse when she found she would not be admitted to train as a veterinary surgeon, she then took a position during World War I as a civil servant. She became interested in entomology, especially in the raising of caterpillars and other larvae.

In 1920, Cheesman met Maxwell Lefroy, then the curator of insects at the London Zoological Society Gardens in Regents Park, who urged her to join him as an unpaid keeper of insects at the zoo. In preparation for this work, she took his course in entomology for the following two years at Imperial College. At the end of four years, she wrote a popular account of insect life for the British Museum.

Four years later, Cheesman was invited to travel with a scientific expedition to the South Pacific. This first voyage was only the beginning of a series of scientific expeditions throughout the Pacific, often undertaken on her own, collecting specimens for the British Museum of Natural History in New Hebrides, New Guinea, Papua New Guinea, and New Caledonia that continued from 1924 to 1955, except during World War II. She began to publish accounts of her collecting expeditions to some popular acclaim. She worked on her collections between expeditions as an honorary associate of the entomological department of the British Museum, Natural History Division (now the British Museum of Natural History). In her seventies and eighties she wrote two accounts of her life of travel and research. She was made a Fellow of the Royal Entomological Society and died in 1969 at the age of ninety.   JH/MBO

PRIMARY SOURCES
Cheesman, Evelyn. *Everyday Doings of Insects.* New York: McBride, 1924. Under Lucy Evelyn.
———. *Hunting Insects in the South Seas.* London: P. Allan, 1932. Under Lucy Evelyn.
———. *Land of the Red Bird.* London: H. Joseph, 1938.
———. *Things Worth While.* London: Hutchinson, 1957. Cheesman's first autobiographical account.
———. *Time Well Spent.* London: Hutchinson, 1960. Her second autobiographical account.

SECONDARY SOURCES
Flora Malesiana 1 (1950): 106.

"Lucy Evelyn Cheesman." *Entomological Monthly Magazine* (1969): 217–219.
[author]. *Madam Dragonfly: Life and Times of Cynthia Longfield.* Describes Longfield's association with Cheesman on one of her voyages and later at the Department of Entomology.
Tinling, M. *Women into the Unknown.* 1969: 85–91.

STANDARD SOURCES
Desmond; *Europa* (under Evelyn Lucy); Uglow 1989.

CHENOWETH, ALICE DREW (1903–)

U.S. physician born in Albany, Mo., 21 February 1903. One brother. Married John Pate. One son. Attended local elementary school; Palmer Junior College, Albany (valedictorian); Northwestern University (B.S. in chemistry, 1924; M.A. in history, 1926); Vanderbilt University (M.D., 1932); Strong Memorial Hospital, internship, pediatrics (1933); Johns Hopkins University Hospital, internship, pediatrics (1934); Philadelphia Children's Hospital, assistant chief resident (1935–1936); University of Pennsylvania, research fellowship (1937). Professional experience: private practice in partnership with John Mitchell (1938–1942?); Department of Health, Louisville, Ky., director of maternal and child health; United States Children's Bureau, Division of Research, later the International Division, consultant, Division of Health Services. Honors and memberships: Phi Beta Kappa, Medical Women's International Association.

Alice Drew Chenoweth, named for both of her grandmothers, was born 21 February 1903 in Albany, Missouri. Her grandmother Drew was seminary-educated and instilled a respect and thirst for knowledge in her son, Alice's father, who was continually frustrated by the necessities of family responsibilities from becoming a doctor. He did become a veterinarian, as did Alice's younger brother. Alice attended the local schools and junior college, graduating valedictorian of her class at Palmer College. On the advice of her chemistry professor at Palmer, she enrolled at Northwestern University as a chemistry major.

In her senior year at Northwestern, Chenoweth first approached her parents about becoming a doctor. Her father, who had always encouraged her desire for education, replied that, if she were a man, nothing would please him more. Taking that for a "no," Chenoweth took her bachelor's "with highest distinction" as a Phi Beta Kappa member and entered the master's program in history. After receiving her master's in 1926, Chenoweth instructed history in a women's college in Montgomery, Alabama, for two years, knowing all the time she would return to school. On a visit in Nashville, Tennessee, Alice met the dean of women at Vanderbilt University, who advised her to pursue her dream of medicine and contacted the dean of the School of Medicine in recommendation. Her father consented with reservations about the harsh treatment he was sure she would receive and doubts about her strength for the profession. On the contrary, she enjoyed her classes thoroughly and was in the first group elected to the medical honor society, consistently earning highest grades in all her studies.

After graduating in 1926, Chenoweth accepted an internship in pediatrics at Strong Memorial Hospital, the teaching hospital of Rochester University, New York. Her second year of internship was spent at Johns Hopkins Hospital. She refused an appointment to serve as chief resident at the Children's Hospital of Philadelphia, preferring to remain assistant chief resident and avoid some of the headaches of chief resident. Soon she accepted a fellowship for research at the University of Pennsylvania, then went into a partnership pediatric practice in Philadelphia. She was married to John Pate on February 12 (1941?) in Radnor, Pennsylvania, and honeymooned in Bermuda before settling in Louisville, Kentucky.

Her husband's connections with the Department of Health of Kentucky helped garner Chenoweth an appointment as director of maternal and child health. She administered the Emergency Maternity and Infant Care program during World War II, consulting with the U.S. Children's Bureau (later the Department of Health, Education, and Welfare). After the war, Pate was moved to Washington, D.C., and Chenoweth accepted a position with the Division of Research in the Children's Bureau and later moved to the international division, where she planned educational and observational programs for fellows from abroad. She spent the last years of professional life in the Division of Health Services in the Children's Bureau, as consultant for state programs.

Alice Chenoweth is a fine example of a woman who overcame doubts and obstacles to combine a life as doctor, wife, and mother most successfully, finding the rewards and satisfaction worth the hardships. JH/MBO

PRIMARY SOURCES
Chenoweth, Alice Drew. In Hellstedt, *Autobiographies.*
———. "Benjamin Franklin in the Pennsylvania Assembly, 1751-1757." Master's thesis. Northwestern University, 1926.
———. *Standards and Progress in Day Care Center Programs.* Rockville, Md.: U.S. Department of Health, Education, and Welfare, Health Services and Mental Health Administration, 1973.

CHESSER, ELIZABETH (SLOAN) (1878–1940)
British physician. Born 1878, probably in Glasgow. Father Samuel Sloan, M.D. Married Stennett Chesser (1902). Two Sons. Educated Queen Margaret College, Glasgow University.

Elizabeth Chesser's father was a Glasgow physician. She followed his example and earned her degrees at Queen Margaret College, Glasgow University. She married a man from Edinburgh and they had two sons. She published extensively.
JH/MBO

PRIMARY SOURCES
Chesser, Elizabeth. *Physiology and Hygiene for Girls' Schools and Colleges.*
———. *Youth: A Book for Two Generations.* New York: E. P. Dutton, 1928.
———. *The Woman Who Knows Herself.* New York: E. P. Dutton, 1929.
———. *Seven Stages of Childhood.* London: H. Jenkins, 1937.
———. *Five Phases of Love.* London: H. Jenkins, 1939.

SECONDARY SOURCES
Manchester Guardian. Obituary notice.

STANDARD SOURCES
Current Biographies, 1940; *WWW.*

CHICK, DAME HARRIETTE (1875–1977)
British physiologist and biochemist. Born 6 January 1875 in Ealing(?), England, to Emma Holley and Samuel Chick. Six siblings. Educated Notting Hill High School; University College, University of London (B.Sc., 1896); postgraduate studies (1896–1899, 1904–1905, D.Sc., 1905?). Professional experience: Hyginia Institute, Vienna and Munich, researcher; Lister Institute of Preventative Medicine, London, researcher (1905–1918); University College, London, fellow (1918); Kinderklinik, University of Vienna, researcher (1919–1922); Department of Nutrition, Lister Institute, head (1923–1958?), researcher (1958–1970). Honors and memberships: Dame of the British Empire (1949); Physiological Society, honorary member (1967).

Harriette Chick was the third daughter (fifth child) of the seven children of Emma Hooley and Samuel Chick. She studied at University College, London, following her sister in a program that gave her a strong interest in science. Graduating in 1896 with a bachelor of science degree, Chick continued in chemistry and bacteriology at a period when those fields were of international importance, taking postgraduate courses between 1896 and 1905, obtaining a doctorate from University College, London, in 1904. She went to Vienna to pursue research at the Hyginia Institute and studied in Munich under Max Gruber. Charles Sherrington, then in Liverpool as professor of physiology, suggested that she apply to the Lister Institute for Preventative Medicine for a Jenner studentship. She received this with the support of the director, Charles Martin, in spite of the opposition of other staff members who did not want a woman colleague. She first worked on mechanisms of disinfection and then in the field of nutrition. An early paper written with Charles Martin involved standardization of disinfectants (the Chick-Martin test). She also collaborated with Martin on protein separation in a series of articles written between 1910 and 1913 in the *Journal of Physiology* and later published a further study as sole author on this topic in *Lancet* (1916). When Casimir Funk joined the Lister Institute in 1911, the attention of the institute turned toward the role of vitamins (a word coined by Funk from the French *vitamine*). Chick also became vitally interested in this topic.

During World War I, Chick was responsible for the preparation of agglutination serum for the diagnosis of typhoid fever and other diseases. Following World War I, it was discovered that widespread malnutrition of both adults and children in Austria resulted in bone and eye pathologies: nutritional osteomalachia in elderly adults, rickets and sometimes keratomalachia in children. Harriette Chick and two other women researchers went to Vienna for three years to study bone and eye diseases and nutrition, sponsored by the Medical Research Council's Committee on Accessory Food Factors as well as by the Lister Institute. They were warmly received by Clemens von Pirquet, head of the Vienna University Kinderklinik, who collaborated on trials of nutritional supplements for his patients. One of the women on Chick's team was the Australian medical researcher Elsie Jean Dalyell, who was working in the Lister Institute supported by a Beit fellowship. Chick would publish on hunger-caused osteomalachia in poor and elderly adults with her. Chick recognized the importance of both sunlight (ultraviolet light) and dietary supplements of cod liver oil in preventing rickets and realized that one could substitute for the other, a link later explained by the identification of vitamin D in cod liver oil and the activation of a precursor to vitamin D by sunlight.

She continued her work on nutrition and vitamins when she returned to London and the Lister Institute. She continued as secretary to the MRC Committee on Accessory Food Factors. Her team of researchers was reorganized as the Department of Nutrition at the Lister Institute and Chick was made head of that department. The group concentrated on standardization of vitamins A, D, and the vitamin B complex. Chick's research focused on the water-soluble vitamin B complex and its introduction into food as a method of improving the health of the British population. She continued this work during World War II. Between 1932 and 1958, her group published forty-eight papers; Chick was the sole author of nineteen of these. She was awarded an honorary doctorate from the University of Manchester in 1933.

In 1932, Chick was honored as a Commander of the British Empire (C.B.E.) and in 1949, she was made a Dame of the British Empire (D.B.E.) for her work on nutrition. At the age of ninety-two she was made an honorary member of the Physiological Society, after a membership of fifty years.

JH/MBO

PRIMARY SOURCES

Chick, Harriette. "The Principles Involved in the Standardisation of Disinfectants and the Influence of Organic Matter upon Germicidal Value." *Journal of Hygiene* 8 (1908): 654–697.

———. "Preparation and Use of Certain Agglutinating Sera." *Lancet* 1 (1916): 857–861.

———. With E. J. Dalyell. "Hunger-osteomalachia in Vienna." *Lancet* 2 (1920): 842–849.

———, et al. "Studies of Rickets in Vienna, 1919–1922." [Medical Research Council] *M.R.C. Reports. Nutrition. Rickets.* London, 1924.

———. *Diet and Climate.* London, 1935.

———. With M. Hume. "The Work of the Accessory Food Factors Committee." *British Medical Bulletin* 12 (1956): 5–8.

SECONDARY SOURCES

Morrissey, Shelagh. "Dame Harriette Chick D.B.E. (1875–1977)." In *Women Physiologists: An Anniversary Celebration of Their Contributions to British Physiology.* ed. Lynn Bindman, et al. London: Portland Press, 1992.

Bibliography of published papers of Harriette Crick in *Annual Reports of the Lister Institute for Preventative Medicine 1928–1958.*

STANDARD SOURCES

DNB; DSB; O'Connor.

CHILD, LYDIA MARIA (FRANCIS) (1802–1880)

U.S. amateur geologist, literary figure, and reformer. Born 11 February 1802 in Medford, Mass., to Susannah (Rand) Francis and David Convers Francis. Five siblings. Married David Lee Child. Educated local "dame school," and Miss Swan's Seminary. Professional experience: Gardiner, Maine, teacher (1820). Died 20 October 1880.

Lydia Maria Francis was the youngest of six children, whose father was a baker. Although she had little formal education, her intellectual development was influenced by her brother, Convers, who was six years older than she, attended Harvard College, and later became a professor in the Divinity School. When Maria was twelve years old, her mother died, and she was raised by a married sister, Mary Rand (Francis) Preston, in Norridgewock, Maine. By this time she was reading Milton, Homer, and Sir Walter Scott. After teaching for a short time in Gardiner, Maine, she joined Convers and his wife in Watertown, Mass. (1820), where he had a Unitarian parish. She decided on a literary career, and wrote a number of successful books and stories. Her publications made her welcome in Boston's literary circles and she continued to improve her knowledge through reading, writing, and discussion. Here she met David Lee Child, an impecunious lawyer, reformer, and editor. Although her family was opposed, the couple married on 19 October 1828. Because David was impractical, Maria increased her publications in order to make ends meet. She became reform-minded in the 1820s after her husband wrote a rousing editorial in defense of the Cherokees against President Jackson. Her ideas became solidified when she met the ardent abolitionist William Lloyd Garrison. In 1833 she published a history of slavery that described its evils in a factual but impelling manner, and it helped attract people to the abolitionist cause. Her popularity at the Boston Athenaeum immediately vanished. David Child, in the meantime, conceived of a number of schemes to make money, all of which failed. The Childs moved to Wayland, Mass., where she continued to write and where she took care of her father until his death. David Child died in 1874, and after his death Maria Child became increasingly reclusive. Her interest in spiritualism increased toward the end of her life. She died of heart disease at seventy-eight in Wayland. John Greenleaf Whittier recited a memorial poem at her funeral and Wendell Phillips provided an oration.

Child was a prolific writer of socially significant books. Although she was not a scientist, in one of these books she showed an interest in geology and produced a book that combined this interest with her social views. In it, Child described Mammoth Cave in Kentucky and provided considerable detail on the geology of the site. In the publication that resulted from her visit she described the geological abilities of Stephen, a mulatto slave who was a tourist guide. In doing so, she not only supported her abolitionist views but documented a contribution of an African American to science. JH/MBO

PRIMARY SOURCES

Child, Lydia Maria. *Appeal in Favor of That Class of Americans Called Africans.* N. p., 1833.
———. "Mammoth Cave." *Anglo-American* 2 (1842): 7–9.
———. *The Letters of Lydia Maria Child.* With a Biographical Introduction by John G. Whittier. Boston: Houghton Mifflin, 1882.
Child's papers are found at Cornell University, the Boston Public Library, and the Massachusetts Historical Society.

SECONDARY SOURCES

Baer, Helene G. *The Heart Is Like Heaven.* Philadelphia: University of Pennsylvania Press, 1964.
Meltzer, Milton. *Tongue of Flame.* New York: Crowell, 1965.

STANDARD SOURCES

Kass-Simon and Farnes; *NAW* (long article by Louis Filler); Uglow 1989 (this article provides a list of secondary materials on the life and works of Child).

CHINCHON, COUNTESS OF (1599–1641)

Spanish/Peruvian learned lady. Born 1599. Professional experience: Vice-queen of Peru. Died 1641.

The Countess is credited by sources such as Mozans and Hurd-Mead with introducing the chinchona bark into Europe. The story states that after being cured of tertian fever in 1638 while living in Peru, she returned to Spain and immediately made its curative properties known. The powder made from the bark was called *Pulvis comitessae*—the countess's powder. Linnaeus named the genus of this tree *Chinchona.* However, a modern paper in the Linnaean Society's *Journal of Botany* debunks the legend with new research. JH/MBO

SECONDARY SOURCES

Journal of Botany 53 (1946).
Markham, Clements R. *A Memoir of the Lady Ana de Osorio, Countess of Chinchon, and Vice-Queen of Peru.* London, 1874.

STANDARD SOURCES

Hurd-Mead 1938; Mozans.

CHINN, MAY EDWARD (1896–1980)

U.S. physician. Born 15 April 1896 in Great Barrington, Mass., to Lulu Ann and William Lafayette. Educated Bordentown Manual and Training Industrial School, New Jersey; Columbia University Teachers College (A.B., 1921); Bellevue Hospital Medical College (M.D., 1926); Columbia University (master's degree in public health, 1933). Professional experience: Harlem Hospital, intern (1927), admitting physician (1940–1978). Private practice in Harlem (1928–1978); Strang Cancer Clinic (1944–1973); Phelps-Stokes Fund, consultant (1978–1980). Honors and memberships: Society of Surgical Oncology. Died December 1980 in New York City.

May Edward Chinn was an African American physician whose mother was half Chickahominy Indian. Showing an early interest in music, she was encouraged by the family of Charles Tiffany for whom her mother worked as a live-in cook. She performed on the piano for black soldiers during

World War I and accompanied the great singer Paul Robeson during the 1920s. Although she began to study music at Columbia University Teachers College, she changed her major to science after a music professor ridiculed her as a black woman studying classical music. She went on to study at Bellevue Hospital Medical College and was the first black woman to graduate. Although she was an intern at Harlem Hospital she was not allowed to hold hospital privileges at that hospital until 1940. In the meantime, she established a private practice in Harlem, where she was forced to practice medicine in her office or in patients' homes. Because health conditions of her Harlem patients were so abysmal, she returned to Columbia University to study public health. Although she was prohibited from establishing formal affiliations with the great New York hospitals, she was invited to join the staff of the Strang Clinic, affiliated with Memorial and New York Infirmary Hospitals, which screened cancer patients. She remained on the staff for the next twenty-nine years. Although she practiced until the age of eighty-two, for the last two years of her life she served as a consultant to the Phelps-Stokes Fund, examining African American students. She died suddenly at Columbia University at a reception honoring a friend. In the last few years of her life her accomplishments were celebrated. JH/MBO

PRIMARY SOURCES
Chinn, May Edward. "Autobiographical Paper," 1977.

SECONDARY SOURCES
Brozan, Nadine. "For a Doctor at 84, A Day to Remember." *New York Times,* 17 May 1980.
Butts, Ellen. *May Chinn: The Best Medicine.* New York: Scientific American Books for Young Readers, 1995. Juvenile literature.
Davis, George. "A Healing Hand in Harlem." *New York Times Magazine,* 22 April 1979: 40 ff.
Ennis, Thomas W. "Obituary: Dr. May Edward Chinn, 84, Long a Harlem Physician." *New York Times,* 3 December 1980.
Hunter-Gault, Charlayne. "Black Women M.D.'s Spirit and Endurance." *New York Times,* 16 November 1977.

STANDARD SOURCES
Notable (long article by Laura Newman).

CHISHOLM, CATHERINE (1878–1952)
British physician. Born 2 January 1878 in Radcliffe, Lancashire, to Mary (Thornley) and Kenneth Mackenzie Chisholm. Never married. Educated privately; Owens College Medical School, Manchester (M.B., Ch.B., 1904; M.D., 1912). Professional experience: Clapham Maternity Hospital, Manchester, and the Eldwick Sanato-

rium, Bingley, Yorkshire, resident; general practice (1906–1908); Manchester High School for Girls and honorary physician to the Chorlton-on-Medlock Dispensary (1908–1919); Northern Hospital, Manchester, honorary physician for children and consultant to the Hope Hospital, Salford (1914–1936); Babies' Hospital, Manchester, founder and consultant (1914–1950). Honors and memberships: C.B.E. (1935); Royal College of Physicians, fellow (1949). Died 21 July 1878.

After Catherine Chisholm received her medical degree and residencies, she entered general practice. However, during successive appointments she found her major interest was in the health of children. She led her colleagues in a campaign against the epidemics of summer diarrhea, which was such a scourge to young children. Her campaign led to the formation of the Babies' Hospital, later the Duchess of York Hospital for Babies in 1914, and the setting up of the first breast-milk bank for sick babies. This hospital was used for training women in both nursing and medicine. In addition to her other appointments, Chisholm was medical officer to the Women Training Students Department of Education (1918–1924) and lecturer on vaccination and on the diseases of children (1923–1948). She published papers on rickets in children and "defective" girls in secondary schools. She was honored by the award of the Commander of the British Empire and by her election to the Fellowship of the Royal College of Physicians. JH/MBO

SECONDARY SOURCES
British Medical Journal no. 4778, 2 August 1952: 287–288. "Catherine Chisholm, C.B.E., M.D., F.B.C.P." Obituary notice.
Lancet 2, 26 July 1952: 178.
Manchester Guardian, 22 July 1952. Obituary notice.
(London) *Times,* 24 July 1952.

STANDARD SOURCES
Munk's Roll, vol. 5, 1955.

CHISHOLM, GRACE EMILY
See Young, Grace Emily Chisholm.

CHMIELEWSKA, IRENE (1905–1987)
Polish biochemist. Born 13 July 1905 in Lodz, Poland. Educated Jakuboswska Gymnasium, Warsaw (graduated 1922); University of Warsaw (graduated 1929, Ph.D., 1934, habilitated, 1939). Professional experience: University of Warsaw, Institute for Organic Chemistry, assistant professor (1947–1951); Institute of Pharmacology, director (1951–1953); chair in biochemistry (from 1958); director of Biochemical Institute (from 1965); pharmaceutical work

during World War II. Honors and memberships: Polish Academy of Sciences, corresponding member; member of the presidium. Died 17 January 1987.

Irene Chmielewska did her academic work at the University of Warsaw, where she received a doctorate in biochemistry in 1934 and habilitated during World War II in 1939. She did research and published prolifically. She held two professorships, one in organic chemistry and the second in biochemistry. Much of her research was on the structure and function of vitamins and the biosynthesis of proteins.

JH/MBO

PRIMARY SOURCES

Chmielewska, Irene. "Sur les colorants des pommes de terre violettes 'Negresse.'" *Bulletin. Societe Chimique de France* series 5, no. 3 (1936): 1575.

———. With others. *Badania nad cialami o dzialaniu antywitamin K* [napisali]. Warsaw: Nakledem Wroclawskiego Towarzystwa Naukowego, 1951.

———. With others. "Structure de la yongonine. Etude spectrographique dans l'ultraviolet et l'infrarouge." *Tétrahedron* 4 (1958): 36.

———. "Oxidative and photosynthetic phosphorylation involving 2-methylquinones." *Biochimica et Biophysica Acta* 39 (1960): 170.

STANDARD SOURCES

Strohmeier; Turkevich and Turkevich; *Soviet Union; WW in Science in Europe.*

CHODAK-GREGORY, HAZEL HAWARD (CUTHBERT) (1886–1952)

British physician. Born 20 July 1886 in London to Marion (Linford) and Goymour Cuthbert. Married Alexis Chodak-Gregory (1916). One son. Educated private school at Eastbourne; University of London (M.B.; B.S., 1911); London (Royal Free Hospital) School of Medicine (M.D., 1913). Professional experience: Children's Hospital, Birmingham, resident surgical and medical officer; Royal Free Hospital, assistant physician (1916–1919); physician (1919–1948?). Concurrent experience: East London Hospital for Children, Shadwell (later the Queen Elizabeth Hospital for Children), children's physician (1926–1946?), chairman of the medical committee, vice-dean (1935–1938); Three Counties Hospital at Arlesley, acting dean and resident physician (1938?–1946). Died 12 January 1952.

Hazel Chodak-Gregory was an imposing woman with a great ability for organization and a love for her work. Her father was an architect, and Hazel was able to enter the Uni-

versity of London and eventually study medicine because of the financial help of her uncle. Graduating in medicine in 1911, she became a resident medical officer at the Children's Hospital, Birmingham. She returned to London and took her medical degree in 1913. In the 1920s, she was appointed physician to the Royal Free Hospital. After holding several positions as assistant physician and physician, she became the assistant physician to the Shadwell Hospital for Children. In 1926 she had a choice to become either senior physician or children's physician at the newly established children's department. She chose the position as children's physician and her new department was very successful.

During the prewar and early war years, she was chairman of the medical committee and then vice-dean of the London School of Medicine for Women. World War II made it necessary to send students to the Three Counties Hospital at Arlesley where she became acting dean and resident physician. In 1946 she was forced to resign because of ill health.

Her professional life was centered in the London School of Medicine for Women and the Royal Free Hospital. She married a physician and had one son who qualified in medicine.

JH/MBO

SECONDARY SOURCES

"Hazel H. Chodak-Gregory, M.D., F.R.C.P." *British Medical Journal* no. 4752, 26 January 1952: 278.

"Hazel Howard Chodak-Gregory, M.D., F.R.C.P.," *Lancet* 1 (1952): 218. Includes photograph.

STANDARD SOURCES

Munk's Roll vol. 5, 1965.

CHRISTEN, SYDNEY MARY (THOMPSON) (ca. 1870–1923)

Irish naturalist and geologist. Born ca. 1870 in Belfast. Married M. Rodolphe Christen. Died July 1923 at Llandudno, Ireland.

Although no exact biographical information is available on Sydney Mary Thompson's birthdate, we know that her family had a house at Macedon, on the shore of Belfast Lough, which became a meeting place for Irish geologists. The Thompsons hosted a gathering of the Geologists' Association in 1895. As a young woman Sydney Mary Thompson cultivated watercolor painting and informally studied both field botany and geology. As an amateur naturalist, she actively supported the Belfast Naturalists' Field Club and organized winter lecture courses concerned with stratigraphy and petrography. In 1900 she married M. Rodolphe Christen who was a Swiss artist. After his death, she produced an illustrated work as a memorial to him.

Stimulated by the work of Percy Kendall on the glacial geology of Yorkshire, Christen's original observations were concerned with the source of glacial material in the deposits of northern Ireland, particularly collecting and naming eratics in order to determine the direction of ice flow. As a Quaternary geologist, Christen studied the glacial deposits of Kerry, Galway, and Ulster. After she married, she lived in the hills near Ballater and continued her interest in geology. Among her many continental visits was a trip to the volcanic region of the Auvergne in 1922.   JH/MBO

PRIMARY SOURCES

Thompson, S. M. "A Plea for Irish Glaciology." *Irish Naturalist* 3 (1894): 30–34.

———. [Report of Conference and Excursion Held at Galway, July 11 to 17, 1895] "II Geology." *Irish Naturalist* (1895): 235–237.

———. "Glacial Geology of Kerry." *Irish Naturalist* 8 (1899): 61.

———. "Report of the Geological Committee." *Belfast Field Club Report* 4 (1901): 115–125; 229–231; 234–235; 302–310; 386–390.

———. "On the Supposed Occurrence of a Patch of White Liss or Rhaectic Rock on the Shore North of Macedon Point, Belfast Lough." *Belfast Field Club Report* 4 (1901): 566–569.

SECONDARY SOURCES

[Cole, Grenville A. J.]. "Madame Christen (Sydney Mary Thompson)." *Geological Magazine* 60, no. 10 (1923): 478–479.

STANDARD SOURCES

Praeger.

CHRISTINA, QUEEN OF SWEDEN
(1626–1689)

Swedish patron of arts and sciences and student of Cartesianism. Born 1626 in Stockholm. Parents: Maria Eleanora, Princess of Brandenburg, and Gustavus II Adolphus, King of Sweden. Educated by tutors. Died in Rome in 1689.

Christina was the only child of King Gustavus II Adolphus (1594–1632), who died when she was only five years old. Sweden was ruled by five regents until Christina came of age and was crowned in 1644. In accordance with the plans left by her father, she was educated as a boy; consequently, her interests were in the areas then considered to be masculine. On becoming queen, she took an active political role but was equally absorbed in being the patron of learned men. Many scholars, including René Descartes, made her court their headquarters.

Christina's desire to convert to Catholicism (proscribed in Sweden) and her unwillingness to marry were the chief reasons for her abdication in 1654. However, recent interpretations cast doubts on the reality of her spiritual conversion. She left the throne to her cousin Charles X Gustavus, publicly declared her Catholicism, and thereafter lived mainly in Rome. She made unsuccessful attempts to become queen of Naples (1657) and to recover the crown of Sweden (1660, 1667), and became involved in church politics. Her palace in Rome was a gathering place for painters, sculptors, musicians, and men of letters, and housed a magnificent library and art collection.

Christina, as a patron of learning, occupied a unique position in the development of seventeenth-century Cartesian science. She corresponded with philosophers and scientists, including the mathematicians Blaise Pascal and Vincenzo Viviani and the physicists Evangelista Torricelli and Alessandro Marchetti. While queen of Sweden, she corresponded with Descartes and at last persuaded him to settle at her court, where he spent the final five months of his life (1649–1650). Her letters and other writings reflect a thorough understanding of Cartesian philosophy. During Descartes's visit to Stockholm, Christina asked him to be the director of a proposed Academy of Philosophy. Ten days before Descartes's death, he presented Christina with his rules for the academy, including the provision that no foreigners could be members. Since this would have excluded Descartes from being the director and other foreign scholars from being members, Christina objected. However, Descartes's death put an end to the project. Descartes is often either credited or blamed for Christina's decision to abandon her national Protestantism. Recent scholarship indicates that he did not have a profound influence on Christina's conversion or her scepticism.

Christina collected books and manuscripts as well as astronomical, mathematical, and geometrical scientific instruments. Shortly after her arrival in Rome, Christina established an academy that was to meet at her home. This group was short-lived, but in 1674 she formed the Accademia Reale of which she was president and patron. The society, with members selected by Christina, included such scientists as Giovanni Borelli. Members would read papers and then discuss them. Christina supported not only her own organization, but other scholarly groups as well. Alchemy was a major interest of Christina's and she collected a wide variety of material on this subject.

Christina's interest in astronomy was perhaps catalyzed by her interest in the work of Gian Domenico Cassini

(1616–1712). The major observatory that she envisioned, however, was never built.   JH/MBO

PRIMARY SOURCES
Christina of Sweden. *Maxims of a Queen.* Selected and translated by Una Birch. London: John Lane, 1907.

SECONDARY SOURCES
Åkerman, Susanna. "The Forms of Queen Christina's Academies." In *The Shapes of Knowledge from the Renaissance to the Enlightenment,* ed. Donald R. Kelley and Richard H. Popkin, 165–188. Dordrecht: Kluwer Academic, 1991.
————. *Queen Christina of Sweden and Her Circle: The Transformation of a 17th-Century Philosophical Libertine.* Brill's Studies in Intellectual History, no. 21. Leiden: Brill, 1991.
Bedini, Silvio A. "Christine of Sweden and the Sciences." In *Making Instruments Count. Essays on Historical Scientific Instruments.* Presented to Gerard L'Estrange Turner, ed. R. G. Anderson, J. A. Benned and W. F. Ryan. 99–117. Cambridge [England]: University Press, 1993.
Descartes, René. *Lettres de Descartes: Où sont traités plusieurs belles questions. Touchant la morale, physique médecine et les mathématiques. Nouvelle édition I.* Paris: Charles Qugot, 1663. Includes correspondence with Christina of Sweden.
Nordstrom, Johan. "Descartes and Queen Christina's Conversion." *Lychnos* (1941): 248–290.

STANDARD SOURCES
DSB.

CHURCH, ELDA RODMAN (MACILVAINE) (1831–?)

U.S. writer. Born 1831 in New York.

Often called a "miscellaneous writer," Church wrote articles and books on many subjects, including women's history and employment, sewing, interior design, and fiction, often set in vacation locales. Church, who often wrote under the name Ella Rodaman also wrote children's books that discussed lives of insects, birds, and other animals as well as books on gardening. Most of these science books were published by the Presbyterian Board of Publication, in Philadelphia.   AEM

PRIMARY SOURCES
Church, Elda Rodman. *Flyers and Crawlers, or Talks about Insects.* Philadelphia: Presbyterian Board of Publication, 1884. In this fictionalized book, Church sets up learning encounters between the main characters, two young girls and a boy, and various insects, with their governess as go-between and interpreter. The governess explains the lives, traits, and physical characteristics of the insects, after reading various books, and quoting them back to the children. The book contains detailed drawings and an index by insect type, including mosquitoes, butterflies, fireflies, and wasps. This book is indicative of Church's style of science writing for children, honest yet friendly.
————. Various titles. Elmridge Series. Philadelphia: Presbyterian Board of Publication, 1885–1887. This series of books concentrates on the activities in and around the house Elmridge, on various science-related subjects. Titles in the series include *Among the Trees at Elmridge, Flower-Talks at Elmridge* (1885), *Little Neighbors at Elmridge* (1887), *In the Hospital at Elmridge* (1887), and *Sunday Evenings at Elmridge* (1887).
————. *Birds and Their Ways.* Philadelphia: Presbyterian Board of Publication, 1886.
————. *Home Animals.* Philadelphia: Presbyterian Board of Publication, 1888.
————. *Some Useful Animals.* Philadelphia: Presbyterian Board of Publication, 1888.

CHUTE, HETTIE MORSE (1888–1962)

U.S. botanist. Born 6 October 1888 in North Platte, Neb. At least one brother. Educated Arcadia University (1916); Toronto University (M.A., 1918); Cornell University (Ph.D., 1929). Professional experience: Westminster Ladies College, Toronto, mathematics and science teacher (1916–1918); Carlyle High School, Saskatchewan, teacher (1918–1920); Colchester County Academy, Truro, Nova Scotia, teacher (1921–1926); Douglass College, Rutgers, instructor (1929–1931), assistant professor (1931–1945), associate professor (1945–1958), professor (1958–1959), emerita professor (1959). Died 22 February 1962.

Born in a sod house in Nebraska, Hettie Chute was a citizen of the United States even though her family had come from Canada. After she received her bachelor's degree, she taught for two years in Toronto. After she received a master's degree, she became principal of a high school in Saskatchewan for two years and then returned to Nova Scotia, where she taught for five years. In 1929, she earned a doctorate at Cornell, where she had an instructorship in botany and worked under Arthur J. Eames. She then took a position at Douglass College, Rutgers, where she spent the remainder of her academic career rising through the ranks to professor, a position that she attained the year before she retired.

Chute was a demanding teacher, and although her college did not support graduate students, her honors undergraduates often produced outstanding papers. Although she continued with her research, most of her time was taken over by her teaching responsibilities. She was also a responsible and effective committee member, an excellent student advisor, worked in faculty governance, an active member of American Association of University Professors, American Association of University Women, Sigma Xi, and Sigma Delta Epsilon, and a loyal participant in community activities. She also belonged to numerous professional organizations, including the Botanical Society of America, American Society of Plant Taxonomists, the Torrey Botanical Club, and the American Institute of Biological Sciences.   JH/MBO

PRIMARY SOURCES

Chute, Hettie Morse. "The Morphology and Anatomy of the Achene." *American Journal of Botany* 17 (1930): 703–723. The published version of her Ph.D. thesis.

———. *Laboratory Outline for General Botany.* Went through four editions.

SECONDARY SOURCES

Small, John A. "Hettie Morse Chute." *Bulletin of the Torrey Botanical Club* 89 (Sept.–Oct. 1962): 331–332. Ann Arbor, Mich.: Edwards Brothers, 1952. Includes a portrait.

STANDARD SOURCES

AMS 5–8, B 9, P&B 10.

CILENTO, LADY PHYLLIS (1894–?)

Australian physician. Born 13 March 1894 to Alice Walker and Charles Thomas McGlew in Sydney, Australia. No siblings. Married Raphael West Cilento (1920). Six children. Educated dame's school in Adelaide; Tormore House girls' school; Adelaide University (M.D.); Adelaide Hospital, surgery intern; Great Ormond Street Hospital for Sick Children, London and Marylebone General Dispensary, postgraduate work. Professional experience: government hospital, Malay; Rabaul, New Guinea, private practice; Brisbane, Australia, private practice (from 1929); helped found the Queensland Mothercraft Association (1932). Honors and memberships: Brisbane Hospital for Sick Children, honorary physician, first lecturer in mothercraft (1930–1934); Royal Brisbane Women's Hospital, lecturer; Australian Federation of Medical Women, president (1939–1948); Creche and Kindergarten Association of Queensland, member, board of management. Weekly radio program on mothercraft and family problems, host (from 1929); weekly newspaper column; weekly television program on family problems, host. Author of several books and journal articles. Retired from practice, 1964. Death date unknown.

Lady Phyllis Cilento was a third-generation Australian. Her father was a grain merchant and salt refiner and her mother a musician. The family of three eventually settled in Adelaide where Phyllis received all of her basic education, through the medical degree she earned at Adelaide University. In medical school, she was the only woman in her class but felt the twenty-one men classmates "tolerated" her well, espe-

cially as she had a car and no one else did. The top male student in the class was Raphael West Cilento, to whom she became engaged in fifth-year medical school. With World War I still raging, Ralph Cilento was activated immediately following graduation and was sent to New Guinea, where he developed the interest in tropical medicine that directed the couple throughout their married life.

Phyllis and Raphael married in March of 1920 and after a brief interlude in Adelaide left for Raphael's position in the colonial service in the Federated Malay States. Cilento reports that she learned a great deal in the way of practical baby care from the Chinese *amah* hired to help with her first child. Soon labeled the "Lady medical officer, Lower Perak," Cilento attended women and children in the government hospital. After a year, Cilento returned to Sydney while her husband took postgraduate training in tropical diseases for the government. During that time she started on a diploma course in public health but was unable to finish. Her interest in nutrition remained and was of value in their next assignment as Raphael Cilento was appointed director of the Institute of Tropical Medicine in New Guinea in 1934. The couple with their two small children settled in Rabaul, where Phyllis started a private general practice, attending Chinese, Malaysians, and Europeans in the colony. Nutritional deficiency diseases were rampant and both Cilentos worked on education and enforcement of the addition of fresh foods to the diets of native children and laborers in particular. In 1935, Raphael Cilento was awarded a knighthood for his work on the health and nutrition of native peoples in the South Pacific.

In 1929, now with four children, the Cilentos settled in Brisbane and Phyllis again established a small part-time medical practice, centered around maternity cases and family care. In 1932, she was instrumental in beginning the Queensland Mothercraft Association, an organization for the education of girls and women in child care and for training home assistants to help mothers. The association worked with baby health centers and established a bureau for the employment of their trained mother's assistants. Cilento was also active during this period with the Australian Federation of Medical Women, serving as president from 1939 to 1948, when she joined her husband in the United States where he was associated with the United Nations. She attended postgraduate classes in "natural childbirth" in the States, while managing the household of six children. After Raphael Cilento retired from the United Nations, the couple returned to Australia and set up a joint general practice.

Phyllis Cilento was a well-known personality to Queensland and greater Australia. From 1929 through the 1940s, she gave child care and family management advice to mothers through a weekly radio program, woman's magazine articles, a weekly newspaper column, and later, a weekly television program. She wrote several books and was one of the early proponents of the Lamaze method. JH/MBO

PRIMARY SOURCES

Cilento, Phyllis. "Lady Phyllis Cilento." In Hellstedt. *Autobiographies.*

CINQUINI, MARIA DEI CONTI CIBRARIO (1905–)

Italian mathematician. Born 6 September 1905 in Genoa, Italy, to Cristina (Botto) and Giulio dei Conti Cibrario. Married Silvio Cinquini (1938). Three children, Giuseppe, Vittoria, Carlo. Educated University of Turin (Ph.D., 1927); Scuola Normale Superiore, Pisa, postgraduate studies (1931). Professional experience: universities of Turin and Pavia, assistant (1928–1947), deputy professor (1936–1947); University of Cagliari, professor (1947–1948); University of Modena, professor (1948–1950); University of Pavia, professor (from 1950). Honors and memberships: Unione Matematica Italiana.

After teaching at several universities, Maria Cinquini became a professor at the University of Pavia. She contributed numerous articles to mathematical reviews. Her husband, Silvio Cinquini, was also a mathematician. Like his future wife, Silvio earned his doctorate at Bologna in 1929 and did postgraduate work at the Scuola Normale Superiore in Pisa at the same time she did. The couple did not marry until 1939 at which time Silvio, and perhaps Maria, got a position at Pavia. The couple collaborated on mathematical papers. Maria contributed over eighty articles to professional journals. Her memberships included the Mathematical Association of Italy, the Lombardy Institute, and the Academy of Sciences and Letters. She was corresponding secretary of the Turin Academy of Sciences. She received the Gold Medal of the Scuola della Cultura and dell'Arte. JH/MBO

PRIMARY SOURCES

Cinquini, Maria del Conti Cibrario. With Silvio Cinquini.
    Equazioni a derivate parziali di tipo iperbolico. Roma: Edizioni Cremonese, 1964.

STANDARD SOURCES

Debus; *World Who's Who of Women.*

CIORANESCU-NENITZESCU, ECATERINA (1909–)

Romanian organic chemist. Born 15 August 1909 in Bucharest. Educated University of Bucharest (Ph.D.). Professional experience: Polytechnic Institute, Bucharest, professor; Center of Organic Chemistry, Bucharest, director (from 1962). Honors and memberships: Rumanian Academy of Sciences, corresponding member and secretary for Chemical Sciences (1963); regular member (1974); national advisory committee of the Socialist-Democratic Union (from 1980).

Organic chemist Ecaterina Cioranescu-Nenitzescu earned her doctorate from the University of Bucharest in organic chemistry and was appointed department head (director) of the Polytechnic Institute, Bucharest. She later became a professor at the institute. She was elected a corresponding member of the Rumanian Academy in 1963 and became a regular member. JH/MBO

STANDARD SOURCES

The Soviet Union; Strohmeier; Turkevich and Turkevich; *WW in Science in Europe.*

CLAPP, CORNELIA MARIA (1849–1934)

U.S. zoologist. Born 17 March 1849 in Montague, Mass., to Eunice (Slate) and Richard Clapp. Five siblings. Educated in local schools; Mount Holyoke Seminary (1868–1871); Anderson School of Natural History, Penikese Island, Buzzard's Bay (1874); Syracuse University (Ph.B., 1888; Ph.D., 1889); University of Chicago (Ph.D., 1896). Professional experience: Mount Holyoke Seminary, teacher (1872–1896); Mount Holyoke College, professor of zoology (1896–1916). Died 31 December 1934 in Mount Dora, Fla.

Cornelia was the oldest of six children of two former teachers. Her father became a farmer and a deacon of the Congregational church. After attending local schools, Clapp entered Mount Holyoke Seminary and completed the three-year course in 1871. She spent one year teaching Latin at a boys' school in Andalusia, Pennsylvania, then joined the staff at Mount Holyoke, at first teaching gymnastics and mathematics. She became interested in natural history through her associate LYDIA SHATTUCK, a science teacher at Holyoke.

After attending Louis Agassiz's Anderson School of Natural History, on Penikese Island in Buzzard's Bay, during the summer of 1874, Clapp devoted herself to promoting the observation-centered method of studying natural history. This summer marked the beginning of her fascination with biology. Although she did not neglect theory, she was primarily interested in field work.

Having qualified by examination, Clapp received bachelor's and doctoral degrees from Syracuse University (1888, 1889). During the period of Mount Holyoke's transformation from a seminary to a college, she took a three-year leave of absence for graduate study at the University of Chicago, where she received a doctorate in 1896. On her return to Holyoke, Clapp became professor of zoology. Clapp was active in the research group that centered around the newly established (1888) Marine Biological Laboratory at Woods Hole, Massachusetts.

After her retirement in 1916, Clapp spent her winters at Mount Dora, Florida (where she was active in town affairs), and her summers at Woods Hole. Mount Holyoke presented her with an honorary doctorate in 1921 and named its new science laboratory for her in 1923. She died of cerebral thrombosis at Mount Dora in 1934.

Although she devoted much of her time to research, particularly at Woods Hole, Clapp published little; hence it is difficult to assess her research achievements. Her involvement in the development of Mount Holyoke College and, especially, her teaching, represent her major contributions to science.   MBO

PRIMARY SOURCES
Clapp, Cornelia. *The Lateral Line System of Batrachus tau.* Boston: Ginn, 1899. Ph.D. thesis.
———. "Some Recollections of the First Summer at Woods Hole." *Collecting Net* 2, no. 4 (1927): 2–10.

SECONDARY SOURCES
Burstyn, Joan N. "Early Women in Education: The Role of the Anderson School of Natural History." *Journal of Education* (Boston University) 159 (1977): 50–64.
Carr, Emma Perry. "One Hundred Years of Science at Mount Holyoke College." *Mount Holyoke Alumnae Quarterly* 20 (1937): 135–138.
Cole, Arthur C. *A Hundred Years of Mount Holyoke College: The Evolution of an Educational Ideal.* New Haven, Conn.: Yale University Press, 1940.

STANDARD SOURCES
AMS 1–4; *NAW*; Ogilvie 1986; Shearer and Shearer 1996.

CLAPPE, LOUISA AMELIA (SMITH) (1819–1906)

U.S. traveler and writer on mining. Born 1819 in Amherst, Mass. Married Fayette Clappe (1848); divorced (1857). Educated Charleston, Mass., Female Seminary; Amherst Academy. Professional experience: San Francisco public schools, teacher (1854–1878). Died 9 February 1906 on the East Coast.

Louisa Amelia Smith Clappe's fame came from the twenty-three letters that she wrote to her sister in New England describing the scenery and local methods and practices of mining. She also included the daily events and concerns of the mining community, Rich Bar, where she and her husband moved because of his ill health. She was born and educated in Amherst, Massachusetts, and married Clappe when

she was twenty-nine years old. She had received $2,500 in an endowment from her family when she turned twenty-one. Her husband, who was five years younger than she, had graduated from Brown University and was prepared to practice medicine when he was bitten by the gold bug. The couple moved to San Francisco, where Fayette Clappe's health reflected their arduous trip around the cape in 1849. Hoping that the mountain air would restore his health, they moved to Rich Bar. In the letters Clappe wrote she calls and signs herself "Dame Shirley," apparently from a shared joke with her sister. These letters are written in an impersonal way, and were meant for publication. When the couple left Rich Bar they moved to San Francisco where their marriage disintegrated. They were divorced in 1857. Louisa remained in San Francisco and taught in the public schools from 1854 to 1878. After 1878, when she retired, she returned to the East Coast until her death in 1906.   JH/MBO

PRIMARY SOURCES
Clappe, Louisa Amelia. *The Shirley Letters from the California Mines, 1851–1852.* New York: Alfred A. Knopf, 1949.

SECONDARY SOURCES
Lloyd, Jon Clark, ed. "The Shirley Letters." *California Geology* 39 (December 1986): 269.

CLARA (CLARE) OF ASSISI, SAINT (1193–1253)

Italian healer. Born 1193. Father Favorino Seisso. Died 1253.

Daughter of Favorino Seisso, Clara of Assisi was a friend of Francis of Assisi, and was a part of the new order of the "Poor Clares" associated with the Franciscans. She cared for the sick and was venerated as a saint.   JH/MBO

STANDARD SOURCES
Echols and Williams; Hurd-Mead 1938; Uglow 1989.

CLARISSE OF ROTOMAGO (OR CLARICE OF ROUEN) (fl. 1312)

French physician. Married Pierre Faverel.

Clarisse of Rotomago was one of the fourteenth-century French midwives who was arrested and excommunicated for practicing medicine. She was excommunicated by the Prior of Sainte-Geneviève in 1312.   JH/MBO

STANDARD SOURCES
Echols and Williams; Hurd-Mead 1938.

CLARK, BERTHA (1878–?)

U.S. physicist. Born 3 May 1878 in Baltimore, Md. Educated Goucher College (A.B., 1900); Bryn Mawr College (1900–1901); Göttingen, Alumnae Association, fellow (1903–1904); Women's Association, fellow (1904–1905); University of Pennsylvania, fellow (1905–1907; Ph.D., 1907). Professional experience: Goucher College, instructor (1901–1903); high school, Philadelphia, head science department (1907–1923). Death date unknown.

Bertha Clark earned her doctorate at the University of Pennsylvania after studying at the University of Göttingen on a fellowship for several years. She did not find a teaching job in a college or university after she got this degree, and spent her career teaching high school in Philadelphia.   JH/MBO

STANDARD SOURCES
AMS 1–8, P 9.

CLARK, FRANCES N. (1894–1987)

U.S. icthyologist. Born 1894 near Omaha, Neb. Never married. Educated San Jose Normal School (1913?); Stanford College (B.A., 1918); University of Michigan (M.A., 1923; Ph.D., 1925). Professional experience: San Jose Junior High School, biology teacher (1918); Professor C. H. Gilbert, research assistant (1919–1921); Bureau of Marine Fisheries of California, Terminal Island, Calif., fisheries researcher (1921–1922), director of marine work (1926–1945), acting head (1946), laboratory director (1942–1956). Honors and memberships: Honorary Research Associate, Scripps Institution of Oceanography (from 1956); American Association of University Women, San Pedro, Calif. Branch, Board of Directors; American Institute of Fishery Research Biologists (AIFRB) banquet of recognition, 23 January 1975. Died 10 February 1987 in La Jolla, Calif.

Frances Clark, sister of Laura Cordelia (Clark) Hubbs, was, like her sister, a working scientist her entire life. Unlike her sister, she held formal positions in science until her retirement in 1956. Born in 1894 on a small farm in Nebraska, she spent her last years in high school in San Jose after her family moved to California. At first she wanted to teach science, and attended the San Jose Normal School. She soon moved instead to Stanford, where her sister was studying mathematics, and took courses in zoology, graduating a year after her sister.

After finishing her undergraduate degree, Clark taught biology for a semester in the San Jose Junior High School, but found she disliked teaching. She then worked with C. H. Gilbert (at Stanford), from whom she learned precise and meticulous methods as a research assistant. Her research led her to take a position as a fisheries researcher for the California State Bureau of Marine Fisheries at Terminal Island, California, where she worked under Will F. Thompson. Here she became interested in the life history of the grunion, a fish being intensely fished at that time and suffering severe depletion. She went back to do further graduate work at Stanford, but then transferred to the University of Michigan, where her sister was located, and began to study marine biology under her brother-in-law, Carl Hubbs. She rapidly obtained her master's degree within a semester and then obtained her doctorate with a dissertation on the life history of the grunion, a classic work that was soon published in sections in the *California Fish and Game Bulletin*.

Clark returned to the California Bureau of Marine Fisheries, and rose to a position as director of the laboratories, publishing articles on grunion, smelt, bass, dolphin, and eel, and displaying a concern for the changing abundance of these marine animals. Her greatest interest was in the pacific sardine, on which she was an authority, studying its weight-length ratio and its seasonal changes, and developing methods for its preservation. She began to supervise the work of younger men in her department, and for a brief period in the mid-1940s served as acting director of the Division of Fisheries. She was the California representative to the Pacific Science Conference of the National Research Council in 1946.

In 1956, Clark retired from the Bureau of Fisheries, but continued to be active in the American Association of University Women, the YWCA, and other organizations. Roger Revelle, Scripps Institution of Oceanography director, suggested that she be made an honorary research associate of this institution upon her retirement. She was honored with a banquet and a gold medal by the American Institute of Fishery Research Biologists at the age of eighty-one. She died twelve years later, only a year before her sister.   JH/MBO

PRIMARY SOURCES

Clark, Frances. "The Life-History of *Leuresthes tenuis*, an Etherine Fish with Tide Controlled Spawning Habits." *Fish Bulletin* 10 (1925): 1–58. Issued by the State Californian Fish and Game Commission.

———. "Life and Habits of the Grunion." Ph.D. diss., University of Michigan, 1926. Clark's thesis director was her brother-in-law, Carl Hubbs.

———. "The Conservation of the Grunion." *California Fish and Game* 12 (1926): 161–166.

———. "The Weight-Length Relationship of the California Sardine (*Sardina caerulea*)." *Division of Fish and Game California, Fish Bulletin* 12 (1928): 1–58.

———. "Maturity of the California Sardine (*Sardina caerulea*). Determined by Ova Diameter Measurements." Issued by the California Division of Fish and Game and California Bureau of Commercial Fisheries, *Fish Bulletin* 42 (1934): 1–99.

———. With Richard S. Crocker. "The Pismo Clam in 1935." *California Fish and Game* 48 (1938).

———. "Analysis of Populations of the Pacific Sardine on the Basis of Vertebral Counts." *California Division of Fish and Game, Fish Bulletin* no. 65 (1947): 1–26.

A bibliography of her papers from 1925 to 1947 is in the file compiled by her sister, Laura Hubbs, along with a brief biography written in 1948 in the Scripps Institution of Oceanography Library archives, in the Carl L. Hubbs papers.

SECONDARY SOURCES

Brandvig, Mary. "Dr. Clark's Name on Fellowship." *Harbor Living,* San Pedro, Calif., 6 March 1969.

Hubbs, Laura. Letter to Winona Bethune, Pacific Biological Station Nanaimo British Columbia, 24 February 1948. Frances Clark folder, Carl L. Hubbs papers. Scripps Institution of Oceanography Library Archives. This letter contains a biography of her sister, Frances Clark.

CLARK, JANET HOWELL (1889–1969)

U.S. physiologist and biophysicist. Born 1 January 1889 to Anne Janet Tucker and William Henry Howell. Married Admont Halsey Clark (July 1917) (d. 1918). Educated Byrn Mawr School (1906); Bryn Mawr College (A.B. in science, mathematics, and physics, 1910); Johns Hopkins University (Ph.D. in physics, 1913). Professional experience: Bryn Mawr, physics faculty; Mt. Wilson Observatory, Calif., fellowship; Smith College, instructor in physics (1916); Johns Hopkins, Department of Hygiene and public health, instructor, assistant, associate professor in physiological hygiene (1918–1932?, 1952–1967); Bryn Mawr School, head (1932–1938). University of Rochester, dean of Women's College and professor of biological sciences (1938–1952). Died 12 February 1969.

Janet Howell Clark was a physiologist and biophysicist who did important research on photobiology, especially the effects of radiation on human beings, including visible and ultraviolet light, infrared, and X-ray radiation. Her father was the eminent physiologist William Henry Howell, professor of physiology at Johns Hopkins Medical School and later director of Johns Hopkins School of Hygiene and Public Health. Janet Howell grew up proud also of her mother's heritage, as daughter of one of General Lee's officers during the Civil War. She attended a Quaker school, Bryn Mawr School, in Bryn Mawr, Pa., and graduated at the top of class in 1906. Having won a scholarship to Bryn Mawr College, she was influenced by president M. Carey Thomas's interest in science. She soon decided to major in physics, and study science and mathematics. Graduating from Bryn Mawr in 1910, she went on to complete a doctorate at Johns Hopkins in physics in 1913, producing a mathematical study of opti-

cal gradings under J. S. Ames and A. J. Anderson. From this point onward she worked on optical phenomena. She then spent two years lecturing in physics at Bryn Mawr and a year with a fellowship from the American Association of University Women at Mt. Wilson Observatory, California, and one year as instructor of physics at Smith. In July 1917, she married Admont Halsey Clark, associate professor of pathology at the Johns Hopkins Medical School. Her one daughter, Anne Janet, was born in May, 1918.

When her husband died at age thirty in the flu epidemic, she returned to live with her parents and began to teach at Johns Hopkins in her father's department of hygiene and public health, as instructor in physiological hygiene in 1918, assistant in 1920, associate in 1923. Her courses emphasized the effects of radiation on human eyesight. She studied visible and ultraviolet light, infrared light, and X-ray radiation. Her other courses on lighting considered appropriate lighting for factories, offices, stores, and schools; and occupational disorders from insufficient lighting (myopia, miner's nystagamus) or excessive lighting (cataract formation among glassblowers, iron smelters, etc.). She then began to concentrate on cataract formation, which she believed to be due to ultraviolet light affecting the lens, precipitating certain proteins. She investigated the amount of ultraviolet light needed to kill pathogenic microorganisms and involved her students in this study. She also studied the positive effects of ultraviolet light in sunlight as a protection against rickets in children.

Clark's important work on the effects of lighting on the eyes was published in 1925. She then began to look at X-ray diffraction patterns produced by muscles, bones, tendons, and related subjects. When her father retired, she became angry that she was not considered as acting head. When no suitable candidate was found, the department was merged with Chemical Hygiene. Clark resigned, but her colleague, ANNA BAETJER, remained and continued publishing in the field of occupational health. At this point, Clark made an interesting career move, and became the head of her secondary school, Bryn Mawr School, from which her daughter was just graduating. Her interest in the education of women in science led her to hold this position through the difficult Depression years. In 1938, she became dean of the Women's College and professor of biological sciences at the University of Rochester (a position equal to that of dean of men). She was an excellent dean and also taught biophysics to graduate students and conducted her own research. With a grant from Jane Coffin Childs Memorial Fund, Clark was able to return to research, and she investigated the effects of radiation on breast tumors in mice. She continued her interest in astronomy as a hobby, lecturing to members of the Wednesday Club, on that subject. When her position as dean of women was downgraded in 1952, placed under the dean of men, Clark left and returned to the School of Hygiene at Johns

Hopkins, where she was given a research laboratory. She lectured on environmental medicine and researched photobiology for the next fifteen years until the age of seventy-eight. She continued her interest in girls' science education and served as a board member of the American Association of University Women. She was a member of a number of professional organizations, especially the American Physiological Society, and served on the photobiology committee of the National Research Council. She also held memberships in American Physical Society and the Optical Society of America. Clark died suddenly, 12 February 1969, at the age of eighty. JH/MBO

PRIMARY SOURCES

[Clark] Howell, Janet. "The Fundamental Law of the Grating." Ph.D. diss., Johns Hopkins University, 1913.

Clark, Janet Howell. *Lighting in Relation to Public Health.* Baltimore: Williams and Wilkins, 1924.

———. "Studies on Radiated Proteins. 1. Coagulation of Albumen by Ultraviolet Light and Heat." *American Journal of Physiology* 73 (1925): 649–666.

———. "Studies on Radiated Proteins. 2. The effect of radiated proteins." *American Journal of Physiology* 113 (1935): 538–547.

A complete bibliography is in American Physiological Society, Bethesda, Md.

SECONDARY SOURCES

Fee, Elizabeth, and Anne Clark Rodman, "Janet Howell Clark, physiologist and biophysicist (1889–1969)." *The Physiologist* 28, no. 5, October 1985. Portrait on cover.

CLARK, JESSIE JANE (1881–1914)

British botanist and horticulturist. Born 25 August 1881. Educated University of London (B.Sc., 1903?); Royal Botanical Gardens, Kew Herbarium, assistant (1909–1913). Died 7 February 1914.

Jessie Jane Carter was educated at the University of London at the beginning of the century and soon after went to work as an assistant in the Kew Herbarium, Royal Botanical Gardens, Kew. She studied abnormal flowers of the genus *Amelanchier,* and published some short pieces in the *Kew Bulletin.* She died at the age of thirty-three. JH/MBO

PRIMARY SOURCES

Carter, Jessie Jane. "Abnormal Flowers of *Amelanchier Spicata.*" *Annals of Botany* 26 (1912): 948–949.

———. Various short pieces. *Kew Bulletin* 1909–1912.

SECONDARY SOURCES

"Jessie Jane Clark." *Kew Bulletin* (1914): 142.

"Jessie Jane Clark." *Journal of the Kew Guild* (1915): 240–241. With portrait.

STANDARD SOURCES

Desmond.

CLARK, LOIS (1884–1967)

U.S. botanist and bryologist. Born 1884 in Charlotte, Mich. Educated Seattle public schools (1898–1903); University of Washington (A.B., 1907); Yale University (graduate study, 1907–1908); University of Minnesota (Ph.D., 1919). Professional experience: Alaska, teacher; Stephens College, Columbia, Mo., teacher; University of Idaho, assistant professor of botany (1923–1928), professor (from 1928); University of Washington, summers, teacher. Reorganized University of Washington herbarium. Died 30 December 1967.

Born in Charlotte, Michigan, Lois Clark moved with her family to Seattle, Washington, when she was young. She attended Seattle public schools and then the University of Washington, where she studied under the bryologist T. B. Frye. After receiving her bachelor's degree, she went to Frye's alma mater, Yale, as a graduate student to study hepatic plants with A. W. Evans (1907–1908). In 1917, she went to the University of Minnesota for her doctorate. Her dissertation was on *Podophyllum peltatum* L. After briefly teaching in Alaska, then at Stephens College in Columbia, where she was acting head 1919–1920, Clark became assistant professor of botany at the University of Idaho and taught during the summer at the University of Washington.

Clark published *Liverworts of the Northwest* (1928) with T. C. Frye and worked with him in the herbarium of the University of Washington. An even more extensive study with Frye appeared almost ten years later—*The Hepaticae of North America* (in five parts, 1937–1947). Clark published outstanding work on the genus *Frullania.* Thirty-five articles appeared under her name alone and sixty in collaboration with Frye and with Ruth Svihla. She collected many specimens and identified those at the University of Washington, including type specimens.

Clark was a member of Sigma Xi and the American Bryological Society, and a Fellow of the AAAS. She died on 30 December 1967. JH/MBO

PRIMARY SOURCES

Clark, Lois. *Acidity of Marine Algae.* Seattle: University of Washington, 1916: 235–236. Puget Sound Biological Station publication.

———. With T. C. Frye. *The Liverworts of the Northwest.* Seattle: University of Washington, Puget Sound Biological Station, 1928. Reprinted from volume 6, 15 December 1827: 1–194.

———. With T. C. Frye. *The Hepaticae of North America* (in five parts). Seattle: University of Washington, 1937, 1947. Publications in biology, vols. 5 and 6.

SECONDARY SOURCES
Bryologist 71, no. 2 (1968): 140–141. Obituary notice with portrait.

CLARK, MAMIE KATHERINE (PHIPPS) (1917–1983)

U.S. psychologist. Born 1917 in Hot Springs, Ark., to Katie F. and Harold H. Phipps. One sibling. Married Kenneth Bancroft Clark (1938). Two children: Kate (born 1940) and Hilton (1943). Educated public schools, Pine Bluff, Ark. (graduated Langston High School, 1934); Howard University (B.S., magna cum laude, 1938); Columbia University (Ph.D., 1943). Professional positions: United States Armed Forces Institute, research psychologist (1945); Riverdale Home for Children in New York, psychologist (1946?); Northside Center for Child Development, director (1946–1979). Died 11 August 1983 in New York City.

Mamie Katherine Phipps's parents were Dr. Harold H. Phipps, originally from St. Kitts in the British West Indies, and Katie F. Phipps, who assisted her husband in his medical practice while rearing Mamie and her younger brother, Harold. The children attended segregated schools in Pine Bluff, Arkansas. Mamie graduated from Langston High School in 1934 and went on to Howard University, where she received a bachelor's with honors in 1938. During her undergraduate years, she did part-time work in the psychology department. Her interest and ambition led her to Columbia University, where in 1938 she married Kenneth Bancroft Clark, who would complete his doctorate in psychology in 1940. She received her doctorate in psychology in 1943. The Clarks had two children: Kate (1940) and Hilton (1943).

Two major influences on Mamie Clark's life were a summer job in the law office of William Houston where early planning began for civil rights cases that challenged the laws requiring and permitting racial segregation. This raised Clark's social consciousness and gave her a grounding in research technique. Also influential were Ruth and Gene (Horowitz) Hartley, who were doing research studies with preschool children in New York City using line drawings of white and black children. Her discussions with them led to the material of her master's thesis, "The Development of Consciousness of Self in Negro Pre-school Children." Early positions held by Mamie Clark were research psychologist at the United States Armed Forces Institute (1945) and psychologist at the Riverdale Home for Children in New York. This work with homeless black girls led to a commitment to continued work in developmental psychology. She established with her husband, Kenneth Clark, the Northside Center for Child Development (1946), and served as its director from 1946 to 1979. Mamie Phipps Clark died 11 August 1983 in New York City.

The research and articles of Mamie and Kenneth Clark were used in several landmark civil rights cases to document the adverse effects of segregation on black children. Her doll research (verifying problems of racial identity and self-esteem in black and minority children) is still discussed and replicated.

Mamie Clark was a member of several boards and advisory groups, such as the American Broadcasting Company, Mount Sinai Medical Center, Museum of Modern Art, Columbia University Teachers College, Institute of Museum Services, New York Public Library. She was president of the Museum Collaborative and a vocal supporter of federal funding of American cultural institutions. She worked with Harlem Youth Opportunities Unlimited and the National Headstart Planning Committee.   JH/MBO

STANDARD SOURCES
O'Connell and Russo 1988; O'Connell and Russo 1990.

CLARK, MARY (JOHNSON) (1895–1969)

See Johnson, Mary.

CLARK, NANCY TALBOT (1825–1901)

U.S. physician. Born 1825 to a New England family of clergymen, physicians, and teachers. Married (1) Champion W. Clark (1845; d. 1848); (2) Amos Binney (1855). Six children. Educated Western Reserve College, Cleveland (M.D., 1852); University of Paris (postgraduate studies, 1854). Professional experience: teacher; Boston, private practice. Died 1901.

Members of Nancy Talbot's family were descendants of the earl of Shrewsbury, who settled in Massachusetts in 1675. They were respected professionals. She married when she was twenty years old, but both her husband and infant daughter died three years later during a typhoid epidemic. Before her marriage, Nancy Clark had been a teacher, so after the death of her husband, she planned to return to teaching. However, she was very interested in medicine. She matriculated at Western Reserve College in Cleveland (Cleveland Medical College) in 1850 and became the first woman to graduate from this institution. She was allowed to enroll because, as a schoolteacher, she needed to comply with a new Massachusetts law requiring that a class in physiology be added to the public school curriculum. She was admitted in 1850 under a new ruling allowing women into the medical school; although the ruling was reversed a year later, Clark was permitted to remain and graduate (1852). She returned to Boston and opened a medical practice rather than return to teaching. In 1853 she applied for membership in the Massachusetts Medical Society, but, while her male classmates were readily accepted, she was rejected.

Clark and her younger brother, Israel Tisdale Talbot, a doctor, went to Europe in 1854 for further study. Upon returning to Boston, Clark met Amos Binney, whose young wife had recently died. The two fell in love and were married the next year. The couple had six children and she gave up her practice in Boston to follow her husband. However, after his death, she returned to Boston and opened a free dispensary for women on Charles Street.   JH/MBO

STANDARD SOURCES
Bonner; Hurd-Mead 1933; Ireland; *LKW*; Lovejoy.

CLARKE, CORA HUIDEKOPER (1851–?)
U.S. botanist and entomologist. Born 9 February 1851 in Meadville, Pa. Educated private schools. Honors and memberships: Massachusetts Horticultural Society; Boston Society of Natural History.

Little information is available on Cora Clarke. She was, however, one of five women who became fellows of the American Association for the Advancement of Science between 1880 and 1884. She did research on caddis-worms, and insect galls. She wrote the book *Mosses of New England* and published on seaweeds. According to Rossiter, Clarke wrote to Hermann Hagen in 1883 about a woman's botanical club in Boston and about this same group to Elizabeth Britton in letters written regularly between 1890 and 1906. A *Boston Sunday Post* article written in 1910(?) ran a story with the headline "Miss Clarke is winning fame as 'Plant Doctor.' "   JH/MBO

PRIMARY SOURCES
Clarke, Cora H. "Description of Two Interesting Houses Made by Native Caddis-fly Larvae." *Proceedings of the Boston Society of Natural History* 22 (1882): 67–71.

———. Letter to Herman Hagen, 30 September 1883, Museum Collection, Museum of Comparative Zoology Archives, Harvard University.

———. "Caddis-worms of Stony Brook." *Psyche* 6 (1891): 153–158.

———. Letters to Elizabeth Britton 1890–1906. In *Elizabeth G. Britton Papers.* New York Botanic Garden Archives.

Letter to Hermann Hagen, 30 September 1883, Museum Collection, Museum of Comparative Zoology Archives, Harvard University.

SECONDARY SOURCES
"Cora H. Clarke." *Psyche Journal of Cambridge Entomological Club* 23 (1916): 94.

Boston Sunday Post, January 1910, 40. Clippings in Archives of Museum of Comparative Zoology Library, Harvard University.

STANDARD SOURCES
AMS 2; Rossiter 1982.

CLARKE, EDITH (1883–1959)
U.S. electrical engineer. Born 10 February 1883 on a farm near Ellicott City, Howard County, Maryland, to Susan Dorsey (Owings) and John Ridgely Clark. Eight siblings. Educated country grade school; Briarley Hall; Vassar College (A.B. mathematics and astronomy, 1908); University of Wisconsin (civil engineering courses, 1911–1912); Hunter College and Columbia University, evening courses in radio; Massachusetts Institute of Technology (M.S., 1919). Professional experience: San Francisco and Huntington, W. Va., math and science teacher; American Telephone and Telegraph Company (AT&T), computing assistant to research engineer George A. Campbell (1912–1918); General Electric Corporation (GE), training and directing women computers (1919–1921), engineer (1922–1945); University of Texas, Austin, professor of electrical engineering (1947–1956). Honors and memberships: American Institute of Electrical Engineers, first female Fellow (1948); Society of Women Engineers, Achievement Award (1954). Died 29 October 1959 in Olney, Md., of a heart attack.

Edith Clarke spent her career in both industry and academia. Born on a Maryland farm, Edith Clarke lost her father when she was seven years old. Her mother continued to run the farm until she too died, five years later. Edith was from a large family, the fifth of seven daughters and the sixth of nine children, three of whom died in childhood. After the death of her parents, a maternal uncle became her guardian, but actually the oldest sister, Mary, cared for the children. Edith, much to the disgust of her relatives, used her inheritance to attend college. After getting her bachelor's degree in astronomy and mathematics (Phi Beta Kappa), she taught high school for several years and decided that teaching was not for her. After an illness that convinced her that she was going to die, she decided to pursue a career that interested her—engineering. She studied civil engineering for a year and then went to work for AT&T as a computer, solving mathematical equations. Computing for engineers was considered appropriate for women with advanced mathematical training. While working for AT&T, Clarke studied radio at Hunter College and electrical engineering at Columbia University in the evenings.

When the United States entered World War I, Clarke entered graduate school at MIT and in 1919 received a master's in electrical engineering, the first woman to earn such a degree. However, after the war, she found that no company would hire a woman engineer, so she took a job at GE in Schenectady, N.Y., training and directing a force of women computers. Unhappy with the job and interested in travel, Clarke spent a year in Turkey teaching. She then returned to GE, this time as an engineer in the Central Station Engineering Department, where she stayed for twenty-three years. She proved to be an innovative engineer, including improvements to long-distance power transmission and the development of the theory of symmetrical component and circuit analysis. She patented her method of regulating the voltage on power transmission lines in 1927 and in 1932 became the first woman to present a paper before the American Institute of Electrical Engineers (AIEE). She published a textbook that included circuit analysis of alternating-current power systems.

Clarke retired from GE in 1945, intending to spend her time on a farm that she had purchased in Howard County, Maryland. However, she accepted a professorship at the University of Texas, and from 1947 to 1956 supervised a number of graduate students and encouraged them to publish their works. She left the University of Texas in 1956 and retired on her farm, where she lived her last years.

JH/MBO

PRIMARY SOURCES

Clarke, Edith. *Circuit Analyses of A-C Power Systems.* Vol. 1. New York: John Wiley & Sons, 1943.

SECONDARY SOURCES

"Edith Clarke Dies, 1954 SWE Award Winner." *Society of Women Engineers Newsletter* (December 1959): 3. Obituary notice.

STANDARD SOURCES

NAW (M) (long article by Terry Kay Rockefeller); *Notable* (long article by Karen Withem).

CLARKE, LILIAN JANE (1866–1934)

British botanist and science educator. Born 27 January 1866 in London. Educated University College, University of London (B.Sc.). Professional experience: James Allen's Girls' School, Dulwich, science mistress (1896–1926). Honors and memberships: Linnean Society, Fellow (1905). Died 12 February 1934.

The British botanist Lilian Jane Clarke was science mistress at the James Allen's Girls' School, Dulwich. Educated at University College, London, she wrote one book, published

after her death, on botany as an experimental science.

JH/MBO

PRIMARY SOURCES

Clarke, Lilian Jane. *Botany as Experimental Science: In Laboratory and Garden.* London: Oxford University Press, 1935.

SECONDARY SOURCES

Delf, E. M. "Dr. Lillian Clarke (1866–1934)." *Journal of Botany* 72 (1934): 112–113. Obituary notice.

Brenchley, Winifred E. "Dr. Lillian Clarke." *Nature* 133 (1934): 439–440. In obituary section.

Proceedings of the Linnean Society 146th session (1933–1934): 150–151. Obituary notice.

"Review of All Plant Science During 1934." *Chronica Botanica* 1 (1935): 163. Obituary notice.

STANDARD SOURCES

Desmond.

CLARKE, LOUISA (LANE) (1812–1883)

British botanist. Born 1812. Married Reverend Thomas Clarke, Woodeaton, Oxfordshire. Died 8 November 1883 at L'Hyereuse, Guernsey, Channel Islands.

Louisa Lane Clarke published a number of popular books on the microscope, the plants of the Channel Islands, and common sea weeds along the British and Channel Island coasts. Her later books went into a number of editions and were published simultaneously in London and New York. She died in Guernsey.

JH/MBO

PRIMARY SOURCES

Clarke, Louisa Lane. *Redstone's Guernsey Guide; or The Stranger's Companion for the Island of Guernsey.* 1841.

———. *The Microscope, Being a Popular Description of the Most Instructive and Beautiful Subjects for Exhibition.* London and New York: Routledge, 1858.

———. *The Common Seaweeds of the British Coast and Channel Islands. With Some Insight into their Structure and Fructifications.* London: F. Warne, 1865.

SECONDARY SOURCES

Ardagh, J. "Louisa Lane Clarke and Her Writings." *Journal of Botany* 66 (1928): 174–175. Notice of Clarke's work.

The Star (Guernsey), 13 November 1883. Obituary notice.

CLAY-JOLLES, TETTJE CLASINA (1881–1972)

Dutch physicist. Born 1881 in Assen, the Netherlands, to Eva Dina Halbertsma and Maurits Aernout Diederik Jolles. Two sisters, Hester and Leida. Married Jacob Clay (1908). One daughter and two sons. Educated Gymnasium at Assen (graduated 1888); University of Leiden (did not complete thesis). Professional experience: Institute of Technology, assistant (1920–1929). Died 1972 in Amsterdam.

Although Tettje Clay-Jolles did not complete her doctoral thesis, she did research in her husband's laboratory. Raising three children occupied her time from 1920. At that time the family accompanied Jacob Clay to Java, where he was appointed professor of physics at the new Institute of Technology, and she worked as an assistant in the physics laboratory. Her student interest in vacuum pumps was rekindled. She also began an editing career, when she edited a volume of lectures by Nobel laureat Hendrik Lorentz. In addition, she typed and edited her husband's papers.

Clay-Jolles worked with her husband on measuring the intensity of atmospheric radiation from 1920 to 1929. This work resulted in advances in the understanding of cosmic radiation. Upon noting that radiation in the ultraviolet solar spectrum varies according to latitude, the couple did research into the causes of this variation. Their conclusion was that ultraviolet penetration related directly to the physics of the upper atmosphere and the ozone layer. They became involved in a dispute with Jan Boerema and Maarten Pieter Vrij, who asserted that tropical ultraviolet penetration existed. By using a cadmium electrocell, Clay and Clay-Jolles demonstrated a relatively weak penetration of ultraviolet light in the tropics. The family returned to the Netherlands in 1929, when Jacob became professor of experimental physics at the University of Amsterdam. Clay-Jolles and Vrij defended their opposing views on ultraviolet penetration in a further published exchange. JH/MBO

PRIMARY SOURCES

Clay-Jolles, Tettje C., ed. *Hendrik Antoon Lorentz, Lessen over theoretische natuurkunde.* Vol. 4, *Thermodynamica.* Leiden: E. J. Brill, 1921.

———. With Jacob Clay. "Measurements of Ultraviolet Sunlight in the Tropics." *Proceedings of the Amsterdam Academy of Sciences* 35 (1933): 69–82, 172–185.

———. "Vergelijking van het ultraviolet zonlicht op Jana en in Europa." *Natuurkundig Tijdschrift voor Nederlandsch-Indië* 93 (1933): 126–138. The exchange between Clay-Jolles and Vrij on the ultraviolet penetration.

SECONDARY SOURCES

Pyenson, Lewis. *Empire of Reason: Exact Sciences in Indonesia, 1840–1940.* New York: E. J. Brill, 1989. Clay-Jolles discussed on pages 120–124, 133–159.

STANDARD SOURCES

Notable (long article by Lewis Pyenson).

CLAYPOLE, AGNES MARY (1870–1954)

U.S. zoologist. Born 1 January 1870 in Bristol, England, to Jane (Trotter) and Edward Waller Claypole. Twin sister, Edith. Married Robert Moody (1903). Educated at home; Buchtel College, Akron, Ohio (Ph.B., 1892); Cornell University (M.S., 1894); University of Chicago (Ph.D., 1896). Professional experience: Wellesley College, instructor in zoology (1896–1898); Cornell University, assistant in histology and embryology (1898–1900); Throop Polytechnic Institute (now California Institute of Technology), instructor (1900–1903); Mills College, Oakland, Calif., lecturer (1918–1923). Died 1954 in Berkeley, Calif.

Although she had a different specialty, Agnes Claypole's career often paralleled that of her identical twin sister, EDITH. Her mother died a few weeks after the twins' birth. Edward Claypole married Katherine B. Trotter of Toronto in 1879 and in that same year he moved his daughters from Bristol, England, to Akron, Ohio, where, after a variety of teaching positions, he taught geology at Buchtel College. Like her sister, Agnes attended Buchtel (Ph.B., 1892) and earned a master's degree from Cornell University (1894). Agnes wrote her thesis on the digestive tract of the Cayuga Lake Lamprey, which was published as the Prize Paper in Animal Histology in the *Proceedings of the American Microscopical Society* (1894). The twins' careers diverged as Agnes attended the University of Chicago and completed a doctoral degree (1896). Her dissertation, "The Embryology and Oogenesis of Anurida Maritima," was published in the *Journal of Morphology* (1898).

For two years Claypole was an instructor in zoology at Wellesley College, followed by an additional two years as an assistant in histology and embryology at Cornell. At Cornell, Claypole was the first woman to teach laboratory classes that were required courses for all students. She found, however, that women had a difficult time advancing in this coeducational institution; they had low status and low pay.

Edward Waller Claypole, Agnes's father, had moved to California to teach at the Throop Polytechnic Institute (now the California Institute of Technology) in Pasadena; in 1900, Claypole left Cornell to assist her father there. After her father's death in 1901, she succeeded him in his appointment at the Throop Institute. In 1903 she married Robert Orton Moody, an instructor in anatomy at the University of California, San Francisco, and temporarily gave up teaching. She returned to teaching in 1918, and she taught at Mills College in Oakland, California, until 1923. JH/MBO

PRIMARY SOURCES

Claypole, Agnes. "The Enteron of the Cayuga Lake Lamprey." *Proceedings of the American Microscopical Society* 16 (1895): 125–164. Master's thesis.

———. *The Embryology and Oogenesis of Anurida maritima (Guer).* Boston: Ginn, 1898. Ph.D. dissertation.

Moody, Agnes Claypole. With Hubbard, Marian E. *In Memoriam: Edith Jane Claypole.* Berkeley, 1915.

STANDARD SOURCES

AMS 1–11; Bailey; *NCAB;* Ogilvie 1986; Rossiter 1982; Shearer and Shearer, *Life Sciences;* Siegel and Finley.

CLAYPOLE, EDITH JANE (1870–1915)

U.S. physiologist and pathologist. Born 1870 in Bristol, England, to Jane (Trotter) and Edward Waller Claypole. Educated at home; Buchtel College, Akron, Ohio (Ph.B., 1892); Cornell University (1892–1893; 1899–1900; M.S., 1893); Massachusetts Institute of Technology (1904); University of California at Los Angeles (M.D., 1904). Professional experience: instructor in physiology and histology, Wellesley College (1894–1899); pathologist, Pasadena, California (1902–1911); research associate, University of California at Los Angeles (1912–1915). Died 27 March 1915 in Berkeley, Calif.

Born in Bristol, England, Edith was the daughter of Edward Waller Claypole, "a well-known man of science" (Moody, 9) and Jane Claypole. She had an identical twin sister, AGNES, and the two girls were similar in interests as well as appearance. When the twins were nine years old, the family moved to Akron, Ohio, where Edward Claypole taught at Buchtel College for sixteen years. The girls were taught at home by their parents and then attended Buchtel (Ph.B., 1892).

After graduate work at Cornell (M.S., 1893), Claypole taught physiology and histology at Wellesley College (1894–1899); during two years of that time (1896–1898) she was acting head of the department of zoology. Agnes Claypole was also an instructor at Wellesley during these years. Although Edith began her work in medicine at Cornell (where she was an assistant in physiology from 1899 to 1901), she went to Pasadena, California, in order to care for her stepmother, who was ill, and continued her education at the University of California, Los Angeles, specializing in pathology (M.D., 1904).

From 1902 to 1911 (at first on a part-time basis while she completed her degree), Claypole was a pathologist in Pasadena and Los Angeles, doing "the routine drudgery in pathology for a group of a half dozen practicing physicians and surgeons" (Moody, 17). In 1912 she joined the department of pathology at the University of California as a volunteer. She was appointed research associate, a position that she held until her death. She died of typhoid fever, contracted during her research on the typhoid bacillus.

Claypole's research was in the area of blood and tissue histology and pathology. Her work on lung pathology and on typhoid immunization was well known. According to one of the practitioners for whom she had worked before 1912,

"she early showed a mental bent towards research, and when she left to enter this field exclusively at the University, the deep regret of the whole office—doctors and assistants alike—at losing her was tempered by the thought that she was now going to have a better opportunity to do the things she liked best to do, and for which she was fitted as few women and men have ever been" (Moody, 17).   JH/MBO

PRIMARY SOURCES
Claypole, Edith. *Human Streptotrichosis and Its Differentiation from Tuberculosis.* Chicago: American Medical Association, 1914.

SECONDARY SOURCES
Moody, Agnes Claypole, and Marian E. Hubbard. *In Memoriam: Edith Jane Claypole.* Berkeley, 1915. Booklet containing a biographical sketch, bibliography, and tributes from friends and colleagues of Edith Claypole.
Science 41 (1915): 527; 754. Obituary notice.

STANDARD SOURCES
AMS 1–2; Bailey; Ogilvie 1986; Rossiter 1982; Shearer and Shearer 1996; Siegel and Finley.

CLEA (fl. 1st–2d centuries C.E.)

Priestess of Isis and Dionysus. Believed to have flourished in the first to the second centuries C.E. Mother or sister, Leontis.

Plutarch is the source of the meager information available on Clea. He reported in his work *On the Virtues of Women* that he had had a long philosophical conversation with her after the death of Leontis, who was probably her mother or sister. He dedicated this work as well as his *De Iside et Osiride* to Clea.   JH/MBO

SECONDARY SOURCES
Griffiths, J. Gwyn. *Plutarch's de Iside et Osiride.* Cambridge: University of Wales Press, 1970. See pages 95 ff., 253 ff.

STANDARD SOURCES
Ménage, Gilles; Kersey.

CLEACHMA (fl. 5th century B.C.E.)

Greek philosopher. Flourished fifth century, B.C.E. Sister of Autocharidas of Lacedemonia.

As is the case with all of the early Greek women philosophers, very little is known about Cleachma. However, she was listed as a woman Pythagorean by Iamblichus. She is considered to be the sister of Autocharidas of Lacedemonia.   JH/MBO

STANDARD SOURCES
Kersey; Ménage.

CLEMENS, MARY KNAPP (STRONG) (1873–1963)

U.S./British/Australian botanist. Born 3 January 1873 near Liberty, N.Y. Married botanist Joseph Clemens (1896). Educated Dickinson Seminary; Wilson College, Pa. Professional experience: British Museum of Natural History, plant collector with J. Clemens (1905–1935). Field Museum, Chicago, plant collector; Museum, Manila, Philippines. Died 1963 in Brisbane, Australia.

Born in Liberty, New York, Mary Strong married Reverend Joseph Clemens, a Methodist minister, who, born in Britain, came to the United States with his family when he was a child. In 1902, he became chaplain to the U.S. Army and was stationed in the Philippines. At the suggestion of a botanist, E. D. Merrill, in Mindinao in 1905 Mary Clemens began collecting plants in the Philippines on a large scale. Joseph Clemens was shipped to France during World War I, and was retired with a disability in 1918. The couple continued to collect plants in eastern Asia and the Malay Islands. Traveling back and forth from the United States (1912–1919) to China (1912–1914), they collected plants in both areas. They made trips to British North Borneo (1915–1917). In 1927 they went to Indochina and Borneo and the Philippines in 1929. They collected specimens in West Java in 1932 and in New Guinea in 1935, where Joseph Clemens died in Finschhafen (1936). Mary Clemens then went to Brisbane, Australia, where she died in 1963.   JH/MBO

SECONDARY SOURCES
"Clemens, Joseph." *Chronica Botanica* 2 (1936): 89–90. Includes photograph of Joseph and Mary Clemens.

STANDARD SOURCES
Barnhart; Desmond.

CLEMENS, EDITH GERTRUDE (SCHWARTZ) (ca. 1877–1971)

U.S. ecologist. Born ca. 1877 in Albany, N.Y. Married Frederic Edward Clements (1900). Educated University of Nebraska (A.B., 1898; Ph.D., 1906). Professional experience: University of Nebraska, assistant botanist (1904–1907); University of Minnesota, instructor (1909–1913); Carnegie Institute of Washington, investigator and illustrator (1918–1941). Died 1971.

Edith Schwartz received both a bachelor's and a doctoral degree from the University of Nebraska. At this university, she met her future husband, ecologist Frederic Clements (1874–1945), who had received his doctorate from Nebraska in 1898. Frederic taught at Nebraska from 1894–1907, and when he became head of the Botany Department at the University of Minnesota in 1907, Edith followed him to that institution, giving up her position as assistant botanist at Nebraska. At the University of Minnesota she became a botany instructor, never advancing beyond that rank during the four years that she taught there. She apparently did not hold a paid position from 1913 until 1918, when she again followed her husband, this time to Washington, D.C., where he became a research associate at the Carnegie Institution of Washington from 1917 until his retirement in 1941. She accepted a position with the Carnegie Institution in 1918 as an investigator and illustrator, a post she held until her retirement in 1941. Her research interests included plant anatomy, taxonomy, and geographic distribution.   JH/MBO

PRIMARY SOURCES
Clements, Edith S. "The Relation of Leaf Structure to Physical Factors." Ph.D. diss., University of Nebraska, 1904.
———. *Rocky Mountain Flowers.* New York: H. W. Wilson, 1914.
———. *Flowers of Mountain and Plain.* White Plains, N.Y.: H. W. Wilson, 1915.
———. "Wild Flowers of the West." *National Geographic,* (May 1927): 566–622.
———. With Frederic E. Clements. *Flower Families and Ancestors.* New York: The H. W. Wilson Co., 1928.
———. *Flowers of Coast and Sierra.* New York: The H. W. Wilson Co., 1928.
———. *Flower Pageant of the Midwest.* Washington, D.C.: Judd and Detweiler, 1939. From *National Geographic,* August 1939.
———. *Flowers of Prairie and Woodland.* New York: Hafner, 1947.
———. *Adventures in Ecology: Half a Million Miles: From Mud to Macadam.* New York: Pageant Press, 1960.
———. *Cryptogamae formationum coloradensium.* New York: New York Botanical Garden, 1972.
Clements, Frederic E., and William Joseph Showalter. "The Family Tree of the Flowers." *National Geographic* (May 1927): 555–563.

STANDARD SOURCES
AMS 3–8, B 9, P&B 10–11.

CLEMENTS, MARGARET (1508–1570)

British natural philosopher. Born 1508. Niece to Sir Thomas More. Married her tutor Dr. John Clements (1531). One daughter, Winifred. Educated in liberal sciences by tutors. Died on 6 July 1570 in Mechlin, Brabant.

Margaret Clements was Sir Thomas More's niece. She was carefully educated in the liberal arts and sciences. She corresponded with humanist Erasmus of Rotterdam, who commended her on the good sense and "chaste Latin" of her epistles. About 1531, she married her tutor, John Clements, and the couple had one daughter. They lavished a great deal of care on her education, and she eventually married William Rastell, a nephew of Sir Thomas More and the greatest lawyer of his time. The Clements left Protestant England for Catholic France to avoid religious persecution. Margaret died there in 1570.   JH/MBO

STANDARD SOURCES
Cyclopaedia; DNB.

CLEOBULINA OF RHODES (fl. 570)
Greek philosopher. Born in Rhodes. Father Cleobulus. Sometimes mentioned as the mother of Thales.

Little information is available on Cleobulina, and some of what is reported is suspect. Diogenes Laertius is the main source for our information on her. He reports that she wrote riddles in hexameter verse, one of which was quoted by Aristotle in his *Poetics* and in his *Rhetoric.* The riddle involves the gluing of brass onto flesh with fire. This feat could be accomplished by creating a vacuum between a brass object and the skin. Aristotle's context for quoting this riddle is to use it as an example of describing a fact in an impossible combination of words. Although real names for things cannot be used to describe such an impossibility, their metaphorical substitutes can be used, e.g., a man gluing brass on another with fire. Ménage interpreted this as referring to the medical application of cupping, in which a vacuum is created to draw blood to the skin's surface. According to Plutarch, Thales praised her as a wise woman who influenced her father Cleobolus to rule Rhodes more fairly.   JH/MBO

SECONDARY SOURCES
Diogenes Laertius. *Lives of the Eminent Philosophers.* Translated by R. D. Hicks. Cambridge: Harvard University Press, 1925.

STANDARD SOURCES
Kersey; Ménage; Waithe.

CLEOPATRA (ca. 5th century B.C.E.)
Physician or alchemist, of unknown nationality (Greek?).

Many different accounts surround the person known as Cleopatra. According to one tradition, she was a physician who was mentioned in the Hippocratic writings; according to a second, she was an alchemist who was a follower of Mary the Jewess. During the Middle Ages the traditions became confused and a third complication was added: the name of Queen Cleopatra of Egypt was linked with the work of both Cleopatra the physician and Cleopatra the alchemist. Although both historians of medicine and historians of alchemy refer to the same ancient sources, their interpretations of these sources depend upon their biases—whether they are searching for a physician or an alchemist. The only connection between the interests of Cleopatra the alchemist and Cleopatra the physician is in their mutual concern with the reproductive process. In the reports of the work of Cleopatra the physician, no more than one ingredient of science, the descriptive element, is apparent. As for Cleopatra the alchemist, although no evidence suggests an originality of approach, she does seem to have integrated the theoretical aspects of alchemy with laboratory experimentation.

JH/MBO

SECONDARY SOURCES
Lindsay, Jack. *The Origins of Alchemy in Graeco-Roman Egypt.* New York: Barnes and Noble, 1976.

STANDARD SOURCES
Lipinska 1930; Uglow 1989.

CLERKE, AGNES MARY (1842–1907)
Anglo-Irish popularizer of astronomy. Born 1842 in Skibbereen, County Cork, western Ireland, to Catherine (Deasy) and John Clerke. Two siblings. Never married. Educated at home by parents. Actonian Prize from the Royal Institution. Honorary member of the Royal Astronomical Society. Died, South Kensington, London, 1907.

Agnes Clerke was born 10 February 1842, at Skibbereen, a small country town in the County Cork, western Ireland. Her older sister, ELLEN MARY (born 1840), was her lifelong companion, with whom she shared many interests, including a fascination with astronomy. Their younger brother, Aubrey St. John, later to become a barrister, was born in 1843. He too was keenly interested in science, winning the first gold medal in mathematics in 1865 at Trinity College, Dublin, and the second gold medal for experimental and natural science.

The Clerke children's love of science was fostered by their father, John, a bank manager, who conducted chemistry experiments in a makeshift laboratory at home and who kept a telescope mounted in the garden. The children were educated entirely at home by their parents due to the lack of suitable local schools. John Clerke instructed them in Latin and Greek, while his Catholic wife, Catherine, a member of the distinguished Deasy family, cultivated in her children an appreciation for music and, as was customary in mixed marriages, assumed the responsibility for their religious education.

Clerke's early education at the hands of her scholarly parents provided her with the joy of learning as well as the ability to conduct private research in order to pursue her scientific interests. By the age of eleven she had mastered Herschel's *Outlines of Astronomy,* which stimulated her to study astronomy in more depth. The Clerke family moved to Dublin in 1861 when the father was appointed court registrar to his brother-in-law Judge Deasy. But starting in 1867, the girls and their mother spent winters in Italy due to Agnes's delicate health, and lived there year round from 1873 to 1877. The sisters spent much of their time in serious study of Italian history and literature, the sciences, and contemporary world affairs, particularly at the magnificent libraries of Florence. Agnes was drawn to Galileo, Renaissance science, and philosophy.

In 1877 the entire Clerke family settled in London, where Agnes (now aged thirty-five) began to pursue a career as a writer. Agnes Clerke's output is daunting and places her in the ranks of the great popularizers of science in the late-Victorian period. The success of *A Popular History of Astronomy during the Nineteenth Century* (1885) first brought her to the attention of the scientific community. Her other major works include *The System of the Stars* (1890), *The Herschels and Modern Astronomy* (1895), *Astronomy* (1898) (which she coauthored), *Problems with Astrophysics* (1903), and *Modern Cosmogonies* (1905). Clerke also churned out scores of essays, mostly on astronomy, for periodicals like the *Edinburgh Review, Knowledge, Observatory,* and *Nature.* For *The Dictionary of National Biography* she composed 150 biographies of famous astronomers; she also submitted entries on astronomers and astronomical subjects to *The Encyclopedia Britannica.* As a result of her labors, Clerke gained partial admission into the male-dominated astronomical world, even though she held no official position at a university or an observatory, and despite the fact that she conducted little original research of her own. Among her correspondents were the Hugginses, Norman Lockyer, David Gill, E. S. Holden of the Lick Observatory in California, and E. C. Pickering of Harvard. Clerke even won her share of scientific honors. In 1892 the Royal Institution awarded her the Actonian Prize for her astronomical works, while the Royal Astronomical Society elected her as honorary member in 1903, an unusual distinction for a woman at the time. She died on 20 January 1907 of pneumonia.

Clerke's significance in the history of science lies in her redefinition of the role of popularizer at a time when an explosion in the growth of knowledge and increasing specialization within science widened the gulf between profes-

sional scientists and the reading public. Often thought of as a historian, both by contemporaries and twentieth-century scholars, Clerke is remembered most for her best-selling *Popular History of Astronomy during the Nineteenth Century,* which required three updated editions (the last appearing in 1902), several reprints, and a German translation. The book is regarded as an authoritative secondary source on the history of nineteenth-century astronomy, in particular the development of the "new astronomy" in the latter half of the century based on the introduction of the spectroscope and camera into astronomical practice.

But Clerke was not merely a historian. She was also a gifted popularizer of science, who possessed the rare ability to communicate clearly the complexities of scientific theory to a popular audience, while synthesizing masses of astronomical information into a coherent whole for professional scientists, who had become so specialized that they could not see the larger connection between their work and other current discoveries in astronomy. After publishing *A Popular History,* Clerke began to work on projects that were not as historical in nature and that were less accessible to a popular audience. Both *System of the Stars* and *Problems in Astrophysics* examined the most recent astronomical research, pointed to the many questions remaining, and suggested work to be done by astronomers to begin answering these questions. In effect, Clerke went beyond the proscribed role of the popularizer who merely reproduced the results of the experts and instructed professional astronomers which lines of research to pursue.

Clerke's work is also distinguished by her attempt to prevent scientists hostile to Christianity from using astronomical theories to undermine the authority of religion in late Victorian culture. In the preface to the first edition of *A Popular History,* she identifies as one of her goals the attempt to help readers to understand how astronomical phenomena reveal the glory of God. She is as awestruck by the design and order in nature as any pre-Darwinian natural theologian. The discoveries of the "new astronomy" testified, in Clerke's opinion, to the complexity and inexhaustible variety of divine creation.

In spelling out the religious implications of the "new astronomy," Clerke adopted the traditional role of the female science writer, concerned with the religious and moral education of the popular reader. But by presenting herself as the interpreter of the larger meaning of recent astronomical discoveries to the experts themselves, she challenged the traditional place for women in science during the Victorian era and ran afoul of some professional scientists, most notably Richard A. Gregory, assistant editor of *Nature.* In his reviews published in *Nature* in 1903 and 1906 of Clerke's more technical works, he launched into a vicious attack on her scientific credentials, arguing that her gender prevented her from engaging in serious scientific work. Clerke's election to the Royal Astronomical Society as an honorary member, a rare distinction for a woman, is proof that many professional astronomers did not agree with Gregory's estimate of her abilities. Clerke's work was also highly regarded by the popular reading audience. Her career therefore points both to the dangers and opportunities that awaited those women who attempted to participate in the scientific enterprise through the route of popularization in the late nineteenth century.   BL

PRIMARY SOURCES

Clerke, Agnes Mary. *A Popular History of Astronomy during the Nineteenth Century.* Edinburgh: Adam and Charles Black, 1885.

————. *The System of the Stars.* London and New York: Longmans, Green, & Co., 1890.

————. *The Herschels and Modern Astronomy.* London, Paris, and Melbourne: Cassell and Company Limited, 1895.

————. *Problems in Astrophysics.* London: Adam and Charles Black, 1903.

————. *Modern Cosmogonies.* London: Adam and Charles Black, 1905.

SECONDARY SOURCES

Brück, Mary T. "Agnes Mary Clerke, Chronicler of Astronomy." *Quarterly Journal of the Royal Astronomical Society* 35 (1994): 59–79.

————. "Companions in Astronomy: Margaret Lindsay Huggins, and Agnes Mary Clerke." *The Irish Astronomical Journal* 20 (1991): 70–77.

————. "Ellen and Agnes Clerke of Skibbereen, Scholars and Writers." *Seanchas Chairbre,* no. 3 (1993): 23–42.

Huggins, Lady. *Agnes Mary Clerke and Ellen Mary Clerke: An Appreciation.* Printed for private circulation, 1907.

Kidwell, Peggy Aldrich. "Women Astronomers in Britain, 1780–1930." *Isis* 75 (1984): 534–546.

Lightman, Bernard. "Constructing Victorian Heavens: Agnes Clerke and the 'New Astronomy.'" In *Natural Eloquence: Women Reinscribe Science,* ed. Barbara Gates and Ann Shteir, 61–75. Madison: University of Wisconsin Press, 1997.

Weitzenhoffer, Kenneth. "The Prolific Pen of Agnes Clerke." *Sky and Telescope* 70, no. 3 (1985): 211–212.

STANDARD SOURCES
DNB.

CLERKE, ELLEN MARY (1840–1906)

Anglo-Irish geographer and popularizer of astronomy. Born 1840 in Skibbereen, County Cork, western Ireland, to Catherine (Deasy) and John Clerke. Two siblings. Never married. Educated at home by parents. Died, South Kensington, London, 1906.

Born on 26 September 1840, Ellen Mary was AGNES CLERKE's older sister and lifelong companion (see Agnes Clerke for biographical details), with whom she shared a fascination with astronomy. Like Agnes, Ellen began to pursue a career as a writer when the entire Clerke family settled in London in 1877.

A prolific writer, she published her essays in a number of influential English journals on a wide variety of topics. For the last twenty years of her life she wrote a weekly leader for *The Tablet,* usually on subjects connected with Catholic missions in foreign countries. She contributed sixty major articles on contemporary social issues, foreign lands, and the Church abroad to the liberal Catholic journal *The Dublin Review,* as well as writing a regular column "Notes of Travel and Exploration," which reported on developments in geography, geology, and anthropology. A member of the Manchester Geographical Society, she wrote essays for its journal. She also produced pieces for *The Cornhill Magazine, Fraser's Magazine,* and *The National Review,* among others.

Though Ellen's specialties were Italian literature and geography, she published two short popular astronomy books, *Jupiter and His System* (1892) and *The Planet Venus* (1893). Science popularization provided one of the few opportunities for women to engage in scientific activity in the latter half of the nineteenth century, when English science was dominated by male professional scientists bent on excluding women, amateurs, and the Anglican clergy. Like her sister, Agnes, Ellen contributed to a significant body of popular works by women which retained strong religious themes in synthetic accounts of contemporary science. Encouraged by the success of her first book outlining the present state of scientists' knowledge of Jupiter, Ellen Clerke's *The Planet Venus* was a far bolder statement of her devoutly Catholic views on the relationship between science and religion. Venus is depicted as one of the most enigmatic objects in space despite its proximity to earth. Clothed in a dense robe of cloud that veils her from the gaze of astronomers, Venus becomes a symbol of the limited powers of science. Later in the book, when she discusses the Star of Bethlehem and argues that no naturalistic explanation can be made to fit the events described in the Gospel narrative—no celestial conjunction of Jupiter, Saturn, or Venus took place—she again puts science in its place so that God and miracles can be accepted. Like Agnes Clerke and her other "sisters in science," Ellen provided a religious alternative to the secular interpretations of professional scientists for a rapidly growing reading public fascinated with the most recent discoveries of modern science.   BL

PRIMARY SOURCES

Clerke, Ellen Mary. "The Planet Mars." *Month* 76 (1872): 185–199.

———. *Jupiter and His System.* London : Edward Stanford, 1892.

———. *The Planet Venus.* London: Witherby and Co., 1893.

SECONDARY SOURCES

Brück, Mary T. "Ellen and Agnes Clerke of Skibbereen, Scholars and Writers." *Seanchas Chairbre,* no. 3 (1993): 23–42.

Huggins, Lady. *Agnes Mary Clerke and Ellen Mary Clerke: An Appreciation.* Printed for private circulation, 1907.

Kidwell, Peggy Aldrich. "Women Astronomers in Britain, 1780–1930." *Isis* 75 (1984): 534–546.

STANDARD SOURCES

DNB (under Agnes Clerke).

PRIMARY SOURCES

Cleve, Astrid. *Zum Pflanzenleben in nordschwedischen Hochgebirgen.* Stockholm: Norstedt, 1901.

———. *Quantitative Plankton Researches in the Skager Rak.* Stockholm: Almquist and Wiksells Boktryckeri, 1917.

———. *Die Diatomeen von Schweden und Finnland.* New York: Stechert-Hafner, 1968.

SECONDARY SOURCES

Fischer-Hjamars, Inga. "Women Scientists in Sweden." In *Women Scientists, The Road to Liberation.* Ed. Derek Richter. London: 1982.

STANDARD SOURCES

Strohmeier.

CLEVE-EULER, ASTRID (1875–1968)

Swedish botanist, chemist, geologist. Born 1875 in Uppsala, Sweden. Father Per T. Cleve, a chemistry professor. Married Hans von Euler-Chelpin (1902; divorced 1912). Five children. Educated University of Uppsala (degree in 1898). Professional experience: University of Stockholm, dozent (1898–1892), honorary professor (1955); girls' secondary school (Mädchenoberschule) (1918–?). Died 1968.

Daughter of a renowned father who was a chemistry professor at Uppsala University, Astrid Cleve studied botany at this institution and earned a degree in 1898 on the germination of a range of Swedish plants. After earning her degree, Cleve went to the University of Stockholm where the academic climate was generally liberal regarding women, and worked as a dozent (assistant professor) in chemistry. During this time she published a paper in inorganic chemistry on lanthanum and selenium.

After four years she married chemist Hans von Euler-Chelpin, whom she assisted in fermentation research, for which he was awarded the Nobel Prize in 1929. The couple had five children. She divorced after ten years and took a position in a girls' secondary school as a teacher. Six years later she worked in forestry where she carried out significant contributions to the chemistry of lignin, a consituent of cellulose in plant cell walls. After a time, Cleve-Euler's interests grew to include the geology of the quarternary, and she wrote a significant article on this subject. She also worked with fossil and recent diatoms. Cleve-Euler published her last work when she was eighty-six years old. Her scientific output was recognized, and she was awarded a title of professor in 1955. Cleve-Euler's son Ulf von Euler won the Nobel Prize in 1970 for his work on chemical transmission.

JH/MBO

CLEVELAND, EMELINE HORTON (1829–1878)

U.S. physician born 22 September 1829 in Ashford, Conn., to Amanda Chaffee and Chauncey Horton. Eight siblings. Educated private tutor; Oberlin College (1850–1853); Female (later Woman's) Medical College of Pennsylvania (M.D., 1855); School of Obstetrics at the Maternité, Paris. Married Giles Butler Cleveland (1854). One son, Arthur (b. 10 February 1865). Professional experience: Women's Medical College, chair of anatomy and histology (1857–1861), professor of obstetrics and diseases of women (from 1861), dean (1872–1874); Pennsylvania Hospital, gynecologist to the department for the insane. Died 8 December 1878 in Philadelphia of tuberculosis.

Emeline was the third daughter and third of nine children of Amanda and Chauncey Horton. The Horton children had private tutors for their early education. Emeline enrolled in Oberlin College (1850–1853) and soon after graduation married (1854) her childhood friend Giles Butler Cleveland, now a Presbyterian minister. They had one son, Arthur, who ultimately became a physician. Emeline entered the Female (later Woman's) Medical College of Pennsylvania in 1853 and received her M.D. in 1855. She planned on a foreign missionary career with her husband but his ill health prevented this (he was an invalid from 1858 until his death). Instead she opened a private practice in the Oneida Valley of New York state where he was preaching and became demonstrator of anatomy at Woman's Medical College in 1856, then chair of anatomy and histology (1857–1861). She was sent to the School of Obstetrics at the Maternité in Paris under the sponsorship of the Quaker women who hoped to establish a hospital for women and children in connection with the medical college in Philadelphia.

Returning to New York, Cleveland became professor of obstetrics and diseases of women at Woman's Medical College of Pennsylvania and was soon asked to be the dean (1872–1874). As dean, she increased enrollment and encouraged women wishing to become medical missionaries. She concurrently served as gynecologist to the department for the insane of the Pennsylvania Hospital.

Cleveland was one of the first women to perform major surgery. She was one of the first professional ovariotomists and the first woman to perform an ovariotomy in Philadelphia. Through her obvious skill and professionalism, she broke down many of the prejudices against women doctors.

Although excluded from the Philadelphia Obstetrical Society, one of her papers was read there by a male colleague and published in their *Transactions,* in 1878. She was a member of the Pennsylvania Medical Association and the Philadelphia Medical Society. JH/MBO

PRIMARY SOURCES
Cleveland, Emeline. *Introductory Lecture on Behalf of the Faculty to the Class of the Female Medical College of Pennsylvania.* Philadelphia: Merrihew and Thompson, printers, 1858.

STANDARD SOURCES
Hurd-Mead 1933; Lovejoy; *NAW* (long article by Patricia Spain Ward).

CLIFFORD, LADY ANNE (1589–1675)

British natural philosopher. Born 30 January 1589 at Skiptoncastle, in Craven. Father George, Earl of Cumberland. Married Richard, Lord Buckhurst, later earl of Dorset. Three sons who died young; two daughters. After Richard's death, married Philip Herbert, earl of Pembroke and Montgomery. No children. Educated by her mother and tutors, including Daniel the Poet. Died 23 March 1675 in Brogham Appleby.

Lady Anne Clifford, the countess of Pembroke, was a seventeenth-century learned lady, whose knowledge was legendary. Her father died when she was only ten years old, but her mother, who was a daughter of the earl of Bedford, insisted that she have an excellent education. One of her tutors was Daniel the poet, to whose memory she later erected a monument. She also erected a monument to Spenser. Her first marriage resulted in three sons who died young and two daughters. After her husband's death, she married again, to Philip Herbert, earl of Pembroke and Montgomery, by whom she had no children. This marriage was very unhappy. The countess, however, spent her time in building hospitals and seeing that churches were repaired or built. After the Restoration she defied Charles II who had recommended a candidate for one of her boroughs. Her defiance won her the admiration of many people.

Truly a Renaissance woman, the countess was well versed in all areas of natural philosophy, and it was said that "she knew how to converse on all subjects from predestination to slea-silk" *(Cyclopaedia).* JH/MBO

STANDARD SOURCES
Cyclopaedia.

CLINCH, PHYLLIS E. M. (1901–1984)

Irish plant physiologist and cytologist. Born 12 September 1901 in Dublin. Educated University of Dublin (B.Sc. 1923; Ph.D. 1928). Professional experience: University College, Galway, Lecturer (1928); University College, Dublin, Professor of Botany (1961–1973). Honors and memberships: Royal Irish Academy; Royal Society of Dublin. Died 19 October 1984, in Teneriffe, Canary Islands.

Phyllis Clinch, an Irish plant physiologist and cytologist, was born in Dublin in 1901 and educated at the University of London, where she received both her bachelor of science and doctor of philosophy degrees. Following this, she lectured in botany at University College Galway in 1928. After a more than thirty-year hiatus, she returned to University College, Dublin, as professor of botany in 1961. She was a member of the Royal Irish Academy and the Royal Society of Dublin, and contributed frequently to these societies. She died in Teneriffe. JH/MBO

SECONDARY SOURCES
Irish Times, 26 October 1984. Obituary notice.
Proceedings of the Royal Irish Academy 76 (1976): 406.
Meenan, James, and Desmond Clarke, eds. *Royal Dublin Society, 1731–1981.* New York: Gill and Macmillan, 1981: 185–206.

STANDARD SOURCES
Desmond.

CLISBY, HARRIET JEMIMA WINIFRED (1830–1931)

British/Australian/U.S. physician and feminist. Born in London. Emigrated to Adelaide, Australia with parents (1838). Educated: Guy's Hospital, London (as nurse); Woman's Medical College of New York (M.D. 1872?). Professional experience: Melbourne, Australia, editor, journalist (1856–1861); Guy's Hospital, private nurse (1860s?); Boston, Mass., private practice (as physician) (1872?–1889). Retired to Geneva, Switzerland. Women's Educational and Industrial Union, Boston, founding member (1880s). Founder of Union des Femmes, Geneva, Switzerland. Died in London, England, 1931.

Harriet Clisby led a varied life before she became a physician in the 1870s. She was born in London but emigrated with her parents to Australia when she was eight years old. There she grew up in Adelaide, where she studied shorthand in preparation for a life as a journalist. At the age of twenty-six, she began to work in Melbourne, editing a magazine written in shorthand. In 1861, she was associated with the publication of the first magazine published by women in Australia, *The Interpreter*. Through her association with this magazine, she came to read about the life of ELIZABETH BLACKWELL, which led her to a career in medicine. First training and practicing as a nurse in London, she was unhappy with her London experiences, and traveled to the United States to study at Elizabeth Blackwell's medical school. She also attended the New York Woman's Medical College and New York Infirmary, which was then under the direction of Blackwell's sister, EMILY BLACKWELL.

After obtaining her medical degree, Clisby went to Boston, where she practiced for about fifteen years. She also became involved in the founding of the Women's Educational and Industrial Union, which trained and placed poor women in domestic work and ran a shop to sell their home crafts.

In her retirement, Clisby moved to Geneva, Switzerland, where she helped to establish a suffrage group, Union des Femmes. She died after she had passed her hundredth birthday in London.   JH/MBO

STANDARD SOURCES
Europa.

CLOTHILDE OF BURGUNDY (d. 544)
French healer. Married Clovis (465–511). Died 544.

Clothilde was a French queen who was married to Clovis. During the Burgundian war, she retired to the monastery of Saint Martin of Tours, where she cared for the sick. She was sainted for her work among the sick.   JH/MBO

SECONDARY SOURCES
Kavanagh, Julia. *The Women of Christianity*. New York: D. Appleton, 1852.
Kurth, Godefroid. *Sainte Clotilde*. Paris: Lecoffre, 1897.

STANDARD SOURCES
Hurd-Mead 1938; Uglow 1989.

COADE, ELEANOR (1733–1821)
British inventor. Born 3 June 1733 in Exeter to Eleanor Enchmarch and George Coade. Never married. Professional experience: draper;

invented and manufactured an artificial stone. Died 16 November 1821.

A considerable amount of controversy surrounded British inventor Eleanor Coade. She claimed to have invented an artificial stone. In 1769 she joined with Daniel Pincot, who was already marketing a form of artificial stone that used a slightly different formula than hers. She dismissed him and appointed John Bacon in his place. Bacon did not last long either; he was supplanted by her cousin John Sealy. Coade's place in the invention of this stone remains unclear.   JH/MBO

STANDARD SOURCES
DNB, Missing Persons.

COATES, SARAH J. (fl. 1850)
U.S. physiologist. Married 1851. At least three children. Professional experience: physiology lecturer; correspondent of William Darlington.

The only information that is available on Sarah Coates comes from Sally Gregory Kohlstedt's article in the January 1978 *Journal of the History of Medicine*. Coates joined many of her contemporaries in offering public lectures for a fee, addressed to women, particularly on the topics of health and physiology. A handbill notice of a series of health lectures by Coates is found in the New York Historical Society. A series of letters by Coates to William Darlington (1782–1863), a retired physician and amateur botanist, survived, and Kohlstedt reprinted several of these letters. Coates's first letter was from 1847 and revealed that she was a single woman who lived at home with her elderly mother. At this time she apparently lived in Ercildoun, a small village in Chester County, Pennsylvania. She explained that her spare time was spent in studying plants and maintaining a herbarium. Apparently encouraged by Darlington, she visited him in Philadelphia to check her plant identifications. For another year they were frequent correspondents, but during the next year there were no letters. After moving to Ohio, Coates took a course from a local physician, probably G. Kersey Thomas, to prepare her as a lecturer and again wrote Darlington to ask his support as a lecturer. Darlington complied with her request, and she apparently had a successful series of lectures. She moved several times to different towns, and her letters indicate that her lectures were successful. However, by July of 1851, she had moved to Minnesota, conducted a small class, and studied the local wildflowers. She was silent for another two years, but in 1853 she wrote to Darlington, explaining that she had married. In her last letter of 1861, she sent Darlington three grass specimens for help in identification and mentioned that she had three children. As far as we know, Darlington did not respond, but by that time he was eighty years old. JH/MBO

PRIMARY SOURCES

Darlington's correspondence is at the New York Historical Society Library and includes the letters from Coates.

SECONDARY SOURCES

Kohlstedt, Sally. "Physiological Lectures for Women: Sarah Coates in Ohio, 1850." *Journal of the History of Medicine and Allied Sciences* 33 (1978): 75–81.

COBB, MARGARET VERA (1884–1963)

U.S. educational psychologist. Born 16 May 1884 in Easthampton, Mass., to Alice Vera (Proctor) and Nathan Augustus Cobb. Six siblings. Never married. Educated local schools in Sydney, Australia, and Worcester, Mass.; Oahu College; Radcliffe College (A.B., 1910); George Washington University (1911–1912); University of Illinois (A.M., 1913); University of Chicago (1915); University of Michigan (1919–1920). Professional experience: Bureau of Social Hygiene and Surgeon General's Office, psychologist (1916–1917); Teacher's College Columbia University, researcher (1921–1925); Children's University School, New York, psychologist and teacher (1926–1927); Harvard University, research associate, supervisor of training of gifted children (1928–1931); New Hampshire National Youth Administration (1936–1941); Community Guidance Center, Manchester, N.H., director (1938–1942) New Hampshire State Employment Service, employment counselor and statistician (1942–1954). Retired 1954. Died 19 November 1963 at Concord, N.H.

Margaret Cobb was the second child in a scientifically oriented family; the Cobb's first child, a son, died shortly before Margaret's birth, thus leaving Margaret as the oldest of the surviving siblings. Her father was a pioneer plant pathologist and nematologist whose career included research on three continents. In 1887, when Margaret was three, N. A. Cobb left a teaching post at Williston Seminary in Easthampton and moved with his wife and three children (Margaret and two younger boys) to Germany, where he earned a doctorate with a dissertation on parasitic and free-living nematodes. In 1889, he went to Australia where he became the first full-time plant pathologist in the British overseas government. The Cobbs had three additional children, all girls, in Australia. In 1905 the Cobbs returned permanently to the United States, moving first to Hawaii and then to Washington, D.C., where Cobb accepted a position in the U.S. Department of Agriculture and developed the new science of nematology.

Growing up in the Cobb family shaped Margaret's attitudes and career. Cobb always had a home laboratory where he did some of his research. Alice Cobb shared her husband's love of science, helped him in his work, and organized the household to support that work. The children, especially the girls, became their father's assistants. In addition, Margaret taught the three younger girls, preparing them for American high schools. Margaret Cobb attended college briefly in Hawaii, then entered Radcliffe College, receiving a bachelor's degree, with honors in biology, in 1910. She moved to the University of Illinois, where her interests turned to educational psychology; she also remained a zoologist, spending some summers at Woods Hole, Massachusetts, and continued to assist her father when needed.

In addition to her work at Illinois, Margaret Cobb had fellowships and/or research positions at several other universities. After earning her master's, she served as an assistant at Illinois in both zoology and education. She became a psychologist for the Bureau of Social Hygiene in Bedford Hills, New York, but moved to the Surgeon General's Office during World War I, where she made a thorough statistical study of available data, including the results of intelligence tests, about army medical officers.

Cobb made many friends, and contemporaries found her fair-minded, keen in argument, enthusiastic, generous, and fond of children. Early in her career, she, sometimes in cooperation with others, published several studies on the use of intelligence tests with children and problems with such tests. She spent much of the 1920s in New York City, where she worked with both Columbia University and the public schools in the training of gifted children. She moved to New Hampshire in 1932 where she served with several state and federal agencies. Her work at the Manchester Community Guidance Center led to a study, *Vocational Outlooks for New Hampshire Youth,* published in 1941. She continued work as a counselor and statistician at the New Hampshire State Employment Service until her retirement in 1954. She was a Fellow of the American Association for the Advancement of Science, and a member of the New Hampshire Academy of Science, the New York Psychological Association, and the New Hampshire Psychological Association. SM

PRIMARY SOURCES

Cobb, Margaret V. "A Preliminary Study of the Inheritance of Arithmetical Abilities." *Journal of Educational Psychology* 8 (1917): 1–20.
———. With Robert M. Yerkes. "Intellectual and Educational Status of the Medical Professions as Represented in the United States Army," *Bulletin of the National Research Council* 8 (1921): 456–532.
———. With E. L. Thorndike, E. O. Bregman, E. Woodyard, and others. *The Measure of Intelligence.* New York: Teachers College, Columbia University, 1926.
———. With L. S. Hollingworth. "Children Clustering at 165

I.Q. and Children Clustering at 145 I.Q. Compared for Three Years in Achievement." *27th Yearbook, National Society for the Study of Education* 2 (1928): 3–33.

———. "Community Guidance Center." In *Vocational Outlooks for New Hampshire Youth: Occupations in Manchester,* by Council of Social Agencies, Manchester, N.H. Community Guidance Center. Manchester: Granite State Press, 1941.

SECONDARY SOURCES
(Concord, N.H.) *Monitor,* 20 November 1963. Obituary notice.
Blanchard Family Papers, Bentley Historical Library, University of Michigan. Contain some of Cobb's letters.

STANDARD SOURCES
AMS 5–8, S&B 9; *Who's Who of American Women.*

COBB, ROSALIE M. KARAPETOFF (b. ca. 1900)

U.S. chemist. Born in Winthrope, Mass. Married 1936. Educated Tufts College (B.S., 1922); MIT (M.S., 1923). Professional experience: MIT, assistant (1923–1924); Larkin Company, Inc., research chemist (1924); Hunt-Rankin Leather Company, research chemist (1924–1926), research director (1926–1951), technical advisor (1951–1965); Lowe Paper Company, Ridgefield, N.J., consultant (from 1965). Death date unknown.

Little information is available about Rosalie Cobb's early life. After earning her master's degree at MIT, she began a research career in industry. She was well respected, winning the Coating and Graphic Arts Division Award of the Technical Association of the Pulp and Paper Industry in 1968. She was a member of the American Chemical Society, and a Fellow of the Technical Association of Pulp and Paper Industry. Her research was on paper sizing and coating, adhesives, lithography, and emulsions.   JH/MBO

STANDARD SOURCES
AMS 5–8, P 9, P&B 10–14.

COBB, ANNE PHILLIPA (1920–1971)

British mathematician. Born 1920. Died 1971.

Anne Philippa Cobbe did research in homological algebra.   JH/MBO

STANDARD SOURCES
Campbell and Grinstein.

COBBE, FRANCES POWER (1822–1904)

Anglo-Irish writer on Darwinism, antivivisectionist, social reformer, woman's rights activist. Born 4 December 1822, in Dublin to Frances (Conway) and Charles Cobbe. Four brothers. Never Married. Educated private ladies' school, Brighton (to 1838). Professional experience: Red Lodge and Ragged Schools, Bristol, assistant (1858–1859); social work with Louise Twining (1859–1862); Daily News, correspondent from Rome and Florence; Echo, columnist (1869–1875); Standard, columnist (1875–1876). Published on women's affairs and other topics with Macmillan and Fraser's Magazine, and Theological Magazine (1860s and 1870s); Zoophile, editor (1883–1884). Died 1904.

Frances Power Cobbe was educated first by governesses at home in Newbridge, Ireland, and then in a ladies' finishing school in Brighton until she was sixteen (in 1838). Her autobiography details the degree to which she was forced to educate herself in history, geometry, and astronomy after her insufficient education. In her early thirties, she wrote and published her first book, *Theory of Intuitive Morals,* and then a second book, *Religious Duty,* that proclaimed her Unitarian beliefs, and corresponded with Theodore Parker. She served as her father's housekeeper following her mother's death, when she was twenty, until his death, when she was thirty-five. Financially independent (although not wealthy), she felt obliged to leave her childhood home when her eldest brother and his wife took it over.

She then traveled throughout Middle East (including Egypt and Jerusalem), publishing her experiences in *Fraser's Magazine,* returning to Italy where she met a number of the English expatriots, including Robert and Elizabeth Barrett Browning and MARY SOMERVILLE. She later lived there for some time. In 1858, Cobbe agreed to assist Mary Carpenter in her Ragged Schools (schools for very poor children) and her Reformatory (the Red Lodge) in Bristol, and then began to work with Louise Twining to improve the workhouses and hospitals for incurables. She also began to read papers before the Social Science Congress on the topic. Later she would publish a more elaborate series of articles on the Poor Law in *Fraser's Magazine* that would be reprinted in her book *Studies: Ethical and Social.* Her *Workhouse Sketches,* printed in the sixties in *Macmillans Magazine* began to earn her a regular income.

When Cobbe was forty, an injury to her leg caused her to give up this social work, and rather bad advice from a series of doctors led her to be suspicious of most of them. She then began to earn her living writing for a series of journals, and wrote a regular column for the *Daily News.* She was invited to contribute to *The Echo* and then in 1876 she moved to the *Standard,* earning her living by journalism in this period. She also began to write books of essays and became interested in Darwinism through her friends and fellow Unitarians, Charles Lyell and his wife. In 1870, she also became a friend of Charles Darwin and his family, who were vacationing in Wales where she lived during the summer with her companion Mary Lloyd. She exchanged letters with Darwin about plant varieties, animal intelligence, and philosophy. She published a series of articles on animal intelligence in the *Quarterly Review,* and later published a review criticizing Darwin's *Descent of Man* because of what she saw as the importance of human morals. This was republished in her book *Darwinism in Morals.* A break came between her and Darwin as well as other Darwinians, including John Tyndall, when she became a proselytizer of antivivisectionism in 1876, in opposition to doctors and physiologists.

She wrote on women's rights as well in the late 1860s and early 1870s, and was encouraged by John Stuart Mill and his stepdaughter HELEN TAYLOR to write for American papers as well on the "woman question." She had early in her journalistic career pointed out the problems of women becoming chronic invalids because of poor medical advice that caused them to avoid regular walks and healthful regimes. In the 1890s, she also objected to experimentation on women in hospitals, writing an important article on human experimentation for the *Daily Chronicle.*

Cobbe gave up her journalistic career in 1875 to establish a society to actively oppose vivisection, later called the Victoria Street Society, obtaining support from individuals like Leslie Stephen, Frances Wedgwood, George Hoggan, and a number of British aristocrats and churchmen, including Cardinal Manning. The question went before Parliament in 1876 and resulted in a bill that limited but did not prohibit animal experimentation. In 1881, Cobbe founded the journal *Zoophile,* which she edited herself from 1883 to June 1884, in tandem with a French journal *Le zoophile.* The French journal did not survive, partly because the French supporters (including Maria Deraismes) were anticlerical and did not subscribe to Cobbe's Christian religious arguments. In 1884, she retired from the management of the journal (which continued), and left London to live with Mary Lloyd in her home, Hengwrt, in Wales. She died there in 1904.

JH/MBO

PRIMARY SOURCES

Cobbe, Frances Power. *The Red Flag in John Bull's Eyes.* London: E. Faithfull, 1863.

————. *Darwinism in Morals and Other Essays.* London: Williams and Norgate, 1872.

————. *The Modern Rack: Papers on Vivisection.* London: Sowan Sonnenschein, 1889.

————. *Life of Frances Power Cobbe by Herself.* 2 vols. London: R. Bentley, 1894.

Cobbe's letters to Darwin are in the Darwin Archive, Cambridge University Library.

STANDARD SOURCES
Uglow 1982; Uglow 1989.

COBBE, MARGARET (fl. 1470)
British midwife.

Margaret Cobbe was the midwife to Elizabeth Woodville, the wife of Edward IV. Through Cobbe we know what a midwife's fees were during that time. She received about ten pounds per year for her services. 　JH/MBO

STANDARD SOURCES
Hurd-Mead 1938.

COCHRAN, DORIS MABEL (1898–1968)
U.S. herpetologist. Born 1898. Educated George Washington University; University of Maryland (Ph.D., 1933). Professional experience: Smithsonian Institution, Division of Reptiles and Batrachians, herpetological aid (1919), assistant curator (1927–1943), associate curator (1943–1956); curator (1956–retirement). Died in 1968.

Doris Mabel Cochran was born in the last years of the nineteenth century and educated at George Washington University. She entered the Smithsonian Institution, Division of Reptiles and Batrachians, first as a herpetological aid in 1919 to the herpetologist Leonhard Stejneger, then as assistant curator in 1927. She went to the University of Maryland while she was working for the Smithsonian to obtain a doctorate in zoology in 1933. Although the head of her department was well over retirement age, a special act of Congress allowed him to stay to an advanced age. Following Stejneger's death in 1943, Cochran was raised to associate curator. But, although she ran the department, she was not made full curator, in spite of her complaints and the support of Waldo Schmitt (nominally her supervisor), because of the objections of individuals at the Smithsonian who "did not like career women." She was finally given the full rank in 1956, after she had been with the Smithsonian for thirty-seven years. Her generosity and kindness to generations of schoolchildren who brought their specimens to her was remembered fondly by her colleagues in the American Society of Icthyologists and Herpetologists. She died in 1968. 　JH/MBO

PRIMARY SOURCES
Cochran, Doris Mable. *Herpetologica* 8, no. 4 (1953). Entire issue.

Doris Mable Cochran Papers, Smithsonian Institution Archives.

Doris Cochran correspondence in Elizabeth Deichmann Papers. In Archives of Museum of Comparative Zoology Library, Harvard University.

SECONDARY SOURCES

Goin, Coleman J. "Doris Mable Cochran, 1898–1968." *Copeia*, no. 3 (1968): 661–62.

STANDARD SOURCES

AMS 5–8, B 9, P&B 10–11; Rossiter 1995 (Rossiter includes a discussion of her fight to improve her governmental salary grade and includes a photograph of Cochran among her collections at the Smithsonian).

COCKBURN, CATHARINE (TROTTER)
(1679–1749)

British social scientist. Born 1679. Father a naval captain. Married a clergyman. Professional experience: playwright; defended John Locke's position.

Catharine Trotter's naval captain father died of plague, and his family was forced to rely on the good offices of relatives to survive. When she was sixteen years old, she had the first of her many plays, a five-act tragedy, produced in London. She moved to Kent and through her acquaintance with Bishop and Mrs. Gilbert met with John Norris and other Cambridge Platonists. This group attacked John Locke's empiricism in his *Essay Concerning Human Understanding*. She published a defense of Locke's position in 1702. Locke traced her through a bookseller and sent her a letter of appreciation. Trotter also sent a copy of her defense to Leibniz. She wrote a second defense of Locke in 1726.   JH/MBO

PRIMARY SOURCES

Trotter, Catharine. *Works of Mrs. Catharine Cockburn*. London: Routledge/Thoemmes Press, 1992. Originally published London, 1751.

SECONDARY SOURCES

Gosse, Edmund. "Catharine Trotter, the Precursor of the Blue-stockings." In *Royal Society of Literature of the United Kingdom*. Transactions, vol. 34, 87–118. London: Adlard, 1916.

McDonald, Lynn. *The Women Founders of the Social Sciences*. Ottawa, Canada: Carleton University Press, 1994.

COCKRELL, WILMATTE (PORTER)
(b. ca. 1876)

U.S. entomologist. Born ca. 1876. Married Theodore D. A. Cockrell (ca. 1899). Educated Stanford University (B.A. ca. 1897). Professional experience: Las Cruces, N.M., high school biology teacher (from 1897); State Preparatory School, Boulder, Colo., biology teacher. Death date unknown.

Wilmatte Porter met Theodore D. A. Cockrell while she was teaching high school biology in Las Cruces, New Mexico. In 1893, the British-born entomologist, his first wife, Annie Fenn, and their infant son had come to Las Cruces, where he became entomologist of the experimental station and professor of entomology and zoology at the Agriculture College. His wife died giving birth to their second son; the first had died as a baby. (His second son died from diphtheria when he was only eight years old.) In Las Cruces, he met Wilmatte Porter, a high school biology teacher, and they married. The Cockrells moved to Boulder, Colorado, where Wilmatte was a biology teacher. According to one of her students, she was an excellent teacher. Wilmatte and Theodore Cockrell worked together on many projects. They spent the summers of 1906 and 1907 collecting fossils.

JH/MBO

SECONDARY SOURCES

Mallis, Arnold. *American Entomologist*. New Brunswick, N.J.: Rutgers University Press, 1971.

Linsley, Gorton E. "Theodore A. Cockrell." *Bulletin of the Brooklyn Entomological Society* 43 (October 1948): 116–118. Theodore Cockrell's obituary notice.

Roher, S. A. "Theodore Dru Alison Cockrell, 1866–1948." *Proceedings of the Entomological Society of Washington* 50 (1948): 103–108. Theodore Cockrell's obituary notice.

COHN, ESSIE WHITE (1902–1963)

U.S. biochemist. Born 23 March 1902 in Pittsburgh, Pa., to Lena (Garfinkel) and Morris White. Married Byron Emanuel Cohn, 10 June 1926. Educated University of Denver (A.B., 1922; M.A., 1923); University of Michigan (graduate work, 1934); University of Chicago (Ph.D. in nutrition, 1936). Professional experience: University of Denver, Department of Chemistry, instructor (1923–1931), assistant professor (1931–1938), associate professor (1938–1941), professor (1942–post 1955?); George Washington University, School of Medicine, visiting professor of biochemistry (1941–1942). Honors and memberships: Colorado-Wyoming Academy of Science, chair of chemical section (1936), executive secretary and editor of journal (1937–1941); Iota Sigma Pi, national president (1948–1951). Dietetic Association, American Chemical Society, member. Died 1963.

Essie White, although born in Pennsylvania, chose to go to the University of Denver in Colorado for her undergraduate and master's degrees. She then began to teach chemistry as an instructor at the university, where she met and married a young physicist, Byron E. Cohn, who was teaching mathematics and physics at the time. After rising to assistant professor, Cohn returned to graduate studies. She studied briefly at the University of Michigan and then obtained her doctorate in nutrition at the University of Chicago, doing research on analytical nutrition studies. Two years later, she was made associate professor in her department. During World War II, while her husband was with the U.S. Naval Ordnance in Washington, Cohn spent a year as a visiting professor in biochemistry at Georgetown University School of Medicine. On her return, she rose to full professor at the University of Denver, where she remained until she died at the age of sixty-one.

Essie White Cohn was active on her campus. She was a faculty advisor to Association of Women Students, an officer in a number of sororities. Cohn did research on analytical nutrition studies, on the effects of sulfa drugs on carbohydrate nutrition, on radioactive tracers, and on the effects of high altitude on growth.   JH/MBO

PRIMARY SOURCES

Cohn, Essie White. "In Vitro and In Vivo Experiments on the Digestibility of Raw and Heat-Treated Egg White." Ph.D. diss., University of Chicago, 1936.

A list of Cohn's publications is in the *Notable American Women* (Unused) files at Schlesinger Library, Radcliffe College.

STANDARD SOURCES

American Women; AMS; NCAB.

COIGNOU, CAROLINE PAULINE MARIE (1865–1932)

British geologist. Born 1865 in Manchester. Educated Convent School; Manchester High School; Newnham College, Cambridge (Natural Science Tripos, Part I, class 3, 1890); Trinity College, Dublin (M.A.). Professional experience: Pendleton High School, assistant mistress (1890–1894); Manchester High School, assistant mistress (1894–1910); West Riding Education Department, examiner (1910–1918); inspector of secondary schools (1918–1927). Died 1 December 1932.

Although Caroline Coignou had little formal training in geology, she passed the Natural Science Tripos and was interested in geology as a hobby as she worked in her positions in various schools. She published a contribution to the *Quarterly Journal of the Geological Society* in 1890.   JH/MBO

PRIMARY SOURCES

Coignou, Caroline. "On a New Species of Cyphaspis from the Carboniferous Rocks of Yorkshire." *Quarterly Journal of the Geological Society* 46 (1890): 421–422.

STANDARD SOURCES

Creese and Creese; *Newnham,* vol. 1.

COLBY, MARTHA GUERNSEY (1899–1952)

U.S. psychologist. Born 22 February 1899 in Montpelier, Idaho. Educated University of Utah (1915–1916); University of Michigan (Ph.D., 1922); University of Vienna (fellow, 1927–1928; 1929–1930); Laura Spelman Rockefeller fellow (1929–1930). Professional experience: University of Michigan, assistant in experimental psychology (1918–1921), assistant professor of social science research (from 1921). Honors and memberships: American Psychological Association; the American Association for the Advancement of Science; the American Eugenics Association; the Michigan Academy of Science; and Sigma Xi.

American psychologist Martha Guernsey Colby attended school in Montpelier, Idaho, graduating from high school at the age of fifteen. After completing one year at the University of Utah and one year at the University of Michigan, she quit school and taught elementary school and music for a year in Ogden, Utah. She returned to the University of Michigan to complete her degrees, ending with a doctorate in psychology. She was only the second woman to receive a doctorate at the University of Michigan. She married a physicist who became a professor at the University of Michigan.

Her mentor at Michigan was W. B. Pillsbury, a theoretician and historian and early student of Tichener; he dominated the department, keeping even the most brilliant of his instructors in his shadow. Martha Colby remained on the staff of the department of psychology from 1921 to 1950, never advancing in rank. Despite the fact that she was awarded honors as an American scientist and received several fellowships that allowed her to visit Europe, her innovative research in child development went relatively unrecognized.

Abroad, Colby worked with Kohler and Wertheimer, gestaltists, in Berlin, and made close friends with Karl and CHARLOTTE BÜHLER in Vienna. She did research at the Institute of Psychology in Vienna, returning on several occasions. When her husband was pressured in 1949 to come to Washington, D.C., to work full-time with the Atomic Energy Commission (AEC), Martha Colby gave up her career to follow him. In 1952, Colby's husband was sent to Europe by the AEC and the couple took advantage of the opportunity to travel. Tragically, on a narrow road in the mountains of Greece, their car went off the road, killing Martha. In a later time, when minds and opportunities were more open to women, Martha Colby would have undoubtedly achieved prominence and recognition for her ideas and skill.   KM

STANDARD SOURCES

AMS 5; Stevens and Gardner.

COLCORD, MABEL (1872–?)

U.S. entomological librarian. Born 24 December 1872 in Boston, Mass. Educated Radcliffe College (A.B., 1905); New York State Library School (B.L.S., 1922). Professional experience: University of Iowa, cataloguer (1902–1903); acting librarian (1903–1904); U.S. Department of Agriculture, Bureau of Entomology and Plant Quarantine (1904–1942). Retired, 1942. National Academy of Science, bibliographer (from 1947). Death date unknown.

Mabel Colcord was a librarian, not an entomologist by training. Nevertheless, she was a member of professional entomological societies and became an expert on the literature of the field. She published an important index to entomological literature.   JH/MBO

PRIMARY SOURCES
Colcord, Mabel. *Check List of Publications on Entomology Issued by the United States Department of Agriculture through 1927.* Washington, D.C.: USDA, 1930.

STANDARD SOURCES
AMS 4–8; Osborn (includes a portrait of Colcord [plate 34]).

COLDEN, JANE (1724–1766)

U.S. botanist. Born 27 March 1724 in New York City to Alice (Christie) and Cadwallader Colden. Nine siblings. Married William Farquhar. One child. Educated at home. Died 10 March 1766 in New York City(?).

Cadwallader Colden, Jane's father, was trained as a physician at the University of Edinburgh and practiced for five years in Philadelphia before he accepted a position as surveyor general for the Province of New York. Cadwallader received an original grant of two thousand acres and later an additional grant of one thousand acres near the present town of Montgomery about ten miles west of Newburgh. He moved his family to this estate, which he called Coldengham, when Jane was four years old; it was there that Jane, the fifth of ten children, grew up.

There was no school near the wilderness for the Colden children, so the task of educating them fell to Alice Colden. From her mother, who possessed skills and interests beyond those of a typical eighteenth-century housewife, Jane received her basic education. From her father, she acquired an interest in botany; for, although Cadwallader Colden had a significant political career—he became lieutenant governor of New York in 1761 and served several times as acting governor—his major enthusiasm was for physical science and botany. He corresponded with the chief European botanists of his day, among them Linnaeus, who arranged for the publication of Colden's "Plantae Coldenghamae" in 1743. For

Jane's use, Colden produced an explication of the principles of botany, in which he translated portions of Linnaeus's works and defined commonly used botanical terms. Although Jane did not learn Latin, she became adept at writing plant descriptions in English and by 1757 had compiled a catalogue of over three hundred local plants. The correspondence of John Bartram and Alexander Garden indicated that they exchanged seeds with Jane. Through her father she met and corresponded with other leading naturalists of the time, including Peter Collinson and John Ellis in England, and J. F. Gronovius and Linnaeus on the Continent.

On 12 March 1759, at the age of thirty-seven, Jane Colden married William Farquhar, a physician who practiced in New York City. Apparently she did not continue her botanical work after her marriage. She died at age forty-one in 1766, the same year in which her only child died.

Colden's botanical work involved classification and cataloguing; she also took ink impressions of leaves and made sketches of living plants. She made large collections of plant specimens and exchanged them with correspondents. According to Peter Collinson, she was "perhaps the only lady that makes profession of the Linnean system." Alexander Garden characterized her work as "extremely accurate."

MBO

PRIMARY SOURCES
Colden, Jane. "Flora Nov.—Eboracensis." British Museum (Natural History) Catalog no. 26, c. 19. Manuscript. Ca. 1753–1758.
———. "Description." *In Essays and Observations, Physical and Literary.* Vol. 2. Edinburgh: G. Hamilton and J. Balfour, 1770. Read before the Edinburgh Philosophical Society and published.
———. Botanic Manuscript. Ed. Elizabeth C. Hall and H.W. Rickett. [New York?]: Garden Society of Orange and Dutchess Counties, 1963. Limited edition of 1500 copies. Includes Colden's notes and illustrations. Fifty-seven descriptions from Colden's "Flora of New York."

SECONDARY SOURCES
Vail, Anne Murray. "Jane Colden, an Early New York Botanist." Contributions from the New York Botanical Garden (1907): 88.

STANDARD SOURCES
DAB; Grinstein 1997 (long article by Katalin Harkányi); *NAW* (long article by Brooke Hindle).

COLE, EMMA J. (1845–1910)

U.S. botanist and high school teacher. Born in Milan, Ohio, in 1845. Never married. Educated Grand Rapids High School; Cor-

nell University. Professional experience: Grand Rapids High School, teacher (1881–1907). Published a flora of Grand Rapids. Died in 1910 in Mexico.

Emma Jane Cole came to Vergennes, Michigan, with her parents when she was very young. She attended high school in Grand Rapids, and then taught in various schools, earning enough to fund her education at Cornell University. She was unable to finish her studies because of her mother's death and returned to Grand Rapids in 1881 to teach high school for the next twenty-six years. During this period, she taught botany at Grand Rapids high school and published a book on the local flora in 1901. She died while collecting plants in Mexico in 1910, following her retirement.

She left a trust to establish a fellowship in botany at the University of Michigan. Her herbarium is at Aquinas College, Grand Rapids, Michigan. JH/MBO

PRIMARY SOURCES
Cole, Emma Jane. *Grand Rapids Flora*. Grand Rapids: A. Van Dort, 1901.

SECONDARY SOURCES
Voss, E. G. "Emma Jane Cole, Founder of a Fellowship in Botany." Unpublished memoir.

COLE, LUELLA (1893–?)
See Pressey, Luella (Cole).

COLE, REBECCA J. (1846–1922)
U.S. African-American physician. Born 1846. Educated Woman's Medical College of Pennsylvania (M.D., 1867). Professional experience: New York, medical care for women and children with EMILY *and* ELIZABETH BLACKWELL; *Philadelphia, same service; Washington, D.C., government-supported medical facility. Died 1922.*

Rebecca Cole was the second African-American woman, after REBECCA LEE, to earn a medical degree. Graduating in 1867 from the Woman's Medical College of Pennsylvania, she worked in New York City with EMILY and ELIZABETH BLACKWELL to provide medical care for women and children. She later moved to Philadelphia to continue the same service. Her last medical position was in Washington, D.C., at a government-supported facility for women and children. JH/MBO

SECONDARY SOURCES
Wertheimer, Barbara Mayer. *We Were There*. New York: Pantheon Books, 1977.

COLLET, CLARA ELIZABETH (1860–1947)
British sociologist. Born 10 September 1860 in London to Jane and Collet Dobson Collet. Educated North London Collegiate School (1873–1878); University College, London (B.A., 1880; Teacher's Diploma and M.A.). Professional experience: University College, London, assistant mistress; Wyggeston Girls' School, Leicester, teacher (1875–1885); worked for Charles Booth (1888–1892); Royal Commission on Labour, assistant commissioner (1892); Board of Trade, labour correspondent (1893–1903); senior investigator (1903–1917); Ministry of Labour (1917–1920); Trade Boards, appointed member (1921–1932); Council of Royal Economic Society (1920–1941).

Clara Collet's career was probably influenced by her father, the editor of the *Diplomatic Review*. At the North London Collegiate School, Collet showed promise as a student. She earned a bachelor's and master's degree from University College, London, and took a teacher's diploma. She won the Joseph Hume Scholarship in Political Economy in 1886. After teaching at Wyggeston High School, Leicester, she left to begin her career in government. During her career, she contributed studies of women's work in East London and secondary education for women. After she had published studies, reports, and surveys on the position and status of working women, she was appointed labour correspondent to the Board of Trade.

Collet provided the first statistical analyses of the position of working women, and was concerned with a broad spectrum of issues surrounding women's status. She was elected a fellow of the Royal Statistical Society in 1893, became a fellow of University College, London, in 1896, and was later a governor of Bedford College and a member of the councils of the Royal Statistical and Royal Economic Societies. JH/MBO

PRIMARY SOURCES
Collet, Clara E. *The Economic Position of Educated Working Women*. London: n.p., 1890.
———. *Educated Working Women*. London: P.S. King, 1902.
———. *Women in Industry*. London: Women's Printing Society, Ltd., 1911.
———. Appendix to *The Private Letter Books of Joseph Collet*. London: Longmans, Green, and Co., 1933.
Various official reports on the economic position of women.

STANDARD SOURCES
Europa; *WWW* 4, 1941–1950.

COLLETT, MARY ELIZABETH (1888–?)

U.S. physiologist. Born 30 July 1888 in Atchison, Kans. Educated Wellesley College (A.B., 1910); University of Pennsylvania (A.M., 1911; Ph.D., 1919); Clark College (1919–1920); Karolinska Institute Sweden (1922–1923); Lund University, Sweden (1923). Professional experience: Brown University, assistant (1911–1912); Carnegie Institute of Technology, researcher (1912–1913), instructor (1913–1917); Clark College, fellow in physiology (1919–1920); Department of Medicine, Buffalo, instructor (1920–1922); American Scandinavian Foundation, fellow, Sweden (1922–1923); Tulane School of Medicine, instructor in physiology (1923–1924); Western Reserve University School of Nursing, assistant professor (1924–1926), associate professor (1926–1931); Flora Stone Mather Collection, biologist (1931–1954). Retired 1954. Death date unknown.

Mary Elizabeth Collett was a physiologist who, after receiving her doctorate from the University of Pennsylvania, studied in Sweden under the auspices of the American Scandinavian Foundation. Returning to the United States in 1923, she held several short posts before getting a position at the Western Reserve School of nursing, where she advanced to associate professor. She spent the last part of her career working with the Flora Stone Mather Collection.

A member of the Physiological Society and the Society of Zoologists, Collett worked on the toxicity of acids and salts, dehydrogenase specificity, minute volume of the heart, basal metabolism, and ovarian hormones.　　　JH/MBO

STANDARD SOURCES
AMS 3–8, B 9, P&B 10.

COLLINS, KATHARINE RICHARDS (1863–?)

U.S. bacteriologist and physician. Born 23 March 1863 in New Albany, Ind. Education: University of Michigan (M.D., 1893). Professional experience: Atlanta, Georgia, medical practice (1894–1902); Rockefeller Institute, fellow (1902–1903); New York Department of Health, bacteriologist and assistant director of research laboratories (1903–1908); Georgia State Board of Health, Atlanta, assistant director (1908–1918); Western Reserve, Department of Pathology, researcher (1918–1919); University of Buffalo, instructor of pathology and bacteriology; Buffalo City Hospital, director of divisional laboratories (1920s); Spartanburg General Hospital, Spartanburg, S.C., director of laboratories (1927?–1940?). Retired before 1944. Honors and memberships: Society of Bacteriology, Society of Immunology, Association for Pathology and Bacteriology, Society for Experimental Biology and Medicine (1910), American Medical Association, Tuberculosis Society. Death date unknown.

Katharine R. Collins obtained her medical degree at the age of thirty from the University of Michigan and then began to practice medicine in Atlanta, Georgia. After seven years in private practice, her experiences in the South inspired her to move into exploring the causes of disease, for she took a fellowship at the Rockefeller Institute from 1902 to 1903, and then began to work for the Department of Health in New York City as a bacteriologist and as assistant director of their bacteriological laboratories. After five years, she returned to Atlanta as assistant director of the Georgia Board of Health, remaining in that position for ten years.

Collins then spent a year of research at Western Reserve in Ohio in the Department of Pathology before she began to teach as an instructor in bacteriology and pathology at Buffalo, New York, while serving as director of laboratories at Buffalo City Hospital. By the late 1920s, she returned to the South, taking a position at the Spartanburg City Hospital in South Carolina. She retired in the early forties to Turnerville, Georgia. Interested in immunology (especially the agglutins) in the causes of dysentery, in studying pneumococci, she was an early member of the Society for Experimental Biology and Medicine (from 1910), an organization begun by Simon Flexner and other founders of the Rockefeller Institute. She was a honorary member of the Georgia Medical Society and a member of the Royal Institute for Public Health, London.　　　JH/MBO

STANDARD SOURCES
AMS 2–7.
Bulletin Société Française d'Histoire de la Medecine.

COLVIN, BRENDA (1897–1981)

British horticulturist, landscape architect, and conservationist. Born 1897 in Simla, India. Educated Swanlea Horticultural College. Professional experience: New Military Town, Aldershot, consultant; Bristol Polytechnic, landscape consultant; power stations, landscape consultant; wasteland restoration. Institute of Landscape Architects, founder (1929); president (1929; 1951–1953). Died 1981.

Brenda Colvin, a British landscape architect and conservationist, was born in Simla, India, during the Raj. She was educated in England, and went to Swanley Horticultural College. She became interested in landscape architecture and founded the Institute of Landscape Architects in 1929, sitting as its first president, and was elected president for a second time in 1951.

She was consultant on many projects including the beautification of power stations, the reservoirs around the River Severen, and the landscaping of Bristol Polytechnic. Colvin had a strong sense of the land and conservation. With Hal Muggeridge as partner, she began to work on plans for wasteland restoration in 1969.　　　JH/MBO

PRIMARY SOURCES

Colvin, Brenda. *Land and Landscape*. London: J. Murray, 1948.

———. With Jaqueline Tyrwhitt. *Trees for Town and Country: A Selection of Sixty Trees Suitable for General Cultivation in England*. 2d ed. London: Lund Humphries, 1949.

SECONDARY SOURCES

Garden (Royal Horticultural Society) (1981): 447–453.

Harvey, S. *Reflections on Landscape*. Aldershot, Hampshire, England: Glower Technical Press, 1987. Brenda Colvin is discussed 139–151, with portrait.

STANDARD SOURCES

Desmond.

COMNENA (COMNENOS), ANNA (1083–1148)

Byzantine physician. Born 1083 probably in Constantinople to Irene and Alexis (Alexios) Comnena (Comnenos). Married Nicephoros Bryennios. Educated at her father's court. Professional experience: ran ten-thousand-bed hospital built by her father. Died 1148, probably in Constantinople.

Anna Comnena reputedly was a brilliant physician, known for her perceptive knowledge of gout. The daughter of Alexis Comnenos, who had built a ten-thousand-bed hospital in Constantinople, Anna studied medicine at her father's court. As was the case with most Byzantine princesses, she was well educated. She not only administered Alexis's hospital, but she also served as the historian of her father's reign. This biography, the *Alexiad*, begun by his son-in-law Nicephoros Bryennios, was continued by Anna and completed not long before her death at the convent founded by her mother in Constantinople. According to Sarton, this book was the first great work exemplifying the Byzantine literary revival. Anna's contribution included the period from 1069 to 1118.

JH/MBO

PRIMARY SOURCES

Comnena, Anna. With Nicephoros Byrennios. *Alexiad*. Trans. Elizabeth A. S. Dawes. London: K. Paul, Trench, Trubner & Co., Ltd., 1928. For a discussion of the texts see Sarton, vol. 2, pt. 1: 250.

SECONDARY SOURCES

Buckler, Georgina. *Anna Comnena*. London: Oxford University Press, 1929.

Macksey, Joan, and Kenneth Macksey. *The Book of Women's Achievements*. New York: Stein and Day, 1976.

Sarton, George. *Introduction to the History of Science*. Vol. 2, *From Rabbi Ben Ezra to Roger Bacon*. Baltimore: Williams & Wilkins, 1931.

STANDARD SOURCES

Hurd-Mead 1938 (vol. 2, pt. 1: 85, 137, 143, 250).

COMSTOCK, ANNA BOTSFORD (1854–1930)

U.S. naturalist. Born 1 September 1854 in Otto, N.Y., to Phebe (Irish) and Marvin Botsford. No siblings. Married John Henry Comstock. Educated in local schools; Chamberlain Institute and Female College, Randolph, N.Y. (1871–1873); Cornell University (1874–1876; B.S., 1885). Professional experience: Cornell University, assistant (1897–1899), assistant professor (1899–1900, 1913–1920), lecturer (1900–1913), professor (1920–1922), summer lecturer (1922–1930), nature study. Died 24 August 1930 in Ithaca, N.Y.

Anna Botsford was the only child of a prosperous Quaker farming couple who imparted to their daughter an interest in studying plants and animals. Her cheerful, undogmatic gifted mother influenced Anna's love of nature. When she arrived at Cornell in 1874, Anna intended to study English and history, but in a class in invertebrate zoology taught by John Henry Comstock (founder of the entomology program at Cornell), she absorbed his enthusiasm for entomology. She left Cornell after two years; in 1878 she and Comstock were married.

In 1879 Henry Comstock was appointed chief entomologist at the U.S. Department of Agriculture. During the couple's two-year stay in Washington, D.C., Anna did clerical, editorial, and laboratory work in her husband's office. On their return to Ithaca, New York (1881), Anna reentered Cornell; she completed her degree in natural history in 1885. A popular figure in university social circles, Anna Comstock was familiar with the complex and often convoluted social structure of the university. She published her observations in 1906 under the pseudonym Marian Lee; entitled *Confessions to a Heathen Idol,* the book came out under her own name in its second printing. During the late 1880s, Comstock studied wood engraving in order to illustrate her husband's work.

Anna Comstock's entry into natural history as a profession came as a result of the agricultural depression of the 1890s. In order to slow down the exodus from the farms to the cities, the New York legislature adopted measures to make farm life more attractive. It appropriated $8,000 for the teaching of nature study in rural schools and designated the College of Agriculture at Cornell to administer the program, under the direction of Liberty Hyde Bailey. One of the early efforts of this extensive program was the publication of a set of *Nature Study Leaflets*. Anna Comstock wrote and illustrated leaflets on birds, trees, and familiar plants and arranged for competent persons to write on other subjects.

In addition to writing the pamphlets, Comstock was active in nature education all over New York. Her reputation as a science educator soon spread; she lectured on nature study at Stanford and Columbia universities, the University of Virginia, and other educational institutions throughout the country. In 1897 she was made an assistant in nature study at Cornell. Two years later she was appointed assistant professor—the first woman to reach professional status at Cornell—to the consternation of some of the college's trustees, who forced her demotion to the status of lecturer in 1900. In 1913 she was again made assistant professor and in 1920 full professor of nature study. Among her honors was designation by the League of Women Voters in 1923 as one of the "twelve living women who have contributed most in their respective fields to the betterment of the world" (Needham, 223). In 1930 Hobart College awarded her the honorary degree of Doctor of Humane Letters.

Anna Comstock made important contributions to the field of scientific illustration. Her superb engravings greatly enhanced Henry Comstock's *Introduction to Entomology* (1888; revised, 1920) and *Manual for the Study of Insects* (1895); her illustrations also appear in her own works. It is, however, in science education that Anna Comstock made her most important contributions. Her work promoting nature study in the schools was very effective, and her publications were important in the popularization of natural history.   JH/MBO

PRIMARY SOURCES

Comstock, Anna. *Handbook of Nature Study for Teachers and Parents, Based on the Cornell Nature Study Leaflets.* Ithaca, N.Y.: Comstock Publishing Co., 1911.

———. *The Nature Notebook Series.* Ithaca, New York: Comstock Publishing Co., 1915.

———. *The Comstocks of Cornell.* Ithaca, N.Y.: Comstock Publishing Co., 1953. Autobiographical.

SECONDARY SOURCES

Needham, James G. "The Lengthened Shadow of a Man and His Wife." I and II. *Scientific Monthly* 62, no. 2 (February 1946): 140–150; no. 3 (March 1946): 219–232. Describes the development of the Department of Entomology at Cornell University. Biographical material on the founders, John Henry and Anna Comstock.

STANDARD SOURCES

AMS 1–4; *NAW* (long article by Kathleen Jacklin); Ogilvie 1986.

COMYNS-LEWER, ETHEL (1861–1946)

British ornithologist. Born 1861 in Dum-Dum, India. Father Major N. D. Garrett, R.A. Married (1) Alexander Comyns (he died in 1890). One son, killed 1914; one daughter. Married (2) S. H. Lewer, J. P. Educated privately. Professional experience: opened first typewriting office in London; The Feathered World, editor. Retired 1935. Died 8 February 1946.

Educated privately, Ethel Garrett married Alexander Comyns; the couple had one son who was killed in World War I and one daughter. After her husband died in 1890, she took over the editorship of *The Feathered World*, becoming the first woman to own, edit, and publish her own paper. This publication dealt mainly with poultry husbandry. Comyns remarried in 1896, this time to publisher and editor S. H. Lewer. Her publications were chiefly popular publications on birds. In *The Feathered World*, she and R. C. Punnett produced a bibliography in a work by Punnett, "Notes on Old Poultry Books."   JH/MBO

PRIMARY SOURCES

Comyns-Lewer, Ethel. With S. H. Lewer. *Poultry Keeping.* London: T. Nelson & Sons, Ltd. [1914].

STANDARD SOURCES

Dorland; *WWW* 4, 1941–1950.

CONE, CLARIBEL (1864–1929)

U.S. pathologist and art collector. Born 14 November 1864 in Jonesboro, Tenn., to Helen Guggenheimer and Hermann Cone. Educated Western High School for Girls (1883); Woman's Medical College of Baltimore (M.D., 1890); Johns Hopkins Medical School (1893); Senckenberg Institute, Frankfurt (1903–1905); Blockley Hospital for the Insane, Philadelphia, intern (1890). Professional experience: Woman's Medical College of Baltimore, Research Pathology Laboratory, instructor (1893–1904), professor of pathology (1904–1910), board of directors (1894–1910). Collector of impressionist art (1901–1929). Died 20 September 1929, Lausanne, Switzerland.

Claribel Cone studied, did research, and taught pathology until she was forty-six, but she is far better known as one of the first and most important American collectors of modern European art with her sister Etta Cone. She was born into a German-Jewish family in Tennessee. Her mother and father, both born in Germany, met after they arrived in the United States. She was the fifth of thirteen children, and one of three daughters. Her father began a wholesale grocery business in Baltimore, but the oldest sons began a textile manufacturing business (Cone Mills) in the late 1880s. This made the family a fortune, part of which came to Claribel Cone.

Cone entered Woman's Medical College of Baltimore in 1887 and received her medical degree in 1890. She then won a competitive internship to the Blockley Hospital for the Insane in Philadelphia, and went back to Baltimore to take additional courses at Johns Hopkins Medical School. She began to do research in the pathology laboratory headed by William H. Welch from 1894 to 1903. Out of this work came two articles on tuberculosis. Cone began to teach pathology at Woman's Medical College in Baltimore, and continued, when in the United States, to serve as a professor of pathology and on its board of directors until 1910 when the college closed. Accompanied by her younger sister, Etta Cone, who took over the household management and first began the collection of important paintings by young modern artists, Cone went to Europe to study and do research at the Senckenberg Institute in Frankfurt during the winters from 1903 to 1905. During the summers, the sisters lived in Paris, as part of the circle surrounding Leo and Gertrude Stein, whom they had known in Baltimore, and their artist friends, Matisse and Picasso.

Although Cone continued to research fatty tissues under normal and pathological conditions and to teach until 1910, her work as a pathologist came virtually to an end even before the beginning of World War I. Caught in Munich, where she was visiting relatives at the start of the war, she remained there until 1921. On her return to Baltimore, she found herself to be a rich woman along with her siblings. Having given up medicine and pathology, she and her sister Etta began to form a private museum and spent their summers in Europe as serious collectors of Cezanne, Renoir, Manet, Picasso, and their friend Matisse. Cone became known not only as a serious patron of the arts in Baltimore, but also for her colorful and eccentric clothing and jewelry.

She died in Lausanne, Switzerland, from pneumonia in early fall, 1929. Her will left her collection to her sister with the understanding that this would eventually form part of the Baltimore Museum of Art. With Etta Cone's addition and a bequest to build a wing on the museum, the Cone collection became one of the great national collections of modern art. Etta Cone published her own catalogue of the collection in 1934.   JH/MBO

SECONDARY SOURCES
Mellow, James R. *Charmed Circle: Gertrude Stein and Company.* New York: Praeger, 1974.
Pollack, Barbara. *The Collectors: Dr. Claribel and Miss Etta Cone.* New York: Bobbs-Merrill, 1962.

STANDARD SOURCES
NAW (long article by Adelyn D. Breeskin).

CONKLIN, MARIE (ECKHARDT) (1908–)

U.S. biologist. Born 30 September 1908 in Derby, Conn. Married George Howard Conklin (1931). One daughter. Educated Welles-ley College (A.B., 1929); University of Wisconsin, Madison (M.S., 1930); Columbia University (Ph.D., 1936). Professional experience: Wellesley College, assistant in botany/bacteriology department (1930–1931); Carnegie Institution of Washington, research associate department of genetics, Cold Spring Harbor (1936–1941); Adelphi College, Garden City, N.Y., instructor through professor (from 1946), chair of department of biology (1953–1966). Honors and memberships: American Association for the Advancement of Science, the Genetics Society of America, the Botanical Society of America, the American Institute of Biological Sciences, the Radiation Research Society, Sigma Xi, and Sigma Delta Epsilon.

Marie Conklin earned her doctorate from Columbia University. After a research position at the Carnegie Institution of Washington, she took a position at Adelphi College, where she advanced from instructor to professor. She became chair of the biology department in 1953. She contributed articles to the *American Journal of Botany,* the *International Journal of Radiation Biology,* and the *Proceedings of the 12th International Congress of Genetics* in Tokyo (1968). Conklin's research interests were eclectic, as can be seen by her memberships. Much of her research, however, was in developmental biology. She published an important monograph on the subject in 1976.   JH/MBO

PRIMARY SOURCES
Conklin, Marie Eckhardt. *Genetic and Biochemical Aspects of the Development of Datura.* Basel: S. Karger, 1976.

STANDARD SOURCES
AMS; WW in America; WW in Education; Who's Who of American Women; World WW of Women.

CONKLIN, RUTH EMELENE (1895–1988)

U.S. physiologist. Born 25 July 1895 in Rochester, N.Y. Educated Mt. Holyoke College (A.B., 1918); University of Rochester (M.S., 1921); Radcliffe College (Ph.D., 1930). Professional experience: University of Rochester, assistant in physiology (1918–1921); Connecticut College, instructor in zoology (1921–1924); Vassar College, assistant professor (1924–1927), associate professor (1937–1944), professor (1944–1946). Died March 1988 in Poughkeepsie, N.Y.

Ruth Conklin spent most of her academic career teaching at Vassar College, where she advanced to full professor. An early member of the American Physiological Society, she did research on the metabolism of newborn infants, and on the physiology of reptile and amphibian lymphatic systems. She also worked on circulatory and respiratory reflexes.   JH/MBO

PRIMARY SOURCES

Conklin, Ruth. "News from Senior Physiologists." *The Physiologist* 20 (February 1977): 29.

STANDARD SOURCES

AMS 5–8, B 9, P&B 10–11.

CONVERSE, JEANNE
(fl. between 1322 and 1327)

French physician. Flourished between 1322 and 1327.

Jeanne Converse was among the approximately five women who were excommunicated for practicing medicine. Like her fellow physician in France, JACOBINA FELICIE, she was prosecuted for practicing medicine without a license.

JH/MBO

STANDARD SOURCES

Hurd-Mead 1938; Lipinska 1900.

CONWAY, ANNE (1631–1679)

British philosopher and savant. Born 1631 in Kensington House (later Palace), London, to Elizabeth (Cradock) and Henage Finch. Four older half-brothers; two older half-sisters; one older sister. Married Edward Conway (later third viscount Conway and Killutag and first earl of Conway) (11 February 1851). One son (died in infancy). Educated at home by tutors; instructed by Henry More and Francis Mercury van Helmont. Professional experience: correspondent of Henry More, Edward Conway, Senior, John Finch, and others; wrote philosophical treatise attacking Cartesian philosophy. Died 16 February 1679 at Ragley Hall, Warwickshire, England.

Anne Conway was one of the remarkable women of the seventeenth century. Unlike MARGARET CAVENDISH, she was not a member of a brilliant circle but rather developed her fame through her role as a pupil of Henry More and later as a disciple of Francis Mercury van Helmont. She wrote a series of brilliant letters to More and others, and prepared at least one philosophical text that was published only after her death.

She was born into a wealthy and aristocratic family who lived in what later became Kensington Palace in London. The youngest daughter of a man who had married twice and had many brilliant and successful sons, she became the favorite of them all. From her youth, her health was fragile, but this did not prevent her from studying both on her own and with the help of tutors, learning Latin, mathematics, and other subjects.

Conway's friendship and correspondence with Henry More began before her marriage at nineteen to Edward Conway through the pupil-tutor relationship of More and her half-brother John Finch at Christ's College, Cambridge. Her brother shared her interests in natural history and natural philosophy and warmly recommended her brilliance to his tutor. At first, More suggested readings to her as a pupil, but as he grew to know her, he became impressed with her wide-ranging intelligence. After her marriage, he became a regular visitor at her house, Ragley Hall. As a Platonist who mixed his interest in Plato with his study of Cartesian philosophy, More encouraged her to read Descartes and comment on his ideas. More and Conway exchanged letters about Descartes and other philosophers over a period of thirty years as More came to treat her not as a pupil or a learned lady but as a fellow philosopher. More also recommended Cambridge tutors to teach her mathematics when her usual method of self-education did not suffice.

Anne Conway had a lifelong struggle with intense headaches, probably migraines, that were treated by a series of famous seventeenth-century doctors, including William Harvey, his student Thomas Willis, and other notable doctors, surgeons, and chemists, but their treatments with heavy amounts of mercury and other chemicals weakened her health. She even sought some relief by seeking to have her skull trepanned in France, but the surgeon was not available, and instead she was bled through her jugular vein, an equally dangerous course.

Even after her one child, a son, was born, her interest in philosophy continued. But her health and spirits were badly affected by her son's death at the age of two from smallpox. Following this, Conway moved for some years to her husband's property in Ireland at Portmore where she had less contact with educated men. She and the local bishop did some investigation into reports of ghosts and other manifestations, which she reported to More.

She returned to Ragley some years later and More put her in touch with the young chemist van Helmont. Conway seems to have hoped that his chemical knowledge might cure her but soon van Helmont became a close friend and constant companion, introducing her to the Kabbalah. Conway became interested in rabbinical learning, a subject that fascinated van Helmont but that More admitted was not part of his knowledge, although he was interested in the subject and developed a cabbalistic circle of scholars.

Van Helmont also introduced her to the community of Quakers and encouraged her to meet George Fox and William Penn. At the end of her life she became a Quaker, to the annoyance of her husband and other family members, who, while tolerant of Conway's interests, found both the Quaker women around her and van Helmont to be sullen and silent. She tried through her husband's influence to improve the life of Quakers in Ireland and England, but succeeded only to a limited degree. More felt himself pushed out of center stage in Conway's intellectual life by van Helmont, seeing little of her on his last visit to Ragley not long before her death, but this did not end the friendship between the two men. When she died, van Helmont had her body preserved in wine so that her husband could see her before her plain and simple burial. Twelve years later, More and van Helmont planned the publication in Amsterdam of Conway's manuscript refuting the Cartesian system. Since there was a direct connection between van Helmont and Leibniz in the 1690s, many scholars have seen this small book not only as prefiguring some of Leibniz's ideas on the monad, but directly influencing them. Leibniz in his writings commented on van Helmont's discussion of both Conway and More, and he himself cited Conway, finding her ideas to resemble his own conclusions by adopting a middle ground between Plato and Democritus.   J H / M B O

PRIMARY SOURCES

Conway, Anne. *Opuscula philosophica quibus continentur principia philosophiae antiquissimae et recentissimae ac philosophiae vulgaris refutatio.* Amsterdam, 1690. Trans. J. C. in London as *The Principles of the Most Ancient and Modern Philosophy.* London, 1692. Published posthumously.

———. *The Principles of the Most Ancient and Modern Philosophy.* Trans. and ed. Allison P. Coudert and Taylor Corse. Cambridge University Press, 1996. A new modern translation of *Opuscula philosophica* for Cambridge Texts in the History of Philosophy. Includes a biographical introduction and bibliography.

———. *The Conway Letters: The Correspondence of Anne, Viscountess Conway, Henry More and Their Friends (1642–1684).* Ed. Marjorie Hope Nicholson. New Haven: Yale University Press, 1930.

———. *Ibid.,* Rev. ed. Ed. Sarah Hutton. Oxford: Clarendon Press; New York: Oxford University Press, 1992. In spite of the title this edition also includes extensive biographical material including her medical history, her relationship with van Helmont, and her conversion to Quaker beliefs.

SECONDARY SOURCES

Gabbey, Alan. "Anne Conway et Henry More: Lettres sur Descartes (1650–1651)." *Archives de philosophie* (Paris) 40 (1977): 379–404.

Hutton, Sarah. "Anne Conway." In *The Cambridge Dictionary of Philosophy,* ed. Robert Audi. Cambridge: Cambridge University Press, 1995. See also Hutton's introduction to the revised edition of *The Conway Letters* above.

Merchant, Carolyn. "The Vitalism of Anne Conway: Its Impact on Leibniz's Concept of the Monad." *Journal of the History of Philosophy* 17 (1979): 255–269.

Popkin, Richard. "The Spiritualistic Cosmologies of Henry More and Anne Conway." In *Henry More (1614–1687):*

Tercentenary Studies, ed. Sarah Hutton. Dordrecht: Kluwer Academic, 1990.

STANDARD SOURCES

REP; Waithe (long article by Louis Frankel).

CONWAY, ELSIE (PHILLIPS) (1902–1992)

British botanist. Born 15 March 1902 in Alford, Cheshire, to Margaret and William Phillips. One sister. Married G. D. Conway (1928). Educated privately by tutors; Queen's School, Chester; University of Liverpool (1919–1922); doctorate (ca. 1924). Professional experience: University of Durham, lecturer (1924–1928); University of Glasgow (1938–1968). Died 15 March 1992 in Aldford, Cheshire.

British botanist Elsie Conway was educated at the University of Liverpool where she took her examinations in botany and chemistry. After attaining her first degree, she spent two years doing research in botany that culminated in a doctoral degree with a dissertation on the anatomy of the Scitaminiaceae. Conway then accepted a position as a lecturer in botany at the University of Durham, a position she held until her marriage in 1928. Ten years later, in 1938, she returned to university teaching, this time at the University of Glasgow, until she retired.

Conway was forty years old when she began an ecological and experimental study on marine algae as a possible source for agar. During World War II, when eastern agar sources were in enemy hands, she supplied an alternative source. Conway also worked on a project on ferns, studying spore production. When she was fifty years old, Conway returned to her studies on algae.

After she retired, she traveled and taught in foreign countries, including time as a visiting professor studying algae at Columbia University, at the University of Otago in New Zealand, and at the University of Vancouver.   J H / M B O

STANDARD SOURCES

Strohmeier.

COOK, A. GRACE (fl. 1915)

British astronomer. Professional experience: British Astronomical Association observer; Meteor Section Society, director (1921–1923).

From 1911 to 1920, M. Davidson was the director of the Meteor Section of the British Astronomical Society, and he depended upon an excellent team of observers, including A. Grace Cook, who were tireless in their work. A. Grace Cook was a director of the Meteor Section Society from

1921 to 1923. Cook was elected to the Royal Astronomical Society in 1915.   JH/MBO

PRIMARY SOURCES
Cook, A. Grace. "Observation of Noval Aquilae on June 8." *Monthly Notices of the Royal Astronomical Society* 78 (January 1918): 569.
———. *Journal of the British Astronomical Association* 30 (1920): 330–331. Obituary notice of Fiammetta Wilson.
———. With J. P. M. Prentice. "Observations of the Meteors of the Arietid Radiant in 1921." *Monthly Notices of the Royal Astronomical Society* 82 (March 1922): 309.

SECONDARY SOURCES
"Cook, A. Grace." *Monthly Notices of the Royal Astronomical Society* 76 (1915): 1. Election notice, RAS.
Kidwell, Peggy Aldrich. "Women Astronomers in Britain, 1780–1930." *Isis* 75 (1984): 534–546.

COOK, MARGARET C. (1899–1968)

U.S. vertebrate paleontologist. Born 1899 in Nebraska. Married Harold Cook. Died 9 August 1968.

Margaret Cook was the wife of Harold Cook, with whom she coauthored a paper on Tertiary vertebrates of Nebraska in 1933. Much of her work after 1933 was incorporated into her husband's papers. After 1962, Margaret's chief concern was to be certain that her husband's dream of establishing a national monument happened. She worked tirelessly to this end, and eventually the Agate Fossil Quarries National Monument, Nebraska, was established.   JH/MBO

PRIMARY SOURCES
Cook, Margaret C. With Harold Cook. "Faunal Lists of the Tertiary Vertebrata of Nebraska and Adjacent Areas." *Nebraska Geological Survey,* paper 5 (1933).

SECONDARY SOURCES
McKenna, Malcolm C. "Margaret C. Cook 1899–1968." *Society of Vertebrate Paleontologists Newsletter,* no. 85 (1969): 59.

STANDARD SOURCES
Sarjeant.

COOKE, ALICE SOPHIA (SMART) (1890–1957)

British botanist. Born 1 June 1890 in London. Father a skilled iron moulder. Two siblings. Married (1) A. S. Bacon (he died in 1916); (2) Henry Cooke (1950). Educated Stepney school; City of London School for Girls (1906–1909); East London College (now Queen Mary College) (B.Sc., 1912). Professional experience: Swindon and North Wilts Secondary School and Technical Institute, temporary appointment as science mistress; Huddersfield Technical College (1914–1920); Brighton Technical College, lecturer; head (1920–1950). FLS (1922). Died 21 May 1957 in Hassocks, Sussex.

Alice Smart was born, educated, and taught in London. After matriculating at the East London College (now Queen Mary College), she was awarded one of the two Drapers Company Scholarships in Science for Women in 1909. Here she worked under the leadership of Professor Fritsch, F.L.S., and obtained a bachelor's degree in botany with subsidiary chemistry in 1912. After a temporary appointment, Smart became assistant lecturer and demonstrator in biology at Huddersfield Technical College. Although she had hoped to have time to work on a higher degree, she found it almost impossible with the heavy teaching load. She did find time to work with T. W. Woodhead in an experiment on spraying to control potato blight.

While at Huddersfield, she met her future husband, Samuel Bacon, a young librarian. After a brief honeymoon in 1916, he went to France, where he was killed in action. In 1920, Smart left Huddersfield to become a lecturer in biology and later head of the department at Brighton Technical College, where she remained for thirty years. Apparently, Smart was a fine teacher, gaining the respect of her classes for her clear lectures and intolerance for second-rate work. Although still burdened with an onerous teaching load, she found time to inspire her students to pursue botanical research. She accompanied her students on field trips on weekends, and passed her great knowledge of the flora of Sussex on to them.

Smart retired from the post of the head of the biology department at Brighton in 1950, and married her colleague Henry Cooke in that same year.

Smart was elected a Fellow of the Linnean Society in 1922. She was a member of the British Bryological Society, the British Ecological Society, the British Mycological Society, the Royal Horticultural Society, the Freshwater Biological Association, and the Brighton and Hove Natural History Society. She traveled extensively through Europe during vacations.   JH/MBO

SECONDARY SOURCES
Gregory, P. H. *Proceedings of the Linnean Society* 169 (1956–1957): 240–241. Obituary notice.
Mycologist (1990): 192. Obituary notice.

STANDARD SOURCES
Desmond.

COOKSON, ISABEL CLIFTON (1893–1973)

Australian palaeobotanist, mycologist, and palynologist. Born 25 December 1893 in Melbourne, Victoria, Australia. Never married. Educated Methodist Ladies' College; University of Melbourne (B.Sc., 1916; D.Sc., 1932). Professional experience: University of Melborne, lecturer (1930–1947); University of Manchester, Leverhulme Research Grant (1948–1949); University of Melbourne, leader, Pollen Research Unit (1949–1966). Died 1 July 1973.

Isabel Clifton Cookson was born in Melbourne, Australia, and educated at the Methodist Ladies' College, and the University of Melbourne, where she received bachelor's and doctoral degrees. As an undergraduate, she specialized in the biological sciences. Her hobby was music and she became a proficient pianist. In 1916 she was awarded a Government Research Scholarship for work on the flora of Australia's Northern Territory, and in December 1916, received the McBain Research Scholarship in biology. In 1917, Cookson earned a First Class Final Honours Scholarship in botany. This scholarship was for her investigation on crown rot in walnut trees in Victoria. Her early work was in botany; however, in 1929 she began to work on Devonian flora in Victoria, receiving grants to study fossil plants in the Tertiary sediments at Yallourn. During her career, Cookson traveled often overseas, most often to Europe and Great Britain. She continued her education through studying fungi with Professor Le Rayner in London and fossil plants with A. C. Seward in Cambridge. On a 1926–1927 visit to England, she collaborated with W. H. Lang in studying the earliest known land plants. In 1933–1934 Cookson received a Grisedale Research Scholarship. In their paper of 1942, W. N. Croft and W. H. Lang honored Cookson by naming a newly created genus for her, *Cooksonia*. Cookson officially retired in 1959, but continued to do research until 1972. She received a number of honors, including memberships in the Royal Society of Victoria and in the Botanical Society of America. A symposium on palynology was conducted in her honor in 1971. Cookson died of cardiac failure in 1973.

Isabel Cookson is best known for her studies of the Tertiary pollen of Australia and the Jurassic to Tertiary dinoflagellate cysts of Australia and Papua. Originally trained in botany, she gradually moved from pure botany to paleobotany. Cookson is considered the founder of the science of palynology in Australia. Later, she turned to the study of fossil microplankton. She again went to Europe to collaborate with A. Eisenack in Germany, S. B. Manum in Norway, and G. Deflandre in France. Her studies of oil basin sedimentology later were of economic importance. She published approximately eighty-six scientific papers, many of which were collaborations with other scientists. Most of these papers were paleobotanical in nature.   CK

SECONDARY SOURCES

Baker, George. "Dr. Isabel Clifton Cookson." *Review of Palaeobotany and Palynology* 16, no. 3 (1973): 133–135.

Morgan, Roger V. "The Cookson Collection: Used and Misused Australian Microplankton." *British Micropalaeontology,* no. 15 (1981): 5–6.

STANDARD SOURCES

Sarjeant.

COOLEY, JACQUELIN SMITH (1883–?)

U.S. botanist. Born 1883. Educated at Randolph-Macon College (A.B., 1906); Virginia Polytechnic Institute (M.S., 1911); Washington University, St. Louis (Ph.D., 1914). Married in 1914. Professional experience: Assistant plant pathologist, Virginia Experiment Station (1911–1912); U.S. Department of Agriculture, scientific assistant, assistant pathologist, associate pathologist, and senior pathologist (1912–1951). Death date unknown.

Jacquelin Cooley was an able botanist who found opportunity for educational and professional advancement within the ranks of the U.S. Department of Agriculture (USDA), the largest single government employer of women professionals in the 1920s. Apparently the agriculture agency was supportive in allowing employees time to obtain advanced degrees, offered good benefits and a wide range of employment possibilities for women. Cooley authored at least twelve publications, and was a member of the American Association for the Advancement of Science and the Botanical Society of America.   JH/MBO

STANDARD SOURCES

AMS 4–8, B 9, P&B 10–11; Bailey; Barnhart.

COOMBS, HELEN COPELAND (1891–1944)

U.S. physiologist. Born 25 July 1891 in St. Joseph, Mo. Educated Columbia University (A.B., 1911; B.S., 1914; A.M., 1915; Ph.D., 1918). Professional experience: Columbia University, assistant in physiology (1917–1918), instructor (1919–1926); Bellevue Hospital Medical College, researcher (1923–1926); Herter Research Fellow in neurology (1926–1927); General Education Board research fellow (1927–1929); New York Homeopathic Medical College instructor in physiology (1929–1932); assistant professor in physiology and biochemistry (1932–1940); Brooklyn College, instructor in physiology (1940–1944). Died Brooklyn, N.Y., 1944.

Born in Missouri, Helen Coombs went to Columbia University, where she remained for her entire education. She received a bachelor's degree, a bachelor of science degree, a master's degree, and a doctorate from the university. During her final year of her doctorate, she also taught physiology as an assistant and then as an instructor for the next seven years, holding a concurrent appointment at the Bellevue Hospital Medical College during the final three years. She was a Sarah Berliner Research Fellow from 1922 to 1923 and a Herter Research Fellow in neurology from 1927 to 1929, during which she was able to explore her research interest in the links between the cardiovascular and nervous systems. From 1929 she taught at the New York Homeopathic Medical College, first as an instructor in physiology and then as assistant professor of physiology and biochemistry until 1940. For the last years of her life, Coombs taught physiology at Brooklyn College. She died in 1944 at the age of fifty-three. She published on the nervous mechanisms of respiration, cerebral anemia, cardiovascular nervous mechanisms, neurophysiology and neuropharmacology, and the relation of calcium and phosphorus metabolism to the nervous system. She was a member of the New York Academy of Science, and the Society for Experimental Biology and Medicine.

JH/MBO

STANDARD SOURCES
AMS 3–7.

COOPER, CLARA CHASSELL (1893–?)

U.S. psychologist. Born 24 March 1893 in Sundance, Wyo. Educated Cornell College, Iowa (A.B., 1912); Iowa State Teacher's College (Di.M., 1913); Northwestern University (A.B., 1912); University of Chicago; Columbia University (Ph.D., 1920). Professional experience: William Woods College, head of department of philosophy and education (1914–1915); Columbia University Teachers College, Horace Mann School, school psychologist; instructor in experimental education; Institute of Educational Research, researcher (1917–1922). Death date unknown.

Clara Cooper spent most of her professional career at Columbia University Teachers College, where she instructed in the experimental school, taught experimental education, and did research at the Institute of Educational Research. She published articles on the psychology of education and was especially interested in religious education.

Cooper was a member of the American Psychological Association and the American Association for the Advancement of Science.

KM

STANDARD SOURCES
Psychological Register, vol. 3, 1932.

COOPER, ELIZABETH MORGAN (1891–1967)

U.S. mathematician. Born 1891. Five siblings who survived her. Educated Radcliffe College (A.B., 1913); Bryn Mawr College (A.M., 1923); University of Illinois (Ph.D., 1930). Professional experience: Baldwin School, Bryn Mawr, Pa., teacher (1913–1927); University of Illinois, teacher (1929–1930); Buckingham School, Cambridge, Mass., principal; Chapin School, N.Y., head of mathematics department; Hunter College, supervisor of mathematics and teacher training (from 1937); Hunter College High School in New York, chair of the mathematics department (to 1958). Retired 1958. Died 17 May 1967.

Elizabeth Cooper used her doctorate in mathematics from the University of Illinois to further secondary school teaching. She taught in well-known preparatory high schools, and for a time was supervisor of mathematics and teacher training at Hunter College. She finished her career at Hunter College High School as chair of the mathematics department. Cooper was a life member of the American Friends Service Committee and founder and president of Newark House of the New Jersey Fellowship for the Aged.

JH/MBO

SECONDARY SOURCES
New York Times, 20 May 1967. Obituary notice.

STANDARD SOURCES
American Women; Campbell and Grinstein.

COOPER, SUSAN FENIMORE (1813–1894)

U.S. writer on natural history and geology. Born 17 April 1813 at Heathcote Hill, Mamaroneck, N.Y., to Susan Augusta De Lancey and James Fenimore Cooper. Three sisters and one brother. Never married. Educated private schools and tutors; studied in Europe (1826–1833). Died 31 December 1894 in Cooperstown, N.Y.

Susan Fenimore Cooper and her four siblings were reared in a supportive environment with parents who emphasized education. Susan was educated in excellent private schools and also by tutors. Her many skills included proficiency in four languages, an excellent grasp of American and European literature and history, and a knowledge of botany and zoology. She also developed skills in music, drawing, and dancing, in addition to social skills learned in Europe. Although Samuel F. B. Morse was rumored to have been a suitor, Cooper never married. In about 1836, the Cooper family moved to Cooperstown (founded by her paternal grandfather) to the old family mansion.

Daughter of the novelist James Fenimore Cooper, Susan wrote a book, *Rural Hours,* published also in Britain as *Journal of a Naturalist,* widely read and praised. She described the annual cycle of life in the New York countryside to provide information on weather, soil, mineral springs, rivers, and other features of the landscape, as well as describing in precise detail local plants and animals.   JH/MBO

PRIMARY SOURCES
Cooper, Susan F. *Rural Hours.* New York: Putnam, 1850.

STANDARD SOURCES
Kass-Simon and Farnes; *NAW* (article by James Franklin Beard).

COOPER, SYBIL (1900–1970)

British physiologist. Born in London January 1900. Father, Sir Edwin Cooper. Married R. S. Creed, (1933). Four children. Educated Kensington High School; Girton College, Cambridge (Natural Science Tripos, 1922); Cambridge University (Ph.D. in physiology, 1927). Professional experience: Cambridge University, research assistant to E. D. Adrian (with studentships) (1922–1927); Oxford University, departmental and university demonstrator in physiology (with Charles Sherrington) (1927–1934), research associate (hon.) (1940–1946), research fellow (1946–1968), emeritus fellow (1968–1970), St Hilda's College, Oxford, lecturer in natural sciences (1941–1945), acting tutor in natural sciences (1943–1945). Died 1970 in car accident.

Sybil Cooper, in contrast to many of her contemporary British women scientists, came from a nonmedical, nonscientific background. Her father was a successful and prosperous architect at the turn of the century in London. Her mother was uneasy about Sybil's decision to attend Girton College, Cambridge. However, with her father's encouragement, Cooper not only entered Girton, but took the Natural Sciences Tripos in 1922. She became fascinated by physiology, especially nerve and muscle physiology then being pursued by E. D. Adrian at Cambridge. She served as his research assistant in the department of physiology, supported by a series of prestigious studentships, as a Girton Yarrow Research Student (1922–1924) and then a George Henry Lewes Student (1924). Cooper received her doctoral degree in 1927. After she had completed her research for this degree, she left Cambridge for Oxford, to work with Charles Sherington in the physiology department. She remained in her positions as departmental, and then university, demonstrator in anatomy until 1934. Concurrently she became a member of St. Hilda's College, first as a research student and then as a research fellow (1926–1934).

While she was university demonstrator, she met her future husband, R. S. Creed, who was a demonstrator in physiology. The two married, and Sybil resigned her position in

order to be with her rapidly growing family. The couple had four children, a daughter (1935), a son (1938), and twin daughters (1939). Financially able to hire domestic help, Sybil returned to research in the department of physiology, although she did not hold a paid position. She taught undergraduates as a lecturer in Natural Science at St. Hilda's until 1945 and then served as acting tutor in natural sciences at Lady Margaret Hall (1943–1945). Her last position was as research fellow (1946–1968). From 1968 until her death in an automobile accident on the way to work, she was an emeritus fellow.

Cooper was one of the fortunate women who was able to continue her scientific career and have a family at the same time. Her private means made this possible. Cooper began her research under Lord Adrian as a graduate student. Before her marriage she worked with J. C. Eccles, C. S. Sherington, and R. Granit on diverse topics. However, after the birth of her children, she continued the work that she had begun in collaboration with her husband on muscle reflexes, and it was in this area that she did her most creative work. Demonstrating great ability in dissecting minute sense organs with intact nerves, she recorded nerve activity. As an excellent histologist, Cooper fixed, stained, and examined the microstructure of the sense organs. Alone and with colleagues, she made advances in understanding how the muscle spindles functioned relative to their structure. In addition to her collaborators mentioned above, Cooper also worked with another group of great physiologists: Peter M. Daniel, David Whitteridge, I. A. Boyd, and Marianne Fillenz.   JH/MBO

PRIMARY SOURCES
Cooper, Sybil. "Conduction of the Nervous Impulse in Narcosis." Ph.D. diss., Cambridge University, 1927.
———. With J. C. Eccles. "The Isometric Responses of Mammalian Muscles." *Journal of Physiology* 69 (1930): 377–385.
———. With P. M. Daniel and D. Whitteridge. "Muscle Spindles and Other Sensory Endings in the Extrinsic Eye Muscles: The Physiology and Anatomy of These Receptors and of Their Connexions with the Brain Stem." *Brain* 78 (1955): 564–584.
———. "The Responses of the Primary and Secondary Endings of Muscle Spindles with Intact Motor Innervation During Applied Stretch." *Journal of Experimental Physiology* 46 (1961): 389–398.
———. With P. M. Daniel. "Muscle Spindles in Man; Their Morphology in the Lumbricals and the Deep Muscles of the Neck." *Brain* 86 (1963): 563–586.

STANDARD SOURCES
Women Physiologists.

COOPER-ELLIS, KATHARINE MURDOCH (1889–?)

U.S. psychologist. Born 15 January 1889 in Pittsburgh, Pa. Educated Columbia University Teachers College (B.S., 1912; A.M., 1913; Ph.D., 1918). Professional experience: Columbia University Teachers College, assistant in educational psychology (1912–1913); extension division, instructor (1917–1920), assistant (1925), lecturer (1919), Carnegie Institute of Technology, instructor of education and psychology (1913–1916); New York School of Social Work, instructor (1918–1920); Punahou School, Honolulu, Hawaii, instructor (1920–1921); Hanahauoli School, Honolulu, director (1922); various other schools in Hawaii (1924); Vocational Service for Juniors, consulting psychologist (1925–1927); consulting psychologist (from 1927). Honors and memberships: the National Committee for Mental Hygiene; the American Psychological Association; the American Association for the Advancement of Science; the National Education Association; and the Association for Applied Psychology. Death date unknown.

Katharine Murdoch Cooper-Ellis earned all three of her degrees from Columbia University Teachers College. One of her major research interests was in race research, and she spent from 1920 to 1924 in Hawaii, doing research on this subject while she was serving as a psychologist in several schools. Her research also included scientific measurement in sewing, achievement quotients, the correlation of mental and physical measures, and mental hygiene. KM

STANDARD SOURCES
AMS 5–6.

COPELAND, LENNIE PHOEBE (1881–1951)

U.S. mathematician. Born 30 March 1881 in Bangor, Maine. Educated University of Maine (B.S., 1904; Sc.D., 1948); Wellesley College (A.M., 1911); University of Pennsylvania (Ph.D., 1913). Professional experience: high school teacher (1905–1910); Wellesley College, instructor in mathematics (1913–1919), assistant professor (1919–1928), associate professor (1928–1937), professor (1937–1946), professor emerita (1946–1951). Honors and memberships: the Mathematics Society; the Mathematics Association; and the New England Association of Teachers of Mathematics, member and president (1928–1930). Died 1951.

Like many early-twentieth-century women, Lennie Copeland owed her career in academia to the advent of the women's colleges. Her bachelor's and doctoral degrees were from state universities, and her master's was from Wellesley College, where she returned to teach. She advanced through the ranks to professor, although she spent a long time at each level. Her research interest was in the algebra of invariants.

JH/MBO

STANDARD SOURCES
American Women; AMS 3–8; Campbell and Grinstein.

CORDIER, MARGUERITE JEANNE (1904–)

French physicist. Born 23 September 1904 in Paris to Eugénie (Charasson) and Louis Cordier. Educated Lycée Fénelon; normal supérieur in Sèvres; University of Paris (Agrégée); teaching qualification; Ph.D. in physics. Professional experience: various French secondary schools, teacher (1929–1946); French Institute in Bucharest, teacher (1946–1949); University of Barcelona, research and teaching (1949–1954); Higher Council for Scientific Research, deputy (1955–1956); University of Rheims, extraordinary professor for physics (from 1957). Honors and memberships: Union of French Academic Women, president; Légion d'honneur; Commandeur des Palmes.

Born in Paris to a pharmacist father, Marguerite Cordier finished her university examinations in the physical sciences, and then became qualified as a teacher. She obtained a doctorate in physics with a work on the solubility of simple ions. She then held teaching and research positions in various institutes. While in Barcelona, Cordier took a year off to work for UNESCO at the University of Caracas. After working in an administrative position for a year, she was appointed extraordinary professor at the University of Rheims.

Her research was on the absorption of molecules and radicals in low temperature ultraviolet fields. She was also the editor of *Informations scientifiques françaises* and *Femmes diplomées.* In addition, she edited a journal for French women academics. JH/MBO

STANDARD SOURCES
Strohmeier; *Who's Who in France; WW in Science in Europe.*

CORI, GERTY THERESA RADNITZ (1896–1957)

Austro-Hungarian/U.S. biochemist. Born 15 August 1896 in Prague to Martha (Neustadt) and Otto Radnitz. Two sisters. Married Carl Cori (1920). One son, Carl Thomas (b. 1936). Educated home; private girls' school (1912); Medical School of the German University of Prague (Carl Ferdinand University) (M.D., 1920). Professional experience: Vienna, Karolinen Children's Hospital, assistant (1920–1922); Buffalo, N.Y., State Institute for the Study of Malignant Disease, assistant pathologist (1922–1925), assistant biochemist (from 1925); Washington University, St. Louis, research fellow (1931–1938), research associate in pharmacology (1938–1942), associate professor of research in biological chemistry and pharmacology (1942–1946), Department of Biochemistry (1946), professor (1947). Honors and memberships: Nobel Prize in medicine and physiology (1947); National Academy of Sciences (1948);

Lasker Award of the American Public Health Association; American Chemical Society, Willard Gibbs Award; American Chemical Society, Garvan Medal (1948). Honorary doctorates: Boston University (1948); Smith College (1949); Yale (1951); Columbia University (1954); University of Rochester (1955); National Conference of Christians and Jews, American Brotherhood Award; Women's National Press Club, Woman of Achievement. Died 26 October 1957 of kidney failure.

In what is now the Czech Republic and was then part of the Austro-Hungarian empire, Gerty Radnitz was born in Prague to a moderately wealthy family. She received her early education through tutors at home and then at a private girls' school at Teschen (graduated 1912). Lacking the requisite courses in Latin, physics, chemistry, and mathematics, when Gerty decided that she wanted to study science, she attained in one year the equivalent of eight years of Latin and five of science and mathematics. She was accepted to the medical school of the University of Prague (Carl Ferdinand University), where to be admitted as a woman was unusual. During her first year at the university, Gerty met her future husband, Carl Cori. The two were immediately drawn to each other. After the first two years at medical school, Carl was drafted into the Austrian army. The war disillusioned the formerly optimistic young man. When the war was over, the couple continued their medical studies and published their first research project on the immune bodies in blood in various diseases. Unhappy with the conditions in postwar Europe, Gerty and Carl emigrated to the United States after graduating from medical school. Carl accepted a position as biochemist at the State Institute for the Study of Malignant Disease (now Roswell Park Memorial Institute). Gerty followed as assistant pathologist with the duty of carrying out examinations of histological specimens. She became assistant biochemist in 1925.

Working as a team throughout their lives, the Coris began their joint research on the metabolism of tumors and then on carbohydrate metabolism. Their colleagues did not see this collaboration as positive. During the time of their first job in the United States, the director of the institute threatened to dismiss Gerty if she continued her collaborative work on the metabolism of tumors with her husband. The demand was ignored, they continued to work together, and the director, having made his statement, appeared to forget it. When Carl Cori was offered a position at the University of Buffalo, he was informed that he could not work with his wife. When Gerty Cori visited the university, she was told that she was interfering with her husband's career and that doing this was "un-American." The Coris became American citizens in 1928. Even though they had done some work on tumors at the cancer institute, their major interest was in carbohydrate metabolism and its regulation. Although the

institute did not question the direction of their research, they felt that their research was not especially relevant to the goals of the institute. Therefore, when Carl was offered the position of chairman of the department of pharmacology at the Washington University School of Medicine, he accepted. Nepotism rules stated that two members of the same family could not be employed. However, Gerty Cori was given a research position at a token salary. They established a laboratory that became a major center for biochemical research. Their students included five future Nobel laureates, Christian de Duve, Arthur Kornberg, Louis Leloir, Severo Ochoa, and Earl Sutherland, Jr. In 1946, Carl Cori became head of the department of biological chemistry and Gerty Cori began to climb the academic ladder. She was not made professor until July 1947, after they jointly received the Nobel Prize. They made two renowned discoveries: that carbohydrates are stored in the liver and muscles and are changed into glucose that can be used by the body; and that certain hormones affect the metabolism of carbohydrates. Glucose is stored in the body, specifically in the liver, in the form of glycogen ("animal starch"). Glycogen is composed of a large number of glucose molecules and is broken down to provide for the body's energy needs. The Coris were interested in the intermediary metabolism of carbohydrates. They postulated that blood glucose is changed to muscle glycogen which then becomes blood lactic acid. Blood lactic acid is then able to form liver glycogen, which completes the cycle by becoming blood glucose when the body needs it. This cycle is known as the Cori cycle, which was proposed in 1929. When they moved to St. Louis, the Coris continued to work on carbohydrates and disproved the current belief that glycogen metabolized glucose by hydrolysis. They demonstrated that the breakdown of glycogen involved the formation of a substance known as glucose-1-phosphate, which was referred to as the Cori ester. The enzyme that catalyzed this reaction was isolated by the Coris and named phosphorylase. This enzyme was involved in both the synthesis and the cleavage of glycogen. They also identified other enzymes and even synthesized glycogen in a test tube in 1939, the first time that this occurred. They used glucose-1-phosphate with phosphorylase and glycogen as a primer, making both linear and branched chain glycogen. Gerty Cori later begun the study of a group of hereditary diseases in which abnormal amounts of glycogen are stored in the body. She determined that disease could be caused by the lack of a specific enzyme.

The Coris shared the Noble Prize for physiology and medicine in 1947 with Bernardo Houssay of Argentina, making Gerty Cori the first woman to win the medicine and physiology Nobel Prize.

Gerty and Carl Cori had one son, Carl Thomas Cori, born in 1936. Typically, she worked in the research laboratory until the last moment before going to the hospital for her son's birth. Always interested in the out-of-doors, she was climbing Snow Mass peak in the summer of 1947, when she began to display the symptoms of myelofibrosis, a rare bone marrow disease. However, she continued to work as hard as ever. Numerous blood transfusions kept her alive for ten years, until she died of kidney failure in 1957.

In the close relationship that existed between the Coris, it was almost impossible to separate and evaluate the contributions of each person. Physicist Mildred Cohn accepted the consensus view of those who knew both of them that they were equally creative. Their differences involved their temperaments. Gerty was energetic and vivacious where Carl was more aloof and easy-going. Cohn noted, however, that he often displayed an excellent sense of humor. They were both hard task masters, who "did not suffer fools gladly." Nevertheless, Gerty was kind and compassionate when somebody needed help. The Coris working as a team were undoubtedly stronger than either one of them would have been alone. JH/MBO

PRIMARY SOURCES
Cori, Gerty. "The Insulin Content of Tumor Tissue." *Journal of Cancer Research* 9 (1925): 408–410.
———. "On the Carbohydrate Metabolism of Adrenalectomized Rats." *Proceedings of the Society of Experimental Biology and Medicine* 24 (1927): 539–541.
———. "The Fate of Sugar in the Animal Body. IV." *Journal of Biological Chemistry* 72 (1927): 597–614.
———. "The Fate of Sugar in the Animal Body. V." *Journal of Biological Chemistry* 72 (1927): 615–625.
———. "Carbohydrate Changes During Anaerobiosis of Mammalian Muscle." *Journal of Biological Chemistry* 96 (1932): 259–269.
———. "Carbohydrate Metabolism." *Annual Review of Biochemistry* 3 (1934): 151–174.
———. "Carbohydrate Metabolism." *Annual Review of Biochemistry* 4 (1935): 183–198.
———. With M. A. Swanson and C. F. Cori. "The Mechanism of Formation of Starch and Glycogen." *Federation Proceedings, Federation of American Societies for Experimental Biology* 4 (1945): 234–241.

STANDARD SOURCES
AMS 6–10; Bailey; *Creative Couples; Current Biography;* Debus; Grinstein 1993; Grinstein 1997; Kass-Simon and Farnes; McGrayne; *NAW* (M) (long article by John Parascandola); *Notable;* Opfell; Rossiter 1982; Siegel and Finley; Uglow 1989.

CORNARO (CORNERO), ELENA (HELENA) LUCRETIA (d. 1685)

Italian natural philosopher and mathematician. Born in Venice. Father Gio Baptista Cornaro. Educated in sciences, languages, and Aristotelian philosophy by tutors; University of Padua (doctorate); University at Rome. Died 1685.

Elena Cornaro exemplified the learned Italian woman who was carefully educated through the care of a family member, most often the father, and who reflected well on her teachers. MARIA AGNESI and LAURA BASSI also demonstrated brilliance after such an education. Gio Baptista Cornaro saw that his daughter was taught languages, sciences, and Aristotelian philosophy. She attended the university of Padua where she may have been the first woman to earn a doctorate. She was also admitted to the University of Rome. She refused to marry, having taking a vow of virginity. Her piety led her to flagellation and fasting. She became a curiosity—a woman savant—and her reputation grew all over Europe. The extremes that she went to in both study and devotion impaired her health and she died young. JH/MBO

STANDARD SOURCES
Cyclopaedia.

CORNELIUS-FURLANI, MARTA (1886–1974)

Italian structural geologist and stratigrapher. Born 4 July 1886. Married Hans Peter Cornelius. Died 19 June 1974.

Marta Cornelius-Furlani undertook studies of the Austrian Alps with her husband, Hans Peter Cornelius. JH/MBO

PRIMARY SOURCES
Cornelius-Furlani, Marta. "Zur Kenntnis der Lienzer Dolomiten und deren Stellung in der ostalpinen Wurzelzone." *Verhandlungen der Schweizerischen Naturforschenden Gesellschaft* 132 (1954): 138–140.
———. With Friedrich Bachmayer. "Die geologische Lage von Wien." *Veroeffentlichungen aus dem Naturhistorischen Museum in Wien* n.s. 3 (1960): 30–32.

SECONDARY SOURCES
Clar, E. "Marta Cornelius-Furlani 4.7.1886–20.6.1974." *Mitteilungen der östen geologischen Gesellschaft in Wien* 68, 163–165.

STANDARD SOURCES
Sarjeant.

CORYNDON, SHIRLEY (CAMERON) (1926–1976)

British zoologist and vertebrate paleontologist. Born 1926. Married (1) Roger Coryndon; (2) Robert Savage. Two daughters. Professional experience: Louis Leakey, research assistant (1949–1963); British Museum (Natural History) (1963–1968); Bristol University (from 1968). Died October 1976.

Shirley Cameron began her work on bones as a radiographer at the Middlesex Hospital in London. She then married Roger Coryndon, the son of a former governor of Kenya. The couple moved to Somalia for two years, where Roger was a police inspector, and then to Kenya. Here, Shirley met the Leakeys and began work at the Coryndon Museum (later the Kenya National Museum). She was a research assistant to Louis S. B. Leakey in Kenya and Tanzania from 1949 to 1963. After the death of her husband in 1963, Coryndon and her daughters returned to London, where she worked at the British Museum of Natural History. She married Robert Savage in 1968, and the couple moved to Bristol. At the university, she organized a new repository for the Bristol vertebrate paleontological collections.

Although she did not have a degree, Coryndon became an excellent mammalian paleontologist. She actively worked at almost all the Miocene and Pleistocene sites in Kenya and Tanzania, including the Olduvai Gorge. These sites were rich with mammalian fossils and she became an expert on fossil hippopotami. After Coryndon went to the British Museum of Natural History, she continued her work on Tertiary faunas, especially hippopotami, from Kenya, Tanzania, and Uganda. She published numerous monographs and articles on East African fossil mammals. After her marriage to Robert Savage, she was associated with the University of Bristol and continued to publish and to work with students.

JH/MBO

PRIMARY SOURCES
Coryndon, Shirley. With H. B. S. Cooke. "Pleistocene Mammals from the Kaiso Formation of Uganda." In *Fossil Vertebrates of Africa*. Vol. 2. New York: Academic Press, 1970.
———. With R. J. G. Savage. "The Origin and Affinities of African Mammal Faunas." In *Organisms and Continents Through Time. Special Papers in Palaeontology* 12 (1973): 121–135. London, Palaeontological Association.
———. "Fossil Hippopotamidae from the Baringo Basin and Relationships within the Gregory Rift, Kenya." In *Geological Background to Fossil Man; Recent Research in the Gregory Rift Valley, East Africa*. Ed. V. J. Maglio and H. B. S. Cooke, 483–495. Cambridge, MA: Harvard University Press, 1978.

SECONDARY SOURCES
Dineley, David L. "Shirley Coryndon 1926–1976." *News Bulletin of the Society of Vertebrate Paleontology* (October 1977): 39–40.

STANDARD SOURCES
Sarjeant.

COSTE BLANCHE, MARIE DE (fl. 1566)

French natural philosopher. Born in Paris. Professional experience: skilled in medicine, physics, and mathematics.

Marie de Coste Blanche was a noted seventeenth-century woman scholar. Her specialties were physics and mathematics, but she was also reputed to be skilled in medicine.

JH/MBO

PRIMARY SOURCES
Coste Blanche, Marie de. *The Nature of the Sun and Earth*. 1566.

STANDARD SOURCES
Harless; Hurd-Mead 1938; Rebière.

COTELLE, SONIA (1896–1945)

Polish/French chemist. Born Sonia Slobodkine 19 June 1896 in Warsaw. Married, later divorced. Educated Sorbonne (bachelor's degree). Professional experience: Marie Curie's laboratory (Institute of Radium), assistant (from 1919); Faculté des Sciences, chemist (1926–1927); Institute of Radium, Prague, Czechoslovakia, research; Iachimow-Jáchymov (now Joachimsthal) Czechoslovakia, researcher. Died 1945, possibly of radiation poisoning.

Sonia Slobodkine studied chemistry at the Sorbonne, where she obtained certificates in general, biological, and applied chemistry. She began work in the Paris Radium Institute under MARIE CURIE in 1919. Cotelle was in charge of the measurement service from 1924 to 1926, at which time she was appointed chemist at the Faculté des Sciences. As a skilled radiochemist, she was sent to Czechoslovakia to set up radium standards. Cotelle worked with polonium, and collaborated with Curie on studies of actinium. With Curie she redetermined the half life of ionium using a method that minimized effects of error in atomic weights. Cotelle used electrolysis to prepare thin samples of radioactive substances for testing. This method allowed determination of polonium's atomic number by X-ray spectrography.

Cotelle became seriously ill with radiation sickness in 1927, probably after accidentally swallowing some polonium solution while pipetting it. She regained her health for a time, but became subject to recurring illnesses caused by exposure to radioactivity, to which she finally succumbed.

MM

PRIMARY SOURCES

Cotelle, Sonia. With M. Curie. "Sur la vie moyenne de l'ionium." *Comptes rendus de l'Academie des Sciences* 190 (1930): 1289–1292.

———. With M. Haïssinsky. "Sur la préparation de couches minces de thorium et d'actinium par électrolyse dans l'alcool éthylique." *Comptes rendus de l'Academie des Sciences* 206 (1938): 1644–1646.

———. With H. Hulubei and Y. Cauchois. "Détermination spectroscopique de numéro atomique du polonium." *Comptes rendus de l'Academie des Sciences* 207 (1938): 1204–1206.

SECONDARY SOURCES

Communication from Ginette Gablot, Directeur Adjoint, Musée et Archives de l'Institut du Radium, Paris.

Curie, Eve. *Madame Curie.* Trans. Vincent Sheean. Garden City, N.Y.: Doubleday, Doran & Co., 1937.

Marie/Irène Curie Correspondence (1905–1934). Paris: Les Éditeurs Français Réunis, 1974.

Reid, Robert. *Marie Curie.* New York: New American Library, 1974.

Róna, Elizabeth. *How It Came About: Radioactivity, Nuclear Physics, Atomic Energy.* Oak Ridge, Tennessee: Oak Ridge Associated Universities, 1978.

COTTER, BRIGID M. (1921–1978)

Irish botanist and chemist. Born 3 January 1921 in Roscommon, Ireland. Educated (B.Sc.). Professional experience: Butter Testing Station, Dublin, Chief Technical Officer. Died 20 November 1978 in Dublin.

Brigid Cotter received a bachelor of science degree. She did research on lichen chemistry and collected a herbarium which is now at the National Botanical Gardens, Glasnevin.

JH/MBO

SECONDARY SOURCES

Irish Naturalist Journal 19 (1979): 445. Obituary notice.

STANDARD SOURCES

Desmond.

COTTON, ENID MARY (1899–1956)

See Jesson, Enid Mary.

COUDREAU, OCTAVIE (fl. 1900)

French explorer and naturalist. Married Henri Coudreau. Professional experience: French Guiana (1894); Province of Pará, northern Brazil, explorer with her husband (1895); further collaborative explorations (1895–1899); Amazonia, official explorer (1899–1906).

Octavie Coudreau was married to the geographer and explorer Henri Coudreau. In 1894, she went to French Guiana under instructions from the colonial minister of France. The next year, 1895, she began a series of collaborations with her husband, Henri, in the Pará in northern Brazil. From 1895 to 1899, the two collaborated on six quarto volumes illustrated by photographs that they had taken. They carefully made charts of the rivers that they had explored. While exploring a tributary of the Amazon, the Trombetas, Henri became ill and died. Octavie remained in the Amazon and finished the book on the subject that had so interested her husband, under the title *Voyage au Trombetas.* The states of Pará and Amazonas employed her to explore a number of other rivers in the vast Amazonian territory. From 1899 to 1896, she worked as an official explorer in the service of Amazonia, enduring incredible hardships. Her explorations contributed a considerable amount to the knowledge of this tropical area.

JH/MBO

PRIMARY SOURCES

Coudreau, Octavie. *Voyage au Trombetas, 7 août 1899–25 novembre 1899.* Paris: A. Lahure, 1900.

———. *Voyage au Cuminá, 20 avril 1900–7 septembre 1900.* Paris: A. Lahure, 1903.

———. *Voyage au Rio Curuá, 20 novembre 1900–7 mars 1901.* Paris: A. Lahure, 1903.

———. *Voyage à la Mapuerá, 21 avril 1901–24 décembre 1901.* Paris: A. Lahure, 1903.

———. *Voyage au Maycurú, 5 juin 1902–12 javier 1903.* Paris: A. Lahure, 1903.

STANDARD SOURCES

Mozans; Uglow 1989.

COWAN, EDWINA ABBOTT (1887–?)

U.S. psychologist. Born 6 January 1887 in Chicago, Ill. Married (1915). Three children. Educated University of Illinois (A.B., 1908; A.M., 1909); University of Chicago (Ph.D., 1913). Professional experience: Vassar College, assistant psychologist (1909–1912); Tulane University, instructor (1913–1915); Friends College, associate professor (1927–1940); Wichita Child Guidance Center, director (1930–1941); visiting consultant, social agencies and schools in Kansas (1941–1949); clinical psychologist with doc-

tors Connell, Street, and Kurth (from 1949). Memberships and fellowships: American Psychological Association, fellow; Kansas Psychological Association, member; Midwest Psychological Association, member. Death date unknown.

Edwina Cowan had a peripatetic career. After receiving her doctorate from the University of Chicago, she went to Vassar where she served as assistant psychologist. She then moved to Tulane. Her marriage in 1915 and the subsequent raising of her family may explain the gap in her career until 1927, when she accepted a position as associate professor at Friends College, a Quaker school. Concurrently, she was director of the Wichita Child Guidance Center. She served as a consultant in many schools and social agencies in Kansas, after she gave up her position at Friends and as director of the Center. She spent the last part of her career as a clinical psychologist for a group of physicians.

Her research interests were in child development and behavior, diagnostic tests for children and adolescents, remedial programs for birth-injured children, and personality adjustment.

K M

STANDARD SOURCES
AMS 3–8.

COX, GERTRUDE MARY (1900–1978)

U.S. statistician. Born 13 January 1900 in Dayton, Iowa, to Emmaline (Maddy) and John William Allen Cox. Never married. Educated Perry High School, Perry, Iowa (graduated 1918); Iowa State College, Ames, Iowa (B.S., 1929; M.S., 1931); University of California, Berkeley (1931–1933). Professional experience: Iowa State College, Statistical Laboratory, assistant to George Snedecor (1933–1939); assistant professor (1939); North Carolina State College, Raleigh, N.C., head of the department of experimental statistics (1940–1945); University of North Carolina and North Carolina State College, director of the Institute of Statistics (1945–1960); Research Triangle Institute in Durham, N.C. (1960–1964); consultant to Egypt and Thailand (from 1964). Died 17 October 1978.

Gertrude Mary Cox was a native of Iowa. After spending several years preparing to become a deaconess in the Methodist Episcopal Church, she entered Iowa State College in Ames, Iowa, where she received bachelor's and master's degrees, the latter in statistics under the department of mathematics. She continued her graduate work at the University of California, but did not write a dissertation, for she returned to Iowa State to work in the new statistical laboratory there and to teach statistics as an assistant professor. Her teaching load was heavy, and she did not have time to com-

plete the dissertation. In 1958, Iowa State conferred upon her the honorary degree of doctor of science. On the recommendation of George W. Snedecor, Cox was hired at North Carolina State College as head of experimental statistics. Cox was successful at obtaining grants for the new program. Cox organized an Institute of Statistics, which combined the statistics programs at the University of North Carolina and North Carolina State College. By developing this collaborative venture, they were able to avoid overlap. She also organized a series of work conferences on a variety of topics and sponsored two summer conferences in the mountains of North Carolina. This work established the institute as an international center. Cox believed that the most important function of the institute was to develop strong statistical programs throughout the South. In 1960, she resigned from the university and became director of the Statistics Section of the Research Triangle Institute in Durham, North Carolina, where she remained until 1964. In 1978, she died of leukemia.

Among her numerous honors were the Oliver Max Gardner award (1959) and the distinguished service award of Gamma Sigma Delta (1960). She was a member and president in 1956 of the American Statistical Association. She was one of the founders of the Biometrics Society in 1947 and editor of the *Biometrics Bulletin* and *Biometrics* from 1945 to 1955. She was the president of this organization in 1969–1970 and was elected an honorary member. A member of the International Statistical Institute, she was its treasurer from 1955 to 1961. She was a Fellow of the Institute of Mathematical Statistics and the American Public Health Association, and an honorary Fellow of the Royal Statistical Society. She was also honorary president of the Statistical Society of the Union of South Africa and an honorary member of the Société Adolphe Quetelet of Brussels.

With her background in psychology and statistics, Cox was well qualified to head an institute of statistics. She was excellent in organizing programs. Her research was in a variety of areas, from agriculture to statistical methodology.

JH/MBO

PRIMARY SOURCES
Cox, Gertrude Mary. With R. C. Eckhardt and W. G. Cochran. "The Analysis of Lattice and Triple Lattice Experiments in Corn Varietal Tests." *Iowa Agricultural Experiment Station Research Bulletin* 281 (1940): 1–66.
———. "Enumeration and Construction of Balanced Incomplete Block Configurations." *Annals of Mathematical Statistics* 11 (1940): 72–85.
———. With William G. Cochran. "Designs of Greenhouse Experiments for Statistical Analysis." *Soil Science* 62 (1946): 87–98.

———. "The Function of Designs of Experiments." *Annals of the New York Academy of Science* 52 (1950): 800–807.

———. With W. S. Conner. "Methodology for Estimating Reliability." *Annals of the Institute of Statistical Mathematics* 16 (1964): 55–67.

SECONDARY SOURCES

Anderson, R. L. "My Experience as a Statistician from the Farm to the University." In *The Making of Statisticians,* edited J. Jagi, 129–148. New York: Springer-Verlag, 1982.

Anderson, R. L., et al. "Gertrude M. Cox—A Modern Pioneer in Statistics." *Biometrics* 35 (1979): 3–7.

Yates, Frank. "Obituary: Gertrude Mary Cox (1900–1978)." *Journal of the Royal Statistical Society* 142, series A (1979): 516–517.

STANDARD SOURCES

Grinstein and Campbell (long article, including bibliography, by Maryjo Nichols); *Notable* (article by Loretta Hall).

COX, RACHEL (DUNAWAY) (1904–)

U.S. psychologist. Born 20 January 1904 in Murray, Ky. Married (1928). Two children. Educated University of Texas (A.B., 1925); Columbia University (A.M., 1930); University of Pennsylvania (Ph.D. in educational psychology, 1943). Professional experience: N.Y. Herald Tribune, editorial assistant (1926–1929); West Side YWCA, teacher and director of education (1929–1935); Walter Reed Hospital and American Red Cross, psychiatric social worker (1944); Bryn Mawr College, lecturer in psychology and education (1944–1945), child study institute director (1944–1970), assistant professor of psychology and education (from 1945), professor (1955–1971), emerita professor (from 1971); clinical psychologist, private practice (from 1973). Concurrent positions: Gaskell House, psychologist; Manchester Royal Infirmary, England, psychologist (1972).

Although Rachel Cox had a varied career before she received her doctorate, she spent most of her career after earning the degree at Bryn Mawr College. At Bryn Mawr she was the recipient of the Lindback Award for distinguished teaching. She published numerous journal articles on longitudinal studies of normal adult personality and studies of the teenage clique from ages thirteen to eighteen. She was a member of the American Psychological Association, the National Association of Social Workers, and the Society for Personality Assessment. She had several postdoctoral fellowships and grants.   K M

PRIMARY SOURCES

Cox, Rachel Dunaway. "Counselors and Their Work: A Study of One Hundred Selected Counselors in the Secondary School." Ph.D. diss., University of Pennsylvania, 1943.

———. *Youth into Maturity: A Study of Men and Women in the First Ten Years after College.* New York: Mental Health Materials Center, 1970.

STANDARD SOURCES

AMS 9–13; Debus.

COYLE, ELIZABETH ELEANOR (1904–1995)

U.S. botanist, bacteriologist, and educator. Born 26 August 1904 in Galion, Ohio, to Lulu Winter and Curtis C. Coyle. Never married. Educated Galion High School (1922); College of Wooster (Ohio) (B.S., 1926); Ohio State University (M.A., 1929; Ph.D., 1935). Professional experience: College of Wooster, instructor through Danforth Professor, Department of Biology (1926–1972). Professor emerita (1972–1995). Died 1 January 1995.

Elizabeth Eleanor (Ibby) Coyle was the descendant of a renowned physician, Charles Lester Coyle, who settled in Galion, Ohio, in 1865. She studied algae in Ohio soils for her doctoral dissertation at Ohio State University in 1935 while serving as an instructor at the College of Wooster. Her entire professional career was in the Department of Biology at the College of Wooster. She served as chairperson from 1963 to 1972. She regularly attended summer studies at various biological stations including the Rocky Mountain Biological Station and the Marine Biological Laboratories at Woods Hole, Mass. Coyle also studied at Columbia University, the University of Hawaii, and Cornell University during summer months, and received a National Science Foundation award for this purpose. Another NSF grant allowed her to study the ecology of algae at the Pymatuning Laboratory of Ecology, Linesville, Pennsylvania, under the auspices of the University of Pittsburgh.

Among Coyle's honors were her election to Phi Beta Kappa, serving as a secretary of their local branch 1943–1973 and as president in 1972 of the triennial council of Phi Beta Kapa. She was an enthusiastic amateur actress throughout her life, and was also active in the Presbyterian church, and various alumnae and faculty clubs, and cofounded the Faculty Club. She also served as a women's dormitory resident for ten years and as an advisor for women students. She joined the Ohio Academy of Sciences in 1927 and was affiliated with the Plant Sciences Section. She died 1 January 1995 at the Wooster Community Hospital, Wooster, Ohio.
                                                     J H / M B O

PRIMARY SOURCES

Coyle, Elizabeth Eleanor. "Algae of Some Ohio Soils." Ph.D. diss., Ohio State University, 1935.

SECONDARY SOURCES

Burk, William R. "Elizabeth Eleanor Coyle (1904–1995)." *Bulletin of the Ohio Academy of Sciences* 95 (1995): 344.

CRAM, ELOISE BLAINE (1896–1957)

U.S. parasitologist. Born 11 June 1896 in Davenport, Iowa, to Mabel (La Venture) and Ralph Warren Cram. Educated University of Chicago (B.S., 1918); George Washington University (M.A., 1922 in parisitology; Ph.D., 1925). Professional experience: Armour & Co., Chicago, bacteriologist (1918–1919); USDA Bureau of Animal Industry, junior zoologist (1920–1924), assistant zoologist (1924–1926), associate zoologist (1926–1929), zoologist (1929–1936); U.S. Public Health Service; National Institutes of Health; Laboratory of Tropical Diseases, Stream Pollution Laboratory, senior zoologist (1936–1956). Honors and memberships: Helminthological Society of Washington, corresponding secretary (1921–1926), president (1927). American Society of Parasitologists council member (1934–1937), president (1956). Died 9 February 1957 in San Diego, Calif.

Eloise Cram was a parasitologist who published more than eighty papers in her field. She studied biology at the University of Chicago and took her first job as a bacteriologist at the meat packing firm of Armour in Chicago. She met B. H. Ransom from the USDA Division of Animal Industry while he was carrying out an investigation of swine ascarids (nonsegmented round worms); he invited her to join his group. Beginning as an apprentice scientist, Cram published her first paper with Ransom the following year on the life history of Ascaris.

In Washington, Cram also began to study for her master's and then her doctorate in parasitology at George Washington University. For sixteen years, she investigated poultry and farm animal parasites. She became an officer and then president of the Helminthological Society of Washington.

As part of a major expansion of the National Institutes of Health, Cram was invited in 1936 to head the Laboratory of Tropical Diseases, and began to investigate human parasites, and then in the forties, to study stream pollution. By the mid-fifties, she was elected president of the American Parasitological Society, and in spite of growing ill health, she gave a memorable and amusing talk on the history and personalities of the American parasitologists. She died six months later in San Diego.

Cram was remembered for a charming personality and the ability to bring enormous energy to her work while remaining considerate of her fellow workers. She was noted for her capacity to overcome difficulties in research and to bring a vigorous persistence to solving perplexing problems.

JH/MBO

PRIMARY SOURCES

Cram, E. B. With B. H. Ransom. "The Course of Micration of Ascaris Larvae." *American Journal of Tropical Medicine* 1 (1921): 129–159.

———. "A New Nematode, *Cylindropharynx ornata*, from the Zebra, with Keys to Related Nematode Parasites of the *Equidae*. *Journal of Agricultural Research* (Washington) 28 (1924): 661–672.

———. "*Cooperia bisonis*, a New Nematode from the Buffalo." *Journal of Agricultural Research* (Washington) 30 (1925): 977–983.

SECONDARY SOURCES

Schwartz, Benjamin. "Eloise Blaine Cram." *Proceedings of the Helminthological Society* 24 (1957): 116–117.

Material in the Schlesinger files, *NAW* (M) unused.

STANDARD SOURCES

AMS 5–8, B 9; Rossiter 1982.

CRAMER, CATHERINE GERTRUDE DU TERTRE SCHRADERS (1665–1746?)

Dutch midwife. Born 1665 in Friesland. Father a pastor. Married (1) Ernst Willem Cramer (d. 1692); (2) Thomas Hight (he died in 1721). Educated by Hendrik van Deventer and Abraham Cyprianus. Professional experience: midwife. Died 1746(?).

Catherine Schraders was married at a young age to a widower with six children. Ernst Willem Cramer was a surgeon and her husband's profession afforded Catherine an opportunity to study obstetrics with two of the best-known teachers in Holland, Hendrik Van Deventer and Abraham Cyprianus. Cyprianus wrote a well-respected book on tubal pregnancies published in 1700. After the death of her husband, Cramer developed a large practice in midwifery. She remarried in 1713, this time to a gold and silversmith. Her second husband died in 1721 and she resumed her practice. She reported that in 1728, when she was seventy-three years old, she cared for seventy-three confinements for which she received 225 gulden plus "something for medicines." She died at the age of ninety-one. During the time of her practice, she had kept detailed records on her patients. She described over four thousand births, including sixty-four pairs of twins and three sets of triplets. This diary was given to the Netherland Medical Association in 1865 and published in 1926.

JH/MBO

PRIMARY SOURCES

Cramer, Catherine. *Het Dagboek van Vrouw Schraders, Een Bijdrage tot de Geschiedenis der Verloskunde in de 17de en 18de Eeuw.* Amsterdam: Door Dr. B.W. Th. Nuyens, arts te

Amsterdam. Overgedrukt uit het Nederl. Tijdschrift voor Geneeskunde, 70th year, No. 18, 1926.

SECONDARY SOURCES
Hurd-Mead 1938.

CRANDALL, ELLA PHILLIPS (1871–1938)

U.S. public health nurse. Born 16 September 1871 in Wellsville, N.Y., to Alice (Phillips) and Herbert A. Crandall. Educated Dayton, Ohio, public schools (graduated high school 1890); Philadelphia General Hospital School of Nursing (graduated two-year course, 1897); New York School of Philanthropy (1909–?). Professional experience: Miami Valley Hospital, Dayton, Ohio, assistant superintendent and first director of school of nursing (1899–1909?); Henry Street Visiting Nurse Service, New York City (1909–1910); Columbia University Teachers College, faculty, graduate nurses' program (1910–1912); National Organization for Public Health Nursing, executive secretary (1912–1920); Committee to Study Community Organization for Self Support for Health Work for Women and Young Children, executive secretary (1921–1922); New York Association for Improving the Condition of the Poor, director (1922); American Child Health Association, associate directory (1922–1925); Payne Fund, executive secretary (1925–1938). Died 24 October 1938 in New York City from pneumonia.

After beginning her career as an administrator in a school of nursing, Ella Crandall became interested in caring for the sick in their homes. This preoccupation led her to become a supervisor in the Henry Street Visiting Nurse Service in New York City founded by LILLIAN WALD, while at the same time enrolling in courses at the New York School of Philanthropy. Crandall joined the faculty at Columbia University Teachers College in the graduate nurses department under MARY ADELAIDE NUTTING and helped to develop courses in public health nursing, a new field in which she soon became a leader. During her time at Columbia, Crandall developed courses in district nursing and health protection. She worked in numerous organizations involved in public health considerations. She became a leading member of a special commission established by the American Nurses Association and the Society of Superintendents of Training Schools for Nurses. Out of the work of this commission, a new organization, the National Organization for Public Health Nursing, was born in 1912, with Crandall as the executive secretary. The purpose of this new organization was to establish professional standards for public health nurses and to improve the quality of their education. Before it could act on this goal, the organization had to make contact with the widely dispersed public health nurses in an attempt to build community. Crandall traveled extensively in her position. She remained with this organization until resigning in 1920. She

had concurrent positions during World War I. Crandall met Frances Payne Bolton, a Cleveland philanthropist who later became a Congresswoman, through her work with the Public Health Nursing organization. Bolton established the Payne Fund to sponsor research and experimentation in education and named Crandall as executive secretary.   JH/MBO

SECONDARY SOURCES
American Journal of Nursing 38 (December 1938): 1406–1409. Obituary notice includes photograph.
Brainard, Annie M. *The Evolution of Public Health Nursing.* Philadelphia: W. B. Saunders Co., 1922.
Gardner, Mary S. *Public Health Nursing.* New York: Macmillan, 1916.

STANDARD SOURCES
NAW (long article by Alma E. Gault).

CRANE, AGNES (1852–?)

British paleontologist and natural historian. Born 1852 in Brighton.

Agnes Crane published on topics in natural history and paleontology from 1877 to 1895. She is important from the standpoint of local history.   JH/MBO

PRIMARY SOURCES
Crane, Agnes. "New Classifications of the Brachiopoda." *Geological Magazine* 10 (1893): 318–323.
———. "The Generic Evolution of the Paleozoic Brachiopoda." *Science* 21, no. 523 (1893): 72–74.

SECONDARY SOURCES
"Crane, Agnes." *British Biographical Archive,* no. 278 (1984). First published in *Who's Who in Kent, Surrey and Sussex, Cox's County Series.* London: Cox, 1911.

STANDARD SOURCES
Creese and Creese.

CRANE, JOCELYN (1909–)

U.S. zoologist. Born 11 June 1909 in St. Louis, Mo. Educated University School for Girls, Chicago (graduated 1926); Smith College (A.B., 1930; honorary M.Sc., 1947). Professional experience: New York Zoological Society, tropical research, from research zoologist to assistant department director (from 1930). Honors and memberships: Society of Woman Geographers; New York Academy of Systematics and Ecology of Deep-Sea Fishes.

Jocelyn Crane was born in St. Louis and had a very peripatetic childhood. Her family moved from St. Louis when she was six, and then moved to eleven different schools all over the United States during her first six grades. When she was in the seventh grade, she was enrolled in the University School for Girls in Chicago. Her fragmented school life did not seem to affect her skills, and at this school she did so well after her first year that the teachers recommended that she skip the eighth grade.

From earliest childhood, Crane knew that she wanted to work with small animals. She decided that she wanted to attend Smith College and major in zoology. She graduated Phi Beta Kappa with highest honors in 1930. After graduation she went to New York City, where she got a job at the Tropical Research Department of the New York Zoological Society. Before she got the job she worked hard to convince William Beebe that she could do the work and she recalled that it took her eighteen months to do so. Her first job took her to the society's Research Laboratories at Nonsuch Island, Bermuda, where Beebe was using his new bathysphere to explore the ocean's depths. From 1930 to 1940, she accompanied Beebe on his explorations and developed a keen interest in fish. She made descents with Beebe in the bathysphere. She published four reports with Beebe on deep sea fishes of Bermuda. She became very interested in animal behavior.

Crane decided not to work on a doctoral degree because she had become so fascinated with small animal behavior that she wanted to do her own research. She stated that she had already done everything that she would be doing in a university laboratory. This decision worked well for her, because she had a position with the Zoological Society. She recognized, however, that the lack of a doctorate might have kept her from getting a different job. She traveled to Kurdistan, where she studied the behavior of various animals. She then went to the department's field station in the Gulf of California and studied crabs, on which she published papers. In 1942, the Tropical Research Department established a temporary field station near Caripito, Venezuela, where Crane studied crabs. She studied the purpose of various coloration in butterflies in the Andes and later in Trinidad. She concluded that color sometimes is used to attract mates. After the end of World War II, Crane returned to Asia and visited the South Pacific and Africa. She received a National Science Foundation grant in the 1950s that made it possible for her to spend a third of her time each year for five years making a worldwide study of Ocypodid crabs.   JH/MBO

PRIMARY SOURCES

Crane, Jocelyn. With William Beebe. *Deep Sea Fishes of the Bermuda Oceanographic Expeditions: Family Melanostomiatidae.* New York: New York Zoological Society, 1939.

———. *Fiddler Crabs of the World.* Princeton, N.J.: Princeton University Press, 1975.

STANDARD SOURCES
AMS B 9, P&B 10–11; Ireland; Yost.

CRANWELL, LUCY MAY (1907–)

New Zealand palynologist. Born 7 August 1907. Married Watson Smith. Educated University of London (M.Sc., D.Sc.); Sweden (1935–1936). Professional experience: Hawaii (1938); University of Arizona (1961–).

Lucy Cranwell's early work was on living pollen and on microfossil assemblages from Antarctica and Chile. She then studied with von Post in Sweden, working on New Zealand pollen diagrams. These diagrams were the first to be produced for the Australasian Quaternary. She worked briefly in Hawaii and then returned to New Zealand. In 1944 she settled in Arizona and began working at the University of Arizona in 1961. She did important research on the distribution of fossil *Nothofagus* in the Pacific region and Antarctica.

JH/MBO

SECONDARY SOURCES

Srivastava, Satish K. "Dr. Lucy M. Cranwell, M.Sc., D.Sc., F.L.S. (London), F.G.S." Fourth International Palynological Conference, Lucknow (1976–1977), *Proceedings* 2 (1980): 392–393.

STANDARD SOURCES
Sarjeant; Hunt Institute (portrait).

CREMER, ERIKA (1900–1996)

German/Austrian physical chemist. Born 20 May 1900 in Munich to Elsbeth (Rothmund) and Professor Max Cremer. Educated high school, Berlin (graduated 1921); University of Berlin (Ph.D. in physical chemistry magna cum laude, 1927; Habilitation (1938). Professional experience: Kaiser Wilhelm Institut für Physikalische Chemie; University of Freiburg, Institut für Physikalische Chemie, scholarship to study in the laboratory of Nobel Laureate, Georg de Hevesy; Berlin, Haber's Institut, studied with Michael Polanyi (until 1933); Kaiser Wilhelm Institut für Chemie in Berlin-Dahlem (1937); University of Innsbruck, Austria, dozent (1940–1971); Physical Chemistry Institute, director (1945); professor (1951). Honors and memberships: Wilhelm Exner Medal (1958); Technical University of Vienna, Johann Josef Ritter von Precht Medal; Austrian Academy of Sciences, Erwin Schrödinger Award (1970); M.S. Tswett Chromatography Award (1974); U.S.S.R. Academy of Sciences, Commemorative M.S. Tswett Medal (1978); Technical University of Berlin (honorary degree); Austrian Academy of Sciences, corresponding membership; Austrian Republic, first-class cross of the Austrian Order for Science and Art. Died 1996.

Erika Cremer's early life was influenced by two world wars. One of the few women to study chemistry at the University of Berlin, Cremer attended lectures by some of the most important scientists of the time: Nobel laureates Fritz Haber (laureate 1918); Walther H. Nernst (laureate 1920); Max von Laue (laureate 1914); Max Planck (laureate 1918); and Albert Einstein (laureate 1921). Cremer completed her doctoral degree, magna cum laude, and then went on to do research and study at a series of laboratories. She studied with Michael Polanyi at Haber's Institut, but Hitler dissolved the institute in 1933, leaving Cremer both unemployed and without research space until 1937, when she joined Nobel laureate Otto Hahn at the Kaiser Wilhelm Institut. She worked at two unpaid positions at three different Kaiser Wilhelm Institutes between 1930 and 1940. She received her Habilitation—inauguration into an academic career after the completion of a second thesis—from the University of Berlin in 1938 and could have expected an academic position. German universities, however, simply did not hire women, and she was told that her academic career was at an end. And so it probably would have been if it had not been for World War II and the shortage of available males it created. Thus the University of Innsbruck hired her, assuming that she would relinquish her job when the men returned from the war.

At Innsbruck, she developed the instrumentation and mathematical theories that made her a pioneer in gas chromatography. The war again interfered, this time not to her benefit. In November 1944, she sent a short publication explaining the new process to *Naturwissenschaften,* noting that the experimental results would be published subsequently. An air raid damaged her laboratory and her experimental facilities were disrupted. She received proofs of the chromatography article from the publisher, corrected, and then returned them. This issue of the journal was never printed and the proofs, plates, and manuscripts were lost. *Chromatographia* published a paper based on Cremer's copy of the corrected proofs thirty years later.

Cremer's German colleagues were stingy in their praise of her work, and her work on gas chromatography was virtually ignored. Only much later, when three men, Anthony Trafford James and Archer John Porter Martin in London and J. Janak in Czechoslovakia, reported on the technique of gas chromatography, was the world interested.

Cremer's earliest research revolved around her doctoral thesis, which she did under Max Bodenstein's supervision. Her conclusion that the kinetics of chloro-hydrogen reactions depended on a chain-type mechanism was an original concept. Bodenstein was an unusual man, who allowed Cremer to publish under her own name alone. Her other research projects were on a variety of subjects. She was

interested in the decomposition of alcohols, using rare earths and other trivalent oxide catalysts. Working with Michael Polanyi on achieving a better understanding of atomic-level reactions, she investigated the transformation of ortho- to para-hydrogen in solid hydrogen. Furthermore, she also demonstrated that solid oxygen could serve as a catalyst in ortho-para transformations.

While she was working on adsorption at Haber's Institut für Chemie and Debye's Institut für Physik, Cremer executed the groundwork that led to her development of gas chromatography. One of her students, using Cremer's theoretical assumptions, built the first gas chromatograph. She and her students continued to develop this method throughout the 1950s and 1960s. Unfortunately, when one reads histories of the development of gas chromatography, Cremer's name is often left out. JH/MBO

PRIMARY SOURCES
Cremer, Erika. "Eine Prüfung der 'Tunneltheorie' der heterogenen Katalyse am Beispiel der Hydrierung von Styrol." *Zeitschrift für Physikalische Chemie* B19 (1932): 443–450.
———. "Adsorption an Oberflachen mit eingefrorenem thermischen Gleichgewicht der aktiven Stellen." *Angewandte Chemie* 51 (1938): 834–835.
———. With R. Müller. "Separation and Determination of Small Quantities of Gases by Chromatography." *Mikrochemie/Mikrochemie Acta* 36/37 (1951): 553–560.
———. With F. Deutscher, P. Fill, et al. "Trennung und Nachweis im Subnanogrammbereich durch Dünnfilm-Chromatographie an Festen Oberflachen." *Journal of Chromatography* 48 (1970): 132–142.

SECONDARY SOURCES
Bobleter, O. "Professor Erika Cremer—A Pioneer in Gas Chromatography." *Chromatographia* 30 (1990): 471–476.
Vogt, Annette. "The Kaiser-Wilhelm-Gesellschaft and the Career Chances for Female Scientists Between 1911 and 1945." Paper for the International Congress for the History of Science, Liège, Belgium, 1997.

STANDARD SOURCES
Debus; Grinstein 1993 (article by Jane A. Miller); Turkevich and Turkevich; *Who's Who of Women.*

CRESPIN, IRENE (1896–1980)

Australian paleontologist. Born 11 November 1896 in Melbourne. Educated University of Melbourne. Professional experience: National Museum, Melbourne, assistant paleontologist (1927–1935); Commonwealth paleontologist (1935–1975). Died 2 January 1980 in Canberra.

Irene Crespin was born and educated in Melbourne. Her first professional position was as assistant palaeontologist to Frederick Chapman of the National Museum in Melbourne. When Chapman died, she succeeded him as commonwealth paleontologist. She moved from Melbourne to Canberra, where she was the only professional micropaleontologist on the Australian mainland. During her time in Canberra, two disastrous fires destroyed thousands of slides and a newly completed manuscript of a catalogue of part of Chapman's Library due for publication in the United States.

Crespin was especially interested in the Tertiary foraminifera, especially the larger ones. These foraminiferans were used at that time by the Dutch micropaleontologists in the Indo-Pacific region for stratigraphic purposes. She also worked with Permian and Cretaceous foraminifera, useful as predictors in the search for oil, coal, and water. When she was working on the larger foraminifera of Papua-New Guinea, western Australia, and Victoria, she made significant contributions to the taxonomy and paleogeography of the Great Australian Basin and of the Permian foraminifera of Australia. She also described the first conodont and the first Devonian foraminifera from Australia. Working under relatively primitive conditions with an obsolete used binocular microscope and other equally antiquated equipment (if any), she still studied thousands of samples and published seventy titles in her own name and another twenty-three with colleagues.

Crespin was involved in a number of scientific societies and received some significant honors. She was a member (and president, 1957) of the Royal Society of Australia (later the Royal Society of Canberra). She was honorary secretary for the Territories Branch of the Geological Society of Australia, and was elected chairman of the Canberra Branch in 1957. She was named an honorary member of this society in 1964. Her other honors include the Coronation Medal (1953) and the Clarke Medal by the Royal Society of New South Wales. She was awarded the Royal Microscopic Society of London's Honorary Fellowship in 1960. In 1960 the University of Melbourne conferred upon her the degree of Doctor of Science *honoris causa.*   CK

PRIMARY SOURCES

Crespin, Irene. "The Larger Foraminifera of the Lower Miocene of Victoria." *Australian Bureau of Mineral Resources Bulletin* 3 (1936): 3–15.

———. "The Genus *Cycloclypeus* in Victoria." *Proceedings of the Royal Society of Victoria* 53, no. 2, n.s. (1941): 301–314.

———. "The Genus *Lepidocyclina* in Victoria." *Proceedings of the Royal Society of Victoria* 55, no. 2 (1943): 157–180.

———. "Some Lower Cretaceous Foraminifera from Bores in the Great Artesian Basin. Northern New South Wales."

Journal of the Proceedings of the Royal Society of New South Wales 78 (1944): 17–23.

———. "Australian Tertiary Microfaunas and their Relationships to Assemblages Elsewhere in the Pacific Region." *Journal of Paleontology* 24 (1950): 421–429.

———. "Some Recent Foraminifera from Vestfold Hills, Antarctica." *Science Reports, Tohoku University* ser. 3, *Mineralogy, Petrology, and Economic Geology* 4 (1960): 19–31.

———. "Recollections on the Growth of Commonwealth Interest in the Geological Sciences." *Records of the Australian Academy of Science* 2, no. 2 (1972): 29–36.

———. "Catalogue of Additional Type and Figured Specimens Other Than Protista in the Commonwealth Palaeontological Collections, Canberra." *Report, Bureau of Mineral Resources, Geology and Geophysics (Australia)*, no. 160 (1974).

SECONDARY SOURCES

"Irene Crespin (1896–1980)." *Micropalaeontology* 27, no. 1 (1981): 94–98. Includes portrait and bibliography.

STANDARD SOURCES

Sarjeant.

CROCKER, LUCRETIA (1829–1886)

U.S. educator and supervisor in natural history. Born 31 December 1829 in Barnstable, Mass., to Lydia E. (Farris) and Henry Crocker. Never married. Educated at the institution that would become the State Normal School at Framingham, Mass. (graduated 1850); attended lectures of Louis Agassiz. Professional experience: normal school teacher (1850–1854); Antioch College, teacher (1857–1859). Honors and memberships: Boston Society of Natural History (one of the first women admitted); American Association for the Advancement of Science. Died 9 October 1886 in Boston, Mass.

Lucretia Crocker grew up in Barnstable and later Boston, Massachusetts, where her father worked in the insurance business. She proved an exceptional student at the pioneering Normal School for Girls in West Newton (later the State Normal School in Framingham), and was asked to stay on after her graduation in 1850 to instruct in geography, mathematics, and the natural sciences. She became acquainted with Harvard naturalist Louis Agassiz and invited him to lecture in her classes. They shared many ideas about teaching nature to children using actual specimens. He allowed her to attend his lectures at Harvard and encouraged her independent study of natural history. She taught astronomy and mathematics for two years at the coeducational Antioch College under Horace Mann before returning to Boston and becoming involved in a variety of educational and reform activities. An apparently self-contained person of quiet demeanor,

Crocker was by all accounts highly influential in educational reform. As a teacher she was exceptional in her scientific demonstrations and her apparent capacity to reach all pupils in class. Her leadership among educators drew on organizational skills, clearly stated goals, and an evident determination to reach students.

As a teacher of teachers in science, Crocker lectured, organized advanced training courses, and wrote textbooks and teaching aids. With Mary L. Hall, she produced a textbook on geography entitled *Our World* (1864) and later, she wrote *Methods of Teaching Geography: Notes on Lessons* (1883) in order to provide even more thorough advice on ways to teach current scientific theories. One year she joined with ELLEN SWALLOW RICHARDS to provide model lectures in twelve local public schools entitled "First Lessons in Minerals." Richards recalled that the practical aspects of the instruction made the lessons successful models of elementary science teaching. Crocker also lectured directly to teachers about natural history subjects.

Some of Crocker's ideas about teaching science in the schools were produced in guidebooks and other materials developed for the Museum of the Boston Society of Natural History. Working with the museum director, Alpheus Hyatt, and local philanthropic women, she extended and enhanced a museum program called the Teachers' School of Science. It provided evening and Saturday classes for teachers in the museum; taught them the most current scientific theories in zoology, geology, geography, and other aspects of the natural sciences; and used museum objects as part of the instruction. Elected among the first group of women on the Boston School Committee, Crocker was soon appointed to supervise the teaching of natural history in the schools. Hyatt acknowledged that she not only helped coordinate the museum programs with the public schools but was also present every Saturday for fourteen years to insure that the activities went well.

Crocker encouraged the informal study of science, organizing the science department of the Society to Encourage Studies at Home, a correspondence school project carried on by the Women's Educational Association of Boston during the 1870s and 1880s. Although she did not publish any scientific papers, Crocker was well informed about science through self study, her attendance in Agassiz's classes, and her participation in the Boston museum's lectures and educational activities. Former students who became active in science noted her capacity to formulate research problems, devise methods for research, and help others analyze their results.

Crocker had many other interests that involved her in the post–Civil War activism of Boston. She was a member in the Unitarian church and helped to organize their network of Sunday school libraries for children. She was on the board of supervisors of the pioneering Horace Mann School for

Deaf-Mutes run by Sarah Fuller. She joined Ednah Dow Cheney as an active member of the New England Freedman's Aid Society and went herself to visit schools for emancipated slaves in the South in 1869. She ran twice for the Boston School Committee, defying conventions that presumed women should not hold public office.

Crocker was herself an active learner as well as teacher, inspiring others by her curiosity and drive to understand, and always persuaded of the importance of understanding science. Active until near the end of her life, she was remembered as an educational leader and honored by numerous memorial statements from former pupils, colleagues in reform, and scientists like Richards and Hyatt. There are virtually no manuscript records of Crocker's work, presumably because she exercised her influence in personal and immediate ways that did not require formal correspondence. There is also relatively little secondary material, with most significant sources being memorials.   SGK

SECONDARY SOURCES

Cheney, Ednah Dow. *Memoirs of Lucretia Crocker and Abby W. May.* Privately printed, 1883. A compilation of memorials for Crocker that provide personal insight. They have only limited biographical information and contain some errors in memory about specific times and events.

Green, Norma Kidd. *A Forgotten Chapter in American Education: Jane Andrews of Newburyport.* Framingham, Ma.: Alumni Association of the State College at Framingham, 1961. Some limited references relating to Crocker's influence on the student Jane Andrews.

Zirngiebel, Frances. "Teachers' School of Science." *Appleton's Popular Science Monthly* 55 (1899): 451–465; 640–652. A useful discussion that documents and may underestimate Crocker's actual work within the Boston Museum of Natural History's program for teachers.

STANDARD SOURCES

ANB; NAW (long article by Norma Kidd Green).

CROLL, HILDA M. (1895–?)

U.S. physiological chemist. Born 31 August 1895 in Lebanon, Pa. Educated University of Illinois (A.B., 1916; A.M., 1917); Yale University (Ph.D., 1925). Professional experience: Woman's Medical College, Chicago (1917–1920); University of Illinois, assistant professor of home economics (from 1925). Death date unknown.

Hilda Croll was awarded her doctoral degree from Yale University. She became an assistant professor at the University of Illinois in 1925. Croll is mentioned in only the fourth edition of *AMS*. Perhaps she married and her additional work is under her married name, or she married and gave up scientific work. She was a member of the Society for Experimental Biology, the Home Economics Association, and the Dietetic Association. She used her chemistry to do research in nutrition, vitamin B in cereal grains, carbohydrate metabolism and diabetic diets, anemia, and intestinal putrefaction.

JH/MBO

STANDARD SOURCES
AMS 4.

CROSBIE, MAY (1880?–1960s)

Irish horticulturalist. Educated Royal Botanic Gardens Glasnevin, student gardener. Professional experience: Robertson's Bulb Farm, manager (1916); Trinity College, Dublin, Botanic Gardens, assistant curator.

It was said of May Crosbie that she was "a most able gardener, if a[n] eccentric and unusual woman" (Desmond). She contributed to *Irish Gardening* and the *Irish Naturalist*.

SECONDARY SOURCES
Nelson, E. C., and E. M. McCracken. *Brightest Jewel: A History of the National Botanic Gardens, Glasnevin, Dublin.* Kilkenny: Boethius, 1987: 202–203.

STANDARD SOURCES
Desmond.

CROSBY, ELIZABETH CAROLINE (1888–1983)

U.S. anatomist. Born 25 October 1888 in Petersburg, Mich., to Frances Kreps and Lewis Frederick Crosby. Never married. Educated Adrian College, Adrian, Mich. (B.S., 1910); University of Chicago (Ph.D., 1915). Professional experience: Petersburg, Mich., Superintendent of Schools (1918–1920); University of Michigan Medical School, instructor (1920–1926); assistant professor (1926–1929), associate professor (1929–1936), professor (1936–1958), professor emerita (1958–1983). Died 28 July 1983.

A native of Michigan, Elizabeth Crosby began her college education there, where she earned a bachelor's degree in mathematics. When she expressed an interest in graduate studies, her mathematics teacher at Adrian College introduced her to C. Judson Herrick of the University of Chicago. Herrick allowed her to take his basic medical anatomy course and his neuroanatomy course at the same time. After she finished her doctorate, Crosby returned to Petersburg, Michigan, to care for her mother. At this time, her career took an unexpected turn; she became a teacher, principal,

and superintendent in the local high school. It was not until her mother died in 1918 that she began to think about her career as an anatomist. She obtained a junior instructorship at the University of Michigan, where she spent her entire academic career. Although she never married, she adopted an eleven-year-old Scots girl, Kathleen. A second girl, Susan McCotter, came to live with them in 1944. She educated both girls. Commitment to her profession and to her girls did not keep Crosby from the literature she loved, especially detective stories and poetry. When she was forced to retire at age sixty-nine, Crosby's friends and colleagues were admonished not to mention her retirement at the party given in her honor. They honored her with a memorial volume in the *Journal of Comparative Neurology*, which contained thirteen research papers from students she had trained. An apparently frail person, Crosby remained productive throughout her ninety-four years. She died in 1983.

Crosby had a heavy teaching load and was paid less than her male colleagues. She seems to have been a work-intoxicated woman, preferring research, advising students, and teaching to travel and other ancillary activities. Not a specialist in a particular part of the nervous system of a particular taxonomic group as were many of her professional colleagues, Crosby's knowledge included the complete neuroanatomy of all members of the subphylum Vertebrata. One of her major interests was in the comparative neuroanatomy of the mammalian midbrain, and she published numerous papers on this subject.

Her clinical and experimental approach to neuroanatomical methodology was sometimes controversial. She coauthored a textbook meant for medical students and graduate students in anatomy in 1962. Crosby's contributions were recognized in the various awards and honorary degrees that she received.

JH/MBO

PRIMARY SOURCES
Crosby, Elizabeth. "The Forebrain of Alligator Mississippiensis." *Journal of Comparative Neurology* 27, no. 3 (1917). Ph.D. dissertation, University of Chicago, 1915.
———. With C. U. Ariens Kappers and G. Carl Huber. *The Comparative Anatomy of the Nervous System of Vertebrates, Including Man.* 2 vols. New York: Macmillan, 1936.
———. With Tryphena Hymphrey and Edward W. Lauer. *Correlative Anatomy of the Nervous System.* New York: Macmillan, 1962.
———, ed. With H. N. Schnitzlien. *Comparative Correlative Neuroanatomy of the Vertebrate Telencephalon.* New York: Macmillan, 1982.

SECONDARY SOURCES
Burns, Scott M. "Elizabeth C. Crosby: A Biography." *Alabama Journal of Medical Sciences* 22 (1985): 317–323.

Herrick, C. Judson. "Elizabeth C. Crosby." *Journal of Comparative Neurology* 112 (1959): 13–17.

Woodburne, Russell T. "Elizabeth Caroline Crosby, 1888–1983." *Anatomical Record* 210 (September 1984): 175–177.

STANDARD SOURCES

AMS 5–8, B 9, P&B 10–12; Debus; *Notable* (article by Jillo Carpenter); Rossiter 1982; Shearer and Shearer 1996.

CROSFIELD, MARGARET CHORLEY (1859–1952)

British stratigrapher and botanist. Born 7 September 1859 in Reigate. Never married. Educated The Mount School, York; Newnham College, Cambridge (1879–1880; 1890–1893; no Tripos). Died 13 October 1952 in Reigate.

Margaret Crosfield made her home in Reigate for ninety-three years. Although she attended Newnham College, her course was interrupted because of ill health. When she returned in 1890, she read only geology. Crosfield was the first woman to be elected a Fellow of the Geological Society (1919). She was also a member of the Palaeontolographical Society (1907–1932) and served on its council several times. She regularly attended the meetings of the British Association for the Advancement of Science. In addition to her geology, Crosfield contributed to the schools of Reigate through serving on the Reigate Education Committee.

At Newnham, she met Margaret Frances Skeat (later Mrs. H. Woods), with whom she surveyed two areas in Wales and published the results. With another collaborator, Mary Sophia Johnston, she studied the Wenlock Limestone of Shropshire. JH/MBO

PRIMARY SOURCES

Crosfield, Margaret Chorley. With Margaret Frances Skeat. "On the Geology of the Neighbourhood of Carmarthen." *Quarterly Journal of the Geological Society of London* 52 (August 1896): 523–541.

———. With Mary Sophia Johnston. "A Study of Ballstone and the Associated Beds in the Wenlock Limestone of Shropshire." *Proceedings of the Geologists' Society* 25 (1914): 193–228.

SECONDARY SOURCES

Johnston, M. S. "Margaret Chorley Crosfield." *Proceedings of the Geologists' Association* 64, no. 1 (1953): 62–63.

STANDARD SOURCES

Newnham, vol. 1.

CSEPREGHYNÉ-MEZNERICS, ILONA (1906–1977)

Hungarian stratigrapher and invertebrate paleontologist. Born Ilona Meznerics, 25 May 1906 in Szabadka, Hungary (today, Subotica, Yugoslavia). Married Dr. Béla Csepreghyné (1945). Educated Szabadka, grade school and first classes of secondary school; Gymnasium for Girls in Budapest (graduated with honors, 1924); University of Budapest, Faculty of Philosophy (high school teacher's diploma in chemistry and physics, 1929); (Ph.D., cum laude, 1930). Professional positions: Vienna, Naturhistorisches Museum, paleontology department (1931–1933); Budapest, high school teacher (1935–1940); Hungarian National Museum of Natural History, Budapest, Geology-Paleontology section, research worker (1940–1948), curator (1948–1951), head of Geology-Paleontology department (1951–1970); State Geological Institute (1971–1973). Retired 1973. Died 14 January 1977 in Budapest, Hungary.

Ilona Meznerics was born in what was at the time Hungary; it later became a part of Yugoslavia. She received her early education in Szabadka, but her family moved to Budapest for her gymnasium education. She graduated from a high school for girls with honors and then attended the University of Budapest, where she studied first chemistry and physics and then geology. As she became more advanced in her studies, she became especially interested in paleontology; she received her doctorate in geology with a focus on paleontology. Her dissertation was entitled "Young Tertiary Features in the [Hungarian] Region Uny-Timnye."

Meznerics received a state stipend (continued as a stipend from a private foundation) to work for three years at the Natural History Museum in Vienna. During this time, she worked in the paleontology department under the direction of F. X. Schaffer, head of the department, and J. von Pia and F. Trauth. She shared an office with Fritz Kautoky, and found his advice very helpful. When she returned to Hungary, she took a job teaching high school. After five years, she finally returned to museum work. She began as a research worker at the Hungarian National Museum; after eight years, she was promoted to Curator. In 1951, she became head of the geology-paleontology department of the museum, where she remained until 1970. In addition to her administrative duties, she was well known for her successful exhibition "The Evolution of Life."

Csepreghyné-Meznerics's main research work was on Tertiary mollusca in several regions of Hungary and Austria. She later worked on Miocene forms, and made a major contribution on Pectinids. Her paper designating the importance of Pectinids for stratigraphy was published in the *Memoirs of the French Geological Society.*

Ilona Csepreghyné-Meznerics continued working after her retirement in 1973. Her last work, the revised volume of the *Lexique stratigraphique,* with her data from Hungary, was not quite completed at her death. She received a number of acknowledgments and awards for her organizational and administrative activities as well as for her scientific work. She became an honorary member of the Hungarian Geological Society and received the coveted title Doctor of Sciences, corresponding to a Soviet system of academic grades, forced onto the Hungarian tradition. During her career, she published at least fifty-three works.   JH/MBO

PRIMARY SOURCES

Csepreghyné-Meznerics, Ilona. "Felhasznált Irodalom." *Az Uny-Tinnye Vidéki környékének Fiatal Harmadkorú üledékek Földtani És Öslenytani Viszonyai. (Bölcsészetdoktori értekezés).* Budapest: Sárkány-nyomda Részvénytársaság, 1930. Includes a bibliography of her works.

———. "Paläontologische Seltenheiten in der Fauna von Szob." *Annals of the National Museum of Hungary.* (1952): 225–231.

———. "La faune tortonienne inférieure des gisements tufiques de la Montagne de Bükk." *Gastropodes: I. Egri Múzeum Évkönyve* 7, kötet (Eger 1969).

SECONDARY SOURCES

Bogsch, Lázló. "Csepreghyné Meznerics, Ilona emlékézete." *Földt. Közl* 107 (1977): 275–281.

Nagy, I. Z. "In Memoriam. Dr. Ilona Csepreghy, née Meznerics (1906–1977)." *Annals of the National Museum of Hungary* 70 (1978): 5–8.

STANDARD SOURCES

Sarjeant.

CUFFE, LADY CHARLOTTE WHEELER (WILLIAMS) (1867–1967)

British/Irish horticulturalist. Born 24 May 1867 in Wimbledon, Surrey. Married Sir Otway Cuffe. Created a botanical garden in Burma and collected and drew plants. Died 8 March 1967 Lyrath, Kilkenny Ireland.

Lady Cuffe went with her husband, a civil engineer, to India and Burma. While in Burma, she created a small botanical garden at Maymyo. Botanist R. E. Cooper became the director after she left Burma in 1921. She went to live in Ireland, where she again constructed a notable garden. Not only was she a fine gardener, but she was also an excellent botanical artist. She is memorialized in the plant *Rhododendron cuffeanum E. C. Nelson.* Her plants, letters, and paintings are in National Botanic Gardens, Dublin.   JH/MBO

SECONDARY SOURCES

Nelson, E. C., and E. M. McCracken. *Brightest Jewel: A History of the National Botanic Gardens, Glasnevin, Dublin.* Kilkenny: Boethius, 1987: 168–171 (includes portrait).

Nelson, E. C., and Brady A. *Irish Gardening and Horticulture.* Dublin: Royal Horticultural Society of Ireland, 1979: 148–149.

STANDARD SOURCES

Desmond.

CULLIS, WINIFRED (1875–1956)

British physiologist. Born June 1875, Gloucester, England. Educated King Edward's High School for Girls, Birmingham; Mason College, Birmingham; Newnham College, Cambridge University (Natural Science Tripos, 1899, 1900, second class); University of London (D.Sc., 1908). Professional experience: girls' school, biology teacher; London School of Medicine for Women (University of London), demonstrator in physiology, lecturer (1901–1908); reader and head of department of physiology (1912–1919); professor of physiology (Jex-Blake Chair) (1919–1945?); Royal Academy of Dancing, physiology and anatomy teacher. Died 1956.

Winifred Cullis, a significant British woman lecturer on physiology in the first half of the century and one of the first six women admitted to the Physiological Society in 1915, has since been almost forgotten. While at Newnham College, Cambridge, she was a student of J. N. Langley, professor of physiology and owner-editor of the *Journal of Physiology.* Cullis took second class honors in the Natural Science Tripos in 1899 and 1900. When Cullis graduated, she went for a year to teach biology in a girls' school. She began to work with T. G. Brodie at the London School of Medicine for Women in 1901 as a demonstrator in physiology, and then a lecturer in 1903. Obtaining a doctorate in science from the University of London in physiology in 1908, she was named reader and head of the department of physiology at the London School of Medicine for Women, and finally succeeded T. G. Brodie four years later.

In 1915, Cullis was one of the first six women admitted to the Physiological Society. Up to that date, she had published a total of eight papers in the *Journal of Physiology* with T. G. Brodie on a variety of topics: urine secretion, intestinal gas metabolism, and innervation of coronary arteries. She continued to be interested in cardiovascular physiology, and published a regular series of studies on this topic with other coworkers until 1936. She also published books on human physiology for a general audience in 1935 and 1949. By 1919 until her retirement in the late 1940s, Cullis was professor of physiology at the London School of Medicine for Women.

During World War II, she traveled extensively for the Ministry of Information to Australasia, North America, and Asia.

Cullis's interests included the physiology of dance, and she taught classes on the anatomy and physiology of movement to the Royal Academy of Dance, on whose board she sat. A believer in university education for women, she also was an early president of the Federation of University Women. She was actively involved in its founding in 1919.   JH/MBO

PRIMARY SOURCES

Cullis, W. C. With E. Tribe. "Distribution of Nerves in the Heart." *Journal of Physiology* (London) 48 (1913): 141–150. Many other papers in that journal; eight before 1915.
———-. *The Body and Its Health.* London: Allen & Unwin, 1935.
———. *Your Body and the Way It Works,* 2d. ed. London: Allen & Unwin, 1950.

SECONDARY SOURCES

British Medical Journal (24 November 1956): 1111–1112. Obituary notice; includes photograph.
Lancet (24 November 1956): 1242. Obituary notice; includes photograph.
The Times, 20 November 1956. Obituary notice.

STANDARD SOURCES

DNB; Newnham Roll; Who Was Who.

CUMMING, LADY GORDON (ELIZA MARIA CAMPBELL) (fl. 1839–1842)
British botanical and geological illustrator. Married.

Lady Gordon Cumming was a geological illustrator and collector. She and her daughter were horticulturists and gardeners who propagated plant hybrids on her husband's Scottish estate. In 1839–1842 she collected systematically ancient fish fossils on this land. Although careful drawings were made of many fossils, Lady Gordon Cumming died before they could be published. Aldrich mentioned that her work provided assistance to Louis Agassiz in his publications of the fish species with which she worked.   JH/MBO

SECONDARY SOURCES

Aldrich, Michele L. "Women in Geology." In Kass-Simon and Farnes.
Andrews, S. M. "Lady Eliza Maria Gordon Cumming." In *Discovery of Fossil Fishes in Scotland up to 1845.* Edinburgh, Royal Scottish Museum.

CUMMINGS, CLARA EATON (1853–1906)
U.S. botanist. Born 13 July 1855 in Plymouth, N.H., to Elmira and Noah Cummings. Educated Plymouth Normal School; Wellesley College (1876–1878). Professional experience: Wellesley College, botanical museum, curator (1878–1879); Wellesley College, instructor in botany (1879–1886), associate professor of cryptogamic botany (1887–1905), Hunnewell Professor of Botany (1905–1906). Honors and memberships: American Association for the Advancement of Science, fellow; Society of Plant Morphology and Physiology, vice-president (1904); Torrey Botanical Club; Boston Society of Natural History; Boston Mycological Club. Died 28 December 1906 in Concord, N.H.

Clara Cummings became a specialist in cryptogamic (spore-producing) flora while a student at Wellesley College. After she completed her studies, she joined its staff. She remained at Wellesley for the rest of her life, except for a year of study in Zurich (1886–1887). Cummings published a catalogue of North American mosses and liverworts (1885) and edited *Decades of North American Lichens* (1892); in the second edition of the latter work, entitled *Lichenes Boreali-Americani* (1894), she initiated a system for the distribution of dried specimens. Her works on the lichens of Alaska and Labrador represent important additions to the systematics of that group. Cautious and conservative, Cummings made taxonomic changes only when the evidence for doing so was overwhelming. Consequently, she made few radical changes, but left behind a body of solid descriptive materials in the field of lichenology.   JH/MBO

PRIMARY SOURCES

Cummings, Clara. *Catalogue of Music and Hepaticae of North America, North of Mexico.* Natick, Mass.: Howard and Stiles, 1885.

SECONDARY SOURCES

Papers are found in the archives of the Margaret Clapp Library, Wellesley College, Wellesley, Mass.
Fink, Bruce. "A Memoir of Clara E. Cummings." *Bryologist* 10 (May 1907): 37–41. Includes a portrait.
Journal of the New York Botanical Garden 9 (March 1908): 63.
Journal of the New York Botanical Garden 12 (June 1911): 125.
Science 25: 77–78. Obituary notice.
Whiting, Sarah F., William H. Niles, and Marion E. Hubbard. "In Memoriam, Clara Eaton Cummings." *College News* 6 (6 February 1907): 1, 7. Includes biographical information.

STANDARD SOURCES

AMS 1; Bailey; Ogilvie 1986.

CUMMINGS, LOUISE DUFFIELD (1870–1947)

Canadian/U.S. mathematician. Born 1870 in Hamilton, Ontario. Educated University of Toronto (B.A., 1895; M.A., 1902); University of Pennsylvania, fellow (1896–1897); University of Chicago (1897–1898); Bryn Mawr College (1899–1900; Ph.D.; 1914). Professional experience: St. Margaret's College, Toronto, mathematics instructor (1901–1902); Vassar College (1902–1915), assistant professor (1915–1919), associate professor (1919–1927), professor (1927–1935), professor emerita (1935–1947). Died 1947.

Although mathematician Louise Duffield Cummings was born in Canada and earned her first two degrees at the University of Toronto, she earned her doctorate at Bryn Mawr College and then spent her entire career at Vassar College. She moved through the academic ranks until she retired as an emerita professor in 1935. Her research was on triad systems on three elements and cyclic systems of points in a binary correspondence. She also worked on the plane figure of seven real lines, heptagonal systems of eight lines in a plane, and the comparison of straight-line nets. JH/MBO

STANDARD SOURCES
AMS 3–7; Grinstein; Grinstein and Campbell.

CUNIO, ISABELLA (13th century)

Italian inventor.

According to Matilda Gage in *Woman as Inventor,* Isabella Cunio may have been the co-inventor, with her twin brother Alexander, of woodblock engraving. When the two were sixteen years old, they are said to have prepared a series of eight pictures representing the actions of Alexander the Great. The designs were executed in relief on blocks of wood, which were then inked and pressed onto paper by hand. If indeed it happened, this represents participation by a woman in a major technological advance. JH/MBO

SECONDARY SOURCES
Gage, Matilda. *Woman as Inventor.* Fayetteville, N.Y.: F. A. Darling, printer, 1870.

STANDARD SOURCES
Ogilvie 1986; *Mothers and Daughters.*

CUNITZ, MARIA (1610–1664)

German astronomer. Born 1610 in Schweidnitz, Silesia to Maria (Scholtz) and Heinrich Cunitz. Married Dr. Elias von Löven. Educated by tutors. Died 1664 in Pitschen, Silesia.

Maria Cunitz, the daughter of a physician who was interested in astrology and astronomy, was tutored by Elias von Löven, a physician whom she later married. During her studies, Cunitz became acquainted with Johannes Kepler's Rudolphine tables (1627). When she compared Kepler's calculations with her own planetary observations and those of her husband, she discovered discrepancies. Finding Kepler's methods of calculation too complex, she published her newly calculated astronomical tables, a compendium in Latin and German for both learned and nonlearned readers, under the title *Urania propitia sive tabulae astronomicae mire faciles, vim hypothesium physicarum a Kepplero proditarum complexae, facillimo calculandi compendio sine ulla logarithmorum mentione phenomenis satisfaci-etes* (1650). In this work, although she detected many mistakes in her original sources, she made numerous new ones herself. The Thirty Years War (1618–1648), in which Silesia was involved throughout most of her life, brought interruptions to her work; for a time she and her husband took refuge in Poland under the protection of Cistercian abbesses, although the two astronomers remained Protestant. After 1648 the couple resumed their correspondence with other scholars, such as Johannes Hevelius, and Cunitz was able to complete her book. IG

PRIMARY SOURCES
Cunitz, Maria. *Urania propitia sive tabulae astronomicae mire faciles, vim hypothesium physicarum à Kepplero . . .* Olsnae Silesiorum, 1650. This work is in the vernacular and in Latin.

SECONDARY SOURCES
Davis, Herman S. "Women Astronomers, 400 A.D.–1750," parts 1 and 2, *Popular Astronomy* 6 (May 1898): 128–138; (June 1898): 211–228.

Guentherodt, Ingrid: "Maria Cunitz und Maria Sibylla Merian: Pionierinnen der deutschen Wissenschaftssprache im 17. Jahrhundert." *Zeitschrift für Germanistische Linguistik* 14 (1986): 23–49.

———. "Urania Propitia (1650)—in zweyerley Sprachen: lateinisch—und deutschsprachiges Compendium der Mathematikerin und Astronomin Maria Cunitz." In *Res Publica Litteraria,* ed. Sebastian Neumeister and Conrad Wiedemann, 619–640. Wiesbaden: Harrassowitz, 1987.

———. "'Dreyfache Verenderung' und 'Wunderbare Verwandelung'. Zu Forschung und Sprache der Naturwissenschaftlerinnen Maria Cunitz (1610–1664) und Maria Sibylla Merian (1657–1717)." In *Deutsche Literatur von Frauen,* ed. Gisela Brinker-Gabler, 1: 197–221. Munich: Beck, 1988.

———. "Kirchlich umstrittene Gelehrte im Wissenschaftsdiskurs der Astronomin Maria Cunitia (1604–1664): Copernicus, Galilei, Kepler." In *Religion und Religiösität im Zeitalter des Barock*, ed. Dieter Breuer, 857–872. Wiesbaden: Harrassowitz, 1995.

———. "Cunitz, Merian, Leporin: das Wagnis der Erkenntnissuche. Kosmos, Tierwelt, Menschenwelt." In *Frauen in der Aufklärung.* Edited by Iris Bubenik-Bauer und Ute Schalz-Laurenz, 173–193. Frankfurt/Main: Helmer, 1995.

———. "Autobiographische Auslassungen: Sprachliche Umwege und nichtsprachliche Verschlüsselungen zu autobiographischen Texten von Maria Cunitz, Maria Sibylla Merian und Dorothea Christiane Erxleben, geb. Leporin." In *Autobiographien von Frauen*, ed. Magdalene Heuser, 135–151. Tübingen: Niemeyer, 1996.

Krupp, E. C. "Astronomical Msings." *Griffith Observer* 39 (May 1975): 8–18.

STANDARD SOURCES
Mozans; Ogilvie 1986; Poggendorff 1, 1863; Schiebinger.

CUNNINGHAM, BESS VIRGINIA (ca. 1896–?)

U.S. educational psychologist. Born in Bethesda, Ohio. Educated Toledo (B.S., 1917); Ohio State University (A.M., 1921); Grace Dodge fellow, Columbia University (1922–1923; Ph.D., 1923). Professional experience: Ohio schools, kindergarten teacher (1903–1917); California State Teachers College, San Francisco, supervisor kindergarten department (1917–1919); Colorado State Teachers College, Greeley, Colo., director kindergarten department (1920); Teachers College, Columbia University, assistant in educational psychology (1921–1923), assistant professor of education and supervisor education clinic (1923–1928), assistant professor (1926–1937); University of Toledo, professor and head of department elementary education (1940–?). Honors and memberships: American Psychological Association, Fellow. Death date unknown.

After moving about in her early years, educational psychologist Bess Cunningham returned to the University of Toledo, in Ohio, where she rose through the ranks as professor and head of the department of elementary education.

Cunningham was interested in tests and measurements, and child psychology and development. She also was interested in parental education and family behavior. She was a member of the American Psychological Association.

JH/MBO

STANDARD SOURCES
AMS 5–8, S&B 9.

CUNNINGHAM, GLADYS STORY (1895–?)

Canadian physician. Born 24 May in Wawanesa, Manitoba, Canada, to a Scottish father and English mother. Four siblings. Married Edison Rainey Cunningham, M.D. (1923). Educated local schools; McGill College, Vancouver (1911–1913); McGill University, Montreal (B.A., 1915); Vancouver General Hospital, nursing student (1917–1918); McGill University, medical student; Manitoba University Medical School (M.D., 1923); Peking Union Medical College, Department of Obstetrics-Gynecology, student; Johns Hopkins Medical School (1927–1928); London School of Medicine, postgraduate training. Professional experience: Chungking, Szechwan province, medical missionary (1923–1925); Chengtu, Szechwan province capital, clinical medicine and teaching (1926–1951); Medical-Dental Faculty, West China Union University, teacher; Peking Union Medical College, researcher in obstetrics and gynecology (1927); Vancouver, Canada, Salvation Army Hospital for Obstetrics-Gynecology and Vancouver General Hospital, where she learned to perform direct blood transfusions (1929); Johns Hopkins Medical School (1937–1938); Vancouver, Canada, private practice (1951–1962). Retired 1962. Honors and memberships: Royal College of Obstetrics and Gynecology, Medical Women's International Association, YWCA, University Women, Soroptimist Club.

Gladys Story was born in Wawanesa, Manitoba, Canada, the third of five children. The Story family moved to Vancouver, British Columbia, in 1910. She attended McGill College, a Vancouver subsidiary of McGill University, for two years after matriculating in high school, then went to Montreal, to McGill University to finish her liberal arts degree. Gladys had from childhood wanted to become a doctor, but her family felt she should be satisfied with the more acceptable woman's role as nurse, so she trained and was "capped" as a nurse through Vancouver General Hospital. Unsatisfied, she worked for a short period as a teacher to earn money for medical school. In 1918, she registered at McGill University, Montreal School of Medicine, following by only three years the first woman graduate in medicine at McGill, Jessie Boyd Scriver.

At McGill, Gladys met Edison Rainey Cunningham, a fellow classmate, and by 1921 they were engaged. Ed Cunningham had already decided to go as a medical missionary to western China where his aunt, Anna Henry, was a practicing physician. Gladys stayed behind to finish her degree, then joined Ed in Szechwan province, China, where they were married in 1923. In 1925, the Cunninghams were moved to Chengtu, the provincial capital and the site of the West China Union University, where they worked in clinical medicine and teaching until 1951. One interruption in their work came in 1927, when a surge of Communist antiforeign sentiment caused the missionaries of Chengtu to be removed; the Cunninghams ended up in Peking where they worked and studied in the Peking Union Medical College. There Gladys worked in the department of obstetrics and gynecology. When they returned to Chengtu, she was put in charge of obstetrics-gynecology in the women's hospital, and served as both teacher and surgeon.

In 1929, the Cunninghams took a sabbatical in Canada where Gladys worked at the Vancouver Salvation Army Hospital and Vancouver General Hospital. Meanwhile, Ed returned to England to acquire his diploma in opthalmological surgery. From 1930 to 1937, they remained at Chengtu, but took another furlough in 1937–1938 and Gladys studied at Johns Hopkins Medical School and at the Postgraduate School of Medicine, London, where she obtained her membership in the Royal College of Obstetrics and Gynecology.

During the war, the provincial capital was moved from Chengtu to Chungking, and in 1945, the Cunninghams and many other civilians were transferred to India and finally shipped overseas. The Cunninghams spent most of a year in Canada, but returned to Chengtu as soon as possible; they left in 1950, following the Communist takeover of West China Union University. They returned to Vancouver, Canada, and set up private practices in their specialties. In June 1962, they retired, and Gladys Cunningham kept busy with volunteer activities with the YMCA, University Women's Club, Soroptimist Club, and family activities. Through all the years as doctor, surgeon, and teacher in China, due to the policy of the United Church missions regarding wives of missionaries, Gladys Cunningham worked without pay. Her service was truly a labor of love for the profession of medicine and for the people of China.

JH/MBO

PRIMARY SOURCES
Cunningham, Gladys S. In Hellstedt, *Autobiographies.*

CUNNINGHAM, SUSAN (1842–1921)

U.S. astronomer. Educated Vassar College (1866–1867); Radcliffe College, Harvard University (1874, 1876); Princeton University (1881); Cambridge University (1877–1879, 1882, 1887); Williams College (1883–1884). No formal degree. Professional positions: Swarthmore College, instructor of mathematics (1869–1872), assistant professor (1872–1874), professor of mathematics and astronomy (1874–1906), professor emerita. Died 1921.

Susan Cunningham entered Vassar College the year after the well-known astronomer MARIA MITCHELL came to Vassar to teach. She spent only one year at Vassar and continued her education piecemeal at Radcliffe, Princeton, Cambridge, and Williams College, apparently without ever getting a formal degree. She was hired by Swarthmore College, where she spent her entire academic career, progressing from instructor to professor. By 1874 she was professor of mathematics and astronomy.

JH/MBO

STANDARD SOURCES
AMS 1–3; Bailey; Mozans; Rossiter 1982.

CURIE, MARIE (MARIA SKLODOWSKA) (1867–1934)

Polish/French physicist/chemist. Born 7 November 1867 in Warsaw to Bronislawa (Boguska) and Wladislaw Sklodowski. Four siblings. Married Pierre Curie. Two daughters, Irene and Eve. Educated government secondary school, Warsaw (graduated 1883); Faculty of Sciences, Sorbonne, Paris (licenciée en physiques, 1893; licenciée en sciences mathematiques, 1894; Doctor of Physical Science, 1903). Professional experience: governess in Poland (1885–1889); Ecole Normale Superieure, Sevres, France, physics teacher (1900–1906); Faculty of Sciences, Sorbonne, assistant professor (1904–1906), professor (1906–1934). Honors and memberships: Nobel Prize in physics, with N. Becquerel and P. Curie (1903); Nobel Prize in chemistry (1912). Died 4 July 1934 in Sancellemoz, Haute Savoie, France.

Maria Sklodowska was born in a Poland controlled by the tsar of Russia. Shortly before Maria's birth, a Polish attempt to overthrow Russian rule failed; the subsequent Russian oppression was brutal. Underground resistance to Russian rule was a constant factor in her early years. Her father, Wladislaw Sklodowski, had obtained a scientific education in Russia. When he returned to Warsaw to teach physics, he married the principal of a girls' boarding school. Although both husband and wife were members of the minor nobility, neither had any money, and they were forced to economize drastically. For the first eight years of the marriage, the family lived in a small apartment furnished by Mme. Sklodowska's school. During that period, their five children, of whom Maria was the youngest, were born. After Maria's birth, Sklodowski took a teaching post at a Warsaw high school for boys, which provided a larger apartment for his family; he obtained an additional job as a school underinspector. As a consequence of the increasing Russianization of Poland, when Maria was six, her father lost his job as underinspector, and the family was obliged to move to a small house where they took in boarders.

Religion and success in school were emphasized in the household. Embittered by the deaths of her sister Zosia, of typhus (1876), and her mother, of tuberculosis (1878), Maria rejected the religious beliefs of her childhood. In 1883, she finished her secondary schooling with a gold medal—the third in the family. She was exhausted by the strain of academic achievement and, at her father's urging, took a year's vacation at her uncle's home in the country.

On returning to Warsaw, Maria Sklodowska allied herself with a coterie of young intellectuals—heirs of the revolutionaries of the 1840s—who met to discuss the ideas of the positivism philosopher Auguste Comte and other advocates of social reform. Girls made up a large part of the membership of this "floating university"—"mostly teenage girls with few responsibilities and time on their hands, young married women with little else to interest them, and the young daughters of successful bourgeois parents" (Reid, 24–25).

Maria sought work as a governess in order to contribute toward her sister Bronia's education before saving money for her own. Her first job was a disaster, for she and her employers developed a mutual dislike. Her second position promised to be more congenial, despite the dullness of provincial life and the necessity for self-repression. "If you could only see my exemplary conduct!" she wrote to a friend. "I go to church every Sunday and holiday, without ever pleading a headache or a cold to get out of it. I hardly ever speak of higher education for women. In a general way I observe, in my talk, the decorum suitable to my position" (quoted in Eve Curie, 65). During her three-year tenure (1886–1889), however, she grew increasingly despondent and prone to illness, as the chance of extricating herself from the provinces seemed ever more remote. She was taken with ideas of social change and spent many hours educating herself. A brief romance with the eldest son of her employers brought her keener unhappiness: because of Sklodowska's inferior position as a governess, the family objected to their marriage; the attachment foundered and soon died. Nevertheless, throughout her governess years, she forced herself to read and study, finding physics and mathematics especially interesting and challenging.

An escape became feasible when Sklodowska's father accepted the directorship of reformatory and was able to send money himself to Bronia, now a medical student in Paris. Sklodowska returned to Warsaw, where she worked as a governess and tutor for two more years. During this period, Bronia married, and invited Maria to come to Paris and share her home while going to school. After hesitating for over a year, Sklodowska accepted. In 1891, she became a student at the Faculty of Sciences of the Sorbonne.

Even though she had studied hard on her own, Sklodowska discovered tremendous gaps in her education in physics and mathematics, which she worked feverishly to repair. The romantic story of her spartan existence in Paris is well known. She left her sister and brother-in-law's apartment for a more convenient, but monastically simple, lodging in the Latin Quarter, where she endured severe cold and hunger, feelingly described in her daughter Eve's account of her life. Biographer Robert Reid, on the other hand, asserts that "a myth has grown up about the poverty of her student days. She *was* poor, but so were most students. Her allowance from Poland was small and had to be divided between tuition fees and the price of life in the garret. When the cost of fuel was high there was little left for food; the main protein cooked over her spirit stove was usually egg. In student history the omelet can probably claim to have sustained more educations than any other stimulant" (Reid, 48). Yet it is apparent that Sklodowska carried self-denial past the ordinary

levels. At one point she almost starved herself until rescued by Bronia's husband. After he and Bronia fed and nursed her back to health, she "began again to live on air" (Eve Curie, 109–110).

In 1893, Sklodowska received her degree in physics from the Sorbonne. She had come to realize the importance of mathematics to a deeper understanding of physics, and therefore, after vacationing in Warsaw, returned to Paris to work on a degree in mathematics. This time the financial situation was easier, for in Warsaw she had been awarded the Alexandrovitch Scholarship for outstanding Polish students who wished to study abroad. The scholarship money supported her for over a year.

During her second year in Paris (1894), Sklodowska met Pierre Curie (1859–1906), who was then laboratory chief at the School of Industrial Physics and Chemistry. Curie was engaged in research in the physics of crystals. Together with his brother, Jacques, he had in 1877 discovered the phenomenon of piezo-electricity—the generation of electricity by certain crystals when deformed by mechanical stress—which was to have important applications in many fields, especially that of electroacoustics. His work during the 1880s had dealt with principles of symmetry, as they applied both to crystallography and to physics as a whole; in 1891, he completed a doctoral dissertation on the magnetic properties of various substances at different temperatures. Curie had scorned to seek his own advancement and had not progressed up the academic ladder. He and Sklodowska, both shy and introverted people, shared the conviction that the scientist must work from entirely disinterested motives.

Marie Sklodowska received her mathematics degree in 1894 and in the following year married Pierre Curie. They honeymooned by bicycling through the Île de France—a vacation pattern that they continued throughout their marriage. Returning to Paris, the couple settled into a routine of work as a team at Pierre's laboratory. In 1897 Marie published her first paper, on the magnetism of tempered steel. An interruption occurred in the form of Marie's pregnancy; their daughter Irene was born in September 1897.

The possibility of giving up her research did not occur to Marie Curie. In addition to recording quantifiable data about little Irene—"April 15, Irène is showing her seventh tooth down on the left" (Eve Curie, 163; Reid, 84)—she began to search for a suitable subject for a doctoral dissertation. Intrigued by Wilhelm Roentgen's discovery of X-rays and by Henri Becquerel's findings on the radiation-emitting properties of uranium salts, both announced in 1896, she and Pierre decided that an investigation into the nature of radioactivity (a term coined by Marie Curie and first used in a joint paper by the Curies in 1898) might serve the purpose.

Postulating that the capacity to emit radiation was an atomic property, Marie Curie proposed to search for additional radioactive substances. Since two uranium ores that she tested, pitchblende and chalcolite, exhibited a much stronger degree of radioactivity than would have been forecast from the quantity of uranium that they contained, she hypothesized the presence of a highly radioactive element.

Pierre Curie, who had been following the results closely, tabled his own projects on crystals to work with his wife. In their partnership, Marie Curie was the chemist, separating and purifying the fractions of pitchblende, and Pierre was the physicist, determining the physical properties of the results. Although they had not yet succeeded in isolating them, the Curies were certain enough of their existence to announce the discovery of two new elements—polonium (named after Marie Curie's native land) and the more active radium—in July and December 1898.

The problem of isolating their theoretical substances was a financial as well as a technical one. Crude pitchblende was expensive. Recognizing that the far cheaper residue—the portion remaining after extraction of the uranium—would suit their needs, the Curies used their savings to buy material from the St. Joachimsthal mines in Bohemia and to have it transported to Paris. A shed with an earth floor, formerly used as a medical school dissecting room, was the location of what proved to be four years of work. This structure "surpassed the most pessimistic expectations of discomfort. In summer, because of its skylights, it was as stifling as a hothouse. In winter one did not know whether to wish for rain or frost; if it rained, the water fell drop by drop, with a soft, nerve-racking noise, on the ground or on the worktables, in places which the physicists had to mark in order to avoid putting apparatus there. If it froze, one froze" (Eve Curie, 169). The physicist Georges Urbain (1872–1938) reported after a visit that he "saw Madame Curie work like a man at the difficult treatments of great quantities of pitchblende." She moved the heavy containers, transferred the contents from one vat to another, and, "using an iron bar almost as big as herself," spent "the whole of a working day stirring the heating and fuming liquids" (Reid, 96).

To Pierre Curie it seemed superfluous to engage in the enormous physical struggle to demonstrate what they already knew. He was "exasperated to see the paltry results to which Marie's exhausting effort had led," (Eve Curie, 174). Nonetheless, in 1902, Marie succeeded in isolating a decigram of radium chloride and making a first determination of the atomic weight of radium, 225.93.

Despite Pierre Curie's impressive research achievements, he was continuously passed over for promotion. In order to help support the family, Marie taught physics at a girls' high school in Sèvres from 1900 to 1906, using what time she had left for research and the preparation of her thesis. The health of both Curies was deteriorating. Though they knew the cause of the burns on their hands, they refused to connect

their general debilitation with exposure to radiation. Not even in Pierre's last paper, written in 1904, on the experimental effects of radioactive emanations on mice and guinea pigs—in which he and two medical colleagues reported that a postmortem examination of the affected animals showed intense pulmonary congestion and modifications of the leukocytes—did he appear to apply these results to his and his wife's symptoms.

Marie Curie defended her doctoral thesis, a comprehensive review of her own and others' research in radioactivity, at the Sorbonne on 25 June 1903. The examination hall was crowded with curiosity seekers as well as family, friends, and colleagues. After the examination, Curie was awarded the degree of Doctor of Physical Science in the University of Paris, with the added accolade of "très honorable."

The year 1903 was one of contrasts for the Curies. Pierre, accompanied by Marie, made a trip to London to present a lecture at the Royal Institution. It was well received and his party tricks with radium especially appreciated. During one demonstration, he spilled a minuscule quantity of radium; fifty years later the level of radioactivity in the building was sufficient to require decontamination. In the same year, Marie lost a child, born prematurely after one of their bicycle rides. During this pregnancy she had been exposed to extremely high doses of radiation.

In December 1903, the Curies and Henri Becquerel were jointly awarded the Nobel Prize for physics—an event that destroyed forever their voluntary isolation. Becquerel went to Stockholm to receive his award, but the Curies, who were both unwell, pleaded uninterruptible teaching schedules as the reason for their absence. It was not until June 1905 that the Curies were able to travel to Sweden, where Pierre gave the lecture required of Nobel recipients.

The year 1904 was less of a burden than its predecessor. A healthy daughter, Eve, was born; Pierre was named occupant of a newly created chair of physics at the Sorbonne. And in the following year, Pierre was elected to the Academy of Sciences. The Curies were continually confronted, however, with the uncomfortable fact that radium experiments had entered the realm of public science. The spectacular nature of radioactivity and its potentially rewarding applications—including the treatment of cancer, which the Curies foresaw as early as 1903—removed some of the Curies' research from the ivory tower. Scrupulous in their belief that the results of scientific research should be in the public domain and equally convinced that investigators would not profit materially from the results of their investigations, the Curies did not take financial advantage of the lucrative radium industry that was growing up around them.

Although by 1906 Pierre's health was wretched, it was not sickness that killed him. On a rainy day in April, while crossing a busy street in his usual state of preoccupation, Pierre

Curie stepped into the path of a horse-drawn wagon and was instantly killed. According to the Curies' daughter Eve, "from the moment when those three words, 'Pierre is dead,' reached [Mme. Curie's] consciousness, a cape of solitude and secrecy fell upon her shoulders forever. Mme. Curie, on that day in April, became not only a widow, but at the same time a pitiful and incurably lonely woman" (Eve Curie, 247).

Within a month of Pierre's death, Marie Curie had returned to work at her laboratory and had been appointed to fill Pierre's vacant chair at the Sorbonne, with the status of assistant professor. She was the first woman in France to receive professorial rank, and within two years became titular professor. Her immediate financial problems were solved, and she had her own facilities for research. She now undertook the defense of her results against the onslaughts of the aging Lord Kelvin (1824–1907), who was never able to accept the implications of the new research on radioactivity. Finding intolerable the idea that atoms were capable of disintegration, he attacked both the Curies' findings and those of Ernest Rutherford (1871–1937) and Frederick Soddy (1877–1956), who, during the first years of the twentieth century, were developing a theory of the radioactive transformation of atoms. When Kelvin questioned the elemental status of radium and polonium, Curie, who had herself expressed some doubts in the case of polonium, began the long purification process again. Although when she finished her work—in 1907, after Kelvin's death—her hypothesis had again been corroborated, the labor had taken a further toll on her health.

During Pierre's lifetime, Marie Curie had been idolized by the public and honored by her colleagues as well. After his death, however, her sometimes icy and haughty manner offended some of her contemporaries. Her originality was questioned by some—notably the physicists Bertram Borden Boltwood (1870–1927) and Ernest Rutherford, who attributed her success more to hard work and tenacity than to any innate creativeness. The lack of colleague support was demonstrated during Curie's attempt to be elected to the Academy of Science in 1911. As soon as she announced her decision to become a candidate, the newspapers seized upon an interesting publicity opportunity. Some articles were effusive in their praise; others claimed that she was seeking credit for work done by her husband. Accusations of unsavory dealings proceeded after she lost the election, by one vote on the first ballot and by two votes on the second. Although Curie pretended indifference, she was hurt badly. Further, the press had developed a taste for probing the secrets of her life.

In the autumn of 1911, reporters uncovered evidence that apparently transformed Curie from a stoic grieving widow—a model of lifelong fidelity and symbol of the ideal partnership between man and woman—to a vicious homewrecker and flaunter of accepted sexual mores. On November 4 the Parisian newspaper *Le Journal* published an article under the headline "A Story of Love: Mme. Curie and Professor Langevin," which purported to prove, on the basis of stolen letters, an adulterous affair between Curie and the eminent physicist Paul Langevin, whom she had known for many years. An international scandal followed. In a recent biography of Curie, Susan Quinn credits the scandal for inspiring Eve Curie to put together her own version of the story very quickly. Quinn noted that when she asked Eve Curie Labouisse in 1988 why she had written the book so quickly she replied that she was "afraid that someone else would do it first and not get it right" (Quinn, 14).

Four days after the appearance of the article, Curie received a telegram informing her that she had been awarded the Nobel Prize for chemistry. The unprecedented award of a second Nobel Prize to the same person was hardly noticed in the newspapers, which had more interesting material to print. The strain of curiosity seekers invading Curie's privacy and that of her children, the publication of large incriminating extracts from the letters, and three resultant duels may have caused a chronic kidney infection to become worse, nearly bringing her death. During the period of recuperation from kidney surgery, she lived in seclusion under the name "Madame Sklodowska."

Curie's reentry into society was gradual. At the request of the English scientist HERTHA AYRTON, whom she had met in 1903 and corresponded with ever since, she signed an international petition requesting the release of three women suffrage leaders who were on a hunger strike in a British jail. For several months in 1912, she stayed with Ayrton in England, incognito, finishing her recuperation. The last entry Curie had made in her notebook on radium standards was dated 7 October 1911; she began to make notes again on 3 December 1912. The Langevin scandal having died away, Curie devoted much of her time to the development of a new research institution to be dedicated entirely to radioactivity. The Institute of Radium was, according to an agreement reached in 1912, to be built jointly by the Pasteur Institute and the Sorbonne and would consist of two parts: one, directed by Marie Curie, was to be devoted to physical and chemical research and to be supported by the university from a government grant; the second, directed by Claude Regaud, was to be used for medical and biological research and to be supported by the Pasteur Institute. Although the building was completed in July 1914, World War I intervened to prevent its occupation by scientists.

Immediately recognizing the need for mobile radiological equipment on the battlefield, Curie approached French government officials with a plan of action. Appointed director of the Red Cross Radiology Service, she solicited money and equipment from individuals and corporations for the establishment of a fleet of X-ray cars. Together with her daughter Irene, Curie visited the battlefields herself and whenever possible established fixed radiological stations. She turned the unused Institute of Radium into a school for training young women in X-ray technique and, again with Irene as assistant, conducted the classes herself.

Although the end of the war signaled Curie's opportunity to resume research, the materials with which to do so were hard to come by in depleted postwar France. One of the greatest deficiencies was the lack of radium itself. More amenable to public compromise in order to attain her ends than had been Pierre, Marie agreed in 1920 to a fundraising proposal by an American journalist, the somewhat brash, but great-hearted, Marie Meloney. Meloney would organize a subscription campaign among American women to provide the institute with the needed radium, and in return Curie would come to America, accompanied by Irene and Eve, to receive it. The campaign succeeded; in May 1921, President Harding presented a gram of radium to her (actually an imitation, since the genuine material was locked up). Her tour of the United States, reception of numerous honorary degrees, and the speeches she gave so tired Curie that the visit was shortened.

Not until the 1920s did the lurking question of the health hazards of radium come to the fore. Workers in Curie's laboratory experienced fatigue and aching limbs. Curie, who had long had sores on the tips of her fingers, was losing her eyesight to cataracts. As the radium industry boomed, cases of sickness and even death among exposed people began to be reported; pernicious anemia and leukemia were diagnosed in radiation laboratory personnel. Curie was confronted with the paradox that radium could both cure and possibly cause cancer. In spite of her own deteriorating physical condition, she was hesitant to admit radium's culpability. Surgery removed her cataracts and she was able to see again. Since her own constitution was remarkably resilient, she remained unconvinced that radium could kill.

During her last years, Marie Curie sought the companionship of her daughters—Irene, her scientific colleague, who in 1926 married the physicist and chemist Frédéric Joliot; and Eve, the nonscientist, who took care of her mother's physical and emotional needs. Often accompanied by one of them, Curie traveled throughout Europe and beyond, giving lectures, attending conferences, and raising money for research. One of her projects was a campaign, sparked by her sister Bronia, to modernize Polish medicine by establishing a radium research institute in Warsaw. Although the physical structure had long been completed, there was still no money to equip the Marie Sklodowska-Curie Institute with radium; in 1928 Marie Meloney agreed to mastermind a second American visit by Curie. The trip was both profitable and timely: Curie received the cash only days before Black Thursday.

Curie continued lecturing at the Sorbonne and supervising the work at her laboratory, although she increasingly yielded authority in the latter to Irene and Frédéric Joliot-Curie. She became active in the League of Nations' International Committee on Intellectual Cooperation and maintained friendships and correspondence with such leading European intellectuals as Albert Einstein.

In 1932, Curie broke her right wrist in a fall in the laboratory. The injury, which did not heal properly, was the beginning of a long decline. It was happily on a day when she was present at the laboratory that Irene and Frédéric Joliot-Curie carried out the momentous experiment in which, by bombarding the nucleus of an aluminum atom with alpha particles, they created a radioactive isotope, thus achieving artificial radioactivity. This was in January 1934. In May, Curie's doctors misdiagnosed her condition as tuberculosis and prescribed a trip to a sanatorium in the mountains. On the way, she developed a high fever. A blood count led to a new diagnosis, a severe form of pernicious anemia. On 4 July 1934, Curie died.

A review of Marie Curie's scientific achievements must, of necessity, address the relationship of her creativity to Pierre's. Did he supply the original ideas and Marie implement them? Was it significant that the original theoretical breakthroughs occurred within his lifetime? Here the assessments of Rutherford and Boltwood must be taken into account. Referring to her *Treatise on Radioactivity* (1910), Rutherford reported in a letter to Boltwood that "in reading her book I could almost think I was reading my own with the extra work of the last few years throwing in to fill up . . . Altogether I feel that the poor woman has labored tremendously, and her volumes will be very useful for a year or two to save the researcher from hunting up his own literature; a saving which I think is not altogether advantageous" (Reid, 168). When Curie received her second Nobel Prize, Boltwood was outraged because the theoretical work of Theodore Richards (1868–1928) on atomic weights had not been honored; instead, Marie Curie had received the reward for what Boltwood considered to be stubborn perseverance rather than theoretical brilliance. He wrote to Rutherford that "Mme. Curie is just what I have always thought she was, a plain darn fool, and you will find it out for certain before long" (Reid, 213). The chemist George Jaffe, who visited the laboratory, assumed that it was Pierre "who introduced the ingenuity into the scientific concepts . . . and the powerful temperament and persistence of Marie that maintained their momentum" (Reid, 91). Curie was aware that critics proclaimed the originality in their work as her husband's. The fact that in their papers it is always "we" whose efforts are described makes it difficult to extricate individual contributions.

In her 1911 Nobel speech, however, Curie made clear by

her use of pronouns what she had contributed. The prize in chemistry was given to Marie Curie "in recognition of her services to the advancement of chemistry by the discovery of the elements radium and polonium, by the isolation of radium and the study of the nature and compounds of this remarkable element" (*Nobel Lectures, Chemistry,* 197). In presenting the historical background to the work, she clarified her priority: "Some 15 years ago the radiation of uranium was discovered by Henri Becquerel, and two years later the study of this phenomenon was extended to other substances, first by me, and then by Pierre Curie and myself" (*Nobel Lectures, Chemistry,* 202).

One of the most significant theoretical assumptions surrounding radioactivity was the postulate that it was an atomic property. In Marie Curie's initial study of the "power of ionization" of uranium rays—that is, their ability to render the air conductor—she used the method of measurement invented by Jacques and Pierre Curie, an "ionization chamber, a curie electrometer, and a piezoelectic quartz" (Eve Curie, 155; Marie Curie, *Radioactive Substances,* 7–11). But it was the conclusion from the measurements that constituted the scientific originality. It is unclear from the original publication whether Marie or Pierre had conceived the idea, for to them at that time it was obviously irrelevant. They concluded that the intensity of radiation is proportional to the quantity of material and that the radiation was not affected either by the chemical state of combination of the uranium or by external factors such as light or temperature. This led to the important theoretical breakthrough that radiation was an atomic property. In 1911 Marie Curie's Nobel Prize lecture made it clear that this idea was hers. "The history of the discovery and the isolation of this substance," she noted, "has furnished proof of my hypothesis that *radioactivity* is an atomic property of matter and can provide a means of seeking new elements" (*Nobel Lectures, Chemistry,* 202–203). In her thesis (1903), she had not used the first person to describe the creation of this hypothesis, writing that "the radio-activity of thorium and uranium compounds appears as an *atomic property*" (Marie Curie, *Radioactive Substances,* 13).

In Pierre Curie's Nobel lecture of 1905, he did not designate individual roles, writing that "radioactivity, therefore, presented itself as an atomic property of uranium and thorium, a substance being all the more radioactive as it was richer in uranium or thorium" (*Nobel Lectures, Physics,* 73–74). From this lecture it is also unclear which one of the pair invented the term "radioactive." "We have called such substances *radioactive,*" he observed (*Nobel Lectures, Physics,* 73). Marie, however, used the first person singular in her 1911 lecture, noting that "all the elements emitting such radiation I have termed *radioactive,* and the new property of matter revealed in this emission thus received the name *radioactivity*"

(*Nobel Lectures, Physics,* 202). In her thesis, she also noted her own part, writing that "I have called *radio-active* those substances which generate emissions of this nature" (Marie Curie, *Radioactive Substances,* 6).

The hypothesis of the atomic nature of radioactivity motivated the long search that resulted in the isolation of polonium and radium. And the imaginative creation of a hypothesis distinguishes the scientist from the ordinary investigator. To be sure, Marie Curie's scientific genius had a second characteristic, perseverance. The labor necessary to substantiate her hypothesis was excruciatingly tedious and demanding. Though to Pierre the inexorable logic of the hypothesis was sufficient proof of its truth, for Marie it was necessary to demonstrate the substances' existence physically as well as hypothetically. Her tenacity in the physical labor of attaining the pure material has contributed to the charge that her part in the Curie team was the less creative one. The evidence indicates, however, that in the discovery of radium Marie Curie contributed both the necessary hypothesis and the perseverance to demonstrate it physically.

In her later work the charge that Marie Curie was more involved in the minutiae of laboratory analyses than in creating new theories has more substance. Her insistence on isolating pure radium and pure polonium is a case in point. In her first effort to isolate radium, she had ended up with very pure radium chloride but not elemental radium. Lord Kelvin's suggestion (1906), that radium was not an element but a molecular compound of lead with a number of helium atoms, had put in jeopardy her own work as well as Rutherford and Soddy's theory of radioactive disintegration. Therefore, Curie began another series of laborious purifications, this time to be sure that she ended up with elemental radium; at the same time, she determined to settle the question of polonium's elemental status as well. Even though this eventually successful process undoubtedly required skill and infinite patience, it did not involve additional suppositions. Similarly, the establishment of a radium standard in 1911, though an important achievement, was not predicated on additional theoretical assumptions.

Marie Curie's most scientifically creative years were indeed those during which she and Pierre shared ideas. Nonetheless, the basic hypotheses—those that guided the future course of investigation into the nature of radioactivity—were hers. Most of her later efforts were spent in elaborating on, refining, and expanding these early ideas.   MBO

PRIMARY SOURCES
Curie, Marie. *Pierre Curie.* Trans. Charlotte and Vernon Kellogg, with introduction by Mrs. William Brown Meloney and autobiographical notes by Marie Curie. New York: Macmillan, 1923.
———. *Radioactivité.* Paris: Herman, 1935.

———. *Radioactive Substances.* New York: Philosophical Society, 1961.

———. *Recherche sur les substances radioactives.* 2d ed., rev. and corr. Paris: Gauthier-Villars, 1904.

SECONDARY SOURCES

Bigland, Eileen. *Marie Curie.* New York: Criterion Books, 1957.

Curie, Eve. *Madame Curie.* Trans. Vincent Sheean. Garden City, N.Y.: Doubleday, Doran and Co., 1938. Biography of Marie Curie by her daughter, Eve. Selective about events included.

Foelsing, Ulla. *Marie Curie: Wegbereiterin einer neuen Naturwissenschaft.* München: Piper, 1990.

Nobel Lectures. Including Presentation Speeches and Laureates' Biographies. Chemistry, 1901–1921. Amsterdam: Elsevier, for the Nobel Foundation, 1966. Includes Marie Curie's lecture, "Radium and the New Concepts in Chemistry." Includes a biography of Curie.

Nobel Lectures. Including Presentation Speeches and Laureates' Biographies. Physics, 1901–1921. Amsterdam: Elsevier, for the Nobel Foundation, 1967. Includes lectures by Henri Becquerel, who shared the 1903 prize with the Curies, and Pierre Curie. Marie did not give a lecture. Includes a biography of Curie.

Pflaum, Rosalynd. *Grand Obsession: Madame Curie and Her World.* New York: Doubleday, 1989.

Quinn, Susan. *Marie Curie: A Life.* New York: Simon and Schuster, 1995.

Reid, Robert. *Marie Curie.* London: William Collins Sons, 1974. A critical biography of Curie.

STANDARD SOURCES

DSB; Grinstein 1993; *Notable* (article by Shari Rudavsky); Ogilvie 1986 (article by Helena Pycior); *Uneasy Careers.*

CURRIE, ETHEL DOBBIE (1899–1963)

Scottish geologist. Born 1899 in Glasgow. Educated Bellahouston Academy and Glasgow University (B.Sc., 1920; Ph.D.; D.Sc.). Professional experience: Hunterian Museum (Glasgow), assistant curator (1920–1962); University of Glasgow, senior lecturer (1920–1962). Honors and memberships: Neill Prize, for the second of the papers on ammonites (1943); Wollaston Fund award (1943); The Royal Society of Edinburgh, one of the first three women to be elected a Fellow (1949); Geological Society (Great Britain), Fellow; Geological Society of Glasgow, first woman to be elected president (1952). Died 24 March 1963 in Glasgow.

After graduation under J. W. Gregory in 1920, Currie was appointed as a demonstrator in his department for a short time and then was appointed assistant curator of the geological collections at the Hunterian Museum, Glasgow, a posi-

tion which she retained for the remainder of her career. Concurrently, she was senior lecturer at the University of Glasgow. Although she did some teaching, her curatorial work was her major interest.

Her research first resulted in a joint paper with J. W. Gregory on fossil echinoids from Persia. Following this paper, she published several other papers on the same subject. She was especially interested in echinoids from Africa, and her detailed descriptions were of great use to systematists. She subsequently published two papers on the growth of ammonite shells. She next moved to a study of the goniatites of the Scottish Carboniferous, a little-studied group of Cephalopods. Collaborating with C. Duncan (Mrs. W. J. McCallien) and H. M. Muir-Woods they published a comprehensive account of the fauna of Skipsey's Marine Band. Another collaboration, this time with J. W. Gregory, resulted in a monograph on the mammalian fossils in the Hunterian Museum from the Scottish glacial and postglacial deposits.

CK

PRIMARY SOURCES

Currie, Ethel Dobbie. "Growth of Ammonite Shells." *Proceedings of the Royal Society of Edinburgh* 61, B (1942).

———. "Growth of Stages in Some Jurassic Ammonites." *Transactions of the Royal Society of Edinburgh* 61 (1944): 171–198.

———. "Scottish Carboniferous Goniatites." *Transactions of the Royal Society of Edinburgh* 62, 1954.

SECONDARY SOURCES

"Ethel D. Currie, D.Sc., Ph.D., F.R.S.E., F.G.S., F.M.A." *Transactions of the Geological Society of Glasgow* 25, pt. 1 (1963): 9. Obituary notice.

[Weir, John]. ["Dr. Ethel Dobbie Currie"]. *Proceedings of the Geological Society of London* 1618 (1965): 112–113.

———. "Ethel Dobbie Currie." *Royal Society of Edinburgh, Year Book* 1964 (1962–1963): 15–17.

CURTIS, DORIS SARAH (MALKIN) (1914–1991)

U.S. geologist. Born 1914 in the Bay Ridge area of Brooklyn, N.Y., to Mary Berkowitz and Meyer Malkin. One sister. Married twice; (1950; 1952), divorced twice. Educated Brooklyn College; Columbia University (Ph.D., 1949). Professional experience: Shell Oil Company (1941–1950; 1960–1979); University of Houston, earth sciences faculty member (1950–1952); University of Oklahoma, faculty member (1954–1959); geology consulting partner (1979–1991). Died 26 May 1991.

Doris Curtis was president of four important organizations in geology: the Geological Society of America, the

American Geological Institute, the Society of Economic Paleontologists and Mineralogists (SEPM), and the SEPM Foundation. She was born, raised, and educated in New York. She graduated from Brooklyn College and earned her doctorate from Columbia University. After receiving her doctorate, she moved to Houston and was eventually hired by Shell Oil Company. From Houston, as the focus of exploration shifted, Curtis moved to Baltimore, Tallahassee, and New Orleans as a stratigrapher and geologist. She left Shell in 1950 to marry a Shell engineer. Because of nepotism rules, she could no longer work for Shell. She began to teach, first at the University of Houston. This marriage ended in divorce in 1952. She remarried, this time to a geologist, and the couple joined the Scripps Institute of Oceanography in La Jolla, California, as associate research geologists. For the American Petroleum Institute Project, number 51, she contributed a comprehensive study of the ostracods of the northwest Gulf of Mexico shelf. Curtis returned to academia in 1954, after completing her work at Scripps. She and her husband moved to Norman, Oklahoma, and she began teaching at the University of Oklahoma. There she proceeded up the academic ranks as instructor, assistant professor, and associate professor, and he worked on research. Curtis was a very popular teacher and her classes were overflowing. She stayed in academia for only five years, at which time she got her second divorce. She returned to Shell in 1959, and remained until 1979. After leaving Shell for the second time, Curtis, with her good friend Dorothy Echols, formed a successful consulting firm. She belonged not only to many professional organizations but to civic organizations as well. An active member of the League of Women Voters, Curtis was president of the Oklahoma chapter, and a member of its environmental quality committee. Her contributions to the petroleum industry and the League of Women Voters caused her to be selected as one of four U.S. delegates for an exchange visit to the Soviet Union.

In early April 1991, Curtis was diagnosed with acute leukemia and entered the M. D. Anderson Cancer Research Institute. Although she seemed to be winning the battle with cancer, she contracted pneumonia and died on May 6.

Curtis wrote over thirty papers on paleoecology, biostratigraphy, ostracods, transgressive-regressive sedimentation, deltaic sedimentation, the source and migration of hydrocarbons in the Cenozoic of the Gulf of Mexico, and time-synchronous sandstone deltas in the Miocene of coastal Louisiana. Curtis, a fine mentor, encouraged young women in geology.
CK

PRIMARY SOURCES

Curtis, Dorothy. "Miocene Deltaic Sedimentation: Modern and Ancient." *Society of Economic Paleontologists and Mineralogists Special Publication* 15 (1970): 293–308.
———. With D. J. Echols. "Paleontologic Evidence for Mid-Miocene Refrigeration, from Sub-Surface Miocene Shales, Louisiana Gulf Coast." *Gulf Coast Association of Geological Societies Transaction* 23 (1973): 422–426.
———. *Finding Deep Sands in the Gulf Coast Tertiary.* Houston Geological Society Continuing Education Committee, Short Course. 1984, 72 pp.
———. "A Conceptual Model for Sources of Oil in Gulf Coast Cenozoic Reservoirs." *Gulf Coast Association of Geological Societies Transaction* 39 (1989): 37–55.

SECONDARY SOURCES

Echols, Dorothy Jung. "Memorial to Doris M. Curtis (1914–1991)." *The Geological Society of America* 23 (1993): 175–183. Obituary notice. Includes portrait and bibliography.
Price, Raymond A. "Doris M. Curtis." *American Association of Petroleum Geologists* 77, no. 11 (1993): 2015–2016.
———. "Tribute to Doris M. Curtis." *Geological Society of America Bulletin* 104, no. 3 (1992): 253–254.

CURTIS, NATALIE (1875–1921)

U.S. anthropologist/ethnomusicologist. Born 26 April 1875 in New York City to Augusta Lawler (Stacey) and Edward Curtis. Five siblings. Married Paul Burlin (25 July 1917). One son. Educated National Conservatory of Music, New York City. Professional experience: anthropological studies of Native American and African American music. Died 23 October 1921.

Natalie Curtis was not trained formally as an anthropologist or an ethnomusicologist. She studied to be a concert pianist, under Arthur Friedheim in New York and Ferruccio Busoni in Berlin. A trip to Arizona caused her to change her goals. She became interested in the disappearing culture of the Native Americans and set about recording their music. At this time, the United States government was pursuing a policy of assimilation, and singing Indian songs in the classrooms was forbidden. Curtis appealed to President Theodore Roosevelt, a family friend, and through his help the strictures were lifted. Recording the music and studying the history of the Indian groups, Curtis found the ceremonial leaders who knew the traditional songs in the ancient languages most helpful. Although she concentrated on southwestern Plains and Pueblo tribes, she studied eighteen tribes from Maine to British Columbia. She first used a phonograph, but replaced it with pencil, paper, and a camera. President Roosevelt provided a dedication for the book that resulted from this work, *The Indians' Book* (1907). In this book, Curtis also wrote about the folklore, poetry, and religious beliefs of the indigenous people. She was always sensitive to their culture, and thus was welcome in Indian villages.

She found African American music equally interesting

and deplored the commercial distortion of their folk songs. She transcribed African American songs in the same careful way that she had the Native American ones. After a study at the Hampton Institute, she published a four-volume collection of songs and spirituals for male quartets, *Hampton Series Negro Folk-Songs.*

Curtis married an artist, Paul Burlin, when she was thirty-two years old. The couple had a son. Her husband was interested in forwarding her career. In 1921, she spoke to an international audience at the Sorbonne on the history of art. Curtis died before her potential could be reached, but her transcriptions are important to students, enabling them to observe changes in this native art.   JH/MBO

PRIMARY SOURCES
Curtis, Natalie. *Songs of Ancient America.* New York: G. Schirmer, ca. 1905.
————. *The Indians' Book.* New York: Harper and Brothers, 1907.
————. "Folk-Songs and the American Indian." *Southern Workman* (September 1915).
————. *Hampton Series Negro Folk-Songs.* New York: G. Schirmer, 1918–1919.

SECONDARY SOURCES
New York Times, 29 October 1921. Obituary notice.

STANDARD SOURCES
NAW (article by Gertrude Kurath); *Woman's Who's Who of America.*

CUSHIER, ELIZABETH (1837–1932)

U.S. physician. Born 1837. Ten siblings (seven survived). Educated local schools; homeopathic college for women; New York Infirmary College for Women (ca. 1869–1872); New York Infirmary for Women and Children, intern; postgraduate study in Zurich. Professional experience: New York Infirmary for Women and Children, physician and surgeon; joined Emily Blackwell in private practice (1882–1900). Retired 1900. Special tasks: worked with the Medical Women's National Association and American Women's Hospitals, and assisted with relief supplies during World War I. Died in 1932.

Elizabeth Cushier was born in 1837, one of eleven children (seven survived; three died in a measles epidemic). She attended both private and public schools before moving to New York, seeking a career in music. There she became interested in medicine and, on the advice of friends, entered a homeopathic college for women; she spent one year there, but found it unsatisfactory. She and a friend heard about ELIZABETH and EMILY BLACKWELL's college connected to the New York Infirmary for Women and Children. They entered (1869?) and found the serious, professional medical education and work they sought. Cushier received her medical diploma in 1872 and entered internship (primarily obstetric service) at the Infirmary of New York. She was partially responsible for moving the infirmary to a larger building (a large house), thus giving the college room to grow into the previous infirmary hospital building. She became interested in normal and pathological histology so went to study with histologist Professor Ebert in Zurich. Cushier spent eighteen months in Europe, then returned to the infirmary as resident physician and surgeon.

In 1882, she left the infirmary and joined Emily Blackwell in private practice, a partnership that lasted eighteen years, keeping her surgical residency at the infirmary. When the infirmary's college closed (after Cornell University opened its medical program to women), its buildings were converted into further hospital space, and an Obstetric and Gynaecological Services Center was opened. Cushier performed vaginal and abdominal hysterectomies, plastic gynecological operations, and Caesarian sections. In 1900, she and Emily Blackwell again went to Europe to travel and rest, giving up their medical practice. Returning, the pair moved to Montclair for winters, having already established a summer home at York Cliffs, Maine. Blackwell died in 1910 and Cushier spent her time in retirement reading, working with the Medical Women's National Association and American Women's Hospitals. She assisted with relief supplies during World War I. She died in 1932 at the age of ninety-four. She had been the leading woman surgeon of her time, an eminently successful practitioner, endocrinologist, and teacher.

JH/MBO

STANDARD SOURCES
Hurd-Mead 1933; Morantz-Sanchez.

CUSHING, HAZEL MORTON (1892–?)

U.S. psychologist. Born 15 March 1892, in Somerville, Mass. Educated Radcliffe College (A.B., 1914); University of Iowa (A.M., 1925); Columbia University, Spelman fellowship (Ph.D., 1929). Professional experience: University of Iowa, assistant (1914–1915), teacher, supervisor, instructor and school psychologist (1914–1928); Ball State Teachers College, associate professor of psychology (1928–1929); University of Rochester, acting professor of education (1929–1934); National Council of Parent Education (1934–1935); Utah State Department of Public Instruction, consultant in family life education (1936–1937); Institute of Child Welfare, Minneapolis [?], Minn., staff member (1937–1939); Spokane and Pullman, Wash., coordinator of family life education (1940–1946). Honors and memberships: American Psychological Association, Fellow; Society for Research in Child Development. Death date unknown.

Psychologist Hazel Morton Cushing was born in Massachusetts and earned her bachelor's degree from Radcliffe. She moved all over the country for her advanced degrees (Iowa and New York) and for her professional positions. From Indiana she took jobs in Utah, Minnesota, and finally in the state of Washington.

Her research interests were in character testing and personality traits. She was also interested in child development and family relations and attitudes.   KM

STANDARD SOURCES
AMS 5–8.

CUSHMAN, FLORENCE (1860–1940)

U.S. astronomer. Born 1860 in Boston, Mass. Educated Charlestown (Mass.) High School (graduated 1877). Astronomer, Harvard College Observatory (1888–1937). Died 1940.

For nearly fifty years, Florence Cushman was a member of the Harvard College Observatory staff, working for much of that time under Edward Pickering (1846–1919). She was especially involved in work on the *Henry Draper Catalogue* (1918–1924), as one of ANNIE JUMP CANNON's assistants. Cushman participated in the painstaking process of observing and classifying stars in this important compilation.   JH/MBO

SECONDARY SOURCES
Jones, Bessie Zaban, and Lyle Gifford Boyd. *The Harvard College Observatory: The First Four Directorships, 1839–1919.* Cambridge, Mass.: Harvard University Press, 1971.

STANDARD SOURCES
Mozans; Ogilvie 1986.

CUTHBERT-BROWNE, GRACE JOHNSTON (1900–)

Scottish-Australian physician. Born 2 January 1900 in Post Glasgow, Scotland, to Captain and Mrs. John Cuthbert. Four older siblings (one died at age three). Emigrated to Sydney, Australia, in 1901. Married Professor F. J. Browne (1951; he died 1963). One stepson. Educated Lindfield College, University of Sydney Medical School (from 1918; M.D.); postgraduate studies in U.S. and Britain (1939); World Health Organization, traveling fellowship (1950). Professional experience: Royal Prince Alfred Hospital, junior assistant in pathology; Royal North Shore Hospital, pathology department; private practice, Pambula; private practice, Eden; Department of Health, New South Wales, director of maternal and baby welfare (1937–1965). In retirement: administrative and consulting work with handicapped children (1965–1970). Honors

and memberships: Australian Medical Association, Fellow (1972); Medical Women's International Association.

Grace Johnston Cuthbert was born in Scotland to a merchant sailor father and teacher/headmistress mother. Throughout her life, her parents encouraged her ambition and supported her education. Captain Cuthbert became chief marine surveyor for a group of insurance companies in Sydney, Australia, a year after Grace's birth, so the family emigrated and settled at Kirribilli Point near Sydney. When Grace was six years old, the family moved to Lindfield; she eventually attended Lindfield College.

World War I caused the Cuthbert family much worry and grief when Grace's closest brother, Niven, was killed. His death delayed Grace's matriculation examinations a year while she remained home with her mother. When she did take the examinations, she was awarded one of the few allowances given annually for the faculty of medicine at Sydney University. She entered her medical studies in 1918 and was appointed, after graduation, junior assistant in the department of pathology. Later, she obtained a position in the pathology department at Royal North Shore Hospital and worked her way to a senior staff position.

Cuthbert's desire was to take a practice in the country and, with her father's financial assistance, she began a private practice in Pambula, a farm community with a district hospital and a small obstetric hospital. She worked this practice for several years before returning to Sydney to take over the practice of a retiring woman physician there, having become intensely interested in obstetrics and the care of the newborn and young child. Cuthbert was the Royal Society honorary medical officer for the welfare of mothers and babies and was also on the staff of the Rachel Forster Hospital until 1937, when she was appointed director of maternal and baby welfare for the Department of Health of New South Wales. In this capacity, she worked to reduce the maternal and newborn death rate by improving prenatal and antenatal care standards and expanding the Baby Health Centers.

In 1950, F. J. Browne was invited by a foundation for Mothers and Babies and the New South Wales government to lecture throughout the country. His textbooks on antenatal care had been a guide and inspiration for Cuthbert since beginning her practice. They met during his lecture series in New South Wales and were married in London in 1951, while Cuthbert was on her traveling fellowship with the World Health Organization. The couple returned to Sydney, where Browne affiliated with three obstetric hospitals and continued to issue textbooks on maternal and newborn care while Cuthbert-Browne continued her practice and administrative duties. When Browne died in 1963, it was a terrible blow to Cuthbert-Browne, but she continued to work, even after her official retirement in 1965. She was honored for her achievements by being voted a Fellow of the Australian Medical Association in 1972.　　　　KM

PRIMARY SOURCES
Cuthbert-Browne, Grace J. In Hellstedt, *Autobiographies.*

CUTLER, CATHERINE (ca. 1784–1866)

British botanist. Born ca. 1784 in Sidmouth?, Devon. Educated privately. Plant collector. Died 15 April 1866 in Exmouth, Devon.

British algologist Catherine Cutler lived in Devon where she collected algae along the coast. Her specimens are now in the British Museum (Natural History). She is memorialized in *Cutleria* Grev. She is remembered in the *Journal of Botany* and the *Botanischer Zeitung* of 1866.　　　　JH/MBO

SECONDARY SOURCES
Botanischer Zeitung (1866): 268. Obituary notice.
Journal of Botany (1866): 238–239. Obituary notice.

STANDARD SOURCES
Desmond.

CZAPLICKA, MARIE ANTOINETTE (d. 1921)

Polish geographer, botanist, and ethnologist. Educated Warsaw in geography. Traveled to Siberia (1914–1915). Professional experience: Oxford and Bristol, lecturer on ethnology. Died 20 May 1921.

Little is known about the Polish geographer, botanist, and ethnologist Czaplicka. After she received her education in geography in Warsaw, she traveled to Siberia where she collected plants. She then went to England where she lectured on ethnology at Oxford and Bristol. Czaplicka was a member of the Botanical Society Exchange Club, which later became the Botanical Society of the British Isles.　　　JH/MBO

PRIMARY SOURCE
Czaplicka, Marie Antoinette. *My Siberian Year.* London: Mills and Boon, 1916.

SECONDARY SOURCES
Botanical Society Exchange Club of the British Isles, Reports. (1921): 356. Obituary notice.
Nature 107 (9 June 1921): 466. Obituary notice.

STANDARD SOURCES
Desmond.

CZECZOTTOWA, HANNA (PERETIATKOWICZA) (1888–?)

Russian/Soviet paleobotanist and phytogeographer. Born 3 January 1888 in St. Petersburg, Russia. Death date unknown.

Hanna Czeczottowa was a paleobotanist phytogeographer who worked in Russia and Poland. In 1939, she completed a two-volume work on the flora and vegetation of Turkey. JH/MBO

PRIMARY SOURCES
Czeczottowa, Hanna. "Diagnoses Planetarum novum in Anatolia septentrionali anno 1925 lectarum." *Acta Societes Botanicorum Poloniae* 9 (1932): 31–45.
———. *A Contribution to the Knowledge of the Flora and Vegetation of Turkey.* 2 vols. Dahlem-Berlin: Verlag des Repertoriums, 1938–1939.

STANDARD SOURCES
Hunt Institute.

D

DALAI, MARIA JOLANDA (TOSONI) (1901–   )

Italian physician. Born 11 October 1901. Eight siblings. Married Giacomo Dalai. Four children. Educated University of Pisa (M.D., 1920?); University of Milan (postgraduate pediatric specialization). Professional experience: Milan, private pediatrician; summer health resorts for delicate children, physician; rural village, attending physician, general practice; Milan, private pediatrician (1950–?); Institute for Human and Eugenic Genetic Research, University of Milan, adviser. Honors and memberships: International Medical Women's Association (president, 1954–1958). Death date unknown.

Maria Jolanda Tosoni was the youngest of nine children of an Italian farm family in which everyone participated fully in the chores associated with producing dairy products, poultry, grains, and vegetables. She credited farm life for her love of botany, zoology, and natural science, and a certain knowledge of anatomy. After having many occasions to observe and listen to the wisdom of the local doctor, who was frequently called to their home to treat chronic bronchitis and other illnesses, she decided as a child to become a doctor. After primary school, Tosoni attended a Catholic boarding school and graduated just at the end of World War I. She took her medical training at the University of Pisa, then received pediatric specialty training at the University of Milan. She set up private pediatric practice in Milan and spent summers at nearby health resorts for delicate children. She married Giacomo Dalai and had four children. When World War II began, her husband went into antiaircraft service and Dalai and her children moved to a country village where she was the only physician left under the age of eighty (the male doctors and hospital surgeon had gone into the army). In 1950, the family returned to Milan for the sake of the children's education, and Dalai entered private pediatric practice again.

From 1950 on, Dalai was very active in the International Medical Women's Association, and founded in 1955 the Seventh International Congress of Medical Women at Gardone.

At that Congress she was elected president of the IMWA (1954–1958). She became an adviser to the Institute for Human and Eugenic Genetic Research, University of Milan, and began working especially in the area of detection and prevention of hereditary illnesses.   JH/MBO

PRIMARY SOURCES
Dalai, Maria. In Hellstedt, Autobiographies.

DALBY, MARY (d. 1978)

British bryologist and veterinary surgeon. Professional experience: Menston and Ilkeley, Yorkshire, veterinary surgeon. Honors and memberships: Wharfedale Naturalists Society, president (1967–1968). Died 15 January 1978.

Mary Dalby was a professional veterinary surgeon, but was a bryologist by avocation. She was president of the Wharfedale Naturalists Society. Her mosses are found at the Bradford Museum in Yorkshire.   JH/MBO

SECONDARY SOURCES
Bulletin Bryological Society 32 (1978): 9. Obituary notice.
Naturalist (1978): 77–78. Obituary notice.

STANDARD SOURCES
Desmond.

DALE, ELIZABETH (1868–?)

British paleobotanist and botanist. Born 1868. Educated Owens College, Manchester; Girton College, Cambridge (Natural Science Tripos, Part II, class 2, 1891). Pfeiffer Research Student (1898–1900). Professional experience: Cambridge Botanical Laboratory, researcher (1898–1914); Balfour Laboratory, demonstrator in botany; Girton, garden steward (1912–1917). Death date unknown.

Elizabeth Dale was primarily a botanist, and most of her journal publications were in that field. However, she has one joint publication in palaeobotany with A. C. Seward in 1900.

JH/MBO

PRIMARY SOURCES

Dale, Elizabeth. *On the Morphology and Cytology of* Aspergillus repens *de Bary.* Berlin: Friedländer & Son, 1909.

———. With Albert Charles Seward. *On the Structure and Affinities of Dipreris, with Notes on the Geological History of the Dipterinae.* London: Dulau, for the Royal Society, 1901.

SECONDARY SOURCES

Creese, Mary R. S., and Thomas M. Creese. "British Women Who Contributed to Research in the Geological Sciences in the Nineteenth Century." *British Journal for the History of Science* 27 (March 1994): 23–54.

STANDARD SOURCES

Girton.

DALLAS, A. E. M. M. (fl. 1924)

British/Scottish physicist. Educated University of Edinburgh (B.Sc.; M.A.); postgraduate research.

As is the case with most women involved in the early days of research on radioactivity, little information is available on Dallas's life. She received her bachelor's and master's degrees probably from the University of Edinburgh. We know that she did postgraduate research at the University of Edinburgh under the physicist Charles G. Barkla. Barkla and Dallas determined the energy of electrons ejected from gases and from metals by X-rays in order to elucidate the processes involved in energy absorption, particularly with respect to quantum theory.

MM

PRIMARY SOURCES

Dallas, A. E. M. M. With Charles G. Barkla. "Notes on Corpuscular Radiation Excited by X-Rays." *Philosophical Magazine* 47 (1924): 1–23.

SECONDARY SOURCES

Siegbahn, Manne. *The Spectroscopy of X-Rays.* Trans. George A. Lindsay. London: Oxford University Press/Humphrey Milford, 1925.

STANDARD SOURCES

Rayner-Canham 1997.

DALLE DONNE, MARIA (1778–1842)

Italian physician. Born 1778 at Roncastaldo, near Bologna. Educated by tutors; University of Bologna. Died 1842.

Maria Dalle Donne, like several other intelligent, young Italian women, was able to use her talents because of the help of a family member. In Dalle Donne's case, the protector was her uncle, who recognized that she was a talented child, took her into his home, and supervised her education. Her tutors persuaded Maria to seek a degree in medicine and surgery so that she could earn her own living. In order to convince skeptics of her knowledge, her teachers arranged for her to undergo a public examination. Emboldened by her successful performance, she requested an additional examination at the University of Bologna, where her spectacular display of expertise resulted in the awarding of a degree in 1799 in philosophy and medicine.

Prospero Ranuzzi, a patron of science convinced of her abilities, awarded Dalle Donne a yearly scholarship and gave her his collection of instruments and his books on medicine. Four years after receiving her degree, she was appointed director of midwives at the University of Bologna and authorized to present lectures in her own house. An excellent teacher, Dalle Donne deplored many of the barbaric practices of ignorant midwives and sought to correct them through education. To apprentice midwives "she was kind and friendly . . . but served as an examiner, not allowing her sympathy to imperil their patients by passing them undeservedly" (Pirami, 154–155). Ability to pay did not determine whom she accepted as students. Dalle Donne supported clever, dedicated, but poor young women who wanted and needed training. She felt a commitment to supply competent midwives to country villages, where obstetrical patients were totally dependent on midwives' skills. In 1829 she received public recognition by being awarded the title of "academic" by the Academia Benedettina. JH/MBO

SECONDARY SOURCES

Pirami, Edmea, "An 18th-Century Woman Physician." *World Medical Journal* 12 (1966): 154–155.

STANDARD SOURCES

Ogilvie 1986.

DAMO (fl. 6th century B.C.E.)

Greek Pythagorean natural philosopher. Reputedly born to Theano and Pythagoras. Educated school of Pythagoras.

The details of Damo's life may be apocryphal, but according to tradition she was the daughter of THEANO and Pythagoras. A story exists that she had custody of Pythagoras's manuscripts and refused to sell them, preferring poverty instead. Pythagoras reputedly had forbidden the spread of his ideas outside of the community, and she was adhering to his wishes.   JH/MBO

STANDARD SOURCES
Kersey; Ménage; Waithe.

DANE, ELISABETH (1903–1984)

German chemist. Born 9 January 1903 in Mayen, Rheinland. Father, Gerhard Dane, a high school teacher. One sister. Never married. Educated Luisengymnasium, Munich (completed 1923); University of Freiburg/Breisgau, Berlin and Munich, additional course of studies (doctorate, Berlin, 1929). Professional experience: University of Munich, Chemical Institute, assistant to Heinrich Wieland (1929–1934); privat dozent (1934); adjunct professor (1941); professor of chemistry and conservator (1942–1968). Honors and memberships: Carl-Duisberg Memorial Award. Died 12 March 1984 in Munich.

Not much is known about the childhood or familial relationships of Elisabeth Dane, daughter of a high school teacher. She received her doctorate in Munich in 1929 for her work on the determination of the constitution of alkaloids in *Lobelia inflata*. Heinrich Wieland directed her thesis. As the first female assistant to a Nobel Prize winner, she took part in one of the most important natural substance research projects of the first half of this century—the determination of the constitution of steroids. For some years she worked on the clarification of the complex ring system of this class of substances. In 1934 she did postdoctoral work on the constitution of bile. At that time, she received her qualification as a university lecturer. She did research on vitamins and hormones and lectured about her work. Beginning in 1939, she directed the chemical practicum and seminar for medical scientists. Although she was not a member of the National Socialist Party and her teacher, Wieland, was known to oppose the "brown regime" in Germany, she was still named professor and "Konservator" in 1942. After World War II, she dedicated herself to the rebuilding of research and teaching at the Chemical Institute of the University of Munich. In 1947 she turned down an offer in the town of Rostock.

A synthesis of complex natural substances like steroids did not seem possible before the World War II. Elisabeth Dane, however, was able to achieve important research results through her brilliant experimental methods. With the aid of a cycloaddition, the so-called Diels-Alder-Reaction, she was able to synthesize the tetracyclical system of steroids. In 1938 she was awarded the Carl-Duisberg prize for the work on female sexual organs that she published with J. Schmidt.

After the war, chemists seized upon the popular field of peptide synthesis and brought their results before an international congress. One can still find references in technical English literature to "Dane's compounds."

Elisabeth Dane was an organic and physiological chemist. She received her doctoral degree from the University of Berlin in 1929 for her thesis, "Beiträge zur Konstitutionsermittlg: Der Nebenalkaloide aus *Lobelia inflata*." An abbreviated version was published with Heinrich Wieland and Walter Koschara in *Liebigs Annalen der Chemie* in the same year.

In spite of her numerous publications, Dane found it difficult to obtain a paying position. After she received her doctoral degree, she assisted Heinrich Wieland on his research for five years and then became a privat dozent, or university lecturer. She obtained a temporary job in 1942 as an adjunct professor. Concurrently, she worked as a conservator, a position involving preservation work.

She published numerous papers in the *Angewandt Chemie, Chemiker-Zeitung, Hoppe-Seylers Zeitung physiologische Chemie,* and *Liebigs Annalen der Chemie*.   SNS

PRIMARY SOURCES
Dane, Elisabeth. With Heinrich Wieland and Walter Koschara. "Über einige Begleitbasen des Lobelins und über die gegenseitigen Beziehungen der Lobelia-Alkaloide." *Justus Liebigs Annalen der Chemie* 473 (1929): 118–126.
———. With others. "Synthesen in der hydroaromatischen Reihe. II. Die Diensynthese von Derivaten des 1-Vinyl-3, 4-dihydro-naphtalins." *Justus Liebigs Annalen der Chemie* 532 (1937): 39–52.
———. "Vitamin-B-Gruppe." *Chemiker-Zeitung* 61 (1937): 145–148.

SECONDARY SOURCES
Chemiker-Zeitung 62 (1938): 425. Short biography.

STANDARD SOURCES
Poggendorff, vol. 7; Strohmeier.

DANIEL, ANNE STURGES (1858–1944)

U.S. physician and public health reformer. Born 21 September 1858 in Buffalo, N.Y., to Marinda (Sturges) and John M. Daniel. Never married. Educated Woman's Medical College of the New York Infirmary (graduated 1879). Professional experience: New York Infirmary, druggist (1879), intern (1880), physician in charge of outpatient service (1881–1940s); New York State Tenement House Commission, investigator (1884); Congressional committee (tenement housing and sweatshop operations) investigator; Women's Prison Association of New York, attending physician. Died 10 August 1944 in New York City of arteriosclerosis.

One of the many early women doctors who dedicated her life to improving the health and living conditions of women and children, Annie Daniel's efforts paved the way for many key reforms. Her teachings in over sixty years of supervising students in outpatient services at the New York Infirmary aroused and inspired hundreds, including SARA JOSEPHINE BAKER, and anticipated such practices as visiting nursing services, child welfare and hygiene services, and hospital social services departments.

Of Scotch-Irish lineage, Daniel's father was a coal and wood merchant. Her mother died while Annie was still a child. Sent to live with relatives in Monticello, New York, Annie took an early interest in biology and the structure of living things. While at the Woman's Medical College of the New York Infirmary, she specialized in obstetrics, gynecology, and pediatrics. Her student training in New York City acquainted her with the poverty, illness, and despair of tenement life, and her perception of the relationship between sickness and social environment aroused in her a desire for reform. She saw that low wages and long, hard working hours led to the lack of sanitation and proper nourishment at the root of much preventable illness. She worked to improve conditions through education concerning hygiene, childcare, and preventive medicine. This work led to her participation in government efforts to study and legislate for changes in the tenement-sweatshop-homework system. She felt that prohibition of tenement homework was essential to raising tenement living standards. As long as female and child labor was necessary to augment low working-class wages, overcrowding, ignorance, poor sanitation, and contagious disease could not be regulated.

A participating member of the Working Women's Society, Daniel was a supporter of the early suffrage movement, and ardently pushed for legislation to improve the status of women. The report she made for the Women's Prison Association of New York (1886) led to a law requiring the employment of matrons in police station houses to supervise female prisoners and destitute lodgers. Her report also urged separate departments for municipal charities and correctional facilities, segregation of novices from confirmed offenders, and higher wages for female facility workers. Working well into her eighties, Annie Daniel contributed greatly to the social medicine movement and to improvement of the tenement population environment. She died in her New York home 10 August 1944.   JH/MBO

SECONDARY SOURCES
Baker, Josephine. *Medical Women's Journal* (September 1944):
   Obituary notice.

STANDARD SOURCES
NAW (article by Roy Lubove).

DANIELS, AMY L. (fl. 1914)
U.S. nutritionist and biochemist. Educated Columbia University (B.A., 1906); Yale University (Ph.D., 1912). Professional experience: University of Missouri, assistant professor of home economics (1911–1914); University of Wisconsin, associate professor (1914–1917); University of Iowa Child Welfare Research Station, professor (1918–1942). Retired, 1942.

Amy Daniels, who earned her doctorate from Yale University, advanced until she received a professorship at the University of Iowa. Previously, she had been an assistant professor at the University of Missouri and an associate professor at the University of Wisconsin. She won the Borden Award in 1939. After she retired (1942), she moved to Avon, Connecticut. Since she is not in the eighth edition of *American Men of Science* (1949) it seems probable that she died before that year.   JH/MBO

STANDARD SOURCES
AMS 3–7; Rossiter 1982.

DANTI OR DANTE, THEODORA (1498–1573)
Italian mathematician and artist. Born 1498 in Perugia. Educated privately. Professional experience: painted small pictures; instructed one of her nephews in mathematics. Died 1573 in Perugia.

Theodora Danti gained a reputation as a female savant. She was known for the small pictures that she painted in the style of Pietro Perugino. She also was an excellent mathematician, and was good enough to teach mathematics to one of her young nephews, who acquired a great reputation for learning as well.   JH/MBO

STANDARD SOURCES
Cyclopedia.

DARWIN, EMMA (WEDGWOOD) (1808–1896)
British amanuensis. Born 1808 in Maer, England, to Elizabeth (Allen) and Joseph Wedgwood II. Five siblings. Married Charles Robert Darwin (29 January 1839). Ten children (seven lived into adulthood). Educated privately. Died 1896.

Although she was not a scientist, nor even a popularizer of science, Emma Darwin deserves a place among the scientists as the major amanuensis, French translator, note transcriber, and copyist of her husband, Charles Darwin, naturalist and theorist of evolution. He also dictated his scientific notes to her when he was ill, and much of his voluminous correspondence is in her hand (either from dictation or from transforming Darwin's cryptic drafts into readable letters). She read French fluently and had no trouble writing it when called upon to answer a formal French correspondent, or translating a letter for Darwin. She also wrote out drafts of his books, although the final copy was done by a copyist.

Emma Darwin's aunt Jessie Allen Sismondi was married to a Swiss economist of some renown, and Emma had visited her in Geneva when she was a young woman, learning to appreciate lively intellectual conversation, although she herself never attempted to shine in that way. One of Darwin's copious notes records Emma observing one nest of slave-making ants while he observed another. But Emma's role was ordinarily limited to the task she preferred, that of Darwin's regular reader (of novels as well as some scientific works when he was ill) and amanuensis. However, she often complained to her children that her hand became tired from writing. She ran her household so as to free Darwin of unpleasant and routine tasks. Her interest in prescribing therapeutic medicines for servants and local people in Down Village may have sparked some of Darwin's later interest in stimulating sensitive and insectiverous plants with a variety of anesthetics and soporifics. She also encouraged her children (five surviving boys, two surviving girls) in their interests, which included botany, insect collecting, and egg collecting, as well as music and literature. She was an excellent musician, and played piano for her family regularly.

Her humor and liveliness came through in her accounts to her children of the daily life of her complicated household. Those aspects of her personality are evident far more clearly in her unpublished letters to her oldest son, William, than to her daughter Henrietta, although it was HENRIETTA DARWIN LITCHFIELD who collected her mother's letters into a book published after her mother's death. Henrietta's view of her mother's intense religious beliefs and excessive concern over her husband's and children's illnesses is somewhat contradicted by these other letters. After her husband's death, Emma Darwin purchased a house in Cambridge, where she lived for part of the year with her daughter Elizabeth (Bessie), close to three of her children's families. The rest of the year she spent at Down with her children and grandchildren visiting her there. She died in 1896 and is buried in Down churchyard.   JH

PRIMARY SOURCES
Litchfield, Henrietta Darwin, ed. *Emma Darwin, Wife of Charles Darwin: A Century of Family Letters.* Cambridge: privately printed, 1904.
Emma Darwin's letters, diaries, and notes for Darwin in her hand along with photographs and portraits are in the Darwin Archive, Cambridge University Library.

SECONDARY SOURCES
Browne, Janet. *Charles Darwin: Voyaging.* Vol. 1. New York: Knopf 1995.

Desmond, Adrian, and James Moore. *Darwin.* London: Michael Joseph, 1992.

DASHKOVA, PRINCESS EKATERINA ROMANOVNA (1743–1810)
Russian cultural figure. Born 28 March 1743 or 1744 in St. Petersburg to Marfa Ivanovna (Surmina) and Roman I. Vorontsov. Four siblings. Married Mikhail I. Dashkov. Three children: Anastasiia, Mikhail, Pavel. Professional experience: Russian Academy of Sciences, director. Died 16 January 1810 in Moscow.

Ekaterina Romanovna Dashkova was born in either 1743 or 1744. Her family was in favor at the imperial court and her godparents were the Empress Elizabeth and her nephew Grand Prince Peter. Dashkova's mother died in 1745 and her father sent her to live with the family of his brother Mikhail Vorontsov who was vice-chancellor of the Russian Empire.

Dashkova was educated according to the standards of the day, concentrating largely on foreign languages and literatures with some reading in philosophy. In 1759, Dashkova married Prince Mikhail Ivanovich Dashkov and had several children: Anastasiia in 1760, Mikhail in 1761 (he died within a year), and Pavel in 1763. In 1764, Dashkova's husband died suddenly, leaving her the title of Princess, but very little else.

Dashkova had, for several years, been close friends with Grand Princess Ekaterina Alekseevna, the future Empress Catherine II, and she claimed to have played a leading role in the coup that brought Catherine to power in June 1762. In any case, she was richly rewarded for her support with a large sum of money. However, relations between Dashkova and the new empress soon deteriorated, and Dashkova withdrew to one of her family estates near Moscow. In 1769, she took her family on a tour of Europe, visiting Prussia, France, Great Britain, and Switzerland, and meeting famous men including Voltaire, Diderot, and Frederick II. On her return to Russia, she was for a time again in Catherine's good graces before the apparently inevitable falling-out occurred. She withdrew again to Moscow, but this time began to write and publish articles and translations into Russian from French and English in the journal *Opyt trudov.*

In 1776, she left with her children for Edinburgh, where she spent three happy years while her son took a university degree there. Upon her return in 1782, Catherine was again glad to see her and named her director of the Russian Academy of Sciences with instructions to restore its affairs to order. The Russian Academy of Sciences had been founded by Peter the Great to promote study of a wide range of scientific, technical, and cultural fields, and had originally included a secondary school and a university. These educational institutions were never really successful and the academy, under Peter's successors, had been badly mismanaged and neglected. Dashkova put the financial affairs of the academy on a sound footing and saw that its publications met their schedule. She renewed the tradition of public lectures on mathematics, physics, mineralogy, and natural history, which proved highly popular. She is also credited with raising professors' salaries and doubling the number of scholarships for students.

In 1783 Dashkova launched publication of a literary magazine, *Sobesednik liubitelei rossiiskago slova*. This limited itself to original works in Russian to which writers like Derzhavin and Fonvizin contributed, as did Dashkova herself and Catherine II. The journal did not last long, and another, *Novye ezhemesiachnye sochineniia,* began in 1786, including science sections which members of the academy were expected to contribute. Another publication was *Russkii teatr,* on the Russian theater.

In the eighteenth century, French was still the language of culture and the court, but Russian, thanks in large part to the efforts of Mikhail Lomonosov (d. 1765), was increasingly becoming a literary language. In 1783, Catherine II founded the Russian Academy to study and popularize the Russian language and Dashkova became its first president. She was responsible for compiling the first Russian etymological dictionary which was published in six volumes between 1789 and 1794. She also established a department of translation to translate the best of foreign books into Russian.

Another quarrel with Catherine led to a leave of absence on Dashkova's part. In 1796 Catherine died and was succeeded by her son Paul. Catherine and Paul had been on the worst possible terms and all Catherine's appointees including Dashkova were dismissed. Paul's reign was short, and when Alexander I came to the throne in 1801, he invited Dashkova to return, but she felt that she was too old. She spent her remaining years on her estate at Troitskoe near Moscow. It was during this period that she dictated her famous memoirs to a young Irish friend Martha Wilmot.

Dashkova was the most prominent nonroyal woman in eighteenth-century Russia. She was by all accounts vain, capricious, and autocratic. She quarreled with almost everyone she came in contact with—including her son and daughter, both of whom she disinherited—and she seems to have bullied the scientists at the Academy of Sciences. Although she did much to improve the condition of the Academy of Sciences, she did it a grave disservice by appointing a very inferior successor when she withdrew on her leave of absence. Perhaps her greatest lasting contribution to Russian science and culture lay in her efforts on behalf of the Russian language as the language of science and the arts and the encouragement she gave to Russian writers and dramatists. She also left invaluable memoirs, voluminous correspondence with many notable people of the day, as well as other work in various genres.   ACH

PRIMARY SOURCES

Dashkova, Ekaterina Romanovna. *Mon histoire.* Memoirs, originally transcribed in French by Martha Wilmot. Various versions and translations exist. The most complete Russian edition is *Zapiski kniagini Dashkovoi* (Memoirs of the Princess Daschkaw, Lady of Honour to Catherine II, Empress of All the Russias). Ed. N. D. Chechulin. St. Petersburg: Izd. A. S. Suvorina, 1907.

SECONDARY SOURCES

Bol'shaia sovetskaia entsiklopediia. 3rd ed. Moscow: Izd-vo "Sovetskaia entsiklopediia," 1973.

Wieczynski, Joseph L., ed. *The Modern Encyclopedia of Russian and Soviet History.* Gulf Breeze, Fla.: Academic International Press, 1979.

DAULTON, AGNES WARNER MCCLELLAND (1867–1944)

U.S. author, illustrator, and lecturer. Born 29 April 1867 in New Philadelphia, Ohio, to Lucy (Warner) and Lewis McClelland. Educated Oberlin College. Married George Daulton (9 December 1890). Professional experience: contributed serials and stories to St. Nicholas, Outlook, *and other magazines; lectured on literature and childhood. Died 5 June 1944 at Woodstock, N.Y.*

Agnes W. Daulton spent her childhood in New Philadelphia, Ohio, and was educated at Oberlin College. Upon marrying George Daulton, also a writer, in 1890, she briefly resided in Chicago before moving to New York City. There she began lecturing on child psychology and literature as well as writing juvenile fiction and books for children concerning nature. Many of her works have been translated into foreign languages. Daulton's nature writings include *Wings and Stings* (1903) and *Autobiography of a Butterfly and Other Stories* (1905). With these stories, Daulton intended to instill in children a compassionate appreciation of nature. To do so, Daulton allowed bees, ants, birds, butterflies, beetles, and flowers to tell their life histories, including details of their everyday life, their allies, and their adversaries. Daulton had an early knowledge of the necessity to preserve wildlife and hoped to hinder its destruction by writing stories that taught children to respect all forms of life, including birds and insects. Although Daulton's stories attribute human characteristics to animals and plant life, they accurately depict their life cycles and are punctuated by the author's realistic sketches of her wildlife subjects.

Daulton's children's works include *Dusk Flyers* (1908), *Fritzi* (1908), *From Sioux to Susan* (1910), *The Gentle Interference of Bab* (1912), *The Marooning of Peggy* (1915), and *Green Gate* (1926). Daulton also contributed serials and stories to various publications and was considered to be an authority on floriculture. An honorary member of the Chicago Women's Club of New York and a member of the Staten Island Women's Club and the Fortnightly Club of Staten Island, Daulton was a supporter of woman suffrage. Daulton died after a long illness at her home, Bittersweet, in Woodstock, New York on 5 June 1944.   CB

PRIMARY SOURCES

Daulton, Agnes. *Wings and Stings.* Illustrated by the author. New York: Rand, McNally & Company, 1903.
———. *Autobiography of a Butterfly and Other Stories.* Illustrated by the author. New York: Rand, McNally & Company, 1905.

STANDARD SOURCES

Who's Who of American Women; WWW(A).

DAVENPORT, GERTRUDE (CROTTY) (1866–1946)

U.S. zoologist. Born 28 February 1866 in Asequa, Colo. Married Charles B. Davenport. Educated University of Kansas (B.S., 1889); Radcliffe College (1892–1894). Professional experience: University of Kansas, instructor (1889–1892); Cold Spring Harbor Laboratory, researcher on microscopic methods (1893–1903).

After Gertrude Crotty earned her bachelor's degree at the University of Kansas, she remained at Kansas until 1892 as an instructor in zoology. She then went to Radcliffe College, where she studied for two years, but apparently did not get a degree. She married Charles B. Davenport, who accepted a position as director of the Carnegie Station for Experimental Evolution at Cold Springs Harbor. At Cold Springs, Gertrude worked on microscopic methods in the biology laboratory. She also served on the women's auxiliary board. After 1903, Gertrude did not hold a paid position, but she and Charles collaborated on many of his publications on experimental evolution. Gertrude Davenport did research on the embryology of the turtle, variation in *Sargatia* and starfish, variations in organisms, and human heredity, all of which complemented her husband's interests.   JH/MBO

PRIMARY SOURCES

Davenport, Gertrude. *The Primitive Streak and Notochordal Canal in Chelonia.* Boston: Ginn, 1896.
———. "Heredity of Skin Pigment in Man." *American Naturalist* 44 (November/December 1910); 641–731.
———. With Charles B. Davenport. *Elements of Zoology.* Rev. ed. New York: Macmillan, 1911.

STANDARD SOURCES

AMS 1–7 (listed as Mrs. Charles B. or Mrs. C. B.); Bailey; Rossiter 1982; Siegel and Finley.

DAVID, FLORENCE N. (1909–)

British/U.S. statistician. Born 23 August 1909 in Hereford, England. Educated University of London (B.Sc., 1931; Ph.D., 1938; D.Sc., 1950). Professional experience: University College London, lecturer through professor of statistics (1935–1967); University of California, Berkeley, professor of statistics (1961–1962; 1964–1965); University of California, Riverside, professor of statistics (from 1967). Concurrent experience: Ministry of Home Security, United Kingdom, senior statistician (1929–1945); U.S. Forest Service, consultant (1963); Pacific State Hospital, Pomona, Calif., consultant (1965).

Although Florence David was born and educated in the United Kingdom, she eventually immigrated to the United States. Her field of statistics was much in demand, and while she was teaching at the University of London, she came to the United States to teach at Berkeley for two one-year appointments. In 1967, she came to the United States permanently as a professor of statistics at the University of California, Riverside. She was a fellow of the American Statistical Society, the Institute for Mathematical Statistics, and the Royal Statistical Society. Her research was on combinatorial and randomization methods and statistical applications.

JH/MBO

STANDARD SOURCES

AMS P&B 11, 12–14.

DAVIDSON, ADA D. (fl. 1893)

U.S. geologist.

Little information is available on Ada Davidson, except that she was from Oberlin, Ohio, and was later a president of the Woman's National Science Club. She spoke at the separate Woman's Department of Geology at the World's Congress of Geology in August 1893. The woman's program at which she spoke was completely separate from the main program, and in fact conflicted with it.   JH/MBO

STANDARD SOURCES

Mozans; Rossiter 1982.

DAVIS, ADELLE (1904–1974)

U.S. nutritionist and writer on food and health. Born 25 February 1904 in Lizton, Indiana, to Harriet (McBollom) and Charles Eugene Davis. Four sisters. Married (1) no information (divorced); (2) George Edward Leisey 1946 (divorced 1953); (3) Frank V. Seiglinger (1960). Two adopted children with Leisley. Educated Lizton High School; Purdue University (1923–1925); University of California, Berkeley (B.A., 1927); Bellevue and Fordham Hospitals,

New York City (dietetics training); University of Southern California (M.S. in biochemistry, 1939). Professional experience: Yonkers, N.Y., public schools, consulting nutritionist (1928–1931). Oakland Calif., private consulting nutritionist (1931–1933); Los Angeles, private consulting nutritionist (1934–1958); popular lecturer, writer, and television guest on nutrition (1947–1973). Died of multiple myeloma, 31 May 1974.

Daisie Adelle Davis was the youngest child of Charles Eugene and Harriet Davis. Her mother became paralyzed ten days after her birth and died seventeen months later, leaving five girls to be raised by their father and an elderly aunt. Living on a farm, the entire family worked hard. When the 4-H Club was formed, Adelle (she dropped the name Daisie, saying it was used too often for cows or pigs) joined and was an active member until she left for college, winning ribbons for bread and canned fruits and vegetables at fairs.

After graduating from Lizton High School, Adelle Davis enrolled at Purdue University to study dietetics. She took odd jobs to help pay expenses and after two years transferred to the University of California at Berkeley, where she received her bachelor's in dietetics in 1927. Davis then moved to New York City to take instruction in hospital dietetics at Bellevue and Fordham hospitals. As a nutritionist at the Judson Health Center in Manhattan's Little Italy, she worked directly with patients and enjoyed the experience so much that she decided against further hospital assignments. She enrolled at the Columbia University Teachers College, but left before the year was out to travel in Europe.

Returning from Europe, Davis moved to Oakland, California, to become a consulting nutritionist at the Alameda County Health Clinic. Two years later, she associated with the William E. Branch clinic in Hollywood and began taking postgraduate classes from the University of Southern California. In 1939, she received a master of science degree in biochemistry and turned full time to her private consulting practice, advising many patients of local physicians who were referred to her. She was convinced that proper nutrition was the key to finding and maintaining good health.

Critical of most cookbooks, Davis took a course in writing, then set out to produce her own cookbook, one that would give practical and tempting recipes for adding nutritious ingredients such as organic fruits and vegetables, whole grains, powdered milk, and brewer's yeast to family meals and that would describe how to prepare food in the best ways for preserving flavors and nutrients. The result of her first efforts was *Let's Cook It Right* in 1947. The cookbook was so well received that she began a second, which concentrated on foods and nutritional advice for pregnant and lactating mothers, as well as for infants and growing children.

When the general public became caught up in the health food movement, Davis was highly sought after as a speaker for television and the lecture circuit.   JH/MBO

PRIMARY SOURCES
Davis, Adelle. *Vitality through Planned Nutrition.* New York: Macmillan, 1942.
———. *Let's Cook It Right.* New York: Harcourt, 1947; revised 1962.
———. *Let's Have Healthy Children.* New York: Harcourt, 1951; revised 1972.
———. *Let's Eat Right to Keep Fit.* New York: Harcourt, 1954.
———. *Let's Get Well.* New York: Harcourt, 1965.

SECONDARY SOURCES
Baker, Ruth. "Encounter with Adelle Davis," *Journal of Nutrition Education* Summer 1972.
Howard, Jane. "Earth Mother to the Food Faddists." *Life* 11 October 1971.
New York Times, 1 June 1974. Obituary notice.
Rynearson, Edward H, "Americans Love Hogwash." *Nutritional Review* July 1974.

STANDARD SOURCES
Current Biography 1973; *NAW*(M) (article by James Harvey Young).

DAVIS, ALICE (ROHDE) (1882–1933)
U.S. biochemist. Born 1882 in Burlington, Iowa. Married H. N. Davis. Educated University of Chicago (B.S., 1903); Johns Hopkins University School of Medicine (M.D., 1910); University of Berlin (1910–1913). Professional experience: Carnegie Institute of Technology, instructor in biochemistry (1913–1914); Johns Hopkins School of Medicine, assistant pharmacologist (1914–1916); University of California, assistant professor of research medicine (1916–1918); University of Pittsburgh, biochemist (1918–1919); Cornell University Medical College (1919–1920). Died 1933.

Alice Rhode Davis received an excellent education both in the United States and abroad and seemed to be developing a career as a research chemist. However, after 1933, she no longer appears in *American Men of Science,* and nothing is recorded about her career after 1920. She was a member of the Society of Biological Chemists, and her research was on the constituents of the blood with special reference to amino acids, sugar, and purines.   JH/MBO

STANDARD SOURCES
AMS 4–5.

DAVIS, FRANCES (ELLIOTT) (ca. 1882–1965)

U.S. nurse and community leader. Born 28 April 1882(?) in Shelby(?), N.C., to Emma and Darryl Elliott. Married William A. Davis. Educated intermittently in Pittsburgh, Pa., public schools; Knoxville (Tenn.) College (graduated 1907); Freedmen's Hospital Training School for Nurses, Washington, D.C. (graduated 1913); Columbia University Teachers College (1929). Professional experience: Henderson, N.C., teacher (1908–1910); Washington, D.C., private duty nursing (1913–1916); Town and Country Nursing (1917); American Red Cross, nurse (from 1918); John A. Andrew Memorial Hospital, director of nurses' training (1919); Dunbar Hospital, Detroit, Mich., organized training school for black nurses (1919–1920); superintendent of nurses and director of nurses' training (1923–1927); Detroit Visiting Nurses' Association (1920; 1935–1940); Detroit Health Department, Child Welfare Division, prenatal, maternal, and child health clinics (1927–1929); Health Department (1929–1932). Inkster, Michigan, established day nursery (1940–1945); Eloise Hospital, Wayne County, Ill., (1945–1951). Died 11 May 1965 in Detroit.

The daughter of a plantation owner and Methodist minister's white daughter and a part-black and part-Cherokee Indian sharecropper, Frances Elliott grew up as an orphan, for her mother died when she was five and her father had fled the area. Her education was intermittent as she moved from one place to another with her guardian. Elliott got the help that she needed to further her education from the Joseph Reed family for whom she had worked as household help. They helped her leave the guardian and go to Knoxville, Tennessee, College, to enter a teacher training program. Although Elliott graduated from this program, she longed to become a nurse, and entered a newly formed training program organized by Knoxville College. Ill health forced her to leave the program, but in the spring of 1910 she enrolled at the Freedmen's Hospital Training School for Nurses in Washington, D.C., from which she graduated. After doing private nursing in Washington, she became the first black nurse to take the Town and Country Nursing Service Course sponsored by the American Red Cross. Her race still precluded her from being accepted fully by the Red Cross. However, she was sent to Jackson, Tennessee, where she provided nursing care and taught the rudiments of sanitation and prenatal care.

In 1917, the United States had entered World War I, and the American Red Cross served as the procurement agency for the Army Nurse Corps. Although the Town and Country Nurses were automatically enrolled as Red Cross Nurses, Davis had not been included because of her race. However, on 2 July 1918, she became the first black nurse to be enrolled. Her major task with the Red Cross was working with the soldiers in training and later nursing victims of the influenza epidemic. Davis herself fell victim to a severe attack of influenza, which left her heart permanently damaged. After the war, she had a variety of nursing jobs, but managed to find time to marry William Davis. Their only child was stillborn.

Frances Davis had always wanted a bachelor's degree. In 1929, with her husband's blessing, she returned to Columbia University Teachers College to complete the degree. However, ill health forced her to leave the program. After her return, the family moved to the Inkster, Michigan, community outside of Detroit. During the Depression, Davis distributed food to Inkster residents from the Ford Motor Plant Commissary. She also convinced Henry Ford to help the Inkster community. Not only did she give freely of her time to help those who needed it, she continued to work with the Detroit Health Department until 1932. At this time she went back to work for the Visiting Nurses' Association to give her more time to do her volunteer work. In 1935, she returned to the Visiting Nurses' Association and worked there until 1940 when she again saw a community need—this time for a nursery in Inkster. She attracted the attention of Eleanor Roosevelt, who obtained money for the enterprise. She worked there until 1951, when she again became ill. After that, Davis remained at home to care for her husband, who died in 1959. Shortly before she was to be honored at the American Red Cross national convention in Detroit, she died of a heart attack on 11 May 1965.   JH/MBO

STANDARD SOURCES
NAW(M) (article by Joyce Ann Elmore).

DAVIS, GRACE EVANGELINE (1870–1955)

U.S. physicist. Born 1871 in North Chelmsford, Mass. Educated Wellesley College (A.B., 1898; M.A., 1908). Professional experience: Wellesley College, instructor (1899–1908), associate professor (1908–1936); associate professor emerita (1936–1955). Died 16 April 1955 in Wellesley, Mass.

Physics professor Grace Evangeline Davis spent her entire academic career at Wellesley. Both her bachelor's and master's degrees were from this college, and she spent thirty-seven years teaching there. She was a physics instructor for nine years, after which she was promoted to associate professor. She remained at this rank until retirement. Davis held memberships in the Physical Society and the Meteorological Society.   JH/MBO

SECONDARY SOURCES
"Professor Grace E. Davis." *New York Times,* 16 April 1955.
    Obituary notice.

STANDARD SOURCES
AMS 3–8, P 9.

DAVIS, KATHARINE BEMENT (1860–1935)

U.S. nutritionist and social reformer. Born Buffalo, N.Y., 15 January 1860 to Frances (Bement) and Oscar Bill Davis. Four siblings. Educated Rochester Free Academy; Vassar (A.B. in food chemistry and nutrition, 1892); Columbia University (1892); University of Chicago (Ph.D. in political economy and sociology, 1900). Traveling fellowship (1898–1899?) University of Berlin; University of Vienna. Professional experience: Dunkirk High School, teacher (1880–1890); Brooklyn Heights Seminary for Girls, teacher; World's Columbian Exposition, Chicago, director of model workingman's home (1893); St. Mary's College Settlement, Philadelphia, director; New York State Reformatory for Women, Bedford Hills, superintendent (1901–1914); New York City, commissioner of corrections (1914–1917); New York State Bureau of Social Hygiene, secretary (1917–1928). Died December 1935 in Pacific Grove, Calif., of arteriosclerosis.

Born 15 January 1860 into an old and respected family, Katharine Bement Davis grew up comfortably but with a middle-class appreciation of the necessity of hard work and a commitment to maintaining those comforts. She enjoyed the benefits of music, dancing, and art lessons, quality public schooling, and participation in family political discussions—led by her grandmother, who spoke out against slavery, drink, and denial of rights for women. Katharine was encouraged by her teachers to continue her interest in chemistry after graduation from high school, but in 1879 the family could not afford to send her off to college. She began teaching at the local high school in Dunkirk in hopes of eventually financing her college education. Studying on her own at night, she finally entered the junior class at Vassar at age thirty.

A desire to work for social change had been instilled in Davis by her civically responsive family; she saw a way to combine that with her talent for chemistry in the field of sanitary science, a relatively new area developed most fully by ELLEN SWALLOW RICHARDS at MIT. Sanitary science combined aspects of public health, chemistry, nutrition, and home economics with a strong sociological dimension. At Vassar, Davis studied food chemistry and continued in related coursework at Columbia University after graduation, while teaching science at the Brooklyn Heights Seminary for Girls. Through her studies at Columbia, Davis obtained an appointment as director of a Chicago World's Fair exhibit on how laborers could live healthier lives on a meager budget. Her exhibit led to an offer of the position of head resident of the College Settlement in Philadelphia. In four tenements of the settlement, Davis created the "model" quarters of her exhibit but remained intellectually unfulfilled. Looking for an area that would afford her the opportunity to pursue her social reform goals and the career goal of entering academia, Davis chose to pursue a doctorate in the science of political economy at the new University of Chicago. Davis received her doctorate in political economy *cum laude* in June of 1900 at the age of forty, the first woman awarded a doctoral degree at the University of Chicago.

Why Davis abandoned the path to teaching in a college or university, the only career in 1900 that absolutely required a doctorate, is unclear. When MARION TALBOT, Dean of Women, and Thorstein Veblen, Davis's political science professor, recommended her for the job of superintendent at the new Bedford Hills Reformatory for Women, Davis accepted. She had no background in criminology, but soon became an active participant in the penal reform movement, which was part of the overall progressive social reform mentality at work in the early 1900s. Davis expanded the "teaching" aspect of rehabilitation to include trades far beyond the domestic skills taught in traditional women's institutions. She viewed Bedford's educational programs as important correctives to the social and economic barriers convicted women faced, and included instruction in farming and construction, arithmetic for accounting, and lectures on law and democracy. She embraced an environmental concept of responsibility for criminal behavior, arguing that the women who broke the law were themselves victims of destructive social and economic forces—poor education, poor public healthcare, inadequate housing, inability to cope with progressive urban life, child labor, and unemployment. She saw that many inmates were mentally retarded, and many were simply illiterate and ignorant due to their social circumstances. When faced with severe overcrowding and an increase in recidivist convicts, Davis searched for a more scientific, rational method of classifying and grouping offenders. Emily Rowland, a Mount Holyoke college psychologist, was brought in during the summer of 1910 to test the inmates and collect data. On the basis of the data, Davis sought and received funding from the New York Foundation to establish a modest psychological laboratory with a temporary psychologist. Determined to fund a permanent research laboratory for the study and classification of female offenders, Davis turned to John D. Rockefeller, Jr., who had expressed an interest in her work previously and who was engaged in forming a Bureau of Social Hygiene to support research into prostitution.

Rockefeller's decision to finance Davis's research facility began a long association between the two. He committed himself to $200,000 to set up the program at Bedford Hills and, under the aegis of the Bureau of Social Hygiene, provided an additional $150,000 for land and buildings adjacent to the existing Bedford property. Davis was installed as one of the original members of the board of the bureau and contributed information to George J. Kneeland's book on prostitution in New York City and to other similar works: Abraham Flexner, *Prostitution in Europe* (1914); Raymond B. Fosdick, *American Police Systems* (1921); H. B. Woolston, *Prostitution in the United States* (1921); Jean Weidensall, *The Mentality of the Criminal Woman* (1916). Under her influence, the bureau gradually expanded its initial studies aimed at palliative measures and entered more clearly into the sex research field. Davis directed an eight-year study of the sex lives of women that resulted in *Factors in the Sex Life of Twenty-Two Hundred Women* (1929), which included a section on lesbianism—a radical inclusion for that time.

In 1914, Davis became the first woman commissioner of correction for New York City and the first woman to hold a cabinet-level office in the history of the city. She soon began to apply her training as a social scientist and her experience using reform psychology to the fifteen prisons in the New York City system. Davis stayed in her position until 1917 in spite of criticism and refusal of the state to support her innovations with permanent legislation. From 1917 until 1928, she served as salaried general secretary of the New York State Bureau of Social Hygiene. Enthusiasm for social reform waned after the United States entered World War I, and, though she continued her campaign against venereal disease and prostitution into the 1920s, Davis was increasingly perceived by other bureau members as an obstructionist. In 1927, after ten years of service, she was fired in a reorganization by Rockefeller and others who felt the original purpose of the bureau had become "outmoded." Davis spent two years consulting and writing before retiring to California with her two sisters, who also never married. In December 1935, she died at age seventy-five of arteriosclerosis.

JH/MBO

PRIMARY SOURCES

Davis, Katharine Bement. "A Study of Prostitutes Committed from New York City to the State Reformatory for Women at Bedford Hills." In *Commercialized Prostitution in New York City,* ed. George Kneeland. New York: Century, 1913.

———. *Delinquency and Mental Defect.* N.p., 1916.

———, director. *Housing Conditions of Employed Women in the Borough of Manhattan: A Study Made by the Bureau of Social Hygiene.* New York: Bureau of Social Hygiene, 1922.

———. *Periodicity of Sex Desire.* St. Louis?: N.p., 1926–1927.

———. *Factors in the Sex Life of Twenty-Two Hundred Women.* New York and London: Harper & Brothers, [ca. 1929].

SECONDARY SOURCES

Bullough, Vern L. "Katharine Bement Davis, Sex Research,

and the Rockefeller Foundation." *Bulletin of the History of Medicine* 62, no. 1 (1988): 78–89.

Fitzpatrick, Ellen. *Endless Crusade: Women Social Scientists and Progressive Reform.* New York and Oxford: Oxford University Press, 1990.

STANDARD SOURCES
LKW.

DAVIS, MARGUERITE (1887–1987)

U.S. biochemist. Born 16 September 1887 in Racine, Wis. Father, Jefferson J. Davis. Never married. Educated University of Wisconsin (1906–1908); Graduate studies (1910–1912?); University of California, Berkeley (B.S., 1910). Professional experience: Squibb Pharmaceutical Company; University of Wisconsin, Department of Chemistry, researcher (from 1912); University of Wisconsin nutritional laboratory, founder; Rutgers University, School of Pharmacy, nutritional laboratory, founder; University of Wisconsin, consultant in biochemistry (1940–1987). Died 19 September 1987 in Racine, WI.

Marguerite Davis never finished her graduate work in biochemistry, but she made a name for herself as the codiscoverer of the nutritional factor vitamin A. She was born in Racine, Wisconsin, and important aspects of her life centered around this city. Her father was a physician, botanist, and professor at the University of Wisconsin. On her mother's side, her grandmother, Amy Davis Winship, had been an active suffragist and social worker. Davis entered the University of Wisconsin in 1906; there, she became interested in science and began to work with her future colleague, the biochemist Elmer Verner McCollum. Halfway through her studies, she left Wisconsin to attend the University of California, Berkeley, completing her bachelor of science degree in 1910. She returned to pursue a master's program in biochemistry, but never finished the degree. Instead she began to work seriously with McCollum to identify nutritional factors in the diet, an important subject at the time. Vitamin B had recently been demonstrated by Danish biochemist, Christian Eljkman. In 1913, Davis and McCollum identified and published on what they termed fat-soluble A and water-soluble B (later renamed vitamins A and B).

Following this major success, Davis became a permanent member of the research staff of the University of Wisconsin, Department of Chemistry, and set up a nutritional laboratory there. Later she went to Rutgers University, where she again founded a nutritional laboratory, this time in the School of Pharmacy. She remained there until her retirement in 1940, when she returned to Racine, serving as consultant to the chemistry department at the university until her death in 1987. Ten years before her death, she was also recognized for her work in civic affairs in Racine. JH/MBO

SECONDARY SOURCES
Racine Journal-Times, 19 September 1987. Obituary notice.

STANDARD SOURCES
Notable (article by George Milte).

DAVIS, OLIVE GRIFFITH STULL (1905–   )

U.S. zoologist. Born 10 February 1905 in Rochester, N.Y. Married Loy E. Davis (1930). Educated Smith College (A.B., 1926); University of Michigan (A.M., 1928; Ph.D., 1929). Professional experience: Hinsdale Museum fellow, Michigan (1927–1929); Syracuse University, teaching fellow (1926–1927); Virginia State Teachers College, Fredericksburg (1929–1930); Museum of Comparative Zoology, Harvard University, national research council fellow (1930–1931); Purdue University, technician (1943), assistant (1943–1953); assistant professor of veterinary anatomy, histology, and embryology (1953–1961), associate professor of veterinary anatomy (from 1961). Concurrent experience: U.S. Department of Agriculture, Bureau of Animal Industry (1943–1950).

Although Olive Stull Davis was trained as a herpetologist, and held fellowships in zoology museums at the University of Michigan and Harvard, much of her work was in veterinary medicine. She was also one of the women employed by the USDA, where she worked as an agent for poultry pathology.

Davis's research interests were varied. From her herpetology days she did research in the taxonomy, physiology, and distribution of snakes. She later worked in poultry pathology, avian leukosis, and cancer research. She was a member of the American Society of Ichthyologists and Herpetologists, the Association of Veterinary Anatomists, and the World Association of Veterinary Anatomists. JH/MBO

PRIMARY SOURCES
Stull, Olive Griffith. *Variations and Relationships in the Snakes of the Genus Pituophis.* Washington, D.C.: U.S. Government Printing Office, 1940.

STANDARD SOURCES
AMS 5–8 (under Olive Stull), B 9, P&B 10–11 (under Olive Davis); Bailey.

DAVIS, ROSE MAY (1894–?)

U.S. chemist. Born 17 November 1894 (possibly 1895) in Cumberland, Md. Educated Chowan College (1912–1914); Southern Conservatory of Music (1914–1916); Trinity College, N.C. (A.B., 1916); University of Virginia (1920–1922); Duke Uni-

versity (M.A., 1927; Ph.D., 1929). Professional experience: Virginia public high school, teacher and chemistry department head (1916–1919); Norfolk, Va., lawyer (1922–1923); Grenada College, professor of chemistry (1923–1924); Limestone College, professor of chemistry and biology (1924–1925); Duke University, teaching fellow and assistant in analytical chemistry (1925–1929); Randolph-Macon Woman's College, adjunct professor of chemistry (1929–1933); Duke University, instructor (1933–1935), research associate (1933–1934); University of New Hampshire, summer visiting professor (1935). I. E. du Pont de Nemours Company (from 1937). Memberships: American Chemical Society; Virginia Academy; and North Carolina Academy.

Rose May Davis had the type of career mobility that was typical of women scientists. She began her career as a high school chemistry teacher, and, after getting more education, she practiced law for a year. She then taught chemistry at two small colleges, and returned to Duke University to work on her master's degree (1927) and doctorate (1929). Her master's thesis was on doubly conjugated ketones and her doctoral dissertation was titled "Investigation of Isoquinoline Alkaloids: Examination of Pictet's Berberine Synthesis." After she received her doctoral degree, she became adjunct professor of chemistry, Randolph-Macon Woman's College (1929–1933). In 1933 she left to become an instructor at Duke University (1933–1935), then research associate, (1933–1934). At this time, Davis left academia and took a job with the legal department of the E. I. du Pont de Nemours company (from 1937).

Her professional interests included Pictet's berberine synthesis; synthesis of alkaloids; reactivity of doubly conjugated unsaturated ketones; catalytic reduction of certain aromatic aldehydes; and dipole moments of certain organic compounds. JH/MBO

PRIMARY SOURCES
Davis, Rose May. "Investivation of Isoquinoline Alkaloids." Ph.D. diss., Duke University, 1929.

STANDARD SOURCES
AMS 5–7.

DAVY, LADY JOANNA CHARLOTTE (FLEMMICH) (1865–1955)

British botanist. Born February 1865 in London. Married. Professional experience: plant collector, plant artist. Died 28 December 1955.

Lady Joanna Charlotte Davy is an example of the importance of the British amateur tradition in botany. She collected and drew plants and in the process discovered a new species, *Carex microglochin,* in the Ben Lawers mountain range, Scottish Highlands, in 1928. She was a friend of the botanist George Claridge Druce and undoubtedly consulted with him about her collections. Her plants are at Oxford, at Kew, and in the collection of J. E. Lousley at Reading University. Her drawings of British orchids are at the British Museum of Natural History. JH/MBO

SECONDARY SOURCES

Lousley, J. E. *Flora of Surrey.* Newton Abbot, England: David & Charles, 1976. Davy is mentioned on page 35.

Proceedings of the Botanical Society of the British Isles (1956): 190–192.

Wild Flower Magazine 407 (1986): 42–46.

STANDARD SOURCES

Desmond.

DAWSON, MARIA (fl. 1898–1901)

British chemist. Educated London (B.Sc.). Exhibition Research Scholar (1851); botanical laboratory.

Very little is known about British chemist Maria Dawson, except that she received a bachelor's degree from London University in 1851 and published three papers in biochemistry between 1898 and 1901. JH/MBO

STANDARD SOURCES

Creese 1991.

DAY, DOROTHY (1896–?)

U.S. plant physiologist. Born 1896. Educated Wellesley College (A.B., 1919); University of Wisconsin (M.A., 1925; Ph.D., plant physiology, 1927); University of Chicago, postgraduate studies (1927); Cornell University (1942–1943). Professional experience: Hood College, instructor in botany and bacteriology (1921–1924); University of Wisconsin, assistant instructor in botany; Mills College, instructor in botany and bacteriology (1927–1928), assistant professor (1928–1929); Smith College, assistant professor (1929–1937), associate professor in botany (1937–1942); Cornell University, assistant (1942–1943); California Central Fibre Corporation, plant physiologist (1943–1944); University of Minnesota, research associate (1944–1946). Quartermaster Corps, Biological Laboratories, microbiologist; Naval Shipyard, Philadelphia, industrial testing laboratory mycologist (1949); MacMurray College, associate professor of biology (1950–1952); Alaska Research Laboratories, microbiological consultant (1952–1954); Bio-Science Information Exchange, professional associate (1953–1955); public school teacher (1955–1957); Westminster College, lecturer in biology (1957–1958); Brigham Young University, visiting professor of botany (1958; 1960).

There seems to be no personal information on Dorothy Day, and her highly peripatetic career provides one with interesting questions but few answers. She was educated at Wellesley College, graduating in 1919. Teaching as an instructor in botany at Hood College from 1921 to 1924, Day earned enough to return to academic work, studying at the University of Wisconsin for a master's degree and then served as an assistant instructor in botany 1924 to 1926 while working towards her doctorate in plant physiology. Not content with that degree, completed in 1927, she went on for postgraduate work at the University of Chicago. From there, she went on to teach botany and bacteriology, first as an instructor and then as an assistant professor between 1928 to 1929 at Mills College.

In the fall of 1929, Day had the opportunity to teach at Smith College, where she remained for the next twelve years, moving from assistant to associate professor of botany between 1929 and 1942. Perhaps feeling that she had few opportunities to do research, she left that position in 1943, to spend a year in postgraduate study at Cornell University, while serving as a research assistant. From Cornell, Day went to work at the California Plant Fibre Corporation as a plant physiologist, and then moved to the University of Minnesota for the next two years, became a microbiologist with the Quartermaster Corps, and from there went to work as a mycologist with the Naval Shipyard in Philadelphia at their industrial testing laboratory. She returned for two years to college teaching as associate professor of biology at MacMurray College (1950–1952).

Over the next ten years, Day was microbiological consultant at the Alaska Research Laboratories, served as a professional associate of the Bio-Sci Information Exchange, taught in the public school system, lectured in biology at Westminster College, and then lectured as a visiting professor of botany at Brigham Young University (1958 and 1960). By this time, she was sixty-four years old. She drops from the lists of the *American Men of Science* after that year. She was a member of a number of professional organizations, including the Botanical Society of America, the American Society of Plant Physiologists, and the Society of Industrial Microbiology, which reflect her interests in plant physiology and industrial microbiology. She also had research interests in plant nutrition and tissue culture. JH/MBO

STANDARD SOURCES

AMS 7–8, B 9, P&B 10–11; Bailey.

DAY, GWENDOLEN HELEN (1883–1967)

British botanist. Born 1883. Professional experience: Bedford Natural History Society and Archaeological Society, president (1935). Died 20 June 1967.

Gwendolen Helen Day was active in local natural history societies. She is an example of a British woman amateur naturalist whose collections and descriptions of plants were useful in understanding the flora of a specific place, in her case Bedfordshire. She contributed to J. G. Dony's *Flora Bedfordshire.* Her herbarium is in the Bedford Natural History and Archaeological Society. JH/MBO

PRIMARY SOURCES
Dony, J. G. *Flora Bedfordshire.* Luton, England: Museum and Art Gallery, 1953. Day was a contributor.

SECONDARY SOURCES
Bedfordshire Naturalist (1965–1967): 46–47. Obituary notice.

STANDARD SOURCES
Desmond.

DAY, MARY ANNA (1852–1924)

U.S. botanical librarian. Educated Academy of Lancaster, MA. Professional experience: public school teacher (1871–1880); public librarian (1887–1892); Harvard University, Gray Herbarium, librarian (1893–1924). Died 1924.

A former schoolteacher, Mary Day was hired in 1893 by the Gray Herbarium at Harvard University as a librarian, although she had no botanical background. Her first task was to verify bibliographical references for the supplement to the *Synoptical Flora of North America.* After this assignment, she became an expert in botanical bibliography. She developed a wide botanical correspondence and over a period of twenty years completed the massive *Card Index of New Genera, Species, and Varieties of American Plants* (about 170,000 cards). The index was produced in quarterly issues of 1,000 to 2,500 cards. She was involved in the editorial work on most of the contributions from the Herbarium. She prepared and published a "list of Local Floras of New England" and "Herbariums of New England" for the New England Botanical Club. She also prepared the index for the journal *Rhodora.* JH/MBO

PRIMARY SOURCES
Day, Mary Anna.z "List of Local Floras of New England." In *The Local Floras of New England.* Cambridge, Mass.: New England Botanical Club, 1899.
———, comp. *Check List of the Plants Contained in* Gray's Manual. 7th ed. Cambridge, Mass.: Gray Herbarium of Harvard University, 1908.

SECONDARY SOURCES
Barnhart, John H. *Biographical Notes upon Botanists.* Boston: G. K. Hall, 1965.

Robinson, B. L. "Miss Day." *Rhodora* 26 (1924): 41–47. Obituary notice; includes photograph of Day.

STANDARD SOURCES
Bailey; Rossiter 1982.

DE ALMANIA, JACQUELINE FELICIA (ca. 1290–1322)

See Felicie, Jacoba.

DE BRÉAUTÉ, ELÉONORE-NELL-SUZANNE (1794–1855)

French astronomer. Born 29 June 1794 in Rouen, France, to Marie and Jean Letellier. Honors and memberships: French academy of science, member. Died 3 February 1855.

Eléonore De Bréauté was born at the end of the eighteenth century. She was the first to observe the comet of 1823 and was instrumental in the construction of a map of Normandy showing different points of elevation. Bréauté Peninsula was named in her honor in 1823. She financed the voyage of the explorer Blosseville to Greenland in 1833. JH/MBO

STANDARD SOURCES
Debus.

DE CHANTAL, MME.

See Sévigné, Marie de Rabutin-Chantal, Marquise de.

DECKER, JANE CYNTHIA (MCLAUGHLIN) (1935–1988)

U.S. botanist. Born 22 June 1935 in Cleveland, Ohio, to Jean and Harold McLaughlin. One brother. Married Henry F. Decker. Three children. Educated Mount Holyoke College (A.B., 1957; M.S., 1958); Yale University (Ph.D., 1961). Professional experience: Bridgewater State College, Mass., instructor (1960–1961); Southern Connecticut State College, instructor (1961–1962); The Ohio State University, instructor (1962–1965), assistant professor; Ohio Wesleyan University, visiting assistant professor (1965–1966), visiting associate professor (1968–1973), assistant professor (1973–1978), associate professor (1978–1982), professor (1982–1988). Died 5 November 1988.

Jane Cynthia McLaughlin was born in Ohio but attended college at Mount Holyoke and Yale University. After marrying Henry Decker while she was in graduate school, she taught for two years in New England. She returned to Ohio to teach at The Ohio State University. After five years at

Ohio State Decker began teaching at Ohio Wesleyan University, as first a visiting assistant and then a visiting associate professor. She then accepted a regular appointment as assistant professor, filling the post left vacant by her husband. Henry Decker left the university to establish Buckeye Bluegrass Farms, Inc., where he conducted experiments on various turf grasses. Jane Decker proceeded to climb the academic ladder, eventually becoming a full professor. Along the way, she convinced the university president that botany and zoology should be separate departments. She also was a great supporter of establishing what became the university's Kraus and Bohannan Nature Preserves. A supporter of Junior Science Fair activities, she was assistant director of the academy's State Science Day starting in 1978. She also promoted women in science as a topic for a workshop. She and her husband published a book on lawn care that resulted from their research. They had three children, Susan J. and twins Emily and Douglas. In November of 1988, Jane Decker died of cancer.

Decker received important awards. She was honored by being named to the Allen Trimble Chair in botany. She received Ohio Wesleyan's highest award for outstanding teaching, the Bishop Herbert Welch Meritorious Teaching Award, presented to her at the commencement program (1988). Decker was an important member of the Ohio Academy of Science and served it in different offices. Her memberships in various scientific organizations included the Botanical Society of America, American Association of Plant Taxonomists, American Fern Society, American Institute of Biological Sciences, American Association for the Advancement of Science, and Sigma Xi.

Her research was on the wood anatomy and phylogeny of tropical plants, *Batidaceae* and *Ochnaceae*. She became interested in using biochemical techniques to classify plants. These techniques required that she master tissue culturing to investigate developmental processes in plants and chromosome banding to determine the nature of genetic diseases.

JH/MBO

PRIMARY SOURCES

Decker, Harry F., and Jane M. Decker. *Lawn Care: A Handbook for Professionals.* Englewood Cliffs, N.J.: Prentice Hall, 1988.

SECONDARY SOURCES

Stuckey, Ronald L. *Women Botanists of Ohio.* Columbus, Ohio: Ronald Stuckey, 1992.

DEFLANDRE-RIGAUD, MARTHE (fl. 1969)

French micropaleontologist and palynologist. Married Georges Deflandre.

Micropaleontologist and palynologist Marthe Deflandre-Rigaud collaborated on research with her husband, Georges Deflandre (1897–1973).

JH/MBO

PRIMARY SOURCES

Deflandre-Rigaud, Marthe. With Georges Deflandre. *Fichier micropaléontologique général, Séries 17 et 18. Nanno fossiles calculaires I et II.* Paris: C.N.R.S., 1967.

———. *Liste chronologique des travaux publiés.* Paris: Laboratoire de Micropaleontologie de l'École Pratique des Hautes Etudes. 5 p. Bibliography complete to April 1969.

STANDARD SOURCES

Sarjeant.

DE FRAINE, ETHEL LOUISE (1879–1918)

British botanist. Born 2 November 1879 in Aylesbury, Buckinghamshire. Educated University of London (D.Sc.). Professional experience: Battersea Polytechnic, lecturer in botany (1910–1913); University of London, Westfield College (1915). Honors and memberships: Fellow of the Linnean Society (1918). Died 25 March 1918 at Falmouth.

Plant anatomist Ethel de Fraine had an active research career of only about ten years. During this time, however, she was very productive, contributing to the knowledge of the relationship between the vascular structure of the stem and that of the primary root and contributing greatly to the knowledge of seedling anatomy. Collaborating with T. G. Hill, she produced a series of four papers in *Annals of Science* on the seedling structure of gymnosperms. Botanist ETHEL SARGANT initiated the school of seedling anatomy to which these publications belong. De Fraine published an independent contribution on the seedling anatomy of the Cactaceae in 1910.

De Fraine concluded that whereas the study of seedlings was important from a taxonomic point of view, it had little to impart to the study of phylogeny. Although she ventured into the realm of fossil botany only once, the paper that she published on the structure and affinities of *Sutcliffia* was important. After taking part in ecological expeditions she published a treatise on the anatomy of *Salicornia* and the common seaside glasswort. Her last publication was in 1916, on the morphology and anatomy of the genus *Statice* as studied from its habitat at Blakeney Point.

JH/MBO

PRIMARY SOURCES

De Fraine, Ethel. With T. G. Hill. "On the Seedling Structure of Gymnosperms I." *Annals of Botany* 22 (1908): 689–712.

———. With T. G. Hill. "On the Seedling Structure of Gymnosperms II." *Annals of Botany* 23 (1909): 189–227.

———. With T. G. Hill. "On the Seedling Structure of Gymnosperms III." *Annals of Botany* 23 (1909): 433–458.

———. With T. G. Hill. "On the Seedling Structure of Gymnosperms IV." *Annals of Botany* 24 (1910): 319–333.

SECONDARY SOURCES
"Notes." *Nature* 101 (25 April 1918): 150–151.

STANDARD SOURCES
Desmond.

DE GORZANO, LEONETTA (b. 14th century)

Italian physician. Born fourteenth century in Turin. Married Giovanni Gorzano.

Leonetta de Gorzano was the wife of Giovanni di Gorzano and practiced as a doctor in Padua and Turin.   JH/MBO

STANDARD SOURCES
Echols and Williams; Hurd-Mead 1938.

DE GRAFFENRIED, MARY CLARE (1849–1921)

U.S. social investigator/statistical compiler. Born 19 May 1849 in Macon, Ga., to Mary Holt (Marsh) and William Kirkland de Graffenried. One younger brother. Educated Weslyan Female College (1865). Professional experience: Georgetown Female Seminary (later Waverley Seminary), teacher of Latin, literature, mathematics (1876–1886); Federal Patent office, copyist (1886); Bureau of Labor, investigator (1886–1888), special investigator (1888–1906). Studied women's working conditions, child labor, industrial safety. Died 26 April 1921 in Washington, D.C., from lethargic encephalitis.

Mary Clare de Graffenried was born in Macon, Georgia, into a family with a connection to eighteenth-century Swiss aristocrats. Her father was a free thinker, a lawyer, and later a colonel in the Confederacy, although he had initially opposed secession. She graduated at the top of her class from Wesleyan Female Seminary in 1865, where she must have received an excellent training in mathematics as well as Latin and literature, since she later taught those subjects. Presumably teaching first in schools in Georgia, she went to Washington, D.C., in 1876, where she taught at Georgetown Female Seminary until 1886. In that year, through the influence of the secretary of the interior, L. Q. C. Lamar, a friend of her father, she obtained a position as a copyist in the U.S. Patent Office and almost immediately afterward moved to the U.S. Department of Labor as an investigator. When this became an independent department, she was appointed a special investigator with nineteen others. She began to investigate conditions of working women and children in the Northeast and South in factories and at home, compiling statistics for the commissioner of labor, Carroll Wright.

An early member of the American Economic Association, de Graffenried began to publish articles in the association's journal; she won a number of prizes for her articles on working women that appeared from 1890 to 1896. She began to get wider attention with articles in the *Century Magazine* on southern women working in cotton mills and illiteracy rates, mixing vivid depictions of difficult situations with objective statistics and facts. In 1892, she was sent to Belgium to investigate industrial education there. Many of her articles first were given as lectures before women's groups like the National Conference of Charities and Corrections, and the Women's Christian Association. She never became active in suffrage or in contemporary social movements, although her information was used for these movements. She entertained widely at her home in Washington. After she retired in 1906, she traveled to Europe, Africa, and Asia. She died in Washington, D.C., in 1921.   JH/MBO

PRIMARY SOURCES
De Graffenried, Mary Clare. "The Needs of Self-Supporting Women." In *Studies in Historical and Political Science,* ed. Herbert Baxter Adams. Baltimore: Johns Hopkins University, 1890.

———. "The Georgia Cracker in the Cotton Mills." *Century Magazine* (February 1892).

———. [On child labor]. *Publications of the American Economics Association* (1890).

———. [On working women]. *Forum,* (1893).

SECONDARY SOURCES
Steelman, Lala Carr. "Mary Clare de Graffenried." In *Studies in the History of the South, 1875–1922.* Publications in History, vol. 3. Ed. John Steelman. Greenville, N.C.: Dept. of History, East Carolina College, 1966.

STANDARD SOURCES
NAW (article by Lala Carr Steelman).

DEICHMANN, ELISABETH (1896–?)

Danish/U.S. marine scientist. Born 12 June 1896 in Copenhagen, Denmark, to Christine (Lund) and Henrik Deichmann. Educated University of Copenhagen (M.Sc. in zoology, 1922); Radcliffe College, Harvard (Ph.D., 1927). Professional experience: Royal Agricultural School zoological laboratory, assistant (1918–1923?); British Museum (1926, 1953); U.S. Bureau of Fisheries, assistant (1928); Museum Comparative Zoology, Harvard, Agassiz Fellow (1929–1930), assistant curator, marine invertebrates

(1930–1942), curator (1942–1961), emerita (1961–1975). *Honors and memberships: Danish government, Freedom Medal (1946); Knight of Dannebrog for zoological work and Danish culture.*

Elisabeth Deichmann was born 12 June 1896 in Copenhagen, Denmark, to a physician father and a mother who was an artist and a member of Danish Royal Art Academy. Elisabeth attended schools in Denmark, receiving a master's degree from the University of Copenhagen in 1922. She was appointed assistant zoologist at the Royal Agricultural College of Copenhagen (under I. E. V. Boas). Receiving a Danish Rask Oersted Foundation grant for research, she spent 1924 at Pacific Grove, California. During 1926, Deichmann worked for the British Museum. She took classes at Radcliffe College to obtain her doctorate (1927), then became assistant zoologist at the U.S. Bureau of Fisheries. She was named Agassiz Fellow at the museum of comparative zoology at Harvard University and became the curator of invertebrates in 1930. She spent the summers of 1931, 1933, and 1936 teaching classes at Stanford University.

Elisabeth Deichmann's specialties were Echinoderms and corals and she was instrumental in classification, discovering several new species herself. She did field work in Cuba, Panama, Mexico, and coastal regions of North America. Much of her research centered on the octocorals and holothurians. She produced over fifty publications and reports.

JH/MBO

PRIMARY SOURCES

Deichmann, Elisabeth. *Holothurians of the Western Part of the Atlantic Ocean.* With twenty-four plates. Cambridge: [Museum of Comparative Zoology, Harvard], 1930.
———. *Alcyonaria of the Western Part of the Atlantic Ocean.* With thirty-seven plates. Cambridge: [Museum of Comparative Zoology, Harvard], 1936.
———. *Notes on Pennatulacea and Holothurioidea Collected by the First and Second Bingham Oceanographic Expeditions 1925–1926.* New Haven, Conn.: Bingham Oceanographic Foundation, 1936.
———. *New Holothurian of the Genus Thyone Collected on the Presidential Cruise of 1938.* Washington, D.C.: Smithsonian Institution, 1939.
———. *Coelenterates Collected on the Presidential Cruise of 1938.* With one plate. Washington: Smithsonian Institution, 1941.
———. *New Species of Thyone s. s., from the Gulf of Mexico: Thyone Mexicana spec. nov.* Baton Rouge: Louisiana State University Press, 1946.
———. *Rediscovery of the Holothurian Holothuria Peruviana Lesson.* New York: American Museum of Natural History, 1952.
———. *Holothurioidea Collected by the Verero III during the Years*

1932 to 1938. Los Angeles: University of Southern California Press, 1941–1957.
———. *Littoral Holothurians of the Bahama Islands.* New York: American Museum of Natural History, 1957.

SECONDARY SOURCES
Levi, Herbert W. "In Memorium: Elisabeth Deichmann (1896–1975)." *Bulletin of Marine Science* 26 (1976): 281–283. Includes long list of references and photograph of Deichmann.

STANDARD SOURCES
AMS 5–8, B 9, P&B 10–12; *NAW* unused.

DÉJERINE-KLUMPKE, AUGUSTA (1859–1927)

U.S./French physician and neuroanatomist. Born 1859 in San Francisco, Calif. Three siblings. Married Jules Déjerine (1892?). One daughter. Educated Lausanne, Switzerland; Faculty of Medicine, Paris (M.D., 1883?). Professional experience: resident (intern) at Bicêtre (1887–1890); Faculté de Médecine, research associate to Jules Déjerine (1890–1923); Invalides Hospital, staff (1914–1927?). Honors and memberships: Académie de Médecine, prize (1885); Société de Biologie, member (1923). Died 1927 in Paris.

Born Augusta Klumpke in San Francisco, one of three remarkable sisters, Augusta moved with her mother, sisters, and brother to Germany and then to Lausanne when she was eleven. She received her baccalaureate in Lausanne and then decided with encouragement from her mother to go to Paris to study medicine, having rejected Zurich because of the presence of so many Russian women nihilists, whom her mother felt would have a bad influence upon her. Her sister DOROTHEA KLUMPKE also went to Paris to study astronomy and work at the Paris observatory.

Klumpke was one of the first women medical students to pass the examination for the *externat* (similar to an American internship) and then petitioned to take the prestigious examination for the *internat* (similar to an American residency) that would allow her to work directly under major faculty members in the Paris hospitals. She had already published two excellent papers in the *Revue medicale* in 1885. Klumpke and Blanche Edwards (later BLANCHE EDWARDS-PILLIET) were finally allowed to take the examinations sponsored by the Assistance Publique in 1887, in spite of the opposition of the medical faculty due to a direct order by Paul Bert, Claude Bernard's former associate, then the Minister of Public Education. Klumpke obtained a high mark, which permitted her to be admitted as a regular *interne* under Dr. Balzer, with whom she did research on subcutaneous injections of insoluble mercurial preparations.

In 1890(?) she began to do research under the neuroanatomist Jules Déjerine, who fell in love with his attractive and intelligent assistant. They married in 1892(?) and completed a study of neuroanatomy in 1895 to which Déjerine attached both their names, explaining in a touching introduction that she had done so much of the work, it was only just to credit her by name. Her husband died in 1917 and one of his students extolled the degree to which husband and wife had worked together, both displaying "knowledge, method, patience, sincerity, and enthusiasm" [avec la savoir, la méthode et la patience, la sincérité, l'enthousiasme] (Andre-Thomas, 418). She published a number of studies under her own name during World War I, extending her interest in neurology to studies of lesions of the brain and to the large trunk nerves caused by projectiles. This work she pursued with her daughter, who began to assist her in her studies. After her husband's death, she created a foundation at the Faculty of Medicine that included a laboratory, a library, and a neurological museum in memory of her husband.

In 1923, Augusta Déjerine was named a member of the Société de Biologie, but this recognition came only after the death of her husband. Nevertheless, she was the first woman to be accepted by that scientific society. She was about to be named to the prestigious Académie de Médecine when she died in 1927.

JH/MBO

PRIMARY SOURCES
Klumpke, Augusta. "Contribution à l'étude des contractures hystériques." *Revue de Médecine* 1885.
———. "Contribution à l'étude de paralysies radiculaires du plexus brachial." *Revue de Médecine* 1885. Prize-winning essay for Académie de Médecine.
Déjerine-Klumpke, Augusta. With Jules Déjerine. *Anatomie des centres nerveuses.* Paris: 1895.

SECONDARY SOURCES
Andre-Thomas, "Jules Déjerine 1849-1917." *Comptes rendus et Memoires de la Société de Biologie* 80 (1917): 120–418.
Déjerine-Klumpke, Augusta. *Madame Déjerine 1859-1924.* Paris: Masson, 1929. Includes portraits and addresses on her death. [Countway 1. Ea. 1929.15.]. Obituary notice.

STANDARD SOURCES
Lipinska 1930.

DE LA CRUZ, JUANA INÉS (1651–1695)

Spanish/Mexican natural philosopher. Born November 1651 near Mexico City. Father Spanish; mother Mexican but of Spanish extraction. Educated by tutors hired by uncle. Died ca. 1695.

Juana Inés De la Cruz was born in Mexico from a Spanish father and a Mexican mother of Spanish extraction. In very early childhood she exhibited a talent for words, and composed poems in Spanish. Recognizing that their child had extraordinary talents, Juana's parents sent her to her uncle's Mexico City home. He supervised her education, and her abilities soon became widely known. The lady of the Viceroy, the Marquis de Mancera, became her patron, and when she was seventeen years old, she was received into the family. An incident is related about Juana reminiscent of those told about Italian prodigies such as MARIA AGNESI. Her patrons, wanting to show off the extraordinary learning of their protégé, invited forty of the most eminent literary personages of the country to examine her in the different branches of learning, including science. The professors questioned her in philosophy, mathematics, history, theology, and poetry. She responded beautifully, but with a characteristic modesty. Like Agnesi, she felt that her learning was unimportant, and became a nun.

De la Cruz is said to have collected a library of four thousand books. She sold these books and used the money for relief of the indigent. Her writings were collected in three quarto volumes.

JH/MBO

PRIMARY SOURCES
De la Cruz, Juana Inés. *Obras.* En Zaragoza: Por Manuel Roman, 1682.

STANDARD SOURCES
Cyclopedia.

DE LAGUNA, FREDERICKA ANNIS LOPEZ DE LEO (1906–)

U.S. anthropologist, ethnologist, and archeologist. Born 3 October 1906 in Ann Arbor, Mich., to Grace Andrus and Theodore de Laguna. One sibling. Educated private progressive schools and Lycée de Jeunes Filles de Versailles; Bryn Mawr (A.B., ca. 1927); Bryn Mawr European Fellowship (1928–1929); Columbia University (Ph.D., 1933). Professional experience: Field researcher and archeologist in Alaska (Yakutat Tlingit), Pima Indian Reservation, Arizona; University of Pennsylvania Museum, American Section, assistant (1931–1934); U.S. Department of Agriculture, U.S. Soil Conservation Service, Associate Soil Conservationist (1936–1937); Bryn Mawr, faculty (1938–1941; 1945–1954), professor of anthropology (1955–1975), department of anthropology, chair (1967–1975), Kenan Professor Emerita (from 1975); U.S. Navy (Waves), Lieutenant Commander (1942–1945). Honors and memberships: National Academy of Sciences, member (from 1975).

Fredericka Annis Lopez de Leo de Laguna is known primarily for combined archeological and ethnological work among the Tlingit cultures of northwestern North America. She was the older child of two philosophers who taught at University of Michigan, Ann Arbor, and then at Bryn Mawr College. Her father had traveled widely as a young man in the Philippines and Japan, and he encouraged her interest in a wide variety of cultures. Her brother, Wallace, became a geologist. Her early education was in a progressive school, Phoebe Anne Thorne School, and she spent a year as a boarder at a girls' school in France while her parents were on sabbatical. She attended Bryn Mawr, graduating in 1927 with a prestigious fellowship for European study, but she first elected to spend a year at Columbia University, studying anthropology with Franz Boas, ELLA DELORIA, GLADYS REICHARD, and RUTH BENEDICT. She then went to London on her fellowship in 1928 and joined a French field school in archeology, where she studied with the famous French anthropologist Henri Breuil in Paris and attended a seminar in London with Bronislaw Malinowski. After traveling to Copenhagen, she excavated for six months in Greenland with the Danish archeologist Therkel Mathiassen.

During the period that she was completing her dissertation at Columbia, de Laguna held low-paying jobs at the University of Pennsylvania Museum, and spent as much time as she could doing archeological research in Alaska with Kaj Birket Smith, locating new sites along the Yukon (1930–1933), which formed the basis of her dissertation in 1934 and her first major publication, *The Archaeology of Cook Inlet, Alaska* (1934). Further work in this area allowed her to combine archeological with ethnological work, as she collected museum specimens and recorded Indian myths. Repeated visits to the Yukon over the next ten years resulted in her second major work, *The Prehistory of Northern North America as Seen from the Yukon* (1947).

In 1936, de Laguna spent some time on the Pima Indian reservation in Arizona for the U.S. Soil Conservation Service, but tensions with the other members forced her to leave. Her receipt of a National Research Council Fellowship allowed her to travel and study at a number of museums and libraries throughout the United States and Canada. During this period de Laguna also wrote two well-received detective stories. She then traveled to Copenhagen to study some of the materials she had collected with her Danish advisors. Determined to be a professional anthropologist, she broke an engagement with an Englishman whom she had met while at Columbia University.

In 1938, de Laguna began to teach at Bryn Mawr College, able only to introduce one course in anthropology. Nevertheless, she set up an archeological summer field school in Arizona for her students. When the United States entered World War II, she joined the navy as part of Women Accepted for Volunteer Emergency Service (Waves). In 1945,

de Laguna returned to Bryn Mawr and helped to organize the department of sociology and anthropology, and then chaired the separate Department of Anthropology in 1967, which included growing numbers of graduate students as well. She continued to publish actively in her field, writing a seminal book on the combined ethnological, archeological, and historical methods used in studying the Tlingit community in 1960, and another, which she considered her finest work, *Under Mount Saint Elias: The History and Culture of the Yakutat Tlingit* (1970). Upon her retirement in 1975, de Laguna was awarded a professorship that allowed her to continue to teach occasionally and do research. The result was her autobiography, *A Voyage to Greenland: A Personal Initiation into Anthropology* (1977).

De Laguna received many prestigious awards and fellowships throughout her career, and also taught as a visiting professor at the University of Pennsylvania from 1947 to 1949 and the University of California, Berkeley, from 1959 to 1960. Throughout her career, she was active in professional organizations, serving as the first vice-president of the Society for American Archaeology, (1949–1950) and guiding the American Anthropological Association through the difficult period 1966–1967 as president. In 1975, de Laguna was elected a fellow of the National Academy of Sciences.

JH/MBO

PRIMARY SOURCES

De Laguna, Fredericka. *The Archaeology of Cook Inlet.* Philadelphia: University of Pennsylvania Press for the University Museum, 1934; Reprint, with a chapter on skeletal material by Bruno Oettiking, New York: AMS Press, 1975.

———. *The Prehistory of Northern North America as Seen from the Yukon.* Society for American Archaeology, Memoir 3. Menasha, Wis.: Society for American Archaeology, 1947.

———. *The Story of a Tlingit Community: A Problem in the Relationship between Archaeological, Ethnological, and Historical Methods.* Bureau of Ethnology Bulletin 172. Washington, D.C.: U.S. Government Printing Office, 1960.

———. *Under Mount Saint Elias: The History and Culture of the Yakutat Tlingit.* Smithsonian Contributions to Anthropology 7 (in three parts). Transcriptions of native music by David P. McAlester. Washington, D.C.: Smithsonian Institution Press, 1972.

———. *A Voyage to Greenland: A Personal Initiation into Anthropology.* New York: W. W. Norton, 1977. De Laguna's autobiography.

SECONDARY SOURCES

McClellan, Catherine. "Fredericka de Laguna." In *Women Anthropologists: A Biographical Dictionary.* Ed. Ute Gacs et al. Westport, Conn.: Greenwood Press, 1988.

STANDARD SOURCES
AMS 5, 6, 8, S&B 9–12, P&B 13; Bailey; Debus.

DE LA MARCHE, MARGUERITE DU TERTRE (1638–1706)

French midwife. Educated privately at the Hôtel Dieu. Professional experience: Hôtel Dieu, "superior midwife."

Marguerite du Tertre de la Marche was one of the best private pupils at the Hôtel Dieu. The school was founded by LOUYSE BOURGEOISE, who had been a pupil of Ambroise Paré, and is credited with introducing new methods of delivery and a more scientific midwifery. De la Marche was the "superior midwife" at the Hôtel Dieu for many years. She reorganized the training of midwives. She insisted that they go through a three-months course and that they be able to manage a delivery without the help of a surgeon. She wrote a book of questions and answers for her pupils to use if they encountered an emergency. It was later enlarged by one of her pupils, Louise Leboursier du Coudray, and was long used as a textbook for midwives.   JH/MBO

PRIMARY SOURCES
De la Marche, Marguerite du Tertre. *Instruction familière et très facile, faite par Questions et Réponses, touchante toutes les choses principales, qu'une Sage femme doit savoir, etc. Composée par Marguer. Du Tertre, Veuve du Sieur de la Marche, Maitresse jurée Sage-femme de la ville de Paris, Hotel Dieu, etc.* Paris: 1677.

STANDARD SOURCES
Hurd-Mead 1938.

DELANEY (OR DELANY), MARY (GRANVILLE), (1700–1788)

British gardener and botanical artist. Born Coulston, Wiltshire, 14 May 1700. Married (1) Alexander Pendarves (1718; he died in 1724); (2) Reverend Patrick Delaney (1743). Died 15 April 1788 in Westminster, London.

This unusual botanical artist and gardener was born Mary Granville in Wiltshire in 1700, the niece of the statesman and art collector Lord Lansdowne. She married Alexander Pendarves, almost forty years her senior, at the age of eighteen. He died six years later. In 1743, she married for the second time, this time an Irish clergyman, Reverend Patrick Delaney, and with him created an outstanding garden at her home at Delville, Dublin Bay. She became well known for creating shell grottoes on Irish estates. In 1768, she returned to England. She was a friend of the DUCHESS OF PORTLAND, MARGARET CAVENDISH BENTINCK with whom she collected and catalogued shells and plants. She was a patron of Fanny Burney and her husband was a good friend of Jonathan Swift.

In her seventies, she began to make unusual flower paper mosaics that carefully represented a wide variety of plants. A collection of almost a thousand of these mosaics are held at the British Museum. She died in Westminster in 1788, at the age of eighty-eight. Her lively letters (1731 to 1768) are widely considered to present an important picture of Georgian Ireland.   JH/MBO

PRIMARY SOURCES
Delaney, Mary. *Autobiography and Correspondence.* 6 vols. Ed. Sarah Chauncey Woolsey. Boston: Roberts Brothers, 1882.
Delany, Mary. *Letters from Georgian Ireland: Correspondence of Mary Delany 1731–1768.* Ed. A. Day. Belfast: Friar's Bush Press, 1991. With portrait.

SECONDARY SOURCES
Vulliamy, C. E. *Aspasia: Life and Letters of . . . Mrs Delaney.* London: G. Bles, 1935.

STANDARD SOURCES
Desmond; *DNB; Larousse;* Shteir.

DE LANGE, CORNELIA CATHARINA (1871–1950)

Dutch physician. Born 1871 in Alkmaar, Holland. Never married. Educated local schools; University of Zurich (chemistry); University of Amsterdam (M.D., 1897). Professional experience: Clinic for women and children, founder (1902); Emme Kinderziekanhuis, Amsterdam, head of infant care (1907–1950); Nederlandsche Bond tot Bescherming van Zuigelingen (the Dutch Confederation for the Protection of Infants), cofounder (1908); medical faculty at the University of Amsterdam, professor (1927–1938). Died 1950.

Perhaps the most successful of women qualifying in medicine before 1900, Cornelia de Lange was the first woman to attain a full professorship in the Faculty of Medicine at the University of Amsterdam. Born in Alkmaar, Holland, in 1871, she was schooled locally then sent by her father to the University of Zurich to study chemistry. Determined to study medicine, she soon changed her courses. After receiving her medical degree from the University of Amsterdam in 1897, she began a general practice, but decided to specialize in pediatrics. With three other women physicians, she founded a clinic for women and children in 1902 and concentrated especially on infant care. She vigorously campaigned for the development of pediatrics as a special field. In 1908, she helped establish the Nederlandsche Bond tot Bescherming van Zuigelingen (the Dutch Confederation for the Protection of Infants) and became a key figure in the infant/child welfare movement in the Netherlands. De Lange was appointed professor of pediatrics at the University of Amsterdam in 1927 and served there for eleven years. During her tenure as professor, she inspired the next generation of pediatricians and produced a large number of professional books, theses, and articles, as well as several popular works on the care and nurture of infants. As a researcher, de Lange made significant contributions in pediatric neurology, undertaking her own pathological and histological studies. In 1933, she described two female Dutch infants with unusual facies and mental retardation; she presented an additional case to the Amsterdam Neurological Society in 1941. The syndrome, a malformation complex comprising severe mental retardation, shortened stature, a characteristic facies and variable reduction defects of the arms, became known as the Cornelia de Lange syndrome. She authored over 250 books and articles.

Like ALETTA JACOBS and Catherine van Tussenbroek, Cornelia de Lange became a doctor in spite of many obstacles within the profession as well as societal and familial disapproval. She developed her own methods of coping, such as helping in 1892 to establish the female debating society Dicendo Discentes Docemus, precursor of the Amsterdam women's student organization. Later, she became an active member of the established major medical societies, though, curiously, never seemed interested in promoting a women's medical society. (The national organization for women doctors was finally created in 1933.) De Lange never aligned herself with women's issues but rather fit herself into the established masculine system, eventually being accepted on a near equal basis. For her participation in the battle to reduce infant mortality and her commitment to improving infant and child health care through her practice and written guides, de Lange received respect and recognition. "A most beloved pediatrician of Amsterdam . . . during the occupation she was an example of courage to us all" (De Knecht-van Eekelen).   JH/MBO

PRIMARY SOURCES
De Lange, C. C. With A. C. Ruys. "Pioneer Medical Women in the Netherlands." *Journal of the American Medical Women's Association* 7 (1952): 99–101.

SECONDARY SOURCES
Beighton, Peter, and Beighton, Greta. *The Man Behind the Syndrome.* Berlin: Springer-Verlag, 1986.
De Knecht-van Eekelen, A. *Cornelia Catharina de Lange (1871–1950).* Nijmegen: Nederlandese Vereniging voor kinderneurologie, 1990. Includes a list of De Lange's publications.

"In Memoriam Cornelia de Lange." *Nederlandsch Tijdschhift voor Geneeskunde* 94, no. 1 (1950): 362–364. Obituary notice.
Marland, Hilary. "'Pioneer Work on All Sides': The First Generations of Women Physicians in the Netherlands, 1879–1930." *Journal of the History of Medicine and Allied Sciences* 50 (1995): 441–447.
Ochme Kinderkrankenschwester 11 (1992): 434–435.

STANDARD SOURCES
Debus; Ireland; Lovejoy.

DELAP, MAUDE JANE (1866–1953)
Irish botanist. Born 7 December 1866 in County Donegal, Ireland. Died 23 July 1953 on Valentia Island, County Kerry, Ireland.

Maude Delap and her sister Constance (1868–1935) studied marine plankton on Valentia Island. They contributed to Reginald Scully's *Flora of County Kerry* (1916).   JH/MBO

PRIMARY SOURCES
Scully, Reginald W. *Flora of County Kerry.* Dublin: Hodges, Figgis, 1916.

SECONDARY SOURCES
Irish Naturalists Journal (1958): 221–222. Includes portrait.
Praeger, R. L. *Some Irish Naturalists.* Dundalk, W. Tempest, 1949.

DELAUNEY, MARGUERITE DE STAËL (1693–1750)
French anatomist. Born 1693.

Marguerite de Staël Delaunay was a French anatomist who was well respected by her colleagues. Her ability to dissect the human body was legendary; the Duchess of Maine declared that she was the daughter of France who best knew the body of man.   JH/MBO

SECONDARY SOURCES
Brunetière. "Etudes sur le xviii siècle." *Revue des deux mondes,* 15 October 1892.

STANDARD SOURCES
Hurd-Mead 1938; Lipinska 1930.

DE LEBRIX, FRANÇOISE (fl. 16th century)
Spanish physician. Father Antoine de Lebrix.

Little is known of the Spanish physician Françoise de Lebrix. She is reported to have substituted for her father, who was a professor of history and rhetoric, at the university of Alcala.   JH/MBO

STANDARD SOURCES
Hurd-Mead 1938; Lipinska 1900; Mozans.

DELF-SMITH, ELLEN MARION (1883–1980)

British Botanist. Born 31 January 1883, probably in East Dulwich, to Catherine Mary (Bridges) and William Herbert Delf. Married Percy John Smith (September 1928). Educated James Allen's Girls' School, East Dulwich; Girton College (1902–1906); Cloth-workers' Scholar; Natural Science Tripos, Pt. 1, Cl. 1 905; Pt. II, Cl. I (Botany 1906); University of London (D.Sc. 1912). Professional experience: Yarrow Research Fellow (1914–1917); Lister Institute, Chelsea, research assistant (1916–1920); Institute of Medical Research, Johannesburg, temporary research fellow (1921); University of London, reader in botany (1921–?); Westfield College, lecturer in botany (1921–1948; department head from 1939). Memberships: S.E. Union of Scientific Societies; South London Botanical Society, life member of Council; Scottish Seaweed Research Association, Advisory Algal Committee, Executive committee member; Association of Women Science Teachers, London Branch, president (1946); Linnean Society, member of Council; Westfield College, London, member of Council. Honors and memberships: Gamble Prize (1912); Association of Former Westfield Students, president (1950–1955); Westfield, Honorary Fellowship; Linnean Society, Fellow (1914). Died 1980.

Ellen Delf was the daughter of an accountant and secretary of East Dulwich. For her undergraduate education, she attended Girton College, Cambridge, where she earned first class passes in both of her Tripos examinations. She held a Cloth-workers' scholarship at Girton, shared the Thérèse Montefiore Memorial Prize, and won the Gamble Prize in 1912 for her essay entitled "The Biology of Transpiration." In 1912 she obtained her doctorate from the University of London and then held both research and teaching positions. While she was a research assistant at the Lister Institute, she did research on the vitamin content of foods, information needed for the campaign in Mesopotamia from 1916 to 1918. In 1921 she became lecturer in botany at Westfield College and head of that department from 1939. She published numerous articles in the *Annals of Botany*, the *Journal of Botany*, *Nature*, the *Journal of Biochemistry*, and others. She also did research at the Joddrell Laboratory at Kew. Her husband was Percy John Smith, an artist who was cited in *Who's Who*.
                                                      JH/MBO

PRIMARY SOURCES
Delf, Ellen Marion. *Studies in Experimental Scurvy: With Special Reference to the Anti-Scorbutic Properties of Some South African*

Food-Stuffs. Johannesburg: Institute of Medical Research, 1921.
———. *The Distribution and Movements of Water in Plants Including Turgor.* London: John Murray, 1928.

SECONDARY SOURCES
Times, 5 March 1980. Obituary notice.

STANDARD SOURCES
Girton.

DELORIA, ELLA CARA (1888–1971)

U.S. anthropologist and linguist. Born 30 January 1888 on Yankton Dakota Reservation, Lake Andes, S.D. to Mary Sully Bordeau and Philip Joseph Deloria. Educated St. Elizabeth's Mission School, Wakpala; All Saints School, Sioux Falls; Oberlin College (1911–1913); Columbia University Teachers College, (B.S., 1915). Professional experience: All Saints School, Sioux Falls, teacher (1915–1922); Haskell Institute (Bureau of Indian Affairs school), Lawrence, Kans., teacher (1923–1925?); American Indian Work, YMCA, New York City, secretary (1925–?); Dakotan languages with Franz Boas and RUTH BENEDICT, Columbia University, informant and teacher (1926–1941); Dakota Sioux reservations, field researcher (1941–1954); St. Elizabeth's School, Wakpala, S.D., director (1955–1958); Sioux Indian Museum, Rapid City, S.D.; W. H. Over Museum, University of South Dakota, Vermillion. Died 1971 in Vermillion, South Dakota.

Now recognized in her own right as an ethnographer and linguist, Ella Cara Deloria began her ethnographic work as an informant on Dakota, Lakota, and Nakota Sioux languages. She was the oldest of four children of Philip Joseph Boudreau (Tipa Sapa or "Black Lodge"), who was the first Native American to become an Episcopal minister. She was born on the Yankton Dakota (Sioux) Reservation, Lake Andes, South Dakota, but spent her formative years on the Hunkpapa and Sihasapa Lakota (Sioux), Standing Rock Reservation. Her father founded St. Elizabeth's Mission on the Standing Rock Reservation, where Ella Deloria attended primary school. As a child, she had little contact with the traditional rituals and ceremonies of Dakota life on the reservation. For secondary school, she attended an Episcopal boarding school in Sioux City, where she won a scholarship to Oberlin College in Ohio. After attending Oberlin for two years (1911–1913), Deloria transferred to Columbia University Teachers College, in New York City, where she obtained a bachelor's degree in 1915. Although she returned to teach at her secondary school, All Saints, in Sioux City, she took the opportunity to introduce an experimental dance and physical education program at Haskell Institute (the Bureau of Indian Affairs boarding school) in Lawrence,

Kansas, in 1923. In the mid-1920s, Deloria moved back to New York City and worked as a secretary for the American Indian work of the National YWCA. Franz Boas soon asked her to teach Dakotan languages to anthropology graduate students as part of his linguistic course in the department of anthropology at Columbia University; this began a collaboration that continued over the next twenty years, resulting in short articles, a major piece of bilingual ethnic folklore, *Dakota Texts* (1932), and the linguistic analyses "Notes on the Dakota" (1933), *Dakota Grammar* (1941), which Boas and Deloria jointly published. Although no published work with RUTH BENEDICT exists, Deloria provided her with materials from the field, as detailed letters now held in the American Philosophica Library attest. Benedict's influence long after her death can be found in the discussion of psychological aspects of Lakotan language in the unpublished Lakota dictionary on which Deloria worked for many years.

At Boas's request, Deloria analyzed the earlier work of scholars who had compiled Dakotan myths from the late nineteenth and early twentieth centuries, interviewing many older people who had provided information for them, and she reported on this work in a series of interesting letters and manuscripts sent to Boas, now held at the American Philosophical Society. She wrote a popular work, *Speaking of Indians* (1944), while she was caring for her father during his long illness; written for a more general readership, it describes the history and life of her people. This book was illustrated by her sister Mary Sully.

From 1962 to 1966, she received funding for her work on a Lakota dictionary, on which she worked until her death in a motel in Vermillion, S.D., in 1971. Unfortunately this and a 392-page manuscript on the Dakota way of life remain unpublished in the Institute of Indian Studies, University of South Dakota. Although she never married, Deloria supported and encouraged her nephews, one of whom, Vine Deloria, Jr., became a well-known writer and critic of Native American and Anglo relations (*Bury My Heart at Wounded Knee*, 1971, and *Custer Died for Your Sins*, 1976).

JH/MBO

PRIMARY SOURCES

Deloria, Ella Cara. *Dakota Texts*. New York: Stechert, 1932.

———. With Franz Boas. *Dakota Grammar.* Memoirs of the National Academy of Sciences no. 23. Washington, D.C.: Government Printing Office, 1941.

———. *Speaking of Indians.* New York: Friendship Press, 1944.

———. "Dakota Way of Life." Unpublished ms, Institute of Indian Studies, University of South Dakota.

———. "Lakota Dictionary." Unpublished ms, Institute of Indian Studies, University of South Dakota.

SECONDARY SOURCES

Murray, Janette K. "Ella Deloria: A Biographical Sketch and Literary Analysis." Ph.D. diss., University of North Dakota, 1974.

STANDARD SOURCES

Gacs (article by Beatrice Medicine); *NAW*(M) (article by Raymond J. Demallie).

DE MARILLAC, LOUISE, MLLE, LE GRAS (1591–1671)

See Marillac, Louise de.

DEMBO, TAMARA (1902–1993)

Russian/U.S. psychologist. Born 28 May 1902 in Baku, Transcaucasia. Never married. Educated Berlin (Ph.D., 1930). Professional experience: State University [Berlin?], research assistant in psychology; Gröningen (1929–1930); Smith College, research associate experimental psychology (1930–1932); Worcester State Hospital, research assistant (1932–1934); Cornell University, research assistant (1934–1935); University of Iowa, research fellow child welfare (1935–1943); Mount Holyoke College, assistant professor (1943–1945); Harvard University, United States Public Health Service Special Research Fellow in Mental Health (1951–1953); Stanford University, acting associate professor of psychology and project director, social-psychological rehabilitation of physically handicapped (1945–1948); New School for Social Research (1948–1950); Clark University, associate professor of psychology (1952–1962), professor, director of psychological development in cerebral palsy (1954–1962), professor of psychology and director, training program in rehabilitation psychology (1962–1972); professor emerita, psychology; social and rehabilitation psychology training program, educational coordinator (1972–1992). Concurrent experience: Veterans Administration, consultant (1953–1992). Honors and memberships: American Psychological Association, member. Died 24 October 1993.

Tamara Dembo was one of the originators of psychological field theory, the interdependence of person and environment. Her research included studies on levels of aspiration, frustration, and aggression; social-emotional relationships; value problems; problems of institutionalized mental patients; and social-psychological rehabilitation. Dembo was born 28 May 1902 in Baku in Transcaucasia to Russian Jewish parents. When she went to the University of Berlin, she was soon active in the research group headed by Kurt Lewin and formed a strong belief in the importance of environment in any psychological equation. For her, as for Lewin, the actor was not a person but a "life space"—a person in a situation. This orientation allowed her to understand more clearly than most the perspective of the disabled, and to succeed brilliantly in her pioneering work in rehabilitation psychology by seeing the environment as "disabling" rather than seeing the person as "handicapped."

Dembo laid the foundation for many concepts of field theory with her doctoral thesis (available in English as *Field Theory as Human Science*, 1976). Constructing a laboratory synthesis of anger she described how negative valences develop on the barriers between the participant and a goal, causing the participant to attempt to leave the field. A secondary "external" barrier was set up that prevented leaving, causing a buildup of tension in the field that eventually broke down the boundaries between reality and fantasy and resulted in an outburst of anger by the participant.

Dembo came to the United States in 1930 to work with Kurt Koffka at Smith College; she decided to remain when political conditions in Germany deteriorated. She worked at the Worcester State Hospital and held research positions at Cornell University and the University of Iowa. She continued to do research in the psychology of emotions, particularly frustration and anger. With Kurt Lewin and Roger Barker, she published *Frustration and Regression: An Experiment with Young Children* (1941). In 1945, Dembo went to Stanford University to direct research projects on the psychological rehabilitation of people who had been blinded or had lost limbs. With Gloria Ladieu Leviton and Beatrice Wright, she helped create the conceptual analysis presented in "Adjustment to Misfortune" (1956).

At Clark University (1953–1972) Dembo worked on problems of psychological rehabilitation, centering her research on children and families of children who have cerebral palsy; later, on improving and enriching the environment of custodial cases. Her efforts to "re-humanize" those whose mental and physical responses were severely impaired taught understanding and sympathy to caretakers and gave them new tools for creatively interacting with their patients. In later years she refined her concept of socio-emotional relationships—dyadic relationships within a given situation. Dembo died 24 October 1993 in Worcester, Massachusetts.   KM

PRIMARY SOURCES

Dembo, Tamara. *Der Ärger als Dynamiches Problem.* Berlin: J. Springer, 1931.

———. With Kurt Lewin and Roger G. Barker. *Frustration and Regression: An Experiment with Young Children.* Iowa City: University of Iowa Press, 1941.

SECONDARY SOURCES

De Rivera, Joseph. "Tamara Dembo (1902–1993)." *American Psychologist* 50 (May 1995): 386. Obituary.

STANDARD SOURCES

AMS 6–8, S&B 10–13; O'Connell and Russo.

DE MILT, CLARA MARIE (1891–1953)

U.S. chemist. Born 8 May 1891 in New Orleans, La. Educated Tulane University (A.B., 1911; M.S., 1921); University of Chicago (Ph.D., 1925). Professional experience: high school teacher (1912–1919); Newcomb College, Tulane University, instructor (1919–1924), assistant professor (1925–1927), and professor of chemistry (from 1930). Honors and memberships: Chemical Society; History of Science Society; American Academy of Science. Died 1953.

Born in New Orleans and educated at Tulane and the University of Chicago, Clara Marie De Milt spent most of her professional career at Newcomb College. She advanced up the academic ladder to the rank of professor in 1930. She was very interested in biography and specialized in seventeenth-, eighteenth-, and nineteenth-century France. Although she taught, wrote, and directed research in the history of chemistry, she also contributed significantly in organic chemistry, which was her special interest. She published on phenyl stearic acid, Grignard's reaction, and diazotization. She wrote and published several instructional manuals on general and qualitative chemistry.

JH/MBO

PRIMARY SOURCES

De Milt, Clara. With Ann Hero Northrup. *Laboratory Outline of General Chemistry.* Ann Arbor, Mich.: Edwards Brothers, 1930.

———. *Laboratory Manual of Preliminary Experiments in Qualitative Analysis.* Norman, Okla.: University Litho Publishers, 1934.

———. *Laboratory Manual of Organic Chemistry.* Norman, Okla.: University Litho Publishers, 1934.

———. With Elsie D. Grueber. *Laboratory Outline of General Chemistry.* Ann Arbor, Mich.: Planographed by Edwards Brothers, 1938.

SECONDARY SOURCES

Anon. "Necrology. Clara M. De Milt." *Chemical and Engineering News* 31 (31 August 1953): 3570.

———. "Recent Deaths. Clara Marle [*sic*] de Milt." *School and Society* 77 (23 May 1953): 334.

Scott, John Mark. "Clara Marie DeMilt (1891–1953)." *Journal of Chemical Education* 31 (August 1954): 419–420.

STANDARD SOURCES

AMS 5–8; Siegel and Finley.

DE MOLE, FANNY ELIZABETH (1835–1866)
British botanist. Born 1 March 1835. Died 26 December 1866 in Burnside, S. Australia.

Fanny De Mole immigrated to Australia in 1856, where she collected plants and published a book on them five years before she died.   JH/MBO

PRIMARY SOURCES
D., F. E. [De Mole, Fanny]. *Wild Flowers of South Australia.* Adelaide, Australia: 1861; Reprint, Carlton, Australia: Queensberry Hill Press, 1981.

SECONDARY SOURCES
Report of the Australian Association for the Advancement of Science (1911): 226.

STANDARD SOURCES
Desmond.

DEMPSEY, SISTER MARY JOSEPH (1856–1939)
U.S. surgical nurse and hospital administrator. Born 14 May 1856 in Salamanca, N.Y., to Mary (Sullivan) and Patrick Dempsey. Six siblings. Christened Julia. Educated at Haverhill Township and Rochester public schools; trained as a teacher; learned nursing from the town's trained nurse. Professional experience: Franciscan nun (1878–1939); schoolteacher (1878–1890); St. Mary's Hospital, surgical nurse (1890–1915); hospital superintendent (1892–1939). Died 29 March 1939 in St. Mary's Hospital, Rochester.

Although Sister Mary Joseph Dempsey was not a scientist herself, her work enabled others to pursue scientific careers. She was born Julia Dempsey to an Irish immigrant couple who had seven children. The family moved from New York to Rochester, Minnesota. After being educated in the local schools, Julia took the vows of a Franciscan nun. She was educated by the order during her novitiate as a teacher. She taught for twelve years before returning to Rochester, which had been devastated by a tornado. The Mother Superior of the convent was convinced that the town needed a hospital, and persuaded Dr. William Mayo (father of the brothers who built the Mayo clinic) to staff the hospital if the sisters built it. Sister Mary Joseph was recalled from Ashland, Kentucky, where she had been teaching, and was taught basic nursing skills by Rochester's only skilled nurse. After two months, she became the head nurse at the hospital and became Dr. Mayo's surgical assistant. Even without formal training, she was an excellent nurse, according to Mayo. He noted that her surgical judgment was equal to that of any medical man and that she ranked first among all of his assistants.

Staffing became increasingly difficult as the hospital grew, so Sister Mary Joseph initiated the St. Mary's School for Nurses. Known as a stern disciplinarian, she also had a keen sense of humor. She refused many honors, insisting that her work was for God and suffering humanity.   JH/MBO

SECONDARY SOURCES
Minneapolis Tribune, 31 March 1939. Obituary notice.
Rochester Post-Bulletin, 30 March 1939. Obituary notice.
St. Mary's Alumnae Quarterly. Special issue on Sister Mary Joseph. May 1939.

STANDARD SOURCES
NAW (article by Robert E. Steller).

DEMUD (fl. ca. 13th century)
German physician.

Only the name of the doctor, Demud, is known. She flourished in Mainz, but nothing is known about her work.
                                           JH/MBO

STANDARD SOURCES
Hurd-Mead 1938.

DENGEL, ANNA MARIA (1892–?)
Austrian medical missionary. Born 1892 in Steeg, Austria, in the Tyrol. Eight siblings. Educated school of the Visitation Sisters; University College, Cork, Ireland; Queen's College Medical School (M.D., 1919). Professional experience: clinic in England, medical assistant; St. Catherine's Hospital, Rawalpindi, India, physician; Medical Mission Sisterhood, founder (1925). Death date unknown.

Anna Maria Dengel was born in Steeg, Austria, in the Tyrol, 1892, the oldest of nine children. She was sent to the boarding school of the Visitation Sisters in Hall, after the death of her mother when Dengel was eight. Impressed by the sisters, she decided on mission work early and studied languages and taught German in Lyons, France, for two years before choosing to study medicine. At the suggestion of AGNES McLAREN, Dengel applied for admission to University College, Cork, Ireland. (McLaren instilled in Dengel the determination to serve in India, for which she needed a British medical diploma.) She finished her premedical work and entered Queen's College Medical School in 1913, receiving her medical degree in 1919. She worked as a medical assistant at a clinic in England until the visa for India came.

Dengel left for Rawalpindi, India, October 1920 for duty at St. Catherine's Hospital. She founded the Medical Mission

Sisterhood in Washington, D.C., in 1925, having traveled to America to raise the funds following World War I, so that there would be a supply of missionaries eligible for full medical practice when the Church officially recognized the need (nuns were prohibited from assisting in many aspects of medicine, such as midwifery, by the rules of the Church; this was overturned in 1936).   JH/MBO

SECONDARY SOURCES
Dengel, Anna Maria. In Hellstedt, *Autobiographies.*

STANDARD SOURCES
Lovejoy.

DENIS, WILLEY GLOVER (1879–?)
U.S. physiologist and chemist. Born 26 February 1879 in New Orleans, La. Educated Tulane (A.B., 1899; A.M., 1902); Bryn Mawr College (1899–1900; fellow, 1902–1903); University of Chicago (Ph.D., 1907). Professional experience: Grinnell College, instructor in analytical chemistry (1907); U.S. Department of Agriculture, assistant chemist, bureau of chemistry (from 1907). Death date unknown.

Willey Denis is an example of a well-educated woman scientist who worked for the U.S. Department of Agriculture. She was a member of the Chemical Society and the Association for Agricultural Chemistry. Her research was on oxidation of aldehydes and ketones. She also worked on methods for analyzing foods and the estimations of tryptophane in proteids. The last edition of *American Men and Women of Science* in which her name appears is the fourth.   JH/MBO

STANDARD SOURCES
AMS 2–4.

DENNETT, MARY WARE (1872–1947)
U.S. psychologist and social activist. Born 1872.

Mary Dennett wrote a treatise for her two sons when they were twelve and fourteen to explain the "facts of life." It was so popular that she gave copies to other mothers until the original was worn out. It came to the attention of the editor of *Medical Reviews of Reviews* and was published in that journal February 1918. She then printed it herself and distributed copies through several agencies, such as the YMCA and YWCA, state welfare and health organizations, and to private individuals who requested it. The U.S. Postal Service declared that it was obscene material, had her arrested, and took her to court in a highly publicized case. The ruling was

against her, but she became a popular and dedicated writer and speaker for socialist causes.   KM

PRIMARY SOURCES
Dennett, Mary Ware. *The Real Point.* New York: National Woman Suffrage Pub. Co., Inc., [1918?].
———. *The Sex Side of Life.* N.p.: privately printed, [ca. 1919].
———. *The Case for Birth Control: With Answers to Questions.* Girard, Kans.: Appeal to Reason, [1919]. The Appeal to Reason pocket series ran 1919–1922 and was a means of disseminating socialist ideas on subjects such as racism, suffrage, marriage and family, birth control, sexually transmitted diseases, labor organization, and so on. Upton Sinclair and H. G. Wells were contributors; E. Haldeman-Julius was editor.
———. *Representative Opinions on "The Sex Side of Life."* N.d. A four-page pamphlet.
———. *The Sex Side of Life: An Explanation for Young People.* With new diagrams and revisions. Astoria, N.Y.: privately printed, 1928.
———. *The Stupidity of Us Humans.* New York: Voluntary Parenthood League, n.d.
———. *Who's Obscene?* New York: Vanguard, 1930. Includes "The Sex Side of life" case, other cases of Post Office suppression, postal service law and legislation.
"Verbatim report of the Town Hall Meeting under the auspices of the Voluntary Parenthood League at which Dr. Marie C. Stopes, of London was chief speaker. October 27, 1921." New York: Voluntary Parenthood League, 1921.

SECONDARY SOURCES
Chen, Constance Marian. *"The Sex Side of Life": Mary Ware Dennett's Pioneering Battle for Birth Control and Sex Education.* New York: New Press, 1996.
Looney, Jane Gray. "The Sex Side of Life: Sexual Education and the Law in early Twentieth Century America." Undergraduate honors thesis, Harvard University 1988.
Records and material concerning the arrest and trial are held by the American Civil Liberties Union, New York.

DENNIS, OLIVE WETZEL (ca. 1880–1957)
U.S. research engineer. Born ca. 1880 in Thurlow, Pa. Father Charles E. Dennis. Educated Baltimore public schools; Goucher College (A.B., Phi Beta Kappa, 1908); Columbia University (M.A.); Harvard University; University of Wisconsin, summer studies (1913–1917); Cornell University (civil engineering degree, 1920). Professional experience: Baltimore and Ohio Railway, railroad engineer, draftsman for bridge engineering (1920), engineer of service (1921–1945), research engineer on president's staff until retirement (1945–1951). Died 1957.

Olive Wetzel Dennis was born in Pennsylvania, studied in the Baltimore public schools, and then went to Goucher College on a four-year scholarship. Goucher gave her a fellowship to pursue her studies at Columbia University where she obtained a master's. She went on to do summer work at Harvard. She attended the University of Wisconsin from 1913 to 1917, and finally received a civil engineering degree from Cornell University in 1920. She was hired by the Baltimore and Ohio Railroad as a draftsman for bridge engineering and went on to serve as an engineer of service from 1921 to 1945. According to Debus, she was the first service engineer in the United States, a position created by the railroad to find a technological means for improving service.

Dennis evaluated passenger service and proposed improvements to railroad cars and designed new equipment and materials for use in passenger cars. She held a number of patents, including a ventilator that could be inserted into the windows of passenger cars to provide air and keep out dust (1927). She also held the patent on blue and white dinnerware for B&O Railroad (1926).

Dennis had a wide variety of interests. She founded B&O Women's Music Club (having studied music at Peabody Conservatory). Her hobby of cryptography led to her presidency of the National Puzzler's League. She was an alumnae trustee of Goucher College, 1937–1940.   JH/MBO

PRIMARY SOURCES
Dennis, Olive Wetzel. *The Cornell Engineer.* Reprinted *B&O Magazine* 35 (January 1949): 22–23. Autobiographical material.

STANDARD SOURCES
NAW unused.

DE NOLDE, HÉLÈNE ALDEGONDE (fl. 1702)
German physician.

Although Hélène Aldegonde de Nolde practiced in Germany it was probably not her birthplace. She was a well-known practicing physician and wrote an important book on practical medicine.   JH/MBO

PRIMARY SOURCES
Aldegonde de Nolde, Hélène. *Medulla medecinae, oder kurzer Begriff, wie man die Medecin recht gebrauchen soll* (The Heart of Medicine, or, Short Concepts on How Medicine Should Be Correctly Used). Wahrendorf, 1702.

STANDARD SOURCES
Hurd-Mead 1938.

DENSMORE, FRANCES THERESA (1867–1957)
U.S. ethnomusicologist. Born 21 May 1867 in Red Wing, Minn., to Sarah Adalaide Greenland and Benjamin Densmore. Two siblings. Never married. Educated local public schools; Oberlin Conservatory of Music (1884–1886); studied piano with Carl Baermann and composition with John K. Paine, Harvard University; studied with Leopold Godlovsky, Chicago (1898). Professional experience: Red Wing and St. Paul, piano teacher and organist (1887–1904?); public lecturer (1893–1906); Bureau of Indian Affairs, researcher (1907–1954); National Archives, consultant (1940–1942); Southwest Museum, research associate in ethnology (1950); University of Florida, consultant in ethnomusic (1954). Honors and memberships: multiple honors and honorary degrees; Society for Ethnomusicology, officer (from 1956). Died 1957.

Frances Densmore became widely known for her transcriptions and later her recordings of Native American music, supplemented by ethnological information and statistical analyses. She came from a well-connected family in Red Wing, Minnesota. Her grandfather was a judge and her father ran the Red Wing Iron Works. After studying music privately, she attended Oberlin Conservatory of Music, where she studied piano, organ, and harmony from 1884 to 1886. After a few years as a piano teacher in Red Wing, she went to Boston to study piano with Carl Baermann and counterpoint with John K. Paine (professor of music at Harvard), and some years later with Leopold Goldowsky in Chicago. She then returned to teaching, adding lectures on musicology.

Interested in American Indian music since hearing the drums and singing from a nearby Sioux encampment as a child, Densmore wrote to ALICE FLETCHER, who had become interested in Omaha Indian music as well as ethnography. Fletcher had just published a study of that music with John C. Fillmore, a well-known musicologist, and Francis La Flesche, an Omaha Indian anthropologist (Fletcher, La Flesche, and Fillmore, 1893), prepared for the Chicago World's fair in 1893. Densmore attended the fair and then wrote to Fletcher, at the suggestion of Fillmore whom she had met through her music professors, receiving strong encouragement to embark on a thorough study of Native American music. She also began to lecture on that subject to music clubs, art institutes, and scientific societies.

With Alice Fletcher serving as teacher, mentor, and friend, Densmore soon began to do her own field studies of Chippewa songs, and transcribed a Sioux song, which became her first publication (1901). In 1905 she traveled with her sister to the White Earth Reservation in Minnesota and transcribed songs of the Chippewa by ear. In 1907, she borrowed a phonograph and recorded songs that she then sent to the Bureau of American Ethnology. They provided her with some funds for further recording, and supplied her with a state-of-the-art Columbia graphaphone for this purpose in 1908. She began a fifty-year association with the BAE from this time onward, and an annual appropriation of $3,000 (a handsome sum at the time) paid not only for her travels but also recompensed her American Indian informants for their time and expertise. In addition to making recordings, Densmore collected musical instruments, herbs used in curing ceremonies, and a wealth of other ethnographic data including photographs. She traveled throughout the United States through British Columbia, Canada, studying the Seminole Indians in Florida, the Pueblo Indians and other southwestern tribes in Arizona and New Mexico, to the Winnebago, Sioux, traveling to the Mandan, Hidatsa, and Nootka in the Northwest Coast, and recording under a wide variety of situations.

She encouraged American and European composers to make use of her materials, and some of them found them an important source of inspiration. She was intrigued at the close association between music and medicine and tried to find out the characteristics of healing songs. Unfortunately, her approach was limited by her classical musical training, and she attempted to render both tempi and harmonies within Western musical scales and bars, unstimulated by the new musical explorations and experiments of modern twentieth-century composers. This became a major weakness of her analytical work, as she tried to make statistical summaries of Indian musical styles based on these transcriptions.

From 1940 to 1942, the wax cylinders on which her recordings were made were transferred to a more permanent base, and made more accessible by placing them in the National Archives, as part of the Archive of American Folksong. During this period, Densmore served as consultant and prepared a handbook for the collection of over three thousand songs from seventy-six tribal groups made between 1907 and 1940. In 1948, she served as a consultant to prepare a series of long-playing records for release to the general public.

Throughout her life, Densmore depended on the assistance of her sister Margaret who gave up her teaching career to accompany Densmore on her trips throughout the country from 1912 until her death in 1947, smoothing her interactions with the many American Indian people with whom she interacted. Densmore never married, and appeared at the end of her life to some observers to be a stereotypical Victorian woman, although her work and her dedication broke through many of the nineteenth-century restrictions that had lain in her way as a young woman.

She remains a seminal figure in American ethnomusicology, supporting the development of the Society for Ethnomusicology in 1956, and serving as one of its first officers. She died the following year in 1957.   JH/MBO

PRIMARY SOURCES

Densmore, Frances. "Chippewa Music." Bureau of American Ethnology (BAE) Bulletin 45. Washington, D.C.: Government Printing Office, 1910.

———. "Teton Sioux Music." Bureau of American Ethnology (BAE) Bulletin 61. Washington, D.C.: Government Printing Office, 1923.

———. "The Use of Music in the Treatment of the Sick by American Indians." *Musical Quarterly* 13 (1927): 555–565.

———. "A Resemblance between Yuman and Pueblo Songs." *American Anthropologist* 34 (1929): 694–700.

———. "Nootka and Quileute Music" BAE Bulletin 124. Washington, D.C.: Government Printing Office, 1938.

———. "Music of Acoma, Isleta, Cochiti and Zuni Pueblos." BAE Bulletin 165. Washington, D.C.: Government Printing Office, 1957.

SECONDARY SOURCES

Hofmann, Charles. *Frances Densmore and American Indian Music: A Memorial Volume.* Vol. 23 of *Contributions from the Museum of the American Indian.* New York: Museum of the American Indian, Heye Foundation, 1968.

Lurie, Nancy O. "Women in Early American Anthropology." In *Pioneers of American Anthropology,* ed. June Helm, 29–81. Seattle: University of Washington Press.

STANDARD SOURCES

Gacs (article by Charlotte Frisbee); *IDA;* Rossiter 1982.

DERICK, CARRIE M. (1862–1941)

Canadian botanist. Born in 1862 in Clarenceville, Quebec. Educated McGill University (B.A., 1890; M.A., 1896); Woods Hole (1895–1897; 1900; 1903; 1912); Royal College of Science, London (1898); Harvard University (1891; 1893; 1894); University of Bonn (1901–1902). Professional experience: McGill University, demonstrator (1891–1895), lecturer (1896–1904), assistant professor (1904–1907), acting head of department (1910–1912), professor, morphology, botany, and genetics (1912–1928); emerita professor (from 1929). Died November 1941.

Carrie Derick received her degrees from McGill University and then rose through the academic ranks to professor. She was the first woman to be on the faculty at McGill. She was especially interested in genetics, eugenics, and education. She conducted research on the holdfasts of the *Rhodophyceae* and on wood-destroying fungi. She was also interested in the nuclear changes in growing seeds and the nuclear differences between resting and active cells. In addition to her scientific work, Derick was active in feminist causes and was president of the Montreal Suffrage Association.   JH/MBO

SECONDARY SOURCES
"Obituary. Dr. Carrie M. Derick." *New York Times* 11 November 1941.

STANDARD SOURCES
AMS 1–5.

DERSCHEID-DELCOURT, MARIE (fl. 1925)
Belgian physician. Educated University of Brussels (M.D., 1893).

Marie Derscheid-Delcourt was one of the first women to graduate from the medical school at Brussels. She won the class gold medal for her work on the congenital dislocation of the hip. She became a physician in Brussels and published a translation in the *Medical Review* (1925) of a Phoenician table of a memorial to an early woman physician, Asyllia Polia.   JH/MBO

STANDARD SOURCES
Hurd-Mead 1938; Lovejoy.

DE STAËL HOLSTEIN, ANNE LOUISE GERMAINE NECKER (1768–1817)
French writer. Born 1768 in Paris to Suzanne (Curchod) and Jacques Necker. Married the Baron of Staël-Holstein. Died 1817.

Anne Germaine Necker was the daughter of Jacques Necker, a rich banker, French minister to Switzerland, and a philanthropist. Her mother SUSANNE NECKER was a great reformer who transformed an old Benedictine convent into a 120-bed hospital, the Hôpital Necker. Suzanne Necker worked tirelessly to suppress slovenly care. Anne Germaine's husband was the Swedish ambassador to Paris. Anne absorbed the characteristics of both parents—her father's talents in politics and finance and her mother's in welfare work and medical sciences. She wrote several books on sociological studies and one psychological romance, *Corinna*.   JH/MBO

PRIMARY SOURCES
De Staël Holstein, Anne. *Corrine, ou, l'Italie.* Philadelphia: A. J. Blocquerst.
———. *De l'Allemagne.* Berlin: Asher, n.d.

STANDARD SOURCES
Hurd-Mead 1938.

DETMERS, FREDERICA (1867–1934)
U.S. botanist. Born 16 January 1867 in Dixon, Ill., to Himke (Heeren) and Henry J. Detmers. Educated Ohio State University (B.S., 1887; M.S., 1891; Ph.D., 1912). *Professional experience: Ohio Agricultural Experimental Station at Wooster, assistant botanist (1889–1892, 1918–1923), systematist (1923); Columbus, Ohio, schools, German teacher (1893–1896) and North High School science teacher (1896–1906); The Ohio State University, Department of Botany, instructor (1906–1914, 1917–1921), assistant professor (1914–1917); University of California at Los Angeles, curator of the herbarium (1923–1934). Died 5 September 1934 in Los Angeles, Calif.*

Frederica Detmers's father was a bacteriologist, veterinarian, and the founder of the College of Veterinary Medicine of The Ohio State University. Her interest in science may have been the result of her intellectual environment. She earned all of her degrees at Ohio State and was the first student to obtain a master's in botany and the second to obtain a doctorate in botany. Her major professor, William A. Kellerman, later hired her as an instructor in the department. She taught courses and worked in the state herbarium. After Kellerman died, John Schaffner replaced him at the herbarium, and she continued to prepare papers.

Detmers studied the rusts of Ohio for her master's thesis; and her doctoral dissertation involved an ecological study of an artificial lake developed out of a large swamp to supply water for the Ohio-Erie Canal built in the 1820s. Her dissertation was completed under the direction of Alfred Dachnowski and was an important early field study, the first of its kind by a woman in Ohio. This study was comprehensive in that it combined data from floristic, ecological, physiographical, and phytogeographical points of view. Detmers published twenty-eight papers on a variety of topics.

                                      JH/MBO

PRIMARY SOURCES
Detmers, Frederica. "A Preliminary List of the Rusts of Ohio." *Annals of the Report of the Ohio Agricultural Experimental Station Bulletin* 44 (1892): 133–140.
———. "An Ecological Study of Buckeye Lake: A Contribution to the Phytogeography of Ohio." *Proceedings of the Ohio State Academy of Science* 5, no. 10 (1912). Special Paper 19: 1–138.
———. "Canada Thistle, *Cirsium arvense* Tourn. Field Thistle, Creeping Thistle." *Ohio Agricultural Experimental Station Bulletin* 414 (1927): 1–45.

SECONDARY SOURCES
Stuckey, Ronald L. "Lois Lampe." Unpublished notes. Collection of Ronald L. Stuckey.
———. *Women Botanists of Ohio Born before 1900.* Columbus, Ohio: The Ohio State University, 1992. Includes portrait.

STANDARD SOURCES
AMS 3–5; Bailey.

DEUTSCH, HELENE ROSENBACK (1884–1982)

Polish/U.S. psychologist, psychoanalyst. Born 9 October 1884 in Przemysl, Galicia (Poland). Three siblings. Married Felix Deutsch (14 April 1912). One child, Martin (b. 29 January 1917). Educated at home and at the private Mrs. Gawronska's School; University of Vienna (M.D., 1913); Wagner-Jauregg Clinic of the University of Vienna Medical School, neurological and psychiatric training (1914–1921). Professional experience: Civilian women's section of the psychiatric department at University of Vienna during World War I, head; Vienna Psychoanalytic Institute, director (1925–1935); Clinic at Massachusetts General Hospital, psychiatric staff (from 1937); Psychoanalytic Institute in Boston, director, training analyst, lecturer. Died 29 March 1982.

Helene Rosenback was born 9 October 1884 in Przemysl, Galicia (Poland), the youngest of four in a cultured family. Her father was a lawyer and eminent scholar of international law. Helene, six years younger than her nearest sibling, was a favorite of her father; he spoiled her and she adored him. There is no doubt that she equally detested her mother, an autocrat and social snob who released her aggressions by physically and mentally abusing her children, especially Helene. The Rosenback children received their early education at home; Helene later attended the private Mrs. Gawronska's School. At age fourteen, she took a job as a weekly columnist for a local newspaper. She was rebellious as an adolescent, proud of her Polish nationality, and involved with the movement to free her "enslaved" country. She flatly refused to be a debutante and, appalled by her parents' opposition to her entry to law school, ran away twice before convincing her father to agree to her plans. She then made him sign a contract as insurance against his changing his mind. During the years spent studying for the Abitur (Gymnasium entrance exam), she became romantically and politically involved with Herman Lieberman, a handsome (married) lawyer and social democrat, who encouraged her ambition and exerted an enormous influence on her life. Rebellious in nature already, Rosenback became an ardent feminist and suffragette, speaking out for the early socialist movement. Wishing to follow in her father's occupation, she applied to the University of Vienna, but was refused: women were not allowed into the law profession. She argued for admission with the administration for two years until they finally relented in 1907. By then she had turned her attention to medicine.

She enrolled in the medical school of Vienna University, originally planning to study pediatrics, but she developed an interest in psychiatry, and spent the last year of her basic medical schooling in Munich under Emil Kraepelin. Also in Munich, she met Felix Deutsch, another medical student, and they married that same year (1912), beginning a happy, supportive relationship that would last fifty-two years, until

Felix Deutsch died in 1964. Having received their medical degrees, the Deutsches moved to Vienna and Helene spent one semester interning in pediatrics before finally deciding on psychiatry as her specialty.

Helene Deutsch spent seven years in neurological and psychiatric service at the Wagner-Jauregg Clinic of the University of Vienna Medical School (1914–1921), working literally as a volunteer while her male counterparts were paid a salary for their clinical services. There is some dispute over the time of Deutsch's first exposure to Freud. Stevens and Gardner date her interest in Freud from ca. 1907, after she read his interpretation of William Jansen's novel *Gradiva*; others believe she discovered Sigmund Freud in 1916 through reading his *Interpretation of Dreams*. At any rate, by 1918, Deutsch had tentatively tried psychoanalysis on some of her own cases and she determined to ally herself with this new radical movement that was especially welcoming to women adherents. Deutsch began attending lectures in psychoanalysis and was one of the first four women analyzed by Freud (1918–1919). She was the second woman admitted to the Vienna Psychoanalytical Society (in 1918, after Hug-Helmuth) and became Freud's personal assistant.

Deutsch established herself as a superior training analyst and teacher. After spending a year in Berlin undergoing personal analysis with Karl Abraham for a bout of depression, she established, with Freud's help, a Viennese duplicate of the Berlin Society's training institute. She directed the Vienna Psychoanalytic Institute for its first ten years and established working relationships with outpatient clinics to insure her graduates of orderly training opportunities. Her husband, Felix Deutsch, assisted in this as he was a leading internist and heart specialist at the University of Vienna Hospital.

The Deutsches maintained a close family relationship, though Helene Deutsch found it difficult to give her son all the attention she wished and still conduct her practice. Many of the psychoanalysts at this time in Europe married each other and so were able to combine career, social, and family lives. The Deutsches hosted a regular Saturday night get-together, which Helene Deutsch called the "Black Cat Card Club" after one of the games they often played.

Felix Deutsch became Freud's personal physician and eventually became an analyst himself. Since both held prominent and responsible positions in the Vienna medical community, the Deutsches were reluctant to join the early immigration of Jewish intelligentsia, but increasing Nazi dominance convinced them to leave.

During the 1920s and 1930s, wealthy Americans had crossed the Atlantic in a steady stream seeking analysis and training in psychoanalysis by the foremost analysts of Europe. Helene Deutsch's caseload in Vienna had become two-thirds American, and she had presented papers to the New

York Psychoanalytic Society as recently as 1930, so when she immigrated to Boston in 1935, an entourage of patients was already waiting. She bought a farm in North Wolfeboro, New Hampshire, and called it "Babayaga"; it became a weekend and summer retreat and a creative outlet. In addition to her private practice, she was director, training analyst, and lecturer for the Psychoanalytic Institute in Boston. In her eighties, she began to cut back her analytic practice, but continued her interest in people and her intellectual vitality. In 1967, she published the monograph *Selected Problems of Adolescence* and supervised the publication of *Neuroses and Character Types* (her 1930 textbook of neuroses plus sixteen of her subsequent clinical papers). She received the Menninger Award in 1962 and was invited to give the Freud Anniversary Lecture at the New York institute in 1967. Her autobiography was finally published in 1973 as *Confrontations with Myself.* Helene Deutsch died 29 March 1982, after several years of intermittent illness.

Deutsch remains one of the most famous women psychoanalysts, partly because of her close association with Sigmund Freud, but largely due to her own independent contributions to the fields of psychology and psychoanalysis. She wrote the first textbook on feminine psychology. While remaining a respectful disciple of Freud, she developed and championed her own theories of what constitutes healthy maleness and femaleness. An ardent feminist, she encouraged independence for women but still felt that motherliness was the natural and normal capacity of women, allowing them to identify with and empathize with others. She was an outstanding clinician and teacher, whose students included a large portion of the next generation of analysts.   JH

PRIMARY SOURCES

Deutsch, Helene. "Psychology of Mistrust" (1921); reprint, "Zur Psychologie des Misstrauens." *Imago* 7 (1930): 71–83.

———. "Über die pathologische Lüge" (On the Pathological Lie). *Internationale Zeitschrift für Psychoanalyse* 12 (1922): 418–433.

———. *Psychoanalyse der weiblichen Sexualfunktionen* (Psychoanalysis of the Sexual Functions of Women). Vienna: International Psychoanalytischer Verlag, 1925.

———. "A Contribution to the Psychology of Sport." *International Journal of Psychoanalysis* 7 (1926): 223–227.

———. *Psychoanalyse der neurosen* (Psychoanalysis of the Neuroses). Vienna: Internationaler psychoanly & ischer verlag, 1930. English edition, London: Leonard & Virginia Woolf at the Hogarth Press and The Institute of Psychoanalysis, 1932. One of the first textbooks of the psychoanalytic movement.

———. "Psychologie der manisch-depressiven Zustände . . ." (The Psychology of the Manic-Depressive States). *Internationale Zeitschrift für Psychoanalyse* 19 (1933): 358–371.

———. "Some Forms of Emotional Disturbance and Their Relation to Schizophrenia." 1934. An early article on the "as if" personality.

———. *Psychology of Women.* 2 vols. New York: Grune & Stratton, 1944–1945. Broke new ground in the understanding of the life cycle and emotional life of women.

———. *Neuroses and Character Types.* New York: International Universities Press, 1965. A new edition of her *Psychoanalysis of the Neuroses* with sixteen subsequent papers added, including an expanded delineation of her famous concept of the "as if" personality (chapter 20).

———. *Selected Problems of Adolescence.* New York: International Universities Press, 1967.

———. *A Psychoanalytic Study of the Myth of Dionysus and Apollo: Two Variants of the Son-Mother Relationship.* New York: International Universities Press, 1969.

———. *Confrontations with Myself.* New York: Norton, 1973. Autobiography.

SECONDARY SOURCES

Roazan, P. *Helene Deutsch: A Psychoanalyst's Life.* New York: Doubleday, 1985. Reprint, New Brunswick, N.J.: Transaction Publishers, 1992.

STANDARD SOURCES

AMS 15; *Encyclopedia of Psychology;* Stevens and Gardner; Uglow 1982.

DE VALERA, MAIRIN (1912–1984)

Irish botanist. Born 12 April 1912 in Dublin to Sinead (Flannagain) and Eamon De Valera. Educated University of Dublin (B.Sc., 1935). Professional experience: University College, University of Dublin, Department of Natural History, assistant lecturer in botany (1947), professor of botany (1962–1977). Died in Galway, 8 August 1984.

Mairin De Valera was the daughter of the famous Irish statesman Eamon De Valera, later head of the Irish Republic. Her mother, a teacher of Irish and supporter of the Gaelic League, became known for her Gaelic fairy tales. Mairin De Valera followed her father's early interest in science (he had been a teacher of mathematics before he moved into politics). She was educated at the University of Dublin, which her father had also attended, receiving her bachelor of science degree in 1935. She began as an assistant to the department of natural history, and then was appointed a lecturer in botany in 1947. From 1962 to 1977, she was professor of botany at the University of Dublin. She died in Galway in 1984.   JH/MBO

PRIMARY SOURCES

De Valera, Mairin. *A Topographical Guide to the Seaweed of Galway Bay: With Some Brief Notes on Other Districts on the West Coast of Ireland.* Dublin: Institute for Industrial Research and Standards, 1958.

———. *Some Aspects of the Problem of the Distribution of Bifucaria bifurcata (Valley) Ross on the Shores of Ireland, North of the Shannon Estuary.* Dublin: Hodges, 1962.

SECONDARY SOURCES
Irish Naturalists Journal 15 (1965): 91.
Irish Naturalists Journal 21 (1985): 377–378. Obituary notice, with portrait.

STANDARD SOURCES
Desmond.

DE VALOIS, MADAME (fl. 13th century)
French healer.

Little is known about Madame de Valois except that she was born to riches and an easy court life. Instead of enjoying what she had, she taught herself medicine and devoted her life to healing the sick. JH/MBO

STANDARD SOURCES
Hurd-Mead 1938.

DE VESIAN, DOROTHY ELLIS (1889–1983)
See also Vesian, Dorothy E. de.
British botanist/biologist. Born 1889. Professional experience: Cheltenham Ladies College, Head of Biology. Died 8 January 1983.

Dorothy Ellis De Vesian became the head of biology at the Cheltenham Ladies College. She collected botanical specimens in Gloucestershire. Her herbarium is in the Gloucester Museum. JH/MBO

SECONDARY SOURCES
Cotteswold Naturalists Field Club 39 (1982–1983): 11–12. Obituary notice.
Watsonia 15 (1984): 57. Obituary notice.

STANDARD SOURCES
Desmond.

DEWEY, JANE MARY (CLARK) (1900–)
U.S. physicist. Born 1900.

A victim of deliberate antifeminism during the Depression, Dewey was replaced at Bryn Mawr by a male crystallographer, A. L. Patterson, in 1935. She was a highly regarded

spectroscopist, former National Research Council Fellow, and associate professor when she was let go. She was subsequently unemployed for four years before obtaining a temporary night job at Hunter College in 1940. There is no further information on her work. JH/MBO

STANDARD SOURCES
AMS 4–8, P&B 10–12; Rossiter 1982.

DE WITT, LYDIA MARIA ADAMS (1859–1928)
U.S. anatomist and pathologist. Born 1 February 1859 in Flint, Mich., to Elizabeth (Walton) and Oscar Adams. Two siblings. Married Alton D. De Witt. One daughter, one son. Educated Michigan State Normal School (finished course in 1886); University of Michigan (M.D., 1898; B.S., 1899); studied at University of Berlin (1906). Professional experience: Washington University, St. Louis, assistant in anatomy (1899–1908); instructor in pathology, University of Berlin (1908?–1910?), assistant professor (1912–1918), associate professor (from 1918) of pathology, University of Chicago. Died 10 March 1928 of chronic high blood pressure and arteriosclerosis.

Lydia Maria Adams was born in Flint, Michigan, to attorney Oscar Adams and Elizabeth (Walton) Adams. Her mother died when Lydia was five and the three children were brought up by Adams's second wife, who was the sister of his first wife. Lydia attended public schools in Flint and after graduating from high school, taught in Michigan public schools. She married a fellow teacher, Alton D. De Witt, at age nineteen (1878) and had two children, Clyde Alton (1879) and Stella Pearl (1880). In 1884, Lydia De Witt entered Ypsilanti Normal College (later Michigan State Normal College), graduating with honors. She went back to teaching as her husband's career progressed. When he was superintendent of schools in South Haven, she was appointed preceptress (1889). Her own thirst for knowledge never abated, and in 1895, Lydia De Witt entered a combined bachelor's and master's course at University of Michigan, finding her niche in microscopic analysis and pathology research.

De Witt, now separated from her husband, was appointed assistant in pathology in 1898 and served as instructor in the department of pathology. She remained several years on the medical faculty at Michigan, taught anatomy and pathology, produced several important research papers, and contributed improvements to histological technique. In response to the rejection of women faculty by both the Faculty Research Club and the Junior [Faculty] Research Club, De Witt formed in 1902 the Women's Research Club, which continues to this day to encourage the work of campus women there. She took a sabbatical year in Berlin in 1906. In 1910 she moved to St. Louis, Missouri, where she spent two years at Washington University and as assistant city pathologist and bacteriologist (St. Louis Department of Health). Areas of De Witt's research included the pathology of tuberculosis; studies of nerve endings in muscles, tendons, and the esophagus; the morphology of kidneys; the pathology of muscle; myosisis ossifans; membranous dysmenorrhea; and the sinoventricular connecting system of the mammalian heart.

In 1912 she was invited by Harry Gideon Wells, professor of pathology at the University of Chicago and director of the newly formed Otho S. A. Sprague Memorial Institute, to join the institute's staff for experimental studies of the chemical treatment of tuberculosis. At the institute, De Witt became principal investigator on a team of top pathologists and organic chemists conducting a longterm series of experiments in possible chemical linkages of dyes and toxic metals in compounds to treat tuberculosis. Although their seemingly promising theory failed to produce an effective treatment, the resulting papers on biochemistry and chemotherapy of tuberculosis contributed to success years later in treating the disease.

De Witt was also associate professor in the department of pathology at the University of Chicago (1918), president of the Chicago Pathological Society (1924–1925), member American Medical Association, Association of American Anatomists (1902), and the Tuberculosis Association. She received an honorary degree from the University of Michigan in 1914. With failing health, she moved in 1926 to live with her daughter in Winter, Texas, and died there 10 March 1928. JH/MBO

PRIMARY SOURCES
De Witt, Lydia Maria. "Morphology and Physiology of Areas of Langerhands in Some Vertebrates." *Journal of Experimental Medicine* 8 (1906): 193–239.
————. "Report of Some Experiments on the Action of *Staphylococcus aureus* on the Klebs-Loeffler Bacillus." *Journal of Infectious Diseases* 10 (1912): 36–42.
————. "The Present Status of Tuberculosis Chemotherapy." *Journal of Laboratory and Clinical Medicine* 1 (1915–1916): 677–684.
————. With Harry Gideon Wells and Esmond R. Long. *Chemistry of Tuberculosis.* Baltimore: Williams & Wilkins, 1923.

SECONDARY SOURCES
Talbott, John H. *A Biographical History of Medicine, Excerpts and Essays on the Men and Their Work.* New York: Grune and Stratton, 1970.

STANDARD SOURCES
AMS 1–4; Bailey; Grinstein 1997 (article by Mary R. S. Creese); *NAW* (article by Esmond R. Long); *NCAB*.

DIANA OF POITIERS (1449–1566)
French medical book collector. Born 1449 in Poitiers, France. Mistress of Henry II. Died 1566.

Diana of Poitiers, the mistress of Henry II of France, collected books and paintings. Her book collection was eclectic, including thirty-six diverse books of theology, geography, natural history, and *belles-lettres.* In her collection were four medical books written by contemporary physicians. These books included Charles Estienne on dissection, Ambroise Paré on the treatment of wounds, Thiérry de Hery on venereal diseases, and Sylvius on human generation and on the diseases of women. The last book contained a dedication to herself. JH/MBO

STANDARD SOURCES
Hurd-Mead 1938; Lipinska 1900.

DICK, GLADYS ROWENA HENRY (1881–1963)
U.S. microbiologist and pathologist. Born 18 December 1881 in Pawnee City, Nebr., to Azelia Henrietta (Edson) and William Chester Henry. Two siblings. Married George Frederick Dick 28 January 1914. Educated public schools, Lincoln, Nebr.; University of Nebraska (B.S., 1900; graduate studies in zoology, 1900–1902). Johns Hopkins Medical School (M.D., 1907; intern, 1908); University of Berlin (postgraduate studies, 1910–1911?). Professional experience: Carney, Nebr., public schools, teacher (1900–1901); Johns Hopkins University Hospital, staff (1909–1910); University of Chicago, researcher (with H. Gideon Wells and George Frederick Dick) (1911–1914); Evanston Hospital, pathologist (1914); John R. McCormick Memorial Institute for Infectious Diseases, microbiologist, pathologist (1914–1953); United States Public Health Service, microbiologist (1918–1919); professional consultant Cradle Society, founder (1918–1953). Died 21 August 1963 in Menlo Park, Calif.

Born and raised in Nebraska, Gladys Rowena (Henry) Dick was the daughter of a former Civil War officer and successful grain dealer and banker. She was the youngest daughter and second of three children. After attending the local public schools in Lincoln, Nebraska, she studied zoology at the University of Nebraska, obtaining her bachelor's degree in 1900. While she taught school for a year, she also did further graduate work in zoology from 1900 to 1902, with the intention of entering medical school. Initially opposed in that aim by her mother, she overcame her mother's objections and entered Johns Hopkins University School of Medicine in 1903.

At Johns Hopkins, Henry convinced the other women medical students to join her in buying a residence, not provided by the university. After receiving her medical degree in 1907, she stayed for a year as an intern and then as part of the medical staff before going to the University of Berlin for postgraduate work in biomedical research. During this period, she also worked on experimental cardiac surgery (with Harvey Cushing) and on blood chemistry with W. G. Mac-Callum and Milton Winternetz.

Moving to Chicago in 1911, Henry became attached to the University of Chicago, doing research on kidney pathochemistry with H. Gideon Wells. Here she also began research on her lifelong interest in scarlet fever etiology with her future husband, George Frederick Dick. She and Dick married 28 January 1914, and settled in Evanston, Ill., later that year. There she continued her work as a pathologist at the Evanston Hospital and began private medical practice. Soon, though, she abandoned this position to join her husband at the John R. McCormick Memorial Institute for Infectious Diseases in Chicago, where she remained until her retirement in 1953.

The Dicks began an intensive study of the hemolytic streptococcus, which they were able to identify in 1923 as the bacterial cause of scarlet fever. They isolated the toxin and established the Dick skin test for determining susceptibility to the infection. In 1924 and 1926, they obtained patents for their toxin and antitoxin methods of production. The patents were censured in the medical press in the United States and the United Kingdom and even criticized by the health organization of the League of Nations as opposed to open research, but the Dicks believed their patents to be a legal device to ensure quality control of the toxin and antitoxin. In 1930, Gladys Dick successfully won an action against Lederle Antitoxin Laboratories. When penicillin and other antibiotics were developed in the 1940s, the antitoxin developed by the Dicks was no longer significant. Nevertheless, the importance of their work in the twenties and early thirties made them contenders for the Nobel Prize in medicine in 1925, and obtained them the Mickle Prize at the University of Toronto in 1926, and a general recognition of their work in practical therapeutics from the University of Edinburgh in 1933.

Gladys Dick turned her attention to polio in the last decade of her active research life. She also founded and served as the major professional consultant to the Cradle Society in Evanston, the first professional organization in America concerned with adoption. She and her husband adopted two children themselves (Rowena Henry and Roger Henry) in 1930. They retired to Palo Alto, California, in 1953, where Gladys Dick became increasingly affected by cerebral arteriosclerosis, dying in 1963 in Menlo Park four years before her husband. JH

PRIMARY SOURCES

Dick, Gladys H. *Journal of the American Medical Association* 81 (1923): 1166–1177.

———. *Journal of the American Medical Association* 82 (1923): 265–266; 301–302; 544–545; 1246–1247.

———. With George F. Dick. "A Skin Test for Susceptibility to Scarlet Fever." *Journal of the American Medical Association* 82 (26 January 1924): 265–266.

———. "Scarlet Fever." *American Journal of Public Health* 14 (1924): 1022–1028.

———. "A Scarlet Fever Antitoxin." *Journal of the American Medical Association* 82 (19 April 1924): 1246–1247.

———. With George F. Dick. "A Method of Recognizing Scarlet Fever Streptococci." *Journal of the American Medical Association* 84 (1925): 802–803.

———. With George F. Dick. "Therapeutic Results with Concentrated Scarlet Fever Antitoxin." *Journal of the American Medical Association* 84 (1925): 803–805.

———. With O. B. Nesbit. "Dick Test and Immunization Against Scarlet Fever." *Journal of the American Medical Association* 84 (1925): 805–807.

———. "The Patents in Scarlet Fever Toxin and Antitoxin." *Journal of the American Medical Association* 88 (23 April 1927): 1341–1342.

———. With George F. Dick. "A Preparation of Toxin Suitable for Oral Immunization Against Scarlet Fever." *Journal of the American Medical Association* 115 (1940): 2155–2156.

SECONDARY SOURCES

"Deaths." *Journal of the American Medical Association* 186, no. 13 (28 December 1963): 1185–1190. Obituary notice.

"Gladys Dick, Scarlet Fever Expert, Dies." *Chicago Tribune,* 23 August 1963. Obituary notice.

"Scarlet Fever Conquers." *Science News-Letter* 12 (22 October 1927): 259. With portrait.

STANDARD SOURCES

AMS 4–6; Bailey; Grinstein 1997 (article by Marilyn R. P. Morgan); *NAW*(M) (article by Lewis P. Ruben); *NCAB;* O'Neill; Rossiter 1982; *WWW*(A).

DICKERSON, MARY CYNTHIA (1866–1923)

U.S. zoologist and herpetologist. Born in 1866. Never married. Educated University of Michigan (1886–1891); University of Chicago (B.S., 1897); Marine Biological Laboratories, Woods Hole (1894; 1897–1898; 1905–1906). Professional experience: high school biology teacher (1891–1895); Providence (R.I.) Normal School, head, department of zoology and botany (1897–1905); Stanford University, instructor (1907–1908); American Museum of Natural History, curator, department of woods and forestry (1908–1910), assistant curator and curator of herpetology (1910–1923). Honors and memberships: New York Academy of Sciences, Fellow. Died 1923.

Mary Cynthia Dickerson was born in 1866. She attended the University of Michigan from 1886 to 1891, leaving before she completed her degree to take a position as a high school biology teacher, a position that she held until 1895. Beginning in the summer of 1894, she attended summer sessions at the Marine Biological Laboratories at Woods Hole. These summers gave her the impetus and encouragement to attend the University of Chicago to complete her degree in 1897. At that point, Dickerson obtained a position as the head of the department of zoology and botany at the normal school in Providence, Rhode Island, instructing would-be teachers on the basics of biological science. During this period, she also published her first book on moths and butterflies (1901).

Dickerson's real interest was in herpetology, and she published a book on North American toads and frogs in 1906, following a further period of time studying at Woods Hole. Her contacts there led her also to join the American Museum of Natural History, where she first worked in the department of woods and forestry and then moved to herpetology, first as assistant and then as full curator from 1910 to 1923. Until her death in 1923, she also made a major contribution as editor of both of the museum's publications, the *American Museum Journal* and *Natural History*. In her scientific work, she emphasized the morphology, developmental history, and ecology of reptiles and amphibians.   JH/MBO

PRIMARY SOURCES

Dickerson, Mary Cynthia. *Moths and Butterflies.* Boston: Ginn & Company, 1901.

———. *The Frog Book: North American Toads and Frogs.* New York: Doubleday, Page & Co., 1906.

STANDARD SOURCES

Bailey; *DSB,* vol. 18 (under Schmidt, Karl Patterson; Schmidt had an assistantship under Dickerson at the Museum of Natural History); *WWW(A),* vol. 1, 1897–1942.

DIETRICH, AMALIE (1821–1891)

German naturalist. Born 1821 in Siebenlehn, Saxony, to Cordel and Gottlieb Nelle. Educated at the village schools. Married Wilhelm Dietrich. One daughter, Charitas. Died 1891.

Amalie Dietrich's mother and father (a purse-maker) were uneducated villagers. Amalie, however, was sent to school, learned how to obtain books, and became an avid reader. She married Wilhelm Dietrich, a "gentleman naturalist," who undertook to teach her the Latin names for plants and the techniques of specimen preparation. The husband's attitude toward his wife soon degenerated into tyranny, according to an account written by their daughter, Charitas (born in 1848). When she discovered that Wilhelm was unfaithful as well, Amalie took the child and went to live with her brother and his wife in Bucharest, earning her living as a maid.

Eventually Amalie Dietrich returned to her husband. More dictatorial than ever, he insisted that she accompany him on long specimen-collecting trips and leave Charitas with whatever stranger agreed to take her. Next he began to send Amalie on the collecting trips while he stayed home. On one such trip—to Holland and Belgium, where she did not know the languages—Amalie became seriously ill and spent many weeks in a hospital. When she arrived home, she found that Wilhelm had left to tutor the sons of a count and had sent Charitas away as a household servant. There were to be no more reconciliations.

Amalie Dietrich decided to try to earn her living by collecting and selling specimens. In Hamburg she met R. A. Meyer, a businessman who was interested in plants. Their meeting was the turning point in her career. Not only did the Meyer family buy her collections, but they befriended her and suggested that Charitas be sent to them to be educated. Through their help, Amalie was employed as a collector by Caesar Godeffroy, who was establishing a museum of the geography, natural history, and ethnology of the South Pacific.

In 1863 Dietrich sailed for Australia; she spent ten years collecting on that continent and in New Guinea. Her letters to her daughter describe her experiences there. She learned to use firearms to collect birds and mammals; she even collected skeletons of Papuan aborigines. She had many setbacks, including a long tropical illness and a fire in which her collections and supplies were destroyed. After she returned home (1873), she lived in Godeffroy's house until his death in 1886.

Dietrich became a popular guest in some of the best Hamburg houses. One of her last triumphs occurred when she attempted to attend an anthropological conference in Berlin from which women were barred. She begged the doorkeeper to let her listen in a corner of the gallery; he spoke to an official, who recognized her name, "brought the old lady in, conducted her past all the rows of the audience, and introduced her to the committee" (Bischoff, 316).

Although no theoretician, Amalie Dietrich was familiar with the Linnaean system of classification and was aware of the advantages and disadvantages of natural and artificial classificatory schemes. Her collections added to the understanding of the flora and fauna of Australia.   MBO

PRIMARY SOURCES

Dietrich, Amalie. *Australische Briefe, with a Biographical Sketch, Exercises, and a Vocabulary.* Ed. Augustin Lodewyck. Melbourne and London: Melbourne University Press in association with Oxford University Press, 1943.

SECONDARY SOURCES
Bischoff, Charitas. *The Hard Road: The Life Story of Amalie Dietrich, Naturalist, 1821–1891.* London: Martin Hopkinson, 1931.

STANDARD SOURCES
Ogilvie 1986; *Uneasy Careers* (article by Ogilvie).

DIGGS, ELLEN IRENE (1906–1998)

U.S. anthropologist. Born 1906 in Monmouth, Ill. Educated Monmouth public school. Attended Monmouth College (1924–1925); University of Minnesota (B.A., 1928); Atlanta University, Ga. (M.A. in sociology, 1933). Professional experience: Atlanta University, research assistant to W. E. B. Dubois (1933–1943); Co-founder with W. E. B. Du Bois of the journal Phylon: A Review of Race and Culture; *University of Havana, Cuba, Roosevelt Fellow (1943–1945); International Exchange Scholar, University of Montevideo, Uruguay (1946–1947); Morgan State College, Baltimore, Md., faculty, then professor, department of sociology and anthropology (1947–1976). Died 1998.*

Recognized for her work on Afro-Latin American culture and society, Irene Diggs contributed important insights into the differences between race relations in Cuba and South America and those in the U.S. She was born into a working-class black family, in the rural town of Monmouth, Illinois, almost at the Iowa border. She graduated at the top of her high school class and received a scholarship that allowed her to attend first Monmouth College for one year (1924–1925) and then to transfer to the University of Minnesota where she received her bachelor's in economics and anthropology in 1928. When her sister married a preacher from Atlanta, Georgia, Diggs accompanied them to Atlanta, where she was impressed by the intellectual stimulation provided in the all-black Atlanta University and decided to pursue a graduate degree there. In her second semester, W. E. B. Du Bois returned to teach there, as professor of economics, sociology, and history. The impact of this distinguished sociologist and historian upon Diggs was profound. She completed her master's degree in sociology under Du Bois in 1933 and continued at the university as his research assistant for the next ten years, helping to research and editing five of his major studies, including *Black Reconstruction* (1935), *Black Folk Then and Now* (1939) and *Dusk of Dawn* (1940). At this time, Diggs cofounded the journal of black history, *Phylon: A Review of Race and Culture,* with Du Bois.

In 1942, she left Atlanta University and traveled to Havana, Cuba, spending the first summer learning the language and then taking up a Roosevelt fellowship at the Institute of International Education at University of Havana (1943–1945). Here she encountered the important anthropologist

Fernando Ortiz, under whom she did important ethnographic field studies, investigating continuities of Yoruban and Dahomeyan African cultural elements transformed within Cuban society. She was also struck by the differences in definitions of race in Cuba's "tri-racial" (white, mulatto, and black) society in contrast to the biracial (white and black) U.S. model, and would later discuss this in terms of both class and race (Diggs, "Attitudes").

By 1946–1947, Diggs had the opportunity to study at the University of Montevideo, Uruguay, as part of the international exchange program between universities, sponsored by the U.S. State Department. Here she continued both archival research and studied the Afro-Urugayan and Afro-Argentinian communities. She became intrigued by all aspects of the culture, including the arts and theater there.

On her return to the United States, Diggs was invited to join the faculty of a black college, Morgan State, in Baltimore, Maryland. Here she would remain for the next twenty-nine years, rising to professor in the department of sociology and anthropology until her retirement in 1976. The heavy teaching load made it difficult to publish book-length monographs, but she managed regularly to produce articles for the *Journal of Negro History, Phylon,* and other journals, as well as to contribute commentary to a variety of radio and television programs.

In 1976, Diggs returned to Cuba as a special visitor to the UN-sponsored International Seminar on Apartheid in South Africa. In 1978, she was honored by the Association of Black Anthropologists, a division of the American Anthropological Association, for her studies on peoples of African descent in the Americas.

JH/MBO

PRIMARY SOURCES
Diggs, E. Irene. "The Negro in the Vice Royalty of Rio de la Plata." *Journal of Negro History* 25, no. 3 (1951): 281–301.
———. "Legacy." *Freedomways: W. E. B. Du Bois Memorial Issue* 5, no. 1 (1951): 18–19.
———. "Attitudes towards Color in South America." *Negro History Bulletin* 34, no. 5 (1971): 107–108.
———. "Cuba before and after Castro." *The News American,* 15 July 1976.

STANDARD SOURCES
Gacs (article by Lynn A. Bolles).

DIMOCK, SUSAN (1847–1875)

U.S. surgeon. Born 24 April 1847 in Washington, D.C., to Henry and Mary Malvina Owens Dimock. No siblings. Never married. Educated home until secondary school; Washington Academy; public school in Sterling, Mass.; New England Hospital (1866); clinicals, Massachusetts General Hospital; University of Zurich (1868–

1871, high honors); Vienna and Paris. Professional experience: New England Hospital for Women and Children, resident physician (from 1873). Died 7 May 1875 at sea.

Susan Dimock's father was the son of a physician, and had attended Bowdoin College, taught school, studied law, and edited a local paper. Her mother taught her daughter (an only child) at home and later opened a school for girls. When Susan was thirteen, she entered Washington Academy, which soon closed because of the beginning of the Civil War. Susan Dimock attended school again briefly in Sterling, Massachusetts, studying Latin among other subjects. Henry Dimock died in the war, and family lost most of its property. To survive, Mary Dimock took in boarders after moving in 1865 to Hopkinton, Massachusetts, where Susan taught school. In response to her interest, a family friend and physician allowed Susan Dimock to accompany him on his calls and borrow his medical books, and incidentally made her known to the doctor MARIE ZAKRZEWSKA, who also began suggesting books for study. Dimock was further encouraged in her studies by her mother; she finally entered the New England Hospital for training in 1866. Dimock's attempt (along with SOPHIA JEX-BLAKE) to enter Harvard Medical School failed, so she began clinical visits at Massachusetts General Hospital. Her intellect and aptitude for medicine so impressed Zakrzewska, LUCY SEWALL, and others, that they advised Dimock to apply to the medical school of the University of Zurich, which had just graduated its first woman medical doctor. Dimock entered in 1868, along with a Swiss woman, Marie Vögtlin, who became a close friend. She graduated with high honors in 1871. She continued her studies in Vienna and Paris, returning to Boston in 1872, one of the best trained of the early women doctors.

Initially Dimock was appointed resident physician and surgeon at the New England Hospital for Women and Children for a three-year term. She took the opportunity to restructure the nursing training program to more closely equal those she had observed in Europe. She handled the management of the hospital and also shared in the patient care and performed most of the surgeries. When her three years were up, the hospital offered her an extension. She consented with the condition that she first be given five months leave during the summer of 1875 to tour Europe, planning a reunion with Marie Vögtlin and other friends from Zurich. She and two friends sailed from New York on 27 April 1875 on the steamer *Schiller*. On the night of 7 May, the ship foundered on the Scilly Islands off the coast of England and nearly all perished, including Dimock. News of her death was a shock to all who had known her and many mourned the loss of her skill and promise. "Among all the bright lives that have been engulfed in this dreadful shipwreck, none is more valuable

than hers . . . both the surgical talents and surgical training of Dr. Dimock are certainly, at the present date, exceptional among women," wrote MARY PUTNAM JACOBI. Dimock's body was returned to Boston for burial.

While medicine was her passion, Susan Dimock was not one-dimensional. She enjoyed art, music, dancing, and travel. She showed little interest in feminism or any reform movement, content to manage a hospital for women and children and limiting her private practice to the treatment of women.

Although refused membership in the Massachusetts Medical Society due to her sex, Dimock was made an honorary member of the North Carolina Medical Society in 1872.

JH/MBO

PRIMARY SOURCES
Dimock, Susan. "Ueber due verschiedenen Formen des Puerperalfiebers." Dissertation, University of Zurich, 1871.
———. Case studies in the *Medical Record,* New York, 1874, 1875.
———. Memoir of Susan Dimock, resident physician of the New England Hospital for Women and Children, Boston, 1875. Schlesinger, Microfilm: History of Women, reel 398, no. 2844. New Haven, Conn.: Research Publications, 1977.

STANDARD SOURCES
Bonner (includes portraits of Suslova, Bokova, Morgan, Dimock, Atkins, Walker, and Vögtlin); *LKW; Lovejoy; NAW* (article by Shirley Phillips Ingebritsen).

DIMSDALE, HELEN EASDALE (BROWN) (1907–1977)

British neurologist. Born 2 July 1907 in Stretford to Ellen Carse and John Harold Brown. Married Wilfrid Dimsdale (1930). One son. Educated Culcheth Hall and Hayes Court; Girton College Cambridge (Natural Science Tripos, first class, 1929); University College Hospital (conjoint diploma, 1933); Cambridge (M.B., B.Chir., 1937); Maida Vale, London, and Chase Farm Hospitals, neuropathology training (1941–1946); (M.A.; M.D., 1949). Professional experience: Windsor, University College Hospital, and Elizabeth Garrett Anderson hospital, house appointments; Elizabeth Garrett Anderson, medical registrar (1938–1939), physician 1946–1952); Maida Vale, physician (1947–1967); Royal Free Hospital, physician (1950–1967). Honors and memberships: Royal College of Physicians, member (1939); Royal Free Hospital, Fellow (1949), council (1961–1963). Died 20 April 1977.

Helen Brown's father was chairman of textile and steel companies and her mother was from a well-known family. After secondary school, Brown went to Girton College, Cambridge, where she earned a first in the Natural Science Tripos. Following this, she went to University College Hospital for clinical studies, where she qualified with a conjoint diploma and passed her MB, Bachelor of Medicine, and B.Chir, Bachelor of Surgery. Interested in neurology and neuropathology, Helen Dimsdale (she married Wilfrid Dimsdale in 1930), now with one son, trained at various hospitals from 1941 to 1946. While she served the Elizabeth Garrett Anderson hospital as a physician, she earned her master's and medical degrees. She also served the Maida Vale and Royal Free Hospitals until poor health forced her to retire.

From 1951 to 1954, Dimsdale was medical tutor at the Royal Free Hospital and taught there as well as at the Institute of Neurology. She was an examiner in neurology for the Diploma of Psychological Medicine at Durham and for the Royal College of Physicians in medical ophthalmology. She published numerous papers during her career. When Dimsdale was appointed to the consultant staff of Maida Vale Hospital, she was the first woman to be appointed to a neurological consultancy in Britain.

Dimsdale proved her administrative abilities when she served as chairman of the planning committee for the new Royal Free Hospital in the 1950s and as treasurer for the Association of British Neurologists (1961–1966). Although during her later years, Dimsdale was plagued by ill health, when she was young, she was an active sportswoman. Her son became an economist and Fellow of Queen's College, Oxford.   JH/MBO

SECONDARY SOURCES
McM., W. H. "Helen Easdale Dimsdale." *Lancet* 1 (1977): 1018.
Times, 23 April 1977. Obituary notice.

STANDARD SOURCES
Munk's Roll, vol. 7, 1984.

DINNERSTEIN, DOROTHY (1923–1993?)

U.S. psychologist. Born 4 April 1923. Educated New School for Social Research (Ph.D., 1951). Professional experience: Swarthmore College, research associate (1952–1959); Rutgers University, professor of psychology (from 1959); Institute Cognitive Studies, member (from 1959). Died 1993?

Dorothy Dinnerstein, a member of the American Psychological Association since 1958, was especially interested in cognitive psychology, specializing in the experimental and descriptive study of cognition. She also worked in psychoanalysis-oriented social philosophy. Gender identities and gender relationships were an important part of her research.
                                                    KM

PRIMARY SOURCES
Dinnerstein, Dorothy. *The Mermaid and the Minotaur: Sexual Arrangements and Human Malaise.* New York: Harper Perennial, 1991.

SECONDARY SOURCES
Women's Review of Books 10, no. 7 (April 1993): 71. Obituary notice.

DI NOVELLA, MARIA (fl. 14th century)

Italian mathematician. Born fourteenth century in Bologna. Father John Andreas. Married John Caldesimus. Educated by her father.

Maria di Novella was educated by her father, a professor at Bologna. She learned mathematics and natural philosophy from him as well as other subjects. It is said that when he was unable to read his lectures to his students, he sent his daughter in his place. Because her beauty was distracting to the scholars, they had a curtain placed in front of her. She was married to John Caldesimus, a canonist, but died shortly after her marriage.   JH/MBO

STANDARD SOURCES
Cyclopedia.

DIOTIMA OF MANTINEA (5th century B.C.E.)

Greek philosopher. Born fifth century B.C.E in Mantinea.

Plato in the *Symposium* describes Diotima as a priestess and a teacher of Socrates. All later references are based on Plato's account. Since Plato did not specify the nature of her knowledge, it cannot be determined whether her purported wisdom took her into the realm of science. She evidenced some interest in at least controlling natural phenomena in her reputed delay of the plague. At any rate, through her pupil Socrates she can be presumed to have exerted some degree of influence on Plato, who, though not a scientist himself, was singularly important in the development of science. JH/MBO

SECONDARY SOURCES
Pauly, August Friedrich von. *Paulys Real-Encyclopädie der classischen Altertumswissenschaft.* Ed. G. Wissowa. Stuttgart: J. B. Metzler, 1894–1919. Vol. 5, part 2, page 1147, gives information on Diotima.
Plato. *Symposium* 201–212. Later references to Diotima are based on this account.

DIX, DOROTHEA LYNDE (1802–1887)

U.S. nursing and mental healthcare reformer. Born 4 April 1802 in Hampden, Maine, to Joseph and Mary (Bigelow) Dix. Never married. Professional experience: Boston, girls' school, director (ca. 1817–1835); directly involved in the creation of thirty-two state mental hospitals. Died 17 July 1887 in Trenton, N.J.

Dorothea Lynde Dix began her professional career by conducting a girls' school in Boston (ca. 1817–1835). This school primarily emphasized the development of moral character. Ill health forced her to give up this school, after which she began a Sunday school class in the East Cambridge, Massachusetts, House of Correction (1841). Her visits to the jails made her aware of the inhuman treatment of the insane as criminals and stimulated her to investigate the treatment of the insane in Massachusetts (1841–1843). She began an effective campaign for the intelligent and humane treatment of the insane by keepers of almshouses and jails. She later realized that state-supported asylums with intelligently trained personnel were necessary, and was responsible for refounding or enlarging state mental hospitals in Massachusetts, Rhode Island, New Jersey, Pennsylvania, and Toronto, Ontario, Canada (1841–1845). She convinced state legislatures to found state hospitals in eleven states (Kentucky, Illinois, Indiana, Tennessee, Missouri, Mississippi, Louisiana, Alabama, South Carolina, North Carolina, and Maryland) from 1845 to 1852. She had submitted to Congress a twelve-million-dollar bill for land to be set aside for taxation to support the care of insane; this bill, however, was vetoed by President Franklin Pierce in 1854. In 1854 to 1857, Dix went to Europe; because of her efforts on behalf of the insane, hospitals were founded on the Isle of Jersey and in Rome. Queen Victoria began a royal commission to investigate the condition of the insane in Scotland. Back in the United States Dix was appointed superintendent of women nurses for the federal government in 1861, and continued activities on behalf of the insane after the Civil War. Dix has been identified with advocacy for the mentally ill. She was directly involved in the creation of thirty-two state mental hospitals and was the inspiration for many more throughout the United States and elsewhere. Though she was not especially interested in psychiatric research, mirroring, instead, the knowledge of her day, she brought about advances in psychiatry by stressing the importance of therapeutic care and by publicizing the plight of the mentally ill. She died in Trenton, New Jersey, 17 July 1887. JH/MBO

PRIMARY SOURCES

Dix's letters on mental health reform are in the New York Public Library.

STANDARD SOURCES

Debus; *NAW* (article by Helen E. Marshall).

DOBROLUBOVA, TATIANA A. (1891–1972)

Russian/Soviet geologist and paleontologist. Born 1891 in Nizhegorod province to a lawyer father and a mother who was an obstetrical physician's assistant. One sibling. Educated Gymnasium (completed 1909) and Highest Women's Courses (first degree diploma, 1915). Professional experience: Institute of Mineral Resources (1934–1936); Paleontological Institute (1936–1972). Died 1972 in Moscow.

Tatiana A. Dobrolubova's father died at an early age, forcing her mother to take care of two children. They first lived in Nizhniy Novgorod and later moved to Moscow. After finishing the Gymnasium, she decided to enter the Highest Women's Courses and finished them in 1915 with a first degree diploma.

Since her time at the Gymnasium, Dobrolubova was interested in geology. At every opportunity she listened to lectures on geological disciplines. From 1921 to 1931, she organized and went on nine large expeditions to the northern Urals. At this time, she decided to become a geologist, and, more specifically, a paleontologist. At the end of this expedition, she and E. D. Soshkina produced a large monograph. By 1931, she was finished with her work on the geological survey and began paleontological research.

Dobrolubova's first jobs were with oil organizations. In the summer of 1934 when an oil institute moved to St. Petersburg, she transferred to a paleontological group in the Institute of Mineral Resources.

However, her real opportunity emerged when she was transferred to the Paleontological Institute, where she worked until the end of her life. The director of the Institute, A. A. Borisyak, was her ardent supporter. In a letter supporting Dobrolubova's petition for a scientific degree, he stressed her remarkable capacity for work. According to Borisyak, she was the best specialist on Carboniferous rugoses in the Soviet Union. He stated that all the collections from geological parties from all over the Soviet Union came to her for identification. This letter resulted in Dobrolubova's being awarded a degree of candidate of geologo-mineralogical sciences without a dissertation.

Dobrolubova produced thirty-nine works, including nine monographs. She was especially interested in corals, and her theoretical conclusions were so original that the Paleontological Institute declined to print them.

Pedagogical work was also a part of Dobrolubova's science. She spent the winter of 1918–1919 teaching in a Gymnasium. From 1920, she trained to be a teacher at the University of Moscow. From January 1922 to 1930, she became an assistant professor in the department of geology. Because of the reorganization of that facility, she moved to the Institute of Chemical Technology, where she taught geological disciplines for five years. Although this position was her last official teaching job, she willingly gave advice to young specialists. She was a member of the Moscow Naturalist's Society and the All-Union Paleontological Society. CK

PRIMARY SOURCES

Dobrolubova, T. A. "Rugosa Corals of the Middle and Upper Carboniferous and Permian of the North Ural." Academy of Sciences USSR, Polar Commission 28 (1936): 77–158. In Russian.

———. "Simple Corals of the Myatshkovo and Podolsk Horizons of the Middle Carboniferous of the Moscow Basin." Academy of Sciences USSR, Inst. Paleozoological 6 (1937): 5–92. In Russian.

———. *Stratigraphical Distribution and Evolution of the Rugosa Corals of the Middle and Upper Carboniferous of the Moscow Basin.* Academy of Sciences USSR, Paleontological Institute 11, 1941. In Russian.

———. With T. A. Kabakovich. *Nekotorye predstaviteli Rugosa srednego i verkhnego karbona Podmoskovnogo basseina.* Trudy Paleontologicheskogo Instituta 14, no. 2, 1948. Moscow: Rossiyskaya Akademiya Nauk, Paleontologicheskiy Institute, 1948. Describes rugose corals, including new genera, species, and varieties from middle and upper Carboniferous localities of the Moscow basin.

———. *Nizhnekamennougolnye kolonialnye chetyrekhluchevye korally Russkoi platformy.* Trudy Paleontologicheskogo Instituta 70, 1958. Moscow: Rossiyskaya Akademiya Nauk, Paleontologicheskiy Institut, 1958. A monographic systematic study of tetracorals (including new species and subspecies) from lower Carboniferous localities of the platform region of European USSR.

———. "New solitary rugose corals from the lower Carboniferous of the Russian platform." In *Novyye vidy paleozoyshikh mshanok i korallov.* Ed. Galina Grigorévna Astronova and I. I. Chudinova. Moscow: Akademiá Nauk SSSR, 1970. In Russian.

STANDARD SOURCES

Nalivkin.

DOBROSCKY, IRENE DOROTHY (1899–?)

U.S. entomologist. Born 27 December 1899 in Yonkers, N.Y. Married Carleton Van de Water. Educated Cornell University (B.S., 1923; Schuyler fellow, 1924; M.S., 1924; Ph.D., 1928). Professional experience: Boyce Thompson Institute, assistant entomologist and plant pathologist (1924–1930); Experimental Station, Association of Hawaiian Pineapple Canners, beneficial insect explorer (1931–1933); consulting entomologist (from 1933). Honors and memberships: Entomological Society of America, Phytopathological Society, New York Entomological Society, member. Death date unknown.

Irene Dobroscky was born and grew up in New York state. When it came time for her to go to college it was natural for her to choose Cornell—both because it was in-state and because of its excellent natural history program. After she received her master's degree and for two years after she earned her doctorate, she worked as an assistant entomologist and plant pathologist at the Boyce Thompson Institute. She then worked for the Institute of Pineapple Canners. Dobroscky was a member of the Entomological Society of America, the Phytopathological Society, and the New York Entomological Society. Her special research interests included the study of insect vectors of plant virus diseases and parasitic insects. JH/MBO

PRIMARY SOURCES

Dobroscky, Irene Dorothy. "Morphology and Cytology of the Digestive System of Cicadula sexnotata (Fallen), the Insect Carrier of Aster Yellows' Virus." Ph.D. diss., Cornell University, 1928.

STANDARD SOURCES

AMS 6–8, P&B 10–11.

DOBROWOLSKA, H. (fl. 1923)

Polish chemist and physicist. Professional experience: Warsaw Academy of Sciences, researcher.

The career of H. Dobrowolska, a Polish researcher, helps to dispel the myth that women did not work in physics. Many women did important research in the early days of radioactivity, but their lives are poorly documented; Dobrowolska is one of them. In order to examine the question of diffusion in the solid state, Dobrowolska and Louis Wertenstein used the sensitive method of scintillation counting to trace diffusion of radioactive elements in noble metals. In addition to diffusion, they suspected that radioactive recoil and artificial disintegration were responsible for some of their results. This work was done at the Radiology Laboratory of the Warsaw Society of Sciences. MM

PRIMARY SOURCES

Dobrowolska, H. With Louis Wertenstein. "Diffusion des éléments radioactifs dans les metaux." *Journal de physique et le radium* 4 (1923): 324–332.

STANDARD SOURCES

Meyer and von Schweidler.

DOBSON, MILDRED E. (d. 1952)

Scottish botanist. Educated St. Andrews University (M.A., 1900). Professional experience: St. Andrews University, demonstrator in botany (summer sessions 1904–1906); St. Winifred's School, Eastbourne, science mistress (1908–1911); St. Andrews University Hall, warden (1911–1936). Died 1952.

Mildred Dobson spent most of her career at St. Andrews University, Saint Andrews, Scotland. After receiving her master's degree there, she served as a demonstrator during the summer session for two years. After spending three years as science mistress at St. Winifred's School, she returned to St. Andrews as warden of University Hall.　　JH/MBO

SECONDARY SOURCES

Macdonald, J. A. *Plant Science and Scientists in St. Andrews.* St. Andrews, Scotland: printed for the author by QUICK print, 1984. Dobson is mentioned on page 29.

STANDARD SOURCES
Desmond.

DOCK, LAVINIA LLOYD (1858–1956)

U.S. nurse, settlement house worker, suffragist. Born 26 February 1858 in Harrisburg, Pa., to Lavinia Lloyd (Bombaugh) and Gilliard Dock. Five siblings. Never married. Educated girls' academy, Harrisburg; Bellevue Hospital, N.Y., School for Nurses (1884–1886). Professional experience: Woman's Mission of New York City Mission and Tract Society, visiting nurse; Bellevue Hospital, night superintendent (1889); Johns Hopkins University Hospital, assistant superintendent of nurses (1890–1893); Columbia University Teachers College, volunteer staff; Cook County Hospital, Illinois Training School, principal (1893–1895); Henry Street Nurses Settlement, nurse (1896–1915); American Journal of Nursing, contributing and foreign editor (1900–1922). Honors and memberships: American Society of Superintendents of Training Schools (cofounder; secretary, 1896–1901); Nurses Associated Alumnae (later American Nurses Association); American New York Women's Trade Union League; National Women's Party; International Council of Nurses (joint founder; secretary, 1899–1922); American Society of Sanitary and Moral Prophylaxis. Died 17 April 1956 in Chambersburg, Pa.

Lavinia Lloyd Dock was born in Harrisburg, Pennsylvania, the second oldest of six children, five of whom were daughters. She attended the local girls' academy and then, at age eighteen, when her mother died, helped her sister raise the other children. All the children inherited enough property to support themselves, but Lavinia's strong social conscience impelled her toward nursing in her late twenties.

Dock went to New York City in 1884, to study nursing at Bellevue Hospital. Here she worked among the sick poor, and graduated in 1886. She then became a visiting nurse with the Woman's Mission of the New York City Mission and Tract Society, and then traveled to disaster sites, assisting in a yellow fever epidemic in Jacksonville, Florida, in 1888 and in the aftermath of the famous Johnstown, Pennsylvania flood. Dock also wrote a book on therapeutic medicines (materia medica) for nurses, which, with the aid of her father and brother (a medical professor) she published in 1890. This book made her name and was adopted as the major nursing text on this subject for the next twenty years.

In late 1890, Dock accepted a position in Baltimore working under Isabel Hampton as assistant superintendent of nurses at Johns Hopkins hospital. She proved to be an excellent teacher of the first-year classes and instructor on the wards. At Johns Hopkins she had as a student Adelaide Nutting, a young woman of her own age who joined with her and Hampton in establishing nursing as a profession. Hampton and Dock spoke at the Chicago World's Fair at an international conference on hospitals; there they called for and eventually had established an organization of nursing superintendents separate from that of the physicians. Dock remained in Chicago as superintendent of the Illinois Training School at Cook County Hospital, where she remained for two years. She decided she did not have the gift for diplomacy required in administration, and she left in 1895, returning to Harrisburg to relieve her sister Mira from her duties as housekeeper so she could study horticulture at the university level.

Dock then returned to New York and joined the Nurses Settlement on Henry Street (also called the Henry Street Settlement House) as part of the community of women around LILLIAN WALD. Here she cared for immigrant poor and met women involved in trade union organizing. She also assisted Isabel Hampton (now Robb) with the development of the Society of Nursing Superintendents, serving as secretary from 1896 to 1901, and helped found the Nurses Associated Alumnae (later the American Nursing Association). Adelaide Nutting, by now superintendent of the Johns Hopkins school of nursing, established postgraduate courses with Hampton Robb at Columbia University Teachers College, where Dock became a volunteer faculty member.

Her major impact on nursing came from her regular column on international questions as a contributing editor to the *American Journal of Nursing* beginning in 1900 and lasting until 1922, as the foreign editor. She also founded the International Council of Nurses with the British nurse Ethel Gordon Fenwick, and served as its secretary from 1900 to 1923, writing an important column that urged European nurses to challenge medical authority. With Nutting she produced a *History of Nursing* in 1907, a book that was rewritten, expanded, and republished through the 1930s.

Dock worked to bring nurses into the labor movement. She also was the only nursing practitioner who worked with physicians to attempt to take action against the spread of venereal disease, and was an early member of the American Society of Sanitary and Moral Prophylaxis. She wrote a manual in 1911, *Hygiene and Morality,* urging the abolition of a double standard of morality, and urged suffrage for women.

Active in both the trade union movement and in the National Women's Party, Dock worked for suffrage, and became a militant suffragist, jailed three times for her participation in demonstrations. Her participation led her to break her ties with the Henry Street Settlement House in 1915. In 1921, she advocated birth control through the *American Journal of Nursing.* In 1922 and 1923, she began to retire from that organization, returning to live with her unmarried sisters in Pennsylvania. Her advocacy of the Equal Rights Amendment made a further rift with her former associates, although she maintained a correspondence with Lillian Wald and Adelaide Nutting. Sales of her *History of Nursing* helped to support her during the Depression. She was rediscovered in 1947 and honored at the International Council of Nurses convention at Atlantic City. She died in Pennsylvania from bronchopneumonia following a fall that broke her hip in 1956. JH/MBO

PRIMARY SOURCES

Dock, Lavinia Lloyd. *Text-book of Materia Medica for Nurses.* New York: G. P. Putnam's Sons, 1890.

———. *Short Papers on Nursing Subjects.* New York: M. L. Longeway, 1900.

———. With Adelaide Nutting. *History of Nursing.* New York: G. P. Putnam's Sons, 1907, 1912.

———. *Hygiene and Morality.* New York: G. P. Putnam's Sons, 1910.

———. "Self-Portrait." (1932). Reprinted, *Nursing Outlook* 25, no. 1 (January 1977): 22–26.

Primary materials, including correspondence and clippings, are in Adelaide Nutting Papers, Columbia University Teachers College; Nursing History Archives, Boston University; and Leonora O'Reilly Papers, Schlesinger Library, Radcliffe College.

SECONDARY SOURCES

Breay, Margaret. With Ethel Gordon Fenwick. *The History of the International Council of Nurses, 1899–1925.* Geneva: International Council of Nurses, 1931.

"Lavinia Lloyd Dock." *Image: Journal of Nursing Schools* 21, no. 2 (1989): 63–68.

New York Times, 18 April 1956. Obituary notice.

Roberts, Mary M. "Lavinia Lloyd Dock: Nurse, Feminist, Internationalist." *American Journal of Nursing* 56 (February 1956): 176–179.

Wald, Lillian D. *The House on Henry Street.* New York: Henry Holt & Co., 1915.

STANDARD SOURCES

NAW(M) (article by Janet Wilson James); *WWW(A).*

DODD, KATHARINE (1892–?)

U.S. physician and pediatrician. Born 24 March 1892 in Providence, R.I. Educated Bryn Mawr College (A.B., 1914); Johns Hopkins University (M.D., 1921). Professional experience: Johns Hopkins Hospital, intern in pediatrics (1921–1922), assistant resident (1922–1923); New Haven Hospital, assistant resident (1923–1924); Boston Psychopathic Hospital, intern (1924–1925); Vanderbilt University Hospital, assistant professor of pediatrics (1925–1928), associate professor (1928–1943); Medical School of Cincinnati, professor (1943–1950); University of Arkansas Medical Center, professor and head of department (from 1952). Death date unknown.

After Katharine Dodd completed her two internships and her residency, she entered academic medicine. After attaining the rank of associate professor at the Vanderbilt University Hospital, she moved to the Medical School of Cincinnati, where she was promoted to professor. Her final move was to the University of Arkansas Medical Center, where she was professor and head of the department.

Dodd was active in many humanitarian and professional groups. She was a member of the Friends Relief Organization and went to Russia as a physician in 1924. She also maintained an association with the U.S. Public Health Service. Her professional affiliations included the American Medical Association (Fellow), Pediatric Society, Academy of Pediatricians, Society for Pediatric Research.

Her major research interest was in fluid and electrolyte balance in children. JH/MBO

STANDARD SOURCES

AMS 5–8, B 9, P&B 10–11.

DODDS, MARY LETITIA (1901–)

U.S. chemist born in 29 March 1901 in Latakia, Syria. Educated University of Pittsburgh (B.S., 1925; M.S., 1927; fellow, 1939–1940; Ph.D., 1940). Professional experience: Mellon Institute, fellow (1928–1935; 1936–?); University of Pittsburgh, Buhl fellow (1940–1941); University of Tennessee, associate nutritionist (1941–1947); Pennsylvania State University, professor of foods and nutrition research (1947–1964); U.S. Department of Agriculture (1964–1965). Honors and memberships: Borden Award (1957).

Mary Letitia Dodds was born in Syria, but was a United States citizen. She earned all three of her degrees at the University of Pittsburgh. After holding two fellowships, she obtained a position at the University of Tennessee as associate nutritionist, where she remained for six years. She then moved to Pennsylvania State University, as professor of food and nutrition research. She retired in 1964, but took a one-year job with the U.S. Department of Agriculture. Dodds was a member of the Chemical Society, the Institute of Nutrition, the Home Economics Association, and the Dietetic Association. She did research into the toxicology of aluminum. She also worked on industrial uses of cane sugar. Dodds studied dental caries and organic synthesis in pharmaceutics and medicine. JH/MBO

STANDARD SOURCES
AMS 6–8, B 9, P&B 10–11.

DODGSON, SARAH ELIZABETH (1857–1921)
British botanist and horticulturist. Born 1857. Married R. O. Backhouse (1854–1940). Professional experience: bred flowers. Died 30 January 1921 at Sutton Court, Hereford.

Sarah Dodgson was a horticulturist who specialized in breeding narcissi, colchicums, hyacinths, and lilies. JH/MBO

SECONDARY SOURCES
Garden History 18 (1990): 62–64. Includes portrait.

STANDARD SOURCES
Desmond.

DODSON, HELEN WALTER (1905–)
See Prince, Helen Walter (Dodson).

DOERING, KATHLEEN CLARA (1900–1970)
U.S. entomologist. Born 8 June 1900 in Cottonwood Falls, Kans. At least three sisters. Educated University of Kansas (A.B., 1922; A.M., 1923; Ph.D., 1929). Professional experience: University of Kansas, assistant instructor, entomology (1922–1924), instructor (1924–1929), assistant professor (1929–1940), associate professor (1940–1966). Retired 1966. Died 21 May 1970 in Ruidoso, N.M.

Little information is available on Kathleen Doering's life. She received all of her degrees from the University of Kansas and

spent her entire teaching career at that institution. While she was working toward her advanced degrees, Doering worked as night librarian in the biology department and did scientific illustrating and research. Doering was a popular freshman and sophomore advisor. After she retired in 1966, Doering went to live with her sisters in Ruidoso, New Mexico. A scholarship fund for deserving students was established in her name at Ruidoso High School.

Her research was on the insect order *Homoptera*. She published a number of papers on this group, mostly taxonomic in nature. JH/MBO

PRIMARY SOURCES
Doering, Kathleen. "Biology and Morphology of *Lepyronia quadrangularis* (Say)." *University of Kansas Science Bulletin* 14 (October 1922): 515–587. This paper was taken from her master's thesis of the same title.
———. "The Genus *Clastoptera* in America North of Mexico." *University of Kansas Science Bulletin* 18, no. 1 (1928): 5–154. Includes twenty-five plates, two of which are colored. This paper was taken from her doctoral dissertation.
———. "A Contribution to the Taxonomy of the Subfamily Issinae in America, North of Mexico (Fulgoridae, Homoptera). Part 4." *University of Kansas Science Bulletin* 27, pt. 1, (1 November 1941): 185–233.
———. "A Revision of Two Genera of North American Cercopidae (Homoptera)." *Journal of the Kansas Entomological Society* 14, nos. 3 and 4 (1941): 102–134.

SECONDARY SOURCES
Bunch, Barry. University of Kansas Archives, Kenneth Spencer Research Library, Correspondence. Information includes a partial bibliography of Doering's publications and a list of faculty publications including Doering's.
"Dr. Kathleen C. Doering." *Kansas Alumni Magazine* 69, no. 3 (November 1970): 15. Obituary notice.

STANDARD SOURCES
Osborn (includes a portrait of Doering [plate 48]).

DOHAN, EDITH HAYWOOD HALL (1877–1943).
U.S. classical archeologist. Born 31 December 1877 in New Haven, Conn., to Mary Jane (Smith) and Ely Ransom Hall. Three siblings. Married Joseph M. Dohan (15 May 1915). Two children. Educated Woodstock (Conn.) Academy; Smith College (A.B., 1899); Bryn Mawr (graduate studies, 1901–1903; Ph.D., 1908); American School of Classical Studies, Athens (1903–1905). Professional experience: Woodstock Academy, teacher (1899–1900); Misses Shipley's School, teacher (1900–1902); Expedition to Cournia, Crete, archeologist (1905); Mount Holyoke College, instructor in classical

archaeology (1908–1912); University of Pennsylvania, expedition to Sphoungaras, Crete, director (summer 1910, 1912); University of Pennsylvania Museum, assistant curator (1912–1915), associate curator (1920–1942), curator of Mediterranean classical archeology (1942–1943); Bryn Mawr College, lecturer in classical archeology (1923–1924; 1926–1927; 1929–1930); Journal of Archaeology, review editor (1932–1943). Died suddenly of coronary sclerosis, 14 July 1943 in Philadelphia.

Edith Hayward Hall Dohan was one of the first American field archeologists. She was born and raised in Connecticut, and attended the school where her father was first a mathematics teacher and then principal. She went on to Smith College where she received her bachelor's in 1899. After teaching for a year at her father's school, she went on to take graduate work in Greek and archeology at Bryn Mawr, while supporting herself by teaching (1901–1903). She then won the Mary E. Garrett Scholarship for European Studies to continue classical archeological studies at the American School of Classical Studies in Athens (1903–1904), and stayed on for a second year after receiving the Agnes Hibben Memorial Fellowship. She had an opportunity then to join an expedition in Crete under another American woman archaeologist, HARRIET BOYD HAWES, who, like Hall, had attended Smith College and the American School of Classical Studies. Here, as part of Hawes's excavation in Gournia, Hall was able to do research on Minoan bronze age decorative arts for her dissertation, completed in 1907. She then received her doctoral degree in 1908 from Bryn Mawr.

For four years after she received her doctoral degree, Hall taught classical archeology at Mount Holyoke, spending two summers in Crete, first assisting and then directing University of Pennsylvania field expeditions, at Sphoungaras in 1910 and at Vokastro in 1912. She wrote about her excavation experience for the university museum journal. She then went to the University of Pennsylvania Museum where she was assistant curator, recataloguing classical antiquities and educating schoolchildren.

In 1915, Hall married Joseph M. Dohan and briefly gave up her museum work while she had two children, a boy and girl. She returned in 1920 when she was appointed associate curator. She also continued to lecture in classical archeology at Bryn Mawr in alternate years from 1923 until 1930, when she took on the review editorship of the *Journal of Archaeology*, which she held until her death. She published over fifty articles in archeological and museum journals.

Dohan turned her attention from prehistoric and classical Greece to the Etruscan materials in the museum, and did detective work using printed documents and field work to unravel the sequences of Etruscan seventh-century tomb groups in Italy, producing an outstanding exhibition shortly before her death in 1942, *Italic Tomb Groups in the University Museum*.

She died suddenly of coronary sclerosis in July 1943 before she could complete her next project on Etruscan bucchero ware. She was buried in Woodstock, Connecticut. JH/MBO

PRIMARY SOURCES
Hall, Edith Haywood. "The Decorative Art of Crete in the Bronze Age." Ph.D. diss., Bryn Mawr, 1907.
———. With others. *Excavations in Eastern Crete, Sphoungaras. Museum Anthropological Publications* 3, (no. 2). Philadelphia: University of Pennsylvania Press, 1912.
———. [Article on excavation life.] *Museum Journal,* University of Pennsylvania Museum. June 1912.
———. With others. *Excavations in Eastern Crete, Vrokastro. Museum Anthropological Publications* 3, no. 3. Philadelphia: University of Pennsylvania Press, 1914.
Dohan, Edith Haywood Hall. *Italic Tomb Groups in the University Museum. Museum Anthropological Publications.* Philadelphia: University of Pennsylvania Press, 1942.

SECONDARY SOURCES
Bolger, Diane L. "Ladies of the Expeditions: Harriet Boyd Hawes and Edith Hall in Mediterranean Archaeology." In *Women in Archaeology,* ed. Cheryl Claasen, 41–50. Philadelphia, University of Pennsylvania Press.
Hanfmann, George M. A. Review of exhibition *Italic Tomb Groups in the University Museum,* by Edith Hayward Hall Dohan. *American Journal of Archaeology* (January–March 1944): 114–116.
Johnson, Franklin P. Review of exhibition *Italic Tomb Groups in the University Museum,* by Edith Hayward Hall Dohan. *Classical Philology* 48 (October 1943): 274–275.
Richter, Gisela A. M., and Mary Hamilton Swindler. "Edith Hayward Hall Dohan." *American Journal of Archaeology* 47 (Oct.–Dec. 1943): 466.

STANDARD SOURCES
NAW (article by Dorothy Burr Thompson).

DOKHMAN, GENRIETTA ISAAKOVNA (1897–?)
Russian geobotanist and phytocenologist. Born 1897 in Kremenchug. Educated Moscow University (candidate of biological sciences, 1937); doctor of biological sciences, 1942). Professional experience: Krupskaia Academy of Communist Education, staff; Institute of Agropedology (1930–1931); Territorial Organizational Research Institute (1931–1932); Moscow University, instructor (1921–1938), lecturer (1938–1946), professor. Death date unknown.

Genrietta Isaakovna Dokhman was born in Kremenchug in 1897. She graduated from the physical-mathematical department of Moscow University and from 1927 to 1930 did post-graduate work there, while acting as an instructor in botany at the Krupskaia Academy of Communist Education.

From 1930 to 1931, she worked as a geobotanist at the Institute of Agropedology and from 1931 to 1932, she was on the staff of the department of territorial organization with the Territorial Organizational Research Institute of the USSR People's Commissariat of Agriculture.

In 1932 Dokhman returned to Moscow University. She worked first as an instructor (to 1938), then lecturer (1938 to 1946), and finally, as a professor and chairman of geobotany of the biological department (from 1946).

Dokhman wrote numerous publications on geobotanical and phytocenological subjects, including classification of steppe vegetation and history of the vegetation of the USSR.

ACH

PRIMARY SOURCES
Dokhman, Genrietta. *Eksperimental'no-fitotsenologicheskie osnovy issledovaniia zlakovo-bobovykh soobitanii.* Moscow: Nauka, 1979.
———. *Lesostep' Evropeiskoi chasti SSSR: k poznaniiu zakonomernostei prirody lesostepi.* Moscow: Nauka, 1968.
———. *Istoriia geobotaniki v Rossii.* Moscow: Nauka, 1973.

STANDARD SOURCES
Debus.

DOLGOPOL DE SAEZ, MATHILDE (1901–1957)

Argentinian vertebrate paleontologist. Born 6 March 1901. Educated Museo de la Plata; Escuela Superior de Ciencias Naturales. Professional experience: Museo de La Plata. Died 29 June 1957.

Argentinian paleontologist Mathilde Dolgopol de Saez worked at the Museo de La Plata. The major part of her research occurred from 1927 to 1940. She published papers on fossil fish and birds.

JH/MBO

PRIMARY SOURCES
Dolgopol de Saez, Mathilde. "Liornis minor: Una nueva especie de ave fósil." *Physis* 1927.
———. "Noticias sobre peces fósiles argentinos." *Notas del Museo de la Plata* 1935.

SECONDARY SOURCES
"Mathilde Dolgopol de Saez." *Ameghiniana* 1, no. 4 (1957): 44. Includes portrait.

STANDARD SOURCES
Sarjeant.

DOLLEY, SARAH READ ADAMSON (1829–1909)

U.S. physician. Born 11 March 1829 in Schuykill Meeting, Chester County, Pa., to Charles Adamson, farmer and storekeeper, and Mary Corson Adamson. Four siblings. Married Dr. Lester Clinton Dolley (1852), three children, one son survived. Educated Friends School in Philadelphia; Central Medical College, Rochester, N.Y. (M.D., 1851); Blockley Hospital, Philadelphia, intern; Hôpital des Enfants Malades, Paris, attended clinics; Prague and Vienna, attended clinics (1875). Professional experience: Woman's Medical College of Pennsylvania, professor of obstetrics (from 1876); Provident Dispensary Association Clinic, Rochester, N.Y., president (from 1877); Blackwell Society, joint organizer (1906). Died 27 December 1909.

Sarah Adamson was born in the Quaker community at Schuykill Meeting, Pennsylvania, to Charles Adamson, farmer and storekeeper, and Mary Corson Adamson. She was the third of five children and the younger of two daughters. The children attended Friends School in Philadelphia, where Sara determined to study medicine. This school provided education to both girls and boys. Both sexes had the opportunity to study science, but in different classes. Her uncle was Dr. Hiram Corson of Plymouth Meeting, Pennsylvania, and, though initially discouraging, he finally acknowledged her determination and allowed her to become a student in his office in preparation for entrance to medical school. Sarah applied to several schools in Philadelphia, becoming one of four to enter the new sectarian medical school, Central Medical College in Rochester, New York. LYDIA FOLGER FOWLER became the school's first woman graduate in June 1850 (the second woman to receive a medical degree in the United States) and Sarah was one (with RACHEL BROOKS GLEASON) of the two women receiving a medical degree at the 1851 commencement.

Sponsored by her uncle, Corson (who became a lifelong supporter and enabler for women physicians) and Isaac Pennypacker, Sarah became an intern at Blockley Hospital, Philadelphia. In 1852, she married Lester Clinton Dolley, professor of anatomy and surgery at the Central Medical College, and returned to Rochester. She combined an active medical practice with a family life, bearing three children but losing two in infancy. Her surviving son, Charles Sumner Dolley, became a marine biologist. Lester Dolley died in 1872; Sarah had begun postgraduate training the year before his death and continued again in the spring and summer of 1875, attending clinics in the Hôpital des Enfants Malades in Paris and also clinics in Prague and Vienna.

Back in America, Dolley spent a year in Philadelphia as professor of obstetrics in the Woman's Medical College of Pennsylvania, then returned to Rochester, where she stayed the remainder of her life. She worked quietly to broaden the opportunities for women in medicine. With a group of women physicians, she opened a dispensary in 1886 for the medical and surgical care of needy women and children, naming it the Provident Dispensary Association. Dolley was its first president. The same women also organized the Practitioners Society, a medical society for women; it changed its name to the Blackwell Medical Society in 1906. The Blackwell Society began the Women's Medical Society of the State of New York in honor of Dolley, holding its annual meetings in Rochester on her birthday until after her death.

Sarah Dolley was active in many venues—reading papers and serving on committees in the Monroe County (N.Y.) Medical Society; organizing the Society of Natural Science in Rochester (for women and men); working to secure positions for women on school boards and other civic positions; serving as president of the Ignorance Club (a group of business and professional women, named to counter the men's Pundits Club). She helped organize Rochester's Woman's Educational and Industrial Union in 1893. Although a friend of Susan B. Anthony, Dolley reserved her political energies for her community, earning the respect and love of local women, and men as well. She died on 27 December 1909, at age ninety.   JH/MBO

STANDARD SOURCES
Hurd-Mead 1933; Lovejoy; *NAW* (article by Genevieve Miller).

DOMBROVSKAIA, IULIIA FOMINICHNA
(1891–?)
Russian pediatrician. Born 11 December 1891 in Elets. Educated Petersburg Women's Medical Institute (M.D., 1913; doctor of medical sciences, 1936). Professional experience: I. M. Sechenov First Moscow Medical Institute, assistant and professor (1916–?), later head of department of children's diseases; Moscow City Department of Mother and Child Care, head (1918–1921); Soviet Academy of Medicine, academician. Honors and memberships: All-Union and Moscow Society of Pediatricians, president; Bulgarian Society of Pediatricians, honorary member; Surkin Czechoslovak Medical Society; Lenin Prize (1970). Death date unknown.

Iuliia Fominichna Dombrovskaia graduated from the Petersburg Women's Medical Institute in 1913. She started work at the children's clinic at the I. M. Sechenov First Moscow Medical Institute in 1916. In 1936, she became a professor and in 1951, director of the clinic. From 1918 to 1921, she was also head of the Moscow City Department of Mother and Child Care. In 1936, she earned the higher degree of doctor of medical sciences.

Dombrovskaia's research was in the field of children's diseases, particularly respiratory disorders, dystrophy, and avitaminosis and child pathology.

Dombrovskaia founded a school of pediatrics. She was active in several pediatric societies and in 1959 was a delegate to the Ninth International Congress of Pediatricians in Montreal. She was the author of numerous publications and the deputy editor of the Pediatrics section of the *Bol'shaia meditsinskaia entsiklopediia*. Dombrovskaia was awarded the Lenin prize in 1970.   ACH

PRIMARY SOURCES
Dombrovskaia, Iuliia Fominichna. *Propedevtika detskikh boleznei.* 3rd ed. Moscow, 1952.
———. *Zabolevanie organov dykhaniia u detei.* Moscow, 1957.

SECONDARY SOURCES
"Dombrovskaia, Iulia Fominichna." *Bol'shaia sovetskaia entsiklopediia.* 3rd ed. Moscow: Izd-vo Sovetskaia entsiklopediia, 1973.
Telberg, Ina, comp. *Who's Who in Soviet Science and Technology.* New York: Telberg Book Co., 1960.

STANDARD SOURCES
Debus.

DONNAY, GABRIELLE (HAMBURGER)
(1920–1987)
German/U.S./Canadian crystallographer. Born 21 March 1920 in Landeshut, Silesia (at that time part of Germany, now in Poland), to a career musician and a textile manufacturer. Married J. D. H. Donnay in 1949. Two sons, Albert and Victor. Educated UCLA (highest honors in chemistry, 1941); MIT (Ph.D., 1949). Professional experience: Carnegie Institution of Washington, Geophysical Laboratory, crystallographer (1949–1969); McGill University, faculty member (1970–1981?). Died 4 April 1987.

Gabrielle (Gai) Hamburger was born in what was then Germany and is now Poland to a musician mother and a textile manufacturer father. She passed the admissions examination to Oxford, but elected to emigrate to the United States at the age of seventeen. She graduated from UCLA with highest honors in chemistry. At that time she had already found crystals fascinating, and was encouraged by a professor, Martin J. Buerger, to find a challenging subject and to continue for her doctorate. She obtained this degree from MIT, and her thesis solved a complicated crystallographic problem that had puzzled others for many years—the noncentrosymmetric rhombohedral structure of tourmaline. After she finished her degree, she went to work for the Carnegie Institution of

Washington, where she met J. D. H. (Jose) Donnay, who was on the staff at the Johns Hopkins University. They married in July 1949 and had a fruitful collaboration for thirty-seven years. When Jose officially retired from Johns Hopkins in 1970, the couple moved to McGill University, which meant Gai Donnay left an experiment-oriented department and joined a field-oriented one. She considered the question of how much crystallography should geologists be taught and published a book on that subject, *Laboratory Manual in Crystallography,* which developed out of her classes at McGill. As she viewed crystallography, it was a common ground where chemists, physicists, biochemists, mineralogists, engineers, and health scientists should meet.

In addition to her scientific work, Donnay became interested in the treatment of women in the predominantly male field of the geological sciences. Although she felt that she personally had been well treated, she recognized that many women had not been so lucky. To correct perceived injustices in the field, she published *Women in the Geological Sciences in Canada.* To commemorate Donnay's retirement from academia the American Crystallographic Society organized a symposium at its 1986 meeting entitled "Women in Crystallography." She was devoted to her husband and her two sons and very proud of their accomplishments. In 1981, physicians informed her that she had cancer, with a life expectancy of eight months. She died in 1987.

Donnay received some highly prized awards for her accomplishments. In 1983 she was awarded the Past Presidents' Medal of the Mineralogical Association of Canada.

Gabrielle Donnay's area of expertise was in crystal chemistry and structural crystallography and Jose Donnay's in the topological and morphological aspects of the structures. She worked on tourmaline and was especially interested in the relationship between the physical properties of a mineral and its structure. She published more than 134 papers in her lifetime, almost half of which were collaborative projects with her husband. The couple became known internationally for their efforts to compile and systematize the findings of all crystallographers. The results were published in *Crystal Data* (1954); the first edition contained 719 pages and the second (1963) 1302 pages. Donnay showed great insight into the various chemical mechanisms that were important in the growth of crystals.   JH/MBO

PRIMARY SOURCES

Donnay, Gabrielle. With M. J. Buerger. "The Determination of the Crystal Structure of Tourmaline." *Acta Crystallographica* 3 (1950): 379–388.

———. With J. D. H. Donnay. *Crystal Geometry: Interpreting Tables for X-Ray Crystallography.* Vol. 2, section 3: 99–158. Birmingham, England: The Kynoch Press, 1959. Page numbers indicate section written by Donnay.

———. With G. Kullerud and J. D. H. Donnay. "Omission Solid Solution in Magnetite: Kenotetrahedral Magnetite." *Zeitschrift für Kristallographie* 128 (1969): 1–17.

———. "Structural Mechanism of Pyroelectricity in Tourmaline." *Acta Crystallographica* A33 (1977): 622–626.

———. With J. D. H. Donnay. "How Much Crystallography Should We Teach Geologists?" *American Mineralogist* 63 (1978): 840–846 (errata 64, 1334).

SECONDARY SOURCES

Martin, Robert F. "Memorial of Gabrielle Donnay (March 21, 1920–April 4, 1987)." *American Mineralogist* 74, nos. 3–4 (1989): 491–493. Includes portrait.

Sherriff, Barbara L., and Shelley Reuter. "Notable Canadian Women in the History of Geology." *Geoscience Canada* 21, no. 3 (1994): 123–125.

DOOLEY, LUCILE (1884–?)

U.S. clinical psychiatrist. Born 12 August 1884 in Stanford, Ky. Educated Randolph-Macon Woman's College (A.B.); University of Tennessee (A.M., 1915); Clark University (Ph.D., 1915); Johns Hopkins University Medical School (M.D., 1922); Vienna Psychoanalytic Institute (1931–1932). Professional experience: St. Elizabeth's Hospital, assistant clinical psychiatrist (1916–1924), associate clinical psychiatrist (1924–1925), medical officer (1925); private practice physician (from 1925); Knoxville Mental Health Center, consultant (from 1957); Washington Psychoanalytic Institution, faculty member. Honors and memberships: American Psychological Association, American Psychiatric Association, American Psychoanalytic Association, Fellow; American Medical Association, American Medical Association of Vienna, member. Death date unknown.

Lucile Dooley's interests were in psychoanalysis, manic depressive psychosis, structure of psychosis, and the psychology of humor and particularly of genius. Her doctoral dissertation at Clark University was "Psychoanalysis of Charlotte Brontë, as a Type of the Woman Genius." She continued psychoanalytic studies of genius and wrote articles on psychosis and on genius.   KM

STANDARD SOURCES

AMS 4–8, B 9, P&B 10–11; Psychological Register, vol. 3, 1932.

DORABIALSKA, ALICJA DOMENICA (1897–1975)

Polish chemist. Born 14 October 1897 in Sosnowiec, Poland. Educated Warsaw (secondary school certificate, 1914); Physical-Mathematical Department, Higher Girl's Course, Moscow (1915–1918); Radium Institute, Paris (1925); University of Warsaw (Ph.D.,

1922). Professional experience: Institute for Physical Chemistry, School of Technology, Warsaw, assistant (1918–1932); School of Technology, Warsaw, docent (1927), department of physical and inorganic chemistry, professor and chair (during World War II); School of Technology, Lwów, assistant professor (from 1934), department of physical and inorganic chemistry, professor and chair (1945–1968), dean of chemical department (1945–1951). Honors and awards: Scientific prize from the city of Lódz (1958); minister for university affairs, prize (1964); official decoration of Poland, bachelor's and commander's cross; Polish Chemical Society, honorary member and president. Died 7 August 1975.

Alicja Dorabialska received her doctorate under the chemist Wojceich Swietosawski with a dissertation on thermochemical investigations on stereoisomerism in ketones. She developed skills in radioactivity research in the Paris laboratory of her compatriot, MARIE CURIE. Later Dorabialska wrote a book on the Curies and coedited a Polish edition of Marie Curie's works.

Dorabialska's main research interests were calorimetry and thermochemistry, radiochemistry, and chemiluminescence. During her career, she worked with many scientists, including a number of women. A prolific writer, Dorabialska authored or edited over 150 works. In addition to her original research, she published numerous review articles as well as biographical articles on Marie Curie and other eastern European scientists. She also compiled a collection of physical chemistry laboratory exercises. Since most of her publications appeared solely in Polish, she was not well known outside of Poland.

Dorabialska's interests extended beyond her professional specialties to history, philosophy, art, and music. A staunch patriot, she participated in the underground during World War II. Dorabialska was well liked and respected by her colleagues, who honored her with a memorial celebration in Lódz in 1980. She died in 1975.   MM

PRIMARY SOURCES

Dorabialska, Alicja. With D. K. Yovanovitch. "Sur une méthod nouvelle pour mesurer l'absorption du rayonnement β et γ du corps radioactifs." *Comptes rendus* 182 (1926): 1459–1461.

———. With W. Swietoslawski. "Le débit de chaleur du polonium." *Comptes rendus* 187 (1929): 988–990.

———. *Promieniotwórczosc naturalna pierwiastków chemicznych* (Natural Radioactivity of Chemical Elements). Warsaw: Pánstwowe Zaktady Wydawn. Szkolnych, 1952.

———. *Jeszcze jedno zycie* (One More Life). Warsaw: PAX, 1972. Autobiography.

SECONDARY SOURCES

Reid, Robert. *Marie Curie.* New York: New American Library, 1974.

"Uroczystos odslonicia Tablicy pamiatkowej ku czci prof. dr Alicij Dorabialskiej w dniu 23–go Maya 1980 roku. (Prof. Dr. Alicja Dorabialska on 23 May 1980.)" *Zeszyty naukowe politechniki lódzkiej Chemia* 38 (1982): 5–12.

"Wspomnienie o prof. dr Alicij Dorabialskiej." *Wiadomosci chemiczne* 31 (1977): 315–324. This obituary contains a bibliography of Dorabialska's publications.

Ziegler, Gillette, ed. Correspondance; Choix de Lettres, (1905–1934) *Marie/Irène Curie.* Paris: Les Éditeurs Français Réunis, 1974.

Records in Institut Curie archives, Paris, assembled by Mme Monique Bordry.

STANDARD SOURCES

Poggendorff, vol. 6, 7b; Rayner-Canham (article by Stephanie Weinsberg-Tekel); Turk and Turk.

DORECK, HERTHA WALBURGER DORIS (SIEVERTS) (1899–1991)

German paleontologist. Born 1899 in Völklingen bei Saarbrücken. Two sisters. Married Walter Doreck. Two daughters. Educated Schulabschluss, Berlin (graduated 1916); Städtischen Oberrealschule Steglitz (certificate, 1921); University of Berlin (doctorate, 1927); University of Innsbruck. Professional experience: Geological-Paleontological Institute of the Technical School in Berlin—Charlottenburg; Geologisch–Mineralogischen Institut der TH Karlsruhe; Anstalt für Angewandte Geologie in Bonn (1930–1935); Preussischen Geologischen Landesanstalt (National Prussian Geological Institute), scientific assistant (1936). Died 30 March 1991.

Hertha Sieverts was born in Völklingen in 1899, the oldest of three girls. Her father was a chemist. She trained as a teacher and received a certificate as a qualified teacher for the lyceum and "middle schools" in Prussia. While she was in school, she had become interested in mathematics and the natural sciences. She began to focus on geology, paleontology, and zoology when she went to the University of Berlin. For a short time she studied at Innsbruck, but then returned to Berlin to work on her doctorate. For this degree she researched the Cretaceous crinoids, under the direction of J. Pompeckj. This experience defined her scientific orientation. After finishing her doctorate in 1927, Sieverts held several short-term positions. However, in 1930, through the recommendation of J. Wanner, she obtained a position at the Institute for Applied Geology in Bonn at a very low salary. Although her work was mostly as a personal assistant to Wanner, she also did independent work with the fossil collection. She remained at this position for five years, at which time she got a training opportunity at the National Prussian Geological Institute in Berlin. In 1936 she was named a scientific assistant. This job entailed mapping and field work and was unusual work for a woman at that time. Her public employment ended in 1936 when she married Walter Doreck and entered the housewife and "private-research" phase of her life. She continued to be active in research and for fourteen years, starting in the mid-1930s, reported on Crinoids in *Zentralblatt,* an international publication. In the early 1950s, Doreck was invited to Lawrence, Kansas, by R. C. Moore, and publicized as the "German Crinoid Expert." She had devised a system of classification for Mesozoic Crinoids that, although never published, was and still is the basis for the systematics of this group. During the last years of her research, Doreck turned to the systematics of the Holothuroideans. During the years she spent as a housewife, she had little time to pursue her research goals. Her husband became seriously ill, and she took care of him until his death in 1972. Doreck's two daughters married and moved away. When she finally had some uninterrupted time to pursue her research she was failing physically, although mentally she was still very keen.

Although the seventy publications that Doreck produced are impressive, she, no doubt, would have published many more if she had not been burdened with household tasks. She gained public recognition by the Paleontological Society, which she joined in 1950, when she was made an honorary member in 1987. JH/MBO

PRIMARY SOURCES
Sieverts, Hertha. "Über die Crinoidengattung *Marsupite.*" *Abhandlungen der Preussischen Geologischer Landesanstale.* n.s., 108 (1927): 73.
————. "Das erste Machaerid aus Deutschland: *Lepidocoleus eifeliensis* n. sp. aus dem rheinischen Mitteldevon." *Zeitschrif der Deutschen Geologischen Gesellschaft* 87 (1935): 683–687.
————. "Crinoiden aus dem Unterkarbon des Oberharzes." *Neues Jahrbuch für Mineralogie, Geologie und Paläontologie* 93 (1951): 117–144.
Sieverts-Doreck, Hertha. "Zur Kenntnis von Balanocrinus württembergicus aus dem schwäbischen Opalinuston (Dogger alpha)." *Jahreshefte des Vereins für Vaterländsiche Naturkunde in Würtemberg* 118–119 (1964): 147–166.
————. "Neue Kronenfunde von Chariocrinus württembergicus, Familie Isocrinidae, aus dem schwäbischen Opalinuston (unteres Aalenium)." *Jahresberichte und Mitteilungen des Oberrheinischen Geologischen Vereines* 65 (1983): 359–381.

SECONDARY SOURCES
Haude, Reimund. "Hertha Doreck, 15.7.1899–30.3.1991." *Palaeontologische Zeitschrift* 66, nos. 1–2 (1992): 1–7.

DORENFELDT, MARGOT (fl. 1923)

German/Norwegian chemist. Married Holtan (1924). Professional experience: Chemical Institute of the University of Christiana, Oslo, researcher.

Margot Dorenfeldt worked at the Chemical Institute of the University of Christiania (Oslo) under the radiochemist ELLEN GLEDITSCH to determine atomic weights of isotopes in Norwegian minerals. Comparing the atomic weights of chlorine from ordinary sodium chloride and from apatite, she found that age and exposure to water had not changed the isotopic proportions, a finding of significance for radioactivity research. Working with Gleditsch and Otto Berg, Dorenfeldt showed that lead produced from uranium by radioactive decay was of lower atomic weight than ordinary lead. After her marriage (ca. 1924), she used the name Dorenfeldt-Holtan.

PRIMARY SOURCES
Dorenfeldt, Margot. "Relative Determination of the Atomic Weight of Chlorine in Bamle Apatite." *Journal of the American Chemical Society* 45 (1923): 1577–1579.
————. With Otto Berg and Ellen Gleditsch. "Determination du poids atomique du mélange isotopique de plomb de la clévéite de Aust-Agder, Norvège." *Journal de chimie physique* 22 (1925): 253–263.

STANDARD SOURCES
Meyer and von Schweidler.

DORETY, ANGELA (fl. 1921)

U.S. botanist. Professional experience: College of St. Elizabeth, Convent Station, N.J., professor.

Sister Angela Dorety was a professor of botany at the College of St. Elizabeth in Convent Station, New Jersey. She was the only Catholic nun to hold a professorship in 1921.
JH/MBO

STANDARD SOURCES
Rossiter 1982.

DORMON, CAROLINE (1888–1971)

U.S. botanist and conservationist. Born 1888 in Briarwood in northwestern Louisiana. Older brothers and older sister. Never married. Educated Judson College, Marion, Ala. (graduated 1907). Professional experience: teacher (1907–1921); Louisiana Department of Conservation, publicity (1921–1923), conservationist (1927–1929). Honors and memberships: Louisiana State University, honorary doctorate. Died 1971.

Born at her parents' summer home, Briarwood, in the hills of northwestern Louisiana, Caroline Dormon grew up in Arcadia, Louisiana. The precocious child loved the outdoors and resented it whenever she felt confined inside. Her only education past high school was at a finishing school, Judson College, in Marion, Alabama. After the death of both of her parents and a tragic fire that destroyed their family home in Arcadia, Dormon and her older sister, Virginia, moved permanently to the old family summer home, Briarwood, in 1918.

Graduating in 1907, Dormon took a teaching position. Stifled by the indoor nature of the job, she transferred to a school in the middle of longleaf virgin pine forests in the hilly Kisatchie area in Natchitoches Parish. The forest was destroyed after a bitter fight when the company that owned the land razed it. This dispute launched Dormon's work with the Louisiana Department of Conservation, but she found the bureaucratic obstacles to progress overwhelming. In 1930, she retired to Briarwood; that same year she was elected to associate membership in the Society of American Foresters.

Back at Briarwood, Dormon spent much of her time painting, photographing, and collecting the wide variety of Louisiana Iris. She corresponded with botanists and often went with them on collecting trips in Louisiana. When the infirmities of age kept her inside, she wrote extensive guides for amateurs. Inspired by RACHEL CARSON's *Silent Spring,* she wrote her last article on the devastating effects of pesticides. Briarwood was preserved as a botanical sanctuary through the Caroline Dormon Foundation.   JH/MBO

PRIMARY SOURCES

Dormon, Caroline. *Forest Trees of Louisiana and How to Know Them.* Baton Rouge, La.: Ramires-Jones Printing Co., 1928.

———. *Louisiana Landscape. State Parks for Louisiana.* Baton Rouge, La.: Louisiana State Park Association, n.d.

———. *Wild Flowers of Louisiana: Including Most of the Herbaceous Wild Flowers of the Gulf States, with the Exception of Mountainous Regions, and the Sub-Tropical Portions of Florida and Texas.* Garden City, N.Y.: Doubleday, Doran, and Co., Inc., 1934.

SECONDARY SOURCES

Moore, Diane M. *The Adventurous Will: Profiles of Memorable Louisiana Women.* Lafayette, La.: Arcadiana Press, 1984.

Snell, David. "The Green World of Carrie Dormon." *Smithsonian* 2 (1972): 28.

STANDARD SOURCES

Bonta.

DOUBLEDAY, NELTJE BLANCHAN (DE GRAFF) (1865–1918)

U.S. nature writer and botanist. Born 23 October 1865 in Chicago, Ill., to Alice (Fair) and (Liverius?) Livinius De Graff. Married Frank Nelson Doubleday, editor and publisher (9 June 1886). Three children. Educated St. John's Academy; Misses Masters School, New York. Professional experience: published widely on various natural history and ethnological topics. Died 21 February 1918 in Canton, China.

Neltje Blanchan De Graff Doubleday, also known as Nellie, was born to a family in Chicago that claimed seventeenth-century Dutch descent. Her father ran a men's clothing store in that city. She was educated in fashionable New York private schools and then married Frank N. Doubleday, the editor and publisher, at the age of twenty-one. They eventually had three children, Felix, Nelson, and Dorothy. A few years after her marriage she began to write on natural history topics under the pseudonym Neltje Blanchan. Her first book was a study of the Piegan Indians, a Blackfoot Plains Indian tribe. She became interested in bird lore, probably influenced by the ornithological writings of FLORENCE MERRIAM BAILEY for the Audubon magazine. Doubleday then published a number of popular books on local birds and birds as prey and predator. Her books were accompanied with illustrations in color from photographs of mounted bird specimens and published by her husband's publishing house, Doubleday, Doran and Company. The first of her bird books, *Bird Neighbors,* was accompanied by an introduction by the naturalist John Burroughs who praised its lively style. The second book, *Birds That Hunt and Are Hunted,* like the first, had some scientific pretensions, listing a large number of bird species in taxonomic order. She wrote other books for children on these topics, and in 1917, rewrote her bird books in a lavishly illustrated edition. She then turned to garden and flower books, writing on wildflowers and on garden design. The gardens described covered large tracts of land like her own garden and those of her immediate wealthy neighbors in Locust Valley near Oyster Bay, Long Island.

Doubleday's professional life sometimes overlapped with that of her husband. Her alarmed reaction, prior to its publication, to Theodore Dreiser's novel on the life of a poor salesgirl, *Sister Carrie,* resulted in a limited printing in 1900 with no advertising by her husband. She and her husband were also active in a variety of social causes, including the Red Cross. Doubleday died in Canton, China in 1918, while accompanying her husband on a special mission for the Red Cross.   JH/MBO

PRIMARY SOURCES

Doubleday, Neltje Blanchan De Graff [Neltje Blanchan,

pseud.]. *Bird Neighbors.* With an introduction by John Bur-
roughs. New York: Doubleday, Doran and Co., 1897.
————. *Birds That Hunt and Are Hunted.* New York: Double-
day, Doran and Co., 1898.
————. *Nature's Garden.* New York: Doubleday, Doran and
Co., 1900.
————. *The American Flower Garden.* New York: Doubleday,
Doran and Co., 1909.
————. *Birds Worth Knowing.* New York: Doubleday, Doran
and Co., 1917.

STANDARD SOURCES
AMS 1–2; Bailey; Grinstein 1997 (article by Keir B. Sterling);
NAW (article by Robert H. Welker); *NCAB*; *WW in Amer-
ica* vol. 9, 1916–1917.

DOUGAL, MARGARET DOUIE (fl. 1885–1909)
*British chemical indexer. Professional experience: Chemical Society,
indexer (1885–1909).*

Little information is available on Margaret Douie Dougal.
However, she indexed the publications of the Chemical Society for fifteen years and was in charge of preparing the collected decennial indices as well. Her contributions to this
major indexing project were evidently appreciated, for Sir
James Dewar acknowledged them in his 1899 Presidential
Address to the society.   JH/MBO

PRIMARY SOURCES
*A Collective Index of the Transactions, Proceedings and Abstracts of the
Chemical Society, for the Period 1873–1912.* 4 vols. London,
n.d. Vols. 1–3 were compiled by Douglas.

SECONDARY SOURCES
Dewar, Sir James. "Presidential Address to the Society, 1899."
Journal of the Chemical Society, Transactions 75 (1899): 1168.

STANDARD SOURCES
Creese 1991.

DOUGLAS, ALICE VIBERT (ca. 1895–1988)
*Canadian astrophysicist. Born 15 December 1895 in Montreal. Ed-
ucated McGill University (bachelor's degree 1919; M.S., 1920;
Ph.D., 1926); Cavendish Laboratory, Cambridge University (postgraduate work). Professional experience: McGill University (ca.
1922–1939); Queen's College, Kingston (1939 until retirement).
Died 2 July 1988 in Kingston, Ontario.*

Alice Vibert Douglas received all three of her degrees from
McGill University. World War I interrupted her studies, but
she returned from war work to complete her bachelor's degree in 1919, followed a year later by her master's. Astrophysics became her primary interest after she attended
Cambridge University for postgraduate work. At Cambridge, she worked with Ernest Rutherford at the Cavendish
Laboratory and with Arthur Eddington. She received her
doctoral degree from McGill in 1926 and remained on its
staff for seventeen years. In 1939, she left McGill to become
dean of women at Queen's University, Kingston.

Douglas had many international interests, representing
Canada at the UNESCO conference in Montevideo,
Uruguay, in 1954, and being active in the International Astronomical Union. In 1947, she became the first Canadian
president of the International Astronomical Union.

Working with John Stuart Foster, she investigated the
spectra of A and B type stars and the Stark effect, using the
seventy-two-inch telescope of the Dominion Astrophysical
Observatory. She published in both popular and professional
journals.   JH/MBO

PRIMARY SOURCES
Douglas, A. Vibert. *The Life of Arthur Stanley Eddington.* London: Nelson, 1956.

SECONDARY SOURCES
Hogg, Helen Sawyer. "A. Vibert Douglas." *Physics Today* 42
(July 1989): 88–89. Obituary notice.

DOVER, MARY VIOLETTE (fl. 1908)
*Canadian/U.S. chemist. Born in Peterborough, Ontario, Canada,
to Frederick and Annette (Wood) Dover. Educated McGill University (B.A., 1898; M.S., 1900); Academy Diploma, Quebec,
1899; University of Breslau (Ph.D., 1908). Professional experience: McGill University, demonstrator in chemistry (1901–1903);
lecture assistant in chemistry (1903–1906) [according to McGill
staff records; AMS has demonstrator in chemistry (1900–1905)];
Mount Holyoke College, instructor (1909–1914); University of
Missouri at Columbia, instructor and later assistant professor
(1915–1928), associate professor (from 1928); Hercules Powder
Company (later Hercules Inc.), chemist (1918–1919). Died probably between 1933 and 1938.*

While at McGill, Dover coauthored a paper on an analytical
reaction used to separate copper, showing previous interpretations were incorrect. She also studied a reaction involving
organic magnesium compounds. During the period 1910–
1917 Dover investigated the separation of cadmium from organic electrolytes, solubilities in nonaqueous solutions, and
the efficiencies of desiccants and of reflux condensers. Subsequent research concerned heats of combustion of oils and
gases, lubricants, and petroleum.

Dover was one of the first women elected to the McGill Physical Society, in 1902. She was a member of the American Association for the Advancement of Science and the American Chemical Society, serving as treasurer of the Missouri section of the latter from 1922 and as vice president from 1932.   MM

PRIMARY SOURCES

Dover, Mary Violette. With James Wallace Walker. "The Iodides of Copper." *Transactions of the Chemical Society of London* 87, part 2 (1905): 1584–1592.

Records in McGill University Archives, Montreal, Quebec.

Records in Trent University Archives, Peterborough, Ontario.

SECONDARY SOURCES

Rayner-Canham, Marelene F., and Geoffrey Rayner-Canham. *Harriet Brooks: Pioneer Nuclear Scientist.* Montreal, Kingston, London, and Buffalo: McGill-Queens University Press, 1992; 1994.

STANDARD SOURCES

AMS 3–5; *Woman's Who's Who of America.*

DOWNEY, JUNE ETTA (1875–1932)

U.S. psychologist. Born 13 July 1875 in Laramie, Wy., to Evangeline (Owen) and Stephen Wheeler Downey. Eight siblings. Never married. Educated Laramie public schools; University Preparatory School, Laramie; University of Wyoming (B.A., 1895); University of Chicago (M.A., 1898; Ph.D., 1907). Professional experience: University of Wyoming, instructor of English and philosophy (1898–1905), professor of English and philosophy (1905–1915), professor of philosophy and psychology (1915–1932). Died 11 October 1932 in Trenton, N.J.

Psychologist June Etta Downey was one of nine children born to a pioneer family in Laramie, Wyoming. Her father, Colonel Stephen Downey, was among the first territorial delegates to Congress from Wyoming and was instrumental in the establishment of the University of Wyoming, where his daughter received a bachelor's in classics in 1895.

After teaching in the Laramie public schools for a year, Downey enrolled at the University of Chicago. At Chicago, she did graduate work in philosophy and psychology, and in 1898 received a master's degree for her thesis on George Berkeley. When she returned to Wyoming, she taught English and philosophy at the university. Downey's interest in psychology germinated during a summer session at Cornell University (1901), where she was introduced to the experimental procedures of Edward Bradford Titchener. His influence was reflected in the courses she later taught in experimental psychology.

In 1905 the University of Wyoming promoted Downey to professional rank, and in 1906 she was awarded a fellowship in the department of psychology at the University of Chicago, from which she received a doctoral degree with honors in 1907. Her dissertation, "Control Processes in Modified Handwriting: An Experimental Study," mentored by James Rowland Angell, was published by the *Psychological Review* in its monographic series.

Upon completion of her degree, Downey was made head of the department of psychology and philosophy at Wyoming, the first woman to head such a department in a state university. An inspiring teacher and a skilled experimentalist, Downey also found time to serve on important university committees. From 1908 until 1916 she was principal of the Department of University Extension, and for many years she chaired the graduate committee. Among the honors she received were membership on the council of the American Psychological Association (1923–1925), fellowship in the American Association for the Advancement of Science, and charter membership in the Society of Experimental Psychologists. Downey was attending the Third International Congress of Eugenics in New York City in 1932 when she was hospitalized with stomach cancer; she died following surgery, at age fifty-seven.

Downey was not associated with a particular school of psychological thought. In fact, her background in philosophy made her skeptical of all systems. One of her major interests was in using handwriting as an indicator of personality differences. She became a world authority on "handedness" and handwriting, studying and conducting experiments in fine muscle behavior (voluntary and involuntary motor controls). Studies on the influence of temperament and emotional states on psychological and motor processes led her into the problems of creativity. She worked with "temperament-trait" testing at a time when most psychologists were concentrating on the measurement of intelligence. In Downey's view of personality, a single trait could not be abstracted from its setting; the personality was an integrated whole.

Downey's studies, resulting in the development of the Individual Will-Temperament Test, enabled the tester to compile a "will-profile" for each case. This work was summarized in *Graphology and Psychology of Handwriting* (1919), *The Will Profile: A Tentative Scale for Measurement of the Volitional Pattern* (1919), and *Will-Temperament and Its Testing* (1924).

Although Downey spent her entire career at remote, unrecognized University of Wyoming, her work earned her international recognition. She published seven books and approximately seventy scholarly papers, reviews, and contributions to encyclopedias and popular magazines. Her literary output included short stories, poems, and plays. Her professional interest in creativity and aesthetics reflected her personal enjoyment of literature, poetry, music, and art.

MBO

PRIMARY SOURCES

Downey, June Etta. *Control Processes in Modified Handwriting: An Experimental Study.* Psychological Review suppl. 37, 1908. Downey's Ph.D. dissertation from the University of Chicago.

———. *The Will Profile: A Tentative Scale Measurement of the Volitional Pattern.* University of Wyoming Bulletin 16, no. 4b (1919).

———. With E. E. Slosson. *Plots and Personalities: A new method of Testing and Training the Creative Imagination.* New York: Century, 1922.

———. *Creative Imagination.* New York: Harcourt Brace; London: Kegan Paul, 1929.

SECONDARY SOURCES

In Memoriam. June Etta Downey, 1875–1932. Laramie: University of Wyoming, 1934. Includes a bibliography of Downey's published and unpublished work.

Uhrbrock, Richard Stephen. "June Etta Downey." *Journal of General Psychology* 9 (1933): 351–364.

STANDARD SOURCES

AMS 2–4; Bailey; *DAB; DNB; NAW;* Ogilvie 1986.

DOWNEY, KATHERINE MELVINA (fl. 1920)

U.S. physicist. Professional experience: University of Minnesota, researcher.

Katherine Melvina Downey is an example of a woman physicist who has essentially been "lost." Nothing is known about her life.

Working at the University of Minnesota, Downey investigated the so-called penetrating radiation, later known as the cosmic rays, and compared the ionization they produced with that produced by gamma rays. Downey developed a differential method to measure ionization produced in a gas.

MM

PRIMARY SOURCES

Downey, K. Melvina. "Variation with Pressure of the Residual Ionization Due to the Penetrating Radiation." *Physical Review* 16 (1920): 420–437.

STANDARD SOURCES

Meyer and von Schweidler.

DOWNIE, DOROTHY G. (1897?–1960)

British/Scottish botanist. Born 1897(?) in Edinburgh. Educated University of Edinburgh (B.Sc., 1917); University of Chicago (1925–1928). Professional experience: W. G. Craib, University of Aberdeen, assistant, lecturer, and reader. Died 23 August 1960.

Dorothy G. Downie was born in Edinburgh around 1897. She studied at the University of Edinburgh, receiving a bachelor of science in 1917. She became assistant to W. G. Craib at the University of Aberdeen. She later became lecturer and reader at Aberdeen. For three years, 1925 to 1928, she went to the University of Chicago to study. She regularly contributed articles on cycads and orchid mycorrhiza to the journal of the Botanical Society of Edinburgh. JH/MBO

PRIMARY SOURCES

Downie, Dorothy G. [Various articles on cycads and orchid mycorrhiza.] *Transactions and Proceedings Botanical Society Edinburgh.*

SECONDARY SOURCES

Transactions Botanical Society Edinburgh 39 (1959–1960): 245–246. Obituary notice.

STANDARD SOURCES

Desmond.

DOWNS, CORNELIA MITCHELL (1892–?)

U.S. microbiologist. Born 20 December 1892 in Kansas City, Kansas to Lily (Campbell) and Henry Mitchell Downs. Never married. Educated University of Kansas (A.B., 1915; A.M., 1920; Ph.D., 1924); University of Chicago, postgraduate work (1920–1921). Professional experience: University of Kansas, professor of bacteriology (1935–1961), Solon Summerfield distinguished professor of microbiology (1961–1963), professor emerita (1963–?). Concurrent experience: Rockefeller Institute, investigator (1939–1940); U.S. Army Chemical Corps, Camp Dietrich, Md., civilian expert, bacteriology (1943–1945); consultant in bacteriology (1945–retirement). Honors and memberships: National Institutes of Health, special fellow, Oxford, England (1959–1960); New York Academy of Science, fellow; bacteriological, immunological societies, member. Death date unknown.

Usually known as Cora, microbiologist Cornelia Downs received her education at the University of Kansas and at the University of Chicago. She returned to teach bacteriology at Kansas, where she remained until retirement. She accepted an endowed chair, the Solong Summerfield distinguished professorship of microbiology, during her last two years of teaching. She published over 100 papers in immunological and bacteriological journals.

JH/MBO

PRIMARY SOURCES

Downs, Cornelia Mitchell. "A Comparison of the Antigenic and Cultural Characteristics of a Number of Strains of *Bacillus typhosus*." *University of Kansas Science Bulletin* 13, no. 15 (1920): 151–164.

———. "Antigenic and Metabolic Studies of *Bacillus typhosus*." *University of Kansas Science Bulletin* 16, no. 1 (1926) 5–89.

Downs, Cornelia. Contributions to the *University of Kansas Science Bulletins* 13 (1922); 16 (1926).

SECONDARY SOURCES

O'Hearn, E. "Cora Mitchell Downs, Pioneer Microbiologist." *ASM News* 40 (1974): 862.

STANDARD SOURCES

AMS 4–8, B 9, P&B 10–11; Barnhart; Debus; *WWW(A)*, vol. 9, 1985–1989.

DRAKE, JUDITH (fl. 1696)

British medical practitioner and writer. Born in Cambridge(?). Father a Cambridge solicitor. At least one brother, James. Educated privately. Professional experience: dispensed medicine; published brother's anatomical text after his death in 1707; wrote on role of women in society.

Little is known about the life of Judith Drake. Her father was a respected solicitor in Cambridge. She was the younger sister of James Drake, physician and political writer, who was a Fellow of the Royal College of Physicians and a Fellow of the Royal Society. According to a recent writer, she and not MARY ASTELL wrote the important feminist text *An Essay in Defence of the Female Sex*. She apparently learned some medicine from her brother, since she was summoned before Sir Hans Sloane in the late seventeenth century for dispensing medicines without the approval of the Royal College of Physicians. She had sufficient medical knowledge to edit and publish her brother's anatomical text after his death in 1707.

JH/MBO

PRIMARY SOURCES

[Drake, Judith]. *An Essay in Defence of the Female Sex*. London: A. Roper and E. Wilkinson and R. Clavel, 1696.

———, ed. *Anatomy*. By James Drake. London, 1707.

STANDARD SOURCES

DNB, Missing Persons; Strohmeier.

DRANT, PATRICIA (HART) (1895–1955)

U.S. dermatologist. Born 27 January 1895 in Grenola, Kans., to James Lafayette and Nora Coombs (Demmitt) Hart. Married (1) Reginald Drant (1 Sept. 1920; divorced); married (2) William Warren Rhodes (18 Aug. 1923; divorced 1949); married (3) James S. Collins (14 June 1952). Educated University of Kansas (B.S., 1918); University of Pennsylvania (M.D., 1920); University of Pennsylvania Graduate Hospital, Philadelphia, graduate studies in dermatology (1921–1922); St. Louis Hospital, Paris, France (1924–1925); Vienna (1925); Budapest (1925). Professional experience: Abington Memorial Hospital, Pennsylvania, dermatologist; Methodist Hospital, Philadelphia, dermatologist; Woman's Hospital, Philadelphia, dermatologist. Honors and memberships: American Academy of Dermatology and Syphilology, diplomate member; American Association for the Advancement of Science, Fellow; American Medical Association, Philadelphia Dermatological Society, Philadelphia County Medical Society, member. Died 3 October 1955.

Patricia Hart Drant was born in Kansas and attended the University of Kansas for her bachelor's degree. After receiving this degree she went to Philadelphia where she studied medicine, receiving her medical degree from the University of Pennsylvania in 1929. She gained additional experience overseas in various hospitals. After she returned to the United States, she practiced dermatology in Philadelphia hospitals. She was a member of many prestigious medical societies.

JH/MBO

STANDARD SOURCES

Debus.

DRAPER, MARY ANNA PALMER (1839–1914)

U.S. benefactor of astronomy. Born 11 September 1839 in Stonington, Conn., to Mary Ann (Suydam) and Courtlandt Palmer. Three siblings. Married Henry Draper. Died 8 December 1914 in New York City.

Mary Anna Palmer was one of four children (the only daughter) of a wealthy real estate investor. She became interested in astronomy through her husband, Henry Draper, whom she married in 1867. Henry Draper was professor of physiology and chemistry at the University of the City of New York (later New York University) and a skilled amateur astronomer, with a special interest in stellar spectroscopy. By aiding him in making observations and by assisting him in the laboratory, Mary Draper became an expert technician. After her husband's death in 1882, Draper established a fund, the Henry Draper Memorial, at the Harvard College Observatory. The money enabled director Edward Pickering to initiate an ambitious program of photographing the spectra of stars and classifying them according to characteristics revealed in the photographs.

In addition to her benefactions to the Harvard Observatory, Draper maintained an interest in the National Academy of Sciences, in 1883 donating to it the Henry Draper Medal, to be awarded for original work in astronomical physics. She was influential in the establishment of the Mount Wilson Observatory in California under the supervision of the newly organized Carnegie Institute (1902). Archeology was another of her interests; she amassed an extensive collection of ancient Near Eastern, Greek, and Roman artifacts.

Draper's generosity made possible the significant advances in the field of stellar spectroscopy that emerged from the Harvard Observatory. Many women were employed as astronomers at the observatory as a consequence of her benevolence.   JH/MBO

PRIMARY SOURCES
Pier, G., and D. Proskey. *Catalogues of Rare Gems, Ancient Greek, Roman, and Other Coins, Amulets, Rosaries, and Other Objects of Archaeological Interest, Collected by the Late Mary Anna Palmer Draper.* New York: American Art Association, 1917.

STANDARD SOURCES
Jones and Boyd; *NAW.*

DREBENEVA-UKHOVA, VARVARA PAVLOVNA (1903–)

Russian entomologist. Born 1903. Educated Moscow University; Timiriazev Research Institute; doctor of biological sciences (1945). Professional experience: Timiriazev Research Institute, ecology department, associate (1925–1930); Ivanovo Medical Institute, department of general biology, assistant (1930–1933); Martsinovskii Institute of Medical Parasitology and Tropical Medicine, staff, later head department of entomology (1933–1963); World Health Organization, expert.

After graduating from the biology department of Moscow University in 1925, Varvara Pavlovna Drebeneva-Ukhova pursued postgraduate studies and was on the staff of the Timiriazev Research Institute until 1930. From 1930 to 1933, she worked as an assistant in the department of general biology at the Ivanovo Medical Institute. In 1933, she moved to the Martsinovskii Institute of Medical Parasitology and Tropical Medicine of the USSR Ministry of Health. Starting as a senior associate, she occupied a series of positions including head of the fly extermination laboratory until 1963, when she became head of the department of entomology.

Drebeneva-Ukhova's principal research has been on experimental and medical entomology, including the structure and development of the female reproductive system of various species of flies, maturation rate of ova, and development of ovarian tubes. She also worked on the ecological classification of flies. Drebeneva-Ukhova was the first in the Soviet Union to use DDT on flies. She also worked as an expert for the World Health Organization.   ACH

PRIMARY SOURCES
Drebeneva-Ukhova, Varvara Pavlovna. *Flies and Their Epidemiological Importance.* 1952.

STANDARD SOURCES
Debus.

DREW, KATHLEEN MARY (1901–1957)

British botanist. Born 1901 in Leigh, Lancashire. Married Wright Baker. Educated Manchester University (B.Sc., 1922; D.Sc., 1939). Professional experience: Manchester University, assistant lecturer in botany; University of California, commonwealth fellowship. Died 14 September 1957 in Manchester.

Kathleen Drew was a distinguished worker in the field of red algae. She spent most of her academic life in the department of cryptogamic botany at the University of Manchester, earning both a bachelor's and doctorate of science from that institution. She was an early Commonwealth Research Fellow. During the time that she held this fellowship, she spent two years in the United States, working at the University of California. During this time, she produced systematic studies and her first substantial monograph, a revision of three genera. She also developed some of the difficult cytological techniques that characterized her later work.

The second period in her work was one in which she introduced cultural and experimental methods into life history studies. This period was initiated by a review of the nuclear and somatic phases in the family of red algae, *Florideae.* She published extensively in scientific journals, including *Phytomorphology* and the *Botanical Review.*

Drew had many research students from all parts of the world, and frequently attended international congresses, many times as an invited speaker. She was one of founders of the British Phycological Society and was its first president.

Drew's marriage to Professor H. Wright Baker was a happy one, and, unlike many women scientists, she continued to maintain her professional interests after her marriage.   JH/MBO

PRIMARY SOURCES
Drew, Kathleen. "Revision of Genera Chantransia, Rhodochorton and Acrochaetium." *University of California Publications in Botany* 14, no. 15 (1928): 139–224, plates 37–48.

SECONDARY SOURCES
British Phycological Bulletin (1958): 1–12. Includes portrait.

Calder, Mary. "Dr. Kathleen M. Drew." *Nature* 180 (1957): 889–890.

———. "Kathleen M. Drew." *Phytomorphology* 7 (1957): 407–408. Includes portrait.

STANDARD SOURCES
Desmond.

DRINKER, KATHERINE (ROTAN) (1889–?)

U.S. physiologist. Born 12 January 1889 in Waco, Tex. Married Cecil Kent Drinker (1910). Two daughters. Educated Bryn Mawr College (A.B., 1910); Woman's Medical College of Pennsylvania (M.D., 1914); Harvard University (1914–1915; 1916–1917; 1921–1923); Johns Hopkins University (1915–1916). Professional experience: Peter Bent Brigham Hospital, Boston, assistant resident physician (1917); Journal of Industrial Hygiene, managing editor (1918–1920); Bryn Mawr College, lecturer in hygiene (1923–1926); School of Public Health, Harvard, research assistant, physiology (1923–1926); medical education work (1937–1947); instructor in public health practice (1939–1946); Monographs in Medicine and Public Health, executive secretary (1939–1947); Office of Scientific Research and Development, research assistant (1941–1942). Death date unknown.

Katherine Drinker earned her medical degree from the Woman's Medical College of Pennsylvania in 1914, four years after she had married Cecil Kent Drinker who earned his medical degree from the University of Pennsylvania in 1913. Both Cecil and Katherine were residents at Peter Bent Brigham Hospital in Boston. Their careers diverged when Katherine took a position as the managing editor for the *Journal of Industrial Hygiene.* Most of her subsequent work was in the field of public health instruction. In the 1920s she, along with her husband, examined women exposed to radium contamination in watch factories. Her results were reexamined by ALICE HAMILTON. Drinker's research interests were in human physiology, the coagulation of blood, blood formation, lung fibrosis, and hygiene of zinc. She was a member of the Physiological Society. JH/MBO

STANDARD SOURCES
AMS 3–8; Debus (under Cecil Kent Drinker, M.D.).

DRUMMOND, MARGARET (1871–?)

Scottish psychologist. Born 15 April 1871 in Edinburgh. Educated University of Edinburgh (A.M., 1897); Cambridge Certificate for Teachers (1896). Professional experience: University of Edinburgh, lecturer in education (from 1929). Death date unknown.

A member of the British Psychological Society, the Educational Institute of Scotland and the Montessori Society, Margaret Drummond spent most of her career in educational work with children and teachers. She was a lecturer in education at the University of Edinburgh. She became chairman of the subcommittee for the "Children's Hour" of the British Broadcasting Corporation. She wrote articles on the Montessori method and preschool education. JH/MBO

PRIMARY SOURCES
Drummond, Margaret. *Dawn of the Mind: An Introduction to Child Psychology.* London: Arnold, 1918.

———. *The Psychology and the Teaching of Number.* London: Harrap, 1922.

———. *Some Contributions to Child Psychology.* London: Arnold; New York: Longmans Green, 1923.

———. With J. Drever. *Psychology of the Preschool Child.* London: Partridge, 1929.

———. *Gateways of Learning: An Educational Psychology Having Special Reference to the First Years of School Life.* London: University of London Press, 1931.

STANDARD SOURCES
Psychological Register, vol. 3, 1932.

DU BOIS, CORA (1903–1991)

U.S. cultural anthropologist. Born 2 October 1903 in Brooklyn, N.Y., to Mattie Schreiber and Jean Jules Du Bois. Educated public schools, Perth Amboy, N.J.; Barnard College (B.A., 1927); Columbia University (M.A. in medieval history, 1928); University of California, Berkeley (Ph.D. in anthropology, 1932). Professional experience: field work among Wintu Indians and other Native American tribes, northern Calif. and Ore. (1932–1935); University of California, Berkeley, teaching fellow and research associate (1930–1935); National Council Research, fellow; Psychological Clinic (Harvard) and New York Psychoanalytic Society (1935–1936); Alor, Indonesia, field worker (1937–1939); Sarah Lawrence College, faculty member (1939–1942); OSS, Indonesian Section, Branch Chief (1942–1945); South East Asian Branch, Division of Research, Office of Intelligence, State Department, chief (1945–1949); World Health Organization, consultant (1950–1951); Institute of International Education, director of research (1951–1954); Harvard University, Radcliffe Zemurray Professor (1954–1969). Bhubaneswar, India, field researcher (1961–1972). Honors and memberships: American Anthropological Association, president (1968); Association of Asian Studies, president (1969–1970); recipient of multiple awards, grants, honors, and eight honorary degrees. Died 1991.

Cora Du Bois, an internationally known anthropologist, was born in Brooklyn, New York, to a Swiss French father and a mother of German origin. Skillful in languages from her early exposure to French and German in her home, she had the opportunity to travel to Europe soon after her high school graduation in Perth Amboy, New Jersey, in 1924, staying with her mother's relatives in Germany. Interested in history, Cora Du Bois studied at Barnard College, receiving her bachelor's in 1927, and went on to study medieval history at Columbia, receiving her master's the following year. A course in anthropology with Franz Boas and RUTH BENE-DICT encouraged her to think about medieval contacts between western Europe and eastern Africa. She went to study under Alfred Kroeber and Robert Lowie at University of California, Berkeley, where she did a dissertation on girls' adolescent rites in the Americas, obtaining her doctorate in 1932. Her first field work was among northern Californian, and Oregonian coastal and Columbia river tribes, one of Kroeber's interests, although Lowie was her principal intellectual guide. This field work was supported by Social Science Research Council Grants; she also had research and teaching fellowships.

In 1935–1936, Du Bois became interested in the links between psychiatry and anthropology and obtained a National Research Council grant to work at the Henry A. Murray Psychological Clinic at Harvard and with Abram Kardiner at the New York Psychoanalytic Society. Following this she studied culture and personality among the Alor, in Indonesia, producing the classic study, *The People of Alor* (1944). During World War II, Du Bois worked for the Office of Strategic Services, heading up the Indonesia research section, and continued related work for the State Department until 1949. Publishing extensively on Southeast Asia, she served as consultant for the World Health Organization, and from 1951 to 1954 directed research for the Institute of International Education. In 1954, Du Bois returned to the academic world with the Radcliffe Zemurray professorship, making her a member of the departments of both anthropology and social relations. From 1961 to 1972, Du Bois conducted a study of sociocultural change in a small town in India (Bhubaneswar in Orissa), directing nine dissertations studying the many aspects of ancient and modern culture there. She received many honors in her lifetime, including honorary degrees from Harvard, Mills, and Mount Holyoke. Du Bois died 7 April 1991 in a nursing home in Brookline, Massachusetts.   JH/MBO

PRIMARY SOURCES

Du Bois, Cora. "Wintu Ethnography." *University of California Publications in American Archaeology and Ethnography* 36 (1935): 1–148.

———. "Some Anthropological Perspectives on Psychoanalysis." *Psycho-analytic Review* 24, no. 3 (1939): 246–263.

———. *The People of Alor.* Minneapolis: University of Minnesota Press, 1944. Reprint, with new chapter, Cambridge, Mass.: Harvard University Press, 1959.

———. *Social Forces in Southeast Asia.* Minneapolis: University of Minnesota Press, 1956.

———. "Studies in an Indian Town." In *Women in the Field.* Ed. Peggy Golde, 1970.

———. "Some Anthropological Hindsights." *Annual Review of Anthropology* 9 (1990): 1–15.

SECONDARY SOURCES

Davis, Eric. "Cora DuBois." *American Anthropologist Newsletter* 32, no. 6 (September 1991): 3. Obituary notice.

STANDARD SOURCES

Debus; Gacs.

DUBUISSON-BROUHA, ADELE (fl. 1937)

Belgian physiologist. Married Marcel Dubuisson. Professional experience: Kaiser Wilhelm Institute of Medical Research, Institute of Physiology, scientific guest.

Adele Dubuisson-Brouha came from Liège, Belgium, to the Max Planck Institute in 1937 with her husband, the professor Marcel Dubuisson. Dubuisson-Brouha worked as a scientific guest from 1937 to 1938 in the Institute of Physiology in the Kaiser Wilhelm Institute of medical research. At this time Nobel Prize–winner Otto Meyerhof was head of the institute.   JH/MBO

SECONDARY SOURCES

Report in *Die Naturwissenschaften* 26 (1938). These annual reports have information on Dubuisson-Brouha.

Vogt, Annette. "The Kaiser-Wilhelm-Gesellschaft and the Career Chances for Female Scientists between 1911 and 1945." Paper given for the International Congress for the History of Science, Liège, Belgium.

DU CHÂTELET, GABRIELLE-EMILIE LE TONNELIER DE BRETEUIL (MARQUISE) (1706–1749)

French writer on natural philosophy. Born 1706 in Paris to Gabrielle-Anne de Froulay and Louis-Nicolas Le Tonnelier de Breteuil, baron of Preuilly. Married Florent-Claude, marquis du Châtelet. Four children (two died in infancy). Educated by tutors. Died 1749 at Lunéville.

Emilie du Châtelet presents a vivid contrast to the forbidding stereotype of the "scientific lady." Spoiled, self-indulgent, a perennial source of gossip in aristocratic circles because of her love affairs—including an enduring relationship with Voltaire—she was also intelligent, perceptive, and industrious. Important in French intellectual history as both popularizer and translator of Newton, she played a significant role too in the integration of Newtonian and Leibnizian ideas in dynamics.

Emilie was the youngest child of Louis-Nicolas Le Tonnelier de Breteuil, chief of protocol at the royal court—a member of the minor nobility and a brilliant busybody with a love for gossip and intrigues—and Anne de Froulay, whose family belonged to the greater nobility. Louis-Nicolas, recognizing that he had produced an exceptionally talented child, deviated from the typical practice of his class of leaving the education of the female children to chance contacts or to a convent's unstimulating seclusion. Perhaps her unprepossessing appearance as well as her abilities led him to "help his clothes-conscious ugly duckling prepare for a life as a spinster" (Edwards 5). Thus, from the age of six or seven, Emilie was surrounded by the best available governesses and tutors.

Emilie's marriage to Florent-Claude, marquis du Châtelet (1725), withstood a succession of lovers, lawsuits, and separations. Her first love affair, with Louis Vincent, marquis de Guébriant, came close to being her last: abandoned, she attempted suicide with "an almost mortal dose of opium" (Besterman, 180).

Because the physical descriptions of Emilie come from biased sources, it is difficult to appraise her fairly. According to the marquise de Créquy, "Mme. du Châtelet had a skin like a nutmeg grater, an uncontrollable passion for pompons, a devastating weakness for gaming, and a violent, although somewhat misplaced, yearning for love." On the other hand, Emilie's male friends invariably found her attractive, one writing of "her beautiful big soft eyes with black brows, her noble, witty and piquant expression" (Mitford, 21). It was after the birth of her third and last child by du Châtelet, when she was twenty-seven years old, that Emilie began to study mathematics seriously. This interest intensified after she became reacquainted in November 1733 with Voltaire, who had been a guest in the Breteuil household when Emilie was a child. Having returned from England saturated with the physics of Newton and the philosophy of Locke, Voltaire had just completed his *Lettres philosophiques* (1733), a work whose ideas so outraged the French regime that it was officially banned.

In du Châtelet, Voltaire found a woman who not only shared his interest in science but was in a position to provide him with a safe retreat from the hostile world. Together they retired to the marquis du Châtelet's estate at Cirey. The tolerant marquis was perfectly content to allow Voltaire to manage the estate in his absence; there were frequent occasions

when all three of them were in residence at the same time. For sixteen years at Cirey, petty intrigues, lawsuits, brilliant fêtes, and dramatic productions were superimposed upon a background of study and intellectual creativity. The principals of the drama, Voltaire and Emilie du Châtelet, were not confined to Cirey, however: separately or together they appeared in Brussels to attend to a long-term lawsuit involving her family, or they used Belgium as a haven on the numerous occasions when reaction to Voltaire's writings forced him to leave France precipitously.

Although the lives of Voltaire and Emilie du Châtelet were seldom on an even keel, their affection for each other remained constant long after their physical relationship ended. Voltaire fell in love with his niece, Marie Louise Denis, and Emilie. du Châtelet fell in love with a young officer, Jean-Grançois, marquis de Saint-Lambert. After the almost forty-three-year-old Emilie discovered that she was pregnant by Saint-Lambert, she and Voltaire conspired to get the marquis du Châtelet to visit Cirey. The strategy succeeded, for when her husband departed three weeks later he was convinced that he was to be a father again. After arranging to spend her confinement at Lunéville, in the palace of Stanislas I, the former king of Poland, Emilie du Châtelet worked desperately to complete her annotated translation of Newton's *Principia,* began in 1744. Complications developed after the birth; Emilie du Châtelet's death was followed a few days later by the death of the baby.

Although Emilie du Châtelet's dominant intellectual pursuits were physics and mathematics, she shared Voltaire's interest in metaphysics and ethics. By 1734, her exposure to the ideas of Pierre Louis Moreau de Maupertuis (1698–1759), Alexis-Claude Clairaut (1713–1765), and Voltaire had converted her to the tenets of Newtonianism. She modified her views, however, after becoming acquainted with the ideas of Leibniz.

During the first half of the eighteenth century, scientists and philosophers considered the systems of Leibniz and Newton incompatible. Although Emilie du Châtelet remained impressed with Newton's analysis, she was dissatisfied with his failure to relate theories in physics and metaphysics. She resolved the conflict after meeting Samuel König, a disciple of Leibniz's interpreter Christian von Wolff (1679–1754). König suggested to her that accepting Leibnizian metaphysics did not preclude accepting Newtonian physical theories if one postulated that these theories were only concerned with the phenomena. Emilie du Châtelet popularized the possibility of a compromise using portions of both systems in her *Institutions de physique,* written as a textbook for her son and published anonymously in 1740 (revised, 1742). An acrimonious quarrel erupted between Emilie du Châtelet and König, shattered their friendship, and set the stage for a controversy about the originality of the work. König claimed the book was only a collection of his lessons. Du Châtelet futilely appealed to Jean Jacques d'Ortous de Mairan (1678–1771), secretary general of the Academie des Sciences. William H. Barber, who carefully examined the question of the originality of the book, concluded that the manuscript of the *Institutions de physique* indicates that although the first chapters were rewritten after du Châtelet's conversion to Leibnizianism, there is no plagiarism of König's teachings.

Before du Châtelet became involved in the Newton-Leibniz controversy, she published a work on the nature of fire. In 1736, the Academie des Sciences announced an essay contest on that subject. Voltaire, planning to enter the competition, established a small chemical laboratory at Cirey for research purposes. Du Châtelet resolved to compete too and prepared her memoir without even Volatire's knowledge. Although neither of them won the prize, Voltaire arranged to have both of their contributions published with those of the winners in 1739. Before her work was published, du Châtelet modified her Newtonian opinions and petitioned the academy to publish a revised version; the academy refused but did allow her to add a series of errata that reflect her acceptance of Leibnizian ideas. In 1744, she published a revised Leibnizian version of her *Dissertation sur la nature et la propagation du feu* and began to translate Newton's *Principia* into French. It was in her annotated translation, published in part in 1756 and in complete form in 1759, that the *Principia* first became available to French readers in their language.

Undoubtedly, Emilie du Châtelet's quick mind grasped many of the complex scientific issues of her day. Love, intrigue, discussion, and dispute intermingled to determine the parameters of her scientific creativity. Her association with Voltaire and his peers assured her exposure to opposing physical and metaphysical views of the universe; yet the social setting of many of their encounters encouraged a superficial, generalized discussion of ideas and discouraged deep or intensive studies. Even though du Châtelet's intellectual achievements went beyond dinner conversation, she never really penetrated the barrier of superficiality to produce original work. Nonetheless, her translation of the *Principia* and her part in the integration of Newtonian and Leibnizian mechanics represent lasting contributions to science. MBO

PRIMARY SOURCES

Du Châtelet, Gabrielle-Emilie. *Institutions de physique.* Paris: Prault fils, 1740. Manifests a conversion to the Leibniz-Wolff philosophy. The first eight chapters indicate ways in which individuals who have embraced certain Newtonian mechanical principles might find epistemological and metaphysical foundations in Leibnizianism.

———. *Les letters de la Marquise du Châtelet* 2 vols. Ed. Theodore Besterman. Geneva: Institut et Musée Voltaire, 1958. Letters, in French, chronologically arranged, with notes and index of names; illustrated.

SECONDARY SOURCES

Barber, William H., et al., eds. "Mme. du Châtelet and Leibnizianism: The Genesis of the Institutions de physique." In *The Age of the Enlightenment: Studies Presented to Theodore Besterman.* Edinburgh: Oliver and Boyd for the University Court of St. Andrew, 1967.

Besterman, Theodore. *Voltaire.* New York: Harcourt Brace and World, 1969. Biography of Voltaire containing considerable information on du Châtelet.

Cohen, I. Bernard. "The French Translation of Isaac Newton's *Philosophiae naturalis principia mathematica* (1756, 1759, 1966)." *Archives internationales d'histoire des sciences* 21 (1968): 261–290. Describes the "mysteries" surrounding Mme. du Châtelet's French translations of Newton's *Principia.*

Edwards, Samuel. *The Divine Mistress.* New York: David McKay, 1970. Popularized biography stressing du Châtelet's relationship with Voltaire.

Hamel, Frank. *An Eighteenth-Century Marquise: A Study of Emilie du Châtelet and Her Times.* New York: James Pott, 1921.

Iltis, Carolyn Merchant. "Madame du Châtelet's Metaphysics and Mechanics." *Studies in the History and Philosophy of Science* 8 (1977): 28–48. More recent publications appear under the name Carolyn Merchant. This is an analysis of Du Châtelet's natural philosophy and mechanics as set forth in the anonymously published *Institutions de physique.*

Maurel, André. *La Marquise du Châtelet: Amie de Voltaire.* Paris: Librairie Hachette, 1930. Biography stressing du Châtelet's relationship with Voltaire.

Mitford, Nancy. *Voltaire in Love.* New York: Harper and Brothers, 1957. Popularized account.

Taton, René. "Madame du Châtelet, traductrice de Newton." *Archives internationales d'histoire des sciences* 22 (1969): 185–209. Discusses circumstances of the genesis of Du Châtelet's translation of the *Principia* and stresses its importance to the development of Newtonianism in France.

Vaillot, René. *Madame du Châtelet.* Paris: Michel, 1978.

Voltaire, François Marie Arouet de. "Mémoires pour servir à la vie de M. de Voltaire." In *Oeuvres complètes de Voltaire.* Vol. 23: 515–521. Paris: Garrier Frères. 1883.

Wade, Ira O. *The Intellectual Development of Voltaire.* Princeton, NJ: Princeton University Press, 1969. Includes du Châtelet's scientific contributions alongside Voltaire's.

———. *Voltaire and Madame du Châtelet: An Essay on the Intellectual Activity at Cirey.* Princeton, N.J.: Princeton University Press, 1941.

STANDARD SOURCES
DSB.

DU COUDRAY, ANGELIQUE (MARGUERITE LE BOURSIER) (1712–1789)

French midwife. Born 1712 in Clermont-Ferrand. Educated Hôtel Dieu School in Paris; licensed as midwife or "accoucheuse," 1740.

Marguerite le Boursier, Angelique du Coudray, published *Abrege de l'art des accouchements avec plusiers observations sur des cas singuliers* in 1759 and her *Oeuvres* in 1773. She was directed by Louis XV to teach in all the provinces at a salary. In the Auvergne, she organized her first class of one hundred pupils. From this beginning, she trained over four hundred pupils in her career. In 1780, she established a course in practical obstetrics at the veterinary school at Alfort. Male surgeons were strongly opposed to her teaching, although her methods were exact and scientific, for she used a model of the female torso and an actual fetus for instruction. Even the Church recognized her work and allowed her to baptize infants. Her expertise was so well accepted that she was often summoned to testify in malpractice cases.   JH/MBO

PRIMARY SOURCES
Du Coudray, Angelique. *Abrege de l'art des accouchements avec plusiers observations sur des cas singuliers.* 1759.
———. *Oeuvres.* 1773.

SECONDARY SOURCES
Hurd-Mead 1938; Uglow 1982.

DUFFIELD, MARY ELIZABETH (ROSENBERG) (1819–1914)

British botanical painter. Born 2 April 1819 in Bath. Father Thomas Elliot Rosenberg. Married William Duffield (1850). Died 13 January 1914.

Mary Elizabeth Rosenberg was born in Bath, the daughter of an artist and drawing master. She married a painter, William Duffield, who specialized in still lifes of fruits and vegetables. She was elected to the Royal Institute of Painters in Water Colors in 1861. She exhibited at the Society of Briths Artists and at the Royal Academy.   JH/MBO

PRIMARY SOURCES
Duffield, Mary Elizabeth. *The Museum of Flowers.* London: R. Groombridge and Sons, 1845.
———. *Art of Flower Painting.* London: Winsor and Newton, 1856. Went through nineteen editions.

Duffield's drawings ar in the Victoria and Albert Museum.

SECONDARY SOURCES
Clayton, Ellen C. *English Female Artists.* 2 vols. London: Tinsley, 1876. See 2:272–273.

STANDARD SOURCES
Desmond; *DNB*; Stafleu; *WWW,* vol. 1, 1897–1915.

DUFFY, ELIZABETH (1904–1970)

U.S. psychologist. Born 6 May 1904 in New Bern, N.C., to Francis and Lida (Patterson) Duffy. Married (1) John T. Baker (13 August 1928; divorced); (2) John E. Bridgers, Jr. (27 August 1938). One daughter, Betsy Elizabeth, with Bridgers. Educated North Carolina College for Women, Greensboro (1921–1925); Columbia University (M.A., 1926), Johns Hopkins University, postgraduate National Research Scholar in Child Development (Ph.D., 1928); Columbia University, national fellow in child development. Professional experience: Sarah Lawrence College, professor of psychology (1929–1937); North Carolina College for Women, Greensboro (1937–?); New York University, part-time visiting professor (1931); Brooklyn College, summer instructor (1937); National Science Foundation, visiting scientist. Honors and awards: Southern Fellowships Fund grantee (1959); Research Council University of N.C., grantee-in-aid (1959–1962, 1964–1966); City of Greensboro for services to Redevelopment Commission, certificate of Meritorious Service (1964). Memberships: American Psychological Association; Society for Research in Psychophysiology; Psychonomic Society; Society for Philosophy and Psychology, Phi Beta Kappa, Sigma Xi; fellow, Society for Research in Child Development; New York Academy of Science (secretary, psychological section 1937). Died of Hodgkin's Disease 19 December 1970.

Elizabeth Duffy was known as Polly. She married twice, the first time to John T. Baker with the marriage ending in divorce. Ten years later, in 1938, she married John Bridgers, and the couple had one daughter. Bridgers was an English professor at the North Carolina College for Women, the institution that Duffy had attended as an undergraduate.

In spite of the fact that Duffy had a Ph.D. from Columbia University and was one of the most popular of the graduate students, she did not take the prescribed path up the academic ladder but moved back and forth basically through grants into different positions.

Her research interests were in theoretical psychology, motor responses as indicators of individual differences, and emotion. She also worked on concepts in descriptive psychology, particularly the idea of activation. Duffy continued to use her maiden name in her publications and professional work.   KM

PRIMARY SOURCES

Duffy, Elizabeth. *Activation and Behavior.* New York: John Wiley & Sons, 1962.

SECONDARY SOURCES

"Elizabeth Bridgers." *Greensboro Daily News.* 20 December 1970. Obituary notice.

STANDARD SOURCES

AMS 5–8, S&B 9–11; Debus; Stevens and Gardner; *Who's Who of American Women.*

DUGES, MARIE-LOUISE

See LaChapelle, Marie Louise.

DU LUYS, GUILLEMETTE (fl. 1479)

French surgeon who flourished in the fifteenth century.

Guillemette du Luys acquired enough medical training to be called into royal service. She was a surgeon in the service of Louis XI of France, and was granted a pecuniary reward by Louis XI in about 1479. She operated the medicinal baths used by the French court. JH/MBO

STANDARD SOURCES

Echols and Williams; Hughes.

DUMÉE, JEANNE (fl. 1680–1685)

French astronomer. Born seventeenth century in Paris.

From childhood, Jeanne Dumée was interested in astronomy. After her soldier husband was killed in battle, leaving her a widow at age seventeen, she pursued astronomical studies and wrote a book explaining the Copernican system. In this work, entitled *Entretiens sur l'opinion de Copernic touchant la mobilité de la terre,* Dumée noted that her purpose was not to support the doctrines of Copernicans, but to discuss the reasons they used to defend themselves. The book apparently has never been published in its entirety. The *Biographie universelle* explains that "on n'a jamais pu trouver ce livre, et l'on doute s'il a été imprime" (12:224). Nevertheless, we know of its contents through an epitome in the *Journal des sçavans.* Critically acclaimed in its own time, the work was praised for treating the "three motions of the earth" *(les trois movements de la terre)* with clarity. By drawing upon analogies between the earth and the other planets, Dumée concluded that it was impossible to conceive of a stationary earth with a celestial sphere revolving around it.

Women of her time, wrote Dumée, considered themselves incapable of study. By her own example she hoped to convince them that "entre le cerveau d'une femme et celui d'un homme il n'y aucune différence" (between the brain of a woman and that of a man there is no difference). JH/MBO

PRIMARY SOURCES

Dumée, Jeanne. "Entretiens sur l'opinion de Copernic touchant la mobilité de la terre, par Mille. Jeanne Dumée de Paris. A Pars, 1680." *Journal des sçavans* 8:304–305 Amsterdam: Pierre le Grand, 1680.

STANDARD SOURCES

Biographie universelle, vol. 6; Debus; Ogilvie 1986; Strohmeier.

DUMMER, ETHEL (STURGES) (1866–1954)

U.S. philanthropist. Born 23 October 1866 in Chicago, Ill., to Mary (Delafield) and George Sturges. Eight siblings. Married William Francis Dummer in 1888. Four daughters, one son (died in infancy). Educated: Kirkland School. Professional experience: wrote articles and financially supported child psychologists, sociologists, and educators. Died 25 February 1954 in Winnetka, Ill.

Ethel Sturges Dummer was the daughter of a banker in Chicago. Although the third child of eight, her two older brothers died in infancy, which made her the oldest child of her surviving siblings (all daughters). Although she had a limited education at the Kirkland School, a private school, this was led by Ellen Gates Starr, a cofounder of JANE ADDAMS's Hull House. Here she acquired a sense of social obligation to the poor and disadvantaged.

After her marriage in 1888 to an associate of her father, William Francis Dummer, and the birth of her four daughters and one son (who died in early infancy), she became interested in early childhood education. Her husband was also interested in educational experiments and used phonetics to teach their daughters to speak by their first birthday.

Beginning in 1908, Dummer joined groups interested in limiting child labor, and became a founding trustee of the Chicago School of Civics and Philanthropy. She began by funding lecture series at the University of Chicago on social problems and by supporting the costs of a study of sanitation in Europe led by Mary MacDowell of the University of Chicago Settlement. She then contributed to the establishment of the Juveline Psychopathic Institute under the directorship of William Healy, who, although a practicing neurologist, was a strong believer in nurture versus nature. With the assistance of AUGUSTA BRONNER, this clinic served as a forerunner of Healey and Bronner's later child guidance clinic that brought together teams of psychiatrists, psychologists, and social workers.

Dummer also became interested in preventing prostitution and in aiding unwed mothers, and supported the work of Mariam van Waters and others in therapeutic detention homes such as El Retiro in Los Angeles. In the 1920s she supported van Waters's surveys and writings on delinquent girls. During this same period, she financially aided the research of the sociologist William I. Thomas (who had lost his position at the University of Chicago), first in his study of *The Unadjusted Girl* (1923) and later in his research with his wife, Dorothy Swaine Thomas, for the study *The Child in America* (1926). In the 1930s, Dummer supported the work of Florence Beaman with retarded and delinquent boys at the Chicago Montefiore School and allowed an educator from Hull House (Neva Boyd) to use her living room to instruct teachers in exercise programs for children.

Dummer became interested as well in the philosophy and the educational experiments of MARY EVEREST BOOLE, the widow of the British mathematician George Boole, who had theories about organized play and the development of logic, and who had developed a number of educational tools to aid mathematical teaching. Dummer not only published her collected writings but she also wrote a small booklet explaining Boole's mixture of Darwinism with religion. She also encouraged her daughter Ethel D. Mintzer to introduce Boole blocks into the school she headed in San Diego, the Francis W. Parker School. Her major writings included philosophical descriptions of the unconscious, introductions to some of the sociological books whose research she supported, and her autobiography in 1937. She died in 1954 of a stroke.   JH/MBO

PRIMARY SOURCES

Dummer, Ethel Sturges. *Mary Everest Boole: A Pioneer Student of the Unconscious.* N.p., 1900.
———. *Why I Think So—The Autobiography of an Hypothesis.* Chicago: Clarke-McElroy, 1937.
———. *The Evolution of a Biological Faith.* Chicago: n.p., 1950.
Papers at Schlesinger Library, Radcliffe.

SECONDARY SOURCES

Healy, William. "In Memorium: Ethel Sturges Dummer, 1866–1954." *American Journal of Orthopsychiatry.* 24 (July 1954): 646–647. Obituary notice.
New York Times, 27 February 1954. Obituary notice.

STANDARD SOURCES

NAW(M) (article by Robert M. Mennel).

DUNBAR, HELEN FLANDERS (1902–1959)

U.S. psychiatrist. Born 14 May 1902 in Chicago, Ill., to Francis William and Edith (Flanders) Dunbar. Married George Henry Soule. One daughter, Marcia Winslow Dunbar-Soule. Educated Bryn Mawr (B.A., 1923); Columbia University (M.A., 1924; Ph.D., 1929; Med.Sc.D., 1935); Union Theological Seminary (B.S., 1927); Yale University (M.D., 1930). Professional experience: General and Psychiatric-Neurological Hospital and Clinic of University of Vienna, travelling fellow; Burghölzli, Zurich, hospitant assistant (1929–1930); College of Physicians and Surgeons, Columbia University, assistant in medicine (1930–1934); Presbyterian Hospital and Vanderbilt Clinic, assistant physician (1931–1934); Columbia University College of Physicians and Surgeons, instructor in psychiatry (1931–1936), associate attending psychiatrist (1936–1949); Presbyterian Hospital and Vanderbilt Clinic, psychosomatic research director (1932–1949); Council for Clinical Training Theology Students, Inc., director and medical advisor (1930–?); New York City Committee on Mental Hygiene and mental hygiene section New York Welfare Council, executive committee member (1936–?); Bellevue Hospital, visiting physician (1935–1937); Greenwich (Conn.) Hospital, associate staff member (1944–1949); New York Psychoanalytic Institution, instructor (1941–1949). Journal of Psychosomatic Medicine, Experimental and Clinical Studies, Monograph Supplements, inaugurator and editor in chief (1938–1947); Psychoanalytic Quarterly, collaborating editor (1938–1940), editor (1939–1940); Acta Psychotherapeutica, Psychosomatica et Orthopaedagogica, editor. Died 1959.

Helen Flanders Dunbar had a varied career. Her scientific interests encompassed many areas, from symbolism to the education of theological students in social and preventive public health problems. She was also interested in the physiological changes accompanying emotions and the psychiatric education of medical students.

Dunbar was a Fellow of the American Medical Association, the New York Academy of Medicine; the American Psychiatric Association; and the International Psychoanalytic Association. She was a member of the Psychopathology Association (and vice-president 1942–1945), the New York Society of Clinical Psychiatry, and the American Committee for the World Federation for Mental Health.   JH/MBO

PRIMARY SOURCES

Dunbar, H. Flanders. *Symbolism in Medieval Thought.* New Haven: Yale University Press, 1929. Ph.D. dissertation.
———. *Emotions and Bodily Changes.* New York: Columbia University Press, 1924. Rev. ed. 1954.
———. *Psychosomatic Diagnosis.* N.P., 1943. Reprint, New York: Johnson Reprint Corp., 1956.
———. *Mind and Body: Psychosomatic Medicine.* New York: Random House, 1947. Rev. ed. 1955.
———. *Synopsis of Psychosomatic Diagnosis and Treatment.* St. Louis: C. V. Mosby Co., 1948.
———. *Your Child's Mind and Body.* New York: Vintage Books, 1949.

―――. *Psychiatry in the Medical Specialties.* New York: Mc-
Graw-Hill, Blakiston Division, 1959.

―――, trans. *Psychopathic Personalities.* By Eugen Kahn. New
Haven: Yale University Press, 1931.

SECONDARY SOURCES

Powell, R. C. "Helen Flanders Dunbar (1902–1959) and a
Holistic Approach to Psychosomatic Problems." *Psychiatric
Quarterly* (1977); (1978).

STANDARD SOURCES

AMS 6–7; Debus; *Encyclopedia of Psychology; NAW*(M); Stevens
and Gardner.

DUNCAN, CATHERINE (GROSS) (1908–1968)

*U.S. mycologist. Born 4 April 1908, Manila, Ind. Educated De
Pauw University, Indiana (A.B., 1931); University of Wisconsin
(M.A., 1933; Ph.D., 1935). Married Robert Gross (1940). One
daughter, Dana. Professional experience: Hood College, Frederick,
Md., assistant professor of botany and bacteriology (1935?–1942);
Forest Products Laboratory, pathologist, eventually principal pathol-
ogist researching wood fungi and insects (1942–1968). Died 24
August 1968.*

Catherine Duncan was a mycologist who was born in the
Midwest and educated at De Pauw University and the University of Wisconsin. At Wisconsin, she specialized in plant
cytology and agricultural bacteriology under Charles E.
Allen and W. D. Frost. Her future husband, Robert E. Duncan, was a fellow student who also studied under Allen.

She taught for seven years at Hood College in Maryland
and then took a position in Madison, Wisconsin with the
Forest Products Laboratory, in December 1942. Although
she was recruited to help with the war effort, she remained
there for the rest of her career. At the time of her death,
Duncan was a principal pathologist in the Section of Wood
Fungi and Insects Research.

Much of Duncan's research was concerned with the microbiological degradation of wood. In her early research she
developed laboratory methods for determining the natural
decay resistance of various species of wood and the usefulness of chemical treatments to protect the less resistant
species from decay. She was involved in the development of
the soil-blocking technique for making assays of the decay-
inhibiting qualities of wood preservatives. Her later work included investigations on the soft-rot fungi, involving their
identification, physiology, the effect of their invasion on different woods, and the development of a method to test for
the resistance of various woods to their attack.

In 1963, Duncan's achievements in research were recognized by the awarding of two postdoctoral fellowships—
one by the Forest Products Laboratory and the other by
the National Science Foundation. With this support, she
studied abroad in the laboratory of the eminent Swiss fungus
physiologist Dr. Frey-Wyssling. In this laboratory, she
worked on developing an immunofluorescent technique that
later allowed her to study the areas of cellulase production
in hyphae and the migration of these enzymes from the
fungihyphae into the surrounding wood. She also worked
on the intercellular movement through wood of typical
wood decay and soft-rot fungi by using fluorescent staining
methods. Duncan was a member of the American Association for the Advancement of Science, the American
Phytopathological Society, and the Botanical Society of
America.

She died in Madison, Wisconsin on 24 August 1968, after
a long illness and was survived by her husband, Robert, and
one daughter, Dana.   JH/MBO

SECONDARY SOURCES

Cowling, Ellis B. "Catherine Gross Duncan, 1908–1968."
Phytopathology 59 (1969): 1777.
Eslyn, W. E. "Catherine Gross Duncan." *Mycologia* 61 (1969):
27–29. Obituary notice, with portrait.

STANDARD SOURCES

NAW unused.

DUNCAN, HELEN (1910–1971)

*U.S. paleontologist. Born 3 May 1910 in Medford, Ore. Never
married. Educated University of Montana (B.A., 1934; M.A.,
1937); University of Cincinnati (1939–1942); Professional experience: U.S. Geological Survey, editor, researcher, paleontologist
(1942–1971). Died 14 August 1971.*

Although Helen Duncan was born in Oregon, she grew up
near Virginia City, Montana, which she considered home.
She attended the University of Montana, where she received
bachelor's and master's degrees in geology. During her time
at the university, Duncan was involved with the purchase of
books for the library. Her master's thesis was published by the
University of Michigan and has become a classic in its field.
After receiving her degree, she moved to the University of
Cincinnati, where she was a graduate student and assistant in
the geology department until 1941 and then in the applied
science research division until 1942. Her first position with
the U.S. Geological Survey was as an editor. She then
worked on a wartime project on fluorspar under James
Steele Williams. When the war was over, she transferred to
the paleontology and stratigraphy branch.

Duncan was active in professional organizations. She was a
member of the subcommission on carboniferous stratigra-

phy of the International Union of the Geological Sciences from 1960 until her death. Her additional international contacts included representing the U.S. Geological Survey at the International Geological Congress in Copenhagen in 1960 and the Sixth Carboniferous Congress in Sheffield, England, in 1967. She served as a member of the Geologic Names Committee of the U.S. Geological Survey from 1957 to 1960. Duncan was a Fellow of the Geological Society of America. Some of the professional organizations to which she belonged: the Paleontological Society, the Palaeontological Association, the American Association for the Advancement of Science, the Society of Systematic Zoology, the Washington Academy of Sciences, and Sigma Xi. She was vice-president and treasurer of the Paleontological Society of Washington and councilor for the Geological Society of Washington.

At the survey, Duncan's specialty was Paleozoic corals. This interest led her to work on Ordovician corals, Hydrozoa, Bryozoa, and archaeocyathids. Her work on corals made this group stratigraphically useful for the first time to field geologists. She produced at least four hundred reports on fossils for fieldmen. Although she published important papers under her own name, she also helped her colleagues identify fossil specimens, receiving acknowledgments in their publications. She died 14 August 1971 after collapsing in 1968 in a London airport on her way home from an international conference on Bryozoa. Her important studies on Ordovician corals and possible origin of *Alcyonaria* were left incomplete at time of death.   JH/MBO

PRIMARY SOURCES

Duncan, Helen M. "Trepstomatous Bryozoa from the Traverse Group of Michigan." *Michigan University Museum Paleontology Contributions* 5, no. 10 (1939): 171–270.

———. With W. H. Easton. "Archimedes and Its Genotype." *Journal of Paleontology* 27, no. 5 (1953): 737–741.

———, et al., eds. "Corals in Cooper GA: Permian Fauna at El Anrimonio, Western Sonora Mexico." *Smithsonian Miscellaneous Collection* 119, no. 2 (1953): 21.

———. "Ordovician and Silurian coral faunas of Western United States." *U.S. Geological Survey Bulletin* 1021-F (1956): 209–256.

———. "*Beghornia,* a New Ordovician Coral Genus." *Journal of Paleontology* 31, no. 3 (1957): 607–615.

———. "Bryozoa Fossils." In McGraw-Hill *Encyclopedia of Science and Technology.* Vol. 2. New York: McGraw-Hill, 356–358.

———. "Bryozoans." In *History of the Redwall Limestone of Northern Arizona. Geological Society America Memoirs No. 114,* ed. E. D. McKee and R. C. Gutschick, chapter 7 (354–434). Boulder, Colo.: Geological Society of America, 1969.

———. With Mackenzie Gordon, Jr. "Biostratigraphy and

Correlation of the Oquirrh Group and Related Rocks in the Oquirrh Mountains, Utah." In *Upper Paleozoic rocks in the Oquirrh Mountains and Bingham mining district, Utah. U.S. Geological Survey Professional Papers 629-A,* ed. Edwin Wilson Tooker and R. J. Roberts, A38–57. Washington, D.C.: U.S. Government Printing Office, 1970.

SECONDARY SOURCES

Aldrich, Michele L. "Women in Paleontology in the United States, 1840–1960." *Earth Sciences History* 1, no. 1 (1982): 14–22.

Flower, Rousseau H., and Jean M. Berden. "Memorial to Helen M. Duncan, 1910–1971." *Geological Society of America Memorials.* 5 (1977): 1–3. Includes bibliography.

DUNCAN, URSULA KATHERINE (1910–1985)

British botanist. Born 17 September 1910 in Kensington, London, to Dorothy Weston and Commander J. A. Duncan. Educated by a governess; University of London (B.A., 1952; M.A., 1956). Honors and memberships: Linnean Society, Fellow; Bloomer Medal; British Lichen Society, honorary membership; University of Dundee, honorary Doctor of Laws. Died 27 January 1985 at Arbroath, Angus.

Ursula Duncan received her early education from a governess, Isobel Leslie. Under her tutelage she passed the entrance school certificate to Cambridge when she was fifteen years old, with a distinction in Greek. She registered as an external student at London University and received both a bachelor's and master's degree in classics. She showed considerable musical talent and became a licentiate of the Royal Academy of Music in 1948. During World War II, she was based in Inverness and worked for the Censorship Department. After her father's death in 1943, she left Inverness and returned to the family home at Parkhill, Arbroath, where she took over the supervision of the family estate.

Duncan was interested in plants from an early age, and was encouraged by her father. Her first interests were the vascular plants. The most difficult groups to classify were always her favorites. After 1939 her interest in the flowering plants waned, and she moved toward the bryophytes and lichens, which presented a special challenge. An excellent field biologist, Duncan was an example of an amateur in the best sense of the word. A member of the Wild Flower Society and the Exchange Club of the British Isles, she corresponded with a wide range of specialists who profited from her many new records, collections, and important field data. In 1980, after many years of collecting data, she published the *Flora of East Ross-shire.* She was also interested in the floras of Angus and the Island of Mull. Her interest in the Isle of Mull stimulated the botany department of the British

Museum (Natural History) to initiate the "flora of Mull" project which she enthusiastically supported.

R. H. Brown of Oxford and W. Watson of Taunton interested Duncan in lichenology. This field suffered an eclipse in Britain between 1945 and 1955, and she was one of the few who kept lichenology alive during that period. She published three books on lichens and contributed records to many other works.

Her next studies were on mosses and liverworts and she became an active member of the British Bryological Society. She always found challenges intriguing and picked an especially difficult group, the Sphagnales, for study. She published an illustrated key to this group.

Duncan was all that a good field botanist should be. She was intuitive, tenacious, and knowledgeable. During her lifetime, she collected a large and important herbarium of vascular plants, which she donated to the Dundee Museum in 1983. Her eyesight began to fail as did her health in general, so she donated her cryptogams to the herbarium of the Royal Botanic Garden, Edinburgh. JH/MBO

PRIMARY SOURCES
Duncan, Ursula. *Guide to the Study of Lichens.* Arbroath: T. Buncle & Co., 1959.

———. *Lichen Illustrations.* Arbroath: T. Buncle & Co., 1963.

———. *An Introduction to British Lichens.* Arbroath: T. Buncle & Co., 1970.

———. *Flora of East Ross-shire.* Edinburgh: Botanical Society of Edinburgh, 1980.

SECONDARY SOURCES
Bulletin of the British Lichen Society 56 (Summer 1985): 19–20.
James, P. W. "Ursula Katherine Duncan." *Lichenologist* 18 (1986): 383–385.

———. "Ursula Katherine Duncan." *Watsonia* 16 (1986): 215–216.

Journal of Bryology 13 (1985): 595–597.

STANDARD SOURCES
Desmond.

DUNHAM, ETHEL COLLINS (1883–1969)

U.S. pediatrician and neonatologist. Born 12 March 1883 in Hartford, Conn., to Alice (Collins) and Samuel G. Dunham. Five siblings. Never married. Educated Hartford High School, Miss Porter's School; Bryn Mawr College (A.B., 1914); Johns Hopkins Medical School (M.D., 1918); Harriet Lane Home, Johns Hopkins Hospital, intern. Professional experience: New Haven Hospital, house officer, department of pediatrics, staff member; New Haven Dispensary, director of outpatient clinic (1919–1935); Yale University Medical School, instructor (1920–1924), associate professor (1924–1927), associate clinical professor (1927–1935), adjunct instructor in clinical pediatrics (1935–1950); U.S. Clinical Bureau, medical officer of neonatal studies (1927–1935), director of child development (1935–1949); World Health Organization, consultant to maternal and child health section (1949–1951). Died 1969.

Born in Hartford, Connecticut, into a business family, where her mother's interest was in art and her father was president of the Hartford Electric Light Company, Ethel Collins Dunham was educated at the local high school and then spent two years at a finishing school, Miss Porter's, in Farmington, Connecticut. After six years of European travel, social activities, and some volunteer social work, she determined to obtain a college education and went to Bryn Mawr, graduating in 1914. She then entered Johns Hopkins Medical School, where she met again MARTHA MAY ELIOT (who had spent a year at Bryn Mawr) who would become her close friend, housemate, and colleague for the rest of her life.

After completing her medical studies, Dunham went to New Haven, where she spent her residency in pediatrics and then joined the staff of the New Haven Hospital, and served as director of the outpatient clinic of the New Haven Dispensary and head of the nursery for newborn infants. The topic of prematurity and newborn babies became a focus for her clinical and research work and she began to write a series of papers on abnormalities and diseases of the very young. She was an instructor, then assistant professor, at Yale; she rose to associate clinical professor in 1927. In that same year, the head of the Children's Bureau in Washington appointed her as medical officer in charge of neonatal studies, but permitted her to continue her studies at her hospital in New Haven. Martha May Eliot had joined her in New Haven as her associate.

In 1933, Dunham presented her detailed report on neonatal morbidity and mortality to the American Pediatric Society, establishing prematurity as the principal cause of death and disease. She was then appointed chairman of a committee on neonatal studies for the society. Two years later, Dunham and Eliot went to Washington, where Dunham was appointed director of research in child development, with Eliot as assistant director, at the United States Children's Bureau. The two women encouraged increased research, the dissemination of information, and the establishment of standards of care to reduce mortality rates in newborns. This was published in important reports on standards of care in 1943, reissued in 1948. In that same year, Dunham issued the manual *Premature Infants* for pediatricians, which included international comparisons from specialized neonatal centers. Under her influence, a model program was developed in which public health nurses and social workers joined pediatricians in offering follow-up care for premature infants. Dunham also published numerous papers in the *American Journal of the Diseases of Children*.

Dunham, again accompanied by Eliot, went to work for the World Health Organization in Switzerland to extend the same kind of measures that they had introduced through the Children's Bureau, encouraging specialized training, and research in the social, economic, as well as medical causes of prematurity. When Eliot received an appointment in 1951 as the new head of the Children's Bureau, replacing Dunham, who retired, Dunham began to do research on infant bearing, rearing, and mothering using primates in primate colonies as her research tools. The two women retired to Cambridge, Mass., in 1957. Dunham died at home of bronchopneumonia in 1969.   JH/MBO

PRIMARY SOURCES
Dunham, Ethel Collins. With Marian M. Crane. *Infant Care.* Washington, D.C.: U.S. Government Printing Office, 1940.
———. *Premature Infants: A Manual for Physicians.* London: Cassell, rev. ed. 1955.
Dunham's letters are in the Children's Bureau, National Archives (1921–1940). Related letters by Martha May Eliot and her oral interview are at the Schlesinger Library archives, Radcliffe College.

SECONDARY SOURCES
New York Times, 14 December 1969. Obituary notice.
Gordon, Harry H. "Presentation of the John Howland Medal and Award of the American Pediatric Society to Ethel G. Dunham." *American Journal of the Diseases of Children* (October 1957).
———. "Perspectives on Neonatology—1975." In *Neonatology: Pathophysiology and Management of the Newborn,* ed. Gordon B. Avery. Philadelphia: Lippincott, 1975.

STANDARD SOURCES
NAW(M) (article by William M. Schmidt).

DUNLOP, JANETTE GILCHRIST (fl. 1916)
Scottish physicist. Educated Edinburgh University (graduated 1914); Carnegie fellowship (1914–1916); teacher training course.

Janette Dunlop graduated from Edinburgh University in 1914. She received a Carnegie fellowship, and worked in Charles Barkla's laboratory studying X-rays until 1916. Under press of teacher shortages during World War I, Dunlop left research to enter a teacher training course.   JH/MBO

PRIMARY SOURCES
Dunlop, Janette. With Charles G. Barkla. "Scattering of X-Rays and Atomic Structure." *Philosophical Magazine* 31 (1916): 222–232.

STANDARD SOURCES
Rayner-Canham 1997.

DUNN, MARY DOUGLAS (1892–1969)
Scottish botanist. Born 1892. Educated St. Andrews (B.Sc., 1914; Ph.D., 1940). Professional experience: St. Andrews University, demonstrator in botany and curator of departmental herbarium.

Mary Douglas was educated at St. Andrews University, Scotland, and then became a demonstrator and curator at that same university.   JH/MBO

SECONDARY SOURCES
Macdonald, J. A. *Plant Science and Scientists in St. Andrews.* St. Andrews, Scotland: printed for the author by QUICK Print, 1984. Dunlop discussed on pages 36–37.

STANDARD SOURCES
Desmond.

DUNN, THELMA BRUMFIELD (1900–   )
U.S. pathologist. Born 6 February 1900 in Pittsylvania County, Va. Married (1929). Three children. Educated Cornell University (A.B., 1922); University of Virginia (M.D., 1926). Professional experience: Bellevue Hospital, New York, intern (1926–1927); University of Virginia, instructor of pathology (1927–1928), assistant professor (1928–1929), acting head of pathology department (1929–1930); George Washington University, volunteer laboratory assistant (1936–1938), assistant (1938–1942); National Cancer Institute, Fellow (1942–1947), pathologist (1947–1970), consultant, Registry Experimental Cancers (1970–?). Death date unknown.

Pathologist Thelma Dunn received her medical degree from the University of Virginia in 1926. While raising her family, she held a variety of professional positions. Her research included the pathologic anatomy of laboratory mice. She was involved in cancer research during much of her career.

Dunn received numerous awards, including an honorary Doctor of Medical Science from the Woman's College of Pennsylvania, an honorary degree from the University of Perugia (1969), and the Federal Women's Award and Distinguished Service Medal from the U.S. Department of Health, Education and Welfare in 1962. She was a Fellow of the

American College of Physicians and of the College of American Pathology. She was a member of the American Society of Pathologists and Bacteriologists and the American Association for Cancer Research.

PRIMARY SOURCES

Dunn, Thelma Brumfield. *The Unseen Fight against Cancer.* Charlottesville: Bates, 1975.

———. Interview for the University of Virginia Oral History Project. University of Virginia Archives, 26 January 1976.

STANDARD SOURCES

AMS 8, B 9, P&B 12.

DUNNING, WILHELMINA FRANCES (1904–)

U.S. biologist and oncologist. Born 12 September 1904 in Topsham, Maine, to A. Evelyn Williams and Fred Jewel Dunning. Educated University of Maine (A.B., 1926); Columbia University (M.A., 1928; Ph.D., 1932). Professional experience: Columbia University, research associate (1930–1941), instructor of pathology (1941–1946), assistant professor of oncology (1946–1950); Wayne University College of Medicine (concurrent) research associate; Detroit Institute for Cancer Research (1933–1950); University of Miami, Coral Gables, Fla., professor of zoology (1950–1952); University of Miami, professor of experimental pathology, director, Cancer Research Laboratory. Honors and memberships: American Association for Cancer Research; American Society of Zoologists; Society for Experimental Biology and Medicine; Society for Growth and Development; New York Academy of Sciences; and Sigma XI.

Wilhelmina Frances Dunning devoted her research life to studies on the etiology and treatment of experimentally induced cancer in mice and rats. She was born and brought up in Maine, and attended the University of Maine, where she received her bachelor's degree in 1926. She went to New York City to Columbia University, where she completed both her master's (1928) and doctorate (1932). During her graduate years, Dunning was a research associate, and she remained in that position for eleven years, until she was made an instructor of pathology during World War II. In 1946, she took a position as research associate at Wayne College of Medicine, Detroit. In 1950, she moved to Florida where, after two years as professor of zoology at the University of Miami, she became director of the Cancer Research Laboratories, where she remained until her retirement in 1968(?). Most of her research centered on induced neoplasms in rats and mice and experimental chemotherapeutic treatment.

JH/MBO

STANDARD SOURCES

AMS 6–8, B 9, P&B 10–14; Debus.

DUPRÉ, MARIE (17th century)

French writer on natural philosophy. Born 17th century. Niece of Roland Desmarets.

Marie Dupré was the niece of a well-known seventeenth-century humanist, Roland Desmarets. Encouraged by her uncle, Dupré studied Greek, Latin, Italian, rhetoric, and philosophy. Through her study of philosophy, she became interested in the works of Descartes, joining in spirit the group of young women who became his disciples. Passionately defending Cartesian ideas from critics, she was christened the "Cartésienne." Dupré published poetry (under the pseudonym Isis) but apparently no scientific works. Two of her contemporaries published works extolling her virtues.

JH/MBO

SECONDARY SOURCES

Nouvelle biographie générale: Depuis les temps les plus reculés jusqu'à nos jours. 46 vols. Paris: Firmin Didot Frères, 1856. Vol. 15, pp. 362–363.

STANDARD SOURCES

Biographie universelle, 12.

DURHAM, MARY EDITH (1863–1944)

British ethnographer, traveler, and popular writer. Born 8 December 1863 in London. Never married. Educated as an artist. Professional experience: exhibited drawings (before 1900); published books on Serbian people, on the Balkans, and on Albania, including tribal life and customs (1904–1928); collected embroidery and garments from Yugoslavia and Albania that formed the Durham Collection; illustrated books with her watercolors, drawings, photographs. Honors and memberships: Royal Anthropological Institute, Fellow. Died 15 November 1944 in London.

Mary Edith Durham (generally called Edith during her lifetime) began her career as an artist. She exhibited some of her drawings and paintings before 1900. She became well known only when she published on her travels through the Balkans, studying manners of customs of different tribal peoples, especially in Montenegro and Albania.

Durham collected information on tribal organization, laws and justice within the tribal groups, tatooing, social ceremonies and customs, and tribal medicine and magical practices. Most of this information was included in her last book, published in 1928. She had earlier become interested in the political issues around the Balkans, and allied herself with the Albanians in their attempts to become a national entity. Her skill as an artist was shown in the watercolors, drawings and photographs with which she illustrated her books.

Durham also collected clothing and embroidery from Yugoslavia and Albania, forming what became the Durham Collection in the Bakfield Museum, Halifax. She made careful notes on these items as well, which appear in a catalogue of her collection. Other artifacts were placed in the Pitt-Rivers Museum, Oxford, and the British Museum. Balkan scholars consider Durham a significant figure.   JH/MBO

PRIMARY SOURCES

Durham, Mary Edith. *Through the Lands of the Serb.* London: E. Arnold, 1904.
———. *The Burden of the Balkans.* London: E. Arnold, 1905.
———. *High Albania.* London: E. Arnold, 1909.
———. *Twenty Years of Balkan Tangle.* London: G. Allen & Unwin, 1920.
———. *Some Tribal Origins: Laws and Customs of the Balkans.* London: G. Allen & Unwin, 1928.

SECONDARY SOURCES

Birkett, Des. *Spinsters Abroad.* Oxford: Oxford University Press, 1989.
Hodgson, John. Introduction to Mary Edith Durham, *High Albania.* London: Virago, 1985.
———. "Edith Durham, Traveller and Publicist." in *Black Lambs and Grey Falcons,* ed. Antonia Young and John Allcock. Bradford: [Bradford University Press], [1991].
Myers, J. L., H. J. Braunholtz, and Beatrice Blackwood. "Mary Edith Durham." *Man* 45 (1945): 21–23. Tributes on her eightieth birthday.
Start, Laura E. *The Durham Collection of Garments and Embroideries from Albania and Yugoslavia.* Halifax: 1939. Includes notes by M. E. Durham.

DUROCHER, MARIE (JOSEFINA MATHILDE) (1809–1893)

French/Brazilian physician. Born 1809 in Paris. Married and widowed. Two children. Educated New Medical School in Rio de Janeiro (M.D., 1834). Private practice. Died 1893.

Although she was born in Paris, Marie Durocher moved to Brazil when she was eight years old. After being widowed and left with two children to support, Marie Durocher decided to become a physician. Influenced by midwife Anne Boivin, Durocher chose obstetrics at the New Medical School in Rio de Janeiro, becoming the first woman to receive a medical degree there (1834). One of the first women doctors in Latin America, she practiced for sixty years, often wearing men's clothes. She was elected to titular membership of the National Academy of Medicine in 1871.   JH/MBO

STANDARD SOURCES

Ireland; *LKW;* Lovejoy; Uglow 1982.

DURYEA, NINA (1868?–1951)

U.S. inventor, novelist, and travel writer. Born ca. 1868. Daughter of Franklin Walker Smith, architect and founder of U.S. YMCA. Married Chester Duryea (1898). One son, Chester B. Duryea, Jr. Died 3 November 1951.

When Nina Duryea married her husband, she did not realize that they would be separated for forty-four years, until he died. Chester Duryea killed his father in 1914, and spent the rest of his life in the hospital for the insane in New York. Nina Duryea lived in England and France before World War I, and began Duryea War Relief, headquartered in Paris. She invented a textile called torso-life that was used during World War II to manufacture army chest protectors. In addition to her inventions, she wrote popular books and plays, including *The House of Seven Gabblers, A Sentimental Dragon, The Voice Unheard,* and *Mallorca the Magnificent.* She died at the age of eighty-three.   JH/MBO

PRIMARY SOURCES

Duryea, Nina. *The House of Seven Gabblers.* New York: D. Appleton and Company, 1911.
———. *The Voice Unheard.* London: Simpkin, Marshall, Hamilton, Kent and Co., [1913].
———. *A Sentimental Dragon.* New York: George H. Doran Company, [1916].
———. *Mallorca the Magnificent.* New York: The Century Co., [1927].

SECONDARY SOURCES

New York Times, 3 November 1951. Obituary notice.

DUTCHER, ADELAIDE (fl. 1901)

U.S. physician and public health worker. Educated at Johns Hopkins University.

While Adelaide Dutcher was in medical school at Johns Hopkins University, she worked with William Osler, head of the department of medicine, on a research project to study environmental causes of tuberculosis. After interviewing 190 outpatients, white and black, who lived in the tenement districts of Baltimore and whose financial condition required them to continue working regardless of their health, she published "Where the Danger Lies in Tuberculosis" in 1900. In the slums of Baltimore, Dutcher identified the elemental problems: crowding, filth, darkness, lack of ventilation, appalling ignorance of the contagiousness of tuberculosis, and carelessness with infectious materials. She thought that education could correct many of the sanitary deficiencies of the poor. On her home visits, Dutcher emphasized the importance of regulations against spitting infected sputum. She urged the organization of a widespread educational campaign about the nature and prevention of tuberculosis. Along with Osler, she understood the impact of environment on transmission of disease and stressed in her study that housing represented a primary source of infection. She reported that many patients stated they became ill only after moving into quarters known to have been occupied previously by victims of the disease. Her study marked the first American investigation to stress the social origins of tuberculosis.   JH/MBO

PRIMARY SOURCES

Dutcher, Adelaide. "Where the Danger lies in Tuberculosis: A Study of the Social and Domestic Relations of Tuberculous Out-Patients." *Philadelphia Medical Journal* 7 (1900): 1031–1032.

SECONDARY SOURCES

Bates, Barbara. *Bargaining for Life: A Social History of Tuberculosis, 1876–1938*. Philadelphia: University of Pennsylvania Press, 1992.

Taylor, Lloyd C., Jr. *The Medical Profession and Social Reform, 1885–1945*. New York: St. Martin's Press, 1974. Dutcher discussed pages 30–32.

DUTTON, BERTHA PAULINE (1903–1994)

U.S. archeologist and anthropologist. Born 1903. Never married. Educated University of Nebraska (B.A., 1935); University of New Mexico (M.A., 1937); Columbia University (Ph.D., 1952). Professional experience: Nebraska, Department of Child Welfare, secretary (1928–1932); University of New Mexico, Department of Anthropology, secretary (1933–1936); Museum of New Mexico, assistant to director Edgar L. Hewett (1936–1939), curator of ethnology (1939–1959), curator of exhibits (1960–1962), Division of Research, head (1962–1965); Museum of Navajo Ceremonial Art, director (1966–1975); University of New Mexico, lecturer, TV courses and adult education (1947–1957). Concurrent experience: archeological digs in Alibates, Texas, Kuaua Pueblo site, Las Madres, N.M. (1933–1965), Bolivia and Peru (1935), Mexico and Guatemala (1953–1954, 1962–1963), Europe (1964), South America (1965), Japan (1968). Honors and memberships: New Mexico State University, Honorary LL.D., 1973. Died in 1994.

Bertha Dutton educated herself by working part-time as a secretary to the Department of Child Welfare in Nebraska while attending the University of Nebraska as a part-time student between 1928 and 1930. She was finally able to finish the degree in 1935 only after she had begun to study archeology in the Southwest. She attended her first archeological dig in 1932, working on a site at Alibates in Texas under Marjorie Lambert. From 1933 to 1935, Dutton

worked as a secretary to the anthropology department of the University of New Mexico, while beginning a master's degree program in anthropology there, which she completed in 1937. In 1935, she was awarded an ALICE FLETCHER Traveling Fellowship, which allowed her to travel to Peru and Bolivia; the same year she was awarded a School of American Research Fellowship. She met Edgar L. Hewett, and took a position with him as his administrative assistant at the new Museum of New Mexico, established at the Palace of the Governors, in Sante Fe. She persuaded him to make her curator of ethnology at the Museum in Santa Fe, where she began to develop collections and create important displays about the American Indians of the Southwest.

Her interest in the education of young women led her to work with the Girl Scout movement from 1946 to 1947, including young Indian girls in her troop of Senior Girl Scouts, leading them on a series of mobile archeological expeditions. She wrote about one of the first expeditions for the museum publication *El Palacio* in 1947. At least one girl became an anthropologist as a result of this training: the ethnobotanist Vorsila Bohrer.

From the late 1940s to the 1950s, Dutton also lectured as an instructor in anthropology on TV and in adult education classes for the University of New Mexico. A Blodgett research fellowship and an award from the American Association of University Women allowed her to do archeological research in Mexico and Guatemala in 1953 and 1954. But in spite of her archeological interests, Dutton remained as the curator of ethnology until 1959, when she was made curator of exhibits and then became head of museum research in 1962, which allowed her to expand her archeological work. She received a Werner Gren Foundation award to excavate the old pueblo of Las Madras in the Galisteo Basin in Mexico and to map out prehistoric pueblo migration patterns into New Mexico.

Retiring from the Museum of New Mexico in 1966, Dutton moved to the Museum of Navaho Ceremonial Art, and served as its director until 1975, when she was seventy-two. Her colleagues, including her first instructor, Marjorie Lambert, honored her with a collection of articles in 1969. She continued to be active on a series of museum and Southwest advisory boards until 1980. Dutton published a very popular book on the Indians of the American Southwest in 1975, and followed that with a book on southwestern Indian myths and legends in 1978.   JH/MBO

PRIMARY SOURCES

Dutton, Bertha. "Leyit Kin, a Small House Ruin in Chaco Canyon, New Mexico." *School of American Research Monograph* no. 1, 5, 1935.

———. "The Navajo Wind Way Ceremonial." *El Palacio* 48, no. 4 (1941): 73–82.

———. *Sun Father's Way: The Kiva Murals of Kuana.* Albuquerque: University of New Mexico Press, 1962.

———. "Mesoamerican Culture Traits Which Appear in the American Southwest." *Proceedings of the 35th International Congress of Americanists* 1 (1964): 481–492.

———. *Indians of the American Southwest.* Englewood Cliffs, N.J.: Prentice-Hall, 1975.

SECONDARY SOURCES

Babcock, Barbara A., and Nancy J. Parezo. *Daughters of the Desert.* 1988. Dutton discussed on pages 134–137, with portrait.

Morris, Elizabeth Ann and Caroline B. Olin. "Bertha Pauline Dutton, 1903–1994." *American Antiquity* 62 (1997): 652–658.

Schroeder, Albert H. *Collected Papers in Honor of Bertha Pauline Dutton.* With contributions from Patrick H. Beckett [et al.]. Albuquerque. Archaeological Society of New Mexico, 1979.

DUTTON, LORAINE ORR (1898–?)

U.S. pathologist. Born 2 August 1989 in Waco, Tex. Educated Texas Christian University (A.B., 1918; M.S. 1921); University of Tennessee (M.D., 1931). Professional experience: United States Public Health Service, field investigator (1918); United States laboratories in Siberia (1918–1919); University of California, teaching fellow (1920); Texas Christian University, instructor in bacteriology (1920–1921); Baptist Memorial Hospital, Memphis, Tenn., assistant director of laboratories (1921–1924); Methodist Hospital, director of laboratories (1924–1929); associated with private clinics and pathological labs (1932–?).

After initially getting a bachelor's and master's degree at Texas Christian University, Lorraine Dutton held a number of positions in public health. She went to the University of Tennessee, where she earned a medical degree in 1931.

Most of her research was on fungi as respiratory allergens. Her special interests were in clinical pathology and allergies. She was a member of the American Medical Association, the Association for the Study of Allergy, and the Medical and Surgical Association of the Southwest.   JH/MBO

STANDARD SOURCES
AMS 4–8.

DYE, MARIE (1891–?)

U.S. home economist and nutritionist. Born 13 September 1891 in Chicago. Educated University of Chicago (B.S., 1914; M.S., 1917; Ph.D., 1933); Michael Reese Hospital, fellow (1921–1922). Professional experience: Starretts School for Girls, Illinois, *teacher (1916–1917); Technical Normal School, teacher (1917–1918); Chicago public high school, teacher (1918–1919); Michigan State College, research associate professor of home economics (1922–1929), professor, dean (from 1929). Death date unknown.*

Marie Dye, who received all three of her degrees from the University of Chicago, was a member of the Chemical Society, the Society of Biological Chemistry, Dietetic Association, Society for Research in Child Development, and the Home Economics Association (secretary, 1921–1933; treasurer, 1942–1944; and president, 1948–1950).

After beginning her career as a secondary school teacher she moved to Michigan State College where she eventually was professor and Dean. Her research topics included basic problems of nutrition, basal metabolism, the relation of vitamin A to chlorophyll content of plants, metabolism in obesity, and the nutritional requirements of children.   JH/MBO

STANDARD SOURCES
Debus.

DYER, HELEN MARIE (1895–?)

U.S. biochemist. Born 26 May 1895 in Georgetown, Washington, D.C., to Florence (Robertson) and Joseph Edwin Dyer. Three siblings. Never married. Educated Goucher College (B.A., 1917); George Washington University (M.S., 1929; Ph.D., 1935). Professional experience: Mount Holyoke College, physiology instructor (1919–1920); U.S. Public Health Service, Hygienic Laboratory, junior and assistant pharmacologist (1920–1928); George Washington University, biochemistry teacher; National Cancer Institute of the National Institute of Health, Bethesda, Md. biochemist (1942–1972). Honors and memberships: Goucher College Achievement and Service Award for Teaching and Researching (1958); Goucher College, honorary D.Sc. (1965); Garvan Medal of the American Chemical Society (1962); Iota Sigma Pi, honorary member (1972). Member of Goucher Alumnae Club of Washington, American Association for the Advancement of Science, American Chemical Society, Sigma Xi, American Association of Biological Chemistry, Institute of Nutrition, American Association for Cancer Research. Death date unknown.

Helen Dyer, one of the early women chemists, made key discoveries in biochemistry, metabolism, and nutrition. Her research was the forerunner of an entirely new concept in biochemistry that had tremendous impact in the medicine field. Dyer made these key discoveries throughout her college and work life, which consisted of lecturing in university classrooms and researching in various laboratories. She did all of this because of the way her teachers inspired her. This inspiration she later returned to her students.

Dyer went to public school and was not particularly interested in science, but took some science-related courses. While attending school, she was active in sports and extracurricular activities. After high school, Dyer went to Goucher College, where she was offered a scholarship. She earned her bachelor's degree in biology with a minor in physiology. Dyer had planned to teach in China, but when World War I broke out in Europe, she returned to Washington and performed war work for the Red Cross and thereafter for the Civil Service Commission.

After the end of World War I, Dyer realized that in order to teach she must further her own learning. She started taking extra courses at Mount Holyoke, where she was offered a job teaching physiology. She decided to return to Washington and took a job in the Chemotherapy Laboratory at the Hygienic Laboratory of the U.S. Public Health Service. Here she was to work, not only on the toxicity of chemotherapeutic drugs in rats and other animals, but also on the activity of those drugs on an organism. All of the work from this research led her to the conclusion that arsenicals and other metals reacted in the body with the sulfhydryl compounds and thus became toxic to both the host tissue and the organism. In 1925, she and Carl Voegtlin began their study on some experimental rat tumors. They learned how these tumors grew and determined their rate of growth. Because of the negative results, this study was not published.

After working at the Hygenic Laboratory for about seven years, Dyer went to George Washington University to do her graduate work. She took organic and biochemistry courses and wrote a thesis, "The Effect of Growth of Rous Sarcoma on the Chemistry of Blood of Young Chicks," in 1929. She decided to stay and teach graduate courses in biochemistry, while working on her doctoral degree under Vincent du Vigneard. Dyer earned her doctorate in 1935 and continued to teach graduate courses in biochemistry and the chemistry of nutrition. Throughout her teaching career, she served as an inspiration to many students at the university.

In 1942, Dyer left George Washington University to return to work under Carl Voegtlin, who was then the head of the National Cancer Institute (NCI) of the National Institute of Health in Bethesda, Maryland. The Civil Service Commission had limited the personnel to one hundred, so Dyer was appointed as a fellow as was one of the other early women biochemists in the group. She continued to study cancer-related biochemistry. She also participated in a group research project, investigating the immunological effect in cancer. This work led her to develop certain techniques for isolating proteins and to conduct research on the effect of protein from an animal's own tumor.

Based on her research and studies, Dyer compiled the first comprehensive index of tumor chemotherapy in 1949. In this index, she discussed the earliest chemical treatments and the evolution and recent developments in tumor chemotherapy. Dyer's index served as one of the most essential aids to the National Cancer Institute in the development of its cancer chemotherapy program. Dyer went on to publish sixty articles on tumor chemotherapy.

While Dyer worked at the National Cancer Institute, she worked in the section called "Nutrition and Chemical Carcinogenosis." Working under Harold Morris, she made significant contributions in the study of cancer. She was the first to synthesize an amino acid antimetabolite. She earned the Garvan Medal in 1962 for her research in biochemistry. This was just one of the numerous awards that Dyer received. She was awarded an honorary degree of doctor of science from Goucher College in 1965; she received the Goucher College Achievement and Service Award for Teaching and Research in 1958; and became a national honorary member of Iota Sigma Pi in 1972. In addition to these awards and honors, Dyer was a member of numerous clubs and societies. She was one of the United States delegates to the International Cancer Congress; head of Goucher Alumnae Club of Washington (1951), and a fellow of the AAAS. Dyer belonged to the American Chemical Society, Sigma Xi, the Polonium Chapter of Iota Sigma Pi, the American Association of Biological Chemistry, the Institute of Nutrition, the Society of Experimental Biology and Medicine, the American Association for Cancer Research, Sigma Delta Epsilon, and numerous other societies.

Dyer continued to be a member of these groups even after her retirement in 1965. Although she was retired due to her age, she did not formally retire until 1972, for she continued active research in the field of cancer causation. She continued to review grants and technical papers for many years.

Dyer was a pioneer in the cancer-related field and she used her knowledge to make contributions. In a 1965 speech, awarding Helen Dyer the honorary degree from Goucher College, the presenter stated that, "in her life and work she has exemplified in high degree three traits . . . that are responsible for the staggering achievement of modern science: intellectual courage and imagination, practical ingenuity and skill and finally undiscouraged persistence and devotion." Because of her devotion to biochemistry, Dyer is a female chemist who has flourished in her work and has made tremendous contributions to her field. NR

PRIMARY SOURCES

Dyer, Helen M. With Joseph H. Roe. "Further Studies on the Blood Chemistry of Hens Bearing the Rous Sarcoma No. 1." *American Journal of Cancer* 18 (1932): 888.
———. "An Index of Tumor Chemotherapy." Washington, D.C.: Government Printing Office, 1950. The first major

work discussing the earliest chemical treatments and developments in tumor chemotherapy.

———. With Margaret G. Kelly. "Cultivation of Tumors in the Anterior Chambers of the Eyes of Guinea Pigs." *Journal of National Cancer Institute* 7 (1946): 177–182.

———. With Harold P. Morris. "An Effect of N-2-Flourenyl-acetamide on the Metabolism of L-Tryptophan in Rats." *Journal of National Cancer Institute* 25 (1961): 315–329.

Roe, Joseph, and Helen Dyer. "Biochemical Studies of Malignant Conditions." *American Journal of Cancer* 15 (1931): 725–731.

SECONDARY SOURCES
Brennan, Mairin. "1962 Garvan Medalist Celebrates 100th Birthday." *Chemical and Engineering News* 73 (29 May 1995): 53.

"Helen Dyer." *Chemical and Engineering News* 40 (6 August 1962): 58.

Roscher, Nina M., and Chinh K. Nguyen. "Helen M. Dyer, a Pioneer in Cancer Research." *Journal of Chemical Education* 63 (1986): 253–255.

Sarada, T. "Doctor Helen M. Dyer, a Pioneer Biochemist." Paper presented at the 178th National Meeting of the American Chemical Society, Washington, D.C., September 1979.

"Trends in Cancer Research through the Years Analyzed." *Buffalo Evening News,* 16 February 1963.

Wisswesser, Wm. J. Letter to ACS Council Committee on Women Chemists, 4 January 1978. Archives of the American Chemical Society(?).

STANDARD SOURCES
AMS 6–8, P 9, P&B 10–11; Grinstein 1993; Shearer and Shearer 1997.

DYLAZANKA, MARIA (1886–1966)
Polish micropaleontologist. Born 1886. Died 1966.

Maria Dylazanka was a Polish micropaleontologist who worked on the Foraminifera.   JH/MBO

SECONDARY SOURCES
Bieda, Franciszek. "Maria Dylazanka (1886–1966)." *Rocznik polskiego Towarzystwa geologicznego.* 40, nos. 3–4 (1971 [1970]): 499–500.

STANDARD SOURCES
Sarjeant.

E

EARLE, MARIE THERESA (VILLIERS) (1836–1925)

British botanical artist and horticulturist. Born 8 June 1836, probably in Hertfordshire. Twin sisters. Married Captain C. W. Earle (1864). Four sons. Educated by governesses; South Kensington and London schools of art. Professional experience: Created a garden in Cobham, Surrey, and wrote extensively on gardens. Died 27 February 1925 in Cobham, Surrey.

Marie Theresa Villiers was born a year after her parents' marriage; her twin sisters arrived the following year. Her interest in gardening came late in her life, although her childhood garden at Hertfordshire may have inspired her subsequent work.

During their marriage of only eight years, Villiers's parents were very much in love, and the family was happy and vibrant. However, upon the death of her father from tuberculosis at Nice in 1843, her mother became withdrawn. Villiers's education was handed over to governesses. Her mother did, however, provide the children with an opportunity to travel, supplying them with a broader education than a schoolroom could dispense. Villiers attended lectures and studied art, becoming a proficient amateur painter. She was especially influenced by William Morris and his *Lectures on Art*.

In 1864, Villiers married Captain C. W. Earle. They lived in Bryanston Square, London, and had three sons. Their home was a center of artistic and intellectual activities. During this time, Maria Earle was not especially interested in gardening. However, after the death of her husband in a bicycle accident, she moved from London to a house called Woodlands in Cobham, Surrey, surrounded by a large block of land. With this raw material, she learned about practical botany, wrote books on the subject, and painted plants. She is best known as the author of *Pot-pourri from a Surrey Garden*. She participated in the activities of the Botanical Exchange Club.

JH/MBO

PRIMARY SOURCES

Earle, Maria Theresa. *Pot-pourri from a Surrey Garden*. London: Smith, Elder, 1897.

———. *More Pot-pourri from a Surrey Garden*. London: Smith, Elder, 1899.

———. *A Third Pot-pourri*. London: Smith, Elder, 1903.

———. *Memoirs and Memories*. London: Smith, Elder, 1911.

———. With E. Case. *Gardening for the Ignorant*. London: Macmillan, 1912.

SECONDARY SOURCES

Gardeners Chronicle 1925: 174. Obituary notice.

Jones, Anna. *Mrs. Earle's Pot-pourri*. London: British Broadcasting Corp.: 1982.

Massingham, Betty. "Mrs. C. W. Earle: An Appreciation." *Gardener's Chronicle* 9 September 1961: 198–199.

"Mrs. C. W. Earle." *Botanical Society Exchange Club of the British Isles, Report* 1925, 846–847. Obituary notice.

STANDARD SOURCES

Desmond; *WWW,* vol. 2, 1916–1928.

EASTWOOD, ALICE (1859–1953)

U.S. botanist. Born 19 January 1859 in Toronto, Canada, to Eliza Jane (Gowdey) and Colin Eastwood. Educated Oshawa Convent, near Toronto; East Denver High School, Denver, Colo., (graduated 1879). Never married. Professional experience: East Denver High School, teacher (1879–1890); California Academy of Sciences, curator of botany (1892–1949). Died 30 October 1953 in San Francisco.

Throughout a childhood fraught with separation, loss, and uncertainty, Alice Eastwood persevered in her quest for knowledge. She was to become the only woman starred for distinction in every volume of *American Men of Science* published during her lifetime. Until she was six years old, she lived on the grounds of the Toronto Asylum for the Insane, where her father was superintendent. When her mother died (1865), her father attempted to establish himself as a storekeeper, placing the three children in the care of his brother, William Eastwood, at the latter's country estate. Allowed to roam freely in the countryside, Alice became interested in plants. Her uncle encouraged her interest, and the two often discussed the flora of the area.

Although the family was reunited for a short time, Eastwood's store was a failure, and he moved to Colorado, taking his son but leaving his two daughters behind to be educated at a convent. Despite the limitations of the convent education, Alice's six years there were useful to her future botanical work, because she spent much of her time with a priest, Father Pugh, who had planted an experimental orchard for use by the convent. She also acquired a love of music from a nun whom she respected.

When Alice was fourteen, her father sent for the girls to join him in Denver. During the construction of their house, Alice worked as a nursemaid for a French family with a large library. Along with the opportunity to read was the chance to study plants when she accompanied the family to the mountains. After the completion of their home, Eastwood kept house for her family and attended public schools. Through her own tenacity and with the help of understanding teachers, she was able to make up for her academic deficiencies and enter high school. Although a further interruption occurred when a financial crisis forced her to take a job in a millinery factory, she kept up with her schoolwork and graduated as valedictorian.

The immediate problem of earning a living forced Eastwood to put aside her ambition to become a botanist and take a job teaching at East Denver High School. By saving from her meager salary, she was able to finance summer collecting expeditions to the Rocky Mountains and to purchase botanical books. The plants she collected on these expeditions became the nucleus of the University of Colorado Herbarium at Boulder.

In 1881, during a visit to the East, Eastwood made a tour of the Gray Herbarium at Harvard University and met its creator, the botanist Asa Gray (1810–1888). Back in Colorado, she was introduced to the British biologist Alfred Russel Wallace (1823–1913), whom she accompanied up the fourteen-thousand-foot Grays Peak during the alpine flowering season of 1887.

A successful small real estate venture improved Eastwood's financial situation and gave her more freedom to travel. On a visit to the California Academy of Sciences in San Francisco in 1890 she met MARY KATHARINE BRANDEGEE, curator of botany at the academy, and her husband. At the Brandegees'

request, she obtained a leave from her teaching position in order to write for their magazine, *Zoe,* and to help organize the academy's herbarium. She returned to Colorado and finished a book, *A Popular Flora of Denver, Colorado,* which she published at her own expense in 1893.

When Katharine Brandegee wrote to Eastwood in the summer of 1892 offering her a $75-per-month salary at the California Academy, Eastwood accepted. Returning to San Francisco in December 1892, she began the task of organizing the botanical collection. The Brandegees left the academy the following year, and Eastwood absorbed both of their jobs—curator of botany and editor of *Zoe.* Her curatorial duties were relieved at intervals by collecting trips. On one of these, a willow-collecting expedition to Dawson, in the Yukon Territory, she made the three-hundred-mile trip from Whitehorse to Dawson in an open carriage on runners over snow and frozen rivers.

Eastwood remained at the academy for fifty-seven years, with only one major interruption. After the earthquake and fire of 1906, which destroyed the academy building, she spent six years studying at the herbaria of the Smithsonian Institution in Washington, the New York Botanical Garden, the Arnold Arboretum in Boston, Kew Gardens and the British Museum in London, Cambridge University, and the Jardin des Plantes in Paris, as part of the work of restoring the San Francisco collection. (It had been through Eastwood's heroism that many of the academy's records and botanical specimens were preserved: consigning her own possessions to the fire, she had saved much of the irreplaceable material of the academy.) When she retired in 1950, she was invited to serve as honorary president of the Seventh International Botanical Congress in Stockholm. The ninety-one-year-old Eastwood flew to Sweden, where she sat in the chair of Carolus Linnaeus—the high point of her trip. Active until the end of her life, Eastwood died in San Francisco at the age of ninety-four.

With very little formal training, Alice Eastwood became one of the most knowledgeable systematic botanists of her time. A specialist in the flowering plants of the Rocky Mountains and California coast, she made important additions to the taxonomic body of knowledge. Moreover, she contributed to the popular literature on plants. Her devoted curatorship made the botanical collection at the California Academy a valued research tool.   MBO

PRIMARY SOURCES

Eastwood, Alice. *A Popular Flora of Denver, Colorado.* San Francisco: Zoe Publishing Co., [1893].

———. Bibliography. *California Academy of Sciences, Proceedings* 25 (1949): xv–xxiv. This volume is dedicated to Eastwood in commemoration of fifty years of service as curator of the department of botany of the California Academy of Sciences. Supplemented by list in the ten-year index, 1932–1966, of *Leaflets of Western Botany* 25 (1968): 114–116.

Correspondence and other papers (from 1906) at the California Academy of Sciences.

SECONDARY SOURCES

Dakin, Susanna Bryant. *The Perennial Adventure: A Tribute to Alice Eastwood, 1859–1953*. San Francisco: California Academy of Sciences, 1954. Biographical information on Eastwood.

"Eastwood, Alice." *New York Times,* 31 October 1953. Obituary notice.

Howell, John T. "Alice Eastwood, 1859–1953." *Taxon* 3 (1954): 98–100.

Science n.s. 40 (4 September, 1914): 341.

Wilson, Carol Green. *Alice Eastwood's Wonderland: The Adventures of a Botanist*. San Francisco: California Academy of Sciences, 1955.

STANDARD SOURCES

AMS 1–8; Bonta; *NAW;* Ogilvie 1986; Shearer and Shearer 1996.

EAVES, ELSIE (1898–1983)

U.S. civil engineer. Educated University of Colorado, Boulder (B.S., 1920). Professional experience: Engineering News Record, Construction Economics Department, manager. Died 27 March 1983 in Roslyn, N.Y.

Elsie Eaves has a number of "firsts" behind her name. She was the first woman to be elected an honorary member of the American Society of Civil Engineers (1979) and the first woman to be elected to this society as an associate member, a fellow, and a life member. Much of her work was concerned with systems thinking. This work was rewarded when she was the first woman to be elected to the American Association of Cost Engineers. She did basic research on indexes and cost trends and developed a nationwide system of collecting, analyzing, and reporting statistical and economic information on construction. This work formed the basis for industry standards. She received many awards for her work on engineering economics. Although her work was not in the area of technical engineering, it was vital to the success of her discipline.   JH/MBO

SECONDARY SOURCES

Trescott, Martha Moore. "Women in the Intellectual Development of Engineering." In Kass-Simon and Farnes, 147–187.

EBERS, EDITH (KNOTE) (1894–1974)

German geologist and geomorphologist. Born 4 December 1894 in Nürnberg to Hermine and Karl Heinrich Knote. Married. Educated University of Munich; University of Heidelberg (doctorate). Professional experience: Bavarian Academy of Science, private researcher. Honors and memberships: German Academy of Academic Graduates, vice-president; Bavarian Nature Conservation Movement, active member; Bavarian Academy of Science, prize winner; Germany Quarternary Geology Union, Quarternary Geology Section, honorary member. Died 13 September 1974.

After Edith Ebers obtained her doctorate, she did not hold a university position, but her work was supported by the Bavarian Academy of Science. She continued working and publishing on the geology of the Quarternary with the academy's support for thirty-five years. She studied glacial erosion, glacial and periglacial deposits, and drumlins. Her numerous publications were well received. Two editions of her major work on alpine geology appeared after her death.

JH/MBO

PRIMARY SOURCES

Ebers, Edith. *Die Eiszeit im Landschaftsbilde des bayerischen Alpenvorlandes.* Munich: C. H. Beck, 1934.

———. *Der Gletschergarten au der deutschen Alpenstrasse.* Remagen: Verlag des Amtes für Landeskunde, 1952.

———. *Felsbilder der Alpen.* Hallein, Austria: H. Nowak, Burgfried Verlag, 1980.

SECONDARY SOURCES

Kürschners Deutscher Gelehrten-Kalender. *Bio-Bibliographisches Verzeichnis deutschsprachiger Wissenschaftler der Gegenwart.* Berlin, 1928–1997.

Vidal, Helmut. "Edith Ebers. 1894–1974." *Eiszeitalter und Gegenwart.* 25 (1974): 289–295.

STANDARD SOURCES

Debus; Strohmeier.

ECCELLO OF LUCANIA
(fl. 5th or 4th century B.C.E.)

Greek/Italian mathematician, natural philosopher. Born Lucania.

Eccello may have been confused with Occello, both of whom are mentioned by Gilles Ménages as Pythagorean philosophers from Lucania. We know nothing of her work, but assume a mathematical interest from her Pythagorean background.   JH/MBO

STANDARD SOURCES

Kersey; Ménage.

ECHECRATIA THE PHILIASIAN
(fl. 5th century B.C.E.)
Greek/Italian mathematician, natural philosopher. Born Philiasia. Father Echecrates.

Diogenes Laertius mentioned Echecrates, the father of Echecratia, as one of the last of the Pythagoreans. Therefore, we can assume that his daughter flourished in the fifth century B.C.E. We are dependent on Ménage for any information about her. He assumes that since she was the daughter of a Pythagorean that she, too, would be a mathematician.

JH/MBO

STANDARD SOURCES
Kersey; Ménage.

ECHOLS, DOROTHY JUNG (1916–1997)
U.S. geologist. Born 1916 in New York City in 1936. Married Leonard S. Echols, Jr. (1941). Four children. Educated New York University (B.S., 1936); Columbia University (M.S., 1938); Washington University (postgraduate work). Professional experience: Houston, Tex., geologist and micropaleontologist (1938–1946); Washington University, St. Louis, laboratory instructor (1948), assistant professor (1960), associate professor (1976); consulting company with Doris Curtis (1982). Died 4 February 1997 in St. Louis, Mo., of lung cancer.

After Dorothy Jung earned her master's degree in geology from Columbia University, she moved to Houston, where she worked until 1946. She met her future husband, Leonard S. Echols, Jr., a research chemist with Shell, whom she married in 1941. The couple had four children. Leonard Echols was transferred to the Wood River Research Center in 1947, and the couple moved to St. Louis, where Dorothy began her teaching career at Washington University. Beginning as a laboratory instructor and working toward a doctoral degree (which she never finished), she slowly progressed to assistant professor and then associate professor. Although she was an excellent teacher, Echols left the university in 1982 to form a consulting company with DORIS CURTIS. She also participated, along with Curtis, as a paleontologist on the Deep Sea Drilling Project aboard the *Glomar Challenger*. Echols produced many research articles on paleontological and geological subjects.

CK

PRIMARY SOURCES
Echols, Dorothy J. With Malkin, D. S. "Marine Sedimentation and Oil Accumulation; II. Regressive Marine Offlap and Overlap-Offlap." *Bulletin of the American Association of Petroleum Geologists* 32, no. 2 (1948): 252–261.
———. With others. "Eocene Stratigraphy, a Key to Produc-

tion [of oil and gas]." *Bulletin of the American Association of Petroleum Geologists* 32, no. 1 (1948): 11–33. Includes illustrations and map.
———. "New Paleozoic Ostracode Genera and Species Reported in Three Russian Publications 1952." *Micropaleontologist* 8, no. 3 (1954): 30–40.
———. With others. "Leg 58 of the Cruises of the Drilling Vessel Glomar Challenger; Yokahama, Japan to Okinawa, Japan; December 1977–January 1978." *Initial Reports of the Deep Sea Drilling Project* 58 (1980): 695–699. Includes illustrations, plates, and a table.

SECONDARY SOURCES
Picou, Edward B., Jr. "Dorothy Jung Echols 1916–1997." *GCSSEPM News* (the newsletter of the Gulf Coast Section Society of Economic Paleontologists and Mineralogists) 44 (July 1997): 9.

ECKERSON, SOPHIA HENNION (d. 1954)
U.S. botanist and plant physiologist. Born in Tappan, N.J., to Ann Hennion and Albert Bogert. Married. Educated Smith College (A.B., 1905; fellow, 1905–1906; A.M. 1907); University of Chicago (Ph.D., 1911). Professional experience: Smith College, assistant first fellow and demonstrator (1908–1909); University of Chicago, assistant plant physiologist (1911–1915), instructor (1916–1920); USDA, Washington, D.C., Bureau of Plant Industry (1919–1921), Cereals Division, physiologist (1921–1922); University of Wisconsin, physiologist and microchemist (1921–1923); Boyce Thompson Institute, N.Y., plant microchemist (1923–1940). Retired 1940. Died 19 July 1954.

Sophia Eckerson's birthdate is unknown. After working in order to help her younger brothers study medicine and art, she entered Smith College as a "mature" student. There, after studying with William Francis Ganong, she received her bachelor's and master's degrees in physiology and microchemistry. Leaving Smith in 1909, she went to the University of Chicago where she earned a doctorate. She remained at the University of Chicago as an assistant plant physiologist and instructor until 1920 when she went to work at the U.S. Department of Agriculture. During her time with the USDA, she also worked as a physiologist and microchemist at the University of Wisconsin. In 1923 she joined the staff of the Boyce Thompson Institute as a plant microchemist, where she remained until retirement.

Early in her career, Eckerson published under the tutelage of Ganong. While still at Smith, she produced in mimeographed form a textbook, "Outlines of Plant Microchemistry." This text was widely used, but she declined to publish it, perhaps out of excessive modesty. Her work as a plant microchemist was widely recognized, and she received a star by her name in *American Men of Science.* She was a member of Phi Beta Kappa, Sigma Xi, and served as chair of the Physiological Section of the Botanical Society of America. Nothing is known of her marriage. After her retirement, she was known for her excellent garden. She died in Pleasant Valley, Connecticut, after a short illness, in July 1954.   JH/MBO

PRIMARY SOURCES

Eckerson, Sophia H. "A Physiological and Chemical Study of After-Ripening." Ph.D. diss., University of Chicago, 1911.

———. "Microchemical Studies of the Progressive Development of the Wheat Plant." *Washington Agricultural Experiment Station Bulletin* 139 (1917): 254–255.

———. "Protein Synthesis by Plants. I. Nitrate Reduction." *Botanical Gazette* 77 (1924): 377–390.

———. "Influence of Phosphorus Deficiency on Metabolism of the Tomato, *Lycopersicon esculentum* Mill." *Contributions from Boyce Thompson Institute* 3 (1931): 197–217.

———. "Conditions Affecting Nitrate Reduction by Plants." *Contributions from Boyce Thompson Institute* 4 (1932): 119–130.

———. "Separation of Cellulose Particles in Membranes of Cotton Fibers by Treatment with Hydrochloric Acid." *Contributions from Boyce Thompson Institute* 6 (1934): 189–203.

SECONDARY SOURCES

Hall, D. L. "Academics, Bluestockings, and Biologists: Women at the University of Chicago, 1892–1932." In *Expanding the Role of Women in the Sciences,* ed. A. M. Briscoe and S. M. Pfafflin, 300–320. New York: New York Academy of Sciences, 1979.

Pfeiffer, Norma E. "Sophia H. Eckerson, Plant Microchemist." *Science* 120 (December 1954): 820–821.

STANDARD SOURCES

American Women 1974; *AMS* 6–8; Bailey; Grinstein 1997 (article by Bonnie Konopak) Rossiter; Shearer and Shearer, *Life Sciences;* Siegel and Finley.

ECKSTORM, FANNIE PEARSON (HARDY) (1865–1946?)

U.S. ornithologist and historian. Born 18 June 1865 in Brewer, Maine, to Emeline Freeman Wheeler Hardy and Manly Hardy. Five siblings. Married Reverend Jacob A. Eckstorm (1893). Two children, Katharine Hardy and Paul. Educated public schools of Brewer; Abbott Academy in Andover, Mass.; Smith College (A.B., 1888). Honors and memberships: University of Maine, honorary master of arts degree (1926). Died 1946(?).

Fannie Hardy graduated from Smith College and five years later married the Reverend Jacob A. Eckstorm of Chicago.

The couple had two children, a daughter who died in 1901 at the age of seven, and a son who became a mining engineer and who died in 1945. Fannie Eckstorm followed her husband to pastorates in Portland, Oregon, Eastport, Maine, and Providence, Rhode Island. When Jacob Eckstorm died in 1899, Fannie Eckstorm returned to her home in Brewer, Maine, where she lived for forty-seven years and worked on her studies of the Maine woods.

Fannie's father, Manly Hardy, was responsible in large part for her interests in natural history. He was an observer of animals and often contributed to *Forest and Stream.* Before his death in 1910, he was recognized as an authority on birds and mammals of the region. Through his business in the fur trade, Manly could tell where a skin was taken by the texture of its fur alone. Thus, Fannie had an apt teacher. She took several long canoe trips into the far north with her father and later used the memories and the detailed scientific notes that she took to write her books on the north woods.

After the death of her husband, Eckstorm kept excellent journals and recalled information about the fauna of the area. A strong believer in the importance of conservation, she was an even stronger believer in the right of the native Maine woodsman to do as he pleased. She was sympathetic with the struggles of the natives when confronted by the local sheriff for illegal actions. She tended to champion unorthodox views on critical problems.   JH/MBO

PRIMARY SOURCES

Eckstorm, Fannie Pearson Hardy. *The Bird Book.* Boston: Heath, 1901.

———. *The Penobscot Man.* Boston: Houghton, Mifflin & Co., 1904.

———. "Thoreau's Maine Woods." *Atlantic Monthly* 102 (August 1908): 244–249.

———. *Indian Place-Names of the Penobscot Valley and the Maine Coast.* Orono: University of Maine Press, 1941.

SECONDARY SOURCES

Ring, Elizabeth. "Fannie Hardy Eckstorm: Maine Woods Historian." *New England Quarterly* 26 (1953): 45–64.

STANDARD SOURCES

AMS 1–2; *DAB; NAW* (article by Janet Wilson James); Siegel and Finley.

EDDY, BERNICE ELAINE (1903–)

U.S. microbiologist. Born 30 September 1903 in Glendale, W.Va. Married (1938). Two children. Educated Marietta College (A.B., 1924); University of Cincinnati (M.S., 1925; Ph.D., 1927). Professional experience: University of Cincinnati, assistant in pediatrics and bacteriology (1928–1929); Davis teaching fellow, bacteriology

(1929–1930); Marine Hospital, U.S. Public Health Service, La., laboratorian leprosarium (1931–1935); National Institutes of Health, associate bacteriologist (1937–1942), bacteriologist (1942–1948), senior bacteriologist (1948–1954), principal bacteriologist (1954–1963), microbiologist (from 1963). Concurrent experience: Cincinnati College of Pharmacy, lecturer (1929–1930). Honors and memberships: American Association for the Advancement of Science, Fellow; American Public Health Association, Fellow; American Society of Microbiologists; American Association of Immunologists; American Society of Tropical Medicine and Hygiene Research.

Bernice Eddy spent the majority of her career working for the National Institutes of Health, advancing from associate bacteriologist through the ranks to principal bacteriologist. Before going to the NIH she worked at a leprosarium in Louisiana for four years.

Her research was on the classification of pneumococci bacteria and the standardization of influenza viruses, vaccines, and adenovirus vaccines. Eddy also worked on hemoglobinophilic bacilli, tuberculin, the poliomyelitis virus, and tumor viruses. She was one of the first to describe the polyoma virus, which was later named the SE polyoma virus in honor of Eddy and her colleague Sarah Stewart.   JH/MBO

PRIMARY SOURCES

Eddy, Bernice E. "Search for Protective Bacteriophage and Enzymatic Agents in Pneumonic Sputums." Ph.D. diss., University of Cincinnati, 1927.

———. *Polyoma Virus.* Virology Monographs. New York: Springer-Verlag, 1969.

STANDARD SOURCES

AMS 7–8, B 9, P&B 10–14; Siegel and Finley; Stanley.

EDGE, ROSALIE BARROW (1881–1962)

U.S. zoologist. Born 1881. Honors and memberships: American Association of Mammalogists, Land Mammals Committee (1945 to 1947); Hawk Mountain Sanctuary Association, president; Emergency Conservation Committee (ECC), founder and chair (founded 1929). Died 1962.

Rosalie Edge was a conservation activist who joined the American Association of Mammalogists in 1930 and promptly joined committees having to do with conservation. In order to protest certain policies of the Audubon Society (specifically, ties between the Audubon Society and arms manufacturers), she founded the Emergency Conservation Committee in 1929. She demanded that groups such as the Pennsylvania Game Commission, *Nature* magazine and the Screen Directors' Guild adhere to the policies she advocated.   JH/MBO

SECONDARY SOURCES

Kaufman, Dawn M., Donald W. Kaufman, and Glennis A. Kaufman. "Women in the Early Years of the American Society of Mammalogists (1919–1949)." *Journal of Mammalogy* 77, no. 3 (1996): 642–654.

EDGELL, BEATRICE (1871–1948)

British psychologist. Born 1871 Tewksbury, Gloucestershire. Educated University College of Wales (B.A., 1894); University of London (1894; M.A., 1898); University of Würzburg (Ph.D., 1901); University of Wales (D.Litt., 1924). Professional experience: University of London, Bedford College, faculty (1897–1944), professor (from 1927). Honors and memberships: British Psychological Society; Aristotelian Society; Mind Association. Died 1948.

Beatrice Edgell was born in Tewksbury, England, and attended University College of Wales, followed by the University of London where she received a master's degree. After two years, she returned to school to take her doctorate in psychology at the University of Würzburg. She wrote articles about memory and contributed to the *Encyclopedia Britannica* (14th ed.). Edgell earned a second doctorate at the University of Wales in 1924. Her book *Mental Life* (1926) was the result of studies reflecting her fascination with mental processes and memory. Edgell's years teaching at Bedford College are considered the golden years of their psychology department.   KM

PRIMARY SOURCES

Edgell, Beatrice. *Mental Life.* London: Methuen, 1926; 2d. ed., 1929.

———. *Ethical Problems.* London: Methuen, 1929.

STANDARD SOURCES

Psychological Register, vol. 3, 1932.

EDGERTON, WINIFRED HARING (1862–1951)

U.S. mathematician. Born 1862. Married to (?) Merrill (1887). Four children. Educated Wellesley College (A.B., 1883); Columbia University (Ph.D., 1886). Professional experience: One of the original board of trustees members of Barnard College. Died 1951.

Winifred Edgerton, later Merrill, was the first woman to earn a doctorate in mathematics at Columbia University. From the time that she applied to Columbia, controversy surrounded her application. Admitted as an exceptional case, she was obliged, according to her son Hamilton Merrill, to dust the astronomical instruments and exert special care not to disturb the male students. One of her former classmates reported that the men in a course of celestial mechanics were sufficiently disturbed by her presence to ask the professor to choose the most difficult textbook he could find. The text was the same one that Edgerton had used at Wellesley, and she did very well in the course. In 1886, when Edgerton finished the work on her degree, women could still not officially be granted degrees. However, she was awarded the degree of Doctor of Philosophy *cum laude* in recognition of her superb work. The year after she graduated she married and in 1888 helped to found Barnard College. She continued to serve on the board of trustees until her husband complained that she was spending far too much time in the offices of two male lawyers.

Her dissertation was inspired by a book by mathematician Benjamin Pierce, *Ideality in the Physical Sciences.* Her topic was the unification of the several systems of mathematical coordinates. JH/MBO

PRIMARY SOURCES

Edgerton, Winifred. "Multiple Integrals: (1) Their Geometrical Interpretation in Cartesian Geometry; in Trilinears and Triplanars; in Tangentials; in Quaternions; and in Modern Geometry. (2) Their Analytical Interpretation in the Theory of Equations using Determinants, Invariants and Co-variants as Instruments in the Investigation." Ph.D. diss., Columbia University, 1886. In Rare Book and Manuscript Library.

SECONDARY SOURCES

Green, Judy, and Jeanne LaDuke. "Contributors to American Mathematics. An Overview and Selection." In Kass-Simon and Farnes.
"Mrs. Merrill, 88, Columbia Pioneer." *New York Times,* 1 April 1933.

EDGEWORTH, MARIA (1767–1849)

Irish novelist and amateur botanist. Born 1767 in Oxfordshire to the first of four wives of Richard Edgeworth who had children by all of his wives. Never married. Died 1849 in Edgeworthstown in County Longford.

Best known as a novelist, Maria Edgeworth wrote the very popular *Castle Rackrent* (1801), *Belinda* (1802), *The Absentee* (1812), and many other novels. She also wrote *Dialogues on Botany: For the Use of Young Persons* (1819), and she was one of the five women admitted as members (honorary) of the Royal Irish Academy.

The Edgeworth family was Anglo-Irish. Maria, although born in England, spent much of her childhood on the family estate at Edgeworthstown, County Longford. Richard Edgeworth, Maria's father, although intended for the bar, studied mechanics instead, and his interest brought him into contact with his contemporary scientific circle. He knew Sir Joseph

Banks, the president of the Royal Society; Captain Cook, the explorer; Nevil Maskelynes, the royal astronomer; and Erasmus Darwin, Charles's grandfather. JH/MBO

PRIMARY SOURCES

Edgeworth, Maria. *Dialogues on Botany: For the Use of Young Persons.* London: R. Hunter, 1819.

SECONDARY SOURCES

Britten, James and Boulger, George. *A Biographical Index of Deceased British and Irish Botanists.* 2d ed. London: Taylor and Frances, 1931. Edgeworth discussed on page 99.
Brück, Mary T. "Maria Edgeworth; Scientific 'Literary Lady.' " *Irish Astronomical Journal* 12, no. 1 (1996): 49–54.

STANDARD SOURCES

DNB, Praeger.

EDINGER, JOHANNA GABRIELLE OTELLIE (TILLY) (1897–1967)

German/U.S. vertebrate paleontologist. Born 13 November 1897, Frankfurt-am-Main, to Anna Goldsmidt and Ludwig E. Edinger. Never married. Educated University of Frankfurt (Dr. Phil. nat., 1921). Professional experience: University of Frankfurt, assistant in the Geology-Paleontology Institute (1920–1927); Naturmuseum Senckenberg, Frankfurt, curator of fossil vertebrates (1927–1938); Museum Comparative Zoology, paleontologist; Harvard University, research associate, research paleontologist (1940–1964), honorary research paleontologist (1964–1968); Guggenheim fellow (1943–1944); Wellesley College, instructor in zoology (1944–1945). Honors and memberships: Paleontologische Gesellschaft; Senckenberg naturf Gesellschaft (honorary); Society of Vertebrate Paleontology (past president); Society for Study of Evolution; American Academy of Arts and Sciences; Wellesley College (1950), University of Giessen (1957), University of Frankfurt (1964), honorary degrees. Died 26 May 1967 in Cambridge, Mass., after being struck by an automobile.

Tilly Edinger, widely respected vertebrate paleontologist and paleoneurologist, was the daughter of Ludwig Edinger, a famous comparative neurologist who helped to found that discipline. Her mother was dedicated to social welfare movements and a bust of her was erected in the local park after her death. Although Edinger's father did not approve of professional careers for women, his death, when she was in her early twenties, may have spurred her to pursue a doctorate in natural sciences at the University of Frankfurt where she studied geology and vertebrate paleontology, completing her degree in 1921 and writing her dissertation on the nothosaurs. She began as an assistant in the Geology and Paleontology Institute at the University of Frankfurt before she finished her degree, and held that position until 1927. She took over as curator of fossil vertebrates at the Senckenberg Natural History Museum in Frankfurt in 1928 and held that position even after the rise of Nazism. Her major work on fossil brains, *Die Fossilen Gehirne,* was published in 1929 and won her international recognition.

From 1934 to 1938, her position became precarious in Germany as a woman of Jewish ancestry. In 1938, although she was protected by the museum director, himself a Nazi until that time, it was discovered that she was still working quietly in the museum and she was expelled from her position. At the same time, her mother's bust was removed from the local park and Edingerstrasse, named after her father, was renamed. Realizing the need to leave Germany, she applied for a visa to Britain, which she obtained in May 1939, just before the outbreak of World War II. In 1940, aided by Alfred S. Romer, Ernst Mayr, and other scientists at Harvard's Museum of Comparative Zoology, she came to Cambridge, Massachusetts, and began to work there as a research associate. Because it was difficult to find sufficient funds to pay her a proper salary, she was urged to teach. For a year (1944–1945), Edinger taught comparative anatomy at Wellesley College, with some success, but her congenital deafness made teaching difficult for her. She returned to the museum and was appointed a research paleontologist. A Guggenheim fellowship (1943–1944) and a grant from the American Association of University Women (1950–1951) helped support her research. In 1948, she completed her major study of horse fossil brains, analyzed from casts made of the interior of skulls (endocasts). She also hoped to bring her German book on fossil brains out in a new edition, but the explosion of work in this field made her limit herself to an extensive bibliography of all the work done on endocasts from fossil skulls. Only parts 1–6 had been completed by the time of her death.

She received a number of honors during her lifetime. Wellesley College awarded her an honorary doctor of science degree in 1950. Subsequently, two German universities, including the University of Frankfurt honored her, and she was inducted as the honorary member of a number of German scientific societies. She was made a member of the Academy of Arts and Sciences, and in 1963–1964, she served as the president of the Society of Vertebrate Paleontology. She never married, but was remembered as a warm friend and colleague and as an outspoken and strong-minded opponent.

Her analysis, according to A. S. Romer and Stephen Jay Gould, helped establish the new field of paleoneurology. She demonstrated that brain evolution was more accurately interpreted directly from fossils rather than from a misleading hierarchy of modern or ancient forms. In the horse brain she showed that the forebrain had evolved several times, inde-

pendently, demonstrating that rates and styles of change varied in different lineages. According to Gould, her work ranks among the dozen or so major figures of modern vertebrate paleontology. On 26 May 1967 she was struck by an automobile, and she died in Cambridge the following day.

JH / MBO

PRIMARY SOURCES

Edinger, Tilly. *Die Fossilen Gehirne.* Berlin: J. Springer, 1929.
———. *Evolution of the Horse Brain.* New York: Geological Society of America, 1944.
———. With A. S. Romer, N. E. Wright, and R. V. Frank. *Bibliography of Fossil Vertebrates Exclusive of North America, 1509–1927.* 2 vols. New York: Geological Society of America, 1962.
———. "Paleoneurology, 1804–1966: An Annotated Bibliography." *Advances in Anatomy, Embryology and Cell Biology* 49, pts. 1–5, 1975. With a foreword by Bryan Patterson on her life.
Edinger's papers are held at the Museum of Comparative Zoology, Harvard University.

SECONDARY SOURCES

A.S.R. [Alfred Sherwood Romer]. "Tilly Edinger." *Society of Vertebrate Paleontology Newsletter* (October 1967): 51–53. With portrait.
Hofer, Helmut. ["In Memoriam Tilly Edinger"] *Gegenbaurs Morophogisches Jahrbuch* 113, no. 2. Includes complete bibliography of her publications.

STANDARD SOURCES

NAW(M) (article by Stephen Jay Gould); *Notable* (article by Sharon F. Suer).

EDKINS, NORA TWEEDY (1890–1977)

British physiologist. Born 1890. Married J. S. Edkins (1919). Educated Bedford College, London (first class honors in physiology, 1914; M.Sc., 1917; D.Sc., 1929). Professional experience: Bedford College, Department of Physiology, demonstrator, reader (1929). Honors and memberships: Physiological Society, member (elected 1927), committee member (1936–1940). Died 1977.

Nora Tweedy Edkins, the sister of MAY TWEEDY MELLANBY, graduated with first class honors in physiology from Bedford College, London, in 1914. She earned her master's degree in 1917. In 1919, she became the second wife of physiologist J. S. Edkins. In 1929, Edkins received her doctorate of science. In this same year, her husband retired from his position as head of the physiology department and Nora succeed him as head. However, she was denied the title of professor because of her sex and remained at the rank of reader. During

World War II, Edkins and MARGARET M. A. MURRAY had the task of supervising the evacuation of her students to Cambridge. She had an excellent reputation as a teacher, for the pass rate of her students was well over 90 percent.

Edkins exhibited considerable skill in technical laboratory work, resulting in a number of papers in collaboration with Margaret Murray. Her particular area of research was on gastric and intestinal absorption. Together, Murray and Edkins demonstrated accelerated gastric absorption of ethyl alcohol in the presence of carbon dioxide. Continuing with the same experimental design, they worked on the absorption of alcohol in the small intestine, demonstrating a slight increase in alcohol absorption but not to the same extent as in the stomach. Edkins also demonstrated that carbohydrates were absorbed from the stomach and that this absorption increased in the presence of alcohol. Many of her experiments were done *in vivo,* with decerebrated cats as well as intact rabbits and cats under anesthesia. She and Murray also did experiments on human volunteers. All of the experiments confirmed the acceleration of gastric absorption in the presence of alcohol.

Murray continued to teach at Bedford after her retirement in 1947. She taught some classes until 1960.　　　JH

PRIMARY SOURCES
Edkins, Nora, and Margaret Murray. "Influence of CO_2 on the Absorption of Alcohol by the Gastric Mucosa." *Journal of Physiology* 59 (1924): 271–275.
———. "The Effect of CO_2 on the Absorption of Alcohol and the Influence of Alcohol on the Diffusion of CO_2 in the Small Intestine." *Journal of Physiology* 62 (1926): 13–16.

STANDARD SOURCES
Women Physiologists.

EDSON, FANNY CARTER (1887–1952)

U.S. petroleum geologist. Born 5 October 1887 in Chicago, Ill., to Cora Belle (Walbridge) and Byron Beach Carter. Two sisters. Married Frank Aaron Edson (divorced). One daughter Eleanor (Edson) Burtnett. Educated public schools Hinsdale, Ill.; University of Wisconsin (bachelor's degree, 1910; master's degree, 1914); University of Oklahoma and Stanford University (graduate work). Professional experience: Roxana Petroleum Corporation, Tulsa, Okla. (later Shell Oil Co.), researcher (1924–1938); private consultant (from 1938); United States Geological Survey stratigrapher (1943–1945); private practice (1946). Died 10 June 1952 in Chillicothe, Ill.

Chicago-born Fanny Carter Edson, one of three daughters of Cora Belle and Byron Carter, was proud of her heritage. Her father, a mechanical engineer, was a University of Wis-

consin graduate whose grandparents had immigrated to Wisconsin from England in 1850. Her mother's ancestors had come even earlier from England to Connecticut. They eventually moved to Wisconsin, where Cora Belle was born; she also attended the University of Wisconsin. Fanny Carter majored in geology at the University of Wisconsin and was married shortly after graduation to Frank Aaron Edson. The marriage, which resulted in one daughter, was not a success; the couple divorced in 1925. She went with her husband, who was also a geologist, to Minnesota, where he was engaged in iron ore exploration. At this time, she saw the need for further education and completed the requirements for a master's degree at the University of Wisconsin. In 1917, the Edsons moved to Duluth, Minnesota, where their daughter, Eleanor, was born. During World War I, Frank Edson worked with the YMCA Field Service, causing him to be away from the family for long periods of time while he visited different army camps. Fanny Edson had various clerical jobs and taught general science in the public schools during this period. In 1921, she and Eleanor joined Frank in Norman, Oklahoma, where he was employed by the Oklahoma Geological Survey. Fanny Edson took graduate courses at the university while she was an instructor in the school of geology. During the academic year 1923–1924, Edson went to Stanford University, where she did special studies under Eliot Blackwelder and Austin Flint Rogers. After the divorce (1925) Edson was solely responsible for rearing her daughter, and accepted a position with Roxana Petroleum Corporation (now part of Shell Oil) in Tulsa, Oklahoma. Edson's duties at Roxana involved examining well samples of subsurface sediments and devising methods of stratigraphic correlation. The oil business was going through a revolution during this period, and science rather than chance was being used more frequently to determine where drilling should occur. Identifiers needed to be established particularly for the deeper oil-bearing formations, for the search for oil continued in ever deeper formations. Edson's task was to characterize these sand and limestone reservoir rocks and to determine their extent. To do this, she established laboratory facilities and procedures in Tulsa where she could detail the broad subdivisions of the stratigraphy and determine mineral assemblages. She supplemented her laboratory work with field studies. The rapid proliferation of oil discoveries kept her busy until the Depression. At this time, Shell downsized its operations, and the Tulsa office was placed directly under Edson's supervision.

After severing her relationship with Shell in 1938, she practiced independently, still maintaining some work in Tulsa. However, in 1940 she moved to Denton, Texas, to help a sister care for their aging parents. After her parents died, she accepted an appointment with the U.S. Geological Survey, where she was stationed first at Tulsa and then at

Denver. During her temporary employment with the survey, she produced two subsurface stratigraphic-structural cross sections of western Kansas and adjoining vicinities.

She resigned from the survey in 1945 and again did private consulting work. In 1946, she retired and lived first in Rome, Illinois, and then in Chillicothe, Illinois, where she lived with her daughter and three grandchildren. Edson published in the *Bulletin of the American Association of Petroleum Geologists,* publications of the Oklahoma Academy of Science, the *Proceedings of the Geological Society of America,* and the *American Mineralogist.*   JH/MBO

PRIMARY SOURCES

Edson, Fannie Carter. *Criteria for the Recognition of Heavy Minerals Occurring in the Mid-Continent Field.* Norman, Okla.: Oklahoma Geological Survey, 1925.

———. *Subsurface Geologic Cross Section from Ford County to Wallace County, Kansas.* Lawrence, Kans.: University of Kansas, 1945.

———. *Subsurface Geologic Cross Section from Ford County, Kansas, to Dallam County, Texas.* Lawrence, Kans.: Kansas Geological Survey, 1947.

SECONDARY SOURCES

Leiser, Jessie Bryan. "Fanny Carter Edson (1887–1952)." *Bulletin of the American Association of Petroleum Geologists* 37, no. 5 (1953): 1182–1186.

EDWARDS, EMMA WARD (1845–1896)

U.S. physician. Born 5 June 1845 in Newark, N.J. Married Arthur M. Edwards (1872). Children. Educated at local schools; Woman's Medical College, New York (M.D., 1870). Professional experience: Woman's Medical College, clinical assistant, dispensary physician and instructor; Newark, N.J., private practice. Honors and memberships: New Jersey State Medical Society, Essex County Medical Society. Died 28 March 1896 of dysentery in Clearwater, Fla.

Emma Ward grew up and was educated in the Newark, New Jersey, area in the normal fashion until she contracted an illness at age seventeen that put her under medical supervision for several years. During that time, she became fascinated with medicine and determined to become a physician. When the Woman's Medical College of the New York Infirmary opened in 1868, she joined the first class and graduated in 1870 as valedictorian. She remained as clinical assistant, dispensary physician, and instructor and also associated with a practicing male physician in New York for a short time. In April 1872, she married Arthur M. Edwards and they moved to Berkeley, California.

Unfortunately, Edwards's husband became incapacitated by illness only six years after their marriage, and the family

moved back to Newark where she had established a core of patients. She returned to her general practice with enormous success. She was a member of the New Jersey State Medical Society and the Essex County Medical Society. Edwards practiced until she retired and moved to Florida, where she died of dysentery in 1896.   JH/MBO

SECONDARY SOURCES

Kelly, Howard A. *Cyclopedia of American Medical Biography,* vol. 1. Philadelphia: W. B. Saunders, 1912.

EDWARDS, LENA FRANCES (1900–)

U.S. obstetrician. Married. Six children. Educated Howard University (M.D.); Freedman's Hospital, intern. Postgraduate training for American Board of Obstetrics and Gynecology examination. Professional experience: Jersey City, N.J., private practice; Margaret Hague Hospital, Jersey City, assistant attending obstetrician, later specialist in obstetrics. Awards: State of New Jersey, Outstanding Black Woman award (1940s).

Lena Frances spent much of her childhood in Washington, D.C., where her father taught dentistry at Howard University. She attended public high school and entered Howard University, eventually receiving her medical degree. She interned at Freedman's Hospital. The day after graduation she married [?] Edwards, M.D., a classmate; they had a total of six children over the years. She took postgraduate training for the American Board of Obstetrics and Gynecology examination. Setting up a private practice in Jersey City, Edwards became assistant attending obstetrician, and later specialist in obstetrics, at the Margaret Hague Hospital. She received the Outstanding Black Woman award from the state of New Jersey.   KM

SECONDARY SOURCES

Knapp, Sally. *Women Doctors Today.* New York: Thomas Y. Crowell Company, 1947.

EDWARDS-PILLIET, BLANCHE (1858–1941)

French physician. Born 24 November 1858 at Milly-La Forêt (Seine et Marne), France, to Amanda (Froc) and George Hugh Edwards. Married Alexandre-Henri Pilliet, 21 February 1891 (he died in 1898). Three children (two daughters, one son). Educated at home by her father; baccalaureate in letters (1877); baccalaureate in sciences (1878); Paris Faculty of Medicine (1878–1882), intern ("externe") (1882–1885), resident ("interne provisoire") (1886–1889); M.D. (1889). Professional experience: intern ("externe") Salpêtrière Hospital (under J.-B. Charcot) (1884–1885); Hôpital des Enfants Assistés, resident ("interne provisoire") under Labadie-Lagrave (1886–1889); private practice (1889–1941); consultant for women employees of the post office (from 1889); Lycée Lamartine, consulting doctor (from 1889); Lycée Victor-Duruy, physician (1893?–1927); Salpêtrière Hospital, professor of nursing instruction (1898–1927); Paris Red Cross, instructor (1914–1917); Puteaux arsenal, physician to female personnel (1917–1919). Honors and memberships: Bronze Medal, Assistance Publique (1889); Faculty of Medicine, laureate (1889); officer of public instruction (1895); Legion of Honor, Chevalier (1924); Ligue pour les Droits des Femmes, vice-president; Ligue des Mères de Famille, founder (1901); Société d'Anthropologie de Paris, titular member; participant in feminist congresses. Died January 1941 in Paris.

Blanche Edwards-Pilliet was the daughter of an English-born but French-educated physician and a French woman, daughter of wealthy farmers near Mélun. As a child, Blanche Edwards spoke English with her father and French with her mother, and was completely bilingual. She also adopted her father's Protestant religion. As a young girl, she accompanied her father on his medical rounds around Milly-La Forêt near Fontainbleu and determined to become a physician herself. The success of ELIZABETH GARRETT ANDERSON, MARY PUTNAM JACOBI, and MADELEINE BRÈS in obtaining medical degrees from the Paris Faculty of Medicine inspired her to follow their example. First, she had to pass the baccalaureate examinations for which there were no formal preparatory schools for girls. Her father prepared her in general studies and science and she successfully passed these examinations in both categories.

As a protected middle-class French girl, she was accompanied to her medical school classes by her father for the first years of her education. She then determined to fight for the right to continue on with her hospital education as an "externe" (the equivalent of the American intern). After some petitioning, she managed to obtain this right in 1884 and joined the service of the distinguished neurologist Jean-Baptiste Charcot at Salpêtrière Hospital. Two years later, she and an American woman, AUGUSTA KLUMPKE (later married to the French neurologist Jules Déjerine) obtained permission to take the examination for the "internat" (equivalent of residency in America) with the support of the scientist and politician Paul Bert, then minister of education. When both young women passed with excellent marks, protests in the medical press and in front of the medical school followed from conservative members of the faculty of medicine and a small group of medical students who objected to women obtaining prized places in the Paris hospitals. Blanche Edwards was made a provisional "interne" to Dr. Labadie-Lagrave at one of the Paris children's hospitals, the Hôpital des Enfants Assistés. Later she reported to a Paris newspaper that her experience was made more pleasant by the presence of her fiancé, Alexandre-Henri Pilliet, a fellow interne.

In the beginning of 1889, Blanche Edwards successfully defended her medical thesis, written on hemiplegia and inspired by her work with Charcot. She then began private medical practice, which she continued for more than fifty years. That same year she entered the Société d'Anthropologie de Paris, where she presented some of her studies on hemiplegia to an audience that included CLÉMENCE ROYER, a fellow member. (Many years later she would be a featured speaker at the centenary of Royer's birth.) Two years after finishing her degree, she married Pilliet and spent seven years combining a very happy marriage with both motherhood and medicine. In 1898, her husband died, leaving her a widow with three children. She took over his position as a professor of nursing instruction at Salpêtrière Hospital.

Blanche Edwards-Pilliet was a strong supporter of middle-class feminism and became an active member of the League for the Rights of Women (Ligue pour les Droits des Femmes). She spoke at a number of feminist conferences in 1889 and 1900 and urged women at these conferences to insist on the expansion of girls' education and to set up their own hospitals on the English model. She continued to agitate for adequate female education well into the twentieth century and urged the creation of women's medical colleges that would provide positions for women professors of medicine. She was a founding member of the Ligue des Mères, which provided health instruction and medical assistance to working women. She was a strong supporter of health and hygiene measures for schoolgirls in her role as consulting physician to two distinguished Paris girls' schools.

Edwards-Pilliet worked much of her life on behalf of women's suffrage, with the exception of the period during World War I, when feminists agreed to put their concerns aside to work for the war effort. The conclusion of that war saw a renewal of their effort, which did not succeed in obtaining the vote until after World War II. Edwards-Pilliet died at the age of eighty-two in Paris during the occupation by Nazi Germany before she could see the positive conclusion of her lifelong endeavors on behalf of women's rights. A respected physician, she was awarded the cross of the Legion of Honor in her sixties and continued to practice into her old age. Her recent biography, which includes charming pictures of her as a young woman physician, was written by two of her grandchildren. J H

PRIMARY SOURCES

Edwards, Blanche. *De l'Hemiplégie dans quelques affections nerveuses.* Paris: Delahaye et Lecrosnier, 1889. This is her published medical thesis, dedicated to her father and to Charcot, for which she was awarded a bronze medal.

———. [Discussions.] *Congrès des Oeuvres et Institutions Feminines.* Paris: Imp. Charles Blot, 1889.

Edwards-Pilliet, Blanche. [Discussion as President of Section "Arts, Lettres, Sciences," 22 June 1900.] *Congrès des Oeuvres et Institutions Feminines,* ed. Mme. Pegaud. Paris: Imp. Charles Blot, 1902, Vol. 4. passim.

———. Series of feminist articles. *La Française* 1906–1911.

SECONDARY SOURCES

Harvey, Joy. "A Focal Point for Feminism, Politics and Science in France: The Clémence Royer Centenary Celebration of 1930." *Osiris,* forthcoming.

Leguay, Françoise, and Claude Barbizet. *Blanche Edwards-Pilliet: Femme et Medecin 1858–1941.* Paris: Editions Cénomane, 1988.

STANDARD SOURCES

Lipinska 1900; Lipinska 1930.

EFIMENKO, ALEKSANDRA IAKOVLEVNA (1848–1918)

Russian ethnographer and historian. Born 30 April 1848 in Vorzuga, Arkhangelsk province, to Iakov I. Stavrovskii, a civil servant, and Elizaveta P. Stavrovskaia. Five siblings. Married Petr Savvich Efimenko. Three daughters: Vera, Aleksandra, Tat'iana; two sons: Taras, Petr. Educated Arkhangelsk women's gymnasium. Professional experience: Kholmogory school, teacher; Bestuzhev Higher Women's Courses, St. Petersburg, teacher, later professor. Died 17 or 18 December 1918 in Volchansk, Ukraine.

Aleksandra Iakovlevna Efimenko was born in a village on the bank of the Vorzuga river, not far from the White Sea. When she was two, her family moved to Arkhangelsk, the nearest cultural and administrative center. Here, her father died, leaving the family in poor economic circumstances. In 1857, Efimenko entered the gymnasium and graduated in 1863, with certification as a teacher. In 1864, she began working as a teacher at a school in Kholmogory some distance from Arkhangelsk. There, in her spare time, Efimenko pursued her education on her own, studying a variety of different subjects but with no real focus.

Life in this northern area was monotonous but it was enlivened by the presence of numerous political exiles who exerted a strong cultural influence. In 1864, an article signed by one of them, Petr Savvich Efimenko, appeared in the Arkhangelsk newspaper laying out a program of ethnographical study and inviting contributions of ethnographical and historical materials from interested members of the public.

Petr Savvich Efimenko (1835–1908) was born in the Crimea and attended university in Kharkov and Moscow. He had been active in student revolutionary circles and, ultimately, was exiled to Kholmogory, where he worked as a clerk in a local government office. During his various wanderings he had developed an interest in ethnography and local history.

Aleksandra decided to pursue his program and soon the young people were working together. Owing to Petr Efimenko's poor health, made worse by the severe climate, Aleksandra began going to the archives and collecting many materials, essentially under his direction.

In 1870, despite Petr's poor health, the young couple decided to get married. This was not an advantageous move for Aleksandra: she lost her job, acquiring in its stead the unpleasant status of exile, subject to police surveillance and control. She now required permission to travel even as far as Arkhangelsk. In the same period, her mother became ill and Petr himself was often too ill to work.

For the next few years, the family's main source of income was articles on ethnography which Aleksandra wrote for newspapers and journals. These attracted attention in the capitals and the young couple began to receive donations from such groups as the Society to Aid Needy Writers and Scholars.

In 1872, the Efimenkos were given permission to leave for a warmer climate. Over the next few years they lived in various cities in the Ukraine, ultimately settling in Kharkov. During this period, three daughters and two sons were born.

Efimenko soon adapted to life in the Ukraine and it became her second home. She was sympathetic to Ukrainian nationalism and wrote an article promoting the use of the Ukrainian language in schools. Besides collecting and studying materials and writing, she was one of the organizers of the historical circle of Kharkov University and took part in many archeological conferences. She also was in much demand as a speaker. In 1902, she was elected a full member of the Moscow Archaeological Society.

Meanwhile, Efimenko's home life became more and more difficult. Petr had fits of increasing severity and two of her daughters, Aleksandra and Vera, were diagnosed with incurable mental illnesses. Both had to be hospitalized; both died. Serious financial problems compounded Efimenko's difficulties.

In 1907, the family moved to St. Petersburg, where Aleksandra Efimenko had been offered a position as teacher at the Bestuzhev Higher Women's Courses. By now, Petr was very ill; he died in 1908. His final illness combined with her teaching responsibilities were very exhausting, but Efimenko found much needed support among her students and colleagues.

In 1910 Kharkov University awarded Efimenko the degree of doctor of history and in the same year, she attained the rank of professor at the Higher Women's Courses. She continued to work there until the courses were closed in 1917 as a result of the Revolution of 1917.

In 1917, Efimenko and her daughter Tat'iana, who by now was a promising young poet, left Petrograd and returned to the Ukraine at the invitation of A. V. Kolokol'tseva, a long-time correspondent of Efimenko's who was the director of a progressive women's gymnasium in Volchansk. Kolokol'tseva offered her a peaceful environment in which to work and the possibility of some teaching.

Efimenko's health was not good and she was unhappy at Volchansk, where she felt very isolated. She hoped to be able to return to Petrograd in spite of the revolutionary situation there. Nevertheless, she completed her final work on the history of the Ukraine.

Meanwhile the civil war had spread to the Ukraine in a particularly virulent form. Besides the struggle between revolutionary and counterrevolutionary forces, there was intervention by Germans, Ukrainian nationalists under Petliura, anarchist bands, and a variety of lawless elements. Sometime on the night of 17 December 1918, Efimenko and Tat'iana were murdered, supposedly by bandits.

Efimenko was the author of over one hundred works, covering a wide range of subjects on ethnography and history of the Arkhangelsk region and the Ukraine. Her reputation was well established during her lifetime and in the period immediately after the Revolution of 1917. In 1930, Kharkov University dedicated a collection of historical publications to her memory. However, after that time, her work, tagged as "bourgeois idealist," fell under a political cloud that did not begin to lift until after the Stalin period.

Efimenko's work is now being reprinted and, with the independence of Ukraine, she is again getting the recognition she deserves.   ACH

PRIMARY SOURCES

Efimenko, Aleksandra Iakovlevna. *Istoriia ukrainskago naroda.* St. Petersburg: Brokgauz-Efron, 1906. Latest reprint, 1990.

———. *Iuzhnaia Rus': ocherki, izsliedovaniia i zamietki.* St. Petersburg: Izd. Ob-va im. T.G. Shevchenka dlia vspomoshchestvovaniia nuzhdaiushchimsia urozhentsam Iuzhnoi Rossii, 1905.

———. *Uchebnik russkoi istorii.* St. Petersburg: Izd. Brokgauza i Efrona, 1909.

SECONDARY SOURCES

Andreevskii, I. E. ed. *Entsiklopedicheskaia slovar'.* St. Petersburg: Tip. I. A. Efron, 1890–1906.

Markov, Polikarp Glebovich. *A. Ia. Efimenko: istorik Ukrainy.* Kiev: Izd-vo Kievskogo gosudarstvennogo universiteta, 1966.

EGGLETON, MARION GRACE (PALMER) (1901–1970)

British physiologist. Born 1901. Married (1) Philip Eggleton; (2) Leonard Bayliss (1939). Educated University College, London as a Bucknill Scholar (B.Sc. with first class honors, 1923); qualified in medicine (1926). Professional experience: University College, London, demonstrator in physiology (1928); University of Edinburgh, (1930–1936); Bedford College, London, (1937–1938); University College, pharmacology department, lecturer, (1938–1943); physiology department, lecturer, senior lecturer, and reader (1944–1966). Died 1970.

Grace Palmer received her education during the interwar years, receiving her bachelor of science in physiology and qualifying in medicine. After qualifying in 1926, she was elected to the Physiological Society in 1927. She had several academic appointments, but returned in 1938 to University College, London, just as the war broke out. Bombing forced the evacuation of the college and the physiology and pharmacology departments were transferred to Leatherhead, Surrey. Grace Eggleton (by this time she had married her first husband, Philip Eggleton) organized the teaching of both pharmacology and physiology during this period. She worked under very trying circumstances. War requirements made the training of medical students a priority. Nevertheless, she was able to do her research through the facilities at the Institute of Physiology at Cardiff.

Eggleton is best known for a discovery she made with her husband Philip. As partners, they discovered an organic phosphate compound in muscle tissue, which decreased as the muscle contracted. This compound was eventually identified as creatine phosphate by Fiske and Subbarow. This discovery was especially significant in understanding the way in which muscles contract. After this initial work, Eggleton became interested in the study of renal function and of the physiological effects of alcohol. Eggleton was not only a fine research physiologist, but also a superb compiler of indexes to books and journals. Among many other indexes, she compiled the cumulative author and subject indexes to the *Journal of Physiology*, covering the issues of the journal published between 1926 and 1970.   JH/MBO

PRIMARY SOURCES

Eggleton, Grace. With Philip Eggleton. "The Inorganic Phosphate and a Labile Form of Organic Phosphate in the Gastrocnemius of the Frog." *Biochemistry Journal* 21 (1927a): 190–195.

———. "The Physiological Significance of 'Phosphagen.'" *Journal of Physiology* 63 (1927b): 55–61.

———. With others. "A Method of Estimating Phosphagen and Some Other Phosphate Compounds in Muscle Tissue." *Journal of Physiology* 68 (1929): 193–211.

———. With others. "The Influence of Diuretics on the Osmotic Work Done and on the Efficiency of the Isolated Kidney of the Dog." *Journal of Physiology* 97 (1940): 363–382.

———. "The Effects of Alcohol on the Central Nervous System." *British Journal of Psychology* 32 (1941): 52–61.

STANDARD SOURCES
Women Physiologists.

EHRENFEST-AFANASSJEWA, TATYANA ALEXEYEVNA (1876–1964)

Russian/Dutch mathematician and mathematical physicist. Born 19 November 1876 in Kiev, Ukraine, to father Alexander Afanassjev, a civil engineer. No siblings. Married Paul Ehrenfest. Four children: Tatyana, Anna, Paul, and Vassily. Educated at normal school and Women's University, St. Petersburg; University of Göttingen. Died 14 April 1964 in Leiden, the Netherlands.

As a young girl, Tatyana Afanassjewa (or Tat'iana Afanas'eva) traveled all over the Russian empire in an observation car with her father, who was chief engineer of the Imperial Railways. After he died, she was raised by her aunt and uncle, Sonya and Peter Afanassjev, the latter a professor at the Polytechnic Institute in St. Petersburg. Afanassjewa completed the mathematics and science curriculum at the normal school in St. Petersburg, then attended the Women's University, where she did exceptionally well in mathematics, studying with Orest D. Chvolsou. She also studied physics with him. Afanassjewa went to the University of Göttingen in 1902, where she attended lectures of Felix Klein and David Hilbert. At that time, women were not permitted to attend the student mathematics club, but an Austrian student, Paul Ehrenfest, convinced the members to change the rules. Afanassjewa and Ehrenfest became acquainted through the mathematics club, and decided to marry.

While Afanassjewa remained in Göttingen, Ehrenfest returned to the University of Vienna to complete his studies. After he received the doctorate (under Ludwig Boltzmann), the couple married in Vienna on 21 December 1904. Because they were of different religions—he was Jewish, she was Russian Orthodox—they were required to renounce their religious ties in order to marry. This action impeded Ehrenfest's search for a position, particularly after they moved to St. Petersburg in 1907. Although Ehrenfest did not obtain an academic appointment, the couple continued their professional activities, participating in an informal physics colloquium and working individually and jointly on mathematics and theoretical physics. Tatyana Ehrenfest-Afanassjewa became involved in the movement to reform mathematics teaching in Russia.

The couple's first child, Tatyana, was born in Vienna in October 1905. The Ehrenfests were devoted parents, who took great interest in their daughter's intellectual development, and arranged for home schooling. The birth of their second child in July 1910 (Anna, called Galya or Galinka) strained the family's financial circumstances. In 1912, Paul Ehrenfest took a position at the University of Leiden. There, Ehrenfest-Afanassjewa continued her work in mathematics and mathematical physics. In 1915, their son Paul was born, followed by Vassily in August 1918. Paul was killed by an avalanche while skiing in the French Alps in 1939.

Sometime during the twenties, Ehrenfest-Afanassjewa returned to Russia, where she taught mathematics and continued to publish papers, although the couple still met occasionally. Her husband became increasingly prone to depression and bizarre behavior. On 25 September 1933, while Ehrenfest-Afanassjewa was teaching mathematics in Moscow, he killed their younger son, then committed suicide. Ehrenfest-Afanassjewa returned to Leiden, where she died on 14 April 1964.

Ehrenfest-Afanassjewa published numerous articles in German, Dutch, Russian, and English language periodicals. Her work, which also included several books, dealt with theoretical physics (statistical mechanics, thermodynamics, kinetic theory, radioactive decay), mathematics (dimensional analysis, probability, geometry) and mathematics and physics pedagogy. By serving as a foil, critic, collaborator, and supporter for her husband, Ehrenfest-Afanassjewa enabled Paul Ehrenfest to probe and productively develop his ideas.

One of the most significant accomplishments of the Ehrenfests was their analysis of statistical mechanics for a prestigious German mathematical encyclopedia, which was later published as a book. Ehrenfest-Afanassjewa's work on probability also was widely noted. MARIA GOEPPERT MAYER used a mathematical device suggested by Ehrenfest-Afanassjewa. Ehrenfest-Afanassjewa was still professionally active in her eighties, when she published books on the foundations of thermodynamics and on mathematics teaching.   MM

PRIMARY SOURCES
Ehrenfest-Afanassjewa, Tatyana Alexeyevna. "Zur Frage über die Konzentrationsschwankungen in radioaktiven Lösungen." *Physikalische Zeitschrift* 14 (1913): 675–676.

———. "Dimensional Analysis Viewed from the Standpoint of the Theory of Similitudes." *Philosophical Magazine* 1 (1926): 257–272.

———. *Die Grundlagen der Thermodynamik.* Leiden: E. J. Brill, 1956.

———. "On the Use of the Notion 'Probability' in Physics." *American Journal of Physics* 26 (1957): 388–392.

———. With Paul Ehrenfest. *The Conceptual Foundations of the Statistical Approach in Mechanics.* Ithaca, N.Y.: Cornell

University Press, 1959. Translated by M. J. Moravcsik from "Begriffe Grundlagen der statischen Auffassung in der Mechanik." In *Encyclopädie der mathematische Wissenschaften*, vol. 4, pt. 2. Leipzig: B. G. Teubner, 1912.

———. *Wiskunde. Didactische opstellen*. Zutphen, Netherlands: Thieme, [1960].

SECONDARY SOURCES

Brush, Stephen G. *Statistical Physics and the Atomic Theory of Matter, from Boyle and Newton to Landau and Onsager*. Princeton, N.J.: Princeton University Press, 1983.

Elasser, Walter M. *Memoirs of a Physicist in the Atomic Age*. New York: Science History Publications; Bristol: Adam Hilger, 1978. Ehrenfest-Afanassjewa discussed on pages 84–85.

Graham, Loren R. *Science in Russia and the Soviet Union*. Cambridge: Cambridge University Press, 1993; 1994.

Highfield, Roger, and Paul Carter. *The Private Lives of Albert Einstein*. New York: St. Martin's Press, 1993; 1994. Ehrenfest-Afanassjewa mentioned on page 142.

Klein, Martin J. *Paul Ehrenfest*. Amsterdam: North Holland Publishing Co., 1970.

Klein, Martin J., A. J. Kox, and Robert Schumann, eds. *The Collected Papers of Albert Einstein. Vol. 5, The Swiss Years: Correspondence, 1902–1914*. Princeton, N.J.: Princeton University Press, 1993.

Sard, Robert D. "Recollections of the Ehrenfest Family." Manuscript, Center for History of Physics, College Park, Md.

van Brakel, J. "The Possible Influence of the Discovery of Radio-active Decay on the Concept of Physical Probability." *Archive for History of Exact Sciences* 31 (1985): 369–385.

Visser, C. "In Memoriam T. Ehrenfest-Afanassjewa." *Leids Universiteitsblad* 1964 (May 8): 5.

———. "In Memoriam T. Ehrenfest-Afanassjewa." *Vernieuwing van Opvoeding en Onderwijs* 22 (June 1964): 217.

STANDARD SOURCES

DSB (under Maria Goeppert-Mayer); Meyer and von Schweidler; *Notable*; Poggendorff 5, 6, 7b.

EICHELBERGER, LILLIAN (1897–?)

U.S. biochemist. Born 2 March 1897 in Macon, Mich., to Huldah (Richards) and Philander W. Eichelberger. Married Ralph Hardin Cannon (11 August 1923). Educated Mississippi State College for Women (B.S., 1914); University of Chicago (M.S., 1919; Ph.D., 1921). Professional experience: University of Chicago, research instructor, department of chemistry (1921–1924); Municipal Tuberculosis Sanitorium, Chicago, chemical research (1924–1927); University of Chicago department of medicine, assistant professor (1929–1944); Office of Scientific Research and Development (OSRD), associate investigator neurogenic shock (1942–1944), associate investigator pharmacology, clinical testing of antimalarial agents (1944–1947). Honors and memberships: citation, OSRD, 1945; American Chemical Society, American Society of Biological Chemists, Society for Experimental Biology and Medicine. Death date unknown.

Lillian Eichelberger was a respected biochemist who earned her two advanced degrees from the University of Chicago. She did research at this university as an assistant professor. While working at the university, she also was an investigator for the Office of Scientific Research and Development. Her studies covered a variety of topics. Tuberculosis was one of her special interests. She also worked on the acid-base balance in the body and the distribution of body water and electrolytes in the soft and hard tissues. She did electrolyte studies on canine homotransplanted hearts and biochemical studies on hypertrophy of heart muscles. On the more clinical side, she studied clinical standardization of many drugs in induced malaria in man, biochemical studies of articular cartilage following disuse by immobilization and by denervation of an extremity.   JH/MBO

PRIMARY SOURCES

Eichelberger, Lillian. "Catalytic Transmutation of Maleic Acid into Fumaric Acid." *Journal of the American Chemical Society* 47 (1925). Eichelberger's Ph.D. dissertation (1921).

STANDARD SOURCES

Debus.

EIGENMANN, ROSA SMITH (1858–1947)

U.S. ichthyologist. Born 7 October 1858 in Monmouth, Ill., to Lucretia (Gray) and Charles Smith. Eight siblings. Married Carl Eigenmann. Five children. Educated Point Loma Seminary, San Diego, Calif.; business college, San Francisco, Calif.; Indiana University (1880–1882); Harvard University (special student, 1887–1888). Died 12 January 1947 in San Diego.

Rosa Smith was the youngest of nine children of a newspaper printer who moved his family to San Diego, California, in 1876. Rosa attended the Point Loma Seminary there and afterward a business college in San Francisco. She became interested in studying plants and animals, in particular the fish of the San Diego area. In 1880, she published her first scientific paper. In the same year she met the noted ichthyologist David Starr Jordan at a meeting of the San Diego Society of Natural History, where, as the society's first woman member, recording secretary, and librarian, she read a paper on her identification of a new species of fish. At Jordan's instigation she attended Indiana University, where he then taught, from

1880 to 1882, traveling through Europe in 1881 with a student group under Jordan's supervision.

In 1887 Rosa Smith married a German ichthyologist, Carl Eigenmann, also a student of Jordan's. She and Eigenmann collaborated on several studies, including research on South American fishes at the Museum of Comparative Zoology at Harvard (1887–1888). During their stay at Harvard, Rosa Eigenmann expanded her knowledge of cryptogamic botany as a special student under William Farlow.

After returning to San Diego in 1888, the Eigenmanns continued joint research at a small biological station that they established. When David Starr Jordan decided to move to Stanford (1891), he invited Carl Eigenmann to replace him at Indiana University as professor of zoology. This move signaled the end of the full collaboration between Carl and Rosa Eigenmann, although she continued to edit his papers. From 1893 Rosa Eigenmann cared for their five children, of whom one was retarded and another became mentally ill. Her home responsibilities kept Eigenmann from taking an active part in university and scientific affairs. The Eigenmanns returned to California in 1926, and Carl died in 1927. Rosa remained in San Diego until her death from myocarditis in 1947.

In the short space of her scientific career, Rosa Eigenmann published twenty papers on her own, chiefly on the taxonomy of the fishes of the San Diego area; a monograph with Joseph Swain on the fishes of Johnson Island in the central Pacific Ocean; and fifteen papers in collaboration with her husband. Her taxonomic studies, especially those coauthored with Carl Eigenmann, represent important contributions to the body of knowledge about the fishes of South America and western North America. Eigenmann was sensitive to the danger of praising second-rate work solely because it was produced by a woman. Excellence in science, she insisted, should be judged by the same standards for both sexes. MBO

PRIMARY SOURCES

Eigenmann, Rosa S. With J. Swaim. "Notes on a Collection of Fishes from Johnson Island, Including Descriptions of Five New Species." *Proceedings, U.S. National Museum* 5 (1883): 119–143.

SECONDARY SOURCES

Dean, Bashford. *A Bibliography of Fishes.* 3 vols. New York: American Museum of Natural History, 1916–1923. Eigenmann's bibliography is found in 1:365–67, 2:463, 3:55.

Martin, Hemme N. "San Diego Woman One of the Earliest Discovers of Pt. Loma Blindfish." *San Diego Union.* 14 June 1935.

"Noted Woman Expert on Fish Dies Here at 88." *San Diego Journal,* 13 January 1947. Obituary notice.

Stejneger, Leonhard. "Carl H. Eigenmann, 1863–1927." *National Academy of Sciences Biographical Memoirs* 18 (1938): 305–336. Discussed in this biography of her husband.

STANDARD SOURCES

NAW (article by Carl L. Hubbs); Ogilvie 1986; Shearer and Shearer 1996.

EIMMART, MARIE CLAIRE (1676–1707)

German astronomer. Father Georg Christoph Eimmart. Educated by her father in astronomy. Married Johann Heinrich Müller (1706). Professional experience: Nuremberg observatory. Died 1707 in childbirth.

Marie Eimmart's father built an observatory in Nuremberg on the city wall. He was the astronomer and director of the Nuremberg Academy of Art from 1699 to 1704. It was through her father that Maria learned French, Latin, mathematics, and drawing. Because of the strength of the crafts tradition in Germany, Eimmart was able to take advantage of the opportunity to train as an apprentice to her father. She had the ability to make exact sketches of the sun and moon and, as Schiebinger reports, made over 250 drawings of phases of the moon. The continuous series that she produced was the basis for a new lunar map. She also made two drawings of the total eclipse of 1706. Although she is sometimes credited with a 1701 book published under her father's name, there is no evidence that she wrote it.

Eimmart's position was further strengthened by her marriage to Johann Heinrich Müller, a physics teacher at a Nuremberg gymnasium and director of her father's observatory since 1705. Her career was cut short when she died in childbirth. JH/MBO

PRIMARY SOURCES

Eimmart, Georg Christoph. *Ichnographia nora contemplationum de sole in desolatis antiquorum philosophorum ruderibus concepta.* Nuremberg: Endteri, 1701. Illustrated by Marie Claire Eimmart.

SECONDARY SOURCES

LaLande, Jérôme de. *Bibliographie astronomique.* Paris: De L'Imprimerie de la République, 1803.

Schiebinger, Londa. *The Mind Has No Sex? Women in the Origins of Modern Science.* Cambridge, Mass.: Harvard University Press, 1989.

STANDARD SOURCES

Poggendorff, vol. 1.

EINSTEIN, ELIZABETH ROBOZ (ca. 1902–)

Hungarian/U.S. biochemist and neuroscientist. Born in Transylvania in Szaszvaros, Hungary (now Orastie, Romania). Father was a rabbi and a teacher. Five siblings. Married Hans Albert Einstein, an engineering professor; no children. Educated University of Vienna and University of Budapest (Ph.D. summa cum laude, 1928). Emigrated to U.S. in 1940. Professional experience: Industrial positions in Hungary and U.S.; California Institute of Technology, research assistant; research associate (1942–1945); University of Wyoming, associate professor (1945–1948); Stanford University, research associate (1948–1952); Georgetown University, associate professor (1952–1958); Veterans Administration hospital, lecturer; Stanford University, associate professor (1958–1959); University of California School of Medicine, San Francisco (from 1959?); University of Bangkok, lecturer on the orient; advertising researcher. Honors and memberships: Georgetown University, Raskob Award (1956); International Congress for Neurochemistry, Milan, Italy, Medaglia d'oro di Milano (1969); Institute of Human Development, University of California, Berkeley.

The daughter of parents who valued education, Elizabeth Roboz grew up in Szaszvaros, Transylvania, Hungary. Her university- and seminary-educated father was the town's chief rabbi and a high school teacher. After her father's death in 1914, the family moved to Nyiregyháza, Hungary, where Roboz's mother struggled to support her six children.

During Roboz's last year of high school, the Hungarian parliament restricted the number of Jewish students who could be accepted to the university. Although she received the grade of excellent in all five subjects in the *Matura* examination, Roboz realized that she might be excluded from the University of Budapest. Since Vienna was then considered one of the outstanding centers of education in Europe, Roboz registered at the University of Vienna, planning to major in chemistry and physics. Roboz received her doctorate *summa cum laude* in 1928, then returned to Hungary, where she was required to repeat examinations in order to have her degree confirmed by the University of Budapest.

With antisemitism on the rise in Hungary, Roboz decided to emigrate. Obtaining an agricultural specialist's visa, she arrived in the United States in 1940. Roboz's brother Karl and two brothers-in-law were killed by Hungarian Nazis; her mother also died during the war. Roboz's surviving siblings joined her in the United States. Later Roboz shared her home in Palo Alto with her sister Edith.

Roboz developed many friendships with her colleagues and their spouses. These included the hydraulic engineer Hans Albert Einstein (son of the physicist Albert Einstein) and his wife, Frieda. After Frieda's death, Einstein increasingly sought Roboz's companionship. Einstein and Roboz were married in Berkeley on 5 June 1959. This happy union of equals ended with Einstein's death on 26 July 1973.

Roboz continued with her work and completed a book on her husband's life. She enjoyed music, cooking, travel, and nature.

As an undergraduate, Roboz worked on plant biochemistry in Zellner's laboratory in Vienna, where she was introduced to the field which would lead to her life's work. After graduation she set up a plant nutrition laboratory for the Hungarian company Agricultural Industry and represented the company at international scientific conferences.

Soon after her arrival in the United States, Roboz found a position with a potato company in Stockton, California, where she again established a laboratory for studying plant nutrition. In 1942, Roboz began working at the California Institute of Technology as assistant to the bioorganic chemist Ari J. Haagen-Smit. There she studied the *Aloe vera* plant and was promoted to research associate. Since Cal Tech did not appoint women as professors, Roboz accepted an associate professorship in chemistry at the University of Wyoming, where she also worked as a research chemist at the College of Engineering. In 1948, Roboz left Wyoming to become a research associate at Stanford University, where she stayed until 1952.

From 1952 to 1958, Roboz, as associate professor in the department of biochemistry, taught biochemistry to medical students at Georgetown University. She also lectured at the Veterans Administration Hospital. While studying neurochemistry in order to teach it to her students, she became interested in multiple sclerosis. Her research at the National Institutes of Health on this disease helped lay the foundations for neurochemistry and led to significant publications and international recognition, including the Raskob Faculty Award for researchers at Catholic universities.

In 1958 Roboz accepted a position as associate professor of medicine at Stanford University. There she taught neurochemistry and led a research group. Her research was supported by NIH, and later by the National Science Foundation, the Multiple Sclerosis Society, and Hartford Foundation. After her marriage, Roboz—now Einstein—moved to the University of California School of Medicine at San Francisco, in order to work closer to home. She continued her research, and taught neurochemistry in the department of neurology. During 1961–1962, she was a SEATO Scholar at the University of Bangkok.

Einstein studied the myelin nerve sheath and isolated the myelin basic protein. She also developed procedures to determine immunoglobulin in cerebrospinal fluid. During her career, Einstein authored or coauthored over ninety publications.

Einstein was honored by the Neurochemical Society in 1978 and by a special edition of *Neurochemical Research* in 1984. The University of California created the Elizabeth Roboz Einstein Fellowship in Neurochemistry and Human

Development in 1982. She was a member of the American Chemical Society, the Society of Experimental Biology and Medicine, and the American Academy of Neurology.

JH/MBO

PRIMARY SOURCES

Einstein, Elizabeth Roboz. With A. Nakao and W. J. Davis. "Basic Proteins from the Acidic Extract of Bovine Spinal Cord." *Biochimica et Biophysica Acta* 130 (1966): 171–179.

———. With H. C. Rauch. "Specific Brain Proteins: A Biochemical and Immunological Review." *Reviews of Neuroscience* 1 (1974): 283–343.

———. "Myelination and Demyelination: Introduction and Comments." *Advances in Experimental Medicine and Biology* 100, ed. J. Pola (1978): 1–16.

———. *Proteins of the Brain and Cerebrospinal Fluid in Health and Disease.* Springfield, Ill.: Charles C. Thomas, 1982.

———. *Hans Albert Einstein: Reminiscences of His Life and Our Life Together.* Iowa City: Iowa Institute of Hydraulic Research, The University of Iowa, 1991.

SECONDARY SOURCES

Neurochemical Research 9 (October 1984). Special issue dedicated to Elizabeth Roboz Einstein.

STANDARD SOURCES

AMS P 9, P&B 10 (under Roboz).

EINSTEIN-MARIC, MILEVA (1875–1948)

Serbian/Swiss physicist. Born 20 December 1875 in Titel, Vojvodina, Austria-Hungary (later Yugoslavia) to Mary (Ruzic) and Milos Maric, a military careerist, later a court clerk. Two siblings. Educated in Vojvodina province, Austria-Hungary; Agram (later called Zagreb). Studied at the normal school, Zurich; the Eidgenössische Polytechnische Schule, Zurich; and the University of Göttingen. Married Albert Einstein. Three children, Lieserl, Hans Albert, and Eduard. Died 4 August 1948 in Zurich.

Shortly after Maric's birth in 1875, her father was discharged from military service and took a position as a court clerk. Her sister, Zora, was born in 1883 and her brother, Milos, in 1885. They were all raised in the Greek Orthodox Church. Mileva Maric spent four years in elementary school in Ruma, Vojvodina province, and completed grammar school in 1890 in nearby Sremska Mitrovica. Through her father's intercession (who by then was at the High Court of Justice in Agram), Maric was allowed to enter the Royal Classical High School in Agram in 1892, where she received excellent grades. Having become interested in mathematics and physics during her previous schooling, Maric requested permission to attend physics lectures, which were restricted to male students. Receiving high recommendations, she was allowed to attend the lectures. Maric graduated in 1894 with the highest grades awarded in mathematics and physics.

Since Swiss universities permitted women to enroll as regular students, Maric went to Zurich the next year, where she studied medicine for a semester. She switched to the mathematical section of the Zurich Eidgenössische Polytechnische Schule in 1896. During the winter semester 1897–1898, Maric studied in Heidelberg under the physicist Philip Lenard, whose lectures she found exciting. She selected a research topic for her diploma in 1900, planning to use it for the doctorate. Although she passed the intermediate examination in 1899, she failed the final examinations twice, in 1900 and in 1901 (under the physical and emotional stress of an unplanned pregnancy). During the summer of 1901, Maric worked in Friedrich Weber's laboratories, where she received an excellent grade. However, she did not like working with Weber (who disliked Einstein), and left without receiving any degree.

Maric met Albert Einstein during her first year at the polytechnic school. Maric and Einstein attended classes and studied together, spending much time reading and discussing classical physics texts. By 1900 they were deeply in love. Marriage was obstructed by Einstein's inability to find a job, coupled with the objections of both sets of parents. The couple's daughter, Lieserl, was born early in 1902 in Novi Sad, where the Marics had a winter home. Einstein, who probably never saw his daughter, finally received a position in the patent office in Bern, where he began working in June 1902. However, Einstein and Maric were not married until 6 January 1903, perhaps because of his parents' objections, or because of a disagreement about whether to keep Lieserl. Although they relinquished their daughter, the Einsteins later had two sons, Hans Albert (born 14 May 1904) and Eduard (born 28 July 1910). In 1909 the family moved to Zurich, where Einstein took a position at the University. His career moves took them to Prague the next year, then back to Zurich in 1912.

During the early years of their marriage, Einstein and Einstein-Maric worked together in the evenings on physics. However, care of the home and children took up much of Einstein-Maric's time, and her husband increasingly sought intellectual companionship with others. He also developed a romantic liaison with his cousin Elsa Einstein Lowenthal, who lived in Berlin. In 1914, against his wife's wishes, Einstein accepted a position there, and the family moved to Berlin. That summer, Einstein-Maric left with their sons for a vacation in Zurich. Soon afterward, World War I erupted, and the separation became permanent. Mileva Einstein-Maric granted Einstein a divorce in 1919. The divorce settlement stipulated that the proceeds of any future Nobel Prize should go to her.

The Einstein's son Hans Albert later became a successful hydraulic engineer and university professor. Eduard, who had been a sickly child, developed a mental illness in his teens from which he never recovered. Mileva Einstein-Maric devoted much time to his care. To supplement the family finances, Einstein-Maric tutored mathematics and gave piano lessons, and may also have taught physics. She experienced severe financial problems in the wake of the Great Depression.

Einstein-Maric suffered from a congenitally dislocated hip, which caused her to limp and eventually led to much pain. Her health deteriorated during the last seven years of her life. She died in Zurich on 4 August 1948.

Since Einstein-Maric left no publications in her own name, and was not employed in a scientific capacity, most historians (with the major exception of her Serbian biographer) have assumed she made no scientific contributions. The belated discovery and publication of early correspondence between Maric and Einstein ignited a controversy over the extent of Maric's contributions to Einstein's early publications. These letters show Maric and Einstein studying together and contain suggestive statements by Einstein, including references to "our work."

Maric must have been unusually intelligent and resourceful to have overcome the barriers to her sex and succeeded so brilliantly in her early studies. Unlike Einstein, who had little patience for detailed work and regular attendance at lectures, she was a conscientious student, who shared her lecture notes and insights with him. Einstein was delighted to have found a partner whom he considered his intellectual equal. Both before and after their marriage, the couple read and discussed physics together. As her domestic cares increased, Einstein-Maric's intellectual contributions decreased, and she redirected her own ambitions toward her husband's career. Although it seems unlikely that Einstein-Maric played a leading role in the genesis of Einstein's early revolutionary ideas, it seems certain she had a greater part in his accomplishments than history has acknowledged. Not only did she provide emotional and domestic support, she made key intellectual contributions during Einstein's most productive period, at the very least by reading and discussing physics with him, by listening to his ideas, and by lending her own suggestions, insights, and analyses.   MM

PRIMARY SOURCES

Einstein, Albert. *Collected Papers.* John Stachel, ed. Princeton, N.J.: Princeton University Press, 1987.

Renn, Jürgen, and Robert Schulmann, eds. *Albert Einstein/Mileva Maric: The Love Letters.* Trans. Shawn Smith. Princeton, N.J.: Princeton University Press, 1992.

SECONDARY SOURCES

Barnett, Carol C. "A Comparative Analysis of Perspectives of Mileva Maric Einstein." Ph.D. diss., Florida State University, 1998.

Clark, Ronald W. *Einstein: The Life and Times.* New York and Cleveland: World Publishing Co., 1971.

Einstein, Elizabeth Roboz. *Hans Albert Einstein: Reminiscences of His Life and Our Life Together.* Iowa City, Iowa: The University of Iowa, 1991. Includes an appendix on Mileva Einstein-Maric by the Serbian physicist Dord Kristic.

Highfield, Roger, and Paul Carter. *The Private Lives of Albert Einstein.* New York: St. Martin's Press, 1994.

Holton, Gerald. "Of Love, Physics and other Passions: The Letters of Albert and Mileva." In two parts: *Physics Today* 47, no. 8 (August 1994): 23–36; 47, no. 9 (September 1994): 37–43.

Kristic, Dord. "The First Woman Theoretical Physicist" (in Serbian). *Collected Papers on History of Education* (Zagreb) 9 (1975): 111.

Medicus, Heinrich A. "The Friendship among Three Singular Men: Einstein and His Swiss Friends Besso and Zangger." *Isis* 85 (1994): 456–478.

Michelmore, Peter. *Einstein: Profile of the Man.* New York: Dodd, Mead and Co., 1962.

Pais, Abraham. *Subtle Is the Lord: The Science and the Life of Albert Einstein.* Oxford, New York, Toronto, Melbourne: Oxford University Press, 1982.

———. *Einstein Lived Here.* Oxford and New York: Clarendon Press, 1994.

Rose, Hillary. *Love, Power, and Marriage: Towards a Feminist Transformation of the Sciences.* Bloomington: Indiana University Press, 1994. See pages 143–144.

Trbuhovic-Gjuric, Desanka. *Im Schatten Albert Einstein: Das tragische Leben der Mileva Einstein-Maric.* Bern: Haupt, 1983.

Troemel-Ploetz, Senta. "Mileva Einstein-Maric: The Woman Who Did Einstein's Mathematics." *Women's Studies International Forum* 13, no. 5 (1990): 415–432.

STANDARD SOURCES
Creative Couples.

EISELE, CAROLYN (d. 1989?)

U.S. mathematician. Born New York City, date unknown. Educated Hunter College (A.B., 1923); Columbia University (A.M., 1925). Professional experience: Hunter College, instructor through professor (1923–1972), professor emerita (1972–1989?). Concurrent experience: American Philosophical Society, research grant (1952–1954, 1964–1967); National Science Foundation, recipient of research grant (1964–1967); International Congress of Mathematics, History of Science, Logic, Methodology, and Philoso-

phy of Science, Hunter College delegate (from 1954); American Council of Learned Societies, recipient of travel grants (1958–1959); Fulbright and Smith-Mundt Awards, screening committee member (1960–1968); John Dewey Foundation, recipient of publication grant (1972); Charles S. Peirce Foundation, secretary (1974). Honors and memberships: American Association for the Advancement of Science, Fellow; New York Academy of Sciences, Fellow; Charles S. Peirce Society (president 1973–1975); American Mathematical Society; Mathematical Association for American Research.

Carolyn Eisele received her bachelor's degree from Hunter College and, after she received a master's degree from the University of Chicago, moved from instructor to professor at Hunter. A recipient of numerous research grants and a member of several professional societies, she did research on the history and philosophy of mathematics and science of the late nineteenth century and the thought of Charles S. Peirce.

JH/MBO

PRIMARY SOURCES

Eisele, Carolyn. "Charles S. Peirce and the Problem of Map-Projection." *Proceedings of the American Philosophical Society* 107, no. 4 (August 1963): 299–307.

———, ed. Charles S. Peirce, *The New Elements of Mathematics. Vol. 1, Arithmetic.* Atlantic Highlands, N.J.: Humanities Press, 1976.

———. *Studies in the Scientific and Mathematical Philosophy of Charles S. Peirce: Essays.* Ed. R. M. Martin. New York: Mouton, 1979.

———, ed. *Historical Perspectives on Peirce's Logic of Science: A History of Science.* New York: Mouton Publishers, 1985.

STANDARD SOURCES
AMS 10–14.

ELAM, CONSTANCE FLIGG (1894–1995)
See Tipper, Constance Fligg (Elam).

ELDERTON, ETHEL (1878–1954)
British eugenicist. Seven siblings. Educated Bedford College for Women (no degree). Professional experience: school teacher (to 1905); Eugenics Records Office, secretary (from 1905); Francis Galton, assistant (from 1905); Galton Research Fellow; Galton Fellow; Galton laboratory assistant professor (to 1923).

Ethel Elderton became interested in eugenics at Bedford College, where she was a student of Alice Lee. Elderton was third in a family of four girls and four boys. Her father earned a first in the Mathematics Tripos at Cambridge and her older brother William Palin Elderton became a distinguished actuary. After the death of her father in 1890, she returned home and taught to help support her younger siblings. Although she did not complete her Bedford degree, she remained interested in mathematics. Elderton was enthusiastic about the eugenist cause, and became Sir Francis Galton's assistant after a recommendation from Alice Lee. She became an assistant to the Eugenics Records Office, was appointed Galton Research Scholar in the Galton Eugenics Laboratory, and was the first Galton Research Fellow. Later she became the Galton Fellow and finally assistant professor in the Galton Laboratory. Elderton thrived on the detailed mathematical computing required in this laboratory.

In the eugenics laboratory, Elderton gathered and processed data on populations. Her work made Sir Francis Galton revise, to some extent, his views on the intellectual inferiority of females. She collected material on the resemblances between different sets of relatives as part of a larger study of the inheritance of ability. One of Elderton's most controversial conclusions dealt with alcoholism. Convinced that it was due to heredity, she concluded that social reforms were useless, and perhaps even harmful. Elderton's statistics were incontrovertible, but her assumptions and those of other early eugenicists, that social problems could be reduced to a set of rigorous measurements, led to much distortion.

Elderton contributed another very interesting study, *The Report on the English Birthrate.* Filled with material about the lives of working men and women, it provides an account with valuable statistics of abortion practices in women in the north of England. However, her interpretation was controversial. Because the English birthrate had been declining, reformers were advocating free milk, free medical attention for mothers, and other social reforms. Elderton, however, saw this kind of "do-gooding" humanitarianism as doing more harm than good.

JH/MBO

PRIMARY SOURCES
Elderton, Ethel. *A First Study of the Influence of Parental Alcoholism on the Physique and Ability of the Offspring.* London: Dulau, 1910.

———. *Report on the English Birthrate: Part I, England North of the Humber.* London: Dulau, 1914.

SECONDARY SOURCES
Love, Rosaleen. "'Alice in Eugenics-Land': Feminism and Eugenics in the Scientific Careers of Alice Lee and Ethel Elderton." *Annals of Science* 36 (1979): 145–158.

ELEANORA, DUCHESS OF MANTUA
(fl. 17th century)
Italian midwife. Born in Mantua? Married Emperor Ferdinand III. Educated lying-in hospital in Vienna.

Eleanora was one of the women mentioned by Harless who studied medicine and midwifery at the lying-in hospital in Vienna. She became an expert *accoucheuse.* JH/MBO

STANDARD SOURCES
Harless; Hurd-Mead 1938.

ELEANORA, DUCHESS OF TROPPAU AND JAGERNDORF (fl. 17th century)
"German" physician and nutritionist.

Eleanora, Duchess of Troppau and Jagerndorf, published several books. The best known of these books, *Secks Bücher auserlesener Artzneyen und Kunstücke fast für aller des menschlichen Leibes, Gebrechen und Krankheiten* (Six Books of Selected Medical Arts and Tricks for All Human Life, Afflictions, and Illnesses), was published in 1600 and reissued in 1613 and 1618. Under a different name, it was reprinted in Leipzig in 1709 and in Nuremberg in 1723. This very popular book contained many herbal remedies. JH/MBO

PRIMARY SOURCES
Eleanora, Duchess of Troppau. *Secks Bücher auserlesener Artzneyen und Kunststücke fast für alle des menschlichen Leibes, Gebrechen und Krankheiten.* Zerbst: Zacharias Deorffern, 1600; 1613; 1618.
———. *Aufgesprungener Granatapfel des cristl. Samariters, oder eröffnete Geheimnisse vieler fortrefflichen Arzneimittel, nebst einer Diast und Kochbuch für Kranke.* Leipzig, 1709; Nuremberg, 1723.

STANDARD SOURCES
Hurd-Mead 1938.

ELEPHANTIS (1st century B.C.E.)
Greek physician of the first century B.C.E.

The name Elephantis was not uncommon in classical times among the *hetaerae,* who often adopted animal names. It seems likely, therefore, that Elephantis was a courtesan, and it is also possible that two or more persons of the same name have been fused together as a single entity. Galen mentions her ability to cure baldness, and Pliny discusses her performance as a midwife and stresses her conflict with Lais. According to Pauly, the original Greek source for the information about Elephantis was a "truly antique Kama-Sutra," a product of "late Alexandrian debauchery."

JH/MBO

SECONDARY SOURCES
Galen. *Opera omnia* 12. Hildesheim: Georg Olms, 1965.
Pliny. *Natural History* 28: 23.81.

STANDARD SOURCES
Ogilvie 1986; Pauly-Wissowa, vol. 5.

ELGOOD, CORNELIA BONTÉ SHELDON (AMOS) (1874–1960)
British physician. Born 1874 to a judge in the Egyptian judicial system. At least one sibling, Sir Maurice Amos. Married Major Percy Elgood (1907). Educated University of London (M.D., 1900). Professional experience: International Quarantine Board of Egypt, member (1901–1902); Alexandria, private practice and outpatient clinic for women and children (1902–1906); Cairo, school administrator (1906–1923). Honors and memberships: Decoration of the Nile (1923); Commander of the British Empire (1939). Died 21 November 1960.

After Sheldon Amos earned her medical degree from London University, she accepted an appointment in Egypt with the International Quarantine Board. Her background probably prepared her for this position as the first woman doctor to be accepted into this service, for her father was a judge in the Egyptian judicial system and her brother, Sir Maurice Amos, was a judicial advisor in this system. Her first appointment was in the Suez at the quarantine hospitals at El-Tor. There she encountered pilgrims returning from Mecca, many with communicable diseases. She produced several papers on dysentery, one of the most common diseases she encountered. After a short stay in the Suez, she was transferred to Alexandria, where she developed a private practice and opened an outpatient clinic for women and children. She was unpaid for her work in this clinic, which was located in a government hospital. After four years in Alexandria Amos was transferred to Cairo. Her charge from the Ministry of Education was to develop and expand a program for the education of girls. At this point, her career slipped into administration. Beginning with three schools with six hundred girl pupils, by 1923 she developed the system into 106 schools with twenty thousand girl pupils. Her medical training served her well in establishing the school system, for she stressed the importance of good sanitation and the avoidance of overcrowding. In Cairo, she met and married Major Percy Elgood.

As she was directing the schools, Elgood also served as a woman medical member on the Countess of Cromer's commission to build the first free children's dispensaries in Egypt. Begun in Cairo and Alexandria, they soon branched out to many parts of the country. Many Egyptian women were trained to be midwives in these institutions. Using her experience in education, Elgood also sponsored Egyptian women to study medicine in Britain, testified before the Balfour Commission on Public Health in Egypt, and served on the board of Victorial Hospital. Even after she retired, the Elgoods remained in Egypt, retiring to Heliopolis. After her husband's death, she continued to live there until 1956, when the Suez crisis forced her to return to England. She lived in London until her death at age eighty-six. JH/MBO

SECONDARY SOURCES
Levin, Beatrice. *Women and Medicine: Pioneers Meeting the Challenge.* Lincoln, Nebr.: Media Publishing, 1988.
"Mrs. Elgood." *Medical Woman's Journal* 30 (October 1923): 309–310.
"Obituary. Bonté S. Elgood, C.B.E., M.B." *British Medical Journal,* 17 December 1960, 1813.

ELION, GERTRUDE BELLE (1918–1999)

U.S. biochemist. Born 23 January 1918 in New York City to Bertha Cohen and Robert Elion. Never married. Educated Hunter College (B.A., 1937); New York University (M.S., 1941); Brooklyn Polytechnic Institute (graduate studies, 1944–1946). Professional experience: New York public schools, substitute high school science teacher (1937–1942); Quaker Maid Company Foods, quality control chemist (1940–1942); Johnson and Johnson, laboratory assistant (1943–1944); Wellcome Research Laboratories, research chemist (1944–1951), senior research chemist (1951–1967), Department of Experimental Therapy, head (1967–1983), scientist emerita and consultant (1983–1999). Concurrent experience: Duke University, research professor of medicine and pharmacology (1983–1999). Honors and memberships: American Chemical Society, Garvan Medal (1968); George Washington University, honorary Ph.D. (1968); Nobel Prize for medicine (with George Herbert Hitchings) (1988); National Medal of Science (1991); National Inventors Hall of Fame; National Academy of Sciences, Fellow; National Women's Hall of Fame; American Association for Cancer Research, president; numerous honorary doctorates. Died 20 February 1999 in Chapel Hill, N.C.

Gertrude Elion had the rare distinction of being honored as an outstanding scientist with the Nobel Prize in medicine. She held only a master's degree in chemistry, although her hundreds of important papers qualified her for a doctorate. Her family on both sides included rabbinical scholars from Eastern Europe who immigrated to New York. Her father trained as a dentist and established a successful career, but lost his money in the Depression.

Elion was an excellent high school student, and went on to attend Hunter College, from which she graduated Phi Beta Kappa, with highest honors in chemistry. She continued on at New York University, completing a master's degree in chemistry while working as a substitute science teacher in the public high schools. Unable to find a research laboratory position, she worked for a while as a quality control biochemist for a supermarket chain. She briefly worked for other commercial laboratories, but found most laboratories unwilling to hire women.

In 1944, aided by the scarcity of male scientists during World War II, Elion found a position as a biochemist at Wellcome Research Laboratories in Tuckahoe, New York. There she met a highly unusual biochemist, George H. Hitchings, with whom she worked for the next forty years.

Elion began to examine the purine bases as part of Hitchings's strategy to follow fundamental research on nucleic acids. He believed that this would not only unravel some of the basic causes for disease but indicate drugs that disrupted the large amount of nucleic acids required by the cells of bacteria, viruses, and tumors. The first successful drug she developed with Hitchings was 6-metacaptopurine (6-MP), which proved to be effective in treating leukemia when combined with other drugs. Another drug, azathioprine, derived from 6-MP, proved highly effective in suppressing the immune system and (as Imuran) allowed kidney and later other organ transplants, and was later used to treat a variety of autoimmune diseases.

Trying to reduce the side effects of 6-MP, Elion examined a drug that reduced the amount of uric acid produced in the body and found that this made an effective drug to help those suffering from kidney disease as well as patients taking radiation or cancer therapies. In the 1960s, Elion's research began to be more independent of Hitchings's work, although they still worked together often. She had been encouraged to write and publish her own papers from the beginning of their collaboration. By 1967, Hitchings moved from active research to serve as vice-president of research, while Elion took over as director of the experimental research division. There, she was able to prove her mettle in directing the development of antiviral agents.

Elion was recognized about the same time that she took over the department by the American Chemical Society, which awarded her its only prize for women scientists, the Garvan Prize. The result of her antiviral investigations would be an anti-herpes drug that also used modified purines: acyclovir. The first really effective anti-herpes drug, acyclovir was announced in the late seventies and released as a drug some years later.

Wellcome, now Burroughs Wellcome, had moved to Chapel Hill, North Carolina, where Elion was able to develop close ties to the academic researchers in the medical faculty at Duke University. When she retired in 1983, she remained as a consultant to her unit at Wellcome, which continued to follow up her and Hitchings's lines of research. They developed the first effective AIDS drug, azidothymidine or AZT.

In retirement, Elion also began to work as a research professor at Duke University, where she took on the occasional student. To her great surprise, she was awarded the Nobel Prize with her former boss, Hitchings. Burroughs Wellcome gave her a matching prize to contribute to charity; she gave it to her college, Hunter, for women's science education. She delighted in the opportunity to support scientific training for women. She was active up to the time of her death at the age of eighty-one in Chapel Hill, North Carolina.   JH/MBO

PRIMARY SOURCES

Elion, Gertrude B. "The Reaction of Guanidine Derivatives with Glucose." M.A. thesis, New York University, 1942.

———. With G. H. Hitchings and E. A. Falco. "Antagonists of Nucleic Acid Derivatives II." *Journal of Biological Chemistry* 185 (1950): 643–649.

———. With G. H. Hitchings. "Studies on Condensed Pyrimidine Systems XI." *Journal of the American Chemical Society* 75 (1953): 4311–4314. One of a long series of articles with this title, sometimes with Hitchings, sometimes by herself.

———. "Condensed Pyrimidine Systems XXI." *Journal of Organic Chemistry* 27 (1962): 2478–2491.

———. *"Some Aspects of Immunosuppression."* Annals of the New York Academy of Sciences 129 (1966): 779–803.

———. With G. H. Hitchings. "Mechanisms of Action of Purine and Pyrimidine Analogs." In *Cancer Chemotherapy: Basic and Clinical Applications,* ed. I. Brodsky and S. B. Kalin, 26–36. New York: Grune and Stratton, 1967.

———. "The Quest for a Cure." *Annual Review of Pharmacology and Toxicology* 33 (1993): 1–23.

SECONDARY SOURCES

Altman, Lawrence, K. "Gertrude Elion, Drug Developer, Dies at 81." *New York Times,* 23 February 1999. Obituary notice with portrait.

McGrayne, Sharon Bertsch. "Gertrude B. Elion." In *Nobel Prize Women in Science: Their Lives, Struggles and Momentous Discoveries.* New York: Birch Lane Press, 1993: 280–303. Includes multiple portraits.

STANDARD SOURCES

AMS 9–19; Grinstein 1993 (article by Miles Goodman; includes a lengthy list of her publications); Grinstein 1997 (article by Miles Goodman); *Notable* (includes portrait); Shearer and Shearer 1995.

ELIOT, MARTHA MAY (1891–1978)

American physician. Born 7 April 1891 in Dorchester, Mass. Never married. Educated Radcliffe College (1913, Phi Beta Kappa); Johns Hopkins Medical College (M.D., 1918; hon. D.H.L., S.Sc., LL.D.). Professional experience: Yale University School of Medicine, instructor of pediatrics (1921–1922), assistant clinical professor (1927–1932), associate clinical professor (1932–1935); Division of Child and Maternal Health, U.S. Department of Health, Education and Welfare, director (1924–1956); World Health Organization, assistant director general (1949–1951); Social Security Administration, U.S. Department of Health, Education and Welfare, chief, children's bureau (1951–1956); Harvard University, School of Public Health, professor of maternal and child health (1957–1960), professor emerita (1960–1978). Died 1978.

Born 7 April 1891 in Dorchester, Massachusetts, Martha Eliot graduated Phi Beta Kappa from Radcliffe College in 1913 and went on to Johns Hopkins Medical College for her medical degree (1918). For the next few years, she taught pediatric medicine in the medical school at Yale University. In 1924, she was named director of the Division of Child and Maternal Health under Grace Abbott. Eliot was responsible for the passage of several child health care bills. The Emergency Maternal and Infant Care Program bill of 1943 provided maternal and child care for the lower-ranking military personnel during wartime conditions. In 1951, Eliot was appointed chief of the United States Children's Bureau and also served the World Health Organization. She was responsible for a study that isolated the causes of rickets in children.

Eliot was an active member of the Academy of Pediatrics, the American Pediatric Society, the Public Health Association, the Society of Research in Child Development, and the Conference on Social Work. Among the many honors Eliot received were honorary degrees from Johns Hopkins University (D.H.L., S.Sc., LL.D.); the *Parent's Magazine* Medal (1948); Lasker Award (1948); Sedgwick Award of the Public Health Association (1958); New York Academy of Medicine Award (1965); Radcliffe College Founders Award (1965). She was chosen as United States representative to the executive board of the United Nations Childrens Fund (1952–1957).   KM

STANDARD SOURCES

AMS 8, B 9, P&B 10–11; *Current Biographies,* 1948; *LKW.*

ELIZABETH OF BOHEMIA (1618–1680)

Bohemian student of natural philosophy. Born in Heidelberg 1618 to Elizabeth, daughter of James I of England, and Frederick V, elector of the Rhine Palatinate and later king of Bohemia. Never married. Died 1618 at Herford, Germany.

Elizabeth of Bohemia was the eldest daughter of Frederick V, Elector Palatine from 1610 to 1623 and briefly king of Bohemia (1619–1620), who had married Elizabeth, daughter of James I of England, in 1613. After her father was deposed, Princess Elizabeth spent her life in exile, first in Holland, at the Hague, where her father maintained the semblance of a royal court, and later in what is now northwestern Germany, where from 1667 she was abbess of a convent at Herford. She maintained a correspondence with Descartes, who dedicated his *Principia philosophiae* (1644) to her, declaring that in her alone were talents for metaphysics and for mathematics united, making possible the proper functioning of the Cartesian system.   JH/MBO

SECONDARY SOURCES
Descartes, René. *Lettres de Descartes: Où sont traitées plusieurs belles questions. Touchant la morale, physique, médecine et les mathématiques.* Rev. ed. Paris: Charles Qugot, 1663. Includes correspondence with Elizabeth.
———. *Principia philosophiae.* Amsterdam: Ludovicum Elzevirium, 1650. Descartes dedicates this work to Elizabeth.

STANDARD SOURCES
Encyclopaedia Britannica.

ELIZABETH OF POLAND, QUEEN OF HUNGARY (ca. 1310–1386)

Polish/Hungarian healer. A.k.a. Elizabeth Lokletek. Born ca. 1310. Father Ladislaus I of Poland. Married Charles I of Hungary. Children. Died 1386.

Daughter of Ladislaus I of Poland, Elizabeth married Charles I of Hungary to cement a Polish/Hungarian alliance. She was the mother of Louis of Anjou, king of Hungary and Poland (b. 1326). Interested in medicine, she invented a treatment for rheumatism made from distilled water and rosemary known as the "water of the queen of Hungary."   JH/MBO

STANDARD SOURCES
Echols and Williams; Hurd-Mead 1938; Lipinska 1900.

ELIZABETH OF PORTUGAL, SAINT (1271–ca. 1336)

Sicilian/Portuguese healer. A.k.a. Isabel of Aragon, Queen of Portugal. Daughter of Constance of Sicily, queen of Aragon and Pedro III of Aragon. Married Diniz of Portugal. One son, Alfonso IV; one daughter, Constance, Queen of Castile.

Unhappily married, Elizabeth devoted her energies to pious activities. She started an orphanage at Coimbra, Portugal,

contributed to hospitals and universities, and founded an agricultural college to prepare girls for marriage to farmers, giving land to the graduates. After her husband died in 1325, Elizabeth donned the habit of the Poor Clares, although she did not take vows. Credited with miraculously restoring the sight of a blind child, she was canonized in 1625. Many miracles have been associated with her shrine at the Convent of Saint Clare in Coimbra.   JH/MBO

SECONDARY SOURCES
Farmer, David Hugh. *Oxford Dictionary of Saints.* Oxford: Clarendon Press, 1978. 129–130.

STANDARD SOURCES
Echols and Williams.

ELIZABETH OF SCHÖNAU (1129–1164)

German healer. Born 1129. Died 1164 at Schönau.

Elizabeth entered the Benedictine double monastery at Schönau as a child. She was known for her healing abilities and as a mystic and proponent of clerical reform.   JH/MBO

STANDARD SOURCES
Echols and Williams.

ELLES, GERTRUDE LILIAN (1872–1960)

British invertebrate paleontologist and stratigrapher. Born 8 October 1872 at Wimbledon to Mary Chesney and Jamison Elles. Five siblings. Educated Wimbledon High School; Newnham College, Cambridge (1891–1895; M.A., 1932; Sc.D., 1949). Professional experience: Newnham College, fellow (1900–1903), lecturer (1904–1936), university reader (1936–1938), reader emerita (1938–1960). Died 18 November 1960 in Helensburgh, Scotland.

Invertebrate paleontologist and stratigrapher, Gertrude Lilian Elles attended Newnham College, where she was a College Scholar. She received a Class 2 rating on Part I of the Natural Science Tripos in 1894 and a Class 1 in Geology in 1895. She held many specialized positions at Newnham, including director of studies in natural science and medicine (1927–1936) and in geography (1927–1933). She was vice-principal of the college from 1925 to 1936 and a member of the council from 1913 to 1922 and again from 1924 to 1943. She was lecturer in geology from 1926 to 1936 and the first woman university reader from 1936 to 1938. After she retired, she became a Cambridge University Reader Emeritus, the first woman to hold this position, a post which she retained until her death.

Elles was one of a family of six. Her father was Scottish and her mother English, so her childhood was divided between Scotland and London. Her broad experiences during this time and her father's business connections with the Far East provided her with an understanding of different cultures and peoples.

She was able to put her broad background into practical use in her chosen field of geology. After she gained first class honors in geology she was awarded a Bathurst Studentship, which she used for study in Sweden. The letters she wrote home were enthusiastic about her experiences.

Under the supervision of Professor Lapworth of Birmingham University, Elles studied graptolites and their use in stratigraphy in the Ordovician and Silurian rocks of the Welsh borderland and Wales. By the time she was thirty years old, she had begun the publication with E. M. R. Wood (DAME ETHEL SHAKESPEAR) of the monumental *Monograph of British Graptolites*. This monograph formed the basis of the work on British graptolites for years to come. In 1922, Elles published an essay in the *Proceedings of the Geologists' Association* in which she gave her ideas on the evolution and classification of graptolites gained from her lifelong study. Although she is best known for her studies of graptolites, she also worked on the metamorphism and structure of the Precambrian rocks of the Scottish Highlands. In 1907 she earned a doctorate in science at the University of Dublin. She received the Murchison Medal of the Geological Society, the first woman to be so honored, in 1919. She was elected Fellow of the Geological Society of London that same year, one of the first group of women admitted, and was a member of its council from 1923 to 1927. She was an honorary Fellow of the Geological Societies of Edinburgh, Liverpool, and China. After Elles became an assistant demonstrator in the Sedgwick Museum and a college lecturer, Newnham became her permanent home. During her vacations, she went to the field, and with map, pick, hammer, and lens, collected her fossils.

Though geology was her major interest, Elles was involved in many subjects, including photography, philosophy, birds, travel, and ethical and social problems. Always interested in music, she attended concerts at King's College Chapel until increasing deafness took away the pleasure. She apparently was rather outspoken, and was not universally loved by members of the Senior Combination Room. During the years of World War I, she was an active member of the Red Cross Society, and in 1915 was a commandant of a small convalescent hospital for soldiers in Newnham Walk. She was named a Member of the British Empire for her services. During the war years, she continued with her teaching in the evenings and kept in touch with college activities.

JH/MBO

PRIMARY SOURCES
Elles, Gertrude Lilian. With E. Mary R. Wood. *A Monograph of British Graptolites*. London: Printed for the Palaeontological Society, 1901–1914.
———. *The Study of Geological Maps*. Cambridge: Cambridge University Press, 1921.
Many articles on paleontology and stratigraphy in the *Quarterly Journal of the Geological Society* and the *Proceedings of the Geologist's Association*.

SECONDARY SOURCES
Bulman, O. M. B. "Gertrude Lilian Elles." *Proceedings of the Geological Society of London* no. 1592 (1961): 143–145.
[King, William B. R.]. "Gertrude Lilian Elles." *Proceedings of the Geologists' Association* 72, pt. 1 (1961): 168–170.
Finney, Stanley C. "Elles, Gertrude Lilian (1872–1960)." In *Biographies of Geologists: Materials for the Study of the History of Geology, Prepared in Geology 851, a Seminar in the History of Geology*, ed. Auréle La Rocque. Sixth Supplement. Columbus: Ohio State University Department of Geology.

STANDARD SOURCES
Newnham, vol. 1; *Newnham Roll*; Sarjeant.

ELLIOTT, CHARLOTTE (1881–1974)

U.S. plant pathologist. Born in 1881. Educated Stanford University (A.B., 1907; A.M., 1913); University of Wisconsin (Ph.D., 1918). Professional experience: high school teacher (1907–1908); South Dakota State Normal School, instructor biology, geography (1908–1912); Brookings State College, botany instructor (1914–1916); USDA, Bureau of Plant Industry, scientific assistant (1918–1922), assistant pathologist (1922–1923), associate pathologist (1923–1940), pathologist (1946). Honors and memberships: Botanical Society of Washington, president (1942).

Most of Charlotte Elliott's career was with the United States Department of Agriculture, after she received her doctoral degree from the University of Wisconsin. During her graduate studies, she worked as a teacher in several schools and colleges.

Elliott's research was on plant pathogens, especially on bacterial and fungal diseases. She contributed five papers to the USDA *Journal of Agricultural Research* and wrote a manual on bacterial plant pathogens. Toward the end of her career she served as president of the Botanical Society of Washington.

JH/MBO

PRIMARY SOURCES
Elliott, Charlotte. *Manual of Bacterial Plant Pathogens*. Waltham, Mass.: Chronica Botanica Co., 1930; 1951.

STANDARD SOURCES
AMS; Bailey; Barnhart; Rossiter 1982.

ELLIS, FLORENCE HAWLEY (1906–1991)

U.S. anthropologist and archeologist. Born 17 September 1906 in Canagnea, Sonora, Mexico, to Amy Roach and Fred Graham Hawley. Married Bruce Ellis (1 June 1950). One daughter, Andrea (later Mrs. Richard Eastin). Educated University of Arizona (A.B., 1927; M.A., 1928); University of Chicago (Ph.D., 1934). Professional experience: University of Arizona, instructor and research associate (1928–1933); University of New Mexico, Sante Fe and Albuquerque, faculty (1934–1937); University of Chicago, associate professor (1937–1942); University of New Mexico, associate (1942–1954), professor of anthropology (1954–retirement); Eckerd College, adjunct professor (1973–1976). Honors and memberships: Society of Ethnohistory, president; Sigma Xi, Phi Beta Kappa, member. Died 1991.

Florence Ellis earned her first two degrees from the University of Arizona in the twenties. She then obtained her doctoral degree in anthropology at the University of Chicago, where she became an associate professor for five years. In 1942, she moved to the University of New Mexico, where she rose to full professor and remained until retirement.

Ellis's major research was on comparative patterns of social organization of southwestern Pueblos, deducing prehistoric culture by analogy to their descendent peoples. She also worked on dating Southwest ruins by tree-ring dating techniques (dendochronology). In the 1950s, she excavated the original Spanish capital of New Mexico and of the largest pueblo ruin, near San Juan. She was active professionally, belonging to a number of anthropological and archeological societies. She was president of the Society of Ethnohistory in 1970. Her honors included memberships in Sigma Xi and Phi Beta Kappa.

JH/MBO

PRIMARY SOURCES
Ellis, Florence Hawley. *The Significance of the Dated Prehistory of Chetro Keti, Chaco Canyon, New Mexico.* Albuquerque: University of New Mexico Press, 1934.
———. *Field Manual of Prehistoric Southwestern Pottery.* Albuquerque: University of New Mexico Press, 1936.
———. *Tree Ring Analysis and Dating in the Mississippi Drainage.* Chicago: University of Chicago Press, 1941.
———. *A Reconstruction of the Basic Jemez Pueblo Pattern of Social Organization.* Albuquerque: University of New Mexico Press, 1964.

SECONDARY SOURCES
Babcock, Barbara A. and Nancy J. Parez. *Daughters of the Desert.* Albuquerque: University of New Mexico Press, 1988.

STANDARD SOURCES
Debus.

ELLISOR, ALVA CHRISTINE (1892–1964)

U.S. stratigrapher. Born 28 April 1892 at Galveston, Tex., to Emma Osterman and William Lee Ellisor, Sr. Four brothers. Never married. Educated Galveston's public schools and Ball High School (valedictorian); University of Texas (B.A., 1915; additional work 1916–1917). Professional experience: Humble Oil and Refining Company, summer assistant (1918), paleontologist (1920), research stratigrapher (1921–1947); University of Kansas, geology teacher (1918–1920). Died 1964.

Alva Ellisor was the only daughter in a family of five children. She was valedictorian of her high school class and accumulated an impressive record at the University of Texas, where she majored in geology. Upon graduation, she taught science at the high school from which she graduated. She then returned to the University of Texas for an additional two years. Although she spent two years teaching at the University of Kansas, her major life work was with the Humble Oil and Refining Company where she worked in three separate stints. The first position was significant even though it was only for a summer (1918) because she was probably the first woman to do geologic work for an oil company (she worked at Cisco Texas for Humble). After a two-year break teaching at Kansas and working for the Kansas Geological Survey, Ellisor was again employed by Humble to organize a new paleontology laboratory at Humble's Houston office. By this time, she was well known as a stratigrapher, and was appointed Humble's first research stratigrapher and paleontologist. She continued this work until her retirement in 1947. After retiring, she traveled to different parts of the world and attended meetings of professional societies. She donated her extensive library to the University of Texas.

Ellisor was twice elected vice-president of the Houston Geological Society (1924 and 1930). She was presented with the Distinguished Geology Alumni Award of the Department of Geology, the University of Texas in 1962. She was a Fellow of the Geological Society of America, a member of the American Association of Petroleum Geologists, the Society of Economic Paleontologists and Mineralogists (vice-president in 1941), and the Paleontological Society.

Ellisor recognized the importance of combining laboratory work with field work. She examined nearly every area of the gulf coast, visiting Pliocene, Miocene, Oligocene, and Cretaceous exposures on the coast. After her first paper (1918) was published, she identified the first Foraminifera ever observed on the Gulf Coast. Although Foraminifera had previously been observed in Florida and in other Tertiary formations throughout the world, this discovery supplied the oil industry with the means to identify these oil-bearing formations where previously they had been dependent on large fossils or fossil fragments. After this discovery, she became Humble's first research stratigrapher and paleontologist. During her career with Humble, Ellisor published numerous papers on the stratigraphy and paleontology of the Gulf Coast. In a 1926 paper, she established that the development of limestone in the Heterostegina zone which is at the surface at Damon Mound and other salt domes underground was of coral reef origin. CK

PRIMARY SOURCES

Ellisor, Alva Christine. "Turritella in the Buda and Georgetown Limestones." *University of Texas Bulletin*, no. 1840 (1918).

———. "Coral Reefs in the Oligocene of Texas." *Houston Geological Society Bulletin* 3 (1926).

———. With Joseph Cushman. "The Foraminiferal Fauna of the Anahuac Formation." *Journal of Paleontology* 19, no. 6 (1945): 545–572.

SECONDARY SOURCES

Teas, L. P. "In Memoriam. Alva Christine Ellisor." *Houston Geological Society Bulletin* 7, no. 6 (1965): 9–10.

———. "Alva Christine Ellisor (1892–1964)." *American Association of Petroleum Geologists Bulletin* 49, no. 4 (1965): 467–471. With portrait.

ELSOM, KATHARINE (O'SHEA) (1903–1996)

U.S. physician, nutritionist. Born 1903. Father Michael Vincent O'Shea. Three siblings. Married physician Kendall Elsom (1928). Two children. Educated University of Wisconsin (Phi Beta Kappa); University of Pennsylvania (M.D.). Professional experience: clinical research on vitamin deficiencies, Philadelphia General Hospital and University of Pennsylvania Hospital; University of Pennsylvania School of Medicine, faculty (1931–1979). Died 14 September 1996.

Katharine O'Shea's father was a professor of education at University of Wisconsin and lectured extensively on the psychology of child development and progressive education. Katharine married a physician who was a gastroenterologist; they had two children.

Interested in the effects of specific vitamins on health, Katharine O'Shea Elsom conducted long-term studies on the effects of vitamin B deficiency and, with her physician husband, researched the relationship of nutritional factors to the control of infection. She taught in various departments of the University of Pennsylvania School of Medicine for forty-eight years. JH/MBO

SECONDARY SOURCES

"Katharine O'Shea Elsom." *Almanac* 43, no. 5 (24 September 1996). Obituary notice.

Knapp, Sally. *Women Doctors Today.* New York: Thomas Y. Crowell Company, 1947.

EMERSON, GLADYS LUDWINA (ANDERSON) (1903–1984)

U.S. biochemist and nutritionist. Born 1 July 1903 in Caldwell, Kans., to Louise (Williams) and Otis Anderson. Married Oliver Huddleston Emerson (1932; divorced 1945). Educated Oklahoma College for Women (A.B. and B.S., 1925); Stanford University (M.A., 1926); University of California (Ph.D., 1932); University of Göttingen, graduate study (1932–1933). Professional experience: Oklahoma College for Women, teaching assistant (1923–1925); Stanford University, assistant (1925–1926); Institute of Experimental Biology, University of California, research associate (1933–1942); visiting lecturer in pharmacology medical school (1945); Sloan-Kettering Institution for Cancer Research, research associate (1950–1953); Merck Institute Therapeutic Research, Rahway, N.J., head, department of animal nutrition, (1942–1946); Sharpe & Dohme Research Labs, director of nutrition (1946–1957); Pennsylvania State College, Marie Curie lecturer (1951); Iowa State College, research lecturer (1952); University of California at Los Angeles, department of Home Economics, professor, chairman (1957–1961), professor of nutrition and public health nutrition, head of division of nutritional sciences, vice chairman, department public health (1962–1971); University of Nebraska, visiting lecturer in biochemistry and nutrition (1958); Office of Scientific Research and Development, researcher (1943–1945). Memberships: liaison and scientific advisory board Q.M. Food and Container Institute (1949–1950); National Research Council, food and nutrition research committee (1952); Food and Nutrition Board (1959–1964); committee dietary allowances (1960–1964); American Board of Nutrition, executive council (from 1959). Rensselaer Polytechnic Institute industrial council, panelist (1955); organizing committee 5th International Congress on Nutrition, Southern California section World Health Organization (1963) delegate to conferences in field; instructor of trainees for Peace Corps (1962–1964). Honors: recipient of Garvan Medal, 1952.

Although Gladys Anderson was born in Caldwell, Kansas, her family moved to Texas, where she spent her childhood. She was an outstanding student, excelling in both mathematics and history. When she was in the seventh grade, the family moved to El Reno, Oklahoma, where her father was the station master for the Rock Island Railroad. Her home life was happy, and her parents encouraged her interest in many different fields.

As an undergraduate at Oklahoma College for Women, Gladys Anderson had a double major. She earned a bachelor of science degree in chemistry and a bachelor of arts in English. Offered assistantships in both chemistry and history at Stanford University, she accepted the history assistantship and earned a master's in history. Her master's thesis was "The Bank Controversy in the Senate, 1833–1834." After becoming head of the history, geography, and citizenship department at an Oklahoma City junior high school (Roosevelt Junior High School), Anderson soon accepted a fellowship in biochemistry and nutrition at the University of California, Berkeley. Her teaching fellowship lasted for three years, but she became a research assistant at Iowa State College for the year 1930–1931. She received her doctorate in animal nutrition and biochemistry with a minor in organic chemistry in 1932, and in that same year married a colleague, Oliver Huddleston Emerson, and became a postdoctoral fellow at the University of Göttingen, where she studied chemistry with Nobel Prize–winning chemist Adolf Windaus. She also worked with Adolf Butenandt, a researcher who studied hormones. She and her husband spent eighteen months (1932–1933) in Göttingen. She had some minor skirmishes with the Nazis because of her outspoken ways. By refusing to salute she displeased an SS officer. However, she formed many useful scientific friendships there.

When Emerson returned to the United States, she worked as a research associate at the Institute of Experimental Biology at the University of California, Berkeley. At Berkeley she studied vitamin E, using wheat germ as her source, and became the first to isolate this vitamin. Leaving Berkeley in 1941 to join the staff at the pharmaceutical firm Merck and Company, Emerson directed research in nutrition and pharmaceuticals. At Merck, she worked with the B vitamin complex, testing her results on laboratory animals, and observing that when rhesus monkeys were deprived of B-6, they developed arteriosclerosis. During World War II, Emerson worked in the U.S. Office of Scientific Research and Development. After the war, she researched the link between diet and cancer at the Sloan Kettering Institute, and eventually became professor of nutrition and vice-chairman of the department of public health at the University of California at Los Angeles.

Emerson was a fellow of the American Association for the Advancement of Science and the New York Academy of Sciences and a member of the American Chemical Society (chairman, women's service committee, 1953–1958) and the American Institute of Nutrition (councillor, 1952–1955; chairman, membership committee, 1964). She was also a member of the Society of Experimental Biology and Medicine (Gordon Research Conference (chairman, vitamins and metabolism, 1952; vice-chairman, 1951) and the Pan American Medical Association (council, 1959–1960). As a member of the International Union of Nutrition Scientists, she was a delegate to the national committee from 1959 through 1962. She held memberships in Sigma Xi, Delta Omega, Sigma Delta Epsilon, Iota Sigma Pi (national president, 1951–1957). Emerson contributed articles to scientific journals and was associate editor of the *Journal of Nutrition* (1952–1956).

She was elected to the Oklahoma Hall of Fame in 1943 and received the Garvan Medal of the American Chemical Society. In 1984, Emerson died of cancer at her home. A Gladys A. Emerson Memorial Fund to aid students in nutritional sciences was established.   JH/MBO

PRIMARY SOURCES

Emerson, Gladys Anderson. "Agnes Fay Morgan and Early Nutrition Discoveries in California." *Federation Proceedings* 36 (May 1977): 1911–1914.

———. "The Effect of Vitamin A Deficiency upon the Urinary Nitrogen Metabolism of the Dog." Ph.D. diss., University of California, Berkeley, 1932.

———. With H. M. Evans. "The Effect of Vitamin E Deficiency upon Growth." *Journal of Nutrition* 14 (1937): 169–178.

———. "Restoration of Fertility in Successively Older Vitamin E-Deficient Female Rats." *Journal of Nutrition* 18 (1939): 501–506.

———. With H. M. Evans. "Growth and Graying of Rats with Total 'Filtrate Factor' and with Pantothenic Acid." *Proceedings of the SEBM* 46 (1941): 445–448.

———. "The Bioassay of Vitamin E." *Journal of Nutrition* 27 (1944): 216–221.

———. "Water-Soluble Vitamins." *Annual Review of Biochemistry* 20 (1951): 559–598.

———. With D. Heyl, M. M. Gaser, et al. "Studies on Carcinolytic Compounds. VI." *Journal of the American Chemical Society* 78 (1956): 4491–4492.

STANDARD SOURCES

Debus; Grinstein 1993 (article by Paris Svoronos); *Notable* (article by John Henry Dreyfuss); *Notable* Suppl.; Siegel and Finley; Vare and Ptacek; Yost.

ENG, HELGA (1875–?)

Norwegian child psychologist. Born 31 May 1875. Educated University of Oslo (1903–1913); University of Leipzig (Ph.D., 1914); University of Halle (1909–1910). Professional experience: University of Oslo, lecturer in educational psychology (1923–1925?); Psychotechnical Institute, Oslo, director (from 1925).

Memberships: Det Norske Videnskaps-Akademie i Oslo; International Association for Psychology and Tecno-Psychology. Death date unknown.

As director of the Psychotechnical Institute in Oslo, Helga Eng had opportunities to publish on her interests. She published numerous articles on emotions in adults and children. Late in her life, Eng became known internationally as a child psychologist.   K M

PRIMARY SOURCES
Eng, Helga. *Begavelsesforskning: I & II* (Research for Gifted Children). Universitets radioforedrag, Serie B. Oslo: Aschehoug, 1930.
————. *The Psychology of Children's Drawing.* London: Kegan Paul; New York: Harcourt, Brace, 1931.

STANDARD SOURCES
Psychological Register.

ENGELBRECHT, MILDRED AMANDA (1899–?)
U.S. bacteriologist. Born 31 July 1899 in Marengo, Ill. Educated University of Wisconsin (A.B., 1927; fellow, 1929–1930; M.S., 1930; Ph.D., 1934). Professional experience: Pelton Clinic, Elgin, Ill., technician (1927–1929); University of Wisconsin, instructor in agricultural bacteriology (1930–1938); University of Alabama, assistant professor (1938–1943), associate professor (1943–1946), professor (from 1947), head of department (from 1950). Death date unknown.

Mildred Engelbrecht was twenty-eight years old before she got her bachelor's degree. From that time on, she made rapid academic progress. After her bachelor's degree, she took two years off, and worked as a technician in a laboratory. She returned to the University of Wisconsin in 1929 as a fellow, and within five years had earned a doctorate. After getting this degree, she stayed on for four more years at Wisconsin, continuing in her position as instructor in agricultural bacteriology. She then took a position at the University of Alabama as assistant professor in bacteriology and physiological chemistry. By 1947, she was a full professor and by 1950, head of the department. Engelbrecht was a fellow of the American Association for the Advancement of Science and a member of the Society of Microbiology, the Public Health Association, and the Royal Society for Health. Her research was on streptococci, especially those found in milk, and in microslide methods for growing organisms.   J H / M B O

STANDARD SOURCES
AMS 6–8, B 9, P&B 10–11.

ERDMANN, RHODA (1870–1935)
German biologist, cytologist. Born 5 December 1870 in Hersfeld/Hessen to Anna Maria (Heldmann), and Heinrich Erdmann, a high school teacher from a family of physicians. Four siblings. Never married. Educated Höhere Mädchenschule of St. John's Cloister, Hamburg (1876–1886); teacher's examination for higher and middle girls' schools (1892); Universities of Berlin, Zurich, Marburg, and Munich, studied philosophy, mathematics, zoology, and botany (1903–1908); Kassel, Realgymnasium, university qualifying examination (abitur) (1907); Berlin, examinations in mathematics, physics, zoology, and botany for the higher teacher's certificate (1909). Habilitation (university lecturer qualification) in protozoology (1920); Habilitation in medicine (1924). Professional experience: Hamburg, teacher (1901–1903); Robert Koch Institute in Berlin, scientific assistant (1909–1913); Yale University, Osborn Zoological Laboratory, research fellow (1913–1919), lecturer in biology (1915–1916); Rockefeller Institute, research associate (1916–1919); Princeton University, research associate (1916–1919); Friederich-Williams University, Berlin, Institut für experimentelle Zellforschung am Krebsforschungsinstitut der Charité (Charité Institute for Experimental Cell and Cancer Research), associate professor of physiology and cell research (1929–1934). Dismissed under "Aryan" laws. Died 23 August 1935 in Berlin.

Rhoda Erdman came from a long line of scientists, surgeons, and physicians on both her mother's and her father's side. Her maternal grandfather, a well-known physician in Hessen-Nassau, had studied spiders and insects for years and wrote marvelous descriptions of them. Her paternal great-grandfather on the father's side, Johann Valentin Erdmann, accompanied Napoleon to Russia as an army surgeon.

Erdmann's father taught at the Hamburg Klosterschule (a high school for girls). After Rhoda and her siblings had graduated from the school, he continued to tutor them in German and history, ensuring their excellent education in the social sciences and humanities. Her father was a well-known free-spirited local politician. He opposed the desire of his daughter to study natural history, believing that a scientific career posed too many difficulties for a woman. As a result, Erdmann attended the course for teachers at the Klosterschule. In 1900 she was employed as a teacher in the Hamburg Experimental School, but left her position in order to qualify as a science teacher in Berlin, planning to teach high school zoology and botany.

Her biological studies in Berlin disappointed her. She was more interested in the functioning of a cell or a muscle than in detailed comparative anatomy, and she complained that the laboratory assistants did not direct students toward practical scientific work, causing too many students to lose interest in further science education. The year her father died (1903), she left the University of Berlin and traveled to the universities of Zurich, Marburg, and Munich to pursue her scientific studies over the next five years. Although it wasn't until 1907 that she passed her university qualifying examination (Abitur) from the Realgymnasium in Kassel, she began to work at the University of Munich, from which she would receive her doctorate. Erdmann received support from the Hamburg board of higher education (Oberschulbehörde) to work at the biology station in Helgoland for two months, and the Naples Zoological Station to pursue experimental cell research for her dissertation—at a time when many scientists were doing morphological studies on fixed preparations.

After Erdmann obtained her doctorate (which, according to Hertwig, exceeded the usual quality of doctoral dissertations), she worked for five years as a scientific assistant at the Robert Koch Institute for Infectious Diseases in Berlin, educating herself further in protozoology and cytology. She also tried to supplement her income through poorly paid literary work at the Fischer-Verlag publishing house. When Richard Goldschmidt in 1912 asked her to provide an index for his journal, *Archiv für Zellforschung,* she replied that she could only take on an additional job if it was well paid.

In 1910, Erdmann demonstrated her excellent background in the relationship between chromosome and cell to write a review of the work of the Göttingen anatomist Friedrich Merkel for the journal *Anatomischen Heften.* In 1913 she wrote the chapter "Berlin's Scientific Institutions" in the book published by Eliza Ichenhäuser that examined various kinds of work available to women: *The Woman's Book: What Women of Berlin Must Know (Frauenbuch Was die Frau von Berlin wissen muss).*

In 1913 the American research scientist Lorande Loss Woodruff caused a great stir when he announced that sexual reproduction was not always necessary in single-celled organisms. He reported that a paramecium could divide asexually up to four thousand times. (This topic of parthenogenesis was also being studied at the same time by Yves Delage in France with the help of another woman, MARIE GOLDSMITH.) Ever since her doctoral dissertation, Erdmann had been studying the importance of sexual reproduction for both nuclear division and death of single-celled organisms. She wrote to Woodruff at the Osborn Zoological Laboratory of Yale University requesting paramecia so that she could investigate parthenogenesis. He was reluctant simply to send her specimens and suggested instead that she should do cytological research under his direction at Yale. She received a grant from the Rockefeller Foundation that enabled her to travel to New Haven. There she worked with Woodruff and solved a number of problems related to parthenogenesis. She also updated her techniques of tissue culture under Ross Harrison, head of the Osborn Labora-

tory at Yale, who had developed new methods of culturing nerve cells. Together with Woodruff she published in medical and biological professional journals in Germany and in the United States (*Biologisches Zentralblatt, Proceedings of the Society for Experimental Biology and Medicine, The Journal of Experimental Zoology*).

In July 1914 she traveled back to Germany by oceanliner, learning in mid-ocean that her country was at war. Held in England, she received an offer from Ross Harrison at Yale to return to the United States as a lecturer, an extraordinary offer since the charter of the university had to be changed to admit her as a woman faculty member. In 1915 she held a position as lecturer in the graduate school of Yale and shortly afterward was named a research associate at the Rockefeller Institute for Medical Research, where she was given the freedom to choose her own research topics. She was provided with a good salary and funds for her scientific work within Harrison's large laboratory. Even though she was able to supervise doctoral students, and taught a course on pathogenic protozoa, she began to hope that soon she could return to Germany and create a laboratory for cell research at the Kaiser-Wilhelm Institute in Berlin. Her tissue culture work developed active cultures for immunizing chickens by inoculating bone marrow. These investigations led to popular misunderstandings in a highly charged anti-German atmosphere. At the end of February 1918, she was forcibly removed from her position and accused of plotting to poison the New Haven drinking water, and of destroying American chickens with a chicken virus that would poison the brains of American soldiers. After four and a half months of detention in the Waverley House in New York (a prison for "wayward girls"), she was released following the intervention of Ross Harrison and American female friends who had paid five thousand dollars in fines, which could only be contributed by nonscientists who had lived in America for at least three generations and had never heard of Erdmann's experiments. Erdmann's health suffered for the rest of her life from the results of this incarceration.

Returning to Germany in 1919, she received over fifty rejections of her job applications. She was particularly disappointed by her former chief at the Robert Koch Institute, Max Hartmann, director of protozoology at the Kaiser-Wilhelm Institute for Biology. She blamed both Hartmann and Carl Correns, the director of the institute, for preventing her from continuing her research. Finally, she was able to obtain a position in Berlin at the Friederich-Williams University Institute for Cancer Research at the Charité Hospital. It was a position without additional personnel and no funding for laboratory equipment. Nevertheless, Erdmann established the first German department for experimental cytology in two empty rooms. She herself provided the most necessary laboratory equipment and the small library, which allowed her to conduct limited research, assisted at first by American funds. Initial research conditions were so bad that she figured that she had lost the first four years for research. Only in April 1930 did her laboratory become formally a university institute for experimental cytology.

Women had, since the formation of the Weimar Republic, been able to qualify for university positions, and Erdmann wrote her dissertation for that qualification (Habilitation) at the University of Berlin in 1920, and qualified a second time in 1924 in medicine. She was not appointed to a teaching post until 1929 when she was named "extraordinary" (associate) professor. Meanwhile both students and coworkers were attracted to the new field and the medical faculty recognized experimental cytology as an interdisciplinary science important to both medical biology and physiology. Erdmann supplied both fields with assistants well-trained in tissue culture. Because she was overloaded with work, her research was shortchanged. Documents in the archives of Humboldt University reflect Erdmann's lifelong fight for material security. She always pointed out in her correspondence with university departments that she had been promised scientific independence on her return to Berlin, a promise not honored for many years. In one document she pointed out that after she lost her position in the United States during World War I, unlike her male colleagues, she received no assistance. In another (1927) she reminded her supervisors that she still earned less than her assistant, convinced that "Prussia does not want to create female associate professors." Although she did finally achieve that position, she continued to work with other women high school and university lecturers and founded a Society for German Women Teaching in Higher Education (Verband deutscher Hochschuldozentinnen).

In 1922, Erdmann published the first German textbook that provided detailed instructions on tissue culture methods and indicated how they might be applied for cancer research. In contrast to Otto Warburg's later famous dictum that the ultimate damage to growing cells that resulted in cancer was due to replaced oxygen respiration, she sought for other metabolic factors, such as nutrition, vitamin A, B complex, D, and blood cholesterol.

In the early thirties, Erdmann's life would once again undergo an extreme change. In 1933, with the rise of Hitler, she was denounced to the Gestapo for helping Jews escape from Nazi Germany. Thrown into jail at Alexanderplatz, she wrote indignantly to the university dean that she had the right to be judged by a university disciplinary committee. The Gestapo reluctantly agreed that she could not be held simply because she was "too much of a democrat." Sadly this is not the end of the story. Stripped of her position under the new "Aryan" laws in 1934, and unable to hold a position of authority as a woman, she died in Berlin in August 1935.

Erdmann was democratic in her scientific work as well her politics. She had benefited from the free flow of ideas with foreign scientists. She in turn had tried to encourage the exchange between several biological and medical disciplines. She encouraged the exchange of new methods and scientific results of tissue culture experiments. In 1919 she founded the journal for experimental cell research, *Archiv für experimentelle Zellforschung,* in which cooperative venture she was able to persuade fourteen colleagues in Europe and the United States to join her, including Harrison at Yale. Many other scientists participated from all over the world, including Japan, and articles appeared in every major Western European language, covering every branch of cytology, including biochemistry, cell physiology, electrophysiology, and radiation biology. This was the only international scientific publication published by a woman. Erdmann also planned several international cell biology congresses, advertising them in the issues of the journal. She promoted the importance of tissue culture studies in biology and cancer research in her lectures and scientific publications until her untimely death.

G V L

PRIMARY SOURCES

Erdmann, Rhoda. "Quantitative Analyse der Zellbestandteile bei normalem, experimentell verändertem und pathologischem Wachstum." *Ergebnisse der Anatomie und Entwicklungsgeschichte* 29, no. 2, 1 (1911): 471–566.

———. "Cytological Observations on the Behavior of Chicken Bone Marrow in Plasma Medium." *The American Journal of Anatomy* 22, no. 1 (1917): 73–125.

———. *Praktikum der Gewebepflege oder Explantation. Besonders der Gewebezüchtung.* Berlin: Julius Springer, 1922. Her introduction to the methods of tissue culture.

———. "Die biologischen Eigenschaften der Krebszelle nach Erfahrunge der Implantation, Explantation un Reimplantation. Karzinoma-Studien I." *Zeitschrift für Krebsforschung* 10 (1923): 322–348.

———. "Typ eines Ausbildungsganges weiblicher Forscher." In *Führende Frauen Europas,* ed. Elga Kern, 35–54. Munich: Ernst Reinhardt, 1927. A description of the difficulties faced by women scientists, and her feeling of frustration in being prevented from pursuing research.

———. "Ist der Krebs eine Stoffwechselerscheinung?" *Centralblatt für Bakteriologie, Parasitenkunde und Infektionskrankheiten* 84, no. 1 (1927): 329–335.

———. "Krebs und Ernährung." *Biologische Heilkunst* 52 (1932): 829–831.

———. "Zahlreich Beiträge in deutschen und amerikanischen Fachzeitschriften 1910–1935." *Archiv für experimentelle Zell-*

forschung 18 (1936): 127–141. This includes both her German and American research papers edited by P. Caffier.

SECONDARY SOURCES

Caffier, Paul. "Rhoda Erdmann." *Archiv für experimentelle Zellforschung* 18 (1936): 127–141. Obituary by her student Caffier in the international publication that Erdmann founded. Erdmann's attempt to get equal opportunity for women in science is belittled as personal oversensitivity.

Hoppe, Brigitte. "Die Institutionalisierung der Zellforschudng in Deutschland durch Rhoda Erdmann." *Biologie Heute* 366, (1989). Pays homage to Erdmann's pioneering scientific work, using extensive American sources from Yale University and the Rockefeller Institute, but does not reflect her concerns about women.

Jank, Dagmar. "Studierende, lehrende un forschende Frauen an der Friedrich-Wilhelms-Universität zu Berlin 1908–1945." *Ausstellungsführer der Universitätsbibliothek der FU Berlin* 20 (1990): 16 ff. A report from the archives of Humboldt University in Berlin which reflects Erdmann's lifelong battle for both a chance to do scientific research and material security.

Koch, Sabine. "Leben und Werk der Zellforscherin Rhoda Erdmann." M.D. diss. Marburg University, 1985. Also excellent on scientific sources, weak about her concern for the opportunities of women scientists.

STANDARD SOURCES

Lexikon der Frau; Strohmeier; *NDB.*

ERDMUTHE, SOPHIE (1644–1675)

German healer and scholar. Born Germany 1644. Father George II of Saxony. Married the Markgraf Christian Ernst of Brandenburg and Bayruth. Princess of Saxony. Died 1675.

Sophie Erdmuthe is an example of a seventeenth-century woman with both medical and scientific interests. She was one of several German healers and scholars of royal blood. One of her special interests was the history of the earth. She wrote a book with the title *Handlung von der Welt Alter,* which appeared in Nuremberg in 1676. JH/MBO

STANDARD SOURCES

Hurd-Mead 1938; Harless; Strohmeier.

ERMOL'EVA, ZINAIDA VISSARIONOVNA (1898–?)

Russian microbiologist and bacteriochemist. Born 24 October 1898 in Frolovo. Educated University of Rostov-on-Don (graduated 1921). Professional experience: North Caucasus Bacteriological In-

stitute, staff member; A. N. Bakh Biochemical Institute of the USSR People's Commissariat of Health, microbiologist; All Union Institute of Experimental Medicine, microbiologist; Institute of Antibiotics of the USSR Ministry of Health, bacteriochemist; Central Postgraduate Medical Institute. Honors and memberships: State Prize (1943); Soviet Academy of Medical Sciences, corresponding member, then academician; Honored Scientist of the Russian Soviet Federated Socialist Republic (1970). Death date unknown.

Zinaida Vissarionovna Ermol'eva was born at Frolovo, a town not far from present-day Volgograd in 1898. She graduated from the University of Rostov-on-Don in 1921 and started work at the North Caucasus Bacteriological Institute there. In 1925, she went to Moscow and worked at the A. N. Bakh Biochemical Institute and the All-Union Institute of Experimental Medicine. From 1947 to 1954, she worked at the Institute of Antibiotics of the Ministry of Health and from 1952, in the department of microbiology at the Central Postgraduate Medical Institute.

Ermol'eva's research was primarily concerned with cholera and antibiotics. In 1931, she developed a treatment using a preparation of lysozyme. She obtained the first Soviet forms of penicillin (1942), streptomycin (1947), as well as Soviet versions of interferon, ekmonovocillin, bicillins, ekmolin, and dipasfen.

She was awarded a State Prize for her work in 1943. In 1945, she was elected a corresponding member of the Soviet Academy of Medical Sciences and became an academician in 1965. In 1970 she was named an Honored Scientist of the Russian Soviet Federated Socialist Republic. She also was awarded two orders of Lenin and other orders and medals.

ACH

PRIMARY SOURCES

Ermol'eva, Zenaida. *Kholera.* Moscow, 1942.
———. *Streptomitsin.* Moscow, 1956.

SECONDARY SOURCES

"Ermol'eva, Zinaida Vissarionovna." *Bol'shaia sovetskaia entsiklopediia.* 3d. ed. Moscow: Izd-vo Sovetskaia entsiklopediia, 1973.

STANDARD SOURCES

Debus.

ERXLEBEN, DOROTHEA CHRISTIANA (LEPORIN) (1715–1762)

German physician. Born 13 November 1715 in Quedlinburg in Saxony to Anna Sophia (Meinecke) and Christian Polycarp Leporin. Four siblings. Married Johann Christian Erxleben. Four children. Educated by physician father; University of Halle (M.D., 1754). Died 13 June 1762 in Quedlinburg.

Reputedly a sickly child, Dorothea Leporin was unable to attend school but listened and absorbed while her physician father tutored her older brother, Christian. Ambitious to study medicine alongside her brother, she read incessantly. As her brother began his schooling at the Quedlinburg preparatory high school for boys, she participated in his lessons there by correspondence. At the same time, she was tutored at home by Pastor Johann Christian Erxleben, whom she later married. At the age of sixteen, she began her medical training with her father, together with her brother, who was preparing for university examinations. As assistant to her father, she showed exceptional skill with patients and soon displayed reliable judgment in diagnosis. As her brother matriculated at the University of Halle, she determined to do the same. As royal university privileges provided for the award of academic honors to men only, Dorothea petitioned King Frederick II of Prussia for permission to pursue a doctor's degree. As she encountered the full impact of her exclusion from the educational system on the basis of her gender she wrote *Gründliche Untersuchung der Ursachen, welche das weibliche Geschlecht vom Studieren abhalten* (A Thorough Examination of the Reasons Why the Female Sex is Barred from [University] Study). This work appeared in 1742 shortly after her petition was granted. The treatise, which was given rave reviews, is a crusade against not only the prejudices that hinder equal educational opportunities for women, but also the prevailing bias against women in general.

Despite the emperor's permission, Dorothea Leporin was not able to pursue her doctorate in Halle. The Prussian-Silesian war forced her father and brother to leave the country, and she directed her father's practice in his absence. In 1744, she married Pastor Johann Erxleben, a widower with five children. By 1752, she had also borne four children of her own. After her father's death in 1747, she took over his medical practice in Quedlinburg. At this time, the completion of her medical doctorate no longer seemed possible. However, as doctors in her area began to feel threatened by the competition and accused her of quackery, Dorothea, then thirty-seven years old and seven months pregnant, took up work on her doctor's degree once again. In January 1754, she submitted her dissertation, written in Latin. After she had passed her examinations with honors, she was finally able, with royal consent, to call herself a *doctor.* On 12 June 1754, at the house of the dean of the School of Medicine at the University of Halle, Erxleben was granted the medical degree, the first full medical degree awarded to a woman by a German university. She was then thirty-nine years old. She died only eight years later of breast cancer at the age of forty-seven.   SNS

PRIMARY SOURCES

Erxleben, Dorothea. *Gründliche Untersuchungen der Ursachen, die das weibliche Geschlecht vom Studiren abhalten.* Berlin, 1742.

———. *Exponents quod nimis cito ac jucunde curare saepius fiat causa minus tutae curationis.* Halle, Magdeburg. Joannis Christian Hilliger, 1754. Her dissertation.

SECONDARY SOURCES

Baudouin, Marcel. *Femmes médecins d'autrefois.* Paris: Librairie Médicale et Scientifique Jules Rousset, 1906.

Brencken, Julia von. *Doktorhut und Weibermütze. Dorothea Erxleben—die erste Ärztin. Biographischer Roman.* Heilbronn: Salzer 1992.

Feyl, Renate. "Dorothea Erxleben." In *Der lautlose Aufbruch: Frauen in der Wissenschaft.* 2d ed. Köln: Kiepenheuer and Witsch, 1944.

Grosse Frauen der Weltgeschichte: Tausend Biographien in Wort und Bild. Wiesbaden: Löwit, 1982.

Meyers Neues Lexikon. Mannheim, Leipzig, Vienna: Meyers-lexikonverlag, 1994.

STANDARD SOURCES

DBE, vol. 3, 1996; Hurd-Mead 1938; Lipinska 1900; NDB, vol. 4; Ogilvie 1986; Strohmeier.

ESAU, KATHERINE (1898–1997)

Russian/U.S. botanist. Born 3 April 1898 in Ekaterinoslav, Russia to Margarethe (Toews) and John J. Esau. Immigrated to U.S. (1923), naturalized (1928). Never married. Educated College of Agriculture, Moscow (1916–1917); College of Agriculture, Berlin (1919–1922); University of California, Berkeley (Ph.D., 1931). Professional experience: Plant Breeder, Spreckels Sugar Company, Oxnar, Calif. (1924–1928); University of California, Davis, assistant (1927–1931), instructor, assistant professor (1931–1943), associate professor (1943–1949), professor (1949–retirement); Agricultural Experimental Station, University of California, junior botanist to associate botanist (1931–1949), botanist (1949–retirement), University of California, Santa Barbara, researcher (1963–1965). Honors and memberships: Guggenheim Foundation Fellow (1940); Botanical Society, president; National Academy of Sciences, Fellow (1973); American Philosophical Society, American Academy of Arts and Sciences, American Association for the Advancement of Science, Phi Beta Kappa, and Sigma Xi, member; honorary degree, Mills College (1962); Prather lecturer at Harvard University (1960); John Wesley Powell lecturer at the American Academy of Arts and Sciences (1973); Swedish Royal Academy. Died 4 June 1997 in Santa Barbara, Calif.

Born in the Ukraine to Mennonite parents, Katherine was educated at a Mennonite school for four years and then attended the gymnasium in Ekaterinoslav from which she graduated in 1916. After graduation, she went to Moscow, where she attended the Golitsin Women's Agricultural College. The Russian Revolution interfered with her education, and the revolutionary government deposed her father as mayor of Ekaterinoslav. In 1918, the Esaus fled from the Bolsheviks, settling in Berlin. Here, Esau continued her education at the Landwirtschaftliche Hochschule, the Berlin Agricultural College, receiving a diploma in 1922. In this year, the family emigrated to Reedly, California, chosen for its large Mennonite population. Esau worked as a housekeeper in Fresno, and looked for a job. She became manager of a seed farm in Oxnard, California, where she learned enough Spanish to communicate with the workers. Spreckles Sugar Company hired her to improve the company's patented curly-top disease-resistant sugar beets. Here she encountered the problem of a viral sugar beet disease, her first work with the topic of plant viruses that would later make her name. The experimental station and its staff was transferred to the School of Agriculture at University of California, Davis. The chair of the botany department there was sufficiently impressed to appoint Esau as an assistant. Esau took the opportunity to enroll in the university, but since Davis did not have a graduate program, she was technically registered at Berkeley, from which she received her doctoral degree. After graduation, she became an instructor in botany and a junior botanist at the Experiment Station of the College of Agriculture at the University of California, Davis, where she slowly rose up the academic ladder, becoming a full professor in 1949. She remained at Davis until 1963, when she moved to the University of California, Santa Barbara, from which she officially retired in 1965. Nevertheless, as an emerita she continued to come into her office until early 1994. She continued as an experimental botanist at the field station well into her seventies.

Much of Esau's research had agricultural implications, but certainly not all of it. She became especially interested in research on the phloem, particularly on the viruses that attacked the phloem alone. Since she had little space at Davis for photomicrography, she bought her own equipment and set up her own darkroom at home. All of her published photomicrographs were developed in this room in the 1940s and 1950s, including the illustrations in the first edition of her classic book, *Plant Anatomy*. In Santa Barbara she was able to work with Vernon I. Cheadle, who had become chancellor there. During her active period she published five books and more than 160 articles.

Esau gave the Faculty Research Lecture at Davis in 1946, was elected to the National Academy of Sciences, president of the Botanical Society of America, received the Merit Certificate for the 50th Anniversary of the Botanical Society of America, the 11th International Botanical Congress Medal in 1969, and foreign membership in the Swedish Royal Academy of Sciences in 1971. She was also awarded honorary doctorates by Mills College and the University of California. Esau continued to do significant work on plant viruses using the electron microscope. She was honored with the National Medal of Honor in 1989. She continued to work on revisions of her texts well into her nineties. In March 1992, an international symposium on plant anatomy was held in her honor at the University of California, Davis. She died at the age of ninety-nine at her home in Santa Barbara, California.

JH/MBO

PRIMARY SOURCES

Esau, Katherine. *Plant Anatomy.* New York: Wiley, 1953.

———. *Anatomy of Seed Plants.* New York: Wiley, 1960.

———. *Plants, Viruses and Insects.* Cambridge: Harvard University Press, 1961.

———. *Vascular Differentiation in Plants.* New York: Holt, Rinehart, and Winston, 1965.

SECONDARY SOURCES

Evert, Ray F. "Katherine Esau." *Plant Science Bulletin* 31 (1985): 33–37.

"Katherine Esau." *New York Times,* 18 June 1997. Obituary notice.

STANDARD SOURCES

American Women 1974; *AMS* 6–18; Bailey; Debus; *Notable* (article by Benedict A. Leerburger); Rossiter 1982; Shearer and Shearer 1996.

ESDORN, ILSE (1897–1985)

German botanist. Born 8 January 1897 in Braunschweig. Educated Herzogin-Elisabeth Lyceum, Braunschweig; pharmacological apprentice; pharmacological preexamination (1918); pharmaceutical state examination (1922); passed her Abitur university entrance examinations and studied pharmacy and botany in Rostock, Leipzig; technical university Braunschweig (1922); Kiel (Ph.D., 1924); Habilitation (postdoctoral university teaching qualification) in botany (1930). Professional experience: Rostock, apothecary's assistant (1918); Botanical Institute of the Technical University, Braunschweig, assistant (1922–1927); Hamburg State Institute for Applied Botany, scientific employee (1927–1932), pharmaceutical studies, teaching position (1932–1938), organized medical botany excursions for medical students (1939–1940), assistant professor (1941); University of Hamburg, department head of Pharmaceutical Studies (1950). Died 1985.

Ilse Esdorn attended a lyceum in Braunschweig, which was an improvement over the ordinary girls' school, and was qualified as a *Realgymnasium*. After that she finished a pharmaceutical apprenticeship in Bergedorf and Braunschweig, passed the pharmaceutical preexamination, and worked as an apothecary's assistant in Rostock. At that time, intense discussions were going on in pharmaceutical publications concerning whether the female help in apothecaries' shops that had been occasioned by the war should continue in times of peace. In 1922, Esdorn passed the pharmaceutical state examination. She belatedly passed the Abitur and began to study pharmacy and botany in Rostock, Leipzig, and in the Technical University in Braunschweig, where she was made an assistant in 1922. In 1925, she graduated in Kiel after writing her dissertation in Braunschweig, on the effects of radiation on plants. She stayed as assistant at the Botanical Institute of the Technical University, Braunschweig. In 1927, Esdorn went to the Hamburg State Institute of Applied Botany as a scientific employee. She habilitated (completed her postdoctoral teaching qualification) in 1930 with thesis research about the hard outer coat of the yellow lupine, concerning the difficult germination of this and other green plants that are used as fertilizer. It was becoming more and more difficult for a woman to maintain a position at the university. From 1932 to 1938 she got a teaching job in pharmakognosie. Starting in 1939, she was asked to organize iatrobotanical excursions for medical students. She sold a pamphlet on wild plants as natural vitamin sources in spring for twenty Pfennig; it was also published in *Die Ärtzin.* In 1940, she was finally terminated from her position as a scientific employee and was taken over by the Reichsinstitut for foreign and colonial forestry in Reinbek. In 1950, she was made head of the department of pharmaceutical studies at the University of Hamburg.

Esdorn published works in phytopathology, germination physiology, plant *rhostoffkund* (plant raw material knowledge), and especially medical botany. GVL

PRIMARY SOURCES

Esdorn, Ilse. "Untersuchungen über Einwirkung von Röntgenstrahlen auf Pflanzen." Dissertation, University of Kiel, 1924.

——. "Untersuchgen über die Hartschaligkeit der gelben Lupine." Habilitation thesis, University of Hamburg, 1930.

——. "Wildpflanzen als natürliche Vitaminträger im Frühling." *Die Ärztin* 16 (1940): 59–61.

——. *Monographien alter Heilpflanzen* (Herausgeberin). 1941.

SECONDARY SOURCES

Algrimm, Ernst-Dietrich. "Nachruf auf Frau Prof. Dr. Esdorn." *Pharmazeutische Zeitung* 180 (1985): 2505.

Köppel, Anna-Pia. *Frauen in den Naturwissenschaften vom Mittelalter bis zur Neuzeit.* Hamburg: Begleitheft zur Ausstellung an der Universität Hamburg, 1985.

STANDARD SOURCES

Lexikon der Frau; Poggendorff, vol. 7.

ETHELDRIDA, QUEEN (ca. 630–660?)

British healer. Born ca. 630. Father Ine, king of East Angles. Married Tonbert.

Many stories circulate about Etheldrida, daughter of the king of the East Angles. One account claims that her dowry from her first husband, Tonbert, was the Island of Ely, where the cathedral is located today. At Ely she was said to have practiced among the nuns teaching them how to cure disease and serve the poor. They attempted to cure lepers. Another report calls her Aethelthryth and says that she was the wife of Ecgfrith, king of Northumbria. This account agrees with the first when it says that she founded the Abbey of Ely and authenticates the first account regarding her medical ability. There are reports of her successfully performing miracles of healing. In Bede's *Ecclesiastical History of England,* he reports that when she was about to die of an abscess in her neck, a monk named Cynefrid was called in. He lanced the abscess, but she died anyway. According to Bede, she believed that God had sent this sickness because she had been vain about her beautiful neck. Sixteen years later, her body was exhumed, and Bede reports that the body was quite sound and that the wound was miraculously cured. As an old man, her father, King Ine, reputedly founded the great Santo Spirito Hospital on the island in the Tiber in Rome. JH/MBO

STANDARD SOURCES

Hurd-Mead 1938.

EUPHEMIA, ABBESS OF WHERWELL (fl. 1226–1257)

British healer. Flourished 1226–1257. Abbess of Wherwell.

Euphemia became Abbess of Wherwell (in Hampshire, England). Medically knowledgeable, and widely known as a mystic, Euphemia is credited for building a water and sewer system under the monastery infirmary. She also designed and supervised construction of new and better convent buildings. JH/MBO

STANDARD SOURCES

Echols and Williams; Hughes; Hurd Mead 1938.

EVANS, ALICE CATHERINE (1881–1975)

U.S. bacteriologist. Born 29 January 1881 in rural Neath, Pa., to parents of Welsh descent. Her father was a surveyor, teacher, and farmer. One older brother. Never married. Educated Susquehanna Collegiate Institute for teachers in Towanda, Pa. (1898–1901); Cornell University (B.S., 1909); University of Wisconsin at Madison (M.S., 1910). Professional experience: Dairy Division of the

Bureau of Animal Industry of the United States Department of Agriculture at the state agricultural experiment station in Madison, Wis., staff researcher (1910–1913); Washington, D.C., office of the Dairy Division of the Bureau of Animal Industry of the USDA, bacteriologist (1913–1918); Hygienic Laboratory of the United States Public Health Service (later National Institutes of Health), senior bacteriologist (1918–1945). Honors and memberships: Woman's Medical College of Pennsylvania, honorary M.D. (1934); Wilson College, honorary Sc.D. (1936); University of Wisconsin at Madison, honorary Sc.D. (1948); Society of American Bacteriologists (now American Society for Microbiology), first woman president (1928). Died 5 September 1975 at age ninety-four, after suffering a stroke in Alexandria, Va.

Bacteriologist Alice Catherine Evans was, in 1913, the first woman scientist to hold a permanent position in the Dairy Division of the Bureau of Animal Industry (BAI) of the United States Department of Agriculture in Washington, D.C. By 1917, she had made what would later be hailed as one of the most significant medical breakthroughs of the first quarter of the twentieth century: the discovery that drinking raw cow's milk and handling infected animals sometimes caused undulant fever, a debilitating, often misdiagnosed, and sometimes fatal human disease, which was later named brucellosis. Soon after, Evans became an indefatigable advocate for the mandatory pasteurization of milk, although she was not immediately successful in her public health crusade because (perhaps foremost) she was a woman scientist, and also because she had neither a doctoral nor a medical degree.

At the annual meeting of the Society of American Bacteriologists in Washington, D.C., in 1917, Evans first reported her discovery that the bacteria *Micrococcus melitensis*, known since the late 1800s to cause what was then called Mediterranean or Malta fever in people who drank raw goat's milk, was closely related to *Bacillus abortus*, which caused the contagious abortion in cattle known as Bang's disease. The *Journal of Infectious Diseases* published her article in July 1918. Years later she recalled that the scientific community's "reaction to [this] paper was almost universal skepticism, usually expressed by the remark that if these organisms were closely related, some other bacteriologist would nave noted it" (Evans, "Memoirs," 1963, 22).

By the late 1920s, brucellosis was recognized worldwide as a threatening and increasingly prevalent disease. Yet it was not until the 1930s that fellow scientists and the United States dairy industry completely acknowledged Evans's discovery and began to pasteurize all milk. As Evans had predicted, cases of brucellosis subsequently decreased. Evans then spent most of her thirty-five-year career as a government-employed scientist researching the genus *Brucella* and the disease it caused. Throughout her career, she published nearly one hundred scientific papers.

Born 29 January 1881 in rural Neath, Pennsylvania, to parents of Welsh descent, Evans had one older brother. Her father was a surveyor, teacher, and farmer. From 1898 to 1901, she attended the Susquehanna Collegiate Institute of Towanda, Pennsylvania, which trained schoolteachers. In a short, unpublished essay titled "Pioneering Women's Basketball," which Evans wrote when she was eighty-two years old, she recalled playing on one of the school's two women's basketball teams. At the turn of the century, the conservative townspeople of Towanda considered basketball such an "unladylike" activity that when Evans dislocated her finger while playing, the country doctor refused to set it, claiming, "If you play basketball, you will have to stand the consequences." Thereafter, Evans's finger remained pain-free but slightly dislocated, "a reminder that if one oversteps conformity, one is apt to have to pay a price" ("Memoirs").

After graduating from the institute, Evans taught elementary school for four years. In 1905 she began a two-year, tuition-free nature study course for rural schoolteachers at the College of Agriculture at Cornell University in Ithaca, New York. Her interest in biology piqued, she continued her undergraduate education at Cornell and earned a bachelor of science degree in agriculture, specializing in bacteriology, in 1909.

Evans was selected to be the first woman to receive a scholarship to pursue a master's degree in bacteriology at the College of Agriculture at the University of Wisconsin at Madison. E. G. Hastings became her advisor. She also studied with Elmer V. McCollum, who taught chemistry of nutrition and later discovered vitamin A. When Evans completed her master of science degree in 1910, McCollum urged her to continue on for a doctorate in chemistry at Wisconsin on a university fellowship. She declined this opportunity because in that era the "Ph.D. degree was not a *sine qua non* for advancement" in the sciences (Evans, "Memoirs," 1963, 10). Many college professors and leading USDA researchers did not have doctorates.

On 1 July 1910, Evans began working for the Dairy Division of the Bureau of Animal Industry of the USDA at the state agricultural experiment station in Madison, Wisconsin. Three years later, she was transferred to the Washington, D.C., office. Evans recollected:

> According to hearsay, when the bad news broke at a meeting of the B.A.I. officials that a woman scientist would be coming to join the staff, they were filled with consternation. In the words of a stenographer who was present, they almost fell off their chairs. (Evans, "Memoirs," 1963, 14).

In 1918, Evans transferred to the Hygienic Laboratory of the United States Public Health Service (later National Institutes of Health), where she also studied epidemic meningitis and influenza. In 1922, Evans became infected with brucellosis. During the next twenty-three years, she had chronic brucellosis and was hospitalized often, sometimes for months at a time.

By the late 1920s, Evans was becoming an increasingly prominent researcher. In 1928, the Society of American Bacteriologists (now American Society for Microbiology) elected her its first woman president. In 1930, she was one of two delegates from the United States to the First International Congress in Microbiology at the Pasteur Institute in Paris. The only other woman delegate at this Congress was LYDIA RABINOVITCH-KEMPNER. In 1939, Evans began research on immunity to streptococcal infection, which she continued until she retired from her position as senior bacteriologist at the National Institutes of Health in 1945. In 1969, she moved to Goodwin House, a retirement home in Alexandria, Virginia. Alice Catherine Evans died on 5 September 1975 at age ninety-four, after suffering a stroke.

SSK

PRIMARY SOURCES

Evans, Alice, "The Large Numbers of *Bacteria abortus* var. *lipolyticus* Which May Be Found in Milk." *Journal of Bacteriology* 2 (1917).

———. "Further Studies on *Bacterium abortus* and Related Diseases." In three parts. *Journal of Infectious Diseases* 22 (1918): 580–593.

———. "Studies on *Brucella (Alkalingenes) melitensis.*" *Hygenic Laboratory Bulletin* 143: (August 1925): 1–63.

———. "Memoirs." Unpublished, 1963. In Alice Catherine Evans Papers, 1908–1965, #2552. Division of Rare and Manuscript Collections, Carl A. Kroch Library, Cornell University.

———. "Memoirs." Unpublished, 1965, revised and expanded from 1963. In Alice Catherine Evans Papers, 1908–1965, #2552. Division of Rare and Manuscript Collections, Carl A. Kroch Library, Cornell University.

———. Papers, 1908–1954, #2552. Division of Rare and Manuscript Collections, Carl A. Kroch Library, Cornell University.

SECONDARY SOURCES

DeKruif, P. "Before You Drink a Glass of Milk: The Story of a Woman's Discovery of a New Disease." *Ladies Home Journal* 46 (September 1929); 8–9; 162; 165–166; 168–169.

MacKaye, M. "Undulant Fever: Are You Unaccountably Tired and Depressed? The Answer May Be in an Innocent Looking Bottle of Unpasteurized Milk." *Ladies Home Journal* 61 (December 1944): 23; 69–70.

Morgan, W. J. B., and M. J. Corbel. [Bibliography of Alice Evans]. *Annali Sclavo* (February 1977). Entire issue on Evans.

STANDARD SOURCES

AMS 4–8, B 9, P&B 10; Bailey; *NAW*(M); *Notable;* O'Hearn; Shearer and Shearer 1995.

EVANS, ALICE MARGARET (1927–1981)

British botanist. Born 12 August 1927 in Penderyn, Breconshire. Educated Aberystwyth (Ph.D.). Professional experience: Welsh Plant Breeding Station, lecturer; Reading University, lecturer; Cambridge University, lecturer in plant breeding and genetics (from 1966). Died 26 March 1981.

Alice Margaret Evans was an academic botanist who was educated in Wales. She ended her career at Cambridge University. She did research on the genetics and breeding of *Phaseolus.*

JH/MBO

SECONDARY SOURCES

Times, 7 April 1981.

STANDARD SOURCES

Desmond.

EVERARD, BARBARA MARY STEYNING (1910–1990)

British botanical artist. Born 27 July 1910. Married. Professional experience: botanical artist in Malaya. Died 12 June 1990 in Barnstaple, Devon.

Barbara Everard's husband was a rubber planter in Malaya, and she spent from 1938 to 1942 and from 1946 to 1950 in that country. While in Malaya, she painted many plants. The Barbara Everard Trust for Orchid Conservation was established in 1986.

JH/MBO

PRIMARY SOURCES

Everard, Barbara, illus. With O. Polunin and A. Huxley. *Flowers of the Mediterranean.* London: Chatto and Windus, 1965.

———, illus. *Wild Flowers of the World.* By B. Morley. New York: Putnam, 1970.

SECONDARY SOURCES

American Orchid Society Bulletin (1989): 680–681.
Orchid Review (1990): 249–250.

STANDARD SOURCES

Desmond.

EVERETT, ALICE (1865–?)

British astronomer. Born 1865. Father Joseph David Everett, Fellow of the Royal Society. Educated Queen's College (now University of Belfast) (first in scholarship examination in science, 1884); Girton College, Cambridge (1886–1889), mathematical Tripos examination senior optime (1889); Royal University of Ireland (B.A. and M.A.). Professional experience: Royal Observatory, computer (1890–1895); Astrophysical Observatory, Potsdam, Germany, visiting astronomer. Death date unknown.

Alice Everett was the daughter of a professor of physics at Queen's College, Belfast. She attended lectures at Queens to prepare for taking the Royal University of Ireland's examinations. She got a first on the scholarship examination at Queen's, which perplexed the university authorities, for women students were not formally recognized. The university lawyers declared women ineligible for scholarships and did not allow Everett's award. Girton College, Cambridge, was the next step in Everett's education. She entered in 1886 and took the mathematical Tripos in 1889, achieving the equivalent rank of senior optime. She received bachelor's and master's degrees with honors in mathematical science from the Royal University of Ireland. After graduation, Everett attained a position as "computer" at the Royal Observatory at Greenwich with a salary of six pounds a month, the maximum salary for this position. Two other women preceded her as computers, Edith Mary Rix and Harriet Maud Furniss. Furniss left in 1891 and Rix in 1892. ANNIE RUSSELL MAUNDER replaced Furniss in 1891 and for a time there were three women computers on the staff at Greenwich.

Upon her appointment in 1890, Everett was assigned to meridian transit work, involving making and reducing observations with the Transit Circle. She joined the photographic department in 1892, where a huge international collaborative project to photograph particular areas of the sky and list stars down to the eleventh magnitude had just begun. In 1893 and 1894, Everett spent her entire working time on the catalog and was involved in every aspect of the project, including observing a portion of the sky two nights a week, making and developing photographs, and measuring the catalogue plates with the astrographic micrometer. Her contributions were recognized in the printed catalog. She also learned to use the zenith telescope, worked with the Sheepshanks equatorial telescope, observed various astronomical phenomena, and took part in some double-star work.

The low salary at Greenwich stimulated Everett to find other work. In spite of excellent recommendations from the Astronomer Royal, she failed to get a position as assistant at the Dunsink Observatory of Trinity College, Dublin. It became vacant a second time and a man who was one of Everett's contemporary computers, ten years younger, got the position at age nineteen. Eventually Everett obtained a three-year appointment at the Astrophysical Observatory in

Potsdam. Following this temporary appointment, she went to Vassar College for one year. James Keeler, director of Lick Observatory, wanted to employ her for his observatory's spectroscopic program, but was unable to find the funds. She then returned to Britain and began a new career in optics.

JH/MBO

PRIMARY SOURCES

Hovestadt, Heinrich. *Jena Glass and Its Scientific and Industrial Applications.* Ed. and trans. Alice Everett. With J. D. Everett. London: Macmillan, 1902.

SECONDARY SOURCES

Brück, Mary T. "Lady Computers at Greenwich in the Early 1890s." *Quarterly Journal of the Royal Astronomical Society* 36 (1995): 83–95.

EVERSHED, MARY ORR (1867–1949)

British astronomer. Born 1867 in Plymouth Hoe to Lucy (Acworth) and Captain Andrew Orr. Educated at home. Married John Evershed. Died 1949 in Sussex.

Although Mary Evershed's formal education was minimal (she was tutored at home), she read widely and traveled to Germany, Italy, and Australia. These experiences sparked her interest in a variety of subjects, including astronomy. While in Florence, she became interested in Dante, a fascination that, combined with a growing interest in astronomy and its history, later resulted in a book, *Dante and the Early Astronomers* (1914). From 1890 to 1895, she lived in Australia with her mother and three sisters. After she returned to England, she joined the recently formed British Astronomical Society and drew on her Australian experience to write *Southern Stars: A Guide to the Constellations Visible in the Southern Hemisphere* (1896).

In 1906, Mary Orr married astronomer John Evershed, and the couple left for the Kodaikanal Observatory in India, where John Evershed was assistant director; he became director in 1911. The partnership between the two resulted in fruitful solar research. A work published in both their names in the *Memoirs of the Kodaikanal Observatory* (1917) discussed the distribution and motion of solar prominences. Mary Evershed published a significant paper on solar prominences in the *Monthly Notices of the Royal Astronomical Society* (1913), in which she concluded that "there can be no doubt that other forces are at work on the Sun's surface besides an eruptive force and gravity." Electric forces acting on ionized gases and the magnetic force that exists in the vicinity of sun spots all contribute, she observed.

In 1923 the Eversheds returned to England. Mary directed the historical section of the British Astronomical

Association from 1930 to 1944. She continued to publish astronomical works, including a bibliographic index to named lunar craters. In 1924, she became a fellow of the Royal Astronomical Society, serving on its library committee for many years. Although neither John nor Mary Evershed made significant theoretical contributions to astronomy, they added important data to the body of astronomical information. In addition, Mary Evershed provided insight into the history of her discipline.   MBO

PRIMARY SOURCES

Evershed, Mary. *Southern Stars: A Guide to the Constellations Visible in the Southern Hemisphere.* London: Gail and Inglis, [1896].

SECONDARY SOURCES

Meadows, A. J. *Greenwich Observatory,* Vol. 2, *Recent History, 1836–1975.* London: Taylor and Francis, 1975.
Melotte, P. J. "Obituary Notice, Mary Evershed." *Journal of the British Astronomical Association* 60 (1950): 86–87.
Thackeray, A. D. "Obituary Notice, Mary Evershed." *Monthly Notices of the Royal Astronomical Society* 110 (1950): 128–129.

EVES, FLORENCE (d. 1911)

British chemist. Birth date unknown. Born in Usbridge. Educated North London Collegiate School; University College, London; Newnham College, Cambridge (1878–1882, Natural Science Tripos Class 1, 1881), Bathurst Student (1881–1882); University of London (B.Sc. with Honors in Botany, Class 1, 1881). Professional experience: Newnham College, demonstrator (1881–1887); Manchester High School, master of arts (1887–1890); St. Leonards School, St. Andrews, science teacher (1891–1892). Head of Women's House and Christian Social Union, Hoxton. Died 11 February 1911.

Florence Eves earned first class honors in the National Science Tripos at Newnham College, Cambridge, and held a Bathurst Studentship. She also earned first class honors in botany at London. She worked as a demonstrator at Newnham for six years before taking positions, first at Manchester High School and then at St. Leonards School at St. Andrews until 1892, when she began to spend most of her time as a worker for social reform. She was head of the Women's House and the Christian Social Union, Hoxton. She published in the *Journal of Physiology.*   JH/MBO

PRIMARY SOURCES

Eves, Florence. With J. N. Langley. "On Certain Conditions Which Influence the Amylolytic Action of Saliva." *Journal of Physiology* 4 (1883–1884): 18–25.

———. "Some Experiments on Liver Ferment." *Journal of Physiology* 5 (1884–1885): 342–351.
———. "On Some Experiments on the Liver Ferment." *Proceedings of the Cambridge Philosophical Society* 5 (1886): 182–183.

STANDARD SOURCES
Newnham, vol. 1.

EWING, ELIZABETH RAYMOND (BURDEN) (1860–1951)

British/Scottish botanist. Born 25 October in Glasgow. Professional experience: plant collector. Died 26 July 1951.

Elizabeth Ewing was president of the Natural History Society of Glasgow in 1919. She also contributed articles to the *Glasgow Naturalist.* Her herbarium, prepared with Peter Ewing, is at the Glasgow Natural History Museum.

JH/MBO

SECONDARY SOURCES
Glasgow Naturalist (1951): 62–63.

STANDARD SOURCES
Desmond.

EYTON, CHARLOTTE (fl. 1860s and 1870s)

British amateur geologist. Born to Elizabeth (Francess) and Thomas Campbell Eyton. Six siblings. Never married.

Charlotte Eyton was an amateur geologist. She absorbed her geological interests from her father, who was a friend of Charles Darwin and a well-known naturalist in Shropshire. She published six notes and papers between 1866 and 1870 in the *Geological Magazine,* as well as a monograph, *Notes on the Geology of North Shropshire.*   JH/MBO

PRIMARY SOURCES

Eyton, Charlotte. *Notes on the Geology of North Shropshire.* London: Robert Hardwicke, 1869.
———. *Flood and Fell* [or *Fell and Flood*]. London, 1872.

SECONDARY SOURCES

Kirk, J. F. *A Supplement to Allibone's Critical Dictionary of English Literature.* 2 vols. Philadelphia: J. P. Lippincott, 1891.

STANDARD SOURCES
Creese and Creese.

F

FABIOLA (d. 399)

Roman physician. Died 399.

Fabiola was the daughter of a patrician Roman family who was converted to Christianity when she was twenty years old and, as one of fifteen female followers of St. Jerome, practiced medicine and offered services free to the indigent. Jerome directed that she establish a hospital and treat rejects from society who were suffering from "loathsome diseases." Part of Fabiola's commitment to her work stemmed from a self-imposed penance. After her first husband died, she remarried, but her second husband died shortly thereafter. She felt that she had sinned by contracting this second marriage and apparently also had misgivings about the frivolity of her youth. Although Fabiola's approach to medicine was pragmatic rather than theoretical, her work illustrates the involvement of early Christian women in medicine.   JH/MBO

STANDARD SOURCES
Hurd-Mead 1938; Ogilvie 1986.

FAGE, WINIFRED E. (fl. 1921)

British chemist and physicist. Educated (B.Sc.). Professional experience: National Physical Laboratory, researcher.

The position of women in the physics laboratories during the early decades of the twentieth century needs to be investigated, especially that of women who held only a bachelor's degree or perhaps no degree at all. Fage is one of many examples of such women. She held a bachelor's degree, and worked at the National Physical laboratory, Great Britain, with E. A. Owen on experiments involving gamma-ray absorption. In a project of practical significance, Fage and Owen compared different methods for determining the radium content of compounds used to make luminescence screens and paint. In another investigation, Fage, Owen, and

Fleming studied absorption and scattering in four different metals in order to elucidate the processes that produce characteristic radiation and the Compton effect.   MM

PRIMARY SOURCES
Fage, Winifred E. With E. A. Owen. "The Estimation of the Radium Content of Radio-active luminous Compounds." *Physical Society of London, Proceedings* 34 (1921): 27–32.
———. With N. Fleming and E. A. Owen. "Absorption and Scattering of Gamma-Rays." *Physical Society of London, Proceedings* 36 (1924): 355–366.

STANDARD SOURCES
Meyer and von Schweidler.

FARENDEN, EMMA (ca. 1800–1880)

British botanist. Born between 1779 and 1881, probably 1800. Never married. Professional experience: schoolmistress. Member Botanical Society (elected July 1845). Died June 1880.

Emma Farenden was a member of the Botanical Society, an organization that aimed to be inclusive rather than exclusive. During the twenty years of the Botanical Society's existence, the total number of members was about four hundred. Of this four hundred, thirty-three were women, but only twenty-five can be identified with any degree of accuracy. Farenden was one of those identified. She lived in Regent's Park, London.   JH/MBO

SECONDARY SOURCES
Allen, D. E. "The Women Members of the Botanical Society of London, 1836–1856." *British Journal for the History of Science* 13 (1980): 240–254.

STANDARD SOURCES
Desmond.

FARNSWORTH, ALICE (1893–1960)

U.S. astronomer. Born 19 October 1893 in Williamsburg, Mass. Educated Mount Holyoke College (A.B., 1916); University of Chicago (M.S., 1916; Ph.D., 1920). Professional experience: Mount Holyoke College, assistant (1920–1922), assistant professor (1922–1928), associate professor (1928–1937), professor (from 1937); J. P. Williston Observatory, director (from 1936). Concurrent experience: University of Chicago, instructor (1925–1926); Lick Observatory, Martin Kellogg fellow (1930–1931). Death date unknown. Died 1 October 1960 in Newton, Mass.

After Alice Farnsworth earned her doctorate from the University of Chicago, she returned to teach at Mount Holyoke, where she had received her bachelor's degree. She moved through the academic ranks at Holyoke, becoming a full professor in 1937. For the year 1930–1931, she was a Martin Kellogg fellow at Lick Observatory. By this time, she was well prepared to be the director of the J. P. Williston Observatory, a post she held concurrently with her professorship. She was a member of the Astronomical Society and the Association of Variable Star Observers (president, 1929–1931). Farnsworth's special research interests were in the relatively new fields of stellar photometry and spectroscopy. She also studied lunar occultations. Her papers are in the Mount Holyoke Archives and Special Collections.   JH/MBO

PRIMARY SOURCES

Farnsworth, Alice. "A Comparison of the Photometric Fields of the 6-Inch Doublet, 24-Inch Reflector, and 40-Inch Refractor of the Yerkes Observatory, with Some Investigation of the Astrometric Field of the Reflector." Ph.D. diss., University of Chicago, 1920.

———. With Rebecca B. Jones. "The Orbit of the Spectroscopic Binary 32 Aquarii." *Lick Observatory Bulletin* (7 September 1932): 48.

STANDARD SOURCES

AMS 4–8, P 9.

FARNSWORTH, VESTA J. (1855–1932)

U.S. writer on hygiene and natural history. Born 15 November 1855 in Poy Sippi, Wis., to Elder and Mrs. P. H. Cady. Died 31 July 1932 in Glendale, Calif.

Vesta J. Farnsworth was the eldest of eleven children born in Wisconsin to Seventh-Day Adventist parents, Elder and Mrs. P. H. Cady. Due to the lack of Seventh-Day Adventist educational institutions at the time, Vesta was educated at home. Following her education, she devoted several years to teaching. Then she pursued evangelical service in Wisconsin, the Dakotas, and Minnesota with her husband, O. A.

Olsen, whom she married in 1877 at the age of twenty-two. Soon after Olsen's death in 1890, she moved to Oakland, California, and became the corresponding secretary for the International Sabbath School Association. In 1893, she married E. W. Farnsworth, a Bible instructor at Union College in College View, Nebraska. Farnsworth returned to evangelical service three years later when she and her husband moved to Australia and subsequently New Zealand. During this time, Farnsworth served as the editor for a publication entitled *Bible Echo.* Eight years later, Farnsworth and her husband traveled extensively in England and the United States before returning to Oakland in 1911. In Oakland, Farnsworth directed the Sabbath School for the California Conference of the Seventh-Day Adventists. In 1893, the Farnsworths moved to their last residence, in Glendale, California.

Although never a mother herself, Farnsworth wrote books for mothers to read to their children about nature and hygiene. Her works were intended to help children become interested in the study of nature and to teach them how to care for their bodies. Additionally, Farnsworth wrote children's stories wherein Christian home life was promoted, including *The Real Home* (1923) and *Stories Mother Told* (1925). Farnsworth's compositions on physiology and nature encouraged children to be mindful of God in order to grow up to be a fine man or woman.

In *The House We Live In* (1900), Farnsworth used a biblical metaphor to liken the body to a house or a temple that must be carefully cleaned and cared for both inside and out. The book was written as a script between a mother and her four children who very much want to learn to care for their bodies and to avoid the negative influence of narcotics and stimulants. Farnsworth included illustrations of the walls of the "home," which show in detail the muscles of the arm and hand. Equally precise are pictures of the bones comprising the ribs, pelvis, and arm. These drawings are accompanied by prose detailing the physiology of body processes. As Farnsworth strictly adhered to the tenets of the Seventh-Day Adventists, the text is often folkloric in nature and is frequently punctuated with warnings about drinking alcohol or smoking cigars. Farnsworth also wrote a book concerning the study of nature entitled *Friends and Foes in Field and Forest,* published in 1913.

Following a brief illness, Farnsworth died at the age of seventy-six on 21 July 1932, at her home in Glendale, California.   CB

PRIMARY SOURCES

Farnsworth, Vesta J. *The House We Live In.* Mountain View, Calif.: Pacific Press Publishing, 1900.

———. *Friends and Foes in Field and Forest.* Payson, Ariz.: Leaves of Autumn Books, 1913.

SECONDARY SOURCES

In Memoriam: Mrs. Vesta J. Farnsworth. Seventh-Day Adventists, 1932.

FARQUHARSON, MARIAN SARAH (RIDLEY) (1846–1912)

British botanist, microscopist, and author. Born 1846 in Hollington (?), Hants. Father Rev. J. Nicholas Ridley. Married Robert F. Ogilvie Farquharson of Haughton, Aberdeenshire. Educated at home and in classes in London. Professional experience: No formal positions. Wrote and spoke on botany and microscopy. Honors and memberships: Scottish Association for Promotion of Women's Public Work, founder and president; Linnean Society, Fellow. Microscopical Society, Fellow. Died 20 April 1912.

Marian Sarah Farquharson was born in 1846. She had no education other than at home and in classes on botany and microscopy that she attended in London. She published a book on British ferns and presented a paper on methods of identifying British mosses in 1885 at the Aberdeen British Association for the Advancement of Science meeting. In 1890, at the International Congress, she presented a paper on the position of women in science and led a movement to obtain equal rights and eligibility for fellowship in scientific societies. At the Glasgow Exhibition of 1901, she spoke on the women's work in science. She was made a fellow of the Linnean Society and the Microscopical Society. She was founder and president of the Scottish Association for Promotion of Women's Public Work. She died in Tillydrine, Kincardine O'Neil, Aberdeenshire, in 1912. JH/MBO

PRIMARY SOURCES

Ridley, Marian Sarah. *A Pocket Guide to British Ferns.* London: D. Bogue, 1881.

Farquharson, Marian Sarah. "On the Identification of the British Mosses." *British Association for the Advancement of Science.* 1885.

———. "The Position of Women in Science." 1890.

———, Marian S. "Women's Suffrage: Should It Be Made a Test Question." Edinburgh National Society for Women's Suffrage, 1901.

SECONDARY SOURCES

"Marian Sarah Farquharson." *Gardeners Chronicle* (1912): 358. Obituary notice.

"Marian Sarah Farquharson." *Proceedings of the Linnean Society* (1911–1912): 45–46. Obituary notice.

STANDARD SOURCES

Desmond; *WWW,* vol. I, 1897–1916.

FARR, WANDA KIRKBRIDE (1895–?)

U.S. biochemist. Born 9 January 1895 in Matamoras, Ohio, to Clara M. and C. Fred Kirkbride. Married (1) Clifford Harrison Farr in 1918 (he died in 1928); and (2) E. C. Faulwetter. One son, Robert. Educated Ohio University (B.S., 1915); Columbia University (M.S., 1918). Professional experience: Kansas State College, instructor in botany (1917–1918); Texas A&M College, research associate (1918–1919); Bernard Skin and Cancer Clinic, St. Louis, research associate (1926–1927); Shaw School of Botany, instructor (1928); Boyce Thompson Institute, investigator in plant physiology (1928–1929); United States Department of Agriculture, cotton researcher (1929–1936); Chemical Foundation cellulose lab, director (1936–1940); American Cyanimid Co., researcher (1940–1943); Celanese Corporation of America, member of research division (1943–1954); University of Maine, associate professor of botany (1957–1964), lecturer in cytochemistry (from 1964). Honors and memberships: the Royal Microscopic Society; the American Association for the Advancement of Science; American Chemical Society; American Botanical Society; Torrey Botanical Club; Society of American Naturalists; New York Academy of Sciences. Death date unknown.

After Wanda Margarite Kirkbride's father died of tuberculosis when she was a child, her role model was her great-grandfather, a physician who taught her to be interested in living things. Although Wanda had first wanted to attend medical school, she was discouraged by her family, who feared that she would be exposed to tuberculosis. She acquiesced and did her undergraduate degree in botany at the Ohio University. She met her husband at Columbia University, while working on her master's degree. Farr had intended to returned to Columbia to work on her doctoral degree, but after Clifford Farr died of a heart condition, she abandoned this project. Clifford Farr was teaching at Washington University in St. Louis when he died. She remained there, teaching her husband's classes. In St. Louis, Farr became knowledgable about new techniques for growing animal cell cultures *in vitro* during the time that she was a research assistant at the Barnard Skin and Cancer Clinic. She received a grant from the National Academy of Sciences to continue the study of root hairs that she and her husband had begun. This work evolved into a position with the U.S. Department of Agriculture at the Boyce Institute as a cotton technologist.

In her research, Farr discovered the origin of cellulose, investigated plant physiology, the formation and structure of plant cell membranes, root hair growth, microscopic analysis, cotton fibers, X-ray diffraction, and microchemical techniques. Her work on cellulose may have been her most important contribution. She showed that cellular inclusions called plastids form this important constituent of plant cell walls. Previous investigators had failed to note this, for certain optical qualities make the plastids seemed to melt into the cytoplasm when they are mounted in water for microscopic studies. The plastids, therefore, become indistinguishable from the surrounding medium. When the plastids fill with the cellulose they have manufactured, the cellulose exerts a great pressure on the walls of the plastids, causing them to explode. The cellulose is then visible, making it seem that it appears magically within the cytoplasm.   JH/MBO

PRIMARY SOURCES

Farr, Wanda. With S. H. Eckerson. "Formation of Cellulose Membranes by Microscopic Particles of Uniform Size in Linear Arrangement." *Contributions of the Boyce Thompson Institute* 6 (1934): 189.

———. "Microscopical and Microchemical Analysis of Material of Plant Origin from Ancient Tombs." *American Journal of Botany* 31 (1944): 9.

SECONDARY SOURCES

"Cellulose Factory Located in Plants." *New York Times,* 27 December 1939.

STANDARD SOURCES

Debus; *Notable* (article by Marc Kusinitz).

FARRAR, LILLIAN KETURAH POND (fl. 1900–1917)

U.S. gynecologist and obstetrician. Educated Boston University (A.B., 1896); Cornell University (M.D., 1900). Professional experience: Woman's Hospital, attending surgeon (from 1917); Cornell University Medical College, assistant professor of obstetrics and gynecology (from 1920); Booth Memorial Hospital, consulting surgeon. Honors and memberships: American Board of Obstetrics & Gynecology, Fellow; Gynecological Society; College of Surgeons (served term as governor); American Medical Association; New York Academy of Medicine.

In 1890 Lillian Farrar was only woman member in the American Gynaecological Society. She worked as surgeon and as radiologist in the Woman's Hospital in New York. A pioneer in radium therapy for cervical cancer, she also did research on the importance of auto blood transfusion in gynecology. An expert in the anatomy of the pelvis, she examined the pros and cons of total abdominal hysterectomies and considered ways to prevent shock. She was a member of the American College of Surgeons, National Association of Gynecology and Obstetrics, an attending surgeon of the Woman's Hospital, and consulting surgeon to the Booth Memorial Hospital. Concurrently, Farrar was assistant professor of obstetrics and gynecology in the Cornell University Medical School.   JH/MBO

STANDARD SOURCES

AMS 5–8, B 9, P&B 10; Hurd-Mead 1933.

FÁTIMA (fl. 10th century)

Moorish astronomer. Born in the 10th century in Madrid. Father ben-Ahmed-el-Magerito (el Madrileño). Educated privately.

The daughter of the Islamic astronomer known as "el Madrileño," Fátima followed in her father's footsteps. Reputedly, she knew Hebrew, Greek, and Latin, as well as Arabic and Spanish. She wrote about astronomy, and her work made her famous in the Moslem circle in Madrid. Her best-known work is *Correcciones de Fátima.* She also helped her father by editing his work, the *Astrolabio,* found in the Library of San Lorenzo del Escorial.   JH/MBO

SECONDARY SOURCES

Robles, Sainz de, and Frederico Carolos, eds. *Ensayo du un Diccionario de Mujeres Celebres.* Madrid, 1959.

STANDARD SOURCES

Strohmeier.

FAUSTINA (fl. 5th century)

Roman healer. Married Emperor Antoninus Pius.

Faustina, the wife of Emperor Antoninus Pius, founded hospitals. Some of the hospitals were public and others were for her slaves and guests. She was greatly interested in the study of medicine.   JH/MBO

STANDARD SOURCES

Hurd-Mead 1938.

FAVILLA (fl. 2d century)

Roman physician. Flourished second century.

Favilla was one of the medical women mentioned by the physician Galen. He praised her remedies for hemoptysis and diarrhea.   JH/MBO

STANDARD SOURCES

Hurd-Mead 1938.

FAWCETT, PHILIPPA GARRETT (1868–1948)

British mathematician. Born 4 April 1868 in Cambridge to Mildred Garrett and Henry Fawcett. Educated Clapham High School; Bedford College; University College, London; Newnham College

(1887–1891); Winworth Scholar; Math Tripos Part I above Senior Wrangler, highest honors in mathematics (1890), Part II, Class 1 (1891); Marion Kennedy Student (1891); M.A. (titulary college degree). Professional experience: Newnham College, lecturer in mathematics (1892–1902), associate (1893–1906), (1907–1922); associate fellow (1917–1919), council member (1905–1915). Other experience: Transvaal Education Department, assistant, organizer of elementary schools after end of Boer War (1902–1905); London Central Council, chief assistant director of education (1905–1924); University College, London, fellow (1918–1948?). Died 10 June 1948.

Philippa Fawcett first attended Bedford and University Colleges, London. Her mother was active on the Newnham College, Cambridge, council from 1881–1909, so naturally wanted her daughter to attend Newnham. Phillipa went to Newnham in 1887, before women could get Cambridge degrees. Philippa was an excellent student. She scored above the Senior Wrangler, the top-scoring male undergraduate, in Part I of the Mathematics Tripos. Her achievement was not officially recognized. The next year she received a first-class pass in Part II of the Tripos.

Fawcett held a number of positions at Newnham, from instructor through associate fellow. In 1905, she was elected to the Newnham Council. Concurrently, she was an assistant in the Transvaal Education Department. She organized elementary schools after the end of the Boer War. In 1905, she became the chief assistant director of education on the London Central Council. In 1918, she became a University College fellow, a post she held until her death.   JH/MBO

PRIMARY SOURCES
Fawcett, Philippa Garrett. "The Electric Strength of Mixtures of Nitrogen and Hydrogen." *Proceedings Royal Society* 56 (1894): 263–271.

SECONDARY SOURCES
Siklos, Stephen. *Philippa Fawcett and the Mathematical Tripos.* Cambridge: Newnham College, 1990.

STANDARD SOURCES
Newnham, vol. 1

FEARN, ANNE WALTER (1867–?)

U.S. physician. Born 1867 at Holly Springs, Miss. Father Colonel Harvey Washington Walter, plantation owner. Many siblings. Educated Presbyterian Day School; Charlotte (N.C.) Female Institute; Woman's Medical College of Pennsylvania (M.D., 1893). Married Dr. John Burrus Fearn (21 April 1896). One daughter, Elizabeth (died at age five). Professional experience: Soochow Woman's Hospital, physician (ca. 1893–1896); Margaret Williamson Hospital for Chinese Women, Shanghai, volunteer physician; Foreign Women's Rescue Home, volunteer physician; founded Fearn Sanitorium, Shanghai (1916–1926). Death date unknown.

Anne Walter Fearn's father, Colonel Harvey Washington Walter, was a wealthy Mississippi plantation owner and was active in the political and social life typical of the Old South. Anne grew up a rather spoiled socialite whose family expected her to follow in the southern lady tradition. Her father died, along with four of his sons, of yellow fever when Anne was about twelve and there was a period of crisis and financial turmoil before an uncle reclaimed the Walter properties and fortune.

In the summer of 1889, after being ill with malaria, Walter went to San Francisco, California, to recuperate and visit her brother Harvey. She was introduced to Dr. Elizabeth M. Yates and became convinced she wanted to become a doctor; her mother responded that if Anne studied medicine, she would no longer recognize her as a daughter. Without finances, Walter embarked on her medical education by studying with Dr. Lucia Lane, then entered Cooper Medical College in San Francisco. To continue her education, she applied for and received a scholarship at Woman's Medical College of Pennsylvania, additional costs being paid for by Yates, her mentor. There she became the protégé of surgeon and obstetrician Joseph Price. Walter apprenticed at his private maternity hospital, Preston Retreat. After graduating, she apprenticed at a major urban maternity hospital.

Walter volunteered to go to China for a temporary (two-to-three-year) stint to replace her friend, Dr. Margaret Polk, while she took care of family problems. Walter thus began her work at the Soochow Woman's Hospital. On 21 April 1896, she married a missionary doctor, John Burrus Fearn. They had one daughter, Elizabeth, who died of amoebic dysentery at age five. Their marriage was marked with dissension and conflict from the beginning (she was nonreligious, he was austere; she was totally committed to her work, he felt that his own medical career should be preeminent). After their daughter died, the Fearns spent a sabbatical in the United States, then John was reassigned to Shangai. Fearn went with him, but was restless and dissatisfied without full-time work. She missed Soochow and tried to fill her life with volunteer charity work. She worked every afternoon at the Margaret Williamson Hospital for Chinese Women. She became associated with anti-opium organizations, and attended the International Opium Conference in Shanghai (1909). Fearn served also as hostess for many semidiplomatic affairs, drawing on her memories of countless balls and parties from her Mississippi high society days. Membership in the American Women's Club gave her another outlet and led to her becoming physician to the Foreign Women's Rescue Home, a treatment and aid facility for the many foreign prostitutes who came to Shanghai to seek their fortunes.

When World War I broke out, Fearn traveled all the way to New York to enlist in the Red Cross, and was disappointed to find that they accepted female nurses and only male doctors. Fearn returned to Shanghai and opened a practice with her old friend Margaret Polk. John Fearn was called to serve as physician in France; while he was away, Fearn set up her own hospital, the Fearn Sanitorium, which offered a wide range of medical services to the area population. John Fearn returned from France to become superintendent of the Shanghai General Hospital, and husband and wife became "rivals in good earnest."

Fearn ran her sanitorium for ten years, until another, larger, hospital was built in the same area. At that time, she closed her hospital reluctantly, because she felt unable to compete for the same clientele without outside financial support. She was also drawn away by her husband's terminal illness and dedicated herself to his needs until his death in 1926. After thirty years in China, Fearn returned to family in America only to find she could not wait to return "home" to China.   KM

PRIMARY SOURCES

Fearn, Anne Walter. *My Days of Strength: An American Woman Doctor's Forty Years in China.* New York: Macmillan, 1939.

SECONDARY SOURCES

Glazer, Penina Migdal, and Miriam Slater. *Unequal Colleagues: The Entrance of Women into the Professions, 1890–1940.* New Brunswick: Rutgers University Press, 1987. Photograph, page 73.

FEDCHENKO, OL'GA ALEKSANDROVNA (1845–1921)

Russian botanist and explorer. Born 30 November 1845. Father Aleksandr Osipovich Armfel'd, professor at Moscow University. Eight siblings. Married Aleksei Pavlovich Fedchenko. One son, Boris. Educated Nikolaevskii Institute. Honors and memberships: Society of Amateur Naturalists, secretary; gold medal, Society of Amateur Naturalists; Russian Geographical Society, silver medal. Died in 1921.

Ol'ga Aleksandrovna Fedchenko was born into the large family of a professor at Moscow University. Her early education took place at home with her five brothers and three sisters. At age eleven, she entered the Nikolaevskii Institute, from which she graduated in 1864 with an excellent knowledge of foreign languages and drawing. Summers spent in a village in the Mozhaisk region awakened her interest in nature at an early age. While still at school, she collected plants,

insects, and birds' eggs. In 1861–1862 she compiled a herbarium of the Mozhaisk region, which the botanist N. N. Kaufman used in his work on Moscow flora.

Ol'ga took her collections to the Zoological Museum in Moscow and made friends with other students of nature. Among these was Aleksei Pavlovich Fedchenko (1844–1873), an enthusiastic naturalist a year older than herself. Aleksei was interested in collecting Diptera at that time and Ol'ga assisted him. During her last year at school, she was admitted to membership in the Society of Amateur Naturalists, founded in 1863 as a forum for students and enthusiasts. The older Society of Naturalists was essentially a specialist organization.

Upon leaving school, Ol'ga translated works from several languages, gave lessons, and made drawings from nature. On 2 July 1867, she married Aleksei Fedchenko. Together, they made several trips to Europe to pursue some of Aleksei's anthropological interests, to meet other scientists, and to prepare themselves for a projected expedition to Turkestan under the auspices of the Society of Amateur Naturalists.

At that time, a trip to Turkestan was not without danger. Some areas, under the control of various khans and beks, had only recently been annexed by the Russian Empire and were not totally pacified. Also there were the natural hazards to contend with. In 1868, the young couple set out on an expedition, which, with several interruptions, lasted three years. They spent time in Samarkand, Iskander-Kul', Tashkent, and Kyzylkum, making observations and collecting a variety of specimens. Ol'ga, in particular, collected botanical specimens and made drawings from nature. A great quantity of material was assembled for what was ultimately to become the monumental *Puteshestvie v Turkestane.*

In 1872, their son, Boris Alekseevich, was born. The following year, Aleksei died in a blizzard on a glacier at Mont Blanc. At that time, serial publication of *Puteshestvie* was in progress and, ultimately, Fedchenko was asked to carry on with the work, a task that took some years. Friends at the Society of Amateur Naturalists also managed to obtain a salary and a pension for her. The correspondence on this subject stresses repeatedly the extent to which Ol'ga had shared her husband's life, interests, and risks.

In 1873 Fedchenko translated Henry Yule's *The History and Geography of the Upper Amu-Darya,* for which she received a silver medal from the Russian Geographical Society. For several years (from 1877), she was secretary of the Society of Amateur Naturalists. In 1884 she worked in the botanical gardens of Moscow University, classifying and organizing the collections. Then, in company with her son, she set out on a series of collecting expeditions to different parts of the Russian Empire (1891–1901). Fedchenko's final expedition was to the Pamirs on the Afghan border; she died in 1921.

Although Fedchenko had no formal education beyond secondary school and never held an official post, her contribution to botany was of the highest order. She was never simply an appendage to her husband. Her interest in nature began years before she met him and was central to their relationship, and she brought up her son, Boris, to share it. It was she who was primarily responsible for the botanical collections and the excellent illustrations. Much of her work was done after Aleksei's death. Her publications on the flora of central Asia, the Crimea, Urals, the Pamirs, and the Caucasus are standard references to this day.   ACH

PRIMARY SOURCES

Fedchenko, Ol'ga Aleksandrovna. *Opredielitel' Pamirskikh rastenii.* St. Petersburg: Typographer K. Mattisena, 1907.

———. *Eremurus; kritische Uebersicht der Gattung.* St. Petersburg, 1909.

———. *Rasteniia Pamira: sobrannyia F.N. Alek'senko v 1901 godu.* St. Petersburg: Typographer Imperatorskoi Akademii Nauk, 1910.

SECONDARY SOURCES

Agafonova, Z. I., and N. A. Khalfin. *A.P. Fedchenko: sbornik dokumentov.* Tashkent: Gosizdat USSR, 1956.

Andreevskii, I. E., ed. *Entsiklopedicheskii slovar'.* St. Petersburg: Typographer I. A. Efron, 1890–1906.

Leonov, Nikolai I. *Aleksei Pavlovich Fedchenko, 1844–1873.* Moscow: Izd-vo Nauka, 1972.

FEICHTINGER, NORA (1890–?)

Austrian biologist. Educated University of Vienna (thesis, 1921). Professional experience: Kaiser Wilhelm Institute for chemistry, assistant in the radioactive physics department (1924–1931); Kaiser Wilhelm Institute for biology, scientific "guest" (1931–1932). Death date unknown.

Little is known about the life of Nora Feichtinger. Educated in Austria, she went to the Kaiser Wilhelm Institute for Chemistry, where she worked under the direction of LISE MEITNER, studying the effects of radiation on different plants. She was listed as one of only ten women assistants in the *Handbook of the Kaiser Wilhelm Gesellschaft* in 1928. She returned to Vienna in 1934, and nothing is known of her from that time forward.   JH/MBO

SECONDARY SOURCES

von Harnack, Adolph, and Richard Ruedy, eds. *Handbook of the Kaiser Wilhelm Society for the Advancement of Science.* Ottawa: National Research Council of Canada, 1928. English translation.

STANDARD SOURCES

Vogt.

FELICIE, JACOBINA (fl. 1322)

Italian physician. Born in Florence. Died in Paris.

Jacobina Felicie was a native of Florence of noble birth. Felicie lived in Paris, where she practiced medicine. An edict dating back to 1220 prohibited any person not a member of the faculty of medicine from practicing. Although technically only unmarried men were eligible for membership, married men were able to circumvent the requirements by studying with a master. According to reports, Felicie also had studied with a master but nevertheless was prosecuted for practicing medicine without a license. After paying her fine, she continued to practice medicine, repeating this process several times. Finally, she was released from custody because of numerous testimonies to her skill. Despite the support of her peers, she lost the battle in the courts, setting a precedent against women practicing medicine in France for many years.   JH/MBO

STANDARD SOURCES

Hurd-Mead 1938; Lipinska 1930; Ogilvie 1986.

FELL, HONOR BRIDGET, DAME (1900–1986)

British cell biologist and mycologist. Born 22 May 1900 in Fowthorpe, Yorkshire, to Alice (Pickersgill-Cunliffe) and Colonel William Fell. Eight siblings. Educated Wychwood School, Oxford; Madras College, St. Andrews (1916–1918); Edinburgh University (B.Sc., 1923; Ph.D., 1924; D.Sc., 1932). Professional experience: Junior Beit Fellow (1924); 4th-year Beit Fellow (1927); Senior Beit Fellow (1928); Messel Research Fellow Royal Society (1943–1967); Royal Society, research professor (from 1963); Strangeways Research Laboratory, director (1929–1970); research worker (1979–1986); University of Cambridge division of immunology, department of pathology, (1970–1979).

Honor Fell was one of nine children of a not very successful farmer and a practical mother who was chiefly responsible for raising the family. Her father probably instilled in Honor a love of nature and of animals. An often told story relates how Honor at age thirteen brought a ferret, Janie, to her sister Barbara's wedding.

Honor's school in Oxford was unusual in that it emphasized the importance of science as well as the classics, history, and literature. She did her early undergraduate work at St. Andrews and then went to Edinburgh University to read zoology. She earned three degrees from this institution. Her superior at Edinburgh, F. A. E. Crew, sent Bridget to

Cambridge to learn a new technique pioneered by T. S. P. Strangeways in his research hospital. Tissue culture was a relatively new art at this time, and he had developed it to the extent that he could study the behavior of living cells on a warm stage. Fell was impressed, and when Strangeways offered her a job as scientific assistant with a grant from the Medical Research Council, she accepted. Her first major study was on chick embryos, examining their cartilage and bones. This work culminated in her first important paper from the Strangeways in 1925, a study of the histogenesis of bone and cartilage in the long bone of embryonic chicks. From this beginning, she used techniques of organ culture to analyze the actions of various agents upon the cells of bone, cartilage, and associated tissues.

The preliminary study was continued, and in 1926 she and Strangeways demonstrated that cartilage would not only grow but would differentiate in culture. Strangeways died in 1926, and Fell was subsequently appointed temporary director. Her accomplishments led to her being appointed director, a position she held for the next forty-one years.

Stimulated by the problems raised by starvation in Europe, Fell began to work with the nutritional importance of vitamin A. It had long been known that both deficiencies and excesses of this vitamin could have deleterious effects, but it was not known how it worked. Edward Mellanby had been doing work on vitamin A and he had the idea that bone culture techniques might be used to study its action on skeletal tissues. He hoped this method would help determine whether vitamin A had a direct action on the bone and cartilage matrix or whether it was mediated by another gland. Fell took up the challenge and identified how vitamin A acts to deplete cellular material. She and John Dingle determined in 1963 that vitamin A both increased the total cellular synthesis and, in doing so, released acid proteases. The released proteases then acted as lysosomal enzymes.

Fell also became interested in the etiology of rheumatoid arthritis. In her search for a cause, she examined the effects of substances such as hydrocortisone on bones and cartilage.

Although Fell retired from Strangeways Research Laboratory in 1970, she continued to be active in scientific research. She returned to Cambridge, Division of Immunology, where her work led to the discovery of interleukin-1. She also returned to Strangeways in 1979, and conducted research on collagen degradation in synovial tissue.

Fell's honors included being named a fellow of the Royal Society (1952), a fellow of Girton College (1955), and Dame Commander of the British Empire (1963). She also received honorary degrees from Harvard University, Cambridge University, and Smith College.   JH/MBO

PRIMARY SOURCES

Fell, Honor. "The Histogenesis of Cartilage and Bone in the Long Bones of the Embryonic Fowl." *Journal of Morphological Physiology* 40 (1925): 417–439.

———. "The Osteogenic Capacity *in Vitro* of Periosteum and Endosteum Isolated from the Limb Skeleton of Fowl Embryos and Young Chicks." *Journal of Anatomy* 66 (1932): 157–180.

———. With E. Mellanby and S. R. Pelc. "Influence of Excess Vitamin A on Organized Tissues Cultivated *in Vitro*." *Journal of Physiology* 133 (1956): 89–100.

———. "The Influence of Hydrocortisone on the Metaplastic Action of Vitamin A on the Epidermis of Embryonic Chicken Skin in Organ Culture." *Journal of Embryological Experimental Morphology* 10 (1962): 389–409.

———. "The Strangeways Research Laboratory and Cellular Interactions." In *Cellular Interactions,* ed. J. T. Dingle and J. L. Gordon. Elsevier/North-Holland, 1981.

SECONDARY SOURCES

Poole, A. Robin, and Arnold I. Caplan. "An Appreciation: Dame Honor Bridget Fell F.R.S." *Developmental Biology* 122 (1987): 297–299.

Vaughn, Janet. "Dame Honor Fell." *Biographical Memoirs of Fellows of the Royal Society* 33 (1987): 235–259.

STANDARD SOURCES

Notable (article by George A. Milite).

FENCHEL, KÄTE (SPERLING) (1905–1983)

German mathematician. Born 21 December 1905 in Berlin to Rusza (Angress) and Otto Sperling. One sister. Married Werner Fenchel. One son, Tom. Educated University of Berlin, Mathematics Institute; pedagogical training. Professional experience: high school teacher (1931–1933); Aarhus University, part-time lecturer (1965–1970). Died 18 or 19 December 1983.

Käte Fenchel was a talented theoretical mathematician whose career was determined by Hitler's race policies. Her father left the family when Käte was very young, putting the family into serious financial straits. She attended a private girls' school as a scholarship student and then attended high school for six years, where she studied Latin, modern languages, mathematics, and physics. Supported by a schoolmate's father, she was able to attend the University of Berlin, where she studied mathematics, philosophy, and physics. She did not encounter sex discrimination at the university, but when she found that a gifted woman friend was unable to get a job because of her sex, she realized that she would have the same difficulties. Therefore, even though she was asked to write a thesis, she declined and supplemented her theoretical education with teacher training in order to qualify herself as a high school teacher. She taught high school for two years, but lost her job in 1933 because she was Jewish. After she was dismissed, she earned some money tutoring nuns who were working on their master's degrees.

In 1933 she and a former fellow student, Werner Fenchel, who was also Jewish, immigrated to Denmark and were married in December 1933. In Denmark, she worked for a Danish mathematics professor as a part-time secretary both to augment the family income and because through correspondence she could help other Jews to emigrate. During this time, she published her first mathematical paper (1937). Her son, Tom, was born in 1940 just when Denmark was occupied by Germany and Danish Jews were deported to German concentration camps. The Fenchels left for Sweden, but returned after the war. Even though she didn't publish during this time, Fenchel was careful to keep up on the current literature. She published two more papers in 1962 and got a part-time lecturer's position in 1965 at Aarhus University. She stayed at Aarhus until she was sixty-five. She published an additional paper in 1978.

Fenchel's research was in pure mathematics, and most of it was concerned with finite nonabelian groups, particularly the nature of odd order groups. One of her papers dealt with "vectormodules," one with conditions that characterize groups of odd order, and another proved that $d_{n-1} = 1$ if and only if the group is identical with its commutator subgroup. Her final paper was concerned with a theorem of Frobenius.

JH/MBO

PRIMARY SOURCES

Fenchel, Käte. "An Everywhere Dense Vectormodule with Discrete One-Dimensional Submodules." *Matematisk Tidsskrift* B (1937): 94–96. In Danish.

———. "Eine Bemerkung über Gruppen ungerader Ordung." *Mathematica Scandinavica* 10 (1962): 182–188.

———. "Beziehungen zwischen der Struktur einer endlichen Gruppe und einer speziellen Darstellung." *Monatshepte Für Mathematik* (1962): 397–409.

———. "On a Theorem of Frobenius." *Mathematica Scandinavica* 42 (1978): 243–250.

SECONDARY SOURCES

Grinstein and Campbell (article by Else Høyrup); *Notable Mathematicians* (article by Annelte Petruso).

FENWICK, FLORENCE (1893–?)

U.S. chemist. Born 11 October 1893 in Green Bay, Wis. Educated University of Michigan (B.S., 1917; M.S., 1920; Ph.D., 1922).

Professional experience: Corning Glass Works, chemist (1918–1919); National Research Council, fellow in chemistry, Yale University (1923–1925), research fellow (1925–1928); U.S. Steel Corporation, physical chemist, research laboratory (from 1928). Death date unknown.

Florence Fenwick spent most of her career in industry, first as a chemist at Corning Glass Works and then at U.S. Steel. She earned all three of her degrees at the University of Michigan. A member of the Chemical Society, she did research in a number of fields, including electrometric analysis, electrode potentials, and ion equilibria. JH/MBO

PRIMARY SOURCES

Fenwick, Florence. *The Theory and Application of Bimetallic Electrode Systems in Electrometric Analysis.* Easton, Pa.: Eschenbach Printing, 1923.

STANDARD SOURCES

AMS 4–5.

FERGUSON, MARGARET CLAY (1863–1951)

U.S. plant geneticist and embryologist. Born 20 August 1863 in Orleans, N.Y., to Hannah (Warner) and Robert Ferguson. Five siblings. Educated Genesee Wesleyan Seminary, Lima, N.Y. (graduated, 1885); Wellesley College (1888–1891); Cornell University (B.S., 1899; Ph.D., 1901). Professional experience: Harcourt Place Seminary, Gambier, Ohio, head of science department (1891–1893); Wellesley College, instructor (1894–1896, 1901–1904), associate professor (1904–1906), professor and head of botany department (1906–1930), research professor (1930–1932), director of greenhouses and gardens (1922–1932). Honors and memberships: American Microscopical Society, vice-president (1914); Botanical Society of America, president (1929); Mount Holyoke College, Honorary D. Sc. (1937); New York Academy of Sciences, Fellow (1943); American Association for the Advancement of Science, Fellow. Died 28 August 1951 in San Diego, Calif.

Margaret Ferguson, one of six children of a farming couple, taught in local public schools from the time she was fourteen years old. During these teaching years, she studied at the Genesee Wesleyan Seminary in Lima, New York, from which she graduated in 1885. From 1888 to 1891, she attended Wellesley College as a special student, combining coursework in botany and chemistry. After two years as head of the science department at a seminary in Ohio, Ferguson returned to Wellesley as an instructor. This was the beginning of a teaching, research, and administrative career at Wellesley that extended over more than four decades, interrupted only by her studies at Cornell, leading to a doctorate in 1901. After serving as head of Wellesley's botany department from 1902 to 1930, Ferguson continued to do research at Wellesley until 1938, when she went to live near relatives in Seneca Castle, New York. Later she lived in Florida and, from 1946, in San Diego, California, where she died of a heart attack.

Margaret Ferguson directed the modernization of both the physical facilities and the curriculum of Wellesley's botany department. She stressed laboratory work and the study of chemistry and physics as essential components of training in botany. Ferguson's research interests evolved throughout her career. From her early study of the physiology of the germination of the spores of basidiomycetous fungi, she moved to research in functional morphology and cytology (her life history of a North American pine became a standard for such life histories). Finally, she became involved in genetics, using *Petunia* as a tool for studying inheritance in higher plants, and publishing on the topic in the 1920s.

Among the honors Ferguson received for her achievements were election as the first woman president of the Botanical Society of America (1929), vice-president of the American Microscopical Society (1914), Fellow of the New York Academy of Sciences (1943), and Fellow of the American Association for the Advancement of Science; starred status in *American Men of Science* beginning with the 1910 edition; an honorable mention (1903) by the Association for Maintaining the American Women's Table at the Zoological Station at Naples; and an honorary doctorate from Mount Holyoke College (1937). MBO

PRIMARY SOURCES

Ferguson, Margaret. "On the Development of the Pollen Tube and the Division of the Generative Nucleus in Certain Species of Pines." Ph.D. diss., Cornell University, 1901.

———. "Contribution to the Knowledge of the Life History of *Pinus* with Special Reference to Sporogenesis, the Development of the Gametophytes and Fertilization." *Proceedings of the Washington Academy of Sciences* 6 (1904): 1–102.

SECONDARY SOURCES

Creighton, Harriet B. "Margaret Clay Ferguson." *Wellesley Alumnae Magazine* 1952: 106.

———. "The Margaret Ferguson Greenhouses." *Wellesley Alumnae Magazine* 1947: 172–173.

Hart, Sophie Chantal. "Margaret Clay Ferguson." *Wellesley Alumnae Magazine* 1947: 408–410.

Morgan, W. J. B., and M. J. Corbel. [Bibliography of Alice Evans]. *Annali Sclavo* February 1977. Issue devoted to Evans.

Rudolph, Emanuel D. "Women in Nineteenth Century Botany." *American Journal of Botany* 69 (1982): 1346–1355.

The Wellesley College Archives contain material on Ferguson.

STANDARD SOURCES

AMS 1–8; Bailey; Barnhart; *NAW*(M) (article by Ann M. Hirsch and Lisa J. Marroni); Ogilvie 1986; O'Hearn; Shearer and Shearer (article by Thura R. Mack) 1996.

FERNALD, GRACE MAXWELL (1879–1950)

U.S. psychologist. Born 29 November 1879 in Clyde, Ohio to Nettie (Barker) and James C. Fernald. Educated Mount Holyoke College (A.B., 1903; A.M., 1905); Bryn Mawr College (1904–1906); University of Chicago (Ph.D., 1907). Professional experience: Bryn Mawr College, assistant in psychology and education (1907–1908); Chicago Psychopathic Institute, assistant director (1909); California State Normal School, Los Angeles, director of the psychology lab (1909–1918); Cincinnati Public Schools (from 1921); University of California, Los Angeles, assistant professor of psychology (1918–1920), associate professor (from 1920), professor (1941–1945), professor emeritus (1945–1950); Brentwood Clinic, director (1945–1950). Concurrent experience: University of California, Los Angeles, Clinical School, director (1921–1945). Honors and memberships: American Psychological Association, Fellow; American Association of Applied Psychology, Fellow; American Association for the Advancement of Science, Fellow; American Board of Professional Psychologists, Diplomat. Died 15 January 1950.

Grace Fernald worked with delinquent and atypical children in the public school systems. She was especially interested in the psychology of special disabilities in reading, spelling, and mathematics. She had practical experience working with these children in the Cincinnati public schools. Her other major research interest was on the Purkinje phenomenon in peripheral vision. KM

PRIMARY SOURCES

Fernald, Grace Maxwell. "The Effect of Achromatic Conditions on the Color Phenomena of Peripheral Vision." *Psychological Monographs* no. 42. Ph.D. dissertation.

———. With William Healy. *Test for Practical Mental Classification.* Lancaster, Pa. and Baltimore: Review Publishing Co., 1911.

———. "The Use of the Benet Scale with Delinquent Children." *Transactions of the International Congress of School Hygiene* 5 (1914): 670–677.

———. *On Certain Language Disabilities: Their Nature and Treatment.* Baltimore: Williams & Wilkins, 1936. Includes section by Helen Keller.

SECONDARY SOURCES

Sulivan, E. B., et al. "Grace Maxwell Fernald 1879–1950." *Psychological Review* 57 (1950): 319–321.

STANDARD SOURCES

AMS 2–8.

FERNALD, MARIA ELIZABETH (SMITH) (1839–1919)

U.S. entomologist. Born 1839 in Monmouth, Maine. Married Charles H. Fernald (1862). One son, Henry. Educated Maine Wesleyan Seminary and Female College. Professional experience: Maine Wesleyan Seminary and Female College, preceptess (1858–1862). Died 1919.

Maria Smith was well-trained at the Maine Wesleyan Seminary and Female College, graduating first in her class. She taught there for a number of years before marrying Charles H. Fernald, an entomologist attached to the University of Maine. Maria Fernald was especially interested in scale insects (Coccidae) and published a study of Coccidae of the world for the Hatch Experimental Station in Massachusetts. Fernald also studied small moths (Tortricidae) and compiled a card catalogue on this topic in the 1870s. She was the first to identify the gypsy moth (1869), which was soon to wreak havoc in the New England woods.

Her influence extended to her son, Henry, himself an entomologist, who later spoke of her skill in catching rare and new species. JH/MBO

PRIMARY SOURCES
Fernald, Mary E. *A Catalogue of Coccidae of the World.* Hatch Experimental Station, Massachusetts, Monograph 68.

SECONDARY SOURCES
Bonta, Marcia Myers. *Women in the Field: America's Pioneering Women Naturalists.* College Station: Texas A & M University Press, 1991.
Carpenter, M. M. "Bibliography of Biographies of Entomologists." *American Midland Naturalist* 33 (1945): 1–116.

STANDARD SOURCES
Osborn.

FERRAND, ELIZABETH M. (1852–1900)

U.S. physician. Born 31 March 1852 in Ann Arbor, Mich., to Francis (Shaw) and Lucretius S. Ferrand. Educated locally; University of Michigan (M.D.). Professional experience: University of Michigan, assistant librarian (1872–1886); Detroit Woman's Hospital, resident physician (1886–1888); Port Huron, Mich., private practice (1888–1900). Honors and memberships: North Eastern District Medical Society (president); Michigan State Medical Society. Died of cancer 17 August 1900 in Port Huron.

Elizabeth Ferrand was trained in medicine at the University of Michigan in the 1880s. In order to finance her studies, she worked in the university's library. She was able to obtain a residency at the Detroit Woman's Hospital for two years, after which she set up practice in Port Huron, Michigan. After only twelve years in practice, Ferrand developed cancer and died at the age of forty-eight. JH/MBO

SECONDARY SOURCES
Kelly, Howard A. *Cyclopedia of American Medical Biography.* Vol. 1. Philadelphia: W. B. Saunders, 1912.

FERRAND, JACQUELINE
See Lelong-Ferrand, Jacqueline.

FERRERO, GINA (LOMBROSO) (1872–1944)

Italian behavioral psychologist. Born 5 October 1872 in Pavia, Italy. Father Cesare Lombroso (1835–1909). Married Guglielmo Ferrero (1871–1942), historian and classicist. Educated Università di Torino (Ph.D., 1896; M.D., 1901). Died 1944.

Gina Lombroso was born in Pavia, Italy. Her father, Cesare Lombroso (1835–1909), was an eminent psychiatrist, anthropometrist, and criminologist. Extremely well known and influential in the positivist prison reform movement of the mid to late nineteenth century, some of his ideas, such as indeterminate sentencing, parole, and juvenile court remain in use today, although his theory that criminal behavior could be traced entirely to physical attributes, then widely accepted, is now ridiculed. His book, *Criminal Man* (reissued by Gina Ferrero in 1911 with a new introduction and a summary of her father's other works) was translated internationally and the "Lombrosian school" served as a basis for anthropometric criminology and psychology into the twentieth century. This "positivist" school held sway against the French school of criminology, which emphasized the role of environment rather than biology in the creation of the criminal—especially in the United States where French works were less readily available in translation.

Gina Lombroso attended the Università di Torino, where she received both doctoral and medical degrees. She married Guglielmo Ferrero (1871–1942), historian and classicist, who coauthored with Cesare Lombroso *La donna delinquente* (The Female Offender) in 1900. During the regime of Mussolini, they moved into democratic Switzerland where many other Italian intellectuals gathered. Gina Ferrero was a member of the Società di l'Igiene Mentale. JH/MBO

PRIMARY SOURCES
Ferrero, Gina. *The Criminal Man According to Cesare Lombroso.* New York: Putnam, 1910.
———. *La vita e le opere di Cesare Lombroso.* Turin: Bocca, 1916; 2d. ed., Bologna: Zanichelli, 1923.
———. *L'anima della donna.* Bologna: Zanichelli, 1919. Many

editions, translated internationally, e.g., New York: Dutton; London: Yonatan Cape; Frankfurt: Siebener-Verlag.

———. *La donna alle prese colla vita.* Bologna: Zanichelli, [1928?].

———. *La donna nella società attuale.* Bologna: Zanichelli; Paris: Payot, [1929?].

———. *Vite di donna.* Bologna: Zanichelli; Paris: Payot; Tokyo: Kenisha Store, [1929?].

———. *Nuove vite di donna.* Bologna: Zanichelli, 1930.

———. *Tragedie del progresso.* Turin: Bocca, 1930; Paris: Payot, 1931; New York: Dutton, 1931.

SECONDARY SOURCES
Harrowitz, Nancy A. *Antisemitism, Misogyny and the Logic of Cultural Difference: Cesare Lombroso and Matilde Serao.* Lincoln: University of Nebraska, 1994.

STANDARD SOURCES
Lovejoy.

FIELDE, ADELE MARION (1839–1916)

U.S. naturalist. Born 30 March 1839 in East Rodman, N.Y. to Sophia (Tiffany) and Leighton Fielde. Never married. Educated New York State Normal College, Albany (teaching certificate, 1860). Professional experience: Long Island, N.Y., public school teacher (1860–1865); Bangkok, Thailand, Baptist missionary teacher, (1866–1872); Swatow, China, Baptist missionary teacher (1873–1883, 1885–1889); Marine Biological Laboratories, evening lecturer (1894–1900); New York City, public lecturer (1893–1907). Seattle, Wash., public lecturer (1907–1915). Honors and memberships: League for Political Education; Philadelphia Academy of Sciences. Died in Seattle, Wash., 21 February 1916.

Adele Marion Fielde grew up in New York state and attended the New York State Normal College at Albany. She took a position on Long Island as a public school teacher, and then planned to marry a young missionary in Thailand. When she found that he had died shortly before her arrival, she joined the Baptist mission in Bangkok, where she worked as a teacher for the next seven years. She returned very briefly to the United States, and then traveled back to the Far East as a missionary teacher in Swatow, China. While there, she became interested in the language and culture, remaining for ten years. By 1883, she decided that, for her role at the mission, she needed training in obstetrics, and she returned to Philadelphia to study at the Woman's Medical College of Philadelphia for two years. At the same time, she took the opportunity to learn more about science through the Philadelphia Academy of Natural Sciences, with which she formed close ties.

Back in China, Fielde prepared a dictionary of the Swatow dialect that was published by the Presbyterian Mission

Board in Shanghai. Two years later, her quarrels with the Baptist Mission Board led her to leave China. Her return voyage lasted two years and took her around the world. Upon her return, she began to lecture to the New York public, following this up with popular books on Chinese culture and Chinese fairy tales.

Fielde began to study insect biology at the Marine Biological Laboratories at Woods Hole, Massachusetts. In the 1880s, she had already been interested in invertebrate biology, but her investigations took a more methodical turn at Woods Hole, and she took the opportunity to give evening lectures on ant behavior, the main topic of her scientific papers.

In 1907, Fielde moved to Seattle, Washington, although she continued to correspond with the Philadelphia Academy of Natural Sciences. Shortly before her death, she found herself engaged in a controversy over the use of antennae as olfactory organs, and she conducted a series of experiments that she believed supported her view that certain segments served as a "nose." She died in Seattle, Washington in her seventy-seventh year.   JH/MBO

PRIMARY SOURCES
Fielde, Adele Marion. *A Corner of Cathay: Studies from Life Among the Chinese.* New York: G. P. Putnam's Sons, 1894.

———. "Experiments with Ants Induced to Swim." *Proceedings of the Philadelphia Academy of Natural Sciences* 55 (1903): 617–624.

———. "Power of Recognition Among Ants." *Biological Bulletin* 7 (1904): 227–250.

———. "The Communal Life of Ants." *Nature Study Review* 1 (1905) 239–250.

———. "On Certain Vesicles Found in the Integument of Ants." *Proceedings of the Philadelphia Academy of Natural Sciences* 67 (1915): 36–39. This includes an account of her controversies over ant antennae, as well as a list of her publications.

SECONDARY SOURCES
Bonta, Marcia Myers. *Women in the Field: America's Pioneering Women Naturalists.* College Station: Texas A & M University Press, 1991.

STANDARD SOURCES
AMS 2; Bailey; Barr; Rossiter 1982; *WWW,* vol. 1.

FIELDING, MARY MARIA (SIMPSON) (fl. early 19th century)

British botanical artist. Married H. B. Fielding (1805–1851).

Mary Maria Fielding married botanist Henry Borron Fielding, who founded the Fielding Curatorship at Oxford and who was a member of the Botanical Society of London. She illustrated her husband's *Sertum Plantarum,* a description of rare and undescribed plants in his herbarium, 1844. Six volumes of her botanical drawings were put up for auction in 1971 at George's in Bristol.   JH/MBO

PRIMARY SOURCES
Fielding, Henry Borron. With G. Gardner. *Sertum plantarum.*
    1844. Illustrations by Mary Maria Fielding.

SECONDARY SOURCES
"Henry Barron Fielding." *Proceedings of the Linnean Society*
    (1852): 188. Obituary notice for Mary Maria Fielding's
    husband mentions her work.

STANDARD SOURCES
Desmond.

FIENNES, CELIA (1662–1741)
British naturalist, horticulturist, and traveler. Born 7 June 1662 in Newton Toney, Wiltshire. Died 10 April 1741 in Hackney, London.

Celia Fiennes traveled through England on horseback and made observations on country houses and their gardens. Her observations included trips between 1685 and 1712.

                                                            JH/MBO

SECONDARY SOURCES
Morris, C., ed. *Journeys of Celia Fiennes.* London: Cresset Press,
    1949.
Northern Gardener 44, no. 2 (1990): 14–15.

STANDARD SOURCES
DNB Missing Persons.

FIESER, MARY (1909–1997)
U.S. organic chemist. Born 1909 in Atchison, Kans., to Julia (Clutz) and Robert Peters. At least one sibling. Married Louis Fieser (1932). Educated at a private girls' school; Bryn Mawr College (A.B., 1930); Harvard College (M.A., 1936). Professional experience: collaborative research with Louis Fieser (1932–1971?). Honors and memberships: Garvan Medal (1971). Died March 1997 in Belmont, Mass.

Mary Fieser was born in Kansas into a well-educated family. Her father was an English professor and her mother, a bookstore owner and manager who had done graduate work in English. Her sister, Ruth, became a mathematics professor.

The family moved to Harrisburg, Pa., where her father took a position at what is now Carnegie-Mellon University.

Mary met her future husband, Louis Fieser, at Bryn Mawr where he was a chemistry instructor. When he left Bryn Mawr for a position at Harvard in 1930, Mary left with him. At Harvard, Mary did research in his laboratory and earned a master's degree. She felt that her marriage was fortuitous for a woman scientist. While she was working on her Harvard degree, her professor of analytical chemistry would not allow her to perform her experiments with the rest of the class; she had to do them in a deserted basement without supervision. After her marriage, she was able to design and perform her own experiments. As a member of Louis Fieser's team, she helped develop a practical method for obtaining large quantities of the antihemorrhagic vitamin K. She also worked on the research of naphthoquinones as antimalarial drugs—work that ultimately contributed to the synthesis of the antimalarial drug lapinone. She studied the chemical causes of cancer, developing methods of synthesizing carcinogenic chemicals for use in medical research. She also contributed to the synthesis of cortisone for use in the treatment of rheumatoid arthritis.

In addition to being a gifted experimental chemist, Mary Fieser was also a gifted writer. She wrote or cowrote numerous texts and reference books. In 1944 she wrote a best-selling textbook, *Organic Chemistry,* and a much used reference book in organic chemistry, *Reagents for Organic Synthesis.*

Fieser's nonacademic interests included organizing games for her husband's research group and setting up contests in horseshoes, ping-pong, and badminton for the graduate students. She and her husband also owned many cats, photographs of which graced her organic chemistry texts.

                                                            JH/MBO

PRIMARY SOURCES
Fieser, Mary Peters. With Louis Fieser. *Organic Chemistry.*
    Boston: D. C. Heath and Company, 1944.
———. With Louis Fieser. *Style Guide for Chemists.* New York:
    Reinhold, 1959.
———. With Louis Fieser. *Reagents for Organic Synthesis.* 16
    vols. New York: John Wiley & Sons, 1967.

SECONDARY SOURCES
"Mary Fieser, Researcher, Writer in Organic Chemistry, Dies
    at Age 87." *Harvard Gazette* (27 March 1997).
Pramer, Stacey. "Mary Fieser: A Transitional Figure in the
    History of Women." *Journal of Chemical Education* 62 (1985):
    186.

STANDARD SOURCES
Notable (article by Donna Olshansky): O'Neill.

FIGNER, VERA (19th century)
Russian physician. Educated University of Zurich. Professional experience: paramedic; midwife.

Born in Russia, Vera Figner became involved in revolutionary causes in her homeland. At the age of nineteen, she traveled across Russia through eastern and central Europe to reach Zurich, where she entered medical school. When she returned to Russia, she got a paramedic's license and practiced for a time as a midwife. However, she became increasingly radicalized even to the extent that she later played a role in the assassination of Alexander II, for which she was sentenced to death.   JH/MBO

STANDARD SOURCES
Bonner 1992.

FINCH, LOUISA (THYNNE), COUNTESS OF AYLESFORD (1760–1832)
British botanist. Born 25 March 1760. Father first marquess of Bath. Married fourth earl of Aylesford (1781). Professional experience: studied Warwickshire plants (1784–1816). Died 28 December 1832 in Warwickshire.

Louisa Finch was an upper-class English woman who enjoyed studying plants. Not only did she study the plants of Warwickshire, she also corresponded with a number of botanists, including W. T. Bree, T. Purton, W. Witheing, and G. Don. She had an excellent collection of 1830 plant drawings which she passed on to the countess of Dartmouth.
                                JH/MBO

PRIMARY SOURCES
Finch's plants are at Oxford. Her manuscripts are at the British Museum of Natural History and sixty-nine of her flower drawings were sold at auction, Sotheby's, 1 November 1973.

SECONDARY SOURCES
Bagnall, J. E. *Flora of Warwickshire.* London: Gurney & Jackson, 1891. Finch mentioned on pages 493–494.
Botanical Society Exchange Club of the British Isles, Report 1914: 49.
Druce, G. C. *Flora of Buckinghamshire.* Arbroath: T. Buncle, 1926. Finch discussed on pages xcv–xcvii. Includes a portrait.
Journal of Botany, 1908: 32.

STANDARD SOURCES
Desmond.

FINDLATER, DORIS (1895–1981)
Irish botanist and horticulturist. Born 27 April 1895. Professional experience: bred daffodils and Nerine. Died 7 December 1981 in Dublin.

Doris Findlater developed different varieties of daffodils. She contributed to the *Yearbook of the Royal Horticultural Society of Ireland.* A plant was named after her, *Daboecia cantabrica* Doris Findlater.   JH/MBO

SECONDARY SOURCES
Moorea 7 (1988): 27–31, Findlater mentioned page 32.
Walsh, W., and E. C. Nelson. *Irish Florilegium II.* New York: Thames and Hudson, 1987. Findlater mentioned pages 158–160. Includes a brief biography.
Yearbook of the Royal Horticultural Society of Ireland 1959: 37.

STANDARD SOURCES
Desmond.

FINKLER, RITA V. (SAPIRO) (1888–1968)
Russian/U.S. endocrinologist. Born in Kherson, Russia. Two sisters. Married. One daughter. Educated University of St. Petersburg, law school (ca. 1908–1910); Woman's Medical College, Philadelphia (M. D., 1915); Philadelphia, internship. Postgraduate training in endocrinology, Berlin and Vienna. Professional experience: Child Federation of Philadelphia, physician; Beth Israel Hospital, Newark, N.J., doctor of pediatrics, gynecology, and obstetrics, chief of endocrine division, Endocrine Service head (1939–1951). Honors and memberships: Committee for the Aid of Displaced Foreign Women Physicians, chairperson. Died 1968.

Rita Sapiro was born into an atmosphere of revolution in Kherson, Russia, and consequently grew up being comfortable with the idea of rebellion and opposition to authority. Many of her relatives spent time in jail because of their outspoken criticism of the oppressive tsarist regime and at eighteen, Sapiro wanted to do something on behalf of the political prisoners and their cause. She entered the University of St. Petersburg with the goal of becoming a lawyer, but after two years found law to be boring, hypocritical, and manipulative. Disillusioned, she spent two years traveling throughout Europe working odd jobs along the way to pay her passage. Sometime during that period she became determined to pursue a scientific profession and settled on experimental medicine as her goal.

Sapiro wrote to her uncle in Philadelphia and emigrated to the United States to attend the Philadelphia Woman's Medical College. She worked as a tutor and translated scientific articles from various European languages into English for the researchers. After the first year, Sapiro's performance was sufficient to win her scholarships. Following her sophomore year, she and a fellow student were married. Because she scored the highest of the several hundred students who took the exam for internship posts, she, now Rita Finkler, was admitted to a Philadelphia hospital over the outraged objection of the male hospital administration and staff, and other interns. To discourage her, the administration assigned Finkler two full-time jobs—laboratory by day and emergency ambulance service at night. In spite of this impossible schedule, Finkler persisted, upheld no doubt by her inborn rebellious and stubborn nature and determination not to seek favor because of her sex. When her lab supervisor caught on to why she was so exhausted, he immediately brought the administration to task and Finkler was afterward treated fairly and was accepted by the others as a "good sport" for not complaining herself.

Finkler's first position was with the Child Federation of Philadelphia, in a health center in the heart of "little Italy" where she gave lectures on preventive care in addition to her general practice. After four years, Finkler moved to Beth Israel Hospital in Newark, New Jersey, serving in pediatrics, gynecology, and obstetrics. The comparatively new field of endocrinology piqued her interest and she took a sabbatical for specialty study in Berlin and Vienna. Returning to Beth Israel Hospital, she soon was placed in charge of the Endocrine Division there and developed a special Endocrine Service that grew steadily under her direction and in response to the increasing applications for hormonal therapy. Finkler was known as an excellent diagnostician, knowledgeable in many areas of medicine, and empathetic and generous with patients and colleagues alike. She traveled and lectured extensively and wrote over thirty-five articles on endocrinology for professional journals.   KM

PRIMARY SOURCES
Finkler, Rita S. "Osteopathies Encountered in the Endocrine Clinic." Scientific exhibit presented at the centennial meeting of the American Medical Association, Atlantic City, N.J., June 1947.

SECONDARY SOURCES
Knapp, Sally Elizabeth. *Women Doctors Today.* New York: Crowell, 1947.

FISCHER, IRENE KAMINKA (1907–)
Austrian/U.S. cartographer and geographer. Born 27 July 1907 in Vienna. Naturalized U.S. citizen. Married (1930). Two children. Educated University of Vienna (M.A., 1931). Professional experience: Geoid Branch, mathematician (1952–1958); geodesist (1958–1962); supervisory geodesist (1962–1965); U.S. Defense Mapping Agency Topographic Center, Geoid branch, supervisory research geodesist (from 1965), chief (from 1962). Honors and memberships: U.S. Department of Army, Meritorius Civilian Performance (1957), Bronze Leaf Cluster (1966), Exceptional Civilian Service (1967); U.S. Department of Defense, Distinguished Civilian Service (1967).

Although Irene Kaminka Fischer was born and educated in Austria, she became a naturalized U.S. citizen. She was married in 1930 and had two children. She apparently did not work outside of the home while the children were young. She began her work with the Geoid Branch and earned regular promotions. Concurrently she was a member of the International Union of Geodesists and Geophysicists from 1954. She received the Meritorious Civilian Performance Award of the Department of the Army (1957), a Bronze Leaf Cluster (1966), a research and development achievement award, an award for Exceptional Civilian Service (1967), and a Distinguished Civilian Service Award, Department of Defense (1967). She conducted research on the figure of the earth, shape of the geoid, parallax and distance of the moon, and geodetic world datum. She also worked on the Fischer ellipsoid, mercury datum for space flights, the Mercury, Gemini, and Apollo projects, deflections at sea, and mean sea level slopes. She was a member of the International Association for Geodetic Research. A memoir of Fisher's life is held at Radcliffe College, Schlesinger Library archives.   JH/MBO

PRIMARY SOURCES
Fischer, Irene. *The Geoid in South America Refered [sic] to Various Systems.* Buenos Aires: Instituto Panamerico de Geografia e Historia.

STANDARD SOURCES
AMS P&B 11 (suppl. 2), 12–14.

FISH, MARGERY (1892–1969)
British botanist and horticulturist. Born August 1892 at Stamford Hill, London. Professional experience: designed gardens. Died March 1969 in East Lambrook, Somerset.

Margery Fish was best known for the gardens that she created at Lambrook Manor and Somerset. She was also a horticultural journalist.   JH/MBO

PRIMARY SOURCES
Fish, Margery. *We Made a Garden.* N.p., 1956.
———. *An All the Year Garden.* N.p., 1958.
———. *Cottage Garden Flowers.* N.p., 1961.

SECONDARY SOURCES

Chivers, S., and S. Woloszynska. *The Cottage Gardener: Margery Fish at East Lambrook Manor.* London: J. Murray, 1990.

Gardener's Chronicle 1969: 383. Obituary notice. Includes portrait.

Macleod, D. *Down-to-Earth Women.* Edinburgh: Blackwood, 1982. See pages 117–128. Includes portrait.

Times 23 March 1969. Obituary notice.

STANDARD SOURCES

Desmond.

FISH, MARIE POLAND (1902–1989)

U.S. ichthyologist, marine biologist, bioacoustician, and oceanographer. Born 22 May 1902. Married Charles J. Fish (1923). Educated Smith College (A.B., 1921); University of Rhode Island (Sc.D., 1966). Professional experience: Carnegie Institution, division of medical research, assistant (1921–1922); New Jersey public schools, teacher (1922); Bureau of Fisheries, hydrobiologist (1923–1927); New York State Conservation Department, senior ichthyologist (1928–1930); Passamaquoddy Bay, investigator (1931–1933); Narragansett Marine Laboratory, R.I., research associate ichthyologist (1937–1939); biological oceanographer (1949–1972); Oceanographic Institute, Woods Hole, ichthyologist (1939–1942, 1947–1949); Rhode Island State College, instructor in zoology; U.S. National Museum, Smithsonian Museum, assistant, division of fishes (1943–1946). Honors and memberships: Society of Women Geographers, member; American Society of Limnology and Oceanography, member; Stamford Museum medal (1963); Sophia Smith Medal (1964); U.S. Navy, Distinguished Public Service Medal (1966). Retired 1972. Died 1 February 1989 in Westport, Conn.

Marie Poland Fish helped the U.S. Navy's antisubmarine vessels distinguish between genuine enemy targets and schools of fish through research in underwater sound detection. She analyzed recordings of more than three hundred species of marine life. For this important work, she was awarded the Navy's Distinguished Public Service Award (1966). For twenty years, she worked for the Office of Naval Research, mostly at the Narrangansett Marine Laboratory in Kingston, Rhode Island.

Fish's research interests centered on underwater sound of biological origin, life histories of marine and freshwater fishes, and the life history of the eel. She studied the ichthyology of the north and south Atlantic, Sargasso Sea, Caribbean Sea, north and south Pacific, Japanese and Indo-Pacific, and the Great Lakes areas. She was a member of numerous professional organizations, among which are the American Society of Ichthyology and Herpetology, the American Society of Limnology and Oceanography, and the Society of Woman Geographers. Her work was recognized by numerous awards: the Stamford Museum Medal in 1963, the first Sophia Smith Medal from Smith College in 1964, the Distinguished Public Service Medal of the U.S. Navy, and the National Federation of Business and Professional Woman's Club Award (1966–1967).   JH/MBO

PRIMARY SOURCES

Fish, Marie Poland. *Sonic Fishes of the Pacific.* Woods Hole, Mass.: Woods Hole Oceanographic Institution, 1949.

———. *Marine Mammals of the Pacific with Particular Reference to the Production of Underwater Sound.* Woods Hole, Mass.: Woods Hole Oceanographic Institution, 1949.

SECONDARY SOURCES

New York Times, 2 February 1989. Obituary notice.

STANDARD SOURCES

AMS 5–8, B 9, P&B 10–13; *Current Biography* 1941; 1989.

FISHENDEN, MARGARET WHITE (1889–1977)

British physicist and engineer. Father R. W. White. One sibling. Married. Educated University of Manchester (B.Sc., 1909; M.Sc., 1910; D.Sc., 1919). Professional experience: University of Manchester, lecturer (1910–1915); Air Pollution Advisory Board, Manchester Corporation, director of research (1916–1922); Imperial College University of London, reader in applied heat, mechanical engineering department. Died 21 October 1977.

Fishenden received her bachelor's degree with first class honors in physics. She was designated a Higgenbottom Scholar in 1907, a Graduate Scholar in 1909, and a Beyer Fellow during 1910–1911. Fishenden conducted research on humidity and ventilation in spinning mills and weaving sheds, and on heat transmission and practical methods of supplying heat. Some of her research was subsidized by the British Iron and Steel Research Association.   MM

PRIMARY SOURCES

Fishenden, Margaret. *The Coal Fire.* Research report for the Manchester Corporation Air Pollution Advisory Board. London: H.M. Stationery Office for the Department of Scientific and Industrial Research, 1920.

———. *House Heating: A General Discussion of the Relative Merits of Coal, Coke, Gas, Electricity, etc., as Alternative Means of Providing for Domestic Heating, Cooking and Hot Water Requirements, with Especial Reference to Economy and Efficiency.* London: H. F. & G. Witherby, 1925.

———. With Owen A. Sanders. *The Calculation of Heat Transmission.* London: H.M. Stationery Office, 1932.

———. With Owen A. Sanders. *An Introduction to Heat Transfer.* Oxford: Clarendon Press, 1957.

SECONDARY SOURCES
Birks, J. B., ed. *Rutherford at Manchester.* London: Heywood & Co., 1962; New York: W. A. Benjamin, 1963.
Rayner-Canham, Marelene F., and Geoffrey W. Rayner-Canham, "Pioneer Women in Nuclear Science." *American Journal of Physics* 58 (1990): 1036–1043.

STANDARD SOURCES
WW, 1974–1975.

FISHER, EDNA MARIE (1897–1954)

U.S. zoologist. Born 1897 in Riverside, Ind. Educated University of California, Berkeley (A.B., 1920; A.M., 1921). Professional experience: University of California, Berkeley, teaching fellow; Museum of Comparative Zoology, assistant curator of osteology (to 1930); San Francisco State College, faculty (1930–1941), associate professor (1941), chair, science department (1941–1944).

Edna Fisher's highest degree was a master's from the University of California, Berkeley. Nevertheless, she had a successful career as a field biologist. After she received her last degree, she remained at Berkeley as a teaching fellow and then she became assistant curator of osteology at the Museum of Vertebrate Zoology, where she remained until 1930. In 1930, she went to San Francisco State College, where she rose to the rank of associate professor in 1941, and also served as department chair during World War II.

She joined the American Society of Mammalogists in 1928, and remained a member until her death. She served on the Life Histories and Ecology Committee of this society from 1943 to 1945. Her scientific interests were broad and included osteology, comparative anatomy, and herpetology, and, most especially, mammalogy. She published nine articles and notes in the *Journal of Mammalogy.* She was especially interested in the natural history, anatomy, and behavior of the sea otter, publishing four papers on this subject. She presented a paper on young sea otters at the annual meeting of the American Society of Mammalogists in 1941.

JH/MBO

PRIMARY SOURCES
Fisher, Edna. "The Early Fauna of Santa Cruz Island, California." *Journal of Mammalogy* 11 (1930): 75–76.
———. "Early Fauna of the Monterey Region, California." *Journal of Mammalogy* 15 (1934): 253.
———. "Habits of the Southern Sea Otter." *Journal of Mammalogy* 20 (1939): 21–36.

SECONDARY SOURCES
Kaufman, Dawn M., Donald W. Kaufman, and Glennis A. Kaufman. "Women in the Early Years of the American Society of Mammalogists (1919–1949)." *Journal of Mammalogy* 77, (1996): 642–654.

STANDARD SOURCES
AMS 5–8.

FISHER, ELIZABETH FLORETTE (1873–1941)

U.S. geologist and geographer. Born 26 November 1873 in Boston, Mass., to Sarah (Cushing) and Charles Fisher. Never married. Educated MIT (S.B, 1896). Professional experience: Wellesley College, geology and geography, instructor (1894–1906), associate professor (1906–1909), professor (1909–1926). Died 25 April 1941.

Elizabeth Florette Fisher graduated from MIT in 1896. She spent her entire career at Wellesley College. She began teaching courses in geology and geography at Wellesley while she was still a student at MIT. The year after she got her degree, she traveled to Russia for the International Geological Congress. She moved up the academic ladder at Wellesley, eventually becoming professor and head of the department of geology and geography. She attained this status with only an undergraduate degree.

In 1918 there was a nationwide oil shortage, and Fisher was hired by an oil company in Kansas to locate oil wells in their north central Texas fields. She was the first woman to be sent out in the field by an oil company to do a survey. After she became emerita at Wellesley, she participated in a geographical survey of coastal Florida.

She was a member of the American Geographic Society and the Boston Society of Natural History.

Her research interests were physiography, commercial and industrial geography, river terraces, oil geology, and conservation. Fisher was a skilled field geologist who studied the oil regions of Texas. One of her students, WINIFRED GOLDRING, would be highly regarded as a paleontologist. JH/MBO

PRIMARY SOURCES
Fisher, Elizabeth F. *Resources and Industries of the United States.* Boston: Ginn and Co., 1919.

SECONDARY SOURCES
Elder, Eleanor S. "Women in Early Geology." *Journal of Geological Education* 30, no. 5 (1982): 287–293.
"Miss Elizabeth F. Fisher." *New York Times,* 3 May 1941.

STANDARD SOURCES
AMS 1–6; *Notable* (article by Miyoko Chu); Sarjeant; *WWW(A).*

FISHER, SARA CAROLYN (1889–?)

U.S. psychologist. Born 17 September 1889 in Bridgeport, Conn. Educated Lombard College (A.B., 1909); University of Illinois (A.M., 1910); Clark University (Ph.D., 1913). Professional experience: Wellesley College, instructor in psychology (1913–1914); Clark University, assistant professor (1914–1915); California State Normal School, Los Angeles, lecturer (1915–1919); University of California at Los Angeles, assistant professor through associate professor of psychology (from 1919); Los Angeles Juvenile Court, psychologist (1921–1929). Honors and memberships: American Psychological Association, Fellow; Society for Psychological Study of Social Issues, member. Death date unknown.

Sara Fisher was a psychologist whose interests were in the area of attitudes and perception. She also worked in social psychology.   KM

PRIMARY SOURCES
Fisher, Sara Carolyn. *The Process of Generalizing Abstraction; and its Product, the General Concept.* Princeton, N.J.: Psychological Review Co., [1916].
———. *Relationships in Attitudes, Opinions, and Values among Family Members.* Berkeley: University of California Press, 1948.

STANDARD SOURCES
AMS 3–8, S&B 9–11.

FITTON, SARAH MARY (fl. 1817–1866)

Irish botanist. Born in Dublin.

Sarah Mary and her sister Elizabeth published *Conversations on Botany* and *The Four Seasons.* She was commemorated by having the genus *Fittonia* named for her.   JH/MBO

PRIMARY SOURCES
Fitton, Sarah Mary, and Elizabeth Fitton. *Conversations on Botany.* London: Printed for Longman, Hurst, Rees, Orme, and Brown, 1817.
———. *The Four Seasons.* London: Griffith and Farran, 1865.

SECONDARY SOURCES
Fussell, G. E. "Some Lady Botanists of the Nineteenth Century. 4. Elizabeth and Sarah Mary Fitton." *The Gardeners' Chronicle: A Weekly Illustrated Journal of Horticulture and Allied Subjects* 130 (1951): 179–181.
Praeger, R. Lloyd. *Some Irish Naturalists: A Biographical Notebook.* Dundalk, W. Tempest: Dundalgan Press, 1949.

FITZGERALD, MABEL PUREFOY (1872–1973)

British physiologist. Born 1872, probably at Preston Candover near Basingstoke. Six siblings. Never married. Educated privately; Oxford University (1897–1898?); University of Copenhagen, studied under Dreyer (1907); Cambridge University, studied with Strangeways; New York University (1915). Professional experience: Oxford University, physiology department, laboratory worker; Rockefeller traveling fellowship (1907–1910?); Edinburgh Infirmary, clinical pathologist (1915); Royal College of Edinburgh Medical School, teacher (1915). Died 1973 in Oxford.

During her entire life, Mabel FitzGerald had aspired to go to medical school. However, circumstances did not allow it. The large FitzGerald family lived at Preston Candover near Basingstoke, Hampshire. Her father was a landowner and farmer. He was also a county councilor and magistrate. Mabel's education and home life were typical for a girl of that period. However, in 1895 both her mother and father died, and the sisters took a house in Oxford, next door to that of the physiologist John Scott Haldane and his wife. Mabel began to educate herself in chemistry and biology by reading Huxley's *Lessons in Elementary Physiology.* Although she took classes at Oxford, women were not allowed to take a degree. She took biology classes from a Mr. Reihaldy, a lecturer at St. Hugh's and Somerville College. She was apparently highly regarded by Francis Gotch, and began to work in the physiology department on the changes in skin during vaccination. Gotch communicated a paper to the Royal Society that was published in her name, on the relative areas of white and grey matter in the spinal cord of the macaque monkey.

FitzGerald studied with a number of well-known physiologists in Copenhagen, Cambridge, Toronto, and the United States. She spent two separate periods in Copenhagen; she also attended lectures in pathology by Ritchie and Almroth Wright, and worked at the Strangeways Laboratory, Cambridge. She published papers in bacteriology and pathology from her research in Copenhagen in 1902, in 1907 from the pathology department at Oxford, and in 1910 from the Rockefeller Institute in New York. A Rockefeller traveling scholarship that she was awarded in 1907 allowed her to go to Toronto, where she worked in Macallum's Biochemical Laboratory. The paper that she produced from her work in Toronto was related to the origin of hydrochloric acid in gastric tubules.

Mabel FitzGerald is best known from her work with J. S. Haldane in 1905 and 1908. She measured the alveolar air of men, women, and children at Oxford. She then studied alveolar carbon dioxide in patients in the Radcliffe Infirmary suffering from respiratory diseases or anemia. In 1911, FitzGerald was in the United States. During this time, Haldane and others went to the top of Pike's Peak with the men on the expedition and studied the process of acclimatization in themselves. FitzGerald did not climb Pike's Peak, but she did travel to mining camps and settlements near the peak to study acclimatization in people who lived at altitudes from five thousand to twelve thousand feet. The results of this expedition and FitzGerald's own work were published separately in the *Philosophical Transactions of the Royal Society* in 1913. FitzGerald remained in the United States and studied people at lower altitudes. She used the Highlands Sanatorium in North Carolina and her results were published in 1915.

The year 1915 marked the end of FitzGerald's publications in physiology. She remained in the United States, where she enrolled at New York University, still hoping to obtain admission to medical school, but the algebra requirement thwarted her ambitions. She returned to the United Kingdom in 1915, for her former pathology teacher asked her to fill a gap caused by World War I. She served as clinical pathologist at the Edinburgh infirmary and teacher in the Royal College's medical school, still without a degree. The medical school goal alluded her, but at age fifty-five, she was still studying anatomy.

Just as women at Oxford could not sit for the official examination and could not take a degree when FitzGerald was there, neither could they join the Physiological Society at the time she was working with Haldane. Because she was in the United States and lost contact with Oxford, she did not seek an Oxford degree or membership in the Physiological Society in the 1920s when the situation was different. She was elected a member of the American Physiological Society.

FitzGerald returned to Oxford in 1930, but did not make contact with physiologists there. In 1961 the physiologists made contact with her. One physiologist noticed her name in the Oxford telephone directory and invited her to the symposium to celebrate the centenary of Haldane's birth. After this, the Oxford physiologists maintained contact with her. When she was 100 years old, she was nominated for the honorary degree of master of arts at Oxford and was elected a member of the Physiological Society. She died at the age of 101 in 1973.   JH

PRIMARY SOURCES

FitzGerald, Mabel, "The Origin of the Hydrochloric Acid in the Gastric Tubules." *Proceedings of the Royal Society* B 83 (1910): 56–93.

———. With J. S. Haldane. "Method for Determining Composition of Alveolar Air." *Journal of Physiology* 32 (1905): 486–494.

———. "The Alveolar Carbonic Acid Pressure in Diseases of the Blood and in Diseases of the Respiratory and Circulatory Systems." *Journal of Pathology and Bacteriology* 14 (1910): 328–343.

———. "The Changes in Breathing and the Blood at Various High Altitudes." *Philosophical Transactions of the Royal Society* B 203 (1913): 185; 351.

SECONDARY SOURCES

Bensley, E. H. "Sir William Osler and Mabel Purefoy Fitzgerald." *Physiologist* 21 (1978): 17–18.

STANDARD SOURCES
O'Connor.

FLAMMEL, PERRENELLE (d. 1397)

French alchemist. Married three times, the third husband being Nicholas Flammel. Died 1397.

In the thirteenth century there had been a revival of alchemy, and as had been the case in earlier times, women were among the ranks of the alchemists. Even though it is apparent that many of these alchemists were charlatans, they still required some knowledge of chemistry to practice their art. In fourteenth-century France, Perrenelle, who had married Nicholas Flammel, a well-to-do scribe, was apparently very sincere in her practice of alchemy. Nicholas Flammel obtained an ancient alchemical manuscript, the Book of Abraham, and he wrote that they became fascinated by the book, and attempted to discern the meaning in the cryptic words. Both Flammels spent twenty-one years consulting people as to the possible meaning. Eventually Nicholas traveled to Spain where he found a Jewish physician, Canche, who explained to him the meaning of the allegorical figures. After the death of Canche, the Flammels began to experiment on their own and claimed to have transmuted mercury into silver. After their first success, they changed mercury into gold. Nicholas explained that Perrenelle was as familiar as he was with the procedures involved. Reports indicate that they made so much money by their alchemical processes that they gave great amounts to charities.   JH/MBO

STANDARD SOURCES
Alic.

FLEMING, AMALIA COUTSOURIS, LADY (1909?–1986)

Greek/British bacteriologist, political activist, and humanitarian. Born ca. 1909 to Greek parents in Constantinople (now Istanbul), Turkey. One brother. Married (1) Manoli Voureka, architect (divorced); (2) Sir Alexander Fleming, Nobel Prize–winner for discovery of penicillin (1953; widowed 1955). Educated University of Athens (M.D., 1938). Professional experience: City hospital of Athens, bacteriologist; Wright-Fleming Institute of Microbiology at

St. Mary's Hospital, London, research assistant (1946–1951, 1953–1967); Evangelismos Hospital, Athens, chief bacteriologist (1951–1952). Honors and memberships: Amnesty International; European Rights Commission; Greek parliament and European parliament. Died 26 February 1986 in Athens, Greece.

Amalia Coutsouris was born in Constantinople (Istanbul), where her physician father had his medical practice and laboratory. When the Turkish authorities confiscated their house and property in 1914, the family (Amalia had one brother, Renos) fled to the Coutsouris homeland, Greece. Amalia eventually entered the University of Athens for her medical degree, specializing in bacteriology; following graduation, she went to work as a bacteriologist in the city hospital of Athens. During this time, she married a Greek architect, Manoli Voureka. During World War II, the couple joined the anti-Nazi underground, working with other Greeks to hide British and Greek officers and arranging escape routes to Egypt. Amalia transcribed and distributed BBC broadcasts and worked on identity cards for Jews to make them appear to be of the Greek Orthodox faith. She and about forty other resistance members were arrested after a colleague identified them under torture by Italian occupation forces. Amalia was confined for six months under sentence of death before being liberated by advancing British troops.

After the war, Amalia's house and laboratory were destroyed and she left her estranged husband and sought new opportunities in bacteriology in Britain. Having obtained a British Council scholarship, she applied at the famous Wright-Fleming Institute of Microbiology at St. Mary's Hospital in London and was accepted on six-months probation. Sir Alexander Fleming was recognized as one of the greatest bacteriologists in the world, having shared the Nobel Prize in medicine and physiology in 1945 for his discovery of penicillin. Amalia Voureka originally asked to work with viruses but, through a fortunate misunderstanding, ended by working directly with Fleming as a research assistant. She was the first woman doctor in his laboratory and he quickly came to appreciate her capabilities. Their first joint study was on streptomycin ("Some Problems in Titration of Streptomycin," *British Medical Journal*, 1947) and Voureka continued at the institute, conducting team and individual research on antibiotics for the next four years. In December 1950, she returned to Greece for the holidays and was offered a job as chief bacteriologist at Evangelismos Hospital in Athens. She accepted the offer and returned to London to await confirmation, not realizing that the shy and reserved Fleming, whose wife had died, was in love with her. A year after she moved to Greece, Fleming came as a delegate to the United Nations Educational Scientific Cultural Organization (UNESCO) conference, confessed his feel-

ings, and proposed marriage, which the divorced Amalia accepted. After a honeymoon in Cuba and the United States, the couple made a home in London and were very happy, but tragically, Alexander Fleming died in 1955, just two years after their marriage, at age seventy-three. The disconsolate Lady Fleming resumed her research, refused the widow's pension from the Wright-Fleming Institute, and returned to Athens.

In 1967, she again felt compelled to take a stand politically when a group of colonels staged a coup that placed Greece under an oppressive military regime. She began a campaign, out of her one-room apartment in Athens, to oppose the regime and condemn the inhumane treatment of political prisoners and their families. She did everything she could to publicize the state of political affairs and helped collect relief funds for the economically deprived families of the prisoners. She was an important personage, and her biting criticism irritated the junta, so that retaliation was inevitable. In the spring of 1970, Lady Fleming testified as a witness for the defense at the trial of thirty-four intellectuals accused of plotting to overthrow the military regime. After the trial, her passport was revoked; it was restored after worldwide protest. She was kept under constant surveillance and many prominent Greek liberals were arrested and held for months without trial while being questioned about their possible links to Fleming. Finally, the authorities were given a reason to arrest Fleming when she and four accomplices were betrayed concerning a plot to aid in the escape of a political prisoner who had been continually tortured as a suspect in an attempt to assassinate Premier George Papadopoulos. After a month of imprisonment, on 27 September 1971, Lady Fleming and the others were brought to trial before a military tribunal. Lady Fleming proudly admitted her guilt and emphasized the cruel treatment the prisoner, Panagoulis, was receiving. She was convicted and sentenced to sixteen months in prison, but given the alternative of deportation and loss of citizenship. She refused deportation, declaring "I am a Greek and I intend to stay" (*Current Biography* 1972), and was placed again in prison. Lady Fleming, who suffered from diabetes and a heart condition, was already weakened from her previous imprisonment and this, along with her heroic stance against violation of human rights, was loudly proclaimed by the world's presses—creating such an embarrassment to the Greek dictator that on 21 October 1971, her sentence was suspended. In November, the police took her, under ruse, to the airport and had her flown to London. At first, she refused to leave the plane but was finally persuaded, and went to live with friends. Though she returned to medical research, she remained a political activist throughout her life, expanding her concern from Greek to world humanitarian causes. She became the first chairman of the Greek committee of Amnesty International and was a member of the

European Rights Commission. At the time of her death in 1986, she was a member of both the Greek and European parliaments. She died in Athens, 26 February 1986.

JH/MBO

SECONDARY SOURCES
Maurois, André. *Life of Alexander Fleming.* London: J. Cape, 1959.

STANDARD SOURCES
Current Biography 1972, 1986 [obit]; Strohmeier.

FLEMING, WILLIAMINA PATON STEVENS (1857–1911)

Scottish/U.S. astronomer. Born 15 May 1857 in Dundee, Scotland, to Mary (Walker) and Robert Stevens. Married James Fleming. One son, Edward Pickering Fleming. Educated public schools, Dundee. Professional experience: Harvard College Observatory, staff member (1881–1911), curator of astronomical photographs (1898–1911). Died 21 May 1911 in Boston.

Williamina Stevens, the daughter of an artisan who earned his living by carving and gilding wood and who experimented with photography, grew up in Dundee, Scotland. She became a pupil-teacher at the age of fourteen and continued to teach in the Dundee schools until her marriage to James Fleming in 1877. The couple emigrated to the United States the next year, settling in Boston. After the disintegration of the marriage (1879), Williamina, who was expecting a child, found work as a maid in the household of Harvard College Observatory director Edward Pickering—a job that proved to be her passport to the world of science. Pickering, impressed by the intellectual capabilities of his maid, offered her part-time employment performing clerical and computing tasks in the observatory. Fleming absorbed more and more responsibility and by 1881 was a permanent member of the staff. In 1886 she took charge of the observatory's new project, the classification of stars on the basis of their photographed spectra. This undertaking was being funded by the Henry Draper Memorial, an endowment established by Draper's widow, Mary. Fleming, in addition to assuming the administration of the program, analyzed many of the photographs herself and supervised the work of the staff of women employed as research assistants.

Fleming was convinced that astronomy was a field in which women should excel, and she became a staunch advocate of women in astronomy. In "A Field for Woman's Work in Astronomy," a paper published in 1893, she described the work of the women at the Harvard Observatory, emphasizing that the Henry Draper Memorial had been made possible by the gift of a woman. In a second essay, she

concluded that women "not only had a natural talent for astronomical work" but "had already made positive contributions to our knowledge of the universe" (Jones and Boyd, 394).

When in 1898 she was named curator of astronomical photographs, Fleming became the first woman to receive a corporation appointment at Harvard. In 1906 she was elected to the Royal Astronomical Society, thereby joining a select fellowship of women—MARGARET HUGGINS, MARY SOMERVILLE, and AGNES CLERKE—so honored. Other distinctions included an honorary fellowship from Wellesley College and the Gold Medal of the Astronomical Society of Mexico. Although her health was poor as she grew older, she continued to work long hours at the Observatory. At her death she left enough material "to fill several quarto volumes of the [*Harvard College Observatory*] *Annals*" (Jones and Boyd, 394–395).

Williamina Fleming arrived at Harvard at the time of Pickering's early experiments in stellar spectroscopy. As she learned more about the field, she became responsible for examining, classifying, and indexing the photographic plates as well as seeing to their physical care. She also served as editor of observatory publications, particularly the *Annals.* Fleming's total commitment to the success of the stellar photographic program, her personal devotion to Pickering, her competence as a technician, and her organizational and supervisory skills cannot be doubted. In addition, she made significant contributions to the discipline of astronomy. She developed a useful classification scheme for stars, organizing them into seventeen categories according to special characteristics. She classified 10,351 stars in the *Draper Catalogue of Stellar Spectra,* published in 1890 as volume 27 of the *Annals of the Harvard College Observatory.* Her work in connection with variable stars and stars having anomalous spectra was of particular importance.

MBO

PRIMARY SOURCES
Fleming, Williamina. "A Field for Woman's Work in Astronomy." *Astronomy and Astrophysics* 12 (1893): 683–689.
———. *A Photographic Study of Variable Stars Forming a Part of the Henry Draper Memorial.* Cambridge, Mass.: The Observatory, 1907.
———. "Stars Having Peculiar Spectra." *Annals of the Harvard College Observatory* 1912: 56.

SECONDARY SOURCES
Cannon, Annie Jump. "Williamina Paton Fleming." *Astrophysical Journal* 34 (1911): 314–317. Obituary notice.
———. "Mrs. W. P. Fleming." *Nature* 86 (1911): 453–454.
———. "Mrs. Fleming." *Scientific American* 104 (1911): 547.
"Fleming, Williamina Paton." *Royal Astronomical Society Monthly Notices* 72 (1912): 261–264.

Gordon, Anne. "Williamina Fleming: 'Women's Work' at the Harvard Observatory." *Women's Studies Newsletter* 6 (1978): 24–27.

Jones, Bessie Zaban, and Lyle Gifford Boyd. *The Harvard College Observatory: The First Four Directorships, 1839–1919.* Cambridge: Harvard University Press, 1971.

Mack, Pamela E. "Strategies and Compromises: Women in Astronomy at Harvard College Observatory, 1870–1920." *Journal for the History of Astronomy* 21 (1990): 65–76.

Pickering, Edward C. "Williamina Paton Fleming: In Memoriam." *Annals of the Harvard College Observatory* 20 October 1911.

Spradley, Joseph L. "The Industrious Mrs. Fleming." *Astronomy* 18 (1990): 48–51.

Thompson, Grace A. "Williamina Paton Fleming." *New England Magazine* 48 (1912): 458–467. Obituary notice.

STANDARD SOURCES
AMS 1–2; *DAB; DSB; NAW;* Ogilvie 1986.

FLETCHER, ALICE CUNNINGHAM (1838–1923)

U.S. ethnologist. Born 15 March 1838 in Havana, Cuba, to Lucia (Jenks) and Thomas Fletcher. Never married. Educated New York City schools. Professional experience: U.S. Indian Bureau and Department of the Interior, special agent (1883–1893); Peabody Museum, Cambridge, Mass., assistant (from 1886) and research fellow (from 1891). Honors and memberships: American Association for the Advancement of Science, Fellow; Woman's Anthropological Society of Washington, president (1903); American Anthropological Association, founding member (1902). Died 6 April 1923 in Washington, D.C.

Alice Fletcher's lawyer father died in 1839 of tuberculosis (he and his wife had left their home in New York for a stay in Cuba for his health's sake at the time of Alice's birth). Her mother's new husband exercised strict control over Alice and her two half-brothers, even refusing to allow Alice to read novels because they were frivolous. After finishing her schooling in New York City and taking a European tour, she began a teaching career in private schools in New York. Various reform movements—especially, in her twenties and thirties, temperance and women's rights—attracted her, and she became active as a lecturer and member of such organizations as Sorosis and the Association for the Advancement of Women.

In the late 1870s, Frederic Ward Putnam, director of the Peabody Museum at Harvard, awakened in Fletcher an interest in archeology and ethnology. She read extensively in these areas, gave public lectures, investigated Indian remains, and became involved in preserving archeological relics. At the same time, she adopted the social cause to which she would henceforth devote most of her energies—the rights of Indians.

After meeting (1879) and becoming a friend of the Omaha Indian Bright Eyes (Susette La Flesche Tibbles), who traveled the country speaking for Indians' rights, Fletcher arranged to live among the Omahas for a time. This experience led her to take up a crusade in Washington for the granting of lands to Indians and for other measures on their behalf. The United States government used Fletcher's expertise in exploring its relationship with the Indians. In 1887, she was appointed by the Department of the Interior to act as its agent in implementing the Dawes Act, a measure providing for the allotment of land, which Fletcher and other humanitarians at the time considered beneficial, although it was later severely criticized for exploiting the Indians.

The young brother of Bright Eyes, Francis La Flesche, became Fletcher's foster son, helping her in both her ethnological research and her reform work. Fletcher spent her last years in Washington with Francis La Flesche and died at the age of eighty-five of a stroke.

Much of Fletcher's original research in ethnology was made possible through her association with Indians with whom she had become friends in the course of her humanitarian efforts. She published over forty scholarly monographs, of which the most significant is *The Omaha Tribe* (1911). She became particularly knowledgeable about the music of the Plains Indians and pioneered the study of Indian music as a scholarly field. As a New World archeologist, she worked to alter the emphasis of the Archaeological Institute of America from the investigation of classical antiquity to that of the Americas. This crusade was, in part, responsible for the institute's establishment of the School of American Research in Santa Fe, New Mexico, in 1908.

Alice Fletcher received numerous honors. She was vice-president of the American Association for the Advancement of Science (1896), president of the Woman's Anthropological Society of Washington (1903), president of the American Folk-Lore Society (1905), and a founder and charter member of the American Anthropological Association (1902).

JH

PRIMARY SOURCES
Fletcher, Alice C., and Francis La Flesche. *The Omaha Tribe.* 27th Annual Report, Bureau of American Ethnology. Washington, D.C.: U.S. Government Printing Office, 1911.

SECONDARY SOURCES
"Alice C. Fletcher." *Buffalo (N.Y.) Courier,* 31 August 1923. Obituary notice.

"Alice C. Fletcher." *Washington Evening Star,* 8 April 1923. Obituary notice.

"Alice Cunningham Fletcher." *The Southern Workman* 51 (1923): 212–213. Obituary notice.

Hough, Walter. "Alice Cunningham Fletcher." *American Anthropologist* n.s. 25 (1923): 254–258. Long obituary report.

La Flesche, Francis. "Alice C. Fletcher." *Science* 58 (1923): 17. Obituary notice.

Mark, Joan T. "Francis La Flesche. The American Indian as Anthropologist." *Isis* 73 (1982): 497–510.

———. *A Stranger in Her Native Land: Alice Fletcher and the American Indians.* Lincoln: University of Nebraska Press, 1988.

STANDARD SOURCES
AMS 1–3; *DAB*; *NAW* (article by Joan Mark).

FLOCK, EUNICE VERNA (1904–)

U.S. biochemist. Born 20 August 1904 in Kellogg, Ind. Educated University of Washington (B.S., 1926); University of Chicago (M.S., 1930; Ph.D. in physiological chemistry, 1935). Professional experience: Mayo Clinic, assistant in physiological chemistry; Mayo Graduate School of Medicine, University of Minnesota, instructor (1936–1939), from assistant professor to professor of biochemistry (1939–1969), emerita professor (from 1969). Honors and memberships: American Chemical Society; Thyroid Association of America; American Society of Biological Chemists; New York Academy of Sciences.

Physiological chemist Eunice Flock received her two higher degrees from the University of Chicago. She spent her career at the University of Minnesota, Rochester, where she proceeded through the academic ranks to professor. Concurrently, she served as a visiting scientist for the Clinical Research Section of the Phoenix Indian Center, where she worked at the National Institute of Arthritis and Metabolic Diseases. Her professional memberships included the American Association for the Advancement of Science, the Thyroid Association of America, the New York Academy of Sciences, the American Chemical Society, and the American Society of Biological Chemists. Her research focused on fat metabolism, amino acids, and various endocrine gland secretions, including thyroxine, serotonin, and epinephrine.

JH/MBO

PRIMARY SOURCES
Flock, Eunice Verna. "A Study of the Phosphorous Compounds in the Liver of the Dog." Ph.D. diss., University of Minnesota, 1935.

STANDARD SOURCES
AMS 6–8, P 9, P&B 10–14; *WWW(A)*, vol. 9.

FLOOD, MARGARET GREER (1896–1921)

Irish botanist. Born 1896 in Dublin. Educated Trinity College, Dublin. Professional experience: National Museum of Dublin, technical assistant (1920). Died 3 May 1921 in Dublin.

Educated at Trinity College, Dublin, Margaret Flood published three papers with A. Henry on London plane, larch, and Douglas firs in the *Proceedings of the Royal Irish Academy.*

JH/MBO

PRIMARY SOURCES
Flood, Margaret. With Augustine Henry. "The Douglas Firs: a Botanical and Silvicultural Description of the Various Species of *Pseudotsuga.*" *Proceedings of the Royal Dublin Society* 35 (1919): 55–66.

———. With A. Henry. "The History of the Dunkeld Hybrid Larch, *Larix eurolepis* with Notes on Other Hybrid Conifers." *Proceedings of the Royal Irish Academy* 35 (1920): 67–92.

SECONDARY SOURCES
Irish Naturalist (1921): 65–67. Obituary notice.
Journal of Botany (1921): 334. Obituary notice.

STANDARD SOURCES
Desmond.

FLORENDO, SOLEDAD ARCEGA (1903–)

Philippine physician. Born 17 October 1903. Four siblings. Married Gerardo Florendo. Two sons, Gerardo and Antonio; two daughters, Maria and Gloria. Educated medical school; National Jewish Hospital, Denver, Colo. (medical-social services and rehabilitation of tuberculosis patients), resident; hospital administration (M.A.). Professional experience: Philippine Tuberculosis Society hospital, Santol Sanatorium, laboratory physician; ward physician, outpatient doctor, physician-at-large to organize the regional and provincial branches of the tuberculosis society. Additional experience: The Crusade (medical informational magazine), chief of health education and information, assistant editor; Antituberculosis Educational and Fund Drive, acting executive secretary; Philippine Department of Health, training officer; Quezon Institute tuberculosis hospital, medical superintendent; Institute of Hygiene and Public Health, lecturer in hospital administration; Philippine State University, Department of Social Work, chair (from 1965); United Nations Mission for the Evaluation of the Family Planning Program for India, member.

Soleda Arcega Florendo's interest in medicine was stimulated by her father (d. 1908), who was at one time a sanitary health inspector and medical aide, and by two uncles, who were pharmacists. She was also impressed by the family physician.

Her mother was a homemaker who engaged in a small retail business.

Before the Americans ended the Spanish colonization of the Philippines, women were not considered worthy of education but were destined to marry, to raise children, and to be active in the church. The Americans introduced universal public education for girls and boys as well as a public health system, which offered better prenatal and general health care for women and new job opportunities. The first degreed women doctors in the Philippines were HONORIA ACOSTA-SISON and Olivia Salamanca, both graduates of Woman's Medical College of Pennsylvania. Salamanca was a crusader against tuberculosis, succumbing to the disease herself, and was Florendo's cousin and role model. Florendo received an award from the Manila Medical Society for her contribution to medical social service in expanding education and home visitation aid to tubercular patients. She spent her life improving health services in the fields of tuberculosis, family welfare, family planning, and hospital administration.

K M

PRIMARY SOURCES
Florendo, Soleda Arcega. In Hellstedt, *Autobiographies*.

FLÜGGE-LOTZ, IRMGARD (1903–1974)

German applied mathematician and engineer. Born 16 July 1903 in Halmeln, Germany, to Dora (Grupe) and Oskar Lotz. One sister. Married Dr. Wilhelm Flügge. Educated elementary school, Frankenthal; high school in Hanover (graduated 1923); Technical University in Hanover, diploma, engineering (1927), doctorate in engineering (1927). Professional experience: Aerodynamische Versuchsanstalt in Göttingen, a research institute, research engineer; Deutsche Versuchsanstalt für Luftfahrt (DVL), consultant in aerodynamics and flight dynamics (1938?–1944). French National Office for Aeronautical Research, Paris, chief of research in theoretical aerodynamics (1946–1948); Stanford University, lecturer in engineering and research supervisor (1948), full professor (1960). Honors and memberships: Society of Women Engineers, Achievement Award (1970); American Institute of Aeronatucis and Astronautics (AIAA), von Kárman lecturer (1971); University of Maryland, Honorary D.Sc. (1973); AIAA, Fellow; Institute of Electrical and Electronic Engineers, senior member; Sigma Xi. Died 22 May 1974.

Irmgard Lotz's childhood experience was difficult, for when her father returned from World War I, his health was broken, and Irmgard had to provide for many of the family's needs. In 1923, she graduated from high school and enrolled in the Technical University in Hanover. From the beginning, she studied applied mathematics with the intention of using mathematics to explain engineering problems. She was the only woman in her class of over a thousand engineering students. During her last two years of working on her doctorate in engineering, Lotz was employed full time as an assistant for practical mathematics and descriptive geometry. Her first job after earning her doctorate was with the Aerodynamisch Versuchsanstalt (AVA), a research institute in Göttingen. She solved the integro-differential equation that had been formulated by Ludwig Prandtl for the spanwise lift distribution of an airplane wing. In 1938, she married Wilhelm Flügge, a civil engineer, who had accepted a new position in Berlin with the Deutsche Versuchsanstalt für Luftfahrt (DVL). Irmgard Flügge-Lotz was offered a position as a consultant in aerodynamics and flight dynamics. After the collapse of Germany, the couple found themselves in the French occupation zone; they were absorbed in the Centre Technique de Wasserburg. They accepted offers to join the newly established French National Office for Aeronautical Research in Paris where Flügge-Lotz served as chief of a research group in theoretical aerodynamics. In 1948, they accepted invitations to come to Stanford, where Flügge was appointed professor but Flügge-Lotz received only the rank of lecturer in engineering mechanics and research supervisor. She taught, conducted research, and advised many graduate students. It was not until 1960 that she was finally appointed full professor, Stanford's first woman professor in engineering. She retired in 1968, and was in constant pain from arthritis until her death at the age of seventy.

Flügge-Lotz received numerous honors, including an honorary doctor of science degree from the University of Maryland (1973) and the Achievement Award by the Society of Women Engineers (1970). She was selected by the American Institute of Aeronautics and Astronautics (AIAA) to give the prestigious von Kármán lecture (1971), the only woman to do so. She was the first woman to be elected fellow of the American Institute of Aeronautics and Astronautics. She was a senior member of the Institute of Electrical and Electronic Engineers, a member of Sigma Xi, and a member of the advisory board of several scientific journals. Flügge-Lotz published over fifty papers and authored two books.

Flügge-Lotz's international reputation was based on her mathematical contributions to aerodynamics and automatic control theory. Her first publication with the AVA in Göttingen, on the method for the calculation of the spanwise lift distribution on wings, was important enough to be called the "Lotz method." She continued to contribute to aerodynamic theory. However her contributions from 1948, when she arrived at Stanford, to her retirement in 1968, were very important. She worked in fluid mechanics and developed numerical methods for solving problems in compressible boundary-layer theory.

JH/MBO

PRIMARY SOURCES

Flügge-Lotz, Irmgard. "Berechnung der Auftriebsverteilung beliebig geformter Flügel." *Zeitschrift für Flugtechnik und Motorluftschiffahrt* 22 (1931): 189–195.

———. *Discontinuous Automatic Control.* Princeton: Princeton University Press, 1953.

———. *Discontinuous and Optimal Control.* New York: McGraw-Hill, 1958.

———. With R. T. Davis. "Second-Order Boundary-Layer Effects in Hypersonic Flow Past Axisymmetric Blunt Bodies." *Journal of Fluid Mechanics* 20 (1964): 593–623.

SECONDARY SOURCES

"A Life Full of Work—the Flügges." *Stanford Engineering News* (May 1969): 68.

New York Times, 23 May 1974. Obituary notice.

STANDARD SOURCES

Grinstein and Campbell (article by John R. Spreiter and Wilhelm Flügge); *NAW*(M); *Notable.*

FOLEY, MARY CECILIA (d. 1925)

British geologist. Educated University College, London (B.Sc., 1891). Professional experience: University of London, staff. Honors and memberships: University College, Morris Prize in Geology (1892); Geologists' Association, council member (1897–1900, 1909–1912). Died 1925.

Mary Cecilia Foley studied at University College, London, under T. G. Bonney. She won the Morris Prize in geology and took her bachelor's degree with honors in geology in 1892. During this same year, she joined the Geologists' Association and served on its council from 1897 to 1900 and 1909 to 1912, the second woman to do so. She held a post at the University of London. She was also interested in social work and spent much of her time working in this field and supporting women's causes.   JH/MBO

SECONDARY SOURCES

E. W. "A New Electrometer, Specially Arranged for Radio-Active Investigations." *Proceedings of the Geologists Association* 37 (1926): 229.

STANDARD SOURCES

Creese and Creese.

FOLMER, HERMINE JACOBA (1882–?)

Dutch geophysicist. Never married. Death date unknown.

The small amount of material available on Hermine Jacoba Folmer indicates that she was an inventor as well as a scientist. While investigating the radioactivity of rocks and of sea water, she developed a highly sensitive electrometer for this work.   JH/MBO

PRIMARY SOURCES

Folmer, Hermine Jacoba. "Researches into the Radio-Activity of the Lake of Rockanje." *Proc. Koniglijke Akademie van Wetenschappen te Amsterdam* 17 (1914): 659.

———. With A. H. Blaauw. *Proc. Koniglijke Akademie van Wetenschappen te Amsterdam* 20, No. 5 (1917).

STANDARD SOURCES

Meyer and von Schweidler.

FOMINA-ZHUKOVSKAIA, EVDOKIIA ALEKSANDROVNA (1860–1894)

Russian chemist. Born 1860 in Lukha (Kostroma province), daughter of a civil servant. Educated Kostroma Women's Teaching Seminary; Samara Women's Gymnasium; University of Geneva (Ph.D.). Worked with Vladimir V. Markovnikov and Nikolai D. Zelinskii. Died in 1894.

Evdokiia Aleksandrovna Fomina-Zhukovskaia was born in Kostroma province in 1860. Her father, a minor civil servant (his rank of collegiate secretary was roughly equivalent to a lieutenant in the navy), died when she was four, leaving the family in precarious financial circumstances. Fomina attended the Kostroma Women's Teaching Seminary and a supplementary course at the Samara Gymnasium (1881) which qualified her to teach as a "domestic tutor." She was not satisfied with this and went to Geneva to continue her education. There she lived on the verge of starvation, giving private lessons while she pursued her studies at the university.

In the laboratory of the chemist Groebe, Fomina conducted research for her dissertation on transformations of xanthone and was awarded the degree of doctor of physical sciences.

Although she was offered a place as assistant in organic chemistry at Geneva, she returned to Russia. In Moscow, despite her qualifications, she could obtain a post only as a mathematics teacher in the junior classes of a private gymnasium. Fortunately, the chemist Vladimir Vasil'evich Markovnikov, who was sympathetic to women students and helped many of them, offered her a position as his private assistant in his laboratory at Moscow University. There she worked with him on cycloheptanone. Later (1893–1894) she assisted Nikolai Dmitrievich Zelinskii in his research on thiophene.

Fomina also took part in work of the Analytic Commission of the Moscow Society of Amateur Naturalists and became a member of the Russian Chemical Society. Years of semi-starvation and overwork took its toll and she died in 1894 at age thirty-four.

Fomina was a talented researcher who succumbed to hardship and privation before she could realize her full potential. However, her contribution was much valued by the chemists in whose laboratories she worked and she certainly holds a rightful place among the early Russian women chemists. ACH

PRIMARY SOURCES

Fomina-Zhukovskaia, Evdokiia. "Recherches sur quelques cominaisons du groupe de l'Euxanthone." Doctoral diss., University of Geneva, ca. 1882.

SECONDARY SOURCES

Musabekov, Iusuf S. *Iuliia Vsevolodovna Lermontove, 1846–1919.* Moscow: Izd-vo "Nauka," 1967.

FONOVITS-SMEREKER, H. (fl. 1919)

Polish?/German physicist.

Next to nothing is known about the physicist, H. Fonovits-Smereker. Not even her nationality is known for certain, but she apparently married a German, Smereker, and hyphenated her name. Fonovits-Smereker made quantitative studies of the ionization produced by alpha rays quantitatively, probably by way of scintillation counting. MM

PRIMARY SOURCES

Fonovits-Smereker, H. *Berichte des Deutschen chemischen Geschellschaft* 128 (1919): 761–.
———. *Berichte des Deutschen chemischen Geschellschaft* 131 (1922): 355–.

STANDARD SOURCES

Meyer and von Schweidler.

FOOT, KATHARINE (1852–?)

U.S. cytologist. Born 14 October 1852 in Geneva, N.Y. Educated private schools; Marine Biological Laboratory, Woods Hole (1892), regular member (1892–1921). Death date unknown.

Although Katharine Foot was apparently a well-respected scientist among her contemporaries (she was starred in the first edition of *AMS*), little is known about her life. She was edu-

cated in private schools, but continued her education at the Marine Biological Laboratory, Woods Hole. However, as far as is known, she was never affiliated with an institution. The *Biological Bulletin* indicates in its annual report that she was a regular member of the laboratory from 1892 and 1921. During this time, she lived in Denver, Colorado; Evanston, Illinois; and New York City. Her listing as a life member began in 1921, and she remained on the roster until 1944. Apparently she lived in London from 1927 to 1938. Her last available address from the *Bulletin* was Camden, South Carolina.

Foot became interested in microscopical observation. Her carefully executed study of the maturation and fertilization of the egg of *Allolobophora fetida* demonstrated her research competence. More important to the history of biology, however, was her use of photography on her research samples. With Ella Strobell, she was one of the first people to use this technique. The resulting photomicrographs are included in the reprinted collection, entitled *Cytological Studies*. Foot and Strobell argued that the chromosomes were too variable in size and form to be considered the specific structures that NETTIE MARIA STEVENS and others postulated that they were. Although Stevens's ideas later were recognized as correct, the use of photographic technology was an important advance. They also invented a method for making very thin sections of specimens at very low temperatures. JH/MBO

PRIMARY SOURCES

Foot, Katharine. With Ellen Strobell. *Cytological Studies, 1894–1917.* 23 pamphlets in one volume. N.p., n.d.
———. "Further Notes on the Egg of *Allolobophora foetida*." *Biological Bulletin* 2 (1898): 143.
———. "Sectioning Paraffine at a Temperature of 25°F." *Biological Bulletin* 9 (1905): 281–286.
———. "Notes on *Pediculus vestimenti*." *Biological Bulletin* 39 (1920): 261.

STANDARD SOURCES

AMS 1–7; In Kass-Simon and Farnes; Ogilvie 1986; Shearer and Shearer 1996.

FORBES, HELENA MADELAIN LAMOND (1900–1959)

British/South African botanist. Born 11 September 1900 in Forfar, Angus. Professional experience: Natal Herbarium, Durban, assistant (1919); Kew (1936–1937); National Herbarium, Pretoria (1938–1940); Natal Herbarium, curator (1940–1945).

Nothing is known about Helena Forbes's education. She was born in England but most of her professional positions were in South Africa. She contributed papers to *Bothalia*.

JH/MBO

STANDARD SOURCES
Desmond; Gunn and Codd.

FORSTER, MARY (fl. 1887)

British geologist. Never married. Professional experience: Bedford College for Women, lecturer (1880s). British Geological Survey, research assistant.

Mary Forster was a coworker of William Topley at the British Geological Survey. She was also a lecturer in geology at Bedford College for Women. She published one paper jointly with Topley.   JH/MBO

PRIMARY SOURCES
Forster, Mary. With William Topley. "Excursion to Belgium and the French Ardennes (1885)." *Proceedings of the Geologists' Association* 9 (1887): 261–286.

STANDARD SOURCES
Creese and Creese.

FOSSEY, DIAN (1932–1985)

U.S. primatologist. Born 1932 in San Francisco to Kitty (Kidd) and George Fossey. Never married. Educated University of California at Davis; San Jose State University (B.A., 1954); Cambridge University (Ph.D., 1974). Professional experience: Kosair Crippled Children's Hospital, Louisville, Ky. (from 1955); L. S. B. Leakey and the Wilkie Brothers Foundations and National Geographic Society, research on gorillas (1967–1980; 1983–1985); Cornell University, visiting associate professor (1980–1983). Died 27 December 1985 in Karisoke, Rwanda.

Dian Fossey had a lonely childhood in San Francisco. Her parents divorced when Dian was six years old. Her mother remarried a wealthy building contractor who was a strict disciplinarian. In her autobiographical book *Gorillas in the Mist,* Dian remembered wanting a pet desperately and being allowed to have only a goldfish. When the goldfish died, she cried for a week.

When she went to the University of California, Davis, Fossey failed chemistry and physics, although she did well in writing and botany. She transferred to San Jose State after two years and earned an bachelor's degree in occupational therapy. Fossey was an excellent equestrian, and her interest in horses drew her to Kentucky, where she became the director of an occupational therapy department in a children's hospital.

After reading George Schaller's book *The Mountain Gorilla: Ecology and Behavior,* Fossey became fascinated by gorillas and took out a bank loan for eight thousand dollars to finance a seven-week safari. When she was in Africa, she met Louis Leakey, the paleoanthropologist. She shattered her ankle on a fossil dig with Leakey, but she was determined to achieve her goal of seeing mountain gorillas. Leakey was impressed by her determination as she climbed a mountain in the Congo (Zaire) using a walking stick. She was rewarded by the sight of six gorillas. Determined to return to Africa, she again met Leakey. This time he was visiting Louisville on a lecture tour. Begging him to hire her to study the mountain gorillas, he told her that she could have a job if she agreed to have a preemptive appendectomy. Fossey immediately agreed and had the surgery performed before Leakey had time to tell her that he had just been testing her resolve.

Funded by the Leakey and the Wilkie Brothers foundations with help from the National Geographic Society, Fossey began her research in the Parc National des Virungas of Zaire, where Schaller had done his research on mountain gorillas. She moved to her permanent site on 24 September 1967 in Rwanda on the slopes of the Virunga Mountains. She called her research area the Karisoke Research Center. Since these gorillas had been harassed by poachers and cattle grazers, their behavior was quite different from Schaller's gorillas. They were much more shy and initially refused any contact with Fossey. Her mission was not only to protect the gorillas from poaching but also to research their habits and write about them. In order to win their confidence, she mimicked their habits. One of her most important successes was when one gorilla, Peanuts, reached out and touched her hand.

Fossey realized that in order to continue getting support for Karisoke, she would need a doctorate. She temporarily left Africa and enrolled at Cambridge University, where she earned a doctoral degree in zoology. Fossey continuously had trouble with poachers. They killed one of her favorite gorillas and later two more animals from her study group were shot and killed while defending their three-year-old son, who was shot in the shoulder. The juvenile also died of his wounds. She mounted a campaign against the tribesmen by raiding their villages.

Suffering from a severe calcium deficiency, Fossey left Africa for the United States and spent three years as a visiting associate professor at Cornell University. During this time she completed her book, *Gorillas in the Mist.* She returned to Karisoke in 1983, but she was no longer funded. Her scientific work was largely over, and she became more of an animal activist than a scientist. This stint in Africa was her last one. She was found murdered in her bedroom at Karisoke. The murder is still unsolved. Although an American, Wayne McGuire, who discovered Fossey's body, and Emmanuel Rwelekana, a Rwandan tracker, were jointly charged by the Rwandan government, there is evidence of a coverup. The Rwandan government recognized her scientific achievement with the highest award it has ever given a foreigner, the Ordre National des Grandes Lacs. Her conservation efforts, no doubt, were important in ensuring that many gorillas were saved.   J H / M B O

PRIMARY SOURCES

Fossey, Dian. "Making Friends with Mountain Gorillas." *National Geographic* (October 1971): 574–585.

——. "The Imperiled Mountain Gorilla." *National Geographic* (April 1981): 501–522.

——. *Gorillas in the Mist*. Boston: Houghton Mifflin Co., 1983.

SECONDARY SOURCES

Brower, Montgomery. "The Strange Death of Dian Fossey." *People* 17 February 1986: 46–54.

Hayes, Harold T. P. *The Dark Romance of Dian Fossey*. New York: Simon and Schuster, 1990.

Kevles, Bettyann. *Watching the Wild Apes: The Primate Studies of Goodall, Fossey, and Galdikas*. New York: Dutton, 1976.

Mowat, Farley. *Woman in the Mists*. New York: Warner Books, 1987.

Montgomery, Sy. *Walking with the Great Apes: Jane Goodall, Dian Fossey, Birute Galdikas*. New York: Houghton Mifflin/Davison, 1991.

Morell, Virginia. "Called Trimates, Three Bold Women Shaped Their Field." *Science* 26 (1993): 420–425.

STANDARD SOURCES

Grinstein 1997 (article by Soraya Ghayourmanesh-Svoronos); *Notable* (article by Cynthia Washam).

FOSSLER, MARY LOUISE (1867–?)

U.S. chemist. Born 14 September 1867 in Lima, Ohio. Educated University of Nebraska (fellow 1897–1899; A.M., 1898); University of Chicago (1900; 1901; 1903; 1927–1928); Northwestern University (Ph.D., 1902). Professional experience: Nebraska public high school principal (1895–1897); University of Nebraska, instructor in chemistry (1899–1908); assistant professor and associate professor of organic and physiological chemistry (1908–1919); University of Southern California, assistant professor (1919–1937), emerita professor (from 1937). Death date unknown.

Mary Louise Fossler earned her doctoral degree from Northwestern University. She began teaching at the University of Nebraska as an instructor in 1899, before she received her doctoral degree, but remained at that rank until 1908. She finally was promoted in 1908, and became an assistant professor and an associate professor at Nebraska. In 1919, she went to California as an assistant professor. She seems to have remained at that rank for eighteen years. She retired in 1937,

and gives her rank at that time as emerita professor, but it seems more likely that she was an emerita assistant professor.

Fossler was a member of the Chemical Society, the American Ornithological Union, the Society of Mammalogists, the Society of Naturalists, the Genetics Society, and the Cooper Ornithological Club. Her research interests were in organic chemistry. She worked on the synthesis of glutaric acids, the separation of alkaloids, and the composition of proteins and their products of dissociation. She also was interested in bacterial food poisoning, the effects of ultraviolet irradiation on antiseptics and disinfectants, the physiological effects of chemical structures, and the colloidal theory of the universe.   J H / M B O

STANDARD SOURCES

AMS 2–8.

FOSTER, JOSEPHINE CURTIS (1889–1941)

U.S. educational psychologist. Born 6 April 1889 in Cambridge, Mass. Educated Wellesley College (A.B., 1910; A.M., 1912); Cornell University (Ph.D., 1915). Professional experience: Smith College, instructor in psychology, education, and mathematics (1912–1913); Boston Psychopathic Hospital, psychologist (1915–1919); University of Minnesota, professor of child welfare and kindergarten and nursery school principal (from 1926). Memberships: Association of Childhood Education, vice-president (1931–1933); National Association of Nursery Education, secretary-treasurer (1935–1937). Died 1941.

Josephine Foster spent most of her career at the University of Minnesota. She was a member of the American Psychological Association, the Association of Childhood Education (vice-president, 1931–1933), and the National Association of Nursery Education (secretary-treasurer, 1935–1937).

Her research interests were in child development, education of children in the nursery school and kindergarten, persistence of interest in young children, fatigue, and learning.

                                            K M

PRIMARY SOURCES

Foster, Josephine Curtis. *Busy Childhood: Guidance through Play and Activity*. New York: Appleton-Century, 1933.

——. *Education in the Kindergarten*. New York: n.p., 1936.

STANDARD SOURCES

AMS 3–6.

FOSTER, MARGARET D. (1895–1970)

U.S. chemist and mineralogist. Born 4 March 1895 in Chicago, Ill., to Minnie MacAuley Foster and the Reverend James Edward Foster. One brother, Robert James. Never married. Educated Illinois College, Jacksonville, Ill. (A.B., 1918); George Washington University

(M.S., 1923); American University (Ph.D., 1936). Professional experience: U.S. Geological Survey Water Resources Branch (1918–1942), Section of Chemistry and Physics (1942–1944), Manhattan Project (from 1942). Laboratory research until 1965. Died 5 November 1970 in Silver Spring, Md.

Margaret (Dot) Foster was born in Chicago into the family of a Presbyterian minister. After her father died in 1910, the family moved to Jacksonville, Illinois, where Dot later attended Jacksonville College. After receiving her bachelor's degree in chemistry, she joined the staff of the United States Geological Survey as the first woman chemist and began what was to be a lifelong career with this institution. During her tenure with the survey, she completed master's and doctoral degrees. Although she officially retired at age seventy, she continued laboratory work until her death at Holy Cross Hospital in Silver Spring, Maryland.

Foster received a number of honors, including an honorary doctor of science degree in 1956 and an Outstanding Alumni Award in 1962 from Illinois College. She was a member of the American Chemical Society and the Geological Society of Washington (secretary, 1945–1946) and a fellow of the Washington Academy of Sciences and the Mineralogical Society of America.

Her first position was with the Water Resources Branch of the survey. After a period of learning techniques of routine water analysis, Foster developed a research project that presented new methods for the quantitative measurements of certain constituents of natural waters. Her first paper on this subject was published in 1923, followed by many more. Of her work on water, she is probably best known for her research on the ground waters of the South Atlantic Coastal Plain and of the Houston-Galveston area. In 1942, Foster transferred to the USGS Section of Chemistry and Physics. She worked for two years in this section, and then was chosen to join the Manhattan Project. Her work with this project resulted in two new quantitative methods for analyzing uranium and thorium. After the conclusion of the Manhattan Project, Foster studied clays, micas, chlorites, and glauconites, working in this field until her final illness. This research resulted in a series of papers. JH/MBO

PRIMARY SOURCES

Foster, Margaret. With W. D. Collins. "Preliminary Examinations of Water Samples." *Industrial Engineering Chemistry* 15 (1923): 1078.

———. "The Chemical Character of the Ground Waters of the South Atlantic Coastal Plain." *Journal of the Washington Academy of Sciences* 27 (1937): 405–412.

———. "Base Exchange and Sulfate Reduction in Salty Waters of the South Atlantic Coastal Plain." *American Association of Petroleum Geologists Bulletin* 26 (1942): 838–851.

———. "Interpretation of the Composition of Vermiculites and Hydrobiotites." *Clays and Clay Minerals* 10 (1963): 70–89.

SECONDARY SOURCES

Fahey, Joseph J. "Memorial of Margaret D. Foster." *The American Mineralogist* 56, nos. 3–4 (1971): 686–690. Includes portrait.

FOUQUET, MARIE DE MAUPEOU, VICOMTESSE DE VAUX (1590–1681)

French healer. Born in 1590. Married Vicomte de Vaux. Wrote book of recipes for unguents and herbal extractions designed to cure "the worst internal and external ills" (1675). Died 1681.

Marie Fouquet de Maupeu is best known for her book of cures that included ointments and herbal teas for both internal and external diseases. This was first published in 1675 and reprinted often during her life and over the next century. The second edition added an ointment for contagious diseases and bore the note that these were all tried by Madame Fouquet. After her death, she was described in the editions as "pious and charitable," and new recipes were added, ostensibly from her memoirs, stressing both that they could successfully cure intractable diseases and were inexpensive to make. JH/MBO

PRIMARY SOURCES

Marie Fouquet de Maupeu. "Recueil de receptes choisies experimentées et approuvées. Contre quantité de maux fort communs tant internes qu'externes inveterés et difficiles à querir." Ville-Franche: Pierre Grandsaigne, 1675. Later editions appear under the title *The Charitable Remedies of Madame Fouquet* (in French).

FOWLER, LYDIA FOLGER (1822–1879)

U.S. physician. Born May 5 1822 in Nantucket, Mass., to Eunice (Macy) and Gideon Folger. Married Lorenzo Fowler. One daughter, Jessie. Educated Nantucket schools; Wheaton Seminary, Norton, Mass. (1838–1839); Central Medical College, Syracuse, and later Rochester, N.Y. (1849–1850). Professional experience: Wheaton Seminary, teacher (1842–1844); Central Medical College, lecturer on anatomy (1850–1852), professor of midwifery and women's and children's diseases (1851–1852); Metropolitan Medical College, New York City, practicing physician and lecturer to women (1852–1860); New York Hygeio-Therapeutic College, instructor in midwifery (1862). Died 26 January 1879 in London, England.

Lydia Folger grew up on Nantucket Island, one of seven children of a businessman and farmer whose family had settled on the island in the seventeenth century. One of Lydia's teachers in the Nantucket schools was the father of astronomer MARIA MITCHELL. Maria and Lydia were distant cousins. Folger studied for a year at Wheaton Seminary (1838–1839) and later taught there (1842–1844).

In 1944, Folger married Lorenzo Fowler (1811–1896), a noted phrenologist who publicized his methods through lecture tours, and through pamphlets and books issued by Fowlers and Wells, a publishing firm he had cofounded. Lydia Fowler herself became a writer and itinerant lecturer, addressing audiences of women on health and phrenology and publishing several books on these subjects. In 1849 she enrolled in Central Medical College, in Syracuse, New York, the first medical institution in the United States to admit women on a regular basis. She became the second American woman (ELIZABETH BLACKWELL was the first) to obtain a medical degree (1850).

While still a student, Fowler had been made head of the school's "Female Department," and after graduation she became demonstrator of anatomy to female students. In 1851, she was promoted to professor of midwifery and diseases of women and children. This position was short-lived, since Central Medical College was dissolved in 1852. From 1852 to 1860 she practiced medicine in New York City and lectured to women at a physiopathic institution, the Metropolitan Medical College. During this time, she became active in a number of reform causes: women's rights, temperance, and the need for women physicians. She traveled to Europe with her husband in 1860–1861 and studied medicine in Paris and London. After another year in New York, where she taught midwifery at the New York Hygeio-Therapeutic College, a hydropathic school, Fowler and her husband moved to London. There she spent the rest of her life, an active participant in various reform movements, particularly temperance. She died in London of pneumonia at age fifty-six.

Lydia Fowler's work was on the periphery of respectability in medicine. Although she was knowledgeable in anatomy and physiology, she was especially interested in phrenology and hydropathic medicine. She was a popularizer and a reformer. Through her lectures and books (for example, *Familiar Lessons on Astronomy* and *Familiar Lessons on Physiology*) she was able to disseminate scientific and medical information to those who might not otherwise have been exposed to it. Yet much of this information, particularly in her later years, involved medical ideas that were not acceptable to most physicians at the time and have since been dismissed. Nonetheless, Fowler did make a lasting contribution to medicine in her support of two areas of reform: the opening of the medical profession to women and the health education of women and children. JH/MBO

PRIMARY SOURCES
Fowler, Lydia Folger. *Familiar Lessons on Astronomy, Designed for the Use of Children and Youth.* New York: Fowlers and Wells, 1848.

———. *Familiar Lessons on Phrenology, Designed for the Use of Schools and Families.* Manchester, England: Heywood, n.d.
———. *Familiar Lessons on Physiology, Designed for the Use of Children and Youth and Families.* New York: Fowlers and Wells, 1848.

SECONDARY SOURCES
Stern, Madeleine. "Lydia Folger Fowler, M.D.: First American Professor of Medicine." *New York State Journal of Medicine* 77 (1977): 1137–1140.
Warner, Deborah Jean. "Science Education for Women in Antebellum America." *Isis* 69 (1978): 58–67.

STANDARD SOURCES
NAW, DAB, Ogilvie 1986.

FOWLER-BILLINGS, KATHARINE STEVENS (1902–1997)

U.S. geologist. Born 12 June 1902 in Little Boar's Head, N.H. to Sarah Farnham (Smith) and William Plumer. Married (1) James W. Lunn (1929); (2) Marland P. Billings (1938). Two children by Billings: George (b. 1939) and Betty (b. 1940). Educated Winsor School (1913–1921); Bryn Mawr College (A.B., 1925); University of Wisconsin (M.A., 1926); Columbia University (Ph.D., 1930). Professional experience: geological mapper of iron ore (1930–1931); Mining company, gold prospector (1932–1933); Wellesley College, instructor in geology (1935–1938); Cardigan Quadrangle, N.H., geological mapper (1935–1937); Monadnock Quadrangle, mapper (1941–1943); Tufts University, instructor in geology (1942–1943); Gorham Quadrangle, geological mapper (1949–1953); Isles of Shoals Quadrangle, geological mapper (1955–1956). Died 17 December 1997.

If one were to look at the *curriculum vitae* of Katharine Fowler-Billings, there would be large gaps in time between jobs. During much of this time, she was gathering data for her geological maps, traveling about the world, and rearing her two children. As a small child, Fowler spent winters in Boston and then attended Winsor School. Her father died in 1918, in the middle of her schooling, but she graduated from Winsor and went on to Bryn Mawr College in 1921. During the summer of 1921 she was a camp counselor and in 1922, she went on a "Grand Tour" of Europe. The next summer she served as an athletic chaperone to three children, and spent the summer after graduation traveling around the western part of the United States. In 1925, Fowler went to the University of Wisconsin to work on her master's degree and spent that summer in the Black Hills and Glacier National Park. After getting her master's degree, Fowler went to Columbia University to work on a doctorate in 1926. She did her thesis fieldwork at the University of

Wyoming field camp (1927) and in the Laramie Mountains (1928). Her mother died during this year.

In 1929, after attending a geological congress in Africa and going on a "Cape to Cairo" trip, Fowler married James "Jock" Lunn in December. In 1930, she took a winter trip to Saint Moritz and then from 1930 to 1933 went to Sierra Leone in West Africa. During her first year in Sierra Leone, she did geological mapping of iron Ore and then from 1932 to 1933 prospected for gold for a mining company. At the end of her African trip, she went to the Gold Coast and Nigeria.

Upon returning home, she did not immediately get a job. However, in 1935 she became an instructor in geology at Wellesley, a position that she held for three years. During her time as instructor, she did geological mapping in the Cardigan Quadrangle in New Hampshire, attended a geological congress in Russia, took a horseback trip across the Caucasus, ascended Mount Fuji, and remarried, this time to geologist Marland P. Billings. This marriage was much more successful, and shortly after the ceremony the couple went mapping in the Mount Washington Quadrangle. Her son, George, was born in 1939 and daughter, Betty, in 1940. However, in 1941 she resumed her mapping, this time in the Monadnock Quadrangle. She took her second academic position from 1942 to 1943 as an instructor at Tufts University. Fowler-Billings apparently spent the next six years raising her family, for she did not resume mapping until 1949, when she mapped the Gorham Quadrangle. She took an extensive western trip with the children in 1954. In 1955, she began geological mapping in the Isles of Shoals Quadrangle which occupied her until 1956. Again there is a gap in her geological activities until 1960, when she attended a geological congress in Copenhagen, followed by extensive travels in Europe.

Fowler-Billings and her husband constructed a retirement home in Bartlett, New Hampshire, in 1965 and throughout the next year, during Marland's sabbatical, they traveled extensively in the Far East, including Taiwan, India, Australia, and New Zealand. They continued to travel during retirement, going to South America, Africa, Alaska, and the Galapagos Islands. They celebrated their golden wedding anniversary by a trip to Bermuda.

During this very full life, Katharine Fowler-Billings managed to produce a number of excellent publications, some as sole author and others as coauthor, often with her husband.

CK

PRIMARY SOURCES

Fowler, Katharine Stevens. "Glacial Drainage Changes in Northeastern United States." Master's thesis, University of Wisconsin at Milwaukee, 1926.

———. "The Anorthosite Area of the Laramie Mountains, Wyoming." Ph.D. diss., Columbia University, 1930.

Fowler-Lunn, Katharine. With Louise Kingsley. "Geology of the Cardigan Quadrangle, N.H." *Geological Society of America Bulletin* 48 (1936) 1363–1386.

———. *The Gold Missus: A Woman Prospector in Sierra Leone.* New York: Norton, 1937.

Fowler-Billings, Katharine. *Sillimanite Deposits in the Monadnock Quadrangle.* New Hampshire State Planning and Development Commission Mineral Resources Survey, part 8. Concord, N.H.: New Hampshire State Planning and Development Commission, 1944. Reprint, 1949. Includes illustrations and maps.

———. "Igneous and Metasedimentary Dikes of the Mount Washington Area, New Hampshire." *Geological Society of America Bulletin* 56 (1944): 1255–1278.

———. "Geology of the Monadnock Quadrangle, New Hampshire." *Geological Survey of America Bulletin* 60 (1949): 1249–1280.

———. With Marland P. Billings. *Geology of the Odiorne Point Area.* Odiorne Point State Park Natural Science and Historical Studies, Information Center, New Hampshire Department of Resources and Economic Development. Concord, N.H., 1973.

———. "The Long Road to Save the Green Hills of Conway, New Hampshire." *Appalachia* 49, no. 1 (1992): 54–59.

———. "Stepping-Stones: The Reminiscences of a Woman Geologist in the Twentieth Century." *Transactions: The Connecticut Academy of Arts and Sciences* 53 (May 1996): 1–244.

STANDARD SOURCES
AMS 6–11; Bailey; Debus.

FOX, RUTH (1895–1989)

U.S. psychiatrist. Born 21 June 1895 in New York City to Adelaide (Gomer) and James Braden Fox. Married McAlister Coleman (1 March 1931). One daughter, Ann. Educated University of Chicago (Ph.B., 1919); Rush Medical College (M.D., 1926). Professional experience: Neurological Institute, New York City, director of laboratories (1934–1938); New York City, private medical practice, specializing in psychiatry (from 1938). Additional experience: National Council on Alcoholism, Inc., medical director (from 1959); New York Department of Mental Hygiene, member, advisory council on alcoholism. Honors and memberships: Malvern Institute for Psychiatric and Alcoholic Studies, citation of merit (1963); American Society for Group Psychotherapy and Psychodrama, award, N.Y. chapter (1963); American Psychiatric and Alcoholic Studies (1963); American Psychiatric Association; New York Academy of Medicine; Association for the Advancement of Psychotherapy; American Academy for Psychoanalysis; American Public Health Association; American Medical Association; Pan American Medical Association, American Medical Women's Association; Rocal Society for Health (England); Society for the Study of

Addiction to Alcohol and Other Drugs (England); American Group Psychotherapy Association, N.Y.; Academy of Sciences; American Orthopsychiatric Association; American Society for Clinical Hypnosis; Society of Clinical and Experimental Hypnosis; and the American Academy of Psychoanalysis, trustee; American Society of Addiction Medicine, founding president. Died 1989.

Psychiatrist Ruth Fox was a member of a very large number of professional organizations, reflecting her wide interests in a variety of fields concerned with psychiatry. However, if we were to pick her major research interest, we would have to chose alcoholism and addiction, its causes and remedies. She was able to apply many of the techniques and ideas that she absorbed from the other fields to the problem of addiction. She also stressed the importance of education in preventing alcoholism. KM

PRIMARY SOURCES
Fox, Ruth. With Peter Lyon. *Alcoholism: Its Scope, Cause and Treatment.* New York: Random House, 1955.
———, ed. *Alcoholism: Behavioral Research and Therapeutic Approaches.* New York: Springer, 1967.

STANDARD SOURCES
Debus.

FRAINE, ETHEL LOUISE DE (1879–1918)
British botanist. Born Aylesbury, Buckinghamshire, 2 November 1879. Educated University of London (D.Sc., 1908?); Linnean Society, fellow (1908). Professional experience: Whitelands Training College, Battersea Polytechnic, lecturer (1910–1913); Westfield College, lecturer 1915. Died Falmouth Cornwall, 25 March 1918.

Ethel Louise de Fraine was born in Aylesbury, Buckinghamshire, 2 November 1879. She was educated at the University of London, receiving her Doctorate in Science around 1908. She was made a fellow of the Linnean Society in 1908, and published articles on the cactus family. After teaching botany at the Whitelands Training College, she then was appointed a lecturer in botany at the Battersea Polytechnic from 1910 to 1913. She then taught at Westfield College in 1915. She died at Falmouth, Cornwall, three years later, at the age of thirty-eight. JH/MBO

PRIMARY SOURCES
Fraine, Ethel Louise de. "Seedling Structures of Certain Cactaceae." *Annals of Botany* (1910): 125–175.

SECONDARY SOURCES
Nature 101 (1918): 150–151. Obituary notice.

STANDARD SOURCES
Desmond.

FRAMPTON, MARY (1773–1846)
British botanist. Born 1773 in Moreton, Dorset. Married. Educated at home. Died 12 November 1846.

Mary Frampton was educated at home. Interested both in plants and in art, she produced five volumes of drawings of Dorset plants which were in the possession of her family. T. B. Salter recognized the importance of her plant records, when he cited them in his botanical appendix to J. Sydenham's *History of Poole.* JH/MBO

PRIMARY SOURCES
Sydenham, J. *History of the Town and County Poole.* London: Whittaker, 1839. Frampton's records are included in this book, page 487.

STANDARD SOURCES
Desmond.

FRANCES OF BRITTANY (fl. 15th century)
French healer. Married (1) Charles VIII; (2) Louis XII. Professional activities: tended the sick during the plague. Died of the plague.

Frances, Duchess of Brittany, was a French medical woman of noble birth. She was apparently the queen of both Charles VIII and Louis XII. She reputedly cared for her bitterest enemy through a long illness, after which she retired to a Carmelite convent, where she cared for the nuns during an epidemic of plague. She herself died of the plague.
JH/MBO

SECONDARY SOURCES
Kavanagh, Julia. *The Women of Christianity.* London: Smith, Elder, 1852.

STANDARD SOURCES
Hurd-Mead 1938.

FRANCINI, ELEONORA CORTI (1904–)
Italian botanist. Born 14 July 1904 in Florence. Educated University of Florence (diploma in natural science), habilitated (1932). Professional experience: University of Florence, botanical institute, research (?–1932); University of Pisa, botanical institute, assistant (1932–1939); University of Bari, teacher, founder of the botanical institute and the botanical gardens (1939–1962); University of

Florence, professor, director of the Tropical African Herbarium and the Center for Electromicroscopy (from 1962); Institute of Botany (Orto Botanico) (1960–1974).

Eleanor Francini was born and educated in Florence. After habilitating in 1932, she went to the University of Pisa as an assistant in the botanical institute there. Leaving Pisa in 1932, she went to the University of Bari for a long period, teaching and founding both a botanical institute and a botanical garden. Francini left Bari in 1962 to return to Florence, where she became a professor at the University of Florence.

Francini studied the embryology of plants, especially the ultrastructure of the gametophytes of the gymnosperms and angiosperms, as well as plants' systematic anatomy. Most of her work was on Mediterranean plants, and she made a number of geobotanical studies, publishing and editing a number of works on the subject. She was awarded a gold medal by the government for her service to teaching, culture, and art. JH/MBO

STANDARD SOURCES
Strohmeier; *WW in Italy* 1994; *WW in Science in Europe* 1967.

FRANÇOISE, MARIE-THÉRÈSE (1903–1989)
French nutritionist. Born 1903 in Paris. Educated Lyceum Victor Duruy in Paris (Baccalaureate, 1920/21); University of Paris, student in mathematics, chemistry, and physics (ca. 1921–1925), (Ph.D., 1929); University of Nancy (habilitated 1937). Professional experience: University of Nancy, assistant in pharmacological research (1935–1938); Section of Pharmacology, professor for medical research (1938–1973). Honors and memberships: Commandeur des Palmes académeiques; Gesellschaft zur Förderung der nationalen Industrie; Chevalier dans l'ordre du Mérite of Italy. Died 6 August 1989.

Marie-Thérèse Françoise was born and educated in Paris. Her doctorate was from the Faculty of Natural Science of the University of Paris. She presented two projects for her doctoral work, a study on the oil of marine animals and another on benzyne and nitrobenzyne. In 1935 she went to University of Nancy as assistant in pharmacological research and habilitated at that university in 1937. At Nancy, she was named professor for medical research for the section of pharmacy, a position that she held until her retirement in 1973. During World War II, Françoise carried on her obligations to the University at Nancy and also taught at Reims and Besançon. At the same time she was engaged in the passive resistance movement and in Red Cross work. In science, her main interests were the oil and fat chemistry of plants and animals. Her research had industrial implications, and she

was chief of a number of boards and commissions that were interested in her work. JH/MBO

STANDARD SOURCES
Strohmeier; *WW in Science in Europe.*

FRANK, MARGARET (1894–?)
U.S. psychologist. Born 24 September 1894 in Columbus, Ohio. Educated Ohio State University (B.S., 1914); University of Chicago (Ph.D., 1930). Professional experience: University of Chicago, research assistant (1930–1932); Douglas Smith Fund, Chicago, psychologist (1933–1939), consulting psychologist (1936–1943); Veterans Administration, personal counselor (from 1946); Illinois Emergency Relief Commission, placement director (1933–1935); Illinois Institute of Technology, instruction technician (1937–1943); Englewood Evening College, instructor (1941–1946); consulting psychologist (1936–1943); Women's Army Corps, Air Force, consulting psychologist (1943–1945); Veterans Administration, consulting psychologist (from 1946), consulting psychologist (from 1951); Meredith Publishing Company, Iowa, consulting editor (1951–1956). Honors and memberships: American Psychological Association, fellow. Memberships: Midwest Psychological Association; Illinois Association of Applied Psychologists. Death date unknown.

Margaret Frank was an applied psychologist, whose research interests were in metabolism and nutrition. During World War II, she was a psychologist for the Women's Army Corps, and after the war worked for the Veteran's Administration and later became a consulting psychologist. KM

STANDARD SOURCES
AMS 6–8, S&B 9–12; *Psychological Register,* 1938.

FRANKLIN, ROSALIND ELSIE (1920–1958)
British crystallographer. Born 25 July 1920 in London to Muriel and Ellis Franklin. Four siblings. Never married. Educated St. Paul's Girls' School, London (graduated 1938); Paris (studied French); Newnham College, Cambridge University (bachelor's, second class 1941; Ph.D., 1945); Professional experience: British Coal Utilization Research Association, physical chemist (1942–1945); Laboratoire Central des Services Chimiques de l'État, Paris, research scientist; King's College, Cambridge, DNA researcher (1951–1953); Birbeck College, research head of tobacco mosaic virus team (1953–1958); Died 16 April 1958.

Rosalind Franklin was the second child and first daughter of Ellis Franklin and Muriel Waley Franklin. The Franklins and the Waleys had been involved in the London Jewish community for four generations. Supported by her mother and aunt but discouraged by her father, Franklin managed to get a university education. Upon entering Newnham College in 1938, she met the physicist Adrienne Weill, who encouraged the work that resulted in her doctoral degree on coals and carbons. She was on the cutting edge of the new field of X-ray crystallography, which revealed the positions of atoms in crystalline structures. Moving from simpler crystals to carbon and biological molecules, Franklin became a very skilled crystallographer. After the end of World War II, Franklin worked in Paris at the Laboratoire Central des Services Chimiques de l'Etat, a position that Weill found for her.

In 1950, Franklin was offered a fellowship at King's College, London, by John Randall, to analyze her expertise in X-ray crystallography. At King's College, she worked with Maurice Wilkins, and the relations between the two rapidly deteriorated. At this time, two laboratories in England were working extensively on the crystalline structures of biological materials, King's College on the structure of DNA, and the Cavendish Laboratory, Cambridge, on the structure of proteins. There was an unspoken agreement between the two laboratories that their two areas would not overlap. Although Wilkins and Franklin were working on DNA, James Watson and Francis Crick from the Cavendish decided that DNA research was more exciting than the protein research in which they were supposedly engaging. Franklin had noted that humidity was an important factor in the quality of her X-ray photographs. At 75 percent humidity, she produced pictures of DNA that she called the "dry A-form," whereas at 95 percent humidity the photographs were less detailed but manifested a cross shape (characteristic of a helical structure). From the "A" form, Franklin concluded that the structure of the molecule could not possibly be a helix. In November 1951, Watson attended a presentation of Franklin's work. He misunderstood Franklin's work, and after reporting to Crick, the two produced a model of the DNA molecule based on this misunderstanding.

Meanwhile, the conflict between Wilkins and Franklin escalated to the extent that they were hardly speaking to each other. Therefore, on an occasion when Watson and Crick visited King's College, Wilkins did not hesitate to show Franklin's photographs to Watson and Crick. After viewing the "B" form that clearly showed the identifying cross, they created the accepted model of the DNA molecule based on the double helical structure.

Franklin was a careful experimenter who was loathe to make theoretical leaps without a mass of corroborating data. On the other hand, Watson and Crick were long on intuitive leaps, but short on data. One look at Franklin's photograph, however, inspired them to create the model that changed twentieth-century biology. Watson and Crick's paper that elicited the Nobel Prize was published in *Nature* in 1953. In

the same issue of *Nature,* Franklin and Raymond Gosling expanded a revised version of their work.

Before these papers were published, Franklin had left King's for Birbeck College, London to work for John Desmond Bernal. She was allowed to bring her fellowship and become head of her own research group, but was not supposed to work on DNA. She did, however, finish her DNA work there, and then began a study of the tobacco mosaic virus.

Franklin was diagnosed with ovarian cancer in the summer of 1956, and underwent three operations and experimental chemotherapy. By this time, she had become friends with Crick and his wife, Odile, traveling through Europe with them and convalescing from her treatments at their home. However, a very private person, she never gave them details of her illness. She died on 16 April 1958 when she was only thirty-seven years old. In 1962, the Nobel Prize for medicine was awarded to Francis Crick, James Watson, and Maurice Wilkins for their work on DNA. Since the Nobel Prize is only given to living individuals, Franklin never received it. Interestingly, the Nobel lectures of the three men (no more than three people can share a Nobel Prize), did not mention Franklin's part in the discovery.　　　JH/MBO

PRIMARY SOURCES

Franklin, Rosalind. "The Physical Chemistry of Solid Organic Colloids with Special Relation to Coal and Related Materials." Ph.D. diss., Cambridge University, 1945.

———. "Crystallite Growth in Graphitizing and Nongraphitizing Carbons." *Proceedings of the Royal Society* 209A (1951): 154.

———. With R. G. Goslin. "Evidence for a 2-Chain Helix in Crystalline Structure of Sodium Deoxyribonucleat." *Nature* 172 (1953): 156–157.

———. "Location of the Ribonucleic Acid in the Tobacco Mosaic Virus Particle." *Nature* 177 (1956): 928–930.

———. With Aaron Klug. "Order-Disorder Transitions in Structures Containing Helical Molecules." *Discussions of the Faraday Society* 25 (1958): 104–110.

SECONDARY SOURCES

Bernal, J. D. "Dr. Rosalind Franklin." *Nature* 182 (19 July 1958): 154.

Klug, Aaron. "Rosalind Franklin and the Discovery of the Structure of DNA." *Nature* 219 (24 August 1968): 808–810; 843–844.

Sayre, Anne. *Rosalind Franklin and DNA.* New York: Norton, 1975.

STANDARD SOURCES

Grinstein 1993 (article by Mary Clarke Miksic); Grinstein 1997 (article by Maureen M. Julian); *Notable.*

FRANTZ, VIRGINIA KNEELAND (1896–1967)

U.S. surgical pathologist and medical educator. Born 1896 in New York City to Yale and Anna Ilsley (Ball) Kneeland. One sibling. Married Angus Macdonald Frantz (1920; divorced 1935). Three children: Virginia Hathaway (1924); Angus Macdonald, Jr. (1927); Andrew Gibson (1930). Educated Brearley School, New York City (1914); Bryn Mawr College (1918); College of Physicians and Surgeons, Columbia University (M.D., 1922); Presbyterian Hospital (Columbia University), surgical internship (1924–1927). Professional experience: Surgical Pathology Laboratory, Presbyterian Hospital, researcher and instructor, later professor of surgery (late 1920s–1962). Honors and memberships: Army-Navy Certificate of Appreciation (1948); New York Pathological Society (president, 1949 and 1950); American Thyroid Association (first woman president, 1961); Elizabeth Blackwell Award, New York Infirmary (1957). Died 23 August 1967 in New York City of cancer.

After Virginia Kneeland graduated from Bryn Mawr College, she attended Columbia University's College of Physicians and Surgeons, where she earned her medical degree.

In the second year of medical school, she married a fellow classmate and had three children, two boys and one girl, although the marriage ended in divorce fifteen years later. She chose to work in surgical pathology where women were few, making her name with studies of pancreatic tumors with the surgeon Allen O. Whipple. The resulting monograph became a standard reference, later published by the Armed Forces Institute of Pathology.

In the 1940s, Frantz worked with a team of researchers using radioactive iodine to identify metastatic thyroid tumors, and helped to introduce this isotope as a treatment. She also produced a major introductory text on surgery that went through four editions between 1946 and 1959. Among her innovative studies was an investigation of cystic disease in female breasts and an award-winning discovery, with Raffaele Lattels, of an absorbable, gauze-like cellulose material for the control of bleeding. For the latter work, she received the Army-Navy Certificate of Appreciation for Civilian Service in 1948.

She received the recognition of her colleagues for her research, but Frantz considered her first commitment to be her students at the College of Physicians and Surgeons. She was made full professor in 1957 and was remembered as a valuable mentor. Although she was sensitive to problems of women physicians, she hesitated to accept the Elizabeth Blackwell award in 1957, wary of its emphasis on her gender rather than her professionalism.

Frantz served her colleagues as president of the New York Pathological Society and as the first woman president of the American Thyroid Association. Even after retirement she continued as a consultant in surgery, until her death from cancer at the age of seventy.   JH/MBO

PRIMARY SOURCES
Frantz, Virginia. "Adenoma of Islet Cells with Hyperinsulinism." *Annals of Surgery* (June 1935): 1299–1335.
———. With Albert S. Keston, et al. "Storage of Radioactive Iodine in a Metastasis from Thyroid Carcinoma." *Science* 95 (April 1942): 362–363.
———. With Harold Dortic Harvey. *Introduction to Surgery.* New York: Oxford University Press, 1946.
———. "An Evaluation of Radioactive Iodine Therapy in Metastatic Thyroid Cancer." *Journal of Clinical Endocrinology* (September 1950): 1084–1991.
———. *Tumors of the Pancreas.* Washington, D.C.: Armed Forces Institute of Pathology, 1959.

SECONDARY SOURCES
New York Times, 24 August 1967. Obituary notice.

STANDARD SOURCES
NAW(M) (article by Allan M Brandt); *NCAB; WWW(A),* vol. 4, 1960–68.

FREEMAN, JOAN MAIE (1918–1998)

Australian/British physicist. Born Perth, Western Australia, 7 January 1918 to Ada Gilham North and Albert Freeman. Married John Jelley (1958). Educated Sydney Church of England Girls' Grammar School; Sydney Technical College; University of Sydney (B.Sc. a double first, 1940; M.Sc., 1942); Newnham College, Cambridge University, College Studentship (1948–1949; Ph.D., 1950). Professional experience: Cavendish Laboratory Cambridge, research assistant (1949–1951); Atomic Energy Research Establishment Harwell, senior science officer (1951–1954); principal science officer (1954–1960); Nuclear Physics Division, group leader (1960–1978). Died 18 March 1998 at Oxford.

Physicist Joan Freeman was a native Australian who spent her career in England. An only child, her childhood, but not her parents' marriage, was relatively happy. She was close to her mother, a musically talented woman who had not come to terms with the poverty caused from the collapse of the great gold boom in the 1900s. Her accountant father was given to spells of rage. In 1922, the family moved to Sydney. After the 1929 crash, Albert Freeman lost his bank job and her mother struggled to make ends meet by running a kindergarten and giving piano lessons. Joan was very successful academically at the Sydney Church of England Grammar School for Girls, and the school allowed her to continue by remitting the fees. Ada Freeman realized that Joan was gifted in mathematics and physics and that the school was not giving her significant experience in these areas. Therefore she took her to physics classes at Sydney Technical College, where she had to be hidden in a cupboard when the inspectors came, and where, as a small girl, she was surrounded by engineering apprentices in a rough part of the city. At the principal's insistence, her mother accompanied her. She passed her Intermediate Certificate Examination (her school leaving examination equivalent to the British O-levels) with seven A's and one B. The B was in chemistry! She won a scholarship to University of Sydney, obtaining a double first in 1940, and was awarded a postgraduate scholarship. At the University, Phyllis Nichol, the second woman to graduate in physics at Sydney, was one of her lecturers. She advised Freeman to take chemistry where employment prospects were slightly greater than in physics.

After she completed her degree, Freeman took a position working on radar at the Government Radiophysics Laboratory near Sydney. Although she did receive her master's degree (completing it in her spare time), it was not possible to earn a doctorate at an Australian university at that time. After the war, she undertook a research project concerning the behavior of low-pressure gas discharges at microwave frequencies. In 1946, after receiving satisfactory results on this project she was awarded a Senior Studentship by the Council for Scientific and Industrial Research. This award allowed her to go to Cambridge University and read for her doctoral degree. She found Newnham College excessively formal after her more casual experience with Australia, and her first year was very disconcerting. The weather was cold and wet and the Cavendish Laboratories where she was to work were in a turmoil with an unfortunate ratio between research students and advisory staff. Advised to join the Nuclear Physics Department, she spent six months trying to find a project. No project had been assigned to her and her supervisor never arrived. After much difficulty, she found a niche for herself with Alex Baxter with whom she teamed up to work on the HT1 accelerator to study short-range alpha particles. By this time she had made many friends and found life in Cambridge very satisfactory. She had intended to go home after she received her doctoral degree, but decided to stay in England. She had been offered a post at Harwell with nuclear physicist Sir John Cockcroft. Her friend John Jelley was also going to work there.

Her decision to join the Van der Graaff accelerator group as a senior scientific officer was a good one. She invited her mother to join her, and lived with her until her mother's death in 1973. In 1958, Freeman married John Jelley, whom she had met in 1948. She retired in 1978 at the age of sixty (the retirement age for women; it was sixty-five for men), but continued as a consultant.

Joan Freeman, her husband, John Jelley, and Roger Blin-Stoyle were awarded the Rutherford Medal for their work on beta-radioactivity of complex nuclei. By 1960, she had become the leader of the Harwell Tandem Accelerator Group that carried out the experimental work and Blin-

Stoyle and his students at Sussex University pursued the theoretical side. Their collaboration on the basic weak interaction theory began in the 1960s. The spontaneous emission of negative or positive electrons from unstable nuclei is known as a manifestation of the four interactions in nature. The other forces are the gravitational, the electromagnetic, and the strong. Although the weak interaction is secondary, its role is still vital in a nuclear reactor.

The Rutherford Medal, awarded for the first time to a woman, was recognition of a life in physics. She also held a Fellowship at the Institute of Physics, one from the American Physical Society, and an honorary doctorate from Sydney University. In her memoirs, *A Passion for Physics* (1991), she indicated that in order to succeed in science a woman needed determination, enthusiasm, and independence of mind.

In order to be with his wife, Jelley took early retirement, and they spent their final years together traveling and sailing until he died in 1997.   JH/MBO

PRIMARY SOURCES
Freeman, Joan. *A Passion for Physics: The Story of a Woman Physicist*. Bristol: Hilger, 1991.

SECONDARY SOURCES
"Joan Freeman." *Times,* 10 April 1998.
Hetzel, Phyllis. *Independent,* 27 March 1998. Obituary notice.

FREIDLINA, RAKHIL' KHATSKELEVNA (1906–)

Russian organic chemist. Born 20 September 1906 at Samoteevichi. Educated Moscow State University. Professional experience: Scientific Research Institute of Insectofungicides, staff; Institute of Fine Chemical Technology, staff; Soviet Academy of Sciences Institute of Organic Chemistry, staff; laboratory in the Institute of Organo-Elemental Compounds, director. Honors and memberships: Soviet Academy of Sciences, corresponding member.

Rakhil' Khatskelevna Freidlina graduated in 1930 from Moscow State University, where she was a student of the Russian chemist A. N. Nesmeianov. From 1930 to 1934 she worked in the Science Research Institute of Insectofungicides. From 1935 to 1939, she worked at the Soviet Academy of Sciences Institute of Organic Chemistry. In 1938 she also began working at the Institute of Fine Chemical Technology, where she remained until 1941, when she returned to the Institute of Organic Chemistry. She remained there until 1954, when she became director of a laboratory at the Institute of Organo-Elemental Compounds. In the same year, she joined the Communist Party.

Freidlina's research included studies on the structure and properties of organic compounds of mercury, arsenic, tin, lead, antimony, zirconium, boron, flourine, and chlorine. She also made discoveries relating to homolytic isomerizations of organic compounds in solution and investigations into the adduct of metallic salts to olefins and acetylenes which led to the establishment of the concept of quasi-complex compounds. Her work on telomerization led to the development of an industrial method for synthesizing intermediate products for the production of the synthetic fibers enanth and pelargon.

Freidlina was elected a corresponding member of the Soviet Academy of Sciences in 1958. She has been awarded three orders and various medals.   ACH

PRIMARY SOURCES

Freidlina, Rakhil' Khatskelevna. "Sinteticheskie metody v oblasti metalloorganicheskikh soedinenii mysh'iaka." In *Sinteticheskie metody v oblasti metalloorganicheskikh soedinenii.* Moscow: Izd-vo Akademii nauk SSSR, 1945.

———. *Telomerization and New Synthetic Materials.* New York: Pergamon Press, 1961.

———. "Metody elementoorganicheskoi khimii." In *Khlor, Alifaticheskie soedineniia.* Moscow: "Nauka," 1973.

SECONDARY SOURCES

Bol'shaia sovetskaia entsiklopediia. 3rd. ed. Moscow: Izd-vo "Sovetskaia entsiklopediia," 1973.

STANDARD SOURCES

Turkevich and Turkevich.

FRENKEL-BRUNSWIK, ELSE (1908–1958)

Polish/U.S. psychologist and psychoanalyst. Born 18 August 1908 in Lemberg, in the Austro-Hungarian Empire, to Helene (Gelernter) and Abraham Frenkel, banker. Two sisters. Married psychology professor Egon Brunswik (9 June 1938; he died 1955). No children. Educated University of Vienna (Ph.D., 1930). Stanford University Center for Advanced Study in the Behavioral Sciences, Fellow (1954–1955); University of Oslo, Fulbright Fellow (1956–1957). Professional experience: Psychological Institute of the University of Vienna, assistant professor (1930–1938); University of California, Berkeley, Institute of Child Welfare, research psychologist (1938–1958); University of California-Berkeley, professor (1957–1958). Died 31 March 1958 in Berkeley, Calif., of overdose of barbital.

Else Frenkel was born 18 August 1908 in Lemberg in what was then the Austro-Hungarian Empire. Her father, Abraham Frenkel, a banker, and mother, Helene (Gelernter) Frenkel, moved the family to Vienna in 1914. Else had an older sister, an extraordinary beauty named Johanna, and a younger sister, Marta (?). Her middle child status and plain-ness contributed to her intellectual achievements, which she soon discovered were appreciated by her father. Little is known of her early education, but she received her higher education at the University of Vienna, earning a doctorate in psychology in 1930 under Karl Bühler. Her dissertation, published in 1931 in *Zeitschrift für Psychologie,* was titled "Atomismus und Mechanismus in der Assoziationspsychologie (Atomism and Mechanism in Association Psychology)."

She joined the faculty at Vienna as a lecturer and researcher and spent part of that time in collaboration with Charlotte Bühler on the longitudinal studies at the Institute of Psychology. Frenkel's later work was greatly influenced by her work with Karl and CHARLOTTE BÜHLER. Another influence was Ernst Kris, an ego psychologist who directed her psychoanalysis. A third major influence in her life was colleague and friend within the Bühler circle, her husband-to-be, Egon Brunswik. The two became caught up in the logical positivism and Unity of Science movements that included Moritz Schlick, Rudolph Carnap, Otto Neurath, and Philipp Frank. In 1937, Else Frenkel, with Edith Weisskopf, published her first book, *Wunsch und Pflicht im Aufbau des menschlichen Lebens* (Wish and Obligation in the Course of Human Life).

When Egon Brunswik returned from a Rockefeller Fellowship in California, the couple were married, and only a few months after the wedding, fled to escape the Nazi *Anschluss,* returning to California where Egon had been offered a post as assistant professor. Else Brunswik became associated with the Institute of Child Welfare in Berkeley and with several other "careers" and she began to write articles and monographs. "Mechanisms of Self-Deception" (1939), published soon after arriving in the United States, related the doctrines of psychoanalysis to everyday life.

Frenkel-Brunswik participated centrally in the early developments of a psychology of personality (with Gordon Allport, Henry Murray, and Gardner Murphy), drawing on her experience and sophistication in both psychoanalysis and the logical positivism of the Vienna circle to champion the scientific respectability of psychoanalytic constructions. She was a pioneer in what later became known as cognitive psychology. She contributed to the development of scales of ethnocentrism and of authoritarianism (the F-scale) and to the study of prejudice, using new methods and testing new hypotheses concerning prejudice. Her specific contribution was the construction and analysis of the semistructured interviews with the subjects of the study. She was a developer of the concept of authoritarian intolerance of ambiguity. In the collaborative book, *The Authoritarian Personality* (1950), she made major contributions in the study of prejudice and antisemitism. She was interested in the sociopolitical psychology of the prejudiced personality in relations with spouse, children, and other people in general, expanding to political and religious views. She focused on the trait of intolerance of ambiguity to isolate and measure, observing that this trait, more basic than authoritarianism, is associated with several distinctive tendencies. Other researchers have since confirmed tolerance versus intolerance of ambiguity as a basic personality and perceptual factor.

In 1950, Frenkel-Brunswik was visiting lecturer at the University of Oslo, Institute for Social Research. In 1954–1955 she was a fellow at the Center for the Advanced Study in the Behavioral Sciences. Her research involved integrative personality theories, longitudinal studies in child development, projective testing, and perception experiments. Because of her early death, she was unable to fully develop the theories she had begun to assess. With the death of her husband in 1955, Frenkel-Brunswik's career literally halted. She ceased her research and writing and fell into deep depression. On 31 March 1958 in Berkeley, California, she committed suicide with an overdose of barbital. JH/MBO

PRIMARY SOURCES

Frenkel-Brunswik, Else, et al. *The Authoritarian Personality.* New York: Harper, 1950.

———. *Psychoanalysis and the Unity of Science.* American Academy of Arts and Sciences in Association with the Institute for the Unity of Science, 1954.

———. *Else Frenkel-Brunswik: Selected Papers.* Ed. Nanette Heiman and Joan Grant. New York: International Universities Press, 1974.

———. *Studien zur Autoritären Persönlichkeit: Ausgewählte Schriften.* Ed. Dietmar Paier. Trans. Bertram F. Malle. Graz: Nausner & Nausner, 1996.

STANDARD SOURCES

NAW(M) (article by M. B. Smith); O'Connell and Russo 1990; Stevens and Gardner; Zuzne.

FREUD, ANNA (1895–1982)

Austrian psychoanalyst. Born 3 December 1895 in Vienna, Austria, to Martha (Bernays) and Sigmund Freud. Five siblings. Never married. Educated teacher training schools in Vienna and England (passed the teacher's examination, 1915); University of Vienna, attended father's courses. Professional experience: Cottage Lyceum, apprentice teacher (1915–1918), teacher (from 1918). Vienna Psychoanalytic Society, member (1922); Vienna Psychoanalytic Society, chair (1925–1938); private practice in child psychoanalysis; Hampstead Center for the Psychoanalytical Study and Treatment of Children, founder. Vienna Institute, lecturer on child analysis. Died 9 October 1982 in London.

Youngest child and youngest of three daughters of famed psychologist and psychoanalyst Sigmund Freud, and Martha

Bernays Freud, Anna Freud was destined to become the caretaker of both her father and of his creation, psychoanalysis. Her professional training was her close association with her father and his associates in the Vienna Psychoanalytic Society. She began analysis by her father in 1918 at age twenty-two and began to attend the weekly scientific meetings of the Vienna Psychoanalytic Society and later on, her father's lectures on dreams and on neuroses at the Vienna University. She presented her paper on "Beating Fantasies and Daydreams" to the society in 1922 and became a full-fledged member. Soon she was accepted on the staff of the Vienna Psychoanalytic Training Institute (headed by HELENE DEUTSCH), and served as secretary. She was a lifetime member of the International Psychoanalytic Association, from 1926 (declined presidency in 1955).

Interested in analysis of children, Anna began a private practice, one of her first patients being the son of a woman who was to become her closest friend and companion, DOROTHY TIFFANY BURLINGHAM. Daughter of millionaire glass manufacturer Louis Comfort Tiffany, Burlingham left America to escape an unhappy marriage and to seek psychological help for her four children. Aware of Anna Freud's work in child analysis, she sought her help in 1925. The friendship between the two women developed rapidly and they soon shared a social as well as professional relationship. Burlingham eventually was analyzed by Sigmund Freud and studied psychoanalysis to become an early and loyal member of both the Vienna Society and the Vienna child analysis school. She and Anna Freud bonded in a supportive "sistership" and partnership, living together after Sigmund Freud's death until Burlingham's own death in 1979, Anna Freud happily taking the role of second mother to the children.

Anna Freud's series of four lectures in child psychoanalysis at the Vienna Psychoanalytic Institute became a book based on the lectures in 1927 and was translated into English in 1929 as *Introduction to the Technique of Child Analysis.* In this work, Freud clearly established the basis for her rejection of the methodology and philosophy of MELANIE KLEIN in child analysis. Freud's view was considered conservative in that it adhered to that of her father regarding the development of the superego, whereas Klein's departed radically. The schism between the two schools of thought in child psychoanalysis divided analysts for many years—the Kleinians based in London, and the Freudians in Vienna.

Because of Nazi occupation, the Freud family relocated to England, Marsefield Gardens, Hampstead, in June 1938. Sigmund Freud lived less than four months following the move. Anna Freud immersed herself in work, seeing patients within a week of her father's funeral, and taking on herself the huge task of organizing and protecting his vast holdings of manuscripts and papers. As soon as Dorothy Burlingham was able to leave America (where she had been detained by the war during a visit to her family) she joined Freud, and the two began pragmatically to respond to a need for which they were particularly suited. The war created a body of young children without adequate housing, food, or, sometimes, parents. In 1941, Burlingham and Freud opened the Children's Rest Center and soon acquired two more homes, one for older children. The homes catered to some 120 children and were staffed with caretakers, psychologists, and volunteers. Besides providing a vital service, the Hampstead Nurseries documented experiences that helped shape fostering and welfare policy, social work, and pediatrics after the war in Britain and in America. Out of the nurseries grew the Hampstead Center for the Psychoanalytical Study and Treatment of Children, which emphasized overall development of the child rather than laying too much stress on obscure preverbal periods. The center also became a training ground for child analysts. Anna Freud directed the clinic until her death in 1982.

The entire psychoanalytic establishment of Europe was virtually destroyed by the Nazis, its leaders and disciples scattered alike. After the war, Anna played an important part in the rebuilding of that network. She was instrumental in bringing many analysts out of Europe and the postwar reconstruction of psychoanalysis was based largely on the work of these refugees in England and America. Her classic work *The Ego and the Mechanisms of Defense* was published in 1936 and is still one of the core works on psychoanalytic ego psychology, extending her father's work on anxiety as a signal function of ego. *The Psychoanalytic Study of the Child,* which appeared in 1945, shortly after Freud resigned from the Psychoanalytic Institute Training Committee, began with a critique and history of Kleinian child analysis. The clash of opposing groups now assembled in Britain because of the war was mollified through compromise. A new training proposal was adapted based on the principle of separate but equal: an A Group of Kleinians; a B Group of Anna Freudians; and a middle group of independents.

Now in her fifties, Freud continued to work ceaselessly, writing, lecturing, and organizing symposia in addition to directing the Hampstead Center. She directed or consulted on the publication of her father's manuscript books and papers. Her seminars on the applications of analytic child psychology to legal issues in the 1960s at Yale University were to have far-reaching consequences. With Albert Solnit, Joseph Goldstein, and Dorothy Burlingham, she cowrote *Beyond the Best Interests of the Child* (1973), *Before the Best Interests of the Child* (1979), and *In the Best Interests of the Child*. This trilogy helped shape child custody legislation in the United States and initiated a controversy over the province of decision making that continues today.

It was not until 1971 that Freud revisited Vienna, where she was given a standing ovation at the 27th International Psychoanalytical Congress. Among the many honors she received were the Dolly Madison Award for Outstanding Service to Children; Austria's Grand Decoration of Honour of Gold; ten honorary scholastic degrees, including University of Chicago, Harvard, Yale, Clark University, University of Sheffield, University of Vienna (M.D., 1972). In March 1982, Freud suffered a stroke which left her with impaired motor and speech abilities. She suffered from longstanding anemia and died 9 October 1982.   JH

PRIMARY SOURCES

Freud, Anna. *Einführung in die Technik der Kinderanalyse: vier Vorträge am Lehrinstitut der Wiener Psychoanalytischen Vereinigung.* Vienna: Internationaler Psychoanalytischer Verlag, 1927. [*Introduction to the Technique of Child Analysis.* Trans. L. Pierce Clark. New York: Nervous and Mental Disease Publishing Co., 1928.]

———. *Einführung in die Psychoanalyse für Pädagogen, vier Vorträge.* Stuttgart: Leipzig: Hippokrates-Verlag, 1930. [*Introduction to Psycho-analysis for Teachers: Four Lectures by Anna Freud.* Trans. Barbara Low. London: Allen & Unwin, 1931.]

———. *The Ego and the Mechanisms of Defense.* Trans. Cecil Baines. London: Hogarth, 1936.

———. With Dorothy Burlingham. *Young Children in War-Time: A Year's Work in a Residential War Nursery.* London: Allen & Unwin, 1942.

———. With Dorothy Burlingham. *War and Children.* [New York: Medical War Books], 1943.

———. With Dorothy Burlingham. *Infants without Families.* London: Allen & Unwin, 1944.

———. *Safeguarding the Emotional Health of our Children: An Inquiry into the Concept of the Rejecting Mother.* New York: Child Welfare League of America, 1962.

———. *Normality and Pathology in Childhood: Assessments of Development.* New York: International Universities Press, 1965.

———. With Joseph Goldstein, et al. *Beyond the Best Interests of the Child* (1973), *Before the Best Interests of the Child* (1979), and *In the Best Interests of the Child* (posthumously). New York: Free Press, 1986.

———. *Anna Freud's Letters to Eva Rosenfeld.* Trans. Mary Weigand; ed. Peter Heller. Madison, Conn.: International University Press, 1992.

SECONDARY SOURCES

Coles, Robert. *Anna Freud: The Dream of Psychoanalysis.* Reading, Mass.: Addison-Wesley, 1992.

Dyer, R. *Her Father's Daughter: The Works of Anna Freud.* New York: Aronson, 1983.

New York Times, 10 October 1982. Obituary notice.

STANDARD SOURCES
Appignanesi; *Current Biography* 1979, 1983; O'Connell and
Russo 1990; Uglow 1982.

FREUND, IDA (1863–1914)

*Austrian/British chemist. Born 5 April 1863, Austria. Orphaned;
brought up by maternal grandparents. Brought to England by uncle,
Ludwig Strauss. Educated state school, Bürgerschule; State Training
College for Women, Vienna (teacher's diploma); Girton College
(Natural Science Tripos Part I, Class 1, 1885; Part II, Physiology, 1886). Professional experience: Cambridge Training College
for Women, lecturer (1886–1887); Newnham College, demonstrator in chemistry (1888–1891), lecturer (1891–1913), associate
(1893–1913), member of council (1896); vacation courses for science teachers at College Laboratory (1897); directed College laboratory, which closed at her retirement. Died 15 May 1914.*

Ida Freund's parents died when she was very young, and she
was brought up by her maternal grandparents in Vienna,
Austria. During her youth, she lost a leg as a result of a cy-
cling accident and disease, and the artificial leg that replaced
it was not very satisfactory. She got around by means of a tri-
cycle worked with her arms. Educated in a Vienna state
school (Bürgerschule) and at the State Training College for
Women in Vienna, she was brought to England by her maternal uncle, Ludwig Strauss, a professional violinist. She had
high praise for the Bürgerschule, which she attended by
choice after her grandparents had sent her to an expensive
but not very good private school.

Freund soon became a naturalized British subject, and
her sympathies and interests were very English, although she
still felt an affection for her native Austria. She attended
Girton College from 1882 through 1886, taking the Natural
Science Tripos in 1885 and 1886, obtaining first class honors in both parts; the second part was in physiology. Considering that she started with only a schoolgirl's knowledge
of English and with no knowledge of Greek or Latin, and
little if any of Euclid and the required algebra, it is a great
tribute to her intelligence and diligence that she passed the
required examinations within the prescribed time and obtained first-class honors in both parts of the Natural Science
Tripos.

After she passed the Tripos, she lectured at the Cambridge
Training College for Women. The rest of her career was
spent at Newnham College, Cambridge, where she rose
from demonstrator to lecturer in chemistry. She remained at
this post until her resignation in 1912 because of ill health.
In effect, she was also director of studies in chemistry and
physics at Newnham. She was associate at Newnham College and then a member of its council. Women students

were not admitted to the Cambridge University laboratory
for elementary chemistry, and all of their practical work for
the Natural Science Tripos had to be conducted in their own
laboratories. Freund arranged a course of practical work for
students, held in the old laboratory. Although the laboratory
was central to Freund's teaching, she did not confine herself
to practical work. Laboratory work was combined with papers and oral instructions. In the third year, Freund added a
course of lectures on chemical theory which traced and illustrated the history of chemical discovery. The substance of
these lectures was published in *The Study of Chemical Composition* (1904). Once the university laboratory was opened to
women students, Freund realized that the Newnham laboratory should be given up.

Freund was considered quite a character. Although she
wrote excellent English, she never mastered the spoken language. A student noted that she would break off a sentence
and say, "Have I got you wiz me in zat?" At another time she
and a student had a mild disagreement and as Freund chastised her she said, "Now, Miss X, have I got you wiz me in
the hydrochloric acid?" Although her sense of humor became legendary, first-year students were terrorized by her
sharp rebukes for silly mistakes. They soon realized, however,
that she had nothing but their best interests at heart. Immediately before the all-important Tripos examination, she
would summon her chemistry students and require them to
do a special study. In 1907, she suggested that her students go
to the laboratory and study the lives of famous chemists.
When they arrived they found large boxes of chocolates
with a different life history and picture of a famous chemist
in each. In another year they were to make a further study of
the periodic table. They found a large periodic table set out
in the laboratory. This table, however, differed from the ordinary periodic table. The elements were iced cakes each with
its name and atomic weight in icing. The numbers were
made of chocolate (Phillips, 71–72).

Ida Freund is best known for her interest in science education. Her two excellent chemistry textbooks show the
breadth of her knowledge. In 1897, she instituted a vacation
course for science teachers at the Newnham College laboratory, which was under her charge. After her retirement, the
laboratory was closed. She arranged for natural science students who had taken their Tripos and had gone to teach in
schools to come to Cambridge to learn how to construct
simple instruments themselves. She taught them to make the
best of the conditions that they had to endure in teaching
and also kept them abreast of progress in the natural sciences.

Freund treated her students in many ways as if they were
her own children. After they left Newnham, she kept in
close personal contact with many of them. Therefore, when
she resigned, her students initiated a fund that expanded after

her death to be used for holiday courses in girls' schools, like the successful one at Newnham Freund had taught. Physics rather than chemistry was the subject that concerned her most in school teaching. She regarded physics as the most fundamental subject and one that was most often neglected in girls' schools—and when it was taught, taught badly. One of the major reasons for this neglect was the expensive equipment required for teaching physics. The outbreak of World War I hindered the collection of further funds; nevertheless, in August 1914, Freund was able to organize a vacation course on mechanics, electricity, and magnetism for women teachers in secondary schools. This course was held at the Cavendish Laboratory with the permission of the professor Sir J. J. Thomason, and taught by the Reverend W. Burton, headmaster of Sir Roger Manwood's School, Sandwich, and late senior science master at The Whitgift School, Croydon. The course was a great success.

Throughout her life, Freund suffered from ill health. Even with the loss of her leg, she would sometimes take long excursions around the neighborhood. Later, she lost the use of one eye after many attempts to save it, and finally died of an "internal" problem, which necessitated an operation that her weak condition did not allow her to survive. She died 15 May 1914 at the age of fifty-one. Freund strongly supported the woman's suffrage movement and left a generous amount in her will to the Women's University Settlement in Southwark. In April 1998 the "Old Laboratory" where she reigned during the early part of the twentieth century was restored as a memorial to Freund and the other Newnham scientists who worked there.   MBO

PRIMARY SOURCES

Freund, Ida. *The Experimental Basis of Chemistry.* Ed. M. B. Thomas and A. Hutchinson. Cambridge: Cambridge University Press, 1920.

———. *The Study of Chemical Composition.* 1904. Reprint, New York: Dover Publications, 1968.

SECONDARY SOURCES

Wilson, H. "Miss Freund." *A Newnham Anthology.* Ed. Ann Phillips. Cambridge: Cambridge University Press, 1979.

Sidgwick, Mrs. "Ida Freund Memorial: Vacation Course for Women Teachers of Physics." Address given by Mrs. Sidgwick at Newnham College on 7 August 1915. Newnham College Archives.

Thomas, M. Beatrice. "The Ida Freund Memorial." In *Newnham College Letter (Newnham College Club).* Cambridge, Mass.: Printed for Private Circulation, 1911.

STANDARD SOURCES

Newnham, vol. 1.

FRIANT, M. (fl. 1930s–1950s)

French comparative anatomist and prehistoric anthropologist. Never married. Professional experience: Muséum National d'Histoire Naturelle, Laboratoire d'Anatomie Comparee, associate director (sous-directrice) (1931?–1956). Honors and memberships: Societe d'Anthropologie, member (1931).

M. Friant was a French comparative anatomist and prehistoric anthropologist. Her research in the early 1930s ranged from the studies of the increasing size of primary schoolgirls in comparison with schoolboys from the Moselle region in the early 1930s, to studies of prehistoric cave mammals found in Vienne, France, by end of that decade.   JH/MBO

PRIMARY SOURCES

Friant, M. "La croissance en taille et en poids des écoliers mosellans de sept à dix ans." *Bulletin et Memoires Société d'Anthropologie (BMSAP)* 20 (1930): 1–3.

———. "La croissance en taille et en poids des écolières mosellans de dix a treize ans." *BMSAP* 1931: 11.

———. "Les écolières de la Moselle . . . entre sept et douze ans et comparisons avec les ecoliers mosellans." *BMSAP* 1931: 17.

———. "Quelques Mammifières moustériens de la grotte des Cottet (Vienne)." *BMSAP* 1939: 175.

FRIEDLANDER, KATE (1895–1949)

Austrian/British psychoanalyst. Educated Berlin Institute (psychoanalysis); London (M.D., 1936?). Honors and memberships: British Psycho-analytic Society (from 1938).

Trained as a psychoanalyst at the Berlin Institute, Kate Friedlander read her membership paper for the Vienna Psychoanalytic Society in March 1933, but left Germany for London at the invitation of Dr. Ernest Jones shortly afterward. She worked closely with Anna Freud and took an active part in the business and discussions of scientific issues of the British Society. She was a founder of the West Sussex Child Guidance Unit and helped to start the Hampstead Child Therapy Training Course, which trained staff for the guidance unit. She was particularly interested in the treatment of juvenile delinquents.   JH/MBO

SECONDARY SOURCES

King, Pearl, and Riccardo Steiner. "Biographical Notes on the Main Participants." In *The Freud-Klein Controversies, 1941–1945,* ed. Pearl King and Riccardo Steiner. New York: Routledge, 1991.

FRIEDMANN, FRIEDERIKE (fl. 1911)

German/Austrian physicist. Educated (doctorate, University of Vienna?). Professional experience: Vienna Institute for Radium Research, researcher.

Friederike Friedmann conducted research at the Vienna Institute for Radium Research on the absorption and range of alpha particles. Her finding that uranium emitted two sets of alpha particles supported the view that uranium consisted of two chemically inseparable components. Friedmann confirmed Karl Herzfeld's theoretical prediction that some alpha particles would exceed their expected range. These experiments were significant for measurements which involved counting particles, an especially popular method and research topic in Vienna.   MM

PRIMARY SOURCES

Friedmann, Friederike. "Bestimmung der Reichweite der α-Strahlen des Poloniums." *Akademie der Wissenschaften, Vienna. Sitzungsberichte 2a* 120 (1911): 1361–1371.

———. "Experimentelle Bestimmung der Schwankungen in der Reichweite bei den einzelnen α-Teilchen." *Akademie der Wissenschaften, Vienna. Sitzungsberichte* 122 (1913): 1269–1280.

SECONDARY SOURCES

Rutherford, Ernest. *Radioactive Substances and Their Radiations.* Cambridge: Cambridge University Press, 1913.

STANDARD SOURCES

Meyer and von Schweidler.

FRIEND, CHARLOTTE (1921–1987)

U.S. microbiologist. Born 11 March 1921 in Lower Manhattan, New York City. Never married. Educated Hunter College (B.A., 1944); Yale University (Ph.D., 1950). Professional experience: U.S. Navy, hematology laboratory, laboratory technician (1944); Sloan-Kettering Institute for Cancer Research, associate member (1946–1966); Department of Cell Biology at Mount Sinai Hospital, professor and director. Died 13 January 1987 of lymphoma.

Charlotte Friend was daughter of Russian immigrants. Her father was a successful businessman. However, after his death, the bulk of his estate was lost in the 1929 stock market crash. Family members were very important to Friend and, for their part, they were supportive of her. She attended Hunter College High School, a tuition-free school for gifted students. During her college years, she worked in a doctor's office. After graduation, she joined the navy, where she worked in the hematology laboratory at the naval hospital in Shoemaker, California. This experience confirmed her goal of becoming a scientist. After she was discharged from the navy, she worked for the Public Health Service for a short time. She did graduate work at Yale University with the help of the G.I. Bill of Rights and earned her doctoral degree in 1950. In 1946, she went to work for Sloan-Kettering Institute, where she remained until 1966, and won awards for her cancer research, including the Alfred Sloan Award in Cancer Research from the American Cancer Society. Friend left Sloan-Kettering in 1966 to become professor and director of the Center for Experimental Cell Biology, Mt. Sinai School of Medicine. She continued her research at Mt. Sinai, where she remained until her death. Her responsibilities were almost entirely in research. This suited her, for she disliked teaching. However, she also disliked applying for grants, a necessary task she forced herself to do. She insisted that Mt. Sinai strike a balance between clinical care and basic scientific research.

A strong supporter of women in the sciences, Friend supported the representation of women in seminars and on committees. She served as a mentor to new researchers and was highly respected by her colleagues. She also became involved in issues such as faculty rights and tenure disputes.

Diagnosed with lymphoma in 1981, Friend kept it a secret for she did not want grant reviewers of manuscripts she had submitted to be influenced. While she was undergoing therapy, she continued her work as usual.

Among her many honors and awards, Friend received the Presidential Medal Centennial Award, Hunter College in 1970, the Virus-Cancer Program Award of the National Institutes of Health (1974), the Prix Griffuel (1979), and an honorary doctorate from Brandeis University (1986).

JH/MBO

PRIMARY SOURCES

Friend, Charlotte. "The Coming of Age of Tumor Virology: Presidential Address." *Cancer Research* 37 (1977): 1255–1263.

SECONDARY SOURCES

Diamond, L. "Charlotte Friend (1921–1987)." *Nature* 326 (1987): 748.

Diamond, L., and S. R. Wolman. "Charlotte Friend, Ph.D., 1921–1987; A Scientist's Life." *Annals of the New York Academy of Sciences* 567 (1989): 1–13.

Rapp, F. "The Friend Legacy: From Mouse to Man." *Annals of the New York Academy of Sciences* 567 (1989): 349–353.

Who's Who in Frontier Science and Technology. Chicago: Marquis, 1984.

STANDARD SOURCES

AMS B 9, P&B 10–14; *Notable;* Shearer and Shearer 1996; *Who's Who of American Women; WW in America,* vol. 9, 1985.

FRITZ, MADELEINE ALBERTA (1896–1990)

Canadian paleontologist. Born 3 November 1896 along Bay of Fundy, Saint John, New Brunswick, Canada. Never married. Educated McGill University, Montreal, (A.B., 1919); University of Toronto (M.A., 1923; Ph.D., 1926). Professional experience: Royal Ontario Museum, associate director (1936–1955), curator of invertebrate paleontology (1955–1957); University of Toronto, professor of paleontology (1956–1967); Royal Ontario Museum, professor emerita in the department of geology and research associate in the department of invertebrate paleontology (1967–1990). Honors and memberships: Geological Association of Canada, Fellow; Geological Society of America, Fellow; Royal Society of Canada, Fellow; Centennial Medal of Canada (1967). Died 20 August 1990.

Born in New Brunswick along the Bay of Fundy, Madeleine Fritz was exposed to tiny marine invertebrates through playing along the seashore. As a child, she sailed around the world with her sea captain father. Her interest in fossil invertebrates developed while she was a student at the University of Toronto.

Fritz was well known for her papers on fossil Bryozoa. She was a member or fellow of a number of societies, including the Geological Association of Canada, the Geological Society of America, and the Paleontological Society. She was the second woman in Canada to be named a Fellow of the Royal Society of Canada (1942), and she received the Centennial Medal of Canada (1967).

JH/MBO

PRIMARY SOURCES

Fritz, Madeleine Alberta. "Hydrozoa, Enchinodermata, Trilobata, and Markings." In Part 3 of *The Stratigraphy and Palaeontology of Toronto and Vicinity.* Toronto: C. W. James for *Ontario Department of Mines,* 1923.

———. "Two Unique Silurian Corals." *Journal of Paleontology* 13, no. 5 (1939).

———. *Bryozoa (mainly Trypostomata) from the Ottawa Formation.* Ottawa: E. Cloutier, 1957.

SECONDARY SOURCES

Monteith, John. "Memorial to Madeleine Alberta Fritz, 1896–1990." *Geological Society of America, Memorials* 23 (1993): 95–98. Includes portrait.

Sherriff, Barbara L., and Shelley Reuter. "Notable Canadian Women in the History of Geology." *Geoscience Canada* 21, no. 3 (1994): 123–125.

FROMM, ERIKA OPPENHEIMER (1910–)

German/American experimental (Gestalt) psychologist. Born 23 December 1910 in Frankfurt, Germany, to Siegfried and Clementine (Stern) Oppenheimer. Two siblings; five half-siblings). Married Paul Fromm (20 July 1928). One daughter. Educated University of Frankfurt, Germany (Ph.D., magna cum laude, 1933); psychoanalytic training, Chicago Institute for Psychoanalysis (late 1940s–early 1950s). Professional experience: Psychiatric Clinic of the University of Amsterdam, research assistant, psychology laboratory; Asylum in Apeldoorn, clinical diagnostician; Michael Reese Hospital, Chicago, psychologist; Northwestern University Medical School, faculty (1954–1961); University of Chicago, professor of psychology (1961–retirement). Honors and memberships: Society of Clinical and Experimental Hypnosis, award for best paper in experimental hypnosis (1965); American Psychological Association, Fellow; American Orthopsychiatric Association (past director); American Association for the Advancement of Science; Society of Clinical and Experimental Hypnosis (past executive secretary); American Society for Clinical Hypnosis; Society for Projective Techniques.

Erika Oppenheimer was born 23 December 1910 in Frankfurt, Germany, the eldest of three children of Siegfried and Clementine (Stern) Oppenheimer, who were Orthodox Jews. Her father, a physician, was widowed when Erika was eight years old. Left with three children, he married his sister-in-law and fathered five more children. As the eldest, Erika took an active part in supervising and entertaining her younger siblings. Very bright, curious, and compassionate, Erika decided early in life that she could have the career she wanted helping others, and still fill the traditional family role. In 1928 she married Paul Fromm. She was trained in experimental psychology under Gestalt theorist Max Wertheimer in Frankfurt, Germany, and received her doctorate *magna cum laude,* at the University of Frankfurt in 1933.

Because of Nazi encroachment, she fled two weeks later to Holland. There she worked as research assistant at the Psychology Laboratory of the Psychiatric Clinic of the University of Amsterdam. She wrote to Wertheimer and Wolfgang Köhler, who had emigrated to the United States, asking for help getting a job in the States. They discouraged her, saying there were no jobs for psychologists, and even advised that she leave the field. Erika continued to work in Amsterdam until early 1938. At that point, the war escalated and it became apparent that Holland would be taken by the Nazis. Erika and Paul Fromm fled to the United States, to Chicago, Illinois, with their daughter, Joan.

Erika Fromm worked briefly at Michael Reese Hospital in Chicago; was on the medical school faculty at Northwestern University (1954–1961); and became professor of psychology at the University of Chicago (1961–retirement), where she conducted clinical research in experimental studies of hypnosis. She took her psychoanalytic training at the Chicago Institute for Psychoanalysis in the late 1940s and early 1950s, but was denied a degree (with others) because of the American Psychoanalytic Association rule that only medical doctors could be psychoanalysts. She campaigned many years for psychologists to be fully admitted as psychoanalysts, helping to form the first Psychologists Interested in the Study of Psychoanalysis (later the APA Division for Psychoanalysis, Division 39). She published *Intelligence—A Dynamic Approach* with L. D. Hartman in 1955. In 1964, she published with Thomas M. French a text on dream interpretation.

Fromm began research into hypnosis and hypnoanalysis partly seeking a means of shortening the lengthy, very expensive therapy process and thereby making it available to more people. She found hypnosis to be a way to access the unconscious more quickly than in psychoanalysis. She noted that when it is pursued by trained experts, hypnosis is a safe way to pierce the unconscious. Fromm published many articles and papers on the subject and taught clinical as well as experimental hypnosis at the University of Chicago and at continuing education workshops across the United States and in Europe.

JH/MBO

PRIMARY SOURCES

Fromm, Erika. With E. Oppenheimer. "Optische versuche über ruhe und bewegung." *Psychologische Forschung* 20 (1934): 1–46.

———. "Spontaneous Auto Hypnotic Age-Regression in a Nocturnal Dream." *International Journal of Clinical and Experimental Hypnosis* 13 (1965): 119–131.

———. "Transference and Countertransference in Hypnoanalysis." *International Journal of Clinical and Experimental Hypnosis* 16 (1972): 77–84.

———. "Ego Activity and Ego Passivity in Hypnosis." *International Journal of Clinical and Experimental Hypnosis* 20 (1972): 238–251.

———. "Selfhypnosis: A New Area of Research." *Psychotherapy: Theory, Research and Practice* 12 (1975): 295–301.

———. "Altered States of Consciousness and Ego Psychology." *Social Service Review* 50 (1976): 557–569.

———. With T. M. French. *Dream Interpretation: A New Approach.* 2d. ed. New York: International Universities Press, 1984. Originally published 1964.

SECONDARY SOURCES

Fass, Margot, and Daniel Brown, eds. *Creative Mastery in Hypnosis and Hypnoanalysis: A Festschrift for Erika Fromm.* Hillsdale, N.J.: Lawrence Erlbaum, 1990.

Quack, Sibylle, ed. *Between Sorrow and Strength: Women Refugees of the Nazi Period.* Washington, D.C.: German Historical Institute, 1995. Fromm discussed pages 249–250, 263–264.

STANDARD SOURCES

Debus; O'Connell and Russo 1988.

FROSTIG, MARIANNE BELLAK (1906–1985)

Austrian/U.S. psychologist. Born 31 March 1906 in Vienna, Austria, to Edda Silberstein and Arnold Bellak. Two siblings. Married Peter Jacob Frostig (neuropsychiatrist) (1924). Two children. Educated University of Vienna, audited courses; College of Social Work Training, Vienna; Hellerau Laxenburg Institute; New School for Social Research, New York City (A.B., 1946); Claremont (Calif.) Graduate School (M.A., 1948); University of Southern California (Ph.D. in educational psychology, 1955). Professional experience: Psychiatric Hospital, Poland, director of rehabilitation (1932–1937); Marianne Frostig Center of Educational Therapy, founder and executive director (1947–1972), emerita executive director (1972–1985); Mount Saint Mary's College, Calif., professor of education (from 1969); Los Angeles County, school psychologist (1949–1955); University of Southern California, clinical professor (1966). Honors and memberships: American Association for the Advancement of Science, Fellow; American Psychological Association, Fellow; American Orthopsychiatric Association, Fellow. Died 1985.

Marianne Bellak was born in Vienna. She and her two younger siblings were educated by governesses, then attended local schools where the precocious Bellak soon became bored and disillusioned. She audited courses at the University of Vienna and became a member of the salon of Karl and CHARLOTTE BÜHLER. When the College of Social Work Training was closed, Bellak transferred to the Hellerau Laxenburg, an institute that taught physical education and rhythmics, which she was to use years later in working with learning-disabled children. At the Hellerau, she worked with August Aichhorn, Hans Hoff, and Paul Schilder (who became the husband of LAURETTA BENDER).

In 1924, Bellak married a Polish neuropsychiatrist, Peter Jacob Frostig, and worked for him in his private practice and in the small private hospital near Warsaw that he administered, from 1929 to 1938. As Frostig's wife, she was able (without degree or credentials) to work in medical laboratories and in rehabilitation and behavior therapy with patients, including schizophrenic patients. Her first child, Anna-Marie, was born in 1933.

In 1939, the Frostigs emigrated to New York where their son was born. Frostig soon realized she would need a degree to continue her work and enrolled at the New School for Social Research in 1945, achieving her bachelor's degree within one year. After the family moved to California, Frostig taught in public schools, then enrolled at Claremont Graduate School, where she resumed her friendship with Charlotte Bühler. Frostig received her master's from Claremont in 1948 and her doctorate from the University of Southern California in 1954 (one year after the death of her husband). At Claremont, Frostig developed an interest in the educability of the mentally retarded and in 1947 began a partnership with Bell

Dubnoff to establish a school for brain-injured children. There they experimented with a wide range of diagnostic tests, educational therapies, and teaching techniques designed to help each child realize his or her full potential. The Marianne Frostig School of Educational Therapy (later the Marianne Frostig Center) developed an interdisciplinary approach to suit Frostig's holistic view. She published several books and her Frostig Developmental Test of Visual Perception was widely used for many years.

Frostig was very influential in special education circles and received many awards and honors, primarily from lay groups such as the Advance Institute for Leadership Personnel in learning disabilities. She was a Fellow of the American Association for the Advancement of Science; Association for Children with Learning Disabilities; American Psychological Association; American Education Research Association; American Orthopsychiatric Association; and Society for Research in Child Development.   JH/MBO

PRIMARY SOURCES

Frostig, Marianne. With Welty Lefever and John R. B. Whittlesey. *Developmental Test of Visual Perception*. Palo Alto, Calif.: Consulting Psychologists Press, 1963.
———. *The Frostig Program for the Development of Visual Perception*. Chicago: Follett, 1964.
———. *Teacher's Guides to Beginning, Intermediate, and Advanced Pictures and Patterns*. Chicago: Follett, 1966–1967.
———. Frostig *Move, Grow, Learn: Movement Education*. Chicago: Follett, 1969.
———. With Phyllis Maslow. *Learning Problems in the Classroom: Prevention and Remediation*. New York: Grune, 1973.

STANDARD SOURCES
AMS S&B 10–13; Stevens and Gardner.

FULFORD, MARGARET HANNAH (1904–)

U.S. botanist. Born 14 June 1904 in Cincinnati, Ohio, to Lotty May (Holloway) and Alfred T. Fulford. Educated University of Cincinnati (B.A., 1926; B.E., 1927; M.A., 1928); Yale University (Ph.D., 1935). Professional experience: University of Cincinnati, instructor (1927–1940), curator of herbarium (1927–1974), assistant professor (1940–1946), associate professor (1946–1954), professor (1954–1974), professor emerita of Botany (from 1974). Honors and memberships: American Association for the Advancement of Science, Fellow; Ohio Academy of Science, Fellow; Indiana Academy of Sciences, Fellow; Guggenheim Fellow (1941–1942); Botanical Society of America, Certificate of Merit; American Association of University Women, Achievement Award.

Margaret Fulford had an important career as a bryologist. She received her first degrees from the University of Cincinnati and her doctorate from Yale University. She taught at the University of Cincinnati, progressing up the academic ladder to professor in 1954. She supervised seven dissertations and thirteen theses.

Fulford was very active in scientific organizations. She belonged to many professional societies, including the American Bryological Society (curator of Hepaticae), American Institute of Biological Sciences, American Society of Plant Taxonomists, Botanical Society of America, British Bryological Society, International Association of Plant Taxonomy, International Association of Plant Morphologists, International Commission for Nomenclature for the International Botanical Congress, Society for the Study of Evolution, and Sigma Xi. She was a Fellow of the American Association for the Advancement of Science, the Indiana Academy of Sciences, and the Ohio Academy of Science. She received the Cincinnati Branch of the American Association of University Women Achievement Award, was a Fellow of the Graduate School, University of Cincinnati, and received the Certificate of Merit from the Botanical Society of America. She was a Daniel Eaton Fellow, Yale University (1931–1932), New York Botanical Garden Scholar (summers 1938–1939), a Guggenheim Fellow (Harvard University, Yale University, and the New York Botanical Garden, 1941–1942), and a Marshall Howe Fellow, New York Botanical Garden (1943–1944). Fulford received four grants from the National Science Foundation and one from the American Philosophical Society and the Ohio Academy of Science.

Fulford's early research was basically taxonomic, including publications of local studies of bryophytes and lichens. However, her systematic concepts have been influenced by her investigations into the morphology, physiology, ecology, and geography of the bryophytes, giving her a complete overview of the group. In her developmental studies, she considered patterns of sporeling development and regeneration in hepatics. In her physiological investigation, she manipulated culture conditions to observe the effects on hepatics. She also studied distribution patterns on the Hepaticae. She noted that disjunct taxa supported the concept of continental drift long before it became fashionable to do so. Fulford is credited with important contributions to the development of modern bryological methods and concepts.

JH/MBO

PRIMARY SOURCES

Fulford, Margaret Hannah. "Sporelings and Vegetative Reproduction in the Genus *Ceratolejeunea*." *Bulletin of the Torrey Botanical Club* 171 (1944): 638–654.
———. "Recent Interpretations of the Hepaticae." *Botanical Review* 14 (1948): 227–273.
———. "Distribution Patterns of the Genera of Leafy Hepaticae of South America." *Evolution* 5 (1951): 243–264.

———. "Sporelings, Gemmalings, and Regeneration in *Isopaches bicrenatus*." *Bryologist* 58 (1955): 317–322.

———. With V. Diller and H. Kersten. "Culture Studies on *Sphaerocarpos* I." *Bryologist* 58 (1955): 173–192.

SECONDARY SOURCES
Stotler, Raymond E. "Margaret H. Fulford—A Tribute." *Bryologist* 90, no. 4 (1987): 285–286. Includes portrait.

STANDARD SOURCES
AMS, 2–6; Stuckey.

FULHAME, ELIZABETH (fl. 1794)
British chemist.

Little is known of Elizabeth Fullhame's life or of the background for her interest in chemistry. In the preface to her *Essay on Combustion* (1794), she explains that her doctor husband and his friends had discussed, but dismissed as impractical, "the possibility of making cloths of gold, silver, and other metals by chemical processes" and that this problem has intrigued her for many years. She "imagined in the beginning, that a few experiments would determine the problem; but experience soon convinced [her], that a very great number indeed were necessary before such an art could be brought to any tolerable degree of perfection" (Fulhame, iii).

Fulhame's original purpose was to find a practical application for her experiments:

Some time after this period, I found the invention was applicable to painting, and would also contribute to facilitate the study of geography: for I have applied it to some maps, the rivers of which I represented in silver, and in the cities in gold. The rivers appearing, as it were, in silver streams, have a most pleasing effect on the sight, and relieve the eye of that painful search for the course, and origin, of rivers, the minutest branches of which can be splendidly represented in this way. (Fulhame, iv)

She soon ventured into the theoretical realm, however, developing her own theory of combustion. Although she accepted Lavoisier's nomenclature, she rejected portions of his theory of combustion. Neither, however, did she find the tenets of the older phlogiston theory acceptable, noting that "combustible bodies do not reduce the metals by giving them phlogiston, as the Phlogistians suppose; nor by uniting with, and separating their oxygen, as the Anti-phlogistians maintain" (Fulhame, iv). To replace these theories, Fulhame posited that when combustion occurs, "one body, at least, is oxygenated, and another restored, at the same time, to its combustible state." Defining oxygenation as the union of oxygen with combustible bodies to their combustible state, she assumed that whenever combustion occurs water is decomposed. Consequently, as one body is oxygenated by the oxygen of the water, the other at the same time is restored to its combustible state by the hydrogen of the water. She concluded "that the hydrogen of water is the only substance that restores bodies to their combustible state," and "that water is the only source of the oxygen, which oxygenates combustible bodies." "This view of combustion," Fulhame asserted, "may serve to show how nature is always the same, and maintains her equilibrium by preserving the same quantities of air and water on the surface of our globe: for as fast as these are consumed in the various processes of combustion, equal quantities are formed, and rise regenerated like the Phoenix from her ashes" (Fulhame, 179–180).

Fear that she would be harshly criticized as a woman engaged in inappropriate activities, almost kept Fulhame from publishing. However, when a respected scientist read portions of her work in 1793 and reacted favorably, she took courage. The *Essay*, published in 1794, established her reputation among contemporary chemists. She was elected an honorary member of the Philadelphia Chemical Society, and her book was reprinted there in 1810. Benjamin Thompson, Count Rumford (1753–1814), repeated the experiments of "the ingenious and lively Mrs. Fulhame on the reduction of gold salts by light" (Partington, 3:708–709).

Elizabeth Fulhame not only participated in the observational-experimental aspects of science, but also developed a theoretical explanation for her observations. She is significant as one of the few women of her time to do both.

JH/MBO

PRIMARY SOURCES
Fulhame, Elizabeth. *An Essay on Combustion with a View to a New Art of Dying and Painting: Wherein the Phlogistic Hypotheses are Proved Erroneous.* London: J. Cooper, 1794.

SECONDARY SOURCES
Partington, J. R. A. *A History of Chemistry.* 4 vols. London: Macmillan, 1962. Includes a bibliography of the various editions of Fulhame's work as well as a listing of secondary references.

FURNESS, CAROLINE ELLEN (1869–1936)
U.S. astronomer. Born 24 June 1869 in Cleveland, Ohio, to Caroline Sarah (Baker) and Henry Benjamin Furness. Never married. Educated Vassar College (A.B., 1891); Columbia University (Ph.D., 1900). Professional experience: high schools in Connecticut and Ohio (1891–1894); Vassar College, assistant, observatory (1894–1898, 1899–1903), instructor in astronomy (1903–

1911), associate professor (1911–1915), director, observatory (from 1911). Honors and memberships: Royal Astronomical Society, Fellow; British Astronomical Association, Fellow; Astronomische Gesellschaft, Fellow; Astronomical Society, member; Association of Variable Star Observers. Died 9 February 1936.

Caroline Furness earned her bachelor's degree from Vassar College, and worked as an assistant at the observatory while working on her doctoral degree at Columbia. After she got this degree, she became an instructor in astronomy and rose through the academic ranks to associate professor. She became director of the observatory as well. Furness spent the summers of 1900–1901 as a research assistant at the Yerkes Observatory, and in 1908 went to the astrophysical laboratory at Gröningen. She was a member of the Astronomical Society and the Association of Variable Star Observers, and a Fellow of the Royal Astronomical Society, the British Astronomical Association, and the Astronomische Gesellschaft. Her research was on the reduction of astronomical photographs, being especially concerned with the reduction of photographs near the North Pole. She also made telescopic observations of asteroids and observed variable stars. Furness was also interested in the history of astronomy. She visited Asian science institutions throughout the world. Probably because of her interest in Asian institutions, she was a delegate to the third Pan-Pacific Congress in Japan in 1926. She was the editor of *Observations of Variable Stars Made at Vassar College* (1901–1912).   JH/MBO

PRIMARY SOURCES

Furness, Caroline. *Catalog of Stars within 1 Degree of the North Pole.* Poughkeepsie, N.Y.: Vassar College Observatory, Ph.D. dissertation. 1900.

———. *Catalog of Stars within 2 Degrees of the North Pole.* Washington, D.C.: Carnegie Institution of Washington, 1905.

———. *Introduction to the Study of Variable Stars.* Boston: Houghton Mifflin, 1915.

STANDARD SOURCES

AMS 1–5; Debus.

FUSS, MARGARITA (1555–1626)

German midwife. Born in Havelberg. Mother a noblewoman and accoucheuse. Married. Educated by her mother; Strasburg and Cologne. Professional experience: midwife. Died 1626 in Havelberg.

Margarita Fuss's mother was a noblewoman and a midwife. After an unfortunate marriage, Margarita was forced to earn a living, so she studied midwifery with her mother. In order to learn more, she went to Strasburg and Cologne. Her fame spread, and she was soon asked to travel to Germany, Holland, and Denmark for consultations in obstetrics. Called "Mother Greta," Fuss adopted a peculiar form of dress, wearing a full red-and-black-striped skirt and a soldier's jacket reminiscent of the Hungarian hussars. She carried a medical bag with the snake of Aesculapius embroidered on it on one arm and in her hand she carried a gold-headed cane. When the weather was cold, she wore a large cape trimmed with yellow fox fur. Her eccentricities were accepted, and she was a notable figure at court. At her death the bells of Havelberg Cathedral were rung in her honor.   JH/MBO

SECONDARY SOURCES

Siebold, Edouard Casper Jacob von. *Essai d'une Histoire de l'Obstétricie.* Trans. F. J. Herrgott. Paris: Steinheil, 1891–1892. Originally published in German.

STANDARD SOURCES

Hurd-Mead 1938.

G

GABLER, ANNA (fl. 1920)

German?/Austrian? physicist. Professional experience: Vienna Institute for Radium Research, researcher.

Little is known about Anna Gabler's life and education. Working at the Vienna Institute for Radium Research, she studied the effects of an electric field on the spatial distribution of radium decay products, which were transported through radioactive recoil and the movements of neutral gas molecules.   MM

PRIMARY SOURCES
Gabler, Anna. "Über die Ausbeute an aktivem Niederschlag des Radiums im elektrischen Felde." *Akademie der Wissenschaften, Vienna. Sitzungsberichte* 129 (1920): 201–220.

STANDARD SOURCES
Meyer and von Schweidler.

GAGE, CATHERINE (1816–1892)

Irish botanist. Born 1816 on Rathlin Island, County Antrim. Died 16 February 1892 on Rathlin Island.

Catherine Gage was known for her collections and drawings of Rathlin Island plants.   JH/MBO

PRIMARY SOURCES
Gage, Catherine. "Plants found in the Island of Rathlin." *Annals and Magazine of Natural History* 5 (1850): 145–146.

SECONDARY SOURCES
Proceedings of the Belfast Naturalist Club 2 (1913): 620.
Irish Naturalist 22 (1913): 26.

STANDARD SOURCES
Barnhart; Desmond; Praeger.

GAGE, SUSANNA PHELPS (1857–1915)

U.S. embryologist and comparative anatomist. Born 26 December 1857 in Morrisville, N.Y., to Mary (Austin) and Henry Phelps. Married Simon Gage (15 December 1881). One son, Henry. Educated Morrisville Union School; Cazenovia (N.Y.) Seminary; Cornell University (Ph.B., 1880). Died 15 October 1915.

Susanna Phelps, the daughter of a businessman and a former schoolteacher, supplemented her educational experience by participating in investigations at the Bermuda Biological Station (1904) and at thze Harvard and Johns Hopkins medical schools (1904–1905). In 1881 she married Simon Gage, who taught histology and embryology at Cornell, and from that time she never held a position of her own. The couple had one son, Henry Phelps Gage, who received a Ph.D. from Cornell. Although Gage was a creative investigator, her work was too often seen as an extension of her husband's.

Susanna Gage engaged in research on the structure of muscle, the comparative morphology of the brain, the development of the human brain, and the comparative anatomy of the nervous system. Her published papers, though few in number, indicate a talent for careful, accurate work. She was an artist as well as a writer, and illustrated scientific papers for her husband and for Burt G. Wilder. Starred in the second edition of *American Men of Science,* she was elected a Fellow of the American Association for the Advancement of Science and of the American Anatomists.

In 1917, two years after Gage's death, her husband and son established the Susanna Phelps Gage Fund for Research in Physics. Even though Gage was a biologist rather than a physicist, they chose physics for the fund, to recognize that she was the first woman to take laboratory work in physics at Cornell.   JH/MBO

PRIMARY SOURCES
Gage, Susanna. "The Intramuscular Endings of Fibres in the Skeletal Muscles of Domestic and Laboratory Animals." In

Proceedings of the American Society of Microscopists, 13th Annual Meeting, 132–139. Washington, D.C.: Judd and Detweiler, 1891.

STANDARD SOURCES
AMS 1–2; Bailey; Barr; Rossiter 1982; Shearer and Shearer 1996.

GAIGE, HELEN (THOMPSON) (1889–1976)

U.S. zoologist. Born 24 November 1889 in Bad Axe, Mich. Married Frederick McMahon Gaige. Educated University of Michigan (A.B., 1909; A.M.; 1910). Professional experience: Museum of Zoology, University of Michigan, assistant (1910–1918), assistant curator of reptiles and amphibians (1918–1923), curator of amphibians (1923–1940); Copeia, editor in chief (from 1937). Died 24 October 1976.

Helen Thompson was born in a small town in Michigan and attended the University of Michigan, where she obtained bachelor's and master's degrees. She then joined the Museum of Zoology at the University of Michigan, where she met her husband, Frederick McMahon Gaige. He joined the museum in 1913 and became director in 1928 and became an instructor and associate professor at the University. Helen Gaige became assistant curator of reptiles and amphibians and then curator of amphibians. As a significant member of the Society of Ichthyology and Herpetology, she became editor in chief of its journal, *Copeia.* Her research concerned the geographical distribution, and habits and life histories of amphibians. In the 1930s, she wrote extensively on Central American amphibians and reptiles. A list of her publications is held at the Museum of Zoology, University of Michigan.

JH/MBO

PRIMARY SOURCES
Thompson, Helen. With Alexander B. Ruthven and Crystal Thompson. The Herpetology of Michigan. Lansing, Mich.: Wynkoop, Hallenbeck, Crawford, 1912.
Gaige, Helen Thompson. The Amphibians and Reptiles Collected by the Bryant Walker Expedition to Schoolcraft County, Michigan. Ann Arbor: University of Michigan, 1915.

STANDARD SOURCES
AMS 3, 7; Rossiter 1982.

GALABERT, RENÉE (fl. 1923)

French physicist. Professional experience: Paris Radium Institute, researcher (1919–1934).

Galabert began working in the Paris Radium Institute under MARIE CURIE in 1919. In 1923, she was put in charge of the institute's Service des Mesures, a position she held until her resignation in January 1934. MM

SECONDARY SOURCES
Joliot-Curie, Irène, ed. *Oeuvres de Marie Sklodowska Curie.* Warsaw: Polish Academy of Sciences, 1954. Galabert mentioned page 604.
Records in archives of the Institut Curie, assembled by Mme. Monique Bordry.

GALINDO, BEATRIX (1473–1535)

Spanish philosopher, teacher of medicine, and Latin teacher. Born 1473. Professional experience: University of Salamanca, professor of Latin and philosophy.

Beatrix Galindo was educated in Italy and was a friend of Queen Isabella of Castille. Queen Isabella was a patron of the university of Salamanca where Beatrix Galindo was a professor of Latin and philosophy (including medicine). Galindo reputedly wore the habit of a nun or abbess. According to Hurd-Mead, she founded a hospital in Madrid, which still exists; her name is inscribed in its record of officials. JH/MBO

SECONDARY SOURCES
Diccionario Manual Enciclopédico de la Lengua Española e Hispano-Americana. Madrid: Editorial "Saturnino Calleja," 1924.
Rashdall, Hastings. *The Universities of Europe in the Middle Ages.* London: Oxford University Press, 1936.

STANDARD SOURCES
Hurd-Mead 1938; Lipinska 1900.

GALVANI, LUCIA (GALEAZZI) (d. ca. 1790)

Italian anatomist and physiologist. Born in Bologna ca. 1740. Father Domenico Galeazzi. Married Luigi Galvani (1760).

Lucia Galeazzi, the daughter of Domenico Galeazzi, Luigi Galvani's teacher, may have aspired to a career at the University of Bologna. This idea was not unheard of, for Bologna was the home of several woman scientists, including LAURA BASSI and ANNA MORANDI MANZOLINI. Lucia's father, who filled the chair of Natural Philosophy at Bologna, was devoted to her, and probably taught her scientific subjects. After Lucia Galeazzi married Galvani, the couple shared her father's home, and the trio organized a local academy, "The Inexperienced." Luigi Galvani set up a laboratory to investigate animal electricity in which Lucia was probably involved. JH/MBO

SECONDARY SOURCES

Fulton, John F., and Harvey Cushing. "A Bibliographical Study of the Galvani and the Aldini Writings on Animal Electricity." *Annals of Science: A Quarterly Review of the History of Science Since the Renaissance.* 1 (July 1936): 239–268.

STANDARD SOURCES

DSB (under Galvani, Luigi).

GAMBLE, ELEANOR ACHESON MCCULLOCH (1868–1933)

U.S. psychologist. Born 2 March 1868 in Cincinnati, Ohio, to Mary McGill and Joseph Gamble. Never married. Educated Wellesley College; Cornell University (Ph.D., 1898); University of Göttingen (1906–1907). Professional experience: Western Female College, teacher, Greek, Latin, and psychology (1889–1890); Plattsburgh Normal School, teacher, Greek and Latin (1891–1895); Wellesley College, instructor (1898–1903), associate professor (1903–1910), professor (1910–1933); director of the psychological laboratory (1908). Died 1933.

Before psychologist Eleanor Gamble earned her doctoral degree from Cornell University, she taught Greek, Latin, and psychology at several small colleges. In 1898, after she received her doctorate, she became an instructor at Wellesley, where she remained for the rest of her career. She progressed through the academic ranks at regular seven-year intervals, becoming professor in 1910. She remained at this rank until her death in the summer of 1933.

Gamble trained a number of other women psychologists, including THELMA ALPER. She was one of the few women psychologists teaching at a women's college at this period to publish experimental studies regularly. Gamble wrote several technical articles on her research area, the processes of memorization. In addition, she did research on smell intensities.

JH/MBO

PRIMARY SOURCES

Gamble, Eleanor Acheson McCulloch. *A Study in Memorizing Various Materials by the Reconstruction Method.* Lancaster, Pa.: The Review Publishing Company, 1909.

———, ed. *Wellesley College Studies in Psychology*, no. 2. Lancaster, Pa., and Baltimore, Md.: The Review Publishing Company, 1916.

SECONDARY SOURCES

Rucknick, C. A. "Eleanor E. M. Gamble." *American Journal of Psychology* 46 (1934): 154–156.

Scarborough, Elizabeth, and Laurel Furumoto. *Untold Lives: The First Generation of Women Psychologists.* New York: Columbia University Press, 1987.

STANDARD SOURCES

AMS 1–5; Bailey; Rossiter 1982; Siegel and Finley; Stevens and Gardner.

GANTT, LOVE ROSA (1875–1935)

U.S. physician and public health worker. Born 29 December 1875 at Camden, S.C., to Lena (Debhrina) and Solomon Hirschmann. Five siblings. Married Robert Joseph Gantt (16 March 1905). No children. Educated public schools of Charleston; Medical College of South Carolina, Charleston (M.D., 1901); New York Ophthalmic and Aural Institute, postgraduate work (Dr. Herman Knapp); Eye and Ear Clinic of New York University. Professional experience: Winthrop College, Rock Hill, S.C., resident physician; private practice as eye, ear, nose, and throat specialist, Spartanburg, S.C., (from 1905). Died in Philadelphia of an embolism 16 November 1935.

Love Rosa Gantt was a highly capable specialist, one of the first women trained in ophthalmic surgery, but is more particularly remembered for her public service and for elevating and strengthening the position of women in medicine. She was instrumental in the passage in 1920 of legislation in South Carolina to provide medical inspection of school children (opposed by the general public as a violation of parental rights and privacy). She was one of the directors of the work of the American Women's Hospitals, a relief organization and traveling dispensary undertaking work in wartime areas and in the southern states. Because of her efforts as president of the American Medical Women's Association, the American Women's Hospitals undertook as its first stateside project a public health program in the southern Appalachians, beginning in Spartanburg County, South Carolina, and extending into North Carolina. The program battled pellagra, tuberculosis, and so on, and later established maternity shelters, health houses, and clinics. During World War I, Gantt served on the board of medical examiners for the draft and organized some five hundred women to serve in Red Cross, Liberty Loan, and hospitality work for soldiers. She was a leader in the establishment (1918) of the state reform school for girls at Campobello, South Carolina, and served as chairman of its board of trustees for ten years. She served on the South Carolina Board of Public Welfare five years and was legislative chairman of the South Carolina Equal Suffrage League. A strong believer in preventive education, she organized and headed the Spartanburg Health League, the Spartanburg Anti-Tuberculosis Association, and the public health and legislation committees of the South Carolina Federation of Women's Clubs.

Gantt was born the second daughter and third of six children of Solomon Hirschmann, a Jew of Austrian birth and a prominent merchant and citizen of Charleston, and Lena

Debhrina, who died when Love Rosa was fourteen. After finishing public school in Charleston, Love Rosa enrolled in 1898 at the Medical College of South Carolina, which had opened its program to women in 1895. She received her medical degree in 1901 and went directly to the New York Ophthalmic and Aural Institute of Herman Knapp to acquire specialty training in diseases and surgery of the eyes, ears, nose, and throat. She also took training at the New York University Eye and Ear Clinic. Returning to South Carolina, she became resident physician at Winthrop College in Rock Hill but left after only one term to marry lawyer Robert Joseph Gantt and move to his home in Spartanburg, South Carolina. There she set up medical practice and began her active and influential involvement in professional, community, and national organizations. Even religion felt her presence, as she organized the Synagogue Ladies' Auxiliary of Congregation B'nai Israel in Spartanburg. (Her husband was Presbyterian but apparently they were able to adhere to their separate religions in accord.) In 1935, she went to the Woman's Medical College Hospital in Philadelphia to be operated on and died there of an embolism, November 16. She was buried in the Jewish cemetery in Spartanburg but her remains were moved some years later to Greenlawn Memorial Gardens. She had no children and was survived by her husband.　　　　　JH/MBO

STANDARD SOURCES
Hurd-Mead 1933; *NAW* (article by Sarah McCulloh Lemmon).

GAPOSCHKIN, CECILIA PAYNE

See Payne-Gaposchkin, Cecilia Helena.

GARDINER, EDITH GERTRUDE (WILLCOCK)

See Willcock, Edith Gertrude.

GARDINER, MARGARET ISABELLA (1860–1944)

British geologist. Born 1860. Father Samuel Rawson Gardiner. Never married. Educated Gower Street School; Bedford College, London; Newnham College, Cambridge (Natural Science Tripos, Part I, Class 2, 1885; Part II, Class 2, 1887). Professional experience: Bathurst Student (1887–1888); St. Leonard's School, St. Andrews, science mistress (1889–1892?); Withington high school, headmistress (1892–1896); Aldeburgh School, founder and first headmistress (1896–1907). Died 2 February 1944.

Margaret Isabella Gardiner was the eldest daughter of the historian Samuel Rawson Gardiner, and through him was descended from Oliver Cromwell. Her mother was the granddaughter of a famous preacher, Edward Irving. She was brought up in London and in the Gower Street School and Bedford College. When she entered Newnham, she specialized in geology.

After she left Newnham, Gardiner became more of an educator than a geologist. She was assistant mistress at St. Leonard's School for Girls, St. Andrews, for about the first four years after leaving Newnham. She was then headmistress at Withington High School and was the founder and first headmistress of Aldeburgh High School. Her goal was to establish a school that would educate girls in the same way boys were educated.

Gardiner did publish two papers in stratigraphy and mineralogy. Gardiner's health failed, and she was forced to retire in 1908, but she had accomplished her goal. When she regained some of her strength, she and a friend settled at Horam in Sussex and built a home there. As the need arose she started the Nursing Association and the Women's Institute. She put into practice what she taught her students was important: service to the community.　　JH/MBO

STANDARD SOURCES
Creese and Creese; *Newnham*, vol. 1; *Newnham Roll*.

GARDNER, ELINOR WIGHT (1892–1981)

British geologist and anthropologist. Born 24 September 1892 in Birmingham to Emilie Montgomery (Atwater) and Guy Huggins Gardner. Educated Edgbaston High School, Birmingham; Newnham College, Cambridge (1912–1916), Natural Science Tripos, Part I, Class 2 (1915), Bathurst Student (1916–1917), M.A. (1926); Waterperry Horticultural School, trainee (1942–1944). Professional experience: Cambridge Associate (1926–1941); Stellenbosch University, South Africa, acting professor (1917–1919); Faiyum Desert, geologist to archeological expeditions (1925–1926, 1927–1928); Kharga Oasis, geologist to archeological expedition (1930–1933); Bedford College, London, lecturer in geology (1926–1930); Lady Margaret Hall, Oxford, research fellow (1930–1936); British Federation of University Women, senior international research fellow (1937–1938); Royal Botanical Gardens, Edinburgh, temporary assistant curator (1938–1941); Lady Margaret Hall, Oxford, director vegetable production (1941–1945); Froebel Educational Institute, Hitchin, garden steward and lecturer (1945–1952).

Elinor Wight Gardner had a checkered career. After serving as a geologist for several archeological expeditions, often with Newnham Research Fellow Gertrude Caton-Thompson, she had several brief temporary academic appointments. However, during the war years she became a trainee at the Waterperry Horticultural School, near Oxford, and thereafter her positions were in botany or horticulture. Her publications, however, stemmed from her earlier geological work.   JH/MBO

PRIMARY SOURCES

Gardner, Elinor Wight. *Some Lacustrine Mollusca from the Faiyum Depression.* Cairo: Imprimérie de l'Institut Français d'Archéologie Orientale, 1932.

———. Numerous papers. *Quarterly Journal of the Geologists' Society.* 1927–1935.

———. Numerous papers. *Geological Magazine.* 1927–1935.

STANDARD SOURCES

Newnham, vol. 1.

GARDNER, JULIA ANNA (1882–1960)

U.S. invertebrate paleontologist and stratigrapher. Born 26 January 1882 in Chamberlain, S.D., to Julia Brackett Gardner and Charles Henry Gardner. Never married. Educated private tutors; Drury Academy, North Adams, Mass.; Bryn Mawr College (graduated 1905; master's degree, 1907); Johns Hopkins University (Ph.D., 1911). Professional experience: Maryland Geological Survey, assistant in paleontology and part-time geologist; U.S. National Museum under contract with the U.S. Geological Survey (1915–1917); Red Cross volunteer (1917–1919); U.S. Geological Survey, paleontologist and geologist (1919 until retirement with several interruptions). Died 15 November 1960 in Bethesda, Md.

Julia Gardner was born in South Dakota and reared by her mother after her physician father died when she was four months old. While in South Dakota, she was tutored privately. She and her mother moved to North Adams, Massachusetts in 1898 and Julia was enrolled in Drury Academy. After she graduated from Drury, she enrolled at Bryn Mawr, where she studied under FLORENCE BASCOM. After graduation, she spent a short time teaching grammar school at Chamberlain, but soon returned to work on her master's degree. At the urging of Bascom, she did her doctoral work at Johns Hopkins University in paleontology under William Clark and Edward Berry, where she was an assistant in paleontology. After she received her doctoral degree, she remained at Hopkins as assistant in paleontology and part-time geologist for the Maryland Geological Survey. In 1915, she began work at the U.S. National Museum under contract with the U.S. Geological Survey to work on the faunas of the Upper Tertiary sediments of the Coastal Plain of Virginia and North Carolina that were the subjects of her dissertation. This work was interrupted by World War I, where Gardner's humanitarian interests caused her to join the Red Cross. She went to France shortly after her mother died in 1917 and remained there until 1919. Her unit was deco-

rated by the French government for its service with distinction and valor. After the close of the war, Gardner joined the U.S. Geological Survey and continued her research on the Coastal Plain. She continued with these studies until her retirement, with several interruptions. During World War II, she joined a newly formed Military Geology Unit of the Geological Survey that described terrain conditions and geologic conditions that would be important in establishing beachheads all over the world. In addition to her knowledge of geology and her skill in map making, Gardner brought to this unit a knowledge of several languages and first-hand familiarity with many of the areas to be surveyed. She joined the U.S. Geological Survey in 1920, where she worked on the stratigrapher and fossils of Gulf and Coastal Plain deposits. In 1946–1947 she was tapped for a tour of duty with the Natural Resources Section of the Headquarters, Supreme Allied Command in Japan. Here she worked with Japanese geologists and biologists, and in addition to providing professional expertise, served as a good-will ambassador.

Gardner was president of the Paleontological Society in 1952 and vice-president of the Geological Society of America, the third woman to be so honored. She was also a member or fellow of the American Association for the Advancement of Science, American Association of Petroleum Geologists, Washington Academy of Sciences, Geological Society of Washington, Phi Beta Kappa, and Sigma Xi. She received the Distinguished Service Medal of the Department of the Interior.

While working for the Maryland Geological Survey, Gardner studied the Molluscan faunas of the Upper Cretaceous of Maryland. This work resulted in two comprehensive papers published by the Maryland survey in 1916, which remain the essential reference work on the Cretaceous of Maryland. Her chief research was on the Coastal Plain that extended from Maryland southward into Mexico. With the exception of her previous work on the Upper Cretaceous mollusks, all of Gardner's work was concerned with Tertiary beds. This interest had begun with her doctoral dissertation (published later as U.S. Geological Survey Professional Paper 199-B), which was concerned with the Upper Tertiary of Virginia and North Carolina. She then extended her work southward into Florida, where she described and illustrated eight hundred species of mollusks. At this time, she moved westward, to the Mississippi Embayment and into Texas. The final phase of her work took her into Mexico across the Rio Grande Embayment. In addition to her publications on these important regions, Gardner published approximately forty other papers. Her study of the collections of Cenozoic fossils made by survey teams to the Western Pacific Islands was left unfinished by her illness and death in 1960.   JH/MBO

PRIMARY SOURCES

Gardner, Julia Anna. *On Certain Families of the Gastropoda from the Miocene and Pliocene of Virginia and North Carolina.* Washington, D.C.: U.S. Government Printing Office, 1911.

———. *The Molluscan Fauna of the Alum Bluff Group of Florida.* Washington, D.C.: U.S. Government Printing Office, 1943–1948.

———. *Mollusca of the Tertiary Formations of Northeastern Mexico.* Baltimore: Waverly Press, 1945.

SECONDARY SOURCES

Sayre, A. Nelson. "Julia Anna Gardner (1882-1960)." *Bulletin of the American Association of Petroleum Geologists* 45, no. 8 (1961): 1418–1421.

STANDARD SOURCES

AMS 3–8, P 9, P&B 10; *NAW*(M) (article by Elaine Brody); *Notable;* Sarjeant.

GARDNER, MARY SEWALL (1871–1961)

U.S. public health nurse. Born 5 February 1871 in Newton, Mass., to Mary (Thornton) and William Sewall Gardner. Educated private schools and by a French governess; Miss Porter's School in Farmington, Conn. (1888–1890); Newport, R.I., Hospital Training School for Nurses (1901–1905). Professional experience: Providence District Nursing Association, superintendent then director of nurses (1905–1931); National Organization of Public Health Nursing, secretary (1912–1913), president (1913–1916); American Red Cross's Town and Country Nursing Service (renamed the Bureau of Public Health Nursing) (1918); American Red Cross Tuberculosis Commission for Italy, chief nurse (1918–1919); International Council of Nurses, chair standing committee on public health nursing (1925–1933). Died 20 February 1961 in Providence, R.I.

Mary Sewall Gardner was an only child whose mother died when she was four years old. Her father remarried and her stepmother, Sarah Gardner, was a physician. Although she was a delicate child, suffering from a severe case of tuberculosis at age sixteen, she lived until she was ninety years old. Gardner obtained her early education in private schools and her well-to-do family provided her with a French governess. After she recovered from tuberculosis, she attended Miss Porter's School in Farmington, Connecticut. After graduating from this school in 1890, she remained at home to care for her invalid stepmother. During this time she also became active in volunteer work. The family moved to Providence, Rhode Island, in 1892, and in 1901, Gardner was finally able to fulfill her own career desires. She entered a training school for nurses, graduating in 1905. Following graduation she took a position with the Providence District Nursing Asso-

ciation (PDNA). Finding this organization abysmally organized, she improved its programs to the extent that it served as a model for other district nursing associations. Always interested in education, Gardner was committed to improving the education of public health nurses, and insisted that they become involved in community planning. Gardner remained with the PDNA as its director until 1931, but took several leaves of absence during which time she became involved in other nursing organizations. A new organization, the National Organization of Public Health Nursing (NOPHN) was begun at the instigation of Gardner and LILLIAN WALD. Gardner served as its secretary and president. In 1918, during another leave time from PDNA, she worked for a short time as director of the American Red Cross's Town and Country Nursing Service. Upon leaving this directorship she undertook several wartime missions. After her first exposure to European public health nursing, she both studied and worked abroad, at one time chairing the standing committee of public health of the International Council of Nurses from 1925 to 1933.

Gardner's *Public Health Nursing* (1916) became a classic. It was revised twice and translated into a number of languages. Gardner was awarded the Walter Burns Saunders Medal for distinguished service to nursing. JH / MBO

PRIMARY SOURCES

Gardner, Mary S. "Problems Met by the District Nurse." *Providence Medical Journal* (March 1913).

———. *Public Health Nursing.* New York: Macmillan, 1916.

———. "A Report of Six Months' Study of the NOPHN." *Public Health Nurse* (July 1926).

———. "Functions of the NOPHN." *Public Health Nursing* (April 1938).

Gardner's papers are located at the Schlesinger Library, Radcliffe College.

SECONDARY SOURCES

"Mary Sewall Gardner." *American Journal Nursing* (April 1961). Obituary notice.

"Mary Sewall Gardner." *Providence Evening Bulletin,* 21 February 1961. Obituary notice.

Nelson, Sophie. "Mary Sewall Gardner." *Nursing Outlook* (December 1953 and January 1954).

STANDARD SOURCES

NAW(M) (article by Ilene Kantrov and Kate Wittenstein).

GARFIELD, VIOLA EDMUNDSON (1899–1983)

U.S. anthropologist. Born 5 December 1899 in Des Moines, Iowa, to Mary Louanna (Dean) and William Henry Edmundson. Five

siblings. *Married Charles Garfield (1924). Educated University of Washington (A.B., 1928; A.M., 1931); Columbia University (Ph.D., 1939). Professional experience: Barnard College, Columbia, assistant in anthropology (1933); U.S. Forest Service, History of Alaskan totem poles (1940–1941); University of Washington, associate (1937–1944), assistant professor (1945–1954), associate professor (1955–1969), professor (1969–1970), emerita professor (1970–1983). Died 1983 in Seattle.*

Viola Edmundson was born in Iowa, but her family moved to Whidby Island off the coast of Seattle, Washington. She started college at the University of Washington in 1919, but financial problems led her to leave the university and attend Bellingham Normal School, where she earned a teaching certificate. For one year she worked for the Bureau of Indian Affairs teaching fourth grade to Tsimshian children in southeastern Alaska. Returning to Seattle, she worked as a secretary for Charles Garfield at the Seattle Chamber of Commerce. A year after his first wife died the couple married (1924). Viola Garfield returned to the University of Washington in 1927. According to her biographer Jay Miller, she received her bachelor's degree in sociology in 1931, but *American Men and Women of Science* places the date at 1928. For her master's degree in anthropology, Garfield worked on the Tsimshian marriage patterns, doing field work in New Metlakatla, Alaska, where she had taught primary school. Now teaching as an junior, part-time member of the department, she entered graduate school at Columbia, taking classes in New York City only during the summers. There she studied under Franz Boas and RUTH BENEDICT. Her dissertation, "Tsimshian Clan and Society," was completed in 1935 although her degree dates from its publication in 1939. Garfield became an assistant professor in the department of anthropology only in 1945 after she had published a number of articles and books. She rose to associate professor in 1945 and was made full professor only a year before her retirement in 1970. Her closest associate at the University was ERNA GUNTHER, who was chair of the department and director of the anthropology museum.

After retirement, Garfield became ill and her heavy smoking contributed to artery blockage, which led to the amputation of both of her legs. At this time in her life, she became interested in issues of the elderly and the disabled. She died on Thanksgiving, 1983.

Although she did not publish extensively, her work is recognized as classic North Pacific ethnography, especially her research on the economics of slavery among the Northwest Indians and her studies of Pacific clans and moieties. She also wrote popular works on totem poles and mythology, not ignoring women's work on basketry, and her major study of Northwest Coast totem poles was republished shortly before her death.   JH/MBO

PRIMARY SOURCES

Garfield, Viola. "Tsimshian Clan and Society." *University of Washington Publications in Anthropology* 7, no. 3 (1939): 167–340.

———. *The Seattle Totem Pole.* Seattle: University of Washington Press, 1940; 1980.

———. "A Research Problem in Northwest Economics." *American Anthropologist* 47, no. 4 (1945): 626–630.

———. "Possibilities of Genetic Relationship in Northern Pacific Moiety Structures." *American Antiquity* 18, no. 3 (1953): 58–61.

———. *The Tsimshian and Their Arts.* Seattle: University of Washington Press, 1966.

SECONDARY SOURCES

Miller, Jay, and Carol M. Eastman. "Viola Edmundson Garfield." In *The Tsimshian and Their Neighbors of the North Pacific Coast,* ed. Miller and Eastman, 311–315. Seattle: University of Washington Press, 1984.

STANDARD SOURCES

AMS 7–12; Gacs.

GARLICK, CONSTANCE (d. 1934)

British botanist. Professional experience: University College School, London, botany teacher. Died in 1934.

Constance Garlick taught botany at University College School in London. She contributed a botanical chapter to P. E. Vizard's *Guide to Hampstead.*   JH/MBO

PRIMARY SOURCES

Garlick, Constance. "Botany of Hampstead." In *Guide to Hampstead,* by P. E. Vizard. London: J. Hewetson, 1898.

SECONDARY SOURCES

Kent, D. H. *History of the Flora of Middlesex.* N.p., 1975. Garlick mentioned on page 25.

STANDARD SOURCES

Desmond.

GARNETT, ALICE (fl. 1924–1968)

British geographer. Professional experience: University of Sheffield (1924–1968). Died 1968(?).

Alice Garnett was a geographer who worked at the University of Sheffield for most of her career. She worked on the geographical interpretation of topographical maps.   JH/MBO

PRIMARY SOURCES

Garnett, Alice. *The Geographical Interpretation of Topographical Maps.* London: Harrap, 1930.

SECONDARY SOURCES

Potter, George, and David L. Lindton. "Professor Alice Garnett." *University of Sheffield Gazette* 48 (1968): 66–68.

STANDARD SOURCES

Sarjeant.

GARNJOBST, LAURA FLORA (1895–1977)

U.S. microbiologist and geneticist. Born near Crofton, Nebr., 6 October 1895, to Augusta Charlotte Dorothy (Peter) and Adolf Friederich Garnjobst. Never married. Educated public schools in Salem, Ore.; Oregon State College (B.S., 1922; M.A., 1927). Stanford University (Ph.D. in biology, 1939); postgraduate study Berlin, Germany, and Plymouth, England (1928–1929). Professional experience: Stanford University, scientific artist and assistant (1930–1934), assistant biologist (1937–1942); U.S. Fish and Wildlife Service, Leetown, W. Va. (1944–1946); Yale University, research assistant (1946–1948); Stanford University, research associate (1948–1957); Rockefeller Institute, associate professor of microbiology (1957–1966). Retired in 1966. Died 31 July 1977 in Corvallis, Ore.

Laura Flora Garnjobst was a microbiologist and geneticist who worked as an assistant and then associate of the Nobel Prize–winner, Edward L. Tatum. Born in 1895, she studied biology at Oregon State College, and after receiving her master's degree went to Berlin and to Plymouth, England, where she did research on aquatic biology. She then went to California, where she worked as a scientific illustrator from 1930 to 1934, working toward her doctorate in biology while serving as an assistant to W. I. Needham at Stanford University. She continued to work with him for three years after receiving her doctorate. In 1942, Garnjobst joined the U.S. Fish and Wildlife Service and worked for two years as an aquatic biologist at Leetown, W.Va.

At Stanford, George Beadle and Edward L. Tatum had begun their study of genetic mutation in the mold *Neurospora crassa* in 1941 that would win them the Nobel Prize in 1958. Garnjobst returned to Stanford to work with Tatum and then continued to serve as his research associate when he moved to Yale for two years. She returned to Stanford where Tatum held a professorship and finally to the Rockefeller Institute, when he was appointed to a position there in 1957. Only at the Rockefeller did she receive an appropriate position as associate professor of microbiology while she continued her research on cell mutation. Even after her retirement in 1967, Garnjobst continued to publish with Tatum on the

genetics of *Neurospora crassa.* Her last publication was in 1970 in *Genetics.* She was the member of many scientific societies, including the Genetics Society and the American Genetic Association. JH/MBO

PRIMARY SOURCES

Garnjobst, Laura Flora. With others. "Vitamin Requirements of *Colpoda duodenaria.*" *Journal of Cellular and Comparative Physiology* (1942).

———. With E. L. Tatum. "A Temperature-Independent Riboflavin-requiring Mutant of *Neurospora crassa.*" *Genetics* (November 1967).

———. With E. L. Tatum. "New Crisp Genes and Crisp-Modifiers in *Neurospora crassa.*" *Genetics* (October 1970).

STANDARD SOURCES

AMS 9–13; *NCAB* (with portrait).

GARRETT, ELIZABETH (1836–1917)

See Anderson, Elizabeth Garrett.

GARRETSON, MARY (WELLECK) (1896–1971)

U.S. invertebrate paleontologist, mining geologist, and journalist. Born 16 December 1896 in Cincinnati, Ohio, to Mary A. (Noble) and Ernest Welleck. Married William Garretson. Two children, Mary Louise and William Welleck Garretson. Educated Girls Latin School (1909–1914); Barnard College (A.B., 1918); Columbia University (M.S., 1919). Professional experience: Young Men's Christian Association, teacher (1921–1923); Brooklyn Children's Museum, assistant; Hunter College, New York City, instructor in geology and student advisor (1946–1951); Haitian-American Resource Company, vice-president (1956–1971). Honors and memberships: Geological Society of America, Fellow; Geological Society of London, Fellow; American Institute of Mining, Metallurgical and Mining Engineers, member; International Society of Economic Geologists, member. Died 8 May 1971 in White Plains, N.Y.

Mary Welleck's father, a journalist, was born in Vienna and came to the United States in 1872. Her mother was a native of Cincinnati and the daughter of a well-known artist. Both parents encouraged Welleck in her intellectual interests. At Barnard College, she received a varied liberal arts education with an emphasis on the sciences. She became enthused by the teaching of Amadeus W. Grabau, who taught both at Barnard and Columbia. After she received her bachelor's degree, she went to Columbia and received a master's degree in geology from that institution, specializing in invertebrate zoology, stratigraphy, and sedimentation. While Welleck was at Columbia, she served as a graduate assistant. At this time she met her future husband and married on 27 September 1922.

She successfully managed a career with her family obligations. She and her husband had two children, a boy and a girl. In her position as a teacher at the YMCA, she planned and taught what may have been the first correspondence course in geology. After this job, she was an assistant at the Brooklyn Children's Museum. Garretson wrote numerous pieces on popular science, including a series of articles for the *New York Tribune* on the geology of New York City. During the war (1943–1945), she did personnel work with the airlines and several industrial organizations. During 1946, she was a research assistant in the Columbia University School of Mines and then became an instructor in geology and student advisor at Hunter College. After 1951, she did consulting work in mining geology and in certain areas of construction engineering. From 1956 until her death, she was vice-president for technology of the Haitian-American Resource Company. After 1957, the Haitian government invited her to serve as a consultant on mineral economics and development.

Mary Garretson was active in the community of Scarsdale, serving as an election inspector. She also was one of the founders of the Westchester County Conservation Association and served on its board of directors from 1933 to 1950.

Garretson was active in several scientific societies. She was a Fellow of both the Geological Society of America and the Geological Society of London. She was a member of the American Institute of Mining, Metallurgical and Petroleum Engineers, the International Society of Economic Geologists, the American Geophysical Union, the Geological Society of China, and the New York Historical Society.

In addition to her popular works, Garretson published several papers and was an important assistant to Amadeus Grabau in writing his *Textbook of Geology*. He gave her credit for her assistance and in the introduction claimed that her help was essential. Garretson is one of the individuals whose life and geological career are inextricably bound.   CK

PRIMARY SOURCES

Garretson, Mary Welleck. "The Cardinal Spines of *Spirifer mucronatus:* Lake Erie Specimen Answers Geological Query." *Hobbies* 17, no. 1 (1936): 12–13.

———. "Color in Trilobites of Trenton Age [N.Y.]." *Science* 117, no. 3027 (1950): 17.

SECONDARY SOURCES

Behre, Charles H., Jr. "Memorial of Mary Welleck Garretson 1896–1971." *Geological Society of America Memorials* 4 (1975): 72–73. With portrait.

STANDARD SOURCES

Sarjeant.

GARROD, DOROTHY ANNE ELIZABETH (1892–1968)

British archeologist and prehistorian. Born 5 May 1892 in London to Laurel Elizabeth (Smith) and Archibald Edward Garrod. Three brothers. Never married. Educated privately; Birklands School, St. Albans; Newnham College, Cambridge (1913–1916, second class degree in history); Oxford University (diploma with distinction in anthropology; 1920–1922); Institut de la Paléontologie Humaine (1922–1924). Professional experience: French Cave Excavations (1924–1926); Newnham College, research fellow (1929–1932); Excavation Mt. Carmel (1929–1934); Newnham College, director of studies (1934–1942); Cambridge University, Disney Chair of Archaeology (1939–1952); Women's Auxiliary Air Force, photographic intelligence officer (1942–1945); excavation, Angles Caves, Vienne, France; retired (1952); excavation Levantine Coast (1952–1957). Died 18 December 1968 in Cambridge.

Dorothy Garrod was the only daughter of Sir Archibald Garrod, well known for his studies of inborn errors of metabolism and eventually Regius Professor of Medicine at Oxford. All three of her brothers died during World War I. She read history at Newnham College. During World War I, she did war work in France. In 1920, she moved to Oxford and worked under R. R. Marett for an Oxford diploma in anthropology. After receiving this diploma with distinction, Garrod went to France on a Mary Ewart scholarship where she studied under Abbé Breuil for two years. She excavated with Breuil in French caves, where she studied the Mousterian culture of the Neanderthals. She wrote her first book in 1926 on the Upper Paleolithic Age in Britain. She then led her first expedition, at Devil's Tower, Gibraltar in 1928, where she found important Neanderthal skull fragments.

From 1929 to 1934, Garrod directed her most important excavation, three caves on Mount Carmel, from which she established an important chronology for over one hundred thousand years, publishing her classic work, *The Stone Age of Mount Carmel* (1937). After returning to Cambridge in 1933, she acted as director of studies at Newnham College until 1942. In 1939, she was made Disney Professor of Archaeology, the first woman professor appointed by Cambridge University. During World War II, she left her teaching post to serve as a section officer in Photographic Intelligence. On her return to the University, Garrod expanded Part II of the Tripos on archeology and anthropology.

Garrod went with Suzanne de St. Mathurin to France to excavate the Angles Cave in Vienne, where she unearthed important Magdalenian sculptures over a period of eleven years. After retirement from teaching, she excavated along the Levantine coast for the next five years, attempting to establish a prehistoric chronology that would parallel that of Mount Carmel. Awarded an honorary Oxford doctorate, Garrod also received honorary degrees from the University of Pennsylvania and two French universities (Toulouse and Poitiers). She was elected Fellow of the British Academy (1952) and appointed Commander of the British Empire in 1965. Her other honors included the Huxley lecture in 1962, and the award of a gold medal from the Society of Antiquaries in 1968, shortly before her death.   JH/MBO

PRIMARY SOURCES
Garrod, Dorothy. *The Upper Paleolithic Age in Britain.* 1926.
———. *The Stone Age of Mount Carmel.* 1937.

STANDARD SOURCES
DNB Missing Persons.

GÀTA, ELENA (STEFANESCU) (1925–1967)

Rumanian soil geologist and geochemist. Born 28 August 1925 in Calarasi. Married G. Gàta. Educated secondary school Bucharest; Faculty of Industrial Chemistry (diploma 1949). Professional experience: Laboratory of Pedology of the Geological Committee, soil geochemist (1949–1962). Honors and memberships: State Institute of Soil Science, Commission for Soil Chemistry, secretary (1960–1964); 8th International Congress, Soil Science, organizer (1964). Died 27 August 1967 in Bucharest.

Elena Stefanescu Gàta's primary education was in Calarasi and she completed her secondary school education in Bucharest. She received a diploma in chemical engineering from the Faculty of Industrial Chemistry. After receiving her diploma, she entered the laboratory of pedology of the State Geological Committee and occupied different functions in the laboratory until she became laboratory director in 1962. From 1953 to 1957, she was principal investigator in a pedological group in the Academy of Sciences.

Gàta was a member of the National Rumanian Society of Soil Analysis of the State Institute of Soil Science. From 1960 to 1964, she was secretary of a Commission for Soil Chemistry at the SISS and actively participated in organizing the 8th International Congress of Soil Science (1964). She introduced into her practice at the laboratory different modern methods of analysis of soil chemistry. In her last years, she did a number of colloidal fractionations on soil sediments. Gàta was an efficient administrator, able to run her laboratories smoothly. She often published jointly with her husband along with other members of her laboratory group. She presented papers at international congresses in thermoanalysis and soil chemistry in Aberdeen in 1965 and Jena in 1967.   JH/MBO

PRIMARY SOURCES
Gàta, Eleana. With G. Gàta. "Determinarea sodiulinui potasiului si calciului cu ajutorul forometrului cu flacara." *Dari de*

Seama Ale Sedintelor, Comitetul de Stat el Geologiei 42 (1954–1955): 273–289.
———. With H. Asvadurov. "Solul silvestru nisipos cu benzi feruginoase din padurea Valea lui Mihai." *Dari de Seama Ale Sedintelor. Comitetul de Stat el Geologiei* 52, no. 1 (1966): 425–441.
———. "Studiul fizico-chimic si mineralogic al solului silvestru brun." *Studii Tehnice si Economice: Institutal de Geologie si Geofizica.* (Bucharest) seris C 17 (1970): 41–56.

SECONDARY SOURCES
Atanasescu, Ruxandra. "Elena Gata (1925–1967)." *Studii Tehnice si Economice: Institutul de Geologie, Serie C. Pedologie* 9 no. 19 (1967): xxi–xxvii. Includes portrait.

GATES, FANNY COOK (1872–1931)

U.S. physicist. Born 26 April 1872 in Waterloo, Iowa, to John Cook and Adelia (St. John) Gates. Educated at Northwestern University (B. Letters 1894; M. Letters 1895); University of Pennsylvania (Ph.D., ca. 1909); postgraduate work at Bryn Mawr (1895–1897); University of Göttingen and Polytechnik Institut Zurich (1897–1898); University of Chicago (summer 1899); McGill University (1902–1903); Cavendish Laboratory, Cambridge (1905). Professional experience: Goucher College, head, department of physics (1898–1911); University of Chicago, researcher, school of education (1911–1913); Grinnell College, associate professor of physics, professor of mental physics and physical hygiene, and dean of women (1913–1916); University of Illinois at Urbana-Champaign, associate professor of physics and dean of women (1916–1918); Y.M.C.A., general secretary (ca. 1918–1920, 1921–1922); Lincoln and Brearley Schools, New York, special teacher of physics (ca. 1920–1921, 1923–1928); Phoebe Ann Thorne School of Bryn Mawr College, headmistress (1922–1923); Roycemore School, Evanston, Ill., physics teacher (1928–1931?). Honors and memberships: American Physical Society, Fellow; American Association for the Advancement of Science, Fellow; Phi Beta Kappa. Died 24 February 1931 in Chicago.

While working in Rutherford's laboratory at McGill, Gates showed that heat volatilized decay products of thorium and radium, but did not destroy them or change their rates of decay. Later others used this principle to partially separate decay products, since these generally volatilized at different temperatures. She also determined that the ionizing action of previously heated quinine sulphate was not due to radioactivity. Gates continued her investigations of quinine sulfate's ionizing power at the Cavendish Laboratory under J. J. Thomson. Her experiments showed the effect was probably due to hydration, rather than to ultraviolet light. Later Gates found that several other substances behaved like quinine sulfate, though to a lesser degree. Heavy teaching and administrative duties, as well as inadequate facilities and equipment, thwarted Gates's desire to continue her research.

During 1909–1911 Gates was education chairman for the Maryland State Federation of Women's Clubs. She was a member of the AAAS, the American Physical Society, the Société de Physique (France), the Association of College Alumnae, and the American Mathematical Society.

JH/MBO

PRIMARY SOURCES

Gates, Fanny. "Effect of Heat on Excited Radioactivity." *Physical Review* 16 (1903): 300–305.

———. Letters to Rutherford, 21 July 1903, 9 April 1904, 20 July 1904, in Rutherford Correspondence, Cambridge University Library Archives.

———. "On the Nature of Certain Radiations from the Sulphate of Quinine." *Physical Review* 18 (1904): 135–145.

———. "The Conductivity of the Air Due to the Sulfate of Quinine." (Abstract.) *Physical Review* 22 (1906): 45–46.

———. "On the Conductivity of the Air Caused by Certain Compounds during Temperature Change." (Abstract.) *Physical Review* 24 (1907): 246.

SECONDARY SOURCES

Heilbron, John. "Physics at McGill in Rutherford's Time." In *Rutherford and Physics at the Turn of the Century,* ed. Mario Bunge and William R. Shea, 42–73. London and New York: Dawson and Science History, 1979.

Rayner-Canham, M. F., and G. W. Rayner-Canham. "Pioneer Women in Nuclear Science." *American Journal of Physics* 58 (1990): 1036–1043.

Rossiter, Margaret W. "'Women's Work' in Science, 1880–1910." *Isis* 71 (1980): 381–398.

Rutherford, Ernest. *Radio-activity.* Cambridge: Cambridge University Press, 1904; 1905.

———. *Radioactive Substances and Their Radiations.* Cambridge: Cambridge University Press, 1913.

STANDARD SOURCES

AMS 1–4; Bailey; Rossiter 1982; Siegel and Finley; *Woman's Who's Who of America.*

GATTY, MARGARET (SCOTT) (1809–1873)

British algologist and botanist. Born 3 June 1809 at Burnham, Essex, to Mrs. Scott (Ryder) and A. J. Scott. Two siblings (a brother who died in infancy and a sister, Horatia). Married Reverend Alfred Gatty (1839) (d. 1903). Five sons: Reginald Alfred, Alfred Scott, Stephen, Horatio Nelson, and one other (name unknown); and five daughters: Juliana, Horatia Katherine Francis, Madge, Undine, and Dot. Educated at home by governess. Published popular and scientific books on nature. Professional experience: edited Aunt Judy's Magazine *(1866–1870). Died 4 October 1873 of a long-term paralytic illness at Ecclesfield, Yorkshire.*

Margaret Gatty, younger sister to Horatia, acted as the elder sister throughout their lifetime. Dr. Scott, their father, recognized Margaret's proclivity to be in charge and was particularly happy to give her numerous responsibilities, including overseeing the Chancery case involving his daughters' inheritance from Grandfather Ryder. Their mother had died when Margaret was two years old and the girls spent their early years living alternately with grandparents, their father, and, in Ecclesfield with their uncle, Reverend Thomas Ryder. Although their education was overseen by governesses, Margaret was happier educating herself. Nevertheless, Dr. Scott had an extensive library, from which he encouraged his daughters to draw, and Gatty became fairly accomplished in the "feminine" arts of piano-playing, pencil-sketching, writing, and translating. In these early years, Scott's academic interests were of a literary nature. On one occasion, she shared her poetry with Margaret Hodgson, friend of Southey, who was impressed with Scott's writing and commented to her that she was "destined to be a worthy competitor in the race for fame" (Maxwell, 33).

In 1837, Scott met Alfred Gatty. Her father took a liking to Gatty, taking pity upon the struggling cleric, who was living on the meager sum of fifty-seven pounds a year from the small parish of Spennithorne, North Yorkshire. Gatty met Margaret Scott and fell in love with her at first sight. Within three days of their meeting, she had accepted his proposal of marriage. While Dr. Scott appreciated Gatty as an intellectual, as a cleric, and perhaps even as a friend, he was not at all keen for his daughter to make such a match. Despite initial tension caused by her father's opposition, friends and family intervened, and the marriage between Gatty and Scott took place on 8 July 1939 at the church of St. Giles-in-the-Fields, London. In the same year, Margaret Gatty's uncle, Thomas Ryder, died, and her uncle Edward Ryder offered the living of Ecclesfield, Yorkshire, to Alfred Gatty for only fourteen years, but the Ecclesfield vicarage became their permanent home.

Between 1839 and 1848, Gatty's literary aspirations were lost in a flurry of activities relating to home and parish. As the wife of a clergyman, Gatty fulfilled many philanthropic and religious duties in the community while continually birthing and raising her own young children. Gatty was strongly affected by her father's death some months after her marriage, and she and Alfred set to work composing the *Recollections of the Life of the Rev. A. J. Scott, DD., Lord Nelson's Chaplain* that would be published in 1842.

In 1848, after the birth of her seventh child, Gatty, suffering from the aftereffects of childbirth and a bronchial condition, was sent to Hastings to recuperate. Her attending doctor introduced her to William Henry Harvey's *Phycologia Britannica* and she was suddenly mesmerized by the sea and its natural treasures. In an early short story entitled "The Dull Watering-Place," published in *The Human Face Divine and Other Tales,* Gatty wrote a thinly veiled autobiographical tale of her discovery of her fascination with seaweeds. From Harvey's guide, she quickly learned of the unbelievable variety of seaweeds on the British coast.

Gatty returned to Ecclesfield, where she began to write collections of children's stories, ostensibly for the extra income they provided for the family. She soon incorporated into her writings both her new discovery of natural history and her strong Christian convictions. In 1855, she began her series, *Parables from Nature,* that taught young children moral and religious values through lessons provided by God via the natural world. Gatty became best known for her *Parables,* which epitomize the continuous tradition of natural theology at midcentury and beyond.

Not content to dabble in botany and algology as an amateur, Gatty, tentatively at first and then with increasing confidence, consulted some of the best known botanists and algologists of her time, as well as many lesser-known specimen collectors, many of whom were women. Gatty not only established long-term connections with men such as William Harvey and George Johnston, but she and her family were invited to spend time with them at their homes. The purpose of such trips was both for holidaying and for talking, collecting, and learning about marine life. Gatty was part of an extensive and influential marine botany network that had been established throughout the British Isles and beyond.

In 1863, Gatty's publisher, George Bell, approached her about writing an introduction to British seaweeds. Although much of the information in Gatty's *British Seaweeds* is, admittedly, drawn from Harvey's *Phycologia Britannica,* Gatty is able to comment knowledgeably upon almost each and every seaweed entry, demonstrating the depth and breadth of her own research. Gatty, as an avid collector, discovered new species of seaweed—*Lepralia gattiana* and *Elachista cambriensis.* She also had several species named after her—*Gattya pinella* and *Gattia spectabilis.* In 1857, she had a short piece published in the *Annals and Magazine of Natural History* on "New Localities for Rare Plants and Zoophytes," quite an achievement for a woman at midcentury.

In later life, Gatty became the editor of the well-known and much loved *Aunt Judy's Magazine.* The magazine was very much a family affair as many of the Gattys published histories and short stories in its pages. Gatty was able to convince several famous children's authors to contribute, including Lewis Carroll. Gatty herself contributed articles on natural history topics, which were later collected in one bound volume, *Waifs and Strays of Natural History.*

While in the last three years of her life, she was affected by a paralysis that eventually took away all her movement and even her speech. Gatty worked feverishly to the last with the close and dedicated assistance of her daughters. They carried her onto the beach so she could watch them gather specimens, they took dictation, copied, illustrated, and helped to organize her later works. Despite her strong religious convictions, Gatty resisted death to the last, wanting more than anything to remain on God's earth, to make neverending discoveries, and to revel in the astounding simplicities and complexities of the marine life that had become her deepest passion. Margaret Gatty is buried in St. Mary's churchyard, Ecclesfield.   SLS

PRIMARY SOURCES

Gatty, Margaret. *Parables from Nature.* London: Bell & Daldy, 1855 (1st series), 1857 (2d series), 1861 (3d series), 1863 (4th series).

———. "New Localities for Rare Plants and Zoophytes." *The Annals and Magazine of Natural History.* 1857.

———. *The Human Face Divine and Other Tales.* London: Bell & Daldy, 1860.

———. *British Seaweeds. Drawn from Professor Harvey's "Phycologia Britannica," with Descriptions, an Amateur's Synopsis, Rules for Laying Out Sea-Weeds, and Order for Arranging Them in the Herbarium, an Appendix of New Species.* 2 vols. London: Bell & Daldy, 1863.

———. *Waifs and Strays of Natural History.* London: Bell & Daldy, 1870.

SECONDARY SOURCES

Drain, Susan. "Marine Botany in the Nineteenth Century: Margaret Gatty, the Lady Amateurs and the Professionals." *Victorian Studies Association Newsletter* 53 (1994): 6–11.

Maxwell, Christabel. *Mrs. Gatty and Mrs. Ewing.* London: Constable & Co., 1949.

STANDARD SOURCES

Barnhart; *DNB;* Desmond; Shteir.

GAW, ESTHER ALLEN (1879–?)

U.S. educator and psychologist. Born 28 December 1879 in Hudson, Ohio. Married; one child. Educated College for Women, Western Reserve University (1900); Sternisches Conservatorium für Musik, Berlin, Germany (1904–1906); State University of Iowa (Ph.D., 1919). Professional experience: Salt Lake City, Utah, music teacher (1900–1915); State University of Iowa, instructor; San Francisco State Teachers College, instructor (1920–1922); Mills College, dean in charge of personnel (1922–1927), associate dean (1923–1927); Ohio State University, dean of women and professor of psychology (1927–1944), dean emerita (from 1944);

Williams Institute, consulting psychologist (1922–1927); Journal of Higher Education, *associate editor (1930–1946). Honors and memberships: National Association of Deans of Women, member; American Psychological Association, member; International Congress of Women Psychologists, member; Sigma Xi, member. Death date unknown.*

Esther Allen Gaw was active in adult education during the period when women students at the university level went from being an exception to being the norm (although still not fully accepted in many departments as equal to the male students). She was born on 28 December 1879 in Hudson, Ohio. She attended the College for Women at Western Reserve University, receiving her bachelor's degree in 1900. Musically talented, she went abroad to the Stern Conservatory of Music, Berlin, Germany (1904–1906), then returned to Ohio where she taught music for some years. She sought a doctorate in psychology at the State University of Iowa, graduated in 1919, and took her first professional position in California at the State Teachers College in San Francisco (1920–1922). Mills College, Oakland, California, offered her the position of associate dean in charge of personnel in 1922; Gaw became an associate professor and associate dean of women in 1923, staying until 1927. At that time, she went to Ohio State University as dean of women and professor of psychology and remained there until her retirement in 1944.

Her primary areas of interest were educational counselling, educational and psychological testing, and measurement of social intelligence on the college level. While at Ohio State, she served as assistant editor of the *Journal of Higher Education,* and wrote numerous articles. She stressed the importance of considering the whole person in preparing young women to meet the challenges of adult professional life and assisted in the development of a program at Ohio State University in which women students had full participation in the academic, social, and governmental life of the university. Gaw was an active member of the American Psychological Association, National Association of Deans of Women, American Association for the Advancement of Science, the International Congress of Women Psychologists, and Sigma Xi.   JH/MBO

PRIMARY SOURCES
Gaw, Esther Allen. Various articles. *Journal of Higher Education.* 1930–1945.

STANDARD SOURCES
AMS 4–8, S&B 9–10.

GAW, FRANCES ISABEL (1897–?)

U.S. psychologist. Born 11 December 1897 in Topeka, Kans. Educated Washburn College, Topeka; Harvard Graduate School of Education and Radcliffe (1920–1921); University of Edinburgh (1922–1923); University of London (Ph.D., 1926). Professional experience: Boston Psychopathic Hospital, staff (1920–1922); Industrial Fatigue Research Board, Great Britain, intern in psychology (1922–1924); National Institute of Industrial Psychology, Great Britain, investigator (1924–1926); University of California, Los Angeles, lecturer in psychology (1927); Department of Psychology and Educational Research, Los Angeles City Schools, supervisor (1927–1929); University of California, instructor; Child Study Department, Seattle public schools, director (from 1929); University of Washington (from 1930). Honors and memberships: American Psychological Association, member; British Psychological Society, member; Western Psychological Association, member. Death date unknown.

Frances Gaw received her education at Washburn College, the Harvard Graduate School of Education, and Radcliffe (1920–1921). She chose to go abroad for her doctorate in psychology, attending first the University of Edinburgh (1922–1923), then the University of London, where she received her doctorate. Returning to the United States, she was an intern in psychology at Boston Psychopathic Hospital (1920–1922), where she worked extensively with the development and administration of tests for evaluating intelligence.

Gaw left the Boston Psychopathic Hospital to work at the National Institute of Industrial Psychology with Cyril Burt, one of the most influential British psychologists of the time. With Winifred Spielman, she conducted a battery of oral and nonverbal performance tests designed to assess basic intelligence, the methodology and results of which are detailed in *A Study in Vocational Guidance* (1926) and in Gaw's *Performance Tests of Intelligence.* This scale of tests had been arranged by the psychologists at the hospital in Boston, and Gaw was considered an authority on their presentation and interpretation. Since the late seventies, Burt was the subject of an enormous scandal in which his research and its results were accused of being faulty and manipulated. Recently the accusations themselves have been questioned and Burt's reputation as one of the founders of British psychological testing somewhat restored. In the process, Gaw's studies have been reanalyzed.

Gaw served as lecturer in psychology at the University of California, Los Angeles, for a year before becoming supervisor for the Department of Psychology and Educational Research, Los Angeles City Schools (1927–1929) and instructor at the University of California. From 1929 until retirement (?), she was director of the Child Study Department of the Seattle Public Schools and was associated with the University of Washington. Her research concentrated on intelligence, intelligence testing, and on vocational guidance. She was a member of the American Psychological Association, the British Psychological Society, and the Western Psychological Association. KM

PRIMARY SOURCES

Gaw, Frances, et al. *A Study in Vocational Guidance Carried Out by the Industrial Fatigue Research Board and the National Institute of Industrial Psychology.* London: H. M. Stationery Office, 1926.

———. With Winifred Spielman. *Performance Tests of Intelligence.* Report no. 31 of Great Britain Industrial Fatigue Research Board. London: H. M. Stationery Office, 1928.

———. With Frank M. Earle, et al. *The Measurement of Manual Dexterities.* London: National Institute of Industrial Psychology, 1930.

SECONDARY SOURCES

Fletcher, Ronald. *Science Ideology and the Media: The Cyril Burt Scandal.* New Brunswick, N.J.: Transaction Publishers, 1991. See pages 60–63, 66, 255, and 361.

Hearnshaw, L. S. *Cyril Burt, Psychologist.* Ithaca, N.Y.: Cornell University Press, 1979.

STANDARD SOURCES

Psychological Register, vol. 2, 1929.

GEIRINGER, HILDA (1893–1973)

Austrian mathematician. Born 28 September 1893 in Vienna, to Martha (Wertheimer) and Ludwig Geiringer. Three siblings. Married (1) Felix Pollaczek (divorced); (2) Richard Martin Edler von Mises. One child by Pollaczek. Educated University of Vienna (Ph.D., 1917). Professional experience: Jahrbuch über die Fortschritte der Mathematik, *editor (1917–1919); University of Berlin, Institute of Applied Mathematics, first assistant (1921–1927), Privatdozent (lecturer) (1930–1933); Institute of Mechanics, Brussels, research assistant (1933); University of Istanbul professor of mathematics (1934–1939); Bryn Mawr College, lecturer (1939–1944); Wheaton College, Norton, Mass., professor and chair (1944–1959). Honors and memberships: Wheaton College, honorary doctor of science; University of Vienna, special presentation on fiftieth jubilee of her graduation; Sigma Xi, American Academy of Arts and Sciences. Died 22 March 1973 in Santa Barbara, Calif.*

Hilda Geiringer was a mathematician who suffered from the Nazi regime. She studied pure mathematics with Wilhelm Wirtinger at the University of Vienna and received a doctorate from this institution. After receiving this degree, she worked for two years under Leon Lichtenstein editing the *Jahrbuch über die Fortschritte der Mathematik,* a review journal. After leaving her editorial job, she went to the Institute of Applied Mathematics at the University of Berlin and became the first assistant to Richard Martin Edler von Mises. While she was in Berlin she had a short (two-year) marriage to a mathematician, Felix Pollaczek, by whom she had a daughter. Her work with von Mises led her away from pure mathematics and toward applied mathematics. In 1927 she was made Privatdozent (lecturer) at the University of Berlin and proposed by the faculty as an associate professor in 1933. No action was taken on the recommendation and she lost her job as Hitler gained more power. Leaving Germany, she took her daughter and went to Belgium as a research associate at the Institute of Mechanics in Brussels. In Brussels, she studied the theory of vibrations. Geiringer stayed for only a year in Belgium and then moved to the University of Istanbul, where she was professor of mathematics. Although in Turkey she was a member of a community of expatriot Germans, she found that she had to learn Turkish in order to present her lectures. After Ataturk died in 1938, Geiringer feared for her safety, and this time she and her daughter went to Bryn Mawr College, where she made friends with ANNA PELL WHEELER. In 1943, she married her former employer and mentor, von Mises, who had also fled Germany. Von Mises was a lecturer at Harvard University at this time, and Geiringer left Bryn Mawr to become professor and chair of the mathematics department at Wheaton College. Although she did not find teaching at a small college stimulating, it gave her an opportunity to spend the weekends with her husband. Richard von Mises died on 14 July 1953 and Geiringer was involved in completing and editing his works. She received a grant to do so and went to Harvard as a research fellow in mathematics. She worked with G. S. Ludford to complete a manuscript of von Mises's from 1955 to 1958. She also worked with J. M. Freudenthal on elasticity. She officially retired from Wheaton in 1958.

Geiringer received a number of honors. The University of Berlin elected her professor emerita with full salary in 1956. In 1960, Wheaton awarded her an honorary doctor of science degree. On the fiftieth jubilee of her graduation she was given a special presentation at the University of Vienna. She was a member of Sigma Xi and a fellow of the American Academy of Arts and Sciences.

In her mathematics, Geiringer made a number of original contributions, first to the theory of multiple trigonometric series and then to the twentieth-century development of Fourier series. Her Berlin contributions were to probability theory and to the mathematical theory of plasticity. During her Wheaton years, Geiringer focused on biometrical problems. JH/MBO

PRIMARY SOURCES

Geiringer, Hilda. "Trigonometrische Doppelreihe." *Monatshefte für Mathematik und Physik* 29 (1918): 65–144.

———. Über eine Randwertaufgabe der Theorie gewöhnlicher linearer Differentialgleichungen zweiter Ordnung." *Mathematische Zeitschrift* 12 (1922): 1–17.

———. *Fondements mathématiques de la théorie des corps plastiques isotropes.* Paris: Gauthier-Villars, 1937.

Geiringer's papers are at the Schlesinger Library, Radcliffe College. Richard von Mises's papers are at the Harvard University Archives.

SECONDARY SOURCES

Fermi, Laura. *Illustrious Immigrants.* Chicago: University of Chicago Press, 1968.

New York Times, 24 March 1973. Obituary notice.

STANDARD SOURCES

Grinstein 1993 (article by Joan L. Richards, including bibliography); *NAW*(M) (article by Joan L. Richards); *Notable.*

GELDART, ALICE MARY (1862–1942)

British botanist. Born 1862. Father, Herbert Decimus Geldart (1831–1902). Never married. Honors and memberships: British Association for the Advancement of Science, Botany and Forestry Section, local secretary (1935–?); Norfolk and Norwich Naturalists' Society, president (1914, 1931), honorary member; Linnean Society, Fellow. Died 4 May 1942 in Thorpe, Norfolk.

Alice Mary Geldart, the daughter of Herbert Decimus Geldart, who was a wine merchant and a member of the Botanical Society of London, not only added to her father's herbarium but became an authority on the history of East Anglia botany. She edited and contributed to the *Transactions of the Norfolk Norwich Naturalists' Society* and was president of this organization in 1914 and 1931. In 1914, her presidential address was "Sir James Edward Smith and Some of His Friends," and in 1931, "The Hookers in Norfolk and Suffolk." She specialized in the study of water plants.

Geldart used her fine botanical library in her research. She contributed a paper to the *Transactions of the Linnean Society* on *Stratiotes aloides*. In order to pursue her research, she also traveled frequently to Aberdeenshire, the Hebrides, the Channel Islands, Devon, and Switzerland.

Geldart's many interests included Egyptology (she was secretary of the local Egyptian Society); music (she was a violinist in the Norwich Philharmonic Society); chess; gardening; leather, metal, and woodwork; and water-color painting. She was also president of the Norfolk and Norwich Library.   JH/MBO

SECONDARY SOURCES

Arber, Agnes. *Water Plants.* Cambridge: Cambridge University Press, 1920. Mentions Geldart's work.

Proceedings of the Linnaean Society 155 (1942–1943): 298–299. Obituary notice.

Transactions of the Norfolk Norwich Naturalists' Society (1943). Obituary notice.

STANDARD SOURCES

Barnhart; Desmond.

GENET-VARCIN, EMILIENNE (fl. 1940s–1970s)

French physical anthropologist. Married. Educated University of Paris (D.Sc.). Professional experience: Bibliothèque Nationale, librarian (1949–?); University of Paris, Faculty of Sciences, chef de Travaux Anthropologiques (ca. 1952); Société d'Anthropologiques (1943–?), Central Bureau (archivist) (1945–?); Bibliotheque Nationale, librarian (1949–?).

Emilienne Genet-Varcin earned her doctoral degree in science from the University of Paris, Faculty of Sciences. She joined the Société d'Anthropologie during World War II in 1943 and soon became archivist of the society. In 1949, she served as a librarian at the Bibliothèque Nationale. She was named head of anthropological work (chef de travaux anthropologiques) at the Faculty of Sciences, Paris. Genet-Varcin published articles on prehistoric human remains in French grottos in the late 1940s into the mid-1950s. Her major book on fossil humans appeared in 1979.   JH/MBO

PRIMARY SOURCES

Genet-Varcin, Emilienne. "Les restes humains de la grotte de Loigne (Lot)." *Bulletin Memoires Société d'Anthropologie (BMSAP)* 9th ser., 10 (1949): 166–177.

———. "Les restes humaines de Solignac-sur-Loire et d'Ours-Mons près Le Puy (Haute Loire)." *BMSAP* 10th ser., 7 (1956): 133–145.

———. *Les Hommes Fossiles.* Paris: Boubée, 1979.

STANDARD SOURCES

DFC.

GENUNG, ELIZABETH FAITH (1883–1975)

U.S. bacteriologist. Born 12 March 1883 in Ithaca, N.Y. Educated New York State Normal School, Courtland, N.Y. (1905); Cornell University (B.S.A., 1911; M.S.A., 1914). Professional experience: Iowa Teachers' College, instructor in bacteriology (1914–1915); Simmons College, instructor (1915–1918); Smith College, instructor, assistant professor (1919–1926), associate professor (from 1926). Honors and memberships: Public Health Association, Fellow; New York Academy of Sciences, Fellow.

Elizabeth Genung was born in New York state and attended the State Normal School. She returned home to attend Cornell, where she earned her bachelor's and master's degrees in bacteriology. After graduation she went as an instructor in bacteriology to Iowa Teachers' College for a year. She returned to the East Coast to teach at Simmons College in Boston for three years. Following her Simmons position, she went to Smith College, where she was appointed an instructor and assistant professor of botany. In 1926, she was made an associate professor of bacteriology.

Her research concerned the cause of color diffusion in Endo's medium and the effect of dyes and chemicals on bacterial growth. Her interests extended to the history of medicine and especially the development of the compound microscope. She was Fellow of the Public Health Association and the New York Academy of Sciences.　JH/MBO

SECONDARY SOURCES
Smith, Eleanor V. *American Society for Microbiology News* (February 1975): 14.

STANDARD SOURCES
AMS 4–8, B 9, P&B 10.

GEPP, ETHEL SAREL (BARTON) (1864–1922)

British botanist. Born 21 August 1864 in Hampton Court Green, Middlesex. Married Anthony Gepp (1902). Educated at school with her brother and at home; studied violin at Leipzig. Professional experience: Department of Botany, British Museum of Natural History; Kew Gardens. Died 6 April 1922 in Torquay, Devonshire.

Ethel (Barton) Gepp married algologist Antony Gepp, who had a bachelor's degree from Cambridge University (1855) and became an assistant in the Botany Department of the British Museum of Natural History. Ethel Gepp also worked in the Botany Department at the museum and at Kew Gardens. Gepp contributed articles to the *Journal of Botany,* the *Journal of the Linnaean Society,* and the *Transactions of the Linnaean Society.* Her plant collection is at the British Museum of Natural History.　JH/MBO

PRIMARY SOURCES
Gepp, Ethel Sarel. *The Genus Halimeda.* Leiden: E. J. Brill, [1901].
———. *List of Marine Algae with a Note on the Fructification of Halimeda.* [London]: Royal Society, 1903.
———. With Anthony Gepp. *The Codiaceae of the Sibaga Expedition, Including a Monograph of Flabellarieae and Udoteae.* Leiden: E. J. Brill, 1911.

SECONDARY SOURCES
Britten, James, and George S. Bougler. *A Biographical Index of Deceased British and Irish Botanists.* 2d. ed. London: 1931.
Journal of Botany 160 (1922): 193–195. Obituary notice.
La Nuova Notarisia, ser. 34 (1923): 47–57.

STANDARD SOURCES
Strohmeier.

GEPPERT, MARIA PIA (1907–1997)

Polish mathematician and biologist. Born 28 May 1907 in Breslau, Poland. Educated University of Breslau, Giessen, and Rome; University of Breslau (doctorate); University of Rome (doctorate, 1936); University of Giessen (habilitated 1942). Professional experience: Kerckhoff-Institut in Bad Nauheim, Abteilungsleiterin (department head); University of Frankfurt, Privatdozentin (assistant professor) (1943–?), ausserplanmässige professor of biometry and mathematical statistics (1951–1966); Technical High School in Darmstadt, instructor (1947–1951); University of Tübingen, professor (1966–1976), emerita (1976). Honors and memberships: International Statistic Institute (from 1951); Société Adolphe Quetelet, corresponding member (1954); Biometric Society, honorary member (1965). Died 25 November 1997.

Maria Geppert applied her mathematical skills to biological problems. Born in Poland, she received her education at several well-known universities, eventually habilitating (earning the right to teach university) at Giessen in 1942. Her ability to use biometrical measures biology, medicine, and population studies eventually earned her a professorship at the University of Tübingen, where she remained until her retirement. She was also active in numerous professional organizations and edited the journals *Biometrie* and *Metron.*　JH/MBO

SECONDARY SOURCES
Boedecker, Elisabeth, and Meyer-Plath, Maria, eds. *50 Jahre Habilitation von Frauen in Deutschland.* Göttingen: O. Swartz, 1974.

STANDARD SOURCES
Strohmeier.

GERMAIN, SOPHIE (1776–1831)

French mathematician. Born 1 April 1776 in Paris to Marie-Madeleine (Gruguelu) and Ambroise-François Germain. Never married. Educated at home; Ecole Centrale des Travaux Publics (later Ecole Polytechnique), Paris (unofficial student, ca. 1794). Died 27 June 1831 in Paris.

Sophie Germain's literary bourgeois father, active in the political events that culminated in the French Revolution, was, for a time, a deputy to the States-General, and was involved in the transformation of that body into the Constituent Assembly. Presumably exposed to a good deal of talk concerning the political and intellectual currents of the time, the young Sophie also made use of her father's extensive library. Here at the age of thirteen she stumbled upon the *Histoire des mathématiques* of J. F. Montucla, and read his account of the death of Archimedes at the hands of the Romans during the siege of Syracuse. Fascinated by the image of a man so preoccupied by his study of geometry that he failed to notice the soldiers' approach, Sophie resolved to make a career of mathematics because it was sufficiently engrossing to obliterate all thoughts of the outside world. She taught herself basic mathematics, Latin, and Greek, becoming proficient enough to read the words of Isaac Newton and of the mathematician Leonhard Euler (1707–1783) in Latin.

Germain's parents disapproved of her mathematical pursuits and did their best to thwart them. According to one story, they tried to prevent her from staying up all night studying by leaving her bedroom without fire or light and removing her clothes from the room after she had gone to bed. After pretending to be asleep, she would arise, wrap herself in quilts and blankets, and study even when the ink was "frozen in her ink-horn" (Mozans).

The unavailability of qualified teachers hampered Germain's early studies. Desiring to take advantage of the newly established Ecole Centrale des Travaux Publics (later the Ecole Polytechnique)—whose faculty included such eminent mathematicians as Joseph Louis Lagrange (1736–1813) and Gaspard Monge (1746–1818)—but unable to attend lectures there because of her sex, she obtained copies of notes taken during the lectures of Lagrange and others. As did the regular students at the end of a term, she submitted a paper to Lagrange, who publicly praised the work and, after he found out who wrote it, offered himself as Germain's mentor.

The support of Lagrange put Germain into direct contact with many of the savants of the time. After reading Karl Friedrich Gauss's *Disquisitions arithmeticae,* she began to correspond with him, under the pseudonym Le Blanc. Once he was aware of her identity, Gauss remarked that although it was rare to find any person who comprehended the mystery of numbers, it was even more surprising to find a woman who did so. Germain also engaged in an extensive correspondence with Adrien Marie Legendre, who incorporated some of her discoveries into the second edition of his book on number theory.

Although, as a largely self-taught mathematician, Germain was frequently hindered by gaps in her knowledge, she produced several important works. Illness curtailed the productivity of her mature years; in 1829 she developed cancer. Often in pain during her last years, she continued both to work and to entertain her friends as long as possible.

Sophie Germain's creativity manifested itself in pure and applied mathematics. Searching for new solutions and plunging boldly into original work, she occasionally went beyond her knowledge. Although the rigor and quality of her proofs suffered accordingly, she nevertheless provided imaginative and provocative solutions to several important problems. One of her contributions was in the area of pure mathematics. A general proof had not—and still has not—been found for "Fermat's last theorem," which postulates that $x^n + y^n = z^n$ has no positive integral solutions if n is an integer greater than 2. Germain showed the impossibility of positive integral solutions if x, y, and z are prime to each other and to n, where n is any prime less than 100. The progress toward a general proof that has been made by twentieth-century mathematicians is built on Germain's theorem.

Sophie Germain made an important contribution to the applied mathematics of acoustics and elasticity in her development of a mathematical model for the vibration of elastic surfaces. This work earned her the grand prize in a competition sponsored by the French Academie des Sciences (1816) and resulted in several publications. In 1808 a German physicist, Ernst Chladni (1756–1824), arrived in Paris and conducted experiments on vibrating elastic plates. He would support a metal or glass plate, of regular shape, horizontally by a stand fastened to its center, sprinkle a fine powder such as sand on it, and set it vibrating by drawing a violin bow rapidly up and down along its edge. The powder would be thrown from the moving points to the nodes—those points that remained at rest. The nodal lines or curves that resulted were the so-called Chladni figures. Germain undertook to analyze them to determine the laws to which they were subject, despite initial discouragement from Lagrange, who asserted that the available mathematical methods were inadequate to the task.

Napoleon, who was very interested in Chladni's experiments, proposed to the Academie des Sciences that it offer a prize to the person who could provide a mathematical theory of the vibrations of elastic surfaces and could relate that theory to experimental results. Germain presented a memoir in 1811, but the prize was awarded to no one. Self-taught in calculus, she had made some avoidable errors; when Lagrange pointed them out, she corrected them and returned to the challenge. The subject was proposed a second time in 1813, and Germain again submitted a solution. Although they awarded her memoir an honorable mention and approved of her comparison between theory and observation, the judges contended that she still had not verified her equation. A third contest was held in 1815. Even though Germain was awarded the grand prize this time, the committee was not entirely satisfied. The acceptance of the prize did not end Germain's work on elastic surfaces. Her continued efforts gave rise to three publications, *Recherche sur la théorie des surfaces élastiques* (1821), *Remarques sur la nature, les bornes et l'étendue de la question des surfaces* (1826), and "Examen des principes qui peuvent conduire à la connaissance des lois de l'equilibre et du mouvements des solides élastiques," *Annales de Chimie* 38 (1828).

In addition to mathematics, Germain took an interest in philosophical subjects, particularly in the idea of the unity of thought. In her *Pensées diverses,* probably written in her youth, she presented brief accounts of the work of past scientists and mathematicians amid her own musings and opinions. In the scholarly *Considérations générales sur l'état des sciences et des lettres,* praised by Auguste Comte, she expounded the theory that there is no essential difference between the sciences and the humanities. Both works were published posthumously.

Sophie Germain's partial success in solving complex mathematical problems illustrates the difficulties faced by an eighteenth-century woman scientist. Although possessed of extraordinary gifts, she was constantly thwarted by her lack of basic mathematical tools. Nevertheless, she managed, often by unorthodox methods, to arrive at solutions to mathematical and physical problems that were both valuable in themselves and stimulating to other investigators.   MBO

PRIMARY SOURCES

Germain, Sophie. *Recherche sur la théorie des surfaces élastiques.* Paris: Courcier, 1821.

———. *Oeuvres philosophiques de Sophie Germain, suivies de pensées et de lettres inedites et precedées d'une notice sur sa vie et ses oeuvres par Hippolyte Stupuy.* Paris: P. Ritti, 1879.

———. *Cinq lettres de Sophie Germain a C. F. Gauss.* Berlin: B. Boncompagni–Ludovici, 1880.

SECONDARY SOURCES

Bidenkapp, Georg. *Sophie Germain, ein weiblicher Denker.* Jena: H. W. Schmidt, G. Tauscher, 1910.

Bucciarelli, L. L., and N. Dworsky. *Sophie Germain: An Essay in the History of the Theory of Elasticity.* Vol. 6, *Studies in the History of Modern Science.* Dordrecht: Reidel, 1980.

Dickson, Leonard Eugene. *History of the Theory of Numbers.* 3 vols. New York: Chelsea, 1951. Vol. 2, pp. 164, 732–735, 763, and 769 contain information about Sophie Germain.

Perl, Teri. *Math Equals: Biographies of Women Mathematicians and Related Activities.* Menlo Park, Calif.: Addison-Wesley, 1978.

Todhunter, Isaac. *A History of the Theory of Elasticity and of the Strength of Materials: From Galilei to Saint-Venant, 1639–1850.* 2 vols. Cambridge: Cambridge University Press, 1886. Discusses circumstances leading to Germain's interest in theories of elasticity. Discusses her work in vol. 1, pp. 147–160.

STANDARD SOURCES
DSB.

GEROULD, ELIZABETH WOOD (1889–1948)

U.S. chemist. Born 1889 in Elmira, N.Y. Educated Colorado College (A.B., 1912; A.M. 1921); Professional experience: Colorado public high school, teacher (1912–1914); Colorado College, instructor in chemistry (1916–1924); Colorado Women's College, (head of chemistry department 1925). Died 1948.

Although she was born in New York state, Elizabeth Wood Gerould went to Colorado for her degrees. She taught high school in Colorado for two years and then became an instructor in chemistry at Colorado College, where she taught for eight years. Gerould then was appointed head of the department of chemistry at Colorado Women's College, where she taught until her death. Her research interest was sanitary chemistry. She was a member of the Colorado/Wyoming Academy of Science.   JH/MBO

STANDARD SOURCES
AMS 5–7.

GERRY, ELOISE B. (1885–1970)

U.S. botanist and forester. Born 12 January 1885 in Boston, Mass. Educated Radcliffe College (A.B., 1908; A.M., 1909); Smith College, fellow (1909–1910; M.S., 1910); University of Wisconsin (Ph.D.– 1921). Professional experience: U.S. Forest Service Forest Products Laboratory, expert (1910–1911); microscopist (1911–1928); senior microscopist (1928–1947). Concurrent experience: University of Wisconsin, lecturer in forest products (1911–1955); emerita lecturer. Honors and memberships: American Association for the Advancement of Science, Fellow; American Chemical Society, member; American Forestry Association, member; Society of American Forestry, member; International Association of Wood Anatomists, member. Died 1970.

The first woman appointed to the professional staff at the Forest Service at Madison, Wisconsin, Eloise Gerry earned her doctorate in plant physiology from the University of Wisconsin. After she received her master's degree from Smith College, she joined the Forest Products Laboratory as a wood microscopist. She remained at this laboratory for her entire career and was appointed forest products technologist in 1947. A skilled preparator of photomicrographs and the cutting of wood specimens, she was highly qualified for her position.

Gerry's first project for this new laboratory was to collect and analyze wood samples from all over the United States. In 1916 she produced a paper on tyloses, the plugging of wood cells that restricts the movement of liquid. She next went to Mississippi and Florida, where she analyzed core samples from living trees for a project on naval stores. From this research she became a nationally recognized expert in naval stores and wrote a handbook on the subject. Her expertise enabled her to be useful during World War II, where she selected wood suitable for packing supplies to be shipped to the armed service in various climates. After the war, she prepared fifty-six reports in the Foreign Wood Series of the Forest Products Laboratory. She published 120 papers in technical and trade journals.

Gerry was a lecturer in forest products at the University of Wisconsin concurrently with her position at the Forest Products Laboratory. She was a member of numerous professional organizations, including the American Association for the Advancement of Science (Fellow), the American Chemical Society, the American Forestry Association, the Society of American Foresters, the Forest History Society, and the International Association of Wood Anatomists.   JH/MBO

PRIMARY SOURCES
Gerry, Eloise B. *Naval Stores Handbook*. Washington, D.C.: U.S. Department of Agriculture, 1935.
Gerry's papers are in the State Historical Society of Wisconsin, Madison.

SECONDARY SOURCES
Journal of Forest History 22 (1978): 192–235.

STANDARD SOURCES
AMS 3–8, B 9, P&B 10; Bailey; Barnhart; *NAW* unused; Rossiter 1982.

GEY, MARGARET LEWIS (fl. 1930)
U.S. virologist and oncologist. Married George Otto Gey (1926). Two children. Professional experience: Johns Hopkins School of Medicine, researcher (1933–ca. 1970).

Oncologist and virologist Margaret Lewis Gey collaborated with her husband, George Otto Gey, a professor of surgery at Johns Hopkins. The couple married 1926 when he was at Columbia Hospital, Milwaukee; they had two children. She collaborated with her husband in cancer research and virology, developing techniques for filming cell growth within test tubes. Some material on George and Margaret Gey is held at the Alan Mason Chesney Medical Archives at Johns Hopkins University.   KM

STANDARD SOURCES
AMS 8 (under George Otto Gey); Rossiter 1982.

GHILIETTA (fl. 13th century)
Italian physician. Flourished thirteenth century. Worked in Venice.

All that is known about Ghilietta is that she was a thirteenth-century medical woman from Venice.   JH/MBO

SECONDARY SOURCES
Hurd-Mead 1938.

GIAMMARINO, PIA (1898–1977)
Italian mineralogist and geochemist. Born 1898. Worked with Uffi-cio Geologico d'Italia. Died 1977.

Little biographical information has been found on Pia Giammarino. She was a mineralogist and geochemist who worked with the Geological Office of Italy.   JH/MBO

SECONDARY SOURCES
Grandi, Lia. "Pia Giammarino." *Bollettino Società Geologica Italiana* 98 (1980): 151.

STANDARD SOURCES
Sarjeant.

GIBBONS, E. JOAN (1902–1988)
British botanist. Born 1902 in Essex. Father Thomas Gibbons, a clergyman. At least three siblings, one brother and two sisters. Professional experience: Lincolnshire Naturalists' Union, botanical secretary (1936–1985), president (1939, 1969?). Honors and memberships: Linnean Society (1969), Fellow. Died 2 December 1988.

Dressed in "sensible clothes" and comfortable shoes, E. Joan Gibbons could often have been seen tramping through the Lincolnshire countryside, recording information about its plants. Although Joan Gibbons was born in Essex, when she was five years old, she moved with her family to an estate that her father had inherited sixteen miles northeast of Lincoln. Stimulated by her rural surroundings and her father's interest in natural history, she went to her first Lincolnshire Naturalists' Union when she was only eleven years old. When she was eighteen, she joined the union, and became botanical secretary in 1936, a position that she held for fifty years. In 1939, she was elected president of that organization, and years later was elected to an unprecedented second term.

Gibbons joined the Botanical Society and Exchange Club of the British Isles (BSBI) in 1946, and was appointed recorder for the two Lincolnshire vice-counties. She continued with these duties for the next forty years. The county of

Lincolnshire's botanical records were in bad shape when Gibbons took over, and when she was finished, they were as good as, and perhaps better than, the records of other counties. During this time, she contributed to the BSBI distribution maps, collected current field records by working her way through all parts of the county, and gathered invaluable information about the past. She not only described the past distribution of plants but made biographical notes about the recorders as well.

Gibbons's major accomplishment was the publication of *The Flora of Lincolnshire* (1985). This work represented the first *Flora* of the county, and was the first full *Flora* of an English county to be written by a woman.

In addition to her botanical work, Gibbons was a "Guider," Assistant County Secretary for twenty-eight years, and County Secretary for handicapped Guides. After the death of her brother in 1972, she moved with her two surviving sisters to Northlands House, Glentwood, where she researched her family's history. She became a prominent member of the Society for Lincolnshire History and Archaeology.   JH/MBO

PRIMARY SOURCES
Gibbons, E. Joan. *Flora of Lincolnshire.* Lincoln: Lincolnshire
    Naturalists' Union, 1975; supplement, 1985.

SECONDARY SOURCES
Transactions of the Lincolnshire Naturalists' Union 22 (1989): 126–
    127. Obituary notice, including portrait.
Watsonia 17 (1989): 507–508. Obituary notice.
Wild Flower Magazine 414 (1989): 38. Obituary notice.

STANDARD SOURCES
Desmond.

GIBBONS, VERNETTE LOIS (1874–?)

U.S. chemist. Born 4 January 1874 in Franklin, N.Y. Educated Mount Holyoke College (B.S., 1896; B.A., 1899); University of Chicago (M.Sc., 1907); Munich University (fellow 1912–1913); Bryn Mawr College (Ph.D., 1914); Harvard (1922). Professional experience: Massachusetts public schools, teacher (1896–1897); Mount Holyoke College, assistant in chemistry (1897–1899), instructor (1899–1901); Wells College, associate professor (1902–1904); Huguenot College, South Africa (1907–1911); Bryn Mawr, Helen Huff Fellow (1914–1915); Mills College, research fellow (1915–1918); National Carbon Company, Ohio, research chemist (1918); National Aniline and Carbon Company, New York, research chemist (1918–1919); Mills College, professor of chemistry (1919–1939), emerita professor (1939–?); Institute of Chemistry, Fellow. Death date unknown.

Vernette Gibbons was born in New York state in 1874 and attended Mount Holyoke College, receiving first a bachelor of science and then a bachelor of arts degree. During this period, she taught for a year in the local public schools and worked as assistant in chemistry at Mount Holyoke, continuing as an instructor for two years beyond her second degree. Wells College hired her as an instructor and she rose to associate professor in 1906 while she was working on her master of science degree at University of Chicago, which was awarded in 1907.

Gibbons then demonstrated an adventurous spirit by taking a position in South Africa at the Huguenot College in 1907; she remained there until 1911. During this period she was also awarded an honorary master of science from the University of Cape of Good Hope (1908). Traveling to Munich, Germany, on a fellowship, she studied from 1912 to 1914 at the University of Munich, and then returned to the States to complete her doctoral degree at Bryn Mawr, receiving the prestigious Helen Huff fellowship for a postgraduate year in 1914–1915. From there, she went from the East to the West Coast, to teach at Mills College for three years, until she took a position as research chemist at an industrial chemical firm, first in Ohio and then in New York state. Mills College brought her back to campus in California in 1919 as full professor of chemistry; she remained there until her retirement, with a brief period studying at Harvard in 1922.

A fellow of the Institute of Chemistry, Vernette Gibbons's research concerned the potentials of metals in non-aqueous solutions of their salts; alcoholic solutions of cadmium salts; and the reproducibility of cadmium electrodes.   JH/MBO

PRIMARY SOURCES
Gibbons, Vernette Lois. *The Potentials of Silver in Nonaqueous
    Solutions of Silver Nitrate.* Easton, Pa.: Eschenball Printing
    Co., 1914. Ph.D. diss.; includes Gibbons's *Vitae.*

STANDARD SOURCES
AMS 3–10.

GIBBS, LILIAN SUZETTE (1870–1925)

British botanist. Born 10 September 1870 in London. Educated Swanley Horticultural College (1891?–1901); Royal College of Science, Department of Botany (1901). Professional experience: Royal College of Science, Department of Botany, research associate. Died 30 January 1925 in Santa Cruz, Teneriffe.

As a young woman, Lilian Suzette Gibbs was interested in mountain flora. Even before she received her degree she collected plants in the mountains of Switzerland and Austria. In

1905 when the British Association for the Advancement of Science met in South Africa, Gibbs collected in Southern Rhodesia, especially at Victoria Falls. Between 1907 and 1950, she collected in the mountains of Fiji, Mount Kenabalu in British North Borneo, in the Arfaq Range in Dutch Northwest New Guinea, the Bellenden-Ker Range in Queensland, and in the Tasmania Mountains. She published memoirs on each of these expeditions in the *Journal of the Linnaean Society,* the *Journal of Botany,* and the *Journal of Ecology.* She brought back collections from each locality (now in the British Museum). She discussed questions of geographical distribution of these plants as well as a systematic account of the collections. She also wrote on the structure and development of flora, published in a series of papers in *Annals of Botany.* She was one of the earliest Fellows of the Linnaean Society and the Royal Microscopical Society. She was also a Fellow of the Royal Geographical Society. She was awarded the Huxley Medal (1910) of the Royal College of Science and the prize for research in natural science. She was especially interested in equal rights for women.   JH/MBO

PRIMARY SOURCES
Gibbs, Lilian Suzette. "A Contribution to the Botany of
    Southern Rhodesia." *Journal of the Linnaean Society* 38 (1906):
    425–494.
———. "A Contribution to the Flora and Plant Formations of
    Mt. Kinabalu and the Highlands of British North Borneo."
    Journal of the Linnaean Society 42 (1914): 1–240.

SECONDARY SOURCES
Nature 115 (1925): 345. Obituary notice.
Proceedings of the Linnean Society (1924–1925); 72–74. Obituary
    notice; includes bibliography.
Rendle, A. B. "Lilian Suzette Gibbs." *Journal of Botany* 63
    (1925): 116–117. Obituary notice; includes bibliography.

STANDARD SOURCES
Barnhart; Desmond.

GIFFORD, ISABELLA (ca. 1823–1891)

British botanist and phycologist. Never married. Born around 1823 in Swansea, Glam. Wrote on marine botany. Died in Minehead, Somerset, 26 December 1891.

Born around 1823 in Swansea, Glamorganshire, Isabella Gifford lived much of her life in Falmouth and then in Minehead, Somerset. She wrote a book on marine botanists in 1848 and contributed plants, primarily specimens of seaweed, to the Somerset Archaeological Society. Sensitive to the contributions of other women botanists, she memorialized ELIZABETH WARREN in 1865 for her zealous and careful collections. She corresponded with the Glasgow professor of botany G. A. Walker Arnott and her letters are included in his correspondence in the British Museum of Natural History. One of her papers appeared in the *Journal of Botany* in 1871. Her plants are at the Taunton Museum. She is memorialized by the algae genus *Giffordia* Batt. She died in 1891 in Somerset.   JH/MBO

PRIMARY SOURCES
Gifford, Isabella. *Marine Botanist.* Brighton: R. Folthorp, 1848;
    3d ed. 1853.
———. "Memorial of Miss [Elizabeth] Warren." *Report of
    Royal Cornwall Polytechnic Society* (1864): 11–14.
———. "Tetraspores of *Seirospora.*" *Journal of Botany* (1871):
    171.
Letters in Walker Arnott Correspondence, British Museum of
    Natural History.

SECONDARY SOURCES
Journal of Botany (1892): 81–83. Obituary notice.
Notarisia (1892): 1396–1399. Obituary notice.

STANDARD SOURCES
Barnhart; Desmond; Shteir.

GILBERT, RUTH (1883–1950?)

U.S. bacteriologist. Born 31 October 1883 in Warren, Conn. Educated Colorado College (A.B., 1907; A.M., 1910); Albany Medical College (Union, N.Y.) (M.D., 1923). Professional experience: Colorado College, instructor in biology (1907–1912); New York Post-graduate Hospital, instructor (1913); New York Woman's Medical College, instructor (1913–1916); New York State Department of Health, bacteriologist (1916–1949).

Connecticut-born Ruth Gilbert earned her undergraduate and master's degrees in Colorado, after which she became an instructor in biology at Colorado College for five years until 1912. She then went to New York City where she was an instructor in biology and simultaneously, was an instructor in New York Woman's Medical College. She then attended the Albany Medical College in New York where she received her medical degree. Even before she received this degree, Gilbert was hired by the new director of the New York State Department of Health in the new Research Division. She worked as the assistant to Augustus B. Wadsworth with MARY KIRKBRIDE, first as bacteriologist and then as assistant director of the diagnostic laboratory from 1921 until she retired in 1949. Part of her work as bacteriologist was to prepare safe vaccines and to study their effectiveness.   JH/MBO

SECONDARY SOURCES

Sexton, Anna M. *A Chronicle of the Division of Laboratories and Research: New York State Department of Health, the First Fifty Years: 1914–1964.* Lunenburg, Vt.: Steinehour Press, 1967.

STANDARD SOURCES

AMS 4–8, B 9, P&B 10; Rossiter 1982.

GILBRETH, LILLIAN EVELYN MOLLER (1878–1972)

U.S. psychologist and management and personnel specialist. Born 24 May 1878 in Oakland, Calif., to Ann and William Moller. Eight siblings. Married Frank Gilbreth (19 October 1904) (d. 1924). Twelve children. Educated University of California at Berkeley (B.Litt. in English literature, 1900); Barnard College (briefly); University of California, Berkeley (M.A. in English literature, 1902); Brown University (Ph.D. in psychology, 1914 [or 1915]). Professional experience: Gilbreth, Inc., co-owner (1904–1924); private management consultant (1924–1972); Bryn Mawr, Rutgers, and Purdue University, visiting lecturer in management (1924–1935); Newark College of Engineering, chair, department of personnel relations (1941–1943); Purdue University, professor of management (1935–1948). University of Wisconsin, professor of management (1955). Concurrent experience: President Hoover's Emergency Committee for Unemployment, member (1930); President's Organization on Unemployment Relief; the International Academy of Management, founding member (1954). Honors and memberships: twenty honorary degrees; Society of Industrial Engineers, honorary member (1921) (this society instituted the Gilbreth Medal in 1931 to reward distinguished contributions to management); American Society of Mechanical Engineers, Management Division Meeting, chair; American Psychological Association, Fellow; Gantt Gold Medal (1944) to Lillian and Frank (posthumously); Hoover Medal for distinguished public service by an engineer (1966; first woman). Honored with commemorative postal stamp in 1987. Died 2 January 1972 in Phoenix, Ariz.

Lillian Moller was the daughter of William Moller, manager of his father-in-law's hardware store and later owner of several shoe stores in San Francisco and Sacramento. Her mother, Ann Moller, managed the household of nine children. Lillian, as first-born, helped out as instructed by her mother, who was in delicate health. Lillian was also influenced by a favorite aunt, Lillian Delger Powell, a psychiatrist and psychoanalyst who studied with Sigmund Freud. Being very shy and terrified of going to public school, Lillian was tutored at home by her parents and private tutors for three years. She read voraciously, and learned French and German and how to play the piano as well as academic subjects. In public school, she found her interests leaned to music and literature; she made excellent grades and wrote poetry for the school paper and composed her own songs and lyrics.

Moller commuted to the University of California at Berkeley, intending to become a teacher. She majored in English literature and studied foreign languages, philosophy, and psychology. She participated in dramatic presentations in an effort to overcome her shyness. At graduation in 1900, she was chosen to be the first woman commencement speaker at Berkeley.

Moller applied to Barnard College (affiliated with Columbia University), wishing to study with Brander Matthews, well-known critic and professor of English literature, but he refused to allow a woman to attend his lectures. While at Barnard, she studied psychology with A. H. Thorndike, but her studies there were cut short when she became seriously ill and returned home. When recovered, she returned to Berkeley where she received a master's in English literature in 1902. Planning to continue for a doctoral degree in English, she took time to tour Europe with a group of other women and en route, in Boston, met Frank Gilbreth, wealthy owner of a successful construction company. He was waiting for her on her return from Europe and assiduously courted her. They were married 19 October 1904. Frank convinced her to change her major to psychology so that she could help him with his business, foreseeing the relation of psychology to management.

Lillian began immediately to work with her husband, encouraging his ideas, critiquing, refining, and improving his management system. They began writing descriptions of their methodology, such as Frank's original experiments in scientific management published in *Motion Study* (1911). With Lillian as partner, Frank gave up the construction business to go into management consultation. They taught management workshops at home in addition to lecturing in schools of engineering and business, consulting, and writing. They wrote *A Primer of Scientific Management* (1912) together, but the editor would not include a woman's name as coauthor. Lillian Gilbreth's *Psychology of Management* (1914) stressed the importance of human relations and the need to recognize the individuality of workers and their needs, psychological as well as physiological. The Gilbreth methods opposed the mechanistic, stop-watch industrial management principles many shops had adopted, following the autocratic standards set by Frederick W. Taylor. While incorporating some of Taylor's time-study methods into their own work, the Gilbreths advocated communication, cooperation, and improved human relations to increase productivity of workers. They endeavored to apply the benefits of scientific management and time and motion study to broader areas of human need, such as hospital and surgical service, rehabilitation of the disabled, and housework. Lillian Gilbreth believed that the tools and workplace should be designed to fit the workers, not vice versa; that workers directly involved in an operation understood best how an operation could be improved; that additional profits accrued by the elimination of wasted time or material should be shared among workers, managers, and owners. Workers would also receive recognition, respect, and reward for contributing ideas to improve the system.

When Frank Gilbreth died in 1924, Lillian was left with twelve children and the responsibility for their support and college expenses. Perfectly knowledgeable of the construction business they had run together, she intended to continue on her own, but was soon frustrated when many clients refused to renew their contracts with a woman. Gilbreth turned again to teaching, recruiting students from as far away as Germany, Belgium, England, and Japan to her workshops in industrial management. Her reputation for efficiency soon brought her requests for consulting services. She redesigned kitchens and household appliances to fit the needs of homemakers and to save them time and energy in performing daily chores. In the area of household management she published *The Home-Maker and Her Job* (1927) and *Management in the Home* (1954). She was hired by Macy's department store in New York City to increase the efficiency of its clerks. Working as a salesperson herself to understand the work flow, she improved the system so successfully that she was asked to stay and train one of the Macy's executives to conduct motion studies and operational analyses.

To handle all the requests for instruction in her methods, Gilbreth began teaching courses in college and universities, including Newark College of Engineering, Bryn Mawr, Rutgers, and Purdue University. In 1935, at age fifty-seven, she was appointed Professor of management at Purdue University, and stayed until "officially" retired at age seventy (1948). She did significant work with people with disabilities and handicaps and developed a model kitchen for the handicapped for the Institute of Rehabilitation Medicine at the New York University Medical Center. In *Normal Lives for the Disabled* (1944), she discusses special equipment and efficient routines for housework. During World War II, when five of her six sons were serving in the armed forces, Gilbreth served as a management consultant in war plants and on military bases at the express request of the government.

Called "Mother of Scientific Management" and "First Lady of Management," Lillian Gilbreth advocated and spread through example and teaching the humanized version of scientific management she and Frank envisioned. J. W. McKenny in 1952 called her the "World's Greatest Woman Engineer" because of her impact on management, her innovations in industrial design, her methodological contributions to time and motion studies, her humanization of

management principles, and her role in integrating the principles of science and management. She wrote eight books and many articles on education, management, and psychology. JH/MBO

PRIMARY SOURCES

Gilbreth, Lillian Evelyn Moller. *Psychology of Management*. New York: Sturgis and Walton, 1914. Provides logical, systematic explanation and defense of her new humanistic practices and principles of management.

———. With Frank Gilbreth. *Fatigue Study: The Elimination of Humanity's Greatest Unnecessary Waste*. New York: Sturgis and Walton, 1916.

———. With Frank Gilbreth. *Applied Motion Study*. New York: Sturgis and Walton, 1917.

———. With Frank Gilbreth. *Motion Study for the Handicapped*. London: Routledge and Sons, Ltd., 1924.

———. *The Quest of the One Best Way*. N.p.: Society of Industrial Engineers, 1924. A biography of her husband Frank, who died the same year.

———. *Living with Our Children*. New York: W. W. Norton and Co., 1928. Combined her philosophical views of home and family life with the principles of psychology and management. (She believed all individuals in a home should be happy and fulfilled, including the wives and mothers—a condition based on the sharing and efficient handling of all household responsibilities.)

———. *The Homemaker and Her Job*. New York: Appleton, 1936.

———. With E. Yost. *Normal Lives for the Disabled*. New York: Macmillan, 1945.

———. With A. B. Cook. *The Foreman in Manpower Management*. New York and London: McGraw-Hill, 1947.

———. *Management in the Home*. New York: Dodd, Mead, 1954.

SECONDARY SOURCES

Yost, E. *Frank and Lillian Gilbreth: Partners for Life*. New Brunswick, N.J.: Rutgers University Press, 1949.

STANDARD SOURCES

Bailey; *Notable*.

GILETTE OF NARBONNE (fl. ca. 1300)

French physician. Flourished ca. 1300. Daughter of physician Gerard of Narbonne.

Gilette took over her father's medical practice after his death. Supposedly she cured the French king of fistula. Boccaccio referred to her as "Donna Medica." JH/MBO

STANDARD SOURCES
Echols and Williams; Hurd-Mead 1938.

GILIANI, ALESSANDRA (1307–1326)

Italian anatomist. Born 1307. Educated University of Bologna. Professional experience: University of Bologna, assistant to Mondino de' Luzzi. Died 26 March 1326.

According to a report in *The History of the Anatomy School in Bologna* quoted in James Walsh's *Medieval Medicine*, Alessandra Giliani was "most valuable as a dissector and assistant to Mondino" (the anatomist Mondino de' Luzzi [ca. 1275–1326]). When she died at age nineteen, "consumed by her labors," a tablet commemorating her work was placed in the hospital church of Santa Maria del Mareto in Florence by her lover Otto Agenius Lustrulanus.

Giliani was the first woman prosector (one who prepares dissections for anatomical demonstrations) to be cited in the historical record. Giliani reputedly devised the technique of injecting blood vessels with dyes, an invaluable aid to anatomists. She drew blood from veins and arteries and refilled them with colored liquids that solidified, so that the paths of the vessels could be traced. Her new technology helped to enhance Mondino's reputation.   JH/MBO

STANDARD SOURCES
Alic; Hughes; Hurd-Mead 1938; Ogilvie 1986; Shearer and Shearer 1996; Walsh.

GILKEY, HELEN MARGARET (1886–1972)

U.S. botanist. Born 6 March 1886 in Montesano, Wash. Educated Oregon State College (B.S., 1907); (M.S., 1911); University of California (Ph.D., 1915?). Professional experience: Oregon State College, assistant botanist (1908–1909); instructor (1909–1911); University of California, assistant in botany (1912); scientific artist (1913–1918); Oregon State College, assistant professor (1919–1927), associate professor (1928–1946), professor (1947); concurrently curator at herbarium (from 1919). Died in 1972.

Helen Gilkey, an authority on truffles, was born and spent her entire career on the West Coast. Educated at Oregon State College, she went to the University of California, where she worked as an assistant in botany and as a scientific artist. Three years after she received her doctorate, she returned to Oregon State College, where she rose through the ranks to full professor of botany in 1947. She concurrently held the position of curator at the Oregon State Herbarium.
JH/MBO

PRIMARY SOURCES
Gilkey, Helen Margaret. *The Most Important Noxious Weeds of Oregon.* Corvallis, Oreg.: Oregon Agricultural College, Extension Service, 1929.
———. With Garland M. Powell. *Handbook of Northwest Flowering Plants.* Portland, Oreg.: Metropolitan Press, [1936].
———. *Northwestern American Plants.* Corvallis, Oreg.: Oregon State College, 1945.

SECONDARY SOURCES
Trapp, James. "Helen Margaret Gilkey." *Micrologia* 67 (1975): 207–213. Obituary notice; includes portrait.

STANDARD SOURCES
AMS 3–8, B 9, P&B 10–11; Barnhart; *NAW*(M) unused.

GILL, JOCELYN RUTH (1916–1984)

U.S. astronomer. Born 29 October 1929 in Flagstaff, Ariz., to Sarah (Bailey) and Thomas B. Gill. Educated Wellesley College (A.B., 1938); University of Chicago (S.M., 1941); University of California, Berkeley, graduate work; teaching assistant (1946–1948); Yale University (Ph.D. in astronomy, 1959). Professional experience: Mount Holyoke College, laboratory assistant and instructor in astronomy (1940–1942), assistant professor (1952–1957); MIT, Radiation Laboratory, staff member (1942–1945); Smith College, from instructor to assistant professor (1945–1952); Arizona State College, associate professor of mathematics and astronomy (1959–1960); Yale University, research assistant in astronomy; Office of Astronomy and Solar Physics, Office of Space Science, National Aeronautics and Space Administration (1960–1961), staff scientist in astronomy and astrophysics (1961–1963), chief in flight science (1963–1966), manned flight experimental office, staff scientist (1966–1968), Program Scientist Manned Flight Experimental Office, Office of Space Science and Application Headquarters, NASA (from 1968). Honors and memberships: American Association for the Advancement of Science, Fellow; American Astronomical Society, member; American Association of Variable Star Observers, member; New York Academy of Sciences, member; Sigma Xi, member. Died 1984.

Jocelyn Gill began her career as an academic scientist, teaching at Smith, Mount Holyoke, and Arizona State colleges. She then began to work for the manned space program and spent her later life as a government employee. She did significant research in NASA's manned space program beginning in 1961. After the former Soviet Union launched Sputnik, there was a great push to catch up, and the U.S. program opened many positions for women in science with expertise in astronomy and astrophysics. Gill was chief of in-flight science from 1963 to 1966 and participated in a solar eclipse flight in 1963. She also worked on the Gemini program.

She was a Fellow of the American Association for the Advancement of Science, and a member of the American Astronomical Society, the American Association of Variable Star Observers, the New York Academy of Science, and Sigma Xi. She received the Federal Women's Award in 1966, representing NASA. Her research was on celestial mechanics, numerical analysis of satellite orbits, and the motion of Neptune's satellite, Triton.   JH/MBO

PRIMARY SOURCES
Gill, Jocelyn. With Helen Dodson and Bernard Howard. *Field Intensity Contours in Generalized Coordinates.* Cambridge, Mass.: Radiation Laboratory, Massachusetts Institute of Technology, 1945.

STANDARD SOURCES
AMS P 9, P&B 10–14; Bailey; Debus; O'Neill.

GILLETT, MARGARET (CLARK) (1878–1962)

British botanist. Born 1878 in Street, Somerset. Married. Education Cambridge University (M.A.). Professional experience: collected plants in South Africa. Died in 1962.

Margaret Clark received a master's degree from Cambridge University. Between 1903 and 1948, she periodically visited Africa, where she collected plants in the Cape and Transvaal. She often accompanied General Jan C. Smuts on these expeditions.   JH/MBO

STANDARD SOURCES
Desmond; Gunn and Codd.

GILMORE, JANE GEORGINA (1887–?)

Irish botanist. Born 2 July 1887 in Ireland. Educated Belfast (B.Sc.). Professional experience: Girls' school in Dublin, botany teacher; St. Andrew's School, Johannesburg, botany teacher; Jeppe High School, senior science mistress (1925). Death date unknown.

Although she was born and educated in northern Ireland, Jane Gilmore used her education in South Africa, where she taught at several places. She collected plants mainly around Johannesburg and left South Africa in 1933.   JH/MBO

STANDARD SOURCES
Desmond; Gunn and Codd.

GILROY, HELEN (TURNBULL) (1887–?)

U.S. physicist. Born 9 May 1887 in Philadelphia, Pa. Married. Educated Bryn Mawr College (A.B., 1909); University of Wisconsin (fellow, 1911–1912; M.A., 1912; 1914); University of Chicago (1915–1917; Huff Fellow, 1920–1921); Cornell University (Ph.D. in physics, 1931). Professional experience: Bryn Mawr College, assistant in physics (1910–1911); demonstrator (1914–1915); Mount Holyoke College, instructor (1912–1914); Vassar College (1917–1920); assistant professor (1921–1924); Lingnan University, assistant professor (?) (1924–1927); professor (1931–1934); Agnes Scott College, assistant professor (?) (1927–1928); Cornell University, assistant (1928–1931), research doctor (1935); Beaver College, professor of physics (1937–1943); Wilson College, instructor (?) (1943–1945), assistant professor (1946–1949), associate professor (1949–1950); Freeman Meteorological Observatory, director (1924–1927). Death date unknown.

Physicist Helen Turnbull Gilroy had a peripatetic career as she moved to various academic posts. Even before she got her doctorate, she worked in numerous places. It was only after she got a position at Wilson College that her career acquired stability. Although information is not available on her marriage, this may be a possible explanation. Her research was on spectroscopy of the extreme ultraviolet and X-ray methods of crystal analysis. She was a member of the physical society and the Association of Physics Teachers.   JH/MBO

PRIMARY SOURCES
Gilroy, Helen Turnbull. *Certain Spectra in the Varadium I Iso-Electronic Sequence.* Minneapolis: n.p., 1931. Ph.D. diss.

STANDARD SOURCES
AMS 3–8, P 9, P&B 10.

GIRAUD, MARTHE (fl. 1921)

French biophysicist. Never married. Professional experience: research on physiological effects of radiation.

Marthe Giraud and her collaborators reported on changes in white and red blood cells and blood pressure accompanying radiation sickness in a patient treated with long-term radiotherapy with X-rays. Subsequent animal experiments indicated that the shock produced in radiation sickness was caused by products from damaged cells that passed into the bloodstream.   MM

PRIMARY SOURCES
Giraud, Marthe. With Gaston Giraud and G. Parès. "La crise hémoclasique du mal des irradiations pénétrantes." *Comptes rendus* 173 (1921): 801–803.

————. "Recherches experimentales sur la genèse de la crise hémoclasique des irradiations intensives." *Comptes rendus* 175 (1922): 186–188.

STANDARD SOURCES
Meyer and von Schweidler.

GITELSON, FRANCES H. (1905–   )

U.S. psychiatrist. Born 19 June 1905 in Chicago. One younger brother. Married Max Gitelson (d. 1965). One child. Educated Northwestern University Medical School (M.D., 1932); Cook County Hospital, Chicago, intern; Institute for Juvenile Research, Chicago, residency in psychiatry (two years); Boston Psychiatric Hospital; attended lectures at the Boston Psychoanalytic Institute, and Chicago Institute. Professional experience: Boston Psychiatric Hospital, psychiatrist; psychoanalysis training analyst (1952–?). Honors and memberships: Omega Alpha, American Psychoanalytic Association, International Psychoanalytic Association.

Frances Gitelson was born in Chicago to middle-class parents who both worked, her father as a mechanic with International Harvester Company, her mother as a teacher in the Chicago public schools. Frances credits her mother for inspiring her to become a doctor, and she weighted her schoolwork with science courses before high school so she would be prepared for medical school. She graduated from Northwestern University Medical School in 1932, then spent a year working in a hospital emergency room before beginning her internship.

During eighteen months of internship, Frances remained undecided on a specialty, then she was assigned to the Psychiatric Hospital and found what she felt was her field. She arranged to have her residency in psychiatry. At the Institute of Juvenile Research, she met Max Gitelson, who was a senior member of the staff, and they became friends. She left the institute to complete her third-year residency at Boston Psychiatric Hospital and to attend lectures at the Boston Psychoanalytic Institute. The couple was married in Boston, but returned to Chicago to practice, both eventually becoming training analysts. Max Gitelson died in 1965, after serving a term as president of the International Psychoanalytic Association, and Frances Gitelson continued her practice and remained active with the IPA, being appointed honorary secretary, and with the American Psychoanalytic Association.   KM

PRIMARY SOURCES
Gitelson, Frances. In Hellstedt, Autobiographies.

GJELLESTAD, GURO ELSE (1914–1972)

Norwegian astrophysicist. Born 11 August 1914 in Bergen, Norway. Educated University of Oslow (diploma in physics, 1950). Professional experience: Mount Wilson Observatory and Yerkes Observatory (1953–1954); Norwegian Institute for Cosmic Physics, researcher (1955–1959); University of Bergen, assistant professor (1959–?). Died 11 January 1972.

Guro Else Gjellestad was thirty-six years old when she earned her diploma in physics. She made up for lost time, doing research on the magnetism of variable stars, doing both observational and theoretical work. She went to two observatories in the United States for two years and then returned to Norway where she conducted research on geomagnetism at the Norwegian Institute for Cosmic Physics. In 1959, she became an assistant professor at the University of Bergen; during this time she did research on paleomagnetism. This was a new field for Norwegian research; Gjellestad collaborated on it with the University of Newcastle. Her initiative resulted in a laboratory for paleomagnetic measurement in Bergen. She dedicated the rest of her short life to this work.   JH/MBO

SECONDARY SOURCES
Jensen, Eberhart. "Guro Else Gjellestad." *Quarterly Journal of the Royal Astronomical Society* 15 (1974): 196.

STANDARD SOURCES
Strohmeier.

GLAGOLEVA-ARKAD'YEVA, ALEKSANDRA ANDREYEVNA (1894–1945)

Russian physicist. Born 28 February 1884. Married Aleksandr Alexsandrovich Glagolev. Educated Moscow University, Faculty of Physics and Mathematics (graduated 1910). Professional experience: Moscow University, Higher Women's Courses, assistant professor physics (1910–1914); Moscow military hospital, X-ray technician (1914–1918); Moscow University, instructor (1918–1930); Second Moscow Medical Institute, researcher (1930–1939). Died 30 October 1945.

Aleksandra Andreyevna was born in Russia in 1884 and educated in the Faculty of Physics and Mathematics under the Higher Women's Courses. After graduation, she became an assistant professor in the Higher Women's Courses. During World War I, she worked in the X-ray department of the military hospital in Moscow. While working in this hospital, she invented a Roentgen stereometer that allowed physicians to locate shrapnel and bullets in the human body. After the Revolution, she taught at Moscow University, and in the

1920s developed an X-ray emitter that allowed her to attain ultra-short wavelengths, upon which she did extensive research. In the 1930s, she was professor in the Second Moscow Medical Institute, but was forced to give up teaching for health reasons. Her collected works were published in 1948.   ACH

PRIMARY SOURCES

Glagoleva-Arkad'yeva, Aleksandra Andreyevna. *Sobraniye trudov (Collected Works)*. Moscow, 1948.

SECONDARY SOURCES

Who Was Who in the USSR. A Biographic Directory Containing 5,015 Biographies of Prominent Soviet Historical Personalities. Ed. Heinrich E. Schulz, Paul K. Urban, Andrew I. Lebed. Metuchen, N.J.: Scarecrow Press, Inc., 1972. Glagoleva-Arkad'yeva discussed page 193.

GLASCOTT, LOUISA S. (fl. 1893–1900)

Irish botanist. Born Alderton, New Ross. Educated Dublin.

Louisa Glascott was the student of A. C. Haddon at Dublin, where she studied Irish Rotifera and published a paper in 1893 dealing with 158 species, 24 of which she claimed were new to science. Her new species were not confirmed by others.   JH/MBO

PRIMARY SOURCES

Glascott, Louisa S. With Gerald Edward Barrett-Hamilton. [Two papers on Wexford flowering plants]. *Irish Naturalist* (1889–1890).
———. *Scientific Proceedings of the Royal Dublin Society* 8 (1893): 29–86.

SECONDARY SOURCES

Praeger, R. Lloyd. *Some Irish Naturalists: A Biographical Note-Book.* Dundalk, W. Tempest: Dundalgan Press, 1949.

GLASGOW, MAUDE (1868–1955)

Irish-born U.S. physician. Born 1868. Educated? (M.D., 1901). Died 1955.

Maude Glasgow came from Northern Ireland to New York City, first working as a nurse, then as a physician. Glasgow fought against blindness in infants caused by venereal disease. She was convinced that education was the way to combat that plague, insisting that promiscuous sexual behavior was intolerable. This "crime" against newborn children could be eliminated by new attitudes, including one that challenged the often held beliefs that sexual activity was nec-

essary for the health of unmarried males. Glasgow asserted that this view was "routed in injustice and founded on male domination."   JH/MBO

PRIMARY SOURCES

Glasgow, Maude. "Maude Glasgow, M.D. (An Autobiography)." *Medical Woman's Journal* 51 (1944): 34–36.
———. *Problems of Sex.* Boston: Christopher, [1949].

SECONDARY SOURCES

Atkinson, Donald T. *Magic, Myth, and Medicine.* Cleveland: The World Publishing Company, 1956. Pages 267–268 consider Glasgow's work.

GLASS, JEWELL JEANETTE (1888–1966)

U.S. mineralogist. Born 24 December 1888 in Daleville, Lauderdale County, Miss., to Julia Ann Vance Glass and Levi Lafayette Glass. Never married. Educated George Washington University (A.B., 1926; M.A., 1929); University of North Carolina (1929–1930); University of Minnesota (summer 1930); Johns Hopkins University (1932–1933). Professional experience: United States Geological Survey, aide in mineralogy, junior assistant, associate, full mineralogist, and geologist (1930–1960); George Washington University, faculty member (from 1960). Died 28 January 1966 in Washington, D.C., and interred at Laurel, Miss.

A native of Mississippi, Glass came to Washington, D.C., to accept a civil service position at the war department. After several years in that department plus several more at the U.S. Department of Agriculture, Glass joined the professional staff of the U.S. Geological Survey in 1930. She progressed through the various ranks of the survey, finally achieving the rank of geologist, with specialties in petrology and mineralogy. After her retirement, Glass joined the faculty of George Washington University where she taught mineralogy.

Glass received numerous honors, including the Department of Interior Meritorious Service Award in 1961. She was a Fellow of the Mineralogical Society of America and the Geological Society of America. She held memberships in the Geological Society of Washington, the Petrologists' Club of Washington, the Virginia Academy of Sciences, the American Geophysical Union, Washington Academy of Sciences, Crystallographic Society of America, and the Mineralogical Society of Great Britain.

Although Jewell Glass was known professionally for her studies of minerals from Colorado, Virginia, South Carolina, Arkansas, Pennsylvania, New Mexico, California, and other states, as well as Puerto Rico, many of her contributions involve teaching others. She was as willing to share her knowledge with elementary school children as she was with her colleagues. Her contributions to both pure science and to the development of mineral resources include studies of beryllium minerals, the discovery of the manganese mineral pyroxmangit in Idaho, and her study of bastnaesite from California, which contributed to the discovery of the largest known deposit of this rare-earth mineral in the world.   CK

PRIMARY SOURCES

Glass, Jewell. "The Pegamite Minerals from near Amelia, Virginia." *American Mineralogist* 20 (1935): 741–768.

———. With S. K. Roy and E. P. Henderson. "The Walters Meteorite." *Fieldiana-Geology* 10 (1962): 539–550.

SECONDARY SOURCES

Jespersen, Anna. "Memorial of Jewell Jeannette Glass." *American Mineralogist* 52, nos. 3–4 (1967): 584–588.

STANDARD SOURCES

Sarjeant.

GLEASON, JOSEPHINE MIXER (1892–1982)

U.S. psychologist. Born October 1892 in North Adams, Mass. Educated Vassar College; Cornell University (Ph.D., 1918). Professional experience: Cornell University, instructor (1918–1929); Vassar College, associate professor of psychology (from 1929). Honors and memberships: American Psychological Association. Died 1982.

Gleason was a member of the department of psychology at Vassar College in 1937 when MARGARET WASHBURN was forced to retire as chairman of the department after suffering several strokes. Gleason had not published sufficiently to be eligible for the position, but she was appointed head of the selection committee. Unfortunately, Gleason chose to ask Edwin Boring, a notorious denigrator of women psychologists, for suggestions, and he opined that while only a man would be suitable for the chair position, the really bright young men would be advised to decline in favor of a university with better facilities. In the end, a man, Lyle Lanier, was chosen. Rossiter cites this as an example of the tremendous resistance, internal and external by both sexes, to appointing women to top positions at the women's colleges (and even more so at coeducational institutions).   JH/MBO

PRIMARY SOURCES

Gleason, Josephine Mixer. An Experimental Study of "Feelings of Relation." Worcester, Mass.: n.p., 1919. Ph.D. diss.

STANDARD SOURCES

AMS 3–8, S&B 9–10; Rossiter 1982.

GLEASON, KATE (1865–1933)

U.S. mechanical engineer. Born 1865. Father William Gleason. Never married. Educated Cornell University (1880s, no degree). Professional experience: Gleason Machine Tools Company; National Bank of East Rochester, president. Died 1933.

Although Kate Gleason attended Cornell University in the 1880s, she never got a degree. When she left Cornell, she went to work for her father's company, the Gleason Machine Tools Company, which was well known for its production of specialized gears. Gleason became famous for her original design of "worm gears." She was the first woman to qualify for full membership in the American Society of Mechanical Engineers (ASME). A very versatile woman, Gleason later became the first woman president of a national bank. According to Alva Matthews, her contributions to engineering thought were great. She is reported to have represented the ASME at international conferences and was a part of an invited delegation that toured the Far East. After her death, her multimillion-dollar estate helped establish the Rochester Institute of Technology.   JH/MBO

SECONDARY SOURCES

Trescott, Martha Moore. "Women in the Intellectual Development of Engineering." In Kass-Simon and Farnes.

GLEASON, RACHEL BROOKS (1820–1905)

U.S. physician. Born 27 November 1820 in Winhall, Vt. Married. Two children (daughter became a physician). Educated Rochester, N.Y. Professional experience: practiced with her husband, Dr. Gleason, in their Vermont infirmary. Died 14 March 1905 in Buffalo, N.Y.

Rachel Brooks married a Vermont doctor who opened an infirmary for invalids in the country. His wife often assisted him and gradually became involved in relaying the symptoms and prescribing treatments. Since the Philadelphia school for women had not yet opened, Dr. Gleason convinced the eclectics assembled in council to allow Rachel to attend their new school at Rochester, New York. One of her two children, a daughter, was educated as a physician.   JH/MBO

PRIMARY SOURCES

Gleason, Rachel Brooks. *Talks to My Patients: Hints on Getting Well and Keeping Well.* New York: Wood and Holbrook, 1870.

SECONDARY SOURCES

Jacobi, Mary Putnam. *Woman's Work in America in Medicine.* New York: Henry Holt Co., 1891.

Kelly, Howard A. *Cyclopedia of American Medical Biography.* Vol. 1. Philadelphia: W. B. Saunders, 1912.

STANDARD SOURCES
Hurd-Mead 1933.

GLEDITSCH, ELLEN (1879–1968)

Norwegian chemist. Born 29 December 1879 in Mandel, Norway, to Petra (Hansen) Gleditsch and Karl Gleditsch, a teacher. Nine siblings. Educated University of Oslo (1901?–1903?); Radium Institute, Paris (1907–1912); University of Paris (Licenciée des Sciences, 1912); Yale University (nonacademic qualification as pharmacist, 1902). Professional experience: University of Oslo, assistant, chemical laboratory (1903–1911), fellow (1911–1916), lecturer (1916–1929), professor of organic chemistry (1929–1946), chairman of chemistry division, professor emerita (1946–1968). Honors and memberships: Norwegian Academy of Science, Nansen prize; honorary doctorates from Smith College (1914), the University of Strasbourg (1948), and the University of Paris (1967); Award of the Legion d'Honneur. Died 6 June 1968 in Oslo.

Ellen Gleditsch grew up in a happy, well-educated family, where she developed a deep sense of responsibility for others. Although she was an outstanding student, women were barred from the university entrance exam, so in 1897 she became an apprentice pharmacist. Later she continued her education at the University of Oslo, where a professor assisted her in obtaining entrance to MARIE CURIE's laboratory.

Curie was impressed by Gleditsch's work, and obtained her services for the industrial production of radium. After her initial five years in Paris, Gleditsch returned to the University of Oslo. She maintained contact with Curie, returning at intervals to work in the Paris laboratory. Gleditsch also continued her friendships with women researchers whom she had met there.

In 1916 Gleditsch was appointed lecturer at the University of Oslo in the new field of radiochemistry, one of the first such chairs in the world. Friendly and cheerful, she was well liked by students and was a supportive mentor. Gleditsch maintained a wide network of professional contacts throughout her life.

During 1924–1928, Gleditsch served as president of the International Federation of Women, an organization she hoped would promote world peace. The next year she became Norway's first female professor of chemistry. Gleditsch was the first woman to receive an honorary doctorate from the Sorbonne.

In Marie Curie's laboratory, Gleditsch tested a claim (by the British chemist William Ramsay) that radiations from radioactive substances could cause transmutation, with negative results. She determined the radium/uranium ratio in minerals of varying age and origin, a test of the transmutation theory of radioactivity and the accuracy of the postu-

lated decay sequence. Gleditsch found significant differences in the ratio, which nevertheless were not large enough to exclude radium's descent from uranium. Her suggested explanations for the discrepancy included the presence of a long-lived intermediate product (which was later confirmed). From her measurements, Gleditsch determined radium's period and decay constant. During 1913–1914, Gleditsch worked at Yale with Bertram B. Boltwood under a fellowship from the American Scandinavian Foundation. In order to shed light on the origin of actinium, Gleditsch determined its ratio to uranium in minerals. She also determined the atomic weight of lead and chlorine isotopes from uranium minerals.

Gleditsch published numerous articles and several books on radioactivity. She also authored a textbook of inorganic chemistry, a biography of the chemist Antoine Lavoisier, and many biographical articles on scientists.   MM

PRIMARY SOURCES

Gleditsch, Ellen. "Sur le lithium dans les minéraux radioactifs." *Comptes rendus* 146 (1908): 331–333.

———. With M. Curie. "Action de l'émanation du radium sur les solutions des sels de cuivre." *Comptes rendus* 147 (1908): 345–349.

———. "Sur le rapport entre l'uranium et le radium dans les minéraux actifs." *Le Radium* 8 (1911): 256–273.

———. "The Life of Radium." *American Journal of Science* 41 (1916): 112–124.

———. With Eva Ramstedt. *Radium og de radioaktive processer.* Kristiana, Norway: Aschehoug, 1917.

Records in Institut Curie archives, assembled by Mme. Monique Bordry.

SECONDARY SOURCES

Badash, Lawrence, ed. *Rutherford and Boltwood: Letters on Radioactivity.* New Haven: Yale University Press, 1969.

Davis, J. L. "The Research School of Marie Curie in the Paris Faculty, 1907–14." *Annals of Science* 52 (1995): 321–355.

Kronen, Torliev, and Alexis Pappas. *Ellen Gleditsch.* Oslo: Aventura, 1987.

Nature 222 (1969): 101. Obituary notice.

Rayner-Canham, Marelene F., and Geoffrey W. Rayner-Canham. "Pioneer Women in Nuclear Science." *American Journal of Physics* 58 (1990): 1036–1043.

Róna, Elizabeth. *How It Came About: Radioactivity, Nuclear Physics, Atomic Energy.* Oak Ridge, Tenn.: Oak Ridge Associated Universities, 1978.

Rutherford, Ernest. *Radioactive Substances and Their Radiations.* Cambridge: Cambridge University Press, 1913.

STANDARD SOURCES

Poggendorff, vols. 5, 6, 7b; Rayner-Canham 1997.

GLUECK, ELEANOR (TOUROFF) (1898–1972)

U.S. criminologist and sociologist. Born 12 April 1898 in New York City. Married Sheldon Glueck (1922). One child. Educated Barnard College, Columbia (B.A., 1920); New York School of Social Work (1921). Harvard University (M.Ed., 1923; Ed.D., 1925; honorary D.Sc., 1958). Professional experience: Harvard University, department of social ethics, researcher in criminology (1925–1928); Harvard Law School, research associate (from 1928), assistant professor (from 1930). Honors and memberships: American Association for the Advancement of Science, Fellow; International Society of Criminologists, Fellow. Died 25 September 1972 in Cambridge, Mass.

Eleanor Glueck was a trustee of the Judge Baker Guidance Center and received recognition for her accomplishments in criminology. She and her husband worked together closely at Harvard Law School. In 1947, she received the Parsons Memorial Award of the United Prison Association of Massachusetts. She was a Fellow of the American Association for the Advancement of Science and the International Society of Criminologists. She conducted research into the causes, prevention, and treatment of delinquency.   JH/MBO

PRIMARY SOURCES
Glueck, Eleanor. With Sheldon Glueck. *Delinquents in the Making.* New York: Harper, 1952.
———. With Sheldon Glueck. *Physique and Delinquency.* New York: Harper, 1956.
———. With Sheldon Glueck. *Predicting Delinquency and Crime.* Cambridge: Harvard University Press, 1959.

STANDARD SOURCES
AMS S&B 9–11.

GOCHOLASHVILI, MARIIA MIKIEVNA (1904–)

Russian plant physiologist. Born 1904 in Tiflis (later Tbilisi), Georgia. Educated agricultural faculty, Tiflis Polytechnic Institute. Professional experience: All-Union Institute of Tea Cultivation, staff; All-Union Institute of Phytoculture, head of laboratory; All-Union Research Institute of Subtropical Crops, staff; Southern Institute for Combatting Plant Pests, head of department of plant physiology, later associate, Batumi Subtropical Botanical Gardens.

Mariia Mikievna Gocholashvili graduated from the agricultural faculty of the Tiflis Polytechnic Institute in 1927. From 1927 to 1929 she worked at the department of plant physiology of the All-Union Institute of Tea Cultivation and in 1929 at the All-Union Institute of Phytoculture. In 1929, she became head of the laboratory of plant physiology at the All-Union Research Institute of Subtropical Crops. In 1931 she was on the staff of the Southern Institute for Combatting Plant Pests, and from 1935 to 1946 she was head of the department of plant physiology at the Batumi Subtropical Botanical Gardens. After 1946, she remained associated with the Botanical Gardens.

Gocholashvili's principal research and publications have been on the winter hardiness and vegetative reproduction of subtropical plants and the study of tea plants.   JH/MBO

PRIMARY SOURCES
Gocholashvili, Mariia Mikievna. *Biological Principles of Tea Plant Cultivation in Georgia.* 1963.

SECONDARY SOURCES
Debus.

GODDING, D. W. (fl. 1847)

Writer, children's science books.

Little information is available on Godding except that she wrote a short geology text for children in 1847.   JH/MBO

PRIMARY SOURCES
Godding, D. W. *First Lessons in Geology: Comprising Its Most Important and Interesting Facts, Simplified to the Understanding of Children.* Hartford: H. S. Parson, 1847.

SECONDARY SOURCES
Aldrich, Michele L. "Women in Geology." In Kass-Simon and Farnes.

GODFERY, HILDA MARGARET (1871–1930)

British botanical artist. Born 1871. Died 17 September 1930 in Guildford, Surrey.

Hilda Godfery was a specialist in drawing orchids. She drew the plates for H. Correvon's *Album des Orchides d'Europe* and M. J. Godfery's *Monograph and Iconograph of Native British Orchidaceae.* Her orchid drawings are at the British Museum of Natural History.   JH/MBO

PRIMARY SOURCES
Correvon, Henry *Album des Orchidées d'Europe.* Geneva: H. Correvon, 1923. Plates by Godfery.
Godfery, M. J. *Monograph and Iconograph of Native British Orchidaceae.* Cambridge: Cambridge University Press, 1933. Plates by Godfery.

SECONDARY SOURCES
Botanical Society Exchange Club of the British Isles, Report (1930): 323. Obituary notice.

Goeppert Mayer, Maria Gertrud Käte

Journal of Botany (1930): 343–344. Obituary notice.
Orchid Review (1930): 341. Obituary notice.

STANDARD SOURCES
Desmond.

GOEPPERT MAYER, MARIA GERTRUD KÄTE (1906–1972)

German/U.S. physicist. Born 28 June 1906 in Kattowitz, Upper Silesia, Germany (now Katowice, Poland) to Maria Wolff and Friedrich Göppert. No siblings. Mother was a teacher before marriage, father became professor of pediatrics at Georgia Augusta University (University of Göttingen) in 1910. Married Joseph Mayer. Two children, Maria Ann (Marianne, Maria Anne) and Peter Conrad. Naturalized U.S. citizen, 1933. Educated at local schools; University of Göttingen (Ph.D., 1930). Professional experience: Johns Hopkins, nominal appointments (1930–1939); Columbia University, instructor(?) (1939–1945), lecturer in chemistry (ca. 1940–1945); Sarah Lawrence College, lecturer, intermittently (1941, 1945–1946); Manhattan Project, researcher (1942–1945); University of Chicago, volunteer associate professor of physics (1946–1960); Metallurgical Laboratory, University of Chicago (later Argonne National Laboratory), consultant; Argonne, senior physicist (1946–1960); University of California at San Diego, professor of physics (1960–1972). Honors and memberships: Nobel Laureate (physics, 1963); National Academy of Sciences; American Philosophical Society; Corresponding Member of the Akademie der Wissenschaften, Heidelberg; American Physical Society, Fellow; American Academy of Arts and Sciences, Fellow; Sigma Xi. Honorary degrees: Russell Sage College, Mount Holyoke College, Smith College, Portland State College, and Ripon College. Died 21(?) February 1972 in La Jolla, Calif.

Maria Göppert was the only child in a well-educated upper-middle-class family. Her mother taught French and piano before her marriage. Her father, who became professor of pediatrics at the University of Göttingen and founded a clinic there, took special pride in being the sixth generation of a family of university professors. Later Goeppert Mayer was pleased to have continued the family tradition.

Friedrich Göppert encouraged his daughter's natural curiosity and adventurousness, and made it clear he would like her to be more than a housewife. She adopted his low opinion of women and women's traditional roles, preferring the company of men throughout her life. Goeppert Mayer claimed later that she found her father, as a scientist, more interesting than her mother. However, she was devoted to her mother, as well as dependent upon her. Goeppert Mayer wrote frequently and visited as often as possible after emigrating to the United States, where she continued her mother's Christmas traditions and gracious entertaining.

Maria Göppert learned the importance of duty while young and presented a reserved, somewhat aristocratic bearing as an adult. She suffered from severe headaches and minor illnesses during her childhood, perhaps in part exacerbated by her parent's high expectations. At the public elementary school for girls, Göppert excelled at languages and mathematics. She entered a private university preparatory school in 1921. The school closed two years later (due to losses suffered in the postwar inflation), before Maria could finish the three-year course. Although she chose to take the university entrance exam (the Abitur) one year early, Göppert passed, and entered the University of Göttingen in 1924 to major in mathematics. Like most of the women students, she began to prepare for a teaching certificate, but found the classes uninteresting. She also considered medicine, but her father argued against it, fearing that she would suffer as he did whenever a patient died.

Göttingen was famous for its mathematics, and was soon to become equally famous for its atomic physics. In 1927, inspired by the theoretical physicist Max Born, Göppert switched to physics. That year her father died unexpectedly. Maria Göppert reacted by resolving to complete her doctorate; Born became her father figure. She was also influenced by the experimentalist James Franck, who later became a family friend. Maria Göppert earned her doctorate in 1930, the same year in which she married the American chemist Joseph Mayer. He had come to Göttingen to work with Born and Franck after receiving his doctorate from the University of California, Berkeley, under Gilbert N. Lewis. Joseph Mayer accepted a position at Johns Hopkins University, and the couple moved to the United States. She anglicized her birth name to Goeppert.

Goeppert Mayer was naturalized before the birth of the couple's daughter, Maria Ann, in the spring of 1933. Their son, Peter Conrad, was born in 1938. The children were unhappy with taking second place to Goeppert Mayer's career, and although both initially studied science in college (Maria Ann began in biology, Peter in physics), they did not pursue scientific careers. Peter become a professor of economics, thus carrying on the Göppert family heritage.

Goeppert Mayer worked for the Manhattan Project and participated in efforts to assist German refugee scientists. Her feelings about the war were ambivalent, due to her German roots and love of family, friends, and colleagues. She made it clear to her children that the war was directed against Hitler, not the German people. After the war, the Mayers monitored research in Germany for the State Department. They also traveled extensively overseas to lecture and attend meetings.

During the war Goeppert Mayer, a heavy smoker, began to experience health problems. In 1956 she lost most of her hearing in one ear. A stroke in 1960 left her partly paralyzed. She died of heart failure on 20 February 1972.

During Goeppert Mayer's time, universities were hesitant to hire women for university positions. A married women experienced additional obstacles, such as anti-nepotism rules, the belief that a married woman would not take her work seriously, and the assumption that her work derived from her husband. Goeppert Mayer dealt with these obstacles by identifying with men at an early age and by ignoring some of her society's expectations.

She also had powerful male allies. Like many other successful women scientists, Goeppert Mayer received much encouragement from key men in her life, beginning with her father. Many colleagues were supportive, such as Born, Franck, Karl Herzfeld, Harold Urey, and Enrico Fermi. Her husband prodded her to complete projects such as her doctorate and her first nuclear shell model papers. Perhaps partly because she worked so long without recognition, Goeppert Mayer was modest about her work and abilities. This diffidence, plus her avoidance of competitiveness in favor of impeccably correct behavior toward her colleagues, also reflects her background as a well-bred young lady of the time.

Some of the difficulties Goeppert Mayer experienced turned to her advantage. Unable to determine her own career path, she seized the opportunities that arose while she followed her husband. Though educated as a mathematical physicist, and equipped with great facility in the Born-Heisenberg matrix formulation of quantum theory, Goeppert Mayer turned to chemical physics when she came to Johns Hopkins. (No one at Johns Hopkins worked on quantum mechanics, but Born had recommended Goeppert Mayer to the physical chemist Karl Herzfeld. With Herzfeld, she did theoretical physical chemistry, working on energy transfer and on the liquid phase. She also worked with her husband to apply quantum mechanics to chemistry. She taught him quantum mechanics, while she learned experimental chemistry from him. Goeppert Mayer's combination of theoretical and practical knowledge was important for her later work on nuclear structure. She also worked briefly with the experimental physicist Robert W. Wood. What was undertaken through necessity led to a deeper appreciation of experiment and understanding of a new field. Goeppert Mayer learned another field new to her, nuclear physics, from Teller and from Fermi while at Columbia and Chicago. The varied strands in her background, both the planned and the unplanned, eventually converged in the studies that earned her the Nobel Prize for her shell model of the nucleus.

Goeppert Mayer's dissertation was a theoretical treatment of two-photon processes (which eventually became experimentally important). She later used the methods of her thesis

to determine the probability of double beta decay. At Johns Hopkins, Goeppert Mayer applied quantum mechanics to chemical physics, working with Karl Herzfeld, Alfred Lee Sklar, and her husband. Particularly noteworthy was her work on benzene's spectrum. The Mayers's 1940 textbook on statistical mechanics grew out of a seminar they gave jointly at Johns Hopkins. Unfortunately, people assumed that Joseph Mayer had done most of the work, so the book did not help Goeppert Mayer's professional reputation. Goeppert Mayer held no academic appointment at Johns Hopkins and received only a token stipend. She was assigned chemistry lectures at Columbia mainly so that she could be listed as holding an academic position in the Mayers' forthcoming book.

In December 1941 Goeppert Mayer accepted a half-time paid teaching position at Sarah Lawrence College, where she developed a unified science course. In the spring of 1942, she joined the Substitute Alloy Materials secret project (whose real goal was to separate U 235 from U 238) directed by Harold Urey. Although her assigned tasks (separation of isotopes, first by using photochemical reactions, then with chemical means) proved to be impractical, Goeppert Mayer's confidence was bolstered by being accepted as a professional worthy of pay and supervisory responsibilities. She also worked with Edward Teller on a project related to nuclear fusion.

After the war, Joseph Mayer accepted a position at the University of Chicago, where Teller, Fermi, Franck, and Urey had decided to relocate. Goeppert Mayer was offered an associate professorship, but (due to anti-nepotism rules) without a salary. Joseph Mayer agreed to lead an institute seminar, which became a means (together with informal conversations with Teller and Fermi) for Goeppert Mayer to learn the newest nuclear physics. In 1946, her former graduate student Robert Sachs invited her to join the theoretical group at the newly created Argonne National Laboratory.

Goeppert Mayer's research with Teller on the origin of the elements led to considerations of the elements' relative abundance. She noticed that the most stable elements contained particular numbers of either protons or neutrons, later called the "magic numbers." Goeppert Mayer read Walter Elasser's almost forgotten 1933 paper on this topic and searched the literature for other clues. Shell models had been considered and discarded earlier, but Goeppert Mayer felt that new evidence strongly supported this notion. In 1948, she published a paper that set out the evidence but provided no theory. A question by Fermi, who was keenly interested in her work, triggered the insight that enabled Goeppert Mayer to solve the theoretical problem. By assuming strong spin–orbit coupling, she was able to calculate energy levels that matched the magic numbers.

Goeppert Mayer delayed publishing her results as a courtesy to several other physicists whom she had heard were working on shell models in the United States. As it turned out, J. H. D. Jensen, Otto Haxel, and Hans E. Suess in Heidelberg published a similar interpretation at about the same time Goeppert Mayer's detailed explanation appeared. Goeppert Mayer and Jensen later became friends and coauthored a book on nuclear shell structure (1955). She worked with Jensen to elaborate the theory and with others to apply it to radioactivity.

In 1959, the Mayers were both offered full paid professorships at the University of California at San Diego. Although Chicago offered her a paid position, the couple moved to California in 1960. Soon afterward, Goeppert Mayer had a stroke. She continued to teach and to work as much as she was able. For the nuclear shell model, Goeppert Mayer and Jensen received half of the physics Nobel Prize for 1963.   JH/MBO

PRIMARY SOURCES

Goeppert Mayer, Maria. With Max Born. "Dynamische Gittertheorie der Kristalle." *Handbuch der Physik* 24, no. 2 (1931): 623–774. 1931.

———. "Double Beta-Disintegration." *Physical Review* 48 (1935): 512–516.

———. With Alfred Lee Sklar. "Calculations of the Lower Excited Levels of Benzene." *Journal of Chemical Physics* 6 (1938): 645–652.

———. With J. Mayer. *Statistical Mechanics.* New York: Wiley, 1940.

———. "On Closed Shells in Nuclei." *Physical Review* 74 (1948): 235–239; 75 (1949): 1969–1970.

———. "Nuclear Configuration in the Spin-Orbit Coupling Model. I. Empirical Evidence; II. Theoretical Considerations." *Physical Review* 78 (1950): 16–23.

———. With J. H. D. Jensen. *Elementary Theory of Nuclear Shell Structure.* New York: John Wiley & Sons, 1955.

Autobiography in the Niels Bohr Library, American Institute of Physics.

Interview with Maria Mayer, conducted by Thomas S. Kuhn, February 1962. Archive for History of Quantum Physics.

Maria Goeppert Mayer Papers, University of California at San Diego Library, special collections.

SECONDARY SOURCES

Dash, Joan. *A Life of One's Own.* New York, Evanston, San Francisco, and London: Harper & Row, 1973. In addition to published sources, Dash used her own interviews of Joseph and Maria Mayer, and unpublished correspondence between Goeppert Mayer and her mother.

Elasser, Walter M. *Memoirs of a Physicist in the Atomic Age.* New York: Science History Publications; Bristol: Adam Hilger, 1978.

Johnson, Karen E. "Maria Goeppert Mayer: Atoms, Molecules and Nuclear Shells." *Physics Today* 39 (1986): 44–49.

Sachs, Robert G. "Maria Goeppert Mayer, 1906–1972." *Biographical Memoirs of the National Academy of Sciences* 50 (1979): 310–328.

———. "Maria Goeppert Mayer, 1906–1972." *Physics Today* 1982: 46–.

Weber, R. L. "Maria Goeppert Mayer, 1906–1972." In *Pioneers of Science: Nobel Prize Winners in Physics,* ed. J. M. A. Lenihan. Bristol: Institute of Physics, 1980.

STANDARD SOURCES

AMS 7–8, P 9, P&B 10–11; Bailey; *DSB,* suppl. 2, vol. 18; Grinstein 1993; Kass-Simon and Farnes; *Notable.*

GOLDFEDER, ANNA (1897–1988)

Polish/U.S. experimental pathologist. Born 25 July 1897 in Poland. Educated University of Prague (D.Sc., 1923). Professional experience: Massaryk University, assistant pathologist (1923–1925), research associate, department of physiology (1925–1928), laboratory for cancer research, director (1928–1931); Lenox Hill Hospital, New York, research fellow (1931–1933); Harvard Medical College, research worker in biological chemistry (1933); Columbia University, College of Physicians and Surgeons, research worker in bacteriology and immunology (1934); Department of Hospitals, New York, head of cancer division (1934–1950), senior biologist (1950–1960), cancer division, principal research scientist and director cancer and radiobiology research laboratory (1960–1977); New York University, adjunct professor of biology, graduate school of arts and sciences and radiobiology research laboratory (from 1977). Honors and memberships: Radiological Society of North America, award (1948); New York Academy of Sciences, Presidential Gold Medal (1978). Died 1988.

A native of Poland, Anna Goldfeder came to the United States in 1931. She had already earned a doctorate of science at the University of Prague and had held several university positions. In the United States, she held several positions as a research worker, but in 1934 began to specialize in cancer research, a subject to which she devoted the rest of her life. In addition to her regular positions, Goldfeder held several concurrent ones. From 1928 to 1929, she was a fellow at the University of Vienna and from 1931 to 1933, a research fellow in cancer research at Lenox Hill Hospital, New York. She was a research fellow in the cancer division of the Department of Hospitals, New York, in 1934. She progressed from research associate to professor at New York University. Goldfeder was a member of the American Association for the Advancement of Science, the Society for Experimental Biology and Medicine, the Radiological Society of North America, the Radiation Research Society, and the American

Association of Cancer Research. Her research was on the relationship between radiation, viral, and chemical carninogenesis, and the genetic properties of a specific inbred strain of mice.   JH/MBO

SECONDARY SOURCES
Baserga, Renato, ed. *Cell Proliferation, Cancer, and Cancer Therapy: A Conference in Honor of Anna Goldfeder.* New York: New York Academy of Sciences, 1982. Includes bibliography.

STANDARD SOURCES
AMS 7–8, B 9, P&B 10–16.

GOLDFRANK, ESTHER SCHIFF (1896–1997)

U.S. anthropologist. Born 1896 in New York City to Matilda (Metzger) and Herman J. Schiff. One brother, Jack. Married (1) Walter S. Goldfrank (he died). One daughter; three stepsons. (2) Karl August Wittfogel. Educated Ethical Culture High School; Barnard College (A.B. in economics, 1918). Professional experience: secretary on Wall Street (1918–1919); secretary to Franz Boas (1919–1922); field work in anthropology. Honors and memberships: American Ethnological Society, secretary-treasurer (1945–1947), president (1948), and editor (1952–1956). Died 23 April 1997 in Mamaroneck, N.Y.

Esther Schiff entered anthropology rather accidentally. The daughter of middle-class parents in New York City, with one brother who died before she was twenty, she majored in economics at Barnard. Upon graduation, she worked as a secretary on Wall Street, and then applied and was accepted for a position as secretary to Franz Boas, chair of the Columbia University anthropology department. While working for Boas, she learned of his intention to go on an anthropological trip to Laguna Pueblo and asked to go along. Boas refused her request, not only for reasons of propriety but because she was totally untrained in anthropological field methods. After engaging the support of ELSIE CLEWS PARSONS, who offered to pay her expenses, and challenging her scandalized parents, she finally convinced Boas to take her with him. With Boas, and later with Parsons, she collected ethnographic data in Laguna. She went on a second trip to Laguna and then went with Boas to Cochiti, New Mexico.

Resigning from her secretarial job in 1922, she planned to devote herself to anthropological studies. However, her plans were interrupted when she met and married a New York businessman, Walter S. Goldfrank, a widower with three young boys. The couple had a daughter, Susan, in 1924, and moved to White Plains, New York. The birth of her daughter did not deter her from field work for very long. In the fall of 1924, with the support of her husband, she left the baby in the care of a nurse and went on a one-month anthropological trip to Isleta Pueblo. After this trip, she decided that being a mother was more important than being an anthropologist. However, in 1935, after her husband died, her stepsons were grown, and her daughter was eleven years old, she returned to Columbia and to anthropology.

With no training beyond her bachelor's degree in economics, Goldfrank's position at Columbia was ambiguous. Although she attended classes, she did not pursue a graduate degree. Her contemporaries, such as MARGARET MEAD, RUTH BENEDICT, and RUTH BUNZEL, all had their doctorates. In spite of her educational handicap, she continued to publish. She met the historian and sinologist Karl August Wittfogel, director of the Chinese History Project at Columbia University. She found his theories on irrigation societies intriguing. The couple married, and Wittfogel encouraged her to pursue a historical approach to explain the differences between the Blood Indians of Canada, the Teton Dakota, and the closely related Blackfoot of the United States. She concluded that the differences were not explicable in terms of aboriginal differences in culture, but instead were a product of the nature of the relationship between the Dakota and the government of the United States and the Blood and the government of Canada. Goldfrank and Benedict differed in their interpretations of the Blood tribe. This disagreement carried over to her work on Pueblo society. Her 1945 article "Socialization, Personality, and the Structure of Pueblo Society" openly contradicted Benedict's view of Pueblo Society. This paper caused a schism in anthropological circles.

In 1943, Goldfrank produced a joint paper with Wittfogel that focused attention on the role of irrigation in the structure of society. She also edited and gathered materials and paintings for Elsie Clews Parson's manuscript "Isleta Paintings." Although the artist of the paintings in this book wanted his name kept secret, after his death, Goldfrank named him and wrote a biography of him, *The Artist of "Isleta Paintings."*   JH

PRIMARY SOURCES
Goldfrank, Esther. "The Social and Ceremonial Organization of Cochiti." *American Anthropological Association Memoir* 33 (1927): 5–129.
———. *Changing Configurations in the Social Organization of a Blackfoot Tribe during the Reserve Period.* American Ethnological Society, monograph 8. New York: J. J. Augustin, 1945.
———. With Karl Wittfogel. "Some Aspects of Pueblo Mythology and Society." *Journal of American Folklore* 56 (219): 17–30.
———. *The Artist of "Isleta Paintings in Pueblo Society.* Smithsonian Contributions to Anthropology, no. 5, Washington, D.C.: Smithsonian Institution, 1967.

SECONDARY SOURCES

Dozier, Edward P. Review of Elsie Clews Parsons's *Isleta Paintings*. *American Anthropologist* 65, no. 4 (1963): 936 ff.

Ortiz, Alfonso. Review of Esther S. Goldfrank's *The Artist of "Isleta Paintings" in Pueblo Society*. *American Anthropologist* 70 (1968): 838.

STANDARD SOURCES

Gacs (article by Gloria Levitas).

GOLDHABER, SULAMITH (1923–1965)

Austrian/U.S. physicist. Born 4 November 1923 in Vienna. Naturalized U.S. citizen 1953. Married Gerson Goldhaber. Children. Educated Hebrew University (M.S.); University of Wisconsin (Ph.D., 1951). Professional experience: University of California, Berkeley, department of physics (1953–1965); concurrently Radiation Laboratory, staff member (1959–1965). Died 11 December 1965 of a brain tumor.

Physicist and molecular spectroscopist Sulamith Goldhaber was born in Vienna and educated in Israel and the United States. She came to the United States to study at the University of Wisconsin. She married Gerson Goldhaber, with whom she later collaborated. Naturalized as a United States citizen, she moved with her husband to the University of California, Berkeley.

She first worked in Bevatron problems using nuclear emulsion techniques. As part of the Goldhaber-Trilling group, Sulamith Goldhaber worked with George Trilling and her husband using hydrogen bubble chambers until the end of her life. She and her associates were world experts on interactions of K+ mesons with nucleons and played important roles in discoveries of several "resonant states," most notably the A mesons. She and her husband first measured the spin of the K meson. They are credited with the first study of the simultaneous production of pairs of resonance states and they devised the "triangle diagram" to aid in such studies.

While Goldhaber was visiting Madras, India, symptoms of a growing brain tumor were detected. She died shortly thereafter. She was seen by her colleagues and friends as a multifaceted woman—mother as well as scientist.

JH/MBO

PRIMARY SOURCES

Goldhaber, Sulamith. With W. Alvarez. "The Lifetime of the Tau-Meson." *Nuovo Cimento* 2 (1955): 344.

——— With W. W. Chupp, G. Goldhaber, W. R. Johnson, and J. E. Lannutti. "K-Meson Mass from a K-Hydrogen Scattering Event." *Physics Review* 99 (1955): 1042.

SECONDARY SOURCES

Alvarez, Luis. "Memorial Tribute to Sulamith Goldhaber." In *Advances in Particle Physics,* ed. R. L. Cool and R. E. Marshak, 2:vii–ix. New York: Interscience Publishers, 1968.

———. "Sulamith Goldhaber." *Physics Today* 19 (February 1966): 101. Obituary notice, including a twenty-three-page bibliography.

GOLDMAN, HETTY (1881–1972)

U.S. archeologist. Born 19 December 1881. Educated Bryn Mawr College (A.B., 1903); Columbia University (1903–1904, 1906–1907); Radcliffe College (Ph.D., 1916). Professional experience: American School of Classical Studies, Fellow (1910–1912); Macmillan Co., manuscript reader (1903–1904); Halae, Greece, excavator (1911–1914, 1921, 1931); Fogg Museum, Harvard, director of excavations, Colophon, Asia Minor (1922, 1925); Eutresis, Greece, researcher (1924–1927); numerous other excavations; Princeton University, Institute of Advanced Studies, scholar (1936 until retirement). Honors and memberships: American Institue of Archaeology, gold medal (1966). Died 4 May 1972 in Princeton, N.J.

Hetty Goldman followed the example of Harriet Boyd. After receiving her doctorate, she, as a fellow of the American School of Classical Studies, became the first woman to lead an officially sanctioned expedition under the auspices of the school. She then participated in a series of brilliant excavations in Asia Minor, Yugoslavia, Greece, and Turkey. She joined the Institute of Advanced Studies at Princeton in 1936, and remained there until retirement. Although she is acknowledged to be an outstanding scholar in her research area and an excellent field archeologist, she was often forgotten in subsequent chronicles.

JH/MBO

PRIMARY SOURCES

Goldman, Hetty. *Excavation at Eutresis.* [Cambridge, Mass.]: Harvard University Press, 1927.

———. "Excavations at Gozlu Kule, Tarsus, 1936." *American Journal of Archaeology* 41 (1937): 262–286.

SECONDARY SOURCES

Williams, Barbara. *Breakthrough: Women in Archaeology.* New York: Walker, 1981.

STANDARD SOURCES

AMS 7–8; Kass-Simon and Farnes; NAW(M) (article by Machted J. Mellink).

GOLDRING, WINIFRED (1888–1971)

U.S. paleontologist. Born 1 February 1888 in Kenwood (near Albany), N.Y., to Mary (Grey) Goldring and Frederick Goldring. Six siblings. Never married. Educated Slingerlands District School; high school associated with the State Normal College for training teachers (now Milne School); Wellesley College (B.A., 1909; M.A., 1912); Johns Hopkins University (1912). Professional experience: Wellesley (instructor in Geology) and assistant instructor in the Teacher's School of Science in Boston (1912–1914); New York State Museum, scientific expert in paleontology (1914), assistant paleontologist (1915–1920), associate paleontologist (1920–1925, 1928–1932), paleobotanist (1925–1928), assistant state paleontologist (1932–1938), provisional state paleontologist (1938–1939), state paleontologist (1939–1954). Honors and memberships: Russell Sage College, honorary D.Sc. (1937); Smith College, honorary D.Sc. (1957); Geological Society of America, officer, vice-president (1921, 1950); Paleontological Society, first woman president (1949); Sigma Delta Epsilon, honorable membership; Paleobotanical Society, member; Paleontological Research Institute, member; American Association for the Advancement of Science, member; American Geophysical Union, member; New York Academy of Sciences, member; New York Historical Association, member; Phi Beta Kappa, member; Sigma Xi, member. Died 30 January 1971.

Winifred Goldring came from a family that was interested in plants both vocationally and avocationally. Her father, Frederick, was trained at Kew Gardens as an orchid grower. When he came to the United States he was well qualified to take charge of the orchid collections at the Erastus Corning estate near Albany. Her mother's father was head gardener at the Corning estate and her mother was a schoolteacher until she married Frederick. The two had seven children, six girls and one boy. When Winifred was two years old, her family moved to Font Grove Road, Slingerlands, New York, and established their own floral business. From this base, Winifred learned to explore the Lower Devonian rocks that were common there. Winifred attended the local school until she was in the tenth grade, when she went to high school in Albany, from which she graduated valedictorian. She attended college at Wellesley, earning a bachelor's degree with honors in 1909 and a master's in 1912. While at Wellesley, she was assistant in geology and geography and took graduate work in geography at Harvard under William Morris Davis. She remained at Wellesley teaching, except for a summer when she took leave to study at Columbia University under Amadeus Grabau.

Most of Goldring's career was at the New York State Museum, where she worked for forty years, retiring in July 1954. In 1914, she began as scientific expert in paleontology and went through a number of ranks, finally becoming state paleontologist in 1939. She received honorary doctorate of science degrees from Russell Sage (1937) and Smith (1957), as well as an honorable membership in Sigma Delta Epsilon. She was elected a Fellow of the Geological Society of

America (elected in 1921 and vice-president in 1950), and was the first woman president of the Paleontological Society (1949). She held memberships in the Paleobotanical Society, the Paleontological Research Institution, the American Association for the Advancement of Science, the Association of American Museums, the American Geophysical Union, the New York Academy of Sciences, the New York Historical Association, Phi Beta Kappa, and Sigma Xi.

Goldring was an advocate for women in geology. She was unhappy with their treatment by many male geologists and paleontologists, and blamed this treatment for the fact that there were few women in the field.

Goldring's main interest was in the museum. She was outspoken in her ideas, impatient with incompetence and meticulous in her own work. She published forty-four titles that ranged over a variety of subjects. She is best known for her popular works, her publications on Devonian Crinoids of New York, and classic quadrangle studies.   JH/MBO

PRIMARY SOURCES
Goldring, Winifred. *The Devonian Crinoids of the State of New York*. Albany: New York State Museum Memoir 16, 1923.
———. *Handbook of Paleontology for Beginners and Amateurs: Pt. 1, The Fossils*. Albany: New York State Museum Handbook 9, 1929. *Pt. 2, The Formations*. Albany: New York State Museum Handbook 10, 1931.
———. *Geology of the Berne Quadrangle*. Albany: New York State Museum Bulletin 303, 1935.
———. *Geology of the Coxsackie Quadrangle, New York*. Albany: New York State Museum Bulletin 332, 1943.

SECONDARY SOURCES
Fisher, Donald W. "Memorial to Winifred Goldring 1888–1971." *Geological Society of America Memorials* 3 (1974): 96–102. Includes a bibliography of Goldring's works.

STANDARD SOURCES
AMS 3–8, P 9, P&B 10; Bailey; *Notable* (article by Joel Schwartz).

GOLDSCHMIDT, FRIEDA (fl. 1929)

German physicist. Professional experience: Berlin researcher.

With the new work on radioactivity, it was not especially far-fetched in the early part of the twentieth century to suspect a sort of modern alchemy. Frieda Goldschmidt's claim to fame occurred when she and two other investigators disproved a claim regarding the production of gold. In response to reports that gold had been produced from mercury subjected to electrical discharges, Goldschmidt and two other investigators, Tiede and Schleede, repeated these experiments at Berlin University's Chemical Institute. Their results suggested that gold was an impurity in the mercury used by the other experimenters. When using twice-distilled mercury, Goldschmidt and her coworkers obtained no gold.   MM

PRIMARY SOURCES

Goldschmidt, Frieda. With Arthur Schleede and Erich Tiede. "Zur Frage der Bildung von Gold aus Quecksilber." *Die Naturwissenschaften* 13 (1925): 745–746.

STANDARD SOURCES

Meyer and von Schweidler.

GOLDSMITH, GRACE ARABELL (1904–1975)

U.S. physician and nutritionist. Born 8 April 1904 in St. Paul, Minn. Educated University of Wisconsin (B.S., 1925); Tulane University (M.D., 1932); University of Minnesota (M.S., 1936). Professional experience: Touro Infirmary, New Orleans, La., intern (1932–1933); Mayo Clinic, fellow in internal medicine (1933–1936); Tulane University, instructor in medicine (1936–1939), assistant professor (1939–1943), associate professor (1943–1949), professor (from 1949); School of Public Health and Tropical Medicine, dean (from 1967). Other professional experience: Nutrition Survey, Newfoundland, member (1944, 1948); Nutrition Foundation, advisory committee (1948–1964); National Research Council, food and nutrition board (1948–1969; chair, 1958–1968); U.S. Public Health Service, member biochemical and nutritional study section (1949–1951), nutritional study section (1959–1963), gastroenterology and nutrition training committee (1966–1970); U.S. Department of Agriculture, food nutrition advisory committee (1951–1963; chair, 1954–1956); Gordon Research Conference on Vitamins and Metabolism, member (1954); Pan-American Sanitation Bureau of Central America and Panama (1954); National Vitamin Foundation, member scientific advisory committee (1955–1958); International Nutrition Congress, organizer and program committee (1960); Conference on Marine Resources and World Nutrition, food and agriculture organizer (1961); Federation of Societies of Experimental Biology, advisory committee (1962–1965); Dairy Industry, science advisory committee (1962–1966); Louisiana State Board of Health, consultant (1962–1967); American Freedom from Hunger Foundation, trustee (1963–1967); MIT, member of the visiting committee in the department of nutrition and food science (1964–1965); President's Science Advisory Committee, panel on world food supply (1966–1967); International Union of Nutrition Scientists, committee on etiology and epidemiology of anemias (from 1967); National Academy of Sciences, National Research Council, chair iron committee, food and nutrition board (1969); National Institutes of Health, national advisor arthritis and metabolic diseases council (1970); Charity Hospital, Louisiana, consulting physician; Touro Infirmary, New Orleans, physician. Honors and memberships: University of Minnesota, award (1964); American Board of Internal Medicine, diplomate; American Board of Nutrition, diplomate; American Medical Association, Goldberger Award (1965); American Institute of Nutrition, Osborn and Mendel Award (1959), president (1963–1964); American Dietetic Association, honorary member; American Association for the Advancement of Science; Society of Experimental Biology and Medicine; American Public Health Association; American College of Physicians; American Dietetic Association; American Society for Clinical Nutrition (president); New York Academy of Sciences. Died 1975.

Although Grace Goldsmith held a medical degree, most of her work was in nutrition, and she did not have a private practice. In addition to her main positions (moving through the academic ranks at Tulane University), she held an overwhelming number of additional jobs in nutrition, from participating in numerous public health committees to serving as a consulting physician. She was also active in professional organizations and held offices in many of them. Her research was in nutrition, specifically the interrelationships of niacin and tryptophan, vitamins of the B-complex, and macrocytic anemia, clinical and laboratory tests for evaluation of nutritional status, and lipid metabolism in humans.   KM

STANDARD SOURCES

AMS 8, B 9, P&B 10–12.

GOLDSMITH, MARIE (1873–1933)

French physiologist and comparative psychologist. Born 19 July 1871 in St. Petersburg. Educated University of Paris, Faculty of Sciences (Licence ès sciences, 1894; Doctorate ès sciences, 1915). Professional experience: University of Paris, Faculty des Sciences, Laboratoire de Physiologie, staff (1894?–1919); L'Année Biologique, general secretary (1902–1924); University of Paris, faculté des sciences, laboratoire de physiologie, researcher (1919–1927); Ecole Pratique des Hautes Etudes, laboratory preparator (1927–1933); Faculté de Médecine, chargée des conferences (seminar leader) (1930–1933). Honors and memberships: Institut général psychologique, Paris; Société zoologique, Paris; Association française pour l'Avancement des Sciences. Died 1933 in Paris.

Marie Goldsmith was a Russian-born, French comparative psychologist and physiologist. As a young woman, she moved to Paris to earn an undergraduate degree in zoology, which she obtained in her early twenties. She began to work in a physiology laboratory and, from 1897, she carried on an extensive correspondence with her fellow exile, the Russian anarchist and evolutionist Peter Kropotkin, whose book on cooperative evolution, *Mutual Aid,* had a considerable influence upon her.

Goldsmith began to work closely with Yves Delage, professor of zoology, anatomy, and comparative physiology at the Faculty of Sciences, University of Paris. When Delage founded a new journal of biology, *L'Année Biologique,* she joined him as the general secretary, a position she held until shortly before his death in 1926. She also coauthored two major publications with Delage, the first on theories of evolution (1909) and the second on parthenogenesis (1913). After his death in 1920, it was she who wrote the major obituary for his journal.

In her forties, she began to qualify herself by completing a doctoral degree from the University of Paris on the comparative physiology and behavior of fish. From this period on, her articles on tropisms, especially the response of marine animals to light, began to appear on a regular basis in the journal of the Academy of Sciences. She continued to publish on psychological evolution in animals and other topics, such as the construction of spider webs, the role of tannin and sugar in parthenogenic sea urchins, as well as on more general topics such as Mendelian evolution. She was attached to the Faculty of Sciences in Delage's laboratory and continued to work as a researcher in the Laboratory of Physiology until 1927, when she moved to a laboratory under the Ecole Pratique des Hautes Etudes, where she served as laboratory preparator.

In the last years of her life, she lectured at the Faculty of Medicine on comparative psychology. In 1929, she traveled to Moscow to observe the apes that NADIE KOHTS was studying at the Zoophysiological Laboratory of the Darwin Museum, reporting on this visit to the Institut Générale Psychologique. Goldsmith died in Paris in her sixtieth year (although some sources give her birth date two years earlier).

JH/MBO

PRIMARY SOURCES

Goldsmith, Marie. With Yves Delage. *Les théories de l'evolution.* Paris: Flammarion, 1909.

———. With Yves Delage. *La Parthénogenèse naturelle et experimentale.* Paris: Flammarion, 1913.

———. "Réactions physiologiques et psychiques des poissons." Paris, 1915. This is the printed version of her thesis, submitted in 1915 to the Faculty of Sciences, University of Paris.

———. "Quelques réactions sensorielles chez le Pouple." *Comptes Rendus Académie des Sciences* 164 (1917): 448–450.

———. "Une contribution à la question des tropismes." *Bulletin Institut général psychologique* 22 (1922): 13–22.

———. *La psychologie comparée.* Paris: Costes, 1927.

SECONDARY SOURCES

Confino, Michael, ed. *Anarchistes en exile: Correspondence inéditéde Pierre Kropotkine à Marie Goldsmith (1897–1917).* Paris:

Institut d'Etudes Slaves, 1995. The first publication of the correspondence between Kropotkin and Goldsmith.

STANDARD SOURCES

DSB (under Yves Delage); *Psychological Register,* vol. 3, 1932.

GOLDTHWAITE, NELLIE ESTHER (1863–1948)

U.S. physiological chemist. Born 4 February 1863 in Jamestown, N.Y. Educated University of Michigan (B.S., 1894); University of Chicago, fellow (1894–1897; Ph.D., 1904). Professional experience: Mount Holyoke College, head chemistry department (1897–1905); Rockefeller Institution, associate in physiological chemistry (1906–1908); University of Illinois, assistant professor, department of household science (1908–1915); University of New Hampshire, head, department of home economics (1915–1916); Colorado Agricultural College, associate professor (1919–1925). Retired 1925.

Like so many women scientists, Nellie Goldthwaite held most of her positions in departments of home economics. Her highest academic position was associate professor. Since she earned a doctorate degree from the University of Chicago, this fact is rather surprising. She spent the years 1916–1919 in Asia. Much of her research was related to home economics, although her early work was in pure physiological chemistry, the substitution of benzhydrol derivatives and bromcyanecetic ether. Later she worked on the chemistry and physics of jelly making, principles of bread making, and chemical composition of Colorado potatoes, all applied subjects.

JH/MBO

PRIMARY SOURCES

Goldthwaite, Nellie Esther. *On Substituted Benzhydrol Derivatives and Bromcyanacetic Ether.* Easton, Pa.: Press of the Chemical Publishing Co., 1903. Ph.D. diss.

STANDARD SOURCES

AMS 2–7; Rossiter 1982.

GOLINEVICH, ELENA MIKHAILOVNA (1901–   )

Russian microbiologist. Born 1901. Educated Kiev Medical Institute (M.D., 1953). Professional experience: laboratory director in hospital; Institute of Experimental Medicine, Leningrad, research worker; All-Union Institute of Experimental Medicine, Moscow; Gamaleia Institute of Experimental Medicine of the Soviet Academy of Medical Sciences, staff. Lenin Prize, 1959.

Elena Mikhailovna Golinevich was born in 1901. She graduated from the Kiev Medical Institute in 1925 and earned her medical degree there in 1953. From 1926 to 1931, she directed a laboratory in a hospital. She worked as a researcher at the Institute of Experimental Medicine in Leningrad (1931 to 1934) and at the All-Union Institute of Experimental Medicine in Moscow (until 1944). She started working at the Gamaleia Institute of Experimental Medicine in 1946 and became laboratory director in 1954.

Golinevich's principal field of research has been rickets and the rickettsial diseases. In 1959 (with the microbiologist Pavel F. Zdrodovskii), she received the Lenin Prize for her definitive work on this subject.   ACH

PRIMARY SOURCES
Golinevich, Elena Mikhailovna. With Pavel F. Zdrodovskii. *The Rickettsial Diseases.* Oxford: Pergamon Press, 1960. Original Russian edition published 1956.

STANDARD SOURCES
Debus.

GOODENOUGH, FLORENCE LAURA (1886–1959)

American developmental psychologist. Born 6 August 1886 in Honesdale, Pa., to Alice and Linus Goodenough. Five sisters and two brothers. Never married. Columbia University (B.S., 1920); Columbia University (M.A., 1921, under Leta Hollingworth); Stanford University (Ph.D. in psychology, 1924, under Lewis Terman). Professional experience: Rutherford and Perth Amboy (New Jersey) public schools, director of research; Lewis Terman's gifted study, chief field psychologist (1921); chief research psychologist (1922–1923); Minneapolis Child Guidance Clinic (1924); University of Minnesota, Child Welfare Institute, research professor (1925–1930), professor of psychology (1931–1947). Died 4 April 1959 in Lakeland, Fla., of a stroke.

Florence Goodenough was a distinguished researcher in child development, test development, and research into the origins of human abilities. Goodenough was educated during a period when developmental psychologists (especially her teacher, Lewis Terman, a student of G. Stanley Hall) stood strongly on the nature side of the nature-nurture question. Early on, she argued for maturation rather than environment as the major factor in determining emotional development of children. In 1939–1940 she published a series of articles defending the concept of fixed intelligence and questioning the role that environmental intervention plays in IQ scores. Another of her early assumptions was that there were innate economic and cultural differences in intelligence and educability. She developed nonverbal intelligence tests for children that were easy to administer, highly reliable, and standardized.

(Now known as the Goodenough-Harris drawing test, following extensive revision by G. and Dale Harris, including addition of a Draw-a-Woman test and a drawing quality score). She was instrumental in training and teaching at the Institute of Child Welfare, University of Minnesota (1925–1930s).

As with many other women in psychology (and other areas), Goodenough was frustrated by sex segregation in the wartime job markets. Opportunities in military personnel selection and training methods, human factors research, military and civilian morale studies, combat neuroses, and so on, were controlled by male-dominated professional committees and social networks. Women were consistently rebuffed in their efforts to participate in the wartime mobilization of psychology, being advised to seek volunteer work in home communities. As president of the National Council of Women Psychologists (NCWP), Goodenough worked to legitimize the group and emphasized the right of women psychologists to equal participation in wartime opportunities. Under her guidance (with such eminent psychologists as HELEN PEAK, THEODORA ABEL, and Gladys C. Schwesinger on her board of directors), the NCWP gained prominence and was invited to send delegates to the all-male Emergency Committee in Psychology, which was a key to obtaining paid employment in military and federal areas. After the war, women were told again to step aside so that returning male military personnel could be fully employed; the desirable positions in business and industry created during the war were generally not available to women, and unemployment for female psychologists climbed to a new high. Although the NCWP continued to push for employment and career opportunities, there was little societal support for the effort.

Goodenough received many professional honors, including presidency of the Society for Research in Child Development, the Division on Childhood and Adolescence of the American Psychological Association, and the National Council of Women Psychologists (1938). She was a member of the American Association for the Advancement of Science; Fellow of the APA.   KM

PRIMARY SOURCES
Goodenough, Florence. *Measurement of Intelligence by Drawings.* Yonkers-on-Hudson, N.Y., and Chicago: World Book Company, 1926. Introduced her "Draw-a-Man" test.

———. *The Kuhlman-Binet Tests for Children of Preschool Age: A Critical Study and Evaluation.* Minneapolis: University of Minnesota Press, 1928.

———. *Anger in Young Children.* Minneapolis: University of Minnesota Press, 1931. Remains a classic in systematic and detailed analyses of emotional development in childhood.

————. *Developmental Psychology.* New York and London: D. Appleton-Century, Inc., 1934. Presented an early argument for a life-span approach to human development and on the integrative and adaptive implications of young children's behavior; as well as the interrelationships of behaviors.

————. With K. M. Maurer and M. J. Van Wagenen. *Minnesota Preschool Scales.* Circle Pines, Minn.: American Guidance Service, 1940.

————. *Mental Testing.* New York: Rinehart, 1949. Analysis of measurement and history of the mental testing movement.

————. *Exceptional Children.* New York: Appleton-Century-Crofts, 1956.

————. With Leona Tyler. *Developmental Psychology.* New York: Appleton-Century-Crofts, 1959.

STANDARD SOURCES
AMS 4–8, S&B 9, Bailey; O'Connell and Russo 1990; Zusne.

GOODRICH, SARAH FRANCES (1851–1917)

U.S. botanist. Born 14 September 1851 in Geneva, Ohio. Educated Geneva Normal School (1872). Geneva schoolteacher (1872–1874). Died 15 March 1917.

Sarah Frances Goodrich was an amateur botanist and plant collector. She became an authority on the local flora of northeastern Ohio and collected large numbers of plants. She deposited many specimens to the herbarium at Western Reserve University, Cleveland, now at the Holden Aboretum; some to the Oberlin College herbarium; and others to Professor William A. Kellerman for the State Herbarium, Columbus. In a local school journal, Goodrich published a list of the scientific and common names of the vascular plants of Ashtabula County, arranged by families. Goodrich was one of five women charter members of the Ohio Academy of Science.   JH/MBO

PRIMARY SOURCES
Goodrich, Sarah Frances. "The Wild Plants of Northeastern Ohio. Preliminary List of the Wild Plants of Ashtabula County." 4 parts. *Western Reserve School Journal* (Geneva, Ohio). 1892–1893.
————. "Grasses of Ashtabula County, Ohio. Part I." *Third Annual Report of the Ohio Academy of Science* (1895): 21–22.

SECONDARY SOURCES
Stuckey, Ronald L. "Sara Frances Goodrich." Unpublished notes.

STANDARD SOURCES
Stuckey.

GOODYEAR, EDITH (1879–1959)

British stratigrapher. Born 8 September 1879 in North Finchley, London. Educated Highbury High School; University College, London (honors degree, 1903). Professional experience: University College, London, assistant to Professor E. J. Garwood (from 1904), honorary assistant lecturer in geology (1930–1944), tutor to women students (from 1926), fellow (1946). Honors and memberships: Geological Society, Fellow (1922); Lyell Fund Award (1927). Died 4 February 1959 in London.

Edith Goodyear lived in London during her entire lifetime. During her time at University College, London, she was awarded the Morris Prize in Geology (1902) and received an honors degree in geology the next year. As E. J. Garwood's assistant, she worked jointly with him on the geology of the Old Radnor district of Wales and the Settle district of Yorkshire. Immediately before Garfield's death, she was working with him on their joint extensive collections of calcareous algae, which she presented to the British Museum (Natural History). Goodyear founded the Garwood Fund, awarded annually by the Geological Society, in his memory. The money was bequeathed to her from the Garwood estate.   CK

PRIMARY SOURCES
Goodyear, Edith. "On the Geology of the Old Radnor District, with Special Reference to an Algal Development in the Woolhope Limestone." *Quarterly Journal of the Geological Society* 74 (1918).
————. "The Lower Carboniferous Succession in the Settle District." *Quarterly Journal of the Geological Society* 80 (1924).

SECONDARY SOURCES
[Muir-Wood, Helen M.] "Edith Goodyear." *Proceedings of the Geological Society of London* 1572 (1959): 147–148.

STANDARD SOURCES
Sarjeant.

GORDON, KATE (1878–1963)

U.S. psychologist. Born 18 February 1878 in Oshkosh, Wisc. Married Ernest Carroll Moore. Educated University of Chicago (Ph.D., 1903); University of Würzburg, alumnae fellow (1903–1904). Professional experience: Mount Holyoke College, instructor of psychology (1904–1906); Columbia University Teachers College, instructor; Bryn Mawr College, associate professor of education (1912–1916); Carnegie Institute of Technology, assistant professor of psychology and education (1916–1919), associate professor (1919–1921); Children's Department, State Board of Control, California, psychologist (1918–1919); University of California at Los Angeles, associate professor of psychology (1922–1934), professor (1934–1948); emerita professor (1948–1963). Honors and memberships: American Psychological Association; American Association for the Advancement of Science. Died 1963.

Kate Gordon was born in Oshkosh, Wisconsin. She enrolled at the University of Chicago in 1896 where she received her doctorate in 1903. Her thesis, *The Psychology of Meaning*, reflected her fascination with the effects of sensory experience and memory on perception of events and interpersonal relations. She continued her education in Europe as an alumnae fellow at the University of Würzburg (1903–1904). After returning to the States, she took the position of instructor of psychology, first at Mount Holyoke College (1904–1906), then at Columbia University Teachers College. Her research concerned color vision of the peripheral retina and aesthetics of color. For four years she served as associate professor of education at Bryn Mawr College (1912–1916), but moved to the Carnegie Institute of Technology as assistant professor of psychology and education, becoming associate professor in 1919. Her early years of research and teaching showed development of theories in memory and attention span, affective memory, and memory for music.

Gordon had consulted for the Children's Department, State Board of Control, California, while still professionally at Carnegie Institute (1918–1919), and in 1922, she moved permanently to California to take a position at the University of California at Los Angeles, advancing from associate professor of psychology to professor, a post she held from 1934 to 1948, when she was named emerita professor. She died in 1963.   KM

PRIMARY SOURCES

Gordon, Kate. *The Psychology of Meaning.* Chicago: University of Chicago Press, 1903.
———. *Esthetics.* New York: Holt, 1909.
———. *Educational Psychology.* New York: Holt, 1917.

STANDARD SOURCES

AMS 1–8, S&B 9; Bailey; *Psychological Register,* vol. 3, 1932.

GORDON, MARIA MATILDA OGILVIE (1864–1939)

See Ogilvie-Gordon, Dame Maria Matilda.

GORINEVSKAYA, VALENTINA VALENTINOVNA (1882–1953)

Russian military surgeon. Born 1882. Educated St. Petersburg Women's Medical Institute (graduated 1908). Professional experience: Peter and Paul Hospital, surgical clinic (1908–1914); military hospital, senior surgeon (1914–1919); Samara University,

professor of general surgery (1919–?); Moscow, Obukh Institute, head of surgical department; Institute of Therapy and Prosthetics, Traumatological Department, surgeon; Central Institute of Postgraduate Medical Training, teacher of surgery; chair of field surgery (1931–1939); military field hospitals, chief surgeon at Khalkin-Gol (1939–?); Main Military Medical Board Soviet Army, senior inspector (1939–1945?). Died 1953.

Valentina Valentinovna Gorinevskaya was the daughter of a physician and physical culture enthusiast. She studied medicine in St. Petersburg and then worked under A. A. Kad'yan and G. I. Turner. At the beginning of World War I, she was the first woman to be appointed senior surgeon in a military hospital. After the war, she held the chair of general surgery at Samara University. Returning to Moscow, she held a series of positions in traumatological clinics teaching field surgery at major Moscow institutes. When World War II began, she served as a surgeon in field hospitals. At the same time, she was a senior medical inspector for the Soviet Army. She was honored as a scientific worker.

Gorinevskaya was one of the first Soviet surgeons to introduce the primary surgical study of wounds from industrial accidents. She pioneered traumatology as a separate branch of surgery and devised treatment in hospitals for lightly wounded soldiers. She published at least ninety books and articles, including books on traumatology, first aid, and comprehensive surgical treatment. She received numerous orders and medals.   JH/MBO

PRIMARY SOURCES

Gorinevskaya, Valentina Valentinovna. *Sovremennyye metody lecheniya ran (Modern Methods of Wound Treatment).* 1942.
———. *Kompleksnoye lecheniye v gospitalyakh dlya legkoranenykh (Comprehensive Treatment in Hospitals for the Lightly Wounded).* 1944.

STANDARD SOURCES

WWW (USSR).

GORIZDRO-KULCZYCKA, ZINAIDA (1884–1949)

Russian vertebrate paleontologist and stratigrapher. Born 1884. Married. Died 1949.

Zinaida Gorizdro-Kulczycka's major research involved a hydrogeological project in the Tien-Shan Mountains, the southern Urals, and the Tashkent region. She also organized expeditions to the Altai Mountains. She married a Polish engineer and settled in Poland, working on Devonian fishes from the Holy Cross Mountains.   JH/MBO

SECONDARY SOURCES
[Malkowski, Stanislaw]. "Zinaida Gorizdro-Kulczycka, 1884–
1949)." *Wladomosci Muzeum Ziemi* (Warsaw) 4 (1948): 412–
415.

STANDARD SOURCES
Sarjeant.

GORSHKOVA, TAT'YANA IVANOVNA (1896–?)
Russian oceanographer. Born 25 January 1896. Educated Moscow University (doctorate, 1921?). Professional experience: State Oceanographic Institute, Plavmornin plan, staff (1921–1950). Death date unknown.

Since her graduation from Moscow University, Gorshkova's research has been associated with the study of the sea. She was invited to take part in Plavmornin plan at the State Oceanographic Institute, where she was exposed to the most talented oceanographers. She completed her work for a doctorate of geophysical sciences under V. I. Vernadskiy. In addition to her research, she also engaged in pedagogic work and taught specialists in geochemistry the origins of oil and the bioproductivity of the waters of the ocean.

Gorshkova received the Order of Lenin and other government awards to honor her contributions. She also received the Certificate of honor of the Geographic Society.

She is well known for her expertise in marine geochemistry and particularly the chemistry of waters and sediments, bottom interstitial solutions, and the organic matter of bottom sediments and suspended matter. She studied the relationship of productivity and the chemical composition of marine sediments. In order to make these contributions, she took part in many expeditions in the seas of the Soviet Union. She also made many methodological advances based on her long experience, and published numerous monographs. Her orientation in all of her studies was consistently biogeochemical. Her methods enabled her to understand the processes on which the productivity of the seas are based.

ACH

SECONDARY SOURCES
Gershanovich, D. Ye. "Tat'yana Ivanovna Gorshkova on her Ninetieth Birthday." *Oceanology* 26, no. 3 (1986): 405–406. Includes portrait.

GÖTZ, IRÉN JULIA (DIENES) (1889–1941)
Hungarian chemist. Born 3 April 1889 in Magyarova, Hungary. Married Laszlo Dienes. Educated University of Budapest (doctorate 1911). Professional experience: Radium Institut, Paris (1911–1912); University of Budapest, lecturer (1919); Cluj University, Romania, lecturer(?) (1922–1928); Berlin, chemical advisor (1928–1931); Nitrogen Research Institute, Moscow, department head (1931?–1939). Died 1941.

After completing a dissertation on radiumemanation (radon), Götz worked in MARIE CURIE's laboratory during 1911–1912. She married in Hungary, then did research on animals at an agricultural station. She also published chemical researches. In 1919, Götz became the first woman lecturer at a Hungarian university. Soon afterward, she escaped from Hungary in the wake of the anti-Communist revolution. Götz taught at the Pharmacological Institute in Cluj, where she did research in electrochemistry and wrote a text on radioactivity and theories of matter. She was a chemical advisor in Berlin for several years, then took a post as a department head at the Nitrogen Research Institute in Moscow. Götz died in 1941. MM

PRIMARY SOURCES
Götz, Iréne. "Über quantitative Bestimmung der Radiumemanation." *Chemiker Zeitung* 35 (1911): 724. Summary.
———. With Jean Danysz. "Sur les rayons b de la radioactivité induite à l'évolution lente." *Le Radium* 9 (1912): 6.
———. *Az elemek átváltozása és a modern anyagfogalom.* Hungary: Korunk, 1926.

SECONDARY SOURCES
Records in archives of the Institut Curie, assembled by Mme. Monique Bordry.
Davis, J. L. "The Research School of Marie Curie in the Paris Faculty, 1907–14." *Annals of Science* 52 (1995): 321–355.

STANDARD SOURCES
Rayner-Canham 1997.

GRACHEVA, YEKATERINA KONSTANTINOVNA (1866–1934)
Russian child psychologist. Born 1866. Professional experience: Asylum for mentally retarded and epileptic children, St. Petersburg, founder (1894); Russian school for mentally retarded children, founder (1898); Russian welfare organization for mentally retarded, founder (1900); courses for training nurses in techniques for caring for mentally retarded children, teacher (1900); Petrograd, lecturer for staff training (1918–1920). Died in 1934.

Yekaterina Konstantinovna Gracheva devoted her life to the education of children with major physical and mental defects. She founded the first Russian asylums and schools for mentally retarded children. She traveled through France, Germany, and Sweden studying the care of the mentally retarded in those countries. When she returned, she sponsored and directed the creation of schools for the mentally retarded in Moscow and other Russian cities. She wrote the first Russian books on the education and training of retarded children, the last of which appeared in 1932. KM

PRIMARY SOURCES
Gracheva, Yekaterina Konstantinovna. *Vospitaniye i obucheniye gluboko otstalogo rebyonka (The Upbringing and Training of Retarded Children).* 1932.

STANDARD SOURCES
WWW (USSR).

GRAHAM, HELEN (TREADWAY) (1890–)

U.S. biochemist. Born 21 July 1890 in Dubuque, Iowa. Married (1916). Two children. Educated Bryn Mawr College (A.B., 1911; M.A., 1912); University of Göttingen (1912–1913); University of Chicago (Ph.D. in chemistry, 1915). Professional experience: Johns Hopkins, assistant pharmacologist (1918); Washington University, St. Louis, instructor (1926–1931), assistant professor (1931–1937), associate professor (1937–1954), professor (1954–1959), emerita professor (from 1959). Death date unknown.

Unlike many women scientists who marry and have children, Helen Treadway Graham's career proceeded relatively smoothly from the time she received her bachelor's degree until she became a professor emerita. She married in 1916, one year after earning her doctorate, and had two children. After a short stint as a pharmacologist at Johns Hopkins University, she took a job as an instructor at Washington University, St. Louis, and moved steadily up the academic ladder. Her longest time at any rank was as associate professor, where she remained for seventeen years. Her major research interests were in the area of nerve physiology. She also worked with the effects of histamines. She was a member of the Society for Pharmacology and the Physiological Society. JH/MBO

STANDARD SOURCES
AMS 3–8, B 9, P&B 10–11; *Who's Who of American Women* (1958–1959).

GRAHAM, MARIA DUNDAS (LADY CALLCOTT) (1785–1842)

See Callcott, Lady Maria Graham.

GRAINGER, JENNIE (ca 1891–1969)

British botanist. Born ca. 1891. Professional experience: schoolmistress, Helme, Yorkshire. Died 15 May 1969.

Jennie Grainger was a mycologist and a schoolmistress at Meltham, Yorkshire. JH/MBO

SECONDARY SOURCES
Naturalist 1969: 106.

STANDARD SOURCES
Desmond.

GRAVATT, ANNIE EVELYN (RATHBUN) (1894–?)

U.S. forest pathologist. Born 15 May 1894 in West Greenwich, R.I. Married George F. Gravatt. Educated Brown University (A.B., 1916; M.S., 1918). Professional experience: U.S. Department of Agriculture, Division of Forest Pathology, Bureau of Plant Industry, from collaborator to associate pathologist and technical education (from 1916). Death date unknown.

After Annie Gravatt received her bachelor's degree, she went to work for the U.S. Department of Agriculture. Two years later, she earned a master's degree. She was one of several women who made careers in the Division of Forest Pathology in this government department. She was on the editorial staff of *Phytopathology,* an important scientific journal, for over ten years. Her research was on plant physiology, the damping off of conifers, and white blister research. From 1926 to 1929, she was the associate editor of *Phytopathology,* and from 1932, coeditor. JH/MBO

PRIMARY SOURCES
Gravatt, Annie Rathbun. "Direct Inoculation of Coniferous Stems with Damping-Off Fungi." *Journal of Agricultural Research* 30 (1925): 327–339.

STANDARD SOURCES
AMS 4–8, B 9, Bailey.

GRAVES, ELIZABETH (RIDDLE) (1916–1972)

U.S. physicist. Born 23 January 1916 in Nashville, Tenn. Mother, Clymetra Riddle. One brother. Married Alvin R. Graves (1937). Three children. Educated University of Chicago (B.S., 1936; Ph.D., 1940?). Professional experience: University of Chicago, Metallurgical Laboratory, researcher (1943); Los Alamos Scientific Laboratory, researcher (1943–1950), group leader (1950–1972). Died 10 January 1972 in Bataan Memorial Hospital, Albuquerque, N.M., of cancer.

Elizabeth Riddle was born in the South and educated at the University of Chicago, where she did both her undergraduate and graduate work. Her dissertation advisor was S. K. Allison and her thesis involved energy release from certain elements. At the beginning of World War II, she began to work with Enrico Fermi at the Metallurgical Laboratory on early work involving the feasibility of a chain reaction that would lead to the creation of an atomic bomb. Soon after, she went to Los Alamos to continue this work. She, her husband, and their three children remained in Los Alamos after the war. He was a division leader from 1948 until his death of a heart attack in 1966. She was a group leader until she was diagnosed with cancer.   JH/MBO

STANDARD SOURCES
AMS 8, P9, P&B 10–12; *NAW* (unused).

GRAY, ETTA (1880–?)

U.S. physician. Professional experience: American Women's Hospitals, service in Serbia, head (1919–1923); Medical Women's National Association, president (1919–1920). Death date unknown.

Etta Gray was active in medical women's associations and served in Serbia and Macedonia, where she performed countless surgeries on the wounded soldiers there. She personally treated more than 1600 cases of trachoma.   KM

SECONDARY SOURCES
Hurd-Mead 1933; Lovejoy.

GRAY, MARIA EMMA (SMITH) (1787–1876)

British botanist. Born 1787 in Greenwich Hospital, London. Father Lieutenant Henry Smith. Married (1) Francis Edward Gray (1812)(d. 1814); (2) John Edward Gray (1826). Two daughters from first marriage. Professional experience: arranged British algae at Kew. Died 9 December 1876 in London.

Maria Gray's father was a lieutenant in the Royal Navy, and she was born at the Greenwich hospital where he was living. She was probably privately educated, but her intellectual interests were broad. She developed a fondness for music as well as an interest in both science and literature, probably through her acquaintance with a number of scientific and literary men. Her first husband died two years after their marriage, leaving her with two daughters. She married a cousin of her first husband who was thirteen years her junior. John Edward Gray was employed as an assistant in the Natural History Department of the British Museum. Since Maria had money of her own, she was able to travel and to allow her husband to travel and visit European naturalists and their collections. This broadening of his knowledge was a factor influencing his appointment in 1840 as keeper of the Zoological Department.

Maria Gray's interests were in mollusks and algae. She arranged and mounted a large part of the Cuming collection of shells at the British Museum. She also etched thousands of plates of marine animals, which were published privately as *Figures of Molluscous Animals.* Maria and her husband spent a long holiday in Ilfracombe collecting algae, and later (in the 1850s) Gray employed for her collection the help of George Johnston of Berwick and W. H. Harvey in Dublin. Her scientific contemporaries were very impressed with her knowledge of both the living and the herbarium specimens. In fact, Sir William Hooker had sufficient confidence in her knowledge to entrust to her the arrangement of the British algae at Kew. J. J. Bennett, Keeper of Botany at the British Museum, invited her to arrange their general collection of algae. She also arranged her own collections and her husband's and both were donated to the Museum of the University of Cambridge. Her husband coined the name *Grayemma* for a newly discovered genus of algae from the Gulf of Mexico to honor her.   JH/MBO

PRIMARY SOURCES
Gray, Maria Emma. *Figures of Molluscous Animals.* London: Privately published, 1857–1874.

SECONDARY SOURCES
Gunther, A. E. *A Century of Zoology at the British Museum.* London: Dawsons, 1975.
Journal of Botany (1866): 45.
Journal of Botany (1877): 32.
Journal of Botany (1891): 191.

STANDARD SOURCES
Desmond; *DNB; Europa.*

GRAY, SUSAN WALTON (1913–1992)

U.S. educational psychologist. Born 5 December 1913 in Rockdale, Tenn. Educated Randolph-Macon Women's College (valedictorian, 1935); George Peabody College (M.A., 1939; Ph.D., 1941). Professional experience: Florida State College for Women, teacher (1942–1945); Peabody College, Vanderbilt University, faculty member, psychology (1945–1978); John F. Kennedy Center for Research on Education and Human Development, cofounder; Demonstration and Research Center for Early Education, founder and director; Early Training Project children and their families, developer of data archive. Honors and memberships: American Board of Examiners in Professional Psychology (School Psychology), diplomate; Southeastern Psychological Association and the American Psychological Association Division of School Psychology, past president; Randolph-Macon Women's College and Peabody College, distinguished alumna awards. Died 30 December 1992.

Susan Walton Gray was born into an affluent Tennessee family that controlled the economy of a small town near Nashville. Her father practiced falconry and raised basset hounds. Growing up on the advantaged side of the gulf between privileged and poor, Susan nevertheless developed a strong sense of social injustice and a determination to improve the odds for achievement and success in poorer communities. She was educated at Randolph-Macon, where she majored in classics but took some courses in psychology (HELEN PEAK was head of the department), then taught fourth grade for a time after graduation. Realizing she needed a greater challenge, she decided to pursue her earlier interest in psychology and entered nearby George Peabody College graduate school in 1938. Her thesis on reminiscence was sent to the *Journal of Experimental Psychology* by her major professor and became the first of her many professional publications. Other research done at Peabody was concerned with the vocational aspirations of young black children (Gray, 1944).

After receiving her doctorate, Gray was appointed to teach at Florida State College for Women in Tallahassee. When the war ended, the president at Peabody, who had been in psychology, asked Gray to return to help build a psychology department. She did so, remaining on faculty thirty-three years. With Julius Seeman and Raymond C. Norris, she started Peabody College's doctoral program in school psychology, and obtained the first federal training grant to support such a program. Her vision of the school psychologist in psychoeducational assessment, classroom consultation, and educational research is described in *The Psychologist in the Schools* (1963). She believed that children dealing with poverty-related adverse social, economic, and environmental circumstances needed a specially structured early education to provide them the motivation and early foundation needed to succeed in public schools. Concerned with the progressive decline of the achievement scores of black children, Gray, with Rupert Klaus, a Murfreesboro, Tennessee, school psychologist, designed a summer educational program for four- and five-year-olds from poor families. She and Klaus studied two different comparison groups of children and their families (one local group and one in another town), in addition to their group receiving early education. Through their study they identified a phenomenon they called "horizontal diffusion": some mothers of children not in the early education group picked up ideas and techniques from conversing with the mothers of the group receiving structured education and were able to improve their own children's scores. Likewise, other children in the same family as those receiving the structured early education benefited by learning from their siblings through "vertical diffusion."

Gray's Early Training Project (ETP) was credited by Sargent Shriver as being the intellectual impetus for Project Head Start, one of the antipoverty programs of the 1960s, which incorporated several innovative aspects of the ETP. Other early education programs also have used Gray's model and included health monitoring, supplemental nutrition, parent participation at school, and home visiting by staff members in addition to classroom teaching. The ETP and several follow-up studies are described in Gray's book *From 3 to 20: The Early Training Project* (1982).

In the 1960s, she collaborated with Nicholas Hobbs and Lloyd Dunn to develop the John F. Kennedy Center for Research on Education and Human Development, one of the original national mental retardation research centers. Later she founded and directed the Demonstration and Research Center for Early Education. She was a part of a national consortium of directors of the experimental early education programs of the 1960s.

After "retirement," Gray developed a computerized data archive that pooled data from twelve early education programs and the longitudinal data from the ETP to create a resource enabling researchers to compare and assess combinations of data in order to discover previously undetected effects.

In private life, Susan Gray was a classical languages scholar, award-winning photographer, patron of fine arts, feminist, and member of several scientific organizations. Professionally she was active in the Southeastern Psychological Association and the American Psychological Association (Division of School Psychology), and was a diplomate of the American Board of Examiners in Professional Psychology (School Psychology). She was given distinguished alumna awards by Randolph-Macon College and Peabody College. The Kennedy Center Experimental School at Peabody College of Vanderbilt University was renamed The Susan Gray School for Children in 1986.   JH/MBO

PRIMARY SOURCES
Gray, Susan Walton. "The Relation of Individual Variability to Intelligence and Emotional Stability." Ph.D. diss., George Peabody College for Teachers, 1941.

———. "Vocational interest of Negro School Children." *Journal of Genetic Psychology* 64 (1944).

———. *The Psychologist in the Schools.* New York: Holt, Rinehart and Winston, 1963.

———. With others. *The Early Training Project: A Handbook of Aims and Activities.* Nashville: George Peabody College, 1965.

———. *Deprivation, Development, and Diffusion.* Nashville: John F. Kennedy Center for Research on Education and Human Development, 1966.

———. *Early Experience in Relation to Cognitive Development.* Nashville: John F. Kennedy Center for Research on Education and Human Development, 1967.

———. *Research, Change, and Social Responsibility: An Illustrative Model from Early Education.* Nashville: John F. Kennedy Center for Research on Education and Human Development, 1967.

———. With Rupert A. Klaus. *The Early Training Project for Disadvantaged Children: A Report after Five Years.* Chicago: University of Chicago Press for the Society for Research in Child Development, 1968.

———. *Selected Longitudinal Studies of Compensatory Education: A Look from the Inside.* Nashville: John F. Kennedy Center for Research on Education and Himan Development, 1969.

———. With Barbara K. Ramsey and Rupert A. Klaus. *From 3 to 20: The Early Training Project.* Baltimore, Md.: University Park Press, 1982.

SECONDARY SOURCES
Haywood, H. Carl. "Susan Walton Gray (1913–1992)." *American Psychologist* 48 (November 1993): 1150.

O'Connell, Agnes N., and Nancy Felipe Russo. *Eminent Women in Psychology.* New York: Human Sciences Press, 1980.

GREACEN, KATHERIN F. (1913–1982)
See Nelson, Katherine Greacen.

GREEN, ARDA ALDEN (1899–1958)
Born 7 May 1899 in Prospect, Pa. Educated University of California, Berkeley (B.S., 1921); Johns Hopkins School of Medicine (M.D., 1927). Professional experience: Harvard University, research fellow (1927–1929), research associate (1929–1941); Radcliffe College, tutor in biochemical sciences (1929–1941); Washington University, Pharmacology, research associate (1941–1945), assistant professor (1942–1945); Cleveland Clinic, Research Division, research staff (1945–1953); Johns Hopkins McCollum-Pratt Institute (1953–1956). Honors and memberships: LeConte Memorial Fellowship (1926); National Research Council, research fellowship (1927–1929); Garvan Medal (posthumous, 1958). Died in Baltimore 22 January 1958, of breast cancer.

Although little is known about her early life, the biochemist Arda Green spent her professional life conducting successful research on enzymes with some of the best research groups in the country. As a young woman, she studied both philosophy and chemistry at the University of California, Berkeley, receiving honors in both fields. She began medical school at Berkeley, as well, but then spent a year in biochemical research at Harvard Medical School, at the suggestion of a professor. While there she worked under the biochemist Edwin J. Cohn, who helped her obtain the LeConte fellowship upon her return to Berkeley. She transferred to Johns Hopkins School of Medicine soon after, working closely with the the biochemist Leonor Michaelis on conductivity of electrolytes within membranes. She completed her degree in 1927.

After graduation from medical school, Green chose a full-time research career. She was awarded a post-doctoral fellowship from the National Research Council and returned to work once more with Edwin Cohn at Harvard Medical School. Two years later, she was made a research associate, investigating hemoglobulin-oxygen equilibrium with Cohn. Later, she moved to the pediatric research laboratory of C. F. McKhann, where she developed methods for isolating blood proteins with her future Cleveland Clinic colleague, Irvine Page. In addition to her research, she began to tutor women students in biochemistry at Radcliffe College.

Green remained in the Boston area until she was offered the opportunity to work with Carl and GERTY CORI in the pharmacology department at Washington University, Saint Louis. This faculty appointment, her first, was as an assistant professor and was concurrent to her research associate position. In the Coris' laboratory, she developed a method for phosphorylase isolation, a method that underlay the Cori team's later success in polysaccharide synthesis, for which they received the Nobel Prize. She also helped to train another future Nobel Prize winner, Edwin Krebs.

When Irvine Page set up his research group at the Cleveland Clinic in the late 1940s, he asked Green to join him and Maurice Rapport. The three discovered and described the neurotransmitter serotonin, revolutionizing the field of neuroscience. With another member of Page's team, F. M. Bumpus, Green studied the proteins involved in renal hypertension.

In the early 1950s, Green returned to Johns Hopkins in order to collaborate with W. D. McElroy at the new McCollum-Pratt Institute. Her careful methods allowed her to successfully purify luciferase, the enzyme that produces bioluminescence in the firefly. Encouraged by this success, she began to investigate bioluminescence in bacteria, until she was forced to limit her research as her health failed due to breast cancer. After three years struggling with the disease and a few months after learning that she would be awarded the Garvan Medal by the American Chemical Society, she died at Sinai Hospital. Her sister accepted her posthumous award. Although she was not sufficiently recognized for her many contributions, fellow scientists credited her meticulous work as an inspiration for their later, prize-winning research.   JH/MBO

PRIMARY SOURCES
Green, Arda A. With Maurice M. Rapport and Irvine H. Page. "Serum Vasoconstrictor (serotonin). IV Isolation and Characterization." *Journal of Biochemical Chemistry* 176 (1948): 1243–1254.

———. With F. M. Bumpus and Irvine H. Page. "Purification of Angiotensin." *Journal of Biological Chemistry* 210 (1954): 281–286.

———. With W. D. McElroy. "Crystalline Firefly Luciferase." *Biochimica et Biophysica Acta* 20 (1956): 170–176.

SECONDARY SOURCES

Colowick, Sidney P. "Arda Alden Green, Protein Chemist." *Science* 128 (1958): 519–521.

Krebs, Edwin G. "Autobiography." In *Les Prix Nobel*, ed. Tore Frangsmyr. Uppsala: The Nobel Foundation, 1922.

STANDARD SOURCES

AMS 7; O'Neill; Shearer and Shearer 1997 (article by Kelly Hensley).

GREEN, MARY LETITIA (1886–1978)

See Sprague, Mary Letitia (Green).

GREEN, VERA MAE (1928–1982)

U.S. anthropologist. Born 6 September 1928 in Chicago. Never married. Educated Chicago public schools; William Penn College (degrees in sociology and psychology); Columbia University (M.A., 1955); University of Arizona (Ph.D., 1969). Professional experience: social welfare jobs in Chicago (early 1950s); United Nations, international community development, educator (1955); United Nations Educational and Cultural Organization, fundamental educator (1956–1963), research assistant, East Harlem and Puerto Rico (from 1963); University of Iowa, faculty member (1969); University of Houston, faculty member (1969–1972); Rutgers University (1972–1976); Latin American Institute of Rutgers, director (1976–1982). Honors and memberships: American Anthropological Association, executive board member; Mid-Atlantic Council for Latin American Studies, executive committee; Quaker Anthropologists, convener; Association of Black Anthropologists, president (1977–1979). Died 1982.

Vera Mae Green is known for her study of family and ethnic relations in the Dutch Antilles and the United States and her work on the development of a methodology for the study of African American anthropology. After receiving her bachelor's degree, Green could not afford to continue in graduate school, so she took several social welfare jobs in Chicago during the early 1950s. Although she liked the idea of helping people, she found the bureaucracy in the social welfare agencies intolerable.

Green moved to New York City in about 1953 and began graduate work in anthropology at Columbia University under the direction of Charles Wagley and Eleanor Padilla.

She studied the relationships among social stress, health, and disease in New York's East Harlem. At Columbia, she came under the tutelage of the noted anthropologist of Native Americans GENE WELTFISH. She earned her master's degree in anthropology in 1955. Wishing to apply her anthropology, Green entered the field of international community development with the United Nations and trained with a mestizo community in Mexico. She also did community development work in India.

She left the United Nations Educational and Cultural Organization and continued to work on the diversity of poverty as one of Oscar Lewis's research assistants in a study of a poor urban area in Puerto Rico and in New York. After she completed this field work, Green went to the University of Illinois where Lewis was a professor. Although Lewis encouraged her to enter the doctoral program in Chicago, E. H. Spicer provided her with the money to enter the program at the University of Arizona. Her field work was done on the Dutch Caribbean island of Aruba. Under the direction of Spicer, she wrote her dissertation, "Aspects of Interethnic Integration in Aruba, Netherlands Antilles." This dissertation reflected her ability to understand interethnic relationships. After receiving her degree, Green taught at both the University of Iowa and the University of Houston before she went to Rutgers, where she remained for the rest of her life.

A committed Quaker, Green was a steadfast advocate of international human rights. She constantly warned against the dangers of oversimplifying cultural relationships. She stressed the importance of understanding the variations seen not only among African Americans, but in all people.

Green was a member of the executive board of the American Anthropological Association, the executive committee of the Mid-Atlantic Council for Latin American Studies, convener of the Quaker Anthropologists, and president of the Association of Black Anthropologists (1977–1979). After her death, her library and papers were given to the Tuskegee Institute.   JH/MBO

PRIMARY SOURCES

Green, Vera. "The Confrontation of Diversity within the Black Community." *Human Organization* 29, no. 4 (1970): 267–272.

———. *Migrants in Aruba*. Assen, Netherlands: Van Corcum, 1974.

———. "Racial vs. Ethnic Factors in Afro-American and Afro-Caribbean Migration." In *Migration, Change and Development: Implications for Ethnic Diversity and Political Conflict*, ed. Helen Safa and Brian DuTroit, 83–96. The Hagues: Mouton, 1975.

———. "U.S. Blacks: The Creation of an Enduring People?" In *Persistent Peoples: Cultural Enclaves in Perspective*, ed.

G. Kushner and C. P. Castile, 69–77. Tucson: University of Arizona Press, 1981.

SECONDARY SOURCES
Cole, Johnett B. "Obituary on Vera Mae Green." *American Anthropologist* 84 (1982): 633–635.

STANDARD SOURCES
Gacs (article by A. Lynn Bolles and Yolanda T. Moses)

GREENE, CATHERINE (LITTLEFIELD) (1755–1814)

U.S. patron of Eli Whitney. Born 17 February 1755 in New Shoreham, R.I., to Phebe (Ray) and John Littlefield. Four siblings. Married (1) Nathanael Greene (d. 1786); (2) Phineas Miller. Five children: George, Martha, Cornelia, Nathaniel, Louisa. Educated at the town school, New Shoreham. Died 2 September 1814 in Dungeness, Ga.

Catherine Littlefield's father represented the town of New Shoreham, on Block Island, in the colonial assembly from 1747 until the Revolution. Catherine, the third of five children, presumably attended the town school. In 1774, she married Nathanael Greene (1742–1786), of Coventry, Rhode Island, who soon became a general under George Washington and a major figure in the Revolutionary War. Catherine Greene was with her husband during most of his campaigns, including the winter of 1777–1778 at Valley Forge. Three of the Greenes' five children were born during the war years.

After the war General Greene was awarded a loyalist estate on the Georgia side of the Savannah River. The family settled at Mulberry Grove, a plantation on the estate, in 1785, but Greene died less than a year later, leaving his wife with five young children and many debts. Two pressing problems were solved when the marquis de Lafayette, her husband's close friend, took on the education of her oldest son in Paris, and when the children's tutor, Phineas Miller, agreed to assume the management of Mulberry Grove.

In 1792, on her way home from her annual summer visit to relatives and friends in Newport, Rhode Island, Catherine Greene traveled with Eli Whitney, a recent Yale graduate whom Phineas Miller had recruited as tutor for a neighboring family. The tutoring job fell through, but Whitney did not return to the North. Observing his inventiveness, Catherine Greene had suggested that he attempt to devise a machine that would strip the seeds from short-staple cotton. Whitney worked for six months in her basement and eventually solved the problem—with design assistance from Greene, it is sometimes claimed. According to Matilda Gage in *Woman as Inventor,* Whitney's initial model, fitted with wooden teeth, "did not do the work well, and Whitney, despairing, was about to throw the work aside, when Mrs. Greene, whose confidence in the ultimate success never wavered, proposed the substitution of wire. (Gage, 4). Whitney tried it, and within ten days a satisfactory model was completed.

In the midst of this process, a tragedy occurred. Greene's eldest son, who had just returned from France, drowned in the Savannah River. Nevertheless, as soon as Whitney finished a working model of his gin (1793), Greene publicized it among her neighbors. This publicity proved disastrous, for copies of the machine had already begun to appear by the time Whitney and his partner Miller, their patent secured (1794), could start large-scale manufacturing. Greene committed all of her resources to the costly legal fight to establish the partners' rights; the litigation dragged on for more than a decade, and although Whitney eventually reestablished title to the invention, he did not profit from it. In 1796, Catherine Greene married Phineas Miller. Four years later, the couple were forced to sell Mulberry Grove to meet legal expanses; they moved to Dungeness, another plantation on the Greene estate. In 1803 Phineas Miller died of a fever. His wife died, also of a fever, in 1814, at the age of fifty-nine.

JH/MBO

SECONDARY SOURCES
Dexter, Elisabeth. *Colonial Women of Affairs: A Study of Women in Business and the Professions in America before 1776.* Boston: Houghton-Mifflin, 1924.
Gage, Matilda. *Woman as Inventor.* Fayetteville, N.Y.: 1870. Information unreliable.

STANDARD SOURCES
NAW (article by Constance McLaughlin Green); Ogilvie 1986.

GREENWOOD, MARION (1862–1932)
See Bidder, Marion Greenwood.

GREGORY, ELIZA STANDERWICK (BARNES) (1840–1932)

British botanist. Born 6 December 1840 in Thrapston, Northhamptonshire. Married. Died 22 March 1932 in Weston-super-Mare.

Eliza Gregory did not begin her botanical work until she was sixty-four years old. At that time she began to study *Viola* at the Botanical Garden in Cambridge, and published a book on them in 1912. She was interested in the variations and mutations in this group. Her book is well illustrated. Her herbarium is at the British Museum of Natural History.

JH/MBO

PRIMARY SOURCES
Gregory, Eliza. *British Violets.* Cambridge: W. Heffer, 1912.

SECONDARY SOURCES
Thompson, H. S. "Eliza Standerwick Gregory (1840–1932)." *Journal of Botany* 70 (1932): 144–145.

STANDARD SOURCES
Desmond; Strohmeier.

GREGORY, EMILY LOVIRA (1840–1897)

U.S. botanist. Born 1840 in Portage, N.Y. Educated Cornell University (B.A., 1881); University of Zurich (Ph.D.). Professional experience: University of Pennsylvania, teaching fellow; Barnard College, lecturer (1890–1895), professor of botany. Died 1897.

In spite of a doctorate from the University of Zurich (she was one of the first American women to be granted a doctorate from a European university), Gregory was unable to find a paid academic position. Because she was independently wealthy, she was able to serve as an unpaid faculty member at the University of Pennsylvania and Barnard College. She went to Europe during four summers to buy the equipment that she needed. In 1886 Gregory became the first woman elected to the American Society of Naturalists, apparently acceptable because of her foreign doctorate. Still, she was not listed in *American Men of Science.*   JH/MBO

SECONDARY SOURCES
"Gregory, Emily." *Science* n.s. 9 (21 April 1899): 598. Obituary notice.
Rudolph, Emanuel D. "Women in Nineteenth Century American Botany: A Generally Unrecognized Constituency." *American Journal of Botany* 69 (1982): 1346–1355.

STANDARD SOURCES
Bailey; Barnhart; Barr; Ogilvie 1986; Rossiter 1982.

GREGORY, EMILY RAY (1863–1946)

*U.S. zoologist. Born 1 November 1863 in Philadelphia to Mary (Jones) and Henry Duval Gregory. Never married. Educated Wellesley College (B.A., 1885); University of Pennsylvania (fellow, 1892–1893; M.A., 1896); University of Chicago (fellow, 1895–1897; Ph.D., 1899). Professional experience: series of Philadelphia private schools for girls, teacher (1885–1888); Uni-*versity of Chicago, assistant in zoology (1897–1899); Wells College, professor of biology (1901–1909); American College for Girls, Constantinople, teacher (1909–1911); University of Akron, instructor (1913–1915); Wellesley and Sweet Briar, substitute teacher (1915–1917); War Trade Board and U.S. Treasury Department (1919–1924). Died 1946.*

Born in Philadelphia, Gregory received her bachelor's degree from Wellesley and then taught in private girls' schools in Philadelphia. She then had a one-year fellowship at the University of Pennsylvania. While she was working on her master's degree, she taught in a Baltimore girls' school. She spent the summers of 1893 through 1895 at Woods Hole. After earning sufficient money, she went to Chicago in 1895 to work on her doctoral degree. She received a fellowship and taught zoology at Chicago as an assistant from 1897 to 1899.

Gregory held the American Women's Table at the Naples Zoological Station in 1899 and 1900. She then took a position at Wells College and then went to Constantinople where she taught in a girls' school. She also taught in Akron, Ohio, and acted as a substitute in Wellesley and Sweet Briar colleges. She moved to Washington, D.C., where she worked for the War Trade Board and then with the U.S. Treasury Department until 1924. Her research involved the origin of the pronephric duct in Selachians, and the development of the excretory system in turtles. She also developed a method for injecting embryos. She returned to Philadelphia near the end of her life.   JH/MBO

PRIMARY SOURCES
Gregory, Emily Ray. *Observations on the Development of Excretory Systems in Turtles.* Jena: G. Fischer, 1900. Ph.D. diss.

STANDARD SOURCES
AMS 2–7; Bailey; Ogilvie 1986; Rossiter 1982; *Women's Who's Who of America.*

GREGORY, LADY ISABELLA AUGUSTA (PERSSE) (1852–1932)

Irish gardener and playwright. Born 15 March 1852 in Roxborough, County, Galway, the daughter of a wealthy landowner. Educated privately. Married Sir William Gregory. One son (killed in World War I). Died 22 May 1932.

Lady Gregory was an important playwright and friend of the poet W. B. Yeats. More of a literary person than a scientist, she still developed a beautiful garden using horticultural principles. She and her husband, Sir William, developed the garden at Coole Park, her husband's home. After her husband's death, she became even more passionately interested in Ireland than she had formerly been. Even though she had been brought up in the Protestant tradition, she learned about Irish peasant life from her Catholic nurse. She was a major figure in the Irish Literary Renaissance and wrote nearly thirty plays. JH/MBO

PRIMARY SOURCES

Gregory, Isabella. *Spreading the News.* Dublin: Maunsel, 1904.
———. *Lady Gregory's Journals.* Ed. Daniel J. Murphy. New York: Oxford University Press, 1978–1984.

SECONDARY SOURCES

Kopper, Edward A. *Lady Isabella Persse Gregory.* Boston: Twayne, 1976.
Malins, Edward G., and Patrick Bowe. *Irish Gardens and Demesnes from 1830.* New York: Rizzoli, 1980.

STANDARD SOURCES

Desmond; *Europa.*

GREGORY, LOUISA CATHERINE (ALLEN) (1848–1920)

U.S. home economist. Born December 1848 in Harristown, Ill., to Amanda (Risk) and David Skillman Allen. Five brothers: Rhodes, Henry, Charles Wesley, Joseph, and E. Wright. Married John Milton Gregory (1879). Educated Macon County District School; State Normal University, North Bloomington, Ill. (1867–1870); summer institutes, including Gannett Institute, series of lectures by MARY BLAKE (1875); Harvard summer course in chemistry (1875); Thomas Henry Huxley's lectures on comparative anatomy, University of London (1876?). Professional experience: Alton (Ill.) High School (1970–1971); County Normal School, Peoria, Ill. (1871–1874). Illinois Industrial University (later University of Illinois), instructor (1874–1877), preceptress (1878), professor (1879–1880). Died 1920.

After having read a book suggested by her future husband, *The American Woman's Home, or Principles of Domestic Science,* (based on an earlier work by Catharine Beecher, *Treatise on Domestic Economy*), Louisa Allen developed a science curriculum for women that stressed the sciences as a basis for domestic economy.

John Milton Gregory was a regent for the newly established land grant institution, Illinois Industrial University. He was convinced of the importance of female education at the university level and actively sought Allen for this position. Allen, raised on a farm and educated as a teacher, did not earn an advanced degree, although she received an honorary master of science from the University of Illinois (1890) and continually upgraded her education by attending various summer institutes and traveling and attending lectures in

Europe. After several teaching positions, Allen, at Gregory's instigation, went to the Illinois Industrial University, which later became the University of Illinois, and remained there for the rest of her teaching career. In 1877, the same year that she became preceptress, the home economics program was absorbed into the College of Natural Science. After only one year as full professor, she resigned from the university in 1880. Her husband resigned as regent that same year. The year after she resigned, the woman's program was integrated into the regular curriculum. In 1890, Elizabeth Bevier was hired to establish a separate home economics department. JH/MBO

STANDARD SOURCES

Arnold; Bailey.

GREGORY, LOUISE HOYT (1880–1954)

U.S. Biologist. Born 21 July 1880 in Princeton, Mass. Educated Vassar (A.B., 1903); Columbia University (A.M., 1907; Ph.D., 1909). Professional experience: Vassar College, assistant in biology (1903–1905), fellow (1905–1907), Barnard College, Columbia, assistant (1908–1909), instructor of zoology (1909–1918), assistant professor (1918–1923), associate professor (1923–1936), professor (1936–1949), emerita professor (1949–1954), associate dean (1932–1948). Died 1(?) November 1954.

Louise Hoyt Gregory began her professional career at Vassar, and then went to Barnard College, Columbia University. After she received her doctorate from Columbia, she became an instructor at that institution. She continued her career trajectory in a traditional male pattern, rising to professor. She served Barnard as associate dean from 1932 to 1948.

Although she was more of a teacher than a researcher, her interests were in the cytology of protozoan conjugation and in the life history of protozoans. JH/MBO

PRIMARY SOURCES

Gregory, Louise Hoyt. "Notes on the Effect of Mechanical Pressure on the Roots of *Vicia Faba.*" *Bulletin of the Torrey Botanical Society* 36 (August 1909) 457–462.

STANDARD SOURCES

AMS 3, 8; Barnhart.

GREIG, MARGARET ELIZABETH (1907–)

Canadian/U.S. pharmacologist. Born 12 March 1907 in Cumberland, Ontario. Educated McGill University (B.A., 1928; Ph.D., 1932); University of Saskatchewan (M.A., 1930). Professional experience: University of Saskatchewan, demonstrator in chemistry (1928–1930); McGill University, assistant cellulose chemist

(1932–1935); Biochemical Research Foundation, Franklin Institute, chemist (1935–1942); Vanderbilt University School of Medicine, from assistant to associate professor, department of pharmacology (1942–1953); Upjohn Company, senior research pharmacologist and section head and senior scientist (1953–1973). Retired 1973. Concurrent experience: Office of Scientific Research and Development (1942–1944); Western Michigan University, adjunct professor in pharmacology (from 1974).

Although Margaret Greig completed all of her education in Canada, she immigrated to the United States, where she first worked at the Franklin Institute and then moved to the Medical School at Vanderbilt University where she progressed from assistant to associate professor. She left Vanderbilt for the Upjohn Company, where she was a senior research pharmacologist, section head, and senior scientist. She remained at Upjohn until she retired. After official retirement, she became an adjunct professor of pharmacology at Western Michigan University. Greig was a member of the Pharmacological Society and a Fellow of the New York Academy of Sciences. Her research was on tumor metabolism, shock from hemorrhage, central nervous system drugs, and allergy and anaphylaxis.   JH/MBO

STANDARD SOURCES
AMS 6–8, B 9, P&B 10–13.

GREISHEIMER, ESTHER MAUD (1891–?)

U.S. physiologist. Born 31 October 1891 in Chillicothe, Ohio. Educated University of Ohio (B.S. 1914); Clark University (fellow 1914-1916; M.A. 1916); University of Chicago (fellow 1916-1918; Ph.D. 1919); University of Minnesota (M.D. 1923). Professional experience: University of Minnesota, instructor in physiology (1918-1921); assistant professor (1923-1931); associate professor (1931-1935); Wellesley College, assistant professor (1921-1922); Woman's Medical College of Pennsylvania, professor (1935-1943); Temple University School of Medicine, professor (1944-1956); Emerita professor, physiology (1956–?). Death date unknown.

Esther Maud Greisheimer was a medical doctor and doctor of philosophy who spent her career in academia. She advanced to associate professor at the University of Minnesota and then moved to the Woman's Medical College of Pennsylvania where she was a professor. For the last twelve years of her teaching career, she was at Temple University Medical School as professor of physiology. Greisheimer was a member of the American Association for the Advancement of Science, the Physiological Society, the American Medical Association, and the Medical Women's Association.

JH/MBO

PRIMARY SOURCES
Greisheimer, Esther Maude. *Physiology and Anatomy.* Philadelphia: Lippincott, 1932.

STANDARD SOURCES
AMS 4–8; B 9, P&B 10–11.

GRIFFIN, HARRIET MADELINE (1903–)

U.S. mathematician. Born 6 April 1903 in Brooklyn, N.Y. Educated Hunter College (A.B., 1925); Columbia University (M.A., 1929); New York University (Ph.D., 1939). Professional experience: Hunter College, mathematics teacher (1926), tutor (1926–1928), instructor (1929–1930); Brooklyn College, faculty (1930–1940); assistant professor (1941–1949), associate professor (1950–1955); professor (from 1956).

Harriet Madeline Griffin received all of her education in New York City and her entire teaching career was spent in that city as well. Although she had a doctorate from New York University, her progress up the academic ladder was very slow. She eventually was promoted to professor. Griffin's research was on abstract algebra, the Abelian quasi-group, and theory of numbers.   JH/MBO

PRIMARY SOURCES
Griffin, Harriet. *Elementary Theory of Numbers.* New York: McGraw-Hill, 1954.

STANDARD SOURCES
AMS 7–8, P 9, P&B 10–11.

GRIFFITHS, AMELIA ELIZABETH (1802–1861)

British botanist. Born 1802 probably in Martinhoe, Devon. Mother Mrs. A. W. Griffiths. Died 1861.

Amelia Griffiths lived in Martinhoe, Devon, and collected plants in Devon. She was a member of the Botanical Society of London. Her plants are at the North Devon Athenaeum, Barnstaple, and Torquay Museums. Her British fungi drawings are in the British Museum of Natural History.

JH/MBO

SECONDARY SOURCES
Phytologist 1 (1844): 521.
Martin, W. K., and G. T. Fraser. *Flora of Devon* 2, no. 1 (1952): 70–71.

STANDARD SOURCES
Desmond.

GRIFFITHS, AMELIA WARREN (ROGERS) (1768–1858)

British botanist. Born 14 January 1768 in Pilton, Devon. Married. Correspondent of W. H. Harvey and R. K. Greville. Died 4 January 1858 in Torquay, Devon.

Amelia Warren Griffiths was called the *facile regina* of British algologists by her correspondent W. H. Harvey. She contributed to *Phytologist* vol. 1, 1844, and contributed plants to O. Blewitt's *Panorama of Torquay*, 1932. Her algae are at the Torquay Museum and the British Museum of Natural History. Her letters are at Kew and in the Berkeley correspondence at the British Museum of Natural History. She had a plant named for her, *Griffitsia Agardh*.   JH/MBO

SECONDARY SOURCES
Harvey, W. H. *Memoir.* London: Bell and Daldy, 1869. See pages 149–150, 158.
Sowerby, J., and J. E. Smith. *English Botany.* London, 1926.

STANDARD SOURCES
Desmond.

GRIGGS, MARY AMERMAN (1886–1962)

U.S. chemist and educator. Born in Somerville, N.J., 11 February 1886, to Mary Sutphin (Craig) and James Lake. Educated Sommerville and Plainfield, N.J. public schools; Vassar College (B.A., 1908); Columbia University (M.A., 1915; Ph.D., 1917). Professional experience: Lederle Laboratories in New York City, analytical chemist (1908–1909); Vassar College, assistant in chemistry (1909–1911), instructor (1911–1913, 1916–1918); Columbia University, instructor in chemistry (1918–1920); Wellesley College, associate professor (1920–1932); professor and chair of the chemistry department (1932–retirement). Honors and memberships: American Chemical Society; New England Association of Colleges and Secondary Schools; American Association of University Women; Sigma Xi. Died 1962 in Wilmington, Del.

After teaching at Vassar and Columbia, Mary Amerman Griggs accepted a position at Wellesley College where she remained for the rest of her career, advancing to professor and chair of the chemistry department. She was awarded fellowships at both Vassar and Columbia, and a grant from Sigma Xi to work on the chemical factors in lead poisoning. She later received an additional grant from Sigma Xi to purchase special equipment for investigating the mineral content of fruits and vegetables. She published extensively on this research. Her other investigations included the use of the Lundegardh spectrographic method, the polarographic study of complex ions, the study of pectin, and the determination of nickel.   JH/MBO

PRIMARY SOURCES
Griggs, Mary Amerman. *The Surface Tension of Mixed Liquids.* Ph.D. diss., Columbia University, 1916.

STANDARD SOURCES
AMS 4–8, P 9, P&B 10; *NCAB.*

GRIGNAN, FRANÇOISE MARGUERITE DE SÉVIGNÉ, COMTESSE DE (1646–1705)

French student of natural philosophy. Born 1646 to Marie de Rabutin-Chantal, marquise de Sévingné, and Henri, marquis de Sévigné. Married François, comte de Grignan, governor of Provence. At least two children who survived infancy. Died 1705 near Marseilles.

Favorite child of the great French woman of letters Mme. de Sévigné, Françoise Marguerite espoused Cartesian philosophy, thus making her of interest to the history of science. Aside from a short time in school with the nuns of Sainte-Marie at Nantes, she was taught by her mother at home. One of Mme. de Sévigné's constant companions, the Abbé de la Mousse, influenced Françoise's intellectual development. A devoted Cartesian, he introduced the child to Descartes's philosophy. Although Françoise too became a devotee of Descartes, "she was bent on more mundane triumphs than philosophy had to offer" (*Encyclopaedia Britannica*, 728). When Francoise married the wealthy forty-year-old comte de Grignan, her doting mother was greatly distressed by the separation and sought to compensate for it by maintaining a voluminous correspondence. Although her mother's letters survive, Françoise's replies were destroyed by her daughter, Pauline (Mme. de Simiane), supposedly from religious motives.

Grignan's Cartesianism led her to "expressions alarming to orthodoxy" (*Encyclopaedia Britannica*, 728). Françoise's numerous miscarriages and malformed surviving children resulted from "the dread truth: that M. de Grignan, having finished off two wives, undoubtedly infected Françoise with venereal disease, so prevalent at that period, and through her his children" (Rabutin-Chantal, 26). She died at the age of fifty-nine of smallpox, the disease that she had tried to escape by not visiting her dying mother.   JH/MBO

PRIMARY SOURCES
Grignan, Françoise Marguerite de Sévigné, comtesse de. *Lettre de Madame de Grignan au Comte de Grignan, son mari.* Paris: Firmin Didot, 1852.

SECONDARY SOURCES
Rabutin-Chantal, Marie de, marquise de Sévigné. *Letters from Madame la Marquise de Sévigné.* Selected, translated, and with

introduction by Violet Hammersley. With a preface by W. Somerset Maugham. London: Secker and Warburg, 1955.

STANDARD SOURCES
Biographie universelle.
Encyclopedia Britannica. 11th ed.
Nouvelle biographie.

GRINNELL, HILDA WOOD (1883–1963)

U.S. natural history contributor. Born 1872. Married Joseph Grinnell. Died 1963.

Hilda Grinnell was a member of the American Society of Mammalogists from 1923 to 1963. Her husband, mammalogist Joseph Grinnell, was a charter member of the society and its tenth president. Her contributions to the *Journal of Mammalogy* were few, two obituaries and a bibliography of C. Hart Merriam. However, the whole story is somewhat different. The very first article to appear in the *Journal of Mammalogy,* "Bats from Mount Whitney, California," was based largely on her work. The credited author, Glover Allen, noted that his brief notes amplified slightly the distributional data published by Hilda Grinnell in her synopsis of the bats of California. In her research, she concentrated on bats and published several other articles in the *Contributions of the Museum of Vertebrate Zoology, University of California.* As much as she pleaded, Hilda Grinnell was never allowed to go on a museum field trip. It was not until 1941 that women were allowed to go on graduate field trips, and this happened only two years after Joseph Grinnell's death. JH/MBO

PRIMARY SOURCES
Grinnell, Hilda Wood. "Synopsis of the Bats of California." *University of California Publications in Zoology* 17 (1918): 223–404.
———. "William Frederic Bade." *Journal of Mammalogy* 18 (1937): 265.
———. "Bibliography of Clinton Hart Merriam." *Journal of Mammalogy* 24 (1943): 436–457.
———. "Edmund Heller: 1875–1939." *Journal of Mammalogy* 28 (1947): 209–218.

SECONDARY SOURCES
Kaufman, Dawn M., Donald W. Kaufman, and Glennis A. Kaufman. "Women in the Early Years of the American Society of Mammalogists (1919–1949)." *Journal of Mammalogy* 77, no. 3 (1996): 642–654.

GRISWOLD, GRACE HALL (1872–1946)

U.S. economic entomologist. Born 14 December 1872 in Taylor's Falls, Minn. Educated Cornell University (B.S., 1918; Ph.D., 1925). Professional experience: Cornell University, research instructor in economic entomology (1924–1941), research associate (1941–1946). Died 1946.

Minnesota-born Grace Griswold went to Ithaca, New York, where she attended Cornell University in her early forties, and earned both bachelor's and doctoral degrees in biology and invertebrate zoology. Inspired by the teaching of John Henry Comstock and the work of his wife ANNA BOTSFORD COMSTOCK, she remained at Cornell, teaching economic entomology. Her research interest centered on the problems of insect infestation of ornamental plants and household insect infestation. In addition she worked on aphid taxonomy. She was made a research associate in 1941 and died five years later. JH/MBO

PRIMARY SOURCES
Griswold, Grace Hall. *Common Insects of the Flower Garden.* Ithaca, N.Y.: New York State College of Agriculture at Cornell University, 1937.
———. *Studies on the Biology of Four Common Carpet Beetles.* Ithaca, N.Y.: Cornell University, 1941.

STANDARD SOURCES
AMS 7; Osborn.

GROMOVA, VERA ISAACOVNA (1891–1973)

Russian zoologist and vertebrate paleontologist. Born 8 March 1891 in Orenburg, Russia. Educated Orenburg Women's Gymnasium (graduated 1908); Petersburg higher girls' courses, division of natural sciences (1908–1912); Moscow higher girls' courses (graduated 1918); doctorate in biological sciences (1946); title of professor (1946). Professional experience: Leningrad Zoological Museum of the Academy of Sciences, researcher (1919–1942); Moscow Paleontological Institute, researcher (1942–1960). Died 21 January 1973 in Moscow.

At the Orenburg Women's Gymnasium, Vera I. Gromova earned a gold medal. After her education, she worked for twenty-three years at the Zoological Museum of the Academy of Sciences in Leningrad, moving through the ranks from preparator to the chief of the osteological section. She left the museum in 1942 and moved to Moscow to join the staff of the Paleontological Institute of the Academy of Sciences of the USSR, where she held the post of the chief of mammals.

Gromova studied the osteological and systematic description of living ungulates, the ancient history of domestic animals, Quaternary mammalian faunas, and the history of separate groups of mammals, chiefly ungulates. She is particularly well known for her monographs on perissodactyls (odd-toed mammals). She had the ability to correlate phylogenetic morphological changes of fossil forms with changes in the environment. She edited the *Mammalia* volume of the *Osnovy Paleontologii* (1962) and directed the publication of four volumes of the *Transactions of the Paleontological Institute* on Tertiary mammals.

The volume of mammalian bones that Gromova studied was immense. During her collecting trips, she supplied bones to many museums, including the Zoological Museum in Leningrad and the Paleontological Museum in Moscow. She also published prolifically, more than one hundred works on horses alone. She insisted that all of the mammals be classified using osteological characteristics.   C K

PRIMARY SOURCES

Gromova, Vera. *The History of Horses in the Old World*. 1949.

———. "Le genre Hipparion." *Annales du centre d'études et de documentation paléontologiques* (Paris), 1955.

———. "Novoye v sistematike i nomenklature drevneyshikh loshadey yevropy" (New Concepts in the Systematics and Nomenclature of Pleistocene Equidae in Europe). *Byulleten' Komissiy po Izucheniyu Chetwertichnogo Perioda* 38 (1972): 126–129.

SECONDARY SOURCES

Gabunia, L., and B. A. Trofimov. "Vera Gromova 1891–1973." *Society of Vertebrate Paleontology News Bulletin* 99 (1973): 64–65.

Nalivkin, D. V. *Our First Women Geologists*. Leningrad: Nauk, 1979. In Russian.

STANDARD SOURCES

Sarjeant.

GRUHN, RUTH (1907–1988)

German/Polish geneticist. Born 7 December 1907 in Opalenitca (now part of Poland). Educated University of Breslau (higher school teaching certificate in mathematics and natural science); doctorate (1938); habilitation (1941). Professional experience: University of Breslau, Division of Heredity, Institute for Animal Research, researcher (?–1942, 1944); University of Göttingen, substitute chair (1942–1943); University of Rostock (1945?–1952); University of Göttingen, Dozentin (assistant professor) (1952–1957), ausserplanmässigen (extraordinary professor) (1957–?). Honors and memberships: Deutschen Studienkommission für Haustiergenetik (German Study Commission for Domestic Animal Genetics) in the European Union for Animal Breeding, member. Died 14 June 1988.

Although Ruth Gruhn passed her teaching examinations in mathematics and natural science, she did not go into secondary school teaching, but took a position doing scientific work with H. F. Krallinger in the Institute for Animal Research Division of Heredity at the University of Breslau. This research resulted in a doctorate, for her project "Uber den Einfluss von Inzucht und Selektion auf das Erbreinwerden von Tierbeständen" (On the Influence of Inbreeding and Selection on Animal Existence). She concerned herself with the breeding methods of poultry and pigs and was interested in answering questions regarding the population genetics of these groups. She brought her considerable mathematical skills to bear upon these questions. This led to her project for habilitation (earning the right to teach university), "Theoretische Grundlagen der Eltern-Nachkommenkordrelation." (Theoretical Foundation of the Parent-Progeny Relationship). For a year, Gruhn represented Krallinger in his chair at Göttingen and then returned to Breslau.

After World War I, Gruhn held a position as a Dozentin at the University of Göttingen and then was promoted to ausserplanmässigen (extraordinary) professor. Her research was very important, especially her work with F. Haring on developing rabbits and pigs for laboratory use through selective breeding. These animals, including a miniature pig, could then be used for serum protein production.   J H / M B O

SECONDARY SOURCES

Glodek, P. "Nachruf für Frau Prof. Dr. Ruth Gruhn." *Züchtungskunde* 61, no. 1 (1989).

STANDARD SOURCES

Strohmeier; *WW in Science in Europe*.

GRUNDY, CLARA (fl. 1870s)

British botanist. Lived in Liverpool. Two sisters.

Little is known of Clara Grundy, although there are numerous records of her plant collection in *Flora of Liverpool* (1872; 1902) and in J. B. L. Warren's *Flora of Cheshire* (1899). Warren termed her the "best lady botanist after Miss [ELIZA] POTTS [1809–1873]" (lxxxii).   J H / M B O

SECONDARY SOURCES

Bulletin of the Liverpool Botanical Society 14 (1967): 33–35. Discusses all three of the Grundy sisters.

Transactions of the Liverpool Botanical Society 1 (1909): 71.

Warren, J. B. L. *Flora of Cheshire*. London and New York: Longmans, Green, 1899.

STANDARD SOURCES

Barnhart; Desmond.

GRUNDY, ELLEN (1815–1894)

British botanist. Born 1815 in Liverpool. Two sisters. Married Francis Boult. Died 18 December 1894.

Born in Liverpool, Ellen Grundy, like CLARA and MARIA ANN, was a noted plant collector. She married Francis Boult, a relative of the husband of her older sister Maria. She began collecting plants of the Liverpool area in her late twenties. Notably, she drew attention to adventive flora from ships' ballast that had been used for road building in the Birkenhead area. She also contributed to the *Flora Liverpool* (1872). She survived her sister Maria Ann by twenty-three years. Her plants are at the Merseyside Museums.   JH/MBO

SECONDARY SOURCES

Bulletin of the Liverpool Botanical Society 14 (1967): 33–35. Discusses all three of the Grundy sisters.
Transactions of the Liverpool Botanical Society 1 (1909): 71.
Warren, J. B. L. *Flora of Cheshire*. London and New York: Longmans, Green, 1899. Grundy mentioned n page lxxviii.

STANDARD SOURCES
Desmond.

GRUNDY, MARIA ANN (1809–1871)

British botanist. Collected plants in Liverpool area. Two sisters. Married Swinton Boult. Died 17 August 1871.

The older sister of Ellen Grundy Boult, Maria Ann, married to Swinton Boult, also collected plants in the Liverpool area and contributed to *Flora Liverpool* (1872). Her plants are also at the Merseyside Museums.   JH/MBO

SECONDARY SOURCES

Bulletin of the Liverpool Botanical Society 14 (1967): 33–35. Discusses all three of the Grundy sisters.
Transactions of the Liverpool Botanical Society (1909): 71.
Warren, J. B. L. *Flora of Cheshire*. London and New York: Longmans, Green, 1899. Grundy mentioned on page lxxviii.

STANDARD SOURCES
Desmond.

GRZIGORZEWSKA, MARJA (1888–?)

Polish psychologist. Born 1888 in Woluca, Poland. Professional experience: Brussels, International Faculty of Pedology (1913–1916); State Institute of Special Education, educator (from 1920); state superior normal school, director (from 1924); Bibljoteka Pedagogiki Leczniczej, editor (from 1924). Death date unknown.

Marja Grzigorzewska's research was on the senses. Her professional memberships included the Scientific Pedagogical Society, the Polish Psychological Society, the Psychological Circle at Warsaw, and the Philosophical Institute of Warsaw.
JH/MBO

STANDARD SOURCES
Psychological Register, 1932.

GSELL, MARIA DOROTHEA HENRICA (GRAF) (1678–1745)

German/Russian natural scientist and painter. Born 1678 in Nuremberg to Maria Sybilla Merian and Johann Anreas Graf. One sister, Johanna Hele (Herold). Married G. Gsell (1717). Educated by parents in painting, natural history, and languages. Professional experienced: worked with her mother and sister in South America (1699–1701). Contributed works to the Court of Peter the Great. Died 1745 in St. Petersburg.

Maria Dorothea Graf was the daughter of the famous naturalist MARIA SYBILLA MERIAN and the painter Johann Andreas Graf. She accompanied her mother and sister on a journey to Surinam, where they spent two years collecting and painting insects and plants. Like her mother, Maria was a gifted painter. After her mother died, she married the painter G. Gsell, who was a member of the court of Peter the Great. She contributed valuable works of her mother's as well as her own paintings to this court.   JH/MBO

STANDARD SOURCES
Strohmeier.

GUALCO, SELLINA (1905–)

Italian endocrinologist. Born in Italy 23 May 1905. Father an engineer. Two older siblings. Never married. Educated locally; higher education certificate at age fourteen; higher education classics diploma (1922); Faculty of Medicine University of Genoa (M.D. with first prize, 1928). Professional experience: Medical Clinic of Genoa, assistant physician; University of Rome, professor of pathology, endocrinology, and orthogenesis; private consultant in the area of endocrine diseases. Honors and memberships: national and international medical organizations.

Sellina Gualco was a precocious student from her elementary school days and knew quite early that she wanted to study some form of medicine, even though her favorite subjects in school were Latin and Greek. Her grandfather was a pharmacist, which influenced her decision to go into medicine. Her father, an engineer and civil servant, expected Sellina to enroll for graduate education in the faculty of literature, but with her mother's help, she enrolled in medicine at the University of Genoa. She received her degree in medicine and surgery in 1928 and was given first prize as the best graduate of the year.

Her interest in the field of endocrinology began in her fourth year in medicine at the Medical Clinic of Genoa, where she studied under Nicola Pende, the founder of the Italian school of endocrinology. That same year, Gualco published the first of over 150 papers involving application of the field of endocrinology to human life. In 1935, Pende invited her to accept the position of professor at the University of Rome to teach pathology, endocrinology, and orthogenesis and to continue her research.　　　JH/MBO

PRIMARY SOURCES

Gualco, Sellina. *La sindrome ipertimica di Pende: studio clinico e terapeutico su 65 casi.* Bologna: Cappelli, 1942.

———. *Corso di biotipologia umana, endocrinologia ed ortogenesi.* Roma: Ferri, 1957.

———. "Gualco, Selliña." In Hellstedt, Autobiographies.

GUARNA, REBECCA (mid-14th century)

Italian teacher of medicine. From the mid-14th century. Taught at Salerno.

The little that is known of Rebecca Guarna indicates that she taught at the famous medical school at Salerno, paid large rents for her offices, and "knew all medicine, herbs, and roots" (Ogilvie). She is said to have written on fevers, urine, and the embryo.　　　JH/MBO

SECONDARY SOURCES

Harington, John, trans. *The School of Salernum: (Regimen salernitanum.)* History of the School of Salernum by Francis R. Packard, M.D., with a note on the prehistory of the *Regimen sanitatis* by Fielding H. Garrison, M.D. New York: Augustus M. Kelley, 1970. Guarna mentioned on page 17.

STANDARD SOURCES

Hurd-Mead 1938; Lipinska 1930; Ogilvie 1986.

GULDBERG, ESTRID (1899–?)

Norwegian gynecologist. Born 6 July 1899 in Göttingen, Germany, to Elisabeth Dalhoff and Alf Guldberg. One sister, five brothers. Married Sigurd Sigmundsen (1893–1964) in 1956. No children. Educated at home until fifth grade; girls' school; gymnasium (graduated 1918); University of Oslo medical school (M.D., 1926); interned at a hospital in Kristiansand; Clinique Tarnier in Paris,

France; a women's clinic in Bergen; and at the Radium Hospital. Certified in obstetrics (September 1933). Professional experience: deputy medical officer in different parts of Norway; private gynecological and obstetrical practice in Oslo (from 1934). Honors and memberships: Norwegian Medical Women's Association, member; Professional Women's Club; Women's League for Peace and Liberty, member and officer. Death date unknown.

Estrid Guldberg was born 6 July 1899 in Göttingen, Germany, to Elisabeth Dalhoff, who was Danish, and Alf Guldberg, a Norwegian. Estrid was born in Göttingen because her father was teaching mathematics there. The family moved to Oslo when Alf Guldberg was appointed lecturer and in 1916 professor of insurance mathematics at the University of Oslo. Their house and estate was called Villa Spes and was built on Nordre Skøyen. Estrid was the eldest of seven children, next a sister and then five brothers. The children did farm chores and Estrid particularly loved horses. Her paternal grandfather was Axel Sopyus Guldberg, a doctor of philosophy in mathematics in a highly educated family which included a sister, Cathinka, who was the first nurse in Norway and founded the Deaconess Institution. When Axel Guldberg died in 1913, the Skøyen estate was sold and the house was acquired by his sister Sia, who had an addition built to Spes, renamed it Fidep and lived there with the Guldberg family. Many foreign and Norwegian intellectuals, mostly mathematicians, visited Fidep, including Albert Einstein and his daughter.

Estrid was taught at home until fifth grade, then attended a girls' school and gymnasium where she graduated in 1918. Unsure of which field to pursue, she consulted with her father, who advised her to choose medicine. She began studies at the University of Oslo medical school with about ten other women who remained her friends for life. Twice she fell in love but did not marry. The medical degree demanded six years of hard work with additional years following her graduation (1926) for internship and specialty training. Guldberg spent six months at a hospital in Kristiansand in the south of Norway and was advised there to take up the specialty of women's diseases. She went to Paris, France, to the Clinique Tarnier but stayed only three months (her French was poor and she was too shy to interact successfully). Returning to Norway, she took posts as deputy medical officer in different parts of the country to gain practical experience. She worked at the women's clinic in Bergen and at the Radium Hospital to be certified as a specialist in obstetrics (1933). Having decided to open a private practice, she returned to her home and family in Oslo. She worked hard day and night to build a gynecologic-obstetric practice, sending her patients to private maternity clinics where she could be called in for delivery (these were expensive and gradually closed in favor of state-run free maternity hospitals).

Her father died in 1936, so Guldberg, her mother, sister (who was a nurse and physiotherapist), and youngest brother lived together throughout the war, suffering much hardship until the armistice of 1945. Guldberg continued to be active in the Medical Society in Oslo, the Gynecologist's Association, the Norwegian Medical Women's Association, the Professional Women's Club and the Women's League for Peace and Liberty—often serving as an officer. After the war she took part in all of the Medical Women's International Association congresses, and wrote a book, *Woman's Menopause—To Be Awaited with Calm,* based on a questionnaire prepared for a congress in Gardone in 1954 that was answered by nine hundred women in Norway. In 1956, Guldberg married a widower with three daughters, Sigurd Sigmundsen (1893–1964). After the deaths of Sigmundsen, her mother, and her sister, Guldberg built a small house behind the garden of Villa Fidep and moved in when she was seventy; she reduced the size of her practice and continued to see patients in her little house. She enjoyed gardening, housekeeping, and visiting with the two brothers still living on the grounds, until her death. KM

PRIMARY SOURCES
Guldberg, Estrid. With Herdis Lund. *Kvinnens overgangsalder; se den rolig i møte.* [Oslo]: Fabritius, 1959. Popular work on menopause based on a questionnaire answered by nine hundred Norwegian women.
———. "Guldberg, Estrid." In Hellstedt, Autobiographies.

GULLETT, LUCY EDITH (1876–1949)

Australian physician. Born in Hawthorn, Victoria. Professional experience: Rachel Forster Hospital for Women and Children in Sydney, Australia, cofounder (1922). Died 1949.

Little is known about Lucy E. Gullett, except that she was cofounder, with Dame Constance d'Arcy, of the Rachel Forster Hospital for Women and Children in Sydney, Australia (1922). Started in a small suburban house, by 1949 the hospital had moved and grown to 120 beds and one of the largest outpatient departments in Sydney. KM

SECONDARY SOURCES
Journal of the American Medical Women's Association 5 (1950): 295.

STANDARD SOURCES
Lovejoy.

GUNDERSEN, HERDIS (1903–)

Norwegian dermatologist. Born 3 July 1903 in Skien, Telemark, Norway. One younger brother. Never married. Educated (M.D.,

1933); *small hospital in central Norway, internship; state hospital; dermatology specialty training (certification 1946); Oslo University scholarship to study in the United States (1947). Professional experience: short-term appointments during the 1940s; National Institute of Public Health, bacteriologist (three years); Oslo Municipal Hospital, assistant dermatologist (1947–1950); private practice (from 1950); Oslo Public Health and Venereal Disease Department (part-time ca. 1959–1973). Honors and memberships: Norwegian Women Doctors' Association, chairperson (1949–1952); Dermatological Association, chairperson (1958–1960); Oslo Medical Association; Norwegian Medical Association.*

Herdis Gundersen was born in Skien, in the ski valley of Telemark, Norway, on 3 July 1903, to a shipping family. When she was four, her only sibling, a brother, was born. The two children moved to Oslo with their mother to live with their maternal grandmother and three uncles after a financial crisis caused by the displacement of sailing vessels by steamships. Eventually, her father and grandfather built a new business in insurance and became quite wealthy. Herdis and her brother were placed in a private elementary school where she did well and enjoyed learning. She became interested in health and medicine early but did not consider medicine as a career until much later on. Gundersen later admitted that in her teens she was lazy and more interested in her social life than in studies, so her grades were not good at her French boarding school or during college. Her mother insisted that she prepare for a career and encouraged her to consider medical school because of a continued interest in medicine (her three uncles were all pharmacists). She and a friend applied to (University of Oslo?) medical school together. Gundersen found the courses very difficult, but enjoyed the practical applications she experienced in hospital assignments. She finally succeeded in receiving her medical degree in 1933 and began a private general practice on the east coast of Norway, partly because hospital jobs, especially for women, were very scarce. After two and a half years in a small practice with a small income, she decided to apply for an internship and was accepted in a small hospital in central Norway. The medical chief and surgeon inspired her with his devotion to his patients and his capacity for ceaseless hard work. During World War II, in the early 1940s, it was again very difficult to get a job in a hospital, and Gundersen took many short-term appointments for income, which had the advantage of giving her experience in several specialties. Her most stable job was at the bacteriological department of the National Institute of Public Health, where she stayed for three years. While there, she decided on dermatology as a specialty, applied for training at the state hospital, and was board certified in 1946. She was awarded a university scholarship to study in the United States, and spent six months in

Chicago, New York, and Rochester, Minnesota, at the Mayo Clinic. In Norway, Gundersen was given a full-time post as assistant dermatologist at the Oslo Municipal Hospital (1947–1950), and began a private practice as well. In 1959, she added a part-time job in the Oslo Public Health and Venereal Disease Department to work specifically with women. She kept this position for fourteen years (to 1972), during which she saw modernization and improvements in treatments and education. Gundersen lectured to medical students on skin diseases and venereal diseases and wrote several papers. She was active in the Norwegian Women Doctors' Association (elected chairperson 1949–1952) and was chairperson of the Dermatological Association (1958–1960). She served on the board of the Oslo Medical Association and was a member of the Norwegian Medical Association. After retiring from the Public Health Department, she retained her private practice. She never married or had children but found that her profession, her good health, and her family gave her a totally fulfilling life.   K M

PRIMARY SOURCES
Gundersen, Herdis. In Hellstedt, *Autobiographies.*

GUNN, MARY DAVIDSON (1899–1989)

British/South African botanist. Born 15 May 1899 in Kerriemuir. Professional experience: Botanical Research Institute, Pretoria, South Africa, clerk (from 1916); later librarian. Died 31 August 1989 in Pretoria.

Mary Davidson Gunn worked with L. E. W. Codd on the flora of southern Africa. She contributed articles to the journal *Bothalia* on the plants that she collected and described in southern Africa. Gunn also collaborated with Codd on a history of botanical literature and biographical accounts of botanists.   J H / M B O

PRIMARY SOURCES
Gunn, Mary E. With L. E. W. Codd. *A Botanical Exploration of Southern Africa: An Illustrated History of Early Botanical Literature on the Cape Flora: Biographical Accounts of the Leading Plant Collectors and Their Activities in Southern Africa from the Days of the East India Company Until Modern Times.* Cape Town: Published for the Botanical Research Institute by A. A. Balkema, 1981.

SECONDARY SOURCES
Bothalia 15 (1985): 127–130. Includes portrait.
Veld and Flora 62 (1976): 31. Includes portrait.

STANDARD SOURCES
Desmond; Gunn and Codd.

GUNTHER, ERNA (1896–1982)

U.S. anthropologist. Born 9 November 1896 in Brooklyn, N.Y. to Susannah (Ehren) and Casper Gunther. No siblings. Married Leslie Spier (1921); divorced (1931). Two children, Robert and Christopher. Educated Barnard College (A.B., 1919); Columbia University (M.A., 1920; Ph.D., 1928). Professional experience: Barnard College, assistant in anthropology (1919–1921); University of Washington, Seattle, lecturer (1923–1924), assistant professor (1929–1941), professor and executive officer of department (1941–1966). Concurrent experience: Washington State Museum, acting director (1929–1930), director (1930–1962); University of Alaska, professor of anthropology (1966–1969). Died 1982.

Erna Gunther was the only child of Susannah (Ehren) and Casper Gunther. Her father had emigrated from Germany, and Erna learned German from him and French from her maternal grandmother, who spoke little English. Even though she majored in English at Barnard, by the time she graduated, she had become interested in anthropology through Franz Boas, from whom she had taken courses. Although Boas was her main mentor, a fellow graduate student, Leslie Spier, whom she married in 1921, also influenced her early anthropological scholarship. The couple moved to Seattle, where Spier taught at the University of Washington and where their two sons were born.

Gunther finished her doctorate in 1928, with the completion of her dissertation, *A Further Analysis of the First Salmon Ceremony.* This work involved the diffusion of cultural traits. She later did research on the Puget Sound Salish, and edited a collection of Puget Sound Salish folktales.

It was not until Gunther and Spier separated in 1930 that Gunther obtained full-time academic employment at the University of Washington. The divorce was actually beneficial to Gunther's career, for Spier negotiated a position for her when he resigned from the university. Being divorced, she also escaped the early-1930s purge of married women from the university's faculty in an austerity move. She remained at the University of Washington for many years, and was chair of anthropology and director of the Washington State Museum on campus. Unwilling to accept mandatory retirement, Gunther resigned from Washington in 1966 to accept the chair of anthropology at the University of Alaska in Fairbanks. She remained there for only three years before returning to Seattle, where she continued her research.

Throughout her career, Gunther suffered from the fact that her topic was unusual; she did not have many peers with whom to discuss her ideas. She is probably best known as an authority on Northwest Indian art. As she matured and developed a broader perspective on anthropology in general, her own interests narrowed. She was less interested in the theoretical and comparative than in the regional and culturally specific.   J H / M B O

PRIMARY SOURCES

Gunther, Erna. "A Further Analysis of the First Salmon Ceremony." *University of Washington Publications in Anthropology* 2 (1928): 129–173.

———. "Ethnobotany of Western Washington." *University of Washington Publications in Anthropology* 10 (1945): 1–62.

———. "The Shaker Religion of the Northwest." In *Indians of the Urban Northwest,* ed. Marian Smith, 37–76. New York: Columbia University Press, 1949.

———. *Indian Life on the Northwest Coast of North America as Seen by the Early Explorers and Fur Traders during the Last Decades of the Eighteenth Century.* Chicago: University of Chicago Press, 1972.

SECONDARY SOURCES

Amoss, Pamela. With Viola Garfield. "Erna Gunther (1896–1982)." *American Anthropologist* 86, no. 2 (1984): 394–399.

STANDARD SOURCES

AMS 5–8, S&B 9–11; Bailey; Debus; Gacs (article by Pamela Amoss).

GUTHRIE, MARY JANE (1895–1975)

U.S. zoologist and cytologist. Born 1895 in New Bloomfield, Mo., to Lula Ella (Lloyd) and George Robert Guthrie. Never married. Educated Columbia High School, Columbia, Mo.; University of Missouri, Columbia (A.B., 1916; A.M., 1918); Bryn Mawr College (Ph.D., 1922). Professional experience: Bryn Mawr College, demonstrator (1918–1920), instructor (1920–1921), fellow in biology (1921–1922); University of Missouri, assistant professor (1922–1927), associate professor (1927–1937), professor (1937–1951), chair, department of zoology (1939–1950); Wayne State University, Pontiac, Mich., department of biology, faculty (1950–1961); Detroit Institute of Cancer Research, research associate (1951–1961). Retired 1961. Died 22 February 1975.

Mary Jane Guthrie was born in a small Missouri town, close to Columbia, Missouri, the home of the University of Missouri. Although she received her first two degrees from Missouri, she went to Bryn Mawr College to work on her doctorate in order to study with zoologist FLORENCE PEEBLES. As a graduate student at Bryn Mawr, she worked as a demonstrator in biology and an instructor before she received a fellowship for her last year. After receiving her doctorate, Guthrie returned to the University of Missouri, where she remained from 1922 to 1950, ascending the academic ladder from assistant to full professor and chair of the department of zoology. However, in 1950, she took a leave of absence from Missouri and went to Michigan, where she was hired to teach biology at Wayne State University, Pontiac, and as a visiting scientist at the Detroit Institute of Cancer Research. Although her post originally was temporary and unsalaried, it was extended and she became a salaried researcher. She did not return to the University of Missouri, and remained at the institute while continuing to teach at Wayne State until her retirement.

During the early part of her career, Guthrie coauthored an important textbook, *General Zoology,* and its accompanying laboratory manual. From 1944 to 1947, she was a member of the editorial board of the *Journal of Morphology.* She became fascinated by cancer research, studying the induction of experimental ovarian tumors. Moving away from tumorigenesis, she worked on locating the origin of renal tumors induced by estrogens in hamsters. She continued to cultivate ovaries *in vitro.* Guthrie encountered gender bias when she attempted to apply for grants. While women were not officially excluded, they had a much more difficult time than men in getting grants.

Although she had little time to contribute to volunteer organizations during her working career, after she retired, Guthrie became a devoted volunteer. She was a member and chair of numerous committees of the Women's Auxiliary of the Pontiac General Hospital, president of the auxiliary, and a member of the Michigan State Board of the Michigan Association of Hospital Auxiliaries, later serving as president of this organization.

JH/MBO

PRIMARY SOURCES

Guthrie, Mary Jane. "Notes on the Seasonal Movements and Habits of Some Cave Bats." *Journal of Mammalogy* 14 (1933a): 1–19.

———. "The Reproductive Cycles of Some Cave Bats." *Journal of Mammalogy* 14 (1933b): 199–216.

STANDARD SOURCES

AMS 4–8, B 9, P&B 10–11; Bailey; Shearer and Shearer 1996.

GUYTON DE MORVEAU, CLAUDINE POULLET PICARDET (ca. 1770–ca. 1820)

French translator of scientific works. Born ca. 1770. Married (1) C. N. Picardet (d. 1794); (2) Louis Bernard, Baron Guyton de Morveau. Died ca. 1820.

Claudine Picardet, left a widow in 1794 by her first husband, a member of the Academy of Dijon, married the chemist Guyton de Morveau (1737–1816) in 1798. Although not a contributor of original work, Mme. Guyton de Morveau made scientific writings more widely accessible through her translations. Among these were the *Mémoires de chymie* of Karl Wilhelm Scheele (1785), the *Traité de charactères extérieurs des fossiles* of Abraham Gottlob Werner (1790), and the "Observation de la longitude du noeud de Mars faite en

Decembre 1873, par M. Bugge," in the *Journal des scavans* (1787). JH/MBO

PRIMARY SOURCES

Scheele, K. W. *Mémoires de chymie de M. C. W. Scheele, tirés des Mémoires de l'Académie Royale des Sciences de Stockholm.* Trans. Claudine Guyton de Morveau. Paris: T. Barrois, 1785.

SECONDARY SOURCES

Lalande, Jérôme. *Bibliographie astronomique avec l'histoire de l'astronomie.* Paris: De l'inaprimerie de la République, 1803.

STANDARD SOURCES

DSB; NBG.

GWYNNE-VAUGHAN, DAME HELEN CHARLOTTE ISABELLA (FRASER) (1879–1967)

British cytologist and mycologist. Born 21 January 1879. Father Captain Hon. A. H. D. Fraser. Eldest daughter. Married David T. Gwynne-Vaughan in 1911 (d. 1915). Educated Cheltenham Ladies College; University of London, King's College (B.Sc., 1904; D.Sc., 1907). Professional experience: University of London, Birkbeck College, Department of Botany, head (1909–1917, 1931–1944), professor of botany (1921–1944), professor emerita (1944–1967). Other experience: Queen Mary's Army Auxiliary Corps, British Armies in France, chief controller (1917–1918); Women's Royal Air Force, commandant (1918–1919); Auxiliary Territorial Services, chief controller (1939–1941). Honors and memberships: Dame of the British Empire (military) (1929); Commander of the British Empire (civil) (1919); Linnean Society, Traill Medal (1920) (for research on protoplasm); Glasgow University honorary degree (LL. D.); Linnean Society, Fellow; Kings College, London, Fellow; Birkbeck College, Fellow. Retired to West Sussex. Died 26 August 1967.

Helen Charlotte Isabella Fraser was born in 1879 and was schooled in the renowned girls' school, Cheltenham. She then went to King's College, where she received her bachelor of science in 1904 and her doctorate in botany in 1907. In 1911, she married a fellow botanist, David T. Gwynne-Vaughan, who was then head of the department of botany at Birkbeck College. (He died at the beginning of World War I after a long illness.) By 1909, Helen Gwynne-Vaughan was appointed head of the department of botany at Birkbeck College at the University of London, a position she held until 1917, when she was made a professor of botany. Her husband went to Queens College, Belfast, and then to Reading, where he held a professorship of botany, in spite of his increasing illness, until his death in 1915.

During World War I, Helen Gwynne-Vaughan was chief controller of one of the women's auxiliary units in France, and then a commandant of the Women's Royal Air Force until the end of the war, for which she was named Dame of the British Empire in 1919. Upon Gwynne-Vaughan's return to her botanical studies, her research on protoplasm won her the Traill medal from the Linnaean Society. With the start of World War II, she was again a chief controller, this time for the Auxiliary Territorial Forces. During this period, she once more served as head of botany, retiring from this and from her professorship in 1944, after which she remained as professor emerita. Primarily interested in the fungi, her honors included an honorary doctorate from Glasgow University and the title of Commander of the British Empire. She was a Fellow of the Linnean Society, of King's College, University of London, and of Birkbeck College. After retiring to West Sussex, she died in 1967.

JH/MBO

PRIMARY SOURCES

Gwynne-Vaughan, Helen. *Fungi.* Cambridge: Cambridge University Press, 1922.

——— With B. Barnes. *Structure and Development of the Fungi.* Cambridge: Cambridge University Press, 1927, 1937.

SECONDARY SOURCES

Discovery (1944): 199–200; 219. Obituary notice, with portrait.

Izzard, Molly. *A Heroine in Her Time, a Life of Dame Helen Gwynne-Vaughan.* London: St Martin's Press, 1969.

Times, 30 August 1967. Obituary notice.

STANDARD SOURCES

DNB; Desmond; Europa; WW, vol. 114 (1962); *WWW,* vol. 6 (1961–1970).

H

HABER-IMMERWAHR, CLARA (1870–1915)

German chemist. Born 21 June 1870 in Polkendorf, Silesia, to Anna Immerwahr (Krohn) and Philipp Immerwahr. Three siblings. Married Fritz Haber (1901). One son, Hermann (1902). Educated Höhere Töchterschule and Lehrerinnenseminar in Breslau; University of Breslau and Bergakademie Clausthal/Harz (Ph.D., 1900) Professional experience: University of Breslau, assistant (1901); course on women's educational associations and workers' education societies, lecturer (1902–1910). Died 2 May 1915 in Berlin.

Clara Immerwahr was born near Breslau, the youngest daughter of an upper-middle-class, liberal, Jewish family. She and her two sisters and one brother grew up in a nationalistic German imperial environment. Her father had studied chemistry in Breslau and Heidelberg and, after he failed at chemical manufacturing, established himself as a big farmer in Silesia. After Clara's mother died of cancer in 1890, her father retired from farming. Clara went to the Lehrerinnenseminar (teacher's college) of Fräulein Hedwig Knittel in Breslau. Clara's uncle, the university professor and gynecologist Wilhelm Freund, demanded in a lecture that women refrain from anything that could conceivably hinder getting or remaining married. Since Clara's sisters were already married at that time, her family was concerned about her single status. Clara refused the marriage proposal of her dancing-school friend, Fritz Haber, described by a woman friend as very smart, but vain and a show-off.

Since there was no girls' *gymnasium* in Prussia at that time, Immerwahr prepared for the Abitur (the high school leaving examination) on her own. At the same time, she attended lectures in experimental physics at the university. Even before she had received permission to pursue her doctorate, she had become a dedicated researcher. Before she finished her doctoral thesis, she had already published on the characteristics of fluorine and fluorine electroplating with her adviser, Richard Abegg. Despite disciplinary disputes with higher-placed colleagues who often called upon authority rather than science in their arguments, Immerwahr gained self-confidence in the sciences, refusing to be called "gnädiges Fraulein" (gracious young lady) because she considered it degrading. In 1900, before women officially were allowed to study in Prussia, she became the first woman in Breslau to earn a doctorate. Numerous women who saw Clara take her examination felt greatly gratified when their colleague received a degree. A question on the gas laws opened her oral examination.

In 1901 Clara finally married Fritz Haber, at that time the Extraordinary Chemistry Professor at the Technischen Hochschule at Karlsruhe. Haber-Immerwahr tried to follow the traditional wifely role. Fritz Haber was ambitious, and she helped him achieve his goals. In 1905, Haber dedicated his book *Thermodynamik technischer Gasreaktionen* to her in appreciation for her cooperation ("zum Dank für stille Mitarbeit zugeeignet"). Haber tried to strengthen his connections to the chemical industry. He complained that this industry was attempting to obtain a monopoly. The Badische Anilin-und Soda Fabrik (BASF) acquired the patent for the lucrative ammonia synthesizing process, the foundation for both explosives and fertilizer. This process was developed in Haber's institute (Hochschulinstitut) and earned him world renown and the Nobel Prize in 1918. Haber-Immerwahr indicated that if he had not been a chemical genius, he would have been a merchant genius. She was bothered by his relationship with money. She blamed the chemical guilds for the many scientific disagreements based on opportunity rather than ideals.

At the same time Haber was establishing himself as a success both in chemistry and in making money, Haber-Immerwahr taught courses for women and girls about chemistry and physics in the household. These courses were forerunners of today's *Volkshochschulen* (community colleges). At that time, Haber-Immerwahr was going her own way and neglected her husband. Rather than representing him with his colleagues, she preferred to sit in the back row. In a letter written to Abegg criticizing scientific research, she expressed her views that success had caused Haber to change and to lose track of other matters that were important in life: "und ich frage mich ob denn die überlegene Intelligenz genügt, den einen Menschen wetvoller als anderen zu machen . . . Fritzens sämtliche Qualitäten ausser dieser einen sind nahe am Eintrocknen und er is sozusagen vor der Zeit alt" (and I ask myself if a superior intellect is enough to make one person more valuable than another . . . Fritz's total qualities except this one are almost dried up and he is, so to speak, old before his time).

When, during World War I, Haber was made chief of the newly established center for chemistry under the war ministry, Haber-Immerwahr considered it a "perversion of science." It was a sign of barbarism, she believed, when a discipline that should give new knowledge for life was corrupted. The first mass-produced poison gas was chlorine, a by-product of the world pace-setting German dye industry. During the war, there was little opportunity for Germany to export its dyes. Therefore, the factories were available for other uses. The Hague Convention had forbade the use of poisonous or suffocating gases in munitions. However, Haber's factories produced the idea of gas bottles from which gas can escape as needed. According to Haber, although both sides were developing poisonous gases, Germany was further advanced than the Allies. The first use of the gas in mass destruction was in Ypern, where the gas was dispersed to a width of six kilometers and a depth of six to nine meters. The French stated their losses at Ypern at eighteen thousand men (25 April 1915), although current estimates are closer to five thousand. Haber was promoted to captain.

After this event, Haber-Immerwahr gave notice at her job. To her, he had shattered her belief that science should be used to promote life to such an extent that she no longer wanted to live. After a carefully calculated plan, she took his service weapon, fired one shot to be certain that it worked, and then fired a lethal shot into her heart.

Family and members of the scientific community attempted a cover-up, by trying to prove that she was the victim of an inherited instability in order to portray her suicide as an irrational reflex and to exclude rational action. In 1991, the German Section of the International Association of Physicians to Stop Atomic War (IPPNW) issued for the first time the Clara Immerwahr Medal against armaments and war and other threats to life. **GVL**

PRIMARY SOURCES

Haber-Immerwahr, Clara. *Beiträge zur Löslichkeitsbestimmung schwerlöslicher Salze des Quecksilbers, Kupfers, Bleis, Cadmiums und Zinks.* Ph.D. diss., University of Breslau, 1900. Despite

precise measurements, Clara Immerwahr thought that the solubility of the products can only be measured approximately because ionic concentrations are only usable as approximate ways to figure the solubility and as a proximate criterion for the sequencing of the solubility. It was important to her that no hasty conclusions be drawn.

———. With Richard Abegg. "Elektrochemische Verhalten von Fluorsilber und Fluor." *Zeitschrift für physikalischer Chemie,* 1900.

———. With Richard Abegg. "Über den Einsfluss des Bindemittels auf den photochemischen Effect in Bromsilberemulsionen und die photochemische Induction." *Sitzungsberich te der Kaiserlichen Akademie der Wissenschaften,* 1900.

SECONDARY SOURCES

Leitner, Gerit von. *Der Fall Clara Immerwahr: Leben für eine humane Wissenschaft.* Munich: Beck, 1993.

———. "Frauenraum Naturwissenschaften? Clara Immerwahr und Gertrud Woker." In *Friedensentwürfe / Positionen von Querdenkern des 10. Jahrhunderst,* ed. Dieter Kinkelbur and Friedhelm Zubke, 47–69. Münster: Agenda, 1995. A historical portrait of the physical chemist.

———, Joachim Zepelin, and Adolf-Henning Frucht. "Die Tragik der verschmähten Liebe. Die Geschichte des deutsch-jüdischen Physikochemmikers und preussischen Patrioten Fritz Haberr." *In Mannheimer Forum 94/95. Ein Panorama der Naturwissenschaften* 63–111. Munich: Piper, 1995.

STANDARD SOURCES

DSB (for Fritz Haber); Poggendorff.

HACCIUS, BARBARA (1914–1983)

German botanist. Born 6 December 1914 in Strassburg (then part of France). Educated Mädchengymnasium in Karlsruhe (Abitur [exam for entering university] 1933); University of Munich, Freiburg, and Halle (doctorate 1939); University of Mainz, habilitated (1950). Professional experience: Studienassessorin (1941–1946); Studienrätin (1946–1949); University of Halle, pedagogical faculty, dozentin (assistant professor 1949–1950); University of Mainz, Botanical Institute, scientific helper (1950–1954); dozentin (1954–1956); ausserplanmässige professorin (1956–1971); university professor and head of section in the Institute for Special Botany (1971–?). Died 29 December 1983 in Mainz, Germany.

Barbara Haccius was born in Strassburg when it was a part of France, but attended school in Germany. She earned her doctorate at the University of Halle with her thesis, "Untersuchungen über die Dedeutung der Distichie für das Verständnis der zerstreuten Blattstellung bei den Dikotylen." During the course of her career she left the university to take a position in the high school in 1941, the *Studienassessorin,* and in 1946 advanced to *Studienrätin.* After five years of this type of work, Haccius returned to the University of Halle, where she joined the pedagogical faculty as a dozent. However, she only remained in this position for a year before going to the University of Mainz as a scientific helper. At Mainz, she habilitated and rose rapidly in this academic environment, being named diätendozentin in 1954, extraordinary professor two years later, and finally university professor and section chair of the Institute for Special Botany.

Much of Haccius's research was on plant embryology, which she used to determine the phylogenetic position of plants. She also worked on regeneration. She published her work in numerous scientific articles and wrote a textbook.

JH/MBO

PRIMARY SOURCES

Haccrus, Barbara. Weitere Untersuchungen zum Verständnis der Zersteuten Blattstellungen bei Dikotylen. Heidelberg: Springer-Verlag, 1950.

SECONDARY SOURCES

Boedecker, Elisabeth and Meyer-Plath, Maria, eds. *50 Jahre Habilitation von Frauen in Deutschland.* Göttingen: O. Schwartz, 1974.

STANDARD SOURCES

Das Deutsche Who's Who; Strohmeier; WW in Science in Europe.

HAGOOD, MARGARET LOYD JARMAN (1907–1963)

U.S. statistician, sociologist, and demographer. Born 26 October 1907 in Newton County, Ga., to Laura Harris (Martin) and Lewis Wilson Jarman. Five siblings. Married Middleton Howard Hagood (1926). One daughter. Educated Emory-at-Oxford in Georgia; Agnes Scott College, Atlanta; Queen's College, Charlotte, N.C. (graduated 1929); Emory University, Atlanta (A.M. in mathematics, 1930); University of North Carolina, Institute for Research in Social Science (Ph.D., 1937). Professional experience: National Park Seminary, College Park, Md., researcher (1930–1934); Institute for Research in Social Science, researcher (1937–1942); U.S. Department of Agriculture, Bureau of Agricultural Economics, researcher (1942–1952); Farm Population and Rural Life Branch of the Agricultural Marketing Service, researcher (1952–1962). Retired, 1962. Died 13 August 1963 in San Diego, Calif., of a heart attack.

Margaret Jarman's father was trained as a mathematician and encouraged his daughter's interest in the subject. After attending Agnes Scott College for a short time, she dropped out in 1926 to marry Middleton Hagood, a man she had known from childhood. Her father had become president of

Queen's College in Charlotte, and Hagood finished her bachelor's degree at that institution. She and her husband moved to Atlanta, where they both attended Emory University, he as a dental student and she as a mathematician. After completing her master's degree, she accepted a position at the National Park Seminary in College Park, Maryland, where she taught for four years. Howard Odum, then head of the Institute for Research in Social Science at the University of North Carolina and a friend of her father, offered her a graduate fellowship in sociology. She became an important member of the group of scholars who collected around Odum. Her mathematical background prepared "Marney," as she was known, for sociological statistics and demography, two rapidly developing fields.

Interestingly, Hagood became involved in a Chapel Hill radical group in the 1930s that in the 1950s was considered suspect by Joseph McCarthy. After the Hagoods had lived apart for several years, they finally divorced in 1936, a year before Hagood finished her dissertation on the fertility patterns of white women in the South. Appointed a research associate in the Institute, she extended her study into a social study into the lives of the wives of white tenant farmers and published this study as a book, *Mothers of the South.* She, another woman sociologist, Harriet Herring, and two photographers from the Farm Security Administration documented the poverty-stricken agricultural life of the Southeast during the Depression. Although this work was exhibited, it was never published.

Hagood moved to statistical studies and demography with her book *Statistics for Sociologists* (1941). During World War II, she moved to the United States Department of Agriculture, where she was associated with a number of bureaus, rising to the head of the Farm Population and Rural Life Branch in 1952.

In 1954, Hagood was elected president of the Population Association of America, and in 1956, of the Rural Sociological Society. Soon after these presidencies, she developed rheumatic heart disease and dramatically reduced her workload, retiring in 1962. The next year she died of a heart attack.

JH/MBO

PRIMARY SOURCES

Hagood, Margaret. *Mothers of the South: Portraiture of White Tenant Farm Women.* Chapel Hill: University of North Carolina Press, 1939.

———. *Statistics for Sociologists.* New York: Reynal and Hitchcock, 1941. Her studies and reports are found at the USDA.

SECONDARY SOURCES

Eldridge, Hope T. "Margaret Jarman Hagood 1907–1963. *Population Index* 30 (January 1964): 30–33. Obituary notice. Includes bibliography of her publications in demography.

"Margaret Jarman Hagood (1908–1963)." *American Statistician* 17 (October 1963): 37. Obituary notice.

Scott, Anne Firor. Introduction to reprint edition of *Mothers of the South*. New York: Norton, 1977.

Taylor, Carl C. "Margaret J. Hagood (1907–63)." *Rural Sociology* 29 (January 1964): 97–98.

STANDARD SOURCES
NAW(M) (article by Anne Firor Scott).

HAHN, DOROTHY ANNA (1876–1950)

U.S. organic chemist. Born 9 April 1876 in Philadelphia, Pa., to Mary (Beaver) and Carl J. Hahn. One sister. Educated Girls' High School, Philadelphia; Florence Baldwin's School, Bryn Mawr, Pa.; Bryn Mawr College (A.B. in chemistry and biology, 1899; graduate work, fellow, 1908?); University of Leipzig, studied organic chemistry (1906–1907); Yale University (Ph.D., 1916). Professional experience: Pennsylvania College for Women, later Chatham College, Pittsburgh, professor of chemistry and biology (1899–1906); Kindergarten College, Pittsburgh, professor (1904–1906); Mount Holyoke College, instructor in organic chemistry (1908–1914), associate professor (1914–1916), professor (1916–1941). Retired 1941. Died 10 December 1950 in South Hadley, Mass., of a heart ailment.

Dorothy Hahn was born in Philadelphia where she grew up. Her father, a clerk and bookkeeper, was born in Germany. After earning her bachelor's degree from Bryn Mawr College, she took a teaching post at Pennsylvania College for Women in Pittsburgh, where she was professor of chemistry and biology. Concurrently, she taught at the Kindergarten College in Pittsburgh. Enticed by the opportunities presented by Arthur Hantzsch at the University of Leipzig, Hahn spent the year 1906–1907 studying organic chemistry in Germany. When she returned to the United States, she did graduate work at Bryn Mawr College as a fellow, under the organic chemist E. P. Kohler. Still without an advanced degree, Hahn obtained a position at Mount Holyoke College. During the academic year 1915–1916, Hahn obtained an American Association of University Women fellowship, which she used to study at Yale Universitiy. She worked with Treat B. Johnson on cyclic polypeptide hydantoins. By the end of her fellowship, she had earned a doctoral degree from Yale.

Hahn was convinced that teaching and research were symbiotic fields. Thus, when she returned to Mount Holyoke, she continued to combine the two with the blessings of department chair, physical chemist EMMA P. CARR. Hahn published extensively in the *Journal of the American Chemical Society* and coauthored books and monographs. Her students were successful in graduate school.

Hahn's interests were not confined to research and teaching. She also enjoyed travel, literature, and international studies. She was a member of the Presbyterian church. She retired in 1941, but remained in South Hadley, where she lived with a long-time friend, Dorothy Fisher, of the Mount Holyoke English department. JH/MBO

PRIMARY SOURCES
Hahn, Dorothy. With Arthur M. Comey. *A Dictionary of Chemical Solubilities, Inorganic.* New York: Macmillan and Co., 1921.

———. With Leroy F. Marek. *The Catalytic Oxidation of Organic Compound in the Vapor Phase.* New York: Chemical Catalog Company, Inc., 1932.

———. With Treat B. Johnson. "Pyrimidines: Their Amono and Aminoöxy Derivatives." *Chemical Reviews* 13 (October 1933): 193–303.

SECONDARY SOURCES
"Dorothy A. Hahn." *Science* 112 (29 December 1950). Obituary notice.

STANDARD SOURCES
AMS 4–8; Bailey, *NAW* (article by Alice G. Renfrew); Shearer and Shearer 1997 (article by Carole B. Shmurak).

HAINAULT, COUNTESS OF (b. 13th century)

French physician. Born thirteenth century. Educated herself in medicine. Practiced in Paris.

The Countess of Hainault is an example of a thirteenth-century medical woman who was licensed to practice in Paris. She was of aristocratic birth and was from a wealthy family. JH/MBO

STANDARD SOURCES
Hurd-Mead 1938.

HALDORSEN, INGER ALIDA (1899–?)

Norwegian physician. Born 19 May 1899 on Bomlo Island off the west coast of Norway. Mother worked as a tailor before her marriage; father was a manufacturer of coach wheels and agricultural machinery. Thirteen siblings and half-siblings. Educated local primary school; six-month boarding school for young people from the country; grammar school; University of Oslo (studied medicine). Professional experience: State School for Midwives, Bergen, senior registrar; private practice (from 1943); children's home, medical superintendent; adviser to the hospital board (1959–1964?). Death date unknown.

Inger Haldorsen was born on a small island off the coast of Norway. Her mother was her father's second wife. He already had seven children by his first wife and then had seven more by his second. Needless to say, it was difficult to support this large family. Nevertheless, when Inger showed an interest in school, even though they could not understand why a woman would want an education, they sacrificed to give her one. She became interested in gynecology and got as much extra training as she could manage. She joined the Norwegian Medical Women's Association in 1934 and became its secretary. As a member, she was eligible to attend an international congress in Edinburgh. She also attended an international course in Paris during the winter of 1937 through 1938. Here she was able to meet members of the Medical Women's International Association from Asia, South America, and Europe.

Upon her return to Bergen, Haldorsen worked as a senior registrar. This post allowed her to practice surgery. With the advent of the German occupation, Haldorsen joined the resistance movement and was interrogated by the Gestapo. She was imprisoned and spent some time in solitary confinement. Before the war was over, she was released, but it was difficult to restart a practice after being away from it for several years. She bicycled to a private hospital where she performed operations. After the war, she became politically active, while maintaining a private practice. She gave talks to women's organizations, held municipal offices, and was a member of committees involving the needs of women and children. She continued to be active in international medical organizations.

Haldorsen became a deputy in Parliament and worked on numerous initiatives to help women and children. She worked on a National Social Insurance Scheme that everybody was required to join after 1956. She was also appointed a member of the Committee of the Norwegian Medical Deput, a government monopoly for the import and export of medicines. She became president of the Norwegian Midwives' Association, a position that she held for six years until she retired. KM

PRIMARY SOURCES
Haldorsen, Inger. In Hellstedt, *Autobiographies*.

HALICKA, ANTONINA (YAROSZEWICZ) (1908–1973)

Lithuanian geologist. Born 1908. Married. Died 1973.

Antonina Halicka originally worked on Lithuanian ore deposits. She settled in Poland in 1945, and became director of the Museum of the Earth. She published her research on Quaternary geology. JH/MBO

SECONDARY SOURCES
"Antonina Halicka." *International Committee on the History of the Geological Sciences Newsletter* 8 (1972): 14–15.

STANDARD SOURCES
Sarjeant.

HALKET, ANN CRONIN (d. 1965)

British botanist. Educated Bedford College (D.Sc.). Linnean Society, elected Fellow (1911), council member (1924–1928). Professional experience: Bedford College for Women, lecturer in Botany.

Ann Cronin Halket earned a doctorate from Bedford College and went on to become a lecturer in botany at the Bedford College for Women. She was elected a fellow of the Linnean Society in 1911. JH/MBO

SECONDARY SOURCES
Proceedings of the Linnean Society 177 (1966): 119.

STANDARD SOURCES
Desmond.

HALKET, LADY ANNE (MURRAY) (1622–1699)

British physician. Born 4 January 1622 in London, into the Scottish family of Robert Murray, descendant of the earl of Tullibardin, and Jane Drummond of the family of the earl of Perth. Privately tutored. Married Sir James Halket on 2 March 1656. Four children, one survived. Died 22 April 1699.

Anne Murray was born into the Scottish family of Robert Murray, descendant of the earl of Tullibardin, and Jane Drummond of the family of the earl of Perth. Robert Murray was instructor to the son of King James I of England, who later became King Charles the first of England, and honored his teacher by naming him provost of Eaton College. Jane Drummond was for a time tutor to the duke of Gloucester and Princess Elizabeth, and was diligent in the education of her own children as well. Anna received tutelage in the usual proper graces and began early to pursue her interest in medicine and surgery. In this area, she became so proficient that her skills were consulted by persons from remote parts of the kingdom; other physicians even sent her patients whose illnesses were beyond their powers to cure.

Murray was pious and graceful, as well as intelligent, and was a loyal Royalist, causing her frequent persecution and suffering. She married Sir James Halket on 2 March 1656 and bore four children, only one of whom (Robert, b. 1660) survived childhood. While pregnant with her first child, she wrote *The Mother's Will to the Unborn Child,* fearing she might die in childbirth. Ballard lists twenty-five collections of her works published as volumes between 1658 and 1699, and mentions another thirty "stitched" books of ten or twelve sheets containing meditations. The bulk of these are religious tracts and meditations; some concern political affairs, some discipline and proper behavior. She was widowed after fourteen years of marriage and lived on to the age of seventy-seven, dying 22 April 1699.   JH/MBO

PRIMARY SOURCES

Halket, Lady Anne. *Meditations and Prayers, upon the First Week; with Objects on Each Day's Creation.* Edinburgh, 1701.

———. *The Life of Lady Halket.* Edinburgh, 1701.

SECONDARY SOURCES

Ballard, George. *Memoirs of Several Ladies of Great Britain, who Have Been Celebrated for Their Writings or Skill in the Learned Languages, Arts and Sciences.* Oxford: Jackson, 1752; rpt., London: Edwards, 1775. Halket discussed on pages 256–262.

Loftis, John ed. *The Memoirs of Anne, Lady Halket and Ann, Lady Fanshawe.* Oxford: Oxford University Press, 1979.

HALL, AGNES C. (1777–1846)

British botanist and miscellaneous writer. Born 1777 in Roxburghshire. Married Robert Hall, a doctor. Died 1 December 1846.

Agnes Hall wrote on many miscellaneous topics, including scientific ones.

PRIMARY SOURCES

Hall, Agnes. *Elements of Botany.* London, 1802.

SECONDARY SOURCES

Gentleman's Magazine 1 (1847): 97.

STANDARD SOURCES

DNB.

HALL, DOROTHY (1896–?)

U.S. chemist. Born 20 September 1896 in Toledo, Ohio. Educated University of Michigan (B.S., 1918; fellow, 1918–1920; Ph.D., 1920). Professional experience: University of Michigan, assistant in analytical chemistry (1917–1919); General Electric Corporation, Schenectady, N.Y., researcher (from 1920). Death date unknown.

After receiving her degrees from the University of Michigan, Dorothy Hall took a position in the research laboratory at General Electric. Her name is listed in only the third edition of *AMS* and no other information is available about her subsequent career.   JH/MBO

PRIMARY SOURCES

Hall, Dorothy. *Electricity and Magnets.* Chicago: Charles E. Merrill, 1946.

STANDARD SOURCES

AMS 3.

HALL, EDITH HAYWARD (1877–1943)

See Dohan, Edith Hayward Hall.

HALL, JULIA BRAINERD (1859–1925)

U.S. chemist and engineer. Born 1859. At least one brother, Charles. Never married. Educated Oberlin College (diploma 1885). Professional experience: Charles Hall's laboratory, assistant. Died 1925.

Julia Hall was one of a category of individuals who collaborate with a family member or teacher, and who seldom get credit for their work. In Hall's case her collaborator was her younger brother, Charles. Brother and sister both attended Oberlin College, Julia matriculating in 1881 and Charles in 1885. Julia was officially enrolled in a "literary course"—which replaced the earlier "ladies' course"—although she, like Charles, took chemistry from Franklin F. Jewett. However, at the end of four years, Julia was only awarded a diploma, while Charles received a degree. Neither Julia nor Charles married and they remained best friends and confidants throughout their lives. Their home in Oberlin served as the location for Charles's laboratory. It was in a woodshed, next to Julia's domain, the kitchen. She assisted him in the laboratory and was vital in developing the process for which Charles is credited: the electrolytic reduction of alumina in a molten bath of cryolite to produce aluminum metal. This is known as the Hall process. It became the basis for the formation of the Pittsburgh Reduction Company, the forerunner of ALCOA, the Aluminum Company of America.

Julia's part in the inventive process was both as an assistant in the experiments and as a competent eyewitness for his experiments. These activities resulted in the issuance of numerous patents. Julia carefully recorded the steps in the inventive process, replete with technical details and the date to substantiate their priority in the inventions. In one notable case, she wrote a "History of C. M. Hall's Aluminum Invention," which assured Hall's victory in the Hall-Héroult patent interference case. In her detailed notes, she was able to establish that Hall had reduced his invention to practice before the French invention had been patented. The witnesses were Charles, Julia, their father, and two of Charles's professors.

She also contacted financiers, and family and friends who might know people willing to back the processes. Julia, however, received little recognition for her part in the team. Charles became very wealthy, while Julia averaged only about eight thousand dollars income from her stocks. Charles did not credit her in his acceptance speech for the Perkins Medal of the American Chemical Society. After the actual production of aluminum was begun, Julia managed the entreprenuerial activities of the entire operation.   JH/MBO

SECONDARY SOURCES
Journal of Chemical Education 54 (1977)

STANDARD SOURCES
Kass-Simon and Farnes (article by Martha Moore Trescott).

HALL, KATE MARION (1861–1918).

British botanist. Born August 1861 in Newmarket, Suffolk. Professional experience: Stepney Museum, curator (1893–1909). Honors and memberships: Linnean Society, Fellow (1905). Died 12 April 1918 in Lingfield, Surrey.

Kate Hall was elected a Fellow of the Linnaean Society in 1905 after she had published on the genus *Tmesipteris.* Shortly thereafter, she became curator of the Stepney Museum (Stepney is a borough of Greater London). She published a popular book, *Nature Rambles in London,* in 1908. An extensive collection of her plants was donated to Queen Mary's College, London. JH/MBO

PRIMARY SOURCES
Hall, Kate. "Tmesipteris." *Proceedings of the Royal Irish Academy* 2 (1891): 1–18.
———. *Nature Rambles in London.* London: Holder and Stoughton, 1908.

SECONDARY SOURCES
Proceedings of the Linnean Society (1917–1918): 61–63. Obituary notice.

STANDARD SOURCES
Desmond.

HALL, ROSETTA SHERWOOD (1865–1951)

U.S. physician. Born 19 September 1865 in Liberty, N.Y., to Phoebe (Gildersleeve) and Rosevelt Rensler Sherwood. Two siblings. Married William James Hall (1892). Two children. Educated Liberty Normal Institute and Oswego State Normal School (graduated 1883); Woman's Medical College of Pennsylvania (M.D., 1889); Nursery and Children's Hospital, Staten Island, intern (1889). Professional experience: Chestnut Ridge (N.Y.) District School, teacher (1883–1886); Madison Street Mission Dispensary, lower Manhattan, physician (1889–1890); founded Baldwin Dispensary in Seoul under the auspices of the Women's Foreign Missionary Society of the Methodist Episcopal Church (1893); Institute for the Blind and Deaf, Pyong Yang, head; Edith Margaret Memorial Wing of the Women's Dispensary, founder (1899); Women's Hospital of Extended Grace, founder (1908); Women's Medical (training) Institute, Seoul, founder (1928). Died 5 April 1951 in Ocean Grove, N.J.

As a young girl, Rosetta Sherwood was influenced by her father's connection to the local Methodist Episcopal Church, where he was an official. She first trained as a teacher and after working at this profession for three years, she was inspired by a visiting lecturer to become a medical missionary. She enrolled in the Woman's Medical College of Pennsylvania and received her medical degree in 1889. After interning on Staten Island, she took a temporary appointment under the Methodist Church to work in a mission dispensary, where she met her future husband, who worked as the medical superintendent of the dispensary. Canadian-born William Hall, who had planned to go as a missionary to China, changed his mind after Sherwood was appointed to a medical missionary position in Seoul, Korea. He joined her in Seoul in 1892, where she was working in a small woman's hospital, and they soon married. They had a son, Sherwood, the following year. The couple was often separated, since he was assigned to establish a new mission in Pyong Yang while she was founding a new dispensary in Seoul. In 1894, they both moved to Pyong Yang, but due to the political unrest that preceded the Sino-Japanese war, they returned to Seoul. While treating wounded soldiers, William Hall contracted typhus and died in Seoul in 1894. Rosetta Hall, pregnant with her second child, returned to New York state, but continued to work raising funds for the Korean mission and serving as an examining physician for a children's mission program in Nyack-on-Hudson and advising would-be medical missionaries at the International Medical Missionary Union. During this period, she edited a biography of her husband.

In 1897, Hall returned to Seoul with her two children and continued her work for the next thirty-five years, first in Pyong Yang and after 1917 in Seoul. Soon after her arrival, her daughter died of amoebic dysentery.

Hall became involved in medical training of Korean women. She arranged for the medical education of Esther Kim Pak in the United States. Esther Kim Pak became the first western-trained woman physician in Korea. Hall also founded a medical school for women in Seoul in 1928. At the age of sixty-eight, Hall returned to the United States, where she continued to lecture and practice medicine. She retired to a rest home for Methodist missionaries in Ocean Grove, New Jersey, where she died.   JH/MBO

PRIMARY SOURCES
Hall, Rosetta, ed. Life of Reverend William James Hall, M.D., 1897.

SECONDARY SOURCES
Hall, Sherwood. *With Stethoscope in Asia: Korea.* 2 vols. McLean, Va.: MCL Associates, 1978. This book by her son includes a bibliography of works by and about Rosetta Hall.

STANDARD SOURCES
Lovejoy; *NAW(M)* (article by Clifton J. Phillips); *WW in New York.*

HALL-BROWN, LUCY (1843–1907)

U.S. physician. Born November 1843 in Holland, Vt. Married R. G. Brown (1891). Educated locally; University of Michigan (1876–1878); postgraduate work in New York and in St. Thomas Hospital, London; Royal Lying-in and Gynecological Hospital, Dresden, intern. Professional experience: Massachusetts Reformatory Prison for Women, assistant physician (1878), resident physician (1879–1883); Vassar College, assistant professor of physiology and hygiene, assistant physician (from 1883); private practice, Brooklyn, N.Y., in association with Eliza M. Mosher (to 1904); visiting lecturer in physiology and hygiene, Japan. Honors and memberships: New York Academy of Medicine, Fellow; Kings County Medical Society, Brooklyn Pathological Society, member. Died 1 August 1907 in Los Angeles, Calif., of valvular heart disease.

Lucy Hall took the medical course at the University of Michigan, graduating in 1878. She served for six months as assistant physician under Eliza M. Mosher at the Massachusetts Reformatory Prison for Women, and then went abroad for postgraduate study, the first woman doctor to gain admittance to clinics in St. Thomas's Hospital, London. After only a month's study in Dresden, she was given an internship at the Royal Lying-in and Gynecological Hospital. While still interning in Dresden, Hall received the call to return to the Reformatory Prison as resident physician. She later declined a request to become Superintendent of the Reformatory. Hall's mentor, Eliza Mosher, when appointed professor of physiology and hygiene, and resident physician of Vassar College in 1883, asked Hall to share her work. The two formed a partnership in practice that lasted until 1904. In 1886, Hall turned to private practice completely and gained a considerable reputation in medical jurisprudence, being recognized and called as an expert witness by various courts in New York, including the Supreme Court.

In 1891, Lucy Hall married R. G. Brown, an electrical engineer. In 1904, the couple moved to Los Angeles, California, for the sake of Hall-Brown's health. They made a visit to Japan where Hall-Brown visited hospitals, schools, missions, prisons, and police courts. She made such an impression on the Japanese officials that she was invited to return on several occasions as visiting lecturer in physiology and hygiene. This was undoubtedly stressful to her already weakened heart, and she died 1 August 1907 in Los Angeles.

Hall-Brown was one of the early women physicians admitted as a Fellow in the New York Academy of Medicine and one of the first American women physicians to be recognized in the Far East. She wrote several articles for professional and popular journals.

JH/MBO

PRIMARY SOURCES
Hall, Lucy. "Inebriety in Women." *Quarterly Journal of Inebriety* (October 1883).
———. "Prison Experiences." *Medico-Legal Journal* (March 1888).
———. "Unsanitary Condition of Country Houses." *Journal of Social Science* (December 1888).

SECONDARY SOURCES
Kelly, Howard A. *Cyclopedia of American Medical Biography.* Philadelphia: Saunders, 1910.

HALLIDAY, NELLIE (1889–?)

U.S. biologist. Born 18 July 1889 in Cincinnati, Ohio. Educated Drexel Institute (1910–1912); Columbia University (B.A., 1925; A.M., 1926; Ph.D., 1930). Professional experience: Cook County Hospital, Chicago, dietitian (1912–1916); Latter Day Saints Hospital, Salt Lake City (1916–1917); American Red Cross, Albania and Turkey, biochemical researcher (1919–1921); U.S. Public Health Service, N.C., biochemical researcher (1921–1922); Columbia University, assistant in biochemistry (1924–1928); Michigan State College, home economics instructor and researcher (1929–1934); Institute for Experimental Biology, Calif., research associate; New England Deaconess Hospital (1937–1938); University of Southern California, biochemical researcher (1938–1941); Mount Zion Hospital, member of staff (from 1941). Death date unknown.

Nellie Halliday earned her two advanced degrees from Columbia University after she had worked as a dietician and for the American Red Cross. She was a member of the Chemical Society, the Institute of Nutrition, and the Society for Experimental Biology. She did research on vitamins in canned goods, the comparative adsorption of vitamins B and G, the stability of the B vitamins, the new vitamin B growth factor for rats, and lipid and carbohydrate metabolism.

JH/MBO

PRIMARY SOURCES
Halliday, Nellie. "Quantitative Comparative Studies of the Adsorption of Vitamins B and G from Protein-Free Milk by Lloyd's Reagant." Ph.D. diss., Columbia University, 1930.

STANDARD SOURCES
AMS 5–8.

HALLOWELL, SUSAN MARIA (1835–1911)

U.S. botanist. Born 25 August 1835 in Bangor, Maine. Educated Colby College (A.M., 1875); Harvard University, summer school (1875–1885); botany laboratories and museums, Europe (1887–1888; 1894–1895). Professional experience: high schools, Portland, Maine, assistant (1853–1854); Bangor, high school teacher (1854–1875); Wellesley College, professor of natural history (1875–1878), professor of botany (1878–1902); emerita professor (from 1902).

Susan Maria Hallowell taught high school for a number of years before she received her bachelor's degree from Colby College. Although she did not enroll in an advanced degree program, she visited numerous European laboratories and museums to absorb the latest knowledge in her field. After teaching high school in Maine until 1875, she won a position on the faculty of Wellesley the year it was founded. She remained at Wellesley until her retirement in 1902. One of her students, MARGARET CLAY FERGUSON, later became an important botanist. Hallowell's research was in histological and physiological botany.   JH/MBO

SECONDARY SOURCES

"Scientific News and Notes." *Science* n.s. 34 (29 December 1911): 911–912.

STANDARD SOURCES

AMS 1–2; Bailey; Barr; Rossiter 1982; Siegel and Finley.

HAMBURGER, ERNA (1911–1988)

Swiss engineer. Born 14 September 1911 in Brussels, Belgium, to Else (Müller) and Frédéric Hamburger. Educated Ecole Supérieure des Jeunes Filles in the Cantonal Gymnasium, Lausanne, Switzerland; University of Lausanne, Engineering School (diploma 1933); doctorate (1937). Professional experience: University of Lausanne, assistant (1937–1938), electronics laboratory, research (1952–1957); Institute for Technical Physics, Division for Industrial Research, Eidgenössischen Technical High School, Zurich, engineering instructor (1938–1941); worked in industry as a developmental engineer (1942–1952); Technischen Hochschule der Schweiz, Lausanne, professor (1957–1988?). Honors and memberships: Internationalen Komittes für Terminologie (International Committee for Terminology), president; Association des femmes universitaires, president (for seven years); Internationalen Akademikerinnenbundes, president (for six years); Association des Femmes de Carrières libérales et commerciales, active member, president (1978); Schweizerischen Elektronischen Vereins (Swiss Electronic Union), honorary member (1979). Died 15 May 1988 in Switzerland.

A female engineer, and even rarer, a full professor, Erna Hamburger was born in Belgium but educated in Switzerland where she earned a doctorate. Although she taught and did research at the University of Lausanne and a technical school, she was very interested in industrial development. She became known for her special apparatus for radio-wave reception. She worked on ultra short waves and a system of optical registration from tone frequencies. After her time in industry, she returned to the University of Lausanne as the head of the laboratory for electronic technique, and became professor of electrometry in 1957. She was the first woman in Switzerland to become a professor at a polytechnic institution.

In 1939, Hamburger joined the army; in 1950, became chief of the telecommunication troops and a year later, the Chief of the technical division. She was active in women's organizations. She died in 1988   JH/MBO

STANDARD SOURCES

Strohmeier; *WW in Switzerland*.

HAMERSTROM, FRANCES (FLINT) (1907–   )

U.S. biologist and ornithologist. Born 1907 in Brookline, Mass., to Helen (Chase) and Lawrence Flint. Three brothers. Married Frederick Hamerstrom. Two children (Alan and Elva); Educated privately and Milton Academy; Smith College; Iowa State College (B.A.); University of Wisconsin (M.A.), Ph.D. Professional experience: University of Michigan, instructor and researcher; Wisconsin Conservation Department, instructor and researcher (1949–1974?).

Born in Brookline, Massachusetts, to a wealthy family, Frances Flint spent her first years in Germany and Europe, where her father consulted as a criminologist. The family returned to the United States at the beginning of World War I. Flint studied at home, went briefly to Smith College, leaving after one year, and for a short time worked as a fashion model. Having met Frederick Hamerstrom at a dance, she married him, and then attended Iowa State College. There she completed her degree in biology, working under Paul Errington. She then accompanied her husband to the University of Wisconsin where they both studied under Aldo Leopold and where she received her master's and doctoral degrees.

She began by studying hawks and owls and then (with her husband) pheasants in Iowa and prairie chickens at the University of Wisconsin. After a few years teaching at the University of Wisconsin, Hamerstrom and her husband left to run a field study for the conservation department of Michigan, the Prairie Chicken Project, which they continued until the mid-1970s. Both husband and wife gained an international reputation for their work and trained many other scientists in field ornithology and conservation. Hamerstrom also continued her own studies of hawks and owls.

In her eighties, Hamerstrom wrote a charming autobiography, *My Double Life,* about her German then American upbringing and her life as she moved from the life of a wealthy debutante to that of a field ornithologist and conservationist. Over the course of her professional career, she wrote ten books and 168 articles. JH/MBO

PRIMARY SOURCES

Hamerstrom, Frances. With Paul L. Errington and Frederick Hamerstrom. "The Great Horned Owl and Its Prey in North-Central United States." *Horned Owl Bulletin.* 1940.

————. *An Eagle to the Sky.* Ames: Iowa State University Press, 1970. Hamerstrom's account of raising and rehabilitating a golden eagle.

————. With Frederick Hamerstrom. *The Prairie Chicken: Highlights of a 22–Year Study of Counts, Behavior, Movements, Turnover and Habitat.* Madison, Wis.: Department of Natural Resources, 1973.

————. *Strictly for Chickens.* Ames: Iowa State University Press, 1980. Hamerstrom's popular account of her work with the prairie chicken.

————. *My Double Life: Memoirs of a Naturalist.* Madison: University of Wisconsin Press, 1994.

STANDARD SOURCES

AMS 10–18; Bailey.

HAMILTON, ALICE (1869–1970)

U.S. pathologist, bacteriologist. Born 27 February 1869 to Montgomery and Gertrude (Pond) Hamilton, Fort Wayne, Ind. Four siblings. Educated University of Michigan Medical School (M.D., 1893); Hospital for Women and Children in Minneapolis and the New England Hospital for Women and Children near Boston, intern; postgraduate training, Munich and Leipzig (1895–1897); Johns Hopkins Medical School (1896–1897); Pasteur Institute (1902). Professional experience: Woman's Medical College of Northwestern University, Chicago, professor of pathology (1897–1902); University of Chicago, research assistant; Memorial Institute for Infectious Diseases, assistant pathologist (from 1902); Occupational Disease Commission of Illinois, director (1908–1910); Labor Commission of the United States Department of Commerce (Department of Labor from 1912)(1910–1919); Department of Industrial Medicine, Medical School of Harvard University, assistant professor (1919–1935); Harvard University, professor emerita (1935–1970). Honors and memberships: Mount Holyoke College, Smith College, University of Michigan, University of Rochester, and Tulane University, honorary degrees; American Association for the Advancement of Science; American Public Health Association; American Medical Association; National Consumers League, president (1945–1946); National Women's Trade Union League; League of Women Voters;

American Association of University Women. Died 22 September 1970.

Alice Hamilton was born 27 February 1869 to Montgomery and Gertrude (Pond) Hamilton in Fort Wayne, Indiana. She and her three sisters and baby brother grew up in a mentally stimulating environment, learning languages, literature, history, and some mathematics informally from their parents and occasional tutors. Alice attended "Miss Porter's" finishing school in Farmington, Connecticut at age seventeen, then began preparatory studies for her chosen profession, medicine. She received her medical degree in 1893 from the coeducational Medical School of the University of Michigan, and interned at the Hospital for Women and Children in Minneapolis and at the New England Hospital for Women and Children near Boston. Hamilton went to Germany for more training in her chosen specialties of bacteriology and pathology.

Returning to the United States, she attended classes at Johns Hopkins Medical School until she received an appointment in pathology at the Woman's Medical School of Northwestern University. Soon after moving to Chicago, Hamilton was accepted as a boarder at Hull House, the famous settlement home of JANE ADDAMS. Here she made many interesting and useful contacts with prominent Chicagoans and visitors and, through her required social service, succeeded in starting Chicago's first baby health center.

Besides teaching, Hamilton carried on research in pathology and bacteriology. When the Women's Medical School closed in 1902, Hamilton spent a year of study at the Pasteur Institute in Paris, returning to Chicago to join the Memorial Institute for Infectious Diseases as assistant to the eminent pathologist Ludwig Hektoen. Typhoid fever was epidemic in Chicago, and Hamilton conducted investigations for the Chicago Health Department, making recommendations that resulted in complete reorganization of the department and acclaim from the Chicago Medical Society for the paper she wrote on flies as contaminating agents of typhoid.

Visiting the neighborhoods around Hull House, Hamilton saw the numbers of immigrant workers sickened by the poisonous fumes they inhaled on their jobs in the steel mills, factories, and foundries. Her investigations proved to Hamilton that similar conditions existed throughout the country, and she began a crusade to educate herself and others on the hazards and toxicities inherent in various trades. In 1910, the governor of Illinois established the Occupational Disease Commission, the first of its kind in the United States. Alice Hamilton was invited to join and later became its managing director. The commission's investigations and reports resulted in legislation for workman's compensation. A paper Hamilton read at the International Congress on Occupational Accidents and Diseases in Brussels, Belgium, came to the attention of the United States Commissioner of Labor (Department of Commerce), who asked her to undertake a national survey. In spite of the fact that this non-salaried post took her to Washington and other parts of the country, she remained at Hull House until 1919, and returned there to work several months out of each year until Jane Addams's death in 1935. She and Addams were delegates together to the peace meeting of the International Congress of Women at The Hague in 1915, to campaign for continued mediation of the crisis in Europe to avoid war. When the United States entered the war, Hamilton served despite her avowed pacifism by studying the munitions industries and observing the effects upon workers of several new poisons.

In 1919, Hamilton was named assistant professor in the new Department of Industrial Medicine at the Medical School of Harvard University, created in part due to the public interest her surveys had aroused. Being the only person qualified for the position, she became the first woman on the faculty at Harvard and had to contend with exclusion from the Harvard Faculty Club and from graduation processions, which remained strictly male. In her sixteen years at Harvard, she was never given a promotion. Since she taught only six months out of the year, she was able to continue her work for the federal government. Two important studies she completed for the Secretary of Labor were a detailed study of the new rayon industry and a study of silicosis and other diseases common to miners. Among the findings that made her a passionate supporter of health insurance and pension plans for workers were the deadly toxicity of lead in many common products such as bathtubs and paint; toxicity of nitrous fumes inhaled by workers in the explosives industry; adverse effects of certain occupations on maternal and fetal health; and others. She was the only female member of the League of Nations Health Committee (1924–1930), for which she visited the Soviet Union (1924). She visited Germany three times: in 1919, she made a study of the famine conditions for the Quakers; in 1933, she went on an exchange fellowship of the Carl Schurz Foundation; in 1938, during the Munich crisis, she went as a U.S. Department of Labor delegate to the Occupational Accidents and Diseases Congress in Frankfurt, and was able to observe the effects of the Nazi government.

Retired from teaching in 1935, Hamilton remained professor emerita of Harvard University and kept active in several organizations. She was a member of the American Association for the Advancement of Science, the American Public Health and Medical Associations, National Consumers League (president 1945–1946), National Women's Trade Union League, League of Women Voters and American Association of Uni-

versity Women. She was given honorary degrees by Mount Holyoke College, Smith College, University of Michigan, University of Rochester, and Tulane University.   JH/MBO

PRIMARY SOURCES

Hamilton, Alice. *Industrial Poisons in the United States.* New York: Macmillan, 1925.

———. *Industrial Toxicology.* New York: Harper and Brothers, 1934.

———. *Exploring the Dangerous Trades: The Autobiography of Alice Hamilton, M.D.* Boston: Little, Brown, 1943.

SECONDARY SOURCES

Fabricant, Noah Daniel. *Why We Became Doctors.* New York: Grune and Stratton, 1954.

Sicherman, Barbara. *Alice Hamilton: A Life in Letters.* Cambridge, Mass.: Harvard University Press, 1984.

STANDARD SOURCES

Current Biography 1946; Hurd-Mead 1933; *LKW;* Lovejoy; *Notable;* Shearer and Shearer 1996; Yost.

HAMILTON, PEGGY-KAY (1922–1959)

U.S. mineralogist. Born 1922. Never married. Vassar College (B.A., 1944); Columbia University (M.A., 1947). Professional experience: Columbia University, research assistant (1947–1959). Died 19 September 1959.

After Peggy-Kay Hamilton earned her master's degree from Columbia University, she chose to remain a full-time research assistant rather than continuing for her doctorate. Paul F. Kerr, with whom she worked, stated that the studies she completed over the years were equivalent to several doctorates, but that she refused to write a thesis and to schedule examinations. Although she could have obtained better-paying and more prestigious positions, Hamilton chose to remain in New York with her beloved family.

Hamilton's first major work concerned the American Petroleum Institute study of reference clay minerals. This institute published a glossary of clay minerals that was largely her work. The optical and X-ray studies from this work were also published. She was also responsible for much of the editorial work involved in this project. Interest in the mineralogy and occurrence of uranium piqued Hamilton's interest in the origin and nature of uranium minerals. As an investigator, she contributed to eleven pamphlets published by the Division of Raw Materials of the Atomic Energy Commission. She also contributed to several papers published in the *American Mineralogist* and the *Bulletin of the Geological Society of America.* A paper on the modes of umohoite, largely the result of her investigation, had been accepted by *American Mineralogist* at the time of her death.

Hamilton was a competent, well-respected mineralogist. She was easily elected a Fellow of the Mineralogical Society of America and of the Geological Society of America. She was a member of Sigma Xi. She died when she was only thirty-nine years old after an operation for brain cancer.   JH/MBO

PRIMARY SOURCES
Hamilton, Peggy-Kay. With P. F. Kerr. "Phosphuranylite at Marysvale, Utah." *U.S. Atomic Energy Commission Annual Report.* 30 June 1952 to 3 April 1953, RME-3046: 52–57.
———. "Umohoite from Cameron, Arizona." *American Mineralogist* 44 (1959): 1248.
Hamilton, Peggy-Kay with Paul F. Kerr, "Glossary of Clay Mineral Names, Preliminary Report No. 1." API Research Project 49, *Clay Mineral Standards.* Ann Arbor, Mich.: University Microfilms International, 1986.

SECONDARY SOURCES
Kerr, Paul F. "Memorial of Peggy-Kay Hamilton." *American Mineralogist* 45, nos. 3–4 (1960): 399–402.

STANDARD SOURCES
NAW unused, Sarjeant.

HAMMER, MARIE SIGNE (1907–   )
Danish natural historian. Born 20 March 1907 to Alma and Niels Jorgensen. Married Ole Hammer (1936). Four children. Educated University of Copenhagen (Ph.D. natural science). Professional experience: published on numerous expeditions.

Marie Signe Hammer was a Danish naturalist, who earned a doctorate in natural science from the University of Copenhagen. Hammer traveled extensively, taking part in expeditions to Iceland, Greenland, Canada, Mexico, the Andes, the Fiji Islands, New Zealand, New Guinea, and Hawaii. She published extensively on these expeditions. She was a member of the Danish Association for Natural History and other organizations.   JH/MBO

PRIMARY SOURCES
Hammer, Marie Signe. *Studies on the Oribatids and Collemboles of Greenland.* Copenhagen: C. A. Reitzel, 1944.
———. *Investigations on the Microfauna of Northern Canada.* Copenhagen: E. Munksgaard, 1952–1953.
———. *Investigations on the Oribatid Fauna of the Andes Mountains.* Copenhagen: I Kommission hos Munksgaard, 1958–1962.

STANDARD SOURCES
Debus.

HANFMANN, EUGENIA (1905–   )
Russian/U.S. psychologist. Born 3 March 1905 in St. Petersburg. Educated University of Jena (Ph.D., 1927). Professional experience: University of Jena, assistant instructor (1928–1930); Smith College, assistant (1930–1932); Worcester State Hospital, research associate (1932–1935); Mount Holyoke College, instructor through assistant professor (1939–1946); Harvard University, lecturer in clinical psychology (1946–1952); Brandeis University, associate professor (1952–1956); professor (1956–1970), Levin Professor (1970–retirement). Honors and memberships: American Psychological Association, Fellow.

Eugenia Hanfmann was born in St. Petersburg, Russia, but was educated in Germany, receiving her doctorate degree in Natural Philosophy from the University of Jena. She then worked as an assistant instructor in psychology at the university until 1930, when she emigrated to the United States and resided in the Boston area. For a few years, she served as a research assistant in the psychology laboratory at Smith College. In 1932, she moved to the Worcester State Hospital to conduct research on dementia praecox (schizophrenia). In 1939, she was appointed as an instructor and then assistant professor in psychology at Mount Holyoke College, from 1939 to 1946, through the war years. During this period, she, like many other psychologists, served the U.S. Government in the Office of Strategic Services (OSS) as a senior instructor in the assessment school. In 1946, she went to teach clinical psychology at Harvard University, where she also served as a consultant to the Russian Research Center, until she was appointed as associate professor at Brandeis in 1952. In the 1960s, she translated the work of psychologist L.W. Vygotsky. She remained at Brandeis for the rest of her academic career, appointed Levin Professor of Psychology in 1970.

Throughout her career, Hanfmann pursued her research interests in the development and pathology of thinking, in visual perception and memory, and in personality studies, including those of national character. In these last interests, she followed her former colleagues in Harvard, who included Henry A. Murray, active in the OSS, and Clyde Kluckhohn, director of the Russian Research Center. She was a Mason in the Scottish Rite in the late 1930s. Her membership in professional organizations included a fellowship in the American Psychological Association and the American Academy of Psychotherapy.
          JH/MBO

PRIMARY SOURCES
Hanfmann, Eugenia. With Jacob Kasanin. *Conceptual Thinking in Schizophrenia.* New York: Nervous and Mental Disease Monographs, 1942.
———. With Gertrude Vakar. *Thought and Language,* ed and trans. by L.S. Vygotsky. Cambridge, Mass.: MIT Press, 1962.

———. *Effective Therapy for College Students.* San Francisco: Jossey-Bass, 1978.

STANDARD SOURCES
O'Connell and Russo 1988; Stevens and Gardner.

HANKS, JANE RICHARDSON (1908–)

U.S. anthropologist and ethnologist. Born 2 August 1908 in Berkeley, Calif., to Leon Josiah Richardson and his wife (née Wilkinson). Married Lucien M. Hanks, Jr. Three sons. Educated University of California, Berkeley (A.B., 1930; Ph.D., 1943). Professional experience: University of California, Berkeley, department of anthropology, teaching assistant (1933–1936); research assistant to MARGARET MEAD *(1940); Office of Naval Intelligence research associate (1943); Bennington College, department of anthropology, lecturer (1944–1945); Cornell Southeast Asia Research Project, Thailand, research associate (1953–1955); Bennington-Cornell Survey of Hill Tribes of North Thailand, associate director (1968–1969, 1973–1974); Peace Corps consultant (1964, 1966); Williams College, visiting professor of anthropology (1968); State University of New York, Albany (1969–1973, 1975–1976). Field experience: Kiowa Reservation, Oklahoma (summer 1935); Blackfoot Reservation (summer 1938); Thailand village communities (1952–1955); Thailand hill tribes (1963–1966, 1973–1974). Honors and memberships: Association for Asian Studies (ASS), Southeast Asia Council, board of directors (1982); ASS Thailand/Laos/Cambodia Studies Group (1985). Fellow, American Anthropological Association, American Ethnological Association, Society of Applied Anthropology.*

The American anthropologist Jane Richardson Hanks had a long and fruitful career that did not rely on formal academic career patterns. She was raised in an academic household, the daughter of a classics professor at University of Califonia, Berkeley. She took some time to study art history abroad during her undergraduate years, but it was only after graduation that she became fascinated by the intermixture of cultures in modern Greece and saw some similarities to the cultural mixes in the American Southwest during the seventeenth century.

Richardson became interested in anthropology, studying with Alfred Kroeber, Robert Lowie, Paul Radin, and others. At the very beginning of her graduate work in 1933, she worked as a teaching assistant in undergraduate courses. She also served as a research assistant to Kroeber in 1934, assisting him in the extension of his study of culture change to women's dress fashions that included insights from her training in art history. The resulting important publication in 1940 generously gave her name as first author. Kroeber also recommended her for her first field work experience with Richard Lesser from Columbia as field director, studying the Kiowa Indians in Oklahoma. Other important researchers included Bernard

Mishkin, Weston LaBarre, and Donald Collier. The Kiowa would provide her with important material for her dissertation.

With a traveling fellowship, Richardson went to Columbia University to work with Richard Lesser. Here she met RUTH BENEDICT, who directed her dissertation on Kiowa law with the Columbia law professor Karl Llewelyn. (Though she completed her dissertation in 1938 and it was published in 1940, her degree was not awarded until 1943, due to her failure to deposit copies of the dissertation.)

After completing her dissertation, Richardson had the opportunity to work in Canada on the Blackfoot reservation as the research assistant of the psychologist Alexander Maslow. An associate of Maslow was the young social psychologist Lucien Hanks, who was also becoming interested in anthropology, a not uncommon fascinatation for psychologists in the 1930s. Robertson and Hanks met and married a few months later and began a long collaborative life together.

The couple went briefly to University of Illinois, Urbana, and then on to Bennington College, where Hanks's husband was based for the rest of his career. Her own career would depend on field work, visiting professorships in the area around Vermont and New York, and field work directorships. The two completed and published their field research on the Blackfoot only after World War II, having been interrupted by the birth of two of her three children between 1940 and 1943.

During the war, Jane Hanks had an opportunity to teach her husband's courses at Bennington while he was with the Office of Strategic Services in Burma. She also assisted first MARGARET MEAD's project on food habits of national minorities while in Urbana and later assisted Ruth Benedict on her "Culture at a Distance" project for the Office of Naval Intelligence, interviewing Dutch nationals in Vermont.

When Lucien Hanks returned from Burma, his interest in Southeast Asia stimulated Jane Hanks to focus her research on that part of the world. Although the two polished their Blackfoot materials into two books in the middle and late forties, they undertook field research in Thailand in the 1950s, studying a Thai village, Bang Cheng. The couple brought their children with them, and Hanks would later comment that the villagers accepted a woman anthropologist more readily if she had children.

The couple continued to do research at Bang Cheng, with Jane Hanks's work focusing increasingly on the culture of food and nutrition in a village entirely dependent on rice cultivation. As did the work of AUDREY RICHARDS in Africa, Hanks's work reflected a worldwide concern with the feeding of populations and the culture as well as the cultivation of food.

In the 1960s, the Hanks began to extend their work to the hill tribes of northern Thailand. Here, under a joint Cornell-Bennington project funded by the National Science Foundation, Hanks served as associate director for an extensive survey that covered the economics, ethnography, and demography of tribes in the midst of social change. She also served as a consultant for the Peace Corps. She returned to Thailand in the seventies, and continued to write on this area in the early eighties. As she aged, she found that her role as an older foreigner allowed her access to wider roles in the Asian communities from which her gender earlier might have limited her. Her work during this period was seen as seminal to those later working in Southeast Asia.

JH/MBO

PRIMARY SOURCES

Richardson Jane. *Law and Status Among the Kiowa Indians.* Monographs of the American Ethnological Society, no. 1. New York: J. J. Augustin, 1940. Her Columbia dissertation.

———. With Alfred L. Kroeber. "Three Centuries of Women's Dress Fashions: A Quantitative Analysis." *University of California Anthropological Records* 5, no. 2 (1940): 111–154. Written while Hanks was Kroeber's research assistant.

Hanks, Jane Richardson. With L. M. Hanks. *Observations on Northern Blackfoot Kinship.* Monographs of the American Ethnological Society, no. 9. New York: J. J. Augustin, 1945.

———. With L. M. Hanks. *Tribe Under Trust.* Toronto: University of Toronto Press, 1949.

———. With Hazel Hauck and Saovanee Sudsaneh. *Food Habits and Nutrient Intakes in a Siamese Rice Village: Studies in Bang Cheng.* Data Paper no. 29, Southeast Asia Program. Ithaca: Cornell University Press, 1958.

———. "Reflections on the Ontogeny of Rice." In *Culture in History: Essays in Honor of Paul Radin,* ed. Stanley Diamond, 298–301. New York: Columbia University, 1960.

———. *Maternity and Its Rituals in Bang Chan.* Data Paper no. 51, Southeast Asia Program. Ithaca: Cornell University, 1963.

———. With L. M. Hanks. "Siamese Tai." In *Ethnic Groups of Mainland Southeast Asia,* ed. Frank LeBar et al., 197–205. New Haven: Human Relations Area Files Press, 1964.

———. "Hill and Valley Peoples of Thailand's Province of Chiengrai: A Changing Relationship." *Proceedings of the Third International Symposium on Asian Studies.* Hong Kong: Asian Research Service, 1981.

SECONDARY SOURCES

Keyes, Charles F., et al. "Commemorating the Work of Lucien and Jane Hanks." *Crossroads: An Interdisciplinary Journal of Southeast Asia Studies* 7, No. 1 (1992). Includes bibliography of Jane Richardson Hanks' work.

STANDARD SOURCES

AMS S&B 11–12, P&B 13; Gacs (article by May Ebihara).

HANSEN, HAZEL D. (1899–1962)

U.S. archeologist. Born 28 September 1899 in San Mateo, Calif., to Marguerite (Charvoz) and Christian William Hansen. Educated Stanford University (B.A., 1920; M.A., 1921; Ph.D., 1926); American School of Classical Studies, Athens (1922–1925); Alice Freeman Palmer Fellowship of the American Association of University Woman (1927–1928). Professional experience: Stanford University, instructor (1928), assistant professor (1931), associate professor (1935), professor (1940–1962). Honors and memberships: Royal Geological Society, Fellow; Stanford Society of the Archaeological Institute of America, founder; honorary citizenship, Skyros, Greece. Died 19 December 1962 in Palo Alto, Calif.

Hazel Hansen received her entire university education at Stanford University with the addition of postgraduate work at the American School of Classical Studies on two separate occasions. Her association with Stanford did not end with her doctoral degree. After returning from Athens in 1928, she accepted a position as instructor in classics. She proceeded through the academic ranks to professor, which she maintained from 1940 until her death. During a sabaticcal year in 1956–1957, she was annual professor at the American School of Classical Studies; she also served as a member of its managing and executive committees.

Hansen became widely recognized as a classical archeologist, especially in the field of Aegean prehistory. Her specialty was the Island of Skyros in the Aegean, where she spent many summers excavating. The Greek government gave her permission to publish her findings, and later asked her to write a guidebook for the Skyros museum. She also became known for her reconstruction of the Cesnola Collection at the Stanford Museum. It consisted of Greek vases and Bronze-Age figurines that had been badly damaged in the earthquake of 1906. Her doctoral thesis, "Early Civilization in Thessaly," was later expanded into a book.

Active in a number of organizations, Hansen founded the Stanford Society of the Archaeological Institute of America, obtained membership for women into Stanford's Faculty Club, was a trustee of American Friends of Greece, a Fellow of the Royal Geological Society, and a member of the American Philological Association. Hansen was honored by the Greek government, which granted her honorary citizenship for her work on Skyros.

JH/MBO

PRIMARY SOURCES

Hansen, Hazel Dorothy. *Early Civilization in Thessaly.* Baltimore: Johns-Hopkins Press, 1933.

STANDARD SOURCES

NCAB (includes portrait).

HANSEN, JULIE MARIE VINTER (1890–1960)

Danish astronomer. Born 20 June 1890 in Copenhagen. Educated University of Copenhagen. Professional experience: University of Copenhagen Observatory, computer; regular assistant (1919–1922); observer (1922–1960). Died 31 July 1960.

During the time that Julie Hansen was a student she held a position as a computer at the University of Copenhagen's Observatory. Apparently a very proficient observer, Hansen advanced rapidly, becoming the first Danish woman to hold a position as a university observer. Hansen spent her entire career at this observatory.

The University of Copenhagen Observatory engaged in classical astronomical activities, mostly observing the motion of asteroids and comets. Hansen was a superb observer, and noted a large number of elements of new comets. Hansen's most important theoretical work was determining the orbits of the asteroids Hector and Achilles; she also determined the orbit of the periodic comet Comas-Sola. JH/MBO

PRIMARY SOURCES

Hansen, Julie Marie Vinter. *Opposition Ephemerides for 1942 of Minor Planets (101) Helena, (103) Hera, (105) Artemis, (119) Althea, (1928) Nemesis, (139) Juewa, (1961) Athor, (179) Klytaemnestra.* Berkley: University of California Press, [1942].

———. *Obeservations of 433 Eros; Observations of the Asteroid 51 Nemausa; Note on Star No. 10263 in the boss General Catalogue.* Berkley: University of Califormia, [1945].

SECONDARY SOURCES

Rasmusen, H. Q. "Julie Marie Vinter Hansen." *Quarterly Journal of the Royal Astronomical Society* 2 (1961): 38–39.

STANDARD SOURCES

Strohmeier.

HANSON, EMMELINE JEAN (1919–1973)

British physiologist. Born 14 November 1919 in Newhall, Derbyshire, to Emily (Rodger) and Tom Hanson. Educated Girls' High School Burton-on-Trent (1930–1938); Bedford College, London (first-class honors in zoology, 1941); University of London (Ph.D., 1951). Professional experience: research student (fellow) (1941–1942); Cambridge, Strangeways Laboratory (1942–1944); Bedford College, demonstrator in zoology (1944–1948); King's College, University of London, Biophysics Research Unit, researcher (1948–1970), professor of biology, (1966–1973); Muscle Biophysics Research Unit, director (1970–1973). Honors and memberships: Royal Society, Fellow (1967). Died 10 August 1973 of Waterhouse-Friderichsen Syndrome.

Jean Hanson was the only child of teacher parents. Her father died when she only a few months old of a cerebral tumor; her mother brought her up by herself, while serving as headmistress of a primary school. Hanson received a Derbyshire Minor Scholarship during her high school years. She followed her family's interest in music and reported on concerts for her school magazine. In her examinations for the Higher School Certificate, she received distinction in all subjects and received two major scholarships. These allowed her to attend Bedford College, London, from 1938 to 1941, graduating with first-class honors in zoology. During World War II, Bedford was evacuated to Cambridge, where Hanson was able to study and work with H. Munro Fox, an outstanding zoologist and Fellow of the Royal Society who had moved to Cambridge from Birmingham. Working with Fox as a research student, she studied the vascular system of annelids, which resulted in a substantial series of papers published between 1945 to 1951. Between 1942 and 1944, she worked at Strangeways Laboratory at Cambridge, studying the mammalian epidermis, which also resulted in publications. An appointment as a demonstrator in zoology at Bedford College from 1944 to 1948 prevented her from completing her doctoral degree until 1951.

In 1948, Sir John Randall, who had just established a Biophysical Research Unit under the Medical Research Council at King's College, London, appointed Hanson to organize and supervise the biological facilities for tissue-culture research. By 1950, she devoted herself to muscle research, a study that occupied her subsequent career. In the course of this research, she went to MIT (1952–1953) and worked with Hugh Huxley and others working on X-ray diffraction studies.

Hanson was elected a Fellow of the Royal Society in 1967 and continued to produce remarkable work until her sudden death from a fulminating meningococcal septicemia of the adrenal cortex in 1973. In her short professional career, she produced over fifty-five articles, ranging from her early studies on annelids and spermatozoa to the forty articles from 1952 to 1973 on structure and function of muscle fibers. She was remembered as an unusual teacher and scientific colleague, working fruitfully with Jack Lowy in her own unit and with Hugh Huxley and many others. According to Randall, her biographer, her formulation and proof of the sliding-filament hypothesis as well as her research into invertebrate smooth-muscle morphology ensures her future reputation. JH/MBO

PRIMARY SOURCES

Hanson, Emmeline Jean. "Formation and Breakdown of Serpulid Tubes." *Nature* 161 (1948): 610.

———. "Changes in the Cross Striation of Myofibrils During Contraction Induced by Adenosine Triphosphate." *Nature* 169 (1952): 530.

─────. With H.E. Huxley. "The Structural Basis of the Contraction Mechanism in Striated Muscle." *Annals of the New York Academy of Sciences* 180 (1959): 403.

─────. With J. Lowy. "Structure and Function of the Contractile Apparatus in the Muscles of Invertebrates." Chapter 9 in Vol. I of *The Structure and Function of Muscles* Ed. G. H. Bourne. New York: Academic Press, 1960.

─────. "Axial Period of Actin Filaments.*" Nature* 213 (1967): 353.

─────. "Evidence from Electron Microscope Studies on Actin Paracrystals Concerning the Origin of the Cross-Striation in the Thin Filaments of Vertebrate Skeletal Muscle." *Proceedings of the Royal Society of London* B, 183, (1973): 39.

SECONDARY SOURCES

Randall, John. "Emmeline Jean Hanson." *Biographical Memoirs of Fellows of the Royal Society* 21 (1975): 313–344. Includes a bibliography of Hanson's works.

STANDARD SOURCES

Women Physiologists; WWW.

HAOYS (LA MERESSE) (fl. 1292)

French healer. Flourished 1292 in Paris.

Haoys, known as la Meresse, was a physician at la Ville de St. Lorenz. She was sufficiently prosperous to pay a seven sous tax in 1292.   JH/MBO

STANDARD SOURCES

Echols and Williams.

HARDCASTLE, FRANCES (1866–1941)

British mathematician. Born 13 August 1866 in Writtle, Essex. Educated Cambridge University (1888–1892); certificate for mathematics; University of London (B.A., 1903). Died 1941.

Frances Hardcastle was born and educated in England. She was the granddaughter of astronomer Sir John Herschel. Hardcastle became certified in mathematics and published in journals in both Great Britain and the United States.   JH/MBO

PRIMARY SOURCES

Hardcastle, Frances. "Observations on the Modern Theory of Point-Groups." *American Mathematical Society Bulletin* 4 (1897?): 12 pp.

─────. "Theorem Concerning the Special Systems of Point-Groups on a Particular type of Base-Curve." *Proceedings of the London Mathematical Society* 29 (1898).

─────. "Present State of the Theory of Point Groups." *British Association Report 1900* (1902).

SECONDARY SOURCES

Whitman, Betsey S. "Women in the American Mathematical Society Before 1900." *Association for Women in Mathematics Newsletter* 13 (July–December 1983): 9–13.

STANDARD SOURCES

Grinstein and Campbell; Poggendorff, vol. 4; Rebière; Siegel and Finley.

HARDESTY, MARY (1905–)

U.S. reproductive biologist. Born 4 October 1905 in San Francisco, Calif. Married William Larkin Duren, Jr. Educated Tulane (A.B., 1926); University of Chicago (M.S., 1929; Ph.D., 1930). Professional experience: Newcomb College, Tulane, teaching fellow in zoology (1926–1927), assistant (1931–1932); University of Chicago (1927–1930); Tulane, independent investigator (from 1931).

Mary Hardesty is listed under her birth name in *American Men of Science* volumes 6 and 7, and under her married name in volume 5. Apparently she changed the way that she wanted to be listed in volume 6, although she remained married. Her paid positions ended with her marriage, but she continued with her research. Nepotism rules would have precluded her from teaching at Tulane, as her husband was a mathematics professor there.

Hardesty's research was on sex in the fowl, and the anatomy, embryology, and endocrine relations of the fowl's comb. She also worked on feather patterns.   JH/MBO

PRIMARY SOURCES

Hardesty, Mary. "The Structural Basis for the Response of the Comb of the Brown Leghorn Fowl to the Sex Hormones." Ph. D. diss.; University of Chicago, 1930.

SECONDARY SOURCES

Hall, Diana Long. "Academics, Blue Stockings, and Biologists: Women at the University of Chicago, 1892–1932." *Annals of the New York Academy of Sciences* 323 (1979).

STANDARD SOURCES

AMS 5–7.

HARDING, ANITA (1953–1995)

British neurogeneticist, physician. Born 1953 in Birmingham. Married P. K. Thomas, M.D. (1977). Educated King Edward VI High School for Girls; Royal Free Hospital Medical School, London (M.B., 1975?); University of London (M.D. in clinical genetics, 1984). Professional experience: University of London, senior lecturer (1986), reader (1987); Institute of Neurology, University of London, professor of clinical neurology (1990–1995); Neurogenetics clinic, National Hospital for Neurology, director. Died 11 September 1995.

Significant for her outstanding work in the new field of neurogenetics, Anita Harding was a leader in that field as well as the first woman professor of clinical neurology in Britain. After finishing her undergraduate medical degree in 1975(?), her first post was as house physician to the neurologist P. K. Thomas, whom she subseqently married and with whom she had a very successful partnership on both the personal and professional levels. She became interested in hereditary nervous diseases, particularly motor and sensory neuropathies, and produced a thesis on this topic that was published as *The Hereditary Ataxias and Related Disorders* (1984), rapidly becoming a classic in the field. She quickly realized the importance of recombinant DNA technology to her research and took further training in molecular genetics at Cardiff, at Massachusetts General Hospital (Boston), and at California Institute of Technology, under leading scientists. Upon return to the Institute of Neurology, she set up a research laboratory in neurogenetics and worked on human mitochondrial disease with her colleagues John Morgan-Hughes and John Clark. Their graduate student Ian Holt began to look for mtDNA mutations in muscle samples from a large series of patients. They were able to demonstrate mtDNA mutations in KearnsSayre syndrome, the first pathogenetic syndrome described (Holt et al. 1988). They also identified the mutation associated with Leigh syndrome, calling this mutation NARP (neurogenic weakness, ataxia and retinitis pigmentosa). They were able to publish the first (and up to now the only) prenatal diagnosis based on mtDNA analysis (Harding et al. 1992).

With these new techniques, Harding set up a diagnostic laboratory, with Mary Davis, for molecular analysis of neurogenetic diseases, one of the largest in the United Kingdom. Her neurogenetics clinic at the National Hospital for Neurology served as a center for the United Kingdom, and her clinical opinion was sought and appreciated by many families sent there for evaluation. She was also an excellent teacher, as testified by the appreciation of the neurologists, geneticists, and neuroscientists whom she trained.

By the time of her death from bowel cancer, 11 September 1995, she had produced more than one hundred papers. Yet she was also a woman of wide interests, including mountain biking and skiing. The testimony of her colleagues and associates in the human genetics community was that she was an exceptional scientist who had made major contributions to the study of hereditary ataxias, peripheral neuropathies, dystonias, and mitochondrial disease.

JH/MBO

PRIMARY SOURCES

Harding, A. E. *The Hereditary Ataxias and Related Disorders.* Clinical Neurology and Neurosurgery Monographs 6. Edinburgh: Churchill Livingstone, 1984.

———. With I. J. Holt, M. G. Sweeney, M. Brockington, and M. B. Davies. "Prenatal Diagnosis of Mitchondrial DNA89932T–G Disease." *American Journal of Human Genetics* 50 (1992): 629–633.

———. With I. J. Holt and others. "A New Mitochondrial Disease Associated with Mitochondrial DNA Heteroplasmy." *American Journal of Human Genetics* 46 (1990): 428–433.

SECONDARY SOURCES

Poulton, J., and S. M. Huson. [Obituary, Anita Harding]. *American Journal of Human Genetics* 58 (1996): 235–236.

HARDWICK, ROSE STANDISH (1868–1939)

U.S. psychologist. Born 11 June 1868 in Weymouth, Mass. Educated Smith College (A.B., 1890, A.M., 1909); Radcliffe College (Ph.D., 1924). Professional experience: Boston Psychopathic Hospital, assistant psychologist (1913–1914); New England Home for Little Wanderers, staff psychologist (from 1915); Habit Clinics, Boston, chief psychologist (from 1925); American School for Physical Education, instructor (1915–1918); Boston YWCA school of domestic science, instructor (1915–1918); Boston School for Physical Education, instructor (1914–1921); lecturer in child psychology (from 1929). Member, American Psychological Association. Died 1939.

Between the time that Rose Hardwick earned her master's and doctoral degrees, she worked as a psychologist at the Boston Psychopathic Hospital and the New England Home for Little Wanderers. After earning her doctorate, she held several teaching positions while she was chief psychologist for the Habit Clinics in Boston. Her research interest was in testing and working with the psychology of visual defects.

KM

PRIMARY SOURCES

Hardwick, Rose Standish. "The Stanford-Binet Intelligence Examination Reinterpreted with Special Reference to Qualitative Differences." Ph. D. diss.; Radcliffe College, 1924.

STANDARD SOURCES
AMS 3–6.

HARDY, HARRIET (1905–1993)

U.S. pathologist. Born 23 September 1905 in Arlington, Mass. Educated Wellesley College (A.B., 1928); Cornell University (M.D., 1932). Professional experience: Philadelphia General Hospital, internship and residency; Northfield Seminary in Massachusetts, school doctor (to 1939); Radcliffe College, college doctor and director of health education (from 1939); Massachusetts General Hospital, clinic of occupational medicine, founder and director (1947–1971); Harvard Medical School, clinical professor (1979–1993). Honors: and memberships: American Medical Women's Association, Woman of the Year (1955). Died 13 October 1993 at Massachusetts General Hospital.

Harriet Hardy started her career as a school doctor. However, in the early 1940s, she began a collaboration with Joseph Aubt to study the effects of lead poisoning. She recognized the dangers inherent in the modern factory to the health of workers. She investigated reports of a strange respiratory disease among workers in the Sylvania and General Electric fluorescent lamp factories in Lynn and Salem, Massachusetts. The symptoms were shortness of breath, coughing, and weight loss. Hardy recognized that it might be occupationally related and after reading reports of research from Russia and Europe, she found a connection to beryllium, a light metal used in the manufacture of fluorescent lamps. The dust or vapor was easily inhaled by factory workers. As she suspected, the outbreak was berylliosis, and she began, through a registry, a system for tracking this and other occupation-related diseases. She established a clinic of occupational medicine at Massachusetts General Hospital in 1947. She was one of the first scientists to recognize a link between asbestos and cancer and was also concerned with the effects of radiation on the human body. Her research also included mercury and lead poisoning and the harmful effects of benzene.

She collaborated with ALICE HAMILTON in 1949, to write a book, *Industrial Toxicology,* and published over one hundred scientific articles during her lifetime. JH/MBO

PRIMARY SOURCES
Hardy, Harriet. With Alice Hamilton. *Industrial Toxicology*. New York: P. B. Hoeber, 1949.

SECONDARY SOURCES
Journal of the American Medical Women's Association (November 1955): 402.
New York Times, 15 October 1993. Obituary notice.

STANDARD SOURCES
Notable (article by Sydney Jones).

HARDY, THORA MARGGRAFF (PLITT) (1902–)

U.S. botanist. Born 31 July 1902 in Switzerland. Married John Ira Hardy (1942). Educated Barnard College, Columbia University (A.B., 1925); University of Chicago (M.S., 1930; Ph.D., 1932). Professional experience: New York City, high school teacher (1925–1929); Hunter College, instructor in botany and plant physiology (1932–1933); Vassar College, instructor in botany (1933–1935); National Bureau of Standards, junior microanalyst (1935–1938); U.S. Department of Agriculture, assistant microanalyst (1938–1939); U.S. Fish and Wildlife Service, assistant, then associate microanalyst (1939–1946); Bureau of Animal Industry, USDA, associate microanalyst (1946–1948); Production and Marketing Administration, grain technologist; Nittany Laboratory, operator (from 1954).

After Thora Marggraff Plitt earned her doctorate, she started in academia as an instructor. In 1935, she saw little chance for advancement, so she took a job in the federal government, first with the U.S. Bureau of Standards, then with the USDA. She continued to work for the government until 1951, when she took a position with the Nittany Laboratory, Lamont, Pennsylvania.

Hardy published under both her birth name and her married name. She published four papers in the *Circular* series of the USDA. She wrote on tests on angora rabbit fur, animal fibers used in brushes, commercial fibers, and feathers from domestic and wild fowl. She was a member of the American Society of Plant Physiologists. Her research interests were plant microchemistry and physiology and microscopic research on commercial furs. JH/MBO

PRIMARY SOURCES
Plitt, Thora M. "Microscopic Methods Used in Identifying Commercial Fibers." Circular of the National Bureau of Standards, no. 423. Washington, D.C.: U.S. Government Printing Office, 1939.
Hardy, Thora M. Plitt. With J.I. Hardy. "Feathers from Domestic and Wild Fowl." Circular of the U.S.D.A., no. 803. Washington, D.C." U.S. Government Printing Office, 1949.

STANDARD SOURCES
AMS 7–8, B 9, P&B 10–11; Bailey; Barnhart.

HARMON, ÉLISE F. (1909–1985)

U.S. engineer. Born 3 September 1909 in Texas. Educated (B.S.); University of Texas (M.S.); George Washington University (graduate studies); University of Maryland (graduate studies). Professional experience: Texas high schools and junior colleges, teacher; Davies Fruit Company, researcher; Pan American Airways, researcher; Standard Oil Company, consultant (1938–1942); Army Ordnance in St.

Louis, Mo. (1942–1945); Naval Research Laboratory, Aircraft and Electrical Division, researcher (1945–1948); National Bureau of Standards Ordnance Division, researcher (from 1948); Aerovox Corporation, researcher (throughout 1950s); American Bosch Arma Corporation, senior engineer of computer development; Autonetics in Anaheim (later North American Rockwell Division (to 1969); Harmon Technical Consultants, director (1969–1985). Honors and memberships: Society of Women Engineers Achievement Award (1956); American Chemical Society; Texas Academy of Sciences; Institute of Radio Engineers. Died 1985.

It was not until 1938 when she accepted a position with the Army Ordnance in St. Louis that Élise Harmon knew what she wanted to do with her life. She had previously taught school and worked at several different jobs but had not found any of them really satisfying. In St. Louis, she found engineering fascinating and knew that it was what she wanted to do for the rest of her life.

Her major engineering contribution was her pioneer work in micro-miniaturization of printed circuitry components. She made an important contribution during World War II, one that allowed American planes to fly above fifteen thousand feet. The carbon brushes that were part of aircraft generators on American planes would disintegrate at higher altitudes, giving an advantage to the more technically advanced German planes, which could fly higher. Harmon devised a method of extending the life of these generator brushes at high altitudes. Later, when she was working at the National Bureau of Standards Ordnance Division, she studied the application of printed circuitry to military equipment. She developed a new methodology to produce printed circuitry for both military and commercial use.

After 1969, Harmon formed her own consulting company, Harmon Technical Consultants, which she directed until her death. She was a member of the American Chemical Society, the Texas Academy of Sciences, and the Institute of Radio Engineers. In 1956, she received the Society of Women Engineers Achievement Award in recognition of her contributions to component and circuit miniaturization.

JH/MBO

SECONDARY SOURCES
"Élise Harmon Receives Award." *Society of Women Engineers Newsletter* (June 1956): 3.

STANDARD SOURCES
Notable (article by Karen Withem).

HARRISON, JANE ELLEN (1850–1928)

British archeologist. Born 9 September 1850 in Yorkshire to Elizabeth (Hawksley) and Charles Harrison. Three sisters. Never married. Educated at home; Cheltenham Ladies College; Newnham College, Cambridge (1874–1879); British Museum, student of archeology (1880–1882). Professional experience: Oxford High School, assistant mistress; British Museum and South Kensington Museum, lecturer, (1882–1887); Newnham College, fellow and lecturer in classical archeology (1899–1922), first Associates' Research Fellow (1900–1903), associate (1893–1916), member of council (1894–1905, 1908–1911). Honors and memberships: Aberdeen University, honorary LL.D.; University of Dublin, honorary D. Litt. Died 15 April 1928.

When Jane Ellen Harrison sat for her Classical Tripos examination in 1879, she was between Class 1 and Class 2. She spent a term at Oxford High School as an assistant mistress. Harrison then studied archeology at the British Museum with Sir C. Newon and then lectured at the British Museum and the South Kensington Museum. She lectured in classical archeology at Newnham and held several positions in the college. In 1915, she studied Russian in Paris and lived in Paris for three years, from 1922 to 1925. She traveled often in Italy, Greece, and France. She published a number of books.

JH/MBO

PRIMARY SOURCES
Harrison, Jane Ellen. *Myths of the Odyssey in Art and Literature.* London: Rivingtons, 1882.
———. *Introductory Studies in Greek Art.* London: Fisher Unwin, 1885.
———. With A. W. Verrall. *Mythology and Monuments of Ancient Athens.* London: Macmillan, 1890.
———. With D. S. MacColl. *Greek Vase Painting.* London: T. F. Unwin, 1894.
———. *Prolegomena to Study of Greek Religion.* Cambridge: University Press, 1903.
———. *Religion of Ancient Greece* London: Constable, 1913.
———. *Ancient Art and Ritual in Home University Library.* London: Williams and Norgate, 1913.
———. *Jane Ellen Harrison: A Portrait from Letters.* London: Merlin, 1959.

SECONDARY SOURCES
Ackerman, Robert. *The Myth and Ritual School: J. G. Frazer and the Cambridge Ritualists.* New York: Garland, 1991.
Hall, Nor. *Those Women.* Dallas, Tex.: Spring Publications, 1988.
Murray, Gilbert. *Jane Ellen Harrison: An Address Delivered at Newnham College, October 27, 1928.* Cambridge, England: Heffer, 1928.
Peacock, Sandra J. *Jane Ellen Harrison: The Mask and the Self.* New Haven: Yale University Press, 1988.

STANDARD SOURCES
Newnham, vol. 1, 1871–1923; *WWW,* vol. 2, 1916–1928.

HARRISON, JANET MITCHELL MARR (DINGWALL) (1893–1971)

British invertebrate paleontologist. Born 15 January 1893 at Newburgh, Fife. Father, David D. Dingwall. Married J. V. Harrison. Educated Edinburgh University (M.A., 1915; B.Sc., 1920); Queen's Street Ladies College, Edinburgh, teacher; Dalkeith High School, staff of University College, Cardiff (1921–1939). Died 19 December 1971 at Oxford.

Janet Dingwall had a successful career in geology before she was married. She received her education at Edinburgh University, where she studied geology under T. J. Jehu. In 1921, she joined the staff of University College, Cardiff, where she taught paleontology, until she married the geologist J. V. Harrison in 1939. Her husband was a university lecturer in the department of geology at Oxford from 1938, and she followed him there. She accompanied her husband on his travels, including a visit to the United States.

Janet Harrison's formal career in geology ended with her marriage, although she continued to attend the annual British Association meetings, the Geologists' Association activities, and to discuss problems with former students. In 1924, she became a member of the Geologists' Association and was a member of its council from 1954 to 1958. While she was at Cardiff, she published a single paper on carboniferous corals.

Harrison died in an Oxford hospital after a car accident.

JH/MBO

PRIMARY SOURCES

Dingwall, Janet Mitchell Marr. "On Cyathoclisia, a New Genus of Carboniferous Coral." *Quarterly Journal of the Geological Society of London* 82 (1926): 12–21.

SECONDARY SOURCES

[Edmonds, J. M.]. "Janet Mitchell Marr Harrison, M.A., B.Sc." *Proceedings of the Geologists' Association* 83, pt. 1 (1972): 112–113.

STANDARD SOURCES

Sarjeant.

HARROWER, MOLLY R. (1906–1999)

South African/U.S. psychologist. Born 25 January 1906 in Johannesburg, South Africa, to Ina May (White) and James Harrower. Married Mortimer Lahm (1955). Educated University of London (diploma in psychology, 1928); Smith College (Ph.D., 1934). Professional experience: Wells College, instructor in psychology (1930–1931); Smith College, research associate (1931–1932); University of London, lecturer (1932–1933); New Jersey College for Women, director of students (1934–1937); Montreal Neurological Institute, chief clinical psychologist (1937–1941); University of Wisconsin, Madison, research associate, department of neuropsychiatry (1941–1944); U.S. Army and Air Force, Surgeon General's Office (1948–1952); Manhattan Children's Center, research director (1952–1954); University of Texas Medical Branch, Galveston, department of psychiatry, visiting lecturer, psychological testing program director; Temple University Medical School, department of psychiatry, associate professor (1957–1959), professor (1959–1964); New School for Social Research, visiting professor (1962–1967); University of Florida, professor (from 1967). Honors and memberships: Rockefeller Medical Foundation, fellow (1938–1942); National Research Council, fellow (1939–1942); Josiah Macy Foundation, fellow (1942–1945); Society for Personality Assessment, Distinguished Contributions Award, (1972); National Multiple Sclerosis Society, Gold Key Award (1972); University of Florida, honorary degree (1981). Died 20 February 1999.

South African–born Molly Harrower received a diploma in psychology from the University of London at the age of twenty-two. In 1930, she went to Wells College as an instructor in psychology. She began to work toward a doctoral degree at Smith College in 1931 and was appointed a research associate. For one year she returned to London to teach as a lecturer. Upon receiving her doctorate, she was appointed director of students at the New Jersey College for Women. She was appointed in 1937 as chief clinical psychologist for the Montreal Neurological Institute, where she remained for the next four years. During this period, Harrower received fellowships from the Rockefeller and the Josiah Macy Foundations. In the early 1940s, she went to the University of Wisconsin, Madison, to the department of neuropsychiatry, taking her Josiah Macy Foundation grant with her. During the postwar period, she worked for the U.S. Department of State and the Surgeon General's Office as a consultant. In 1952, she moved to New York, where she became the research director for the Manhattan Childrens' Center. Harrower became a professor at Temple University, where she remained until 1967, when she moved to the University of Florida. She served as editor for the American Psychologist Lecture Series (1944–?). She was a member of the advisory board of the National Multiple Sclerosis Society from 1952 and served as a consultant to the Veterans Administration from 1970.

Harrower's research emphasized group testing methods, multiple sclerosis, and the area of perception, especially Gestalt perception. In her late seventies, Harrower wrote a book on the Gestalt psychologist Kurt Koffka. She died at the age of 93 in Gainesville, Florida.

JH/MBO

PRIMARY SOURCES

Harrower, Molly. *The Psychologist at Work.* London and New York: Kegan Paul & Harper Bros., 1937.

———. *Appraising Personality.* New York: Norton, 1952.

———. *Personality Change and Development as Measured by the Projective Techniques.* New York: Grune, 1958.

———. *The Practice of Clinical Psychology.* Springfield, Ill.: C. C. Thomas, 1961.

———. *Psychodiagnostic Testing: An Empirical Approach.* Springfield, Ill.: C.C. Thomas, 1965.

———. *Kurt Koffka: An Unwitting Self Portrait.* Gainsville: University Presses of Florida, 1983.

SECONDARY SOURCES
The Gainesville Sun, 22 February 1999.

STANDARD SOURCES
AMS S&B 9–12; O'Connell and Russo 1988; Stevens and Gardner.

HART, ESTHER HASTING (1862–1940)

U.S. entomological artist. Born 1862. Married entomologist Charles A. Hart. Educated art schools. Professional experience: U.S. Bureau of Entomology, illustrator. Died 1940.

Esther Hart worked for the U.S. Bureau of Entomology after she completed art school. She contributed many illustrations for the bureau's articles.   JH/MBO

STANDARD SOURCES
Osborn (includes a portrait, plate 51).

HART, HELEN (1900–1971)

U.S. plant pathologist. Born 1900. Educated Lawrence College (1918–1920); University of Minnesota (B.A., 1922; A.M., 1924; Ph. D., 1929). Professional experience: U.S. Department of Agriculture, division of cereal crops and diseases, researcher (1923–1933); University of Minnesota, part-time instructor in plant pathology (1924–1933), instructor (1933–1937), assistant professor (1940–1944), associate professor (1944–1947), professor (1947–1966). Phytopathology, associate editor (1938–1940), editor in chief (1944–1951). Honors and memberships: Phytopathological Society, president (1955–1956); Elvin Stakman award for work on cereal diseases (1963); Phytopathological Society, Fellow; American Association for the Advancement of Science, Fellow. Died 1971.

Helen Hart was the first woman to be president of the American Phytopathological Society. She attended Lawrence College for two years and then moved to the University of Minnesota, where she received all three of her degrees. Shortly before she received her master's degree, she was hired by the United States Department of Agriculture and the following year taught part-time as an instructor at the University of Minnesota. While she was at the USDA, she worked on the important problem of cereal rusts, a problem that also concerned the department of plant pathology. For a year in the late 1930s she became an exchange assistant at the University of Halle in Belgium. After two years as associate editor of *Phytopathology,* the important journal on plant disease, she became an assistant professor; she became associate professor at the same time as her appointment as editor-in-chief of that journal. She received a major award for her work on cereal disease and became a Fellow of the American Phytopathological Society as well as of the American Association for the Advancement of Science.

                                                JH/MBO

PRIMARY SOURCES
Hart, Helen. *Morphological and Physciological Studeis on Stem Rust Resistance in Wheat.* Washington, D.C., U.S. Government Printing Office, 1931. Based on her Ph. D. dissertation.

SECONDARY SOURCES
Phytopathology 61 (1971): 1151. Obituary notice, with portrait.

STANDARD SOURCES
Bailey.

HART, J. B. (fl. 1886)

British amateur paleontologist and natural historian. Married W. E. Hart.

Little information is available on J. B. Hart, except that she was married and spent much of her time in India. She published five papers on topics in natural history in the *Journal of the Bombay Natural History Society.* She published one paper in paleontology in 1886.   JH/MBO

STANDARD SOURCES
Creese and Creese.

HARTT, CONSTANCE ENDICOTT (1900–)

U.S. plant physiologist. Born 2 November 1900 in Passaic, N.J., to Claudine (Millington) and George leBaron Hartt. Educated Mount Holyoke College (A.B., 1922); University of Chicago (S.M., 1924; Ph.D., 1928). Professional experience: North Carolina College for Women, instructor (1922–1924); St. Lawrence University, instructor (1925–1930); Connecticut College for Women, assistant professor of botany (1930–1931); Hawaiian Sugar Planters Association, experimental station, sugarcane physiology researcher (1931–1963), senior physiologist (1959–1963); University of Hawaii, assistant professor (1932). Honors and memberships: Hawaiian Botanical Gardens

Foundation, secretary (from 1959); Hawaiian Sugar Technologists, distinguished service award (1963); American Association for the Advancement of Science, Fellow; Hawaiian Botanical Society, honorary life member; American Association of University Women, research fellow (1931), Honolulu chapter president; American Society of Plant Physiologists, member; Botanical Society of America, member.

From her early professional positions, it would appear that Constance Hartt would have continued in academia. However, she went to Hawaii, and became involved in studying the physiology of the sugarcane plant. She worked for the Sugar Planters Association and advanced to the position of senior physiologist.

Hartt's research on the sugarcane plant involved the effects of potassium deficiency on the plants. She also worked on phosphorus nutrition, the mechanism of photosynthesis and factors affecting it, and the translocation of photosynthate and factors affecting it, including temperature, intensity, and quality of light. A fellowship for women studying science at the graduate level is awarded yearly in her name at the University of Hawaii.   JH/MBO

PRIMARY SOURCES
Hartt, Constance Endicott. *Some Effects of Potassium upon the Growth of Sugar Cane and upon the Absorption and Migration of Ash Constituents.* Lancaster, Pa.: n.p., 1934.
———. *The Plant Ecology of Mauna Kea, Hawaii.* Mauna Kea: n.p., 1940.

STANDARD SOURCES
AMS 5–9, B 9, P&B 10–11; Debus.

HARVEY, ELIZABETH (ca. 1797–1873)
British botanist. Born ca. 1797, probably in Edinburgh. Father Admiral Sir John Harvey. Professional experience: collected natural history items. Honors and memberships: Botanical Society of London; Botanical Society of Edinburgh. Died 1873 in London.

Elizabeth Harvey spent much of her life in Edinburgh and in Deal, Kent, and amassed a large natural history collection including numerous shells. Most of her surviving specimens were from Deal, but some collected in Scotland in 1845–1846 survived. She was a member of the Botanical Society of London and of the Botanical Society of Edinburgh.

There is some question about the accuracy of Harvey's records, for in a 1847 *Phytologist* article by H. C. Watson "On the Credit-Worthiness of the Labels Distributed from the Botanical Society of London," a statement accuses "one lady-botanist, of well-known name" of mingling specimens from different localities. D. E. Allen noted in *Watsonia* that he

found a note in Watson's handwriting that identified the lady as Miss Elizabeth Harvey. Allen concluded that although Watson may have been too harsh in his criticisms, localities on Harvey's labels should still be treated with some scepticism.

JH/MBO

PRIMARY SOURCES
Harvey's plants are at Bolton Museum, Edinburgh; her shells are at the University Museum, Oxford.

SECONDARY SOURCES
Allen, D. E. "Records of Elizabeth Harvey." *Watsonia* 14 (1982): 67–68.
Cowell, M. H. *A Floral Guide for East Kent.* Faversham: W. Ratcliffe, 1839. Many of Harvey's Deal, East Kent, finds were reported by Cowell.

STANDARD SOURCES
Desmond.

HARVEY, ETHEL NICHOLSON BROWNE (1885–1965)
U.S. embryologist and cell biologist. Born 1885 in Baltimore, Md., to Jennie and Bennet Browne. Four siblings. Married Edmund Newton Harvey (1916). Two sons. Educated Bryn Mawr School; Woman's College of Baltimore (A.B. 1906); Columbia University (A.M., 1907; Ph.D., 1913). Professional experience: Dana Hall School, Wellesley, Mass.: instructor in biology; Hopkins Marine Station, University of California, Sarah Berliner Fellow (1914–1915); Cornell Medical College, assistant in histology (1915–1916), part-time researcher (1916–1927); Washington Square College, New York University, researcher (1928–1931); Princeton University, independent researcher (1931–1959). Died 2 September 1965.

Ethel Nicholson Browne was born the youngest of three girls and two boys to parents who believed that girls and boys should receive equivalent educations. She graduated from the Bryn Mawr School, a school devoted entirely to preparing girls for college. While she was working on her degrees at Columbia University, she held a number of teaching positions and fellowships in order to support herself. During the summers, beginning in 1906, she studied at the Marine Biological Laboratory at Woods Hole, Massachusetts, where she worked on aquatic insects. One fellowship was from Goucher College (1906–1907), where she had received her bachelor's degree the previous year, from the Society for the Promotion of University Educaton for Women (1911–1912). After she received her doctorate under Edmund Beecher Wilson on spermatogenesis in an aquatic insect, she was awarded the Berliner Fellowship. This fellowship was intended to be used in Berlin, but since this was during World War I, she used it to attend the University of California's Hopkins Marine Station.

On 12 March 1916, Ethel Browne married an assistant professor, Edmund Newton Harvey, at Princeton. The couple had two sons, one born in 1916 and the other in 1922, and it became clear that her family henceforth would have priority over her career. Since she had a considerable amount of help with the children, she was able to continue with her research part-time; however, she never held a tenure-track position nor was supported by a university. She was given space in Edwin Conklin's laboratory at Princeton and Princeton paid her summer fees at the Marine Biological Laboratory, where she shared space with her husband until 1962. In 1925 to 1926 and in 1932, Harvey went to the Naples Marine Station as a member of the American Women's Table, established by IDA HYDE. Between 1933 and 1937, she was also awarded use of the Jacques Loeb Memorial Table. Harvey also performed research at marine stations at Japan, Bermuda, and North Carolina. Without an academic home it was difficult to get grants; however, she was awarded a grant from the American Philosophical Society in 1937.

The road to Ethel Browne Harvey's international reputation began when, as a predoctoral fellow, she worked with T. H. Morgan at Columbia. This early work was in embryology, reflecting Morgan's interests at this time. She published a paper in 1909 on this research, "The Production of New Hydranths in *Hydra* by the Insertion of Small Grafts." This work preceded the work of Hans Spemann and HILDE MANGOLD on organizers. As was common during this period, her interest shifted from embryology to the role of the nucleus in heredity. Her major professor, Edmund Beecher Wilson, may have been instrumental in her changed interests. Wilson and NETTIE MARIA STEVENS tentatively demonstrated that a particular trait could be traced to a specific chromosome, the sex chromosome. If this idea were to hold true, then the chromosomal theory of inheritance would gain support. During the years that she worked at Princeton, Browne made most of her significant contributions. In an article entitled "Cleavage without Nuclei," she described centrifuging the egg to redistribute its contents. Her research suggested that cleavage could occur in an unfertilized enucleated egg, and that the early cleavage stages could occur without input from either the maternal or paternal nucleus. Much of her work was done on sea urchins, and she published a paper that became a standard reference for scientists working on sea urchin embryology. Her research was controversial in some circles, for her work was considered to be an interference in the life process. It opened up the possibility that life could be created in the laboratory. JH/MBO

PRIMARY SOURCES

Browne, Ethel. "The Production of New Hydranths in Hydra by the Insertion of Small Grafts." *Journal of Experimental Biology* 7 (1909): 1–23.

———. "A Study of the Male Germ Cells in *Notonecta*." *Journal of Experimental Zoology* (January 1913).

Harvey, Ethel Browne. "Cleavage without Nuclei." *Science* 82 (1935): 277.

———. *The American Arbacia and Other Sea Urchins*. Princeton: Princeton University Press, 1956.

STANDARD SOURCES

AMS 3–8, B 9, P&B 10; Kass-Simon; *NAW(M)* (article by Donna J. Haraway); Shearer and Shearer 1996.

HARWOOD, MARGARET (1885–1979)

U.S. astronomer. Born 19 March 1885 in Littleton, Mass., to Emelie Augusta (Green) and Herbert Joseph Harwood. Educated Radcliffe College (A.B., 1907); University of California (A.M., 1916). Professional experience: Harvard College Observatory, computer and assistant (1907–1912), visiting astronomer (from 1967); Nantucket Maria Mitchell Association, resident fellow (1912–1916), director of the observatory (1915–1951); International Astronomical Union Bibliography of Astronomical Literature published in the U.S.A. from 1881–1898, bibliographer (1961–1967); Mt. Wilson Observatory, Carnegie Institution (1923–1924); MIT Radiation Laboratory, staff member (1944–1946); Radcliffe Institute, visiting research fellow (from 1970). Honors and memberships: American Astronomical Society, Annie J. Cannon Award (1961); International Astronomical Union; American Association of Variable Star Observers; British Astronomical Association, and Royal Astronomical Society. Died 1979.

In 1903, Margaret Harwood entered Radcliffe College where she studied physics, chemistry, and mathematics. Inspired by Arthur Searle, in whose household she boarded, she overcame her fear of astronomy. She attended regular class lectures, read in theoretical astronomy, and practiced computing orbits of comets. She was allowed to use the fifteen–inch refractor at the observatory, and gained much practical knowledge from ANNIE JUMP CANNON and HENRIETTA SWAN LEAVITT. Immediately after graduating from Radcliffe, she joined the staff of the observatory. She was on the regular Harvard College Observatory staff for only five years. However, she spent almost half of every year there while directing her own observatory at Nantucket.

During her first year at the observatory, Harwood assisted Searle in computing observations of the zones assigned to Harvard for the revision of the Southern Durchmusterung, read proofs for a volume of the *Annals,* and helped prepare photometric measures made with the meridian photometer for publication. Other research interests included observation of variable stars and measuring long-period variables.

In 1912, Harwood received the first thousand-dollar Astronomical Fellowship of the Nantucket Maria Mitchell Association. The terms of the fellowship required her to spend one half year at Nantucket and the other at one of the larger observatories for research and study. She spent most of her half years at Harvard, with the exception of one year at the Lick Observatory and the University of California, during which time she earned a master's degree. She began investigations of the light curves of Eros in 1914, using both the Harvard plates and her own photographs from the Maria Mitchell Observatory. In 1916, she became the permanent director of this observatory, a position that she held until retirement in 1957. One of her other tasks was to complete a bibliography of all American articles on astronomy published between 1881 and 1889 on behalf of the International Astronomical Union.

During the time that she was director of the observatory, Harwood published studies on 65 known and 354 new variables in or near the Scutum Cloud. These publications were based on plates from the Maria Mitchell Observatory, Harvard, and Leiden Collections.   JH/MBO

PRIMARY SOURCES
Harwood, Margaret. "Bond Zones of Faint Equatorial Stars." *Annals of the Astronomical Observatory of Harvard College* 75, no. 1 (1912). Harwood studied the Bond Zones of faint stars one degree north of the equator. These had been observed by both George Bond and his father between 1852 and 1859. Pickering assigned her to study this subject.

STANDARD SOURCES
AMS 3–8, P 9, P&B 10–12; Bailey; Jones and Boyd; Shearer and Shearer 1997, *Who's Who of American Women.*

HASLETT, DAME CAROLINE (1895–1957)
British electrical engineer. Born 17 August 1895 in Sussex, England, eldest daughter to Robert and Caroline Sarah (Holmes) Haslett. Educated locally. Left high school to take a job at the outbreak of World War I; studied engineering (qualifed in engineering; qualified in electrical engineering). Professional experience: Cochran Boiler Company, clerk, production worker; Women's Engineering Society 1919, secretary; WES journal, The Woman Engineer, *founder and editor; Electrical Association for Women, director (1924); conference on power, Berlin, delegate (1930); Washington World Power Conference, delegate (1936); Institution of Electrical Engineers, companion (1934, first woman to be admitted); Royal Institution, member; British Ministry of Labor during World War II, adviser; Hosiery Working Party (government fact-finding commission), chairman; British Electricity Authority, member (1947); Crawley-Three Bridges New Town Development Corporation, member; British Federation of Business and Professional Women, president (several terms); International Federation of Business and Professional Women, president (1950); London School of Economics and Political Science, governor; Bedford College for Women, governor; King's College of Household and Social Science, council member; Administrative Staff College, court of governors, member; Comité de l'Organization Scientifique, member; several professional women's journals and handbooks, founder and editor. Honors and memeberships: Dame of the British Empire (1947); Justice of the Peace for the County of London (1950); only woman included in* Who Runs Britain?, *a symposium of leaders of fourteen aspects of British life (1949). Died 4 January 1957.*

Dame Caroline Haslett was a dynamic woman and engineer who was largely responsible for the opening of the light engineering industry to women in England. Her superb executive and organizational skills put her in positions where she could influence engineering education opportunities for women and promote production of household appliances to aid housewives. She was active in the suffrage movement and crusaded persuasively for equal training and employment opportunities for women in engineering after the wars (when many women who had held positions in both production and management were being laid off in favor of men returning from military service). She served as president of the International Federation of Business and Professional Women, which worked for the reestablishment of business and professional women's federations in war-torn European countries, and fought for removal of discrimination against women.

This remarkable woman had an inauspicious start, born into the modest home of railroad engineer Robert Haslett and his wife Caroline Sarah (Holmes) on 17 August 1895. Caroline attended local schools, but left high school when wartime vacancies created job openings for women. Beginning in a clerical post at the Cochran Boiler Company, Haslett became interested in the possibilities of engineering applications for the home and decided to become an engineer herself. She asked to be transferred to production and worked in the the plant for five years while she qualified first as engineer, then as electrical engineer. In 1919, Haslett became affiliated with a new organization formed to work toward promoting highly trained women in engineering—the Women's Engineering Society (WES). She founded and edited for many years the society's journal, *The Woman Engineer.* She used her persuasive logic to convince employers that women had special aptitudes for light engineering work and to show the various engineering institutions that women deserved to be admitted.

The WES founded the Electrical Association for Women to promote training and jobs for women in the field of electrical engineering; Haslett was its director for over twenty five years (from 1924). Over time, the association has grown to an organization of over ninety branches and provides scholarships and traveling fellowships through an endowed trust named for Caroline Haslett. Through her work with this and other industrial organizations, Haslett earned her reputation as an engineer, executive, and organizer. In 1930, she was named the only woman delegate to a conference on power in Berlin; in 1936, she was one of two women delegates to the Washington World Power Conference. She was the first woman to be made a Companion (member) of the Institution of Electrical Engineers (1934). Recognized for her expertise in training, she was asked to develop a simplified course in engineering and electricity for the Home Office and the Board of Education and was an adviser of women's training during World War II. As she toured the industrial plants throughout Britain, she pleaded the case of women workers, analyzing their capabilities, arguing for equal pay for equal work, and for continued opportunities after the war. She visited the United States to study the participation of American women in the industrial work force.

At the end of the war, the Board of Trade nominated Haslett to be chair of the Hosiery Working Party, a factfinding committee set up to study various industries. In 1947, Dame Haslett (so honored in 1947) was appointed to the Central Electricity Authority, a board formed to manage the British electrical industry (1947–1956) and was named to the Crawley-Three Bridges New Town Development Corporation which was to design and build a model of the satellite towns proposed to alleviate the overcrowding of big cities (1947–1955). She also served on a committee of the Ministry of Works and chaired a committee of the Ministry of Fuel and Power.

Haslett visited the United States again in 1944 as president and representative of the British Federation of Business and Professional Women. She was elected president of the International Federation of Business and Professional Women at its meeting in London in 1950 (she served till 1956), lending her years of experience to its campaign for equal education and work opportunities for women. The same year, she was named a Justice of the Peace for the County of London. Haslett spoke at many national and international meetings and convocations (including the United Nations) of her belief that there was little difference in the natural abilities of men and women, only in their psychological approach, and argued that both approaches were valid and necessary in solving postwar problems.

Haslett's capacity for achievement was awesome. Besides serving on many government boards and committees of soci-

eties in the industrial sector, she connected with the educational sector by serving on the governing boards of several colleges. She contributed papers and articles to professional engineering and industrial journals, founding and editing *The Electrical Age* (a journal), editing *The Electrical Handbook for Women*, writing *Household Electricity, Munitions Girl,* and *Problems Have No Sex.* She was the only woman included in the 1949 edition of *Who Runs Britain?,* a symposium of leaders of fourteen aspects of British life. Never married, Haslett enjoyed relaxing with golf, motoring, and gardening. Her club was the Forum. She died 4 January 1957. The Institution of Electrical Engineering named their trust aftr Haslett following her death. Her papers are in their archives.

JH/MBO

PRIMARY SOURCES
Haslett, Caroline. With Elsie E. Edwards. *Household Electricity.* London: English Universities Press, [1939].
———. *Munitions girl: A Handbook for the Women of the Industrial Army.* London: English Universities Press, [1942].
———, ed. *The Electrical Handbook for Women.* Edited for the The Electrical Association for Women. London: Hodder & Stoughton, Ltd., 1934; rpt., London: English Universities Press, 1956.

SECONDARY SOURCES
Eastman, Crystal. "Caroline Haslett and the Women Engineers." In *Crystal Eastman on Women and the Revolution,* ed. Blanche Wiesen Cook. New York: Oxford University Press, 1978.

STANDARD SOURCES
Current Biography 1940–1950; *DNB; Europa; International WW; WWW,* vol. 5, 1951–1960.

HASSALL, BESSIE FLORENCE (CORY) (1883–1954)

British botanical artist. Married. Died 15 September 1954 at Oxford.

Bessie Hassall sketched plants and was an active member of the Botanical Society of the British Isles.   JH/MBO

SECONDARY SOURCES
Proceedings of the Botanical Society of the British Isles (1955): 413.

STANDARD SOURCES
Desmond.

HASTINGS, BARBARA, MARCHIONESS OF (1810–1858)

British collector of fossil vertebrates. Born 1810. Father Henry Edward Yelverton, Baron Grey of Ruthin. Married (1) George Augustus Rawdon Hastings (he died 1844); (2) Captain Hastings Reginald Henry. Four children by first marriage; one by the second. Died 1858.

Barbara Hastings compiled a superb collection of fossil specimens from Britain and Europe currently housed in the British Museum. While she was married to her first husband, she collected some fossil materials herself from the Hordle and Beacon Cliffs on the Hampshire coast, and bought others from dealers. When her first husband died in 1844 she remarried in 1845 and settled at Efford House, between Milford and Lymington. She continued her collecting with a passion, and enlisted the help of local people. These collections resulted in her paper of 1847 that was presented at the British Association for the Advancement of Science meeting at Oxford by a male scientist, immediately followed by Richard Owen's discussion of the same fossils. At this same meeting she exhibited a turtle shell and crocodile fossils. At that meeting Richard Owen proposed to name her fossil skull discovery *Crocodilus hastingsiae.*

In addition to collecting fossil vertebrates, Hastings published works on Eocene stratigraphy. She was interested in fossils not only for their curiosity value but was concerned with the wider picture. By preparing colored, scale-drawn sections of the beds on which she based her main papers, she was able to record the stratigraphic locations of her fossils. A meticulously careful collector, she recognized the danger of accidentally destroying and obscuring specimens that revealed much of the history of life in the Eocene. In her 1853 paper, she noted that her purpose was to provide data on which to build a comprehensive picture of Tertiary stratigraphy. She recognized that local observations provided the basis from which a complete picture could eventually be built. Hastings corresponded with many scientists of the period, including Edward Forbes, Alexander Falconer, William Buckland, and Charles Lyell. Her most extensive correspondence was with Richard Owen, a total of sixty-four letters. She sold her collections to the British Museum (Natural History) in 1851.

JH/MBO

PRIMARY SOURCES
Hastings, Barbara, Marchioness of. "On the Freshwater Eocene Beds of Hordle Cliff, Hampshire." *Report British Association for the Advancement of Science* (1848): 63–64. Read by secretary at meeting in Oxford 1847.

———. "On the Tertiary Beds of Hordwell, Hampshire." *Philosophical Magazine* 6 (1853): 1–11.

———. "Description géologique des falaises d'Hordle, et sur la côte de Hampshire en Angleterre." *Bulletin de la Société Géologique de France* n.s. 9 (1851–1852): 191–203.

"On the Freshwater Eocene Beds of Hordle Cliff, Hampshire." *Report British Association for the Advancement of Science* (1848): 63–64. Read by secretary at meeting in Oxford 1847.

Letters in Richard Owen Collection (1846–1854), British Natural History Museum Archives.

SECONDARY SOURCES
Edwards, Nicholas. "The Hastings Collection (Fossil Vertebrates): History of Additions Made by the Marchioness of Hastings Between 1845–1851 from the Upper Eocene Beds at Hordle Cliff, Hampshire." *Journal of the Society for the Bibliography of Natural History* 5, no. 1 (1970): 340–343.

Gruber, Jacob W. "Richard Owen and his Correspondents: 'My Dear Owen.'" In *Richard Owen Commemoration,* ed. Jacob W. Gruber and John Thackery, 54–55. London: Natural History Publications, 1992.

Owen, Richard. "On the Fossils Obtained by the Marchioness of Hastings from the Freshwater Eocene Beds of Hordle Cliffs." *Report of the British Association for the Advancement of Science* (1848): 65–66. Read at meeting, Oxford 1847.

Wilson, G., and A. Geikie. *Memoir of Edward Forbes.* London: Macmillan and Edmonston Co., 1861.

STANDARD SOURCES
Creese and Creese; Sarjeant.

HATHAWAY, MILLICENT LOUISE (1898–1974)

U.S. nutritionist and physiological chemist. Educated Wells College (A.B., 1920); University of Buffalo (A.M., 1920); University of Chicago (Ph.D., 1932). Professional experience: Cedarville College, science and mathematics teacher (1920–1921); small college, teacher (1921–1922); high school teacher (1922–1924); University of Buffalo, assistant in chemistry (1924–1925); Science Survey, instructor (1925–1929); University of Chicago, assistant in biochemistry (1931–1933); University of Michigan(?), assistant physiologist, College of Medicine (1933–1935), associate in home economics (1935–1937); Battle Creek College, professor of physiology (1937–1938); Cornell University, instructor through associate professor (1938–1946); U.S. Department of Agriculture, Bureau of Nutrition and Home Economics, nutrition specialist (1946–1962); Howard University, professor of home economics (1962–1966). Honors and memberships: Home Economics Association, Borden Award (1947); American Institute of Nutrition, member; American Association for the Advancement of Science, Fellow. Died 1974.

Milicent Hathaway, after receiving her bachelor's degree from Wells, taught science and mathematics in several small colleges and a high school. She returned to study chemistry at the University of Buffalo, where she received a master's degree while serving as an assistant in the chemistry department. After receiving her master's, she taught a science survey course for four years. In 1931, Hathaway studied biochemistry at the University of Chicago and after receiving her doctoral degree continued as an assistant in the chemistry department there. She then moved to the College of Medicine of the University of Illinois (?) for two years and was made an associate in home economics until 1937. After teaching at another small college, she went to the home economics department of Cornell University, where she remained for the next eight years, rising through the ranks from instructor through associate professor. Like many other women in her day, she went from Cornell to the U.S. Department of Agriculture in the postwar period. She remained there as nutrition specialist until 1962, when she was appointed professor of home economics at Howard University, from which she retired in 1966.

Hathaway published a number of papers on her research on citric acid metabolism, sterols, and human metabolism of essential vitamins and minerals. JH/MBO

PRIMARY SOURCE
Hathaway, Millicent Louise, *Provitamin D Potencies, Absorption Spectrta, and Chemical Studies of Heat-Treated Cholesterol.* Baltimore: n.p., 1935, Ph.D. dissertation.

———. *Heights and Weights of Children and Youth in the United States.* Washington, D.C.: Institute of Home Economics, U.S. Agricultural Research Service, U.S. Government Printing Office., 1957.

SECONDARY SOURCES
Long, Diana Hall. "Academics, Bluestockings, and Biologists." In *Annals of the New York Academy of Sciences,* vol. 323, ed. A. M. Briscoe and Sheila Pfallin. 1979.

STANDARD SOURCES
AMS 6–11; Bailey; Debus.

HATSHEPSUT, QUEEN (d. 1468 B.C.E.)
Egyptian queen. Daughter of eighteenth-dynasty Pharaoh Thutmose I. Married half-brother Thutmose II. Stepmother of Thutmose III. Reigned 1486–1468 B.C.E.

Queen Hatshepsut ruled Egypt as pharaoh, relegating her husband to a minor position. After his death, she continued to rule as regent for her stepson Thutmose III for twenty-two years. During her peaceful reign, she developed the resources of Egypt, reviving the mining industry at Sinai and building a famous temple at Deir el Bahari in western Thebes. She sent a botanical expedition in search of medicinal plants.

SECONDARY SOURCES
New Columbia Ency, S.V. "Hatshepsut" and "Thutmose I." New York: Columbia University Press, 1975.

STANDARD SOURCES
Alic.

HAUSSER, ISOLDE (GANSWINDT) (1889–1951)
German technical and biomedical physicist. Born 7 December 1889 in Berlin to Anna Minna Fritzsche and Hermann Ganswindt. Sixteen siblings. Married Karl Wilhelm Hausser (1887–1933) in 1918. One son, Karl Herrmann (1919). Educated private higher girls' education, Muncipal Higher Educations for Girls, sciences branch (Realgymnasium); Berlin University (Ph.D. in physics, 1914). Professional experience: Gesellschaft für drahtlose Telegraphie-Telefunken GmbH Berlin, technical physicist, head of laboratory group for vacuum tubes; Kaiser Wilhelm/Max Planck Institut (KWI) für Medizinische Forschung (Institute for Medical Research), Heidelberg, research scientist. Honors and memberships: Scientific Council (Wissenschaftlicher Rat) of the Kaiser Wilhelm Gesellschaft (KWG). Died 5 October 1951.

Isolde Ganswindt was the fourth of sixteen children; two elder brothers died at birth. Hermann Ganswindt, her father, was an ambitious, but not very successful inventor-entrepreneur. Her mother had, as was the case with most bourgeois women in imperial Germany, no profession outside of the home. As an autodidact in engineering, Ganswindt designed coaches for various purposes, flying apparatuses, and conceptualized space cruisers. His techno-scientific inclinations and the workshop premises constituted the educational background that may have influenced Isolde in her future career choice.

Since most education for girls deserving of the name at the turn of the century was private and expensive—the German state institutionalized it only in 1908—Ganswindt's parents were farsighted enough to enroll Isolde at a private school. From 1903 until 1909 she was a pupil at the municipal science and realities-oriented *Realgymnasium* (secondary school) for girls, following a curriculum that went beyond the usual arts-based girls' education. In 1909 she took her *Abitur,* thus becoming qualified to matriculate at a German university. Only one year before, the Prussian state, as the last of the German states, had allowed women officially to become regular students at universities.

As one of the forty-one women of roughly seven hundred students, Ganswindt enrolled in the summer of 1909 in physics, mathematics, and philosophy at Berlin University. The physicists Max Planck, Heinrich Rubens, and Arthur Wehnelt were among her teachers, the latter specializing in research on early types of vacuum tubes. Here she may have first become interested in the subject that was to become important in her later career. In 1914 she earned a doctorate with a thesis on the generation and detection of short electrical waves, based on experimental work.

Since her large family lived on a consistently low budget, with war approaching in August 1914, Ganswindt decided to take up a position in the research laboratory for vacuum tubes at the Gesellschaft für Drahtlose Telegraphie-Telefunken GmbH, which then specialized in wireless technology. She soon became head of a research group working on the fledgling vacuum tube technology involving a new means to generate continuous electromagnetic high-frequency waves. Tubes for radio-receiving purposes were soon mass-produced by Telefunken when they turned out to be indispensable in military operations at the western front from 1917 to 1918. A few years later, they were to revolutionize the communications industry. Ganswindt's work centered on vacuum control and measurement and resulted in tubes becoming more durable goods. She also tested radio equipment for use on the front and conducted radio experiments on U-boats and on airplanes.

In 1918, Ganswindt married the physicist Karl Wilhelm Hausser, a colleague at the Telefunken laboratory. Due to a fire and possibly to poisonous gases deriving from the neighboring film plant, Hausser had a miscarriage shortly after her marriage. In June 1919, she gave birth to a son, her only child, who became a physicist.

When her husband became professor and director of the Kaiser Wilhelm Institut für Medizinische Forschung (Institute for Medical Research), founded the same year, Isolde Hausser gave up her well-paid, responsible industrial position to join him at Heidelberg. She became research assistant and head of the electrical department at her husband's institute. She may have consoled herself with the possibility of pursuing her academic career and eventually reaching professorship herself. Unfortunately, her husband died of cancer in 1933, becoming a late victim of X-ray work conducted during World War I.

Walther Bothe, one of the first nuclear physicists in Germany, succeeded Karl Wilhelm Hausser at the institute in 1934. With the ensuing reorganization, Isolde Hausser's position as a relatively independent researcher at the institute became precarious. Friction and misunderstanding turned the years until Hausser's death in 1951 into a period of an unceasing "war of nerves" and perpetual quarreling for laboratory room, trained assistant staff, and the delineation and marking of fields of work. Hausser insisted on her work contract from 1930, which guaranteed her responsibilities. Yet the new head insisted on his authority. In 1935, the president of the KWG intervened and Hausser's former position was more or less restored. Her future field of work, biological physicals, crystallized. Her superior, Bothe, however,

would only have her department work under the name of "*Abteilung Dr. Isolde Hausser,*" fearing to call it programmatically "*Abteilung für biologische Physik*" (Department of Biological Physics) because it gave the impression that Hausser was the only scientist at the institute to work in that field.

Nevertheless, Hausser continued her research after her husband's death, first by taking up his studies on light erythemaes and the formation of pigment, on sun burning, and on light absorption and double bonds. Then she conducted a series of measurements leading to a better understanding of the composition of muscle substance. She developed a method to define simultaneously the dielectric constant and the conductivity of conductive substances, which shed light on understanding muscle contraction. She worked on the constitution of chemical behavior of organic compounds using modern physical methods. She did experiments on banana skins and human skin which have similar absorption characteristics. Finally, around 1936–1937, she discovered the specific action of longwave ultraviolet.

In 1938, Isolde Hausser was elected a member of the scientific council of the KWG, albeit with the opposition of her superior Bothe and two other eminent scientists on "grounds of standard" in academic performance. Only two other women held this distinction, the physicist LISE MEITNER, who had to emigrate from Germany that year because of the Nazi anti-Jewish politics, and the other, the Swiss neurophysiologist Cécile Vogt.

During the mid-1930s, Hausser again became interested in what was by then called ultrashort waves. Thus she took up earlier work on the generation of short electromagnetic waves and vacuum tubes. Shortwave therapy had become of interest to medical researchers and physicians, who applied it to many medical subfields and to almost all organs and various clinical syndromes. This part of the electromagnetic wave spectrum had also become of interest to radio practitioners and to the military in the form of radar.

From about 1942, Hausser's work became instrumental in the Nazi war effort. Her department contributed to the radar research program, a fact that led the Allied Forces in 1945 to accuse her of collaboration in "war research." In early 1946, Hausser was allowed to continue her work because she intended to focus on physical therapy, a field judged of public medical interest by the Allies.

Possibly under the impression that she herself was suffering from cancer, Hauser began to work on ultrasound action on tumors, and continued her earlier work on the structural problems of organic chemistry.

She lived and worked with her son Karl Hermann, who, in the meantime, had become a physicist. Her last paper on the photochemistry of solutions of finite thickness was a co-production, but appeared only after she died in December 1951.

The immediate postwar years brought unemployment, malnutrition, and general hardship to most Germans. Hausser's health continued to decline. In a letter to a friend in 1949, she contemplated the situation of women in academia. By this time she was the head of a research institute within the renamed Max Planck Gesellschaft (formerly KWG). She explained that heavier demands were put on women and they were more criticized than men: "It looks like a wonder to me that after the collapse of 1945, I have been able to conquer that position I hold and even enlarge upon it in time . . . but I had to give my utmost."

Isolde Hausser was one of the first generation of women in Germany who were formally admitted to study at the university (1908), but whose desire to apply their newly gained knowledge to pursue academic careers was still not accepted by German society as a whole. Hausser paid a high price for her independence and her recognition as a scientist, which she gained largely as a lone fighter.   M F

PRIMARY SOURCES

Hausser, Isolde. With H. Rukop. "Die Schwingungserzeugungdurch Rückkopplung vermittelst der Anoden-Gitter-Kapazität bei der Hochvakuum-Eingitterröhre." *Telefunken-Zeitung* 25 (1922): 3–24.

———. "Das dielektrische Verhalten organischer zwitterionen unter besonderer Berücksichtigung von Molekülen der Hirn- und Nervensubstanz." *Sitzungsberichte der Heidelberger Akademie der Wissenschaften.* Mathematisch-naturwissenschaftliche Klasse (Jahrgang 1935): 6. Abhandlung.

———. With A. Überle. "Lichtbräunung an Fruchtschalen im UV-und sichtbaren Spektralbereich." *Die Naturwissenschaften* 26 (1938): 323–330.

———. Über Einzel—und Kombinationswirkungen des kurzwelligen und langwelligen UV bei Bestrahlung der menschlichen Hauat." *Die Naturwissenschaften* 27 (1939): 563–566.

———. "Ultrakurzwellen: Physik, Technik und Anwendungsgebiete." *Sitzungsberichte der Heidelberger Akademie der Wissenschaften.* Mathematisch-naturwissenschaftliche Klasse (Jahrgang 1939): 4. Abhandlung.

SECONDARY SOURCES

Fuchs, Margot. "Isolde Hausser (7.12.1889–5.10.1951), Technische Physikerin und Wissenschafterin am Kaiser-Wilhelm-/Max-Planck-Institut für Medizinische Forschung, Heidelberg." *Berichte zur Wissenschaftsgeschichte* 17 (1994): 201–215.

"Hausser, Isolde." *Neue Deutsche Biographie,* vol. 8. Verlag Duncker and Humblot, Berlin: 1969.

"Hausser, Isolde." *Kürschners Deutscher Gelehrten-Kalender.* 7th ed. Berlin and New York: Walter de Gruyter, 1950.

"Hausser, Isolde." *Lexikon der Frau,* vol. 1.

"Hausser, Isolde." *Grosse Frauen der Weltgeschichte: Tausend Biographien in Wort und Bild.* Murnau, Munich, Innsbruck, Basel: Verlag Sebastian Lux, ca. 1958.

Kuhn, Richard. "25 Jahre Max-Planck-Institut für Medizinische Forschung in Heidelberg." *Mitteilungen der Max-Planck-Gesellschaft zur Förderung der Wissenschaften* 2 (1955): 69–100.

STANDARD SOURCES
Poggendorf, vol. 7a, 1932–1953.

HAWES, HARRIET (BOYD) (1871–1945)

U.S. archeologist. Born 11 October 1871 in Boston, Mass., to Harriet (Wheeler) and Alexander Boyd. Married Charles Hawes. Two children: Alexander and Mary. Educated public schools, Boston; boarding school, Morristown, N.J.; Prospect Hill School, Greenfield, Mass. (1885–1888); Smith College (B.A., 1892; M.A., 1901). Professional experience: classics teacher, girls' school in Wilmington, Del. (1893–1896); instructor, Greek archeology and modern Greek, Smith College (1900–1906); lecturer on pre-Christian art, Wellesley College (1920–1936). Died 31 March 1945 in Washington, D.C.

Harriet Boyd's mother died when she was a baby; she grew up in a masculine household whose other members were her father (a leather merchant) and her four older brothers. Among her brothers she was particularly close to Alexander, Jr., whose interest in ancient history she absorbed. After attending various public and private schools in Massachusetts and New Jersey, Boyd enrolled at Smith College, receiving a bachelor's in 1892.

Boyd taught classics to private students in North Carolina and at a girls' school in Delaware for several years, then took up graduate work at the American School of Classical Studies in Athens (1896–1900). During the final spring and summer of her stay in Greece, she did excavations on Crete, discovering several tomb sites from the Iron Age, which provided the subject for her master's thesis, submitted to Smith College in 1901. Boyd taught at Smith for the next six years, but during this period returned several times to Crete to do field work. At Gournia, she discovered and supervised the excavation of a Minoan Early Bronze Age town site (1901–1904). She described her findings in several publications and in a national lecture tour in 1902.

In 1906, Boyd married Charles Hawes, a British anthropologist whom she had met in Crete. Their two children were born in 1906 and 1910. The family lived for two years in Madison, Wisconsin (1907–1909), where Charles Hawes taught at the university, and then, on his taking a teaching post at Dartmouth College, they moved to Hanover, New Hampshire (1910–1917). During World War I, Harriet Hawes, who had served as a volunteer nurse in Thessaly in the Greco-Turkish War (1897) and in Florida in the Spanish-American War (1898), worked in a Serbian army hospital camp on Corfu and participated in relief and hospital work in France. Her social activism later manifested itself in her support of Norman Thomas for president in 1932, and her aid to striking shoe workers in Massachusetts in 1933. From 1919 to 1936, Hawes lived in Boston and Cambridge, while her husband was assistant director of the Boston Museum of Fine Arts. She resumed her own career and taught at Wellesley College from 1920 to 1936. In that year, the Haweses retired to a farm in Alexandria, Virginia. Harriet Hawes died in Washington, D.C., at age seventy-three.

Hawes contributed to the knowledge of the Minoan civilization in Crete. She discovered new sites, supervised their excavation, and published her findings. Although basically a classicist, Hawes used scientific methods to locate and excavate sites. Her work expanded the data available on early civilizations. JH/MBO

PRIMARY SOURCES

Hawes, Harriet. *Gournia, Vasiliki and Other Prehistoric Sites on the Isthmus of Hierapetra, Crete.* Philadelphia: American Exploration Society, 1908.

Harriet Boyd Hawes Collection. Smith College Archives. Material on Hawes includes biography, correspondence, journals, publications, and information on her war work.

SECONDARY SOURCES

Bolger, Diane L. "Ladies of the Expedition: Harriet Boyd Hawes and Edith Hall." In *Women in Archaeology*, ed. Cheryl Claassen. Philadelphia: University of Pennsylvania Press, 1994.

STANDARD SOURCES

Bailey; *DAB* suppl.; *NAW;* Ogilvie 1986.

HAWKES, JACQUETTA (HOPKINS) (1910–1996)

British archeologist and writer. Born 10 August 1910 in Cambridge, England. Married (1) Christopher Hawkes (1933), had one son, Nicholas, divorced; (2) J. B. Priestley (1953; he died 1983). Educated Cambridge University (1932?). Professional experience: field research, Palestine and England; United Nations Educational, Scientific and Cultural Organization (UNESCO), United Kingdom Commission, founder (1947); Festival of Britain, archeological adviser (1951); writer of popular books on archeology (1951–1971). Died 19 (?) March 1996 in Cheltenham General Hospital, London.

Jacquetta Hopkins was born in Cambridge, England, surrounded by academic excitement and a sense of history. She went to Cambridge University and graduated with a degree in

archeology and anthropology at a time when excitement about the spectacular finds in Egypt was at its height.

Hopkins married her first husband, Christopher Hawkes, who took her on expeditions to Palestine and to digs in England. During the war, Hawkes showed her administrative ability in several government posts. Immediately after the war she founded the United Kingdom Commission of the United Nations Educational, Scientific and Cultural Organization (UNESCO). A conference for UNESCO in Mexico City in 1947 introduced her to J. B. Priestley. Although the two felt immediately attracted, she waited for some years to divorce her husband and marry Priestley.

During the Festival of Britain, Hawkes served as archeological adviser, and recorded her experiences in a book illustrated by Henry Moore, *A Land* (1951). She continued to publish popular books on archeology over the next thirty years. She also wrote with Priestley the play *Dragon's Mouth,* produced off Broadway in 1955. She wrote science fiction, as well, and one autobiographical novel, *A Quest for Love* (1981). In her sixties, she published archeological atlases on ancient human history along with popular books on Egypt. Priestley died in 1984, and Hawkes survived him by twelve years, living in a small town, Chipping Camden in the Cotswolds in England. JH/MBO

PRIMARY SOURCES

Hawkes, Jacquetta. *A Land*. Illustrated by Henry Moore. London: Cresset Press, 1951.

———. With J. B. Priestley. *Dragon's Mouth*. In *Famous Plays of Today,* London: S. French, 1953. A play produced in New York City, 1955.

———. With Christopher Hawkes. *Prehistoric Britain*. Middleton: Penguin, 1958.

———. "The Achievements of Paleolithic Man." In *Man before History,* ed. Gabel Creighton, 21–35. Englewood Cliffs, N.J.: Prentice-Hall, 1965.

———. "The City of Croesus." *Harvard Today* (1965): 14–148.

———. *Prehistory*. New York: New American Library, 1965.

———. *King of the Two Lands: The Pharoah Akhenaten.* London: Random House, 1966.

———. *A Quest for Love.* London: Braziller, 1981. Her autobiographical novel.

SECONDARY SOURCES

Collins, Diana. *Time and the Priestleys.* London, A. Sutton, 1994. A double biography of Jacquetta Hawkes and J. B. Priestley.

Gusow, Mel. "Jacquetta Hawkes." *New York Times,* 21 March 1996. Obituary notice with portrait.

STANDARD SOURCES

Kass-Simon and Farnes (article by Cyntha Irwin-Williams).

HAWKINS, KATE (ca. 1896–1989)

British horticulturist. Born around 1896 in Herefordshire. Professional experience: gardener at Royal Botanic Garden, Edinburgh; designed gardens. Died 7 May 1989.

Kate Hawkins trained and worked with horticulturists Percy Cane and BRENDA COLVIN. She became a gardener at the Royal Botanic Garden, Edinburgh, and designed gardens, primarily in Scotland.   JH/MBO

SECONDARY SOURCES
Gardener's Historical Society Newsletter 27 (1989): 28.

STANDARD SOURCES
Desmond.

HAWKINS, MARY ESTHER (SIBTHORP) (fl. 19th century)

British botanist. Father H. W. Sibthorp (1712–1797). Married J. Hawkins (1761–1841).

Mary Esther Hawkins and her husband collected plants in many seemingly inaccessible places.   JH/MBO

SECONDARY SOURCES
Polwhele, Richard. *Language, Literature and Literary Characters of Cornwall.* London, 1806. Hawkins discussed on pages 121–123.

STANDARD SOURCES
Desmond.

HAWN MIRABILE, MARGARET H. (1915–1982)

U.S. petroleum geologist. Born 17 August 1915 in Dover, Idaho. Married (1) Andrew E. Hawn (d. 1972); (2) Charles Mirabile. One son, Earl Duane Hawn. Educated University of Chicago (B.S., 1938). Professional experience: Roland and Wilson of Centralia, Ill. (geologist, 1939); many additional jobs in the oil exploration business; independent consulting. Died 23 December 1982 in Denver, Colo.

Margaret H. Hawn Mirabile was born in Denver, Colorado, and earned a bachelor of science degree in geology from the University of Chicago. Although she began a graduate program, she was able to complete only one year because of financial considerations. When Hawn Mirabile got her first position as a geologist with Roland and Wilson of Centralia, Illinois, it was extremely rare for a woman to be employed in geology and even more unusual to find one in the oil exploration area. After getting this job, she proceeded to work for a number of other companies, including Allied Oil Production Co., W. C. McBride. Inc., William E. Brubeck, Indiana Farm Bureau Cooperative Association, Inc., R. K. Petroleum, Spartan Petroleum, Robert L. Dayson, and the T. W. George Estate.

Alongside her first husband, Andrew E. Hawn, a landman, she worked as an independent consultant. Andrew died in 1972, and she continued independent consulting until 1977. Much of her work during this period was in Texas, Michigan, and Oklahoma. From 1977 to 1982, she worked for an independent of Evansville, Indiana, Richard Beeson. Her hobbies included collecting minerals and fossils, hiking, swimming, breeding English Setters, and horse training. She did not live long after her September 1982 marriage to Charles Mirabile, for she died of a heart attack on December 23 of that same year.

Hawn Mirabile was a member of the American Institute of Professional Geologists, the Rocky Mountain Association of Geologists, the Indiana-Kentucky Geological Survey (president 1980–1981), and past president of the Illinois Geological Society. She was active in the American Association of Petroleum Geologists and was president of the Eastern Section and alternate delegate during 1981–1982.

Hawn Mirabile was an excellent field petroleum geologist. In oil exploration, she made a number of important discoveries in Illinois, Indiana, Kentucky, Colorado, and other states. Her work was practical, not theoretical, but she was extremely knowledgable about finding oil deposits.

CK

PRIMARY SOURCES
Hawn Mirabile, Margaret H. With others. *Geology and Petroleum Production of the Illinois Basin.*

SECONDARY SOURCES
Kaveny, Bridget, and Robert J. Berven. "Margaret H. Hawn Mirabile (1915–1982)." *Bulletin of the American Association of Petroleum Geologists* 67, no. 3 (1983): 881. Includes portrait.

STANDARD SOURCES
Sarjeant.

HAYES, ELLEN AMANDA (1851–1930)

U.S. mathematician and educator. Born 23 September 1851, to Ruth Rebecca (Wolcott) and Charles Coleman Hayes. Five siblings. Never married. Educated Oberlin College (A.B., 1878). Professional experience: Adrian College, Michigan, principal of the women's department (1878); Wellesley College (1879–1882), assistant professor (1882–1883), associate professor (1883–1888), professor and head of math-

ematics department (1888–1897), head of applied mathematics (1897–1916); Vineyard Shore School for women workers in industry, teacher (1929–1930). Died 27 October 1930 in West Park, N.Y.

Amanda Hayes's unconventional childhood led to an unconventional career. As a child she spent time gardening on her grandparents' farm in Ohio, and was allowed more freedom than most girls at that time. Climbing trees, swimming, and skating were allowed, although, to her disgust, horseback riding was not. Her mother was a teacher who had graduated from the Granville Female Academy, and she taught the children the Latin names of plants, and ways to identify them. Astronomy was another of Hayes's interests encouraged by her mother. She was the oldest of four girls and two boys and was a leader in childhood activities. Her primary education was at a one-room ungraded public school.

After teaching at a country school to earn money for college, Hayes entered Oberlin's preparatory department in 1872 and was admitted as a freshman in 1875. Her career began after she received her bachelor's degree in 1878, when she became a mathematics teacher at Wellesley College. Although she moved up the academic ladder to professor she became a controversial teacher, and upon her retirement was not appointed professor emerita. Her views were unorthodox and, as an adult, she did not affiliate with any religion and seldom attended college chapel. She also refused to wear the long skirts that were fashionable, and was on the cutting edge of many social concerns. These causes included women's issues such as suffrage and dress reform and the temperance movement, as well as labor reform, and various socialist causes. An outspoken political radical, Hayes supported the labor union movement and preached the right of workers to share in profits. In 1912, she was the Socialist Party candidate for Secretary of State in Massachusetts—of course, in those days before women's suffrage, no woman could vote for her. She helped raise money for Russian orphans during the anticommunist mania in the United States, and wrote and published a monthly journal, *The Relay,* that discussed current events as well as various scientific subjects. At the age of seventy-six, she was arrested for marching in protest against the execution of Nicola Sacco and Bartolomeo Vanzetti, and became a defendant in the American Civil Liberties Union's (ACLU) test case regarding the legality of the arrests. She won the case on appeal. In 1930, she read a paper entitled "Is Science Becoming Religious?" at the New York ACLU meeting. The year before her death, she moved to West Park, New York, to teach in a new school for women workers in industry.

Hayes was, indeed, a social radical, and her political activities took considerable time from her mathematical work. Most of her publications in mathematics were pedagogical.

She published four textbooks. Her standards were predictably high, and over half of the students who used her new trigonometry book received D's or F's. Many students, nevertheless, appreciated her teaching. She had several original ideas in astronomy, a subject that interested her especially. She studied at the Leander McCormick Observatory at the University of Virginia where she determined the orbit of an asteroid, Minor Planet 267. In an article in *Science,* she suggested that a newly discovered Comet *a* could be an asteroid. She urged girls and women to study science and mathematics and was critical of the elective system, which allowed girls to avoid these subjects.   JH/MBO

PRIMARY SOURCES
Hayes, Ellen Amanda. *Lessons on Higher Algebra.* Boston: F. I. Brown, 1891.
———. *Elementary Trigonometry.* Boston: J. S. Cushing & Co., 1896.
———. "Comet *a* 1904." *Science* 19 (27 May 1904): 833–834.
———. "Women and Scientific Research." *Science* 32 (16 December 1910): 864–866.
Archives at Wellesley College.

SECONDARY SOURCES
Gordon, Geraldine. "Ellen Hayes: 1851–1930." *The Wellesley Magazine* (February 1931): 151–152.

STANDARD SOURCES
Bailey; Grinstein and Campbell (article by Ann Moskol).

HAYNER, LUCY JULIA (1898–1971)

U.S. physicist. Born 15 January 1898 in Haynerville, N.Y. Married Bernhard Kurrelmeyer (1927). One son. Educate Barnard College, Columbia University (A.B., 1919; A.M., 1920; Ph.D., 1925); Barnard College, Columbia, fellowship (1924–1925). Professional experience: Columbia University, assistant in physics (1920–1924; 1929–1931), instructor (1931–1940), associate (1940–1946), assistant professor (1946–1952), associate professor (1952–1963), professor (from 1963); General Electric Company, physicist (1925–1928). Died in 1971.

Lucy Hayner earned all three of her degrees at Columbia University and spent most of her career there, with the exception of the three years when she worked at General Electric with KATHARINE BLODGETT and Irving Langmuir. While at General Electric, she worked on problems of electron emission in vacuum tubes.

She returned to Columbia, teaching in the Ernest Kempton Adams Laboratory, which she headed for many years until her retirement in 1966. She designed and constructed a circular slide rule of a twenty–inch diameter with very precise Braille markings, making it possible for blind students to equal the exactness of seeing students. She was involved in research in atomic and electron physics, sometimes working jointly with her husband.

She was a member of the Physical Society, she worked on the time of persistence of radiation in mercury vapor, shot effects at about one hundred kilocycles, dielectric constants of gases, and the recombination spectrum in mercury. JH/MBO

PRIMARY SOURCES
Hayner, Lucy Julia. *The Persistence of the Radiation Excited in Mercury Vapor.* Corning, N.Y.: n.p., 1925. Ph.D. dissertation.

SECONDARY SOURCES
New York Times, 25 September 1971. Obituary notice.

STANDARD SOURCES
AMS 5–8, P 9, P&B 10–11; Rossiter 1982.

HAYWARD, IDA MARGARET (1872–1949)
British botanist. Born 1872 in Trowbridge, Wiltshire. Honors and memberships: Fellow, Linnean Society, (1910); Fellow, Botanical Society of Edenburgh, (1913). Died 2 October 1949 in Galashiels, Scotland.

Ida Hayward's interest in adventitious flora was sparked by the connection of her family with the woolen trade. Her uncle, William Sanderson, had observed great problems from prickly fruits and seeds in imported wool from Australia, New Zealand, and South America that survived drastic treatment in the woolen mills. Her father suggested to her the alien (non-native) plants around the river Tweed were important, where many of the plants from the wool process were washed and, subsequently, germinated. Hayward did an exhaustive survey of these plants, which was published with the botanist Claridge Druce. Whereas Druce did most of the identification, Hayward did the collecting and included many important observations. They even show the penetration of some of the fruits into the skin of the sheep. The herbarium on which the book was based was given to the Royal Botanic Garden, Edinburgh. Her work on aliens came to an end when a new wool-cleaning process was developed, and she turned to a study of the natural history of the Scottish Borders. She became interested in photography, and gave popular lectures on the scenery and plants of the area. She traveled to South America and South Africa and secured excellent records of botanical subjects.
JH/MBO

PRIMARY SOURCES
Hayward, Ida, with Claridge Druce. *The Adventive Flora of Tweedside.* Arbroath: T. Buncle, 1919.

SECONDARY SOURCES
Smith, William Wright. "Ida Margaret Hayward." *Proceedings of the Linnaean Society* 162 (1949–1950): 105–106.
Watsonia 1, no. 5 (1950): 324.

HAYWOOD, CHARLOTTE (1898?–1971)
U.S. marine physiologist. Born around 1898. Educated Mount Holyoke College (A.B., 1919); Brown University (M.A.); University of Pennsylvania (Ph.D.). Professional experience: Mount Holyoke, faculty (1921–1924, 1930–1961), department of physiology, chair (from 1940); Vassar College, instructor of physiology (1924–1927). Died 1971.

Charlotte Haywood's physician father came from a patrician New England family. As a child, she accompanied his buggy as he visited his patients. After obtaining a bachelor's degree from Mount Holyoke College, Haywood went to Brown University, where she earned a master's degree. Upon receiving this degree, she went to the University of Pennsylvania, where she received a doctoral degree. Having completed this degree, she joined the Mount Holyoke faculty as an instructor of physiology. After three years at Holyoke, she taught at Vassar College for three years as an instructor in physiology. After spending a short time teaching at Brown, she returned to Mount Holyoke where she began an association with ABBY TURNER who remained her mentor and who caried on CORNELIA CLAPP's scientific tradition.

Haywood spent most summers, except for those spent in European laboratories, at the Marine Biological Laboratory at Woods Hole, beginning in 1924, when she came as a physiology student. She was a member of Marine Biological Laboratory (MBL.) Corporation from 1928 to 1971, attending meetings until 1970. She expressed her love of flowers through photography.

Haywood was one of the first members of American Physiological Society. A list of her publications from the MBL includes articles on carbon dioxide effects on cells; on fish liver metabolism; effects of argon on sea urchin egg cleavage at high pressure. Doing research at the University of Rochester for the U.S. Navy, Haywood studied the physiological effects of deep sea diving. She obtained a 1958 Public Health Service grant to study effects of increased carbon dioxide on respiration of women. JH/MBO

PRIMARY SOURCES
Haywood, Charlotte. "Carbon Dioxide as a Narcotic Agent . . . The Effect of Carbon Dioxide upon the Contraction of

Striated Muscle of the Frog." *Biological Bulletin* 53, no. 6 (1927): 450–464.

———. With W. S. Root. "A Quantitative Study of the Effect of Carbon Dioxide upon the Cleavage Rate of the Arbacia Egg." *Biological Bulletin* 59 (1930): 63–70.

———. With R. Höber. "The Permeability of the Frog Liver to Certain Lipoid Insoluable Substances" (abstract). *Biological Bulletin* 69 (1935): 340.

SECONDARY SOURCES
Smith, Curtis J. "Charlotte Haywood." *Annual Report Marine Biological Laboratory*, 1971?

STANDARD SOURCES
AMS 5–8, P&B 10–11; *NAW* unused.

HAZEN, ELIZABETH LEE (1885–1975)

U.S. mycolgist and microbiologist. Born 24 August 1885 in Rich, Miss., to Maggie (Harper) and William Edgar Hazen. Adopted by aunt and uncle. Two siblings. Educated rural public schools of Lula, Miss.; Mississippi Industrial Institute and College (now Mississipi University for Women) (B.S., 1910); Columbia University (M.S., 1917; Ph.D., 1927). Professional experience: Jackson (Miss.), High School, teacher (1910–1916?); Bacterial Diagnosis Laboratory, Division of Laboratories and Research, New York State Department of Health, New York City Branch, director (1931–1973); Albany Medical College, associate professor (concurrent appointment from 1958). Honors and memberships: Squibb Award in Chemotherapy (with Rachel Fuller Brown) (1955); honorary doctorates from Hobart College and William Smith College; Rhoda Benham Award, Medical Mycological Society of the Americas (with Rachel Brown) (1972); Chemical Pioneer Award, American Institute of Chemists (with Rachel Brown); posthumously inducted into National Inventors Hall of Fame (with Rachel Brown). Died 24 June 1975 in Seattle, Wash., of acute cardiac arrhythmia.

Both of Elizabeth Lee Hazen's Mississippi cotton farmer parents died before she was four years old. She and her brother (who died at the age of four) were adopted by an aunt and uncle. Hazen graduated with a bachelor of science degree and a certificate in dressmaking from what later became Mississippi University for Women. After graduation, she taught physics and biology for six years. As her interest in bacteriology accelerated, she decided to continue her education at Columbia University, where she earned a master's degree. After 1917, Hazen worked for a time at the army diagnostic laboratories and directed the bacteriological laboratory at a West Virginia hospital. During this time, she continued work for her doctoral degree from Columbia, which she earned at the age of forty-two. Hazen joined the Division of Laboratories and Research of the New York State Department of

Health in 1931, where she analyzed vaccines and serums and conducted microbiological research on infectious diseases.

During her early tenure with the department of health, Hazen traced outbreaks of anthrax and tularemia to their source. She is credited with being the first in North America to implicate *Clostridium botulinum* Type E toxin to deaths blamed on imported canned fish. Her interest in fungal diseases occurred at this time while working with RUTH GILBERT on moniliasis (candidiasis). Hazen set out to find a naturally occurring antifungal antibiotic that would be safe for human use. With children and members of the armed forces especially in mind, she noted that the accepted treatments were too toxic. She proceeded by creating a library of fungal cultures and slides. She tested two pathogenic fungi, *Candida albicans* and *Cryptococcus neoformans* against organisms from soil samples that she had screened for antifungal qualities. She began a fruitful collaboration with chemist RACHEL FULLER BROWN. Brown would extract, isolate, and purify the antifungal substance within the cultures that Hazen had made and return them to her for additional testing. Hazen isolated a streptomyces culture in a soil sample that relinquished two antifungal antibiotics. The first appeared to be identical with an existing substance, cycloheximide, which was used to inhibit fungal growth on golf course greens, but was too toxic to be used on humans. However, the second agent was a previously discovered antibiotic that prolonged the lives of mice infected with *C. neoformans*. It also proved to be potent against *C. albicans* and fourteen other fungi, including pathogenic forms. Hazen and Brown called the extracted substance Fungicidin. Hazen named the microorganism from which it was derived *Streptomyces noursei* in honor of the Nourse family on whose property the sample was found. Hazen insisted that no conclusion could be reached about Fungicidin's safety for humans, based on animal trials. E. R. Squibb and Sons first contacted Hazen about producing the material commercially. Hazen insisted that she shepherd the invention through its patenting in 1957 under the name Nystatin with the Research Corporation of New York. Squibb produced the drug under the name Mycostatin.

After being approved by the Federal Drug Administration, Nystatin proved effective against *Candida* infections, oral, vaginal, and skin. It was also useful in combating monilial infections of the intestinal tract. These infections sometimes developed after antibacterial antibiotics allowed the fungi to proliferate, particularly after intestinal surgery. It has proved effective in combating fungal infection in other species and is used to control fungal infections in fowl, in trees afflicted with Dutch Elm disease, and to protect bananas during shipment. One of its most exotic uses was in the restoration of paintings damaged by mildew. In 1958, Hazen accepted an associate professorship at Albany Medical College, while continuing to collaborate with Brown and work with the division of public health. At this time she recommenced her study on *Microsporum audouini,* the causative agent of scalp ringworm. Along with Frank Curtis Reed, she produced a textbook, *Laboratory Identification of Pathogenic Fungi Simplified.* She was a guest investigator in the Columbia University Medical Mycology Laboratory in 1960, where she gave scholarly lectures and also provided help to young research students.

The work of Hazen and Brown was widely recognized. Among many awards and honorary degrees, they received a singular honor, when, in 1994, they became the second and third woman to be inducted into the National Inventors Hall of Fame. They used the money, over $13 million in royalties, from the patent of Nystatin, to support the Research Corporation's own grant programs and to support basic research in biochemistry, microbiology, and immunology. Brown-Hazen funds were used to strengthen academic programs in the sciences and, in particular, those programs that advanced women's participation in sciences. The fund lasted until 1976, and was the most important support for research in medical mycology in the United States.   JH/MBO

PRIMARY SOURCES

Hazen, Elizabeth Lee. "General and Local Immunity to Ricin." *Journal of Immunology* 13 (1927): 171–218.

———. With Rachel Brown. "Two Antifungal Agents Produced by a Soil Actinommycete." *Science* 112 (1950): 423.

———. With Frank Curtis Reed. *Laboratory Identification of Pathogenic Fungi Simplified.* Springfield, Ill.: Charles C. Thomas, 1955.

The papers of Elizabeth Hazen and Rachel Brown are held at the Schlesinger Library, Radcliffe College.

SECONDARY SOURCES

Bacon, W. Stevenson. "Elizabeth Lee Hazen, 1885–1975." *Mycologia* 68 (1976): 961–969.

Baldwin, Richard S. *The Fungus Fighters: Two Women Scientists and Their Discovery.* Ithaca, N.Y.: Cornell University Press, 1981.

STANDARD SOURCES

Bailey; *Mothers and Daughters; NAW(M)* (article by Lewis P. Rubin); *Notable;* O'Hearn; Shearer and Shearer 1996.

HAZLETT, OLIVE CLIO (1890–1974)

U.S. mathematician. Educated Radcliffe College (A.B., 1912); University of Chicago (M.S., 1913; Ph.D., 1915). Professional experience: Bryn Mawr College, associate in mathematics (1916–1918); Mount Holyoke College, assistant professor (1918–1924), associate professor (1924–1925); University of Illinois, assistant professor (1925–1929), associate professor (1929–1959). Died 1974.

Olive Hazlett, an expert in linear algebra, earned her advanced degrees at the University of Chicago. After receiving her doctoral degree, she taught at Bryn Mawr College as an associate in mathematics. From Bryn Mawr, she moved to Mount Holyoke, progressing from assistant professor to associate professor. In 1925, she moved to the University of Illinois in order to have more research time. This move meant that she started again as an assistant professor. Rossiter mentions her difficulties at the University of Illinois and her lengthy mental illness. During 1928–1929, Hazlett studied in Italy, Switzerland, and Germany on a Guggenheim fellowship. The fellowship was extended for an additional year, during which time she was promoted to associate professor, a rank she retained until her retirement.

Active in professional societies, Hazlett was associate editor of the *Transactions of the American Mathematical Society* and served on its council from 1926 to 1928. She was elected a Fellow of the American Association for the Advancement of Science and was a member of the American Mathematical Society and the New York Academy of Sciences.

Hazlett's major research interest was in linear algebra and in modular invariants. She published a number of papers in these areas   JH/MBO

SECONDARY SOURCES

New York Times, 12 March 1974. Obituary notice.

STANDARD SOURCES

AMS 4–7; Bailey; Kass-Simon and Farnes (includes photograph); *Notable Mathematicians; Rossiter 1982.*

HEARST, PHOEBE (APPERSON) (1842–1919)

U.S. philanthropist. Born 3 December 1842 in Franklin County, Mo. to Drucilla (Whitmire) and Randolph Walker Apperson. Two siblings. Married George Hearst (1862). One child, William Randolph. Educated local school; St. James, Mo., school. Died 13 April 1919.

Although Phoebe Apperson Hearst was not a scientist herself, her philanthropic activities made many scientific ventures possible, particularly in the field of anthropology. Born into a Missouri farm family and with little formal education, she met and married George Hearst, twenty-two years her senior, and went with him to San Francisco. The couple's only child, William Randolph, was born in 1863. In San Francisco, Phoebe Hearst soon learned the art of gracious entertaining. Her self-improvement activities included studying architecture, music, and French. Travel, often with her young son, rounded out her education. Although George Hearst began his career in mining, his fortune grew as he expanded into oil, real estate, newspaper publishing, and politics.

After a brief but wrenching period of financial reverses when they were forced to sell their house, Phoebe Hearst began to concentrate on various philanthropic activities. During the time her husband was a senator from California and the couple lived in Washington, D.C., she donated much time and money to educational projects. However, as early as 1895, she became interested in archeology and anthropology, contributing to the support of various expeditions. In that year she financed an expedition to excavate a site in Florida where an ancient civilization had been reported. From this beginning, she financed expeditions to Italy, Mexico, Russia, and Egypt. Her interest was also personal, for she visited one of the excavation sites in Egypt. Hearst specified that artifacts collected from these excavations be deposited at the University of California. In order to have a proper place to store these items, Hearst gave money for the establishment of a university museum (1901). She also gave money to establish a department of anthropology at the University of California. But before she made the large investment, she solicited advice from anthropologist ZELIA NUTTALL, whom she had helped with certain of Nuttall's pet projects. Hearst's interest in anthropology included friendships with some of the foremost women anthropologists of the period. Nuttall brought ALICE FLETCHER and Phoebe Hearst together.   JH/MBO

SECONDARY SOURCES

Black, Winifred. *The Life and Personality of Phoebe Apperson Hearst.* San Francisco: Printed for W. R. Hearst and J. H. Nash, 1928.

Mark, Joan. *A Stranger in Her Native Land: Alice Fletcher and the American Indians.* Lincoln: University of Nebraska Press, 1988. Discusses the relationship between Hearst, Fletcher, and Nuttall on page 282 ff.

STANDARD SOURCES

NAW (article by Rodman Wilson Paul).

HEATH, DAISY WINIFRED (1875–1954)

U.S. geology editor and indexer. Born 29 May 1875 in Hartford, Conn., to Susan Elizabeth Morehouse Heath and Alfred Russell Heath. At least one sister, Lilian. Never married. Educated Cornell University (Ph.D., 1900). Died 27 August 1954 in Tulsa, Okla.

Daisy Heath was not a professional geologist in the usual sense, but she applied her skills to editing journals and producing indexes for the *Journal of Geology* and the *Bulletin of the American Association of Petroleum Geologists.*

Born in Hartford, Connecticut, Heath moved as a two-and-a-half-year-old child to Danbury, Connecticut, and then to Brooklyn, where her father was employed by Funk and Wagnalls. In 1891, they moved to Staten Island. Heath at-

tended Cornell, where she earned a bachelor of philosophy degree, then remained for a year to study English. When the Heath family moved to Chicago in 1900, Daisy took stenographic courses and then held positions with several businesses. After the death of her parents, she found a more compatible position. At this time, T. C. Chamberlin was editing a new journal to be published by the University of Chicago Press. She assisted various geology professors with secretarial and editorial work. She already had English and editing skills and in 1908 amd 1909 took Wallace W. Atwood's and Rollin Chamberlin's courses in geology to improve her knowledge of this field. She remained connected with the department of geology and the *Journal of Geology* for twenty years. In 1922, Heath changed positions, serving as editorial secretary for the American Association of Petroleum Geologists' *Bulletin.* In 1926, the AAPG established its headquarters in Tulsa, Oklahoma, and the next year the *Bulletin* printing was moved to that city. Daisy Heath had been living with her sister in Chicago and the two moved to Tulsa where Daisy became the full-time editorial secretary.

Heath's work, although primarily with the *Bulletin,* also included editing papers of the symposia and occasional books published by the association. She also compiled the annual and comprehensive ten-year indexes for this journal; these three indexes appeared in 1927, 1937, and 1945. She was working on the next index when she died with an unfinished page remaining in her typewriter. Heath enjoyed landscape painting, playing the piano, flying, and church work. Although she was never a member of the AAPG, Heath's work was very important in the history of geology.   CK

SECONDARY SOURCES

Hull, J. P. D. "Daisy Winifred Heath (1875–1954)." *Bulletin of the American Association of Petroleum Geologists* 30, no. 1, (1955): 144–147.

STANDARD SOURCES

Sarjeant.

HEBB, CATHERINE OLDING (1911–1978)

Canadian/British physiologist. Born in Chester, Nova Scotia, to Clara (Olding) and Arthur Morison Hebb. Three brothers. Educated: Dalhousie University (A.B., 1932; M.A., 1933); McGill University (Ph.D., 1937). Professional experience: McGill University postdoctoral fellowship (1937–1938); Edinburgh University, Department of Physiology, junior fellow (1938–1941), research fellow (funded by Air Ministry) (1941–1945); Cambridge University, Physiological Laboratory, junior fellow (1941–1946); University of Edinburgh, university lecturer (1946–1951); Agricultural Research Council Institute of Animal Physiology, Department of Physiology, researcher (1952–1960),

Sub-Department of Chemical Physiology, head (1960–1965), Department of Physiology, head (1966–1971), researcher (1972–1976). Retired 1976. Honors and memberships: Banting Research Fellowship (1933); Hosmer Research Fellowship (1937); Beit Memorial Junior Fellowship (1938–1941); Beit Fourth Year Fellowship (1945); Lucy Cavendish College, Cambridge, Fellow (1968); Cambridge University, honorary degree (1968); Institute of Biology, Fellow; Physiological Society, Fellow, committee member (1963–1967). Editorial boards: Journal of Physiology (1961–1965), Quarterly Journal of Physiology (1951–1964), International Review of Neurobiology (1958–1977), Journal of Neurochemistry (1962–1968). Died 1978.

Catherine Olding Hebb, a Canadian-British physiologist, was born into a family living in Chester, Nova Scotia, where both of her parents practiced as physicians. Her older brother, Donald Oldring Hebb, also became a notable physiologist and psychologist at McGill University. Hebb initially followed in her brother's footsteps, attending Dalhousie University and studying biology, staying on to take a master's in pharmacology. She won scholarships throughout her undergraduate career, and then fellowships that funded her graduate work in physiology with B. P. Babkin, a pupil of Pavlov. During this period, she published her first notable paper, with Babkin, on the presence of glucose in the salivary glands after treatment with adrenaline.

After obtaining her doctorate, Hebb was awarded a Beit fellowship. She left Canada to move to the department of physiology at Edinburgh University, where she began a long and fruitful collaboration with I. de Burgh Daly on pulmonary physiology. She also did some teaching in the department, and served as a senior medical lecturer to the Polish medical faculty, in exile in Edinburgh. LILIAN MARY PICKFORD was a lecturer in the Edinburgh department at the same time, researching the effects of acetylcholine on urinary flow. Soon after World War II broke out, Daly's laboratory began to do research for the Air Ministry into the effects of decompression as an aspect of high-altitude flying and also on the effects of phosogene gas on the lungs. Much of this remained classified and unpublished.

After the war, Hebb took her postponed fourth year Beit Memorial Fellowship to go to Cambridge, where she worked with Feldberg on acetylcholine synthesis and became deeply interested in ACh effects on the physiology of nerves. On her return to Edinburgh as a university lecturer, she began to do more extensive research on acetycholine metabolism, and soon resigned her lectureship to join Daly in the Agricultural Research Council Institute at Babraham in his new physiology department. There she did extensive biochemical and physiological work on ACh as a neurotransmitter.

After five years, Daly asked Hebb to head the subdepartment of chemical physiology, and in 1965, she took over as head of the Department of Physiology. She was a very effective head, but soon showed signs of developing Parkinsonism, and she resigned her position as head at the age of sixty-three because of ill health. She continued to do research on her chosen subjects for the next five years. She was elected a Fellow of Lucy Cavendish College, Cambridge, and also awarded an honorary master's from Cambridge.

During her research life, Hebb had been very active on the publication board of many physiology and neuroscience journals. She was sympathetic to the problems of Eastern European scientists as an outgrowth of her experiences with Babkin and the Polish medical faculty, and her first-hand encounters with other Polish scientists during a trip to Warsaw. She was generous in her support of their attempts to publish.

Hebb had a close friendship with an Edinburgh woman, Irene Roddick, who joined her in Babraham. The two shared a house together, where Hebb often entertained her colleagues. Hebb was generous in her support of other scientists, and proposed a loan fund to be created out of funds raised for her retirement to serve as bridging grants for colleagues awaiting grants to come through.

Just before her death, two universities in Canada, McGill and Edmonton, were planning to award her honorary degrees. The delay at McGill (because her brother was still dean) prevented the award being bestowed in time.   JH/MBO

PRIMARY SOURCES

Hebb, Catherine O. With I. de Burgh Daly et al. "Evaluation of Bronchomotor and Pulmonary Vasomotor Activity by Means of Perfused Living Animal under Negative Pressure Ventilation." *Quarterly Journal of Experimental Physiology* 31 (1942): 227–262.

———. With B. N. Smallman. "Intracellular Distribution of Choline Acetylase." *Journal of Physiology* 134: (1956) 385–392.

———. With V. P. Whittaker. "Intracellular Distribution of Acetylcholine and Choline Acetylase." *Journal of Physiology* 142 (1958): 187–196.

———. With I. de Burgh Daly. *Pulmonary and Bronchial Vascular Systems.* Monographs of the Physiological Society, no. 16. London: Edward Arnold, 1966.

———. "Biosynthesis of Acetylcholine in Nervous Tissue." *Physiological Reviews* 52 (1972): 918–987.

STANDARD SOURCES
Women Physiologists.

HEBEL, MEDICIENNE (fl. 1397)
German healer. Flourished 1397.

This fourteenth-century German physician, Hebel, was one of fifteen medical women licensed to practice in Frankfurt-am-Main.   JH/MBO

HECKTER, MARIA (0000–0000)
See Strassmann, Maria C. Heckter.

HEDGES, FLORENCE (1878–?)
U.S. botanist. Born 24 August 1878 in Lansing, Mich. Educated University of Michigan (A.B., 1901). Professional experience: University of Michigan, assistant botanist (1901–1902); U.S. Department of Agriculture, Bureau of Plant Industry, assistant expert (1902), scientific assistant (1903–1909), assistant pathologist (1909–1927), associate pathologist (1927–1944). Retired 1944. Death date unknown.

Florence Hedges had only a bachelor's degree, but she managed to pursue a satisfying career with the U.S. Department of Agriculture, as did many other women. She was a member of the Phytopathology Society and the Botanical Society of Washington. She was treasurer of the latter organization in 1925. Her general research topic was bacteriology and she worked specifically on bacterial diseases of leguminous plants and diseases of citrus trees.

JH/MBO

PRIMARY SOURCE
Hedges, Florence. *A Knot of Citrus Trees Caused by Sphaeropsis Tumefaciens.* Washington, D.C.: U. S. Government Printing Office, 1912.

STANDARD SOURCES
AMS 3–8.

HEDWIG OF SILESIA, SAINT (1174–1243)
German/Polish healer. Born 1174. Married Duke Henry of Silesia. Several children. Educated convent of Franken, Germany. Died 1243.

At age thirteen, Hedwig married Duke Henry of Silesia. Although she lost her first two children, she eventually had several more, some of whom assisted her in the hospitals and convents she founded. Especially interested in helping lepers, she was credited with miracles of healing. Supposedly she brought a hanged man back to life. Hedwig died in 1243 and was canonized by 1267.

JH/MBO

SECONDARY SOURCES
Echols and Williams.

HEERMANN, MARGARETA (1898–1957)
Hungarian geologist. Born 1898 in Kantorjanosi, Hungary. Father, estate agent. Two siblings, one older brother, Julius, and one younger sister. Educated University of Budapest (diploma, 1918?); University of Budapest, doctorate (1952?). Professional experience: private school and various city schools, teacher (1923); Hungarian National Museum, botany department, researcher, (1929–1934), mineralogic-petrographic department, researcher, (from 1934). Died 8 September 1958.

Margareta Heermann, the daughter of an estate agent who saw to it that his three children were well educated, had a difficult life. Both Margareta and her older brother, Julius, studied at the University of Budapest. Her younger sister was consumptive and remained at her parents' home. At the university, Margareta first studied mathematics and physics and then natural sciences and geography. In 1918, her father and mother died of Spanish influenza and her brother died in 1920 "in tragic circumstances." These deaths made Margareta the sole caretaker for her increasingly sick sister. She taught in various city schools, after which she went to Belgium to supervise Hungarian children at a recovery spa there from 1923 to 1925. She returned home and again taught in private schools and was active in administrative work for the council for trade-school instruction (1926–1928). In 1929, her sister died, and Heermann received her first museum position. At first she was involved with administrative work in the botanical department but in 1934 moved to the mineralogic-petrographic department, where she remained for the rest of her career. On the basis of her doctoral dissertation, "Contributons to the Knowledge of Eruptive Rocks of the Bükk Mountain," she passed her doctoral examinations *summa cum laude* in Mineralogy-Petrography, Geology, and Botany. In recognition for her petrographic studies, she also obtained the *Kandidaten* title in geologic and mineralogic sciences.

Much of Heermann's research was on mineral deposits in Hungary, which would be important for ore prospecting. Although from the 1950s onward, she began to investigate sedimentary rock, she always returned to her favorite theme, the investigation of magma rock. She attained valuable results in micromineralogic research of sedimentary rocks. She established in her first sedimentary petrographic work the marine origins of glauconite-bearing sandstone of Ipolytarnoc. She published many articles on her studies of the Pannonian sand, found at the foot of the Bükk and Matra mountains. She carefully studied the mineral content of these sands. She also carried on micromineralogic research on the material in mine deposits

CK

SECONDARY SOURCES

Todady, L. "Erinnerung an Margareta Herrmann (1898–1957)." *Annales Historico-Naturales Musei Nationalis Hungarici* n.s. 9, no. 50 (1958): 7–10.

HEFFERAN, MARY (1873–?)

U.S. bacteriologist. Born 24 June 1873 in Eastmanville, Mich. Educated Wellesley College (A.B., 1896; A.M., 1898); University of Chicago (fellow; 1899–1902; Ph.D., 1903). Professional experience: Bacteriological Museum, Chicago, curator (1903–1904), assistant and curator (1904–1910).

After Mary Hefferan earned her doctoral degree from the University of Chicago, she became a curator at the Bacteriological Museum, Chicago. She did research on zoological grafting, red chromogenic organisms, agglutinative relations in a group of non-pathenogenic organisms, *Bacillus bulgaricus,* and *Anopheles* in Michigan.   JH/MBO

PRIMARY SOURCES

Hefferan, Mary. "Variation in the Teeth of Nereis." *Biological Bulletin* 2, no. 3 (1900).
———. *A Comparative and Experimental Study of Bacilli Producing Red Pigment.* Jena: G. Fischer, 1904.

STANDARD SOURCES

AMS 1–7; Bailey.

HEIDBREDER, EDNA FRANCES (1890–1985)

U.S. psychologist. Born 1 May 1890 in Quincy, Ill., to Mathilda Emelie (Meyer) and William Henry Heidbreder. Four siblings. Educated Knox College (A.B., 1911); University of Wisconsin (A.M., 1918); Columbia University (Ph.D. in psychology, 1924). Professional experience: University of Minnesota, instructor of psychology (1923–1926), assistant professor (1926–1928), associate professor (1928–1934); Wellesley College, professor of psychology (1945–1955); emerita professor (from 1955); Radcliffe College, Radcliffe Seminars (1955–1961); Journal of Abnormal & Social Psychology, associate editor; American Psychological Association representative to the National Research Council (1944–1947). Honors and memberships: American Association for the Advancement of Science (president, section of psychology, 1947); American Psychological Association, Fellow (member, Council of Directors, 1940, 1942–1944, and president, Division on General Psychology, 1950); Sigma Xi; Eastern Psychological Association, Fellow (president, 1944); New York Academy of Sciences, Fellow. Died 19 February 1985.

Edna Heidbreder was born and raised in Quincy, Illinois, in a family of German descent. She was the third of five children. Edna graduated from Quincy High in 1907 and went on to Knox College, a small, liberal arts college in Galesburg, Illinois, to receive her bachelor's degree. She was an outstanding student—honors in both Latin and biology, Phi Beta Kappa, commencement speaker, and at least two of her teachers at Knox encouraged her to pursue a graduate degree. However, she returned to Quincy to teach high school. During those years she was busy with her high school students and social and community activities, but continued to read in philosophy and psychology—areas that had intrigued her at Knox and raised questions in her mind for which she sought answers. At some point, Heidbreder decided to return to college, chosing the University of Wisconsin, which had been strongly recommended to her by her philosophy/psychology professor at Knox. Working for her master's degree (1918), Heidbreder studied experimental psychology with Joseph Jastrow. The young graduate student who directed her experimental lab was Clark Hull, who later became a renowned learning theorist. Heidbreder credits Hull with stimulating her thinking on theories of concept formation. In 1921, seeking to broaden her exposure to different approaches to psychology, she traveled to New York City and Columbia University to begin work toward a doctorate in psychology (1924). At Columbia, she studied with R. S. Woodworth, H. L. Hollingworth, A. T. Poffenberger, H. E. Garrett, and John Dewey. Her doctoral dissertation was entitled, "An Experimental Study of Thinking."

Heidbreder's first professional position was at the University of Minnesota, where she remained for ten years, teaching and conducting experiments. Several of the theories that were central to her life's work germinated at Minnesota. She began her experiments on the attainment of concepts; she worked on aspects of the thinking process and problem solving; she conducted studies that included introversion, extroversion, and inferiority attitudes as measured by rating scales. She participated in the publication of *The Minnesota Mechanical Ability Tests.* Perhaps most important, she wrote her book *Seven Psychologies* (1933). This history and analysis of seven systems of psychology was praised by Edwin G. Boring, the preeminent historian of psychology, "for range, clarity, and lack of bias, this book is without peer among the very few that exist." It has been used as a text by more generations of psychologists than any other unrevised book and has been in continuous print since 1933. Mary Henle and John Sullivan wrote of *Seven Psychologies* in a review in 1973 that "the astonishing thing about reading this volume today is the impression that one is reading a *contemporary* book," due perhaps to the fact that Heidbreder exposed the innermost core of each system; the essence that remains at the base of subsequent changes.

In 1934, Heidbreder accepted a teaching position at Wellesley College, where she remained until her retirement in 1955. She was ideal successor to the pioneering ELEANOR GAMBLE, and was vitally interested in encouraging and improving education for women. A resourceful and stimulating teacher, she also continued her research on the attainment of concepts, which she published as a series of nine articles between 1946 and 1955. Her detailed investigations of stimulus variables in concept formation inspired others by exposing the complexity of cognitive response and raising questions for further study. She published several papers on systematic psychology, which were evaluations of contributions to psychological theory.

In 1971, Heidbreder was elected the first honorary member of Cheiron, the International Society for the History of the Behavioral and Social Sciences. Several of her papers as well as a bibliography of all her published works to 1972 appeared in *Historical Conceptions of Psychology* (1973), edited by Mary Henle, J. Jaynes, and J. J. Sullivan, and dedicated to Heidbreder. She was one of thirty-seven persons honored in 1967 at the American Psychological Association's seventy-fifth anniversary celebration with a certificate for "a distinguished lifetime's contribution to psychology as a science and as a profession." Edna Heidbreder died in Bedford, Massachusetts, 19 February 1985, just short of her ninety-fifth birthday.

K M

PRIMARY SOURCES

Heidbreder, Edna. *An Experimental Study of Thinking.* Archives of psychology, no. 73. New York, 1924.
———, ed. With D. G. Paterson, R. M. Elliott, D. Anderson, and H. Toops. *The Minnesota Mechanical Ability Tests.* Minneapolis: University at Minnesota Press, 1930.
———. *Seven Psychologies.* New York: Century, 1933.
———. With others. "The Attainment of Concepts Series." "I: Terminology and Methodology" and "II: The Problem." *Journal of General Psychology* 35 (1946); "III: The Process." *Journal of Psychology* 24 (1947); "IV: Regularities and Levels." *Journal of Psychology* 25 (1948); "V: Critical Features and Contexts." *Journal of Psychology* 26 (1948); "VI: Exploratory Experiments on Conceptualization at Perceptual Levels." *Journal of Psychology* 26 (1948); "VII: Conceptual Achievements during Card-Sorting." *Journal of Psychology* 27 (1949); "VIII: Conceptualization of Verbally Indicated Instances." *Journal of Psychology* 27 (1949); "IX: Semantic Efficiency and Concept-Attainment." *Journal of Psychology* 40 (1955).
———. *Historical Conceptions of Psychology.* New York: Springer, 1973. Edited by Mary Henle, J. Jaynes, and J. J. Sullivan and dedicated to Heidbreder, this is a selection of Heidbreder's essays and bibliography of her works.

SECONDARY SOURCES

Furumoto, Laurel. "Edna Heidbreder: Systematic and Cognitive Psychologist." *Psychology of Women Quarterly* 5 (1980): 94–102.
Henle, Mary. "Edna Heidbreder (1890–1985)." *American Psychologist* 42 (1987): 94–95. Obituary notice.
Henle, M., and J. Sullivan. "Seven Psychologies Revisited." *Journal of the History of the Behavioral Sciences,* 10 (1974): 40–46.
Kimble, G. A., M. Wertheimer, and C. L. White, eds. *Portraits of Pioneers in Psychology.* Washington, D.C.: American Psychology Association, 1991. Heidbreder discussed on pages 293–305.

STANDARD SOURCES

AMS 4–8, S&B 9–11; Debus; O'Connell and Russo 1990; *Psychological Register,* 1932.

HEIMANN, BERTA (fl. 1914)

German physicist and chemist. Professional experience: Physical-Chemical Institute, Berlin University, researcher.

ELLEN GLEDITSCH's finding of discrepancies in the ratio of radium to uranium in minerals prompted reassessments by other chemists. Working at Berlin University's Physical-Chemical Institute, Heimann and the prominent chemist Willy Marckwald determined the ratio of radium to uranium in pitchblendes from various sources. They found this ratio to be constant, in agreement with the disintegration theory of radioactivity. Heimann also determined the half life of thorium.

M M

PRIMARY SOURCES

Heimann, Berta. With Willy Marckwald. "Über den Radiumgehalt von Pechblende." *Jahrbuch der Radioaktivität und Elektronik* 10 (1913): 299–323.
———. With Willy Marckwald. *Physikalische Zeitschrift* 14 (1913): 303–305.
———. "Über die Lebensdauer des Thoriums." *Akademie der Wissenschaften, Vienna. Sitzungsberichte 2a* 123 (1914): 1369–1372.

STANDARD SOURCES

Meyer and von Schweidler.

HEIMANN, PAULA (1899–1982)

German/British psychoanalyst. Born 1899. Educated Berlin Institute of Psychoanalysis; University of London (M.D.?, 1937). Analyzed by Theodor Reik. Honors and memberships: Berlin Psycho-Analytic Society, associate member (1932). Died 1982.

German born and educated, Paula Heimann trained at the Berlin Institute of Psychoanalysis, where she was analyzed by Theodor Reik. She fled Germany in 1933 and went to London at the invitation of Ernest Jones, Freud's major English disciple. In that same year she was elected an associate member of the British Psychoanalytical Society. Unlike many psychoanalysts in Britain, she trained in medicine at the University of London. She was analyzed by MELANIE KLEIN, who had broken away from the Freudian group. Heimann became Klein's loyal supporter in the often vituperative controversy with the Freudians. She became one of the presenters of the Kleinian point of view during the scientific controversies of the 1940s. She became a training analyst in 1944 and played an important role in the society, becoming Joint Training Secretary with Hedwig Hoffer in 1954.

In her later years, Heimann broke with Klein, following a dispute over Klein's methods. She became an independent following this disagreement. JH/MBO

PRIMARY SOURCES

Heimann, Paula. *About Children and Children-No-Longer: Collected Papers 1942–1980, Paula Heimann.* Ed. Margret Tonnesmann. London: New York: Routledge, 1989 (New Library of Psychoanalysis, vol.10).

SECONDARY SOURCES

King, Pearl, and Riccardo Steiner, eds. *The Freud-Klein Controversies, 1941–1945.* London: Tavistock/Routledge, 1991.

HEIM-VÖGTLIN, MARIE (1845–1916)

Swiss physician. Born 1845 in Aargau, Switzerland, to Henriette (Benker) and Pfarrer Julius Vögtlin. Married Albert Heim. Educated by her parents; Herrnhuter Institut Montmirail bei Neuenburg; University of Zurich (1868–1874; doctorate 1874). Professional experience: Brugger Kinderhospital, assistant; Armenschule, assistant; Leipzig and Dresden, assistant physician (1874–?); private practice for women and children, Zurich; participated in the opening of the Zurich Women's Hospital (1901). Died 7 November 1916 in Zürich.

Marie Heim-Vögtlin was a pioneer woman physician. There was a good deal of opposition to her entry into the University of Zurich, but in 1868 she became the first Swiss woman to enter the Faculty of Medicine at the University of Zurich. Six years later, she became the first Swiss woman to pass the state medical examination, a feat that she accomplished with honors. Her dissertation, "Ueber den Befund der Genitalien im Wochenbett," earned her a doctoral degree.

Although the exact date is not known, Vögtlin married her colleague Albert Heim after she earned her degree. She opened a successful private practice for women and children,

and when the Zurich Women's Hospital opened in 1901 she was a staunch supporter. Most of her writings are popular works for women and children. JH/MBO

SECONDARY SOURCES

Oelsner, Elise. *Die Leistung der deutschen Frau in den letzten vierhundert Jahren.* Guhrau, 1894.

Siebel, Johanna. *Das Leben von Frau Dr. Marie Heim-Vögtlin, der ersten Schweizer Aerztin (1845–1916).* Leipzig: Rascher, 1925.

STANDARD SOURCES

Strohmeier.

HEINLEIN, JULIA ELIZABETH HEIL (1895–?)

U.S. child psychologist. Born 9 October 1895 in Baltimore, Md. Married (1927). Educated Johns Hopkins (B.S.,1926; A.M., 1928; Ph.D., 1929). Professional experience: Florida State University, assistant professor of child psychology (1930–1935), director of university nursery school (1935–1937, 1943–1947); Berea College, assistant professor of psychology (1948–1950); Nebraska Wesleyan, associate professor (1950–1952); University of North Carolina, Greensboro, assistant professor (1952–1959), associate professor (1959–1962), emerita associate professor (1962–1982).

Julia Heinlein, a child psychologist, was born at the end of the nineteenth century. She did her undergraduate and graduate training at Johns Hopkins University near her home in Baltimore. She obtained a prestigious Laura Spelman Rockefeller Foundation Fellowship from 1927 to 1928 to study psychology at the master's level. The same year that she began her graduate work she was married. She continued for her doctoral degree, which she received the following year.

Her research interests centered on child creativity, emotional adjustment, and manipulative skills. It was not surprising that when she went to teach at Florida State University, she became director of the nursery school there as well. This position allowed Heinlein and her students to study child development. When she left Florida State, she had a series of temporary positions until she was appointed assistant professor of psychology at the University of North Carolina, Greensboro. Here she progressed up the academic ladder to her highest position, associate professor, retiring emerita from this position in 1962. She continued to serve the university with vocational counseling until 1966. She was a Fellow of the American Psychological Association and a member of the Society for Research in Child Development and the International Council of Psychologists. KM

PRIMARY SOURCES

Heinlein, Julia. *Preferential Manipulation in Children.* Ph.D. diss., Johns Hopkins University, 1930.

———. *Study of Dexterity in Children.* In Comparative Psychology, monographs.

———. With Christian Paul Heinlein. "What Is the Role of ESP in Objective Testing at the College Level?" *Journal of Psychology* 46 (1958): 319–328.

STANDARD SOURCES

AMS 5–8, S&B 9–11.

HÉLÈNE, DUCHESS OF AOSTA
(fl. 19th century)

Belgian/Italian botanist. Flourished nineteenth century. Collected plants in Africa.

Hélène, Duchess of Aosta, collected plants in many parts of Africa, including areas around Lake Banguelo, Lake Kivu, and Lake Tanganyika, Lake Albert-Edouard, Lake Albert, and Lake Victoria. She also collected in the Congo, around the Nile river, and in Abyssinia. Hélène collected six new species. A series of printed drawings in the herbarium of the Jardin Botanique de l'État includes these new species that were described in 1913 by L. Buscalioni and R. Muschler. The drawings were published in a work by Maurizio Piscicelli in 1913.

JH/MBO

SECONDARY SOURCES

Buscalioni, L., and R. Muschler. *Engler's Botanische Jahrbuch* 49, nos. 3–5 (March and June 1913).

Pisicelli, Maurizio. *Nella Regione dei Lagni Equatoriali.* Naples: L. Pierro, 1913.

Schubert, B. G. and G. Troupin. *Taxon* 4 (1955): 94–96.

HELLMAN, JOHANNA (1889–?)

German/Swedish physician. Swedish citizenship (1945). Born 14 June 1889 in Nuremberg, Germany. One sister. Never married. One adopted child. Educated public school for girls; private school; University of Berlin; University of Kiel (M.D., 1914). Professional experience: Kiel University Hospital, replacing heads of various departments at municipal hospitals (1921–1929); private hospital in Berlin, surgeon (from 1929); Professor Sauerbruch's assistant (1929?-1932); Salvation Army Hospital, director (1932–1938); Surgical Hospital of Eskilstuna, Sweden, assistant (1944–1947); general surgical practice (from 1947); private practice (1950–1986). Death date unknown.

Born in Germany, Johanna Hellman earned a medical degree from the University of Kiel. She had first studied in Berlin and attended Professor R. Virchow's lectures. While attend-ing a lecture in surgery, she became certain that her goal was to be a surgeon. Surgery was an area with few women practitioners, and Hellman was told that a woman surgeon had no future whatever. Nevertheless the director of the University Surgical Hospital accepted her. While she continued with her surgical training, she worked in the hospital, gaining experience in all aspects of patient care. After World War I broke out, she remained at the hospital, passed her final licensing examination, and wrote her doctoral thesis. With the head surgeon, she began to perform major operations. During this time, Hellman became a substitute for the heads of various municipal hospitals. In 1920, she joined the Northwest German Surgical Society, and in 1925 became the first female member of the German Society for Surgery. As an assistant in a university hospital, she lived in the hospital proper for fifteen years.

Hellman accepted a position in a private hospital in Berlin in 1929, but was unhappy with the work. When she was offered a position as the assistant to the director of the university outpatient clinic, she accepted it. During vacations, she was a substitute in the municipal hospitals of Lauben and Warmbrunn and finally opened her own private practice in Berlin as a specialist in surgery, urology, and roentgenology. She applied for positions in various municipal hospitals in Berlin, but the politicians objected to her political views. She became the director of a Salvation Army Hospital in Berlin, where she remained until 1938, when she resigned because of the Nazi discrimination laws.

Hellman emigrated to Sweden, but as a refugee was not able to work in her field. She spent the time learning Swedish and caring for other people's children. When one of the families had a fourth child, they left its care entirely to Hellman. She adopted the little girl many years later. In 1944, she finally was allowed to work, and given an assistantship in the surgical hospital of Eskilstuna. Finally, in 1947, she was authorized to have a general surgical practice. It took many years for her reputation to win her patients. In spite of everything, she succeeded in building up a considerable practice. At the age of eighty-six, she was still actively practicing medicine.

KM

PRIMARY SOURCES

Hellman, Johanna. In Hellstedt, Autobiographies.

HELLSTEDT, LEONE MCGREGOR (1900–)

Canadian/Swedish physician. Born 19 January 1900 on a farm just outside Carnduff (Northwest Territories) to Mary (Roadhouse) and Matthew McGregor. Two surviving siblings. Married Folke Hellstedt (1932). Two children: one daughter and one son. Educated: one-room school, Tilston, Manitoba; home schooled; school in Alberta; Calgary high school; teacher's training school (graduated at top of class); University of Alberta (M.D., 1925); University of Minnesota (Ph.D., 1929); Zurich, psychoanalytic training (passed licensing examination); license in Sweden (1937). Professional experience: country schoolteacher; psychoanalyst (from ca. 1938)

Born in Canada's Northwest Territories, Leone McGregor moved often with her family, first to Tilston, Manitoba, then to a new town in Alberta where there was no school. Her mother home-schooled her until a new school was opened. The teacher was excellent and prepared her to enter the tenth grade at twelve years of age in Calgary, where the family had by then moved. She passed her senior matriculation when she was fifteen. She had to convince the principal to bend the rules and accept her at the teachers' training school, for the entrance age was eighteen. After she graduated, she took a job as a teacher in a country school.

McGregor began medical school at the University of Alberta in 1919, and graduated in 1925. She won the Gold Medal for the highest average percentage in all subjects during her six years. Just before she was due to graduate, the authorities informed their class that no internships were available in Canada because of the Depression. She was offered a fellowship at the University of Minnesota to work on a doctorate in pathology. After she earned this degree, she was awarded a National Research Council Fellowship at Harvard under Frank Mallory. In 1930, Mallory recommended her as an assistant to Simon Flexner at the Rockefeller Foundation. In the interview with Flexner, she told him of her wish to see Europe before she settled down. He arranged for her to go to Hamburg to work with Theodore Fahr, an expert on kidney disease. McGregor's research was also on kidney disease.

In Hamburg at the home of the Canadian trade commissioner, she met her future husband, a broad-minded Swedish economist and director of a large Swedish factory located outside of Hamburg. They married, and the couple moved to Stockholm, where his head office was located. In Sweden, Hellstedt realized that there were too many doctors; clinical pathology did not exist and research in pathology was of no importance.

With the full support of her husband, she decided to train to be a psychoanalyst. Since she could not get this training in Sweden, she arranged to work at the Neurology Clinic in Zurich and to start her training analysis with Gustav Bally. She took Carl Jung's lecture course. She returned to Sweden and asked the authorities for permission to qualify. Although they granted her credit for previous work, she was still forced to repeat the two last years of medicine. Hellstedt claimed that this was the only injustice that she suffered in her medical life. She finally received her license in 1937, one of only three foreign physicians to apply for legitimation in Sweden.

In 1937 the Hellstedts' daughter, Monica, was born and in 1939 a son, Donald, followed. After World War II broke out, Swedish analysts returned to Sweden and the Swedish Psychoanalytical Association was founded. Hellstedt continued her education in the field, and gradually became an analyst. She was admitted to membership in the International Association of Psychoanalysts and soon developed a full-time practice.

Hellstedt became involved with the Medical Women's International Association. She was president-elect in Vienna in 1968 and president in Melbourne in 1970–1972. Her husband died of cancer in 1969 and she had several surgeries on her hip. Her family thrived; her son was in business administration and her daughter in pediatrics, and she had five grandchildren. On 28 May 1977 she was awarded the honorary degree of doctor of science by the University of Alberta in Edmonton, Canada.   JH/MBO

PRIMARY SOURCES
Hellstedt, Leone McGregor. In Hellstedt, Autobiographies.

HÉLOISE (ca. 1100–1164)

French natural historian, mathematician, and medical administrator. Born 1098 or 1101 according to sources. Educated by Peter Abelard. Professional experience: abbess of the convent of the Paraclete. Died 15 May 1164.

During the time she was living in the home of her uncle Fulbert, a canon of the Cathedral of Notre Dame in Paris, Heloise's uncle employed the young philosopher, Peter Abelard, to educate his seventeen-year-old niece. Unsurpassed by even Romeo and Juliet as one of the most famous love stories of all times, Heloise became pregnant and went to a convent in Brittany where she gave birth to a son, Atrolabe. She and Abelard secretly married, but her distraught family ordered Abelard castrated and Heloise sent to a convent at Argenteuil. Abelard, a brilliant but controversial philosopher, retired to the monastery of St. Denis outside Paris.

When the convent at Argenteuil was dispersed, Heloise went to the community of Paraclete, near Nogent-sur Seine. Abelard gave Heloise and the nuns property, and Heloise became the convent's abbess. Most of what we know of Heloise comes from her letters to Abelard. They establish that she was a learned woman, although there is some doubt about the authenticity of the letters. She was buried beside Abelard at the Paraclete, but the remains of both were removed to the Père-Lachaise cemetery in Paris.   JH/MBO

SECONDARY SOURCES

Dronke, Peter. *Women Writers of the Middle Ages: A Critical Study of Texts from Perpetua (+203) to Marguerite Porete (+1310).* Cambridge: Cambridge University Press, 1984.

Gilson, Etienne. *Heloise and Abelard.* Ann Arbor, Mich.: University of Michigan Press, 1960.

Klapisch-Zuber, Christiane, ed. *Silences of the Middle Ages: A History of Women in the West,* Vol. 2. Cambridge, Mass.: Belknap Press, 1992.

STANDARD SOURCES

Alic; Echols and Williams; Hurd-Mead 1938; Shearer and Shearer 1996.

HENDERSON, NELLIE FRATER (1885–1952)

U.S. botanist and educator. Born 30 November 1885 in Belmont County, Ohio, to Margaret (Frater) and Thomas Henderson. Married Carl Edmund Strickler (1934). Educated Franklin College, New Athens, Ohio (Ph.B., 1908); The Ohio State University (B.A, 1912; M.A, 1916). Professional experience: Jennings Seminary, Aurora, Ill., teacher; high schools at Little Rock, Ark., Marietta; and Martins Ferry, Ohio, teacher. East High School Columbus, Ohio, teacher. Honors and memberships: Sigma Xi (1925), Sigma Delta Epsilon (1927), Pi Lambda Theta (1928), member; Oklahoma Academy of Science, Fellow. Died 29 March 1952 in Wheeling, West Virginia.

Henderson's professional life was spent teaching high school. After brief teaching stints in Illinois, Little Rock, and two small towns in Ohio, she returned to Columbus, Ohio, where she taught at East High School until retirement. She was elected to Sigma Xi (1925), Sigma Delta Epsilon (1927), and Pi Lambda Theta (1928), all scientific honor societies. She was a Fellow of the Ohio Academy of Sciences.

Although she was chiefly an educator, she is important for her extensive study of mosses. She made the first attempt to develop a moss flora of Ohio that included keys and descriptions of the taxa. While she was a student at Ohio State and later when she returned to teach, she was involved with John Schaffne's project on the vascular flora of Ohio, which resulted in the publication of several papers in the *Ohio Journal of Science.* During school vacations, she worked at the State Herbarium, preparing descriptions and keys to the orders, families, genera, and species of Ohio mosses. Her culminating work was a *Check List of Ohio Mosses* (1930), which was never published.   JH/MBO

PRIMARY SOURCES

Henderson, Nellie Frater. "Ohio Mosses, Polytrichiales." *Ohio Journal of Science* (1925): 177–182.

———. "Ohio Mosses, Bryales." *Ohio Journal of Science* 27 (1927): 1–18.

SECONDARY SOURCES

Stuckey, Ronald L. "Nellie Frater Henderson." Unpublished notes.

———. *Women Botanists of Ohio Born Before 1900.* Columbus, Ohio: The Ohio State University, 1992. With portrait.

HENDRICKS, EILEEN M. (1888–1978)

British stratigrapher. Born 1888. Educated Queens University, Belfast (degree?, 1921). Professional experience: Queens University, Belfast (one year). Died 1978.

Eileen M. Lind Hendricks held only one appointment, at Queens University, Belfast, and that for only one year. However, she was known for her research on the geology of Cornwall and, particularly, on the killas.   JH/MBO

SECONDARY SOURCES

H., M. R. "Dr. E. M. Lind Hendricks (1888–1978)." *Geological Society of London, List of Fellows and Members* (1983): 251.

STANDARD SOURCES

Sarjeant.

HENNEL, CORA BARBARA (1886–1947)

U.S. mathematician. Born 21 January 1886 in Evansville, Ind., to Anna Mary (Thuman) and Joseph Hennel. Educated University of Indiana (A.B.; A.M.; Ph.D.). Professional experience: Indiana University, professor of mathematics. Honors and memberships: American Association of University Women; American Association of University Professors; Mathematical Association of America; American Mathematic Society; Indiana Academy of Science; Corda Fratres Association of Cosmopolitan Clubs. Died 26 June 1947.

Cora Hennel earned all three of her degrees from the University of Indiana. She was a member of Phi Beta Kappa, Sigma Xi, Mortar Board, and Pi Lambda Theta. Her earlier professional positions were at the University of Indiana. She became a professor of mathematics there at the age of forty, and when she died she was considered one of the outstanding teachers at the university. Hennel also endowed a mathematics scholarship for undergraduates.   JH/MBO

PRIMARY SOURCES

Hennel, Cora Barbara. *Transformations and Invariants Connected with Linear Homogeneous Difference Equations and Other Functional Equations.* Baltimore: n.p., 1913.

———. With Harold T. Davis. *A Course in General Mathematics.* Bloomington, Ind.: n.p., 1925.

SECONDARY SOURCES

American Women 1935–1940: A Composite Biographical Dictionary. Howes, Durwood, ed. Detroit: Gale Research, 1981.

STANDARD SOURCES

Grinstein and Campbell

HENREY, BLANCHE ELIZABETH EDITH (1906–1983)

British botanist and bibliographer. Born 7 February 1906 in Brentford, Middlesex. Died 9 March 1983.

Blanche Henrey began her career as a photographer of flowers and trees, using her photographs to illustrate three popular books between 1937 and 1944. She began to seriously collect bibliographic sources on British botanical and horticultural literature before the nineteenth century, and published a three-volume work on this field. A final book appeared three years after her death on the life of an eighteenth-century gardener, Thomas Knowlton, based on his letters.

Henrey was awarded the Veitch Gold Medal of the Royal Horticultural Society in 1976. In 1979, she received the prestigious triennial bibliography prize of the International League of Antiquarian Booksellers, as well as the H. H. Bloomer Award from the Linnaean Society for those who have made important contributions to natural knowledge.

JH/MBO

PRIMARY SOURCES

Henrey, Blanche. *Flower Portraits.* London: Country Life, 1937.

———. *Trees and Shrubs Throughout the Year.* London: L. Drummond, Ltd., 1944.

———. *British Botanical and Horticultural Literature before 1800.* 3 vols. London: Oxford University Press, 1975.

———. *No Ordinary Gardener.* London: British Museum of Natural History, 1986.

Manuscripts and photographs are at the British Museum of Natural History.

SECONDARY SOURCES

Antiquarian Book Monthly Review 10 (1983): 189. Obituary notice with portrait.

Taxon 32 (August 1983): 531. Obituary notice.

Times, 14 March 1983. Obituary notice.

STANDARD SOURCES

Desmond.

HENRY, CAROLINE (ORRIDGE) (d. 1894)

British botanical collector. Married Augustine Henry. Died 1894.

Caroline Henry accompanied her husband, a medical officer of the Maritime Custom Service, to China, where they collected plants in order to study Chinese *materia medica.* She continued her collections in Japan as well as Colorado, where she collected plants with her sister-in-law, Mary Henry. After her death in 1894, her husband became an authority on Chinese *materia medica* and a professor of forestry at University of Dublin. The botanist Hemsley named a plant after Caroline, *Carolinella henryi* (the plant is now *Primula henryi*). Her plants are at the Royal Botanical Gardens, Kew.   JH/MBO

SECONDARY SOURCES

Hooker, William Jackson. *Icones Plantarum.* 1902. New York: Stechert-Nafner, 1966, reprint.

Ewan, Joseph, ed. *Biographical Dictionary of Rocky Mountain Naturalists.* Utrecht: Bohn, Sheltema, & Holkena, 1981.

STANDARD SOURCES

Desmond.

HENSHAW, JULIA WILMOTTE (1869–1937)

English/Canadian botanist. Born 1869 in Shropshire. Married Charles Henshaw. Honors and memberships: Royal Geographic Society, Fellow. Died 20 November 1937 in Vancouver of a heart ailment.

Julia Henshaw was born in England, but did most of her creative botanical work in Canada. She lived in Vancouver and wrote on mountain wildflowers. She wrote early field guides, based on her observations and collecting in the American West. She was a columnist and book reviewer for the *Vancouver Sun.*   JH/MBO

PRIMARY SOURCES

Henshaw, Julia. *Mountain Wild Flowers of Canada: A Simple and Popular Guide to the Names and Descriptions of the Flowers That Bloom above the Clouds.* Toronto: William Briggs, 1906.

———. *Wild Flowers of the North American Mountains.* New York: R. M. McBride, 1915.

SECONDARY SOURCES

Daily Telegraph, 10 November 1937. Obituary notice.

Ewan, Joseph, ed. *Biographical Dictionary of Rocky Mountain Naturalists.* 1981.

New York Times, 21 November 1937. Obituary notice.

HEPPENSTALL, CAROLINE A. (d. 1991?)

U.S. zoologist. Professional experience: Carnegie Museum, Pittsburgh, Pa. Honors and memberships: American Society of Mammalogists (1941–1991). Died 1991.

Caroline Heppenstall was a life member of the American Society of Mammalogists (AMS). Her duties at the Carnegie Museum in Pittsburgh, included teaching young workers how to prepare specimens. She also did mammal surveys in Pennsylvania. These surveys eventualy resulted in a coauthored book, *Mammals of Pennsylvania*. She was unanimously elected treasurer of the AMS in 1953, the first woman to be elected an officer of the society. She was elected to the board of directors and served from 1957 to 1959, the second woman in that position. Always interested in bats, Heppenstall authored two short papers about them in the *Journal of Mammalogy*.   JH/MBO

PRIMARY SOURCES

Heppenstall, C. A. "A Possible Bat Migration." *Journal of Mammalogy* 41 (1960): 509.

SECONDARY SOURCES

Kaufman, Dawn M., Donald W. Kaufman, and Glennis A. Kaufman. "Women in the Early Years of the American Society of Mammalogists (1919–1949)." *Journal of Mammalogy* 77, no. 3 (1996): 642–654.

HERFORD, ETHILDA B. MEAKIN (1872–1956)

British physician and psychotherapist. Born 6 December 1872 in Surrey to Ann (Budgett) and Edward Meakin. Married O. G. Herford (1907). Three sons, one daughter. Educated University College, London (M.B., B.S.); Royal Free Hospital; postgraduate study in Berlin, Munich, Vienna, Budapest. Professional experience: British Hospital for the Treatment of Mental Disorders, physician; London Clinic of Psychoanalysis, physician; Maudsley Hospital, psychological researcher; psychotherapist, consultant, private practice. Died 26 August 1956.

Physician and psychotherapist, Ethilda Herford was born in Surrey and attended University College, London, where she received both a bachelor of medicine and a bachelor of science degree. She interned at Royal Free Hospital and did postgraduate work in major clinical centers in Germany and Austria. Before she became interested psychiatry and psychoanalysis, she had studied diseases of the ovary. By the 1920s, she was doing research and publishing in the field of psychoanalysis and mental hygiene.   KM

PRIMARY SOURCES

Herford, Ethilda. *Ovarian Cysts and Their Origin.*
———. *Sixteen Unselected Cases of Hebosteotomy.* 1911.
———. *The Infantile Mind and Its Relation to Social Problems.*
———. *Mental Hygiene.* N.p., 1928.

STANDARD SOURCES
WWW, vol. 3, 1951–1960.

HERRAD OF HOHENBURG (d. 1195)

German/French natural philosopher. Flourished 1160s. Educated by nuns at convent in Hohenburg. Professional experience: abbess of the convent of Hohenburg. Died in 1195.

Also known as Herrad of Landsberg, she was sent to Hohenberg as a girl to study. She remained and became abbess of the Hohenberg convent on Mount St. Odile in Alsace in 1167. She was also chief physician and by 1187 had built a large hospital on the convent grounds. She wrote *Hortus Deliciarum* (Garden of Delights), an encyclopedia of religion, history, astronomy, geography, philosophy, natural history, and medical botany, between 1160 and 1170, making additional entries until 1190. Herrad wrote the technical terms in both Latin and German so that the encyclopedia could be used as a teaching text for her nuns, and illustrated it herself. It was considered of great artistic value but the only manuscript copy was destroyed in the 1870 siege of Strasbourg. A copy of large portions of the original made by an early-nineteenth-century scholar survived.

In the Augustinian convent, the nuns enjoyed considerable freedom and the *Hortus Deliciarum* provides a detailed picture of their lives. Although there was no known contact between Herrad and HILDEGARD OF BINGEN, their lives and writings bear many resemblances. Herrad's microcosmic concepts and illustrations were similar to Hildegard's. She explained the antipodean inversion of two climates, dividing the world into two temperate and two tropical zones. She also explored the relationship of the winds to the four elements and their effects on the four humors regulating human behavior. *Hortus* included an illustration of the signs of the zodiac and a table for determining festival days, working out the dates for Easter and the day of the week of Christmas for a cycle of 532 years, from 1175 to 1706.   JH/MBO

PRIMARY SOURCES

Herrad. *Hortus deliciarum.* N.p., n.d.

SECONDARY SOURCES

Dronke, Peter. *Women Writers of the Middle Ages: A Critical Study of Texts from Perpetua (+203) to Marguerite*

Porete (+1310). Cambridge: Cambridge University Press, 1984.

Katzenellbogen, Adolf. *Allegories of the Virtues and Vices in Medieval Art: From Early Christian Times to the Thirteenth Century.* Medieval Academy Reprints for Teaching, no. 4. Toronto: University of Toronto Press, 1989.

Klapisch-Zuber, Christiane, ed. *Silences of the Middle Ages: A History of Women in the West.* Vol. 2. Cambridge, Mass.: Belknap Press, 1992.

Schmidt, Charles. *Herrad of Landsberg, Abbess of Hohenburg, ca. 1130–1195.* Strasbourg: J. H. E. Heitz, [1897].

STANDARD SOURCES
Alic; Echols and Williams; Shearer and Shearer 1996.

HERRICK, CHRISTINE (TERHUNE) (1859–?)

U.S. home economist. Born 13 June 1859 at Newark, N.J. to Mary Virginia (Hawes) and Reverend Edward Payson Terhune. Married James Frederick Herrick. Educated in English literature and Anglo-Saxon philology. Professional experience: New England schoolteacher and writer. Death date unknown.

Christine Terhune Herrick was influenced by her mother's idea that a woman should be able to support herself in case of necessity. She, threfore, was educated in English literature and Anglo-Saxon philology and taught for a short time in New England. Her husband, James Frederick Herrick, was the editor of the *Springfield Republican,* and encouraged his wife to write. She had not shown any particular gift for writing as a girl, but contributed an article to a magazine while she was living in Springfield, Massachusetts, and with the support of her husband completed a series of articles on housekeeping topics for a newspaper syndicate. Her first article was "The Wastes of the Household." She published articles in the *Ladies Home Journal, Demorest's Monthly Magazine, Harper's Bazaar, Harper's Weekly, Good Housekeeping,* and *The Christian Union.* Several of these series have appeared as books.

JH/MBO

SECONDARY SOURCES
"Herrick, Christine (Terhune)." *National Cyclopaedia of American Biography.* New York: James T. White, 1900.

STANDARD SOURCES
Bailey.

HERRICK, JULIA FRANCES (1893–?)

U.S. physiologist and biophysicist. Born 14 September 1893 in North Saint Paul, Minn. Educated University of Minnesota (1913–1919, A.B., M.A.; Ph.D. in biophysics, 1931). Professional experience: Pub-

lic schools, Minnesota, teacher (1915–1920); Rockford College, assistant professor of physics (1922–1927); Mayo Foundation, associate (1931–1934); University of Minnesota, assistant professor, experimental medicine (1934–1942); Signal Corps Engineering Laboratory, associate physicist and radio engineer (1942–1946); University of Minnesota, associate professor (1946–1958), professor (1958–1959), emerita professor (from 1959); University of Wisconsin Medical School, Cardiovascular Research Laboratory, research associate (1959–1960); Vista Lab, California Institute of Technology, senior scientist (1960–1964), consultant (1964–1965); Interscience Research Institute, senior research scientist (from 1967). Death date unknown.

Biophysicist Julia Herrick had a long and varied career, extending for years after she retired from her professorial position at the University of Minnesota. As a young woman she supported herself throughout her undergraduate and early graduate education by teaching in the Minnesota public schools. A grant from the Mayo Foundation provided financial help as she worked for her doctoral degree. After she received this degree in 1931, she became an associate with the Mayo Foundation, and by 1934 had begun her career at the University of Minnesota as an assistant professor. This trajectory was interrupted between 1942 and 1946, when she worked for the U.S. Signal Corps Engineering Laboratory as an associate physicist and radio engineer during World War II. She returned to Minnesota in 1946 and proceeded up the academic ladder. However, her progress was not rapid, for she spent twelve years as an associate professor and was promoted to full professor only the year before she retired from the university. Retirement meant little to Herrick, who accepted a number of experience as senior scientist for several institutions.

Herrick was a member of the American Association for the Advancement of Science, the American Physical Society, the American Physiological Society, the Institute of Electrical and Electronic Engineering, the Biophysics Society, and the American Association of Physicists in Medicine. Her research was quite varied, including topics such as circulation, microwave diathermy, biological aspects of ultrasonics, physiological thermometry, and radio direction finding. JH/MBO

PRIMARY SOURCE
Herrick, Julia Frances. With Edward James Baldes. *The Thermos-Strohmuhr Method of Measuring Blood Flow.* N.p., 1932.

STANDARD SOURCES
AMS B 9, P&B 12.

HERRICK, SOPHIA MCILVAINE (BLEDSOE) (1837–1919)

U.S. microscopist. Born 26 March 1837 in Gambier, Ohio, to Harriet (Bledsoe) and Albert Taylor. Married James B. Herrick (1860).

Educated at Miss Coxe's School, Cincinnnati, and Cooper Institute, Dayton, Ohio. Professional experience: Baltimore, Md., schoolteacher, principal (1868–1872); Southern Review *(Baltimore), associate editor (1875–1878);* Scribner's Magazine *and its successor,* The Century Magazine, *editorial staff (1878–1907). Died 1919.*

Sophia Herrick was born and educated in Ohio. She married at the age of twenty-three. She began to teach in the Baltimore schools and served as principal. When her father, Albert T. Bledsoe, became an editor of the *Southern Review* in Baltimore, Maryland, she joined him on the staff. In 1878, she joined the editorial staff of *Scribner's*, remaining until 1907, through its name change to *The Century Magazine*. Herrick described her scientific investigations as a microscopist in numerous popular articles that she illustrated herself. Toward the end of her life, she lived in Plainfield, New Jersey.   JH/MBO

PRIMARY SOURCES

Herrick, Sophia. *Chapters in Plant Life*. New York: American Book Co., 1885.

———. *The Earth in Past Ages*. New York: Harper, 1888.

———. *Wonders of Plant Life*. New York: G. P. Putnam's Sons, 1883.

SECONDARY SOURCES

Adams, O. "Sophia Herrick." *A Dictionary of American Authors*. Boston: Houghton Mifflin 1897.

STANDARD SOURCES

Appleton's Cyclopedia. 1888;
WWW(A), vol. 1, 1897–1942.

HERSCHEL, CAROLINE LUCRETIA (1750–1848)

German astronomer. Born 16 March 1750 in Hanover to Anna (Moritzen) and Isaac Herschel. Five siblings. Never married. Educated at home. Died 9 January 1848 in Hanover.

Caroline Herschel's father, an oboist with the Hanoverian Foot Guards, lacked formal schooling himself but strove to provide an education for his six children. Much to the displeasure of Anna Herschel, whose interest focused exclusively on daily housekeeping requirements, conversation in the Herschel house tended toward the philosophical. Although Anna Herschel reluctantly accepted the need to educate her sons, she utterly rejected the possibility for the two girls. The eldest daughter, Sophia, was twenty-three years older than Caroline and accepted her mother's values without question. Caroline, on the other hand, was fascinated by the subjects discussed by her father and brothers. Whenever pos-

sible, Isaac Herschel included Caroline in their discussions, as well as in the musical instruction he gave to the boys. It was her father who brought about her introduction to astronomy: a "great admirer" of that science, he took her "on a clear frosty night into the street, to make me acquainted with several of the beautiful constellations, after we had been gazing at a comet which was then visible" (Lubbock, 5).

From 1757 to 1760, Caroline's father was away with the Hanoverian army, fighting the French; her brother William emigrated to England to pursue a musical career. During this period, her mother was in control. Caroline attended an inferior school run by the garrison, and a special knitting school. Her remaining time was occupied by knitting stockings for her brothers and father and writing letters for her illiterate mother. She also wrote letters "for many a poor soldier's wife in our neighborhood to her husband in the camp; for it ought to be remembered that in the beginning of the last century, very few women, when they left country schools, had been taught to write" M. C. Herschel, 11).

Isaac Herschel returned in 1760 broken in health; he died in 1767. Unrelieved by his presence, Caroline's drudging existence under the rule of her mother and eldest brother, Jacob, became intolerable. William, her favorite brother, was now employed as an organist and orchestra leader in Bath. After learning of Caroline's plight from another brother, Alexander, he determined to fetch her away to England and train her as a professional singer. Over the protests of both her mother and Jacob, who felt he would be inconvenienced by the loss of a free servant, Caroline left with William in 1772.

Herschel's new life in England was something of a disappointment. William had less time and attention to give her than she had hoped. Still, lessons in English, singing, arithmetic, and bookkeeping kept her occupied; and she and William "by way of relaxation . . . talked of Astronomy and the fine constellations with whom I had made acquaintance during the fine nights we spent on den Postwagen travelling through Holland" (Lubbock, 50). Meals were occasions when William devoted himself to his sister's education. At the seven o'clock breakfast so detested by the late-rising Herschel, William gave her lessons in mathematics, entitled "Little Lessons for Lina." From the playful first attempts they progressed through algebra, geometry, and trigonometry. After she had acquired sufficient skill in spherical trigonometry to put it to practical use, Herschel showed no desire to proceed further. Abstract mathematics for its own sake had little appeal for her.

William Herschel's hobby, astronomy, occupied more and more of his time. Fascinated by the unproved stellar region, he concluded that a systematic survey of the entire heavens was needed. In order to begin his tasks, he had to equip himself with the proper instruments. Herschel reluctantly helped him construct a telescope, begrudging the time taken away from her music. William's granddaughter Constance Lubbock noted in *The Herschel Chronicle* that "it required all Caroline's devotion to overcome the dismay with which she found herself swept along in such an unexpected direction" (65). Her fastidious nature was sorely challenged. According to Lubbock, Herschel later recalled, "Every leisure moment was eagerly snatched at for some resuming some work which was in progress, without taking time or changing dress, and many a lace ruffle . . . was torn or bespattered by molten pitch & c . . . I was even obliged to feed him by putting the vitals by bits into his mouth;—this was once the case when at the finishing of a 7 feet mirror he had not left his hands from it for 16 hours together" (Lubbock, 67–68). Herschel's work moved from caring for William to "sometimes lending a hand." Grinding and polishing mirrors, copying catalogues and tables, and offering assistance with whatever task called for it, she soon became indispensable to William.

William Herschel was catapulted into fame in 1781 by his discovery of a new "comet," later recognized as a planet. The sighting of "Georgium sidus," as William Herschel named the body (it was later called Uranus), signaled the beginning of the end of his musical career. His friends at the Royal Society arranged for him to show his telescopes to the royal family. George III was so impressed that he awarded William Herschel a stipend of two hundred pounds per year—a modest income, but sufficient to enable him to give up music and devote his entire energies to astronomy. Caroline Herschel's brief but successful career as an oratorio singer also came to an end; in 1782, she and William left Bath for the neighborhood of Windsor Castle, having found there a house where they could set up their telescopes. For want of anything better to do and to win her brother's approbation, Herschel became increasingly involved in astronomy. William encouraged her and gave her a small refracting telescope with which she could "sweep for comets." Industrious, she continued observing—discovering three new nebulae in 1783—and gradually became more proficient. As a reward for her diligence, William presented her with a new instrument, the one she called her "Newtonian small sweeper." Her opportunities to use it, however, were limited by her duty to William: "it could hardly be expected to meet with any Comets in that part of the heavens where I swept, for I generally chose my situation by the side of my Brother's instrument that I might be ready to run to the clock or to write down memorandums." By the beginning of December 1783, Herschel had become "entirely attached to the writing desk and had seldom an opportunity of using my newly acquired instruments" (Lubbock, 150–151).

Only when William was away from home did Herschel have the chance to work on her own. It was during these times that she discovered eight comets over the period 1786–1797. After her discovery of the first comet, she became the pet of the astronomical community. Her growing fame had a practical result, for in 1787 she was granted a salary of fifty pounds per year by the king, as official recompense for her work as William's assistant. This sum, the first money she had ever earned herself, was an intoxicating triumph.

The comparative serenity of Herschel's existence was disrupted by William's marriage to Mary Pitt in 1788. The loss of her privileged position in the life of her brother brought great pain. Eventually she grew fond of her sister-in-law and, penitent over remarks she had made in her journal about the marriage, destroyed every page dating from this period of her life.

Shortly after she had discovered her last comet in 1797, Herschel embarked upon a new task—one for which her qualities of perseverance, accuracy, and attention to detail perfectly suited her. The star catalogue of the first Astronomer Royal, John Flamsteed (1646–1719), was very difficult to use because the original observations were published in a separate volume from the catalogue. William Herschel had discovered numerous discrepancies between the catalogue and his own observations. He badly needed a cross-index in order to trace these differences, but was unwilling to devote "the labor and time required for making a proper index" at the expense of his more exciting pursuits. Still, he wrote, "I found the indispensable necessity of having this index recur so forcibly, that I recommended it to my Sister to undertake the arduous task" (Sidgewick, 160; Lubbock, 256). Caroline accepted his suggestion. The resultant *Catalogue of Stars* was published by the Royal Society in 1798 and contained an index to "*every* observation of *every* star made by Flamsteed," an enumeration of errata, and a list "of upwards of 560 stars that are *not inserted* in the British Catalogue" (Baily, 388–389).

Not until after William's death did Herschel again become deeply involved, independently or semi-independently, in an astronomical project. She was always available, however, to assist William in his work and to follow his orders. After years of failing health, William Herschel died in 1822. Feeling that England without William would be unbearable, Herschel made an impulsive decision to return to her native Hanover—a decision she constantly regretted. The one person who could even begin to replace William in her affections, his son, John (1792–1871), had begun a distinguished career as an astronomer, physicist, and chemist. Herschel took a keen interest in his work and was sustained through her later years by his letters and visits from England. For his use she compiled a new catalogue of nebulae, arranged in zones, from material in William's multivolume *Book of Sweeps* and *Catalogue of 2,500 Nebulae*. This work, indispensable to John Herschel's investigations, was never published; yet she received recognition for it in the form of a gold medal awarded by the Royal Astronomical Society in 1828.

Among her contemporaries, Caroline Herschel had become a legend. Anyone of any scientific eminence who passed through Hanover stopped to visit her. In 1835, she and MARY SOMERVILLE became the first women to be awarded honorary memberships in the Royal Society. (The only other woman made an honorary member before the twentieth century was Anne Sheepshanks, in 1862.) In 1838, she was elected to membership in the Royal Irish Academy. Two years before her death, Herschel received a letter from Alexander von Humboldt informing her that "His Majesty the King [of Prussia], in recognition of the valuable service rendered to Astronomy by you, as the fellow worker of your immortal brother, wishes to convey to you in his name the large Gold Medal for science" (M. C. Herschel, 336–337). Although from the time she left England in 1822, Herschel expected to die at any moment, she survived most of her contemporaries and many of her juniors. At the age of ninety-seven years and ten months she died on 9 January 1848, and was buried with a lock of her beloved William's hair.

It is possible to be an important contributor to science without being a scientist, for science must transcend the mere collection of data by adding the critical element of interpretation. The contributions of Caroline Herschel to the science of astronomy were considerable. As an observer, she added to the total of astronomical facts available to the scientist. Beside her eight comets (five of which can properly be credited to her), she located several new nebulae and star clusters. Speculation, however, as to the nature of comets or of the nebulae was left to William. She seldom displayed curiosity about the objects of her discoveries. Even her interest in mathematics was pragmatic; she learned well what was necessary for the work William set her to, but showed no propensity toward mathematics for its own sake. Her second contribution to the science of astronomy was the skilled and accurate transcription and reduction of astronomical data. Love of her brother was the stimulus behind Caroline Herschel's achievements in astronomy. Barred from the ranks of creative astronomers by both inadequate training and a disinclination for abstract concepts, she substituted other qualities, notably accuracy and perseverance, which assured her a place in the history of astronomy.   MBO

PRIMARY SOURCES

Herschel, Caroline. "An Account of a New Comet: In a Letter from Miss Caroline Herschel to Charles Blagden, M.D., Sec. R. R." *Philosophical Transactions of the Royal Society of London* 77 (1787): 105.

———. "An Account of the Discovery of a Comet: In a Letter from Miss Caroline Herschel to Joseph Planta, Esq.,

Sec. R.S." *Philosophical Transactions of the Royal Society of London* 84 (1794): 1.

———. "Account of the Discovery of a New Comet: In a Letter to Sir Joseph Banks, Bart., K.B., P.R.S." *Philosophical Transactions of the Royal Society of London* 86 (1797): 131–134.

SECONDARY SOURCES

A Kempis, Mary Thomas. "Caroline Herschel." *Scripta mathematica* 21 (1955): 246–247.

Ashton, Helen, and Katherine Davies. *I Had a Sister*. London: Lovat Dickson, [1937]. A study of four famous sisters of famous men: Cassandra Austen, Caroline Herschel, Mary Lamb, and Dorothy Wordsworth.

Baily, Francis. *An Account of the Revd. John Flamsteed, the First-Astronomer-Royal: Compiled from His Own Manuscripts, and Other Authentic Documents, Never Before Published. To Which Is Added His British Catalogue of Stars, Corrected and Enlarged.* London: W. Clowes and Sons, 1835.

———. "A Catalogue of the Positions (in 1690) of 564 Stars Observed by Flamsteed, but not Inserted in His British Catalogue; Together with Some Remarks on Flamsteed's Observations." *Memoirs of the Royal Astronomical Society* 4 (1830): 129–164.

Faujas de Saint Fond, Barthelemy. *A Journey through England and Scotland to the Hebrides in 1784.* Ed. Sir Archibald Geikie, rev. ed. of English translation. 2 vols. Glasgow: Hugh Hopkins, 1907. Travel journal in which the traveler describes his first encounter with C. Herschel. See volume 1, pages 63–64.

Herschel, Mary Cornwalis. *Memoir and Correspondence of Caroline Herschel.* New York: Appleton, 1876.

Lubbock, Constance A. *The Herschel Chronicle: The Life-Story of William Herschel and His Sister Caroline Herschel.* Cambridge: Cambridge University Press, 1933.

Ogilvie, Marilyn Bailey. "Caroline Herschel's Contributions to Astronomy." *Annals of Science* 32 (1975): 149–161.

Sidgewick, J. B. *William Herschel, Explorer of the Heavens.* London: Faber and Faber, 1953.

South, James, Esq. "An Address Delivered at the Annual General Meeting of the Astronomical Society of London, on February 8, 1829, on Presenting the Honorary Medal to Miss Caroline Herschel." *Memoirs of the Royal Astronomical Society* 3 (1829): 409–412.

STANDARD SOURCES

Debus; *DNB; DSB;* Ogilvie 1986.

HERSENDE, ABBESS OF FONTEVRAULT
(fl. 1090–1120s)

French abbess, healer. Flourished 1090–1120s. Professional experience: first superior of the mission foundation of Fontevrault by Robert of Arbrissel.

Thanks to Hersende's abilities, the abbey of Fontevrault remained in the charge of female superiors. Hersende was interested in medicine, attended patients, and taught nuns to be healers and nurses. MBO

SECONDARY SOURCES
Echols and Williams.

HERSKOVITS, FRANCES S. (SHAPIRO)
(1897–1972)

U.S. cultural anthropologist. Born 1897. Married Melville J. Herskovits (1924; he died 1963). One daughter, Jean Frances (b. 1935). Professonal experience: collaborated in anthropological research and publications with husband. Died 4 May 1972 in Evanston, Ill.

Although little personal detail is known about the life of Frances Herskovits before she married, she is recalled as a full participant in the research and writing of the celebrated anthropologist Melville J. Herskovits. Raised in a Jewish family, probably in New York, even her education is not recalled in any biographical source. MARGARET MEAD recalled the attractive bohemian apartment of Frances and Melville Herskovits in the 1920s while he was a graduate student in anthropology at Columbia and later while he was teaching there as a lecturer. The couple spent a brief period at Howard University where they deepened their interest in what Melville Herskovits would call "cultural retention" by African Americans of African culture. They soon moved to Northwestern University, where Melville Herskovits rose rapidly to associate professor of anthropology, and by the mid-thirties to head of the department of anthropology, which he also founded. In the summers, the couple traveled first to the Caribbean (in 1928, then later in the thirties and forties) and then to West Africa to do field reseach on the Dahomean and Surinam cultures where their skill with a number of European languages proved useful. Frances Herskovits carried out such a highly collaborative research program with her husband, that it almost is impossible to tell who did what research.

The two were prolific in their publication of major studies of African, African-Caribbean and African American culture. Mead recalled that the couple had an unusual manner of working, each writing half the chapters of a book in draft form, and then editing the other half. This merging of their research and publication meant that although Melville Her-

skovits was careful to credit Frances's work jointly with his own, the anthropological community made no attempt to offer her independent recognition, even after his death. This contrasts with the careful crediting by their husbands of the independent contributions of MARIE CURIE and GERTY CORI.

Three other factors may have played a part in Herskovits's lack of independent recognition. One was the existence of nepotism rules that prevented a wife from being hired in her husband's department. The second was the culture of the time that encouraged women to submerge their independent contributions to their husband's work. The third was the existence of antisemitism, to which Frances was quite sensitive and which she believed had prevented her husband from gaining the full recognition that she felt he deserved.

From the early 1950s, Melville Herskovits created the first program of African American Studies in an American university at Northwestern. He died in the early sixties. After the death of her husband, Frances Herskovits was encouraged by colleagues and friends to bring together selections of their joint articles in new edited volumes. These, although edited by Frances Herskovits with a foreword by her, do not illuminate her own participation with the exception of the original footnotes recognizing her participation in the research and writing.

The publication of a major biography of her husband in the *Biographical Memoir* of the National Academy of Sciences, recognized Frances as "a professional anthropologist in her own right" and referred to her contributions to her husband's work as going far beyond the books they coauthored (Goldberg 1971).

Just before her death at the age of seventy-four, Frances Herskovits's second edited volume, *Cultural Relativism*, was in press. Her daughter, Jean Herskovits, continued her interest in her parents' work as a professor of African history at the State University of New York, Purchase, studying and publishing on Africa and African American subjects.

JH/MBO

PRIMARY SOURCES
Herskovits, Frances S. With M. J. Herskovits. "An Outline of Dahomean Religious Beliefs." *Memoirs of the American Anthropolgical Association* 41 (1933): 7–77.
———. With M. J. Herskovits. *Rebel Destiny: Among the Bush Negroes of Dutch Guiana.* New York: Whittlesey House (McGraw Hill), 1934.
———. With M. J. Herskovits. *Suriname Folklore.* New York: Columbia University Press, 1936.
———. With M. J. Herskovits. *Trinidad Village.* New York: Alfred Knopf, 1947.
———. With M. J. Herskovits. *Dahomean Narrative: A Cross-Cultural Analysis.* Evanston: Northwestern University Press, 1958.

———, ed. *The New World Negro,* by M. J. Herskovits. Indiana University Press, 1966. Includes introduction by Frances Herskovits.

SECONDARY SOURCES
Goldberg, Joseph H. "Melville J. Herskovits." *Biographical Memoirs National Academy of Sciences* 42 (1971): 65–93.
"Mrs. Frances Herskovits." *New York Times,* 8 May 1972. Gives no personal information about her family, early life, or education.
Simpson, George Eaton. *Melville J. Herskovits.* New York: Columbia University Press, 1973. Includes Margaret Mead's recollections and a discussion of the Herskovits's perception of anti-semitism.

STANDARD SOURCES
Debus (under Melville Herskovits); Rossiter 1982.

HERTWIG, PAULA (1889–1983)

German geneticist and biologist. Born 11 October 1889 in Berlin. Father Oskar Hertwig (1849–1922). Educated University of Berlin (Ph.D., 1916; habilitation, 1919). Professional experience: University of Berlin, Institute of Genetics, assistant; Medical Faculty of Berlin, teacher of human heredity (1946); Institute of Biology, Halle, director (1948), professor of general biology and genetics, honorary promotion to the medical faculty. Died in 1983 in Villingen.

Paula Hertwig was the first woman who habilitated at the University of Berlin, achieving a postdoctoral lecturing qualification. She was the daughter of the biologist Oskar Hertwig, who published extensively. She studied biology in Berlin from 1909. In 1913 she worked for a few months in the zoological station in Naples. Her thesis was on radiation experiments on fish embryos. In 1919, her second thesis to qualify as a lecturer concerned research on the results of radiation, which became her lifelong concern: "Durch Radiumbestrahlun hervorgerufene Veränderungen in den Keimteilungsvorgängen. Probleme der Geschlectsumwandlung." She was *privat-dozent* (assistant professor) of general biology and heredity in the agricultural faculty *(landwirtschaftlichen fakultät).*

The first attempt in 1925 to promote her to a professorship failed, although the faculty certified that her scientific achievements should qualify her to be given an official professorship. She was then made an unoffical professor. In 1927, Hertwig was named unoffical extraordinary professor in the Institute of Medicine faculty of biology and anatomy, which was founded by her late father. Reluctantly, the rector of Berlin University sent on an application of the Medical Faculty in September, 1939, to name Paula Hertwig *ausserplanmässigen* (extraordinary) professor in the Reichs Ministry

for science and education. The application was refused since Paula Hertwig was politically unreliable. From 1918 to 1932 she was a member of the German People's Party (Deutschen Volkspartei) and from March until June 1933, of the State's Party, Deutsche Staatspartei. In November 1939 she was named scientific assistant in the Institute of Heredity and Husbandry (Vererbuns-und-Züchtungsforschung). When she found out that her teaching certificate was going to be taken away, she protested in January 1940 to the ministry and contacted the rector. She wrote that "this occupation of University Teacher has always meant a great deal to me, since I value the honor of being a member of Berlin University because of tradition and of personal connections I have always valued it most highly and because I have been committed with gusto and love and maybe some success to show young people the way to scientific work." She made concessions vis-à-vis the National Socialist authorities by declaring that she had received in 1938 a National Socialist Award, the "Treudienstehrenzeichen" and was a member of National Socialist organizations, the Dozentenbundes and the Hochschulgemeinschaft of German women in the Altherrenbund of the German Dozentinnen. In April 1938, she received an upaid job in order to have the teaching continue and half a year later she got paid. She was informed that she was not be named *ausserplanmässigen professor.*

Paula Hertwig's ground-breaking work regarding questions in genetics and embryological damage is little known.

GVL

PRIMARY SOURCES
Hertwig, Paula. "Partielle Keimschädigung durch Radium-u.Röntgenstrahlen." In *Handbuch der Vererbungswissenschaft,* ed. E. Baur and M. Hartmann. Vol. 3. Berlin: Gebrüder Borntraeger, 1927.
———. "Regulation von Wachstum, Entwicklung u. Regeneration durch Umweltfaktoren." In *Handbuch der normalen pathologischen Physiologie.* Vol. 16. Berlin: J. Springer, 1930.
———. "Artbastarde bei Tieren." In *Handbuch der Vererbungswissenschaft.* Vol. 2. Berlin: Borntraeger, 1936.
———. "Mutationen bei den Säugetieren und die Frage ihrer Entstehung durch kurzwellige Strahlen uind Keimgifte." In *Handbuch der Erbbiologie des Mencschen.* Berlin: J. Springer, 1940.
———. "Strahlenschäden und Strahlenschutz im zellulären Bereich." *Berichte über der Verhandlungen der Sächsischen Akademie der Wissenschaften zu Leipzig, mathematisch-naturwissenschaftliche Klasse* 102, no. 6 (1957): 1–43.

SECONDARY SOURCES
Jank, Dagmar. *Studierende, lehrende und forschende Frauen an der Friedrich-Wilhelms-Universität zu Berlin 1908–1945.*

Ausstellungsführer ed. Ulla Bock u. Dagmar Jank 15f. Berlin: University Library of the Free University of Berlin, 1990.

STANDARD SOURCES
Lexikon der Frau.

HERTZ, MATHILDE (1891–1975)

German zoologist. Professional experience: Max Planck Institute for Biology (formerly the Kaiser Wilhelm Institute), "miscellaneous co-worker" (1927–1929), assistant (1929–1935); University of Berlin, privat-dozent (assistant professor, 1930–1933).

During 1928 when Mathilde Hertz worked at the Kaiser Wilhelm Institute for Biology there were seven women among seventeen assistants. By 1936, she was the only woman among nine assistants. She was a *privat-dozent* (assistant professor) at the University of Berlin in zoology until 1933 when she lost the position because of the Nazis' position against Jewish scientists. Because of the support of Max Planck, she was able to remain at the Max Planck Institute until 1935, when she emigrated to Cambridge, England. Her scientific career ended at that point.   JH/MBO

SECONDARY SOURCES
Handbook of the KWG (1928): 195; *Handbook of the KWG* 1 (1936): 174.

Jaeger, Siegfried. "Vom erklärbaren, doch ungeklärten Abbruch einer Karriere-Die Tierpsychologin und Sinnesphysiologin Mathilde Hertz (1891–1975)." In *Untersuchungen zur Geschichte der Psychologie und der Psychotechnik,* ed. Horst Gundlach, 228–262. Munich and Vienna: Profil Verlag, 1996.

STANDARD SOURCES
Vogt.

HERWERDEN, MARIANNE VAN (1874–1934)

Dutch physiologist and geneticist. Born 16 February 1874 in the Netherlands. Educated gymnasium; medical school (graduated 1897), doctorate (1905, cum laude). Professional experience: University of Utrecht, assistant to C. A. Pekelharing (1908–1918); lecturer (from 1922). Died 26 January 1934.

Marianne van Herwerden finished the gymnasium in 1897 and began medical school that same year. In 1905, she was awarded a doctorate (cum laude), and in 1908 became the assistant of C. A. Pekelharing, professor of physiology at the University of Utrecht. Although she was a successful teacher and published extensively on topics such as menstrual cycle, she remained Pekelharing's assistant, this despite the fact that such a position was usually a stepping-stone to advancement. Pekelharing resigned in 1918, and there are some reports that Herwerden was considered as his successor. Others noted that the resistance of the male professors of the medical faculty was so great that she was passed by. She was appointed lecturer in 1922 and ended her career at that rank. Herwerden died on 26 January 1934.   JH/MBO

PRIMARY SOURCES
Herwerden, Maria Anna van. Bijdrage tot de Kennis van menstrueelen cyclus en puerperium. Leiden: n.p., 1905.

SECONDARY SOURCES
Lindeboom, G. A. *Dutch Medical Biography: A Biographical Dictionary of Dutch Physicians and Surgeons, 1475–1975.* Amsterdam: Rodopi, 1984.

Offereins, Marianne I. C. *Vrouwen Miniaturen. Biografische Schetsen uit de Exacte Vakken.* Utrecht: A. Kwadraat, 1996.

Stamhuis, Ida H. "A Female Contribution to Early Genetics: Tine Tammes and Mendel's Laws for Continuous Characters." *Journal of the History of Biology* 28 (1995): 495–531.

Tammes, Time. "Die Bedeutung von Dr. Maria Anna van Herwerden für die Genetik und die Eugenetik." *Genetica* 18 (1936): 3–9.

STANDARD SOURCES
Strohmeier.

HERXHEIMER, FRANZISKA (fl. 1912)

German? physicist and chemist. Professional experience: University of Leipzig, Physical Institute, researcher.

Working at the Physical Institute of the University of Leipzig under Wiener and W. Möbius, Herxheimer made photometric measurements in gases and in liquids which confirmed Rayleigh's theory of dispersion.   MM

PRIMARY SOURCES
Herxheimer, Franziska. "Über die Zerstreuung des Lichtes in trüben Mitteln." *Physikalische Zeitschrift* 13 (1912): 1106–1112.

HESLOP, MARY KINGDON (ca. 1884–ca. 1954)

British mineralogist, igneous petrologist, and geographer. Born in Egypt in about 1884. Professional experience: brief appointments at Kings

College Newcastle-on-Tyne; Bedford College, London; school teaching in Newcastle-on-Tyne; University of Leeds; Kenton Lodge Training College, Newcastle-on-Tyne (1923–1950). Died around 1954.

After numerous short appointments at different colleges and universities, Heslop spent twenty-seven years at the Kenton Lodge Training College, Newcastle-on-Tyne. She studied the igneous dykes of northern England.   JH/MBO

SECONDARY SOURCES
[Smythe, J. A.]. "Mary Kingdon Heslop." *Proceedings of the Geological Society of London* no. 1529 (1955): 139–140.

STANDARD SOURCES
Sarjeant.

HESSE, FANNY (1850–1934)
Dutch microbiologist. Born 1850.

Fanny Hesse was a Dutch microbiologist who introduced agar agar into bacteriology. Agar agar is a medium used in growing bacteria, and is very important in the laboratory culturing of such organisms.   JH/MBO

SECONDARY SOURCES
Hitchens, Arthur Parker, and Morris Likind. "The Introduction of Agar Agar into Bacteriology." *Journal of Bacteriology* 37 (1939): 485–495.

STANDARD SOURCES
Høyrup.

HETZER, HILDEGARD (1899–?)
Austrian educational psychologist. Born 9 June 1899 in Vienna. Educated University of Vienna (Ph.D., 1927). Professional experience: University of Vienna, Psychological Institute, assistant professor (1926–1931); Pedagogical Academy, Elbing, teacher and researcher (1926–1931), professor of psychology (1931). Death date unknown.

Educational and child psychologist Hildegard Hetzer was trained in Vienna and taught at the University of Vienna, Psychological Institute. In 1926 she went to the Pedagogical Academy in Elbing, then a part of Prussia (now Poland) where she became a professor in 1931. She was a member of the German Society for Experimental Psychology and published many articles on child development and education, some with the child psychologist CHARLOTTE BÜHLER.   KM

PRIMARY SOURCES
Hetzer, Hildegard. With Charlotte Bühler. *Kleinkinder tests: entwicklungs tests.* Leipzig: J.A. Barth, 1932.
————, et al. *Kinderspiel im Freien.* Munich: E. Reinhardt, 1966.

STANDARD SOURCES
Psychological Register, 1932.

HEVELIUS, ELISABETHA KOOPMAN (1647–1693)
Polish astronomer. Born around 1647. Married Johannes Hevelius. Three daughters. Died 1693 in Danzig.

Elisabetha, the well-educated daughter of a wealthy merchant, became the second wife of the astronomer Johannes Hevelius (1611–1687) in 1663. Before he was an astronomer, Hevelius was a brewer. His first wife managed the brewery, leaving Hevelius free to pursue his major interest, astronomy. After the death of his first wife, Hevelius married Elisabetha Koopman, who was already interested in astronomy. Thirty-six years younger than her husband, she aided him in running his observatory in Danzig. In addition to acting as hostess to many visiting astronomers, she helped with observations and, after Hevelius's death, edited many of his unpublished writings, most notably the *Prodromus astronomiae* (1690), a catalogue of over sixteen hundred stars and their positions.

Elisabetha Hevelius was significant in the history of astronomy, illustrating the importance of the guild wife. Although in proper guild tradition she served as her husband's chief assistant (all guild masters were required to have one), she was allowed a more important role because the observatory was in the home rather than in the university.   JH/MBO

PRIMARY SOURCES
Hevelius, Johannes. *Prodromus astronomiae.* Danzig, 1690. The work in which Elisabetha played a most important role.

SECONDARY SOURCES
Schiebinger, Londa. *The Mind Has No Sex: Women in the Origins of Modern Science.* Cambridge: Harvard University Press, 1989. See pages 79, 81–82, and 83.

STANDARD SOURCES
DSB (under Johannes Hevelius); Ogilvie 1986.

HEWER, DOROTHY (d. 1948)

British botanist. Educated Bedford College, London (B.Sc.). Professional activities: founded herb farm. Died 1948.

After Dorothy Hewer earned a bachelor of science degree from Bedford College, London, she founded an herb farm. She wrote a book on growing herbs.   JH/MBO

PRIMARY SOURCES
Hewer, Dorothy. *Practical Herb Growing*. London: G. Bell, 1941.

SECONDARY SOURCES
McCleod, D. *Down-to-Earth Women*. Edinburgh: Blackwood, 1982. Hewer mentioned on page 72.
Sanecki, K. *History of English Herb Gardening*. England: Ward Lock, 1992. Hewer mentioned on page 90.

STANDARD SOURCES
Desmond.

HEWITT, DOROTHY CARLETON (1905–1984)

U.S. biologist. Born 1905 in Middletown, Conn. Married R. C. Hutchinson (1933). Three children. Educated Mount Holyoke College (A.B., 1927); Yale University (Ph.D., 1932). Professional experience: Albertus Magnus College, instructor comparative anatomy (1932); Index Wistar Institute, editor; Abstract Card Service, editor. Honors and memberships: Mount Holyoke College, honorary degree (1977). Died 1984.

Dorothy Hewitt's name is found in only two editions of *AMS*. Yet Ross G. Harrison of Yale considered her be one of the best students that Bryn Mawr had graduated. The preference for male teachers made it very difficult for a woman to get a position. Hewitt worked at Albertus Magnus for a year and then became the editor of the Index of the Wistar Institute. Her husband, Robert Cranford Hutchinson, had been a fellow at Yale when Dorothy was there and was at the Wistar Institute from 1931 to 1936. Around 1943 she became active in the peace and civil rights movement and continued these activities until her death in 1984. Her papers are held in the Swarthmore Peace Collection, Swarthmore College.

Hewitt's research area was in experimental morphology, and she worked on the embryology of xenoplastically transplanted amphibian organs.   JH/MBO

PRIMARY SOURCES
Hewitt, Dorothy Carlton. "Xenoplastic Transplantation of Amphibian Eye Rudiments." Ph.D. diss., Yale University, 1932.

STANDARD SOURCES
AMS 6–7; Rossiter 1982.

HIBBARD, HOPE (1893–1988)

U.S. zoologist. Born 1893 in Altoona, Pa., to Mary (Schofield) Hibbard and Herbert Wade Hibbard. Educated University of Missouri (B.A., 1916; M.A., 1918); Bryn Mawr College (Ph.D., 1921); Sorbonne (Ph.D., 1928). Professional experience: Bryn Mawr College, demonstrator in biology (1919–1920); Elmira College in New York, associate professor (1921–1925); Sorbonne, Berliner Fellow (1925–1926); International Education Board Fellow (1927–1928); Oberlin College, assistant professor (1928–1930), associate professor (1930–1933), professor (1933–1961), chair department of zoology (1954–1958), professor emerita (1961–1988). Died 12 May 1988.

Hope Hibbard was raised by her father and stepmother, Mary Davis, after her mother died when Hibbard was two years old. The family moved from Pennsylvania to Minneapolis, where Hibbard's father was professor of mechanical engineering on the faculties of the University of Minnesota and Cornell University. In 1909, her father took a position at the University of Missouri. Hibbard received both her bachelor's and master's degrees from this institution. After receiving her master's degree, she went to Bryn Mawr College to work on her doctorate. Her dissertation, on sea urchin egg fertilization, earned her a doctorate in 1921. For four years she took a teaching job at Elmira College in rural New York. Dissatisfied after this time, she applied for and received a fellowship from the American Association of University Women to do research in Paris. She began a study of oogenesis in frog eggs at the Laboratory of Anatomy and Comparative Histology at the Sorbonne. Her fellowship was extended for an additional year and a small stipend that she received from a teaching assistantship enabled her to stay for a third year. At the end of this year, she was awarded a second doctorate by the Sorbonne. Hibbard returned to the United States to a job at Oberlin College, where she moved through the academic ranks rapidly.

In the 1930s, Hibbard published papers on the histology of limpets, earthworms, squid, and silkworms. Probably her most important work was on the Golgi apparatus. She produced a definitive literature review on the subject that is still cited. Hindered in her work by lack of equipment, specifically an electron microscope, she was frustrated with the impossibility of seeing the fine structure of this cytoplasmic inclusion. After she retired, Oberlin acquired such an instrument, which was, fittingly enough, dedicated to her.

After Hibbard retired, she cared for her stepmother until she died in 1967. At this point, Hibbard began to travel extensively. She was politically active: she rode a bus from

Oberlin to the United Nations to attend a nuclear disarmament rally; was active in the American Association of University Women; and founded the Oberlin Chapter of the League of Women Voters. Apparently an excellent teacher, she was devoted to her students and was determined to give them the tools that they would need for a successful career. She also exhibited personal courage when less than five weeks after she had cancerous lung removed she gave the introductory biology lecture. A singular honor came to Hibbard when she was elected Adelia A. Field Johnson Professorship. This professorship was established in 1898 by contributors who wanted to assure that Oberlin would have a woman professor on its faculty.

JH/MBO

PRIMARY SOURCES

Hibbard, Hope. "Cytoplasmic Inclusion in the Egg of Echinarachnius Parma." Ph.D. dissertation, Bryn Mawr College, 1922.

SECONDARY SOURCES

Egloff, David. "Memorial Minute: Hope Hibbard." *Oberlin Alumni Magazine* (Fall 1988): 54–55.

STANDARD SOURCES

AMS 4–11; Rossiter 1982; Shearer and Shearer 1996.

HICKEY, AMANDA SANFORD (1838–1894)

U.S. physician. Born 28 August 1838 in New Bedford, Mass. Married Patrick Hickey (1884). Educated Friend's Academy, Union Springs, N.Y.; Woman's Medical College, Philadelphia, Pa. (M.D., 1870); New England Hospital, Boston, Mass., intern; University of Michigan, Ann Arbor (graduated 1871); postgraduate work in Paris and London (1879). Professional experience: Auburn, N.Y., private practice; Auburn City Hospital, staff physician and surgeon (1880?–1894). Honors and memberships: Medical Society of the State of New York, member. Died 17 October 1894 from pneumonia.

Amanda Sanford had a great desire to study medicine and planted a market garden to sell for funds to enter the Woman's Medical College in Philadelphia. After gaining her medical degree in 1870, she interned one summer in surgery at the New England Hospital in Boston, then entered the University of Michigan for a second degree, and was the first woman graduated from that institution (1871). She settled in Auburn, N.Y., and developed a substantial practice. She spent 1879 studying in Paris and London.

A member of the original staff of the Auburn City Hospital, Sanford gained a reputation as an outstanding surgeon, performing intra-abdominal surgery with above average success. A maternity hospital in Auburn was named in her

honor. In 1884, she married Patrick Hickey and continued her practice until her death in 1884 of pneumonia, which she contracted after performing a laborious operation in an overheated room.

JH/MBO

STANDARD SOURCES

Cyclopedia AMB.

HICKS, BEATRICE ALICE (1919–1979)

U.S. engineer. Born 2 January 1919 in Orange, N.J. to Florence (Neben) and William Hicks. Married Rodney Chipp (1948). Educated Newark College of Engineering (B.S., 1939); studied electrical engineering (1939–1943); Stevens Institute of Technology (M.S., 1949). Professional experience: Western Electric, technician (1942); engineer (1942?–1945); Newark Controls Co., chief engineer (1945), vice-president (1946), president (1955). Honors and memberships: Society of Women Engineers, cofounder and first president (1950), board member (1952–1953), trustee (1960–1964); Mademoiselle magazine, Woman of the Year in Business (1952); U.S. delegate to the Tenth International Management Congress in Sao Paulo, Brazil (1954); Eleventh International Management Congress in Paris (1957); Project Ambassador sponsored by National Society of Professional Engineers (1959); Achievement Award of the Society of Women Engineers (1963); Rensselaer Polytechnic Institute, honorary doctorate. Died 1979.

Beatrice Hicks was one of the few women to become an engineer. Her father, an engineer and founder of the Newark Controls Co., was, no doubt, greatly influential in her choice of a profession. At the age of thirteen she decided that she would become an engineer after her father took her to the Empire State Building and the George Washington Bridge and explained that the structures had been designed by engineers. She was encouraged to get her degree in engineering and after completing it, studied electrical engineering further. Her first position was at Western Electric, where, in spite of her degree, she was hired only as a technician. She spent not even a year at this position, for her supervisor lobbied for the title of engineer with a salary increase for her. She remained at Western Electric for three years, when she joined her father's firm. Again, her family connections were helpful, for she soon became chief engineer, and a year later, vice-president. In 1955 she became president of the company. In the meantime, she had married engineer Rodney Chipp and earned a master of science degree in physics.

Hicks was active in numerous organizations, but was especially important in her role as a cofounder and officer of the Society of Women Engineers. In 1965 she became the first woman named an honorary doctor of engineering from Rensselaer Polytechnic Institute.

JH/MBO

SECONDARY SOURCES
Withem, Karen. "Beatrice Hicks, Society's First President, Dies." *Society of Women Engineers Newsletter* (November/December 1979): 5.

STANDARD SOURCES
Bailey; *Notable* (article by Karen Withem).

HIGGINS, VERA (COCKBURN) (1892–1968)

British botanist/physicist. Born 15 January 1892 in London to Frances Margaret and William Cockburn. Married William Frederick Higgins (1 June 1920). Educated Addiscombe High School; Croham Hurst School; Newnham College, Cambridge (1912–1916; Natural Science Tripos, Part I, class 2; Part II, class 3, physics); Muriel Edwards prize winner (1915); (M.A., 1924). Professional position: National Physical Laboratory, scientific officer (1916–1920). Editorships: Journal of the Cactus and Succulent Society, Great Britain, editor (1935). Alpine Garden Society Bulletin, editor. Honors and memberships: Linnean Society, Fellow (1945); Victoria Medal of Honor (1946). Died 1968.

Vera Higgins was educated at Newnham College, where she studied physics. Upon graduation, she was a scientific officer at the National Physical Laboratory. Botany for her began as a hobby but gradually became her major research interest. She collected and drew plants and wrote books on plants. She worked mostly on succulents and cacti. Her Cambridge drawings are at the Royal Horticultural Society.

JH/MBO

PRIMARY SOURCES
Higgins, Vera. *Naming of Plants*. London: E. Arnold & Co., 1937.
———. *Study of Cacti*. London: Blandford Press, Ltd., 1933. 2d ed., 1946.
———. *Succulent Plants Illustrated*. London: Blandford Press, Ltd., 1949.
———. *Succulents in Cultivation*. London: Blandford Press, Ltd., 1960.
———. *Crassulas in Cultivation*. London: Blandford Press, Ltd., 1964.

SECONDARY SOURCES
Gardener's Chronicle 101 (1937): 180.
Gardener's Chronicle 150 (1961): 379. Includes portrait.
Gardener's Chronicle 164 (1968) 27–28. Obituary notice.
Journal of the Royal Horticultural Society (1969): 187–188. Obituary notice.
Journal of the Cactus Succulent Society, Great Britain, (1969): 1. Obituary notice

STANDARD SOURCES
Desmond; Newnham (includes portrait).

HIGHTOWER, RUBY USHER (1880–?)

U.S. mathematician. Born 1880 near Covington, Ga. Educated Shorter College (A.B.); University of Chicago; London University; University of Georgia (A.M., 1919); University of Missouri (1924–1925; Ph.D., 1927). Professional experience: Alabama Normal College, professor; Harden College, professor; Shorter College, professor. Death date unknown.

Ruby Hightower earned a doctorate at the University of Missouri. The dates when she taught at the three small colleges are unknown. Hightower was a member of the Mathematical Association and her research was on the theory of numbers.

JH/MBO

PRIMARY SOURCES
Hightower, Ruby U. *On the Classification of the Elements of a Ring*. Lancaster, Pa.: Lancaster Press, [1927?].

STANDARD SOURCES
AMS 4–8, P 9.

HILDEGARD OF BINGEN (1098–1179 or 1180)

German cosmologist, natural philosopher, and writer on medicine. Born 1098 in Böckelheim, Mainz, to Mechtilde and Hildebert. At least ten siblings. Educated at the convent of Disibodenberg. Professional experience: Abbess of Disibodenberg (1136–1145) and Bingen (1145– ca. 1179). Died Rupertsberg, near Bingen, ca. 1179.

Hildegard of Bingen was the tenth child of Mechtilde (about whom nothing is known) and Hildebert of Vermersheim, a member of the landed gentry and a knight in attendance on Meginhard, Count of Sponheim. Sources disagree over her place of birth, giving it variously as Bermersheim, Germany, Böckelheim, and simply the Rhineland. During her childhood she was subject to visions and extrasensory phenomena. She later stated that she found "divine testimony" at age five. Much of her childhood was spent vacillating between the ideal reality of her visions and the perceptual reality of her senses. As a delicate seven-year-old, Hildegard spent much of her time in a dream world. She was educated at the convent of Disibodenberg on the Nahe River, where she was trained to care for the sick. Some sources indicate that Hildegard learned to read and write in German; others indicate that she was literate in Latin, whereas some insist that she was dependent on scribes to record her ideas.

When Abbess Jutta of Disibodenberg died, Hildegard succeeded her in 1136. Declaring the convent's facilities inadequate, and pleading a mandate from God for a move, she and eighteen sisters relocated to a new convent on the Rupertsberg near Bingen. The move generated considerable controversy, and Hildegard responded by becoming ill and, according to reports, lay prostrate for several years. After her recovery, she was assaulted by a new round of visions. She was careful to explain that these visions came to her when she was in a profoundly serious mood. She explained that the visions began by a bright white light that spread over the objects around her.

Hildegard corresponded with both ecclesiastical and temporal leaders. Pope Eugenius read a portion of her *Scivias* in 1148 (the work was completed in 1151), which described her cosmology and the place of humans within it. She and Eugenius carried on a lengthy correspondence. She also corresponded with other important clerics, including Bernard of Clairvaux—the mystic founder of the order of the Knights Templar—and Popes Anastasius IV, Adrian IV, and Alexander III. She also corresponded with the rulers Frederick Barbarossa, Conrad II, and Henry II of England, and became involved in several important political crises. If threats and cajolery were necessary to get her way, Hildegard did not hesitate. Feminist sources indicate that Hildegard tailored her rhetoric to appeal to the gender of those to whom she was writing. The language of her appeals to powerful men differed from that used in letters to women.

Hildegard died at the age of eighty-one in either 1179 or 1180. Three attempts under three different popes were made to have her canonized. Even though she is referred to as Saint Hildegard and is included in the *Acta sanctorum,* she was never officially made a saint, for the investigators concluded that either the miraculous cures attributed to her were insufficiently miraculous or they were not properly attested to.

In evaluating Hildegard's contributions to science, it is important to consider her work in the context of the Middle Ages. She, as did many of her contemporaries, made no distinction among physical events, ethical truths, and mystical experience. Various sources have tried to portray Hildegard's work as either a forerunner of modern ideas or as so consumed by mysticism that she has no importance in the history of science. Those who would make her modern credit her with presaging "the beautiful discoveries of Cesalpino and Harvey and later discoveries regarding 'the alternation of the seasons'" (Mozans, 169–170). She did not, as one writer asserted, anticipate the theory of universal gravitation. On the opposite end of the spectrum, Hildegard's work cannot be dismissed as mystical nonsense. Her works are similar neither to ancient nor to modern science and must be understood as a medieval phenomenon immersed in a medieval milieu.

In her five major writings, Hildegard not only dwelt upon spiritual matters but provided theoretical solutions for physical observations. They must not be dismissed because her "scientific method" used "visions from God." Visions, under different names, have always been part of science. Today,

these visions are called theories or intuition. Hildegard used terms such as divine inspiration, embarrassing to twentieth-century scientists, but very much a part of a medieval scientific vocabulary. Both theoretical and practical aspects of science are found in Hildegard's writings, although the theoretical predominate, as in the *Scivias,* the *Liber vitae meritorum,* and the *Liber divinorum operum.* In these three books, she discusses the origin of the cosmos and the interrelationships among its components. In the *Causae et curae* and the *Physica,* she emphasized the practical aspects of science as she described plants, animals, and minerals and their relationship to humankind's well-being. MBO

PRIMARY SOURCES

Hildegard of Bingen. *Welt und Mensch: Das Buch "De operatione Dei," aus dem Genter Kodex (Liber divinorum operum).* Trans. and ed. Maura Böckeler. Salzburg: Otto Müller, 1954. This theoretical work on cosmology shows the evolution of Hildegard's ideas from the earlier *Scivias.* An English translation, *Hildegard of Bingen's Book of Divine Works, with Letters and Songs,* ed. Matthew Fox (Santa Fe, N.M.: Bear and Company, 1987) is available.

———. *Wisse die Wege—Scivias—nach dem Originaltext des illuminierten Rupertsberger Kodex, der Wiesbadener Landesbibliothek.* Trans. and ed. Maura Böckeler. Salzburg: Otto Müller, 1954. Hildegard's early theoretical work on cosmology. An English translation, *Scivias by Hildegard of Bingen: The English Translation from the Critical Latin Edition,* trans. Bruce Hozeski (Santa Fe, N.M.: Bear and Company) is available.

———. *Heilkunde: Das Buch von dem Grund und Wessen und der Heilung der Krankheiten (Causae et curae).* Trans. Heinrich Schipperges. Salzburg: Otto Müller, 1957. The first section is theoretical and considers the origin of the universe and its components. The final section is concerned with practical applications of "nature knowledge" and helped establish Hildegard's reputation as a physician.

———. *Naturkunde: Das Buch von dem inneren Wesen der verschiedenen Naturen in der Schöpfung (Physica).* Ed. Peter Riethe. Salzburg: Otto Müller, 1959. Some sources question the authenticity of this work. It is one of the works from which Hildegard's reputation as a physician was derived.

———. *Der Mensch in der Verantwortung: Das Buch der Lebensverd enste (Liber vitae meritorum).* Trans. and ed. by Heinrich Schipperges. Salzburg: Otto Müller, 1972. This book was composed in 1158 when Hildegard was sixty years old. She reported that God instructed her to compile this book, which contained a collection of moral admonitions. The only Latin edition is found in J. B. Pitra's *Analecta sanctae Hildegardis* (Monte Cassino, 1882). Although not complete, J. P. Migne, ed., *Patrologia latina,* vol. 197: *S. Hildegardis abbatissae opera omnia* (Paris: Garnier, 1882) is the most convenient source for the writings of Hildegard. In addition, it supplies biographical information from the *Acta sanctorum* as well as a biography by the monks Godefrid and Theodoric, who were scribes who may have transcribed Hildegard's work.

SECONDARY SOURCES

Ahlgren, Gillian T. W. "Visions and Rhetorical Strategy in the Letters of Hildegard of Bingen." In *Dear Sister: Medieval Women and the Epistolary Genre,* ed. Karen Cherewatud and Ulrike Wiethaus, 46–63. Philadelphia: University of Pennsylvania Press, 1993. Uses the letters of Hildegard as an opportunity to analyze the interplay of religious experience, prophetic authority, and rhetorical skill in the life of a twelfth-century visionary. Argues that because of the precarious position of medieval women in society, Hildegard was concerned with the way her visions would be received by her male contemporaries. Assumes that Hildegard consciously developed rhetorical strategies to express her visions in her personal correspondence, and the literary formulae which she used depended on the gender and socio-religious status of the recipient.

Allen, Prudence. "Hildegard of Bingen's Philosophy of Sex Identity." *Thought* 64 (1989): 231–241.

Breindl, Ellen. *Das Grosse Gesundheitsbuch der Hl. Hildegard von Bingen: Leben und Wirken einen bedeutenden Frau des Glaubens: Ratschlage und Rezepte für ein gesundes Leben.* Aschaffenburg: Pattloch, 1983. Divided into five parts. The first is biographical. The second includes a discussion of her major philosophical works and how they fit into the philosophy of the middle ages. The third describes her botanical works, including plates, many in color, of the most important plants described by Hildegard. Part four lists the plants in alphabetical order. Part five gives practical advice on the use of plants. With bibliography, index, and Illustrations.

Cadden, Joan. "It Takes All Kinds: Sexuality and Gender Differences in Hildegard of Bingen's Book of Compound Medicine." *Traditio* 40 (1984): 149–174.

Engbring, Gertrude M. "Saint Hildegard, Twelfth Century Physician." *Bulletin of the History of Medicine* 8 (1940): 770–784.

Fischer, Hermann. *Die Heilige Hildegard von Bingen. Die erste deutsche Naturforcherin und Artzin. Ihr Leben und Werk.* Munich: Verlag der Munchner Drucke, 1927. A critical study in German of the life and works of Hildegard. Good bibliography of secondary sources.

Flanagan, Sabina. *Hildegard of Bingen, 1098–1179: A Visionary Life.* New York: Routledge, 1989.

Hertzka, G. *So heilt Gott: die Medizin der hl. Hildegard von Bingen als neues Naturheilverfahren.* Stein am Rhein: Christiana Verlag, 1972.

Singer, Charles, ed. "The Scientific Views and Visions of Saint Hildegard (1098–1180)." In *Studies in the History and Method of Science,* 1–55. Oxford: Clarendon Press, 1917.

———. "The Visions of Hildegard of Bingen." In *From Magic to Science: Essays on the Scientific Twilight.* New York: Boni and Liveright, 1928. Gives an account of the life, writings, and visions of Hildegard. Illustrates the mystical-magical point of view typical of the Middle Ages. Includes plates, figures, and a few notes.

Strehlow, W., and G. Hertzka. *Hildegard of Bingen's Medicine.* Translated by K. A. Strehlow. Santa Fe, N.M.: Bear & Co., 1988.

Thorndike, Lynn. "Saint Hildegard of Bingen, 1098–1179." In *A History of Magic and Experimental Science During the First Thirteen Centuries of Our Era,* 124–154. London: Macmillan, 1923. A well-documented account of Hildegard's life, the influence of her predecessors, and the interaction between science and religion in her writings.

STANDARD SOURCES
DSB; Ogilvie 1986.

HILDRETH, GERTRUDE HOWELL (1898–1984)

U.S. psychologist. Born 11 October 1898 in Terre Haute, Ind. Educated Northwestern Univesity; University of Illinois (A.M., 1921); Columbia University (Ph.D., 1925). Professional experience: public schools in Oklahoma, psychologist (1921–1923); Columbia University, Lincoln School of Teachers College, instructor(?) (1925–1945); Brooklyn College, assistant professor to professor of education (1949–1965); American University, Beirut, visiting professor (1964–1968). Memberships: American Psychological Association; American Association for the Advancement of Science; American Educational Research Association. Death date unknown.

Gertrude Hildreth was born in the Midwest and educated at Northwestern University and the University of Illinois. She earned her master's degree from the latter institution. After receiving this degree she took her first professional position as a psychologist in the public schools of Oklahoma. Two years later she returned to graduate studies at Teachers College, Columbia University, where she received her doctoral degree three years later. She remained in New York teaching at Columbia until 1949, when she was appointed assistant professor of education at Brooklyn College, rising through the ranks to full professor. From 1964 to 1968 she spent time as a visiting professor at the American University in Beirut.

During her professional career she developed educational measurement tests for children and published on gifted and talented children. Her papers and her test collection can be found at Princeton University.   JH/MBO

PRIMARY SOURCES
Hildreth, Gertrude. *Psychological Service for School Problems.* Yonkers, N.Y.: World Book, 1930.

———. With S. F. Bayne and F. B. Graham. *Metropolitan Achievement Test. Primary Batteries I and II.* Yonkers, N.Y.: World Book Co., 1931, 1932.

———. *Introduction to the Gifted.* New York: McGraw-Hill, 1965.

SECONDARY SOURCES
Schmidt, C. *Guide to G. Hildreth Papers and Test Collection.* (Princeton).

STANDARD SOURCES
AMS 4–6, S&B 9–11; *Psychological Register,* vol. 3.

HILGARD, JOSEPHINE ROHRS (1906–1989)

U.S. psychiatrist, psychologist, and psychoanalyst. Born 12 March 1906 in Napoleon, Ohio, to Edna Belden (Balsely) and Henry F. Rohrs. Married Ernest R. Hilgard 19 September 1931. One son and one daughter. Educated public high school, Napoleon (graduated 1924); Radcliffe College; Smith College (magna cum laude, Phi Beta Kappa, 1928); Yale University (Ph.D. in child psychology, 1933); Stanford Medical School (M.D., 1940); Institute for Juvenile Research, Chicago (1940–1942); Chicago Institute of Psychoanalysis (1940–1944). Professional experience: Chestnut Lodge, Washington, D.C. (1942–1945). San Francisco Child Guidance Clinic of Childrens Hospital, director (1945–1947?); Stanford University School of Medicine, clinical professor of psychiatry (1947–?); Stanford University Department of Psychology, hypnosis laboratory, research associate. Honors and memberships: Society for Clinical and Experimental Hypnosis Bernard B. Raginsky Award; International Society of Hypnosis, Benjamin Franklin Gold Medal for Excellence (1985); American Psychiatric Association, Fellow; American Psychological Association, member. Died 16 May 1989 in Palo Alto, Calif.

Josephine Rohrs was born in Napoleon, Ohio, where her father was local school board president. She was valedictorian of her high school. She began her higher education at Radcliffe College, but transferred after a year to Smith College where she graduated magna cum laude and Phi Beta Kappa in 1928. She received her doctorate in child psychology at Yale University (1933), where Arnold Gesell supervised her dissertation research.

At Yale, she met Ernest R. Hilgard, whom she married on 19 September 1931. Two years later they moved to California, where Ernest accepted a position at Stanford University. Josephine Hilgard entered Stanford Medical School and received her medical degree in 1940. Moving to Chicago with her husband and young son, Henry, born in 1936, she received a Rockefeller Fellowship at the Institute for Juvenile Research (1940–1942), where she worked with Franz Alexander. She received a training psychoanalysis from Margaret Gerard and extended her psychoanalytical

training at the Chicago Institute of Psychoanalysis (1940–1944). When the family moved to Washington, D.C., Hilgard obtained a professional position at nearby Chestnut Lodge, where she worked with Frieda Fromm Reichman and Harry Stack Sullivan from 1942 to 1945. Daughter Elizabeth Ann was born in 1944. Working with severely emotionally disturbed adolescents at the lodge stimulated Hilgard to study a variety of developmental issues.

Hilgard conducted research on psychotic episodes relating to the death of a parent, "anniversary reaction," using both clinical observations and long-term archival investigation. After the Hilgards moved to Palo Alto, she was appointed professor of clinical psychiatry at the Stanford Medical School and also conducted research at the hypnosis laboratory. This involved interviews with hundreds of Stanford undergraduates who had participated in the laboratory's ongoing research program as reported in her book *Personality and Hypnosis: A Study of Imaginative Involvement.* Her other books concerned hypnotic analgesia: *Hypnosis in the Relief of Pain* (1975), coauthored with her husband, and *The Hypnotherapy of Pain in Children with Cancer* (1984), written with Samuel LeBaron.

Among her many awards was one from the Society for Clinical and Experimental Hypnosis, the Bernard B. Raginsky Award, for excellence in teaching and research in hypnosis (1982). The International Society of Hypnosis awarded her its Benjamin Franklin Gold Medal (1985). She was a fellow of the American Psychiatric Association. The American Psychological Association held a special symposium in Hilgard's honor in 1985 at its ninety-third annual convention. She died 16 May 1989 in Palo Alto, California.   JH/MBO

PRIMARY SOURCES
Hilgard, Josephine Rohrs. *The Effect of Early and Delayed Practice on Memory and Motor Performances Studied by the Method of Co-Twin Control; from the Clinic of Child Development, Yale University.* Worcester, Mass.: Clark University Press, 1934.

———. *Personality and Hypnosis: A Study of Imaginative Involvement.* Chicago: University of Chicago Press, 1970. 2d ed., 1979.

———. With Ernest R. Hilgard. *Hypnosis in the Relief of Pain.* Los Altos, Calif.: Kaufmann, 1975. Rev. ed., 1983.

———. With Samuel LeBaron. *Hypnotherapy of Pain in Children with Cancer.* Los Altos, Calif.: Kaufmann, 1984.

SECONDARY SOURCES
Bowers, Kenneth S. "Josephine R. Hilgard (1906–1989)." *American Psychologist* 45 (1990): 1382. Obituary notice.

STANDARD SOURCES
Stevens and Gardner.

HILL, DOROTHY (1907–1997)

Australian invertebrate paleontologist and stratigrapher. Born 10 September 1907 in Brisbane to Sarah Jane (Kington) and Robert Samson Hill. Educated Brisbane Girls Grammar School (1920–1924); University of Queensland (B.Sc., 1928, first class honors; M.Sc., 1930; D.Sc., 1942); Cambridge University (Ph.D., 1932). Professional experience: University of Queensland, research fellow (1937–1942); Department of Geology, lecturer (1945?–1956), chief lecturer (1956–1958), research professor (1959), professor (1960–1972). Honors and memberships: Royal Society of Queensland, honorary secretary (1938–1942), member of the council (1947–1950), president (1949); Great Barrier Reef Committee, honorary secretary (1946–1955); Australian/New Zealand Association for the Advancement of Science, president of Section C at the Dunedin Meeting (1957); Geological Society of Australia, journal editor (1958–1964); Australian Academy of Science, fellow (1956); Geological Society of London, Lyell Medal (1964); Royal Society of London, Fellow (1965); Royal Society of New South Wales, Fellow (1966); ANZAAS, Mueller Medal (1967). Died 23 April 1997 in Brisbane.

Dorothy Hill won an open scholarship to the University of Queensland from the Brisbane Girls Grammar School in 1925 and graduated with first class honors in geology and mineralogy. She was able to continue her education because she won a University Gold Medal for outstanding merit and a Scholarship for the Encouragement of Original Research. During her postgraduate work at Queensland, she studied the stratigraphy, structure, and relationships of the Brisbane Valley's Mesozoic rocks. Her interests became focused on paleontology when she accidentally discovered a rich coral fauna in the carboniferous limestone of the Mundubbera area. She won a Foundation Travelling Scholarship to Cambridge University in 1930, where she earned her doctoral degree. She remained at Cambridge for seven years. During that time, she was elected to a research fellowship at Newnham College. Under the mentorship of two leading geologists, W. D. Lang and Stanley Smith, she was awarded a Senior Studentship of the Exhibition of 1851, which allowed her to continue doing research at the Sedgwick Museum for two more years.

By the time she returned to Australia, her reputation as a world authority on rugose corals was established. At this time she took up a post at the University of Queensland, a Council of Scientific and Industrial Research Fellowship. She worked on Paleozoic corals from all over Australia from 1937 to 1942. However, in 1942, World War II was moving closer to Australia, so she joined the WRANS as Operations Staff Officer. After the war, she continued her career in the Department of Geology at the University of Queensland, where she passed through the academic ranks to full professor.

Hill was a good citizen of the geological community, serving in many societies. She held a number of offices in the Royal Society of Queensland, including being elected the first woman president of the society. She was also the first woman to be elected to the fellowship of the Australian Academy of Science. In addition to many other honors, including the Lyell Medal, she was elected a Fellow of the Royal Society.

Although Dorothy Hill's research was chiefly on the Carboniferous corals of Australia and Scotland, she also worked on other invertebrate groups and on the geology of Queensland. She published prolifically, especially on Australian Paleozoic Corals. Although her most important work has been in paleontology, she has also made significant contributions in the areas of stratigraphy, sedimentation, and regional geology.

C K

PRIMARY SOURCES

Hill, Dorothy. "The Stratigraphical Relationship of the Shales about Esk to the Sediments of the Ipswich Basin." *Proceedings of the Royal Society of Queensland* 41 (1930): 162–191.

———. "The Permian Corals of Western Australia." *Journal of the Proceedings of the Royal Society of Western Australia* 23 (1937): 43–63.

———. "The Silurian Rugosa of the Yass-Bowning District, N.S.W." *Proceedings of the Linnaean Society of New South Wales* 65 (1940): 388–420.

———. With J. W. Wells. "Cnidaria-General Features." In *Treatise on Invertebrate Paleontology. Part F, Coelenterata*, ed. R. C. Moore. Lawrence, Kans.: Geological Society of America and University of Kansas Press, F67, 1956. This chapter, which contains contributions from Hill and Wells, is a part of a series of twelve publications from the Geological Society of America and the University of Kansas Press.

SECONDARY SOURCES

Denmead, A. K. "Portrait of a Scientist: Dorothy Hill." *Earth Science Review* 8 (1972): 351–363. Includes a photograph.

———. "Professor Dorothy Hill." In *Stratigraphy and Paleontology; Essays in Honor of Dorothy Hill*, ed. K. S. W. Campbell, v–vii. Canberra, Australia: Australian National University Press, 1969. Obituary notice.

Dorothy Hill Jubilee Memoir: Proceedings of a Meeting Organised by the Association of Australian Paleontologists, a Specialist Group of the Geological Society of Australia, Inc. at the University of Queensland, 9 & 10 September 1982. J. Roberts and P. A. Jell, eds. Sydney, Australia: Association of Australian Palaeontologists, 1983. Includes a chronological listing of events in her career. Also contains a selected bibliography of secondary as well as her own writings.

"Obituary. Dorothy Hill AC, CBE." *Australian Geologist* 103 (30 June 1997): 50.

STANDARD SOURCES
Sarjeant.

HILL, JUSTINA HAMILTON (1893–?)

U.S. bacteriologist. Born 1 October 1893 in Washington, D.C., to Jennie Justina (Robinson) and Robert T. Hill. Educated Miss Capen's School for Girls, Northampton, Mass.; Smith College (A.B., 1916); University of Michigan (M.S., 1917). Professional experience: Red Cross worker (1917–1918); Near East Relief, relief worker; Johns Hopkins University School of Medicine, Brady Urological Institute, associate in bacteriology (1920–1921); instructor and associate in urology (from 1922). Death date unknown.

Although Justina Hill received an honorary doctorate of science from Smith College, she did not have an earned doctorate. Nevertheless, she was able to become head of the bacteriological laboratory at the Brady Institute of the Johns Hopkins Medical School and at that time was probably the only female associate in urology. After she finished her degree, she wanted to go overseas with the American Red Cross to contribute her scientific knowledge, but was refused because she was too young. She joined the Red Cross, nevertheless, and was stationed at Spartanburg, South Carolina, where she ran a bacteriological laboratory. She remained there for fifteen months and then went with a Smith College Unit to the Near East, where she ran a laboratory for five thousand refugees. Upon returning to the United States, Hill was made an associate in bacteriology at the Brady Urological Institute and two years later an instructor in urology. She added the title of associate in urology. She published numerous technical articles in medical journals as well as popular books on bacteriology. Her papers are in the Alan Chesney Medical Archives at Johns Hopkins University.

JH/MBO

PRIMARY SOURCES
Hill, Justina. *Germs and the Man.* New York: G. P. Putnam's Sons, 1940. A popular book that Karl Menninger called the best popular presentation that had yet appeared.

SECONDARY SOURCES
Time, 13 January 1941.

STANDARD SOURCES
AMS 5–8; *Current Biography* 1941.

HILL, MARY ELLIOTT (1907–1969)

U.S. analytical chemist. Born 5 January 1907 in Norfolk, Va. Married (1927). One child. Educated Virginia State College (B.S., 1929); University of Pennsylvania (M.S., 1941). Professional experience: Science Laboratory School, Virginia State College, instructor (1930–1932; 1939–1942); Hampton Institute, assistant professor (1934–1935; 1937–1938); Bennett College, chemist (1942–1943); Tennessee State University, associate professor (1944–1962); Kentucky State College (from 1962). Died 1969.

Analytical chemist Mary Elliott Hill held several different jobs early in her career. However, after she earned her master's degree (she did not get a doctoral degree), she spent eighteen years at Tennessee State University where she was acting department head in 1951. In 1962, she left Tennessee State for Kentucky State College, where she remained for the rest of her career. She was a member of the Chemical Society and the National Institute of Science. Hill's research was on ultraviolet spectrophotometry; titrations in nonaqueous solutions, synthesis and properties of monomeric and dimeric ketones, Grignard reagents, and unsaturated ethers.

JH/MBO

STANDARD SOURCES
AMS P 9, P&B 10–11.

HINES, MARION (1889–?)

U.S. neuroanatomist. Born 11 June 1889 in Carthage, Mo. Married. Educated Smith College (A.B., 1913); honorary Sc.D. (1943); University of Chicago (Ph.D. in neurology, 1917); University of London (1920); Cambridge University (1923–1924); Würzburg (1930). Professional experience: University of Chicago, assistant in anatomy (1915–1917), associate (1917–1918), instructor (1918–1924), assistant professor (1924–1925); Johns Hopkins University, associate (1925–1930), associate professor (1930–1947), director of postgraduate training grant in neuroanatomy (1960–1965); Emory University, professor of experimental medicine, school of medicine (1947–1959), emerita professor (1959–1965). Death date unknown.

Neuroanatomist Marion Hines had an excellent education. After completing her undergraduate work at Smith College, she went to the University of Chicago where she held an assistantship and then got her doctoral degree. She traveled abroad, spending a part of a year at the University of London, a year at Cambridge, and another year at Würzburg. She advanced to assistant professor at the University of Chicago before she left for Johns Hopkins University, where she became an associate professor. In 1947, she went to the Emory

Medical School as a full professor. She remained at Emory for twelve years until retirement. Upon retirement, Hines received a grant at Hopkins on the training of postgraduates.

Her papers are in the Alan Chesney Medical Archives at Johns Hopkins University. Some correspondence with FLORENCE SABIN is held at the American Philosophical Library, Philadelphia.   JH/MBO

PRIMARY SOURCES

Hines, Marion. "The Development and Regression of Reflexes: Postures and Progression in the Young Macaque." *Carnegie Institution* 30 (1942): 153–209.

STANDARD SOURCES

AMS 3–8, B 9, P&B 10–11.

HINMAN, ALICE HAMLIN (1869?–1934)

U.S. psychologist. Born 20 December 1869(?) in Constantinople, Turkey. Married Edgar L. Hinman. Educated Wellesley College (A.B., 1893) and Cornell University (Ph.D., 1897). Professional experience: Mount Holyoke College, professor of psychology (1897); University of Nebraska, psychology and ethics faculty (from 1898); Lincoln, Nebraska, Board of Education (1907–1919; chairman, 1910). Died 24 April 1934.

Alice Hamlin Hinman was a qualified psychologist whose greatest contribution was in the area of public education. After receiving her doctorate at Cornell, she taught psychology at Mount Holyoke College for one year before marrying Edgar Hinman, the head of the department of philosophy and psychology at the University of Nebraska. Once in Lincoln, she joined the university faculty, teaching psychology and ethics. Her membership and influence on the Lincoln Board of Education from 1907 to 1919 resulted in the public school system's evolution from backwoods to a model of progressive education. She had great skills in dealing with people and used this talent in a wide range of local, national, and international service organizations. Hinman taught in various schools at various times and continued to study and write journal articles in her areas of interest: memory, hypnotism, and infant psychology.   KM

STANDARD SOURCES

AMS 1–5; *NCAB* (with photograph); Siegel and Finley.

HINRICHS, MARIE AGNES (1892–1979)

U.S. physiologist and zoologist. Born 22 September 1892 in Chilcago, Ill. Educated Lake Forest College (1917); University of Chicago (Ph.D. in zoology, 1923; Rush Medical School, M.D.,

1934). Professional experience: Chicago elementary schools, teacher (1912–1915); Vassar College, instructor in zoology (1920–1921); Nela Research Lab, assistant (1922–1924); University of Chicago, national research fellow (1924–1926), research associate in physiology (1926–1934); Southern Illinois University, associate professor and department head (1935–1938), professor of physiology and hygiene and department head (1938–1949), professor of physiology and department head (1949–1952), head of student health service (1935–1949); University of Illinois, health service physician (1949–1952), associate professor of health education (1952–1954); Chicago Public Schools, director, Bureau of Health Services (1953–?); Journal of School Health, editor in chief. Attended marine biology lab at Woods Hole. Honors and memberships: Public Health Association, Fellow; Association of Health, member; Physical Education & Recreation Society, member; Physiological Society, member; American Medical Association, member; Society of Experimental Biology, member; Sigma Delta Epsilon, member; American School Health Association award (1962, 1969); Southern Illinois University Distinguished Service Award (1979).

Like so many women scientists, Marie Hinrichs held a variety of positions. From what started out to be a purely academic career at Southern Illinois University, where she held the rank of professor and head of the department, she moved on to become head of the student health service and then a health service physician. She moved back to an academic post for four years and then became director of the Bureau of Health Services for the Chicago Public School System and editor-in-chief of the *Journal of Public Health*.

Her research centered on the effects of ultraviolet radiation and visible radiation on living matter, especially developing embryos. She also studied akaloids and their effects on lower animals. Reflecting her versatility, she also studied student health facilities.   JH/MBO

PRIMARY SOURCES

Hinrichs, Marie A. With Philip O.C. Johnson. *Heart Rhythms in Frog and Turtle as Affected by Ultraviolet Point Radiation.* N.p.: Society for Experimental Biology and Medicine, 1930.

———. With George Warrick. *Ultraviolet Point Radiation in the Production of Arrhythmias in the Heart of Chick Embryo.* N.p.: Society for Experimental Biology and Medicine, 1931.

STANDARD SOURCES

AMS 4–8, B 9, P&B 10–14.

HIRSCHFELD-TIBURTIUS, HENRIETTE (PAGELSEN) (1834–1911)

German dentist. Born 1834 in Westerland on the island of Sylt. Father a clergyman. Studied in America under her widowed name,

Henriette Hirschfeld. Second marriage in 1872 to Oberstabsarzt Carl Tibertius. Two children. Educated Dental College of Philadelphia (D.D.S., 1869). Professional experience: Women and children's dentist in Berlin; Poliklinik für Frauen (Outpatient Clinic for Women) in Berlin, cofounder with Franziska Tibertius and Emilie Lehmus (1887). Honors and memberhips: Executive Committee to the World Exposition in Chicago, member (1893). Died 24 October 1911 in Berlin.

When Henriette Hirschfeld (born Pagelsen) lost her husband, she took a job in Berlin as a housekeeper. Due to unsuccessful, drawn-out treatments she underwent for painful tooth problems, her interest in dentistry was awakened. She received technical training and, after numerous requests, was granted permission by the Ministry of Education and Arts to open a dental practice in Berlin. She was required, however, to show proof of her training at an accredited institution. She decided to attempt to become accredited in America and studied dentistry from 1867 to 1869 at the Dental College in Philadelphia. The wife of James Truman, the only professor to take an interest in Hirschfeld, was active in the American Women's Movement. Hirschfeld lacked Latin and had to complete these course requirements before she received her doctor's degree in 1869. Although she had an opportunity to remain in Philadelphia, she returned to Germany to open her own practice. The first female dentist to practice in Germany, Hirschfeld offered a *Zahnatelier* (dental office) for women and children. Working with a hand drill required strength and dexterity. Such innovations as pedal-driven drills and the hydralic dental chair were first introduced in 1875. Hirschfeld's basic principle of dentistry was to avoid tooth extraction and preserve the tooth whenever possible. She also emphasized adherence to oral hygiene, and introduced preventative dentistry to fight cavities, which she called the "mass grave of the peoples' health" and a source of infection. Only in 1883 did dental check-ups become required in school and in the military.

In 1872, the busy dentist married Oberstabarzt Dr. Carl Tibertius, a captain in the medical corps. She continued to practice dentistry after the birth of her two children, feeling that they needed an independent and active mother. Her engagement in the field of social work accompanied her into old age. Alongside her demanding dental practice, an energetic interest in community work blossomed. She was especially involved with "morally endangered" and young "wayward" women and their children, as well as with efforts to educate maids and servants. She was on the board of two homes for women in Berlin (the Heimathauses für Stellung suchende Mädchen and the Heimstätte Berlin). Together with Lina Morgenstern she founded a women's club to help educate minors discharged from prison and "neglected"

girls, then still later, she cofounded the Frauenclub 1900. She advised both EMILIE LEHMUS and her own sister-in-law, FRANZISKA TIBURTIUS, to study medicine in Switzerland. Both returned as doctors of medicine and founded the Poliklinik für Frauen in 1887 with enthusiastic support from Hirschfeld-Tiburtius. The Polikinik für Frauen, (Outpatient Clinic for Women) on Alter Schönhauser Strasse, later became the Klinik weiblicher Ärzte (Clinic for Women's Medicine), Karl-Schrader-Strasse 10. This clinic gave preference to women without financial means or health insurance.

In 1887, the Royal Supreme Court of Berlin decided that only certificates of qualification for the German Reich could be fully recognized and titled. An effort was made to discredit American colleges and Swiss universities as refugee centers for women where a "lowering of standards" existed.

In 1902, Henriette Hirschfeld-Tiburtius retired from her practice, passing her patients on to Elisabeth von Widekind.

GVL

SECONDARY SOURCES

Feyl, Renate. *Der lautlost Aufbruch. Frauen in der Wissenschaft.* Darmstadt und Neuwied: Luchterhand, 1983. Berlin: Verlag Neues Leben, 1984. Hirschfeld-Tiburtius discussed on pages 131–145.

Schelenz, H. *Frauen im Reiche Äskulaps.* Leipzig: Ernst Günther's Verlog, 1900.

Schönfeld, W. *Frauen in der abendländischen Heilkunst.* Stuttgart: Enke, 1974. Hirschfeld-Tiburtius mentioned on page 147.

STANDARD SOURCES

Lexikon der Frau.

HITCHCOCK, FANNY RYSAM MULFORD (1851–?)

U.S. chemist. Educated University of Pennsylvania (Ph.D., 1894). Death date unknown.

Nothing is known of Fanny Hitchcock's early life, or what she did professionally after she got her doctorate from the University of Pennsylvania in 1894. She was, however, a member of the Chemical Society, the Mathematics Society, and the Torrey Botanical Club. She was elected a Fellow of the New York Academy of Science. Her research was on the effect of high temperature on minerals, the chemistry of iron ores, and the origin of disease in the pineapple plant.

JH/MBO

STANDARD SOURCES

AMS 1–3.

HITCHCOCK, ORRA WHITE (1796–1863)

U.S. geological illustrator. Born 1796 in Amherst, Mass, to Jarib White. Married Edward Hitchock (1821). Eight children. Professional experience: Deerfield Academy, assistant instructor (to 1821). Died 1863.

Orra White Hitchcock was a geological illustrator. She was the wife of Edward Hitchcock (1793–1864), a professor and then president of Amherst College and the first state geologist of Massachusetts in the 1830s and 1840s. Orra Hitchcock's atlas of plates accompanied Edward Hitchcock's reports. Her drawings illustrate several conventions of the time. Human figures or houses are often included in her scenic plates to convey scale. Her technical plates are not as detailed as are those of some of the later artists and do not convey scale as successfully.

Her and her husband's papers are in the archives at Amherst College.   JH/MBO

PRIMARY SOURCES

Hitchcock, Edward. *Final Report of the Geology of Massachusetts.* Amherst: J. S. and C. Adams, 1841. Includes Orra White Hitchcock's illustrations.

SECONDARY SOURCES

Marche, Theresa A. "Orra White Hitchcock: A Virtuous Woman." *Working Papers in Art Education* 10 (1991): 40–52.

STANDARD SOURCES

Michele L. Aldrich (article by). In Kass-Simon and Farnes.

HITCHENS, ADA FLORENCE R. (1891–?)

British-Scottish chemist. Born 1891 in Devon, England, to William Hedley Hitchins, a supervisor of Customs and Excise. Educated Campbelltown, Scotland; University of Glasgow (B.Sc., 1913). Professional experience: University of Glasgow, researcher (1913); Aberdeen University, researcher (1914–1916), Carnegie Scholar (1914–1915); British Admiralty, researcher (from 1916); Sheffield, England, chemist; Oxford University, technical assistant (1921), research assistant (1922–1927); Kenya, government assayer and chemist (1932–1946). Death date unknown.

Ada Hitchens began research with the well-known radiochemist Frederick Soddy while she was at the University of Glasgow. Together they determined the half life of ionium (an isotope of thorium). When Soddy moved to Aberdeen University, Hitchens obtained a research scholarship there. She took over research that led to the identification of a new element, protactinium. She also prepared radium standards to be used for calibrating laboratory instruments and contributed to determinations of the atomic weight of radiolead.

During World War I, Hitchens worked for the government on steel analysis. Afterward, she obtained a position with a steel manufacturer in Sheffield. In 1921 Hitchens became Soddy's assistant at the University of Oxford, where she extracted radium from ores and determined the ratios of various isotopes of thorium in minerals.

Hitchens moved to Kenya, where her family had emigrated. She joined the colonial government's mining and geological department, where she performed assays and other chemical work for the mining industry.   MM

PRIMARY SOURCES

Hitchens, Ada. With Frederick Soddy. "The Relation between Uranium and Radium. Part VII. The Life-Period of Ionium." *Philosophical Magazine* 30 (1915): 209–219.

———. With Frederick Soddy. "The Relation between Uranium and Radium. Part VIII. The Period of Ionium and the Ionium-Thorium Ratio in Colorado Carnotite and Joachimsthal Pitchblende." *Philosophical Magazine* 47 (1924): 1148–1158.

STANDARD SOURCES

Meyer and von Schweidler; Rayner-Canham 1997.

HITZENBERGER, ANNALIESE (1905–)

Austrian physician. Born 30 March 1905 in Vienna. Married Karl Hitzenberger (1928). Four children: two boys and two girls. Educated at home; primary school (from third grade); Marienberg Convent near Bregenz; Gymnasium; University of Vienna (M.D., 1931). Professional experience: Vienna General Hospital, internal medicine department (1931–1933); private practice (from 1941).

Outside influences were very important in the life and career of Annaliese Hitzenberger. When she was born, the Hapsburg empire in Austria was very powerful, but with the assassination of Archduke Ferdinand, the heir to the Austrian throne, in 1913, Austria moved rapidly toward World War I. Annaliese's mother home-schooled her from the time she was six. When she was eight, she was finally allowed to go to a primary school. However, her enjoyment in being with other children did not last, for it was when she was eight that Ferdinand was assassinated. The family left Vienna for Bregenz on Lake Constance, which meant more home schooling. After an additional year, she was sent to a Marienberg Convent near Bregenz, where she went to school with other children again. Although the wartime conditions were very unpleasant, she graduated from the school and opted to attend the gymnasium rather than the traditional girls' school.

After graduation from the gymnasium, when it came time to decide on a career, acting and writing vied with medicine. To her parents' displeasure, she decided on medicine. They forbade her to study medicine, so she studied philology and history for a year. The next year she pretended to continue with these studies, while actually taking medical courses. When she finally confessed to her parents, they were quite displeased. Her academic career had its ups and downs, but she performed adequately. During her courses, she met the head of the department, Karl Hitzenberger, who appeared stern at first, but the couple later fell in love and married. She completed her examinations in spite of two pregnancies. She then practiced in the clinic and worked in the adjacent internal medical department of the Vienna General Hospital until the third month of her third pregnancy. She suffered from tubercular pleurisy and gave up working.

Meanwhile, the political conditions in Austria worsened and a fascist government came to power. In 1936, the Hitzenbergers' fourth child was born and Karl was appointed chief medical officer of the Rudolf hospital. His health was compromised by a number of factors, and he died in 1941 at the age of forty-eight, leaving Annaliese with four children between five and twelve years old to support. Because many male doctors had been called into the military, she was able to successfully manage her husband's medical practice. Her father had died, but her mother forgot her animosity toward her daughter's career and cared for the children while Hitzenberger worked.

Hitzenberger decided that avoiding politics was wrong, so she joined the Socialist Party. She was vice-president of the Association of Austrian Medical Women for many years and then became president in 1974. She was also active in the Medical Women's International Association and edited the *Vienna Medical Journal.*   K M

PRIMARY SOURCES
Hitzenberger, Annaliese. In Hellstedt, *Autobiographies.*

HOARE, SARAH (ca. 1767–1855)
British botanist. Born around 1767 in Bristol. Professional experience: wrote popular books on botany. Died 14 April 1855 in Bath.

Little is known about Sarah Hoare except the titles and contents of her books.   JH/MBO

PRIMARY SOURCES
Hoare, Sarah. *A Poem on the Pleasures and Advantages of Botanical Pursuits.* Bristol: Philip Roses, 1825.

———. *Poems on Conchology and Botany.* London: Simpkin & Marshall, 1831.

SECONDARY SOURCES
Smith, J. *Catalogue of Friends' Books* 1 (1867): 955–956.

STANDARD SOURCES
Desmond.

HOBBY, GLADYS LOUNSBURY (1910–1993)
U.S. microbiologist. Born 19 November 1910 in New York City. Educated Vassar College (A.B., 1931); Columbia University (M.A., 1932; Ph.D., 1935). Professional experience: Columbia Medical School, research team (1934–1943); Presbyterian Hospital in New York City (1934–1943); Pfizer Pharmaceuticals, New York City, researcher (1944–1959); Veteran's Administration Hospital, East Orange, N.J., chief of research (1959–1977); Cornell Medical College, assistant researcher; clinical professor in public health (to 1977). Honors and memberships: American Association for the Advancement of Science; American Academy of Microbiology; American Society of Microbiology. Died 4 July 1993 in Pennsylvania.

Gladys Hobby worked on discovering ways to manufacture large amounts of penicillin to be used in treating war wounded. As a part of a research team at the Columbia Medical School, she worked on perfecting the extraction of penicillin. She left Columbia for Pfizer Pharmaceuticals, where she did research on streptomycin and other antibiotics to discover how these antimicrobial drugs worked. As chief of research at the Veteran's Administration Hospital in East Orange, New Jersey, she worked on chronic infectious diseases.

In 1977, Hobby retired. During retirement, she became a consultant and a freelance science writer. At this time she wrote a book, *Penicillin: Meeting the Challenge,* which told the story of the movement of the drug from the laboratory to the clinic.

Hobby was the author of over two hundred articles and founded and edited the journal *Antimicrobial Agents and Chemotherapy.* She was a member of the American Association for the Advancement of Science, the American Academy of Microbiology, and the American Society of Microbiology.   JH/MBO

PRIMARY SOURCES
Hobby, Gladys Lounsbury. *Penicillin: Meeting the Challenge.* New Haven: Yale University Press, 1985.

SECONDARY SOURCES

Saxon, Wolfgang. "Gladys Hobby, 82, Pioneer in Bringing Penicillin to Public." *New York Times*, 9 July 1993. Obituary notice.

STANDARD SOURCES

Notable (article by Denise Adams Arnold).

HOBY, LADY MARGARET DAKINS
(1571–1633)

British amateur physician. Married three times before she was twenty-five years old. Third husband: Sir Thomas Posthumous Hoby.

Lady Hoby left a diary that gives insight into the way she treated her patients on her estate. She was not afraid to perform surgery and often attempted difficult procedures.

JH/MBO

PRIMARY SOURCES

Hoby, Margaret Dakins, Diary of Margaret Hoby, 1599–1605. Ed. Dorothy Meads. London: G. Routledge & Sons, 1930.

———. The Private Life of an Elizabethan Lady: The Diary of Lady Margaret Hoby, 1599–1605. Ed. Joanna Moody. Stroud, Gloucestershire: Sutton, 1998.

SECONDARY SOURCES

Hannay, Margaret P. "'How I These Studies Prize'": The Countess of Pembroke and Elizabethan Science. In *Women, Science and Medicine, 1500–1700*. Ed. Lynette Hunter and Sarah Hutton. Stroud, Gloucestershire: Sutton, 1997.

STANDARD SOURCES

Hurd-Mead 1938.

HODGKIN, DOROTHY MARY CROWFOOT
(1910–1994)

British crystallographer. Born 12 May 1910 in Cairo, Egypt, to Grace Mary (Hood) and John Winter Crowfoot. Two sisters. Married Thomas Hodgkin. Three children, two sons and one daughter. Educated Sir John Leman School (Beccles); Somerville College, Oxford (1928–?). Professional experience: Somerville College, Oxford, fellow (1936–1977); Wolfson College, Oxford, professor emerita (1977–1983); Royal Society, Wolfson Research Professor (1960–1977); Bristol University, chancellor (1970–1988). Honors and memberships: Royal Society, Fellow, British Association for the Advancement of Science, Fellow (1977–1978); Pugwash Conference on Science and World Affairs (1975–?); Royal Netherlands Academy of Science and Letters; American Academy of Arts and Sciences, Bavarian Academy; Austrian Academy; Yugoslav Academy of Sciences; Ghana Academy of Sciences; Puerto Rico Academy of Sciences; Australian Academy of Sciences; Leopoldina Academy of Sciences; Norwegian Academy of Sciences; Indian Academy of Sciences, foreign member; National Academy of Science (US); USSR Academy of Sciences, honorary member (1976); Somerville College, Oxford; Linacre College, Oxford; Girton College, Cambridge; Newnham College, Cambridge; honorary fellowships: Leeds, Manchester, Cambridge, Sussex, Ghana, Hull, East Anglia, London, Delhi, Harvard, Exeter, Kent, Mount Sinai, Bath, Brown, Chicago, Warwick, Oxford, St. Andrews, Bristol, Dalhousie, Zagreb, York, Open University, Modena, honorary doctorates, Royal Medal of the Royal Society (1957); Nobel Prize for Chemistry (1964); Copley Medal of the Royal Society (1976); Mikhail Lomonosov Gold Medal (1982); Dimitrov Prize (1984); Lenin Peace Prize (1987). Died 29 July 1994.

The daughter of a classical scholar and archeologist, Dorothy Crowfoot was born in Cairo, where her father was an inspector for the British Ministry of Education. She had some practical archeological experience herself, for before she left to study chemistry at Somerville College, Oxford, she helped her parents excavate Byzantine churches in the Transjordan. She left Oxford in 1932 to study with J. D. Bernal at Cambridge, where he had begun to work on sterols. There she studied preparations of vitamin B-1, vitamin D, and several sex hormones. In 1934, they took the first single crystal photographs of a protein, the digestive enzyme pepsin. Crowfoot then returned to Oxford, where she began a crystal analysis of the halogen derivatives of cholesterol. At Oxford, she missed the excitement of Bernal's Cambridge laboratory and returned whenever it was possible.

In 1937 Crowfoot married historian Thomas Hodgkin, who became active in African studies at Oxford and Ghana. They often lived apart, keeping two households, one in England and the other in Africa. The couple had three children. When her Nobel Prize was announced in 1964, she was in Accra, Ghana, with her husband. Her three children were all working overseas. Luke was teaching mathematics, Elizabeth was on the faculty of a girls' school in Zambia, and Toby was in voluntary service in India. During the previous year, Thomas Hodgkin's cousin, Alan, had shared the Nobel Prize in physiology and medicine.

In 1942, Hodgkin began to obtain crystalline degradation products of penicillin. Structural information was critical if penicillin were to be synthesized, for it was needed urgently during World War II. This project involved cooperation between crystallographers and biochemists, something that seldom happened. They determined the essential chemical structure by the summer of 1945. From penicillin, Hodgkin turned to the study of vitamin B-12, important in understanding pernicious anemia. Hodgkin and others again cooperated to discover its structure, a feat that had been thought impossible. In 1964, Hodgkin received the Nobel

Prize in chemistry for her work in determining the structure of these biochemical compounds of primary importance. After receiving the Nobel Prize, she made her third important discovery: the determination of the structure of the protein insulin.   JH/MBO

PRIMARY SOURCES
Hodgkin, Dorothy. "The X-Ray Analysis of Complicated Molecules." *Science* 150 (1965): 979–988.

SECONDARY SOURCES
Ferry, Georgia. *Dorothy Hodgkin: A Life.* London: Granta, 1998.

STANDARD SOURCES
Notable; Shearer and Shearer 1997.
Kass-Simon and Farnes (article by Maureen M. Julian).

HODGSON, ELIZA AMY (1889–1983)

New Zealand botanist. Professional activities: structure and taxonomy of New Zealand liverworts. Honors and memberships: Massey University, Palmerston North, New Zealand (honorary D.Sc., 1976); Royal Society of New Zealand, Fellow; Linnean Society, Fellow. Died 7 January 1983.

Eliza Hodgson lived in Wairoa, New Zealand, where she died at the age of ninety-four. Her publications on New Zealand liverworts are considered excellent, and she laid the foundation for future studies on these plants.   JH/MBO

PRIMARY SOURCES
Hodgson, Eliza Amy. "Hepatics from the Subantarctic Islands of New Zealand, including 'Cape Expedition' Collections from the Aukland and Campbell Islands." *Records of the Dominion Museum* (Wellington) 4 (1962): 101–132.

SECONDARY SOURCES
Campbell, Ella. "Eliza Amy Hodgson." *Taxon* 32 (August 1983): 531–532.

HODGSON, ELIZABETH (1814–1877)

British amateur geologist. Born 1814 in Ulverston, Lancashire (?) Died 1877.

Elizabeth Hodgson of Ulverston, Lancashire, published eight papers on the geology of the Lake District. These papers appeared in the *Quarterly Journal of the Geological Society* in 1863; she wrote others that appeared in the *Geological Magazine* over the next seven years on topics including paleontology and glaciology.   JH/MBO

SECONDARY SOURCES
"Hodgson, Elizabeth (1814–1877)." *Journal of Botany* 16 (1878): 64.

STANDARD SOURCES
Creese and Creese.

HOFFLEIT, ELLEN DORRIT (1907–)

U.S. astronomer. Born 12 March 1907 in Florence, Ala. At least one brother. Educated Radcliffe College (A.B., 1928; M.A., 1932; Ph.D., 1938). Professional experience: Harvard University Observatory, assistant (1929–1938), research associate (1938–1943), astronomer (1948–1956); Ballistic Research Laboratory, Aberdeen Proving Grounds, Md., mathematician (1943–1948); Maria Mitchell Observatory, (1956–1978); Yale University Observatory, senior research astronomer (1969–1975). Honors and memberships: Radcliffe Graduate Society, distinguished achievement award (1964); American Association for the Advancement of Science, Fellow; American Association of Variable Star Observers, vice-president (1958–1960), president (1961–1963); International Astronomical Union; American Astronomical Society; American Astronomical Society, George van Biesbroeck Prize (1989); Annenberg Foundation Prize (1993); Connecticut Women's Hall of Fame, inductee (1998); Connecticut Woman of Distinction (1999). Still living as of 1999.

Ellen Dorrit Hoffleit's interest in astronomy reached back to her childhood when she and her mother, the daughter of an East Prussian physics professor, observed a spectacular Perseid meteor shower on an August evening after the end of World War I. Born in Alabama, Hoffleit grew up in New Castle, Pennsylvania. She earned all three of her degrees from Radcliffe College. As an undergraduate, she prepared to teach high school geometry and graduated cum laude. After graduation, she took a position as a research assistant at the Harvard College Observatory. In this position, she compared photographic plates to find new variable stars and determined their light curves. She discovered about 1,000 new southern-sky variable stars.

While working on the variable star project, Hoffleit took courses at Harvard toward her master's degree. Her work was outstanding, and in 1933 Observatory Director Harlow Shapley encouraged her to get a Ph.D. degree. Energized by his confidence in her ability, Hoffleit completed a doctoral thesis on the spectroscopic absolute magnitudes of stars, winning an award for the best original work. After she earned her Ph.D. she was appointed research associate. However, during World War II and in the immediate postwar period, she took a position as a mathematician at the Aberdeen Proving Grounds Ballistic Research Laboratory in Maryland. She found the military mentality made life unpleasant for a female scientist. After the end of World War II, she helped with the V-2 rocket project.

Hoffleit returned to the Harvard Observatory in 1948 as an astronomer. However, after Shapley retired in 1952, she did not get along well with the observatory's new director, Donald H. Menzel, who thought her type of research was obsolete. Hoffleit left in 1956 to become director of the Maria Mitchell Observatory, an appointment that was only for the summer months. In honor of MARIA MITCHELL, she used the observatory's resources to fund summer jobs for women undergraduates who were doing variable star research. Many women astronomers began their careers in this program.

In 1969, Hoffleit became the senior research astronomer at the Yale Observatory, where she remained until she retired in 1975. She retired from the Maria Mitchell Observatory in 1978, but continued to work there into her nineties.

Hoffleit held a number of concurrent positions, including lecturer at Wellesley College during 1955–1956, Astronomical Observatory, Pasteur Institute in Strassbourg, France in 1976. Hoffleit's research was on variable stars, stellar spectra, proper motions, meteors, and galactic structure. In March 1997, a meeting of astronomers was held at Yale University in honor of Hoffleit's ninetieth birthday.   JH/MBO

PRIMARY SOURCES

Hoffleit, Dorrit. *Bibliography on Meteoric Dust with Brief Abstracts.* Cambridge, Mass.: Harvard College Observatory, 1952.

———. *Catalogue of the Positions and Proper Motions of Stars Between Declinations -30° and -35° Reduced to the Equinox of 1950 Without Applying Proper Motions.* New Haven: The Observatory, 1967.

———. *The Bright Star Catalogue.* 4th ed. rev. New Haven, Conn.: Yale University Observatory, 1982.

SECONDARY SOURCES

Levy, David H. "Astronomy's First Lady." *Sky and Telescope* (February, 1999), 89–94?.

STANDARD SOURCES

AMS 7–8, P 9, P&B 10–14; Shearer and Shearer 1997.

HOFMANN, ELISE (1889–1955)

Austrian paleontologist and palynologist. Born 1889. Educated University of Vienna (doctorate, 1924). Professional experience: University of Vienna, teacher and researcher. Died 14 March 1955.

According to an obituary account, Hofmann's entire life was devoted to her science. After teaching in Viennese schools, she studied plant anatomy and histology under the 607Viennese master Molisch, who referred to her as his most talented student. She received her doctorate in botany

in 1924. After receiving this degree, she became more deeply involved in the university's "research circle." Even though World War II caused her much anguish, Hofmann worked diligently to rebuild the lectureship in paleobotany at the University of Vienna. She was greatly honored by an appointment to a professorial chair in paleobotany at the University of Graz. However, she turned down the appointment because she was convinced that she was indispensable to the University of Vienna. An inspiring teacher and caring advisor, Hofmann was the major professor for many dissertations in paleobotany.

Hofmann gave lectures and papers in the area of paleobotany to many organizations. She also attended many international meetings and was well thought of by her colleagues.

She pioneered micropaleontologic pollen analysis, a field that was introduced in Austria. In one of her works she was able to demonstrate the existence of a number of "new" spore forms, previously suspected by Eduard Suess, considered the master of alpine geology. She also discovered fossilized pollen grains from the lignite of the Hausruck area in upper Austria. With her work on the coal forms, she moved from the theoretical to more practical applications.   JH/MBO

PRIMARY SOURCES

Hofmann, Elise. "Fossile Gewebe unter dem Mikroskop." *Mikroskopie* 2 (1947): 9–12.

———. "Das Flyschproblem im Lichte der Pollenanalyse." *Phyton* (1948): 1.

———. "Pollenkörner im Oberkreideflysch von Muntigl bei Salzburg (Palynological Conference, Stockholm, 7 November 1950)." *Proceedings of the Seventh International Botanical Congress, Stockholm.* Stockholm: Almquist & Wiksell, 1954.

SECONDARY SOURCES

Kühn, Othmar. "Elise Hofmann." *Osterreichische Hochschulzeitung* 7, no. 8 (1957): 2.

Klaus, W. "Abschied von Elise Hofmann." *Grana palynologia* 1, no. 2 (1956): 115–118.

Kühn, Othmar. "Elise Hofmann." *Mitteilungen Geologische Gesessellschaft in Wien* 49 (1956): 357–364. Includes portrait.

STANDARD SOURCES

Sarjeant.

HOGG, HELEN SAWYER (1905–1993)

Canadian astronomer. Born 1 August 1905 in Lowell, Mass., to Carrie Myra (Sprague) and Edward Everett Sawyer. Married (1) Frank Scott Hogg (d. 1951); (2) Francis E. L. Priestley in 1985 (d. 1988). Three children, two sons and one daughter. Educated Mount Holyoke College and University of Leithbridge (A.B.);

McMaster University and universities of Toronto and Waterloo; St. Mary's University, Nova Scotia; Radcliffe College (M.A.); Harvard College Observatory (Ph.D., 1931). Professional experience: Harvard College Observatory, Pickering fellow (1926–1930); Smith College, lecturer (1927); Mount Holyoke College, lecturer (1930–1931), assistant, associate professor, chair of the department of astronomy; University of Toronto, department of astronomy, David Dunlap Observatory, research associate (1936–1993), assistant professor (1951–1955), associate professor (1955–1957), professor (1957–1976), professor emerita (from 1976). Honors and memberships: Annie J. Cannon Prize (American Astronomical Society); Radcliffe Graduate Achievement Medal (1967); Centennial Medal (1967); Rittenhouse Silver Medal (1967); Silver Jubilee Medal (1977); Klumpke-Roberts Medal (Astronomical Society of the Pacific, 1983); Sanford Fleming Medal (Royal Canadian Institute, 1985); Helen Sawyer Hogg Observatory, National Museum of Science and Technology, Ottawa (dedicated 1989). Died 28 January in Richmond Hill, Ontario.

Astronomer Helen Sawyer Priestley grew up in an intellectually stimulating home. Although she graduated from high school when she was sixteen years old, she was not allowed to attend college immediately because of her age. The following year, she went to Mount Holyoke College, where she graduated Phi Beta Kappa. While she was a graduate student at Radcliffe College, she published her first paper in astronomy (1927). After she received her doctorate, she married astronomer Frank Scott Hogg, who accepted a position in British Columbia. With a stipend and observatory privileges, Helen Hogg photographed star clusters and found a total of 138 new variable stars. She became fascinated by variable stars, and studying them became her lifetime occupation. After both she and her husband were given positions at the University of Toronto, she continued her work on variable stars, publishing a catalogue of over 1,000 globular star clusters in 1949. She collaborated with Frank Hogg, but he was the one who held the paying position at the Dominion Astrophysical Observatory in British Columbia. She eventually received the rank of professor at the the University of Toronto's David Dunlap Observatory. That same year, she was elected president of the Royal Astronomical Society of Canada (1951), then named honorary president (1977–1981) and honorary member (1987).

JH/MBO

PRIMARY SOURCES

Hogg, Helen Sawyer. *Man and His World: The Noranda Lectures.* Toronto: University of Toronto Press, 1968.

———. *Out of Old Books.* Toronto: David Dunlap Observatory, 1974.

———. *The Stars Belong to Everyone: How to Enjoy Astronomy.* Toronto: Doubleday, 1976.

SECONDARY SOURCES

"Hogg-Priestley, Helen Battles Sawyer." *The International Who's Who of Women.* London: Europa Publications Ltd., 1992.

STANDARD SOURCES

Kass-Simon and Farnes (article by Pamela E. Mack); *LKW Notable.*

HOGGAN, ISMÉ ALDYTH (1899–1936)

British/U.S. botanist. Born 23 March 1899. Educated Cambridge University (B.A., 1922; M.Sc., 1924); University of Wisconsin, fellow (1924; M.S., 1925; Ph.D., 1927). Professional experience: University of Wisconsin, assistant in horticulture (1925–1928), research associate (1928–1930), instructor (1930–1933), assistant professor (1933–1936). Died Madison, Wis., 28 December 1936.

After receiving her degrees at Cambridge, Ismé Hoggan came to the United States as a fellow at the University of Wisconsin. She obtained a Cambridge master of science degree in 1924 (or 1925). She earned a master of science degree from the University of Wisconsin in 1925 and a doctorate in 1927. She remained at Wisconsin until her death, holding several positions at that institution. In addition to her academic positions, Hoggan was an agent for the Bureau of Plant Industry, U.S. Department of Agriculture, from 1930. Her research was in mycology and she contributed to *Phytopathology.* She was a member of the British Mycological Society. Hoggan died in 1936 at the early age of thirty-seven.

JH/MBO

STANDARD SOURCES

AMS 5; Desmond.

HOHL, LEONORA ANITA (1909–1997)

U.S. microbiologist. Born 9 March 1909. Married Edwin Strohmaier. Educated University of California (A.B., 1931; Ph.D., 1939); University of Michigan, Newcombe fellow (1933–1935; A.M., 1934). Professional experience: University of California, Berkeley, general assistant in the herbarium (1931–1932), teaching assistant, botany (1932–1933), assistant, fruit products (1935–1940), lecturer in home economics (1941–1943); College of Agriculture experimental station, instructor in food technology and assistant mycologist (1943); (associate mycologist (1943–1948); Roma Wine Co., Fresno (1940–1941). Died 30 June 1997 in Oakland, Calif.

Leonora Hohl received her degrees from the University of California and the University of Michigan. She held several positions at the University of California and in addition was the mycologist for the Peerless Yeast Co. and Acme Brewery. She was a member of the Institute for Food Technology, the

California Academy of Sciences, and the Pasteur Society of Northern California.

Her research in association with Maynard Jocelyn at the College of Agriculture at Berkeley, was on freezing preservation of fruits and vegetables, histological changes resulting from food processing, the physiology and taxonomy of yeasts, general microbiology, and the acid metabolism of the yeast *Saccharomyces cereviseae.*   JH/MBO

PRIMARY SOURCES

Hohl, Leonora A. With Maynard Jocelyn. *The Commercial Freezing of Fruit Products.* Berkeley, California Agricultural Experiment Station, College of Agriculture, University of California, 1948.

STANDARD SOURCES

AMS 7–8.

HOKE, CALM (MORRISON) (1887–?)

U.S. chemist and metallurgist. Born 25 August 1887 in Chicago, Ill. Married 1927. Educated Hunter College (A.B., 1908); Wittenberg College (1909); University of Chicago (1910–1911); Columbia University (A.M., 1913); New York University (1923). Professional experience: Harriman Research Laboratory, New York, laboratory assistant (1911–1912); Jewelers Technical Advice Co., New York, chemist and salesperson (1913–1917), advertising manager and chemist (from 1919); Columbia University assistant chemist (1917–1919); Hoke, Inc., New York City, vice-president and consulting chemist (1926–1934). Death date unknown.

Calm Hoke was a chemist who used her degrees in industry. After holding several positions, she became vice-president and consulting chemist at Hoke, Inc., a family business. She was a member of the Chemical Society, the Electrochemical Society, a Fellow of the Institute of Chemistry (councilor, 1923–1927), and the Institute of Mineralogy and Metallurgy, England. Her interests were practical: refining precious metal wastes, melting and working platinum, electroplating and finishing precious metals, and designing controls for compressed gases.   JH/MBO

STANDARD SOURCES

AMS 5–8.

HOL, JACOBA BRIGITTA LOUISA (1886–?)

Dutch geographer. Born 21 September 1886 in Antwerp to Maria Theresia (Koene) and Richard Hol. Educated University of Utrecht (Ph.D. in science). Professional experience: University of Tilburg, instructor higher Catholic studies (1914–1946); University of

Utrecht, professor of geography, physics, and geomorphology; director of the Institute of Geography (1946–1958). Honors and memberships: Royal Netherlands Geographical Society, member; Belgian Society of Geographic Study, member; Geographic Society of the Netherlands, member; Collegium Studiosorum Veritas, member; Royal Belgian Society for Geography, member; Geological Society of Belgium, member; Adelbert Society, member. Death date unknown.

Jacoba Hol earned her doctorate from the University of Utrecht. Her first professional position was not related to geography. She served as an instructor in higher Catholic studies for a number of years. However, in 1946, she got a position at the University of Utrecht that utilized her skills. She was a member of the Royal Netherlands Geographical Society, the Belgian Society of Geographic study, the Geographic Society of the Netherlands, Collegium Studiosorum Veritas, the Royal Belgian Society for Geography, the Geological Society of Belgium, and the Adelbert Society, among others.   JH/MBO

PRIMARY SOURCES

Hol, Jacoba Brigitta Louisa. *Beiträge zur Hydrographie der Ardennen.* Frankfurt, 1914.

———. *De Geomorfologische Landschappen van Nederland.* Zwolle: Erven J. J. Tijl, 1959.

STANDARD SOURCES

Debus.

HOLLEY, MARY AUSTIN (fl. 1833)

U.S. geologist.

Mary Austin Holley was one of several women who reported on geological phenomena in their neighborhoods or during their travels. When she was at Transylvania University in Kentucky, she had learned geology from Constantine Rafinesque. She included a map that showed topographic features and the locations of mines.   JH/MBO

PRIMARY SOURCES

Holley, Mary A. *Texas, Observations, Historical, Geographical, and Descriptive.* Baltimore: Armstrong and Plaskitt, 1833.

STANDARD SOURCES

Kass-Simon and Farnes (article by Michele L Aldrich).

HOLLINGWORTH, LETA ANNA STETTER (1886–1939)

U.S. educational psychologist. Born 25 May 1886 near Chadron, Neb., to Margaret Elinor (Danley) and John G. Stetter. Two sisters.

Educated Valentine, Nebr. high school; University of Nebraska (B.A., 1906); Columbia University (M.A., 1913; certificate in educational psychology; Ph.D., 1916). Married Harry Levi Hollingworth 31 December 1908. No children. Professional experience: Clinic for Atypical Children, New York City, psychologist (1913–1916); Bellevue Hospital, psychopathic service, clinical psychologist (1915–1916); Columbia University Teachers College, instructor of educational psychology (1916–1928), professor of education (1929–1938). Died 27 November 1939 of cancer at Columbia-Presbyterian Medical Center in New York City; buried in Lincoln, Nebr.

Leta Stetter Hollingworth rose from an inauspicious beginning and years of intellectual lassitude to become a distinguished authority in the areas of psychology of women and in the education of the "exceptional" child. She was born in a dugout on a homestead near Chadron, Nebraska; in 1890, her childhood was interrupted by the death of her gentle, educated mother, Margaret Elinor. John Stetter was a restless man without a steady vocation and left his three girls to be reared by their maternal grandparents who were also homesteading in the Nebraska frontier. Stetter was twelve when her father remarried and took his daughters to live with him and a hostile stepmother in Valentine, Nebraska. Hoping to become a writer, Stetter entered University of Nebraska, majoring in literature and creative writing, but also qualified for a teaching certificate (1906). She taught in high schools for two years before her classmate at Nebraska convinced her to marry him and move to New York City where he was a graduate student at Columbia University. Harry Levi Hollingworth subsequently became a professor of psychology at Columbia and the couple spent the remainder of their lives in New York.

Hampered by lack of a market for her writings and ineligibility as a married women to teach in the New York schools, Hollingworth spent several restless years during which her interests turned more and more to the problems of education and the position of women in society. When she was able to return to classes, she specialized in education and sociology, receiving her master of arts from Columbia and a certificate in educational psychology from Columbia University Teachers College. While working on her doctoral degree, she worked at Bellevue Hospital, New York City, in the new area of clinical psychology. In 1916, Hollingworth completed her doctoral degree with her dissertation, *Functional Periodicity*, which tested the mental and motor abilities of women both during and outside of the menstrual period, as contrasted to the abilities of men. She found no evidence of a feminine cycle of impairment. In other studies, she challenged the prevalent theory that there was an inherent greater variability in the male which made him capable of more intellectual accomplishment. Hollingworth attributed any differences to sociological rather than biological limita-

tions of women. Her objective and careful testing in measuring and comparing sexual factors in selected traits and types of performance significantly strengthened the case for educational and professional equality. Leta and Harry Hollingworth both supported the suffrage movement, but she thought the reform of attitudes regarding women more important than the vote.

Hollingworth first worked primarily in a clinical setting, but later moved to the educational arena, studying mental and emotional abnormality, frequency of inferior grades of intelligence as related to sex, and gifted children. A major discovery and concern of hers was that giftedness does not preclude maladjustment (see *Gifted Children*). She became a champion of special education for gifted children and of improved standards of test administration and of test administrators in clinical psychology. She set up a guidance laboratory at Columbia University Teachers College for educational and psychological counseling. In 1936, the New York City Board of Education established Speyer School, an experimental school, and appointed Hollingworth director of research. Her observations and studies there led her to describe the social isolation experienced by the child functioning at a mental level far above his contemporaries, and to develop the concept of an "optimum intelligence" for total adjustment (between 125 and 155 IQ on the Stanford-Binet scale). Her data and notes were presented in a book posthumously completed and published, *Children above 180 I.Q.*, in 1942.

Active in professional and community organizations, Hollingworth helped found the American Association of Clinical Psychology in 1917. She acted as scientific authority in the renowned feminist club Heterodoxy in New York City, and was a member of the American Psychological and National Education associations. She served as associate editor of the *Journal of Genetic Psychology; Genetic Psychology Monographs;* and *Journal of Juvenile Research;* and was a consulting editor to *The Nation's Schools*. Leta and Harry Hollingworth both received honorary doctorates from the University of Nebraska (1938). Leta Hollingworth died of cancer at age fifty-three, and was buried in Wyuka Cemetery, Lincoln, Nebraska. A year later, Columbia University Teachers College held a conference on education of the gifted in her honor   JH/MBO

PRIMARY SOURCES

Hollingworth, Leta. *Psychology of Subnormal Children.* New York: Macmillan, 1920.

———. *Gifted Children; Their Nature and Nurture.* New York: Macmillan, 1926.

———. *Psychology of the Adolescent.* New York: Appleton, 1928; London: King, 1930.

———. *Children above 180 I.Q.* Yonkers, N.Y.: World Book, 1942 (posthumously published).

SECONDARY SOURCES

Hollingworth, H.L. *Leta Stetter Hollingworth.* University of Nebraska Press, 1943.

Kimble, G. A., M. Wertheimer, and C. L. White. *Portraits of Pioneers in Psychology.* Washington, D.C.: American Psychological Association, 1991.

STANDARD SOURCES

AMS 3–6; Bailey; *NAW* (article by Victoria S. Roemele); *Psychological Register,* vol. 3, 1932; Uglow 1982; Zusne.

HOLM, ESTHER (ABERDEEN) (1904–1984)

U.S. geologist and paleontologist. Born 6 January 1904 in Chicago, Ill. Married Donald August Holm. Educated Northwestern University (bachelor's degree, 1928; M.S., 1931); University of Chicago (Ph.D., 1937). Professional experience: Northwestern University, tutor in geology (1931–1933); Milwaukee-Downer College, instructor in geology (1934–1935); Wellesley College, instructor (1936), assistant professor (to 1942); U.S. Geological Survey, Military Geology Unit, researcher (1942–1965); Astro Geology Branch, researcher (1965–1971). Died 4 May 1984.

As a child, Esther Aberdeen spent time on the beaches of Lake Michigan, where she became interested in the sands and water-smoothed pebbles that she found there. Her father was a trainman. Her mother apparently encouraged her to attend a university, so she entered Northwestern University, supporting herself by working as a stenographer in an advertising company. Graduating in 1928, she worked a year in the YWCA in St. Joseph, Michigan, and then returned to graduate school at Northwestern, where she earned a master of science degree in 1931. She remained at Northwestern as a tutor from 1931 to 1933, when she entered the University of Chicago to work on her doctoral degree. Money was always short, so she took a year off to teach geology at Milwaukee-Downer College. She completed her doctorate in paleontology in 1937. In 1936, Aberdeen accepted a job as instructor of geology at Wellesley College, and after she finished her degree was promoted to assistant professor. She remained at Wellesley until 1942, when she joined the newly formed Military Geology Unit of the U.S. Geological Survey. She remained at this job throughout the war, and was stationed in several different localities, including Japan. She stayed in Japan until June 1948, when she returned to Washington. While attending the 19th International Geological Congress in Algiers, Aberdeen met Donald Holm, a senior geologist with the Arabian American Oil Company. They were married in 1953 and Esther Holm took leave from the survey and went to Saudi Arabia. She became interested in Arabian horses, and brought several to Arizona, where they retired. Holm retired from the survey in 1971.

She spent three and a half years before her death in a nursing home. She was honored by the Department of the Interior, which presented her with its Distinguished Service Medal.

The fact that Holm published few papers does not mean that she did not do significant research. She wrote dozens of reports for the Corps of Engineers while in the Military Geology Branch, and many of the reports she prepared for the lunar project were never formally published. The course of her career was dictated by the war. Although she began as an academic, entering the Military Geology Unit changed the type of research she was doing. From paleontological work specializing on diatoms, she turned to applied geology. Her new interest involved providing information about terrains and mapping them. After the war she continued the same kind of work—this time on the lunar landscape.   JH/MBO

PRIMARY SOURCES

Aberdeen, Esther. With Margaret F. Boos. "Indian Creek Plutons of the Front Range, Colorado." *Proceedings of the Geological Society of America.* (1936): 66–67.

———. "Radiolarian Fauna of the Caballos Formation, Marathon Basin, Texas." *Journal of Paleontology* 14, no. 2 (1940): 127–139.

Holm, Esther Aberdeen. With L. C. Rowan and J. F. McCauley. "Lunar Terrain Mapping and Relative-Roughness Analysis." *U.S. Geological Survey Professional Paper* 599–G (1971): 28 pp.

SECONDARY SOURCES

Whitmore, Frank C., Jr. "Memorial to Esther Aberdeen Holm, 1904–1984." *Geological Society of America, Memorials* 21 (1991): 9–12.

HOLMES, MARY EMILEE (1849–?)

U.S. paleontologist. Born 10 April 1849 in Chester, Ohio. Educated Rockford College (A.B., 1868); University of Michigan (A.M., 1887; Ph.D., 1888). Professional experience: Manitowoc, Wisc., instructor in natural sciences (1869–1870); Rockford College, professor (1871–1882). Death date unknown.

Mary Emilee Holmes earned a doctoral degree at the University of Michigan in 1888, an early date for a woman to get that degree. She was a member of the Geologists Society and worked on the Branchiopoda. She also did research in botany and general nature study. Active in the Presbyterian church, Holmes was president of the Presbyterian Home Mission Society of the Freeport Presbytery, Illinois, and secretary of the Synodical Home Mission Society (1883). She edited and published the journal *Freedmen's Bulletin* (1885–?).   JH/MBO

STANDARD SOURCES

AMS 1–2.

HOLTON, PAMELA MARGARET (WATSON-WILLIAMS) (1923–1977)

British physiologist. Born 13 August 1923 at Bristol to Cresten Margaret (Boase) and Eric Watson-Williams. Married Francis Arthus Holton (4 July 1945). Two sons; two daughters. Educated Clifton High School, Bristol; Newnham College, Cambridge (1942–1944; National Science Tripos, Part I, class 2, 1944; M.A., 1949), associate (1964–1977), associate fellow (1973–1976); Somerville College, Oxford (Ph.D., 1950). Professional experience: Oxford University department of pharmacy, demonstrator (1947–1949); Cambridge University, Physiological Laboratory, research worker, Junior Beit Fellow (1951–1953); Royal Society, Foulerton Research Fellow (1953–1955); Saint Mary's Hospital Medical School, London, researcher (1955–1969), reader in physiology (1969–1977); University of California, visiting researcher (1966–1967).

Pamela Margaret Watson-Williams took only Part I of the Natural Science Tripos at Newnham, because she spent the last years of World War II (1944–1945) working for the admiralty. After the war, she married Francis Holton, a research scientist. From 1947 to 1949 (sources differ slightly on dates), Pamela Holton worked in the department of physiology, Oxford, and was also a research student under J. H. Burn. With Burn she studied the standardization of hormones affecting pancreatic secretion, and enzymes and drugs related to the neurotransmitters acetylcholine and noradrenaline. She returned to Cambridge after earning a doctoral degree, continuing her research on adrenaline and vasodilation. She received two important fellowships to support her research, the Beit Memorial Junior Research Fellowship and a Foulerton Research Fellowship from the Royal Society. When Francis Holton was at the Molteno Institute and Pamela Holton at the Physiological Laboratory, the two collaborated. Their funding came both from Cambridge University and Research Council grants to each of them separately. This collaboration resulted in two joint papers. She published five other papers during her postgraduate time at Cambridge, both alone and in collaboration with other investigators.

Holton left Cambridge for St. Mary's Hospital Medical School, London, as a senior lecturer, where she spent the rest of her career. She spent a sabbatical year at the University of California, Berkeley, where she investigated asthma-induced exercise (Medical Center in San Francisco) and gastric blood flow (University of California, Berkeley).

Holton led a research team at St. Mary's that worked on gastric blood flow and gastric secretions. Many consider her most important contribution to be this work in gastric physiology. In 1969, Holton was promoted to reader. Shortly before this promotion, she became very interested in new teaching methods in physiology, and she developed courses at the University of London. She also was on the University

of London Audio-Visual Sub-Committee of the Board of Studies in Physiology and the Education Sub-Committee of the Physiological Society. She used the University of London Audio-Visual Sub-Committee to compile a catalogue of films for teaching together with critical assessments of each film. The Audio-Visual Sub-Committee also produced a book of learning objectives for physiology and developed a bank of multiple-choice questions for examinations. She also developed self-instructional materials in medical physiology that were distributed throughout the world through the British Life Assurance Trust (BLAT). The incentive for this project was to develop materials that would help students who had failed their examinations the first time. Often, these students needed to learn the material for the first time, through self-instructional materials. The project was supported by the Nuffield Foundation.

When Pamela Holton died at the age of cancer at age fifty-three, she left husband Francis and four children, who were between fifteen and twenty-four years of age. JH/MBO

PRIMARY SOURCES

Holton, Pamela. With B. P. Curwain. "The Effects of Isoprenaline and Adrenaline on Pentagastrin-Stimulated Gastric Acid Secretion and Mucosal Flow in the Dog." *British Journal of Pharmacology* 46 (1972): 225–233.

———. With B. P. Curwain. "The Measurement of Dog Gastric Mucosal Blood Flow by Radioactive Aniline Clearance Compared with Amidopyrine Clearance." *Journal of Physiology* (London) 229 (1973): 115–131.

———, ed. "Catecholamines and Gastric Secretion." In *International Encyclopaedia of Pharmacology and Therapeutics,* section 39A, vol. 1: 287–315. Oxford: Pergamon Press, Ltd., 1973.

———. With J. Spencer. "Acid Secretion by Guinea Pig Isolated Stomach." *Journal of Physiology* (London) 255 (1976): 465–479.

STANDARD SOURCES

Newnham; Women Physiologists (article by Lynn Bindman).

HOMER, ANNIE (1882–1953)

British biochemist. Born 3 December 1882 at West Bromwich. Educated King Edward VI High School, Birmingham; Newnham College, Cambridge (1902–1905; clothworkers' scholar; Natural Science Tripos, Parts I and II, chemistry, class 1, 1904–1905; M.A., 1926); University of Toronto (D.Sc., 1913). Professional experience: Newnham College, Bathurst Student (1905–1907), associates' research fellow (1907–1910), associate (1907–1923), demonstrator (1907–1911); Beit Memorial Fellow for medical research (1910–1914); University of Toronto, medical research fellow and demonstrator in biochemistry (1914–1915); Toronto

University, assistant director antitoxin laboratory and assistant chemist at Dominion Experimental Farm, Ottawa (1915–1916); Lister Institute and University College, London, physiological laboratory, researcher (1916–1921); development of oil, potash, etc., in Palestine (from 1921).

Annie Homer was a research fellow at Newnham College, Cambridge, from 1907 to 1910. She earned a first-class pass in Part II of her Tripos examination and remained at Newnham as a Bathurst student. Since women could not get Cambridge University degrees at that time, she went to the University of Toronto, where she earned a doctoral degree. Remaining in Canada as a fellow and demonstrator at the university, she then became the assistant director of the antitoxin laboratory at the university and assistant chemist at the Dominion Experimental Farm, Ottawa. In 1916, she returned to England to reorganize the commercial production of antitoxins for war purposes. She was an assistant at the Lister Institute until 1921, when she went to Palestine to work for the development of oil and potash. She also negotiated for the British government during World War II.

Homer was a Fellow of the Royal Institute of Chemistry. She published extensively in the *Journal of the Chemical Society* and the *Biochemical Journal*. JH/MBO

STANDARD SOURCES
Newnham.

HOOBLER, ICIE GERTRUDE MACY (1892–1984)

U.S. physiological chemist. Born 1892 in Missouri. Educated Randolph-Macon Woman's College (A.B.); Yale University (Ph.D.?). Professional experience: West Pennsylvania Hospital, researcher; Merrill-Palmer School for Motherhood and Child Development, Detroit, researcher (1923); Children's Fund of Michigan Laboratory, researcher (to 1954). Retired 1954. Died 1984.

After Icie Hoobler received her bachelor's degree from Randolph-Macon College, she was encouraged by her adviser, Jules Stieglitz, to teach before she went on to graduate school. She taught in a position that Stieglitz found for her at the University of Colorado. At Colorado, she became interested in physiological chemistry, and went to Yale to study with Lafayette Mendel. Women were not allowed to teach at Yale, but were provided with research assistantships. Hoobler's assignment was to determine the possible toxicity and food value of cotton seeds which had been substituted for wheat flour during the war. She discovered that a poison in the seeds, gossypol, sickened the animals that were fed cottonseeds. Mendel encouraged her to work in the health sciences, because he was convinced that women could make a special

contribution in this area. At his instigation, Hoobler analyzed human milk and studied the nutrition of mothers and children.

Her first professional position was at West Pennsylvania Hospital, where she analyzed fetuses for calcium and magnesium and compared the composition of the bloods of mothers and their newborn babies. After she left Pennsylvania, Hoobler went to California, where she worked with AGNES FAY MORGAN. In 1923, she went to the Merrill Palmer School for Motherhood and Child Development in Detroit, and finally to the Children's Fund of Michigan Laboratory, where she remained until her retirement.

Hoobler and her group of scientists studied the effect of nutrition on both mother and child. She determined the nutritional requirements of both pregnant and nursing mothers and of infants and children. She demonstrated the effect on infant health of maternal malnutrition, even before the conception of the child. Other research indicated the need for vitamin D. She studied amino acids in foods and the standardization of vitamins B and C. JH/MBO

PRIMARY SOURCES
Macy, Icie G. "Composition of Human Colostrum and Milk." *American Journal of Diseases of Children* 78 (1948): 589.
Hoobler, Icie G. Macy. With Helen A. Hunscher. "An Evaluation of Maternal Nitrogen and Mineral Needs during Embryonic and Infant Development." *American Journal of Obstetrics and Gynecology* 68 (1954): 878.
———. With Harold C. Mack. "Implications of Nutrition in the Life Cycle of Women." *American Journal of Obstetrics and Gynecology* 68 (1954): 131.
———. *Boundless Horizons: Portrait of a Pioneer Woman Scientist.* Smithtown, N.Y.: Exposition Press, 1982. Autobiography.

SECONDARY SOURCES
Cavanaugh, Margaret A. "Contributions of Icie Macy Hoobler to Chemistry." Paper presented at the 178th National Meeting of the American Chemical Society, September 1979.

STANDARD SOURCES
AMS P&B 12–13; Kass-Simon and Farnes (article by Jane Miller).

HOOKER, FRANCES HARRIET HENSLOW (1825–1874)

British botanist. Born 30 April 1825 in Cambridge to Harriet Jenyns and John Stevens Henslow. Four siblings. Married J. D. Hooker (1851). Six sons; two daughters. Died 1874.

Frances Harriet Henslow was the wife of the botanist Joseph Dalton Hooker and the daughter of the botanist John

Stevens Henslow. The mother of eight children and always in poor health, Hooker still had time to translate E. Le Maout and J. Decaisne's *Traité de Botanique* in 1873. She also translated French works for Charles Darwin. In his correspondence with Darwin, J. D. Hooker voiced his concern about his wife's health. Her sister was the botanist LADY ANN HENSLOW BARNARD.   JH/MBO

SECONDARY SOURCES

Allan, Mea. *Hookers of Kew, 1785–1911*. London: Joseph, 1967.
Garden 6 (1874): 486. Obituary notice.
Gardener's Chronicle 2 (1874): 661. Obituary notice.
Journal of Botany (1874): 383. Obituary notice.

STANDARD SOURCES

Desmond.

HOOKER, HENRIETTA EDGECOMB (1851–?)

U.S. botanist. Born 12 December 1851 in Gardiner, Maine. Educated Mount Holyoke College; Syracuse University (Ph.D., 1889); Woods Hole; MIT; University of Berlin. Professional experience: Vermont public schools, teacher (1869–1870); Academy of West Charleston, Vt., teacher (1870–1871); Mount Holyoke College, professor of botany (1873–1908), emerita professor (from 1908). Death date unknown.

Henrietta Edgecomb Hooker did her undergraduate work at Mount Holyoke College and returned to teach at that institution. One of her interests was completing historical sketches of Mount Holyoke. She was a member of the Torrey Botanical Club and the International Association of Botanists. Her research was on the morphology and embryology of Cuscuta.   JH/MBO

STANDARD SOURCES

AMS 1–4.

HOOKER, MARJORIE (1908–1976)

U.S. mineralogist, petrologist, and bibliographer. Born 10 May 1908 in Flushing, N.Y. Two sisters, Elsie A. Hooker and Vera Hooker Heidrich. Educated Hunter College, New York City; Syracuse University (master's degree). Professional experience: U.S. State Department, mineral specialist (1943–1947); U.S. Geological Survey, researcher and bibliographer (1947–1976). Honors and memberships: American Association for the Advancement of Science, Fellow; Minerological Society of America (treasurer, 1958–1968); Washington Academy of Sciences; Geological Society of London, member. Died 4 May 1976 in Washington, D.C.

Marjorie Hooker earned a master's degree from Syracuse University. While working on this degree (1937–1943), she served as departmental and research assistant in mineralogy. During the middle of this time period (June to October 1942) she worked for the Army-Navy Munitions Board in Washington, D.C., as a technical assistant. In 1943, Hooker became a mineral specialist with the U.S. Department of State. After four years with this department, she moved to the U.S. Geological Survey, where she spent the rest of her working life. Most of her work involved scientific bibliography. Hooker was active in the community and was a gracious host to visitors, both native and foreign.

Hooker was a Fellow of the American Association for the Advancement of Science, the Geological Society of America, the Mineralogical Society of America (treasurer 1958–1968), the Washington Academy of Sciences, and the Geological Society of London. She was a member of many other geological and mineralogical societies from all over the world. International in outlook, she was a delegate to four International Geological Congresses and five General Meetings of the International Mineralogical Association. She was one of the first of three distinguished alumni of the geology department of Syracuse University to received the Alexander Winchell Award, presented annually to outstanding alumni for professional contributions. Syracuse also established the Marjorie Hooker Award, which is given annually to support the research of an outstanding student.

Although Hooker did not do much original research, she produced valuable data for geologists and mineralogists. Her contributions included abstracting geological literature, compiling data on rock composition, and correlating international chemical data on granitic rocks. Since 1969 she organized abstracts from the United States for *Mineralogical Abstracts,* resulting in sixty-four papers. While working with the survey, Hooker was responsible for rock analyses. Hooker developed new programs in mineralogical and petrological studies, corresponded extensively with geologists from all over the world, and organized international conferences.

                                            JH/MBO

PRIMARY SOURCES

Hooker, Marjorie. "Bibliography of North American Geology, 1949." *U.S. Geological Survey Bulletin* 977 (1951): 273 pp.
———. "Annotated Bibliography of North American Geology, 1950." *U.S. Geological Survey Bulletin* 985 (1952): 394 pp.
———, Pieter C. Zwaan, and Ole V. Petersen, eds. *World Directory of Mineral Collections. International Mineralogical Association.* 1963, 240 pp.

SECONDARY SOURCES

Jespersen, Anna. "Memorial to Marjorie Hooker, 1908–1976." *Geological Society of America Memorials* 8 (1978): 1–4. Includes a portrait and bibliography.

Hopkins, Esther (Burton)

STANDARD SOURCES
Sarjeant.

HOPKINS, ESTHER (BURTON) (1815–1897)

British botanist. Born 18 November 1815.

Esther Hopkins lived in Bath, and was active in botanical collecting. She discovered a new species, *Potamogeton decipiens.* She was active in the London Botanical Exchange groups. She contributed to H. C. Watson's *Topographical Botany.* Her herbarium was in the possession of D. M. Atkinson, Royal Infirmary at Glasgow   JH/MBO

PRIMARY SOURCES
Watson, H. C. *Topographical Botany.* London: B. Quaritch 1883.
    Hopkins was a contributor.

SECONDARY SOURCES
Botanical Society and Exchange Club of the British Isles Report
    (1866): 13.
Glasgow Naturalist 20 (1980): 53.

STANDARD SOURCES
Desmond.

HOPPER, GRACE (BREWSTER MURRAY) (1906–1992)

U.S. mathematician and computer science specialist. Born 9 December 1906 in New York City to Mary Campbell (Van Horne) Hopper and Walter Fletcher Murray. Two siblings. Married Vincent Foster Hopper (1930; divorced 1945). Educated Vassar College (B.A., 1928); Yale University (M.A., 1930; Ph.D., 1934). Professional experience: Vassar College, assistant in mathematics, associate professor; New York University, Courant Institute, Vassar Faculty Fellowship (1941); Women Accepted for Voluntary Emergency Service (WAVES), lieutenant (1943–1946); U.S. Naval Reserve (USNR), captain (1973), commodore (1983), and rear-admiral (1986); Harvard University Research Fellow, applied physics computation laboratory (1946–1949); Eckert-Mauchly Computer Corporation (later Univac Corporation and eventually a division of Sperry-Rand), Philadelphia, senior mathematician (1949–1950), senior programmer (1950–1959), UNIVAC systems engineer, director of automatic programming, Sperry Rand Corporation staff scientist (1959–1971). University of Pennsylvania, member of the adjunct faculty at the Moore School of Electrical Engineering (from 1959). Honors and memberships: Phi Beta Kappa; Sigma Xi; Institute of Electrical and Electronics Engineers, Fellow; Society of Women Engineers Achievement Award; Data Processing Management Association "Man-of-the-Year" Award. Died 1 January 1992 in Arlington, Va.

Grace Hopper's experience included academics, the military, and finally a private company. Her parents believed that girls should have the same educational opportunities as boys and encouraged their daughter when she wanted to study mathematics at Vassar. After a successful undergraduate career, she earned a doctorate at Yale and returned to Vassar to teach. She took a leave of absence from Vassar and joined the Women Accepted for Voluntary Emergency Service (WAVES), where she was commissioned lieutenant, junior-grade, and was assigned to the Bureau of Ordnance Computation Project at Harvard University. Her job there involved programming one of the early digital computers, the Mark I. As a research fellow at Harvard after the war, Hopper worked on the Mark II and III computers for the U.S. Navy. She continued her affiliation with the navy through the reserves and was promoted to commander in 1957. In 1949 she joined the Eckert-Mauchly Computer Corporation and was involved in the development of the first Binac and later Univac I. Although the company was absorbed first by Remington-Rand and then by Sperry, she remained with it. Much of work involved designing software for digital computers that span three computer generations.

Hopper is probably best known for her development of the computer language COBOL. However, it had numerous antecedents. At first she devised computer solutions to war-related problems. She conceived of a piece of tape on which three letters were typed to represent each set of instructions. From this basic idea came the first compiler, the A-O system. During the 1950s, she gained experience with mathematical languages by supervising what may have been the first compiler of AT-3, an early mathematical language, subsequently renamed MATHEMATIC. She went on to play a leading role in the development of commercial programming languages. Her team developed FLOW-MATIC, one of the early English-language data processing compilers and an antecedent of COBOL. COBOL was an especially innovative development in that it utilized an English-like language that could be written by someone who had no knowledge of the computer's internal workings.

Although the navy enforced its mandatory retirement age of sixty for Hopper in 1966, she was assigned to the U.S. Naval Data Automation Command (NDAC) on "temporary" active duty. She was given the task of standardizing the navy's computer languages, and spent the last twenty years of her active career standardizing the computers at the Pentagon. An act of Congress promoted the retired Hopper to captain in 1973, and to commodore in 1983. A special presidential decree appointed her to rear-admiral in 1986. She was deactivated in the summer of 1986.

Hopper was a team worker. She was able through persistence to make many technological innovations palatable. Although she claimed that she was too busy to look for gender bias, she also noted that she would like to have been a civil engineer but in 1928, there were no openings for female engineers. Her honors include Phi Beta Kappa, Sigma Xi, Fellow of the Institute of Electrical and Electronics Engineers, the Achievement Award of the Society of Women Engineers and the "Man-of-the-Year" Award of the Data Processing Management Association. She received honorary doctorates from at least ten universities and presented lectures all over the world. Her influential position in the computer industry encouraged other women to go into the field.

JH/MBO

PRIMARY SOURCES

Hopper, Grace Brewster Murray. "The Education of a Computer." In *Proceedings of the Association for Computing Machinery (Meeting Jointly Sponsored by the Association for Computing Machinery and the Mellon Institute in Pittsburgh, PA, May 2 and 3, 1952)*, 243–249. Pittsburgh: Richard Rimbach Association, 1952.

———. "Standardization of High Level Programming Languages." *Data Processing* 14 (June 1969): 329–335.

———. "Future Possibilities: Data, Hardware, Software, and People." In *Naval Tactical Command and Control*, ed. Gordon R. Nagler. Washington, D.C.: Armed Forces Communication and Electronics Association International Press, 1985.

SECONDARY SOURCES

Annual Obituary, 1992, The. Detroit: St James Press, 1993.

"Grace Murray Hopper." *Association for Computing Machinery '71: A Quarter Century Review* (1971): iii–iv.

Mace, Scott. "'Mother of COBOL'—Still Thinkin', Still Workin'." *Infoworld* 18 (1983): 29–31.

Mitchell, Carmen Lois. "The Contributions of Grace Murray Hopper to Computer Science and Computer Education." Ph.D. diss., University of North Texas, 1995.

Tropp, Henry S. "Grace Hopper: The Youthful Teacher of Us All." *Abacus* 2, no. 1 (1984): 7–18.

Whitelaw, Nancy. *Grace Hopper: Programming Pioneer.* New York: Scientific American Books for Young Readers, 1995. Juvenile literature.

Zientara, Marguerite. "Capt. Grace M. Hopper and the Genesis of Programming Languages." In *The History of Computing: A Biographical Portrait of the Visionaries Who Shaped the Destiny of the Computer Industry.* Part 11, 51–53. Framingham, Mass.: C. W. Communications, Inc.

STANDARD SOURCES

Grinstein and Campbell (article by Amy C. King and Tina Schalch); *Notable.*

HORENBURG, ANNA ELIZABETH VON (fl. 1564)

German midwife. Professional experience: official obstetrician of Braunschweig.

Anna Elizabeth von Horenburg worked in Braunschweig, where she was the official obstetrician. Her services were much in demand. In 1564, Conrad Gesner published a chapter on women's diseases in his encyclopedia for von Horenburg and her contemporaries. She wrote a textbook that was used in northern Germany.

JH/MBO

STANDARD SOURCES
Hurd-Mead 1938.

HORNEY, KAREN CLEMENTINE (DANIELSEN) (1885–1952)

German physician and psychoanalyst. Born 16 September 1885 in Hamburg, Germany, to Clotilde (van Ronzelen) and Bernt Danielsen. Married Oskar Horney. Three daughters. Educated University of Freiburg; University of Göttingen; University of Berlin (1911–1915; M.D., 1913); studied psychoanalysis with Karl Abraham (1913–1915). Professional experience: Berlin Sanitorium, resident physician (1915–1918); military neuropsychiatric hospital, physician (during World War I); Neurological Outpatient Clinic, Berlin, physician; Berlin Psychoanalytic Institute, psychoanalyst (1920–1932); Chicago Institute for Psychoanalysis, assistant director (1932–1934); New School for Social Research, New York, lecturer (1934–1952); American Institute of Psychoanalysis, cofounder and dean (1941–1952). Concurrent experience: Association for the Advancement of Psychoanalysis, cofounder; American Journal of Psychoanalysis, editor. Died 4 December 1952 in New York City of abdominal cancer.

Karen Danielsen was born in a suburb of Hamburg, Germany, the daughter of a Norwegian sea captain, Bernt Henrik Wackels Danielsen, and a Dutch mother, Clotilde Marie (van Ronzelen). Clotilde was Danielsen's second wife and eighteen years his junior; their temperaments were vastly different and eventually their discord resulted in separation. Karen had an older brother, Bernt, and four much older step-siblings from her father's first marriage. Her intelligence was obvious at an early age and her mother was proud and encouraged Karen. Her father, however, did not approve of education for women, and denigrated her abilities and discouraged her desire to become a doctor to the point of initially refusing permission and tuition for her to attend the *Realgymnasium*.

In 1906, Danielsen and her mother (now separated from her husband) left for the University of Freiburg. There Danielsen excelled both academically and socially and met Oskar Horney, a handsome and brilliant economics major. They began a continuous correspondence that lasted while he finished his studies at the University of Brunswick. In 1908, both entered the University of Göttingen, where they were married in 1909. Karen Horney was able from the start to combine marriage with work and continued her medical studies, finishing at the University of Berlin in 1911, the year her first daughter, Bridgitte, was born. She attended the universities of Freiburg, Göttingen, and Berlin, and received her medical degree at Berlin in 1915. Her second daughter, Marianne, had been born in 1913 and daughter Renate was born the year she graduated. In 1911, while in medical school, Horney became interested in psychoanalysis and joined the Berlin Psychoanalytic Society headed by Karl Abraham. She remained in therapy with Abraham for another two years and had her first introduction to various theories of psychology, including Freud's mechanistic concepts.

While accepting some tenets of the classical theory and having the utmost respect for Freud, she challenged Freud's pessimistic view of human nature. In her first psychoanalytic paper in 1917, she spoke of the potential for lifelong growth, an ideal she would achieve in her own life. By 1919, she had begun her private practice as a "Specialist in psychoanalysis," and by 1920 was working at the Psychoanalytic Institute of the Berlin Society as head of curriculum and training. She began to focus more on feminine psychology, lecturing on issues of importance to women and teaching classes relating to women's psychic nature. Increasingly bold, she challenged many of Freud's concepts. Rejecting the theory of primacy of biological and sexual factors in personality development and interpersonal relations, she theorized that women really envied not the penis but the superior position of men in society. She chastised the developers of psychoanalysis for being androcentric and believed that cultural factors were more responsible for perpetuating the subordinate role of females in society than any actual feelings of inferiority on women's part. Her most significant seminal papers on feminine psychology were written between 1922 and 1929.

Horney separated from her husband in 1926. Perhaps as a coping strategy, Horney made personal conflicts the focus of her theoretical work between 1926 and 1932, publishing six papers on marital problems in that time. She also dealt with the problems of raising adolescents, reflective of her own experiences. When Franz Alexander at the Institute for Psychoanalysis in Chicago offered her a job as assistant director in 1932, Horney emigrated to the United States, where she began to develop a theory of personality and new concepts of neuroses. After two years in Chicago, she moved to New York to work at the New School for Social Research and at the New York Psychoanalytic Institute. In New York she would write her most significant and controversial books.

Her *The Neurotic Personality of Our Time* (1937) advanced

three strategies for coping with anxiety: moving toward others (compliance), against others (aggression), or away from others (withdrawal). In normal behavior there is integration of all three. She believed that the cultural context of a behavior can be crucial in defining whether the behavior is neurotic in one case or adaptive in another. She suggested that clinging to one parent demonstrated not the Oedipus complex, but a disturbed parent-child relationship. She stressed that the role of a child's insecurity and feeling of isolation and the resulting search for security and feeling of superiority were possible sources of neurosis.

Horney's book *New Ways in Psychoanalysis* (1939) sought to clarify various concepts in psychoanalytic theory and explained her own attitude and where she agreed or differed with others. Her reinterpretation of Freudian concepts resulted in a professional uproar which precipitated her resignation from the New York Psychoanalytic Society in 1941. That same year she was one of the founders of the Association for the Advancement of Psychoanalysis and of the American Institute of Psychoanalysis, where she served as dean until her death in 1952. She was also editor of the *American Journal of Psychoanalysis*.

Horney was teacher, therapist, neo-Freudian, prolific writer, humanist, and feminist, with a wide range of interests and a full social life. One of her last journeys was to Japan to pursue an interest in Zen Buddhism. She has the distinction of being the only woman whose theory is detailed in textbooks on personality. Her contributions to theorists in various fields are innumerable in that she opened the door to holistic thinking and freedom from the mechanistic structure. She died 4 December 1952, in New York City, of abdominal cancer.

JH/MBO

PRIMARY SOURCES
Horney, Karen. *The Neurotic Personality of Our Time*. New York: Norton, 1937.
———. *New Ways in Psychoanalysis*. New York: Norton, 1939.
———. *Self-Analysis*. New York: Norton, 1942.
———. *Our Inner Conflicts*. New York: Norton, 1945.
———. *Neurosis and Human Growth*. New York: Norton, 1950.
plus many journal articles and papers.

SECONDARY SOURCES
O'Connell, Agnes. "Karen Horney: Theorist in Psychoanalysis and Feminine Psychology." *Psychology of Women Quarterly* 5 (1980): 81–93.
Rubens, Jack L. *Karen Horney: Gentle Rebel of Psychoanalysis*. New York: Dial Press, 1978.

STANDARD SOURCES
Current Biography 1941; O'Connell and Russo 1988; O'Connell and Russo 1990; Uglow 1982; Zusne.

HOROWITZ, STEPHANIE (1887–1940)

Polish/Austrian chemist. Born 17 April 1877 in Warsaw to Leopold Horowitz, an artist. Educated University of Vienna (Ph.D., 1914) and the Institute for Radium Research, Vienna. Professional experience: Institute for Radium Research, Vienna. Died 1940.

Horowitz worked in Vienna (and perhaps also in Prague) with the chemist Otto Hönigschmid to determine the atomic weight of radiolead. Their work was of great theoretical importance, as it verified the prediction (from the disintegration theory of radioactivity and the theory of isotopes) that lead in uranium minerals would have a lower weight than ordinary lead. Horowitz and Hönigschmid also found that a thorium-ionium mixture gave the same spectra as pure thorium, but had a different weight, thus confirming that thorium and ionium were isotopic.

After World War I, Horowitz returned to Warsaw. She was killed by the Nazis in 1940.   MM

PRIMARY SOURCES

Horowitz, Stephanie. With O. Hönigschmid. "Sur le poids atomique du plomb de la pechblende." *Comptes rendus* 158 (1914): 1796–1798; errata, 1948.
———. With O. Hönigschmid. "Über das Atomgewicht des 'Uransbleis'. II. Mitteilung." *Monatshefte für Chemie und verwandte Teile anderer Wissenschaftlichen* 36 (1915): 335–380.
———. With O. Hönigschmid. "Revision des Atomgewichtes des Thoriums. Analyse des Thoriumbromids." *Monatshefte für Chemie und verwandte Teile anderer Wissenschaftlichen* 37 (1916): 305–334.
———. With O. Hönigschmid. "Zur Kenntnis des Atomgewichtes des Ioniums." *Monatshefte für Chemie und verwandte Teile anderer Wissenschaftlichen* 37 (1916): 335–345.

SECONDARY SOURCES

Anders, Oswald U. "The Place of Isotopes in the Periodic Table." *Journal of Chemical Education* 41 (1964): 522–525.
Malley, Marjorie. *From Hyperphosphorescence to Nuclear Decay: A History of the Early Years of Radioactivity, 1896–1914.* Ph.D. diss., University of California, Berkeley, 1976.
Paneth, Fritz. "Über die Arbeit des Instituts für Radiumforschung." *Die Naturwissenschaften* 3 (1915): 437–443.

STANDARD SOURCES

Meyer and von Schweidler; Rayner-Canham 1997.

HOUGH, MARGARET JEAN RINGIER (1903–1961)

U.S. vertebrate paleontologist. Born 10 June 1903 in St. Louis, Mo. Married Elliot Hough, later divorced. One daughter. Educated St. Louis primary and secondary schools; University of *Missouri; University of Chicago (B.S., 1929; M.S., 1942; Ph.D., 1946). Professional experience: American and National Museums under auspices of the Geological Society of America, researcher; Geological Survey, researcher (1949–1960); Long Island University, professor of biology (1960–1961). Died 1961 in Chicago.*

Margaret Jean Ringier was born in St. Louis, Missouri, where she attended primary and secondary school. She attended the University of Missouri, where she met a journalism student, Elliot Hough, and married him before completing her degree. Jean Hough followed her husband to Chicago, where he was employed by a Chicago newspaper. She went to the university there and obtained her bachelor's degree in 1929, and immediately embarked upon postgraduate work in vertebrate paleontology under Alfred Romer. The marriage began to collapse, worsened considerably after the birth of a daughter, and finally ended in divorce in 1939. Hough was dismayed when Elliot died shortly after the divorce. Her way of dealing with crisis was to become intensely involved in work. She supported herself by working as an assistant at the Chicago Natural History Museum and as an instructor in midwestern colleges. After a while, she reentered graduate school and obtained her master's (1942) and doctoral (1946) degrees. After receiving her doctorate, Hough worked at both the American and the National Museums under a Geological Society of America grant, worked in the U.S. Geological survey, and was assistant professor of biology at Long Island University just prior to her death.

Hough was an expert on fossil vertebrates and did field work in the Northern Plains and Rockies states. Most of her research was on the Carnivora. However, she also published papers on Eocene and Oligocene faunas and on Tertiary marsupials and insectivores.   JH/MBO

SECONDARY SOURCES

Patterson, Bryan. "Margaret Jean Ringier Hough (1903–1961)." *Society of Vertebrate Paleontology News Bulletin* (1961): 36.

STANDARD SOURCES

Kass-Simon and Farnes (article by Michele L. Aldrich)

HOWARD, LOUISE ERNESTINE (MATTHAEI), LADY (1880–1969)

British classicist and ecologist. Born 26 December 1880 in Kensington, London, to Louise Henriette Elizabeth Sueur and Carl Hermann Ernst Matthaei. Two sisters. Married Sir Albert Howard, M.A., Fellow of the Linnean Society. Educated South Hampton High School; North London College School; Newnham College, Cambridge (Part I, class 1, 1898; Part II, class 1 botany, 1899),

Classical Tripos first in both parts (1903–1904), exhibitioner (1897–1899). Professional experience: Newnham, Bathurst Student (1900–1902), Resident Fellow (1903–1905), demonstrator in chemistry (1900–1905), lecturer and director of classical studies (1909–1916); International Review, *assistant editor (1918–1920); International Labour Office, Geneva, agricultural service (1920–1924), chief of section (from 1924).*

Louise Ernestine Matthaei took firsts in the Tripos at Newnham College. She earned a first-class pass in botany in 1899 and later sat for the Classical Tripos, where she earned first-class passes. She married Sir Albert Howard, the widower of Gabrielle, her older sister. Gabrielle had been a botanist. Howard was adamant in his opposition to chemical pesticides. He also stressed the importance of an ecological outlook, that plants must be studied together with their environments. The couple worked together, and published books reflecting their ideas. Louise Howard published over 150 works.

Howard hoped to see a world without frontiers where there would be a free exchange between the nations of the direct and indirect products of sunlight.　　JH/MBO

PRIMARY SOURCES
Howard, Louise. *Studies in Greek Tragedy.* Cambridge: The University Press, 1918.
———. *Labour in Agriculture: an International Survey.* London: Oxford University Press, 1935.
———. *The Soil and Health.* New York: Devin-Adair, 1947.
———. *The Earth's Green Carpet.* Emmaus, Pa.: Rodale Press, 1947.

STANDARD SOURCES
Desmond; *DNB Missing Persons;* Newnham.

HOWARD BECKMAN, RUTH WINIFRED (1900–)

U.S. psychologist. Born 25 March 1900 in Washington, D.C. Married Albert Sidney Beckman (1934). Educated Simmons College (B.S., 1921; National Urban League fellow; M.S., 1926); Columbia University, Spelman Foundation fellow (1929–1930); University of Minnesota, Spelman Foundation fellow (Ph.D., 1934); University of Chicago, postdoctoral fellow (1942–1943; 1955). Professional experience: Illinois Institute for Juvenile Research, clinical psychology intern (1935–1936); Center for Psychological Services, codirector (1940–1964), director (from 1964). Honors and memberships: American Psychological Society, member; Society for the Psychological Study of Social Issues, member; International Reading Association, member.

After receiving her doctorate in child development and psychology in 1934, Howard worked for a year as a clinical psychology intern at the Illinois Institute for Juvenile Research. She then went to the Center for Psychological Services, where she remained for the rest of her career, first as codirector, and, from 1964, as director. Concurrently, she was a psychologist for the Provident Shop School of Nursing from 1940 to 1966, a consultant for Waters College and Kentucky State College in 1948, a lecturer in the Evanston Public Schools from 1953 to 1955, a reading therapist for the reading clinic, University of Chicago, in 1955, a psychologist for the McKinley Center for Retarded Children during 1964–1965, and the Lincoln Center for Retarded Children from 1966. She also worked with the Head Start Program, the Worthington-Hurst Association (1966–1968), and the Mental Health Division of the Chicago Board of Health from 1967. She was a member of the American Psychological Society, the Society for the Psychological Study of Social Issues, and the International Reading Association.

Howard's research interests were in child development, individual differences, genetics, and mental retardation. She was the author of a number of journal articles　　KM

STANDARD SOURCES
AMS S&B 12; O'Connell and Russo 1988.

HOWARD WYLDE, HILDEGARDE (1901–1997)

U.S. paleontologist, specialist in fossil birds, and writer. Born 3 April 1901 in Washington, D.C., to Hattie Sterling (Case) and Clifford Howard. Only child. Married Henry Anson Wylde (1908–1983) 6 February 1930. No children. Educated University of California, Berkeley (B.A., 1924; M.A., 1926; Ph.D. in zoology, 1928). Professional experience: Natural History Museum of Los Angeles County, curator of avian paleontology (1939–1950), chief curator of science (1951–1961); emerita chief curator (from 1974). Honors and memberships: Brewster Memorial Award, American Ornithological Union (1953); Guggenheim research fellowship (1962–1963); Distinguished California Scientist Award, California Academy of Sciences (1973); American Association for the Advancement of Science, Fellow; Society of Vertebrate Paleontology, honorary member; Geological Society of America, Fellow; Cooper Ornithological Society, honorary member; American Ornithological Union, Fellow; Phi Beta Kappa, Phi Sigma, Sigma Xi, member.

Hildegarde Howard Wylde was born 3 April 1901 in Washington, D.C., the only child of Hattie Sterling Case and Clifford Howard. Hildegarde's mother was a gifted musician and composer. Her father studied law, and served for fifteen years (1891–1905) as stenographer for the District of Columbia. He also wrote profusely, producing articles for magazines and newspapers along with numerous books, one of which he dedicated to his young daughter. In September 1906, five-year-old Hildegarde moved with her parents to Los Angeles, where her father became a Hollywood screenwriter for the legendary director Cecil B. De Mille. An ardent champion of the women's suffrage movement, Clifford Howard was a delegate to the 1912 convention in Washington, D.C. Hildegarde did not openly champion women's rights as her father did, but throughout her life believed in the inherent equality of women.

Hildegarde Howard completed elementary school in the Los Angeles School District. In 1920 she enrolled at the Southern Branch of the University of California in Los Angeles (now known as the University of California at Los Angeles, or UCLA), then a two-year college. Having grown up in a family where life centered around creative arts, Howard had little inclination for science. Her original goal was to be a writer like her father. During her two years at UCLA, she was strongly influenced by her biology teacher, Pirie Davidson, and decided on biology as a major. In 1921, Howard began volunteer work at the Los Angeles County Museum (now called the Natural History Museum of Los Angeles County). Her first position was cleaning fossil bones from the Rancho La Brea Tar Pits for Chester Stock, a well-known mammalian paleontologist and then professor at UC Berkeley. While continuing and completing her studies at Berkeley, Howard worked in the summers as an assistant in zoology at UCLA, and as a research associate at the Los Angeles County Museum. In 1923, her first scientific paper was published in an international high school natural history bulletin.

At Berkeley and in Los Angeles, Howard was greatly influenced in her studies by scientists such as Lloye Miller, Chester Stock, William Diller Matthew, Joseph Grinnell, and William G. Burt. Lloye Miller, a vertebrate paleontologist specializing in Rancho La Brea fossils, was chairman of the biology department at UCLA. Affectionately called "Padre" by his students, Miller was especially inspirational to Hildegarde Howard in her scientific and philosophical outlook. Their professional collaboration and friendship lasted a lifetime.

Howard's lifelong enthusiasm for avian paleontology began in earnest in 1924 when she initiated her study of the fossil birds from Rancho La Brea. Howard obtained credit toward her master's degree from Berkeley for her research on the California turkey from Rancho La Brea. This study became the basis of her first major scientific publication. In summer 1924 she began work at the Los Angeles County Museum as a paid "day laborer." Howard stated that the most memorable part of this period in her life was meeting her future husband, Henry Anson Wylde, while both worked in the basement of the museum sorting La Brea fossils. Seven years Hildegarde's junior and an aspiring artist, Wylde went on to become the chief of exhibits at the Los Angeles County Museum. He died in 1983. Already a published scientist at the time of her marriage in 1930, Howard continued to use her maiden name in her professional life.

In 1928, Howard completed her doctoral dissertation at Berkeley on fossil birds from the Emeryville Shell Mound of Southern California. Her dissertation has become a classic in its field, a model for careful comparative research, and remains the principle reference of its kind. In the same year, Howard began full-time work at the Los Angeles County Museum, but not until February 1929 did she assume her first permanent position there as a junior clerk. Despite the unassuming title, she was in reality a curator and the first true specialist in paleornithology. She went on to become curator of avian paleontology (1939–1950), and chief curator of the division of science (1951–1961) at the Natural History Museum of Los Angeles County. Paleontology was dominated by men during most of her lifetime, but Howard felt she was an equal among equals. A pioneer and acknowledged expert in the field of paleornithology, she received due respect and admiration from her colleagues.

In 1951, Hildegarde Howard accepted the position of chief curator at the museum reluctantly, fearing that an outside person would be placed in charge of the science division with an adverse impact on the program. She was responsible for enlarging the science division with important additions to the professional staff. Howard had the ability to work harmoniously with her staff; tension and conflict were minimal.

Howard was not only an eminent scientist and administrator, but also found time to influence the professional careers of several other paleontologists. One such is Patricia Vickers Rich, a paleontologist now living in Australia, who specializes in Cenozoic fossil birds. Others are Laurie Bryant, an environmental geologist and paleontologist with the Bureau of Land Management in Montana, and Theodore Downs, a paleontologist specializing in Neogene mammals who started out as an ornithologist. Brought to the Los Angeles County Museum in 1952 by Howard, Downs assumed the position of chief curator of science at the museum in 1961 after Howard's retirement.

Howard's meticulous and prolific research on fossil birds contributed significantly to the status of her institution as a major research center. As a testimonial to her work and influence, in 1980 the Natural History Museum of Los Angeles County named in her honor the Hildegarde Howard Cenozoic Hall, an exhibition gallery devoted to a display of vertebrate fossils from the geologic period to which Howard devoted a lifetime of study. In 1973, the California Academy of Sciences honored Howard as a Distinguished California

Scientist, and featured a special exhibit of her works. Howard's lifelong interest in the fossils from the Rancho La Brea Tar Pits led her to champion the scientific, educational, and historical aspects of the Rancho La Brea site in nearby Hancock Park. A handsome building, the George L. Page Museum, was erected at the site in 1978 largely due to the pioneering efforts of Chester Stock and Hildegarde Howard.

Research was Howard's foremost passion. After retirement, Howard had a complete office set up in her home so she could continue her work, with weekly trips to the museum to compare specimens. A wealth of previously collected, unstudied, and often uncataloged fossil material from Rancho La Brea and elsewhere was at her fingertips, enough for several lifetimes of study. Her research routine throughout her career was simple and unvarying. Working mainly with a pair of calipers, Howard carefully measured each bone and jotted the information in a notebook, then evaluated the variability within each species before coming to any firm conclusions. Characterized by caution, restraint, and meticulous thoroughness, her research continues to amaze scientists with its accuracy, since her methods are considered outmoded and quite inadequate by today's standards. Her pioneering work is often cited by current avian paleontologists, demonstrating her continued prominence as a first-rate research scientist.

Howard's research focused on two main areas: the fossil birds of Rancho La Brea, and the Tertiary marine birds of southern California. She also did work on cave deposits from the western states, and Pliocene and Miocene fauna of Mexico. Howard's important works include several papers on the flightless diving auks of the genus *Mancalla*, the first of which was published in 1939. She described the most primitive form known of these birds, the late Miocene *Praemancalla lagunensis*, in 1968. Through Howard's careful work it is now possible to visualize the evolution of these flightless marine birds over the past forty thousand years. She also described the "toothed" odontopterygiforms of the genus *Osteodontornis*, the bony teeth being a specialized feature in these remarkable birds. Howard's most singular achievement centers around her correct diagnosis of a group of flightless diving birds belonging to the family Plotoptredae, which she described from only the humeral end of a coracoid. During her career, starting in 1924, Howard named at least twenty-three extinct species and six genera of birds, and recommended the establishment of two new families and one new order of fossil birds. Averaging three publications a year over the span of fifty years, she published well into her eighties, producing more than 140 scientific works as well as many articles of a nontechnical nature. One of the fortunate few who spent a lifetime doing work that she loved, Hidegarde Howard is the preeminent student of paleornithology. MLR

PRIMARY SOURCES

Campbell, Kenneth E., Jr., ed. "Papers in Avian Paleontology honoring Hildegarde Howard." In *Contributions to Science, Natural History Museum of Los Angeles County*, 330 (15 September 1970).

Chester Stock Papers, George L. Page Museum, Hancock Park, California.

Hildegarde Howard Papers, archives, George L. Page Museum, Hancock Park, California.

Hildegarde Howard Papers, archives, Natural History Museum of Los Angeles County, Los Angeles, California.

Hildegarde Howard, Personal Papers, Laguna Hills, California.

Personal interview with Hildegarde Howard, May 1994, Laguna Hills, California.

HOWE AKELEY, DELIA JULIA DENNING (1872?–1970)

U.S. photographer, explorer, museum collector, and preparator. Married Carl Akeley (1902; divorced 1923); married Warren D. Howe (1939). Professional experience: Chicago Field Museum, collector. Died 22 May 1970 in Daytona Beach, Fl.

Carl Akeley's first wife, Delia, accompanied him on museum collecting trips to Africa, collecting flora for the dramatic Chicago Field Museum exhibit. She went on expeditions to Africa in 1904–1905, 1909, 1910, and 1911. It was she and not he who shot the largest elephant for the field museum. World War I interrupted their explorations. She divorced Akeley on grounds of cruelty in 1923; he remarried Mary Lee Jobe almost immediately. Delia Akeley supposedly discovered new species of duiker antelopes and birds, but this is not confirmed. She did, however, prepare habitat groups with Carl Akeley and was a proficient photographer and game hunter.

She continued her own work under the auspices of the Brooklyn Museum after her divorce, and went to Africa to study pygmies in the Ituri forest. She wrote no scholarly accounts, but published a popular book on an African monkey with her own photographs. Her second book was *Jungle Portraits*. She outlived her second husband, whom she married in 1939, and subsequently faded into obscurity. She published a number of popular articles from 1927 to 1930. She died in Daytona Beach, Florida. JH/MBO

PRIMARY SOURCES

Howe, Delia Julia. *JT, Jr., the Biography of an African Monkey*. New York: Macmillan, 1928. Includes her own photographs.

———. *Jungle Portraits.* New York: Macmillan, 1930. Many photographs.

STANDARD SOURCES
NAW unused.

HOWES, ETHEL DENCH PUFFER (1872–1950)

U.S. psychologist. Born 10 October 1872 in Framingham, Mass. Married. At least one child, Benjamin T. Howes. Educated Smith College (A.B., 1891); Berlin and Freiburg universities (1895–1897); Radcliffe (Ph.D., 1902). Professional experience: Keene, N.H., high school teacher (1891–1892); Smith College, instructor in mathematics (1892–1895), director of instruction for coordination of women's interests (from 1925), lecturer in sociology (1928–1931); Radcliffe College, assistant psychologist (1898– 1906); Wellesley College, instructor and assistant professor in philosophy (1901–1906); Simmons College, psychologist (1904– 1906). Honors and memberships: starred in second edition of American Men of Science (1910). Died 1950.

Psychologist Ethel Howes taught high school for a year immediately after she graduated from Smith College. After leaving her high school teaching position, she returned to Smith College as an instructor in mathematics, where she remained until she decided to continue her studies in Germany. When she returned to the United States, she worked on her doctorate at Radcliffe College. During this time she served as an assistant psychologist. She then went to Wellesley, where she became a philosophy instructor, and finally to Simmons College, where she was the psychologist.

Considered in 1910 to be one of the top one thousand American scientists by *American Men of Science,* Ethel Dench Puffer Howes was a woman of many interests. She was concerned with symmetry and aesthetics, which she treated in her book *The Psychology of Beauty* (1905), and with the quality of life of women. She founded the Institute for the Coordination of Women's Interests at Smith College in 1925 to develop methods of combining efficient home management with intellectual endeavors. While she did not depart from the Victorian edict that women should be wives and mothers first, she did strive to find ways for women to escape their confined world. She designed a nursery program using the mothers' shared time and talents, which enabled the women to have some time to themselves and gave the children a supervised social and educational experience. Howes was a member of the Psychological Association and the Philosophical Association.

KM

PRIMARY SOURCES
Howes, Ethel Dench Puffer. *The Psychology of Beauty.* Boston and New York: Houghton, Mifflin and Company, 1905.

———. *How to Start a Co-operative Nursery. Prepared for the Home Administration Bureau, Woman's Home Companion.* New York: Crowell Publishing Co., [1923?].
———. *Progress of the Institute for the Co-ordination of Women's Interests: Report at Alumnae Conference October 12, 1928.* Northampton, Mass.: Smith College, 1928.
———. with Dorothea Beach. *The Co-operative Nursery School; What It Can Do For Parents: an Experimental Demonstration of the Institute for the Co-ordination of Women's Interests.* Northampton, Mass.: Smith College, 1928.

SECONDARY SOURCES
Kimble, G. A., M. Wertheimer, and C. L. White, eds. *Portraits of Pioneers in Psychology.* Washington, D.C.: American Psychological Assocation, 1991.
Scarborough, Elizabeth and Laurel Furumoto. *Untold Lives.* New York: Columbia University Press, 1987. Howes discussed on pages 71–90.

STANDARD SOURCES
AMS 2–5; Bailey; Siegel and Finley.

HOWITT, MARY (BOTHAM) (1799–1888)

British writer and naturalist. Born 12 March 1799 (or 10 March 1797, depending on source) in Coleford, Gloucestershire, to Anne (Wood) and Samuel Botham. Married William Howitt (16 April 1821). Children. Educated at home. Professional experience: studied British plants. Died 30 January 1888 in Rome.

Mary Howitt was an eclectic writer, including among her many interests children's books, translation of Swedish and Danish works, and other popular works. Much of her work was done in conjunction with her husband. They were so close, that friends called them "William and Mary." His death in 1879 and her oldest daughter's death in 1884 caused her intense sorrow. Among her eclectic interests was natural history, about which she published several books.

JH/MBO

PRIMARY SOURCES
Howitt, Mary. *Sketches of Natural History.* Boston: T. H. Carter, 1834. In verse.
———. *Wood Leighton, or a Year in the Country.* London: J. Green, 1836.
———. *Birds and Flowers and Other Country Things.* London: J. Green, 1838.
———. *Our Four-Footed Friends.* London: S. W. Partridge, [1862 ?], 1867.
———. *Mary Howitt, an Autobiography.* Ed. Margaret Howitt. 2 vols. 1889.

SECONDARY SOURCES

Good Words. Monthly Journal (1886). Howitt mentioned on pages 52, 172, 330, 394, 592.

Hale, Sarah Josepha Buell. *Woman's Record.* New York: Harper & Bros., 1853. Hewitt mentioned on pages 699–702.

STANDARD SOURCES

Desmond; *DNB.*

HROSWITHA OF GANDERSHEIM (935–ca. 999)

German canoness, dramatist, healer. Born 935. Educated in Greek and Latin. Canoness of Benedictine abbey of Gandersheim. Died 999.

Hroswitha was the first recognized medieval dramatist. Canoness at the Benedictine abbey of Gandersheim, she wrote saints' legends, at least six comedies, and the *Gesta Ottonis,* a history of Otto the Great. She was also knowledgeable about herbal medicines and treated some patients.   JH/MBO

STANDARD SOURCES

Echols and Williams.

HUBBARD, MARIAN ELIZABETH (1868–?)

U.S. zoologist. Born 31 August 1868 in McGregor, Iowa. Educated University of Chicago (B.S., 1894); University of California (1902–1903). Professional experience: Wisconsin high school, assistant (1889–1903); Wellesley College, instructor (1894–1901), assistant professor (1901–1917), professor (1917–1937), emerita professor (from 1937). Death date unknown.

Marian Hubbard's career trajectory is interesting, because the only degree that she earned was a bachelor's. She did do postgraduate work at the University of California, but there is no indication that it resulted in a degree. She then progressed through the academic ranks from instructor to professor at Wellesley. She worked on the heredity of variations in the grain beetle *Silvanus* and the embryology of the chick. She correlated protective devices in salamanders and studied nesting bluebirds.   JH/MBO

PRIMARY SOURCES

Hubbard, Marian Elizabeth. *Correlated Protective Devices in Some California Salamanders.* Berkeley: The University Press, 1903.

STANDARD SOURCES

AMS 1–8.

HUBBARD, RUTH MARILLA (1902–1982)

U.S. clinical psychologist. Born 22 September 1902 in Charleston, Ill. Educated Oberlin College (A.B., 1924); University of Minnesota (A.M., 1925; Ph.D., 1927). Professional experience: University of Minnesota, teaching fellow (1924–1927); Columbia University Teachers College, Laura Spelman Rockefeller fellow in child development (1927–1928); Child Guidance Clinic, Cleveland, psychologist (1928–1930); Rochester [NY?] (1930–1934); Kalamazoo (Mich.) State Hospital, psychologist and instructor (1934–1935); Family Service Society, Detroit, psychologist (1935–1948); U.S. Veterans Administration Hospital, chief clinical psychologist (from 1948); Case Western University, lecturer, graduate school for applied social sciences (1929–1930); University of Michigan, lecturer, institute of public and social administration (1936, 1939–1948); Wayne State University, lecturer, school of public affairs and social work. Honors and memberships: American Psychological Association, Fellow; American Association for the Advancement of Science; Association of Social Workers; Sigma Xi. Died 20 December 1982.

Ruth Hubbard worked chiefly as a clinical psychologist while lecturing at schools of social sciences, nursing, public and social administration, and public affairs and social work. Her research centered around tests and measurements. She was involved with interest tests and worked on the reliability of infant tests. She also worked on factors that affected improvement in children in child guidance clinics as well as psychotherapy with psychotic patients.

She was a member of the American Psychological Association, the American Association for the Advancement of Science, the Association of Social Workers, and Sigma Xi.

KM

STANDARD SOURCES

AMS 5–8, S&B 9–11; *Psychological Register,* vol. 3, 1932.

HUBBS, LAURA CORNELIA (CLARK) (1893–1988)

U.S. mathematician and research ichthyologist. Born 26 March 1893 near Omaha, Nebr. One sister. Married Carl Leavitt Hubbs (1918). Three children (one daughter; two sons). Educated public schools in Nebraska and California; Stanford College (B.A., 1915; M.A. in mathematics, 1918). Professional experience: Stanford University, instructor of mathematics (1916–1918); University of Michigan, Museum of Zoology, (unpaid) cataloguer (1920–1944); Scripps Institution of Oceanography, (unpaid) associate (1944–1979); library affiliate (1979–1983?); research expeditions in zoology and marine biology, field associate and photographer (1922–1973?). Honors and memberships: Mission Bay Research Institute (Sea World) named Carl and Laura Hubbs Sea World Research Institute, 24 May 1977. Died La Jolla, Calif., 24 June 1988.

Laura Cornelia Clark was born on a small farm near Omaha, Nebraska, and educated in the public schools near there until 1910 when her family moved to San Jose, California. She and her younger sister Frances Clark then completed their high school years in San Jose. Both sisters went on to Stanford College, although Frances first attended the San Jose Normal School. Laura was interested in mathematics and prepared for a career as a mathematics teacher by taking first a bachelor's and then a master's degree. While accompanying her sister on a biology field trip at Stanford, she met the zoologist Carl Leavitt Hubbs, one year her junior; a few years later she married him. For a year after obtaining her master's degree, she taught mathematics to the non-science students at Stanford.

After Carl completed his master's, the couple moved to Ann Arbor, where he was appointed curator of the Museum of Zoology. Once her three children were old enough to go along on research trips, the entire family would spend holidays collecting specimens for the museum from 1922 to 1943. Her two sons entered the field of biology, and her daughter married a distinguished biologist she met on a field trip, in spite of her claim that she had disliked the trips as a child.

In 1944, Carl Hubbs was appointed professor of biology at Scripps Insitution of Oceanography in La Jolla, Calif., and the couple returned to California. The family lived in La Jolla first in the Community House and then in the Director's House of the Scripps Institution. Finally in 1954 they moved to their own house. Laura Hubbs continued to work full-time as an unpaid associate of Scripps, doing all the statistical calculations for Hubbs's papers and coauthoring at least nineteen of the seven hundred papers he published, especially those on the hybridization of fishes. Photographs of Carl and Laura Hubbs show her actively collecting fish, participating in field trips, and organizing his files. In the late 1940s through the 1950s they made monthly visits to Baja, California, to measure ocean temperatures and collect fish. Rosa Fish Eigenmann was an associate of Hubbs. They also shared an interest in early Aztec and Mayan culture. Laura Hubbs was responsible for organizing his library of books and reprints, which numbered eighty-eight thousand, maintaining her office in the SIO archives after Carl's death in order to finish her job organizing his archives. Both during his lifetime and afterward, her role as his partner in research was widely recognized. An article from the French journal *Cybium*, the bulletin of the French Society of Icthyology, commented on the manner in which the entire family, including Laura Hubbs, her son-in-law, Robert Miller, and her children formed the "Hubbs tribe" of taxonomists.   JH

PRIMARY SOURCES

Hubbs, Laura. With C. L. Hubbs. "Increased Growth in Hybrid Sunfishes." 1931.

———. With C. L. Hubbs and R. R. Miller. "Hydrographic History and Relict Fishes of the North Central Great Basin." San Francisco: California Academy of Sciences, 1974.

SECONDARY SOURCES

Bauchot, M. L. "Carl L. Hubbs 1894–1979." *Cybium, Bulletin de la Société Française d'Ichtyologie* 3rd ser. 9 (1980): 3–4.

Cox, Anne. "Laura Hubbs—At His side, Not in His Shadow." *Seacoast* 2 (May 1981): 11–15.

"Laura Clark Hubbs, 95, Passes away June 24." *La Jolla Light*, 11 July 1988. Obituary notice with portrait. Two pages.

"Laura Clark Hubbs." *The Tribune (San Diego)*, 28 June 1988.

"Laura Clark Hubbs, Dies at 95." Press Release, Scripps Institution of Oceanography, USCD News, 1988.

Miller, Frances Hubbs. "The Scientific Publications of Carl Leavitt Hubbs, Bibliography and Index: 1915–1981." San Diego: Hubbs-Sea-World Research Institute, 1981. Hubbs's joint papers with her husband are listed.

Shaw, Marjorie. "Laura Clark Hubbs 1893–1988." *Zoonooz* 62 (1988): 16. With three portraits.

STANDARD SOURCES

AMS 6–8.

HUDSON, HILDA PHOEBE (1881–1965)

British mathematician. Educated Cambridge University (1900–1904); University of Berlin (1904–1905); Bryn Mawr College, Bryn Mawr, Pa. (1910–1911); University of Dublin (D.Sc., 1913). Professional experience: Newnham College, Cambridge, lecturer (1905–1913), research fellow (1910–1913); West Hampshire Technical Institute, lecturer (1913–1917). Honors and memberships: London Mathematical Society, member of council (1917–1925).

British mathematician Hilda Hudson was educated in three countries: England, Germany, and the United States. She earned a doctoral degree from the University of Dublin. She published in many mathematical journals and she wrote the article on a new survey of universal knowledge for the sixth edition of the *Encylopaedia Britannica* (1865) and the article on curves in the twenty-first edition, 1965.   JH/MBO

PRIMARY SOURCES

Hudson, Hilda Phoebe. "On the 3–3 Birational Transformat in Three Dimensions." *Proceedings of the London Mathematical Society* 9 and 10 (September 1910–1911).

———. "On Cubic Birational Space-Transformats." *American Journal of Mathematics* 34 (8 September 1912).

———. "The Product of Two Quadro-Quadric Space Transformats." *American Journal of Mathematics* 35 (6 September 1913).

———. "Linear Dependency of the Schur Quadrics of a Cubic Surface." *The Journal of the London Mathematical Society* 1 (2 September 1926).

STANDARD SOURCES
Grinstein and Campbell; Poggendorff, vols. 5–1, 6–2, and 7b–4.

HUG-HELLMUTH, HERMINE VON (1871–1924)

Austrian psychoanalyst. Born 31 August 1871 to Ludovika (Achelpohl) and Ritter Hugo von Hugenstein. One sister. Educated Vienna, teaching certificate (1904); University of Vienna (Ph.D., physics, 1909). Professional experience: psychoanalytic training analysis (1910–1913). Honors and memberships: Vienna Psychoanalytical Society, member (1913); International Congress of Psychoanalysis, member. Murdered 9 September 1924.

Hermine von Hug-Hellmuth was the "first child analyst," and influenced both ANNA FREUD and MELANIE KLEIN. She was the first woman to be accepted as a full member of the Vienna Psychoanalytic Society. Although she never married, she raised the illegitimate son of her sister, whom she later adopted. On 9 September 1924 the adolescent boy murderd his adoptive mother, Hug-Hellmuth. After the murder, HELENE DEUTSCH suggested that Hug-Hellmuth brought it upon herself by conducting experiments in child raising upon the boy. Another controversy surrounding Hug-Hellmuth is that a book that she published, *A Young Girl's Diary*, was castigated as a fraud—the autobiography not of a patient but of Hug-Hellmuth herself.
K M

PRIMARY SOURCES
Hug-Hellmuth, Hermine. *Aus dem Seelenlebendes Kindes; eine Psychoanalytische Studie.* Leipzig: F. Deuticke, 1921.

SECONDARY SOURCES
Maclean, George, and Ulrich Rappen. *Hermine Hug-Helmuth: Her Life and Work.* New York: Routledge, 1991.

STANDARD SOURCES
Stevens and Gardner.

HUGGINS, MARGARET LINDSAY (MURRAY) (1848–1915)

Irish astronomer. Born 1848 in Dublin to John Murray. Married William Huggins. Educated at home and for a time at a school in Brighton, England. Died 1915.

A woman of cosmopolitan tastes and varied talents, Margaret Huggins collaborated with her husband, a former businessman who had made his hobby of astronomical spectroscopy into a second career, in preparing an atlas of stellar spectra and in studying binary stars, nebulae, and Wolf-Rayet stars.

Margaret's mother died when she was a young child. After her father, a Dublin lawyer, remarried, she was left by herself much of the time. During this period she was grateful for the attention of her grandfather, who spent many evening hours teaching her to recognize the constellations. From this early exposure she became interested in astronomy, studying the heavens with homemade instruments. An article in the magazine *Good Words* inspired her to construct a spectroscope. William Huggins (1824–1910), who was engaged in pioneering work in stellar spectroscopy, was impressed by Margaret's interests and abilities. They were married in 1875 and thereafter worked together as astronomers.

Another enthusiasm they shared was music. William Huggins owned a Stradivarius violin, which he played as Margaret Huggins accompanied him on the piano or organ. Violins and their history interested them both, and Margaret Huggins published an account of the life and work of the Brescian violin maker Giovanni Paolo Maggini. An accommplished painter and an expert on antique furniture, Margaret Huggins was also a superb letter writer. Her correspondence documents the multifaceted life of a nineteenth-century Renaissance woman.

The common interest in spectroscopy that brought the Hugginses together persisted throughout their careers. Although she is often characterized as his assistant, skilled at photographic manipulations and visual observations, William considered Margaret's work significant on its own. Later memoirs were issued under their joint names. Margaret Huggins participated in an investigation of the spectrum of the Orion nebula, contributed visual observations of the spectrum of Nova Aurigae, was the joint author of *Atlas of Representative Stellar Spectra* (1899), and participated in the editing of *The Scientific Papers of Sir William Huggins* (1909).

Margaret Huggins's comment on women in science reflects an attitude that merits further investigation. She wrote,

> I find that men welcome women scientists provided they have the proper knowledge. It is absurd to suppose that anyone can have useful knowledge of any subject without a great deal of study. When women have really taken the pains to fit themselves to assist or to do original work, scientific men are willing to treat them as equals. It is a matter of sufficient knowledge. That there is any wish to throw hindrances in the way of women who wish to pursue science I do not for a moment believe. The lady doctors had a great

fight, it is true, but that is old history now, and there were special ancient prejudices involved. ("Lady Margaret Huggins")

Apparently Huggins was not reflecting on equal privileges as evidenced from her own experience. Because women were not allowed to become regular fellows of the Royal Astronomical Society, she was elected an honorary member in 1903.

There is little doubt that Margaret Huggins added to the bulk of astronomical data and worked well as part of a team with her husband. She represents the diligent, sensitive nineteenth-century intellectual woman at her best.   MBO

PRIMARY SOURCES
Huggins, Margaret Lindsey. *Gio: Paolo Maggini, His Life and Work, compiled and edited from material collected and contributed by William Ebsworth Hill and his sons William, Arthur, and Alfred Hill.* London: W. E. Hill and Sons, 1892.

———.*Agnes Mary Clerke and Ellen Mary Clerke: An Appreciation.* Privately printed, 1907. Information on the lives and works of Agnes and Ellen Clerke.

———. *"Kepler." A Biography.* London: Hazell Watson and Viney, [n.d.].

Huggins, William. *The Scientific Papers of Sir William Huggins and Lady Huggins.* London: W. Wesley and Son, 1909.

Huggins, William, and Margaret Huggins. *An Atlas of Representative Stellar Spectra from 4870 to 3300, Together with a Discussion of the Evolutional Order of the Stars, and the Interpretation of Their Spectra. Preceded by a Short History of the Observatory and Its Work.* London: W. Wesley and Son, 1899.

SECONDARY SOURCES
Brück, Mary T. "Companions in Astronomy. Margaret Lindsey Huggins and Agnes Mary Clerke." *Irish Astronomical Journal* 20 (1991): 70–77.

Kidwell, Peggy Aldrich. "Women Astronomers in Britain, 1780–1930." *Isis* 75 (1984): 534–546.

"Lady Margaret Huggins." *Monthly Notices of the Royal Astronomical Society* 76 (February 1916): 278–284. Obituary notice.

STANDARD SOURCES
Uneasy Careers.

HUGHES, ELLEN KENT (1893–?)

Australian physician. Born 29 March 1893 in Australia to an English mother and Australian (of Scots descent) father. Six siblings: two brothers and four sisters. Married (1) Paul Loubet (died three months after marriage); (2) Garde Wilson. One son by Loubet; four children by Wilson. Educated Ruyton School in Kew (graduated 1907); Melbourne University (1913–1918?). Professional experience: Queen Victoria Hospital, house doctor; Hospital for Sick Children, Brisbane; Mitchell, physician; Kingaroy in Queensland, private practice for seven years; Armidale Hospital, physician. Honors and memberships: Armidale, freeman of the city; cathedral council; Member of the British Empire. Death date unknown.

Ellen Hughes's life exemplifies the problems that any physician, male or female, would have had during the first half of the twentieth century in Australia. While growing up, she helped her physician father in his practice and finished her degree at Melbourne University, where there were three other women in her class. World War I broke out during her medical schooling, and she had to go home to take care of the younger children. She married a Frenchman who was becoming qualified at the children's hospital. He died three months after they were married, leaving Hughes pregnant. She had to combat her father's prejudice that a single mother should not care for her baby; he wanted to adopt her son, but she refused and arranged for his care while she was a resident at the Hospital for Sick Children in Brisbane. Her experience during the influenza epidemic was traumatic. She moved shortly afterward to establish a practice at Mitchell, four hundred miles west of Brisbane. She married Garde Wilson in Mitchell, and the couple had four children.

Hughes worked full time in general practice in several places and found that being a woman had no adverse influence on her practice. She published many papers in the *Medical Journal of Australia*.   JH/MBO

PRIMARY SOURCES
Hughes, Ellen Kent. In Hellstedt, Autobiographies.

HUGHES, MARY CAROLINE (WESTON) (fl. 1888)

British geologist. Father Rev. G. F. Weston, honorary Canon of Carlisle. Married Thomas McKenny Hughes.

Mary Caroline Weston married Thomas McKenny Hughes, professor of geology at Cambridge, in 1882. She had one publication in paleontology (1888) and coauthored a monograph, *Cambridgeshire* (1909), with her husband.   JH/MBO

PRIMARY SOURCES
Hughes, Mary Caroline. "On the Mollusca of the Pleistocene Gravels in the Neighbourhood of Cambridge." *Geological Magazine,* n.s. 5 (May 1888): 193–207.

———. With Thomas McKenny Hughes. *Cambridgeshire.* Cambridge: University Press, 1909.

SECONDARY SOURCES

"Thomas McKenny Hughes." *Geological Magazine* 54 (1917): 334–335. Obituary notice for husband.

STANDARD SOURCES

Creese and Creese.

HUGHES-SCHRADER, SALLY PERIS (1895–?)

U.S. cytologist/zoologist. Born 25 January 1895 in Hubbard, Ore. Married Franz Schrader 1920. Educated Grinnell College (B.S., 1917); Columbia University (Ph.D. in zoology, 1924). Professional experience: Grinnell College, instructor in zoology (1917–1919); Barnard College, Columbia University, lecturer (1919–1921), member of science faculty (1941–1947), research associate in cytology (1947–1958; 1959–1972); Bryn Mawr College, demonstrator in biology (1922–1924); instructor (1924–1930); Sarah Lawrence College, science faculty member (1931–1941); Duke University, emerita research associate in cytology (from 1972). Death date unknown.

Most of Sally Hughes-Schrader's career was spent as a research cytologist. Although she was on the faculty of several colleges and universities, she did not seem to consistently advance up the academic ladder. She held several concurrent experience; she was a corporate member of the Marine Biological Laboratory, Woods Hole, in 1925; a Berliner Fellow of the American Association of University Women in 1929–1930; the Duke University Hargitt Fellow in zoology (1961–1962); and visiting professor (1962–1965). She was a member of the American Society of Zoologists and the Genetics Society of America, and a Fellow of the American Academy of Arts and Sciences. Her research was on the cranial nerves and ganglia of fishes and amphibians; cytology; chromosome structure, behavior, and evolution; and the chromosome cytology of *Neuroptera*.   JH/MBO

PRIMARY SOURCES

Schrader, Sally Hughes. With Franz Schrader. "Morality in Pike-Perch Eggs in Hatcheries." Report. U.S. Commission on Fisheries. Appendix 5. 1922.

———. "Reproduction in *Acroschismus Wheeleri Pierce*." *Journal of Morphology and Phisiology* 39 (1924) 157–205.

SECONDARY SOURCES

Manning, Kenneth R. *Black Apollo of Science.* Oxford: Oxford University Press, 1983. Sally Hughes-Schrader discussed on pages 67–74, based on an interview with her from 7 July 1977.

STANDARD SOURCES

AMS 4–8, B 9, P&B 10–14.

HUGONNAI-WARTHA, VILMA (1847–1922)

Hungarian physician born in 1847, daughter of a count. Married (1) Gyorgy Szillassy (1865), one child who died at age six; (2) Vince Wartha. Educated medical classes in Zurich (passed M.D. exam, received certificate 1879). Died 1922.

Reared and tutored in a privileged household, Vilma Hugonnai was married at age eighteen to Gyorgy Szillassy. The couple had one child, who died at age six, a tragedy that awakened Hugonnai's interest in medicine, especially pediatrics. She began her study of medicine in 1872 while living in Zurich; published two papers, one on tracheotomy in diphtheria and one on the treatment of burns. She passed the oral examination to complete a medical degree in February 1879, but as a woman she was allowed only a midwife's certificate.

She returned to Budapest to become assistant to a professor, Vince Wartha, whom she later married. Her research contributed knowledge to Hungarian medicine. In 1897 the Ministry of Culture recognized her Zurich degree and allowed her to practice as a doctor in Hungary (although women were required to practice in association with a male doctor until 1913). Her example and encouragement helped improve the status of women.   KM

STANDARD SOURCES

Uglow 1989.

HUMMEL, KATHARINE PATTEE (1904–)

U.S. biologist. Born 2 October 1904 in St. Paul, Minn. Educated Carleton College (B.A., 1926); University of Minnesota (M.A., 1927); Cornell University (Ph.D. in histology and embryology, 1934). Professional experience: Carleton College, instructor in zoology (1927–1932); Mount Holyoke College, instructor (1935–1936); Cornell University, research instructor in animal nutrition (1936–1937); New Jersey College for Women, Rutgers, (1939–1941), assistant professor (1941–1943); Jackson Memorial Laboratory, staff scientist (from 1943). Honors and memberships: Society of Zoologists, member; Association of Anatomists, member; Association for Cancer Research, member.

Katharine Hummel's progress toward her degrees was steady. After she finished her master's degree at Minnesota, Carleton hired her as an instructor. After she got her doctorate from Cornell, she had a one-year job at Mount Holyoke as an instructor. Her succeeding university jobs were all of short duration. At the New Jersey College for Women, where she remained for four years, she was acting head of the department of zoology from 1942 to 1943. As a staff scientist at the Jackson Memorial Laboratory, Hummel worked on developmental anomalies and various topics in experimental biology. She was a member of the Society of Zoologists, the Association of Anatomists, and the Association for Cancer Research. JH/MBO

PRIMARY SOURCES
Hummel, Katharine Pattee. "Cestodes of Reptiles." M.A. thesis, University of Minnesota, 1927.

STANDARD SOURCES
AMS 6–8, B 9, P&B 10–11.

HUNSCHER, HELEN ALVINA (1904–)

U.S. nutritionist. Born 5 August 1904 in Gates Mill, Ohio. Married (?) Wilkinson (1939). Educated Ohio State University (A.B., 1925); University of Chicago (Ph.D., 1932); American Board of Nutritionists (diploma). Professional experience: Merrill-Palmer School and Children's Hospital, Michigan, assistant nutritionist (1928–1929), instructor in home economics (1930–1931); Children's Fund of Michigan, research associate (1931–1937), professor of home economics and department head (1937–1963), professor of nutrition and chemistry (1963–1974); Case Western Reserve University, emerita professor of nutrition and consultant (from 1974). Honors and memberships: American Chemical Society; American Home Economics Association; American Public Health Association; Society for Experimental Biology and Medicine; Society of Research in Child Development, Fellow.

As did many women, Helen Hunscher decided on a scientific career that had applications for "women's work." After earning her doctoral degree from the University of Chicago and becoming a board-certified nutritionist, she taught her subject. Concurrently, she was a lecturer at Wayne State University from 1931 to 1937. Hunscher was a member of several professional organizations, including the American Chemical Society, the American Home Economics Association, the American Public Health Association, the Society for Experimental Biology and Medicine, and a Fellow of the Society of Research in Child Development. Her research was on the vitamin content and chemistry of human milk, mineral metabolism of women during pregnancy and lactation, mineral and nitrogen metabolism of children, and skeletal maturity and nutrition. JH/MBO

STANDARD SOURCES
AMS 5–8, B 9, P&B 10–13.

HUNT, CAROLINE LOUISA (1865–1927)

U.S. home economist. Born 23 August 1865 in Chicago, Ill. Educated Northwestern University (A.B., 1888). Professional experi-
ence: Lewis Institute, teacher domestic economy (1896–1901); University of Wisconsin, professor (1903–1908); U.S. Department of Agriculture, office of home economics, specialist (1909–1924), bureau of home economics, administrator (1924–1927). Died 1927.

Although Caroline Hunt did not hold an advanced degree, she was typical of a woman who used her interest and education in the acceptable field of home economics. She used her education both in teaching and working in the U.S. Department of Agriculture, where so many other women who were interested in science worked. JH/MBO

STANDARD SOURCES
AMS 3–4.

HUNT, EVA VERBITSKY (1934–1980)

Argentinian/U.S. anthropologist. Born 12 April 1934 in Buenos Aires, Argentina, to Josefa (Plotkin) and Alejandro Verbitsky. One brother. Married Robert Hunt (1960). One daughter, born 1965. Educated Universidad Femina, Mexico City (A.B., 1953); Escuela Nacionál de Antropología; University of Chicago (Ph.D., 1962). Field work: Cuicatec Indians, Oaxaca, Mexico (1954, 1963–1964); Juxtlahuaca Indians, Mixtec, Oaxaca, Mexico (1955); Tzeltal Indians, Chiapas Project, Mexico (1959). Professional experience: Escuela Nacionál de Antropología, research assistant (1953–1957); Northwestern University, Department of Anthropology, research associate, instructor (1961–1962); National Science Foundation funded researcher (1963–1964); University of Chicago, Department of Anthropology, teacher (1965–1969); Boston University, Department of Anthropology, assistant to associate professor (1969–1980). Honors and memberships: American Anthropological Association, Fellow; honored in posthumous session of the AAA (1964). Died 1980.

Eva Verbitsky was brought up in a lively intellectual family in Buenos Aires. Her parents, both second-generation Jewish intellectuals in Argentina, gave her a sound education. Verbitsky came from a line of strong women who held professional positions: her mother was in education, her grandmother had practiced as a physician. At first, Verbitsky was mainly interested in painting, and showed some skill in that direction that she continued to display throughout her life.

When she was in her adolescent years, Verbitsky's father was at odds with the Peron government, and moved his family to Mexico City. There, Eva entered the Universidad Femina, and, after finishing her bachelor's degree, entered the graduate school of anthropology, Escuela Nacionál de Antropología. During this period of her life, she worked as a research assistant to two anthropologists, Roberto Weitlaner, who introduced her to field research in Oaxaca with the Cuicatec Indians, and Kimball Romney, a graduate student from Harvard who encouraged her to continue her graduate studies at the University of Chicago.

Verbitsky knew little English, but Chicago was very welcoming since Sol Tax was developing an important Mexican research project, the Chiapas Project. She was allowed to prepare her papers and exams in Spanish until she mastered the English language. She went to Mexico to study two Tzeltal villages as part of the Chiapas project, and this investigation served as the subject for her dissertation. Three years after she entered Chicago, she met and married a graduate student in anthropology at Northwestern, Robert Hunt, with whom she began a close and fruitful personal and intellectual collaboration. By this time, she had mastered English well enough to serve as research associate to Paul Bohannan at Northwestern and teach a course on kinship for him.

The two young anthropologists decided to return to the area in Oaxaca, to study the Cuicatec Indians for their postdoctoral work. They obtained a National Science Foundation grant to do archival research and to do field reseach for the next ten months. Soon after Eva Hunt returned, she gave birth to her only daughter; in the fall of that same year, she began to teach undergraduate courses at University of Chicago. She also continued to expand her own knowledge through the seminars given by Victor Turner and Terrance Turner on myth and ritual. She was stimulated to redirect her own thinking toward symbolic anthropolgy while retaining an interest in Levi-Strauss's structuralism. The Hunts continued their field work in Oaxaca but they began to reject the community-based studies and insisted on regional studies that investigated the conflicts that arose between the Indian culture and the educational, judicial, and economic institutions of the Mexican state. Eva Hunt's anthropology was seen as groundbreaking in this approach.

In 1969, the two anthropologists moved to the Boston area, where Eva Hunt took up a position at Boston University and Robert Hunt at Brandeis. She soon rose to associate professor and stimulated the thinking and the methodological approach of her devoted students. Her major study, *The Transformation of the Hummingbird*, examined the "archaeology of symbols" in the ritual MesoAmerican poem to which she brought ethnographic, ethnohistorical, and archeological analysis. In the mid-seventies, Eva Hunt was stricken with cancer, from which she died five years later after a courageous struggle. She left unpublished a book-length manuscript "The Buried Bell: Variation and Orthodoxy in a Mexican Village," which included a dramatic account of a Cuicatec woman healer performing a curing ritual. She was memorialized four years later by a special session at the American Anthropological Association.   JH/MBO

PRIMARY SOURCES

Hunt, Eva Verbitsky. "The Meaning of Kinship in San Juan: Geneological and Social Models." *Ethnohistory* 8 (1969): 37–54.

———. "Irrigation and the Socio-Political Organization of the Cuicatec Cacicazgos." In *Prehistory of the Teahuacan Valley*, ed. Richard MacNeish and Fred Johnson, 162–257. Austin: University of Texas Press, 1972.

———. "Conciousness of Conformation and Submission: The Symbolic Dimension of Indian Mexican Political Interaction." In *Symbol and Politics in Communal Ideology*, ed. S. F. Moore and B. Myerhoff. Ithaca, N.Y.: Cornell University Press, 1974.

———. With Robert Hunt. "Canal Irrigation and Local Social Organization." *Current Anthropology* 17 (1976): 389–411.

———. *The Transformation of the Hummingbird: Transformations of a Zincantecan Myth*. Ithaca, N.Y.: Cornell University Press, 1977.

SECONDARY SOURCES

Bohannan, Paul. "Obituary: Eva Verbitsky Hunt." *American Anthropologist* 83, no. 4 (1981): 892–894.

STANDARD SOURCES

AMS; Gacs (article by Judith Friedlander).

HUNT, HARRIOT KEZIA (1805–1875)

U.S. physician and reformer. Born 9 November 1805 in Boston, Mass., to Kezia (Wentworth) and Joab Hunt. One younger sister. Never married. Educated in neighborhood home-based school; studied anatomy and physiology with Dr. and Mrs. Mott; opened her own school in 1827; Female Medical College of Philadelphia, honorary medical degree (1853). Professional experience: local general medicine practice. Died of Bright's disease 2 January 1875 in Boston.

Sometimes referred to as the first woman to practice medicine in the United States, Harriot Kezia Hunt achieved success through self-education, compassion, and common sense. Her entreaties to enter Harvard Medical School were twice refused, once in 1847 and a second time in 1850. For decades she worked for the advancement of women and raised money and support for their medical education. She was daughter of Joab and Kezia Hunt, both of old New England families, and was educated at home and at private schools run by local women, known as "dame schools." She and her younger sister, Sarah, were encouraged to read widely and take an interest in public affairs. Harriot began her own school in 1827, shortly before her father died suddenly.

In 1830, Hunt became ill with a tubercular disease, which continued despite the ministrations of conventional doctors.

Desperate for a cure, the sisters consulted Dr. and Mrs. Mott, who came to Boston in 1833 advertising themselves as physicians. Their homeopathic approach proved successful and the Hunt sisters both began to study anatomy and physiology with the Motts, who were determined to learn the science of prevention. With the encouragement of their mother, the sisters spent every free moment reading and studying and gradually built up a steady practice, mostly of women and children. Their treatments, given with patience and sympathetic kindness, consisted basically of attention to diet and sanitation, bathing, moderate exercise, adequate rest, and fresh air. In 1843, Hunt, convinced of the preventive value of education, organized a Ladies' Physiological Society and began a career of public lectures in physiology and campaigned for improved health and hygiene.

After Sarah Hunt married, and after the death of their mother, Harriot applied for admittance (1847) to Harvard University Medical School, writing Dean Oliver Wendell Holmes, who was agreeable to the experiment himself but was overruled as the governing board deemed it "inexpedient." In 1850 Hunt was given permission to attend lectures at Harvard, but a riot by enrolled students opposed to the admission of a woman (and three blacks) obliged her to withdraw. The publicity engendered by the riot had one positive effect: in 1853, the Female Medical College of Pennsylvania presented her an honorary medical degree (she had then practised medicine for eighteen years).

Through her patients, Hunt learned of the widespread injustices and discriminations toward working women and joined the campaign for reform, including remuneration for domestic labor. She championed every woman's right to education and a career. She spoke for abolition of slavery and racial inequality. She attended the first Women's Rights Convention at Worcester, Massachusetts, in 1850 and became a friend to many of the leaders of the women's rights movement. She became interested in mental illness and tried to combat women's nervous diseases by helping them toward self-esteem, again seeing education and opportunities for intellectual advancement as a key issue. Beginning in 1852, Hunt accompanied her annual tax payment with a written protest against paying taxes without having the vote. In 1853, she petitioned the Massachusetts constitutional convention for equal educational rights for women and helped to found a school of design for women in Boston to prepare them for jobs in the clothing industry. She kept up her medical practice and was still consulting cases when she died of Bright's disease in Boston in January 1875. Her model of determination and benevolent concern as well as her outspoken challenge to male exclusivity in medicine helped pave the road for the first generation of university-trained women doctors.

JH/MBO

PRIMARY SOURCES

Hunt, Harriot K. *Glances and Glimpses; or, Fifty Years Social, Including Twenty Years Professional Life.* Boston: J. P. Jewett and Company [etc.], 1856. Rpt., New York: Source Book Press, 1970. Hunt's autobiography.

STANDARD SOURCES

AMS S&B 9–10; Hurd-Mead 1933; Lovejoy; *NAW* (article by Alice Felt Tyler); Uglow 1982.

HURLER, GERTRUD (ZACH) (1889–1965)

German pediatrician. 1 September 1889 at Taberwiese in the district of Rastenburg, Prussia. Father general practice physician. Married veterinary surgeon Konrad Hurler in 1914. Two children: one daughter; one son. Educated Königsberg; University of Munich (M.D.); Hauner Children's Hospital, postgraduate training. Professional experience: private pediatric practice in Neuhausen (1919–1965). Died 1965.

Gertrud Zach was born in Prussia, where her father was a general practitioner. She was educated in Königsberg and completed her medical degree at the University of Munich. She took additional training for a pediatric specialty after she married and had a daughter, Elizabeth, who eventually studied medicine herself. Zach's husband was Konrad Hurler, a veterinary surgeon whom she inspired to obtain a medical qualification after their marriage in 1914. Their son, Franz Gustav, born in 1921, was killed in World War II.

During her pediatric training at Hauner Children's Hospital, Hurler published an account of two infants displaying a syndrome of corneal clouding, dwarfing skeletal dysplasia, spinal malalignment, and mental retardation. Although the report had been presented to the Munich Pediatric Society by her chief, Professor von Pfaundler, the disorder, previously called gargoylism or lipochondrodystrophy, became known as Hurler Syndrome. The Hurler family settled in Neuhausen in 1919 and Gertrud opened a private practice in pediatrics, which she attended actively until her death at age seventy-six in 1965.

Hurler is described as an exceptional clinician, well loved by her patients and active in her profession and community. She was associated with the local orphanage, served on many medical committees, and was a pioneer in the establishment of a maternal postnatal service.

KM

PRIMARY SOURCES

Hurler, G. "Ueber einen Typ multipler Abartungen, vorwiegend am Skelettsystem." *Zournal Kinderheilk* 24 (1919): 220.

SECONDARY SOURCES

Beighton, Peter, and Greta Beighton. *The Man Behind the Syndrome.* New York: Springer-Verlag, 1986.

HURLOCK, ELIZABETH BERGNER (1898–?)

U.S. psychologist. Born 4 July 1898 in Harrisburg, Pa. Married 1931. Two children. Educated Bryn Mawr College (A.B., 1919; A.M., 1922); Columbia University (Ph.D., 1924). Professional experience: New York and Pennsylvania schools, teacher (1919–1921); Columbia University, instructor in psychology (1924–1940), associate professor (1940–1946); University of Pennsylvania (from 1949). Death date unknown.

Elizabeth Hurlock was born in Pennsylvania and received her first two degrees from Bryn Mawr College. She did not marry until seven years after she attained her doctoral degree from Columbia University and had begun to rise through the academic ranks at the University of Pennsylvania.

Interested in child and adolescent psychology, Hurlock wrote five books, over thirty-five articles, and eighteen text films on these subjects. She was a member of the American Psychological Association, the Gerontological Society, and Sigma Xi. She edited the first issue of *Teaching of Psychology* in November 1950.   KM

PRIMARY SOURCES

Bergner, Elizabeth. *The Psychology of Dress.* Ronald, 1929.

Hurlock, Elizabeth. *Child Development.* New York: McGraw-Hill, 1942.

———. *Adolescent Development.* New York: McGraw-Hill, 1949.

———. *Child Growth and Development.* New York: McGraw-Hill, 1949.

———. *Developmental Psychology,* 2d ed. New York: McGraw-Hill, 1959.

———. *Personality Development.* New York: McGraw-Hill, 1973.

STANDARD SOURCES

AMS 4–8, S&B 9–13; *Psychological Register,* vol. 3, 1932.

HURSTON, ZORA NEALE (1903–1960)

U.S. cultural anthropologist, folklorist, and writer. Born 7 January 1903 in Eatonville, Fla. Seven siblings. Father Rev. John Hurston. Married (1) Herbert Sheen (1927; divorced); (2) Albert Price III (1939; divorced). Educated Morgan Academy (1918); Howard University Preparatory Academy (1918); Howard College (A.A., 1920); Columbia University, Barnard College (A.B. 1925); Columbia graduate work in anthropology (1928–1935). Professional experience: Federal Works Progress Administration (WPA), Federal Theatre Project, dramatic coach (1934–1936); field work in Jamaica and Haiti (1936), and Honduras (1948); North Carolina College for Negroes, University of North Carolina, and Florida Normal College, lecturer and drama teacher (1941–1943). Honors and memberships: Rosenwald grants (1928–1932); Guggenheim fellowship (1936); Morgan College, honorary degree; Howard University, honorary degree. Died 1960 in St. Lucie County, Fla.

Zora Neale Hurston was an unusually gifted anthropologist, folklorist, and writer. She was born in Florida to a preacher and carpenter father; her mother instilled in her a desire to change her life. After a variety of circumstances that led her to Baltimore as the maid to a traveling Gilbert and Sullivan troupe, Hurston entered a school in Baltimore. Soon after she graduated, she had the chance to do college preparatory work at Howard University. She continued on to an associate of arts degree, became interested in the work of members of the Black Renaissance, and began to study anthropology.

Sponsored by the writer Fannie Hurst, Hurston was one of the first African-American women to enter Barnard College, where she met Franz Boas, who encouraged her to collect southern folklore as part of the work toward her bachelor's degree. During this period, she also married and divorced her first husband. Her folklore research formed the basis of her book *Mules and Men,* with an introduction by Franz Boas. With grants that included a Rosenwald fellowship, she was able to continue on in graduate work with the encouragement of RUTH BENEDICT. Her work also appeared in the *Journal of American Folklore.* During this period, she also collaborated with the poet Langston Hughes on theatrical versions of her folk tales, and worked with the Federal Theatre Project as a dramatic coach to earn a living.

Unable to obtain further Rosenwald grants to do her graduate research on voodoo ritual in Jamaica and Haiti, her studies were slowed down until she managed to obtain a Guggenheim fellowship in 1936. Her resulting study, *Tell My Horse,* which included a description of her induction into voodoo cults, was challenged upon publication two years later by some scholars, in spite of its warm reception by the public and Melville Herskovits. During this time, she made another unsuccessful marriage and wrote her famous autobiography.

Feeling rejected by the scholarly community, she obtained drama positions at a series of black colleges. She made another attempt to obtain grants to do research in Honduras World War II, hoping to unearth a lost Mayan temple. She wrote a final novel in Honduras in the postwar period exploring the role of white women in the South, but this was badly received.

From this time on, Hurston experienced great difficulties. Her later novels were rejected and she became ill and isolated. She entered a welfare home in Florida in 1959 following a stroke and died the following year. There is some suggestion by Mikell, one of her biographers, that she was far older than her published age, which may explain her rapid decline. In the seventies, most of her books were reprinted. Biographies and appreciations by women writers like Alice Walker have led to her recent appreciation as a fine writer and scholar.   JH/MBO

PRIMARY SOURCES
Hurston, Zora Neale. "Cudjo's Own Story of the Last African Slaver." *Journal of Negro History* 12 (1927): 648–663.
———. "Dance Songs and Folk Tales from the Bahamas." *Journal of American Folklore* 43 (1930): 294–312.
———. "Characteristics of Negro Expression"; "Conversions and Visions"; "The Sermon." In *Negro: An Anthology,* ed. Nancy Cunard. London: Wishart, 1934.
———. *Mules and Men.* Philadelphia: J. B. Lippincott, 1935. With an introduction by Franz Boas. Hurston's southern folklore collection.
———. *Their Eyes Were Watching God.* Philadelphia: J. B. Lippincott, 1937. The classic novel of black experience.
———. *Tell My Horse.* Philadelphia: J. B. Lippincott, 1938. An account of her experiences of voodoo in Haiti and Jamaica.
———. *Dust Tracks on a Road.* Philadelphia: J. B. Lippincott, 1942. Hurston's autobiography.

SECONDARY SOURCES
Hemenway, Robert E. *Zora Neale Hurston: A Literary Biography.* Urbana: University of Illinois Press, 1977.
Walker, Alice, ed. *I Love Myself When I Am Laughing: A Zora Neale Hurston Reader.* New York: Feminist Press, 1979.

STANDARD SOURCES
Bailey; Gacs (article by Gwendolyn Mikell).

HUSSEY, ANNA MARIA (REED) (d. pre-1859)
British botanist. Married. Died before 1859.

Little is known of British botanist Anna Maria Hussey. Her interests were in British fungi, and she published one book on the subject. She lived in Hayes, Kent, and her correspondence is found in the Berkeley correspondence at the British Museum of Natural History.   JH/MBO

PRIMARY SOURCES
Hussey, Anna Maria Reed. *Illustrations of British Mycology.* London: Reeve, Benham, and Reeve, 1847–1855.

STANDARD SOURCES
Desmond.

HUSSEY, PRISCILLA BUTLER (1894–?)
U.S. entomologist. Born 24 January 1894 in Bowling Green, Fla. Educated University of Michigan (A.B., 1919); Smith College (A.M., 1921); Radcliffe College (Sc.D., 1923). Professional experience: University of Michigan, assistant in zoology (1917–1919); Smith College, curator in zoology (1919–1921); New York University, instructor in zoology (1923–1927); Battle Creek College, assistant professor (1917–1928); Louisiana State Normal College (Natchitoches, La.), associate professor, professor (from 1928). Death date unknown.

While Priscilla Hussey was working on her bachelor's degree at the University of Michigan, she worked as an assistant in zoology and while she was working on her master's degree at Smith, she served as curator. After earning her doctorate of science degree, she was a zoology instructor at New York University for four years and then moved to Battle Creek College as an assistant professor for a year. She then moved to Louisiana State Normal College as an associate professor and soon advanced to full professor. Her research was in entomology (including economic entomology, microtechnique, and embryology). She also worked with trematode parasites, mostly of insects.   JH/MBO

PRIMARY SOURCES
Hussey, Priscilla Butler. *A Taxonomic List of Some Plants of Economic Importance.* Lancaster, Pa.: The Science Press Printing Co., 1939.

SECONDARY SOURCES
Osborn, Herbert. *A Brief History of Entomology. Including Time of Demosthenes and Aristotle to Modern Times with Over Five Hundred Portraits.* Columbus, Ohio: The Spahr & Glenn Co., 1952. Includes a portrait of Hussey (plate 32).

STANDARD SOURCES
AMS 4–7.

HUTCHINS, ELLEN (1785–1815)
Irish cryptogamic botanist. Born 17 March 1785 at Ballylickey House, Bantry Bay, Ireland, to Elinor (d. 1814), only child and heir of Arthur Hutchins of Thomastown and Cregane Castle, Limerick, and Thomas Hutchins (1735–1787), magistrate. Twenty siblings but only six survived. Never married. Educated in Dublin. Died 9 February 1815 at Ardnagashel House, Bantry Bay, Ireland.

Ellen Hutchins gained a formidable reputation among early nineteenth-century men of science for her capacity to find cryptogamic plants, her beautifully preserved specimens, and her skillful botanical drawings. However, like many women of the period, she was reluctant to see her name in print. Only after forming a close epistolary friendship with the eminent botanist Dawson Turner of Yarmouth (Norfolk, England), was she persuaded to allow her name to appear as the collector of specimens she provided for Turner's *Fuci* (1808–1819), which also included six of her drawings of seaweeds; James Sowerby and James Edward Smith's *English Botany* (1790–1814); Lewis Weston Dillwyn's *British Confervae* (1802–1809); and William Jackson Hooker's *British Jungermanniae* (1812–1816).

When Hooker began to publish his monograph in 1812, he privately expressed concerns that Hutchins's discoveries would overwhelm the work and was fearful of encouraging even more prolific contributions from her. As it was, Hooker opened his monograph with *Jungermannia hutchinsiae,* a new species found by Hutchins, and acknowledged her discovery of Bantry Bay habitats for almost half the species described in the work. Hutchins was also honored by the botanist Robert Brown, who named a genus of alpine plants *Hutchinsia* in 1812. The president of the Linnaean Society of London, James Edward Smith, claimed that she could find almost anything.

Hutchins had begun her botanical work because of illness and she continued to pursue it despite increasing physical and psychological pain. Her health first began to fail when she was completing her education. While receiving treatment in the Dublin home of a family friend and physician, Dr. Whitley Stokes, she met the botanist James Townsend Mackay, and began to read botanical works in Stokes's library. Botany was regarded as a perfect pursuit for sickly individuals because of its combination of outdoor exercise and indoor occupation. On returning home to Ballylickey, Hutchins not only laid out her own garden but also collected algae, mosses, liverworts, and lichens along the shores of Bantry Bay and in the surrounding mountains. By 1806, she was sending fine specimens of seaweeds and other algae to Mackay, who, in turn, forwarded rare discoveries to Dawson Turner at Yarmouth. Deeply impressed by what he received, Turner began a correspondence with Hutchins that was to inspire and sustain her for the remainder of her life. Initially he explained the complex classificatory systems of cryptogamic plants and overcame Hutchins's isolation by sending books and named specimens. By 1809, the botanist Lewis Weston Dillwyn, who visited Hutchins at Ballylickey, noted in his diary that "Miss Hutchins amazed me by the extent & depth of her botanical knowledge" (Lyne, "Dillwyn's Visit to Waterford," 94).

Hutchins's botanical achievements were made despite her poor health and a troubled domestic life. The youngest daughter and second youngest child of twenty-one children, she devoted much of her time to caring for her brother Thomas, paralyzed following an accident, and nursing her elderly mother. Hutchins's troubles became acute in 1813 when she and her mother moved to Bandon, thirty miles from Bantry Bay, after her oldest brother Emanuel took possession of Ballylickey House and drove them out. In Bandon, Hutchins became desperately ill and barely able to care for her mother, who died on 22 March 1814. By May 1814, Hutchins was back in Bantry Bay, living at Ardnagashel, the estate belonging to another brother, Arthur. Although mercury treatment for a liver complaint reduced Hutchins to a "mere skeleton," her physician believed she would recover. Her cousin, the botanist Thomas Taylor, however, thought this unlikely given the proximity to her brother Emanuel. Hutchins herself attributed her mental and physical suffering to family disputes. As her illness worsened, she relied more and more on Turner's friendship, claiming that their correspondence was the one source of happiness in her life. She died on 9 February 1815, shortly before her thirtieth birthday.

Despite never meeting Hutchins in person, Turner deeply mourned her death. In the concluding volume of his works on seaweeds, he lamented his loss and paid tribute to Hutchins, celebrating their shared love of botany and poetry by quoting from James Hurdis's 1794 poem "Tears of Affliction: A Poem Occasioned by the Death of a Sister Tenderly Beloved." Aware of the value of her botanical collections, Hutchins bequeathed her herbarium to Turner. Following Hutchins's death, however, the fate of her collection was thrown into doubt when fighting broke out between two of her brothers, one of whom attempted to seize Ballylickey House with forty armed men. Eventually Hutchins's specimens and drawings were safely shipped to Turner, who ensured their continued use by botanists.　AS

PRIMARY SOURCES
Ellen Hutchins to Dawson Turner, letters, Trinity College, Cambridge, England.
Dawson Turner to Ellen Hutchins, letters, Royal Botanic Gardens, Kew, England.

SECONDARY SOURCES
Bevan, John. "Miss Ellen Hutchins (1785–1815) and the Garden at Ardnagashel, Bantry, County Cork." *Moorea* 3 (1984): 1–10.
Burke's Landed Gentry of Ireland, 4th ed. London: Burke's Peerage, 1958.
Chesney, Helena C. G. "The Young Lady of the Lichens." In *Stars, Shells and Bluebells: Women Scientists and Pioneers,* ed.

Mary Mulvihill and Patricia Deevy, 28–39. Dublin: Women in Technology and Science (WITS), 1997.

Knowles, Matilda C. "The Lichens of Ireland." *Proceedings of the Royal Irish Academy* 38B (1929): 179–434. Hutchins mentioned on page 182.

Lett, H. W. "Census Report on the Mosses of Ireland." *Proceedings of the Royal Irish Academy* 38B (1915): 65–166. Hutchins mentioned on pages 70–71.

Lyne, Gerard J. "Lewis Dillwyn's Visit to Kerry, 1809." *Journal of the Kerry Archaeological and Historical Society* nos. 15–16 (1982–1983): 83–111. Hutchins discussed on pages 86–87.

———. "Lewis Dillwyn's Visit to Waterford, Cork and Tipperary in 1809." *Journal of the Cork Historical and Archaeological Society* 91 (1986): 85–104. Hutchins discussed on pages 93–94.

Lyne, Gerard J., and M. E. Mitchell. "A Scientific Tour through Munster: The Travels of Joseph Woods, Architect and Botanist, in 1809." *North Munster Antiquarian Journal* 27 (1985): 15–61. Hutchins mentioned on page 27.

Nelson, E. Charles. *An Irish Flower Garden.* Kilkenny, Ireland: Boethius Press, 1984.

Pearson, W. H. "Ellen Hutchins—A Biographical Sketch." *The Bryologist* 21 (1918): 78–80.

Turner, Dawson. *Fuci: or, Coloured Figures and Descriptions of the Plants Referred by Botanists to the Genus Fucus.* 4 vols. London: 1808–1819. See especially volume 4, 1819, p. 152.

STANDARD SOURCES
Desmond.

HUTCHINSON, DOROTHY (HEWITT) (1905–)

See Hewitt, Dorothy.

HUTTON, LADY ISABEL EMILIE (d. 1960)

Scottish/British physician. Born late nineteenth century. Father, James Emilie. Married Sir Thomas Jacomb Hutton (1921). Educated Edinburgh Ladies' College; Edinburgh University (M.D. with honors, 1912); Munich, Vienna, etc., postgraduate studies. Professional experience: Royal Sick Children's Hospital, Edinburgh, resident physician; Stirling District Mental Hospital, pathologist; Royal Mental Hospital, Edinburgh, physician; British Hospital for Mental and Nervous Disorders, consultant psychiatrist; World War I, physician in the army (1914–1918); Scottish Women's Hospital in Macedonia and Serbia (1915–1920); Lady Muriel Paget Hospital, Sebastopol, Crimea, commanding officer; director of Indian Red Cross Welfare Service (1945). Honors and memberships: Royal Society of Medicine, Fellow; White Eagle Award of Serbia; Croix de Guerre, France; St. Anne of Russia award; Commander of the *Order of St. John; St. Sava of Serbia; Royal Red Cross, Serbia; C.B.E. (Order of the British Empire) 1948; Royal Medico-Psychological Association, member (1939–1945). Died 11 January 1960.*

Isabel Hutton specialized in the study and treatment of mental and nervous diseases. She made a name for herself in both world wars. Her contributions were recognized by her awards from Serbia, France, Russia, and Great Britain. In addition to her medical work, she found time to enjoy music, the ballet, and learning languages. She was a member of the University Women's Club. She published many articles in professional journals in addition to her books.   JH/MBO

PRIMARY SOURCES
Hutton, Isabel. *The Hygiene of Marriage.* London: Heinemann, 1923.

———. *With a Woman's Unit in Salonika, Serbia and Sebastopol.* London: Williams & Norgate, 1928.

———. *Mental Disorders in Modern Life.* London: Heinemann, 1940.

———. *Woman's Change of Life.* London: Heinemann, 1958.

STANDARD SOURCES
WWW, 1951–1960.

HYDE, IDA HENRIETTA (1857–1945)

U.S. physiologist. Born 8 September 1857 in Davenport, Iowa, to Babette (Loewenthal) and Meyer Heidenheimer. Higher education, University of Illinois (1881–1882); Cornell University (B.S., 1891); Bryn Mawr College (1891–1893); University of Strassburg (1893–ca. 1895); University of Heidelberg (Ph.D., 1896). Professional experience: Irwin Research Fellow, Radcliffe College (1896–1897); University of Kansas, associate professor (1898–1905), professor (1905–1920). Died 22 August 1945 in Berkeley, Calif.

Ida Hyde's German parents shortened their name, Heidenheimer, after settling in the United States. The father was a merchant; there were two daughters and a son. When she was sixteen years old, Ida was apprenticed to a millinery establishment in Chicago. During the seven years of her work there, she read, studied, and attended classes at the Chicago Athenaeum, a school for working people. At the age of twenty-four, she spent one year at the University of Illinois. Depleted finances, however, caused an interruption in her higher education, and for seven years she taught in the Chicago public schools.

After this teaching experience, Hyde returned to college, this time to Cornell, where she earned a bachelor of science degree (1891). She continued her education at Bryn Mawr

College, studying under the physiologist Jacques Loeb (1859–1924) and the zoologist Thomas Hunt Morgan (1866–1945). In 1893 she was invited to do research in the zoology department at the University of Strassburg in Germany; a fellowship from the Association of Collegiate Alumnae (later the American Association of University Women) enabled her to accept the invitation.

Because of opposition to women earning the doctorate at Strassburg, Hyde was unable to take the doctoral examination. At Heidelberg, however, she was allowed to pursue a degree, although even here she was hindered by the prejudice of the well-known physiologist Wilhelm Küne, under whom she wanted to study. Other faculty members supported her, and in 1896 she became the first woman to receive a doctoral degree from Heidelberg University. Before returning to the United States, Hyde did research in marine biology at the Heidelberg Table of the Naples Zoological Station and in physiology at the University of Bern, Switzerland.

During her year as Irwin Research Fellow at Radcliffe College (1896–1897), Hyde worked with the physiologist William Townsend Porter at the Harvard Medical School; she was the first woman to do research at that institution. Her experience at the Naples Zoological Station having interested her in providing a similar opportunity for other women scientists, she led the effort to establish the Naples Table Association for Promoting Scientific Research by Women.

In 1898 Hyde went to the University of Kansas as associate professor of physiology. After the university established a separate department of physiology in 1905, Hyde was promoted to professor. She earned an outstanding reputation as a teacher and continued her own education as well—at the University of Liverpool (summer 1904) and at the Rush Medical College in Chicago (summers 1908–1912). During many summers, Hyman conducted research in marine physiology at the Marine Biological Laboratory at Woods Hole, Massachusetts. During 1922–1923, having retired from the University of Kansas, she conducted research on the effects of radium at Heidelberg University. Hyde was the first woman elected to membership in the American Physiological Society (1902). She spent her last years in California and died in Berkeley at the age of eighty-eight of a cerebral hemorrhage.

Hyde's research dealt with the physiology of the circulatory, respiratory, and nervous systems of both vertebrates and invertebrates. She was especially interested in the developing embryo. Known for the scrupulous precision of her experimental methods, she developed microtechniques by which she could investigate a single cell.   MBO

PRIMARY SOURCES
Hyde, Ida. *Entwicklungsgeschichte einiger Scyphomedusen.* Leipzig: W. Englemann, 1894.

———. "The Effect of Distention of the Ventricle on the Flow of Blood through the Walls of the Heart." *American Journal of Physiology* 1 (1898): 215–224.
———. *Outlines of Experimental Physiology.* Lawrence: University of Kansas Press, 1905.
———. "A Study of the Respiratory and Cardiac Activities and Blood Pressure in the Skate Following Intravenous Injection of Salt Solutions." *University of Kansas Science Bulletin* 5, no. 4 (1911): 27–63.
———. "The Development of a Tunicate without Nerves." *University of Kansas Science Bulletin* 9, no. 15 (1915): 175–179.
———. "Before Women Were Human Beings." *Journal of the American Association of University Women* (June 1938): 226–236.

SECONDARY SOURCES
Sloan, Jan Butin. "The Founding of the Naples Table Association for Promoting Scientific Research by Women, 1897." *Signs: Journal of Women in Culture and Society* 4 (1978): 208–216.

STANDARD SOURCES
NAW; Notable; Ogilvie 1986.

HYMAN, LIBBIE HENRIETTA (1888–1969)

U.S. zoologist. Born 1888 in Des Moines, Iowa, to Sabina and Joseph Hyman. Three brothers. Never married. Educated local high school (graduated 1905); University of Chicago (B.S., 1910; Ph.D., 1915). Professional experience: University of Chicago, research assistant for Charles Manning Child (1915–1931); independent scholar (1931–1969). Honors and memberships: National Academy of Sciences, Daniel Giraud Medal (1955); Linnean Society of London, Gold Medal (1960); American Museum of Natural History, Gold Medal; University of Chicago, honorary doctorate; Coe College, honorary doctorate; Upsala College, honorary doctorate; American Society of Zoologists, president (1953); Society of Systematic Zoology, president (1959). Died 20 August 1969 of Parkinson's disease.

Born of Jewish Polish immigrant parents, Libbie Hyman grew up in Fort Dodge, Iowa, where her father owned an unprofitable clothing store. She became interested in biology as a child, and collected butterflies and plants from the woods surrounding Fort Dodge. An excellent student, Hyman graduated valedictorian in 1905. After graduation, she took additional courses in science and German until she was no longer eligible for these courses. Her first job was pasting labels onto boxes at the local Mother's Rolled Oats Factory. Her German teacher, Mary Crawford, was dismayed at this waste of talent and helped her get a scholarship at the University of Chicago. Although the scholarship paid for her tuition, she worked as a cashier in the Women's Commons and lived with her aunt and uncle to pay her room and board. After Hyman's father died in 1907, her mother and brothers moved to Chicago. Libbie lived with her mother, who disapproved of her career choice, until she died in 1929.

Hyman's first major was botany, but she changed to chemistry when she perceived antisemitism in the botany department. However, finding living things more of interest, she changed her major to zoology in her junior year. Encouraged by Mary Blount, a doctoral candidate who was in charge of the elementary zoology laboratory, Hyman took Charles Manning Child's invertebrate zoology class during her senior year. So impressed was Child by her abilities that he suggested she attend graduate school. After she received her bachelor's degree in zoology, she became Child's graduate student. Hyman replaced Blount as the laboratory assistant in zoology and comparative vertebrate anatomy. This experience led her to write two very successful and financially remunerative laboratory manuals. The royalties on these early works made her financially independent.

Hyman continued to work as Child's laboratory assistant after she received her doctorate. She remained in this position for sixteen years doing the experimental work on planarians and hydroids in an attempt to support Child's ideas on physiological gradients. Hyman, however, never found experimental biology as interesting as taxonomic work. Because she was secure financially, after the sixteen years she was able to resign and pursue her goal: a major monograph on the invertebrates. She moved to New York City near the American Museum to work on this grand project. She worked at home until 1937, when she received an unpaid research appointment at the American Museum that provided her with office space, library access, and a laboratory. Never using an assistant, Hyman spent the next thirty years working on her multivolume treatise. During this time she continued to study and publish on the morphology, physiology, and taxonomy of the invertebrates. The last volume of the incomplete set of *The Invertebrates* was published in 1967. Debilitating Parkinson's disease kept her from working on the additional volumes. She died in 1969, almost completely immobile.

Hyman took over the editorship of *Systematic Zoology* from 1959 to 1963. She was a member of many scientific societies and was vice-president of the American Society of Zoologists in 1953 and president of the Society of Systematic Zoology in 1959. Her honors included honorary doctorates from the University of Chicago, Goucher College, Coe College, and Upsala College. In addition to her two gold medals she became the first woman to be awarded the Daniel Giraud Medal from the National Academy of Sciences.   JH/MBO

PRIMARY SOURCES
Hyman, Libbie H. *A Laboratory Manual for Elementary Zoology*. Chicago: University of Chicago Press, 1919.
———. *A Laboratory Manual for Comparative Anatomy*. Chicago: University of Chicago Press, 1922.
———. *The Invertebrates*. 6 vols. New York: McGraw-Hill, 1940–1967.
———. *Comparative Vertebrate Anatomy*. Chicago: University of Chicago Press, 1942.

SECONDARY SOURCES
Stunkard, Horace W. "In Memoriam, Libbie Henrietta Hyman, 1888–1969." In *Biology of the Turbellaria* (Libbie H. Hyman Memorial Volume), ix-xii. New York: McGraw-Hill, 1974.
Yost, Edna. *American Women of Science*. Philadelphia: Frederick A. Stukio, 1943.

STANDARD SOURCES
Notable; Shearer and Shearer 1996.

HYNES, SARAH (1860–1938)

Australian botanist. Born 1860. Educated University of Sydney (B.A., 1891). Professional experience: Sydney Botanic Gardens, staff.

Little is known about Sarah Hynes's life and work. After earning her bachelor's degree from the University of Sydney, she took a position at the Sydney Botanic Gardens.   JH/MBO

SECONDARY SOURCES
Proceedings of the Linnean Society of New South Wales 64 (1939): 1. Obituary notice.
Sydney Morning Herald, 30 May 1938. Obituary notice.

STANDARD SOURCES
Desmond.

HYPATIA OF ALEXANDRIA (ca. 370–415)

Alexandrian mathematician and philosopher. Born ca. 370 in Alexandria, Egypt, to Theon of Alexandria. Probably never married. Educated at the museum and Neoplatonic school at Alexandria. Teacher at the Neoplatonic school, Alexandria.

The mathematician Hypatia of Alexandria was the victim of a spectacularly brutal murder at the hands of a mob. The violent nature of the crime as well as its subtle political and religious overtones encouraged both friends and enemies to remember her. Not surprisingly, all of the reports place more emphasis on the social impact of her life than on her contributions to science and mathematics. The early accounts that have supplied the bulk of the source material for derivative works are the *Ecclesiastical History* of the fifth-century historian of Constantinople, Socrates Scholasticus (b. ca. 380), and two compilations: the tenth- or eleventh-century *Suidas,* a lexicon-encyclopedia containing excerpts from earlier Greek writers; and the *Bibliotheca* of the ninth-century theologian Photius. In addition, the popular but notoriously inaccurate report of the Byzantine chronicler Johannes Malalas has often been used as a source. The last of the Greek Church historians to comment on Hypatia was Nicephorus Callistus (fl. 1320–1330). Although his *Ecclesiasticae historiae,* covering church history until 610, is unreliable, it is still frequently referred to by scholars of Hypatia.

Hypatia was the daughter of Theon of Alexandria, a mathematician-astronomer attached to the museum at Alexandria. Several accounts describe him as the director of that institution, but there is no consensus. Most scholars agree that Hypatia's early education included mathematics and astronomy and probably occurred at the museum. Although she was also well known as a Neoplatonist, the circumstances of her introduction to this doctrine are less certain. Most sources assume that she received her training in the Neoplatonic school at Alexandria, since she later became a teacher in that institution. An assertion in the *Suidas* forms the basis for dating her assumption of the directorship of the school at C.E. 400, when she was thirty-one years old (*Suidas;* Hoche, 644).

According to Socrates Scholasticus, not only was Hypatia well known in her native land, but her widespread fame attracted students from afar. One of her most famous disciples was Synesius, later bishop of Ptolemas, with whom she carried on an extended correspondence and who became an excellent public relations agent for her. In spite of reports to the contrary, the best evidence indicates that Hypatia was never married.

The *Suidas* records that "she was torn apart by the Alexandrians and her body was outraged and scattered throughout the whole city." It gives the reason for this atrocity as envy on the part of Bishop Cyril of Alexandria over "her wisdom exceeding all bounds and especially in the things concerning astronomy" (*Suidas* 166:644). Although all the sources basically agree concerning the circumstances of her death, they disagree about the reasons for the murder. Some, like the *Suidas,* assume that Bishop Cyril was so jealous of her popularity that he contrived the murder; another theory casts Hypatia as a scapegoat, a victim of political rivalry between the Roman prefect Orestes, a great admirer of Hypatia, and Cyril, who wished to extend his authority over secular as well as religious areas. Still other accounts blame the murder on "the inherent insolent and seditious nature of the Alexandrians," which led them to riot at the slightest provocation (*Suidas* 166:644).

Later writers continued to speculate on the part that Cyril and the church played in Hypatia's demise. Catholic partisans insisted that Cyril was completely innocent and unjustly maligned by biased reporters. Protestant writers were vehement

in denouncing Cyril; "a Bishop, a Patriarch, nay a Saint was the contriver of so horrid a deed, and his Clergy the executioners of his implacable fury" (Toland, 129–130). These and other conflicting interpretations will always surround Hypatia's death.

Tradition indicates that Hypatia wrote books on mathematics, lectured on a variety of subjects, and invented mechanical devices. Although it is assumed from a report by Hesychius in *Suidas* that she wrote at least three books, no fragments of her writings remain. According to Hesychius, she wrote a commentary on Diophantus. Several secondary authors considered it possible that Hypatia wrote Theon's commentary on the third book of Ptolemy's *Almagest.* Her lectures covered astronomy and mathematics as well as the philosophies of Plato and Aristotle. Synesius, in his letters, depicts her mechanical and technological talents. He refers to two mechanical devices, a hydrometer and a silver astrolabe, as having been invented by himself with Hypatia's aid.

Hypatia of Alexandria was an intriguing figure—a woman whose philosophical acumen was reputed to have surpassed that of the best known men of her time, a woman of legendary Athena-like beauty and virtue, and a woman whose fame was assured by her martyrdom. Even without her writings, enough information has been available to tempt secondary writers to consider and expand upon the data contained in the earliest sources. The terse ancient accounts are often ambiguous and lend themselves to a variety of interpretations, each tending to buttress the particular bias of the interpreter.   MBO

SECONDARY SOURCES

Coolidge, Julian L. "Six Female Mathematicians." *Scripta mathematica: A Quarterly Journal Devoted to the Philosophy, History, and Expository Treatment of Mathematics* 17 (1951): 20–31.

Hesychius of Miletus. *Onomatologi.* Ed. Johannes Flach. Leipzig: Teubner, 1822. Hesychius, a Greek chronicler and biographer, produced information on Hypatia within a biographical compendium. The original work is lost, but fragments are found in the works of Photius and in the *Suidas.*

Hoche, Richard. "Hypatia die Tochter Theons." *Philologus.* 1860.

Malalas, Johannes. *Chronographia ex recensione.* Bonn: Ludwig Dindorf, 1831. Byzantine chronicler often used as a source for Hypatia.

Meyer, Wolfgang Alexander. *Hypatia von Alexandria: Ein Beitrag zur Geschichte des Neuplatonismus.* Heidelberg: Georg Weiss, 1886. A scholarly work on Hypatia.

Nicephorus, Saint (Nicephorus Callistus Xanthopuli). "Ecclesiasticae historiae." In *Patrologiae cursus completus. Series Graeca, CXLV-CXLVI, libri XVII, caput xvi,* 1106–1107. Ed. J. P. Migne. Paris 1865. The last of the Greek Church historians to comment on Hypatia. Commentary in both Greek and Latin. Not reliable.

Philostorgius. *The Ecclesiastical History of Philostorgius: As Epito-mized by Photius, Patriarch of Constantinople*. Trans. Edward Walford. London: Henry G. Bohn, 1853. Important source for Hypatia because Philostorgius was her contemporary. The epitome by Photius, the only record of Philostorgius's work, is biased because Photius disapproved of the Arian ideas of Philostorgius.

Photius. *The Library of Photius*. Trans. J. H. Freese. London: Society for Promoting Christian Knowledge, 1920. English translation of *Bibliotheca ex recensione* (ed. J. Bekker, Berlin: 1824). Work of a ninth-century theologian who supplied information on Hypatia.

Richeson, A. W. "Hypatia of Alexandria." *National Mathematics Magazine* 15 (October 1940–May 1941): 74–82.

Socrates Scholasticus. *The Ecclesiastical History*. Ed. A. C. Zeno. In *A Select Library of Nicene and Post-Nicene Fathers of the Chris-tian Church*, vol. 2: *Socrates, Sozomenus*, vii–xvii. Ed. Philip Schaff and Henry Wace. 2d series. Grand Rapids, Mich.: W. B. Erdmans, 1952. Information on Hypatia by this fifth-century historian of Constantinople.

Suidas. Vol. I, parts 1–4 of Teubner's *Lexicographi graeci*. Ed. Ada Adler. Stuttgart: Teubner, 1971. *Suidas* is the name not of an author but of the lexicon. Contains information, often relying on second- and third-hand sources, on Hypatia.

Synesius. *Opera quae exctant omnia*. Ed. Theodorus Mopsuis-tenus. In *Patrologiae cursus completus*. Series Graeca. Ed. J. P. Migne. Vol. 66, 1330–1538. Paris: J. P. Migne. Letters of Hypatia's former student and lifetime disciple, Synesius.

Toland, John. *Tetradymus. Hypatia: Or the History of a Most Beauti-ful, Most Vertuous, Most Learned, and Every Way Accomplish'd Lady; Who Was Torn to Pieces by the Clergy of Alexandria, to Gratify the Pride, Emulation, and Cruelty of Their Archbishop, Commonly but Undeservedly Stil'd St. Cyril*. London: 1720. In *An Historical Account of the Life and Writings of the Eminently Famous John Toland*. London: J. Roberts, 1722. Anticlerical panegyric on Hypatia.

Wernsdorf, Johann Christian. *Dissertation academica. I. de Hypatia philosopha Alexandrina; II. de Hypatia speciatim de ejus caede; III. de Hypatia, speciatim de causis caedis ejus; IV. de Hypa-tia, speciatim de Cyrillo Episc. in causa tumultus Alexandrini caedisque Hypatiae contra G. Arnoldum et. J. Tolandum defenso*. Wittenberg: I, J. D. Rittero; II, R. E. Scheffler; III, C. B. Acoluthus; IV, A. L. F. Drechsel, 1747–1748. Established Hypatia's birth date of 370 C.E., the one accepted by most writers.

Wolf, Stephan. *Hypatia die philosophin von Alexandrien. Ihr Leben, Wirken und Lebensend, nach den Quellenschriften dargestellt*. Vienna: Alfred Hölder, 1879. Interpretations later criticized by Meyer.

STANDARD SOURCES
DSB; Ogilvie 1986.

I

IANOVSKAIA, SOF'IA ALEKSANDROVNA (1896–1966)

Russian mathematician. Born 31 January 1896 in Pruzhany. Father Aleksandr Neimark. Educated Odessa gymnasium; Higher School for Women, Odessa; Institute of Red Professors in Moscow; Moscow University (Ph.D., 1935). Professional experience: Moscow State University, faculty member, professor; Perm University, professor; Moscow State University, seminar on mathematical logic, director, chair of department of mathematical logic. Honors and memberships: Order of Lenin. Died 24 October 1966.

Little is known about Sof'ia Aleksandrovna Ianovskaia's childhood. She was born at Pruzhany in Poland (now in Belarus), but was quite young when her family moved to Odessa. There she received a classical education and studied mathematics under several well-known teachers. The revolution of 1917 interrupted her studies and she became active in the Bolshevik wing of the Communist Party in various capacities.

In 1924 Ianovskaia turned her attention back to her earlier interest in mathematics and entered the Institute of Red Professors in Moscow. By 1931 she was a professor at Moscow State University. She received her doctorate from the mechanical-mathematical faculty without having to defend a thesis in 1935. During World War II, Ianovskaia was evacuated to Perm, where she taught at the university, returning in 1943 to Moscow, where she directed the seminar on mathematical logic at Moscow State University. In 1946, she began teaching mathematical logic in the philosophy department also. In 1959, a department of mathematical logic was created at Moscow State University and she became its first chair.

A devoted Marxist-Leninist, Ianovskaia used mathematical logic as a weapon of ideological warfare against bourgeois idealist philosophy. However, she refused to compromise her theories to satisfy the demands of Soviet dialecticians and was often criticized for this.

Stalin's "Letter on Marxism and Linguistics" (1950), in which he wrote that language was not class-dependent, heralded a change of approach to the subject: it became ideologically possible to separate mathematical logic as a science from its bourgeois originators. Ianovskaia was now free to develop a program of mathematical logic without fear of political reprisal. She was an influential teacher, a number of her students achieving worldwide recognition.

Ianovskaia wrote widely on many mathematical subjects, but particularly on the development of mathematical methodology and the history of logic. Of particular note are her two studies on the history of mathematical logic in the USSR (1948 and 1959). By the time of her death in 1966, the study of mathematical logic was fully accepted and already being developed by a new generation. Ianovskaia was awarded the Order of Lenin in 1951 for her services to mathematics.

ACH

PRIMARY SOURCES

Ianovskaja, Sof'ja Alekxandrova. "The Contemporary Crisis in the Foundations of Mathematics." *Estestvoznanie i Marksizma* 2 (1930).

———. "Paradoxes of Mathematics." *Big Soviet Encyclopedia* vol. 44, 1939.

———. "Foundations of Mathematics and Mathematical Logic." In *Matematika v SSSR za Tridcat Let 1917–1947,* eds. A. G. Kurosha, A. I. Markushevicka, and P. K. Pasherskogo 11–45. Moscow and Leningrad, 1948.

———. "Osnovaniia matematiki i matematicheskaia logika." In *Matematika v CCCR za 30 let.* 11–45. Moscow: Gosizdat, 1948.

———. "Matematicheskaia logika i osnovaniia matematiki." In *Matematika v CCCR za 40 let, 1917–1957.* Vol. 1, 13–120. Moscow: Fizmatgiz, 1959.

———. "Mathematic Logic and Foundations of Mathematics." In *Matematika v. SSSR za sorok let 1917–1957.* Ed. A. G.

Kurosh, 13–120. Moscow and Leningrad: Gos. Izd.-vo
fiziko-matematicheskoi lit-ry, 1959.

———. *Metodicheskie problemy nauk.* Moscow: Mysl', 1972.

SECONDARY SOURCES

Anellis, Irving H. "History of Philosophy of Mathematics in
the USSR, Javskaja to Barabashev." In *Philosophic Sovietology,*
Ed. T. J. Blakeley and E. Swiderski. Sovietica vol. 50. Dordrecht: Reidel Publishing 1987.

Bashmakova, I. G. "Sof'ia Aleksandrovna Ianovskaia (k semi-
desiatiletiiu so dnia rozhdeniia)." *Uspekhi matematicheskikh
nauk* 21, no. 3 (1966): 239–247.

Bochenski, Josef M. "S. A. Janovskaja." *Studies in Soviet Thought*
7 (1967): 66–67.

Borodin, A. I. and A. S. Bugai. "Sof'ja Alexsandrovna
Janovskaja" (in Russian). In *Biograficheskii Slovar' Dejatelei v
oblasti Matematiki,* ed. A. I. Borodin and A. S. Bugai, 555–
556. Kiev: Radjanska Shkola, 1977.

Kline, George. Review of Ianovskaia 1948. *Journal of Symbolic
Logic* 16 (1951): 46–48.

STANDARD SOURCES

Grinstein and Campbell 1993 (article by Irving H. Anellis).

IBBETSON, AGNES (THOMSON) (1757–1823)

*British botanist. Born 1757 in London. Father Andrew Thomson.
Married a barrister, James Ibbetson. Educated finishing school. Professional experience: correspondent of leading botanists; published
more than fifty papers in* Nicholson's Journal *and the* Philosophical Magazine. *Honors and memberships: Bath and West of
England Society, honorary and corresponding member (1814). Died
February 1823 at Exmouth near Devon.*

Agnes Ibbetson has the rare distinction of being one of the
only women botanists who regularly published in the scientific journals of the first two decades of the nineteenth century. Her early life was apparently one of fashionable pursuits
until the illness and subsequent death of her husband, a barrister in London, in 1790. Soon after, she moved to Exmouth near Devon to live with a sister. Here she spent a
quiet and studious life, collecting and studying plants.

Using a single lens microscope, occasionally supplemented with a compound and a solar microscope, she began
to investigate plant physiology, carefully drawing and re-
drawing what she observed. She soon devoted her life to the
pursuit of botany, working for many hours a day. Beginning
in 1809, she published her findings in the recently established *Nicholson's Journal of Natural Philosophy, Chemistry and
the Arts.* This was the first of twenty further contributions to
the journal, in the form of letters to the editor.

Although very careful in her dissections, using "as many
different sorts as a surgeon," Ibbetson was criticized by some
of her contemporaries who felt that the high magnifying
power of her single lens microscope had led her into error.
She did not hesitate to challenge, in turn, the famous
botanists of her day, such as Jussieu and Knight. Urged by
one of her correspondents, James Bostock, who was both a
botanist and physician, she sent her "Phytology," an exposition of her philosophy of botany, to Sir James E. Smith, a
Fellow of the Royal Society, in the hopes of publishing her
work in the prestigious *Philosophical Transactions.* Smith answered her kindly but unfavorably and she felt deeply discouraged. She attempted, unsuccessfully, to gain another
hearing from him on the grounds that the experiments she
had outlined, if not her drawings, had proven her claims.
Among the ideas she promoted was the denial of "perspira-
tion" or transpiration of plants and the suggestion that an
early form of the embryo was formed in the interior of the
root of the plant and moved up into the stem.

Nevertheless, Ibbetson continued to investigate and to
publish a further thirty or so articles in the *Philosophical Magazine* and in the *Annals of Philosophy.* She became interested
in agriculture and wrote on the use of particular plants
suited to local soils, the judicious use of manures, and the
enrichment of soils by using burned weeds as well as the addition of lime. In her fifties, she was admitted as a corresponding and honorary member of a local agricultural
society, but in the custom of the day, as a woman, she could
not present her own papers. Ibbetson was sufficiently recognized to have extracts from her articles appear in translation
in French and Italian scientific journals, but she was never
able to have her longer works published. They remain in
manuscript in the Natural History Museum and the Linnaean Society. She was memorialized by the plant *Ibbetsonia
genistoides* (now *Cyclopia genistoides*).   JH/MBO

PRIMARY SOURCES

Ibbetson, Agnes. "On the Interior Buds of All Plants." *Nicholson's Journal* 33 (1810): 10, 177.

———. "On the Adapting of Plants to the Soil and Not the
Soil to the Plants." *Correspondence of the Bath and West of
England Society* 14 (1816): 136–159.

———. "On the Death of Plants." *Annals of Philosophy.* 11
(1818): 252–262.

———. "On the Action of Lime on Animal and Vegetable
Substances." *Annals of Philosophy* 14 (1819): 125–129.

Ibbetson's manuscript "Botanical Treatise" is included in five
volumes of manuscript and drawings in the Botany Library,
Natural History Museum, London. Her manuscript "Phytology" and her correspondence to James E. Smith are in the
Linnaean Society Library.

STANDARD SOURCES
DNB; Shteir.

IDE, GLADYS GENEVRA (1888–?)

U.S. educational psychologist. Born 4 October 1888 in Trent, S.D. Educated University of Washington (Seattle) (A.B., A.M., 1914); University of Pennsylvania (Ph.D., 1918). Professional experience: Washington, Idaho, and Oregon, public school teacher (1906–1913); University of Washington, instructor (1914–1915); Drexel Institute, Philadelphia (1918–1920); Temple University, lecturer (1921–1930); Pennsylvania State College, instructor (1924–1928); University of Pennsylvania, summer instructor (1921); Philadelphia public schools, Division of Special Education, director (from 1928). Honors and memberships: American Psychological Association. Death date unknown.

Born and educated in the West, Gladys Ide went east to the University of Pennsylvania for her doctorate. After she received this degree, she began her career in this part of the United States, where she remained. Ide eventually became director of the Division of Special Education for the public schools in Philadelphia. Although she was listed in the fourth edition of *AMS*, she was not in later editions. JH/MBO

STANDARD SOURCES
AMS 4; *Psychological Register*, vol. 3, 1932.

ILG, FRANCES LILLIAN (1902–1981)

U.S. pediatrician. Born 11 October 1902 in Oak Park, Ill., to Lennore (Peterson) and Joseph Ilg. Never married. Educated Wellesley College (B.A., 1925); Cornell Medical School (M.D., 1929); St. Mary's Hospital for Children, pediatric intern; postgraduate training, Stockholm, Sweden (1936–1937). Professional experience: New England Hospital for Women and Children, Boston (1931–1932); Yale University Clinic of Child Development, visiting pediatrician (1932); Clinic of Child Development, research assistant (1933); assistant professor of child development (1937–1947); Yale University, research associate (1947–1970). Died 26 July 1981 in Manitowish Waters, Wis.

Frances Ilg graduated from Wellesley College and earned a medical degree at Cornell Medical School, New York City, New York (1929), interning in pediatrics at St. Mary's Hospital for Children. She took a year's leave to study child health facilities in Stockholm, Sweden, and while there, adopted a daughter, Tordis Kristen. She never married. She returned to Yale as assistant professor of child development.

Ilg was an associate of Arnold Gesell, LOUISE BATES AMES, and others at Yale University Clinic of Child Development, later known as the Gesell Institute of Human Development.

This was one of the most progressive child-study laboratories in the nation and provided ample opportunities for study of newborn through preschool children. Out of her association at the clinic came Ilg's first collaboration with Gesell and Ames, *Infant and Child in the Culture of Today*. When the Yale Clinic affiliated with the New Canaan (Connecticut) Country School, the team was able to extend its studies to older children. They educated the parents of the children according to the developmental point of view and taught them to report day-to-day observations that concerned the mechanism of the growth process. More than fifty children from five to nine years (along with a number of ten-year-olds) were included, and their case studies were analyzed in great detail. *The Child from Five to Ten* was the result of this collaboration. These two books were tremendously popular with postwar modern middle-class families concerned with raising healthy, "normal" children. They gave practical guidance and reassurance of typical normal growth patterns and fluctuations. After Gesell retired in 1950 at age seventy, Ilg and Ames founded the Gesell Institute of Child Development to carry on the Gesell programs, with Gesell acting as consultant until his death in 1961.

With Louise Ames, Ilg wrote the popular syndicated newspaper column, "Child Behavior," which appeared in over fifty newspapers nationwide. It was primarily a question and answer column that centered on development of children from infancy through their teens and gave advice on basic child-rearing as well as on specific behavior problems. The book *Child Behavior* was an outgrowth of the column and was the first Gesell publication to address specific behavior problems of children. In 1956, in *Youth: The Years from Ten to Sixteen*, Gesell, Ilg, and Ames reported several thousand adolescent behavior patterns they had identified and codified in forty areas of behavior drawn from the study of a select group of eighty-three boys and eighty-two girls. The book was criticized as being too narrow in focus, but the team felt they had succeeded in describing patterns of a "normal" adolescent (delinquent and neurotic children not being covered by their program).

Ilg authored or coauthored over twenty books on behavior patterns of children. She retired in 1970 but continued to write and lecture. She died 26 July 1981 in Manitowish Waters, Wisconsin. KM

PRIMARY SOURCES
Ilg, Frances Lillian. With Arnold Gesell and Louise Ames. *Infant and Child in the Culture of Today*. New York: Harper, 1943.

———. With Arnold Gesell and Louise Ames. *The Child from Five to Ten*. New York: Harper, 1946.

———. With Louise Ames. *Child Behavior*. New York: Harper and Brothers, 1955.

————. With Arnold Gesell and Louise Ames. *Youth: The Years from Ten to Sixteen*. New York: Harper and Brothers, 1956.

SECONDARY SOURCES
New York Times, 28 July 1981. Obituary notice.

STANDARD SOURCES
Current Biography, 1956; 1981 (obituary notice).

INGLIS, ELSIE (MAUDE) (1846–1917)

Scottish physician and surgeon. Born 1864 at a Himalayan hill station. Father in the Indian civil service. Seven siblings. Educated Edinburgh School of Medicine for Women and Medical College for Women, Glasgow (M.D. 1899). Professional experience: Elsie Inglis Hospital for Women and Children in Edinburgh, founder; Scottish Women's Hospitals for war service, founder; Serbia field hospital, surgeon (1915–1917). Died 25 November 1917 at Newcastle.

Elsie Inglis was born into a family in which personal suffering and heroics were expected. Descended from Robert the Bruce, her great-grandfather was an early emigrant to South Carolina, where he built a small fortune and died in a duel in defense of his loyalty to the British Crown; her father spent years in the civil service in India and Tasmania. Elsie was born in 1864 at a Himalayan hill station in India, one of eight children, and was tutored and well schooled. She attended the Edinburgh School of Medicine for Women (founded by SOPHIA JEX-BLAKE), but defected to Glasgow where she promoted, with her father's support, a rival medical college for women and won the right to study surgery with men. In 1892, she passed the Scottish Triple Qualification: licentiate of the Royal College of Physicians of Edinburgh, the Royal College of Surgeons of Edinburgh, and the Royal Faculty of Physicians and Surgeons of Glasgow. She spent several years in London and Dublin, then returned to University of Edinburgh to receive a medical degree in 1899. She attended clinics in Germany, Vienna, New York, Chicago, and the Mayo Clinic in Minnesota. She founded with Jessie MacGregor the Maternity Center and Free Hospital for Women and Children, a hospital that later became the Elsie Inglis Hospital, run by women physicians in Scotland.

An outspoken suffragist, Inglis lectured throughout Scotland. In 1914, at the beginning of World War I, supported by the Federated Women's Suffrage Societies of Scotland, she founded and led the Scottish Women's Hospitals (SWH). She proposed to send women's medical teams onto the battlefields. Her ideas spread throughout the United Kingdom, and were taken up by the National Union of Women's Suffrage Societies. More than two million dollars was raised to finance this project.

The British War Office rejected the Scottish women's medical teams, but the French government welcomed them. They immediately sent two units into the combat zone and another unit, headed by Inglis, to Serbia, where they had to deal with both wounded men and an epidemic of typhoid fever. Other Allied governments also accepted the offer of hospital units run by women's medical teams and fourteen such units were mobilized. Inglis's Serbian unit stayed with the wounded when Austrians and Bulgars invaded. Even as prisoners, they continued to treat the Serbian and Austrian wounded until they were sent back to Britain in February 1916. Inglis soon organized the return of her team to Russia where they served until 1917 when she pulled out her units to avoid the impending Bolshevik Revolution. She died at Newcastle the day after her return to England.

Inglis claimed she had only two passions: "suffrage and surgery." She is memorialized through the Elsie Inglis Unit of the Scottish Women's Hospitals; a children's home in Yugoslavia; and a wing of the Royal Infirmary of Edinburgh.

JH/MBO

SECONDARY SOURCES
Lawrence, M. A. *Shadow of Swords: A Biography of Elsie Inglis*. London: Michael Joseph, 1971.

STANDARD SOURCES
Concise Universal Biography; *Europa*; *LKW*; Lovejoy; Uglow 1982.

IRWIN, MARIAN (1889–?)

U.S. physiologist. Born 1889 in Tokyo, Japan. Married Winthrop John van Leuven Osterhaut (27 February 1933). Educated Bryn Mawr College (A.B., 1913); Radcliffe College (Ph.D., 1919). Professional experience: Radcliffe College, National Research Council fellow (1923–1925); Rockefeller Institute, associate, department of general physiology (1925–1933), emerita associate (from 1933). Death date unknown.

Marian Irwin was born in Tokyo, Japan, but was educated in the United States. While she was a graduate student at Radcliffe she met her future husband, physiologist W. J. V. Osterhaut, then a professor at Harvard. After obtaining her degree examining the effects of electrolytes on sensory stimulation and respiration, she obtained a National Research Council fellowship. At the same time that Osterhaut moved to the Rockefeller Institute, Marian obtained a position there and remained in the medical research division until her marriage to Osterhaut in 1933, the second marriage for her husband.

Two years before her husband's death, Irwin turned his papers over to the American Philosophical Society. Her own papers and manuscripts as well as a volume of her reprints are held at the Rockefeller University.   JH/MBO

PRIMARY SOURCES

Irwin, Marian. "Effect of Electrolytes and Non-electrolytes on Organisms in Relation to Sensory Stimulation and Respiration." Ph.D. diss., Radcliffe College, 1919.

Rockefeller University has her bibliography, a volume of reprints, some manuscripts, and a folder of correspondence.

STANDARD SOURCES

AMS 4–7; Debus (under Osterhout); *NAW* unused.

ISAACS, SUSAN SUTHERLAND (FAIRHURST) (1885–1948)

British psychologist. Born 24 May 1885 in Bolton, England. Educated Victoria University of Manchester; University of Cambridge (1912–1913). Professional experience: University of Manchester, lecturer in psychology; University of London, lecturer (1916–1920); London County Council Education Committee, lecturer in psychology and educational method (1920–1922); Malting House School, Cambridge, principal (1924–1927); London Institute of Education, director of the Department of Child Development (1933–1943). Died 1948.

British psychologist Susan Isaacs was educated at the Victoria University of Manchester and Cambridge University. She held positions as lecturer in psychology at the universities of Manchester and London. After leaving the University of London, she took a position at the London Council of Education Committee, where she was a lecturer in psychology and educational method. She spent the last ten years of her active career as director of the Department of Child Development at the London Institute of Education.

Isaacs held a number of editorial positions. She was assistant editor for the *British Journal of Psychology* in 1921, an editorial board member of *Educational Psychology*, editorial board member of the *British Journal of Educational Psychology* from 1931 to 1948, and a board member of *Medical Psychology* from 1936 to 1948. She was a member of the British Psychological Society [Honorary Joint Secretary of Education Section (1919–1921), Honorary Secretary of Committee for Research in Education (1921–1927); Chairman of Education Section (1928–31)]; the British Psychoanalytical Society, and the Royal Anthropological Institute.

Isaacs first was analyzed by Flugel and later (in 1927) by JOAN RIVIERE. She did her pioneering research in child development while she was principal of the Malting House School. The London Institute of Education became one of

three major centers of child psychology under her leadership. She worked closely with MELANIE KLEIN during the controversies with ANNA FREUD over the early development of the child. She followed Melanie Klein's theories and criticized Piaget's dating of developmental stages. A progressive educator with an emphasis on spontaneity, she criticized exaggerated notions of freedom. She explained that a child needed a settled framework of control and routine. She was elected to the Board and Council and the Training Committee of the British Psychoanalytic Society and served on the Ad Hoc Committee on Training along with Melanie Klein. Isaacs wrote fourteen books.   JH/MBO

PRIMARY SOURCES

Isaacs, Susan. *Introduction to Psychology.* London: Metheun, 1921.

———. *The Nursery Years.* London: Routledge, 1929.

———. *Intellectual Growth of Young Children.* London: Routledge, 1930.

———. *The Children We Teach: Seven to Eleven Years.* London: University of London Press, 1932.

———. *Social Development of the Young.* London: Routledge, 1933.

———. *Troubles of Children and Parents.* New York: Vanguard [1948].

SECONDARY SOURCES

Gardner, Dorothy E. M. *Susan Isaacs.* London: Methuen, 1969. Includes bibliography.

King, Pearl, and Riccardo Steiner, ed. *The Freud-Klein Controversies, 1941–1945.* London and New York: Tavistock/Routledge, 1991. Isaacs mentioned on page xiv.

Smith, Lydia Averell Hurd. *To Understand and To Help: The Life and Work of Susan Isaacs (1885–1948).* Rutherford, N.J.: Farleigh Dickinson University Press, 1985.

STANDARD SOURCES

Europa; Psychological Register, vol. 3, 1932; Uglow 1982; *WWW,* vol. 4, 1941–1955.

IUSUPOVA, SARADZHAN MIKHAILOVNA (1910–1966)

Russian geochemist. Born 18 May 1910. Educated at Uzbek University, Samarkand. Professional experience: Tadzhik University, Stalinabad, lecturer, professor. Tadzhik Academy of Sciences, member. Died 17 May 1966.

Saradzhan Mikhailovna Iusupova graduated from Uzbek University in Samarkand in 1935. From 1948 to 1949, she was a lecturer at Tadzhik University, becoming a professor in 1949. Iusupova conducted X-ray structural research on colloid minerals, especially clays, and she also studied the geochemistry of celestite and other mineral resources and mineral springs of the Tadzhik Soviet Socialist Republic.   ACH

PRIMARY SOURCES

Iusupova, Saradzhan Mikhailovna. *Koloidno-khimicheskie svoistva glin Uzbekistana.* 1941.

———. *Mineralogicheskie osobennosti liossov Srednei Azii.* 1951.

STANDARD SOURCES

WWW (USSR).

IVANOVA, ELENA ALEKSEEVNA (1901–   )

Russian geologist, stratigrapher, and paleontologist. Born 1901 in Moscow. Father A. P. Ivanov. Educated gymnasium; Moscow Highest Women's Courses (1918–1924); Geologo-mineralogical sciences, candidate degree (1938); defended thesis for doctorate in biological sciences (1948). Professional experience: Moscow Department of the Geological Committee (later Moscow Geological Establishment), collector, then work superintendent (1924–1930); chief of the party (1930–1934); All-Union Scientific Research Institute of Raw Minerals, researcher (1934); Paleontological Institute, researcher (1934–1938); Paleozoic Commission of the Academy of Sciences of the USSR, secretary (1939); Paleontological Institute, scientific secretary (1940–1944), deputy director (during World War II).

Elena Alekseevna Ivanova's background was important to her success as a geologist. Her father, although from a peasant family, finished Moscow University, worked as a geologist, a teacher, and finally as a professor in Moscow University. Each summer, Elena Alekseevna traveled with her father to exposures of the Upper Carboniferous of Moscow suburbs and collected fauna. During these trips she asked him questions about their finds and he answered them. In 1918 when she entered the Highest Women's Courses, which in 1919 became a part of Moscow University, she heard lectures in botany and other subjects, but she was especially interested in geology and did practical work in her father's geology class. His credo was to "forget the book; learn to read nature!" Elena dropped botany and switched to geology and paleontology. In 1924, when she finished the university, she worked in geological survey parties of the Moscow department of the Geological Committee, eventually becoming chief of the party. In this position she led geological surveys of the Moscow suburbs. Her father had been working on a monograph, but in 1932 became ill and died in the beginning of 1933. Ivanova completed the monograph that he had begun.

For one year she worked at the Paleontological Laboratory of All-Union Scientific Research Institute of Raw Minerals, but soon moved to the Paleontological Institute. She received a candidate's degree of geologo-mineralogical sciences in 1938 and in 1948 defended her thesis for a doctoral degree in biological sciences. One of Ivanova's interests was organizational work. She was a secretary for the Paleozoic Commission of the Academy of Sciences of the USSR and later a scientific secretary in the Paleontological Institute. When World War II began, she was appointed deputy director of the Paleontological Institute and was responsible for evacuating the collections to Alma-Ata. This time-consuming work meant that she had little time for science. At the end of 1943, Ivanova returned to Moscow, and she could again concentrate on her scientific work.

Ivanova's scientific interests were in paleoecology, evolution and morphology, and stratigraphy. Any one of these three areas could represent a lifetime work. In paleoecology she used brachiopods to demonstrate the development and geographic spreading of organisms with their environment. She did her first work in this area from 1937 and the more complete work in 1949 that resulted in her doctoral dissertation. She moved from the more particular to the more general and dealt with many faunal groups in her works from 1958 to 1964. In her work on evolution and morphology, Ivanova concentrated on brachiopods again. Her first work in this area was published in 1937, and more complete results in articles of 1959 and 1967. She produced a monograph in 1972. She worked on the stratigraphy of the Middle and Upper Carboniferous deposits throughout her career, although her first paleontological work, which was published in 1936, was a description of productids of the Upper and Middle Carboniferous of the Moscow suburbs.

She published over 78 works including a monograph *Development of Fauna in Connection with Conditions of Existence* (translated title) that was translated into French and published in Paris in 1960.

In 1950, the Paleontological Institute, like the other Institutes of the Academy of Sciences of the USSR, was ordered by the government to do more work in the east of the country—in Siberia. In response to the directive, Ivanova left her favorite working site, the Podmoscovnaya depression, and went to the dense forests of Western Siberia for eight years. For two years, she worked in the remote Podkamennaya Tunguska, three years in the Minussinskaya and Tuvinskaya depressions, and three years in Kuzbas. She published her results quickly, and in 1955 and 1958 produced large summary works on the fauna, ecology, and stratigraphy of the Ordovician. She continued to work in the field, going to Podoliya in 1961, to the Northern Urals in 1963–1964, to Podmoscovie in 1966, and to the Bashkir Autonomous Soviet Socialist Republic and Orenburg area in 1967. Her last field trip was in 1973, when she prepared the expedition to Podmoscovie for the International Congress on the Carboniferous.

During the 1960s, Ivanova published four works of which three are monographs. In the 1970s she published twelve works, including two monographs, both of which are very important: *Enforcement into the Study of Spiriferida* and *Composition, System, and Phylogeny of the Order Spiriferida* (in Russian). Ivanova's international connections were very important. She exchanged publications and corresponded with ninety paleontologists from eighteen different countries.   CK

PRIMARY SOURCES

Ivanova, Elena A. *Biostratigrafiya srednego i verkhnego karbona Podmoskovnoi kotloviny*. Moscow: Rossiyskaya Akademiya Nauk. Paleontologicheskiy Institut, 1947. A description of the stratigraphic and faunal facies of middle and upper Devonian deposits of the Moscow basin, with special reference to the evolution of brachiopod fauna.

———. *Usloviya suschestvovaniya, obraz zhizni i istoriya razvitiya nekotorykh brakhiopod srednego i verkhnego karbona Podmoskovnoi kotloviny*. Moscow: Rossiyskaya Akademiya Nauk, Paleontologicheskiy Institut, 1949. A monographic study of the habitat, manner of living, migration, and evolution of middle and upper Carboniferous brachiopods of the Moscow basin.

———. *Ontogenez nekotorykh kamennougolnykh brakhiopod*. Trudy Paleontologicheskogo Instituta, 20 (1949): 243–265. Discusses the ontogenetic development and relations of Carboniferous brachiopods belonging to the Protremata and the Telotremata.

———. *Stratigrafiya srednego i verkhnego karbona zapadnoi chasti Moskovskoi sineklizy (Razvitie fauny sredne- i verkh nekamennougolnogo morya zapadnoi chasti Moskovskoi sineklizy v svyazi s ego istoriei kniga 1)*. Moscow: Rossiyskaya Akademiya Nauk, Paleontologicheskiy Institut, 1955. A monographic study of the detailed stratigraphy of middle and upper Carboniferous deposits of the western part of the Moscow basin.

———. *Nastavlenie po izucheniyu brakhiopod*. Akademiya Nauk SSSR, Paleontological Institute, Nastavleniya Sboru i Izuch. Iskopaem. Organichesk. Ostatkov: 10, 1963. A manual of methods of collecting and studying fossil brachiopods.

SECONDARY SOURCES

Nalivkin, D. V. *Our First Women Geologists*. Leningrad: Nauka, 1979. In Russian.

IVES, MARGARET (1903–)

U.S. psychologist. Born 10 April 1903 in Detroit, Mich. Father Augustus Wright Ives. One brother. Never married. Educated Vassar College (A.B., 1924); University of Michigan (M.A., 1929; Ph.D., 1938). Professional experience: Elizabeth, N.J., schoolteacher (1924–1928); Wayne County Clinic for Child Study, De-

troit, Mich., clinical psychologist (1929–1932); Henry Ford Hospital, Detroit, associate psychologist (1935–1942); St. Elizabeth's Hospital, Washington, D.C., psychologist (1943–1951), director of psychological services (1951–1972), associate director of psychology (1972–1973); American Board of Professional Psychologists, executive director (1977–1981). Concurrent experience: George Washington University, lecturer in psychology (1946–1955), professorial lecturer (1955–1970); U.S. Civil Service Commission, Rating Panel for Psychologists, member (1954–1968); American Board of Professional Psychologists, executive director (1977–1981). Honors: U.S. Department of Health, Education and Welfare, Super Service Award (1964); Harold Hildreth Memorial Award (1974). American Psychological Association, Fellow. Memberships: American Association for the Advancement of Science; Society for Personality Assessment; International Council of Psychologists; Association of World Federation for Mental Health.

Margaret Ives was the daughter of a psychiatrist who was a professor of neurology and psychiatry at the Detroit College of Medicine (later Wayne State University). As a young woman, her mother had taught school. At her mother's suggestion, she attended Vassar College, where she studied with MARGARET FLOY WASHBURN. In her senior year, she wrote a paper with Washburn which was published in the *American Journal of Psychology*. Upon graduating from Vassar, Ives accepted a teaching position in New Jersey. This school was a special institution that worked with fourteen- and fifteen-year-old working-class dropouts. During this period, Ives also demonstrated for the Equal Rights Amendment.

Ives left teaching in 1928 to enter graduate school in psychology. Just before she received her master's degree, she took a position at the Wayne County Clinic for Child Study, which was associated with the juvenile court, where she worked for three years as a psychologist. In 1932, she returned to graduate school with a fellowship from Vassar, where her major professor was Carl R. Brown. She wrote her dissertation on visual perception while working as a psychologist at the Henry Ford Hospital in Detroit. Finding that her salary was sixty percent of that of her male colleagues even after she received her degree, and experiencing other examples of gender discrimination, she determined to find another position. After taking the Civil Service examination, she was recruited as a psychologist at St. Elizabeth's Hospital in Washington, D.C., a large federal psychiatric institution. There she taught nurses psychology and tested maximum security patients. She began to testify as an expert witness in court trials where the rulings concerning the acceptability of psychology as an expert field was being modified. Ives supervised the psychological services until shortly before her retirement, when, because of decentralization, her title was reduced to associate director. For many years she served on the D.C. Board for Psychological Examiners.

Ives taught a course for several years at George Washington University on clinical assessment. Most of the recognition she received occurred only when she reached the age of sixty and was elected to high positions in her professional organizations. She was also recognized with service awards and awards for her work in forensic psychology.

Although she ostensibly had retired in 1973, Ives was asked to serve as executive officer of the American Board of Professional Psychologists. During her tenure, she dealt with questions of certification and excellence determination. In 1981 she had the opportunity to go to China as part of a delegation in a "People to People International Mental Health Project," which she found to be a stimulating and satisfying opportunity.

In her old age she expressed some regrets at the lack of a family and children, but believed that her choice allowed her to have a professional career without concerns about raising young children. In her late seventies she still maintained a small private practice, although she was never able to return to her early interest in experimental psychology.   JH/MBO

PRIMARY SOURCES

Ives, Margaret. With M. F. Washburn. "Memory Revival of Emotions as a Test of Emotional and Phlegmatic Temperaments." *American Journal of Psychology* 36 (1925): 459–460.

———. "The Flight of Colors, Following Intense Brief Stimulation of the Eye." Ph.D. diss., University of Michigan, 1938.

———. "Interrelationship of Clinical Psychology and Psychiatry." *Journal of Clinical Psychology* 2 (1946): 146–150.

———. With Arthur H. Brayfield, et al. "Testimony before the Senate Subcommittee on Constitutional Rights of the Committee on the Judiciary." *American Psychologist* 20 (1965): 898–901.

———. "Psychology at Saint Elizabeth's Hospital, 1907–1970." *Professional Psychology* 1 (1970): 155–158.

SECONDARY SOURCES

Some records of her work at St. Elizabeth's Hospital (1950–1972) are held in the hospital's archives.

STANDARD SOURCES

AMS B 9, S&B 9, 11–13, P&B 10; O'Connell and Russo 1988; O'Connell and Russo 1990.

IWANOWSKA, WILHELMINA (1905–1999)

Polish astronomer. Born 2 September 1905 in Wilna, Lithuania. Educated University of Wilna (graduated 1929), doctorate in astronomy (1933); habilitated (1937). Professional experience: observatory at Wilna, assistant (1927–1937); University of Wilna, dozentin (assistant professor) (1937–1939); oberschullehrerin, secondary school teacher (1939–1945); University of Thorn (Torun), Poland, assistant professor (1945–1948), ordinary professor of astrophysics (1948–1979); Observatory in Piwnice bei Thorn, leader of an observatory team; Astronomical Institute, director (1969–1979). Memberships and fellowships: Polish Academy of Sciences, corresponding member; International Astronomical Union, vice-president (1973–1979); Royal Astronomical Society of London, Fellow; Royal Society of Canada, Fellow; Société Royale des Sciences, Liége, Fellow; Nicolaus Copernicus University, honorary doctorate (1973). Died 16 May 1999.

Polish, Lithuanian-born astronomer Wilhelmina Iwanowska was educated at the University of Wilna, which is also where she held her first professional positions. During World War II she left Wilna to teach at a secondary school, but when the war was over she returned to university work, this time at the University of Thorn (Torun), now called Nicolaus Copernicus University, where she spent the remainder of her career. In addition to her university responsibilities, she was the leader of an observatory team and the director of the Astronomical Institute. Most of her scientific work involved spectroscopic measurements; she also worked on the structure of stars.   JH/MBO

SECONDARY SOURCES

"Pani Professor Wilhelmina Iwanowska." *Urania Postepy Astronomii* 4, no. 682 (1999). Obituary notice.

STANDARD SOURCES

Strohmeier; *WW in Science in Europe.*

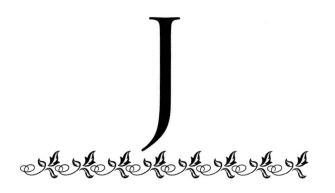

JACOBI, MARY CORINNA PUTNAM
(1842–1906)

U.S. physician. Born 31 August 1842 in England to U.S. parents Victorine (Haven) and George Palmer Putnam. Eight siblings. Married Abraham Jacobi (1873). Two surviving children. Educated New York College of Pharmacy (1863?); Woman's Medical College of Pennsylvania (M.D., 1864?); Paris Medical Hospitals, postgraduate study (1866–1867); University of Paris, School of Medicine (M.D., 1871). Professional experience: New England Hospital for Women, intern (1864–1865); New York Woman's Medical College and New York Infirmary, lecturer in materia medica (1871–1873), professor of materia medica (1873–1898?); New York Infirmary for Women and Children, staff physician (1873–1901?). Concurrent experience: Columbia University, College of Physicians and Surgeons, lecturer in diseases of children (1883–1884); Mount Sinai Hospital, New York, Dispensary for Women and Children, founder and staff member (1873–1893?). St. Marks Hospital, visiting physician (1893–1900?). Honors and memberships: University of Paris, Faculty of Medicine, bronze medal (1872); Harvard University Medical School, Boylston Prize (1876). Member of New York Academy of Medicine, New York Pathological Society, New York Neurological Society, New York County Medical Society. Died 10 June 1906 in New York City from a brain tumor.

Mary Putnam Jacobi, a pioneer American clinical physician and research scientist, was born in England to American parents. Her father was the publisher George Palmer Putnam, who shortly after her birth returned to Staten Island and then Westchester County, New York, where most of his other children were born. Putnam was educated primarily at home, but attended a local private school, and then a public school in Manhattan. Interested in science and medicine from a very young age, she studied chemistry at the New York College of Pharmacy, graduating in 1863. She went on to study medicine at the Woman's Medical College of Pennsylvania, graduating with a medical degree in the following year.

In the midst of the Civil War, Putnam rushed to Louisiana to nurse her soldier brother, George Haven, back to health and then went to help her sister, who was teaching former slaves in the early Reconstruction period. Moving to Boston to spend a year at the New England Hospital for Women under Dr. Marie Elizabeth Kazrzewska, she felt the experience to be frustrating, perhaps because there was no call for her research skills. At the suggestion of ELIZABETH BLACKWELL, she went to Paris in 1866, deciding to experience the renowned Paris medical clinics first hand. She was granted permission, as a physician, to do postdoctoral work, going from hospital to hospital, attending clinical rounds and clinical lectures and performing autopsies. She recorded accounts of the Paris clinics and clinical debates in letters to her family and in regular reports on Paris medicine that she wrote for the *New York Medical Record,* as its anonymous Paris correspondent.

By late in 1867, she decided to attempt to enter the Paris School of Medicine and, with the help of the Ministry of Education, the administration of the medical school, and the American ambassador, she finally managed to open the door for women. She immediately wrote to ELIZABETH GARRETT (ANDERSON), who also entered at the same time, as did a Russian doctor, Dr. Goncharov, and a French woman, MADELEINE BRÈS. By early 1868, she began to attend the faculty lectures and prepare for a series of examinations.

Delighted with the intellectual excitement of her experience, Putnam regretted only the lack of facilities for medical research in chemistry, but tried to supplement this lack with studies at the Collège de France.

During this period, she moved into the apartment of a family of gentle anarchists, Elie and Elisée Reclus and their wives, whose radical ideas had an important influence on her later concern about problems of gender and class. The Franco-Prussian war of 1870 and the consequent siege of Paris slowed down her medical education, while the proclamation of the third French Republic and the subsequent revolutionary uprising fired her imagination. Her attempts to persuade her father that the Paris Commune was not the work of fanatics went unheeded, although her experiences were later published by her sister, Ruth Putnam. She managed to save Elisée Reclus, a geographer and explorer, from prison and exile by searching for him throughout Paris and initiating a petition campaign to save him, signed by a remarkable number of English and U.S. scientists and politicians.

Renewing her medical studies after the end of the commune, she finished her work by 1871 with a thesis on fatty degeneration in various clinical disorders, "De la graisse neutre et des acides gras," which was awarded a bronze medal. She had originally dedicated it to the "one member of the faculty of medicine who voted to admit me," but was persuaded to remove this comment from later copies of the thesis as being unfair to those not asked to vote.

Elizabeth and Emily Blackwell had already invited her to join the medical faculty of the Woman's Medical College of the New York Infirmary to teach therapeutics (materia medica). Although Putnam at first found her students dull after Paris, and had to relearn the U.S. medical style, she soon became an excellent although highly demanding teacher. She arrived to teach in 1871 and was shortly afterward elected to the New York Pathological Society and the County Medical Society at the instigation of the excellent German physician and pediatrician Abraham Jacobi, whom she would marry in 1873.

The next decade was a happy and profitable one, as her son and daughter were born and she was able to teach, practice, and write. In 1873, Putnam Jacobi founded a medical dispensary for women and children at Mount Sinai Hospital, which continued to have a female staff even after she left it. She was asked by a committee of women to enter a competition for a Harvard Medical School prize on the topic of menstruation. Answering the misogynist claims of Edward Clarke about the physiological inability of women to compete, Putnam Jacobi argued that difficult menstruation was often related to poor health, and cited statistics indicating that more than a third of the women interviewed experienced no monthly discomfort. The award of the Boylston prize to a woman physician was hailed by many as a significant step, especially pleasant because the Harvard Medical School categorically refused to admit women.

Between 1879 and 1882, Putnam Jacobi published a total of twenty-two papers on topics that ranged from diseases of women and children to research in neuropathology. In 1882, she was one of the first lecturers at the New York Post-Graduate School of Medicine on children's diseases, urging further research on fetal pathology and the physiology of the child. The death of her son in the summer of 1883 put pressure on her marriage and made her question her profession, especially because her husband, a noted pediatrician, was a specialist in diphtheria, from which her child died. His re-

fusal to accept bacterial contamination as a cause of diphtheria, in contrast to his wife, also put them at odds. She encouraged her student ANNA WESSELS WILLIAMS to study bacteriology; Williams was later responsible for developing a successful strain for a diphtheria vaccine.

In 1891, Putnam Jacobi wrote an important account of women in medicine that was unequaled for its time. Shortly after, always aware of the need for women to work together, she saw in the arguments against votes for women the same arguments that had been urged against women physicians. She spoke before the New York legislature in that year on behalf of women's suffrage and the next year wrote a lengthy book on the topic, which she defended in correspondence against the arguments of her husband's close friend, the politician Carl Schurz.

Her energetic intellectual and physical life was slowed radically as she began to experience the first symptoms of a brain tumor that would disable and then kill her ten years later. At first aware only of headaches and a lessening energy, she was confined to her chair for the last three years of her life. With characteristic candor, she wrote up her own diagnosis that has been preserved in files at the New York Academy of Medicine. A memorial service held in 1906 by women from a number of different fields testified to her influence.   JH

PRIMARY SOURCES

Putnam, Mary. "De la graisse neutre et des acides gras." Thesis, Faculté de Médicine, Paris: 1871.

Jacobi, Mary Putnam. *The Question of Rest for Women during Menstruation.* New York: G.P. Putnam's Sons, 1877. She counters Edward Clarke's suggestion that women are disabled by normal cycles from professional careers and even higher education.

———. *The Value of Life.* New York: G. P. Putnam's Sons, 1879.

———. "Women in Medicine." In *Woman's Work in America.* Ed. Annie N. Meyer, 139–205. New York: Holt, 1891. One of the most comprehensive and interesting contemporary accounts of the entrance of women into the medical profession. She includes some statistics as well.

———. *Common Sense Applied to Woman's Suffrage.* New York: G. P. Putnam's Sons, 1894.

———. *Mary Putnam Jacobi: A Pathfinder in Medicine,* ed. Committee of Women Physicians. New York: Putnam, 1925. Original scientific papers and lectures by Mary Putnam Jacobi with front matter taken from her memorial service by significant physicians.

Schlesinger Library, Radcliffe College, holds most of the surviving archival materials, including autobiographical fragments, some unpublished stories, and published and unpublished letters. The New York Academy of Medicine holds a copy of her thesis and materials from her memorial service.

SECONDARY SOURCES

Abrams, Ruth J. *Send Us a Lady Physician*. New York: Norton, 1985.

Harvey, Joy. "Medicine and Politics: Dr. Mary Putnam Jacobi and the Paris Commune." In "Women and Revolution," ed. J. Diamond, special issue. *Dialectical Anthropology* 15 (1990): 107–117. Discusses the radicalization of Mary Putnam Jacobi and its relationship to her later feminism.

———. "'La Visite: Mary Putnam Jacobi and the French Medical Clinics." In *French Medical Culture in the Nineteenth Century*, ed. Ann La Berge and Mordecai Feingold. Amsterdam and Atlanta: Wellcome Series in the History of Medicine, Clio Medica 1994. Discusses Mary Putnam Jacobi's experiences in the Paris Hospital Clinics.

———. "Clanging Eagles: The Marriage and Collaboration between Two Nineteenth Century Physicians, Mary Putnam Jacobi and Abraham Jacobi." In *Collaborative Couples in the Sciences*, ed. H. Pycior, N. Slack, and P. Abir-Am, 185–197; 325–327. New Brunswick, New Jersey: Rutgers University Press, 1996. A critical look at the interaction between the couple.

Putnam, Ruth, ed. *Mary Putnam Jacobi, Life and Letters*. New York: Putnam, 1925. This contains much of her correspondence, including letters to her family no longer available in repositories. Her sister was the editor and has shortened or edited some letters.

Sanchez, Regina Morantz. *Sympathy and Science: Women Physicians in American Science*. New York: Oxford University Press, 1985.

Truax, Rhonda. *The Doctors Jacobi*. Boston: Little Brown, 1952. A popular account, this book incorporates material from interviews with her daughter.

STANDARD SOURCES

Concise Universal Biography; Hurd-Mead 1933; Lovejoy; McHenry, Robert, *Liberty's Women;* Lubove; *NAW;* O'Neill.

JACOBINA MEDICA OF BOLOGNA (fl. 1304)

Italian physician. Flourished 1304. Daughter of a doctor, Bartholomew.

Jacobina Medica of Bologna practiced medicine in Bologna and was called a great surgeon by a male contemporary.

JH/MBO

STANDARD SOURCES

Echols and Williams; Hurd Mead 1938; Lipinska 1900.

JACOBS, ALETTA HENRIETTA (1851–1929)

Dutch physician. Born 1851. Father Abraham Jacobs. Ten siblings. Educated local schools; the University of Groningen (qualified in medicine, 1878). Married Carel Victor Gerritsen (1892; d. 1905). Professional experience: Amsterdam, private practice; opened a free clinic for women and children and a birth control clinic (1882–1904). Left medicine in 1904 to pursue social and peace concerns. Died 1929.

Aletta Jacobs was one of the pioneering women in medicine in the Netherlands, a country significantly slow both in the admittance of women to university medical schools and in the amount of interest shown by women in medical professions. One of ten children who lived past infancy in the relatively poor family of a country doctor, Abraham Jacobs, she was educated at home, then in a local finishing school. She was initially refused entrance to medical school but was qualified as an apprentice dispenser. Encouraged by her father, she then wrote to J. R. Thorbecke, Minister of Public Affairs, who replied that she could attend the University of Gröningen. She studied there from 1874 to 1879, meeting with enormous hostility from men, but becoming the first qualified woman doctor in the Netherlands. Returning to Amsterdam, she joined her father's practice and then worked on her own, running a free surgery for the poor with courses on hygiene and child care. Her first priority was to help women and she mixed medicine and social service from the start of her practice. After visiting England and encountering the work and philosophy of such "radicals" as Charles Drysdale, ANNIE BESANT, and Charles Bradlaugh, she began Europe's first systematically organized birth control clinic (1882) in Amsterdam—advocating effective and simple contraception. Her "Dutch pessary" and clinical work became a source of inspiration for birth control reformers in other countries, including MARGARET SANGER and Norman Haire. She married Carel Victor Gerritsen (d. 1905), a reforming journalist and politician, in 1892.

Jacobs also was involved in campaigns to improve the status of women in society, advocating shorter working hours, protective legislation concerning safety at work (for all workers); education and counseling on venereal disease and sex; abolition of state-regulated prostitution; penal reform; marriage law reform; and suffrage. She began the Association for Women's Suffrage (1894); initiated the international suffrage movement in Washington, D.C. (1902) and in Berlin (1904). In 1904, Jacobs gave up her medical practice of twenty-five years and devoted herself fully to her concerns with women's emancipation and the peace movement. In 1911 she toured with Carrie Catt; she led in the peace movement during World War I with JANE ADDAMS; worked for the International Alliance of Women after suffrage was achieved in the Netherlands in 1919, and was particularly concerned with the rights of women in Asia. She died in 1929.

KM

SECONDARY SOURCES

Marland, Hilary. "'Pioneer Work on all Sides': The First Generations of Women Physicians in the Netherlands, 1879–

1930." *Journal of the History of Medicine and Allied Sciences* 50 (30 October 1995): 441–447.

STANDARD SOURCES
Uglow 1982.

JACOBSON, CLARA (1887–?)

U.S. physician and physiologist. Born 21 July 1887. Educated University of Chicago (B.S., 1909; fellow, 1910–1911; Ph.D., 1916); Rush Medical College (M.D., 1913). Professional experience: Cook County Hospital, intern (1914–1915); Municipal Tuberculosis Sanitarium, Grand Crossing Dispensary, physician in charge (from 1917). Honors and memberships: American Medical Association; Chicago Pathology Society. Death date unknown.

Clara Jacobson took all of her degrees except her medical doctorate (which she earned at Rush Medical College) at the University of Chicago. Her scientific interests were concentrated on the glands of internal secretion, the endocrine glands. She was also interested in the etiology and treatment of tuberculosis. JH/MBO

STANDARD SOURCES
AMS 3–4.

JACOPA OF PASSAU (fl. 1474)

Austrian/Italian physician. Flourished 1474.

Jacoba of Passau was licensed to practice during the plague outbreak of 1474 in Florence. JH/MBO

STANDARD SOURCES
Echols and Williams; Hurd-Mead 1938; Lipinska 1900.

JACSON, MARIA ELIZABETH (1755–1829)

British botanist. Born 1755 in Bebington, Cheshire. Two siblings. Never married. Educated at home. Professional activities: Published series of popular and didactic botanical books. Died 10 October 1829.

Maria Jacson's mother belonged to the Fitzherbert family; her father was educated for the clergy at St. John's College, Cambridge. He became rector of Bebington and then Tarporleyi, Cheshire. Jacson had one older brother and an older sister, Frances Margaretta. Their father died in 1808, and the two sisters apparently lived with him until his death. Jacson had no formal access to botanical training, but came into contact with botanists through the family network. According to Shteir, clerical families were known for encouraging their daughters to study botany because of its spiritual value.

Through her family, she met Sir Brooke Boothby of Ashbourne Hall, Derbyshire, who was a cousin on her mother's side. Boothby belonged to a literary circle that included Erasmus Darwin among others. Jacson probably met Darwin through Boothby. Darwin served as a patron for her first book, and mentioned Jacson in his *The Botanic Garden* as well as the *Zoonomia*. Both Darwin and Boothby wrote Maria Jacson a letter praising the manuscript of her *Botanic Garden,* a commendation that helped the sale of the book. Erasmus Darwin was one of three eighteenth-century writers who developed a plan for the education of women that included science within its curriculum. In his *Plan for the Conduct of Female Education* (1797), he recommends the *Botanical Dialogues.*

Maria Jacson wrote the *Botanical Dialogues* when she was forty-two years old. During the 1790s, women authors found additional opportunities to write and publish books. Many constraints still applied to women authors; the dialogue was a common format used by eighteenth-century authors. Jane Marcet used it, as did PRISCILLA WAKEFIELD. Jacson began by using this format, and *Botanical Dialogues* is cast as a narrative wherein the mother, Hortensia, attempts to educate her daughters and sons. The book was dull and long and didn't go beyond a first edition. Pedagogical works did not seem to suit Jacson's style. In her later books, she left the didactic dialogue for a more discursive form, which seemed to suit her better. All of her works were published anonymously. JH/MBO

PRIMARY SOURCES
[Jacson, Maria Elizabeth.] *Botanical Dialogues: Between Hortensia and Her Four Children.* London: Joseph Johnson, 1797.
———. *Botanical Lectures.* London: Joseph Johnson, 1804.
———. *Sketches of Physiology of Vegetable Life.* London: John Hatchard, 1811.
———. *The Florist's Manual.* London: Henry Colburn, 1816.

SECONDARY SOURCES
Shteir, Ann B. "Botanical Dialogues: Maria Jacson and Women's Popular Science Writing in England." *Eighteenth Century Studies* 23 (1990): 301–317.

STANDARD SOURCES
Desmond.

JAHODA, MARIE (1907–)

Austrian/English/U.S. psychologist. Born 26 January 1907 in Vienna to Betty and Carl Jahoda. Three siblings: two brothers and one sister. Married (1) Paul Lazarsfeld (1927; separated early 1930s); (2) Austen H. Albu (1958). One daughter, Lottie (b. 1930). Educated Realgymnasium (1926); Pedagogical Academy of Vienna (teaching diploma, 1928); University of Vienna (Ph.D. in psychology, 1933); Pinsent-Darwin Studentship at Cambridge

University (1938–1941). Professional experience: Wirtschaftspsychologische Forschungsstelle, director (1933–1936); Society for the Protection of Science and Learning, researcher, mining community in South Wales (1937–1938); British Ministry of Information, Wartime Social Survey, conductor of study of civilian morale; daily radio broadcasts to Austria, writer and presenter (1938–1943); National Institute for Social and Economic Research, researcher on the British economy (1943–1945); American Jewish Committee, member, research department (1945–1948); Columbia University, Bureau of Applied Research, conductor of study of interracial housing (1948–1949); New York University, associate professor, later professor of social psychology (1949–1958); Research Center for Human Relations, associate director, later director (1949–1958); Brunel College, London, research fellow (1958?), professor (1962–1965); University of Sussex, developer and chair, department of social psychology (1965–1973). Retired 1973. Honors and memberships: British Association for the Advancement of Science, president of Section X, the Social Sciences; Universities of Leiscester, Sussex, Brement, and Stirling, honorary degrees; American Psychological Association, Award for Distinguished Contributions to Psychology in the Public Interest (1979); Psychological Study of Social Issues, Kurt Lewin Memorial Award (1980); Council of the British Psychological Society, honorary Fellow.

Marie Jahoda carved out a career in three countries: Austria, England, and the United States. Born and educated in Austria of Jewish parents, Jahoda began her career taking over her ex-husband's position as director of the Wirtschaftspsychologische Forschungsstelle, where she remained for three years. Jahoda was a political activist and a member of the underground. She was arrested, imprisoned, and eventually expelled from Austria in 1937. Her major publication from this period was a book entitled *Die Arbeitslosen von Marienthal,* in which she studied the small village of Marienthal during the years of the Great Depression, when most of those in the community were unemployed. She concluded unexpectedly that unemployment and its corollary, economic deprivation, led not to revolutionary tendencies but to resignation and passivity. With the decrease in the quality of their physical lives, residents contracted their wants and lowered their expectations.

After Jahoda was expelled from Austria, the general secretary of the British Institute of Sociology, Alexander Farquharson invited her to England, where she studied another community, one in South Wales. The project, sponsored by the Friends (Quakers), suggested that the unemployed work as part of an organization that produced goods for their own consumption. Johoda lived in this community for four months, during which time her findings did not support the assumptions of the project sponsors. During the time that Jahoda was in Wales, Hitler's troops occupied Austria, where her family was still living. Through a friend, Lord Forrester, a code was arranged whereby she could communicate with

her family. Her family escaped through English sponsorship immediately before the outbreak of the war. In recognition of her study of the unemployed in Marienthal, Jahoda was awarded a three-year Pinsent Darwin Studentship at Cambridge University to conduct a study of factory workers. At the close of this fellowship she worked with the British Ministry of Information as a member of the Wartime Social Survey, an organization established to study civilian morale. In response to the ministry's refusal to accept one of their findings (that one of the causes of poor morale was the emphasis by government planners on carrots as the everyday available vegetable), the entire team resigned. Jahoda accepted an assignment to make daily radio broadcasts to Austria from a secret radio station. She, along with two other Austrians, researched, prepared, and presented the reports. Her last position in England was to study the British economy for the National Institute for Social and Economic Research.

Toward the end of the war, Jahoda secured passage on a troop ship in order to be reunited with her daughter, who was in the United States. In the United States, she first was employed in the Research Department of the American Jewish Committee. She stayed there for three years and published several studies on prejudice. She then moved to the Bureau of Applied Social Research at Columbia University for a year, where she studied the role of interracial contact in improving race relations in interracial housing. New York University hired Jahoda as an associate professor and associate director of the Research Center for Human Relations. She was later promoted to professor and director. Her research during this time made her an internationally known personage in social psychology. She published an important textbook, *Research Methods in Social Relations,* field studies on the effect of the suppression of political opinion by loyalty oaths and employment blacklisting , and the conceptual clarification of the idea of mental health.

Another stage in Jahoda's life began in 1958 when she married an engineer and prominent Labour Party member of Parliament, Austen H. Albu. She returned to England with her new husband, and accepted an appointment at Brunel College. She advanced to professor and was entrusted with developing a new psychology department. She designed and introduced a new four-year program for psychology students, where six months of each year was devoted to academic study and six months to work assignments. During her time at Brunel, she also began a series of studies analyzing the relationship of psychoanalysis to psychology. In 1965, Jahoda was invited to develop and chair a department of social psychology at the University of Sussex. This department was the first department of social psychology in the United Kingdom.

Although Jahoda formally retired at the age of sixty-six in 1973, she continued with her research and in the succeeding fifteen years authored two books, coedited three others, and published twenty-three articles and book chapters. JH/MBO

PRIMARY SOURCES

Jahoda, Maria. "Some Socio-Psychological Problems of Factory Life." *British Journal of Psychology* 31, part 3 (1941): 193–206.

———. With E. Cooper. "The Evasion of Propaganda: How Prejudiced People Respond to Anti-Prejudice Propaganda." *Journal of Psychology* 23 (1947): 15–25.

———. "Toward a Social Psychology of Mental Health." In *Problems of Infancy and Childhood,* ed. M. J. E. Senn. New York: Josiah Macy, Jr. Foundation, 1950.

———. With S. W. Cook. "Security Measures and Freedom of Thought: An Exploratory Study of the Impact of Loyalty and Security Programs." *Yale Law Journal* 61 (1952): 295–333.

———. "Prejudice: A Psychoanalytic Interpretation." In *Races of Man,* ed. S. M. Cole. London: British Museum (Natural History), 1960.

———. "Some Notes on the Influence of Psychoanalytic Ideas on American Psychology." *Human Relations* 16 (1963): 111–129.

———. With P. F. Lazarsfeld and H. Zeisel. *Marienthal: The Sociography of an Unemployed Community.* London: Tavistock, 1972. From the early study *Die Arbeitslosen von Marienthal* (Leipzig: Hirzel, 1933).

———. *Employment and Unemployment: A Social-Psychological Analysis.* Cambridge: Cambridge University Press, 1982.

STANDARD SOURCES

O'Connell and Russo 1990 (article by Stuart W. Cook); Stevens and Gardner.

JAMES, LUCY JONES (1823–1895)

British botanist. Born 1823. Died 20 December 1895.

Lucy Jones James was a member of the Botanical Society of London and collected plants around Denham, Buckinghamshire, where she lived. JH/MBO

STANDARD SOURCES

Desmond.

JANAKI AMMAL, EDAVALETH KAKKAT (1897–?)

Indian botanist and cytogeneticist. Born 4 November 1897. Educated University of Michigan (Ph.D., 1931; LL.D., 1956). Professional experience: Women's Christian College, Madras, instructor; Maharaja's College of Science, Trivandrum, instructor; Sugarcane Research Station, Coimbatore, geneticist; Royal Horticultural Society, London, cytologist; Reorganization of the Botanical Survey of India, Calcutta, officer on special duty and director; Central Botanical Laboratory, Botanical Survey of India, Allahabad, researcher; Cytogenetics Discipline, officer on special duty and chairman; Regional Research Laboratory, Jammu, researcher; University of Kashmir, professor of botany; Bhabha Atomic Energy Center, Bombay, emerita scientist; Center of Advanced Studies in Botany, University of Madras, emerita scientist. Honors and memberships: Linnean Society, Fellow; Royal Geographical Society; Genetical Society of England; Genetical Society of America; Royal Horticultural Society; Botanical Society of India (secretary, 1935–1938; president, 1961–1964); Sigma Xi; British Association for the Advancement of Science; Birbai Sahni Medal (1961); Padma Shri (1977); Indian National Science Academy (elected 1957). Death date unknown.

Edavaleth Kakkat Janaki Ammal had a varied career. It is difficult to decipher the order of her professional positions, as the one source jumbles them together. She reorganized and directed the Botanical Survey of India. She become well known for her work on cytogenetical studies on sugar cane and eggplant. She traced the evolution of these crops and worked with the Babha Atomic Energy Centre, Bombay, probably studying genetic mutation. In her sixties, she was president of the Botanical Society of India, and she was awarded a number of medals and other prizes. Janaki Ammal was one of the few women members of the Indian National Science Academy. JH/MBO

PRIMARY SOURCES

Janaki Ammal, Edavaleth Kakkat. *Chromosome Atlas of the Cultivated Plants.* London: Allen & Unwin, 1945.

SECONDARY SOURCES

Fellows of the Indian National Science Academy 1935–1984. New Delhi, Indian National Science Academy, 1984.

JANSSEN, MME. (fl. 1880s)

French astronomer. Married astronomer Pierre Jules César Janssen (1824–1907). One daughter. Professional experience: assisted her husband as secretary on his astronomical journeys.

Little is known about the wife of Pierre Jules Janssen (the French astronomer based at the observatory at Meudon). Not even her first name is given in major biographical accounts. However, she is said to have assisted him as a secretary on his multiple journeys as head of major astronomical expeditions. He traveled throughout the world (including expeditions to Japan, South America, the Himalayas, and the Pacific islands to observe the transit of Venus, alpha rays in the spectrum of Mars, and eclipses of the sun). *Ciel et Terre,* the journal of the sociète belge d'astronomie (Brussels), includes information about Jules Janssen and his wife, mentioning that both she and her daughter helped prepare for Janssen's and his associates' yearly expeditions to the astronomical observatory he built on the summit of Mount Blanc. Mme. Janssen's more than two hundred letters to her husband were presented to the Institut de France by her daughter, Antionette. JH/MBO

SECONDARY SOURCES
Pluvinel, A. De la Baume. "Jules César Janssen." *Astrophysical Journal* 28 (1908): 89–99.

STANDARD SOURCES
Rebière.

JEANES, ALLENE ROSALIND (1906–1995)

U.S. chemist. Born 19 July 1906 in Waco, Texas, to Viola (Herring) and Largus Elonzo Jeanes. One sibling. Never married. Educated Baylor University (B.A., 1928); University of California (M.A., 1929); University of Illinois (Ph.D., 1938). Professional experience: Texas, teacher (1929); Athens College, head of department of science (1930–1935); University of Illinois, instructor of chemistry (1936–1937); National Bureau of Standards, research chemist (1940–1941). Honors and memberships: Distinguished Service Award to Northern Regional Research Laboratory (NRRL) Dextran Team (1956); Garvan Medal, American Chemical Society (1956); Federal Women's Award, U.S. Civil Service Commission (1962); Outstanding Alumna Award, Baylor University (1968); Superior Service Award to Biopolymer Research Team (1968); American Chemical Society, Sigma Xi, and Iota Sigma Pi, member. Died 11 December 1995 at Urbana, Ill.

Allene Jeanes was a woman chemist who, despite the low number of female scientists at the time, was able to succeed and contribute to the chemistry field. Through her research, Jeanes influenced others, who in return helped her contribute the discoveries she made. She worked her way up from high school, to college, to graduate school, and to the career field, making a difference in everything that she did.

Jeanes grew up in Waco, Texas. Her father was a switchman, and later yardmaster, for the Cotton Belt Route of the St. Louis Southwestern Railroad. She graduated with honors from Waco High School in 1924 and continued to live in Texas to attend Baylor University, where she studied chemistry and graduated in 1929 *summa cum laude* with departmental honors and a bachelor's degree in organic chemistry. She went to the University of California at Berkeley to earn her master's degree, then found herself back in Texas teaching mathematics at a high school (1929). She moved soon

after to Alabama, where she taught biology, chemistry, and physics at Athens College from 1930 to 1935 and served as the head of the department of science.

Jeanes returned to school, to the University of Illinois, where she earned her doctorate in organic chemistry in 1938. She worked with Roger Adams and earned the first of her ten patents (1941). This patent was on phenanedicarboxylic anhydrides. Jeanes encountered many barriers as a result of being a woman. She was not able to pursue her desire to do pharmaceutical research because of discrimination and the economic depression. Despite these obstacles, Jeanes found an opportunity to work in Claude Hudson's laboratory at the National Institutes of Health, by accepting one of the first Corn Industry Research Foundation Fellowships. Jeanes's work with Hudson was on a new technique of periodate oxidation of starches. She was able to apply this technique in her research with Horace Isbell after she moved to the National Bureau of Standards (now the National Institute of Standards and Technology).

Jeanes did not stay long at the National Bureau of Standards. She moved to Peoria, Illinois, in 1941 after the United States Department of Agriculture opened the Northern Regional Research Laboratory (NRRL). She stayed at NRRL throughout the balance of her career, continuing to research and to write for many years after her retirement.

In 1950, Jeanes was one of the first to propose that the NRRL undertake an active part in the investigation of dextrans as a blood plasma volume expander. From her research on dextrans, she published her first bibliography on dextrans, which she updated in 1978. Much of the early work reflected her own careful experimentation technique. In recognition of this research, she became the first woman honored with the Distinguished Service Award given by the Department of Agriculture (1953). In 1956, Jeanes received more recognition for her research with dextrans by being honored as the recipient of the Garvan Medal. With the Garvan Medal, she was recognized by the American Chemical Society "for her leadership in the pioneering chemical research on dextrans and in the development of blood volume expander." This work also found its way later into commercial application. Jeanes made significant contributions to the knowledge of the structure of starch and other polysaccharides, and she developed assay methods for carbohydrates and their derivatives and degradation process. A former associate wrote in a 1956 *Chemical and Engineering News* article, "by her own accomplishments in research, by the training of her assistants, and above all, by the high standards of her work and ideals, she has influenced those who know and have worked with her."

Jeanes went on to receive more honors in her field. In 1956 she won the Distinguished Service Award of the United States Department of Agriculture for her research team. They also received several patents for their group work on dextrans. Jeanes received the Federal Women's Award of the U.S. Civil Service Commission for her high level of achievement in scientific research. Other honors include the Superior Service Award from the U.S. Department of Agriculture awarded to her Biopolymer Research Team (1968). It was received for their "outstanding creativity and highly significant microbiological chemical and engineering team research resulting in the discovery, development, and industrial acceptance and commercialization of a new industrial gum of cereal grain origin." Jeanes continued her gum studies, which led to a series of papers on the properties and applications that were useful to the microbial gum industry developing in the United States. She indicated that the new techniques could provide a better picture of the structure of many of the dextrans produced by various strains of bacteria, which could lead to a better understanding of the immunochemical interactions. Jeanes's final paper, published in 1986, reviewed the work done up to that time.

Jeanes made numerous contributions to the chemistry world. Her honors reflect only a few of her many discoveries. After becoming associated with the U.S. Department of Agriculture, her ensuing thirty-five years of research at the NRRL resulted in two major scientific and industrial developments, over sixty publications, twenty-four presentations, and ten patents. Not only did she receive recognition for her work from the U.S. government, but she also received international recognition through honors and awards for her contributions to the chemistry field. Doing all of this research took a great deal of time and energy for Jeanes—more so since she was female and getting people on her research team was difficult. However, once Jeanes proved herself and showed the chemistry world that she knew what she was talking about, colleagues were not hard to find.

Working for the chemistry field was not Jeanes's only passion. She had many cultural pursuits in her life. She belonged to the Amateur Musical Club and the Knife and Fork Club in Peoria. At the same time, she enjoyed classical music, ballet, and foreign cooking and tailoring. These were just some of the hobbies that made Jeanes a unique chemist. Unique in that, as a female, she was able to make a difference in the chemistry world and left her mark even after her death on 11 December 1995 in Urbana, Illinois.   N R

PRIMARY SOURCES

Jeanes, Allene. With Charles A. Wilham. "Periodate Oxidation of Dextran." *Journal of the American Chemical Society* 72 (1950): 2655–2657. This paper is one of many on her early work on dextrans.

———. "Young Women: Define Your Individual Identity and Plan Its Continuous Nurture." Waco, Texas: Laurel Society, Baylor University. 1968.

———. "Microbial Polysaccharides." *Encyclopedia of Polymer Science and Technology* 8 (1968): 693–711. A review of what Jeanes and her coworkers had discovered up to that time about microbial polysaccharides.

———, ed. With John E. Hodge, ed. *Physiological Effects of Food Carbohydrates.* Washington, D.C.: American Chemical Society, 1975. This volume resulted from a symposium on this topic that took place at the American Chemical Society in 1974, sponsored by the Division of Carbohydrate Chemistry of the Division and Food Chemistry.

———. "Dextran Bibliography. Extensive Coverage of Research Literature (Exclusive of Clinical) and Patents, 1861–1976." Washington, D.C.: United States Department of Agriculture, 1978. Jeanes had published in 1950 an earlier bibliography on dextrans. It was 13 pages long. She updated it in 1967, at which point it was 92 pages long. The 1978 version excludes clinical work and is 368 pages long.

———. "Immunochemical and Related Interactions with Dextrans as Reviewed in Terms of Improved Structural Information." *Molecular Immunology* 23 (1986): 999–1028. Jeanes's final paper, in which she analyzes all of the work known up to that time on the structure of the dextrans and their interactions.

SECONDARY SOURCES

"Allene R. Jeanes." *Chemical and Engineering News* 34, no. 17 (1956): 1984.

Jennings, Bojan Hamlin. *Carbohydrates—Not for Eating: Allene Jeanes Curriculum.* Norton, Mass.: Chemistry Department, Wheaton College, 1982.

Sandford, Paul A. "Allene R. Jeanes." *Carbohydrate Research* 66 (1978): 3–5.

STANDARD SOURCES

AMS 7–8, P 9, P&B 10–12; Shearer and Shearer 1997.

JEKYLL, GERTRUDE (1843–1932)

British horticulturist, landscape architect, and garden designer. Born 29 November 1843 in London to Julia (Hammersley) and Edward Joseph Hill Jekyll. Six siblings. Educated at home; Kensington School of Art (1861–1863). Died 8 December 1932 in Godalming, Surrey.

Gertrude Jekyll was a pioneer of the informal style of gardening. Born into an intellectual and artistic family, she received her early education at home. During her youth, she traveled in Greece, Italy, and Algeria, where she studied the flora and drew plants in their natural habitats. She became known as an interior decorator. After suffering from progressive myopia, she gave up painting, embroidery, and other close work, and concentrated on gardening. She met Sir

Edwin Lutyens, a young man with similar interests, and together they drove around Surrey getting ideas for gardens. She designed numerous gardens, often collaborating with Sir Edwin. Some of her gardens, such as Hestercombe in Somerset, Lindisfarne in Northumberland, and Upton Gray in Hampshire, have been restored. She was awarded the Victoria Medal of Honour of the Royal Horticultural Society as well as its Veitchian Gold Medal. The Massachusetts Horticultural Society awarded her its G.R. White Gold Medal.

JH/MBO

PRIMARY SOURCES

Jekyll, Gertrude. *Wood and Garden.* London: Longmans, Green and Co., 1899.

———. *Home and Garden.* London: Longmans, Green and Co., 1900.

———. *Some English Gardens.* London: Longmans, Green and Co., 1904.

———. *Annuals and Biennials.* London: Scribner, 1916.

SECONDARY SOURCES

Brown, Jane. *Gardens of a Golden Afternoon.* Harmondsworth, Middlesex, England: Viking, 1982. Includes a list of Jekyll's commissions.

STANDARD SOURCES

Desmond; *DNB Missing Persons; WWW,* vol. 3, 1929–1940.

JENSEN, ESTELLE LOUISE (1888–?)

U.S. plant pathologist. Born 25 May 1888 in Minneapolis, Minn. Married Elvin Charles Stakman. Educated University of Minnesota (A.B., 1909; fellow, 1911–1912); Smith College (A.M., 1910). Professional experience: South Dakota, high school teacher (1910–1911); Forest Products Laboratory, Wisconsin, xylotomist, (1912–1913); University of Minnesota, instructor (1913–1917); Minnesota Experimental Station, mycologist (1913–1917). Death date unknown.

Louise Jensen was a plant pathologist, as was her husband, Elvin C. Stakman, who headed the plant pathology department at the University of Minnesota. Both she and her husband were interested in mycology. Her specialty was imperfect fungi on cereals.

JH/MBO

PRIMARY SOURCES

Stakman, Louise J. "A Helminthosporium Disease of Wheat and Rye. *Agricultural Experiment Station Bulletin,* University of Minnesota; reprint; St. Paul, Minn.: University Farm, 1920.

STANDARD SOURCES

AMS 3–7; Bailey.

JÉRÉMINE, ELISABETH (TSCHERNAIEFF) (1879–1964)

Russian petrologist. Born 28 October 1879 in Kamenka, Russia. Married Constantin Jérémine. Educated Women's University, St. Petersburg; University of Lausanne (Ph.D., 1911?). Professional experience: Women's University, Saint Petersburg(?), assistant to the chair of petrography, F. J. Loewinson-Lessing; Sorbonnne researcher; l'Institut de Géologie Appliquée de Nancy, Paris researcher. Died 10 March 1964 in Zurzach.

Born in Russia, Elisabeth Jérémine attended the Women's University, St. Petersburg, where she got a good general background in literature and the arts. She then became an assistant to the chair of petrography, F. J. Loewinson-Lessing, who was a great advocate for women's education. He became Jérémine's mentor and published her first memoirs of the *Comptes rendus* with him in 1905 and 1907. Loewinson-Lessing also arranged for her to obtain financial support to attend International Congresses. On one of these trips she met Maurice Lugeon, then a young professor at the University of Lausanne, who invited her to prepare a doctoral dissertation under his supervision, which was published in 1911. Lugeon's laboratory, while small, was well respected, and Jérémine's reputation began to be known. However, she returned to Russia where she participated under the direction of the mineralogist and geochemist A. Fersman, in an expedition that he organized on the peninsula of Kola to study the geology and petrography, and to note minerals and their locations.

With the advent of the Russian Revolution, she again left Russia, this time under a false name, in order to seek asylum in France. On arriving in France, she was welcomed into the geology laboratory of Albert Michel-Lévy, to initiate students into the techniques of observing thin sheets of rock under the microscope. During this time she met a colleague, Juliette Pfender, who became her close friend until her death. The Sorbonne and the laboratory of mineralogy represented her base of operations. She collaborated with a number of geologists, including François Antoine Alfred Lacroix (1863–1948). After several years, she accepted a position at the institute of applied geology of Nancy.

Jérémine was an indefatigable worker, equally at home in the laboratory and in the field. She studied rocks and meteors from different parts of the world, including Canada, Chad, Cameroons, Portugal, Mali, Niger, Kenya, Algeria, Madagascar, and Tahiti, and was able to describe them within their geological context. During her life she published over 115 papers.

JH/MBO

PRIMARY SOURCES

Jérémine, Elisabeth. Les bassins fermés des Préalpes. *Bulletin de la Société Vaudoise des Sciences Naturelles* 47 (1911): 465–533.

SECONDARY SOURCES

Orcel, Jean. "Elisabeth Jérémine (1879–1964)." *Bulletin de la Société Geologique de France*, ser. 7, 7, no. 4 (1965): 608–614.

JERMOLIEVA, ZINAIDA VISSARIONOVNA (1898–1974)

Russian microbiologist and bacteriologist. Born 12 October 1898 in Frolowo, Russia. Educated University of Rostow on the Don (graduated 1921). Professional experience: Bacteriological Institution of the North Caucasus (1921–ca. 1936); Biochemical Institute, professor of microbiology and bacteriological chemistry (ca. 1921–1952); Health Ministry of the USSR, Antibiotic Institute (ca. 1921–1952); High School for Physicians, professor (1952–?). Honors and memberships: Medical Academy of Science of the USSR, corresponding member; Stalin Prize recipient (1943); Order of Lenin, recipient twice. Died 1974.

Zinaida Vissarionovna Jermolieva studied at the University of Rostow, but what type of degree she received is unclear. Much of her research revolved around treatments of cholera with different antibiotics. Her important published works were on cholera, penicillin, and streptomycin. Her research earned her several important awards. JH/MBO

STANDARD SOURCES

Strohmeier; *WW in Soviet Science*.

JESSON, ENID MARY (1899–1956)

British botanist. Born 1 May 1889 in Malvern, Australia. Married A. D. Cotton (1915). Died 19 April 1956 in Farham Common, Buckinghamshire.

Enid Jesson was born in Australia but moved to England. She contributed textual material to *Curtis's Botanical Magazine* in 1916. She also contributed to E. F. Vallentin's *Illustrations of Flowering Plants of the Falkland Islands*. JH/MBO

PRIMARY SOURCES

Jesson, Enid Mary. Contribution of text in *Curtis's Botanical Magazine* 1916, 8690.

Vallentin, E. F. *Illustrations of the Flowering Plants and Ferns of the Falkland Islands with Descriptions by Mrs. E. M. Cotton*. Ashford, Kent: L. Reeve, 1921.

STANDARD SOURCES

Desmond.

JEX-BLAKE, SOPHIA (1840–1912)

British pioneer physician. Born 21 January 1840 at Hastings, England, to Maria (Cubitt) and Thomas Jex-Blake. Two siblings who survived infancy. Educated Queens College, London (1858–1861); studied under Lucy Sewell and Elizabeth Blackwell in U.S. (1865–1868); University of Edinburgh (1869–1873). Professional experience: founder, London School of Medicine for Women (1874); practicing physician in Edinburgh (1878–1899); founder, Edinburgh Women's Hospital (1885) and Edinburgh School of Medicine for Women (1886). Died 7 January 1912 at Rotherfield, Sussex.

Sophia Jex-Blake was the youngest of six children of Thomas and Maria Jex-Blake, only three of whom survived childhood. Her father was a solicitor (known as a proctor) at Doctors Commons. Her father was fifty and her mother thirty-nine when Sophia was born. Her parents were evangelical Anglicans who encouraged serious reading and frowned upon frivolity. Despite the austerity, Sophia was close to her parents. Sophia was schooled at home by her parents until she was eight years old, when she was sent to boarding school. Boarding school and Sophia did not agree: during eight years, she changed boarding schools six times, exhibiting the feisty nature that was her lifelong trademark. When Jex-Blake left boarding school for the last time, she pondered possible occupations. Most options, including marriage, did not appeal to her, but she found that Queen's College, London, appealed to her. She took a full course load of subjects: astronomy, church history, English, French, history, mathematics, natural philosophy, and theology. While she was at Queens, Jex-Blake began to tutor students with deficiencies, a situation abhorred by her father when he found that she was paid for the work. After a break with her close friend, Octavia Hill, Jex-Blake met ELIZABETH GARRETT ANDERSON, who was also hunting a fulfilling career. Jex-Blake, unsuccessfully, tried to help Garret in her quest for admission to the medical school at Edinburgh University. After a tour of the United States (1865–1868), Jex-Blake decided to study medicine (1866). During this trip she met Dr. LUCY SEWALL; their association developed into a lifelong friendship.

The abrasive Jex-Blake spent most of her life fighting for a career in medicine for herself and for other women. In 1868 she began a program of study under Dr. ELIZABETH BLACKWELL in New York, but had to abandon it the following year when her father's death brought her back to England. Jex-Blake now sought a medical school that would allow her to complete her education. She first applied to the University of London, "of whose liberality one heard so much, and was told by the Registrar that the existing charter had been purposely so worded as to exclude the possibility of examining women for medical degrees, and that under the Charter nothing whatever could be done in their favor" (Jex-Blake, *Medical Women*, 72). Then began a strenuous campaign for acceptance at the University of Edinburgh, during which she found both "kind and liberal friends among the Professors" and bitter opponents—such as the medical professor

Dr. Laycock, who "calmly told me, when I called on him, that he could not imagine *any decent woman* wishing to study medicine—as for *any lady,* that was out of the question" (Jex-Blake, *Medical Women,* 72).

The majority of the professors, however, were neutral. Although reluctant to alter the status quo, they did not have any violent objections. At last the university senate passed a resolution that would allow women to study medicine in special classes "confined entirely to women . . . Four other ladies and myself were, in October 1869, admitted provisionally to the usual preliminary examination in Arts, prescribed for medical students entering the University" (Jex-Blake, *Medical Women,* 78).

The women attended classes and did very well. In fact, one of them won an important distinction, the Hope Scholarship, which, however, was "wrested from the successful candidate and given over her head to the fifth student on the list, who had the good fortune to be a man" (Jex-Blake, *Medical Women,* 82). The situation deteriorated to the point where no instructor could be found to teach the women a separate class in anatomy. Finally, a recognized "extra-mural" teacher of anatomy, Dr. Handyside, agreed to allow them to attend his regular class. Another obstacle was encountered when they were refused permission to study at the Royal Infirmary, a necessary step toward completing the medical degree. During the time when the women were attempting to get this decision reversed, some of the male medical students "took every opportunity of practicing the petty annoyances that occur to thoroughly ill-bred lads, such as shutting the doors in our faces, ostentatiously crowding into the seats we usually occupied, bursting into horse-laughs and howls when we approached—as if a conspiracy had been formed to make our position as uncomfortable as might be." These students also signed a petition against admitting the women to the infirmary. The conflict was brought to a head when a mob "comprising some dozen of the lowest class of our fellow-students at Surgeon's Hall, with many more of the same class from the University, a certain number of street rowdies, and some hundreds of gaping spectators," blocked the entrance to Surgeon's Hall as the women approached. A small group of students took the women's side, and a riot ensued (90–92).

The publicity afforded the riot helped bring about a turn in popular opinion. Indignation became a factor as people learned of the denial of the Hope Scholarship, the riot at Surgeon's Hall, and the exclusion of women from the Royal Infirmary. Nonetheless, when in 1871 Jex-Blake had the temerity to bring an action for libel against a member of the university staff whom she accused of leading the riot, she was awarded a farthing in damages and had a legal bill of nearly a thousand pounds to pay.

Even with their improved public image, conditions for the women students at Edinburgh continued to worsen. Those lecturers who had been permitting women to attend their classes were no longer allowed to do so. Obstacle after obstacle was erected. Finally, "on January 8, 1872, the University Court declared that they could not make any arrangements to enable us to pursue our studies with a view to a degree but that, *if we would altogether give up the question of graduation,* and be content with certificates of proficiency, they would try to meet our views" (Jex-Blake, *Medical Women,* 136). Jex-Blake and her compatriots responded by bringing suit against the university for breach of its implied contract to enable them to win degrees. After a judgment against them (1873) they attacked the legal question in Parliament. Three years of fighting brought victory in the Russell Gurney Enabling Act (1876), which allowed medical examining bodies to test women.

Meanwhile, Jex-Blake had founded the London School of Medicine for Women (1874), with a staff of respected lecturers. She herself was granted the legal right to practice medicine in Great Britain by the Irish College of Physicians in 1877. She began practicing in Edinburgh in 1878, founded the Women's Hospital there in 1885, and in 1886 organized the Edinburgh School of Medicine for Women.

The differences in personality between Sophia Jex-Blake, the aggressive, flamboyant fighter, and Elizabeth Garrett Anderson, the quiet, persistent diplomat, often led to disagreement between them as the best ways of attaining their common goal, opening the medical profession to women. Hurt feelings and misunderstandings especially attended the development of the London School of Medicine for Women. Although the school had been established by Jex-Blake, and had even been opposed in print by Anderson, it was Anderson and not Jex-Blake who was named dean in 1883. Jex-Blake retired from active work in 1899 and settled in Rotherfield, Sussex, where she died in 1912. Her courage and tenacity had hastened the acceptance of women in British medical schools; and in her chronicle of her own and earlier women's experiences, *Medical Women* (1886), she had made an important contribution to the history of medicine.

MBO

PRIMARY SOURCES

Jex-Blake, Sophia. *Medical Women: A Thesis and a History.* Edinburgh: Oliphant, Anderson, and Ferrier, 1886. The first section is a brief history of women in medicine. The second discusses Jex-Blake's own admission to medical school.

———. "Medicine as a Profession for Women." In *Woman's Work and Woman's Culture,* ed. Josephine Butler. London: Macmillan, 1957.

SECONDARY SOURCES

Roberts, Shirley. *Sophia Jex-Blake: A Woman Pioneer in Nineteenth-Century Medical Reform.* London: Routledge, 1993. An excellent biographical source.

Todd, Margaret. *The Life of Sophia Jex-Blake.* London: Macmillan, 1918.

STANDARD SOURCES
DNB suppl. 3; Ogilvie 1986; Shearer and Shearer 1996 (article by Carol Brooks Norris).

JEŽOWKSA-TRZEBIATOWSKA, BOGUSLAWA (1908–)

Polish chemist. Born 19 November 1908 in Stanislawów, Poland. Educated mathematics and scientific gymnasium in Lemberg (Lwow) (graduated 1926); Polytechnischen Hochschule technical college (Engineering diploma 1932; habilitated 1951). Professional experience: Polytechnischen Hochschule, assistant (1932–1937); Polish Chemical Society, Lembert division, secretary (1937–1939); Firma Galikol (1939–1945); University of Breslau and the Polytechnischen Hochschule Breslau, Institute of Inorganic and Analytical Chemistry, research (1946–1948), faculty of natural sciences, head of general chemistry (1948–1951), teacher of inorganic chemistry (1951–1958), dean of her field (1958–1962); Institute for Low Temperature and Structural Research of the Polish Academy of Science, leader (1978–). Honors and memberships: Polish Academy of Science, corresponding member (1964), ordinary member (1967); International European Congress for Molecular Spectroscopy, president (1972, 1977); Academy of Wissenschaften of the DDR, member; Universities of Moscow, Pressberg, and Breslau, honorary degrees.

Boguslawa Ježowksa-Trzebiatowska received her engineering diploma in 1932 at the Polytechnical College for Chemistry in Lemberg. For five years she was an assistant at the Polytechnical College and for another two years was secretary of the Lemberg division of the Polish Chemical Society. During the war she worked for a firm, the *Firma Galikol,* and after the war became director of the Institute for Inorganic and Analytical Chemistry of the Polytechnical College in Breslau and the University of Breslau. She later became the head of the division of general chemistry in the natural science faculty. Ježowksa-Trzebiatowska habilitated in 1951 and in the same year was named to the chair of the inorganic chemistry department. She later became chair of the chemistry of the rare elements department. In 1958 she became dean of her field.

For her research she was involved with the theory and structure of chemical compounds. She was a specialist in the field of spectroscopy, radiospectroscopy, and magnetochemistry. JH/MBO

STANDARD SOURCES
Strohmeier; *WW in Science in Europe; WW in Soviet Science* 1960.

JHIRAD, JERUSHA (1891–?)

Indian physician. Born 21 March 1891 in the Bene-Israel community of India. Seven siblings (four sisters and three brothers). Married. Children. Educated high school for girls at Poona; Bombay(?) medical studies (qualified in 1912); London School of Medicine for Women (M.B., B.S.); London University (M.D. in obstetrics and gynecology, 1919). Professional experience: Private practice in Bombay (1912–1914); consultant practice (1919–1920); small hospital in Gangalore, in charge of maternity unit (1920–1924); Bombay, honorary posts (1924–1928); medical officer (1928–1971). Honors and memberships: Padma Shree, an Indian award for distinction. Death date unknown.

Jerusha Jhirad was born in a Jewish community in India, about 120 miles south of Bombay and reputedly one of the lost tribes of Israel. Her family was well educated—her mother's youngest sister was the first university graduate among the Bene-Israel community and her father studied at the medical college. Apparently he never finished medical school, for after Jhirad's grandfather acquired a coffee estate in Mysore, her father ran it, until the crop was decimated by disease. Her father went north to find employment and her mother developed rheumatoid arthritis. Jhirad was sent to a high school for girls at Poona.

Part of her motivation for studying medicine occurred after her seventeen-year-old sister delivered premature twins and was gravely ill after the birth. Her life was saved by a woman physician. Jhirad developed a life plan, which involved study in London and being in charge of Cama hospital. She qualified in Bombay in 1912 and set up a private practice there. However, she was awarded a Tata loan scholarship to study in London and later became the first woman to be awarded the Government of India scholarship. At the London School of Medicine for Women, she obtained bachelors of medicine and science degrees and then went to the University of London to study for a doctor of medicine degree. After obtaining this degree in 1919, Jhirad returned to India.

Hoping to realize the second part of her plan, to be in charge of Cama Hospital, she went to Bombay. Since there were no openings at Cama, she set up a consultant practice, and after a year went to a small hospital in Gangalore, where she was in charge of the maternity unit. With social workers, she formed a child welfare council to organize clinics and feeding centers.

Returning to Bombay in 1924, she found that honorary posts were available and worked there until 1928, when she was appointed medical officer of the hospital, the first Indian to hold that post. She worked at this hospital until retirement. In addition to her medical and administrative responsibilities, she opened a postgraduate library at the hospital and persuaded the government to provide grants for subscriptions to current journals. She was examiner for the medical degree at Bombay, Poona, and Madras universities for many years. She was active in a number of medical organizations. KM

PRIMARY SOURCES

Jhirad, Jerusha. In Hellstedt, *Autobiographies.*

JOHANNA (JOHANNE, JOANNA) (fl. 1408)
British physician. Flourished 1408 in Westminster.

The name Johanna appears in the Westminster Abbey Infirmarer's Rolls as being paid for various medicines. She is referred to as "Johanne, Leech," and again "Johanne Leche, Mulieri" to remove any suspicion that this might be a man. The title "leech" rather than "apothecaria" would strongly suggest medical practice. JH/MBO

SECONDARY SOURCES

Talbot, Charles and Hammond, E. H. *Medical Practitioners in Medieval England: A Biographical Register.* London: Wellcome Medical Historical Library, 1965. Johanna discussed on page 100.

JOHNSON, DOROTHY DURFEE MONTGOMERY (1909–)
U.S. physicist. Born 3 May 1909 in Rochester, N.Y., to Abigail (Leroy) and Charles G. Durfee. Married (1) Carol Montgomery (1 June 1933; he died 1950); (2) Thomas H. Johnson (1965). Two children (with Montgomery); one boy and one girl. Educated Vassar College (A.B., 1930); Yale University (M.S., 1932; Ph.D. in physics, 1951). Professional experience: Yale University, assistant in physics (1931–1932), researcher (1940–1941); MIT Radiation Laboratory, researcher (1941–1945), research associate (1946–1951); Massachusetts Institute of Technology, researcher (1942–1946); Hollins College, associate professor of physics and head physics department (1952–1966). Retired 1966.

After her undergraduate education at Vassar College, Dorothy Johnson attended Yale University, where she received both a master's and a doctoral degree. While working on her master's, she was an assistant in physics. She married in 1933, and probably took courses and did research for her doctorate during the years for which explicit information is unavailable. From 1940 to 1941, she was a research assistant at Yale. After this assistantship, she took a position at MIT in the radiation lab but returned to Yale where she was a research associate for five years. After she received her doctorate, she took a position at Hollins College, as professor of physics and head of the physics department.

Johnson was a member of the American Association of Physics teachers and a Fellow of the American Physical Society. Her research was in spectroscopy and cosmic radiation. JH/MBO

STANDARD SOURCES

AMS P&B 12.

JOHNSON, HILDEGARDE (BINDER) (1908–)
German/U.S. geographer. Born 20 August 1908 in Berlin to Emma (Gartenschlager) and Albert Wilhelm Binder. Married Palmer O. Johnson (20 August 1936). Two children. Educated University of Berlin (M.A.; Ph.D., 1933); University of Munich (D.Sc.). Immigrated to U.S. (1936); naturalized (1944). Professional experience: Manchester, England, high school teacher (1934); Macalester College, Minneapolis, geography faculty (1947–1968), department chair (1955). Concurrent experience: University of Georgia, Michigan, California, and Washington, visiting professor. Honors and memberships: Minnesota Council for Social Studies (1956–1960); Minnesota Governor's Council for Atomic Development, member; American/Canadian Association of Geographers; American Geographical Society; Minnesota Academy of Science.

Hildegard Binder was born and educated in Germany. She obtained her doctorate of science from the University of Munich. She left Germany after the imposition of Nazi antisemitic laws and moved to England. After teaching at the secondary school level in Manchester for a year, she moved to the United States, where she held a position at Mills College. She married that same year and had two children. She appears not to have worked until after World War II, when her children were in school. She then obtained a position at Macalester College in Minneapolis and remained there until her retirement. Binder was a visiting professor at a number of universities in the fifties. She served on the Minnesota Governor's Council for Atomic Development and was a member of the Minnesota Academy of Science.

Johnson was very interested in site selection in original settlements, and she was intrigued by the choice of watersheds by different culture groups. She studied pioneer settlements in the American Midwest as well as the significance of original site selection for development in Africa. JH/MBO

PRIMARY SOURCES

Johnson, Hildegarde. *Carta Marina; World Geography in Strassburg, 1925.* Minneapolis: University of Minnesota Press, 1963.

JOHNSON, MARY (1895–1969)
British chemist. Born 14 January 1895 in Sunderland to Betsy Eleanor (Burdis) and John Wright Johnson. Married Leslie Marshall

Clark (27 February 1926). Two daughters, Jean Mary (b. 1927) and Honor Margaret (b. 1935). Educated Oxford Local Examination (Junior, first class, 1909; Senior, second class, 1910); London Matriculation (first class, 1911); Cambridge Higher Local Examination (from Sunderland Bede Collegiate Girls School, 1912; repeated 1913); Newnham College Cambridge, Natural Science Tripos (Part I, Second class, 1916); Part II, Chemistry first class, 1917). Professional experience: Bathurst Research Studentship, Newnham (1917–1918); Institute of Chemistry, associate (from 1918); Mary Bateson Research Fellowship, Newnham (1922–1923). Died 26 April 1969 in Cambridge.

Mary Johnson's career trajectory was not unusual for a woman of her time. She seemed to be proceeding toward a career as a research chemist but then married and did little chemistry thereafter.

After less than sterling results on her examinations, Johnson was accepted into Newnham, where she showed a great deal of promise. She only got second class honors on the first part of the (Natural Sciences) Tripos. However, her father and only brother had been killed in December of the previous year, and surely that affected her performance. On part two of the Tripos, she earned first class honors, and was the only person so placed in the university—including all of the men. At that time, women could not be registered for a doctoral degree, but she received a Bathurst Research Fellowship and then was an associate at the Institute of Chemistry. In 1922, she held a research fellowship at Newnham but resigned it after she became engaged to L. M. Clark. She taught at the College Laboratories at Newnham, was on its governing body from 1924 to 1928, and was an associate from 1925 to 1939.

As far as her family has been able to ascertain, Johnson published only one paper under her own name. However, they believe that she wrote one of the official histories of the first world war—one on high temperature gas furnaces. This and other papers were apparently published under the name of William Hobson Mills (1873–1959). The one paper that she is known to have written was published in 1921 in the *Transactions of the Society of Chemical Industry.* Johnson was senior in the Chemical Laboratory. The story is that her future husband, junior to her in the laboratory, came to work beside her when she answered a query about which young man she would like to work opposite her on the bench. She replied that she did not care as "long as he is a good tidy clean worker." The couple married in 1926.

At the beginning of World War II, Leslie Clark was running a research laboratory for ICI Alkali. He said that she was a better chemist than he, and that he would have her in the laboratory "like a shot" if it were not for the children. Later in the war she taught chemistry briefly to the sixth form at Howells School in North Wales. When it looked as if it would be possible for her to begin research again, she had a massive stroke in 1945, which disabled her mentally.

JH/MBO

PRIMARY SOURCES
Johnson, Mary. "Dyestuffs of the Pyrazolone Series." *Transactions of the Society of Chemical Industry* 40, no. 15 (1921): 176T–178T.

SECONDARY SOURCES
Vitae compiled by Professor Margaret Spufford, daughter of Mary Johnson. Newnham College Archives, 1998.

JOHNSON, MINNIE MAY (1896–1970)
U.S. botanist and horticulturalist. Born 1896 in McConnellsville, Ohio. Father, William Johnson. Educated University of Ohio (B.S.Ed., 1922); The Ohio State University (M.Sc., 1926; Ph.D., 1929). Stephens College, Columbia, Mo., instructor in biology and founder and director of the greenhouse. Died 3 March 1970 in Columbia, Missouri.

Minnie May Johnson is best known for her creation of the greenhouse at Stephens College. The greenhouse was used as a laboratory for her classes, in particular her floriculture class. A skilled photographer, Johnson won prizes for her photographs in nationwide contests.

She was a member of the Botanical Society of America, Pi Lambda Theta, Sigma Delta Epsilon, Sigma Xi, and Kappa Alpha Mu.

JH/MBO

PRIMARY SOURCES
Johnson, Minnie May. "The Gasteromycetae of Ohio: Puffballs, Birds'-Nest Fungi and Stinkhorns." *Ohio Biological Survey Bulletin No. 22* 4, no. 7 (1929): 271–352.
———. "Check List of Fleshy Fungi Collected in West-Central Illinois." *Transactions of the Illinois Academy of Science* 45: 27–30.

SECONDARY SOURCES
"Minnie May Johnson." Biographical background for the Office of Information, Stephens College, Columbia, Mo. Stephens College Archives, from the Collection of Ronald L. Stuckey.
Stephens Life. Articles on Minnie Mae Johnson, 22 October 1959; 19 February 1970. Stephens College Archives, from the collection of Ronald L. Stuckey.
Press release from Office of Information, Stephens College, Columbia, Mo. Biographical notice on Johnson's death, published in the Columbia *Missourian* and *The Columbia Daily Tribune,* 3 March 1970. Stephens College Archives, from the collection of Ronald L. Stuckey.

JOHNSTON, MARY SOPHIA (1875–1955)

British geologist, geomorphologist, and paleontologist. Born 29 October 1875 at Folkestone. Father the Reverend W. A. Johnston. Educated privately. Studied at one of the London colleges. Professional experience: University of Durham, reader in chemistry and mineralogy (1832–1855). Died 23 January 1955.

Little is known of Johnston's early life. She was born at Folkestone, and after the death of her minister father, she and her mother went to live on Wimbledon Hill. While she was being privately educated, she became interested in geology and joined the Geologists' Association in 1898. She was active in the association, becoming illustrations secretary (1910–1925), a position that required her to maintain the association's albums of geological photographs. She was librarian from 1932 to 1936, and a council member. As a reward for her service to the society, she was elected an honorary member in 1939.

Johnston became increasingly involved in geological activities, although she was obliged to remain an amateur. Traveling widely, she attended international geological congresses in Spain, France, South Africa, and the United States, and the British Association's meeting in Canada, and visited New Zealand and Egypt, where she was able to expand her collections. Johnston published notes on the geology of Spain, France, the Balearic Islands, and the volcanoes of New Zealand. She also published on the volcanoes of New Zealand (a ten-page paper in German), stromatoporoids, a Jurassic fish, and the Silurian stratigraphy of Shropshire.

Johnston was a woman who very well may have liked to become a professional geologist if the opportunity had been there. Since it was not, she contented herself with amateur status while comporting herself like a professional.   CK

PRIMARY SOURCES
Johnston, Mary Sophia. "Some Geological Notes on Central France." *Geological Magazine* 38 (1901): 59–65.
———. "On a . . . Jurassic Ganoid Fish." *Geological Magazine* 16 (1909): 309–311.
———. With M. C. Crosfield. "A Study of Ballstone and the Associated Beds in the Wenlock Limestone." *Proceedings of the Geologists' Association* 25 (1914): 193–228.
———. "On *Labechia rotunda,* a New Species of Stromatoporoid, from the Wenlock Limestone." *Geological Magazine* 2 (1915): 433–434.
———. "Geological Notes on Spain and Majorca." *Proceedings of the Liverpool Geological Society* (1927).

SECONDARY SOURCES
[Deighton, Thomas H.]. "Miss Mary Sophia Johnston." *Proceedings of the Geological Society of London,* no. 1529 (1955): 141–142.

L., A. L. "Mary Sophia Johnston." *Proceedings of the Geologists' Association* 67 (1956): 197–199.

STANDARD SOURCES
Sarjeant.

JOLIOT-CURIE, IRÈNE (1897–1956)

French physicist. Born 12 September 1897 in Paris, France to Marie Sklodowska Curie and Pierre Curie, physicists. One sibling. Married Frédéric Joliot. Two children, Hélène and Pierre. Educated at home; Collège Sévigné, Paris (baccalaureate, 1914); University of Paris (the Sorbonne; licencée, 1920; D.Sc., 1925). Professional experience: army nurse (1914–1918); Radium Institute, preparator (1918), assistant (1923), head of work (research) (1932), director (1946–1956); Under-Secretary of State for scientific research (1936); Sorbonne, professor (1937–1956); Commissioner for Atomic Energy (1946–1951). Honors and memberships: honorary doctorates from the Universities of Edinburg, Oslo, Sofia, New Delhi, Lublin, and Cracow; Medals of French Recognition and the Society of Civil Engineers, and the Joykissen Mokerjee gold medal; prizes from the Monaco Academy of Sciences and the Paris National Academy of Medicine. (With Frédéric Joliot-Curie) Nobel Prize, 1935; medals from Italian Society of Sciences, U.S. Academy of Sciences, Columbia University, and Paris Academy of Sciences; Henri-Wilde prize and Marquet prize, Paris Academy of Sciences. Died 17 March 1956 in Paris.

The eldest daughter of Nobel-prize-winning parents, Irène Curie grew up in an educated, unconventional home. Soon after Irène's birth, her widowed grandfather, Eugène Curie, moved into the home, where he helped to raise his granddaughter and served as her mentor until his death, in 1910. From him she took her lifelong socialist and anticlerical views. When Pierre Curie was killed in an accident in 1906, Marie Curie tried to keep the information from her children. Irène Curie grew up under the pall cast by her mother's chronic depression and ill health, without having been given the opportunity to grieve her father's death. After her grandfather's death, Irène Curie became increasingly attached to her mother, whom she admired greatly.

A believer in the beneficial effects of fresh air and physical exercise, Marie Curie arranged for Irène and her younger sister, Eve, to participate in various sports and outdoor activities. She ensured that they would learn Polish by hiring governesses from her native country. Dissatisfied with the public schools, Curie and some of her friends organized a floating cooperative school for their children. Here Irène was introduced to experimental physics and chemistry, received a broad educational foundation, and made lifelong friendships.

Irène Curie attended the Collège Sévigné, then continued her studies at the Sorbonne, earning a degree in physics and mathematics. During World War I, she volunteered at the front as an army nurse, where she worked with the mobile X-ray units organized by her mother.

After the war, Curie began working at the Radium Institute, under her mother's directorship, where she remained for the duration of her scientific career. When Frédéric Joliot entered the laboratory, Irène Curie introduced him to procedures used to study radioactivity. Although the shy, socially inept Curie and the charming, spirited Joliot seemed quite different externally, they shared deeply held values and interests. Curie and Joliot married in 1926. Their children Hélène (born in 1927) and Pierre (born in 1932) eventually chose careers in physics.

Although Joliot-Curie supported democratic and feminist political ideals throughout her life, she did not enjoy the political work necessary to implement them. During part of 1936, she served as France's under-secretary of state for scientific research, resigning after she found herself unsuited for the position. Joliot-Curie remained in Paris during the German occupation, attempting to preserve the Radium Institute's research and materials, but she did not become involved with the political activities that occupied her husband. As a member of the Resistance and of the Communist Party, Frédéric Joliot-Curie was forced to go underground in 1944, while his wife and children escaped to Switzerland.

Heavy exposure to radiation gradually eroded Joliot-Curie's health. After years of intermittent illness and increasing fatigue, she succumbed to leukemia in 1956.

Joliot-Curie was a member of the Polish Academy of Sciences, a corresponding member of the Belgian Royal Academy of Medicine and the U.S.S.R. and Berlin academies of science, and an honorary member of the Indian Academy of Sciences, the Indian Chemical Society, and the Grand Ducal Institute of Luxembourg. Although she applied several times to the French Academy of Sciences, she was refused admission because of her sex.

Joliot-Curie's early research concerned radiations from radioactive substances, particularly the alpha rays of polonium, which became her doctoral topic. This interest continued throughout her career, and formed the departure for the Joliot-Curie collaboration, which contributed to four major discoveries in the thirties: the neutron, the positron, artificial radioactivity, and nuclear fission. Although the couple were disappointed by their failure to identify the neutron and the positron, their recognition in 1934 of artificial radioactivity (produced by alpha-ray bombardment of aluminum and boron) brought them worldwide renown. Within a remarkably short time they were awarded the Nobel Prize for chemistry, in 1935.

The discovery of artificial radioactivity led to experiments to determine whether neutrons would also produce this effect. Researchers expected the products to be heavier than uranium. Working with a student (Paul Savich), Joliot-Curie identified a short-lived product produced by neutron bom-

bardment of uranium which behaved like actinium, an element that is lighter than uranium. It was while trying to disprove this finding of Joliot-Curie and Savich that Otto Hahn and Fritz Strassmann, with input from their exiled partner Lise Meitner, realized that the radioactive products of neutron bombardment were fission products of uranium.

After the war, Joliot-Curie's investigations included applications of artificial radioactivity and of alpha rays. She published a practical text on the radioelements in 1946.   MM

PRIMARY SOURCES

Joliot-Curie, Irène. *Les radioéléments naturels: Propriétés chimiques, préparation, dosage.* Paris: Hermann, 1946.

Joliot-Curie, Frédéric et Irène. *Oeuvres scientifiques complètes.* Paris: Presses Universitaires de France, 1961.

Gillette Ziegler. *Correspondance. Choix de lettres, 1905–1934 [de] Marie [et] Irène Curie.* Paris: Editéurs Français Réunis, 1974.

SECONDARY SOURCES

Cotton, Eugénie. *Les Curies et la radioactivité.* Paris: Seghers, 1963.

Curie, Eve. *Madame Curie.* Trans. by Vincent Sheean. Garden City, N.Y.: Doubleday, Doran & Co., 1937.

McKown, Robin. *She Lived for Science: Iréne Joliot-Curie.* New York: Messner, 1961.

Pflaum, Rosalind. *Grand Obsession: Madame Curie and Her World.* New York: Doubleday, 1989.

Quinn, Susan. *Marie Curie: A Life.* New York: Simon and Schuster, 1995.

Reid, Robert. *Marie Curie.* New York: New American Library, 1974.

Wasson, Tyler, ed. *Nobel Prize Winners.* New York: H. W. Wilson Co., 1987.

STANDARD SOURCES

Creative Couples; DSB 7; Grinstein 1993; Kass-Simon and Farnes; McGrayne; *Notable;* Poggendorff, vol. 76; Rayner-Canham 1997 (article by E. Tina Crossfield).

JONAS, ANNA I. (1881–1974)

See Stose, Anna Isabel (Jonas).

JONES, AMANDA THEODOSIA (1835–1914)

U.S. inventor and spiritualist. Born 19 October 1835 in East Bloomfield, N.Y., to Mary Alma (Mott) and Henry Jones. Educated public schools; Buffalo High School; East Aurora (N.Y.) Academy; classes in education. Professional experience: country schoolteacher (1850– 1854); freelance writer; editor; patenter of oil burners (1880, 1904, 1912, 1914); Woman's Canning and Preserve Company, Chicago, co-founder (1890). Died 31 March 1914 in Brooklyn, N.Y. of influenza.

A convinced spiritualist as well as a poet, editor, and inventor, Amanda Theodosia began to teach in country schools in New York at the age of fifteen. She wrote poetry for various publications, including Frank Leslie's *Illustrated Newspaper*, from the age of twenty-five. She believed her actions were directed by her "spiritual guardian," and under this direction she moved to Chicago at the age of thirty-four, where she worked in an editorial capacity for a group of journals.

In her late thirties, Jones began to turn to invention, working with LeRoy Cooley of Albany, a relative by marriage of one of her sisters. Together they produced a patent for a vacuum canning process. In 1873, Jones was issued five further patents, some with Cooley and others in her own name. The Jones process (also termed the Pure Food Vacuum Preserving Process) became the standard canning process in the United States. Unable to found a canning company at the time, she was successful in founding the Woman's Canning and Preserving Company in Chicago some seventeen years later, an enterprise that had only women as stockholders. It was successful until 1921, but Jones was excluded from the board after 1893.

Meanwhile, convinced her psychic abilities were urging her to continue in a new field, she developed a new method for heating furnaces with an oil burner, for which she obtained a patent in 1880. While in the oil fields of Pennsylvania, she founded a working women's home in Bradford. She was unable to finance her invention, but later described it in articles for *Engineering and Steam Engineering* in the early twentieth century, obtaining further patents during those years.

Jones also returned to her canning experiments, and obtained further patents for canning, for a vacuum process of food drying, and for an easy-opening tin can. At the same time, she published poetry and short articles in *Century Magazine* and other journals while living with one of her sisters. She also published collected books of poetry. At the age of sixty-five, she published an autobiography detailing her psychic as well as her practical life, a story that William James, in his role as an officer of the Society for Psychical Research, had encouraged her to tell. She died of influenza in her apartment in Brooklyn at the age of seventy-eight, and was buried in the same plot with her brother in Cleveland, Ohio.

JH/MBO

PRIMARY SOURCES

Jones, Amanda Theodosia. *A Psychic Autobiography*. New York: Greaves, [ca. 1910].

STANDARD SOURCES

Mothers and Daughters; NAW (article by Mary Tolford Wilson); *Woman's Who's Who of America*.

JONES, EVA ELIZABETH (1898–?)

U.S. comparative pathologist and zoologist. Born 12 September 1898, in Ottawa, Kans., to Mary (Redmond) and Edward Archbold Jones. Educated Radcliffe College (A.B., 1920; Ph.D., 1930); University of Maine (M.A., 1924). Professional experience: Cold Springs Harbor, Station for Experimental Evolution, research fellow (1920–1922); University of Maine, instructor (1924–1925); Radcliffe College (Harvard University), research assistant (1926–1927), fellow (1927–1928), departmental research fellow (1930–1934); Wellesley College, faculty (1934–1949), professor of zoology (1949–1964), emerita professor (from 1964); Simmons College, instructor (1936–1937). Concurrent experience: Free Hospital for Women, Brookline, Mass., researcher; Fearing Research Laboratory, research fellow (1934–1938); National Cancer Institute, special research fellow (1947–1948; 1955–1956); Children's Cancer Research Foundation, researcher (from 1964). Honors and memberships: Wellesley College Harbison Award (1956–1957); American Association for the Advancement of Science, Fellow; Phi Beta Kappa member; Sigma Xi member.

Born in Kansas, Eva Elizabeth Jones was educated at Radcliffe College, graduating in 1920. She was encouraged to continue her studies in zoology at Cold Spring Harbor, in the laboratory for experimental evolution, where she worked as an assistant from 1920 to 1922. At that point, she moved to the University of Maine, where Raymond Pearl and ALICE BORING were on the faculty. She served as an instructor in the Maine Department of Zoology for a year after she received her master's degree, studying parasitic diseases in birds, and then returned again to Cambridge, Massachusetts, to pursue a doctoral degree at Radcliffe College in the biology laboratories of Harvard University. She wrote her thesis on coccidiosis (a fungal disease) in chickens, obtaining research fellowships from the college and the department during this period and for four years following the award of her degree (1930–1934).

At the age of thirty-six, Jones began to teach zoology at Wellesley College, where she remained for the rest of her professional teaching career, except for a year (1936–1937) when she taught at Simmons College in Boston. In the thirties, Jones became interested in cancer, and held a research appointment concurrently during those early teaching years in the Fearing Research Laboratory at the Woman's Free Hospital in Brookline, Massachusetts. In the 1940s, she did research with the National Cancer Institute, where she did experimental studies on cancer in mice. She was made full professor of zoology in 1949, and served as chair of her department from 1949 to 1955, retiring from Wellesley in 1964 at the age of sixty-six, when she was named an emerita professor.

After her retirement, Jones's research continued. She was a research associate of the Children's Cancer Fund from 1964 until after 1968, with an office and laboratory in the Jimmy Fund Building.   JH/MBO

PRIMARY SOURCES

Jones, Eva Elizabeth, "Size as a Species Characteristic in Coccidia: Variation under Diverse Conditions of Infection." Ph.D. diss., Radcliffe College, 1930.

STANDARD SOURCES

AMS 4–8, B 9, P&B 10–12; Debus.

JONES, KATHARINE, VISCOUNTESS RANELAGH (1613–1691)

British learned lady. Born in Cork, Ireland, to Katharine (Fenton) and Richard Boyle, first Earl of Cork. Thirteen siblings. Sister of scientist Robert Boyle. Married Arthur Jones (later Viscount Ranelagh) in 1630. Three daughters; one son. Educated privately in languages and philosophy (including Hebrew). Hired Henry Oldenberg (Secretary of the Royal Society) and John Milton to tutor her son. Professional experience: built experimental laboratory for her brother, Robert Boyle (1668). Died 23 December 1691 in London.

Katharine Jones, Viscountess Ranelagh, was an unusual woman of intellect and spirit, who supported many of the scientists of her era. Born in Youghal, Ireland, she married at the age of seventeen and had four children, but seems to have lived apart from her drunken husband after the birth of their son, moving to London in 1641. In her London home in Pall Mall, she provided a center for an unusual group of Irish Protestants and scientific figures. She hired both the poet John Milton and the German emigré scientist Henry Oldenberg to tutor her son. She also became interested in contemporary scientific and philosophical debates, serving as a patron to individuals like Benjamin Worsley, Samuel Hartlib, John Dury, and others. She was a supporter of the Parliament during the 1640s, but also interceded on behalf of her Royalist friends. After the Restoration of Charles II, she successfully appealed to the court for moderation toward nonconformists, such as some of the Quakers in her circle.

One of her most important influences was on her younger brother, Robert, who became an eminent scientist and a significant member of the Royal Society of London. Henry Oldenberg was secretary of this society. Boyle later dedicated one of his collections of occasional pieces to her as "Sophonia, my dearest sister." She had welcomed him often to her house in London in the 1640s and visited him in Oxford in the 1650s. She built a laboratory for Boyle in her house in 1668 after he left Oxford, and he continued to carry out important experiments. When she died in 1691, he wrote her eulogy, calling her one of the great women of the age. His claim that her death had broken his heart was verified by his own death one week later. The brother and sister were buried near each other in the chancel of St. Martin's in the Fields.   JH/MBO

SECONDARY SOURCES

Maddison, R. E. W. *Life of the Honourable Robert Boyle.* London: Taylor and Francis, 1969.

Masson, Flora. *Robert Boyle: A Biography.* London: Constable & Company, 1914. Includes a number of quotations from Katharine Jones's letters to Boyle.

Webster, Charles. *The Great Instauration. Science, Medicine and Reform.* New York: Holmes & Meier, 1975.

STANDARD SOURCES

Europa.

JONES, LORELLA MARGARET (1943–1995)

U.S. physicist. Born Toronto, Ontario, 22 February 1943 to F. Shirley (Patterson) and Donald Cecil Jones. Educated Radcliffe College (A.B., 1964); California Institute of Technology (M.Sc., 1966; Ph.D., 1968). Professional experience: postdoctoral fellow and instructor (1967–1968); University of Illinois, Urbana, assistant professor (1968–1970), associate professor (1970–1978), professor (1978–1995). Honors and memberships: American Physics Society (division of particles and fields), Fellow; American Associaton of University Professors, chapter president (1989–1991). Died Livermore, Calif., 9 February 1995.

Lorella Margaret Jones was born in Canada during World War II, and came with her parents to the United States during the postwar period when she was three years old. She was educated at Radcliffe College, Harvard University, and went from there to California Institute of Technology, where she studied physics for both her master's and doctoral degrees. She went to teach physics at the University of Illinois, Urbana, in the late sixties and remained there, rising to full professor at the young age of thirty-five. Her research centered on particles and fields. She developed educational physics software and was a Fellow of the American Physics Society. She died at Livermore, California, just before her fifty-second birthday.   JH/MBO

PRIMARY SOURCES

Jones, Lorella M. *An Introduction to Mathematical Methods of Physics.* Menlo Park, Calif.: Benjamin/Cummings, 1979.

———. With Dennis J. Kane. "Student Evaluation of Computer-Based Instruction in a Large University mechanics Course." *American Journal of Physics* 62 (1994): 832–836.

STANDARD SOURCES

WWW(A), vol. II, 1993–1996.

JONES, MARY AMANDA DIXON (1828?–1908)

U.S. physician and gynecologist. Married John Quincy Adams Jones, a Maryland lawyer (separated late 1870s?). Three children. Educated New York Hygeio-Therapeutic College (M.D., 1862); preceptorship (three months) with Mary Putnam Jacobi (1873); Woman's Medical College of Pennsylvania, completed course (1875); Post-Graduate Medical School and Hospital in New York City (training in gynecology). Professional experience: practiced privately in Brooklyn (1862–1872); Women's Dispensary and Hospital of Brooklyn, chief medical officer (from 1882). Died 1908.

Mary Amanda Dixon was born around 1828 and apparently received the standard education for females of her day, which would include classical languages, literature, some basic mathematics, and natural and physical sciences. She married John Quincy Adams Jones, a Maryland lawyer, and bore three children. She and her husband later separated. She taught courses in physiology at various female seminaries then entered the New York Hygeio-Therapeutic College, from which she received a medical degree in 1862. She practiced medicine privately in Brooklyn for a decade and during that time became interested in women's diseases and the "new" field of gynecology. Seeking surgical training, Jones passed a three-month preceptorship with MARY PUTNAM JACOBI in New York in 1873 and completed a course of study at Woman's Medical College of Pennsylvania in 1875. She spent the next year studying pathology with Charles Heitzman, and developed great proficiency in microscopic analysis. Her postgraduate surgical training was received at the Post-Graduate Medical School and Hospital in New York City, following which she became the chief medical officer with the Women's Dispensary and Hospital of Brooklyn (1882).

During all this, she successfully raised her three children. Charles Dixon Jones received his medical degree and became his mother's colleague and surgical assistant. Her second son became an Episcopal minister after graduating from Harvard in 1881; her daughter unfortunately died in her twenties.

Amanda Jones was active in coediting or guest editing the mainstream medical periodicals of her time, such as *Philadelphia Times and Register* (weekly), *Woman's Medical Journal,* and *American Journal of Surgery and Gynecology.* She wrote articles for the *Medical Record,* the *New York Medical Journal, American Journal of Obstetrics and Diseases of Women and Children, Buffalo Medical Surgical Journal, Annals of Gynecology and Pediatry,* and also for the *British Gynaecological Journal.*

In 1892, Jones sued the Brooklyn *Eagle* newspaper for libel after the paper ran a series of articles hinting at financial improprieties at her Brooklyn hospital and implying medical irresponsibility in forcing "unnecessary operations on unsuspecting women." Jones was by then a nationally known

ovariotomist; a "pioneer whose operative innovations and contributions to the cellular pathology of the female reproductive system were known to, and taken seriously by, male colleagues in the United States and abroad" (Morantz-Sanchez, 542–543). She lost her suit, had to close the hospital in Brooklyn, and devoted the rest of her career (she was sixty-four) to her microscopical studies in pathology.   K M

SECONDARY SOURCES

Morantz-Sanchez, Regina. "Surgical Career of Mary Amanda Dixon Jones." *Bulletin of the History of Medicine* 69, no. 4 (Winter 1995): 542–568.

Physicians and Surgeons of America: A Collection of Biographical Sketches of the Regular Medical Profession. Ed. Irving A. Watson. Concord, N.H.: Republican Press, 1896.

JONES, MARY COVER (1896–1987)

U.S. psychologist. Born 1 September 1896 in Johnstown, Pa. Married (1920) psychologist Harold Ellis Jones (1894–1960). Two daughters. Educated Vassar College; Columbia University (M.A., 1920; Ph.D. in psychology, 1926); Laura Spelman Rockefeller Fellow (1921–1923). Professional experience: Columbia University, research associate in child development (1922–1926); National Research Fellow in Child Development (1925–1927); Institute of Child Welfare, University of California, research associate; California State Department of Education (1927); University of California, Berkeley, research associate, Institute of Human Development (1927–1960), assistant professor (1952–1955), associate professor (1955–1959), professor (1959–1960), emerita research associate in child development (1960–1987), private consultant in developmental psychology (1969–1987); Stanford University, research associate in psychology (1961–1965). Died 22 July 1987 in Santa Barbara, Calif.

Mary Cover's career choices, like those of many other professional women of her era, were often based on a strong belief in woman's primary responsibility to husband and family. Throughout a pioneering professional career that produced major scholarly achievements on several fronts, she maintained the traditionally feminine attributes of warmth, nurturance, and affiliation. Her devotion to Harold Jones (including support of his career goals) and her two daughters probably retarded her rate of advancement and undoubtedly influenced her choice of appointments, but she never saw them as negative or as compromising her career satisfaction.

After a rather slow start at Vassar College (where MARGARET FLOY WASHBURN taught psychology), she became intrigued with the possibilities of conditioned learning after hearing a lecture by John B. Watson, which described an experiment in which a child was conditioned to fear. Mary Cover perceived the same approach might be used to remove fear and began her landmark thinking and research in positive conditioning. She entered Columbia University in 1919, and received her master's in 1920. That same year she met and married Harold Ellis Jones, a fellow student of psychology at Columbia. Within six years they had two daughters, Barbara and Lesley. While in graduate school, Mary Cover began looking at methods of developmental conditioning and worked under the guidance of John Watson to conduct and publish a study on behavioral therapy as a means of deconditioning fear *(The Case of Peter)*, which established her reputation as a developmental psychologist. Juggling family and coursework, Mary Jones finished her doctoral requirements in 1926. Her dissertation concerned research on the development of behavior patterns, such as visual pursuit, during infancy.

When Harold Jones was offered a position at Berkeley as director of research in 1927, Mary Jones took the position offered to her as research associate. Soon she was involved in setting up the nursery school for child development studies. NANCY BAYLEY and Jean Macfarlane were hired as administrators of the first two longitudinal studies, the Berkeley Growth Study and the Berkeley Guidance Study. In 1932, Mary and Harold Jones together designed the third longitudinal study (Oakland Growth Studies), whose years of carefully documented data have spawned many research projects on aspects of behavior resulting from developmental factors. Jones herself published over one hundred articles based on the longitudinal data. Among these is a highly regarded series of studies on the behavioral correlates and long-term consequences of early and late physical maturing.

Mary Jones became a lecturer in the Department of Psychology at the University of California, Berkeley, in 1946, was appointed assistant professor of education in 1956, and became full professor in 1959. The same warmth and enthusiasm that enabled her to bond closely with her longitudinal subjects made her a popular and stimulating teacher; both Mary and Harold were noted for their innovative classroom methods and supportive encouragement of their students. Together they produced the first television course on developmental psychology.

Harold Ellis Jones died in 1960, shortly after the couple retired. The loss of the primary person in both her personal and professional lives could have been devastating, but Jones's courage and affiliative abilities enabled her to enter a new phase of productive work to offset her grief. For the next four years she joined Nevitt Sanford at Stanford University at the Institute for the Study of Human Problems in a study of alcohol problems. She was able to combine data collected during the Oakland Growth Study with the Stanford research to discern patterns of personality exhibited before the onset of drinking problems. She remained involved with the Institute of Human Development as consultant to the Intergenerational Studies into her eighties.

Mary Cover Jones received many awards including the G. Stanley Hall Award of the American Psychological Association Developmental Psychology Division (1968) and the Fortieth Anniversary Award from the Institute of Human Development, University of California, Berkeley (1969). She was an active member and fellow of the American Psychological Association, the Society for Research in Child Development; and the Geront Society. She died 22 July 1987 in Santa Barbara, California, having worked on the Oakland Growth Study, lectured, and counseled until her last few months.

KM

PRIMARY SOURCES

Jones, Mary Cover. *The Development of Early Behavior Patterns in Young Children.* New York: 1926.

———. *A Laboratory Study of Fear: The Case of Peter.* N.p., 1929.

———. "The Nursery School in Relation to the Health of the Pre-school Child." *Hospital Social Service* 21 (1930): 142–148.

———. With Barbara Stoddard Burks. *Personality Development in Childhood: A Survey of Problems, Methods and Experimental Findings.* Washington, D.C.: Society for Research in Child Development, National Research Council, 1936.

———. With Nancy Bayley. "Physical Maturing among Boys as Related to Behavior." *Journal of Educational Psychology* 41 (1950): 129–148.

———. "Personality Correlates and Antecedents of Drinking Patterns in Adult Males." *Journal of Consulting and Clinical Psychology* 32, no. 1 (1968): 2–12.

———. "Personality Correlates and Antecedents of Drinking Patterns in Women." *Journal of Consulting and Clinical Psychology* 36, no. 1 (1971): 61–69.

———, ed. With others. *The Course of Human Development: Selected Papers from the Longitudinal Studies.* Waltham, Mass.: Xerox, [1971].

SECONDARY SOURCES

Eichorn, Dorothy and Paul Mussen. "Mary Cover Jones (1896–1987)." *American Psychologist* (October 1988): 818.

STANDARD SOURCES

AMS 5–8, S&B 9, 10, 11 (suppl. 1), 12–13; O'Connell and Russo 1990 (article by Deana Dorman Logan); *Psychological Register*, vol. 2.

JORDAN, LOUISE (1908–1966)

U.S. geologist. Born 3 January 1908 in Joplin, Mo., to Anna and Fred A. Jordan. Never married. Educated Port Henry, N.Y., High School (graduated 1925); Wellesley College (B.A., 1929); MIT (M.S., 1931; Ph.D., 1939). Professional experience: American College for Girls, Instanbul, Turkey, instructor (1931–1933); Maden Tetkik ve Arama Enstitüsü, researcher (1935–1938);

Anzac Oil Company, researcher (1938–1941); Sun Oil Company (1941–1950); Florida Geological Survey, researcher (1950–1951); private consulting geologist (1951–1955); Oklahoma Geological Survey, researcher (1955–1966). Died 22 November 1966 in Oklahoma City.

Louise Jordan's father was a mining engineer, and a frequent traveler who took his family with him. Thus, Louise was introduced early to different parts of the world. She graduated from high school at Port Henry, New York, and then attended Wellesley College, where she received a bachelor's degree in geology and chemistry in 1929. She then earned a master of science degree at MIT in 1931. At this time, she took a position teaching physics at the American College for Girls in Instanbul, Turkey. She returned to the United States in 1933 and became a part-time instructor in geology and geography at Mount Holyoke College while she was working on her doctoral dissertation.

In 1935, Jordan returned to Turkey, where she worked as a stratigrapher and micropaleontologist for the Turkish government. She returned to the United States in 1938 and worked as a geologist with the Anzac Oil Company at Coleman, Texas. She received her doctoral degree from MIT in 1939 for her dissertation "A Study of the Miocene Foraminifera from Jamaica, the Dominican Republic, the Republics of Panama, Costa Rica and Haiti." She was micropaleontologist and stratigrapher for nine years with the Sun Oil Company. From 1950 until 1955, she was a consulting geologist. In 1955 she joined the Oklahoma Geological Survey staff at the University of Oklahoma, Norman, where she remained until her death.

Jordan had two distinct sides to her personality. On first acquaintance, colleagues found her somewhat forbidding, but on later encounters, she would appear to be a warm, gracious person. She demanded academic rigor, insisted on what she considered to be "objectivity," and constantly worked to ensure the accuracy of her own work and that of her students. Shoddy workmanship was not tolerated, and she was blunt in expressing her opinions to those who had not done their best work. As she directed the work of many graduate students, they found her a demanding dissertation advisor, but one who became as involved in the project as the students themselves. She died after a long and painful illness in 1966.

Jordan was involved in geological societies at both the local and national level. She was the fourteenth recipient of honorary membership in the Oklahoma City Geological Society, and was a member of both the American Association of Petroleum Geologists and the Society of Economic Paleontologists and Mineralogists. In 1963, she became a charter member of the American Institute of Professional Geologists and of the Oklahoma Section of the National Association of Geology Teachers, and was chairman of the Eighth and Ninth Biennial Geological Symposia held at the University of Oklahoma in 1963 and 1966. She also attended many international conferences.   CK

SECONDARY SOURCES
[Nicholson, Alexander]. "Louise Jordan, 1908–1966." *Oklahoma Geology Notes* (1967): 3–8. Includes portrait.
Nicholson, Alexander. "Louise Jordan, 1908–1966." *The American Association of Petroleum Geologists Bulletin* 52, no. 10 (October 1968): 2058–2059. Includes portrait.

JORDAN, SARA CLAUDIA (MURRAY) (1884–1959)

U.S. physician, specializing in gastroenterology. Born 20 October 1884 in Newton, Mass., to Marla (Stuart) and Patrick Andrew Murray. Married (1) Sebastian Jordan (14 January 1913; divorced 1921); (2) Penfield Mowrer (1935). One daughter by Jordan, Mary. Educated Newton public schools; Radcliffe College (A.B., 1904); University of Munich (Ph.D. in classical philology, 1908); Tufts Medical School (M.D., 1921). Professional experience: Worcester Memorial Hospital, intern (1922); Adelphi Academy, teacher (1911–1912); Lahey Clinic, head of gastroenterology (1923–1958); private and group practice, Boston (1922–1958). Honors and memberships: Editorial Board Chair, Gastroenterology (1956–1958); Smith College, honorary D.Sc. (1945?); Tufts College, honorary D.Sc. (1956); Jane Addams Medal (1952); Gastroenterology Association, Julius Friedenwald Medal (1952); Gastroenterology Association, president (1943–1944); American College of Physicians, Fellow. Died 21 November 1959 of cancer of the colon in New England Baptist Hospital, Boston, Mass.

Sara Murray Jordan, well known as a gastroenterologist at the Lahey Clinic, began her education with a Munich doctorate in classical philology. She met and married a young German while studying abroad, but after the birth of her daughter, she returned to the United States. After a lengthy separation during World War I, they were divorced. Soon after returning to the United States, Jordan entered Tufts Medical School to study medicine, although she was thirty-three at the time. She graduated at the top of her class, having impressed the young Frank H. Lahey, with whom she wrote her first paper on a new test of thyroid function. At his suggestion, she did her residency in Chicago, where she worked under Bertram Sippey, a specialist in gastroenterology.

On her return to Boston, Jordan joined Lahey and an unusual group of other doctors to begin a new kind of group practice, while also holding down her own private practice in her home in Brookline where she was raising her young daughter. She moved to the new Lahey Clinic in 1926 when the clinic opened its own building, and remained there as an important authority on diseases of the gastrointestinal tract.

She recommended a conservative approach to peptic ulcers and other stress-related diseases, emphasizing rest, recreation, and dietary changes rather than surgery. She was urged to write a popular book, *Good Food for Bad Stomachs* with Sheila Hibben, the culinary expert at *The New Yorker,* after the well-known editor, Harold Ross, became her patient. She was widely praised for her medical knowledge and received both medical and popular awards for her work, including a number of honorary degrees. On her retirement, Jordan began to write a popular syndicated column, "Health and Happiness," but within a year she diagnosed her own cancer of the colon and died of the disease in one of the three hospitals at which she worked in Boston.   KM

PRIMARY SOURCES
Jordan, Sara M. With Frank H. Lahey. "Basal Metabolism as an Index of Treatment in the Diagnosis of Thyroid Disease." *Boston Surgical and Medical Journal* (1921): 348–358.
———. With Sheila Hibben. *Good Food for Bad Stomachs.* New York: Doubleday, 1951.
———. "The Woman Doctor Today." *Radcliffe Quarterly* (August 1954): 27–29.

SECONDARY SOURCES
Boston Globe, 22 November 1959.
New York Times, 22 November 1959.

STANDARD SOURCES
NAW(M) (article by Barbara Gutmann Rosenkrantz); *WWW(A),* vol. 3, 1951–1960.

JORDAN-LLOYD, DOROTHY (1889–1946)
British biochemist. Born 1 May 1889 in Birmingham to Marian Hampson (Simpson) and George Jordan-Lloyd. Three siblings. Educated King Edward VI High School, Birmingham; Cambridge University, Newnham College (Natural Science Tripos, Part I, class 1, 1910; Part II, class 1, 1912; fellow, 1913–1921; M.A., 1925); London University (B.Sc., 1910; D.Sc., 1916). Professional experience: Medical Research Committee (later Council), bacteriologist (1914–1920); British Leather Manufacturers Federation, staff, then director (1921–1928). Honors and memberships: Bathurst Student (scholarship) Newnham (1912–1914); Royal Institute of Chemists, vice-president; Tanners' Council of America, Fraser Moffat Muir Medal (1939). Died 21 November 1946.

Dorothy Jordan-Lloyd was educated at a girls' high school in Birmingham, and went from there to Newnham College, Cambridge, on a Bathurst student scholarship. At Newnham she studied for the Natural Science Tripos, and received first-class honors. She was a Newnham College Fellow for some years while also studying for a London University

bachelor's and doctorate of science. Women could earn degrees at London, whereas they could not get an official degree from Cambridge until much later. During World War I, she worked for the Medical Research Committee as a bacteriologist and later joined the British Leather Manufacturers Federation as a scientist and then as a director. Jordan-Lloyd published an important book on the chemistry of the proteins in leather, a publication that later earned her the Fraser Muir Moffat Medal awarded by the Tanners' Council of America for distinguished contributions to leather chemistry. She served as the vice-president of the Royal Institute of Chemists. In addition to her scientific interests, she was a mountain climber and an excellent horsewoman.   JH/MBO

PRIMARY SOURCES
Jordan-Lloyd, Dorothy. *The Chemistry of the Proteins.* Philadelphia: Blakiston's Son, 1926.
———. "The Problem of Gel Structure." In *Colloid Chemistry,* ed. J. Alexander. New York: Chemical Catalog Company, 1926.
———. "The Proteins." In *Recent Advances in Analytical Chemistry,* vol. 1, ed. C. A. Mitchell. Philadelphia: Blakiston's Son, 1930.
———. Planned and contributed to *Progress in Leather Science 1920–1945.* 3 vols. London: British Leather Manufacturers' Research Association, 1946–1948.

STANDARD SOURCES
Europa; Newnham, vol. 1.

JOSLIN, LULU BROADBENT (1883–?)
U.S. physicist. Born 12 October 1883 in Attleboro, Mass. Educated Brown University (A.B., 1905; A.M., 1906). Professional experience: Smith College, assistant in physics (1907–1909); Goucher College, instructor (from 1909). Death date unknown.

Lulu Joslin's name appears in only the second edition of *American Men of Science.* Although she was still teaching at Goucher when this edition was produced, it is not known whether she pursued her teaching and research. She was an associate member of the Physical Society. She studied nucleation and ionization of the atmosphere of Providence, Rhode Island.

JH/MBO

STANDARD SOURCES
AMS 2.

JOSSELYN, IRENE (MILLIKEN) (1904–1978)
U.S. psychiatrist. Born 19 January 1904 in La Grange, Ill., to Hattie (Fagersten) and Orris J. Milliken. Married (1) Livingston Josselyn (29 August 1931; he died in April 1957); (2) Eugene F.

Englehard (27 October 1960). One daughter. Educated Rockford College (B.A., 1925); Smith College (M.S., 1926); University of Chicago (M.D., 1934); Chicago Institute for Psychoanalysis (post-graduate work, 1941–1945). Professional experience: Women and Children's Hospital, Chicago, intern (1934); Institute for Juvenile Research and Psychiatric and Neurological Institute of Illinois, resident (1935–1936); University of Illinois, College of Medicine, faculty (1938–1939); University of Chicago, School of Social Service Administration (1948–1949); Chicago Institute of Psychoanalysis (1950–1961); committee on child analysis, and training and medical director child care course (1957–1960); Herrick House, consulting psychiatrist (1941–1959); Michael Reese Hospital, Chicago, psychiatric administrator and researcher (1959–1961); Southern California Psychoanalytic Institute, analyst (from 1962); Arizona State University School of Social Work, Phoenix (from 1963); University of Southern California, Los Angeles, clinical professor of child psychiatry (from 1964).

Psychiatrist Irene Josselyn had an exceptionally busy career holding several positions concurrently. Her research interests were in child psychiatry, psychosomatic illnesses in children, and the psychological effects of chronic illness. She held a diploma from the American Board of Psychiatrists and Neurologists (1959), was a member of the American Medical Association, the Psychoanalytic Association, the Psychiatric Association, and the Academy of Child Psychiatrists. She was editor of the journal of the American Academy of Child Psychiatrists. In addition to her books, she published extensively on adolescent problems, working mothers, unwed mothers, and the role of parents.   KM

PRIMARY SOURCES
Josselyn, Irene Milliken. *Psychosocial Development of Children.*
    New York: Family Service Association of America, [1948].
————. *The Adolescent and His World.* New York: Family Service Association of America, 1952.
————. *The Happy Child.* New York: Random House, 1955.

STANDARD SOURCES
AMS P&B 10, 11; Debus.

JOTEYKO, JOSÉPHINE (1866–1929)

*Polish experimental physiologist. Born 29 January 1866 in Pocsu-jki near Kiev, Poland. Educated Varsovie secondary school (baccalaureate); University of Geneva (science studies); Brussels Faculty of Medicine; University of Paris, Faculty of Medicine (M.D., 1896). Professional experience: Brussels, Institute Solvay, experimental physiologist (1897–1903); Université Libre of Brussels, Kasimir Laboratory of Psychology, head of work (research) (1903–1921); Revue psychologique, Brussels, editor (1908). Concurrent experience: Collège de France, lecturer (1916); University of Paris, Sor-*bonne, lecturer (1917–1918); Université de Lyon, lecturer (summer 1917; 1918); Faculté internationale de pédologie, Brussels, founder (1912); Warsaw, Poland, laboratory of psychophysics, researcher (1921–1929). Honors and memberships: Académie des Sciences, Paris, laureate; Académie Royale de Médecine, Brussels, laureate; Association des Chemistes de sucrérie de Frances et des Colonies, gold medal (1905); Société Royale des Sciences Médicales et Naturelles, Brussels, laureate and corresponding member; Société Belge de Neurologie, vice-president (1904–1905), president (1905–1906); Philosophical Society of Lwow (Poland). Died 1929 in Warsaw, Poland.

Josephine Joteyko was born near Kiev on a large property, but her family moved to Warsaw when she was a little girl to provide her with a good education. There she was educated up to the level of the baccalaureate (her secondary school training). She then went to Geneva, where she began her university education, specializing in science. From Geneva she went to Brussels to begin her medical training. In the late nineteenth century, Brussels provided some of the best background for both biological and physiological training.

After a year in Brussels, Joteyko moved to the Medical School in Paris, where the anatomy and physiology of the nervous system was taught by major figures. She studied with the physiologist Charles Richet, completing her thesis on the physiology of muscle fatigue in 1896. After finishing her degree, she returned to Brussels, where she accepted a position at the Institute Solvay. She then served as the head of the psychophysiological laboratory and lectured at the Free University of Brussels (Université Libre). She remained at this institute for over fifteen years, studying muscular contraction, electrophysiology. Publishing regularly with other physiologists, her work included some volumes published with M. Stevanowska on pain. Her articles appeared in important French and Belgian journals and won her awards from the Academy of Sciences of Paris and the Royal Academy of Medicine in Brussels. She also studied the effect of various chemical substances on muscles, earning a gold medal for her work.

Becoming interested in vegetarianism, Joteyko did some research on the effect of a vegetarian diet on work, a study that MÉLANIE LIPINSKA, her compatriot, used in connection with her clinical studies on vegetarianism and intellectual work. She participated regularly at conferences throughout the French-speaking world, and edited the *Revue psychophysique* in Brussels for some years. During this period she also collaborated on Richet's *Dictionary of Physiology*, and wrote for many other psychological journals and reviews. During World War I, Joteyko gave lectures in Paris and Lyon, which were published in a series of books on work fatigue. In Brussels she also founded a pedagogical institute, the Faculté Internationale de Pédologie (*sic*).

When Poland became an independent country in 1921, Joteyko decided to return to Warsaw and throw herself into the reestablishment of teaching and science in her native country. She lived very simply, establishing a small laboratory in Warsaw, and began to assist with pedagogy in Poland. There she was visited by some of her famous teachers and colleagues, including Charles Richet and her friend and countrywoman Lipinska, but died in comparative poverty.

JH/MBO

PRIMARY SOURCES

Joteyko, Josephine. "Fatigue musculaire." Faculté de Médecine, Paris, 1896. Medical thesis directed by Charles Richet.

———. *Education de la memoire et de l'attention.* Paris: Doin, 1909.

———. *Cours de pédologie: anthropométrie, psychologie expérimentale, Pédologie expérimentale.* 3 vols. Brussels: 1912.

———. *La science du travail et son organisation.* Paris: Alcan, 1917.

STANDARD SOURCES

Lipinska 1930.

JOYCE, MARGARET ELIZABETH (fl. 1900s)
Irish botanist. Married. Lived in St. Cleran's, Craughwell, County Galway.

Margaret Joyce collected plants in County Galway, Ireland. She was a correspondent of A. G. More.

JH/MBO

SECONDARY SOURCES

Moffat, C. B. (ed.). *Life and Letters of Alexander Goodman More.* Dublin: Hodges, Figgis & Co., 1898. Joyce discussed on pages 377–381.

Proceedings of the Royal Irish Academy 7 (1901): cxxv.

STANDARD SOURCES

Desmond.

JUHN, MARY (fl. 1923–1965)
Austrian/U.S. reproductive endocrinologist. Born Vienna, Austria; naturalized U.S. citizen. Married 1936. Educated Zurich University (B.Sc., 1916; Ph.D. in zoology, 1923). Professional experience: Whitman Laboratory for Experimental Zoology, Chicago, assistant (1923–1928), research associate (1928–1938); University of Maryland, associate research professor in poultry husbandry (1938–1945), research professor (1945–1965). Retired 1965.

Although Mary Juhn was born in Austria and educated in Switzerland, she immigrated to the United States and be-

came a naturalized citizen. She retired as research professor in 1965. She was a member of the American Association for the Advancement of Science, the Society of Zoologists, the Society for Experimental Biology, the Genetic Association, and the Association of Anatomy. She studied the embryology of reptiles and birds, hormones in birds, gradients and asymmetries in plumage, and plumages as indicators of hormonal and other states.

JH/MBO

STANDARD SOURCES

AMS 5–8, B 9, P&B 10–11.

JULIAN, HESTER FORBES (PENGELLY) (1865?–?)
British geology popularizer. Born in Torquay to Lydia (Spriggs) and William Pengelly, Fellow of the Royal Society (geologist). Educated private schools Torquay; Clevedon; Ladies' College, Cheltenham. Married Henry Forbes Julian 30 October 1902 (he died in 1912). Professional expereince: published biographies of both her father and her husband. Death date unknown.

Youngest daughter of her father's second marriage, Hester Pengelly was educated at private schools and in the renowned girls' secondary school, the Ladies' College, Cheltenham. She was very proud of having been taught mathematics and geology by her father, a well-known geologist, a Fellow of the Royal Society. Her father, much older than Hester Pengelly's mother, had married for the second time in the late 1850s. He had also founded the Devonshire Association and the Torquay Natural History Society, and after his death his Devonian fossil collection was presented to Oxford.

As a young woman, Hester Pengelly followed her father's extensive explorations of Devonshire caves with great interest. She was attracted to a young geologist, metallurgist Henry Forbes Julian, after her father's death, marrying him in 1902. She then began to assist her husband, traveling with him and the British Association for the Advancement of Science to South Africa and to the United States, where husband and wife examined geological collections. In 1909, the two traveled to Canada on the occasion of the joint Canadian and British Association at the University of Manitoba. Henry Forbes Julian was now a member of the British Association General Committee as well as of the Chemistry Section B and the Engineering Section G, and worked professionally as a consultant to Butters Corporation. In a number of regions of Canada, Julian's husband examined and debated the origin of various ores. They also viewed the glaciers in British Columbia and visited the fossil beds near Lake Louise, and he then visited mining centers in Canada and the United States.

During her husband's later absence to Canada and the United States, she attended sessions of the Royal Society, especially when her father's geological work was discussed, and sent copies of abstracts of other papers to her husband. Again they attended the British Association in Sheffield, and his wife took notes on the meetings. The decision to hold a meeting of the association in Australia in 1914 was enthusiastically seconded by Forbes Julian. Hester Julian gave talks at the Devonshire Association (primarily in reference to her father's work). In 1912, Forbes Julian died aboard the Titanic in another trip to America. Following his death, Hester Julian devoted herself to books memorializing both her father and her husband.   JH/MBO

PRIMARY SOURCES

Forbes, Hester. *A Memoir of William Pengelly.* London: Charles Griffin and Company; Philadelphia: J. B. Lippincott, 1897.

————. *Memorials of Henry Forbes Julian.* London: Charles Griffin and Company; Philadelphia: J. B. Lippincott, 1914.

SECONDARY SOURCES

Bricaud, Isabelle. *Saintes et pouliches.* Paris: Albin Michel, 1985.

JUSTIN, MARGARET M. (1889–1967)

U.S. home economist and nutritionist. Born 15 June 1889 in Agra, Kans. Never married. Educated Kansas State College (B.S., 1909); Columbia University (M.S., 1915); Yale University, Susan Rhoda Cutler Fellow and American Association of University Women Fellow (1922–1923; Ph.D., 1923). Professional experience: Bennett Academy, Mathison, Miss., settlement worker (1909–1913 or 1910–1914); Michigan State College, district leader home demonstration agents (1915–1918); YMCA Canteen Service overseas (1918–1919); School of Home Economics, Kansas State College, *dean (1923–1954), emerita dean (from 1954). Honors and memberships: American Association for the Advancement of Science, Fellow; Omicron Nu, past president; Fulbright to Holland as consultant in home economics. Died 10 June 1967 in Manhattan, Kans.*

Margaret M. Justin was best known as dean of the Kansas State College School of Home Economics. She was first educated at Kansas State. After receiving her bachelor's degree, she went to Mississippi as a settlement worker. Four years later, she returned to the Midwest, where she worked for four years as a home economics specialist while working toward a Columbia University master's degree. After working at the end of World War I with the YMCA's canteen service, Justin went to Yale to study home economics. On receiving her degree, she returned to Kansas State as dean of the School of Home Economics. She remained there for thirty years, except for a year when she traveled to Holland on a Fulbright as a consultant in home economics. In the forties and fifties, she published a series of popular books on home economics.   JH/MBO

PRIMARY SOURCES

Justin, Margaret. With L. O. Rust. *Problems in Home Living.* Philadelphia: J. B. Lippincott, [1929]. Rev. ed., 1953.

————. With L. F. Barker and L. O. Rust. *Our Share in the Home.* Chicago: J. B. Lippincott, [1945].

————. With L. O. Rust and G. Vail. *Foods.* New York: Mifflin, 1933.

STANDARD SOURCES

AMS 4–8, B 9, P&B 10; Rossiter 1982; *WWW(A)*, vol. 5, 1969–1973.

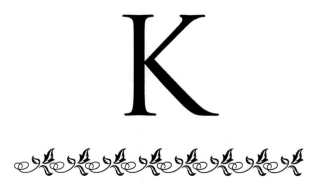

K

KAAN, HELEN WARTON (1897–?)

U.S. zoologist. Born 4 July 1897 in Brookline, Mass., to Mary Moore (Dunbar) and George Warton Kaan. Educated Mount Holyoke College (A.B., 1919); Yale University (Ph.D., 1925). Professional experience: Wheaton College, instructor (1919–1921, 1927–1928); Yale University, fellow (1921?–1925); New York University Medical School (Bellevue Hospital), staff (1925–1927); Wellesley College, department of zoology, assistant through associate professor (1927?–1944?). Death date unknown.

Helen Kaan was a U.S. zoologist who spent her entire life in the New England and New York area. She was born in Brookline, Massachusetts, and went from there to Mount Holyoke College. After receiving her undergraduate degree, she went to teach at Wheaton College and then obtained a fellowship at Yale that allowed her to earn her doctoral degree. In the mid-twenties, she worked for two years as an anatomist at Bellevue Hospital under the New York Medical School.

A few years after obtaining her doctoral degree, Kaan was appointed as an assistant professor at Wellesley College, where she rose through the ranks to associate professor of zoology. She was a member of the American Association of Anatomists and the American Association of University Women.   JH/MBO

STANDARD SOURCES
American Women; AMS 4–8, 89, P&B 10–11.

KABERRY, PHYLLIS MARY (1910–1977)

British anthropologist. Born 1910 in California of English parents. Educated University of Sydney (B.A., 1933; M.A, first class, 1935). University of London, London School of Economics (Ph.D., 1939). Field Work: Australia, Kimberley (1934–1936); New Guinea, Sepik River (Abelam) (1939–1941); Africa, Camaroons (Bamenda, Nbo) (1945–1946, 1947–1948, 1958, 1960,

1963). Professional experience: London School of Economics, research assistant (1936–1939); Sydney University, department of anthropology, honorary assistant lecturer (1940–1941); International Institute of International Affairs, researcher (1943–1945); International Research Institute, African research (1945–1946, 1947–1948); University of London, University College, department of anthropology, lecturer (1948–1950), reader (1951–1977), honorary reader (1977). Honors and memberships: Stirling International Fellowship (1941); Yale University Carnegie Fellowship (1942); Rivers Memorial Medal for fieldwork (1957); Liverhulme Fellowship (1958); Wellcome Medal for Applied Anthropology (with Sally Chilver) (1960). Died 30 November 1977 in London.

Phyllis Kaberry was an American-born British anthropologist, raised in Sydney, Australia. She was unusual in emphasizing, for her entire career, the important role of women in traditional societies, studying aboriginal Australia and women in Africa and New Guinea. She first studied at Sydney University with Raymond Firth, but A.P. Elkin suggested she study the position of Aboriginal women in the Kimberleys, where she spent eighteen months. She received her master's degree with first-class honors and then went to the London School of Economics where she worked as a research assistant for AUDREY RICHARDS. Her doctoral dissertation, under Bronislaw Malinowki, continued her work on women, appearing in book form the same year as *Aboriginal Women: Sacred and Profane.*

Kaberry was awarded a fellowship by the Australian National Research Council, to study the Abelam tribe of New Guinea, which was under Australian control. Given only an honorary teaching position at Sidney, she then obtained fellowships that sent her to Yale University to write up her field materials. She also collated and edited Malinowski's unpublished papers, following his death in 1942; the book appeared in the immediate postwar period. In 1943, wishing to do something for the war effort, she returned to London, to work at the Royal Institute of International Affairs at Chatham House doing research on colonial affairs, much as her former mentor Audrey Richards was doing.

Immediately following the war, Kaberry began to study the Bamenda people of the (British-controlled) Cameroons with support from the International African Institute and the colonial Nigerian government. The result was another important book, *Women of the Grassfields,* which discussed the control of women over the crops they produced. She also became a lecturer at University College, London, promoted to a readership by 1951. Although burdened by heavy teaching and administration responsibilities, Kaberry returned to the field following the award of two medals for her outstanding fieldwork and applied research, the Rivers Memorial Medal (1958) and the Wellcome Medal for Applied Anthropology (1960). With some additional small grants, she went back to study the Bamenda and collaborated extensively with E. M. (Sally) Chilver to develop a comparative study of political systems.

Kaberry's willingness to collaborate with other rising women anthropologists is shown by her coediting with Mary Douglas (also her former student) a volume of essays on Africa dedicated to Daryll Forde (*Man in Africa*). She retired from University College London as an honorary research fellow (1977), but her unexpected death cut short what promised to be an active period of retirement.

JH/MBO

PRIMARY SOURCES

Kaberry, Phyllis Mary. *Aboriginal Women: Sacred and Profane.* London: Routledge, 1939.

———. *Women of the Grassfields: Study of the Economic Position of Women in Bamenda, British Cameroons.* Colonial Research Publications no 14. London: Her Majesty's Stationery Office, 1952. Rep. 1969.

———. "Nsaw Political Conceptions." *Man* 59 (1959): 206.

———. With E.M. (Sally) Chilver. "From Tribute to Tax in a Tikar Chiefdom." *Africa* 30 (1960): 1–19. The first of twelve articles written in collaboration with Chilver over ten years.

———, ed. With Mary Douglas. *Man in Africa.* London: Tavistock.

SECONDARY SOURCES

Chilver, E. M. "Phyllis Kaberry." *Royal Anthropological Institute Newsletter (RAIN)* (1978): 24.

Firth, Raymond. "Phyllis Kaberry 1910–1977." *Africa* 48 (1978): 296–297.

STANDARD SOURCES

Gacs (article by Catherine H. Berndt); *IDA.*

KABLICK [KABLIKOVÁ], JOSEPHINE (ETTEL) (1787–1863)

Bohemian botanist and paleontologist. Born 9 March 1787 in Hohenhelbe, Bohemia. Father (?) Ettel. Married Adalbert Kablik (1806) in Hohenhelbe, Bohemia. Professional experience: Collected plants and made herbaria; collected fossil animals. Died 21 July 1863 in Hohenhelbe, Bohemia.

A collector akin to MARIA MERIAN, Josephine Kablick's reputation was widespread. Unlike Merian, however, she apparently did not publish anything nor was she known for her artistic ability. According to Mozans, she studied under "the best-known botanists of her time" (Mozans), but no details are available about her education. She collected plants enthusiastically, especially lichens, and compiled her own herbarium. Not only did she add to her own herbarium, she made plant collections for schools, colleges, museums, and learned societies. Kablick contributed over twenty-five thousand specimens to the Pflanzentausch-Anstalt of Opitz. She was known for her willingness to collaborate with individuals and institutions. Kablick's second interest was in paleontology. She collected fossil animals and plants, several of which are named after her. A vigorous, healthy woman, she was not deterred in her collecting by bad weather. Enjoying field work, Kablick would traipse through forest and climb high mountains in order to search for new species of plants and fossils. Apparently Kablick's husband, Adalbert Kablik, a pharmacologist and zoologist, was supportive of his wife's occupation. He, too, loved to study nature, and he and his wife collaborated on their natural history project for fifty years.

JH/MBO

SECONDARY SOURCES

Oesterreich Botanische Zeitschritt 10 (1860): 1–6. Includes portrait.

Oesterreich Botanische Zeitschritt 13 (1863): 206, 334, 337. Obituary notice.

STANDARD SOURCES

Barnhardt (as Kablik); Ireland; Mozans; Stafleu and Cowan (as Kablíková)

KACZOROWSKA, ZOFIA (1902–)

Polish geographer and climatologist. Educated University of Warsaw, Faculty of Natural Science and Mathematics (doctorate). Professional experience: Meteorological Office, Warsaw scientific worker (1932–1939); Academy of Agriculture, Warsaw, scientific assistant and adjunct instructor (1945–1951); Geographical Institute, University of Warsaw, adjunct and associate professor of climatology (from 1951).

Zofia Kaczorowska was educated at the University of Warsaw and remained in that city throughout her career. She began as a scientific worker and then as a scientific assistant and adjunct instructor at the Academy of Agriculture in Warsaw. She then became an adjunct and associate professor at the Department of Climatology of the Geographical Institute, University of Warsaw. She became head of the section on climate of Poland in the Geographical Institute's department of climatology.   JH/MBO

PRIMARY SOURCES
Kaczorowska, Zofia. "Przyczny meteorologiczne letniche wezbrán Wisly" (Meteorological Causes of the Summer Floods of the Vistula River). *Pracé PIM* 2, (Warsaw) 1933.
————. "Opady w. Polsce w przekroju wieloletnum" (Precipitation in Poland in long-period averages.) *Pracé Geograficzne no. 33 Instytut Geografii Polskiej Akademii Nauk.* (Warsaw) 1962.

STANDARD SOURCES
Turkevich and Turkevich.

KAHN, IDA (fl. 1890s)
Chinese physician. Educated University of Michigan (M.D., 1888?). Professional experience: mission hospital, Nanjing(?), China.

Like Mary Stone, with whom she was educated in medicine, Ida Kahn was a Chinese woman who came to the United States to study medicine at the University of Michigan. She returned to China to practice successfully in a mission hospital in Nanjing.   JH/MBO

SECONDARY SOURCES
Burton, M. E. *Notable Women of China.* New York: Fleming H. Revell, 1912.

STANDARD SOURCES
Hurd-Mead 1933; Lovejoy.

KALTENBEINER, VICTORINE (fl. 1777)
Swiss midwife. Lived in Lucerne. Professional positions: taught midwifery to both men and women in Lucerne. Translated textbook of Johan van Hoorn.

Little information is available on the Swiss midwife Victorine Kaltenbeiner. We do know that she taught midwifery to large coeducational classes in Lucerne using a textbook by the Swedish obstetrician Johan van Hoorn that she herself had translated. He was known for his successes in cases of version, face-presentation, and placenta praevia. Kaltenbeiner made annotations and additions to the text from her own experiences.   JH/MBO

PRIMARY SOURCES
Hoorn, Johan van. *Die zwei wohlbelohnten Wehemütter Siphra und Pua, oder Anleitung zur Hebammenkunst.* Trans. Victorine Kaltenbeiner. Lucerne, 1777. Includes Kaltenbeiner's annotations and additions to the text.

STANDARD SOURCES
Harless; Hurd-Mead 1938.

KANE, LADY KATHERINE SOPHIA (BAILY) (1811–1886)
Irish botanist. Born 11 March 1811. As Katherine Baily, first woman member of the Botanical Society of Edinburgh (1836). Married Sir Robert John Kane in 1838. Died 25 February 1886 in Dublin.

Lady Katherine Sophia Kane wrote an *Irish Flora* in 1833 with her gardener at Glasnevin, John White. The book was reissued in 1845. She also published on conifer cultivation in Ireland. Her husband, Sir Robert John Kane, was appointed by Sir Robert Peel to a commission to study the potato blight at the beginning of the Irish potato famine.   JH/MBO

PRIMARY SOURCES
[Kane, Katherine Sophia]. *The Irish Flora: Comprising the Phaenogamous Plants and Ferns.* Dublin: Hodges and Smith; London: Longman, Rees; Edinburgh: Maclachlan and Stewart, 1833. Rpt., 1845. Published anonymously. Assisted by John White.
Kane, Lady Katherine Sophia. [On conifer cultivation]. *Irish Farmer's and Gardener's Magazine* 1834.

SECONDARY SOURCES
Colgan, Nathaniel. *Flora County Dublin.* Dublin: Hodges, Figgis, 1904. Kane mentioned page xxvii.
Garden History 6 (1960): 41–42.
Scully, Reginald W. *Flora County Kerry.* Dublin: Hodges, Figgis, 1916. Kane mentioned page xiii.

STANDARD SOURCES
Desmond; *DNB;* Praeger.

KANOUSE, BESSIE BERNICE (1889–1969)
U.S. botanist. Born 21 November 1889, Quincy, Mich. Educated University of Michigan (B.A., 1922; M.S., 1923; Ph.D., 1926). Professional experience: Michigan Public Schools, teacher (1908–1912); Indiana Public Schools, teacher (1915–1918); New Jersey Public Schools, teacher (1917–1921); University of Michigan, herbarium assistant (1922–1923), assistant curator (1926–1928),

curator and assistant to director (1932–1955?). Honors and memberships: American Association for the Advancement of Science, Fellow; Sigma Xi, member; University of Michigan Women's Research Club, president. Died 1969.

Bessie Bernice Kanouse was raised and educated in Michigan. She spent her early professional years as a public school teacher and supervisor in Michigan, Indiana, and New Jersey. She returned to study at the Unversity of Michigan in her late twenties, continuing on to complete a doctorate at age thirty-seven. She began to work at the herbarium after she completed her undergraduate degree, remaining there as assistant curator. Following the award of her doctoral degree, she was made curator as well as assistant to the director of the university herbarium, with a research speciality in mycology.

JH/MBO

SECONDARY SOURCES
"Bessie Bernice Kanouse." *Michigan Botanist* 8 (1969): 187–188. Obituary notice.

STANDARD SOURCES
American Women 1974.

KARAMIHAILOVA, ELIZABETH/ELIZAVETA [KARA-MICHAILOVA] (1897–1968)

Bulgarian physicist. Born 3 September 1897 in Vienna to Mary (Slade) and Ivan Karamihailov. Mother a musician, father a surgeon. Never married. Educated in Sophia, Bulgaria; University of Vienna (D.Phil., 1922). Professional experience: Institut für Radiumforschung, researcher (1922–1935); Cambridge University, Yarrow Scientific Research Fellow (1935–1939); Sophia University, associate professor, Department of Atomic Physics, chair (from 1945); Physics Institute, Bulgarian Academy of Sciences, senior researcher, laboratory head, professor. Died 22 May 1968.

Karamihailova was raised in a cultured and intellectual home, first in Vienna, then (from 1909) in Sophia. After completing secondary school she enrolled at the University of Vienna. Her thesis research was performed at the Vienna Radium Institute under Karl Przibram. She then pursued studies on radioactivity, particularly on the use of the scintillation method for registering alpha particles and protons. Together with Hans Pettersson, she devised a method to separate the effects of these two kinds of particles. In addition to Przibram and Pettersson, Karamihailova worked with several of the women researchers at the institute.

In 1935, Karamihailova was awarded a fellowship for women scientists which enabled her to work at the Cavendish laboratory under Ernest Rutherford. Her researches included determinations of the energy of gamma rays and studies of ionization in gases. Karamihailova then returned to Bulgaria, where she taught at Sophia University and did research on radioactivity and cosmic rays.

After the Communist takeover, Karamihailova's activities were restricted because of her well-known anti-Communist views. During the fifties she was put in charge of the radioactivity and spectroscopy laboratory of the Bulgarian Academy of Sciences Physics Institute. There she investigated the radioactivity of rocks, soils, and waters. Some of this research was pursued jointly with medical researchers.

MM

PRIMARY SOURCES
Karamichailova, Elizabeth. With Hans Petterson. "The Brightness of Scintillations from H-particles and from α-particles." *Nature* 113 (1924): 715.
———. With Berta Karlik. "Zur Kenntnis der Szintillationsmethode." *Zeitschrift für Physik* 48 (1928): 765–783.
———. "The Total Energy of the G-radiation Emitted from the Active Deposit of Actinium." *Cambridge Philosophical Society Proceedings* 34 (1938): 429–434.

SECONDARY SOURCES
Sir James Chadwick, ed. *The Collected Papers of Lord Rutherford of Nelson.* Vol. 3, plate. London: Allen and Unwin, 1965.

STANDARD SOURCES
Meyer and von Schweidler; Rayner-Canham 1997.

KARDYMOWICZOWA, IRENA (1899–1980)

Lithuanian igneous and metamorphic petrologist. Born 1899. Educated University of Vilno (1930–1946?); University of Torun (1947–1949); Museum of the Earth and State Geological Institute (1949–1965).

Irena Kardymowiczowa first worked in her native Lithuania, studying the Volhynian crystalline massif. She then settled in Poland in 1947, where she studied the volcanic rocks of the Pieniny Mountains, Lower Silesia, and the petrology of lamprophyres and dolerites.

JH/MBO

SECONDARY SOURCES
Radlicz, Krzysztof. "Irena Kardymowiczowa (1899–1980)." *Rocznik Polskiego Towarzystwa Geologic Znego,* 51, nos. 3–4 (1981): 611–615.

STANDARD SOURCES
Sarjeant.

KARLIK, BERTA (1904–1990)

Austrian physicist. Born 24 January 1904 in Vienna. Studied at University of Vienna (Ph.D., 1928); Institute for Radium Research, Vienna; Royal Institution, London, and Cambridge University (1930–1931); Radium Institute, Paris (1927, 1939). Professional experience: Institute for Radium Research, Vienna, assistant (1933), director (from 1945); University of Vienna, associate professor (1950), professor (from 1956). Honors and memberships: Austrian Academy of Sciences, member; Austrian Academy of Sciences, Haitinger Prize; City of Vienna, culture prize; Wilhelm Exner Medal, 1954. Died 4 February 1990.

Berta Karlik did her doctoral research under Stefan Meyer, director of the Vienna Radium Institute. Her first publications concerned the luminescent scintillations produced in zinc sulfide by alpha particles, which researchers used to count particles. These studies led to investigations of fluorescence and fluorescence spectra and of the scintillatization capabilities of other substances. Karlik and Frederick Hernegger used fluorescence to detect uranium in sea water, which enabled them to determine its radium content as well. Karlik also measured the helium contained in salt deposits and samples, useful for determining their content of radium and other radioactive substances. In 1943 Karlik and Traude Bernert detected natural isotopes of element 85 (astatine, previously known only as an artificial element) formed from branching β-decay. Karlik's work was honored with several prizes.   MM

PRIMARY SOURCES

Karlik, Berta. "Abhängigkeit der Szintillationen von der Beschaggenheit des Zinksulfids und des Wesens des Szintillat.-Vorganges." *Akademie der Wissenschaften, Wien, Sitzungsberichte* (2a) 136 (1927): 531–561.

———. With Friedrich Hernegger. *Uranium in Sea-Water.* Göteborg, 1935 (Göteborgs k. vetensk. och vitterh. samhälles Handlinger 5, Ser. B, 4, 12).

———. With Traude Bernert. "Element 85 in den natürlichen Zerfallsreihen." *Zeitschrift für physikalische Chemie* 123 (1944): 51–72.

———. "Radon und Isotope." In R. Fresenius and G. Jander, *Handbuch der analytische Chemie* 3 (1949): 98–120.

SECONDARY SOURCES

Glasstone, Samuel. *Sourcebook on Atomic Energy.* Princeton, N.J., etc.: D. Van Nostrand, 1950.

Róna, Elizabeth. *How It Came About: Radioactivity, Nuclear Physics, Atomic Energy.* Oak Ridge, Tenn.: Oak Ridge Associated Universities, 1978. Karlik mentioned pages 33, 53, 64.

STANDARD SOURCES

Kass-Simon and Farnes; Meyer and von Schweidler; Poggendorff, vol. 7a; Rayner-Canham 1997; Turkevich and Turkevich.

KARP, CAROL RUTH (VANDER VELDE) (1926–1972)

U.S. mathematician and logician. Born 10 August 1926 in Forest Grove, Mich., to Janet (Keizer) and Peter Nelson Vander Velde. Two brothers. Married Arthur L. Karp. Educated Manchester College, North Manchester, Ind. (graduated with distinction, 1948); Michigan State College (M.A., 1950); University of Southern California (Ph.D., 1959). Professional experience: New Mexico College of Agricultural and Mechanical Arts (now New Mexico State University), instructor (1953–1954); University of California, Berkeley, teaching assistant and graduate student (1954–1956); University of Maryland (instructor 1958, assistant professor 1960; associate professor 1963; full professor 1966). Died 20 August 1972.

Although Carol Vander Velde's family was very conservative, forbidding dancing and movie-going, they encouraged their children to attend college. Vander Velde attended a small Brethren college in North Manchester, Indiana, and then enrolled in a graduate program in mathematics at Michigan State College. She had become a fine violist and following receipt of this degree traveled around the country as a violist in an all-women orchestra. She moved to California in 1951 and enrolled in the doctoral program at the University of Southern California. She married Arthur L. Karp in 1952. She received her doctorate from Southern California in 1959, but spent many of the intervening years elsewhere. During the academic year 1953–1954, Karp was an instructor at the New Mexico College of Agricultural and Mechanical Arts. Her thesis advisor, Leon Henkin, had moved to the University of California, Berkeley, in 1953, and Karp followed him there in 1954. She moved to Japan with her husband in 1957 and in 1958 returned to the United States to a position as instructor.

After she received her degree the next year, she was promoted to assistant professor (1960) and climbed the academic ladder rapidly thereafter. Karp became the nucleus for a group of logicians at Maryland and was influential in bringing many of the most important logicians to the Maryland Mathematics Colloquium and Logic Seminar. Karp was known for the high standards she demanded of her graduate students. She also directed a National Science Foundation sponsored Undergraduate Research Program. She was a highly respected member of the international logic community, published regularly, participated in conferences, and gave invited addresses throughout much of North America and Europe. In 1969, Karp found that she had breast cancer; she died in 1972.

Karp's field of research, infinitary logic, has, thanks to Karp and Leon Henkin, become a well-established area within mathematical logic. Karp's monograph was the first systematic exposition.   JH/MBO

PRIMARY SOURCES

Karp, Carol. "Languages with Expressions of Infinite Length." Ph.D. diss., University of Southern California, 1959.
———. *Languages with Expressions of Infinite Length.* Amsterdam: North-Holland, 1964.
———. "Nonaxiomatizability Results for Infinitary Systems." *Journal of Symbolic Logic* 32 (1967): 367–384.

SECONDARY SOURCES

López-Escobar, E. G. K. "Introduction." In *Infinitary Logic: In Memoriam Carol Karp,* ed. D. W. Kueker, 1–16. Springer Lecture Notes in Mathematics, vol. 492. New York: Springer-Verlag, 1975.
Williams, Mary B. [Obituary.] *Association for Women in Mathematics Newsletter* 3, no. 1 (January–February 1973): 2–3.

STANDARD SOURCES

Grinstein and Campbell (article by Judy Green).

KARPOWICZ, LUDMILA (1903–)

Polish botanist and ecologist. Educated University of Warsaw (doctorate). Professional experience: Botanical Garden Warsaw, director.

Ludmila Karpowicz earned a doctorate from the University of Warsaw and then became the director of the botanical garden.   JH/MBO

PRIMARY SOURCES

Karpowicz, Ludmila. *Rhaponticum carthamoide (Willd.) Iljin.* Warsaw: Panstowe Wydawn. Nauk, 1963.

STANDARD SOURCES

Turkevich and Turkevich.

KARRER, ANNIE MAY HURD (1893–?)

U.S. plant physiologist. Born 28 July 1893 in La Conner, Wash. Married Sebastian Karrer (1923). Educated University of Washington (A.B., 1915; 1917); University of California, Berkeley (Ph.D., 1918). Professional experience: University of Washington, teaching assistant (1915–1916); Bureau of Plant Industry, U.S. Department of Plant Industry, researcher (1918–1924; associate plant physiologist (1924–1944); plant physiologist (1944–1949).

Annie May Hurd Karrer joined the United States Department of Agriculture in 1918, the same year in which she got her doctoral degree from the University of California, Berkeley. While she was at the Bureau of Plant Industry, the division of the USDA where Karrer worked, she published sixteen reports in the USDA series. Karrer's area of specialization was the improvement of cereal crops and the control of cereal diseases.

Karrer was a member of the American Association for the Advancement of Science, the American Society of Plant Physiologists, the Botanical Society of America, and the Botanical Society of Washington.   JH/MBO

PRIMARY SOURCES

Karrer, Annie May Hurd. *USDA Reports.* Published 16 reports.

STANDARD SOURCES

AMS 3–8 (in vol. 3, included as Annie Hurd); Bailey; Barnhart.

KASHEVAROVA-RUDNEVA, VARVARA ALEKSANDROVNA (1842–1899)

Russian physician. Born 1842 in Belorussia. Married (1) Nikolai S. Kashevarov; (2) Mikhail M. Rudnev. Educated at Princess Elena Pavlovna course for midwives in St. Petersburg; Kalinkinskii Hospital; St. Petersburg Medical Surgical Academy (degree of physician, 1868; doctor of medicine, 1876). Professional experience: worked in Botkin's Clinic in St. Petersburg; assistant to M.M. Rudnev; private practice at Aleksandrovka. Died at Staraia Russ in 1899.

Varvara Aleksandrovna Kashevarova-Rudneva, the first woman to become a doctor in a Russian medical school, started life as an illiterate Jewish orphan living as household help in the family of a poor teacher. As a young teenager, she decided to run away to St. Petersburg. Falling ill with typhus on the way, she spent three months in the hospital. When she recovered, she was given a letter of recommendation to a family in St. Petersburg, where she again did housework but was allowed to learn to read with the children of the family. At fifteen, her patron married her off to Nikolai Stepanovich Kashevarov, a merchant twenty years her senior. Although her husband had agreed that he would allow her to study, he did not keep his word, and Kashevarova soon left him. By this time, she had made up her mind to study medicine and she enrolled in the course for midwives at the Princess Elena Pavlovna Lying-in Home. She finished the two-year course successfully in eight months in 1862.

As the result of a chance meeting, Kashevarova obtained a small stipend as midwife for Bashkir troops in the Orenburg military region. The Bashkirs were Moslems and their women could not be treated by men. The authorities, considering that it would be desirable for a midwife to know how to treat syphilis, a growing scourge at that time, suggested that Kashevarova take a course on this treatment at the Kalinkinskii hospital. Kashevarova was accepted in this course (although not without some difficulty), but soon began to feel that it would be better if she had a complete medical education; she decided to try to enroll in the Medical Surgical Academy. At that time there were several women attending as auditors.

It took eight months to obtain permission, and she would probably not have succeeded had it not been for the support of the Orenburg governor, who was still paying her stipend, and the minister of war, Miliutin, who believed that women specializing in women and children's complaints could help alleviate the shortage of doctors. In the autumn of 1863, Kashevarova entered the Medical Surgical Academy as the only fully enrolled female student.

In 1864, the auditors were expelled, and Kashevarova remained. This put her at the center of controversy and unpleasantness, but she refused to become involved and worked hard at her studies. Further difficulties arose over whether she would be allowed to take the midcourse examinations that would entitle her to continue studying for a diploma. The diploma carried with it the right to academic rank, which was not permitted to women. A compromise was finally reached whereby she could receive the diploma without the rank.

Kashevarova passed her courses with distinction and was given a monetary reward by her sponsors in Orenburg. This enabled her to spend the summer in clinics in Prague and Vienna where she took the opportunity to learn German.

In her third year, Kashevarova began to work with Mikhail Matveevich Rudnev, and in 1868 read a paper on her research to the Society of Russian Physicians in St. Petersburg. Problems about her stipend arose, but again Miliutin and the governor of Orenburg supported her. She finished her examinations with distinction and was awarded the degree of physician.

She now had her diploma but without the rank that normally would have accompanied it in the case of male students. She did not have the right to work in a military hospital. Ironically, the only hospitals in Orenburg were military ones and she could not work there. Instead she was invited to work in the clinic of Sergei Petrovich Botkin. At the same time, she decided to study for the higher degree of doctor of medicine, which required, among other things, a mastery of Latin. By 1869, she had learned Latin and passed the preliminary examinations and only her dissertation remained.

In 1870, her marriage with Kashevarov was dissolved and she married Rudnev. Still unable to secure a post, she did research in his pathology laboratory and assisted him in his teaching.

Kashevarova-Rudneva was determined to write her dissertation, but again the authorities put obstacles in her way. She could not obtain permission to work in a maternity hospital and an attempt to work in the St. Petersburg Foundling Home was also unsuccessful.

In 1873, she requested permission to defend her dissertation, but withdrew the request as the controversy it aroused might have jeopardized the existence of the women's medical courses, which had only just been established on an experimental basis.

In 1876, her dissertation on the initial stages of cancer of the uterus was completed and she had published five scientific studies. The Women's Medical Courses were now permanently established and Kashevarova again requested permission to defend her thesis, which, this time, was granted. In May 1878, she brilliantly defended her thesis before a large audience and thus became the first woman to receive a diploma as doctor of medicine in Russia.

Kashevarova-Rudneva's ambition had been to become a member of the teaching faculty of the Women's Medical Courses, but in spite of having every qualification, her application was denied. Professors had greater rank and prestige than physicians and those in power had no intention of allowing women into this privileged group. In 1877, her application to go to the Turkish war front as a doctor was denied on similar grounds.

In 1878, Rudnev died. This was a tragedy for Kashevarova-Rudneva in every sense. Not only had she lost her beloved husband and the opportunities his laboratory had afforded for her research work, but she also lost the protection her marriage had provided. Also, unfortunately, Rudnev's death coincided with a backlash against the populist movement and the women physicians who were seen as connected with it.

Kashevarova-Rudneva was now subject to personal attack in, among other things, a serial novel published in *Novoe vremia*. Although a lawsuit against the writer and publisher was successful, it did not end the criticism. It was claimed that Rudnev had indulged in favoritism, that they had lived together before their marriage, but worse than that was the accusation that, despite having received years of support for her medical education from the Bashkir people in Orenburg, she had never spent a day in their service.

At this point Kashevarova-Rudneva found all doors closed to her. She had enemies, she was overqualified for many positions, and she was Jewish at a period when antisemitism was strong. Kashevarova-Rudneva withdrew from St. Petersburg and bought a piece of land near Kharkov. There she lived for eight years, treating the local peasantry and writing. Later, she bought a house in the village of Staraia Russ near St. Petersburg, where she opened a private practice. She died there in 1899.

Of all the women physicians of the period, Kashevarova had probably the most obstacles to overcome. Unlike the majority of her coevals who were of the gentry class, she came from a poor background and had the further disadvantage of being Jewish. That her admittance to the Medical Surgical Academy was an exception to the rule was held against her, and she had no natural allies in the populist and feminist movements.

It was only in her last years and after her death that her extraordinary achievements were recognized and publicly honored by Russian medical societies. She was the first woman doctor to be trained in Russia, she contributed to the study of cancer of the uterus, she wrote books on hygiene for women, and conducted an exemplary private medical practice. It is of note that over a dozen obituaries were published after her death and, in the Soviet period, two biographies.   ACH

PRIMARY SOURCES
Kashevarova-Rudneva, Varvara Aleksandrovna. *Gigiena zhenskogo organizma vo vsekh fazisakh zhizni.* 2d ed. St. Petersburg: n.p., 1892.

STANDARD SOURCES
Tuve.

KATHERINE, LA SURGIENE (THE SURGEON) (ca. 1286)
British physician and surgeon. Flourished around 1286 in London. Father Thomas the Surgeon. At least one brother, William.

Katherine "la surgiene," was the daughter of Thomas the Surgeon. Her brother, William, was also a surgeon. The extent of her practice is unknown.   JH/MBO

SECONDARY SOURCES
Talbot, Charles and Eugene Ash Hammond. *Medical Practitioners in Medieval England: A Biographical Register.* London: Wellcome Medical Historical Library, 1965. Katherine mentioned on page 200.

KATZ, ROSA HEINE (1885–?)
Russian/German psychologist. Born 9 April 1885 in Odessa. Educated Frauenuniversität (women's university) in Odessa; Universität Göttingen (Ph.D., 1913). Professional positions: Staatlichen Volkshochschule für Mädchen, docent (from 1923). Memberships: Deutsche Gesellchaft für Psychologie. Death date unknown.

Rosa Katz received her advanced training at the Odessa Women's University. She moved to Germany and obtained a

doctorate in psychology at the University of Göttingen. She wrote numerous scholarly journal articles.   JH/MBO

STANDARD SOURCES
Psychological Register, vol. 3, 1932.

KAYE-SMITH, A. DULCIE (d. 1955)
British botanist. Professional activities: Secretary Hastings Natural History Society (1926–1950). Died 1955.

A. Dulcie Kaye-Smith was an amateur botanist who was the long-time secretary of the Hastings Natural History Society. She was a contributor to A. H. Wolley-Dod's *Flora of Sussex* (1937).   JH/MBO

PRIMARY SOURCES
Wolley-Dod, A. H. *Flora of Sussex.* Hastings: n.p., 1937. Kaye-Smith was a contributor.

SECONDARY SOURCES
"A. Dulcie Kaye-Smith." *Hastings and East Sussex Naturalist* 8 (1956): 157.

STANDARD SOURCES
Desmond.

KEELER, HARRIET LOUISE (1833–1921)
U.S. botanist. Born 28 July 1844 in South Kortright, N.Y. Educated Oberlin College (A.B., 1870; A.M., honorary, 1900); Western Reserve (LL.D., 1913). Died 12 February 1921 in Clifton Springs, NY.

Harriet Louise Keeler was an Oberlin-trained botanist. She was recognized with honorary degrees from Oberlin and from Western Reserve.   JH/MBO

STANDARD SOURCES
Barnhart; *Who's Who of American Women.*

KEEN, ANGELINE MYRA (1905–   )
U.S. paleontologist. Born 23 May 1905 in Colorado Springs, Colo., to Mary (Thurston) and Ernest B. Keen. Educated Colorado College (A.B., 1930); Stanford University (M.A., 1931); University of California, Berkeley (Ph.D., 1934). Professional experience: Stanford, research associate (1934–1936), curator of paleontology (1936–post-1968), faculty member (1954–1965), professor of paleontology (from 1965). Concurrent positions: Paleontological Research Institute, consultant. Honors and memberships: Guggen-

heim Fellow (1965–1966); Paleontological Society, Fellow; Geological Society of America, Fellow; California Academy of Sciences, Fellow; Malacological Society of America, past president.

The research paleontologist Angelina Keen was born in Colorado and received her first degree from Colorado College. She then traveled to the west coast, where she became intrigued by living and fossil marine shells. She earned a master's degree at Stanford, and then went on to do a doctoral degree at University of California, Berkeley.

Keen returned to Stanford to take up a curatorship of paleontology at the university museum, publishing a number of articles and a series of books and articles on marine fossil and living molluscs from the west coast of the Americas. She became a member of the Stanford faculty in the mid-fifties and was raised to the rank of professor by 1965. She also was a consultant to the Paleontological Research Institute.

JH/MBO

PRIMARY SOURCES
Keen, A. Myra. With Herdis Benson. *California Tertiary Marine Mollusca.* N.p., 1944.
———. *Sea Shells of Tropical West America.* Stanford, Calif.: Stanford University Press, 1958.
———. *Marine Molluscan Genera of Western North America.* Stanford, Calif.: Stanford University Press, 1963.

STANDARD SOURCES
Debus.

KEENEY, DOROTHEA LILIAN (1896–?)

U.S. botanist. Born 2 May 1896 in Elmira, N.Y. Educated Syracuse University (A.B., 1917; M.A., 1918; Ph.D., 1932). Professional experience: Drew Seminary, Carmel, N.Y., biology teacher (1918–1920); Hwa Nan College, Foochow, China, biology department, head (1920–1926); Syracuse University, assistant in botany (1917–1918); instructor (1927–1932). Death date unknown.

Dorothea Keeney obtained all three of her degrees from Syracuse University. After teaching biology for two years at Drew Seminary, following the completion of her master's degree, she went to Foochow, China. There, Keeney was head of biology for six years, finding an opportunity she could not have found at home. On her return to the United States, she was an instructor in botany at Syracuse University while working toward her doctoral degree, and doing research on nitrogen fixation.

JH/MBO

STANDARD SOURCES
AMS 5–7.

KEIL, ELIZABETH MARBARETA (d. 1699)

German midwife. Professional experience: midwife. Died 1699.

Elizabeth Keil wrote a respected work on midwivery.

JH/MBO

STANDARD SOURCES
Hurd-Mead 1938.

KEIL, ELSA MARIE (1906–)

U.S. zoologist. Born 2 March 1906 in New Rochelle, N.Y., to Anna Marie (Ahrens) and William Keil. Married Ferdinand J. Sichel 1937. Educated Elmira College (B.S., 1927); Brown University (M.S., 1929); Woods Hole, Marine Biological Laboratory (summers). Professional experience: Brown University, department of zoology, teaching fellow and assistant; Rutgers University (New Jersey College for Women), department of biology, assistant professor (1929–1934), assistant professor (1934–1939); Vermont State Normal School (1939–1943); St. Michaels College, faculty member; Trinity College, professor of biology (from 1943); Woods Hole, Marine Biological Laboratories, Chemistry Department, summer staff. Honors and memberships: Corporation Member, Woods Hole, Marine Biological Laboratories.

Elsa Keil was educated at Elmira College in New York State and went from there to study for an advanced degree in zoology at Brown University. While there, she worked as a teaching fellow and assistant in the zoology department. During the summers, she went, as did many women biologists, to the Marine Biological Laboratories in Woods Hole, where she first studied and then taught. Eventually she would become a Corporation Member, which gave her voting rights. She taught in the biology department of the New Jersey Woman's College, part of Rutgers University, until she met and married Ferdinand J. Sichel, a Canadian-born physiologist. The two biologists moved to Vermont, where he held a position in the biology department of the University of Vermont, rising through the ranks to full professor and chairman. Because of the nepotism rules, she taught biology to teachers at the Vermont State Normal School and then at St. Michaels, part of Trinity College, from 1943, as professor of biology. Her research focused on regeneration in flatworms, the effect of cations on muscle regeneration and growth and micrurgical studies on invertebrate and vertebrate muscles.

JH/MBO

PRIMARY SOURCES
Keil, Elsa Marie. "Regeneration in *Polychoerus caudatus* Mark." M.A. thesis, Brown University, Providence, R.I., 1929.

STANDARD SOURCES
American Women; AMS 7–9B (in 9B under Sichel, Elsa Keil).

KEITH, MARCIA ANNA (1859–1950)

U.S. physicist. Born 1859 in Brockton, Mass., to Mary Ann (Cary) and Arza Keith. Educated Mount Holyoke College (B.S., 1892); Worcester Polytechnic Institute (special student, 1887, 1889); University of Berlin (1897–1898); University of Chicago (summer, 1901). Professional experience: Mount Holyoke College, instructor in mathematics and physics (1885–1889), head of physics department (1889–1903); firm of Herbert Keith, New York, assistant engineer (1906–1908). Died 1950 in Braintree, Mass.

Marcia Keith, one of the founders of the American Physical Society, began her teaching career in the public schools of Massachusetts (1876–1879). From 1883 to 1885, she was a science instructor at the Michigan Seminary and from 1885 to 1888, a mathematics instructor at Mount Holyoke. She became the first full-time instructor in the physics department at Mount Holyoke and was head of this department from 1889 to 1903. She later worked as an engineer for the firm of Herbert Keith in New York City. Marcia Keith was not a research physicist. Her importance to the history of science lies in the teaching of physics to a group of young women and in her role in establishing the American Physical Society in 1899.   JH/MBO

STANDARD SOURCES
AMS 1–8; Bailey; Ogilvie 1986; Rossiter 1982.

KELDYSH, LIUDMILA VSEVOLODOVNA (1904–)

Russian mathematician. Born 11 March 1904 in Orenburg. Father Vsevolod Keldysh, construction specialist. Educated Moscow University (doctor of physical-mathematical sciences, 1941). Professional experience: Moscow Aviation Institute, staff; Mathematical Institute of the Soviet Academy of Sciences, director; Physical-Mathematical Institute, director.

Liudmila Vsevolodovna Keldysh was a member of a family that had produced several distinguished scientists. Her father, Vsevolod Keldysh, was a well-known specialist in technical aspects of construction. She graduated from the University of Moscow in 1925. From 1930 to 1934, she was on the staff of the Moscow Aviation Institute; from 1934 she worked at the Mathematical Institute of the Soviet Academy of Sciences, becoming a senior associate in 1948 and from 1941 also the director of the Physical-Mathematical Institute. Sources are reticent on the subject of Keldysh's personal life.

However, as a recipient of the Maternity Medal (second class), she was evidently the mother of a sizable family.

Keldysh specialized in set theory and topology. Her earliest work was on the descriptive theory of sets, especially the structure of B-sets. Later, she became interested in continuous mappings of various classes. This involved such problems as the construction of a monotonic open mapping of a cube onto a cube of greater dimension.

In the beginning of the 1960s, Keldysh turned to research in geometric topology. This complex field concerns itself with topological and piecewise linear embeddings and homeomorphisms, particularly the embeddings of polyhedra and manifolds. Keldysh introduced the concept of the smooth continuum, otherwise known as the cell continuum, as a tool in these calculations.

Keldysh's work has been much admired for its elegance and she has inspired a number of students. She was awarded the order of the Red Flag of Labor for her work.   ACH

PRIMARY SOURCES
Keldysh, Liudmila Vsevolodovna. "Struktura B-mnozhestv." *Akademia Nauk SSSR. Matematicheskii Innstitut.* Trudy 17 (1945): 1–76.
———. "Preobrazhenie monotonnykh neprivodimykh otobrazhenii v monotonno-otkrytoe otobrazhenie kuba na kub bol'shei razmerosti." *Doklady Akademia nauk* 114, no. 3 (1957): 472–475.
———. Topological Imbeddings in Euclidean Space. Providence, R.I.: AMS, 1968.

SECONDARY SOURCES
Aleksandrov, P. S., et al. "Liudmila Vsevolodovna Keldysh." *Uspekhi matematicheskikh nauk* 29, no. 4m (1974): 187–192. Includes list of published papers. Trans. in *Russian Mathematical Surveys* 29, no. 4 (1974): 155–161.

STANDARD SOURCES
Debus; *WW in Soviet Science* 1966.

KELLER, IDA AUGUSTA (1866–1932)

German-born U.S. botanist and plant physiologist. Born 11 June 1866 in Darmstadt, Germany. Educated University of Zurich (doctorate, 1890). Professional experience: Bryn Mawr College, lecturer (1891–1892); Bryn Mawr High School for Girls, Philadelphia, teacher (from 1893). Philadelphia, herbarium curator. Honors and memberships: Philadelphia Botanical Club. American Society of Naturalists; American Association for the Advancement of Science, Fellow (1926). Died 10 September 1932 in Aquatong, Bucks County, Pa.

Ida Augusta Keller was born in Darmstadt, Germany, and obtained her botanical training from the University of Zurich, Switzerland, in the late 1890s—a time when many women were traveling to Zurich to obtain advanced degrees. On completing her degree, Keller moved to Pennsylvania where she lectured for a year at Bryn Mawr College and then moved to the Bryn Mawr High School for Girls in Philadelphia, where she taught botany for many years. She was a herbarium curator in Philadelphia and a Fellow of the American Association for the Association of Science.

JH/MBO

PRIMARY SOURCES

Keller, Ida A. "The Phenomenon of Fertilization in the Flowers of *Monada fistulosa.*" *Philadelphia Academy Natural Sciences, Proceedings* (1892): 452–454.

———. "The Glandular Hairs of *Brasenia peltata.*" *Philadelphia Academy Natural Sciences, Proceedings* (1893): 188–193.

———. "Notes on the Cross-Fertilization of Flowers by Insects." *Philadelphia Academy Natural Sciences, Proceedings* (1896): 555–561.

———. "The Coloring Matter of the Aril of *Cleastrus sandens.*" *American Journal of Pharmacy* 68 (1896): 183–186.

———. "Notes on Hyacinth Roots." *Philadelphia Academy Natural Sciences, Proceedings* (1900): 438–440.

STANDARD SOURCES

AMS 1–4; Bailey; Stafleu and Cowan.

KELLERMAN, STELLA VICTORIA (DENNIS) (1855–1936)

U.S. botanist. Born 25 July 1855 in Amanda, Ohio. Father Anthony Dennis. Married William A. Kellerman in 1876. Three children. Educated Academy at Cedar Hill, Fairfield County, Ohio, female academy (graduated). Died 21 July 1936 in San Diego, Calif.

Stella Victoria Kellerman was married to a botanist with a doctorate, but lacked formal botanical training herself. It was her husband, William, who suggested after they had traveled to the universities of Göttingen and Zurich that Kellerman might aid him by taking drawing lessons. When they returned to the United States Kellerman, sporting a new doctoral degree from Göttingen, took a one-year job at the State College of Agriculture and Mechanic Arts, Lexington, Kentucky. After the year passed, the family, which now included a son and a daughter, moved in with Stella Kellerman's parents in Amanda, Ohio, where William wrote a textbook, *Elements of Botany.* He praised Stella's contribution in the preface, noting that she had aided him in the entire preparation of the book. She contributed a number of original illustrations which she had prepared. In the fall of 1883, William Kellerman accepted a position at the Kansas State Agricultural College (now Kansas State University). In the book that he published in 1884 he also praised his wife's contributions. Together they published two papers on the vascular flora of Kansas, both of which emphasized the use of keys in identification. The rest of Kellerman's career was spent at The Ohio State University.

Through time, Kellerman's botanical expertise increased and she began to study critically the many morphological variations in the leaves. She presented a paper on the subject at the annual meeting of the Kansas Academy of Science (1889), which was published a year later in the Academy's *Transactions.* Stella Kellerman moved with her husband when he accepted the position of chairman of the newly established biology department at The Ohio State University. In Ohio she continued to study morphological variation and evolution in leaves of vascular plants and wrote several substantive papers on the subject. She also worked with her husband on projects such as revising his textbook. She had some interesting ideas on the origin of corn, and is given credit for being the first investigator to point out that the present-day ear of the corn plant is homologous to the central spike of the tassel. Both Kellermans were interested in introducing non-botanists to the state's flora. They collected specimens for the state herbarium, founded by William and developed with the department of botany. They published an important checklist providing the results of their studies on non-indigenous vascular plants of Ohio. This important work was described in a short notice in the *Asa Gray Bulletin* (1900).

On 8 March 1908 William Kellerman died of "pernicious malarial fever" in Guatemala while on a plant collecting expedition. Although Stella Kellerman remained active in a number of other activities, she did not continue with botanical work.

JH/MBO

PRIMARY SOURCES

Kellerman, Stella Victoria. "The Probable Differentiation of the Ear and Tassel in the Indian Corn." *Vick's Illustrated Monthly Magazine* 18 (1894): 19.

———. "Some Rare Leaves of *Liriodendron tulipifera.*" *Meehan's Monthly* 18 (1896): 104–105.

———. "Observations [of leaf variation] on a Hop Vine." *Vick's Illustrated Monthly Magazine* 21 (1898): 1141.

———. With William Kellerman. "The Non-Indigenous Flora of Ohio." *Journal of the Columbus Horticultural Society* 15 (1900): 30–54.

SECONDARY SOURCES
Stuckey, Ronald L. "Botanical and Horticultural Contributions
   of Mrs. William A. Kellerman (Stella Victoria [Dennis]
   Kellerman) 1855–1936." *The Michigan Botanist* 31 (1992):
   123–142. Portrait and bibliography. Well researched and
   provides understanding of this little-known botanist.

STANDARD SOURCES
Stuckey.

KELLEY, LOUISE (1894–?)

*U.S. organic chemist. Born 10 October 1894 in Franklin, N.H.
Educated Mount Holyoke College (A.B., 1916; M.A., 1918);
Cornell University (doctorate, 1920); University of Graz, postdoctoral study (1929). Professional experience: Mount Holyoke
College, assistant in chemistry (1916–1917); Wheaton College,
instructor (1917–1918); Goucher College, assistant professor
(1920–1923), associate professor (1923–1930), professor (1930–
1959), emerita professor (from 1959). Concurrent positions: National Defense Research Committee and Office of Scientific Research
and Development, technical aide (1942–1946); Chemical Reviews, assistant editor (1929–1959), Journal of Physical Chemistry, editor (1937–1951). Honors and memberships: Sage Fellow,
Cornell (1918–1919); Du Pont and Wooley Fellowships, Cornell
(1919–1920); Presidential Certificate of Merit (1948); Manufacturing Chemical Association Award (1959); Goucher College honorary doctorate (1959); Fellow, Institute of Chemistry, Chemical
Society. Death date unknown.*

Louise Kelley was an organic chemist who attended Mount
Holyoke College for both her undergraduate and master's
degrees. During this period she worked as an assistant in
chemistry in the Mount Holyoke laboratory and as an instructor at Wheaton College. After obtaining her doctoral
degree at Cornell, she began to teach at Goucher College,
and was made an associate professor three years later. In
1929, she went to Europe to do postdoctoral work at the
University of Graz. On her return, she was made a full professor and also began to serve as assistant editor of the
Chemistry Society journal *Chemical Reviews,* and later as the
editor of the *Journal of Physical Chemistry.*

   During World War II, Kelley served as a technical aide to
the National Defense Research Committee and the Office
of Scientific Research and Development, for which she was
recognized with a Presidential Merit Award. In the year of
her retirement, a number of honors came her way, including
the Manufacturing Chemical Society Award and an honorary doctorate from Goucher College. She was made an
emerita professor by Goucher and soon after retired to her
native town of Franklin, New Hampshire.   JH/MBO

PRIMARY SOURCES
Kelley, Louise. With George Albert Hill. *Organic Chemistry.*
   Philadelphia: Blakiston's Son, 1932.

STANDARD SOURCES
AMS 4–8, P 9, P&B 10; Rossiter 1982.

KELLOGG, LOUISE (1879–1967)

*U.S. mammalogist. Born 27 August 1879 in Oakland, Calif., to
Anita and Charles Winslow Kellogg. Four siblings. Educated University of California, Berkeley (A.B., 1901). Professional experience: series of collecting expeditions from 1908 until 1949 with
Annie Alexander. Died 1967.*

Louise Kellogg was born to an affluent family in Oakland,
California. During her youth, she showed little interest in
natural history subjects. At the University of California, she
earned a degree in classics and found her time occupied with
the usual activities of young women of her social class.
However, her father, an officer of Tubbs Cordage in San
Francisco, was a founder of the Cordelia Shooting Club, a
duck club in California. Luckily for Kellogg's later career, he
taught her how to shoot and to fish. When ANNIE ALEXAN-
DER was searching for a companion to accompany her on an
Alaskan expedition in 1908, Kellogg, thirteen years younger,
agreed to go. This expedition was a success for both of them,
and they formed a team that endured for over forty years.
They trapped animals in the American West and Alaska for
the new Museum of Vertebrate Zoology at the University of
California. They even set up housekeeping together on a
farm that they bought in the California Suisun marshes on
Grizzly Island. Mammalogists such as E. Raymond Hall attested to Kellogg's importance to the discipline. During the
later part of her life, she turned to botanical collecting. Her
last fieldtrip to Baja, California, was in 1960 when she was
eighty years old. She was honored by having a subspecies of
bird, *Lagopus rupestris kelloggae* (Grinell, 1910) and a species
of plant, *Acacia kelloggiana,* named for her.   JH/MBO

SECONDARY SOURCES
Kaufman, Dawn M., Donald W. Kaufman, and Glennis A.
   Kaufman. "Women in the Early Years of the American
   Society of Mammalogists (1919–1949)." *Journal of Mammal-
   ogy* 77, no. 33: 642–654.
Smith, Felisa A., and James H. Brown. "The Changing Role of
   Women in North American Mammalogy." *Journal of Mam-
   malogy* 77, no. 3 (1996): 609–612.
Smith, Felisa A., and Dawn M. Kaufman. "A Quantitative
   Analysis of the Contributions of Female Mammalogists
   from 1919 to 1994." *Journal of Mammalogy* 77, no. 3 (1996):
   613–628.

Stein, B. R. "Women in Mammalogy: The Early Years." *Journal of Mammalogy* 77, no. 3, 1996.

STANDARD SOURCES
Bonta.

KELLOR, FRANCES A. (1873–1952)

U.S. sociologist. Born 20 October 1873 in Columbus, Ohio, to Mary (Sprau) and Daniel Kellor. Educated Cornell Law School (LL.B., 1897); University of Chicago, graduate studies in sociology (1898–1900); New York Summer School of Philanthropy. Professional experience: College Settlement Association, fellow (1902); Inter-Municipal Household Research, secretary; State Commission of Immigration, secretary (1908–1910); New York Bureau of Industries and Immigration, administrator (1910). Honors and memberships: League for the Protection of Coloured Women (later part of Urban League), founder (1907); Progressive Party, National Service Committee, chair (1912); Immigrants in America Review, *co-founder and editor (1915–1916); Pan American Union, executive board member; American Arbitration Association, vice-president (1926–1952). Died 4 January 1952 in New York City.*

Frances Kellor was a U.S. sociologist interested in race and gender issues. She had links to JANE ADDAMS, and the reformers Emily Greene Balch and Edith Abbott. She studied at Cornell Law School and the University of Chicago, where she took graduate courses in sociology. She became interested in juvenile crime and black immigration and published on those subjects.

In 1905, Kellor moved to New York City, where she lived with the social reformers Mary and Margaret Dreier. Three years later, she was appointed secretary of the New York State Immigration Commission, where she helped establish the Bureau of Industries and Immigration, which she directed. The bureau established language classes and promoted job safety.

Kellor was active in Theodore Roosevelt's bid for the presidency with the Progressive Party, and directed his interest toward the urban immigrant. She continued her interest in black women coming from the South, and helped to establish a group that became part of the Urban League.

During World War I, Kellor was caught up in the fear shared by many Americans that immigration threatened the survival of the United States. Her solution was to educate and "Americanize" the new immigrants through the Americanization Committee and her work with the Inter-Racial Council and the Association of Foreign Language Newspapers, of which she was the director.

For the last part of her life, she worked with organizations for industrial arbitration. She also supported the League of

Nations and later the Pan-American Union. She died at the age of seventy-eight in New York City.   JH/MBO

PRIMARY SOURCES
Kellor, Frances A. *Experimental Sociology*. New York: Macmillan, 1901.
———. "Criminal Sociology: The American Versus the Latin School." *Arena* 23 (1900): 301–307.
———. *Out of Work*. New York: G. P. Putnam's Sons, 1904. Rev. ed., 1915.
———. "Colored Women's Associations." *Colored American Magazine* 9 (1909): 695–699.
———. *Immigrants and the Future*. New York: Macmillan, 1920.
———. With Antonia Hatvany. *Security against War*. 2 vols. New York: Macmillan, 1924.
———. *Arbitration in the New Industrial Society*. New York: McGraw Hill, 1934.
Kellor's manuscripts and letters are in the Library of Congress, manuscript collections.

SECONDARY SOURCES
Deegan, Mary Jo. "Frances A. Kellor (1873–1952)." In *Women in Sociology*, ed. Mary Jo Deegan. Westport, Conn.: Greenwood Press, 1991.

STANDARD SOURCES
NAW (M) (article by Lucille O'Connell).

KELLY, AGNES (fl. 1900)

British geologist. Born in Australia. Educated Bedford College for Women and University College, London (graduated 1897); University of Munich (graduated ca. 1899; Ph.D., 1900). Professional experience: Oxford University, research with H.A. Miers.

Agnes Kelly was born in Australia and went to England with her parents when she was three years old. She began her university education at Bedford College for Women in 1892, and five years later graduated from University College, London. In 1899, Kelly presented a proposal for a doctoral thesis. She was the first woman to earn a doctorate at the University of Munich, followed by her fellow mineralogist MARIA MATILDA OGILVIE GORDON. Kelly's doctoral examination on 25 July 1900 was rigorous, but she performed admirably.

Kelly's dissertation was titled "Beiträge zur mineralogischen Kenntniss der Kalkausscheidungen im Theirreich" (Contribution to Mineralogical Knowledge of the Analysis of the Calcium Deposits in the Animal Kingdom). She continued to work on the boundaries between mineralogy and zoology. Returning to England, Kelly worked with H. A. Miers at Oxford University. She published two papers on mineralogy, one in 1900 and another in 1901.   JH/MBO

PRIMARY SOURCES

Kelly, Agnes. "Beiträge zur mineralogischen Kenntniss der Kalkausscheidungen im Theirreich." Jena: n.p., 1901. Doctoral dissertation.

STANDARD SOURCES

Creese and Creese; Strohmeier.

KELLY, ISABEL TRUESDELL (1906–1983)

U.S. anthropologist and archeologist. Born 4 January 1906 in Santa Cruz, Calif., to Alice (Gardner) and Thomas William Kelly. Educated Santa Cruz High School; University of California, Berkeley (A.B., 1926; M.A., 1927; Ph.D., 1932). Field work: Southern Paiute (1932–1934); Mexico, Culican, Sinaloa, excavations (1935), archeological survey (1939–1947); Arizona, Hodges Ruin (Hohokan) excavation. western Mexico, archeological and ethnological work (1948–1980). Professional experiences: National Research Fellow in Biological Sciences (1932–1934); University of California, research associate (1930–1935), teaching assistant (1936); Gila Pueblo, Globe, Ariz., researcher (1937–1938); Institute for Andean Research, director of west Mexican archeological field research (1939–1945); Institute of Social Anthropology (Smithsonian), Mexico City branch, ethnologist in charge (1946–1951); Institute of Inter-American Affairs (later Agency for International Development, Health Division, anthropologist (1952–1960); Arizona State Museum, research consultant (in Mexico) (1960–1976). Honors and memberships: National Research Fellow, California and Santa Fe, N.M. (1933–1935); Gila Foundation research grant (1937–1939); Guggenheim Memorial Foundation Fellow (1940); Rockefeller Foundation, Werner-Gren and National Geographic Society grants and fellowships (1960–1980); American Anthropological Association, executive council (1931–1942). Died in Mexico, 1983.

Isabel Kelly studied anthropology and archeology at the University of California, Berkeley, under Albert Kroeber, Robert Lowie, and others, but her real mentor was Carl Sauer, an important geographer. She finished her doctoral degree about the same time as CORA DU BOIS.

With a National Science fellowship, Kelly began an ethnogeographic study of the Southern Paiute. This work has continued to be of value. In 1935, she went to Mexico for the first time to direct an excavation at Culiacan, Sinoloa, under the direction of Albert Kroeber and Carl Sauer. She returned early the next year to serve Carl Sauer as a teaching assistant for a term, and then went to excavate Hodges Ruin, a Hohokam site in the Southwest.

By 1939, Kelly returned to Mexico with encouragement from Sauer, though with only minimal funds. She managed to survey archeological sites through much of western Mexico with the aid of grants from the Guggenheim, Carnegie

Institute, and the American Philosophical Society. By the end of the war years, she obtained a brief stint as a librarian in the U.S. Information Service in Mexico City, and the next year joined the Smithsonian Insitute of Social Anthropology (ISA), teaching in the Escuela Nacional di Antropologia and continuing her research, this time among the Totonac people in Veracruz. As the ISA turned its interest to public health, Kelly changed her research to this area.

When the Smithsonian closed the ISA in 1951, Kelly joined the U.S. government-sponsored Institute of Inter-American Affairs, which preceeded the Agency for International Development (AID). Here again she studied public health clinics in Mexico and Bolivia. As the agency began to require long absences from Mexico to complete research in far-flung places, including Pakistan, she left and turned again to foundation support. With grants from the Rockefeller Foundation and Werner-Gren, she was able to return to her former archeological research in Mexico and to write up her data.

Through much of her career, Kelly did not have the kind of encouragement from her anthropology department in Berkeley she expected, and she initially resented some of Kroeber's attitudes toward women. Other anthropologists, such as Albert Kidder and Carl Sauer, both felt she deserved an appropriate position in a U.S. university. Given that this was not forthcoming, Kelly succeeded in accomplishing an enormous amount of work, which has caused her to be considered the "mother of west Mexican archeology." For her earlier work on the Paiute and on a Hohokam site, she is also included as one of the "Daughters of the Desert," in the conference and exhibit of that name held in Tucson, Arizona, in 1988.   JH/MBO

PRIMARY SOURCES

Kelly, Isabel T. "Southern Paiute Bands." *California University Publications in American Archaeology and Ethnology* 31 (1934): 67–210.

———. *Excavations at Culican, Sinaloa.* Berkeley: University of California Press, 1945.

———. *Excavations at Apatzingan.* New York: Viking Fund Publications in Anthropology, no. 7, 1947.

———. *Public Opinion and the Xochimilco Health Center.* Washington D.C.: Institute of Social Anthropology, Smithsonian Institute, 1952.

———. "Seven Colima Tombs: An Interpretation of Ceramic Content." Studies in Mesoamerica 3. *Contributions of the University of California Research Facility* 26 (1978): 1–26.

SECONDARY SOURCES

Babcock, Barbara A. and Nancy J. Parezo. "Isabel Kelly, 1906–1984 [sic]." In *Daughters of the Desert: Women Anthropologists and the Native American Southwest, 1880–1980.* University of New Mexico Press, 1988.

Buzaljko, Grace Wilson. "Isabel Kelly: From Museum Anthropologist to Archaeologist." *Museum Anthropology* 17, no. 2 (1993): 41–48.

STANDARD SOURCES

AMS 6–8; S&B 19–12, P&B 13; Gacs (article by Patricia J. Knobloch; includes portrait); Rossiter 1995.

KELLY, MARGARET G. (1906–)

U.S. pharmacologist. Born 8 October 1906 in Minneapolis, Minn. Married Roger W. O'Gara (1955). Educated George Washington University (B.A., 1941; M.S., 1945; Ph.D. in pharmacology, 1951). Professional experience: National Institutes of Health, National Cancer Institute, biochemist (1941–1949), pharmacologist (1949–post-1960). Memberships: Society of Pharmacology, American Cancer Research.

Margaret G. Kelly was a research pharmacologist, trained at George Washington University. She spent her working life attached to the National Cancer Institute, part of the National Institutes of Health, first as a biochemist and then as a pharmacologist. Her research topics included the pharmacology of pharmoclastic drugs, carcinogenesis, and the study of various cancer chemotherapies. JH/MBO

PRIMARY SOURCES

Kelly, Margaret G. "Nutritional Requirements of Normal and Malignant Cells." M.A. thesis, George Washington University, 1945. Typescript.

STANDARD SOURCES

AMS, B 9, P&B 10–11.

KELLY, MARGARET W. (1886–1968)

U.S. chemist. Born 6 January 1886 in Oakland, Pa. Educated Mount Holyoke College (A.B., 1909); Columbia University (A.M., 1920; Ph.D., 1923). Professional experience: Pennsylvania Public Schools, teacher (1910–1918); Columbia University, assistant in chemistry (1920–1924, 1925–1928); Mount Holyoke College, assistant professor (1924–1925, 1928–1929); Vassar College, assistant professor (1929–1930), associate professor (1930–1932); Connecticut College, associate professor (1932–1946), professor (1946–1952), emerita professor (1952–1968). Memberships: Chemical Society. Died 1968.

Margaret W. Kelly obtained her advanced degrees in chemistry from Columbia University in the 1920s, during which period she also served as an assistant in chemistry. She also

continued as an assistant after she obtained her doctoral degree until she was appointed an assistant professor at Mount Holyoke. After this stint of teaching ended, she returned to work as an assistant until she was appointed as an assistant professor at Vassar College, rising to the position of associate professor. She then went to Connecticut College, where she rose to full professor by 1946. She retired as an emerita professor in 1952 and died some sixteen years later. Her research was in colloidal chemistry, proteins, tanning materials, aluminium oxychloride hydrosols, the chemical analysis of steels for boron content, and fixation of tannins by hidepowder. JH/MBO

PRIMARY SOURCES

Kelly, Margaret W. "The Fixation of Vegetable Tannins by Hide Substance." Ph.D. diss., Columbia University, 1923.

STANDARD SOURCES

AMS 4–8, P&B 9–10.

KENDALL, CLARIBEL (1889–1965)

U.S. mathematician. Born 23 January 1889 in Denver, Colo., to Emma (Reily) Kendall and Charles M. Kendall. One sibling. Never married. Educated Denver public schools; University of Colorado (B.A. and B.Ed., 1912; M.A., 1914); University of Chicago (Ph.D., 1922). Professional experience: University of Colorado, instructor (1913–1921), assistant professor (1921–1928), professor (1944–1957). Died 1965.

Claribel Kendall was born and received the majority of her education in Colorado, although she received her doctorate from the University of Chicago. Her entire career was at the University of Colorado, where she slowly rose up the academic ladder to full professor. Male members of the department progressed much more rapidly. She was active in the Christian Science Church and left a substantial amount of money to it. She was secretary for the Colorado Chapter of Phi Beta Kappa for over thirty years, and upon her death left five thousand dollars to the chapter, which still gives the Claribel Kendall award. She enjoyed outdoor activities, particularly hiking and jeep driving through back mountain trails. After retirement, she lived in Boulder until her death in 1965.

Kendall was not a productive research mathematician. She was, however, a dedicated mathematics teacher. She directed ten master's theses, eight of which were by women. In addition to her master's thesis and doctoral dissertation, she posed and solved problems that appeared in the problems section of the *American Mathematical Monthly*. She was one of the founders of the Rocky Mountain Section of the Mathematical Association of America. JH/MBO

PRIMARY SOURCES

Kendall, Claribel. "Preassociative Syzygies in Linear Algebra." Master's thesis, University of Colorado, 1914.

———. "Congruences Determined by a Given Surface." *American Journal of Mathematics* 45 (1923): 25–41.

SECONDARY SOURCES

Jones, Burton W., and Wolfgang Thron. *A History of the Mathematics Departments of the University of Colorado.* Boulder, Colo.: N.p., 1979.

STANDARD SOURCES

Grinstein and Campbell (article by Ruth Rebekka Struik).

KENDRICK, PEARL (LUELLA) (1890–1980)

U.S. physician and microbiologist. Born 24 August 1890 in Wheaton, Illinois. Educated Syracuse University (B.S., 1914); Johns Hopkins University (Sc.D. in immunology, 1932). Professional experience: New York public schools, teacher and principal (1914–1919); New York State Department of Health, researcher (1919–1920); Michigan State Department of Health Labs, microbiologist (1920–1926), associate director (1926–1951); Department of Epidemiology, School of Public Health, Michigan, lecturer (1951–1960), emerita professor (from 1960); Health Department of Mexico, consultant (1940–1942); Blodgett Hospital, Grand Rapids, Mich., honorary staff member. Fellow: American Association for the Advancement of Science; Society of Bacteriologists. Member: American Public Health Association; Academy of Microbiology; New York Academy of Medicine. Honorary member, Society of Microbiologists, Panama, and Clinical Laboratories Association, Mexico. Died in 1980.

After teaching briefly, Pearl Kendrick was associated with state health organizations the remainder of her stellar career. As associate director of the Michigan State Department of Health Labs, Kendrick and her coworker, Grace Eldening, developed a pertussis (whooping cough) vaccine, which became available for mass production by 1939. From this vaccine, Kendrick proceeded to develop the standard DPT (diphtheria, whooping cough, and tetanus) immunization, which virtually eradicated those diseases from the Western world. Other research was concerned with the serology of syphilis, antigenicity studies in bacteriophage, and multiple antigens.

She contributed many articles to the professional literature and was active in professional organizations. At various times, she consulted for the World Health Organization, serving on the whooping cough immunization committee (1949–1959), as delegate to the WHO conference in Dubrovnik (1952), and on the immunology delegation to Russia (1962–1963). She consulted for the United Nations International Childrens Emergency Fund, working on the UNICEF immunization projects for Panama, Chile, Colombia, Venzuela, and Brazil (among others), and the program for pertussis vaccination in Mexico. A woman who shunned publicity, Kendrick received little public recognition for her discoveries, which saved millions of children from suffering devastating disease.   JH/MBO

STANDARD SOURCES

AMS P&B 11; Uglow 1989.

KENNARD, MARGARET ALICE (1899–?)

U.S./Canadian neurophysiologist. Born 25 Sept 1899 in Brookline, Mass. Educated Bryn Mawr College (A.B., 1922); Cornell Medical School (M.D., 1930). Professional experience: Yale Medical School, instructor in physiology; Rockefeller Fellow, Europe (1934–1936); New York University, associate professor of neuroanatomy and neurophysiology (1944–1948); University of British Columbia Medical School, Department of Neurological Research, physiologist (from 1951). Honors and memberships: Physiological Society; Neurological Association; Psychiatric Association; Association for Research in Nervous and Mental Diseases. Death date unknown.

Margaret Kennard earned her bachelor's degree at Bryn Mawr College and her M.D. at Cornell University. After her internship she entered academic medicine, teaching and doing research at Yale for eleven years. She then spent two years doing research at hospitals in Europe on a Rockefeller fellowship in neurophysiology. After she returned from Europe, Kennard accepted a position at the New York University Medical School as an associate professor. Leaving the East Coast in 1948, she accepted a position in experimental surgery at a medical school in Oregon for two years, after which she moved to the Medical School at the University of British Columbia to do neurological research. Her last position was with the State of Oregon's Mental Health Research Institute.

Kennard's research varied from physiological and anatomical studies to psychiatric ones. She was especially interested in the neurophysiological causes of psychiatric disorders.   JH/MBO

PRIMARY SOURCES

Kennard, Margaret. "The Syndrome of the Premotor Cortex in Man: Impairment of Skilled Movements, Forced Grasping, Spasticity, and Vasomotor Disturbance." *Brain* 57 (1934): 69–84.

STANDARD SOURCES

AMS 6–8, B 9, P&B 10.

KENNEDY, CORNELIA (1881–?)

U.S. agricultural biochemist. Born 3 February 1880 in Eau Claire, Wisc. to Georgeanna Francis (Atkinson) and Donald Kennedy. Educated University of Minnesota (B.A., 1903); University of Wisconsin (M.A., 1913); Johns Hopkins University (Ph.D., 1919). Professional experience: Washburn-Crosby Flour Mills, assistant chemist (1903–1908); University of Minnesota, instructor in agricultural chemistry (1908–1914), associate professor of agricultural chemistry (1930–1948). Concurrent position: Minnesota Experimental Station, assistant agricultural chemist (1908–1948). Retired 1948. Honors and memberships: Sarah Berliner Fellowship (to Johns Hopkins); Sigma Xi; American Association for the Advancement of Science, Fellow; American Society of Biological Chemists; American Institute of Nutrition. Death date unknown.

Cornelia Kennedy was born in Wisconsin, went to Minnesota for her bachelor's degree, and returned ten years later to obtain her Master's degree at the University of Wisconsin. Between those two periods, she took a position as an assistant chemist to the Washburn-Crosby Flour Mills. From the period that she returned to the University of Minnesota to study for her master's degree, she began to teach as an instructor in agricultural chemistry, taking a concurrent position as an assistant agricultural chemist at the Minnesota Agricultural Experimental Station, a position she held for the next thirty-two years. She was almost forty years old when she earned her doctorate at Johns Hopkins, after receiving a Sarah Berliner fellowship. She returned to the University of Minnesota and rose from assistant to associate professor of agricultural chemistry, while also working at the field station. She retired in 1949.   JH/MBO

PRIMARY SOURCES
Kennedy, Cornelia. With Harold Paul Morris. *Fundamental Food Requirements for the Growth of the Rat. VII: An Experimental Study of Inheritance as a Factor Influencing Food Utilization in the Rat.* St. Paul: University Farm, [1933?].

STANDARD SOURCES
American Women; AMS 6–8, P 9; Rossiter 1982.

KENNY, ELIZABETH (SISTER KENNY) (1886–1952)

Australian nurse. Born Kellys Gully, near Warialda, New South Wales, to Mary Moore and Michael Kenny. Four siblings. Never married. Educated Nobby, Queensland, where she attended primary school. Professional experience: established small hospital at Clifton (1912); Australian Army Nursing Service (1915–1919); private nursing (1919–1933); opened series of clinics to treat paralysis (1933–1940). Honors and memberships: Rutgers University, New York University, and the University of Rochester, honorary degrees. Died 30 November 1952 at Toowoomba, Queensland.

Elizabeth Kenny, who developed an unorthodox method of treating the paralysis resulting from poliomyelitis, apparently had no formal training in nursing. She must, however, have had an early interest in the subject, for she established a small hospital in 1912. However, her interest in working with paralyzed patients began while she was a member of the Australian Army Nursing Service. During her trips back to Australia with soldiers who had contacted encephalitis she practiced her new therapy of passively moving the affected limbs.

Upon her discharge from the army she did private nursing, and encountered her first case of poliomyelitis. She used her method successfully, and the patient recovered fully. With the aid of voluntary subscriptions she opened a clinic in Townsville to treat victims of paralysis. Other clinics followed—Carshalton, England in 1937 and Minneapolis, Minnesota. She demonstrated her techniques in many different countries.

Many physicians were opposed to Kenny's methods, asserting that moving the limbs—instead of the traditional rigid splinting—would cause deformities and muscle injury. Possibly because of her lack of medical training, the medical community was unwilling to accept the results of her new method. Kenny never took money for treating a patient and only treated patients in association with a physician.

Kenny's work was widely accepted in the United States, and a special Act of Congress was passed in 1950 that allowed her to enter and leave the country without a visa. Her work was recognized by a motion picture made of her life during her lifetime. Elizabeth Kenny headed the American Institute of Public Opinion's 1951 survey to determine which woman was held in highest esteem by the American public. She returned to Queensland from the United States in 1952 and died that same year.   JH/MBO

PRIMARY SOURCES
Kenny, Elizabeth. *The Treatment of Infantile Paralysis in the Acute Stage.* Minneapolis: Bruce Publishing, 1941.
———. With Martha Ostenso. *And They Shall Walk: the Life Story of Sister Elizabeth Kenny.* New York: Dodd, Mead & Company, 1943.

SECONDARY SOURCES
Pohl, John Florian M. *The Kenny Concept of Infantile Paralysis and Its Treatment.* Minneapolis: Bruce, 1943.

STANDARD SOURCES
DNB; Europa.

KENT, ELIZABETH (fl. 1820–1840s)

British botanical writer. Sister-in-law of romantic writer, journalist Leigh Hunt. Wrote regular column on botany for Magazine of Natural History *(1820s). Gave lessons in botany; governess (1845–1855?). Died after 1860.*

Elizabeth Kent was an English romanticist who combined her knowledge of botany with horticultural information and literary references. Her sister, Marianne, was married to Leigh Hunt, friend of the poet Shelley. Kent was a major correspondent of Hunt. She began writing in 1818, and continued to make her living writing popular books such as *Flora Domestica* (with some suggestions from Hunt), *Sylvan Sketches,* and a series in the *Magazine of Natural History* in the late 1820s. Later in life, when these sources dried up, Kent lived as a governess to a wealthy family and ended her life in poverty depending on the generosity of her nephews and small literary grants. She died sometime after 1860.

JH/MBO

PRIMARY SOURCES
Kent, Elizabeth. *Flora Domestica, or the Portable Flower-Garden.* London: Taylor and Hussey, 1823.
———. *Sylvan Sketches, or a Companion to the Park and Shrubbery.* London: Taylor and Hessey, 1825.
———, ed. *Synoptical Compendium of British Botany.* By John Galpine. London: S. Bagster, 1834. Updates Galpine with a comparison of the Linnaean and Jussieuan systems of classification.

SECONDARY SOURCES
Tatchell, Molly. *Leigh Hunt and His Family in Hammersmith.* London: Hammersmith Local History Group, 1969.

STANDARD SOURCES
Desmond; Shteir.

KENT, ELIZABETH ISIS POGSON (fl. 19th century)

British astronomer. Flourished in the nineteenth century.

In 1886, Kent was nominated as a Fellow of the Royal Astronomical Society. After two attorneys rendered contradicting opinions about the legality of women fellows, Kent's nomination was withdrawn. She worked at the Madras Observatory from 1873 to 1896, originally as assistant astronomer and then as meteorological observer. JH/MBO

SECONDARY SOURCES
Kidwell, Peggy Aldrich. "Women Astronomers in Britain, 1780–1930." *Isis* 75 (1984): 534–546.

KENT, GRACE HELEN (1875–1973)

U.S. clinical psychologist. Born 6 June 1875 in Michigan City, Ind. Educated Grinnell College; University of Iowa (M.A., 1904); Harvard University (1905–1906); George Washington University (Ph.D., 1915). Professional experience: Philadelphia Hospital for the Insane, psychological intern (1906–1907); Kings Park State Hospital, New York, psychologist (1907–1910); St. Elizabeth's Hospital, Washington, D.C., psychologist (1910–1911); Warren State Hospital, Pennsylvania, psychologist (1911–1912); South Carolina State Training School, psychologist (1920–1922); Worcester (Mass.) State Hospital, psychologist (1922–1926); Danvers State Hospital, psychologist (1928–1946); University of Miami, Florida, visiting professor (1947–1948). American Psychological Association, member; American Association for the Advancement of Science, Fellow. Died 18 September 1973 in Silver Spring, Md.

After Grace Kent got her master's degree from the University of Iowa, she worked at the Philadelphia Hospital for the Insane as an intern and then in several hospitals in the East. Eventually, she went back to school to work on her doctorate at George Washington University. She then moved to the South, where she held various positions as a psychologist. She published numerous articles on association in insanity, habit formation in *dementia praecox,* occupations for the insane, performance tests, and tests of special abilities. KM

STANDARD SOURCES
AMS 3–8, S&B 9; Stevens and Gardner; Zusne.

KENT, KATE PECK (1914–1987)

U.S. museum archeological textile specialist. Born 1914. Educated: University of Denver (A.B., 1934); Columbia University (graduate studies 1935–1937; 1940–1942); University of Arizona (M.A., 1950). Professional experience: Barnard College, Columbia, graduate assistant in anthropology (1936–37); Museum of Northern Arizona, assistant (1940); Denver Art Museum, assitant curator of Indian art (1942–1944); University of Denver, instructor through associate professor (1950–1978), Department of Anthropology, department chair (1973–1978); School of American Research, Santa Fe, research curator; Museum of International Folk Art, senior research associate (1984–1987). Honors and memberships: Denver Art Museum, student fellowship (1934–1935); Columbia University, resident scholarship (1935–36); American Philosophical Society, fellowship (1952); University of Denver grants (1966–1967; 1969–1970); School of American Research (1978–1979). National Endowment for the Arts grant (1980–1983). Died 1987.

Kate Peck Kent was interested in material culture from her earliest work as a student fellow at the Denver Art Museum under the director, Frederic Douglas. She then went to work with GLADYS REICHARD at Columbia University, working as her graduate assistant at Barnard, but did not obtain her degree. Her failure to complete the degree at that time probably resulted from her realization that the study of arts and crafts of indigenous peoples was outside mainstream anthropology.

Kent then returned to Denver Art Museum, where she began to study textile fragments from Tonto Ruins at Douglas's request. She worked for a time as assistant curator and soon became an expert on ancient textiles. After completing a master's degree at the University of Arizona, she began to teach at the University of Denver, eventually rising to associate professor.

From the 1940s on, Kent published a series of articles and books on prehistoric and modern Pueblo and Navajo weaving. After her retirement from teaching in 1978, she went to Santa Fe to study the textiles at the School of American Research and the International Folk Art Museum.   JH/MBO

PRIMARY SOURCES

Kent, Kate Peck. "Notes on the Weaving of Prehistoric Pueblo Textiles." *Plateau* 14 (1941): 1–11.

———. *Montezuma Caste Archaeology. Part II: Texiltes. Southwest Monuments Association Technical Series.* 3 (1954): 2–102.

———. "The Cultivation and Weaving of Cotton in the Prehistoric Southwestern United States." *Transactions of the American Philosophical Society.* New ser. 47 (1957): 457–732.

———. *Prehistoric Textiles of the Southwest.* Albuquerque: University of New Mexico Press, 1983.

SECONDARY SOURCES

Babcock, Barbara A., and Nancy J. Parezo. "Kate Peck Kent 1914–1987." In *Daughters of the Desert: Women Anthropologists and the Native American Southwest, 1880–1980.* Albuquerque: University of New Mexico Press, 1988. Includes portrait.

"Kate Peck Kent." *American Anthropologist* 190 (1988).

KENYON, KATHLEEN MARY (1906–1978)

British archeologist. Born 5 January 1906 in London, England. Father, Sir Frederic Kenyon. Educated St. Paul's School for Girls. Oxford, Somerville College. Field experience: Great Zimbabwe, assistant (1929); Verulamium (near St. Albans), assistant (1930–1935); Samaria, Palestine, assistant (1931–1934); Sabratha, North Africa, director (1948–1949, 1951); Jerusalem excavations, director (Mound of Jericho, 1952–1959), Jerusalem excavations project, director (1962–1967). Professional experience: University of London, Institute of Archaeology, acting director and first secretary (1939?–1945), lecturer (1948–1962); British School of Archaeology, Jerusalem, honorary director (1951–1957); Oxford University, St. Hugh's College, principal (1962–1973). Died 24 August 1978 in Erbistock, Wrexham, England, from a stroke.

Kathleen Kenyon was a distinguished British archeologist noted for her work on the tower of Jericho. The elder daughter of Sir Frederick Kenyon, the director and principal librarian at the British Museum, she went from St. Paul's School for Girls (where she was head girl) to read history at Somerville College, Oxford. While at Oxford, she was the first head of the Oxford University Archaeological Association. She obtained her first archeological experience working as an assistant to Gertrude Caton-Thompson at the British Association archeological dig, Great Zimbabwe (then part of Southern Rhodesia). Fired with this new experience, she continued to study under R. E. M. (Mortimer) Wheeler at the Roman site of Verulamium in England. Wheeler was the first to develop stratigraphic techniques including careful labeling of every level and drawing the sections of each trench. When Kenyon had the opportunity to work in Palestine in the early thirties, she attempted to bring Wheeler's technique to the Levant as an assistant at the excavations directed by J. W. Crowfoot, sponsored by the British School of Archaeology in Jerusalem, but found this difficult to integrate into the older style of archeology that relied upon pottery types for dating. Returning to England, Kenyon directed a number of ancient Romano-British excavations under Wheeler in Leicestershire and Shropshire and then at Southwark in London and at Sutton Wells in Herefordshire.

During the war years, she helped to establish the Institute of Archaeology at the University of London, and was its first secretary and the acting director while also serving in the Red Cross. From 1948 to 1968, she lectured on Palestinian archeology at the Institute. During this period, she also taught archeological techniques in the field.

By 1951, with new funds for excavations in Palestine, Kenyon was named honorary director of the British School of Archaeology. She began to work at the site of Jericho, and carfully studied the mound with what became known as the Wheeler-Kenyon technique, applying a grid of five-meter squares with small teams working within each square. The materials unearthed dated back to around 8,000 B.C.E. and gave very important evidence of a continuously occupied site.

Kenyon's results made her a world-renowned figure. In 1962, Kenyon was made principal of St. Hugh's College at Oxford. Although she began a final excavation in Jerusalem, the complications of her other obligations and the problems of the site diminished the importance of this last excavation, while the Six-Day War effectively put an end to the excavation. In 1973, Kenyon retired from Oxford to her family home in Wrexham. In 1978, her former students prepared a *festschrift* of writings in her honor. She died only a few months later from a stroke at her home.   JH/MBO

PRIMARY SOURCES

Kenyon, Kathleen. "Sketch of the Exploration and Settlement of the East Coast of Africa." In *The Zimbabwe Culture*, ed. Gertrude Caton-Thompson. Oxford: Clarendon Press, 1931.

———. *Verulamium Theatre Excavations.* 1935.

———. *Excavations at Sabratha.* London: Society for the Promotion of Roman Studies, 1948–1951.

———. *Beginning in Archaeology.* London: Phoenix House, 1952. Rev. ed., New York: Praeger, 1961.

———. *Excavations at Jericho.* Vol. 1. London: British School of Archaeology, 1960; Volume 2, 1965.

———. *Digging Up Jerusalem.* New York: Praeger, 1974.

SECONDARY SOURCES

Callaway, Joseph A. "Dame Kathleen M Kenyon." *Biblical Archaeologist* 42, no. 2 (1979): 122–125.

Moorey, Peter R. S., and Peter Parr, eds. *Archaeology in the Levant: Essays for Kathleen Kenyon.* Warminster, England: Arts and Phillips, 1978.

STANDARD SOURCES

Europa.

KERLING, LOUISE CATHARINA PETRONELLA (1900–)

Dutch botanist. Born 19 July 1900. Educated Univeristy of Leiden; Rijks-Universiteit, Utrecht (Ph.D., 1928). Professional experience: school in Indonesia, biology teacher; Agricultural University, Wageningen, research worker; Universities of Utrecht and Amsterdam, professor; Willie Commelin Scholten, Baarn, phytopathology laboratory director.

Lousie Kerling obtained her doctorate from the Rijks-Universiteit in Utrecht. After a term as a biology teacher in Indonesia, she took a position as a research worker at the Agricultural University in Wageningen. Appointed professor at the Universities of Utrecht and Amsterdam, she wrote on the anatomy and diseases of plants. JH/MBO

PRIMARY SOURCES

Kerling, L. C. P. "De anatomische bouw van bladvlekken." Rijks Universiteit, Utrecht. 1928.

———. "Het overgaan met zaad van de Amerikaanse vaatziekte van erwten" (Seed transmission of fusarium wilt of peas). *Tijdschrift over Plantenziekten* 58 (1952): 236–239.

———. "Beschadiging en schimmelaantasting bij erwten als gevolgen van nachtvorst." *Tijdschrift over Plantenziekten* 58 (1952): 29–54.

STANDARD SOURCES

Turkevich and Turkevich.

KEUR, DOROTHY LOUISE (STROUSE) (1904–)

U.S. anthropologist. Born 14 February in New York City. Married John Y. Keur (1928). Educated Morris High School; Hunter College (B.A., 1925); Columbia University (M.A., 1928; Ph.D., 1941); School of American Research, Santa Fe (Summers). Professional experience: Hunter College, Department of Botany, laboratory assistant (1925–1928); Department of Anthropology, instructor (1928–1940), assistant professor (1940–1947), associate professor (1947–1957), professor (1957–1965). Field experience: Big Bead Mesa, N.M. (1939, 1940); Gobernador, N.M. (1944?); Anderen Village, Netherlands (1951–1952); Dutch Winward Islands (St. Maarten, Saba, St. Eustatius) (1956). Retired 1965. Honors and memberships: New Mexico Governor's Award for Historic Preservation (April 1986); American Ethnological Society, secretary-treasurer (1947–1949), president (1955); New York Academy of Sciences, Fellow.

Dorothy Strouse was born in New York City and moved soon after to Morris Park, New York, where she went to high school. Her parents had no higher education, but her mother, who was a strong Protestant, wanted her daughter to become a missionary. Supported by her teachers who found her very bright, Strouse went to Hunter College, then tuition-free.

At Hunter, Strouse became the favorite pupil of Edward S. Burgess, a botany professor who had begun to teach a few courses in anthropology. She graduated *summa cum laude* and Phi Beta Kappa, and took a position as a laboratory assistant in botany to Burgess, which included tours to the American Museum of Natural History to view the anthropological collections. There she met Henry F. Osborn, who encouraged her to continue her studies in anthropology.

She went to Columbia to pursue a master's degree, taking summer and part-time course work, earning a master's for her study of the origins of maize under Franz Boas and the botanist Carlton Curtis. After she received her degree, Strouse was promoted to instructor in anthropology at Hunter. The same year, she married John Y. Keur, the son of Dutch immigrants who was studying forestry at Yale and who went on to earn a doctorate in biology at Columbia. The two formed a close intellectual as well as personal partnership, and later did research together in Holland and in the Dutch West Indies.

Dorothy Keur continued to advance her graduate studies in anthropology, studying archeology under Duncan Strong, and spending summers at the School of American Research in Santa Fe, New Mexico. She took a sabbatical year to complete an archeological study of Big Bead Mesa, an early Navajo site, north of Santa Fe. For this, she was awarded her doctoral degree at Columbia in 1941, a year after she had advanced to assistant professor at Hunter.

Working with her husband, from whom she had learned both Dutch and a good deal about Dutch culture, Keur began to study Dutch villages in Holland and later the Dutch Caribbean. She published two books with her husband, *The Deeply Rooted* and *Winward Children*. By this time a tenured professor at Hunter, Keur served as an officer and president of the American Ethnological Society, and was made a Fellow of the New York Academy of Sciences.

In the 1980s, Keur was honored for her earlier work on the Southwest in the conference "Daughters of the Desert," held in Tucson that also honored Elsie Parsons, FLORENCE ELLIS, ISABEL KELLY, and others. Although Keur retired from Hunter College in 1965, she continued to lecture and to be active in her profession.   JH/MBO

PRIMARY SOURCES
Keur, Dorothy L. *Big Bead Mesa: An Archaeological Study of Navaho Archaeology*. Memoirs of the Society for American Archaeology, Memoir no. 1. Menasha, Wisc.: Society for American Archaeology, 1941.
———. "A Chapter in Navaho-Pueblo Relations." *American Antiquity* 10 (1944): 75–86.
———. With John Y. Keur. *The Deeply Rooted: A Study of Drents Community in the Netherlands*. American Ethnological Society, Monograph 25. Assen: Van Gorcum, 1955. This also appeared in a Dutch edition the same year.
———. With John Y. Keur. *Winward Children: A Study in Human Ecology of the Three Dutch Winward Islands*. Assen, the Netherlands: Van Gorcun, 1960.

SECONDARY SOURCES
Babcock, Barbara A., and Nancy J. Parezo. "Dorothy Louise Keur 1904–." In *Daughters of the Desert: Women Anthropologists and the Native American Southwest, 1880–1980*. Albuquerque: University of New Mexico Press, 1988. Includes portrait.

STANDARD SOURCES
AMS 7–8, S&B 9–12; Gacs (article by Alice James).

KHARUZINA, VERA NIKOLAEVNA (1866–1931)

Russian ethnographer. Born 29 September 1866 in Moscow. Three brothers. Educated Berlin and Paris. Professional experience: lecturer, Moscow Higher Women's Courses and Archaeological Institute; Moscow University, professor. Died 17 May 1931.

Vera Nikolaevna Kharuzina was the first woman professor of ethnography in Russia. She was the younger sister of three talented ethnographers, Mikhail, Aleksei, and Nikolai Kharuzin. Of the three, Nikolai was the most eminent and the closest in age to Kharuzina. She accompanied him on expeditions to the Olenek and Arkhangel'sk provinces, to the Altai, the Baltic area, and Barabin Steppe, the Crimea and the Caucasus.

From 1907 to 1923, Kharuzina taught ethnography, first at the Higher Women's Courses and the Archaeological Institute in Moscow; later, as a professor at Moscow University.

Kharuzina and her brothers belonged to the school of ethnography known in Soviet scholarship as "evolutionary," to distinguish it from earlier romantic and later Marxist approaches. The object of research tended to be cultural phenomena as opposed to individual tribes or peoples. These phenomena were seen as progressing from simpler to more complex forms in a manner somewhat analogous to Darwinian evolution of species. From this point of view, of two phenomena, the simplest must always precede the more complicated. To ethnographers of this school, the economic aspects of the life of a people played a lesser role than it would in the later Soviet period.

The Kharuzins as a family collected a wealth of materials and made a substantial contribution to many aspects of Russian ethnography. Kharuzina's particular contribution was in the area of religious belief, spiritual culture, and folklore.

Besides her own scientific publications, she was responsible for editing her brother Nikolai's course of lectures after his death in 1900, and was also the author of a number of popular works.   ACH

PRIMARY SOURCES
Kharuzina, Vera Nikolaevna. "K voprosu o pochitanii ognia." *Etnograficheskoe obozrenie* 3, no. 4 (1906).
———. *Vvedenie v etnografiiu*. 3d ed. 1941. Course of lectures.

SECONDARY SOURCES
Tokarev, Sergei A. *Istoriia russkoi etnografii*. Moscow: Nauka, 1966.
Vredenskii, B.A., ed. *Bol'shaia sovetskaia entsiklopediia*. 3d ed. Moscow: Izd-vo "Sovetskaia entsiklopediia," 1973.

STANDARD SOURCES
WWW (USSR).

KIELAN-JAWOROWSKA, ZOFIA (1925–)

Polish paleontologist and geologist. Exact birth date unknown. Married Zbigniew Jaworowski. One son, Mariusz. Educated Secret Polish High School in Warsaw (graduated 1943); Secret Warsaw

University (1944); Warsaw University (master's degree in zoological sciences, 1949); (Ph.D. in paleontology, 1956). Professional experience: Institute of Paleobiology of the Polish Academy of Sciences, docent (1956), senior scientist (1956–1961), director (from 1961); University of Warsaw, professor (1961).

Zofia Kielan-Jaworowska was the first woman to serve in the International Union of Geological Sciences (IUGS) Executive Committee. Born in Poland, she began her education during the German occupation of that country. During this time, all high schools and universities were closed down, but she was one of a group of students and teachers who worked in secret, at the so-called Secret Polish High School and Secret Warsaw University. In 1944, her studies were interrupted when she was captured as a prisoner of war (she was a soldier in the Home Army and had taken part in the Scouts' movement, which supported the Warsaw uprising) and sent to a camp in Pruszkow near Warsaw. After the war was over, she studied zoology and paleontology at Warsaw University under Roman Kozlowski, a well-known paleontologist and a supportive mentor to Kielan. After she earned a master's degree in zoology, she continued her studies and received her doctorate in paleontology. She held concurrent positions at the Polish Academy of Sciences' Institute of Paleobiology and the University of Warsaw, where she was first a docent and later professor. Kielan married Zbigniew Jaworowski, professor of radiobiology in the Central Laboratory for Radiological Protection in Warsaw in 1958 and the following year gave birth to a son.

Kielan-Jaworowska's research interests revolved around three separate time periods. From the late 1940s to 1950s, she worked on Devonian, Cambrian, and Ordovician trilobites. From 1958 to about 1964, she studied the Paleozoic jaw apparatus of polychaete annelids. After the mid-1960s, she changed her focus dramatically and worked on vertebrates, especially Mesozoic mammals. In 1974, she was awarded the Polish State Prize for her work on Cretaceous mammals.

Kielan-Jaworowska was the vice-president of IUGS, president of the Polish National Committee on Evolutionary Biology, and an editor of *Palaeontologia Polonica*. She was a member of the Polish Academy of Sciences, the Presidium of the Academy, the Polish Geological Society, the Polish Zoological Society, the American Palaeontological Society, Sigma Xi, and the Scientific Research Society (U.S.). And she was an honorary member of the (U.S.) Society of Vertebrate Paleontology, and of the Polish Copernicus Society of Naturalists. JH/MBO

PRIMARY SOURCES
Kielan-Jaworowska, Zofia. "Upper Ordovician Trilobites from Poland and Some Related Forms from Bohemia and Scandinavia." *Palaeontologia Polonica* 11 (1959): 1–198.

———. "Polychaete Jaw Apparatuses from the Ordovician and Silurian of Poland and a Comparison with Modern Forms." *Palaeontologia Polonica* 16 (1966): 1–152.

SECONDARY SOURCES
"Zofia Kielan-Jaworowska of Poland." *Episodes* 2 (1981): 51.

STANDARD SOURCES
Debus.

KIL, CHUNG-HEE (1899–1990)

Korean physician. Born 3 February 1899 in Seoul, Korea, to Mr. and Mrs. Hyun-Suk Kil. Two siblings. Married Tak-Won Kim. Three children. Educated Tokyo Women's Medical College (M.D., 1923). Professional experience: with her husband and Rosetta Hall founded the Chosen Women's Medical Training Institute (later the Seoul Women's Medical Training Institute); private practice in Korea (1939–1964). Retired 1964. Emigrated to the United States (1979). Died 1990 in Cheltenham, Pa.

Chung-Hee Kil was beset by a number of obstacles in her path to becoming a physician in Korea. Although education of women was discouraged in Korea, Kil's parents encouraged her to obtain a formal education. Japan, however, had annexed Korea in 1910, and had repressive rules regarding Koreans and education, even forbidding them to speak their own language. In spite of the prejudices of the Japanese, Kil graduated from the Tokyo Women's Medical College with a medical degree. She was especially suspect among her classmates, for she had participated in the Declaration of Korean Independence on 1 March 1919, and pledged to fight for independence by swearing an oath in her own blood.

Kil returned to Korea and began her internship at the Chosen Government General Hospital (now Seoul National University Hospital). She married Tak-Won Kim, a specialist in internal medicine. The couple separated for three years to pursue further education—she returned to Japan and he went to Beijing. When they returned they met a missionary physician from New York State, ROSETTA HALL. Hall impressed upon the couple the need for women physicians in Korea, for many women died unnecessarily because of their hesitation to call in a male physician. The three of them, Hall, Kil, and Kim, founded the Chosen Women's Medical Training Institute. After Hall retired in 1933, Kil and her husband expanded the curriculum so that the courses taught there were equivalent to those at one-year premedical and four-year medical colleges. A hospital was attached to the institute.

Funding for the institute was always a problem, because of the hostility of the Korean establishment. However, it was the Japanese governor-general who had the ultimate say in decisions regarding the institute, and he had even suppressed preexisting institutions for male Koreans. In spite of the problems, the institute (with its new name, the Seoul Women's Medical Training Institute) survived and grew. In 1938, the institute was elevated to a college, and once this happened, Kil and Kim were prohibited from joining the faculty because of their anti-Japanese activities. The Japanese took over the college and favored Japanese students over Korean. Tak-Won Kim died in 1939, and Kil continued to practice medicine in Korea for the next twenty-five years. During the same time, she was an instructor at the Ewha Woman's University and raised her two daughters and one son. The daughters became doctors and emigrated to the United States.

Kil received a number of honors in her native Korea. She served as president of the Korean Women's Medical Association as well as being the chief physician for the Korean royal family. The Korean minister of public health recognized Kil for her contributions to medical education in Korea in 1959. In 1960, she was recognized by the city of Seoul as a dedicated public servant, and in 1961 was recognized by the Ewha Woman's University as a pioneer in the medical education of women.

Kil retired from medicine in 1964 and in 1979 emigrated to the United States to be with her daughter. In 1980 she established a fellowship to promote scientific education at Korea University College of Medicine, which allows graduates of this college to study medicine in the United States. She published her autobiography in 1981, which provides information on the education of women in medicine in Korea.   JH/MBO

PRIMARY SOURCES

Kil, Chung-Hee. In Hellstedt, *Autobiographies.*

SECONDARY SOURCES

Kim, Sangduk. "Women's Medical Training Institute, 1928–1938." *Korean Journal of Medical History* 1 (1993): 80–84.

STANDARD SOURCES

Shearer and Shearer 1996 (article by Sangduk Kim).

KING, ANASTASIA KATHLEEN (MURPHY) (1894–1978)

Irish botanist. Born 1894 in Dublin. Honors and memberships: Dublin Naturalists Field Club (1944), president (1955). Died in 28 March 1978 in Mount Merrion.

The Irish botanist Anastasia Kathleen King was born in Dublin and lived there for most of her life. She became a member of the Dublin Naturalists Field Club when she was in her fifties and became its president ten years later. She studied Irish bryophytes and discovered the moss *Meesia tristicia* in County Mayo in 1957. She had many articles published in *Irish Naturalists Journal.*   JH/MBO

PRIMARY SOURCES

King, Anastasia Kathleen. "Supplement to Colgan's Flora of the County Dublin." In *Flora County Dublin,* ed. Neal Colgan. Dublin: Stationery Office, 1961.

SECONDARY SOURCES

"Anastasia Kathleen King." *Irish Naturalists Journal* 19 (1975): 130.
Bulletin Irish Biogeographical Society (1979): 75–80. Obituary notice.

STANDARD SOURCES

Desmond.

KING, GEORGINA (1845–1932)

Australian anthropologist, stratigrapher, and economic geologist. Born 1845. Died 1932.

King is noted for her controversial writings connecting anthropology to economic geology.   JH/MBO

PRIMARY SOURCES

King, Georgina. *The Mineral Wealth of New South Wales and Other Lands and Countries.* 1895.

SECONDARY SOURCES

Branagan, David F. "Georgina King: Geological Prophet or Lost?" *University of Sydney Archives Rec.* 10, no. 2 (1982): 4–9.
Bygott, Ursula. "Georgina King—Amateur Geologist and Anthropologist—1845–1932." *University of Sydney Archives Rec.* 9, no. 2 (1982): 11–18.

STANDARD SOURCES

Sarjeant.

KING, HELEN DEAN (1869–1955)

U.S. biologist. Born 27 September 1869 in Owego, N.Y. to Leonora (Dean) and George King. Two siblings. Never married. Educated Owego Free Academy (graduated, 1877); Vassar College (B.A., 1892); Bryn Mawr College (Ph.D., 1899). Professional experience: Bryn Mawr College, assistant in biology; University of Pennsylvania, fellow in biology (1906–1908); Wistar Institute of Anatomy and Biology, Philadelphia, assistant in anatomy (1908–

1913), assistant professor of anatomy (1913–1927), professor of embryology (1927–1949). Died 9 March 1955 in Philadelphia.

Helen Dean King was the elder of two daughters born to George and Leonora King, both of whose families had been long established in Owego as owners of leather companies. Like her father, Helen graduated from the Owego Free Academy, apparently in 1887, although her name is not on the list of graduates for that year. After leaving the academy, she attended Vassar College, from which she graduated in 1892.

As were so many women biologists in the early twentieth century, King was exposed to the ideas of Thomas Hunt Morgan at Bryn Mawr College, where she did her doctoral work. She majored in morphology under Morgan and minored in physiology and paleontology under J. W. Warren and FLORENCE BASCOM. After completing her doctoral degree at Bryn Mawr, King remained at the college for five years as an assistant in biology (1899–1904). From 1906 to 1908, she worked with E. G. Conklin at the University of Pennsylvania. In 1908 she took a teaching post at the Wistar Institute of Anatomy and Biology in Philadelphia, then under the scientific directorship of H. H. Donaldson. She stayed there for over forty years, progressing from assistant to assistant professor (1913–1927), and to professor of embryology from 1927 until her retirement in 1949. She served on the institute's advisory board for twenty-four years, was editor of its bibliographic service for thirteen years, and was associate editor of the *Journal of Morphology and Physiology* for three years.

King published prolifically. Her early papers reflect the interests of Morgan at that time in regeneration and developmental anatomy. King focused, however, on the effects of close inbreeding after she began to work at the Wistar Institute. In order to obtain and maintain as uniform a stock as possible, King undertook a series of inbreeding experiments on albino rats beginning in 1909. She used brother-sister matings, selected the healthiest litters, and published a complete analysis of many phases of growth and activity in the inbred animals. By 1918, she had reached the twenty-fifth generation. King noted that there had been almost universal prejudice against inbreeding. In her first three papers on the subject, she considered the effects of inbreeding on body weight, fertility, constitutional vigor, and sex ratios. She concluded that the inbred animals compared favorably with the stock albinos.

King's results captured the imagination of newspapers reporters, who implied that she considered incest taboos unnecessary. Under the headline "Dr. King Quizzed on Kin Marriage Theory: Home Folk Shocked by Advocacy of Human Inbreeding," a newspaper article in 1922 began,

"All sorts and varieties of letters are pouring into the office of Dr. Helen D. King, member of the faculty of the University of Pennsylvania and research scholars of Wistar Institute. The last but not the least finding its way to the office of the woman who recently made public some of her results of experiments on rats, showing, she said, that consanguineous marriages under proper laws and conditions would improve the race, is that of a Los Angeles spinster, who asks Doctor King to find her a husband." (Ogilvie 1986)

To insure a prompt reply, the article continued, the Californian had enclosed a stamped, self-addressed envelope. Some of the responses were violent, such as that from a "Christian and a student" at Clark University who wrote that "he wished someone would kill her, and if they didn't he would do it himself."

Commenting on her sensationalized findings, King asserted that although her inbred strain was superior in body size, fertility, and longevity, "I do not claim that this superiority is due solely to the fact that the animals were inbred, neither do I wish to assert that, in general, inbreeding is better than outbreeding for building up and maintaining the general vigor of a race." Certain benefits, she continued, result from both inbreeding and outbreeding, for each has its merits and can be useful for bringing out the best in any stock. She did conclude from her experiments, however, "that even in mammals the closest form of inbreeding possible, *i.e.,* the mating of brother and sister from the same litter, is not necessarily injurious either to the fertility or to the constitutional vigor of a race even when they continued for many generations." Success or failure in inbreeding experiments, she believed, depends on the "character of the stock that is inbred, on the manner in which the breeding animals are selected, and on the environmental conditions under which the animals are reared" (Ogilvie 1986).

King's second important contribution to science involved the domestication of the Norway rat. She began this project in 1919 and continued working on it until she retired. Her study of the life processes in these rats involved the cataloguing of a large series of mutants that appeared throughout the study. Again, the impact of her work extended beyond the scientific community into the popular mind. A newspaper announced that King "has succeeded in producing several generations of gray rats in the experimental laboratory in spite of the theory that wild rats would not breed in captivity and has noted differences in each successive generation, which show that natural evolution can be simulated in the laboratory." The amazed reporter had stood "in wonder, not at the beauty of the rat, but at the spectacle of a woman holding a rat in the palm of her hand," and had found it difficult to "believe that one of the greatest authorities on rats in the country is a very human and thoroughly feminine woman" (Ogilvie 1986). People were fascinated by reports of curly-haired rats, waltzing rats, and chocolate-colored rats.

King's work in animal husbandry helped make it possible to maintain pure strains of laboratory animal; her isolation of various mutant forms provided strains for studying specific characteristics.

In 1932 King was awarded the Ellen Richards Research Prize of the Association to Aid Scientific Research for Women. After a very productive career, King died in Philadelphia at the age of eighty-five.   MBO

PRIMARY SOURCES
King, Helen Dean. "Regeneration in *Asterias vulgaris.*" *Archiv für Entwicklungsmechanik der Organismen* 7, no. 2 (1900): 351–436.
———. "Studies on Inbreeding. I. The Effects of Inbreeding on the Growth and Variability in the Body Weight of the Albino Rat." *Journal of Experimental Zoology* 26, no. 1 (1918): 1–54.
———. "Studies on Inbreeding. II. The Effects of Inbreeding on the Growth and Variability in the Body Weight of the Albino Rat." *Journal of Experimental Zoology* 26, no. 2 (1918): 335–378.
———. "Studies on Inbreeding. III. The Effects of Inbreeding with Selection, on the Sex Ratio of the Albino Rat." *Journal of Experimental Zoology* 27, no. 1 (October 1918): 1–35.
———. "Studies on Inbreeding. IV. A Further Study of the Effects of Inbreeding on the Growth and Variability in the Body Weight of the Albino Rat." *Journal of Experimental Zoology* 29 (August 1919): 1–54.

SECONDARY SOURCES
Rossiter, Margaret. "Women Scientists in America before 1920." *American Scientist* 62 (1974): 312–323.

STANDARD SOURCES
AMS 1–8; Bailey; *DSB*, supplement 2; Ogilvie 1986; Shearer and Shearer 1996 (article by Ann Lindell).

KING, JESSIE LUELLA (1882–?)
U.S. physiologist. Born 19 October 1882 in Richmond, Ind., to Edward and Mary (Evans) King. Educated Earlham College (B.S., 1904); Cornell University (Ph.D., 1911). Professional experience: Pratt Institute, Department of Physiology, associate and instructor (1905–1908); Goucher College, instructor in physiology (1911–1915), associate professor of physiology (1915–1919); professor of physiology (1919–1947), emerita professor (from 1947). Death date unknown.

Jessie King was born in Richmond, Indiana, and attended Earlham College. Before she completed her dissertation at Cornell University, she taught physiology as an associate instructor at Pratt Institute of Art in New York Universty for three years. She began to teach at Goucher College as an instructor in physiology and rose in the ranks to become professor of physiology in 1919. She remained at Goucher until she retired as an emerita professor in the late 1940s.

A Quaker as well as a socialist, King took her commitment to peace seriously in the 1930s as a member of the Women's International League for Peace and Freedom.
JH/MBO

STANDARD SOURCES
American Women; AMS 9, B 11; Rossiter 1982.

KING, LOUISA BOYD (YEOMANS) (1863–1948)
U.S. horticulturist and landscape architect. Born 17 October 1863, probably in Washington, N.J. Father Alfred Yeomans. Four siblings. Married Francis King. Three children. Educated private schools. Honors and memberships: Massachusetts Horticultural Society, George Robert White Medal for Eminent Service in Horticulture; Garden Club of America, Medal of Honor; National Home Planting Bureau, Distinguished Service Award. Died 16 January 1948.

Louisa Yeomans was the third of five children of Presbyterian minister Alfred Yeomans and his wife. She was educated in private schools, and, when she was twenty-six years old, married Francis King of Chicago. The young couple spent the first years of their marriage at the home of her husband's mother. Much of her horticultural education occurred at that time, for her mother-in-law was a superb gardener, versed in both theoretical and practical aspects of gardening. In 1902, the Kings moved to their own home, Orchard House, in Alma, Michigan. King began to correspond with the writers she had read in her mother-in-law's library, and began writing for magazines such as *Garden Magazine, House Beautiful,* and *Country Life.* Her first book, *The Well-Considered Garden,* documented her beginner's attempts at planning and establishing a garden. After the popularity of her books, she became interested in garden clubs. Although there were a few garden clubs in the eastern states, there were none in the other states. In 1913, at a luncheon meeting in Philadelphia, the Garden Club of America was established, with King as one of four vice-presidents. The idea ballooned, and clubs were established all over the country. She insisted that the clubs provide help to members with an overall purpose of education. In addition to her work in the Garden Club of America, King was instrumental in the formation of the Women's National Farm and Garden Association (1914), and served as its first president. Through the association, university women investigating business and professional opportunities for women in horticultural and other agricultural fields helped farm women who were isolated come together for matters of mutual interest. This organization became especially important during World War I, when women often had to manage the farms. After King's husband died in 1927, she sold Orchard House, and moved to Kingstree, a house in South Hartsford, New York, where she renovated the old gardens and built new ones.

King was awarded the George Robert White Medal for eminent service in horticulture by the trustees of the Massachusetts Horticultural Society, the Medal of Honor of the Garden Clubs of America, and the Distinguished Service Award of the National Home Planting Bureau.　JH/MBO

PRIMARY SOURCES
King, Louisa. *The Well-Considered Garden.* New York: Charles Scribner's, 1915.
———. *From a New Garden.* New York: Alfred A. Knopf, 1930.

SECONDARY SOURCES
Hollingsworth, Buckner. "Mrs. Francis King, 1863–1948: Gardner's Guide and Friend." In *Her Garden Was Her Delight.* New York: Macmillan, 1930.

STANDARD SOURCES
WWW(A); NAW; Shearer and Shearer 1996 (article by Carol W. Cubberley).

KING, MARTHA (1803–1897)

Irish-born New Zealand botanical illustrator. Born circa 1803 in Cork. Emigrated to New Zealand with sister and brother (1840). Professional experience: Wellington Horticultural and Botanical Society, commisioned illustrator (1842). Died 1897 in New Zealand.

Martha King was born in Cork, Ireland, and emigrated to New Zealand when she was in her late thirties, along with her sister and brother. She moved first to Wanganui and, four years later, to New Plymouth. An excellent illustrator, she was commisioned by the Wellington Horticultural and Botanical Society to draw the local flora. Five of these drawings were included in a book on New Zealand flora by E. J. Wakefield.　JH/MBO

PRIMARY SOURCES
Wakefield, E. J. *Illustrations to Adventure in New Zealand.* London: Smith, Elder, and Cornhill, 1845. Includes five of Martha King's drawings.

SECONDARY SOURCES
Sampson, F. B. *Early New Zealand Botanical Art.* Aukland: Reed Methuen, 1985. King discussed on pages 83–84.

STANDARD SOURCES
Desmond.

KING, SUSAN (RAYMOND) (1892–?)

U.S. astronomer. Born 1892. Married Harold S. King (1922). Educated Smith College (A.B., 1913); Harvard (Radcliffe College) (A.M., 1919). Professional experience: Smith College, demonstrator in astronomy (1913–1915); Nantucket Maria Mitchell Association, fellow (1915–1917); Smith College, instructor (1917–1922); Leavitts Almanac, N.H., computer (1922–1942); Yale Observatory, researcher (1943–1945); Smith College, instructor of astronomy and mathematics (1943–1945). Death date unknown.

Susan Raymond was trained in mathematics and astronomy at Smith College, receiving her bachelor's degree in 1913. Made a fellow of the Nantucket Maria Mitchell Association from 1915 to 1917, she studied astronomy and mathematics at Harvard University, and then returned to Smith as an instructor in astronomy from 1917 to 1922. During this period, she was awarded her master's degree by Radcliffe College, since all women's graduate degrees were then awarded not by Harvard but by Radcliffe.

In 1922, she married a chemist, Harold S. King, who obtained a teaching position in chemistry at Dalhousie University, Halifax, Nova Scotia, which he held until 1942. Susan King found a position as computer for the Leavitt Almanac Company in New Hampshire. During World War II, her husband left his teaching position in Canada to work with the U.S. Army chemical ordnance in the southern states. Susan King took the opportunity to return to New England to do research at Yale Observatory and to teach astronomy and mathematics again at Smith College. Her husband's continued work with the U.S. Army Chemical Corps in Maryland as scientist and technical advisor in the postwar period apparently ended her own teaching and research career. King's research had been on variable stars and celestial mechanics.

　JH/MBO

PRIMARY SOURCES
King, Susan Raymond. "The Photographic Light Curve of B.D. +18° 318b." Smith College, M.A. thesis, 1919.

STANDARD SOURCES
AMS 4–8, P 9, P&B 10.

KINGSLEY, LOUISE (1899–1968)

U.S. geologist. Born 14 August 1899 in Binghamton, N.Y. Educated Smith College (B.A., 1922; M.A., 1924); Bryn Mawr College (Ph.D., 1931). Professional experience: Wellesley College, geology instructor (1930–1934), assistant professor (1934–1939), associate professor (1939–1951), professor (from 1951). Honors and memberships: Geological Society, Fellow; Sigma Xi, member; New York Academy of Science, member. Died 1968.

Geologist Louise Kingsley received all of her education at two of the "Seven Sisters" colleges, with bachelor's and master's degrees from Smith, and a doctorate from Bryn Mawr. She continued this pattern in her professional life, teaching exclusively at Wellesley College.

As a specialist in field geology and petrology, Kingsley pursued research on cauldron subsidence. In her research, she concentrated on the Ossipee Mountains, the Cardigan Quadrangle, and the White Mountains of New Hampshire. She collected fossils in Kansas and investigated new techniques in submarine topography in Alaska.   JH/MBO

SECONDARY SOURCES
Fins, Alice. *Women in Science.* Skokie, Ill.: VGM Career Horizons, 1979.

STANDARD SOURCES
AMS 5–8, P 9, P&B 10–11.

KINGSLEY, MARY HENRIETTA (1862–1900)

English explorer and natural history collector. Born in 1862. Father George Kingsley. Explored and collected in West Africa materials for British Museum. Died in South Africa in 1900.

Mary Kingsley had little formal education. Her father had been deeply interested in anthropology and natural history, and she had read widely in those fields. Some of this interest may have ben stimulated by her uncle, the writer and clergyman Charles Kingsley. When her parents died in 1892, she began to travel, first to the Canary Islands and then to West Africa. She explored the Calabar and Ogowe rivers on her second voyage and climbed the highest mountain in the Cameroons in West Africa, the second European climber to do so. On her journeys, Kingsley collected insects, fish, reptiles, and plants for the British Museum.

Kingsley became a celebrity on her return to England. Her collections were analyzed by curators at the British Museum as appendixes to her important book *Travels in West*

Africa (1896). She published her second book, *West African Studies,* three years later (1899). She championed African causes and considered taxes on the Sierra Leone protectorate unfair. She suggested that West Africa be administered by traders in association with the native African people. When the Boer War began, she traveled to South Africa to nurse prisoners, and she died from enteric fever in South Africa at the age of thirty-eight. At her request, she was buried at sea. After her death, the journal *Africa* was dedicated to her. Curiously, she remained a Victorian middle-class woman in her disapproval of women on bicycles and of women's suffrage.   JH/MBO

PRIMARY SOURCES
Kingsley, Mary Henrietta. *Travels in West Africa.* London: Macmillian and Co., 1896. Appendix III included a report by Dr. A. Gunther on her collections of reptiles and fishes. Appendix IV included a report by N. F. King on her collection of insects.
———. *West African Studies.* London: Macmillian and Co., 1899.

SECONDARY SOURCES
Blyden, Woodward M. *The African Society and Miss Mary Kingsley.* London: J. Scott, 1901. Includes some correspondence in which she described conditions observed among African tribal people.
Campbell, Olwen. *Mary Kingsley: A Victorian in the Jungle.* London: Methuen, 1957.
Frank, Katherine. *A Voyager Out: The Life of Mary Kingsley.* Boston: Houghton Mifflin, 1986. More on her earlier life as well as her life in Africa.
Sweeney, Patricia E. *Biographies of British Women, an Annotated Bibliography.* Santa Barbara, Calif., and London, England: ABC-Clio, 1993.

STANDARD SOURCES
Desmond; Uglow 1989.

KIRBY, ELIZABETH (1823–1873)

British botanist. Born 15 December 1823 in Leicester. Sisters, including older sister Mary Kirby Gregg, with whom she collaborated. Died June 1873 in Leicester.

Kirby, like her sister Mary Kirby Gregg, was an amateur botanist. She was also a lucid writer, and did some of the writing for three books by Mary.   JH/MBO

PRIMARY SOURCES:
Kirby, Elizabeth. With Mary Kirby. *Flora of Leicestershire; Comprising the Flowering Plants and the Ferns Indigenous to the*

County. Arranged on the Natural System. London: Hamilton, Adams, and Co. Paternoster Row, 1850.

————. With Mary Kirby. *Plants of the Land and Water.* London: Jarrold and Sons, 1857.

————. With Mary Kirby. *Chapters on Trees: A Popular Account of Their Nature and Uses.* London: Cassell, Petter and Galpin, 1873.

KIRCH, CHRISTINE (ca. 1696–1782)

German astronomer. Born circa 1696 in Berlin to Maria (Winkelmann) and Gottfried Kirch. Brother, Christfried. Sister Margaretha. Never married. Died 1782 in Berlin.

Christine was the daughter of astronomers Maria and Gottfried Kirch and the sister of astronomer Christfried Kirch. She and her sister Margaretha were trained in astronomy from the age of ten, and both worked as assistants to their brother. Christine was the older and did the calculations for Christfried. After the deaths of her parents, she calculated the annual almanac and ephemeris for the Berlin Academy of Sciences and assisted her brother Christfried in his observations and calculations. After Christfried's death, Christine continued to prepare the academy calendar until her own death.   JH/MBO

SECONDARY SOURCES
Davis, Herman S. "Women Astronomers." *Popular Astronomy* 6 (May 1898): 128–138; (June 1898): 211–228.
Schiebinger, Londa. *The Mind Has No Sex? Women in the Origins of Modern Science.* Cambridge, Mass.: Harvard University Press, 1989. Contains an excellent discussion of Kirch.

STANDARD SOURCES
Bibliographie astronomique; DSB; Rebière.

KIRCH, MARGARETHA (b. ca. 1700)

German astronomer. Born circa 1700 in Berlin to Maria (Winkelmann) and Gottfried Kirch. Brother, Christfried. Sister, Christine. Never married.

Margaretha was the younger daughter of Maria and Gottfried Kirch. Like her sister, Christine, she worked for her brother Christfried as his assistant.   JH/MBO

SECONDARY SOURCES
Schiebinger, Londa. *The Mind Has No Sex? Women in the Origins of Modern Science.* Cambridge, Mass.: Harvard University Press, 1989.

KIRCH, MARIA MARGARETHA WINKELMANN (1670–1720)

German astronomer. Born 1670 at Panitsch, near Leipzig. Father Lutheran minister. Married Gottfried Kirch. At least three children: Christfried, Christine, and Margaretha. Professional experience: assistant to her husband, the astronomer to the Berlin Academy of Sciences; independent calendar maker. Died 1720 in Berlin.

Maria Margaretha Winkelmann's Lutheran clergyman father provided her with a good education, and a self-taught amateur astronomer, Christoph Arnold of Sommerfeld, near Leipzig, who was known as the "astronomical peasant," inspired her interest in astronomy. Therefore, she was already a respected astronomer before her marriage in 1692 to her other teacher, the astronomer Gottfried Kirch (1639–1710). Gottfried Kirch had served as an informal apprentice at Hevelius's private observatory at Danzig and studied mathematics at the University of Jena at Arnold's house. It probably occurred to Winkelmann that she, by marrying Kirch, increased her chances of continuing in astronomy. The marriage also benefited Kirch, who had been married previously; he now obtained both a housewife and an astronomical assistant. As her husband's assistant, Kirch made observations and performed the calculations necessary for the production of Gottfried's calendars and ephemerides. The couple's children, Christfried (1694–1740), Christine (ca. 1696–1782), and Margaretha (b. ca. 1700) became astronomers as well.

In 1702 Maria Kirch discovered a comet. Since the comet was reported in Gottfried's and not Maria's name (possibly because she was not conversant with Latin, the language of the *Acta eruditorum,* Germany's scientific journal), the discovery was often attributed to him. Although the Gottfried did not mention Kirch's part in the discovery in the original report, in a report published in 1710 he explained that she observed the comet. She published three astrological pamphlets between 1709 and 1711. She also predicted the appearance of a new comet in another pamphlet and the work was favorably reviewed in the *Acta eruditorum* in 1712. She also was active in calendar production.

When her husband died, Kirch proposed that she replace him as astronomer at the Academy of Sciences in Berlin. This proposal was not unusual for, as Londa Schiebinger has noted, it was a well-established principle that the widow might carry out her husband's profession after his death. Hence, there were no problems when Kirch continued her former work. The difficulty arose when she attempted to secure an appointment as the academy astronomer. Although she was supported by Leibniz, her candidacy was rejected. Schiebinger noted that the conflict did not occur solely because Kirch was a woman, although her gender certainly was a factor, but because of the position of the academy astronomer. The astronomer was a university-educated mathematician, but he was also, as a calendar maker, an artisan. It was acceptable for a non-university-educated woman to occupy the artisan part of the dichotomy, but unacceptable for her to hold the institutional title.

After working in several observatories following the death of her husband, she joined her son Christfried, who had been appointed astronomer of the Berlin Observatory (1716). She remained in Berlin for the rest of her life, calculating calendars for various German cities.　　　MBO

SECONDARY SOURCES
Allgemeine deutsche Biographie. 56 vols. Leipzig: Duncker and Humblot, 1875–1912.
Schiebinger, Londa. *The Mind Has No Sex? Women in the Origins of Modern Science.* Cambridge, Mass.: Harvard University Press, 1989. Contains an excellent discussion of Kirch.

STANDARD SOURCES
DSB; Lalande (Kirch discussed on page 359); Rebière.

KIRKBRIDE, MARY BUTLER (1874–?)
U.S. bacteriologist. Born Philadelphia, Pa., 15 June 1874. Educated University of Pennsylvania (1897–1906); Harvard University (1909); Cornell University (1909–1910); Columbia University (1910–1914). Professional experience: Philadelphia Polyclinic and College of Graduate Medicine, assistant to director (1899–1909); New York State Department of Health, assistant bacteriologist (1914–1916), bacteriologist (1916–1930), assistant director in charge of antitoxin, serum, and vaccine laboratories (1930–1932), associate director, antitoxins (1932–1946). Concurrent positions: U.S. Army Surgeon General, consultant (1944). Awards and honors: Rockefeller Institute grant (1910–1912); New York State Association of Public Health Laboratories, Gold Medal (1935); Smith College, honorary D.Sc. (1932); Public Health Association, Fellow. Honors and memberships: Society for Experimental Biology; New York Public Health Laboratories Association, secretary-treasurer. Retired 1946. Death date unknown.

Although Mary Butler Kirkbride was well trained as a bacteriologist, she never completed a formal degree. From the age of twenty-three to thirty-two she took classes in biology and bacteriology at the University of Pennsylvania while holding a position as assistant to the director of the Philadelphia Polyclinic and College of Graduate Medicine. She then studied at Harvard University, and in 1910 she obtained a Rockefeller Institute grant that allowed her to extend her studies at Columbia University, which she then continued over four years. In 1914, she received her first professional appointment in the New York State Department of Health as an assistant bacteriologist, rising to bacteriologist by 1916. By 1930 she was in charge of antitoxin, serum, and vaccine laboratories, first as assistant director and then, from 1932 to 1946, as associate director. In 1944, she also served as consultant to the U.S. Surgeon General's office.

In 1932, Smith College acknowledged Kirkbride's contributions to public health with an honorary Doctor of Science degree and three years later the New York State Association of Public Health Laboratories awarded her its gold medal. She was active in this professional association, serving as its secretary-treasurer from 1922 until her retirement in 1946.　　　JH/MBO

STANDARD SOURCES
AMS 9 B; Rossiter 1982.

KIRKHAM, NELLIE (d. 1979)
British mining historian, poet, playwright, and broadcaster. Married J. H. D. Myatt. Died 1979.

Nellie Kirkham wrote extensively on the history of the mines of the Peak District of Derbyshire and Staffordshire.　　　JH/MBO

PRIMARY SOURCES
Kirkham, Nellie. *Derbyshire Lead Mining through the Centuries.* Truro: Barton, 1968.

SECONDARY SOURCES
Nash, Douglas A. "Miss Nellie Kirkham. (Mrs. J. H. D. Myatt)—an Obituary." *Bulletin of the Peak District Mines Historical Society* 7, no. 4 (1979): 195–198.

STANDARD SOURCES
Sarjeant.

KITTRELL, FLEMMIE PANSY (1904–1980)
U.S. nutritionist and educator. Born 25 December 1904 in Henderson, North Carolina to Alice (Mills) and James Lee Kittrell. Seven siblings. Educated Hampton (Va.) Institute (B.S., 1928); Cornell University (M.A., 1930; Ph.D., 1938). Professional experience: Bennett College, home economics teacher (1928–?); Hampton Institute, dean of women and head, home economics department (1940–1944); Howard University, Washington, D.C., faculty, head of home economics department (1944–1972); emerita professor (from 1972); Cornell Visiting Senior Fellow (1974–1976);

Moton Center Senior Research Fellow (1977); Fulbright lecturer in India (1978). Honors and memberships: Hampton University, outstanding alumna (1955); National Council of Negro Women, Scroll of Honor (1961); Cornell University, achievement award (1968); University of North Carolina, Greensboro, honorary degree (1974); American Home Economics Association, scholarship fund in honor of her career. Died 3 October 1980 of cardiac arrest.

Nutritionist Flemmie Pansy Kittrell was born to parents who both had African American and Cherokee ancestors. They stressed the importance of education to their children. Kittrell's first job was at Bennett College in 1928, and she returned to this college after she obtained her doctoral degree. Her next teaching job was at Hampton Institute, where she remained until she went to Howard University in 1944. During her career at Howard, she broadened the concept of home economics to include additional fields such as child development. Although she remained at Howard until retirement in 1972, she engaged in many international studies. She carried out a nutritional survey of Liberia sponsored by the United States government, received a Fulbright award in 1950 leading to work with Baroda University in India to develop an educational plan for nutritional research, returned to India to teach home economics and nutritional seminars (1953), headed a team that traveled to Japan and Hawaii to conduct research on home economics in these countries (1957), and led three tours to West Africa, Central Africa, and Guinea (between 1957 and 1961). Although she retired from Howard in 1972, she continued to be active in her field. Kittrell was the recipient of numerous honors.

JH/MBO

SECONDARY SOURCES

Kessler, James H. *Distinguished African American Scientists of the Twentieth Century.* Phoenix: Onyx Press, 1996. With portrait.

Sammons, Vivian O. *Blacks in Science and Medicine.* New York: Hemisphere Publishing, 1990. Kittrell discussed pages 143–144.

STANDARD SOURCES

NBAW; Notable (article by Leonard Bruno).

KLEEGMAN, SOPHIA (1901–1971)

Russian/U.S. physician, gynecologist. Born 8 July 1901 in Kiev, Russia, to Elka (Siergutz) and Israel Kleegman. Seven siblings (four brothers died in childhood). Naturalized 1923. Married Dr. John H. Sillman. Two children. Educated New York University and Bellevue Hospital Medical College (later the New York University College of Medicine) (M.D., 1924). Professional experience: Chicago Lying-In Hospital, resident (1924); gynecology and obstetrics, private practice; New York University College of Medicine, fac-

ulty of obstetrics and gynecology (from 1929); Bellevue Hospital, attending staff (from 1929); clinical professor of obstetrics and gynecology (from 1953). Concurrent positions: New York State Planned Parenthood Association, medical director (1936–1961); Eastern Planned Parenthood League, medical consultant. Honors and memberships: New Women's Medical Association of New York, president (1942–1944); American Association of Marriage Counselors (1960); New York University Medical Alumni Association, first woman president. Died 26 September 1971 in New York from cancer.

Born in Russia, Sophia Kleegman was able to immigrate to the United States because her two older sisters, Mary and Rae, earned passage money for their younger sisters and parents by working in a garment industry sweatshop in the Lower East Side of New York. Four of the Kleegman sons had died in Russia. The two younger girls, Sophia and Anna, were encouraged to become professionals. Both were exempt from household chores while the two older girls, Mary and Rae, and their Talmudic scholar father supported them. Their mother took in boarders.

In 1920, Sophia became a member of the second coeducational class of what later became the New York University College of Medicine. She followed the path of her sister Anna in becoming an obstetrician and gynecologist. While practicing privately, she became the first woman appointed to the New York University College of Medicine. By 1953, she had become a full professor. After her marriage in 1932 to an orthodontist who worked on the growth and development of the jaw, she gave up her private practice to minimize night duties. The couple had two children, Frederick Holden, born in 1937, and Anne Marice, born in 1941.

Kleegman became interested in problems of infertility in both men and women, helping to dispel the notion that only women were responsible for childlessness. She also became involved in the psychological aspects of sexual dysfunction. Although her work in the social aspects of medicine is what she is generally known for, she added the endometrial aspiration test, which extended the diagnostic value of George Papanicolau's smear test for cervical cancer.

An advocate of birth control and Planned Parenthood clinics, Kleegman supported the clinic established in New York by MARGARET SANGER. She was convinced that premarital counseling would save many marriages, and stressed the importance of the education of the physician in these matters. After Kleegman's death from cancer, her friends and patients established the Sophia J. Kleegman professorship in human reproduction at the NYU Medical Center.

JH/MBO

PRIMARY SOURCES

Kleegman, Sophia. "Medical and Social Aspects of Birth Control." *Journal-Lancet,* Minneapolis, 15 November 1935.

————. "Recent Advances in the Diagnosis and Treatment of Sterility." *Medical Woman's Journal* (January 1939).

————. Contributor to J. V. Meigs and S. Sturgis, eds. *Progress in Gynecology*. 2 vols. London: Heinemann, 1946; 1950.

————. Contributor to R. J. Lowrie, ed. *Gynecology*. Springfield, Ill.: Thomas, 1952.

————. "Therapeutic Donor Insemination." *Fertility and Sterility* (January–February 1954).

————. With Sherwin Kaufman. *Infertility in Women*. Philadelphia: F. A. Davis, 1966.

SECONDARY SOURCES
New York Daily News, 27 September 1971. Obituary notice.
New York Times, 27 September 1971. Obituary notice.
Singer, Joy Daniels. *My Mother, the Doctor*. New York: Dutton, 1970. By Kleegman's daughter.

STANDARD SOURCES
NAW(M) (article by Deborah Dwork); *WWW(A)*, vol. 5, 1973.

KLEIN, MARTHE (fl. 1919–1921)
Educated Institut Curie (1919–1921).

Klein worked with Marie Curie to set up infirmaries for X-ray diagnostic imaging.   MM

PRIMARY SOURCES
Records in Institut Curie archives, assembled by Mme. Monique Bordry.

SECONDARY SOURCES
Correspondence; Choix des lettres, 1905–1934. Marie [et] Irène Curie. Paris: Les Éditeurs Francais Réunis, 1974.

KLEIN, MELANIE (REIZES) (1882–1960)
Austrian/British psychoanalyst. Born 30 March 1882 in Vienna, Austria. Father medical practitioner. Three siblings, two of whom died young. Married Arthur Klein (1903). Three children. Educated Budapest and Berlin, trained as analyst. Professional experience: Berlin Psychoanalytical Institute, child therapist (1921); British Psychoanalytic Society, therapist (1927); British Psychoanalytic Society, Training Committee (1929); practice in psychoanalysis and research (1921–1960?). Died 22 September 1960 in London.

Melanie Klein, the noted Austrian/British child psychoanalyst, was the youngest of four children (one of her sisters and a brother died young). She married a cousin, Arthur Klein, an industrialist, when she was twenty-one, and then had three children. She divorced her husband in 1923 after she had embarked upon her analytical training.

When she was in her mid-thirties, Klein trained as a Freudian analyst in Budapest with the encouragement of Sandor Ferenczi. She began to work in his clinic with children and then moved to Berlin, where she was further encouraged and analyzed by Karl Abraham. Soon after she had begun to work with Ferenczi, she delivered her first paper on the development of the child for the Hungarian Psychoanalytic Society. She then moved to Berlin and practiced as a child therapist at the Berlin Psychoanalytical Institute until 1925, when she was encouraged by Alix Strachey to lecture on her theories of child psychotherapy at the London Psycho-Analytic Society. Ernst Jones then invited her to move to London, where, after a few years, she joined the Institute of Psycho-Analysis as a training analyst.

Klein studied problems of character and personality by analysis of progressively deeper levels of the unconscious. She and HERMINE VON HUG-HELLMUTH were among the first to apply the psychoanalytic technique to small children using play techniques now adopted in child guidance clinics. Klein believed human personality to be determined in the first four months of life and to be characterized by aggressive and libidinal aspects directed toward the mother. She also assumed the infant to have a rich fantasy life at an early stage. She placed the development of the superego in infancy and recognized that fear and aggressive tendencies were present in children between the ages of one and two. She argued that these were important for understanding deviant development and she used play therapy extensively in her analysis.

Klein's approach to clinical work with children was more acceptable to the British than it had been to the Berlin Society, and her influence in the British Society grew along with her criticism of basic Freudian analytical methods, especially regarding the child patient. Although she saw herself as more in keeping with Freud's own radical descriptions, this approach placed her in direct conflict with his daughter, ANNA FREUD, who was working in the field of child analysis in Vienna.

Klein was recognized as a training analyst and was elected a member of the London Training Committee, making regular contributions of papers to the society. After Hitler's invasion of Austria, Viennese analysts (including both Sigmund and Anna Freud) escaped to London with the help of members of the British Society. The ambivalence or outright opposition to Klein's ideas by Anna Freud and her supporters heightened the spirit of controversy within the society. Areas of difference in theory and technique focused on early development of sexuality, especially in the female, the genesis of the superego and its relation to the Oedipus complex, the concept of the death instinct, and the technique of child analysis.

In order to prevent a damaging split in the British Society for Psychoanalysis, the society developed parallel systems of training, which included Klein's modifications while retaining the essential structure of psychoanalysis. Klein's daughter Melitta (later Schmideberg) joined her in London after her own analytical training and became first a co-contributor, later a bitter opponent of her mother in the British Society controversies.

Klein expanded the range of patients who could be psychoanalyzed to include those with severe mental disorders, even psychotic and schizophrenic patients. She also contributed important studies on the psychological bases of ethics, thinking, group relations, and aesthetics.   KM

PRIMARY SOURCES

Klein, Melanie. *Die Psychoanalyse des Kindes.* Vienna: Internationaler Psychoanalytischer Verlag, 1932.

———. *The Psychoanalysis of Children.* London: L. & Virginia Woolf at the Hogarth Press and the Institute of Psychoanalysis, 1932.

———. *Contributions to Psychoanalysis 1921–1945.* London: Hogarth Press, 1948.

———, ed. *New Directions in Psychoanalysis.* London: Tavistock, 1955.

———. *Our Adult World and its Roots in Infancy.* London: Tavistock, 1960.

———. *Psychoanalysis of Children.* New York: Grove Press, 1960.

———. *The Writings of Melanie Klein.* Ed. Roger Money-Kryle. 4 vols. London: The Hogarth Press and the Institute of Psycho-Analysis, 1975.

SECONDARY SOURCES

King, Pearl, and Riccardo Steiner, *The Freud-Klein Controversies, 1941–1945.* London and New York: Tavistock/Routledge, 1991.

Grosskurth, P. *Melanie Klein: Her World and Her Work.* London: Hodder & Stoughton, 1986.

STANDARD SOURCES

Appignanesi; *DNB;* Uglow 1982; Zusne.

KLETNOVA, E. N. (1869–post-1925)

Russian archeologist. Born 1869 near Smolensk, daughter of small landowner. Educated in music; Moscow Archaeological Institute. Professional experience: Smolensk State University, professor. Died in emigration after 1925.

E. N. Kletnova was born in 1869 in the Viazemsk region of Smolensk province into a family of small landowners. She received an excellent education in music and translated operas for the musical publisher P. F. Iurgenson.

In 1908, Kletnova became interested in the archeological research that the Moscow Archaeological Society was doing at the Smiadinsk Monastery; a nunnery was planned for the site and the work had to be performed expeditiously. With other local amateur archeologists, she took some part in this research, and became so enthusiastic about archeology that she enrolled in the course at the Moscow Archaeological Institute as a student of V. A. Gorodtsov.

After she had completed the course, Kletnova began personally conducting excavations in the Viazemsk and Smolensk areas. Her archeological knowledge was not great at this time, and her efforts were apparently amateurish. However, correspondence with the Petersburg archeologist A. A. Spitsyn encouraged her to try to improve her methods.

During the Revolution, life became very difficult for Kletnova. As a member of the landowning class, she was accused of exploiting the peasants. Ultimately, it became impossible for her to carry on with her research and she was obliged to pack up her by now extensive collection and transport it to Smolensk.

In 1918, the Smolensk State University was opened and Kletnova was appointed professor of archeology. She energetically carried on her studies of the archeology of the Smolensk region and published a local history journal, *Smolenskaia Nov',* for which she wrote articles about archeology, ethnography, and folklore. She worked hard to preserve historical monuments, a particularly difficult task at a time when there was a strong reaction against religion and many church buildings were being destroyed. However, Kletnova could not adapt to the difficult postrevolutionary conditions. She donated her collection to Smolensk State University and emigrated. She died in emigration some time after 1925.

For all her weaknesses as an archeologist, Kletnova was distinguished by an unbounded enthusiasm for the history, folklore, and archeology of the Smolensk region. She was the first archeologist of any note to undertake major studies of the area. Her work on the Little Church of the Smiadyn Monastery is the only source of information on this monument. All present-day knowledge of the archeology of the burial mounds (*kurgany*) along the Viaz'ma River is based on her work. Her valuable collection is still in the possession of the Smolensk State University. Contemporary Russian archeologists are again giving her credit for her service to the archeology of the region.   ACH

PRIMARY SOURCES

Kletnova, E. N., ed. *Smolenskaia Nov'.* Published in Smolensk in the early postrevolutionary period.

SECONDARY SOURCES

Sukhova, O. A. "Vospitannitsa Moskovskogo Arkheologicheskogo Instituta, pervyi smolenskii arkheolog, E. N. Kletnova." In *Uvarovskie chteniia*, 9–11. Murom: Muromskaia gorodskaia tip., 1990.

KLIENEBERGER-NOBEL, EMMY (1892–1985)

German / British bacteriologist and microbiologist. Born 25 February 1892 in Frankfurt, Germany, to Sophie (Hamberger) and (Abraham) Adolf Klieneberger. Three siblings. Married Edmund Nobel (1944). Educated teacher-training college (certified 1911); Unterprima of the Schillerschule (1911–1913); University of Göttingen (1913–1914); Goethe University, Frankfurt (Ph.D., 1917); University of London (Ph.D., 1942; D.Sc.). Professional experience: Nolden School for Girls, Dresden, teacher (1919–1922); Hygiene Institute, Frankfurt, researcher (1922–1933); Lister Institute, London, researcher (1933–1962); retired 1962. Honors and memberships: Robert Koch Institute, honorary member (1967); German Society for Bacteriology and Hygiene, corresponding member (1967); International Organization for Mycoplasmology, honorary member with an award lectureship established in her name; Robert Koch Medal for her achievements in microbiology. Died 1985.

Antisemitism drove Emmy Klieneberger from her native Germany to England, although her parents, "free thinkers," had her baptized. Following her early education, she entered a teacher-training college and became certified. However, after completing her certification she decided to attend university classes instead of teaching. After studying mathematics and Latin at the Schillerschule, she attended lectures in mathematics and the sciences at the University of Göttingen. An illness and the advent of World War I drove her away from Göttingen, and she returned home to Frankfurt where she attended Goethe University and earned a doctorate in botany with mathematics and zoology as areas of special interest. After receiving the degree, she worked part-time in the zoology laboratory at Goethe University, attended additional mathematics lectures at Göttingen, and passed the certification examination to become a teacher in the higher schools. She used this certification for only one teaching job. Although she enjoyed teaching, she missed the laboratory work and found a position as a bacteriologist at the Hygiene Institute in Frankfurt. Although she knew little about bacteriology when she began, by 1930 she had become a member of the German Society for Hygiene and Bacteriology and a member of the institute's medical faculty.

The rise of antisemitism with Hitler's ascent to power caused extreme hardship to the Klieneberger family. One brother and one sister committed suicide following their persecution; Klieneberger's other brother emigrated to South America. Klieneberger emigrated to England, where she secured a position at London's Lister Institute; she worked there for the remainder of her career. She obtained a second doctor of philosophy degree and a doctor of science degree from London University and then was appointed a full member of the Lister Institute staff. She met and married a sixty-year-old pediatrician from Vienna, Edmund Nobel. Two years after the marriage, Edmund Nobel died. After the death of her husband, Klieneberger-Nobel worked for a year at the Hygiene Institute in Zurich. She retired in October 1962 and died at the age of ninety-three.

Her creative research was chiefly in the area of mycoplasma. The genus *Mycoplasma*, which lacked a cell wall, appeared in some respects to be intermediate between bacteria and viruses. She discovered a variant, known as the "L-form," which she named for the Lister Institute.

Recognizing that there were variants within the mycoplasma, Klieneberger-Nobel developed a medium to grow the mycoplasma that caused an unusual strain of bronchopneumonia in rodents. She found that after incubating for several days, colonies had grown that were similar to those of the well-known pleuropneumonia and agalactia. New morphological forms were found in dogs as well as rodents, and a saprophytic strain was found in sewage and soil.

Dr. Albert Sabin in the United States had described a "rolling disease" that resulted from a toxoplasma infection of mouse brains. After Klieneberger-Nobel had written to Sabin, he sent her freeze-dried brains of infected mice. She successfully grew cultures from his samples in her special medium and shared her results with Sabin. Before her work could be published in the *Lancet,* Sabin published his results in *Science,* neglecting to mention Klieneberger-Nobel's part in his results. With George M. Findlay of the Welcome Bureau for Scientific Research, she had identified a mycoplasma in the brains of mice exhibiting the "rolling disease." They examined a disease of rats, polyarthritis, and found that when fluid from the joints of the infected rats was grown on her medium, mycoplasma colonies resulted. They then were able to recreate the situation in the rats by injecting a medium suspension and the mycoplasma, demonstrating that the causative agent was the mycoplasma (*Mycoplasma arthritides*). Klieneberger-Nobel identified other mycoplasma diseases. Her work led to the later isolation of *Mycoplasma pneummoniae* in humans.

JH / MBO

PRIMARY SOURCES

Klieneberger, E. "Über die Grösse und Beschaffenheit der Zellkerne mit besonderer B erucksichtigung der Systematik." Ph.D. diss., Goethe University, Frankfurt am Main, 1917.

———. "The Colonial Development of the Organisms of Pleuropneumonia and Agalactia on Serum Agar and Variations of the Morphology Under Different Conditions of

Growth." *Journal of Pathology and Bacteriology* 39 (1934): 409–420.

———. With G. M. Findley, F. O. MacCallum, et al. "Rolling Disease. New Symptoms in Mice Associated with a Pleuropneumonia-like Organism." *Lancet* 235 (1938): 1511–1513.

Klieneberger-Nobel, Emmy. *Memoirs.* London: Academic Press, 1980.

SECONDARY SOURCES
Chick, Harriette, et al. *War on Disease.* London: Deutsch, 1971.
Tully, Joseph G. "Foreword." In *Memoirs,* by Emmy Klieneberger-Nobel. London: Academic Press, 1980.

STANDARD SOURCES
Grinstein 1997 (article by Gary E. Rice).

KLINE, VIRGINIA HARRIETT (1910–1959)

U.S. stratigrapher and geologist. Born 14 July 1910 in Coleman, Mich., the daughter of Abbie Young Kline and Ray Kline. Two brothers, Harland Kline and Robert Kline. Never married. Educated Michigan State College (B.S., 1931); University of Michigan (M.A., 1933; Ph.D., 1935; B.A. in library science, 1942). Professional experience: geologist for various oil companies: Michigan Oil Exploration Company, Chapman Minerals Corporation in Lansing, Mich., and Sohio Producing Comnpany, Owensboro, Ky.; North Dakota Geological Survey, Grand Forks, N.D., stratigrapher; University of Michigan, Civil Engineering School, librarian; University of Mississippi, associate professor of geology; Mississippi Geological Survey, assistant geologist (1942–1943); Office of the Petroleum Administration for War, assistant petroleum analyst (1943–1944); Illinois State Geological Survey, associate geologist in the Oil and Gas Section (1944–1959). Honors and memberships: Fellow, Geological Society of America; member, American Association of Petroleum Geologists, Illinois Geological Society, and Illinois Academy of Science. Died 5 February 1959 in Urbana, Ill.

Virginia Harriett Kline was born in Michigan, and received her bachelor of science degree from Michigan State College. All of her graduate education was done at the University of Michigan. After she received her doctoral degree in geology in 1935, she worked as a geologist for several oil companies. Then she returned to the university to attend library school; she received a bachelor's degree in library science in 1942. After she received her library degree, Kline worked briefly as librarian for the Civil Engineering School at the University of Michigan. For the 1942–1943 school year, she was associate professor of geology and assistant geologist with the Mississippi Geological Survey, University of Mississippi. In 1943, she moved to Chicago to become assistant petroleum analyst for the Petroleum Administration for War. She stayed with the Petroleum Administration for about a year and a

half, at which time she moved to the Illinois State Geological Survey, in Urbana, where she was associate geologist in the Oil and Gas Section. She remained with the survey until her death, which occurred after a period of ill health.

Kline was a good stratigrapher, participating both in field work and in the analysis of the field work. She published a number of papers. In her last job with the Illinois State Geological Survey, she compiled the yearly reports on oil and gas developments in Illinois and evaluated the new discoveries. She issued monthly reports on oil and gas drilling and mapped the pay zones of most of the Illinois oil-producing regions.   CK

PRIMARY SOURCES
Kline, Virginia Harriett. "Stratigraphy of North Dakota." *American Association of Petroleum Geologists Bulletin* 16 (1942): 336–379.
———. "Clay County Fossils—Midway Foraminifera and Ostracoda." *Mississippi Geological Survey Bulletin* 53, part 3 (1944).
———. With Alfred H. Bell. "Oil and Gas Development in Illinois in 1947." *American Institute of Mining and Metallurgical Engineers, Statistics of Oil and Gas Development and Production* 1948: 49–99. These joint reports are published for each year that Kline worked for the Illinois Survey, 1942 to 1959.

SECONDARY SOURCES
"Memorial, Virginia Harriett Kline (1910–1959)." *American Association of Petroleum Geologists Bulletin* 44, no. 1 (1960): 113–114. Includes portrait.
Oros, Margaret O. "Memorial to Virginia Harriett Kline (1910–1959)." *Proceedings of the Geological Society of America.* Annual Report for 1960 (February 1962): 115–118.

KLOSTERMAN, MARY JO (1955–1994)

U.S. geologist. Born 29 May 1955 in Fargo, N.D. Five siblings. Married to James Klosterman. Two children, Andrea and William. Educated Gonzaga University, Spokane, Wash.; University of North Dakota (B.A., 1978); Louisiana State University (1981). Professional experience: Exxon Production Research Company, reservoir quality analyst (1981–1986); Exxon Company International, researcher (1986–1993); Exxon Exporation Company CIS group, researcher (1993–1994). Died 2 July 1994 near Charlotte, N.C.

Mary Jo Klosterman was born in North Dakota and received a bachelor's degree with a major in geology and a minor in English. An excellent student, she was awarded the Sigma Gamma Epsilon Society's W. A. Tarr Award. She then went to Louisiana to do graduate work and earned her master's degree in geology from Louisiana State University. She and her husband, Jim, had two children, and Mary Jo was very active in civic and school affairs. She was among the thirty-seven people killed on 2 July 1994, in the crash of a US Air DC-9 during a thunderstorm near Charlotte, North Carolina, on her way home after attending a conference at the University of South Carolina.

Her significance to geology was oriented more toward management (of both data and people) than toward research. As a group leader for Exxon Production Research Company, she was involved in changing reservoir quality prediction techniques to an integrated, quantitative approach. She proposed integrating different data types to extend the range of observations on reservoir quality. She also advocated assessing the data within a sequence-stratigraphic framework.

After transferring to Exxon Company International, Klosterman was involved in several Central and South American projects, including one in Trinidad, working in the field and immersing herself in its culture, geology, and flora and fauna. She applied her geological expertise to select drill sites and used her cultural understanding to help the project members from Trinidad feel more at home in Houston. Her final job at Exxon with the Exxon Exploration Company was to coordinate two joint technical studies between Exxon and the State Oil Company of Azerbaijan. She completed her report shortly before her death.　　C K

PRIMARY SOURCES

Klosterman, M. J. With F. D. Holland. "Paleontologic Sites in North Dakota (through 1976)." *REAP Reports* (1977): 77–83.

———. With T. A. Cross. "Primary Submarine Cements and Neomorphic Spar in a Stromatolitic-Bound Phylloid Algal Bioherm, Laborcita Formation (Wolfcampian). Sacramento Mountains, New Mexico, USA." In *Phanerozoic Stromatolites: Case Histories,* ed. Claude Monty, 60–73. Berlin: Springer Verlag, 1981.

———. With others. "Geochemical Characterization of Lithofacies and Organic Facies in Cretaceous Organic-Rich Rocks from Trinidad, East Venezuela Basin." *Organic Geochemistry* 22, nos. 3–5 (1994): 441–459.

SECONDARY SOURCES

Ajdukiewicz, Joanna, Churck Wielchowsky, Pinar O. Yilmaz, and Jonelle Glosch. "Mary Jo Klosterman (1955–1994)." *American Association of Petroleum Geologists.* November 1994, 78: 1800–1803.

KLUCKHOHN, FLORENCE ROCKWOOD (1905–)

U.S. sociologist and psychologist. Born 14 January 1905 in Illinois to Florence (McLaughlin) and Homer Garfield Rockwood. Married (1) Clyde Kluckhohn (he died in 1960); (2) George E. Taylor. One

son, Richard Rockwood Kluckhohn. Educated Wisconsin (A.B., 1927); Harvard (Radcliffe) (Ph.D., 1941). Professional experience: Wellesley College, Department of Sociology, assistant professor (1940–1948); Harvard University Department of Social Relations, lecturer and research associate (1948–1968). Concurrent experience: Office of War Information, research analyst (1944–1945). Group for the Advancement of Psychiatric Publications, consultant (1949–1965). Children's Medical Center, staff (1956–1961). Honors and memberships: Sociological Association; American Anthopological Association; Society for Applied Anthropology; Academy of Politics and Social Sciences.

Florence Rockwood was born in the Midwest and went to the University of Wisconsin for her undergraduate degree. After meeting and marrying the anthropologist Clyde Kluckhohn, she began to pursue a doctoral degree in sociology at Radcliffe College (Harvard University). During World War II, her husband was named deputy head of the Office of War Information (OWI) for the War Department during the period that Florence worked for the OWI. He was a member of the anthropology department and had close ties with members of the Department of Social Relations, within which Florence Kluckhohn was a faculty member and a research associate. Even after his death in 1960, she remained at Harvard with a connection to the Department of Social Relations.

Florence Kluckhohn was also interested in issues of mental health in children and began to work with the Children's Medical Center in Boston. She developed theory and research methods for analysis and variations in the basic values of human beings of different societies. She used these theories for testing methods for research on family systems, educational systems, emotional maladjustments, and mental illness, as well for the anthropological concerns of cultural integration and change.

Kluckhohn's one son, Richard Rockwood Kluckhohn, followed his father's profession by studying anthropology and becoming a professor in the field. Some years after her first husband's death, Kluckhohn married for the second time and moved to Seattle, Washington, relinquishing her professional connections.　　K M

PRIMARY SOURCES

Kluckhohn, Florence. *American Family: Past and Present.* Chicago: Delphian Society, 1952.

———. With Fred L. Strodbeck. *Variations in Value Orientations.* Evanston, Ill.: Row, Peterson, [1961].

STANDARD SOURCES

AMS S&B 10, 11; Debus; Stevens and Gardner.

KLUMPKE, DOROTHEA (1861–1942)

See Roberts, Dorothea Klumpke.

KNAKE, ELSE (1901–1973)

German biochemist. Born 1901. Educated University of Berlin Medical School (1929); University of Berlin, habilitation (1940). Professional experience: University of Berlin, medical faculty (1929–1943); Kaiser Wilhelm Institute, Department for Tissue Culture, researcher (1943–1945), Department of Physical Chemistry and Electrochemistry, visiting scientist (1945–1948), Department of Cell Physiology, researcher (1948–1950); Department for Tissue Research, researcher (1950–1953), (Kaiser Wilhelm Institute becomes the Max Planck Institute in 1955) Department of Comparative and Pathological Genetics, researcher (1953–1960); Max Planck Institute in Berlin-Dahlem, researcher (1956–1963).

Else Knake was one of many women who worked at the Kaiser Wilhelm Institute. After she habilitated in 1940, she was qualified for such a research position, and she remained there throughout her career, even after it became the Max-Planck Institute. JH/MBO

STANDARD SOURCES
Vogt.

KNIGHT, MARGARET (1838–1914)

U.S. inventor. Born 1838 in York, Maine, to Hannah (Teal) and James Knight. Educated local schools, Manchester, N.H. Died 1914 in Framingham, Mass.

Inventor Margaret Knight received little formal education. From the beginning she was interested in mechanical devices, and her favorite toys were woodworking tools. After spending most of her childhood in Manchester, New Hampshire, where her brothers worked for a cotton textile mill, she moved to Springfield, Massachusetts. Here, while working in a shop that produced paper bags, she devised the first of her inventions to be patented, a mechanism that enabled a paper-feeding machine to fold square-bottomed bags.

Having conceived the idea for the mechanism in 1867, Knight took two years to perfect it; and when in 1869 she traveled to Boston to supervise the manufacturing of the final model, she allowed it to be seen by another inventor, who quickly devised his own model and applied for a patent. The ensuing priority dispute was decided in Knight's favor in 1870. During the 1880s and 1890s, while living in Ashland and then Framingham, Massachusetts, she invented numerous household devices, machines for shoe cutting, a window frame and sash, and a numbering mechanism. In her final years, Knight concentrated on heavy machinery, devising a series of components for rotary engines and motors.

As an inventor, Knight concerned herself with the application of science rather than the development of theories. Her limited education did not provide her with the capacity to understand the mechanical principles behind her work. Both the number of her inventions and her predominant interest in heavy machinery, however, make her unique among women inventors. JH/MBO

STANDARD SOURCES
Mozans; *NAW* (article by Robert W. Lovett); Uglow 1989.

KNOPF, ELEANORA FRANCES (BLISS) (1883–1974)

U.S. petrologist, stratigrapher, and structural geologist. Born 15 July 1883 in Rosemont, Pa., to Mary (Anderson) and General Tasker Howard Bliss. Married Adolph Knopf. Educated private school adjacent to Bryn Mawr, Florence Baldwin School (graduated 1904); Bryn Mawr College (A.B., 1904; A.M.; Ph.D., 1912); Johns Hopkins, postdoctoral fellowship (1912). Professional experience: U.S. Geological Survey, researcher (1912–1955). Died 21 January 1974 in Menlo Park, Calif., of arteriosclerosis.

Eleanora Frances Bliss was born in Pennsylvania, the daughter of a career army officer. Both of her parents were accomplished linguists. She attended college at Bryn Mawr, where she received a bachelor's degree in chemistry and a master's degree in geology. She served as assistant curator in the Geological Museum and as a demonstrator in Bryn Mawr's geological laboratory while she did graduate work with FLORENCE BASCOM culminating in a doctoral degree in 1912. Thanks to Bascom, she received a postdoctoral fellowship in geology at Johns Hopkins. Bascom also helped her get work with the United States Geological Survey, where she remained for forty-three years. Bliss married Adolph Knopf in 1920 and moved with him to New Haven, Connecticut, where he had been appointed professor at Yale. Although she had no children of her own, she served as a mother to Knopf's three children.

Like Florence Bascom, Knopf studied petrology. She and ANNA I. JONAS STOSE prepared a joint dissertation on the Doe Run-Avondale region west of Bryn Mawr. Along with Stose, Knopf was involved in the controversy over the dating of the Wissahickon formation, which led to estrangement with Bascom. Much of Knopf's work was done in collaboration with Stose, although the personalities of the two women were very different. Whereas Stose was abrasive, Knopf was mild. She dropped out of the dispute with Bascom, although some hard feelings remained. She also studied the geology of the Taconic region of New York and neighboring New England states.   JH/MBO

PRIMARY SOURCES

Bliss, Eleanor F., and Anna I. Jonas. "Relation of the Wissahickon Mica Gneiss to the Shenandoah Limestone and Octoraro Schist of the Doe Run and Avondale Region, Chester County, Pennsylvania." U.S.G.S. Professional Paper 98. *Shorter Contributions to General Geology, 1916* (1917): 9–34.

———. "Stratigraphy of the Crystalline Schists of Pennsylvania and Maryland." *American Journal of Science* 5th ser., 5 (1923): 40–62.

———. With Louis M. Prindle. "Geology of the Taconic Quadrangle." *American Journal of Science* 24 (1932): 257–302.

SECONDARY SOURCES

Arnold, Lois B. "The Wissahickon Controversy: Florence Bascom vs. Her Students." *Earth Sciences History* 2, no. 2 (1983): 130–142.

Rodgers, John. "Memorial to Eleanora Bliss Knopf 1883–1974." *Geological Society of America Memorials* 6, 1977: 1–4. Includes portrait.

STANDARD SOURCES

Bailey; *NAW*(M) (article by Michelle L. Aldrich); *Notable;* Sarjeant.

KNOTT-TER MEER, ILSE (1899–?)

German engineer. Born 1899 in Hanover to Paula (Behrens) and Gustav Ter Meer. Married Karl Knott (1925). Educated girls higher school (gymnasium course); Oberprima eines Jungengymnasiums (first division of the highest form); Technischen Hochschule in Hanover (1920–1924), engineering diploma (1924?). Professional experience: independent bureau, engineer (1925–?). Honors and memberships: Club of German Engineers, organizer (1930); Ausschluss Frauen im Ingenieurberuf, Hamburg (1955).

Ilse Ter Meer's father was an engineer and director of a machine factory. She studied at a girls' higher school and then was in the first division of the highest form in a gymnasium. Earlier, her father supported the technical capabilities of his daughter through a gift of a steam engine. She became especially interested in the cars in her father's workshop, and in 1917 she became one of the first women to get a driver's license. In 1920, she began studying at the Technical high school, where she remained for four and a half years. She became the first woman to earn an engineering diploma. Shortly after receiving this diploma she married her colleague Karl Knott and went to Aachen with him. In Aachen she worked with an independent bureau. She was active in a num-

ber of organizations, and was the first woman in the Union of German Engineers (Verein Deutscher Ingenieure).   JH/MBO

SECONDARY SOURCES

Fuchs, Margot. *Wie die Väter so die Töchter. Frauenstudium an der Technische Hochschule.* Munich: N.p., 1994.

STANDARD SOURCES

Strohmeier.

KNOWLES, MATILDA CULLEN (1864–1933)

Irish botanist. Born 31 January 1864 in Ballymena County, Antrim. Father William Knowles. One sister, Catherine. Never married. Educated Royal College of Science and Art in Dublin (1896–1900). Professional experience: National Museum of Science and Art, botanist; College of Science and Art, assistant to head of botany department; National Museum of Science and Art, curator, national herbarium. Died 27 April 1933 in Dublin.

Matilda Knowles and her sister, Catherine, spent a large part of their childhood under the direction and tutelage of their father, William Knowles, an insurance agent who was an active and enthusiastic naturalist. Together, they attended the meetings and lectures of the Belfast Naturalists Field Club, taking part in excursions and field trips. There, Matilda met Robert Lloyd Praeger, who became the best-known Irish naturalist of his generation and her lifelong friend. Encouraged by their father, both girls attended natural science classes at the Royal College of Science and Art in Dublin, and Matilda Knowles remained at the College after her graduation to work at the National Museum of Science and Art (National Museum of Ireland after 1921). Five years later, she became assistant to Thomas Johnson, head of the botany department. When Johnson retired in 1923, Knowles took complete charge of the botanical collections and, assisted by Margaret Buchanan, spent the remainder of her life caring for and adding to the collections. She died in Dublin 27 April 1933.

While at the Museum, Knowles published many papers on botanical subjects. *The Handlist of Irish Flowering Plants and Ferns* (1910), generally attributed to Johnson, was almost entirely written by Knowles. In 1908, Lorrain Smith of the British Museum invited Knowles to join with the most notable naturalists of England, Ireland, and Europe in preparing a comprehensive natural history of Clare Island, County Mayo. Subsequent to this work, Knowles became devoted to the study of lichens.

Matilda Knowles made a unique addition to the botanical history of Ireland by concentrating on a particular and difficult group of plants. Her major work, *The Lichens of Ireland,* added over a hundred species of lichen to the Irish list and recorded the distribution of the eight hundred species found in that country. During the period she managed the national herbarium, its excellence made it a prime research facility for botanists from all parts of the world, many of whom corresponded with Knowles regularly and sent her specimens.

JH/MBO

PRIMARY SOURCES

Knowles, Matilda. "The Lichens of Ireland." *Proceedings of the Royal Irish Academy. Section B: Biological, Geological, and Chemical Science* 38, no. 12 (1929): 179–434.

SECONDARY SOURCES

Mollan, Charles, William Davis, and Brendan Finucane, eds. *More People and Places in Irish Science and Technology.* Dublin: Royal Irish Academy, 1990.

Praeger, R. Lloyd. "Matilda Cullen Knowles." *Irish Naturalists' Journal* 4 (1933): 191–193.

———. *Some Irish Naturalists: A Biographical Note-Book.* Dundalk: Dundalgan Press, 1949.

KNOWLES, RUTH SHELDON (1915–1996)

U.S. writer on petroleum geology. Born 1915 in Oklahoma. Married and divorced. Four children. Professional experience: independent petroleum writer; Mexican government, oil property inspector (1938); Mexican government, surveyor of oil fields and refiners (1939–1941); U.S. Department of the Interior, petroleum specialist (1941–1942); Venezuelan government advisor and consultant (1942); independent correspondent, New York City and Asia (1965–1975). Honors and memberships: American Women of Radio and Television, Woman of the Year; Theta Sigma Phi (national professional society for women in journalism), Outstanding Woman Writer; Women's Economic Round Table of New York, founding member; Indonesian Cultural Foundation, board of directors. Died 2 September 1996 in New York City of heart failure.

Although Ruth Sheldon Knowles was not a geologist, she had a broad understanding of the field. The granddaughter and daughter of independent oilmen, she was acquainted with the legendary figures of oil exploration such as Everette DeGolyer and Wallace Pratt. She chronicled many of the oil discoveries throughout the world from the rainforests of Asia and South America to the desert conditions of the Middle East and North Africa. She wrote several best-selling books and numerous articles in popular magazines.

Before she was thirty years old, Knowles was invited by the Mexican government to travel to remote parts of the country as a petroleum writer. In 1938 she was the first foreigner to be allowed to inspect the petroleum properties after they were expropriated by the government, and in 1939, the Mexican government retained her to make a survey of its oil fields and refineries. Secretary of the Interior Harold Ickes appointed Knowles as a petroleum specialist, in which capacity she was sent to South America to make the first U.S. government strategic oil and production capability survey. At the end of 1942, Knowles left the Petroleum Administration for War and went to work as a consultant for the Venezuelan government and assisted it in conveying its interests on the world market.

It was unusual to find a woman who was able to move freely in the male-dominated world Knowles inhabited. Her facility with languages and ability to communicate with people of different cultures made her popular with such world figures as King Faisal of Saudi Arabia, Prime Minister Golda Meier of Israel, President Suharto of Indonesia, President Thieu of South Vietnam, and Fidel Castro and Che Guevarra of Cuba.

Knowles spent the years 1965 to 1975 traveling between Asia and her home in New York City. As a single mother, she had to work to support her four children. Never fearing danger, she went to remote rice paddies and rainforests to research her stories and made friends everywhere she went. She was made an honorary member of the U.S. Special Forces Green Berets.

During the last part of her life she was highly sought after as a lecturer. An excellent lecturer, she spoke on college campuses throughout the United States, and gave special short courses to over five thousand social studies teachers for their continuing education credits. She also wrote and narrated television and radio programs for educational networks. Her series on the history and development of oil was broadcast in international markets. Knowles was an important public relations agent for the oil countries, ably defending them against many charges from environmentalists.

Knowles received a number of awards, including the "Woman of the Year" award of the American Women of Radio and Television. She was also selected as Oklahoma's outstanding woman writer by the national professional society for women in journalism, Theta Sigma Phi. She was a founding member of the Women's Economic Round Table of New York and the Indonesian Cultural Foundation, where she served on the board of directors for many years.

Even though she had suffered a stroke that left her paralyzed, she was still working on projects involving help for poor but promising villagers in oil-rich countries when she died in 1996. She had also written a manuscript on how to cope successfully with negative problems and people when personal catastrophies strike. Her oldest daughter, Nora, saw to its publication.

CK

PRIMARY SOURCES

Knowles, Ruth Sheldon. *The Greatest Gamblers: The Epic of American Oil Exploration.* New York: McGraw Hill, 1959.

———. *Indonesia Today: The Nation That Helps Itself.* Los Angeles: Nash, 1973.

———. *America's Energy Famine.* Norman: University of Oklahoma Press, 1980.

———. *The First Pictorial History of the American Oil and Gas Industry.* Athens: Ohio University Press, 1983.

SECONDARY SOURCES

"Mrs. Ruth Sheldon Knowles Lecture Tour. Background Information." American Petroleum Institute, Washington, D.C.

"Ruth Sheldon Knowles: Poet Laureate of the High Rollers." *Geophysics: The Leading Edge of Exploration* 3 (February 1984): 34–35.

KNULL, DOROTHY J. (fl. 1939)

U.S. entomologist. Married Josef Nissley Knull.

Dorothy Knull was the wife of the curator of insects at Ohio State University. She wrote numerous articles on the Homoptera, especially the family Cicadellidae. Knull also assisted entomologist Herbert Osborn with his book on meadow insects.   JH/MBO

PRIMARY SOURCES

Osborn, Herbert. Assisted by Dorothy J. Knull. *Meadow and Pasture Insects.* Columbus, OH: Educator's Press, [1939].

STANDARD SOURCES

Osborn (includes portrait).

KOBEL, MARIA (1897–1996)

German biochemist. Born 5 August 1897 in Liegnitz (Silesia) into a family of teachers. Many siblings. Educated University of Breslau (Wroclaw) (doctorate, 1921). Professional experience: Kaiser Wilhelm Institute for Biochemistry, substitute director (1928), Department of Tobacco Research, director (1928–1936); Hoffman House, Berlin, collaborator; Beilstein Edition, Berlin, researcher; Frankfurt am Main, researcher (1945–1946).

Maria Kobel was born into a family with many children to teacher parents. She later noted that it was not unusual for a girl to study chemistry at that time. Her mother had supported her, wanting her as a woman to have a vocation and to be independent. After she completed her dissertation, "Über die in der Literatur als 'Glyoxylharstoff' bezeichneten Stoffe," in Breslau, she traveled to Berlin. Since she had one of the best graduation records, she thought it was natural to get one of the much sought-after places in the Kaiser Wilhelm Institute. Carl Neuberg, the director of the Kaiser Wilhelm Institute for Biochemistry, obviously had an open mind and was not troubled by prejudices in his dealings with female scientists. He had been a professor at the agricultural university since 1914, and since 1919 held an honorary professorship in biochemistry at Berlin University. He promoted several women, including his daughter Irene (1932). He furthered Kobel's career during the 1920s. After he had been able to open a research department in tobacco research in the institute where the chemical processes of tobacco fermentation were to be studied, he was able to get Kobel to lead that department, first in 1928 as his substitute and a year later on her own. The financing of this department, however, remained a problem, since the KWG was hampered by the drastic savings measures of the Weimar Republic in the second half of the 1920s. After Carl Neuberg was ousted in 1933, the Department for Tobacco research came under such financial pressure that it was closed in 1936. The books of the Max Planck Gesellschaft (MPG), including the yearbook that appeared for the fifty-year jubilee, do not speak to the further life of the department chief. The article concerning the institute covered the department in detail, but did not mention the leader once.

After Kobel left the KWG, she worked in the Hoffman House laboratory working on chemical questions surrounding fermentation. She wrote several articles for the three-volume standard work, *Methoden der Fermentforschung.*

When the Hoffman House was destroyed by bombs, the Beilstein group was taken out of Berlin and ended up in Frankfurt am Main. Kobel remained one of the editors until she retired. She died a few days after her ninety-ninth birthday.   JH/MBO

PRIMARY SOURCES

Kobel, Maria. "Einfache Ester der Phosphorsäure." *Methoden der Fermentforschung* 1 (Leipzig 1941): 68–73.

———. "Modifizierte Gärformen." *Methoden der Fermentforschung* 3 (1941): 2173–2196.

SECONDARY SOURCES

Vogt, Annette. "Die Kaiser-Wilhelm-Gesellschaft wagte es: Frauen als Alteilungsleiterinne." In *Aller Männerkultur zum Trotz: Frauen in Mathematik un Naturwissenschaftern,* ed. Renate Tobies. Campus Verlag: Frankfurt, 1997.

STANDARD SOURCES

Poggendorff, vol. 7.

KOCH, HELEN LOIS (1895–1977)

U.S. developmental psychologist. Born 26 August 1895 in Blue Island, Ill. Educated University of Chicago (Ph.B., 1918), fellow (Ph.D., 1921). Postgraduate fellowships and grants: "effect of family on child personality," City of Chicago Schools (1946–1960); "twin and twin relationships," Schools of Illinois (1960–1966). Professional experience: University of Texas, instructor in educational psychology (1921–1922), adjunct professor (1923–1924), associate professor (1925–1926), professor (1927–1928), graduate professor (1929–1939); University of Chicago, associate professor of child psychology (1939–1945), professor (1945–1960), University of Chicago Nursery School, director (1933?-1958), emerita professor of Child Psychology (from 1960). Honors and memberships: G. Stanley Hall Medal; American Psychological Association, Fellow; Society for Research in Child Development, Fellow, president (1931); Association for Childhood Education, Fellow; Association of Applied Psychology, Fellow; Division of Developmental Psychology, member. Died 14 July 1977.

Educational psychologist Helen Koch was born and educated in Illinois. For her first job after she earned her doctoral degree she went to Austin, Texas, where she rose to the rank of professor at the University of Texas. However, she returned to Chicago in 1939 as an associate professor at the University and after six years was promoted to professor. Concurrently, she was the director of the University of Chicago Nursery School. Koch's interests in children's concerns spread into the community. She was a member of numerous committees on child care, including a review committee on personnel of the Office of Civil Defense nurseries from 1942 to 1945. She also worked with training child care aides from 1942 to 1947. She was the recipient of the G. Stanley Hall Medal and was a member of the Division of Developmental Psychology and the American Psychology Association. She was a Fellow of the American Psychology Association, the Society for Research in Child Development (president, 1937), the Association for Childhood Education, and the Association of Applied Psychology.

Koch's research interests were in personality studies of children and families. Her specialty was the relationship between twins and the psychological development of twins.

JH/MBO

PRIMARY SOURCES
Koch, Helen. "Attitudes of Young Children Toward Their Peers as Related to Certain Characteristics of Their Siblings." Washington, D.C.: American Psychological Association, 1956.
———. *Twins and Twin Relations.* Chicago: University of Chicago Press, 1966.
———. *Collected Papers in Child Psychology.* N.p. [196?]. A volume of selected papers reprinted by Koch's students.

SECONDARY SOURCES
American Psychologist (September 1977): 786. Obituary notice.

STANDARD SOURCES
AMS 4–8, S&B 9–12; Rossiter 1995.

KOCH, MARIE LOUISE (1899–?)

U.S. medical bacteriologist. Born 16 June 1899 in Baltimore, Md. to Gertrude (Brossel) and Charles J. Koch. Married (1) C. E. McGulgan (1 June 1922; divorced November 1934); (2) D. A. Sprosty (20 February 1937). One child. Educated Johns Hopkins University (A.B., 1921; M.S., 1935; Ph.D., 1949). Professional experience: Edgewood Arsenal, Md., Chemical Warfare Service, junior toxicologist (1921–1923); Boston Lying-In Hospital, associate bacteriologist (1923–1924); Hynson, Westcott, and Dunning, Md.; bacteriologist (1935–1937); Johns Hopkins Medical School, assistant in medical bacteriology and immunology (1944–1949); Marquette University School of Medicine, assistant professor of microbiology and immunology (from 1949). Concurrent positions: Veterans Administration Center, Wood, Wisc. Death date unknown.

Marie Louise Koch, born in Baltimore, Maryland, completed all of her education at Johns Hopkins University. Her first professional position, obtained as soon as she completed her bachelor's degree, was with the chemical warfare division of the Edgeware Arsenal in Maryland. She then obtained a position as a bacteriologist in the Boston Lying-In Hospital. She had married in 1934 and had a daughter, Dorothy. (This marriage ended in divorce.) After a ten-year pause (probably during the early years of marriage and childraising), she returned to Johns Hopkins for further study in 1934, completing her master's degree by 1935. From there, she took a position as bacteriologist with a Maryland firm.

Koch remarried in 1937 and she returned to Hopkins to pursue a doctorate in medical bacteriology from 1944 to 1949, during which period she held an assistantship in medical bacteriology and immunology. After she received her doctorate, she moved to Wisconsin and was appointed an assistant professor of microbiology and immunology at Marquette School of Medicine in 1949. Concurrently, she held a position as a bacteriologist in the Veterans Administration Center in Wood, Wisconsin, from 1950.

Koch's research initially centered on a study of differential media for isolation of the diphtheria bacillus and for isolation of gonococcus. She also investigated the correlation of phases of the menstrual cycle with the successful recovery of gonococci from cervical secretions. Later she focused on the susceptibility of members of the genera *Staphylococcus* and *Streptococcus* to different antibiotics. Her memberships in professional organizations included the Public Health Association and the Association of Professional Biologists.

JH/MBO

STANDARD SOURCES
AMS B 9, P&B 10–11; Debus.

KOCHANOWSKÁ, ADÉLA (1907–)

Czechoslovakian physicist. Born 8 March 1907 in Ostrava, Czechoslovakia. Educated Charles University, Prague (Dr. rer nat. 1931; lecturer qualification, 1947; D.Sc., 1957). Professional experience: University of Prague(?), professor (1960–?). Honors: Badge for Services to Reconstruction (1953); State Prize (1953).

Adéla Kochanowská attended Charles University in Prague from 1926 until 1930, obtaining a doctorate in natural sciences in 1931. World War II interrupted her studies, but she was qualified to teach at a university by 1947. She was awarded a number of prizes by the socialist state in 1953. In 1960, she became a full university professor.   JH/MBO

SECONDARY SOURCES
Stritbiwsjum Juliusz, ed. *Who's Who in the Socialist Countries of Europe.* 3 vols. Munich, New York, London, and Paris: K.G. Saur, 1989. Kochanowská discussed in volume 2, page 573.

STANDARD SOURCES
Debus.

KOCHINA, PELAGEIA IAKOVLEVNA (1899–?)

Russian mathematician. Born 13 May 1899 in Astrakhan, daughter of Iakov Stepanov Polubarinov, an accountant, and Anisiia Panteleimonovna Polubarinova. Three siblings. Married Nikolai E. Kochin. Two daughters, Ira and Nina. Educated at gymnasium in Astrakhan; Pokrovskii Women's Gymnasium in St. Petersburg; Petrograd University. Professional experience: Main Geophysical Observatory, staff; Institute of Transportation in Leningrad, teacher; Institute of Civil Aviation Engineering, teacher; Leningrad University, professor; Steklov Mathematical Institute, Moscow, senior research associate; Institute of Mechanics of the Soviet Academy of Sciences, researcher; Institute of Hydrodynamics of the Siberian branch of the Soviet Academy of Sciences, researcher; Institute of Problems of Mechanics of the Soviet Academy of Sciences, researcher. Honors and memberships: Soviet Academy of Sciences, corresponding member (1946) and academician (1958); State Prize (1946); four Orders of Lenin. Death date unknown.

Pelageia Iakovlevna Kochina (or Polubarinova-Kochina) was one of Russia's leading woman scientists. She was born in

Astrakhan, the daughter of an accountant who was so concerned about his children's education that he moved the family to St. Petersburg in order to give them better opportunities.

Pelageia Iakovlevna's father died in 1918 and, to support her mother, sister, and younger brother, she went to work in the Main Geophysical Laboratory, while studying at Petrograd University. This was a very difficult period: Russia was in the grip of a civil war and Iakovlevna's younger sister died of tuberculosis, which she also contracted, but she persisted with her education.

When she graduated in 1921, Iakovlevna continued working for A. A. Fridman, a specialist in hydrodynamics, in the division of theoretical meteorology at the Main Geophysical Laboratory. There she met her future husband, Nikolai Efgrafovich Kochin. They were married in 1925 and had two daughters, Ira and Nina.

After the birth of her daughters, Kochina left the Main Geophysical Laboratory. During the years 1925 to 1931, she taught at a high school for workers and at the Institute of Transportation. From 1931 to 1934, she taught at the Institute of Civil Aviation Engineering; in 1934, she was appointed professor at Leningrad University.

In 1935, Nikolai Kochin was appointed head of the division of mathematics at the Steklov Mathematics Institute in Moscow and the family moved to Moscow. There Kochina also found work in the Mathematics Institute as a senior research associate. In 1939, the institute became part of the newly established Institute of Mechanics of the Academy of Sciences, and Kochin was named an academician of the Soviet Academy of Sciences: part of the government reorganization and expansion of the old academy along Communist Party lines. For a time, during World War II, Kochina and her daughters were evacuated to Kazan; but they returned to Moscow after the tide of the war turned at Stalingrad. Kochin remained in Moscow.

In 1944, Kochin died. Kochina continued his course of lectures and also taught, first at the Hydrometeorological and Aircraft Building Institute, and later at the Aviation Industry Academy of the University of Moscow. In 1948, she became the director of the division of hydromechanics, within the Institute of Mechanics.

In 1959, at age sixty, Kochina volunteered to go to Siberia to help establish the Siberian branch of the Academy of Sciences at Novosibirsk. This involved leaving her children and grandchildren in Moscow and living under primitive conditions in the severe Siberian climate while the new branch of the academy was under construction. She was a member of its praesidium and also director of the department of applied hydrodynamics at the Hydrodynamics Institute and head of the department of theoretical mechanics at the University of Novosibirsk.

In 1970, Kochina returned to Moscow, where she became director of the section for mathematical methods of mechanics at the Institute for Problems in Mechanics.

Although originally trained as a pure mathematician, Kochina's main contributions to science were applications of mathematics to hydrodynamics. The Soviet government encouraged the use of applied mathematics to solve the many technical problems with which it was confronted in its efforts to develop and industrialize the country. In 1940, Kochina completed and defended her doctoral dissertation on theoretical aspects of filtration of water in ground soil, receiving the degree of doctor of physical and mathematical sciences (the third woman to receive this degree).

During her long career, Kochina was one of the leading scientists in the development of irrigation and hydroelectric projects in Central Asia and Azerbaijan, and she made many visits to those areas. Kochina continued to do research in this area and also on the hydrodynamics of freeflowing currents and the theory of tides.

Kochina was also interested in the history of mathematics and mechanics, particularly in the life and work of the Russian mathematician SOF'IA KOVALEVSKAIA, about whom she wrote several articles and a biography, as well as editing two volumes of her correspondence. She also wrote a definitive study of Nikolai Kochin's work in dynamic meteorology, hydrodynamics, aerodynamics, and theoretical mechanics, and helped publish his collected works.

Kochina was, in the highest degree, politically orthodox, and she served as a deputy in the Leningrad (city) Soviet, the Moscow (city) Soviet and the Supreme Soviet of the Russian Republic. Kochina was elected a corresponding member of the Academy of Sciences in 1946 and an academician in 1958. She was awarded the State Prize in 1946. She also received four Orders of Lenin, the Order of the Red Banner of Labor, and other medals. In 1969, she was named a Hero of Socialist Labor.   ACH

PRIMARY SOURCES

Kochina, Pelageia Iakovlevna. *Zhizn i deiatel'nost' S. V. Kovalevskoi (1850–1891).* Moscow: Izd-vo Akademii nauk SSSR, 1950.

——. *Teoriia dvizheniia gruntovykh vod.* Moscow: Gos. izd-vo teckniko-teoret. lit-ry, 1952.

——. *Dinamika sploshnoi sredy.* Vol. 2. Novosibirsk: 1969.

SECONDARY SOURCES

Bol'shaia sovetskaia entsiklopediia. 3d ed. Moscow: Izdvo "Sovetskaia entsiklopediia," 1973.

STANDARD SOURCES

Grinstein and Campbell (article by George W. Phillips); *Notable.*

KOHLER, ELSA (1879–?)

Austrian psychologist. Born 1879 in Lemberg, Poland. Educated University of Grenoble (diplome de hautes etudes de langue et de littérature français, 1909); University of Vienna (1909–1911; Ph.D., 1926). Professional experience: Pädagogisches Institut Wien, dozentin (assistant professor) (from 1924); Bunderserziechungsanstalt für Mädchen, Vienna III, faculty (from 1909). Death date unknown.

Psychologist Elsa Kohler was a member of the Deutsche Gesellschaft für Psychologie, the Oesterreichische paedogogische Gesellschaft, and the Fédération Internationale des Professeurs de Langues vivantes (Paris).   JH/MBO

STANDARD SOURCES

Psychological Register, vol. 2, 1929.

KOHN, HEDWIG (1887–1964)

German/U.S. physicist. Born 5 April 1887 in Breslau, Germany (now in Poland). At least one brother. Educated in local schools; University of Breslau (Ph.D., 1913; Dr. Phil. Habil., 1930). Professional experience: Physical Institute, assistant (1917–1930); University of Breslau, lecturer (1930–1933); Lichtklimatisches Observatorium, Arosa, Switzerland, industrial consultant and researcher (1934–1938); Woman's College, University of North Carolina, Greensboro, instructor (1941?–1942); Duke University, summer researcher (1941, 1942, 1943); Wellesley College, lecturer (1942–1945), associate professor (1945–1948), professor (1948–1952), emerita professor (from 1952); Duke University, research associate of physics (from 1952); honorary associate professor emerita (1956); honorary professor emerita, Germany (1954). Died 26 November 1964 in Durham, N.C.

Hedwig Kohn earned her Ph.D. in physics under Otto Lummer, a physicist well known for his work on black body radiation, optics, and illumination technology. Her dissertation on spectral emission produced in flames colored by metallic salts reportedly ended a twenty-year controversy. By her careful work Kohn showed that these spectral lines followed Kirchhoff's law for temperature dependent radiation, and thus were not caused by chemical luminescence.

Kohn published papers on optical radiation, pyrometry, and spectroscopy, and collaborated with Lummer in his book on illumination technology. She also supervised many students. Because of her sex, Kohn was not allowed to qualify as an academic lecturer until 1930. For her *Habilitationsschrift* (the dissertation necessary to qualify as an academic lecturer), Kohn submitted three important articles she had written for the volume in optics in the eleventh edition of *Müller-Pouillets Lehrbuch der Physik,* edited by Lummer.

After the Nazis came to power, Kohn, a Jew, lost her position, but she was able to remain at the Institute under industrial auspices until March 1938. It was difficult for her to decide to leave Germany. Kohn's brother eventually died in a concentration camp, while the cousin and friend with whom she lived committed suicide. She herself barely escaped in time, arriving in Stockholm in 1940 where the emigré physicist LISE MEITNER helped her obtain a U.S. visa. She then traveled through Siberia and Japan to the United States. Kohn was naturalized in 1946. Together with other friends who had immigrated to the United States, Kohn sent numerous care packages to friends in Germany after the war.

Several prominent physicists testified after the war that Kohn's "spectral photometric work, because of the great care and adept research arrangement, are the best in the world." These evaluations, prompted by inquiries from the German government, led to the award of a retroactive honorary professorship, allegedly intended to make amends for the interruption of Kohn's career by the Nazi regime.

At Wellesley, Kohn struggled to pursue research with limited resources, while sparking interest in science among her students. Upon reaching retirement age, she was able to supplement her inadequate pension by earnings from a position at Duke University.

Kohn's work was of both theoretical and practical significance. She was a member of the American Physical Society, the Optical Society of America, the American Association of Physics Teachers, and Sigma Xi.   JH/MBO

PRIMARY SOURCES
Kohn, Hedwig. "Über das Wesen der Emission der in Flammen leuchtenden Metalldämpf." Ph.D. diss., University of Breslau, 1913.
———. With M. Guckel. "Untersucheng am Kohlelichtbogen; Dampfdruckbestimmung des C." *Zeitschrift für Physik.* 27 (1924): 305–357. Includes a determination of vapor pressure and heat of sublimation of carbon.
———. Chapter "Photometrie" (pp. 1104–1320). In *Müller-Pouillets Lehrbuch der Physik,* ed. Otto Lummer. Braunschweig: Friedrick Vieweg & Sohn, [1926?].
———. "Intensitätsmessungen an den Hauptseriendubletts der Alkalimetalle." *Physikalische Zeitschrift* 27, (1926).
———. "Methode zur Bestimmung der Zahl angeregter Atomzustände." *Physikalische Zeitschrift* 29 (January 1928): 49–52.
———. *Photometrie.* Sonderdruck aus Müller-Pouillet, vol. 2. Braunschweig: Friedr, Vieweg & Sohn Akt.-Ges. Dr. Hedwig Kohn, Breslau. Inscribed to J. Franck, December 1929.
———. "Umkehrmessungen an Spektrallinien zur Bestimmung der Gesamtabsorption und der Besetzungszahlen angeregter Atomzustände." *Physikalische Zeitschrift* 33 (1932): 957–963.

———. With H. J. Hübner. "Intensitätsmessungen an Hauptserienmitgliedern von Rb und Cs." *Physikalische Zeitschrift* 34 (1933): 278–282.
———. With Hertha Sponer. "Absorption Spectrum of 1,2,4 Trichlorobenzene in the Near Ultraviolet." *Journal of the Optical Society of America* 39 (1949): 75–85.
———. With Einar Hinnov. "Optical Cross Sections from Intensity-Density Measurements." *Journal of the Optical Society of America* 44 (1957): 156–162.
Notes from an oral interview of Kohn, 7 June 1962. Archive for the History of Quantum Physics.

SECONDARY SOURCES
Lummer, Otto. *Grundlagen, Ziele und Grenzen der Leuchttechnik.* Munich: Oldenbourg, 1923.
Physics Today 18 (January 1965): 154–155. Obituary notice.
Rider, Robin E. "Alarm and Opportunity: Emigration of Mathematicians and Physicists to Britain and the United States, 1933–1945." *Historical Studies in the Physical Sciences* 15 (1984): 107–176, on 109 n. 14, 174.
Schaefer, Clemens. "Hedwig Kohn 70 Jahre." *Physikalische Blätter* 13 (1957): 224–225.
Sime, Ruth. *Lise Meitner: A Life in Physics.* Berkeley, Los Angeles, and London: University of California Press, 1996.

STANDARD SOURCES
AMS 7–10.

KOHTS, NADIE (LADYCHIN) (fl. 1920s)
Russian comparative psychologist. Flourished 1920s–1930s. Married. Darwin Museum, Moscow, Zoopsychological Laboratory, director (1918–1939?).

Little information is available on the life of Nadie Kohts, listed in some of her articles as Nadia Ladychin-Kohts. She worked on sensory discrimination and perception in chimpanzees, using a small colony developed at the Darwin Museum, Moscow, where she was director of the Zoopsychological Laboratory in the 1920s and 1930s. Her work is cited in various writings of the primatologist and psychologist Robert Yerkes, and more recently by Emily Hahn and Donna Haraway.   JH/MBO

PRIMARY SOURCES
Kohts, Nadia. *Untersuchngen uber die Erkenntniss fahrigkeiten des Schimpansen aus dem zoopsychologischen Laboratorium des Museum Darwinianum im Moskau.* Moscow: N.p., 1923.
———. "Infant Ape and Human Child." *Scientific Reports of the Moscow Darwin Museum* 3 (1936): 524–591.

SECONDARY SOURCES

Hahn, Emily. *Eve and the Apes.* New York: Weidenfeld and
Nicholson, 1988. Kohts discussed on pages 173–178.

Haraway, Donna. *Primate Visions: Gender, Race and Nature in the
World of Modern Science.* Haraway gives a nod, on pages 22
and 298, in the direction of Kohts's early work on the mind
of apes.

KOLACZKOWSKA, MARIA (1885–1977)

*Polish mineralogist and crystallographer. Born 1885. Professional
positions: Polytechnic and Mineralogical Laboratory, Warsaw; University of Warsaw until 1939; Nicholas Copernicus University,
Torun, from 1947. Died 1977.*

Maria Kolaczkowska was a mineralogist and crystallographer
whose last position was at the University of Torun.

                                                    JH/MBO

PRIMARY SOURCES

Kolaczkowska, Maria. "Badania rentgenologiczne naturalnego i
syntetycznego kaliofilitu oraz jego pochodnych; etudes
roentgenoscopiques sur la kaliophilite et sur l'alunite naturelle et synthetique." *Archiwum Mineralogiczne* 13 (1937):
92–97.

————. "Mikroskopische Untersuchungen des Meteorits von
Lowicz; badania mikroskopowe meteory; tulowickiego."
Archiwum Mineralogiczne 14 (1938): 47–56.

SECONDARY SOURCES

Laszkiewicz, Antoni. "Maria Kolaczkowska (1885–1977)."
*Rocznik Polskiego Towarzystwa Geologicznego (Annales de la
Société Géologique de Pologne)* 47, no. 4 (1977): 639–642.

STANDARD SOURCES

Sarjeant.

KOMAROVSKY, MIRRA (1905–)

*Russian/U.S. sociologist. Born 1905 in the Cacausus, Russia, to
Anna (Steinberg) and Manuel Komarovsky. Naturalized (1933).
Married (1) ? (1926, divorced 1928); (2) Marcus A. Heyman
(1940). Educated privately (in Russia); Barnard College (A.B.,
1926; M.A., 1936?); Columbia University (Ph.D., 1940). Professional experience: Skidmore College, instructor (1926–1928);
Yale Institute for Human Relations, researcher (1928–1933); Columbia Council for Research in Social Sciences, research assistant
(1933–1936?); International Institute for Social Research, research
associate (1936–1938?); Barnard College, part-time instructor in
sociology (1938–1940), instructor (1940–1945); assistant professor (1945–1948); associate professor (1948–1953), professor and
chair of department (1953–1970), emerita lecturer (1970–1974);*
*Columbia University, School of General Studies, researcher (1974–
1977); Women's Studies, chair (1978), emerita professor and special lecturer (1979–1990?). New School for Social Research, visiting professor (1975–1978); City College of New York, visiting
professor. Honors and Memberships: Barnard College Caroline
Durer fellowship for graduate study (1926); Eastern Sociological
Association, vice-president (1949), president (1955); The American Sociological Review, associate editor (1957–1965); American Sociological Association, Section on the Family, chair (1956–
1966); council member (1966–1969, 1973–1974), vice-president (1970–1972), president (1972); Distinguished Alumna
Award, Barnard College (1976); American Sociological Association, Jesse Bernard Award (1977); Eastern Sociological Association,
Merit Award (1977); Barnard College, Emily Gregory Award
(1977); Barnard Medal of Distinction (1983); Columbia University, honorary doctorate (1979); National Council on Family Relations, Burgess Award (1986); Commonwealth Award (1990).*

Mirra Komarovsky was born in Russia, but came to the
United States with her family as a teenager in the 1920s. She
began to study anthropology under Franz Boas and RUTH
BENEDICT and a group of women economists, as well as with
the sociologist William Ogburn at Barnard College. She received a prestigious award from her college to continue her
graduate work and then made a disastrous first marriage. She
began to teach at Skidmore College, but eventually left her
husband and went to New Haven to work as a research assistant in the Yale Institute for Human Relations. After a few
years, she went to work with George Lundberg on the Westchester Leisure Project under a Columbia social science
council grant, which resulted in the publication of her first
book *Leisure: A Suburban Study,* with Lundberg and Mary
McInerny.

In the mid-thirties, Komarovsky returned to graduate
study to work first under Ogburn and then under Paul
Lazarfield, who directed her doctoral dissertation on the effects of unemployment on the family, published as *The Unemployed Man and His Family* (1940). She began to teach
undergraudates at Barnard, at first part-time, then as a full-time instructor until after World War II. Her experiences as
a woman and a foreigner made her aware of gender issues.
She later spoke about the decision to look at women's issues
and sex roles as exacting a price, and slowing down her
advancement.

Komarovsky's new marriage in 1940 to a successful businessman gave her the support to continue. Her book also
began to receive good reviews, although there were also critical ones. She continued to produce a number of articles on
the contradictions within women's sex roles, but remained at
the rank of assistant professor until the age of forty-two.

With the arrival of a new energetic woman president
at Barnard, Millicent MacIntosh, Komarovsky began to

advance through the ranks, obtaining tenure and then the position of full professor in 1954. She was chair of her department until her retirement.

Her studies that advocated women's access to public spheres and the inclusion of men in domestic duties, *Women in the Modern World,* was in advance of its time and failed to have a great effect. Nevertheless, Komarovsky became influential as a teacher and within her profession until the revival of the feminist movement in the seventies brought her wide recognition and numerous honors from both her university and her professional associations. She continued to turn out important books on masculinity as well as on women's issues, and advocated the feminist study of men. Komarovsky included not only statistical studies but psychological and anthropological elements in her analyses. She was the first head of Women's Studies at Columbia and remained an active lecturer into the 1990s.

JH/MBO

PRIMARY SOURCES

Komarovsky, Mirra. With George Lundberg and Mary Alice McIverny. *Leisure: A Suburban Study.* New York: Columbia University Press, 1934.

————. *The Unemployed Man and His Family.* New York: Dryden Press, 1940. Her Columbia dissertation.

————. "Cultural Contraditions and Sex Roles." *American Journal of Sociology* 51 (1946): 184–189.

————. *Women in the Modern World: Their Education and Their Dilemmas.* Boston: Little, Brown, 1953.

————. *Dilemmas of Masculinity: A Study of College Youth.* New York: W. W. Norton, 1976.

————. *Women in College: Shaping New Feminine Identity.* New York: Basic Books, 1985.

SECONDARY SOURCES

Reinharz, Shulamit. "Mirra Komaraovsky." In *Women in Sociology: A Bio-Bibliographic Sourcebook,* ed. Mary Jo Deegan, 239–248. New York, Westport Conn.: Greenwood Press.

STANDARD SOURCES
O'Neill.

KOPROWSKA, IRENA GRASBERG (1917–)
Polish/U.S. physician. Born 12 May 1917 in Warsaw, Poland. Married Hilary Koprowski (14 July 1938). Two sons. Educated Warsaw School of Medicine (M.D., 1939). Professional experience: Cornell University, research assistant, pathology (1945–1946), research assistant, pharmacology and anatomy (1949–1950); Public Health Research Institute of the City of New York, Inc., assistant pathologist (1946–1947), research fellow and associate in anatomy (1950–1954); New York Infirmary, researcher (1947–1949); New York University Medical School, assistant professor of pathol- ogy; *King's County Hospital, N.Y., director of cytology (1954–1957); New York Society of Clinical Pathologists, consultant; Hahnemann Medical College, Philadelphia, associate professor through professor; Hahnemann Hospital, director of cytological laboratory; Temple University Health Sciences Center, director of cytological services, professor of pathology (from 1970). Concurrent positions: Cornell University Medical College, research fellow (1949–1954); U.S. Public Health Service research grants (from 1954); Runyon Memorial Fund Grant recipient (1955–1956); American Cancer Society, grant recipient (1958–1961); lecturer, France, Poland, India, and Iran; World Health Organization, consultant (from 1962).*

Irena Grasberg Koprowska was a native of Poland, where she earned her doctoral degree. She married a fellow medical student at the University of Warsaw. He later was a discoverer of the living virus vaccine against rabies, hog cholera, yellow fever, and poliomyelitis. The couple came to the United States, where Koprowska held several positions at Cornell University. She then worked for the Research Institute of the City of New York for two different times, and held several other positions in New York.

Koprowska moved from associate professor to professor at the Hahnemann Medical College, Philadelphia, and during the same time was director of the cytological laboratory at the Hahnemann Hospital. Her husband was director of the Wistar Institute. The couple then moved to Temple University, where Koprowska was professor of pathology and director of the Cytological Service at the Health Sciences Center there. In addition to her regular jobs, she held a number of concurrent positions. She was a member of the American Association for the Advancement of Science, the American Society of Clinical Pathologists, the American Society of Experimental Pathology, and the American Medical Association, and a Fellow of the College of American Pathologists.

Koprowska specialized in studies of progressive morphologic cellular changes, especially endoplastic progression in human beings, mice, and in tissue culture systems. She also worked in cancer research, experimental pathology, and exfoliative cytology.

KM

STANDARD SOURCES
AMS P&B 14; *Current Biography* 1968.

KORN, DORIS ELFRIEDE (1904–)
German mineralogist. Born 30 May 1904 in Zwickau, Germany, to Elsa (Junghanns) and Otto Korn. Married Benno Schachner (28 August 1938). One daughter. Educated University of Heidelberg (Ph.D. in natural sciences); University of Aix-la-Chapelle (France), (Agregé, 1933). Professional experience: professor (1949–1968?); Minerology Institute, Aachen, Germany, director. Honors

and memberships: German Mineralogy Association, German Geological Association, French Geological Society, American Mineralogical Association.

Doris Elfriede Korn was a German mineralogist who conducted research and published on the structure of minerals and ores, the mechanism of mineral formation, and the genesis of veins of minerals. She obtained her doctorate at the University of Heidelberg and then did her agregation (the highest competitive examination for teachers in France) at the University of Aix-la-Chapelle, which qualified her to teach in French universities. By 1949, she was a full professor, and by 1968, she was director of the Mineralogy Institute in Aachen, Germany.   JH/MBO

STANDARD SOURCES
Debus.

KOROBEINIKOVA, IULIIA IVANOVNA (1883–1950)

Russian plant selectionist. Born 17 June 1883 in Blagoveshchenk-on-Amur. Educated Stebut Women's Higher Agricultural Courses, Petrograd. Professional experience: explorer, Amur region; Kharkov Experimental Agricultural Station, staff; Agricultural Department, Amur Land Board, head; geobotanical research department, Primor'ie settlement, head; selection department, Ukrainian Institute of Grain Farming, assistant professor; Kharkov Selection Station, associate. Died 1 April 1950.

Iuliia Ivanovna Korobeinikova graduated from Stebut Women's Higher Agricultural Courses in 1917. During 1911 and 1912, she took part in an exploration of the Amur region. From 1912 to 1924, she worked at Kharkov Experimental Agricultural Station. In 1924 she became head of the agricultural department of the Amur Land Board, and from 1927 to 1930 was head of the geobotanical research department of the Primor'ie settlement. From 1930 to 1932, she was assistant professor at the selection department of the Ukrainian Institute of Grain Farming, and from 1933 to her death in 1950 was associated with the Kharkov Selection Station.

Her research was primarily concerned with wheat breeding. She established that there is no connection between the planting depth of the bushing node of winter wheat and its winter resistance.   ACH

PRIMARY SOURCES
Korobeinikova, Iuliia Ivanovna. *Sorta ozimoi pshenitsy selektsii Kharkovskoi opytnoi stantsii.* N.p., 1937.
———. *Glubina zaleganiia uzla kushcheniia i ee sviazi s zimostoikost'iu u raznykh sortov ozimoi pshenitsy.* N.p., 1947.

STANDARD SOURCES
WWW (USSR).

KORRINGA, MARJORIE K. (1943–1974)

U. S. igneous petrologist, vulcanologist and structural geologist. Born 1943. One sibling. Married twice, but single at time of death. Educated High School Averill Park, New York (graduated 1960); Radcliffe College (B.A. 1964); Stanford University (Ph.D. 1972). Professional experience: University of Nevada, geological consultant to David B. Slemmons; Woodward-Clyde Consultants. Died 8 September 1974.

Marjorie Korringa graduated from Radcliffe College in 1964 with a bachelor's in geology. In 1972, she received a doctorate in geology from Stanford University, working in volcanic petrology. For her dissertation, she researched the geologic history and volcanic phenomena at the linear vent area of the Soldier Meadow Tuff, an ash-flow sheet in northwestern Nevada. After receiving her degree, she served as a geological consultant to David B. Slemmons at the University of Nevada. She worked with another University of Nevada geologist, Donald C. Noble, on volcanic petrology in western North America and Peru. She expanded her interests to include problems involved in active faulting and landslides. She worked with Woodward-Clyde Consultants for the rest of her life, evaluating active faults. She was important in studies of the Alyeska fault for the Trans-Alaska pipeline. She was working on a number of projects at the time of her death, including a study of nuclear reactor siting in California, a study of the Managua earthquake and related faults for the Nicaraguan government, and a nuclear reactor project in Italy. In addition to designing the scope of these projects, she also interpreted the imagery. She was becoming more involved with the managerial functions at Woodward-Clyde and was chair of the Geology-Seismology-Geophysics Planning Committee immediately before she died.

Korringa's life ended on TWA flight 841, which crashed into the Ionian Sea between Athens and Rome. The investigation indicates that the crash was caused by a bomb on board. Korringa was on her way to Rome after spending time with her parents in Greece. She had presented a paper in Zurich at the International Symposium on Recent Crustal Movements.   CK

PRIMARY SOURCES
Korringa, Marjorie K. With D. C. Noble. "Ash-Flow Eruption from a Linear Vent Area without Caldera Collapse." *Geological Society of America Abstracts with Programs* 2, no. 2 (1970): 108–109.

———. "Vent Area of the Soldier Meadow Tuff, and Ash-Flow Sheet in Northwestern Nevada." Ph.D. diss., Stanford University, 1972.

———. With D. C. Noble. "Genetic Significance of Chemical, Isotopic, and Petrographic Features of Some Peralkaline Salic Rocks from the Island of Pantellaria." *Earth and Planetary Science Letters* 17 (1972): 258–262.

———. With others. "Highly Differentiated Subalkaline Rhyolite from Glass Mountain, Mono County, California." *Geological Society of America Bulletin* 83, no. 4 (1973): 1179–1184.

———. "Linear Vent Area of the Soldier Meadow Tuff, and Ash-Flow Sheet in Northwestern Nevada." *Geological Society of America Bulletin* 84, no. 12 (1973): 3849–3866.

SECONDARY SOURCES
Packer, Duane R., William R. Dickinson, and Kathryn M. Nichols. "Memorial to Marjorie K. Korringa, 1943–1974." *Geological Society of America Memorials* 6 (1977): 1–3. Includes portrait.

STANDARD SOURCES
Sarjeant.

KORSHUNOVA, OLGA STEPANOVNA (1909–)

Russian microbiologist. Born 1909 in Moscow to Vera (Sokolova) and Stepan Aelksandrovitch Korshunov. Educated Moscow University (undergraduate degree, 1930; M.D., 1946). Professional positions: Metchnikov Institute, Moscow, staff (1931–1937); All-Union Instittute for Experimental Medicine, staff (1938–1942); Scientific Research Control Institute, Moscow, head of experimental production department (1943–1945); U.S.S.R. Academy of Medicine, Gamaleya Institute of Epidemiology and Microbiology, microbiologist (1946–post-1968). Honors and memberships: State Medal for Labor Value.

Olga Korshunova was a Russian (Soviet) microbiologist who researched rickettsial diseases, isolating the blood from patients, and from their vectors, ticks and fleas. Educated at Moscow University, she also studied medicine and microbiology. As a recent undergraduate, she worked first at the Metchnikov Institute in Moscow and then at the All-Union Institute for Experimental Medicine. During World War II, she was made head of the experimental production department of the Scientific Research Control Institute. After the war, she entered the Gamaleya Institute of Epidemiology and Microbiology, a wing of the Academy of Medicine. There she did research on tick-borne typhus, and epidemic outbreaks of nephroso-nephritis in the South Ukraine and adjoining areas. She was awarded the State Medal for Labor Value.   JH/MBO

PRIMARY SOURCES
Korshunova, Olga Stepanovna. With Zhmajeva Pltonkovskaya. *Ixodid Vectors of Rickettsial Diseases.* Moscow: N.p., 1952.

———. *Human Disease with Natural Foci.* Moscow: N.p., 1960

———. With Zhmajeva Pltonkovskaya. *Experimental Findings on Tick-Borne Typhus in the Krasnoyarskaya Territory.* Moscow: N.p., 1966.

STANDARD SOURCES
Debus.

KOSHLAND, MARIAN (ELLIOTT) (1921–1997)

U.S. immunologist and molecular biologist. Born New Haven, Conn., 25 October 1921. Married Daniel Edward Koshland, Jr., in 1945. Five children. Educated Vassar College (A.B., 1942); University of Chicago (M.S., 1943; Ph.D. in Bacteriology, 1949). Professional experience: University of Chicago Cholera Project, assistant (1943–1945); University of Colorado, Commission on Air-Borne Diseases (1943–1944); Manhattan District (atom bomb project), Tennessee, junior chemist (1945–1946); Brookhaven National Labs (1953–1965); University of California, Berkeley, professor of bacteriology and immunology (1970–1997); department chair (1983–1997). Honors and memberships: National Institutes of Health, R.E. Dyer Lecturer; Harvard Fellow in immunology and bacteriology (1949–1951). NSF board (1976–1982); American Association of Immunologists (president, 1982–1983); member of National Academy of Sciences, American Society of Biological Chemists, and American Academy of Microbiologists. Died 30 October 1997.

Marian Elliott was educated at Vassar College and went on to earn a master's and doctoral degree in bacteriology at the University of Chicago, where her future husband, Daniel E. Koshland, was studying biochemistry. During World War II, she worked first with the University of Chicago cholera project and then with the government group studing air-borne diseases. By 1943, she joined the so-called Manhattan District in Tennessee, connected to the group of the Manhattan Project working on the atom bomb, which her husband directed. The two married in 1945 and had five children. In 1949, the couple went to Harvard, where she was a fellow in immunology while her husband was a fellow in biochemistry for two years. Koshland and her husband both joined the Brookhaven Laboratories in the 1950s, and remained until the mid-sixties. At this point, her husband joined the University of California, Berkeley, but she was able to be appointed to the faculty as a full professor only in the 1970s when the antinepotism rules were relaxed and the antidiscrimination laws made her appointment possible. She was not sympathetic to feminism, however, nor was she remembered as helpful to other women faculty members.

Before her death in 1997, Koshland served as president of the American Association of Immunologists and was honored by an appointment to the National Academy of Sciences. Her research included the mechanism of antibody biosynthesis, lymphokine regulation of immunoglobulin gene expression, mechanisms of lymphokine signaling of B lymphocytes, the roles of K chain and IgM in differentiation of antibody-forming cells. She also studied the genetic control of J chain and heavy chain synthesis as she moved into molecular biology.

JH/MBO

SECONDARY SOURCES
New York Times, 30 October 1997. Obituary.

STANDARD SOURCES
AMS B 9, P&B 10–18; Bailey.

KOVALEVSKAIA, SOFIA VASILYEVNA (1850–1891)

Russian mathematician. Born 1850 in Moscow to Yelizaveta (Shubert) and Vasily Korvin-Krukovsky. Married Vladimir Kovalevsky. One daughter, Foufie. Educated by tutors; "underground university," St. Petersburg; University of Heidelberg (1869–1871); studied under Karl Weierstrassin, Berlin (1871–1874); University of Stockholm, professor. Died 1891 in Stockholm.

Both Sofia Kovalevskaia's mother and her father, an artillery general, were members of the Russian nobility. Sofia and her two sisters spent most of their childhood at the Krukovsky country estate at Palabino, cared for and educated by nursemaids, governesses, and tutors. In her *Recollections of Childhood,* Kovalevskia described her strained relationship with her parents—particularly her mother, who preferred her eldest and youngest daughters, Aniuta and Fedya, to Sofia, the middle one.

Sofia obtained her early education from a Polish tutor, Iosif Malevich, who was convinced that his "talented pupil could occupy a prominent position in the literary world." He was, however, less ecstatic about her progress in arithmetic. Margaret Smith, her English governess, also contributed to her education. Although Sofia complained of having no companions her own age, her lesson-filled days included several diversions including writing poetry and playing ball.

Two of Sofia's uncles influenced her intellectual development. Her father's eccentric oldest brother, Piotr, loved to read and discuss the latest scientific speculations. Sofia was often his sounding board. From her mother's brother she absorbed an interest in natural history.

A family friend, Nikolai Tyrtov (1822–1888), who was a physics teacher at the St. Petersburg naval school, recognized Sofia's gifts. He advised her father to have her taught higher mathematics during her visits to St. Petersburg with her mother and older sister.

Russian young people during Sofia's youth were rebelling against established ideas and among their causes was the emancipation of women. "An epidemic seemed to seize upon the children—especially the girls—an epidemic of fleeing from the parental roof. In our immediate neighborhood, through God's mercy, all was well so far; but rumors reached us from other places; the daughter, now of this, now of that landed proprietor had run away; this one abroad, the other to Petersburg to the 'nihilists'" (*Recollections,* 93). Aniuta, who had earlier declined to study anything, began to read and absorb radical ideas. She secretly sent a manuscript to Feodor Dostoevsky, who agreed to publish it in his journal. During a visit to St. Petersburg, both sisters became good friends of Dostoevsky; indeed, he fell in love with Aniuta, a love that was not reciprocated. To complete the triangle, Sofia became infatuated with Dostoevsky and jealous of her sister. The affair was resolved when Dostoevsky left St. Petersburg and wrote that he was marrying someone else.

Sofia, as the little sister, slipped into Aniuta's social circle, where, because of her evident keenness and quickness of perception, she was accepted by the older students. "We were so enthusiastic about the new ideas," she recalled, "so sure that the present social state could not continue long. We pictured to ourselves the glorious period of liberty and universal enlightenment of which we dreamed, and in which we firmly believed" (*Recollections,* 161). In spite of this stimulating intellectual atmosphere, the lack of opportunity for formal study plagued Sofia. As a woman she could not matriculate at the university; nevertheless she worked under some competent teachers. During 1867 and 1868 she studied with Alexander Strannolyubsky (1839–1903), a mathematics teacher at the naval school and an ardent supporter of both popular education and education for women. In addition, she attended advanced courses for women that were conducted in private homes. Among the prominent scholars who gave lectures free of charge was the chemist Dmitri Mendeleev (1834–1907). Craving additional education, Sofia approached P. L. Chebyshev (1821–1894), who headed the Russian Mathematical School, and asked for permission to attend his lectures. When he refused, she decided to leave Russia and study at a foreign university.

A new custom was becoming increasingly common in Russia. In order to go abroad to study, a woman would contract a marriage of convenience with a man who was also planning to attend a foreign school. Trusting that if one of them married and left Russia, their father would allow the other to go along, Aniuta and Sofia sought a suitable young man and found him in a clever young geology student named Vladimir Kovalevsky. He agreed on condition that

Sofia be the bride. As they knew it might be impossible to convince the general that the younger daughter should marry first, the sisters decided to force the issue by creating a scandal. Sofia disappeared; and when her father asked where she was, he was presented with a note that read, "Father, I am with Vladimir, and beg you will no longer oppose our marriage" (*Recollections,* 169). That evening General Krukovsky brought both Sofia and Vladimir back to dinner and introduced Vladimir as Sofia's fiancé.

After spending six months in St. Petersburg, Sofia and Vladimir Kovalevsky left for Heidelberg in 1869, he to study geology and she, mathematics. Shortly after matriculation at the university, they made a trip to England, where they met George Eliot, Charles Darwin, and Herbert Spencer. In Heidelberg the Kovalevskys and a woman friend of Sofia's shared lodgings, and for a time an innocent harmony prevailed. The situation soon changed, however, as suspicion and jealousy developed among the three. Kovalevsky moved out and went to Jena and then to Munich to study. Throughout this time of tension in her private life, Sofia Kovalevskaia's reputation as a scholar was spreading.

Kovalevskaia went to Berlin in the autumn of 1871 to continue her studies under Karl Weierstrass (1815–1897). At first doubtful about her abilities, he soon became her chief supporter. Since as a woman Kovalevskaia could not be admitted to university lectures, Weierstrass tutored her privately for four years. Her stay in Berlin was difficult, both physically and emotionally. Both she and the friend with whom she lived were impractical. They had miserable lodgings, cheating servants, and poor food, and neither of them knew how to remedy the situation. Moreover, Sofia began to realize the peculiarity of her relationship with her husband—who had followed her to Berlin but had left her and moved in with her friend from Heidelberg. She worked to exhaustion at mathematics, but even that no longer gave her pleasure.

In 1874 Kovalevskaia received her doctorate in absentia from the University of Göttingen. Her qualifications for the degree were three treatises written under the guidance of Weierstrass. Finding that despite her credentials she was unable to find a teaching position in a European university, she returned to Russia. Here she was reunited both with her own family—she became especially close to her father, whose sudden death from an aneurysm greatly disturbed her—and with her husband, with whom she "glided into a full relationship." Their only daughter, Foufie, later a student of medicine and translator of literary works into Russian, was born in 1878.

For several years, Kovalevskaia committed herself as wholeheartedly to a brilliant social life as she had before to mathematics. She neglected to answer the letters of her old teacher and benefactor Weierstrass—including one in which he asked her to deny the rumor current in Berlin that she

had become a society woman and had abandoned mathematics. Meanwhile her husband, attempting to remedy the effects of living beyond their means, became involved with an unscrupulous speculation. He was disgraced and committed suicide by drinking an entire bottle of chloroform in 1883.

Following her husband's death, Kovalevskaia approached Weierstrass for help. He arranged for her to send a mathematical treatise to an eminent disciple of his, Gösta Mittag-Leffler of the University of Stockholm. Mittag-Leffler was interested in the "woman question" and wanted to secure the "first great woman mathematician" for the new university. Kovalevskaia was appointed lecturer in mathematics in 1883. She found herself in the middle of a dispute between the "old guard" (angered that a university position was given to a woman) and "young Sweden" (insistent on the equality of women). She, however, took it all calmly, and was not upset when she found out that notices of her lectures, put up by students in their union in Uppsala, had been defaced by the professors. Kovalevskaia secured a five-year appointment as a professor in 1884, and in 1889 was given a life professorship.

She soon, however, found Stockholm dull and provincial. As much time as could be spared from her teaching duties was spent away from Sweden and in the great European capitals. Because of the illness of her sister Aniuta, Kovalevskaia also made many trips back to Russia. Aniuta's death of an inflammation of the lungs affected her profoundly.

One positive element of Kovalevsky's life in Stockholm was her close friendship with Mittag-Leffler's sister, Anna Carlotta, who later contributed a life of Kovalevskaia to the volume containing the latter's *Recollections.* In 1887, the two women collaborated on a play, *The Struggle for Happiness,* which enjoyed a modest success in Moscow. During the time that she was engaged in literary efforts, Kovalevskaia utterly lost interest in mathematics.

Kovalevskaia believed that she had predictive abilities. The year 1888, she foretold, would bring her to the peak of her success and happiness. It was in this year that she received the Prix Bordin of the French Academy of Sciences for her paper on the rotation of a solid body about a fixed point. During the time when she was working on the prize-winning essay, however, her personal life was again racked by conflict. She had fallen in love with a Russian historian, Maxim Kovalevsky (not related to her husband), who had come to Stockholm in 1888 after being discharged from the University of Moscow for political reasons. As usual, Kovalevskaia was demanding and jealous. In addition, there was the conflict with her work. Kovalevskaia was convinced that his love was "chilled" by seeing her so successful. Yet she was unwilling to give up her professorship, follow him to Paris—where he had received a permanent teaching post—and "become merely a wife."

During the period when her turbulent relationship with Maxim Kovalevsky had apparently suffered its final "shipwreck," Kovalevskaia spent much of her time in literary composition. She wrote a series of autobiographical novels, *The University Lecturer, The Nihilist, The Woman Nihilist, A Story of the Riviera,* and *The Sisters Raevsky.* The relationship that was supposedly over must have been rekindled, however, for Kovalevskaia spent the Christmas holidays of 1890–1891 with Maxim at his villa in France. It is probable that they planned to be married in the spring. Returning to Stockholm in late January 1891, Kovalevskaia became badly chilled before she arrived at Stockholm, but insisted on giving her lectures anyway. The chill developed into pneumonia, and Kovalevskaia died on February 10, three weeks after her forty-first birthday.

The three research papers that Kovalevskaia completed for her doctorate in 1874 were on partial differential equations, Abelian integrals, and the rings of Saturn. Although all three were important, the first is considered particularly significant by mathematicians. In this paper, published in 1875, Kovalevsky added to the work of Augustin Louis Cauchy (1789–1857) in the solution of partial differential equations. By adducing new examples, she gave his work a more generalized form. The result is known as the Cauchy-Kovalevsky theorem.

Kovalevskaia's second doctoral paper dealt with the so-called Abelian integrals. Niels Henrik Abel (1802–1829) had died shortly after he had begun his research, and Weierstrass and his students were left with the task of developing a general theory. Kovalevskaia's contribution, published in 1884, demonstrated the possibility of expressing certain types of Abelian integrals in terms of simpler elliptic integrals.

In her third paper (published in 1883), Kovalevskaia studied the form of Saturn's rings. Laplace had worked on the problem and had concluded that certain cross sections of the rings were elliptical, whereas Kovalevskaia proved that they were egg-shaped ovals symmetric relative to a single axis. She also considered the problem of the stability of motion of liquid bodies that are ring-shaped.

The paper for which Kovalevskaia won the Prix Bordin, "Sur le problème de la rotation d'un corps solide autour d'un point fixe" (published in 1889), involved complex analysis and nonelementary integrals. She generalized the work of Leonhard Euler (1707–1783), Simeon Denis Poisson (1781–1840), and Joseph Louis Lagrange (1736–1813), who had considered simpler cases where a rigid, symmetrical body rotates about a fixed point. Kovalevskaia treated asymmetric bodies, and, according to the *Dictionary of Scientific Biography,* "her solution was so general that no new case of rotatory motion about a fixed point has been researched to date" (479). Subsequent research on the subject earned her a prize

from the Swedish Academy of Sciences in 1889. In the same year she was made a member of the Russian Academy of Sciences.

Brilliant, complex, and troubled, Sonya Kovalevskaia was a creative mathematician of the highest order. Though guided by Weierstrass in her choice of problems to address, she produced solutions to the problems that were thoroughly original.   MBO

PRIMARY SOURCES

Kovalevskaia, Sofia. "Zur Theorie der partiellen Differential-gleichungen," *Journal für die reine und angewandte Mathematik* 80 (1875): 1–32.

———. "Zusätze und Bemerkungen zu Laplaces Untersuchungen über die Gestalt der Saturnsringe." *Astronomische Nachrichten* 3 (1883): 37–48.

———. "Über die Reduction einer bestimmten Klasse Abelscher Integrale dritten Ranges auf elliptische Integrale." *Acta Mathematica* 4 (1884): 393–414.

———. "Sur le problème de la rotation d'un corps solide autour d'un point fixe." *Acta Mathematica* 12 (1889): 177–232.

———. *Recollections of Childhood.* Trans. Isabel F. Hapgood; with a biography by Anna Carlotta Leffler. Trans. A. M. Clife Bayley. With biographical notes by Lily Wolffsohn. New York: Century, 1895.

SECONDARY SOURCES

Coolidge, Julian L. "Six Female Mathematicians." *Scripta Mathematica* 17 (March–June 1951): 20–31.

Koblitz, Ann Hibner. *A Convergence of Lives: Sofia Kovalevskaia, Scientist, Writer, Revolutionary.* Boston: Birkhäuser, 1983. This fine biography of Kovalevskaia has been reprinted with a new preface in 1993 by Rutgers University Press.

Mittag-Leffler, G. "Zur Biographie von Weierstrass." *Acta Mathematica.* 35 (1912). A biographical sketch with bibliography of Kovalevskaia.

Osen, Lynn M. *Women in Mathematics.* Cambridge, Mass.: MIT Press, 1975.

Polubarinova, P. *Sophia Vasilyevna Kovalevskaya: Her Life and Work.* Trans. P. Ludwick. Moscow: Foreign Languages Publishing House, 1957.

STANDARD SOURCES

DSB; Ogilvie 1986.

KOVRIGINA, MARIIA DMITRIEVNA (1910–)

Russian physician and public health administrator. Born July 1910 in Troitskoe, Perm province, to Dmitrii Vasil'evich and Varvara Ivanovna Kovrigin, peasants. At least six siblings. Two daughters:

Taniia, Svetlana (adopted niece). Educated at local schools; "worker's faculty" in Sverdlovsk; Sverdlovsk Medical Institute. Worked at Cheliabinsk City Hospital; health inspector, Cheliabinsk area; director of evacuees during war; Commissariat of Health, Moscow, deputy; Minister of Health of the RSFSR; First deputy Minister of Health of the USSR; Minister of Health of the USSR; Institute of Advanced Training for Physicians, Moscow, director. Honorary doctorate, Warsaw, 1980.

Mariia Dmitrievna Kovrigina, born in a field during the haying season, was the seventh (living) child of a hardworking Siberian peasant family. The area where the Kovrigins lived changed hands several times during the civil war. Kovrigina's older brothers were in the Red Army and her father was arrested, which left the family for a time in a difficult position without adult male workers.

Kovrigina's parents had always dreamed of giving their children an education and, despite difficulties, managed to send the eight-year-old Kovrigina to the local *semiletka* (seven-year) school where she remained for six years.

In 1924, at age fourteen, Kovrigina joined the Komsomol and was soon a leader and organizer, first in her village and later in the whole region. Among other activities, Kovrigina was involved in setting up the first pioneer camp for children in her region.

In 1930, Kovrigina enrolled in the "worker's faculty" or *rabfak* of the Sverdlovsk Medical Institute, but soon found that her education was inadequate. With the help of sympathetic professors, Kovrigina worked hard to catch up and was able to enter the Sverdlovsk Medical Institute in the autumn of 1931.

In 1936, Kovrigina graduated and was assigned to the Cheliabinsk City Hospital. Although she had originally hoped to treat patients, she was sent to work in administration. She became a health inspector, then the deputy director of the preventive medicine administration. In this post she was responsible for nearly twenty large cities and industrial centers including Cheliabinsk and Magnitogorsk.

In 1939, Kovrigina went on a course in neuropathology in Kazan, but, although she was invited to stay on and work for a higher degree, her employers in Cheliabinsk would not agree to it. However, she was allowed to work part of the time in the psychiatric section of the hospital.

In 1940, Kovrigina was moved into party work at the Cheliabinsk District Committee of the Communist Party, first as an instructor and then as head of the sector of education and health. When war began, Kovrigina was appointed deputy responsible for health, education, social security, and culture. She was personally responsible for the reception and organization of evacuees. This was a gargantuan task: in the first year of the war alone, it involved receiving and arrang-

ing for the care of thirty-three thousand children as well as numerous adults, many of whom had lost all their possessions or required medical treatment.

Early in September 1942, Kovrigina was summoned to Moscow as deputy of the Commissariat of Health of the Soviet Union with special responsibility for the health of children and women. To take up this post, Kovrigina had to leave her daughter, Taniia, born earlier in the year, behind with her sister. During this period, Kovrigina became a spokesperson on health matters for the government. She gave radio talks, dispensing advice on health and nutrition, and urging mothers to get their children inoculated against diphtheria and smallpox and to breastfeed infants.

Besides an overwhelming amount of work, the war brought personal losses to Kovrigina. Her niece, Svetlana, was left an orphan under harrowing circumstances and Kovrigina adopted her.

During the 1950s, Kovrigina moved upward through a rapid series of appointments. In 1950, she was appointed Minister of Health of the Russian Republic; in 1953, First Deputy Minister of Health of the Soviet Union and in 1954, she became Minister of Health of the Soviet Union, the first woman to hold this post. In 1959, Kovrigina retired to a less stressful position as director of the Central Institute of Advanced Training for Physicians in Moscow, following VERA PAVLOVNA LEBEDEVA in that post.

Although Kovrigina did not set out to become an administrator, her aptitude for this kind of work was recognized by others very early in her career. A loyal party member (she became a member of the Central Committee of the Communist Party in 1952), she rarely refused to go where the party wished to send her. The war made enormous demands on her but, having sent the men to the front, also provided unusual scope for her organizational talents and realistic common sense. Kovrigina loved children and was genuinely concerned for their welfare. During her period in high office, she made serious attempts to rationalize aspects of the public health delivery system in a practical way.

Kovrigina made several trips abroad to conferences and as a member of delegations and she obviously enjoyed meeting people of all kinds. She was also responsible for inviting a commission of American physicians (including the heart specialist Paul Dudley White) to visit Russia in 1956. Kovrigina received an honorary doctorate from the University of Warsaw in 1980.   ACH

PRIMARY SOURCES
Kovrigina, Mariia Dmitrievna. *Usovershenstvovanie vrachei.*
    Moscow: N.p., 1968.
———. *V neoplatnom dolgu.* Moscow: Politizdat, 1985. Autobiography.

STANDARD SOURCES
Lovejoy.

KOZLOVA, OL'GA GRIGORIYEVNA (1931–1970)

Soviet oceanologist and geologist. Born 23 June 1931 in Kukharevovillage, Smolensk Province. Educated Moscow State University (graduated 1956; Ph.D., 1962). Staff member of the Geology Department of the P. P. Shirshov Institute of Oceanology of the USSR Academy of Science. Died 3 March 1970.

Little is available on Ol'ga Kozlova's early life. After she graduated from Moscow State University's Biology and Soil Faculty, she worked for the Oceanology Institute. She was apparently popular with her colleagues, leaving them bereft when she died suddenly at age thirty-nine.

Her major research interest was diatoms. She studied these organisms in the suspensions and sediments of the Indian sector of the Antarctic. This study was the basis of her candidate dissertation, which she successfully defended in 1962. She continued to study diatoms, this time in the tropical regions of the Indian Ocean, and published many papers on her research. She was a member of a geological team that went to the Indian Ocean in 1967, and as head of the team in 1969 to the Pacific. Her work on diatoms is significant for the methods of diatom analysis that she established as well as standards for oceanographic practice. JH/MBO

PRIMARY SOURCES
Kozlova, O. A. "Redkie zemli v plavikovykh shpatakh razlichnykh mestorozhdenii SSSR." *Geokhimiya* 1 (1957): 46–56.
———. "Diatoma and Silicoflagellates in Suspension and Floor Sediments of the Pacific Ocean." *International Geology Review* 9 (1967): 1322–1342.
———. "Diatoms in Suspension and in Bottom Sediments in the Southern Indian and Pacific Oceans." *Antarctica Ecology* 1 (1970): 148–153. Scientific Committee on Antarctic Research. New York: Academic Press, [1970?].
———. "Growth Conditions on the Shape and Imperfections of Crystals." *Moscow University Geology Bulletin* 36 (1981): 9–19.
———. "Deformation Microstructures of Sphalerite in Pyrite-Polymetal Deposits of Rudnyi Altai (According to Electron Microscope Data)." *Moscow University Geology Bulletin* 41 (1986): 34–41.

SECONDARY SOURCES
"In Memory of Ol'ga Grigoriyevna Kozlova." *Oceanology* 10, no. 3 (1970): 435–436.

KRASNOSEL'SKAIA, TAT'IANA ABRAMOVNA (1884–1950)

Russian plant physiologist. Born 1 January 1884 in St. Petersburg. Educated Petersburg Higher Women's Courses (1904); St. Petersburg University (1912). Professional experience: Petersburg Agricultural Courses, assistant professor (1907–1909); Petersburg Higher Women's Courses, assistant professor (1909–1914); Tiflis Higher Women's Courses, lecturer (1914–1919); Transcaucasian University, lecturer; Tiflis Botanical Garden, associate; Krasnodar Agricultural Institute, lecturer (1919–1921); Leningrad Institute of Textile Crops, lecturer (1921–1925); All-Union Phytological Research Institute, researcher (1925–1935); Saratov Agricultural Institute, professor (1935–1937); Lenin Teachers' Training Institute, Moscow, professor (1938–1950). Died 17 February 1950 in Moscow.

Tat'iana Abramovna Krasnosel'skaia graduated from the faculty of physics and mathematics of the Bestuzhev Higher Women's Courses in St. Petersburg in 1904. She passed the state examinations as an external student in 1910 and obtained a master's degree from St. Petersburg University in 1912.

From 1905 to 1914, she held assistant professorships in botany departments at Petersburg University, Petersburg Agricultural Courses, and Petersburg Higher Women's Courses.

In 1914, Krasnosel'skaia moved to Tiflis as a lecturer at the Tiflis Higher Women's Courses and the Transcaucasian University, and an associate of the Tiflis Botanical Garden. From 1919 to 1921, she was a lecturer at the Krasnodar Agricultural Institute.

In 1921 she returned to her birthplace, now renamed Leningrad, where she worked as a lecturer at several institutes including the Leningrad Institute of Textile Crops and the Leningrad Timber Institute. From 1925 to 1935 she also conducted research at the Laboratory of Plant Physiology of the All-Union Phytological Research Institute. From 1935 to 1937 she was a professor and head of the department of plant physiology and microbiology at the Saratov Agricultural Institute. In 1938 she became head of the department of botany at the Lenin Teachers' Training Institute in Moscow, where she remained until her death in 1950.

Krasnosel'skaia's principal research was on the growth and development of plants and included such aspects as respiration and fermentation, water economy and drought resistance, photosynthesis, and the influence of trace elements. She also wrote on the history of plant physiology, and translated works by Hans Molisch, J. Lilian, and [?] Clarke into Russian as well as editing several agricultural and biological dictionaries. ACH

PRIMARY SOURCES
Krasnosel'skaia, Tat'iana Abramovna. *Dykhanie i brozhenie plesnevykh gribov na tverdom substrate.* Moscow: 1904.

———. *Novye dannye po fiziologii prorasteniia semian.* Moscow: 1929.

———. With others. *Anglo-russkii sel'skokhoziaistvennyi slovar'.* Moscow: Gostekhizdat, 1944.

STANDARD SOURCES
WWW (USSR).

KRASNOW, FRANCES (ca. 1894–?)

U.S. biochemist. Born New York City, 1894. Married Marcus Thou (25 December 1930). One child (b. 1933). Educated Barnard College (B.A., 1917); Columbia University (M.A., 1917; Ph.D., 1922). Professional experience: Columbia University, Department of Biological Chemistry, instructor and investigator; Guggenheim Dental Clinic, School for Dental Hygiene, assistant director, head of biochemical-bacteriological laboratory (1932–?), consulting biochemist-bacteriologist (1935–?); Universal Research Laboratories, researcher (1952–1955); Universal Coatings Inc., research director (from 1955). Honors and memberships: State of New York fellowship; Vanderbilt Clinic Tuberculosis Fellowship; Phi Beta Kappa; Sigma Xi; Society for Experimental Biology and Medicine; Society of American Bacteriologists; International Association for Dental Research (New York section, editor). Death date unknown.

Frances Krasnow was born around 1894, and attended Barnard College, continuing on to obtain her master's and Ph.D. in biological chemistry at Columbia. She worked during this period as an instructor and an investigator in the Department of Biological Chemistry. In 1930, Krasnow married an industrial chemist; they had a child three years later.

Krasnow obtained a series of grants including the Vanderbilt Clinic Tuberculosis Fellowship. Her work began to shift to bacteriology in dental research when she obtained a position at the School for Dental Hygiene of the Guggenheim Dental Clinic as assistant director and the head of their bacteriological and biochemical laboratory. She studied the effects of nutrition on dental health and correlated general metabolic levels with tooth condition. In the early 1950s, she became the director of a research firm that produced materials for dentists. In the mid-1950s, she became the head of research at a related firm producing tooth coverings.

JH/MBO

STANDARD SOURCES
American Women 1974; *AMS* 7–8, P9; Debus.

KRAUS RAGINS, IDA (1894–?)

Russian-born U.S. chemist. Born in Russia, 10 October 1894, to Bernard and Gertrude Kraus. Married Oscar B. Ragins (19 May 1924). One daughter; one son. Educated University of Chicago (A.B., 1918; M.S., 1919; Ph.D., 1924). Professional experience: University of Chicago, department of chemistry, assistant in quantitative analysis (1915–1918); Oklahoma College for Women, teacher (1919–1920); University of Chicago, instructor in biochemistry (1924–1937); Cook County Hospital, senior chemist (1937–1946); Northwestern Medical School, senior chemist in experimental medicine (1946–1949); Chicago College of Osteopathy, head of biochemistry department (from 1949). Death date unknown.

Ida Kraus was born in Russia and moved to the United States with her parents. She attended the University of Chicago for all her degrees, obtaining her doctorate in chemistry at the age of thirty-two. In that same year she married a physician, Oscar B. Ragins, and had two children: a daughter, Naomi, born in 1926, and three years later, a son, Herzl, named after the founder of the Zionist movement.

After she obtained her degree, Kraus Ragins taught as an instructor in biochemistry for thirteen years until the late 1930s, when she obtained a position as the senior chemist at the Cook County Hospital in Chicago. Here her research focused on protein specificity reactions while she continued her studies of amino acids. In the early 1940s, she moved to Northwestern Medical School, where she was a senior chemist in experimental medicine. In 1949, she was made the head of the Department of Biochemistry at the Chicago College of Osteopathy.

JH/MBO

SECONDARY SOURCES
Hall, Diana Long. "Academics, Bluestockings and Biologists: Women at the University of Chicago, 1892–1932." In ed. A. M. Briscoe and Sheila M. Pfallin. "Expanding the Role of Women in the Sciences," Special issue. *Annals of New York Academy of Sciences* 323 (1979).

STANDARD SOURCES
American Women; AMS 7, P 9 (under Ragins).

KROEBER, THEODORA KRACAW (1897–1979)

U.S. anthropologist and writer. Born 24 March 1897 in Denver, Colo., to Phebe (Johnston) and Charles Kracaw. Two siblings. Married (1) Clifton Spencer Brown (1920) (d. 1923); (2) Alfred Kroeber (June 1926); (3) John H. Quinn (1969). Two sons by Brown; one daughter and one son by Kroeber. Educated University of California at Berkeley (A.B., 1919, cum laude; M.A. in psychology 1920; anthropology graduate studies, 1924–1926). Professional experience: University of California, regent (1977). Died 1979.

Enrolled in University of California at Berkeley in 1915, Theodora Kracaw completed her studies in 1919. The next year, she married Clifton Spencer Brown, a graduate student in law at the University of California, Berkeley. In spite of Clifton's poor health, the couple had two sons, Clifton, Jr,. and Theodore. Her first husband died in Santa Fe, New Mexico, in October 1923 and Theodora returned to Berkeley the following year to study anthropology, attending the seminars of the outstanding anthropologist Alfred Kroeber, who had set up a department at Berkeley. By 1926, the two were married, traveling to Peru for their honeymoon while he supervised an archeological expedition and she catalogued potsherds and identified specimens. Alfred Kroeber had been briefly married to Henriette Rothschild, who had died of tuberculosis in 1913. Although her husband encouraged Theodora Kroeber to continue her doctoral work, she never finished her degree. He also adopted her two children from her previous marriage. The couple proceeded to have two children of their own as well, Karl and Ursula. Their daughter, Ursula LeGuin, became a famous science fiction writer noted for incorporating anthropological insights into her writing. All three sons became academics.

Not until Alfred Kroeber retired and they had grown children did Theodora Kroeber begin to write seriously. In 1955–1956, the couple spent a year at the Center for Advanced Studies in Behavioral Sciences at Stanford, where she wrote a full-length novel about Telluride that was never published. Kroeber also accompanied her husband in the late 1950s on visits to the Klamath River and to the Mohave Desert. In 1959, Kroeber wrote *The Inland Whale*, with the central motif based on a Yurok legend. In spite of the inspiration Kroeber derived from her husband's research, the only truly collaborative works the Kroebers completed were articles on the analyses of English poetry in the early 1960s.

In the late 1950s, Kroeber began to write her best-known book, an account of Ishi, the sole survivor of the California Indian Yahi tribe. In 1911, he was found starving in the Sacramento Valley of Oroville and brought to the university museum, where he demonstrated his hunting and craft survival skills for five years, until he died of tuberculosis. Although she never met Ishi, Kroeber wrote a remarkable book on the clash between the two cultures. This book was published as *Ishi in Two Worlds* (1961), a best-seller in the United States and translated into nine languages. Alfred Kroeber had died in 1960 before its highly successful publication and reviews. She rewrote *Ishi* for children in 1964, but found the topic of death difficult to discuss for young Americans who are usually protected from any knowledge of this subject. Kroeber next wrote a biography of her husband in 1970 and then published some of his unpublished Yurok myths with a foreword six years later. She collaborated with Robert F. Heizer, a young anthropologist and friend, on two books that presented photographic and pictorial histories of the early Western and Native American Indians.

In 1969, Kroeber married an artist and psychotherapist more than forty-three years her junior, a topic she discussed frankly in an article and in a series of interviews for the University of California, Berkeley, oral history project. Appointed a regent of University of California, Berkeley, she protested nuclear weapons research at the university two years before her death. Although she held no formal positions in anthropology, she was considered by many anthropologists to be an unusually sensitive interpreter of one culture to another.   JH/MBO

PRIMARY SOURCES
Kroeber, Theodora Kracaw. *The Inland Whale.* Bloomington: Indiana University Press, 1959.

———. *Ishi: Last of His Tribe. A Biography of the Last Wild Indian in North America.* Berkeley: University of California Press, 1961.

———. *Alfred Kroeber: A Personal Configuration.* Berkeley: University of California Press, 1970.

STANDARD SOURCES
Gacs (article by Grace Wilson Buzaljko).

KROGH, BIRTHE MARIE (JORGENSEN) (1874–1943)
Danish physician, research physiologist, and nutritionist. Born 25 December 1874 in Vosegaard, Island of Fyn, Denmark, to Ane and Anders Jorgen Jorgensen. Married August Krogh, 24 March 1904; four surviving children (one boy; three girls). Educated Miss (Nathalie) Zahl's School (1898–1901); University of Copenhagen (medical degree, 1907; Dr. Med., 1914). Professional experience: Blegdams Hospital, intern (1907–1908); Rigs Hospital, clinical assistant (1914–1915); private practice (1910–1941?); University of Copenhagen, medical faculty, censor in physiology (1919–?); Zoophysical Laboratory, University of Copenhagen, scientist (1928–1941?); lecturer in home economics (1923–?). Honors and memberships: Tagea Brandt Rejselgat (travel grant for women) 1930. Died 25 March 1943.

Marie Jorgensen was raised on a farm on a beautiful peninsula in Denmark one of nine children, only four of whom survived tuberculosis. From her early childhood, she determined to study to become a doctor, but only at the age of twenty-four did her family allow her to enter a school (Miss Zahl's) that had recently begun to prepare young women for university entrance examinations. She continued her medical studies at the University of Copenhagen where she met August Krogh, the future Nobel Prize–winner, while studying physiology with him. After they married in 1904, she continued her medical studies, finishing her degree in 1907.

Like Oskar and CÉCILE VOGT, they then began a lifelong collaboration.

Soon after Marie Krogh completed her degree, the Kroghs spent the summer in Greenland, performing an arduous experiment together on the respiration and gas exchange of Eskimos who ate an exclusively meat diet. They set up a small respiration chamber especially for this purpose, studying two individuals at a time, feeding the subjects a meat diet, and sampling oxygen input and carbon dioxide output as well as amounts of nitrogen in urine and feces. The results (inconclusive) were not published until 1913, but the work established their future interest in human and animal respiration and exercise physiology and her particular interest in nutrition.

The Krogh's first children (twin boys) were born prematurely in October 1908, only one of whom survived. For the next two years, Krogh worked closely with her husband (in the laboratory of his former professor and then in the plant physiology laboratory), publishing seven papers on gas diffusion in the lungs, following experiments in which husband and wife served as experimental subjects performing normal and forced breathing. During this period, Krogh also began a medical practice which she continued throughout her life, her clincal work helping to support the family before her husband earned a significant income. Three years later she bore a stillborn son, a daughter was born in 1913, and two other daughters in 1917 and 1918. (The youngest daughter, Bodil [Krogh] Schmidt-Nielsen also became an outstanding physiologist, and wrote a biography of her mother and father.) Continuing some of the respiration work on her own, Marie Krogh produced a doctor of medicine dissertation in 1914, "The Diffusion of Gasses through the Lungs of Man." She was the fourth Danish woman to receive an advanced (doctoral) degree in medicine, which required a dissertation on a scientific subject.

Marie Krogh also became interested in thyroid disease and its effect on metabolic rate, publishing studies on this and on other metabolic diseases, soon to be her major clinical speciality. When she developed diabetes in the early 1920s, the interest of husband and wife was stimulated in the new work on insulin therapy derived from swine pancreas. August Krogh had become widely known throughout the world following his Nobel Prize work on capillary function in 1922. While visiting in the United States and Canada, he arranged to cooperate with J. J. R. Macleod and his group in Toronto to develop insulin production in Denmark. The result was a technique developed by August Krogh and his associate H. C. Hagedorn resulting in a pharmaceutical company whose profits went back into physiological and endocrinological research. They also were able to produce sufficient amounts of insulin within a year to supply the hospitals (and, inci-

dently, Marie Krogh). A number of women scientists as well as men came to work in the zoophysical laboratory, including ABBY TURNER, Beverly Carrier (later Seeborn), and RUTH CONKLIN and HILDE LEVI, most of them with August Krogh and his collaborators.

During this period, Marie Krogh began to teach home economics to young women and struggled to have the subject accepted by the University of Copenhagen. She served as an examiner in physiology to the Medical Faculty from 1919. She soon became very well known in Denmark for her work on nutrition, while continuing to see patients and working as a senior scientist in the new Zoophysical Laboratory (directed by her husband and funded in part by the University and the Rockefeller Foundation). In the 1920s, she conducted research on vitamin deficiencies and popularized the importance of good nutrition for the health of the Danish population. In 1930, she received a prestigious traveling grant (the Tagaea Brandt award), which allowed her to study malnutrition in children in the Canary Islands in 1931 and to attend the International Congress of Physiology in Italy in 1932. Her husband chose not to go because he disapproved of Mussolini's fascist government. In 1939, as World War II was approaching, the Kroghs went for three months to Swarthmore College in the United States, where August Krogh lectured on physiology.

Three of the Krogh children worked at one point or another with their parents in physiology, although at first the youngest daughter, Bodil, trained and then practiced as a dentist, following her older sister's career. In the early forties, during the German occupation of Denmark, Marie Krogh developed breast cancer. She died in 1943.   JH/MBO

PRIMARY SOURCES

Krogh, Marie. With August Krogh. "Versuche uber die Diffusion von Kohlenoxyd durch die Lungen des Menschen." *Zentralblatt für Physiologie* 23 (1909).

———. With August Krogh. "On the Tension of Gases in the Arterial Blood. The Mechanism of Gas-Exchange. I." *Skandinavisches Archiv für Physiologie* 23 (1910). The first of seven papers on the topic of gas exchange published in this journal 1909–1910.

———. With August Krogh. "A Study of the Diet and Metabolism of Eskimos Undertaken in 1908 on an Expedition to Greenland." *Medd om Gronland* 51 (1913). Includes data from the study of metabolism of the Greenland Eskimo.

———. "The Diffusion of Gases through the Lungs of Man." In Danish. Dr. Med. diss., University of Copenhagen Medical School, 1914.

———. "The Diffusion of Gases through the Lungs of Man." *Journal of Physiology* 49 (1915): 271–300. A publication based on her medical dissertation.

————. "Patalogiske forandringer i hvilestofskiftet" (Pathological changes in resting metabolic rate). *Ugeskrift for Laeger* (1920): 537–577.

————. With Clara Black, Estrid Hein, and Kis Jacobsen. *Kvindelige Akademikere, 1875–1925.* Copenhagen: Glydendalske Boghandel, Nordisk Forlag, 1925.

SECONDARY SOURCES

Fredericia, L. S. "Marie Krogh, December 25, 1874–March 25, 1943." *Akademiet for de teknikske videnskaber.* Copenhagen, 1943. Obituary notice.

Schmidt-Nielsen, Bodil. *August and Marie Krogh: Lives in Science.* New York and Oxford: American Physiological Society, 1995.

KRUPSKAIA, NADEZHDA KONSTANTINOVNA (1869–1939)

Russian educator and political figure. Born 26 February 1869 in St. Petersburg to Elizaveta (Tistrova) and Konstantin Ignat'evich Krupskii, a military officer. Married Vladimir I. Ul'ianov (Lenin). Educated Obolenskii Female Gymnasium; Bestuzhev Higher Women's Courses. Professional experience: Obolenskii Female Gymnasium, teaching assistant; Commissariat of Education (Narkompros), official; Central Committee for Political Education, chair; Scientific Methods Section of the State Academic Council of Narkompros, chair. Honors and memberships: Soviet Academy of Sciences, honorary member. Died 27 February 1939.

Nadezhda Konstantinovna Krupskaia suffered injustice from an early age as the result of her father's misfortunes as a military officer put to trial for unclear reasons in 1874. Although his name was eventually cleared, the family encountered long-term financial difficulties.

Krupskaia completed the Obolenskii Female Gymnasium in 1887 and remained there until 1891 as a part-time teaching assistant. In 1889 she enrolled in the Bestuzhev Higher Women's Courses, but dropped out the next year. At this time she began studying Marxist theory and joined a Marxist circle in St. Petersburg.

In 1891, she began to teach evening and weekend schools for factory workers. In 1894, Krupskaia first met Vladimir Il'ich Ul'ianov, later famous under the name of Lenin. In 1896, she was arrested as a result of her political activities and in 1898 sentenced to three years of exile in Ufa, Bashkiria. Lenin, exiled in Shushenskoe, Siberia, asked her to join him there, and the authorities granted permission on condition that they would be married when she arrived. The couple were married in 1898.

During this period of exile, Krupskaia wrote her first pamphlet, *The Woman Worker.* From 1901 to 1905, Krupskaia and Lenin lived in Munich, London, and Geneva, where they were both involved in political activity. Like Lenin, Krupskaia had a number of revolutionary pseudonyms, including Artamonova, Frei, Gallilei, Katia, Lenina, Minoga, Onegina, Ryba, Rybkina, Sharko, and Sablina. Krupskaia acted as assistant to her husband and secretary for the Marxist periodical *Iskra.* Later, after the split between the Russian Social Democratic Labor Party into Bolshevik and Menshevik factions, she served as secretary to *Vpered,* the Bolshevik journal established by Lenin. After the revolution of 1905, they returned to Russia, but left again for Western Europe in 1907. Although, in general, Krupskaia was not a Marxist theorist like Lenin, in 1915 she wrote a treatise on education entitled *Narodnoe obrazovanie i demokratiia,* in which she attempted to develop a Marxist theory of education.

The March revolution of 1917 forced out the old regime and in its place a provisional government under Alexander Kerensky was formed. This made it possible for Lenin and Krupskaia to return to Russia. Although the revolution had started without him, Lenin and the Bolsheviks soon defeated the weak provisional government, and in November 1917, the Bolshevik Party took power. At first Krupskaia occupied a minor position in the Bolshevik Party secretariat but after the Soviet Republic was established, she became an official of the Commissariat of Education (Narkompros). With A. V. Lunacharskii and M. N. Pokrovskii, she developed the educational policies and practices of the new state. She was particularly interested in eradicating illiteracy and developing polytechnic and antireligious education. She acted as chair of the Central Committee of Political Education in 1920 and chair of the Scientific Methods Section of the State Academic Council of Narkompros, and traveled widely in the Soviet Union on behalf of education.

In May 1922, Lenin suffered his first stroke and Krupskaia abandoned her public activities to nurse and assist him. Although he hoped to return to politics, a second stroke in December made him ineffective.

Lenin died in January 1924. Without him, Krupskaia was essentially excluded from politics. Although she remained a celebrity, she had no power to oppose Stalin's policies. She devoted the remaining years of her life to preserving the memory of Lenin and writing on education and children. She was a strong supporter of the family and favored Stalin's policies that outlawed abortion and restricted divorce. She was also interested in women's rights.

Although Krupskaia is known mainly as a revolutionary and the wife of Lenin, she made a significant contribution to the development of education in a country that, at the time of the revolution of 1917, was largely illiterate. Aware of how extremely backward the country was, she was much concerned with the promotion of scientific education. In the Stalin period, the importance of her role in education was downplayed but revived in the post-Stalin period. Undoubtedly it will be reevaluated again in the post-Soviet period.   ACH

PRIMARY SOURCES

Krupskaia, Nadezhda Konstantinovna. *Narodnoe obrazovanie i demokratii.* Izvestiya 3. Berlin: Gos. izd-vo RSFSR, 1921.
————. *Pedagogicheskie sochineniia.* 11 vols. Moscow: N.p., 1957–1963.
————. *O professional'n-otekhnicheskoi podgotovke kvalifitsirovannoi sily.* Moscow: Vysshaia shkola, 1974.

SECONDARY SOURCES

Wieczynski, Joseph L., ed. *The Modern Encyclopedia of Russian and Soviet History.* Gulf Breeze, Fla.: Academic International Press, 1979.

KRUTIKHOVSKAIA, ZINAIDA ALEKSANDROVNA (1916–1986)

Soviet geologist. Born 16 October 1916 in village of Kargopol, Kurgan province, the daughter of schoolteachers. Educated Sverdlovsk Mining Institute (1938); Ukrainian Institute of Geophysics (Ph.D., 1971). Professional experience: Institute of Geology, coal deposit prospector in the Urals; Institute of Geophysics of the Ukrainian Academy of Sciences, researcher of iron ore in the Ukraine (1938–1958); Institute of Geophysics (later the Department of the Permanent Geomagnetic Field), founder and later head of the laboratory of magnetic prospecting (1961–1981). Honors and memberships: Scientific Committee of the Academy of Sciences of the USSR on geomagneticism; Ukrainian section of the scientific editorial council of the Ministry of Geology of the USSR; Geophysical Journal, editorial board; State Prize of the Ukrainian Soviet (1972); Order of the Badge of Merit; honorary title of Meritorious Scientific Worker of the Ukrainian SSR. Died 28 December 1986.

From her second position after her graduation from the Sverdlovsk Mining Institute until her death, Zinaida Aleksandrovna Krutikhovskaia specialized in studying the earth's magnetism. Immediately after graduation, she worked for the Institute of Geology, where she prospected for coal in the Ural mountains and iron ore in the Ukraine. In the Ukraine, she was involved in the discovery of the major deposits of the Kremenchug iron ore district. She founded the laboratory of magnetic prospecting in the Institute of Geophysics, which subsequently became the Department of the Permanent Geomagnetic Field, which she headed until 1981 and for which she was a consultant for the rest of her life. The State Prize of the Ukrainian SSR, which she won in

1972, was presented to her for her work on the development and introduction of a procedure for geologic mapping, prospecting, and study of the structure of the deep-seated deposits of the Ukrainian iron ore province. Her research contributed to the understanding of the structure and development of the earth's crust and the location of minerals in it. She was a prolific writer, and produced over 160 published articles and nine monographs.

Krutikhovskaia was a member of numerous professional organizations. She collaborated widely with the academies of science of the socialist countries, which allowed her to work on regional magnetic anomalies originating at a great depth. Not only did Krutikhovskaia make important contributions to geomagnetic research, but she also devoted ten years to teaching in the Kiev Geological Prospecting Technical Institute, where she supervised postgraduate students.   CK

SECONDARY SOURCES

"In Memory of Zinaida Aleksandrovna Krutikhovskaya." *Geophysical Journal* 9, no. 3 (1990): 467–469.

KUNDE, MARGARETHE META H. (1888–?)

German/U.S. physiologist. Born 12 February 1888 in Germany. Naturalized U.S. citizen 1922. Educated University of Nebraska (A.B., 1917; B.Sc., 1919); University of Chicago (Ph.D., 1923); Rush College of Medicine (M.D., 1925). Professional experience: University of Chicago, assistant in physiology (1919–1922), instructor (1922–1925), associate (1925–1926), Smith Fellow (1926), instructor in medicine (1927–1929), assistant professor (1930–1932), professor of physiology (1932–1936); Northwestern Medical School, instructor in medicine (1941–post-1968); Chicago Maternity Center, endocrine clinic staff (1941); Cook County Hospital, clinical assistant (1942); Chicago Wesley Hospital, assistant attending physician; practicing physician (1936–post-1968). Honors and memberships: National Research Council, Fellow (1923); University of Chicago, Smith Fellow (1926); American Medical Society, Fellow; Society for Experimental Biology and Medicine, member; Endocrine Society, member. Death date unknown.

Margarethe Meta Kunde was born in Germany and came to the United States at an early age. She attended the University of Nebraska, where she obtained both a bachelor of arts and a bachelor of science degree. From Nebraska she went to the University of Chicago where she worked toward a doctoral degree in physiology, researching the effects of prolonged fasting on the basal metabolic rate system. At the same time she was an assistant in the laboratory and, after she obtained her degree, continued to teach in the field.

With a National Research Council Fellowship, Kunde went to the Rush College of Medicine in Chicago for a medical degree. She continued to teach at the University of Chicago as an instructor and assistant professor of medicine. She then became a professor of physiology at the medical school until 1936, when she began to develop her private practice. She maintained her teaching of medicine at Northwestern Medical School beginning in the 1940s, while continuing her interest in the clinical aspects of endocrinology.

Kunde was briefly on the staff of the Endocrine Clinic of the Chicago Maternity Center, and followed research as a member of the Society of Endocrinology. JH/MBO

STANDARD SOURCES
AMS 8, B 9, P&B 10–11, suppl. 4.